THE NATIONAL ROLL OF THE GREAT WAR.

The National Roll of the Great War

One of the most sought-after sets of reference books of the First World War is the *National Roll of the Great War*. The National Publishing Company attempted, shortly after hostilities ceased, to compile a brief biography of as many participants in the War as possible. The vast majority of entries refer to combatants who survived the Great War and the *National Roll* is often the only source of information available. Fourteen volumes were completed on a regional basis; **the Naval & Military Press has compiled a fifteenth volume which contains an alphabetic index to the fourteen now republished volumes**.

The National Roll - complete 15 vol. set	ISBN: 1 847340 33 4	£285.00
Section I – London	ISBN: 1 847340 34 2	£22.00
Section II – London	ISBN: 1 847340 35 0	£22.00
Section III – London	ISBN: 1 847340 36 9	£22.00
Section IV – Southampton	ISBN: 1 847340 37 7	£22.00
Section V – Luton	ISBN: 1 847340 38 5	£22.00
Section VI – Birmingham	ISBN: 1 847340 39 3	£22.00
Section VII – London	ISBN: 1 847340 40 7	£22.00
Section VIII – Leeds	ISBN: 1 847340 41 5	£22.00
Section IX – Bradford	ISBN: 1 847340 42 3	£22.00
Section X – Portsmouth	ISBN: 1 847340 43 1	£22.00
Section XI – Manchester	ISBN: 1 847340 44 X	£22.00
Section XII – Bedford & Northampton	ISBN: 1 847340 45 8	£22.00
Section XIII – London	ISBN: 1 847340 46 6	£22.00
Section XIV – Salford	ISBN: 1 847340 47 4	£22.00
Section XV – Index to all 14 volumes	ISBN: 1 847340 48 2	£22.00

The Naval & Military Press Ltd

Unit 10, Ridgewood Industrial Park, Uckfield,
East Sussex, TN22 5QE, England
Tel: 01825 749494   Fax: 01825 765701
www.naval-military-press.com
www.military-genealogy.com

THE NATIONAL ROLL
OF THE GREAT WAR
1914-1918

CONTAINED WITHIN
THE PAGES OF THIS
VOLUME WILL BE
FOUND THE NAMES
AND RECORDS OF
SERVICE OF THOSE
WHO HELPED TO
SECURE VICTORY FOR
THE EMPIRE DURING
THE GREAT WAR OF
1914-1918.

THE
NAVAL &
MILITARY
PRESS LTD
2006

Published by

The Naval & Military Press Ltd

Unit 10, Ridgewood Industrial Park,

Uckfield, East Sussex,

TN22 5QE England

Tel: +44 (0) 1825 749494

Fax: +44 (0) 1825 765701

www.naval-military-press.com

www.military-genealogy.com

© The Naval & Military Press Ltd 2006

FOREWORD

AND SHORT OUTLINE OF THE PART
PLAYED BY BRITAIN IN THE GREAT WAR.

WHEN we quietly consider what the Great War, with its gains and losses, its cares and anxieties, has taught us, we are at once struck by the splendid heroism of all who took part in it. Many by reason of special qualities of mind or soul stand out more prominently than the rest ; but the names and deeds of others, who toiled no less meritoriously, are officially left unsung.

Yet it is well, if only for purely personal and family reasons, that there should be some abiding record of the self-sacrificing services of all men and women who answered their Country's call in her hour of need, and who, whether on land, or sea, or in the air, in hospital, or camp, or workshop, were ready to lay down life itself, if need be, that Britain might live and Right prevail over Might.

It is for this reason primarily that the present " National Roll of the Great War " was projected. In these pages will be found records of devotion and patriotism of which the individual, the family, and the nation have every reason to be proud.

1914. This foreword, besides recording our gratitude to all who toiled for the Empire, may also serve a subsidiary purpose by providing a sketch of the part which Britain played in the war which burst on the World in the Summer of 1914. Space does not allow us to follow the course of the negotiations which preceded the outbreak, or to explain the aims of Germany. Suffice it to say that her long projected design of rushing through Belgium on France in one overwhelming flood was foiled by the gallantry of the Allies in August and September. Our share in that struggle is told in the records of " The Contemptible Little Army " that fought at Mons, the Marne, the Aisne and Ypres.

1915. Our campaign in 1915 opened with the Battle of Neuve Chapelle, and in quick succession followed those at St. Eloi, Hill 60, Ypres, and Festubert. In the Autumn we gained a temporary success at Loos, and at one time Lens was almost ours, but when Winter set in, our lines were much the same as they had been a year before. We now began to realize, in a way we had not done hitherto, the greatness of the task to which we had set our hands. Our failure in the East had taught us the lesson that in the West and on the Sea lay our hopes of victory.

1916
Early in 1916 the fortune of war swayed for and against us at Loos, Ypres and Vimy Ridge, while the Germans were making their great effort at Verdun. Their protracted attack on that fortress failed, while their attempt to take command of the Sea was crushed by our Naval victory in the Battle of Jutland. Our great effort in 1916 was the Somme Offensive, which opened in July, and continued with varying success until November

1917.
Early in 1917 we reaped to some extent the benefit of our efforts of the preceding year, and a German retirement on a long line of the front took place, which by the middle of March gave us Bapaume and Péronne. On Easter Monday we attacked along the Vimy Ridge, and before Arras. Monchy-le-Preux was captured, Bailleul and several villages near Lens fell into our hands, and by May 17th we had taken Bullecourt. In June came our victory at Messines, and from July to November we fought the series of engagements round St. Julien, Pilkem, Hooge, Polygon Wood and Passchendaele, which go by the name of the third Battle of Ypres. At the same time severe fighting was going on near Lens, and this was followed in November and December by the first Battle of Cambrai, which opened auspiciously, but left us with little gained in the end.

1918.
The year 1918 opened with the great German Offensive, which was designed to end the struggle before the full weight of the American help could tell in our favour. It broke upon the Allied lines between the Scarpe and the Oise on March 21st, and for a time carried everything before it ; but Arras and Amiens remained in our possession. On April 9th the Germans made another effort on the Lys front, from La Bassée to Armentières. Desperate fighting occurred around Bailleul, Passchendaele, Kemmel and Givenchy, but in spite of our severe losses, Ludendorff failed to break through.

At the end of May the Germans made yet another attempt along the Aisne, and captured Soissons, Dormans and many villages. Their last effort began on July 15th along the Marne, east and west of Rheims. They achieved some success at first, but on July 18th the Allied counter-stroke began. Blow followed blow in quick succession, and Soissons and Beaumont-Hamel, that had been lost in the Spring, were now recovered. On August 21st the Battle of Bapaume opened, and concurrently with it the Battle of the Scarpe was going on. Towards the end of September the Battles of Cambrai and Ypres began, and our victories began seriously to jeopardise the enemy's lines of communication Eastwards. Le Cateau was entered on October 10th ; Ostend, Lille and Douai fell into Allied hands and within a few days the Belgian coast was freed. In November our successes still continued in the Battle of the Sambre, and the enemy retreated rapidly towards Mons and Maubeuge. Mons was entered at dawn on November 11th, 1918, and at 11 a.m. fighting ceased.

GALLIPOLI.
During 1915 we anxiously followed the course of our venture in the Dardanelles. Weighty reasons prompted it, and we hoped that our combined forces would be able to make their way to Constantinople, and by so doing would relieve the pressure on Russia, as well as remove the danger that threatened Egypt.

Unhappily, however, the successes at Anzac and Krithia and the later landing at Suvla Bay could not be followed up ; the Naval forces could not force their way through the Narrows ; and reluctantly we had to admit failure and evacuate the Peninsula.

EGYPT.

Early in the war the Turks made several unsuccessful attacks on the Canal Zone, while on the Western Frontiers of Egypt the Senussi were repulsed at Mersa, Matruh and Agagia. In August 1916 another Turkish attack was crushed at Romani, and six months later the enemy were again defeated at Magdhaba and Rafa. Henceforward Egypt became the base for offensive operations against the Turks in Palestine. Gaza was first attacked in March 1917, and again in April, but it was not captured until November, after General Allenby had previously taken Beersheba. Shortly afterwards Jaffa fell into our hands, and on December 9th Jerusalem surrendered, to be followed by Jericho in February. Hostilities were resumed in September, 1918, and by the end of October we were masters of Acre, Haifa, Damascus, Tripolis and Aleppo.

MESOPOTAMIA

Indian detachments reached Mesopotamia in November 1914, and occupied Basra and Kurma on the Tigris. Amara, higher up the river, was captured in June 1915, and Kut-el-Amara in September. General Townshend's forces then proceeded towards Baghdad, but their way was barred at Ctesiphon, and finding it impossible to break through the Turkish lines they retired on Kut, where in April 1916 they surrendered. In December 1916 a better organised offensive began, which in 1917 and 1918 captured Kut, Baghdad, Tekrit and Mosul.

SALONIKA.

Our troops on this front came from Gallipoli in December 1915, too late to stem the Bulgarian Advance against Serbia, but in August 1916 they began a general offensive along the Doiran front, and in September advanced across the Struma. Before the close of the year Monastir was recovered. In 1917 we were mainly concerned in the Doiran Advance, and in 1918 in a similar operation along the Vardar, which on September 30th ended in the victory of the Allies and the Armistice with Bulgaria.

AFRICA.

The Germans in Togoland were overcome by August 27th, 1914, while those in the Cameroons held out only one month longer. German South-West Africa proved more difficult to reduce owing to political complications, but it eventually surrendered to General Botha in July 1915. In East Africa the Germans kept up the struggle with success whilst hostilities continued in Europe, and ceased fighting on November 14th, 1918, in compliance with the terms of the Armistice.

THE NAVY.

The work of the Navy throughout the war was of boundless importance. Not only did she take command of the Seas in August 1914, but she kept it to the end. Of the Battles of Heligoland, Coronel and the Falkland Islands in 1914, the Dogger Bank and the Dardanelles in 1915, Jutland in 1916, the bombardments of Zeebrugge and Ostend in 1917, and the raids on Zeebrugge and Durazzo in 1918 the public have full information ; but of the smaller engagements in almost all waters of the globe, few have as yet any accurate knowledge.

ROYAL AIR FORCE. Still less do we know, except in a general way, of the work of the Royal Air Force, which arose in 1918 from the union of the R.F.C. and the R.N.A.S. Handicapped at first by lack of men and material, they soon became a highly efficient body, and proved of incalculable value to both the Army and the Navy. The heroic deeds of Major McCudden, Captain Leefe Robinson, Captain Ball, Lieutenant Warneford and many others, will for ever live in our memory.

The National Roll makes no claim to being a complete book of reference—in fact no such record could be compiled—but it may safely claim to supply a wonderful memorial of splendid services, truly worthy of the thankful remembrance of a grateful Empire.

To all who, by their Faith and Courage, helped to bring Victory to our Arms, we dedicate this book.

THE EDITOR.

1, York Place, Baker Street,
London, W.1.

THE NATIONAL ROLL OF THE
1914   GREAT WAR   1918

SECTION XI

A

ABBOTT, A., Private, East Lancashire Regiment.
He volunteered in March 1915, and six months later proceeded to the Western Front, where he fought in the Battles of Loos, Ypres and Albert, and then, contracting rheumatic fever, was invalided to England in 1916. On his recovery he was sent to Mesopotamia and was in action at Kut-el-Amara and on the Tigris. After seven months' service on the Eastern Front he was transferred to India, and contracted fever and was in hospital in Bombay. He returned to England in 1919, and was demobilised in May of the same year, holding the 1914-15 Star, and the General Service and Victory Medals.
38, Higher Chatham Street, Chorlton-on-Medlock, Manchester. Z1000

ABBOTT, J., Pte., 6th K.O. (Royal Lancaster Regt.)
He was already serving in the Army when war broke out in August 1914, and at once proceeded with the first Expeditionary Force to the Western Front. After taking a prominent part in the Battle of Mons, he was unhappily killed during the Retreat in August 1914. He was entitled to the Mons Star, and the General Service and Victory Medals.
"A costly sacrifice upon the altar of freedom."
11, Ogden Street, Hulme, Manchester. TZ9016

ABBOTT, R., Private, Cheshire Regiment.
Joining in December 1917, he proceeded to France in the following May and took part in many of the principal battles during the Retreat and Allied Advance, entering Mons at dawn on November 11th, 1918. He afterwards proceeded with the Army of Occupation to Germany, and served there until September 1919, when he returned to England and was demobilised. He holds the General Service and Victory Medals. 27, Sun Street, Newton Heath, Manchester. 9774

ABBOTT, W., Private, 2nd Manchester Regiment.
He volunteered in November 1914, and after training at Cleethorpes, was drafted overseas in December 1915. During his service on the Western Front he was in action at Loos, St. Eloi, Albert and Vimy Ridge, but fell fighting in the Battle of the Somme on July 2nd, 1916. He was entitled to the 1914-15 Star, and the General Service and Victory Medals.
"A valiant soldier with undaunted heart, he breasted life's last hill."
87, Blackthorn Street, Ardwick, Manchester. Z7755B

ABEL, W., Private, R.M.L.I.
He volunteered in September 1914, and embarking for the Dardanelles in the following March, took part in the Landing at Gallipoli and the Battle of Cape Helles, and was in action until the Evacuation of the Peninsula. Transferred to Egypt in January 1916 he was engaged on important duties at Alexandria, Cairo, Port Said and Port Suez, and in the following March proceeded to France, subsequently fighting in engagements at Ypres, Béthune and Arras. In September of the same year he was posted to H.M.S. "Cæsar," which vessel was stationed in the Bermuda Islands, at Malta, Brindisi and the Bosphorus. He was demobilised in November 1919, and holds the 1914-15 Star, and the General Service and Victory Medals.
62, Downing Street, Ardwick Green, Manchester. Z9775-6B

ABERNETHY, J. Private, Loyal N. Lancashire Regt.
Volunteering in August 1914, he embarked for Egypt in the following May, and took part in fighting at Katia. Transferred to Mesopotamia in July 1916, he fought in several engagements, and in November of the succeeding year proceeded to India, subsequently being engaged on important duties in the Punjab until the close of hostilities. He was demobilised in May 1919, and holds the 1914-15 Star, and the General Service and Victory Medals.
4, Whittaker Street, Gorton, Manchester. Z9777

ABRAHAM, R.. Gunner, R.F.A.
Volunteering in May 1915, he was three months later sent to the Western Front. There he did excellent work as a gunner in numerous important engagements, including those on the Somme and at Albert, St. Eloi, Arras, Bullecourt, Ypres, Cambrai and Bapaume. Whilst serving in France he suffered severely from shell-shock and died from the effects in January 1919. He was entitled to the 1914-15 Star, and the General Service and Victory Medals.
"Whilst we remember, the sacrifice is not in vain."
8, Ernest Street, Ancoats, Manchester. Z6032A

ABRAHAMS, J., Corporal, 11th Manchester Regt.
Volunteering in December 1914, he four months later proceeded to Gallipoli, where he was in action at Krithia, Suvla Bay and Chunuk Bair. After the Evacuation of the Peninsula he was sent to France in June 1916, but was killed whilst taking part in heavy fighting at the Battle of the Somme in September 1916. He was entitled to the 1914-15 Star, and the General Service and Victory Medals.
" A valiant soldier, with undaunted heart, he breasted life's last hill."
22, White Street, Hulme, Manchester. Z1001

ACHESON, J. E., Private, 8th Manchester Regt.
He volunteered in May 1915, and after undergoing a period of training served at various stations, where he was engaged on duties of great importance. He was unable to obtain his transfer to a theatre of war on account of ill-health, but, nevertheless, rendered valuable services with his unit until invalided from the Army in June 1917.
63, Welcomb Street, Hulme, Manchester. Z11620

ACKERLEY, R. H., Driver, R.F.A.
At the outbreak of war he was mobilised at once and proceeded with the First Expeditionary Force to France, where he fought in the Battles of Mons, Le Cateau, the Marne, the Aisne, Ypres, Neuve Chapelle, St. Eloi, Hill 60 and Loos. He was then transferred to Mesopotamia, and in this theatre of war was in action at Kut, Um-el-Hannah and Sanna-i-Yat and on the Tigris, but contracting malaria, was sent to hospital in India. On his recovery he was sent back to the Western Front and took part in fierce fighting in the Aisne, Marne and Cambrai sectors. He was discharged in July 1919, and holds the Mons Star, and the General Service and Victory Medals.
4, Rex Street, Jackson Street, Hulme, Manchester. Z1002

ACKERS, J., Private, 22nd Manchester Regiment.
Volunteering in November 1914, he proceeded to France in the following October, and was in action at Loos, La Bassée, Arras and Albert. He was unfortunately killed on July 1st, 1916, during the opening phase of the Somme Offensive, and was entitled to the 1914-15 Star, and the General Service and Victory Medals.
" His name liveth for evermore."
25, Marcer Street, Ancoats, Manchester. Z9778

ACKROYD, A., Driver, R.F.A.
Mobilised in August 1914, he was immediately drafted to France with the First Expeditionary Force and served in the Battle of, and through the Retreat from, Mons. He was also in action at the Battles of Le Cateau, La Bassée, Neuve Chapelle, St. Eloi, Hill 60, Festubert and Loos, and in November 1915 was sent home for his discharge, time-expired. He holds the Mons Star, and the General Service and Victory Medals.
10, Stretton Street, Collyhurst, Manchester. Z10279B

ACTON, E., Pte., Argyll and Sutherland Highlanders.
He volunteered in September 1914, and crossing to France in the following May, took part in several important engagements until wounded in the Battle of Loos in September 1915. Returning to the forward areas on recovery, he was wounded for the second time in the Somme Offensive in September 1916, but after treatment was engaged with his unit in several operations. Wounded in the Battle of Arras in April 1917, he was sent to hospital at the Base and evacuated to England a month later. After convalescence he served on home defence duties, and demobilised in April 1919, holds the 1914-15 Star, and the General Service and Victory Medals.
4, Duke Street, Miles Platting, Manchester. Z10081C

ADAMS, C., Private, 3rd York and Lancaster Regt.
A Reservist, he was called up at the outbreak of war and drafted overseas in November 1914. Whilst serving on the Western Front he saw heavy fighting at St. Eloi, Festubert, Vimy Ridge, the Somme, Beaumont-Hamel, Arras and Cambrai and in the Retreat and Advance of 1918. He was wounded on three occasions—at Armentières, Oppy Wood and the Somme—and in consequence was invalided to England in March 1918. He was eventually discharged in March 1919, and holds the 1914 Star, and the General Service and Victory Medals.
18, Cornwall Street, New Cross, Manchester. Z9017

ADAMS, H., Corporal, King's (Liverpool Regt.)
Having previously served in the South African campaign, he rejoined the Army in August 1914, and proceeded in the following December to France. There he fought in important engagements at La Bassée, Ypres and Neuve Chapelle, and was severely wounded at Givenchy and invalided to England. On his discharge from hospital he was retained on home service and was eventually discharged in March 1920, holding the Queen's and King's South African Medals, 1914 Star, and the General Service and Victory Medals.
12, Wesley Street, Ardwick, Manchester.   Z1005

ADAMS, J., Private, 24th Manchester Regiment.
In August 1914 he volunteered, and two months later was sent to the Western Front, where he was engaged in fierce fighting at Armentières, Ypres, Neuve Chapelle, Vermelles, the Somme, the Ancre, the Aisne and Havrincourt. He was badly wounded at Ypres in November 1914, and suffered the loss of his left eye. He was invalided out of the Army in June 1918, and holds the 1914 Star, and the General Service and Victory Medals.
10, Johnson Street, Ancoats, Manchester.   TZ9019

ADAMS, J., Lieut., 12th Manchester Regiment.
At the outbreak of hostilities in August 1914, he volunteered and in December 1915 proceeded to France, where he served for eleven months. During that time he was in action in numerous engagements, including those at Loos, St. Eloi, Albert and Vimy Ridge, and was wounded in the Battle of the Somme in 1916. Later he was invalided to England and after a protracted hospital treatment was retained on home service until December 1918, when he was demobilised, holding the 1914–15 Star, and the General Service and Victory Medals.
7, Florence Street, Moss Side, Manchester.   Z1004A

ADAMS, L. J., Corporal, 2/7th Manchester Regt.
He joined in September 1916, and after a course of training was drafted to the Western Front four months later. There he took part in the Battles of Arras, Bullecourt, Messines and Ypres and was wounded and gassed at Nieuport. After rejoining his unit he was in action at Cambrai and in the final decisive engagements of the war. Demobilised in February 1919, he holds the General Service and Victory Medals.
29, Parkfield Avenue, Rusholme, Manchester.   Z1003

ADAMS, S., 2nd Lieut., Sherwood Foresters.
He volunteered for active service in August 1914, but was retained on important duties in England until January 1916, when he was drafted overseas. During his service in France he was in action in the Loos, St. Eloi and Albert sectors, and whilst taking a conspicuous part in fierce fighting at Vimy Ridge was wounded. On his recovery he performed valuable work as a Despatch rider to the Tank Corps. Demobilised in March 1919, he holds the General Service and Victory Medals.
7, Florence Street, Moss Side, Manchester.   Z1004B

ADAMS, T., Private, 3rd Welch Regiment.
He volunteered in May 1915, but on conclusion of his training was unable to procure a transfer to a theatre of war. He was therefore retained on home defence, and throughout the period of his service was stationed at Cardiff, where he was engaged in general camp duties, and also in guarding prisoners of war. In July 1916 he was discharged from the Army as medically unfit for further service.
11, Stand Street, Ancoats, Manchester.   TZ9018

ADAMS, W., Private, 1/8th Manchester Regiment.
Volunteering in July 1915, he proceeded nine months later to Egypt, where he saw service at Alexandria, Kantara, Hill 70 and El Arish. After eleven months in the East he was transferred to the Western Front and took an active part in the Battles of Ypres, Passchendaele, Cambrai, the Somme and Epéhy. He was demobilised in July 1919, and holds the General Service and Victory Medals.
9, Stand Street, Ancoats, Manchester.   TZ9020

ADAMSON, J., Bombardier, 38th Divn., R.F.A.
Volunteering in April 1915, he was sent to Egypt in January 1917, and after only a month's service there was drafted to the Western Front. There he took an active part in the Battles of Arras, Vimy Ridge, Bullecourt, Ypres, Passchendaele and Lens, and was severely wounded in action at Cambrai in November 1917. He was in consequence discharged from the Army in October 1918 as medically unfit for further military duties and holds the General Service and Victory Medals.
54, George Street, Hulme, Manchester.   Z1006

ADDERLEY, W. H., Gunner, M.G.C.
He joined the Army in April 1917, and in the following September was drafted to the Western Front, where he experienced fierce fighting in engagements in the Ypres, Cambrai and Somme sectors. After the Armistice he passed into Germany with the Army of Occupation and served there until September 1919, when he proceeded to Ireland. He was stationed at Cork until his demobilisation in March 1920, and holds the General Service and Victory Medals.
55, Markham Street, Ardwick, Manchester.   Z1007

ADDISON, G., Sapper, R.E.
Volunteering in August 1914, he was on conclusion of his training sent to the Western Front in November 1915. In this theatre of war he saw heavy fighting at Loos, St. Eloi, Albert, Vimy Ridge and the Somme, and sustained wounds in the Battle of Arras, which necessitated his being sent back to England. On recovery he proceeded to Palestine, and there was in action at Gaza, Jericho and Jerusalem. In May 1919 he returned home and was demobilised, holding the 1914–15 Star, and the General Service and Victory Medals.
1, Chell Street, Longsight, Manchester.   Z1008

ADDY, H., Corporal, Royal Scots Fusiliers.
He volunteered in August 1914, and in the following March was drafted to India. Here he was engaged at Bangalore on important garrison and training duties until April 1918, and then returned to England, where he did similar work until demobilised in November 1919. He holds the General Service Medal.
19, Back Hadfield Street, Ancoats, Manchester.   Z9402

ADEY, J. W., Private, 11th Manchester Regiment.
Volunteering in April 1915, he embarked for Egypt a month later, and took part in the defence of the Suez Canal and in fighting at Katia. Later he was transferred to France, and was in action in many important engagements, including those at Nieuport, La Bassée, Loos, and Arras. Owing to a severe wound he was invalided home and discharged in May 1918, and holds the General Service and Victory Medals.
12, Summer Street, Chorlton-on-Medlock, Manchester.   Z9780A

ADSHEAD, C. W., Private, 1/8th Manchester Regt.
He volunteered for active service in October 1915, and seven months later proceeded to Egypt. During his eight months' service there, he took part in engagements on the Suez Canal and in the desert, and in January 1917 was transferred to the Western Front. There he was in action in different sectors, and fought at Havrincourt and Ypres, but was severely wounded in action at Nieuport. His wounds ultimately resulted in the loss of his left arm, and in consequence he was invalided out of the Army in November 1918. He holds the General Service and Victory Medals.
212, Morton Street, Longsight, Manchester.   Z1010

ADSHEAD, J., Pte., King's Own Scottish Borderers.
A month after the outbreak of war he volunteered, and in the following June proceeded to the Western Front, where he saw heavy fighting in numerous sectors, and was wounded at Loos. After three months in hospital he rejoined his unit, but was unhappily killed in the Battle of the Somme in July 1916. He was entitled to the 1914–15 Star, and the General Service and Victory Medals.
"Whilst we remember, the sacrifice is not in vain."
14, Sorrell Street, Hulme, Manchester.   Z1009B

AFFLECK, C., Private, 2nd Manchester Regiment.
He volunteered in September 1914, and in May of the following year was drafted to France. In this theatre of war he was in action at Hill 60, Ypres and Festubert, but whilst engaged in fierce fighting at Loos was unfortunately killed on February 5th, 1916. He was entitled to the 1914–15 Star, and the General Service and Victory Medals.
"He died the noblest death a man may die,
Fighting for God and right and liberty."
121, Cross Street, Bradford, Manchester.   Z9021

AGGER, H., Sapper, R.E.
He joined in February 1917, after being engaged on work of National importance, and was drafted to France. He was stationed at Calais and in the surrounding district, and during his service in the Army carried out the duties assigned to him with the greatest ability. He was demobilised in October 1919, and holds the General Service and Victory Medals.
27, Elizabeth Street, Openshaw, Manchester.   Z1011

AIMSON, F., Bombardier, R.G.A.
At the outbreak of hostilities he volunteered, and in June 1915 proceeded overseas. Whilst serving on the Western Front he was in action in numerous important engagements, and was wounded. He served at Beaumont-Hamel and on the Somme and also in the Retreat and Advance of 1918. After the war terminated he proceeded with the Army of Occupation to Germany and was stationed at Cologne and Bonn. Demobilised in January 1919, he holds the 1914–15 Star, and the General Service and Victory Medals.
11, Hampton Place, Erskine Street, Hulme, Manchester.   TZ1012

AIMSON, W., Gunner, R.F.A.
Having originally enlisted in 1900, he proceeded at the outbreak of war to France, where he took part in heavy fighting in numerous engagements. In 1915 he landed in Gallipoli and served throughout the campaign there and was then drafted back to the Western Front, where he fought in the Battles of the Somme and Ypres and also in the Allied Advance of 1918. He was discharged in March 1919, and holds the 1914 Star, and the General Service and Victory Medals.
15, Lincoln Street, Longsight, Manchester.   TZ1013

AINSWORTH, H., Pte., 2nd North Staffordshire Regt.
He was already serving in the Army when war broke out, but was retained on important work in England until March 1917. He was then sent to Afghanistan and took an active part in the campaign there, but was severely wounded in action. After receiving treatment in various hospitals, he was sent back to England, and there discharged in January 1920, He holds the General Service, Victory and India General Service Medals (with clasp, Afghanistan, N.W. Frontier 1919). 12, Alderley Street, Hulme, Manchester. Z1014

AINSWORTH, T., Private, Manchester Regiment.
Volunteering in January 1916, he embarked for France three months later and fought in the Battles of the Somme and Ypres, where in October 1917 he was badly wounded. On recovery, however, he returned to the line, but in the following August was again wounded at St. Quentin. He was demobilised in September 1919, and holds the General Service and Victory Medals.
14, John Street, Miles Platting, Manchester. Z9781

AINSWORTH, W., Private, Lancashire Fusiliers.
Already in the Army at the outbreak of war in August 1914, he was drafted to the Western Front in the following January, and took a prominent part in the Battles of Neuve Chapelle, Ypres II and Loos. He was gassed in action at La Bassée in May 1915, and in the following September was sent home and discharged, time-expired. He holds the 1914-15 Star, and the General Service and Victory Medals.
4, Heelis Street, Rochdale Road, Manchester. Z10280

AKID, A., Private, Labour Corps.
He joined in June 1916, and in February of the following year was drafted to France, where he was engaged on important duties in various sectors of the Front. He took an active part in the Battles of Ypres, Cambrai, Armentières, Havrincourt and Epéhy and many other engagements and was also stationed for a time at Rouen. Demobilised in January 1919, he holds the General Service and Victory Medals.
42, Fullford Street, Old Trafford, Manchester. Z116621

ALDCROFT, F., Private, Royal Scots Regiment and Seaforth Highlanders.
He volunteered in January 1915, and after a course of training was a year later drafted to the Western Front, where after fighting in numerous engagements, he was wounded and gassed at Meteren in September 1918. After the Armistice he proceeded with the Army of Occupation to Germany, and was stationed there until his demobilisation in May 1920. He holds the General Service and Victory Medals.
29, John Street, Rusholme, Manchester. Z1015A

ALDCROFT, H., Private, Manchester Regiment.
He joined in April 1916, and in the following month was drafted to the Western Front. There he saw heavy fighting in various sectors of the line, and was sent to hospital in August 1917, suffering from septic poisoning. He was eventually invalided to England, and was discharged from the Army in September 1918 as medically unfit for further military service. He holds the General Service and Victory Medals.
29, John Street, Rusholme, Manchester. Z1015B

ALDCROFT, J., Private, 6th Manchester Regiment.
Volunteering in November 1914, he was on completion of his training in the following year sent to the Western Front, where he fought in the Battles of Ypres, Albert, Loos, the Somme and Cambrai, and was twice wounded in action. He also served in the final engagements of the war, and remained in France until March 1919, when he was demobilised, holding the 1914-15 Star, and the General Service and Victory Medals. 32, Byron Street, Hulme, Manchester. Z1016

ALDERSON, G., Pte., K.O. (Royal Lancaster Regt.)
Volunteering in August 1914 he proceeded in the following January to France and fought in the engagement at Ploegsteert Wood. He was invalided home owing to nervous breakdown as a result of shell-shock, and after hospital treatment was discharged in July 1916. He holds the 1914-15 Star, and the General Service and Victory Medals.
102, Ronald Street, Miles Platting, Manchester. Z9403

ALDERSON, G., Private, 2nd Sherwood Foresters.
Volunteering in August 1914, he was engaged on duties of an important nature until January 1916, when crossing to France, he fought in the Battles of the Somme, Ypres, Loos, Nieuport, La Bassée and Givenchy. He was unhappily killed in action at Arras on August 28th, 1918, and was entitled to the General Service and Victory Medals.
"The path of duty was the way to glory."
19, Saville Street, Miles Platting, Manchester. Z9782

ALDERSON, W. B., Corporal, 7th King's Shropshire Light Infantry.
He joined in 1918, and later in the same year was drafted to the Western Front, where he took severe fighting in the Arras, Cambrai, Lens, Lille and Bullecourt sectors. In 1919 his health broke down and he was detained in hospital, both in France and also at Antwerp. He was demobilised in November 1919, and holds the General Service and Victory Medals. 5, Curzon Street, Gorton, Manchester. Z11458

ALDGATE, B., Private, Royal Welch Fusiliers.
He volunteered at the commencement of hostilities, and crossing to France shortly afterwards took part in the final operations of the Retreat from Mons and the Battles of the Marne and the Aisne. In October 1914, he contracted a severe illness and invalided home to hospital, was discharged as medically unfit a month later. He holds the Mons Star, and the General Service and Victory Medals.
45, Milton Street, West Gorton, Manchester. Z9783

ALDRED, J., Pte., King's (Shropshire Light Infy).
Joining in May 1918, he proceeded to France in the following October, and after taking part in the final operations, which led to the conclusion of hostilities in November of that year, was sent with the Army of Occupation to Germany. He was demobilised in August 1919, and holds the General Service and Victory Medals. 45, Sycamore Street, Newton, Manchester.

ALEXANDER, B., Sapper, R.E. Z9784A
Volunteering in September 1915, he embarked for Egypt in the following August and was engaged on important duties in connection with operations on the Suez Canal and at Agagia and Rafa. Transferred to France in November 1917, he served in the same capacity at Ypres and Passchendaele, where he was so severely gassed as to necessitate his return to England for hospital treatment. Later he was re-drafted to the Western Front, and remained there until the close of hostilities. He was demobilised in February 1919, and holds the General Service and Victory Medals.
50, Nayor Street, Oldham Road, Manchester. Z9785

ALKER, A., Lance Corporal, 3rd Manchester Regt.
Volunteering in December 1915, he was engaged on important home duties until May 1917, when crossing to France he fought at St. Quentin, Cambrai and Havrincourt Wood, where he was wounded in October 1918. Evacuated to England, he underwent hospital treatment, and was eventually demobilised in February 1919. He holds the General Service and Victory Medals.
127, Mill Street, Ancoats, Manchester. Z9786

ALLAN, G. A. (M.M.), Pte., 6th Manchester Regt.
When war broke out he volunteered for active service, and in October 1914 was drafted to the Western Front. In this theatre of war he was engaged in fierce fighting at Ypres, Loos, Vermelles and the Ancre, and was awarded the Military Medal for conspicuous bravery in a Lewis gun attack on the German trenches at Messines in July 1917. He was wounded in action. He was demobilised in February 1919, and also holds the 1914 Star, and the General Service and Victory Medals. 45, Lyme St., Chorlton-on-Medlock, Manchester. Z1017

ALLAN, J., Sapper, R.E.
He joined the Army in September 1916, and in the following February was drafted overseas. Whilst serving on the Western Front he took an active part in numerous engagements and was in action on the Ancre and at Arras, Messines, Ypres, Passchendaele, Cambrai I, the Aisne, the Marne, Amiens, Bapaume and Cambrai II. He remained in France until January 1919, when he was demobilised, holding the General Service and Victory Medals.
1, Sorrell Street, Hulme, Manchester. Z8413B

ALLAN, J., Private, 9th Manchester Regiment.
He volunteered in September 1914, and embarking for the Dardanelles a year later, fought in several engagements on the Gallipoli Peninsula. Transferred to France in May 1916, he was in action at Vimy Ridge and on the Somme, where he was severely wounded. On recovery, he was drafted to Salonika, but after a short period of service there, returned to the Western Front, and was in action until the close of hostilities. He was demobilised in February 1919, and holds the 1914-15 Star, and the General Service and Victory Medals.
13, Kertch Street, Ancoats, Manchester. Z9789

ALLATT, H., Private, 8th Manchester Regiment.
He volunteered in December 1914, and on completion of his training was engaged on special guard duties at prisoners of war camps in various places. He was not successful in [obtaining his transfer overseas but rendered valuable services until his demobilisation in January 1919.
29, Dalton Street, Collyhurst, Manchester. Z10281A

ALLATT, T. H., Private, South Wales Borderers.
He joined in October 1918, immediately on attaining military age, and on completion of a period of training was sent to the Army of Occupation in Germany four months later. He did consistently good work with his unit at Cologne and Bonn, until his demobilisation in March 1920.
29, Dalton Street, Collyhurst, Manchester. Z10281B

ALLCOCK, J., Private, Loyal N. Lancashire Regt.
Joining in June 1916, he served at Felixstowe before proceeding to Mesopotamia in March 1917. In that theatre of war he took part in many important engagements, including those at Kut-el-Amara, Baghdad and on the Tigris. After the close of hostilities he was stationed at Baghdad and engaged on important garrison duties. On his return to England he was demobilised in October 1919, and holds the General Service and Victory Medals.
34, Cuttell Street, Bradford, Manchester. Z11402

ALLCROFT, W. A., Gunner, R.F.A.
He joined in March 1918, but was not successful in procuring a transfer overseas before the cessation of hostilities, and was retained on home service until July 1919. He was then drafted to India and stationed at Lucknow, where he was employed on important garrison duties, which he performed in a very able manner. In 1920 he was still serving in the Army. 33, Hamilton Street, Hulme, Manchester. Z1018

ALLEN, A., Corporal, 102nd Labour Corps.
Joining in November 1916, he was after a period of training, four months later, drafted overseas. Whilst serving on the Western Front he was in action at Ypres and the Marne, and also performed valuable work in repairing roads in the various sectors of the war zone. In August 1919 he was demobilised, and holds the General Service and Victory Medals. 26, Butler Street, Greenheys, Manchester. Z1021B

ALLEN, C. J., Sergeant, 7th East Lancashire Regt.
He volunteered in September 1914, and in the following June crossed to France, where he took part in much heavy fighting. He was in action on the Somme, and was severely wounded at Ypres in July 1917. He was invalided home in consequence, and after lengthy treatment was discharged as medically unfit in March 1918. He holds the 1914–15 Star, and the General Service and Victory Medals. 5, Linson Street, Bradford, Manchester. Z9405

ALLEN, E., Private, 18th Manchester Regiment.
Volunteering in August 1914, he embarked for France in September, and fought in engagements at Loos, the Somme, Ypres, La Bassée and Vimy Ridge. He was unfortunately killed on May 9th, 1917, whilst saving the life of a comrade, and was entitled to the 1914 Star, and the General Service and Victory Medals.
"Greater love hath no man than this, that a man lay down his life for his friends."
3, Whittaker Street, Gordon, Manchester. Z9787

ALLEN, F., Private, 2nd Manchester Regiment.
He was serving in India at the outbreak of hostilities, and in the following November landed in France, where he fought in the Battle of La Bassée. After only one month's service on the Western Front he was unhappily killed in action at Givenchy on December 22nd, 1914. He was entitled to the 1914 Star, and the General Service and Victory Medals.
"A costly sacrifice upon the altar of freedom."
85, Norton Street, West Gorton, Manchester. Z1019B

ALLEN, F. H., Private, 1st Manchester Regiment.
Joining in May 1917, he, three months later, proceeded to the Western Front and fought in many engagements, including that at Lens, during which he was wounded. On his recovery he was drafted to Italy and took an active part in the offensive on the Piave. In August 1919 he was discharged, and holds the General Service and Victory Medals. 26, Butler Street, Greenheys, Manchester. Z1021A

ALLEN, H., Private, 12th Manchester Regt., and Driver, R.E.
He volunteered in December 1914, and after training at Bovington Camp and Winchester, was drafted overseas in July 1915. During his service in France he was in action at St. Eloi, Dickebusch, Hooge, "Sanctuary Wood," Menin Road, Ypres and Armentières. In April 1916 he was transferred to the R.E. as a driver, and served at Arras, Bailleul and Nieppe Forest in 1918. Later in the year he was stationed at Rouen and Dieppe, and was demobilised in April 1919, holding the 1914–15 Star, and the General Service and Victory Medals.
15, Franchise Street, North Ardwick, Manchester. X1022A

ALLEN, H., L/Corporal, Lancashire Fusiliers.
A Reservist, he was called up when war broke out in August 1914, and at once proceeded with the First Expeditionary Force to France, where he was engaged in fierce fighting at Mons, the Marne, the Aisne, La Bassée, Ypres and Neuve Chapelle. During the second Battle of Ypres he was gassed, and after receiving treatment at numerous hospitals was eventually invalided out of the Army in February 1917, holding the Mons Star, and the General Service and Victory Medals. 85, Norton Street, West Gorton, Manchester. Z1019A

ALLEN, H. J., Driver, R.F.A.
He was called up from the Reserve when war was declared, and at once proceeded to France with the first Expeditionary Force. He took part in the Battle of Mons, and after only one month's service was killed in action during the Retreat from Mons on September 17th, 1914. He was entitled to the Mons Star, and the General Service and Victory Medals.
"Great deeds cannot die."
33, Boundary Street, Newton, Manchester. Z9023

ALLEN, J., Private, 2/7th Manchester Regiment.
He volunteered in September 1915, and proceeding to France in March 1916, fought at Vermelles, Ploegsteert Wood, the Somme, Arras, and Cambrai. He also served throughout the Retreat and Allied Advance of 1918, and was demobilised on his return to England in January of the following year. He holds the General Service and Victory Medals. 57, Milton Street, West Gorton, Manchester. Z9788

ALLEN, J., Driver, M.G.C.
He volunteered in November 1915, and after training at Grantham and Clipstone, was fourteen months later drafted to Salonika. In this theatre of war he served for over two years, and during that time was engaged in fierce fighting in operations on the Doiran and the Vardar fronts. Whilst in the East he suffered from malaria, and returned to England in April 1919, when he was demobilised, holding the General Service and Victory Medals. 40, Somerset Place, Colleyhurst, Manchester. Z9022

ALLEN, J. H., Private, 2/8th Manchester Regiment.
Volunteering in October 1914, he embarked for the Western Front in the following August and fought in the Battles of Albert, the Somme, and Beaumont-Hamel. Transferred to Egypt in January 1917, he later served in the Advance across Palestine, during which he took part in the Battles of Gaza, and the Capture of Jerusalem, Jericho, and Aleppo. Returning home, he was demobilised in March 1919, and holds the 1914–15 Star, and the General Service and Victory Medals. 7, Rennie Street, West Gorton, Manchester. Z9790

ALLEN, J. W., Private, 8th Manchester Regiment.
When war was declared he was called up from the Reserve, and in February 1915 proceeded to Gallipoli, where he took part in the Landing and in the three Battles of Krithia. He fell fighting at Achi Baba on June 21st, 1915, and was entitled to the 1914–15 Star, and the General Service and Victory Medals. "Nobly striving,
He nobly fell that we might live."
28, Neptune Street, Ancoats, Manchester. Z6033A

ALLEN, M., Private, King's Own Scottish Borderers.
He volunteered in October 1914, and in the following year after completing his training was drafted to the Dardanelles in the "Royal Edward." He unfortunately lost his life when this vessel was sunk by a German submarine on August 14th, 1915, and was entitled to the 1914–15 Star, and the General Service and Victory Medals.
"Thinking that remembrance, though unspoken, may reach him where he sleeps."
14, Roe Street, Ancoats, Manchester. Z9404

ALLEN, R., Cpl., 6th Dragoon Guards (Carabiniers).
He volunteered in September 1914, and in June of the following year sailed for France. Whilst there he saw much fighting, and was in action at Armentières, Ypres, and many other engagements. He was invalided home and discharged through ill-health due to his service in November 1918. He holds the 1914–15 Star, and the General Service and Victory Medals. 16, Holbeck Street, Oldham Road, Manchester. Z9406

ALLEN, W., Corporal, 7th Manchester Regiment.
Volunteering in August 1914, he proceeded to Egypt in February of the following year, and was thence transferred to Gallipoli in April 1915. There he saw much severe fighting until wounded in action, and invalided to hospital in England. After his recovery he was retained on important duties at various stations at home, until demobilised in January 1919, and holds the 1914–15 Star, and the General Service and Victory Medals. 4, Bright Street, Hulme, Manchester. Z11622

ALLERTON, B., L/Cpl., 2nd East Lancashire Regt.
He volunteered in September 1914, and on completion of his training was eight months later sent to the Western Front. There he saw service in the Battles of Loos, St. Eloi, Vimy Ridge, the Somme, Arras, Messines, and Lens, and was unhappily killed in action in April 1918. He was entitled to the 1914–15 Star, and the General Service and Victory Medals.
"And doubtless he went in splendid company."
16, Silk Street, Hulme, Manchester. Z9024

ALLISON, J., Private, 18th Manchester Regiment.
Volunteering in August 1914, he was after a course of training, six months later drafted to the Western Front. There he was in action during important engagements at Neuve Chapelle, Hill 60, and Loos, and fell fighting at St. Eloi in May 1916. He was entitled to the 1914–15 Star, and the General Service and Victory Medals.
"He died the noblest death a man may die,
Fighting for God and right and liberty."
77, Cawder Street, Hulme, Manchester. Z1023

ALLITT, C. F., Pte., K.O. (Royal Lancaster Regt.)
He volunteered in February 1915, and in the following April proceeded overseas. After only one month's service on the Western Front he was wounded and gassed, whilst fighting at Hill 60, and was invalided to England. He, in consequence, received his discharge from the Army in December 1917, being no longer fit for further military duties, and holds the 1914–15 Star, and the General Service and Victory Medals. 22, Henry Street, West Gorton, Manchester. Z1024

ALLMAN, G., Pte., Loyal North Lancashire Regt.
Volunteering in August 1914, he was in the following year drafted to Gallipoli, and after taking part in the campaign there, was sent to Salonika. On this front he saw heavy fighting in numerous important engagements, including those in the Dorian, Vardar, and Struma sectors. He was later transferred to Egypt, and served there until July 1918. In 1920 he was still serving in the Army, and holds the 1914–15 Star, and the General Service and Victory Medals.
18, Spurgeon Street, West Gorton, Manchester. Z9025

ALLMARK, F., Gunner, R.F.A.
Being already in the Army when war broke out he was at once sent to France, and took an active part in the Battles of Mons, the Marne, the Aisne, Ypres, Neuve Chapelle, and Loos. In March 1916 he was discharged as a time-expired man, and holds the Mons Star, and the General Service and Victory Medals. From April 1916 until the close of hostilities he rendered valuable services at Messrs. Galloway's, and was engaged on the important work of making shells.
41, Marsland Street, Ardwick, Manchester. Z1025

ALLTREE, J. E., Sapper, R.E.
On the outbreak of hostilities he was mobilised, and proceeded at once with the first Expeditionary Force to France. There he experienced fierce fighting in the Battles of Mons, Le Cateau, the Marne, the Aisne, Ypres, Neuve Chapelle, St. Eloi, Hill 60, Ypres II, Festubert, and Loos, and whilst in action on the Somme, he was severely wounded. Crippled for life by his injuries he was discharged from the Army in July 1919, and holds the Mons Star, and the General Service and Victory Medals.
15, Dale Street, Stockport Road, Manchester. X1026C

ALLWOOD, C., Private, 4th Manchester Regiment.
He volunteered in February 1915, and a year later embarked for Egypt, where he took part in the defence of the Suez Canal, subsequently participating in the Advance across Palestine. Later he saw service in Salonika, and was in action on the Doiran, Struma, and Vardar fronts. He was demobilised in December 1918 after his return home, and holds the General Service and Victory Medals.
Montague Street, Collyhurst, Manchester. Z9792

ALMOND, J., Corporal, R.M.L.I.
He was already serving when war broke out, and in 1915 proceeded in H.M.S. "Majestic" to the Dardanelles, where he was in action until the Evacuation. He was then posted to "M27," and in this vessel was engaged in bombarding the German lines on the Belgian Coast. He also rendered valuable services on patrol work in the North Sea, and in 1920 was still serving. He holds the 1914 Star, and the General Service and Victory Medals.
45, Ashover Street, Ardwick, Manchester. Z1028

ALMOND, W., Pioneer, R.E.
He volunteered in March 1915, and the following month proceeded to Gallipoli, where he was in action at Krithia and Suvla Bay, and took part in heavy fighting until the Evacuation. He was then transferred to the Egyptian Front, where he did good work in engagements on the Suez Canal, and at Agagia, Sollum, Katia, El Fasher, and Romani. Later he was sent to France, fought in the Battles of Arras, Ypres III, and the Marne II, and in the Advance of 1918 was wounded. He was demobilised in February 1919, and holds the 1914–15 Star, and the General Service and Victory Medals.
12, Edlin Street, Morton Street, Longsight, Manchester. Z1027

ALTY, D., Private, South Wales Borderers.
He joined in March 1916, but was not successful in procuring a transfer overseas before hostilities ceased. He was engaged on important duties in England, until the Armistice, and then he proceeded to Germany, where he was employed on responsible guard duties. Later he was transferred to Ireland, and was eventually demobilised in April 1920.
19, Hughes Street, Ardwick, Manchester. Z1029

AMBROSE, J., Private, 77th Labour Corps.
Volunteering in February 1916, he proceeded to France in the same month, and attached to the Royal Engineers was engaged on important railway duties at Cambrai, La Bassée, Arras, Vimy Ridge, Hill 60, and Festubert. In June 1918, he was gassed, but after receiving treatment returned to the line and served until the close of hostilities. He was demobilised in February 1919, and holds the General Service and Victory Medals.
20, Wilkinson Street, Collyhurst, Manchester. Z9793

AMBROSE, M. J., 1st Air Mechanic, R.A.F.
He joined in August 1916, and after his training was engaged on important duties as a fitter and gun-mounter at various stations. He was not successful in obtaining his transfer to a theatre of war before the termination of hostilities, but nevertheless did valuable work until demobilised in February 1919. 19, Rigel Street, Ancoats, Manchester. Z9794

ANCOATS, C., Private, 2nd King's Liverpool Regt.
He volunteered in November 1914, and was retained in England on duties of an important nature until March 1916. He then proceeded to Egypt and did excellent work at Suez, Sollum, Katia, and Romani. Afterwards in Salonika he saw severe fighting on the Struma and Vardar fronts, and suffered much from malaria. After his return to England he was demobilised in March 1919, and holds the General Service and Victory Medals. 2, Law Street, Rochdale Road Manchester. Z9407

ANDERSON, C., Private, Royal Scots.
He volunteered in August 1914, and on completion of his training was engaged on important duties with his unit in Scotland and England. Owing to his being medically unfit he was unsuccessful in obtaining a transfer overseas, but rendered valuable services until his demobilisation in January 1919. 9, Frederick Place, Rochdale Road, Manchester. Z11867A

ANDERSON, E., A.B., R.N., H.M.S. "Lord Nelson."
He volunteered in October 1914, and after a course of training was posted to H.M.S. "Lord Nelson," in which vessel he was engaged on patrol duty in the North Sea for two years. He then proceeded to the Ægean Sea, and rendered valuable services on convoy and patrol work until the termination of the war. In 1920 he was still serving in the Navy, and holds the 1914–15 Star, and the General Service and Victory Medals. 2, Rumford Place, Chorlton-on-Medlock, Manchester. X1030

ANDERSON, G. A., Pte., 12th Lancashire Fusiliers.
In May 1916 he joined the Army, and later in the same year proceeded to Salonika. In this theatre of war he served for nearly two years and during that time was in action at Monastir, and in the Advance on the Doiran front. In August 1918 he was sent to France, and there took an active part in fighting at Havrincourt, Epéhy, Cambrai, and Ypres, and was present at the entry into Mons. Demobilised in March 1919, he holds the General Service and Victory Medals. 5, Peter Street, Ardwick, Manchester. Z1034

ANDERSON, J., Gunner, R.F.A.
He volunteered in August 1914, and in the following May proceeded to Gallipoli. There he was in action at Anzac Cove, and Walker's Ridge, and was then invalided home with enteric. On his recovery he was sent to France in July 1916, and saw heavy fighting in the Béthune and Armentières sectors until 1917, when he was transferred to the Italian Front, where he fought in numerous engagements, and took part in the Piave Offensive. In February 1918 he returned to the Western Front, and was present in the final Allied Advance. Demobilised in February 1919, he holds the 1914–15 Star, and the General Service and Victory Medals. 3, Picking Street, Hulme, Manchester. Z1036

ANDERSON, J., Private, 8th Manchester Regt. and Sapper, R.E.
He joined the Manchester Regiment in May 1917, and served with this unit in numerous engagements on the Western Front until March 1918, when he was transferred to the Royal Engineers. He then took part in heavy fighting in the final Retreat and Advance, and after the Armistice entered into Germany with the Army of Occupation. He was demobilised in February 1919, and holds the General Service and Victory Medals. 2, Rosamond Place, Chorlton-on-Medlock, Manchester. Z1035A

ANDERSON, J., Pte., Loyal North Lancashire Regt.
He was already serving when war broke out, and immediately proceeded to France, where he fought in the Battles of Mons, the Marne, the Aisne, La Bassée, Ypres, Neuve Chapelle, Festubert, Albert, the Somme, Arras, Ypres III, and Cambrai, and was also in action in the Retreat and Advance of 1918. He was wounded on two occasions, and was discharged in February 1920, holding the Mons Star, and the General Service and Victory Medals. 31, Gregory Street, West Gorton, Manchester. Z1032

ANDERSON, J. T., Private, Lancashire Fusiliers.
Joining in May 1916, he was on completion of his training at Colchester drafted overseas in February 1917. Whilst serving in France he took an active part in engagements in the La Bassée, Givenchy, Ypres, Passchendaele, and Cambrai sectors, but was wounded and taken prisoner during the Battle of the Somme in March 1918. He was kept in captivity at Crossen, and employed in the coal mines. On his release in December 1918, he returned to England, and was demobilised, holding the General Service and Victory Medals. 68, Norton Street, West Gorton, Manchester. Z1033

ANDERSON, P., Corporal, 23rd Manchester Regt.
Volunteering in December 1914, he was engaged on important home duties until January 1916, when crossing to France, he fought at Armentières, and the Somme, where he was severely wounded. On recovery, he rejoined his unit, and was in action until the close of hostilities. He was demobilised in January 1919, and holds the General Service and Victory Medals. 115, Mills Street, Ancoats, Manchester. Z9795

ANDERSON, T., Private, 2nd Manchester Regiment.
Mobilised at the declaration of war, he crossed to France in September 1914, and a month later was severely wounded at La Bassée. Evacuated to England for hospital treatment, he was invalided out of the Service in November of the succeeding year, and holds the 1914 Star, and the General Service and Victory Medals. 29, Wrigley Street, West Gorton, Manchester. Z9796

ANDERSON, W., Private, 10th Border Regiment.

Volunteering at the outbreak of war, he proceeded to France early in 1915, and subsequently fought in engagements at Arras, Peronne, and the Somme, where in July 1916, he was wounded. He was under treatment at a Base hospital until the following May, when he was evacuated to England, and in January 1918, was discharged as medically unfit. He holds the 1914-15 Star, and the General Service and Victory Medals
57, Lime Street, Miles Platting, Manchester.   Z9797

ANDERTON, A., L/Cpl., 1st King's (Liverpool Regt.).

He volunteered in September 1914, and proceeding to France in the following May, played a prominent part in the Battles of Loos, the Somme, Ypres (III), and Cambrai, where he was unhappily killed in action on November 30th, 1917. He was entitled to the 1914-15 Star, and the General Service and Victory Medals.
"He died the noblest death a man may die,
Fighting for God and right and liberty."
18, Higham Street, Oldham Road, Manchester.   Z11868B

ANDERTON, G., Private, 1st Manchester Regiment.

Volunteering in November 1914, he was drafted to the Dardanelles in the following year, and took part in much severe fighting on the Gallipoli Peninsula. He laid down his life for King and Country on January 8th, 1916, during the Evacuation, and was entitled to the 1914-15 Star, and the General Service and Victory Medals.
"His memory is cherished with pride."
18, Higham Street, Oldham Road, Manchester.   Z11868A

ANDERTON, J. E., Private, 2nd Border Regiment.

He volunteered in October 1914, and seven months later was drafted to Egypt, where he was stationed at Khartoum until August 1915. He then proceeded to Gallipoli, and was present at the Landing at Suvla Bay, but being wounded in action there, was invalided to England. In January 1916 he proceeded to France, and in this theatre of war took part in the Battle of the Somme, but unfortunately fell fighting at Albert on July 1st, 1916. He was entitled to the 1914-15 Star, and the General Service and Victory Medals.
"His life for his Country, his soul to God."
27, Fenn Street, Hulme, Manchester.   Z1037

ANDERTON, T., Sergt., 12th Manchester Regiment.

Volunteering in September 1914, he proceeded to France in the following March, and served there for three years. During that time he was in action in numerous engagements, including the Battles of Ypres, Loos, Albert, Vimy Ridge, the Somme, Arras, and Ypres III. In May 1918 he was transferred to Italy, and served with distinction on the Piave front. He was demobilised in February 1919, and holds the 1914-15 Star, and the General Service and Victory Medals.
22, Dearden Street, Hulme, Manchester.   TZ1038

ANDREW, C. A., Private, Royal Fusiliers.

In April 1915 he volunteered for active service, and six months later was sent to the Western Front. There he was engaged in fierce fighting in the Loos, Vimy Ridge, Somme, Beaucourt, Arras, and Bullecourt sectors, and was wounded in the Battle of Ypres. He was invalided to England, and in August 1917 was discharged from the Army as medically unfit for further service, holding the 1914-15 Star, and the General Service and Victory Medals.
2, Ridley Grove, Greenheys, Manchester.   Z1041

ANDREW, C. H., Q.M.S., 7th Manchester Regiment.

At the outbreak of war, he volunteered, and a month later proceeded to Egypt, where he saw service on the Suez Canal, and in the desert. He then went to Gallipoli, and was in action at Krithia I, II and III, and Suvla Bay. He was sent back to England with dysentery, but on his recovery was drafted to the Western Front, where he took a conspicuous part in operations in the Somme, Arras, Ypres, Marne, Cambrai, and Le Cateau sectors. Demobilised in February 1919, he holds the 1914-15 Star, and the General Service and Victory Medals.
41, Cottenham Street, Chorlton-on-Medlock, Manchester.   Z1040

ANDREW, J., Private, Manchester Regiment.

Mobilised from the Army Reserve on the declaration of war, he was drafted to France in September 1914, and was almost immediately in action with his Battalion. He was wounded in the Battle of Ypres on November 11th, 1914, and on recovery fought at Albert, Messines, Cambrai, and in several other engagements until the termination of hostilities. Demobilised in January 1919, he holds the 1914 Star, and the General Service and Victory Medals.
24, Holland Street, Newton, Manchester.   Z9799

ANDREW, T., Sergt., R.A.F. and 6th Manchester Regt.

He joined in May 1916, and being drafted on completion of his training to France in the following September, served with the Royal Air Force at Arras. After only a month on the Western Front he was sent back to England, and was employed on testing aircraft, which responsible work he carried out with the greatest skill and ability. He was demobilised in March 1919, and holds the General Service and Victory Medals.
64, Upper Duke Street, Hulme, Manchester.   Z1039

ANDREWS, G. P., Private, Border Regiment.

He volunteered in January 1916, and seven months later proceeded to the Western Front, where he fought in the Battle of Messines. During his service in France he was chiefly employed on pioneer and trench repairing work, and in February 1918 was sent to hospital at Rouen, suffering from fever. On his recovery he was placed in charge of the camp theatre for the six months prior to his demobilisation in September 1919. He holds the General Service and Victory Medals.
40, Exeter Street, Ardwick, Manchester.   Z1043

ANDREWS, J. H., Private, Manchester Regiment.

Volunteering in October 1915, he was unsuccessful in procuring a transfer overseas, and was retained on home service throughout the period of hostilities. He was stationed at Heaton Park and Whitchurch until August 1916, when he was sent to a munition works at Bradford, where he was employed on important work, and rendered most valuable services to the Country. He was demobilised in January 1919.
111, Devon Street, Ardwick, Manchester.   Z1044

ANDREWS, H., Sergeant, Royal Welch Fusiliers.

Volunteering in May 1915, he was sent overseas in the following year, and saw active service on the Western Front. He was in action in the Battles of the Somme and Arras, and in the third Battle of Ypres was severely wounded on July 31st, 1917. Sent home owing to his injuries, he was admitted to Stepping Hill War Hospital, Stockport, where he died on December 9th, 1917. He was entitled to the General Service and Victory Medals.
"Courage, bright hopes, and a myriad dreams, splendidly given."
22, Adelaide Street, Bradford, Manchester.   Z9798

ANDREWS, M., Private, Royal Welch Fusiliers.

Joining in June 1917, he completed his training and was sent in the same year to Gibraltar. There he was engaged on garrison, guard, and patrol duties, and rendered valuable services for over two years. Returning home for demobilisation in November 1919, he holds the General Service Medal.
174, Cobden Street, Ancoats, Manchester.   Z9800

ANDREWS, T. W., Gunner, R.F.A.

In August 1914 he volunteered, but was retained on important work in England until January 1916, when he was sent overseas. During his service in France he did good work with his Battery in engagements at Loos, Albert, the Somme, Arras and Vimy Ridge, but was unfortunately killed in action at Ypres on July 5th, 1917. He was entitled to the General Service and Victory Medals.
"The path of duty was the way to glory."
55, Hinckley Street, Bradford, Manchester.   Z1042

ANGOLD, H. W., Private, 2nd Manchester Regt.

He was already serving in the Army at the outbreak of hostilities, and accordingly proceeded in August 1914 with the first Expeditionary Force to the Western Front. There he took an active part in heavy fighting at Mons, but received a severe wound at Le Cateau, which resulted in the loss of his left leg. He was sent back to England and subsequently invalided out of the Army in December 1915, holding the Mons Star, and the General Service and Victory Medals.
15, Cawdor Street, Hulme, Manchester.   TZ1045

ANGUS, A., Private, Tank Corps.

He joined in October 1916, and on completion of his training was seven months later drafted to France, where he rendered valuable services in the workshops. Later he was in action at Ypres, Passchendaele, Arras, Albert, and the Somme, and also in the final decisive engagements of the war. After the Armistice he proceeded with the Army of Occupation to Germany, where he served until demobilised in September 1919. He holds the General Service and Victory Medals.
43, Granville Street, Chorlton-on-Medlock, Manchester.   Z1046

ANKERS, T., Rifleman, 3rd Rifle Brigade.

Volunteering in September 1914 he was in the following January drafted to the Western Front, where he served for four years. During that time he was in action in the Battles of Neuve Chapelle, Hill 60, Ypres, Festubert, Loos, Albert, the Somme, Arras, Bullecourt, Messines, Ypres III, and Cambrai, and was also engaged in heavy fighting in the final Retreat and Advance. Demobilised in February 1919, he holds the 1914-15 Star, and the General Service and Victory Medals.
84, Henry Street, West Gorton, Manchester.   Z1049

ANKERS, W., Lance Corporal, R.E.

He joined in April 1916, and completed two years' training and service before being drafted to the Western Front. He played an important part in several engagements during the Retreat and Advance of 1918, notably those at Amiens, the Somme, Bapaume, Havrincourt, Cambrai, and Le Cateau. He was demobilised in February 1919, but unhappily died of pneumonia on the 18th of the same month. He was entitled to the General Service and Victory Medals.
"Great deeds cannot die."
85, Henry Street, West Gorton, Manchester.   Z1050

ANKERS, W., Sapper, R.E.

Volunteering in November 1914, he proceeded to the Dardanelles in the following June, and saw much fighting, notably at Cape Helles. Early in 1916 he was sent to the Western Front, and there was engaged chiefly on constructional work in the Ypres salient. After rendering valuable services he was demobilised in January 1919, and holds the 1914-15 Star, and the General Service and Victory Medals.
39, Randolph Street, Ardwick, Manchester. Z1048

ANKERS, W. R., Private, 2/7th Manchester Regt.

Six months after volunteering in September 1915, he was drafted to the Western Front. In that theatre of war he was in action at St. Eloi, Albert, Vimy Ridge, Arras, Messines, Ypres, the Somme, Havrincourt, Cambrai, and Le Cateau, but was in hospital for a short time as the result of an accident. He was eventually demobilised in January 1919, and holds the General Service and Victory Medals.
6, Milton Square, Lingard Street, Hulme, Manchester. Z1047

ANNABLE, R., Corporal, 25th Manchester Regt.

Volunteering in November 1915, he was drafted to the Western Front ten months later and was there in action at Arras and Bullecourt. Having been severely wounded in August 1917 during the third Battle of Ypres, he was invalided to England, and after hospital treatment, was retained at home until February 1919, when he was demobilised. He holds the General Service and Victory Medals.
90, Henry Street, West Gorton, Manchester. Z1051

ANNABLE, T. H., Corporal, R.A.M.C.

Having volunteered in March 1915, he was sent to the Western Front in February 1917, and was employed as a stretcher-bearer in the Field. He served in the La Bassée, Givenchy, Festubert, Béthune, Ypres, Passchendaele, Cambrai, and Lens sectors, but was gassed in September 1918, and invalided home. After hospital treatment he was discharged in December 1918, and holds the General Service and Victory Medals.
2, Dennison Street, Rusholme, Manchester. TZ1052

ANNIS, J., Sergeant, Lancashire Fusiliers,

Mobilised in August 1914, he was at once drafted to France, where he served with distinction at Mons, and in the Battles of the Marne, and the Aisne. In January 1915 he was sent home for special duties at Hull, and rendered valuable services there until March 1918. He was then again drafted to the Western Front, but was unhappily killed in action in the following month during the Retreat. He was entitled to the Mons Star, and the General Service and Victory Medals.
"Nobly striving, he nobly fell that we might live."
2, Seal Street, Collyhurst, Manchester. Z10282

ANNISON, J., Corporal. R.A.M.C.

Volunteering in August 1915, he was engaged after a period of training at various hospitals on important duties as orderly. He was not able to obtain a transfer overseas before hostilities ended, but rendered very valuable services until demobilised in February 1919.
8, Linson Street, Bradford, Manchester. Z9408

ANNISON, J. T., Private, Royal Fusiliers.

He joined in 1916, and crossing to the Western Front in the following year, fought at Arras, Armentiéres, Bourlon Wood, and Cambrai. He was then sent to Italy, but after a short period of service, he returned to France in 1918, in time to take part in the Retreat and Advance of that year. On the termination of hostilities he proceeded into Germany with the Army of Occupation. He returned home for demobilisation in 1919, and holds the General Service and Victory Medals.
17, Pierce Street, Ancoats, Manchester. Z9801A

ANNISON, W., Private, R.A.S.C.

Joining in 1916, he completed his training and was engaged on important transport duties with his unit at various depôts. He was unable to secure his transfer to a theatre of war before hostilities ceased, but was sent to Ireland, where he rendered valuable services. He was demobilised in 1919.
17, Pierce Street, Ancoats, Manchester. Z9801B

ANSLOW, J., Private, R.A.S.C.

He joined the Royal Army Veterinary Corps in May 1917, and in October was sent to France, where he served at Le Havre, and Calais. Transferred to the Royal Warwickshire Regiment, he was stationed at Wittes and Guizancourt, but rejoined the Royal Army Veterinary Corps. He was later sent to the Royal Army Service Corps, with which unit he remained until his return home in January 1919. He was demobilised in the following November, and holds the General Service and Victory Medals. 7, Riall Street, Hulme, Manchester. Z1053

ANTHONY, W. C. G., Private, 4th North Staffordshire Regiment.

He volunteered in December 1915, and on completing a period of training in June of the following year, was drafted to the Western Front. There he saw severe fighting in various sectors, took part in the Battles of the Somme, Arras, Ypres, and Cambrai, and many other important engagements, and was wounded in action at Amiens in August 1918. He was finally demobilised in January 1920, and holds the General Service and Victory Medals.
31, Heald Avenue, Rusholme, Manchester. Z11624

ANTLEY, R., Private, 4th Manchester Regiment.

Volunteering in December 1914, he was sent to France in the following April and served there for nearly four years. During that period he took part in the Battles of Ypres, Loos, Albert, the Somme and Beaucourt, but was wounded at Arras. He remained in hospital until February 1919, where he was demobilised, holding the 1914-15 Star, and the General Service and Victory Medals.
17, Dougall Street, Hulme, Manchester. Z1054

ANTLEY, R., Private, Manchester Regiment.

Volunteering in August 1914, he was drafted overseas a year later and served in France until the end of the war. During this period he took part in many important engagements, including those on the Somme, at Arras, Ypres, and Cambrai, and in the Retreat and Advance of 1918, and was wounded three times. He holds the 1914-15 Star, and the General Service and Victory Medals, and was demobilised in January, 1919. 17, Dougall Street, Hulme, Manchester. Z9802

APPLEBY, G., Corporal, R.F.A.

He volunteered in August 1914, and in the following month proceeded to the Western Front, where he was in action in numerous important engagements. Whilst taking part in the Battle of the Somme he was severely wounded in July 1916, and was invalided home. Discharged owing to wounds in February 1917, he holds the 1914 Star, and the General Service and Victory Medals.
51, Princess Street, Rusholme, Manchester. Z1055

APPLETON, E., Driver, R.F.A.

He volunteered at the outbreak of war, and a year later was sent to France, where he served for nearly four years. During that period he fought at Loos, St. Eloi, Albert, Vimy Ridge, the Somme I (where he was wounded in October 1916), Ypres III, Cambrai I, the Somme II, Cambrai II and Ypres IV, and remained in France until his demobilisation in April 1919. He holds the 1914-15 Star, and the General Service and Victory Medals.
16, Riga Street, City Road, Hulme, Manchester. Z1056

APPLETON, T., Pte., 10th King's (Liverpool Regt.), (Liverpool Scottish).

He joined in 1918, and landing on the Western Front in the same year saw heavy fighting in the final stages of the German Offensive and the subsequent Allied Advance. Returning to England for demobilisation in March 1919, he rejoined the Colours two months later, and returning to France was engaged on special duties at Dunkirk. He was discharged on account of service in February 1920, and holds the General Service and Victory Medals.
9, Heaton Street, Ardwick, Manchester. Z9803A

APPLETON, W. J., Private, M.G.C.

He was mobilised when war broke out, and embarking for France in 1915, fought in the Battles of Ypres, Loos, St. Eloi, the Somme, and was wounded. Rejoining his unit on recovery he was in action in several engagements until taken prisoner in 1917. He was repatriated from Germany in 1919, and in the same year proceeded to Russia with the British Military Mission with which he served at Archangel for six months. Demobilised on his return to England in May 1920, he holds the 1914-15 Star, and the General Service and Victory Medals.
9, Heaton Street, Ardwick, Manchester. Z9803B

APPLIN, W., Private, Monmouthshire Regiment.

Volunteering in February 1915, he completed his training and was sent to Ireland. Transferred to the Royal Defence Corps in 1916, he was employed on garrison duty and rendered valuable services until, returning home, he was demobilised from Heaton Park in February 1919.
32, Downs Street, Openshaw, Manchester. Z1057

ARCHER, A. G., Private, Welch Regiment.

Volunteering in November 1914, he was sent to France in the following April and fought in the Battles of Hill 60, Ypres, Festubert and Loos, where he was severely wounded. He was in hospital at first in Rouen and later in Manchester and owing to his injuries was eventually discharged in December 1915. He holds the 1914-15 Star, and the General Service and Victory Medals.
4, Edlin Street, Morton Street, West Gorton, Manchester. Z1058

ARCHER, J., Private, Lancashire Fusiliers.

He joined in June 1917, and in the following year was drafted to the Western Front, where he rendered valuable services with his unit on the Somme and at Beaucourt, Givenchy and Epinoy. He was in hospital for a time at Tréport, and was demobilised in April 1919, holding the General Service and Victory Medals. 70, Parker St., Bradford, Manchester. Z11866

ARCHER, T., Private, Manchester Regiment and York and Lancaster Regiment.

He volunteered in February 1915, but was retained on home service until November 1916, when he was drafted to the Western Front. There he was in action on the Somme and the Ancre and at Beaucourt, and was wounded in the Battle of Arras, unfortunately succumbing to his injuries on March 21st, 1917. He was entitled to the General Service and Victory Medals. "His life for his Country."
14, Bednal Street, Miles Platting, Manchester. Z11459

ARDRON, F., Private, 9th Border Regiment.
He volunteered in July 1915, and eight months later proceeded to Egypt, where he saw much severe fighting. After taking part in engagements at Sollum, Katia, El Fasher, Romani, Magdhaba and Rafa, he was sent into Palestine, and there took part in the Battles of Gaza and Aleppo and the capture of Jerusalem, Jericho and Tripoli. Returning home in December 1918, he was demobilised in the following February and holds the General Service and Victory Medals.
14, Russell Street, Moss Side, Manchester. Z11625A

ARDRON, R., Private, 9th Border Regiment.
He joined in September 1917, and in January of the following year was drafted to Salonika, where he saw much severe fighting. He took part in many important engagements on the Doiran and Vardar fronts and also suffered from dysentery and malaria whilst overseas. He returned home in July 1919, and two months later was demobilised. holding the General Service and Victory Medals.
14, Russell Street, Moss Side, Manchester. Z11625B

ARDRON, W., Gunner, R.G.A.
He joined in December 1916, and after completing his training served at various stations, where he was engaged on important clerical duties in the pay office. He was not successful in obtaining his transfer to a theatre of war, but, nevertheless, rendered valuable services with his Battery until November 1919, when he was demobilised.
14, Russell Street, Moss Side, Manchester. Z11626

ARKWRIGHT, H., Private, 8th Manchester Regt.
Volunteering in January 1915, he completed his training and was retained on important duties with his unit at various stations. Though unable to obtain his transfer overseas, he did valuable work and was demobilised in July 1919.
30, Napier Street, Ardwick, Manchester. Z1059

ARKWRIGHT, W., Private, 3rd Manchester Regt.
He volunteered in September.1914, and proceeding to France two months later, served in various parts of the line until sent to Gallipoli in August 1915. After taking part in the Landing at Suvla Bay he was engaged in various operations on the Peninsula, and was wounded in the following November and sent to hospital. On recovery he returned to the Western Front in July 1916, and fought in the Battles of the Somme, Arras, Bullecourt, Messines, Ypres and Cambrai. Sent home owing to illness he received medical treatment, and was invalided out of the Service in September 1918. He holds the 1914 Star, and the General Service and Victory Medals.
7, Jersey Street Dwellings, Ancoats, Manchester. Z9805

ARMIN, C., Private, 2nd Manchester Regiment.
He volunteered in January 1915, and in the following October proceeded to the Salonika Front, where he served in the Vardar and Doiran engagements and the advance across the Struma, and was wounded. Sent to France in August 1916, he fought on the Ancre, at Arras, Messines, Lens, Cambrai, Bapaume and the Scarpe. He was demobilised in May 1919, and holds the 1914-15 Star, and the General Service and Victory Medals.
29, Prescott Street, West Gorton, Manchester. Z1061

ARMIN, J. C., Private, 12th Manchester Regiment.
Having enlisted in January 1914, he proceeded to France in September and took a prominent part in numerous engagements, including the Battles of La Bassée, Ypres, Hill 60, Loos, the Somme, Arras, Cambrai, Amiens and the Selle. He was severely wounded at Loos, and was invalided home, but, recovering, returned to France and fought on until the end of the war. He was discharged in May 1919, and holds the 1914 Star, and the General Service and Victory Medals.
14, Wigley Street, Ardwick, Manchester. Z1060

ARMITAGE, D., Private, East Lancashire Regt.
In August 1914 he volunteered and thirteen months later proceeded to the Western Front, and was in action at Vermelles and Albert. He was wounded at Vimy Ridge in 1916, and on his recovery saw heavy fighting on the Somme and at Bullecourt and Ypres. In April 1917 he was drafted to Salonika and played an active part in engagements on the Doiran and the Vardar fronts. Returning to England in March 1919, he was demobilised, and holds the 1914-15 Star, and the General Service and Victory Medals.
18, Newman Street, Ancoats, Manchester. Z9026

ARMITAGE, F., L/Cpl., 9th South Lancashire Regt.
He volunteered in September 1914, and in the following December was drafted overseas. After three months' service on the Western Front he was sent to Salonika, where he was in action in the Doiran, Struma, Monastir and Vardar sectors. He was wounded whilst fighting on the Doiran front in November 1917, and was sent to the Canadian Hospital. He returned to England in April 1919, and was then demobilised, holding the 1914 Star, and the General Service and Victory Medals.
29, Churchill Street, Openshaw, Manchester. TZ9027

ARMITAGE, R. E., Gunner, R.F.A.
He volunteered in August 1914, and after a period of training proceeded to Egypt. There he took part in severe fighting on the Suez Canal, and later transferred to the Dardanelles, participated in the Landing at Suvla Bay. Returning to Egypt, he was in action at Mersa-Matruh, Agagia, and Sollum,

and was then sent to France, where he took part in further fighting, was gassed at Vimy Ridge, and was subsequently wounded on the Somme in 1918. After spending some time in hospital in France, he was sent home and eventually demobilised in September 1919, holding the 1914-15 Star, and the General Service and Victory Medals.
78, George Street, Hulme, Manchester. Z1062

ARMITAGE, T., Private, 11th Lancashire Fusiliers.
Volunteering in August 1914, he embarked for the Western Front in July 1915, and was engaged in heavy fighting on the Somme. He gave his life for King and Country on April 25th, 1916, and was entitled to the 1914-15 Star, and the General Service and Victory Medals.
"Nobly striving,
He nobly fell that we might live."
69, Branson Street, Ancoats, Manchester. Z9806

ARMSDEN, R., Private, Bedfordshire Regiment.
Mobilised at the outbreak of hostilities in August 1914, he was for some time engaged on important duties in connection with the training of recruits. Subsequently he was sent to Ireland and was stationed at the Curragh. He was not successful in obtaining a transfer to a theatre of war, but, nevertheless, rendered valuable services until he was discharged in February 1919.
68, Ruskin Avenue, Moss Side, Manchester. Z1069

ARMSTON, W. E., Pte., 10th Royal Warwickshire Regiment.
He volunteered in July 1915, and was employed on special duties on patrol boats and transports between Southampton, Boulogne and Havre, until March 1917, when he was drafted to the Western Front. During six months' service in this theatre of war, he took part in the Battles of Arras, Ypres, and Cambrai, where he was severely wounded in November 1917. As a result he was evacuated to England, and after spending a considerable time in hospitals and undergoing several operations, he was eventually discharged in May 1919. He holds the 1914-15 Star, and the General Service and Victory Medals.
9, Walnut Street, Hulme, Manchester. TZ1063

ARMSTRONG, G., Sergt.-Major, R.F.A.
Enlisting in 1903, he was stationed in India, when war broke out and sailed for France in October 1914. He took an active part in the Battles of La Bassée, Neuve Chapelle, Hill 60, Albert, the Somme, Bullecourt and Cambrai, and served with his Battery in several other engagements until the conclusion of hostilities. He was demobilised in March 1919, and holds the 1914 Star, and the General Service and Victory Medals.
15, Canning Street, Ancoats, Manchester. Z9807

ARMSTRONG, J., Corporal, 2nd Manchester Regt.
Volunteering in February 1915, he was drafted in the following August to Gallipoli. There he took part in heavy fighting at Krithia and during the Evacuation of the Peninsula, after which he was sent to France. In this theatre of war he was in action at Ypres and Hooge, and was wounded on the Somme. Invalided home as a result, he recovered, returned to France, and was again wounded. In 1920 he was serving in Mesopotamia, and holds the 1914-15 Star, and the General Service and Victory Medals.
16, Olive Grove, Hulme, Manchester. Z1066

ARMSTRONG, J. C., Corporal, 9th Northumberland Fusiliers.
He volunteered in June 1915, and in the following October was sent to Salonika. After taking part in several engagements he was transferred to Egypt, where he served until admitted to hospital on account of ill-health. Upon his recovery he was transferred to France, where he participated in the Battles of the Somme, Arras, Cambrai, Ypres and other severe engagements, prior to being killed in action on the Lys on April 14th, 1918. He was entitled to the 1914-15 Star, and the General Service and Victory Medals.
"Whilst we remember, the sacrifice is not in vain."
161, Warde Street, Hulme, Manchester. Z1067

ARMSTRONG, J. E., Air Mechanic, R.A.F.
He joined in November 1917, but was not successful in obtaining a transfer to a theatre of war. Retained at home, he was employed testing machine guns, important work which demanded a high degree of technical skill, and he rendered valuable services until he was demobilised in January 1919.
54, Piggott Street, Greenheys, Manchester. Z1068

ARMSTRONG, J. H., Pte., 1/8th Manchester Regt.
Already serving at the outbreak of war in August 1914, he was shortly afterwards drafted to Gallipoli. There he was wounded during the Battle of Cape Helles, and was later gassed in action in August 1915. Admitted to hospital at Cairo, he remained there until the following October, after which he served on the Suez Canal. Returning home he was discharged in July 1916, but rejoined a few months afterwards, and was eventually demobilised in February 1919, holding the 1914-15 Star, and the General Service and Victory Medals.
5, Milton Street, Bradford, Manchester. TZ1064A

ARMSTRONG, W., Private, King's (Liverpool Regt).
He volunteered in August 1914, and in the following February crossed to the Western Front, where he was almost immediately in action in the Battle of Neuve Chapelle, in the course of which he was wounded in March 1915. Invalided home he received treatment and sent to Egypt four months later, served at Alexandria and Cairo, until drafted to Salonika in January 1916. During the Balkan campaign he fought in the Battle of the Vardar, the advance on the Struma and Lake Doiran, and in the capture of Monastir. Returning home for demobilisation in February 1919, he holds the 1914-15 Star, and the General Service and Victory Medals.
10, Howarth Street, Chorlton-on-Medlock, Manchester. Z9808

ARMSTRONG, W. F., Pte., King's (Liverpool Regt.)
Serving when war broke out in August 1914, he was sent to France in January 1915, During his service overseas he took part in many important engagements, including the Battles of Loos, and Arras, and was gassed in action. He was subsequently admitted to hospital suffering from neurasthenia and was eventually discharged in October 1919 as unfit for further service. He holds the 1914-15 Star, and the General Service and Victory Medals.
5, Amy Street, Openshaw, Manchester. Z1065

ARNOLD, A., Private, Royal Fusiliers.
He joined in April 1917, and was retained at home on duties of an important nature until May 1918, when he was drafted to France. There he took a prominent part with his unit in strenuous fighting in many sectors, prior to being killed in action at Albert in August 1918. He was entitled to the General Service and Victory Medals.
" His life for his Country."
34, Kippax Street, Moss Side, Manchester. Z1071

ARNOLD, A., Sergt., 1/8th Manchester Regiment.
When war broke out he was already serving, but was retained on important duties at home until March 1917, when he obtained a transfer overseas. Whilst on the Western Front he took a prominent part in important engagements at Bullecourt, Ypres, the Somme, Bapaume, Havrincourt and Amiens, and was wounded in action at Cambrai in September 1918. He was discharged in March 1919, and holds the General Service and Victory Medals.
1, Beecher Street, Queen's Park, Manchester. Z11460

ARNOLD, C. W., Private, 2/6th Manchester Regt.
Joining in August 1916, he proceeded in the following March to the Western Front. In this theatre of war he participated in heavy engagements at Arras, Vimy Ridge and Bullecourt doing excellent work, but was unhappily killed in action at La Bassée, on May 4th, 1917. He was buried at Cambrai, and was entitled to the General Service and Victory Medals.
" Great deeds cannot die."
24, Wenlock Street, Hulme, Manchester. Z1070

ARNOTT, G., Sapper, R.E.
He volunteered in May 1915, and early in the following year was sent to Egypt, where he served on the Suez Canal and at Mersa Matruh, Agagia, Katia, and Romani, before being transferred in February 1917, to the Western Front. There he served at Ypres, and as the result of being gassed, spent some time in hospital at Rouen. Upon his recovery he was employed on important duties at Cambrai, on the Somme, and on the Marne, and was demobilised in February 1919, holding the General Service and Victory Medals.
14, Lime Street, Hulme, Manchester. Z1072

ARRANDALE, J., L/Cpl., 12th Manchester Regt.
He volunteered in August 1914, ad after a period of training proceeded to the Western Front in July of the following year. After taking part in engagements at Loos, Neuve Chapelle and Hooge, he fell fighting at the Battle of the Somme on July 12th, 1916. He was entitled to the 1914-15 Star, and the General Service and Victory Medals.
" Whilst we remember, the sacrifice is not in vain."
5, Rocester Street, Harpurhey, Manchester. Z11461

ARRANDALE, J., Pte., K.O. (Royal Lancaster Regt.)
Volunteering in October 1914, he was retained on home defence duties until July 1916, when he proceeded to Mesopotamia. During his service in this theatre of war he was in action at Kirkuk and in many other important engagements. He also took an active part in the capture of Baghdad and remained there until 1919, when he returned home. He was demobilised in April of that year, and holds the General Service and Victory Medals.
5, Rocester Street, Harpurhey, Manchester. Z11462

ARROWSMITH, G., Pte., 2nd South Lancashire Regt.
Volunteering in October 1914, he was drafted a month later to France. There he took part in the Battles of La Bassée, Ypres, Neuve Chapelle, St. Eloi and Hill 60, and performed consistently good work. In June 1915 he was sent to Egypt, and saw service at Alexandria, Cairo, Sollum, Katia, and against the Senussi Arabs. Afterwards he served at Jaffa, Rafa, Gaza and Jerusalem in Palestine. During his service overseas he was wounded in action, and was demobilised on his return home in July 1919. He holds the 1914 Star, and the General Service and Victory Medals.
37, Hancock Street, Rusholme, Manchester. Z1073

ARTHINGTON, H., Pte., 15th Lancashire Fusiliers.
He volunteered in August 1914, and in the following May was sent to Egypt, where he took part in heavy fighting on the Suez Canal. He then proceeded to the Dardanelles and was present at the Landing at Suvla Bay. After the Evacuation of the Gallipoli Peninsula he returned to Egypt, but after being in action at Katia, was transferred to the Western Front and fought on the Somme and at Ypres and Joncourt, where he was unfortunately killed on September 30th, 1918. He was entitled to the 1914-15 Star, and the General Service and Victory Medals.
" A costly sacrifice upon the altar of freedom."
29, Greenhough Street, Ancoats, Manchester. Z9409

ARTHUR, G., Lieutenant, M.G.C.
Volunteering in September 1915, he proceeded in the following January to the Western Front There, in the Battle of the Somme, he was sent back to England and received a commission. He returned to France in May 1917, and was wounded at Ypres shortly afterwards. On his recovery he was drafted to Syria, and took a prominent part in engagements at Beyrout and Aleppo. He was twice mentioned in Despatches for gallantry in the Field, and was demobilised in April 1919, a month after his return home, holding the General Service and Victory Medals.
40, Mallow Street, Hulme, Manchester. Z9028

ASCROFT, J., Private, 1/7th Lancashire Fusiliers.
He joined in April 1916, and was employed on important duties at various home stations until July 1917, when he proceeded to France. In this theatre of war he took part in numerous important engagements, including the Battle of Ypres and the Retreat and Advance of 1918. He was wounded at Nieuport, but remained overseas until March 1919, when he returned home and was demobilised, holding the General Service and Victory Medals.
90, Redvers Street, Ardwick, Manchester. Z1074

ASHCROFT. R., Private, Royal Dublin Fusiliers.
He joined in November 1917, but was not successful in obtaining a transfer to a theatre of war. Whilst stationed at Hull, Hartlepool and Aldershot, he was employed on important duties in connection with home defence, and rendered valuable services. In February 1919, he was sent to Constantinople, where he was still serving in 1920.
36, Nellie Street, Ardwick, Manchester. Z1091

ASHCROFT, R,, Private, King's (Liverpool Regt.)
Joining in February 1916, he was sent two months later to France, where he was in action on the Aisne and at Amiens, Ypres and Arras. Proceeding to Italy in June 1918 he was employed on guard duties until the following December, when he was sent to Germany to join the Army of Occupation. Returning home in November 1919, he was demobilised, and holds the General Service and Victory Medals.
36, Nellie Street, Ardwick, Manchester. Z1075

ASHCROFT, T. H., Private, 3rd Lancashire Fusiliers.
Volunteering in January 1915, he proceeded to the Dardanelles five months afterwards and saw heavy fighting. Severely wounded during the third attack on Krithia on June 4th, he remained in hospital until October 1917, but on his release from hospital contracted enteric and was sent to Malta. Later he was invalided home and discharged as unfit in August 1917. He holds the 1914-15 Star, and the General Service and Victory Medals.
18, Robert Street, West Gorton, Manchester. Z1076

ASHFORD, J. W., Private, Lincolnshire Regiment.
Volunteering in September 1914, he was quickly drafted to the Western Front. Whilst in this theatre of war he was in action at the Battles of Neuve Chapelle, St. Eloi, Hill 60, Ypres (II), the Somme, Arras, Vimy Ridge, Bullecourt, Ypres (III), and Cambrai. He was then invalided home as the result of a breakdown in health, and was discharged as medically unfit in December 1918, holding the 1914-15 Star, and the General Service and Victory Medals.
48, Richardson Street, Collyhurst, Manchester. Z10283

ASHLEY, A., Private, 2nd Cheshire Regiment.
He volunteered in June 1915, and nine months later was drafted to Egypt. After taking part in the Suez Canal engagements he proceeded to Palestine, and there fought in the Battles of Gaza and was also in action round Jerusalem. In June 1917 he was transferred to Salonika, where he served until after the close of hostilities, engaged on important guard duties. In April 1919 he returned to England and was demobilised, holding the General Service and Victory Medals.
54, George Street, Newton, Manchester. Z9029

ASHLEY, H., Private, Loyal N. Lancashire Regt.
He joined in March 1917, and two months later was drafted to France. He only served there until August 9th in the same year, when he made the supreme sacrifice, being killed in action. He was buried at Westlock Ridge Cemetery, and was entitled to the General Service and Victory Medals.
" Great deeds cannot die ;
They, with the sun and moon renew their light for ever."
100, Walmer Street, Rusholme, Manchester. Z1077

ASHLEY, W. G., Private, King's (Shropshire Light Infantry), and 48th T.R.B.
Joining in November 1916 on becoming fit enough, he was retained in England after the completion of his training and was employed on important duties, until his health broke down. He spent some time in hospital and was eventually discharged in April 1917.
34, Armitage Street, Ardwick, Manchester. Z1078

ASHMORE, F., Corporal, King's Own (Royal Lancaster Regiment and R.E.
He joined in March 1917, and three months later proceeded to Mesopotamia, where he served for nearly three years. During that time he worked on the railways at Marjel with the R.E., and after the cessation of hostilities performed excellent work in the Military Police at Baghdad. On his return to England in April 1920 he was demobilised, and holds the General Service and Victory Medals.
63, Lynn Street, West Gorton, Manchester. TZ6034

ASHMORE, G., Private, 16th Manchester Regt.
Volunteering in September 1914, he was sent to France a year later, and fought in the Battles of Loos, Albert, Vimy Ridge, Arras, Ypres, Cambrai and Amiens. In the course of his three and a half years' service on the Western Front he was gassed in the Ancre sector. Demobilised in February 1919 he holds the 1914-15 Star, and the General Service and Victory Medals.
54, Cheetham Street, Lower Openshaw, Manchester. Z1079

ASHTON, A., Corporal, King's (Liverpool Regt.)
He joined in March 1917, and was soon drafted to France. There he took part in the Battles of Arras, Vimy Ridge, Ypres, Cambrai, the Somme and the Marne, and in the Retreat and Advance of 1918, and was gassed on the Somme in April. He was demobilised in November 1919, and holds the General Service and Victory Medals.
41, Hazel Street, Hulme, Manchester. Z1080

ASHTON, C. H., Corporal, 8th Manchester Regt.
Volunteering in August 1914, he completed his training and was sent to Grimsby, where he was employed on guarding the docks. Subsequently he served in various other capacities, especially as a drill Instructor, and was in April 1915 discharged as unfit for further military services.
139, Everton Road, Chorlton-on-Medlock, Manchester. Z1082

ASHTON. E., Private, East Lancashire Regiment.
Volunteering in September 1914, he was sent to France a year later and saw heavy fighting at Albert, Givenchy and on the Somme. He was then drafted to Salonika in November 1916, and was in action on Lake Doiran, but owing to illness was admitted to hospital at Malta. Rejoining his unit in the Balkans on recovery he was later invalided home on account of bad health and after treatment proceeded to the Western Front in May 1918, and served there in the concluding stages of the war. He was demobilised in March 1919, and holds the 1914-15 Star, and the General Service and Victory Medals.
54, South Porter Street, Ancoats, Manchester. Z9809

ASHTON. G., Private, 2nd Manchester Regiment.
Joining in December 1916, he embarked in the following year for France, where he saw much fighting. During the Retreat in March 1918, he was wounded and taken prisoner and held in captivity until after the Armistice. Later he proceeded to India and took part in the operations on the North West Frontier, where he was again wounded and taken prisoner. In September 1920 he was released and in December of that year was still serving. He holds the General Service and Victory Medals, and the India General Service (with clasp Afghanistan, N.W. Frontier 1919).
26, Higher Duke Street, Miles Platting, Manchester. TZ9410

ASHTON, H., Private, 8th Manchester Regiment.
He volunteered for active service in January 1915, but was unsuccessful in obtaining a transfer overseas. He was retained on Home Defence and stationed at Morecambe, Redcar, Lulworth, Colchester and Cromer, where he was employed as a transport driver. Later he rendered valuable services in connection with agricultural work at Selby and Driffield, and was eventually demobilised in February 1919.
28, Brougham Street, West Gorton, Manchester. Z9030

ASHTON, H., Private, 2/5th Manchester Regiment.
Joining in March 1916, he was on conclusion of his training drafted overseas in the following September. During his service on the Western Front he was engaged in heavy fighting in various sectors of the line, and was in action at Arras, Ypres, Cambrai and also in the Retreat and Advance prior to the close of hostilities. He was demobilised in January 1919, and holds the General Service and Victory Medals.
15, Neptune Street, Ancoats, Manchester. Z6035

ASHTON, H., Corporal, 1st Manchester Regiment.
A Reservist, he was called to the Colours in August 1914, and in the following December was sent to France, where he played a prominent part in the Battles of Neuve Chapelle, Hill 60, Ypres (II) and Festubert. In September 1915 he was transferred to Mesopotamia and was unfortunately killed in action at Kut-el-Amara on December 3rd of the same year. He

was entitled to the 1914-15 Star, and the General Service and Victory Medals.
"The path of duty was the way to glory."
3, Phelan Street, Collyhurst, Manchester. Z10284A

ASHTON, J., Private, 13th Welch Regiment.
He volunteered in September 1914, and proceeding to France in the following May fought in the Battle of Festubert, and in several engagements in the Ypres sector. He fell fighting on April 24th, 1916, and was buried in the British Cemetery at Fins, near Péronne. He was entitled to the 1914-15 Star, and the General Service and Victory Medals.
"He passed out of the sight of men by the path of duty and self-sacrifice."
39, Albion Terrace, Varley Street, Manchester. Z9810

ASHTON, J., Driver, R.F.A.
Joining in April 1917, he was drafted overseas six months later and served with his Battery in various sectors of the Western Front. He did good work during the Battles of Cambrai, and the Somme, and in several others, until the end of hostilities, when he proceeded into Germany with the Army of Occupation. After upwards of a year's service on the Rhine, he returned home for demobilisation in October 1919, and holds the General Service and Victory Medals.
16, James Street, Bradford, Manchester. Z9811

ASHTON, J. W., Private, Lancashire Fusiliers.
Volunteering in September 1914, he was sent to the Western Front in January of the following year, and fought at St. Eloi, Loos, Vermelles, the Somme, Arras and Messines. He was wounded at Loos in August 1917, but after a time in hospital rejoined his unit and took part in the Battles of Cambrai and the Aisne. He was demobilised in February 1919, and holds the 1914-15 Star, and the General Service and Victory Medals.
45, Sawley Street, Beswick, Manchester. Z1081

ASHTON, M., Private, 8th Welch Regiment.
He volunteered in August 1914, and in June 1915 was drafted to Gallipoli, where he was in action in the Suvla Bay Landing. In December 1915, however, he was invalided home with enteric fever, and on his recovery sent to the Western Front in June 1916. In this theatre of war he took part in the Battles of the Somme and Ypres, but was sent back to England suffering with trench fever, and was discharged in consequence in January 1919. He holds the 1914-15 Star, and the General Service and Victory Medals.
428, Ashton New Road, Bradford, Manchester. TZ9032

ASHTON, T., Private, 23rd Manchester Regiment.
He volunteered in November 1914, but was retained on Home Service until January 1916, when he was sent to the Western Front. There he took an active part in engagements at Albert, Ploegsteert Wood, the Somme and Arras, but was invalided to England in July 1918, suffering from heart trouble. He was in consequence discharged as medically unfit for further military duties later in the same month, and holds the General Service and Victory Medals. Z9031
3, Johnson's Buildings, Every Street, Ancoats, Manchester.

ASHTON, T., Private, S. Lancashire Regiment.
Volunteering in November 1914, he proceeded three months later to the Western Front, where he took part in the Battle of Ypres. After a year's service in France he was invalided to England suffering from epilepsy brought on by concussion, and in consequence was discharged from the Army in April 1916, as medically unfit for further military duties. He holds the 1914-15 Star, and the General Service and Victory Medals.
25, Higher Duke Street, Miles Platting, Manchester. TZ6036

ASHTON, W. H., Sergt., 1st King's (Liverpool Regt.)
A month after volunteering in August 1914 ,he proceeded to France and fought in the Battles of the Marne, the Aisne, Hill 60, Ypres and Vimy Ridge. He spent some time in hospital, owing to wounds received at Arras in May 1917, and rheumatism. Transferred to the Labour Corps, he did valuable work, but had again to enter hospital. He was demobilised in March 1919, and holds the 1914 Star, and the General Service and Victory Medals.
24, Hardman Street, City Road, Hulme, Manchester. Z1083

ASHTON, W. W., Private, King's (Liverpool Regt.)
He joined in May 1917, and was quickly drafted to the Western Front, where he saw much severe fighting. He laid down his life for King and Country at the Battle of Ypres on September 16th, 1917, and was entitled to the General Service and Victory Medals.
"A costly sacrifice upon the altar of freedom."
3, Phelan Street, Collyhurst, Manchester. Z10284B

ASHWORTH, J., Driver, R.A.S.C. (M.T.)
He joined in June 1916, and early in the following year crossed to France, where he was engaged in the transport of troops and food to the trenches. He served at Bullecourt, Arras, Siegfried Line, Ypres, Passchendaele, and Lens, and in November 1917 was drafted to Italy. There he was engaged on similar duties at Camposanpiero, Cittadella, and Treviso. After returning to France and fighting at Bapaume, Havrincourt, and Le Cateau, he was demobilised in September 1919, and holds the General Service and Victory Medals.
38, George Street, Hulme, Manchester. Z1086

ASHWORTH, N. B., Private, 2/7th Lancashire Fusiliers and Sapper, R.E.

He volunteered in September 1914, but was unable to obtain his transfer overseas, and was stationed at various places in England, especially on the East Coast. He was discharged owing to heart trouble in March 1917, but re-enlisted in the Royal Engineers later, and was drafted to France, where he served at Calais on transport work, until finally discharged in March 1919. He holds the General Service and Victory Medals.
5, Clipping Street, Longsight, Manchester. Z1087

ASHWORTH, R., Pte., 6th South Lancashire Regt.

Volunteering in April 1915, he was drafted in September to Gallipoli, and saw heavy fighting there. Early in 1916 he proceeded to Mesopotamia, and was in action at Kut, Um-el-Hannah, and Sanna-i-Yat, and at the occupation of Baghdad and Tekrit. Although he suffered from malaria he remained with his unit practically the whole time until his return home in August 1919. He was demobilised in that month, and holds the 1914-15 Star, and the General Service and Victory Medals.
6, Edmund Street, Openshaw, Manchester. Z1085

ASHWORTH, S., Corporal, 12th Manchester Regt.

He volunteered at the outbreak of war, and in the following May was sent to France, where he fought at Loos, Albert, and the Somme. He was wounded at Arras in May 1917, after taking part in engagements at Beaumont-Hamel and Beaucourt on the Ancre front, and was invalided home. Returning five months later to the firing line, he was unhappily killed at Ypres on September 7th, 1917. He was entitled to the 1914-15 Star, and the General Service and Victory Medals.
"A costly sacrifice upon the altar of freedom."
33, Lythgoe Street, Moss Side, Manchester. Z1088

ASHWORTH, W., Private, 11th Manchester Regt.

A year after volunteering in August 1914, he reached Gallipoli, and took part in the Suvla Bay Landing, during which he was wounded. After being in hospital in Alexandria, he returned to England, but was sent to Mesopotamia shortly afterwards, and served at Kut and Baghdad. Demobilised in March 1919, after landing in England, he holds the 1914-15 Star, and the General Service and Victory Medals.
11, Dawsons Buildings, off King Street, Manchester. Z1084

ASHWORTH, W. H., Pte., 3rd K. (Liverpool Regt.)

Volunteering in March 1915, he crossed to the Western Front two months later and fought at the Battles of Ypres and Loos. In June 1916 he was sent to Salonika, but contracted malaria, and was invalided home eighteen months afterwards. He was eventually demobilised in February 1919, and holds the 1914-15 Star, and the General Service and Victory Medals.
12, Williams Street, Hulme, Manchester. Z1089

ASPINALL, T., Corporal, Lancashire Fusiliers.

He volunteered in September 1914, and served on home defence duties with his Battalion until February 1916, when he was drafted to France. There he was almost immediately in action at Loos, and was wounded on the Somme in June 1916. Sent home for treatment, he returned to the Western Front in the following December, and took part in the Battles of Arras, Ypres, and Passchendaele, and wounded for the second time in August 1917, was invalided to England. After being in hospital for some months he was discharged as medically unfit in March 1918, and holds the General Service and Victory Medals. 27, Francisco Street, Collyhurst, Manchester. Z9812

ASTBURY, W., Private, R.A.V.C.

When he attained the necessary age in February 1917, he joined the Royal Army Veterinary Corps, and was stationed at the Remount Depôt at Ormskirk. There he did much valuable work, but was badly kicked by a horse. He was unable to obtain his transfer overseas before the cessation of hostilities, and was demobilised in November 1919.
8, Hey Street, Bradford, Manchester. Z1090

ASTIN, H., Pte., Manchester Regt. (Ardwick Bn.)

He volunteered in January 1915, and completed his training. He was unable to proceed overseas but was stationed at Morecambe, and engaged on important work. Unfortunately he contracted typhoid fever, and was discharged as unfit in consequence in May 1917.
14, Franchise Street, Ardwick, Manchester. Z1092B

ASTLEY, F., Private, M.G.C.

He was retained in England for a year before being sent to Salonika in November 1916. Whilst in the Balkans he saw much heavy fighting, but was wounded on the Doiran front in April 1917. He also suffered badly from malaria, and was eventually demobilised in April 1919 after his return home, holding the General Service and Victory Medals.
22, Fleeson Street, Rusholme, Manchester. Z1093

ATHERTON, F. Private, R.A.S.C.

He joined in November 1916, and in the following month crossed to France, where he served as a turner, and was engaged in the repair of transport waggons. He was in action at Arras, Messines, Ypres, and Cambrai, and in the Retreat and Advance of 1918, and served in Germany with the Army of Occupation until his demobilisation in November 1919. He holds the General Service and Victory Medals.
9, Churchfield Street, Openshaw, Manchester. Z1094

ATHERTON, J., Sapper, R.E.

Volunteering in August 1914, he was sent overseas in the following year, and saw service in various theatres of war. Landing on the Western Front he served in the Battles of Neuve Chapelle, St. Eloi, Hill 60, Festubert, and Loos, and then proceeded to Egypt. After a period of service during operations in the Canal zone, and at Mersa Matruh, he returned to France, where he did good work in connection with the Battles of Arras, Vimy Ridge, Messines, Lens, and in those of the Retreat and Advance of 1918, and was wounded. Demobilised in March 1919, he holds the 1914-15 Star, and the General Service and Victory Medals.
22, Pilling Street, Newton Heath, Manchester. Z9813

ATHERTON, W. H., 8th South Lancashire Regt.

He joined in September 1916, and in the following month was drafted overseas. He served on the Western Front for about two years, and during that time was wounded at Arras, and after his recovery, again at Passchendaele. On November 4th, 1918, he was unfortunately killed in action. He was entitled to the General Service and Victory Medals.
"Whilst we remember the sacrifice is not in vain."
30, Riga Street, City Road, Hulme, Manchester. Z1095

ATKIN, G. W., Private, Labour Corps.

Volunteering in November 1915, he completed his training at Prees Heath, and was then transferred to the Royal Welch Fusiliers, with which Regiment he served at stations at home. Being unfit for foreign service he was sent to the Labour Corps, and was eventually demobilised in January 1919, from Heaton Park.
15, Thomas Street, West Gorton, Manchester. Z1096

ATKINS, H., Private, 2/8th Manchester Regiment.

In August 1914 he volunteered for active service, but was retained on important duties in England throughout the period of hostilities. He served at numerous important home stations, including Southport, Crowborough, Maidstone, and Rochester. where he was employed in the band, until demobilised in January 1919.
44, Milton Street, West Gorton, Manchester. Z3500

ATKINS, H. E., Private, 1/8th Manchester Regt.

He volunteered at the outbreak of war, and in the following year was sent to the Dardanelles, where he took part in the Suvla Bay Landing, and was wounded. After also serving for a time in Egypt, he was invalided home, and discharged through wounds in May 1916. He subsequently joined the Royal Marine Light Infantry in March 1919, and a month later was sent to France, from where he was demobilised in January 1920. He holds the 1914-15 Star, and the General Service and Victory Medals.
243, Moreton Street, Longsight, Manchester. Z1097

ATKINS, S., Private, South Lancashire Regiment.

He volunteered in August 1914, and in September of the following year crossed to France, where he was engaged with his unit in the Battles of Albert, Ploegsteert Wood, the Somme, Vimy Ridge, Messines, Passchendaele, and Lens. He was badly gassed on the Somme, and on recovery rejoined his Battalion, with which he took part in several further operations until the close of the war. Returning home for demobilisation in March 1919, he holds the 1914-15 Star, and the General Service and Victory Medals.
93, Great Jackson Street, West Gorton, Manchester. Z9814

ATKINSON, A., L/Corporal, Welch Regiment.

Volunteering in April 1915, he embarked for the Western Front a month later, and was in action in the Battles of Hill 60, Ypres, Albert, the Somme, Arras, and Bullecourt, where he was wounded in June 1917. He returned to the trenches on recovery, and fought at Lens and Cambrai, and was again wounded in the Battle of the Somme in March 1918. After convalescence he saw heavy fighting in the concluding stages of the war, and returning to England was demobilised in January 1919. He holds the 1914-15 Star, and the General Service and Victory Medals.
30, Gray Street, Ancoats, Manchester. Z9815

ATKINSON, A. E., Pte., 6th King's Own Scottish Borderers.

He volunteered in August 1914, and in the following May was drafted to the Western Front, where he played an important part in the Battles of Ypres (II), Festubert, Loos, Albert, the Somme, Arras, Messines, and Ypres (III), and in the Retreat and Advance of 1918. He holds the 1914-15 Star, and the General Service and Victory Medals, and was demobilised in January 1919.
3, Dalton Street, Collyhurst, Manchester. Z10285

ATKINSON, D., Private, 18th Manchester Regiment.

Volunteering in January 1915, he was eleven months later sent to France, where he fought at Loos, in the Battles of the Somme, Arras, Bullecourt, Ypres, and Cambrai, and in the Retreat and Advance of 1918. Severely injured at Havrincourt Wood, in September 1918, he was invalided home and four months later was demobilised, holding the 1914-15 Star, and the General Service and Victory Medals.
18, Berwick Street, Chorlton-on-Medlock, Manchester. Z1098

ATKINSON, D., Private, 8th Manchester Regiment.
He volunteered in August 1914, and proceeding overseas in September of the following year served in various parts of France and Flanders. He took part in the Battles of Loos, St. Eloi, Albert, the Somme, Arras, Bullecourt, and Ypres, in which last he was wounded in November 1917, and admitted to hospital. After treatment he rejoined his Battalion, with which he went into action in several engagements, including those at Havrincourt, and on the Lys, during the Allied Advance of 1918. He holds the 1914–15 Star, and the General Service and Victory Medals.
20, Gray Street, Ancoats, Manchester.   Z9816

ATKINSON, E., Private, 1/4th Cheshire Regiment.
He joined in March 1918, and after completing his training, was drafted to France in the following August. He took part in heavy fighting during the concluding stages of the war, and was wounded at Kemmel Hill. After serving for a time with the Army of Occupation, he was demobilised in October 1919, and holds the General Service and Victory Medals.
9, Harper Place, Hulme, Manchester.   Z1099

ATKINSON, G., Private, 1st Cheshire Regiment.
He volunteered at the outbreak of war, and completed a period of training and service in the United Kingdom before being sent to Salonika in January 1916. After remaining there for five months he was drafted to Egypt, but, having been wounded at Gaza in 1917, was invalided home. He was eventually demobilised in January 1919, and holds the General Service and Victory Medals.
46, Frances Street, Chorlton-on-Medlock, Manchester. X1101

ATKINSON, H., Private, 2/7th Lancashire Fusiliers.
He joined in March 1917, and three months later crossed to the Western Front, where he fought at Messines, Ypres, Bullecourt, and Cambrai. He was wounded badly and taken prisoner in March 1918 during the second Battle of the Somme. Repatriated after the Armistice, he was demobilised in November 1918, and holds the General Service and Victory Medals.
46, Blackthorn Street, Ardwick, Manchester.   Z1100

ATKINSON, J., L/Corporal, 4th, 1st, and 12th Manchester Regiment.
Joining in March 1916, he was sent to France in July and went straight into action in the Battle of the Somme. He later fought on the Ancre front, but being badly wounded at Arras in April 1917, was invalided home. On recovery he returned to the firing line, and was in action in the Battles of the Somme II, Aisne II, and Marne II, and in the Retreat of 1918. He was unhappily killed in the subsequent Advance on August 25th. He was entitled to the General Service and Victory Medals.
"Whilst we remember, the sacrifice is not in vain."
23, Chell Street, Longsight, Manchester.   Z1102

ATKINSON, J., Private, East Lancashire Regiment.
He volunteered in November 1915, and was kept in England until May 1916. Proceeding in that month to France, he was wounded in July during the Somme Offensive, and invalided home after being in hospital in France. Early in 1918 he returned to France, but in May was a second time wounded on the Somme. Again sent home, he was eventually demobilised in November 1919, and holds the General Service and Victory Medals.
7, Crissey Street, Queen's Road, Manchester.   Z11973A

ATKINSON, T. E., Corporal, R.E.
He joined in July 1917, and after completing his training was engaged on important coastal defence duties in the South-East of England, and rendered valuable services. He was unable to obtain his transfer overseas before the conclusion of hostilities, owing to physical unfitness for general service, and was discharged in consequence in December 1918.
13, Irlam Street, Miles Platting, Manchester.   Z9817

ATKINSON, W., Private, 8th Manchester Regt.
He volunteered in June 1915, and after a course of training was drafted overseas seven months later. Whilst serving on the Western Front he fought in many engagements of importance, including those at Vermelles, Albert, the Somme, Messines, Bullecourt, the Marne, Amiens, and Bapaume. He served in France until demobilised in March 1919, and holds the General Service and Victory Medals.
36, Whitfield Street, Chorlton-on-Medlock, Manchester.   Z11463

ATKINSON, W. H., Rflmn., Cameronians (Scottish Rifles).
He joined in May 1917, and in the following February landed on the Western Front, where he was engaged in heavy fighting in the German Offensive. Taking part in the subsequent Allied Advance he was gassed and wounded in October 1918, and after treatment was retained on special duties for over a year after hostilities ceased. He was demobilised in December 1919, and holds the General Service and Victory Medals.
4, Duke Street, Miles Platting, Manchester.   Z10081B

ATKINSON, W. T., Driver, R.A.S.C. (M.T.)
Shortly after volunteering in May 1915, he was drafted to the Western Front, where he was engaged in conveying ammunition to the forward areas in various sectors. He was injured in an accident in July 1916, during the Somme Offensive, and after his recovery, took an active part in the Battles of Vimy Ridge, and Ypres, and other engagements. He was finally invalided from the Army in October 1917, suffering from debility, and holds the 1914–15 Star, and the General Service and Victory Medals.
33, Allen Street, Hulme, Manchester.   Z11627

ATTENBOROUGH, E., A.B., Merchant Service.
He was already serving at the outbreak of hostilities, and until September 1918 was engaged in the transport of troops between Alexandria, France, and England. In September 1918 his eyesight was injured in a collision, and he was discharged three months later after a period in Liverpool. He holds the General Service and Mercantile Marine War Medals.
22, Walnut Street, Hulme, Manchester.   Z1103

AUST, T., Corporal, 2nd South Lancashire Regt.
He enlisted in 1912, and at the commencement of war was drafted with his Regiment to France. During the Retreat from Mons he was wounded and taken prisoner. He was held in captivity at Friedricksfeld until after the Armistice, and after his release was discharged as time-expired in April 1919. He holds the Mons Star, and the General Service and Victory Medals. 60A, Vine Street, Newton Heath, Manchester. Z9411

AUSTERBEERY, A., Cpl., 21st Manchester Regt.
Joining in April 1916, three months later he landed in France and was in action in several engagements in the Somme Offensive, in the Ypres salient, and at Cambrai, after which he was drafted to Italy. In that theatre of war he took part in several operations, including the advance on the Piave, and on the conclusion of hostilities returned to England. He was demobilised in February 1919, and holds the General Service and Victory Medals.
3, King Street, Hulme, Manchester.   Z9818A

AUSTIN, G., Private, King's (Liverpool Regiment).
He joined in March 1918, and was retained on work in England until June 1919, when he was sent to France. From there he proceeded to Germany, and served with the Army of Occupation, attached to a Trench Mortar Battery. He returned home and was demobilised in October 1919.
44, New Bank Street, Ardwick, Manchester.   Z1105A

AUSTIN, R., Private, 3rd Gordon Highlanders.
Volunteering in April 1915, he was sent to the Western Front in July, and saw much heavy fighting. He fought at Loos, La Bassée, Givenchy, Festubert, Ypres, Passchendaele, Cambrai, and Lens, but was wounded at Loos in January 1916. After hospital treatment he returned to France in April 1916, but was unhappily killed on the Somme in July 1918. He was entitled to the 1914–15 Star, and the General Service and Victory Medals.
"His life for his Country, his soul to God."
12, Dennison Street, Rusholme, Manchester.   Z1104

AUSTIN, W., Private, East Lancashire Regt.
Volunteering in May 1915, he was sent to France seven months afterwards. He played a prominent part in the heavy fighting at Loos, St. Eloi, Albert, and Vimy Ridge, but was unhappily killed in action in July 1916 during the Battle of the Somme. He was entitled to the 1914–15 Star, and the General Service and Victory Medals.
"He died the noblest death a man may die,
Fighting for God, and right and liberty."
44, New Bank Street, Ardwick, Manchester.   Z1105B

AVERILL, J., Private, 1st Royal Berkshire Regt.
He joined in January 1918, and after two months training at Barrow-in-Furness was drafted overseas. Whilst serving on the Western Front he was engaged in fierce fighting in various sectors of the line, and did good work with his unit in the Battles of the Somme, Amiens, Bapaume, Ypres, and Cambrai. He remained in France until December 1918, when he was demobilised, holding the General Service and Victory Medals.
29, Susan Street, Rochdale Road, Manchester.   Z9033

AVERILL, W. T., Private, 2nd Lancashire Fusiliers.
A month after the outbreak of hostilities he volunteered, and on conclusion of his training was drafted overseas, in September 1915. During his service on the Western Front, he was in action in numerous important engagements, including those at Ypres, Loos, St. Eloi, Albert, the Somme, Ypres III, Cambrai, Bapaume, Havrincourt and Le Cateau. He was demobilised in February 1919, and holds the 1914–15 Star, and the General Service and Victory Medals.
18, Susan Street, Rochdale Road, Manchester.   Z9034

AYERS, A., Private, 3rd Welch Regiment.
Mobilised from the Reserve in August 1914, he proceeded with the British Expeditionary force to France, and fought at Mons, La Bassée, and many subsequent battles. In March 1916 he was drafted to Egypt and did good work at Alexandria on garrison and outpost duty until the following August, when he was sent to Salonika and served on the Doiran front. He was invalided home in December with malaria, and after receiving hospital treatment was discharged as medically unfit in October 1917. He holds the Mons Star, and the General Service and Victory Medals.
64, Teignmouth Street, Collyhurst, Manchester.   9412

B

BACON, A. E., Corporal, R.A.S.C.
He volunteered in October 1914, and in March 1915 proceeded to France, where he was employed on transport work until April 1916, when he was sent back to hospital in England. On his recovery he was drafted to Salonika, and served there for nine months, at the end of which time he proceeded to Egypt. Later he was in action in Palestine, and was attached to the Canal Transport Corps. He returned to England in April 1919, and was demobilised, holding the 1914-15 Star, and the General Service and Victory Medals.
20, Milton Street, Bradford, Manchester. TZ9035

BADGER, H. W., Private, 23rd Lancashire Fusiliers.
He joined in March 1916, and after training at Cleethorpes was sent to France, where he saw fierce fighting on the Ancre, and at Arras, Ypres and Passchendaele, and was wounded in action in January 1917. He was taken prisoner at Cambrai, and sent to Germany, where he was employed on farm work until released from captivity in January 1919. He was demobilised in August 1919, and holds the General Service and Victory Medals.
8, Drinkwater Street, Harpurhey, Manchester. Z11403

BAGELEY, J., Private, Lancashire Fusiliers.
He joined in August 1917, and was retained on special duties with his unit in the North of England. Owing to ill-health he was unable to proceed overseas, but nevertheless rendered valuable services until he was discharged in June 1918 as physically unfit.
23, Gorse Street, Hulme, Manchester. Z1106

BAGGOLEY, R., Private, 18th Manchester Regt.
He volunteered in January 1915, and after a period of training was drafted to France later in the same year. There he took part in heavy fighting in various sectors and was in action at many engagements of importance, including the Battles of Ypres, Cambrai II and St. Quentin. He also saw service in Italy, and returning to England after the cessation of hostilities was demobilised in February 1919, holding the 1914-15 Star, and the General Service and Victory Medals.
24, Seymour Street, Hulme, Manchester. Z1108

BAGGOLEY, R. H., Pte., 3rd Lancs. Fus. and R.E.
He volunteered in October 1914, and was retained on special duties with the Lancashire Fusiliers until June 1916, when he was discharged. He was called up again, and after being posted to the Royal Engineers, proceeded to France in January 1917. There he was engaged on important duties in many sectors, and saw service at Arras, Vimy Ridge and Ypres, and during the Retreat and Advance of 1918. After the Armistice he was sent to Germany, where he did duty with the Army of Occupation on the Rhine. He holds the General Service and Victory Medals, and was demobilised in February 1919. 14, Dearden Street, Hulme, Manchester, Z1107

BAGNALL, E., Driver, R.F.A.
He was already serving in the Army when war was declared in August 1914, and immediately proceeded with the First Expeditionary Force to France, and fought in the Battle of Mons. He was also in action at La Bassée, Ypres, Neuve Chapelle, the Somme, Arras, Vimy Ridge, Nieuport and Givenchy. In February 1919 he was discharged, and holds the Mons Star. and the General Service and Victory Medals.
64, Victoria Square, Oldham Road, Manchester. Z9036

BAGNALL, J., L/Corporal, Lancashire Fusiliers.
Joining in April 1916, he proceeded in the following November to the Western Front and took part in the Battles of Ypres, the Somme, Cambrai, and many other engagements until January 1918, when he was transferred to the Tank Corps. He also fought in the Battles of Arras, St. Quentin, Le Cateau and Passchendaele, and in the Retreat and Advance of 1918, after which he proceeded with the Army of Occupation into Germany and served on the Rhine until his demobilisation in August 1919. He holds the General Service and Victory Medals. 45, Gardner Street, West Gorton, Manchester. Z9819

BAGOT, R., Pte., King's Own (Royal Lancaster Regt.)
He enlisted in February 1903, and was drafted in September 1914 to France. In this theatre of war he saw heavy fighting on the Aisne, and at Armentières, La Bassée, Ypres I and II, and Hill 60. Invalided home in January 1915, owing to ill-health, he received hospital treatment, and was discharged in consequence in February of the succeeding year as medically unfit for further service. He holds the 1914 Star, and the General Service and Victory Medals.
12, Park Street, West Gorton, Manchester. Z9820

BAGOT, R., Private, King's Own (Royal Lancaster Regiment), and Air Mechanic, R.A.F.
Volunteering in August 1914, he was drafted two months later to the Western Front, where he served in various parts of the line until the close of hostilities. During this period he fought in several engagements, including those at La Bassée, Ypres, Armentières, Hill 60, Festubert, Vermelles, Vimy Ridge, the Somme, Arras, Bullecourt, Cambrai, and the Marne. Returning home for his demobilisation in September

1919, he holds the 1914-Star, and the General Service and Victory Medals.
12, Park Street, West Gorton, Manchester. Z9821

BAGULY, H., Private, R.A.M.C.
He joined in October 1917, and was retained on important duties at various stations in England. He was unable to obtain his transfer to a theatre of war, but nevertheless rendered valuable services at the East Leeds Hospital, until his demobilisation in April 1919.
12, Mercer Street, Hulme, Manchester. Z1109

BAILEY, A. E., Sapper, R.E.
He volunteered in June 1915, and was retained with his unit in England during the first period of his service. He was drafted to the Western Front in April 1917, and rendered valuable services at many engagements of importance, including the Battles of Vimy Ridge, Messines, Ypres and Passchendaele, and was slightly gassed, Returning to England after the Armistice he was eventually demobilised in March 1919, and holds the General Service and Victory Medals. TZ1110
51, Georges Avenue, Chester Road, Hulme, Manchester.

BAILEY, D., Private, Black Watch.
He joined in July 1918, and after a course of training was later in the same year drafted to the Western Front. There he was engaged in heavy fighting, principally in the Arras sector. After the close of hostilities he was sent to Calais, and employed in the food supply depôt, and also rendered valuable services to the wounded on the trains passing through that town. He was demobilised in January 1919, and holds the General Service and Victory Medals.
105, Butterworth Street, Bradford, Manchester. Z9037

BAILEY, E., Gunner, R.G.A.
Mobilised at the outbreak of war in August 1914, he was immediately drafted to France, where he took part in the Battle of Mons, and the subsequent Retreat. He was also in action with his Battery at the Battles of La Bassée, Ypres, Neuve Chapelle, Festubert, Albert, the Somme, Arras and Cambrai. He was also present during the Retreat and Advance of 1918, and after the Armistice did duty with the Army of Occupation on the Rhine. He was discharged in April 1919, and holds the Mons Star, and the General Service and Victory Medals.
42, Hewitt Street, Openshaw, Manchester. Z1111

BAILEY, F., Private, 1/7th Manchester Regiment.
He was already in the Army at the outbreak of war in August 1914, and proceeded to Egypt in the following month with the 42nd Division, and was stationed at Khartoum. He was transferred to France in March 1917, and later took part in many engagements, including those at La Bassée, Ypres and Nieuport, and was gassed in the Arras sector. He holds the 1914 Star, and the General Service and Victory Medals, and was discharged as time-expired in February 1919.
9, Hibbert Street, Hulme, Manchester. Z1115

BAILEY, G., Private, South Lancashire Regiment.
He volunteered in April 1915, and early in the following year proceeded to France, where he took part in many important engagements. He saw much heavy fighting in various sectors, and also took part in the engagements at La Bassée, Festubert, Arras and Albert. He was badly wounded in action on October 2nd, 1916, and unfortunately died the following day. He was entitled to the General Service and Victory Medals.
"A valiant Soldier, with undaunted heart he breasted life's last hill."
91, Norton Street, West Gorton, Manchester. Z1118

BAILEY, G. W., Private, 2/6th Manchester Regt.
He joined in August 1916, and in the following March proceeded to France, where he was in action at many engagements, including the Battles of Arras, Messines, Passchendaele and Cambrai. He was wounded and taken prisoner at the second Battle of the Somme on March 21st 1918, and unhappily died in captivity four days later. He was entitled to the General Service and Victory Medals.
"Whilst we remember, the sacrifice is not in vain."
33, John Street, Hulme Manchester. TZ1112

BAILEY, H., Corporal, 2nd East Lancashire Regt.
He volunteered in April 1915, and crossing to the Western Front in the following March, fought in many important engagements, including the Battles of the Somme, Ypres and Nieuport. He gave his life for the freedom of England on the Field of Battle on August 4th, 1916, and was buried in Béthune Cemetery. He was entitled to the 1914-15 Star, and the General Service and Victory Medals.
"The path of duty was the way to glory."
37, Copestick Street, Ancoats, Manchester. Z9823A

BAILEY, J., Sergt., 3rd K.O. (Royal Lancaster Regt.)
Volunteering at the outbreak of war in August 1914, he completed a period of training, and was drafted to Mesopotamia in April of the following year. There he took a distinguished part in many engagements, including those at Kut-el-Amara and Sanna-i-Yat, and was killed in action on April 9th, 1916. He was entitled to the 1914-15 Star, and the General Service and Victory Medals.
"A costly sacrifice upon the altar of freedom."
12, Dorset Street, West Gorton, Manchester. Z1119

BAILEY, J., Private, 2nd Sherwood Foresters.
Mobilised in August 1914, he was immediately drafted to the
Western Front, where he took part in the fighting at Mons.
After serving also through the Battle of the Aisne and other
engagements, he was taken prisoner at La Bassée, in October
1914, and held in captivity in Germany until the cessation
of hostilities, was forced during this time to work on the land.
He was discharged in March 1919, and holds the Mons Star,
and the General Service and Victory Medals.
5, Singleton Buildings, Garlor Street, Miles Platting, Manchester.   Z11628

BAILEY. J., Driver, R.F.A. (T.M.B.)
He volunteered in August 1914, and was drafted to France
in January of the following year. In this theatre of war
he was in action with his Battery at many important engagements, including the Battles of Neuve Chapelle, Loos, La
Bassée, Ypres, the Somme and Cambrai, and was wounded.
He holds the 1914-15 Star, and the General Service and Victory Medals, and was demobilised in April 1919.
42, Markham Street, Ardwick, Manchester.   Z1114

BAILEY, J., Pte., King's Own (Royal Lancaster Regt.)
He volunteered in September 1914, and was retained on important work in England during the period of his service. He
was stationed at Lancaster and Ramsey, but in October 1915
after only thirteen months service in the Army was discharged
as medically unfit for further military duties.   Z6037A
2, Pitt Street. Chapel Street, Ancoats, Manchester.

BAILEY, J., Private, King's (Liverpool Regiment.)
Joining in October 1916, he was three months later drafted
overseas. During his service on the Western Front he was
in action at Arras, Bullecourt, Ypres, Cambrai, the Somme,
Bapaume, and the Marne, and fell fighting gallantly in September 1918. He was entitled to the General Service and
Victory Medals.
" He passed out of the sight of men by the path of duty and
     self-scarifice."
2, Pitt Street, Chapel Street, Ancoats, Manchester.   Z6037B

BAILEY, J. W., Private, 9th Cheshire Regiment.
Joining in March 1917, he embarked in the following February
for the Western Front, and saw heavy fighting in various
parts of the line, notably at La Bassée. He was unfortunately
reported missing on March 27th 1918, and later presumed
to have been killed in action on that date. He was entitled
to the General Service and Victory Medals.
                  " Nobly striving,
          He nobly fell that we might live."
37, Copestick Street, Ancoats, Manchester.   Z9823B

BAILEY, N., Private, 1st King's (Liverpool Regt.)
Volunteering in July 1915, he embarked in December of the
same year for France, and whilst there saw much heavy
fighting. He was in action at Loos, St. Eloi, the Somme,
Arras, Ypres, Cambrai, and many other engagements in the
final Offensives until hostilities ceased, and was wounded.
He was demobilised in March 1919, and holds the 1914-15
Star, and the General Service and Victory Medals.
7, Clay Street, Newton Heath, Manchester.   Z9413

BAILEY, T., Driver, R.F.A.
He volunteered in September 1915, and crossing to France
in the following December, fought with his Battery in the
Battles of the Somme and Ypres. He also took part in several
engagements during the Retreat and Advance of 1918, and
after the Armistice proceeded to Germany with the Army of
Occupation. Returning home for demobilisation in May 1919,
he holds the 1914-15 Star, and the General Service and Victory
Medals.
353, Mill Street, Bradford, Manchester.   Z9822

BAILEY, W., Private, South Lancashire Regiment.
He volunteered in May 1915, and was retained on important
duties with an Aircraft Section. He was unable to obtain
his transfer overseas owing to ill-health, but nevertheless,
did consistently good work until his discharge in March 1918.
113, Margaret Street, W. Gorton, Manchester.   Z1117

BAILEY, W., Private, King's (Liverpool Regiment.)
Volunteering in September 1914, he was unable to procure
a transfer overseas owing to ill-health. He served at West
Kirby and Prees Heath, at which stations he was engaged on
important guard duties, which he fulfilled in a very capable
manner. In 1915 his health broke down and he was sent to
hospital, and in consequence was discharged from the Army
as medically unfit in July 1915.
47, Elliott Street, Bradford, Manchester.   TZ11404

BAILEY, W., Pte., K.O. (Royal Lancaster Regt.)
He volunteered in August 1914, and after a period of training
was drafted to the Dardanelles in June of the following year.
He took part in the Landing at Suvla Bay, and the fighting
at Chunuk Bair and after the Evacuation was transferred
to Mesopotamia. In this theatre of war he was in action at
Kut-el-Amara, Um-el-Hannah and Sanna-i-Yat, and was
killed in action on April 9th, 1916. He was entitled to the
1914-15 Star, and the General Service and Victory Medals.
          " He died the noblest death a man may die."
21, Arthur Street, Hulme, Manchester.   Z1116

BAILEY, W. T., Driver, R.F.A.
He volunteered in January 1915, and five months later proceeded to the Western Front, where he was in action with
his Battery at many important engagements. He took part
in much heavy fighting in various sectors, and was present
at the Battles of Loos, Albert, the Somme, Beaucourt and
Arras, and rendered valuable services during the Retreat
and Advance of 1918. He holds the 1914-15 Star, and the
General Service and Victory Medals, and was demobilised
in January 1919.
32, Parkfield Avenue, Rusholme, Manchester.   TZ1113

BAILIFF, W., Pte., K.O. (Royal Lancaster Regt.)
Volunteering in November 1914, he proceeded overseas in
the following November, and landed at Salonika. In this
theatre of war he took part in the Advance across the Struma,
the capture of Monastir, and in heavy fighting on the Dorian
front until July 1917. Transferred to the Western Front
in the succeeding month he fought in several engagements,
and was unhappily killed in the Battle of Passchendaele in
October 1917. He was entitled to the 1914-15 Star, and the
General Service and Victory Medals.
          " His name liveth for evermore."
2, Osborne Street, Oldham Road, Manchester.   Z9824

BAINBRIDGE, A., Private, Royal Welch Fusiliers.
He joined in December 1916, and in March of the following
year was drafted to France. There he took part in much
severe fighting in various sectors, and was wounded at Arras
in April 1917 by a sniper. He was invalided to England, and
was discharged from hospital in November 1917 as physically
unfit for further service. He holds the General Service and
Victory Medals.
51, Upton Street, Chorlton-on-Medlock, Manchester.   Z1120

BAINBRIDGE, A., Private, 19th Manchester Regt.
He volunteered in September 1914, and after a period of
training was drafted to the Western Front in November of
the following year. In this theatre of war he took part in
many important engagements, including the Battles of Hill 60,
Loos and Vimy Ridge, and was gassed on the Somme. He
again went into action four months later and was reported
missing and presumed killed in September 1918. He was
entitled to the 1914-15 Star, and the General Service and
Victory Medals.
          " The path of duty was the way to glory."   Z1121
11, Mornington Street, Chorlton-on-Medlock, Manchester.

BAINES, A., Private, Northumberland Fusiliers.
He joined in January 1916, and after a course of training
was engaged for a time on various important duties. Soon
afterwards he was discharged from the Army in order to take
up munition work of National importance at Messrs. Peacocks,
Gorton, where he rendered valuable services until the Armistice. 1, Bowden Street, Newton Heath, Manchester. Z9414

BAINES, T., Private, 12th King's (Liverpool Regt.)
He volunteered in October 1914, and in the following March
proceeded to France. There he took part in many notable
battles, including those at Ypres, Festubert, Albert, the
Somme, Arras, Bullecourt, Cambrai and the Retreat and
Advance of 1918, during which time he was wounded. Demobilised in January 1919, he holds the 1914-15 Star, and
the General Service and Victory Medals.
36, Teignmouth Street, Collyhurst, Manchester.   Z9415

BAIRD, E., Private, Royal Dublin Fusiliers.
He joined in September 1916, but was unsuccessful in securing a transfer to the war zone. He was stationed at various
important depôts in Ireland and throughout the period of
his service performed excellent work. He was discharged
from the Army in 1918, but re-enlisted in December 1919,
and proceeded to India, where he was still serving in 1920.
93, Jersey Street Dwellings, Manchester.   Z11464

BAIRD, J., Company Quarter-Master-Sergeant, R.E.
He volunteered in January 1916, and later in the same year
proceeded to Salonika, where he rendered distinguished
services in engagements on the Doiran front. He was later
transferred to Egypt and Palestine and in Febraury 1918
embarked for France. In this theatre of war he was engaged
on constructional work and was demobilised in March 1919,
holding the General Service and Victory Medals.
59, Upton Street, Charlton-on-Medlock, Manchester. Z1122A

BAIRD, J., Air Mechanic, R.A.F
He joined in July 1918, but owing to his being medically
unfit for service overseas was retained on important duties
with his Squadron at various stations in England. He,
nevertheless, rendered valuable services until January 1919,
when he was demobilised.
59, Upton Street, Chorlton-on-Medlock, Manchester. Z1122B

BAKER, C., Private, King's (Liverpool Regiment).
Joining in March 1916, he proceeded in the following July
to France, where during the fierce fighting on the Somme
he was killed in action in September 1916. He was entitled
to the General Service and Victory Medals.
" Honour to the immortal dead, who gave their youth that
     the world might grow old in peace."
5, Bright Street, Rochdale Road, Manchester.   Z9416A

BAKER, C. W. R., Pte., 1/7th Lancashire Fusiliers.
He volunteered in May 1915, and after training at various
stations was drafted to Egypt in January 1916. There he
saw service on the Suez Canal, and later was in action at the
Battles of Gaza in Palestine. He also took part in the fighting
at Romani, and in March 1917 proceeded to France, where
he made the supreme sacrifice, being killed in action at
Péronne on May 2nd, 1917. He was entitled to the General
Service and Victory Medals.
" The path of duty was the way to glory."
10, Ferry Street, Ardwick, Manchester. Z1123

BAKER, J., Private, 2/7th Manchester Regiment.
He joined in May 1916, and in the following January proceeded to the Western Front, where he did good work with
his unit in engagements at Arras, Ypres, Bullecourt, Messines
and Cambrai. Whilst fighting in the Retreat of 1918 he was
killed in action on March 21st. He was entitled to the General
Service and Victory Medals.
" His life for his Country, his soul to God."
13, Pownall Street, Hulme, Manchester. Z9038

BAKER, J., C.S.M., 11th Manchester Regiment.
Volunteering in August 1914, he was drafted to the Dardanelles
early in the following year, and served with distinction at
the Landing at Cape Helles, the Battles of Krithia and the
Landing at Suvla Bay, where he was wounded in August
1915. After the Evacuation of the Gallipoli Peninsula, he
proceeded to the Western Front, and was badly wounded
in action during the Somme Offensive in October 1918. He
was invalided home and after hospital treatment in Sussex,
was discharged as medically unfit for further service in July
1917, holding the 1914-15 Star, and the General Service and
Victory Medals.
33, Dickens Street, Queen's Road, Manchester. Z10286

BAKER, R., Private, Royal Welch Fusiliers.
He volunteered in October 1914, and in June of the following
year embarked for France, where he served till the end of
the war. He was in action at Loos, the Somme, Arras,
Ypres, Cambrai and in many other notable battles until the
close of hostilities. In 1920 he was serving in Mesopotamia,
and holds the 1914-15 Star, and the General Service and
Victory Medals.
5, Bright Street, Rochdale Road, Manchester. Z9416B

BAKEWELL, L. M. (Mrs.), Special War Worker.
This lady volunteered her services in September 1914, and
was engaged on the production of shells. She was later
appointed shell examiner at the Belsize Munition Works,
and did consistently good work until June 1918, when she
relinquished her duties.
33, Bunyan Street, Ardwick, Manchester. Z1124

BALDWIN, F., Capt., 56th Labour Battalion.
He was gazetted in March 1916, and three months later
proceeded to France, where he rendered distinguished services
in many sectors. On one occasion he and his men were in
action with picks and shovels during a German break through.
He was accidentally gassed when removing gas syphons to
new positions. He holds the General Service and Victory
Medals, and was demobilised in August 1919.
114, Tamworth, Street, Hulme, Manchester. Z1130A

BALDWIN, J., Sergt., 2nd East Lancashire Regt.
He volunteered in November 1914, and was shortly afterwards
drafted to the Western Front, where he played a distinguished
part in the fighting in many sectors. He was in action at
the Battles of the Aisne, Ypres, Neuve Chapelle, Festubert,
Loos, Albert, Vermelles, Vimy Ridge, the Somme, Beaumont-
Hamel, the Ancre and Arras. He holds the 1914 Star, and
the General Service and Victory Medals, and was demobilised
in December 1919. He had served sixteen years in India
before the great war.
9, Ribston Street, Hulme, Manchester. Z1129

BALDWIN, W., Private, Royal Fusiliers.
He volunteered in September 1914, and early in the following
year proceeded to the Dardanelles, where he was in action
during the Landing at Suvla Bay, and was wounded. Invalided to Malta he was sent on his recovery to Salonika, and
saw much service. In 1916 he was drafted to Egypt, and was
engaged on important garrison duties until his return to
England for demobilisation in July 1919. He holds the 1914-
15 Star, and the General Service and Victory Medals.
114, Tamworth Street, Hulme, Manchester. Z1130B

BALL, A., Private, 16th Lancashire Fusiliers.
Volunteering in November 1914, he was sent a year later to
France, where he was in action in various sectors of the Front.
He fought in the Battles of Loos, Albert and Vimy Ridge,
and was severely wounded on the Somme. He was invalided
to England, and unfortunately succumbed to his injuries
in August 1916. He was entitled to the 1914-15 Star, and
the General Service and Victory Medals.
" He joined the great white company of valiant souls."
42, Lostock Street, Miles Plating, Manchester. Z9039

BALL, A. H., Private, 1st Manchester Regiment.
A time-serving Soldier, he was in India when war broke out in
August 1914, and immediately embarked for France, There
he took part in many important engagements, including the
Battles of Ypres, Neuve Chapelle, Hill 60, and Loos. In
December 1915 he was transferred to Mesopotamia, where
he saw much fighting at Kut-el-Amara, Um-el-Hannah and
various other places, but was unfortunately killed in action
at Kut in March 1916. He was entitled to the 1914 Star,
and the General Service and Victory Medals.
" Great deeds cannot die."
9, Fountain Street, City Road, Hulme, Manchseter. TZ1125

BALL, J., Pte., King's Own (Royal Lancaster Regt.
He joined in February 1918, on attaining military age, but
owing to his having met with an accident was unable to obtain
his transfer to a theatre of war. He, nevertheless, rendered
valuable services at various important stations, and was
demobilised in October 1919.
6, Olive Grove, Hulme, Manchester. Z1126

BALL, J., Private, King's (Liverpool Regiment).
He joined in May 1916, and after training at Whitchurch,
proceeded in the following month to the Western Front.
In this theatre of war he served with the Labour Corps,
principally in the Somme, Passchendaele and Cambrai sectors.
He remained in France until April 1919, when he returned
home and was demobilised, holding the General Service and
Victory Medals.
50, Gibbon Street, Bradford, Manchester. Z9040

BALL, R., Private, 21st Manchester Regiment.
He volunteered in August 1914, and after a period of training
was drafted to the Western Front, where he was in action at
many important engagements, including the Battles of Loos,
Albert and Vimy Ridge. He was wounded during the Somme
Offensive in July 1916, and was invalided to England and
eventually discharged in August 1917 as physically unfit for
further service. He holds the 1914-15 Star, and the General
Service and Victory Medals.
3, Arbury Street, Hulme, Manchester. Z1127

BALL, W. M., Corporal, R.F.A.
He volunteered in September 1914, and was drafted to the
Western Front in August 1915, after doing duty in Ireland.
He took a prominent part in many important engagements,
including those at Loos and St. Eloi, but made the supreme
sacrifice on April 24th, 1916, being killed in action on the
Ypres front. He was entitled to the 1914-15 Star, and the
General Service and Victory Medals.
" Whilst we remember, the sacrifice is not in vain."
9, Cheltenham Street, Chorlton-on-Medlock, Manchester.
Z1128C

BALLINGALL, W., Private, West Riding Regt.
Joining in 1917, he shortly afterwards proceeded to the
Western Front, and served in many sectors. He was in action
at Armentières, Bullecourt, the Somme, Ypres, and numerous
other places until hostilities ceased, and was wounded. Returning home in 1919 he was demobilised, and holds the
General Service and Victory Medals.
9, Elizabeth Street, Ancoats, Manchester. TZ9417B

BAMBER, G., Sergt., 12th Manchester Regt. and R.E.
Volunteering in October 1914, he was sent to France in May
of the following year, and played a distinguished part in
many engagements. He was in action at the Battles of
Loos, St. Eloi, Albert, Vimy Ridge and the Somme, and after
being invalided to England through wounds, returned to
the Western Front and took part in the fighting on the Passchendaele and Cambrai fronts. He holds the 1914-15 Star,
and the General Service and Victory Medals, and was demobilised in January 1919.
186, Viaduct Street, Ardwick, Manchester. Z1132

BAMBER, T., Private, Royal Welch Fusiliers.
He joined in July 1917, and after serving in Ireland for some
time, proceeded in March 1918 to France, where he took part
in the Retreat and Advance of that year, being in action on
the Somme and at Havrincourt and Epéhy. After the
Armistice he was sent to Germany, and served with the Army
of Occupation on the Rhine. He holds the General Service
and Victory Medals, and was demobilised in February 1919.
46, Gorton Street, Ardwick, Manchester. Z1131

BAMFORD, G., Bombardier, R.F.A.
He volunteered in September 1914, and after a course of
training was sent to the East in June of the following year.
There he was in action at many engagements, both in Egypt
and Palestine, and rendered valuable services at the Battles
of Gaza and Jaffa, the taking of Jerusalem and the capture
of Jericho. He was demobilised in March 1919 on his return
home, and holds the 1914-15 Star, and the General Service
and Victory Medals.
24, Shipley Street, Longsight, Manchester. Z1133

BAMFORD, H., Corporal, 2nd Lancashire Fusiliers.
He volunteered in September 1914, and three months later was drafted to the Western Front, where he played a prominent part in much severe fighting. After taking part in the Battles of Ypres and the Somme, he was unfortunately killed in action on May 3rd, 1917. He was entitled to the 1914–15 Star, and the General Service and Victory Medals.
" A valiant Soldier, with undaunted heart he breasted life's last hill."
1, Virginia Street, Rochdale Road, Manchester.   Z10287A

BAMFORD, J., Private, Suffolk Regiment.
He volunteered in September 1914, and on completion of his training was sent overseas in February 1916. During his period of service on the Western Front he fought in numerous sectors and was in action at Albert, Armentières, Arras, Bailleul, Langemarck, Fontaine, and was wounded. He served in France until November 1918. and was demobilised in the following March, holding the General Service and Victory Medals.
17, Mytton Street, Chapman Street, Hulme, Manchester.
   Z9041

BANCROFT, J. W., Private, 1st Manchester Regt.
He volunteered in January 1916, and in June of the following year proceeded to France, where he took part in many engagements of importance, and for four months saw much active service on the Ypres front. He was also in action during the Retreat and Advance of 1918, and was wounded on the Somme. He holds the General Service and Victory Medals, and was demobilised in September 1919.
39, Caton Street, Hulme, Manchester.   Z1134

BANCROFT, P., Sergt., 8th Border Regiment.
He volunteered in January 1915, and proceeded to France in the following December. There he played a distinguished part in many engagements, and was in action at St. Eloi, Ypres, Albert, Vermelles, Vimy Ridge, the Somme, Beaumont-Hamel, the Ancre and Bullecort. He was invalided to hospital, owing to ill-health, and later did duty on Headquarter Staff at Rouen, until his demobilisation in May 1919. He holds the 1914–15 Star, and the General Service and Victory Medals.
44, Buckingham Street, Moss Side, Manchester.   Z1135

BANKS, E., Pte., King's Own (Royal Lancaster Regt.)
He volunteered in June 1915, and after undergoing a period of training, was drafted to France in May of the following year. There he took part in many important engagements, including those at La Bassée, Givenchy, Festubert, Albert, Arras and Loos, and was wounded in August 1916. Invalided to England in consequence, he was discharged in September 1917, as physically unfit for further service, and holds the General Service and Victory Medals.
65, Norton Street, West Gorton, Manchester.   Z1136

BANKS, J., L/Corporal, Inniskilling Fusiliers.
He volunteered in December 1914, and five months later was drafted to France, where he served at Loos, Neuve Chapelle, Nieuport, Armentières, Ploegsteert Wood. the Somme, Arras, La Bassée, Hill 60, Festubert, Vermelles, Beaumont-Hamel, Beaucourt, Albert, St. Eloi, Vimy Ridge and Ypres. He was unhappily killed in action in June 1917, and was entitled to the 1914–15 Star, and the General Service and Victory Medals.
" A costly sacrifice upon the altar of freedom."
16, John Street, Bradford, Manchester.   X11869

BANKS, J., Pte., Loyal North Lancashire Regt.
Volunteering in September 1914, he completed a period of training and was sent to the Western Front in August of the following year. In this theatre of war he took part in much heavy fighting, and was in action at the Battles of Loos, the Somme, the Ancre, Arras and Vimy Ridge. His health failing, he returned to England, and was discharged in September 1917 as medically unfit. He holds the 1914–15 Star, and the General Service and Victory Medals.
17, Gay Street, Jackson Street, Hulme, Manchseter.   TZ1137A

BANKS, J., Private, South Lancashire Regiment.
He volunteered in September 1914, and three months later proceeded to the Western Front, where he took part in many important engagements in various sectors. He was in action at the Battles of Neuve Chapelle, Hill 60 and Ypres II, but was unfortunately killed during the German attack on Loos, in January 1916. He was entitled to the 1914–15 Star, and the General Service and Victory Medals.
" His life for his Country, his soul to God."
17, Gay Street, Jackson Street, Hulme, Manchester.   TZ1137B

BANKS, W. J., Corporal, R.E.
He volunteered in May 1915, and four months later proceeded to France, where he was engaged on important duties in connection with the construction of railways. Later he was sent to the East and did work of a similar nature in Egypt and Palestine. He holds the 1914–15 Star, and the General Service and Victory Medals, and on his return home was demobilised in April 1919.
17, Wycliffe Street, Ardwick, Manchester.   Z1138

BANNISTER, A. E., Pte., South Lancashire Regt.
He volunteered in September 1914, and on completion of his training was sent to Salonika, where he saw severe fighting on the Struma, Doiran and Vardar fronts, and during the General Advance of 1918. Remaining in the East until March 1919, he was then sent home and a month later was demobilised, holding the 1914–15 Star, and the General Service and Victory Medals.
63, Hamilton Street, Collyhurst, Manchester.   Z10238

BANNON, E., Sergt., 6th Manchester Regiment.
Volunteering in September 1914, he proceeded to France in March 1917, and played a distinguished part in many engagements. He was in action at the Battles of St. Quentin, Passchendaele, the Somme and Cambrai, and during the Retreat and Advance of 1918, and was wounded on the Marne. He returned to England after the Armistice, and was demobilised in February 1919, holding the General Service and Victory Medals.
24, Chapman Street, Hulme, Manchester.   Z1139

BANTON, J., Sergt., R.G.A.
He joined in June 1917, and was shortly afterwards drafted to Mesopotamia, where he played a distinguished part in the fighting in this theatre of war. He also saw service in Palestine, and rendered valuable services during the capture of Jericho, Tripoli and Aleppo. He unfortunately died in hospital on October 26th, 1919, after contracting influenza. He was entitled to the General Service and Victory Medals.
" His memory is cherished with pride."
21, Melbourne Street, Hulme, Manchester.   Z1140

BARBER, G. H. (M.M.), Pte., 2/7th King's (Liverpool Regt.) and M.G.C.
He volunteered in October 1915, and was five months later drafted to the Western Front, where he took an active part in the Battles of Loos, St. Eloi, St. Quentin, Arras, Ypres and the Somme. He was wounded in action at Ypres, and the Somme, and whilst fighting in the latter engagement was awarded the Military Medal for conspicuous bravery in the Field during a German attack. After the close of the war he rejoined for two years, and in 1920 was still serving in the Army. He also holds the General Service and Victory Medals.
113, Edensor Street, Beswick, Manchester.   Z9042A

BARBER, J., C.S.M., Lancashire Fusiliers.
He volunteered at the outbreak of war in August 1914, and proceeded to France in February of the following year. He played a conspicuous part in the fighting on the Somme, and was wounded. After being invalided home he returned to the Western Front and was stationed at Dunkirk, where he was engaged on general superintending duties until his demobilisation in March 1919. He holds the 1914–15 Star, and the General Service and Victory Medals.
6, Geoffery Street, Chorlton-on-Medlock, Manchester,   Z1141

BARBER, J. H., Corporal, 16th Manchester Regt.
A month after the outbreak of hostilities he volunteered for active service, but was not successful in obtaining a transfer to a theatre of war. He was retained on important duties in England and performed excellent work with the Military Police at Altcar, Chester, Ripon, Blackpool and Prees Heath. In December 1918, he was discharged from the Army on account of bronchitis.
113, Edensor Street, Beswick, Manchester.   Z9042B

BARCLAY, T., Corporal, Manchester Regiment.
Volunteering in August 1914, he was drafted to Mesopotamia in June 1917, and took part in engagements at Kut, where he was wounded, and on the Tigris. In July 1918 he was transferred to Palestine, but after being in action at Jaffa and Jerusalem, proceeded to Egypt. There he served at Kantara, Cairo and Alexandria, and rendered valuable services in quelling the riots in 1919. Returning to England in December 1919 he was demobilised, holding the General Service and Victory Medals.
83, Dale Street, Miles Platting, Manchester.   Z9043

BARDSLEY, D., Private, 3rd South Wales Borderers.
Joining in March 1916, he completed his training and was sent in the following March to France. In this theatre of war he took part in several engagements, notably those at Arras, Ypres III, and Cambrai, where he was wounded in November 1917. Evacuated to England, he received protracted medical treatment, and was eventually demobilised in March 1919. He holds the General Service and Victory Medals.
12, Dyson Street, Varle Street, Miles Platting, Manchester.   Z9827A

BARDSLEY, G., Driver, R.A.S.C.
He volunteered in August 1914, and served at home until 1916, when he was drafted to Salonika. In this theatre of war he was employed for a short period on the General Headquarters Staff, and also took part in several operations on the Bulgarian front, and was present at the capture of Monastir in December 1916. On the cessation of hostilities he returned home for demobilisation in 1919, and holds the General Service and Victory Medals.
127, Morton Street, Longsight, Manchester.   Z9826

BARDSLEY. G., Private, 2nd Border Regiment.
He was serving with the Militia at the outbreak of hostilities and was drafted in November of the same year to France, where he served until the end of the war. During this period he fought in several engagements, including the Battles of Neuve Chapelle, Hill 60, Festubert, La Bassée, Ypres II and III, Arras and Cambrai, during the German Offensive and at Amiens and Le Cateau in the subsequent Allied Advance of 1918. He was demobilised in April 1919, and holds the 1914–15 Star, and the General Service and Victory Medals.
12, Dyson Street, Varley Street, Miles Platting, Manchester.
Z9827B

BARDSLEY, H., L/Corporal, 21st Manchester Regt.
Volunteering in January 1915, he was retained on special duties with his unit at important stations in England, owing to his being physically unfit for service overseas. He was, however, discharged from the Army in the following July, and was engaged on work of National importance until the cessation of hostilities. He was still working for Messrs. John Hetheringtons, of Ancoats, Manchester, in 1920.
64, Brunt Street, Rusholme, Manchester.
Z1142

BARDSLEY, J., Private, 9th Border Regiment.
Volunteering in November 1914, he was drafted in the following August to the Western Front, where he fought in the Battle of Loos, and other engagements, until transferred to Salonika two months later. In this theatre of war he took part in fighting on the Doiran front, and in the Advance across the Struma and Vardar. He was also present at the capture of Monastir, and on the conclusion of hostilities returned home for his demobilisation in February 1919. He holds the 1914–15 Star, and the General Service and Victory Medals.
12, Dyson Street, Varley Street, Miles Platting, Manchester.
Z9828

BARDSLEY, R., Private, R.M.L.I., and Labour Corps.
He joined in July 1916, and was sent in the following month to France. There he was stationed at Dieppe and engaged on important duties in connection with the loading and unloading of vessels. He rendered valuable services throughout the war, and returned home for his demobilisation in March 1919. He holds the General Service and Victory Medals.
12, Dyson Street, Varley Street, Miles Platting, Manchester.
Z9827C

BARKER, A., Private, R.A.S.C.
He joined in June 1916, and shortly afterwards crossed to France, where he served during many important engagements. He was present at Loos, the Somme, Arras, Ypres and Albert, and rendered valuable services until demobilised in January 1919. He holds the General Service and Victory Medals.
85, Woodward Street, Ancoats, Manchester.
TZ9419

BARKER, A., Private, Essex Regiment.
He volunteered in September 1914, and was engaged on Coast defence until April 1916, when he proceeded to the Egyptian front. After taking part in engagements at Katia, Romani and Magdhaba, he was sent to Palestine and was again in action at Gaza and Jerusalem. He served overseas until May 1919, when he returned to England, and being demobilised a month later, holds the General Service and Victory Medals.
198, Victoria Square, Ancoats, Manchester.
Z9044

BARKER, C., Private, 1st Manchester Regiment.
He volunteered in August 1914, and proceeding to France shortly afterwards, took part in heavy fighting in the Battles of Ypres and Neuve Chapelle. He gave his life for King and Country on March 21st, 1915, and was entitled to the 1914 Star, and the General Service and Victory Medals.
" A valiant Soldier, with undaunted heart he breasted life's last hill."
54, York Street, Chorlton-on-Medlock, Manchester. Z9829

BARKER, E., Private, 4th Seaforth Highlanders.
He volunteered in January 1915, and after a period of training was drafted to France, where he took part in much severe fighting during his service on the Western Front. He made the supreme sacrifice in May 1915, being killed in action at the Battle of Hill 60, and was entitled to the 1914–15 Star, and the General Service and Victory Medals.
" He died the noblest death a man may die."
47, Clayton Street, Hulme, Manchester. Z1143A

BARKER, G. E., Private, Manchester Regiment, and Air Mechanic, R.A.F.
He volunteered in July 1915, and in the following December was sent to France, where he fought at Albert, Ypres, the Somme, Arras, Beaumont-Hamel and Cambrai, and was wounded in action at St. Quentin in April 1917. He was invalided home and on the way to England the hospital ship " Donegal " was torpedoed. He was discharged as medically unfit in November 1917 but some time later joined the R.A.F. and served at Blandford and Birmingham, until demobilised in April 1919. He holds the 1914–15 Star, and the General Service and Victory Medals.
8, Boundary Street, Newton, Manchester. Z9045

BARKER, F., Private, R.A.S.C.
He joined in April 1918, and was retained at various stations in England after completing his training. In 1919 he was sent to France, where he acted as a Despatch Rider, and was also engaged on duties of importance at the General Headquarter Staff. He was still serving in 1920.
47, Clayton Street, Hulme, Manchester. Z1143B

BARKER, H., Private, 7th Lancashire Fusiliers.
Volunteering in November 1915, he completed his training and was engaged on important duties with his Battalion, and redered valuable services. Contracting illness he was sent to Cambridge Hospital, Aldershot, and after treatment was discharged as medically unfit for further service in October 1916.
11, Birch Street, Bradford, Manchester. Z9830

BARKER, J. S., Private, Royal Berkshire Regiment.
He joined in May 1918, and after a few weeks' training proceeded to France, where he took part in the heavy fighting during the Retreat, and was severely wounded at Cambrai, in the Advance of 1918. He was invalided home, and eventually discharged in January 1919, holding the General Service and Victory Medals.
92, Gibson Street, Ardwick, Manchester. Z1144B

BARKER, J. W., Private, 8th Lancashire Fusiliers.
He volunteered in September 1914, and sailing for Gallipoli in the following year, served in various operations on the Peninsula until invalided to hospital in November 1915, owing to illness. On recovery he was engaged on home service duties, and in June 1918 crossed to France, where he saw heavy fighting during the Retreat and Advance of that year. Demobilised in July 1919, he holds the 1914–15 Star, and the General Service and Victory Medals.
60, Clayton Street, Chorlton Road, Manchester. Z9831

BARKER, S., Private. 11th King's Own (Royal Lancaster Regiment.)
He volunteered in June 1915, and after completing his training served at various stations on important duties with his unit. Owing to medical unfitness he was not able to obtain a transfer to a fighting unit, and in 1917 was discharged, after rendering much valuable service.
1, Elizabeth Ann Street, Manchester. Z9418

BARKER, S., Corporal, Manchester Regiment.
In 1916 he joined the Army, and was retained on important duties in England during the period of hostilities. Throughout his three years' service he performed excellent work with the Military Police at Southport, Manchester, Wigan, Holyhead, Preston, Waterloo, Liverpool, Altcar and also in Ireland. He was eventually demobilised in 1919.
3, Duncan Street, Ancoats, Manchester. Z6038

BARKER, T., Private, K.O. (Royal Lancaster Regt.)
Volunteering in August 1914, he was drafted to France in the following February and took part in many engagements of importance. He saw much heavy fighting in various sectors, being in action at the Battles of Neuve Chapelle, Hill 60, Loos, Albert, Vimy Ridge, the Somme and Arras, and contracted trench fever. He was invalided to England, and was discharged in November 1917, as physically unfit for further military service. He holds the 1914–15 Star, and the General Service and Victory Medals.
9, Hancock Street, Rusholme, Manchester. Z1145

BARLOW, A., Driver, R.F.A.
He was mobilised at the outbreak of war in August 1914, and was immediately drafted to the Western Front, where he took part in the Retreat from Mons. He was also in action with his Battery at many subsequent engagements, including the Battles of the Aisne, La Bassée, Ypres, St. Eloi, Loos and Albert, and was wounded. After five months in hospital he returned to France, and was soon engaged in further heavy fighting at Beaucourt, Arras, Vimy Ridge and Messines, and was again wounded. He eventually returned to England, and was discharged as physically unfit in January 1918, holding the Mons Star, and the General Service and Victory Medals.
22, Franchise Street, Ardwick, Manchester. Z1146

BARLOW, A., Private, 22nd Manchester Regt.
He volunteered in October 1914, and after a period of training was drafted to the Western Front in November 1915. In this theatre of war he took part in many important engagements, including the Battles of St. Eloi and Loos, and was reported missing, and later presumed killed in action on the Somme in July 1916. He was entitled to the 1914–15 Star, and the General Service and Victory Medals.
" His memory is cherished with pride."
17, Everton Road, Chorlton-on-Medlock, Manchester. Z1149C

BARLOW, A. J., Private, 11th Lancashire Fusiliers.
He volunteered in August 1914, but being unfit for active service, he was not able to secure a transfer overseas. He was engaged in Home Defence, and was chiefly employed on important guard duties at Codford, Bournemouth, Aldershot and Sutton, at which stations he carried out his work in a highly capable manner. In January 1919 he was demobilised.
6, Spurgeon Street, West Gorton, Manchester. Z9046

BARLOW, C., Private, Welch Regiment.
Joining in March 1916, he crossed to France in the following December, and there took part in many important engagements. He was in action at Arras, Ypres, and Cambrai, and later was engaged with the Labour Corps on various important duties until demobilised in October 1919. He holds the General Service and Victory Medals.
8, Shears Street, Newton Heath, Manchester. Z9420

BARLOW, C. F., Pte., 17th Manchester Regiment.
Volunteering in August 1914, he proceeded to France in September of the following year and was in action in various important sectors. He saw much severe fighting at Ploegsteert Wood, Vimy Ridge, and the Somme, and was wounded. In February 1917 he was transferred to Mesopotamia, and took part in the Battle of Kut, and the capture of Tekrit. Returning to England after the Armistice, he was demobilised in March 1919, and holds the 1914-15 Star, and the General Service and Victory Medals.
9, Mather Street, Hulme, Manchester. TZ1151A

BARLOW, E., Private, 9th Welch Regiment.
Volunteering in February 1915, he embarked for the Western Front in the following April, and fought at St. Eloi, Albert, Vimy Ridge, in the Somme Offensive and at Arras. He was gassed in the Battle of Ypres in July 1917, and on recovery was in action at Passchendaele, and in numerous engagements in the Retreat and Advance of 1918. Returning home in December of that year, he was demobilised a month later, and holds the General Service and Victory Medals.
29, Montague Street, Collyhurst, Manchester. Z9832

BARLOW, E., Sapper, R.E.
Volunteering in September 1914, he was drafted to the Dardanelles in the following year and saw much severe fighting on the Gallipoli Peninsula. After the Evacuation, he proceeded to Egypt, but was soon transferred to the Western Front, where he fought at La Bassée. He was unfortunately killed in action on April 7th, 1918, and was entitled to the 1914-15 Star, and the General Service and Victory Medals.
"His life for his Country, his soul to God."
12, Whitley Street, Collyhurst, Manchester. Z11870B

BARLOW, F. A., Captain, 12th Manchester Regt.
Joining in April 1917, he was drafted to the Western Front two months later and there saw much severe fighting in various sectors. He took a distinguished part in the Battles of Cambrai, Bapaume, Havrincourt and Le Cateau, and many other important engagements in this theatre of war, and was wounded in action at Passchendaele in August 1917. He was demobilised in November 1919, and holds the General Service and Victory Medals.
58, Russell Street, Moss Side, Manchester. Z11630

BARLOW, G. E., Driver, R.F.A.
Volunteering in August 1914, he proceeded a month later to Egypt, where he was in action an the Suez Canal, and at Katia, El Fasher, Romani and Magdhaba, and was wounded at Mersa Matruh. Whilst serving in Palestine, he took part in fighting at Gaza and Jerusalem. In June 1918 he was drafted to France, and in this theatre of war was in action in the Battles of the Marne, Bapaume and Havrincourt, and was again wounded. He was demobilised in February 1919, and holds the 1914-15 Star, and the General Service and Victory Medals.
5, Garden Place, Ancoats, Manchester. Z9048B

BARLOW, H., Private, 2nd South Lancashire Regt.
He volunteered in August 1914, and two months later was sent to the Western Front. There he saw heavy fighting at Ypres, Festubert and Loos, and was wounded in the later engagement. On returning to the firing line he was again in action at St. Eloi, Vimy Ridge, the Somme, Messines, Lens and Ypres. In October 1918 he was sent back to England suffering from dysentery, and on his discharge from hospital served at Ripon until demobilised in February 1919, holding the 1914 Star, and the General Service and Victory Medals.
23, Ogden Street, Hulme, Manchester. TZ9047

BARLOW, H., Private, 14th South Lancashire Regt.
He joined in June 1918, but owing to his being physically unfit was retained on important duties at various stations on the East Coast. Though unable to proceed to a theatre of war he nevertheless rendered valuable services, and was demobilised in February 1919.
17, Everton Road, Chorlton-on-Medlock, Manchester. Z1149B

BARLOW, H., Driver, R.F.A.
He volunteered in June 1915, and two months later proceeded to France, where he took part in the Battles of St. Eloi, Loos and Vimy Ridge. He acted as gun team driver and was engaged taking up ammunition to the forward areas. He also saw service in Egypt for a short time and was demobilised in May 1919, on his return, holding the 1914-15 Star, and the General Service and Victory Medals.
132, South Street, Longsight, Manchester. Z1147B

BARLOW, J., Private, 2nd Manchester Regiment.
He joined in March 1917, and after a short period of training was drafted to the Western Front, where he was engaged in heavy fighting in various sectors. He was also in action at

Festubert and was wounded in action in the third Battle of Ypres. Returning to England, he was transferred to the Royal Air Force, and did duty with his Squadron until his discharge in February 1918 as physically unfit. He holds the General Service and Victory Medals.
15, Jones Street, Hulme, Manchester. Z1153

BARLOW, J., Private, R.A.S.C.
He joined in June 1916, and crossing to France two months later was engaged on important transport duties in the forward areas. He did good work in the Battles of the Somme, the Ancre, Arras, Ypres, Lens and Cambrai, in those of the German Offensive, and at Amiens and other places in the subsequent Allied Advance of 1918. After the Armistice he was sent into Germany with the Army of Occupation, and returning to England for demobilisation in December 1918, holds the General Service and Victory Medals.
70, Great Jackson Street, West Gorton, Manchester. Z9833

BARLOW, J., Private, Royal Welch Fusiliers.
He volunteered in February 1915, and first did duty in Ireland. In August, however, he was drafted to Salonika, and after seeing service in this theatre of war proceeded to Mesopotamia, where he took part in many important engagements. He holds the 1914-15 Star, and the General Service and Victory Medals, and was demobilised on his return home in April 1920.
22, William Street, Hulme, Manchester. Z1152

BARLOW, J. (M.M.), Corporal, Rifle Brigade.
Volunteering in November 1914, he proceeded to France in July of the following year. There he played a prominent part in many engagements, including the Battles of the Somme, Messines, Passchendaele and Cambrai, and was wounded in action at Ypres. He also took part in the Retreat and Advance of 1918, and was awarded the Military Medal for conspicuous bravery and devotion to duty in the Field. He also holds the 1914-15 Star, and the General Service and Victory Medals, and was demobilised in March 1919.
37, Marsland Street, Ardwick, Manchester. Z1150

BARLOW, J., Private, R.A.M.C.
He volunteered in May 1915, and after a period of training was drafted to France, where he did consistently good work with his Corps. He was present at the Battles of the Somme, Ypres and Cambrai, and suffered from gas poisoning. He was later transferred to Italy, and saw active service on the Piave. Returning to England after the Armistice, he was demobilised in February 1919, and holds the General Service and Victory Medals.
3, Emily Street, Ardwick, Manchester. Z1148

BARLOW, J. A., Gunner, R.G.A.
Joining in December 1916, he completed his training and was engaged with his Battery on important duties at various depôts. He did excellent work but was unable to secure his transfer to a theatre of war before the conclusion of hostilities, owing to medical unfitness for general service. He was demobilised in September 1919.
6, Pine Street, Gorton, Manchester. Z9834

BARLOW, J. H., Private, 17th Manchester Regt.
He volunteered in August 1914, and after undergoing a period of training was drafted to the Western Front in September 1915. There he took part in many important engagements including those at Loos, Albert and Vimy Ridge, and made the supreme sacrifice, being killed on the Somme in action on March 14th, 1916. He was entitled to the 1914-15 Star, and the General Service and Victory Medals.
"Whilst we remember, the sacrifice is not in vain."
9, Mather Street, Hulme, Manchester. TZ1151B

BARLOW, J. H., Private, Royal Welch Fusiliers.
He joined in January 1917, and after training for three months was drafted to Mesopotamia, where he took a prominent part in many important engagements, including the capture of Amara. He also saw service in Palestine and was twice wounded. He holds the General Service and Victory Medals, and was demobilised in January 1919, after his return home.
17, Everton Road, Chorlton-on-Medlock, Manchester. Z1149A

BARLOW, J. W., Private, R.A.M.C.
He was already in the Army at the outbreak of war in August 1914, and proceeded to Egypt in the following month. He later saw service on the Gallipoli Peninsula, and was engaged on important duties with the Red Cross at the Battle of Krithia, and the attack on Achi-Baba. He was unfortunately killed by an enemy sniper in July 1915. He was entitled to the 1914-15 Star, and the General Service and Victory Medals.
"His life for his Country, his soul to God."
40, Carter Terrace, Greenheys, Manchester. Z1154B

BARLOW, R., Private, R.A.S.C.
Volunteering in September 1914, he was retained in England on important transport duties at various stations, and was unable to obtain his transfer overseas on account of his being medically unfit. He nevertheless rendered valuable services, and was discharged in November 1917. Unfortunately through contracting consumption he died in November 1919.
"His memory is cherished with pride."
3, Jones Street, Hulme, Manchester. Z1155

BARLOW, R., Driver, R.A.S.C.

He volunteered at the outbreak of war in August 1914, and in July of the following year proceeded to the Western Front, where he was engaged on important duties in various sectors. He also took an active part in the Battles of Loos, Albert, the Somme, Messines, Passchendaele, Cambrai and the Marne, and many other engagements in this theatre of war. Demobilised shortly after the cessation of hostilities in November 1918, he holds the 1914–15 Star, and the General Service and Victory Medals.

11, Oak Street, Hulme, Manchester. Z11631

BARLOW, R. A., Private, Royal Welch Fusiliers.

He volunteered in June 1915, and four months later was sent overseas. During his service on the Western Front he took an active part in the heavy fighting at St. Eloi, Vermelles, the Somme, and the Ancre, and was unhappily killed in action in July 1916. He was entitled to the 1914–15 Star, and the General Service and Victory Medals.

"Nobly striving,
He nobly fell that we might live."

5, Garden Place, Ancoats, Manchester, Z9048A

BARLOW, T. E., L/Corporal, 7th Manchester Regt.

Volunteering in February 1915, he was retained in England with his unit during the first part of his service, and in February 1917 was drafted to France. There he took part in many important engagements, including the Battles of Arras and Vimy Ridge, but was unfortunately killed during an enemy bombardment in May 1917. He was entitled to the General Service and Victory Medals.

"He joined the great white company of valiant souls."

40, Carter Terrace, Greenheys, Manchester. Z1154A

BARLOW, T. W., Private, R.A.S.C. (M.T.)

He volunteered in August 1914, and in the following year proceeded to the Dardanelles, where he was engaged on important duties on the Gallipoli Peninsula. He was badly wounded during the Landing at Suvla Bay in August 1915, and invalided to England, was discharged in December 1916, as physically unfit for further service. He holds the 1914–15 Star, and the General Service and Victory Medals.

15, Heron Street, Hulme, Manchester. Z1156

BARLOW, W., Driver, R.F.A.

He volunteered in November 1915, and after a period of training was drafted to France in August 1916. He was in action with his Battery at many important engagements, and suffered severely from trench fever at Ypres. He was eventually invalided to England, and after spending some time in various hospitals, was demobilised in January 1919. He holds the General Service and Victory Medals.

132, South Street, Longsight, Manchester. Z1147A

BARLOW, W., L/Corporal, 1st Manchester Regt.

Enlisting in September 1909, he was stationed in India when war broke out, and sailing for France in September 1914, fought in several engagements until wounded at La Bassée in the following November. On recovery he was in action in the Somme Offensive, and in 1917 was again wounded at Arras. After treatment he served in the Battles of Ypres, Passchendaele, Cambrai and the Somme II, and wounded in this last engagement was invalided home to hospital in June 1918. Subsequently discharged as medically unfit for further service in December 1918, he holds the 1914 Star, and the General Service and Victory Medals.

27, Cookson Street, Ancoats, Manchester. Z9835

BARLOW, W., Private, Lancashire Fusiliers.

Having previously served in the South African War, he volunteered at the outbreak of hostilities in August 1914, but whilst training in Dorsetshire contracted enteric fever. He was in consequence discharged from the Army in July 1915, but unfortunately died a month later.

"His memory is cherished with pride."

20, Montague Street, Collyhurst, Manchester. Z9049

BARNBROOK, E., C.S.M., 2nd S. Staffordshire Regt.

He volunteered in August 1914, and was engaged on special duties as an Instructor in physical training and bayonet fighting. Owing to the important nature of his duties, he was unsuccessful in obtaining his transfer overseas, but carried out his responsible work in a very efficient manner, and rendered valuable services until demobilised in March 1919.

24, Romily Street, Queen sRoad, Manchester. Z10289

BARNES, A., Private, Lancashire Fusiliers.

He volunteered in November 1914, and crossing to the Western Front in the following August, was in action in several engagements in the Ypres sector, at Albert, Vimy Ridge, and in the Somme Offensive. He fell fighting on July 15th, 1916, and was buried near Vimy Ridge. He was entitled to the 1914–15 Star, and the General Service and Victory Medals.

"Whilst we remember, the sacrifice is not in vain."

31, Chatham Street, Bradford, Manchester. Z9836A

BARNES, A. H.. Private, 3rd Manchester Regiment.

Volunteering in July 1915, he completed a period of training, and was drafted to France in January of the following year. There he took part in much severe fighting in various sectors, including Vimy Ridge, the Somme, the Ancre, Arras and Pass-

chendaele. He was also in action during the Retreat and Advance of 1918, and after the Armistice returned to England and was demobilised in February 1919, holding the General Service and Victory Medals. TZ1157

3, Milton Square, Lingard Street, Hulme, Manchester.

BARNES, G. A., Private, Royal Welch Fusiliers.

Volunteering in May 1915, he was drafted to the Western Front in the following year, and was first in action during the German attacks on Loos, St. Eloi and Albert. He also took part in the Battles of Vermelles, Ploegsteert, the Somme, Bullecourt, Messines, Lens, Cambrai, the Aisne III, Amiens, Bapaume, Epéhy and Havrincourt, and was twice wounded. He holds the General Service and Victory Medals, and was demobilised in February 1919.

3, Roberts Street, Newton Heath, Manchester. Z11871

BARNES, H., Bombardier, R.F.A.

He volunteered in January 1915, and in May was drafted to the Western Front, where he played a prominent part with his Battery in much severe fighting. He was in action at the Battles of Festubert, Loos, Albert, the Somme, Bullecourt, Ypres III and Cambrai, and also throughout the Retreat and Advance of 1918. Returning to England in February 1919, he holds the 1914–15 Star, and the General Service and Victory Medals.

11, Dickens Street, Queens Road, Manchester. Z10290

BARNES, H. V., Private, Lancashire Fusiliers.

He volunteered in August 1914, and three months later proceeded to France, where he took part in many engagements of importance. He saw much severe fighting in various sectors, notably at the Battles of Ypres, Neuve Chapelle, Loos and Armentières, and was wounded on five occasions. He holds the 1914 Star, and the General Service and Victory Medals. and was demobilised in April 1919.

19, Ribstone Street, Hulme, Manchester. TZ1158

BARNES, J., Sapper, R.E.

Volunteering in September 1914, he was drafted overseas in the following July, and served in various parts of France and Flanders. He was engaged on important duties in connection with operations in the forward areas, and was gassed during heavy fighting in the Ypres salient. Sent home, suffering from gas-poisoning, he was under treatment at Alma Park War Hospital, Manchester, and was ultimately invalided out of the Service in February 1917. He holds the 1914–15 Star, and the General Service and Victory Medals.

31, Chatham Street, Bradford, Manchester. Z9836B

BARNES, J., Private, Lancashire Fusiliers.

He volunteered in August 1914, and shortly afterwards proceeded to France, where he was in action at the second Battle of Ypres, and other engagements of importance and was wounded. After being invalided home he was drafted to Mesopotamia in October 1915, and served with the Kut Relief force, with which he fought at Sanna-i-Yat, and on the Tigris. Returning to England, he was demobilised in March 1919, and holds the 1914–15 Star, and the General Service and Victory Medals.

43, Ann Street, Hulme, Manchester. Z1159

BARNES, P. E., Private, Northumberland Fusiliers.

Volunteering in December 1914, he was shortly afterwards drafted to Mesopotamia. He took part in the heavy fighting during the Advance in this theatre of war, but was unhappily drowned in the River Tigris near Kut-el-Amara in March 1917. He was entitled to the 1914–15 Star, and the General Service and Victory Medals.

"His memory is cherished with pride."

67, Princess Street, Rusholme, Manchester. Z1160B

BARNES, R., Pte., King's Shropshire Light Infantry.

He volunteered in August 1914, and a month later was drafted overseas. He served on the Western Front for twelve months, and during that time was in action at La Bassée, Ypres I and II, Neuve Chapelle, Hill 60, Lens and Vimy Ridge, and was wounded on the Somme in September 1915. In consequence he was discharged from the Army as medically unfit in June 1916. and holds the 1914 Star, and the General Service and Victory Medals.

7, Kertch Street, Ancoats, Manchester. Z8881

BARNES, S., Private, Cheshire Regiment.

Volunteering in June 1915, he embarked for Mesopotamia in the following September, and took part in engagements at Kut-el-Amara, Um-el-Hannah, Sanna-i-Yat, the British success on the Tigris, and the capture of Baghdad. After the close of hostilities, he was engaged on important duties until September 1919, when he returned to England, and a month later was demobilised. He holds the 1914–15 Star, and the General Service and Victory Medals.

30, Heyrod Street, Ancoats, Manchester. Z9837

BARNES, S., Private, 1/5th Manchester Regiment.

He volunteered in January 1916, and after three months' training at various camps, was drafted to France. He saw much heavy fighting in various sectors of the Front, and was severely wounded in the Advance of 1918. He spent some time in hospital, and was demobilised in January 1919, holding the General Service and Victory Medals.

67, Princess Street, Rusholme, Manchester. Z1160A

BARNES, S., Driver, R.A.S.C.
Joining in March 1916, he was in the following June sent to the Western Front, where he took part in fierce fighting in the Battles of the Somme, Vimy Ridge, Arras, Ypres, Bullecourt, Cambrai, Havrincourt, Bapaume, the Marne and the Aisne. He was wounded in action at Cambrai in September 1918, and on his recovery continued to serve in France until November 1919, when he was demobilised, holding the General Service and Victory Medals.
18, Portugal Street, Ancoats, Manchester. Z8882

BARNETT, D. L. W. (M.M.) Sergt., King's Royal Rifles.
He volunteered in August 1915, and in the following November was drafted to France. During his service on the Western Front he fought at Loos, Albert, Vimy Ridge, and the Somme, where he was wounded and gassed in action. After his recovery he was sent to Salonika in February 1917, and whilst there did excellent service on the Doiran front until December 1917, when he was again drafted to France and took part in the Battles of the Marne, Bapaume, Cambrai, during the Offensives of 1918. He was awarded the Military Medal for conspicuous bravery in the Field, and also holds the 1914-15 Star, and the General Service and Victory Medals. In February 1919 he was demobilised.
13, Hoylake Street, West Gorton, Manchester. Z10519A

BARNETT, H., Private, Lancashire Fusiliers.
He volunteered in November 1914, and on completion of his training was drafted six months later to Egypt. There he took part in the engagements on the Suez Canal, and at Sollum, and whilst being conveyed to hospital in Alexandria was wounded by a sniper. He unhappily succumbed to his injuries in Malta hospital in August 1916, and was entitled to the 1914-15 Star, and the General Service and Victory Medals.
"The path of duty was the way to glory."
3, Elvington Street, Hulme, Manchester. Z8883

BARNETT, J., L./Corporal, King's Own (Royal Lancaster Regt.) and Royal Welch Fusiliers.
He volunteered at the outbreak of war, and after the completion of his training at various stations was drafted to Gibraltar in November 1914. Whilst there he was engaged on important duties as a librarian, for three years, but owing to severe illness he was invalided home and discharged as medically unfit for further duty in November 1917. He holds the General Service Medal.
13, Hoylake Street, West Gorton, Manchester. Z10519B

BARNETT, M. K. (Miss), Special War Worker.
During the war this lady was engaged for three months by Messrs. Armstrong, Whitworth & Co., on important munition duties, as a shell-steel tester, and afterwards held a responsible post for over three years at the Belsize Motor Works, Manchester. She carried out her duties with efficiency, and to the entire satisfaction of both firms.
13, Hoylake Street, West Gorton, Manchester. Z10518B

BARNETT, P. J., Guardsman, 2nd Grenadier Guards.
He volunteered in November 1915, and in the following August was drafted to the Western Front. Whilst overseas he fought in the Battles of the Somme, the Ancre, Arras, Ypres, Cambrai, and in the chief engagements in the Retreat and Advance of 1918, up to the close of hostilities. He returned home, and was demobilised in February 1919, and holds the General Service and Victory Medals.
13, Hoylake Street, West Gorton, Manchester. Z10518A

BARNETT, W., Corporal, R.A.S.C. (M.T.)
He volunteered in September 1914, and two months later proceeded to France, where he was engaged in taking ammunition and food stuffs to the forward areas. In August 1916 he was transferred to Mesopotamia, and did consistently good work of a similar character in that theatre of war. He holds the 1914 Star, and the General Service and Victory Medals, and on his return home was demobilised in April 1919.
24, Ann Street, Hulme, Manchester. Z1161

BARNSHAW, J. J., Private, 20th Manchester Regt.
Volunteering in November 1914, he proceeded overseas a year later. During his service on the Western Front he was in action in various sectors, and fought in the Battles of Loos, St. Eloi, Vimy Ridge and Albert. He was unhappily killed on the Somme front on June 11th 1916. He was entitled to the 1914-15 Star, and the General Service and Victory Medals.
"A valiant soldier, with undaunted heart he breasted life's last hill,"
6, Ward Street, Oldham Road, Manchester. Z8884

BARNSLEY, F., Driver, R.F.A.
Volunteering in May 1915, he was sent to France later in the same year, and was in action with his Battery at many important engagements. He was present at the Battles of Ypres, Arras, Amiens, Havrincourt, Beaumont-Hamel and Cambrai, and was wounded on the Somme. He holds the 1914-15 Star, and the General Service and Victory Medals, and was demobilised in April 1919.
57, New York Street, Chorlton-on-Medlock, Manchester. X1164B

BARNSLEY, H., Driver, R.F.A.
He volunteered in May 1915, and after training at various stations in England, was sent to France in October 1916. There he took part with his Battery in many important engagements, notably those at Hill 60, Ypres II and III, Vimy Ridge, La Bassée, Givenchy and the Somme, and was wounded at Ypres II, and on the Somme. He also rendered valuable services during the Retreat and Advance of 1918, and was gassed. He holds the General Service and Victory Medals, and was demobilised in May 1919.
6, William Street, West Gorton, Manchester. Z1163

BARNSLEY, W., Private, 1/7th Manchester Regt.
He volunteered in August 1914, and in the following month proceeded to the Eastern theatre of war, where he saw service on the Suez front, and in the desert. In May 1915, he was transferred to the Dardanelles and took part in much heavy fighting on the Gallipoli Peninsula, including the Battles of Krithia, Suvla Bay and Chunuk Bair. After the Evacuation he saw further service in Egypt, and in January 1918 fought at the Battles of Ypres and Cambrai on the Western Front. He proceeded later to Germany, and did duty with the Army of Occupation on the Rhine. He holds the 1914-15 Star, and the General Service and Victory Medals, and was demobilised in April 1919.
57, New York Street, Chorlton-on-Medlock, Manchester. Z1162

BARNSLEY, W., Private, 17th Manchester Regt.
Mobilised at the outbreak of war in August 1914, he was drafted to Egypt in the following month, and saw active service there. He was later transferred to the Dardanelles, and took part in the Landing on the Gallipoli Peninsula, and early in 1917 proceeded to France. In this theatre of war he was in action at many engagements, including the Battles of Ypres, the Somme, Amiens, Havrincourt, Arras and Cambrai. He holds the 1914-15 Star, and the General Service and Victory Medals, and was demobilised in April 1919. X1164A
57, New York Street, Chorlton-on-Medlock, Manchester.

BARON, H. K., Private, 2nd Manchester Regiment.
He joined in June 1916, and after a period of training was drafted to the Western Front in the following November. There he took part in much heavy fighting, and was in action at Beaumont-Hamel, Beaucourt, Arras, Vimy Ridge, Bullecourt, Ypres and Cambrai, and was wounded. He was in consequence invalided home and eventually discharged in October 1918, as physically unfit for further service, holding the General Service and Victory Medals.
38, Dryden Street, Chorlton-on-Medlock, Manchester. Z1165

BARON, J., Air Mechanic, R.A.F. (late R.F.C.)
He volunteered in October 1915, and embarking for the Western Front in the following February, served with his Squadron engaged on important duties of a highly technical nature. In the course of his service he was present during operations at Loos, Neuve Chapelle, Albert and Arras, and was invalided home to hospital owing to an accident at Ypres in May 1918. After receiving medical treatment, he was discharged in December of that year, and holds the General Service and Victory Medals.
76, Lind Street, Ancoats, Manchester. Z9825

BARR, F., Driver, R.G.A.
He volunteered in May 1915, and after undergoing a period of training was drafted to the Westren Front in June 1916. In this theatre of war he was in action with his Battery at many engagements of importance, including those at Arras, Messines, Ypres, Passchendaele and Cambrai and in the Retreat and Advance of 1918. He holds the General Service and Victory Medals, and was demobilised in February 1919.
17, Carter Street, Greenheys, Manchester. Z1166B

BARR, P. J., Bombardier, R.G.A.
Volunteering in September 1915, he proceeded to France in the following June, and took part in many important engagements. He was in action with his Battery at the Battles of Arras, Vimy Ridge and Ypres III, but having met with an accident at Loos in August 1917, was invalided home and eventually discharged in January 1919. He holds the General Service and Victory Medals.
38, Clifford Street, Chorlton-on-Medlock, Manchester. Z1166C

BARR, S., Driver, R.G.A.
He volunteered in December 1915, and in July 1916, proceeded to the Western Front. There he took part in many important engagements, and was in action with his Battery at the Battles of Vimy Ridge, Arras, Hill 70, Ypres III, Lens, and Cambrai. He also rendered valuable services during the Retreat and Advance of 1918, and was demobilised in February 1919, holding the General Service and Victory Medals.
38, Clifford Street, Chorlton-on-Medlock, Manchester. Z1166A

BARRACLOUGH, H., Air Mechanic, R.A.F.
He joined in June 1918, and after a period of training, was engaged on special duties in connection with the repair and cleaning of motors. He was unsuccessful in obtaining his transfer overseas, but did consistently good work until April 1919, when he was discharged as medically unfit for further service, owing to heart disease.
389, Collyhurst Road, Collyhurst, Manchester. Z10291

BARRATT, C., Corporal, R.A.M.C.

Volunteering in November 1914, he proceeded to Egypt in September of the following year, and saw active service in the Suez Canal, and at Mersa-Matruh. In December 1917 he was transferred to the Western Front, and did good work on the Somme, the Lys, the Aisne, the Marne, Ypres and Havrincourt, during the Retreat and Advance of 1918, and was wounded just before the Armistice. He holds the 1914-15 Star, and the General Service and Victory Medals, and was demobilised in February 1919.

9, Craven Street, Preston Street, Hulme, Manchester. Z11767

BARRATT, F., L/Cpl., 13th West Riding Regt.

He volunteered in December 1915, and on completing his training in the following year was drafted to the Western Front. In this theatre of war he took part in many engagements, including those on the Somme, at Ypres, and in the Advance of 1918. He was demobilised in March 1919, and holds the General Service and Victory Medals.

4, Sarah Street, Bradford, Manchester. Z1319

BARRATT, P., Pte., K.O. (Royal Lancaster Regt.)

Volunteering in November 1915, he completed his training and proceeded overseas in the following November. Landing at Salonika he took part in several engagements on the Doiran front, the Advance across the Struma and Vardar, and the capture of Monastir. Invalided home in August 1918, owing to ill-health, he underwent hospital treatment, and on recovery was retained on important Home Service duties until the cessation of hostilities. He was demobilised in March 1919, and holds the General Service and Victory Medals.

87, Elliott Street, Bradford, Manchester. Z9838

BARRETT, B., Private, King's (Liverpool Regt.)

He volunteered in August 1914, and was retained with his unit in England during the first part of his service. He was drafted to France in December 1916, and saw service on the Ancre front and at the Battles of Vimy Ridge, Lens and Cambrai. He was wounded in November 1917, and returning to England was discharged in the following month as physically unfit for further service. He holds the General Service and Victory Medals. 17 Davies Street, Hulme, Manchester. Z1170

BARRETT, E. H., Private, 2nd Worcestershire Regt., and R.A.M.C.

He volunteered in April 1915, and four months later proceeded to the Western Front, where he took part in many important engagements, and did good work on the lines of communication in the Loos, St. Eloi, Vimy Ridge and Somme sectors. He was later transferred to the R.A.M.C., and rendered valuable services until invalided home with shell-shock. He was discharged in September 1916 as unfit, and holds the 1914-15 Star, and the General Service and Victory Medals.

41, Caythorpe Street, Moss Side, Manchester. Z1172

BARRETT, H. J., Private, 4th Manchester Regiment.

Volunteering in May 1915, he was drafted to France in the following September, and after being in action at the Battles of Albert, the Somme, Beaucourt, Vimy Ridge and Arras, was wounded at the third Battle of Ypres. He was invalided home and eventually discharged as unfit in June 1918. He holds the 1914-15 Star, and the General Service and Victory Medals. 3, Peter Street, Openshaw, Manchester. Z1169

BARRETT, M., Pte., 1st Loyal N. Lancashire Regt.

He joined in December 1917, and after a period of service in England was drafted to France in July 1918. He took part in engagements at Havrincourt, the Selle, and the Sambre' during the Advance of 1918, and after the Armistice proceeded to Germany, where he did duty with the Army of Occupation at Cologne. He holds the General Service and Victory Medals, and was demobilised in October 1919.

21, Meadow Street, Ardwick, Manchester. TZ1168

BARRETT, P., Private, Royal Irish Fusiliers.

He volunteered in September 1914, and was drafted to France in March of the following year. There he was soon in action at the second Battle of Ypres, and was gassed. He subsequently took part in the fighting on the Somme and Ancre front, and was taken prisoner at St. Quentin in March 1917, and retained in Germany until the beginning of 1919. He was eventually demobilised in August 1919, and holds the 1914-15 Star, and the General Service and Victory Medals. 17, Davies Street, Hulme, Manchester. Z1173

BARRETT, T., L/Cpl, 7th and 10th Seaforth H'ldrs.

He joined in November 1916, and embarking in the following January for France, served in different parts of the line during operations on the Somme, and Ancre. He also took part in many other important engagements, including those at Arras, Bullecourt, Messines, Cambrai, and Passchendaele, but was unfortunately killed during operations at Wytschaete on April 18th, 1918. He was entitled to the General Service and Victory Medals. "His name liveth for evermore." 14, Ranson Street, Ancoats, Manchester. Z9839

BARRETT, W., Sapper, R.E.

Volunteering in March 1915, he proceeded to the Western Front in the following November, and was engaged on important duties in connection with the construction of roads and pontoon building. He also took part in the Battles of Loos, the Somme, Arras and Messines, and was unfortunately killed in action at Ypres in July 1917. He was entitled to the 1914-15 Star, and the General Service and Victory Medals. "The path of duty was the way to glory." 71, Taylor Street, Bradford, Manchester. Z1171

BARROW, H. J., Driver, 56th Brigade R.F.A.

He volunteered in August 1914, and after a period of service in England was drafted to the Dardanelles in August of the following year. There he was engaged with his Battery in much heavy fighting, and after the Evacuation of the Gallipoli Peninsula was transferred to Mesopotamia in March 1916. He was invalided to India in July 1917, but later returned to Mesopotamia, where he again saw much active service. He was also in action at Baku in Russia before returning to England for demobilisation in May 1919, and holds the 1914-15 Star, and the General Service and Victory Medals.

2, Stamford Street, Hulme, Manchester. Z1174

BARROW, J., Private, 2nd Lancashire Fusiliers.

He was mobilised in August 1914, and two months later was drafted to France, where he took part in the Battles of Ypres and Hooge before being badly wounded in action at Ypres in June 1915. Invalided to England, he was discharged March 1916, but in the following December was recalled to the Colours, and did duty with the R.G.A. In July 1917, however, he was finally discharged as medically unfit for further service, and holds the 1914 Star, and the General Service and Victory Medals.

43, Windsor Street, Collyhurst, Manchester. Z10292

BARROW, J., Private, 11th Lancashire Fusiliers.

In November 1914 he volunteered, and in the following August proceeded overseas. Whilst serving in France he was engaged in fierce fighting, principally in the Loos sector until December 1915. He was then sent to Salonika, but on the journey out was taken ill and died from pneumonia in Alexandria on December 23rd, 1915. He was entitled to the 1914-15 Star, and the General Service and Victory Medals. "He joined the great white company of valiant souls." 1, Metcalfe Street, Miles Platting, Manchester. TZ6039

BARROW, J. H., Private, 6th Manchester Regiment.

Volunteering in September 1915, he was engaged on important duties on the Coast until June 1917, when he was drafted to France, where he was retained at the Base at Calais. He returned to England after the Armistice, and was demobilised in January 1919, holding the General Service and Victory Medals. 6, Mary Street, Hulme, Manchester. Z1175

BARROW, W., Private, Royal Welch Fusiliers.

He volunteered in October 1915, and after a period of training was drafted to Egypt in October of the following year. He was stationed at Alexandria and Cairo, and in March 1917 was sent to Sollum, where he served for nearly two years. Returning to England, he was demobilised in February 1919, and holds the South African, General Service and Victory Medals.

109, Heald Grove, Rusholme, Manchester. Z1176

BARRY, E., Private, 4th K.O. (Royal Lancaster Regt.)

He volunteered in November 1914, and crossing to the Western Front two months later, took part in heavy fighting in the Battles of Neuve Chapelle, and St. Eloi. After only a few weeks' active service he was unhappily killed in the second Battle of Ypres on May 5th, 1915. He was entitled to the 1914-15 Star, and the General Service and Victory Medals. "A costly sacrifice upon the altar of freedom." 16, Boslam Street, Ancoats, Manchester. Z9840

BARRY, J., Private, Labour Corps.

He joined in September 1916, and was retained on special duties at various stations in England. He was unable to obtain his transfer to a theatre of war, but nevertheless, rendered valuable services until his demobilisation in March 1919. 6, Lord Street, Hulme, Manchester. Z1177A

BARRY, T., Corporal, 1st South Lancashire Regt.

He joined in January 1917, and in February of the following year was drafted to the Western Front, where he played a prominent part in many important engagements during the Retreat and Advance of 1918, notably the Battle of the Marne. He was both gassed and wounded, and after the Armistice proceeded to Ireland, where in 1920 he was still serving. He holds the General Service and Victory Medals.

6, Lord Street, Hulme, Manchester. Z1177B

BARTLEY, W. E., Private, South Lancashire Regt.

Volunteering in March 1915, he was sent in the following August to the Dardanelles, where he took part in various operations until the Evacuation of the Peninsula. In August 1916 he was drafted to Mesopotamia, and in this theatre of war was engaged in heavy fighting during the attempted Relief of Kut until September 1917, when he was again transferred to the Western Front. He fought in the Battle of Cambrai and many others during the Retreat and Advance of 1918, and returned home for his demobilisation in March 1919. He holds the 1914-15 Star, and the General Service and Victory Medals.

61, Able Street, Collyhurst, Manchester. Z9841

BARTON, A. E., Private, 1st Manchester Regiment.
Mobilised from the Reserve at the outbreak of war he proceeded with the first Expeditionary Force to France, and fought in the Retreat from Mons and the Battles of the Marne, the Aisne and Ypres, where he was wounded. On his recovery he was drafted to Mesopotamia and took part in the fighting near Kut for General Townshend's Relief, and on the Tigris. He unfortunately contracted an illness from which he died on May 3rd, 1916. He was entitled to the Mons Star, and the General Service and Victory Medals.
" His life for his Country, his soul to God."
8, Wragley Street, Miles Platting, Manchester. Z9423

BARTON, J., Private, 11th Border Regiment.
Joining in March 1917, he was drafted to France four months later, and took part in several important engagements. He was reported missing on December 2nd, 1917, at Passchendaele, and later was presumed to have been killed in action. He was entitled to the General Service and Victory Medals.
" A costly sacrifice upon the altar of freedom."
22, Adelaide Street, Hulme, Manchester. .Z1179A

BARTON, R., Private, 10th Sherwood Foresters.
He joined in October 1917, and was drafted to France in April of the following year. There he took part in the Battle of the Somme II, Bapaume, Thiepval and Cambrai, and was in action during the Advance of 1918. He returned to England after the Armistice, and was demobilised in February 1919, holding the General Service and Victory Medals.
22, Adelaide Street, Hulme, Manchester. Z1179B

BARTON, S., Private, South Lancashire Regiment.
He volunteered in June 1915, and in the following November proceeded to France, where he took part in various important engagements, including the Battles of Ypres and Loos, and was wounded in the Somme Offensive of 1916. He returned to his unit shortly afterwards, but almost at once made the supreme sacrifice, being killed in action at Beaumont-Hamel on August 28th, 1916. He was entitled to the 1914–15 Star, and the General Service and Victory Medals. Z1178
" Whilst we remember, the sacrifice is not in vain."
17, Hampton Place, Erskine Street, Hulme, Manchester.

BARTON, W., Private, South Lancashire Regiment.
Mobilised in August 1914, he at once proceeded to the Western Front, where he served for over two years. During that period he took an active part in the Battles of Mons, Le Cateau, the Marne, Neuve Chapelle, Ypres, and Passchendaele, and was severely wounded on the Somme. He was discharged in consequence in April 1917, and holds the Mons Star, and the General Service and Victory Medals.
31, Congon Street, Ancoats, Manchester. Z6040

BASFORD, J., Sergt., Lancashire Fusiliers.
He volunteered in 1916, and drafted in February of the following year to the Western Front, was in action in various parts of the line. After only a few weeks' service he was unhappily killed in action at Mametz Wood in the Somme area on April 1st, 1917. He was entitled to the General Service and Victory Medals.
" His memory is cherished with pride."
231, Morton Street, Longsight, Manchester. Z9842

BASHAM, G. W., Private, Royal Welch Fusiliers.
Joining in April 1918, he was sent in the following August to the Western Front. In this theatre of war he fought in many important engagements during the Allied Advance of that year, notably those at Amiens, Armentières, Cambrai and the Somme. After the Armistice he was engaged on important duties guarding prisoners of war until their return home. He was demobilised in January 1920, and holds the General Service and Victory Medals.
14, Hewitt Street, Gorton, Manchester. Z9843

BASSNETT, T., Private, 19th Royal Fusiliers.
He volunteered in June 1915, and was drafted to France five months later after a period of training. He was unfortunately killed in a dug-out at La Bassée by the explosion of a shell in January 1916, and was buried near Cambrai. He was entitled to the 1914–15 Star, and the General Service and Victory Medals.
" A valiant Soldier, with undaunted heart he breasted life's last hill. TZ1180
8, Nuttall Street, Chorlton-on-Medlock, Manchester.

BATE, D. H., Corporal, 22nd Manchester Regt.
He joined in August 1916, and after a period of training was drafted to the Western Front, where he played a prominent part in many engagements. He saw much severe fighting in various sectors, and was in action at the Battles of Ypres and Cambrai. In December 1917, after a bout of fever, he was transferred to Italy, and was attached to a Labour Battalion. He holds the General Service and Victory Medals, and was demobilised in May 1919.
21, Lythgoe Street, Moss Side, Manchester. Z1181B

BATEMAN, G., Driver, R.E. and Private, East Lancashire Regt.
He volunteered in June 1915, and five months later was sent to Egypt, where he performed valuable work in constructing

railways in the Mersa Matruh, Agagia, Katia, El Fasher, Romani and Magdhaba districts. In March 1917 he was drafted to France, and was once more engaged in construction work in the Arras sector. Whilst supplying Bullecourt with water he was gassed, and was sent to hospital for three months, at the end of which time he was retained on Home Service at Conway until demobilised in March 1919. He holds the 1914–15 Star, and the General Service and Victory Medals.
22, Pownall Street, Hulme, Manchester. Z8885

BATEMAN, R., R.S.M., 12th Lancashire Fusiliers.
He volunteered in September 1914, and after rendering valuable services in England, proceeded to Salonika in December 1915. He played a conspicuous part in the general Offensive of 1916, was in action on the Doiran and Vardar fronts, and was later transferred to the Western Front, where he served at Bapaume, Havrincourt, and Le Cateau during the Retreat and Advance of 1918. He later proceeded to Germany after the Armistice and did duty with the Army of Occupation on the Rhine. He holds the 1914–15 Star, and the General Service and Victory Medals, and was demobilised in March 1919.
87, Old Elm Street, Chorlton-on-Medlock, Manchester.
X1182B

BATES, A. (M.M.), Pte., K.O. (Royal Lancaster Regt.)
He enlisted in May 1910 and in September 1914 was sent to France, where he took part in the fighting at La Bassée, Armentières, Ypres, Hill 60, Festubert, Loos, Vermelles, Vimy Ridge and the Somme, and was wounded. In January 1917 he was transferred to Salonika, and served in the Advance on the Doiran and Vardar fronts, and was gassed. He holds the Military Medal, awarded for conspicuous gallantry in carrying Despatches through heavy shell-fire at Vimy Ridge, the 1914 Star, and the General Service and Victory Medals, and the Greek Cross, 2nd Class, and was invalided home and discharged in February 1918 as medically unfit for further service. 5, Thompson Street, W. Gorton, Manchester. Z9844

BATES, A., Corporal, Shropshire Dragoons.
He volunteered in April 1915, and was drafted to the East early in the following year. He saw service in Egypt and Palestine, and played a distinguished part in various engagements, including the Battles of Gaza, and was present at the entry into Jerusalem. He was transferred to France in May 1918, and served in the Advance of 1918. He holds the General Service and Victory Medals, and was demobilised in February 1919.
14, Moulton Street, Hulme, Manchester. Z1189

BATES, A., Gunner, R.F.A. and R.H.A.
He joined in August 1916, and after having completed his training was retained at Middlesborough on important duties in connection with the defence of the East Coast, against attacks of the enemy. He was not successful in obtaining his transfer overseas before hostilities ceased, but rendered valuable services, until demobilised in April 1919
18, Cross Street, Newton Heath, Manchester. Z9424

BATES, C. V. H., Pte., 1st K.O. (Royal Lancaster Regt.)
He was called up from the Reserve at the outbreak of war in August 1914, and proceeded to the Western Front with the British Expeditionary Force. There he took part in the Battle of Mons and the subsequent Retreat and was also in action at the Battles of the Marne, the Aisne, La Bassée and Ypres, and was wounded. He was invalided to England and honourably discharged in February 1915, being no longer physically fit for service, and holds the Mons Star, and the General Service and Victory Medals.
41, Albemarle Street, Moss Side, Manchester. Z1183

BATES, J., L/Corporal, 8th Manchester Regiment.
He volunteered in August 1914, and after a period of training was drafted to the Dardanelles in April of the following year. There he took part in much heavy fighting on the Gallipoli Peninsula until the Evacuation in December 1915, when he was transferred to Egypt. After taking part in many engagements in this theatre of war, including those at El-Fasher and Romani, he proceeded to France and fought at the Battles of Ypres, Passchendaele and Havrincourt. He was demobilised in February 1919, and holds the 1914–15 Star, and the General Service and Victory Medals.
19, Devonshire Street, Hulme, Manchester. TZ1187

BATES, J., Private, K.O. (Y.L.I.)
He volunteered in January 1915, and in June of the same year proceeded to France, where after three months' service he was killed in action at Ypres on August 31st, 1915. He was entitled to the 1914–15 Star, and the General Service and Victory Medals.
" His life for his Country, his soul to God."
73, Vine Street, Newton Heath, Manchester. Z9425A

BATES, L. (Miss), Special War Worker.
This lady volunteered her services in November 1917, and was engaged on the important duty of testing fuses for shells. She rendered valuable services whilst in the employ of the Government at City Hall, Manchester, and did not relinquish her duties, which she carried out in a highly commendable manner, until March 1919. Z1185B
23, Granville, Street, Chorlton-on-Medlock, Manchester.

BATES, P., Private, 1/8th Lancashire Fusiliers.

He volunteered in August 1914, and, on completing his training in the following year, proceeded to France, where he saw severe fighting in various sectors of the Front. He took part in the Battles of Loos, Albert, the Somme, Arras, Vimy Ridge, Ypres, Passchendaele and Cambrai, and other important engagements, fought also in the Retreat and Advance of 1918, and was wounded in action. He was demobilised in February 1919, and holds the 1914–15 Star, and the General Service and Victory Medals.

48, Barrack Street, Hulme, Manchester. Z11632

BATES, P., Private, King's (Liverpool Regiment).

He volunteered in September 1914, and after a period of training proceeded in the following March to the Western Front. There he participated in the Battles of Neuve Chapelle, Hill 60, Festubert, Loos, Vimy Ridge, and the Somme, where he was unfortunately killed in action on July 23rd 1916. He was entitled to the 1914–15 Star, and the General Service and Victory Medals.

" The path of duty was the way to glory."

279, Hamilton Street, Collyhurst, Manchester. Z8886

BATES, R., Private, Manchester Regiment.

Joining in January 1917, he embarked for France in the following July, and whilst there saw much active service. He took part in the fighting at Ypres, Cambrai and in the Retreat and Advance of 1918, but through causes due to his service was discharged in September of that year. He holds the General Service and Victory Medals.

73, Vine Street, Newton Heath, Manchester. Z9425B

BATES, R., Private, 8th Manchester Regiment.

He volunteered in September 1915, and in June of the following year was sent to Egypt with the Royal Army Ordnance Corps as a metal sorter. Here he rendered excellent service until 1918, when he was invalided home owing to illness, and after a period in hospital was discharged as medically unfit for further service. Later he unfortunately died on May 14th, 1920, and was entitled to the General Service and Victory Medals.

" His memory is cherished with pride."

2, Wesley Street, Gorton, Manchester. Z9845

BATES, T., Private, R.A.S.C.

He joined in April 1918, and later in the same year was sent to France. Here he was engaged at Abbeville, Paris, Rouen and Calais, on the repair of motor cars, and rendered excellent services. After the Armistice he proceeded with the Army of Occupation to Germany. He was demobilised in April 1920, and holds the General Service and Victory Medals.

9, Truro Street, West Gorton, Manchester. Z9846

BATES, V., Cpl., 8th Manchester Regt. and R.A.S.C.

Volunteering in November 1915, he was not medically fit for transfer to a theatre of war. Retained at home he was stationed successively at Oswestry, Southport, Liverpool and Worcester, engaged on various duties of an important nature. He was later transferred to the Royal Army Service Corps, and was employed looking after horses until he was demobilised in February 1919.

6, Johnsons Buildings, Ancoats, Manchester. Z8887

BATES, W., Private, South Lancashire Fusiliers.

Volunteering in August 1914, he was sent to France in September of the following year and took part in the fighting on the Somme and Ancre fronts, and at Arras, Bullecourt, Messines, Ypres, Cambrai, Bapaume and Havrincourt. He was demobilised in February 1919, and holds the Queen's South African Medals, and the 1914–15 Star, and the General Service and Victory Medals.

23, Irlam Street, Miles Platting, Manchester. Z9847

BATES, W., Private, 16th Lancashire Fusiliers.

He volunteered in November 1914, and proceeded to France in February of the following year. There he took part in many important engagements, including the Battles of Hill 60, Festubert, Loos and Vimy Ridge, and was wounded during the Somme Offensive in 1916. He was invalided to England, and eventually discharged in September 1917, as physically unfit for further service, and holds the 1914–15 Star, and the General Service and Victory Medals.

26, Parkfield Avenue, Rusholme, Manchester. TZ1188

BATES, W., Private, 7th Manchester Regiment.

Volunteering in March 1915, he underwent a period of training and was drafted to the Western Front in March 1917. In this theatre of war he was in action at numerous engagements, including those at Arras, Bullecourt, Ypres and Cambrai, and later took part in fighting at Havrincourt and Cambrai II, during the Retreat and Advance of 1918. He proceeded to Germany after the Armistice, and did duty with the Army of Occupation on the Rhine until his return to England for demobilisation in July 1919. He holds the General Service and Victory Medals.

12, Violet Street, Hulme, Manchester. Z1186

BATES, W., Corporal, R.E., and Tank Corps.

After working at Trafford Park on munitions of war, he joined the Royal Engineers in October 1916, and was later transferred to the Tank Corps. He took part in engagements at

Ypres, Messines, Passchendaele and Cambrai, and rendered valuable services during the Retreat and Advance of 1918. He holds the General Service and Victory Medals, and was demobilised in March 1919.

110, Marsland Street, Ardwick, Manchester. TZ1184

BATES, W. H., Special War Worker.

He volunteered his services at the outbreak of war in August 1914, and was engaged in the testing of cables at Old Trafford, Manchester, where he did good work throughout the period of the war. He was, however, accidentally killed by a live cable on November 10th 1919, at Oliver's Cable Works.

23, Granville Street, Chorlton-on-Medlock, Manchester. Z1185A

BATLEY, W. B., Private, 6th Royal Irish Fusiliers.

Volunteering in August 1914, he was drafted to the Dardanelles in the following year and took part in the fighting at Krithia and Suvla Bay, and was wounded. After the Evacuation of the Peninsula, he was transferred to Salonika, where he was in action on the Doiran and Struma fronts. In April 1917 he was invalided home through wounds, and in May of the following year was discharged as medically unfit for further service. He holds the 1914–15 Star, and the General Service and Victory Medals.

55, Bath Street, Miles Platting, Manchester. Z9848

BATLEY, W. H., Private, R.A.S.C.

He volunteered in March 1915, and later in the same year was drafted to France. In this theatre of war he served at Neuve Chapelle, Loos, Ypres, Festubert, the Somme and the Marne, and performed consistently good work, whilst engaged on important duties. Returning home after the Armistice, he was eventually demobilised in August 1919, and holds the 1914–15 Star, and the General Service and Victory Medals.

13, Charlton Street, Collyhurst, Manchester. Z8888

BATT, G. S. W, Private., 7th Manchester Regiment.

Joining in November 1916, he was drafted to the Western Front after three months' training, and there saw much severe fighting. He served through the Battles of Arras, Vimy Ridge, Ypres, Cambrai, the Somme, Amiens and Le Cateau, and many other important engagements in various sectors, and also took part in the march into Germany. He was demobilised on his return home in January 1919, and holds the General Service and Victory Medals.

11, Edgeley Street, Ardwick, Manchester. Z11634

BATT, R. M., Private, East Lancashire Regiment.

He volunteered in May 1915, and after undergoing a period of training, served at various stations, where he was engaged on duties of great importance. He was not successful in obtaining his transfer to a theatre of war, but later, was sent to Ireland, where he did much useful work with his unit, and in 1920 was still serving.

11, Edgeley Street, Ardwick, Manchester. Z11633

BATTEN, J., Private, 4th Yorkshire Regiment.

He volunteered in October 1915, and after his training was engaged on important coastal defence duties, and later in guarding German prisoners. He rendered valuable services, but was not successful in obtaining his transfer overseas prior to the cessation of hostilities. He was demobilised in December 1919.

16, Hampden Street, West Gorton, Manchester. Z9849

BATTMAN, A. N., Private, 14th Manchester Regt.

He joined in February 1916, and in the following August was sent to Mesopotamia, where he took part in the fighting at Kut and Baghdad. He was then invalided home through ill-health contracted whilst in the East, but on his recovery was drafted to France. In this theatre of war he fought at Cambrai, the Somme, and in the Retreat and Advance of 1918, during which he was severely wounded. He was invalided home, and in March 1919 was discharged, holding the General Service and Victory Medals.

43, Lord Street, Openshaw, Manchester. Z9426

BATTY, J. W., Private, 21st Manchester Regiment.

He volunteered in May 1915, and three months later proceeded to the Western Front, where he took part in many important engagements. He was in action at the Battles of Loos, Albert, Vermelles and Vimy Ridge, but was unfortunately killed on July 23rd, 1916, during the Somme Offensive. He was entitled to the 1914–15 Star, and the General Service and Victory Medals.

" Great deeds cannot die."

197, Earle Street, Longsight, Manchester. Z1190

BAXENDALE, E. (M.M.) Private, 25th Manchester Regiment, and 7th Lancashire Fusiliers.

Volunteering in May 1915, he proceeded four months later to the Western Front. There he played a prominent part with his unit in many important engagements, including the Battles of Loos, St. Eloi, Vimy Ridge, Arras, the Somme I, Ypres III, and the Somme II, and was wounded at Amiens in August 1918. He was awarded the Military Medal and bar, for bravery and consistent devotion to duty in the Field, and when demobilised in January 1919, was also entitled to the 1914–15 Star, and the General Service and Victory Medals.

4, Cheltenham Street, Collyhurst, Manchester. Z8889

BAXENDALE, G. E., Sergt., 9th S. Lancashire Regt.
He volunteered in August 1914, and in due course proceeded to France. He was transferred to Salonika in October 1915, and saw service in this theatre of war, but unfortunately contracted malaria and was invalided to Malta. He spent some considerable time in hospital, and in January 1919 was sent to South Russia. He eventually returned to England, and was demobilised in March 1920, holding the 1914–15 Star, and the General Service and Victory Medals.
32, Allen Street, Hulme, Manchester.   Z1191

BAXTER, J., Private, Lancashire Fusiliers.
He volunteered at the outbreak of hostilities, and after his training was sent to France in March 1915. He was unfortunately killed in action at La Bassée on the 15th of that month, and was entitled to the 1914–15 Star, and the General Service and Victory Medals.
"His memory is cherished with pride."
42, Burns Street, Bradford, Manchester.   Z9850A

BAXTER, J., Sergeant, Northumberland Fusiliers.
He joined in June 1916, and two months later proceeded to the Western Front, where he played a distinguished part in many engagements, including the Battles of Beaumont-Hamel, Vimy Ridge, Arras and Cambrai. He was also in action during the Retreat and Advance of 1918, and after the Armistice was sent to Germany, where he did duty with the Army of Occupation on the Rhine. He was demobilised in July 1919, and holds the General Service and Victory Medals.
26, Stamford Street, Hulme, Manchester.   Z1192

BAYLEY, A., Private, 4th East Surrey Regiment.
He joined in July 1917, and on the completion of his training was drafted to France. During his service overseas, he was in action on the Somme front, and at Albert, Bullecourt, and Cambrai, and was wounded. He remained on the Western Front until after the cessation of hostilities, and was demobilised on his return home in 1919, holding the General Service and Victory Medals.
21, Worsley Street, Oldham Road, Manchester.   Z8890

BAYLIS, C. A., Corpl., King's (Liverpool Regiment.)
Joining in July 1916, he completed a period of training and was drafted to the Western Front in January of the following year. In this theatre of war he rendered valuable services at Etaples, but owing to ill-health returned to England and was discharged in May 1918, as physically unfit. He holds the General Service and Victory Medals.
12, Copinger Street, Greenheys, Manchester.   Z1193

BEARDSALL, A., Private, 4th East Yorkshire Regt.
He joined in August 1916, and in the following October was drafted to India, where he was engaged on garrison duty until August 1918. He then returned to England, and in the following February was demobilised, holding the General Service Medal.
95, Montague Street, Collyhurst, Manchester.   Z9851

BEARPARK, H., L/Corporal, R.E.
He volunteered in April 1915, and in September of the same year was drafted to the Western Front, where he served in many important engagements. He was engaged on important work in various sectors, including Loos, Vimy Ridge, Albert and Passchendaele, and took part in the Retreat and Advance of 1918, at Amiens and on the Somme. He holds the 1914–15 Star, and the General Service and Victory Medals, and was demobilised in February 1919.
146, Hartington Street, Moss Side, Manchester.   TZ1194

BEATTIE, J., Private, Lancashire Fusiliers.
Volunteering in September 1914, he was drafted in the following year to the Dardanelles, and during the Landing at Suvla Bay was severely wounded. He was invalided to hospital, and after receiving treatment was discharged in January 1916, as medically unfit for further service. He holds the 1914–15 Star, and the General Service and Victory Medals.
7, Garratt Street, Manchester.   Z9427

BEAUMONT, E., Corporal, 1st Manchester Regt.
He volunteered in September 1914, and in the following year was sent to Mesopotamia. Here he saw much fighting at Kut, and Es Sinn, and in many minor engagements, and was later drafted to France. Whilst in this theatre of war he fought at Ypres and Passchendaele, but was invalided home, and subsequently discharged through causes due to his service in December 1917. He holds the 1914–15 Star, and the General Service and Victory Medals.
8, Heath Street, Ancoats, Manchester.   Z9428

BEAUMONT, P. (M.M.), Corporal, M.G.C.
Volunteering in August 1915, he was drafted to France in the following June and took part in the engagements on the Somme, and at Arras, Bullecourt, Lens and Cambrai. In November 1917 he was awarded the Military Medal for conspicuous gallantry in holding a position with a machine gun for three days. Later he was wounded and severely gassed. Returning to England in April 1919, he was demobilised, holding in addition to the Military Medal, the General Service and Victory Medals.
40, Great Jackson Street, West Gorton, Manchester.   Z9852

BEAUMONT, W., Rflmn., King's Royal Rifle Corps.
Volunteering at the outbreak of hostilities, he was drafted to the Western Front in January 1915, and took part in the fighting at Neuve Chapelle, Hill 60, Ypres, Loos, Vimy Ridge, the Somme, Arras, Bullecourt and Havrincourt. During his service he was wounded four times, and in March 1918 was taken prisoner at St. Quentin. He was held in captivity until after the Armistice and was then released. Returning to England he was demobilised in April 1919, holding the 1914–15 Star, and the General Service and Victory Medals.
7, Brougham Place, West Gorton, Manchester.   Z9853

BEBBINGTON, F., Corporal, 2nd Manchester Regt.
He volunteered in October 1915, and in March of the following year proceeded to France. There he played a prominent part in numerous important engagements, including the Battles of Loos, St. Eloi, Albert, Vermelles, Ploegsteert Wood, the Somme, Arras, Ypres, and Cambrai, and was also in action during the Retreat and Advance of 1918. He was demobilised in March 1919, and holds the General Service and Victory Medals.
5, Dawson Street, West Gorton, Manchester.   Z1195

BECK, T., Private, Labour Corps.
He joined in February 1917, and was shortly afterwards sent to France, where he did valuable work. He was principally engaged on important duties in the Arras sector until May 1919, when he returned home and was demobilised. He holds the General Service and Victory Medals.
4, Juno Street, Newton Heath, Manchester.   Z9429

BECKWITH, J. W., Special War Worker.
He volunteered in August 1914, and was engaged on work of National importance at the United Brass Founders and Engineering Co., Cornbrook, where he acted as foreman in the shell department. He did consistently good work throughout the period of hostilities, and relinquished his duties in November 1918.
7, Alphonsus Street, Old Trafford, Manchester.   Z1196

BEDDOES, E., Sergt., R.E.
Volunteering in April 1915, he was drafted to France four months later, and was engaged on important constructional work. He was also present at many important engagements, including those at Vimy Ridge, Ypres, and the Somme, and was wounded on two occasions. After serving in the Retreat and Advance of 1918, and until his demobilisation in May 1920 he was placed in charge of the R.E. Workshops at Rouen. He holds the 1914–15 Star, and the General Service and Victory Medals.
26, Ripon Street, Greenheys, Manchester.   Z1197

BEDDOWS, H., L/Corporal, Manchester Regiment.
He volunteered in October 1915, and in the following June was drafted to Egypt. Here he served until March 1917, when he was transferred to the Western Front, where he took part in the Battle of Ypres, and was wounded during the Retreat of March 1918. After a period in hospital he rejoined his unit, and fought in the Advance, during which he was wounded for the second time. Returning to England he was demobilised in February 1919, and holds the General Service and Victory Medals.
11, Marple Street, Miles Platting, Manchester.   Z9854

BEDDOWS, L., Private, 8th Manchester Regiment.
He volunteered in January 1915, and shortly afterwards proceeded to Egypt, where he saw active service. He was later transferred to the Dardanelles and was badly wounded during heavy fighting on the Gallipoli Peninsula. He was invalided to Malta, but unhappily died of his wounds on October 8th 1915. He was entitled to the 1914–15 Star, and the General Service and Victory Medals.
"His memory is cherished with pride."
10, William Street, West Gorton, Manchester.   Z1198

BEER, W. (Sen.), Sapper, R.E.
He volunteered in August 1915, and first did duty with the Manchester Regiment. He was later transferred to the Royal Engineers, and was engaged on special duties at important stations in England. He was unable to obtain his transfer overseas, but nevertheless rendered valuable services until his demobilisation in May 1919.
101, Marsland Street, Ardwick, Manchester.   Z1199

BEER, W., Private, 1/7th Manchester Regiment.
He was mobilised in August 1914, and in September of the same year was drafted to Egypt with the 42nd Division, and saw service in that theatre of war. He was later transferred to the Dardanelles and took part in much heavy fighting at Cape Helles, Achi-Baba and Krithia, and was invalided home. After again serving in Egypt he was transferred to France, and was in action at the Battles of Ypres and Bullecourt, and the Retreat and Advance of 1918. He holds the 1914–15 Star, and the General Service and Victory Medals, and was demobilised in February 1919.
101, Marsland Street, Ardwick, Manchester.   Z1200

BEHAN, G. W., Private, 1/7th Manchester Regt.
He volunteered in August 1914, and in the following April was drafted to the Dardanelles, where he took part in the Landings at Cape Helles and Suvla Bay, and in the Evacuation of the Gallipoli Peninsula, during which he was wounded in action in January 1916. As a result he was invalided home, and discharged in April 1916 as medically unfit for further service. He holds the 1914–15 Star, and the General Service and Victory Medals.
20, Olive Street, Hulme, Manchester. Z11635

BEHENNA, G., Driver, R.A.S.C.
He volunteered in April 1915, and in June of the following year was sent to France, where he was present at the Battles of the Somme and Cambrai, and served in the Retreat and Advance of 1918. After the cessation of hostilities he returned to England, and in February 1919 was demobilised, holding the General Service and Victory Medals.
1, Sycamore Street, Gorton, Manchester. Z9855

BELL, A., Private, 1/7th Manchester Regiment.
He volunteered in August 1914, and after completing his training in the following April, was drafted to the Dardanelles, where he took part in much severe fighting. He died gloriously on the Field of Battle at Krithia III on June 4th, 1915, and was entitled to the 1914–15 Star, and the General Service and Victory Medals.
"The path of duty was the way to glory."
19, Halton Street, Hulme, Manchester. Z11636

BELL, A., Private, 3rd Border Regiment.
Volunteering in December 1914, he was drafted to Gallipoli in the following May, and was in action in the first and second Battles of Krithia, and at Suvla Bay, where he was severely wounded. He was invalided home, and in September 1917 was discharged as medically unfit for further service. He holds the 1914–15 Star, and the General Service and Victory Medals.
48, Beaumont Street, Beswick, Manchester. Z9856

BELL, C., Private, K.O. (Royal Lancaster Regt.)
He joined in January 1917, and four months later proceeded to France, where he took part in many important engagements and saw much heavy fighting in various sectors. He was in action at Passchendaele, Lens and Cambrai, and made the supreme sacrifice, being killed on November 5th 1917. He was entitled to the General Service and Victory Medals.
"And doubtless he went in splendid company."
39, Wood Street, Hulme, Manchester. Z1204

BELL, C., Private, 7th and 12th Lancashire Fusiliers.
He volunteered in September 1914, and in the following year was sent to France. Shortly afterwards he proceeded to Salonika, where he was in action on the Vardar and Doiran fronts. In 1918 he returned to France and was engaged in the Loos, Passchendaele and Cambrai sectors. He was demobilised in January 1919, and holds the 1914–15 Star, and the General Service and Victory Medals.
5, Nancy Street, Chester Road, Manchester. Z9857

BELL, D., Private, R.A.S.C. and Labour Corps.
He volunteered in September 1915, and was drafted to France in January of the following year. He did consistently good work in this theatre of war, but was unfortunately wounded by shell-fire in the vicinity of Valenciennes on October 19th, 1918, and died from his injuries on March 17th of the following year. He was entitled to the General Service and Victory Medals.
"His memory is cherished with pride."
2, Swailes Street, Chorlton-on-Medlock, Manchester. TX1206B

BELL, G., Private, 6th South Lancashire Regiment.
Volunteering in December 1915, he was drafted overseas shortly afterwards. During his service in Mesopotamia, he took part in engagements at Kut, Sanna-i-Yat, and on the Tigris, and also served as a machine gunner. He returned home, and was demobilised in February 1919, holding the 1914–15 Star, and the General Service and Victory Medals.
19, Halton Street, Hulme, Manchester. Z11637

BELL, G. E., Private, North Staffordshire Regt.
He was mobilised at the outbreak of hostilities, and in the following month was drafted to the Western Front. During his service in France he took part in much heavy fighting in many engagements, including those at the Marne, La Bassée, Ypres, St. Éloi, Hill 60, Loos, Vimy Ridge, the Somme, Arras, Messines, and Ypres. He was also in action in the Retreat of 1918, and was wounded in the Advance. He returned home and was demobilised in October 1919, and holds the 1914 Star, and the General Service and Victory Medals.
12, Worrall Street, Collyhurst, Manchester. Z10320A

BELL, G. W., Private, Northumberland Fusiliers.
He joined in February 1916, and in the following November was sent to France, where he took part in many important engagements. He was in action at the Battles of Beaumont-Hamel, Arras and Bullecourt, and was taken prisoner during the fighting at Ypres III in July 1917. He was repatriated after the Armistice, and eventually demobilised in December 1918, holding the General Service and Victory Medals. He re-joined the Army, and in 1920 was serving in Mesopotamia.
27, Arthur Street, Hulme, Manchester. Z1208

BELL, H., Private, Manchester Regiment.
He volunteered in May 1915, and after being drafted to Egypt in the following year was in action at Siwa. In May 1917 he was transferred to France and took part in the Battles of Ypres and Cambrai, and in the Retreat and Advance of 1918. He was demobilised in January 1919, and holds the General Service and Victory Medals.
27, Dougill Street, Hulme, Manchester. Z9858

BELL, H., Private, Sherwood Foresters.
He volunteered in March 1915, and after completing a period of training was sent to France, where he did good work in connection with transport. He was present at the Battles of Albert, Vimy Ridge, the Somme, Arras, Bullecourt, Ypres III, and in the Retreat and Advance of 1918, and Cambrai, and was eventually demobilised in March 1919, holding the 1914–15 Star, and the General Service and Victory Medals.
13, Cedar Street, Hulme, Manchester. Z1209

BELL, J., Private, 3rd Loyal N. Lancashire Regt.
Mobilised in August 1914, he was at once ordered to France, where he took part in the Battle of Mons, and the subsequent Retreat, and also in the Battles of the Marne, the Aisne, La Bassée, where he was wounded and Neuve Chapelle. In April 1915, he was transferred to Gallipoli, and was wounded in action at Suvla Bay. Returning later to France, he was in action on the Somme, and at Arras and Cambrai, and was wounded and taken prisoner in November 1917. Interned in Germany until the Armistice, he was then repatriated and demobilised in January 1919, holds the Mons Star, and the General Service and Victory Medals.
4, Heyrod Street, Ancoats, Manchester. Z8891

BELL, J., Private, East Lancashire Regiment.
He volunteered in September 1914, and in the following year proceeded to France, where he took part in the Battles of Loos, the Somme, Arras, Ypres and Cambrai, and in other engagements of importance in various sectors, and was severely wounded at Grandcourt during his service. He was demobilised in January 1919, and holds the 1914–15 Star, and the General Service and Victory Medals.
24, Belleek Street, Hulme, Manchester. Z1210

BELL, J., Private, 2nd Manchester Regiment, and Middlesex Regiment.
He volunteered in August 1914, and after serving in England for a time proceeded to India in February 1916. He was stationed at Allahabad, and was engaged on important garrison and other duties. He later saw service in China and Siberia, and was invalided home suffering from heart trouble. He holds the General Service and Victory Medals, and was demobilised in May 1919.
18, Gomm Street, Ardwick, Manchester. Z1205

BELL, J., L/Corpl., King's Own (Scottish Borderers).
He joined in June 1917, and three months later was drafted to France, where he was in action at many important engagements, including those at Cambrai, and during the Retreat of 1918. He was wounded in the second Battle of the Somme, and invalided to England and in consequence was discharged in November 1919, as unfit for further service. He holds the General Service and Victory Medals. Z1203A
5, Callender Street, Chorlton-on-Medlock, Manchester.

BELL, J. A., Private, Border Regiment.
He volunteered in September 1914, and in August of the following year was drafted to France, where he took part in the fighting at Loos. He was transferred to Salonika in November 1915, and was in action on the Doiran and Struma fronts, and at Monastir, but was wounded at the Battle of Vardar II, He returned to England for demobilisation in April 1919, and holds the 1914–15 Star, and the General Service and Victory Medals. 7, Anthony Street, Ardwick, Manchester. TZ1212–13A

BELL, J. R., Private, East Surrey Regiment.
He joined in June 1916, and later in the same year was drafted to France, where he was in action at Albert, the Somme, Arras, Ypres and Cambrai. He also took part in the Retreat and Advance of 1918, and after the Armistice proceeded with the Army of Occupation to Germany. He was demobilised in October 1919, after his return home from Cologne, and holds the General Service and Victory Medals.
39, Parker Street, Ardwick, Manchester. Z9859B

BELL, P., Private, Labour Corps.
Joining in May 1916, he was drafted to France in the following July, and did valuable service at the Somme, the Ancre, Arras, Bullecourt, Ypres, Lens and Cambrai. In November 1917 he was taken prisoner, and after internment in Germany for over a year returned home and was demobilised in January 1919, holding the General Service and Victory Medals.
1, Blomeley Street, Miles Platting, Manchester. Z9860

BELL, T., Private, King's Own (Scottish Borderers).
He volunteered in September 1914, and in the following May was drafted to the Western Front, where he was in action in many important sectors. He was unfortunately wounded by shell-fire, which eventually resulted in the loss of both his legs. He holds the 1914–15 Star, and the General Service and Victory Medals, and was discharged in September 1916. 50, Canning Street, Hulme, Manchester. Z1214

BELL, R., Private, 22nd Manchester Regiment.
From December 1915, until 1918, he was working on high explosives at the Bradford Gas Works, Manchester, and then joined the Army. In July 1918 he proceeded to France, and after serving on the Ypres front was drafted to Italy. There he took part in heavy fighting on the Piave, and after the close of hostilities was sent to Austria with the Army of Occupation. He was demobilised in February 1919, and holds the Gerenal Service and Victory Medals.
11, Class Street, Beswick, Manchester. TZ11465

BELL, R., Driver, R.F.A.
Volunteering in January 1915, he was shortly afterwards drafted to France, where he was in action with his Battery at many important engagements. He saw service at the Battles of Ypres II, Albert, the Somme, Arras, Vimy Ridge and Cambrai, and was sent to hospital suffering from pneumonia. He was eventually demobilised in May 1919, and holds the 1914-15 Star, and the General Service and Victory Medals.
31, Bark Street, Hulme, Manchester. TZ1211

BELL, W., Private, 7th Manchester Regiment.
He joined in May 1918, and later in the same year was drafted to France, where he was in action at the Selle River Bridgeheads, Normal Forest, and other places. After six mnoths' service guarding prisoners of war he returned home in November 1919, and was demobilised, holding the General Service and Victory Medals.
39, Parker Street, Ardwick, Manchester. Z9859A

BELL, W., Private, 22nd Manchester Regiment.
Joining in November 1916, he was sent to France later in the following month and was in action at Arras, Vimy Ridge and Ypres. He was wounded on one occasion and was taken prisoner in 1917. On his release after the Armistice he returned home and was discharged after hospital treatment at Blackburn, as medically unfit for further service in April 1919. He holds the General Service and Victory Medals.
20, Hampden Street, West Gorton, Manchester. Z9861

BELL, W., Pte. (M.M.) King's Own Scottish Borderers.
He volunteered in November 1915, and was shortly afterwards drafted to the Western Front, where he took part in many important engagements in various sectors, and was both wounded and gassed. He was awarded the Military Medal, whilst acting as a runner for conspicuous bravery and devotion fo duty on Passchendaele Ridge, and also holds the General Service and Victory Medals. He was demobilised in March 1919.
2, Swailes Street, Chorlton-on-Medlock, Manchester. TX1206A

BELL, W., Private, Royal Welch Fusiliers.
Volunteering in August 1915 he crossed to France in January of the following year, and whilst there saw much severe fighting. He took part in the Battles of the Somme, Arras, Ypres, Cambrai, and in the Retreat and Advance of 1918, and also did good work at Nieuport and Dunkirk. Returning to England in January 1919 he was demobilised, and holds the General Service and Victory Medals.
101, Naylor Street, Oldham Road, Mamchester. Z9430

BELL, W., Gunner, R.G.A.
He volunteered in October 1914, but was medically unfit for transfer to a theatre of war. Retained at home, he was stationed near Weymouth and at Gosport, and whilst engaged on important duties in connection with home defence, rendered valuable services. He was later admitted to hospital in Gosport on account of ill-health, and was eventually discharged in December 1918.
44, Ogden Street, Hulme, Manchester. TZ8892

BELL, W. A., Gunner, R.F.A.
Volunteering in August 1915, he completed a course of training and was sent to the Western Front in March 1917. He was in action at La Bassée, Givenchy, Festubert, Béthune, Nieuport and Ypres III. and was invalided home owing to heart trouble. He holds the General Service and Victory Medals, and was demobilised in March 1919.
14, Bakewell Street, Ardwick, Manchester. Z1201

BELL, W. G., Driver, R.A.S.C. (M.T.)
He joined in June 1916, and in July of the following year proceeded to France, where he was engaged on important transport duties in many sectors. He did consistently good work as a driver at Abbeville, St. Owen, Cambrai, Amiens, Bapaume, Havrincourt and Le Cateau, and was demobilised in June 1919, holding the General Service and Victory Medals.
36, Gregory Street, West Gorton, Manchester. Z1202

BELL, W. H., Private, 11th South Wales Borderers.
He joined in February 1917, and in December of that year was drafted to France. In this theatre of war he took a prominent part in many engagements, including the Battles of Ypres, Arras, Cambrai, and the Somme and Beaumont-Hamel, and was wounded at Vimy Ridge. He eventually returned to England, and was demobilised in January 1919, holding the General Service and Victory Medals.
2, Norseman Street, Ardwick, Manchester. Z1207

BELLAMY, J., Driver, R.F.A.
He joined in 1916, and afterwards proceeded to the Western Front, where he served with his Battery at Albert and Cambrai, and on the Somme front. Gassed in an action during the Advance in September 1918, he was invalided home and after some time in hospital at Hereford and Blackpool, was stationed at Whittingham until April 1919, when he was demobilised, holding the General Service and Victory Medals.
24, Marlow Street, Longsight, Manchester. Z8893

BELLFIELD, W., Sapper, R.E.
Joining in May 1917, he was drafted to France in the following September, and played an important part in the Battle of Cambrai. He was badly wounded in action on the Somme during the Retreat in April 1918, and spent some time in hospital in France. He was eventually demobilised in December 1919, two months after returning to England, and holds the General Service and Victory Medals.
7, Royds Street, Longsight, Manchester. Z1215

BELLINGHAM, F., Private, 21st Welch Regiment.
He volunteered in March 1915, and was quickly drafted to France. In this seat of war he took part in several engagements, including the Battles of Ypres, Bullecourt and Cambrai. Later he was transferred to the King's Liverpool Regiment, thence to the Labour Corps, and after the cessation of hostilities, went to Germany with the Army of Occupation, and served there until his demobilisation in September 1919. He holds the 1914-15 Star, and the General Service and Victory Medals.
86, Book Street, Hulme, Manchester. Z11638

BENNELL, W., Pte., K.O. (Royal Lancaster Regt.)
Mobilised at the outbreak of war in August 1914, he was soon afterwards sent to France. There he took part in the Battles of Ypres, Loos, Albert, Vimy Ridge, and the Somme, before being transferred to Egypt in December 1916. After serving for some time on the Suez Canal, he was wounded in action at Mersa Matruh, and sent to hospital at Malta. Later evacuated to England he was in hospital in London, and upon his recovery served at home stations, guarding prisoners of war until he was discharged in July 1919. He holds the Mons Star, and the General Service and Victory Medals.
22, Ogden Street, Hulme, Manchester. TZ8894

BENNELL, W., Pte., K.O. (Royal Lancaster Regt.)
He volunteered in February 1915, and in the following July proceeded to France. There he took part in many important engagements, including the Battles of Loos, Albert, the Somme, Arras, Ypres, Cambrai, the Somme II, and in the Retreat and Advance of 1918. After hostilities ceased, he went to Germany with the Army of Occupation, and served there until his demobilisation in January 1919. He holds the 1914-15 Star, and the General Service and Victory Medals.
40, Lancaster Street, Hulme, Manchester. Z11640

BENNETT, A., Private, 1st E. Lancashire Regiment.
Already in the Army at the outbreak of war he proceeded with his Regiment to France, and fought at Mons, Ploegsteert, Ypres, Hill 60, St. Eloi and Zonnebeke. Later he was drafted to Mesopotamia, and took part in important operations of Kut, Baghdad, and on the Tigris. After remaining in the East until hostilities ceased he returned home and was demobilised in May 1919, holding the Mons Star, and the General Service and Victory Medals.
164, Mill Street, Ancoats, Manchester. Z9863

BENNETT, A., Pte., 1st K.O. (Royal Lancaster Regt.)
He volunteered in May 1915, and underwent a period at training prior to his being drafted to the Western Front. There he took part in the Battles of Arras, Ypres III, Passchendaele, and the Somme II, and in heavy fighting during the Retreat and Advance of 1918. He was also present at the entry into Mons on Armistice Day, and was demobilised in February 1919. He holds the General Service and Victory Medals.
101, Silver Street, Hulme, Manchester. TZ11639

BENNETT, C., Private, Durham Light Infantry.
Joining in May 1917, he was retained for special duty in England until April of the following year. He then embarked for France, and whilst there took part in the severe fighting in the Retreat and Advance of 1918, and in October was badly gassed. After being invalided home, he was demobilised in November 1919, and holds the General Service and Victory Medals.
12, Clayton Street, Newtown, Manchester. Z9864

BENNETT, G., Private, 9th Manchester Regiment.
He volunteered in September 1914, and in January of the following year was drafted to France. He was in action at Neuve Chapelle, Ypres, the Somme, Arras, Cambrai, and in the Retreat and subsequent Allied Advance of 1918, and was gassed. He was demobilised in April 1919, after his return home and holds the 1914-15 Star, and the General Service and Victory Medals.
74, Teignmouth Street, Collyhurst, Manchester. Z9431

BENNETT, G., L/Corporal, 19th Manchester Regt.

He volunteered in September 1915, and in the following March proceeded to the Western Front. In this theatre of war, he was in action at Neuve Chapelle, Ypres and La Bassée, and did excellent work before he fell fighting at Poelcapelle on October 4th, 1917. He was buried at Ypres, and was entitled to the General Service and Victory Medals.
" Thinking that remembrance, though unspoken, may reach him where he sleeps."
3, Baker Street, Ardwick, Manchester.   Z8896B

BENNETT, H., Private, R.A.S.C.

He joined in January 1916, and early in the following year proceeded to France, where he saw much service. He was present during the engagements at Ypres, Arras, Messines, Givenchy, and after the Armistice proceeded with the Army of Occupation into Germany. After returning home he was demobilised in November 1919, and holds the General Service and Victory Medals.
5, Schofield Street, Ancoats, Manchester.   Z9865

BENNETT, H. J., Private, R.A.M.C.

He joined in May 1917, and in the following September crossed to the Western Front, where he was engaged as orderly at the 54th General Hospital. He was invalided home in December 1917, and after his recovery rendered valuable medical service in Gloucestershire until demobilised in February 1919. He holds the General Service and Victory Medals.
203, Cobden Street, Ancoats, Manchester.   Z9432

BENNETT, J., Private, R.A.S.C.

Joining in 1916, he was not successful in his efforts to obtain a transfer to a theatre of war owing to ill-health. He, however, rendered valuable services whilst employed on various duties of an important nature at Grove Park and other places until he was discharged in December 1918.
14, Oram Street, Miles Platting, Manchester.   Z8895

BENNETT, J., Private, 21st Manchester Regiment.

He volunteered in April 1915, and proceeded overseas in the following March. During his service on the Western Front he was in action at Loos, Neuve Chapelle, Ypres, Passchendaele, Cambrai, and on the Somme, where he was wounded. Later serving in Italy, he took part in heavy fighting on the Piave front, and was again wounded. He was demobilised on his return home in February 1919, and holds the General Service and Victory Medals.
3, Baker Street, Ardwick, Manchester.   Z8896A

BENNETT, J., Sapper, R.E.

Volunteering in March 1915, he was drafted six months later to France. In this theatre of war he served with his Company at Loos, St. Eloi, Albert, Arras, Bullecourt, Lens, Cambrai, Bapaume, Le Cateau, and on the Aisne, and did good work whilst employed on important duties. He was demobilised on his return home in February 1919, and holds the 1914–15 Star, and the General Service and Victory Medals.
46, Prescott Street, West Gorton, Manchester.   Z8897

BENNETT, J., Private, 18th King's (Liverpool Regt.)

He volunteered in July 1915, and after a period of training was drafted to Salonika in November of the following year. There he took part in many engagements on the Doiran and Vardar fronts, and was in hospital for some time with malaria. In June 1918 he was transferred to France, and after much heavy fighting in this theatre of war, he returned to England, and was demobilised in February 1919, holding the General Service and Victory Medals.
13, Lime Street, Hulme, Manchester.   Z1217

BENNETT, J., L/Corporal, Lancashire Fusiliers.

Volunteering in January 1915, he was drafted to France in the following November, and whilst there took part in much heavy fighting at the Somme and Arras. He was unhappily killed in action on June 21st, 1917, and was entitled to the 1914–15 Star, and the General Service and Victory Medals.
" A valiant Soldier, with undaunted heart he breasted life's last hill."
4, Abel Street, Collyhurst, Manchester.   Z9866

BENNETT, J., L/Corporal, King's (Liverpool Regt.)

He volunteered in April 1915, but was discharged in the following June as medically unfit. In March 1917 he was again called up, and in the same month was drafted to France, where he served in many sectors of the Front until January 1918. He then returned to England, and was engaged on important hospital duties until demobilised in August 1919. He holds the General Service and Victory Medals.
12, Victoria Street, Miles Platting, Manchester.   Z9867

BENNETT, L., Bombardier, R.G.A.

Volunteering in May 1915, he was sent to France in July 1916, and played a prominent part in the Battles of the Somme, Arras, Ypres III, Lens and Cambrai I. He was also in action at the Battles of Amiens, Bapaume, Cambrai II and Ypres IV, during the Retreat and Advance of 1918. He returned to England for demobilisation in December 1919, after a period of service on the German Frontier, and holds the General Service and Victory Medals.
2, Ridley Grove, Greenheys, Manchester.   Z1218

BENNETT, S., Pte., 4th K.O. (Royal Lancaster Regt)

Mobilised in August 1914, he proceeded to France with the 1st Expeditionary Force, and took part in the Battles of Mons, La Bassée, Ypres, and the Somme before being wounded at Nieuport. After hospital treatment at the Base, he rejoined his unit, and was in action at Givenchy and Arras. He received his discharge in January 1919, and holds the Mons Star, and the General Service and Victory Medals.
4, Barnes Place, Ancoats, Manchester.   Z11925A

BENNETT, W., Private, 5th Manchester Regiment.

He joined in May 1916, and in the following January was drafted to Egypt, where he served for four months. He then proceeded to France, and was in action at Vimy Ridge, Messines, Ypres, Cambrai, and the Retreat and Allied Advance of 1918. After the Armistice he proceeded with the Army of Occupation into Germany, where he remained until demobilised in September 1919. He holds the General Service and Victory Medals.
6, Howard Street, Ancoats, Manchester.   Z9868

BENNETT, W. A., Air Mechanic, R.A.F.

He joined in February 1917, but owing to his being medically unfit for service overseas was retained with his Squadron on special duties at important stations in England. He nevertheless rendered valuable services, and was discharged in January 1918, as unfit for further duty.
2A, Pleasant View, Ardwick, Manchester.   Z1216

BENNETT, W. F., Farrier-Sergeant, R.F.A.

He volunteered in August 1914, and in the following June proceeded to Egypt, where he rendered valuable services with his Battery at Mersa-Matruh, Agayia and Sollum, and in other engagements in the Suez Canal zone. In July 1916 he was transferred to India, and after a period of duty at Jubbulpore, unfortunately contracted fever and died at Bombay on December 1st 1917. He was entitled to the 1914–15 Star, and the General Service and Victory Medals.
" His memory is cherished with pride."
70, Dorset Street, Hulme, Manchester.   Z1219

BENNION, C., Private, 23rd Manchester Regiment.

Volunteering in January 1915, he was drafted early in the following year to France, and whilst there saw much heavy fighting. He took part in the Battles of the Somme, Arras, Ypres and Cambrai, where he was severely wounded. After being invalided home and receiving hospital treatment he was discharged in December 1918, as medically unfit for further service. He holds the General Service and Victory Medals.
105, Beaumont Street, Beswick, Manchester.   Z9869

BENSON, A., Corporal, 8th Manchester Regiment.

Volunteering in May 1915, he proceeded to Egypt in February 1916, and saw service on the Suez Canal, and at Romani and Katia. He was transferred to the Western Front in March 1917, and played a prominent part in many engagements, including the Battles of Vimy Ridge, Ypres III, Lens, Cambrai, the Sambre and the Selle, and was badly wounded in action during the Advance of 1918. He holds the General Service and Victory Medals, and was demobilised in February 1919.
20, Wigley Street, Ardwick, Manchester.   Z1221

BENSON, H., Sergeant, R.E.

He joined in May 1916, and was quickly drafted to France. There he saw much heavy fighting on the Somme, at Bullecourt, Ypres, Cambrai, and in the Retreat and Advance of 1918. After hostilities ceased, he went into Germany with the Army of Occupation, and in 1920 was still with his Regiment on garrison duties at Kantara in Egypt. He holds the General Service and Victory Medals.
17, Green Street, Gorton, Manchester.   Z1320

BENSON, J. S., Captain, Royal Fusiliers.

He volunteered in April 1915, and in August was drafted to France, where he played a distinguished part in heavy fighting at St. Eloi and Festubert. He was also in action at the Battles of Loos, Vermelles, the Somme, Arras and Cambrai. In August 1916 he was badly wounded, and later was recommended for the Military Cross for conspicuous bravery in rescuing a fellow officer under heavy fire. Demobilised in February 1919, he holds the 1914–15 Star, and the General Service and Victory Medals.
23, Solent Street, Beswick, Manchester.   Z1222

BENSON, R., Gunner, R.G.A.

He volunteered in August 1914, and in the following April was sent to the Dardanelles, where he took part in the Landings at Cape Helles and Suvla Bay, and in the Battles of Krithia I, II and III, and Chunuk Bair. After the Evacuation of the Gallipoli Peninsula, he was transferred to Egypt, and saw heavy fighting at Agayia, Sollum, El Fasher and Romani. In April 1917 he was invalided home with defective eyesight caused by wounds received in action at Suvla Bay in August 1915, and spent some time in hospitals at Fulham. He was eventually demobilised in January 1919, and holds the 1914–15 Star, and the General Service and Victory Medals.
1, Bury Street, City Road, Hulme, Manchester.   TZ1220

BENT, C. (D.C.M.) Sergeant, Lancashire Fusiliers.
Mobilised at the outbreak of war in August 1914, he proceeded to Egypt in the following month, and was in action on the Suez Canal. In 1915 he was drafted to the Dardanelles, and was awarded the Distinguished Conduct Medal for conspicuous bravery and devotion to duty on the Gallipoli Peninsula. He also saw service on the Western Front, and was in action at the Battle of Ypres III, Passchendaele, Nieuport, the Somme and Havrincourt. In addition to the Distinguished Conduct Medals, he holds the 1914–15 Star, and the General Service and Victory Medals, and was demobilised in January 1919. 16, Milton Street, Longsight, Manchester.   Z1223

BENT, W., L/Corporal, K.O. (Royal Lancaster Regt.)
When war broke out he was already serving in the Army, and at once proceeded with the First Expeditionary Force to France. There he fought in the Battles of Mons and Ypres, and was wounded at Festubert in May 1915. On his recovery, he was drafted to Egypt, and after serving at Alexandria, Cairo, Khartoum, the Sudan and Port Said, was sent to Palestine, where he took part in engagements at Jaffa and Jerusalem. On returning to England he was discharged in March 1919, and holds the Mons Star, and the General Service and Victory Medals.
179, Victoria Square, Ancoats, Manchester.   Z11405

BENTICK, H., Private, Labour Corps.
He joined in January 1918, and was first engaged on special work with the Labour Corps. Later, however he was transferred to the 24th Cheshire Regiment, and although unsuccessful in obtaining his transfer overseas, rendered valuable services with his unit until his demobilisation in January 1919.
13, Bloom Street, Hulme, Manchester.   TZ1224

BENTLEY, E., 1st Class Stoker, R.N.
He enlisted in 1902, and at the outbreak of war in August 1914 was sent to Belgium with the Royal Naval Division, and was taken prisoner at Antwerp. During his captivity he suffered many hardships. After a short time in Doeberitz Camp, he was forced to repair trenches on the German front in Russia, where he was often under heavy fire, worked at the docks at Libau on the Baltic Coast, and also down the coal mines in Saxony. He was repatriated and discharged in March 1919, and holds the 1914 Star, and the General Service and Victory Medals. 34, Brunt Street, Rusholme, Manchester.   Z1226

BENTLEY, J., Private, King's (Liverpool Regiment.)
He joined in April 1916, and after a period of training was retained on duties of an important nature in England. After hostilities ended he was drafted to the Army of Occupation in Germany, and until demobilised in September 1919, rendered valuable service at Bonn, Cologne and other important towns. 122, Hamilton Street, Collyhurst, Manchester. Z9871

BENTLEY, S., Private, Lancashire Fusiliers.
He volunteered in August 1915, and in February of the following year was drafted to France, where he acted as a Lewis gunner. He took part in many important engagements, including the Battles of Vimy Ridge, the Somme, Messines and Ypres, and was killed in action in November 1917. He was entitled to the General Service and Victory Medals.
"He died the noblest death a man may die."
20, Abbey Field Street, Openshaw, Manchester.   Z1225

BERESFORD, J. T., Private, 23rd Manchester Regt.
Volunteering in November 1914 he was sent to France in the following October. Whilst in this theatre of war he saw much heavy fighting and was in action at Albert, Ploegsteert Wood, the Somme, Arras and Messines. In July 1917, in consequence of being wounded he was invalided home, and after receiving hospital treatment was discharged as medically unfit for further service in October 1918. He holds the 1914–15 Star, and the General Service and Victory Medals.
62, Heyrod Street, Ancoats, Manchester.   Z9872

BERESFORD, R., Private, Royal Fusiliers.
He joined in April 1917, and after a course of training was engaged on important duties with his unit. He was not successful in securing his transfer overseas, and owing to being under military age was discharged in September of the same year. 91, Egerton Street, West Gorton, Manchester. Z9873A

BERESFORD, R., Pioneer, R.E.
Volunteering in June 1915, he was drafted overseas in the following month, and whilst in France saw much service. He was present during the engagements at Festubert, Loos, the Somme, Arras, Bullcourt and Messines, but in December 1917 was sent home and discharged as medically unfit for further service. He holds the 1914–15 Star, and the General Service and Victory Medals.
91, Egerton Street, West Gorton, Manchester.   Z9873B

BERGIN, E., Corporal, King's Royal Rifle Corps.
He volunteered in August 1914, and after a period of training proceeded to France, where he took part in the Battles of Loos, and in much heavy fighting on the Ypres and Ancre fronts. He made the supreme sacrifice, being killed in action on the Somme on May 25th 1917. He was entitled to the 1914–15 Star, and the General Service and Victory Medals.
"Whilst we remember the sacrifice is not in vain."
40, Fielden Street, Oldham Road, Manchester,   Z11641

BERRA, A., Private, 20th Lancashire Fusiliers.
He volunteered in May 1915, and in the following January proceeded to the Western Front. There he played a prominent part in many important engagements, including Neuve Chapelle, the Somme, Arras, Ypres, Bapaume, Amiens, Péronne, Havrincourt, Cambrai and Le Cateau, and performed excellent work. He was demobilised in February 1919, holding the General Service and Victory Medals.
18, Pomfret Street, West Gorton, Manchester.   Z8898

BERRISFORD, J., Private, R.A.M.C.
Volunteering in November 1915, he was drafted to Egypt in May 1916, and acted as nursing orderly in the R.A.M.C., and did consistently good work. He was stationed at Kantara with the 24th Military Hospital during the whole period of hostilities, and returning to England was demobilised in August 1919, holding the General Service and Victory Medals.
13, Guy Street, Ardwick, Manchester.   Z1227

BERRY, A. (Miss), Special War Worker.
This lady volunteered her services in 1918, and was engaged at the Newton Street Post Office, Manchester, as a sorter, thus releasing a man for the Army. She did consistently good work until 1919, when she relinquished her duties.
73, Dalton Street, Hulme, Manchester.   Z1229

BERRY, H., Gunner (Signaller), R.G.A.
He joined in June 1916, and on completion of his training, first saw active service in Italy. Later, however, he was sent to Palestine, and took part in the third Battle of Gaza, and in other important engagements under General Allenby until May 1918. He was then drafted to the Western Front, where he was in action at the Battles of Amiens and Cambrai, and at the entry into Mons on Armistice Day. During his overseas service he was three times gassed, and after the cessation of hostilities, was stationed at Bonn with the Army of Occupation. He was demobilised in April 1919, and holds the General Service and Victory Medals.
23, Cuba Street, Hulme, Manchester.   Z1231

BERRY, J., Private, King's (Liverpool Regiment).
He joined in November 1916, and was drafted to the Western Front in the following month. Whilst in this theatre of war he was engaged on special duties with a Labour Battalion in various sectors, and rendered valuable services until after the cessation of hostilities. He returned to England for demobilisation in September 1919, and holds the General Service and Victory Medals.
54, Canning Street, Hulme, Manchester.   Z1232

BERRY, J., Private, Sherwood Foresters.
Volunteering in February 1915, he was sent to France in the following March and first saw heavy fighting at Loos and St. Eloi. He was also in action at the Battles of Albert and Vimy Ridge, where he was badly wounded. After hospital treatment at Boulogne and Stockport, he returned to the Western Front, and took part in the Battles of Ypres III, the Somme II, Cambrai II, and Le Cateau II, and was gassed. Demobilised in January 1919, he holds the General Service and Victory Medals.
49, Frame Street, Chorlton-on-Medlock, Manchester.   Z1230

BERRY, J. E., L/Corporal, Manchester Regiment.
Volunteering in August 1914, he was sent in the following May to India, and after serving in several skirmishes on the Afghan Frontier, was transferred to China. He assisted to quell the Chinese outbreak in Singapore in 1917, and was later drafted to Egypt, and was serving in Alexandria in January 1919, during the Students' riots. He was afterwards invalided home on account of ill-health, and admitted to hospital in Halifax, remained there until he was discharged from the Army in May 1919, holding the General Service and Victory Medals.
8, Coleman Street, Miles Platting, Manchester.   Z8899

BERRY, R. A., Corporal, 1/6th Essex Regiment.
Volunteering in November 1915, he first served in the Manchester Regiment as a signalling instructor and was drafted to Egypt after his transfer to the Essex Regiment. He saw much active service in the East and played a prominent part in the fighting on the Suez, and later in Palestine, where he was in action at the Battles of Gaza. He made the supreme sacrifice on December 2nd, 1917, when he was killed in heavy fighting on the Anga River. He was entitled to the General Service and Victory Medals.
"A costly sacrifice upon the altar of freedom."
13, Cowesby Street, Moss Side, Manchester.   Z1228

BERRY, T. H., Private, 1/6th Manchester Regiment.
He joined in November 1916, and two months later was drafted to France. After serving for two months in this theatre of war, he was sent to Egypt, but returned to France a few weeks later, and was wounded in action at Arras. He spent three months in hospital in Rouen, and on his recovery rejoined his unit, and participated in heavy fighting at Ypres, Cambrai, and on the Marne. Invalided home in July 1918, suffering from gas-poisoning, he was sent to hospital in Plymouth, and later served at Heaton Park before being demobilised in February 1919. He holds the General Service and Victory Medals.
11, Lingard Street, Hulme, Manchester.   Z6365A

BERRY, T. W., Private, Durham Light Infantry, and Sapper, R.E.
He volunteered in October 1915, and in June of the following year was drafted to France, where he fought in the Battle of the Somme. He was also in action in many other engagements, including those at Loos, Lens and Passchendaele. He returned to England in 1919, and was demobilised in March of that year, holding the General Service and Victory Medals.
36, Harvest Street, West Gorton, Manchester. Z9874

BERTENSHAW, J. (M.M.), Sergt.-Major, Lancashire Fusiliers, and M.G.C.
He was already serving at the outbreak of hostilities, and was at once ordered to the Western Front, where he fought in the Battle of Mons. He was also in action in the Battles of the Somme, Loos, Messines and Arras, during which he was wounded. On returning to the firing line he served at Cambrai and in the Retreat and Advance of 1918. He was awarded the Military Medal for conspicuous bravery in the Field at Cambrai, and was discharged in February 1919, also holding the Mons Star, and the General Service and Victory Medals.
6, Wilson Street, Bradford, Manchester. Z11406

BEST, J., Private, Royal Defence Corps.
He volunteered in January 1915, and after a period of training was engaged on special guard duties at various important stations. He rendered valuable services with his unit for nearly two years, but was admitted to hospital at Warrington with heart disease, and unhappily died there on September 29th 1916.
"His memory is cherished with pride."
22, Derby Street, Ardwick, Manchester. TZ1237

BESWICK, A., Sapper, R.E.
He joined in November 1916, but owing to ill-health was unable to procure a transfer overseas. He was stationed at Sandwich for a time, and then proceeded to Chepstow, where he rendered most valuable services in the shipbuilding yards, in connection with the repair and construction of transports. He was demobilised from Heaton Park in February 1919.
24, Werneth Street, Harpurhey, Manchester. Z11466

BESWICK, C., Private, 22nd Manchester Regiment.
He joined in April 1916, and in the following year was drafted to the Western Front, where he took part in the Battle of Cambrai, and was wounded and made prisoner of war. He was held in captivity behind the German lines and was forced to work as a labourer. He was released after the Armistice, and demobilised in September 1919, holding the General Service and Victory Medals.
41, Fenwick Street, Hulme, Manchester. Z11642C

BESWICK, C., Private, 1/8th King's (Liverpool Regt.)
Volunteering in May 1915, he was sent on active service in the following August, and whilst on the Western Front took part in the Battles of the Somme, Arras and Ypres III, and was wounded in action. In February 1918 he was transferred to North Russia, and served at Archangel under General Ironside. He was demobilised in September 1919, and holds the General Service and Victory Medals.
71, Henry Street, Ardwick, Manchester. Z11872

BESWICK, F., Pte., 2nd York and Lancaster Regt.
Joining in March 1916, he proceeded overseas in the following October. During his service on the Western Front he took part in several engagements, including the Battles of Arras, Bullecourt, Messines, Passchendaele, Cambrai, and on the Somme (II), where he was badly wounded in March 1918. As a result he was discharged in November 1919 as medically unfit for further service, and holds the General Service and Victory Medals.
41, Fenwick Street, Hulme, Manchester. Z11642A

BESWICK, G., Pte., R.A.M.C. (1/2nd E. Lancashire Field Ambulance).
He was mobilised with the Territorials in August 1914, and proceeded to Egypt in the following month. Early in 1915, he was transferred to the Gallipoli Peninsula, and was wounded by a sniper in July of that year. After six weeks in hospital, he returned to Gallipoli, and was again wounded by a sniper during the Evacuation in January 1916. He remained in hospital at Cairo for nine months, but on his recovery was sent to France, where he saw much severe fighting until hostilities ceased. He was demobilised in February 1919, and holds the 1914–15 Star, and the General Service and Victory Medals.
134, South Street, Longsight, Manchester. Z1236

BESWICK, H., Private, Lancashire Fusiliers.
Volunteering in August 1914, he was engaged on important duties in England until October 1916. He was then drafted to the Western Front, and immediately went into action on the Somme. On November 23rd, seven weeks after landing in France, he laid down his life for King and Country at Beaumont-Hamel. He was entitled to the General Service and Victory Medals.
"The path of duty was the way to glory."
55, Caton Street, Hulme, Manchester. Z1234

BESWICK, H., Private, 8th Manchester Regiment.
Volunteering in September 1915 he was retained in England for his training until January 1916. He then proceeded to France and fought in the Battles of Vermelles, the Somme, Arras, Bullecourt, Ypres, Cambrai, the Marne, and many others until hostilities ended. He returned home, and was demobilised in October 1919, holding the General Service and Victory Medals.
170, Teignmouth Street, Rochdale Road, Manchester. Z9433

BESWICK, J., Sergt., K.O. (Royal Lancaster Regt.)
Mobilised in August 1914, he was drafted to France in the following month, and played a distinguished part in the Battles of the Marne, the Aisne, La Bassée, Ypres, and Neuve Chapelle. In May 1915 he was transferred to Mesopotamia, where he was in action at Amara, Kut-el-Amara, Sanna-i-Yat I, before being wounded on the Tigris in June 1916. He was invalided to Malta, and on recovery proceeded to India in December 1918, and was engaged on special duties until his return to England for discharge in January 1920. He holds the 1914 Star, and the General Service and Victory Medals.
9, Ernest Street, Morton Street, Longsight, Manchester. Z1235

BESWICK, J., Private, 1st Manchester Regiment.
Prior to the war he had served for five years, and in October 1914, proceeded to France. A few weeks later he was unfortunately killed in action at Givenchy on December 21st, 1914. He was entitled to the 1914 Star, and the General Service and Victory Medals.
"His life for his Country, his soul to God."
37, Lawrence Street, West Gorton, Manchester. Z9875

BESWICK, R., Private, 1st East Lancashire Regt.
He was mobilised at the outbreak of war in August 1914, and was immediately drafted to France. There he took part in much severe fighting, and was present at many of the early battles of the war. He was unfortunately killed in action at Poperinghe on May 13th 1915, and was entitled to the 1914 Star, and the General Service and Victory Medals.
"He died the noblest death a man may die."
14, Fleetwood Street, Ancoats, Manchester. TZ1233

BESWICK, W., Private, 2/4th Seaforth Highlanders.
He volunteered in January 1915, and was quickly drafted to France, where he took part in the Battle of Neuve Chapelle. He died gloriously on the field of Battle near Hill 60 on May 9th, 1915, and was entitled to the 1914–15 Star, and the General Service and Victory Medals.
"A costly sacrifice upon the altar of freedom."
41, Fenwick Street, Hulme, Manchester. Z11642B

BETTLES, A., Rifleman, Rifle Brigade.
He volunteered in April 1915, and in December of the same year was drafted to the Western Front, where he took part in many important engagements. He was in action at Albert, Ploegsteert Wood, the Somme, Beaumont-Hamel, Arras, Bullecourt, Ypres, and Cambrai, and made the supreme sacrifice on April 22nd, 1918, when he was killed in action on the Lys. He was entitled to the 1914–15 Star, and the General Service and Victory Medals.
"Great deeds cannot die."
2, Little Rumford Street, Chorlton-on-Medlock, Manchester. Z1238

BEVAN, I. (Mrs.), Special War Worker.
During the war this lady was engaged on work of National importance at Heath Hall, Dumfries, Scotland. She was employed on canteen work, and carried out her arduous duties in a highly commendable manner.
48, Mawson Street, Chorlton-on-Medlock, Manchester. Z11643

BEVINS, A., Private, 21st Manchester Regiment.
He joined in February 1916, and on completion of a period of training was in the following November drafted overseas. During his service on the Western Front, he experienced fierce fighting in the Somme sector. In February 1917 he was transferred to Italy, and in that theatre of war took part in many important engagements. He was demobilised in December 1918, and holds the General Service and Victory Medals.
3, St. Ann Street, Bradford, Manchester. Z11873

BEVINS, J., Private, Lancashire Fusiliers.
Volunteering in January 1915 he completed a period of training and was drafted to the Western Front in June 1917. There he took part in many important engagements, including the Battles of Ypres, La Bassée, and Cambrai, and rendered valuable services during the Retreat and Advance of 1918. After the Armistice he proceeded to Germany, where he did duty with the Army of Occupation on the Rhine. He holds the General Service and Victory Medals, and was demobilised in March 1919.
33, Lord Street, Openshaw, Manchester. Z1239

BEVINS, W., Driver, R.A.S.C. (M.T.)
He joined in September 1917, and in the following month proceeded to the Western Front, where he was engaged on important transport duties in many sectors. He was present at many engagements, including the Battles of Ypres, the Somme, Arras, Bapaume, and Cambrai, and did consistently good work during the Retreat and Advance of 1918. He holds the General Service and Victory Medals, and was demobilised in January 1919.
34, Ryder Street, Bradford, Manchester.   Z1240A

BICKERDYKE, J., Private, 8th Manchester Regt.
He volunteered in October 1914, and during the first part of his service, did consistently good work at various stations in England. He was drafted to France in January 1917, and took part in many important engagements in this theatre of war. He was severely wounded on the Ancre front, and after being invalided to England, was discharged in March 1918, as physically unfit for further service. He holds the General Service and Victory Medals.
11, Hayfield Street, Ardwick, Manchester.   Z1241B

BICKERDYKE, W., Pte., 8th Manchester Regt.
Volunteering in October 1914, he was engaged on important defence duties on the East Coast, and on special work on Salisbury Plain until early in March 1918. He then proceeded to France, but, ten days after landing, was unhappily killed in action on March 23rd, 1918, during the second Battle of the Somme. He was entitled to the General Service and Victory Medals.
          "The path of duty was the way to glory."
11, Hayfield Street, Ardwick, Manchester.   Z1241A

BICKERS, J. R., Private, M.G.C.
Volunteering in August 1914, he was quickly drafted to Egypt, where he saw heavy fighting in the Suez Canal zone. Later, however, he was transferred to the Dardanelles, and took part in many important engagements, during the course of which he was wounded in June 1915 at the Battle of Krithia. After the Evacuation of the Gallipoli Peninsula he proceeded to the Western Front, and was in action at Ypres, and La Bassée. Demobilised in April 1919, he holds the 1914–15 Star, and the General Service and Victory Medals.
36, Windsor Street, Collyhurst, Manchester.   Z10293

BICKERSTAFF, T., Pte., 4th South Lancashire Regt.
He joined in July 1917, and on completion of his training was engaged on special work in England until April 1918. He was then sent to Dublin in Ireland for garrison duty, and rendered valuable services with his unit. He was unsuccessful in obtaining his transfer to a theatre of war, and was demobilised in February 1919.
170, Heald Grove, Rusholme, Manchester.   Z1242

BICKERTON, H., Private, 8th Manchester Regt.
He volunteered in September 1914, but owing to his being medically unfit for service overseas, was retained in England on important engineering work at various stations. He nevertheless did consistently good work, and was discharged in July 1918 as no longer physically fit for military service.
19, Power Street, Ardwick, Manchester.   Z1243

BIGGS, C. T., Pte., Queen's (Royal West Surrey Regt.)
Volunteering in September 1914, he was sent to France in the following January, and after a short period of heavy fighting, was badly wounded in action at the Battle of Festubert in May 1915. He was invalided to England, but on his recovery four months later, was transferred to the Middlesex Regiment, and engaged on important garrison duties at Chatham until July 1916. He was then invalided from the Army through the effects of his wounds, and holds the 1914–15 Star, and the General Service and Victory Medals.
3, Marie Street, Openshaw, Manchester.   Z1244

BILLINGHAM, R., Air Mechanic, R.A.F.
Joining in July 1917, he was stationed at Farnborough, Blandford, Kimmel Park, and in London, Surrey, and Ireland, engaged on important duties which demanded a high degree of technical skill. He was not successful in obtaining a transfer overseas, but nevertheless rendered valuable services until he was demobilised in July 1919.
19, Clare Street, Chorlton-on-Medlock, Manchester.   Z8900

BILLINGS, H., Private, Border Regiment.
He volunteered in August 1914, and after a period of training, was drafted to Mesopotamia in June 1915. There he took part in much heavy fighting, and was present at numerous engagements, including the Battles of Kut-el-Amara, and the capture of Baghdad. He unhappily died in France in February 1919, on his way home and was entitled to the 1914–15 Star, and the General Service and Victory Medals.
          "His memory is cherished with pride."
12, Clifford Street, Lower Openshaw, Manchester.   Z1245B

BILLINGS, J., Private, 8th Manchester Regiment.
He was mobilised with the Territorials in August 1914, and after a period of important duties in England, was drafted to the Western Front in May 1917, and took part in much heavy fighting in various sectors. He was in action at the Battles of the Somme, Arras, Ypres, Givenchy, and Cambrai, and later

in the Retreat and Advance of 1918, and suffered from gas poisoning. He proceeded to Germany after the Armistice, and did duty with the Army of Occupation on the Rhine. Returning to England, he was demobilised in June 1919, holding the General Service and Victory Medals.
12, Clifford Street, Lower Openshaw, Manchester.   Z1245A

BILLINGTON, J., Pte., K.O. (Scottish Borders).
He volunteered in August 1914, and in the following November proceeded to the Western Front. He was in action at Neuve Chapelle, Ypres, the Somme, Passchendaele, and the Retreat and Advance of 1918, and also served for a time at Nieuport, and Dunkirk. Demobilised in February 1919, he holds the 1914 Star, and the General Service and Victory Medals.
12, Pollard Street East, Ancoats, Manchester.   Z9876

BILLINGTON, W., Gunner, R.F.A.
Having previously served for twelve years with the Colours, he re-enlisted in August 1914, and was at once ordered to France. There he took part with his Battery in the Retreat from Mons, and the Battles of Neuve Chapelle, Loos, La Bassée, Festubert, Arras, Ypres, and Cambrai. He was wounded in action on the Somme in September 1918, and sent to hospital at the Base, being eventually evacuated to England. He was demobilised in January 1919, and holds the Mons Star, and the General Service and Victory Medals.
36, Randolph Street, Openshaw, Manchester.   Z8910

BINGHAM, A., Gunner, R.F.A.
He was already in the Army at the outbreak of war in August 1914, and in September was drafted to Egypt, where he saw active service. In 1915 he was transferred to the Dardanelles, and took part in much heavy fighting at the Landing on the Gallipoli Peninsula, and was in action at Cape Helles, Krithia, and Achi-Baba. He proceeded to France after the Evacuation and was engaged in the fighting at Ypres, Passchendaele, Cambrai, and on the Somme, and was severely wounded and gassed. He was invalided home, and eventually discharged in February 1919, and holds the 1914–15 Star, and the General Service and Victory Medals.
21, Gibson Street, Ardwick, Manchester.   Z1249

BINGHAM, F., Gunner, R.F.A.
He volunteered in February 1915, and first served with the 8th Manchester Regiment. On being transferred to the Royal Field Artillery, he proceeded to Egypt, but was quickly sent to the Dardanelles, and took part in the Landing at Suvla Bay, and in further heavy fighting until the Evacuation of the Gallipoli Peninsula. He was then drafted to France, where he was in action at the Battles of the Somme (I and II), Arras, Vimy Ridge, Ypres, and Cambrai, and in the Retreat and Advance of 1918. He was badly wounded on the Somme, was discharged as medically unfit for further service, holding the 1914–15 Star, and the General Service and Victory Medals.
21, Gibson Street, Ardwick, Manchester.   Z1247

BINGHAM, G. W., Private, King's (Liverpool Regt.)
Joining in January 1917, he was quickly drafted to the Western Front, where he played an important part in the Battles of Arras, Bullecourt, Ypres (III), Lens, the Aisne (II), Havrincourt and Le Cateau, and in other engagements during the Retreat and Advance of 1918. He was demobilised in November 1919, and holds the General Service and Victory Medals.
156, Crossley Street, Gorton, Manchester.   Z1248

BINGHAM, W. J., Private, 12th Manchester Regt.
He volunteered in February 1915, and after training for three months, proceeded to the Western Front. There he took part in numerous engagements, including the Battles of Ypres, Festubert, Loos, the Somme, Arras, Messines and Cambrai, and later was in action during the Retreat and Advance of 1918. He was sent to Germany after the Armistice and did duty with the Army of Occupation until his return to England for demobilisation in January 1919. He holds the 1914–15 Star, and the General Service and Victory Medals.
1, Derby Street, Ardwick, Manchester.   Z1246

BIRCH, C. J., Private, Manchester Regiment.
He volunteered in August 1914, and after a period of duty at various home stations, was sent to India in February 1916. He was then stationed at Allahabad, and was engaged on important guard and outpost work. In June 1918 he was transferred to Russia, where he rendered valuable services with his unit until his demobilisation in May 1919. He holds the General Service and Victory Medals.
99, Ryder Street, Collyhurst, Manchester.   Z10294

BIRCH, F., Private, 22nd Manchester Regiment.
He volunteered in November 1914, and was retained at home on important duties until November 1915, when he proceeded to the Western Front. In this theatre of war, he was in action at Albert and Vimy Ridge, and did good work until he was unhappily killed in action on July 1st, 1916, the first day of the Battle of the Somme. He was entitled to the 1914–15 Star, and the General Service and Victory Medals.
          "Nobly striving,
          He nobly fell that we might live."
18, Juniper Street, Hulme, Manchester.   Z8902

BIRCH, J., Corporal, R.A.S.C. (M.T.)

He joined in February 1916, and after a period of service in England was sent to France early in 1917. Whilst on the Western Front he played an active part in the Battles of Arras, Vimy Ridge, Passchendaele, Cambrai, Havrincourt and Le Cateau. He returned to England for demobilisation in February 1920, and holds the General Service and Victory Medals.

13, Industrial Street, Stockport Road, Chorlton-on-Medlock, Manchester. Z1250

BIRCH, W., Private, Middlesex Regiment.

He volunteered in March 1915, but owing to his being physically unfit for service overseas, was retained on important garrison duties on the East Coast. He nevertheless rendered valuable services until his demobilisation in November 1919.

58, Dudley Street, Stretford, Manchester. Z1252

BIRCH, W. H., Air Mechanic, R.A.F.

He joined in January 1917, and on completion of his train ng was engaged on special duties of an important nature with a Kite Balloon Section. He was unsuccessful in obtaining his transfer overseas, but rendered valuable services at various stations until his demobilisation in March, 1919.

15, Tunstall Street, Longsight, Manchester. Z1251

BIRCHALL, P., Private, 8th Lancashire Fusiliers.

He was mobilised in August 1914, and in the following March was drafted to Gallipoli. There he participated in heavy fighting at Krithia and was severely wounded at Suvla Bay in August 1915. Evacuated to England, he was admitted to hospital in London, and after being detained there for a long period was eventually invalided out of the Service in August 1918, holding the 1914-15 Star, and the General Service and Victory Medals.

214, Victoria Square, Oldham Road, Manchester. Z8903

BIRCHENOUGH, F., Private, Labour Corps.

Joining in March 1917, he proceeded to France one week later, and was engaged on the important duty of taking ammunition to forward areas. He rendered valuable services at the Battles of Messines, Ypres, and Hill 60, and was wounded. He was then invalided home and eventually discharged in May 1918, as unfit for further service, and holds the General Service and Victory Medals.

11, Coalbrook Street, Ardwick, Manchester. Z1253

BIRD, C. H., Sergeant, 12th Lancashire Fusiliers.

He volunteered in September 1914, and in the follwoing year embarked for France. Whilst there he took part in the Battles of Hill 60, Ypres, Festubert, the Somme, Arras, Bullecourt, Messines, Lens and Cambrai. He also did good work in Salonika and Italy, returning home for demobilisation in February 1919. He holds the 1914-15 Star, and the General Service and Victory Medals.

29, Grimshaw Lane, Newton Heath, Manchester. Z9877

BIRD, F. W., Private, 1/8th Manchester Regiment.

He volunteered in August 1914, and early in the following year was drafted to the Dardanelles, where he was engaged in much heavy fighting on the Gallipoli Peninsula and was in action at the Battles of Krithia (I, II, and III), the Landing at Suvla Bay and the capture of Chunuk-Bair. He contracted dysentery, and after being invalided to hospital at Alexandria, returned to England, and was discharged in March 1917, as physically unfit for further service. He holds the 1914-15 Star, and the General Service and Victory Medals.

33, Riga Street, City Road, Hulme, Manchester. Z1255

BIRD, H., Private, M.G.C.

He joined in April 1918, and after a brief period of training, was drafted to Palestine, where he played a prominent part in the heavy fighting during the Advance of General Allenby's Forces. He was present at the capture of Tripoli and Aleppo, and was in hospital with malaria for a time at Jaffa. Demobilised in February 1920, he holds the General Service and Victory Medals.

18, Bickley Street, Moss Side, Manchester. Z1254

BIRD, J., Private, 1/5th King's Liverpool Regiment.

He joined in January 1917, and underwent a short period of training prior to his being drafted to France. Whilst in this theatre of war he took part in several engagements, including those at Ypres (III), Passchendaele, Cambrai and in the Retreat and Advance of 1918. He was discharged in December 1918 as medically unfit for further duty, and holds the General Service and Victory Medals.

424, Mills Street, Bradford, Manchester. Z1321

BIRD, J., Private, Border Regiment.

He volunteered in August 1914, and in December of the same year was sent to France, where he took part in many important engagements. He was in action at St. Eloi, Hill 60, Loos, Vimy Ridge, Arras, Bullecourt, Lens and Cambrai, and during his service was wounded three times. He was invalided home, and in July 1918 was discharged as unfit for further service. He holds the 1914-15 Star, and the General Service and Victory Medals.

9, Cymbal Street, Ancoats, Manchester. Z9879

BIRD, P., Private, Royal Irish Fusiliers.

Volunteering in February 1915 he was sent to the Western Front in the following May. He was in action during many engagements, including those at Festubert, Albert, the Somme, Arras, Messines, Cambrai, and was taken prisoner in the Retreat in March 1918. Released after the Armistice, he was subsequently demobilised in March 1919, and holds the 1914-15 Star, and the General Service and Victory Medals.

61, Kemp Street, Ancoats, Manchester. TZ9434

BIRDS, H., Private, Lancashire Fusiliers.

Volunteering in November 1915, he proceeded to France in August of the following year. Whilst in this theatre of war he fought in many notable engagements, including those at Ypres and Cambrai and in the Retreat and subsequent Allied Advance of 1918. He holds the General Service and Victory Medals, and in September 1919 was demobilised.

121, Jersey Street Dwellings, Ancoats, Manchester. Z9878

BIRTLES, H., Gunner, R.M.A.

Mobilised at the outbreak of war, in August 1914, he was immediately drafted to France, and took part in the Battle of Mons and the subsequent Retreat. He was later in action at Ypres and served for a short period on anti-aircraft duties. During the course of hostilities he also saw service at sea, and was present at many engagements, but shortly after his discharge in May 1918, died through the effects of gas poisoning sustained in France. He was entitled to the Mons Star, and the General Service and Victory Medals.

" His memory is cherished with pride."

19, Greenhill Street, Chorlton-on-Medlock, Manchester. Z1256

BLACK, G. S., Pte., 12th Bn. Lancashire Fusiliers.

Volunteering in September 1914, he proceeded in March of the following year to France, and there saw much fighting in the Ypres sector. In 1916 he was drafted to Salonika, where he did much valuable service. While in the East he contracted malaria, in consequence of which he was invalided to Jersey. He was eventually demobilised in March 1919, and holds the 1914-15 Star, and the General Service and Victory Medals.

2, Louisa Street, West Gorton, Manchester. Z9880B

BLACK, J., Private, Lancashire Fusiliers.

Volunteering in February 1915, he was sent to France in the following November and was first in action during the heavy fighting at St. Eloi. Later he took part in the Battles of the Somme, Arras, Vimy Ridge, Bullecourt, Ypres (III), Cambrai, Havrincourt and Le Cateau. He was wounded in action during the Somme Offensive in July 1916, and was eventually demobilised in February 1919, holding the 1914-15 Star, and the General Service and Victory Medals.

5, Devonport Street, Rochdale Road, Manchester. Z1029S

BLACK, M. (Mrs.), Special War Worker.

From April 1916 until December 1918 this lady held an important position at Messrs. Brooks and Doxey's Works, Manchester. She was engaged as a fuse tester and carried out her responsible duties in a highly efficient manner.

2, Louisa Street, West Gorton, Manchester. Z9880A

BLACKBAND, J. H., Corpl., 2nd E. Lancashire Regt.

Joining in September 1916, he proceeded overseas in the following year. During his service on the Western Front he saw much heavy fighting at Bullecourt, Ypres (III), Passchendaele, Cambrai and in the Retreat and Advance of 1918. He was demobilised in December 1919, and holds the General Service and Victory Medals.

26, Milton Street, West Gorton, Manchester. Z1322

BLACKLEY, J., Corporal, R.A.M.C.

Volunteering in September 1914, he proceeded in July of the following year to the Western Front. In this theatre of war he served with the 51st Field Ambulance attached to the 17th Division, at Albert, Ploegsteert, Beaumont-Hamel, Arras, Bullecourt, Ypres and Cambrai, and rendered valuable service until he returned home in February 1919, and was demobilised, holding the 1914-15 Star, and the General Service and Victory Medals.

46, Harrison Street, Ancoats, Manchester. Z8904

BLACKSHAW, J. W., Private, Manchester Regiment.

Having previously served in the South African campaign, he rejoined in November 1914, although he had had his right leg amputated as the result of being wounded in action at Ladysmith. He was first engaged on the instruction of recruits, but later rendered valuable services as a batman until invalided from the Army in September 1915. He holds the Queen's South African Medal.

4, Fleeson Street, Rusholme, Manchester. Z1257

BLACKWELL, J. E., Driver, R.F.A.

Volunteering in September 1915, he was drafted to the Western Front on completion of his training and took part in the Battles of the Somme, Arras, Bullecourt, Ypres (III), He was badly wounded in action in November 1917, and was invalided home, but on his recovery did consistently good work until his demobilisation in January 1919, holding the General Service and Victory Medals.

29, Dicken's Street, Queen's Road, Manchester. Z10296

BLAGBROUGH, W. J., Pte., 11th Manchester Regt.
Volunteering in September 1914, he underwent a period of training and was drafted to the Dardanelles in September of the following year. There he took part in important engagements until the Evacuation of the Peninsula and was sent home suffering from dysentery. In May 1917 he was drafted to France and was in action at Cambrai, the Somme (II) and Havrincourt Wood and was gassed. He was eventually discharged in June 1919 as unfit for further service, and holds the 1914–15 Star, and the General Service and Victory Medals.
49, Melbourne Street, Hulme, Manchester. Z1258

BLAGG, A., Private, 23rd Manchester Regiment.
He volunteered in November 1914, and after a period of training and service in England, was drafted to the Western Front in January 1916. There he took part in many important engagements and was gassed. After recovery he was transferred to the Royal Army Ordnance Corps and did consistently good work until his demobilisation in July 1919. He holds the General Service and Victory Medals.
14, Stone Place, Rusholme, Manchester. Z1259A

BLAGG, J. W., Private, 23rd Manchester Regiment.
He volunteered in November 1914 and proceeded to France after a period of training. There he was in action at many important engagements, and during a raid by the enemy, was killed by shell-fire at Neuve Chapelle in May 1916. He was entitled to the 1914–15 Star, and the General Service and Victory Medals.
"His life for his Country, his soul to God."
14, Stone Place, Rusholme, Manchester. Z1259B

BLAIN, F., L/Corporal, R.E.
He joined in September 1918, and was retained on special duties in connection with motor transport and locomotive driving. He did consistently good work, but was unable to obtain his transfer to a theatre of war before the cessation of hostilities, and was demobilised in September 1919.
17, Bonsall Street, Hulme, Manchester. Z1260

BLAIR, F. H., Private, King's (Liverpool Regt.)
Joining in September 1917, he was drafted in the following month to the Western Front. There he took part in many important engagements in the last stages of the war, including those at Cambrai, the Somme, Bapaume, the Scarpe and Le Cateau. Demobilised in June 1919, he holds the General Service and Victory Medals.
15, Ellen Street, West Gorton, Manchester. Z9881

BLAIR, S., Rifleman, Rifle Brigade.
He volunteered in August 1914, but after a period of training was sent to munition work at Messrs. Hansronalds Ltd., Burnage. Owing to his being a skilled mechanic he was retained on this work throughout hostilities and rendered valuable services. He was demobilised in November 1918.
16, Chatsworth Street, Hulme, Manchester. Z11644

BLAIR, W., Private, 4th Manchester Regiment.
Volunteering in November 1914, he was retained on important duties in England until January 1916, when he obtained a transfer overseas. During his service on the Western Front he experienced fierce fighting in many sectors, and was unhappily killed in action at the Battle of the Somme on July 1st, 1916. He was entitled to the General Service and Victory Medals.
"A costly sacrifice upon the altar of freedom."
12, Fleetwood Street, Ancoats, Manchester. Z11609

BLAIR, W., Private, South Lancashire Regiment.
Joining in August 1917, he was retained on important duties in England and Ireland until September of the following year. He was then drafted to the Western Front and took part in the Battles of Havrincourt and Cambrai (II) before being unhappily killed in action at Le Cateau on October 8th, 1918. He was entitled to the General Service and Victory Medals. "Great deeds cannot die."
3, Hinckley Street, Bradford, Manchester. Z1261

BLAKE, J. R., Pte., K.O. (Royal Lancaster Regt.)
Volunteering in December 1914 he was drafted to France in February of the following year and took part in many important engagements. He was in action at the Battles of St. Eloi, Loos, Vermelles and the Somme, and was wounded at Lens in August 1917. He was invalided home and on his recovery proceeded to the East, where he saw service in Egypt and Palestine, taking part in the Offensive under General Allenby, during which he was in action at Jericho, Tripoli and Aleppo. He holds the 1914–15 Star, and the General Service and Victory Medals, and was demobilised in November 1919.
59, Lyme Street, Chorlton-on-Medlock, Manchester. Z1262

BLAKE, J. W., Private, 4th Manchester Regiment.
He volunteered in August 1914, and was retained in England on duties of an important nature until March 1916. He was then drafted to the East and saw much service in Egypt and Palestine, at Kantara and Gaza. After returning home he was demobilised in May 1919, and holds the General Service and Victory Medals.
10, School Street, West Gorton, Manchester. Z9882

BLAKE, T. H., Driver, R.A.S.C.
He joined in July 1916, and was engaged on important transport duties with his unit at Aldershot for two years. He was then sent to the Western Front and took an active part in the Battle of the Sambre during the Advance of 1918. After the cessation of hostilities he proceeded to Germany with the Army of Occupation and served there until his demobilisation in November 1919, holding the General Service and Victory Medals.
16, Eskrigge Street, Ardwick, Manchester. Z11874

BLAKELEY, A. (M.S.M.), Pte., King's Own (Royal Lancaster Regt.)
Mobilised at the outbreak of war in August 1914, he was shortly afterwards drafted to France and took part in the Battles of the Marne, the Aisne, La Bassée, Ypres, Neuve Chapelle, Hill 60, Loos, Vimy Ridge, the Somme and Arras. He suffered from gas poisoning at the third Battle of Ypres, and was sent home, but on his recovery returned to his unit and was in action until the cessation of hostilities. He was awarded the Meritorious Service Medal for devotion to duty in the Field, and also holds the 1914 Star, and the General Service and Victory Medals. He was discharged in February 1919.
6, Hyde View, Grey Street, West Gorton, Manchester. Z1263

BLAKELEY, B., Private, Manchester Regiment.
Volunteering in August 1914, he was sent to France four months later and was wounded in action at the Battle of Neuve Chapelle in March 1915. On his recovery he proceeded to the Dardanelles and took part in much severe fighting there until the Evacuation of the Gallipoli Peninsula in January 1916. He was then again sent to France, where he took part in the Battles of the Somme, Arras, Ypres and Cambrai and in the Retreat and Advance of 1918. Demobilised in December 1919, he holds the 1914–15 Star, and the General Service and Victory Medals.
65, Fitzgeorge Street, Collyhurst, Manchester. Z10297

BLAKELEY, W., Trooper, Duke of Lancaster's Own Dragoons.
He volunteered in December 1914, and on completion of his training, first served with the Military Police in Scotland. Later he was transferred to the Northumberland Fusiliers and sent to Ireland, where he did consistently good work on garrison duty at Belfast and Tralee. He was unsuccessful in obtaining his transfer to a theatre of war, and was demobilised in February 1919.
14, New Lorne Street, Moss Side, Manchester. Z1264

BLAKEWAY, F., Cpl., 11th Durham Light Infantry.
He volunteered in September 1914, and was drafted to France in July of the following year. In this theatre of war he took part in many important engagements, including the Battles of Loos, Albert, the Somme, Beaumont-Hamel, Arras, Ypres, and Cambrai, and was wounded on two occasions. He was also in action during the Retreat and Advance of 1918, and died of bronchial pneumonia on February 23rd, 1919. He was entitled to the 1914–15 Star, and the General Service and Victory Medals.
"His memory is cherished with pride."
27, Bangor Street, Hulme, Manchester. TZ1265-66B

BLAKEWAY, J. A., Pte., 7th Manchester Regiment.
He joined in March 1916, and four months later proceeded to the Western Front, where he took part in the Somme Offensive. He was unfortunately killed in action in November 1916 at Beaumont-Hamel, four months after his landing in France, and was entitled to the General Service and Victory Medals.
"And doubtless he went in splendid company."
27, Bangor Street, Hulme, Manchester. TZ1265-66C

BLAKEWAY, R., Special War Worker.
In 1914 he offered his services at Messrs. Storey's, Manchester, and was engaged on important duties in connection with the manufacture of heavy shells for two years. He then went to Messrs. Levensteins, where he assisted in the production of asphyxiating gasses and did consistently good work until hostilities ceased. Unfortunately he developed stomach poisoning as a result of his work, and this, along with mental worry and strain, caused his death in April 1919.
"Steals on the ear the distant triumph song."
27, Bangor Street, Hulme, Manchester. TZ1265-66E

BLAKEWAY, S., Pte., 13th King's (Liverpool Regt.)
Volunteering in September 1914, he completed a period of training and was sent to France in October of the following year. He was soon in action in this theatre of war, and after only three weeks' service made the supreme sacrifice in the same month, being killed during heavy fighting in the Loos sector. He was entitled to the 1914–15 Star, and the General Service and Victory Medals.
"Whilst we remember, the sacrifice is not in vain."
27, Bangor Street, Hulme, Manchester. TZ1265-66D

BLAKEWAY, W. H., Private, Labour Corps.

He joined in March 1917, and was immediately drafted to France, where he was present at many engagements of importance, including those at Ypres and Cambrai. He did consistently good work during the Retreat and Advance of 1918, and was gassed at Ploegsteert Wood in September of that year. He was entitled to the General Service and Victory Medals. and was discharged in October 1918 as medically unfit, but unhappily died from the effects of gas-poisoning in January 1920.
" A valiant soldier, with undaunted heart, he breasted life's last hill."
27, Bangor Street, Hulme, Manchester.   TZ1265-66A

BLANCHARD, G., Pte., 21st Manchester Regt.

He joined in November 1916, and in February of the following year was drafted to France, where he took part in much heavy fighting in various sectors. He was badly gassed at Vimy Ridge in April 1917, and after being invalided home to England was discharged in January 1918 as physically unfit for further service. He holds the General Service and Victory Medals.
66, Ridgway Street, Moss Side, Manchester.   Z1268

BLANCHARD, S. A., Driver, R.E.

He joined in March 1918, and later proceeded to the Western Front, where he was engaged on important duties in various sectors. He was present at the Battles of Ypres, the Somme and Cambrai, and during the Retreat and Advance of 1918, rendered valuable services. After the cessation of hostilities he was sent to Germany, where he did duty with the Army of Occupation at Cologne. He holds the General Service and Victory Medals, and was demobilised in March 1920.
162, Hartington Street, Moss Side, Manchester.   TZ1267

BLANEY, H., Private, 19th Manchester Regiment.

He volunteered in September 1914, and did consistently good work in England during the first part of his service. In 1916 he proceeded to France, where he was in action at the Battles of the Somme, Arras and Passchendaele, and was wounded. He returned to England and was discharged in October 1918 as medically unfit, and holds the General Service and Victory Medals.
15, Kenmare Street, Chorlton-on-Medlock, Manchester.   X1269-70B

BLANTERN, W. H., Driver, R.E.

He volunteered in May 1915, and in April of the following year was sent to Egypt, where he was in action at Katia, El Fasher and Romani. In March 1917 he was transferred to the Western Front and saw heavy fighting at Zillebeke, Zonnebeke, Monchy and Dickebusch. He also took part in the Battles of Arras, Ypres (III) and Cambrai (I and II), and was gassed near Bailleul in September 1918. Demobilised in January 1919, he holds the General Service and Victory Medals. 35, Orchard Street, Greenheys, Manchester. Z1271

BLATCHFORD, J. A., Bombardier, R.F.A.

Mobilised in August 1914, he crossed in the same month to France and served in many sectors of the Front on the lines of communication, especially at the Marne and the Aisne, La Bassée, Ypres, Loos, the Somme, Arras, Cambrai and the chief operations of 1918 until hostilities ceased. He was demobilised in September 1919, and holds the 1914–15 Star, and the General Service and Victory Medals.
30, Kendell Street, Bradford, Manchester.   Z9883

BLATHERWICK, G., Sapper, R.E.

He volunteered in November 1915, and after a period of training was drafted to Egypt in June 1916, and saw heavy fighting on the Suez Canal and at Romani and Magdhaba. In March 1917 he was transferred to the Western Front, where he took part in many important engagements, including the Battles of Arras, Messines, Ypres, Cambrai, the Somme and Bapaume. He was sent to hospital suffering from eczema, and was ultimately demobilised in December 1918, holding the General Service and Victory Medals.
9, Haughton Street, Bradford, Manchester.   Z1272A

BLATHERWICK, G. E., Sapper, R.E.

Volunteering in November 1915, he was drafted to Egypt in the following January and took part in many engagements, including those at Gaza, Sollum, Katia and El Fasher. In April 1917 he was transferred to the Western Front, where he did consistently good work at the Battles of Ypres and Cambrai and later in the Retreat and Advance of 1918. He holds the General Service and Victory Medals, and was demobilised in January 1919.
49, Redvers Street, Ardwick, Manchester.   Z1273

BLEASDALE, F. C., Private, King's Shropshire Light Infantry.

He volunteered in May 1915, and served for some time in Ireland, engaged on various duties of an important nature. Later proceeding to France, he was in action on the Somme front and at Passchendaele and Ypres, and was wounded at Cambrai in September 1918. After the Armistice he was sent to Germany and served with the Army of Occupation until February 1919. He was then demobilised, holding the General Service and Victory Medals.
56, Chadwick Street, West Gorton, Manchester.   Z8905

BLEASDALE, J., Private, 1st Border Regiment.

He volunteered in November 1914, and on completing his training in the following May, was drafted to the Dardanelles. There he took part in severe fighting at Krithia (III) and in the Landing at Suvla Bay. He was unfortunately killed in action at Chunuk Bair on August 21st, 1915, and was entitled to the 1914-15 Star, and the General Service and Victory Medals.   " He died the noblest death a man may die, Fighting for God and right and liberty."
56, Russell Street, Moss Side, Manchester.   Z11645

BLICK, R., Corporal, R.A.P.C.

He joined in July 1917, and first rendered valuable services on the clerical staff of the Pay Corps at Preston, Blackheath and Purfleet. He was unsuccessful in obtaining his transfer overseas during hostilities, but in May 1919, was sent to France and did consistently good work in a Chinese Savings Bank at Noyelles until his demobilisation in the following August.
127, Hartington Street, Moss Side, Manchester.   TZ1274

BLOCKLEY, W., Driver, R.A.S.C.

He joined in October 1916, and two months later was drafted to the Western Front, where he was engaged on important transport duties in many sectors. He was present at the Battles of Arras, Vimy Ridge, Bullecourt, Ypres and Cambrai, and rendered valuable services during the Retreat and Advance of 1918. He holds the General Service and Victory Medals, and was demobilised in February 1919.   Z1275
19, Blossom Avenue, Chorlton-on-Medlock, Manchester.

BLOOR, E., Private, Lancashire Fusiliers.

Volunteering in August 1915, he proceeded to the Western Front in January of the following year and took part in engagements at Loos, St. Eloi, Albert, Vimy Ridge and on the Somme, and suffered from shell-shock. He was discharged in November 1916, but rejoined in January 1917, and saw further active service at Arras and Ypres. He again suffered from shell-shock and was finally discharged in January 1919, holding the General Service and Victory Medals.
11, Gay Street, Jackson Street, Hulme, Manchester.   TZ1276

BLOW, R., Private, 22nd Manchester Regiment.

He volunteered in November 1914, and after undergoing a period of training, was drafted to India in February 1916. There he was engaged on important garrison and other duties until January 1918, when he was transferred to Palestine and saw much severe fighting during the Advance on Aleppo under General Allenby. He returned to England, and was demobilised in May 1919, holding the General Service and Victory Medals. 19, Dawson Street, West Gorton, Manchester. Z1277

BLUNT, W., Private, 11th Manchester Regiment.

He enlisted in May 1914, and eight months after the outbreak of war in the following August, was sent to France, where he took part in the Battles of Neuve Chapelle and Loos before being wounded during the Somme Offensive in July 1916. He was invalided to hospital in Liverpool, and on his recovery in the following November returned to the Western Front, and was in action at the Battles of Arras, Ypres, Passchendaele, La Bassée and Albert, and in the Retreat and Advance of 1918. He holds the 1914-15 Star, and the General Service and Victory Medals, and was discharged in November 1918.
93, Harold Street, Bradford, Manchester.   Z1278

BLYTON, J., Private, Labour Corps.

He joined in June 1917, and was retained on important duties in various parts of England in connection with horse transport and agriculture. He was unable to obtain his transfer overseas, but, nevertheless, rendered valuable services and was demobilised in May 1919.
4, Blossom Avenue, Chorlton-on-Medlock, Manchester.   Z1279

BOAM, S., Private, South Lancashire Regiment.

He volunteered in April 1915, and in December of the same year embarked for France. He took part in the Battles of the Somme and Ypres, and gave his life for King and Country during the fighting at Messines Ridge on June 10th, 1917. He was entitled to the 1914–15 Star, and the General Service and Victory Medals.
5, Herbert Street, Bradford, Manchester.   TZ9435

BOARDMAN, G. L., Private, 1/8th Manchester Regt.

He volunteered in August 1914, and in May of the following year was sent to the Gallipoli Peninsula. After taking part in much severe fighting, he was badly wounded in action at the third Battle of Krithia in August 1914, and was invalided home. On his recovery he was transferred to Class W, Army Reserve, and rendered valuable services as a cleaner at the Hyde Road Depôt Car Sheds in Manchester. He holds the 1914–15 Star, and the General Service and Victory Medals.
21, Teak Street, Beswick, Manchester.   Z1281

BOARDMAN, J., Private, 8th Manchester Regiment.

He joined in May 1916, and two months later was drafted to France, where he took part in many important engagements. He was in action at the Battles of Arras, Messines, Lens and Cambrai and made the supreme sacrifice in April 1918, when he was killed in action on the Somme. He was entitled to the General Service and Victory Medals.
" His life for his Country, his soul to God."
13, Beswick Street, Ardwick, Manchester.   Z1280

BOARDMAN, J., Sapper, R.E.
He joined in May 1916, and six months later proceeded overseas. During his service on the Western Front he performed excellent work in the construction of pontoons and trenches, and was engaged in severe fighting in the Somme, Arras, Messines, Vimy Ridge, Passchendaele and Cambrai sectors, and in the Retreat and Advance of 1918. He was wounded in action in 1917, and after the Armistice proceeded into Germany with the Army of Occupation. Demobilised in September 1919, he holds the General Service and Victory Medals.
24, Lancashire Street, Newton Heath, Manchester.　　Z9884

BOARDMAN, J. H., Private, 8th E. Lancashire Regt.
Volunteering in October 1914, he was sent to the Western Front in July 1915, and during his service in France was in action on the Somme and at Arras, and was wounded at both engagements. On his discharge from hospital he was sent back to the firing line and was killed at Rheims during a German attack on that town. He was entitled to the 1914–15 Star, and the General Service and Victory Medals.
"A costly sacrifice upon the altar of freedom."
13, Howarth Street, Bradford, Manchester.　　Z9885

BODEN, C. H., Private, 13th Manchester Regiment.
Joining in March 1916, he was sent to Salonika on completion of his training in the following September. Whilst in the Balkan theatre of war, he saw much severe fighting on the Doiran front, and in Bulgaria. After hostilities ceased, he served with the Army of Occupation in Turkey until October 1919, when he came home for demobilisation. He holds the General Service and Victory Medals.
24, Overton Street, Hulme, Manchester.　　Z1282

BODEN, T., Private, R.A.O.C.
He joined in January 1917, and two months later was sent to France, where he was engaged on important mechanical duties in a traavelling workshop. He was present at engagements at Armentières, the Somme, La Bassée, Festubert, Givenchy, and Lille, and after the Armistice proceeded to Germany, where he did duty with the Army of Occupation. He holds the General Service and Victory Medals, and was demobilised in November 1919.
3, Lord Street, Openshaw, Manchester.　　TZ1283

BODGERS, H. T., Private, South Wales Borderers.
He joined in October 1916, and in December was drafted to France. There he took part in many important engagements, including those at Arras, Vimy Ridge, and Messines, and was gassed and wounded. In August 1917 he was transferred to Mesopotamia, but owing to ill-health, took no part in actual fighting in this theatre of war. He was eventually discharged in September 1918, and holds the General Service and Victory Medals.
81, Grey Street, West Gorton, Manchester.　　Z1284

BODY, W., Pte., Lancashire Fusiliers and Labour Corps.
He joined in March 1917, and five months later was sent to France. There he took part in heavy fighting at Ypres, and shortly afterwards was invalided home on account of ill-health. Upon his recovery, he was transferred to the Labour Corps, and returning to France did good work whilst employed on railways, until November 1919. Demobilised on returning home, he holds the General Service and Victory Medals.
17, Sidney Street, Bradford, Manchester.　　TZ8906

BOFF, C., Private, East Lancashire Regiment.
He volunteered in August 1914, and five months later proceeded to the Western Front, and there saw heavy fighting in important engagements, including those at Neuve Chapelle and St. Eloi. He was wounded in action at Ypres in April 1915, and invalided to England, was subsequently discharged as unfit for further service in January 1916. He holds the 1914–15 Star, General Service and Victory Medals.
2, Times Street, Newton Heath, Manchester.　　Z9886

BOGEN, J., Bombardier, R.F.A.
Volunteering in August 1914, he was drafted to Egypt in the following February, but two months later, proceeded to the Dardanelles, and took part in the Landing at Cape Helles. He was also in action at the Battle of Krithia, and in other severe fighting until the Evacuation of the Gallipoli Peninsula in January 1916. Returning then to Egypt, he served there for some time, but eventually proceeded to Palestine, where he played an important part in the Battles of Gaza (I, II, and III), the Capture of Jerusalem and Tripoli, and in the Advance under General Allenby. He was discharged owing to ill-health in May 1919, and holds the 1914–15 Star, and the General Service and Victory Medals.
11, Shepley Street, Harpurhey, Manchester.　　Z10298

BOGG, F., A.B., Royal Navy.
He joined in April 1918, and immediately proceeded to the North Sea, where he was engaged on the important duty of mine-sweeping off the Coast of Scotland. He did consistently good work until the cessation of hostilities, and returning to port, was demobilised in March 1919, holding the General Service and Victory Medals.
19, Leigh Place, Stockport Road, Manchester.　　TZ1285B

BOGG, W., H., Gunner, R.F.A.
He volunteered in April 1915, and after undergoing a period of training was drafted to France in November 1916. There he took part in many important engagements, and was in action at the Battles of Beaumont-Hamel, Arras, Vimy Ridge, Ypres, and Cambrai, but was unfortunately killed on the Somme front on August 27th, 1918, during the Advance of that year. He was entitled to the General Service and Victory Medals.
"Great deeds cannot die."
19, Leigh Place, Stockport Road, Manchester.　　TZ1285A

BOLAS, C., Private, King's (Liverpool Regiment).
He joined in October 1916, and in January of the following year proceeded to France, where he was in action at Albert, Loos, and Ypres. In November 1917 he was transferred to the Royal Army Medical Corps, and served at the 4th and 26th General hospitals on the Western Front. He did consistently good work at Cambrai, and during the Retreat and Advance of 1918, and was demobilised in October 1919, holding the General Service and Victory Medals.
33, Avon Street, Chorlton-on-Medlock, Manchester.　　Z1286A

BOLAS, G., Private, 8th Manchester Regiment.
Mobilised with the Territorials in August 1914, he was drafted to Egypt in the following month, where he saw service with the 42nd Division. He was stationed at Alexandria and Cairo, and later took part in the fighting on the Suez Canal. He was wounded in action and invalided home, and was discharged in December 1916, as physically unfit for further service. He holds the 1914–15 Star, and the General Service and Victory Medals.
33, Avon Street, Chorlton-on-Medlock, Manchester.　　Z1286C

BOLD, A. P., Pte., Leicestershire (Prince Albert's Own) Hussars.
He volunteered in January 1916, and at the end of the year was drafted to France (after being wounded in the riots in Dublin in 1916). He saw much active service on the Western Front, and was present at the Battles of Arras and Ypres, and was again wounded. He returned to France in December 1917, and fought at the second Battle of the Somme, and was gassed. He was again invalided to England, and was eventually demobilised in January 1919, holding the General Service and Victory Medals.
2, Hazel Grove, Longsight, Manchester.　　TZ1287

BOLLARD, J., Corporal, R.A.V.C.
He volunteered in December 1914, and in January of the following year embarked for France. He was present during the Battles of Neuve Chapelle, Hill 60, Festubert, Beaumont-Hamel, Bullecourt, Ypres, and was later sent to Calais, where he was unfortunately killed by a kick from a horse on May 13th, 1918. He was entitled to the 1914–15 Star, and the General Service and Victory Medals.
"He passed out of the sight of men by the path of duty and self-sacrifice."
16, Leigh Street East, Ancoats, Manchester.　　Z9436

BOLSOVER, C., Pte., 7th Manchester Regt. and King's (Liverpool Regt.)
He volunteered in December 1915, and proceeded to France in February 1917, after being engaged on important duties in England. He saw much severe fighting on the Western Front, and was in action at the Battles of Ypres, Armentières, Albert, and Messines, and was then transferred to Italy, where he fought on the Piave. He was invalided home through ill-health, and was eventually discharged in April 1918, as medically unfit. He holds the General Service and Victory Medals.
45, Allen Street, Hulme, Manchester.　　Z1288

BOLTON, C. R., Sapper, R.E.
Volunteering in August 1914, he was drafted in the following May to the Western Front. In this theatre of war, he served with his Company at Ypres, Festubert, Ploegsteert Wood, the Somme, and also at Beaucourt, Arras, and Cambrai, employed on various duties of an important nature. He remained overseas, and rendered excellent services until May 1919, when he was demobilised, holding the 1914–15 Star, and the General Service and Victory Medals.
13, Hardy Street, West Gorton, Manchester.　　Z8907

BOLTON, T. (D.C.M.), C.S.M., 5th Royal Irish Fusiliers.
Volunteering in September 1914, he was sent to Gallipoli in the following August and played a prominent part in the Landing at Suvla Bay, and in the Capture of Chunuk Bair. After the Evacuation of the Peninsula, he was sent to Egypt, where he was in action at Katia, El Fasher, Romani, and Magdhaba before proceeding to Palestine. Whilst with General Allenby's Forces he took part in the three Battles of Gaza and other important engagements. In May 1918 he was transferred to the Western Front, and fought in the Battles of the Marne (II), the Aisne (III), Bapaume, Havrincourt, Cambrai (II), and Le Cateau (II). He was awarded the Distinguished Conduct Medal for conspicuous gallantry at Katia in 1916, and was several times mentioned in Despatches. He also holds the 1914–15 Star, and the General Service and Victory Medals, and was demobilised in February 1919.
26, St. Clement's Place, Grey Street, West Gorton, Manchester.　　Z1290

BOLTON, F. J., Private, 2/4th Royal Scots.
He volunteered in January 1915, and after a period of training was sent to Ireland, where he was engaged on important duties as a farrier. He was unable to obtain a transfer to a theatre of war owing to his being medically unfit, but rendered valuable services until his discharge in March 1918.
4, Oak Street, Hulme, Manchester. TZ11646

BOLTON, H., Private, Royal Defence Corps.
He volunteered in December 1914, and was engaged on important guard duties at various stations in England. He rendered valuable services throughout the period of the war, and was eventually demobilised in March 1919.
36, Bell Street, Openshaw, Manchester. Z1289

BOND, A. (Mrs.), Special War Worker.
This lady volunteered her services in February 1915, and was engaged on work of National importance at the Westinghouse Company, Didsbury, Manchester. She did consistently good work in connection with the making of base plates for shells, and relinquished her duties in November 1919.
38, Dalton Street, Hulme, Manchester. Z1291B

BOND, A., Private, 7th Seaforth Highlanders.
Volunteering in January 1915, he was sent to France in July 1916. He served on the Western Front for over two years, and during that time took an active part in fierce fighting in various sectors, and was wounded on three occasions, at Arras, Kemmel, and Ypres. He was invalided to England in October 1918, and was in hospital until the following July, when he was demobilised, holding the General Service and Victory Medals.
28, Clayton Street, Bradford Road, Manchester. Z9887

BOND, E., Private, Border Regiment.
He joined in March 1916, and two months later was drafted to France. In this theatre of war he took part in many engagements, including the Battles of Vimy Ridge, the Somme, Arras, Bullecourt, Ypres, Lens, Cambrai, Bapaume, the Aisne (III), the Marne (II), and Le Cateau (II), and was gassed in action in October 1917. He was demobilised in October 1920, and holds the General Service and Victory Medals.
3, Irlam Street, Miles Platting, Manchester. TZ11647

BOND, F., Rifleman, 8th Rifle Brigade.
He volunteered in 1915, and in the same year was drafted to France where he took part in the fierce fighting round Ypres, Hill 60, Neuve Chapelle, and Loos. In the following year he was in action in the Somme Offensive, and was twice wounded, but on his recovery resumed his place in the line, and fought gallantly at Mericourt, Avion, and Lens. He was discharged in 1917 in consequence of his service and holds the 1914-15 Star, and the General Service and Victory Medals.
14, Elizabeth Ann Street, Manchester. Z9437

BOND, F. (M.M.) L/Corpl., 2nd Royal Fusiliers.
When war broke out he was already serving and was at once ordered to the Western Front. There he fought in the Battles of Mons, Le Cateau, the Marne, La Bassée, Ypres, Festubert, Vermelles, Arras, Bullecourt, Lens, and Cambrai, and was wounded in action in 1915, and again in November 1916, during the Somme engagement. He was awarded the Military Medal for great bravery in carrying Despatches through a heavy bombardment on the Somme, and also holds the Mons Star, and the General Service and Victory Medals. He was discharged in August 1917, through wounds.
10, Brougham Place, West Gorton, Manchester. Z9888

BOND, H., Private, 1/6th Welch Regiment.
He joined in January 1918, and in the following August proceeded to the Western Front, where he took part in heavy fighting at La Bassée. He was invalided to Boulogne shortly afterwards suffering from trench feet, but on his recovery went into Germany with the Army of Occupation, and served there until his demobilisation in December 1919. He holds the General Service and Victory Medals.
28, Clayton Street, Bradford Road, Manchester. Z11648

BOND, J., Private, 1/7th West Riding Regiment.
Joining in January 1917, he completed a period of training, and was sent to France in February of the following year. There he took part in important engagements in various sectors, including the Battles of the Somme, Passchendaele, and Cambrai, and was wounded. After four months in hospital, he rejoined his unit and rendered valuable services until his demobilisation in August 1919. He holds the General Service and Victory Medals.
18, Riga Street, City Road, Hulme, Manchester.. Z1292B

BOND, R., Private, Manchester Regiment.
He volunteered in August 1915, and in January of the following year was drafted to France, where he took part in many important engagements. He was in action at the Battles of Loos, St. Eloi, Vimy Ridge, the Somme, Arras, Passchendaele and Cambrai, and was wounded. On his recovery he was transferred for duty with the Labour Corps, and returning to England, was demobilised in February 1919. He holds the General Service and Victory Medals.
18, Riga Street, City Road, Hulme, Manchester. Z1292A

BOND, W. E., Engine Room Artificer, R.N. H.M.S. P67.
He volunteered in June 1915 in the Royal Naval Division as an A.B., but was shortly afterwards transferred to the Royal Navy as an engine-room artificer. In this capacity he served at sea in H.M.S. "Amphitrite" and "Zealandia," and on land at Portsmouth, and in the Isle of Wight. After also being engaged on important duties in H.M.S. "P67" he eventually returned to shore, and was demobilised in February 1919. He holds the 1914-15 Star, and the General Service and Victory Medals.
4, Smedley Road, Cheetham, Manchester. Z11467

BOND, W. F., Corporal, R.F.A.
Volunteering in August 1914, he was drafted to Salonika in the following year, and played a prominent part in the fighting on the Struma and Vardar fronts. He rendered valuable services with his Battery during the period of hostilities, and was demobilised in April 1919, holding the 1914-15 Star, and the General Service and Victory Medals.
38, Dalton Street, Hulme, Manchester. Z1291A

BONHAM, E. Mrs., (née McKenna), Nurse, British Red Cross Society.
She joined in July 1918, as a voluntary assistant, and served at the Blakeley Institute, where she was engaged on various responsible duties. She did much useful work during the period of hostilities, her services being highly valued, and was demobilised shortly after the signing of the Armistice in November 1918.
49, Garden Street, Ardwick, Manchester. Z1293B

BONHAM, J., Private, 4th Manchester Regiment.
He volunteered in January 1915, and six months later was drafted to the Western Front, where he took part in many important engagements, including the Battles of the Somme and Cambrai. He was wounded in action in July and October 1916, again in December 1917, and in the following March was taken prisoner. Whilst in captivity he was forced to load munitions immediately behind the line, and suffered much at the hands of the Germans. Repatriated in November 1918, he was demobilised two months later, and holds the 1914-15 Star, and the General Service and Victory Medals.
49, Garden Street, Ardwick, Manchester. Z1293A

BONIFACE, J., Private, 4th Connaught Rangers, and 7/8th Inniskilling Fusiliers.
He volunteered in August 1914, and proceeding to the Dardanelles in the following April, took part in the Landings at Cape Helles and Suvla Bay, and in the three Battles of Krithia. On the Evacuation of the Gallipoli Peninsula in January 1916, he was sent to Salonika, where he was in action on the Doiran and Struma fronts. In August of the same year he was invalided to Malta with malaria, but in April 1917, was drafted to France, and fought at the Battles of Arras, Ypres, Cambrai, Havrincourt, and Le Cateau. Demobilised in March 1919, he holds the 1914-15 Star, and the General Service and Victory Medals.
140, Viaduct Street, Ardwick, Manchester. Z1294

BOOMER, G,, Private, 2nd Manchester Regiment, and Driver, R.A.S.C.
He volunteered in August 1914, and in April of the following year proceeded to France. There he participated in strenuous fighting at La Bassée, Béthune, Givenchy, Festubert, Beaumont-Hamel, and the Somme. He was later transferred to the Royal Army Service Corps, and did valuable work whilst employed as a transport driver in various sectors. Invalided home in March 1918, suffering from gas-poisoning, he was in hospital in Lincoln and Manchester, prior to being demobilised in March 1919. He holds the 1914-15 Star, and the General Service and Victory Medals.
84, Lind Street, Ancoats, Manchester. Z8908

BOON, G., Pte., Royal Fusiliers, and Labour Corps.
He joined in October 1916, and was drafted to the Western Front in the following year. There he took part in many important engagements, including the Battles of Arras and Croiselles, and was sent to hospital suffering from wounds. He was later transferred to the Labour Corps, and rendered valuable services until the Armistice. He holds the General Service and Victory Medals, and was demobilised in March 1919.
16, York Street, Stage Offices, London West, Manchester. Z1295

BOOTH, A., Private, 2nd Border Regiment.
He enlisted in September 1913, and when war was declared was sent with the First Expeditionary Force to France. There he was engaged in action at Mons, Le Cateau, the Marne, the Aisne, La Bassée, Ypres I, Neuve Chapelle, St. Eloi, Hill 60, Ypres II, Festubert, the Somme, Arras, Bullecourt and Messines. In August 1917 he was drafted to Salonika, where he served on the Vardar front. In December 1918 he returned to England, and was discharged from the Army in May 1919, as medically unfit as the result of dysentery, and malaria, contracted when serving in the East. He holds the Mons Star, and the General Service and Victory Medals.
69, Bath Street, Miles Platting, Manchester. Z9891

BOOTH, A., Private, 1/5th York and Lancaster Regt.
Joining in September 1916, he was drafted to France four
months later, and during his service on the Western Front,
took part in the Battles of Arras, Bullecourt, Messines, Ypres,
and Cambrai, and in the Retreat and Advance of 1918. He
was gassed in action at the third Battle of Ypres in July 1917.
Demobilised in March 1919, he holds the General Service and
Victory Medals.
61, Dalton Street, Collyhurst, Manchester.   Z10299

BOOTH, A. J., Pioneer, R.E.
He volunteered in April 1915, and was shortly afterwards
drafted to France, where he saw much service. He did
valuable work in the Somme, Arras, Ypres, and Cambrai
sectors on the lines of communication. After returning home
he was demobilised in April 1919, holding the 1914–15 Star,
and the General Service and Victory Medals.
27, Clay Street, Newton Heath, Manchester.   Z9438

BOOTH, C., Private, 2nd Lancashire Fusiliers.
He joined in February 1918, and after a short training was
engaged on important duties at various stations. Owing to
the early cessation of hostilities, he was unable to obtain a
transfer overseas, but rendered valuable services. In 1920
he was on garrison duty at Lahore in India.
42, Green Street, Gorton, Manchester.   TZ1323

BOOTH, E., Driver, R.A.S.C. (M.T.)
Volunteering at the outbreak of war in August 1914, he was
sent two months later to the Western Front. In this theatre
of hostilities he served at Neuve Chapelle, Hill 60, Ypres, and
Cambrai, and on the Somme, Marne, and Ancre fronts, and
was wounded in March 1915. He remained overseas doing
consistently good work until after the cessation of fighting,
and was demobilised on his return home in February 1919,
holding the 1914–15 Star, and the General Service and Victory
Medals. 52, Gibbon Street, Bradford, Manchester.   Z8909

BOOTH, F., Driver, R.F.A.
He volunteered in December 1914, and in the following year
proceeded to France, where he served for twelve months.
During that time he saw heavy fighting at Ypres, Festubert,
Hill 60, St. Eloi, Neuve Chapelle, and Mericourt. In 1916
he was transferred to the Italian front, and after taking part
in numerous engagements was wounded in action on the
Austrian Frontier. Demobilised in 1919, he holds the 1914–15
Star, and the General Service and Victory Medals.
47, Kemp Street, Manchester.   Z9892A

BOOTH, F., Private, 11th Lancashire Fusiliers.
Volunteering in November 1914, he underwent a period of
training, and was drafted to France in September 1915. In
this theatre of war he took part in many important engagements, including the Battles of Loos, the Somme, La Bassée,
Givenchy, Festubert, Lens, Cambrai, and Ypres, and was
wounded in action and gassed. He returned to his depôt and
was eventually demobilised in February 1919, holding the
1914–15 Star, and the General Service and Victory Medals.
29, Lindum Street, Rusholme, Manchester.   Z1297

BOOTH, F., Private, 21st Manchester Regiment.
He volunteered in November 1914, and underwent a period
of training prior to his being drafted to France. There he was
in action in several engagements, including those at St. Quentin,
Ypres, Albert, and Arras, and after the cessation of hostilities,
took part in the march to Cologne. He was demobilised in
April, 1919, and holds the 1914–15 Star, and the General Service
and Victory Medals.
6, Groom Street, Ancoats, Manchester.   Z11649

BOOTH, G., Corporal, Royal Lancashire Fusiliers.
He volunteered in May 1915, and three months later proceeded
to the Western Front, where he was in action at the Battles
of Loos and Albert. He did consistently good work until
July 1916, when he was unhappily killed during the Offensive
on the Somme. He was entitled to the 1914–15 Star, and the
General Service and Victory Medals.
"His life for his Country, his soul to God."
48, York Street, Hulme, Manchester.   Z1298

BOOTH, J., Pte., Duke of Cornwall's Light Infantry.
He joined in February 1917, and after a course of training
served through the Irish Rebellion at Belfast. In January 1918
he proceeded to Italy, but after only a month's service there was
drafted to the Western Front. In this theatre of war he experienced fierce fighting at Cambrai, and in the final decisive
engagements of the war. He remained in France until March
1920, and was demobilised a month later, holding the General
Service and Victory Medals.
35, Brunswick Street, West Gorton, Manchester.   TZ6041

BOOTH, J., Private, 2nd Manchester Regiment.
Volunteering in January 1915, he was later in the same year
drafted overseas. Whilst serving on the Western Front he
took an active part in engagements at St. Quentin, Ypres,
Fœstubert, St. Eloi, and Passchendaele, and was wounded at
Arras in 1916. On rejoining his unit he was in action on the
Somme, and at Cambrai, Albert, and Bourlon Wood, and was
again wounded at Cambrai in 1918. He was demobilised in
1919, and holds the 1914–15 Star, and the General Service and
Victory Medals. 47, Kemp Street, Manchester.   Z9892B

**BOOTH, H. G., Private, South Wales Borderers, and
Air Mechanic, R.A.F.**
Volunteering in May 1915, he proceeded in September of the
following year to France and fought on the Somme, but after
three months' service was sent to England for munition work
of National importance. In December 1917, he returned to
the fighting area and took part in the Battle of Cambrai, and
other engagements until drafted with the Royal Air Force to
Italy. There he was in action on the Piave, and on one
occasion was badly injured in a fire. After returning to
England, he unfortunately died in February 1919, and was
entitled to the General Service and Victory Medals.
"Whilst we remember, the sacrifice is not in vain."
33, Ainsworth Street, West Gorton, Manchester.   Z9439

BOOTH, J. A., Private, Lancashire Fusiliers.
Volunteering in September 1914, he proceeded to the Dardanelles in the following March and took part in the Landings
at Cape Helles and Suvla Bay. In August 1915 he was severely
wounded and taken prisoner, and whilst in captivity, received
a bayonet wound from one of his Turkish guards. Repatriated
after the cessation of hostilities, he was demobilised in March
1919, and holds the 1914–15 Star, and the General Service and
Victory Medals.
9, Butler Street, Greenheys, Manchester.   Z1299

BOOTH, J. W., A.B., R.N., H.M.S. "Euryalus."
He volunteered in August 1914, and on completion of his
training took an active part in the Battle of Heligoland. In
May 1915, he proceeded to the Dardanelles and during the
campaign there was engaged on patrol work, and in the transport of troops to the scene of activities. After the Evacuation
he served in various seas, and was also in action in the Battle
of Jutland in May 1916. He was demobilised in June 1919,
and holds the 1914–15 Star, and the General Service and
Victory Medals.
18, Edith Street, West Gorton, Manchester.   Z9893

BOOTH, M., L/Corporal, 3rd Manchester Regiment.
He volunteered in October 1915, but proved to be unfit for
active service. He was retained on home defence, and stationed
at Cleethorpes, where he carried out the various duties assigned
to him with great ability. In December 1917, he was invalided
out of the Army, suffering from bronchitis, and died from that
complaint on April 13th, 1919.
"His memory is cherished with pride."
16, Heyrod Street, Ancoats, Manchester.   Z8910

BOOTH, R., Private, King's (Liverpool Regiment).
He joined the Army in August 1918, and after training at
Oswestry proceeded in the following October to the Western
Front. There he took an active part in the final victorious
engagements, and after the close of hostilities was sent with
the Army of Occupation to Germany, where he was stationed
until demobilised in January 1920. He holds the General
Service and Victory Medals.
1, Thomas Street, West Gorton, Manchester.   Z5791B

BOOTH, R., Sergt., 2nd Manchester Regiment.
Volunteering in August 1914, he proceeded to France in
November, and served with distinction at the Battles of Ypres
(1914 and 1915), and Hill 60. He was badly wounded in action
in May 1915, and was invalided home, but on his recovery
returned to the Western Front, and took part in the Battles
of Albert, the Somme, Arras, Vimy Ridge, Ypres (III) (where
he was gassed), the Somme (II), and Cambrai. He was
demobilised in March 1919, and holds the 1914 Star, and the
General Service and Victory Medals.
23, Dixon Street, Hulme, Manchester.   Z1300

BOOTH, R. A., Corporal, R.A.S.C.
He volunteered in October 1914, and in January of the following year was drafted to France, where he was engaged on
important transport duties in various sectors of the front. He
was badly wounded and sent to hospital in England, and on
recovery, from November 1917 did consistently good work
until his demobilisation in April 1919. He holds the 1914–15
Star, and the General Service and Victory Medals.
56, Longridge Street, Longsight, Manchester.   Z1296

BOOTH, S. D., Private, 18th Manchester Regiment.
Volunteering in September 1914, he proceeded to the Western
Front in February of the following year and took part in the
second Battle of Ypres. He was also in action during the
Somme Offensive, and made the supreme sacrifice, being
killed on July 31st, 1916. He was entitled to the 1914–15
Star, and the General Service and Victory Medals.
"Great deeds cannot die."
24, Stott Street, Hulme, Manchester.   Z1302

BOOTH, W., Private, 18th Royal Irish Regiment.
Mobilised in August 1914, he proceeded to France with the
first Expeditionary Force, and took part in the Battles of Mons
and Le Cateau. During the subsequent Retreat from Mons,
he was wounded in action and taken prisoner, and whilst in
captivity suffered many hardships in Doeberitz Camp. He was
repatriated in January 1919, and after two months in Bangour
Hospital, Edinburgh, was discharged in March, holding the
Mons Star, and the General Service and Victory Medals.
16, Craven Street, Preston Street, Hulme, Manchester.   Z1303

BOOTH, R. L., Private, Northumberland Fusiliers.
Volunteering in September 1914, he was engaged on important duties at home stations until early in 1916, when he was sent on active service. Whilst in Mesopotamia, he took part in much severe fighting, and was present at the Capture of Tripoli. He contracted malarial fever, and was invalided to India, but on his recovery, was in action against the Afghans on the North Western Frontier. Demobilised in October 1919, he holds the General Service and Victory Medals, and the India General Service Medal (with clasp Afghanistan, North West Frontier 1919).
15, Avenham Street, Hulme, Manchester. Z1301

BOOTH, W., Sergt., 8th Royal Welch Fusiliers.
He volunteered in August 1914, and in the following year was drafted to Gallipoli, where he played a prominent part in the Suvla Bay Landing. He served throughout the campaign, and then proceeded to India, and was engaged on important garrison duties at Bombay, and other stations until December 1919. Whilst in the East he suffered from malaria, and on his return to England was demobilised in January 1920, holding the 1914-15 Star, and the General Service and Victory Medals.
1, Thomas Street, West Gorton, Manchester. Z5791A

BOOTH, W., Private, 13th Manchester Regiment.
He volunteered in January 1915, and in August was drafted to Salonika, where he was in action on the Doiran and Vardar fronts until March 1918. He was then transferred to France, and was engaged on trench and bridge construction with the Labour Corps in that theatre of war. He holds the 1914-15 Star, and the General Service and Victory Medals, and was demobilised in February 1919.
24, Apsley Grove, Ardwick, Manchester. Z1304B

BOOTH, W. J., Corporal, R.F.A.
He volunteered in August 1914, and was shortly afterwards drafted to the Western Front, where he saw much severe fighting at La Bassée, Neuve Chapelle, Hill 60, Ypres, Loos, the Somme, and Arras. He was unfortunately killed in action at Dickebusch in August 1917, and was entitled to the 1914 Star, and the General Service and Victory Medals.
"His life for his Country, his soul to God."
38, Nelson Street, Bradford, Manchester. Z1324

BORLAND, J., Private, Border Regiment and 9th Gordon Highlanders.
He volunteered in August 1914, and proceeded to France in January of the following year. He took part in many important engagements, including the Battles of Neuve Chapelle, Ypres, and Festubert, and was wounded at Fricourt in April 1916. He was invalided home and later transferred to the Gordon Highlanders, and again proceeded to the Western Front in March 1918. After taking part in the Retreat and Advance of 1918 he returned to England, and was demobilised in January 1919, holding the 1914-15 Star, and the General Service and Victory Medals.
13, Anthony Street, Ardwick, Manchester. Z1305

BORTOFT, J., Driver, R.F.A.
He was mobilised in August 1914, and immediately proceeded to Egypt, where he served with the 42nd Division at Alexandria and Cairo. After taking part in engagements on the Suez Canal at Ismailia, and Kantara, he was drafted to the Western Front in March 1917, and did good work with his Battery at Arras, Messines, Ypres, and Cambrai, and in the Retreat and Advance of 1918. He was discharged in February 1919, and holds the 1914-15 Star, and the General Service and Victory Medals. 5, Brown Street, Miles Platting, Manchester. Z11468

BOSANKO, W. H. Pte., 2nd K.O. (Liverpool Regt.)
Volunteering in August 1914, in the following year he proceeded to Gallipoli, and after serving throughout the campaign there, was sent to Egypt. He was in action at Katia, and was then transferred to France, where he saw heavy fighting at Ypres, the Somme, and Givenchy. In July 1916 he was drafted to Salonika, and in this theatre of war saw service in numerous engagements, including those at Kut. He was invalided to England in December 1918, and demobilised in the same month, holding the 1914-15 Star, and the General Service and Victory Medals. 1, Mary Street, Ancoats, Manchester. Z8911

BOSTOCK, E., L/Corporal, 2nd Lancashire Fusiliers.
He volunteered in August 1914, and in February 1915 was drafted to France. After taking part in the Battles of Neuve Chapelle, and Hill 60, he was gassed at Ypres, and invalided to England. On his discharge from hospital, he was sent to India in May 1916, and was employed on garrison duties on the Afghanistan Frontier until October 1917. He then proceeded to Mesopotamia, where he served at Kut and Mosul, and was taken to Kut Hospital suffering with dysentery. In April 1919 he returned home, and was demobilised, holding the 1914-15 Star, and the General Service and Victory Medals.
24, Beaumont Street, Beswick, Manchester. Z9889

BOSTOCK, F., Sapper, R.E.
Having previously served for twenty-one years he again volunteered in January 1915, and in the following March was drafted to France, where he took part in numerous engagements, including those at Loos, Ypres, the Somme, La Bassée, Givenchy, Arras, and the Retreat and Advance of 1915. He was

demobilised in January 1919, and holds the 1914-15 Star, and the General Service and Victory Medals.
24, Fletcher Street, Newton Heath, Manchester. Z9440

BOSTOCK, J., L/Corporal, 20th Manchester Regt.
He volunteered in January 1915, and at the end of the same year was drafted to the Western Front, where he played an important part in the Battle of the Somme. Unfortunately he was badly wounded in action at Givenchy in September 1916, and was invalided home. After hospital treatment in London, he was discharged in April 1917, as medically unfit for further service, and holds the 1914-15 Star, and the General Service and Victory Medals.
41, Back Mount Street, Harpurhey, Manchester. Z10300

BOSWELL, D., Private, K.O. (Royal Lancaster Regt.)
Joining in November 1918, he was sent to Liverpool for a course of training, on the conclusion of which he was drafted to Ireland. Stationed at Cork throughout the period of his service in the Army, he was engaged on important guard duties, which he fulfilled with great ability, and was demobilised in Dublin in October 1919.
1, Park Street, West Gorton, Manchester. Z10666B

BOSWELL, E., Private, 1st Cheshire Regiment.
He joined in March 1916, and seven months later was drafted to the Western Front. There he was in action in the Battles of the Somme, the Ancre, Arras, Bullecourt, Ypres, Cambrai, and the Aisne, and died gloriously on the Field of Battle at Havrincourt in September 1918. He was entitled to the General Service and Victory Medals.
"Great deeds cannot die."
1, Park Street, West Gorton, Manchester. Z10666A

BOTCHETT, C. A., Private, King's (Shropshire Light Infantry).
He joined in May 1916, and proceeded to Ireland, where he served for two years at Fermoy, and was then drafted to the Western Front. There he took an active part in many important engagements, and was in action at Lens, Cambrai, and Bapaume, and in the Retreat and Advance of 1918. He remained in France until his demobilisation in January 1919, and holds the General Service and Victory Medals.
27, Ainsworth Street, West Gorton, Manchester. Z8912

BOTTOMLEY, I. H., Gunner, R.G.A.
He volunteered in August 1914, and in the following November was drafted to France. Later, however, he was transferred to Salonika, and was wounded in action during the Landing. He was invalided to hospital at Alexandria, but, on his recovery, rendered valuable services as an Instructor at the Imperial School of Gunnery in Egypt. Demobilised in March 1919, he holds the 1914 Star, and the General Service and Victory Medals.
16, Holt Terrace, Longsight, Manchester. Z1306

BOTTOMLEY, J., Pte., 2/7th Lancashire Fusiliers.
He volunteered in October 1915, and on completion of his training was engaged on important work with his unit in England for three years, during which time he rendered valuable services. In October 1918 he was sent to Russia for special duty, and remained there until his demobilisation in July 1919. He holds the General Service and Victory Medals.
19, Dalton Street, Collyhurst, Manchester. Z10301

BOTTOMLEY, J., Sergeant, R.G.A.
He joined in April 1916, and after rendering valuable services on the East Coast for two years, was drafted to the Western Front, where he took part in important engagements in many sectors, including those of Cambrai, Ypres, Bullecourt. He was also in action during the Retreat and Advance of 1918, and was demobilised in January 1919, holding the General Service and Victory Medals.
161, Acomb Street, Moss Side, Manchester. Z1308

BOTTOMLEY, S., Corporal, R.A.V.C.
Joining in September 1916, he was shortly afterwards drafted to the Western Front, where he did consistently good work at Boulogne, Le Havre, Rouen, Ypres, and Cambrai. He was also present during the Retreat and Advance of 1918, and after the Armistice proceeded to Germany, where he served with the Army of Occupation at Cologne on the Rhine. He was demobilised in May 1919, and holds the General Service and Victory Medals. 10, Green Street, Gorton, Manchester. Z1307

BOTTOMS. E., Rifleman, Rifle Brigade.
He volunteered for active service in September 1914, and was stationed at Aldershot, where he was employed on important work. In December 1914, after only three months' service in the Army he was discharged at Elstead, as medically unfit for further military duties.
5, Rigg Street, Gorton, Manchester. Z9890A

BOULTON, A., Private, 1st North Staffordshire Regt.
Mobilised at the outbreak of war in August 1914, he was drafted to France shortly afterwards, and was in action at the Battle of the Aisne, before being wounded at Armentières in October 1914. He was invalided home, and was transferred later to the Royal Engineers, with which unit he did consistently good work in England until the cessation of hostilities. He holds the 1914 Star, and the General Service and Victory Medals, and was discharged in February 1919.
19, Adelaide Street, Hulme, Manchester. Z1309A

BOULTON, J., Bombardier, R.G.A.

He joined in November 1916, and rendered valuable services on the East Coast, where he was engaged on important anti-aircraft duties. In March 1918, he was drafted to India with the Royal Garrison Artillery, and did garrison and other duties until his return to England for demobilisation in March 1919. He holds the General Service and Victory Medals.
41, Ossory Street, Rusholme, Manchester.   Z1310

BOURKE, J., Private, Royal Welch Fusiliers.

Joining in April 1917, he was on conclusion of his training ten months later, drafted overseas. Whilst serving on the Western Front he was in action principally in the Lys Sector, and fell fighting after only three months' active service in May 1918. He was entitled to the General Service and Victory Medals.
    "He died the noblest death a man may die,
        Fighting for God and right, and liberty."
13, Williams Place, Ancoats, Manchester.   Z8913B

BOUSTEAD, R., Private, 1/7th Manchester Regt.

He enlisted in May 1908, and at the outbreak of war in August 1914, was sent on special duties to the Soudan. Later, however, he proceeded to the Dardanelles, and saw much severe fighting but in September 1915, contracted dysentery, and was invalided home. After hospital treatment in Sussex, he was discharged in May 1916 as medically unfit for further service, and holds the 1914–15 Star, and the General Service and Victory Medals.
48, Princess Street, Rusholme, Manchester.   Z1311A

BOUSTEAD, R., Private, Manchester Regiment.

He volunteered in September 1914, and after a period of training, was drafted to France in September of the following year. He was wounded in action during the Somme Offensive of July 1916, and was invalided to England. On his recovery, he was sent to Salonika, where he took part in many engagements, and was again wounded and finally discharged in November 1918, as physically unfit for further service. He holds the 1914–15 Star, and the General Service and Victory Medals.
48, Princess Street, Rusholme, Manchester.   Z1311B

BOWATER, L., Pte., 1st K.O. (Royal Lancaster Regt.)

He joined in 1918, and was retained on special duties with his unit at important stations in England and Ireland. He was unable to obtain his transfer to a theatre of war, but nevertheless rendered valuable services until his demobilisation in November 1919.
40, Etruria Street, Longsight, Manchester.   Z1312

BOWCOCK, J., Private, 7th Border Regiment.

He joined in February 1916, and three months later proceeded to the Western Front, where he was engaged in the Battles of the Somme, Arras, and Messines, and was wounded at Ypres. He was sent to hospital in Etaples, and later to Birmingham, and on his return to the Front took an active part in the Battle of the Marne, and in the final Allied Advance of 1918. He was demobilised in June 1919, and holds the General Service and Victory Medals.
12, Lilford Street, West Gorton, Manchester.   Z8914

BOWDEN, H., Pte., King's Shropshire Light Infty.

He joined in March 1916, and five months later proceeded to the Western Front, where he took part in many important engagements, including the Battles of the Somme, Ypres, and Arras, and was later in action during the Retreat and Advance of 1918. He returned to England after the Armistice, and was demobilised in January 1919, holding the General Service and Victory Medals.
Hampden Street, Ardwick, Manchester.   Z1314B

BOWDEN, J. W., Private, King's (Liverpool Regt.)

He volunteered in February 1915, and after a period of training was drafted to the Western Front, where he was in action in many important sectors. He saw much heavy fighting at St. Eloi, Albert, Vimy Ridge, the Somme, Arras, Ypres, and Cambrai, and was wounded. He was also in action at Havrincourt and Le Cateau, during the Retreat and Advance of 1918, and was demobilised in September of the following year, holding the General Service and Victory Medals.   Z1315
3, Auburn Place, Moor Street, Rusholme, Manchester.

BOWDEN, W., Gunner, R.F.A.

He volunteered in August 1915, and was shortly afterwards drafted to France, where he was in action with his Battery at various engagements. He made the supreme sacrifice in November 1916, being killed in action on the Somme. He was entitled to the 1914–15 Star, and the General Service and Victory Medals.
        "The path of duty was the way to glory."
18, Mary Street, Hulme, Manchester.   Z1316

BOWDEN, W. H., Sergt., 16th Manchester Regt.

Volunteering in January 1915, he did consistently good work in England during the first part of his service, but in April 1917 proceeded to France. There he took a distinguished part in many important engagements including the Battles of Bullecourt and Messines, and was killed in action on July 31st

1917, at Sanctuary Wood, Ypres, while in charge of Lewis gunners. He was entitled to the General Service and Victory Medals.   "A costly sacrifice upon the altar of freedom."
36, Molyneux Street, Longsight, Manchester.   Z1313

BOWE,, K., Corporal, Tank Corps.

He volunteered in August 1914, and was drafted to the Western Front in January of the following year. There he played a prominent part in many engagements including the Battles of Neuve Chapelle, Loos, the Somme, Beaumont-Hamel, Messines, and Cambrai. He was wounded in June 1917 on Messines Ridge, and later at the third Battle of Ypres in September. He holds the 1914–15 Star, and the General Service and Victory Medals, and was demobilised in May 1919.
36, Edge Street, Hulme, Manchester.   Z1318

BOWEN, F., Private, Labour Corps.

He joined in September 1918, and was engaged on various farms on important agricultural duties. Owing to the early cessation of hostilities he was unable to proceed overseas, but rendered valuable services until his demobilisation in October 1919.
49, Crosscliffe Street, Moss Side, Manchester.   Z1330

BOWEN, J., Sergt., R.A.S.C. (M.T.)

He was mobilised in August 1914, and in the following month proceeded to France, where he was engaged on important staff and transport duties in many sectors. He did consistently good work during the whole period of hostilities, and was discharged in November 1919, holding the 1914 Star, and the General Service and Victory Medals.
7, Geoffrey Street, Chorlton-on-Medlock, Manchester.   X1371

BOWEN, P., Sergt., M.G.C.

Having previously served for twelve years in the Army, he rejoined in October 1915, and two months later was sent to France. There he was in action principally in the Somme sector until 1917, when he returned to England, and was stationed at Colchester. In June 1918 he was drafted to Russia, where he took a prominent part in heavy fighting on the Murmansk Coast. Returning home in August 1919, he was demobilised a month later, and holds the 1914–15 Star, and the General Service and Victory Medals.
20, Harrowby Street, Collyhurst, Manchester.   Z9894

BOWEN, W., Private, 18th Lancashire Fusiliers.

He volunteered in January 1915, and in the following year proceeded to the Western Front. In this theatre of war he took part in several engagements, including the Battles of the Somme, Arras, Ypres III, and Passchendaele, and was wounded in action in July 1916. He was demobilised in January 1919, and holds the General Service and Victory Medals.
33, Worsley Street, Oldham Road, Manchester.   Z11650

BOWER, A., Pte., King's Own (Yorkshire Light Infy.)

He joined in May 1917, and in the following November was drafted to France, where he took part in the fighting at Cambrai I, the Somme II, and was twice wounded in action. He was taken prisoner in March 1918, and held in captivity in Germany for several months. After the Armistice he was released and returned home for his demobilisation in November 1919. He holds the General Service and Victory Medals.
23, Arthur Street, Seadley, Pendleton, Manchester.   C999

BOWERS, D., Private, M.G.C.

Joining in August 1917, he was drafted to France in the following April. In this theatre of war he took part in many engagements, including those on the Somme, and at Cambrai, and was taken prisoner in May 1918. He was held in captivity in Germany, being forced to work in the mills at Metz until he was released after the Armistice. He was demobilised in September 1919, and holds the General Service and Victory Medals.
18, Gresham Street, Ashton Old, Openshaw, Manchester.
                                                       Z1332

BOWES, J. Gunner, R.G.A.

He volunteered in October 1914, and a year later was sent to the Western Front. Whilst serving there he was in action at Loos, Vimy Ridge, Ypres, the Somme, the Marne and Cambrai, and in the final Allied Advance. He was both wounded and gassed, but remained in France until April 1919, being employed in the transport of supplies. Demobilised in April 1919, he holds the 1914–15 Star, and the General Service and Victory Medals.
5, Duke Street, Bradford, Manchester.   Z9895

BOWES, J. F., Private, East Lancashire Regt.

He joined in March 1916, and served at Southport until September 1917, when he was drafted overseas. During his service in France he experienced severe fighting at Lens and Cambrai, and was unfortunately killed in action at the Battle of the Somme on April 11th 1918. He was entitled to the General Service and Victory Medals.
    "A valiant Soldier, with undaunted heart he breasted life's
                last hill."
42, Howarth Street, Chorlton-on-Medlock, Manchester.   Z9896

BOWES, P. A., Private, 17th Manchester Regt.
Volunteering in September 1914, he proceeded to France in the following year. Whilst on the Western Front he saw much fighting at La Bassée, Givenchy, Loos, Arras, and on the Somme, where he was badly wounded, and consequently invalided to hospital in England. On his recovery he was transferred to the R.A.F., and served at various stations until his demobilisation in February 1919. He holds the 1914-15 Star, and the General Service and Victory Medals.
63, Granville Street, Chorlton-on-Medlock, Manchester.
Z1333

BOWES, S., Private, 8th Manchester Regiment.
He volunteered in August 1914, and a month later was sent to the Western Front, but after only a few months' service in this theatre of war was drafted to Gallipoli. There he took an active part in the Landing on the Peninsula and fell fighting at Krithia in August 1915. He was entitled to the 1914 Star, and the General Service and Victory Medals.
"He died the noblest death a man may die,
  Fighting for God, and right, and liberty."
15, Tonge Street, Ancoats, Manchester.
Z9897

BOWKER, E. R., Sergt., 3rd Manchester Regiment.
Having previously served in the South African Campaign, he volunteered in November 1914, and was retained at home for some time as an Instructor in musketry. Later he was drafted to France, and saw much heavy fighting at Monchy, where he was severely wounded. He died in hospital on April 28th, 1917, as a result of his wounds, and was buried at Étaples. He was entitled to the 1914-15 Star, and the General Service and Victory Medals.
"Thinking that remembrance, though unspoken, may reach him where he sleeps."
80, Percival Street, Chorlton-on-Medlock, Manchester.
Z1337

BOWKER, J., Private, Cheshire Regiment.
He joined in April 1916, and in the following October was drafted to France, where he took part in much heavy fighting in many sectors. He was wounded and taken prisoner at Passchendaele, and was held in captivity in Germany, suffering many hardships. He was released after the Armistice, and sent to hospital in London, and was later discharged as medically unfit for further duty in March 1919. He holds the General Service and Victory Medals.
34, Ridgway Street, Moss Side, Manchester.
Z1334A

BOWKER, R., Private, 8th Manchester Regiment.
He joined in August 1918, but owing to the early cessation of hostilities, was not drafted overseas. He was therefore engaged on important duties with his unit, and did consistently good work until his demobilisation in January 1919.
43, High Sheffield Street, Ardwick, Manchester.
X1336

BOWKER, R., Pte., K.O. (Royal Lancaster Regt.)
He volunteered in August 1914, and in the following April was drafted to the Dardanelles, where he took part in much heavy fighting at Suvla Bay and was badly wounded. In consequence he was invalided to Malta, but on his recovery saw much severe fighting in Mesopotamia, was present at the capture of Baghdad and was twice wounded in action. He returned home and was engaged on despatch work until his demobilisation in February 1919. He holds the 1914-15 Star, and the General Service and Victory Medals.
25, Worrington Street, Hulme, Manchester.
TZ1335

BOWKER, S., Private, Durham Light Infantry.
He joined in September 1916, and underwent a period of training prior to his being drafted overseas. Whilst on the Western Front he took part in many engagements, and was badly gassed and wounded in action. As a result, he was invalided home and on his recovery, was retained on important duties until his demobilisation in July 1919. He holds the General Service and Victory Medals.
34, Ridgway Street, Moss Side, Manchester.
Z1334B

BOWKER, T., Private, 12th King's (Liverpool Regt.)
He volunteered shortly after the outbreak of war, and in September 1914 was sent to France, where he took part in the Battle of Ypres. Whilst fighting on the Somme in 1916, he was wounded and sent to hospital in Bournemouth. On his discharge he returned to the Western Front, and served in the final decisive engagements of the war. He was demobilised in January 1919, holding the 1914 Star, and the General Service and Victory Medals.
12, Boardman Street, Harpurhey, Manchester.
Z11469

BOWLER, H., Gunner, R.G.A.
Volunteering in September 1915, he was drafted overseas in the following December. During his service on the Western Front he took part in many engagements, including those at Loos, Albert, Vimy Ridge, the Somme, Arras, Ypres, the Somme II, the Marne II, and in the Retreat and Advance of 1918, being slightly gassed in action. He was demobilised in February 1919, and holds the 1914-15 Star, and the General Service and Victory Medals.
35, Wellbeck Street, Chorlton-on-Medlock, Manchester.
Z1339

BOWLER, W., Private, 19th Manchester Regiment.
He joined in March 1917, and two months later was drafted to France, where he took part in the fighting at Ypres and on the Somme II. Later he was attached to the M.G.C., and was engaged as a signaller during the Retreat and Advance of 1918. He was demobilised in October 1919 and holds the General Service and Victory Medals.
8, Mornington Street, Chorlton-on-Medlock, Manchester.
Z1338

BOWLES, D., Private, King's (Liverpool Regiment).
He joined in October 1916, and in the following year was drafted to France, where he took part in much severe fighting and was wounded and gassed. He returned home and was demobilised in March 1919, holding the General Service and Victory Medals. He died from the after effects of gas poisoning on May 31st, 1920, and was buried at Bradford Cemetery.
"His memory is cherished with pride."
15, Whitley Street, Rochdale Road, Manchester.
Z9441B

BOWLES, T., Gunner, R.F.A.
Having joined in March 1916, he was sent to France in the following year and took part in numerous engagements. He was unfortunately killed in action at the Battle of Ypres on December 1st, 1917, and was entitled to the General Service and Victory Medals.
"He passed out of the sight of men by the path of duty and self-sacrifice."
15, Whitley Street, Rochdale Road, Manchester.
Z9441A

BOWLES, W., Private, King's (Liverpool Regt.)
He joined in April 1916, and in the following January was sent to France. Badly wounded in action at the 3rd Battle of Ypres in July 1917, he was invalided to England, but on his recovery, returned to the Western Front in March 1918. He was then wounded and taken prisoner at Festubert in the following month and was held in captivity in Germany until December 1918. He holds the General Service and Victory Medals, and was demobilised in January 1919.
35, Fitzgeorge Street, Collyhurst, Manchester.
Z10302

BOWMAN, J. W., Private, Royal Sussex Regiment.
Volunteering in August 1915, he was retained on important duties in England until October 1917, when he proceeded overseas. Whilst serving on the Western Front, he was in action in the Ypres sector, and was wounded there in December 1917. He unhappily succumbed to his injuries on January 29th, 1918, and was entitled to the General Service and Victory Medals.
"Whilst we remember, the sacrifice is not in vain."
228, Cobden Street, Ancoats, Manchester.
Z9898

BOWMAN, R., Driver, R.E.
Volunteering in May 1915, he was drafted overseas in the following January. Whilst in Salonika he saw much heavy fighting on the Vardar and Struma fronts until the cessation of hostilities. He unfortunately contracted malarial fever, and in consequence was invalided home, and was demobilised in 1919. He holds the General Service and Victory Medals.
21, Hancock Street, Rusholme, Manchester.
Z1341

BOWNES, W. T., Private, 6th Manchester Regiment.
He volunteered in August 1914, and underwent a period of training prior to his being drafted overseas. He saw much fighting in Egypt, where he was twice wounded in action, but on his recovery he again took part in engagements in Abyssinia, until hostilities ceased. He returned home and was demobilised in March 1919, holding the General Service and Victory Medals.
18, Apsley Square, Ardwick, Manchester.
X1340

BOWNES, W. T., Pte., 1st and 6th Manchester Regt.
He joined the Army in January 1913, and after the outbreak of war proceeded to Egypt, and thence to the Dardanelles. Here he took part in the Landing at Cape Helles, and in the engagements at Krithia, being wounded in action and invalided to Malta. Later he was sent home and served on important duties until his demobilisation in March 1919. He holds the 1914-15 Star, and the General Service and Victory Medals.
18, Apsley Square, Ardwick, Manchester.
Z1342

BOWTELL, E. W., Sapper, R.E.
He volunteered in January 1916, and on completing his training in the following year was drafted to France. There he was engaged on important duties as an Instructor at Abbeville, and rendered valuable services. He suffered from trench feet, and was invalided to hospital, and finally demobilised in January 1919. He holds the General Service and Victory Medals.
42, Haydon Avenue, Moss Side, Manchester.
Z1343

BOX, W. E., Private, K.O. (Royal Lancaster Regt.)
Volunteering in 1914, he was eventually drafted overseas, and saw much severe fighting on the Galliopli Peninsula. After the Evacuation, he was transferred to the Western Front, where he was badly wounded in action. As a result he unfortunately had to have one of his legs amputated, and was invalided from the Army in 1919. He holds the 1914-15 Star, and the General Service and Victory Medals.
2, Halifax Street, Chorlton-on-Medlock, Manchester. X1345A

BOX, C. H., Sergeant, R.F.A.
He volunteered in 1914, and after his training was retained on important duties in England for some time. He was eventually drafted to the Western Front, and played a prominent part with his Battery in much severe fighting. In 1919 he was demobilised, and holds the General Service and Victory Medals.
2, Halifax Street, Chorlton-on-Medlock, Manchester. X1345B

BOYD, C. F., Private, 8th Loyal N. Lancashire Regt.
Joining in February 1916, he was six months later ordered to the Western Front. There he was in action in various sectors, and fought in engagements at La Bassée, Ploegsteert Wood, Armentières. He was severely wounded in the Battle of the Somme in 1918, and invalided to England, eventually being discharged as medically unfit in February 1919. He holds the General Service and Victory Medals.
27, Moreton Street, Longsight, Manchester. Z9899

BOYD, E., Private, 1st Manchester Regiment.
He volunteered in February 1915, and eleven months later proceeded overseas to the Egyptian theatre of war. There he saw service at Katia, and was later ordered to Mesopotamia, where he was engaged in action at Kut, Basra and Amara. He returned to England in July 1919, and was demobilised, but later rejoined the Army for a further period of three years. He holds the General Service and Victory Medals.
29, Dearden Street, Ancoats, Manchester. Z9900A

BOYD, J., Private, 6th East Lancashire Regiment.
Volunteering in November 1914, he was on completion of his training in June 1915, drafted to Gallipoli. During the Landing at Suvla Bay he was wounded and sent to hospital in Egypt, but on his return to the Peninsula served in further fighting until the Evacuation. In February 1916, he was sent to Mesopotamia, served with the relief force, and took part in severe fighting until the close of hostilities. He was again wounded in May 1916, and on his return to England was demobilised in March 1919, holding the 1914-15 Star, and the General Service and Victory Medals.
9, Ross Street, West Gorton, Manchester. Z10868B

BOYD, J., Private, 6th South Lancashire Regiment.
He volunteered in November 1914, and on completion of his training at Liverpool was drafted overseas in January 1915. He served in Mesopotamia for four years, and during that period was engaged in fierce fighting at Amara, Kut, Sanna-i-Yat, and on the Tigris. In February 1919 he returned to England and was demobilised a month later, holding the 1914-15 Star and the General Service and Victory Medals.
16, Drinkwater Street, Harpurhey, Manchester. Z11407

BOYD, R., Private, 9th Lancashire Fusiliers.
Volunteering in August 1914, he was on completion of his training a year later sent to Egypt. He was then ordered to Gallipoli, and after taking part in severe fighting, was killed in action on August 21st, 1915, after only a fortnight's active service on the Peninsula. He was entitled to the 1914-15 Star, and the General Service and Victory Medals.
"Honour to the immortal dead, who gave their youth that the world might grow old in peace."
29, Dearden Street, Ancoats, Manchester. Z9900B

BOYLE, J., Pte., Cheshire Regt., and Pioneer, R.E.
He volunteered in December 1915, and in March of the following year was drafted to the Western Front, where he took part in numerous important engagements and saw heavy fighting at Fricourt, the Somme and St. Eloi. He was invalided to England in December 1916, and subsequently discharged as medically unfit for further service in September 1918. He holds the General Service and Victory Medals.
2, Mary Ellen Street, Collyhurst, Manchester. Z9901

BOYLE, J., Sapper, R.E.
He volunteered in May 1915, and in the following January was drafted to the Western Front, where he was badly wounded in action at Ypres in November 1916. He was invalided to England and on his recovery, was retained on important duties with his unit until his demobilisation in April 1919 He holds the General Service and Victory Medals.
14, Bonsall Street, Hulme, Manchester. Z1346

BOYLE, W., Sapper, R.E.
When war broke out in August 1914 he was already serving, and was at once ordered overseas. During his service on the Western Front, he fought in the famous Battles of Mons, Ypres, the Somme, Nieuport, La Bassée, Givenchy, Arras and Cambrai. He remained in France until January 1919, when he was discharged, holding the Mons Star, and the General Service and Victory Medals.
17, Railway Street, Oldham Road, Manchester. Z9902

BOYNE, T., Private, 13th Manchester Regiment.
Volunteering in January 1915, he was drafted to Salonika later in the same year, and took part in the heavy fighting on the Vardar, Struma and Doiran fronts, and at the recapture of Monastir. He was wounded in action in April 1917, and in August 1918 was transferred to the Western Front, where he was again wounded a month later at Havrincourt Wood. In January 1919 he was demobilised, and holds the 1914-15 Star, and the General Service and Victory Medals.
29, Mark Lane, Chorlton-on-Medlock, Manchester. Z1347

BRABIN, J., Sergeant, R.F.A.
He enlisted in the Army in 1899, and served in the Boer war, and at the outbreak of war in August 1914 was stationed in India. He returned to England, and performed excellent work in drilling recruits at Aldershot. In October 1914, however, he was discharged as medically unfit for further military duties, and holds the Queen's and King's South African Medals, and General Service Medal.
11, Nuttall Street, Openshaw, Manchester. Z1348

BRACEGIRDLE, J., Private, M.G.C.
He joined in June 1917, and after training at Mansfield and Northampton, was drafted overseas four months later. Whilst serving on the Western Front, he experienced fierce fighting in different sectors, and was wounded in the Battle of Cambrai. On his discharge from Etaples Hospital he was principally engaged in guarding prisoners of war. He was demobilised in February 1919, and holds the General Service and Victory Medals.
59, Beaumont Street, Beswick, Manchester. Z9904B

BRACEGIRDLE, R., Private, 12th Manchester Regt.
He volunteered in September 1914, and after training at Ashton was two months later drafted overseas. During his service in France he fought in the Battles of the Marne, Le Cateau, Ypres and La Bassée and was unfortunately killed in action during the Battle of the Somme on July 7th, 1916. He was entitled to the 1914 Star, and the General Service and Victory Medals.
"A costly sacrifice upon the altar of freedom."
32, Fielden Street, Oldham Road, Manchester. Z8915A

BRACEGIRDLE, W., Private, Welch Regiment.
He volunteered in May 1915, and in the following September proceeded to Salonika, where he served for eighteen months. During that time he took part in the capture of Monastir, and whilst engaged in heavy fighting on the Doiran front was wounded and gassed in March 1917. A year later he was sent to France and fell fighting at Kemmel Hill on April 16th, 1918. He was entitled to the 1914-15 Star, and the General Service and Victory Medals.
"Whilst we remember, the sacrifice is not in vain."
59, Beaumont Street, Beswick, Manchester. Z9904A

BRACKENRIDGE, J. T., Driver, R.A.S.C.
He joined the Army in June 1917, but on account of his age, was not successful in procuring a transfer to a theatre of war. He was retained on home defence and stationed in London, and throughout the period of his service performed his duties in a highly capable manner. In February 1919 he was demobilised.
1, Amy Street, Openshaw, Manchester. Z5790

BRACKIN, T. W., Private, 1/8th, 5th and 9th Manchester Regiment.
He volunteered in October 1914, and first saw active service in the Dardanelles in the following April. He took part in the Landing at Cape Helles and in the Battles of Krithia. In June 1915 he was invalided to Egypt suffering from typhoid fever, but on his recovery, fought at El Fasher, Romani and Magdhaba. He was transferred to the Western Front in December 1916, and took part in the Battles of Arras, and Ypres, where he was wounded and gassed. After hospital treatment at Etaples, he rejoined his unit and was in action at the Battles of Havrincourt and Cambrai in 1918. Demobilised in February 1919, he holds the 1914-15 Star, and the General Service and Victory Medals.
25, Industrial Street, Stockport Road, Chorlton-on-Medlock, Manchester. Z1349

BRADBURY, D., Gunner, R.F.A.
He volunteered in August 1914, and after a period of service in England, was drafted to the Western Front in May 1916. Whilst in this theatre of war he took part in the Battles of the Somme, the Ancre, Arras, Passchendaele, Lens, Amiens and Le Cateau. He was demobilised in November 1919, and holds the General Service and Victory Medals.
11, Cleveland Street, West Gorton, Manchester. Z1350

BRADBURY, G., Private, 2/4th King's Shropshire Light Infantry.
He joined in May 1916, but, owing to his being medically unfit for transfer overseas, was retained on important duties with his unit until the following September, when he was invalided from the Army. He then rendered valuable services on work of National importance at a large munition factory until November 1918.
135, Clopton Street, Hulme, Manchester. Z1351B

BRADBURY, H., Private, 1st Manchester Regt.
At the outbreak of hostilities in August 1914, he was already serving, and in March 1915 proceeded to the Western Front. There he saw heavy fighting in the Neuve Chapelle, Ypres, Festubert, Somme, Arras, Cambrai and La Bassée sectors, and was wounded in action. He was later transferred to the Royal Scots Fusiliers, and in 1920 was still serving with that Regiment. He holds the 1914-15 Star, and the General Service and Victory Medals.
160, Harrold Street, Bradford, Manchester. Z11470

BRADBURY, J., Private, 2/7th Lancashire Fusiliers.
He joined in June 1917, and in the following September was drafted to France, where he was badly wounded in action at Passchendaele and invalided to England two months later. On his recovery he was medically unfit for transfer overseas, and was therefore engaged on home duties until his demobilisation in April 1920. He holds the General Service and Victory Medals.
135, Clopton Street, Hulme, Manchester.   Z1351A

BRADBURY, W., Private, King's (Liverpool Regt.)
He volunteered in August 1914, and was eventually drafted to France in December 1915. During his service on the Western Front he took part in the Battles of the Somme, Messines, Ypres and Passchendaele. He also served through the Retreat and Advance of 1918, until badly wounded in action at the second Battle of Le Cateau. As a result he was invalided from the Army in November 1918, and holds the 1914-15 Star, and the General Service and Victory Medals.
14, Rose View, Longsight, Manchester.   Z1352

BRADBURY, W., Private, Lancashire Fusiliers.
Volunteering in October 1914, he proceeded overseas in September of the following year. During his twelve months' service on the Western Front, he was in action in various sectors until severely wounded in the Battle of the Somme in 1916. He was invalided to England, and on his recovery was retained on home service until demobilised in March 1919, holding the 1914-15 Star, and the General Service and Victory Medals.
52, Montague Street, Collyhurst, Manchester.   Z8916

BRADDOCK, F. S., Private, R.A.S.C.
Volunteering in November 1915, he was sent to France three months later and was chiefly engaged as a wheelwright. He, however, was also employed in carrying supplies to the forward areas in the St. Eloi, Vermelles, the Somme, the Ancre, Arras and Cambrai sectors. He was demobilised in June 1919, and holds the General Service and Victory Medals.
28, Lyme Street, Chorlton-on-Medlock, Manchester.   Z1353

BRADEN, A. E., Private, R.A.S.C.
He volunteered in December 1915, and was engaged with his unit on important duties as a mechanical engineer until September 1917, when he was drafted to France. There he did excellent work at St. Omer, Hazebrouck, the Somme and other parts. He was demobilised in December 1919, after his return home, and holds the General Service and Victory Medals.
31, Bedford Street, Moss Side, Manchester.   Z9442B

BRADER, H., Sergt., 10th King's (Liverpool Regt., Liverpool Scottish).
He was mobilised in August 1914, and for a period of two years rendered valuable services with the R.A.M.C. at Whitworth Street Hospital. He was then transferred to the K.(L.R.) and proceeded to France, where he took part in the Battles at Arras, Lens, Cambrai, Armentières and Albert. In November 1918 he was discharged, and holds the General Service, Victory, and Long Service and Good Conduct Medals.
11, Tranmere Street, Gorton, Manchester.   TZ1354

BRADFORD, G. J., Pte., 2/6th North Staffordshire Regiment.
Joining in May 1916, he was employed on important duties in England until March 1918, when he was sent to the Western Front. There he served in numerous important engagements, including those at Arras, Soissons and Loos, and was also in action during the Retreat and Advance of 1918. Remaining in France until August 1919, he was demobilised at Ripon a month later, and holds the General Service and Victory Medals.
14, Williams Place, Ancoats, Manchester.   Z8917

BRADLEY, A., Pte., 16th (The Queen's) Lancers.
After joining in March 1917, he was sent to Egypt in the following year. He contracted fever and dysentery, and was in hospital in Cairo for a considerable time. In 1920 he was still serving in Egypt, and holds the General Service and Victory Medals.
31, Iron Street, Miles Platting, Manchester.   Z9443D

BRADLEY, C., Private, 21st Manchester Regiment.
He volunteered in October 1914, but after a period of service at Salford, was discharged in March 1915, in order to take up work of National importance. He was then engaged as a driller to the manufacture of hand grenades at Messrs. Mabbot and Co., Polland Street, Manchester, where he rendered valuable services until the cessation of hostilities.
1, Harper Street, Longsight, Manchester.   Z1355

BRADLEY, D., Driver, R.F.A.
He joined the R.F.A. in April 1916, and after training at Preston and Kinmel Park was a year later drafted to France. In this theatre of war he performed good work with his Battery at Arras, Ypres, Cambrai, the Somme, the Marne, Albert, Amiens and Le Cateau. After the termination of the war he was stationed in France until demobilised in January 1919, holding the General Service and Victory Medals.
48, Gibbon Street, Bradford, Manchester.   Z8918

BRADLEY, D., Pte., K.O. (Royal Lancaster Regt.)
He volunteered in August 1914, and in April of the following year was drafted to France, where he took part in the severe fighting at the Somme and Albert. He was unfortunately killed in action in the Somme sector on November 15th, 1916, and was entitled to the 1914-15 Star, and the General Service and Victory Medals.
"Honour to the immortal dead, who gave their youth that the world might grow old in peace."
31, Iron Street, Miles Platting, Manchester.   Z9443A

BRADLEY, H., Private, 16th Manchester Regt.
He volunteered in May 1915, and after his training was sent to France, where he took part in the severe fighting on the Somme, and was wounded. After being invalided home, he served at Cleethorps till he was demobilised in March 1919, holding the 1914-15 Star, and the General Service and Victory Medals.
31, Iron Street, Miles Platting, Manchester.   Z9443C

BRADLEY, H., Private, King's (Liverpool Regt.)
He joined in May 1917, but on completion of his training was not successful in procuring a transfer to the fighting areas. He served at Oswestry, Warrington and Chester, at which stations he performed the various duties assigned to him in a highly capable manner, and in February 1919 was demobilised from Heaton Park.
555, Collyhurst Road, Manchester.   Z11471

BRADLEY, H., Pte., 1st Royal Scots Fusiliers.
He volunteered in April 1915, and in August of the following year was drafted to France. During his service on the Western Front he took part in the Battles of Beaumont-Hamel, Beaucourt and the Ancre, before being seriously wounded in action at Arras in April 1917. Unfortunately he had to suffer amputation of his right leg, and after treatment in various hospitals in France and England, was invalided from the Service in July 1918. He holds the General Service and Victory Medals.
2, Brunswick Street, Hulme, Manchester.   Z1358

BRADLEY, S., Pte., 8th Loyal North Lancashire Regt.
Joining in May 1916, he proceeded to France in August and played a prominent part in the Battles of Beaumont-Hamel, Arras, Messines, Ypres and Cambrai. In January 1918 he was invalided to Netley Military Hospital, owing to a nervous breakdown, and was discharged medically unfit, in July of the same year. He holds the General Service and Victory Medals. 30, Guy Street, Ardwick, Manchester.   Z1356

BRADLEY, T., Sergt., 8th Manchester Regiment.
He volunteered in September 1914, and after his training at Southport and Crowborough, was drafted to France in 1915. Shortly afterwards he was sent to the Dardanelles, where he did much good work. In consequence of malaria he was invalided to Egypt, but on his recovery returned to the Western Front in 1916, and took part in many important engagements until the cessation of hostilities. He was demobilised in March 1919, and holds the 1914-15 Star, and the General Service and Victory Medals.
31, Iron Street, Miles Platting, Manchester.   Z9443B

BRADLEY, W., Private, 1/8th Manchester Regt.
He volunteered in September 1914, and was quickly drafted to Egypt, where he was in action during heavy fighting with the Turks in the Suez Canal zone. He contracted enteric fever and was invalided to hospital in Gibraltar, where he unfortunately died in November 1915. He was entitled to the 1914-15 Star, and the General Service and Victory Medals.
"His memory is cherished with pride."
18, William Street, Ardwick, Manchester.   Z1357

BRADSHAW, A., Pte., Loyal North Lancashire Regt.
He volunteered in January 1915, and four months later was drafted to the Western Front, where he took part in the Battles of Hill 60, Festubert, Ypres, Loos, Albert and Vimy Ridge (1916). He laid down his life for King and Country during the Somme Offensive in July 1916, and was entitled to the 1914-15 Star, and the General Service and Victory Medals
"Nobly striving,
He nobly fell that we might live."
39, Rylance Street, Ardwick, Manchester.   Z1359

BRADSHAW, H., Air Mechanic, R.A.F.
Volunteering in November 1914, he was retained on important duties, which called for a high degree of technical skill at various aerodromes in England. In January 1918 he was transferred to the Western Front, and saw heavy fighting at Ypres, Passchendaele, Nieuport and on the Somme. He was demobilised in February 1919, and holds the General Service and Victory Medals.
27, Churnett Street, Collyhurst, Manchester.   Z10303

BRADSHAW, H. J., Driver, R.A.S.C.
He volunteered in September 1914, and after a period of service in England was drafted to France in July 1916. Whilst on the Western Front, he was engaged as a motor ambulance driver and saw heavy fighting in the Somme, Vimy Ridge and the Sambre sectors. He was demobilised in April 1919, and holds the General Service and Victory Medals.
4, Elton Street, Chorlton-on-Medlock, Manchester.   Z1361

BRADSHAW, A., Private, 22nd Manchester Regt.
Four months after volunteering, he was drafted to the Western Front in May 1915, and took part in the Battles of Loos, Vermelles, the Somme, the Ancre and Messines, and in heavy fighting at Beaumont-Hamel, Beaucourt and Passchendaele. He laid down his life for King and Country at Ypres on September 24th, 1917, and was entitled to the 1914-15 Star, and the General Service and Victory Medals.
" The path of duty was the way to glory."
8, Hulton Street, Brooks Bar, Manchester. Z11651B

BRADSHAW, E., Private, R.A.M.C.
He was mobilised in August 1914, and proceeding to France with the 1st Expeditionary Force, served as a stretcher bearer at the Battle of Mons and in the subsequent Retreat, and at the Battles of Le Cateau, La Bassée, Ypres, Neuve Chapelle, Festubert and Albert. He then acted as a nursing orderly on an ambulance train, running between Boulogne and Marseilles, and in May 1918 proceeded to Italy on similar duties. He received his discharge in July 1919, and holds the Mons Star, and the General Service and Victory Medals.
8, Hulton Street, Brooks Bar, Manchester. Z11651A

BRADSHAW, J., Private, 2nd Manchester Regt.
When war was declared in August 1914, he volunteered and five months later was drafted overseas. Whilst serving in France he was in action in different sectors of the Front, and did good work with his unit at Ypres, the Somme, and Arras. He was unhappily killed in action in December 1915, and was entitled to the 1914-15 Star, and the General Service and Victory Medals.
" A valiant Soldier, with undaunted heart he breasted life's last hill." 4, Marsh Street, Ancoats, Manchester. Z9903

BRADSHAW, J. H., Private, Labour Corps.
He volunteered in January 1916, and two months later was drafted to the Western Front, where he was engaged on important trench digging and wiring duties in Belgium until May 1918. He was then moved into France and carried out salvage work in the Bapaume and Amiens sectors. In February 1919 he was demobilised, and holds the General Service and Victory Medals.
11, Spruce Street, Hulme, Manchester. Z1360

BRADSHAW, T., Private, R.A.M.C.
Volunteering in 1915, he was engaged on important medical duties at Colchester throughout the whole period of hostilities. Although unsuccessful in obtaining his transfer overseas, he nevertheless, rendered valuable services with his unit until his demobilisation in 1919.
14, Hancock Street, Rusholme, Manchester. Z1362A

BRADSHAW, W., Rifleman, 11th Rifle Brigade.
Having volunteered in August 1914, he was drafted to France in July of the following year, and took part in the Battles of the Somme, Arras, Ypres and Cambrai. He was also in action throughout the Retreat and Advance of 1918, and was demobilised in December of that year, holding the 1914-15 Star, and the General Service and Victory Medals.
41, Fitzgeorge Street, Collyhurst, Manchester. Z10304A

BRADSHAW, W., Private, South Wales Borderers.
He joined in August 1916, and in April of the following year was drafted to the Western Front, where he played an important part in the Battles of Arras, Ypres and Cambrai, and in the Retreat and Advance of 1918. He was twice wounded in action on the Somme in July 1917, and in March of the following year. In November 1918 he was invalided home with pneumonia, and was eventually demobilised in November 1919, holding the General Service and Victory Medals.
41, Fitzgeorge Street, Collyhurst, Manchester. Z10304B

BRADSHAW, W., Private, 2nd Manchester Regt.
He joined in March 1916, and in June was drafted to the Western Front. During his service in this theatre of war he took part in much severe fighting in various sectors and did consistently good work with his unit. He was demobilised in February 1919, and holds the General Service and Victory Medals. 14, Hancock Street Rusholme, Manchester. Z1362B

BRADSHAW, W., Bombardier, R.F.A.
Volunteering in May 1915, he was sent to the Dardanelles in the following July, and took part in the Landing at Suvla Bay. After the Evacuation of the Gallipoli Peninsula, he was transferred to Egypt, and fought at Sollum, Jiffjaffa, Katia, Romani and Magdhaba. In June 1917 he was drafted to the Western Front, where he was in action at the Battles of Ypres, Lens, Cambrai, the Somme (II) and the Marne (II), and in the Retreat and Advance of 1918. He was mentioned in Despatches for conspicuous gallantry, and was demobilised in February 1919, holding the 1914-15 Star, and the General Service and Victory Medals.
11, Gorse Street, Hulme, Manchester. Z1363

BRADWELL, C. S., Special War Worker.
In April 1915, he offered his services for work of National importance at Messrs. Armstrong and Whitworths, Manchester, where he was engaged in preparing the steel for manufacture into shells. He carried out his responsible duties in a very skilful manner throughout the whole period of hostilities. 66, William St., West Gorton, Manchester. Z1364

BRADY, D., Rifleman, 2nd Rifle Brigade.
A month after war was declared he volunteered, and in March 1915 proceeded overseas. Whilst serving on the Western Front he was wounded in action at Neuve Chapelle, and on his return to the firing line took part in the Battle of Hill 60. He was again wounded at Ypres, and also taken prisoner and kept in captivity until the close of hostilities. On his release he was demobilised in January 1919, and holds the 1914-15 Star, and the General Service and Victory Medals.
54, Sandal Street, Newton, Manchester. Z8919

BRADY, J., A.B., Royal Navy.
Volunteering in August 1915, he was sent to the North Sea, and was engaged on special duties during important Naval operations. He served on board H.M.S. " Caterham," " Shakespeare " and " Drake " and was in the last-named vessel when she was torpedoed off the North Coast of Ireland in October 1917. Fortunately he was rescued and later served in the Baltic against the Bolsheviks. In 1920 he was still at sea, and holds the General Service and Victory Medals.
23, Hamilton Street, Collyhurst, Manchester. Z10305B

BRADY, J., Private, King's Own Scottish Borderers.
He volunteered in October 1915, and in January of the following year was sent to France and was in action at Loos, Vimy Ridge, the Somme, Arras, Bullecourt, Messines, Ypres, Passchendaele and Cambrai. He also took part in the Retreat and Advance of 1918. In 1920 he was serving in India, and holds the General Service and Victory Medals.
5, Stonehewer Street, Ancoats, Manchester. Z9444B

BRADY, P., Private, Manchester Regiment.
He enlisted in April 1914, and on completion of his training, was engaged on important duties at various home stations. He was unsuccessful in obtaining his transfer overseas, but did consistently good work with his unit until October 1917, when he was discharged as medically unfit for further service.
23, Hamilton Street, Collyhurst, Manchester. Z10305A

BRAITHWAITE, T. (M.M.) Private, 1/7th Manchester Regiment.
He volunteered in May 1915, and in the following April was sent to Egypt, where he was in action at Katia before being transferred to France. Whilst on the Western Front he played a prominent part in the Battles of the Ancre, the Aisne (III), Bapaume, Havrincourt and Cambrai and was wounded in July 1917. During his service in Egypt he was in hospital at Port Said, suffering from fever. He was awarded the Military Medal for conspicuous gallantry in a bombing raid, and also holds the General Service and Victory Medals. He was demobilised on his return to England in March 1919.
11, Watson Street, Hulme, Manchester. Z1365

BRAMHALL, J. W., Private, 1/5th Border Regt.
He joined in January 1917, and in the following October was drafted to the Western Front, where he took part in the Battles of Cambrai, the Somme, Havrincourt and Ypres (IV), when he was wounded in action by a sniper in September 1918. He also took part in the Advance into Germany, and was demobilised in November 1919, holding the General Service and Victory Medals. 158, PalmerstonSt.,Beswick, Manchester.Z1367

BRAMHALL, W., Corporal, R.A.S.C. (M.T.)
Mobilised in August 1914, he was sent to France three months later and was present at the Battles of La Bassée, Ypres, Festubert and Loos. Early in 1916 he was transferred to Egypt, where he was engaged on special duties taking supplies to the forward areas, and later proceeded to Palestine. In this last theatre of war he carried out important work in connection with the prisoners of war. He was discharged in February 1918, and holds the 1914 Star, and the General Service and Victory Medals.
158, Palmerston Street, Beswick, Manchester. Z1366

BRAMLEY, J., Private, 8th Lancashire Fusiliers.
Volunteering in August 1914, he was sent to France in December 1916, and was transferred to the Manchester Regiment. He then took part in the Battles of Arras, Ypres, the Somme, Bapaume, Cambrai and Le Cateau, and in other engagements during the Retreat and Advance of 1918. He was demobilised in March 1919, and holds the General Service and Victory Medals. 39, Cedar Street, Hulme, Manchester. Z1368

BRAMMER, J., Gunner, R.F.A.
He joined in 1906, and at the outbreak of war in August 1914, was serving in India, but was immediately drafted to France. After being wounded in action at Ypres, he was transferred to Egypt in October 1915, and later proceeded to Salonika, where he took part in the heavy fighting on the Doiran front. He received his discharge in January 1919, and holds the 1914 Star, and the General Service and Victory Medals. 12, Birch Street, Ardwick, Manchester. Z1369

BRAMWELL, W. E., Private, Labour Corps.
He joined in May 1917, and was quickly drafted to France, where he was engaged on road construction and police duties in the Ypres, Passchendaele and Cambrai sectors. He was also present during the Retreat until June 1918, when he was invalided home (as a result of a breakdown in health) and discharged. He holds the General Service and Victory Medals.
32, Percy Street, Hulme, Manchester. Z1370

BRANAGAN, C., Pte., King's (Liverpool Regt.)
He joined in January 1917, and on conclusion of his training was ten months later sent overseas. During his year's service on the Western Front, he played an active part in engagements at Ypres, Armentières and Cambrai, and was severely wounded at Lille in October 1918. He was sent back to England, and after protracted hospital treatment at Birmingham and Manchester was discharged from the Army in March 1920, holding the General Service and Victory Medals.
11, Clayton Street, Newtown, Manchester. Z9005A

BRANAGAN, C. W., Private, Lancashire Fusiliers.
Joining in August 1917, he proceeded four months later to the Western Front. He served in this theatre of war for eleven months, and during that period was in action in the Retreat of 1918, and also performed excellent work with his unit in the final victorious engagements of the war. He was released from the Army in November 1918, on compassionate grounds, and holds the General Service and Victory Medals.
11, Clayton Street, Newtown, Manchester. Z9005B

BRANNAN, F., Cpl., 9th East Lancashire Regt.
Volunteering in September 1914, he was sent to Salonika twelve months later, and after taking part in the Serbian Retreat, unfortunatley died from dysentery on December 22nd, 1915. He was entitled to the 1914-15 Star, and the General Service and Victory Medals.
"His memory is cherished with pride."
12, George Street, Moss Side, Manchester. Z1371

BRANNICK, W., Pte., Loyal North Lancashire Regt.
He enlisted in August 1913, and when war broke out a year later, was at once ordered to the Western Front. There he fought in the Battles of Mons, La Bassée and Ypres, and was taken prisoner in December 1916. He remained in captivity at Wittenberg Camp until January 1919, and was employed in a sugar factory. He was discharged from the Army in August 1919 after his release, and holds the Mons Star, and the General Service and Victory Medals.
1, Marple Street, Ancoats, Manchester. Z9907

BRANNIGAN, A., Sapper, 330th R.E.
He volunteered in January 1916, and after a period of training was ordered to the Western Front. During his service there he was engaged in severe fighting at Amiens, Zillebeke, Bapaume, Dickebusch, Gauche Wood, and in many other important engagements, and was wounded in action. He was demobilised in July 1919, and holds the General Service and Victory Medals.
15, Key West Street, Beswick, Manchester. Z9906

BRANNON, J. W., Private, Border Regiment.
Joining in October 1917, he was drafted to the Western Front in the following March, and was in action on the Somme, before being taken prisoner at Festubert in April 1918. Whilst in captivity he was forced to carry ammunition behind the German lines until the cessation of hostilities. He was demobilised in February 1919, and holds the General Service and Victory Medals.
52, Blackthorn Street, Ardwick, Manchester. Z1372

BRASSINGTON, B., Pte., 14th King's (Liverpool Regt.)
He volunteered in April 1915, and in the following June proceeded to Salonika, where he served for over three years. During that period he took an active part in many engagements, and was in action on the Vardar, and Doiran fronts. He contracted malaria whilst serving in the East, and received treatment at various hospitals in Salonika. In February 1919 he was invalided out of the Army, and holds the 1914-15 Star, and the General Service and Victory Medals.
13, Wrigley Street, West Gorton, Manchester. Z9908

BRATBY, E. W., Pte., 1/8th Manchester Regiment.
When war broke out he volunteered, and later was sent to Egypt, but after serving at Alexandria and Cairo proceeded to Gallipoli. He was wounded during the campaign there and after the Evacuation of the Peninsula was transferred to France. There he fought at Vimy Ridge, and was again wounded on the Somme. On returning to the firing line he was in action at Bullecourt, Ypres and Cambrai, and in the Retreat and Advance of 1918. Demobilised in February 1919, he holds the 1914-15 Star, and the General Service and Victory Medals.
23, Dawson Street, West Gorton, Manchester. Z9909

BRATT, G., Private, Royal Welch Fusiliers.
He joined the Army in November 1916, and on completion of a period of training was three months later drafted to Palestine. In this theatre of war he took an important part in numerous engagements, and was unfortunately killed in action at Beersheba in November 1917. He was entitled to the General Service and Victory Medals.
"His life for his Country."
1, Gray Street, Ancoats, Manchester. Z9910

BRAY, F., Sapper, R.E.
He volunteered in November 1915, and in the following April proceeded to Egypt and served on the Suez Canal until February 1917, when he was transferred to the Western Front. There he was in action at Vimy Ridge and Ypres, and being gassed in the latter engagement, was sent back to England for

hospital treatment. On his return to France he took part in heavy fighting at Bapaume and Havrincourt and was eventually demobilised in February 1919, holding the General Service and Victory Medals.
14, Kingston Street, Hulme, Manchester. Z8920

BRAYFORD, T., Driver, R.A.S.C.
Volunteering in April 1915, he trained at Aldershot and Aylesbury, and seven months later was sent overseas. Whilst serving on the Western Front he was in action in the Loos and St. Eloi sectors, and was severely wounded at the latter place in February 1916. He was invalided to England and unhappily succumbed to his injuries on March 9th, 1916. He was entitled to the 1914-15 Star, and the General Service and Victory Medals.
"A costly sacrifice upon the altar of freedom."
18, Kendall Street, Bradford, Manchester. Z9911

BRECKELL, J. H., Private, King's Own Yorkshire Light Infantry.
He joined in January 1917, and was quickly drafted to the Western Front, where he saw much severe fighting. He was in action at the Battles of Arras, Ypres and Cambrai, and througout the Retreat and Advance of 1918. He remained in France until October 1919, when he was sent home for demobilisation, and holds the General Service and Victory Medals.
3, Seal Street, Collyhurst, Manchester. Z10306

BREEZE. J., H., Rifleman, Rifle Brigade.
Volunteering in September 1914, he was sent to France in the following May, and played a prominent part in the Battles of Ypres, Festubert, Albert, the Somme, Arras, Messines, Passchendaele and Cambrai. He was wounded in action on the Somme in March 1918, and was invalided home, but, after an operation in Grangethorpe Hospital, Manchester, unfortunately died on September 28th, 1919. He was entitled to the 1914-15 Star, and the General Service and Victory Medals.
"And doubtless he went in splendid company."
9, Gotha Street, Ardwick, Manchester. Z1373

BREMNER, E. A., Private, R.A.S.C. (M.T.)
He volunteered in November 1915, and was quickly drafted to France, where he was engaged on important transport duties in the Loos, St. Eloi, the Somme, Passchendaele and Cambrai sectors. He was chiefly employed in carrying wounded to various field hospitals. In May 1919 he was demobilised, and holds the 1914-15 Star, and the General Service and Victory Medals.
10, Chipping Street, Longsight, Manchester. Z1374

BRENNAN, C. H., Private, 5th Lancashire Fusiliers.
He joined in April 1917, and in the following September was drafted to the Western Front, where he was in action at the Battles of Cambrai and the Somme, and in the Retreat and Advance of 1918. He also took part in the march to the German Frontier, and was demobilised in February 1919, holding the General Service and Victory Medals.
8, Cross Street, Hulme, Manchester. Z1378B

BRENNAN, J., Private, R.A.M.C. (T.F.)
Mobilised with the Territorials in August 1914, he first saw active service with the 3rd East Lancashire Field Ambulance in Gallipoli, where he took part in the Landing in April 1915, and in the capture of Chunuk Bair. After the Evacuation of the Peninsula, he was transferred to the Western Front, and was in action at Guillemont, Péronne and Epéhy, where he was gassed in August 1917. In May 1918 he was transferred to Italy, but two months later returned to the Western Front, and was engaged on an ambulance train until February 1919. He was demobilised in March, and holds the 1914-15 Star, and the General Service and Victory Medals.
3, Marcus Grove, Rusholme, Manchester. Z1375

BRENNAN, J. (Miss), Special War Worker.
In April 1916, this lady took up work of National importance at the Westinghouse, Salford, and was engaged on the manufacture of munitions there until June 1917. She then went to Messrs, Mantlebury's, White City, where she was employed in the aeroplane fitting and finishing shops. She rendered valuable services throughout, and relinquished her duties in December 1918.
29, Mawson Street, Ardwick Green, Manchester. TX1377A

BRENNAN, J. W., Air Mechanic, R.A.F.
He joined in 1918, but on account of his age, was unable to procure a transfer overseas. He was, however, stationed at Lincoln throughout the period of his service, and employed on work requiring exceptional technical knowledge and skill, and was eventually demobilised in 1919.
25, Pierce Street, Ancoats, Manchester. Z9912A

BRENNAN, P., Air Mechanic, R.A.F.
He joined in March 1917, and on completion of his training was engaged on important duties, which called for a high degree of technical skill. Although he was unsuccessful in obtaining his transfer overseas, he nevertheless did much good work with his Squadron at various aerodromes until his demobilisation in May 1919.
6, Brunswick Street, Hulme, Manchester. Z1376

BRENNAN, P., Private, 16th Manchester Regiment.
He volunteered in September 1914, and early in the following year was drafted to the Western Front, where he played a prominent part in the Battles of Neuve Chapelle, Ypres, Albert and Vimy Ridge (1916). Unfortunately, he was killed in action on the Somme in July 1916, during a bombing raid, and was entitled to the 1914-15 Star, and the General Service and Victory Medals.
"A valiant Soldier, with undaunted heart he breasted life's last hill."
8, Cross Street, Hulme, Manchester. Z1378A

BRENNAN, T., Private, 1st Manchester Regiment.
Volunteering in November 1914, he was six months later drafted to Mesopotamia, where he was in action in many engagements. He took an active part in heavy fighting at Amara, Kut-el-Amara, Sanna-i-Yat, and the Tigris. Whilst serving on the Eastern Front he contracted malaria, and was in hospital at Amara and Alexandria. On returning to England, he was demobilised in June 1919, and holds the 1914-15 Star, and the General Service and Victory Medals.
137, Suddell Street, Ancoats, Manchester. Z8921

BRENNAN, T., Private, 2nd Manchester Regiment.
Mobilised in August 1914, he was at once drafted to the Western Front, and took part in the Battles of Mons, Le Cateau, La Bassée and Ypres. He was badly wounded in action in the La Bassée sector in December 1914, and was invalided home. On his recovery he was sent to Egypt in 1916, and remained there until his discharge in March 1919, holding the Mons Star, and the General Service and Victory Medals.
16, Windsor Street, Rochdale Road, Manchester. Z10307

BRENNAN, W., Private, 15th Lancashire Fusiliers.
He volunteered in September 1914, and twelve months later was drafted to the Western Front, where he rendered valuable services with his unit in various sectors, and was wounded in action by a sniper in November 1917. As a result, he was invalided from the Army in March 1918, and holds the 1914-15 Star, and the General Service and Victory Medals.
29, Mawson Street, Ardwick Green, Manchester. TZ1377B

BRERETON, J., Sergeant, 2nd Manchester Regt.
Volunteering in January 1915, he proceeded three months later to the Western Front. There he took a prominent part in important engagements at St. Eloi, Ypres, the Somme, St. Quentin, Arras, La Bassée, and whilst fighting in the Advance of 1918, was wounded. He was invalided to England, and on his recovery served at Cleethorpes and Yarmouth, at which stations he performed excellent work as an instructor. Demobilised in February 1919, he holds the 1914-15 Star, and the General Service and Victory Medals.
9, Howard Street, Ancoats, Manchester. Z9913

BRERTON, E., Private, 14th King's Own (Royal Lancaster Regiment).
He volunteered in August 1914, and later in the same year was drafted overseas. During his service on the Western Front he experienced fierce fighting in many engagements, and was also in action at Dickebusch, Ypres, and the Somme. He was gassed whilst in France, and invalided home in 1916, and in 1918 was discharged as unfit for further military duties. He holds the 1914 Star, and the General Service and Victory Medals.
11, Linson Street, Bradford, Manchester. Z9914

BRERETON, G., A.B., Royal Navy, H.M.S. "Donegal."
He volunteered in September 1914, and after training at Portsmouth was posted to H.M.S. "Donegal." In this vessel he performed excellent work as a gunner in the North Sea, but in July 1916 was severely injured, and was in hospital for five months. On returning to duty he served in H.M.S. "Unity," and was engaged in mine-sweeping in the North Sea. He was demobilised in March 1919, and holds the 1914-15 Star, and the General Service and Victory Medals.
42, Burns Street, Bradford, Manchester. Z9850B

BRETT, H., Private, 1st Border Regiment.
He joined in August 1916, and was quickly drafted to France, where he played a prominent part in heavy fighting at Ypres, and St. Eloi, before being taken seriously ill. After hospital treatment in France and at Canterbury, he was transferred to the Royal Air Force, with which unit he rendered valuable services until his demobilisation in February 1919, holding the General Service and Victory Medals.
7, Halton Street, Hulme, Manchester. Z11652

BRETT, J. D., Special War Worker.
For over four years he was employed on work of National importance at Ashbury's Munition Works, Manchester. He was engaged on special duties in connection with fitting gun carriages, and carried out his responsible and arduous work with the greatest ability. He did not relinquish his position until August 1919.
28, Gardner Street, West Gorton, Manchester. Z9915

BRETT, S., Private, Royal Welch Fusiliers.
He volunteered in June 1915, and was posted to the Royal Welch Fusiliers, but on being sent overseas was transferred to the Labour Corps. Whilst on the Western Front, he did good work with his unit in many sectors of the line, and saw heavy fighting in various engagements. He remained in France until demobilised in June 1919, holding the General Service and Victory Medals.
19, Martha Street, Bradford, Manchester. TZ11610C

BREWER, E., Private, 9th Border Regiment.
He volunteered in August 1914, and in June of the following year was sent overseas. Whilst serving in France he saw heavy fighting in the Loos sector, and then proceeded in August 1915 to Salonika. During his service there he was engaged chiefly on the Vardar front, until June 1918, when he returned home. He was then retained on home service until demobilised in January 1920, and holds the 1914-15 Star, and the General Service and Victory Medals.
198, Gorton Lane, Gorton, Manchester. Z9916

BREWER, R., L/Corporal, 13th Manchester Regt.
Volunteering in September 1914 in the following year he was drafted to France, and thence to Salonika, and was in action on the Vardar and Struma fronts, and at Monastir. In July 1918 he returned to France and took part in the Advance of that year. He was demobilised in January 1919, and holds the 1914-15 Star, and the General Service and Victory Medals.
31, Almond Street, Collyhurst, Manchester. Z9445

BREWERTON, H., Private, R.A.M.C.
A Reservist, he was called to the Colours in August 1914, and was drafted to France in the following month. He played an active part in the Battles of La Bassée, Ypres, Neuve Chapelle, Hill 60, Loos, Albert and the Somme, and in March 1917 was sent home for his discharge as time-expired. He holds the 1914 Star, and the General Service and Victory Medals.
33, Alder Street, Hulme, Manchester. Z1379

BREWSTER, A., Sergeant, 3rd Grenadier Guards.
Mobilised in August 1914, he was quickly drafted to the Western Front, where he served with distinction at the Battles of the Aisne, La Bassée, Ypres, Neuve Chapelle, St. Eloi, Hill 60, Loos, the Somme, Ypres (III), and Passchendaele, and was wounded in action in April 1915. He laid down his life for King and Country on the Somme on April 12th, 1918, and was entitled to the 1914 Star, and the General Service and Victory Medals.
"Great deeds cannot die: They, with the sun and moon renew their light for ever."
13, Carmen Street, Ardwick, Manchester. Z1381B

BREWSTER, A., Gunner, R.G.A.
He joined in March 1917, and six months later was drafted to Palestine, where he was wounded in action at the third Battle of Gaza in November 1917, but, on his recovery, was present at the capture of Jerusalem and Jericho, and in the Advance under General Allenby's Forces. He was demobilised in February 1919, and holds the General Service and Victory Medals.
13, Carmen Street, Ardwick, Manchester. Z1380

BREWSTER, A., Guardsman, Grenadier Guards.
He joined in April 1916, and four months later was drafted to the Western Front, where he was wounded during heavy fighting at Arras. He laid down his life for King and Country, in the same sector at the commencement of the Retreat, on March 23rd, 1918. He was entitled to the General Service and Victory Medals.
"The path of duty was the way to glory."
29, St. Ann Street, Bradford, Manchester. Z11875

BREWSTER, S., Private, 2nd Lancashire Fusiliers.
Mobilised in August 1914, he was immediately drafted to the Western Front, where he took part in the fighting at Mons. He also served through the Battles of Le Cateau, the Marne, La Bassée, Ypres, Neuve Chapelle, Hill 60, and Festubert, was wounded in action at Loos in October 1915, and was in hospital at Rouen. On his recovery he rejoined his unit, and after fighting at Albert, was unhappily killed in action on the Somme on October 12th, 1916. He was entitled to the Mons Star, and the General Service and Victory Medals.
"A costly sacrifice upon the altar of freedom."
13, Carmen Street, Ardwick, Manchester. Z1381A

BRIDDOCK, W., Pte., 3rd Manchester Regt. and King's (Liverpool Regt.)
He volunteered in September 1914, and in March of the following year was drafted to the Western Front, where he took part in the Battle of Ypres, and several minor engagements. He died gloriously on the Field of Battle at Loos on September 25th, 1915. He was entitled to the 1914-15 Star, and the General Service and Victory Medals.
"Honour to the immortal dead, who gave their youth that the world might grow old in peace."
13, Hampton Place, Erskine Street, Hulme, Manchester. Z1382

BRIDDON, G., Pte., Manchester Regt. and Pioneer, R.E.
He volunteered in January 1915, and was retained at various stations, where he was engaged on important duties as a drill instructor. He was not successful in obtaining his transfer to a theatre of war, but nevertheless, rendered very valuable services with his unit until November 1917, when he was invalided from the Army.
14, Hayfield, Street, Ardwick, Manchester. Z1384

BRIDDON, J. J., Rflmn., King's Royal Rifle Corps.
Volunteering in September 1914, he proceeded to the Western Front after three months' training, and there took part in the Battles of Neuve Chapelle, Ypres, and Loos, and other important engagements. In December 1915, he was transferred to Salonika, where he was again in action on the Doiran and Struma fronts, and at Monastir. He returned home in December 1918, and in the following February was demobilised, holding the 1914–15 Star, and the General Service and Victory Medals.
6, Hayfield Street, Ardwick, Manchester. Z1383

BRIDDON, L., Gunner, R.F.A.
He joined in 1916, and later in the same year was ordered to the Western Front, where he did good work with his Battery in many engagements. He was in action at Ypres, Festubert, Hill 60, the Somme, Vimy Ridge, Cambrai, and Mericourt. Whilst fighting on the Arras front he was severely wounded, and succumbed to his injuries shortly afterwards. He was entitled to the General Service and Victory Medals.
" The path of duty was the way to glory."
35, Piercy Street, Ancoats, Manchester. Z9917

BRIDGE, J., Private, 26th Manchester Regiment.
He volunteered for active service in September 1914, and sixteen months later was drafted overseas. During his four months service on the Western Front he did good work with his unit at Loos and St. Eloi, and was severely wounded in action at Albert. He was sent back to England, and invalided out of the Army in July 1916, holding the General Service and Victory Medals.
14, Kirtch Street, Ancoats, Manchester. Z8922

BRIDGEMAN, J., Sergt., 21st Manchester Regt.
Shortly after volunteering in August 1914, he was drafted to the Western Front, where he saw severe fighting in various sectors and was wounded in action. He took part in the Battles of Ypres, Neuve Chapelle, Hill 60, and Loos, and other important engagements until transferred to Italy, where he was wounded and taken prisoner on the Asiago Plateau. Held in captivity until after the cessation of hostilities, he was finally discharged in March 1919, holding the 1914 Star, and the General Service and Victory Medals.
3, Thomas Street, Hulme, Manchester. Z1386

BRIDGEMAN, J. E., Pte., 8th (King's Royal Irish) Hussars.
He was mobilised in August 1914, and was drafted to the Western Front in time to take part in the Retreat from Mons. After fighting also in the Battles of La Bassée, Ypres, Loos, Vimy Ridge, and the Somme, and many other important engagements, he was invalided home in January 1918. He was discharged as medically unfit for further service in July of that year, and holds the Mons Star, and the General Service and Victory Medals.
23, Phillip's Street, Hulme, Manchester. TZ1385

BRIDGEWOOD, T., Pte., 8th Manchester Regt.
Already in the Territorials when war broke out in August 1914, he proceeded to Egypt in the following month, and there served at various stations. In April 1915 he was transferred to the Dardanelles, where he took part in the first Landing at Gallipoli and fought in the Battles of Krithia. He was unhappily reported missing, and later killed in action on June 12th, 1915. He was entitled to the 1914–15 Star, and the General Service and Victory Medals.
" The path of duty was the way to glory."
38, Pump Street, Hulme, Manchester. Z1387

BRIERLEY, C., Private, 19th Manchester Regt.
Volunteering in August 1915, he was sent to France in March 1916. During his service on the Western Front he saw much severe fighting at St. Eloi, Vimy Ridge, and Albert, and was unfortunately killed in action at the Battle of the Somme on July 23rd, 1916. He was entitled to the General Service and Victory Medals.
" He died the noblest death a man may die,
Fighting for God and right and liberty."
22, Teer Street, Ancoats, Manchester. Z9918A

BRIERLEY, G., Rflmn., King's Royal Rifle Corps.
Joining in November 1917, he proceeded to the Western Front in the following July, and was seriously wounded in action a month later at Arras. After being operated on at a Base hospital, he was invalided home, and after further treatment at Leeds, was discharged in September 1918 as medically unfit for service. He holds the General Service and Victory Medals.
2, Cowper Street, Bradford, Manchester. TZ11653

BRIERLEY, J., Driver, R.F.A.
Shortly after volunteering in September 1915, he was drafted to the Western Front, where he saw severe fighting in various sectors, and took part in the Battles of Ypres and Passchendaele, and other engagements. He fell in action at Dickebusch on November 24th, 1917. He was entitled to the 1914–15 Star, and the General Service and Victory Medals.
2, Cowper Street, Bradford, Manchester. Z1325

BRIERLEY, J., Sapper, R.E.
Joining in April 1917, he was drafted to France in the following month, and there served in various sectors of the Front. He was engaged chiefly in conveying food to the forward areas and served at Ypres, La Bassée, Givenchy, Nieuport, Nieppe Forest, and Kemmel before being invalided home in October. After being for a time in hospital at Sheffield, he was demobilised in October 1919, holding the General Service and Victory Medals.
6, Wilson Street, Chester Road, Hulme, Manchester. Z1388

BRIERS, A., Private, 6th Lancashire Fusiliers.
Volunteering in August 1914, he was retained on important work at home until April 1916, when he was drafted to the Western Front. Whilst in action in the Battle of the Somme, he was severely wounded, and in consequence was rendered unfit for further fighting. On his discharge from hospital he performed valuable work as an orderly in one of the Base hospitals. He was demobilised in March 1919, and holds the General Service and Victory Medals.
33, Carisbrook Street, Harpurhey, Manchester. Z11472A

BRIERS, F., Private, 18th Lancashire Fusiliers.
He volunteered in January 1915, and in the following December was sent to the Western Front, where he was in action in the Battles of Loos, the Somme, Albert and Messines. During the German Offensive in March 1918, he was wounded and taken prisoner, and during his captivity endured many hardships. After the Armistice he was released, and was demobilised in August 1919, holding the 1914–15 Star, and the General Service and Victory Medals.
33, Carisbrook Street, Harpurhey, Manchester. Z11472B

BRIGGS, H., Private, 2nd Manchester Regiment.
Volunteering in August 1914, he was drafted to the Western Front in the following December, and there saw severe fighting in various sectors. He took part in the Battles of Hill 60, Ypres, Albert, the Somme, Arras, Cambrai, Bapaume, Amiens, Havrincourt, and Le Cateau, and many minor engagements, until the cessation of hostilities. He was demobilised in February 1919, and holds the 1914–15 Star, and the General Service and Victory Medals.
44, Nelson Street, Bradford, Manchester. Z1326

BRIGGS, J., Driver, R.F.A.
He joined in March 1917, and after two months' training, was sent to the Western Front, where he took part in many important engagements during the Retreat and Advance. After the cessation of hostilities he was sent with the Army of Occupation into Germany, and was there stationed at Cologne until his return home for demobilisation in September 1919. He holds the General Service and Victory Medals.
23, Teak Street, Beswick, Manchester. Z1389

BRIGHT, W., Private, R.A.S.C.
Mobilised in August 1914 he was shortly afterwards sent to France, and was engaged on important transport duties at Mons, La Bassée, Ypres, Givenchy, Loos, Vimy Ridge, the Somme, and Arras. After the cessation of hostilities he returned home, and in January 1919 was demobilised, holding the 1914–15 Star, and the General Service and Victory Medals.
35, Flower Street, Ancoats, Manchester. Z9446

BRINDLE, F., Private, Labour Corps.
He joined in June 1916, but on account of a physical disability was medically unfit for transfer overseas. He was engaged at his civil occupation as a joiner and rendered valuable services with his unit at various home stations until his demobilisation in January 1919.
181, Broadfield Road, Moss Side, Manchester. Z11654

BRINDLEY, J. T., Pte., King's (Liverpool Regt.)
He was mobilised in August 1914, and immediately drafted to France, where he took part in the Battles of Mons, and was wounded. On his recovery he fought at the Battles of Ypres (I) and (II), and Loos, and was again seriously wounded in action. In December 1915 he was discharged as medically unfit for further service, but on September 3rd, 1918, unfortunately died at home from the effects of his wounds. He was entitled to the Mons Star, and the General Service and Victory Medals.
" His memory is cherished with pride."
28, Brown Street, Ancoats, Manchester. Z11876

BRINDLEY, J., Corporal, 2nd Lancashire Fusiliers.
He volunteered at the outbreak of war in August 1914, and on completion of his training was engaged on special guard and escort duties at various home stations. Owing to medical unfitness, he was not transferred to a theatre of war, but did consistently good work with his unit until invalided from the Army with heart disease in January 1918.
8, Hurlbutt Street, Hulme, Manchester. Z11655

BRINE, D., Sapper, R.E.

He joined in February 1917, and was quickly drafted to France, where he played an active part in the Battles of Arras, Vimy Ridge, Bullecourt, Messines, Ypres (III), Cambrai, the Marne (II), Amiens, Bapaume, and Havrincourt. He returned to England for demobilisation in October 1919, and holds the General Service and Victory Medals.

25A, Sherwood Street, Rochdale Road, Manchester. Z10308

BRISKE, F., Private, Royal Welch Fusiliers.

He joined in September 1916, and after a period of training was drafted to France, where he fought at Loos, Bray, Amiens, and La Bassée, before being badly wounded and gassed on the Somme in August 1918. He was invalided to hospital in Liverpool, and was eventually demobilised in January 1919, holding the General Service and Victory Medals.

32, Whiteley Street, Rochdale Road, Manchester. Z11877

BRITTAIN, J., Pte., 1st King's Shropshire Light Infty.

Mobilised in August 1914, he was at once ordered to France, where he took part in the Battle of Mons and the subsequent Retreat. He was later in action on the Somme front, and at Ypres, La Bassée, Nieuport, Loos, Arras, and in other sectors, and rendered valuable services until he was killed in action on March 21st, 1918. He was entitled to the Mons Star, and the General Service and Victory Medals.

"Steals on the ear the distant triumph song."
46, Clare Street, Chorlton-on-Medlock, Manchester. Z8923

BROAD, H., Sergeant, 28th Manchester Regiment.

He joined in June 1916, and after completing a term of training served at various stations, where he was engaged on important clerical duties. He was unable to obtain his transfer to a theatre of war, but nevertheless rendered valuable services with his unit until September 1919, when he was demobilised.

31, Birch Street, West Gorton, Manchester. Z1390

BROADBENT, A., Corporal, R.E.

Mobilised in August 1914, he was immediately drafted to the Western Front, where he served through the Battle of Mons, and the subsequent Retreat. He also took an active part in the Battles of Ypres and Neuve Chapelle, was severely wounded in action on October 1915, and invalided home. He was recommended for decoration for bravery displayed in rescuing the wounded at Hill 60, in May 1915, and holds the Mons Star, and the General Service and Victory Medals. He was discharged in August 1916 as medically unfit for further service.

24, Gore Street, Greenheys, Manchester. Z1391

BROADBENT, E., Private, 1/8th King's Own Scottish Borderers.

He volunteered in September 1914, and ten months later proceeded to France, where he fought in the Battles of Loos and the Somme. He was wounded in action in April 1917, and unfortunately died of his injuries at the Casualty Clearing Station at Arras on April 25th, 1917. He was entitled to the 1914–15 Star, and the General Service and Victory Medals.

"His life for his Country, his soul to God."
10, Matilda Street, Ancoats, Manchester. Z9919

BROADBENT, H., C.S.M., 4th Royal Scots.

He volunteered in October 1914, and in June of the following year, proceeded to Egypt, where he fought in the capture of El Fasher and Magdhaba, and in other engagements. In November 1917 he was transferred to the Western Front, and there took a prominent part in the Battles of the Somme, the Marne, Bapaume, and Ypres, and the entry into Mons at dawn of Armistice day. He was demobilised in March 1919, and holds the 1914–15 Star, and the General Service and Victory Medals. 42, Phillips Street, Hulme, Manchester. Z1393

BROADBENT, T., Private, 4th King's Own Royal Lancaster Regiment.

He volunteered in August 1914, and in June of the following year was sent to the Western Front. Whilst in this theatre of war he fought in many important engagements, including the Battles of Albert, Ploegsteert Wood, and Vermelles, and was wounded in action in October 1916, during the Somme Offensive. He was demobilised in February 1919, and holds the 1914–15 Star, and the General Service and Victory Medals.

10, John Street, Openshaw, Manchester. Z1392

BROADHEAD, A., Private, South Wales Borderers.

In April 1918 he joined the Army, but was unable to procure a transfer to a theatre of war, before the cessation of hostilities. In 1919, however, he was sent to Germany, and served with the Army of Occupation until drafted at a later date to Ireland, where he was stationed in County Down. He was demobilised in September 1919.

185, Thornton Street, Manchester. Z11473B

BROADHEAD, W., Private, King's (Liverpool Regt.)

He joined in January 1917, and in the following year proceeded to Egypt, where he took an active part in repulsing the Turkish attacks on the Suez Canal. He also experienced severe fighting at Mersa Matruh, and on the termination of the war was engaged in important guard duties. He returned home in 1919, and was demobilised in January 1920, holding the General Service and Victory Medals.

185, Thornton Street, Manchester. Z11473A

BROWNHILL, A., Private, 1st Cheshire Regiment.

Shortly after the outbreak of war he volunteered, and in January 1915 he was sent to France where, after taking part in the Battles of Hill 60, Ypres, and the Somme, he was wounded at Arras in 1917. On returning to the firing line he was in action at Cambrai, and was again wounded at Arras in 1918. He was invalided to England, and was eventually demobilised in May 1919, holding the 1914–15 Star, and the General Service and Victory Medals.

6, Hilton Street, Harpurhey, Manchester. Z11474

BROADHURST, G., Private, 1st Manchester Regt.

Having enlisted in January 1908, he was already in the Army when war broke out in August 1914, and one month later, was drafted to the Western Front, where he took part in many important engagements. In December 1915 he was transferred to Mesopotamia, and was mortally wounded in action near Baghdad, dying in hospital on June 21st, 1916. He was entitled to the 1914 Star, and the General Service and Victory Medals. "Steals on the ear the distant triumph song."

1, Horsley Street, Chorlton-on-Medlock, Manchester. Z1394

BROADHURST, H., L/Corporal, 6th Lancashire Regiment, and 1/4th East Lancashire Regt.

He volunteered in August 1914, and shortly afterwards was drafted to Egypt, whence he proceeded in the following year to the Dardanelles. There he saw much severe fighting at Cape Helles, and wounded in action at Suvla Bay, returned to Egypt, and was afterwards transferred to the Western Front. He took part in many important engagements in this theatre of war, was gassed at Havrincourt, and taken prisoner on the Somme in March 1918. Held in captivity until the cessation of hostilities, he was finally demobilised in March 1919, and holds the 1914–15 Star, and the General Service and Victory Medals. 3, Newman Street, Ancoats, Manchester. X1395

BROADHURST, V. (M.S.M.), Sergeant, R.E.

Volunteering in June 1915 he was sent to France later in the same year, and took part in numerous engagements, including those at Vermelles, Albert, the Somme, Ypres, Cambrai, Lens, Bapaume, and Le Cateau. He was awarded the Meritorious Service Medal for extricating his men from a poison gas area, and also holds the 1914–15 Star, and the General Service and Victory Medals. He was demobilised in February 1919.

61, Kemp Street, Ancoats, Manchester. Z9447

BROADHURST, W., Private, M.G.C.

He volunteered in August 1914, and in the following year was drafted to the Western Front, and was in action at Neuve Chapelle, Hill 60, Ypres, Loos, St. Eloi, Vimy Ridge, Bullecourt, Messines, the Aisne, the Marne, and Bapaume. He was demobilised in November 1919, and holds the 1914–15 Star, and the General Service and Victory Medals.

4, Brief Street, Ancoats, Manchester. Z9448

BROADHURST, W. H., Private, Lancashire Fusiliers.

Volunteering in August 1914, he proceeded in May 1915 to Gallipoli, but after serving at Krithia, Achi Baba, and Suvla Bay, was invalided to England. In May 1916 he was sent to France, and fought in engagements at the Somme, Arras, and Ypres. He was severely wounded at Loos, and taken prisoner, and unhappily succumbed to his injuries in April 1918. He was mentioned in Despatches for bravery in the Field, and devotion to duty, and was entitled to the 1914–15 Star, and the General Service and Victory Medals.

"Great deeds cannot die."
33, Hope Street, Bradford, Manchester. Z9920

BROADY, J., L/Corporal, R.A.S.C.

He volunteered in January 1915, and a year later was ordered to the Western Front, where he was in action at Loos, the Somme, Arras, Ypres, Givenchy, Nieuport, Cambrai, and Delville Wood, and was present during the Entry into Mons. After the Armistice he proceeded with the Army of Occupation to Germany, and served there until demobilised in July 1919. He holds the General Service and Victory Medals.

2, Railway Street, Oldham Road, Manchester. Z9921

BROBBIN, J., Pte., S. Lancashire Regt., and M.G.C.

Volunteering in January 1915, he proceeded six months later to Gallipoli, where he took part in severe fighting at Suvla Bay and Chunuk Bair. At the end of the Campaign on the Peninsula, he was sent to Mesopotamia, and was in action at Kut, Um-el-Hannah, the Tigris, and Baghdad. Whilst in the East he contracted malaria and enteric, and was sent to hospital in India. On his return home he was demobilised in May 1919, and holds the 1914–15 Star, and the General Service and Victory Medals.

37, Cyrus Street, Ancoats, Manchester. Z9922

BROCKBANK, A., Driver, R.F.A.

Two months after joining in February 1917, he was drafted to the Western Front, where he saw severe fighting in various sectors. He took part in the Battles of Cambrai, the Somme, and the Marne, and many minor engagements, fought also in the Retreat and Advance of 1918, and was wounded in action. He was demobilised in March 1919, and holds the General Service and Victory Medals.

3, Aden Street, Ardwick, Manchester. Z1397B

BROCKBANK, H. H., Gunner (Signaller) R.F.A.
He joined in December 1916, having previously been engaged on work of National importance, and, after completing a period of training was retained on special duties at various stations. Unable to obtain his transfer to the Front, he nevertheless, rendered valuable services with his Battery until February 1919, when he was demobilised.
10, Shrewbridge Street, West Gorton, Manchester. TZ1396

BROCKWELL, W., Private Lancashire Fusiliers.
He enlisted in 1913 and seven months after the outbreak of war in August 1914, proceeded to the Western Front, where he took part in the Battles of Neuve Chapelle and Hill 60, and several minor engagements. He fell fighting in the second Battle of Ypres in May 1915. He was entitled to the 1914–15 Star, and the General Service and Victory Medals.
"Whilst we remember, the sacrifice is not in vain."
3, Aden Street, Ardwick, Manchester. Z1397A

BRODERICK, J., Pte., R.M.L.I., and Labour Corps.
After working on munitions at Trafford Park for some considerable time, he joined the Army in February 1918, and a month later was sent to France. During his service overseas, he was stationed at Dunkirk and performed consistently good work whilst employed unloading ships, and on various other duties in connection with transport. He was demobilised in March 1919, and holds the General Service and Victory Medals.
16, Vance Street, Oldham Road, Manchester. Z8924

BRODERICK, J. (D.C.M.), Sapper, R.E.
Mobilised in August 1914, he proceeded to Egypt in March of the following year, and was thence transferred to Gallipoli in the following month. There he took part in the Landing at Cape Helles, and, engaged on various important duties, was present at the Battles of Krithia, the Landing at Suvla Bay, and the capture of Chunuk Bair. He unhappily fell in action in August 1915. He had been awarded the Distinguished Conduct Medal, and a Serbian decoration for conspicuous bravery in the Field, was mentioned in Dispatches for distinguished service in Gallipoli, and was entitled also to the 1914–15 Star, and the General Service and Victory Medals.
"His memory is cherished with pride." Z1398A
19, Higher Ormond Street, Chorlton-on-Medlock, Manchester

BRODERICK, W., Private, Cheshire Regt. and Worcestershire Regiment.
He joined in April 1917, and twelve months later was drafted to the Western Front, where he saw severe fighting in various sectors. He took part in the Battles of the Somme, the Aisne, Bapaume and Ypres and other important engagements, served also through the Retreat and Advance of 1918, and was wounded in action. He was invalided from the Army in December 1918, and holds the General Service and Victory Medals. 1398B
19, Higher Ormond Street, Chorlton-on-Medlock, Manchester.

BROGAN, E., Private, 11th Manchester Regiment.
Volunteering in August 1914, he was sent in the following year to the Dardanelles, where he took part in the Landing at Suvla Bay, and the action at Chunuk Bair. In 1916 he was transferred to France and was engaged in the fighting at St. Eloi, Albert, the Somme, Ploegsteert Wood, Arras, Bullecourt, Cambrai and in many other engagements, and was wounded. He was demobilised in 1919, and holds the 1914–15 Star, and the General Service and Victory Medals.
23, Baguley Street, Miles Platting, Manchester. Z9450

BROGAN, J., Rifleman, Rifle Brigade.
He volunteered in September 1914, and in the following year was drafted to France, and took part in the Battle of Ypres. He fell fighting at Loos on January 14th, 1916, and was entitled to the 1914–15 Star, and the General Service and Victory Medals.
"And doubtless he went in splendid company."
12, Wragley Street, Miles Platting, Manchester. Z9449B

BROGAN, J. H., Driver, R.F.A.
On attaining military age he joined the Army in June 1918 after having been employed by the Bradford Colliery Company in supplying coal to the various munition factories in Manchester. He was unsuccessful in obtaining a transfer to the war zone, but nevertheless, performed excellent work as a driver at Prees Heath and Bettersfield Park, until demobilised in July 1919. 4, Duke Street, Bradford, Manchester. Z9923

BROGAN, W., Private, 1st Manchester Regt. and Sapper, R.E.
Having previously served in the South African campaign he volunteered in August 1914, and proceeded overseas in the same year. Whilst serving on the Western Front he fought at La Bassée, Ypres, Givenchy, St. Vaast, Laventie, and Neuve Chapelle. In 1915 he was sent to Mesopotamia, where he took part in fierce fighting at Es Sinn. He was later transferred to India and served at Poona, Bangalore and Raman. He was invalided home in 1918, and in consequence was discharged as medically unfit in August 1918. He holds the Queen's and King's South African Medals, 1914 Star, and the General Service and Victory Medals.
18, Granville Place, Ancoats, Manchester. Z9924

BROGDEN, H., Private, Lancashire Fusiliers.
Joining in July 1916, he was drafted to the Western Front in the following December and there saw much heavy fighting He took part in many important engagements in this theatre of war, including the Battles of the Ancre, Arras, Vimy Ridge, Messines, Ypres, Cambrai, the Somme, the Aisne, the Marne and Havrincourt. He was demobilised in March 1919, and holds the General Service and Victory Medals.
24, George's Avenue, Chester Road, Hulme, Manchester. Z2400B

BROGDEN, N., Private, 5th Manchester Regiment.
He volunteered in August 1917, and after three months' training proceeded to the Western Front. Whilst in this theatre of war he saw much heavy fighting, took part in the Battles of St. Eloi, Albert, Ploegsteert Wood and the Somme and other engagements, and was gassed and wounded in action. He was for some months in hospital before being invalided from the Army in February 1918, and holds the 1914–15 Star, and the General Service and Victory Medals.
44, Boardman Street, Ardwick, Manchester. Z1399

BROMLEY, R., Driver, R.A.S.C.
After volunteering in December 1914, he was retained on important duties at home until January 1917, when he proceeded to the Western Front. There, engaged in conveying food and ammunition to the forward areas, he was present at the Battles of Arras, Ypres, Passchendaele and Cambrai, served also through the Retreat and Advance of 1918 and was gassed in August of that year. He was demobilised in July 1919, and holds the General Service and Victory Medals.
19, Hancock Street, Rusholme, Manchester. Z2401

BROOKBANK, A., Private, R.A.S.C.
He volunteered in September 1914, and after training at Liverpool was later in the same year drafted to the Western Front, where he rendered valuable services in conveying ammunition to the firing line. He was engaged in fierce fighting in the Somme, Passchendaele, the Ancre, Arras and Cambrai sectors and served in France until November 1918. Demobilised in January 1919, he holds the 1914 Star, and the General Service and Victory Medals.
175, Brook Street, Miles Platting, Manchester. TZ6042

BROOKES, A., Private, R.A.S.C.
He joined in April 1916, and after a period of training was engaged on important transport duties, conveying remounts to France. He rendered very valuable services with his Company during the period of hostilities, and was finally demobilised in April 1919. He holds the General Service and Victory Medals.
22, Collin's Street, Hulme, Manchester. Z2402

BROOKES, A., Corporal, 19th Welch Regiment.
He joined in May 1916, and seven months later was drafted to the war zone. During his service on the Western Front he took an active part in severe fighting at Arras, Bullecourt, Ypres and Cambrai, and was wounded at the Battle of the Somme in May 1918. Sent back to hospital in England, he was subsequently demobilised in December 1918, holding the General Service and Victory Medals.
24, Lowe Street, Oldham Road, Manchester. Z9925

BROOKES, E., Private, 7th Lancashire Fusiliers.
Volunteering in April 1915, he was drafted to Gallipoli in October of the same year and there saw much severe fighting at Suvla Bay, Salt Lake, Chocolate Hill and many other places. He made the supreme sacrifice, falling in action on December 9th, 1915, during the Evacuation of the Peninsula. He was entitled to the 1914–15 Star, and the General Service and Victory Medals.
"He joined the great white company of valiant souls."
3, Alpha Street, Hulme, Manchester. Z2403

BROOKES, H., Corporal, 1/7th Manchester Regt.
He volunteered in August 1914, and was retained on important duties at home until April 1916, when he was drafted to Egypt. There he took part in the fighting at Katia, El Fasher and Romani and other important engagements before being transferred to France in March 1917. He fought in the Battles of Arras, Bullecourt and Ypres, and gassed in action, was invalided home. He was discharged in August 1917 as medically unfit for further service, and holds the General Service and Victory Medals.
66, Howarth Street, High Street, Chorlton-on-Medlock, Manchester. Z2404

BROOKES, R., Sergt., 1st Cheshire Regiment.
When war was declared he was mobilised and proceeded with the First Expeditionary Force to France. There he fought with distinction in the Battles of Mons, Ypres and the Somme. In 1917 he was transferred to the Italian front, but after a year's service there returned to France and fell fighting on August 21st, 1918. He was mentioned in Despatches for conspicuous gallantry in the Field and was awarded the Belgian Croix de Guerre. He was also entitled to the Mons Star, and the General Service and Victory Medals.
"Great deeds cannot die:
They with the sun and moon renew their light for ever."
15, Ross Street, West Gorton, Manchester. Z9926

BROOKES, W., Private, East Surrey Regiment.
Joining in April 1916, he was retained on home service until November 1917, when he was sent to the Western Front. During his service in this theatre of war he was in action in the 1918 Retreat, and also took part in the final engagements of the war. He contracted trench fever, and was in consequence discharged from the Army in December 1918, holding the General Service and Victory Medals.
47, Burn Street, Bradford, Manchester. Z9927

BROOKS, S., Rifleman, 4th Rifle Brigade.
He volunteered in October 1914, and in the same month was sent to France, where he took part in the fierce fighting at La Bassée and Ypres. He was unfortunately killed in action at the Battle of Neuve Chapelle on March 6th, 1915, and was entitled to the 1914 Star, and the General Service and Victory Medals.
"Courage, bright hopes, and a myriad dreams, splendidly given."
16, Bright Street, Rochdale Road, Manchester. Z9451

BROOKS, T. H., Private, 7th Manchester Regiment.
He volunteered in January 1916, and after a brief period of training was engaged on important duties at various stations, where he rendered valuable services with his unit. Unable owing to ill-health to obtain his transfer to a theatre of war, he was invalided from the Army in May 1916.
22, St. Clements Place, Grey Street, Manchester. Z2406

BROOKS, W., Rifleman, 8th Rifle Brigade.
Volunteering in August 1914, he was drafted to the Western Front in May of the following year, and there fought in various sectors. He took part in the Battles of Ypres, Albert, Ploegsteert Wood, Vimy Ridge, the Somme, Arras, Passchendaele and Cambrai and other engagements and served also through the Retreat and Advance of 1918. He was demobilised in February 1919, and holds the 1914–15 Star, and the General Service and Victory Medals.
67, Earl Street, Longsight, Manchester. Z2405

BROOM, T., Private, 13th Manchester Regiment.
He volunteered in November 1915, and in the following October proceeded to Salonika. In this theatre of war he took part in severe fighting near Monastir, and in several engagements on the Doiran front, where he was wounded in May 1917. Evacuated to England, he remained in hospital in London until June 1918, when he was invalided out of the Army as unfit for further service, holding the General Service and Victory Medals.
25, Gladstone Street, West Gorton, Manchester. Z8925

BROOME, G., Private, 2/1st E. Lancashire Regt., and R.A.M.C.
Joining in July 1916, he was drafted to France in the following December and there served in various ssctors of the Front. He was engaged on important duties whilst in this theatre of war, and was for a time undergoing treatment in hospital at Boulogne. He was demobilised in July 1919, and holds the General Service and Victory Medals.
26, Nelson Street, Bradford, Manchester. Z2408

BROOME, J. H., Private, Manchester Regiment.
He enlisted in the Army in 1909, and after seeing service at various places proceeded to the Western Front in June 1915. During two years' service in that theatre of war he fought at different parts of the Ypres Salient, at Arras, Bullecourt, and during the Somme Offensive, and was wounded no less than seven times. In consequence of these injuries he was invalided home and discharged as unfit for further service. He holds the 1914–15 Star, and the General Service and Victory Medals.
10, Castleton Street, Bradford, Manchester. Z9933

BROOME, W., Private, R.M.L.I.
He joined in July 1916, and on completing his training in January of the following year proceeded to sea on board a submarine, in which he served in the Mediterranean Sea for a considerable period, chiefly off the coast of Malta. He holds the General Service and Victory Medals, and in 1920 was still at sea in East Indian waters.
21, Dearden Street, Hulme, Manchester. Z2407

BROOMER, C., Bombardier, R.F.A.
He was mobilised in August 1914, and in May 1915 was drafted to Egypt, where he took part in numerous engagements, including that at Romani. In February 1917 he was transferred to the Western Front, where he did excellent work with his Battery at Ypres, and in the Retreat and Advance of 1918. He served in France until April 1919, when he was discharged, holding the 1914–15 Star, and the General Service and Victory Medals.
39, Albion Street, Miles Platting, Manchester. Z9928

BROOMHEAD, R., Sapper, R.E.
Joining in January 1917, he proceeded to the Western Front in the following month and there served in various sectors. He took an active part in the Battles of Ypres and Cambrai and many other important engagements in this theatre of war and served also through the Retreat and Advance of 1918. He was demobilised in February 1919, and holds the General Service and Victory Medals.,
46, Meadow Street, Ardwick, Manchester. Z2409

BROOMHEAD, T., Private, 2nd Manchester Regt.
When war was declared in August 1914, he was already serving in the Army and accordingly at once proceeded with the First Expeditionary Force to the Western Front. He was unhappily killed during the heavy fighting in October 1914, after having taken part in the Retreat from Mons. He was entitled to the Mons Star, and the General Service and Victory Medals.
"Great deeds cannot die,
They with the sun and moon renew their light for ever."
2, Stanley Street, Hulme, Manchester. Z8926A

BROTHERDALE, J., Private, 23rd Manchester Regt.
He volunteered in November 1914, and a year later was drafted overseas. During his service on the Western Front he took an active part in engagements in the Ypres sector, and was gassed at the Battle of the Somme. On returning to the firing line he was engaged in severe fighting at Arras, Nieuport and La Bassée. He was demobilised in January 1919, and holds the 1914–15 Star, and the General Service and Victory Medals.
8, Schofield Street, Ancoats, Manchester. Z9929

BROTHERTON, J., Private, Lancashire Fusiliers.
Mobilised at the outbreak of war in August 1914, he was immediately drafted to the Western Front and took part in the Battle of, and the Retreat from, Mons and the Battles of Le Cateau, the Marne, the Aisne and Ypres (I and II). He was then badly wounded in action and invalided to hospital at Woolwich. On his recovery he returned to France and rendered valuable services whilst engaged on special duties at Etaples. He was discharged in February 1919, and holds the Mons Star, and the General Service and Victory Medals.
7, Hamilton Street, Hulme, Manchester. Z11657

BROTHERTON, T. J., Pt., 1st King's Liverpool Regt.
He volunteered in January 1915, and in the following May was drafted to the Western Front. There he took part in the Battles of Ypres, Loos and the Somme, and was twice wounded in action and finally invalided home. On his recovery he was engaged on important agricultural duties until his demobilisation in April 1919. He holds the 1914–15 Star, and the General Service and Victory Medals.
14, Blossom Street, Hulme, Manchester. TZ2410

BROTHERTON, W., L/Corpl., K. (Liverpool Regt.)
He joined in September 1916, and on completion of his training was drafted to the Western Front early in 1917, and took a prominent part in the Battles of Arras (where he was wounded in action), Lens, Cambrai, the Marne (II) and Le Cateau (II). He was demobilised on his return to England in January 1919, and holds the General Service and Victory Medals.
56, Charlton Street, Collyhurst, Manchester. Z11656

BROUGHAM, E. (Miss) Special War Worker.
During the war this lady was engaged on canteen duties at one of the munition factories. She rendered valuable services whilst carrying out her duties in a highly commendable manner for four years. She relinquished her work in January 1919.
41, Francis Street, Chorlton-on-Medlock, Manchester. X2412B

BROUGHAM, Eva., Special War Worker.
During the war this lady rendered valuable services on work of National importance. In June 1915 she went to the National Shell Factory at Manchester and carried out arduous duties on a hydraulic press, in connection with the manufacture of munitions. She gave every satisfaction until January 1919, when she relinquished her duties. X2412A
41, Francis Street, Chorlton-on-Medlock, Manchester.

BROUGHAM, W., Engineer, Merchant Service.
He was already in the Mercantile Marine at the outbreak of war in August 1914, and during hostilities was engaged on important duties in the English Channel and the Mediterranean, carrying foodstuffs and troops. He also made several journeys to Canada and served on board s.s. "Manchester Mariner," "Manchester Miller," "Manchester Commerce" and "Inventor," being attacked by an enemy submarine, whilst in the last-named vessel in January 1917. In May 1919 he resumed his pre-war duties in the Merchant Service, and holds the General Service and Mercantile Marine War Medals.
22, Alder Street, Hulme, Manchester. Z2411

BROUGHTON, J., Private, 9th S. Lancashire Regt.
Volunteering in April 1915, he was sent to Salonika at the end of the same year and took part in the Landing. He was afterwards in action during heavy fighting on the Struma, Vardar and Doiran fronts and at Monastir, but was unfortunately killed at the second Battle of the Vardar in September 1918. He was entitled to the 1914–15 Star, and the General Service and Victory Medals.
"His life for his Country, his soul to God."
5, Charles Street, Bradford, Manchester. TZ2413

BROWN, A., Driver, R.F.A.

He joined in January 1918, on attaining military age, but whilst in training at Preston, was found to be suffering from a defective heart, and was therefore discharged in the following April, as medically unfit for further service.
15, Eskrindge Street, Ardwick, Manchester. Z2415B

BROWN, A., Private, Royal Scots.

He volunteered in March 1915, and three months later proceeded to the Western Front, where he played a prominent part in the Battles of Loos, the Somme and Arras, during which engagement he was badly wounded in action in April 1917. He was invalided home, but after a period of hospital treatment in Kent, was sent on important duties to Glasgow. He holds the 1914–15 Star, and the General Service and Victory Medals and was demobilised in March 1919.
51, Caroline Street, Hulme, Manchester. TZ2422

BROWN, A., Private, 13th Manchester Regiment.

Having volunteered in August 1914, he was drafted to France in the following year. In January 1916 he was transferred to Salonika, where he took part in engagements on the Doiran, Struma and Monastir fronts. In 1918 he returned to France and was in action at Amiens and Bapaume and was wounded and invalided home. He was demobilised in January 1919, and holds the 1914–15 Star, and the General Service and Victory Medals.
27, Pearson Street, Newton Heath, Manchester. Z9452

BROWN, A. F.W., Private, Loyal N. Lancashire Regt.

He volunteered in January 1915, and in the following November was drafted to Mesopotamia. After taking part in the heavy fighting during the attempt to relieve Kut, he was unhappily killed in action in April 1916. He was entitled to the 1914–15 Star, and the General Service and Victory Medals.
" Nobly striving,
He nobly fell that we might live."
10, Holt Street, Longsight, Manchester. Z2421

BROWN, A. J., Driver, R.A.S.C.

Volunteering in September 1915, he was quickly drafted to the Western Front, where he was engaged on important transport duties in the forward areas and saw heavy fighting at the Battles of Ypres, Beaumont-Hamel, Bullecourt and the Somme (II) and in the Retreat and Advance of 1918. After the Armistice he served in Germany with the Army of Occupation until his return home for demobilisation in January 1919, and holds the 1914–15 Star, and the General Service and Victory Medals.
19, Robson Street, Hulme, Manchester. Z2423

BROWN, B., Private, 13th Manchester Regiment.

He volunteered in August 1914, and proceeded to France in the following year. Whilst on the Western Front he took part in the Battles of Ypres (II), Loos, Givenchy, the Somme, Arras and St. Quentin. He was then transferred to Mesopotamia and served at Kut, but later returned to France and fought at Ypres. He holds the 1914–15 Star and the General Service and Victory Medals, and was demobilised in March 1919.
40, Nelson Street, Rochdale Road, Manchester. Z11878

BROWN, C., Private, R.A.S.C. (M.T.)

He joined in April 1916, and in the following September was sent to Mesopotamia, where he was engaged on important transport duties. He remained in this theatre of war till December 1919, when he returned to England, and in the following months was demobilised. He holds the General Service and Victory Medals.
83, Nicholson Street, Rochdale Road, Manchester. Z9454

BROWN, E., Private, 1/8th Argyll and Sutherland Highlanders.

He volunteered for active service in April 1915, and on completion of his training was eight months later sent to the Western Front, where he served for only four months. He saw heavy fighting at Ypres and was unfortunately killed in action there on April 9th, 1916. He was entitled to the 1914–15 Star, and the General Service and Victory Medals.
" Nobly striving,
He nobly fell that we might live."
13, Higham Street, Miles Platting, Manchester. Z9930

BROWN, E. A., Private, 2/6th Manchester Regt.

He joined in August 1916, and five months later was sent on active service. Whilst on the Western Front he took part in the Battles of Ypres, Lens, Passchendaele, Cambrai, the Somme and Béthune and in heavy fighting at Festubert, Loos, Givenchy and La Bassée. In June 1918 he was invalided home, and after hospital treatment at Ipswich and Manchester, was eventually demobilised in March 1919, holding the General Service and Victory Medals.
7, Lindum Street, Rusholme, Manchester. TZ2424

BROWN, F., Private, 6th Border Regiment.

Volunteering in November 1914, he was in the following June sent to Gallipoli. There he saw heavy fighting at Suvla Bay and Chunuk Bair, and after the Evacuation proceeded to Egypt. On this front he took part in engagements at Sollum, Katia and El Fasher and in August 1916 was transferred to France. He served on the Western Front until after the close of hostilities and was in action at Arras, Bullecourt, Ypres, Cambrai and in the Retreat and Advance of 1918. Demobilised in March 1919, he holds the 1914–15 Star, and the General Service and Victory Medals.
88, Heyrod Street, Ancoats, Manchester. Z9931

BROWN, F., Sapper, R.E.

Volunteering in October 1914, he proceeded in January of the following year to the Western Front. There he was in action in engagements at Neuve Chapelle, Ypres, Loos, St. Eloi, Vermelles, the Somme, Arras, Messines, Cambrai, the Marne and the Sambre. He served in France until December 1918, when he was demobilised, holding the 1914–15 Star, and the General Service and Victory Medals.
4, School Street, Bradford, Manchester. X11879

BROWN, F. W., Private, 23rd Manchester Regt.

He volunteered in the Bantam Battalion in November 1914, and was drafted to the Western Front in January 1916. After taking part in the Battles of the Somme and Arras, he was badly wounded in action at the Battle of Messines in May 1917, and was invalided home. He was in hospital at Guildford for fifteen months and was then discharged as medically unfit for further service in July 1918, holding the General Service and Victory Medals.
9, Chatsworth Street, Hulme, Manchester. Z11658

BROWN, F. W., Air Mechanic, R.A.F.

He joined in April 1918, and after a period of training was engaged on special work in connection with the fitting and repairing of machine guns on aeroplanes. He was unsuccessful in obtaining his transfer overseas but rendered valuable services with his Squadron until his demobilisation in January 1919.
47, Henry Street, Ardwick, Manchester. Z11887

BROWN, G., Private, 21st Manchester Regiment.

Volunteering in January 1915, he was drafted to France in the following November and took part in heavy fighting at Loos, Albert and Vimy Ridge and in the Battle of the Somme. He laid down his life for King and Country at the Battle of Arras on May 12th, 1917, and was entitled to the 1914–15 Star, and the General Service and Victory Medals.
" A costly sacrifice upon the altar of freedom."
12, Belleek Street, Hulme, Manchester. Z2430A

BROWN, G., Pte., Duke of Cornwall's Light Infantry.

He joined in February 1917, and early in the following year was drafted to the Western Front, where he took part in much severe fighting during the Retreat and Advance of 1918. He died gloriously on the Field of Battle on September 29th, 1918, and was entitled to the General Service and Victory Medals.
" Great deeds cannot die:
They with the sun and moon renew their light for ever."
6, Lamb Street, Richmond Grove, Longsight, Manchester
Z2414

BROWN, G. H., Pte., King's Shropshire Light Infy.

Four months after volunteering in April 1915, he was drafted to the Western Front, where he took part in the Battles of Loos, the Somme, the Ancre, Arras, Vimy Ridge, Messines, Ypres, Cambrai and the Marne (II). He was also in action during the Retreat and Advance of 1918, and whilst in France was wounded on the Somme in July 1916, at Arras in the following year and on the Marne in August 1918. He was invalided to England in October 1918, and was eventually demobilised in February 1919, holding the 1914–15 Star, and the General Service and Victory Medals.
9, Hyde View, Grey Street, Ardwick, Manchester. Z2425

BROWN, G. H., Private, Manchester Regiment.

Joining in May 1917, he was on conclusion of a period of training seven months later, drafted to Salonika, where he served for fifteen months. During that time he was in action in numerous engagements and took an active part in fierce fighting on the Struma and the Doiran fronts. On his return to England in March 1919, he re-enlisted for a further period of service, and holds the General Service and Victory Medals.
63, Jersey Street Dwellings, Ancoats, Manchester. Z8927

BROWN, J., Sergt., 1/7th Manchester Regiment.

Mobilised with the Territorials in August 1914, he was sent to Egypt in the following month and served at Khartoum until April 1915, when he was drafted to the Dardanelles. Whilst on the Gallipoli Peninsula he took part in the Landings at Cape Helles and Suvla Bay and in the three Battles of Krithia, being slightly wounded in action during the second engagement. After the Evacuation he proceeded to the Western Front, where he took part in the heavy fighting at Loos and Albert, the Battles of the Somme, Arras, Bullecourt, Ypres, Lens, Cambrai, the Marne and Bapaume and during the Retreat and Advance of 1918. He was wounded in action on the Somme and gassed at Ypres. In February 1917 he was demobilised and holds the 1914–15 Star, and the General Service and Victory Medals.
31, Walnut Street, Hulme, Manchester. TZ2427

BROWN, H., Private, North Staffordshire Regiment.
He volunteered in August 1915, and on completion of his training was sent to France in the following February. During his service on the Western Front he saw much severe fighting in the Ypres and Armentières sectors and was badly wounded in action in September 1918. Invalided to England, he was in hospital at Manchester before being discharged as medically unfit for further service in February 1919. He holds the General Service and Victory Medals.
2, Forest Street, Erskine Street, Hulme, Manchester. Z2426

BROWN, J., Private, 2nd Devonshire Regiment.
Volunteering in January 1915, he was sent to the Western Front four months later and took a prominent part in the Battles of Loos, Albert, the Somme, the Ancre, Arras and Vimy Ridge. He laid down his life for King and Country at Messines in June 1917 whilst on wiring operations after the attack, and was entitled to the 1914-15 Star, and the General Service and Victory Medals.
"Nobly striving, he nobly fell that we might live."
10, Chatsworth Street, Hulme, Manchester. Z11659

BROWN, J., L/Cpl., 1st K.O. (Royal Lancaster Regt.)
A Reservist, he was called to the Colours at the outbreak of war in August 1914, and after taking part in the Battle of Mons, was taken prisoner at Le Cateau in the same month. During his captivity in Germany he suffered many hardships, and was forced to work in the fields. He was released after the Armistice, and eventually discharged in March 1919, holding the Mons Star, and the General Service and Victory Medals.
11, Blackburn Street, Marple Street, Hulme, Manchester. Z2428

BROWN, J., Private, Army Cyclist Corps.
He joined in June 1917, and in the following year proceeded overseas. During his service on the Western Front he was engaged in carrying Despatches, and also took part in operations on the Aisne and the Marne, and was in action in the Retreat of 1918. After the Armistice he was stationed at Boulogne and served with the Regimental Staff at the Demobilisation Centre until December 1919, when he was himself demobilised, holding the General Service and Victory Medals.
79, Dale Street, Miles Platting, Manchester. Z8928

BROWN, J., Private, 1st Manchester Regiment.
Volunteering in July 1915, he was sent to Mesopotamia in the following January and saw severe fighting at Kut-el-Amara, Um-el-Hannah, Sanna-i-Yat and on the Tigris. In February 1917 he was transferred to Palestine and took part in the Battles of Gaza and the capture of Jerusalem, Jericho and Aleppo with General Allenby's Forces. He was demobilised in July 1919, and holds the General Service and Victory Medals.
3, Platt Street, Moss Side, Manchester. Z2429

BROWN, J., Private, South Lancashire Regiment.
He joined in February 1917, and in the following December was drafted to the Western Front, where he was transferred to the 18th Manchester Regiment and was taken prisoner at Ypres in the same month. During his captivity at Dülmen in Germany, he suffered many privations and was repatriated in February 1919. He was then immediately demobilised, and holds the General Service and Victory Medals.
12, Pump Street, Hulme, Manchester. Z2431A

BROWN, J., Gunner, R.F.A. (T.F.)
Volunteering in May 1915, he was drafted to the Western Front twelve months later and took part in much severe fighting at Dickebusch, St. Julien, St. Jean and on the Yser Canal before being badly wounded at Ypres in June 1917. After treatment in hospital at St. Omer until May 1918, he was invalided home to Ilford and Liverpool, and was discharged as medically unfit for further service, holding the General Service and Victory Medals.
9, Chipping Street, Longsight, Manchester. Z2432

BROWN, J., C.S.M., Loyal North Lancashire Regt.
He volunteered at the outbreak of war in August 1914, and proceeded overseas in the following year. During his service on the Western Front he played a conspicuous part in engagements at Hill 60, Ypres, Festubert, Albert, Vimy Ridge, the Somme, Arras, Cambrai, Armentières, Havrincourt and Avions but was unhappily killed in action on November 11th, 1918, half an hour before the Armistice came into force. He was entitled to the 1914-15 Star, and the General Service and Victory Medals.
"He passed out of the sight of men by the path of duty and self-sacrifice."
25, Pierce Street, Ancoats, Manchester. Z9912B

BROWN, J., Sergt., K.O. (Royal Lancaster Regt.)
In August 1914 he volunteered, and in the following year proceeded to Gallipoli, where he took a prominent part in very severe fighting. He was in action at Suvla Bay and other engagements, and was unfortunately killed in action late in 1915 just before the Evacuation of the Peninsula. He was entitled to the 1914-15 Star, and the General Service and Victory Medals.
"Courage, bright hopes, and a myriad dreams splendidly given."
25, Pierce Street, Ancoats, Manchester. Z9912C

BROWN, J., Private, King's (Liverpool Regiment).
He joined in April 1916, but proving to be medically unfit for active service, was not successful in obtaining a transfer to a theatre of war. He was stationed at Oswestry during his period of service and carried out his various duties with great ability. He was discharged from the Army in June 1918 as medically unfit for further military duties.
117, Mills Street, Ancoats, Manchester. Z9932

BROWN, J. E., Private, 2nd Manchester Regiment.
Volunteering in February 1915, he was under orders for India on completion of a period of training, but, owing to his being subject to epileptic fits, was retained on important duties at home until April 1916, when he was invalided from the Army.
12, Pump Street, Hulme, Manchester. Z2431B

BROWN, J. E., Private, Argyll and Sutherland Highlanders.
Volunteering in January 1915, he was drafted to France in the following December and was in action at Loos and at the Battles of Albert, Vimy Ridge and the Somme, before being killed in December 1916. He was entitled to the 1914-15 Star, and the General Service and Victory Medals.
"He died the noblest death a man may die,
Fighting for God and right and liberty."
12, Belleek Street, Hulme, Manchester. Z2430B

BROWN, J. R., Private, Lancashire Fusiliers.
He volunteered in November 1914, and after a period of service in England, was drafted to the Western Front, where he was in action at Festubert, at the Battles of the Somme, Arras, Ypres, St. Quentin and Cambrai, and in the Retreat and Advance of 1918. After three years in France he was demobilised in March 1919, and holds the General Service and Victory Medals.
6, Pump Street, Hulme, Manchester. Z2433

BROWN, J. W., Sapper, R.E.
He joined in August 1918, but owing to the early cessation of hostilities was not able to obtain his transfer overseas. He was therefore engaged on important duties as a fitter and did consistently good work with his unit at various stations until his demobilisation in January 1919.
47, Henry Street, Ardwick, Manchester. Z11888

BROWN, L., Corporal, 3rd Manchester Regiment.
He volunteered in March 1915, and in May was drafted to the Western Front, where he played a conspicuous part in the Battles of Loos, St. Eloi (1916), the Somme, Arras, Ypres, Bapaume, Havrincourt, and Cambrai. He was wounded in action at Bapaume and Cambrai, and was invalided home in November 1918. After hospital treatment at Sheffield, Doncaster, and Higher Broughton, he was discharged in December 1918, holding the 1914-15 Star, and the General Service and Victory Medals.
155, Rosebery Street, Moss Side, Manchester. Z2417

BROWN, P., Corporal, Military Mounted Police.
He volunteered in the 4th (Queen's Own) Hussars in September 1914, but in January 1916 was transferred to the Military Mounted Police and drafted to France. Whilst on the Western Front he was engaged on important duties in the Somme, Ypres, Arras, Albert, La Bassée, Givenchy, Festubert, Lens, and Cambrai sectors. He also served in the Retreat and Advance of 1918, and after the cessation of hostilities, proceeded to Germany with the Army of Occupation. He was demobilised in September 1919, and holds the General Service and Victory Medals.
159, Hartington Street, Moss Side, Manchester. Z2434

BROWN, P., Private, 19th (Queen Alexandra's Own Royal) Hussars.
He joined in November 1917, and on completion of his training, was engaged on important garrison duties with his Squadron in Ireland. Although unsuccessful in obtaining his transfer to a theatre of war, he rendered valuable services as a trumpeter until February 1919, when he was demobilised.
7, Back Pump Street, Hulme, Manchester. Z11660

BROWN, R. (Miss), Special War Worker.
She offered her services in April 1916 at Messrs. Vickers, White-Lund, near Morecambe, and did consistently good work in the T.N.T. department until the following August, when she was forced to relinquish her duties owing to T.N.T. poisoning, for which she was under treatment several months.
10, Emma Street, Ardwick, Manchester. Z2420

BROWN, S. J., Private, 14th Royal Welch Fusiliers.
He joined in November 1917, and on completion of his training in the following April, proceeded to France. There he took part in many important engagements on various sectors of the front, and was gassed in action at Fins near Epéhy, during the Advance of 1918. He was demobilised in February 1920, and holds the General Service and Victory Medals.
52, Robert Street, Chorlton-on-Medlock, Manchester. X11661

BROWN, T. E., Private, R.A.S.C. (M.T.)

He volunteered in June 1915, and later in the same year was sent to Egypt, where he was stationed at Cairo, Alexandria, and Kantara. Afterwards he proceeded to Palestine, and was engaged on important transport duties at Gaza, and Jericho, and in the Advance to Jerusalem. He was demobilised in May 1919, and holds the 1914-15 Star, and the General Service and Victory Medals.

6, St. George's Buildings, Rochdale Road, Manchester. Z9455

BROWN, W., Private, Bedfordshire Regiment.

In May 1916 he joined the Army, and after six months' training was drafted overseas in the following November. Whilst serving on the Western Front, he was in action in many sectors of the line, and was severely wounded at Bertincourt in March 1918. He was sent to hospital in France, and later to England, and was eventually demobilised in February 1919, holding the General Service and Victory Medals.

12, Malpas Street, Bradford, Manchester. Z8929

BROWN, W., Pioneer, R.E.

He joined in June 1917, and in the following February was drafted to France, where he was chiefly engaged as a signaller on the lines running between the trenches and Divisional Headquarters. He played an active part in the Battles of the Somme (II), and Amiens, and in the Retreat and Advance of 1918. In January 1919, he was demobilised, and holds the General Service and Victory Medals.

12, Sessay Street, Hancock Street, Hulme, Manchester. Z2437

BROWN, W., Gunner, Tank Corps.

He joined in June 1916, and in December was drafted to France. During his service on the Western Front, he took part in many important engagements, including the Battles of Ypres, Passchendaele, and Cambrai, and was wounded in action. He was demobilised in January 1919, and holds the General Service and Victory Medals. X2435-36B

47, Robert Street, Chorlton-on-Medlock, Manchester.

BROWN, W. Private, 1/8th Manchester Regiment.

Volunteering in January 1915, he was sent to the Western Front in the following November, and first took part in heavy fighting at Loos, and St. Eloi early in 1916. He also served at the Battles of Albert, Vimy Ridge, the Somme, and the Ancre, where he was unhappily killed in action in January 1917. He was entitled to the 1914-15 Star, and the General Service and Victory Medals.

" The path of duty was the way to glory."

15, Eskrigge Street, Ardwick, Manchester. Z2415A

BROWN, W. A., Private, King's (Liverpool Regt.)

Joining in April 1918, he was medically unfit for transfer overseas, and was therefore retained on important duties at prisoner of war camps in Wales. He rendered valuable services in this capacity until his demobilisation in November 1919.

41, Gorton Road, Lower Openshaw, Manchester. Z2416

BROWN, W. J., Private, 11th Manchester Regiment.

Volunteering in May 1915, he first saw active service in the following August, when he took part in the Landing at Suvla Bay in the Dardanelles, and the Capture of Chunuk Bair. After the Evacuation of the Gallipoli Peninsula, he served on the Suez Canal defences for a short time before proceeding to the Western Front, where he was in action at the Battles of the Somme, Arras, Messines, Ypres, and Cambrai. He was badly wounded at Hulluch in June 1918, and as a result, lost his left ear. In September 1918 he was invalided from the Service, and holds the 1914-15 Star, and the General Service and Victory Medals.

28, Garibaldi Street, Ardwick, Manchester. Z2438

BROWN, W. R., Sergeant, 1st Manchester Regt.

He enlisted in April 1903, and at the outbreak of war in August 1914, was stationed in India, whence he immediately embarked for France. Whilst on the Western Front, he served with distinction at the Battles of La Bassée, Ypres, Hill 60 (where he was wounded in action), Loos, Vermelles, the Somme, Arras, and Cambrai. In 1920 he was still serving, and holds the 1914 Star, and the General Service and Victory Medals.

108, Thomas Street, West Gorton, Manchester. Z2418-9A

BROWNE, S., Private, 2nd E. Lancashire Regiment.

Having volunteered in September 1914, he was drafted to France in the following year, and was in action at Ypres, Festubert, Loos, St. Eloi, Albert, Vimy Ridge, and the Somme, where he was wounded. He was invalided home, and after a period in hospital was discharged, owing to his injuries, in August 1918. He holds the 1914-15 Star, and the General Service and Victory Medals.

4, Mansfield Street, Oldham Road, Manchester. TZ9453

BROWNE, T., Rifleman, 4th Cameronians (Scottish Rifles).

Mobilised in August 1914, he immediately proceeded to France and took part in the Battles of Mons, Le Cateau, the Marne, the Aisne, La Bassée, Ypres, and Neuve Chapelle, where he was badly wounded in action in March 1915. After hospital treatment at Versailles and in Scotland, he was eventually

discharged as medically unfit for further service, and holds the Mons Star, and the General Service and Victory Medals.

20, Birch Street, Moss Side, Manchester. Z2439

BROWNHILL, T., Corpl., 2nd Lancashire Fusiliers.

A Reservist, he was called to the Colours in August 1914, and immediately drafted to France, but, after taking a prominent part in the Battle of Mons, was unfortunately killed in action during the Retreat early in September. He was entitled to the Mons Star, and the General Service and Victory Medals.

" Nobly striving,
He nobly fell that we might live."

42, Oliver Street, Bradford, Manchester. Z2440

BRUCE, H., Pte. (Signaller), 5th King's (L'pool Regt.)

He joined in January 1918, but being under age for transfer overseas, was engaged on important duties with his unit in Wales, and at Aldershot, and rendered valuable services until his demobilisation in December 1919.

58, Lingard Street, Hulme, Manchester. Z2442B

BRUCE, J., Private, Royal Fusiliers.

He volunteered in October 1914, and proceeding in January 1916 to France, took part in heavy fighting at Loos, the Somme, and Arras. He was then transferred to the Labour Corps, and sent to Italy, where he rendered valuable services in the construction of roads and trenches. After taking part in the Offensive on the Piave, his health broke down and he was sent back to England. Demobilised in January 1919, he holds the General Service and Victory Medals.

5, Albion Terrace, Miles Platting, Manchester. Z6043

BRUCE, J., Private, R.A.S.C.

He volunteered in September 1914, and after a period of training was engaged on important transport duties at Aldershot until March 1915. He was then discharged as medically unfit for further service, owing to a physical infirmity.

12, Major Street, Ardwick, Manchester. Z2441

BRUCE, W., Private, 2/6th Manchester Regiment.

He joined in August 1916, and four months later was drafted to the Western Front, where he played a prominent part in the Battles of the Ancre, Arras, Bullecourt, Messines, Ypres, Cambrai, and the Aisne. He was also in action during the Retreat and Advance until August 1918, when he was badly gassed in the Marne sector. After hospital treatment at Etaples and Manchester, he was invalided from the Service in November 1918, and holds the General Service and Victory Medals.

58, Lingard Street, Hulme, Manchester. Z2442A

BRUMBILL, H., Rflmn., 1st Cameronians (Scottish Rifles).

When war was declared in 1914, he was already serving, and was at once ordered overseas with the First Expeditionary Force. He took an active part in fierce fighting at Mons, the Marne, and the Aisne, but sustaining severe injuries was invalided home, and subsequently discharged as medically unfit for further service in December 1914. He holds the Mons Star, and the General Service and Victory Medals.

38, Heyrod Street, Ancoats, Manchester. Z9934

BRUMFITT, H., Private, 17th Manchester Regiment.

He volunteered in August 1914, and early in the following year was drafted to France, where he took part in the Battles of Neuve Chapelle, Hill 60, Ypres, Loos, and Albert, before being badly wounded in action on the Somme in June 1916. He was invalided to hospital at Stockport, but, on his recovery, was again sent to the Western Front, and was seriously wounded at the Battle of Arras in April 1917. Unfortunately he had to suffer amputation of his right leg, and after treatment at Colchester and Brighton, was invalided from the Service in June 1918, holding the 1914-15 Star, and the General Service and Victory Medals.

14, Harrowby Street, Hulme, Manchester. Z2443

BRUNT, R., Sergt., Manchester Regiment.

Four months after volunteering, he was drafted to France in December 1915, and served with distinction at Ypres, and at the Battles of the Somme and Ypres (1917). He made the supreme sacrifice on April 4th, 1918, when he was killed in action during the Retreat. He was entitled to the 1914-15 Star, and the General Service and Victory Medals.

" A valiant soldier, with undaunted heart he breasted life's last hill."

5, Small Street, Ardwick, Manchester. Z24444

BRUNTON, G. F., Private, 1st Border Regiment.

Volunteering in August 1914, he first saw active service in the Dardanelles, where he took part in the Landing at Cape Helles in April 1915, and in heavy fighting in Gallipoli until the Evacuation of the Peninsula. He was then in action at the Battles of Beaumont-Hamel, Bullecourt, Ypres, and the Somme (II), in the Retreat and Advance of 1918 on the Western Front. Whilst overseas he was wounded, but remaining with his unit, proceeded to Germany with the Army of Occupation. He was eventually demobilised in April 1919, and holds the 1914-15 Star, and the General Service and Victory Medals.

11, Barrack Street, Hulme, Manchester. Z2445

BRYAN, H., Private, 2nd Royal Irish Regiment.
He joined in July 1917, and after a period of training at Queenstown proceeded in April 1918 to France. There he performed valuable work as a despatch carrier, but was unfortunately killed in action in the Battle of the Somme on May 28th, 1918. He was entitled to the General Service and Victory Medals.
"Nobly striving,
He nobly fell that we might live."
25, Cransworth Street, Chorlton-on-Medlock, Manchester.
Z2446A

BRYAN, J. T., Private, East Lancashire Regiment.
He volunteered in January 1915, and on completion of his training at Preston was drafted overseas in the following year. During his service on the Western Front he was wounded in the Battle of Ypres, and invalided to hospital in London. On his recovery he returned to France, but was unhappily killed in action on July 1st, 1916, during the Somme Offensive. He was entitled to the General Service and Victory Medals.
"His life for his Country, his soul to God."
12, Pratley Street, Ravald Street, Ancoats.
Z10890

BRYAN, T., Private, 1/8th Manchester Regiment.
When war was declared he volunteered, and a month later was sent to Egypt. After serving at Alexandria and in Cyprus, he proceeded to Gallipoli, and was in action at Cape Helles and Krithia, but fell fighting at Achi Baba in June 1915. He was entitled to the 1914-15 Star, and the General Service and Victory Medals.
"Honour to the immortal dead, who gave their youth that the world might grow old in peace."
25, Cransworth Street, Chorlton-on-Medlock, Manchester.
Z2464B

BRYANT, L., Private, R.A.M.C.
He joined in March 1917, and after training at Blackpool was in the following year sent to Egypt. There he served in the hospital at Alexandria, and rendered valuable services to the wounded, until the close of hostilities. In June 1919, he re-enlisted for a further period of two years, and in 1920 was serving at Alexandria. He holds the General Service and Victory Medals.
131, Edensor Street, Beswick, Manchester.
Z8996B

BRYANT, W., Private, Manchester Regiment.
He joined in November 1916, and in the following February was drafted to the Western Front, where he took part in the Battles of Arras, Ypres, and Cambrai, and was wounded in action at the last-named engagement in November 1917. He was invalided home to hospital at Canterbury, and was eventually discharged in August 1918 as medically unfit for further service, holding the General Service and Victory Medals.
23, Seal Street, Collyhurst, Manchester.
Z10309

BRYCE, G., Private, 2nd Argyll and Sutherland Highlanders.
He enlisted in February 1901, and took part in the latter stages of the South African Campaign. At the outbreak of war in August 1914, he was immediately drafted to France, where he took part in the Battles of Mons and Le Cateau, being taken prisoner during the latter engagement. Whilst in captivity he suffered many hardships, and was poisoned by the food given at Doeberitz Camp. He was repatriated and discharged in December 1918, but shortly afterwards, died from the effects of his treatment in Germany. He already held the Queen's and King's South African Medals, and was entitled to the Mons Star, and the General Service and Victory Medals.
"A costly sacrifice upon the altar of freedom."
51, Rusholme Road, Chorlton-on-Medlock, Manchester.
TX2448B

BRYCE, H., Corporal, King's (Liverpool Regiment).
He joined in February 1916, and after his training was engaged on important duties with his unit at various stations in England. He was not successful in obtaining his transfer overseas during hostilities, but, in May 1919, was sent to France, and rendered valuable services, whilst attached to a Chinese Labour Battalion at Noyelles. He was demobilised in November 1919.
51, Rusholme Road, Chorlton-on-Medlock, Manchester.
TX2447

BRYCE, J., Sapper, R.E.
He joined in August 1917, and on completion of his training was engaged on special duties with the Inland Water Transport at Chepstow. He was not successful in obtaining his transfer overseas, but nevertheless did much good work until his demobilisation in December 1918.
51, Rusholme Road, Chortlon-on-Medlock, Manchester.
TX2448A

BRYNING, T. H., Private, Highland Light Infantry.
Volunteering in February 1915, he underwent a period of training, and was then engaged on special duties in England and Scotland. He rendered valuable services, but owing to medical unfitness, was unsuccessful in obtaining his transfer overseas, and was demobilised in April 1919.
2, Phelan Street, Collyhurst, Manchester.
Z10310

BUCK, F., A.B., Royal Navy.
He joined in July 1917, and after a period of training was posted to H.M.S. "Impregnable" at Devonport. Later he proceeded to Russia on special service, and was eventually sent to the Bosphorus, where his ship cruised off Constantinople until August 1919. In 1920 he was serving on board H.M.S. "Revenge" in home waters, and holds the General Service and Victory Medals.
40, Margaret Street, West Gorton, Manchester.
Z2449

BUCKLAND, C. R., Corporal, 7th (Princess Royal's) Dragoon Guards.
A Reservist, he was called to the Colours in August 1914, and immediately drafted to the Western Front, where he was engaged on important duties with the horses of his unit. He was invalided home in the following October, and after a period of service in England was discharged in November 1915 as medically unfit for further military duty. He holds the 1914 Star, and the General Service and Victory Medals.
8, Clayton Street, Hulme, Manchester.
Z2450

BUCKLEY, A., L/Corporal, 2nd Border Regiment.
Already in the Army at the outbreak of war, he was drafted to France in August 1914, and took part in the Battles of the Aisne, Ypres (I), Neuve Chapelle, Ypres (II), Loos, Albert, and the Somme, and was wounded at Beaumont-Hamel. Invalided to England, he spent six months in hospital, and then returned to the Western Front, where he was in action at the Battles of Ypres (III), Cambrai, and the Somme (II), and was again wounded at the 2nd Battle of Cambrai in the Advance of 1918. He was once more invalided home, and was eventually discharged in December 1919, holding the 1914 Star, and the General Service and Victory Medals.
10, Matlock Place, Hulme, Manchester.
Z11662

BUCKLEY, T., Private, 1st Manchester Regiment.
He enlisted in November 1910, and when war broke out in August 1914, was stationed in India, but immediately sailed for France with the 1st Indian Expeditionary Force. On landing in France he went into action at Givenchy, and later took part in the Battles of La Bassée, Ypres, Neuve Chapelle, Hill 60, and Festubert. In December 1915 he was transferred to Mesopotamia, where he was in action at Kut-el-Amara, and Baghdad, and was wounded at Dajalia Redoubt in April 1917. He was discharged to the Reserve in January 1919, and holds the 1914 Star, and the General Service and Victory Medals.
118, Thomas Street, West Gorton, Manchester.
Z2454

BUCKLEY, J., T., Pte., Loyal N. Lancashire Regt.
Mobilised in August 1914, he proceeded to France with the 1st Expeditionary Force, and took part in the Retreat from Mons, and the Battles of the Marne, and the Aisne. He was unfortunately reported missing in October 1914, and is now presumed to have been killed in action. He was entitled to the Mons Star, and the General Service and Victory Medals.
"Thinking that remembrance, though unspoken, may reach him where he sleeps."
13, Higher Chatham Street, Chorlton-on-Medlock, Manchester.
Z2453A

BUCKLEY, J. T., Corporal Shoeing Smith, R.F.A.
He volunteered in August 1914, and early in the following year was sent to Egypt, but quickly proceeded to Salonika. Whilst in this theatre of war, he took part in the Retreat from Bulgaria in November 1915, and was also in action in many important engagements on the Vardar, Doiran, and Struma fronts. He was demobilised in May 1919, and holds the 1914-15 Star, and the General Service and Victory Medals.
41, Garden Street, Ardwick, Manchester.
Z2456

BUCKLEY, R. W., Private, 2nd Manchester Regt.
He joined in November 1917, and two months later was drafted to the Western Front, where he took part in the Battles of the Somme (II), the Aisne (III), the Marne (II), the Scarpe and Cambrai (II). In February 1919 he was transferred to Mesopotamia, where he was still serving in 1920, and holds the General Service and Victory Medals.
86, Margaret Street, West Gorton, Manchester.
Z2452

BUCKLEY, W., Private, King's (Liverpool Regt.)
He was mobilised in August 1914, and proceeding to France immediately, took part in the Battle in the Retreat from Mons. He was also in action at the Battles of the Marne, La Bassée, Ypres, Loos, the Somme, and Arras, and at the entry into Mons on Armistice Day. After the cessation of hostilities, he went to Germany with the Army of Occupation, and in 1920 was still serving. He holds the Mons Star, and the General Service and Victory Medals.
35, Dixon Street, Hulme, Manchester.
TZ2451

BUCKLEY, W., Private, Lancashire Fusiliers.
Joining in May 1917, he was drafted to France three months later and played a prominent part in the Battles of Passchendaele, Lens, and Cambrai, and in the Retreat and Advance of 1918. After hostilities ceased, he proceeded to Germany, and served with the Army of Occupation until November 1919, when he was demobilised, holding the General Service and Victory Medals.
111, Marsland Street, Ardwick, Manchester.
Z2455

BUDSWORTH, T. E., Corpl., E. Lancashire Regt.

He volunteered at the outbreak of hostilities, and was immediately drafted overseas. During his service on the Western Front he fought in the Retreat from Mons, and other engagements. He made the supreme sacrifice on September 21st, 1915, at the 2nd Battle of Ypres, and was entitled to the Mons Star, and the General Service and Victory Medals.

" Nobly striving, he nobly fell that we might live."

8, Mary's Place, Ancoats, Manchester. Z11889

BULLEN, G. W., Gunner, R.G.A.

He joined in May 1916, and in the following July was sent to France, where he took part in the fighting at Vermelles, the Somme, Arras, Bullecourt, Lens, the Marne, and the Lys. He was demobilised in February 1919, and holds the General Service and Victory Medals.

5, Teignmouth Street, Rochdale Road, Manchester. Z9456

BULLOCK, J. R., Private, Royal Irish Fusiliers.

He joined in February 1917, and on completion of his training was engaged on important garrison duties at Cork and Belfast in Ireland. He was unsuccessful in obtaining his transfer overseas, but did consistently good work with his unit until his discharge as medically unfit for further service in March 1918. 10, Hancock Street, Rusholme, Manchester. Z2457

BULLOUGH, F., Pte., King's Shropshire Light Infy.

He joined in May 1918, and two months later was drafted to the Western Front, where he took part in the 2nd Battle of Cambrai, and in heavy fighting during the Advance of 1918, He was wounded in action, and was eventually demobilised in October 1919, holding the General Service and Victory Medals.

11, Worrall Street, Collyhurst, Manchester. Z10311

BULWICH, J., Private, Labour Corps.

He joined in July 1918, and was not successful in procuring a transfer overseas before the termination of the war. He was retained in England on important duties, and stationed at Pembroke, where he was chiefly employed on the roads and bridges which work he performed in a very able manner. After five months service in the Army he was demobilised in December 1918.

3, Twemlow Street, Rochdale Road, Manchester. Z8930

BUNN, S., Private, King's (Liverpool Regiment.)

He volunteered in June 1915, and five months later was drafted to France, where he took part in the Battles of the Somme, Messines, Ypres, and Givenchy, and was wounded. He was also in action in the Retreat and Advance of 1918 until taken prisoner at Meteren. He was eventually released from captivity, and demobilised in March 1919, holding the 1914–15 Star, and the General Service and Victory Medals.

5, Harrop Street, Openshaw, Manchester. Z2458

BUNNER, T. F., Private, 1/8th Manchester Regt.

He volunteered in October 1914, and seven months later proceeded to Egypt, where he served for nearly two years. During that time he saw heavy fighting on the Suez Canal, and at Katia, and was then sent to the Western Front. There he was in action in engagements at Ypres, the Somme, La Bassée and Nieuport, and served in France until demobilised in February 1919, holding the 1914–15 Star, and the General Service and Victory Medals.

37, Lomas Street, Ancoats, Manchester. Z6044

BUNTING, J. F., Private, 2/7th Manchester Regt.

Joining in September 1916, he was drafted early in the following year to the Western Front. In this theatre of hostilities he was in action at La Bassée, Nieuport, Ypres, Hill 60, Neuve Chapelle, Cambrai, Amiens, Fresnoy, and Charleroi, and performed consistently good work. Returning home after the signing of the Armistice, he was eventually demobilised in 1919 and holds the General Service and Victory Medals.

55, Granville Place, Ancoats, Manchester. Z9935

BURBIDGE, C. E., Sapper, R.E.

He joined in June 1918 on attaining military age, having been previously engaged on work of National importance at Messrs. Mallison and Eckersley's, in connection with the manufacture of shell, grenade, and aerial torpedo boxes since September 1914. He was not drafted overseas until 1919, when he was sent to Egypt, and rendered valuable services there until his demobilisation in April 1920.

33, Garden Street, Ardwick, Manchester. Z2459A

BURBIDGE, E., Special War Worker.

During the whole period of hostilities, he was engaged on work of National importance at Messrs. Mallison and Eckersley's. He carried out his responsible duties in a very able manner, and rendered valuable services to his country until he relinquished his work in 1919.

33, Garden Street, Ardwick, Manchester. Z2459B

BURDETT, G. S. T., Pte., 3rd Royal Sussex Regt.

Volunteering in July 1915, he was drafted to the Western Front in the following March, and was first engaged on the Headquarters' Staff of the 33rd Labour Battalion at Lestrem. Later he took part in the Battle of Arras, but was invalided home through illness in August 1917. After hospital treatment in London, he was discharged as medically unfit for further service in July 1918, and holds the General Service and Victory Medals.

12, Craig Street, Miles Platting, Manchester. Z10312

BURDETT, R., Private, R.A.S.C.

He volunteered in May 1915, and after a period of training proceeded in the following February to Mesopotamia. There he served at Kut-el-Amara, and was employed at that place, and in other sectors on various duties of an important nature. During his service overseas, he did excellent work, and was demobilised on his return home in January 1919, holding the General Service and Victory Medals.

12, Summer Street, Chorlton-on-Medlock, Manchester. Z9780B

BURGESS, A., Pte., 2nd East Yorkshire Regiment.

Joining in June 1917, he was sent to France five months later. In this theatre of war, he was in action at Amiens, Cambrai, and on the Somme, and afterwards proceeding to India, served for a brief period in Bombay. He was later sent to Mesopotamia, where he assisted in quelling several Arab disturbances. He was still serving with the Colours in 1920, and was stationed at Baghdad, holding the General Service and Victory Medals.

44, Hewitt Street, Gorton, Manchester. Z9936

BURGESS, F., Private, North Staffordshire Regt.

Joining in February 1917, he proceeded ten months later to the Western Front, where he was engaged in severe fighting at Ypres, Spielbeke, Sanctuary Wood, and Beaucourt. He was gassed at Zillebeke, and in consequence was invalided to England, but on his recovery was sent to Ireland, where he served until demobilised in September 1919. He holds the General Service and Victory Medals.

15, Elias Street, Manchester. Z11475

BURGESS, H., Private, Manchester Regiment, and King's (Liverpool Regiment).

He volunteered in August 1915, and in the following March proceeded to Egypt. After participating in severe fighting near the Suez Canal, he was sent into Palestine, and was in action at Gaza, Jerusalem, and Jericho. During his service overseas he performed very good work and was demobilised on his return home in April 1919, holding the General Service and Victory Medals.

4, Anthony Street, West Gorton, Manchester. Z8931

BURGESS, J., Sapper, R.E.

He joined in June 1916, and on conclusion of his training was drafted overseas in the following December. Whilst serving on the Western Front, he took an active part in numerous engagements, including the Battles of Arras, Bullecourt, Messines, Ypres, Passchendaele, Cambrai, and Bapaume, and was wounded at Le Cateau in October 1918. He was demobilised in January 1919, holding the General Service and Victory Medals.

8, Williams Place, Ancoats, Manchester. Z11408

BURGESS, J., L/Corporal, 1st Royal Fusiliers.

He joined in August 1916, and in the following March was drafted to France. Here he took a prominent part in heavy fighting on the Somme front, and at Ypres, and La Bassée, after which he was sent to Italy. In this theatre of war, he was in action in several important engagements, and later returning to France, served there until the Armistice. He then proceeded to Germany, and served with the Army of Occupation in Cologne until June 1919, when he returned home. In 1920 he was still in the Army, and, stationed in Ireland, holds the General Service and Victory Medals.

30, Whalley Street, Ancoats, Manchester. Z9937

BURGESS, J. G., Corporal, M.G.C.

He volunteered in February 1915, and first served with the Manchester Regiment, but was later transferred to the Machine Gun Corps, and proceeded to France in June 1916. After only a month's service on the Western Front, he was badly wounded in action during the Somme Offensive of July 1916. He was invalided to hospital in Manchester, and on his recovery was stationed at Grantham until September 1917. He was then put on munition work, at which he remained until discharged from the Army in October 1918, holding the General Service and Victory Medals.

136, Victoria Street, Longsight, Manchester. Z2460

BURGESS, P., Stoker, R.N.

He was called up from the Reserve in August 1914, and saw service with the Royal Naval Division at Antwerp. Later he proceeded to the Dardanelles on board H.M.S. " Europa," and took part in the Landing at Gallipoli. He was afterwards transferred to H.M.S. " Foresight," and was engaged on important patrol duties in the Mediterranean Sea. In April 1919 he was discharged, and holds the 1914 Star, and the General Service (with 3 clasps), and Victory Medals.

16, Milne Street, West Gorton, Manchester. Z11663

BURGESS, W. B., Corporal, R.A.S.C.

Volunteering in February 1915, he was quickly drafted to the Western Front, where he rendered valuable services as a despatch rider. He took an active part in the Battles of Neuve Chapelle, St. Eloi, Ypres, Festubert, Albert, the Somme, Arras, Bullecourt, Passchendaele and Cambrai, and in the Retreat and Advance of 1918. He was demobilised in February 1919, and holds the 1914–15 Star, and the General Service and Victory Medals.

18, Callender Street, Chorlton-on-Medlock, Manchester. Z2461

BURGOYNE, J., Corporal, King's (Liverpool Regt.)

Volunteering in August 1914, he was drafted to France early in the following year and was in action on the Somme and at Arras, Messines, Passchendaele and Ypres. He was wounded and taken prisoner at Armentières and was sent to Germany. Here he remained in captivity until after the Armistice, when he was released, and returning home was demobilised in April 1919, holding the 1914–15 Star, and the General Service and Victory Medals.

128, Cross Street, Bradford, Manchester.   TZ9457

BURGOYNE, P., Private, 17th Lancashire Fusiliers.

He volunteered in September 1914, and was drafted to France in December 1915. Whilst on the Western Front he took part in the heavy fighting at Loos and St. Eloi early in 1916, and in the Battles of the Somme, Arras and Ypres. He was also in action during the Retreat and Advance of 1918, and was in hospital in Boulogne for some time. Demobilised in January 1919, he holds the 1914–15 Star, and the General Service and Victory Medals.

6, Arbury Street, Hulme, Manchester.   Z2462

BURKE, J., Private, 23rd Manchester Regiment and 22nd Lancashire Fusiliers.

Volunteering in January 1915, he was drafted towards the end of the same year to France, where he took part in heavy fighting at Loos, St. Eloi, Albert and Vimy Ridge, was wounded on the Somme in July 1916. As a result he was invalided home, but upon his recovery, returned to France and participated in further fighting at Amiens, Bapaume and Havrincourt, before he was killed in action at Cambrai on September 27th, 1918. He was entitled to the 1914–15 Star, and the General Service and Victory Medals.

"Honour to the immortal dead who gave their youth that the world might grow old in peace."

49, Cheltenham Street, Collyhurst, Manchester.   Z8932

BURKE, J., Private, 51st Cheshire Regiment.

Joining in May 1918, he was not successful in obtaining a transfer to a theatre of war. Retained on home service, he was sent to Ireland, and whilst stationed at the Curragh and in other places, was employed with his unit on garrison and other duties of an important nature. He performed consistently good work until he was demobilised in May 1920.

10, Ross Street, West Gorton, Manchester.   Z9938

BURKE, J., Private, 9th Lancashire Fusiliers.

He volunteered in September 1914, and after a period of training at Grantham, proceeded in the following July to the Dardanelles. In this theatre of war he took part in strenuous fighting at Suvla Bay and was reported wounded and missing after an engagement on August 21st, 1915. He was later presumed to have been killed on that date, and was entitled to the 1914–15 Star, and the General Service and Victory Medals.

"Courage, bright hopes, and a myriad dreams, splendidly given."

57, Masonic Street, Oldham Road, Manchester.   Z8933

BURKE, J., Private, 1st Manchester Regiment.

He was mobilised in August 1914, and was drafted to the Western Front. There he saw much active service, taking part in the Battles of Mons, the Somme, Ypres and Arras, and was wounded in May 1917. On his recovery he returned to France and was again in action until the cessation of hostilities, when he proceeded to Germany and served with the Army of Occupation until discharged in June 1919. He holds the Mons Star, and the General Service and Victory Medals.   12, Brown Street, Ancoats, Manchester.   Z11890

BURKE, J. F., Private, 4th Manchester Regiment.

Mobilised in August 1914, he was immediately drafted to the Western Front and took part in the Battle of Mons and the subsequent Retreat. He was also in action at the Battles of the Marne, the Aisne and Ypres (I) before being badly wounded and gassed at the second Battle of Ypres in May 1915. After long treatment in hospital he was eventually invalided from the Army in October 1918, and holds the Mons Star, and the General Service and Victory Medals.

15, Davies Street, Hulme, Manchester.   TZ2463

BURKE, J. M., Private, 5th Manchester Regiment.

He volunteered in September 1914, and in the following year was sent to Gallipoli, where he was in action at Suvla Bay and Chunuk Bair. Later transferred to France, he was in action on the Somme and Ancre fronts, and at Arras, Ypres, Cambrai and Havrincourt, and was wounded. As a result, he was evacuated to England and sent to hospital at Warrington, where he remained until he was invalided out of the Service in September 1918 as unfit for further service. He holds the 1914–15 Star, and the General Service and Victory Medals.   33, Savoy Street, West Gorton, Manchester.   Z9939

BURKE, J. W., Sergt., Royal Fusiliers and South Lancashire Regiment.

Four months after volunteering in September 1914, he was drafted to the Western Front, where he served with distinction at the Battles of Hill 60, Loos, the Somme and Arras and was badly wounded in action at the third Battle of Ypres in July

1917. He was invalided home, and on his recovery was transferred to the transport Battalion of his unit, and was engaged on important duties at Salford Docks until his demobilisation in December 1918. He holds the 1914–15 Star, and the General Service and Victory Medals.

78, Birch Street, Ardwick, Manchester.   Z2464

BURKE, T., C.S.M., 16th Manchester Regiment.

Having previously served in the South African campaign, he rejoined in September 1914, and proceeded to France in March 1915. He took a distinguished part in the Battles of Neuve Chapelle, the Somme, Cambrai and the Aisne (III), and in the Retreat and Advance of 1918. After the cessation of hostilities he proceeded to Germany with the Army of Occupation, and was eventually demobilised in March 1919. He holds the Queen's and King's South African Medals, the 1914–15 Star, and the General Service and Victory Medals.

15, Abbey Street, Hulme, Manchester.   Z2465

BURKE, W., Private, 5th Manchester Regiment.

He joined in September 1916, and in the following year was drafted to the Western Front. Here he took part in the fighting at Cambrai and Nieuport, and was wounded and gassed. He was invalided home and was discharged in October 1917 as medically unfit for further service, holding the General Service and Victory Medals.

11, Heath Street, Ancoats, Manchester.   Z9453

BURLEY, G., Private, Cheshire Regiment.

He joined in February 1917, and in the following September proceeded to Egypt. There he was employed with his unit on various duties of an important nature whilst stationed at Alexandria and Cairo. For some time he was engaged on guard duties at an internment compound, and performed good work until he returned home for demobilisation in March 1919, holding the General Service and Victory Medals.

1, Booth Street, Newton, Manchester.   Z9940

BURNEY, J., Private, Royal Scots.

Volunteering in December 1914, he was drafted to France after a brief training and played a prominent part in many important engagements, including the Battles of Neuve Chapelle, Hill 60, Festubert, Loos, the Somme and Ypres (III). He was demobilised in February 1919, and holds the 1914–15 Star, and the General Service and Victory Medals.

6, William's Place, Grey Street, Ancoats, Manchester.   X2466

BURNHAM, J. S., Private, 21st Manchester Regt.

Volunteering in November 1914, he was drafted to the Western Front twelve months later and was in action at Fonceque-villers, Carnoy and Mametz during the Somme Offensive of July 1916. He was then invalided home suffering from debility, and after treatment in the 4th London General Hospital, was discharged as medically unfit for further service in October 1916. He holds the 1914–15 Star, and the General Service and Victory Medals.

15, Myrtle Grove, Ardwick, Manchester.   Z2467

BURNS, A., Sergt., 8th Manchester Regiment.

Volunteering in August 1914, he was sent to the Dardanelles in August 1915, and took part in the Landing at Suvla Bay. After the Evacuation of the Gallipoli Peninsula he was transferred to Mesopotamia, but was later drafted to Egypt. Eventually proceeding to the Western Front, he took a prominent part in the third Battle of Ypres, and was wounded in action at the commencement of the Retreat of March 1918. He was in hospital in France and on his recovery was sent to England, where he carried out important duties as a Sergeant-Instructor until his demobilisation in December 1918, holding the 1914–15 Star, and the General Service and Victory Medals.   19, Down Street, Ardwick, Manchester.   Z2471A

BURNS, E., Private, 8th Manchester Regiment.

Having volunteered in August 1914, he was sent to France in the following October, and was afterwards transferred to Gallipoli, where he took part in the Landing at Suvla Bay, and the Battle of Krithia, and was wounded and invalided home. He was discharged in July 1916 owing to his injuries and holds the 1914 Star, and the General Service and Victory Medals.

14, Carruthers Street, Ancoats, Manchester.   Z9462

BURNS, F., Corporal, R.A.S.C. (M.T.)

He volunteered in September 1915, and early in the following year was drafted to France, where he served on the Somme, and at Messines Ridge, Arras and Ypres. Invalided home as the result of being wounded in July 1917, he later returned to France, and was employed in various sectors until the termination of hostilities. He was demobilised in 1919, and holds the General Service and Victory Medals.

8, Bradley Buildings, Oldham Road, Manchester.   Z9941

BURNS, F., Private, 3rd Manchester Regiment.

He volunteered in August 1914, and in March of the following year was drafted to France and thence to Mesopotamia. Hence he took part in the fighting at Kut-el-Amara, and was wounded. He was invalided home and after a period in hospital was discharged as medically unfit for further service in January 1917. He holds the 1914–15 Star, and the General Service and Victory Medals.

129, Cobden Street, Bradford, Manchester.   Z9461

BURNS, G., Driver, R.A.S.C. (M.T.)
Volunteering in January 1915, he was drafted twelve months later to the Western Front, where he served for three years. During this time, he was engaged as a motor transport driver at St. Eloi, Vimy Ridge, on the Somme front, and at Bullecourt, Messines Ridge, Ypres, Passchendaele, and Cambrai. He was demobilised in February 1919, and holds the General Service and Victory Medals.
35, Hewitt Street, Gorton, Manchester. Z9942

BURNS, J. (D.C.M.) Corpl., 2nd Manchester Regt.
Mobilised in August 1914, he was at once drafted to France, where he participated in the Battle of Mons and the subsequent Retreat, and also in the Battles of the Aisne and the Marne. He later took part in strenuous fighting on the Somme and at Ypres, Hill 60, Passchendaele and Cambrai, and was wounded in action at Ypres. He was awarded the Distinguished Conduct Medal for conspicuous gallantry at Hill 60 in saving an officer's life, and on being discharged in March 1919, was also entitled to the Mons Star and the General Service and Victory Medals.
19, Ryder Street, Bradford, Manchester. Z9944

BURNS, J., Private, 1/8th Manchester Regiment.
He volunteered in September 1914, and in the following November was sent to Egypt. There he was employed on important duties at Alexandria and Cairo, until May 1915, when he was transferred to Gallipoli. After two months service in this theatre of hostilities he was severely wounded at Krithia, and sent to hospital at Malta. Later evacuated to England, he was for some time in hospital at Dundee, and was eventually discharged in February 1916, as unfit for further service. He holds the 1914-15 Star, and the General Service and Victory Medals.
10, Branson Street, Ancoats, Manchester. Z9943

BURNS, J., Pte., 2nd (Garr. Bn.) King's (L'pool Regt.)
He joined in December 1916, and in the following October was drafted to Salonika. In this theatre of war he took part in several important engagements on the Doiran and Struma fronts, and did good work. After the Armistice he served in Turkey until October 1919, engaged on garrison and other duties, and was demobilised on his return home in the following month, holding the General Service and Victory Medals 74, Lind Street, Ancoats, Manchester. Z9945

BURNS, J. (M.M.) Sapper, R.E.
A serving Soldier, he was drafted to France in January 1915, and played a prominent part in the Battles of Ypres, Festubert, Loos, Albert, the Somme, Arras and Cambrai, and in the Retreat of 1918. He was four times wounded in action, and on the last occasion, in March 1918, was invalided home, being eventually discharged in March 1919. He was awarded the Military Medal for conspicuous bravery at Loos in 1916, and also holds the 1914-15 Star, and the General Service and Victory Medals. 134, Clopton St., Hulme, Manchester. Z2475

BURNS, J., Private, 20th Manchester Regiment.
He volunteered in September 1914, and in the following June proceeded to France. During his service in this theatre of war he took an active part in many important engagements, including the Battles of Loos, the Somme (I), Arras, Messines and Passchendaele, where he was unfortunately killed in action on October 10th, 1917. He was entitled to the 1914-15 Star, and the General Service and Victory Medals.
"His life for his Country, his soul to God."
10, Lord Street, Hulme, Manchester. Z11664

BURNS, J., Private, 6th South Lancashire Regt.
He volunteered in November 1915, and was quickly drafted to the Western Front, where he was in action at the Battles of Albert, the Somme, Arras, Vimy Ridge and Messines, before being invalided home suffering from dysentery in June 1917. He was discharged as medically unfit for further service in the same month, and holds the 1914-15 Star, and the General Service and Victory Medals.
20, Baxter Street, Hulme, Manchester. Z2468B

BURNS, J., Private, 1/7th Royal Welch Fusiliers.
Joining in April 1916, he was sent to Egypt on completion of his training, but later proceeded to Palestine, where he took part in the Battles of Gaza, the capture of Jerusalem and in other important engagements during the Advance of General Allenby's Forces. He also served for a time in Cyprus, and was demobilised in November 1919, holding the General Service and Victory Medals.
7, Clegg Street, Rochdale Road, Manchester. Z10313

BURNS, J., Sergt., 12th King's (Liverpool Regt.)
He joined in February 1916, and seven months later was drafted to the Western Front, where he served with distinction at the Battles of Beaumont-Hamel, Arras, Vimy Ridge, Messines and Ypres. During the last-named engagement he was severely wounded in action and taken prisoner in 1917, and unfortunately, whilst in captivity in Germany, suffered amputation of his left arm at Aachen Hospital. He was released and discharged in February 1919, and holds the General Service and Victory Medals.
8, Culvert Street, Rochdale Road, Manchester. Z10314

BURNS, J., Private, 4th King's (Liverpool Regt.)
He volunteered in February 1915, and three months later was drafted to France. There he played a prominent part in severe actions at Ypres, Festubert, Neuve Chapelle, and Lens, and was wounded on the Somme front in October 1916. As a result he was invalided home, but upon his recovery returned to France, where he participated in further fighting at Armentières, Bullecourt, Cambrai and Arras. He was gassed in action in 1918, and again invalided home, but eventually demobilised in February 1919, holding the 1914-15 Star, and the General Service and Victory Medals.
Junction Street, Ancoats, Manchester. Z8934

BURNS, J., Pte., 1st K.O. (Royal Lancaster Regt.)
Mobilised in August 1914, he was drafted in the following October to the Western Front. In this theatre of hostilities he took part with his unit in the Battles of Ypres, and Neuve Chapelle, and rendered excellent service before he fell gloriously on the Field of Battle at Hill 60, on May 24th, 1915. He was entitled to the 1914 Star, and the General Service and Victory Medals.
"Whilst we remember, the sacrifice is not in vain."
20, Milton Street, Hulme, Manchester. Z4630C

BURNS, J., Private, 8th Manchester Regiment.
Volunteering in August 1914, he was sent to Gallipoli in May of the following year. Here he took part in the Landing at Suvla Bay, the Battle of Krithia, the capture of Chunuk Bair and the Evacuation. He was demobilised in March 1919, and holds the 1914-15 Star, and the General Service and Victory Medals.
14, Carruthers Street, Ancoats, Manchester. Z9463

BURNS, J., Private, 2nd Lancashire Fusiliers.
Having enlisted in 1899, he was called up from the Reserve at the outbreak of war in August 1914, and was immediately drafted to the Western Front. After fighting in the Retreat from Mons and other important engagements, he was wounded in action at St. Julien early in 1915, and sent to hospital at Rouen. He rejoined his unit, however, on his recovery, and was again wounded near Ypres in July of the same year. Invalided home he was in hospital at Chatham until April 1916, when he was discharged as medically unfit for further service, and holds the Mons Star, and the General Service and Victory Medals.
19, Buxton Street, Chorlton-on-Medlock, Manchester. Z2472B

BURNS, J. A., L/Corporal, 16th Manchester Regt.
Shortly after volunteering in January 1915, he proceeded to the Western Front, where after fighting in many important engagements, he was wounded in action on the Somme in July 1916, and sent to hospital at the Base. He rejoined his unit on his recovery, but was again wounded at Ypres in 1917, and was for a time in hospital. Wounded in action a third time, he was invalided home, but later returned to France, where he was taken prisoner during the Retreat of March 1918. He unhappily died whilst in captivity in Germany on July 27th, 1918. He was entitled to the 1914-15 Star, and the General Service and Victory Medals.
"His life for his Country, his soul to God."
19, Down Street, Ardwick, Manchester. Z2471B

BURNS, L., Private, 4th K.O. (R. Lancaster Regt).
Mobilised in August 1914, he was immediately drafted to the Western Front, where he served through the Retreat from Mons, and was wounded in action. After taking part also in the Battles of the Marne and La Bassée, he was taken prisoner at Hill 60, and held in captivity until after the cessation of hostilities, was forced during this time to work on the land. He was discharged in June 1919, and holds the Mons Star, and the General Service and Victory Medals.
20, Baxter Street, Hulme, Manchester. Z2468A

BURNS, M., Private, K.O. (Royal Lancaster Regt.)
Mobilised in August 1914, he proceeded to France with the 1st Expeditionary Force, and took part in the Battles of Mons, Le Cateau, the Marne, the Aisne, La Bassée, and Hill 60, where he laid down his life for King and Country on May 2nd, 1915. He was entitled to the Mons Star, and the General Service and Victory Medals.
"A costly sacrifice upon the altar of freedom."
24, Hamilton Street, Collyhurst, Manchester. Z10315

BURNS, R., Private, 6th S. Lancashire Regiment.
He volunteered in August 1914, and twelve months later was sent to Egypt, where he saw much severe fighting. After serving through engagements at Messa Matruh, Sollum, Katia, El Fasher and Magdhaba, he took part in the Advance into Palestine, and fought in the Battles of Gaza and the capture of Jerusalem, Tripoli and Aleppo. Returning home in December 1918, he was demobilised in the following month, and holds the 1914-15 Star, and the General Service and Victory Medals.
7, Briar Street, Hulme, Manchester. TZ2470

BURNS, R., Private, Lancashire Fusiliers.
Mobilised in August 1914, he was drafted to Gallipoli twelve months later, and there took part in the Landing at Suvla Bay. After seeing much severe fighting in this seat of operations, he was transferred on the Evacuation of the Peninsula to Egypt, whence he proceeded to France in June 1916. There he fought in the Battles of the Somme, the Ancre and Passchendaele, and many minor engagements, and was severely gassed whilst in action. He was for a considerable period in hospital at Boulogne and Leeds, before being invalided from the Army in August 1918, and holds the 1914-15 Star, and the General Service and Victory Medals.
2, Pine Street, City Road, Hulme, Manchester.   Z2473

BURNS, T., Pte., 1st K.O. (Royal Lancaster Regt.)
Called up from the Reserve in August 1914, he at once proceeded to France and there fought in the Battle of Mons and through the Retreat, and in the Battles of the Marne, the Aisne, La Bassée and Loos, after which he was sent to Salonika. After a few months' service on the Vardar Front, he was invalided home on account of ill-health, and was eventually discharged in November 1916, holding the Mons Star, and the General Service and Victory Medals.
31, Bosham Street, Ancoats, Manchester.   Z9946

BURNS, T., Private, 6th Essex Regiment.
He volunteered in December 1915, and was engaged on important duties with his unit till June 1917, when he was drafted to Egypt, and thence to Palestine. He took part in the Battle of Gaza and the capture of Jerusalem, and returning home after the cessation of hostilities was demobilised in November 1919, holding the General Service and Victory Medals.
8, Raw Street, Collyhurst, Manchester.   Z9459

BURNS, T., A.B., Royal Naval Division.
Having previously served for ten years, he was called up from the Reserve at the outbreak of war in August 1914, and was shortly afterwards drafted to the Western Front. There he took part in the Defence of Antwerp and taken prisoner in October 1914, was held in captivity at Doberitz until after the cessation of hostilities, and during this time was forced to work in a wood factory. He was finally discharged in December 1919, and holds the 1914 Star, and the General Service and Victory Medals.
37, Lord Street, Openshaw, Manchester.   TZ2469

BURNS, T. A., Private, 2nd Border Regiment.
Mobilised in August 1914, he proceeded to the Western Front in the following month, and there took part in many important engagements, including the Battles of the Marne, Ypres, Loos, Albert and Vimy Ridge. He was unfortunately reported missing, presumed to have been killed in action on the Somme in July 1916. He was entitled to the 1914 Star, and the General Service and Victory Medals.   Z2474
"And doubtless he went in splendid company."
15, Clarendon Place, Chorlton-on-Medlock, Manchester.

BURNS, T. H., Private, 16th Manchester Regiment.
He joined in January 1916, and in the following March was drafted to the Western Front, and took part in important engagements. He was unfortunately killed in action on the Somme on July 31st, 1916, and was entitled to the General Service and Victory Medals.
"He joined the great white company of valiant souls."
25, Sand Street, Collyhurst, Manchester.   Z9460

BURROWS, A., Private, 8th Manchester Regiment and King's (Liverpool Regiment).
After volunteering in June 1915, he underwent a period of training prior to being drafted to the Western Front in 1917. Whilst in this theatre of war he fought in many important engagements, including the Battles of Arras, Ypres, Passchendaele, the Somme and Armentières, served also through the Retreat and Advance of 1918, and was for a time attached to the Military Police. He was demobilised in March 1919, and holds the General Service and Victory Medals.
95, Birch Street, Ardwick, Manchester.   Z2477

BURROWS, A. S., Private, Labour Corps.
He joined in January 1918, and after completing a period of training, served at various stations, where he was engaged on duties of a highly important nature. He was not successful in obtaining his transfer to a theatre of war, but nevertheless, rendered valuable services until February 1919, when he was demobilised.
84, Platt Street, Moss Side, Manchester.   Z2476

BURROWS, E., Corporal, 2/6th Manchester Regt.
He joined in May 1916, and in March of the following year proceeded to France, where he saw severe fighting in various sectors of the Front. He took part in the Battles of Ypres and the Somme, and many other important engagements in this theatre of war and finally returned home for demobilisation in September 1919. He holds the General Service and Victory Medals.
12, Cotsworth Street, Moss Side, Manchester.   Z2478

BURROWS, I., Private, 7th Manchester Regiment.
He volunteered in January 1915, and after undergoing a period of training, was engaged on important duties at various stations where he rendered valuable services with his unit. He was

unable to obtain his transfer overseas on account of deafness, and in August 1916 was invalided out of the Army.
117, Dale Street, Hulme, Manchester.   TZ2479

BURROWS, J. R., Rifleman, 3rd Rifle Brigade.
He volunteered in the early days of the war, and after a brief training at Winchester was drafted to the Western Front. In this theatre of hostilities he at once participated in heavy fighting and was severely wounded on the Marne on September 3rd, 1914, unfortunately dying on the same day from the effects of his injuries. He was entitled to the 1914 Star, and the General Service and Victory Medals.
"Whilst we remember the sacrifice is not in vain."
84, Thornton Street, Collyhurst, Manchester.   Z9947

BURROWS, W., Shoeing-Smith, R.F.A.
He volunteered in August 1914. and in the following month was drafted to Egypt. Whilst in this seat of operations, he was engaged on important duties at Kantara and various other stations, and rendered very valuable services with his Battery until his return home in December 1916. He was finally demobilised in February 1919, and holds the 1914-15 Star, and the General Service and Victory Medals.
4, Solent Street, Ardwick, Manchester.   Z2480

BURT, W. M., Private, East Lancashire Regiment.
Volunteering in September 1914, he was sent twelve months afterwards to France, and after a time took part in the Battle of Loos. Transferred to Salonika, he was in action on the Doiran and Struma fronts, and was wounded on the Vardar front in September 1916, Upon his recovery he rejoined his unit, and took part in heavy fighting at Monastir and on the Vardar front. Returning home in February 1919, he was demobilised in the following month, and holds the 1914-15 Star, and the General Service and Victory Medals.
118, Hamilton Street, Collyhurst, Manchester.   Z9948

BURTON, A. E., Corporal, 12th Manchester Regt.
He volunteered in August 1914, and ten months later was drafted to the Western Front, where he served for eight months. During that time he was in action principally in the Ypres and Ploegsteert Wood Sectors. In August 1915 he was wounded at Ypres, and in the following October suffered from shell-shock. Shortly afterwards he was transferred to the York and Lancaster Regiment, and served with that unit until demobilised in February 1919, holding the 1914-15 Star, and the General Service and Victory Medals.
2, Beecher Street, Queen's Park, Manchester.   Z11476

BURTON, E., Gunner, R.F.A.
Volunteering in August 1914, he proceeded overseas in the following year. During his service on the Western Front he took part in much serious fighting at Loos, St. Eloi, Albert, Vimy Ridge, the Somme, Arras, Ypres, Cambrai, the Marne (II) and Le Cateau (II). He was demobilised in June 1919, and holds the 1914-15 Star, and the General Service and Victory Medals.
3, Pomfort Street, West Gorton, Manchester.   Z8935

BURTON, J., Private, 16th Lancashire Fusiliers.
He volunteered in November 1914, and after a period of training, was drafted to the Western Front twelve months later. There he took part in the Battle of St. Eloi and many other important engagements until severely wounded in action at Albert, and invalided home in 1916. He was for a considerable period in hospital, before being invalided from the Army in April 1918, and holds the 1914-15 Star, and the General Service and Victory Medals.
11, Hibbert Street, Hulme, Manchester.   Z2481B

BURTON, J., Pte., 2/7th Royal Warwickshire Regt.
He joined in June 1917, and shortly afterwards was sent to the Western Front. During his service in this theatre of war he took part in the heavy fighting at Cambrai and on the Somme (II), but was badly wounded in action in March 1918, and was invalided to hospital and later sent to England. He unfortunately suffered amputation of his left leg, and was discharged in July 1919, holding the General Service and Victory Medals.
3, Phoenix Street, Hulme, Manchester.   Z11665

BURTON, R. C., Pte., K.O. (Royal Lancaster Regt.)
Having previously served for nine years in India, he was drafted to the Western Front immediately on the outbreak of war in August 1914, and was there wounded in action and taken prisoner during the fighting at Mons. Held in captivity in Germany until after the cessation of hostilities, he was finally discharged in March 1919, holding the Mons Star, and the General Service and Victory Medals.   Z2482
10, Coleman Street, Erskine Street, Hulme, Manchester.

BUSHBY, F. H., Private, 23rd Manchester Regt.
He volunteered in November 1914, and was retained at various stations in England until January 1916, when he was drafted to the Western Front. There, after seeing much heavy fighting in various sectors, he was severely wounded in action in April 1916, and invalided home. He was discharged as medically unfit for further service in November 1917, and holds the General Service and Victory Medals.
162, Earl Street, Longsight, Manchester.   Z2483A

BUSHE, W., Sergt., R.A.S.C. (M.T.)

He volunteered in 1914, and in the following year was drafted to France. In this theatre of war he served at Ypres, Passchendaele, and Neuve Chapelle, and was wounded. In 1917 he was sent to Italy and was again wounded, and admitted to hospital. Later evacuated to England, he was eventually demobilised in 1919, and holds the 1914-15 Star, and the General Service and Victory Medals.
74, Bridge Street, Chorlton-on-Medlock, Manchester. Z9949A

BUSHELL, D., Private, Manchester Regiment.

He volunteered in May 1915, and in April of the following year was sent to Egypt, where he served at Kantara, El-Arish and Cairo. Later, however, he was transferred to the Western Front and took part in the Battles of the Somme, Arras, Messines and Ypres, and in the Retreat and Advance of 1918. He was twice wounded—on the Somme in 1916, and at Ypres in 1917, and was also gassed at Messines in the same year. Demobilised in February 1919 he holds the General Service and Victory Medals.
7, Worth Street, Rochdale Road, Manchester. Z10316

BUSHELL, W., Pte., 2nd K.O. (R. Lancaster Regt.)

Having enlisted in July 1906, he was already serving in India when war was declared in August 1914, and was there engaged on important garrison duties at various stations. In January 1915 he was transferred to the Western Front, where he saw much severe fighting in the Ypres sector until invalided home in April of the same year. He was invalided from the Army in May 1915, and holds the 1914-15 Star, and the General Service and Victory Medals.
95, Stott Street, Hulme, Manchester. Z2484

BUTLER, E., Private. East Lancashire Regiment.

Joining in November 1916, he was drafted to the Western Front on completion of his training in May of the following year, and there saw severe fighting in various sectors. He took part in many important engagements, and was twice wounded in action—at the third Battle of Ypres and at Amiens in August 1918, and was for a time in hospital in France and England. On his recovery in January 1919, he returned to the Western Front, but was again invalided home and was for five months in hospital. He was finally demobilised in November 1919, and holds the General Service and Victory Medals. X2485B
44, Grosvenor Street, Chorlton-on-Medlock, Manchester.

BUTLER, E., Private, King's (Liverpool Regiment).

He volunteered in August 1915, and a month later was sent on active service. Whilst on the Western Front he took part in the Battles of Loos, Albert, Somme (I), and the Ancre. He was then invalided home, and discharged as medically unfit for further duty in November 1916, and holds the 1914-15 Star, and the General Service and Victory Medals. He now suffers from consumption as a result of his war service.
5, Edgely Street, Ardwick, Manchester. Z11666

BUTLER, J., Sapper, R.E.

He was engaged on work of National importance from August 1914 until he joined the Army in March 1917. Proceeding to France in February 1918, he served on the Somme and at Amiens, Epéhy, Bray and Mons, engaged on various duties of an important nature, and performed consistently good work. He was demobilised in March 1919, and holds the General Service and Victory Medals.
34, Lind Street, Ancoats, Manchester. Z9950

BUTLER, J., Private, 51st King's (Liverpool Regt.) and R.A.V.C., and 20th Hampshire Regiment.

He joined in December 1917, and after completing a period of training, served at various stations, where he was engaged on duties of great importance. He was unable to obtain his transfer to a theatre of war, but did good work with his unit until April 1919, when he was invalided from the Army. He re-enlisted, however, in August of that year, and was drafted to France, where he served at Rouen until finally discharged as medically unfit for further service in April 1920. Z2485A
44, Grosvenor Street, Chorlton-on-Medlock, Manchester.

BUTLER, W., Special War Worker.

He had previously served in the Royal Navy on board H.M.S. "Albemarle" during the Boxer risings in China, but after the outbreak of war in August 1914, was no longer eligible for active service. He was consequently engaged on work of great importance at the National Projectile Factory, Lancaster, where, employed on various responsible duties, he rendered valuable services during the period of hostilities.
37, Lingmoor Street, Chorlton-on-Medlock, Manchester. X2487

BUTTERFIELD, J., L/Cpl., 9th Lancashire Fusiliers.

He volunteered in August 1914, and in the following year proceeded to Gallipoli, where he was wounded in action during the Landing at Suvla Bay. After the Evacuation of the Peninsula he was transferred to the Western Front, where he took part in the Somme Offensive of 1916, and was again wounded. He fell fighting on August 16th, 1917, whilst in action on the Somme.

He was entitled to the 1914-15 Star, and the General Service and Victory Medals.
"He joined the great white company of valiant souls."
7, Richmond Street, Ardwick, Manchester. Z2488

BUTTERS, H. F., Private, 18th Welch Regiment.

He joined in February 1917, and in the following December, was drafted to the Western Front, where he saw much severe fighting, taking part in many important engagements. He made the supreme sacrifice, falling in action at Blairville during the Retreat of March 1918. He was entitled to the General Service and Victory Medals.
"Courage, bright hopes, and a myriad dreams, splendidly given."
20, Chapman Street, Hulme, Manchester.. Z2493

BUTTERWORTH, E., Pte., 2nd Lancashire Fusiliers.

Two months after joining in May 1917, he was drafted to the Western Front, where he took part in the Battles of Passchendaele, Lens, Cambrai, the Somme, and Amiens, and many minor engagements, and also fought in the Retreat of 1918. He died gloriously on the field of battle near Havrincourt in September 1918. He was entitled to the General Service and Victory Medals.
"Steals on the ear the distant triumph song."
157, Hartington Street, Moss Side, Manchester. Z2489

BUTTERWORTH, F., Pte, 9th S. Lancashire Regt.

He volunteered in March 1915, and on completing his training in the following August was drafted to Salonika. In this seat of operations he took part in much fighting on the Vardar, Doiran and Struma fronts, and at the recapture of Monastir. He returned home after hostilities ceased and was demobilised in March 1919, holding the 1914-15 Star, and the General Service and Victory Medals.
19, Gadley Street, Ancoats, Manchester. Z8936

BUTTERWORTH, G., L/Cpl., Royal Scots Fusiliers.

He volunteered in October 1915, and in July of the following year proceeded to the Western Front, where he took part in the Somme Offensive, and was wounded in action. Invalided home he returned to France, however, on his recovery in November 1917, and fought in the Battles of Cambrai, the Somme, the Aisne and the Marne, and was again wounded at Bapaume in August 1918, and gassed. He was finally demobilised in January 1919, and holds the General Service and Victory Medals.
4, Molyneux Street, Longsight, Manchester. Z2490

BUTTERWORTH, H., Private, L.N. Lancs. Regt.

Volunteering in September 1914, he was drafted to the Western Front in February of the following year, and was there wounded in action in the second Battle of Ypres. He was invalided home, but on his recovery, returned to France and took part in the Battles of the Somme and Ypres, and other important engagements, fought also in the Retreat and Advance of 1918, and was again wounded. He was demobilised in March 1919, and holds the 1914-15 Star, and the General Service and Victory Medals.
9, Kelsall Street, West Gorton, Manchester. Z2491

BUTTERWORTH, H., Air Mechanic, R.A.F.

He joined in April 1918, and on completing his training in October of the same year was sent to the Western Front, where he served at Arras, Albert, La Bassée, the Somme, Cambrai, Ypres, and many other places. After the cessation of hostilities he proceeded into Germany, and was there stationed at Bonn with the Army of Occupation. He was demobilised on returning home in August 1919, and holds the General Service and Victory Medals.
157, Hartington Street, Moss Side, Manchester. Z2492

BUTTERWORTH, J., Private, Manchester Regt.

Volunteering in August 1914, he proceeded in the following January to the Dardanelles. In this theatre of war he took part in the Landing and subsequent Battle of Suvla Bay, and was severely wounded. Invalided home as a result, he spent some time in hospital, and was eventually discharged in June 1916, as unfit for further service, holding the 1914-15 Star, and the General Service and Victory Medals.
290, Mill Street, Bradford, Manchester. Z9951

BUTTERWORTH, J., Private, 6th Manchester Regt.

He volunteered in November 1915, and seven months later was sent to Egypt. After serving at Alexandria, Ismaila and Sinai, he was drafted to France, and there participated in strenuous fighting at Arras, Bullecourt, Messines, Ypres, Pass-Sinai, he was drafted to France, and there participated in chendaele, Nieuport and Cambrai. During his service overseas, he rendered excellent service and was demobilised in February 1919, holding the General Service and Victory Medals.
88, Mills Street, Ancoats, Manchester. Z9952

BUTTERWORTH, W.S., Pte., K.O. (R.Lancaster Regt.)

He volunteered in August 1914, and did consistently good work with his unit until the following January. He was then discharged as medically unfit for further service as the result of a serious accident he had met with whilst following his civilian occupation at the Westinghouse, Manchester.
104, Chester Street, Hulme, Manchester. TZ8937

BUXTON, T., Drummer, 2nd King's (L'pool Regt.)
He joined the Army in August 1911, and after the outbreak of war in August 1914, was drafted to France, where he fought at Loos, Albert, Vimy Ridge, the Somme and Messines, and was wounded in action. On his recovery, he proceeded to Mesopotamia, and saw much fighting at Kut, and at the capture of Baghdad. He returned home in June 1918, and was discharged in April 1920, holding the 1914–15 Star, and the General Service and Victory Medals.
2, Cross Street East, Ancoats, Manchester.   TZ8938

BUZZA, A., Private, 1/7th Manchester Regt.
He volunteered in December 1914, and in April of the following year was drafted to Gallipoli, where he took part in the Landing at Cape Helles, and in the Battles of Krithia, and the fighting at Suvla Bay. In August 1915 he was sent to hospital at Cairo, and afterwards served through the engagements at Agayia, Sollum and Romani. He was invalided home in December 1916, suffering from enteric fever, but on his recovery proceeded to the Western Front, and took part in the Battles of Arras, Vimy Ridge, Ypres and Cambrai. He unfortunately contracted pneumonia and died in hospital in France on May 3rd 1918. He was entitled to the 1914–15 Star, and the General Service and Victory Medals.
"His memory is cherished with pride."
90, Chell Street, Longsight, Manchester.   Z2494A

BUZZA, H., Private, 1/8th Manchester Regt.
He volunteered in August 1914, and shortly afterwards proceeded to Egypt, where he served at various stations until April 1915. He was then transferred to the Dardanelles, and took part in the first Landing at Gallipoli, where he saw much severe fighting. He unhappily fell in action in the third Battle of Krithia on June 4th, 1915. He was entitled to the 1914–15 Star, and the General Service and Victory Medals.
"Honour to the immortal dead who gave their youth that the world might grow old in peace."
90, Chell Street, Longsight, Manchester.   Z2494B

BUZZA, J., Sergt., 18th Manchester Regiment.
He volunteered in September 1914, and was retained at various stations in England until November 1915, when he was drafted to the Western Front. There he saw much heavy fighting in the Somme sector, was twice wounded in action at Suzanne, and as a result has lost his left eye. He was for a considerable period in hospital in France and England, before being invalided from the Army in September 1916, and holds the 1914–15 Star, and the General Service and Victory Medals.
16, Bark Street, Hulme, Manchester.   TZ2495

BYRAM, W., Private, 13th Manchester Regiment.
Volunteering in December 1914, he was drafted to the Western Front in September of the following year, and there took part in the Battle of Loos and many minor engagements. In February 1916 he was transferred to Salonika, where he saw severe fighting on the Doiran, Struma and Vardar fronts, and suffered from malaria. He was demobilised on his return home in March 1919, and holds the 1914–15 Star, and the General Service and Victory Medals.
99, Earl Street, Longsight, Manchester.   Z2496

BYRNE, J., Private, Royal Munster Fusiliers.
He re-enlisted in December 1914, and in September of the following year was sent to France, where he saw severe fighting in various sectors of the Front. He took part in the Battles of Loos, Albert, Vimy Ridge, the Somme, Arras, Passchendaele and Cambrai, and many other important engagements, and was for a time in hospital suffering from rheumatism amd malaria. He was demobilised in February 1919, and holds the 1914–15 Star, and the General Service and Victory Medals.
13, Stone St., Chester Road, Hulme, Manchester.   TZ2497

BYRNE, J., Pte., 8th (King's Royal Irish) Hussars.
Mobilised in August 1914, he was quickly sent to the Western Front, where he played an important part in the Battles of Neuve Chapelle, Hill 60, the Somme, Bullecourt, Messines and Ypres (III). He was three times wounded in action at Neuve Chapelle in March 1915, at Hill 60 in the following month, and on the Somme in November 1916. In July 1917 he was invalided home and after hospital treatment in London was discharged as medically unfit for further service, holding the 1914 Star, and the General Service and Victory Medals.
17, Baird Street, Chapel Street, Ancoats, Manchester. Z8940

BYRNE, J., Private, Labour Corps.
He volunteered in December 1915, and after undergoing a period of training served at various stations, where he was engaged on duties of a highly important nature. He was unable to obtain his transfer to a theatre of war, but nevertheless rendered valuable services with his Company until April 1918, when he was invalided from the Army.
19, Adelaide Street, Hulme, Manchester.   Z1309B

BYRNE, J. E., Private, Manchester Regiment.
He volunteered in June 1915, and after a short period of training proceeded to the Western Front. There he saw much heavy fighting on the Somme, and at Bullecourt, where he was badly wounded in action in May 1917, and consequently was invalided to England. On his recovery he was retained

on home service until his discharge as medically unfit for further duty in September 1918. He holds the 1914–15 Star, and the General Service and Victory Medals.
9, Abbott Street, Rochdale Road, Manchester.   Z8941

BYRNE, M., Private, Royal Fusiliers.
Volunteering in October 1915, he was drafted three months afterwards to France. There he was in action at Loos, Albert, Vimy Ridge, and on the Somme, and was wounded at Arras in April 1917. Invalided home, he spent some time in hospital at Leeds, and upon his recovery returned to France, where he was again in action on the Somme, and at Havrincourt and Le Cateau before he was unhappily killed in action on November 3rd 1918. He was entitled to the General Service and Victory Medals.
"His life for his Country."
20, Howarth Street, Bradford, Manchester.   Z9953

BYRNE, T., Private, Manchester Regiment.
He volunteered in December 1915, and in the following year was drafted to the Western Front. In this theatre of war he took part in many important engagements, including Passchendaele Ridge, and the Somme, and was wounded. He was demobilised on his return home in February 1919, and holds the General Service and Victory Medals.
18, Whitehead Street, Collyhurst, Manchester.   Z9954

BYRNE, T., L/Corporal, Royal Irish Rifles.
Having enlisted in 1911, he was already serving in India when war broke out in August 1914, and two months later was transferred to the Western Front. There he saw much severe fighting, taking part in many important engagements, and was three times wounded in action in 1914, at Neuve Chapelle and at Ypres in 1917. He was finally invalided from the Army in November 1918, and holds the 1914 Star, and the General Service and Victory Medals.
4, Horsley Street, Chorlton-on-Medlock, Manchester. TX2498

BYRNE, T. H., Private, Lancashire Fusiliers.
He volunteered in August 1914, and in the following July was drafted to Egypt, and thence to the Dardanelles, where he saw much fighting at the Landing at Suvla Bay. He suffered from shell-shock, and was invalided to Mudros, but on his recovery proceeded to France and served with the R.E. on important duties in the Somme, Arras and Ypres sectors. He was demobilised in November 1919, and holds the 1914–15 Star, and the General Service and Victory Medals.
86, Naylor Street, Newton, Manchester.   Z8939

BYROM, G., Private, King's (Liverpool Regiment).
He joined in March 1917, and in February of the following year proceeded to the Western Front, where he saw severe fighting in various sectors. He took part in the Battles of Amiens, Bapaume, Cambrai and Le Cateau, and many minor engagements, and was wounded in action at St. Quentin early in November 1918. He was for six weeks in hospital at Bath, before being demobilised in March 1919, and holds the General Service and Victory Medals.
6, Spencer Street, City Road, Hulme, Manchester.   TZ2499

BYRON, C. F., Private, 23rd Cheshire Regiment.
A Reservist, he was called up at the outbreak of war, and at once ordered to France. There he was in action in the Battles of Mons, the Marne, La Bassée, Ypres, Neuve Chapelle, Loos, the Somme, Arras, Cambrai, and fell fighting in the Somme Offensive in August 1918. He was entitled to the Mons Star, and the General Service and Victory Medals.
"A valiant Soldier, with undaunted heart he breasted life's last hill."
122, Cobden Street, Ancoats, Manchester.   Z11477

C

CADMAN, E., Private, 11th King's (Liverpool Regt.)
He volunteered in November 1914, and in 1915 proceeded to France, where he saw heavy fighting in various sectors of the Front, and was in action at Ypres, the Somme, Arras and St. Quentin. He was wounded in March 1918, and sent back to hospital in Glasgow. He rejoined his unit in time to take part in the final operations prior to the cessation of hostilities, and was demobilised in March 1919, holding the 1914–15 Star, and the General Service and Victory Medals.
50, Booth Street East, Chorlton-on-Medlock, Manchester. Z3502

CADMAN, J., Private, 1st Manchester Regiment.
Volunteering in January 1915, he proceeded four months later to the Dardanelles, where he was engaged in heavy fighting at Krithia, Achi-Baba and Suvla Bay. After the Evacuation he was invalided home until July 1916, when he was drafted to Mesopotamia. He remained in this theatre of war for twelve months, and served in Basra, Kut and Baghdad but was taken ill, and died in July 1917. He was entitled to the 1914–15 Star, and the General Service and Victory Medals.
"His memory is cherished with pride."
90, Birch Street, Ardwick, Manchester.   Z3501

CADMAN, J., Private, Lancashire Fusiliers.

He volunteered in September 1914, and in the following April proceeded to Gallipoli, where after fighting in the three Battles of Krithia he was wounded during the Landing at Suvla Bay. After protracted hospital treatment in Mudros and England, he was drafted to the Western Front in July 1917, and took part in numerous engagements and in the Allied Advance of 1918. After the Armistice he entered Germany with the Army of Occupation, and was demobilised in July 1919, holding the 1914–15 Star, and the General Service and Victory Medals.

40, Coral Street, Chorlton-on-Medlock, Manchester.   TX3503

CADYWOULD, G. H., Private, R.A.M.C.

He volunteered in August 1914, and served at various stations until July 1915, when he proceeded to France, and took part in the engagements at Ypres, Armentières and the Somme. Owing to ill-health he was invalided to England, but on his recovery was sent to Egypt. He served with the R.A.M.C. at Kantara and Alexandria until demobilised in May 1919, holding the 1914–15 Star, and the General Service and Victory Medals.   Z9955

54, Howarth Street, Chorlton-on-Medlock, Manchester.

CAFFREY, D. J., Private, 2nd Manchester Regt.

In October 1915, he volunteered, and in the following year was drafted overseas. Whilst serving in France he was in action at Arras, La Bassée, Givenchy, Festubert, Béthune, Ypres, Passchendaele, Cambrai, Le Cateau and the Sambre, and was present during the entry into Mons. He remained in France until his demobilisation in March 1919, and holds the General Service and Victory Medals.

40, Markham Street, Ardwick, Manchester.   Z3504

CAFFREY, J., Private, 1st Loyal N. Lancs. Regt.

Having previously served in the Army, he re-enlisted in August 1914, and five months later was sent to France, where he participated in engagements at Neuve Chapelle and Ypres, and was wounded at Festubert in May 1915. He was sent back to England, but after his recovery proceeded to Egypt, where he was engaged in making Army boots and was stationed at Alexandria, Cairo, and in Palestine. Returning home, he was demobilised in February 1919, and holds the 1914–15 Star, and the General Service and Victory Medals.

61, Hyde Street, Hulme, Manchester.   Z3505

CAHILL, H., Private, 1st Manchester Regiment.

He joined in March 1916, and in the following year was drafted to Mesopotamia, where he was in action during the capture of Tekrit. He served on this front until July 1918, when he was sent to Palestine, and there took part in the September Offensive, eventually going forward to Aleppo. In January 1919, he was drafted to Cairo, and did good work in quelling the riots. Returning to England two months later, he was demobilised in May 1919, and holds the General Service and Victory Medals.

15, Erskine Street, Hulme, Manchester.   Z3506

CAHILL, W., Private, 8th Manchester Regiment.

He volunteered in September 1914, and was retained on important duties with his unit at various stations until July 1915. He then proceeded to the Dardanelles, and took part in the engagements at Krithia and Akaba, and was wounded and invalided to Cairo, where he served until transferred to Palestine. He was then in action at Gaza, and at the capture of Jerusalem. He was demobilised in June 1919, holding the 1914–15 Star, and the General Service and Victory Medals.

5, Douro Street, Newton Heath, Manchester.   Z9956

CAIN, E., Sapper, R.E.

Volunteering in March 1915, he proceeded six months later to France. There he rendered valuable services in building bridges, and whilst in action in various sectors was also employed as a bomb-thrower. On July 2nd, 1916, after only nine months' active service he fell fighting in the Battle of the Somme. He was entitled to the 1914–15 Star, and the General Service and Victory Medals.

" Nobly striving,
He nobly fell that we might live."

39, Longridge Street, Longsight, Manchester.   Z3508

CAIN, H., Driver, R.A.S.C. (M.T.)

He joined in July 1916, and after a period of training proceeded to the Western Front in November 1917. Throughout his period of service in France he was stationed at St. Paul, was employed as a motor driver, and also as an iron turner, and for a time was employed in guarding prisoners of war. He was demobilised in December 1918, and holds the General Service and Victory Medals.

6, Baxter Street, Hulme, Manchester.   TZ3510

CAIN, J., Private, 1st Manchester Regiment.

He volunteered in July 1915, and on completion of his training in the following year was drafted to Mesopotamia. There he was engaged in fierce fighting in several engagements, but contracting malaria, he died in July 1916. He was entitled to the General Service and Victory Medals.

" Thinking that remembrance, though unspoken, may reach him where he sleeps."

161, Crossley Street, Gorton, Manchester.   Z3507

CAIN, J. M., Pte., King's (L'pool Regt.) and Spr., R.E.

He was called up from the Reserve in August 1914, and immediately proceeded to France, where he took part in the Battles of the Aisne, the Marne, La Bassée and Ypres, and was wounded at Loos, and gassed at St. Eloi in April 1916. He was in consequence discharged in October 1917. Six months later, however, he rejoined as a Sapper in the R.E., was again drafted to the Western Front, and was in action at Ploegsteert and Armentières. He was discharged in February 1919, holding the 1914 Star, and the General Service and Victory Medals.

11, Gotha Street, Ardwick, Manchester.   TZ3509

CAIN, J. T., Sapper, R.E.

He volunteered in August 1914, and in the following January embarked for France. Whilst overseas he was engaged on important road-making and bridge-building operations in connection with many great battles, especially those at Ypres, the Somme, Passchendaele and Messines. He was invalided home owing to ill-health in February 1918, and was discharged as medically unfit for further duty in the following April. He holds the 1914–15 Star, and the General Service and Victory Medals   16, Crook Street, Miles Platting, Manchester. Z10521

CAIN, M., Private, Machine Gun Corps.

He volunteered in November 1914, and after a period of training was drafted to Gallipoli, where he took part in the Landing at Suvla Bay, and other engagements until the Evacuation of the Peninsula. Later he was sent to the Western Front, and saw much heavy fighting at the Battles of Albert, the Somme (I), Beaumont-Hamel and Cambrai and was wounded. On his recovery he again went into action, but after a few months was unfortunately killed on March 21st, 1918. He was entitled to the 1914–15 Star, and the General Service and Victory Medals.

" His life for his Country, his soul to God."

3, Truro Street, West Gorton, Manchester.   Z9957

CAIN, M. J., Private, R.A.M.C.

He joined in June 1916, and was retained on important duties as a nursing orderly at Chisleton Hospital. Owing to his being over-age he was not able to obtain a transfer to a theatre of war, but rendered valuable services until demobilised in February 1919.

4, Matlock Place, Hulme, Manchester.   Z11667

CAIN, J., Rifleman, 10th Scottish Rifles.

At the outbreak of war, he volunteered, and in the following March was drafted overseas. During his service on the Western Front he took part in heavy fighting at Loos, Festubert, Albert, the Somme, Beaucourt, Beaumont-Hamel, Arras, Ypres and Cambrai, and was also in action in the Retreat and Advance of 1918. Demobilised in March 1919, he holds the 1914–15 Star, and the General Service and Victory Medals. 37, Derby Street, Ardwick, Manchester.   Z3511

CAIN, W. T., King's (Liverpool Regiment).

He volunteered in August 1914, at the outbreak of hostilities, and proceeded to France early in the following year. During his service on the Western Front he took part in the fierce fighting at the Battles of Neuve Chapelle, Ypres, Festubert, and Loos, where he was killed in action on September 25th, 1915. He was entitled to the 1914–15 Star, and the General Service and Victory Medals.

" His memory is cherished with pride."

52, Hewitt Street, Gorton, Manchester.   Z9958

CAINE, J., Pioneer, R.E.

He volunteered in October 1915, and was quickly drafted to Salonika, where he took part in the fighting on the Doiran front. Later he was transferred to the Western Front, and saw much service in various sectors until September 1917, when he was invalided to England. He was discharged as medically unfit in October 1917, and holds the 1914–15 Star, and the General Service and Victory Medals.

19, Laurence Street, Gorton, Manchester.   Z9959

CAIRNS, J., Private, Lancashire Fusiliers.

He volunteered in July 1915, and after a period of training was retained on important duties with his unit. Later, however, he was sent to France, and did good work as a bomber. He took part in the Battles of the Somme (I), Arras and Passchendaele, and was twice wounded.—at Arras in April 1917, and Passchendaele in November 1917, and on the second occasion was invalided home. After his recovery he served at Liverpool with the Labour Corps, until demobilised in March 1919. He holds the General Service and Victory Medals.

2, Albion Terrace, Miles Platting, Manchester.   Z11668

CALDER, D., Sergeant, 12th Lancashire Fusiliers.

Volunteering in September 1914, he was a year later sent to France, but after serving there for six months was drafted to Salonika. There he took a prominent part in fighting on the Doiran front, and was also engaged on transport work. However, owing to malaria, his health broke down, and he was sent to the Base until August 1918, when he again proceeded to the Western Front, and was employed on important guard duties until demobilised in April 1919. He holds the 1914–15 Star, and the General Service and Victory Medals.

18, Swain Street, Coupland Street, Chorlton-on-Medlock, Manchester.   Z3512

CALDWELL, D., Private, S. Lancashire Regiment.
Volunteering in August 1914, he proceeded overseas in February 1915. Whilst serving on the Western Front he was in action at Hill 60, Ypres and Festubert, but unfortunately on August 2nd, 1915, died of tuberculosis, contracted through trench fever. He was entitled to the 1914-15 Star, and the General Service and Victory Medals.
"His memory is cherished with pride."
6, Woburn Place, Chorlton-on-Medlock, Manchester. X3513

CALDWELL, J., Private, R.A.V.C.
Volunteering in 1915, he proceeded overseas after a period of training. Whilst on the Western Front he was engaged on important duties and was present during much fighting at Arras, Albert, Cambrai and Lens. He was demobilised in 1919, and holds the General Service and Victory Medals.
85, Junction Street, Ancoats, Manchester. Z8942A

CALDWELL, J., L/Cpl., 1st Loyal N. Lancs. Regt.
He volunteered in February 1915, and four months later was sent to the Western Front, where he was engaged in heavy fighting at Loos, Albert and Béthune. In June 1916 he was sent back to England, and was employed at Baxendale's Lead Works. He rendered valuable services as a lead roller during the most critical moments of the war, and was not demobilised until March 1919. He holds the 1914-15 Star, and the General Service and Victory Medals.
26, Adelaide Street, Hulme, Manchester. Z3514

CALE, A., Private, Lancashire Fusiliers.
He joined in March 1916, and in the following December was drafted to France. During his service on the Western Front he took part in the fighting at Loos, Ypres, the Somme, and was wounded at Delville Wood in 1917. He was sent to hospital at Rouen, but after his recovery rejoined his unit, and was in action at Arras, and was wounded for the second time at Messines Ridge. He was invalided to England, but later proceeded to Germany with the Army of Occupation, and was stationed at Cologne until November 1919, when he returned home and was demobilised. He holds the General Service and Victory Medals.
4, Morris Street, Ancoats. Manchester. TZ9464

CALLAGHAN, P., Private, 13th Manchester Regt.
He volunteered in September 1914, and a year later was sent to France, where he saw heavy fighting in the Albert sector. In January 1916, he was transferred to Salonika, and took part in the Battles on the Doiran and Struma, and at Monastir, but was taken prisoner by the Bulgars in 1917. During his captivity he was made to do the duties of a labourer. He was released in 1919, and sent home suffering from malaria and dysentery, and was demobilised in April of that year, holding the 1914-15 Star, and the General Service and Victory Medals.
6, Brice Street, Hulme, Manchester. TZ3515

CALLAGHAN, T., Private, 21st Cheshire Regiment.
He volunteered in April 1915, and in the following January was drafted to the Western Front. He took an active part in many engagements, including the Battles of Givenchy and the Somme, and was gassed in December 1916, and invalided to hospital. He was discharged in April 1917, as medically unfit for further military service, and holds the General Service and Victory Medals.
11, Rome Street, Oldham Road, Manchester. Z9960

CALLAGHAN, T., Private, 1st East Lancs. Regt.
Joining in September 1916, he quickly proceeded to the Western Front, where he took part in many engagements, including those on the Somme, and at Ypres, and was taken prisoner in August 1917. He was held in captivity in Germany and suffered many privations. After the Armistice, he was released, and returned home for his demobilisation in March 1919. He holds the General Service and Victory Medals.
15, Milton Street, Ancoats, Manchester. Z8943

CALLAGHAN, T., L/Cpl., 1st K.O.(R.Lancaster Regt.)
He was mobilised at the outbreak of war in August 1914, and at once proceeded with the First Expeditionary Force to the Western Front, where he fought in the Battle of Mons. Whilst in action at Le Cateau in 1914 he was taken prisoner, and employed on agricultural work by the Germans until after the Armistice. In December 1918 he was released, and returning to England was discharged in March 1919, holding the Mons Star, and the General Service and Victory Medals.
12, Dorset Street West, Gorton, Manchester. Z3516

CALLAN, W., Private, 13th Manchester Regiment.
Volunteering in September 1914, he was a year later drafted to France, where he took part in the Battle of Loos. He was then transferred to Salonika, and during over two years service there was engaged in heavy fighting on the Vardar and Doiran fronts. In March 1918 he returned to the Western Front, and served there until March 1919, when he was demobilised, holding the 1914-15 Star, and the General Service and Victory Medals.
92, Margaret Street, West Gorton, Manchester. Z3517

CALLAN, W. J., Private, East Yorkshire Regiment.
He joined in March 1917, and on completion of his training, was drafted to the Western Front early in the following year. After a short period of heavy fighting during the Retreat, he was wounded and taken prisoner at the Battle of the Aisne (III) in May 1918, and was held in captivity until the cessation of hostilities. He was eventually demobilised in December 1919, and holds the General Service and Victory Medals.
17, William Street, Ancoats, Manchester. Z11669

CALOW, G. F., L/Cpl., 1st East Lancashire Regt.
He was mobilised in August 1914, and proceeding with the First Expeditionary Force to France was taken prisoner in the Battle of Mons. During his captivity he was employed in the Iron Works at Westphalia, and was accidentally knocked down by a railway truck and succumbed to his injuries on August 12th, 1916. He was entitled to the Mons Star, and the General Service and Victory Medals.
"Great deeds cannot die."
7, Myrtle Grove, Ardwick, Manchester. Z6279

CALVERT, A., Private, R.A.M.C.
Volunteering in October 1915, he was drafted to France in the following March. Whilst on the Western Front he rendered valuable services as a stretcher bearer at the Battles of Albert and the Somme. He was then transferred to Egypt, but on the voyage East, was unfortunately drowned when the "Transylvania" was torpedoed in the Mediterranean on May 4th, 1917. He was entitled to the General Service and Victory Medals.
"His life for his Country, his soul to God."
13, Prospect Street, Hulme, Manchester. TZ11670

CALVERT, H., Sergt., Loyal North Lancashire Regt.
He volunteered in August 1914, and was drafted overseas in the following year. Whilst on the Western Front he took part in many important engagements, including the Battles of Loos, Albert, the Somme, Bullecourt and Arras. He made the supreme sacrifice being killed in action at Ypres on August 4th, 1917. He was entitled to the 1914-15 Star, and the General Service and Victory Medals.
"Whilst we remember, the sacrifice is not in vain."
13, Jane Street, West Gorton, Manchester. Z8944

CALVERT, T. A., Private, 18th Manchester Regt.
A month after the outbreak of hostilities he volunteered, and in October 1915 was drafted to the Western Front. There he was in fierce fighting at Neuve Chapelle, Loos, La Bassée and Ypres, and was unhappily killed in action during the Battle of the Somme on July 9th, 1916. He was entitled to the 1914-15 Star, and the General Service and Victory Medals.
"Honour to the immortal dead who gave their youth that the world might grow old in peace."
9, Walmer Place, Longsight, Manchester. Z3518

CALVERT, W., Private, 1st Manchester Regiment.
He volunteered in November 1914, and in February 1916 was sent to India, where he was employed on garrison duties at important stations. Later he proceeded to Hong Kong, and afterwards to Vladivostock, and was engaged on responsible guard duties until December 1918, when he returned to China for two months, but being unable to stand the climate was sent back to England, and demobilised in March 1919, holding the General Service and Victory Medals.
146, Heald Grove, Rusholme, Manchester. Z3519

CAMERON, B., Private, Lancashire Fusiliers.
He was mobilised at the outbreak of war, and in the following year was sent to the Dardanelles. There he took part in the Landing at Gallipoli and the Battle of Krithia, and was severely wounded. As a result he unfortunately died on May 5th, 1915, and was entitled to the 1914-15 Star, and the General Service and Victory Medals.
"And doubtless he went in splendid company."
4, Harrold Street, Bradford, Manchester. Z11891

CAMPBELL, A., Gunner, R.G.A.
He joined in March 1916, and was at first employed on the output of shells at Messrs. Cary's, Red Bank, Manchester. In June 1918, however, he was sent to France, and took part in the Battles of Cambrai, where he was gassed in action, Ypres and Le Cateau, and was present at the entry into Mons on Armistice Day. Afterwards he proceeded to Germany and served with the Forces on the Rhine until September 1919, when he returned to England and was demobilised. He holds the General Service and Victory Medals.
145, Ludell Street, Rochdale Road, Manchester. Z9465

CAMPBELL, F., Private, Border Regiment.
He joined in April 1917, and in the following July was drafted to France. Whilst overseas he fought in numerous engagements, including those at Arras, Ypres, and Passchendaele. He returned to England in December 1917. and was engaged on important duties at several stations until June 1919, when he was demobilised. He holds the General Service and Victory Medals.
3, Worrall Street, Collyhurst, Manchester. Z10522

CAMPBELL, G. W., L/Cpl., Royal Welch Fusiliers.

He joined in September 1917, on attaining military age, and in January of the following year was drafted to the Western Front. During his service in France he fought in the Battles of Bapaume, Cambrai, Havrincourt and Ypres, where he was severely wounded in action in September 1918. He was invalided home in consequence, and after his recovery, was sent to Ireland. In 1920 he was serving in India with the Lancashire Fusiliers, and holds the General Service and Victory Medals.
15, Belmont Street, Collyhurst, Manchester. Z10523

CAMPBELL, H., Private, 88th Labour Corps.

He joined in February 1917, and a month later was sent to France, where he was in action at Bullecourt, Messines and Cambrai, and in the final engagements of the war. He did excellent work mending roads in various sectors of the Western Front, and during the last period of his service was engaged in guarding prisoners of war in Belgium. Demobilised in October 1919, he holds the General Service and Victory Medals.
201, Earl Street, Longsight, Manchester. Z3522A

CAMPBELL, H., Bugler, 15th Highland Light Infy.

Volunteering in September 1914, he proceeded in March 1917 to the Palestine front, where he fought in the Battle of Gaza, and later was wounded in action on Hesi Ridge, and sent to hospital at Cairo. On his recovery he was drafted to France, and whilst engaged in heavy fighting was again wounded at Arras in August 1918. He was demobilised in February 1919, and holds the General Service and Victory Medals.
9, Jackson Street, Ardwick, Manchester. Z3520

CAMPBELL, J., Private, 3rd Manchester Regiment.

Volunteering in August 1915, during the course of training he sustained severe injuries in an accident, and was unfortunately unable to continue his service, and was discharged as physically unfit for further duty in August 1916.
8, Holbeck Street, Oldham Road, Manchester. Z9466

CAMPBELL, J. V., Private, 2/4th Royal Scots Regt.

In November 1914 he volunteered for active service, and in August 1916 proceeded overseas. Whilst serving on the Western Front he took an active part in engagements in various sectors, and was unfortunately killed in action in the Battle of the Somme on October 30th, 1916. He was entitled to the General Service and Victory Medals. "Nobly striving,
He nobly fell that we might live."
201, Earl Street, Longsight, Manchester. Z3522B

CAMPBELL, P., C.S.M., 6th Leinster Regt.

He was already serving when war broke out in August 1914, but on account of his age was unable to procure a transfer to a theatre of war. He served at various important stations in Ireland throughout the period of hostilities, and performed very valuable work as a drill instructor. After twenty one years' service in the Army, he was discharged in January 1919.
40, Higher Chatham Street, Chorlton-on-Medlock. Z3521A

CAMPBELL, P., Corporal, 1st Leinster Regiment.

He volunteered in March 1915, and was employed as a Lewis gun instructor in Ireland until September 1916. He was then drafted to Salonika, and was in action on the Struma and the Doiran front. He was later transferred to Egypt and took an active part in engagements on the Suez Canal and afterwards in Palestine, at Jerusalem and Jericho. He was still serving in the Army in 1920, and holds the General Service and Victory Medals. Z3521B
40, Higher Chatham Street, Chorlton-on-Medlock, Manchester.

CAMPBELL, R., Private, Royal Sussex, and Manchester Regiments and R.D.C.

Having previously fought in the South African campaign, he re-enlisted in August 1914, and was stationed in Scotland until May 1916, when he proceeded to Egypt. During his service in this seat of war he took part in most of the engagements, and returned to England in February 1919. He was demobilised in March 1919, and holds the Queen's and King's South African Medals (with clasps Elandslaagte, and Defence of Ladysmith), and the General Service and Victory Medals.
38, Harrowby Street, Collyhurst, Manchester. Z9961

CAMPBELL, T. J., Private, Royal Fusiliers.

He joined in July 1916, and on completion of his training was drafted to the Western Front, where he played a prominent part in heavy fighting on the Ancre and at the Battles of Arras, Bullecourt, Ypres and Cambrai. He laid down his life for King and Country during the last-named engagement in November 1917, and was entitled to the General Service and Victory Medals.
"A costly sacrifice upon the altar of freedom."
37, Eliza Ann Street, Rochdale Road, Manchester. Z9962

CAMPBELL, W., Private, South Lancashire Regt.

He volunteered in October 1914, and in the following February was drafted to France. Whilst in this theatre of war he took part in the fighting at Neuve Chapelle, and Hill 60, where he was severely wounded in May 1915. He was sent to hospital in England, and after receiving medical treatment was invalided out of the Service in June 1916. He holds the 1914-15 Star, and the General Service and Victory Medals.
94, Woodward Street, Ancoats, Manchester. Z9467

CAMPION, E. P., Private, 2nd West Riding Regt.

Volunteering in October 1914, he was sent a month later to the Western Front, and fought in the engagements at Ypres, Neuve Chapelle, Loos and Albert, but was taken to hospital at Rouen, suffering from frost-bite. On rejoining his unit he took an active part in severe fighting in the Somme, Arras, Ypres, Cambrai and Le Cateau sectors, and in the final engagements of the war. He was demobilised in February 1919, and holds the 1914 Star, and the General Service and Victory Medals. 70, Stott Street, Hulme, Manchester. Z3523

CANING, W. Private, King's (Liverpool Regiment).

Joining in April 1916, he was drafted to the Western Front in the following month. He saw much severe fighting in this theatre of war, and was in action at the Battles of Vermelles, Somme (I), Ancre, Beaumont-Hamel, Arras, Bullecourt, Ypres (III) and Cambrai, and in the Retreat and Advance of 1918. He was demobilised in February 1920, and holds the General Service and Victory Medals.
67, Montague Street, Manchester. Z9963

CANNON, E. (M.M.) Private, 8th Manchester Regt.

Joining in May 1916, he proceeded to France in the same year and played a prominent part in the Battles of the Somme (I), Arras, Bullecourt, Messines, Ypres, Passchendaele and Cambrai, and in the Retreat and Advance of 1918. He was wounded in action at Bullecourt in 1917, and at the same time was awarded the Military Medal for conspicuous bravery and devotion to duty. He also holds the General Service and Victory Medals, and was demobilised in January 1919.
142, Hamilton Street, Collyhurst, Manchester. Z9964A

CANNON, P., Private, South Lancashire Regiment.

He volunteered in May 1915, and after a period of training was retained on important guard and transport duties at various stations. He was unsuccessful in obtaining his transfer to a theatre of war before the cessation of hostilities, but, nevertheless, rendered valuable services until demobilised in January 1919.
142, Hamilton Street, Collyhurst, Manchester. Z9964B

CANTWELL, J., Private, 9th Manchester Regiment.

He volunteered in September 1914, and in the following July proceeded to France, where he was in action in the Neuve Chapelle, Ypres, Somme, La Bassée and Albert sectors. In 1916 he was transferred to Salonika and saw heavy fighting on the Doiran front and in the Bulgarian mountains, until July 1918, when he was sent back to the Western Front. After fighting at Lens and Cambrai he was unhappily killed in action on the Somme in October 1918. He was entitled to the 1914-15 Star, and the General Service and Victory Medals.
"Courage, bright hopes and a myriad dreams, splendidly given."
50, Gore Street, Greenheys, Manchester. TZ3524

CAPELLA. A., Private, Lancashire Fusiliers.

He volunteered in October 1914, and after completing his training was sent overseas. During his service on the Western Front, he took part in the Battles of Ypres, Loos, Albert and the Somme (I), where he was unhappily killed in action on July 1st, 1916. He was entitled to the 1914-15 Star, and the General Service and Victory Medals.
"He died the noblest death a man may die,
Fighting for God, and right and liberty."
16, Francisco Street, Collyhurst, Manchester. Z9965

CAPPER, A., Private, Royal Welch Fusiliers.

He enlisted in November 1913, and three months after the outbreak of war was sent overseas. Whilst serving in France he took part in engagements at Ypres, Loos and Messines, and was wounded in action at Cambrai. He was in consequence discharged from the Army in February 1918, as medically unfit for further military service, and holds the 1914 Star, and the General Service and Victory Medals.
40, Inkerman Grove, Greenheys, Manchester. Z3526

CAPPER, A., Private, 7/9th King's Liverpool Regt.

Joining in September 1916, he was retained on home service until July 1918, when he succeeded in obtaining a transfer to the Western Front. There he was in action at Amiens, Bapaume, Havrincourt and Cambrai, and was wounded at Le Cateau in October 1918. In January 1919 he was discharged as unfit for further service, and holds the General Service and Victory Medals.
4, Instruction Place, Rusholme. Manchester. Z3525A

CAPPER, W. F., Private, 9th E. Lancashire Regt.

He volunteered in September 1914, and nine months later was drafted to Salonika, where he served for fifteen months. During this time he was in action in numerous engagements, including those on the Vardar and Doiran fronts, and fell fighting on the Struma on September 13th, 1916. He was entitled to the 1914-15 Star, and the General Service and Victory Medals.
"A costly sacrifice upon the altar of freedom."
4, Instruction Place, Rusholme, Manchester. Z3525B

CARDEN, W., Sapper, R.E.
Volunteering for active service in August 1915, he was drafted overseas seventeen months later. During his service in France he took part in heavy fighting in different sectors of the Front, and was in action at Arras, Vimy Ridge, Bullecourt and Messines. He was invalided to England in July 1917, suffering from a nervous breakdown, and in consequence was discharged from the Army two months later, holding the General Service and Victory Medals.
111, Earl Street, Longsight, Manchester. Z3527

CARDIN, J. F., A.B., Royal Navy.
He was already serving at the outbreak of hostilities in August 1914, and was in action with the Mediterranean Fleet during the Dardanelles campaign. After his ship was torpedoed he was transferred to H.M.S. "Ramillies" and took an active part in important operations. In 1920 he was still serving in the Navy, and holds the 1914-15 Star, and the General Service and Victory Medals. Z3528
57, Cambridge Street, Chorlton-on-Medlock, Manchester.

CARDIN, W., Pte., 8th Manchester Regt., and 42nd East Lancashire Regt.
He was mobilised in August 1914, and a month later proceeded to Egypt where he served for some months before being drafted to Gallipoli. There he took part in fierce fighting in several engagements, and was wounded in the Battle of Krithia and invalided to Malta. Later he proceeded to England and was discharged in February 1917 as a time expired man, holding the 1914-15 Star, and the General Service and Victory Medals.
19, Robinson Street, Hulme, Manchester. Z3529

CAREY, A., Sergeant, Labour Corps.
Volunteering in August 1914, he proceeded to France in the following February, and did conspicuously good work during the Battles of Hill 60, Loos and Vermelles. He was then transferred to Egypt and saw heavy fighting at Katia, El Fasher, Magdhaba and Rafa before being sent to Palestine, where he took an active part in the Battles of Gaza and in the capture of Jerusalem. He was demobilised in August 1920, and holds the 1914-15 Star, and the General Service and Victory Medals.
171, Victoria Square, Oldham Road, Manchester. Z8945

CAREY, J., Mechanic, R.A.F.
He joined in May 1917, and was engaged at various stations on work which called for a high degree of technical skill. He rendered valuable services, and was demobilised after the Armistice, but rejoined the R.A.M.C. later, and proceeded to Germany, where he served with the Army of Occupation. He was finally demobilised in September 1920.
13, Day Street, Butler Street, Manchester. Z8946

CAREY, R., Pte., R.A.S.C. and King's (L'pool Regt.)
He joined the Army in July 1917, and was not successful in obtaining a transfer to the fighting zone. He was retained on Home Service and when transferred to the R.A.S.C. was stationed at Barry, Swansea and Bettersfield, where he rendered valuable assistance in looking after supplies, and forage for the horses. He was eventually demobilised in November 1919.
16, Clifford Street, Lower Openshaw, Manchester. Z3530

CAREY, S., Private, 2nd King's (Liverpool Regt.)
He volunteered in May 1915, and in October of the same year proceeded to the East, where he took part in the first Landing at Salonika. He afterwards saw much severe fighting, taking part in important engagements on the Vardar, Doiran and Struma fronts, and was also present at the recapture of Monastir. He was sent home and invalided from the Service in September 1918, suffering from malaria, and unhappily died of pneumonia on May 14th, of the following year. He was entitled to the 1914-15 Star, and the General Service and Victory Medals.
"He joined the great white company of valiant souls."
112, Beaumont Street, Beswick, Manchester. Z9966

CAREY, W. H., Private, K.O. (R. Lancaster Regt.)
Volunteering in August 1914, he proceeded overseas in the following July. Whilst on the Western Front he served in engagements at Loos, Neuve Chapelle, Hill 60, St. Eloi, Ypres, Festubert, Givenchy, La Bassée, Albert, the Somme (I), Beaucourt, Beaumont-Hamel, Ypres (III), Passchendaele and the Somme (II). He was gassed during an attack on La Bassée in 1915, and was demobilised in March 1919, holding the 1914-15 Star, and the General Service and Victory Medals.
16, Sutherland Street, Hulme, Manchester. Z3531

CARLIN, J., Driver, R.F.A.
He volunteered in January 1915, and in the following April was sent to the Western Front, where he fought in the Battles of Festubert, Loos, Albert and the Somme. In June 1917 he was transferred to Salonika and took an active part in heavy fighting during the Advance on the Vardar front. In 1919 he returned to England and was demobilised in June of that year, holding the 1914-15 Star, and the General Service and Victory Medals.
85, Bickley Street, Moss Side, Manchester. Z3522

CARLISLE, S., Private, Royal Fusiliers.
He volunteered in August 1915, and in the following December was drafted to Salonika. Whilst in this theatre of war he took part in much of the heavy fighting on the Vardar and Doiran fronts, and was wounded in action in May 1916. He returned to England in February 1919, after the close of hostilities, and was demobilised in March, holding the 1914-15 Star, and the General Service and Victory Medals.
22, Dickens Street, Miles Platting, Manchester. Z10524

CARLISLE, W. (O.B.E.), Lieut. and Q.M., 17th Sussex Regiment.
He volunteered in August 1914, and in June 1915 proceeded to France, where he fought with distinction in the Battles of Loos, Albert, the Somme, Ypres and Passchendaele, and was wounded in action and also gassed. In November 1917 he was drafted to Italy, where he held the rank of Quarter-Master and served on the Asiago Plateau for fifteen months. He was demobilised in February 1920. He was mentioned in Despatches on three occasions, and was awarded the O.B.E. for valuable services rendered. He also holds the 1914-15 Star, and the General Service and Victory Medals.
171, Lloyd Street, Greenheys, Manchester. Z3533

CARMICHAEL, J. A. (M.M.), C.S.M., 4th King's (Liverpool Regiment).
He volunteered in August 1914, and five months later was sent to the Western Front. There he fought with distinction at Armentières, the Somme, Arras and Douai, and was unfortunately killed in action at Polygon Wood, on September 27th, 1917. He was awarded the Military Medal for conspicuous gallantry in the Field, and also received a Russian Decoration. He was entitled to the 1914-15 Star, and the General Service and Victory Medals.
"Great deeds cannot die."
10, Adelaide Road, Bradford, Manchester. Z11881A

CARMICHAEL, W., Private, Border Regiment.
After volunteering in August 1914, he was retained on important coastal defence duties at various stations until September 1917, when he was drafted to the Western Front. There he saw severe fighting in various sectors, and took part in the Battles of Ypres, Cambrai, the Marne and Bapaume, and many other engagements until the cessation of hostilities. Demobilised in February 1919, he holds the General Service and Victory Medals.
20, Aspden Street, Ancoats, Manchester. Z9967

CARNEY, J., Private, Royal Irish Fusiliers.
He volunteered in August 1914, and in April of the following year, was drafted to the Dardanelles, where, after taking part in the Landing at Cape Helles, he fought in the Battles of Krithia and at Suvla Bay. On the Evacuation of Gallipoli he was transferred to Salonika and there saw severe fighting on the Doiran and Struma fronts, and at Monastir. He was for three months in hospital at Alexandria, suffering from dysentery and finally returned home and was invalided from the Army in April 1918. He holds the 1914-15 Star, and the General Service and Victory Medals.
35, Zinc Street, Rochdale Road, Manchester. Z9968

CARNEY, T., Corporal, 20th Manchester Regt. and King's (Liverpool Regiment).
Volunteering in August 1915, he proceeded four months later to France, and was in action in the Neuve Chapelle, Somme, Ypres and Passchendaele sectors. His health then broke down, and he was sent back to England until September 1917, when he returned to the Western Front as a Lewis gunner in the King's (Liverpool Regiment), with which he carried out excellent work at Cambrai and Ypres (III), and in the final victorious engagements of the war. Demobilised in April 1920, he holds the 1914-15 Star, and the General Service and Victory Medals.
11, Anthony Street, Ardwick, Manchester. Z3534

CARR, J., Private, 1/6th Manchester Regiment.
He joined in September 1916, and after a period of training was drafted in February of the following year to the Western Front. There he took part in important engagements in various sectors, including the Battles of Arras, Bullecourt, Ypres, the Marne, Havrincourt and Le Cateau, and was wounded in action on the Somme in the Retreat of March 1918. He was demobilised in January 1919, and holds the General Service and Victory Medals.
25, Park Street, West Gorton, Manchester. Z9969

CARR, J., Bombardier, R.G.A.
He volunteered in March 1915, and embarked for France in February of the following year. During his service on the Western Front he was wounded and gassed in the Ypres salient in August 1917, and was sent to hospital at St. Omer. After his recovery he rejoined his unit, and was again wounded in action near Cambrai, in April 1918, and invalided to hospital at Wimereux. He afterwards returned to the firing line and was present at the memorable entry into Mons at dawn on Armistice Day. He was demobilised after his return to England in April 1919, and holds the General Service and Victory Medals.
195, Cobden Street, Ancoats, Manchester. Z9468

CARR, J., Driver, R.A.S.C.

He volunteered in November 1914, but was retained on Home Service until January 1917. When he proceeded to France. There he was attached to the Road Construction Company, of the R.E. and served with this Corps at Ypres, the Somme, Bapaume and Armentières. He also took an active part in the Allied Advance of 1918, and after the Armistice served in Germany with the Army of Occupation. He was demobilised in April 1919, and holds the General Service and Victory Medals.

75, Crondall Street, Moss Side, Manchester.   Z3535

CARR, W., Private, Lancashire Fusiliers.

Volunteering in July 1915, he was on completion of his training drafted to the Western Front, where he was engaged in fierce fighting at Loos, Neuve Chapelle and Albert, and was wounded and taken prisoner during the Battle of the Somme in October 1916. Throughout the period of his captivity he was employed on a farm in Germany, and on his release returned to England and was demobilised in February 1919, holding the 1914–15 Star, and the General Service and Victory Medals.

38, Gresham Street, Lower Openshaw, Manchester.   Z3536

CARR, W., Private, Manchester Regiment.

Called up from the Reserve in August 1914, he was sent to France with the first Expeditionary Force, and took part in the Battle of and the Retreat from Mons. He was wounded in action in October 1914, and was invalided home. On his recovery he served with the Military Police until October 1915, when he was drafted to Egypt. Whilst in this theatre of war, he saw much severe fighting in the Suez Canal and Sinai Desert zones, and was later stationed at Cairo and Kantara until the cessation of hostilities. Demobilised in March 1919, he holds the Queen's South African Medals, the Mons Star, and the General Service and Victory Medals.

80, Princess Street, Bradford, Manchester.   Z8948

CARRINGTON, R., Private, Cheshire Regiment.

He joined in July 1916, and after a period of training in Ireland proceeded to France. There he served as a Lewis gunner and saw much heavy fighting at Ypres, Cambrai, the Somme (II) and in the Retreat and Advance of 1918, and was gassed in action. After hostilities ceased he went to Germany with the Army of Occupation, where he served until his demobilisation in February 1919. He holds the General Service and Victory Medals.

3, Abbey Field Street, Openshaw, Manchester.   Z8949

CARRINGTON, S., Private, 8th Manchester Regt.

In August 1914 he volunteered, and in September 1915 was drafted to France, where he served for three years. During that time he saw much heavy fighting, and was severely wounded on two occasions. He was in action at Vermelles and Amiens, and in various other sectors, and in August 1918 was invalided to England and retained on Home Service until demobilised in February 1919, holding the 1914–15 Star, and the General Service and Victory Medals.

2, Union Street, Rusholme, Manchester.   Z3537

CARROLE, L., Private, Lancashire Fusiliers.

He was mobilised in August 1914, and at once proceeded to the Western Front, where he was in action at Mons, Loos, the Somme and Cambrai, and took an active part in the Advance of 1918. During this period of service in France he was wounded on four occasions and also gassed. He was eventually discharged from the Army in May 1919, and holds the Mons Star, and the General Service and Victory Medals. 7, Romeo Street, Ardwick, Manchester.   Z3538

CARROLL, A., Pte. 6th K.O. (R. Lancaster Regt.)

He volunteered in September 1914, and proceeded to Mesopotamia nine months later. During his service in this theatre of war he was in action at the Battles of Kut (I), Ctesiphon, Kut-el-Amara, Um-el-Hannah, Sanna-i-yat, Kut (II) and Ramadich and at the capture of Baghdad and Tekrit. He holds the 1914–15 Star, and the General Service and Victory Medals, and was demobilised in February 1919.

29, Meadow Street, Ardwick, Manchester.   Z11671

CARROLL, A., Private, 2nd Manchester Regiment.

When war was declared in 1914, he was called up from the Reserve, and immediately proceeded to France, where after fighting at Mons and Ypres, he was wounded at Hill 60. On returning to the firing line, he was in action at Arras, Messines, Ypres and Cambrai and in the Retreat and Advance of 1918, and was again wounded at Ypres. He served on the Western Front until discharged in February 1919, and holds the Mons Star, and the General Service and Victory Medals.

40, Crissey Street, Miles Platting, Manchester.   Z11478

CARROLL, E., Driver, R.F.A.

He was mobilised in August 1914, and was shortly afterwards drafted to France. There he took part in the Battles of Ypres (I), Neuve Chapelle, Givenchy, Laventie, Festubert, the Somme, the Ancre, Ypres (III) and Passchendaele. In 1917 he was transferred to Italy and saw much fighting on the Asiago Plateau and on the Piave. He returned home and was discharged in March 1919, holding the 1914 Star, and the General Service and Victory Medals.

86, Long Street, Ancoats, Manchester.   Z8950

CARROLL, E., Private, 7th Manchester Regiment.

He joined in February 1916, and was retained at home on important duties until June 1917, when he was drafted to France. In this theatre of war he took part in several important engagements, including the Battles of Ypres, and Cambrai, and was unfortunately killed in action on the Marne on June 23rd, 1918. He was entitled to the General Service and Victory Medals.

"Nobly striving,
He nobly fell that we might live."

87, Earl Street, Longsight, Manchester.   Z3540A

CARROLL, F., L/Corpl, 9th E. Lancashire Regiment.

He volunteered in September 1914, and in the following July proceeded to Salonika. There he took part in strenuous fighting on the Doiran, Struma and Vardar fronts, and was also in action at Monastir. Whilst home on leave he was admitted to Redcar Red Barn Hospital, suffering from malaria and pneumonia, from the effects of which he unhappily died on February 10th, 1919. He was entitled to the 1914–15 Star, and the General Service and Victory Medals.

"He passed out of the sight of men by the path of duty and self-sacrifice."

87, Earl Street, Longsight, Manchester.   Z3540B

CARROLL, F., Private, 7th E. Yorkshire Regiment.

Volunteering in December 1915, he was employed on important duties at various home stations until September 1917, when he was sent to France. During his service overseas he participated in several important engagements, including actions on the Ancre front and at Riencourt and Gouzeaucourt, where he was wounded in September 1918. Returning home in January 1919, he was demobilised a month later, and holds the General Service and Victory Medals.

95, Halston Street, Hulme, Manchester.   Z3541

CARROLL, J., Rifleman, King's Royal Rifle Corps.

He volunteered at the outbreak of war in August 1914, and in the following January proceeded to the Western Front. There he took part in several important engagements, including the Battles of Ypres, Festubert and Loos, and did good work until he unfortunately died in June 1915. He was entitled to the 1914–15 Star, and the General Service and Victory Medals.

"Courage, bright hopes, and a myriad dreams, splendidly given."

77, Chester Street, Chorlton-on-Medlock, Manchester.   Z3543

CARROLL, J., Driver, R.F.A.

He joined in February 1918, and after undergoing a period of training, served at various stations, where he was engaged on important duties as a driver. He was not successful in his efforts to obtain his transfer to a theatre of war, but nevertheless, did much useful work with his Battery until December 1918, when he was demobilised.

23, Garrick Street, Ancoats, Manchester.   Z9970

CARROLL, J., Pte. K.O. (R. Lancaster Regt.)

He volunteered in July 1915, and whilst undergoing training at Aldershot, was severely injured in an accident and was in hospital at Cambridge until December 1915, when he was invalided from the Army. He unfortunately died on October 9th, 1916.

"Thinking that remembrance, though unspoken, may reach him where he sleeps."

16, Rigel Street, Ancoats, Manchester.   Z9971A

CARROLL, J., Private, 5th Border Regiment.

He joined in March 1917, and on completion of a period of training in September of that year, proceeded to the Western Front, where he saw severe fighting in various sectors. He took part in the Battle of Cambrai and many other important engagements, fought also in the Retreat and Advance of 1918, and after the cessation of hostilities, served with the Army of Occupation in Germany. He was demobilised on his return home in October 1919, and holds the General Service and Victory Medals.

16, Rigel Street, Ancoats, Manchester.   Z9971B

CARROLL, J., Private, Manchester Regiment.

Having enlisted in August 1908, he was already in the Army when war broke out six years later, and was immediately drafted to the Western Front, where he fought in the Retreat from Mons. He also took part in many other important engagements until severely wounded in action in the second Battle of Ypres, was sent to hospital at Manchester. He was invalided from the Army in September 1916, and holds the Mons Star, and the General Service and Victory Medals.

23, Clayton Road, Bradford, Manchester.   Z9972

CARROLL, J., Private, Border Regiment.

He volunteered in April 1915, and later in the same year was sent to France. Whilst on this front he fought in many engagements, and was wounded in the vicinity of Ypres in February 1916. He was subsequently invalided home and discharged as medically unfit for further service in February 1917. He holds the 1914–15 Star, and the General Service and Victory Medals.

6, Windsor Street, Rochdale Road, Manchester.   Z10525

CARROLL, J. J., Private, 8th Manchester Regiment.
He volunteered in February 1915, and in the following August
was drafted to the Dardanelles, where he saw much severe
fighting. After the Evacuation of the Gallipoli Peninsula
he was transferred to France and took part in the Battles of
the Somme, Arras, Ypres, Passchendaele and Cambrai.
He was demobilised in March 1919, and holds the 1914–15
Star, and the General Service and Victory Medals.
4, Kertch Street, Ancoats, Manchester.   Z8951

CARROLL, J. W., Private, 2nd Manchester Regt.
Volunteering in August 1914, he proceeded to the Western
Front on completing his training in November of that year,
and there saw much severe fighting in various sectors. After
taking part in the Battles of La Bassée and Ypres he was
invalided to hospital at Lincoln in February 1915, suffering
from fever, but on his recovery was drafted to Salonika.
There he took part in important engagements on the Doiran
and Struma fronts, finally returning home for demobilisation
in May 1919. He holds the 1914 Star, and the General Service
and Victory Medals.
94, Lind Street, Ancoats. Manchester.   Z9973

CARROLL, M., Private, Border Regiment.
He volunteered in September 1914, and in the following March
was sent to the Dardanelles. There he took part in several
severe actions, and was wounded and invalided home. After
spending some time in hospital at Manchester, he was drafted
to France, saw further fighting and was again wounded.
Evacuated to England, he was admitted to hospital and eventually discharged in March 1918, holding the 1914–15 Star,
and the General Service and Victory Medals.
6, Nelson Place, Rusholme, Manchester.   Z3544

CARROLL, P., Private, Lancashire Fusiliers.
He joined in June 1916, and in February of the following
year proceeded to the Western Front, where he saw much
severe fighting on the Somme, and in various other sectors.
He died gloriously on the Field of Battle at Cambrai on November 11th, 1917. He was entitled to the General Service and
Victory Medals.
    "He died the noblest death a man may die,
    Fighting for God, and right, and liberty."
4, Chapman Square, Bradford, Manchester.   Z8952

CARROLL, R., Gunner, R.F.A.
Mobilised in August 1914, he proceeded in the following
February to Egypt. There he was in action on the Suez
Canal, and at Katia and Romani, after which he was transferred to France. In this theatre of war he took part in heavy
fighting at Passchendaele, and on the Somme front, and in
July 1918 was invalided home on account of ill-health. He
was subsequently demobilised in February 1919, and holds
the 1914–15 Star, and the General Service and Victory Medals.
17, Nuttall Street, Chorlton-on-Medlock, Manchester. Z3542

CARROLL, W., Pte., 9th Northumberland Fusiliers.
He volunteered in January 1915, and six months later was
drafted to the Western Front. During his service overseas,
he took part in strenuous fighting at Loos, Albert, Vermelles,
Ploegsteert Wood, and the Somme, and was wounded in July
1916. Invalided home, he was admitted to hospital in Lincoln,
where he remained until October 1917, when he was discharged
as unfit for further service. He holds the 1914–15 Star, and
the General Service and Victory Medals.
7, Hardy Street, West Gorton, Manchester.   Z3539

**CARSON, A. M., Pte., 10th Border Regt., and 3/8th
Manchester Regt.**
Volunteering in November 1914, he underwent his training
at Southend, and Hamilton, Scotland, after which he was
stationed at Salisbury Plain, Southport, and Codford, engaged
on police and other important duties. Medically unfit for
transfer overseas, he nevertheless rendered valuable services
at home, until he was invalided out of the Army in January
1917.
25, St. Clements Place, West Gorton, Manchester.   Z3547

CARSON, D., Private, Manchester Regiment.
He volunteered in November 1915, and in the following May
proceeded to France. During three months' service in this
theatre of hostilities he took part in heavy engagements at
Vimy Ridge, and on the Somme front, where he was severely
wounded. He unfortunately died in hospital at Rouen in
August 1916, from the effects of his wounds, and was buried
in the military cemetery there. He was entitled to the General
Service and Victory Medals.
    "His memory is cherished with pride."
11, Walmer Place, Longsight, Manchester.   Z3545

CARSON, G., Private, South Lancashire Regiment.
He joined in January 1916, and six months later was drafted
to India. There he was employed with his unit on garrison
and other important duties at various stations, and performed
uniformly good work. He subsequently contracted malaria,
and being invalided home, was eventually discharged in August
1919, holding the General Service and Victory Medals.
204, New Bank Street, Longsight, Manchester.   Z3546

CARTER, A., Private, Loyal N. Lancs. Regiment.
He volunteered in August 1914, and towards the end of the
same year was sent to France. There he took part in the
Battles of Neuve Chapelle, Hill 60, Ypres (II), Loos, Vimy
Ridge, Somme (I), Arras, Ypres (II) and Cambrai, and was
unfortunately killed in action on the Somme front on June
21st, 1918. He was entitled to the 1914–15 Star, and the
General Service and Victory Medals.
    "A costly sacrifice upon the altar of freedom."
4, Albany Street, Ardwick, Manchester.   Z3548–51

CARTER, C., Stoker, R.N., H.M.S. "Pembroke."
He was mobilised from the Reserve in August 1914, and soon
afterwards took part in the defence of Antwerp. In April
of the following year he proceeded to the Dardanelles, and was
present at the Naval operations there until the Evacuation
of the Peninsula. He then returned to home waters, where
he was engaged on important duties during the remaining
period of the war. He was demobilised in January 1919,
and holds the 1914–15 Star, and the General Service (with
four clasps) and Victory Medals.
27, Limer Street, Rochdale Road, Manchester.   Z10526

CARTER, E., Sapper, R.E.
He joined in August 1916, and after completing his training
was retained on important duties in England until February
1918, when he was drafted to the Western Front. There he
was engaged on road-making and bridge-building at Ypres
and Cambrai, and in various other sectors, was stationed also
at Boulogne, and took an active part in the Retreat and Advance of 1918. He afterwards served with the Army of Occupation in Germany, finally returning home in August 1919,
for demobilisation in the following month. He holds the
General Service and Victory Medals.
48, Ryder Street, Bradford, Manchester.   Z9974

CARTER, F., Private, 18th Manchester Regiment.
Volunteering in March 1915, he was drafted to the Western
Front twelve months later, and there took part in various
important engagements. He made the supreme sacrifice,
falling in action on July 1st, 1916, during the Advance on the
Somme. He was entitled to the General Service and Victory
Medals.   "Great deeds cannot die:
They with the sun and moon, renew their light for ever."
53, Gunson Street, Ancoats, Manchester.   Z8953A

CARTER, G. W., L/Corporal, R.A.M.C.
He volunteered in September 1914, and in August of the
following year was sent to Gallipoli. Whilst there he did
good service in the Landing at Suvla Bay, and in the capture
of Chunuk Bair. After the Evacuation of the Peninsula
he was drafted to the Western Front, and served in the Battles
of the Somme, Passchendaele and Cambrai, and was wounded
in October 1918 at Poelcapelle. He returned home and was
demobilised in June 1919, and holds the 1914–15 Star, and
the General Service and Victory Medals.
58, Inkerman Street, Collyhurst, Manchester.   Z10527

CARTER, J., Corporal, R.A.F.
He joined in May 1916, but was not successful in obtaining
a transfer to a theatre of war. Retained at home, he was
stationed at the Army Experimental Station, Orford Ness,
and was employed on important duties which demanded a high
degree of technical skill. He rendered valuable services
until he was demobilised in October 1919.
40, Lime Bank Street, Ardwick, Manchester.   Z3552

CARTER, J. P., Private, R.N.D. and Sapper, R.E.
He volunteered in June 1915, and underwent a period of
training prior to being drafted to the Western Front in April
of the following year. There he saw much fighting in
various sectors and took part in the Battles of Albert, Vimy
Ridge, the Somme, the Ancre, Bullecourt, Ypres, Passchendaele,
Lys, Amiens, Havrincourt and Epéhy, and many minor engagements. He was demobilised on his return home in February
1919, and holds the General Service and Victory Medals.
35, Carver Street, Chorlton-on-Medlock, Manchester.   TZ8954

CARTER, J. W., Private, R.A.M.C.
He volunteered in November 1915, and after completing a
period of training, served at various stations, where he was
engaged on duties of great importance. He was unable to
obtain his transfer overseas on account of ill-health, and was
for a considerable period in hospital, where he underwent
several operations, before being invalided from the Army in
July 1919.
53, Gunson Street, Ancoats, Manchester.   Z8953B

CARTER, J. W., Private, 17th Royal Sussex Regt.
Joining in July 1917, he was retained at home on important
duties until August 1918, and was then drafted to France.
There he participated in severe fighting at La Bassée, Givenchy,
Festubert, Arras and Lille, and did good work until the ter-
mination of hostilities. He returned home in March 1919,
and was demobilised, holding the General Service and Victory
Medals. 29, Halsbury Street, Longsight, Manchester.   Z3549

CARTER, J. W., L/Corporal, R.A.M.C.
He volunteered in November 1915, and after his training was retained at Dartford on important general hospital duties. He rendered valuable services, but was not successful in obtaining his transfer overseas before the cessation of hostilities. He was demobilised in October 1919.
89, Ryder Street, Collyhurst, Manchester. Z10528A

CARTER, P., Private, 13th Manchester Regiment.
He volunteered in September 1914, and in the following year proceeded to Salonika, where he saw much severe fighting. He took part in the re-capture of Monastir, and in many other important engagements on the Doiran, Struma and Vardar fronts until the cessation of hostilities. He finally returned to England for demobilisation in March 1919, and holds the 1914–15 Star, and the General Service and Victory Medals.
28, Branson Street, Ancoats, Manchester. Z9975

CARTER, R., Sergt., R.A.V.C.
Two months after volunteering in April 1915, he was drafted to the Western Front, where, attached to the R.F.A., he was engaged on important duties in various sectors. He was present at the Battles of Loos, the Somme, Messines, Ypres and Cambrai, and many other engagements and also took an active part in the Retreat and Advance of 1918. He afterwards served with the Army of Occupation in Germany until his demobilisation in March 1919, and holds the 1914–15 Star, and the General Service and Victory Medals.
114, Clifton Street, Bradford, Manchester. Z6045

CARTER, W., Private, Border Regiment.
Volunteering in August 1914, he proceeded in the following January to the Western Front. There he took part in many important engagements, including the Battles of Festubert, Ypres, Loos and the Somme, where he suffered from shell-shock, and was in consequence invalided home in August 1917. Upon his recovery he was transferred to the Military Police, and was eventually demobilised in December 1918. He holds the 1914–15 Star, and the General Service and Victory Medals.
12, Harper Street, Longsight, Manchester. Z3550

CARTEY, R., Private, 13th Manchester Regiment.
He volunteered in January 1915, and on completing three months' training, was drafted to the Western Front, where he took part in the Battles of Ypres and the Somme, and engagements at Nieuport, and many other places. He was afterwards transferred to Mesopotamia, and there served at Kut and was later with his unit in Italy, before returning home for demobilisation in February 1920. He holds the 1914–15 Star, and the General Service and Victory Medals.
9, Milton Street, Ancoats, Manchester. Z8955

CARTHY, F., L/Corporal, K.O. (R. Lancaster Regt.)
He volunteered in November 1915, and three months afterwards was sent to France. In this theatre of war he took part in heavy fighting at Loos, St. Eloi, Ploegsteert Wood, the Somme, Arras, Vimy Ridge, Lens and Ypres. He was severely wounded at Cambrai in November 1917, and evacuated to England was admitted to hospital at Newmarket. Eventually demobilised in September 1919, he holds the General Service and Victory Medals.
108, Thomas Street, West Gorton, Manchester. Z2418–9B

CARTLEDGE, G., Private, 1st Lancashire Fusiliers.
A serving soldier, he was stationed in India at the outbreak of war in August 1914, and in the following April was sent to the Dardanelles. There he took part in heavy fighting, and was later transferred to the Western Front. In this theatre of war he was in action at Ypres and at Bullecourt, where he fell fighting on July 31st, 1916. He was entitled to the 1914–15 Star, and the General Service and Victory Medals.
91, Chester Street, Hulme, Manchester. TZ3553

CARTWRIGHT, E., Private, 2/4th Yorkshire Regt.
He joined in September 1916, but was not medically fit for service in a theatre of war. Stationed for some time at Northallerton, he was subsequently attached to the Labour Corps, and was employed at a Government Pumping Station. Whilst thus engaged, he performed consistently good work, and was demobilised in March 1919.
11, Roy Street, Ardwick, Manchester. Z3554A

CARTWRIGHT, E., Pte., K.O. (R. Lancaster Regt.)
Joining in March 1917, he was sent after a period of training to Ireland, where he was stationed at Fermoy, and employed on garrison and other important duties. He proceeded later to Salonika, and there took part in several engagements on the Vardar front. Invalided home on account of having contracted malaria, he was eventually demobilised in November 1919, and holds the General Service and Victory Medals.
11, Roy Street, Ardwick, Manchester. Z3554B

CARTWRIGHT, T., Sergt., 1st Cheshire Regiment.
He was mobilised in August 1914, and immediately proceeded to France with the First Expeditionary Force. After serving with distinction through the Retreat from Mons, and in the strenuous fighting during the early days of the war, he died gloriously on the Field of Battle at La Bassée on November 16th, 1914. He was entitled to the Mons Star, and the General Service and Victory Medals.
81, Silver Street, Hulme, Manchester. TZ11672

CARTY, J., Private, 1st East Lancashire Regiment.
Four months after volunteering in January 1915, he was drafted to the Western Front, where he took part in the Battles of Hill 60, Ypres and Festubert, and many minor engagements. In August 1915, however, he was invalided home, suffering from consumption, and in November of that year was discharged as medically unfit for further service. He unhappily died on December 21st, 1919. He was entitled to the 1914–15 Star, and the General Service and Victory Medals.
" His memory is cherished with pride."
6, Grantham Street, West Gorton, Manchester. Z9976A

CARTY, J., Private, R.A.V.C.
He joined in November 1917, and after undergoing a period of training served at various stations, where he was engaged on duties of great importance. He was not successful in his efforts to obtain his transfer overseas, but nevertheless, rendered very valuable services with his Company until November 1919, when he was demobilised.
6, Grantham Street, West Gorton, Manchester. Z9977

CARVEL, T., Driver, R.E.
He joined in July 1917, and after a period of training was drafted in June of the following year to Russia. There he was engaged on important transport duties at Archangel, and many other places, and did much useful work until his return to England for demobilisation in August 1919. He holds the General Service and Victory Medals.
14, Gray Street, Ancoats, Manchester. Z9978

CASEY, J., Private, 8th Manchester Regiment.
He volunteered in October 1914, and in May of the following year proceeded to the Dardanelles, where after taking part in the Landing at Cape Helles, he fought in the Battles of Krithia and Achi Baba. On the Evacuation of the Gallipoli Peninsula, he was sent to Egypt, and served on the Suez Canal until transferred to the Western Front in March 1917. There he took part in the Battles of Vimy Ridge, Ypres and Passchendaele, and many other engagements, and also served through the Retreat and Advance of 1918. He was demobilised in February 1919, and holds the 1914–15 Star, and the General Service and Victory Medals.
2, Vale Street, North Porter Street, Miles Platting, Manchester. Z9979

CASEY, J., Private, K.O. (R. Lancaster Regt.), and Pioneer, R.E.
He joined in January 1916, and after serving for some time at Prees Heath was transferred to the Royal Engineers. Stationed at Chepstow, he was employed as a pioneer, and was subsequently engaged on special work in connection with laying water pipes at other stations. He was not successful in obtaining a transfer to a theatre of war, but rendered valuable services at home until he was demobilised in February 1919.
17, Claremont Street, Chorlton-on-Medlock. Manchester. Z3555

CASEY, M., Private, 2nd Lancashire Fusiliers.
He volunteered in January 1916, and in the following month was drafted to Gibraltar. There he was engaged on important garrison duties for three years, and during this period rendered very valuable services with his unit. He finally returned home for demobilisation in February 1919, and holds the General Service and Victory Medals.
113, Jersey Dwellings, Ancoats, Manchester. Z9980

CASEY, M., Private, 1/7th Manchester Regiment.
He volunteered in May 1915, and four months later was sent to Gallipoli, where he served until the close of hostilities there. In January 1916, he proceeded to Egypt, and after serving at Alexandria, Khartoum, the Sudan and El Arish was transferred to France. On this front he took part in fierce fighting at La Bassée, Ypres and Nieuport, and was wounded in action at Havrincourt in October 1917. In consequence he was invalided out of the Army in January 1918, holding the 1914–15 Star, and the General Service and Victory Medals.
131, Jersey Street Dwellings, Ancoats, Manchester. Z11292B

CASEY, P. F., L/Corporal, Royal Munster Fusiliers.
He volunteered in March 1915, and two months later proceeded to France. There he played a prominent part in heavy fighting at Ypres and Loos, and was severely wounded and gassed. He was invalided home, and admitted to hospital in Reading, and owing to gas-posioning, lost the sight of his left eye, being eventually discharged in 1917 as unfit for further service. He holds the 1914–15 Star, and the General Service and Victory Medals.
5, Charlotte Street, Chorlton-on-Medlock, Manchester. Z3556

CASEY, R., Private, 4th East Yorkshire Regiment.
He volunteered for active service in September 1915, and on completion of a period of training in Yorkshire was drafted overseas in October 1916. He served in the West Indies for eighteen months, and during that time was employed on important garrison duties at Hamilton. In April 1918 he returned to England suffering from fever, and was eventually demobilised in January 1919, holding the General Service and Victory Medals.
121, Montague Street, Collyhurst, Manchester. Z11479

CASEY, W., Private, 9th Lancashire Fusiliers.
Mobilised in August 1914, he proceeded twelve months later to the Dardanelles. After taking part in heavy fighting at Suvla Bay, he was sent to Egypt, where he was in action at El Cantara. In July 1916, he was transferred to France, and saw further fighting on the Somme, and at Beaumont-Hamel, Arras, Ypres, Bapaume, Havrincourt, Cambrai, and the Ancre. He was wounded at Passchendaele in August 1917, but remained overseas until March 1919, when he returned home and was demobilised, holding the 1914-15 Star, and the General Service and Victory Medals.
17, Foster Street, City Road, Hulme, Manchester. Z3557

CASH, D., Private, Manchester Regiment.
He joined in June 1917, but was not successful in obtaining a transfer to a theatre of hostilities. Retained at home, he was stationed at Derby, Gloucester, Salisbury Plain, Aldershot, and London, and was employed on various duties of an important nature. He performed consistently good work until he was demobilised in November 1919.
9, Fenn Street, Hulme, Manchester. Z3558

CASHIAN, J., Corporal, 1st Cheshire Regiment.
Already serving in August 1914, he was at once ordered to France, where he participated in the Battle of Mons, and the subsequent Retreat. He later took part in the Battles of Le Cateau, La Bassée, Ypres, Neuve Chapelle, Loos, Vimy Ridge, Arras and Cambrai and during over four years' service on the Western Front, was twice wounded at Loos in October 1915, and on the Somme in September 1916. In 1920 he was serving at Colchester, and holds the Mons Star, and the General Service and Victory Medals.
13, Hazel Street, Hulme, Manchester. Z3559

CASHION, J., Private, 2nd Manchester Regiment.
He volunteered in January 1915, and after four months' training proceeded to the Western Front, where he saw severe fighting in various sectors. He took part in the Battles of Ypres, Passchendaele and Cambrai, and many other important engagements, fought also in the Retreat and Advance of 1918, and was three times wounded in action on the Somme—in July 1916, in September of the following year, and again twelve months later. Demobilised in March 1919, he holds the 1914-15 Star, and the General Service and Victory Medals.
11, Wilkinson Street, Rochdale Road, Manchester. Z9981

CASPER, J., Private, 8th Manchester Regiment.
Joining in March 1916, he was drafted to the Western Front on completing his training in September of that year, and there saw much severe fighting. After taking part in the Battles of Vimy Ridge, and the Somme, and other engagements in various sectors he was taken prisoner, and held in captivity until after the cessation of hostilities. Demobilised on his release in January 1919, he holds the General Service and Victory Medals.
11, Stand Street, Ancoats, Manchester. TZ9018B

CASSERLEY, J., Private, 7th Manchester Regiment.
Volunteering in August 1914, he was drafted to Egypt in the following month and served there until he proceeded to Gallipoli in March 1915. He was in action in the Battles of Krithia and was wounded, and after the Evacuation of the Peninsula embarked for France. He fought at Ypres, and throughout the Retreat and Advance of 1918, and was twice wounded. He was demobilised in March 1919, and holds the 1914-15 Star, and the General Service and Victory Medals.
46, Lower Chatham Street, Chorlton-on-Medlock, Manchester. Z3560

CASSIDY, J., Private, Lancashire Fusiliers.
He joined in September 1917, and three months later proceeded to the Western Front. Whilst in this theatre of war, he saw severe fighting in various sectors, took part in the Battles of Lys, Bapaume, Havrincourt and Cambrai, and many other engagements, and also served through the Retreat and Advance of 1918. He was demobilised in October 1919, and holds the General Service and Victory Medals.
41, Long Street, Ancoats, Manchester. TZ8956

CASSIDY, L. C., Private, 8th Manchester Regiment.
Volunteering in May 1915, he was drafted to the Western Front in July of that year, and there saw severe fighting in various sectors. Engaged chiefly as a despatch-rider, he took part also in the Battles of Vermelles, Arras, Bullecourt, Ypres, Cambrai, the Aisne and Havrincourt, and other engagements, and was wounded in action in November 1917. He was demobilised in January 1919, and holds the 1914-15 Star, and the General Service and Victory Medals.
5, Newby Street, Ancoats, Manchester. Z8958

CASSIDY, P., Corpl., S. Wales Borderers, and M.G.C.
He volunteered in May 1915, and in August of the following year was drafted to the Western Front. There he took part in many important engagements in various sectors, including the Battles of the Somme, Arras, Cambrai and Amiens, and was twice wounded in action—at Loos in November 1916, and at Bullecourt in August 1918. He was for a time in hos-

pital at Manchester, before being demobilised in April 1919, and holds the General Service and Victory Medals.
7, Marple Street, Openshaw, Manchester. Z8957

CASTLE, J., Private, 3rd Manchester Regiment.
He volunteered at the outbreak of war in August 1914, but was not medically fit for service in a theatre of war. Whilst stationed at Cleethorpes, he was employed with his unit on various duties in connection with home defence, and did excellent work until he was invalided out of the Service in May 1915. 68, Roseberry Street, Gorton, Manchester. Z3561

CATLIN, J., Private, 6th East Lancashire Regiment.
He volunteered in September 1914, and after a period of training at Blackpool was sent to Lancaster, and later to Salisbury Plain. There he was engaged on various duties of an important nature, and did good work until he was discharged in November 1914, as unfit for military service.
14, Solent Street, Ardwick, Manchester. Z3562

CATLIN, J., Private, 1/8th Lancashire Fusiliers.
Volunteering in August 1914, he was drafted in the following December to the Western Front. There he took part in the Battles of Neuve Chapelle, Ypres, Festubert, Loos, the Somme, Arras and Cambrai, and in heavy fighting at Havrincourt, Bapaume and Le Cateau, during the Retreat and Advance of 1918. He was demobilised on his return home in January 1919, and holds the 1914-15 Star, and the General Service and Victory Medals.
2, Dougal Street, Hulme, Manchester. Z3563

CATLING, F., Private, Lancashire Fusiliers.
Three months after joining in August 1916, he was drafted to France, where he saw severe fighting in various sectors of the Front. After taking part in the Battle of Bullecourt, and many other important engagements, he was severely wounded in action at Ypres in December 1917, and invalided to hospital in Scotland. He was finally discharged as medically unfit for further service in September 1918, and holds the General Service and Victory Medals.
55, Abbott Street, Rochdale Road, Manchester. Z8960

CATLOW, H. W., Sergeant, 15th Royal Scots.
Having volunteered in October 1914, he was sent early in the following year to France. In this theatre of war he at once took part in heavy fighting, and was wounded at Neuve Chapelle in March 1915, and invalided home. Upon his recovery he returned to the Western Front, and was in action at Vimy Ridge, Arras, and the Somme. Subsequently evacuated to England on account of ill-health, he served in Ireland and Scotland prior to being demobilised in February 1919. He holds the 1914-15 Star, and the General Service and Victory Medals.
27, Ossory Street, Rusholme, Manchester. Z3564C

CATLOW, R., Lieutenant, 21st Manchester Regt.
He joined in July 1916, and a few months later proceeded to France. After a few months' service in this theatre of war he returned home in order to train for a Commission, and eventually returned to France as a Second Lieutenant. He subsequently was transferred to Italy, and served on the Piave front until October 1919, when he returned home for demobilisation. He holds the General Service and Victory Medals. 27, Ossory Street, Rusholme, Manchester. Z3564A

CATLOW, W. L., Private, 1st Royal Fusiliers.
Joining in May 1916, he was sent after a brief training to the Western Front. There he took part with his unit in severe fighting in various sectors until March 1917, when he was invalided home on account of ill-health. Upon his recovery he returned to France, and saw further fighting before he made the supreme sacrifice, being killed in action at Ypres in July 1917. He was entitled to the General Service and Victory Medals.
"Thinking that remembrance, though unspoken, may reach him where he sleeps."
27, Ossory Street, Moss Side, Manchester. Z3564B

CATON, J., Private, 4th Border Regiment.
He volunteered in September 1915, and a month later was drafted to India. There he was stationed at Rangoon, and in other places, engaged with his unit on garrison, escort, and other important duties. He performed consistently good work until he returned home and was demobilised in July 1919. He holds the General Service and Victory Medals.
10, Park Street, Hulme, Manchester. Z3565

CAUDWELL, J., Driver, R.F.A.
Volunteering in January 1915, he was sent in the following August to the Western Front. In this theatre of war he was in action at Loos, on the Somme and at Ypres. He subsequently took part with his Battery in many engagements during the Retreat and Advance of 1918, and was again in action on the Somme front, and also on the Marne. Returning home after the cessation of hostilities, he was demobilised in February 1919, and holds the 1914-15 Star, and the General Service and Victory Medals.
7, Allen Street, Hulme, Manchester. Z3566

CAUNCE, G., Sergt., Border Regt. and M.F.P.

A serving soldier, he returned from India shortly after the outbreak of war in August 1914, and was later drafted to Gallipoli, where he took part in heavy fighting, and was wounded at Krithia in June 1915. He was invalided home, and upon his recovery was sent to Aldershot, where he served as Sergeant in the Military Foot Police until May 1919. He was later sent back to the Border Regiment, and returned to India, where he was still serving in 1920. He holds the 1914-15 Star, and the General Service and Victory Medals.
51, Stott Street, Hulme, Manchester. Z3567

CAUSER, J., Private, 8th Manchester Regiment.

He volunteered in June 1915, and in the following August was drafted to the Western Front. There he took part in several engagements, including the Battles of Ypres, the Somme and Messines, where he was taken prisoner. He was held in captivity in Germany, being forced to work as a labourer, and suffered many privations. He was released after the Armistice and returned home for his demobilisation in December 1918. He holds the 1914-15 Star, and the General Service and Victory Medals.
13, Linson Street, Bradford, Manchester. Z9986

CAUSSIDIERE, F. A., Pte., 6th Manchester Regt.

He volunteered in August 1915, and in November of the following year proceeded to Salonika. There he took part in heavy fighting on various fronts, and did excellent work until May 1918, when he was transferred to the Western Front. In this theatre of war he saw further fighting, and was wounded :t Le Cateau. Invalided home he spent some time in hospital at Bournemouth, after which he served in Ireland until he was demobilised in March 1919, holding the General Service and Victory Medals.
62, Stockton Street, Moss Side, Manchester. TZ3568

CAVANAGH, C. H., Pte., 19th Lancashire Fusiliers.

He volunteered at the outbreak of war in August 1914, and in July of the following year, was drafted to Gallipoli, where he saw severe fighting at Suvla Bay, and various other places. He also served for a time in Egypt, on the Suez Canal, before being transferred to the Western Front in March 1916. There, after taking part in the Battles of the Somme and Passchendaele and many other engagements, he was wounded in action at Ypres in October 1918, and invalided home. He was demobilised in March 1919, and holds the 1914-15 Star, and the General Service and Victory Medals.
26, Fielden Street, Oldham Street, Manchester. Z8959

CAVANAGH, E., Private, 4th Manchester Regt.

He joined in March 1916, and three months later was drafted to France, where he fought in the Somme Offensive of that summer. Wounded at Ypres he was invalided to England, and served at various stations there until his discharge from the Army on account of medical unfitness in November 1917. He holds the General Service and Victory Medals.
2, Bonsall Street, Hulme, Manchester. Z3570

CAVANAGH, F., L/Cpl., 7th Manchester Regt.

He volunteered in August 1914, and on completion of his training was drafted to Gallipoli, where he took a prominent part in the Landing at Cape Helles, and in the three Battles of Krithia. He made the supreme sacrifice in June 1915, when he was killed in action during a bayonet charge. He was entitled to the 1914-15 Star, and the General Service and Victory Medals. " The path of duty was the way to glory."
18, Hamilton Street, Hulme, Manchester. Z11673B

CAVANAGH, J., Private, 18th Lancashire Fusiliers.

Volunteering in February 1915, he landed in France a year later, and was in action in the Battles of Albert, the Somme, Arras, Bullecourt, Messines, Ypres, and Cambrai. He was also engaged in heavy fighting throughout the Retreat and Advance of 1918, and returning home after the Armistice was demobilised in March 1919. He holds the General Service and Victory Medals.
3, Dickens Street, Queen's Road, Manchester. Z10529

CAVANAGH, P., Private, 2nd Welch Regiment.

He volunteered in November 1915, and in the following June proceeded to France, where he fought in the Somme Offensive and was wounded. He also served at Beaumont-Hamel, Beaucourt, Arras, Bullecourt, Messines, Ypres, Passchendaele and Cambrai, was gassed at Armentières during the Retreat in April 1918, and was taken prisoner on the Selle shortly afterwards. He was employed behind the German lines unloading barges and platelaying and after his release was demobilised in February 1919. He holds the General Service and Victory Medals.
44, Bell Street, Openshaw, Manchester. Z3569

CAVANAGH, T., Private, King's (Liverpool Regt.)

He joined in June 1918, and two months later was in action on the Western Front, where he took part in several important engagements during the Advance, particularly the Battles of Bapaume and Cambrai (II.). After hostilities ceased he served in Germany with the Army of Occupation until his demobilisation in November 1919. He holds the General Service and Victory Medals.
18, Hamilton Street, Hulme, Manchester. Z11673A

CAVANAGH, W., Pte., K.O. (R. Lancaster Regt.)

He volunteered in August 1914, and proceeding to the Western Front in the following March, was unfortunately taken prisoner two months later. During his long captivity in Germany, he suffered much privation and was eventually repatriated in January 1919. He was then demobilised, and holds the 1914-15 Star, and the General Service and Victory Medals.
26, Aspden Street, Ancoats, Manchester. Z9982

CAVENEY, E. D., Private, 3rd Manchester Regt.

He joined in August 1916, and after a period of training was engaged on important duties at various stations with his unit. He was unable to obtain a transfer overseas, but rendered valuable services until his demobilisation in January 1919. 17, Flower Street, Ancoats, Manchester. ₁Z9983

CAVENEY, W., Private, 2nd Manchester Regt.

Already serving in the Army, he was sent to France in June 1915, and fought at Loos, Ypres and Neuve Chapelle. Later he was sent to Mesopotamia and was in action during heavy fighting at Kut and Amara. Returning home, he was discharged in May 1916, having served for seven years in the Regular Army, and holds the 1914-15 Star, and the General Service and Victory Medals.
47, Markham Street, Ardwick, Manchester. Z3571

CAWLEY, A., Private, Manchester Regiment.

He joined in February 1917, on attaining military age, and was engaged on important duties at various stations with his unit. After hostilities ceased, he was drafted to Egypt and rendered valuable services there until he returned home for his demobilisation in February 1920.
42, Ryder Street, Bradford, Manchester. Z9985

CAWLEY, B., L/Cpl., 1/7th Manchester Regiment.

He volunteered in August 1914, and was shortly afterwards drafted to Egypt, where he was engaged on important duties until 1915. He was then transferred to the Dardanelles and made the supreme sacrifice, being killed in action at the Landing at Suvla Bay in August 1915. He was entitled to the 1914-15 Star, and the General Service and Victory Medals.
" He died the noblest death a man may die,
Fighting for God, and right and liberty." Z9984B
15, Retford Street, Chorlton-on-Medlock, Manchester.

CAWLEY, F., Private, 5th Manchester Regiment.

Volunteering in March 1915, he completed his training and was drafted to the Western Front in August 1917. He went into action at Ypres, but was unhappily killed in October during the desperate struggle for the possession of Passchendaele Ridge. He was entitled to the General Service and Victory Medals.
" Thinking that remembrance, though unspoken, may reach him where he sleeps."
6, Cedar Street, Hulme, Manchester. Z3572

CAWLEY, H., Pte., Argyll and Sutherland Highl'drs.

He volunteered in 1915, and later in the same year proceeded to the Western Front. There he took part in several engagements, including the Battles of Ypres and the Somme, where he was badly wounded in action in 1916. As a result, he was invalided home, but on his recovery returned to France and fought in the Retreat and Advance of 1918, being again wounded in action. He was demobilised in 1919, and holds the 1914-15 Star, and the General Service and Victory Medals.
15, Retford Street, Chorlton-on-Medlock, Manchester. Z9984A

CAYTON, W., Private, King's (Liverpool Regt.)

He joined in May 1917, and served in the King's (Liverpool Regiment), Lancashire Fusiliers and R.A.S.C. at different stations in the United Kingdom. He was engaged on important duties, particularly transport work, but was wounded during an air-raid on Woolwich about ten months before his discharge, which took place in March 1919.
26, Mount Street, Hulme, Manchester. Z3573

CERVI, B., Pte., 7th King's Own Scottish Borderers.

Volunteering in September 1914, he completed a brief period of training and proceeded to the Western Front two months later. He saw heavy fighting, but made the last great sacrifice being killed in action in September 1915, at the Battle of Loos. He was entitled to the 1914-15 Star, and the General Service and Victory Medals. Z3574
" His life for his Country, his soul to God."
7, Leamington Avenue, Chorlton-on-Medlock, Manchester.

CHADD, F., Pte., R.A.M.C., and R₂ Welch Fusiliers.

He volunteered in November 1915, and from August of the following year, served in H.M.H.S. " Herefordshire," " Assaye " and " Dunluce Castle," engaged in conveying the wounded from the Eastern theatres of war. In April 1918, he was transferred to the Royal Welch Fusiliers and drafted to Palestine, where he was stationed at Gaza, Jerusalem and various other places. He afterwards served in Egypt until his return home for demobilisation in July 1919, and holds the General Service and Victory Medals.
32, Husband Street, Manchester. Z8961

CHADWICK, F., Private (Driver) M.G.C.
He joined in April 1916, and a year later was drafted to the Western Front, where he took an important part in several engagements. Whilst overseas he fought at Arras, Bullecourt, Ypres and Cambrai and during the Retreat and Advance of 1918 was in action at Amiens, Thiepval, St. Quentin, Cambrai and Ypres. He was demobilised in August 1919, and holds the General Service and Victory Medals.
8, Alder Street, Hulme, Manchester. Z3578

CHADWICK, G., Sapper, R.E.
Volunteering in February 1915, he was sent to the Western Front later in the year and served at Monchy, Arras, Albert, the Somme, Ypres, Maricourt, Fricourt, Oppy and Ginchy. Severely wounded at Ginchy in October 1916, he was invalided home, and after hospital treatment, was discharged as unfit in October 1917. He holds the 1914–15 Star, and the General Service and Victory Medals.
12, Gomm Street, Ardwick, Manchester. Z3575

CHADWICK, G., Gunner, R.F.A·
He volunteered in May 1915, and in the following August proceeded overseas. Whilst on the Western Front he took part in several engagements, including the Battles of Ypres and the Somme, where he was wounded and invalided home in 1916. On his recovery he returned to France and was in action at Cambrai, but after a month, was transferred to India and served on important garrison duties until after hostilities ceased. He returned home and was demobilised in December 1919, holding the 1914–15 Star, and the General Service and Victory Medals.
21, Alderman Street, Ardwick, Manchester. Z9987

CHADWICK, J., Private, East Lancashire Regiment.
He volunteered in September 1914, and after completing his training, was drafted to the Western Front. There he took part in the Battles of Loos, Vimy Ridge and the Somme, where he was reported missing and later killed in action in October 1916. He was entitled to the 1914–15 Star, and the General Service and Victory Medals.
"A valiant Soldier, with undaunted heart, he breasted life's last hill."
12, Perrin Street, Ancoats, Manchester. Z9988

CHADWICK, J., Pte., 2/5th Durham Light Infantry.
He joined in July 1916, and four months afterwards reached the Balkans. There he was employed on the lines of communication, guarding stores and doing work in the docks. Whilst at Karissa he was in hospital with malaria and later at Kalamata. He was invalided home and served in England until his demobilisation in January 1919. He holds the General Service and Victory Medals. Z3576
2, Gay Street, off Jackson Street, Hulme, Manchester.

CHADWICK, J., Private, 2nd Manchester Regiment.
A Reservist, he was called to the Colours when war broke out in August 1914, and in December of that year was drafted to the Western Front, where he took part in the Battles of Neuve Chapelle, Ypres, Loos, Albert, Ploegsteert Wood, the Somme, Arras and Messines. He unfortunately fell fighting on September 23rd, 1917, at the third Battle of Ypres. He was entitled to the 1914–15 Star, and the General Service and Victory Medals.
"Whilst we remember, the sacrifice is not in vain."
5, Heyrod Street, Ancoats, Manchester. Z8962

CHADWICK, J. J., Air Mechanic, R.A.F.
He joined in June 1916, and after completing his training was stationed at various aerodromes on the South and East Coasts with his Squadron on important duties. He was unsuccessful in obtaining his transfer to a theatre of war prior to the cessation of hostilities, but rendered excellent services, until demobilised in February 1919.
21, Burton Street, Rochdale Road, Manchester. Z10530

CHADWICK, T. W., Private, Loyal N. Lancs. Regt.
He volunteered in September 1914, and after a period of training was engaged at various stations on important duties. He was also employed at Messrs. Richard Johnson's Wire Works in Bradford and rendered valuable services until his demobilisation in December 1918.
93, Montague Street, Manchester. Z9989

CHADWICK, W., Air Mechanic, R.A.F.
He joined in April 1918, and was shortly afterwards drafted to France. There he was engaged on important duties in the repair shops at Wimereux and Marquise, and was employed on work which called for a high degree of technical skill. He was demobilised in February 1919, and holds the General Service and Victory Medals.
32, Howarth Street, Bradford, Manchester. Z9990

CHADWICK, W., Gunner, Tank Corps.
Joining in August 1917, he was drafted to France in the following October and fought in the first Battle of Cambrai. He also served with distinction in the important engagements during the Retreat and Advance of 1918 and subsequently was stationed in Cologne with the Army of Occupation. He was demobilised in April 1920, and holds the General Service and Victory Medals.
21, Gotha Street, Ardwick, Manchester. Z3577

CHALLINOR, A., Rifleman, Rifle Brigade.
He was mobilised in August 1914, and immediately drafted to France. In this theatre of war he fought at the Battle of Mons, and in the subsequent Retreat, and the Battles of the Marne, the Aisne, Ypres, Loos and the Somme, where he was badly gassed. As a result he was invalided home and discharged in May 1917 as medically unfit for further service. He holds the Soudan Medal, the Queen's and King's South African Medals, the Mons Star, and the General Service and Victory Medals.
39, Alice Street, Bradford, Manchester. Z9991A

CHALLONER, W. (D.C.M.) Sergt., 1st K.O. (Royal Lancaster Regt.)
He volunteered at the outbreak of war and at the end of 1914 crossed to France, where he saw severe fighting. In August 1915 he proceeded to the Dardanelles and was in action at Suvla Bay. After the Evacuation of Gallipoli he was sent to Mesopotamia and was present at the capture of Baghdad, where he was twice wounded and was awarded the D.C.M. for conspicuous gallantry whilst in charge of a raiding party. Owing to his wounds, he was invalided first to India and then home, and after a period in hospital, and acting as an instructor, he was demobilised in March 1919. He also holds the 1914–15 Star, and the General Service and Victory Medals.
77, York Street, Hulme, Manchester. Z3579

CHALONER, E., Private, Labour Corps.
Volunteering in May 1915, he completed his training, but was unable to obtain his transfer overseas. He was stationed at Blackpool, where he was employed as a batman and on other work, and after rendering valuable services, was demobilised in January 1919.
7, Bangor Street, Hulme, Manchester. Z3580B

CHALONER, H., Private, 8th Manchester Regiment.
He volunteered in August 1914, and was later drafted to France. After taking part in the Battles of Neuve Chapelle, St. Eloi, Ypres (II) and Albert, he was badly wounded at Vimy Ridge and spent six months in hospital at Ramsgate. On his recovery he returned to the Western Front and was in action at the Battles of Bullecourt, Ypres (III), Cambrai and the Somme (II), where he was again badly wounded and invalided home. In January 1919, he was discharged as medically unfit for further service, and holds the 1914–15 Star, and the General Service and Victory Medals.
48, Lancaster Street, Hulme, Manchester. Z11674

CHALONER, R., Sapper, R.E.
Two months after joining in June 1916 he embarked for France, where he was employed on important duties with his Corps. Whilst in France he was stationed at Le Havre, Marseilles and Trouville and served as a bricklayer. He was also placed in charge of German prisoners whilst on fatigue. Discharged in November 1918, he holds the General Service and Victory Medals.
7, Bangor Street, Hulme, Manchester. Z3580A

CHAMBERLAIN, L., Pte., 2nd Leicestershire Regt.
He was already in the Army when war broke out in August 1914, and was immediately drafted to the Western Front, where he took part in the Battles of Mons and was severely wounded in October. As a result he was invalided home and unfortunately suffered amputation of an arm. He was finally discharged in 1915, and holds the Mons Star, and the General Service and Victory Medals.
40, Granville Place, Ancoats, Manchester. Z9992

CHAMBERLAIN, W., Driver, R.F.A.
Mobilised in August 1914, he was immediately drafted to the Western Front, where he took part in the fighting at Mons. He also served through the Battles of Le Cateau, the Marne, Ypres, Neuve Chapelle, St. Eloi, Hill 60, Loos, the Somme, Arras, Messines and Cambrai and many other engagements, and fought in the Retreat and Advance of 1918. He was discharged in January 1919, and holds the Mons Star, and the General Service and Victory Medals.
3, Long Street, Ancoats, Manchester. Z6046

CHAMBERS, A., Driver, R.F.A.
He joined in April 1918, and after completing a period of training served at various stations, where he was engaged on duties of a highly important nature. He was not successful in obtaining his transfer to a theatre of war, but, nevertheless, rendered valuable services with his Battery until January 1919, when he was demobilised.
18, Heyrod Street, Ancoats, Manchester. Z8963

CHAMBERS, J., Private, R.A.S.C. (M.T.)
He joined in December 1917, and after the completion of his training was drafted three months later to Ireland, where he was stationed at Dublin and the Curragh and was engaged on work with the Mechanical Transport. Though unable to proceed to a theatre of war, he did good work until his demobilisation in October. 1919
47, Burnley Street, Bradford Road, Miles Platting, Manchester. Z3581

CHANDLER, R. H., Bombardier, R.G.A.
Volunteering in August 1915, he crossed to the Western Front at the end of the year and was in action in different sectors. He played an important part in the fighting at Albert, Vermelles, Vimy Ridge, the Somme, Bullecourt, Ypres, Passchendaele, Cambrai, Amiens, Le Cateau and the Sambre, and was present at the entry into Mons. Demobilised in January 1919, he holds the 1914-15 Star, and the General Service and Victory Medals.
27, Dudley Street, Stretford, Manchester. Z3582

CHANTRELL, B., Private, 5th Lancashire Fusiliers.
Volunteering in August 1914, he proceeded with the 42nd Division to Egypt in the following month and later took part in the Landing at Cape Helles and in the fighting round Krithia and Achi Baba during the Gallipoli campaign. After the Evacuation he returned to Egypt and was wounded at Kantara. He later served in France and was wounded at Arras. He was discharged in consequence in November 1917, and holds the 1914-15 Star, and the General Service and Victory Medals.
28, Herbert Street, Ardwick, Manchester. Z3583

CHAPELL, A., Private, 1st Manchester Regiment.
Volunteering in March 1915, he was drafted to Egypt in the following year. In this seat of operations he took part in engagements at Katia, El Fasher, Magdhaba and Siwa. Later he proceeded to Palestine, where he was in action at the Battles of Gaza (I, II and III) and the capture of Jerusalem and Jericho with General Allenby's forces. He returned home and was demobilised in February 1919, holding the General Service and Victory Medals.
5, Cathcart Street, Ancoats, Manchester. Z9993

CHAPMAN, J., Private, Royal Scots.
Volunteering in December 1914, he was drafted to France in January 1916, and was in action on the Arras front, where he was wounded. He was sent to hospital at Rouen and later to England. After his recovery he rejoined his unit in France and was again wounded in action at Armentières and invalided home to hospital. Subsequently he served in Ireland until his demobilisation in December 1918. He holds the General Service and Victory Medals.
21, Iron Street, Miles Platting, Manchester. Z9469

CHAPMAN, J. W., Pte., 9th Lancashire Fusiliers.
A year after volunteering in August 1914, he was sent to Gallipoli and took part in the Landing at Suvla Bay, the fighting on Chunuk Bair and the Evacuation of the Peninsula. He then served in Egypt and was in action on the Suez Canal and in the Sinaitic Peninsula. He was sent to France in June 1916, and was wounded during the first Battle of the Somme in September. Later he was transferred to the R.A.F. and served with a Balloon Section until discharged as unfit in March 1918. He holds the 1914-15 Star, and the General Service and Victory Medals.
6, Melbourne Place, Hulme, Manchester. TZ3585

CHAPMAN, L., Corporal, 16th Manchester Regt.
He volunteered in January 1915, and in February of the following year was drafted to the Western Front, where he saw much severe fighting in various sectors. He gave his life for King and Country, falling in action on July 1st, 1916, during the Advance on the Somme. He was entitled to the General Service and Victory Medals.
"Honour to the immortal dead who gave their youth that the world might grow old in peace."
9, Lindum Street, Rusholme, Manchester. TZ7736A

CHAPMAN, S. B., Corporal, 51st Welch Regiment.
He joined in January 1918, but was not successful in obtaining a transfer to a theatre of war before the termination of hostilities. He, however, proceeded to Germany in February 1919, and served with the Army of Occupation until the following August, when he was sent to Ireland, where he remained until demobilised in March 1920.
25, Glebe Street, Gorton, Manchester. Z3584

CHAPPLES, W., Private, 8th Manchester Regiment.
Joining in October 1916, he was drafted to the Western Front after three months' training, and there saw severe fighting in various sectors. He took part in the Battles of Arras, Bullecourt, Messines, Ypres and the Somme, and many other important engagements, and also served through the Retreat and Advance of 1918. He was demobilised on his return home in July 1919, and holds the General Service and Victory Medals.
108, Jersey Street Dwellings, Ancoats, Manchester. Z8964

CHARLES, W., Pte., North Staffordshire Regt. and Manchester Regt.
Joining in January 1916, he was drafted in the following June to the Western Front. There he took part in the Battles of the Somme and Ypres, where he was wounded. As a result, he was evacuated to England and after spending some time in hospitals at Keighley and Grangethorpe, was eventually invalided out of the Service in January 1918, holding the General Service and Victory Medals.
91, Robert Street, West Gorton, Manchester. Z3586

CHARLESWORTH, G., Pte., York & Lancaster Regt.
Joining in June 1916, he proceeded four months later to the Western Front, where he took an active part in engagements at Hébuterne, Thiepval and Sailly. In January 1917 he was sent back to England suffering from pleurisy, and four months later was discharged from the Army as medically unfit for further military duties. He holds the General Service and Victory Medals.
161, Morton Street, Longsight, Manchester. Z11611

CHARLTON, A., L/Corporal, 2nd Border Regt.
He joined in August 1918, on attaining military age, and after a period of training was sent to Ireland, where he was engaged on many important duties. He rendered valuable services, and in 1920 was still on duty there.
15, Adair Street, Ancoats, Manchester. Z9994

CHARNOCK, L., Private, 13th Manchester Regt.
He volunteered in August 1914, and on completing his training in the following August was drafted to the Western Front, where he saw much heavy fighting. He made the supreme sacrifice, being killed in action at Loos on October 5th, 1915. He was entitled to the 1914-15 Star, and the General Service and Victory Medals.
"Whilst we remember, the sacrifice is not in vain."
34, Wood Street, Bradford, Manchester. Z9995A

CHARNOCK, R., Private, 17th Manchester Regt.
He joined in October 1916, and three months later was sent to France. In this theatre of war he took part in several important engagements, including Arras, Messines and the Ancre, and was wounded and taken prisoner at St. Eloi in April 1918. Retained in captivity in Germany until after the Armistice, he was then repatriated, and, demobilised in March 1919, holds the General Service and Victory Medals.
109, Bell Street, Openshaw, Manchester. Z3587

CHARTERS, W., L/Cpl., 7th King's (L'pool Regt.)
He joined in June 1916, and was sent to the Western Front two months later. He was in action in many important engagements, including the Battles of Beaumont-Hamel, Arras, Bullecourt and Ypres. Severely gassed in August 1917, he returned to England, and after receiving hospital treatment at Bournemouth, was demobilised in October 1919. He holds the General Service and Victory Medals.
52, Phelan Street, Collyhurst, Manchester. Z10531

CHASE, P. (D.C.M.), Sergt.-Major, 2/7th Lancs. Fus.
He volunteered in November 1914, and in the following April was drafted to France. There he played a distinguished part with his unit in heavy fighting at Ypres, and was wounded. After spending three months in hospital, he rejoined his unit and participated in further fighting on the Ancre and Somme fronts, and at Arras, Ypres and Cambrai. Taken prisoner in May 1918, he was interned in Germany until the cessation of hostilities, when he was released. He was awarded the Distinguished Conduct Medal for gallantry and consistent good work under heavy shell-fire at Ypres, and when he was demobilised in February 1920, was also entitled to the 1914-15 Star, and the General Service and Victory Medals.
26, North Street, Hulme, Manchester. Z3588

CHATTERTON, J. C., Pte., 1st Manchester Regt.
He joined in February 1918, but was not successful in obtaining a transfer overseas owing to the termination of hostilities. Stationed in County Cork, he was employed with his unit on garrison and other important duties, and rendered excellent service. He was still serving with the Colours in 1920.
2, Daniel Street, Hulme, Manchester. Z3589

CHATTERTON, L., Pte., 9th Loyal N. Lancs. Regt.
He enlisted in June 1914, and after the outbreak of war two months later was retained on important duties in England until August 1916. He was then drafted to the Western Front, where he took part in many engagements, including the Battles of Arras, Messines, Passchendaele and the Somme, and also fought in the Retreat and Advance of 1918. He was discharged in January 1919, and holds the General Service and Victory Medals.
84, Newcastle Street, Hulme, Manchester. Z8965

CHATTERTON, R. J., Pte., 2nd Manchester Regt.
He volunteered in September 1914, and on completion of his training was in January of the following year drafted to the Western Front, where he served for over three years. During that period he was engaged in severe fighting in the Hill 60, Ypres, Albert, Bullecourt, Arras, Cambrai, Marne and Bapaume sectors. In 1920 he was still serving in the Army, and holds the 1914-15 Star, and the General Service and Victory Medals. 9, Ernest Street, Ancoats, Manchester. Z11480

CHEETHAM, H., Pte., 2nd King's (Liverpool Regt.)
He joined in March 1917, and seven months later was drafted to Salonika, where he took part in many important engagements on the Struma and Vardar fronts and saw heavy fighting until the cessation of hostilities. He also served for a time in Constantinople with the Army of Occupation, and was demobilised in April 1920, holding the General Service and Victory Medals.
1, Truro Street, West Gorton, Manchester. Z9996

CHEETHAM, H., Private, 6th Manchester Regt.

Having volunteered in February 1915, he was drafted two months later to the Western Front. In this theatre of war he took part in heavy fighting at Ypres, Albert and Vermelles, and was gassed in action. He subsequently proceeded to Palestine and was in action at Magdhaba, Rafa and Gaza, and did exceedingly good work. Returning home, he was eventually demobilised in February 1919, and holds the 1914-15 Star, and the General Service and Victory Medals.

12, Etruria Street, Longsight, Manchester. Z3591

CHEETHAM, W., L/Corporal, Military Foot Police.

He volunteered in May 1915, and after training proceeded to France in August of the same year. He did good service in many forward areas on that front, and in the Ypres sector, near Loos and St. Eloi, in the Somme and Ancre regions, and about Lens and Bullecourt. Following up the Advance of 1918 he did service at Bapaume, Cambrai and Le Cateau, and after the Armistice was demobilised in August 1919. He holds the 1914-15 Star, and the General Service and Victory Medals.

11, Margaret Street, West Gorton, Manchester. Z3590

CHESNEY, J., Private, Army Cyclist Corps.

Joining in June 1917, he was drafted to the Western Front on completing his training in November of that year, and there saw much severe fighting. He took part in many important engagements during the Retreat and Advance of 1918, and after the cessation of hostilities, served on the Headquarter Staff at Le Cateau. He was demobilised on returning home in March 1919, and holds the General Service and Victory Medals. 7, Heyrod Street, Ancoats, Manchester. Z8966

CHESSBROUGH, J., Private, Royal Fusiliers.

He joined in April 1916, and in the following June was drafted to the Western Front. During his service overseas he fought in various engagements, including those at Ypres and Nieuport. He gave his life for the freedom of England whilst in action in the Somme sector on November 4th, 1918, and was entitled to the General Service and Victory Medals.

"A valiant Soldier, with undaunted heart he breasted life's last hill."

52, Flower Street, Ancoats, Manchester. Z9470A

CHESSHYRE, F., Driver, R.A.S.C.

He joined in July 1916, and proceeding to France two months later, was engaged on important transport duties in the forward areas during the Battles of the Somme, Bullecourt, Ypres (III), Cambrai, Amiens and Havrincourt. In September 1918 he was sent to the Base at Boulogne for special work with the horses, and was eventually demobilised in May 1919, holding the General Service and Victory Medals.

8, George Street, Moss Side, Manchester. Z11675

CHESTERS, W., Gunner, R.F.A.

He volunteered in September 1914, and after a period of training in Ireland was sent to France in August of the following year. He saw much heavy fighting with his Battery at Loos, Arras and La Bassée, and was also engaged in the Battle of Ypres (III), including Passchendaele Ridge, where he was severely wounded. After being under hospital treatment in Scotland, he was, on his recovery sent to Ireland, and demobilised from there in January 1919. He holds the 1914-15 Star, and the General Service and Victory Medals.

38, Markham Street, Ardwick, Manchester. Z3592

CHESWORTH, F., Private, 1/8th Manchester Regt.

After volunteering in November 1914, he passed through his training, and was drafted in the next year to the Dardanelles, where he took part in most of the important Battles on the Gallipoli Peninsula. After the Evacuation he was transferred to Egypt, and fought in the engagement at Katia on the Egyptian frontier. In 1917 he was sent to France, and was in action at Havrincourt Wood, Gommecourt and Festubert. In February 1918 he was found unfit for further service, and was discharged on that account. He holds the 1914-15 Star, and the General Service and Victory Medals.

36, Carey Street, Hulme, Manchester. Z3593

CHETWOOD, J., Private, 4th Royal Fusiliers.

Volunteering in May 1915, he was drafted to France later in the same year and took part in much severe fighting. He was in action at the Battles of Cambrai and Havrincourt (where he was wounded and gassed), and in other important engagements during the Retreat and Advance of 1918. He holds the 1914-15 Star, and the General Service and Victory Medals, and was demobilised in 1919.

25, Spire Street, Ardwick, Manchester. Z9997

CHILTON, C., Corporal, 8th Manchester Regiment.

Shortly after volunteering in August 1914, he was drafted to Egypt, whence he proceeded to the Dardanelles in the following year. There he saw much severe fighting at Suvla Bay and many other places until the Evacuation of the Gallipoli Peninsula, was wounded in action in August 1915, and afterwards was transferred to the Western Front. There he was engaged on important duties in various sectors, finally returning home for demobilisation in March 1919. He holds the 1914-15 Star, and the General Service and Victory Medals.

49, Stonehewer Street, Rochdale Road, Manchester. Z8967

CHILTON, S., Corporal, R.E.

He volunteered in August 1914, and after a period of training, was sent to France in the following June. He did good service in the Battles of Loos, Somme I, Messines Ridge, and Ypres III, and carried on the important, and often dangerous work of his Corps in many other battle areas. In spite of being twice gassed in two of the earlier engagements, and being attacked with trench fever, he served on after hospital treatment through the final stages of the war, and was not demobilised until June 1919. He holds the 1914-15 Star, and the General Service and Victory Medals.

6, Ernest Street, Morton Street, Manchester. Z3594

CHORLEY, P., Sapper, R.E.

Volunteering in August 1914, he was sent to Gallipoli in the following July, and was engaged in heavy fighting at W. Beach, and in other parts of the line. After the Evacuation he proceeded to Egypt, and served in the canal zone, and at various other stations until January 1917, when he embarked for France. He was present at many engagements of note, and in November 1917 returned to England, where he was employed on important munition work for three months. He returned to France in November 1918, and afterwards was drafted to Germany where he was still serving in 1920 with the Army of Occupation. He holds the 1914-15 Star, and the General Service and Victory Medals.

9, Pollitt Place, West Gorton, Manchester. Z10532

CHORLTON, J., L., Private, 8th E. Lancashire Regt.

He volunteered in November 1914, and proceeded to France in he following February. He took part in the trench fighting at Neuve Chapelle, Loos, La Bassée, and Albert, also afterwards at Arras, and on the Somme, where he was wounded in January 1916. Suffering also from trench feet, he was sent first to a Base hospital, and afterwards to England for treatment, and was finally discharged in January 1917, as unfit for further service. He holds the 1914-15 Star, and the General Service and Victory Medals.

54, Gorton Street, Ardwick, Manchester. Z3595

CHORLTON, P., Private, 18th Manchester Regiment.

He joined in July 1917, and after training proceeded to France in the following December. He served through the Retreat and Advance of 1918, being in engagements at Havrincourt and Cambrai II, and many other actions up to the Armistice, after which he remained in France until shortly before his demobilisation in October 1919. He holds the General Service and Victory Medals.

98, Church Street, Hulme, Manchester. Z3596

CHRISTIAN, A., Private, King's (Liverpool Regt.)

He joined in February 1917, and was sent to a depôt in North Wales for training, then with his unit to Ireland. He rendered valuable services, but owing to a physical disability, was not successful in obtaining his transfer overseas before the Armistice, and after serving in Ireland was transferred to the East Coast of England for defence work, and later in March 1919, to the Army of Occupation in Germany, from which, on hi return to England, he was demobilised in September 1919.

13, Dryden Street, Longsight, Manchester. Z3598A

CHRISTIAN, E., Private, 3rd Manchester Regiment.

He was mobilised from the Reserve at the outbreak of hostilities and in September 1914 was drafted to France. Whilst overseas he took part in much of the heavy fighting at La Bassée, Ypres, Neuve Chapelle, Hill 60, and Festubert. He was invalided home in June 1915, owing to ill-health, and was discharged as medically unfit for further service in November of the same year. Later he died in August 1916, and was entitled to the 1914 Star, and the General Service and Victory Medals.

"His memory is cherished with pride."

66, Woodward Street, Ancoats, Manchester. Z9471B

CHRISTIAN, J., Gunner, R.F.A.

He volunteered in May 1915, and after a period of training was drafted to Egypt, whence after five months' service there he was transferred in March 1916 to the Western Front. There he was in action in many important engagements, but was unfortunately killed at Poperinghe in July 1917. He was entitled to the 1914-15 Star, and the General Service and Victory Medals.

"Whilst we remember the sacrifice is not in vain."

13, Dryden Street, Longsight, Manchester. Z3598B

CHRISTIAN, J., Private, 1st Lancashire Fusiliers.

He was mobilised from the Reserve in August 1914, and in the following year was drafted to Gallipoli, and took part in the Landing at Suvla Bay. He died gloriously on the Field of Action at the third Battle of Krithia in June 1915, and was entitled to the 1914-15 Star, and the General Service and Victory Medals.

"Thinking that remembrance, though unspoken, may reach him where he sleeps."

66, Woodward Street, Ancoats, Manchester. Z9471A

CHRYSTAL, J., Sergeant, 9th Manchester Regiment.
Having previously served in the Boer War, he re-enlisted in September 1914, and was engaged on important duties as a machine-gun Instructor until he proceeded to the Dardanelles, where he took part in the Battles of Krithia, and Achi-Baba. After the Evacuation of the Peninsula, he served at Kantara and El Arish in Egypt before being transferred to the Western Front in March 1917. After taking part in heavy fighting at Havrincourt, he was engaged on the anti-aircraft defences at Boulogne, and rendered valuable services. He holds the Queen's South African Medal, the 1914–15 Star, and the General Service and Victory Medals, and was demobilised in February 1919.
17, Elliott Street, Bradford, Manchester. Z9998

CHURM, J. W., Corporal, Rifle Brigade.
He volunteered in August 1914, and in the following February was sent to France, where he took part in the Battles of Loos, the Somme, the Ancre, Arras, Ypres, Passchendaele, and Cambrai. Early in 1918 he was transferred to the Labour Corps, and rendered valuable services throughout the Retreat and Advance of 1918. He was gassed in action at Arras in 1915. Demobilised in February 1919, he holds the 1914–15 Star, and the General Service and Victory Medals.
19, Francisco Street, Collyhurst, Manchester. Z9999

CIRCUIT, L. F., Private, King's (Liverpool Regt.)
He joined in April 1917, and was later drafted to the Western Front. He saw heavy fighting at Arras, and in the Battles of Ypres III, and Cambrai, after which he was transferred to the Royal Air Force, and did duty in it on mechanical and electrical repair of aircraft until his demobilisation in April 1919. He holds the General Service and Victory Medals.
236, Viaduct Street, Ardwick, Manchester. Z3599A

CLANCY, J., Private, East Yorkshire Regiment.
Having enlisted in 1907, he was sent to France early in 1915, and fought at Neuve Chapelle, St. Eloi, and Hill 60. Later he took part in engagements at Festubert, Loos, Albert, and Vimy Ridge, also in the 1st Battle of the Somme, and in action near Arras, Bullecourt, and Lens. During this long period of fighting he was both wounded and gassed, but served on through the Retreat and Advance of 1918, until the Armistice, after which he was transferred to the Royal Engineers, in which Corps he was still serving in 1920. He holds the 1914–15 Star, and the General Service and Victory Medals.
20, Walnut Street, Hulme, Manchester. Z4600A

CLANCY, J., Gunner, R.F.A.
He volunteered in January 1915, and after training, was drafted to France in the following September. He at once fought in the Battle of Loos, in which he was wounded, but recovered, and was in an engagement on the Somme. After two months in France he was transferred to Salonika, where he took part in the Doiran Advance, and later in two actions on the Vardar River, which concluded the Campaign on that front. Returning to England after the Armistice, he was demobilised in February 1919, and holds the 1914–15 Star, and the General Service and Victory Medals.
20, Walnut Street, Hulme, Manchester. Z4600C

CLANCY, J., Private, R.A.S.C. (M.T.)
He volunteered on the outbreak of war, and was sent to France before the end of 1914. He did fine service as a Despatch rider between different places in the fighting areas, notably on the Somme front, and near Arras and Cambrai. During his difficult and dangerous duties he was twice wounded, once at Arras, and once at Albert, and carrying on his work to the end of the war, was demobilised in June 1919, and holds the 1914–15 Star, and the General Service and Victory Medals.
20, Walnut Street, Hulme, Manchester. Z4600D

CLANCY, T., Private, 2nd East Yorkshire Regt.
He joined in August 1916, and served with his unit at various places in the United Kingdom. He rendered valuable services, but was not successful, owing to defective eyesight, in obtaining his transfer overseas before the cessation of hostilities, and was eventually demobilised in March 1919.
20, Walnut Street, Hulme, Manchester. Z4600B

CLAPHAM, H. E., Cpl., 2/6th Manchester Regt. (T.F.)
He volunteered at the outbreak of hostilities, and went through training at various places in England, but, being barely of military age to proceed at once overseas, was not sent to France until March 1917. He then fought at Arras, also in the Battles of Ypres III, and Cambrai, and serving through the Retreat and Advance of 1918, was eventually demobilised in February 1919. He holds the General Service and Victory Medals.
67, Bedford Street, Moss Side, Manchester. TZ4601B TZ4602B

CLAPHAM, T., L/Cpl., 6th Manchester Regt. (T.F.)
Having enlisted in April 1914, he was mobilised on the outbreak of war, and saw service on many different fronts in Egypt, from August 1914 to April 1915, then in Gallipoli, where he took part in the first Landing, the Krithia Battles, and the Cape Helles attack. After the Evacuation he returned to Egypt, where he served round Ismailia, and in the actions at Kantara, and El Arish. In March 1917 he was transferred to France and fought at Arras, and in the Battle of Ypres III, in which he was severely wounded, and being passed to hospital

in England remained under treatment until discharged in March 1919. He holds the 1914–15 Star, and the General Service and Victory Medals.
67, Bedford Street, Moss Side, Manchester. TZ4601A TZ4602A

CLARE, A., Private, 1st Manchester Regiment.
He joined in July 1917, and was sent in the following October to the Egyptian front, where he took part in the Advance on Jerusalem, and was present at its capture, and also that of Jericho. In July 1918 he was wounded near Kantara, and after treatment at a hospital in Alexandria, was invalided to England, and discharged in January 1919. He holds the General Service and Victory Medals.
28, Mallow Street, Hulme, Manchester. Z4605

CLARE, A., Private, 2nd Manchester Regiment.
He volunteered in April 1915, and after training, proceeded to France in the following December. He took part in heavy fighting at Loos, St. Eloi, Albert, and Vimy Ridge in 1916, also in the Somme Offensive of that summer. Later he fought in the Battles of Arras, Ypres III, and Cambrai I, and served through the Retreat and Advance of 1918, being in action on the Marne, at Cambrai again, and Le Cateau. On his return home after the Armistice he was demobilised in February 1919, and holds the 1914–15 Star, and the General Service and Victory Medals.
35, Bishop Street, Moss Side, Manchester. Z4603B

CLARE, J. H.. Gunner, R.F.A.
After volunteering in September 1915, he passed through a short training, and proceeded with his Battery to France in the following November. He was soon involved in heavy fighting in the Ypres sector, where he was wounded, but after treatment at a Base hospital, recovered, and took part in the Somme Offensive of 1916, and later in the Battle of Ypres III, in which he was badly gassed, and being evacuated to hospital in England, was finally discharged in August 1919. He holds the 1914–15 Star, and the General Service and Victory Medals.
60, York Street, Hulme, Manchester. Z4604

CLARE, J. R., Pte., K.O. (Royal Lancaster Regt.)
After volunteering in August 1914, he proceeded to France the next month, and saw heavy fighting in the great Battles of the Marne and Aisne, also at La Bassée, in the desperate struggles at Ypres, and later at St. Eloi, Hill 60, and Loos. He took part in an action at Vimy Ridge, and later in the Somme Offensive, during which in July 1916 he died gloriously on the Field of Battle. He was entitled to the 1914 Star, and the General Service and Victory Medals.
"And doubtless he went in splendid company."
35, Bishop Street, Moss Side, Manchester. Z4603A

CLARK, A., Quarter-Master Sergt., Tank Corps.
He joined in 1916, and served in his Corps at a large training centre in the South of England. He rendered valuable services, but was not successful in obtaining his transfer overseas before the cessation of hostilities, and after doing valuable work, was demobilised at the end of 1918.
42, Greville Street, Rusholme, Manchester. Z4609B

CLARK, H. W., Q.M.S., 6th Manchester Regiment.
He volunteered in August 1914, and after a long period of training and service in England, proceeded to France in September 1917. During his service on that Front in January 1918, he suffered from shell-shock and trench fever, and was passed to hospital in England; after treatment at various places he was discharged in the same year as unfit for further service, and holds the General Service and Victory Medals.
42, Greville Street, Rusholme, Manchester. Z4609A

CLARK, J., Sapper, R.E.
Volunteering in November 1915, he was drafted to the Western Front in the following month, and there took part in severe fighting at Ypres, Loos, Hooge, Arras, and many other places. He made the supreme sacrifice, falling in action in July 1916, during the Advance on the Somme. He was entitled to the 1914–15 Star, and the General Service and Victory Medals.
"The path of duty was the way to glory."
7, Pollitt Street, West Gorton, Manchester. Z10008

CLARK, J., Private, East Lancashire Regiment.
Volunteering in May 1915 at the age of 17 years, he was drafted to France in the following September, and served as a Lewis gunner in many important engagements. He took part in the Battles of the Somme, Arras, Ypres, Passchendaele, Cambrai (I), and in the Retreat, and was in action at the 2nd Battle of Cambrai in October 1918, during the Advance. After the cessation of hostilities, he proceeded to Germany with the Army of Occupation, and served there until his demobilisation in February 1919. He holds the 1914–15 Star, and the General Service and Victory Medals.
13, Douro Street, Newton Heath, Manchester. Z10000

CLARK, J. W., Private, 8th Manchester Regiment.
A veteran Soldier, who had seen service in the South African War, he joined on the outbreak of war, and did valuable work in coast defence and other duties during the first year of the war. In May 1915 he unfortunately contracted illness which resulted in his being invalided out of the Service in that same month. 5, Hughes Street, Ardwick, Manchester. Z4607

CLARK, R., L/Corporal, 2nd Manchester Regiment.
He volunteered in October 1914, and was sent to France in the following February. He saw heavy fighting in the Battles of Hill 60, and Ypres II, also in actions at St. Eloi, and Albert. Later he took part in the Somme Offensive, and fought at Beaumont-Hamel, Beaucourt, and Messines Ridge. He then unfortunately contracted illness, and being invalided home in July 1917, was discharged, after treatment at various hospitals in December 1918. He holds the 1914-15 Star, and the General Service and Victory Medals.
96, Church Street, Hulme, Manchester. TZ4606

CLARK, T. H., Private, Royal Fusiliers.
He volunteered in September 1914, and in June of the following year was drafted to the Dardanelles, where he was wounded in action during the Landing at Suvla Bay in August 1915. After the Evacuation of the Gallipoli Peninsula, he served in Egypt until December 1916, when he was transferred to the Western Front. He then took part in the Battles of Arras, Ypres, and Cambrai, and in the Retreat and Advance of 1918. He was demobilised in February 1919, and holds the 1914-15 Star, and the General Service and Victory Medals.
55, Thomas Street, Miles Platting, Manchester. Z10001A

CLARK, W. H., Gunner, R.F.A.
He joined in March 1918, and on completion of his training was drafted to the Western Front in time to take part in the final stages of the Advance of that year. He saw nearly three months' severe fighting in various sectors, and was sent home in March 1919. In 1920 he was still serving, and holds the General Service and Victory Medals.
55, Thomas Street, Miles Platting, Manchester. Z10001B

CLARK, W. H., Corporal, 16th Manchester Regt.
After volunteering in November 1915, he was sent in the following March to Mesopotamia, where he took part in the operations for the Relief of Kut, and later in the Battle of Kut-el-Amara. In February 1918, he was transferred to France, and fought through the Retreat and Advance on the Somme, being in actions at Bapaume, Amiens, Cambrai, and Le Cateau. After the Armistice he was in the Army of Occupation on the Rhine, and was finally demobilised in September 1919. He holds the General Service and Victory Medals.
56, Canning Street, Hulme, Manchester. Z4610

CLARKE, A., Cpl., Manchester Regt. and R.A.M.C.
After volunteering in January 1916, he was sent to France in the following May, and at once engaged in the trench fighting of that period. In August of the same year he was severely wounded, and after treatment at a hospital in England, was transferred in November to the Royal Army Medical Corps, in which he did much useful work as a hospital orderly, until his demobilisation in September 1919. He holds the General Service and Victory Medals.
6, Grove Place, Longsight, Manchester. Z4622

CLARKE, A. A., Private, 2/6th Manchester Regt.
After volunteering in April 1915, he proceeded to France in the following August, and saw heavy fighting near Vimy Ridge, and in the Somme Offensive, in the course of which he was gassed, but recovered and fought again on the Ancre Front, also in very many engagements during the Retreat and Advance of 1918, notably those of the Marne and Aisne, Ypres IV, and Le Cateau II. After the Armistice he returned home, and was demobilised in March 1919. He holds the 1914-15 Star, and the General Service and Victory Medals.
1, Lofas Street, Moss Side, Manchester. Z4628

CLARKE, C. E., Gunner, R.G.A.
He volunteered in October 1914, and twelve months later was drafted to the Western Front, where he served with the 50th Heavy Battery. He took part in the Battles of the Somme, Baeumont-Hamel, High Wood, Ypres, Passchendaele, and Cambrai, and in heavy fighting at Nieuport, Dunkirk, and during the Retreat and Advance of 1918. He holds the 1914-15 Star, and the General Service and Victory Medals, and was demobilised in June 1919.
21, Buxton Street, West Gorton, Manchester. Z10002

CLARKE, E., Private, 22nd Manchester Regiment.
He volunteered in September 1914, and after a period of training and service in England, was drafted to France in November 1915. He saw fighting in the Somme Offensive, in which he was wounded, and after recovery, sustained another wound on the same front in 1917. As a result he was evacuated to hospital in England in May, and discharged on account of wounds in October of the same year. He holds the 1914-15 Star, and the General Service and Victory Medals.
4, Pump Street, Hulme, Manchester. Z4626

CLARKE, E., Private, 2nd Royal Welch Fusiliers.
Volunteering in January 1915, he was drafted to the Western Front on completing his training in June of that year, and there saw much severe fighting, taking part in important engagements in various sectors. He died gloriously on the Field of Battle at Loos on January 27th, 1916. He was entitled to the 1914-15 Star, and the General Service and Victory Medals.
"He joined the great white company of valiant souls."
6, Neptune Street, Ancoats, Manchester. Z6047

CLARKE, E., Private, 4th King's (L'pool Regt.)
Mobilised in August 1914, he was at once drafted to the Western Front, where he played a prominent part in the Battles of Mons, Ypres, La Bassée, Neuve Chapelle, and the Somme. He was sent home in September 1916, owing to a breakdown in health, and was discharged as medically unfit for further service, holding the Mons Star, and the General Service and Victory Medals. 24, Flower St., Ancoats, Manchester. Z10003

CLARKE, E. J., Private, 9th S. Lancashire Regt.
After volunteering in March 1915, he proceeded to France in the following September, and took part in heavy fighting at Loos, and other places. He was very shortly afterwards transferred to Salonika, where he was engaged in the Offensive on the Doiran front, and many other of the subsequent actions in that region. Continuing his service there until the end of the war, he was demobilised in March 1919, and holds the 1914-15 Star, and the General Service and Victory Medals.
5, Amy Street, Longsight, Manchester. Z4620

CLARKE, E. V., Private, R.M.L.I.
He volunteered in January 1916, and after training, proceeded in the following September to France, where he at once saw heavy fighting on the Somme. On April 28th, 1917, in an engagement near Oppy Wood, he was reported missing, and afterwards officially presumed killed, thus giving his life for King and Country. He was entitled to the General Service and Victory Medals. "Whilst we remember, the sacrifice is not in vain."
20, Milton Street, Hulme, Manchester. Z4630B

CLARKE, F., Private, 9th Border Regiment.
Volunteering at the outbreak of war in August 1914, he proceeded to the Western Front in June of the following year, and there served in the Battle of Loos, and many minor engagements. In October 1915, however, he was transferred to the East, and after taking part in the first Landing at Salonika, saw much severe fighting on the Vardar front. He returned to France in January 1919, and there served in various sectors until demobilised in June of that year. He holds the 1914-15 Star, and the General Service and Victory Medals.
10, Dawson Street, West Gorton, Manchester. Z10004

CLARKE, F., Private, Lancashire Fusiliers.
He volunteered in August 1914, and in the following June was drafted to the Dardanelles. During his service in Gallipoli he was severely wounded in the third Battle of Krithia in June 1915, and invalided to hospital in Cairo. After his recovery he proceeded to the Western Front in 1917, and was again wounded in action, and was sent to hospital in England. He was discharged as medically unfit for further duty in May 1918, and holds the 1914-15 Star, and the General Service and Victory Medals. 21, Fraser Street, Manchester. Z9472

CLARKE, F., Private, 1st Lancashire Fusiliers.
Volunteering in August 1914, he was sent to France in the following month, and fought at La Bassée, and in the desperate Battle of Ypres I, in which he was wounded, and sent to hospital in England on recovery. In May 1915 he proceeded to Gallipoli, and took part in the Suvla Bay Landing. After the Evacuation, he was invalided home suffering from dysentery, but returned to France in February 1916, and was in action at Vimy Ridge, and later in the 1st Battle of the Somme. In this he sustained another wound, and being passed to hospital in England, was finally discharged after his hard service, in May 1918, on account of wounds. He holds the 1914 Star, and the General Service and Victory Medals.
5, Briar Street, Hulme, Manchester. Z4623

CLARKE, F. T., Private, Cheshire Regiment.
He joined in May 1917, and served with his unit at various stations in the United Kingdom. He rendered valuable services, but, owing to a physical disability, was not successful in obtaining his transfer overseas before the cessation of hostilities, and after doing much good work in the carrying out of varied duties, was eventually demobilised in November 1919.
85, Bedford Street, Hulme, Manchester. TZ4621

CLARKE, F. P., Private, 7th Manchester Regiment.
After volunteering in August 1914, he went through his training and was drafted in August 1915 to the Dardanelles. Here he was wounded in an early engagement, and after being sent to hospital in England was transferred to Egypt, where he served for fifteen months, and then proceeded to France. He was in action on the Somme front, and later in April 1917, was badly wounded at Gommecourt. This wound resulted in the amputation of a leg, and he was finally discharged from hospital in England in March 1918. He holds the 1914-15 Star, and the General Service and Victory Medals.
43, Caroline Street, Hulme, Manchester. Z4625

CLARKE, G., Private, 2nd Manchester Regiment.
He re-enlisted in February 1915, and after completing a period of training, served at various stations, where he was engaged on duties of great importance. He was unable to obtain his transfer to a theatre of war, but nevertheless rendered very valuable services with his unit. He was unfortunately severely wounded in the bombardment of Felixstowe, and was consequently invalided from the Army in October 1918. He holds the Queen's and King's South African Medals.
25, Irlam Street, Miles Platting, Manchester. Z10006

CLARKE, F. W., L/Corporal, 4th Manchester Regt.

He volunteered in January 1915, and proceeded to Gallipoli in the following April. He took part in the famous Landing on the Peninsula, and also in the Krithia Battles, and the Suvla Bay operations. In December 1916 he was transferred to France, and fought at Arras, and in the Battle of Vimy Ridge in April 1917. Being severely wounded in this engage· ment he was sent to hospital in England, and after treatment, was discharged as unfit for further service in January 1918. He holds the 1914–15 Star, and the General Service and Victory Medals. 7, Conch Terrace, Gorton, Manchester. Z4619

CLARKE, H., Private, Manchester Regiment.

He volunteered in September 1914, and being sent for training to various stations in England, proceeded to the Western Front in November 1915. He took part in heavy fighting at Loos, St. Eloi, and Albert. During an action at Vermelles, in May 1916, he died gloriously on the Field of Battle, and was entitled to the 1914–15 Star, and the General Service and Victory Medals. His body lies in Vermelles Cemetery.
" His life for his Country."   Z4624
15, Moor Street, Winslow Road, Rusholme, Manchester.

CLARKE, H., Corporal, 1st Lancashire Fusiliers.

He volunteered in August 1914, and in the following year was sent to Gallipoli. During his service in this theatre of war he took part in the Battles of Krithia, and was wounded and sent to Egypt, and later to England. On his recovery he proceeded to the Western Front, and was in action in many important engagements until July 1916, when he was wounded on the Somme. He was demobilised in March 1919, and holds the 1914–15 Star, and the General Service and Victory Medals.
14, Dickson Street, West Gorton, Manchester. Z11892

CLARKE, H., Private, Royal Welch Fusiliers.

After volunteering in September 1914, he underwent training, and was drafted to the Western Front in the following January. He saw heavy fighting at St. Eloi, and in the Battles of Ypres II, and Loos, and also at Vermelles, and on the Ancre front. Later he fought at Arras, and Lens, near which place he was badly gassed in August 1917, and also disabled by a wound in the arm. After long treatment at a Base hospital he was demobilised in August 1919, and holds the 1914–15 Star, and the General Service and Victory Medals.
26, Thomas Street, West Gorton, Manchester. TZ4615

CLARKE, H., Private, 11th Manchester Regiment.

Mobilised on the outbreak of war, he proceeded to France with the Expeditionary Force, and took part in the fighting at Mons, and at Le Cateau in the Great Retreat, also in the Battles of the Marne and Ypres I. Later, in 1916, he was in action at St. Eloi, and at Albert, where he was seriously wounded, and being invalided to a hospital in England, was eventually discharged as unfit for further service in November 1917. He holds the Mons Star, and the General Service and Victory Medals. 4, Watson Street, Hulme, Manchester. Z4632

CLARKE, J., Private, 10th King's (Liverpool Regt.)

He joined in January 1917, and after his training was drafted to France in the following July. During his service on the Western Front he fought at Arras, Ypres, and Givenchy, and in the second Battle of the Somme, and in many of the engagements which followed until the Armistice was signed. He holds the General Service and Victory Medals, and was demobilised in February 1919.
41, Pilling Street, Newton Heath, Manchester. Z9473B

CLARKE, J., Private, 6th Manchester Regiment.

He volunteered in 1915, and after undergoing a period of training, was retained on important duties at various stations. Owing to ill-health, he was unable to obtain his transfer to the front, but nevertheless, rendered valuable services with his unit until discharged in 1916, as medically unfit for further service. He has unhappily died since.
" Steals on the ear the distant triumph song."
5, Monroe Street, Chorton-on-Medlock, Manchester. Z10007B

CLARKE, J., Sapper, R.E.

Volunteering in August 1914, he proceeded at once to Egypt, and in the following February saw fighting on the Suez Canal, and later at Mersa Matruh, Agagia, Sollum, and Romani, where he was wounded. After being evacuated for treatment to a hospital in England, he recovered, and proceeded to the fighting line in France in January 1917. Here he took part in the Battles of Arras, Ypres, III, and Cambrai I, and fought through the Retreat and Advance of 1918, being in action at Havrincourt, and again at Cambrai. After the Armistice he returned home, and was demobilised in February 1919. He holds the 1914–15 Star, and the General Service and Victory Medals.
2, George's Avenue, Chester Road, Hulme, Manchester. Z4631

CLARKE, J., Pte., Loyal North Lancashire Regt.

He joined in May 1916, and proceeded to France in the following August, in time to take his part in the Somme Offensive, and in the actions on the Ancre front which succeeded it, notably those of Beaumont-Hamel, and Beaucourt. He afterwards fought at Arras, Bullecourt, Messines Ridge, and in the Battle of Ypres III, also at Cambrai. He served through the Retreat and Advance of 1918, fighting at Cambrai again, and at Le

Cateau, up to the time of the Armistice, after which he was demob-ilised in January 1919, and holds the General Service and Victory Medals. 94, Bold Street, Moss Side, Manchester. Z4629

CLARKE, J., Sergt., 3rd King's (Liverpool Regt.)

A Reservist, he was called to the Colours when war was declared in August 1914, and was immediately drafted to the Western Front, where he was wounded in action during the fighting at Mons. Invalided home, he served, after his recovery, at various stations, where he was engaged in instructing recruits and on other important duties. He was discharged in March 1916, time-expired, and holds the Mons Star, and the General Service and Victory Medals.
30, Nelson Street, Bradford, Manchester. Z6048

CLARKE, J., Private, 2nd Manchester Regiment.

Mobilised at the commencement of hostilities he at once proceeded to France, and fought in the Retreat from Mons, and was wounded and taken prisoner at Le Cateau on August 26th, 1914. He was held in captivity in various camps in Germany, until the cessation of the war, and after being repatriated was demobilised in February 1919. He holds the Mons Star, and the General Service and Victory Medals.
49, Dalton Street, Collyhurst, Manchester. Z10533

CLARKE, J. T., Private, 1/4th Dorsetshire Regt.

He joined in December 1916, and proceeded, after training, to India in the following April. From there he was shortly afterwards transferred to Mesopotamia and then back to India, being chiefly engaged in the important duty of carrying Despatches to and from the General Headquarters in those two countries. He was eventually demobilised in June 1919, and holds the General Service and Victory Medals.
17, Bangor Street, Hulme, Manchester. Z4611

CLARKE, J. T., Private, 8th Border Regiment.

He joined in April 1917, and proceeded to the Western Front in the following July. He fought in the Battle of Cambrai (I) and later in the Retreat on the Somme and the third Battle of the Aisne, in which he was wounded and taken prisoner on May 27th, 1918. Being released after the Armistice, he did duty at a prisoners of war camp in Wales until demobilised in December 1919. He holds the General Service and Victory Medals. 27, Raglan Street, Hulme, Manchester. TZ4613

CLARKE, J. W., Private, Lancashire Fusiliers.

After volunteering in November 1914, he passed through a considerable period of training and service in England and was drafted to France in September 1916. He took part in engagements on the Somme, in the Ypres sector and at Cambrai ; later was in the Retreat and Advance of 1918, through which he served until the Armistice, and was subsequently demobilised in March 1919. He holds the General Service and Victory Medals.
36, Clifford Street, Lower Openshaw, Manchester. Z4614

CLARKE, M., Private, 2nd Manchester Regiment.

After volunteering in July 1915, he passed through a considerable period of training and service in England, and was drafted to the Western Front in November 1917. He took part in the Retreat and Advance of 1918, being in actions on the Aisne, and the Marne, and also at Bapaume and in the second Battle of Cambrai. In this engagement he was badly wounded, and after suffering the loss of a leg by amputation, was passed to hospital in England, and eventually discharged in July 1919. He holds the General Service and Victory Medals.
10, Wilberforce Terrace, Hulme, Manchester. Z4627

CLARKE, R. W., Special War Worker.

Having volunteered in May 1915 for work of National importance, he was employed at Iron Works connected with a shipyard during the whole of the rest of the war. He rendered valuable services, being chiefly engaged in manipu-lating the cranes at these works. He was discharged in November 1918.
36, Gorton Street, Ardwick, Manchester.   Z4617

CLARKE, R. W., Private, 7th Manchester Regt. and R.A.S.C.

He joined in January 1917, and after undergoing six months' training, served at various stations, where he was engaged on duties of great importance. He was medically unfit for service overseas and was consequently unable to obtain his transfer to a theatre of war, but did good work with his unit until his demobilisation in February 1919.
13, Dora Street, Rochdale Road, Manchester. Z8968

CLARKE, T., Driver, R.A.S.C. (M.T.)

After volunteering in April 1915, he passed through his training and proceeded to the Western Front in the following August. Here he carried out the valuable duties of supply in many forward areas of the Battle front, notably near Loos, on the Somme, at Messines and Passchendaele Ridges and in the Retreat and Advance of 1918, showing both courage and coolness in the performance of his difficult and often dangerous task. He served on until the Armistice, and after it, and was finally demobilised in June 1919. He holds the 1914–15 Star, and the General Service and Victory Medals.
144, Blackthorn Street, Ardwick, Manchester. Z4618

CLARKE, M., Pte., 2nd King's (Liverpool Regt.)
He volunteered in August 1914, and after his training served at various stations on important garrison duties with his unit. He rendered valuable services, but was not successful in obtaining a transfer overseas before the termination of hostilities. He was demobilised in March 1919.
41, Pilling Street, Manchester.   Z9473A

CLARKE, W., Private, R.A.S.C.
He volunteered in June 1915, and after training was sent to Egypt in the following December. He did good work in transport at the engagements of Agagia, Romani and Magdhaba, and was afterwards, at the end of 1916, transferred to Mesopotamia, where he continued his service in the actions at Kut, Baghdad and Tekrit. He then unfortunately contracted malarial fever, and after being sent to hospital in India, was invalided to England and finally demobilised, convalescent, in July 1919. He holds the 1914–15 Star, and the General Service and Victory Medals.
493, Claremont Road, Rusholme, Macnhester.   Z4612

CLARKE, W., Pte., Loyal North Lancashire Regt.
He volunteered in 1914, and on completing his training in the following year was drafted to the Dardanelles, where he took part in the Landing at Suvla Bay. On the Evacuation of the Peninsula, he was transferred to Mesopotamia and was there severely wounded in action at Kut and invalided home in 1916. He unfortunately died in hospital on November 14th of that year. He was entitled to the 1914–15 Star, and the General Service and Victory Medals.
"A costly sacrifice upon the altar of freedom."
11, Evans Street, Chorlton-on-Medlock, Manchester. Z10009A

CLARKE, W., Pte., Loyal North Lancashire Regt.
Volunteering soon after the outbreak of war, he was sent for training to a Southern depôt and proceeded to France in November 1915. He took part in the Somme Offensive, during which he was wounded, but recovered and fought at Arras and in July 1917 in the Battle of Ypres (III), in which he was again wounded, and unluckily taken prisoner. On his release after the Armistice, he was demobilised in December 1918, and holds the 1914–15 Star, and the General Service and Victory Medals.
73, Birch Street, Ardwick, Manchester.   Z4616

CLARKSON, T. V., Pte., Royal Welch Fusiliers.
He joined in May 1916, and proceeded to France in the following August, in time to take part in the later stages of the Somme Offensive. He afterwards fought at Beaumont-Hamel, at Arras, and in the Battles of Viny and Messines Ridges and Ypres (III). Later he was engaged in the fight of Cambrai (I), in which he was severely wounded, and being invalided home remained under hospital treatment until demobilised in January 1919. He holds the General Service and Victory Medals.
4, Greenhill Street, Chorlton-on-Medlock, Manchester. TZ4633

CLAYPOLE, T., Rifleman, K.R.R.C.
When war broke out he was already serving, and at once proceeded to France, where he fought in the Battles of Mons, Ypres, Hill 60, St. Eloi and Festubert. In 1916 he was sent to Salonika and later to Egypt, where he served until his return to the Western Front in 1918. He then saw heavy fighting in the Amiens, Cambrai, Somme, Arras, Bullecourt Armentières and Albert sectors, and was discharged in February 1919, holding the Mons Star, and the General Service and Victory Medals.
39, Alexandra Place, Manchester.   Z11409A Z11444A

CLAYTON, A. P., Corporal, 7th Manchester Regt.
After volunteering in January 1915, he passed through his training and was drafted to the Egyptian front in the following November. He took part in actions at Agagia, Sollum, Katia and El Fasher, and in August 1916, was transferred to Salonika, where he was engaged in all the operations on that front, including the Doiran Offensive, the Battle on the Struma, the capture of Monastir, the final success on the Vardar. He then unfortunately contracted malaria, and other illnesses, to which he succumbed in hospital at Salonika on October 10th, 1918, thus giving his life for his Country. He was entitled to the 1914–15 Star and the General Service and Victory Medals.
"Thinking that remembrance, though unspoken, may reach him where he sleeps."
18, New Lorne Street, Moss Side, Manchester. Z4634A

CLAYTON, E., L/Corporal, R.E.
Volunteering in August 1914, he was drafted to Egypt in the following month and there served on the Suez Canal until transferred to Gallipoli in time to take part in the Landing at Suvla Bay. He returned to Egypt, however, on the Evacuation of the Peninsula, and after fighting in engagements at Sollum, Jifjaffa and Romani, proceeded into Palestine. In April 1917 he was sent to the Western Front, where he saw heavy fighting at La Bassée, Festubert, Nieuport and many other places and was severely wounded in action in the third Battle of Ypres in September 1917. He was mentioned in Despatches for distinguished service in the Field in that engagement, and holds the 1914–15 Star, and the General

Service and Victory Medals. He was invalided from the Army in March 1918.
24, King Street, Hulme, Manchester.   Z10010

CLAYTON, G., Sapper, R.E.
He volunteered in June 1915, and in January of the following year, was drafted to Egypt. Whilst in this seat of operations he served through many important engagements, including those on the Suez Canal and at Agagia, Sollum, Katia and Romani, and afterwards took part in the Advance into Palestine. Invalided home in October 1917, suffering from fever, he was discharged in March of the following year, as medically unfit for further service, and holds the General Service and Victory Medals.
24, King Street, Hulme, Manchester.   Z10011

CLAYTON, H., Sergt., 2nd Manchester Regiment.
He volunteered in January 1916, and proceeded to France in the following June. He took part in the Somme Offensive and in the fighting on the Ancre front, whcih followed it. He afterwards fought at Arras, and in the Battles of Viny Ridge and Ypres (III), in the last of which he was wounded. After being sent to a hospital in England for twelve months, he returned to France and did duty guarding German prisoners of war. He was demobilised in March 1919, and holds the General Service and Victory Medals.
18, New Lorne Street, Moss Side, Manchester.   Z4634B

CLAYTON, J., Rifleman, 2nd Cameronians (Scottish Rifles).
He joined in September 1916, and in April 1918, after much valuable service at home stations, was drafted to France. He fought through the German Offensive and subsequent Allied Advance of 1918, and returning home after the Armistice, was demobilised in March 1919. He holds the General Service and Victory Medals.
97, Fitzgeorge Street, Collyhurst, Manchester.   Z10534

CLAYTON, T., Private, Lancashire Fusiliers.
Shortly after volunteering in January 1915, he was drafted to the Western Front, where he saw severe fighting in various sectors. He took part in the Battles of Festubert, Loos and Albert, and in engagements at Givenchy and many other places until severely gasssd at Arras and admitted to hospital at Rouen. He was also for a time in hospital at Manchester, but on his recovery, rejoined his unit in France. He was demobilised in March 1919, and holds the 1914–15 Star, and the General Service and Victory Medals.
119, Cobden Street, Bradford, Manchester.   Z8969

CLAYTON, W., Rifleman, Rifle Brigade.
After volunteering in 1914, he underwent a period of training prior to being drafted to the Western Front in May 1916. He saw much severe fighting in various sectors, whilst in this theatre of war, and took part in the Battles of the Somme, Bullecourt and Cambrai and many other important engagements. He died gloriously on the Field of Battle on March 21st, 1918, during the Allied Retreat. He was entitled to the General Service and Victory Medals.
147, Morton Street, Longsight, Manchester.   Z10012

CLAYTON, W. N., Pte., Royal Army Cyclist Corps.
He joined in October 1916, and was sent for training to a depôt in North Wales. He then served with his Corps at various stations in the United Kingdom. He rendered valuable services, but was not successful in obtaining his transfer overseas before the cessation of hostilities, and was eventually demobilised in October 1919.
245, Morton Street, Longsight, Manchester.   Z4635

CLEARY, J., Private, 52nd King's (Liverpool Regt.)
He joined in February 1918, and went through his training in England. After the Armistice he was sent to the Army of Occupation in Germany, and served at many places on the Rhine on garrison and guard duties, until his return to England, and his subsequent demobilisation in November 1919.
44, Queens Street, Higher Ardwick, Manchester.   Z4636

CLEARY, J. E., Private, Lancashire Fusiliers.
He volunteered in August 1914, but was retained on important duties at home until February 1916. Proceeding to France in that month, he took part in the Battles of the Somme (where he was wounded in July 1916), Ypres and Cambrai, the Marne (II), and the Aisne (III), and in much strenuous fighting during the Retreat and Advance of 1918. He holds the General Service and Victory Medals, and was demobilised in July 1920. 26, Strand, St. Ancoats, Manchester. TZ1166

CLEARY, J. E., Private, 8th Manchester Regiment.
After volunteering in August 1914, he passed through his training and was sent in the following October to Salonika. Here he was in action in the first engagement on the Vardar River, where he was wounded, but on recovery, took part later in the Advance on the Doiran front and the Struma River Battle. He was then transferred to France in January 1917 and fought on the Ancre front, later at Bullecourt, Lens and Cambrai, also in the Advance of 1918, in the Ypres sector, where he was again wounded. Being sent to hospital in England, he was demobilised in February 1919, and holds the 1914–15 Star, and the General Service and Victory Medals.
80, Thomas Street, West Gorton, Manchester.   Z4637

CLEASBY, R. B., Private, 2nd Manchester Regt.

He joined in March 1917, but was not successful in obtaining a transfer overseas before the cessation of hostilities. During the war he was engaged on important work in Ireland, and in February 1919 proceeded to Mesopotamia, where he was wounded eight months later. He was taken to hospital at Baghdad, and in 1920 was still serving in the Army.
7, Alton Street, Harpurhey, Manchester. Z11481

CLEGG, G., Private, Lancashire Fusiliers.

Having previously served in the South African campaign, he volunteered in August 1914, and in March 1915 proceeded to France. Thence, after taking part in the Battle of Loos, he was in action on the Vardar, Doiran and Struma fronts and at Monastir, later advancing into Servia, he took part in heavy fighting in the Balkan Mountains. He was invalided home in May 1917, and served at Ripon until discharged in May 1918, holding the Queen's and King's South African Medals, 1914–15 Star, and the General Service and Victory Medals. 51, Craven Street, Cheetham, Manchester. Z11410

CLEGG, G. E., Private, East Lancashire Regiment.

He volunteered at the outbreak of war, and in August 1915 was drafted to the Western Front. Whilst in France he fought in many important engagements, including those at Albert, the Somme, Arras, Vimy Ridge and Bullecourt. He died gloriously on the Field of Battle at Ypres in August 1917, and was buried in the Popéringhe Cemetery. He was entitled to the 1914–15 Star, and the General Service and Victory Medals.
'His life for his Country, his soul to God."
79, Kemp Street, Ancoats, Manchester. TZ9474

CLEGG, H., Private, 6th Manchester Regiment.

Having volunteered soon after the outbreak of war, he went through his training, and was sent in April 1915 to Gallipoli. where he took part in the famous landing and the subsequent operations, including Suvla Bay. After the Evacuation he proceeded to Egypt in February 1916, and fought in all the actions of that year on the Palestine front, including Romani and Magdhaba. He was then transferred to France, and was in the Battle of Cambrai and the Retreat and Advance of 1918. After the Armistice he was demobilised in February 1919, and holds the 1914–15 Star, and the General Service and Victory Medals.
11, Bremner Street, Chorlton-on-Medlock, Manchester. Z4638

CLEGG, H., Sergeant, Royal Army Pay Corps.

He joined in November 1916, and did valuable work with his unit in England. He was not successful in obtaining his transfer overseas, but carried out his important duties at a Western Pay depôt during the rest of the war, and after the Armistice, being not demobilised until December 1919.
37, Roberts Street, Chorlton-on-Medlock, Manchester. X4639

CLEGG, J., Bombardier, R.F.A.

Having volunteered in August 1914, he was sent for training to a north-western depôt in England, and then proceeded to Egypt, where he was in action on the Suez Canal, and afterwards to Gallipoli, where he took part in the Suvla Bay operation and other engagements. In February 1916 he returned to England, and was transferred to the Royal Air Force, in which he worked as a mechanic, until demobilised in March 1919. He holds the 1914–15 Star, and the General Service and Victory Medals.
132, Thomas Street, Miles Platting, Manchester. Z1327

CLEGG, J.(D.C.M.) L/Corpl., 2nd Lancs. Fus. and R.E.

Having enlisted in 1907, he was already in the Army when war broke out in August 1914, and was immediately drafted to the Western Front, where he fought in the Battle of Mons and the subsequent Retreat. He also took part in the Battles of the Marne, La Bassée, Ypres, Loos, the Somme, Arras and Cambrai, and many minor engagements, serving as a Signaller to his Battalion, and was wounded in action in the Retreat of 1918. He was awarded the Distinguished Conduct Medal for conspicuous gallantry and devotion to duty displayed in carrying Despatches under heavy fire in the third Battle of Ypres, and holds also the Mons Star, and the General Service and Victory Medals. He was discharged in February 1919.
24, Perrin Street, Ancoats, Manchester. Z10013

CLEGG, J., Private, 8th Manchester Regiment.

He volunteered in September 1914, and in August of the following year was drafted to Gallipoli, where after taking part in the Landing at Suvla Bay, he saw much severe fighting and was wounded in action. On the Evacuation of the Peninsula, he was transferred to the Western Front and there fought in engagements in various sectors until wounded a second time in October 1917. He was invalided home, but on his recovery returned to France in time to serve through the Advance of 1918. Finally demobilised in June 1919, he holds the 1914–15 Star, and the General Service and Victory Medals.
1, Jackson Place, Longsight, Manchester. Z10014A

CLEGG, J. E., 7th South Wales Borderers.

Volunteering in April 1915, he was drafted in March 1917 to the Western Front. There he was in action at Arras, Bullecourt, Messines and Ypres and proceeded to Salonika in May 1918. In this theatre of war he took part in numerous

engagements and eventually entered Bulgaria. Returning to England in April 1919, he was demobilised, and holds the General Service and Victory Medals.
21, Derby Street, Ardwick, Manchester. Z6268

CLEGG, R. T., Private, R.A.M.C.

He joined in September 1916, and on completing his training in January of the following year, was drafted to the Western Front. Whilst in this theatre of war he was engaged on important duties in various sectors and also took an active part in the Battle of the Ancre and many other engagements. He was invalided home in March 1917, and in July of the following year was discharged as medically unfit for further service. He holds the General Service and Victory Medals.
79, Irlam Street, Miles Platting, Manchester. Z10015

CLEGG, W., Private, 7th Loyal N. Lancs. Regt.

Shortly after volunteering in 1914, he was drafted to Egypt, where he served at various stations until transferred to the Western Front early in 1916. There, after taking part in the Battles of Albert and the Somme and many other important engagements, he fell fighting at Ypres on July 18th, 1917. He was entitled to the 1914–15 Star, and the General Service and Victory Medals.
" Whilst we remember, the sacrifice is not in vain."
5, Monroe Street, Chorlton-on-Medlock, Manchester. Z10007A

CLEGG, W. H., Private, 21st Manchester Regiment.

He joined in March 1917, and after five months' training proceeded to the Western Front, where he saw much severe fighting in the Ypres sector. He made the supreme sacrifice, being killed in action on October 31st, 1917, only two months after landing in France. He was entitled to the General Service and Victory Medals. Z10014B
" He died the noblest death a man may die,
Fighting for God and right and liberty."
1, Jackson Place, Morton Street, Longsight, Manchester.

CLEWES, J., Private, 2nd Border Regiment.

Shortly after volunteering in August 1914, he was drafted to the Western Front, where he took part in the first Battle of Ypres and in many minor engagements. He died gloriously on the Field of Battle at Neuve Chapelle on March 11th, 1915. He was entitled to the 1914–15 Star, and the General Service and Victory Medals.   " Great deeds cannot die:
They, with the sun and moon renew their light for ever."
27, Stewart Street, Gorton, Manchester. Z10016

CLEWS, A. V., L/Corporal, 20th Manchester Regt.

After volunteering in November 1915, he proceeded after a period of training to the Western Front in the following April. He took part in the great Offensive on the Somme which commenced in July of that year. During which, at Guillemont, on August 28th, 1916, he gave his life for King and Country. He was entitled to the General Service and Victory Medals.
" A valiant Soldier, with undaunted heart, he breasted life's last hill."
37, James' Street, Moss Side, Manchester. Z4640E

CLEWS, D., Gunner, R.G.A.

He volunteered in April 1915, and after training and service in England, was drafted to the Western Front in the following April in time to take part in the Somme Offensive of July 1916. He afterwards fought at Arras and Ypres, and at Bapaume in the Retreat of 1918. After serving to the end of the campaign, he was attacked by illness in February 1919, invalided home and discharged in March of that year. He holds the General Service and Victory Medals.
37, James Street, Moss Side, Manchester. Z4640A

CLEWS, E., Sergt., 11th Manchester Regiment.

After volunteering in March 1915, he was sent to Gallipoli, and took part in the Suvla Bay Landing. After the Evacuation he was transferred to the Western Front and fought in the Somme Offensive, doing good service in his responsible rank. Later he was engaged at Lens and Ypres, and went through the Retreat and Advance of 1918, being finally demobilised in May 1919. He holds the 1914–15 Star, and the General Service and Victory Medals.
37, James Street, Moss Side, Manchester. Z4640C

CLEWS, F. R., L/Corporal, R.A.S.C.

He joined in June 1917, and although he did not see actual fighting, shares the fine record of his family. After training and service in England, he was sent in January 1920 to the Army of Occupation on the Rhine, where he was still serving later in that year.
37, James Street, Moss Side, Manchester. Z4640D

CLEWS, J., Corporal, Manchester Regiment.

He volunteered in May 1915, and was drafted to the Western Front the following September. He at once saw heavy fighting in the Battle of Loos, after which he was attacked with illness, and invalided home, but returned to France in September 1916, and took part in engagements at Arras, in the Ypres sector, at Beaumont-Hamel, and in the final Advance of 1918. After the Armistice he was demobilised in January 1919, and holds the 1914–15 Star, and the General Service and Victory Medals.
37, James Street, Moss Side, Manchester. Z4640B

CLIFF, A., Pte., 1st King's Shropshire Light Infantry.
He joined in March 1917, and after training proceeded to the Western Front in the following December in time to take part in the Battle of Cambrai, in which he was badly gassed. Being invalided home, he underwent treatment at a Midland hospital, and on recovery was sent to Aden, where he was still serving in 1920. He holds the General Service and Victory Medals. 183, Earl Street, Longsight, Manchester   Z4642

CLIFF, H., Private, 7th Manchester Regiment.
Volunteering soon after the outbreak of war, he was at once sent to Egypt and did garrison duty at Alexandria. He was afterwards transferred to Gallipoli and took part in the famous Landing, also in the third Battle of Krithia, in which he was wounded on June 4th, 1915. On recovery he proceeded to France and fought in the Battles of the Somme (I), Messines Ridge, and Cambrai (I), as well as in the Retreat and Advance of 1918 until the Armistice, after which he was, on his return to England, demobilised in February 1919. He holds the 1914-15 Star, and the General Service and Victory Medals. 191, Earl Street, Longsight, Manchester   Z4643

CLIFF, R., Private, 2nd Manchester Regiment.
He volunteered in December 1914, and after a short period of training was drafted to France in the following March. There he took part in the three important Battles of Neuve Chapelle, Ypres (II) and Loos, in the last of which he was wounded and unluckily taken prisoner. After three years' imprisonment in Germany, he was on his release, demobilised in June 1919, and holds the 1914-15 Star, and the General Service and Victory Medals.
36, Robson Street, Hulme, Manchester.   Z4641

CLIFF, W., Corporal, Northumberland Fusiliers.
He joined in February 1917, and proceeded almost immediately to the Western Front, where he took part in the great Battle of Vimy Ridge. Afterwards, in helping to stem the German Advance of 1918, on March 21st, he died gloriously on the Field of Battle at Bullecourt. He was entitled to the General Service and Victory Medals.
"His memory is cherished with pride."
91, Bickley Street, Moss Side, Manchester.   Z4644

CLIFFE, W., Private, 2nd Royal Welch Fusiliers.
He joined in June 1918, but was unsuccessful in procuring a transfer to the war zone before the termination of the war. He, however, rendered valuable services in connection with coast defence, and in July 1919 was drafted to Salonika. There he was engaged in guarding prisoners of war, but contracted malaria, and was in hospital for five months. On his return home he was demobilised in January 1920, holding the General Service Medal.
7, Nelson Place, Rusholme, Manchester.   Z6710

CLIFFORD, A., Pte., King's Own Scottish Borderers.
He volunteered in October 1914, and being sent almost immediately to France, took part in the desperate Battle of Ypres (I), and afterwards those of Neuve Chapelle and Loos. In this last engagement in September 1915, he gave his life for the freedom of England. He was entitled to the 1914 Star, and the General Service and Victory Medals.
"The path of duty was the way to glory."
52, York Street, Hulme, Manchester.   Z4646

CLIFFORD, P., Private, Royal Welch Fusiliers.
He joined in May 1916, and after a short period of training proceeded to France in the following September. He took part in action during that Autumn, and in the next Spring also in the Battle of Vimy Ridge. Here, in April 1917, he gave his life for King and Country, dying gloriously on the Field, and was entitled to the General Service and Victory Medals. His body lies in the Cemetery at Arras.
"Great deeds cannot die."
8, Chell Street, Longsight, Manchester.   Z4645B

CLIMO, J. H., Private, 1st Lancashire Fusiliers.
He joined in February 1918, on attaining military age, and after training and service at various stations in England, was not successful in obtaining his transfer overseas, but was sent later to Ireland, where he rendered valuable services on garrison and other duties, on which he was still engaged in 1920.
7, Anthony Street, Ardwick, Manchester.   TZ1212B TZ1213B

CLINE, C., Private, East Lancashire Regiment.
He volunteered in April 1915, and after his training was retained on important duties at various stations until June 1918. He was then drafted to the Western Front, where he saw severe fighting at Vimy Ridge and in other sectors until wounded in action in August 1918, and invalided to hospital at Sheffield. He was demobilised in May 1919, and holds the General Service and Victory Medals.
8, Newton Street, Openshaw, Manchester.   Z5755

CLINE, W., Sapper, R.E.
Having volunteered immediately after the outbreak of war, he went through his training and proceeded to France in January 1915. He rendered valuable services in the Battle of Ypres (II), in which he was wounded, and after his recovery, in those of Somme (I) and Ypres (III), being gassed in the

last engagement. He also served through the Retreat and Advance of 1918 until the Armistice. After his demobilisation in February 1919, he re-enlisted and while serving with his Corps in France was unfortunately drowned by accident, in the Froissy Canal. His body lies in the Cemetery at Péronne. He was entitled to the 1914-15 Star, and the General Service and Victory Medals.
"Thinking that remembrance, though unspoken, may reach him where he sleeps."
100, Robert Street, West Gorton, Manchester.   TZ4647

CLOAD, L., Private, Lancashire Fusiliers.
He joined in September 1917, and served with his unit at various stations in England. He rendered valuable services, but was not successful in obtaining his transfer overseas before the cessation of hostilities, and after carrying out well a variety of military duties, was demobilised in December 1918. 6, Tunstall St., Longsight, Manchester.   TZ4648

CLORAN, P., Private, 3rd Manchester Regiment.
He volunteered at the outbreak of war in August 1914, and in April of the following year was drafted to the Dardanelles. There he took part in the Landing at Cape Helles, and afterwards fought in the Battles of Krithia, at Suvla Bay and in the capture of Chunuk Bair. Returning home on the Evacuation of the Gallipoli Peninsula, he was finally invalided from the Army in June 1918, suffering from enteric fever. He holds the 1914-15 Star, and the General Service and Victory Medals.
5, Linacre Street, Oldham Road, Manchester.   Z10017

CLORLEY, D., Pte., Loyal North Lancashire Regt.
Two months after volunteering in September 1915 he proceeded to France, where he saw severe fighting in various sectors of the Front and took part in engagements at St. Eloi, Loos and Vermelles. He fell in action at Vimy Ridge in October 1916, during the Somme Offensive. He was entitled to the 1914-15 Star, and the General Service and Victory Medals.
"His life for his Country, his soul to God."
3, Thompson Street, West Gorton Manchester.   Z10018

CLOUDSDALE, H. L., Private, M.G.C.
He joined in August 1916, and in January 1918 was drafted to France. During his service on the Western Front he was engaged on important duties in guarding German prisoners at various camps, including those at Boulogne, Ypres, Cambrai and Bullecourt. He returned home and was demobilised in January 1919, and holds the General Service and Victory Medals
38, Parkfield Avenue, Rusholme, Manchester.   Z9475

CLOUGH, S., R.S.M., 7th Manchester Regiment.
Mobilised with the Territorials in August 1914, he proceeded to Egypt in the following month and served in the Soudan until May 1915. He was then drafted to Gallipoli, but returned to Egypt on the Evacuation of the Peninsula and took a prominent part in engagements at Katia and Romani. In February 1917 he was transferred to the Western Front, where he fought at Bullecourt, Lens, St. Quentin and Havrincourt. He was mentioned in Despatches for distinguished service in Egypt in October 1916, and in France in March 1918, and was awarded the Belgian Croix de Guerre for conspicuous gallantry in the Field at Nieuport in February 1918. Holding also the 1914-15 Star, and the General Service, Victory and Territorial Efficiency Medals, he was discharged in March 1919.
9, Sun Street, Newton Heath, Manchester.   Z10019

CLOWES, J., Pte., 7th Manchester Regt., and R.D.C.
He volunteered in November 1914, and after completing a period of training served at various stations, where he was engaged in guarding prisoners of war and on various other important duties. He was not successful in obtaining his transfer to a theatre of war, but, nevertheless, rendered valuable services with his unit until March 1919, when he was demobilised. 7, Margaret Street, Ancoats, Manchester.   Z10020

CLOWREY, F., Private, Northumberland Fusiliers.
Volunteering in August 1914, he was eventually drafted to France in May 1916, but three months later was badly wounded at Arras. Invalided to England, he underwent treatment at Liverpool and then returned to the Western Front, where he was again wounded at the Battle of Arras in April 1917. After being in hospital at the Base, he rejoined his unit, but was unfortunately badly wounded for the third time later in the same year on the Somme. He was once more invalided home, and on his recovery was discharged in December 1918, in order to take up his former occupation as a miner. He holds the General Service and Victory Medals.
34, Harrold Street, Bradford, Manchester.   Z11677

CLOY, H., A.B., Royal Navy.
After joining in June 1918, he served on patrol work on the home seas for the remainder of the war, and was then posted to H.M.S. "Allido." This ship was employed as a submarine tender, and aboard it he was still serving in 1920. He holds the General Service and Victory Medals.
9, Settle Street, Hulme, Manchester   Z4649A

CLOY, H., C.S.M., 1/6th Manchester Regiment.
Mobilised on the outbreak of war, he proceeded to Egypt in September 1914, and in the next April took part in the famous Landing at Gallipoli, and afterwards in that of Suvla Bay. In this last operation, on August 7th, 1915, he gave his life for King and Country, and was entitled to the 1914–15 Star, and the General Service and Victory Medals.
"His name liveth for evermore."
9, Settle Street, Hulme, Manchester. Z4649B

CLUCAS, H., L/Corporal, 8th King's (L'pool Regt.)
Volunteering in August 1914, he was trained at Liverpool and Bedford, and was then drafted overseas in May 1915. During his service on the Western Front, he took an active part in engagements at La Bassée, Givenchy, Festubert, Béthune, Laventie, and the Somme. He was severely wounded in action at Albert in August 1916, and in consequence was invalided out of the Army two months later, holding the 1914–15 Star, and the General Service and Victory Medals.
45, Southwell Street, Harpurhey, Manchester. Z11482

CLUEARD, G. L., Driver, R.A.S.C.
He volunteered in November 1914, and after training with his Corps, was sent to France in August of the next year. He did good service in supply in many engagements in the forward areas, notably at Loos, on the Somme, at Bullecourt, in the Ypres Sector, and at Cambrai. After serving right through the final stages of the war, he was demobilised in February 1919, and holds the 1914–15 Star, and the General Service and Victory Medals.
162, Earl Street, Longsight, Manchester. Z2483B

CLULOW, E., Private, Manchester Regt., and K.O. (Royal Lancaster Regiment.)
He joined in May 1916, and proceeded to France in the following November. Soon after his arrival on the Front he was transferred to the King's Own Royal Lancaster Regiment, and in this unit, fought on the Ancre, at Messines Ridge, and in the Battle of Ypres III. In this last engagements on July 12th, 1917, he was mortally wounded in the Field, and died of his wounds the same day, thus giving his life for the great cause. He was entitled to the General Service and Victory Medals.
"A costly sacrifice upon the altar of freedom."
26, Marsland Street, Ardwick, Manchester. Z4651

CLULOW, H., Private, 18th Manchester Regiment.
He volunteered in March 1915, and after passing through a considerable period of training and service in England, was drafted to France in July 1916, in time to take part in the great Offensive on the Somme. He afterwards fought on the Ancre Front, and at Beaucourt, Arras, and Vimy Ridge, also in the Battle of Ypres III, in which he was wounded, and, suffering also from trench fever, was sent to a Base hospital. On recovery he joined in the Ypres Sector, and was badly gassed there. After some months in hospital he was finally demobilised in October 1919, and holds the General Service and Victory Medals.
23, Buckingham Street, Moss Side, Manchester. Z4650

CLULOW, W., Private, South Lancashire Regiment.
Shortly after volunteering in July 1915, he proceeded to France, where he saw severe fighting in various sectors of the Front. He took part in the Battles of Loos, Vimy Ridge, and Messines, and many other important engagements until wounded in action, and sent to hospital at the Base. On his recovery, however, he re-joined his unit, and was again in action until the cessation of hostilities. Demobilised in January 1919, he holds the 1914–15 Star, and the General Service and Victory Medals.
16, Whittaker Street, Gorton, Manchester. Z10021

COATES, A., Private, Labour Corps.
He joined in March 1916, and was sent to France in the following September. He did good service in his Corps in connection with various engagements in the forward areas, notably on the Ancre front, and at Beaucourt, Bullecourt, Lens, and Cambrai, being employed in road repairs, trench digging, and many other useful duties. He served on to the time of the Armistice, and after it, and was not demobilised until November 1919. He holds the General Service and Victory Medals.
10, Hilton Street, Lower Openshaw, Manchester. Z4653A

COATES, A., Private, Royal Welch Fusiliers.
He joined in March 1917, and served with his unit at many different stations in the United Kingdom. He rendered valuable services, but was not successful in obtaining his transfer overseas before the cessation of hostilities, and after doing much valuable garrison and guard work, was demobilised in January 1919.
10, Hilton Street, Lower Openshaw, Manchester. Z4653B

COATES, C., Private, 13th King's (Liverpool Regt.)
He joined in June 1918, and was drafted to France in the following August, in time to take part in the victorious Advance, during which he was in action at Cambrai and Le Cateau. After the cessation of hostilities he proceeded to Germany, and concluded his service in the Army of Occupation on the Rhine, being eventually demobilised in October 1919. He holds the General Service and Victory Medals.
16, Rumford Street, Hulme, Manchester. TZ4654

COATES, G. R., Private, 2nd Manchester Regt., and Sapper, R.E.
He volunteered in August 1915, and in March of the following year, proceeded to Egypt, where he took part in the Battle of Katia, and the Capture of El Fasher. In May 1916, however, he was transferred to Salonika, and there served at the re-capture of Monastir, and saw much severe fighting on the Doiran front. He was sent to the Western Front in January 1918, and fought in the Battles of the Somme, the Aisne, Bapaume, and the Scarpe, and other engagements in various sectors. He was demobilised in February 1919, and holds the General Service and Victory Medals.
14, Park Street, West Gorton, Manchester. Z10022

COATES, J. W., Private, 5th South Lancashire Regt.
A month after the outbreak of war he volunteered, and in February 1915 was ordered to the Western Front. There he was engaged in fierce fighting in many engagements, including those at Neuve Chapelle, St. Eloi, Hill 60, Ypres, Loos, and Vimy Ridge, but was wounded in the Battle of the Somme in September 1916, and in consequence was discharged as medically unfit for further service in October 1916. He holds the 1914–15 Star, and the General Service and Victory Medals.
73, Long Street, Ancoats, Manchester. Z11411A

COATES, R. E., Private, 7th Lancashire Fusiliers.
Volunteering in March 1915, he served at various stations until he proceeded to the Western Front in February 1917. He was in action at Vimy Ridge, and in other engagements of note, and was severely wounded in May 1917. After returning home he received hospital treatment, and was finally invalided out of the Service in November 1917. He holds the General Service and Victory Medals.
18, Stretton Street, Rochdale Road, Manchester. Z10535

COATES, S., Corporal, R.A.S.C.
Mobilised on the outbreak of war, he proceeded to France with the Expeditionary Force, and rendered valuable services in the Retreat from Mons, being attached for supply purposes to a Siege Battery. He continued to carry out his difficult, and often dangerous duties in connection with many other engagements, at Ypres, Hill 60, Loos, and on the Somme. In operations near Arras in April 1917, he was badly injured by an accident, and sent to hospital in England. After several months' treatment he resumed his service in France, and carried it on right through the final stages until the Armistice, after which he was demobilised in January 1919, and holds the Mons Star, and the General Service and Victory Medals.
4, Platt Street, Moss Side, Manchester. Z4652

COBAIN, W., Private, Tank Corps.
He joined in February 1916, and after training in this novel arm of the Service, proceeded to France in March 1917. He took his part in the Battles of Ypres III, and Cambrai I, and was gassed near Amiens, but shared in the great Advance of 1918, being in action at Havrincourt, Epéhy, Cambrai (a second time) and Le Cateau. Returning home after the Armistice, he was demobilised in January 1919, and holds the General Service and Victory Medals.
23, Edge Street, Hulme, Manchester. TZ4655

COBB, C., Private, 8th Lincolnshire Regiment.
He volunteered in October 1915, and was drafted to France in the following February. Here he saw much hard service, being in actions at Loos, St. Eloi, Albert, and Vimy Ridge, also in the Somme Offensive of July in which he was wounded, but on recovery fought again on the Ancre Front, and at Beaucourt. In April 1917, he fell fighting at Arras, and was entitled to the General Service and Victory Medals.
"His life for his Country, his soul to God."
20, Holt Street, Morton Street, Longsight, Manchester. Z4656

COBB, C. H., Driver, R.F.A.
He volunteered in 1915, and later in the same year was drafted to the Western Front, whence he proceeded shortly afterwards to Mesopotamia. There he took part in the Relief of Kut, and the Capture of Baghdad, and many other important engagements until the cessation of hostilities. He finally returned home for demobilisation in February 1920, and holds the 1914–15 Star, and the General Service and Victory Medals.
9, Norbury Street, Longsight, Manchester. Z10023

COBB, J. (M.M.), L/Corporal, R.A.S.C.
He joined in August 1916, and went to France in the following December. He did good service on a caterpillar tractor taking heavy guns to the front in many different engagements. He was gassed and wounded at Arras in April 1917, but after treatment at a Base hospital rejoined, and took part in many other actions, being awarded the Military Medal for conspicuous bravery in the Field. In December 1918, he unfortunately contracted influenza and succumbed to the complaint in a Base hospital on the 13th of that month. In addition to the Military Medal he holds the General Service and Victory Medals.
"He joined the great white company of valiant souls."
46, Brunt Street, Rusholme, Manchester. Z4657

COBURN, J., Private, R.A.M.C.
After volunteering in May 1915, he passed through training and service in England, and was sent to the Eastern front in January 1917. He did good service on hospital ships, conveying wounded from Mesopotamia and Egypt to Bombay, and doing orderly's work in hospital there until his return to England and his demobilisation in June 1919. He holds the General Service and Victory Medals.
179, Broadfield Road, Moss Side, Manchester.   TZ4658

COCHRANE, W. J., Cpl., 8th Manchester Regt.
After volunteering in 1915, he went through his training, and proceeded to the Egyptian front in November 1915. After being engaged on the Suez Canal he was transferred to Gallipoli, and took part in the famous Landing at Cape Helles, and afterwards at Suvla Bay. Being then invalided home with fever, he recovered, and was sent to the Western Front. In October 1916 he was reported missing at Grandcourt, and later officially presumed killed. He was entitled to the 1914–15 Star, and the General Service and Victory Medals.
"His life for his Country, his soul to God."
59, Dorset Street, Hulme, Manchester.   Z4660A

COCKCROFT, W. Driver, R.A.S.C.
After volunteering in January 1915, he was sent for training to various centres in England, and proceeded to France in August 1916. He did good service in the Somme Offensive, on the Ancre front, and at Arras, and Vimy and Messines Ridges. Later he took part in the Battles of Ypres III, and Cambrai I, and carried on the valuable work of supply through all the final stages of the war. He was demobilised in May 1919, and holds the General Service and Victory Medals.
7, Brookside, City Road, Manchester.   Z4661

COCKERHAM, S., Private, R.A.M.C.
He volunteered in April 1915, and after training was sent to the Egyptian front in May 1916. He did good work as hospital orderly in the 19th General Hospital at Alexandria, and also in the telephone office there. Later, he unfortunately contracted dysentery, and after a long period of treatment was invalided home, and eventually demobilised in July 1919. He holds the General Service and Victory Medals.
4, Rex Street, Jackson Street, Hulme, Manchester.   Z4659

COCKING, W., Private, 8th Manchester Regiment.
He joined in June 1917, and four months later proceeded to the Western Front, where he took part in the second Battle of the Somme, and many minor engagements. He then served with a Labour Battalion in the Cambrai Sector, and was afterwards engaged on important duties with the 11th Grave Registration unit until November 1919. He returned home for demobilisation in that month, and holds the General Service and Victory Medals.
46, Cowcill Street, Chorlton-on-Medlock, Manchester.   Z8970

COE, G., Gunner, R.G.A.
He volunteered in November 1914, and after going through a considerable period of training and service in England, was sent in January 1916, to Mesopotamia, where he took part in the operations at Kut, Um-el-Hamah, and Sanna-i-Yat. In July 1917 he was attacked with fever, and being sent to hospitals in Bombay, Alexandria, and afterwards many in England, was finally discharged in February 1919, and holds the General Service and Victory Medals.
59, Dorset Street, Hulme, Manchester.   Z4660B

COE, J., Private, 2nd Wiltshire Regiment.
Volunteering in January 1916, he was drafted to the Western Front on completion of two months' training, and there took part in severe fighting at Loos, Nieuport, and in various other sectors. Wounded in action at Ypres, he was invalided home in January 1917, but on his recovery returned to France, and was again in action. On the cessation of hostilities, he re-engaged for a further period of four years, and in 1920 was still with his unit in Hong-Kong. He holds the General Service and Victory Medals.
35, Neill Street, Gorton, Manchester.   Z10024A

COGHLAN, A., Special War Worker.
He volunteered in October 1915 for work of National importance, and found employment in a large steel manufactory. Here he remained throughout the war, being employed chiefly as a fitter, showing both skill and industry, and was discharged in November 1918, after the Armistice.
11, Turner Street, Lower Openshaw, Manchester.   Z4663

COGLAN, E., Private, 8th Manchester Regiment.
He volunteered in July 1915, and served with his unit at many stations in the United Kingdom. He rendered valuable services, but was not successful in obtaining his transfer overseas, and after doing much useful work in coast defence and other duties was discharged on account of service in January 1918.
10, Wilson Street, Bradford, Manchester.   Z1328

COGLAN, T., Private, 3rd Border Regiment.
He joined in March 1917, and proceeded to France in the following July. He at once took part in the Battle of Ypres III, including Passchendaele, where he was gassed in September, and sent to a Base hospital. On recovery he fought near

Givenchy and Festubert, and in the Retreat and Advance of 1918. He was demobilised in November 1919, and holds the General Service and Victory Medals.
18, William Street, West Gorton, Manchester.   Z4662

COLBRIDGE, J., Private, Manchester Regiment.
He volunteered in August 1914, and proceeded to France in the following October. He took part in the 1st Battle of Ypres, and in actions near Arras, and Passchendaele Ridge, in the course of which he was three times wounded. On his recovery he fought again, and in October 1917, gave his life for his Country near Cambrai. He was entitled to the 1914 Star, and the General Service and Victory Medals.
"A costly sacrifice upon the altar of freedom."
8, Marsland Street, Ardwick, Manchester.   Z4664A

COLDHAM, B., Private, 3rd Manchester Regiment.
He joined in March 1916, and served with his unit at a northern station. Here he unfortunately developed rheumatism, and after long treatment in hospital, was discharged as unfit for further service in September 1917.
29, Foster Street, City Road, Hulme, Manchester.   Z4665

COLE, A. A., Driver, R.F.A.
After volunteering in April 1915, he went through training, and proceeded with his Battery to France in the following April. He was at once engaged in the Ypres sector, and later took part in the Capture of Vimy Ridge, and in actions near Béthune, Passchendaele Ridge, and Havrincourt. He afterwards served through the Retreat and Advance of 1918 until the Armistice, and was demobilised in March 1919. He holds the General Service and Victory Medals.
26, Moulton Street, Hulme, Manchester.   Z4667

COLE, J. H., Gunner, R.F.A.
He joined in May 1916, and was sent, after training, to the Western Front in the following February. He took part in heavy fighting at Arras, Bullecourt, Messines and Passchendaele Ridges, and in the 1st Battle of Cambrai, in which he was gassed in November 1917. After some months of hospital treatment, he was discharged as unfit for further service in December 1919, and holds the General Service and Victory Medals.
35, Albemarle Street, Moss Side, Manchester.   Z4666

COLEBOURN, J., Rifleman, Rifle Brigade.
Volunteering in September 1914, he was sent to the Western Front in the following May. Whilst in France he fought in several actions in the Ypres sector, and was reported missing after an engagement in July 1915. It was subsequently officially notified that he had been killed in action on that date. He was entitled to the 1914–15 Star, and the General Service and Victory Medals.
"A costly sacrifice upon the altar of freedom."
11, Nicholson Street, Rochdale Road, Manchester.   Z9477

COLEBOURN, J., Gunner, R.H.A. and R.F.A.
He joined in April 1917, and in September of the following year proceeded to France, where he took part in the final operations of the Advance of 1918, notably in the Ypres sector. He returned home and was demobilised in June 1919, and holds the General Service and Victory Medals.
77, Nicholson Street, Rochdale Road, Manchester.   Z9476

COLEBOURN, W., Bombardier, R.F.A.
After volunteering in May 1915, he proceeded in the following December to the Egyptian front, from which, three months afterwards, he was transferred to France. Here he did good service with an ammunition column, and also in the capacity of despatch rider, in engagements on the Somme, where he was wounded, and later at Vimy Ridge, and in the Retreat and Advance of 1918. He was demobilised in May 1919, and holds the General Service and Victory Medals.
16, Sadler Street, Moss Side, Manchester.   Z4668

COLECLIFFE, J. (M.M.), Sergt., R.A.M.C.
After volunteering at the outbreak of war, he proceeded to France in the following January, and did good service with his Corps at the Battles of Neuve Chapelle, and Ypres II, and later in actions at Albert, in the Somme Offensive, on the Ancre front, and at Cambrai. He continued to serve through the Retreat and Advance of 1918, and in the course of these operations was awarded the Military Medal for special gallantry in attending to wounded in the Field. He was demobilised in March 1919, and holds, in addition to the Military Medal, the 1914 Star, the General Service and Victory Medals.
16, Ridley Grove, Greenheys, Manchester.   Z4670

COLESBY, F., Private, Manchester Regiment.
He joined in October 1916, and was drafted to France in the following December. He fought in the Ypres sector, where he was wounded, but after six months' treatment at a hospital in Wales, recovered, and rejoining his unit, fought in the Retreat and Advance of 1918 up to the time of the Armistice. Returning to England soon after the cessation of hostilities, he was demobilised in January 1919, and holds the General Service and Victory Medals.
123, Devon Street, Ardwick, Manchester.   Z4669

COLEY, A., Pte., King's Own Scottish Borderers.
Volunteering in September 1914, he went through training, and was drafted to the Western Front, in the following July. He took part in heavy fighting at Loos and La Bassée, where he was wounded, and on recovery, was sent to Egypt. Here he was in action on the Suez Canal, and served through the operations which concluded with the capture of Jerusalem and Jericho. After this he returned to France and fought through the final stages of the war, being eventually in the Army of Occupation on the Rhine. He was demobilised in September 1919, and holds the 1914-15 Star and the General Service and Victory Medals.
28, Ashover Street, Ardwick, Manchester. Z4671

COLL, J., Private, 1st King's (Liverpool Regiment).
Having enlisted in January 1913, he was drafted to the Western Front six months after the outbreak of war in August of the following year. After taking part in the Battles of Neuve Chapelle, Ypres, Festubert, Loos, Vimy Ridge, and Albert, and many minor engagements, he was taken prisoner at Guillemont during the Somme Offensive of 1916. Held in captivity until December 1918, he was forced to do farm work during this period in Westphalia and Poland. He holds the 1914-15 Star, and the General Service and Victory Medals, and in 1920 was still with his unit.
59, Barlow Street, Bradford, Manchester. Z6049

COLLEY, W. J., Private, 1/7th Manchester Regiment.
He volunteered in November 1915, and was sent to Egypt in the following July. After nine months' service there he was transferred to the Western Front and took part in the Battle of Cambrai I, also later in the Retreat and Advance of 1918. During the latter on September 28th, 1918, he gave his life for the great cause in the 2nd Battle of Cambrai, and was entitled to the General Service and Victory Medals.
"Nobly striving,
He nobly fell that we might live."
44, Victoria Street, Longsight, Manchester. Z4672

COLLIER, B. C., Private, 1st Lancashire Fusiliers.
He volunteered at the outbreak of war in August 1914, and after undergoing a period of training, was drafted in the following year to the Dardanelles, where he saw severe fighting. He was unfortunately killed in action in Gallipoli on June 4th, 1915. He was entitled to the 1914-15 Star, and the General Service and Victory Medals.
"Thinking that remembrance, though unspoken, may reach him where he sleeps."
20, Whitehead Street, Collyhurst, Manchester. Z10025

COLLIER, F. J., Private, King's (Liverpool Regt.)
He joined in August 1916, and proceeded to France in the following January. After taking part in the Battle of Ypres III, he was made divisional stretcher bearer for four divisions, but, unfortunately, soon after this was taken with severe illness, and being evacuated to a hospital in England, was discharged in February 1919. He holds the General Service and Victory Medals. 17, Naylor Street, Hulme, Manchester. Z4677

COLLIER, H., Private, Middlesex Regiment.
He joined in February 1917, and served with his unit at many different stations in England. He rendered valuable services, but was not successful in obtaining his transfer overseas before the cessation of hostilities, and was discharged, as being the only support of his family at home, in October 1918.
14, Dryden Street, Longsight, Manchester. Z4673

COLLIER, J., Private, 14th Royal Welch Fusiliers.
He joined in June 1917, and after his training embarked for France later in the same year. After taking part in several important engagements in the Retreat and Advance he was reported missing in September 1918. In the following month he was officially announced as having been killed in action at that time, and was entitled to the General Service and Victory Medals. "His life for his Country, his soul to God."
81, Garratt Street, Miles Platting, Manchester. Z9478

COLLIER, J., L/Corporal, Labour Corps.
He volunteered in the Manchester Regiment in November 1914 and twelve months later was drafted to France, where he played a prominent part in the Battles of the Somme and Arras. In October 1917, he was invalided home with trench fever, and after hospital treatment at Sheffield, was transferred to the Labour Corps in March 1918. He then rendered valuable services with this unit in the South of England until March 1919, when he was demobilised, holding the 1914-15 Star, and the General Service and Victory Medals.
13, Ashmore Street, West Gorton, Manchester. Z11678

COLLIER, J. H., Private, Lancashire Fusiliers.
He volunteered in June 1915, and in January of the following year, was drafted to Egypt, where he saw much severe fighting. After taking part in engagements at Agagia, and Katia, and in the Capture of El Fasher, and Magdhaba, he proceeded into Palestine and fought in the Battles of Gaza, and the Capture of Jerusalem. In February 1918, however, he was transferred to the Western Front, where he served through the Battles of the Lys, the Marne, Bapaume, and Ypres, and other engagements until the cessation of hostilities. Demobilised in March 1919, he holds the General Service and Victory Medals.
54, School Street West Gorton, Manchester. Z10026

COLLIER, J. W., Private, 7th Lancashire Fusiliers.
Mobilised on the outbreak of war, he proceeded to France with the Expeditionary Force, and took part in the Retreat from Mons, being in action at Le Cateau, and later on the Marne, at La Bassée, and in the desperate struggle of Ypres I. On April 2nd, 1915, he gave his life for King and Country in the Battle of Hill 60, and was entitled to the Mons Star, and the General Service and Victory Medals.
"He died the noblest death a man may die,
Fighting for God and right and liberty."
51, Oliver Street, Openshaw, Manchester. Z4675

COLLIER, S., Private, 8th Manchester Regiment.
He volunteered in December 1915, and served with his unit at various stations in the United Kingdom. He rendered valuable services, but owing to ill-health, was not successful in obtaining his transfer overseas, and after doing good guard work on the East Coast, was discharged on medical grounds, in November 1917.
31, Sawley Street, Beswick, Manchester. Z4678

COLLIER, W., Private, R.A.S.C., and M.G.C.
Volunteering in May 1915, he trained with the Army Service Corps, and being afterwards transferred to the Machine Gun Corps, proceeded to France in May 1917. Here he took part in actions at Arras, in the 3rd Battle of Ypres, and in the Retreat and Advance of 1918 up to the time of the Armistice. Returning to England soon afterwards, he was demobilised in February 1919, and holds the General Service and Victory Medals. 44, Byron Street, Hulme, Manchester. Z4674

COLLIER, W., A.B., Royal Navy.
Volunteering in August 1914, he was posted to a minesweeping vessel in the following October, and did good service in this difficult duty in the North Sea. He afterwards took part in the Naval actions off the Dogger Bank, and the Narrows in H.M.S. "Elysian." Later he was transferred to H.M.S. "Glory II," for duty on the Russian Coast, where he was also engaged in mine-sweeping. He holds the 1914-15 Star, and the General Service and Victory Medals, and was demobilised in August 1919.
7, Buckingham Street, Moss Side, Manchester. Z4676

COLLINGE, J., Corporal, South Lancashire Regt.
Volunteering in September 1914, he was drafted to France in August of the following year, and was in action at Loos, Vimy Ridge, the Somme, Arras, Messines and Cambrai. He gave his life for King and Country on March 24th, 1918, during the opening stages of the German Offensive. He was entitled to the 1914-15 Star, and the General Service and Victory Medals. "Great deeds cannot die."
46, Buckley Street, Rochdale Road, Manchester. Z10537

COLLINS, A., Pte., 16th Manchester Regt., and M.G.C.
He volunteered in June 1915, and in the following March, proceeded to the Western Front, where he saw severe fighting in various sectors. He took part in the Battles of St. Eloi, Albert, the Somme, Arras, Bullecourt, Ypres, Passchendaele and Cambrai, and many minor engagements until taken prisoner on the Somme during the Retreat of 1918. He was held in captivity in Bavaria until after the cessation of hostilities, and during this time was compelled to work on the railways. He was demobilised in April 1919, and holds the General Service and Victory Medals.
42, Gorton Street, Ardwick, Manchester. Z4680

COLLINS, E., L/Corporal, Military Police.
He volunteered in January 1915, and after undergoing a period of training, served at various stations, where he was engaged on important coastal defence duties. He was not successful in obtaining his transfer to a theatre of war, but nevertheless, rendered valuable services with his unit until August 1919, when he was demobilised.
33, Whitfield Street, Chorlton-on-Medlock, Manchester. Z8971

COLLINS, G., Private, South Wales Borderers.
Two months after volunteering in June 1915, he was drafted to France, where he saw heavy fighting in various sectors of the Front. He took part in the Battles of Albert, the Somme, Arras, Lys, the Marne, Amiens, and Bapaume, and many other important engagements, and was severely wounded in action at Cambrai. After a considerable period in hospital, he was invalided from the Army in October 1919, holding the 1914-15 Star, and the General Service and Victory Medals.
7, Armour Street, Ancoats, Manchester. Z10027

COLLINS, H., Private, Manchester Regiment, and North Staffordshire Regiment.
He volunteered in August 1914, and in October of the following year, was sent to France, where he saw much severe fighting. He took part in many important engagements in various sectors of the Front, including the Battles of Loos, the Somme, Ypres, and Cambrai, served also through the Retreat and Advance of 1918, and was among the troops to enter Mons at dawn of Armistice Day. He was demobilised in November 1919, and holds the 1914-15 Star, and the General Service and Victory Medals. 45, Markham Street, Ardwick, Manchester. Z4682

COLLINS, J., Private, 8th Manchester Regiment.

Mobilised from the Reserve at the commencement of hostilities, he was sent to Gallipoli in the following March, and was in action in the first Landing, the Battles of Krithia, and Suvla Bay, and in many other engagements. After the Evacuation of the Peninsula he embarked for France, and fought at Albert, the Somme, Arras, Ypres, Cambrai, and throughout the Retreat and Advance of 1918, and was twice wounded. He was demobilised in January 1919, and holds the 1914-15 Star, and the General Service and Victory Medals.
25, Phelan Street, Collyhurst, Manchester.   Z10536

COLLINS, J., Guardsman, 1st Grenadier Guards.

Mobilised at the outbreak of war, he was drafted to the Western Front in October 1914, and was in action in the first Battle of Ypres, where he was wounded and taken prisoner. He was held in captivity in Germany until January 1919, and after returning home was demobilised in the following September. He holds the 1914 Star, and the General Service and Victory Medals. 8, Clifford Street, West Gorton. Manchester. Z10520

COLLINS, J., Private, Labour Corps.

Volunteering in January 1916, he proceeded to the Western Front in the following month, and was there engaged on important duties on the Somme until September of that year. He was then sent home on account of defective eyesight, and was retained at various stations in England until January 1918, when he was invalided from the Army. He holds the General Service and Victory Medals.
27, Kingston Street, Hulme, Manchester.   Z8972

COLLINS, J., Private, 11th Manchester Regiment.

He volunteered in August 1914, and was engaged on important duties in England for twelve months. He then proceeded to Gallipoli, but was unfortunately killed in action during the Landing at Suvla Bay on August 6th, 1915. He was entitled to the 1914-15 Star, and the General Service and Victory Medals.
"His life for his Country, his soul to God."
46, Lancaster Street, Hulme, Manchester.   Z11679

COLLINS, J. J., Pte., Loyal North Lancashire Regt.

Joining in January 1916, he was drafted to the Western Front in the following December. Whilst in France he saw much active service, and fought in the engagements on the Ancre, at the Capture of Vimy Ridge, and at Bullecourt, Lens, the Somme, Amiens, and Bapaume. He was demobilised after his return to England in November 1919, and holds the General Service and Victory Medals.
11, Teignmouth Street, Rochdale Road, Manchester. Z9479

COLLINS, R. L., Private, 9th Border Regiment.

He volunteered in October 1914, and underwent a period of training prior to being drafted to Salonika in the following year. There he saw much severe fighting on the Doiran, Vardar, and Struma fronts, and was also engaged in conveying food to the forward areas. He unhappily died of fever whilst on his way home on June 5th, 1919, and was buried in a military cemetery in Greece. He was entitled to the 1914-15 Star, and the General Service and Victory Medals.
"A costly sacrifice upon the altar of freedom."
94, Norton Street, West Gorton, Manchester.   Z4681

COLLINS, S., Leading Stoker, R.N.

He volunteered in November 1914, and in February of the following year was posted to H.M.S. "Leviathan," on board which vessel he was on patrol and escort duties in many waters. He was engaged chiefly in convoying troops from the Colonies to England, and rendered valuable services until May 1920, when he was discharged. He holds the 1914-15 Star, and the General Service and Victory Medals.
9, Bedson Street, Bradford, Manchester.   Z6050

COLLINS, S. P., Royal Marine Labour Corps.

Shortly after joining in April 1917, he was drafted to the Western Front, where he was engaged in unloading transports and on various other important duties at Le Havre, and Calais. He rendered very valuable services with his Company until April 1918, when he was discharged, and holds the General Service and Victory Medals.
20, Milton Street, Hulme, Manchester.   Z4630A

COLLINS, T., Driver, R.A.S.C. (M.T.)

Joining in May 1916, he proceeded to the Western Front in the following month and there served in the Somme sector, where he was severely wounded in action. Suffering also from shell-shock, he was invalided home, and after his recovery was stationed at Hitchin until July 1918, when he was discharged as medically unfit for further service. He holds the General Service and Victory Medals.
25, Walnut Street, Hulme, Manchester.   Z4683

COLLINS, W., Special War Worker.

Throughout the period of hostilities he was engaged on important Government work with Messrs. Coop and Rothwell of Manchester. There he was employed on transport duties, conveying ammunition to the docks for shipment to the various theatres of war, and rendered very valuable services until his discharge in November 1919.
8, Emma Street, Ardwick, Manchester.   Z4679

COLLINS, W. E., Private, 1/4th King's (Shropshire Light Infantry).

He joined in April 1918, and on completing his training in September of that year, was drafted to the Western Front, where he saw much severe fighting. He took part in many important engagements during the Allied Advance and finally returned to England for demobilisation in February 1919. He holds the General Service and Victory Medals.
Bedson Street, Bradford, Manchester.   Z6051

COLLINS, W. H. (M.M.), Pte., 1st Wiltshire Regt.

He volunteered in 1915, and on completing his training in the following year was drafted to the Western Front. Whilst in this theatre of war, he saw severe fighting in various sectors, took part in the first Battle of the Somme and many other important engagements, and also served through the Advance of 1918. He was awarded the Military Medal for conspicuous bravery displayed in tending the wounded under heavy shell-fire in November of that year, and holding also the General Service and Victory Medals was demobilised in 1919.
2, Slack Place, Hyde Road, Ardwick, Manchester.   Z10028

COLWELL, W., Private, R.A.M.C.

He joined in November 1916, and after a period of training served at various stations, where he was engaged on duties of great importance. He was unable to obtain his transfer to a theatre of war on account of defective eyesight, but in April 1919 was drafted to Egypt, where he served for twelve months. He was demobilised on his return home in April 1920.
25, Lower Chatham Street, Chorlton-cn-Medlock, Manchester.   Z4684

COLWICK, W., Private, 1st Border Regiment.

He joined in June 1916, and in November of the following year proceeded to the Western Front, where he took part in the Battles of Cambrai and the Somme, and several other important engagements. He died gloriously on the Field of Battle at Meteren in April 1918, and was buried at Hazebrouck. He was entitled to the General Service and Victory Medals.
"And doubtless he went in splendid company."
27, Law Street, Rochdale Road, Manchester.   Z10029

COMAR, W., Air Mechanic, R.A.F.

He joined in July 1917, and after completing a period of training, served at various stations, where he was engaged on important duties which required a high degree of technical skill. He was unable to obtain his transfer to the Front, but, nevertheless, rendered valuable services with his Squadron until January 1919, when he was demobilised.
88, Tame Street, Ancoats, Manchester.   TZ8973

COMPTON, H., Air Mechanic, R.A.F.

He joined in August 1916, and after completing a term of training, served at various stations, where he was engaged on duties of a highly technical nature. He was not successful in his efforts to obtain his transfer overseas, but, nevertheless, rendered valuable services with his Squadron until November 1919, when he was demobilised.
8, Dryden Street, Chorlton-on-Medlock, Manchester.   Z4685

CONDON, D., Gunner, R.F.A.

He volunteered at the outbreak of war in August 1914, and in May of the following year proceeded to Egypt, where he served on the Suez Canal. In February 1917, however, he was transferred to the Western Front, and there after taking part in the Battles of Ypres and the Somme and other important engagements, he was severely wounded in action. After a considerable period in hospital, he was invalided from the Army in September 1919, holding the 1914-15 Star, and the General Service and Victory Medals.
28, Neill Street, Gorton, Manchester.   Z10030

CONDRON, J., L/Corporal, 7/th Rifle Brigade.

Volunteering in August 1914, he was drafted to the Western Front in May of the following year, and there saw severe fighting in various sectors. He took part in the Battles of Ypres, Albert, Ploegsteert Wood, the Somme, Arras, Vimy Ridge, Messines, Ypres and Passchendaele and many minor engagements, and fought also in the Retreat and Advance of 1918. He was demobilised in February 1919, and holds the 1914-15 Star, and the General Service and Victory Medals.
34, Napier Street, Ardwick, Manchester.   Z4686

CONDUIT, G., Private, 8th Manchester Regiment.

Shortly after volunteering in August 1914, he was drafted to Egypt, where he served on the Suez Canal. In April of the following year was transferred to Gallipoli and there, after taking part in the Landing at Cape Helles, fought in the Battles of Krithia and at Suvla Bay. He proceeded to India on the Evacuation of the Peninsula, and was there engaged on garrison duties, and was in hospital for a time suffering from tuberculosis. He was also in hospital in China, before being invalided from the Army on his return home in September 1919, and holds the 1914-15 Star, and the General Service and Victory Medals.
16, Garden Walks, Ardwick, Manchester.   Z4687

CONLEY, F., Private, 4th Cheshire Regiment.
He joined in July 1917, and, after completing a period of
training, served at various stations, where he was engaged
on important clerical duties. Although unsuccessful in his
efforts to obtain his transfer to a theatre of war he rendered
very valuable services with his unit until December 1919,
when he was demobilised.
9, Whitby Street, Ancoats, Manchester. Z8974

CONLEY, J., Pte., Loyal North Lancashire Regt.
He volunteered in September 1914, and in April of the following
year was drafted to Gallipoli, where, after taking part in the
Landing at Cape Helles, he fought in the Battles of Krithia
and at Achi Baba and Suvla Bay. In November 1915 he
was invalided to hospital at Alexandria, suffering from dysentery, and finally returned home and was discharged as
medically unfit for further service in June 1916. He holds
the 1914-15 Star, and the General Service and Victory Medals.
41, Newcastle Street, Hulme, Manchester. Z8975

CONLEY, J. T., Sergt., Royal Welch Fusiliers.
He had previously served in the South African war, and in
August 1914 was drafted to Gibraltar, where he was engaged
on important guard duties and as a training instructor. He
rendered valuable services throughout the period of hostilities,
and was demobilised after his return to England in February
1919. He holds the General Service Medal.
28, Roe Street, Ancoats, Manchester. Z9480

CONNELL, E., Private, 1/8th Manchester Regt.
Volunteering in August 1914, he proceeded to the Dardanelles
in the following year, and there, after taking part in the first
Landing at Gallipoli, fought in the Battles of Krithia. He
contracted enteric fever, and in September 1915 was invalided
to hospital at Cairo and thence to England, but on his recovery
in September 1916, was drafted to the Western Front. There
he took part in the Battles of Arras, Bullecourt, Messines,
Ypres, Cambrai, Havrincourt and Le Cateau, and also served
through the Retreat and Advance of 1918. He was demobilised in March 1919, and holds the 1914-15 Star, and the
General Service and Victory Medals.
20, Meridian Street, Higher Ardwick, Manchester. Z4688

**CONNELL, F., Private, 16th King's (Liverpool Regt.)
and Labour Corps.**
He volunteered in June 1915, and after a period of service in
England was drafted to the Western Front, where he did
consistently good work on the lines of communication in the
Passchendaele, Dickebusch, Poperinghe and Nieuport sectors.
He was badly gassed in October 1917, and as a result was
invalided from the Army in the following January, holding
the General Service and Victory Medals.
32, Law Street, Rochdale Road, Manchester. Z8976

CONNER, F., Gunner, R.F.A.
Volunteering in August 1915, he landed in France in the following March and was in action at St. Eloi, Vimy Ridge, the
Somme, Arras, Bullecourt, Messines, Ypres and Cambrai.
He was also engaged in much heavy fighting in the German
and Allied Offensives of 1918, and after returning home after
the Armistice was demobilised in February 1919. He holds
the General Service and Victory Medals.
23, Crook Street, Harpurhey, Manchester. Z10538B

CONNER, J., Private, 7th Manchester Regiment.
He volunteered in August 1915, and was sent to France twelve
months later. After only a few weeks of service he was
unfortunately killed in action on October 2nd, 1916, during
the first Battle of the Somme. He was entitled to the General
Service and Victory Medals.
"The path of duty was the way to glory."
23, Crook Street, Harpurhey, Manchester. Z10538A

CONNOLLY, M., Private, Labour Corps.
He joined in February 1918, and on completion of his training
was engaged on important duties with his unit at various
stations. Owing to being medically unfit he was unsuccessful
in obtaining a transfer to a theatre of war, but, nevertheless,
rendered valuable services until discharged in July 1918.
58, Loom Street, Ancoats, Manchester. Z8977

CONNOLLY, T., Private, 20th Manchester Regt.
Volunteering in November 1915, he embarked for the Western
Front in the following November, and during his service in
France fought at Beaumont-Hamel, Bullecourt, where he
was wounded, Ypres and Passchendaele. In October 1917 he
proceeded to Italy, and was in action in the operations on the
Piave. Later he returned to the Western Front in August
1918, and serving in many engagements in the final Advance
was wounded for the second time in the following October
at St. Quentin. He returned home and was demobilised in
March 1919, and holds the General Service and Victory Medals.
8, League Street, Rochdale Road, Manchester. Z9481

**CONNOLLY, W. Private, 23rd Manchester Regt.,
and Royal Inniskilling Fusiliers.**
He volunteered in December 1915, and in June of the succeeding year was drafted overseas. Whilst in France he saw
active service in the Battles of the Somme, Arras, Ypres,

Cambrai and Nieuport. He was severely wounded in August
1918, at Nieppe Forest, and was invalided home to hospital
in the following month. He holds the General Service and
Victory Medals, and was demobilised in March 1919.
16, Ardsley Street, Oldham Road, Manchester. TZ9482

CONNOLLY, W. T., Special War Worker.
For three and a half years of the war he was engaged on work
of National importance at Messrs. A. V. Roe's, not being
eligible for service with the Colours on account of ill-health.
He was employed on various responsible duties in connection
with the construction of aeroplanes and rendered valuable
service until after the cessation of hostilities.
29, Dalten Street, Hulme, Manchester. Z4689

CONNOR, C., Corporal, 13th Manchester Regiment.
He was mobilised at the outbreak of war, and was almost
immediately drafted to France, where he took part in the
Retreat from Mons. He also served at Neuve Chapelle,
St. Eloi, Hill 60, and Festubert, and later in 1915 was sent to
the Balkan front. Whilst in this theatre of war he fought
in the operations on the Vardar and was severely wounded
in action, sustaining the loss of one of his eyes. He was
invalided to hospital in England, and was subsequently
demobilised in April 1919. He holds the Mons Star, and the
General Service and Victory Medals.
43, Elizabeth Street, Ancoats, Manchester. Z9483

CONNOR, D., Private, 1st Border Regiment.
Volunteering in April 1915, he was drafted to Gallipoli in
the following May, and took part in the Landing at Suvla
Bay, and in the fighting at Chocolate Hill, and the Evacuation
of the Peninsula. In March 1916 he proceeded to the Western
Front, where he was in action at Vermelles and Albert, and
severely wounded in the Battle of the Somme in July of the
same year. He was invalided home to hospital, and discharged
as medically unfit for further service in February 1918. He
holds the 1914-15 Star, and the General Service and Victory
Medals. 60, Woodward Street, Ancoats, Manchester. Z9484

CONNOR, E. (Senior) Air Mechanic, R.A.F.
Having previously been engaged on work of National importance in connection with the construction of aircraft, he joined
in October 1918, and after completing a short period of training
was engaged on clerical duties at various stations. Owing
to the early cessation of hostilities he was unable to obtain his
transfer overseas, but did good work with his Squadron until
January 1919, when he was demobilised.
25, Sadler Street, Moss Side, Manchester. Z4690B

**CONNOR, E. (Junior), Private, 4th King's Own
(Royal Lancaster Regiment).**
He joined in September 1916, and after undergoing a term of
training, was sent to Ireland, where he was engaged on important duties as a Lewis gunner at various stations. He
was not successful in obtaining his transfer to a theatre of
war, but, nevertheless, rendered valuable services with his
unit until discharged in November 1918.
25, Sadler Street, Moss Side, Manchester. Z4690A

CONNOR, F., Private, Manchester Regiment.
After volunteering in September 1914, he underwent a period
of training prior to being drafted to the Western Front in
November of the following year. There he saw severe fighting
in various sectors, took part in the Battles of the Somme,
Arras and Bullecourt and other important engagements,
and was wounded in action. Invalided home in August 1918,
he was finally demobilised in January of the following year,
and holds the 1914-15 Star, and the General Service and
Victory Medals.
38, Rusholme Grove, Rusholme, Manchester. Z10031A

CONNOR, G., Private, Royal Fusiliers.
He joined in September 1916, and six months later proceeded
to France, where he saw severe fighting in various sectors
of the Front. After taking part in the Battles of Arras and
Cambrai and many other important engagements, he was
severely gassed whilst in action in May 1918, and invalided
to hospital at Liverpool. He was finally demobilised in
February 1919, and holds the General Service and Victory
Medals.
10, Lime Street, Miles Platting, Manchester. Z10032-3B

CONNOR, G. W. (M.M.), Cpl., 11th Manchester Regt.
Mobilised in August 1914, he was immediately drafted to the
Western Front, where after fighting in the Battle of Mons and
the subsequent Retreat, he took part in the Battles of the
Marne and the Aisne and was wounded in action at Ypres
in November 1914. He was invalided home, but on his re-
covery, proceeded to Gallipoli, and there took part in the
Landing at Suvla Bay, and was again wounded. On the
Evacuation of the Peninsula he returned to France and fought
in the Battles of Vimy Ridge, Passchendaele, Cambrai, the
Somme, the Marne and Havrincourt. He was awarded the
Military Medal for conspicuous bravery displayed in the Field
on the Sambre in November 1918, and holding also the Mons
Star, and the General Service and Victory Medals, was discharged in February 1919.
24, Riga Street, City Road, Hulme, Manchester. Z4693

CONNOR, H., Private, East Lancashire Regiment.

He joined in December 1917, and in June of the following year proceeded to the Western Front. Whilst in this theatre of war he saw severe fighting in various sectors and took part in several important engagements during the Allied Advance until July 30th, 1918, when he fell in action, after only seven weeks' active service. He was entitled to the General Service and Victory Medals.   "Nobly striving,
                          He nobly fell that we might live."
31, Thomas Street, Miles Platting, Manchester.   Z10034

CONNOR, J., Private, Royal Fusiliers.

Volunteering in January 1916, he was drafted to the Western Front six months later, and there saw much severe fighting. He was unfortunately reported missing, and later killed in action, in October 1916, during the Somme Offensive, after only three months' overseas service. He was entitled to the General Service and Victory Medals.
"He passed out of the sight of men by the path of duty and self-sacrifice."
38, Rusholme Grove, Rusholme, Manchester.   Z10031B

CONNOR, J., Sergeant, Lancashire Fusiliers.

He volunteered in September 1914, and in October of the following year proceeded to France, where he saw heavy fighting in various sectors of the Front. He took part in the Battles of Vimy Ridge, Albert and the Somme, and many minor engagements until severely wounded in action in July 1916. He was for a considerable time in hospital at Portsmouth, before being invalided from the Army in July 1917, and holds the 1914-15 Star, and the General Service and Victory Medals.
148, Harold Street, Bradford, Manchester.   Z4691

CONNOR, M., Private, Labour Corps, and R.A.S.C.

Shortly after volunteering in October 1915, he proceeded to the Western Front, where he was engaged on various important duties at the docks, at Boulogne and Marseilles. He was for a time in hospital in France, before being invalided home in November 1918, and was finally discharged as medically unfit for further service in March of the following year. He holds the 1914-15 Star, and the General Service and Victory Medals.
21, Elton Street, Chorlton-on-Medlock, Manchester.   Z4692

CONNOR, W., Private, 4th South Wales Borderers.

He joined in August 1918, and after completing a short period of training, served at various stations, where he was engaged in guarding prisoners of war, and on other important duties. Owing to the early cessation of hostilities, he was unable to obtain his transfer to the Front, but rendered valuable services with his unit until November 1919, when he was demobilised.
25, Sadler Street, Moss Side, Manchester.   Z4690C

CONROY, E., Private, 1st Manchester Regiment.

A Reservist, he was called to the Colours in August 1914, and in November of that year was drafted to the Western Front, where he saw much severe fighting. He made the supreme sacrifice, falling in action on December 21st, 1914, in the first Battle of Ypres, where he was buried. He was entitled to the 1914-15 Star, and the General Service and Victory Medals.
"He joined the great white company of valiant souls."
12, Linacre Street, Oldham Road, Manchester.   Z10035

CONROY, J., Private, Loyal North Lancashire Regt.

When war broke out in August 1914, he volunteered and a month later proceeded overseas. Whilst serving on the Western Front he saw heavy fighting in various engagements, but was taken prisoner at Polygon Wood in December 1914. He remained in captivity throughout the remaining period of hostilities, and on his release in November 1918 was demobilised, holding the 1914 Star, and the General Service and Victory Medals.
10, Adelaide Street, Bradford, Manchester.   X11881B

CONROY, J., Private, 12th Manchester Regiment.

Volunteering in September 1914, he proceeded to France two months later and there saw severe fighting in various sectors of the Front, took part in the Battle of Loos and other important engagements, and was wounded in action. In January 1916, however, he was transferred to Salonika, but was shortly afterwards invalided to hospital at Malta, suffering from dysentery and malaria. He finally returned home and was demobilised in December 1918, and holds the 1914 Star, and the General Service and Victory Medals.
16, Neill Street, Gorton, Manchester.   Z10036

CONROY, W., Private, Lancashire Fusiliers.

He volunteered in August 1914, and in August 1915 proceeded to Gallipoli, where he took part in the Suvla Bay Landing, and subsequent engagements prior to the Evacuation of the Peninsula. In June 1916 he was transferred to France, and was severely wounded in the Battle of the Somme a month later. He was invalided to England, and discharged as medically unfit for further duty in May 1917, holding the 1914-15 Star, and the General Service and Victory Medals.
10, Houghton Street, Collyhurst, Manchester.   Z11378B

CONSTABLE, R. J., 1st Air Mechanic, R.A.F.

He volunteered in July 1915, and on completion of a term of training was engaged on duties of great importance at various stations. Unable to obtain his transfer to a theatre of war on account of ill-health, he nevertheless rendered very valuable services with his Squadron until his demobilisation in March 1919. 3, Holt Terrace, Longsight, Manchester.   Z4694

CONSTERDINE, F., Pte., 9th South Lancashire Regt.

Volunteering in March 1915, he landed in France in the following August, and was in action in the Battles of Loos and the Somme. He was later transferred to Salonika and fought in many engagements on various fronts. During his service in the Balkans he contracted malaria. After returning home he was demobilised in March 1919, but died from the after effects of malaria on July 31st, 1920. He was entitled to the 1914-15 Star, and the General Service and Victory Medals.
"His memory is cherished with pride."
41, Goodier Street, Harpurhey, Manchester.   Z10539

CONWAY, C., Private, King's (Liverpool Regt.)

He joined in June 1918, and in the following month embarked for Egypt. On the Palestine front he fought in many engagements during the final British Advance into Syria, and was present at the capture of Tripoli and Aleppo. After his return to England he was demobilised in April 1920, and holds the General Service and Victory Medals.
486, Collyhurst Road, Rochdale Road, Manchester.   Z10540

CONWAY, K. L., Pte., Manchester Regt. and Labour Corps.

He volunteered in November 1914, and twelve months later was drafted to the Western Front, where he took part in the Battles of Arras and Bullecourt and many minor engagements until December 1917. He was then transferred to Italy and was there engaged on various important duties with the Labour Corps until after the cessation of hostilities. He was demobilised on returning home in February 1919, and holds the 1914-15 Star, and the General Service and Victory Medals.
77, Cobden Street, Ancoats, Manchester.   Z10037

CONWELL, T. H., Private, M.G.C.

He joined in April 1917, and on completion of his training in February of the following year, proceeded to the Western Front. There he took part in the second Battle of the Somme, saw heavy fighting at La Bassée and many other places, and was severely wounded in action at Arras in September 1918. He was for some time in hospital at Boulogne and Orpington, before being demobilised in February 1919, and holds the General Service and Victory Medals.
37, Sycamore Street, Newton, Manchester.   Z10038

COOK, A., Private, 8th Manchester Regiment.

Volunteering in August 1914, he proceeded to Egypt on completing a brief period of training, and there served on the Suez Canal. In April 1915, he was transferred to Gallipoli, where, after taking part in the Landing at Cape Helles, he saw much severe fighting. He unhappily fell in action in the third Battle of Krithia on June 5th, 1915. He was entitled to the 1914-15 Star, and the General Service and Victory Medals.   "The path of duty was the way to glory."
9, Hinckley Street, Bradford, Manchester.   Z4695

COOK, E., Gunner, R.F.A.

He volunteered shortly after the outbreak of war in August 1914, and in the following December was drafted to the Western Front, where he saw much severe fighting at Armentières, and took part in the Battles of Ypres and the Somme. Later in 1916 he was transferred to Salonika and was in action during the Advance across the Struma. He was demobilised in June 1919, and holds the 1914-15 Star, and the General Service and Victory Medals.
80, Junction Street, Ancoats, Manchester.   Z8978

COOK, G., Private, 6th Manchester Regiment.

He joined in November 1916, and after a period of training, was engaged at various stations on important duties with his unit. He was not successful in obtaining a transfer overseas, but rendered valuable services until his demobilisation in November 1919.
3, Taunton Street, Ancoats, Manchester.   Z10040

COOK, H., Private, 18th Manchester Regiment.

He volunteered in October 1915, and was drafted to France in November of the following year. He was in action in the Battles of Arras, Ypres, Passchendaele and Cambrai, and was wounded and gassed in the second Battle of the Somme in March 1918. Returning home he received hospital treatment and was demobilised in July 1919, holding the General Service and Victory Medals.
107, Naylor Street, Oldham Road, Manchester.   Z9485

COOK, J., Sergt., Buffs (East Kent Regiment).

He volunteered in September 1914, and after a period of training, was retained on important duties at various stations until 1918, when he was drafted to the Western Front. There he saw much severe fighting in various sectors and was wounded in action in the Allied Advance. He was demobilised on his return home in 1919, and holds the General Service and Victory Medals.
46, Greville Street, Rusholme, Manchester.   Z4696A

COOK, J., Private, K.O. (Royal Lancaster Regt.)

He was serving in India when war broke out in August 1914, and was quickly drafted to the Western Front. There he took part in the Battles of La Bassée, Ypres, Loos, Hooge and the Somme, and was wounded in action. On his recovery he was transferred to Salonika and saw much heavy fighting on the Vardar, Struma and Doiran fronts. He returned home and was discharged in November 1918, holding the 1914 Star, and the General Service and Victory Medals.

63, Sycamore Street, Manchester.   Z10041

COOKE, A., Private, 8th Manchester Regiment.

Shortly after volunteering in August 1914, he was drafted to Egypt, where he served at Alexandria and Cairo until April 1915. He was then transferred to Gallipoli, where he took part in the Landing at Cape Helles and fought also in the Battles of Krithia.. He died gloriously on the Field of Battle near Achi Baba on June 4th, 1915. He was entitled to the 1914-15 Star, and the General Service and Victory Medals.

"Whilst we remember, the sacrifice is not in vain."

9, Hinckley Street, Bradford, Manchester.   Z4699

COOKE, E., Private, 1st Manchester Regiment.

He volunteered in August 1914, and on completing his training in the following January was drafted to France. There he took part in the Battles of Neuve Chapelle, St. Eloi, Hill 60, Ypres (II), Loos, Bullecourt, Ypres (III), Passchendaele and Cambrai, and was twice wounded in action. He was unfortunately killed at St. Quentin in October 1918, and was entitled to the 1914-15 Star, and the General Service and Victory Medals.

"He died the noblest death a many may die,
Fighting for God, and right, and liberty."

16, Dawson Street, West Gorton, Manchester.   Z10042

COOKE, J., Private, Labour Corps.

He joined in March 1916, and in the following month proceeded to the Western Front, where he served in several sectors. Engaged on various important duties, he was present at the Battles of the Somme, Arras, Ypres and Cambrai, and took an active part also in the Retreat and Advance of 1918. He was demobilised in March 1919, and holds the General Service and Victory Medals.

13, Jack Street, Ardwick, Manchester.   Z4698B

COOKE, J. H., Gunner, R.F.A.

Joining in April 1916, he was drafted to the Western Front on completing a period of training in November of the same year. There he saw much severe fighting, taking part in the Battle of Vimy Ridge, and many minor engagements until invalided home in April 1917, suffering from trench fever. He was discharged in December 1918, as medically unfit for further service, and holds the General Service and Victory Medals.   59, Caton Street, Hulme, Manchester.   Z4697

COOKE, R., Private, 1/8th Manchester Regiment.

He volunteered in October 1914, and in the following year was drafted to the Dardanelles, where he saw much heavy fighting at Cape Helles. Later he proceeded to Egypt, and was in action on the Sinai Peninsula, but in 1917 was sent to the Western Front. There he fought at the Battles of Arras, Albert, Lens and the Somme, and in other important engagements. He was demobilised in 1919, and holds the 1914-15 Star, and the General Service and Victory Medals.

49, Thornton Street, Manchester.   Z10043

COOKE, T., Private, Lancashire Fusiliers.

He joined in August 1916, and two months later was drafted to the Western Front. There he was attached to the 6th Leicestershire Regiment, and took part in the Battles of the Somme, Arras and Messines, where he was wounded in 1917. On his recovery he returned to his unit and saw much fighting at Cambrai, and in the Retreat. He was unfortunately killed in action in March 1918, and was entitled to the General Service and Victory Medals.

"A costly sacrifice upon the altar of freedom."

4, Howard Street, Ancoats, Manchester.   Z10044

COOKSON, E., Private, 2nd Manchester Regiment.

He volunteered in August 1914, and in the following March was drafted to France, where he saw service in various sectors of the Front. He fought in many important engagements, including the Battles of Ypres, Festubert, Loos, St. Eloi, Albert and Somme (I), where he was wounded. He was invalided to England, and finally discharged in April 1917 as medically unfit for further service. He holds the 1914-15 Star, and the General Service and Victory Medals.

6, Dora Street, Rochdale Road, Manchester.   Z8979

COOKSON, F., Worker, Q.M.A.A.C.

She joined in June 1918, and was shortly afterwards drafted to France where she was stationed at Le Havre. She was engaged on important duties as a cook and rendered valuable services, whilst carrying out her work in a highly commendable manner. She was demobilised in November 1919, and holds the General Service and Victory Medals.

34, Crossley Street, Gorton, Manchester.   Z10045

COOMBES, J., Private, Loyal N. Lancashire Regt., and Sapper, R.E.

He joined in July 1917, and in February of the following year, proceeded to the Western Front, where he served on the railways, conveying ammunition to the forward areas at Ypres, the Somme and Cambrai, and in various other sectors. He unhappily fell in action at Ypres on July 24th, 1918. He was entitled to the General Service and Victory Medals.

"And doubtless he went in splendid company."

8, Buxton Street, West Gorton, Manchester.   Z10039A

COOMBES, J., Driver, R.F.A.

Volunteering in November 1914, he was drafted overseas in the following August. Whilst on the Western Front he took part in several engagements, including the Battles of Loos, Ypres, the Somme and Cambrai, where he was gassed in action in November 1917. As a result he was invalided home, but on his recovery, returned to France and fought in the Retreat and Advance of 1918. He was demobilised in April 1919, and holds the 1914-15 Star, and the General Service and Victory Medals.

8, Buxton Street, West Gorton, Manchester.   Z10039B

COOMBES, W. H., Private, 1st Loyal N. Lancs. Regt.

He volunteered in November 1914, and was sent to France in the following month. He was in action in the Battles of Neuve Chapelle, Loos, Albert, the Somme, Beaucourt, Cambrai and throughout the German and Allied Offensives of 1918, and was wounded. He was transferred to Class W, Army Reserve on November 27th, 1918, to enable him to resume his pre-war occupation as a miner. He holds the 1914-15 Star, and the General Service and Victory Medals.

20, Pearson Street, Newton Heath, Manchester.   Z9486

COONEY, J., Private, 11th Royal Warwickshire Regt.

He joined in July 1916, and underwent a period of training prior to his being drafted to the Western Front, where he took part in the Retreat and Advance of 1918. He made the supreme sacrifice being killed in action at Havrincourt Wood in September 1918, and was buried near Cambrai. He was entitled to the General Service and Victory Medals.

"Honour to the immortal dead, who gave their youth that the world might grow old in peace."

10, Haigh Street, West Gorton, Manchester.   Z10047C

COONEY, J., Private, Loyal N. Lancs. Regt.

He volunteered in August 1914, and on completing his training in the following May, was drafted to the Western Front, where he took part in several engagements, including that of Ypres. He died gloriously on the Field of Battle, at Loos, on September 25th, 1915, and was entitled to the 1914-15 Star, and the General Service and Victory Medals.

"His life for his Country, his soul to God."

10, Wilkinson Street, Collyhurst, Manchester.   Z10046

COONEY, W., Private, M.G.C.

He was called up from the Reserve in August 1914, and immediately drafted to France. In this theatre of war he took part in the Battles of Mons, Ypres (I), Neuve Chapelle, Ypres (II), the Somme, Arras, Ypres (III), Cambrai and in the Retreat and Advance of 1918. He was discharged in March 1919, and holds the Mons Star, and the General Service and Victory Medals.

10, Haigh Street, West Gorton, Manchester.   Z10047A

COONEY, William, Private, 2nd Lancashire Fusiliers.

Volunteering in November 1915, he was drafted to France in the following year. In this theatre of war he took part in several engagements, but was unfortunately killed in action at Vimy Ridge on April 11th, 1917. He was entitled to the General Service and Victory Medals.

"The path of duty was the way to glory."

10, Haigh Street, West Gorton, Manchester.   Z10047B

COOP, H., Private, Cheshire Regiment.

He volunteered in August 1914, and in the following year was drafted to France, where he fought at the Battles of Neuve Chapelle and Loos, and was twice wounded in action. As a result he was invalided home but on his recovery, was sent to Africa, thence to India. After three months' garrison duty, he proceeded to Egypt, and later took part in much fighting in Palestine at Gaza, the capture of Tripoli, and in engagements at Aleppo, and in the Advance with General Allenby's Forces. He returned home and was discharged in 1919, holding the 1914-15 Star, and the General Service and Victory Medals.

8, Norbury Street, Longsight, Manchester.   Z10048B

COOP, V., Private, 2nd Royal Scots.

He volunteered in January 1915. and in the following September, was drafted to Egypt, where he served at Sollum until transferred to the Western Front in July 1916. There, after taking part in the Battles of the Somme, the Ancre, Arras, Ypres and Cambrai and many other engagements, he was taken prisoner and despite several attempts to escape, was held in captivity until after the cessation of hostilities. He was demobilised in March 1919, and holds the 1914-15 Star, and the General Service and Victory Medals.

104, Old Elm Street, Ardwick, Manchester.   X5700

COOP, W., Private, Welch Regiment.
He volunteered in 1915, and after a period of training was attached to the Army Cyclist Corps, and engaged at various stations on important duties with his unit. He was unable to obtain a transfer overseas owing to his being medically unfit, but rendered valuable services until his discharge in 1917.
8, Norbury Street, Longsight, Manchester.   Z10048A

COOPER, A., C.Q.M.S., Manchester Regiment.
Volunteering in January 1915, he was drafted overseas in the following year. Whilst on the Western Front he took a prominent part in the Battle of the Somme, and was severely wounded, losing the sight of his right eye. In consequence he was invalided home, and on his recovery served with the Labour Corps on important duties until his demobilisation in September 1919. He holds the General Service and Victory Medals.
17, Crondall Street, Moss Side, Manchester.   Z10049

COOPER, A., Private, 11th Manchester Regiment.
Three months after joining in March 1917, he was drafted to the Western Front, where he took part in many important engagements in various sectors. He made the supreme sacrifice, falling in action in the third Battle of Ypres in October 1917. He was entitled to the General Service and Victory Medals.
" He passed out of the sight of men by the path of duty and self-sacrifice."
13, Brookside, City Road, Hulme, Manchester.   Z5703

COOPER, A. T., Private, 4th Lancashire Fusiliers.
Mobilised at the commencement of hostilities, he was drafted to Gallipoli in April 1915, and fought in the Landing at Cape Helles, the Battles of Krithia, and was wounded at Suvla Bay in the following August. Returning home he received hospital treatment and was invalided out of the Service in October 1915. He holds the 1914–15 Star, and the General Service and Victory Medals.
24, Pearson Street, Newton Heath, Manchester.   Z9487

COOPER, F., Private, 8th Manchester Regiment.
He volunteered in September 1914, and early in the following year was sent to the Dardanelles, where he took part in the Landings at Cape Helles and Suvla Bay, the three Battles of Krithia, and was wounded during the Evacuation of the Gallipoli Peninsula in January 1916. On his recovery he was engaged on garrison duties at Alexandria and Cairo until December 1916, when he was transferred to the Western Front and was in action at the Battles of Arras (in which engagement he was a second time wounded), Ypres and Cambrai, and was wounded a third time in the Ypres sector. In July 1918 he was invalided home, and three months later was discharged medically unfit, holding the 1914–15 Star, and the General Service and Victory Medals.
24, Prescott Street, West Gorton, Manchester.   Z8980

COOPER, G., Private, Manchester Regiment.
He joined in March 1917, and was shortly afterwards drafted to France. Whilst in this theatre of war he took part in much heavy fighting, including that at the Battle of Ypres (II), and in the Retreat and Advance of 1918. He returned home and was demobilised in February 1919, holding the General Service and Victory Medals.
1, Higher Duke Street, Miles Platting, Manchester.   TZ6052

COOPER, J., Corporal, R.A.M.C.
He volunteered in January 1915, and in the following month proceeded to France, where he served as a stretcher-bearer in various sectors of the Front. He took an active part in the Battles of Ypres, Festubert, Albert, the Somme, Arras, Cambrai and Amiens, and other important engagements, and also served through the Retreat and Advance of 1918. He was demobilised in February 1919, and holds the 1914–15 Star, and the General Service and Victory Medals.
91, Parkfield Street, Rusholme, Manchester.   Z5705

COOPER, J., Spr., R.E., and Pte., 10th K.O. (Y.L.I.)
Having attested in December 1915, he was called to the Colours in June of the following year, and in January 1917 was drafted to the Western Front, where he took part in the Battle of Arras and other important engagements. He fell fighting at Passchendaele on October 4th 1917. He was entitled to the General Service and Victory Medals.
" His life for his Country, his soul to God."
15, Franchise Street North, Ardwick, Manchester.   Z1022B

COOPER, J., Corporal, R.E.
Volunteering in October 1914, he was quickly drafted to the Western Front, where he played a prominent part in the Battles of Ypres, Neuve Chapelle, St. Eloi, Hill 60, Festubert, the Somme, Arras, Bullecourt, Cambrai, and in the Retreat and Advance of 1918. He was demobilised on his return to England in May 1919, and holds the 1914 Star, and the General Service and Victory Medals.
35, Redvers Street, Ardwick, Manchester.   Z5701

COOPER, J. B., Private, Worcestershire Regiment.
He joined the King's Shropshire Light Infantry in March 1916, and five months later was drafted to France, where he was transferred to the Worcestershire Regiment. After taking part in much severe fighting during the Somme Offensive he laid down his life for King and Country on October 9th, 1916. He was entitled to the General Service and Victory Medals. " A costly sacrifice upon the altar of freedom."
81, South Street, Longsight, Manchester.   Z5702A

COOPER, R. W., Pioneer, R.E.
He volunteered in January 1915, and in the following November was drafted to the Western Front, where he saw much severe fighting at Ypres. Later he was transferred to a Trench Mortar Battery, and served with a special gas company. He was gassed in action during the Retreat of March 1918, and was invalided home, but on his recovery returned to France, and served there until his demobilisation in February 1919. On March 6th 1919 he unfortunately died from the effects of gas poisoning, and was entitled to the 1914–15 Star, and the General Service and Victory Medals.
" Great deeds cannot die."
81, South Street, Longsight, Manchester.   Z5702B

COOPER, T., Private, Manchester Regiment.
He volunteered in June 1915, and after a period of training, was drafted to the Western Front. There he played a prominent part in many engagements, including the Battles of St. Eloi, Albert, Vimy Ridge, and the Somme, where he was unhappily killed in action in July 1916. He was entitled to the General Service and Victory Medals.
" A valiant Soldier, with undaunted heart he breasted life's last hill."
188, Victoria Square, Ancoats, Manchester.   TZ8981

COOPER, W., Pioneer, R.E.
Joining the Royal Fusiliers in May 1916, he was sent to France three months later, and was then transferred to a special Gas Company of the R.E., and served with a Trench Mortar Battery. He was wounded in action at Ypres in 1917, and was sent to a Base Hospital, but on his recovery, rejoined his unit, and was again in action in the Ypres sector. Demobilised in May 1919, he holds the General Service and Victory Medals.
81, South Street, Longsight, Manchester.   Z5702C

COOPER, Wm., Private, King's (Liverpool Regt.)
Volunteering in May 1915, he was quickly drafted to France, where he took part in the Battles of Loos, the Somme, Arras, Vimy Ridge, Messines, Ypres and Cambrai. He suffered severely from rheumatism and trench fever, and was invalided home in January 1918. After a period of hospital treatment in Cheshire he was discharged as medically unfit for further service and holds the 1914–15 Star, and the General Service and Victory Medals.
115, Devon Street, Ardwick, Manchester.   Z5704

COOPER, W., Private, Royal Fusiliers.
Three months after joining, he was sent to France in October 1916, and whilst in this theatre of war took part in the Battles of the Somme and Ypres. He was badly gassed in action during the Retreat of March 1918, and was invalided home. After hospital treatment in Manchester, he was discharged, medically unfit, in January 1919, and holds the General Service and Victory Medals.
115, Devon Street, Ardwick, Manchester.   Z5706

COPE, C., Sergt., 22nd Manchester Regiment.
He joined in 1918, but was unsuccessful in obtaining his transfer to a theatre of war during hostilities. In June 1919, however, he proceeded to Egypt, where he rendered valuable services until March 1920, when he was demobilised. Whilst in the Army he gained rapid promotion to Sergeant for his consistently good work.
57, Rochdale Road, Manchester.   Z8982

COPE, J. T., Gunner, R.F.A.
He volunteered in January 1915, and in the following August was sent to France, where he took part in heavy fighting at Festubert, St. Eloi and Albert, and was in action at the Battles of the Somme, Arras, Messines and Cambrai. He was wounded in April 1918, and invalided home to hospital near Stockport, but on his recovery returned to the Western Front four months later and served through the final stages of the Advance. He was demobilised in July 1919, and holds the 1914–15 Star, and the General Service and Victory Medals.
52, Newcastle Street, Hulme, Manchester.   Z8983

COPELAND, E., Driver, R.A.S.C.
He was mobilised from the Reserve in August 1914, and proceeding to France immediately, served through the Retreat from Mons. He also took an active part in the Battles of the Marne, Ypres, Loos, and the Somme, and during the Retreat and Advance of 1918, acted as a stretcher-bearer. He was discharged in January 1919, and holds the Mons Star, and the General Service and Victory Medals.
48, Earl Street, Longsight, Manchester.   Z5707C

COPELAND, F., Private, 21st Manchester Regt.
Volunteering in September 1915, he was drafted to the Western Front in the following May, but after only two months' active service, died gloriously on the Field of Battle at the commencement of the Somme Offensive on July 1st, 1916. He was entitled to the General Service and Victory Medals.
" Steals on the ear the distant triumph song."
7, Stonehewer Street, Rochdale Road, Manchester.   Z11680A

COPELAND, N., Gunner, R.F.A.

He volunteered in May 1915, and after a period of service in England was sent to France in March 1917. After taking part in the Battles of Arras, Bullecourt, Ypres and Passchendaele, he was unhappily killed in action at Cambrai in November 1917. He had been previously gassed in action, and was entitled to the General Service and Victory Medals.

" He joined the great white company of valiant souls."

48, Earl Street, Longsight, Manchester. Z5707A

COPELAND, R., Sergt., 1/8th Lancashire Fusiliers.

Mobilised with the Territorials in August 1914, he was immediately drafted to Egypt, and after being in action on the Suez Canal, was sent to the Dardanelles, where he took part in the Battles of Krithia, and the Landing at Suvla Bay. After the Evacuation of the Gallipoli Peninsula, he again served in Egypt until March 1917. He was then transferred to the Western Front, and played a conspicuous part in the Battles of Ypres (III), the Somme (II) and La Bassée. Whilst overseas, he was twice wounded in action—in June 1915 on Gallipoli, and in April 1918 on the Somme, when he was invalided home. In December 1918 he was discharged as medically unfit for further service, and holds the 1914–15 Star, and the General Service and Victory Medals.

7, Stonehewer Street, Rochdale Road, Manchester. Z11680C

COPELAND, W., Pte., 1/4th King's Shropshire Light Infantry.

He enlisted in March 1914, and after the outbreak of war in the following August was engaged on important duties in England and Wales until October 1917. He then proceeded to the Western Front, where he was in action at Ypres, Albert, Cambrai and La Bassée, and also took part in the strenuous fighting during the Retreat and Advance of 1918. He was discharged in January 1919, and holds the General Service and Victory Medals.

7, Stonehewer Street, Rochdale Road, Manchester. Z11680B

COPELAND, W., Pte., King's (Liverpool Regiment).

Volunteering in August 1914, he was drafted to the Western Front in the following March, and took part in the Battles of Neuve Chapelle, Ypres, Loos, the Somme, Arras and Cambrai. He was invalided home in August 1918, and then served in Ireland until his demobilisation in March 1919, holding the 1914–15 Star, and the General Service and Victory Medals.

48, Earl Street, Longsight, Manchester. Z5707B

COPLEY, A. E., Pte., K.O. (Y.L.I.)

He volunteered at the declaration of war, and sent to France in February of the following year fought at Neuve Chapelle. He was unfortunately killed in action at St. Eloi in March 1915, and was entitled to the 1914–15 Star, and the General Service and Victory Medals.

" Steals on the ear the distant triumph song."

3, Aspell Street, Newton Heath, Manchester. Z9488

COPPELLA, A., Private, R.A.M.C.

He joined in August 1916, and after completing a term of training was engaged on important duties with his unit at various stations in England and Scotland. He was unsuccessful in obtaining his transfer to a theatre of war, but nevertheless, rendered valuable services until demobilised in August 1919. 44, Masonic Street, Oldham Road, Manchester. Z8984

COPPIN, S., Private, Lancashire Fusiliers.

He joined in June 1917, and six months later was sent on active service. Whilst on the Western Front he played a prominent part in the Battle of the Somme, but was unfortunately killed in action in the Lys sector in April 1918. He was entitled to the General Service and Victory Medals.

" Nobly striving,
He nobly fell that we might live."

20, Thomas Street, West Gorton, Manchester. Z5708

CORBISHLEY, F., Private, 8th Manchester Regt.

He volunteered in June 1915, and twelve months later was drafted to Egypt, where he was in action in the Suez Canal zone. In March 1917 he was transferred to the Western Front and took part in the Battles of Ypres and Passchendaele, and in heavy fighting at Dunkirk and on the Somme. He was gassed in action in September 1917, and was invalided home. Demobilised in March 1919, he holds the General Service and Victory Medals.

35, William Street, West Gorton, Manchester. Z5709

CORCORAN, C., Private, 18th Manchester Regt.

He volunteered in November 1915, and after a period of training was drafted to the Western Front. There he saw much active service, and took part in the Battles of the Somme and Arras. He was gassed and wounded in June 1917, near Ypres, and was sent to hospital. On his recovery he served on important duties in England until discharged in April 1918, and holds the 1914–15 Star, and the General Service and Victory Medals.

29, Higham Street, Miles Platting, Manchester. Z11894

CORCORAN, J., Sapper, R.E. (Signal Section).

He volunteered in January 1916, and in the following May proceeded to France, where he took part in several engagements, including those at Ypres and Armentières. He was invalided home suffering from ill-health, and was discharged in August 1916, as medically unfit for further service. He holds the General Service and Victory Medals.

11, Cathcart Street, Ancoats, Manchester. Z10050

CORCORAN, J., Private, Lancashire Fusiliers.

He volunteered at the outbreak of hostilities in August 1914, and was immediately drafted to the Western Front. During his service in this theatre of war he took part in much heavy fighting at La Bassée, Armentières, Hill 60, Ypres, Festubert and Vimy Ridge, where he was killed in action, and was buried in the British Cemetery in October 1916. He was entitled to the Mons Star, and the General Service and Victory Medals.

" Whilst we remember, the sacrifice is not in vain."

1, Ernest Street, Ancoats, Manchester. Z6053

CORDING, J., Private, 2nd Manchester Regiment.

He enlisted in March 1913, and was sent to France in August 1914. He was wounded in action at the Battle of Mons, but on his recovery, took part in the Battles of Ypres, St. Eloi and Loos. In 1915 he was transferred to Mesopotamia, where he fought at Kut-el-Amara and Sanna-i-Yat before being sent to Egypt, and taking part in the Battles of Romani and El Fasher. Later he proceeded to Palestine, and served at Gaza, Jerusalem, Jericho and Aleppo, during the Advance of General Allenby's forces. In June 1920 he was placed on the Reserve, and holds the Mons Star, and the General Service and Victory Medals.

51, Barlow Street, Bradford, Manchester. Z5710

CORDING, T., Private, 11th King's (Liverpool Regt.)

He joined in February 1917, and was soon drafted to the Western Front, where he was in action at the Battles of Passchendaele, Cambrai, the Somme (II), St. Quentin and Amiens. Later he was attached to the 88th Labour Battalion for special work in the forward areas, and was eventually demobilised in November 1919, holding the General Service and Victory Medals.

51, Barlow Street, Bradford, Manchester. Z6054

CORDINGLEY, G., Pte., K.O. (Royal Lancaster Regt.)

Mobilised in August 1914, he was quickly sent to France, where he took part in the Battles of the Marne, the Aisne, Armentières, La Bassée, Ypres and Neuve Chapelle. He laid down his life for King and Country at St. Julien in May 1915, and was entitled to the 1914 Star, and the General Service and Victory Medals.

" Great deeds cannot die."

23, Marple Street, Ardwick, Manchester. Z5711

CORE, H., L/Corporal, 29th Royal Fusiliers.

He joined in June 1917, and three months later proceeded to the Western Front, where he played a prominent part in the Battles of the Somme (II), the Marne (II) and Amiens, and in the Retreat and Advance of 1918. He was wounded in action whilst in France, and also served with the 755th Labour Battalion. Demobilised in February 1920, he holds the General Service and Victory Medals. Z5712

40, Cranworth Street, Chorlton-on-Medlock, Manchester.

CORE, T., Worker, British Red Cross Society.

He joined in March 1915, and during the war was engaged on important duties conveying wounded from ambulance trains to the various hospitals in Manchester. He also rendered valuable services as an orderly at the Whitworth Street, Nell Lane and London Road Hospitals, and relinquished his duties in April 1919.

8, Talbot Street, Beswick, Manchester. Z5713

CORESMITH, J., Driver, R.A.S.C.

After volunteering in October 1914, he underwent a period of training prior to being drafted to Salonika in the following year. There he was engaged on important duties on the Struma front until February 1916, and was then transferred to the Western Front, where he was again in action. He took part in the Battles of Vermelles, Vimy Ridge, the Somme and Cambrai, and many other engagements, and also fought in the Retreat and Advance of 1918. He was demobilised in February 1919, and holds the 1914–15 Star, and the General Service and Victory Medals.

56, Heald Avenue, Rusholme, Manchester. Z11681

CORFIELD, R., Corporal, R.A.M.C.

Having already served fourteen years in the Army, he was sent to France at the outbreak of war in August 1914, and was taken prisoner during the Retreat from Mons. In June 1915 he was released as an exchanged prisoner, and did duty for a time on board a hospital ship bringing wounded from Egypt. Later, however, he returned to the Western Front, and was present at the Battles of the Somme, Arras and Ypres. He returned to England for his discharge on the expiration of his term of service in June 1917, and holds the Mons Star, and the General Service and Victory Medals.

50, George Street, Newton, Manchester. Z8985

CORK, W. T., Private, R.A.V.C.

He joined in September 1916, and on completion of his training was stationed at Woolwich, where he was engaged on important duties tending sick horses. Although unsuccessful in obtaining his transfer overseas, he rendered valuable services until his demobilisation in January 1919.
1, Erskridge Street, Ardwick, Manchester.   Z5714

CORKIN, H., Private, 7th Norfolk Regiment.

Three months after joining the Army, he was drafted to France in February 1917, and took part in the Battles of Arras, Bullecourt, Cambrai, the Somme, Havrincourt (where he was wounded in action) and Le Cateau. He also fought in other important engagements during the Retreat and Advance of 1918, and was demobilised in April 1919, holding the General Service and Victory Medals.
17, Melbourne Street, Hulme, Manchester.   Z5715

CORLESS, F., Private, 2nd Manchester Regiment.

He joined in April 1916, and in the following December proceeded to the Western Front, where he played a prominent part in the Battles of Arras, Bullecourt, Ypres, and Cambrai (I and II), and in the Retreat and Advance of 1918. He was invalided home sick in October 1918, but in March 1919, was sent to Ireland. Eight months later he was drafted to Mesopotamia, and in 1920 was stationed at Baghdad. He holds the General Service and Victory Medals.
24, Cedar Street, Hulme, Manchester.   Z5716

CORLESS, H., Gunner, R.F.A.

Volunteering in August 1914, he was drafted overseas three months later, During his service on the Western Front he took part in several engagements, including the Battles of Ypres (I), Neuve Chapelle, Hill 60, Loos, Albert, Vimy Ridge, the Somme, Ypres (III), Cambrai and the Lys, and was wounded in action. He was demobilised in March 1919, and holds the 1914 Star, and the General Service and Victory Medals.
2, Sandall Place, Ardwick, Manchester.   Z10051

CORLESS, T., Sergeant, 22nd Manchester Regiment.

Volunteering in August 1914, he was drafted to France in the following January and served with distinction at the Battles of St. Eloi, Loos, Albert, and the Somme, where he was badly wounded in action. He was invalided home, and unfortunately lost the sight of his left eye, but after nine months in hospital was sent to Italy in November 1917. In this theatre of war he fought on the Asiago Plateau, and on the Piave. He was discharged in February 1919, and holds the 1914-15 Star, and the General Service and Victory Medals.
214, Morton Street, Longsight, Manchester.   Z5717

CORNER, A., Private, 2nd Manchester Regiment.

Joining in July 1917, he completed his training, and was then engaged on special duties as an orderly at various stations in England, Scotland and Wales. He was unsuccessful in obtaining his transfer overseas but rendered valuable services until February 1920, when he was invalided from the Army owing to general debility.
22, Harrold Street, Miles Platting, Manchester.   Z8986

CORNER, A., Pte., 4th K.O. (Royal Lancaster Regt.)

He volunteered in January 1915, and three months later was drafted to the Western Front, where he played an important part in the Battles of Festubert, Albert and Ploegsteert. He died gloriously on the Field of Battle during the Somme Offensive in July 1916, and was entitled to the 1914-15 Star, and the General Service and Victory Medals.
"Nobly striving,
He nobly fell that we might live."
36, Coalbrook Street, Ardwick, Manchester.   TZ8987A

CORNER, J., Pte., 4th K.O. (Royal Lancaster Regt.)

He joined in April 1918, and on completion of his training was engaged on special garrison and fatigue duties in various parts of England and Ireland. He did consistently good work with his unit until May 1919, when he was invalided from the Army owing to defective hearing.
22, Harrold Street, Miles Platting, Manchester.   TZ8987B

CORNS, J., Private, Welch Regiment.

He joined in May 1917, and in the following March was drafted to the Western Front, where he saw much strenuous fighting during the Retreat and Advance of 1918. He took part in the Battles of the Somme (II) and the Marne (II), in engagements in the Arras and Passchendaele sectors and was gassed in action at St. Quentin in October 1918. After the cessation of hostilities, he served at Cologne with the Army of Occupation and was eventually demobilised in April 1919, holding the General Service and Victory Medals.
16, Marple Street, Openshaw, Manchester.   Z8988

CORNS, S., Private, 16th South Lancashire Regt.

He joined in January 1917, and on completion of his training was engaged for a time on important transport work. Later, however, his did duty with the Military Police, but owing to a serious break-down in health, was invalided from the Army in August 1918, after rendering valuable services.
16, Marple Street, Openshaw, Manchester.   Z8989

CORRY, F., Private, 7th Manchester Regiment.

Volunteering in November 1914, he was sent to the Gallipoli theatre of war in the following June, but after taking part in

the Landing at Suvla Bay, was invalided home with malaria in September 1915. On his recovery, he was engaged on important duties in England until July 1918, when he was drafted to France. Whilst on the Western Front he was in action at the Battle of Amiens, Bapaume, Havrincourt, Cambrai (II), and Ypres (IV), and was badly wounded at Le Cateau in October 1918. Again invalided home, he was discharged as medically unfit for further service in December 1919, and holds the 1914-15 Star, and the General Service and Victory Medals.   44, Tame Street, Ancoats, Manchester.   TZ8990

COSGROVE, C., Private, 7th Gordon Highlanders.

He volunteered in February 1915, and was shortly afterwards drafted to the Western Front. In this theatre of war he took part in the Battles of Hill 60, Ypres, Festubert, Loos, Albert, Vermelles and the Somme. He suffered from shell-shock, and was invalided home and discharged in October 1916, as medically unfit for further service. He holds the 1914-15 Star, and the General Service and Victory Medals.
9, Wrigley Street, West Gorton, Manchester.   Z10052

COSGROVE, F., Private, 11th Manchester Regt.

He volunteered in April 1915, and proceeding to Gallipoli in the following September, was in action there in many engagements. After the Evacuation of the Peninsula he was sent to France, and fought in the Battles of the Somme and Arras, but owing to ill-health he was invalided home in April 1917, and received hospital treatment. On his recovery he served at various depôts on important duties until demobilised in March 1919. He holds the 1914-15 Star, and the General Service and Victory Medals.
22, Phelan Street, Collyhurst, Manchester.   Z10541

COSGROVE, G., Bombardier, R.F.A.

Volunteering in March 1915, he was sent to France in the following October, and after taking part in the heavy fighting at Loos and Albert in 1916, was in action at the Battles of the Somme, Arras, Messines, Ypres and Passchendaele, and in the Retreat and Advance of 1918. He was demobilised in March 1919, and holds the 1914-15 Star, and the General Service and Victory Medals.
134, Morton Street, Longsight, Manchester.   Z5718

COSGROVE, L. W., Pte., South Lancashire Regt., Royal Welch Fusiliers and Welch Regt.

He volunteered in November 1915, and after a period of service in England was drafted to France in June 1918. He was in action on the Somme and at Albert (where he was wounded), Mametz Wood and Le Cateau, during the Retreat and Advance of that year. Demobilised on returning home in March 1919, he holds the General Service and Victory Medals.
12, Ryder Street, Bradford, Manchester.   Z5719

COSGROVE, W., Private, Royal Scots.

Volunteering in August 1915, he landed in France in the following March, and was in action at St. Eloi. He was afterwards taken prisoner near Loos, and was held in captivity in Germany until the termination of hostilities. After being repatriated he was demobilised in February 1919, and holds the General Service and Victory Medals.
125, Ryder Street, Collyhurst, Manchester.   Z10542

COSTA, W., Private, 16th Manchester Regiment.

He volunteered in September 1914, and during his period of training at Heaton Park unfortunately met with an accident which caused his discharge in May 1915. He rendered valuable services during his nine months in the Army.
5, Irlam Street, Miles Platting, Manchester.   Z10053

COSTELLO, W. C., Gunner, R.G.A.

He volunteered in October 1914, and in the following year was drafted to the Western Front, where he played an important part in the Battles of Loos, Albert, Vimy Ridge, the Somme (I), Arras, Lens, Cambrai and the Somme (II), and in heavy fighting during the Retreat and Advance of 1918. After hostilities ceased, he marched into Germany with the Army of Occupation and was demobilised in February 1919, holding the 1914-15 Star, and the General Service and Victory Medals.
118, Newcastle Street, Hulme, Manchester.   Z8991

COTT, J. (M.M.), Sergt., K.O. (R. Lancaster Regt.)

He volunteered in August 1914, and twelve months later was drafted to the Western Front, where he served with distinction at the Battles of Loos, the Somme, Arras, Ypres and Cambrai. He was wounded in action during the Somme Offensive in July 1916, and in the same year was awarded the Military Medal for conspicuous bravery and devotion to duty in the Field. He also holds the 1914-15 Star, and the General Service and Victory Medals, and was demobilised in April 1919.
14, James Street, Moss Side, Manchester.   Z5720

COULTHARD, G. W., Private, Manchester Regt.

Volunteering in September 1915, he proceeded overseas in the following April. During his service in France, he served as a Lewis Gunner, and took part in engagements on the Ancre and at Arras, Vimy Ridge, Bullecourt and Messines. He died gloriously on the Field of Battle at Cambrai on May 4th 1918, and was entitled to the General Service and Victory Medals.
"Great deeds cannot die:
They, with the sun and moon renew their light for ever."
19, Hope Street, Bradford, Manchester.   Z10054A

COULTHARD, T., Private, South Lancashire Regt.
He joined in November 1917, and after a period of training was engaged at various stations on important duties with his unit. Owing to the early cessation of hostilities, he was unable to obtain a transfer overseas, but rendered valuable services until his demobilisation in December 1919.
19, Hope Street, Bradford, Manchester. Z10054B

COUNSELL, W., Private, 1/4th Dorsetshire Regt.
He volunteered in November 1914, and in the following July was drafted to Salonika, where he took part in the Landing, and the first Battle of the Vardar, and was wounded in action near Monastir in December 1915. In May 1916 he was transferred to Mesopotamia, and served at Kut-el-Amara, and in other important engagements during the Advance. He was demobilised in March 1919, and holds the 1914-15 Star, and the General Service and Victory Medals.
44, Henry Street, West Gorton, Manchester. Z5721

COUPE, J., Sapper, R.E.
He joined in August 1917, and was quickly drafted to France. In this theatre of war he took part in several engagements, and was badly gassed in action and consequently invalided home in November 1917. He was discharged as medically unfit for further service in April 1918, and holds the General Service and Victory Medals.
18, Boslam Street, Ancoats, Manchester. Z10055

COURTENEY, T., Pte., 8th K.O. (R. Lancaster Regt.)
He volunteered in November 1914, and in September of the following year was drafted to the Western Front, where he played a prominent part in the Battles of Loos, Albert, Vermelles, Ploegsteert, the Somme (when he was wounded in action in July 1916), Bullecourt, and Cambrai, and in the Retreat and Advance of 1918. He was demobilised in February 1919, and holds the 1914-15 Star, and the General Service and Victory Medals.
19, Myrtle Grove, Ardwick, Manchester. Z5722

COURTNEY, John, Pte., K.O. (R. Lancaster Regt.)
Volunteering in August 1914, he was sent to France in the following November and took part in heavy fighting at La Bassée, Armentières and Arras. He was also in action at the Battles of Ypres and Hill 60, where he was badly gassed. He was invalided home, and in February 1917 was discharged as medically unfit for further service, holding the 1914-15 Star, and the General Service and Victory Medals.
18, Clifford Street, Lower Openshaw, Manchester. Z5723C

COURTNEY, Joseph, Private, Welch Regiment.
He joined in March 1917, and after a period of home service, was drafted to France in April 1918. He took part in the Battles of the Somme and the Marne, and in other important engagements during the Retreat and Advance of 1918, but was unhappily killed in action at St. Quentin in September of the same year. He was entitled to the General Service and Victory Medals.
"And doubtless he went in splendid company."
18, Clifford Street, Lower Openshaw, Manchester. Z5723B

COURTNEY, L., Private, South Lancashire Regt.
Volunteering in August 1915, he was sent to Mesopotamia in the following May and took part in heavy fighting at Kut-el-Amara, where he was badly wounded in action. On his recovery, he rejoined his unit and was present at the capture of Baghdad, and during the Advance to Mosul. He returned to England for his demobilisation in April 1919, and holds the General Service and Victory Medals.
18, Clifford Street, Lower Openshaw, Manchester. Z5723A

COVER, R. P., Pte., Loyal North Lancashire Regt.
He volunteered in August 1914, and in the following June proceeding to the Western Front, saw heavy fighting at Festubert, Givenchy and Bazentin-le-Petit. Severely wounded on July 6th, 1916 during the first British Offensive on the Somme, he returned home and after receiving hospital treatment was discharged as unfit for further military service in March 1917. He holds the 1914-15 Star, and the General Service and Victory Medals.
348, Oldham Road, Failsworth, near Manchester. Z9489

COVERDALE, C., Pte., King's Own Scottish Borderers.
When war was declared in August 1914, he volunteered, and after a period of training was drafted overseas six months later. Whilst serving on the Western Front he saw heavy fighting in different sectors of the line until wounded in the Battle of Loos in September 1915. He was invalided home, and in consequence discharged from the Army as medically unfit in May 1916. He holds the 1914-15 Star, and the General Service and Victory Medals.
208, Cheltenham Street, Collyhurst, Manchester. Z11483

COWAN, C. E., Private, Royal Defence Corps.
He joined in August 1916, and throughout his service did consistently good work whilst engaged on guard duties at Liverpool Docks, over munition works at Litherland and at prisoner of war camps in the Isle of Man. In January 1919 he was invalided from the Service owing to bronchitis and valvular disease of the heart.
44, Riga Street, City Road, Hulme, Manchester. TZ7034B

COWAN, J., Corporal, R.A.M.C.
Mobilised in August 1914, he first saw active service in Egypt, where he was stationed at Cairo and Alexandria. Early in 1915, he proceeded to the Dardanelles and took part in the Gallipoli campaign. After the Evacuation of the Peninsula, he was transferred to the Western Front, where he was in action at the Battles of the Somme, Arras and Cambrai. He was then invalided home suffering from the effects of malaria, but later proceeded to Archangel in Russia. He was eventually discharged in September 1919, and holds the 1914-15 Star, and the General Service and Victory Medals.
99, Broadfield Road, Moss Side, Manchester. Z5724B

COWAN, J. W., Pte., 19th King's (Liverpool Regt.)
Joining in April 1916, he was drafted to France three months later. Whilst overseas he took part in the Battles of Beaumont-Hamel, Arras and St. Quentin, where he was wounded and taken prisoner in 1917. He was held in captivity in Germany about eighteen months, and suffered many privations. After the Armistice he was released and returned home and was demobilised in August 1919. He holds the General Service and Victory Medals.
19, Bath Street, Miles Platting, Manchester. Z10056

COWBURN, A. G., Pte., 19th Manchester Regt.
He volunteered in September 1914, and in the following November was drafted to France, where he saw much severe fighting. He took part in the Battle of the Somme, but was reported missing in October 1916, and is now presumed to have been killed in action at Flers in that month. He was entitled to the 1914-15 Star, and the General Service and Victory Medals.
"Honour to the immortal dead who gave their youth that the world might grow old in peace." Z5725B
47, Cambridge Street, Chorlton-on-Medlock, Manchester.

COWEN, T., Pte., 8th K.O. (Royal Lancaster Regt).
He volunteered in September 1914, and completing his training served at various stations with his unit, on important duties. Owing to ill-health he did not obtain his transfer overseas, and was invalided out in May 1916. He subsequently died in February 1917.
"Steals on the ear the distant triumph song."
22, Law Street, Rochdale Road, Manchester. Z9490

COWIN, J., Private, Labour Corps.
Joining in March 1917, he was sent to France in the following month and whilst on the Western Front, was engaged on important duties in the forward areas. He was present at the Battles of Bullecourt, Messines, Ypres, Passchendaele and Cambrai, and in the Retreat and Advance of 1918. Demobilised in February 1919, he holds the General Service and Victory Medals. 14, Newark Avenue, Rusholme, Manchester. Z5726

COWLEY, G., Private, 2/8th Manchester Regiment.
He volunteered in June 1915, but owing to his being medically unfit, was not eligible for transfer overseas. He was therefore engaged on special duties with his unit at various stations until July 1916, when he was invalided from the Army suffering from heart disease.
40, Gorton Street, Ardwick, Manchester. Z5727

COWLEY, T., Private, 2nd Border Regiment.
Volunteering in October 1914, he landed in France two months later, and was in action in the Battle of Neuve Chapelle. He died gloriously on the Field at La Bassée on May 16th, 1915. He was entitled to the 1914-15 Star, and the General Service and Victory Medals.
"A costly sacrifice upon the altar of freedom."
24, Heelis Street, Rochdale Road, Manchester. Z10543

COWLISHAW, W. E. Pte., King's Own (R.L. Regt.)
He attested under the Derby scheme in December 1915, but was not called to the Colours until July 1918. He was then retained on important guard duties as prisoner of war camps and rendered valuable services until his demobilisation in June 1919.
50, Lindum Street, Rusholme, Manchester. Z5728

COX, E., Sergt., 4th Manchester Regiment.
He volunteered in November 1915, and twelve months later was drafted to the Western Front, where he served with distinction at the Battles of the Ancre, Arras, Messines and the Somme (II) and at Havrincourt, the Selle and the Sambre, during the Retreat and Advance of 1918. He was demobilised in March 1919, and holds the General Service and Victory Medals. 7, Bloom Street, Hulme, Manchester. TZ5729

COX, G. H., Private, 8th South Lancashire Regt.
He volunteered in March 1915, and nine months later was drafted to the Western Front. After taking part in heavy fighting at St. Eloi, Albert and Vermelles, he was unfortunately killed in action on July 15th, 1916, during the Somme Offensive. He was entitled to the 1914-15 Star, and the General Service and Victory Medals.
"Great deeds cannot die:
They with the sun and moon renew their light for ever."
6, Chapel Street, Ancoats, Manchester. Z8992A

COX, G., Private, 1st Cambridgeshire Regt. (T.F.)
He volunteered in September 1914, and early in the following year was drafted to the Western Front, where he took part in the Battles of Neuve Chapelle, St. Eloi, Ypres, Hill 60, Festubert, Loos, Albert and the Somme, and was twice wounded in action. He was invalided to hospital in Nottingham, and was eventually discharged in February 1919, holding the 1914–15 Star, and the General Service and Victory Medals.
32, Oliver Street, Bradford, Manchester. Z5732

COX, J. E., Private, 1/7th Manchester Regiment.
Mobilised in August 1914, he was quickly drafted to Egypt and was engaged on garrison duties at Khartoum until the commencement of the Gallipoli campaign. He then took part in the Landing at Cape Helles and in the 1st and 2nd Battles of Krithia, and made the supreme sacrifice on May 31st, 1915. He was entitled to the 1914–15 Star, and the General Service and Victory Medals.
"The path of duty was the way to glory."
91, Victoria Square, Oldham Road, Manchester. TZ8993A

COX, T., Private, Highland Light Infantry.
Mobilised in August 1914, he was sent to France with the first Expeditionary Force. During his service on the Western Front he played a prominent part in the Battles of Mons, the Aisne, Ypres, St. Julien and the Somme, and was twice wounded in action. He received his discharge in 1919, and holds the Mons Star, and the General Service and Victory Medals. TX5730
5, Melbourne Street, Chorlton-on-Medlock, Manchester.

COX, T. H., Private, K.O. (Y.L.I.)
Volunteering in October 1915, he was sent to France in January 1916, and after taking part in heavy fighting at Loos, St. Eloi and Albert, was gassed in action at the Battle of the Somme in July 1916. He was invalided to hospital in Leeds, but on his recovery returned to the Western Front, and was in action at the Battles of Arras (where he was wounded), Ypres, Cambrai, the Somme (II) and Le Cateau. He was finally demobilised in February 1919, and holds the General Service and Victory Medals.
33, Hastings Street, Chorlton-on-Medlock, Manchester. Z5731

COX, T. W., Private, South Wales Borderers.
Volunteering in October 1914, he was drafted to France on completion of his training in the following March. During his service on the Western Front, he took part in the Battles of Hill 60, Ypres (II), Albert, the Somme and Cambrai, and in the Retreat and Advance of 1918. He was wounded in action at Ypres in May 1916, and again on the Somme in July 1916. He holds the 1914–15 Star, and the General Service and Victory Medals, and was demobilised in March 1919.
6, Chapel Street, Ancoats, Manchester. Z8992B

COYLE, J., A.B., Royal Navy, H.M.S. "Lion."
He was mobilised in August 1914, and quickly proceeded to sea on board H.M.S. "Lion," with which ship he took part in the Battles of Heligoland Bight, the Falkland Islands, the Dogger Bank and Jutland. He was also engaged on special mining and submarine work, and rendered valuable services throughout hostilities. He holds the 1914–15 Star, and the General Service (with four clasps) and Victory Medals, and was discharged in March 1919.
19, Baird Street, Chapel Street, Ancoats, Manchester. Z8994

COYNE, A., Private, 13th Manchester Regt.
He volunteered in September 1915, and in November of the following year, was sent to Salonika, where he took part in the recapture of Monastir and in heavy fighting on the Doiran and Vardar fronts. He was unhappily killed in action in November 1918, and was entitled to the General Service and Victory Medals.
"His life for his Country, his soul to God."
28, William Street, Hulme, Manchester. Z5733

COYNE, M. J., Private, 23rd Manchester Regiment.
He volunteered in December 1915, and in the following year proceeded to the Western Front. There he served with the Labour Corps and was engaged on important duties on the Somme and at Passchendaele and Cambrai. He was demobilised in September 1919, and holds the General Service and Victory Medals.
26, Law Street, Rochdale Road, Manchester. Z10057

CRABTREE, F., Private, 16th Manchester Regt.
Volunteering early in August 1914, he was sent to France in November 1916. Whilst on the Western Front he took part in the Battles of the Somme, Arras, Vimy Ridge, Ypres and Passchendaele and in the Retreat and Advance of 1918. He was also in action during heavy fighting at Loos in March 1916, and was wounded in July of that year. Demobilised in May 1919, he holds the 1914–15 Star, and the General Service and Victory Medals.
15, Cresswell Street, Ardwick Green, Manchester. X5734

CRARGEN, E., Private, Manchester Regiment.
He volunteered in February 1915, and in the following year was drafted to France. Whilst in this theatre of war he took part in engagements at Arras, and on the Somme, where he was badly wounded in action. As a result he was invalided

home, and discharged in October 1917 as medically unfit for further service. He holds the 1914–15 Star, and the General Service and Victory Medals.
15, Fisher Street, Newton, Manchester. Z10058A

CRAIG, H. B., Private, 19th Manchester Regiment.
He volunteered in 1915, and on completing his training in the following year was drafted to France. There he took part in several engagements, including those at Ypres, Albert and Armentières, and was wounded in action. On his recovery he returned to his unit and was unfortunately killed in action in July 1916. He was entitled to the General Service and Victory Medals.
"He joined the great white company of valiant souls."
63, Kirk Street, Ancoats, Manchester. Z10059

CRAIG, J. V., Private, King's (Liverpool Regiment).
Mobilised in August 1914, he was quickly drafted to the Western Front, where he played a prominent part in the Battles of the Marne, the Aisne, Ypres (1914 and 1915), Hill 60, Loos, the Somme, the Ancre, Vimy Ridge, Cambrai and Le Cateau (1918). He was discharged in December 1918, and holds the 1914 Star, and the General Service and Victory Medals.
5, Platt Street, Moss Side, Manchester. Z5735

CRAIG, R., Corporal, Lancashire Fusiliers.
Volunteering in November 1914, he was sent to France two months later, and took part in the Battles of Neuve Chapelle, St. Eloi, Ypres, Albert, the Somme and the Marne (II). He was wounded at Ypres in 1915, gassed at Albert in the following year and again badly wounded on the Marne in July 1918, on which occasion he was invalided home. After a long period of hospital treatment in Norfolk and Stockport, he was discharged in February 1919, and holds the 1914–15 Star, and the General Service and Victory Medals.
33, Hulme Street, Chorlton-on-Medlock, Manchester. Z5736

CRAINE, T., Corporal, Royal Scots.
He joined in October 1917, but owing to his being medically unfit for marching, was retained on important garrison duties in Ireland. After six months' valuable service, during which time he gained quick promotion to Corporal, he was invalided from the Army in March 1918. Z5737
3, Humphrey Street, Chorlton-on-Medlock, Manchester.

CRANE, F., L/Corporal, 7th Manchester Regiment.
Volunteering in August 1914, he was drafted to the Dardanelles early in the following year, and after taking a prominent part in the Landing at Cape Helles on the Gallipoli Peninsula, was unfortunately killed in action at the 3rd Battle of Krithia on June 4th, 1915. He was entitled to the 1914–15 Star, and the General Service and Victory Medals.
"He died the noblest death a man may die,
Fighting for God, and right, and liberty."
13, Morton Street, Chorlton-on-Medlock, Manchester. X5738A

CRANE, H., Rifleman, 1st K.R.R.C.
He was mobilised in August 1914, and was soon drafted to France. During his service on the Western Front, he took part in the Battles of Ypres, Neuve Chapelle, Loos, Ploegsteert, the Somme, Arras, Messines and Passchendaele. He was three times wounded in action, twice at Ypres and on the last occasion at Passchendaele, when he was invalided home and eventually discharged, medically unfit, in February 1918. He holds the 1914 Star, and the General Service and Victory Medals.
13, Morton Street, Chorlton-on-Medlock, Manchester. X5738C

CRANE, J. J., Private, 1st Manchester Regiment.
He volunteered in October 1914, and was quickly drafted to the Western Front, where he took part in the Battle of Loos and other important engagements. At the end of 1915 he was transferred to Mesopotamia and was in action at the Battle of Kut. Invalided to England he was discharged in 1917, and holds the 1914–15 Star, and the General Service and Victory Medals.
12, Morton Street, Chorlton-on-Medlock, Manchester. X5738E

CRANE, T. (M.M.), Pte., 2nd, 22nd Manchester Regt.
Volunteering in August 1914, he was sent to France four months later and played a prominent part in the Battles of Hill 60, Ypres, Albert, the Somme and Bullecourt, where he was gassed and wounded in action in May 1917. He was awarded the Military Medal for conspicuous bravery and devotion to duty at Croisilles, when he carried two wounded officers and fourteen other ranks to safety under heavy shell-fire. He was eventually demobilised in March 1919, and also holds the 1914–15 Star, and the General Service and Victory Medals. Z5739
14, Clarendon Place, Chorlton-on-Medlock, Manchester.

CRANE, T.A., Pte., 6th Manchester Regt. and Spr., R.E.
Mobilised in August 1914, he was quickly sent to France, where he played a prominent part in the Battles of Ypres, Neuve Chapelle, Festubert, Loos, the Somme, Arras, Messines and Passchendaele. He was wounded in action at Festubert, on the Somme in July 1916, and at Arras in 1917. He holds the 1914 Star, and the General Service and Victory Medals, and was discharged in 1919.
13, Morton Street, Chorlton-on-Medlock, Manchester. X5738D

CRANE, W., Private, 7th Manchester Regt. (T.F.)
Mobilised with the Territorials in August 1914, he first saw active service in the Dardanelles, where he took part in the Landing at Cape Helles, and in the Battles of Krithia, being wounded in action in the second engagement. After the Evacuation of the Gallipoli Peninsula, he was transferred to the Western Front, and took part in the Battles of Messines, Ypres and Passchendaele (where he was again wounded) and in the Retreat and Advance of 1918, being wounded for the third time at the Battle of the Marne (II). He was demobilised in 1919, and holds the 1914-15 Star, and the General Service, Victory, and the Territorial Long Service Medals.
13, Morton Street, Chorlton-on-Medlock, Manchester. X5738B

CRANK, T., 2nd Lieut., 3rd Loyal N. Lancs. Regt.
He was mobilised in August 1914, and proceeding to France immediately, took part in the Battle of Mons, and in the subsequent Retreat, He was also in action at the Battles of the Marne, the Aisne, La Bassée, Ypres (I), Neuve Chapelle, Hill 60, Ypres (II) (where he was gassed), Arras, Bullecourt and Cambrai, and in the Retreat until May 1918. He was mentioned in Despatches for conspicuous bravery at Hill 60, in May 1915, when he brought in wounded under heavy fire, and was discharged in January 1919, holding the Mons Star, and the General Service and Victory Medals.
32, Milton Street, West Gorton, Manchester. Z1329

CRANSTON, W., Private, 1st E. Lancashire Regt.
Volunteering in August 1914, he was sent to Egypt before proceeding to the Dardanelles in April 1915. He took part in the Landing at Cape Helles, and in heavy fighting on the Gallipoli Peninsula until the Evacuation in January 1916. He was then transferred to the Western Front, where he was in action at the Battles of Albert, the Somme, Arras, Vimy Ridge, Ypres, Cambrai and Le Cateau and in other engagements during the Retreat and Advance of 1915. After the Armistice he served in Germany with the Army of Occupation until February 1919, when he was demobilised, holding the 1914-15 Star, and the General Service and Victory Medals.
23, Ely Street, Hulme, Manchester. TZ5740B

CRAVEN, A., Sapper, R.E.
He joined in June 1916, and six months later was drafted to the Western Front, where he played an active part in the Battles of Arras, Messines, Ypres, Passchendaele and Cambrai. He was unfortunately killed in action near Béthune on April 20th, 1918, and was entitled to the General Service and Victory Medals. "The path of duty was the way to glory."
29, Hazel Street, Hulme, Manchester. TZ5741

CRAVEN, A., Private, 19th Manchester Regiment.
Volunteering in September 1914, he was drafted to France in November of the following year, but after taking part in heavy fighting at Ypres, died gloriously on the Field of Battle during the Somme Offensive in July 1916. He was entitled to the 1914-15 Star, and the General Service and Victory Medals. "His memory is cherished with pride."
10, River Place, Hulme, Manchester. Z5742

CRAVEN, J., Pte., R.A.S.C. and 13th Middlesex Regt.
Volunteering in October 1914, he was drafted to the Western Front in the following month and there served in various sectors. He took part in the Battles of La Bassée, Ypres, Neuve Chapelle, Hill 60, the Somme, Arras, Messines, Cambrai the Aisne, the Marne and Amiens, and many minor engagements and was twice wounded in action, at Loos in October 1915, and on the Somme in March 1918. He was demobilised in April 1919, and holds the 1914 Star, and the General Service and Victory Medals.
27, Hyde Street, Hulme, Manchester. Z5743

CRAWFORD, A., Private, 3rd Border Regiment.
He joined in February 1917, and after three months' training proceeded to the Western Front. There, attached to the Labour Corps, he served in many sectors, and engaged on various important duties, rendered valuable services until his return to England for demobilisation in January 1919. He holds the General Service and Victory Medals.
16, Anson Street, Hulme, Manchester. Z5745

CRAWFORD, J., Private, 15th Lancashire Fusiliers.
He volunteered in September 1914, and in November of the following year after completing his training was sent to France, where he fought in the Battles of the Somme, Arras, Messines and Ypres. He was also engaged in much heavy fighting throughout the German Offensive and Allied Advance of 1918. After returning home he was demobilised in May 1919, and holds the 1914-15 Star, and the General Service and Victory Medals.
12, Susan Street, Rochdale Road, Manchester. Z10544

CRAWFORD, J. B., Private, 2nd Royal Scots.
Volunteering in January 1915, he was drafted to the Western Front in the following April, and there saw severe fighting in various sectors. He took part in the Battles of Ypres, Loos, St. Eloi and Albert, was wounded in action on the Somme and was for a time in hospital at Etaples. On his

recovery, however, he rejoined his unit and was again in action at Vimy Ridge, Ypres and Cambrai and was gassed on the Somme in March 1918. Invalided home, he was demobilised in February 1919, and holds the 1914-15 Star, and the General Service and Victory Medals.
10, Webster Street, Greenheys, Manchester. Z5744

CRAWFORD, R., Private, Lancashire Fusiliers.
Joining in April 1916, he was drafted to Salonika in the following September. Whilst in this seat of operations he took part in much fighting on the Vardar, Struma and Doiran fronts, but in 1917 was transferred to France. There he fought at Ypres, Passchendaele, Cambrai and in the Retreat and Advance of 1918. After hostilities ceased he went into Germany with the Army of Occupation and served there until his demobilisation in September 1919. He holds the General Service and Victory Medals.
2, Pratley Street, Ancoats, Manchester. Z10060

CRAWFORD, S., Private, Labour Corps.
He joined in June 1916, and in December of that year was sent to the Western Front, where he was engaged on important duties in various sectors. He was present at the Battles of Arras, Bullecourt and Ypres and other important engagements until wounded in action at Cambrai in November 1917, and invalided home. He was discharged in May 1918 as medically unfit for further service, and holds the General Service and Victory Medals.
30, Mark Street, Hulme, Manchester. Z5746

CREGAN, T., Private, 5th Manchester Regiment.
He volunteered in January 1915, but owing to his being medically unfit for immediate transfer overseas, was engaged on important garrison duties at various home stations. In March 1918, however, he was drafted to France, where he took part in the Battles of the Somme (II) and Ypres (IV) with the Cheshire Regiment, and was wounded in action during the latter engagement in September 1918. He was demobilised in March 1919, and holds the General Service and Victory Medals.
34, Somerset Place, Collyhurst, Manchester. Z8995

CREIGHTON, F. A., Private, 7th Manchester Regt.
He volunteered in May 1915, and underwent a period of training prior to being drafted to Egypt in April of the following year. There he served for twelve months at Cairo and Khartoum before being transferred to the Western Front, where he took part in the Battles of Messines and Cambrai. He fought also in the Retreat of 1918, and was so severely wounded in action at Bapaume in August of that year as to necessitate the amputation of his left arm. He was invalided from the Army in October 1918, and holds the General Service and Victory Medals.
15, Cedar Street, Hulme, Manchester. Z5747

CREIGHTON, J., Pioneer, R.E.
He joined in April 1917, and after completing a term of training served at various stations, where he was engaged on duties of a highly important nature. He was not successful in obtaining his transfer to a theatre of war, but nevertheless, rendered valuable services with his Company until January 1919, when he was demobilised.
26, Cedar Street, Hulme, Manchester. Z5748B

CREIGHTON, T. H., Private, 7th Manchester Regt.
He volunteered in May 1915, and in January of the following year, proceeded to Egypt, where he was engaged on important duties at Alexandria and Katia. He was also in hospital for a time at Cairo and was finally invalided home and discharged as medically unfit for further service in August 1916. He holds the General Service and Victory Medals.
26, Cedar Street, Hulme, Manchester. Z5748

CRESSWELL, A., Private, Manchester Regiment.
He volunteered in September 1915, and in the following April was drafted to the Western Front, where, after taking part in the Battles of Albert, Vimy Ridge, the Somme and Bullecourt he was wounded in action at Ypres. Invalided home, he proceeded to Italy on his recovery in 1917, and shortly afterwards returned to France in time to fight in the Retreat and Advance of 1918. He holds the General Service and Victory Medals, and was demobilised in March 1919.
10, Crayton Street, Hulme, Manchester. Z5750

CRESSWELL, C., Private, 1/7th Lancashire Fusiliers.
Volunteering in August 1914, he was drafted to Gallipoli in April of the following year and there, after taking part in the Landing at Cape Helles, fought in the Battles of Krithia and was wounded in action at Suvla Bay. He was invalided home and was for a considerable period in hospital, suffering also from malaria and dysentery, before being discharged as medically unfit for further service in December 1916. He unhappily died on June 7th, 1917. He was entitled to the 1914-15 Star, and the General Service and Victory Medals. "His memory is cherished with pride."
6, Foster Street, City Road, Hulme, Manchester. Z5751

CRESSWELL, R., Private, 9th Cheshire Regiment.
He volunteered in September 1914, and in July of the following year proceeded to France, where he saw severe fighting in various sectors of the Front. After taking part in engagements at Ypres, Festubert and La Bassée, he was severely injured whilst playing football at Givenchy in December 1915, and was invalided to hospital at Lincoln. He was discharged in May 1916 as medically unfit for further service, and holds the 1914–15 Star, and the General Service and Victory Medals.
32, Ferneley Street, Hulme, Manchester.   Z5752

CRESWELL, G., Private, 16th S. Lancashire Regt.
He volunteered in May 1915, and in the following February sailed for France, where he fought at Albert, Ploegsteert and the Somme. Transferred to Salonika in February 1917 he saw much fighting on the Vardar front and took part in the final Allied Advance in this theatre of war. Returning to England he was demobilised in February 1919, and holds the General Service and Victory Medals.
20, Teignmouth Street, Collyhurst, Manchester.   Z9492

CREWE, E. J., Driver, R.G.A.
Two months after joining in January 1917, he was drafted to the Western Front, where he saw much severe fighting in various sectors. He served through the Battles of Arras, Messines, Ypres, the Marne, Havrincourt and Cambrai and many other engagements in this theatre of war, and also took part in the Retreat and Advance of 1918. He was demobilised in March 1919, and holds the General Service and Victory Medals.
10, Stockton Street, Chorlton-on-Medlock, Manchester.   Z5749

CRIBBIN, H., Private, Border Regiment.
He volunteered in 1914, and underwent a period of training prior to his being drafted to France in the following year. There he took part in the Battles of Ypres, Arras and the Somme, and was wounded in action in 1917. On his recovery he returned to his unit, was in action in the Advance of 1918 and was taken prisoner of war. He was held in captivity in Germany at Gefangenenlager, where he was engaged in farming. After the Armistice, he was released and returned home for his demobilisation in 1919. He holds the General Service and Victory Medals.
15, Richmond Street, Ardwick, Manchester.   Z10061

CRIGHTON, E. T., Driver, R.F.A.
Mobilised in August 1914, he was immediately drafted to France and was wounded in action at the Battle of Mons. After treatment in a Casualty Clearing Station, he rejoined his Battery, and took part in the Battles of the Marne, the Aisne, Ypres (I), Neuve Chapelle, Hill 60, and Ypres (II). In November 1915 he was discharged, time-expired, but rejoining early in 1917, returned to the Western Front and fought in the Battles of Arras, the Somme (II), Bapaume, Havrincourt and Le Cateau (II). He was demobilised in December 1918, and holds the Mons Star, and the General Service and Victory Medals.   131, Edensor Street, Beswick, Manchester.   Z8996B

CRIGHTON, W., Private, 1st Manchester Regt.
He volunteered in January 1915, and after completing a period of training was drafted to Mesopotamia, where he took part in much heavy fighting, including the capture of Amara, and the Battles of Kut-el-Amara and Um-el-Hannah. He was wounded in action in March 1916, and invalided to England. He was demobilised in March 1919, and holds the 1914–15 Star, and the General Service and Victory Medals.
5, Clyde Street, Ancoats, Manchester.   Z10062

CRIMES, W. R. (M.M.) Private, Manchester Regt.
Volunteering in April 1915, he was drafted to the Western Front in the following December, and there, after much severe fighting, was wounded in action on the Somme. He was invalided home, but on his recovery, returned to France in 1917, and took part in the Battles of Ypres, and Passchendaele, and was again wounded. He was awarded the Military Medal for conspicuous bravery displayed in holding a machine-gun post, single-handed, under heavy fire, and holding also the 1914–15 Star, and the General Service and Victory Medals, was demobilised in January 1919.
8, Rose Street, Old Trafford, Manchester.   Z5753

CRIMMINS, P., Private, East Yorkshire Regiment.
He volunteered in January 1915, and shortly afterwards was drafted to India, where he was engaged on important garrison duties at Peshawar, and various other stations. Later he proceeded to Mesopotamia, where, in 1920 he was still with his unit at Baghdad. He holds the General Service and Victory Medals.
39, Roseberry Street, Gorton, Manchester.   Z5754

CROASDALE, W., Rifleman, King's R. Rifle Corps.
He volunteered in March 1915, and was sent to the Western Front in the following August. He fought on the Somme, and at Ypres, Albert, Bullecourt, and many engagements during the German and Allied Offensives of 1918. Returning home after the Armistice he was demobilised in February 1919, and holds the 1914–15 Star, and the General Service and Victory Medals.
174, Barmouth Street, Bradford, Manchester.   Z9493

CROFT, J., Driver, R.A.S.C.
He volunteered in August 1914, and in the following March proceeded to the Western Front. During his service in this theatre of war he saw much heavy fighting, and took an active part in the Battles of Hill 60, Loos, Albert, Vermelles, the Somme, Arras, Vimy Ridge, Ypres, the Aisne, Bapaume and Le Cateau. He was demobilised in June 1919, and holds the 1914–15 Star, and the General Service and Victory Medals.
16, Spencer Street, Ancoats, Manchester.   Z10063

CROFT, R., Private, Royal Defence Corps.
He volunteered in February 1915, and on completion of his training served at various stations with his unit. He was engaged on important guard duties at prisoner of war camps during the period of hostilities, and rendered very valuable services until demobilised in February 1919.
11, Garrick Street, Ancoats, Manchester.   Z10064B

CROFTON, W., Private, Manchester Regiment.
Already in the Army when war broke out in August 1914, he was immediately drafted to the Western Front, where, after fighting at Mons, he took part in the Battles of Le Cateau, the Marne, La Bassée, Neuve Chapelle and St. Eloi. He was killed in action in May 1915, during the second Battle of Ypres. He held the Queen's and King's South African Medals, and was entitled to the Mons Star, and the General Service and Victory Medals.
    "Steals on the ear the distant triumph song."
33, Patchett Street, Hulme, Manchester.   Z5756

CROFTS, A., Sapper, R.E.
Joining in January 1917, he proceeded to France four months later, and served on the Somme and Cambrai fronts on important duties connected with road and bridge construction and repairs. He saw much severe fighting during the Retreat and Advance of 1918, and returning to England after the Armistice, was demobilised in May 1919. He holds the General Service and Victory Medals.
97, Inkerman Street, Collyhurst, Manchester.   Z10545

CROLLA, H., Private, 4th Manchester Regiment.
Mobilised at the commencement of hostilities, he was stationed with his unit at various depôts on important duties. Owing to ill-health he was unsuccessful in obtaining his transfer overseas, but rendered valuable services until discharged as unfit for further duty in 1915.
9, Elizabeth Street, Ancoats, Manchester.   TZ9417A

CROMBELHOLME, D., Pte., 21st and 6th M/C Regt.
He volunteered in January 1915, and in October of that year proceeded to the Western Front, where he took part in many important engagements, including the Battles of Loos, Albert and the Somme. He fell fighting on the Ancre front on January 11th 1917, and was buried at Albert. He was entitled to the 1914–15 Star, and the General Service and Victory Medals.
    "Thinking that remembrance though unspoken, may reach him where he sleeps."
19, John Street, Hulme, Manchester.   TZ5757

CROMPTON, G., Driver, R.F.A.
Shortly after volunteering in August 1914, he was drafted to Egypt, whence he proceeded in April of the following year to Gallipoli. He saw much severe fighting in this seat of operations until the Evacuation of the Peninsula, and then returned to Egypt, where he served at various stations until February 1917. He was then transferred to the Western Front, and took part in the Battles of Arras, Vimy Ridge, Passchendaele, Cambrai, the Somme, Bapaume and St. Quentin, and was gassed at Ypres in July 1917. He was demobilised in May 1919, and holds the 1914–15 Star, and the General Service and Victory Medals.
10, Viaduct Street, Ardwick, Manchester.   Z5758

CROMPTON, J., Private, 20th Manchester Regt.
He volunteered in 1915, and later in the same year was drafted to the Western Front, where he saw much severe fighting at St. Eloi, Ypres, Festubert, Hill 60, Albert, Armentières, Arras and Vimy Ridge. He made the supreme sacrifice during the Somme Offensive in July 1916, and was entitled to the 1914–15 Star, and the General Service and Victory Medals.
    "His life for his Country, his soul to God."
4, Catherine Street, Manchester.   Z8997

CROMPTON, J., Private, 1st Lancashire Fusiliers.
He volunteered in September 1914, and in the following year was drafted to the Dardanelles, where he took part in the Battles of Krithia and Chunuk Bair, the Landing at Suvla Bay, and in other important engagements until the Evacuation of the Gallipoli Peninsula. Later he proceeded to the Western Front, and saw service at Neuve Chapelle, Hill 60, Loos, and in the Somme sector, where he was unfortunately killed in action in April 1916. He was entitled to the 1914–15 Star, and the General Service and Victory Medals.
    "And doubtless he went in splendid company."
9, Roberts Street, Newton Heath, Manchester.   Z10065

CRONE, J., Private, King's (Liverpool Regiment).
He joined in February 1917, and after three months' training was drafted to the Western Front. Whilst in this theatre of war he saw much severe fighting and took part in the Battles of Cambrai, the Somme, Bapaume and Havrincourt, and many other engagements until the cessation of hostilities. He was then sent with the Army of Occupation into Germany, and finally returned home for demobilisation in November 1919. He holds the General Service and Victory Medals.
68, Phillips Street, Hulme, Manchester. Z5759

CRONSHAW., A. E., Private, 2nd Manchester Regt.
He volunteered in January 1916, and in June of that year was drafted to the Western Front, where he saw severe fighting in various sectors. He took part in the Battles of the Somme, the Ancre, Arras, Vimy Ridge, Ypres, Passchendaele, Amiens and Le Cateau and many other engagements until the signing of the Armistice, when he was sent with the Army of Occupation into Germany. He was demobilised on his return home in July 1919, and holds the General Service and Victory Medals.
29, Birch Street, Hulme, Manchester. Z5760

CRONSHAW, D., Private, King's (Liverpool Regt.)
He volunteered in August 1914, at the outbreak of hostilities, and after a period of training was drafted to Egypt. Later he proceeded to Palestine, where he took part in the Battles of Gaza, and was also present at the capture of Jerusalem, and other important engagements. Remaining in this seat of war until April 1919, he was then demobilised, holding the 1914-15 Star, and the General Service and Victory Medals.
133, Cobden Street, Ancoats, Manchester. Z10066

CRONSHAW, J., Private, 2nd Manchester Regt.
A serving Soldier, he was drafted to the Western Front at the outbreak of war, and fought in the Retreat from Mons, and in the Battle of Le Cateau. He was killed in action on September 25th, 1914, during the concluding stages of the Retreat, and was entitled to the Mons Star, and the General Service and Victory Medals.
"His life for his Country, his soul to God."
23, Daniel Street, Ancoats, Manchester. Z9494

CRONSHAW, J., Pte., 6th York and Lancaster Regt.
He volunteered in December 1915, and on completion of his training was engaged on important duties at home until June 1916, when he obtained a transfer overseas. During his nine months' service on the Western Front he was engaged in fierce fighting in the Somme, Arras and Cambrai sectors. He was demobilised in May 1919, and holds the General Service and Victory Medals.
23, Duke Street, Miles Platting, Manchester. Z10278

CRONSHAW, R., Private, Royal Welch Fusiliers.
He volunteered in December 1915, and landing in France in the following March was in action in the Battles of the Somme, Bullecourt, Messines and Passchendaele, and throughout the German Offensives of 1918. Wounded in September during the Allied Advance he returned to England, and after receiving hospital treatment was invalided out of the Service in January 1919. He holds the General Service and Victory Medals.
8, Phelan Street, Collyhurst, Manchester. Z10546

CROPPER, H., Pte., 9th North Staffordshire Regt.
Joining in February 1917, he underwent a period of training prior to being sent to France in the following October. He saw much severe fighting at Passchendaele, took part in the Battles of Cambrai, the Somme (II), and the Marne (II), and was unhappily killed in action on November 4th, 1918. He was entitled to the General Service and Victory Medals.
"A costly sacrifice upon the altar of freedom."
49, Sandal Street, Newton, Manchester. Z8998

CROPPER, J., Private, 22nd Manchester Regiment.
He joined in May 1916, and in July was drafted to the Western Front, where he played a prominent part in the Battles of the Somme, Arras, Vimy Ridge and Bullecourt. He laid down his life for King and Country at the third Battle of Ypres in October 1917, and was entitled to the General Service and Victory Medals. "His memory is cherished with pride."
26, Rhodes Street, Miles Platting, Manchester. Z8999

CROSBY, H., Sergt., R.G.A.
He joined in April 1916, and in March of the following year was drafted to the Western Front, where he saw much severe fighting. He took part in the Battles of Arras, Bullecourt, Messines, Ypres and Passchendaele, served also through the Retreat and Advance of 1918, and was gassed at Cambrai in November 1917. Later he served with the Army of Occupation in Germany, finally returning home for demobilisation in September 1919. He holds the General Service and Victory Medals. 22, Napier Street, Ardwick, Manchester. Z5761

CROSBY, S., Private, 2nd Manchester Regiment.
He volunteered in December 1915, and twelve months later was drafted to the Western Front. There he saw much severe fighting in various sectors, took part in the Battles of Ypres, Passchendaele, the Somme and Havrincourt and other engagements and was wounded in action in February 1918, and sent to hospital at Boulogne. He was demobilised in January 1920 and holds the General Service and Victory Medals.
21, William Street, West Gorton, Manchester. Z5762

CROSBY, W., Private, 2nd Manchester Regiment.
Volunteering July 1915, he was drafted to the Western Front in December of that year, and there saw much severe fighting in various sectors. He took part in many important engagements in this theatre of war, and was three times wounded in action—at Loos in March 1916, at Ypres, and again on the Somme in December 1917. He was demobilised in December 1919, and holds the 1914-15 Star, and the General Service and Victory Medals. 32, William St., Hulme, Manchester. Z5763

CROSS, H., Private, M.G.C.
He joined in April 1917, and after his training was drafted to the Western Front, where he was wounded in action at Arras, and invalided home. On his recovery, he returned to France, and later took part in the Advance into Germany. After a period of service at Cologne with the Army of Occupation, he was demobilised in February 1920, and holds the General Service and Victory Medals.
11, Groom Street, Ancoats, Manchester. Z10067

CROSS, W., Private, King's (Liverpool Regiment).
Having previously served in the South African campaign, he re-enlisted in August 1914, and served at various stations on Coast Defence duties. In November 1915, he was drafted to Egypt, and there served at Alexandria. He was later sent to Salonika, and took part in the Advance across the Struma, and the capture of Monastir. He was invalided home on account of ill-health, and finally discharged as medically unfit for further service in November 1917, holding the Queen's South African Medal, the 1914-15 Star, and the General Service and Victory Medals.
32, Cookson Street, Ancoats, Manchester. Z10068

CROSSFIELD, T., Driver, R.A.S.C.
Volunteering in November 1914, he was drafted to the Western Front six months later, and there took an active part in the Battles of Ypres, and Festubert, and was wounded in action at Loos. In December 1915, he was transferred to Salonika, where he served on the Doiran and Struma fronts until his return home in October 1918. He was demobilised in February 1919, and holds the 1914-15 Star, and the General Service and Victory Medals. 70, Ducie St., Longsight, Manchester. Z5764

CROSSLEY, F., Private, 1st Manchester Regiment.
He joined in July 1918, and on completion of a period of training in November of that year, was drafted to the Western Front. There he was engaged in guarding prisoners of war, and on other important duties at Rouen, Boulogne, Le Havre and Etaples, finally returning home for demobilisation in November 1919. 22, Hardy St., West Gorton, Manchester. Z5768

CROSSLEY, G., Private, Royal Scots.
He volunteered in January 1915, and after completing a short period of training served at various stations, where he was engaged on duties of great importance. Owing to ill-health, he was unable to obtain his transfer to a theatre of war, and was finally invalided from the Army in June 1915.
39, Byron Street, Hulme, Manchester. Z5766

CROSSLEY, J. H., Pte., 17th (Duke of Cambridge's Own) Lancers.
He joined in September 1917, and was shortly afterwards drafted to the Western Front, where he saw much active service. He took part in engagements in various sectors, and fought in the Battles of Cambrai (I), Somme (II), the Aisne (III), the Marne (II), Bapaume and Ypres (IV). He was demobilised in October 1919, and holds the General Service and Victory Medals.
10, Mozart Street, Ancoats, Manchester. Z10069

CROSSLEY, J., Driver, R.F.A.
Volunteering at the commencement of hostilities, he was sent to the Western Front in October 1914, and fought at La Bassée, Ypres, and Loos. He gave his life for the freedom of England at Albert in June 1916, and was entitled to the 1914 Star, and the General Service and Victory Medals.
"Whilst we remember, the sacrifice is not in vain."
39, Buckley Street, Rochdale Road, Manchester. Z10547

CROSSLEY, J. W., Private, Manchester Regiment.
He volunteered in January 1916, and in the following June was drafted to France, where he saw severe fighting in various sectors of the Front. He served through the Battles of Cambrai, Bapaume and Havrincourt, and other engagements, took part also in the Retreat and Advance of 1918, and was three times wounded in action—on the Somme, and at Messines and Epéhy. He was demobilised in February 1919, and holds the General Service and Victory Medals.
28, Berwick Street, Chorlton-on-Medlock, Manchester. Z5765

CROSSLEY, R., Private, Manchester Regiment.
Volunteering in January 1916, he was engaged on important duties at home stations for twelve months before being sent to France. He then took part in the Battles of Ypres (III), Passchendaele and Cambrai, and in heavy fighting at La Bassée and Festubert, and during the Retreat and Advance of 1918. He was wounded in action on the Somme in September 1918, and was invalided to hospital in Wales. Demobilised in February 1919, he holds the General Service and Victory Medals.
28, Wardle Street, Newton, Manchester. Z9000

CROSSLEY, S. M., Driver, R.A.S.C. (M.T.)
Joining in October 1916, he proceeded to Salonika on completing two months' training, and was there engaged on important transport duties. He took an active part in engagements on the Doiran and Vardar fronts, and was also present at the capture of Monastir. He returned home in November 1919, and in the following January was demobilised, holding the General Service and Victory Medals.
10, Gregory Street, West Gorton, Manchester.   Z5767

CROSSLEY, W. H., Gunner, R.F.A.
Volunteering in August 1914, he was soon drafted to the Western Front and took part in the Battles of Neuve Chapelle, St. Eloi, Hill 60, Ypres, Festubert, Loos, the Somme, the Ancre, Arras, Bullecourt (where the Siegfried Line was captured), Amiens, Bapaume and Havrincourt. He was wounded in action in 1916, and was eventually demobilised in 1919, holding the 1914–15 Star, and the General Service and Victory Medals.
2, Pilling Street, Newton Heath, Manchester.   Z10070

CROSSWAITE, J. H., Private, Royal Welch Fusiilers.
He volunteered in August 1915, and twelve months later was drafted to the Western Front, where he fought in various sectors. He took part in the Battles of the Somme, Arras, Ypres and Cambrai, and other important engagements, served also through the Retreat af 1918, and was wounded in action at Havrincourt in September of that year. He was demobilised in February 1919, and holds the General Service and Victory Medals.
26, Marple Street, Ardwick, Manchester.   Z5769

CROUCHER, W. H., Sergt., 11th E. Lancs. Regt.
He volunteered in November 1915, and twelve months later was sent to the Western Front, where he saw severe fighting in various sectors. He took part in the Battles of Arras, and many other engagements, served also through the Retreat and Advance of 1918, and was twice wounded in action—at Vimy Ridge in April 1917, and at Gommecourt in March 1918. He was demobilised in March 1919, and holds the General Service and Victory Medals.
28, Guy Street, Ardwick, Manchester.   Z5770

CROWLEY, E., Private, Royal Dublin Fusiliers.
He joined in November 1916, and after his training served at various stations until January 1918, when he proceeded to the Western Front. There he saw much heavy fighting at Cambrai and in other sectors, until severely wounded in action in the Allies' Retreat. He unhappily died of wounds in April 1918. He was entitled to the General Service and Victory Medals. "Whilst we remember, the sacrifice is not in vain."
27, Carter Terrace, Greenheys, Manchester.   TZ5771

CROWLEY, S., Pte., King's Own (Lancaster Regt.)
He joined in April 1917, and on completion of his training was drafted overseas in the following February. During his service on the Western Front he took part in heavy fighting at Givenchy and La Bassée, where he was badly wounded and invalided to hospital in March 1918. He was demobilised in November 1919, and holds the General Service and Victory Medals.   11, Iles Street, Oldham Road, Manchester.   Z10071

CROWTHER, A., Pte., K.O. (Royal Lancaster Regt.)
Volunteering in September 1914, he proceeded to the Western Front in February of the following year, and there took part in many important engagements in various sectors. He died gloriously on the Field of Battle at Delville Wood in July 1916, during the Advance on the Somme. He was entitled to the 1914–15 Star, and the General Service and Victory Medals.
"A valiant Soldier, with undaunted heart he breasted life's last hill."
6, Waldon Street, Longsight, Manchester.   Z11682A

CROWTHER, A. C., Sergeant, S. Lancashire Regt.
Volunteering in May 1915, he proceeded to the Western Front on completing his training in November of that year, and there saw heavy fighting in various sectors. After taking part in many important engagements, he was severely wounded in action in the third Battle of Ypres in July 1917, and was for some months in hospital at Brighton. He was invalided from the Army in March 1918, and holds the 1914–15 Star, and the General Service and Victory Medals.
6, Waldon Street, Longsight, Manchester.   Z11682B

CROWTHER, G. W., 1st Air Mechanic, R.A.F.
He joined in January 1917, and on completion of his training was engaged on important duties which demanded a high degree of technical skill. Owing to medical unfitness, he was not drafted overseas, but did consistently good work with his Squadron until his demobilisation in January 1919.
32, Fielden Street, Oldham Road, Manchester.   Z8915B

CROWTHER, R., Private, 11th Lancashire Fusiliers.
He volunteered in August 1914, and after a period of training and important duties in England was drafted to France in September 1915. He took part in the Battle of Loos, but was then unfortunately killed in action at Hill 60, in January 1916. He was entitled to the 1914–15 Star, and the General Service and Victory Medals.
"And doubtless he went in splendid company."
30, Rhodes Street, Miles Platting, Manchester.   TZ9001

CROZIER, James, Private, 2nd Manchester Regt.
A Reservist, he was called to the Colours at the outbreak of war in August 1914, and proceeded to the Western Front in the following January. After taking part in the Battles of Neuve Chapelle, Ypres (II) and Festubert, he was transferred to Mesopotamia in October 1915, but was unfortunately killed in action on March 3rd, 1916, during the attempt to relieve the besieged garrison in Kut-el-Amara. He was entitled to the 1914–15 Star, and the General Service and Victory Medals.
"The path of duty was the way to glory."
108, Tame Street, Ancoats, Manchester.   Z9003

CROZIER, John, Sergeant, 2nd Grenadier Guards.
A serving soldier, he was drafted to France at the outbreak of war in August 1916, and served with distinction in the Battles of Mons and Le Cateau, and in the Retreat from Mons, during which he was wounded in action. On his recovery, he took part in the Battles of Ypres (I), Neuve Chapelle, Hill 60, Loos, Albert, the Somme, Arras, Bullecourt, Ypres (III), Passchendaele and Cambrai, and was badly wounded on the Somme in March 1918. Invalided to England, he was discharged as medically unfit in the following October, and holds the Mons Star, and the General Service and Victory Medals.
108, Tame Street, Ancoats, Manchester.   Z9004B

CROZIER, J., Private, 3rd (King's Own) Hussars.
He joined in September 1917, and on completion of his training was engaged on important garrison duties at various home stations. Although unsuccessful in obtaining his transfer overseas, he rendered valuable services with his unit until his demobilisation in January 1919.
108, Tame Street, Ancoats, Manchester.   Z9002

CROZIER, L. (Mrs.), Corporal, Q.M.A.A.C.
She volunteered in June 1915, and rendered valuable services at Caterham, Shoreham, Abbey Wood and Woolwich. She was in charge of a working party of cooks, and carried out her responsible duties in a very exemplary manner, until her demobilisation in October 1918.
108, Tame Street, Ancoats, Manchester.   Z9004A

CRUISE, T., Guardsman, Grenadier Guards.
He volunteered in August 1914, and was engaged at the Guards Depôt in London. He rendered valuable services, but unfortunately contracted bronchitis, and was finally discharged in November 1915, as medically unfit for further duty.
110, Chester Road, Hulme, Manchester.   TZ9005

CRUMLEY, H., Private, King's (Shropshire L.I.)
He joined in May 1918, and after completing a period of training, served at various stations, where he was engaged on duties of great importance. He was unable to obtain his transfer overseas before the cessation of hostilities, but later proceeded with the Army of Occupation to Germany, where he served for five months. He was demobilised on his return home in April 1919.
85, Dale Street, Hulme, Manchester.   Z5772

CUDDY, H., Private, 2nd Lancashire Fusiliers.
Already in the Army when war broke out, he was immediately sent to France with the First Expeditionary Force. There he served throughout the Battle and Retreat from Mons, and later took part in the Battles of Loos, Somme (I), Arras, Messines and Ypres. He served with the Transport section in the Retreat and Advance of 1918, and was also present at the Advance into Germany. He was discharged in March 1919, after ten years' service, and holds the Mons Star, and the General Service and Victory Medals.
11, Francisco Street, Collyhurst, Manchester.   Z10072

CUFF, E. J., Private, 1/8th King's (Liverpool Regt.)
Volunteering in May 1915, he was drafted to the Western Front three months later and there took part in the Battles of Loos, St. Eloi, Albert, Vimy Ridge, the Somme, Beaucourt, Arras and Messines, and many minor engagements. He fell fighting at the third Battle of Ypres in July 1917. He was entitled to the 1914–15 Star, and the General Service and Victory Medals.
"His memory is cherished with pride."
2, Albany Street, Ardwick, Manchester.   Z5773

CULLEN, C., Private, Manchester Regiment.
He volunteered in July 1915, and on completion of his training was drafted six months later to the Western Front. There he did good work with his unit in many important engagements, including those at St. Eloi, Loos and Vimy Ridge, and fell fighting in the Battle of the Somme on July 1st, 1916. He was entitled to the General Service and Victory Medals.
"His life for his Country."
24, Wood Street, Harpurhey, Manchester.   Z11210B

CULLEN, F., Private, 4th King's (Liverpool Regt.)
Joining in August 1916, he was sent to France in the following month and there saw severe fighting in various sectors of the Front. He took part in the Battles of the Ancre, Arras, Messines, Ypres and Cambrai and other engagements, and was gassed, wounded in action and taken prisoner on the Somme in March 1918. Held in captivity in Germany until after the cessation of hostilities, he was finally demobilised in September 1919, and holds the General Service and Victory Medals.
41, Orchard Street, Greenheys, Manchester.   Z5774

CULLEN, R., Corporal, Lancashire Fusiliers.
He volunteered in June 1915, and proceeding to the Western Front later in the same year, took a prominent part in the Battles of Loos, Albert, the Somme, Arras, Vimy Ridge, Bullecourt, Messines, Ypres (III), Passchendaele, Cambrai and Amiens, and in the Retreat and Advance of 1918. He was demobilised in May 1919, and holds the 1914–15 Star, and the General Service and Victory Medals.
29, Halton Street, Ancoats, Manchester.   Z10073

CULLEN, T., Private, 2nd Manchester Regiment.
Mobilised in August 1914, he was drafted to the Western Front in time to take part in the Retreat from Mons. He saw much heavy fighting in various other sectors until severely wounded in action in the first Battle of Ypres. He was invalided home in December 1914, and was discharged as medically unfit for further service in July 1915, and holds the Mons Star, and the General Service and Victory Medals.
8, Hibbert Street, Hulme, Manchester.   Z5775

CULLEY, C. H., Private, Royal Berkshire Regiment.
Volunteering in September 1914, he proceeded to France in the following July. In this theatre of war he took part in several engagements, including the first Battle of the Somme, where he was wounded in 1916. As a result he was invalided home and discharged as medically unfit in September 1916. He holds the 1914–15 Star, and the General Service and Victory Medals.
11, Zena Street, Ancoats, Manchester.   Z9006

CULLEY, H., Private, Loyal North Lancashire Regt.
He was mobilised in August 1914, and was immediately drafted to the Western Front, where he tok part in the fighting at Mons. He also served through the Battles of Le Cateau, La Bassée, Ypres, Loos, Albert, the Somme, Arras and Cambrai and other engagements, fought also in the Retreat and Advance of 1918, and was gassed at Ypres. He was discharged in April 1919, and holds the Mons Star, and the General Service and Victory Medals.
38, Gorton Street, Ardwick, Manchester.   Z5776

CULLEY, J. H., Pte. (Signaller), Manchester Regt.
He volunteered in September 1914, and in the following year proceeded to France, where he was wounded in action at Ypres. As a result he was sent to the Base, but on his recovery, returned to his unit and played a prominent part in the Battle of the Somme, but was again wounded in July 1916. He was invalided home, and after hospital treatment in Wales, returned to the Western Front, where he was wounded on two other occasions. He was twice mentioned in Despatches for conspicuous bravery in repairing telephone wires under heavy shell-fire. He holds the 1914–15 Star, and the General Service and Victory Medals, and was demobilised in April 1919. 11, Zena Street, Ancoats, Manchester.   Z9007

CULLEY, J. W., Lieut., 2nd Manchester Regiment.
He volunteered in March 1915, and in September of that year was drafted to the Western Front. Whilst in this theatre of war, he took part in many important engagements, including the Battles of Albert, Vimy Ridge, Arras, Bullecourt and Cambrai, and was twice wounded in action on the Somme—in July 1916, and again in April 1918. He was invalided from the Army in March 1919, and holds the 1914–15 Star, and the General Service and Victory Medals.
23, Etruria Street, Longsight, Manchester.   Z5777

CUMBERBIRCH, E., Pte., 2nd Loyal N. Lancs. Regt.
He volunteered in August 1914, and in January 1915 proceeded to France, where he was in action at Armentières, Bullecourt, Ypres, Passchendaele, the Somme, Cambrai, and in the 1918 Retreat and Advance. He was wounded at Havrincourt in September 1918, and was demobilised in the following year. Shortly afterwards he re-enlisted for a further period of service, and holds the 1914-15 Star, and the General Service and Victory Medals.
36, Hood Street, Ancoats, Manchester.   Z11412

CUMERFORD, T., Private, 1st Manchester Regiment.
Volunteering in August 1914, he sailed for France in the following March and was in action in the Battles of Ypres and Loos, and was wounded. On his recovery he proceeded to Mesopotamia and fought at Kut and in many other engagements and was again wounded. Returning to France he was engaged in heavy fighting on the Somme and at Ypres and Passchendaele and during the Retreat and Advance. In September 1918 he was wounded, and returning to England, received hospital treatment. Subsequently he was demobilised in February 1919, and holds the 1914–15 Star, and the General Service and Victory Medals.
13, League Street, Rochdale Road, Manchester.   Z9495

CUMMING, F., Private, 19th Manchester Regiment.
He joined in August 1916, and on completing his training in the following January, was drafted to the Western Front. In this seat of war he took part in engagements on the Ancre and at Arras, where he was badly wounded and consequently invalided home. He was discharged in September 1917 as medically unfit for further service, and holds the General Service and Victory Medals.
2, Carver Street, Hulme, Manchester   Z9008B

CUMMING, A., Driver, R.A.S.C.
He volunteered in November 1914, and in the following year was drafted to France. There he was engaged on important duties conveying supplies to the forward areas during the Battles of Loos, the Somme, Passchendaele, Lens, Bapaume and Havrincourt. He contracted influenza and in consequence was invalided home and was demobilised in March 1919. He rejoined shortly afterwards and returned to France, where he served until he again contracted influenza and was finally demobilised in May 1920. He holds the 1914–15 Star, and the General Service and Victory Medals.
2, Carver Street, Hulme, Manchester.   Z9008A

CUMMINGS, C., Private, 2nd East Lancashire Regt.
He volunteered in September 1914, and proceeded to France in the following February. During his service in this theatre of war he took part in much heavy fighting in various sectors of the Front, including the Battles of Loos, the Somme and Messines. After the cessation of hostilities, he returned to England and was demobilised in March 1919, holding the 1914–15 Star, and the General Service and Victory Medals.
10, Lawrence Street, Gorton, Manchester.   Z10075

CUMMINGS, L., Corporal, King's (Liverpool Regt.)
Joining in February 1916, he was first retained on important duties with his unit at various stations. He then proceeded to the Western Front and took an active part in many important engagements, including the Battles of Arras, Messines, Ypres (III), Cambrai, and the Retreat and Advance of 1918. After the Armistice he proceeded to Germany with the Army of Occupation and saw service there until he returned to England, and was demobilised in September 1919, holding the General Service and Victory Medals.
26, Cookson Street, Ancoats, Manchester.   Z10074

CUMMINGS, R., Private, East Yorkshire Regiment.
He joined in May 1916, and on completing a term of training in the following November, was drafted to India. There he was engaged on important garrison duties at Calcutta and various other stations, and rendered valuable services with his unit until August 1919, when he returned home for demobilisation. He holds the General Service and Victory Medals.
32, Robson Street, Hulme, Manchester.   Z5778

CUMMINGS, W., Private, Lancashire Fusiliers.
He joined in July 1916, and underwent a period of training prior to his being drafted to France. Here he took part in several engagements, including the Battles of Arras, Bullecourt, Messines, Ypres, Passchendaele and Cambrai, and in the Retreat and Advance of 1918, and was gassed and twice wounded in action. He was demobilised in February 1919, and holds the General Service and Victory Medals.
107, Hamilton Street, Collyhurst, Manchester.   Z9009

CUMMINS, J., Private, 2nd Manchester Regiment.
Mobilised at the outbreak of war in August 1914, he proceeded to France with the First Expeditionary Force and took part in much severe fighting before being seriously wounded in the spine at the Battle of Neuve Chapelle. He was invalided from the Army in October 1915, and after a lingering illness, unfortunately died from the effects of his wounds on December 20th, 1918. He was entitled to the 1914 Star, and the General Service and Victory Medals.
" A costly sacrifice upon the altar of freedom."
10, Lawrence Street, Gorton, Manchester.   Z10076

CUNDALL, J., Rifleman, 1st Rifle Brigade.
He volunteered at the outbreak of hostilities in August 1914, and shortly afterwards proceeded to the Western Front. During his service in this seat of war, he took part in the Battles of Neuve Chapelle, Hill 60 and Ypres. He was unfortunately killed in action on April 27th, 1915, and was entitled to the 1914–15 Star, and the General Service and Victory Medals.
" Whilst we remember, the sacrifice is not in vain."
12, Anderton Street, West Gorton, Manchester.   Z10077C

CUNDALL, Jane (Miss), Special War Worker.
In May 1915, this lady volunteered for work of National importance, and was engaged at Messrs. Brooks and Doxeys' Munition Factory. Her duties chiefly consisted of testing fuses and varnishing shells. She rendered valuable services until December 1916, when she relinquished her duties.
12, Anderton Street, West Gorton, Manchester.   Z10077B

CUNDALL, L. R. (Miss), Special War Worker.
This lady volunteered for work of National importance in August 1915, and for a period of three years during the war, was engaged at Messrs. Manns' Munition Factory, Leeds. Her duties consisted in examining the shells, and she rendered very valuable services until December 1918.
12, Anderton Street, West Gorton, Manchester.   Z10077D

CUNDALL, W. (Miss), Special War Worker.
For nearly three years during the period of hostilities this lady was engaged on work of National importance. She was employed by Messrs. Brooks and Doxeys' on the output of munitions, and rendered valuable services until February, 1919, when she relinquished her responsible duties.
12, Anderton Street, West Gorton, Manchester.   Z10077A

CUNLIFFE, H., Private, Manchester Regiment.
He volunteered in November 1914, and in the following July
was drafted to the Dardanelles, where he took part in the
Landing at Suvla Bay and the capture of Chunuk Bair. After
the Evacuation of the Gallipoli Peninsula, he was sent to
Egypt and saw service there until transferred to the Western
Front, and was in action in the Somme and Ancre sectors.
Invalided to England, he was discharged as medically unfit
for further service in February 1917, and holds the 1914-15
Star, and the General Service and Victory Medals.
41, Alice Street, Bradford, Manchester.   Z10078

CUNLIFFE, J., Private, R.M.L.I.
He volunteered in April 1915, and in the following month
was posted to H.M.S. "Virginia," attached to the Grand
Fleet in the North Sea. He was afterwards engaged in escorting American troops to and from Europe in H.M.S. "Caesar"
and in August 1917 was posted to H.M.S. "Triad" for duty
in the Mediterranean and Black Seas. In August 1919 he
was transferred to H.M.S. "Highflyer," on board which
vessel he was still serving in East Indian waters in 1920.
He holds the 1914-15 Star and the General Service and
Victory Medals.
131, Armitage Street, Ardwick, Manchester.   Z5780

CUNLIFFE, T. E., Private, 21st Manchester Regt.
He joined in January 1917, and in the following October was
drafted to the Western Front, where he played a prominent
part in the Battles of Cambrai, the Lys, the Aisne (III),
Amiens, Bapaume and Ypres (IV), and was wounded in
action at the second Battle of Cambrai in October 1918.
Returning to England in February 1919, he was then demobilised, and holds the General Service and Victory Medals.
49, Irlam Street, Miles Platting, Manchester.   Z10079

CUNLIFFE, W. Private, R.M.L.I.
He joined in April 1917, and was afterwards engaged as a
fireman in s.s. "Spen," "Manchester Importer" and "Vicker-
ston" and other vessels, plying chiefly to and from France.
He was for a time in hospital at Calais and in England, and was
finally discharged as medically unfit for further service in
May 1918. He holds the General Service and Victory Medals.
131, Armitage Street, Ardwick, Manchester.   Z5779

CUNNINGHAM, M., Private, 22nd Manchester Regt.
He volunteered in January 1915, and was engaged on important duties at various stations with his unit. He was
unable to obtain a transfer overseas owing to his being medically
unfit, but rendered valuable services until his discharge in
October 1917. 20, Tame Street, Ancoats, Manchester. Z9010

CUNNINGHAM, T., Pte., 3rd (King's Own) Hussars.
He joined in March 1916, and underwent a period of training
in Ireland prior to his being drafted to France. In this
theatre of war he took part in several engagements, including
the Battles of Ypres, Albert, the Somme and Passchendaele.
He was demobilised in November 1919, and holds the General
Service and Victory Medals.
37, Stonehewer Street, Rochdale Road, Manchester.   Z9011

CURLEY, G. W., Pte., 9th and 12th Lancs. Fusiliers.
Volunteering in August 1914, he first saw active service at
the Landing at Cape Helles in April 1915. He also took
part in the three Battles of Krithia, the Landing at Suvla
Bay and the capture of Chocolate Hill. After the Evacuation
of the Gallipoli Peninsula, he was sent to Salonika, where he
saw much heavy fighting on the Vardar, Doiran and Struma
fronts. In December 1917 he was transferred to France and
was in action at the Battles of the Somme (II), Amiens,
Bapaume and Le Cateau (II). He was wounded at Suvla
Bay in August 1915, and was eventually demobilised in February 1919, holding the 1914-15 Star, and the General Service and Victory Medals.
21, Nancy Street, Chester Road, Hulme, Manchester. Z10080B

CURLEY, J. T., Private, 23rd Cheshire Regiment.
Joining in November 1917, he was sent to the Western Front
shortly after the commencement of the Retreat in the following
year and took part in much severe fighting at Armentières,
the Nieppe Forest and Lille. He returned home for demobilisation in November 1919, and holds the General Service
and Victory Medals.
21, Nancy Street, Chester Road, Hulme, Manchester. Z10080A

CURLEY, M., Private, 1/8th Manchester Regiment.
Volunteering in August 1914, he was drafted to Egypt on
completing his training. In this seat of operations he took
part in the attacks on the Suez Canal and later proceeded to
the Dardanelles, where he saw much heavy fighting and was
badly wounded at Krithia. As a result, he was invalided
home and finally discharged in August 1916 as medically
unfit for further service. He holds the 1914-15 Star, and the
General Service and Victory Medals.
29, Baird Street, Chapel Street, Ancoats, Manchester. Z9012

**CURLEY, T., Private, Manchester Regt., and Air
Mechanic, R.A.F. (late R.F.C.)**
He volunteered in August 1914, and in March of the following
year was drafted to Egypt, whence he proceeded shortly
afterwards to the Dardanelles. There he was wounded in

action at the Landing at Suvla Bay and was sent to hospital
at Malta and finally invalided home. After his recovery
he served at various stations with the R.A.F. until demobilised
in February 1919, holding the 1914-15 Star, and the General
Service and Victory Medals.
38, Downs Street, Openshaw, Manchester.   Z5781

CURLEY, T., Special War Worker.
During the whole period of hostilities he was engaged on
responsible work at the Gaythorne Gas Works, being exempt
from service with the Colours on account of the National
importance of his duties. There, employed chiefly as a stoker,
he rendered very valuable services throughout the war.
59, Dalton Street, Hulme, Manchester.   Z5782A

CURRAN, F., Private, 11th Royal Scots.
He was mobilised in August 1914, and was shortly afterwards
drafted to the Western Front, where he took part in the
Battles of La Bassée, Ypres, Neuve Chapelle, Hill 60 and
Festubert. He made the supreme sacrifice, being killed in
action at Loos in September 1915. He was entitled to the
1914-15 Star, and the General Service and Victory Medals.
"His life for his Country, his soul to God."
9, New Murray Street, Oldham Road, Manchester. Z9013A

CURRAN, F., Private, 1st Manchester Regiment.
Volunteering in August 1914, he was drafted to the Western
Front in the following December and after taking part in
much severe fighting in the Ypres sector, was unfortunately
killed in action at the Battle of Hill 60 on April 26th, 1915.
He was entitled to the 1914-15 Star, and the General Service
and Victory Medals.
"He died the noblest death a man may die,
Fighting for God and right and liberty."
4, Duke Street, Miles Platting, Manchester.   Z10081A

CURRAN, H., Gunner, R.F.A.
Mobilised at the outbreak of war in August 1914, he was
immediately drafted to the Western Front, where he fought
in the Battle of Mons and the subsequent Retreat and also
took part in the Battles of Le Cateau, the Marne, La Bassée,
Ypres, Givenchy, Neuve Chapelle and Festubert. He was
unhappily killed in an air-raid on La Bassée on March 1st,
1916. He was entitled to the Mons Star, and the General
Service and Victory Medals.
"A costly sacrifice upon the altar of freedom."
104, George Street, Moss Side, Manchester.   Z5784

CURRAN, J., Private, 19th Royal Welch Fusiliers.
He volunteered in May 1915, and in June of the following
year landed in France and was in action in many parts of the
line. He fought at Havrincourt, the Somme, the Ancre,
Arras, Vimy Ridge and Ypres and throughout the Retreat
of 1918. In October of that year he was transferred to Italy
and served at various stations until he returned home and was
demobilised in March 1919. He holds the General Service and
Victory Medals.
7, Acorn Street, Rochdale Road, Manchester.   Z9496

CURRAN, R. Private, Labour Corps.
He joined in April 1916, and two months later proceeded to
the Western Front. In this theatre of war he was engaged
on many important duties in various sectors, including those
of Ypres, the Somme, Arras and Bapaume. He was demobilised in April 1919, and holds the General Service and Victory
Medals. 25, Higher Duke Street, Manchester.   TZ6055

CURRAN, T., Private, 15th Lancashire Fusiliers.
He joined in December 1916, and in the following March was
drafted to the Western Front. There he took part in the
Battles of Messines, Ypres, Lens, Cambrai, the Aisne (II)
and in the Retreat and Advance of 1918. He was unfortunately
killed in action in the Ypres sector on September 6th, 1918,
and was entitled to the General Service and Victory Medals.
"Great deeds cannot die."
34, Pownall Street, Hulme, Manchester.   Z9014

CURRAN, T., Private, 2/6th Manchester Regiment.
He volunteered in November 1914, and in January of the
following year proceeded to the Western Front, where he
served in various sectors. He took part in many important
engagements in this theatre of war, was wounded in action
on the Somme and at Ypres, taken prisoner at Givenchy in
March 1918 and again wounded behind the German lines.
Held in captivity until after the cessation of hostilities, he
was demobilised on his release in February 1919, and holds
the 1914-15 Star, and the General Service and Victory Medals.
18, Pump Street, Hulme, Manchester.   Z5783

CURRAN, W., Private, 10th Manchester Regiment.
He volunteered in January 1915, and in the following March
embarked for Gallipoli, where he fought in many engagements. After the Evacuation of the Peninsula, he was
transferred to France and was in action in the Battles of the
Somme, Arras and Ypres, where he was wounded in November
1917. On his recovery, rejoining his unit, he was engaged in
heavy fighting throughout the Retreat and Advance of 1918.
He was demobilised in February 1919, and holds the 1914-15
Star, and the General Service and Victory Medals.
48, Teignmouth Street, Collyhurst, Manchester.   Z9497

CURRIE, P., Private, 16th Manchester Regiment.

He joined in January 1918, and on completion of a period of training in the following May, was drafted to the Western Front, where he saw severe fighting in various sectors. He was for three months in hospital in France suffering from trench feet, and was finally demobilised in November 1919. He holds the General Service and Victory Medals.

182, Acomb Street, Moss Side, Manchester. Z5785B

CURRIE, R. G., Sergt., 13th Cycle Signal Corps and R.A.F.

Volunteering in November 1914, he was drafted to the Western Front in August of the following year, and there saw severe fighting in various sectors. After taking part in the Battles of Loos, Vermelles and the Ancre and many other engagements, he was in hospital for a considerable period suffering from trench fever. In March 1918 he was transferred to the R.A.F. and served in Ireland until his demobilisation in February 1919. He holds the 1914-15 Star, and the General Service and Victory Medals.

182, Acomb Street, Moss Side, Manchester. Z5785A

CURRY, H., Private, R.A.M.C.

He volunteered in August 1914, and after twelve months' training in various hospitals, was drafted to the Western Front. Whilst in this theatre of war he rendered valuable services on the lines of communication in the Somme, Cambrai and Passchendaele sectors. He was demobilised on his return home in February 1919, and holds the 1914-15 Star, and the General Service and Victory Medals.

75, Branson Street, Ancoats, Manchester. Z10082

CURRY, M., Private, South Lancashire Regimentt.

He joined in September 1916, and two months later was drafted to Mesopotamia. During his service in this theatre of war, he did consistently good work with his unit in many important engagements, including the operations against Kut-el-Amara, and was attached to the Loyal North Lancs. Regiment throughout the Advance beyond Baghdad. He was demobilised in March 1919, and holds the General Service and Victory Medals. 304, Mill Street, Bradford, Manchester. Z10083

CURTIS, G., Private, East Lancashire Regiment.

He volunteered in April 1915, and underwent a period of training prior to his being drafted to Mesopotamia. In this seat of operations he saw much heavy fighting and was unfortunately killed in action in April 1916. He was entitled to the 1914-15 Star, and the General Service and Victory Medals.

" The path of duty was the way to glory."

16, Charlton Street, Collyhurst, Manchester. Z9015B

CURTIS, W., Private, East Lancashire Regiment.

Volunteering in September 1914, he was drafted overseas early in the following year. Whilst on the Western Front he took part in several engagements, including the Battles of Neuve Chapelle, Festubert, the Somme, the Marne (II) and Cambrai (II), where he was wounded in action in September 1918. He was demobilised in September 1919, and holds the 1914-15 Star, and the General Service and Victory Medals. 16, Charlton Street, Collyhurst, Manchester. Z9015A

CUSHION, A., Private, Manchester Regiment.

He volunteered in May 1915, and underwent a period of training prior to his being drafted to France. There he saw much heavy fighting, and was in action at the Battles of Ypres (III), Passchendaele, Cambrai and Lens, and in the Retreat and Advance of 1918. He was demobilised in January 1919, and holds the General Service and Victory Medals. 18, Long Street, Ancoats, Manchester. Z6056D

CUSHION, C., Private, 9th Lancashire Fusiliers.

He volunteered in August 1914, and in the following year was drafted to the Dardanelles. In this seat of operations he took part in much severe fighting, was badly wounded in action at Krithia in June 1915, and consequently was invalided to Egypt. On his recovery, he was engaged on various important duties in Egypt, where he remained until his demobilisation in July 1919. He holds the 1914-15 Star, and the General Service and Victory Medals. 18, Long Street, Ancoats, Manchester. Z6056C

CUSHION, J., Private, 11th Lancashire Fusiliers.

Volunteering in August 1914, he was engaged on important duties and rendered valuable services for about four months. Owing to medical unfitness he was discharged in December 1914, and unfortunately died at home some time afterwards.

" His memory is cherished with pride."

18, Long Street, Ancoats, Manchester. Z6056A

CUSHION, T., Private, 11th Lancashire Fusiliers.

He volunteered in September 1914, and in the following year was drafted to France, where he took part in many engagements, including those at Loos, and St. Eloi. He made the supreme sacrifice, being killed in action at Vimy Ridge on May 19th, 1916. He was entitled to the 1914-15 Star, and the General Service and Victory Medals.

" His life for his Country, his soul to God."

18, Long Street, Ancoats, Manchester. Z6056B

CUSICK, T., Private, Tank Corps.

He volunteered in 1914, and on completing his training in the following year, proceeded to the Western Front, where he served in various sectors with the Yeomanry. After taking part in the Battles of Neuve Chapelle, Hill 60, Ypres and Festubert, he was transferred to the Tank Corps, and was again in action in the Somme sector and in the Battles of Arras and Ypres and other engagements. He was finally demobilised in 1919, and holds the 1914-15 Star, and the General Service and Victory Medals.

122, Victoria Square, Manchester. TZ11683

CUSWORTH, F., L/Corporal, R.E.

Joining in July 1916, he proceeded to the Western Front on completing three months' training, and was there engaged on important duties as a charge hand on the railways at Dieppe and various other places. He took an active part in engagements near St. Quentin in March 1918, and finally returned home in December of that year. He was demobilised in March 1919, and holds the General Service and Victory Medals.

32, Myrtle Grove, Ardwick, Manchester. Z5786

CUTHBERT, F. L., Pte., 2/4th East Yorkshire Regt.

Joining in 1916, he underwent a period of training and was then sent to Bermuda on important garrison duties. He was unsuccessful in obtaining his transfer to an actual fighting area, but rendered valuable services with his unit until his demobilisation in March 1919. He holds the General Service Medal.

10, Brunswick Street, West Gorton, Manchester. Z10084

CUTLER, A., Private, 11th Manchester Regiment.

He volunteered in August 1914, and in February of the following year proceeded to Egypt, where he served on the Suez Canal. He was shortly afterwards transferred to the Dardanelles and saw much severe fighting in Gallipoli until the Evacuation of the Peninsula, when he was drafted to the Western Front. There he took part in the Battle of the Somme and was unfortunately killed in action at Ypres in October 1917. He was entitled to the 1914-15 Star, and the General Service and Victory Medals.

" Great deeds cannot die."

3, Chapel Grove, Openshaw, Manchester. Z5787

CUTNER, E. W., Sapper, R.E.

He joined in May 1917, and after passing the trade test at Woolwich, was engaged on important duties as a crane driver at Richborough. Although unsuccessful in obtaining his transfer overseas, he rendered valuable services with his unit until January 1919, when he was demobilised.

5, Wrigley Street, West Gorton, Manchester. Z10085

CUTTING, A. E., Special War Worker.

For four and a half years he was engaged on work of National importance at Messrs. Finnigan's, Salford, and Messrs. Crossley's, Manchester. Employed first in making leather equipment, he was afterwards engaged on responsible duties in connection with the construction of aeroplanes, and rendered very valuable services until his discharge in July 1919.

21, Bremner Street, Ardwick, Manchester. Z5788

CUTTING, H. S., Private, East Yorkshire Regiment.

Volunteering in June 1915, he was sent to France in the following August and first saw heavy fighting at St. Eloi and Albert. He also took part in the Battles of Ploegsteert Wood, the Somme, Arras, Messines, the Lys and Amiens, where he was unfortunately killed in action in August 1918. He was entitled to the 1914-15 Star, and the General Service and Victory Medals.

" Nobly striving,
He nobly fell that we might live."

18, Gray Street, Ancoats, Manchester. Z10086

D

DAGOSTINO, A. (M.M.), Pte., 22nd Manchester Regt.

He joined in November 1916, and was drafted to France two months later. He was in action in the Battles of Bullecourt, Ypres and Passchendaele and in November 1917 was transferred to Italy. He fought in many engagements on the Piave and on the Asiago Plateaux, and in November 1918 was awarded the Military Medal for conspicuous gallantry and devotion to duty in the Field. Returning home he was demobilised in December 1919, and in addition to the Military Medal holds the General Service and Victory Medals.

21, Sanitary Street, Oldham Road, Manchester. Z9050A

DAGOSTINO, C., Private, 1/4th Cheshire Regiment.

Volunteering in November 1914, he was eventually drafted to Egypt in August 1916, but later proceeded to Palestine and was present at the fall of Jerusalem. In March 1918 he was transferred to the Western Front, where he took part in many important engagements during the Retreat and Advance, including the Battles of Ypres and Cambrai, and was wounded and gassed in action. He holds the General Service and Victory Medals, and was demobilised in March 1919.

23, Jersey Street Dwellings, Ancoats, Manchester. Z10087

DAGOSTINO, D., Private, 8th Royal Scots.
He joined in March 1916, and embarked for France in the following July. He was in action in the Battles of the Somme, Arras, Ypres, Cambrai and throughout the German and Allied Offensives of 1918. During his service overseas he was twice wounded, and after the Armistice proceeded with the Army of Occupation into Germany. He was stationed at Cologne until he returned home and was demobilised in September 1919. He holds the General Service and Victory Medals.
21, Sanitary Street, Oldham Road, Manchester.   Z9050B

DALE, A., Private, R.A.S.C.
Volunteering in November 1915, he was drafted to Salonika in the following August, and was engaged in important transport duties on the Doiran, Struma and Vardar fronts. He saw heavy fighting during the final Allied Advance in this theatre of war, and returning home after the Armistice, was demobilised in May 1919. He holds the General Service and Victory Medals.
43, Wardle Street, Holland Street, Manchester.   TZ9051

DALE, A., Private, Border Regiment.
Volunteering in June 1915, he completed his training and was retained at various stations on guard and other important duties. He was unsuccessful in obtaining his transfer overseas prior to the cessation of hostilities, but rendered valuable services until demobilised in March 1919.
6, Hancock Street, Rochdale Road, Manchester.   Z10548B

DALE, A. G., Private, 28th Manchester Regiment.
He joined in December 1916, and two months later proceeded overseas. Whilst in France he was in action in engagements at Arras, Albert, Bray, the Somme, Ypres, Lens, Cambrai and Loos and during his service on the Western Front was wounded on two occasions. In 1920 he was still serving, and holds the General Service and Victory Medals.
10, Lloyd Street, Rusholme, Manchester.   Z5794B

DALE, A. G., Drummer, 9th Loyal N. Lancs. Regt.
In September 1914, he volunteered, and after training at Tidworth, Bournemouth and Aldershot, proceeded overseas in January 1915. Whilst on the Western Front he saw heavy fighting in the Ypres sector, and was severely wounded in action at Loos in March 1916. He was sent back to England, and subsequently discharged as unfit for further service in May 1917, holding the 1914–15 Star, and the General Service and Victory Medals.
37, Crissey Street, Queen's Park, Manchester.   Z11484

DALE, A. W., L/Corporal, 15th Royal Scots.
He volunteered in October 1914, and after training at Edinburgh, he was in November 1915 drafted to the Western Front. There he was in action at Loos, Neuve Chapelle, Arras, Albert and the Somme, but was unhappily killed whilst fighting at Beaucourt on July 1st, 1916. He was entitled to the 1914–15 Star, and the General Service and Victory Medals.
" A valiant soldier, with undaunted heart, he breasted life's last hill." 8, Norway Street, Ardwick, Manchester. Z5793

DALE, F., L/Corporal, R.A.M.C.
Volunteering in November 1915, he was unsuccessful in obtaining a transfer to a theatre of war, and was retained in England throughout the period of hostilities. He rendered very valuable services at the second Western General Hospital at Manchester, where he carried out the responsible duties of chief technical assistant in the laboratories, and was demobilised in April 1919.
10, Lloyd Street, Rusholme, Manchester.   Z5794A

DALE, J., Driver, R.F.A.
He volunteered in January 1915, and proceeding to France in the following November, was in action in the Battles of Vimy Ridge, the Somme, Arras, Ypres and Cambrai. He also was engaged in heavy fighting during the German Offensive and Allied Advance of 1918. He was demobilised in May 1919, and holds the 1914–15 Star, and the General Service and Victory Medals.
63, Ainsworth Street, West Gorton, Manchester.   Z9052

DALE, J., Private, 2nd K.O. (Royal Lancaster Regt.)
He joined in October 1918, and was engaged on important duties at Dublin until the close of the war. After the Armistice he rejoined for a period of three years, and was drafted to Burma, where he was still serving in 1920.
6, Hancock Street, Rochdale Road, Manchester.   Z10548A

DALE, J. E., Private, King's (Liverpool Regiment).
Joining in April 1918, he could not obtain a transfer overseas before the termination of the war, but was retained on home service. In February 1919, however, he was drafted to France and later to Germany, where he was engaged on important garrison duties, until his demobilisation in November 1919.
11, Lingmoor Street, Chorlton-on-Medlock, Manchester.
X1026A

DALE, J. M. C. (M.M.) Staff-Sergeant, R.A.M.C.
At the outbreak of war he volunteered, but was retained on important work in England until April 1916, when he was sent to France and attached to a field ambulance. He served at Ypres, Arras, the Somme and Cambrai, and in the final engagements of the war. In 1918 he was awarded the Military

Medal for conspicuous gallantry in the Field, and was demobilised in January 1919, also holding the General Service and Victory Medals.
247, Morton Street, Longsight, Manchester.   Z5792

DALE, J. W., Driver, R.F.A.
He volunteered in October 1914, and five months later was drafted to the Western Front, where he took part in heavy fighting at Ypres and was gassed. On rejoining his Battery he was in action at Loos, Albert, Vimy Ridge, Messines, Ypres III, Passchendaele, and Cambrai, and in the final Retreat and Advance of 1918. After the Armistice he entered Germany with the Army of Occupation, and served at Cologne until demobilised in January 1920, holding the 1914–15 Star, and the General Service and Victory Medals.   Z1026B
11, Lingmoor Street, Chorlton-on-Medlock, Manchester.

DALE, W., Driver, R.A.S.C.
Volunteering in January 1915 he completed his training and was retained at various depôts with his unit on important transport duties. Owing to ill-health he did not obtain his transfer overseas and ultimately was invalided out of the Service in May 1917, after rendering much valuable service.
60, Birtles Street, Collyhurst, Manchester.   Z10549

DALEY, P., Private, Manchester Regiment.
Volunteering in September 1914, in the following April he was sent to the Dardanelles, where he took part in the Landing at Cape Helles, and in the subsequent fighting until the Evacuation of Gallipoli. Proceeding to Egypt, he served at Cairo for some months, and then embarked for France, where he was in action in the Loos sector, and at Vimy Ridge. He died gloriously on the Field of Battle in November 1916, during the first Battle of the Somme. He was entitled to the 1914–15 Star, and the General Service and Victory Medals.
" Great deeds cannot die."
19, Lever Street, Bradford, Manchester.   TZ9053

DALTON, R. H., Private, K.O.(Royal Lancaster Regt.)
He volunteered in August 1914, and in the following June was drafted to the Dardanelles, where he took part in the Landing at Suvla Bay, and in heavy fighting until the Evacuation of the Gallipoli Peninsula in January 1916. He then proceeded to Mesopotamia, and served in that theatre of war until the cessation of hostilities. Demobilised in March 1919, he holds the 1914–15 Star, and the General Service and Victory Medals.
38, Able Street, Collyhurst, Manchester.   Z10088

DALY, J., Private, Royal Irish Fusiliers.
Volunteering in August 1914, he was drafted in the following April to Gallipoli, where he served throughout the campaign there, and fought at Krithia I, II, and III, and Suvla Bay. After the Evacuation he proceeded with the relief force to Mesopotamia, and was in action at Sanna-i-Yat, and Kut-el-Amara. In January 1917 he was sent to France, and took an active part in engagements on the Marne, and at Passchendaele, and Le Cateau. Demobilised in June 1919, he holds the 1914–15 Star, and the General Service and Victory Medals.
32, Stockton Street, Chorlton-on-Medlock, Manchester. Z5795

DANCE, H., Pte., King's Own (Royal Lancaster Regt.)
He volunteered in November 1914, but was unable to procure a transfer overseas on account of defective eyesight. He was stationed on Salisbury Plain, and at Aldershot for nearly three years, and was then transferred to the military police, with whom he did excellent work at Wareham and Bournemouth. In February 1918 he was discharged from the Army as unfit for further service.
4, Small Street, Ardwick, Manchester.   Z5796

DANCE, T., Private, Lancashire Fusiliers.
Volunteering in June 1915, he was drafted overseas in January 1916. During his service in France he saw heavy fighting in numerous sectors of the Front, and was in action in the Battles of the Somme and Ypres. In August 1918, he was gassed and invalided to Edinburgh, where he remained in hospital until his discharge in December 1918. He holds the General Service and Victory Medals.
18, Higher Duke Street, Miles Platting, Manchester.   Z6057

DANIEL, C. W., Private, 2nd Manchester and 20th Middlesex Regiments.
He volunteered in December 1915, and four months later was sent to the Western Front. There he was in action at Albert, Vimy Ridge, the Somme, and the Ancre, and was wounded at Arras, and invalided to England. On his recovery he returned to France, and experienced fierce fighting in the Passchendaele and Cambrai sectors. He was demobilised in March 1919, and holds the General Service and Victory Medals.
29, Garibaldi Street, Ardwick, Manchester.   Z5797

DANIEL, G., Private, 8th Cheshire Regiment.
Volunteering in April 1915, he proceeded seven months later to Egypt, where he served for five months. During that time he took an active part in engagements at Jiffjaffa, but was unfortunately killed in action at Katia on April 18th, 1916. He was entitled to the 1914–15 Star, and the General Service and Victory Medals.
" He died the noblest death a man may die,
Fighting for God and right and liberty."
20, Abram Street, Hulme, Manchester.   Z5798

DANIEL, J., Private, 18th Manchester Regiment.
He volunteered in November 1915, and after training at Grantham was sent to France in the following January. He was in action at Hill 60, Ypres, Loos, St. Eloi, and Albert, and fell fighting at Vermelles on May 11th, 1916, after only four months' active service. He was entitled to the 1914-15 Star, and the General Service and Victory Medals.
" Great deeds cannot die ;
They, with the sun and moon renew their light for ever."
32, Augustus Street, Brooks Bar, Manchester. Z5799A

DANIEL, J., L/Corporal, K.O. (Y.L.I.)
He volunteered in April 1915, and in the following July was drafted to France, where he served in engagements at Ypres, Loos, St. Eloi, Albert, Vimy Ridge, and the Somme, and, wounded at Arras, was invalided to England. Six months later he was again in the firing line at Passchendaele, Cambrai, and the Marne and was once more wounded at Ypres, and sent back to hospital in Liverpool. He was demobilised in February 1919, and holds the 1914-15 Star, and the General Service and Victory Medals.
32, Augustus Street, Brooks Bar, Manchester. Z5799B

DANNATT, T. L., Pte., Northumberland Fusiliers.
Joining in September 1917, he was drafted to the Western Front in May of the following year, and during the Retreat and Advance of 1918, saw much severe fighting in the Merville, Estaires, and Cambrai sectors. He was demobilised on his return to England in October 1919, and holds the General Service and Victory Medals.
110, Edensor Street, Bradford, Manchester. Z10089

DANSON, R., Sergt., Lancashire Fusiliers.
He enlisted in the Army in May 1919, and in the following October was drafted to Ireland, where he served for a short time. He later proceeded to India, where he was employed on important garrison duties, and was still serving in 1920.
3, Somerset Square, Ardwick, Manchester. X5800B

DANSON, S., Private, 8th Manchester Regiment.
He volunteered for active service in September 1915, and on completion of a period of training was drafted in June 1916, to the Western Front, where he took an active part in numerous important engagements in various sectors of the line. He was wounded in action on two occasions, and also suffered from trench fever. He was demobilised in 1919, and holds the General Service and Victory Medals.
3, Somerset Square, Ardwick, Manchester. X5800A

DARBY, J. W., Private, 7th East Lancashire Regt.
Volunteering in October 1914, he was quickly drafted to the Western Front, and played a prominent part in the Battles of Neuve Chapelle, St. Eloi (where he was wounded in March 1915), and Loos. He laid down his life for King and Country at Hill 60 in January 1916, and was entitled to the 1914-15 Star, and the General Service and Victory Medals.
" Honour to the immortal dead, who gave their youth that the world might grow old in peace."
6, Grantham Street, West Gorton, Manchester. Z9976B

DARLINGTON, H., Pte., 2nd Lancashire Fusiliers and Tank Corps.
He volunteered in August 1914, and two months later proceeded overseas. Whilst serving on the Western Front he saw heavy fighting at La Bassée, Ypres, Ploegsteert, the Somme, Beaumont-Hamel, Arras, and Messines, and was wounded on two occasions, and also gassed. After joining the Tank Corps in 1917, he was in action at Cambrai. Demobilised in January, he holds the 1914 Star, and the General Service and Victory Medals.
15, Cheltenham Street, Chorlton-on-Medlock, Manchester. X5801

DARNBROUGH, S. W., Corporal, R.A.M.C.
He joined the Army in October 1916, and a year later was drafted to Russia, and stationed at Archangel. For nearly two years he was employed at the 85th General Hospital there, and during that time performed excellent work as a nursing orderly. In July 1919 he returned to England, and a month later was demobilised, holding the General Service and Victory Medals. 14, Derby Street, Ardwick, Manchester. Z5802

DAVENPORT, A. (M.M.), Sergt., Lancs. Fusiliers.
When war broke out he volunteered, but was retained on important duties in England until 1917, when he obtained a transfer to the Western Front. There he fought with distinction in numerous important engagements, and was twice wounded in action at Roisel. In March 1918, he was taken prisoner, and on his release in May of the following year returned home and was demobilised. He was awarded the Military Medal for conspicuous gallantry in the Field, and also holds the General Service and Victory Medals.
8, Ella Street, Harpurhey, Manchester. Z11485

DAVENPORT, B. A., Corporal, Lancashire Fusiliers.
Volunteering in September 1914, he was on completion of his training in May 1915 drafted overseas. During his service on the Western Front he took an active part in numerous engagements, including those at Loos, Neuve Chapelle, Vimy Ridge, St. Eloi, St. Pol, Ploegsteert Wood, the Somme, Arras, Bullecourt, Messines, Ypres, and Nouvillion. He was also in action in the Retreat and Advance of 1918, and was demobilised in

February 1919, holding the 1914-15 Star, and the General Service and Victory Medals.
51, Hendham Vale, Collyhurst, Manchester. Z11486C

DAVENPORT, C., Private, 1st Manchester Regt.
He volunteered in August 1914, and a month later was sent to France, where he fought in the Battles of the Marne, La Bassée, Ypres, Neuve Chapelle, Hill 60, and Festubert. In December 1915, he was drafted to Mesopotamia, and took part in engagements at Kut-el-Amara, but on February 9th,1917, fell fighting at Kut II. He was entitled to the 1914 Star, and the General Service and Victory Medals.
" His life for his Country."
10, Somerset Square, Ardwick, Manchester. Z5806

DAVENPORT, C., Private, 8th Manchester Regt.
Volunteering in April 1915, he was a month later drafted to the Western Front, where he was in action at Ypres, Festubert, and Loos, but in December 1915, was transferred to Mesopotamia. In this theatre of war he saw fierce fighting at Um-el-Hannah and Sanna-i-Yat, and was unhappily killed in action at Kut in January 1917. He was entitled to the 1914-15 Star, and the General Service and Victory Medals.
" Great deeds cannot die."
35, Garibaldi Street, Ardwick, Manchester. Z5804B

DAVENPORT, C. S., Private, R.A.M.C.
He was mobilised in August 1914, and at once proceeded with the first Expeditionary Force to the Western Front. In this theatre of war, he was in action in the Battles of Mons, Le Cateau, La Bassée, Ypres, St. Eloi, Hill 60, Festubert, and Loos. Owing to ill-health he was discharged from the Army as medically unfit in February 1917, and holds the Mons Star, and the General Service and Victory Medals.
51, Hendham Vale, Collyhurst, Manchester. Z11486A

DAVENPORT, J., Sapper, R.E.
He joined in January 1917, and a month later was drafted to the Western Front, where he was at first employed in guarding railways. Later, he took an active part in engagements at Arras, Ypres, Cambrai, the Somme, Bapaume, Havrincourt, and Le Cateau, and remained in France until July 1919, when he was demobilised, holding the General Service and Victory Medals.
26, Callender Street, Chorlton-on-Medlock, Manchester. Z5807

DAVENPORT, J., Private, Welch Regiment.
He volunteered in October 1915, and after a period of training proceeded five months later to the Western Front, where he served for three years. During that time he took part in engagements in different sectors of the line, and was also in action at Albert, Vimy Ridge, the Somme I, Arras, Ypres, Cambrai, the Somme II, Bapaume, Havrincourt, and Le Cateau. Demobilised in March 1919, he holds the General Service and Victory Medals.
35, Garibaldi Street, Ardwick, Manchester. Z5805

DAVENPORT, J., Private, 8th Manchester Regt.
He volunteered in October 1914, and was retained until November 1916, on various important duties in England. He then crossed to France and fought in many important engagements, including those at the Ancre, Vimy Ridge, Bullecourt, Ypres, where he was wounded, and in the Retreat and Advance of 1918. After returning to England he was demobilised in February 1919, and holds the General Service and Victory Medals. 5, Phelan Street, Collyhurst, Manchester. Z10553

DAVENPORT, J. A., Private, 13th Manchester Regt.
Volunteering in November 1914, he proceeded in the following year to France, where he fought at Neuve Chapelle, St. Eloi, Hill 60, and Ypres. He took part in the Landing at Salonika in 1915, and was in action on the Doiran front until August 1916, when he was invalided to England with heart trouble. After receiving treatment at numerous hospitals, he was eventually discharged in January 1919, and holds the 1914-15 Star, and the General Service and Victory Medals.
36, Wenlock Street, Hulme, Manchester. Z5809

DAVENPORT, S., Corporal, 3rd Lancashire Fusiliers.
When war broke out he volunteered, and in May 1915 was drafted to the Western Front. There he experienced fierce fighting at Loos, St. Eloi, and Albert, and was wounded in the Battle of the Somme. On his recovery he returned to the firing line, and took an active part in engagements at Arras, Ypres, Cambrai, the Somme, the Marne, and Le Cateau. He was demobilised in February 1919, and holds the 1914-15 Star, and the General Service and Victory Medals.
35, Garibaldi Street, Ardwick, Manchester. Z5804A

DAVENPORT, W., Private, 15th S. Lancs. Regt.
He volunteered in April 1915, and proceeding to Gallipoli in the following December, was in action during the Evacuation of the Peninsula. He then was drafted to Mesopotamia, and whilst taking part in the Capture of Kut was wounded. On his recovery he saw heavy fighting on the Tigris, and in 1916 was transferred to Salonika, where he served at Monastir. Returning to England in April 1917, he unfortunately died from influenza at Barrow-in-Furness on July 1st, 1918. He was entitled to the 1914-15 Star, and the General Service and Victory Medals. " His memory is cherished with pride."
7, Melbourne Street, Hulme, Manchester. Z5808

DAVEY, S. E., Sergt., 1/5th Duke of Cornwall's Light Infantry.
Volunteering in December 1915, he proceeded in the following May to France where he took a conspicuous part in fierce fighting at Vimy Ridge, the Somme, Arras, Ypres, and Passchendaele, and was wounded at Cambrai in 1917. On returning to the firing line he was in action at Havrincourt, Epéhy, and Cambrai, and after the Armistice was employed on important garrison and guard duties at Namur until September 1919, when he was demobilised, holding the General Service and Victory Medals.
221, Earl Street, Longsight, Manchester.   Z5810

DAVIDSON, E., Rflmn., 1st Cameronians (Scottish Rifles).
A Reservist, he was called to the Colours in August 1914, and shortly afterwards was drafted to the Western Front, where he took part in the Battles of Neuve Chapelle, Ypres (II), Festubert, Loos, and Albert. He died gloriously on the Field of Battle on July 15th, 1916, during the Somme Offensive, and was entitled to the 1914-15 Star, and the General Service and Victory Medals.
" A valiant Soldier, with undaunted heart he breasted life's last hill."
34, Bath Street, Miles Platting, Manchester.   Z10090

DAVIDSON, J. S., Private, 1/4th R. Scots Fusiliers.
Joining in February 1916, he was retained on home service for two years, and was then drafted overseas. Whilst serving in France he saw heavy fighting in the Arras, Albert, Cambrai, Ypres, Passchendaele, the Somme, and Kemmel sectors, and was wounded at Bullecourt in March 1918. On rejoining his unit he was again in action at Cambrai, and was gassed and invalided to England. In February 1919 he was demobilised, and holds the General Service and Victory Medals.
45, Cowesby Street, Moss Side, Manchester.   TZ5811 .

DAVIDSON, W., Driver, R.H.A.
Volunteering in November 1914, he embarked for the Western Front three months later and fought in many parts of the line, including the Arras, Ypres, Cambrai, and Somme sectors. In 1917 he sailed for India, where he was engaged on garrison duties at various stations until the cessation of hostilities. Returning to England, he was demobilised in December 1919, and holds the 1914-15 Star, and the General Service and Victory Medals.
23, Neptune Street, Ancoats, Manchester.   Z9054

DAVIDSON, W., Private, 2nd Border Regiment.
Shortly after volunteering in September 1914, he was drafted to the Western Front, where he saw severe fighting in various sectors. He took part in the Battles of Ypres, the Ancre, Passchendaele and Cambrai, and many other important engagements in this theatre of war, and was wounded in action on the Somme in 1916. He was demobilised in April 1919, and holds the 1914 Star, and the General Service and Victory Medals.
1, Vine Street, Newton, Manchester.   Z11684

DAVIES, A., Private, 2nd Manchester Regiment.
Mobilised in August 1914, he quickly proceeded to the Western Front, and took a prominent part in the Battles of Armentières, La Bassée, Ypres, St. Eloi, Hill 60, Loos, and Albert, where he was badly wounded in action. As a result, he lost the sight of his left eye, and after hospital treatment, was invalided from the Army in June 1916, holding the 1914 Star, and the General Service and Victory Medals.
27, Spencer Street, Ancoats, Manchester.   Z10091

DAVIES, A., Private, Lancashire Fusiliers.
He joined in June 1916, and in the following December was sent to the Western Front, where he served for sixteen months. During that time he took part in many engagements, and was twice wounded in action. He was engaged in fierce fighting at Messines, Arras, La Bassée, and in many other sectors of the line. He was invalided to England in April 1918, and eventually demobilised in December of that year, holding the General Service and Victory Medals.
2, Avenham Street, Hulme, Manchester.   Z5823

DAVIES, A., Corporal, Lancashire Fusiliers.
In September 1914, he volunteered, and a year later proceeded to Egypt, where he was in action in numerous important engagements. In March 1916 he was sent to hospital for two months, suffering from dysentery, but at the end of that time returned to his unit, and did excellent work until June 1919, when he returned to England and was demobilised, holding the 1914-15 Star, and the General Service and Victory Medals.
172, Palmerston Street, Beswick, Manchester.   Z5820

DAVIES, A., Private, Royal Scots Fusiliers.
Joining in January 1917, he was on completion of his training at Edinburgh, sent in the following July to the Western Front. There he took an active part in important engagements at Arras, Ypres, Cambrai, the Scarpe, and the Sambre, and served in France until his demobilisation in February 1919. He holds the General Service and Victory Medals.
4, Tonge Street, Ardwick, Manchester.   Z5818B

DAVIES, A., Air Mechanic, R.A.F.
He volunteered in December 1915, and after passing the necessary tests proceeded in the following March to the Western Front. In this theatre of war he served at various aerodromes, engaged on important duties which demanded a high degree of technical skill. He performed exceedingly good work, until invalided home on account of ill-health, and after spending some time in hospital at Liverpool, was demobilised in February 1919, holding the General Service and Victory Medals.
54, Nelson Street, Bradford, Manchester.   Z5814

DAVIES, A. E., L/Corporal, East Lancashire Regt.
Volunteering in January 1915, he was drafted two months later to France. There he played a prominent part with his unit in strenuous fighting at Neuve Chapelle, St. Eloi, Hill 60, Ypres, Festubert, Loos, and Albert, and was reported missing after a heavy engagement at Vimy Ridge on May 27th, 1916. He was later presumed to have died on June 11th of the same year, and was entitled to the 1914-15 Star, and the General Service and Victory Medals.
" His life for his Country."
4, Edmund Street, Openshaw, Manchester.   Z5812

DAVIES, C. H., Sergeant, 6th Manchester Regiment.
He volunteered in September 1914, but was found to be medically unfit for transfer to a theatre of war. Retained at home he was stationed at Southport, Ramsgate, and Tunbridge Wells, employed training recruits, and rendered very valuable services until he was demobilised in February 1919.
3, Rose Street, Old Trafford, Manchester.   Z5821

DAVIES, C. W., Gunner, R.F.A.
He joined in April 1918, and was sent to France in the following August. During his service overseas, he was in action with his Battery at Bapaume, Amiens, Havrincourt, and Cambrai, and did excellent work. After the Armistice, he proceeded into Germany with the Army of Occupation, and served on the Rhine until February 1919, when he returned home, and was demobilised, holding the General Service and Victory Medals.
40, Edensor Street, Beswick, Manchester.   Z5815

DAVIES, D., L/Corporal, 8th Manchester Regiment.
Joining in November 1916, he was drafted four months afterwards to the Western Front. There he participated in several important engagements, including Messines Ridge, Passchendaele Ridge, Cambrai, and Havrincourt, and was wounded in December 1917, during a bombing raid near Cambrai. Returning home after the cessation of hostilities, he was demobilised in February 1919, and holds the General Service and Victory Medals.
10, John Street, Hulme, Manchester.   Z5819

DAVIES, D., Sapper, R.E.
He joined in March 1917, and after nine months' training was drafted to the Western Front. Whilst in this theatre of war, he took an active part in the Battles of the Somme, the Marne, and Cambrai, and in the Retreat and Advance of 1918. During the latter period of hostilities, he was engaged on special Tank Corps Work, and rendered valuable services. He holds the General Service and Victory Medals, and was demobilised in April 1919.
62, Beaumont Street, Beswick, Manchester.   Z10092

DAVIES, E., Private, Loyal N. Lancashire Regiment.
Joining in June 1917, he was drafted to the Western Front in the following November, and was in action in various parts of the line. He fought in many important engagements in the Retreat and Advance of 1918, and was wounded in the second Battle of Le Cateau in October. Returning home he received hospital treatment, and was discharged as unfit for further service in March 1919. He holds the General Service and Victory Medals.
56, Birtles Street, Collyhurst, Manchester.   Z10552C

DAVIES, E. (Mrs.), Special War Worker.
This lady volunteered for work of National importance, and from December 1915, until January 1918, was employed at Messrs. William Aytons', making shells. She subsequently was engaged making parts for aeroplanes at Messrs. Masons', Levenshulme, until November 1918. During the whole period of her service she did excellent work, completely satisfying her employers.
5, Grove Place, Longsight, Manchester.   Z5829

DAVIES, F. (M.M.), Private, 2nd Manchester Regt.
Volunteering in January 1915, he embarked for France in the following October, and was in action in the Battles of Albert, Ploegsteert, the Somme, Arras, and Ypres, but was wounded at Passchendaele. On his recovery he rejoined his unit and fought throughout the German and Allied Offensives of 1918. He was awarded the Military Medal for conspicuous gallantry and devotion to duty in the Field in securing wounded under heavy fire. After the Armistice he proceeded to Germany with the Army of Occupation, and served at Bonu until he returned home, and was demobilised in March 1919. In addition to the Military Medal, he holds the 1914-15 Star, and the General Service and Victory Medals.
4, Gatley Street, Ancoats, Manchester.   Z9055

DAVIES, E. T., Corporal, R.E.

When war broke out he volunteered for active service, and served with the Rifle Brigade at Aldershot for seven months, but was then discharged from the Army. He re-enlisted, however, in September 1915, in the Manchester Regiment, and was stationed at Southport and Ripon until 1917, when he joined the Royal Engineers. He was not successful in obtaining a transfer overseas, but did excellent work with his Battery until demobilised in February 1919.

25, Baguley Street, Miles Platting, Manchester.   Z9499

DAVIES, F., Private, Labour Corps.

He joined in March 1917, and a few weeks later was drafted to France. During his service in this theatre of war, he served with his Company at Arras, Bullecourt, Messines Ridge, Ypres, and Cambrai, and performed consistently good work, engaged in carrying rations to the front line, and also in road repairing. He returned home for demobilisation in October, 1919, and holds the General Service and Victory Medals.

8, New Street, West Gorton, Manchester.   Z5816

DAVIES, G., Private, R.A.S.C. (M.T.)

Joining in October 1916, he proceeded in the following May to Palestine. There he was attached to the anti-aircraft service, and performed very good work whilst engaged on motor transport duties. He served at Beersheba, Jerusalem, Jericho, Damascus, and other places, until January 1920, when he returned home, and was demobilised, holding the General Service and Victory Medals.

12, Thornhill Street, Hulme, Manchester.   TZ5822

DAVIES, G., Private, Manchester Regiment.

He volunteered in January 1915, and embarked for the Dardanelles in the following August. He was in action at the Landing at Suvla Bay, and in many other engagements of note. After the Evacuation of the Peninsula he was sent to France, and fought at Vimy Ridge, the Somme, Arras, Messines, Ypres, Passchendaele, Cambrai, and throughout the Retreat and Advance of 1918. He was demobilised in April 1919, and holds the 1914-15 Star, and the General Service and Victory Medals.

119, Ryder Street, Collyhurst, Manchester.   Z10550

DAVIES, G. T., Rifleman, 4th Rifle Brigade.

He volunteered in September 1914, and later in the same year was drafted to the Western Front, where he was wounded in action at Armentières, and sent to hospital at the Base. On his recovery he proceeded to Salonika, and served in this theatre of war until he contracted malaria. He was invalided home, and was subsequently demobilised in March 1919, holding the 1914-15 Star, and the General Service and Victory Medals.

12, Garratt Street, Newton, Manchester.   Z9498

DAVIES, J., L/Corporal, 15th Royal Scots.

He volunteered in October 1914, and during his training was engaged on guard and other important duties at Edinburgh Castle. Owing to ill-health he was not successful in obtaining his transfer overseas, but rendered valuable services until invalided out in May 1915. He subsequently died on September 7th 1920.

"His memory is cherished with pride."

60, Inkermann Street, Collyhurst, Manchester.   Z10551

DAVIES, J., Pioneer, R.E. (Signals).

He joined in January 1917, and completing his training, was stationed at various military centres on important duties with his unit. He was unsuccessful in obtaining his transfer overseas, but rendered valuable services until demobilised in January 1919.

111, Hamilton Street, Collyhurst, Manchester.   Z9056

DAVIES, J., Private, 11th Lancashire Fusiliers.

Mobilised in August 1914, he was soon drafted to the Western Front, and played an important part in the Battles of Ypres, St. Eloi, Loos, Albert, Ploegsteert Wood, Vimy Ridge, and the Somme He laid down his life for King and Country at La Bassée, at the end of 1916, and was entitled to the 1914 Star, and the General Service and Victory Medals.

"The path of duty was the way to glory."

24, Hinde Street, Gorton, Manchester.   Z10093

DAVIES, J., Pte., 8th Manchester Regt. and R.D.C.

He volunteered in September 1914, and in August of the following year proceeded to the Dardanelles. After taking part in several engagements there, he was sent to Salonika, and was wounded during heavy fighting on the Vardar front. Invalided home, he was later stationed in Ireland, where he was employed on guard and other important duties. He was demobilised in February 1919, and holds the 1914-15 Star, and the General Service and Victory Medals.

4, Tonge Street, Ardwick, Manchester.   Z5818A

DAVIES, J. H., Private, 15th Welch Regiment.

He joined in October 1916, and on completion of his training was drafted to the Western Front, where he took part in the 3rd Battle of Ypres, and in heavy fighting in other important sectors. He died gloriously on the Field of Battle on the Somme on May 3rd, 1918, during the Retreat. He was entitled to the General Service and Victory Medals.

"And doubtless he went in splendid company."

1, July Street, Chorlton-on-Medlock, Manchester.   Z10094

DAVIES, J. J., Private, 3rd Lancashire Fusiliers.

He joined in June 1917, and later in the same year was drafted to the Western Front, where he took part in severe fighting at Armentières, La Bassée, Arras, Cambrai, Albert, St. Eloi, and Montauban, and in the Retreat and Advance of 1918. Later he was sent to Egypt, and was transferred to the 25th King's (Liverpool Regiment), with which unit he served at Port Said until his return to England for demobilisation in 1920. He holds the General Service and Victory Medals.

52, Granville Place, Ancoats, Manchester.   Z10095

DAVIES, M. G., Gunner (Signaller), R.F.A.

He joined in May 1917, and later proceeding to the Western Front, served there until the termination of hostilities. He was in action on the Somme front during the Retreat of 1918, and fought at Amiens and Bapaume during the Advance in the same year. After the Armistice he was sent to Germany, where he served with the Army of Occupation, and was demobilised on his return home in October 1919. He holds the General Service and Victory Medals.

9, Russell Square, Hyde Street, Hulme, Manchester.   Z5824

DAVIES, R. V., Private, King's (Liverpool Regt.)

Volunteering in May 1915, he was shortly afterwards sent to France. There he participated in strenuous fighting at Ypres, Festubert, Loos, Albert, and Vimy Ridge, and did excellent work, until he fell in action on the Somme in April 1917. He was entitled to the 1914-15 Star, and the General Service and Victory Medals.

"Whilst we remember the sacrifice is not in vain."

16, Rosebery Street, Moss Side, Manchester.   TZ5830

DAVIES, S., Pte., 2nd K.O. (Royal Lancaster Regt.)

Mobilised at the commencement of hostilities he was at once drafted to the Western Front, and was in action in many of the earliest operations of the war. He died gloriously on the Field of Battle during the Retreat from Mons, and was entitled to the Mons Star, and the General Service and Victory Medals.

"His life for his Country, his soul to God."

56, Birtles Street, Collyhurst, Manchester.   Z10552A

DAVIES, T., Pte., 1st Loyal North Lancaster Regt.)

A serving Soldier, mobilised at the commencement of hostilities he was drafted to Gallipoli in April 1915, and after taking part in the Landing at Cape Helles, fought in the first and second Battles of Krithia, Chunuk Bair, and in many other engagements until the Evacuation of the Peninsula. Proceeding to France in February 1916, he was in action on the Somme, at Ypres, Cambrai, and throughout the Retreat and Advance of 1918. In 1920 he was serving at Malta, and holds the 1914-15 Star, and the General Service and Victory Medals.

132, Tame Street, Ancoats, Manchester.   Z9057

DAVIES, T. J., Private, Royal Welch Fusiliers.

Joining in September 1917, he was drafted to France in the following December. During his service overseas he took part in heavy fighting on the Somme and Marne fronts, and at Cambrai, where he was wounded in October 1918. As a result, he was evacuated to England, and after spending some time in hospital at Leicester, was eventually demobilised in March 1919. He holds the General Service and Victory Medals.

77, Edensor Street, Beswick, Manchester.   Z5813B

DAVIES, W. (M.M.), Private, Manchester Regt.

He volunteered in December 1914, and three months later was sent to the Western Front, where he was in action at Ypres, Loos, the Somme, Bullecourt, Havrincourt and Cambrai, and was wounded at Vimy Ridge. On returning to the firing line he took part in heavy fighting in the final Retreat and Advance of 1918, and was again wounded. He was awarded the Military Medal for conspicuous bravery in the Field, carrying Despatches under heavy shell-fire. In January 1919 he was demobilised, and also holds the 1914-15 Star, and the General Service and Victory Medals.

17, Churchfield Street, Openshaw, Manchester.   Z9500

DAVIES, W., Rifleman, Rifle Brigade.

Volunteering in September 1914, he proceeded to France in July 1915, and took part in the Battles of the Somme (at Beaumont-Hamel), Arras and Ypres. He was wounded and taken prisoner at Arras in March 1918 and was held in captivity at Mannheim in Germany. In May 1918 he was released as an exchanged prisoner, and was invalided from the Army in the same month. He holds the 1914-15 Star, and the General Service and Victory Medals.

51, Ryder Street, Bradford, Manchester.   Z10096

DAVIES, W., Cpl., 1st Loyal North Lancaster Regt.

Mobilised at the outbreak of war, he proceeded immediately to France and fought in the Retreat from Mons and the Battles of Ypres, the Somme and Arras. He was also engaged in much heavy fighting throughout the German Offensive and Allied Advance of 1918, and during his service overseas was wounded on three occasions. He was demobilised in February 1919, after returning home, and holds the Mons Star, and the General Service and Victory Medals.

56, Birtles Street, Collyhurst, Manchester.   Z10552B

DAVIES, W., 2nd Air Mechanic, R.A.F.

He joined in April 1917, and after a period of training proceeded to the Western Front. There he served in various aerodromes, and was employed on important duties which demanded a high degree of technical skill. He rendered valuable services until January 1919, when he returned home, and was demobilised, holding the General Service and Victory Medals. 151, Morton St., Longsight, Manchester.　　Z5817

DAVIES, W., Private, Royal Berkshire Regiment.

Joining in April 1918, he was drafted in the following June to France. In this theatre of war he was in action at Bapaume, Amiens and in other sectors during the Advance prior to the signing of the Armistice, and was gassed in action at Le Cateau. Invalided home, he was three months in hospital, and was eventually demobilised in March 1919, holding the General Service and Victory Medals. 21, Avenham Street, Hulme, Manchester.　　Z5826

DAVIES, W., Pte., King's Shropshire Light Infantry and Trooper, West Somerset Dragoons.

He joined in March 1916, and after a period of training in Norfolk, was stationed at Whitchurch, and at the Curragh. He was not successful in obtaining a transfer to a theatre of war, but performed consistently good work whilst engaged on various duties of an important nature at home, until he was demobilised in September 1919. 44, Botham Street, Moss Side, Manchester.　　Z5827

DAVIS, B., Private, 6th Manchester Regiment.

He volunteered in October 1914, but was unable to procure a transfer to a fighting area. He was retained on home defence, and rendered very valuable services at Yarmouth, Lowestoft and other important stations. In May 1917 he was wounded during an air-raid over Shorncliffe, and in consequence was invalided out of the Army three months later. 4, Twemlow Street, Rochdale Road, Manchester.　Z11487

DAVIS, D. R., Private, 21st Manchester Regiment.

He volunteered in September 1914, and in the following July proceeded to France, where he took a prominent part in the fightiig at Armentières, St. Eloi, Albert and Vimy Ridge. Wounded on the Somme in July 1916, he recovered and was sent to Italy, where he served on the Piave. He was demobilised in March 1919, after his return home, and holds the 1914–15 Star, and the General Service and Victory Medals. 16, Stockton Street, Chorlton-on-Medlock, Manchester. Z5828

DAVIS, E. H., Rifleman, K.R.R.C.

He was mobilised in August 1914, and proceeded to France immediately. During his service on the Western Front he played a prominent part in the Battles of La Bassée, Ypres (I), Neuve Chapelle, St. Eloi, Ypres (II), Hill 60, Loos, the Somme, Arras, Vimy Eidge, Bullecourt and Cambrai. He was also in action throughout the Retreat and Advance of 1918, and was three times wounded. He holds the 1914 Star, and the General Service and Victory Medals, and was discharged in March 1919. 51, Hewitt Street, Gorton, Manchester.　Z10097B

DAVIS, P. F., Private, 19th King's (Liverpool Regt.)

He volunteered at the outbreak of war in August 1914, and in the following May was drafted to the Western Front. In this theatre of war he took part in many important engagements in various sectors in France and Belgium, including the Battles of Ypres, Arras, and Cambrai and was unfortunately killed in action at Ypres on October 8th, 1917. He was entitled to the 1914–15 Star, and the General Service and Victory Medals.
"Great deeds cannot die."
91, Halston Street, Hulme, Manchester.　　Z5825

DAVIS, Mrs., Worker, Q.M.A.A.C.

She joined in August 1916, and was quickly sent to France, where she was engaged on special duties at St. Valeriè, Etaples, Calais, Abbeville and Cambrai. She rendered valuable services with her unit until February 1919, when she was demobilised, holding the General Service and Victory Medals. 51, Hewitt Street, Gorton, Manchester.　　Z10097A

DAWES, F. J., Gunner, R.F.A.

He volunteered in November 1915, but was retained at his employment on the railway until he was called up for service in September 1917. Shortly afterwards, proceeding to France, he was in action at Arras, Havrincourt, Cambrai and Loos, and was later stationed at Douai. During his service overseas, he did valuable work, and was demobilised on his return home in May 1919, holding the General Service and Victory Medals. 8, Oldenburg Street, Longsight, Manchester.　　Z5831

DAWKES, A. Private, Manchester Regiment.

He joined in August 1916, and in the following April landed in France, where he was engaged in heavy fighting in many parts of the line, including the Arras sector. He gave his life for the freedom of England in October 1917 at Ypres. He was entitled to the General Service and Victory Medals.
"A costly sacrifice upon the altar of freedom."
110, Montague Street, Collyhurst, Manchester.　　Z9058

DAWSON, C. J., Trooper 7th (Princess Royal's) D.G.

He enlisted as a boy in 1902, and had served with his Regiment in India, China, West Africa and Egypt, prior to the outbreak of war in August 1914, when he was immediately ordered to France. There he took part in the Retreat from Mons and the Battles of the Marne, the Aisne, La Bassée, and Neuve Chapelle, where he was wounded. He was consequently discharged in May 1916, and holds the Mons Star, and the General Service and Victory Medals. 36, Ossory Street, Rusholme, Manchester.　　Z5835

DAWSON, F., Private, 15th Lancashire Fusiliers.

He volunteered in August 1914, and two months later was drafted to the Western Front. In this theatre of war he played a prominent part in the Battles of La Bassée, Neuve Chapelle, Ypres (II), Loos, Vimy Ridge and the Somme, but was unfortunately killed in July 1916. He was entitled to the 1914 Star, and the General Service and Victory Medals.
"His memory is cherished with pride."
2, Oldenburg Street, Longsight, Manchester.　　Z5832A

DAWSON, F. B., Gr., R.N.R., H.M.S. "Caledonian."

Mobilised in August 1914, he was posted to H.M.S. "Ionian," carrying munitions and foodstuffs from America, and was serving in this vessel when she was sunk by a submarine off the Coast of Wales on October 20th, 1917. He was rescued, and later served in H.M.S. "Caledonian," engaged on similar duties until August 1919, when he was discharged, holding the 1914–15 Star, and the General Service and Victory Medals. 2, Oldenburg Street, Levenshulme, Manchester. Z5832B

DAWSON, G., Gunner, R.G.A

Already in the Army, he was sent in September 1914 to Egypt. After service at Alexandria and Cairo he proceeded later to the Dardanelles, where he took part in severe fighting at Cape Helles, Krithia and Achi Baba. He was invalided home through ill-health, but in April 1918, after his recovery, was drafted to France and fought at Ypres, Cambrai and other engagements in the Retreat and Advance of 1918, during which he was wounded. He returned to England in February 1919, and was demobilised, holding in addition to the Queen's and King's South African Medals, the 1914–15 Star, and the General Service and Victory Medals. 20, Belmont Street, Collyhurst, Manchester.　　Z10554

DAWSON, G., Driver, R.E.

He volunteered in October 1914, and in the following year proceeded to France. There he served with his unit at Ypres, on the Somme front, and at Péronne and Cambrai, and performed uniformly good work. Invalided home, suffering from gas poisoning, he was for some time in hospital at Runcorn, and was eventually demobilised in February 1919. He holds the 1914–15 Star, and the General Service and Victory Medals. 4, Leonard Street, Openshaw, Manchester.　　Z5834

DAWSON, J., Private, King's (Liverpool Regiment).

Volunteering in September 1914, he was drafted in the following February to Egypt. After two months' service there, he was sent to Salonika, where he was employed with his unit on garrison and other duties of an important nature. He remained overseas until March 1919, when he returned home and was demobilised, holding the 1914–15 Star, and the General Service and Victory Medals. 1, Charles Street, Bradford, Manchester.　　TZ6058

DAWSON, J. A., Pte., Manchester Regt.,and R.A.S.C.

He volunteered in May 1915, and was retained at home on important duties until March 1917, when he was sent to France. There he served at Arras and Ypres, until the following November, when he was invalided home on account of ill-health and admitted to hospital in Sheffield. Upon his recovery, he was stationed at Heaton Park, and Romsey, Hants, until he was demobilised in May 1919, and holds the General Service and Victory Medals. 17, Clayburn Street, Hulme, Manchester.　　Z5837

DAWSON, M.A., Private, West Riding Regiment.

He joined the Army in November 1917, and in May of the following year was sent to the Western Front. There he did good work with his unit in engagements in the Aisne, Marne and Ypres sectors. He was wounded in action at La Cateau in October 1918, and sent to hospital in France. On his recovery, he was engaged in guarding prisoners of war in Germany, until demobilised in September 1919. He holds the General Service and Victory Medals. 67, Park Street, Hulme, Manchester.　　Z5836

DAWSON, T., Private, M.G.C.

He volunteered in October 1915, and early in the following year was sent to France. There he played a prominent part in heavy fighting at Ypres, Polygoneveld, Arras, and on the Somme, and was gassed in action in May 1918. As a result he was invalided home, and after recovering, served at the Machine Gun Corps Depôt, Alnwick, until he was demobilised in February 1919, holding the General Service and Victory Medals. 36, Stott Street, Hulme, Manchester.　　Z5838

DAWSON, P. Sapper, R.E.

He joined in March 1917, but was not successful in obtaining a transfer to a theatre of war. Retained at home, he served at Chatham, Bovington Camp, Salisbury Plain, Wool Camp, Christchurch, and Bournemouth, and was engaged on various duties of an important nature. He did exceedingly good work until he was demobilised in March 1919.

15, Teak Street, Beswick, Manchester. TZ5833

DAY, A., Driver, R.E.

He volunteered in March 1915, and in November of the same year embarked for France. There he rendered valuable service during the Battles of the Somme, Ypres, Kemmel, Passchendaele, Soissons and many other engagements in the offensives of 1918. In November 1918 he was discharged through illness due to his service, and holds the 1914–15 Star, and the General Service and Victory Medals.

32, Alexandra Street, Rochdale Road, Manchester. Z10555

DAY, R., A.B., Royal Navy.

He joined in July 1917, and in the following month was posted to H.M.S. "Cornwall." On board this vessel he was engaged on important escort duties in the Atlantic Ocean, plying between England and Canada, and rendered very valuable services. He was demobilised in January 1919, and holds the General Service and Victory Medals.

1, Burns Street, Bradford, Manchester. Z11685

DAY, W. A., Private, 8th King's (Liverpool Regt.) Liverpool Irish.

He volunteered in May 1915, and twelve months later was drafted to France, where he took part in heavy fighting on the Somme and Ancre fronts, and was taken prisoner. After spending seven months in captivity in Germany, he was repatriated, and was eventually demobilised in January 1919, holding the General Service and Victory Medals.

5, Tempest Street, Ardwick, Manchester. Z11612

DEAKIN, A., Private, 1st Lancashire Fusiliers.

Volunteering in August 1914, he was dratted to Gallipoli in the following June, but after taking part in heavy fighting during the Landing and subsequent Evacuation, was invalided home on account of ill-health. Upon his recovery he was sent to France and employed on police duties until February 1919, when he returned to England, and was demobilised in February 1919, holding the 1914–15 Star, and the General Service and Victory Medals.

6, Oliver Street, Bradford, Manchester. Z5839

DEAKIN, G., Private, R.A.O.C.

He joined in June 1917, and on completion of his training was engaged on important duties with his unit at various home stations. He rendered valuable services until July 1918, when he was discharged as medically unfit owing to heart disease.

73, Cromwell Avenue, Manley Park, Manchester. Z10098

DEAKIN, H., Air Mechanic, R.A.F.

He joined in October 1918, and completing his training was stationed at various depôts on important duties with his unit. He did not obtain his transfer overseas prior to the cessation of hostilities, but proceeded to France in April 1919, and served at St. Omer and Ypres. Returning home, he was demobilised in September 1919.

37, Amsworth Street, West Gorton, Manchester. Z9059B

DEAKIN, J., Air Mechanic, R.A.F.

Until joining in October 1918, he was employed at Armstrong-Whitworth's Works on the manufacture of armour plate. Completing his training he was engaged at various stations on important duties in connection with the defence of the South-east Coast against attacks by hostile air-craft. He did not obtain his transfer to a theatre of war prior to the cessation of hostilities, but rendered excellent services until demobilised in October 1919.

37, Ainsworth Street, West Gorton, Manchester. Z9059A

DEAKIN, R., Sapper, R.E.

He joined in September 1916, and proceeding later to France, served at Arras, Vimy Ridge, Bullecourt, Ypres, Passchendaele and Cambrai, and on the Somme and Marne fronts. Employed on various duties of an important nature, he rendered excellent service, and subsequently was similarly engaged at Amiens and Lille during the Advance of 1918. He was demobilised in September 1919, and holds the General Service and Victory Medals.

22, Birch Street, Hulme, Manchester. Z5840

DEAKIN, W., Sapper, R.E.

Volunteering in November 1915, he was drafted to Egypt five months later, and was engaged on special bridge construction work there until March 1917. He was then transferred to the Western Front, where he saw service fighting in the Ypres sector and during the Retreat and Advance of 1918. Demobilised on returning to England in March 1919, he holds the General Service and Victory Medals.

35, Albion Street, Miles Platting, Manchester. Z10099

DEAN, A. P., Private, R.A.S.C.

Joining in April 1916, he was retained on home service until 1918, when he proceeded overseas. Whilst on the Western Front he took part in severe fighting in the Ypres, Neuve Chapelle, St. Eloi, Aire, Cambrai, Arras and Albert sectors. He remained in France until 1919, and was demobilised in June of that year, holding the General Service and Victory Medals.

79, Elisabeth Ann Street, Manchester. Z9501

DEAN, C., Private, 3rd East Lancashire Regiment.

He joined in June 1916, and completed his training before being sent to France in the following January. Whilst in that theatre of war he took a prominent part in the Battles of Arras, Vimy Ridge, Bullecourt, Messines, Ypres and Cambrai, and was taken prisoner at Armentières in March 1918. Released after the Armistice, he was demobilised in August 1919, and holds the General Service and Victory Medals.

26, Geoffrey Street, Chorlton-on-Medlock, Manchester. Z5842

DEAN, C., Sergt., 7th East Lancashire Regiment.

Volunteering in September 1914, he was drafted to France early in the following year and served with distinction at the Battle of Neuve Chapelle, Festubert, Loos (where he was wounded in September 1915), Albert and the Somme, and was again wounded at La Boiselle in 1916. On this occasion he was invalided home, but returning to the Western Front on his recovery in 1917, again saw heavy fighting and was gassed during the Advance in 1918. He was demobilised in April 1919, and holds the 1914–15 Star, and the General Service and Victory Medals.

6, Ward Street, Gorton, Manchester. Z10100

DEAN, F., Private, 9th East Lancashire Regiment.

Volunteering in September 1914, he was sent to the Western Front in April 1915, but only served there fourteen months. He was then sent to Salonika, and after serving with distinction on the Doiran and Vardar fronts, was killed in action on September 19th, 1918, during the second Battle of the Vardar. He was buried at Salonika and was entitled to the 1914–15 Star, and the General Service and Victory Medals.

"Thinking that remembrance, though unspoken, may reach him where he sleeps."

8, Shrewbridge Street, West Gorton, Manchester. Z5843d

DEAN, G., Private, 1/8th Lancashire Fusiliers.

Eight months after volunteering in August 1914, he reached Gallipoli and took part in the Landing on the Peninsula. After serving with distinction in the operations on Achi Baba, he contracted enteric and was invalided home in June 1915. Four months later he was discharged as unfit and holds the 1914–15 Star, and the General Service and Victory Medals.

1, Newton Street, Hulme, Manchester. Z5844

DEAN, J., Corporal, Manchester Regiment.

Volunteering in November 1914, he was sent to the Western Front in the following July and was in action in the Battle of the Somme, and was wounded. On recovery he rejoined his Regiment and fought at Ypres, Passchendaele and in many engagements in the Retreat of 1918. Gassed in April 1918, he was admitted into hospital, and subsequently returned to England. He was demobilised in February 1919, and holds the 1914–15 Star, and the General Service and Victory Medals.

1, Iron Street, Bradford Road, Newton, Manchester. Z9060

DEAN, J., Private, 1/8th Manchester Regiment.

He joined in September 1916, and in the following January was drafted to the Western Front. Whilst in this theatre of war, he took part in many important engagements, including the Battles of Ypres and Cambrai, and was twice wounded in action. He was demobilised in November 1919, and holds the General Service and Victory Medals.

1, Greenshaw Street, West Gorton, Manchester. Z10101

DEAN, J., Private, 3rd King's (Liverpool Regiment).

Joining in February 1916, he was drafted to Salonika on completing his training in November of that year, and there took part in the recapture of Monastir and other engagements on the Doiran and Struma fronts. In December 1917, however, he was invalided home, suffering from malaria, but on his recovery in March of the following year, proceeded to the Western Front. There he fought in the Battle of Havrincourt and other engagements, served also through the Retreat and Advance of 1918 and was wounded in action at Le Cateau in October of that year. He was finally demobilised in August 1919, and holds the General Service and Victory Medals.

18, Walter Street, Hulme, Manchester. Z11686

DEAN, J., Private, K.O. (Royal Lancaster Regt.)

He volunteered in September 1914, and after more than a year's service in England, was sent to Salonika in October 1915. There he played a prominent part in the first and second Battles of the Vardar and the advance on the Doiran front, but owing to ill-health had to spend a month in hospital at the Base. Returning to the line, he resumed his duties and eventually reached England in March 1919, when he was demobilised. He holds the 1914–15 Star, and the General Service and Victory Medals.

1, Nuttall Street, Hulme, Manchester. Z5845

DEAN, J. E., Gunner, R.F.A.

Volunteering in May 1915, he was quickly sent to France and went into action at Ypres. He was then sent to the Base and employed as an instructor in gunnery for the remainder of the war. After rendering valuable services in this capacity, he was eventually demobilised in January 1919, and holds the 1914-15 Star, and the General Service and Victory Medals.
30, Robson Street, Hulme, Manchester.   Z5846

DEAN, R., Rflmn., 10th Cameronians (Scottish Rifles).

He volunteered in September 1914, and nine months later proceeded to the Western Front, where he was wounded in September during the Battle of Loos. Subsequently he saw heavy fighting at Arras, but received a second wound, and was gassed during the great Somme Offensive in July 1916. Attached to the Labour Corps on his recovery, he was engaged on salvage work and served on the Marne and at Amiens. He was demobilised in May 1919, and holds the 1914-15 Star, and the General Service and Victory Medals.
3, Charles Street, Bradford, Manchester.   Z5841

DEANE, W. N., Sapper, R.E.

He joined in September 1916, and completing his training was stationed at various depôts with his unit on guard and other important duties. He was not successful in obtaining his transfer overseas prior to the cessation of hostilities, but rendered valuable services until demobilised in December 1918.
84, Harrowby Street, Collyhurst, Manchester.   Z9061

DEARDEN, E., A.B., R.N., H.M.S. "Delhi."

He enlisted in July 1912, and during the war served in H.M.S. "Delhi" off the Coasts of Germany, Russia, the Canary Islands and Mexico. He was also engaged in laying mines in the North Atlantic. He performed valuable work throughout the duration of hostilities, and in 1920 was stationed at Chatham. He holds the 1914-15 Star, and the General Service and Victory Medals.
27, Walmer Street, Rusholme, Manchester.   Z5848

DEARDEN, F., Corporal, 6th Manchester Regiment.

He volunteered in February 1915, and eleven months later proceeded to Egypt, where he served on the Suez Canal and at Mersa Matruh, Agagia, Sollum, Katia, El Fasher, Romani and Magdhaba. In February 1917 he was invalided to England with heart trouble, but two months later was drafted to France, and there took an active part in heavy fighting at Ypres, the Somme, Arras, La Bassée and Albert. From August 1918 until his demobilisation a year later, he was employed on garrison duty in Wales, and holds the General Service and Victory Medals.
3, Beech Street, Hulme, Manchester.   Z5861

DEARDEN, J. W., Tpr., Westmoreland and Cumberland Hussars.

He joined in 1916, and in the following year was drafted to the Western Front. Whilst in that theatre of war he fought in the Ypres sector and was also in action during the Retreat and subsequent Advance in 1918. Returning home, he was demobilised in March 1919, and holds the General Service and Victory Medals.
70, Greville Street, Rusholme, Manchester.   Z5847

D'EATH, J. H., Pte. (Signr.), 1/8th Manchester Regt.

Volunteering in March 1915, he was drafted to Gallipoli in the following October, and fought in many engagements. After the evacuation of Gallipoli he proceeded to Egypt and saw much fighting during the advance across the Sinai Peninsula. In March 1917 he was transferred to France, and was in action at Epéhy, Ypres and Havriucourt, and was gassed. On his recovery he rejoined his unit and served throughout the Retreat and Advance of 1918. He was demobilised in February 1919, and holds the 1914-15 Star, and the General Service and Victory Medals.
29, Raglan Street, Ancoats, Manchester.   Z9062

DEBIO, A., Private, 21st Manchester Regiment.

He joined in October 1916, and was drafted to the Western Front in the following January. He was in action at Beaumont Hamel, Beaucourt and Arras, and in November 1917 was transferred to Italy. He was engaged in heavy fighting on the Piave and Asiago Plateaux and took part in the final Allied Advance in this theatre of war. During his active service he was twice wounded, once in France and once in Italy. He was demobilised in February 1919, and holds the General Service and Victory Medals.
24, Shelmerdine Street, Collyhurst, Manchester.   Z9063

DE BOTTE, L. M., Pte., 10th Royal Dublin Fusiliers.

Volunteering in October 1915, he proceeded to Ireland in the following April and took part in quelling the Rebellion. Two months later he was drafted to France and served as a Lewis gunner during the Somme Offensive. He also fought at Beaumont-Hamel, Arras, Albert, Ypres and the Ancre, and was wounded. Invalided home with trench feet, he was discharged as unfit in April 1918, and holds the General Service and Victory Medals.
53, Ducie Street, Longsight, Manchester.   Z5849

DEGNAN, J., Private, M.G.C.

He volunteered in August 1914, and proceeded to the Western Front in the following January. He saw much severe fighting at Armentières and Albert, and took part in the Battles of Ypres and the Somme, where he was wounded in action in July 1916. After hospital treatment at Rouen, he rejoined his unit and died gloriously on the Field of Battle at Arras on May 7th, 1917. He was entitled to the 1914-15 Star, and the General Service and Victory Medals.
"His life for his Country, his soul to God."
14, George Street, Newton, Manchester.   Z10102

DELANEY, H., Corporal, 8th Manchester Regiment.

He volunteered in September 1914, and after a course of training was drafted to France in the following year. During his service in this theatre of war he fought at Neuve Chapelle, Hill 60, Festubert, Albert and Vimy Ridge, and was wounded twice. He was taken prisoner in March 1918 during the German attack and was held in captivity until after the Armistice. After returning home, he was demobilised in October 1919, and holds the 1914-15 Star, and the General Service and Victory Medals.
28, Stonehewer Street, Rochdale Road, Manchester.   Z10556B

DELANEY, W. H., Corporal, 22nd Manchester Regt.

Volunteering in September 1914, he was engaged after the completion of his training at various stations on important band duties with his unit. He rendered valuable services throughout, but was not successful in obtaining his transfer overseas, and in April 1918 was discharged.
29, Stonehewer Street, Rochdale Road, Manchester.   Z10556A

DELL, F. C., Driver, R.A.S.C. (M.T.)

He joined in July 1916, and a year later was sent to Mesopotamia, where he took part in operations at Um-el-Hannah and Sanna-i-Yat during the Kut campaign. He also served at Baghdad, the Persian Hills, Tekrit and Mosul. Returning home, he was demobilised in August 1919, and holds the General Service and Victory Medals.
12, Russell Street, Moss Side, Manchester.   TZ5850

DENMAN, H., Private, 1st Loyal N. Lancashire Regt.

Joining in March 1917, he completed his training and was retained at various stations in England with his unit. He was unable to obtain his transfer overseas before the cessation of hostilities, but in March 1919 was sent to Malta, where he was still serving in 1920.
20, Brunswick Street, Hulme, Manchester.   Z5851

DENNIS, J., Private, 2nd King's (Liverpool Regt.)

Mobilised at the outbreak of hostilities in August 1914, he was immediately sent overseas. During his service on the Western Front, he took part in the Retreat from Mons. He was also in action at La Bassée, Ypres, the Somme and other important engagements until the cessation of hostilities. He was demobilised in January 1919, and holds the Mons Star, and the General Service and Victory Medals.
17, Gilson Street, Newton Heath, Manchester.   Z11895

DENNON, G. D., Private, 1st Manchester Regiment.

He joined in September 1918, but was not able to obtain his transfer to a theatre of war, when he had completed his training. He, however, rendered valuable services whilst stationed at various camps in England, and was ultimately demobilised in November 1919.
5, Ashbury Street, Openshaw, Manchester.   TZ5852B

DENNON, T., Private, Loyal N. Lancashire Regt.

Six months after volunteering in December 1914, he was sent to Mesopotamia and served there for a little over a year. He fought at Amara, Kut-el-Amara and Um-el-Hannah and on the Tigris, but in August 1916 was drafted to India. After being engaged on garrison duties at Calcutta for some time, he returned home and was demobilised in April 1919. He holds the 1914-15 Star, and the General Service and Victory Medals.
4, Ashbury Street, Openshaw, Manchester.   TZ5852A

DENSON, J., Private, 20th Cheshire Regt.

He volunteered in June 1915, and proceeding to France a year later, took a prominent part in the great Somme Offensive. He also fought on the Ancre front and in the Battles of Arras, Messines, Lens, the Lys, Cambrai and Le Cateau. He was demobilised in January 1919, and holds the General Service and Victory Medals.
19, Jackson Street, Ardwick, Manchester.   Z5853B

DENSON, W., Private, 10th Cheshire Regiment.

Volunteering in November 1914, he proceeded to France early in the following year and took part in the Battles of St. Eloi, Hill 60, Festubert and Loos. He was severely wounded during the Somme Offensive and was invalided home with shell-shock. Discharged later as unfit, he holds the 1914-15 Star, and the General Service and Victory Medals.
19, Jackson Street, Ardwick, Manchester.   Z5853A

DENT, A., Q.M.S., 19th Manchester Regiment.

After volunteering in September 1914, he was retained at home for some time, but was eventually sent to France in December 1915. He was in action at Loos, Neuve-Chapelle, Ypres, the Somme, Arras, Albert, and Cambrai, and also in the Retreat and Advance of 1918. He was demobilised in February 1919, and holds the 1914-15 Star, and the General Service and Victory Medals.

13, Bremner Street, Ardwick, Manchester.   Z5854B

DENT, F., L/Corporal, South Lancashire Regt.

Volunteering in September 1914, he proceeded a year later to the Western Front, and fought at Neuve-Chapelle. He also took part in the Battle of Loos, but on July 3rd was badly wounded during the Somme Offensive of 1916, and succumbed to his injuries three days later. He was entitled to the 1914-15 Star, and the General Service and Victory Medals.

"Nobly striving.
"He nobly fought that we might live."

13, Bremner Street, Ardwick, Manchester.   Z5854A

DENTITH, A., Private, 1st Manchester Regiment.

Volunteering in August 1914, he was sent to France in the following December and played a prominent part in the Battles of Neuve Chapelle, Hill 60, Ypres, Festubert, Loos, and Vermelles, where he was badly gassed in action in May 1916. He was invalided home, and after seven months in hospital was discharged as medically unfit for further service in December 1916, holding the 1914-15 Star, and the General Service and Victory Medals.

29, Stanley Street, West Gorton, Manchester.   Z10104

DENTON, H., Private, 2nd Border Regiment.

He joined in April 1916, and four months afterwards embarked for France. There he played a prominent part in the great Offensive on the Somme, but on January 10th, 1917, gave his life for King and Country on the Ancre front. He was entitled to the General Service and Victory Medals.

"Great deeds cannot die;
They, with the sun and moon renew their light for ever."

5, Milton Street, Bradford, Manchester.   TZ1064B

DENTON, J., Corporal, 20th Manchester Regiment.

Volunteering in August 1915, he was sent to the Western Front in June of the following year, and went into action at Delville Wood during the Somme Offensive. Wounded at Givenchy in September 1916, he spent some time in hospital in France and England, and was then transferred to the Labour Corps, and stationed at Boulogne. Demobilised in March 1919, he holds the General Service and Victory Medals.

23, Taylor Street, Bradford, Manchester.   TZ6059

DENTON, W., Bombardier, R.G.A.

Having enlisted in August 1913, he did not proceed overseas until February 1915. On reaching the Western Front he was in action at Ypres, Festubert, Loos, Albert, Vermelles, the Somme, Arras, the Ancre, Cambrai, Bapaume, and Le Cateau. He was invalided home in March 1917, owing to dysentery and ear trouble, but returned to the line in 1918. He was discharged in July 1919, and holds the 1914-15 Star, and the General Service and Victory Medals.

16, Margaret Street, West Gorton, Manchester.   Z5855

DENTON, V., Private, 3rd Cheshire Regiment.

Volunteering at the declaration of war, he was drafted to the Dardanelles in the following year, and fought in many engagements of note. After the Evacuation of the Peninsula he proceeded to Egypt, and served at various stations. Owing to ill-health he returned home, and after receiving hospital treatment he was not passed fit for further service overseas, and was engaged on important duties at Brunner Chemical Works until demobilised in January 1919. He holds the 1914-15 Star, and the General Service and Victory Medals.

64, Naylor Street, Oldham Road, Manchester.   Z9064

DERBYSHIRE, C., L/Cpl., 2nd K.O.(R. Lancaster Regt.)

Volunteering at the outbreak of war, he completed his training and was sent to France in January. There he played an important part in the Battles of Neuve Chapelle, and Hill 60, but was wounded and taken prisoner in April 1915 during the second Battle of Ypres. On August 20th, 1916, he unhappily died whilst in a German internment camp. He was entitled to the 1914-15 Star, and the General Service and Victory Medals.

"Thinking that remembrance, though unspoken, may reach him where he sleeps."

127, Edensor Street, Beswick, Manchester.   Z5856A

DERBYSHIRE, J., Pte., 7th K.O. (R. Lancaster Regt.)

He volunteered in December 1915, and reached France in June 1916, in time to take part in the Somme Offensive. During the next year he fought at Arras, Vimy Ridge, Ypres III, Lens and Cambrai, and in 1918 was in action at the Battles of the Aisne III, Amiens, Ypres IV, and Le Cateau II. After serving in Germany from November 1918 until April 1920, he was demobilised, and holds the General Service and Victory Medals.

8, Clement Street, Hulme, Manchester.   Z5859

DERBYSHIRE, J. W., Private, 21st Cheshire Regt.

He joined in August 1916, and two months later embarked for the Western Front. After serving at Neuve Chapelle, he fought in the Battle of the Somme and engagements at Havrincourt, Beaumont-Hamel, La Bassée, Givenchy, Albert, Oppy, Trones Wood, and Cambrai, and in the Retreat and Advance of 1918, during which he was in action on the Somme, and at Le Cateau. Demobilised in March 1919, he holds the General Service and Victory Medals.

16, King Street, Ardwick, Manchester.   Z5858

DERBYSHIRE, J. W., Rifleman, Rifle Brigade.

He volunteered in January 1915, and five months later proceeded to Egypt. He served in this theatre of war for over two years, and during that time was in action on the Suez, and at Katia, El Fasher, and Romani. He was in January 1918, transferred to France, where he took part in the Battles of the Somme, and the Marne, and during the final Advance was wounded. Sent back to England, he was discharged in November 1918, and holds the 1914-15 Star, and the General Service and Victory Medals.

127, Edensor Street, Beswick, Manchester.   Z5856B

DERBYSHIRE, R., Sergt., 5/6th Royal Scots.

Volunteering in January 1915, he was sent to Egypt in the following August and served with distinction against the Senussi Arabs. In March 1916 he was transferred to the Western Front, where he took part in the Battles of the Somme, Passchendaele, Le Cateau, and the Sambre and in other important engagements during the Retreat and Advance of 1918. He holds the 1914-15 Star, and the General Service and Victory Medals, and was demobilised in January 1919.

512, Mill Street, Bradford, Manchester.   Z10105

DERBYSHIRE, R., Private, Border Regiment.

In November 1914, he volunteered, and in the following July was sent to the Western Front, where he took part in the Battles of Loos, the Somme and Ypres, and was wounded on three occasions. He also saw fierce fighting in the Retreat of 1918 and was in action during the final victorious engagements of the war. He was demobilised in July 1919, and holds the 1914-15 Star, and the General Service and Victory Medals.

61, Thomas Street, West Gorton, Manchester.   Z5857

DERBYSHIRE, T., Pte., 2nd Lancashire Fusiliers.

Mobilised at the outbreak of war, he proceeded to France in August 1914, and took a prominent part in the Battles of Mons, La Cateau, the Marne, the Aisne, Ypres (I), Neuve Chapelle, Hill 60, Ypres (II), Loos, the Somme (I), Arras, Ypres (III), and Cambrai. He was badly wounded in action during the 2nd Battle of the Somme in March 1918, and was invalided home. In January 1919 he was discharged as medically unfit for further service and holds the Mons Star, and the General Service and Victory Medals.

6, New Murray Street, Oldham Road, Manchester.   Z10106

DERBYSHIRE, T., Pte., 7th Gordon Highlanders.

He volunteered in January 1915, and in May 1915 proceeded to the Western Front. There he served at Richbourg, Festubert, Laventie, the Somme, and Mametz Wood, and in November 1916, was invalided home for nine months. On his return to France he was in action in engagements at Cambrai and Ypres, and also in the Retreat in 1918. He was demobilised in January 1919, and holds the 1914-15 Star, and the General Service and Victory Medals.

15, Higham Street, Miles Platting, Manchester.   Z9502

DERBYSHIRE, T. E., Stoker, R.N.R.

He was serving off the coasts of West Africa when war was declared in August 1914, and took part in minor naval operations in these waters, whilst on board H.M.S. "Highflyer." In March 1916 he was sent home and discharged as medically unfit for further service and holds the 1914-15 Star, and the General Service (with clasps 1914-15-16), and Victory Medals.

24, School Street, West Gorton, Manchester.   Z10107

DERBYSHIRE, W., L/Corporal, M.G.C.

He attested in November 1915, but was engaged on work of National importance until called up in June 1917. After his training he proceeded to France, and did good work as a gunner, in engagements at Passchendaele, Ypres, and Cambrai. He was invalided home in March 1918, and on his recovery served with the Motor Battalion of the Machine Gun Corps in England until demobilised in July 1919, holding the General Service and Victory Medals.

11, Latimer Street, Longsight, Manchester.   Z5860

DERRICK, W., Sapper, R.E.

Volunteering in July 1915, he was on completion of his training sent to Grimsby where he was employed on important guard duties at the Docks. In July 1916 he proceeded to the Western Front, and rendered valuable services in building bridges and pontoons in different sectors of the war zone. He was demobilised in April 1919, and holds the General Service and Victory Medals.

9, Crawshaw Street, York Street, Chorlton-on-Medlock, Manchester   Z5862

DERRY, S., Private, 100th Labour Corps.
He joined in February 1917, and after a course of training was later in the same year drafted to the Western Front, where he took part in heavy fighting in the La Bassée, Loos, Arras, and Vimy sectors. During his two years' service in France, he was chiefly employed in repairing and maintaining the railway tracks, and was demobilised in November 1919. He holds the General Service and Victory Medals. TX5863
12, New York Street, Chorlton-on-Medlock, Manchester.

DERVIN, J., Gunner, R.F.A.
Mobilised from the Reserve at the commencement of hostilities, he served at various stations, until drafted to Egypt in May 1917. On the Palestine front he fought in many engagements, including the Battles of Gaza, and the operations resulting in the capture of Jerusalem. He was in action in various sectors and took part in the final British Advance into Syria in 1918. Returning home, he was demobilised in May 1919, and holds the General Service and Victory Medals.
140, Tame Street, Ancoats, Manchester. Z9065

DEVANEY, S., Corporal, 8th Border Regiment.
Volunteering in October 1914, he embarked for the Western Front in the following September and fought in the Battles of Loos, St. Eloi, Albert, Vimy Ridge, and the Somme. He was also in action at Arras, and Messines, and was reported wounded and missing in April 1918, during the Allied Advance. Subsequently he was reported to have been taken prisoner, and was held in captivity until December 1918. Repatriated, he was demobilised in March 1919, and holds the 1914-15 Star, and the General Service and Victory Medals.
76, Newcastle Street, Hulme, Manchester. Z9066

DEVINE, J., Sapper, R.E.
He joined in October 1916, and in the following January was drafted to the Western Front, where he was engaged on special road and pontoon construction work. He took an active part in the Battles of Arras, Messines, Ypres (III) (where he was wounded), and Cambrai, and in the Retreat and Advance of 1918. After the cessation of hostilities, he proceeded to Germany with the Army of Occupation and served on the Rhine until demobilised in September 1919, holding the General Service and Victory Medals.
23, Hope Street, Bradford, Manchester. Z10108

DEVLIN, W., Private, 7th East Lancashire Regt.
Volunteering in September 1914, he proceeded to France early in the following year, and took part in the Battles of Neuve Chapelle, Ypres, and Festubert, before being badly wounded in action in July 1915. He was invalided to hospital in Scotland, and on his recovery returned to the Western Front, and saw much further heavy fighting. He holds the 1914-15 Star, and the General Service and Victory Medals, and was demobilised in March 1919.
42, Hinde Street, Gorton, Manchester. Z10103

DEWHIRST, H., Private, 2nd Lancashire Fusiliers.
Volunteering in January 1916, he was almost at once ordered to the Western Front, and was wounded in the Battle of Ypres. On returning to his unit, he was engaged in severe fighting at Arras, Nieuport, La Bassée, and Vimy Ridge, was again wounded at Passchendaele, and sent to hospital in England, and discharged as medically unfit for further service in October 1918. He holds the General Service and Victory Medals.
18, Padgate Street, Ancoats, Manchester. TZ9503

DEWHURST, F., L/Corporal, 21st Manchester Regt.
Volunteering in October 1915, he proceeded to France five months later, and first saw heavy fighting at St. Eloi. He also took part in the Battles of Vermelles, the Somme, the Ancre, Vimy Ridge, Bullecourt, Ypres (III), Cambrai, the Marne (II), and Havrincourt. He was twice wounded in action—at Vermelles in May 1916, and at Ypres in October 1917. He holds the General Service and Victory Medals, and was demobilised in August 1919.
11, James Street, West Gorton, Manchester. Z10109

DEWHURST, W., Gunner, R.F.A.
Volunteering in August 1914, he proceeded in the following year to Gallipoli, where he was in action at Krithia and Anzac. After the Evacuation he was sent to Salonika and took part in fierce fighting on the Dorian front, and later was transferred to Palestine, where he did good work with his Battery until the cessation of hostilities. He was wounded on one occasion and in 1920 was still serving in the Army. He holds the 1914-15 Star, and the General Service and Victory Medals.
6, Abbey Grove, Hulme, Manchester. Z5864

DEWSNUP, E., Pte., Argyll and Sutherland H'ldrs.
He volunteered in January 1915, and later in the same year was drafted overseas. After taking part in numerous engagements on the Western Front, he was wounded in the Battle of Ypres, and sent back to hospital in England. On his recovery he returned to France, and saw heavy fighting until the close of hostilities, but in March 1919 was accidentally drowned in Belgium. He was entitled to the 1914-15 Star, and the General Service and Victory Medals.
"His memory is cherished with pride."
8, Bruton Street, Moss Side, Manchester. Z5865B

DEWSNUP, F. (M.M.), Private, Border Regiment.
He volunteered in January 1915, and ten months later was sent to the Western Front, where he was wounded in the Battle of the Somme. On rejoining his unit he took part in numerous other engagements, and was in action at Ypres and Messines. In June 1917 he was awarded the Military Medal for conspicuous gallantry in the Field, and also holds the 1914-15 Star, and the General Service and Victory Medals. He was demobilised in June 1919. 8, Bruton Street, Moss Side, Manchester. Z5865A

DEWSNUP, J., A.B., Royal Navy.
At the outbreak of war he was already serving in the Navy, and in August 1914, was posted to a destroyer. Throughout the period of hostilities, he performed valuable work in patrolling the North Sea with destroyer flotillas. In 1920 he was still serving, and holds the 1914-15 Star, and the General Service and Victory Medals.
8, Bruton Street, Moss Side, Manchester. Z5865D

DEWSNUP, N., L/Corporal, Royal Naval Division.
Volunteering in February 1915, he was on completion of his training, five months later, drafted overseas. Whilst serving in Gallipoli, he took an active part in the Suvla Bay Landing and was in heavy fighting until the Evacuation. He then proceeded to Palestine, and was in action in the Offensive of 1918. Returning to England in July 1919, he was demobilised, and holds the 1914-15 Star, and the General Service and Victory Medals.
8, Bruton Street, Moss Side, Manchester. Z5865C

DEXTER, W. H., Private, R.A.S.C.
He joined in April 1917, and after a course of training was in in the following September sent overseas. He served on the Western Front for nearly two years, and during that time was in action in different sectors of the line, and fought in the Battles of Cambrai, the Somme, the Aisne, and the Marne. In August 1919, he was demobilised, and holds the General Service and Victory Medals.
21, Davies Street, Hulme, Manchester. Z5866

DEY, W., Private, R.A.V.C., and West Riding Regt.
He volunteered in August 1914, and in the following June proceeded to France, and saw heavy fighting at Loos, Vimy Ridge, and the Somme. In October 1916 he was transferred to the Italian front, and took an active part in the engagements on the Piave. He served in this theatre of war until December 1918, when he was demobilised, holding the 1914-15 Star, and the General Service and Victory Medals.
11, Churchfield Street, Openshaw, Manchester. TZ9504

DIAMOND, A., Private, Lancashire Fusiliers, and Loyal N. Lancashire Regiment.
He volunteered in July 1915, and in the following November was drafted to the Western Front, where he took an active part in engagements at Loos, Albert, and Vimy Ridge, and was wounded in the Battle of the Somme. He was in consequence invalided out of the Army in October 1916, but rejoined in June 1918, and was stationed in Dublin until demobilised in March 1919. He holds the 1914-15 Star, and the General Service and Victory Medals.
12, Nesbit Street, Hulme, Manchester. Z5867

DICKENS, T., Private, 8th Manchester Regiment.
Joining in June 1916, he, seven months later proceeded to Mesopotamia, where he was engaged in fierce fighting at Kut, Baghdad, and Ramadieh, and was wounded at Tekrit in November 1917. On his recovery he was sent out to Palestine, and did good work in the operations at Tripoli and Aleppo, and served there until June 1919, when he returned to England. He was demobilised a month later, and holds the General Service and Victory Medals.
9, Derby Street, Ardwick, Manchester. Z5874

DICKENSON, H., Private, 6th Manchester Regt.
An ex-soldier who had previously served throughout the South African War, he rejoined in August 1914, and was engaged on important guard duty over a large munition factory until August 1916. He was then employed in guarding German prisoners' detention camps, and rendered valuable services until his demobilisation in January 1919.
42, Ogden Street, Hulme, Manchester. TZ9067

DICKENSON, J. R., Private, South Wales Borderers.
He joined in August 1918, on attaining military age, but on account of bad health was unable to procure a transfer overseas. Throughout his service in the Army he was stationed at Reepham, and rendered valuable services in guarding prisoners of war. He was eventually demobilised in October 1919.
96, Rutland Street, Hulme, Manchester. Z5873

DICKINSON, G. T., Rifleman, Rifle Brigade.
He was mobilised at the outbreak of hostilities, and was almost immediately drafted to France, where he took part in the Retreat from Mons. He gave his life for the freedom of England in the Battle of Le Cateau on August 26th, 1914, and was entitled to the Mons Star, and the General Service and Victory Medals.
"Courage, bright hopes, and a myriad dreams, splendidly given."
19, Randolph Street, Openshaw, Manchester. Z9068

DICKINSON, J., Wheeler, R.A.S.C.

When war broke out he was already serving in the Army, but was retained on home service until February 1916, when he was drafted to the Western Front. There he served for over three years, and during that period was in action in the Battles of the Ancre, Beaumont-Hamel, Beaucourt, the Somme, Arras, Vimy Ridge, Bullecourt, Ypres, Lens, Cambrai, Amiens, Bapaume, and Havrincourt. He was discharged in May 1919, and holds the General Service and Victory Medals.
167, Hartington Street, Moss Side, Manchester. TZ5872

DICKINSON, J., Private, S. Lancashire Regiment.

He joined the Army in June 1916, but on account of his age was unable to procure a transfer to a theatre of war. He served at Kinmel Park, Birkenhead, Glasgow, and Barrow, and in all these stations, carried out the various duties assigned to him with the greatest ability, and was eventually demobilised in January, 1919.
13, Durham Place, Hulme, Manchester. Z5868

DICKINSON, J., Private, 2/8th Manchester Regt.

Volunteering in August 1914, he was retained on important duties in England until March 1917, when he proceeded to France. In this theatre of war he was in action at Ypres, Passchendaele, Cambrai, St. Quentin, Nieuport, the Somme, Havrincourt, Epéhy, and was wounded whilst fighting at Loos in August 1918. He was demobilised in March 1919, and holds the General Service and Victory Medals.
34, Hardy Street, West Gorton, Manchester. TZ5871

DICKINSON, J., Private, 1st Royal Irish Fusiliers.

He volunteered in September 1914, and ten months later proceeded to France, where he fought in the Battle of Loos. In October 1915, he was drafted to Salonika, and was in action at Monastir, and on the Doiran front. After nearly three years' service in this theatre of war he was invalided to England, suffering from malaria, and was discharged as unfit for further service in December 1918. He holds the 1914-15 Star, and the General Service and Victory Medals.
3, Jack Street, Ardwick, Manchester. Z5870A

DICKINSON, J. A., Private, 1/7th Manchester Regt.

He was mobilised in August 1914, and at once proceeded to Egypt where he was engaged in garrison duties at Alexandria for six months, and was then transferred to Gallipoli. After serving at Suvla Bay, he was in action until the Evacuation, and was once more sent to the Egyptian front, where he fought at Sollum, Katia, El Fasher, Romani, Magdhaba, Rafa, Gaza, and Jerusalem. In February 1918, he was sent to France, and served in the final Retreat and Advance, and was wounded at Albert in the following August. He was in consequence discharged from the Army in March 1919, and holds the 1914-15 Star, and the General Service and Victory Medals.
7, Sykes Street, Reddish, Manchester. Z5869

DICKINSON, N., Private, 7th Manchester Regiment.

Joining in September 1916, he was drafted overseas six months later. Whilst serving in France he saw heavy fighting at Arras, Vimy Ridge, and Bullecourt, was wounded at Ypres, and was sent back to hospital in England. He returned, however, to the firing line in May 1918, and took an active part in the final engagements of the war. Demobilised in February 1919, he holds the General Service and Victory Medals.
20, Dearden Street, Hulme, Manchester. TZ5876

DICKINSON, R., Sergt., 14th Manchester Regiment.

Volunteering in January 1915, he was retained after the completion of his training at Lichfield, Stafford, and other stations, on important bombing duties. He rendered very valuable services as chief bombing instructor, but was not successful in obtaining his transfer overseas before hostilities ceased. In January 1919, he was demobilised.
45, Alma Street, Queen's Park, Manchester. Z10558

DICKINSON, T. W., Private, R.A.M.C.

He joined the Army, but proved to be medically unfit for service overseas. He served in the Royal Army Medical Corps for nearly three years, and during that time did excellent work as a doctor's orderly in the operating theatre at Belmont War Hospital in Surrey, carrying out his responsible duties in a very able manner. He was demobilised in October 1919.
7, Halsbury Street, Longsight, Manchester. Z5875

DICKINSON, W., Corporal, 1st Lancashire Fusiliers.

He joined in October 1917, and after a period of training was a year later drafted to the Western Front, where he took an active part in the final decisive engagements of the war. He was in action at Le Cateau, the Selle, and the Sambre, and was present during the entry into Mons. In June 1919, he proceeded to Ireland, and was employed on garrison duties. In 1920 he was still serving in the Army, and holds the General Service and Victory Medals.
3, Jack Street, Ardwick, Manchester. Z5870B

DICKINSON, W., Private, Lancashire Fusiliers.

He volunteered in May 1915, and in the following November was drafted to France. During his service on the Western Front he took part in the heavy fighting at Albert, on the Somme, and at Arras, and was wounded in the third Battle of Ypres. After his recovery he rejoined his unit, and was again wounded, and also gassed in action in August 1918. He was

invalided home to hospital, and was later demobilised in January 1919. He holds the 1914-15 Star, and the General Service and Victory Medals.
9, Somerset Place, Collyhurst, Manchester. Z9069

DICKINSON, W. E., Corporal, 62nd M.G.C.

Joining in June 1916, he was on conclusion of his training drafted overseas in March 1917. During his service on the Western Front, he was engaged in heavy fighting in the Battles of Arras, Vimy Ridge, Messines, Ypres, Cambrai I, the Somme, the Marne, Bapaume, Havrincourt, and Cambrai II, and remained in France until demobilised in February 1919. He holds the General Service and Victory Medals.
6, Lingard Street, Hulme, Manchester. Z5877

DILLON, E., Private, Manchester Regiment.

Having volunteered in January 1915, he was sent to France in the following November, and played an important part with his unit in the Battles of the Somme, and Ypres (III). In April 1918 he was taken seriously ill, and was in hospital at Le Havre for seven months. He holds the 1914-15 Star, and the General Service and Victory Medals, and was demobilised in January 1919.
43, Clayton Street, Ancoats, Manchester. Z10110

DILLON, H. J., Private, 1/7th Manchester Regt.

He volunteered in August 1914, and eight months later proceeded to Gallipoli, where after fighting in the three Battles of Krithia he was unhappily killed in action after only two months' active service on June 4th, 1915. He was entitled to the 1914-15 Star, and the General Service and Victory Medals.
"Honour to the immortal dead who gave their youth that the world might grow old in peace."
10, Freeman Street, Hulme, Manchester. Z5878A

DILLON, J., Private, 10th Royal Dublin Fusiliers.

He was already serving, when war broke out, and at once proceeded to France. There he took an active part in the Battles of Mons, the Marne, the Aisne, La Bassée, Ypres I, Neuve Chapelle, Ypres II, Albert, the Somme, Arras, Bullecourt, and Cambrai, and was unfortunately killed in action during an engagement on the Somme on March 22nd, 1918. He was entitled to the Mons Star, and the General Service and Victory Medals. "A costly sacrifice upon the altar of freedom."
16, Henry Street, Ardwick, Manchester. Z5880

DILLON, J. H., Private, 1/7th Manchester Regt.

In August 1914, he volunteered for active service, and in April 1915 was drafted to Gallipoli. There he saw heavy fighting in several engagements, and was severely wounded in the second Battle of Krithia in May 1915. He was sent to hospital in Alexandria, and from thence to England, and was subsequently invalided out of the Army in February 1917. He holds the 1914-15 Star, and the General Service and Victory Medals.
10, Freeman Street, Hulme, Manchester. Z5878B

DILLON, P., Private, Labour Corps.

A month after the outbreak of hostilities he volunteered, and in May 1915, proceeded to the Western Front, where he fought in the Battles of Loos, the Somme, Ypres, Arras, and Cambrai, and was also in action in the Retreat and Advance of 1918. He was wounded on three occasions, and remained in France until demobilised in March 1919. He holds the 1914-15 Star, and the General Service and Victory Medals.
19, Berwick Street, Chorlton-on-Medlock, Manchester. Z5879

DILLON, P., Sapper, R.E.

Mobilised with the Territorials in August 1914, he was quickly drafted to Egypt and served there until the opening of the Dardanelles Campaign. He then took part in the Landing at Cape Helles, and the Battles of Krithia, where he was wounded and invalided home in June 1915. In August 1916 he was sent to Salonika, and saw much severe fighting there until February 1918, when he was transferred to the Western Front, and was in action at the Battles of the Somme (II), and Cambria (II), and in the Retreat and Advance. He holds the 1914-15 Star, and the General Service and Victory Medals, and was demobilised in March 1919.
4, Longridge Street, Longsight, Manchester. Z10111

DILLON, R., Corporal, 2nd Manchester Regiment.

He was mobilised in August 1914, and was almost immediately drafted to France. During his service overseas he took part in the Retreat from Mons, and in the Battles of La Bassée, Ypres, Givenchy, and Festubert, where he was wounded. After his recovery he was again in action on the Somme, and in various other sectors, and was gassed. He was invalided home to hospital suffering from the effects of gas poisoning, and was discharged in April 1919. He holds the Mons Star, and the General Service and Victory Medals.
34, Nelson Street, Rochdale Road, Manchester. Z9070

DILLON, T., Rifleman, K.R.R.C.

He volunteered in September 1914, and four months later was drafted to the Western Front, where he saw heavy fighting at Neuve Chapelle. He was mortally wounded at Hill 60, and succumbed to his injuries in May 1915, at the 2nd Canadian Stationary Hospital. He was entitled to the 1914-15 Star, and the General Service and Victory Medals.
"Nobly striving, he nobly fell that we might live."
16, Watson Street, Hulme, Manchester. Z5881

DIMELOE, J., Private, 3/7th Manchester Regiment.
Volunteering in December 1915, he proceeded a year later to the Western Front. In this theatre of war he took part in numerous important engagements in different sectors of the line, and was in action at Arras, Vimy Ridge, Bullecourt, Messines, Ypres, Passchendaele, the Somme, and Havrincourt. In February 1919, he was demobilised, and holds the General Service and Victory Medals.
39, Dale Street, Hulme, Manchester.   Z5882

DINSDALE, G., Private, 7th Manchester Regiment.
He volunteered for active service on the outbreak of war, but was retained on home service until August 1915, when he was drafted to Gallipoli. There, after fighting in several engagements he was unhappily killed in action at Suvla Bay in October 1915. He was entitled to the 1914–15 Star, and the General Service and Victory Medals.
" His life for his Country, his soul to God."
18, Mary Street, Hulme, Manchester.   Z5883

DINSDALE, H., Pte., K.O. (Royal Lancaster Regt.)
Having enlisted in 1907, he was already serving in India when war broke out in August 1914, and returned home in December of that year. He was then immediately drafted to the Western Front, where, after much severe fighting, he was killed in action on May 8th, 1915, at the second Battle of Ypres. He was entitled to the 1914–15 Star, and the General Service and Victory Medals.
" Whilst we remember, the sacrifice is not in vain."
244, Thornton Street, Collyhurst, Manchester.   Z10112A

DINSDALE, H., Pte., 3rd Northumberland Fusiliers.
Volunteering in November 1914, he was employed on various duties at home stations until February 1916, when he proceeded to Mesopotamia. In this theatre of war, he served at Basra and other places, and was later sent to India. Prior to returning home, he spent some time in hospital at Darjeeling, and was subsequently demobilised in March 1919, holding the General Service and Victory Medals.
28, Lawrence Street, West Gorton, Manchester.   Z11298

DINSDALE, R., Private, 7th Manchester Regiment.
He volunteered in January 1915, and in November of that year was drafted to France, where he saw severe fighting in various sectors of the Front. He took part in the Somme Offensive, and in engagements at Festubert and many other places, and was wounded in action at Delville Wood in July 1916. Demobilised in February 1919, he holds the 1914-15 Star, and the General Service and Victory Medals.
244, Thornton Street, Collyhurst, Manchester.   Z10112B

DITCHFIELD, G. W., A.B., Royal Navy.
He volunteered in October 1915, and was stationed at the Crystal Palace and Devonport until December of the following year, when he was posted to H.M.S. " City of London." He was attached to the Grand Fleet in the North Sea until his ship was torpedoed and was then transferred to H.M.S. " Lightfoot " for duty in the Persian Gulf. He was demobilised in March 1919, and holds the General Service Medal (with two clasps), and Victory Medal.
53, Branson Street, Ancoats, Manchester.   Z10113

DITCHFIELD, T., Private, 3rd Manchester Regiment and 1st Class Stoker, R.N.
Volunteering in August 1914, he proceeded to the Western Front in November of that year, and there took part in the Battles of Ypres, Neuve Chapelle and Hill 60, and was wounded in action at Loos. Invalided from the Army in December 1915, he afterwards enlisted in the Navy and was posted to H.M.S. " Caesar," for duty in West Indian waters. He also served in H.M.S. " Abercrombie " before his demobilisation in June 1919, and holds the 1914–15 Star, and the General Service (with two clasps), and Victory Medals.
39, Branson Street, Ancoats, Manchester.   Z10114

DIXON, E., Private, K.O. (Royal Lancaster Regt.)
Volunteering in April 1915, he was on completion of his training four months later, drafted to Gallipoli. Whilst taking part in the Suvla Bay Landing he was taken prisoner, and during his captivity worked in a sugar factory, and later in a wood factory in Bulgaria. After the close of hostilities he was released, and returning to England was demobilised in March 1919, holding the 1914–15 Star, and the General Service and Victory Medals.
10, Shrewbridge Street, West Gorton, Manchester.   TZ5886

DIXON, E., Pte., 1/10th Liverpool Scottish Regt.
He joined in October 1917, and five months' later was sent overseas. During his service on the Western Front, he took an active part in many engagements of importance during the Allied Advance, and was in action at Amiens, Epéhy and Cambrai (II), during which battle he was badly gassed and sent to hospital in Sheffield. He was eventually demobilised in October 1919, and holds the General Service and Victory Medals.   Z5725A
47, Cambridge Street, Chorlton-on Medlock, Manchester.

DIXON, G., Gunner, M.G.C.
Joining in October 1916 he was drafted overseas in the following April, but after only a month's service on the Western Front was transferred to Italy. There he was engaged in

heavy fighting in actions on the Piave (I and II), Asiago Plateaux and Mount Grappa. Whilst on this front he was sent to Genoa, suffering with frost-bite, and was retained in hospital there until after the Armistice. Demobilised in October 1919, he holds the General Service and Victory Medals.
57, Mawson Street, Chorlton-on-Medlock, Manchester. Z5887

DIXON, J., Gunner, R.G.A.
He joined in June 1916, and proving to be unsuccessful in procuring a transfer overseas, was retained on important duties in England. During his service in the Army he was stationed at Dover, Shrewsbury, and Ramsgate, and rendered valuable services in connection with anti-aircraft guns. He was demobilised in January 1919.
13, Jobling Street, Bradford, Manchester.   Z6060

DIXON, J., Sergt., 12th Lancashire Fusiliers.
Volunteering in September 1914, he proceeded to France in August 1915, and served there for four months. During that time he fought in the Battles of Loos and in the Ypres and Somme sectors. He was then transferred to Salonika where, he fought with distinction on the Vardar and Doiran fronts, and took a prominent part in the re-capture of Monastir. He was severely wounded in action on the Vardar, and in consequence was discharged from the Army as medically unfit in October 1917. He holds the 1914–15 Star, and the General Service and Victory Medals.
40, Owen Street, Hulme Manchester.   Z5889

DIXON, J., Private, Royal Welch Fusiliers.
He joined in September 1917, on attaining military age, and in the following January proceeded to France. As a Lewis gunner he took part in the Battle of Cambrai, the second Battle of the Somme, and in the Retreat and Advance of 1918, and was badly wounded in August of that year. He was invalided home, and after hospital treatment was discharged as medically unfit for further duty in December 1918. He holds the General Service and Victory Medals.
13, Worth Street, Rochdale Road, Manchester.   Z10560B

DIXON, J. (M.M.), Private, 11th Royal Fusiliers.
He volunteered in May 1915, and in December of the same year crossed to France, where he fought with distinction at the Somme, Ypres and other engagements until hostilities ceased. He also acted as despatch carrier, and was awarded the Military Medal for conspicuous bravery in delivering messages under heavy fire during the Battle of the Somme. In addition he holds the 1914–15 Star, and the General Service and Victory Medals, and in February 1919 was demobilised.
5, Virginia Street, Rochdale Road, Manchester.   Z10559

DIXON, J., Rifleman, 8th Rifle Brigade.
Mobilised in August 1914, he proceeded in the following month to the Western Front and fought in engagements at La Bassée, Ypres (during which he was wounded), Hill 60, Loos and Albert. In the Battle of the Somme he was again severely wounded and invalided to England. After receiving treatment in various hospitals, he was eventually discharged from the Army as medically unfit in January 1919, and holds the 1914 Star, and the General Service and Victory Medals.
58, Church Street, Hulme, Manchester.   Z5884B

DIXON, J. A., Pte., 23rd King's (Liverpool Regt.)
He joined in June 1917, but on conclusion of his training was unable to obtain a transfer to a theatre of war. He served in the Army for over two years, and during that time was employed in Wales on agricultural work, which he performed in a very able manner. He was demobilised in October 1919. 58, Church Street, Hulme, Manchester.   Z5884A

DIXON, J. E., Staff-Sergt., R.A.M.C.
He volunteered at the outbreak of war in August 1914, and after his training served at various stations, where he was engaged on duties of a highly important nature. He was not successful in obtaining his transfer to a theatre of war, but, nevertheless, rendered very valuable services until his demobilisation in August 1919. He re-enlisted, however, shortly afterwards and proceeded to Mesopotamia, where he was still serving at Amara in 1920.
1, Fletcher Square, Hulme, Manchester.   Z11687

DIXON, J. H., Gunner, R.F.A.
He volunteered in July 1915, and a year later was drafted to the Western Front, where he did good work with his Battery at Beaumont-Hamel, Beaucourt, Bullecourt, Ypres and Passchendaele, and was gassed at Cambrai. On returning to the firing line, he was in action during the final important engagements of the war, and was demobilised in February 1919, holding the General Service and Victory Medals.
23, Mark Lane, Chorlton-on-Medlock, Manchester.   Z5888

DIXON, J. L., Corporal, King's Shropshire L.I.
A Reservist, he was called to the Colours in August 1914, and was immediately drafted to the Western Front, where he saw severe fighting in various sectors. He took part in the Battles of Ypres, Albert, the Somme and many other important engagements in this theatre of war, and after the cessation of hostilities, served with the Army of Occupation at Cologne. He was discharged on his return home in February 1919, and holds the 1914 Star, and the General Service and Victory Medals.   112, Cobden Street, Ancoats, Manchester. Z10115

DIXON, R., Private, 8th Manchester Regiment.
Mobilised on the declaration of war he was retained on important duties in England until 1915. He then was sent to the Dardanelles, where he saw much fighting at Cape Helles, Krithia and Achi Baba, and was wounded. On his recovery after hospital treatment at home he proceeded to France and served with the Labour Corps in many sectors of the Front on road making and other important duties, and was present during the Battles of Messines, Ypres, Passchendaele, Cambrai, and in the Retreat and Advance of 1918. In March 1919 he was demobilised, holding the 1914-15 Star, and the General Service and Victory Medals.
13, Worth Street, Rochdale Road, Manchester. Z10560A

DIXON, W., Private, 19th Welch Regiment.
He volunteered in May 1915, and six months later proceeded to the Western Front. There he took part in strenuous fighting at Albert, Laventie, Messines Ridge, Amiens and Bapaume, and was gassed in action at Givenchy in July 1916. He was evacuated to England shortly afterwards, and was invalided out of the Service in January 1917, in consequence of gas poisoning. He holds the 1914-15 Star, and the General Service and Victory Medals.
25, Middlewood Street, Harpurhey, Manchester. Z11489

DIXON, W., L/Corporal, Lancashire Fusiliers.
Joining in January 1916, he was fourteen months later sent to the Western Front. In this theatre of war he experienced fierce fighting in engagements at Bullecourt, Ypres and Passchendaele, but was unfortunately killed in action at Cambrai on October 21st, 1917. He was entitled to the General Service and Victory Medals.
"He passed out of the sight of men by the path of duty and self-sacrifice."
38, Milton Street, West Gorton, Manchester. Z5885B

DOBIE, W. W., Private, Manchester Regiment.
He joined in August 1918, and prior to that date, was engaged on work of National importance at Messrs. Crossley Bros.' Munition Works. After serving at Aldershot and Cleethorpes, he proceeded to Egypt in February 1919, and was stationed at Cairo, where he was employed on the Regimental Staff, in the Officers' Quarters. Returning to England in March 1920, he was demobilised.
42, Ryder Street, Bradford, Manchester. Z5890

DOBSON, F., Private, 2nd Manchester Regiment.
Volunteering in March 1915, he was drafted overseas in September of the same year. During his service on the Western Front he acted as a bomber and took part in the engagements at Loos, the Somme, Arras, Ypres, Cambrai and in the Retreat and Advance of 1918, and was three times wounded. He was demobilised in February 1919, and holds the 1914-15 Star, and the General Service and Victory Medals.
8, Crook Street, Miles Platting, Manchester. Z10561

DOBSON, R., Pte., King's Own (Royal Lancaster Rgt.)
Mobilised in August 1914, he was at once drafted to the Western Front, where he took part in the Retreat from Mons, and the Battles of the Marne, La Bassée and Ypres, and was three times wounded. During the Battle of Neuve Chapelle in March 1915, he was wounded for the fourth time, admitted to hospital in Rouen and later evacuated to England. He was eventually discharged in 1917, as unfit for further service, and holds the Mons Star, and the General Service and Victory Medals. 7, Dorrington Street, Hulme, Manchester. TZ5891

DODD, G. W., Staff-Sergt.-Major, R.A.S.C.
He volunteered in April, 1915 and in the following December proceeded to Egypt. In this theatre of war he served at Cairo, Mersa Matruh, Zazazig and Assiont, engaged on various duties of an important nature and rendered excellent services He subsequently was in action in an engagement against the Turks at Romani, prior to his return home for demobilisation in July 1919. He holds the 1914-15 Star, and the General Service and Victory Medals.
53, Baker Street, Longsight, Manchester. Z5892

DODD, H., Pte., King's Own (Royal Lancaster Rgt.)
Having previously fought in the South African campaign, he re-enlisted in August 1914, and in January of the following year was drafted to the Western Front. After taking part in the second Battle of Ypres, he was blown up by an explosion at Hill 60, and was admitted to hospital. On his recovery, however, he rejoined his unit, was again in action on the Somme and at Ypres, and was afterwards attached to the Labour Corps. He was demobilised in February 1919, and holds the 1914-15 Star, and the General Service and Victory Medals. 19, Elliott Street, Bradford, Manchester. Z10116

DODD, J., L/Corporal, South Lancashire Regiment.
He volunteered in January 1915, and in August reached France, where he was wounded at the Battle of Loos in the next month. Returning to the line, he was wounded in August 1916 during the great Somme Offensive, and was invalided home. Again in action, he was captured in May 1918 and taken to Germany. On his release after the Armistice, he was demobilised in February 1919, and holds the 1914-15 Star, and the General Service and Victory Medals.
7, Crissey Street, Queen's Road, Manchester. Z11973B

DODD, J., Private, 23rd Manchester Regiment.
He joined in February 1916, and during his training served at Liverpool, Kinmel Park, and Oswestry. Drafted to the Western Front in June 1916 he at once took part in heavy fighting, but had only been overseas for a few weeks when he made the supreme sacrifice, being killed in action on the Somme in July 1916. He was entitled to the General Service and Victory Medals.
"Whilst we remember, the sacrifice is not in vain."
4, Bury Street, City Road, Hulme, Manchester. Z5894A

DODD, R., Private, 8th Manchester Regiment.
He volunteered in November 1915, and was drafted to France in March 1917. Whilst overseas he took part in the fighting at Ypres, Arras and Passchendaele, and in various subsequent engagements in the Retreat and Advance of 1918. He was wounded at Bapaume in August of that year, and was demobilised after his return to England in April 1919. He holds the General Service and Victory Medals.
15, Holt Street, Chorlton-on-Medlock, Manchester. Z9071

DODD, T., Private, Loyal North Lancashire Regt.
He volunteered in September 1914, and twelve months later proceeded to the Western Front, where he saw much severe fighting until wounded in action on the Somme in July 1916. Invalided home, he returned to France, however, on his recovery, and was wounded a second time on the Somme in March 1917. He afterwards took part in the Retreat and Advance of 1918, and was finally demobilised in December of that year. He holds the 1914-15 Star, and the General Service and Victory Medals.
21, Whyatt Street, Bradford, Manchester. TZ11688

DODD, W. Private, 4th King's (Liverpool Regt.)
Joining in September 1916, he proceeded in October of the following year to France. There he took part in the Battle of Cambrai, where he was gassed, and in the second Battle of the Somme, where he was wounded and gassed. After spending three months in hospital at Etaples, he rejoined his unit and was in action in various sectors during the Retreat and Advance of 1918. Demobilised on his return home in December 1918, he holds the General Service and Victory Medals.
4, Bury Street, City Road, Hulme, Manchester. Z5894B

DODD, W. E., Private, King's (Liverpool Regt.)
Mobilised in August 1914, he was immediately ordered to France, and took part in the Battle of Mons and the subsequent Retreat. He later participated in the Battles of Ypres, Neuve Chapelle, La Bassée, Festubert, Cambrai, the Somme, and Passchendaele, and was wounded at Cambrai in November 1917. Evacuated to England, he was for some time in hospital at Manchester and Leeds, being eventually discharged in May 1919, holding the Mons Star, and the General Service and Victory Medals.
19, Halsbury Street, Longsight, Manchester. Z5893

DODDS, L. H., Private, 13th Manchester Regiment.
He volunteered in September 1914, but was medically unfit for transfer to a theatre of war. Retained at home, he was stationed at Ripon, Redmines Camp, Sheffield, and Wakefield, and performed consistently good work whilst engaged on various duties of an important nature. He was eventually invalided out of the Army in June 1918.
32, Derby Street, Ardwick, Manchester. Z5895

DODSON, A., Private, 23rd Manchester Regiment.
Volunteering in September 1915, he proceeded in the following June to the Western Front. After taking part in heavy fighting at Arras, he was sent to the Base on account of being under age, and was engaged on various duties until August 1917. Sent to Chester, he was released from the Colours for agricultural work, and was later demobilised in March 1919, holding the General Service and Victory Medals.
23, New Bank Street, Ardwick, Manchester. Z5896

DOHERTY, M., Driver, R.F.A.
He volunteered in September 1914, and in the following year was sent to France. In this seat of war he took part in many important engagements, including the Battles of Loos and the Somme. He was wounded in action in December 1916, and on his recovery rejoined his Battery and saw further service taking part in the fighting at Givenchy and Ypres. After the cessation of hostilities he returned to England and was demobilised in December 1918. He holds the 1914-15 Star, and the General Service and Victory Medals.
25, Butterworth Street, Bradford, Manchester. Z11896

DOHERTY, T., Private, 2nd Border Regiment.
Called up from the Reserve at the outbreak of war in August 1914, he at once proceeded to France, where he participated in the Battle of Mons and the subsequent Retreat. After taking a prominent part in further fighting, he fell gloriously on the Field of Battle at Ypres on December 1st, 1914. He was entitled to the Mons Star, and the General Service and Victory Medals.
"His life for his Country."
107, Norton Street, West Gorton, Manchester. Z5897

DOLAN, J., Private, Manchester Regt., K.O. (Royal Lancaster Regt.) and Lancashire Fusiliers.
Joining in September 1916, he was drafted in the following April to the Western Front. In this theatre of war he took part in several important engagements, including actions at La Bassée, Festubert, and Bapaume, and fought in various sectors during the Advance of 1918, being twice wounded. After the Armistice he served with the Army of Occupation in Germany until October 1919, when he returned home and was demobilised, holding the General Service and Victory Medals. 8, Aden Street, Ardwick, Manchester. Z5898

DOLAN, J., Private, Royal Welch Fusiliers.
He volunteered in April 1915, and was retained at home on important duties until May 1916, when he was sent to France. There he was wounded in action on the Somme two months later, and after spending some time in hospital at Rouen rejoined his unit, and saw further fighting at Arras and Ypres, where he was again wounded. He subsequently served on the Marne and at Cambrai, and was demobilised on returning home in February 1919. He holds the General Service and Victory Medals.
49, Armitage Street, Ardwick, Manchester. Z5899

DOLAN, J., L/Corporal, 1st Manchester Regiment.
Serving in India at the outbreak of war in August 1914, he was at once ordered to the Western Front. On the way there he disembarked in Egypt, and eventually arrived in France in September 1914. On the Western Front he at once took part in heavy fighting, and was unfortunately killed in action at Givenchy on December 21st, 1914. He was entitled to the 1914 Star, and the General Service and Victory Medals.
"Great deeds cannot die."
8, Horace Street, Green Lane, Ardwick, Manchester. Z5900

DOLAN, J., L/Corporal, 11th Manchester Regiment.
Volunteering in August 1915, he proceeded to Egypt after two months' training, but was shortly afterwards transferred to the Western Front. There he took part in important engagements in various sectors, including the Battles of the Somme, Arras and Cambrai, and fought also in the Retreat and Advance of 1918. He unhappily fell in action on October 9th, 1918. He was entitled to the 1914-15 Star, and the General Service and Victory Medals.
"Honour to the immortal dead, who gave their youth that the world might grow old in peace."
8, Handel Street, Miles Platting, Manchester. Z10117B

DOLAN, N., Private, 20th Lancashire Fusiliers.
He volunteered in August 1914, and after completing a brief period of training, served at various stations, where he was engaged on duties of great importance. He was unable to obtain his transfer overseas on account of ill-health, but, nevertheless, rendered valuable services with his unit until invalided from the Army in February 1915. He was afterwards engaged in making gas-masks at the Premier Rubber Works, until the cessation of hostilities.
21, Iles Street, Oldham Road, Manchester. Z10118B

DOLAN, S. H., Corporal, R.E.
He volunteered in September 1914, and was employed on various duties at home stations until August 1916, when he was sent to Egypt. There he served at Romani and Magdhaba, and was later admitted to hospital suffering from fever. Upon his recovery he was transferred to France, and served on the Ancre front, and at Arras, Bullecourt and Lens. Though gassed in action at Ypres in July 1918 he remained overseas until January 1919, when he was demobilised, holding the General Service and Victory Medals.
6, Ribston Street, Hulme, Manchester. Z5901

DOLEMAN, A., Private, 16th Manchester Regiment.
Volunteering in September 1914, he was retained at home on important duties until November 1915, and then proceeded to France. In this theatre of war he took part in several important engagements, and rendered excellent service until he was unhappily killed at Maricourt on Feburary 29th, 1916, whilst carrying rations. He was entitled to the 1914-15 Star, and the General Service and Victory Medals.
"His memory is cherished with pride."
13, Melbourne Street, Hulme, Manchester. Z5902B

DOLEMAN, J. E., Sergt., 12th Manchester Regiment.
He volunteered in September 1914, and in the following July was drafted to the Western Front. There he played a prominent part with his unit in the Battle of Loos, and in severe fighting in other sectors, and fell gloriously in action in Sanctuary Wood, on January 3rd, 1916. He was entitled to the 1914-15 Star, and the General Service and Victory Medals.
"Nobly striving,
He nobly fell that we might live."
13, Melbourne Street, Hulme, Manchester. Z5902A

DOLEMAN, R., Sergt., Armoured Car Section.
He joined in March 1917, and two months later was sent to Mesopotamia. In this theatre of hostilities he took a conspicuous part in strenuous fighting at Kut and near Baghdad.

Subsequently proceeding to Palestine he again saw heavy fighting near Jerusalem and was present at the capture of Jericho. For some months he was in hospital suffering from enteric, and was demobilised on his return home in October 1919, holding the General Service and Victory Medals.
36, Birch Street, West Gorton, Manchester. Z5903

DONALD, G. S., Private, Royal Welch Fusiliers.
He joined in April 1916, and proceeded to the Western Front in February of the following year. There he took part in much of the severe fighting at Arras, Ypres, Cambrai and the Somme, and in many later engagements in the Retreat and the Advance of 1918. After the Armistice was signed he entered Germany with the Army of Occupation, and served with the Rhine Forces until September 1919, when he returned to England and was demobilised. He holds the General Service and Victory Medals.
20, Malpas Street, Bradford, Manchester. TZ9072

DONALDSON, J. F., Cpl., K.O. (R. Lancaster Regt.)
He volunteered in December 1914, and in September of the following year proceeded to the Western Front, where he saw much severe fighting until November 1915. He was then transferred to Salonika, but was shortly afterwards admitted to hospital at Malta, suffering from malaria. On his recovery, however, he returned to Salonika, and was in action on the Doiran front until invalided home. He was finally demobilised in February 1919, and holds the 1914-15 Star, and the General Service and Victory Medals.
8, South Porter Street, Ancoats, Manchester. Z10119

DONBAVAND, S. W., Private, 1st Manchester Regt.
Joining in May 1917, he proceeded in the following July to India. There he was employed with his unit on garrison and other important duties at Bombay. Delhi and Calcutta, but in May 1918 was transferred to Egypt, where he took part in fighting at Jericho, Tripoli and Aleppo. He returned home in April 1919, and when demobilised a month later was entitled to the General Service and Victory Medals.
33, Teak Street, Beswick, Manchester. Z5904

DONIGAN, W., Private, 12th Manchester Regt., and Sapper, R.E.
He volunteered in August 1914, and two months afterwards was sent to France, where he at once took part in heavy fighting and was gassed at Ypres. Upon his recovery he rejoined his unit, and participated in further fighting on the Somme front and at Armentières, Cambrai, Passchendaele and Vimy Ridge. He was subsequently transferred to the Royal Engineers, and was employed on important duties until demobilised in February 1919, holding the 1914 Star, and the General Service and Victory Medals.
15, Clegg Street, Hulme, Manchester. Z5906

DONLY, J., 1st Air Mechanic, R.A.F.
He joined in February 1918, and after his training served at various stations on important duties, which demanded a high degree of technical skill. He rendered valuable services, but was not successful in obtaining a transfer overseas before the cessation of hostilities, and was demobilised in May 1919.
50, Fielden Street, Oldham Road, Manchester. Z9074

DONNELLY, A., Private, 11th Lancashire Fusiliers.
He volunteered in September 1914, and twelve months later was drafted to the Western Front. Whilst in this theatre of war he saw severe fighting in various sectors, took part in the Battles of Albert, Vermelles, the Somme, Arras, Bullecourt and Bapaume, and many other engagements, and was wounded in action in October 1915. Demobilised in April 1919, he holds the 1914-15 Star, and the General Service and Victory Medals.
11, Osborne Street, Oldham Road, Manchester. Z10121

DONNELLY, E., Private, 1st Manchester Regiment.
He volunteered in August 1914, and in June of the following year was sent to the Dardanelles, where he saw severe fighting at Suvla Bay, and Chocolate Hill, and took part in the capture of Chunuk Bair. On the Evacuation of the Peninsula he was transferred to Mesopotamia and there fought at Sanna-i-Yat and Baghdad, and was twice wounded in action—at Kut in February 1917, and at Samara in April of that year. He was afterwards engaged on garrison duties in India until his return home for demobilisation in February 1920, and holds the 1914-15 Star, and the General Service and Victory Medals.
20, Ardsley Street, Oldham Road, Manchester. Z10122

DONNELLY, J., Pte., K.O. (Royal Lancaster Regt.)
Mobilised in August 1914, he was immediately drafted to the Western Front, where he participated in the Battle of Mons and the Retreat. He also took part in the Battles of Le Cateau, the Marne, the Aisne, La Bassée, Ypres, Neuve Chapelle, and St. Eloi, and was gassed in action at La Bassée in September 1915. As a result he was evacuated to hospital at Cheltenham, and eventually invalided out of the Service in February 1916, holding the Mons Star, and the General Service and Victory Medals.
56, Dorset Street, Hulme, Manchester. Z5905

DONNELLY, T. H., Private, Cheshire Regiment.
Shortly after joining in June 1916, he was drafted to the Western Front, where he took part in the Battles of the Somme, Arras, Ypres and Cambrai, and many minor engagements. In February 1918, however, he was transferred to Italy, where he was again in action on the Piave and the Asiago Plateaux until the cessation of hostilities. He afterwards proceeded to Egypt, and also served in Syria and Palestine, before returning home for demobilisation in February 1920. He holds the General Service and Victory Medals.
8, Ardley Street, Miles Platting, Manchester.   Z10123

DONNELLY, W., Private, 23rd Manchester Regt.
He volunteered in January 1915, and in the following May embarked for France, where he took part in the fighting at Albert and Vermelles, and was severely wounded in the Battle of the Somme in September 1916. He was invalided home to hospital, and was subsequently discharged as medically unfit for further military service in November 1917. He holds the 1914-15 Star, and the General Service and Victory Medals.
24, Tame Street, Ancoats, Manchester.   Z9073

DONOHUE, E., Pte., K.O. (Royal Lancaster Regt.)
Volunteering in August 1914, he proceeded to the Western Front two months later, and was there wounded in action and taken prisoner, after only a few days' active service. Held in captivity for over four years at Ruhleben and other prison camps, he was finally invalided from the Army on his release in December 1918. He holds the 1914 Star, and the General Service and Victory Medals.
4, Lime Street, Bradford, Manchester.   Z10124

DONOHUE, J., Private, 8th Manchester Regiment.
Volunteering in September 1914, he was drafted in the following April to Gallipoli. In this theatre of war, he took part in the Battles of Krithia and in strenuous fighting at Suvla Bay. Contracting dysentery, he was sent to hospital at Alexandria and later invalided home. After spending some time in hospital at Leicester, he was attached to the Labour Corps, and did good work whilst employed on various duties at different home stations. Demobilised in March 1919 he holds the 1914-15 Star, and the General Service and Victory Medals.
9, Davies Street, Hulme, Manchester.   Z5907

DONOHUE, T., Private, 2nd Manchester Regiment.
A Reservist, he was called to the Colours at the outbreak of war in August 1914, and shortly afterwards was drafted to the Western Front, where he took part in the Retreat from Mons. He also fought in the Battles of Ypres, Neuve Chapelle, St. Eloi, Hill 60, Festubert, Vimy Ridge, the Somme, Arras and Cambrai, and many minor engagements, and suffered from shell-shock whilst overseas. He was discharged on his return home in 1919, and holds the Mons Star, and the General Service and Victory Medals.
51, Thornton Street, Manchester.   Z10120

DOODSON, E., Pte., Argyll and Sutherland H'ldrs.
He volunteered in January 1915, and towards the end of the same year proceeded to France. There he took part in heavy engagements at Loos, Neuve Chapelle, and Arras, where he was wounded in July 1916. Invalided home, he was sent to hospital at Wareham, and returning later to France, participated in severe fighting at Albert, Vimy Ridge, Ypres, Passchendaele, Cambrai, La Bassée, Givenchy and on the Somme. Wounded again in October 1918, he was evacuated to England, and was eventually demobilised in January 1919, holding the 1914-15 Star, and the General Service and Victory Medals.
19, Baker Street, Ardwick, Manchester.   Z5909

DOODSON, R., Pte., 9th K.O. (Royal Lancaster Regt.)
Volunteering in September 1914, he was sent twelve months later to Salonika. In this theatre of war he took part in many important engagements, and was in action on the Doiran, Struma and Vardar fronts, and also in severe fighting at Monastir. He remained overseas until December 1918, and was demobilised a month later, holding the 1914-15 Star, and the General Service and Victory Medals.
54, Derby Street, Ardwick, Manchester.   TZ5908

DOODSON, T., Private, Royal Welch Fusiliers.
He joined in August 1916, and after a brief training was drafted to the Western Front. During his service overseas he was in action at Beaumont-Hamel, Beaucourt, Arras, Vimy Ridge, Bullecourt, Messines Ridge, Ypres, and Cambrai. He performed consistently good work until the cessation of hostilities, and was demobilised on his return home in January 1919. He holds the General Service and Victory Medals.
20, Mary Street, Higher Ardwick, Manchester.   Z5910

DOODSON, T., Private, 1/6th Welch Regiment.
Joining in January 1918, he proceeded in the following June to France, where he played a prominent part in severe fighting at Givenchy and La Bassée during the Advance of 1918. After the Armistice, he served with the Army of Occupation in Germany, and remained there until October 1919. He then returned home and was demobilised, holding the General Service and Victory Medals.
20, Mary Street, Ardwick, Manchester.   TX5911

DOOLAN, J., Private, K.O. (Royal Lancaster Regt.)
He volunteered in February 1915, and two months later was sent to France. There he was in action at Ypres, Loos, and in other sectors until he was transferred to Mesopotamia in March 1916. In this theatre of hostilities he took part in heavy fighting on various fronts, and did good work until he returned home for demobilisation in December 1918, holding the 1914-15 Star, and the General Service and Victory Medals. 8, Picking Street, Hulme, Manchester.   TZ5912

DOOLER, R. J., L/Corporal, 1/7th Manchester Regt.
Volunteering in August 1914, he was sent in the following month to Egypt. After taking part in severe fighting near the Suez Canal and at Mersa Matruh, where he was attached to the Camel Corps, he was drafted to the Dardanelles, and soon afterwards fell in action at Suvla Bay on June 4th, 1915. He was entitled to the 1914-15 Star, and the General Service and Victory Medals.
"Whilst we remember, the sacrifice is not in vain."
16, Luke Street, Collyhurst, Manchester.   Z11490

DOOLEY, A., Private, K.O. (Royal Lancaster Regt.)
He joined in June 1916, and after two months' training was drafted to France, where he saw severe fighting in various sectors of the Front. After taking part in the Battles of the Somme, Arras, Bullecourt and Messines, and many minor engagements, he was taken prisoner at Bapaume in August 1918, and held in captivity until after the cessation of hostilities. He was finally demobilised in August 1919, and holds the General Service and Victory Medals.
32, Gray Street, Ancoats, Manchester.   Z10125

DOOLEY, C. H., Private, 1/6th Manchester Regt.
He volunteered in September 1914, and on completing his training in April of the following year was drafted to Gallipoli, where he was severely wounded in action in the Landing at Cape Helles. Invalided home he was for some time in hospital before being discharged in January 1916, as medically unfit for further service, and holds the 1914-15 Star, and the General Service and Victory Medals.
25, Hora Street, Bradford, Manchester.   Z10126

DOOLEY, M., Private, 13th Manchester Regiment.
Volunteering in September 1914, he was drafted a year later to Salonika, where he took part in strenuous fighting at Monastir, and on the Doiran and Struma fronts. In May 1917, he was transferred to France, and after participating in further fighting at Bullecourt, was unfortunately killed in action at Ypres on August 18th, 1917. He was entitled to the 1914-15 Star, and the General Service and Victory Medals.
"A costly sacrifice upon the altar of freedom."
4, Hardy Street, West Gorton, Manchester.   Z5913

DORAN, E., Private, Border Regiment.
He volunteered in August 1915, and after his training was engaged on important guard duties with his unit at his depôt. His health unhappily broke down, and he was invalided to hospital, and discharged as medically unfit for further service in January 1916. He died in June 1920 from the effects of illness contracted whilst in the Army.
"His memory is cherished with pride."
36, Lostock Street, Miles Platting, Manchester.   Z9075

DORAN, J. F., Private, 1st Manchester Regiment.
He enlisted in July 1914, and in April of the following year was drafted to the Western Front, where he saw severe fighting in various sectors. After taking part in the Battles of Ypres and Festubert, and other engagements in this theatre of war he was transferred in 1916 to Mesopotamia, where he was shortly afterwards wounded in action. Invalided to India, he returned to Mesopotamia, however, on his recovery and was a second time wounded and sent to hospital in India. He afterwards re-joined his unit at Baghdad, and finally returned home for demobilisation in September 1919. He holds the 1914-15 Star, and the General Service and Victory Medals.
9, Ward Street, Gorton, Manchester.   Z10127

DORAN, T., Private, 3rd Manchester Regiment.
Volunteering in August 1914, he proceeded to the Western Front in the following month, and there took part in important engagements at Laventie, and in various other sectors. He was afterwards in action in the Balkan Campaign, before being invalided to hospital at Liverpool and finally discharged in March 1917, as medically unfit for further service. He holds the 1914 Star, and the General Service and Victory Medals.
6, Lawrence Street, Gorton, Manchester.   Z10128

DORBER, F., Gunner, R.F.A.
He volunteered in September 1914, and was employed at home on various duties until May 1916, when he proceeded to France. In this theatre of hostilities he served with his Battery on the Somme front, and at Neuve Chapelle, Arras and Ypres, and performed consistently good work. He was demobilised on his return home in May 1919, and holds the General Service and Victory Medals.
24, John Street, Ardwick, Manchester.   Z5914

DORRICOTT, T., Private, K.O. (R. Lancaster Regt.)
He joined in November 1918, and after a period of training was sent in the following April to Dublin. Whilst stationed there he was attached to the Labour Corps, and rendered excellent service, employed on transport duties. He spent some time in hospital as the result of an accident, and was eventually demobilised in November 1919.
8, Union Street, Rusholme, Manchester. Z5915

DORSETT, G., Air Mechanic, R.A.F.
He joined in August 1916, and was retained on important duties in England until July 1917, when he proceeded to the Western Front. There he served in various sectors on duties of a highly technical nature, and took part also in the Retreat of 1918. He returned home for demobilisation in April 1919, and holds the General Service and Victory Medals.
9, Mytton Street, Hulme, Manchester. Z11689

DORWARD, W., Private, 20th Manchester Regt.
Volunteering in May 1915, he was seven months later drafted overseas. Whilst serving on the Western Front he was engaged in fierce fighting in the Battles of Loos, St. Eloi, Vimy Ridge and Vermelles, and was unfortunately killed in action at Givenchy on August 27th, 1916. He was entitled to the 1914-15 Star, and the General Service and Victory Medals.
"Whilst we remember, the sacrifice is not in vain."
42, Armitage Street, Ardwick, Manchester. Z5803

DOUGLAS, A., A.B., Royal Navy.
He volunteered in April 1915, and was posted to H.M.S. "Roxburgh," on board which vessel he was engaged on patrol duties with the Grand Fleet iu the North Sea. He took part in the Battle of Jutland, in a Cruiser engagement at Heligoland Bight, and in many minor actions. He unhappily died of influenza in July 1918, and was buried at sea. He was entitled to the 1914-15 Star, and the General Service (with six clasps) and Victory Medals.
"His life for his Country, his soul to God."
8, Aspden Street, Ancoats, Manchester. Z10129

DOUGLAS, R., Sergt., 3rd Lancashire Fusiliers.
Volunteering at the outbreak of war in August 1914, he was drafted in the following month to the Western Front. There he played a conspicuous part in the Battles of the Marne, the Aisne, La Bassée, Ypres (I), Neuve Chappelle St. Eloi, Hill 60, Ypres (II), Loos, Vimy Ridge, and the Somme. He spent some time in hospital as the result of being gassed, and later, transferred to the Labour Corps, was employed on important duties until he was invalided out of the Service on account of ill-health in August 1917. He holds the 1914 Star and the General Service and Victory Medals.
5, Fountain Street, City Road, Hulme, Manchester. Z5916

DOUGLAS, W. Private, King's (Liverpool Regt.)
He volunteered in August 1915, and four months later proceeded to Salonika. In this theatre of war he was in action on the Doiran and Struma fronts, and took part in the Battles of the Vardar. He was wounded in action in April 1917, but remained overseas until February 1919, and was demobilised on his arrival home in the following month, holding the 1914-15 Star, and the General Service and Victory Medals. TZ5917
61, George's Avenue, Chester Road, Hulme, Manchester.

DOUTHWAITE, H., Pte., Royal Welch Fusiliers.
He joined in December 1916, and in May of the following year was drafted to the Western Front, where he saw severe fighting in various sectors. He was afterwards engaged on transport work and other important duties, and rendered valuable services with his unit until his return home for demobilisation in March 1920. He holds the General Service and Victory Medals. 9, Aspden Street, Ancoats, Manchester. Z10130

DOVE, A., Private, R.A.S.C.
Volunteering in November 1914, he served at Southport and Colchester, employed on important duties until March 1917, when he was sent to France. In this theatre of hostilities he was stationed at La Bassée, Béthune, Nieuport, Dunkirk, Ypres, Passchendaele, and the Somme, and did good work whilst engaged on various duties. He was later admitted to hospital, owing to ill-health, and eventually invalided out of the Army in July 1919. He holds the General Service and Victory Medals.
14, Wilson Street, Ardwick, Manchester. Z5918

DOVER, R., Sapper, R.E.
He joined the Army in January 1914, and after the outbreak of war in the following August was retained on important duties at home stations until 1915, when he proceeded to France. There he took part in the Battles of Ypres, the Somme, Cambrai and La Bassée, and was wounded in action. He was discharged in 1919, and holds the 1914-15 Star, and the General Service and Victory Medals.
265, Morton Street, Longsight, Manchester. Z10131A

DOVER, D. M., Private, Manchester Regiment.
He joined in September 1917, and was engaged at various stations on important duties with his unit. After hostilities ceased, he proceeded to Palestine and served on garrison duties at Jaffa. He returned home and was demobilised in 1920. 265, Morton Street, Longsight, Manchester. Z10131B

DOVEY, H., Rifleman, 3rd Rifle Brigade.
Volunteering in September 1914, he was sent to France in the following December, and saw service at Neuve Chapelle, St. Eloi, Hill 60, Ypres, Loos, Albert and Vimy Ridge. He gave his life for his King and Country at Guillemont on August 21st, 1916, and was entitled to the 1914-15 Star, and the General Service and Victory Medals.
"Great deeds cannot die:
They, with the sun and moon renew their light for ever."
8, Lilford Street, West Gorton, Manchester. Z9076

DOWDALL, G., Private, 4th East Lancashire Regt.
Having previously taken part in the South African Campaign, he was called up from the Reserve in August 1914, and proceeded to France with the First Expeditionary Force. He took part in the Battle of Mons, and was taken prisoner during the subsequent Retreat. Whilst in captivity in Germany he was employed on agricultural work in various prison camps, and was repatriated after the Armistice. He was discharged in January 1919, and holds the Mons Star, and the General Service and Victory Medals, in addition to the Queen's and King's South African Medals.
7, Abbey Field Street, Openshaw, Manchester. Z5919

DOWDING, C. S., Pte., Loyal North Lancashire Regt.
He volunteered in September 1915, and in August of the following year was drafted to the Western Front. In this theatre of war he took part in heavy fighting at Ypres, but had only served overseas for a few months when he fell in action on the Somme on December 25th, 1916, and was buried in the Military Cemetery at Ploegsteert. He was entitled to the General Service and Victory Medals.
"The path of duty was the way to glory."
6, Walmer Place, Longsight, Manchester. Z5920

DOWLEY, A. S., Chief Petty Officer, R.N.
Having enlisted as a boy, he was sent to sea at the outbreak of war and proceeded iu 1915 to Gallipoli, where he was wounded. On his recovery he was engaged in bringing food from America to England. He was discharged in March 1920, and holds the 1914-15 Star, and the General Service and Victory Medals.
5, Kay Street, Chorlton-on-Medlock, Manchester. TX5924A

DOWLEY, N. W.(Miss),Stewardess, Merchant Service.
This lady joined in October 1917, and served as a stewardess in the s.s. "Eupion," engaged on important duties between New York and England, and was in this vessel when attacked by an enemy submarine. She rendered valuable services until she was discharged in April 1918.
5, Kay Street, Chorlton-on-Medlock, Manchester. TX5924B

DOWLING, L., Private, M.G.C.
Volunteering in January 1915, he proceeded overseas in the following year. During his service on the Western Front he took part in several engagements, including the Battles of Ypres, the Somme, and Vimy Ridge and was gassed in action. In consequence he was invalided to the Base, but on his recovery returned to his unit, and saw much fighting at Arras, Givenchy and Delville Wood. He was demobilised in February 1919, and holds the General Service and Victory Medals.
16, Rowe Street, Oldham Road, Manchester. Z10132

DOWNES, F., Private, King's (Liverpool Regiment).
He joined in April 1918, but owing to his being under age could not procure his transfer overseas. He was, however, retained in England, and engaged on important duties with his unit until he was demobilised in September 1919.
1, Castleton Street, Gorton, Manchester. TZ5922

DOWNEY, A., Driver, R.F.A.
Joining in April 1916, he did not proceed to France until September 1917. Whilst on the Western Front he fought in the Battle of Cambrai and during the Retreat and Advance of 1918 was in action on the Somme, and at Cambrai, Bapaume and Havrincourt. He was demobilised in September 1919, and holds the General Service and Victory Medals.
15, Potter Street, Hulme, Manchester. Z5923

DOWNING, J., 2nd Monmouthshire Regiment.
He joined in June 1916, and in the following November proceeded to France. In this theatre of war he took part in several engagements, including the Battles of Beaucourt, the Ancre, Bullecourt, Arras and Vimy Ridge, and was badly wounded at Dickebusch. As a result he was invalided home, and finally discharged in April 1918, as medically unfit for further service. He holds the General Service and Victory Medals.
15, Grantham Street, West Gorton, Manchester. Z10133

DOWNING, J. E., Private, R.A.V.C.
He joined in November 1916, and two months later embarked for France. There he served in the Ancre, Arras, Vimy, Ypres, Cambrai, Marne, Havrincourt and Le Cateau sectors, and was engaged on the lines of communication attending to horses. Demobilised in August 1919, he holds the General Service and Victory Medals.
59, Caythorpe Street, Moss Side, Manchester. Z5926

DOWNING, T. M., Private, 20th Lancashire Fusiliers.
Volunteering in June 1915, he was sent to France six months later, and fought at Neuve Chapelle, Ypres, La Bassée, Givenchy, Festubert, and the Somme. During the Offensive on the Somme, he was unhappily killed on July 23rd, 1916. He was entitled to the General Service and Victory Medals.
"His life for his Country, his soul to God."
7, Hancock Street, Rusholme, Manchester.   TZ5921

DOWNING, W. H., Air Mechanic, R.A.F.
He volunteered in May 1915, but was discharged as unfit owing to heart-trouble. Subsequently he rejoined, and in 1916 was sent to Italy, where he was engaged on duties of a highly technical nature in different sectors. Returning home, he was demobilised in May 1919, and holds the General Service and Victory Medals.
38, Caroline Street, Hulme, Manchester.   Z5925

DOWNS, A., Private, 3rd Manchester Regiment.
He volunteered in December 1915, and in July of the following year was drafted to the Western Front, where he saw much heavy fighting. He was severely wounded in action in the Somme Offensive, and in October 1916 was invalided home, suffering also from shell-shock. He was for some months in hospital in England, before being discharged as medically unfit for further service in April 1917, and holds the General Service and Victory Medals.
4, Phillips Street, Hulme, Manchester.   Z11690

DOWNS, J., Sapper, R.E. (Signals).
He joined in June 1916, and towards the end of the same year proceeded with the 56th Division Signal Service to France. There he was employed as a Field Linesman on communications and served on the Somme front, also at Armentières, Ypres, Cambrai, Mons and in various sectors during the Retreat and Advance of 1918. He was demobilised in January 1919, and holds the General Service and Victory Medals.
9, Cranworth Street, Chorlton-on-Medlock, Manchester.
                                                       Z11613A

DOWNS, J., Private, 1/7th Manchester Regiment.
He volunteered in December 1914, and in the following August was drafted to the Dardanelles, where he served until after the Evacuation. He was then sent to Egypt, and was in action at Gaza, El Kantara and El Arish, before he was transferred to France with the 42nd Division in February 1917. On the Western Front he took part in heavy fighting at Havrincourt, Ypres, Passchendaele, Cambrai and La Bassée, and was demobilised on returning home in February 1919. He holds the 1914-15 Star, and the General Service and Victory Medals.
9, Cranworth Street, Chorlton-on-Medlock, Manchester.
                                                       Z11613B

DOYLE, A., Private, King's (Liverpool Regt.)
He joined in February 1916, after having worked on munitions, and three weeks later crossed to France. There he took part in the Somme Offensive, and the Battles of Ypres, Passchendaele and Cambrai, and also fought during the Retreat and Advance of 1918. He also served for a time with the Army of Occupation in Germany, and was demobilised in November 1919, holding the General Service and Victory Medals.
15, Anthony Street, Ardwick, Manchester.   Z5929

DOYLE, A., Leading Seaman Gunner, R.N., H.M.S. "Excellent."
Volunteering in December 1915, he was sent to sea in H.M.S. "Victory VI" and took a prominent part in the Battle of Jutland, during which he was wounded. He was also engaged on patrol work in the North Sea and Atlantic in H.M.S. "Montigua," "Excellent" and "President III." He was demobilised in July 1919, and holds the General Service and Victory Medals.
6, Hewitt Street, Openshaw, Manchester.   Z5928

DOYLE, F., Private, 6th Battalion Royal Scots.
He volunteered in February 1915, and after the completion of his training was sent to Egypt in 1916, and later in the same year proceeded to France. There he fought in the Battles of Loos and Ypres, and after being badly wounded, was invalided home. On his recovery he was engaged in the production of munitions until demobilised in May 1919. He holds the General Service and Victory Medals.
159, Cheltenham Street, Collyhurst, Manchester.   Z10562

DOYLE, H. P., Private, Yorkshire Regiment and Durham Light Infantry.
Seven months after volunteering in September 1914, he proceeded to the Dardanelles, but was wounded during the Landing at Gallipoli. After a period in hospital at Nottingham, he was sent to Salonika, and there served on the Doiran, Struma and Monastir fronts. He unfortunately contracted malaria and was treated at Alexandria. Returning home he was demobilised in March 1919, and holds the 1914-15 Star, and the General Service and Victory Medals.
11, Garden Walks, Ardwick, Manchester.   Z5927

DOYLE, J., Sapper, R.E.
He joined in February 1918, and after a period of training was engaged at various stations on important duties with his unit. Owing to the early cessation of hostilities, he was unable to obtain a transfer overseas, but rendered valuable services until his demobilisation in November 1919.
33, Boslam Street, Ancoats, Manchester.   Z10134

DOYLE, J. G., Private, King's (Liverpool Regt.)
He volunteered in 1915, and in the succeeding year embarked for France, where he served until 1918. During that time he fought in the Battle of Ypres (III), and was also in action at Loos, Armentières and Vimy Ridge. Wounded at La Bassée, he was sent home and spent some time in hospital at Cardiff before being discharged as unfit in 1919. He holds the General Service and Victory Medals.
23, Byrom Street, Longsight, Manchester.   Z5930

DOYLE, J. J., Private, 20th Manchester Regiment.
Volunteering in November 1914, he proceeded in the following October to the Western Front. In this theatre of war he played a prominent part in the Battles of the Somme, Arras and Ypres, and other important engagements, and was twice wounded—at Albert in April 1916, and on the Somme three months later. He was demobilised in March 1919, and holds the 1914-15 Star, and the General Service and Victory Medals.
14, Alma Street, Collyhurst, Manchester.   Z11491

DOYLE, W., Private, 23rd Manchester Regiment.
Volunteering in November 1915, he embarked for France in May of the following year, and took part in the heavy fighting on the Somme. He was unhappily killed in action there on July 21st, 1916, and was buried at La Neuville. He was entitled to the General Service and Victory Medals.
"He died the noblest death a man may die, Fighting for God, and right, and liberty."
28, Dalton Street, Collyhurst, Manchester.   Z10563

DRANE, J., Private, Border Regiment.
Volunteering in October 1914, he was drafted to France in June of the following year, and whilst overseas was severely wounded in action at Ypres, after fighting at Loos, Vermelles and St. Eloi. He was invalided home to hospital, and after receiving medical treatment was discharged as physically disabled for further duty in June 1916. He holds the 1914-15 Star, and the General Service and Victory Medals.
17, Victoria Square, Ancoats, Manchester.   Z9077

DRAPER, E., Sergt., 8th Manchester Regiment.
He volunteered in September 1914, and in July 1916 was sent to France, where he fought in the Battle of the Somme, and was wounded in action. After his recovery he was again wounded at Arras in May 1917, and was later transferred to the Royal Air Force, and subsequently invalided home to hospital. He holds the General Service and Victory Medals, and was discharged as medically unfit for further service, owing to ill-health in September 1920.
137, Victoria Square, Ancoats, Manchester.   TZ9078

DRAPER, W., Private, K.O. Scottish Borderers.
Volunteering at the outbreak of war, he was sent to the Dardanelles in the following August, but was badly wounded. After being in hospital in Birmingham, he proceeded to France, where he served in the Loos, St. Eloi and Albert sectors, but was reported missing, and later killed in action on the Somme on July 31st, 1916. He was entitled to the 1914-15 Star, and the General Service and Victory Medals.
"Great deeds never die."
42, King Street, Ardwick, Manchester.   Z5931

DREW, R., Private, Manchester Regiment.
Volunteering in November 1915, he was sent eight months later to France, and after taking part in the Battles of Beaumont-Hamel, the Somme, Arras and Bullecourt, was wounded at Messines. On his recovery, he proceeded to Egypt, and served at Cairo, Alexandria, Khartoum and Kantara. Transferred to Italy in October 1918, he was wounded in action, and sent back to England. He was demobilised in February 1919, and holds the General Service and Victory Medals.
4, Juno Street, Ancoats, Manchester·   Z9505

DREW, S. E. (Mrs.), Special War Worker.
During the war this lady was engaged on work of National importance at Messrs. Armstrong and Whitworth's, Manchester. She worked on the manufacture of shells and carried out her difficult duties in an efficient manner, and rendered valuable services until November 1918.
12, Buxton Street, West Gorton, Manchester.   Z10135

DRINKROW, J. W., Sapper, R.E.
He joined in November 1916, and five months later embarked for France, where he served in the Ypres, St. Quentin, Arras and Albert sectors. Gassed at Albert in March 1918, he was sent two months afterwards to Palestine, and was stationed at Gaza and Romani. Returning to England, he was demobilised in March 1919, and holds the General Service and Victory Medals.
3, Mytton Street, Hulme, Manchester.   Z5932

DRINKWATER, E., Private, 2nd Manchester Regt.
He was mobilised at the outbreak of hostilities, and was almost immediately drafted to France, where he served in the memorable Battle of Mons. He made the supreme sacrifice during the subsequent Retreat in September 1914, and was entitled to the Mons Star, and the General Service and Victory Medals.
" He died the noblest death a man may die,
   Fighting for God, and right, and liberty."
18, Kingston Street, Hulme, Manchester.   Z9079

DRINKWATER, W., Pte., K.O. (R. Lancaster Regt.)
He joined in October 1917, and in the following March was drafted to the Western Front. Whilst in this theatre of war he took part in the Retreat and Advance, and was wounded in action at La Bassée in August 1918, and consequently was invalided home. He was discharged in February 1919, as medically unfit for further service and holds the General Service and Victory Medals.
25, Albion Street, Miles Platting, Manchester.   Z10136

DRIVER, R., Sapper, R.E.
He volunteered in September 1915, and eight months later was drafted to Egypt, where he served on the Suez Canal, and the Sinai Peninsula, and also at Kantara. He afterwards took part in the Advance into Palestine, and fought in the Battles of Gaza. He was for a short time in hospital at Alexandria, before returning home for demobilisation in July 1919, and holds the General Service and Victory Medals.
52, Gore Street, Greenheys, Manchester.   Z11691

DRIVER, R., 1st Air Mechanic, R.A.F.
He joined in February 1918, having previously been engaged on important Government work during the earlier part of the war. After his training he served with the Irish Command Squadron, and was employed on skilled motor and aero-fitting duties. He rendered valuable services, and was demobilised in November 1919.
15, Sarah Ann Street, Beswick, Manchester.   TZ9080

DRUMMOND, M., C.Q.M.S., 4th K.O. (R. Lancaster Regiment).
He volunteered in August 1914, and was engaged at various stations on important duties with his unit. He was not successful in obtaining a transfer overseas, but rendered valuable services until his discharge in June 1916, as medically unfit for further duty.
16, Elizabeth Street, West Gorton, Manchester.   Z10137

DUCKWORTH, J., Private, M.G.C.
Seven months after joining in June 1916, he was drafted to the Western Front, and took part in many important engagements. He fought in the Battles of Ypres (III), Cambrai, Arras and the Somme (II), but was wounded in Belgium. Re-joining his unit, he, however, continued to serve until the cessation of hostilities. Demobilised in February 1919, he holds the General Service and Victory Medals.
17, Mount Street, Hulme, Manchester.   Z5933

DUDDLE, A., Driver, R.A.S.C. (M.T.)
He joined in December 1917, and was quickly drafted to Mesopotamia. In this theatre of war he was engaged on important duties with the Mechanical Transport at Kut, Baghdad, Um-el-Hannah and Basra. He returned home, and was demobilised in March 1920, holding the General Service and Victory Medals.
57, Irlam Street, Miles Platting, Manchester.   Z10138

DUDSON, A., Private, 16th Lancashire Fusiliers.
Volunteering in November 1914, he was drafted in the following year to France, where he saw much hard fighting. He was in action at Neuve Chapelle, Hill 60, Ypres, Loos, St. Eloi, the Ancre, Arras, Messines, Lens and Albert, where he was severely wounded in 1917. After being invalided home he was discharged in February 1918, as medically unfit for further duty, and holds the 1914-15 Star, and the General Service and Victory Medals.
54, Bugley Street, St. Michaels, Manchester.   Z10564

DUFFEY, T., Private, 1st Loyal N. Lancashire Regt.
Volunteering at the commencement of hostilities, he was immediately sent to France. In this theatre of war he took part in the heavy fighting at the Battles of Mons and La Bassée, and was wounded. Later he returned to France, and served at Ypres, the Somme, and Messines. He remained in this seat of war until after the conclusion of hostilities, and in January 1919 was demobilised, holding the Mons Star, and the General Service and Victory Medals.
7, Frederick Street, Rochdale Road, Manchester.   Z11897

DUFFIELD, A. F., Gunner, R.G.A.
He was mobilised in August 1914, and immediately drafted to the Western Front. There he took part in the Battles of Mons, Le Cateau, the Marne, La Bassée, Ypres (I), Neuve Chapelle, Loos, Vimy Ridge, Ypres (II), the Somme, Ypres (III), Cambrai, and in the Retreat and Advance of 1918, when he was wounded in action. He was discharged in March 1919, and holds the Mons Star, and the General Service and Victory Medals.
1, Sun Street, Newton Heath, Manchester.   Z10139A

DUFFY, C. G., Private, Seaforth Highlanders.
He joined in June 1916, and on completion of his training was drafted to the Western Front, where he took part in many important engagements. He was gassed in action at Beaumont-Hamel, but after hospital treatment at Étaples, rejoined his unit, and saw further heavy fighting until the cessation of hostilities. He holds the General Service and Victory Medals, and was demobilised in February 1920.
4, Wilson Street, Ancoats, Manchester.   Z10140A

DUFFY, D. E., Cpl., Loyal North Lancashire Regt.
At the outbreak of war in August 1914, he was stationed in India, but proceeded to France with the first Indian Expeditionary Force, and was badly wounded in action at the Battle of Ypres (I). He was invalided home, and on his recovery was engaged on special duties at his Regimental depôt. He received his discharge in December 1918, and holds the 1914 Star, and the General Service and Victory Medals.
4, Wilson Street, Ancoats, Manchester.   Z10140C

DUFFY, H., Pte., 3rd Manchester Regt. and 1st King's (Liverpool Regt.)
Volunteering in November 1914, he proceeded to France in March of the following year, and whilst there took part in much severe fighting. He was in action at St. Eloi, Ypres and Loos, and was unfortunately killed on the Somme in July 1916. He was entitled to the 1914-15 Star, and the General Service and Victory Medals.
" Thinking that remembrance, though unspoken, may reach
   him where he sleeps."
15, Limer Street, Rochdale Road, Manchester.   Z10565

DUFFY, J. F., Corporal, Manchester Regiment.
He volunteered in August 1914, and on completion of his training was drafted to Mesopotamia, where he played a prominent part in much severe fighting. He was badly wounded in action at Kut-el-Amara, and was invalided to hospital at Allahabad in India. After long treatment he unfortunately died from the effects of his wounds on June 22nd, 1918, and was entitled to the 1914-15 Star, and the General Service and Victory Medals.
" A costly sacrifice upon the altar of freedom."
4, Wilson Street, Ancoats, Manchester.   Z10140B

DUFFY, J. W., Private, Lancashire Fusiliers.
Volunteering in August 1914, he proceeded to France in the following July, and fought at Beaumont-Hamel and Beaucourt in the Somme Offensive of 1916. He also took part in the Battles of Arras, Ypres (III), and Passchendaele, and the capture of Vimy Ridge, but was wounded during the second Battle of the Somme. Invalided home, he remained in hospital until his demobilisation in December 1918, and holds the 1914-15 Star, and the General Service and Victory Medals.
12, Birch Street, Hulme, Manchester.   Z5934

DUFFY, T., Driver, R.A.S.C.
He volunteered in September 1914, and in May of the following year embarked for France, where he was engaged in taking ammunition up the lines during the Battles of Ypres (II), Loos, Albert, the Somme, Arras, Cambrai, Havrincourt and Le Cateau. He was sent home in July 1918, and remained in England until March 1919, when he was demobilised, holding the 1914-15 Star, and the General Service and Victory Medals.
18, Church Street, Hulme, Manchester.   Z5935A

DUFFY, T., Pte., R.A.S.C. and 1st Manchester Regt.
Volunteering in January 1915, he proceeded to Egypt later in the year, but in 1916 was admitted to hospital with fever and septic poisoning. Subsequently he served at Kantara, Gaza and Jerusalem, and returned home in April 1918. He was discharged in May 1918, and holds the 1914-15 Star, and the General Service and Victory Medals.
8, Allen Street, Hulme, Manchester.   Z5936

DUGDALE, C., Air Mechanic, R.A.F.
He joined in February 1916, but was not successful in obtaining a transfer to a theatre of war. Retained on home service, he was stationed at Catterick and Glasgow, and did excellent work whilst engaged on important duties which demanded a high degree of technical skill, until he was demobilised in February 1919.
12, Milton Street, West Gorton, Manchester.   TZ11413

DUGDALE, F. (M.M.), Cpl., 1/6th Manchester Regt.
Volunteering in January 1915, he was sent to Egypt in the following March, and was in action on the Suez Canal. He also took part in the Landing at Suvla Bay on the Gallipoli Peninsula, and after the Evacuation, was transferred to the Western Front. He then served with distinction at the Battles of the Somme and Arras, and in heavy fighting at La Bassée and Nieuport. He was awarded the Military Medal for conspicuous bravery and devotion to duty at Bihucourt and Bucquoy. In 1920 he was stationed in Ireland, and also holds the 1914-15 Star, and the General Service and Victory Medals.
20, Flower Street, Ancoats, Manchester.   Z10141A

DUGDALE, J., Private, 11th Manchester Regt.
Volunteering in August 1914, he was drafted to France in the following January. During his service on the Western Front, he took part in the Battles of Ypres, Loos and the Somme, in heavy fighting at La Bassée and Nieuport, and was badly wounded in action at the Battle of Arras. He was invalided home and after hospital treatment was discharged as medically unfit for further service in December 1917, holding the 1914-15 Star, and the General Service and Victory Medals.
20, Flower Street, Ancoats, Manchester.　Z10141B

DUGDALE, J., Pte., 1/7th Royal Welch Fusiliers.
He joined in February 1917, and after completing his training, was sent a year later to Egypt, where he was stationed at Alexandria. Later he served in the Army Printing and Stationery Department at Mustapha, and afterwards was sent to Kantara. Returning home, he was demobilised in April 1920, and holds the General Service and Victory Medals.
10, Cobden Street, Hulme, Manchester.　TZ5937

DUGGAN, P., Private, 3rd South Lancashire Regt.
Volunteering in August 1914, he was drafted to the Western Front in March of the following year, and there saw severe fighting in various sectors. He took part in the Battles of Festubert, Loos, the Somme, Messines, Cambrai and Havrincourt, and other important engagements, and was also among the troops to enter Mons at dawn of Armistice Day. He was afterwards sent with the Army of Occupation into Germany, where he was stationed at Cologne until his return home for demobilisation in June 1919. He holds the 1914-15 Star, and the General Service and Victory Medals.
14, Back Pump Street, Hulme, Manchester.　Z11692

DUGGATT, W., Private, South Wales Borderers.
Joining in May 1918, he completed his training and served with his unit in Suffolk, until after the Armistice. He was then sent to Germany and was engaged with the Army of Occupation for four months. Drafted to Ireland, he was demobilised from there in March 1919.
111, Devon Street, Ardwick, Manchester.　Z5938

DUMBLETON, J. H., Pte., 8th E. Lancashire Regt.
Volunteering in May 1915, he was drafted later in the same year to the Western Front, where he served for seven months. During that period he fought in engagements at St. Eloi, Albert and Ploegsteert Wood, but was unfortunately killed in action in the Battle of the Somme on July 15th, 1916. He was entitled to the 1914-15 Star, and the General Service and Victory Medals.
"Whilst we remember, the sacrifice is not in vain."
44, Teignmouth Street, Collyhurst, Manchester.　Z9506

DUMPHREY, J., Private, 26th Middlesex Regt.
He joined in April 1916, and in the following October was drafted to Salonika, where he was in almost continuous action on the Doiran front until January 1918, when he was sent to Russia. Here he served in the Minsk sector with the Transport, and was engaged on important duties until his return to England. He was demobilised in December of the same year, and holds the General Service and Victory Medals.　50, Newcastle Street, Hulme, Manchester.　Z9081

DUMVILLE, N., Private, R.A.O.C.
He joined in July 1916, and after a period of training was sent to Salonika in the following March. Whilst in this theatre of war he was transferred to the Royal Army Veterinary Corps and rendered valuable services with this unit during the Balkan campaign. He was demobilised in November 1919, and holds the General Service and Victory Medals.
65, Eliza Ann Street, Collyhurst, Manchester.　Z10147

DUNBAR, T., Private, 15th Lancashire Fusiliers.
Volunteering in September 1914, he was soon sent to the Western Front, and fought in the Battle of La Bassée. Later he took a prominent part in the fighting at Thiepval, Beaumont-Hamel, Cambrai and St. Quentin, and saw service in other sectors. He was demobilised in March 1919 after his return to England, and holds the 1914 Star, and the General Service and Victory Medals.
17, Robert Street, Chorlton-on-Medlock, Manchester.　X5939

DUNBAR, W. H., Sergt., 31st M.G.C.
He was retained at home for some time after volunteering in August 1914, and in May 1916 was drafted to the Western Front. During nearly three years' service in that theatre of war he played a distinguished part in the Battles of Vimy Ridge, the Somme (I), the Ancre, Arras, Bullecourt and the Somme (II), and in the Retreat and Advance of 1918. He was demobilised in March 1919, and holds the General Service and Victory Medals.
24, Prescott Street, Hulme, Manchester.　TZ5940

DUNCAN, E., Private, 2nd Border Regiment.
In February 1917 he joined the Westmoreland and Cumberland Hussars, and in August was drafted to France, where he served in the Battle of Ypres and was transferred to the Border Regiment. In December 1917 he was sent to Italy and after fighting on the Piave was employed on H.Q. Staff. He was demobilised in January 1919, and holds the General Service and Victory Medals.
20, Herbert Street, Ardwick, Manchester.　Z5941

DUNEASE, T., Private, 28th Labour Corps.
He volunteered in October 1915, and three months later was drafted to Salonika. He served in this theatre of war for over two years and during that time took part in severe fighting on the Doiran front. In September 1917 he contracted malaria and later was invalided to England, and discharged from the Army as medically unfit for further service in March 1918. He holds the 1914-15 Star, and the General Service and Victory Medals.
52, Teignmouth Street, Collyhurst, Manchester.　Z9507

DUNFORD, G. A., Private, Manchester Regiment.
Enlisting in 1913, he was sent to France with the 1st Expeditionary Force at the outbreak of war, in August 1914, and took part in the Battle of, and the Retreat from, Mons. He was also in action at the Battles of Le Cateau, the Marne, the Aisne, La Bassée, Ypres (I and II), Loos and the Somme, and was twice wounded. In May 1917 he was transferred to the M.G.C., and, sent to Palestine, took part in the Battles of Gaza and the capture of Jaffa and Jerusalem, where he was wounded for the third time. He received his discharge in July 1920, and holds the Mons Star, and the General Service and Victory Medals.
40, Cookson Street, Ancoats, Manchester.　Z10142

DUNKERLEY, C., Private, R.A.M.C.
Volunteering shortly after the outbreak of hostilities, he completed his training and served at various stations on important duties with his unit. He did valuable work in the course of his home service and succeeded in obtaining his transfer overseas early in 1917. He saw much heavy fighting during that year on the Western Front, but owing to continued ill-health was invalided home in January 1918. After some months' hospital treatment, he was discharged in August of that year, and holds the General Service and Victory Medals.　C10143

DUNKERLEY, D., Pte., Manchester Rgt., and R.A.M.C.
He volunteered in September 1914, and later was sent to Egypt, where he served until February 1915, when he was sent home on account of defective eyesight, and invalided out of the Army a month later. He subsequently joined the R.A.M.C., and proceeding to France served at Neuve Chapelle, Ypres, La Bassée, and on the Somme, where he was gassed in July 1916. Eventually demobilised in February 1919, he holds the 1914-15 Star, and the General Service and Victory Medals.
42, Marcer Street, Ancoats, Manchester.　Z10143

DUNKERLEY, G. H., Pte., Royal Welsh Fusiliers.
He joined in October 1916, and drafted to the Western Front in the succeeding year, was wounded at Bullecourt. On his recovery, he rejoined and fought at La Bassée and Cambrai, but was a second time wounded at Le Cateau during the victorious Advance. After treatment, he was discharged as unfit in July 1919, and holds the General Service and Victory Medals.
33, Down Street, Openshaw, Manchester.　Z5942

DUNKERLEY, W., Gunner, R.F.A.
Having volunteered in September 1915, he was drafted to France in December and played a prominent part in the Battles of the Somme, the Ancre, Arras, Vimy Ridge, Bullecourt, Ypres (III), Cambrai, Bapaume and Havrincourt. He returned to England for his demobilisation in May 1919, and holds the 1914-15 Star, and the General Service and Victory Medals.
79, Irlam Street, Miles Platting, Manchester.　Z10144

DUNLOP, D., Corporal, R.F.A.
He volunteered in August 1914, and in the following September was drafted to France. After taking part in the engagements at Loos, Laventie, Ypres, Fromelles, the Somme, the Ancre and Passchendaele he proceeded in November 1917 to Italy, and was in action on the Asiago Plateau, and in the great Offensive on the Piave. He returned home after the Armistice was signed in November 1918, and was demobilised in the following February. He holds the 1914-15 Star, and the General Service and Victory Medals.
28, Kirk Street, Ancoats, Manchester.　Z9082

DUNN, J., Private, 21st Cheshire Regiment.
He joined in October 1916, and in the following December was drafted overseas. During his service on the Western Front he took part in many notable battles, including those of the Somme, Ypres and Passchendaele, and the leading operations in the Offensives of 1918. After returning home he was demobilised in March 1919, and holds the General Service and Victory Medals.
48, Anslow Street, Rochdale Road, Manchester.　Z10566

DUNN, J. R., Sapper, R.E.
He volunteered in March 1915, and in the following year, after completing his training, crossed to France. There he did excellent work in many important engagements, including those at the Somme, Arras, Bullecourt, Cambrai and the Retreat and Advance of 1918. He was demobilised in February 1919, after returning home, and holds the General Service and Victory Medals.
30, Dalton Street, Collyhurst, Manchester.　Z10567

DUNN, L., Private, 9th Lancashire Fusiliers.

Volunteering in August 1914, he was engaged for a year on duties of an important nature in England. In August 1915 he was drafted to the Dardanelles and took part in the fighting at Suvla Bay and Chocolate Hill, where he was wounded. After his recovery he proceeded to France in January 1917, and was in action at Ypres and Armentières, when he again was wounded. After being invalided home and receiving hospital treatment he was discharged as unfit for further service in November 1918, and holds the 1914-15 Star, and the General Service and Victory Medals.

16, Hancock Street, Rochdale Road, Manchester.   Z10568

DUNN, R., Corporal, 8th Manchester Regiment.

Mobilised with the Reservists in August 1914, he at once proceeded to Egypt and was stationed at Cairo and Alexandria until July 1915. He was then sent to France and fought at Albert, the Somme and Arras. Wounded at Vimy Ridge in April 1917, he was invalided home and after treatment in Manchester was discharged as unfit in December 1917. He holds the 1914-15 Star, and the General Service and Victory Medals.

37, Green Street, Gorton, Manchester.   Z5943

DUNN, T., L/Corporal, York and Lancaster Regt.

He joined in June 1916, and proceeded to the Western Front in the following October. After serving with distinction at the Battle of Arras, he laid down his life for King and Country in the same sector on June 15th, 1917. He was entitled to the General Service and Victory Medals.

"Nobly striving,
He nobly fell that we might live."

175, Montague Street, Collyhurst, Manchester.   Z10145

DUNN, W., Private, King's (Liverpool Regiment).

After serving on important Government work at Messrs Hardman and Holden's on an acid plant, he joined the Army in June 1918. In May of the following year he was drafted to Egypt, and was engaged on important guard duties until February 1920, when he returned to England and was demobilised. 48, George Street, Newton, Manchester.   Z9083

DUNNE, J., Private, Royal Defence Corps.

He volunteered in September 1914, and on completion of his training, was sent to London, where he rendered valuable services in connection with the anti-aircraft defences of the city. Unfortunately he met with a serious accident, and after a period of hospital treatment, was discharged as medically unfit for further duty in November 1916.

9, Heatley Street, Miles Platting, Manchester.   Z10146

DUNSTAN, F., Private, R.M.L.I.

He joined in 1917, and served in H.M.S. "Canopus" and "Elro," attached to the Grand Fleet in the North Sea. He was chiefly engaged on patrol duties off the coast of Belgium and served also in other waters and did much useful work until his return home for demobilisation in 1919. He holds the General Service and Victory Medals.

19, Oram Street, Manchester.   Z11693

DUTTON, A., Pte., 8th Royal Welch Fusiliers.

He volunteered in August 1915, and was soon sent to Mesopotamia, where he took a prominent part in the capture of Nasiriyeh. He served with the force which made the famous dash for Baghdad and was captured at Kut. Interned in Constantinople, he was repatriated after the Armistice and returned home. Demobilised in April 1919, he holds the 1914-15 Star, and the General Service and Victory Medals.

17, Halton Street, Hulme, Manchester.   Z5947

DUTTON, A., Sergt., R.F.A.

Mobilised in August 1914, he first served at Southport as a gunnery instructor and later in Shropshire in a similar capacity. He was unable to proceed overseas, but rendered valuable services before being discharged as medically unfit for further service in April 1917.

18, Ross Place, Ardwick, Manchester.   Z5944

DUTTON, F., Private, 22nd Manchester Regiment.

Volunteering in August 1915, he was drafted overseas in the following November. Whilst serving on the Western Front he saw heavy fighting in the Somme sector, and was wounded in action at High Wood, and sent to hospital at Etaples, and eventually to England. In June 1917 he proceeded to the Italian Front, where he served until demobilised in August 1919, holding the 1914-15 Star, and the General Service and Victory Medals.

60, Higham Street, Miles Platting, Manchester.   Z9508

DUTTON, F., Private, 18th Welch Regiment.

Volunteering in March 1915, he was drafted to the Western Front twelve months later, and after taking part in the Battles of Vermelles, the Somme (I), Arras, Vimy Ridge, Messines, Lens and Cambrai, was unfortunately killed in action at the 2nd Battle of the Somme in March 1918. He was entitled to the General Service and Victory Medals.

"He died the noblest death a man may die,
Fighting for God and, right, and liberty."

28, School Street, West Gorton, Manchester.   Z10148

DUTTON, L., L/Corporal, Manchester Regiment.

He joined in January 1916, and in March of the following year was drafted to France. Whilst overseas he fought at Arras, Ypres and St. Quentin, and in various engagements during the Retreat and Advance of 1918. He holds the General Service and Victory Medals, and was demobilised in April 1919.

34, Rochdale Road Dwellings, Manchester.   Z9084

DUTTON, T., Pioneer, R.E.

Volunteering in September 1915, he was sent to France and went straight into action at Loos. He later served at Albert, Ploegsteert, the Somme, Arras, Bullecourt and Ypres, but meeting with an accident, was invalided home in November 1918, and discharged as unfit three months afterwards. He holds the 1914-15 Star, and the General Service and Victory Medals.   14, Napier Street, Ardwick, Manchester.   Z5946

DUTTON, T. J., Pte., 7th and 22nd Manchester Regt.

He volunteered in November 1914, and a year later proceeded to France, where he played a prominent part in numerous engagements, including the Battles of the Somme, Albert, Arras, Ypres and Messines, and was wounded at Cambrai in November 1917. He also served in the Retreat and Advance of 1918, and was demobilised in November 1919, holding the 1914-15 Star, and the General Service and Victory Medals.

37, Greenheys Lane, Moss Side, Manchester.   Z5945

DUTTON, T. S., Private, 8th Manchester Regiment.

He joined in July 1917, and in the following October embarked for France. There he fought with distinction in the Battles of Cambrai, the Lys, the Marne (II), the Scarpe, and Ypres, where he was wounded, and in the Retreat and Advance of 1918. After also serving with the Army of Occupation on the Rhine he was demobilised in February 1919, and holds the General Service and Victory Medals.

9, Septre Street, Greenheys, Manchester.   Z5948

DUTTON, W., Air Mechanic, R.A.F.

He joined the R.A.F. in February 1917, and after training at Aldershot and Barking was not successful in obtaining a transfer to the war zone. He was stationed at Lowestoft and Yarmouth, and throughout his period of service, performed valuable work in connection with Coastal defence. He was demobilised in March 1919.

166, Teignmouth Street, Rochdale Road, Manchester.   Z9509

DUTTON, W., Private, Lancashire Fusiliers.

Volunteering in 1914, he proceeded to France in the following year, and played a prominent part in the Battles of Ypres (II), and Somme (I), during which he was wounded. On his recovery he returned to the Western Front, and served in the Retreat and Advance of 1918. He was demobilised in March 1919, and holds the 1914-15 Star, and the General Service and Victory Medals.   Z5949

26, Booth Street East, Chorlton-on-Medlock, Manchester.

DYER, D., Gunner, R.G.A.

He joined in August 1916, and five months afterwards was drafted to France, where he took part in the Battles of the Ancre, Arras, Messines and Ypres (III). In November 1917 he was transferred to Italy, and was in action with his Battery during the heavy fighting on the Asiago Plateau and the Piave. He was demobilised in February 1919, and holds the General Service and Victory Medals.

18, Branson Street, Ancoats, Manchester.   Z10149

DYER, J., Private, 1st Lancashire Fusiliers.

He volunteered in August 1914, and in the next May proceeded to Gallipoli, where he fought at the Battle of Krithia (III), and at Chocolate Hill, and was wounded at Suvla Bay in August 1915. After treatment at home, he was transferred to the Labour Corps, and served at Andover. He was demobilised in April 1919, and holds the 1914-15 Star, and the General Service and Victory Medals.

4, Lord Street, Hulme, Manchester.   TZ5950

DYSON, P., Private, K.O. (Royal Lancaster Regt.)

He volunteered in September 1914, and in the following January was drafted overseas. Whilst in France he fought in many important engagements, including those at Armentières and St. Eloi, but was invalided home, suffering from heart trouble, brought on by shell-shock. After receiving medical treatment in hospital he was discharged as unfit for further duty in April 1916, and holds the 1914-15 Star, and the General Service and Victory Medals.

9, Lucas Street, Openshaw, Manchester.   Z9085

DYSON, W. G., Private, 6th Cheshire Regiment.

He joined in November 1916, and after completing his training was retained at various stations in England with his unit, and engaged on signalling duties. Though unable to obtain his transfer overseas, he did good work before being demobilised in September 1919.

2, Gladstone Street, Brook's Bar, Manchester.   TZ5951

E

EADSFORTH, G., Pte., 8th Manchester Regiment.
He volunteered in November 1914, and drafted to France in the following year, was in action at Loos, Vermelles, the Somme, Bullecourt, Ypres, Cambrai, Lens and was three times wounded. He was invalided home, and after a period in hospital, was discharged unfit for further service in August 1918. He holds the 1914–15 Star, and the General Service and Victory Medals.
53, Slater Street, Ancoats, Manchester. Z10150

EAKINS, J. E., Sapper, R.E.
Joining in March 1916, he was drafted five months later to France. In this theatre of hostilities he served at Beaumont-Hamel, Beaucourt, Arras, Bullecourt, Ypres and Cambrai, engaged on various duties of an important nature. After the Armistice he served in Germany with the Army of Occupation until October 1919, when he was demobilised, holding the General Service and Victory Medals.
21, Wrigley Street, West Gorton, Manchester. Z11414

EARDLEY, A., Pte., 1/5th Loyal N. Lancashire Regt.
Volunteering in September 1914, he was drafted to Egypt twelve months later, and was there engaged on important duties at various places. He was in hospital for a time at Alexandria, and in August 1916 was invalided home, but on his recovery proceeded to the Western Front. There he took part in engagements in various sectors, and was twice wounded in action. Again invalided home, he was finally discharged in March 1919, as medically unfit for further service. He holds the 1914–15 Star, and the General Service and Victory Medals. 6, Union Street, Rusholme, Manchester. Z5953

EARDLEY, J., Private, 7th Manchester Regiment.
Having enlisted in 1904, he was mobilised when war broke out in August 1914, and in the following month proceeded to Egypt. Later, however, he was transferred to Gallipoli, where, after taking part in the Landing at Cape Helles, he fought in the Battles of Krithia. He was unhappily reported missing, and presumed to have been killed in action on June 4th, 1915. He was entitled to the 1914–15 Star, and the General Service and Victory Medals.
"His life for his Country, his soul to God."
18, Carter Terrace, Greenheys, Manchester. Z5952

EARLEY, H. E., Sergt., R.E.
He volunteered in March 1915, and was drafted to Egypt in June of the following year. After taking part in engagements at Romani and various other places, he was transferred in March 1917 to the Western Front, where he fought in the Battles of Cambrai, Havrincourt, Epéhy, Le Cateau and the Sambre. He was demobilised on his return home in February 1919, and holds the General Service and Victory Medals.
17, Dorrington Street, Hulme, Manchester. TZ5954

EARNSHAW, G. H., Corporal, Royal Fusiliers.
He joined in January 1917, and after completing a period of training served at various stations, where he was engaged in guarding prisoners of war and on other important duties. He was unable to obtain his transfer to a theatre of war, but, nevertheless, rendered valuable services with his unit until February 1920, when he was demobilised.
32, Rose Street, Greenheys, Manchester. Z5957B

EARNSHAW, J., Pte., K.O. (Royal Lancaster Regt.)
He volunteered in October 1914, and in March of the following year was drafted to Egypt, whence he proceeded shortly afterwards to the Dardanelles. Taking part in the Landing at Suvla Bay, he was severely wounded in action in August 1915, and invalided home. He was for a considerable time in hospital before being discharged as medically unfit for further service in January 1916, and holds the 1914–15 Star, and the General Service and Victory Medals.
28, Gresham Street, Openshaw, Manchester. Z5955

EARNSHAW, J. W., Sergt., R.A.S.C.
Mobilised in August 1914, he was immediately drafted to the Western Front, where he served through the fighting at Mons. He also took an active part in the Battles of Le Cateau, the Marne, the Aisne, the Somme, Passchendaele and Cambrai, and many other important engagements in various sectors. He was discharged in May 1919, and holds the Mons Star, and the General Service and Victory Medals.
33, Charles Street, Bradford, Manchester. Z5956

EARNSHAW, R. A., Private, Welch Regiment.
He volunteered in September 1914, and in November of the following year proceeded to the Dardanelles, where he saw much severe fighting, and was wounded in action. Rendered deaf through gun-fire, he was for a considerable period in hospital at various places, and was finally sent home and invalided from the Army in March 1920. He holds the 1914–15 Star, and the General Service and Victory Medals.
30, Rose Street, Greenheys, Manchester. Z5957

EARP, W., Sergt., Lancashire Fusiliers.
After volunteering in July 1915, he underwent a period of training prior to being drafted to the Western Front in March 1917. There he saw severe fighting at La Bassée, Festubert

and Béthune, took part also in the third Battle of Ypres and was gassed at Givenchy in November 1917. He was invalided home and was for a time in hospital before being demobilised in March 1919. He holds the General Service and Victory Medals. 46, Markham Street, Ardwick, Manchester. Z5958

EASON, F., Private, 2nd Manchester Regiment.
Mobilised in August 1914, he was immediately drafted to the Western Front, where he saw much severe fighting. He took part in the Battles of the Marne, the Aisne, La Bassée, Ypres, St. Eloi, Hill 60, Loos, the Somme, Arras, Messines, Cambrai and Bapaume, and many other engagements in various sectors until the cessation of hostilities. He was discharged in November 1919, and holds the 1914 Star, and the General Service and Victory Medals.
5, Pine Street, Erskine Street, Hulme, Manchester. TZ5959

EASTHAM, T. E., Private, South Lancashire Regt.
He volunteered in September 1914, and in the following year was drafted to France, where he took part in the fighting at Albert and Arras. In October 1915 he was transferred to Salonika, and was in action on the Doiran and Vardar fronts, at Monastir, and was twice wounded. He remained in this theatre of war till April 1919, when he returned home and was demobilised, holding the 1914–15 Star, and the General Service and Victory Medals.
41, Elliott Street, Bradford, Manchester. Z10151

EASTHOPE, A., L/Corporal, Seaforth Highlanders.
He volunteered in November 1915, and in the following year proceeded to the Western Front, where he fought in various sectors. After taking part in the Advance on the Somme, he was severely wounded in action on the Ancre front, and invalided home in December 1916. He was discharged as medically unfit for further service in December 1918, and holds the General Service and Victory Medals.
6 Back Hawthorne Street, Ardwick, Manchester. Z5960

EASTWOOD, A., Private, R.A.M.C.
Volunteering in June 1915, he was sent to France later in that year, and was engaged on important duties with his unit at Loos, St. Eloi and Festubert. Owing to ill-health he was invalided to England, and after receiving hospital treatment was discharged as medically unfit for further service in April 1916. He holds the 1914–15 Star, and the General Service and Victory Medals.
11, Monday Street, Oldham Road, Manchester. Z10152

EASTWOOD, A., Private, 18th Manchester Regt.
He was in the Merchant Service at the outbreak of war, and was engaged in transporting troops across the Channel until July 1916, when he joined the Army. During his service on the Western Front he was gassed and wounded in action in the third Battle of Ypres in July 1917, and was sent to a Base Hospital in France. In December of the same year he proceeded to Italy, and took part in the Operations on the Piave, returning later to France and remaining there until after the cessation of hostilities. He holds the 1914–15 Star, and the General Service and Victory Medals, and in 1920 was still with the Colours.
10, Emma Street, West Gorton, Manchester. Z9086

EASTWOOD, B., Driver, R.F.A.
He was mobilised in August 1914, and was immediately sent to the Western Front, where he took part in the fighting at Mons, and also served through the Battles of Le Cateau, the Aisne, Neuve Chapelle, Ypres, Loos, Albert and Vimy Ridge. He died gloriously on the Field of Battle on the Somme on October 27th, 1917. He was entitled to the Mons Star, and the General Service and Victory Medals. Z5962
"Steals on the ear the distant triumph song."
37, Cambridge Street, Chorlton-on-Medlock, Manchester.

EASTWOOD, F., Gunner, R.F.A.
A Reservist, he was mobilised at the outbreak of war, and proceeded to France with the first Expeditionary Force, with which he took part in the Retreat from Mons. He was also in action in the Battles of the Marne, the Aisne, Ypres, Neuve Chapelle, and Hill 60, and was wounded at Loos. In February 1916 he was discharged as time-expired, and was subsequently engaged on work for the Admiralty until the Armistice was signed. He holds the Mons Star, and the General Service and Victory Medals.
36, Ainsworth Street, West Gorton, Manchester. Z9087

EASTWOOD, H., Sergt.-Major, Sherwood Foresters.
Mobilised in August 1914, he was drafted to the Western Front in time to take a prominent part in the Battle of Mons and the subsequent Retreat, during which he was wounded in action. After six months in hospital he re-joined his unit and fought in the Battles of Ypres, St. Eloi and Albert, and was again wounded at Ploegsteert Wood. Invalided home, he returned to France, however, on his recovery and was wounded a third time on the Marne. He was finally invalided from the Army in February 1919, and holds the Mons Star, and the General Service and Victory Medals.
9, Charlotte Street, Chorlton-on-Medlock, Manchester. Z5961

EATON, A. J., Driver, R.F.A.
He volunteered in May 1915, and in March of the following year was drafted to France, where he saw severe fighting in various sectors of the Front. He took part in the Battles of Arras, Bullecourt, Messines, Ypres and Cambrai, and many minor engagements, and fought also in the Retreat and Advance of 1918. He was demobilised in March 1919, and holds the General Service and Victory Medals.
9, Teak Street, Beswick, Manchester.   Z5965

EATON, E., Private, 15th Royal Scots.
He volunteered in October 1914, and was engaged with his unit on important duties until January 1916, when he was drafted to France. He was engaged in heavy fighting at Loos, St. Eloi, the Somme, Arras, Messines, Cambrai, and was wounded. He also served throughout the Retreat and Advance of 1918, and was demobilised in March 1919, holding the General Service and Victory Medals.
60, Inkerman Street, Collyhurst, Manchester.   Z10569

EATON, J., Air Mechanic, R.A.F.
He joined in December 1917, and after completing his training served at various stations, where he was engaged on duties of a highly technical nature. Unable to obtain his transfer to a theatre of war, he nevertheless rendered valuable services with his Squadron until February 1919, when he was demobilised.
3, Mark Lane, Chorlton-on-Medlock, Manchester.   Z5963

EATON, J. T., Bombardier, R.F.A.
He volunteered in August 1915, and in April 1916 was drafted to Egypt, where he took part in the engagements at Katia, Romani and Magdhaba, and various other places. He was for three months in hospital suffering from dysentery, and later was transferred to India, where he was engaged on garrison duties. He returned home for demobilisation in November 1919, and holds the General Service and Victory Medals.
43, Hulme, Street Chorlton-on-Medlock, Manchester.   Z5964

EATON, T., Private, 12th East Surrey Regiment.
He joined in May 1917, and shortly afterwards proceeded to the Western Front, where he saw much severe fighting. He took part in engagements at Ypres, Passchendaele, Kemmel Hill, Ploegsteert Wood, and many other places in various sectors, and fought also in the Advance of 1918, and was wounded in action in September of that year. Demobilised in December 1918, he holds the General Service and Victory Medals.
48, Burns Street, Bradford, Manchester.   TZ11694

EATON, W., Private, 3rd Manchester Regiment.
He joined in June 1916, and in the following month was sent to France and was in action at the Somme, Beaumont-Hamel, Arras, Vimy Ridge and La Bassée. He was killed in action at the Battle of Ypres on July 31st, 1917, and was buried at that place. He was entitled to the General Service and Victory Medals.
"Whilst we remember, the sacrifice is not in vain."
12, Churnett Street, Collyhurst, Manchester.   Z10570

EBBS, G., Special War Worker.
Being too old for service with the Colours, he was engaged on work of National importance on the Northern Canal Control during the whole period of hostilities. Employed on various important duties in connection with the shipment of goods to and from the various theatres of war, he rendered very valuable services throughout.
35, Alder Street, Hulme, Manchester.   TZ5966

ECCLES, A. H., Sergt., R.F.A.
He volunteered in September 1915, and was retained on important duties with his Battery at various stations until September 1917, when he proceeded to the Western Front, and served in various sectors. He took part in many important engagements, and was wounded during the Offensive of 1918. He was demobilised in February 1919, and holds the General Service and Victory Medals.
12, Whiteley Street, Rochdale Road, Manchester.   Z11870A

ECCLES, H., Private, 19th Royal Welch Fusiliers.
He volunteered in May 1915, and in June of the following year was drafted to the Western Front. Whilst in this theatre of war he saw severe fighting in various sectors, and took part in many important engagements during the Advance on the Somme. He was sent home, and invalided from the Army in August 1917, and holds the General Service and Victory Medals.
8, Mary Street, Hulme, Manchester.   Z5967

ECKERSLEY, C., Private, 1st Manchester Regt.
He was mobilised in August 1914, and in the same month was drafted to France. Whilst on the Western Front he fought at Ypres, Neuve Chapelle, Festubert and Givenchy, and in January 1916 proceeded to Mesopotamia, where he was in action at Kut-el-Amara, and the capture of Baghdad, and in various other engagements. He was finally sent to Egypt in April 1918, and served with General Allenby's forces in the great Offensive in Palestine. He was mentioned in Despatches for his conspicuous gallantry in action during the Palestine campaign, and holds the 1914-15 Star, and the General Service and Victory Medals. He was demobilised after his return to England in March 1919.
75, Jersey Street Dwellings, Ancoats, Manchester.   Z9088

ECKERSLEY, J., Private, 1st Lancashire Fusiliers.
Volunteering in September 1914, he was sent to the Dardanelles in the following year and was in action in many engagements of note, and was wounded. He was invalided home, and after receiving hospital treatment, was discharged in August 1915, owing to his injuries, holding the 1914-15 Star, and the General Service and Victory Medals.   Z10571
32, Windsor Street, Rochdale Road, Collyhurst, Manchester.

ECKFORD, J. W., Pte., East Lancashire Regt. and Royal Marine Labour Corps.
He volunteered in February 1915, and after his training served at various stations in England until April 1916, when he was invalided from the Army. Later he re-enlisted, however, and in January 1918 was drafted to France, where he was engaged on important duties at Boulogne and Ostend. He was demobilised in February 1919, and holds the General Service and Victory Medals.
23, Helsby Street, Ardwick, Manchester.   Z5968A

ECKFORD, W., Private, Welch Regiment.
He volunteered in April 1915, and in July of the following year was drafted to the Western Front, where he took part in the Battles of the Somme, and the Ancre. Invalided home in February 1917, he afterwards proceeded to Egypt, where, attached to the Royal Engineers as a pioneer, he served on the Suez Canal, and at Kantara and Cairo. He was demobilised on his return home in June 1919, and holds the General Service and Victory Medals.
23, Helsby Street, Ardwick, Manchester.   Z5968B

ECTCHELLS, J., Private, 1/5th Border Regiment.
In November 1917, he joined, and seven months later was drafted to the Western Front. There he took an active part in severe fighting in different sectors, and was in action at Ypres, Kemmel, the Somme, Vermelles, Lille and La Bassée. After the Armistice he proceeded to Germany with the Army of Occupation, and was stationed at Bonn until demobilised in January 1920, holding the General Service and Victory Medals. 102, Hadfield St., Collyhurst, Manchester. Z9510

EDDLESTON, D., L/Cpl., Queen's Own (Royal West Kent Regt.)
Joining in February 1916, he was drafted to the Western Front in the following May, and there saw much severe fighting. He took part in the Battles of the Somme, and other engagements until transferred to Italy later in 1917. He returned to France, however, in time to serve through the Retreat and Advance of 1918, and after the cessation of hostilities was sent with the Army of Occupation to Germany. He was demobilised on returning home in March 1919, and holds the General Service and Victory Medals.
69, South Street, Longsight, Manchester.   Z5969B

EDDLESTON, F., Cpl., Lancashire Fusiliers and 10th East Yorkshire Regt.
He joined in June 1918, and after a short period of training was engaged on important duties with his unit at various stations. He was unable to obtain his transfer overseas before the cessation of hostilities, but in January 1919 was drafted to France, where he was engaged in guarding prisoners of war. He returned home for demobilisation in October 1919. 69, South Street, Longsight, Manchester.   Z5969A

EDDLESTON, W., Private, M.G.C.
Volunteering in August 1915, he was drafted to Salonika four months later, and there saw much severe fighting. He took part in many important engagements on the Struma and Doiran fronts, and was also present at the re-capture of Monastir. He was demobilised on his return to England in February 1919, and holds the 1914-15 Star, and the General Service and Victory Medals.   Z5970
9, Charlotte Street, Chorlton-on-Medlock, Manchester.

EDEN, J., Private, 11th Manchester Regiment.
He joined in June 1916, and in December of that year proceeded to the Western Front. There he saw severe fighting in various sectors, took part in the Battles of Arras, Ypres and Cambrai, and other engagements, and served also through the Retreat and Advance of 1918. He was demobilised in January 1919, and holds the General Service and Victory Medals. 7, Hewitt Street, Openshaw, Manchester. TZ5971

EDGAR, A., Pte., King's Own Scottish Borderers.
He was mobilised at the outbreak of war, and was almost immediately drafted to France, where he took part in the Retreat from Mons, and was wounded in September 1914. He was invalided home and discharged in October 1915, but rejoined in the Royal Scots, and returned to the Western Front. He then served in the Battle of the Somme, and was again wounded in July 1916, was sent back to England, and admitted into hospital. After receiving medical treatment he was ultimately discharged as unfit for further military duty in June 1917, and holds the Mons Star, and the General Service and Victory Medals.
9, New Murray Street, Oldham Road, Manchester.   Z9013B

EDGE, J. H., Stoker, R.N.

He volunteered in July 1915, and during the war served in H.M.S. " Carnarvon." He was engaged on escort and convoy duties between England and Canada until January 1919. He rendered excellent services throughout, and was demobilised in March 1919. He holds the 1914–15 Star, and the General Service and Victory Medals.
4, Virginia Street, Rochdale Road, Manchester.   Z10572

EDGE, W., Driver, R.H.A.

Volunteering in November 1914, he was drafted to France in the following April. Whilst overseas he did good work as a driver at Hill 60, Ypres, Festubert, Loos, Vimy Ridge, the Somme, Arras, Bullecourt, Messines, Passchendaele and Cambrai, and was also in action during engagements in the Retreat and Advance of 1918. He holds the 1914–15 Star, and the General Service and Victory Medals, and was demobilised in March 1919.
38, Temple Street, Chorlton-on-Medlock, Manchester.   Z9089

EDISBURY, A., Private, 8th Manchester Regiment.

He volunteered at the outbreak of war in August 1914, and after completing a term of training, served at various stations, where he was engaged on duties of great importance. He was not successful in obtaining his transfer to the Front, but, nevertheless, rendered valuable services with his unit until March 1919, when he was demobilised.
17, Gotha Street, Ardwick, Manchester.   Z5972

EDISS, A., Gunner, R.H.A.

He volunteered at the outbreak of war in August 1914, and in March of the following year proceeded to Mesopotamia. He saw much severe fighting in this seat of operations, took part in numerous engagements at Kut, Sanna-i-Yat, Ramadieh, Khan Baghdadie and the Persian Gulf, and was present at the Relief of Kut, and the capture of Baghdad. Returning home in January 1919, he was demobilised in April of that year, and holds the 1914–15 Star, and the General Service and Victory Medals.
12, Hulton Street, Brooks Bar, Manchester.   Z11695A

EDISS, E., Pte., 1st K.O. (Royal Lancaster Regt.)

Mobilised in August 1914, he was immediately drafted to the Western Front, where he took part in the Battles of Mons and Le Cateau. He was wounded in action and taken prisoner in the Retreat from Mons, and was held in captivity for over four years at Wittenberg, where he was forced to work in a blacksmith's shop. He was finally discharged in January 1919, and holds the Mons Star, and the General Service and Victory Medals.
12, Hulton Street, Brooks Bar, Manchester.   Z11695B

EDISS, E. (M.M.), Gunner, R.F.A.

Joining in November 1916, he was sent to the Western Front four months later, and there saw severe fighting in various sectors. He took part in the Battles of Messines, Ypres, Passchendaele, Cambrai, the Somme, Bapaume, Havrincourt, and the Sambre, and other engagements, and was among the troops to enter Mons at dawn of Armistice Day. He afterwards served with the Army of Occupation in Germany, before returning home for demobilisation in December 1919. He was awarded the Military Medal for conspicuous bravery displayed in the Field at Menin Road, in August 1917, and holds also the General Service and Victory Medals.
12, Hulton Street, Brooks Bar, Manchester.   Z11695C

EDMONDS, A., Private, King's (Liverpool Regt.)

He joined in June 1916, and after his training was retained on home service in Dublin and Co. Cork, where he was employed on important garrison duties. In July 1918 he was transferred to the Army Reserve in order to take up work of National importance in Messrs. Johnson's Wire Works, Manchester.
16, Pearson Street, Newton Heath, Manchester.   Z9511

EDMONDS, S., Private, Royal Naval Division.

He joined in August 1916, and in the following January was drafted to France, where he saw much service. He fought at Ypres, Cambrai, St. Quentin, and on the Somme, and was wounded at the beginning of the Allied Advance in August 1918. He was invalided home to hospital, and after prolonged medical treatment was demobilised in January 1919. He holds the General Service and Victory Medals.
14, Cobden Street, Hulme, Manchester.   TZ9090

EDMUND, J., Private, Manchester Regiment, and Lancashire Fusiliers.

Joining in June 1916, he was sent to France in January of the following year, and took part in the fighting at the Ancre, Arras and Ypres. He was unfortunately killed in action in August 1917. He was entitled to the General Service and Victory Medals.   " His life for his Country."
25, Churnett Street, Collyhurst, Manchester.   Z10573

EDWARD, J., L/Corporal, Lancashire Fusiliers.

Volunteering in August 1914, he was drafted to the Western Front on completing his training in February of the following year, and there took part in the Battles of the Somme, Arras and Ypres, and many other important engagements. He returned home in September 1917, and was afterwards retained on important duties in England until his demobilisation in

December 1918. He holds the 1914–15 Star, and the General Service and Victory Medals.
156, Montague Street, Collyhurst, Manchester.   Z11696

EDWARDS, A., Private, Welch Regiment.

Joining in August 1917, he proceeded to the Western Front in the following November, and there saw severe fighting in various sectors. He took part in the Battles of Cambrai, the Somme, the Marne, Havrincourt and Le Cateau, and other engagements, and also served through the Retreat and Advance of 1918. He was demobilised in November 1919, and holds the General Service and Victory Medals.
135, Blackthorn Street, Ardwick, Manchester.   Z5978

EDWARDS, E., Pte., K.O. (Royal Lancaster Regt.)

He volunteered in May 1915, and in January of the following year was drafted to India. There he was engaged on important garrison duties at Bombay, Bangalore, and various other stations and rendered valuable services with his unit. He was demobilised on returning home in October 1920, and holds the General Service and Victory Medals.
15, Matlock Street, Ardwick, Manchester.   Z5973

EDWARDS, E., Sergt., Lancashire Fusiliers.

He volunteered in August 1914, and a month later was ordered to Egypt, but after serving there for a few months was sent to Gallipoli. In this campaign he took a prominent part in fighting at Suvla Bay, and after the Evacuation of the Peninsula was invalided home. In September 1916 he proceeded to France, and was in action at Ypres, and in the Allied Advance of 1918. He was wounded on two occasions whilst on the Western Front, and was demobilised in March 1919, holding the 1914–15 Star, and the General Service and Victory Medals.   82, Ravald St., Miles Platting, Manchester.   Z9512

EDWARDS, E., Private, 18th Manchester Regt.

Four months after joining in August 1916, he proceeded to the Western Front, where he saw much severe fighting in various sectors. Mortally wounded in action on the Somme, he died at a Casualty Clearing Station on May 3rd, 1917. He was entitled to the General Service and Victory Medals.
" A valiant Soldier, with undaunted heart he breasted life's last hill."
4, William Street, West Gorton, Manchester.   Z5975

EDWARDS, F., Private, 1/8th Manchester Regt.

He joined in July 1916, and in January of the following year proceeded to Egypt, where he was stationed on the Suez Canal, and at Sollum until March 1917. He was then transferred to the Western Front, and took part in the Battle of Ypres, and many minor engagements. He fell fighting in the first Battle of Cambrai on December 11th 1917. He was entitled to the General Service and Victory Medals.
" Thinking that remembrance, though unspoken, may reach him where he sleeps."
44, George Street, Hulme, Manchester.   Z5977

EDWARDS, G., Private, 3rd Manchester Regiment.

He volunteered in February 1915, and in January of the following year was drafted to France, where he saw severe fighting in various sectors of the Front. After taking part in the Battles of Albert and Vimy Ridge, and minor engagements, he was sent home and invalided from the Army in July 1916. He holds the General Service and Victory Medals.
18, Ducie Avenue, Chorlton-on-Medlock, Manchester.   Z5979

EDWARDS, H., Private, 8th Manchester Regt.

He volunteered in November 1915, and in the following July proceeded to Egypt, where he was in action at Romani and El Arish, and was also stationed at Kantara for a time. In February 1917, he was drafted to France, and took part in many important engagements, including those at Ypres and Nieuport, where he was severely wounded. He was invalided to hospital and afterwards to England, and on recovery rejoined his unit in September 1918, but was discharged as medically unfit for further duty in the following month. He holds the General Service and Victory Medals.
41, Ogden Street, Hulme, Manchester.   TZ9091

EDWARDS, H., Pte., King's Own Scottish Borderers.

He volunteered in August 1914, and early in the following year was sent to the Dardanelles. He took part in the Landing at Cape Helles, in the Battle of Krithia, and was severely wounded during an attack on Achi Baba. He was invalided home and discharged as unfit for further service in July 1916, and holds the 1914–15 Star, and the General Service and Victory Medals.
7, Hope Street, Bradford, Manchester.   Z10153

EDWARDS, J., Private, 8th Manchester Regiment, and King's (Liverpool Regiment).

He volunteered in August 1914, but did not proceed overseas until February 1917, on account of ill-health. During his service on the Western Front, he took part in several important engagements, including Bullecourt and Messines Ridge, before he fell fighting at Lens in September 1917. He was entitled to the General Service and Victory Medals.
" His life for his Country."
59, Carisbrooke Street, Harpurhey, Manchester.   Z11492

EDWARDS, J., Private, K.O. (Royal Lancaster Regt.)
Volunteering at the outbreak of war, he proceeded overseas in June 1915, and whilst in France fought in various engagements. He was in action at Loos and Vimy Ridge, and was severely wounded in the Battle of the Somme in July 1916. Invalided home to hospital, he was later discharged as medically unfit for further duty in April 1917, and holds the 1914-15 Star, and the General Service and Victory Medals.
76, Princess Street, Bradford, Manchester.   Z9092

EDWARDS, J., Private, 1/7th Manchester Regt.
Volunteering in May 1915, he proceeded to Egypt on completion of his training in the following August. After taking part in engagements at Mersa Matruh and Agagia, he was transferred to the Western Front, where he fought in the Battles of Bullecourt, Ypres and the Somme,, and also served through the Retreat and Advance of 1918. He was demobilised in February 1919, and holds the 1914-15 Star, and the General Service and Victory Medals.
80, Park Street, Hulme, Manchester.   Z5976

EDWARDS, J., Private, 1st Duke of Cornwall's L. I.
He joined in March 1917, and in April of the following year was drafted to the Western Front, where he saw much severe fighting. He made the supreme sacrifice, falling in action at St. Quentin on April 24th, 1918, only a few days after landing in France. He was entitled to the General Service and Victory Medals.
        "A costly sacrifice upon the altar of freedom."
162, Heald Grove, Rusholme, Manchester.   Z5981A

EDWARDS, J., Driver, R.A.S.C.
Volunteering in December 1914, he was drafted to the Western Front in the following month, and there served in various sectors, conveying food and ammunition to the forward areas. He was present at the Battles of Hill 60, Ypres, Albert, the Somme, Arras, Passchendaele and Cambrai, served also through the Retreat and Advance of 1918, and was gassed in September 1915. He was demobilised in December 1918, and holds the 1914-15 Star, and the General Service and Victory Medals.
23, Brunt Street, Rusholme, Manchester.   TZ5982

EDWARDS, J. T., L/Corpl., 8th Manchester Regt.
Shortly after volunteering in August 1914, he was drafted to Egypt, whence he proceeded to Gallipoli in the following year. He saw much severe fighting in this seat of operations, being wounded in action in the third Battle of Krithia, and on the Evacuation of the Peninsula, was transferred to the Western Front. There he took part in the Battles of Arras, Ypres and Cambrai, and also served through the Retreat and Advance of 1918. He was demobilised in February 1919, and holds the 1914-15 Star, and the General Service and Victory Medals.
3, Tipper Street, Hulme, Manchester.   Z5984

EDWARDS, R., Corporal, 8th Manchester Regt.
After volunteering in August 1914, he underwent a period of training prior to being drafted to the Western Front in June 1916. There he took part in the Battles of the Somme, Ypres, Passchendaele and Cambrai, and many other important engagements, and was wounded in action in December 1917, and invalided home. He returned to France, however, on his recovery and fought in the Retreat and Advance of 1918. He was demobilised in February 1919, and holds the General Service and Victory Medals.
5, Harold Street, Bradford, Manchester.   Z5974

EDWARDS, R. S., Sergt., 8th Manchester Regt.
He volunteered in August 1915, and was engaged on instructional duties till January 1918, when he was drafted to the Western Front. He was in action in many important engagements during the Retreat and Advance of 1918, and returning home after the Armistice was demobilised in February 1919, holding the General Service and Victory Medals.
45, Fitzgeorge Street, Collyhurst, Manchester.   Z10574

EDWARDS, T., L/Corporal, Cheshire Regiment.
He joined in March 1917, and after undergoing a period of training, served at various stations, where he was engaged on duties of great importance. Owing to ill-health he was not successful in obtaining his transfer to a theatre of war, but, nevertheless, rendered valuable services with his unit until March 1919, when he was demobilised.
162, Heald Grove, Rusholme, Manchester.   Z5981B

EDWARDS, T., Pte., King's Own Scottish Borderers.
Volunteering in August 1914, he was drafted to France in April of the following year, and was in action at St. Eloi, Hill 60, Ypres and Festubert. He gave his life for King and Country on September 25th, 1915. He was entitled to the 1914-15 Star, and the General Service and Victory Medals.
        "Great deeds cannot die."
64, Granville Street, Ancoats, Manchester.   Z10154-5

EDWARDS, T. Private, Royal Welch Fusiliers.
He joined in October 1916, and three months later was sent to France. There he was in action at Cambrai ,Arras, Albert, Mericourt, Ypres, Hill 60, St. Eloi and Kemmel, and on the Somme. Gassed in action, he was invalided home, and was eventually demobilised in December 1918, holding the General Service and Victory Medals.
24, Alexandra Place, Manchester.   Z11493

EDWARDS, T., Private, 1/8th Manchester Regt.
He joined in July 1916, and during his service on the Western Front, fought in the Somme sector, and at Arras, Ypres and Passchendaele. He also served at Méricourt, Bullecourt, Cambrai, Armentières, and in various later engagements, and gave his life for King and Country at Bapaume on August 28th, 1918. He was entitled to the General Service and Victory Medals.
"A valiant Soldier, with undaunted heart he breasted life's last hill."
3, Alexandra Place, Manchester.   Z9093

EDWARDS, W., Private, R.A.M.C.
He volunteered in October 1914, and was eventually drafted to France in March 1916. Whilst on the Western Front he served as a stretcher-bearer, and took part in the Battles of Albert, Ploegsteert,the Somme, Arras, Bullecourt, Ypres, and Cambrai (where he was gassed in November 1917), and in the Retreat and Advance of 1918. After the cessation of hostilities he served on the Rhine with the Army of Occupation, and was demobilised in November 1919, holding the General Service and Victory Medals.
15, Gotta Street, Ardwick, Manchester.   Z5983

EDWARDS, W., Private, Seaforth Highlanders.
He volunteered in October 1915, and in January of the following year was drafted to Mesopotamia, where he took part in the capture of Kut. In 1917 he was transferred to India, and was engaged at Poona, Bangalore, and other stations on garrison duties. Returning home, he was demobilised in November 1919, and holds the General Service and Victory Medals.
125, Jersey Street, Ancoats, Manchester.   Z10156

EDWARDS, W. H., Private, Border Regiment.
He volunteered in August 1914, and twelve months later was sent to the Dardanelles. where he took part in the Suvla Bay Landing, and was wounded in action. In November 1915 he was transferred to the Western Front, and fought at the Battles of the Somme (where he was again wounded), Arras, Ypres, and Cambrai. During the last-named engagement he was a third time wounded, and was taken prisoner. Released from captivity in March 1919, he was then demobilised, and holds the 1914-15 Star, and the General Service and Victory Medals.
16, Shakespeare Street, Bradford, Manchester.   Z6029

EGAN, H., Private, 12th Manchester Regiment.
He was mobilised from the Reserve in August 1914, and proceeding to France immediately, took part in the Battles of Mons and Le Cateau, and in the Retreat from Mons, during which he was wounded in action. After hospital treatment at Oxford, he returned to the Western Front, and fought at the Battles of Neuve Chapelle, where he was again wounded, and sent to hospital in Calais. On his recovery, he rejoined his unit, and served in the Battles of the Somme and Cambrai, and in the Retreat and Advance of 1918, being wounded in action a third time. After a period of service with the Army of Occupation in Germany, he was placed on the Reserve, holding the Mons Star, and the General Service and Victory Medals.   20, Daniel Street, Hulme, Manchester.   Z5986

EGAN, J., Pte., King's Shropshire Light Infantry.
He volunteered in August 1914, but being overage for service in a theatre of war, was retained on important duties with his unit at Shrewsbury, and in Wales. He did consistently good work on the land until his demobilisation in January 1919.   36, Ashover Street, Ardwick, Manchester.   Z5985

EGAN, J., Gunner, R.F.A.
He was mobilised in August 1914, and shortly afterwards sent to France, fought in the Retreat from Mons, the Battles of La Bassée, Ypres and many other important engagements, and was wounded. He returned to England and after a period in hospital was invalided out of the Service in March 1917. He holds the Mons Star, and the General Service and Victory Medals.   13, Flower Street, Ancoats, Manchester.   Z10157

EGAN, P. (M.M.), Pte., King's Own Scottish B'ders.
He volunteered in 1914, and in the following year was drafted overseas. Whilst serving on the Western Front he was in action at Ypres, Hill 60, Festubert, St. Eloi, Neuve Chapelle, Méricourt, and La Bassée. He proceeded to Egypt in 1916, and served there until 1919, when returning home, he was demobilised. He was awarded the Military Medal for conspicuous gallantry in the Field, and also holds the 1914-15 Star, and the General Service and Victory Medals.
37, Elizabeth Street, Ancoats, Manchester.   Z9513

EGERTON, A., Private, 1st Manchester Regiment.
He joined in November 1916, and proceeded to India in January of the following year. After serving for twelve months in this country he was transferred to Singapore, where he was engaged on important duties till February 1920, when he returned home and was demobilised, holding the General Service and Victory Medals.
40, Harvest Street, West Gorton, Manchester.   Z10158

ELFORD, J., Private, 1/8th Manchester Regiment.
He volunteered in August 1914, and after a period of training
was engaged on important duties at various stations, where he
rendered valuable services until March 1915. He was then
invalided from the Army as medically unfit for further military
duty. 17, Brown Street, Ancoats, Manchester. Z5987

ELFORD, W., Private, 6th Manchester Regt. and Gunner, R.F.A.
He volunteered in May 1915, but on completion of his training
was discharged as medically unfit. In January 1917, however,
he rejoined, and in the following month was sent to France,
where he took part in the Battles of Arras and Ypres. He
was then admitted to the 22nd Canadian Hospital with
trench fever, and in September 1917 was invalided to Chatham
Military Hospital. On his recovery he served at Ripon until
his demobilisation in February 1919, holding the General
Service and Victory Medals.
28, Nelson Street, Bradford, Manchester. Z6030

ELGER, A., Private, Labour Corps.
He joined in February 1918, but being medically unfit for
transfer to the theatre of war, was retained on important
work in England until July 1919. He was then sent to the
Army of Occupation in Germany, where he rendered valuable
services until his demobilisation in March 1920.
58, Sewerby Street, Moss Side, Manchester. Z5988

ELKES, J., Cpl., Loyal North Lancashire Regt.
Volunteering in January 1915, he was, on completion of his
training six months later, sent to the Western Front. There
he performed excellent work as a Lewis gunner in important
engagements on the Somme and at Arras, Vimy Ridge, Ypres,
Messines, and Cambrai, and also took part in the Advance
prior to the cessation of hostilities. He was wounded on three
occasions and was demobilised in February 1919, holding the
1914–15 Star, and the General Service and Victory Medals.
49, Robert Street, Newton Heath, Manchester. Z9514

ELKIN, P., Private, North Staffordshire Regiment.
Volunteering in September 1914, he was sent to the Dardanelles in November 1915, but after two months' heavy fighting
on the Gallipoli Peninsula, was invalided home suffering from
dysentery. In March 1916 he was transferred to the South
Staffordshire Regiment, and proceeding to France, was wounded in action during the Somme Offensive in November 1916.
On his recovery he rejoined his unit, and was wounded and
gassed at the Battle of Cambrai in November 1917. Whilst
on the Western Front, he was also in action at Neuve Chapelle,
Hill 60 and Ypres. He was discharged medically unfit in
December 1917, and holds the 1914–15 Star, and the General
Service and Victory Medals.
11, Boston Street, Hulme, Manchester. Z5989

ELLERAY, C., Pte., 6th Northumberland Fusiliers.
He joined in February 1917, and in the following December
was drafted to the Western Front, where he took part in the
Battles of St. Quentin, La Bassée, the Marne, Amiens and
Bapaume, and in other important engagements during the
Retreat and Advance of 1918. Demobilised in February
1919, he holds the General Service and Victory Medals.
51, Peel Street, Eccles, Manchester. Z5990

ELLERY, J. J., Sapper, R.E.
He volunteered in 1915, and later in the same year was sent
to France, where he took part in numerous engagements.
He was in action at Neuve Chapelle, Loos and Béthune,
where he was wounded. On recovery, rejoining his unit, he
served throughout the Retreat and Advance of 1918, and
returning home after the Armistice was demobilised in January
1919. He holds the 1914–15 Star, and the General Service
and Victory Medals.
20, Retford Street, Chorlton-on-Medlock, Manchester. Z10159

ELLIOTT, A., Driver, R.A.S.C.
He enlisted in December 1903, and at the outbreak of war in
August 1914, was sent to France, where he was engaged in
assisting the wounded during the Retreat from Mons and the
Battle of the Marne. He was serving at the Battles of Neuve
Chapelle, St. Eloi, Albert, the Somme, the Ancre, Arras,
Vimy Ridge, Cambrai and Bapaume, and was badly wounded
in action at Bohain in October 1918. He received his discharge
in March 1919, and holds the Mons Star, and the General
Service and Victory Medals.
20, Craven Street, Hulme, Manchester. Z5992

ELLIOTT, J. H., Pte., Arygll and Sutherland Hldrs.
He volunteered in January 1915, and was quickly drafted to
the Western Front, where he played a prominent part in
the Battles of Neuve Chapelle, St. Eloi, Ypres, Festubert,
Loos and the Somme. Later in 1916 he was sent to England
and engaged on important Government work in a large
munition factory in Dudley. He was eventually demobilised
in May 1919, and holds the 1914–15 Star, and the General
Service and Victory Medals.
29, Brunswick Street, West Gorton, Manchester. TZ5991B

ELLIOTT, W. H., Private, Gloucester Regiment.
He joined in July 1917, and after his training was completed
in the following September, served at various stations on
important duties on the coast. He rendered valuable services,
but was unable to secure a transfer abroad owing to defective
eyesight, and was demobilised in February 1919.
22, Cheltenham Street, Collyhurst, Manchester. Z9095

ELLIS, A. E., Pte., 1st King's Shropshire Light Infy.
He joined in May 1918, and in the following September was
drafted to the Western Front, but after taking part in the
Battle of Havrincourt, was badly wounded in action at the
Battle of Cambrai in October 1918. He was invalided to
England, and after twelve months in hospital near Blackburn,
was discharged in October 1919 as medically unfit for further
service, holding the General Service and Victory Medals.
3, Guy Street, Ardwick, Manchester. Z5994

ELLIS, B. W., Private, King's (Liverpool Regiment.)
He volunteered in October 1915 and in the following May was
drafted to the Western Front, where he played a prominent
part as a Signaller in the Battles of the Somme, Messines,
Ypres and Cambrai, and in the Retreat and Advance of 1918.
He was wounded and gassed at Ypres in 1917, and was finally
demobilised in March 1919, holding the General Service and
Victory Medals.
73, Elliott Street, Bradford, Manchester. Z5999

ELLIS, E., Sapper, R.E.
Joining in March 1917, he was drafted to France on the
completion of his training in March of the following year.
Whilst on the Western Front he was stationed at Rouen and
was engaged in guarding German prisoners until June 1918,
when, owing to heart trouble, he was invalided home and
discharged as medically unfit for further service. He died
from his complaint in February 1920, and was entitled to the
General Service and Victory Medals.
"Whilst we remember, the sacrifice is not in vain."
38, Henry Street, West Gorton, Manchester. Z9099B Z9100B

ELLIS, G. A., Private, Training Reserve Battalion.
He joined in April 1916, and was in training when his health
unfortunately broke down. He was sent to a sanatorium
suffering from tuberculosis, and invalided out of the Service
in August 1917. He died from the effects of his disease on
September 17th, 1919.
"He joined the great white company of valiant souls."
7, Class Street, Beswick, Manchester. TZ9096

ELLIS, H., Gunner, R.F.A.
Volunteering in January 1915, he was later drafted to France
and was in action at Albert and in the Battle of Loos. In
December 1915 he was transferred to Salonika, where he took
part in the heavy fighting on the Doiran, Struma and Vardar
fronts. He was demobilised in April 1919, and holds the
1914–15 Star, and the General Service and Victory Medals.
8, Humphrey Street, Chorlton-on-Medlock, Manchester.
Z5998

ELLIS, J. (D.C.M.), Driver, R.A.S.C.
He volunteered in September 1914, and in the following
September was drafted overseas. During his service in
France he served in the Loos, Albert, Somme, Arras, Bulle-
court, Messines, Ypres, Cambrai, Havrincourt and Bapaume
sectors. He was demobilised after his return to England in
May 1919, and holds the 1914–15 Star, and the General
Service and Victory Medals.
18, Paris Street, Ancoats, Manchester. TZ9098

ELLIS, J., Gunner, R.G.A.
He volunteered in June 1915, and in the following November
was sent to India. Whilst in this country he was engaged on
garrison and other important duties at Bombay, and rendered
valuable services until discharged in December 1919. He
holds the 1914–15 Star, and the General Service and Victory
Medals.
67, Henry Street, Ardwick, Manchester. Z11898

ELLIS, J., Sapper, R.E.
He volunteered in October 1915, and in the following March
was drafted to France, where he served at Albert, and was
wounded in July 1916 at the Battle of the Somme. On
recovery he again went into action during operations at Ypres
and Cambrai and in the Retreat and Advance of 1918. He
was demobilised in January of the following year and holds
the General Service and Victory Medals.
38, Henry Street, West Gorton, Manchester. Z9099C Z9100C

ELLIS, J., Gunner, R.F.A.
He was mobilised from the Reserve in August 1914, and was
almost immediately drafted to France, where he was in action
in the Retreat from Mons. He also served with the guns in
the Battles of the Marne, the Aisne, La Bassée, Ypres, Neuve
Chapelle, Loos, Albert and the Somme, and after an engagement at Arras suffered severely from shell-shock. He was
invalided out of the Service on this account in April 1917, and
holds the Mons Star, and the General Service and Victory
Medals. 63, Halston Street, Hulme, Manchester. TZ9097

ELLIS, J., Private, 13th Manchester Regiment.
He volunteered in September 1914, and eight months later was drafted to France, where he saw much severe fighting until October 1915. He was then transferred to Salonika and was in action on the Doiran, Struma and the Vardar fronts. Demobilised in March 1919, he holds the 1914–15 Star, and the General Service and Victory Medals.
37, Francis Street, Chorlton-on-Medlock, Manchester.
TX5993

ELLIS, J., Private, Cheshire Regiment.
He volunteered in August 1915, and was retained on important duties in England until May 1916. He was then posted for duty with the Mercantile Marine and made several journeys across the Atlantic on board s.s. "Plumley" and "Boxleaf," between Montreal and England. Whilst on the last-named vessel she was mined, but succeeded in keeping afloat. In 1920 he was still serving, and holds the General Service and Victory Medals.
16, Shrewbridge Street, West Gorton, Manchester. Z5995

ELLIS, R., Private, R.A.S.C. (M.T.)
From August 1914 until March 1915, he did duty with the Merchant Service, and was on board the s.s. "Falaba" when she was torpedoed, but although over 100 lives were lost, he was fortunately rescued. He then joined the R.A.S.C. and was quickly sent to France, where he was engaged on transport work in the forward areas during the Battles of Ypres, Loos and Arras, and was wounded in action. As a result, he was invalided from the Army in August 1918, and holds the 1914–15 Star, and the General Service, Victory, and the Mercantile Marine War Medals.
9, Maskell Street, Chorlton-on-Medlock, Manchester. X5997

ELLIS, R., L/Corporal, 1/8th Manchester Regiment.
Mobilised in August 1914, he was sent to Egypt in the following month and served in the Suez Canal zone until transferred to the Dardanelles, where he was wounded in action in June 1915. He was invalided to England, but on his recovery was sent to the Western Front and took part in the Battles of the Somme, Ypres, Passchendaele and Cambrai, and in heavy fighting at Loos, Neuve Chapelle and La Bassée. He was demobilised in March 1919, and holds the 1914–15 Star, and the General Service and Victory Medals.
66, Gresham Street, Lower Openshaw, Manchester. Z6000

ELLIS, R. H., Gunner, R.G.A.
Volunteering in October 1915, he proceeded to France in May of the following year, and whilst on the Western Front fought in engagements on the Somme and at Beaucourt, Bullecourt and Messines. He died gloriously on the Field of Battle at Ypres on August 11th, 1917, and was entitled to the General Service and Victory Medals.
"His life for his Country, his soul to God."
38, Henry Street, West Gorton, Manchester. Z9099B Z9100B

ELLIS, W., Sapper, R.E.
He joined in April 1918, and in the following October proceeded to France, where he was engaged on important duties in connection with the operations, and was frequently in the forward areas, notably at Le Cateau and on the Selle. He was present at the entry into Mons on Armistice Day, and afterwards advanced into Germany with the Army of Occupation and was stationed on the Rhine. He was demobilised in February 1920, and holds the General Service and Victory Medals.
38, Henry Street, West Gorton, Manchester. Z9099A Z9100A

ELLIS, W., Private, 1st King's (Liverpool Regt.)
He joined in September 1918, and completing his training was engaged at various stations on important duties with his unit. He rendered valuable services, but owing to defective eyesight was discharged as medically unfit for further service in December 1918.
34, Boslam Street, Ancoats, Manchester. Z10162

ELLIS, W., Private, Labour Corps.
Joining in October 1916, he was sent to France in the following year, and was engaged on important duties at Boulogne and other Bases. After the Armistice he proceeded with the Army of Occupation to Germany, and served there until he returned home, and was demobilised in February 1920. He holds the General Service and Victory Medals.
8, Whitehead Street, Collyhurst, Manchester. Z10160

ELLIS, W., Private, 4th King's (Liverpool Regt.)
Volunteering in January 1916, he was drafted to France in the following April, and was in action on the Somme, at Arras, Ypres, La Bassée, Givenchy, and was wounded. On his recovery he rejoined his unit and fought throughout the Retreat and Advance of 1918. He returned home after the Armistice, and was demobilised in February 1919, holding the General Service and Victory Medals.
8, Flower Street, Ancoats, Manchester. Z10161

ELLISON, J., Driver, R.F.A.
He volunteered in May 1915, and was quickly drafted to Egypt, but in August 1915 was transferred to the Gallipoli Peninsula, and served at the Landing at Suvla Bay and in the Evacuation in January 1916. He then returned to Egypt and was in action at Romani, Magdhaba and Rafa. Later he took part in the three Battles of Gaza and the capture of Jerusalem, Jericho and Aleppo during the advance of General Allenby's Forces in Palestine. He holds the 1914–15 Star, and the General Service and Victory Medals, and was demobilised in March 1919.
106, Henry Street, West Gorton, Manchester. Z6001

ELLISON, J., Private, 14th Manchester Regiment.
He joined in March 1916, and in the following July was drafted to the Western Front, where he was in action in many parts of the line. He gave his life for the freedom of England in the Battle of the Somme on October 10th, 1916. He was entitled to the General Service and Victory Medals.
"His life for his Country, his soul to God."
6, Hiram Street, Ancoats, Manchester. Z10163B

ELLWOOD, R., Guardsman, 2nd Grenadier Guards.
Volunteering in January 1915, he was drafted to France twelve months later and played a prominent part in the Battles of the Somme and in heavy fighting at Beaumont-Hamel and Ypres. He was badly wounded in action at Flers in September 1916, and was invalided home. After treatment in a hospital at Croydon, he was discharged in September 1917 as medically unfit for further service, and holds the General Service and Victory Medals.
92, Heald Place, Rusholme, Manchester. Z6005

ELMA, H. T., Private, R.A.S.C.
He volunteered in August 1914, and on completion of his training was engaged on important duties with his unit at various stations. Owing to a defective heart, he was not drafted overseas, and after rendering valuable services was invalided from the Army in August 1917. Z6002
31, Stockton Street, Chorlton-on-Medlock, Manchester.

ELPHICK, G., Cpl., King's (Liverpool Regiment).
Volunteering in January 1915, he was drafted to France in June and played a prominent part in much heavy fighting. He was severely wounded in action in October 1916, during the Somme Offensive, and was invalided home. After a period of hospital treatment at Colchester, he was discharged as medically unfit for further service in January 1917, and holds the 1914–15 Star, and the General Service and Victory Medals.
6, Amy Street, Openshaw, Manchester. Z6003

ELSE, E., Private, R.A.M.C.
Volunteering in November 1914, he first saw active service with the 1/3 E. Lancs. Field Ambulance in the Dardanelles, where he saw much severe fighting in the Krithia sector on Gallipoli until December 1915, and was wounded in action. He then proceeded to Egypt and served in the Suez Canal zone, but owing to his suffering from neurasthenia, was discharged as medically unfit in September 1916. He holds the 1914–15 Star, and the General Service and Victory Medals.
13, Tranmere Street, Hulme, Manchester. Z6004A

ELSE, G., Corporal, R.A.M.C.
He joined in January 1917, and in the following May was sent to France, but after a month's service at Etaples, was invalided to England, owing to a breakdown in health. Eventually he was drafted to Egypt in May 1918, and did conspicuously good work at the 88th General Hospital at Cairo until March 1920, when he was sent home for demobilisation. He holds the General Service and Victory Medals.
13, Tranmere Street, Hulme, Manchester. Z6004B

EMBERTON, W., Pte., 8th and 20th Lancashire Fus.
He volunteered in June 1915, and in February of the following year was drafted to the Western Front, where he took part in heavy fighting at Richebourg, Neuve Chapelle, Laventie and Albert, before being invalided home in August 1916. On his recovery, he proceeded to Mesopotamia, and after a period of service there was transferred to Salonika and fought in the Balkan campaign. At the cessation of hostilities he went to Constantinople with the Army of Occupation, and was eventually demobilised in April 1919, holding the General Service and Victory Medals.
7, Clegg Street, Hulme, Manchester. Z6006

EMBLOW, J., Private, 7th Manchester Regt. and King's (Liverpool Regt.)
Volunteering in September 1914, he was eventually drafted to France in October 1916. During his service on the Western Front, he was in action at Loos, Neuve Chapelle, Ypres, Beaumont-Hamel, La Bassée, Givenchy and Festubert. He was invalided home in April 1918, and three months later was discharged as medically unfit for further service, holding the General Service and Victory Medals. Z6007
82, Higher Chatham Street, Chorlton-on-Medlock, Manchester.

EMBURY, E., Gunner, R.F.A.
Joining in March 1916, he was drafted to the Western Front in April 1917. Whilst in this theatre of war he took part in the Battles of Arras, Epéhy, Cambrai and Maubeuge, and was gassed in action at Hill 60 in July 1917. He was demobilised in March 1919, and holds the General Service and Victory Medals. 96, Radnor Street, Hulme, Manchester. Z6008

EMETT, E., Private, 2nd Cheshire Regiment.

He joined in May 1918, and completing his training, served on important duties at various stations. In September of the following year he proceeded to the Army of Occupation at Constantinople, where he remained until October 1920, when he was invalided home to hospital. He was still serving in the Army later in the same year.

12, Anderton Street, West Gorton, Manchester.   Z10077E

EMMETT, J., 1st Air Mechanic, R.A.F. (late R.F.C.)

Volunteering in June 1915, he was drafted to the Western Front on completion of his training in the following October, and there served at Boulogne. He was engaged on duties of a highly technical nature in the workshops whilst in France, and after the cessation of hostilities, was sent with the Army of Occupation into Germany. He was demobilised on his return home in August 1919, and holds the 1914–15 Star, and the General Service and Victory Medals.

115, Broadfield Road, Moss Side, Manchester.   TZ6009

EMSLIE, G., Private, Essex Regt. and R.A.S.C.

A Reservist, he was mobilised at the outbreak of hostilities, and was almost immediately sent to the Western Front. During his service in France he took part in the Retreat from Mons and in the Battle of the Marne, Ypres (I and II), the Somme and Arras and in many subsequent operations. He was discharged in March 1919, and holds the Mons Star, and the General Service and Victory Medals.

4, Luke Street, Collyhurst, Manchester.   Z9094

ENGLAND, F., Private, Manchester Regiment.

He volunteered in November 1915, and drafted to Egypt in the following June, served at various stations in the Canal zone. In April 1917 he proceeded to the Western Front, and fought in various engagements, including that at Givenchy. He gave his life for King and Country in the third Battle of Ypres on September 8th, 1917, and was entitled to the General Service and Victory Medals.

"A costly sacrifice upon the altar of freedom."

92, Lind Street, Ancoats, Manchester.   Z10164A

ENGLAND, T., Private, 12th Manchester Regt.

He joined in May 1918, and in the following September embarked for France and served in many parts of the line. He died gloriously on the Field of Battle on October 18th, 1918, during the Allied Advance. He was entitled to the General Service and Victory Medals.

"Honour to the immortal dead who gave their youth that the world might grow old in peace."

92, Lind Street, Ancoats, Manchester.   Z10164B

ENNIS, A., Corporal, 1st King's (Liverpool Regt.)

He volunteered in December 1915, and after a period of training was drafted overseas in August 1916. During his service on the Western Front he took an active part in numerous engagements in different sectors of the line, saw severe fighting at Ypres, Passchendaele, Amiens and Bapaume and was gassed at Ypres. He was demobilised in March 1919, and holds the General Service and Victory Medals.

20, Grange Street, Bradford, Manchester.   Z9515

ENNIS, T., Private, Lancashire Fusiliers.

He volunteered in September 1914, and in the following month was drafted overseas. During his service in France he fought in the engagements at La Bassée, Festubert, Béthune and many others, and was taken prisoner at Givenchy in April 1918. He was held in captivity until the cessation of hostilities and then was repatriated according to the terms of the Armistice. He was demobilised in May 1919, and holds the General Service and Victory Medals.

7, Wilkinson Street, Rochdale Rd., Manchester.   Z10165

ENTWISTLE, A., Rifleman, Rifle Brigade.

Volunteering in August 1914, he was sent to the Western Front in May of the following year, and saw much service. He was in action at Festubert, Givenchy, Loos, Ypres, Vimy Ridge, Arras and Passchendaele, but developing heart trouble was invalided home to hospital in August 1917. After rejoining his unit at Winchester, he was subsequently discharged as medically unfit for further duty in October of the same year, and holds the 1914–15 Star, and the General Service and Victory Medals.

13, Anthony Street, West Gorton, Manchester.   Z9101

ENTWISTLE, G., Pte., 8th South Lancashire Regt.

Volunteering in September 1914, he was drafted to the Western Front in the following February, and in this theatre of war participated in the Battles of Neuve Chapelle, Hill 60, and Loos. He did good work until he was unfortunately killed in action on the Somme in June 1916. He was entitled to the 1914–15 Star, and the General Service and Victory Medals.

"Great deeds cannot die."

29, Drinkwater Street, Harpurhey, Manchester.   Z11415

ENTWISTLE, J., Q.M.S., R.A.F. (late R.N.A.S.)

Mobilised in August 1914, he was immediately drafted to the Western Front, where he took part in the fighting at Mons. He also served through the Battles of Le Cateau, Ypres and Armentières and other engagements until gassed at Ypres and invalided home. He was for a time in hospital, and after his recovery, was engaged on duties of great importance with the R.A.F. at various stations. He was finally discharged in April 1919, and holds the Mons Star, and the General Service and Victory Medals.

7, Walter Street, Ardwick, Manchester.   Z11697

ENTWISTLE, J., Private, R.M.L.I.

He volunteered in September 1914, and proceeded to France with the 1st Motor Battalion (Canadians) in December of the same year. He was then transferred to the Royal Marines and fought at Passchendaele, on the Somme, at Cambrai, Amiens, Bapaume, and in the second Battle of Cambrai. Returning home, he was demobilised in February 1919, and holds the 1914–15 Star, and the General Service and Victory Medals.

44, Gibbon Street, Bradford, Manchester.   Z9102

ENTWISTLE, J. R., Private, 1/8th Manchester Regt.

He volunteered in August 1914, and after a period of training was drafted to Gallipoli in April of the following year, and there took part in the Battles of Krithia. He made the supreme sacrifice, falling in action at Suvla Bay in August 1915. He was entitled to the 1914–15 Star, and the General Service and Victory Medals.

"He died the noblest death a man may die,
Fighting for God and right and liberty."

24, Vulcan Street, Ardwick, Manchester.   Z6015

ENTWISTLE, P., Private, Middlesex Regiment.

Volunteering at the commencement of hostilities, he proceeded to France, and was in action in the Battles of the Marne, the Aisne, and Hill 60. He was wounded and gassed at Ypres in April 1915, and returning to England received hospital treatment. He was invalided out of the Service in August 1916, and holds the 1914–15 Star, and the General Service and Victory Medals.

36, Duke Street, Miles Platting, Manchester.   Z10166

ENTWISTLE, R., Pte., 2/6th N. Staffordshire Regt.

He joined in April 1917, and in March of the following year proceeded to France, where he saw severe fighting in various sectors of the Front. After taking part in engagements at Ypres and Passchendaele, he was taken prisoner at Kemmel Hill and held in captivity behind the German lines until the cessation of hostilities. He was finally demobilised in November 1919, and holds the General Service and Victory Medals.

30, Wilson Street, Ardwick, Manchester.   TZ6010

ENTWISTLE, S., Private, 9th Manchester Regiment.

He was mobilised at the outbreak of hostilities and proceeding in September 1914 to Egypt, was stationed at Suez and Cairo. He was then drafted to the Dardanelles and took part in the Landing at Cape Helles, in the fighting at Krithia and in the Evacuation of the Peninsula. He returned to Egypt, but after being in action at Katia in April 1916, was sent to the Western Front, where he served at Ypres, Passchendaele and Cambrai and in the Retreat and Advance of 1918. He holds the 1914–15 Star, and the General Service and Victory Medals, and was discharged in March 1919.

99, Cross Street, Bradford, Manchester.   Z9103

ESKEY, G., Private, King's (Liverpool Regiment).

Volunteering in September 1914, he proceeded to the Western Front after three months' training and there saw much heavy fighting. He took part in the Battles of Neuve Chapelle, Hill 60, Ypres, the Somme and the Ancre and many other engagements until February 1917, when he was severely wounded in action and sent home. He was invalided from the Army in July 1917, and holds the 1914–15 Star, and the General Service and Victory Medals.

18, Gorton Place, Longsight, Manchester.   Z6016

ETCHELLS, E. G., Sergt., King's (Liverpool Regt.)

Volunteering in September 1914, he was shortly afterwards drafted to the Western Front, where he saw much severe fighting. After taking part in the Battles of Ypres, St. Eloi, Loos and the Somme and many other engagements, he was invalided to hospital at Birmingham in March 1918, suffering from shell-shock. He afterwards served in Ireland until demobilised in February 1919, and holds the 1914–15 Star, and the General Service and Victory Medals.

43, Lancaster Street, Hulme, Manchester.   TZ5980

ETCHELLS, J., Private, Lancashire Fusiliers.

He volunteered in August 1914, and in April of the following year he was drafted to Gallipoli, where he took part in the Landing at Cape Helles. After serving through the Battles of Krithia, he was wounded in action at Achi Baba, sent to hospital at Malta and thence invalided to England. He was discharged as medically unfit for further service in January 1916, and holds the 1914–15 Star, and the General Service and Victory Medals.

27, Phœnix Street, Hulme, Manchester.   Z6014

ETCHELLS, J., Private, 1st Manchester Regiment.
Mobilised in August 1914, he was shortly afterwards drafted
to the Western Front, where he took part in the Battles of the
Marne, the Aisne, Neuve Chapelle, Hill 60, Loos, St. Eloi,
the Somme and Arras and was wounded in action. Later he
was transferred to Mesopotamia and there saw much severe
fighting, and was again wounded at the capture of Baghdad.
He was in hospital for a time at Bombay, before returning
home for discharge in October 1919, and holds the 1914 Star,
and the General Service and Victory Medals.
76, Armitage Street, Ardwick, Manchester.   X6013

ETCHELLS, J., Private, 1st Manchester Regiment.
He was mobilised in August 1914, and was immediately drafted
to the Western Front, where he fought in the Battle of Mons
and the subsequent Retreat. He also took part in the Battles
of Le Cateau, the Marne, the Aisne, La Bassée, Ypres, Neuve
Chapelle, Hill 60 and Loos before being transferred to Mesopotamia in November 1915. There he was in action at Kut,
Sanna-i-Yat and many other places until wounded in action
and invalided to hospital at Bombay. On his recovery he
served in China on police duty until his return home for discharge in November 1919. He holds the Mons Star, and the
General Service and Victory Medals.
10, Garden Walks, Ardwick, Manchester.   Z6011

ETCHELLS, J. W., Private, 13th Manchester Regt.
Volunteering in August 1914, he was drafted to the Western
Front in February of the following year and there saw much
severe fighting. He took part in the Battles of St. Eloi,
Loos, Vimy Ridge and Albert and many other engagements in
various sectors, and was wounded in action at Ypres in May
1915. In November 1916 he was transferred to Salonika
and there fought on the Doiran and Vardar fronts, and was
again wounded. He was invalided home and finally demobilised in April 1919, holding the 1914-15 Star, and the General
Service and Victory Medals.
76, Armitage Street, Ardwick, Manchester.   Z6012

ETHERALL, C. H., Private, 2nd Manchester Regt.
He volunteered in 1914, and after his training was completed,
served at various stations on important duties with his unit.
He rendered valuable services, but was unable to secure a
transfer overseas before the cessation of hostilities. He was
demobilised in 1919.
17, Evans Street, Chorlton-on-Medlock, Manchester. Z10167

ETHERALL, D., Corporal, 2nd Manchester Regt.
Mobilised at the commencement of hostilities, he proceeded
to France, and fought in the Retreat from Mons, the Battles
of Neuve Chapelle and Ypres. Wounded and taken prisoner
in the first Battle of the Somme, he was held in captivity
until the close of hostilities. Repatriated, he was demobilised
in 1919, and holds the Mons Star, and the General Service
and Victory Medals.
7, Evans Street, Chorlton-on-Medlock, Manchester. Z10168

ETTERY, T., Corporal, Rifle Brigade.
Volunteering in July 1915, he was drafted to France in the
following month and saw much active service. He fought
at Albert, Vimy Ridge and was wounded and again in action
in the Battle of the Somme in July 1916. After his recovery
he took part in the engagements at Arras, Ypres, Cambrai,
and was engaged in heavy fighting throughout the Retreat
and Advance of 1918. He returned home, and was demobilised in March 1919, holding the 1914-15 Star, and the
General Service and Victory Medals.
3, Teer Street, Ancoats, Manchester.   Z10169

EVANS, A., L/Corporal, 23rd Manchester Regiment.
He volunteered in October 1914, and was retained at various
stations at home until January 1916, when he was drafted
to the Western Front. There, after taking part in many
important engagements in various sectors, he was severely
wounded in action and invalided home, suffering also from
shell-shock. He was for a considerable period in hospital at
Birmingham, and was finally demobilised in December 1918,
holding the General Service and Victory Medals.
15, Nelson Place, Rusholme, Manchester.   Z6017

EVANS, A., Drummer, 6th Lancashire Fusiliers.
He joined in July 1917, and after completing a period of
training, served at various stations, where he was engaged on
duties of great importance. Unable to obtain his transfer
to a theatre of war, he nevertheless rendered valuable services
with his unit until September 1919, when he was demobilised.
10, Lythgoe Street, Moss Side, Manchester.   Z6018A

EVANS, E. A., Pte. (Signaller), 1/7th Lancs. Fusiliers.
He volunteered in May 1915, and twelve months later was
drafted to Egypt, where he served at Cairo, Kantara and
many other places. In January 1917 he was transferred to
the Western Front and there took part in many important
engagements, including the Battles of Arras, Vimy Ridge,
Passchendaele and the Somme. He fell fighting at Havrincourt in March 1918. He was entitled to the General Service
and Victory Medals.
"He joined the great white company of valiant souls."
143, Rosebery Street, Moss Side, Manchester.   Z6024

EVANS, C. H., Private, Royal Welch Fusiliers.
He joined in February 1918, and after undergoing a period of
training was engaged on important garrison duties at various
stations in Ireland. He was not successful in obtaining his
transfer overseas, but, nevertheless, rendered valuable services
with his unit until his demobilisation in September 1919.
17, Myrtle Grove, Ardwick, Manchester.   Z6022

EVANS, F., Private, Royal Welch Fusiliers.
From the outbreak of hostilities until 1916 he was training
for the Navy, and then was discharged. Joining the Royal
Welch Fusiliers he proceeded to Egypt in 1917, and was
torpedoed en route, but fortunately was saved. He saw much
service at various stations in the Canal zone, and later was in
action in many engagements on the Palestine front, and was
twice wounded. Returning home he was demobilised in
August 1919, and holds the General Service and Victory
Medals. 22, Worth St., St. Michaels, Manchester. Z10575

EVANS, F. H., Private, 1/6th Manchester Regt.
Volunteering in April 1915, he proceeded to Egypt in the
following October, and was thence transferred to Gallipoli,
where he saw much severe fighting during the Evacuation of
the Peninsula. Later he was drafted to the Western Front,
and there took part in the Battles of Arras, Bullecourt and
Ypres, served also through the Retreat and Advance of 1918,
and was wounded in action at Passchendaele in September
1917. He was demobilised in March 1919, and holds the 1914-
15 Star, and the General Service and Victory Medals.
70, Derby Street, Ardwick, Manchester.   TZ6020

EVANS, F. W., A.B., R.N., H.M.S. "Halcyon."
Volunteering in September 1914, he was posted to H.M.S.
"Halcyon" and in this vessel fought in the Battle of the
Dogger Bank. Transferred in August 1915 to H.M.S. "Ches-
ter," he was in action during the Battle of Jutland, and later
was engaged on escort and patrol duties in the North Sea.
Returning to shore, he was demobilised in February 1919, and
holds the 1914-15 Star, and the General Service and Victory
Medals. 52, Gorton Street, Ardwick, Manchester. Z9104

EVANS, H., Sergt., 10th Manchester Regiment.
Volunteering in September 1914, he was retained on important
work in England until February 1917, when he proceeded to
the Western Front. There he played a prominent part in
operations at Givenchy, Nieuport, and Ypres. During this
last engagement he was wounded and sent to England, and
after his recovery was engaged on home service until demobilised in January 1919, holding the General Service and Victory
Medals.
11, Marsden Street, Newton Heath, Manchester.   Z9516

EVANS, J., Private, 8th Manchester Regiment.
He volunteered in May 1915, and in January of the following
year proceeded to Egypt, where he took part in engagements
at Katia and various other places. In January 1917 he was
transferred to the Western Front, where he was unhappily
killed in action at Béthune on December 13th of that year. He
was entitled to the General Service and Victory Medals.
"Courage, bright hopes, and a myriad dreams, splendidly
given."
3, Fairhaven Street, West Gorton, Manchester.   6031A

EVANS, J. F., Private, 18th Manchester Regiment.
He joined in August 1916, and in January of the following year
was drafted to the Western Front. There he took part in
many important engagements, including the Battles of Messines
and Ypres, and was so severely wounded at Passchendaele as
to necessitate the amputation of his right arm. He was
recommended for decoration for bravery in the Field, and holding the General Service and Victory Medals was invalided from
the Army in June 1918.
36, Rumford Street, Hulme, Manchester.   Z6026A

**EVANS, J. H., Sergt., 8th and 22nd Manchester
Regt. and 8th King's (Liverpool Regt.)**
He volunteered in December 1915, and in March 1917, was
drafted to the Western Front, where he saw severe fighting
in various sectors, taking part in the Battles of Ypres and
Passchendaele, and many minor engagements. He also served
with the 4th Royal Welch Fusiliers, the Royal Engineers, and
the 287th Prisoners of War Company, with which he was
stationed at St. Omer until his demobilisation in May 1919.
He holds the General Service and Victory Medals.   TX6025
116, Cottenham Street, Chorlton-on-Medlock, Manchester.

EVANS, P., Private, Lancashire Fusiliers.
He volunteered in August 1914, and in April of the following
year was drafted to the Dardanelles, where he took part in the
Landing at Cape Helles, and in the subsequent operations until
the Evacuation of the Peninsula. In May 1916 he proceeded
to France, and was gassed in the third Battle of Ypres. After
his recovery he served throughout the German Offensive and
Allied Advance of 1918. He was demobilised in February
1919, and holds the 1914-15 Star, and the General Service
and Victory Medals.
44, Richardson Street, Collyhurst, Manchester.   Z10576

EVANS, J. S., Pte., Loyal North Lancashire Regt.
Volunteering in January 1915, he proceeded to France in June of the same year. Whilst overseas he fought at Ypres and Festubert, and died gloriously on the Field of Battle at Loos on September 25th, 1915. He was entitled to the 1914–15 Star, and the General Service and Victory Medals.
" Courage, bright hopes, and a myriad dreams splendidly given." 19, Long Street, Ancoats, Manchester.   Z10170

EVANS, R. H., Private, 2/6th Manchester Regt.
He joined in July 1916, and in December of the following year proceeded to France, where he saw severe fighting in various sectors of the Front. After taking part in the Battles of the Somme, and the Lys, he was severely wounded in action and gassed near Arras in April 1918, and was invalided home. He afterwards served in Ireland until his demobilisation in March 1920, and holds the General Service and Victory Medals. 4, George's Avenue, Chester Road, Hulme, Manchester. Z6019

EVANS, S. R., Driver, R.G.A.
Joining in February 1916, he was drafted to the Western Front in the following October, and there served as a despatch-rider in various sectors. After taking part in many important engagements in the Somme sector, he was wounded in action at Vimy Ridge, and invalided home. He returned to France on his recovery, however, and was in action until the cessation of hostilities. He holds the General Service and Victory Medals, and was demobilised in February 1919.
3, Fairhaven Street, West Gorton, Manchester.   6031B

EVANS, T., Gunner, R.G.A.
He joined in December 1916, and in the following February was drafted to India, where he was engaged on important garrison duties at Rawal Pindi, and at various stations on the North West Frontier. He returned to England, and was demobilised in March 1919, and holds the General Service Medal. 7, Rosebery Street, Moss Side, Manchester. Z10171

EVANS, T., Sergt., 13th King's (Liverpool Regt.)
He volunteered in November 1914, and in the following September was drafted to France. Whilst there he fought at Loos, where he was wounded, Vermelles, Vimy Ridge, and the Somme, and was again severely wounded in November 1916, and invalided home to hospital. In January of the following year he proceeded to India, and was engaged on important garrison duties at Lahore, Lucknow, and Bangalore. He returned home and was demobilised in November 1919, and holds the 1914–15 Star, and the General Service and Victory Medals.
23, Brougham Street, West Gorton, Manchester.   Z10172

EVANS, T., Private, King's (Liverpool Regiment).
He joined in April 1918, and after a period of training was engaged on important duties at various stations, not being able to obtain his transfer to a theatre of war on account of his youth. In December 1918, however, he proceeded to Germany, where he served at Bonn with the Army of Occupation until his return home for demobilisation in December 1919. 36, Rumford Street, Hulme, Manchester. Z6026B

EVANS, W., Driver, R.F.A.
He volunteered in December 1914, and after his training was completed was drafted to France in July of the following year. He was in action in the Battles of the Somme, the Ancre Guillemont, Arras, Ypres, Cambrai, and throughout the German and Allied Offensives of 1918. He returned to England, and was demobilised in January 1919, and holds the 1914–15 Star, and the General Service and Victory Medals.
99, Kendall Street, Bradford, Manchester.   Z10173

EVANS, W., Private, Manchester Regiment.
He volunteered in December 1914, and after undergoing a period of training, served at various stations, where he was engaged on duties of a highly important nature. Unable, owing to ill-health, to obtain his transfer overseas, he nevertheless rendered valuable services with his unit until invalided from the Army in January 1918.
10, Lythgoe Street, Moss Side, Manchester.   Z6018B

EVANS, W. Private, R.M.L.I.
He volunteered in October 1914, and in the following year was drafted to Gallipoli, where he took part in the Battles of Krithia, saw severe fighting at Suvla Bay, and was present at the Capture of Chunuk Bair. On the Evacuation of the Peninsula he was transferred to the Western Front, where he was again in action at Beaumont-Hamel, Beaucourt, the Ancre, Arras, and Cambrai. He was sent home and invalided from the Service in May 1918, on account of a fractured ankle, and holds the 1914–15 Star, and the General Service and Victory Medals. 55, Wood Street, Hulme, Manchester. TZ6023B

EVERALL, A., L/Cpl., 8th Lancashire Fusiliers.
He volunteered in January 1915, and in April of the following year proceeded to Egypt, where he fought in the engagements at Katia, El Fasher, Romani, and Magdhaba, and was in

hospital for a time at Cairo. He was afterwards transferred to the Western Front, and there took part in the Battles of Arras, Ypres, Cambrai, the Somme, and Le Cateau. He was demobilised in February 1919, and holds the General Service and Victory Medals.
8, Hibbert Street, Rusholme, Manchester.   Z6027A

EVERALL, S., Private, R.A.S.C.
He joined in February 1917, and after his training was engaged on important duties at various stations. He was not successful in obtaining his transfer to a theatre of war, but, nevertheless, rendered very valuable services with his Company until November 1919, when he was demobilised.
8, Hibbert Street, Rusholme, Manchester.   Z6027B

EXLEY, A., Private, 19th Manchester Regiment.
Two months after volunteering in August 1915, he was drafted to the Western Front, where he took part in the Battles of Albert, Ploegsteert Wood, the Somme, and Arras, and other engagements. He fell fighting at Ypres on November 27th, 1917, and was buried on the Menin Road. He was entitled to the 1914–15 Star, and the General Service and Victory Medals.
" He passed out of the sight of men by the path of duty and self-sacrifice."
8, Gresham Street, Openshaw, Manchester.   Z6021

EXTON, J.W., A.B., R.N., H.M.S. "King Edward VII."
Having enlisted in September 1913, he went to sea at the outbreak of war and fought in the Battle of the Bight of Heligoland. Nearly three months later he played a prominent part in the destruction of Von Spee's Squadron off the Falkland Islands, and then returned to the North Sea, where he was in action at the Battle of Jutland, and was engaged on patrol duties. He was in H.M.S. " King Edward VII," when she was sunk on January 6th 1916, but was luckily rescued. He also served in H.M. Ships " Edinburgh Castle," " Cyclops," " Powerful," " Impregnable," and " Royal Arthur," and was not discharged until January 1920. He holds the 1914–15 Star, and the General Service and Victory Medals.
86, Victoria Square, Oldham Road, Manchester.   TZ9105

EYCOTT, J. J. (M.S.M.), Staff-Sergt.-Major, R.A.S.C.
A serving Soldier since August 1898, he was sent to the Western Front soon after the outbreak of hostilities, and served in many important engagements, including the Battles of Neuve Chapelle, St. Eloi, Festubert, and Cambrai, and in operations in the Retreat and Advance of 1918. After the Armistice he proceeded to Germany with the Army of Occupation, and was stationed on the Rhine until August 1919. He won the Meritorious Service Medal for his consistently good work, and devotion to duty throughout the war, and also holds the Queen's and King's South African Medals, the 1914 Star, and the General Service and Victory Medals. In 1920 he was serving in Ireland.
28, Halston Street, Hulme, Manchester.   Z9106

EYRE, C., Gunner, R.F.A.
Volunteering in June 1915, he served at various depôts until proceeding to the Western Front in March 1917. He fought in the Battles of Ypres, Passchendaele, and throughout the German Offensive and subsequent Allied Advance of 1918. Returning home he was demobilised in April 1919, and holds the General Service and Victory Medals.
8, Duke Street, Bradford, Manchester.   Z10174

EYRE, F., Private, 3rd King's (Liverpool Regiment).
In May 1917 he joined the Army, and after serving in Cork for four months was drafted overseas. Whilst on the Western Front he was engaged in severe fighting in the Ancre, Bapaume, Amiens, Ypres, Lille, Cambrai, and Le Cateau sectors. He remained in France until his demobilisation in February 1919, and holds the General Service and Victory Medals.
36, Vine Street, Newton Heath, Manchester.   Z9517

EYRES, C., Private, K.O. (Royal Lancaster Regt.)
Volunteering in February 1915, he proceeded to the Western Front on completing his training in the following July, and there saw severe fighting in various sectors. After taking part in many important engagements, he was badly gassed at Ypres, and was in hospital at Rouen and Plymouth. He was invalided from the Army in May 1916, and holds the 1914–15 Star, and the General Service and Victory Medals.
42, Dark Lane, Ardwick, Manchester.   Z6028

EYRES, W., Private, King's (Liverpool Regiment).
He joined in November 1916, and in the following June proceeded to the Western Front. Whilst overseas he fought at Arras, Ypres, Cambrai, the Somme, and was wounded in the second Battle of the Marne in August 1918. After his recovery he was again in action at Ypres and Havrincourt, and returning home after the Armistice was demobilised in October 1919. He holds the General Service and Victory Medals.
13, Broughton Street, Ancoats, Manchester.   Z10175

F

FAGAN, J. H., Private, 1/16th Manchester Regt.
He volunteered in April 1915, and in June of the following year embarked for France. Whilst there he fought in many important engagements, including those of the Somme, Arras, and Ypres, where he was killed in action on November 6th, 1917. He was entitled to the General Service and Victory Medals.
" He passed out of the sight of men by the path of duty and self-sacrifice."
10, Ward Street, Oldham Road, Manchester.   Z9107

FAIRBANK, A., Pte., K.O. (Royal Lancaster Regt.)
He was mobilised in August 1914, and was immediately sent to France, where he took part in the Retreat from Mons, and in the Battles of Ypres, and Neuve Chapelle. He was drafted to Egypt in 1916, and served in the Advance over the Desert and the Sinai Peninsula. He afterwards returned to France and took part in the Battles of Ypres and Passchendaele, and the Retreat of 1918. During his service he was twice wounded. He was taken prisoner on the Somme in March, and was employed by the enemy on various duties behind their lines, till he was sent to internment camps in Germany. On his release he returned to England, and was demobilised in March 1919, holding the Mons Star, and the General Service and Victory Medals.
35, Heaton Street, Ardwick, Manchester.   Z10176

FAIRCLOUGH, G. E., Pte., 2/5th Manchester Regt.
Joining in September 1916, he was first engaged on important duties in England, but eventually proceeded to France in March 1918. During his service on the Western Front he was in action at Festubert, La Bassée, Nieuport, and Ypres, and was taken prisoner at St. Quentin. Whilst in captivity he was forced to work in a foundry at Mannheim and Heiberg. Demobilised in March 1919, he holds the General Service and Victory Medals. 26, Eskrigge St., Ardwick, Manchester. Z6061

FAIRCLOUGH, R., Driver, R.A.S.C. (M.T.)
He joined in January 1918, after having been engaged on work of National importance. First as driver on transport work, and then with the Manchester Ship Canal in connection with the supply of food. After joining the Royal Army Service Corps he served in London, and later in Ireland, where he carried out excellent work in his section. In August 1918 his health broke down, and he was invalided out of the Army.
43, Francisco Street, Collyhurst, Manchester.   Z9518

FAIRFIELD, H., Gunner, R.G.A.
He joined in May 1916, and in the following year was drafted to the Western Front, where he took part in the Battles of Arras, Bullecourt, Vimy Ridge, Ypres, and Cambrai. He also served in the Retreat and Advance of 1918, and was gassed. He was demobilised in January 1919, and holds the General Service and Victory Medals.
128, Thomas Street, West Gorton, Manchester.   Z10177

FAIRHURST, W., Private, 7th Manchester Regt., and Labour Corps.
Volunteering in September 1914, he was sent to France twelve months later and took part in the Battles of Arras, Ypres, Passchendaele, St. Quentin, and Cambrai. In 1917 he was transferred to the Labour Corps, and was unfortunately killed near Arras in June 1918. He was entitled to the 1914–15 Star, and the General Service and Victory Medals.
" His memory is cherished with pride."
9, Tipper Street, Hulme, Manchester.   Z6062

FALEY, T., L/Corporal, 2nd Manchester Regiment.
He volunteered in September 1915, and in the following February crossed to France. During his service in this theatre of war he took part in many engagements, including those on the Somme, and was wounded. In March 1917 he was sent to the East, and served with the forces in the Advance on Jerusalem and Jericho. Demobilised in August 1919 after his return home, he holds the General Service and Victory Medals. 120, Tame St., Ancoats, Manchester.   Z9108

FALLON, J. F., Private, South Lancashire Regt.
Mobilised in August 1914, he proceeded to France with the first Expeditionary Force, and took part in the Battle of Mons, and the subsequent Retreat. He was also in action at the Battles of La Bassée, Ypres (1914– 15), St. Eloi, Loos, Albert, and Vimy Ridge, before being badly wounded on the Somme in October 1916. He was invalided to hospital in Newcastle, and was finally discharged as medically unfit in March 1917, holding the Mons Star, and the General Service and Victory Medals.
56, Piggott Street, Greenheys, Manchester.   Z6063

FANNING, A., Private, 9th Lancashire Fusiliers.
He was mobilised in August 1914, and a month later proceeded to France, where he took part in the Battles of Hill 60, Loos, Vermelles, and the Somme. He laid down his life for King and Country at Lens in August 1917, and was entitled to the 1914 Star, and the General Service and Victory Medals.
" A valiant soldier, with undaunted heart he breasted life's last hill."
16, Dalton Street, Longsight, Manchester.   Z6064A

FARADAY, G., Private, Labour Corps.
He joined in March 1917, and was soon sent to France, where he was engaged on important duties in the forward areas, repairing roads, bridges, and trenches. After the Armistice he served with the Army of Occupation in Germany until his demobilisation in October 1919, holding the General Service and Victory Medals.
3, Dalton Street, Longsight, Manchester.   Z6065

FARLEY, J., Private, 22nd Manchester Regiment.
He volunteered in December 1914, and eleven months later was ordered to the Western Front, where he was in action at Villers, Albert, Ploegsteert Wood, the Somme, Beaucourt, and Beaumont-Hamel. In September 1917, he was sent to hospital at St. Omer, and two months later was invalided home with muscular rheumatism. In consequence he was discharged as medically unfit for further service in April 1918, and holds the 1914–15 Star, and the General Service and Victory Medals.
40, Leigh Street East, Ancoats, Manchester.   Z9516

FARLEY, S., Bombardier, R.F.A.
He volunteered in August 1914, and in the following October embarked for Egypt, later proceeding to Mesopotamia, and taking part in the operations at Kut, Um-el-Hannah, and on the Tigris. He was unfortunately wounded and sent into hospital at Alexandria. He returned to England in May 1919, and in the following June was demobilised, holding the General Service and Victory Medals.
43, Newcastle Street, Hulme, Manchester.   Z9109

FARLEY, W., Sergt., K.O. (Royal Lancaster Regt.)
Prior to the outbreak of war in August 1914, he had served in the Army for twenty-eight years, and in January 1915, re-enlisted. Throughout the period of hostilities he performed valuable work in training recruits at the depôt at Lancaster, but was discharged in February 1919, suffering with heart trouble, and in November 1920 unhappily died.
2, Bright Street, Rochdale Road, Manchester.   Z9520

FARNWORTH, A, Private, E. Lancashire Regiment.
Joining in November 1917, he was drafted to France three months later, and took a prominent part in the Battles of the Somme, the Marne, Bapaume, Havrincourt, and Ypres, during the Retreat and Advance of 1918. He was invalided home in November 1918, owing to a breakdown in health, and was eventually discharged in November 1919, holding the General Service and Victory Medals.
42, Garibaldi St, Ardwick, Manchester.   Z6067

FARNWORTH, T., Pte., K.O.(Royal Lancaster Regt.)
He joined in October 1916, and after a period of service in England and Wales, was drafted to France in January 1918. He took part in the second Battle of the Somme, and was badly wounded in action in March 1918. Invalided home, after a period of treatment in hospital at Amiens, he was discharged in July 1918 as medically unfit for further service, and holds the General Service and Victory Medals.
8, Hamlet Street, Ardwick, Manchester.   Z6066

FARRAND, B., L/Corporal, 23rd Manchester Regt.
He volunteered in December 1914, and three months later was sent to France, where he played a prominent part in the Battles of Neuve Chapelle, Ypres (II), Festubert, Vermelles, Ploegsteert, the Somme, Arras, Ypres (III), and Cambrai. He died gloriously on the Field of Battle at Amiens on August 10th, 1918, and was entitled to the 1914-15 Star, and the General Service and Victory Medals.
" Nobly striving,
He nobly fell that we might live."
47, Derby Street, Ardwick, Manchester.   Z6068

FARRELL, C., Private, 26th Manchester Regiment.
He joined early in 1916, but after a short period of training was found to be medically unfit for military service, and was therefore invalided from the Army in July of the same year.
1, Peel Street, Chorlton-on-Medlock, Manchester.   X607A

FARRELL, J., Private, 8th Manchester Regiment.
Volunteering in August 1914, he was sent to the Dardanelles in the following April. After taking part in the first Landing on the Gallipoli Peninsula, and in the first and second Battles of Krithia, he laid down his life for King and Country at the third Battle of Krithia on June 4th, 1915. He was entitled to the 1914-15 Star, and the General Service and Victory Medals.
" A costly sacrifice upon the altar of freedom."
180, Viaduct Street, Ardwick, Manchester.   Z6071A

FARRELL, L., Pte., 1/4th Loyal N. Lancs. Regt.
He volunteered in November 1915, and after a period of duty in England, was drafted to France early in 1917. Whilst on the Western Front he was in action at Ypres, La Bassée, Festubert, Givenchy, and Lille, and after the Armistice, served in Germany with the Army of Occupation until March 1919. He was then invalided home, and was in hospital at Manchester until his discharge in August 1919, holding the General Service and Victory Medals.
8, Dyson Street, Miles Platting, Manchester.   Z6069

FARRELL, R., Private, South Lancashire Regt.
He volunteered in August 1914, and first saw active service at the Landing at Salonika in October 1915. He afterwards took part in heavy fighting on the Doiran and the Struma fronts, and was badly wounded in action. He was invalided home to hospital at Bristol, and was eventually discharged as medically unfit in September 1916. He also suffered from malaria, and holds the 1914–15 Star, and the General Service and Victory Medals.
180, Viaduct Street, Ardwick, Manchester.   Z6070B

FARRELLY, J. J., Sergt., R.F.A.
He volunteered in June 1915, and five months later was sent to France. During his service overseas, he was employed on clerical duties of an important nature, and did excellent work, whilst in the Loos, Vermelles, Arras, Cambrai, Messines, and Somme sectors. He was demobilised in June 1919, and holds the 1914–15 Star, and the General Service and Victory Medals.
36, Sanitary Street, Oldham, Road, Manchester.   Z11494

FARRELLY, J. V., Pte., 14th King's (L'pool Regt.)
Volunteering in September 1914, he was drafted to Salonika in the following year, and took part in the Landing. He also fought at the Battle of Machine Gun Hill in the Vardar sector, and was unfortunately killed in action in September 1916. He was entitled to the 1914–15 Star, and the General Service and Victory Medals.
"And doubtless he went in splendid company."
12, Brampton Street, Ardwick, Manchester.   X6072

FARRICKER, F. W., Pte., K.O. (R. Lancaster Regt.)
He volunteered in August 1914, and in the following April was drafted to the Western Front. Unfortunately, after only a short period of active service, he was killed in action at the Battle of Hill 60 on April 24th, 1915. He was entitled to the 1914–15 Star, and the General Service and Victory Medals.
"He died the noblest death a man may die,
Fighting for God and right and liberty."
8, Ashbury Street, Openshaw, Manchester.   TZ6073B

FARRICKER, J., Pte., Argyll and Sutherland Hldrs.
He volunteered in February 1915, and three months later was drafted to the Western Front, where he played a prominent part in the Battles of Festubert and Ypres. In July 1915, owing to a severe attack of bronchitis, he was invalided home, and, after a period of hospital treatment and convalescence, was discharged as medically unfit for further service in September 1917. He holds the 1914–15 Star, and the General Service and Victory Medals.
44, Cowper Street, Bradford, Manchester.   X6074

FARRINGTON, A., Sergt., R.F.A.
He enlisted in November 1899, and at the commencement of war was drafted to the Western Front, where he fought during the Retreat from Mons, and the subsequent Battles. He was also in action at Ypres, on the Somme, and was twice wounded. When hostilities ceased, he proceeded with the Army of Occupation into Germany, and in 1920 was still serving. He holds the Mons Star, and the General Service and Victory Medals.
22, Fielden Street, Oldham Road, Manchester.   Z9110

FARRINGTON, J., Stoker, R.N.
He was in the Royal Navy at the outbreak of war, having joined in 1909, and served in H.M.S. "Bellona" and "Sentinel." In September 1914 he proceeded with the Royal Naval Division to Antwerp, where he took part in various operations. In June 1916, he joined H.M.S. "Drake," which was torpedoed off the coast of Ireland in October 1917. He was discharged in August 1918, in consequence of his services, and holds the 1914 Star, and the General Service and Victory Medals.
29, Dawson Street, West Gorton, Manchester.   Z10178

FARRINGTON, J., Private, Army Cyclist Corps.
He volunteered in October 1914, and in November of the following year proceeded to France, where he was in action at Vermelles, Loos, the Somme, the Ancre, Arras, Messines, Bullecourt, Ypres, Cambrai, the Aisne, and the Marne. He was badly wounded on the Somme in 1916, and also at Cambrai in October 1918. He was demobilised in January 1919, and holds the 1914–15 Star, and the General Service and Victory Medals.
32, School Street, West Gorton, Manchester.   Z10179

FARRINGTON, L., Private, Devonshire Regiment.
Joining in February 1916 he was sent to Egypt in December of the following year, and during the voyage out his ship was twice torpedoed, but he was saved. He did good service at Alexandria, and was later transferred to France, where he took part in the Battle of Ypres, and the final engagements in the Advance of 1918. He was demobilised in March 1919, after returning home, and holds the General Service and Victory Medals.
17, Douro Street, Newton Heath, Manchester.   Z10180A

FARRINGTON, W., Private, R.A.S.C.
Volunteering in August 1914, he was drafted to France in the following December, and was engaged on important transport duties at Ypres, Loos, the Somme, and Messines. He also did excellent work as an Army cook. He was unfortunately

killed in action at Lens in August 1917, and was entitled to the 1914–15 Star, and the General Service and Victory Medals.
"The path of duty was the way to glory."
17, Douro Street, Newton Heath, Manchester.   Z10180B

FARROW, G., Pte., 10th K.O. (R. Lancaster Regt.)
He joined in June 1917, and was sent to France in the following year. He was in action at Trônes Wood, and was afterwards engaged on hospital sanitation duties. He contracted fever and was invalided home, but on his recovery he returned to France. He was demobilised in November 1919, and holds the General Service and Victory Medals.
24, Glee Street, Ancoats, Manchester.   Z10181

FARROW, J. E., Private, King's (Liverpool Regt.)
He volunteered in August 1914, and in the following May was sent to France, where he saw much heavy fighting, and was in action at Loos, Ypres, and Vimy Ridge, amongst other places. Severely wounded he was invalided home, and after receiving hospital treatment was discharged as medically unfit in March 1918. He holds the 1914–15 Star, and the General Service and Victory Medals.
74, Naylor Street, Oldham Road, Manchester.   Z9111

FAULKNER, A., Private, Royal Defence Corps.
After having been rejected owing to medical unfitness on several previous attempts to enlist, he succeeded in joining the Royal Defence Corps in 1918, but, after a short period of valuable services, was once more discharged as medically unfit in December of the same year.
11, East View, West Gorton, Manchester.   Z6075

FAULKNER, A., Private, 2/4th Yorkshire Regt.
He volunteered in January 1915, and in the following March sailed for France, where he took part in the fighting at Hill 60, Ypres, and Loos. He was unhappily killed in action at St. Eloi by a shell, and was entitled to the 1914–15 Star, and the General Service and Victory Medals.
"A costly sacrifice upon the altar of freedom."
2, Cross Street East, Ancoats, Manchester.   Z9112

FAULKNER, D., Special Constable.
He joined the Manchester Special Constabulary in February 1916, and during the remaining period of hostilities rendered valuable services, being continually on duty at night in the event of air raids. He was demobilised in September 1919.
5, Avenham Street, Hulme, Manchester.   Z6078

FAULKNER, D., Private, East Lancashire Regt.
Volunteering in November 1914, he was drafted in the following June to the Western Front. Whilst there he fought at La Bassée, Loos, and Albert, and gave his life for King and Country in the Battle of the Somme on July 15th, 1916. He was entitled to the 1914–15 Star, and the General Service and Victory Medals.
"His memory is cherished with pride."
37, Baker Street, Ardwick, Manchester.   Z9113

FAULKNER, J., Private, 5th Manchester Regt.
Joining in February 1917, he served after a period of training at various stations on important guard and other duties. Owing to medical unfitness he was not able to obtain a transfer overseas, but rendered valuable services until demobilised in January 1919.
9, Hardy Street, West Gorton, Manchester.   Z9114

FAULKNER, J., Driver, R.A.S.C.
He volunteered in November 1914, and in the following September was sent to France, but after two months' service in the Albert sector, was transferred to Salonika. He then played an active part in heavy fighting on the Doiran and Struma fronts, and was wounded in May 1916. After hospital treatment, however, he was again in action, and was present at the recapture of Monastir. In May 1918 he was invalided home with malarial fever, and three months later was discharged as medically unfit. He holds the 1914–15 Star, and the General Service and Victory Medals.
216, Morton Street, Longsight, Manchester.   Z6077A

FAULKNER, J., Private, 17th Manchester Regt.
He volunteered in September 1914, and twelve months later was drafted to France, and was in action at Loos, St. Eloi, Albert, and on the Somme, where he was wounded and invalided home. On his recovery he returned to the Western Front, and fought at the Battles of Arras and Ypres, where he was unhappily killed in action on October 9th, 1917. He was entitled to the 1914–15 Star, and the General Service and Victory Medals.   "Great deeds cannot die."
216, Morton Street, Longsight, Manchester.   Z6077B

FAULKNER, T., Private, R.A.S.C.
He joined in October 1917, and two months later proceeded to the Western Front, where he was engaged on important transport duties in the forward areas. He saw much heavy fighting in the Passchendaele and Somme sectors, and was eventually invalided from the Army, owing to defective eyesight, in May 1919. He holds the General Service and Victory Medals. 216, Morton St., Longsight, Manchester.   Z6077C

FAWCETT, E., Private, 2nd Manchester Regiment.
He volunteered in April 1915, and in the following June was sent to Gallipoli, where he saw much severe fighting until the Evacuation of the Peninsula in January 1916. He was then transferred to the Western Front, and was in action at Loos, Albert, Vimy Ridge, the Somme, Arras, Ypres (III), Cambrai, Bapaume, and Le Cateau, and in the Retreat and Advance of 1918. Demobilised in January 1919, he holds the 1914-15 Star, and the General Service and Victory Medals.
17, Rylance Street, Ardwick, Manchester.   Z6079

FAWCETT, J. W., Private, Labour Corps.
He volunteered in 1915, and after his training was retained at Chester and Cardiff on important duties with his unit. He rendered valuable services, but was not successful in obtaining his transfer overseas before the cessation of hostilities. He was demobilised in 1919.
74, Bridge Street, Chorlton-on-Medlock, Manchester. Z9949B

FAWLEY, T., Private, Labour Corps.
He joined in May 1918, and in August of the same year proceeded to France. He was chiefly engaged on constructional work in the Ypres and Arras sectors, remaining there until his return home for demobilisation in March 1919. He holds the General Service and Victory Medals.
10, Sydney Street, Bradford, Manchester.   Z9115

FAY, W., L/Corporal, K.O. (Y.L.I.)
Having joined in October 1917, he was drafted to France in the following May, and took part in numerous engagements in the Retreat and Advance of 1918, including that at Cambrai. He was unfortunately killed in action there on September 12th, 1918, and was entitled to the General Service and Victory Medals.   "His memory is cherished with pride."
7, Hooley Street, Ancoats, Manchester.   Z10182

FEAREY, J. L., Private, R.A.S.C. (M.T.)
He joined in February 1918, and after his training was engaged on important duties with his unit. He was employed as a motor driver, and rendered valuable services, but was not successful in obtaining his transfer overseas before the cessation of hostilities. He was demobilised in March 1919.
71, Irlam Street, Miles Platting, Manchester.   Z10183

FEARNCLOUGH, S., Private, 1st Manchester Regt.
He joined immediately on attaining military age early in November 1918, and after a short period of training, served at various stations, where he was engaged on duties of great importance. Although unable to obtain his transfer overseas on account of the early cessation of hostilities, he nevertheless rendered valuable services with his unit until October 1919, when he was demobilised.
39, Victoria Street, Longsight, Manchester.   Z6080

FEEHAN, J., Private, 22nd Manchester Regiment.
He volunteered in November 1914, and twelve months later, was drafted to the Western Front, where he saw severe fighting in various sectors. After taking part in several important engagements, he was sent home and invalided from the Army in April 1916, suffering from the effects of pneumonia. He holds the 1914-15 Star, and the General Service and Victory Medals.   73, Stott Street, Hulme, Manchester.   Z6081

FELLOWES, W., Pte., 3rd Northumberland Fusiliers.
Mobilised in August 1914, he was immediately drafted to the Western Front, where he took part in the fighting at Mons. He also served through the Battles of the Marne, Armentières, Ypres, Loos, Vermelles, the Somme, Arras, and Bullecourt, and was twice wounded in action—on the Aisne in September 1914, and at Hill 60 in the following April. He was invalided from the Army in July 1917, and holds the Mons Star, and the General Service and Victory Medals.
184, Crossley Street, Gorton, Manchester.   Z6082

FELSTEAD, C. R., Private, 25th Manchester Regt.
Joining in February 1916, he was drafted to the Western Front in the following May, and there saw much severe fighting. He made the supreme sacrifice, falling in action in the Advance on the Somme on July 1st, 1916. He was entitled to the General Service and Victory Medals.
"Nobly striving,
He nobly fell that we might live."
17, Neptune Street, Ancoats, Manchester.   Z6076

FENTON, J., Sapper, R.E.
He joined in May 1916, and after undergoing a period training, was retained at various stations, where he was engaged on important clerical duties. He was not successful in obtaining his transfer to a theatre of war, but, nevertheless, rendered valuable services with his Company until March 1919, when he was demobilised.
109, Teignmouth Street, Rochdale Road, Manchester. Z11698

FENTON, J., Private, 1st Queen's Own (Royal West Kent Regiment).
He joined in August 1916, and later in the same year after completing his training was sent to France where he was in action at La Bassée, Nieuport, and Vimy Ridge. He after-

wards proceeded to India and served at Agra and Calcutta. He was still serving there in 1920, and holds the General Service and Victory Medals.
9, Broughton Street, Ancoats, Manchester.   Z10184

FERGUSON, J., Private, 1st Manchester Regiment.
He volunteered in October 1914, and in April of the following year was sent to France, where he took part in the fighting at Hill 60, Ypres, Loos, and Vimy Ridge. He was wounded there and invalided home, but on his recovery he returned to France and was transferred to the King's Liverpool Regiment (Labour Battalion), and served at Arras, Messines, Passchendaele and Cambrai. Owing to illness he was invalided home and was discharged in March 1918, on account of disabilities. He holds the 1914-15 Star, and the General Service and Victory Medals.
20, Copper Street, Rochdale Road, Manchester.   Z10577

FERGUSON, J. (M.M. and Bar), Sergt. 2nd Manchester Regiment.
Already in the Army when war broke out in August 1914, he was immediately drafted to the Western Front, where he fought in the Retreat from Mons. He also took part in the Battles of the Marne, the Aisne, La Bassée, Ypres, Festubert, the Somme, Arras, Bullecourt, Messines, and Passchendaele, and other engagements, and was wounded in action near Albert in September 1918, and on one other occasion. He was awarded the Military Medal for conspicuous gallantry in the field near Albert in July 1916, the Bar for bravery at Beaumont-Hamel in the following November, and the Croix de Guerre for distinguished conduct at Nieuport in the Advance of 1918. He also holds the Mons Star, and the General Service and Victory Medals, and was discharged in March 1919.
76, Halston Street, Hulme, Manchester.   Z6083

FERGUSON, J., Sergt., 12th Manchester Regiment.
Volunteering in January 1915, he was drafted to the Western Front in the following August, and there saw severe fighting in various sectors. He took part in the Battles of Loos, and Cambrai, and many other engagements, served also through the Retreat and Advance of 1918, and was twice wounded in action—on the Somme, and at Arras. He was demobilised in February 1919, and holds the 1914-15 Star, and the General Service and Victory Medals.
8, Cowell's Buildings, Ardwick, Manchester.   Z6084

FERGUSON, S., Driver, R.A.S.C. (M.T.)
He was mobilised in December 1914, and immediately proceeded overseas. During his four years' service on the Western Front, he was chiefly employed in conveying supplies to the fighting line. He also took part in heavy fighting at Ypres, Loos, the Somme, Arras, Passchendaele, and Cambrai, and was wounded during the Retreat of March 1918. He was invalided to England, and discharged in March 1919, holding the 1914 Star, and the General Service and Victory Medals.
43, Robert Street, Newton Heath, Manchester.   Z9522

FERNELEY, J., Gunner, R.G.A.
He joined the Royal Field Artillery in February 1917, and after eleven weeks' training was transferred to the Royal Garrison Artillery, and was at once drafted to the Western Front. In this theatre of war he was in action at Messines, Ypres, Passchendaele, and in other engagements until gassed at Béthune in April 1918. On his recovery he acted as clerk to the Education Officer of the 47th London Division until demobilised in January 1919. He holds the General Service and Victory Medals. 39, Sloane Street, Brooks Bar, Manchester.   TZ9521

FERNS, M., Private, 1st Manchester Regiment.
He volunteered in October 1914, and in April of the following year proceeded to France. He was engaged as a bomber, and took part in the Battles of Hill 60, Ypres, and Loos. In February 1916 he was transferred to Mesopotamia, and while serving there was in action at Kut-el-Amara, and Baghdad. He was demobilised in January 1919, and holds the 1914-15 Star, and the General Service and Victory Medals.
14, Perrin Street, Ancoats, Manchester.   Z10185

FERRISS, G. R., Driver, R.F.A.
He volunteered in 1914, and on completing his training in the following year, proceeded to France, where he saw severe fighting in various sectors of the Front. He took part in the Battles of Neuve Chapelle, Hill 60, Ypres, Festubert, and Cambrai, and many other important engagements, and was gassed at Ypres. He was demobilised in 1919, and holds the 1914-15 Star, and the General Service and Victory Medals.
13, Malage Street, Ancoats, Manchester.   Z6085

FETHERSTON, T., Corporal, Lancashire Fusiliers.
Mobilised in August 1914, he was immediately drafted to the Western Front, where he took part in the Battle of Mons, and the subsequent Retreat. He also served through the Battles of the Marne, Ypres, Loos, Vimy Ridge, and the Somme, and other engagements, and was gassed and wounded in action. Invalided home, he was for some time in hospital before being discharged in February 1919, and holds the Mons Star, and the General Service and Victory Medals.
12, Billington Street, Chorlton-on-Medlock, Manchester. Z6086

FEWTRELL, R., Pte., K.O. (R. Lancaster Regt.)
Volunteering in December 1915, he was retained at home until June 1917, when he proceeded to France. There he took part in heavy fighting at Ypres, and Passchendaele, and was wounded at Armentières in April 1918. Wounded for the second time a month later, in action on the Marne, he was invalided home, and upon his recovery was sent to Constantinople where he was employed on garrison duties until he returned home for demobilisation in April 1920. He holds the General Service and Victory Medals.
23, Geoffrey Street, Chorlton-on-Medlock, Manchester. Z6087

FIDDLER, G., Gunner, R.F.A.
He volunteered in August 1914, and in March of the following year was drafted to the Western Front, whence, later in 1915, he proceeded to Salonika. There saw much severe fighting on the Vardar, Doiran, and Struma fronts, took part in the re-capture of Monastir, and was for a time in hospital suffering from malaria. He was demobilised on his return home in January 1919, and holds the 1914–15 Star, and the General Service and Victory Medals.
10, Towson Street, Russell Street, Hulme, Manchester. TZ6088

FIDDLER, J., Private, 2nd Manchester Regiment.
Volunteering in August 1914, he proceeded to the Western Front in March of the following year, and there took part in the Battles of Hill 60, Ypres, Loos, and Vimy Ridge, and other engagements. Mortally wounded in action on the Somme, he unhappily died in hospital at Southampton on July 11th, 1916. He was entitled to the 1914–15 Star, and the General Service and Victory Medals.
"And doubtless he went in splendid company."
10, Towson Street, Russell Street, Hulme, Manchester. TZ6089

FIDLER, T. H., Private, 5th Manchester Regt.
He volunteered in March 1915, and after three months' training was drafted to the Western Front, where he saw much heavy fighting. He took part in the Battles of Loos, St. Eloi, the Somme, Arras, and Bullecourt, and was severely wounded in action in July 1917, and invalided home. After twelve months in hospital he was discharged in September 1918 as medically unfit for further service, and holds the 1914–15 Star, and the General Service and Victory Medals.
32, Nellie Street, Ardwick, Manchester. Z6090

FIELD, H., Drummer, 2nd Manchester Regiment.
Joining in March 1918, he was engaged in the Aldershot District on important duties with his unit. He was not successful in obtaining his transfer overseas before hostilities ceased, but rendered valuable services, till he was demobilised in November 1919.
21, Cornbrook Park Road, Stretford, Manchester. Z10186–7B

FIELD, T., 1st Air Mechanic, R.A.F.
He volunteered in April 1915, and on completion of his training at Farnborough, was three months later sent to the Western Front. There he served at St. Omer, Boulogne, and other important stations, where he rendered valuable services in connection with the construction and repair of aircraft. He was demobilised in February 1919, and holds the 1914–15 Star, and the General Service and Victory Medals.
24, Brass Street, Rochdale Road, Manchester. Z9523

FIELDEN, W., Private, 6th Manchester Regiment.
He volunteered in July 1915, and in January of the following year, was drafted to Egypt, where he fought in engagements at Agagia, Sollum, Katia, and Romani. Later he was transferred to the Western Front, and there, after taking part in the Battles of Bullecourt, Messines, and Ypres, fell in action near Cambrai on October 9th, 1917. He was entitled to the General Service and Victory Medals.
"His memory is cherished with pride."
9, Ash Street, Hulme, Manchester. Z6091

FIELDHOUSE, J. W., Stoker 1st Class, R.N.
He joined the Navy in 1912, and after the outbreak of war did valuable service in H.M.S. "Queen Mary," which was engaged on important duties in the North Sea. He was unfortunately killed in action at the Battle of Jutland on May 31st, 1916, and was entitled to the 1914–15 Star, and the General Service and Victory Medals.
"A costly sacrifice upon the altar of freedom."
23, Lime Street, Miles Platting, Manchester. Z10188

FIELDHOUSE, S., Rifleman, K.R.R.C.
Volunteering in August 1914, he proceeded to France a year later. He took part in numerous engagements of importance, including that at Arras, and though twice wounded, continued his service till the close of hostilities. He returned home and was demobilised in February 1919, holding the 1914–15 Star, and the General Service and Victory Medals.
6, Exton Street, Miles Platting, Manchester. Z10189

FIELDING, C., Private, 6th Border Regiment.
Volunteering in August 1914, he proceeded in the following year to the Dardanelles, and took part in the landing and Evacuation of the Peninsula. Afterwards he was drafted to France and fought in many Battles, including those of Vimy Ridge, the Somme, Arras, Ypres, and Cambrai, where he was wounded. He was invalided to hospital, and in January 1919 was dis-

charged as unfit, holding the 1914–15 Star, and the General Service and Victory Medals.
250, Hamilton Street, Collyhurst, Manchester. Z9116A

FIELDING, C. F., Cpl., 4th Royal Welch Fusiliers.
He volunteered in June 1915, and in January of the following year was drafted to the Western Front. After taking part in the fighting at Neuve Chapelle, and the Somme, he was sent home in August 1916, on account of being under age. He was afterwards engaged on important duties with his unit, and was accidentally injured at Folkestone. He was demobilised in March 1919, and holds the General Service and Victory Medals. 22, King Street, Hulme, Manchester. Z10190

FIELDING, E., Pte., 1st East Lancashire Regt.
A serving soldier, at the outbreak of war in August 1914, he was at once ordered to the Western Front, where he took part in the Battle of Mons, and the subsequent Retreat, and was wounded at La Bassée in the following September. Invalided home, he was in hospital for some time at Plymouth, and in October 1915, was sent to Gallipoli. There he saw further fighting, and after two months in this theatre of war was killed in action on December 19th, 1915. He was entitled to the Mons Star, and the General Service and Victory Medals.
"The path of duty was the way to glory."
36, Dyson Street, Miles Platting, Manchester. Z11495A

FIELDING, F., Private, Border Regiment.
Volunteering in April 1915, he was drafted in the same month to the Dardanelles, and took part in the Landing and subsequent Evacuation of the Peninsula. Later he proceeded to France, but after fighting at Vimy Ridge, was unfortunately killed in action on the Somme on July 1st, 1916. He was entitled to the 1914–15 Star, and the General Service and Victory Medals.
"He died the noblest death a man may die.
Fighting for God and right and liberty."
250, Hamilton Street, Collyhurst, Manchester. Z9116B

FIELDING, G., Pte., 3rd Lancashire Fusiliers and 2nd South Lancashire Regt.
He volunteered in July 1915, and later in the same year was drafted to France. He took part in the fighting at Nieuport, Loos, the Somme, Arras, Ypres, Amiens, Bapaume, Havrincourt, and other engagements until hostilities ended, and was gassed. He returned home, and was demobilised in May 1919, holding the 1914–15 Star, and the General Service and Victory Medals.
18, Romiley Street, Queen's Road, Manchester. Z10579

FIELDING, J., Sergt., Lancashire Fusiliers.
Mobilised in August 1914, he was drafted a month later to Egypt, where he served for a short period on the Suez Canal before being sent to Gallipoli. In this theatre of war he took part in the Battles of Cape Helles and Suvla Bay, and was wounded in June 1915. Sent to hospital at Alexandria, he later served in Palestine at Gaza and Jerusalem, and was again wounded. He was still serving in 1920, and holds the Mons Star, and the General Service and Victory Medals.
36, Dyson Street, Miles Platting, Manchester. Z11495B

FIELDING, R., Driver, R.F.A.
Mobilised in August 1914, he was immediately drafted to the Western Front, where he served through the Retreat from Mons. He also took part in the Battles of the Marne, the Aisne, La Bassée, and Ypres, and other engagements until severely wounded in an accident and invalided home. He was discharged in December 1915 as medically unfit for further service, and holds the Mons Star, and the General Service and Victory Medals.
24, Franchise Street North, Ardwick, Manchester. Z6092

FIELDING, W., Sapper, R.E.
He joined in January 1917, and two months afterwards proceeded to France. In this theatre of hostilities he served at Ypres, Passchendaele, and on the Somme front, performing consistently good work until after the termination of fighting. In 1920 he was still in the Army, stationed at York, and holds the General Service and Victory Medals.
36, Dyson Street, Miles Platting, Manchester. Z11495C

FILDES, J., Rifleman, 4th Rifle Brigade.
He volunteered in September 1914, and proceeding to the Western Front in March of the following year was in action at St. Eloi and Ypres. Being severely wounded in both legs he was invalided home, and after a period in hospital was discharged, owing to his injuries, in July 1916. He holds the 1914–15 Star, and the General Service and Victory Medals.
40, Harrowby Street, Collyhurst, Manchester. Z10191

FILDES, J. J., Private, 1/8th Manchester Regiment.
Shortly after volunteering in August 1914, he proceeded to Egypt, where he served on the Suez Canal until transferred to Gallipoli in April of the following year. There he took part in the Landing at Cape Helles, and was severely wounded in action in the third Battle of Krithia. He was sent to hospital at Alexandria, and afterwards returned to England, where he underwent nine operations before being invalided from the Army in December 1916. He holds the 1914–15 Star, and the General Service and Victory Medals.
21, Marple Street, Ardwick, Manchester. Z6093

FILDES, J. T., Driver, R.A.S.C. (M.T.)

Volunteering in October 1915, he proceeded in March of the following year to Egypt, where he did good work with his unit in engagements at Katia, El Fasher, Magdhaba, and Rafa. Whilst serving in Palestine he took an active part in the severe fighting at Gaza, Jerusalem, Jericho, Tripoli, and Aleppo. On his return to England he was demobilised in July 1919, and holds the General Service and Victory Medals.

62, Teignmouth Street, Collyhurst, Manchester.   Z9524

FINCH, J., L/Corporal, 1st Manchester Regiment.

When war was declared in August 1914, he was called up from the Reserve, and at once ordered to the Western Front, where he was in action at Mons, Le Cateau, the Marne, La Bassée, and Givenchy. He was then drafted to Mesopotamia, but unfortunately died of fever on the voyage in H.M.S. " Tigris " in April 1916. He was entitled to the Mons Star, and the General Service and Victory Medals.

" His memory is cherished with pride."

137, Parker Street, Bradford, Manchester.   TZ9525B

FINCH, W., Private, 21st Manchester Regiment.

He volunteered in November 1915, and two months later was drafted to the Western Front, where he served for fifteen months. During that period he was engaged in fierce fighting at Ypres, Beaumont-Hamel, the Somme, and St. Léger, and was severely wounded in action at Croisilles in April 1917. He was invalided home, and subsequently discharged as medically unfit for further service in November of that year, holding the General Service and Victory Medals.

137, Parker Street, Bradford, Manchester.   TZ9525A

FINCH, W. J., Corporal, R.G.A.

Volunteering in September 1914, he was sent to Malta in March of the following year and served on garrison duty as a 1st class gunner. In September 1917 he was transferred to France where he took part in the Battles of Lens and Cambrai, and the Somme, and also served in the Retreat and Advance of 1918, and was wounded. He was demobilised in July 1919, and holds the General Service and Victory Medals.   Z10580

41, Worth Street, off Butler Street, Rochdale Road, Manchester.

FINCHETT, J., Bandsman, Duke of Lancaster's Own Dragoons.

He volunteered at the outbreak of war in August 1914, and after a period of training, served at various stations, where he was engaged on duties of great importance. He was unable to obtain his transfer to the front, but nevertheless, rendered valuable services until March 1916, when he was discharged in order to take up Government work as a fitter at Messrs. Mitchell and Shackelton's.

118, Cowesby Street, Moss Side, Manchester.   Z11699

FINDLAW, F., L/Corporal, R.A.M.C.

He volunteered in June 1915, and in March of the following year was drafted to the Western Front, where he saw severe fighting in various sectors. He took an active part in the Battles of Arras, Bullecourt, Cambrai, the Somme, and Le Cateau, and other engagements and served also through the Retreat and Advance of 1918. He afterwards served with the Army of Occupation in Germany until his return home for demobilisation in January 1919. He holds the General Service and Victory Medals.

14, Matlock Place, Hulme, Manchester.   Z6094

FINDLOW, J. H., Private, 8th Manchester Regt.

He volunteered in October 1914, and was engaged with his unit on important duties till February 1916, when he was sent to France. He was in action near Loos, and St. Eloi, and in the Battles of Albert, the Somme, Beaumont-Hamel and Arras. He was badly wounded and gassed, and after a period in hospital at Rouen and Eastbourne, he was discharged, owing to his injuries, in November 1918. He holds the General Service and Victory Medals.

25, Edensor Street, Beswick, Manchester.   Z10192

FINLAY, G., Gunner, R.G.A.

Volunteering in November 1915, he proceeded to France after two months' training, and there saw severe fighting in various sectors of the Front. He took part in the Battles of Vimy Ridge and the Ancre, and many other important engagements until gassed in action and sent to hospital at Le Havre. He re-joined his Battery later, however, but was finally invalided from the Army in November 1919, holding the General Service and Victory Medals.

50, Poplar Street, Ardwick, Manchester.   Z6096

FINLEY, H. W., Driver, R.A.S.C.

Mobilised in August 1914, he was retained on important duties in England until August 1916, when he was drafted to Salonika. There he took an active part in many important engagements on the Doiran and Struma fronts, and was also present at the re-capture of Monastir. He was finally invalided home, and discharged in January 1919, and holds the General Service and Victory Medals.

28, Clifford Street, Lower Openshaw, Manchester.   Z6095

FINLEY, W. H., Gunner, R.F.A.

He volunteered in 1915, and after completing a period of training later in the same year, was drafted to the Western Front, where he took part in important engagements in various sectors. He died gloriously on the Field of Battle at Ypres on July 13th, 1917. He was entitled to the 1914-15 Star, and the General Service and Victory Medals.

" Honour to the immortal dead, who gave their youth that the world might grow old in peace."

7, Peel Street, Chorlton-on-Medlock, Manchester.   X6097

FINNEY, A. Private, 1/10th Manchester Regiment.

He joined in January 1918, and in August of that year was drafted to the Western Front, where he saw much severe fighting. He made the supreme sacrifice, falling in action in the fourth Battle of Ypres on September 28th, 1918. He was entitled to the General Service and Victory Medals.

" A valiant Soldier, with undaunted heart he breasted life's last hill."

23, Teak Street, Beswick, Manchester.   TZ6100

FINNEY, R., Sapper, R.E.

Volunteering in April 1915, he was sent to France in June, and took an active part in the Battles of Loos, Vermelles, the Somme, Arras, and Cambrai. He was gassed in action at Loos, and was wounded at Ypres in November 1915. Demobilised in January 1919, he holds the 1914-15 Star, and the General Service and Victory Medals.

5, Hughes Street, Ardwick, Manchester.   Z6098

FINNEY, W., A.B., Royal Navy, H.M.S. " Glorious."

Joining in May 1916, he was posted to H.M.S. " Glorious," in which vessel he took an active part in the Battle of Jutland, and was severely wounded. He was sent into hospital at Portsmouth, and after receiving treatment was invalided from the Navy in November 1918. He holds the General Service and Victory Medals.

3, Harry Street, London Road, Manchester.   Z9117

FINNIGAN. E., A.B., Royal Navy.

He was already in the Navy when war was declared in August 1914, and was afterwards attached to the Grand Fleet in the North Sea, where he was engaged on various important duties. He took part in many destroyer actions in these waters until the cessation of hostilities and was finally discharged in February 1919. He holds the 1914-15 Star, and the General Service and Victory Medals.

10, Homer Street, Chorlton-on-Medlock, Manchester. TX11700A

FINNERTY, M. J., Private, 8th Manchester Regt.

Volunteering in August 1914, he first saw active service at the Landing at Suvla Bay, where he was wounded in action in August 1915. He was admitted into hospital at Alexandria, but in October 1915, was invalided to Southport. On his recovery he was retained on special duties as an orderly until his demobilisation in February 1919, and holds the 1914-15 Star, and the General Service and Victory Medals.

26, Daniel Street, Hulme, Manchester.   Z6099

FIRBY, A. M., Gunner, R.F.A.

He joined in July 1916, and in December of the same year was drafted to the Western Front, where he was in action at the Ancre, Arras, Bullecourt, Messines, Ypres, Passchendaele, Cambrai, and in the Retreat and Advance of 1918. During his service overseas he was once wounded. He was demobilised in June 1919, and holds the General Service and Victory Medals.

3, Hamilton Street, Collyhurst, Manchester.   Z10581

FIRSTBROOK, J., Private, 10th King's (Liverpool Regiment) Liverpool Scottish.

Joining in June 1918 on attaining military age, he was sent to France in November 1918. He served for a time at Brussels and Antwerp on various important duties, and later was stationed at Cologne. Returning to England he was demobilised in October 1919.

13, Gladstone Street, West Gorton, Manchester.   Z9118

FIRTH, R., Rifleman, 2nd Cameronians (Scottish Rifles).

He enlisted in 1912, and in November 1914 he was drafted to the Western Front. He took part in the Battles of La Bassée and Ypres, and fell fighting gallantly at Neuve Chapelle on March 10th, 1915. He was entitled to the 1914 Star, and the General Service and Victory Medals.

" He died the noblest death a man may die, Fighting for God and right and liberty."

56, Knightly Street, Rochdale Road, Manchester. Z10582A

FIRTH, W., Gunner, R.G.A.

He joined in August 1917, and in January of the following year after completing his training, was sent to France. He was in action at the Somme, the Marne, Ypres, Havrincourt, Cambrai, and Le Cateau. He returned home and was demobilised in January 1919, holding the General Service and Victory Medals.

56, Knightly Street, Rochdale Road, Manchester. Z10582B

FISH, T., Private, 1st Border Regiment.
Joining in July 1916, he was drafted to France in January of the following year. He took part in numerous engagements of importance, including those at Arras, Ypres, Combles, Passchendaele, Armentières, Cambrai, and Bourlon Woods. He also served with the Flying Column in the Retreat and Advance of 1918, and was gassed in July. He was demobilised in October 1919, and holds the General Service and Victory Medals.
Thornton Street, Manchester. Z10193

FISHBURN, T., Private, 52nd Manchester Regt.
He joined in June 1918, and after completing his training was retained on important duties with his unit. He was engaged in the East Coast Defence, and rendered valuable services, but was unsuccessful in obtaining his transfer overseas before the cessation of hostilities. He was demobilised in January 1919.
43, Cyrus Street, Ancoats, Manchester. Z10194

FISHER, G. A., Private, 3rd Manchester Regt.
Volunteering in August 1914, he was sent to France in the following January, and took part in the Battles of Ypres and Festubert before being wounded in action and invalided home. On his recovery he was drafted to Mesopotamia, but a few months afterwards was again invalided to England, after being in action at Kut and Amara. Later, however, he was sent to Palestine and was in action at the three Battles of Gaza, and at the capture of Jerusalem and Jericho. Demobilised in July 1919, he holds the 1914–15 Star, and the General Service and Victory Medals.
30, Bedale Street, Hulme, Manchester. Z6101

FISHER, H., Corporal, 12th Cheshire Regiment.
He volunteered in June 1915, and in August of the following year was sent to Salonika, where he played a prominent part in much severe fighting in the Balkans, particularly on the Doiran front, and in the Advance across the Vardar. He was demobilised in March 1919, and holds the General Service and Victory Medals.
7, Harper Place, Hulme, Manchester. Z6104

FISHER, J., Pioneer, R.E.
He volunteered in September 1915, and was soon drafted overseas. During his service on the Western Front he was in action at Loos, Albert and on the Somme, and was wounded at Beaucourt in October 1916. A month later he was discharged on account of his age, and holds the 1914–15 Star, and the General Service and Victory Medals.
40, Napier Street, Ardwick, Manchester. Z6103

FISHER, J., Gunner, R.F.A.
He volunteered in September 1914, and in the following November was sent to the Western Front. There he took a prominent part with his Battery in many important engagements, including La Bassée, Ypres, Hill 60, St. Eloi, Loos, Vimy Ridge, the Somme, Arras, Bullecourt, Messines and Cambrai. After four and a half years' excellent service overseas, he was demobilised in May 1919, and holds the 1914–15 Star, and the General Service and Victory Medals.
100, Long Street, Ancoats, Manchester. Z11416C

FISHER, J. W., Private, 16th Manchester Regt.
He volunteered in June 1915, and five months later was sent to France, where he took part in the Battle of the Somme, and was wounded in action in July 1916. He was invalided home, but after hospital treatment at Manchester, was again sent to France and fought in the Arras, Vimy Ridge and St. Quentin sectors during the Retreat and Advance of 1918. He was demobilised in March 1919, and holds the 1914–15 Star, and the General Service and Victory Medals.
40, Napier Street, Ardwick, Manchester. Z6102

FISHER, R., Private, 1st Welch Regiment.
Joining in February 1917, he was drafted four months later to France. In this theatre of war he took part in strenuous fighting at Arras, Bullecourt, Ypres, Messines, Passchendaele, Cambrai, and in many sectors during the Retreat and Advance of 1918. He performed consistently good work until he was wounded at Cambrai in October 1918. Demobilised in April 1919, he holds the General Service and Victory Medals.
100, Long Street, Ancoats, Manchester. Z11416B

FISHER, W., Private, 8th Manchester Regiment.
He volunteered in January 1915, and after a period of training served at Southport and Ardwick, engaged on various duties of an important nature. In September 1915, he was released from the Colours in order to take up work of National importance, and until the termination of hostilities was employed on munitions at Messrs. Mather and Platts', Miles Platting, and rendered valuable services.
100, Long Street, Ancoats, Manchester. Z11416A

FISHWHICK, C , Private, Manchester Regiment.
He joined in May 1917, and after a course of training served on important duties at various stations with his unit. He was not successful in obtaining his transfer overseas before hostilities ceased, but in March 1919 proceeded to Germany, and served with the Army of Occupation on the Rhine. In January 1920 he was demobilised.
185, Victoria Square, Ancoats, Manchester. TZ9119

FISK, W. (M.M.), Private, R.A.M.C.
Mobilised in August 1914, he was immediately drafted to France and took part in the Battles of Mons, the Marne, La Bassée, Ypres (I), Neuve Chapelle, Hill 60, Ypres (II), the Somme, Arras, Ypres (III) and Cambrai, where he was awarded the Military Medal for conspicuous bravery and devotion to duty in the Field. He was unfortunately killed in action on the Somme on March 21st, 1918, and was also entitled to the Mons Star, and the General Service and Victory Medals.
" A costly sacrifice upon the altar of freedom."
216, Viaduct Street, Ardwick, Manchester. Z6105

FITTON, J., Pioneer, R.E.
He joined in February 1916, and after completing his training was engaged at Aldershot, Salisbury and other stations on important guard, patrol and police duties. He rendered valuable services, but was not successful in obtaining his transfer to a theatre of war before hostilities ceased, and was discharged in November 1918.
103, Ryder Street, Collyhurst, Manchester. Z10584A

FITTON, T., Signalman, R.N.
He volunteered in May 1915, and served in H.M.S. " Laertes," " Doris " " Lowestoft," " Lord Nelson " and " Sandfly." In October 1915 he proceeded to the North Sea and was engaged on escort, mine-laying and transport duties. In January 1916 he was transferred to the Mediterranean, where he was employed on similar work and remained till December 1918. He was demobilised in February 1919, and holds the 1914–15 Star, the General Service (with four Clasps), and the Victory Medals. 361, Collyhurst Road, Collyhurst, Manchester. Z10583

FITZGERALD, G. A., Pte., 13th Manchester Regt.
He volunteered in September 1914, and a year later was drafted to the Western Front. Two months afterwards he was sent to Salonika, where he took an active part in many engagements of importance, and lost his left hand and part of his right in consequence of severe wounds received in action. On his voyage home in October 1917, his vessel H.M.H.S. " Gurka " was torpedoed off Malta, but no lives were lost, and he reached England in safety. After much hospital treatment he was discharged in November 1918, as unfit for further duty, and holds the 1914–15 Star, and the General Service and Victory Medals. 90, Lind Street, Ancoats, Manchester. Z10195B

FITZGERALD, T., Pte., King's Own Shropshire Light Infantry and K.O. (R. Lancaster Regt.)
He joined in August 1917, and after a course of training was engaged at various stations on important guard and other duties. He was not successful in obtaining his transfer overseas before hostilities ceased, but rendered very valuable services until demobilised in November 1919.
90, Lind Street, Ancoats, Manchester. Z10195C

FITZGERALD, T. J., Pte., 21st Manchester Regt.
He volunteered in October 1914, and was soon drafted to France, where he took part in the Battles of Neuve Chapelle, Hill 60, Ypres (II), Festubert, Loos, Albert, Vimy Ridge, the Somme, Ypres (III), and in the Retreat and Advance of 1918. He was wounded in action at the second Battle of Ypres in 1915, and was demobilised in May 1919, holding the 1914–15 Star, and the General Service and Victory Medals.
32, Ribston Street, Hulme, Manchester. Z6106

FITZGERALD, T. M., Sergt., 3rd Lancashire Fuslrs.
He volunteered in September 1914, and was retained at various stations as drill instructor. Owing to being over military age he could not obtain his transfer to a fighting front, and after rendering valuable services at Conway, Prees Heath, and other training camps was discharged in April 1919.
90, Lind Street, Ancoats, Manchester. Z10195A

FITZPATRICK, F., Pte., 21st Manchester Regt.
Volunteering in November 1914, he was engaged after a period of training at Grantham, Ripon, and other stations on important duties with his unit. He was not successful in obtaining his transfer overseas on account of physical disability, and in February 1919 was demobilised, after rendering valuable services throughout.
48, Phelan Street, Collyhurst, Manchester. Z10585

FITZPATRICK, J., Stoker, R.N.
Joining in July 1917, he was later posted to H.M.S. " Tiger," in which he did good service with the Home Fleet until the end of the war. He holds the General Service and Victory Medals, and in 1920 was still in the Navy.
12, Wood Street, Harpurhey, Manchester. Z10586

FITZPATRICK, J., Sergt., Lancashire Fusiliers.
Volunteering in November 1914, he proceeded to France in the following July, and whilst there fought in many notable battles. He was wounded at Loos, but on his recovery returned to the trenches, and fought at Vermelles, Albert, and the Somme, when he was again wounded. After rejoining his unit he took part in the Battles of Arras, Vimy Ridge, Bullecourt, Ypres, the Aisne, Bapaume and other important operations in the Retreat and Advance of 1918. He was demobilised at Heaton Park in April 1919, and holds the 1914–15 Star, and the General Service and Victory Medals.
8, Purdon Street, Ancoats, Manchester. Z10196

FITZPATRICK, J. M., Pte., 7th Manchester Regt.
Volunteering in September 1914, he was drafted to France twelve months later, and whilst in this theatre of war took part in the Battles of Loos, Albert, the Somme, Arras, Vimy Ridge, Bullecourt, Ypres, Cambrai and Amiens, and in the Retreat and Advance of 1918. He was demobilised in February 1919, after serving in Germany for a time, and holds the 1914–15 Star, and the General Service and Victory Medals.
16, Albert Street, Rusholme, Manchester.   Z6107

FITZSIMMONS, A., Pte., 6th S. Lancashire Regt.
Volunteering in September 1914, he proceeded in the following June to Gallipoli, where he was wounded two months later in action at Cape Helles. After spending some time in hospital at Alexandria, he served at Zagizig, and in the Soudan, and later proceeding into Palestine was in action at Jerusalem, Jaffa, and Bethlehem. He was demobilised on returning home in February 1919, and holds the 1914–15 Star and the General Service and Victory Medals.
17, Williams Place, Ancoats, Manchester.   Z11417B

FITZSIMMONS, R., Private, 11th Manchester Regt.
Volunteering in May 1915, he proceeded to Egypt in October of that year, and there took part in engagements at Sollum, Katia, and various other places. In May 1916, however, he was transferred to the Western Front, where he was unhappily killed in action on October 4th of the same year, during the Somme Offensive, and was buried at Courcelette. He was entitled to the 1914–15 Star, and the General Service and Victory Medals.
"Whilst we remember, the sacrifice is not in vain."
4, Peter Street, Hulme, Manchester.   Z11701

FITZSIMMONS, W., Private, Royal Scots.
He volunteered in August 1914, and in the following February was sent to the Western Front, where he took part in the Battles of Ypres, Loos, the Somme and Vimy Ridge. He was badly wounded in action in the last-named engagement, and was invalided home. In December 1918 he was demobilised, and holds the 1914–15 Star, and the General Service and Victory Medals.
29, Roseberry Street, Gorton, Manchester.   TZ6108

FITZWATER W., Trooper, 2nd Life Guards.
He joined in May 1918, on attaining military age, and was sent for training at Windsor and Caterham. He was unsuccessful in obtaining his transfer overseas, but nevertheless, did consistently good work, and in 1920 was still serving.
60, Avon Street, Chorlton-on-Medlock, Manchester.   Z6109B

FLAHERTY, M., Gunner, R.F.A.
Volunteering in August 1915, he was sent to France in the following October, and first took part in heavy fighting at Neuve Chapelle in 1916. Later he was in action at the Battles of the Somme, Arras, Ypres, St. Quentin and Monchy, and was wounded in March 1918, during the Retreat. He was invalided to England, but on his recovery returned to France in time to serve at Cambrai and Maubeuge during the Advance. He was demobilised in August 1919, and holds the 1914–15 Star, and the General Service and Victory Medals.
30, Lawrence Street, Ardwick, Manchester.   X6110

FLANAGAN, D., Sergt., R.A.S.C.
He volunteered in August 1914, and in May of the following year was sent to the Western Front, where he remained for nearly four years. During this period he served at Ploegsteert Wood, La Bassée, Festubert, Arras, Bray, Amiens, Albert, and on the Somme. He was engaged on various duties of an important nature, and did excellent work until he was demobilised in February 1919, holding the 1914–15 Star, and the General Service and Victory Medals.
3, Southwell Street, Harpurhey, Manchester.   Z11496

FLANAGAN, J., Private, 8th Manchester Regiment.
Volunteering in August 1914, he proceeded in the following month to Egypt, where he saw service at Suez, and in the Desert. He was sent in April 1915 to the Dardanelles, where he took part in the Battles of Krithia, and was wounded. On his recovery he was drafted to the Western Front, and served with the Labour Corps on the lines of communication in the Cambrai sector, until demobilised in February 1919. He holds the 1914–15 Star, and the General Service and Victory Medals.
54, Sycamore Street, Oldham Road, Manchester.   Z10198

FLANAGAN, W., Pte., 25th King's (Liverpool Regt.)
Volunteering in August 1915, he was sent to France in March of the following year, and whilst there fought in many notable engagements. He was in action at Ypres, and on the Somme, and after hostilities ceased proceeded to Germany with the Army of Occupation. Demobilised in March 1920, he holds the General Service and Victory Medals.
3, Mary Place, Ancoats, Manchester.   TZ9120

FLANNAGAN, T., Private, South Lancashire Regt.
He joined in November 1916, and seven months later was drafted to the Western Front, where he took part in the Battles of Ypres, and in the heavy fighting at Vimy Ridge. He was badly gassed in action in September 1917, and was sent to hospital in Torquay. In March 1918 he was invalided from the Army and holds the General Service and Victory Medals.
28, Wood Street, Hulme, Manchester.   Z6111

FLANNERY, T., Private, 14th (King's) Hussars.
He enlisted in March 1911, and in November 1915, proceeded to Mesopotamia, where he served throughout the war. He took a promnient part in the operations at Baghdad and Kut, and in many other engagements in this theatre of war, and suffered from malaria during his service. Returning home, he was discharged in May 1919, and holds the 1914–15 Star, and the General Service and Victory Medals.
13, Alfred Street, Collyhurst, Manchester.   Z9121

FLAWN, A., Sergt., R.F.A.
A time-serving soldier, he was immediately drafted to the Western Front at the outbreak of war, but was unfortunately killed near Mons on August 26th, 1914. He was entitled to the Mons Star, and the General Service and Victory Medals.
"He died the noblest death a man may die,
    Fighting for God and right, and liberty."
5, Kay Street, Ardwick, Manchester.   X6112

FLEET, C., Private, 2nd Cheshire Regiment.
He re-enlisted in August 1914, and almost immediately proceeded with the First Expeditionary Force to France. There he was in action in the Battles of Mons, Ypres and Neuve Chapelle, and fell fighting at the second Battle of Ypres in May 1915. He was entitled to the Mons Star, and the General Service and Victory Medals.
"A valiant Soldier, with undaunted heart he breasted life's last hill."
11, Turner Street, Rusholme, Manchester.   Z9526

FLEMING, J., Driver, R.A.S.C.
He volunteered in January 1916, and in the following December was drafted to the Western Front, where he was wounded in action during the Battle of Arras in April 1917. At the end of the same year he was transferred to Italy, and was engaged on special duties there until March 1918, when he was sent to Palestine, and was present at the capture of Tripoli and Aleppo. He also served at Jerusalem and Jericho for a time, and was demobilised in April 1920, holding the General Service and Victory Medals.
8, Mill Street, Bradford, Manchester.   Z6113

FLEMING, J., Private, 13th Manchester Regiment.
Volunteering in January 1915, he was drafted in the following September to France, and took part in heavy fighting in Champagne, where he was wounded. Upon his recovery, he was transferred to Salonika, and in this theatre of war served until January 1919, when he returned home. During his service overseas he did good work, and was demobilised in February 1919. He holds the 1914–15 Star, and the General Service and Victory Medals.
220, Cheltenham Street, Collyhurst, Manchester.   Z11497

FLEMING, S., Private, King's (Liverpool) Regt.
He joined in October 1917, and in the following May was drafted to the Western Front, where he was in action at Arras until August 1918. He was then badly wounded and invalided home, but on his recovery served for four months at Cork in Ireland. Demobilised in November 1919, he holds the General Service and Victory Medals.
10, Pump Street, Hulme, Manchester.   Z6114

FLEMMING, W., Private, Loyal N. Lancs. Regt.
He volunteered in September 1914, and in October of the following year was drafted to the Western Front, where he took part in the Battles of Vermelles, Ploegsteert, and the Somme. He laid down his life for King and Country at Armentières on December 3rd, 1916, and was entitled to the 1914–15 Star, and the General Service and Victory Medals.
"The path of duty was the way to glory."
13, Hazel Street, Hulme, Manchester.   TZ6115

FLETCHER, F., Private, 8th Manchester Regiment.
Volunteering in December 1915, he was sent to France in April 1916, and was almost immediately wounded in action at Albert, After three months in hospital in France, he rejoined his unit, and was taken prisoner on the Somme in November 1916. During his captivity he suffered many hardships, and was eventually repatriated and discharged in December 1918. He holds the General Service and Victory Medals.
13, Bradshaw Street, Hulme, Manchester.   Z6116

FLETCHER, G., L/Corporal, 20th Manchester Regt.
He volunteered in November 1914, and twelve months later was drafted to France, and was first in action during the heavy fighting at Loos and Vimy Ridge. He also took part in the Battles of the Somme, Arras and Ypres before proceeding to Italy, where he served in the operations on the Piave. Demobilised in February 1919, he holds the 1914–15 Star, and the General Service and Victory Medals.
7, Hinckley Street, Bradford, Manchester.   Z6117A

FLETCHER, H., Gunner, R.F.A.
Volunteering in March 1915, he crossed to France in the same year, and fought at Loos, the Somme, and in many other engagements of importance until hostilities ended. In June 1919 he was demobilised, holding the General Service and Victory Medals.
5, Dunstan Buildings, Chester Road, Manchester.   Z10201

FLETCHER, H., Private, 2/7th Manchester Regt.
He volunteered in December 1914, and after a period of duty in England, was sent to France in February 1917, and took part in the Battles of Vimy Ridge, Messines and Ypres. In January 1918, he was invalided home suffering from hernia, and was in hospital at Birmingham. On his recovery, he joined the 2/7th Durham Light Infantry, and in the following October was sent to Russia, where he served on special duties until his demobilisation in June 1919. He holds the General Service and Victory Medals.
25, Chell Street, Longsight, Manchester.   Z6119

FLETCHER, H. (M.M.), Gunner, R.G.A.
Volunteering in August 1914, he was sent to France in the following November, and took part in the Battles of Ypres, Neuve Chapelle, St. Eloi, Festubert, the Somme, Arras, Vimy Ridge, Passchendaele and Cambrai. He was awarded the Military Medal for conspicuous bravery and devotion to duty at Ypres in January 1915, when he repaired telephone wires under heavy shell-fire. He also holds the 1914 Star, and the General Service and Victory Medals, and was demobilised in February 1919.
22, Thomas Street, West Gorton, Manchester.   TZ6118

FLETCHER, L. W., Pte., 7th Lancashire Fusiliers.
Volunteering in November 1914, he was drafted to France in the following year. Whilst in this theatre of war he took part in many Battles, including those of the Somme, Arras, Vimy Ridge, Ypres and Cambrai, and in the Retreat and Advance of 1918, and was wounded three times. Demobilised in February 1919, he holds the 1914–15 Star, and the General Service and Victory Medals.
5, Heyrod Street, Ancoats, Manchester.   Z9123

FLETCHER, J., Driver, R.A.S.C. (M.T.)
Volunteering in March 1915, he was drafted to France in May and was present at the Battles of Ypres (1915 and 1917), Loos, the Somme (1916 and 1918), Arras, Vimy Ridge, Cambrai, Bapaume and Le Cateau. He was demobilised on returning to England in March 1919, and holds the 1914–15 Star, and the General Service and Victory Medals.
31, Geoffrey Street, Chorlton-on-Medlock Manchester.   Z6121

FLETCHER, S. J., Special War Worker.
In October 1914, he volunteered for work of National importance, and until the cessation of hostilities was employed as charge hand at the Westinghouse Works, Manchester. There he was engaged making shells and tanks, and rendered very valuable services.
52, Bengal Street, Ancoats, Manchester.   Z11418

FLETCHER, T., Sergt., 1/4th Seaforth Highlanders.
He volunteered in January 1915, and for a time was retained for duty in England. In March 1916 he proceeded overseas, and was in action at Neuve Chapelle, Hill 60, Ypres, Loos, and the Somme, and was wounded. On recovery he returned to the trenches, but was taken prisoner at Cambrai, and interned in Holland until after the war. Demobilised in March 1919, after his return home, he holds the 1914–15 Star, and the General Service and Victory Medals.
23, Marple Street, Openshaw, Manchester.   Z9122

FLETCHER, W., Sergt., East Lancashire Regiment.
Joining in March 1916, he proceeded in July of the following year to France, where he saw much fighting. Amongst other places he was in action at Messines Ridge, Ypres, Cambrai, and in the Retreat and Advance, after which he was invalided home through ill-health. He was demobilised in August 1919, and holds the General Service and Victory Medals.
1A, Cambrian Street, Ancoats, Manchester.   Z9124

FLETCHER, W., Private, R.A.S.C. (M.T.)
He volunteered in November 1915, and owing to the important nature of his trade as a steel miller, was retained on important duties at various R.A.S.C. depôts, and rendered valuable services. In February 1919 he re-enlisted for a period of three year, and in 1920 was stationed at Fulham with the 369th M.T. Company.
106, Tiverton Street, Ardwick, Manchester.   X6120

FLETCHER, W., Private, 51st Manchester Regt.
He joined immediately on attaining military age in March 1918, but was not successful in obtaining his transfer overseas during hostilities. In March 1919, however, he was sent to the Army of Occupation in Germany, and rendered valuable services on the Rhine for nearly eight months. He was demobilised in October 1919.
7, Hinckley Street, Bradford, Manchester.   Z6117B

FLINT, C., Private, K.O. (Royal Lancaster Regt.)
Volunteering in March 1915, he proceeded in the following September to Gallipoli, and served there until the Evacuation of the Peninsula. Afterwards he was drafted to Mesopotamia, and took part in the operations at Kut, Um-el-Hannah, and was unfortunately killed in action at Sanna-i-Yat on April 10th, 1916. He was entitled to the 1914–15 Star, and the General Service and Victory Medals.
"The path of duty was the way to glory."
61, Milton Street, West Gorton Manchester.   Z10818B

FLINT, F., Private, 10th Manchester Regiment.
He volunteered in January 1916, and in the following month proceeded to the Western Front, where he saw severe fighting in various sectors. After taking part in the Battles of Vimy Ridge and Ypres, he was taken prisoner at Cambrai and held in captivity in Germany until after the cessation of hostilities. He was demobilised in March 1919, and holds the General Service and Victory Medals.
8, Park Place, Hulme, Manchester.   Z6122

FLINT, J. R., Pte., Welch Regt. and Lancs. Fusiliers.
He joined in July 1918, and after a period of training was retained on important duties in England until drafted to India. There he was engaged on garrison duties at Lahore and various other stations, and in 1920 was still with his unit. He holds the General Service and Victory Medals.
39, Gresham Street, Openshaw, Manchester.   Z6125

FLINT, R., Private, 2nd Manchester Regiment.
Volunteering in August 1914, he proceeded to the Western Front after two months training, and there took part in the first Battle of Ypres, and many minor engagements, and was wounded in action at Hill 60 in April 1915. Invalided home, he was drafted to Italy on his recovery and was in action in this theatre of war until the cessation of hostilities. He was demobilised on his return home in March 1919, and holds the 1914 Star, and the General Service and Victory Medals.
23, Marie Street, Openshaw, Manchester.   TZ6124

FLINT, W., Air Mechanic, R.A.F.
He joined in June 1917, and after completing a period of training served at various stations, where he was engaged on duties of a highly technical nature. He was not successful in obtaining his transfer to a theatre of war, but nevertheless, rendered valuable services with his Squadron until February 1920, when he was demobilised.
4, Woodhouse Street, Openshaw, Manchester.   Z6123

FLITCROFT, H., Private, Labour Corps.
Two months after joining in May 1916, he was drafted to the Western Front, where he was engaged on important duties in various sectors. He served at Boulogne, and many other places, and was also present at the Battles of the Somme, Cambrai, Amiens and Bapaume, before his return to England for demobilisation in December 1918. He holds the General Service and Victory Medals.
6, Eskrigge Street, Ardwick, Manchester.   Z6126

FLITCROFT, W., Private, K.O. (R. Lancaster Regt.)
Mobilised in August 1914, he was immediately drafted to the Western Front, where he fought in the Retreat from Mons, and also took part in the Battles of La Bassée, Neuve Chapelle and Hill 60, and many minor engagements. He died gloriously on the Field of Battle at Ypres in May 1915. He was entitled to the Mons Star, and the General Service and Victory Medals.
"Whilst we remember, the sacrifice is not in vain."
6, Eskrigge Street, Ardwick, Manchester.   Z6127

FLOCKHART, A., Private, Gordon Highlanders.
He volunteered in 1915, and later in the same year was drafted to France. Whilst overseas he took part in the Battles of Ypres, the Somme and Passchendaele, and was severely wounded in action in 1917. He was invalided home in consequence, and after much treatment was discharged as physically unfit for further duty in February 1918. He holds the 1914–15 Star, and the General Service and Victory Medals.
43, Herbert Street, Ardwick, Manchester.   Z10203

FLYNN, J., Corporal, R.F.A.
He volunteered in August 1915, and in January of the following year was drafted to the Western Front, where he saw severe fighting in various sectors. He took part in the Battles of Albert, Arras, Ypres, Passchendaele and many other important engagements in this theatre of war until the cessation of hostilities. He was demobilised in April 1919, and holds the General Service and Victory Medals.
4, Broom Street, Ardwick Manchester.   Z6128

FLYNN, J. J., Private, 8th Border Regiment.
He volunteered in August 1915, and two months later was sent overseas. During his service in the Western theatre of war he saw heavy fighting at Loos, Albert, the Somme, Arras, Bullecourt, Ypres and Cambrai, but was unhappily killed in action in the second Battle of the Somme on April 17th, 1918. He was entitled to the 1914–15 Star, and the General Service and Victory Medals.
"A costly sacrifice upon the altar of freedom."
126, Teignmouth Street, Collyhurst, Manchester.   Z9527A

FLYNN, P., Private, 1st Manchester Regiment.
Mobilised at the outbreak of hostilities, he was immediately drafted to France, where he took part in the Retreat from Mons. He also served gallantly at Le Cateau, Neuve Chapelle, St. Eloi, Hill 60, Ypres, and the Somme, and was severely wounded in the head in the fierce fighting at Loos. He holds the 1914–15 Star, and the General Service and Victory Medals, and was demobilised in February 1919.
12, Worth Street, St. Michael's, Manchester.   Z10588

FLYNN, T., Private, 1/6th Manchester Regiment.
Joining the Army in February 1916, he proceeded in the following May to the Western Front. There he served in various sectors of the fighting zone, and was in action in the Battles of the Somme (I), Arras, Ypres, and the Somme (II). During the latter engagement he was severely wounded, and in consequence was discharged as medically unfit for further military duties in September 1918. He holds the General Service and Victory Medals.
126, Teignmouth Street, Collyhurst, Manchester. Z9527B

FLYNN, T., Corporal, 15th Royal Welch Fusiliers.
He volunteered in March 1915, and after undergoing a period of training was engaged on important duties at various stations. He was too old for service overseas, and was consequently unable to obtain his transfer to a theatre of war, but did much useful work with his unit until November 1919, when he was demobilised.
2, Argyle Street, Marple Street, Hulme, Manchester. TZ6129

FLYNN, W., Private, 16th Manchester Regiment.
He volunteered in July 1915, and in the following October was drafted to the Western Front, where he served throughout the war. He took part in the Battles of the Somme, Ypres and Arras, and many other engagements until hostilities ceased. Returning home he was demobilised in November 1919, and holds the General Service and Victory Medals.
14, Mary Place, Ancoats, Manchester. Z9125

FODEN, W., Sergt., 7th Manchester Regiment.
Mobilised in August 1914, he was drafted to Egypt in the following month and there served until April 1915. He was then transferred to the Dardanelles, where, after taking part in the Landing at Cape Helles, he fought in the Battles of Krithia and Achi Baba, and was wounded in action. Invalided home, he afterwards served as an instructor until February 1917, when he proceeded to the Western Front, and took part in the Battles of Arras, Ypres and Cambrai and the Allies' Retreat. He fell fighting at Havrincourt on September 27th, 1918, during the Advance. He was entitled to the 1914-15 Star, and the General Service and Victory Medals.
"His memory is cherished with pride."
14, Claremont Street, Chorlton-on-Medlock, Manchester. Z6130A

FODEN, W., Private, Border Regiment.
He volunteered in December 1915, and in August of the following year was sent to the Western Front, where, after taking part in the Somme Offensive, he was wounded in action in December 1916, and invalided home. He returned to France however, on his recovery in September 1917, and there fought at Passchendaele, and was wounded a second time at Cambrai in December of that year. Being sent to England, he again returned to the Western Front in July 1918, and was a third time wounded at Havrincourt during the Advance. He was finally demobilised in February 1919, and holds the General Service and Victory Medals. Z6130B
14, Claremont Street, Chorlton-on-Medlock, Manchester.

FOGARTY, D., Private, 8th Manchester Regiment.
Volunteering at the declaration of war he was drafted to the Western Front in September 1914, and fought in the Battles of Ypres, La Bassée, Hill 60, Vimy Ridge and Arras. He was unfortunately killed in action in October 1917, at Ypres, and was entitled to the 1914 Star, and the General Service and Victory Medals.
"Great deeds cannot die:
They with the sun and moon renew their light for ever."
11, Monday Street, Oldham Road, Manchester. Z10204

FOGARTY, R., Private, East Lancashire Regiment.
He volunteered in September 1914, and drafted to the Western Front in the following February, fought at Hill 60, Ypres and Festubert, and was wounded. On his recovery he was sent to Salonika, and saw much service on the Doiran front, and was again wounded. Later, returning to France he was engaged in heavy fighting in many parts of the line and wounded at Cambrai in October 1917, was invalided to England. After receiving hospital treatment he was discharged in September 1918, and holds the 1914-15 Star, and the General Service and Victory Medals.
57, Slater Street, Ancoats, Manchester. Z10205

FOGELL, D., Private, Lancashire Fusiliers.
Volunteering in February 1916, he was sent to France three months later, and fought in the Battles of Vimy Ridge, the Somme, Bullecourt and Cambrai. He was also in action in many engagements during the German and Allied Offensives of 1918, and returning home after the Armistice, was demobilised in April 1919. He holds the General Service and Victory Medals.
22, Tonge Street, Ancoats, Manchester. Z10206

FOGG, J. E., Private, Manchester Regiment.
He volunteered in November 1915, and completing his training was stationed at various depôts on important duties with his unit. Owing to ill-health he was unsuccessful in obtaining his transfer to a theatre of war, but rendered valuable services until invalided out in November 1917.
17, Albion Street, Miles Platting, Manchester. Z10207

FOGG, H., Private, M.G.C.
After volunteering in July 1915, he underwent a period of training prior to being drafted to Mesopotamia. There he saw much severe fighting, and took part in engagements at Kut, Sanna-i-Yat, and on the Tigris, and also served at the capture of Baghdad. He returned home for demobilisation in May 1919, and holds the General Service and Victory Medals.
18, Higher Chatham Street, Chorlton-on-Medlock, Manchester. Z6131

FOGG, W., Private, 8th Manchester Regiment.
He joined in October 1916, and five months later proceeded to France, where he saw severe fighting in various sectors of the Front. He took part in the Battles of Passchendaele, and the Somme, and engagements at La Bassée, Nieuport, and many other places, and also served through the Retreat and Advance of 1918. Returning home on the cessation of hostilities, he was demobilised in April 1919, and holds the General Service and Victory Medals.
47, Denton Street, Hulme, Manchester. Z6132

FOLEY, E., Private, 3rd Manchester Regiment.
Joining in August 1916, he landed in France three months later, and was engaged in heavy fighting in many parts of the line. He fought on the Ancre, and at Arras, and was wounded in the third Battle of Ypres. Returning to England, he received hospital treatment, and ultimately was discharged as medically unfit for further service in November 1917. He holds the General Service and Victory Medals.
13, Wilkinson Street, Rochdale Road, Manchester. Z10208

FOLEY, J., Sergt., Royal Irish Fusiliers.
Having enlisted in February 1888, he was already in the Army when war was declared in August 1914, and was retained at various stations until April 1916. He was then drafted to India, where he served at Bombay on garrison duties, and also engaged in conducting prisoners of war to internment camps at Poona, Calcutta and elsewhere. He returned home and was invalided from the Army in April 1917, and holds the General Service and Victory Medals.
4, Bloom Street, Hulme, Manchester. TZ6135

FOLEY, J., Private, 18th Manchester Regiment.
He volunteered in April 1915, and in December of that year was drafted to the Western Front. Whilst in this theatre of war he took part in many important engagements in various sectors, and was wounded in action and taken prisoner at Albert in May 1916. Held in captivity in Germany until after the cessation of hostilities, he was forced during this period to work on the railways, and was finally demobilised on his release in December 1918. He holds the 1914-15 Star, and the General Service and Victory Medals.
21, Gore Street, Greenheys, Manchester. TZ6134

FOLEY, R. W., Driver, R.A.S.C.
Mobilised in August 1914, he shortly afterwards proceeded to the Western Front, where he was engaged on conveying food and ammunition to the forward areas. He was present at the Battles of Ypres, the Somme and Arras, and many other important engagements in various sectors until invalided home in March 1918. He was discharged in October of that year as medically unfit for further service, and holds the Queen's and King's South African Medals, the 1914 Star, and the General Service and Victory Medals.
26, Glebe Street, Gorton, Manchester. Z6133

FONE, T., Corporal, Cheshire Regiment.
He enlisted in April 1906, and when war broke out was on Indian service. In January 1915, he was drafted to France, and during the fighting at Loos was wounded, on recovery returning to the trenches. He then fought on the Somme, Ypres and Cambrai, where he was again wounded and invalided home, being discharged as medically unfit in March 1918. He holds the 1914-15 Star, and the General Service and Victory Medals. 1, Gleave Street, West Gorton, Manchester. Z9126

FOOTITT, W. S., Gunner, R.F.A.
Volunteering in March 1915, he proceeded to the Western Front later in that year and fought in the Battles of Ypres, Festubert and Vimy Ridge. He was wounded at Mametz Wood during the first Battle of the Somme, and was invalided to England for treatment. On his recovery he was drafted to Italy, and saw much fighting, serving throughout the final Allied Advance in this theatre of war. He returned home, and was demobilised in 1919, and holds the 1914-15 Star, and the General Service and Victory Medals.
90, Kemp Street, Manchester. Z10209

FORAN, W., Private, South Lancashire Regiment.
He volunteered in August 1914, and until April of the following year was retained on home duties, in the course of which he was wounded in a bomb explosion. He later proceeded to Gallipoli, and took part in the operations at Suvla Bay and various other places during that campaign. He was invalided home through ill-health, but on recovery was drafted to France, where he fought in many notable battles, including Ypres, Arras, the Somme and Cambrai, and was twice wounded. Demobilised in February 1919, he holds the 1914-15 Star, and the General Service and Victory Medals.
1, Alfred Street, Collyhurst, Manchester. Z912

FORD, A., Rifleman, Rifle Brigade.
Volunteering in September 1914, he was drafted to the Western Front in the following December, and there saw much severe fighting. He made the supreme sacrifice, falling in action at La Bassée on February 6th, 1915. He was entitled to the 1914-15 Star, and the General Service and Victory Medals.
"He died the noblest death a man may die,
Fighting for God, and right, and liberty."
199, Broadfield Road, Moss Side, Manchester. TZ6137A

FORD, E., Corporal, King's (Liverpool Regiment.)
He joined in April 1916, and in March of the following year proceeded to the Western Front. There he saw severe fighting in various sectors, took part in the Battle of Bullecourt and other important engagements, and was wounded in action at Cambrai in November 1917. Sent home, he was finally invalided from the Army in March 1918, and holds the General Service and Victory Medals.
88, Erskine Street, Hulme, Manchester. Z6138

FORD, F., Driver, R.F.A.
He volunteered at the commencement of war, and was shortly afterwards sent to France, where he fought in the Retreat from Mons, and many of the subsequent battles until November 1915. He was then drafted to Mesopotamia, and was in action at Kut, Sanna-i-Yat, and on the Tigris, remaining in the East until his return home for demobilisation in April 1919. He holds the Mons Star, and the General Service and Victory Medals. 33, Sycamore Street, Manchester. Z9128

FORD, J., Gunner, R.F.A.
Volunteering in January 1915, he was drafted to Egypt on completion of four months' training, and there saw much severe fighting. He was present at the capture of El Fasher and Magdhaba, and taking part in the Advance into Palestine, served also at Jerusalem. In November 1917, he was transferred to the Western Front, and there contracted influenza, and unhappily died in hospital in January 1918, and was buried at Cambrai. He was entitled to the 1914-15 Star, and the General Service and Victory Medals.
"A costly sacrifice upon the altar of freedom."
12, William Street, Ardwick, Manchester. Z6136

FORD, S., Private, 22nd Manchester Regiment.
He volunteered in September 1915, and in January of the following year, proceeded to the Western Front, where he was engaged on transport duties, conveying food and ammunition to the lines. He also took part in the Battles of the Somme, and many other important engagements in various sectors until transferred to Italy in 1917. He finally returned home for demobilisation in March 1919, and holds the General Service and Victory Medals.
199, Broadfield Road, Moss Side, Manchester. TZ6137B

FORD, W. J., Pte., E. Lancs. Regt. and Cheshire Regt.
Four months after volunteering in January 1915, he was drafted to the Western Front, where he saw fighting in various sectors. After taking part in the Battles of Ypres, Festubert, Loos and Vimy Ridge, he was wounded in action on the Somme, and invalided home. He returned to France, however, on his recovery, and was again in action at Messines, Cambrai, and many other places until again sent home, suffering from bronchitis. He was finally demobilised in March 1919, and holds the 1914-15 Star, and the General Service and Victory Medals. 1, Hyde View, Ardwick, Manchester. Z6139

FORDEN, T., Private, Labour Corps.
He joined in June 1916, and after completing a short period of training proceeded to the Western Front. There, engaged on important duties in various sectors, he took part also in the Battles of Arras, Vimy Ridge and Cambrai, and was gassed. He returned home for demobilisation in January 1919, and holds the General Service and Victory Medals.
28, James Street, Moss Side, Manchester. Z6140

FOREST, E., Private, Border Regiment.
Volunteering in January 1915, he was sent to the Western Front later in the same year, and fought at Arras, and the Somme, and in many engagements during the German and Allied Offensives of 1918, and was wounded five times. He was demobilised in 1919, and holds the 1914-15 Star, and the General Service and Victory Medals. Z10210
4, Lamb Street, off Richmond Grove, Longsight, Manchester.

FORKERT, W. F., Private, Manchester Regiment.
He joined in August 1917, and in December of that year was drafted to the Western Front, where he saw much severe fighting. He took part in the Battles of Cambrai, and many other important engagements in various sectors until wounded in action and invalided home in August 1918. He afterwards served on coastal defence duties in England, until discharged in August 1919, and holds the General Service and Victory Medals. 112, Marsland Street, Ardwick, Manchester. TZ6142

FORREST, J., Private, 23rd Manchester Regiment.
He volunteered in November 1914, and in January 1916 was drafted to the Western Front, where he took part in the Battles of Albert, the Somme, Arras, Vimy Ridge, Messines, Ypres, the Marne, Amiens, Bapaume and Cambrai (II). He was gassed in action and spent some time in hospital. Demobilised in April 1919, he holds the General Service and Victory Medals.
6, Stockton Street, Chorlton-on-Medlock, Manchester. Z6143

FORREST, F. C., Private, 21st Manchester Regt.
Joining early in 1917, he was drafted to the Western Front on completing his training in May of that year, and there saw much severe fighting. He died gloriously on the Field of Battle at Messines on July 1st, 1917, after only a few weeks' active service. He was entitled to the General Service and Victory Medals. "Great deeds cannot die:
They with the sun and moon renew their light for ever."
42, Ardwick Green, Chorlton-on-Medlock, Manchester. X6144

FORREST, J., Private, King's (Liverpool Regiment).
He volunteered in September 1914, and in the following year was drafted to France, and thence to Salonika, where after a short time he was sent into hospital. He was later sent to Malta and finally to Queen Mary's Hospital, England. On recovery he was transferred to the 75th T.R.B., and subsequently to the Monmouth Regiment, and the R.A.F. Demobilised in April 1919, he holds the 1914-15 Star, and the General Service and Victory Medals.
10, Queen Street, Bradford, Manchester. TZ9129

FORSHAW, G. W., Private, 9th Manchester Regt.
He joined in February 1917, and four months later was drafted to the Western Front, where he took part in the Battles of Ypres and Passchendaele, and was gassed in action on the Somme in December 1917. He was invalided to hospital at Colchester, and was discharged in March 1918, as medically unfit for further service, holding the General Service and Victory Medals.
11, Carmen Street, Ardwick, Manchester. Z6145

FORSHAW, J. H., Private, 16th Manchester Regt.
Volunteering in November 1915, he was sent to France in the following June and was in action with his unit at the Battles of the Somme (at Beaumont-Hamel, Beaucourt and Albert), Ypres and Passchendaele, where he was taken prisoner in August 1917. During his captivity at Giessen in Germany, he was forced to work on the land. He was eventually repatriated and demobilised in December 1918, and holds the General Service and Victory Medals.
52, Markham Street, Ardwick, Manchester. Z6146

FORSTER, J., L/Corporal, 2nd Cheshire Regiment.
He volunteered in August 1914, and in the following April was drafted to France, but a month later was badly wounded in action at the Battle of Ypres, having his left knee-cap blown away. He was invalided home, and after eight months in hospital near Blackburn, was discharged in January 1916, as medically unfit for further service, holding the 1914-15 Star, and the General Service and Victory Medals.
215, Earl Street, Longsight, Manchester. Z6147

FORSTER, R., Guardsman, Grenadier Guards.
He volunteered in January 1915, and in the following year was drafted to France, where he was badly wounded in action in October 1916, during the Somme Offensive. He was invalided home and after hospital treatment in Edinburgh and London, was discharged in March 1917, as medically unfit for further service. He holds the General Service and Victory Medals.
103, South Street, Longsight, Manchester. Z6151

FORTH, G., Private, 3rd Lancashire Fusiliers.
He joined in July 1917, and on completion of his training was engaged on important guard duties at various stations. He was unsuccessful in obtaining his transfer overseas, but rendered valuable services with his unit until his demobilisation in October 1919.
168, Hartington Street, Moss Side, Manchester. TZ6148

FORTH, W., Private, Manchester Regiment.
He joined in March 1916, and after three months' training was drafted to the Western Front, where he took part in much severe fighting, and was wounded in action in November 1917. After hospital treatment at Reading, he returned to France in March 1918, and was wounded a second time on the Somme in the following August. He was again sent home, and was in hospital near Blackburn, being eventually discharged as medically unfit in June 1919. He holds the General Service and Victory Medals.
1, John Street, Moss Side, Manchester. Z6149

FOSBROOK, F., Private, Border Regt. and R.A.S.C.
He volunteered in November 1914, and embarking for the Western Front in August of the following year was in action in the Battles of Loos, St. Eloi, the Somme, Arras, Ypres and Cambrai. He saw much service throughout the Retreat and Advance of 1918, and returning home after the cessation of hostilities was demobilised in March 1919. He holds the 1914-15 Star, and the General Service and Victory Medals.
115, Kendall Street, Bradford, Manchester. Z10211

FOSTER, H., Sapper, R.E.
He volunteered in September 1914, and after a period of training was engaged on important guard duties on the East Coast until October 1915. He was then discharged in order to take up work of National importance on munitions at Heaton Park, where he rendered valuable services during the remainder of hostilities.
13, Matthew Street, Ardwick, Manchester. Z6125

FOSTER, L., Sapper, R.E.
A Reservist, he was called up when war broke out in August 1914, and was immediately ordered to France. He was in action at Mons, the Marne, the Aisne, Ypres, Loos,, the Somme, Arras and Cambrai, and in the Retreat and Advance of 1918, and was present during the triumphal entry into Mons. After the Armistice he was invalided home suffering from the effects of gas, and was discharged in April 1915, holding the Mons Star, and the General Service and Victory Medals.
12, Wragley Street, Miles Platting, Manchester.   Z9449A

FOSTER, P., Air Mechanic, R.A.F.
He joined in July 1918, and on completion of his training was engaged on important duties at various aerodromes. He was medically unfit for transfer overseas, but nevertheless rendered valuable services which called for a high degree of technical skill until his demobilisation in November 1919.
3, Fountain Street, City Road, Hulme, Manchester. Z6150B

FOSTER, R. W., Stoker Petty Officer, R.N.
He was mobilised from the Royal Fleet Reserve in August 1914, and was sent to the North Sea on board H.M.S. "Victorious." After four months on patrol there, he was transferred to H.M.S. "Caesar," in which ship he took part in the Naval operations during the Gallipoli campaign. After the Evacuation of the Peninsula, he returned to the Grand Fleet in the North Sea, and was in action at the Battle of Jutland. He was discharged in March 1919, and holds the 1914–15 Star, and the General Service and Victory Medals.
4, Carlisle Street, Hulme, Manchester.   TZ6153

FOULDS, R., Special War Worker.
He offered his services for work of National importance, and throughout the war was engaged on the manufacture of barbed wire at Messrs. R. Johnson's Wire Works. He rendered excellent services, discharging his duties throughout in a most satisfactory and efficient manner.
7, Haigh Street, West Gorton, Manchester.   Z10212

FOULKES, F., Engine Room Artificer, R.N.
He joined in June 1916, and during the war saw service in H.M.S. "Nessus" and "Marvel." He was in action in the Battle of Heligoland Bight and the Falkland Isles, and was afterwards engaged on various important duties in the North Sea until hostilities ended. Later he was present at the surrender and internment of the German Fleet at Scapa Flow. Demobilised in February 1919, he holds the General Service and Victory Medals.
8, Norway Street, Ardwick, Manchester.   Z9130

FOULKES, J., Private, Manchester Regiment.
He volunteered in January 1915, and in the following month was sent to the Western Front, and fought in the engagements at Neuve Chapelle and St. Eloi. After only two months' service in the Army he was unfortunately killed in action in March 1915. He was entitled to the 1914–15 Star, and the General Service and Victory Medals.
"He died the noblest death a man may die,
Fighting for God, and right, and liberty."
85, Teignmouth Street, Rochdale Road, Manchester. Z9528

FOULKES, W., Pte., 8th Lancashire Fusiliers (T.F.)
Mobilised with the Territorials in August 1914, he was immediately sent to Egypt where e served until April 1915. He was then transferred to the Dardanelles and took part in the Landings at Cape Helles and Suvla Bay, and in the Battles of Krithia. After the Evacuation of the Peninsula, he had one month's leave in England before proceeding to France, where he was in action with the M.G.C., at the Battles of the Somme, Arras, Ypres and Cambrai, and in the Retreat and Advance of 1918. Demobilised in March 1919, he holds the 1914–15 Star, and the General Service and Victory Medals.
2, Crayton Street, Hulme Manchester.   Z6154

FOUND, A., Sapper, Royal Marine Engineers.
He joined in January 1918, but owing to his being too old for transfer overseas, was retained on important guard duties and also in the workshops, building ships at Chatham and Shoreham. He rendered valuable services in this capacity until his demobilisation in February 1919.
14, King Street, Ardwick, Manchester.   Z6155

FOWLER, G., Private, 8th King's (Liverpool Regt.)
He volunteered in July 1915, and two months later landed in France, where he was in action in the Battles of Loos, Ploegsteert, the Somme, Arras and Ypres. He gave his life for King and Country in the fighting at Cambrai in November 1917, and was entitled to the 1914–15 Star, and the General Service and Victory Medals.
"His life for his Country, his soul to God."
39, Elizabeth Street, West Gorton, Manchester.   Z10213

FOWLER, H., Private, 13th Manchester Regiment.
He volunteered in March 1915, and four months later was drafted to the Western Front, where he was in action at Neuve Chapelle and Albert, before proceeding to Mesopotamia. He then took part in the operations for the Relief of Kut, and in other engagements on the Tigris. Later he proceeded to China, served also at Singapore, and in the Straits Settle-

ments. Whilst overseas, he was twice wounded in action. Demobilised in February 1920, he holds the 1914–15 Star, and the General Service and Victory Medals.
11, Sandown Street, Ardwick, Manchester.   Z6156

FOWLER, J., Private, Lancashire Fusiliers.
Volunteering at the commencement of hostilities, he proceeded to Gallipoli in April 1915, and was engaged in heavy fighting in many parts of the line. After the Evacuation of the Peninsula he was sent to Salonika, and fought in many engagements on the Vardar and Doiran fronts. Later, owing to ill-health, he was invalided to Alexandria, and died there in September 1916. He was entitled to the 1914–15 Star, and the General Service and Victory Medals.
"His memory is cherished with pride."
8, Edith Street, West Gorton, Manchester.   Z10214A

FOX, A., Private, R.M.L.I.
Volunteering in August 1914, he was posted to H.M.S. "Russell" on completing his training, and in 1915 was sent to the Dardanelles. He was wounded in the fighting at West Beach, and was invalided to Malta. On his recovery he was drafted to France, and was in action at Vimy Ridge, the Somme, Arras, and Ypres. Gassed during the fighting in 1918, he returned home and after receiving hospital treatment served at various depôts until demobilised in March 1919. He holds the 1914–15 Star, and the General Service and Victory Medals.
42, Granville Place, Ancoats, Manchester.   Z10215

FOX, A., Private, 9th Lancashire Fusiliers.
Volunteering in April 1915, he proceeded to France in the following October, but a month later was transferred to Salonika, where he was in action on the Doiran and Struma fronts until February 1918. He was then invalided home to Manchester, but in August returned to the Western Front, and was taken prisoner at Ypres in the following month. Eventually demobilised in March 1919, he holds the 1914–15 Star, and the General Service and Victory Medals.
34, William Street, West Gorton, Manchester.   Z6157

FOX, E., Private, 15th Lancashire Fusiliers.
He joined in April 1917, and in the following March was drafted to the Western Front, where he was in action at Ypres, Albert, and Cambrai during the Retreat and Advance of 1918. He later took part in the march to the Rhine, and was demobilised in December 1919, holding the General Service and Victory Medals.
32, Riall Street, Hulme, Manchester.   Z6160

FOX, G. F., Gunner, R.G.A.
He volunteered in October 1914, and in the following February was drafted to France, where he took part in much of the heavy fighting. He was also in action at Hill 60, Festubert, Ypres, Loos, St. Eloi, the Somme, Arras, Cambrai and Amiens, where he was wounded in July 1918. He was demobilised in March 1919, and holds the 1914–15 Star, and the General Service and Victory Medals.
1, Wovenden Street, Bradford, Manchester.   Z9131

FOX, J. (D.C.M.) Corporal, 4th King's (L'pool Regt.)
He joined in March 1917, and three months later was drafted to the Western Front, where he played a prominent part in heavy fighting at Ypres, Nieuport, Bailleul and Meteren, and was taken prisoner in April 1918. Whilst in captivity he was forced to do fatigue work in the forward areas and was gassed. Before being captured he was awarded the Distinguished Conduct Medal for conspicuous bravery and devotion to duty, when as a private, he took command of his platoon on the death of his Officer, and captured a German pill-box. He was demobilised in September 1919, and also holds the General Service and Victory Medals.
30, Durham Place, Hulme, Manchester.   Z6163

FOX, R. H., Rifleman, Rifle Brigade.
He volunteered in September 1914, and three months later was sent to France, where he played a prominent part in the Battles of Ypres, Hill 60, Ploegsteert, the Somme, Cambrai and St. Quentin. He was wounded in action on the Somme and twice during the Retreat and Advance of 1918. Demobilised in January 1919, he holds the 1914–15 Star, and the General Service and Victory Medals.
69, Ainsworth Street, West Gorton, Manchester.   Z6161

FOX, R. H., Rifleman, 5th Rifle Brigade.
Three months after volunteering in September 1914, he was sent to France, and was in action at Hill 60, Festubert, Loos, Vimy Ridge, and on the Somme, where he was wounded in July 1916. Invalided home he was sent to hospital in Northampton, and upon his recovery returned to France, saw further service in Arras and Ypres, and was again wounded in August 1917. After spending some time in hospital at Etaples. he rejoined his unit, and was wounded for the third time in March 1918, on the Somme. He later took part in heavy fighting at Havrincourt and Le Cateau, and was demobilised in February 1919, holds the 1914–15 Star, and the General Service and Victory Medals.
71, Nelson Street, Bradford, Manchester.   TZ11419

FOX, T., Private, 1st Kings (Liverpool Regiment).

He joined in November 1916, and four months later was drafted to the Western Front, where he fought at the Battles of Ypres and Cambrai, in which latter engagement he was wounded. After hospital treatment in Bristol and Manchester, he returned to France and was in action during the Retreat and Advance, being again wounded in September 1918. He was demobilised in February 1919, and holds the General Service and Victory Medals.

38, Gorton Road, Lower Openshaw, Manchester.   TZ6158

FOX, W., Corporal, R.F.A.

He volunteered in October 1914, and rendered valuable services with his Battery at Athlone in Ireland until July 1915. He was then transferred to Class W, Army Reserve, and went to work at the British Dyes Factory, Huddersfield, where he was engaged on responsible duties as foreman in the mustard and chemical gas shell-making department. He relinquished these duties in July 1919.

15, Mark Lane, Chorlton-on-Medlock, Manchester.   Z6162

FOX, W., Private, Lancashire Fusiliers.

He was mobilised in August 1914, and immediately drafted to France, where he fought at the Battle of, and in the Retreat from, Mons. Later he proceeded to the Dardanelles, and was wounded in action during severe fighting on the Gallipoli Peninsula. After the Evacuation, he returned to the Western Front, and took part in the Battles of the Somme and Ypres before being accidentally killed whilst serving with the Royal Engineers in December 1918. He was entitled to the Mons Star, and the General Service and Victory Medals.

" His memory is cherished with pride."

101, Chester Street, Hulme, Manchester.   Z6164

FOXLEY, J. R., Private, R.A.M.C.

He joined in July 1917, and after a period of training, was engaged on important duties at various hospitals in England, Scotland, and Wales. Owing to his low medical category, he was unfit for transfer overseas, but rendered valuable services until his demobilisation in July 1919.

9, Blackburn Street, Hulme, Manchester.   Z6165

FOXTON, S., Private, 2/7th Manchester Regiment.

He volunteered in January 1916, and was drafted to France in March of the following year. After only a month's service in this theatre of war, he laid down his life for King and Country at the Battle of Arras on April 15th, 1917. He was entitled to the General Service and Victory Medals.

" The path of duty was the way to glory."

473, Claremont Road, Rusholme, Manchester.   Z6166

FOY, E., 1st Air Mechanic, R.A.F.

He joined in February 1918, and after completing his training, was engaged on special duties with the transport section at various aerodromes in England. He was not successful in obtaining his transfer overseas, but rendered valuable services until his demobilisation in January 1919.

20, Parkfield Avenue, Rusholme, Manchester.   TZ6167

FOY, E., Gunner, R.F.A.

He volunteered in April 1915, and was drafted to France in the following year. During his service with C Battery 307th Brigade on the Western Front, he took part in the Battles of the Somme, Arras, Ypres, Lens, and Cambrai, and in the Retreat and Advance of 1918. He was demobilised in January 1919, and holds the General Service and Victory Medals.

43, Marsland Street, Ardwick, Manchester.   Z6159

FOY, J., Private, South Lancashire Regiment.

He volunteered in August 1914, but whilst in training near Liverpool, was taken seriously ill with pneumonia and unfortunately died at home on October 6th, 1914.

" Steals on the ear the distant triumph song."

27, Lord Street, Hulme, Manchester.   Z6168A

FOY, J., Private, 1/6th Manchester Regiment.

He joined in September 1917, and in the following April was drafted to the Western Front, where he saw much severe fighting during the Retreat and Advance of 1918, and was in action at the Battles of Bapaume, Havrincourt, Cambrai and Le Cateau. He was demobilised in February 1919, and holds the General Service and Victory Medals.

27, Lord Street, Hulme, Manchester.   Z6168C

FOY, J. H., Private, King's (Liverpool Regiment).

He joined in February 1917, and in the following July was sent to the Western Front, where he took part in the Battles of Cambrai and the Somme and in the Retreat and Advance of 1918. He died gloriously on the Field of Battle at Riencourt on September 1st, 1918, and was entitled to the General Service and Victory Medals.

" A costly sacrifice upon the altar of freedom."

27, Lord Street, Hulme, Manchester.   Z6168B

FOY, W., L/Sergt., 2nd Manchester Regiment.

Mobilised in August 1914, he was immediately sent to France, and after taking part in the Battle of Mons was wounded in action during the subsequent Retreat. He was invalided to England, but on his recovery was again sent to the Western Front and took part in the Battles of St. Eloi, Ypres (II),

Ploegsteert and the Somme, where he was badly wounded. Once more invalided home, he was eventually transferred to the R.A.F., but unfortunately became totally blind, and was discharged in November 1918. He holds the Mons Star, and the General Service and Victory Medals.

17, Stanley Street, Hulme, Manchester.   Z6169

FOYSTER, T., Gunner, R.F.A.

He joined in August 1917, and after a course of training served at various stations on important transport duties. Owing to medical unfitness he was not able to obtain a transfer overseas, but rendered valuable services until discharged in September 1920

3, Clifford Street, West Gorton, Manchester.   Z9132

FOZZARD, M., Gunner, R.G.A.

He volunteered in November 1915, and in the following January proceeded with the 100th Siege Battery to France, where he served with distinction. He was present during the fighting at Loos, the Somme, Arras, Ypres and Cambrai and in the Retreat and Advance of 1918, and was wounded. He was awarded the Croix de Guerre for successfully getting through the enemy lines under heavy shell-fire, with Despatches to the French Forces, at Ypres, and in addition holds the General Service and Victory Medals. Returning home, he was demobilised in March 1919.

24, Enoch Street, Miles Platting, Manchester.   TZ9133

FRADLEY, J., Pte., Loyal North Lancashire Regt.

He volunteered in August 1914, and twelve months later was drafted to the Western Front, where, after only a few weeks' fighting, he was unfortunately killed in action at the Battle of Loos on September 25th, 1915. He was entitled to the 1914-15 Star, and the General Service and Victory Medals.

" He died the noblest death a man may die,
    Fighting for God and right and liberty."

7, Old Street, Ardwick, Manchester.   TX6170

FRAIN, W., Private, Lancashire Fusiliers.

He volunteered in August 1914, and for a time was retained in England on duties of an important nature. In June 1915 he crossed to France and took part in many important engagements including those on the Somme, and was twice wounded. He was invalided home and after receiving hospital treatment was discharged in November 1917 as medically unfit. He holds the 1914-15 Star, and the General Service and Victory Medals.

138, Victoria Square, Ancoats, Manchester.   TZ9134

FRANCE, C., Private, Cheshire Regiment.

He volunteered in August 1915, and after a period of duty in England was drafted to the Western Front in October 1917. He took part in the Battles of Ypres and Cambrai and in heavy fighting at Arras, Givenchy and in the Retreat and Advance of 1918. In January 1919 he was invalided to Scotland, and was demobilised in the following month, holding the General Service and Victory Medals.

22, Hope Street, Hulme, Manchester.   Z6171

FRANCIS, H., Driver, R.A.S.C. (M.T.)

Volunteering in June 1915, he was drafted to the Western Front two months later and served in the Battles of Loos, Vermelles, the Somme, Ypres and Cambrai. He was engaged on important transport duties throughout the German Offensive and Allied Advance of 1918, and rendered excellent services. He was demobilised in January 1919, and holds the 1914-15 Star, and the General Service and Victory Medals.

17, Apollo Street, Ancoats, Manchester.   Z10216

FRANCIS, R. A., Pte., R.A.M.C. and Sapper, R.E.

He volunteered in August 1914, and in the following April was drafted to Gallipoli, where he was in action at the Landing at Suvla Bay and in heavy fighting on the Peninsula. After the Evacuation, he was transferred to France and carried out important duties as a despatch rider until his demobilisation in February 1919. He holds the 1914-15 Star, and the General Service and Victory Medals.

32, Dalton Street, Hulme, Manchester.   Z6172

FRANCIS, W., Private, 2nd Manchester Regiment.

Mobilised in August 1914, he was immediately drafted to the Western Front, where he took part in the Battle of Mons and the subsequent Retreat. He also served at the Battles of Le Cateau (I), La Bassée and Ypres (I). He was unhappily killed in action at the Battle of Neuve Chapelle in March 1915. and was entitled to the Mons Star, and the General Service and Victory Medals.

" Whilst we remember, the sacrifice is not in vain."

2, Middlewood Street, Hulme, Manchester.   Z6173

FRANCIS, W., Driver, R.F.A.

Two months after volunteering in September 1915, he was drafted to France, where he saw severe fighting in various sectors of the Front. He served through the Battles of Albert, Vimy Ridge, the Somme, Arras, Messines, Ypres, Cambrai, Amiens and Bapaume, and many other important engagements, and also took part in the march into Germany. Demobilised on his return home in September 1919, he holds the 1914-15 Star, and the General Service and Victory Medals.

7, School Street, Bradford, Manchester.   Z11702

FRANK, J., Corporal, 1/7th Manchester Regiment.
He volunteered in August 1914, and in the following April was sent to Gallipoli. There he took part in the Battle of Krithia (III), and was wounded and sent to Malta. He was afterwards sent to England for convalescence. On his recovery he proceeded to France and took part in the Retreat and Advance of 1918, and was again wounded twice. Demobilised in February 1919, on his return home, he holds the 1914-15 Star, and the General Service and Victory Medals.
85, Dalton Street, Hulme, Manchester. Z6174

FRANKISH, H., Private, Lancashire Fusiliers.
Volunteering in September 1914, he was sent to France in the following August, and was in action in the Battles of Ypres and the Somme, and was wounded. He also was engaged in heavy fighting throughout the German Offensive and Allied Advance of 1918, and returning home after the signing of the Armistice, was demobilised in 1919. He holds the 1914-15 Star, and the General Service and Victory Medals.
105, Morton Street, Longsight, Manchester. Z10217

FRANKLIN, A. (M.M.), L/Cpl., R. Inniskilling Fus.
Volunteering in April 1915, he sailed for France in the following December with the South Lancashire Regiment. During the fighting at Albert he was wounded and invalided to hospital in England, on recovery returning to the trenches. He was awarded the Military Medal for conspicuous gallantry in delivering messages under heavy shell-fire during the Advance of 1918, and also holds the 1914-15 Star, and the General Service and Victory Medals. In December 1918 he was demobilised.
5, Herbert Street, Bradford, Manchester. Z9135

FRANKLIN, B., Private, 2nd Cheshire Regiment.
Volunteering in April 1915, he was drafted to France in the following July and took part in heavy fighting at Kemmel and Wulverghem and in the Battle of Loos. Later he was transferred to Egypt, and after serving for a time at Alexandria, was drafted to Salonika, where he was again in action. He was discharged in August 1918, and holds the 1914-15 Star, and the General Service and Victory Medals.
25, Lomas Street, Ancoats, Manchester. Z6175B

FRANKLIN, J., Corporal, 1st Cheshire Regiment.
He volunteered in January 1915, and in the following May proceeded to Egypt and later to the Dardanelles, where he was in action at W. Beach and Suvla Bay. After the Evacuation of the Peninsula he was drafted to Mesopotamia and fought at Amara and Kut, was present at the capture of Baghdad and took part in the final British Advance to Mosul. Returning home, he was demobilised in November 1919, and holds the 1914-15 Star, and the General Service and Victory Medals.
15, Lomas Street, Ancoats, Manchester. Z10218

FRANKLIN, J., Private, 2nd Cheshire Regiment.
He volunteered in April 1915, and six months later was drafted to Mesopotamia, where he took part in the Relief of Kut operations. Later he was transferred to Palestine and was in action at Siwa, the three Battles of Gaza and the capture of Jericho, Jerusalem and Tripoli. In February 1919 he proceeded to India and served at Bombay and Calcutta until the following October, when he returned to England. Demobilised in November 1919, he holds the 1914-15 Star, and the General Service and Victory Medals.
25, Lomas Street, Ancoats, Manchester. Z6175A

FRANKLIN, J C., Private, Buffs (East Kent Regt.)
He volunteered in November 1915, and embarking for France in the following June was in action in many parts of the line. He fought in the Battles of Arras, Ypres and Cambrai and throughout the German and Allied Offensives of 1918, and was wounded. He was demobilised in March 1919, and holds the General Service and Victory Medals.
150, Hamilton Street, Collyhurst, Manchester. Z10219

FRANKLIN, T., Private, 8th Manchester Regiment.
He was called up from the Reserve in August 1914, and was quickly drafted to Egypt, where he served with the 42nd Division. He was afterwards sent to the Dardanelles, took part in the Landing at Gallipoli and the fighting at Cape Helles, Krithia and Acha Baba, and was severely wounded in October 1915. Invalided home, he served in England until his discharge in July 1918. He holds the 1914-15 Star, and the General Service and Victory Medals.
34, Bunyan Street, Ardwick, Manchester. Z6176

FRANKS, J., Sapper, R.E.
He volunteered in October 1915, and proceeded to France in March 1917. Whilst in this theatre of war he took part in the severe fighting at Beaucourt and Beaumont-Hamel on the Somme. He was later in action at Vimy Ridge, Bullecourt, Messines, Cambrai, and in the Retreat and Advance of 1918 and was chiefly occupied as a wireman. Demobilised in August 1919, he holds the General Service and Victory Medals.
27, Birch Street, West Gorton, Manchester. TZ6177

FRANTER, W., Private, 8th Black Watch.
He joined in February 1916, and in the following May was drafted to the Western Front, where he took part in the Battle of the Somme, and was wounded in October 1916. He was then sent to the Base, but on his recovery, took part in the Battle of Arras and the Retreat and Advance of 1918, and was again wounded in August. He was demobilised on his return to England in August 1919, holding the General Service and Victory Medals.
3, Leo Street, Ardwick, Manchester. Z6178

FRASER, G., Private, 13th Manchester Regiment.
Volunteering in September 1914, he was drafted to the Western Front in the following February. There he was in action at the Battles of Neuve Chapelle, Ypres (II) and Loos (I). He was also present at the Landing at Salonika and in the Battles on the Vardar front. Later he was invalided to Malta, where he contracted fever and was invalided to hospital at Stockport. On his recovery he rendered valuable services with the R.A.F as a mechanic and was stationed at Farnborough until discharged in February 1918. He holds the 1914-15 Star, and the General Service and Victory Medals.
8, Mallow Street, Hulme, Manchester. Z6179

FREAKES, A., Private, Border Regiment.
He joined in August 1917, and first served with the Manchester Regiment on important guard and regimental duties at Cleethorpes. Later he was transferred to the Border Regiment and sent to France in December 1918, eventually proceeding to Germany with the Army of Occupation. He did consistently good work with his unit on the Rhine until his demobilisation in September 1919.
98, Hillkirk Street, Ardwick, Manchester. Z6180

FREDERICK, A., Private, 11th Manchester Regt.
He joined in October 1916, and was drafted to the Western Front in the following year. He was in action at Passchendaele and Cambrai and throughout the Retreat and Advance of 1918 and was wounded. Returning to England, he was demobilised in December 1919, and holds the General Service and Victory Medals.
60, Clayton Street, Chorlton Road, Manchester. Z10220B

FREDERICK, W. H., Pte., South Wales Borderers.
Joining in March 1917, he proceeded to the Western Front in the following year and fought in many engagements during the German Offensive and Allied Advance of 1918. After the Armistice drafted to Germany, he served at various stations with the Army of Occupation until returning home. He was demobilised in September 1919, holding the General Service and Victory Medals.
60, Clayton Street, Chorlton Road, Manchester. Z10220A

FREEL, T., Private, R.A.S.C.
He volunteered in January 1915, and six weeks later was drafted to the Western Front, where he was engaged on important transport duties until December 1915. He was then invalided home suffering severely from bronchitis and asthma, and after hospital treatment at Nantwich, was discharged as medically unfit for further service in June 1916. Unfortunately he never recovered from his illness and died at home on March 7th, 1920. He was entitled to the 1914-15 Star, and the General Service and Victory Medals.
"His memory is cherished with pride."
2, Clayburn Street, Hulme, Manchester. Z6181

FREEMAN, G., Private, Manchester Regiment, and Army Cyclist Corps.
Volunteering in November 1914, he was sent to France twelve months later with the Army Cyclist Corps and was engaged on important duties as a despatch rider. He saw much severe fighting at Mailley-Maillet and was wounded at Albert in February 1916. After hospital treatment at Rouen and Huddersfield, he was discharged in the following July as medically unfit for further service. He holds the 1914-15 Star, and the General Service and Victory Medals.
14, Gresham Street, Openshaw, Manchester. Z6182

FRENCH, J., Private, Lancashire Fusiliers.
Joining in November 1917, he landed in France in the following May, and was in action in many engagements in the German Offensive. Taken prisoner, he was held in captivity until the close of hostilities and then was repatriated. He was demobilised in October 1919, and holds the General Service and Victory Medals.
83, Ryder Street, Collyhurst, Manchester. Z10589B

FRENCH, J., Sergt., 2nd Lancashire Fusiliers.
Mobilised in August 1914, he was at once ordered to the Western Front, where he took part in the Battles of Mons and subsequent Retreat. He later played a conspicuous part in the Battles of the Aisne, Le Cateau, La Bassée, Ypres, Neuve Chapelle and Loos, where he was gassed and as a result, invalided home. After staying some time in hospital at Epsom, he was drafted to Nigeria, and was still serving with the Colours in 1920. He holds the Mons Star, and the General Service and Victory Medals.
18, Stonehewer Street, Ancoats, Manchester. Z9529/30A

FRITH, G. H., Air Mechanic, R A.F.
He joined in May 1917, and twelve months later was drafted to the East. Whilst in Egypt, he was engaged on important aircraft duties on the Nile and in the Desert and also carried out structural and mechanical work with his Squadron. He rendered valuable services until his return home for demobilisation in November 1919, and holds the General Service and Victory Medals.
19, Churchill Street, Stockport Road, Chorlton-on-Medlock, Manchester. Z6183

FRITH, J., L/Corporal, 18th Manchester Regiment.
He volunteered in September 1914, and in October of the following year was drafted to the Western Front, where he took part in the Battles of Albert, Ploegsteert, the Somme, Arras, Vimy Ridge, Messines and Ypres. Unfortunately he was killed in action on August 1st, 1917, and was entitled to the 1914-15 Star, and the General Service and Victory Medals.
" The path of duty was the way to glory."
50, Redvers Street, Ardwick, Manchester. Z6185

FRITH, W. J., Trooper, 1st Middlesex) Duke of Cambridge's) Hussars.
He volunteered in November 1915, and in the following July was sent to Egypt, where he was in action at Jifjaffa. Later he took part in the Advance of General Allenby's Forces through Palestine and was present at the capture of Damascus. He was demobilised in June 1919, and holds the General Service and Victory Medals.
15, Greenhill Street, Chorlton-on-Medlock, Manchester. Z6184

FROBISHER, J., Sergt., Royal Fusiliers.
He volunteered in November 1914, and two months later was drafted to France. In this theatre of war he participated in , the second and third Battles of Ypres and the Battle of the Somme, and was later in action in many sectors during the Retreat and Advance of 1918. He rendered excellent service during the time he served overseas, and demobilised in February 1919, holds the 1914-15 Star, and the General Service and Victory Medals.
62, Burnley Street, Ancoats, Manchester. Z9531

FROBISHER, W., Private, 22nd Manchester Regt.
Volunteering in November 1914, he was eventually drafted to the Western Front in March 1916, and took part in the Battles of Ploegsteert, the Somme, Arras, Bullecourt and Ypres. He was also in action during the Retreat and Advance of 1918, and returning to England in February 1919, was then demobilised, holding the General Service and Victory Medals.
32, Milton Street, West Gorton, Manchester. TZ6186

FRODSHAM, G., Guardsman, Grenadier Guards.
He joined in March 1916, and six months later was drafted to the Western Front, where he saw much severe fighting. He was in hospital for two months suffering from trench fever, and on his recovery, returned to the transport of his unit on special duty. After the cessation of hostilities, he served with the Army of Occupation in Germany until July 1919, and in the following month was demobilised, holding the General Service and Victory Medals.
35, Ridgway Street, Moss Side, Manchester. Z6141

FROGGART, J., Gunner, R.H.A.
At the outbreak of war in August 1914, he was stationed in India, and in the following February was drafted to Egypt, where he was in action at Kantara. Later, he proceeded to Palestine, but after a period of heavy fighting during the Advance of General Allenby's Forces, returned to Egypt, and in 1920 was serving at Cairo. He holds the 1914-15 Star, and the General Service and Victory Medals.
17, Alma Street, Hulme, Manchester. Z6187

FROGGATT, B. G., Private, 17th Manchester Regt.
Volunteering at the commencement of hostilities, he embarked for France in November 1914, and was in action in the Battles of Ypres, St. Eloi, and Loos, where he was severely wounded. Invalided home, he received hospital treatment and was discharged as medically unfit for further service in February 1916. He holds the 1914-15 Star, and the General Service and Victory Medals.
12, Albany Street, Ardwick, Manchester. Z10221

FROGGATT, H., Pte., 4th King's (Liverpool Regt.)
He volunteered in December 1915, but was retained on important duties in England until March 1918. He was then sent to France and played a prominent part in the Battle of Cambrai (I) and in much severe fighting during the Retreat and Advance of 1918. Returning home in November 1919, he was demobilised, and holds the General Service and Victory Medals. 56, Libby St., Lower Openshaw, Manchester. Z6188

FROGGATT, S., Cpl., 10th Lancashire Fusiliers.
Volunteering in August 1914, he proceeded in the following January to the Western Front. There he played a prominent part with his unit in many important engagements, including Ypres, Neuve Chapelle and Loos, and received a severe wound, which involved the loss of his right eye. He remained overseas until February 1919, when he was demobilised, holding the 1914-15 Star, and the General Service and Victory Medals. 74, Nicholson St., Rochdale Road, Manchester. Z9532

FROGGATT, S., Special War Worker.
In December 1914, he offered his services at Messrs. Galloways', Bennett Street, Ardwick, where he was engaged on special Admiralty work in connection with the construction of mines. He carried out this important and dangerous duties in a very skilful manner until the cessation of hostilities.
14, Emma Street, Ardwick, Manchester. Z6189

FROST, A., Private, 2nd East Lancashire Regiment.
He volunteered in September 1914, and in the following January landed in France, where he fought at Ypres, Loos, and the Somme. He was unfortunately killed in action at Zillebeke on July 31st, 1917, and was entitled to the 1914-15 Star, and the General Service and Victory Medals.
" Steals on the ear the distant triumph song."
11, Saville Street, Miles Platting, Manchester. Z10222

FROST, A., Private, East Lancashire Regiment.
Volunteering in September 1914, and drafted to France in the following March, he was engaged in heavy fighting in various sectors, being in action in the Battles of St. Eloi, Vimy Ridge, the Somme, Arras and Bullecourt. He gave his life for the freedom of England on July 31st, 1916, during the third Battle of Ypres, and was entitled to the 1914-15 Star, and the General Service and Victory Medals.
" Courage, bright hopes and myriad dreams, splendidly given."
19, Crook Street, Harpurhey, Manchester. Z10590B

FROST, A., Private, South Lancashire Regiment.
He volunteered in April 1915, and in the following October was drafted to Mesopotamia. In this seat of operations he took part in many important engagements, but was severely wounded in action, and unfortunately died through the effects of his wounds near Kut on January 12th, 1917. He was entitled to the 1914-15 Star, and the General Service and Victory Medals.
" Thinking that remembrance, though unspoken, may reach him where he sleeps."
17, Burns Street, Bradford, Manchester. Z11704A

FROST, A., Driver, R.F.A.
He joined in April 1917, and after a period of training was engaged at various stations on important duties with his unit. He was unable to obtain a transfer overseas before the cessation of hostilities, but rendered valuable services until his demobilisation in December 1918.
17, Burns Street, Bradford, Manchester. Z11704B

FROST, E., Private, South Wales Borderers.
Joining in January 1917, he was drafted overseas in the following July. Whilst on the Western Front he took part in the Battles of Ypres (III), Passchendaele, the Somme (II), Havrincourt and in the Retreat and Advance of 1918. He was then engaged on special duties at Albert until demobilised in December 1919, and holds the General Service and Victory Medals.
49, Bedford Street, Hulme, Manchester. Z11703

FROST, E., Worker, Q.M.A.A.C.
She joined in June 1916, and after a period of service in England, was sent to France in May 1918. She then did consistently good work as an assistant in the stores department of a depôt at Rouen, and remained there until her demobilisation in September 1919. She holds the General Service and Victory Medals.
39, Byron Street, Hulme, Manchester. Z6190

FROST, W., Guardsman, 5th Grenadier Guards.
He joined in July 1916, and on completion of his training was engaged on important duties with his unit at various stations. Owing to a defective heart he was not fit for transfer overseas, and after rendering valuable services, was invalided from the Army in October 1916.
38, Gregory Street, West Gorton, Manchester. Z6191

FRYER, F., Driver, R.F.A.
Volunteering in August 1914, he sailed for Malta three months later and was engaged there on important duties until proceeding to Salonika in October 1915. He saw much fighting on the Vardar front, and contracting malaria was invalided to Malta. On his recovery he was sent to France in November 1917 and was in action at Cambrai and throughout the Retreat and Advance of 1918. After the Armistice he served with the Army of Occupation in Germany until demobilised in April 1919. He holds the 1914-15 Star, and the General Service and Victory Medals.
68, Gunson Street, Miles Platting, Manchester. Z10223

FRYERS, J., Sergt., 2nd K.O. (R. Lancaster Regt.)
He was mobilised in August 1914, and in the following month was drafted to the Western Front. There he played a prominent part in the Battles of La Bassée, Ypres (I) and Hill 60, where he was badly wounded in May 1915 and invalided home. On his recovery he returned to France and fought at Cambrai, Bapaume and Le Cateau (II). He was discharged in February 1919, and holds the 1914 Star, and the General Service and Victory Medals.
18, Peter Street, Hulme, Manchester. Z11705

FULLAM, G., Pte., King's Own Scottish Borderers.

He volunteered in August 1914, and in May of the following year was drafted to France. In this theatre of war he only served for a few months, for after taking part in the Battle of Festubert, he was killed in action at Loos in September 1915, and buried in the British cemetery there. He was entitled to the General Service and Victory Medals.

"A costly sacrifice upon the altar of freedom."

15, Teignmouth Street, Collyhurst, Manchester.   Z9422A

FULLER, A. E., Private, Durham Light Infantry.

He joined in May 1917, and four months later was drafted to the Western Front, where he took part in the Retreat of 1918. After two months heavy fighting during the subsequent Advance, he gallantly fell in action in September 1918. He was entitled to the General Service and Victory Medals.

"His memory is cherished with pride."

67, Robert Street, West Gorton, Manchester.   Z6192A

FULLER, T., Bombardier, R.F.A.

Volunteering in August 1914, he eventually proceeded to the Western Front in July 1916, and immediately went into action at the Battle of the Somme. Later he took part in the Battle of Ypres and in the Retreat of 1918, but unfortunately, was killed at Meteren on July 19th of the same year. He was entitled to the General Service and Victory Medals.

"The path of duty was the way to glory."

67, Robert Street, West Forton, Manchester.   Z6192B

FURBER, A., Corporal-Farrier, R.A.S.C.

Volunteering in May 1915, he was sent to Salonika in the following year and saw much severe fighting on the Doiran front. He was in hospital with malarial fever for some time, but on recovery, rejoined his unit, and in October 1917 was engaged on the lines of communication in the Somme, Cambrai and Passchendaele sectors. He was demobilised in May 1919, and holds the General Service and Victory Medals.

40, Lythgoe Street, Moss Side, Manchester.   Z6194B

FURBER, J. K., Private, 7th Manchester Regiment.

He volunteered in October 1915, and in the following May was drafted to Egypt, where he was in action at Katia and Romani. In February 1917 he was transferred to the Western Front and took part in the Battles of the Ancre, Ypres, Cambrai, the Somme (II) and Bapaume, where he was badly wounded in August 1918. After hospital treatment in France and England, he was demobilised in April 1919, and holds the General Service and Victory Medals.

40, Lythgoe Street, Moss Side, Manchester.   TZ6193

FURBER, W. A., L/Corporal, 1st Manchester Regt.

Volunteering in August 1914, he proceeded to France in the following April, and after taking part in the Battles of Hill 60, Ypres, Festubert and Loos, was transferred to Mesopotamia in December 1915. He was in action at Um-el-Hannah and Kut-el-Amara, where he was reported missing on March 8th, 1916. He is now presumed to have been killed in action on that date, and was entitled to the 1914-15 Star, and the General Service and Victory Medals.

"Nobly striving,

He nobly fell that we might live."

40, Lythgoe Street, Moss Side, Manchester.   Z6194A

FURNESS, J. A., Driver, R.A.S.C. (M.T.)

He volunteered in December 1914, and was quickly drafted to France, where he was engaged on important transport duties in the forward areas. In May 1915 he was invalided home with gastritis and was in hospital at Warrington for six months. In September 1916 he was sent to Mesopotamia and saw much severe fighting, being wounded in action. He was demobilised in September 1919, and holds the 1914-15 Star, and the General Service and Victory Medals.

132, South Street, Longsight, Manchester.   Z6195

FURNIFER, J., Private, 6th Manchester Regiment.

Volunteering in November 1914, he was eventually drafted to France in January 1917, and took part in the Battles of the Ancre, Arras, Ypres and the Somme (II), where he was so seriously wounded in March 1918 as to necessitate the amputation of his right leg. After hospital treatment at Rouen and in London, he was invalided from the Army in June 1919 and holds the General Service and Victory Medals.

125, Edensor Street, Beswick, Manchester.   Z6196

FURNIFER, W., Private, 16th Manchester Regt.

He volunteered in September 1914, and in October of the following year was drafted overseas. Whilst in France he took part in the fighting at Loos, Ypres, Hill 60 and Festubert, and was wounded and invalided home. After receiving hospital treatment he rejoined his unit, but was shortly afterwards sent to hospital again. In October 1917 he was discharged, but in February of the following year died from the effects of his injuries. He was entitled to the 1914-15 Star, and the General Service and Victory Medals.

"His life for his Country, his soul to God."

7, Imlay Street, Newton Heath, Manchester.   Z9136

FYNES, H., Air Mechanic, R.A.F.

He joined in April 1917, and on completion of his training was engaged on important duties with his Squadron at various aerodromes. He was not sent overseas until October 1919, when he was drafted to Germany and rendered valuable services with the Air Control Commission at Berlin until his demobilisation in October 1920.

9, Hewitt Street, Openshaw, Manchester.   TZ6197

G

GAFFIN, W., Private, King's Own Scottish Borderers.

He volunteered in September 1914, and on completion of his training at Borden Camp, was in July 1915 sent to the Western Front. There he served in several engagements, but was unfortunately killed in action at Loos on September 21st, 1915. He was entitled to the 1914-15 Star, and the General Service and Victory Medals.

"A valiant Soldier with undaunted heart he breasted life's last hill."

9, Groom Street, Ancoats, Manchester.   Z10224

GALE, H. B., Private, 4th South Lancashire Regt.

He volunteered in November 1915, and was engaged in guarding the coast at various important stations until June 1917, when he was drafted to the Western Front. There after taking part in several engagements, he fell fighting at Lens in August 1917. He was entitled to the General Service and Victory Medals.

"Thinking that remembrance though unspoken, may reach him where he sleeps."

48, Wigley Street, Ardwick, Manchester.   Z6199

GALE, J. H., Private, 3rd Manchester Regiment.

He joined in June 1916, and two months later proceeded to the Western Front, where he was in action in the Ancre, Arras, Ypres, Passchendaele, Cambrai, and the Sambre sectors. He was wounded at Loos in January 1918, and sent back to England, but after undergoing an operation, returned to France, and was engaged in guarding prisoners of war. Demobilised in November 1919, he holds the General Service and Victory Medals.

48, Wigley Street, Ardwick, Manchester.   Z6198

GALE, S. R., Corporal, M.G.C.

Volunteering in January 1915, he was drafted overseas two months later, and during his service on the Western Front, took part in the important Battles of Ypres, Festubert, the Somme, Arras, Bullecourt, Messines, Lens, Cambrai, Havrincourt, and the Aisne. He remained in France until February 1919, when he was demobilised, holding the 1914-15 Star, and the General Service and Victory Medals.

76, Paget Street, Rochdale Road, Manchester.   Z10591

GALLAGHER, J., Private, 9th Lancashire Fusiliers.

In August 1914, he volunteered, and in the following April being sent to Gallipoli, served throughout the Campaign there, and fought at Krithia I, II, and III, Suvla Bay, and Chunuk Bair. After the Evacuation he was drafted to Egypt, and served at Kartara and Hill 40. In July 1916, he was transferred to the Western Front, and saw fierce fighting at Arras, and Bapaume, and was wounded in the Battle of the Somme in 1918. He was demobilised in December 1918, and holds the 1914-15 Star, and the General Service and Victory Medals.

42, Haughton Street, Bradford, Manchester.   Z6200

GALLAGHER, J. J., Private, 12th Manchester Regt.

At the outbreak of war in 1914 he volunteered, and in the following year proceeded overseas. Whilst serving in France he was in action at Ypres, the Somme, Arras, Albert, Cambrai, and in the Retreat of 1918. He was wounded at Albert during the Advance in July 1918, and sent back to England, where he remained in hospital until discharged as medically unfit for further service in May 1919. He holds the 1914-15 Star, and the General Service and Victory Medals.

4, Evans Street, Chorlton-on-Medlock, Manchester.   Z10225

GALLAGHAR, R., Gunner, R.F.A.

He volunteered in April 1915, but was unable to procure a transfer overseas. He was however retained on home defence, and stationed at Salisbury, where he fulfilled his duties in a highly capable manner. In December 1916, he was discharged from the Army as medically unfit for further military service.

28, Anslow Street, Rochdale Road, Manchester.   Z10592

GALLIMORE, G., Private, 8th Manchester Regt.

At the outbreak of hostilities in August 1914, he was already serving in the Army, and proceeded in June 1915 to Gallipoli, but was wounded a fortnight later during an engagement at Cape Helles. He was sent to Mudros, and on his recovery returned to the firing line, but contracted dysentery, and was invalided to Cairo, and eventually to England, where he was discharged as medically unfit for further service in December 1916. He holds the 1914-15 Star, and the General Service and Victory Medals.

35, Pownall Street, Hulme, Manchester.   Z6201

GALLIMORE, S., Private, 1st E. Lancashire Regt.

He enlisted in 1910, and four months after war broke out was drafted to the Western Front, where he took an active part in the three Battles of Ypres, and Passchendaele, and was wounded in action on two occasions. Sent to hospital at Rouen, he returned in November 1916 to the firing line, and served on the Ypres front until the Armistice. He was demobilised in March 1919, and holds the 1914 Star, and the General Service and Victory Medals.

12, Halsbury Street, Longsight, Manchester. Z6202

GALLOWAY, W., Drvr.,R.A.S.C. (Remount Section).

He joined in June 1916, and was chiefly employed as a rough rider in England, and in taking remounts to Le Havre and Rouen. In January 1918 he was attached to the Royal Army Veterinary Corps, and the Royal Field Artillery Remounts, and did valuable work breaking in limber mules and horses. After nearly three years' service he was demobilised in May 1919, and holds the General Service and Victory Medals.

51, Pownall Street, Hulme, Manchester. Z6203A

GALLOWAY, W., Private, R.A.S.C.

Joining in September 1916, he was on completion of his training drafted to the Western Front. There he was stationed at a Remount Depôt in Rouen, and throughout the period of his service was engaged in taking horses to the firing line, chiefly in the Ypres, Cambrai, and Somme sectors. In December 1918 he was demobilised, and holds the General Service and Victory Medals.

6, King Street, Ardwick, Manchester. Z6204

GALVIN, C. W., Private, R.A.S.C.

He joined in December 1916, and on conclusion of his training at Bath, was three months later sent to France, where he served for nearly two years. During that period he rendered most valuable services as a clerk on the head-quarter staff at Rouen. He was demobilised in February 1919, and holds the General Service and Victory Medals.

1, Bradbury Street, Ancoats, Manchester. Z10226A

GALVIN, H., Private, 5th Cameron Highlanders.

He volunteered in August 1914, and after a course of training was in April of the following year drafted overseas. Whilst serving on the Western Front, he experienced fierce fighting at La Bassée, Givenchy, and Béthune, and was killed in action at Loos on September 25th, 1915. He was entitled to the 1914–15 Star, and the General Service and Victory Medals.

"Whilst we remember the sacrifice is not in vain."

1, Bradbury Street, Ancoats, Manchester. Z10226B

GANDY, J., Private, South Lancashire Regiment.

When war broke out in August 1914, he volunteered, but was unable to procure a transfer overseas, and owing to defective eyesight was discharged in the same year, after serving at Bedford, Bristol, and Shepstone. He subsequently rejoined, and after a few months' service at Bristol and Colchester, was again discharged in November 1917, on account of his bad sight.

7, Lillian Square Ardwick, Manchester. Z6205

GARDNER, A., Private, 1/7th Manchester Regt.

Volunteering in May 1915, he proceeded eight months later to Mesopotamia, where he took an active part in severe fighting until 1917. He was then transferred to the Western Front, and was in action at Ypres, Passchendaele, and Nieuport, and also in the final victorious engagements of the war. He served in France until demobilised in February 1919, and holds the General Service and Victory Medals.

11, Richmond Street, Ardwick, Manchester. Z10227

GARDNER, C., 2nd South Wales Borderers.

He volunteered in September 1915, and after a period of training was drafted overseas in the following March. Whilst serving on the Western Front, he took part in numerous engagements, and was wounded in the Battles of Arras and Cambrai. He was also in action in other sectors of the line, and saw heavy fighting on the Somme, and at Amiens and Epéhy, before being demobilised in March 1919. He holds the General Service and Victory Medals.

6, Deyne Avenue, Rusholme, Manchester. TZ6207

GARDNER, E. H., Gunner, R.G.A.

Volunteering in December 1915, he was unsuccessful in procuring a transfer overseas before the termination of the war, and was stationed at Derby for some time, and employed as a cook. He was then sent to Winchester, where he did good work as a gunner. In April 1918 he was admitted to hospital with heart trouble, and was eventually demobilised in January 1919.

24, Apsley Grove, Ardwick, Manchester. Z1304A

GARDNER, R. R., L/Cpl., 11th Loyal N. Lancs. Regt.

When war was declared in August 1914, he volunteered for active service, and six months later was ordered to the Western Front. There he took an active part in engagements at Ypres, La Bassée, and Loos, and fell fighting at Ypres on June 7th, 1917. He was entitled to the 1914–15 Star, and the General Service and Victory Medals.

"His life for his Country."

75, Sycamore Street, Newton, Manchester. Z10228B

GARDNER, W., Corporal, 20th Manchester Regt.

He joined in October 1916, and in July 1917 was sent to the Western Front, where he served for four months. During that time he was in action at Ypres and Passchendaele, and was then transferred to Italy, where he took part in engagements on the Piave, and Asiago Plateaux. After the close of hostilities, he returned to France, and served there until demobilised in November 1919. He holds the General Service and Victory Medals.

75, Sycamore Street, Newton, Manchester. Z10228A

GARDNER, W., Private, Labour Corps.

Volunteering in November 1915, he was stationed at various depôts until drafted to France in August 1917. He was engaged on important constructional duties in the advanced areas and was almost continuously under fire. Invalided home in August 1918, he received hospital treatment, and on his recovery was transferred to the Royal Army Service Corps, with which he served until demobilised in October 1919. He holds the General Service and Victory Medals.

13, Enoch Street, Miles Platting, Manchester. Z9137

GARDNER, W. E., Private, 1/7th Manchester Regt.

In August 1914 he was mobilised, proceeding a month later to Egypt, went into action on the Suez Canal and in the Desert. In April 1915 he was sent to Gallipoli, and fought in the three battles of Krithia, and at Suvla Bay. After the Evacuation he was transferred to France, where he was in heavy fighting at Loos, Albert, the Somme, the Ancre, Arras, Messines, Ypres, and Cambrai, and was killed in action during the second battle of Cambrai, on September 27th, 1918. He was entitled to the 1914–15 Star, and the General Service and Victory Medals.

"His memory is cherished with pride."

14, Hyde View, Grey Street, West Gorton, Manchester. Z6206

GARDOM, J. W., Bombardier, R.F.A.

He volunteered in September 1914, and six months later was sent to the Western Front, where he took an active part in engagements at Hill 60, Ypres, Festubert, Loos, and the Somme. In October 1916, he was recalled under Class W Army Reserve, and employed on the Midland Railway at Derby. He holds the 1914–15 Star, and the General Service and Victory Medals.

47, St. John's Road, Longsight, Manchester. Z6208

GARFORD, J., Cpl., 3rd Loyal N. Lancashire Regt.

Volunteering in September 1914, he was on conclusion of his training two months later drafted to the Western Front, where he only served for two months. During that time he fought in the Battle of Ypres, and was severely wounded in action in January 1915, and invalided to England. On leaving hospital he was sent to Felixstowe, and served there until demobilised in March 1919, holding the 1914 Star, and the General Service and Victory Medals.

12, Stanley Street, Hulme, Manchester. Z6209

GARLAND, H., Tpr., Q.O. (Oxfordshire Hussars).

He joined in October 1916, and served in Ireland until March 1918, when he was drafted to the Western Front. In this theatre of war he took part in engagements at Cambrai and the Somme, and performed excellent work with his unit in the Retreat and Advance of 1918. He was demobilised in February 1919, and holds the General Service and Victory Medals.

17, Perrin Street, Ancoats, Manchester. Z10229

GARLINGE, W. G., A.B., R.N., H.M.S. "Lennox."

He enlisted in the Navy in 1908, and after war broke out served in the North Sea in H.M.S. "Lennox," "Loyal," and "Laurel," with which he was engaged in laying mines. He took an active part in several important engagements and was in action in the Battles of Falkland Isles, Dogger Bank, and Jutland. He was discharged from Chatham in June 1919, and holds the 1914–15 Star, and the General Service and Victory Medals. He had also been awarded a medal for gallantry at sea, in December 1911.

13, Poplar Street, Ardwick, Manchester. Z6210A

GARMORY, D., 1st Air Mechanic, R.A.F.

He joined in November 1917, but being unsuccessful in obtaining a transfer overseas was retained on Home service, and stationed at Farnborough, Ascot, and Norwich. He was engaged on the construction of aircraft, which work, requiring great technical skill, he carried out with the greatest ability until he was demobilised in March 1919.

11, Lingard Street, Hulme, Manchester. Z6365B

GARNER, J., Private, 23rd Manchester Regiment.

Volunteering in November 1914, he was after a course of training drafted to India, where he served for two years, carrying out important garrison duties at Bombay, Allahabad, and Bangalore. In April 1918 he was sent to the Palestine front, and there took part in fierce fighting near Jerusalem, Jericho, and Aleppo, until the Armistice. Returning to England in January 1919, he was demobilised, and holds the General Service and Victory Medals.

10, Hardy Street, West Gorton, Manchester. Z6211

GARNER, C. V., Driver, R.A.S.C. (H.T.)

He joined in March 1917, and two months later was drafted to Italy. In this theatre of war, he was employed carrying supplies to the front line on the Piave front, and the Asiago Plateau, and did excellent work. In December 1918, he was sent to France and served at Ypres, and Cambrai until February 1919, when he returned home. He was demobilised a month later, and holds the General Service and Victory Medals.
11, Heyrod Street, Ancoats, Manchester.   Z11614

GARNER, W., Private, Cheshire Regiment.

He joined in November 1916, and on conclusion of his training at Prees Heath, was drafted overseas a month later. Whilst serving on the Western Front, he took part in important engagements, in different sectors of the line, and saw heavy fighting on the Ancre, and at Arras, Ypres, Cambrai, the Somme, Amiens, and Bapaume, and whilst at Cambrai suffered from shell-shock. He was demobilised in December 1918, and holds the General Service and Victory Medals.
43, Middlewood Street, Harpurhey, Manchester.   Z11498

GARNER, W. A., Gunner, R.G.A.

He volunteered in June 1915, but was unable to procure a transfer overseas before the cessation of hostilities. He was retained on Home Service and was stationed at Southport, in Wales, and also at Chelmsford. He was subsequently transferred to the Anti-Aircraft section, and rendered valuable services in the Isle of Wight, until demobilised in January 1919.
61, Burn Street, Bradford, Manchester.   Z10230

GARNETT, E., Corporal, 7th Royal Welch Fusiliers.

At the outbreak of hostilities in August 1914, he volunteered, but did not succeed in procuring a transfer to a theatre of war. During the first twelve months of his service he was employed on important clerical duties at the headquarters in Newtown, and after that acted as an officers' servant until his demobilisation in 1919.
12, Link Street, Longsight, Manchester.   Z6212

GARNETT, J. H. (M.S.M.), C.S.M., R.E.

He volunteered in August 1914, and early in the following year was drafted to the Dardanelles, where he saw much heavy fighting at Cape Helles, Suvla Bay, Chunuk Bair, and at the Evacuation of the Gallipoli Peninsula. He was then transferred to France, and played a prominent part in the Battles of the Somme (II), Amiens, Bapaume, and Havrincourt, where he was gassed in action in September 1918. He was awarded the Meritorious Service Medal for continuously good work throughout hostilities, also holds the 1914-15 Star, and the General Service and Victory Medals, and was demobilised in January 1919.
63, Russell Street, Moss Side, Manchester.   Z11706A

GARRATT, H., Private, King's (Liverpool Regt.)

He volunteered in April 1915, and in the following December, was sent to the Western Front, where he was in action at Loos, St.Eloi, Albert, Vimy Ridge, the Somme, the Ancre, Beaumont-Hamel, and Beaucourt. Wounded at Arras in 1917, he was sent to hospital in Rouen, and on his recovery joined the Labour Corps, and was employed first as a cook, and then in guarding prisoners of war until demobilised in March 1919. He holds the 1914-15 Star, and the General Service and Victory Medals.
30, Trentham Street, Chester Road, Hulme, Manchester. Z6213

GARRATT, J., Pte., K.O. (Royal Lancaster Regt.)

Volunteering in August 1914, he was seven months later drafted to France, but, being wounded in the Battles of Ypres, was invalided to England. In October 1915, however, he proceeded to Egypt, and saw service on the Suez Canal, at Mersa Matruh, Agagia, Sollum, Katia, and Romani. On reaching Palestine he was in action at Rafa, Gaza I, II, and III, Jericho, Tripoli, and Aleppo. Returning to England in June 1919 he was demobilised, and holds the 1914-15 Star, and the General Service and Victory Medals.
30, Trentham Street, Chester Road, Hulme, Manchester.Z6214

GARRETT, J., Private, 1/6th Manchester Regiment.

Volunteering in December 1915, he was drafted to the Western Front in the following October, and was in action in many parts of the line. He fought in the Battles of the Ancre, Arras, Vimy Ridge, Ypres, and throughout the German Offensives and Allied Advance of 1918, and was wounded. He was demobilised in March 1919, and holds the General Service and Victory Medals.
3, Worsley Street, Oldham Road, Manchester.   Z9138

GARRITY, J., Special War Worker.

When war broke out, he was working at Messrs. Armstrong and Whitworth's, and as he was employed on work of National importance, could not be released for military service. Throughout the period of hostilities he was engaged in the manufacture of munitions, and rendered most valuable services to his Country in the most critical moments of the war.
27, Helsby Street, Ardwick, Manchester.   Z6215A

GARRY, J.,Pte.,King's (L'pool Regt.) and Essex Regt.

Volunteering in August 1914, he was on completion of his training five months later sent overseas. Whilst serving on the Western Front, he took an active part in many important engagements in different sectors of the line, including the Battles of Ypres, the Somme, and Cambrai, and was wounded in action on three occasions. He was demobilised in January 1919, and holds the 1914-15 Star, and the General Service and Victory Medals.
22, Gardner Street, West Gorton, Manchester.   Z10231

GARSIDE, R., Private, 1st Gloucestershire Regt.

Volunteering in June 1915, he was trained at Bristol and Gravesend, and in March 1916 proceeded to the Western Front. He experienced fierce fighting in many engagements, including those in the Albert and Ypres sectors. In August 1916 he was wounded at Ypres, and sent to hospital at Rouen, and finally to Glasgow, from whence he was discharged in February 1917 as unfit for further military service. He holds the General Service and Victory Medals.
24, Glee Street, Ancoats, Manchester.   Z10232

GARSIDE, R., Sergt., 1/8th Manchester Regiment.

He volunteered in August 1914, and a month later was drafted to Egypt, where he was in action on the Suez Canal. He was then sent to Gallipoli, and was wounded there in June 1915. A month later he returned to the firing line and fought at Suvla Bay, after which he proceeded to France and took a prominent part in fighting at Nieuport, Ypres, Passchendaele, the Somme, Bullecourt, and Havrincourt. He was invalided to England suffering from trench fever, and was subsequently demobilised in January 1919, holding the 1914-15 Star, and the General Service and Victory Medals.
22, Gorton Street, Ardwick, Manchester.   Z6216

GARSTANG, G., Private, Manchester Regiment.

A month after the outbreak of war he volunteered, and in August 1915, proceeded to Egypt, where he served for six months. Transferred to the Western Front, he was in action during the Battles of the Somme and Ypres, and in the Retreat of 1918, and also fought in the final decisive engagements of the war. He was demobilised in October 1919, and holds the 1914-15 Star, and the General Service and Victory Medals.
155, Heald Grove, Rusholme, Manchester.   Z6217

GARTLEY, M., Private, K.O. Scottish Borderers.

He volunteered in August 1914, and two months later was ordered overseas. During his service on the Western Front he saw heavy fighting at La Bassée, Ypres, St. Eloi, Festubert, Loos, Vermelles, Albert, and Armentières. He was later invalided to England, suffering from severe shell-shock, and in consequence was discharged as medically unfit in May 1916. He holds the 1914 Star, and the General Service and Victory Medals.
31, Burton Street, Rochdale Road, Manchester.   Z10593

GARTSIDE, J. W., Private, Royal Welch Fusiliers.

Enlisting in January 1912, he was drafted to France in August 1914, but after taking part in the Battle of, and the Retreat from, Mons, and the Battles of Le Cateau, the Marne, and the Aisne, was wounded at Armentières in May 1915. He was invalided home, and on his recovery in the following December was sent to Egypt, where he was in action in the Suez Canal zone, and the Desert. Early in 1916, however, he returned to the Western Front, and was badly wounded in the Ypres sector. He was again invalided home, and in June 1917, was discharged as medically unfit for further service, holding the Mons Star, and the General Service and Victory Medals.
44, Fielden Street, Oldham Road, Manchester.   Z11707

GARVAN, C., Driver, R.A.S.C. (M.T.)

Joining in September 1916, he was on completion of a course of training drafted overseas in March 1917, and served in Salonika for nearly two years. During that time he took part in numerous important engagements, and also fought in the two Battles of the Vardar. Returning to England in February 1919, he was demobilised eight months later, and holds the General Service and Victory Medals.
23, Albemarle Street, Moss Side, Manchester.   Z6218A

GARVAN, E. C., Private, 19th Manchester Regt.

He volunteered in January 1915, and ten months later was drafted to the Western Front, where he was in action in engagements at St. Eloi, Albert, Vermelles, the Somme, Arras, Bullecourt, Messines, Ypres, and Cambrai. He was taken prisoner at St. Quentin in March 1918, and sent to Chemnitz, where he was employed on work in connection with the coal mines. After the Armistice he was released and subsequently demobilised in March 1919, holding the 1914-15 Star, and the General Service and Victory Medals.
23, Albemarle Street, Moss Side, Manchester.   Z6218B

GARVEY, A., Private, 1st Manchester Regiment.

Volunteering in August 1914, he was a month later drafted to Egypt, where he served in the engagements on the Suez Canal before proceeding to Gallipoli. There he fought at Suvla Bay, and throughout the remainder of the Campaign, and was then transferred to France, where he was in action at La Bassée, Nieuport, Ypres, Passchendaele, and the Somme. He was demobilised in October 1919, and holds the 1914-15 Star, and the General Service and Victory Medals.
14, Spurgeon Street, West Gorton, Manchester.   Z6219

GASKELL, A. E., Private, 22nd Manchester Regt.
Volunteering in November 1914, he was sent twelve months later to France, where he was in action at Loos, Albert, Beaumont-Hamel, and on the Somme front. He was afterwards transferred to Italy, and then took part in heavy fighting on the Piave. Demobilised on his return home in February 1919, he holds the 1914-15 Star, and the General Service and Victory Medals.
41, Grosvenor Street, Newton Heath, Manchester.   Z9533

GASKELL, H., Private, R.A.O.C.
He volunteered in March 1915, and two months later was drafted to the Western Front, where he fought in the Battle of Festubert. In August 1915 he proceeded to Salonika, and took part in engagements on the Doiran front, at Monastir, on the Struma, and in the Advance on the Vardar. He returned to England in May 1919, and was demobilised, holding the 1914-15 Star, and the General Service and Victory Medals.
18, Derby Street, Ardwick, Manchester.   Z6221

GASKELL, J. R., Staff-Sergt., 3rd Manchester Regt.
He volunteered in January 1915, but was retained on important duties in England throughout the period of hostilities. For over twelve months he rendered valuable services as Instructor to cadets at Ripon and Durham University. In 1916 he was sent to the Senior Command Officers' School, Brocton, and in the following year was employed on the head-quarters staff at the N.C.O. School at Fulford. He was eventually demobilised in January 1919.
3, Whitland Street, Queen's Park, Manchester.   Z11499

GATE, A. E., Gunner, R.F.A.
Volunteering in September 1914, he proceeded in January 1916, to the Egyptian front, and was engaged in fierce fighting on the Suez Canal, and at Mersa Matruh, and Agagia. He was transferred to France in 1917, and in this theatre of war, was in action at Arras, Bullecourt, Ypres, and Cambrai, and in the Retreat and Advance of 1918. After the Armistice he entered Germany with the Army of Occupation, and was stationed at Cologne, until demobilised in April 1919, holding the General Service and Victory Medals.
66, Milton Street, West Gorton, Manchester.   Z6222

GATEHOUSE, W., Sapper, R.E.
He joined in March 1916, but was medically unfit for transfer to a theatre of war. Retained at home, he served successively at Sandwich and Dover, and performed consistently good work whilst engaged on important duties in connection with home defence. He was demobilised in February 1919.
36, Cross Street, Newton Heath, Manchester.   Z9534

GATLEY, W., Private, Royal Fusiliers.
Volunteering in July 1915, he proceeded three months later to Salonika, but after serving on the Doiran front, was taken prisoner in November 1915, and sent to Philippopolis, where he remained until after the cessation of hostilities. During his captivity he was employed in a tobacco factory, and on his release returned to England, and was demobilised in December 1919. He holds the 1914-15 Star, and the General Service and Victory Medals.
14, Morna Street, Ardwick, Manchester.   Z10233

GAUNT, R. (M.M.), L/Corporal, R.F.A.
He volunteered in January 1915, and in the following August was sent to France. In this theatre of war he fought in important engagements at Mailly, the Somme, Arras, Ypres, and La Bassée, and was wounded in action on two occasions. He was awarded the Military Medal for conspicuous gallantry in the Field at Arras. In March 1919 he was demobilised, and also holds the 1914-15 Star, and the General Service and Victory Medals.
1, Great Jones Street, West Gorton, Manchester.   Z10235

GAUNT, T. A., Sergt., R.A.S.C.
He volunteered in April 1915, but was retained on responsible work in England until February 1916, when he succeeded in securing a transfer overseas. He was drafted to the Western Front, and stationed at Calais, where he was employed on important clerical duties in connection with the food depôts at the Docks. Demobilised in December 1918 he holds the General Service and Victory Medals.
52, William Street, West Gorton, Manchester.   Z6224

GAUNT, W., Driver, R.F.A.
He attested under the Derby Scheme in 1915, and being called up in January 1917, was four months later sent to the Western Front. There he served with an ammunition column, was in action at Ypres, Passchendaele, and Cambrai, and in the final Allied Advance, and was wounded. After the close of hostilities he proceeded with the Army of Occupation to Germany, and was demobilised in September 1919, holding the General Service and Victory Medals.
54, Earl Street, Longsight, Manchester.   Z6223

GAVEN, J. F., Private, 6th Manchester Regiment.
In September 1914 he volunteered, and in March 1916 was drafted to Egypt, where he saw heavy fighting at Katia, El Fasher, Romani, and Magdhaba. In 1917 his health broke down, and he was sent to hospital, first at Alexandria, and then at Bombay for treatment. In April of that year he was discharged from the Army as medically unfit for further military service, and holds the General Service and Victory Medals.
86, Armitage Street, Ardwick, Manchester.   Z6225

GEE, B., Private, Lancashire Fusiliers, and Air Mechanic, R.A.F.
Mobilised in August 1914, he at once proceeded to Egypt, and served there for sixteen months. During that time he took an active part in engagements on the Suez Canal, at Agagia, Katia, and Romani, and was then sent to the Western Front with the Royal Air Force. He did good work with the 28th Squadron at Ypres, and Lille, and was demobilised in February 1919, holding the 1914-15 Star, and the General Service and Victory Medals.
24, Lancaster Street, Hulme, Manchester.   Z6227

GEE, J., Gunner, R.G.A.
He volunteered in October 1914, and in the following April proceeded to Singapore, where he was employed on important garrison duties. Sent a year later to France, he was in action on the Somme, and at Arras, and Ypres, and was severely wounded at Passchendaele. On rejoining his Battery, he took part in engagements at Cambrai, and also served in the Retreat and Advance of 1918. He was demobilised in February 1919, and holds the 1914-15 Star, and the General Service and Victory Medals.
37, Berwick Street, Chorlton-on-Medlock, Manchester.   Z6226

GEE, R., Private, 6th South Lancashire Regiment.
Volunteering in April 1915, he was five months later drafted to Mesopotamia, where with the Relief Force, he took an active part in heavy fighting at Kut. He was later reported missing and subsequently killed on April 9th, 1916. He was entitled to the 1914-15 Star, and the General Service and Victory Medals.
"Honour to the immortal dead who gave their youth that the world might grow old in peace."
23, Hadfield Street, Chorlton-on-Medlock, Manchester.   Z6228

GEE, R., Pte., King's Shropshire Light Infantry.
He joined in May 1918, but was not successful in obtaining a transfer to a theatre of war before the close of hostilities. He was stationed at Shrewsbury, and later in Ireland, at Cork and Fermoy, and rendered valuable services as a first-class signaller, until his demobilisation in September 1919.
2, Longworth Street, Hulme, Manchester.   Z6229

GEORGE, A. M., Worker, Q.M.A.A.C.
She joined in November 1917, and at once proceeded to the Western Front, where she was employed on important clerical work at St. Omer and Calais. She served in France for ten months, and at the end of that time returned to England, suffering from shell-shock, as the result of air raids. She was eventually demobilised in January 1919, and holds the General Service and Victory Medals.
47, Cowesby Street, Moss Side, Manchester.   Z10594

GEORGE, B., Pte., 55th King's (Liverpool Regt.)
Volunteering in August 1915, he proceeded in April 1917 to the Western Front, and fought in the Battles of Arras, Vimy Ridge, but was wounded at Ypres, and invalided to England. On returning to France, he saw service at Havrincourt and Cambrai, and in the final engagements of the war. After the Armistice he entered Germany with the Army of Occupation, and was demobilised in February 1919, holding the General Service and Victory Medals.
16, Marsland Street, Chorlton-on-Medlock, Manchester.   Z6231

GEORGE, E. F., Guardsman, Coldstream Guards.
He volunteered in August 1915, and ten months later proceeded overseas. Whilst serving in France he saw heavy fighting in the Somme, Guillemont, Beaumont-Hamel, Beaucourt, Ypres, Passchendaele, La Bassée, Arras, Albert, and Cambrai sectors, and was wounded in the Battle of the Somme. After the cessation of hostilities he was sent to Germany with the Army of Occupation, and was stationed at Cologne until demobilised in March 1919. He holds the General Service and Victory Medals.
15, Emma Street, Ardwick, Manchester.   Z6230

GEORGE, T., Pte., Loyal North Lancashire Regt.
He volunteered in January 1915, and four months later proceeded overseas. During his service on the Western Front he was in action at Festubert, Loos, Albert, the Somme, Bullecourt, Ypres, Cambrai, Bapaume, and La Bassée, and fell fighting at Cambrai in October 1918. He was entitled to the 1914-15 Star, and the General Service and Victory Medals.
"His life for his Country."
35, Edinburgh Street, Miles Platting, Manchester.   Z10237

GERRARD, E., Private, Lancashire Fusiliers.
Volunteering in September 1914, he proceeded to the Western Front in October 1915, and whilst fighting in the Battle of the Somme in 1916 was wounded, and sent back to England. On his recovery he returned to his unit in France and took part in numerous other engagements until again wounded in May 1917. He was demobilised in March 1919, and holds the 1914-15 Star, and the General Service and Victory Medals.
108, South Street, Longsight, Manchester.   Z6233

GERRARD, G. F., Air Mechanic, R.A.F.

He joined in June 1916, and after training at Reading was drafted six months later to the Western Front, where he was stationed at St. Omer, and employed in the Royal Air Force workshops, carrying out the important duties of a rigger, until the close of hostilities when he proceeded to Germany with the Army of Occupation. He was demobilised in October 1919, and holds the General Service and Victory Medals.

3, Plymouth Street, Chorlton-on-Medlock, Manchester. Z6232

GERRARD, T., Corporal, R.E.

Volunteering in August 1914, he was drafted in January 1916 to the Western Front, where he served for three years. During that time he took an active part in engagements in the Ypres, Arras, Lens, Mericourt, Avion, Armentières, Oppy, Bourlon Wood, Viny Ridge, La Bassée, and Hill 60 sectors, and was gassed at Passchendaele. He was demobilised in February 1919, and holds the General Service and Victory Medals.

11, Lever Street, Gorton, Manchester. Z10238

GERRITY, J., Private, 23rd Manchester Regiment.

Volunteering in July 1915, he proceeded in the following April to the Western Front. There he was in action in engagements at Albert, Ploegsteert, Vermelles, and the Somme, but as the result of being gassed in the Battle of Arras in March 1917, was discharged from the Army in the same month, as medically unfit for further service. He holds the General Service and Victory Medals.

21, Pitt Street, Ancoats, Manchester. Z6234

GERRITY, J., Gunner, R.F.A.

He volunteered in October 1915, and on completion of his training was drafted overseas in December 1916. During his two years' service on the Western Front, he did good work with his Battery in the Battles of the Ancre, Arras, Messines, and Ypres, and was also in action in the 1918 Retreat, and in the final Allied Advance. In December 1918 he was demobilised, holding the General Service and Victory Medals.

8, Grafton Street, Longsight, Manchester. Z6235

GETHING, G., Gunner, R.F.A.

He joined in April 1918, but was unsuccessful in procuring a transfer to the fighting area, before the close of the war. He was stationed at Liverpool and Whitchurch, and carried out the various duties assigned to him in a very able manner. After a year's service in the Army he was demobilised in April 1919.

12, Albion Street, Miles Platting, Manchester. Z10239

GIBBONS, H., Private, 52nd Cheshire Regiment.

In May 1918 he joined the Army, but was retained on home service until after the close of hostilities. In April 1919, however, he was sent to Germany with the Army of Occupation, and was engaged on important garrison duties at Cologne and Bonn for four month. He was demobilised from Prees Heath in January 1920.

9, Grantham Street, West Gorton, Manchester. Z10240

GIBBONS, J., Private, 3rd East Lancashire Regt.

A month after the outbreak of war he volunteered, and in the following May was sent to France, where he was in action at Festubert, Loos, Ypres, Vimy Ridge, the Somme I, Arras, Ypres, the Somme II, and Le Cateau, and took part in fierce fighting during the engagements prior to the termination of hostilities. He was demobilised in January 1919, and holds the 1914–15 Star, and the General Service and Victory Medals.

20, Bradshaw Street, Hulme, Manchester. Z6236

GIBBONS, M. Pte., King's (L'pool Regt.) and Spr., R.E.

He volunteered in November 1915, and two months later was drafted to France, where he was transferred to the Royal Engineers. After working on the railways for two months he was sent up to the firing line, and was in action at Vimy Ridge, the Somme, Beaumont-Hamel, Beaucourt, Arras, Ypres, Passchendaele, Bullecourt, Lens, Cambrai, the Somme II, and Le Cateau. He was demobilised in March 1919, and holds the General Service and Victory Medals.

16, Wenlock Street, Hulme, Manchester. Z6237

GIBBONS, P., Private, 9th South Lancashire Regt.

A month after the outbreak of war he volunteered, and in November 1915 was sent to France, where during his four months service he was in action at St. Eloi and Loos. In March 1916 he was transferred to Salonika, and did good work with his unit on the Doiran and the Struma fronts, and in the Capture of Monastir. He contracted malaria, and was sent to hospital at Malta, whence he was discharged as unfit for further service in March 1918. He holds the 1914–15 Star, and the General Service and Victory Medals.

58, Branson Street, Ancoats, Manchester. Z10241

GIBBONS, T., Private, 2nd Manchester Regiment.

Mobilised in August 1914, he was at once ordered to France, where he participated in the Battle of Mons and the subsequent Retreat. He also took part in the Battles of the Marne, the Aisne, Le Cateau, La Bassée, Ypres, Hill 60, Loos, St. Eloi, the Somme, Arras and Cambrai, serving on the Western Front during the whole period of hostilities. Discharged in March 1919, he holds the Mons Star, and the General Service and Victory Medals.

20, Brass Street, Rochdale Road, Manchester. Z9535

GIBLIN, J., Pte., K.O. (Royal Lancaster Regt.)

He joined in June 1916, and in the following October was sent to the Western Front, where after taking an active part in the fighting on the Somme, and at Albert, and Beaumont-Hamel, he was unhappily killed in action at Beaucourt in December 1916. He was entitled to the General Service and Victory Medals.

"A valiant soldier, with undaunted heart he breasted life's last hill."

39, Naylor Street, Hulme, Manchester. TZ6238

GIBSON, G. F., Pioneer, R.E.

He joined in May 1917, and early in the following year proceeded to France. There he was employed on various duties at Albert, Vimy Ridge, Ypres, and Passchendaele, and did excellent work. After the Armistice, he served in Germany with the Army of Occupation until October 1919, when he was demobilised, holding the General Service and Victory Medals.

16, Vine Street, Newton Heath, Manchester. Z9536

GIBSON, H., Writer, R.N., H.M.S. "Cyclops."

He volunteered in December 1915, and was posted to H.M.S. "Cyclops." In this vessel he served off the Orkney Islands and with the Grand Fleet in the North Sea, and rendered valuable services whilst employed on important duties. He was discharged on account of ill-health in May 1918, and holds the General Service and Victory Medals.

152, Barmouth Street, Bradford, Manchester. Z9537

GIBSON, H., Private, Labour Corps.

Joining in June 1917, he was almost immediately sent out to the Western Front, and attached to the Labour Corps, with which he fulfilled his various duties in a highly capable way. Whilst serving in France he contracted pleurisy, and unhappily died in March 1919, of that illness. He was entitled to the General Service and Victory Medals.

"Thinking that remembrance, though unspoken, may reach him where he sleeps."

10, Ravensdale Road, Rusholme, Manchester. Z6241A

GIBSON, J., Private, 29th Manchester Regiment.

He volunteered in November 1915, but on completion of his training was unsuccessful in procuring a transfer overseas. He was, however, retained on home service, and served at Southport and Altcar and performed the duties allotted to him with great ability. In December 1916 he was sent to Nottingham, and was there employed as a cook until discharged a year later, as medically unfit for further military service.

8, Stott Street, Hulme, Manchester. Z6243

GIBSON, J., Stoker, R.N., H.M.S. "Edgar."

He joined in January 1918, and after training at Plymouth was posted to H.M.S. "Edgar" two months later. He served in this vessel for nearly a year, and during that time rendered valuable services on the North Sea until demobilised in January 1919. He holds the General Service and Victory Medals.

14, Whyatt Street, Bradford, Manchester. TZ6239

GIBSON, J., Sergt., 1st Manchester Regiment.

He was already serving when war broke out, and in October 1914 proceeded to France, where he was in action at Ypres and Loos, and was wounded at La Bassée. In August 1915 he was sent to Mesopotamia, and took a prominent part in the attempted relief of Kut, and in fighting on the Tigris, and at Kut-el-Amara, and was wounded on two occasions. He returned to England in April 1920, and was discharged after thirteen years service in the Army. He holds the 1914 Star, and the General Service and Victory Medals.

10, Whitfield Street, Ardwick, Manchester. Z6240

GIBSON, P., Private, 10th Lancashire Fusiliers.

He volunteered in March 1915, and later in the same year was drafted to the Western Front. There he took an active part in engagements at Ypres, Passchendaele, Arras, Albert, Lens, Cambrai, St. Eloi, Neuve Chapelle, and Armentières, and was wounded in action at the Somme in 1917, and again at St. Vaast in 1918. He was demobilised in February 1919, and holds the 1914–15 Star, and the General Service and Victory Medals. 39, Granville Place, Ancoats, Manchester. Z10242

GIBSON, W., Private, 43rd Royal Fusiliers.

Volunteering in August 1914, he proceeded to France on the completion of his training in September 1915. Whilst on the Western Front he saw service at Armentières, Guillemont, and Vimy Ridge, and was wounded on the Somme. On his recovery he returned to the firing line, and was in action at St. Eloi, Albert, Arras, Bullecourt, and Amiens, and in the Retreat and Advance of 1918. Demobilised in February 1919, he holds the 1914–15 Star, and the General Service and Victory Medals.

26, Hewitt Street, Gorton, Manchester. Z10243

GIBSON, W., Private, 8th Manchester Regiment.

Having previously served in the South African Campaign he was called up from the Reserve at the outbreak of hostilities in August 1914, but on account of his age was not drafted overseas. He was retained on home service, and performed valuable guard duties on the railways, until his health broke down, and he was invalided out of the Army in 1915. He holds the India General Service (with clasp Burma), and the Queen's and King's South Africa Medals.

8, Morton Street, Chorlton-on-Medlock, Manchester. TX6242

GIDLEY, C., Private, 11th Manchester Regiment.
He volunteered in December 1914, and in April 1915 was drafted to Gallipoli, where he saw service in the three Battles of Krithia, Suvla Bay, and Chocolate Hill, and was wounded. In February 1916 he was sent to Egypt, and was in action on the Suez Canal, at Kantara, and the Sinai Desert. He proceeded to France in June 1916, and took an active part in engagements on the Somme and at Beaumont-Hamel, Passchendaele, Cambrai, Albert, the Ancre, Bapaume, and Havrincourt, and was again wounded at Pozières. He was demobilised in July 1919, and holds the 1914–15 Star, and the General Service and Victory Medals.
20, Wright Street, Oldham Road, Manchester.   Z10244

GILBERT, H., Private, 2nd Manchester Regiment.
He volunteered in May 1915, and after a course of training at Heaton Park and Southport, was drafted overseas in February 1916. During his three years' service on the Western Front he performed excellent work as a food transport driver in the St. Eloi, Albert, Vimy Ridge, Somme, Bullecourt, Ypres, Passchendaele and Cambrai sectors. He was demobilised in February 1919, and holds the General Service and Victory Medals.
38, Dyson Street, Miles Platting, Manchester.   Z11500B

GILBERT, T., Private, 2nd South Lancashire Regt.
Volunteering in July 1915, he proceeded two months later to the Western Front. In this theatre of war he was engaged in fierce fighting at Albert, Ploegsteert Wood, Vermelles, the Somme, Beaumont-Hamel, Arras, Messines, Ypres, and Passchendaele, and was severely wounded at Cambrai. He was in consequence invalided out of the Army in September 1918, and holds the 1914–15 Star, and the General Service and Victory Medals. 10, Dalton Street, Collyhurst, Manchester. Z10595

GILBERT, W. H., Private, Cheshire Regiment.
Joining in May 1918, he trained in Wales, and four months later was sent to the Western Front. There he was engaged in severe fighting, principally in the Somme sector, and after the Armistice was signed proceeded with the Army of Occupation to Germany. He served there until May 1919, when he was drafted to Ireland. In 1920 he was still serving in the Army, and holds the General Service and Victory Medals.
38, Dyson Street, Miles Platting, Manchester.   Z11500A

GILBODY, J. A., Driver, R.F.A.
Mobilised in August 1914, he proceeded at once to the Western Front, and fought in the Battles of Mons, Neuve Chapelle, St. Eloi, Loos, Albert, the Somme, and Cambrai. He was wounded on three occasions, and in consequence was discharged from the Army as medically unfit for further service in April 1918. He holds the Mons Star, and the General Service and Victory Medals.
1, Heron Street, Hulme, Manchester.   Z6244

GILCHRIST, W., Guardsman, Grenadier Guards.
He volunteered in March 1915, and after training at Chelsea proceeded overseas in September 1916. During his service on the Western Front, he took an active part in fierce fighting in the Ypres sector, but in December 1916, he was sent to England suffering from trench feet, and remained in hospital for eight months. At the end of that time he was retained on home service at Chelsea until demobilised in March 1919, holding the General Service and Victory Medals.
66, Bennett Street, Ardwick, Manchester.   Z6245

GILDEA, E., Private, R.A.M.C.
He joined in March 1917, and a month later proceeded to France, where he was stationed at Rouen, and attached to the Royal Air Force Medical Corps. Throughout the period of his service he was engaged on important duties which he performed in an extremely able manner, and was not demobilised until September 1919. He holds the General Service and Victory Medals. 6, Bonsall Street, Hulme, Manchester.   Z6248

GILDEA, F., Private, Manchester Regt.
Volunteering in September 1914, he was eighteen months later drafted to the Western Front, and after fighting in the Somme and the Ancre sectors, was transferred to Italy in November 1916. He served in this theatre of war for over two years, and during that time was in action on the Piave and the Asiago Plateaux, and was wounded. He was demobilised in February 1919, and holds the General Service and Victory Medals.   Z6246
25, Higher Chatham Street, Chorlton-on-Medlock, Manchester.

GILDEA, W., Private, 12th Manchester Regiment.
In November 1915, he volunteered, and in the following March proceeded to the Western Front. There he saw heavy fighting at St. Eloi, Albert, Vimy Ridge, and the Ancre, and was severely wounded in the Battle of Arras, which resulted in the loss of his right leg. He was in consequence discharged from the Army in September 1918, and holds the General Service and Victory Medals. 25, Lavender Street, Hulme, Manchester.   Z6247

GILES, E., Private, King's (Liverpool Regiment).
He volunteered in November 1915, and three months later was drafted overseas. During his service in France he saw heavy fighting at Loos, Vimy Ridge, the Somme, Messines,

and Cambrai, and in the Retreat of 1918. In April of that year he was gassed, and invalided home, and in June was discharged from the Army as medically unfit for further military duties. He holds the General Service and Victory Medals.
6, Hope Street, Bradford, Manchester.   Z10245B

GILES, J., Private, South Lancashire Regiment.
He joined in December 1916, after having already been engaged in the manufacture of barbed wire with Messrs. Johnston and Nephew, Manchester. In February 1917 he proceeded to the Western Front, and fought in engagements at Ypres, Passchendaele, Messines, and Cambrai, and in the final Allied Advance. After the Armistice he entered Germany with the Army of Occupation, and was demobilised in January 1919, holding the General Service and Victory Medals.
6, Hope Street, Bradford, Manchester.   Z10245A

GILES, J. H., Corporal, 7th Manchester Regiment.
He volunteered in September 1914, and in the following July proceeded to Gallipoli, but after taking part in the fighting at Suvla Bay, was sent back to England suffering from dysentery. On his recovery he was stationed at Oswestry, and in Ireland, and the day after the Armistice was declared, was drafted to France, where he served with the Labour Corps at Ypres and Mons until demobilised in February 1919. He holds the 1914–15 Star, and the General Service and Victory Medals.
11, Orvil Street, Hancock, Street, Hulme, Manchester. Z6249

GILL, R., Private, R.A.S.C. (M.T.)
He joined in May 1916, and two months later was sent to the Western Front, where he served for nearly three years. During that time he performed excellent work with his unit in engagements at Vimy Ridge, the Somme, the Ancre, Arras, Bullecourt, Messines, Ypres, Cambrai, the Marne, Bapaume, and Havrincourt. He was still serving in the Army in 1920, and holds the General Service and Victory Medals.
50, Sherwood Street, Rochdale Road, Manchester. Z10596

GILFOYLE, W., Sapper, R.E.
Joining in June 1916, he completed his training and was eleven months later drafted to the Western Front, where he was in action in engagements at Bullecourt and Messines. He fell fighting in the Battle of Ypres on October 6th 1917, and was entitled to the General Service and Victory Medals.
"He died the noblest death a man may die,
Fighting for God and right and liberty."
12, Callender Street, Chorlton-on-Medlock, Manchester. Z6250

GILL, A. T., Private, 2nd Royal Scots.
He volunteered in November 1914, and after his training served at various important home stations before proceeding in March 1917 to France. There he was engaged in fierce fighting in different sectors, and was in action at Bullecourt and Ypres. After the Battle of the Somme he was reported missing, and later reported to have been killed on May 3rd, 1917. He was entitled to the General Service and Victory Medals.
"Whilst we remember the sacrifice is not in vain."
2, Ripon Street, Greenheys, Manchester.   Z6251A

GILL, J. D., Private, 3rd Cheshire Regiment.
He volunteered for active service in April 1915, but after two months' training he was found to be suffering from chest trouble and was discharged from the Army in June 1915 as medically unfit for further military duties.
11, Coburg Place, Rusholme, Manchester.   Z6253

GILL, J. H., Private, Royal Marine Engineers.
He joined in March 1918, but was unsuccessful in procuring a transfer to a theatre of war. After his training he proceeded to Chatham, and later to Southwick, and in this district rendered valuable services as an engine driver until demobilised in February 1919.
29, Fenn Street, Hulme, Manchester.   Z6252

GILL, M., Private, King's Shropshire Light Infantry.
He joined the Army in November 1917, and four months later was drafted to the Western Front, where he took part in operations on the Aisne and the Marne. He was wounded in the latter engagement, and sent to hospital in Rouen for five months, but at the end of that period he rejoined his unit, and was in action at Havrincourt, Cambrai, and Le Cateau. He remained in France until demobilised in September 1919, and holds the General Service and Victory Medals.
19, Gay Street, Jackson Street, Hulme, Manchester. Z6261

GILL, W., L/Corporal, 2nd Manchester Regiment.
At the outbreak of war in 1914, he was mobilised, and at once proceeded with the first Expeditionary Force to France, where he took part in the Battle of Mons, and in several other engagements. After only two months' active service he was unfortunately killed in action at La Bassée in October 1914. He was entitled to the Mons Star, and the General Service and Victory Medals.
"Great deeds cannot die."
10, Mary Street, Hulme, Manchester.   Z6254

GILL, W., Pioneer, R.E.
He joined in March 1916, and two months later embarked for France, where he was in action on the Somme, at Arras, and Bullecourt. Owing to ill-health he was invalided home, and after receiving hospital treatment was discharged as unfit for further service in September 1918. He holds the General Service and Victory Medals.
5, Newby Street, Ancoats, Manchester. Z9139

GILLAND, E., Private, 1/7th Royal Welch Fusiliers.
He volunteered in June 1915, and ten months later was drafted to Palestine, where he was engaged in fierce fighting during the three Battles of Gaza, and near Jerusalem. He also took part in the Capture of Jericho, and was in action in General Allenby's Offensive in September 1918. In February 1919 he was demobilised after his return home, and holds the General Service and Victory Medals.
47, Robert Street, Chorlton-on-Medlock, Manchester.
X2435A X2436A

GILLAND, J. T., Private, 1/6th Manchester Regt.
He volunteered in August 1914, and a month later proceeded to Egypt. Afterwards he was sent to Gallipoli and served throughout the Campaign there. In 1917 he was drafted to the Western Front, and after fighting in numerous engagements was unhappily killed in action at Bapaume on September 2nd, 1918. He was entitled to the 1914-15 Star, and the General Service and Victory Medals. X2435C X2436C
"A costly sacrifice upon the altar of freedom."
47, Robert Street, Chorlton-on-Medlock, Manchester.

GILLAND, W., Private, 3/7th Manchester Regt.
Volunteering in September 1915, he was in the following year drafted to Salonika, where he took part in the Allied Offensive on the Doiran front. After serving in Egypt for a short time, he was sent to France, and there fought in the Battles of Ypres, Passchendaele and Cambrai, and in the Retreat and Advance of 1918. After the Armistice he entered Germany with the Army of Occupation, and was eventually demobilised in March 1919, holding the General Service and Victory Medals.
47, Robert Street, Chorlton-on-Medlock, Manchester.
X2435E X2436E

GILLENEY, J. F., Gunner, R.G.A.
He volunteered in August 1914, but was retained on home service until March 1917, when he was sent overseas. Whilst serving in France, he was in action at Arras, Vimy Ridge, Bullecourt, Passchendaele, and Cambrai, and in the final engagements of the war. He was gassed at St. Omer in October 1918, but served in France until demobilised in February 1919, holding the General Service and Victory Medals.
30, Coach Terrace, Longsight, Manchester. Z6255

GILLIBRAND, D. J., Private, Welch Regiment.
Volunteering in May 1915, he was a month later drafted to Gallipoli, and whilst engaged in heavy fighting in the Battle of Krithia was severely wounded. Invalided home he was in consequence discharged as medically unfit for further military service in May 1916, and holds the 1914-15 Star, and the General Service and Victory Medals.
4, Erskine Street, Ardwick, Manchester. Z6257

GILLIBRAND, J., Private, 8th Welch Regiment.
He volunteered in May 1915, and proceeding overseas four months later served in the Gallipoli Campaign. After the Evacuation he was sent to Mesopotamia, and was in action at Sanna-i-Yat, Kut-el-Amara, and during the capture of Baghdad. After the Armistice he was drafted to Egypt, and thence to Salonika, and finally to Constantinople, where he served until June 1919, when returning to England he was demobilised, holding the 1914-15 Star, and the General Service and Victory Medals.
104, Marsland Street, Ardwick, Manchester. Z6256

GILLIBRAND, R., Staff-Sergt., Border Regiment.
He volunteered in October 1914, and in March of the following year was sent to Gallipoli, where he saw service at the Landing, and at Krithia, and Suvla Bay. After the Evacuation of the Peninsula he took part in heavy fighting on the Suez Canal, and was later drafted to France. There he fought with distinction in the Battles of the Somme I, Arras, Ypres, Cambrai, the Somme II, Amiens, Le Cateau, and Ypres III, and was wounded on three occasions. He was demobilised in February 1919, and holds the 1914-15 Star, and the General Service and Victory Medals.
58, Beaumont St., Beswick, Manchester. Z10246

GILLIGAN, C., L/Corporal, 1/8th Manchester Regt.
He volunteered in August 1914, and in the following month was sent to Egypt, where he saw service on the Suez Canal. Proceeding to Gallipoli in April 1915, he fought in the three Battles of Krithia, and was then invalided to England suffering from rheumatism. He returned to Egypt in 1916, and was in action at Romani, Magdhaba, and Rafa, and on being sent to Palestine, saw heavy fighting at Gaza, Jerusalem, and Jericho. Returning to England in July 1919, he was demobilised, and holds the 1914-15 Star, and the General Service and Victory Medals. 46, Armitage St., Ardwick, Manchester. Z6259

GILLIGAN, J., Sapper, R.E.
Volunteering in March 1915, he was not able to procure a transfer overseas after completing his training. He was retained on home defence with his unit and during his period of service performed excellent work in connection with searchlights, until he was eventually demobilised in March 1919.
69, Leach Street, Gorton, Manchester. TZ6258

GILLIGAN, L., Private, 21st Cheshire Regiment.
Joining in June 1916, he was drafted four months later to the Western Front, where he served for three years. During this period, he was in action on the Somme front, at La Bassée, Bray, and Cambrai, and also took part in many engagements during the Retreat and Advance of 1918. Demobilised on returning home in October 1919, he holds the General Service and Victory Medals.
8, Strand Street, Ancoats, Manchester. Z9538B

GILLIGAN, T., Private, Lancashire Fusiliers.
He volunteered in February 1915, and in the following June was drafted to Gallipoli, where he took part in heavy fighting at Suvla Bay, and was wounded in August 1915. Upon his recovery he was transferred to France, but, after participating in the Battle of Vimy Ridge, was unfortunately killed in action on July 1st, 1916, during the Battle of the Somme. He was entitled to the 1914-15 Star, and the General Service and Victory Medals. "The path of duty was the way to glory."
8, Strand Street, Ancoats, Manchester. Z9538A

GILLIN, P., Private, 26th Manchester Regiment.
He volunteered in January 1915, but owing to ill-health was unable to secure a transfer to a theatre of war. He was retained on Home Defence, and stationed at Heaton Park, Whitchurch and Southport, where he rendered most valuable services. In December 1916, he received his discharge from the Army, being no longer fit for further military duties.
6, Flower Street, Ancoats, Manchester. Z10247

GILMAN, J., Private, 4th Manchester Regiment.
Volunteering in September 1914, he landed in France in November of the following year, and was in action at Vermelles, and Vimy Ridge. He gave his life for King and Country on July 1st, 1916, in the first Battle of the Somme. He was entitled to the 1914-15 Star, and the General Service and Victory Medals.
"Whilst we remember, the sacrifice is not in vain."
25, John Street, Hulme, Manchester. TZ7212B

GILMAN, T., Sergt., 4th Manchester Regt., and R.G.A.
He was mobilised in August 1914, and at once proceeded with the First Expeditionary Force to the Western Front, where he was engaged in fierce fighting at Ypres, Hill 60, the Somme, Arras and Guillincourt, and was wounded in action and gassed. He was later transferred to the R.G.A., and did excellent work as a gunner. He also served in Ireland, and in August 1919 was discharged, holding the 1914 Star, and the General Service and Victory Medals.
82, Higher Temple Street, Chorlton-on-Medlock, Manchester. X6260

GILMARTIN, J., Private, R.A.V.C.
Volunteering in August 1914, he was on completion of his training drafted overseas six months later. Whilst serving on the Western Front, he was in action in various sectors of the line, and took part in engagements at Ypres, the Somme, Nieuport, La Bassée, Arras and Givenchy. Remaining in France until February 1918, he was eventually demobilised in January 1919, and holds the 1914-15 Star, and the General Service and Victory Medals.
12, Unity Street, Ancoats, Manchester. Z6262

GILSON, J. T., Guardsman, Grenadier Guards.
Volunteering in October 1914, he was drafted to the Western Front four months afterwards. During his service in this theatre of war, he took part in the Battles of Ypres and Hill 60, and fell fighting at Albert during the first Battle of the Somme. He was entitled to the 1914-15 Star, and the General Service and Victory Medals.
"He passed out of the sight of men by the path of duty and self-sacrifice."
29, Marsden Street, Newton Heath, Manchester. Z9539

GILSON, R., Private, 1/8th Manchester Regiment.
Volunteering at the commencement of hostilities, he was drafted to Egypt shortly afterwards, and fought in many engagements during the Advance across the Sinai Peninsula. In 1917 transferred to France he was in action on the Somme, at Ypres, and throughout the Retreat and Advance of 1918, and was wounded. He was demobilised in April 1919, and holds the 1914-15 Star, and the General Service and Victory Medals. 12, Hope Street, Ardwick, Manchester. Z9140

GITTINS, E., Pte., 18th King's (Liverpool Regt.)
He volunteered in December 1915, and after a period of training was three months later drafted to the Western Front. There he was in action at Albert, Vimy Ridge, the Somme, Beaumont-Hamel, Mailly, Arras and Ypres, and was wounded at Messines in April 1918, and invalided to England. After treatment in various hospitals he was eventually demobilised in February 1919, and holds the General Service and Victory Medals.
78, Armitage Street, Ardwick, Manchester. Z6263

GLADWELL, T. (M.M.), Cpl., 36th Northumberland Fusiliers.

Volunteering in March 1915, he was engaged on important duties at home for three years, and was then drafted to the Western Front. There he was in action in many engagements, and took an active part in the final Allied Advance. He was awarded the Military Medal for exceptional bravery in bringing in the wounded under heavy shell-fire at Le Cateau in October 1918. He was demobilised in February 1919, and also holds the General Service and Victory Medals.
38, Alma Street, Collyhurst, Manchester.   Z11501

GLASGOW, G., Driver, R.A.S.C.

Volunteering in November 1914, he was retained on important duties in England until March 1917, when he was drafted to the Western Front, where he was chiefly engaged in transporting food and ammunition to the forward lines. He was in action in engagements on the Somme and the Marne, and also in the Retreat and Advance of 1918, and after the Armistice served with the Army of Occupation in Germany. He was demobilised in June 1919, and holds the General Service and Victory Medals.
17, Sandown Street, Ardwick, Manchester.   Z6264B

GLASGOW, S., Pte., Q.M.A.A.C. and Women's Legion.

She joined the Women's Legion in June 1917, but was afterwards transferred to the Q.M.A.A.C. and served at Catterick and Derby. She was engaged at the stations as a waitress in the officers' mess and carried out her duties with great ability. She was not demobilised until January 1920.
17, Sandown Street, Ardwick, Manchester.   Z6264A

GLASGOW, W., Q.M.S., K.O. (R. Lancaster Regt.)

He volunteered in August 1914, and in the following June proceeded to Gallipoli, where he was engaged in fierce fighting at Krithia and Suvla Bay. After the Evacuation of the Peninsula, he was sent to Mesopotamia and took part in engagements at Kut, the Tigris and Baghdad. He served in this theatre of war until after the close of hostilities, and returning to England in January 1919, was demobilised, holding the 1914–15 Star, and the General Service and Victory Medals.
17, Sandown Street, Ardwick, Manchester.   Z6264C

GLASSER, F. H., Private, R.A.S.C.

Having previously served in the Boer War, he joined the Army in August 1916, and five months later was sent to France, where he saw heavy fighting at Arras, Vimy Ridge, Passchendaele, Cambrai, the Ancre, the Aisne, the Marne, Havrincourt and Cambrai (II). He returned home on leave in October 1919, but contracted pneumonia and died in West Didsbury Hospital in the following month. He was entitled to the Queen's and King's South African Medals and the General Service and Victory Medals.
"He joined the great white company of valiant souls."
35, Wood Street, Hulme, Manchester.   Z6265

GLEAVE, G., Cpl., A/Sergt., 1st Manchester Regt.

When war broke out he was already serving, and was sent to France in September 1914. There he fought in the Battles of La Bassée and Ypres, and was then invalided to England suffering from trench feet and illness. In August 1915 he was drafted to Gallipoli, where he played a conspicuous part in the Suvla Bay Landing, and in the other engagements of the campaign. He returned to France in July 1916, and was in action at Bullecourt, Arras, Vimy Ridge, but was wounded at Messines and sent back to England. On his recovery he was retained on home service until May 1919, when he was discharged, holding the 1914–15 Star, and the General Service and Victory Medals.
9, Fletcher Street, Hulme, Manchester.   Z6266A

GLEAVE, J., Private, Sherwood Foresters.

He volunteered in November 1915, and was drafted in the following August to the Western Front, but after serving at Ypres, Albert, Arras and the Somme, was invalided to England with trench fever in January 1917. Fourteen months later he returned to France and was severely wounded in action at Albert and sent to hospital in Blackburn. He was still receiving treatment in 1920, and holds the General Service and Victory Medals.
32, Brunt Street, Rusholme, Manchester.   Z6267

GLEAVE, J. W., Gunner, R.G.A.

Joining in May 1918, he was a month later drafted overseas, where he served for a year. Whilst on the Western Front he did excellent work as a gunner in important engagements on the Marne and at Bapaume, Havrincourt and Le Cateau and advanced into Germany with the Army of Occupation. He was demobilised in July 1919, and holds the General Service and Victory Medals.
501, Mill Street, Bradford, Manchester.   Z10248

GLEAVE, T., Private, R.A.M.C.

Volunteering in November 1914, he was after a period of training stationed at Colchester and Southport, and performed excellent work as a hospital orderly. In February 1917 he was sent to France, and served at Le Havre, Rouen, Boulogne,

Etaples and Bullecourt. He was attached to the E. Lancs. Field Ambulance, and rendered valuable services at the Field dressing stations on the Somme front. He was demobilised in June 1919, and holds the General Service and Victory Medals.
9, Fletcher Street, Hulme, Manchester.   Z6266B

GLEDHILL, G. H., Private, Labour Corps.

He joined in July 1918, and was later sent to France. There he served with his Company on the Somme front and at Cambrai, Arras, Albert and Lens, performing consistently good work whilst engaged on various duties of an important nature. He was demobilised in March 1919, and holds the General Service and Victory Medals.
44, Elizabeth Ann Street, Manchester.   Z9540

GLENNON, P., Private, Manchester Regiment.

He volunteered in May 1915, and seven months later proceeded overseas. Whilst serving in the Western theatre of war he was wounded in the Battle of the Somme in 1916, and sent to the Base hospital. On his recovery he saw heavy fighting at Ypres, in the 1918 Retreat and also in the final decisive engagements of the war. He was again wounded in September 1918, and was demobilised in May 1919, holding the 1914–15 Star, and the General Service and Victory Medals.
20, Wainwright Street, Ancoats, Manchester.   Z10249

GLENNON, T., Pte., 1st South Lancashire Regt.

He volunteered for active service in April 1915, and on completion of his training four months later proceeded to the Western Front, where he was engaged in heavy fighting in several engagements. After only six months' service in France, he was unhappily killed in action at Loos in February 1916. He was entitled to the 1914–15 Star, and the General Service and Victory Medals.
"His life for his Country, his soul to God."
37, Hancock Street, Rusholme, Manchester.   Z6269

GLEW, W., Corporal, 20th Manchester Regiment.

Volunteering in November 1914, he was drafted overseas thirteen months later. During his service on the Western Front he was in action in various engagements, including that at St. Eloi, but fell fighting at Albert on May 8th, 1916. He was entitled to the General Service and Victory Medals.
Nobly striving,
"He nobly died that we might live."
22, Coach Terrace, Longsight, Manchester.   TZ6270

GLOAG, J., Private, 1st Loyal N. Lancashire Regt.

In May 1918 he joined, but on completion of his training at the Curragh, was unsuccessful in obtaining a transfer overseas. He was, however, engaged on important guard duties on the Irish Coast until demobilised in March 1919. He later rejoined for a further period of two years and was sent to Malta, where he was employed on garrison work at St. Andrew's Barracks.
24, Edensor Street, Beswick, Manchester.   Z10250

GLOAG, L., Private, 10th Manchester Regiment.

He volunteered in January 1916, and later in the same year was ordered to the Western Front. There he was in action in the Albert, Somme, Ancre, Bullecourt, Siegfried, Passchendaele, Lens, Armentières and Cambrai sectors, but was unfortunately killed in action in October 1917. He was entitled to the General Service and Victory Medals.
"A costly sacrifice upon the altar of freedom."
Buckley Street, St. Michaels, Manchester.   Z10597

GLOVER, J. S., Pte., 20th Manchester Regiment.

He volunteered in November 1914, and after a period of training was twelve months later drafted to the Western Front. In July 1916 whilst engaged on duties in the cookhouse at Trones Wood, he was wounded, as a result of a shell exploding, and whilst fighting in the Battle of the Somme was again wounded. On his recovery he was transferred to Italy, where he served until demobilised in February 1919. He holds the 1914–15 Star, and the General Service and Victory Medals.
75, Percival Street, Chorlton-on-Medlock, Manchester. TZ6272

GLOVER, W. J., Private, 6th Manchester Regt.

In August 1914, he volunteered, but being unable to procure a transfer overseas, was retained on home service throughout the period of hostilities. He served at Morecambe, and also at important stations in Ireland, and was engaged on responsible garrison duties until he was demobilised in February 1919. 44, Lancaster Street, Hulme, Manchester.   Z6271

GLYNN, J. A., Private, 1/9th Manchester Regt.

He volunteered in November 1914, and in the following June embarked for Gallipoli, where after taking part in the Landing at Suvla Bay, he fought in many engagements of note. After the Evacuation of the Peninsula he proceeded to France, and was in action in the Battles of the Somme, Arras, Ypres, Passchendaele and throughout the Offensives of 1918. He was demobilised in May 1919, and holds the 1914–15 Star, and the General Service and Victory Medals.
220, Victoria Square, Oldham Road, Manchester.   TZ9141

GLYNN, J., Private, 2nd Manchester Regiment.
Joining in August 1916, he was on account of ill-health unfit for active service. He served at Colchester, Bury St. Edmunds and Lowestoft, and performed his duties at these stations with great ability. He was discharged from the Army in May 1917 as medically unfit for further military service.
1, Virginia Street, Rochdale Road, Manchester. Z10287B

GODDARD, J.(M.M.) Sergt., 13th King's (L'pool Rgt.)
Volunteering in August 1914, he was drafted to France in the following May and fought in the Battles of Loos, Arras, Ypres and Lens. He was awarded the Military Medal for conspicuous gallantry in rescuing wounded under fire at Ypres. He was in action in many engagements during the Retreat and Advance of 1918, and returning home after the Armistice was demobilised in January 1919. In addition to the Military Medal, he holds the 1914–15 Star, and the General Service and Victory Medals.
13, Jackson Street, Miles Platting, Manchester. Z9142

GODDARD, J., Rifleman, 21st Rifle Brigade.
He volunteered in August 1914, and in the following May was drafted to Mesopotamia. There he was in action at Kut-el-Amara and Baghdad, after which he was sent to Palestine. In this theatre of war he took part in strenuous fighting at Magdhaba, Rafa, Gaza and near Jerusalem, and was present at the capture of that city as well as of Jericho, Tripoli and Aleppo. Demobilised on returning home in May 1919, he holds the 1914–15 Star, and the General Service and Victory Medals.
70, Irlam Street, Miles Platting, Manchester. Z9541

GODDARD, W. L., Rifleman, K.R.R.C.
He enlisted in the Army in 1913, and accordingly, when war broke out, immediately proceeded to France, where he took part in fierce fighting at Mons, the Marne, the Aisne, Ypres, St. Eloi, the Somme, Bullecourt, Hermies, Mailly, Serre, Arras and Trones Wood. He was wounded in action on three occasions, and in consequence was invalided out of the Army in December 1917. He holds the Mons Star, and the General Service and Victory Medals.
56, Dorset Street, Hulme, Manchester. Z6273

GODFREY, F., Corporal, R.A.O.C.
He volunteered in December 1916, and served in his Corps at a depôt in England. He rendered valuable services, but, owing to medical unfitness, was not successful in obtaining his transfer overseas before the cessation of hostilities, and after doing good work, was finally demobilised in December 1919. 16, Ivy Grove, Hulme, Manchester. Z6276

GODFREY, L., Private, 1/8th Manchester Regt.
When war was declared in August 1914, he was already serving, and was immediately ordered to Egypt, where he took part in engagements on the Suez Canal, and at Katia. In February 1917 he was transferred to the Western Front, but after fighting in the Ypres sector, returned to Preston, whence he was discharged as a time-expired man in April 1918. He holds the 1914–15 Star, and the General Service and Victory Medals.
41, Neill Street, Gorton, Manchester. Z10251

GODFREY, T. A., Private, 17th Manchester Regt.
He volunteered in June 1915, and after training, proceeded to France, in the following February. He saw heavy fighting in the Somme Offensive, on the Ancre front, at Arras and at Passchendaele Ridge. He was then, in November 1917, transferred to Italy, where he fought on the Piave and the Asiago Plateaux. He was afterwards attacked with illness, and being sent to England, underwent treatment at various hospitals until his final discharge in September 1919. He holds the General Service and Victory Medals. Z6274–5
16, Holt Street, Morton Street, Longsight, Manchester.

GODWIN, G., Private, 6th Manchester Regiment.
Volunteering in June 1915, he underwent training at Southport and was later sent to Egypt, where he served for some time before being transferred to France. There he took part in several important engagements, including those at Givenchy, La Bassée, and on the Somme front, and being wounded in March 1918, was invalided home and admitted to hospital in Liverpool. He was eventually demobilised in February 1919, and holds the General Service and Victory Medals.
4, Whitley Street, Rochdale Road, Manchester. Z9542

GODWIN, T. E., Gunner, R.H.A.
He volunteered on the outbreak of war, and was sent to France early in November 1914, in time to take part in the desperate Battle of Ypres (I). He afterwards fought in almost all the important engagements of the war, including Neuve Chapelle, Loos, Somme (I), Arras and Messines Ridge. Later he was in action at Cambrai, also at Bapaume in the Retreat on the Somme, and at Le Cateau in the subsequent Advance. After the Armistice he joined the Army of Occupation on the Rhine, and was finally demobilised in April 1919. He holds the 1914 Star, and the General Service and Victory Medals.
15, Broom Street, Ardwick, Manchester. Z6277

GOLDWICK, H., Private, 7th Manchester Regiment.
He volunteered in January 1915, and on completion of his training was sent to Egypt, where he took part in the engagements on the Suez Canal and at Katia. Later he was transferred to the Western Front, and served at La Bassée, Loos and Arras, but in May 1918 he was taken prisoner at the Battle of Aisne (III). After the cessation of hostilities he was released and demobilised in December 1918. He rejoined in June 1919, and served for a further period of twelve months, and was finally discharged in January 1920, holding the 1914–15 Star, and the General Service and Victory Medals.
110, Victoria Square, Oldham Road, Manchester. Z11899

GOLTON, F. E., Sapper, R.E. (Signal Section).
He joined in May 1917, and in the following January was drafted to France, where he took part in several engagements during the Retreat and Advance, including the Somme (II), the Aisne (III), Bapaume, Cambrai (II), and Le Cateau (II), and was wounded in action in March 1918. After hostilities ceased he went into Germany with the Army of Occupation, and served there until his demobilisation in March 1920. He holds the General Service and Victory Medals.
11, Rumford Street, Hulme, Manchester. TZ11709A

GOLTON, I. H., Private, 1/7th Manchester Regt.
He was mobilised in August 1914, and in the following month drafted to Egypt, where he was stationed at Khartoum and took part in several small engagements on the Nile. Later he was sent to the Dardanelles and saw much severe fighting at the Landing at Gallipoli. He was invalided home in December 1915, and discharged time-expired, but on his recovery, rejoined and was again sent to Egypt. Proceeding to France, he was unfortunately killed in action at Havrincourt Wood in May 1917. He was entitled to the 1914–15 Star, and the General Service and Victory Medals.
"A costly sacrifice upon the altar of freedom."
11, Rumford Street, Hulme, Manchester. TZ11709B

GOLTON, J. H., Private, 7th Manchester Regiment.
Volunteering at the outbreak of hostilities, he proceeded to Egypt in the following September, and after being stationed at Khartoum and Alexandria, was sent to Gallipoli, where he took part in the famous Landing, and in many subsequent engagements. After the Evacuation he was transferred to France, and saw fighting in the Somme Offensive of 1916, and at Arras in 1917. Here he was badly wounded and on May 25th, succumbed to his wounds. He was entitled to the 1914–15 Star, and the General Service and Victory Medals.
"His name liveth for evermore."
3, Botham Street, Moss Side, Manchester. Z6280

GOMERSHALL, H., Pte, 14th Worcestershire Regt.
He joined in August 1917, and after training proceeded to France in the following April, and did service near Lille, Lens and St. Quentin. Later he took part in the great Advance to the Rhine, at the end of which, in December 1918, he was unfortunately attacked with pneumonia, and being invalided home remained under treatment in hospital until his discharge in February 1919. He holds the General Service and Victory Medals. 64, Rutland Street, Hulme, Manchester. TZ6281

GOODFELLOW, R. A. (M.M.) 1st King's (Liverpool Regiment).
He volunteered in February 1915, and was sent to France in the following June. He fought in the heavy battles of Loos, Somme (I), Arras and Cambrai, and also took part in the great Advance of 1918, during which at Ayette, on July 29th, 1918, he won the Military Medal for bravery in connection with a raid on the enemy's outposts. After the Armistice he served in the Army of Occupation on the Rhine, and was finally demobilised in March 1919, and holds in addition to the Military Medal, the 1914–15 Star, and the General Service and Victory Medals.
5, Goldschmidt St., Chorlton-on-Medlock, Manchester. Z6282

GOODFELLOW, W., Private, 8th Manchester Regt.
He volunteered in November 1915, and after a period of training and service in England was drafted to France in December 1916. He served in the trenches near Arras for six weeks, and being then transferred to the Light Railway Section, continued in the same region driving the engine on the railway, which brought ammunition and supplies up to the fighting line and the wounded back from it. While engaged in this duty he was killed by a shell in June 1918, thus giving his life for his Country. He was entitled to the General Service and Victory Medals. Z6282B
"He joined the great white company of valiant souls."
5, Goldschmidt Street, Chorlton-on-Medlock, Manchester.

GOODLIFFE, W., Private, 9th Welch Regiment.
He volunteered in May 1915, and after a short period of training proceeded to France in the following November. He fought in the Ypres sector, and afterwards took part in the great Somme Offensive. During this, in July 1916, at Contalmaison, he was severely wounded and reported missing, and afterwards officially presumed killed, thus giving his life for the great cause. He was entitled to the 1914–15 Star, and the General Service and Victory Medals.
15, Durham Place, Hulme, Manchester. Z6283

GOODMAN, H., Pte., 1st King's (Liverpool Regt.)
He volunteered in January 1915, and after training was
drafted to the Western Front in the following December.
He took part in actions at Loos, in the Ypres sector, on the
Somme and at Givenchy, where he was wounded and invalided
to hospital in England. On recovery he returned to France
and was again wounded at Guillemont, but after treatment
at a Base hospital, rejoined and fought in the great Advance
of 1918, in which he was again wounded at Cambrai. He
was later discharged from hospital in December 1918, and
holds the 1914-15 Star, and the General Service and Victory
Medals.
15, Kensington Street, Moss Side, Manchester.   Z6284

GOODMAN, M., Sapper, R.E.
He volunteered in August 1914, and after training was sent
in April of the following year to Gallipoli, where he took part
in the famous Landing, and in the three Krithia Battles which
succeeded it, also in the attack on Chunuk Bair and the Suvla
Bay action. After this he proceeded to Cairo in Egypt, and was
invalided home from there suffering from dysentery, but on
recovery was drafted to France in February 1917, and was
in action at Arras, Passchendaele and Cambrai, also in the
Retreat and Advance of 1918, at Bapaume and Epéhy. He
was finally demobilised in March 1919, and holds the 1914-15
Star, and the General Service and Victory Medals.
31, Devonshire Street, Hulme, Manchester.   TZ6285

GOODWIN, G. W., Driver, R.A.S.C. (M.T.)
He volunteered in November 1914, and was quickly drafted
to France. There he took an active part with the Mechanical
Transport in engagements at La Bassée, Ypres, Neuve Chapelle,
Ypres (II), Festubert, Loos, Albert, Vermelles, Ploegsteert,
Vimy Ridge, the Somme, Beaucourt and Arras, and was
wounded in action at Passchendaele. As a result he was
invalided to hospital at Calais, but on his recovery rejoined
his unit and was again in action at Bapaume and Cambrai
(II), during the Retreat and Advance of 1918. He was demobilised in April 1919, and holds the 1914-15 Star, and the
General Service and Victory Medals.
28, Platt Street, Moss Side, Manchester.   Z11708

GOODWIN, J., Private, M.G.C.
He volunteered in May 1915, and five months later was drafted
to the Dardanelles. Wounded in severe fighting during the
Evacuation, he was invalided home, and after spending some
time in hospital at Bournemouth, was sent to the Western
Front. He took part in the Battle of Arras, was again wounded in June 1917, and as a result was evacuated to England,
being subsequently discharged in October 1918 as unfit for
further service. He holds the 1914-15 Star, and the General
Service and Victory Medals.
70, Gibbon Street, Bradford Manchester.   Z9543

GOODWIN, J., Private, Manchester Regiment.
He volunteered in September 1914, and was sent for training
to a Northern centre until the following December, when he
was discharged, in order to take up work of National importance. This he carried out as a coal getter in a Yorkshire
Colliery until the end of the war.
102, Prince Street, Ardwick, Manchester.   Z6286

GOODWIN, T., L/Cpl., 10th Lancashire Fusiliers.
He volunteered in August 1914, and after training, proceeded
to France in the following July. He did good service in
the Machine-gun section of his Battalion at Ypres, and Loos,
and being severely wounded at Hooge in November 1915,
was transferred to the Hospital Ship "Anglia," which was
sunk by an enemy mine, and he was drowned, thus giving his
life for his Country. He was entitled to the 1914-15 Star,
and the General Service and Victory Medals.
"A costly sacrifice upon the altar of freedom."
12, Sefton Street, Longsight, Manchester.   Z6287

GOODWIN, T., Private, 3rd Manchester Regiment.
A Reservist, mobilised at the outbreak of hostilities, he proceeded to France, and was in action in the Battles of Ypres
and Hill 60, where he was severely wounded. On his recovery
he embarked for Gallipoli, and was engaged in heavy fighting
there until the Evacuation of the Peninsula. He then returned
to France and fought in many parts of the line, and was buried
by the explosion of a shell. Returning home he received
hospital treatment, and served at various stations until
discharged in June 1919. He holds the 1914-15 Star, and the
General Service and Victory Medals.
1, Ravenglass Street, Miles Platting, Manchester.   Z9143

GOODWIN, W., Private, 7th Gordon Highlanders.
He volunteered in January 1915, and in the following May was
drafted to the Western Front. In this theatre of war he played
a prominent part in the Battles of Hill 60, Ypres, Loos, Vimy
Ridge, the Somme, and Cambrai, and was severely wounded
in March 1918, having his right foot blown off by a shell.
Invalided home, he was eventually discharged in May 1919,
and holds the 1914-15 Star, and the General Service and
Victory Medals.
6, Walter Street, Hulme, Manchester.   TZ6288

GORDON, C. H., Private, King's (Liverpool Regt.)
He joined in July 1916, but was medically unfit for service
overseas. Retained on home service, he was engaged with
his unit on duties of an important nature at Prescot, Pembroke
Dock, Cardiff, and other places, and performed consistently
good work until he was demobilised in April 1919.
6, Clayburn Street, Hulme, Manchester.   Z6289

GORDON, J., L/Cpl. (Blacksmith), R.A.S.C. (M.T.)
Volunteering in November 1915, he proceeded early in the
following year to France. There he served at Albert, Ploegsteert Wood, Beaucourt, Arras, Ypres, Cambrai and the Somme
and did excellent work whilst employed as a blacksmith. He
remained overseas for some time after the termination of
hostilities, and was demobilised in September 1919, holding
the General Service and Victory Medals.
47, Redvers Street, Ardwick, Manchester.   Z6290

GORDON, W., Private, 4th Manchester Regiment.
He volunteered in August 1914, and on completion of his
training proceeded to France. There he took part in many
important engagements in various sectors of the Front,
notably in the Battles of the Somme, Arras, Ypres, and Cambrai, where he was wounded in action in November 1917.
On his recovery he returned to France and served until the
cessation of hostilities. He was discharged in March 1919,
and holds the General Service and Victory Medals.
6, St, Clements Place, Ancoats, Manchester.   Z11900

GORDON, W. J., Rifleman, 7th Rifle Brigade
He volunteered in August 1914, and in the following year was
sent to France. During his service in this theatre of war he
saw much heavy fighting, and was in action at the Battles of
Ypres, Loos, Vimy Ridge, Somme (I), Arras and Messines.
He remained in this seat of war until after the cessation of
hostilities, and was demobilised in February 1919, holding
the 1914-15 Star, and the General Service and Victory Medals.
42, Brown Street, Ancoats, Manchester.   Z11901

GORE, E., Gunner, R.G.A.
He volunteered in November 1915, and was retained on important duties at home until June 1917, when he was sent to
the Western Front. During his service there he was in action
at Arras and Nieuport, and was wounded at Ypres. On
rejoining his Battery he saw severe fighting in the Retreat and
Advance of 1918, and after the cessation of hostilities entered
Germany with the Army of Occupation. He was demobilised
in September 1919, and holds the General Service and Victory
Medals.
31, Abel Street, Collyhurst, Manchester.   Z10252

GORMAN, H., Sergt., Lancashire Fusiliers.
He volunteered in May 1915, and towards the end of the same
year was drafted to France. During his service in this theatre
of war, he played a conspicuous part in strenuous fighting at
Loos, Neuve Chapelle, Ypres, the Somme and Passchendaele
Ridge, and was five times wounded. After the Armistice
he proceeded into Germany with the Army of Occupation
and served on the Rhine until April 1919, when he returned
home and was demobilised. He holds the 1914-15 Star,
and the General Service and Victory Medals.
54, Gresham Street, Openshaw, Manchester.   Z6291

GORMAN, J., Rifleman, K.R.R.C.
He volunteered in October 1914, and in the same year proceeded
to France. During his service on the Western Front he was
in action at La Bassée, Ypres, Neuve Chapelle, Hill 60, St.
Eloi, Festubert, the Somme, Albert, Arras, Vimy Ridge, Lens,
Loos, Cambrai, Armentières, Bourlon Wood, St. Quentin,
Avion, Mericourt, and Epéhy, and was gassed at Loos in
1915. He was demobilised in 1919 and holds the 1914 Star,
and the General Service and Victory Medals.
86, Kemp Street, Manchester.   Z10253

GORMLEY, T. B., Corporal, Border Regiment.
Volunteering in November 1914, he proceeded in the following
April to Gallipoli. There he took part in heavy fighting
during the Landing and Evacuation, after which he served
for some time at Lemnos. Later, transferred to the Western
Front, he was in action at Albert, Ploegsteert Wood, the Somme
and Arras, was wounded at Messines and was invalided home.
Upon his recovery he returned to France, was again in action
on the Marne, and at Amiens, and was wounded for the second
time. Evacuated to England he spent some time in hospital
and was eventually demobilised in January 1919, holding the
1914-15 Star, and the General Service and Victory Medals.
32, Hancock Street, Rusholme, Manchester.   Z6292

GORNALL, J., Pte., K.O. (R. Lancaster Regt.)
He joined in September 1918, and completing his training
served at various stations in the united Kingdom with his
unit. Engaged on important duties he rendered valuable
services, but was not successful in obtaining his transfer overseas prior to the cessation of hostilities. He was demobilised
in November 1919.
14, Charlton Street, Collyhurst, Manchester.   Z9144

GORST, J., Private, Border Regiment.
Mobilised at the commencement of hostilities he was drafted to France and fought in the Retreat from Mons, the Battles of the Marne, Givenchy and Festubert. He was unfortunately killed in action in July 1916, during the first Battle of the Somme. He was entitled to the Mons Star, and the General Service and Victory Medals.
"A valiant Soldier, with undaunted heart he breasted life's last hill."
105, Cobden Street, Ancoats, Manchester. Z9145

GOSLING, C., Pte., Manchester Regt. and Spr., R.E.
He volunteered in September 1914, and served at Crowborough until March 1916, when he was sent to France. In this theatre of war, he took part in several important engagements, including the Battles of the Somme, Arras and Ypres, where he was wounded. Upon his recovery, he was transferred to the Royal Engineers, and whilst serving at Cambrai, and in other sectors, did good work in erecting bridges. He was demobilised in January 1919, and, holds the General Service and Victory Medals.
78, Queen Street, Bradford, Manchester. Z6294

GOSLING, J., Corporal, East Lancashire Regiment.
He volunteered in June 1915, and served with the Red Cross Society and later with the East Lancashire Regiment. He rendered most valuable services in conveying the wounded to the various hospitals, and also performed excellent work as a hospital orderly. He was not successful in procuring a transfer to the fighting areas, and was eventually demobilised in April 1920.
17, Great Jones Street, West Gorton, Manchester. Z10254

GOSLING, L., Driver, R.A.S.C. (M.T.)
He joined in July 1918, and three months later was drafted to the Western Front. During his service overseas, he was stationed at Passchendaele, and in other places, and performed consistently good work whilst employed as a motor driver. Returning home in May 1919, he was then demobilised and holds the General Service and Victory Medals.
32, Boden Street, Ardwick, Manchester. Z6293

GOTT, J., Sapper, R.E.
Volunteering in April 1915, he was sent in the following July to France. There he served through severe fighting at Loos, Albert, and Vimy Ridge, and rendered excellent services until he was wounded on the Somme and invalided home. After spending some time in hospital at Boscombe, he was discharged in September 1916, as unfit for further service, and holds the 1914-15 Star, and the General Service and Victory Medals.
23, Link Street, Longsight, Manchester. Z6295A

GOTT, R. E., Corporal, 1/8th Manchester Regiment.
He volunteered in April 1915, and after a period of training proceeded later in the same year to the Western Front. In this theatre of war he played a prominent part in many important engagements in various sectors in France and Belgium, and did excellent work. He was demobilised in February 1919, and holds the 1914-15 Star, and the General Service and Victory Medals.
23, Link Street, Longsight, Manchester. Z6295B

GOUGH, J., 1st Air Mechanic, R.A.F.
He volunteered in December 1915, and after a period of training, was engaged at various stations on duties which demanded a high degree of technical skill. He was unable to obtain a transfer overseas, but rendered valuable services with his Squadron until his demobilisation in May 1919.
6, Jones Street, Chorlton-on-Medlock, Manchester. Z11710

GOUGH, T., Sergt., R.F.A.
Volunteering in May 1915, he was shortly afterwards sent to France. There he took a conspicuous part with his Battery in actions on the Somme front, and at Beaucourt, Arras, Ypres, Lens, Amiens, Cambrai, and Le Cateau. After the Armistice he proceeded into Germany and served with the Army of Occupation until February 1919, when he returned home and was demobilised. He holds the 1914-15 Star, and the General Service and Victory Medals. Z6296
24, Humphrey Street, Chorlton-on-Medlock, Manchester.

GOUGH, W., Private, Manchester Regiment.
He volunteered in March 1915, and towards the end of the same year proceeded to France, where he participated in several severe engagements, and did good work until he was invalided home on account of ill-health. After spending some time in hospital in Dublin, he was drafted to Salonika, and later contracting malaria was admitted to hospital. Evacuated to England, he remained in hospital in Pendleton until he was invalided out of the Service in February 1918, holding the 1914-15 Star, and the General Service and Victory Medals.
130, Lowe Street, Miles Platting, Manchester. Z6220

GOUGH, W., Driver, R.A.S.C.
He volunteered in April 1915, and after his training was engaged at various stations on important duties for some time. In 1917, however, he was drafted to Salonika, and served at the supply depôts until hostilities ceased, when he went to Constantinople on transport work. He returned home and was demobilised in December 1919, holding the General Service and Victory Medals.
6, Rowland Street, Moston, Manchester. Z11711

GOUGH, W., Private, 6th Cheshire Regiment.
Volunteering in 1914, he was drafted a year later to the Western Front, and was in action during the Battle of the Somme, and at Ploegsteert Wood, Albert and Ypres, where he was wounded. He was later wounded for the second time on the Somme front, and evacuated to England, and was admitted to hospital in London, being eventually invalided out of the Army in 1917, holding the 1914-15 Star, and the General Service and Victory Medals. 81, Morston Street, Longsight, Manchester. Z6297

GOULDBOURN, R., Private, Lancashire Fusiliers, and Pioneer, R.E.
He volunteered in March 1915, but was found to be medically unfit for transfer overseas, and retained at home, was engaged for some time on garrison duties at Prees Heath. Subsequently serving with the Royal Engineers, he rendered valuable services employed on sound locating work in connection with enemy air raids until he was discharged in January 1917, on account of ill-health. 10, Herbert St., Ardwick, Manchester. Z6298

GOULDEN, E., Private, 10th Dublin Fusiliers.
He joined in May 1916, and in the following August was drafted overseas. Whilst on the Western Front he took part in fierce fighting at Beaumont-Hamel, Beaucourt (during which engagement he was wounded), Arras, Vimy Ridge and Bullecourt. He was again wounded at Cambrai in September 1918, and invalided to England, and subsequently demobilised a year later, holding the General Service and Victory Medals.
7, Rigel Street, Ancoats, Manchester. Z10255

GOULDEN, F., Private, 21st Manchester Regiment.
He joined in April 1917, and embarked for France in the following August. He was engaged in heavy fighting in many parts of the line, and took part in several important engagements. He was killed in action on October 27th, 1917 at Passchendaele, and was entitled to the General Service and Victory Medals.
"And doubtless he went in splendid company."
53, Stonehewer Road, Rochdale Road, Manchester. Z9146

GOULDEN, J., Driver, R.F.A.
Volunteering in January 1915, he proceeded in the following July to France. There he was in action with his Battery at Loos, Neuve Chapelle, Hill 60, Ypres, Armentières, the Somme, Arras, Cambrai, Dickebusch and Bapaume, and was gassed on three occasions. He rendered excellent service whilst overseas, and was demobilised on his return home in April 1919, holding the 1914-15 Star, and the General Service and Victory Medals.
74, Walker Street, Oldham Road, Manchester. TZ9544

GOULDING, H., Private, 8th Manchester Regiment.
Mobilised with the Territorial Force in August 1914, he was sent two months later to Egypt. There he was wounded whilst taking part in heavy fighting at Mersa Matruh, and invalided home, was sent to hospital at Leicester. Upon his recovery, he returned to Egypt, and served at Alexandria until February 1917, when he was transferred to France. In this theatre of war, he was in action at Arras, Bullecourt, Ypres, Cambrai, Havrincourt, Bapaume and Le Cateau. After the Armistice he served in Belgium until June 1919, when he was demobilised, holding the 1914-15 Star, and the General Service and Victory Medals. 45, Hyde Street, Hulme, Manchester. TZ6299

GOULSON, F., Private, Loyal North Lancs. Regt.
He volunteered in November 1914, and later proceeding to France, was in action at Neuve Chapelle, St. Eloi, Ypres, Festubert and Loos. He did very good work until he was admitted to hospital suffering from gas poisoning and shell-shock, and on being evacuated to England, spent some time in hospital at Leicester and Holyhead. He was eventually invalided out of the Service in October 1916, and holds the 1914-15 Star, and the General Service and Victory Medals.
22, Geoffrey Street, Chorlton-on-Medlock, Manchester. Z6300-1

GOWER, V., Private, Royal Welch Fusiliers.
Mobilised in August 1914, he was sent in the following month to France, where he took part in the Battles of the Aisne, Ypres (I), Neuve Chapelle, Hill 60, Vimy Ridge, Arras and the Somme, and was wounded at Ypres (III). Invalided home, he was sent to hospital at Frodsham, and later transferred to the King's Shropshire Light Infantry, proceeded to Palestine, and participated in severe fighting near Jerusalem prior to the capture of that city. In 1918 he returned to France, and saw further fighting, but was eventually killed in action at St. Venant in the Merville sector. He was entitled to the 1914 Star, and the General Service and Victory Medals.
"His life for his Country."
228, Morton Street, Longsight, Manchester. Z6302

GRABURN, W., Leading Seaman, R.N., H.M. Submarine, "K 15."
He was serving in the Royal Navy at the outbreak of war in August 1914, and was posted to H.M.S. "Malaya." He participated in the Battles of the Falkland Islands and Jutland, and also in heavy fighting off Zeebrugge. He was subsequently employed on convoy and other duties, and transferred to H.M. Submarine K15, was serving at Rosyth in 1920. He holds the 1914-15 Star, and the General Service and Victory Medals.
15, Stafford Street, Hulme, Manchester. TZ6303

GRACE, B., Private, 6th Manchester Regiment.
Volunteering in July 1915, he proceeded in January 1916 to Egypt, where he was attached to the 42nd Division, and served at Kantara and El Arish. A year later he was transferred to the Western Front, and was in action at Ypres, Cambrai and Havrincourt. He also took part in the final Allied Advance prior to the close of hostilities. Demobilised in March 1919, he holds the General Service and Victory Medals.
22, Howarth Street, Chorlton-on-Medlock, Manchester. Z10256

GRACE, J., Private, Loyal North Lancashire Regt.
He joined the Army in November 1916, and seven months later was sent overseas. He served on the Western Front for nearly two years, and during that time was in action in important engagements at Ypres, Lens, Cambrai, Havrincourt, the Marne and the Aisne, and was wounded at Bapaume in August 1918. He remained in France until demobilised in January 1919, and holds the General Service and Victory Medals.
23, Tubal Street, Ancoats, Manchester. Z10599

GRACE, J., Private, 23rd Manchester Regiment.
Volunteering at the outbreak of hostilities, he proceeded to the Western Front in December 1915, and fought in the Battles of the Somme, Albert, St. Eloi, Arras, Ypres and Cambrai. He also was engaged in heavy fighting throughout the German and Allied Offensives of 1918. He was demobilised in February 1919, and holds the 1914-15 Star, and the General Service and Victory Medals.
23, Tubal Street, Ancoats, Manchester. Z9147

GRADY, R., Private, Loyal N. Lancashire Regt.
He volunteered in October 1914, and landed in France in the following August. He was in action in the Battles of Loos, Albert, the Somme and Arras, and was severely wounded at the third Battle of Ypres in July 1917. Returning home, he received hospital treatment, and finally was invalided out of the Service in December 1917. He holds the 1914-15 Star, and the General Service and Victory Medals.
93, Dale Street, Miles Platting, Manchester. TZ9358B

GRAHAM, A., Private, 8th Manchester Regiment.
He joined in October 1916, and was afterwards sent to the Western Front. In this theatre of hostilities he was attached to a Trench Mortar Battery, and took part in heavy fighting at Vimy, Messines and Passchendaele Ridges, was wounded at the latter place, and later gassed at Cambrai. After the Armistice, he was employed escorting prisoners, and was demobilised in March 1919, holding the General Service and Victory Medals.
17, Whatmough Street, Newton, Manchester. Z9545

GRAHAM, J. E., Corporal, Royal Irish Fusiliers.
Volunteering in August 1914, he crossed to France in the next month, and fought in the Battles of La Bassée, Ypres (I), Neuve Chapelle, Hill 60, Ypres (II), Loos, Albert, Vimy Ridge, and the Somme, where he was wounded. Invalided first to a hospital at Boulogne, and then to the Military Hospital, Guildford, he underwent treatment, and in December 1916, was discharged as medically unfit for further service. He holds the 1914 Star, and the General Service and Victory Medals.
13, Edlin Street, Morton Street, Longsight, Manchester. Z6304

GRAHAM, J. H., Private, 1st Lancashire Fusiliers.
He volunteered in August 1914, and embarking for the Dardanelles in the following April took part in the first Landing at Gallipoli, in which he was severely wounded. He was invalided to England, and on recovery was transferred to France in August 1916, and fought in the Somme Offensive, and at Arras, but was unfortunately killed in action at Monchyle-Prieux on May 29th, 1917. He was entitled to the 1914-15 Star, and the General Service and Victory Medals.
"A costly sacrifice upon the altar of freedom."
44, Hewitt Street, Openshaw, Manchester. Z6307

GRAHAM, J. P., Private, 2nd Manchester Regt.
Mobilised at the commencement of hostilities he proceeded to the Western Front, and fought in the Retreat from Mons, and the Battles of Ypres, and Hill 60. He was also in action on the Somme, at Arras, Cambrai, and throughout the German and Allied Offensives of 1918, and was wounded. He was demobilised in April 1919, and holds the 1914-15 Star, and the General Service and Victory Medals.
46, Somerset Place, Oldham Road, Manchester. Z9149

GRAHAM, J. W., Driver, R.A.S.C.
He was in the Army at the outbreak of war, having enlisted in 1905, and crossing to France in February 1915, fought at Neuve Chapelle, Ypres and Arras. Whilst in action on the Somme in 1916 he contracted a severe illness, and evacuated to England underwent eight months treatment at the Netley Red Cross Hospital. On recovery he was engaged on important duties with his unit until demobilised in January 1919. He holds the 1914-15 Star, and the General Service and Victory Medals.
7, Leamington Street, Chorlton-on-Medlock, Manchester. Z6306

GRAHAM, R., Private, 12th Lancashire Fusiliers.
Volunteering in September 1914, in the following August he embarked for France, and was in action in the Battle of Loos.

Transferred to Salonika in November 1915 he fought in many engagements on the Struma, Vardar and Doiran fronts, and contracting fever returned to England for treatment. On his recovery he again proceeded to the Western Front, and served throughout the Retreat and Advance of 1918. He was demobilised in January 1919, and holds the 1914-15 Star, and the General Service and Victory Medals.
53, Wardle Street, Holland Street, Newton, Manchester. Z9150

GRAHAM, W. V., Private, 13th East Lancs. Regt.
Joining in October 1917, he crossed to France in the following March and fought in the second Battle of the Somme. After taking part in many engagements in the Retreat of 1918, he fell fighting at Nieppe Wood in August of that year, during the subsequent Allied Advance. He was entitled to the General Service and Victory Medals.
"The path of duty was the way to glory."
46, New Bank Street, Ardwick, Manchester. Z6305

GRAINGER, G., Private, Royal Fusiliers.
He joined in January 1917, and in the following November proceeded to the Western Front, where he was in action in many parts of the line. He fought at Ypres, on the Somme, and at Givenchy, but owing to ill-health was invalided home. After receiving hospital treatment he was discharged as unfit for further service in February 1919, and holds the General Service and Victory Medals.
68, Clarence Street, Miles Platting, Manchester. Z9151

GRANGER, E. S., Private, 8th Manchester Regt.
Volunteering in August 1914, he embarked for Egypt in September of that year, and served on that front in operations in the Canal zone, and later in the Advance through Palestine. During the Advance on Jerusalem in December 1917, he was so severely wounded, as to necessitate his return to England, and after six months' hospital treatment, was demobilised in March 1919. He holds the 1914-15 Star, and the General Service and Victory Medals.
32, Rose Street, Greenheys, Manchester. Z6308

GRANT, J., Private, 2nd Manchester Regiment.
He volunteered in July 1915, and later in the same year proceeded to France. There he took part in much fighting at the Battles of Albert, Vimy Ridge, the Somme, Beaumont-Hamel, Bullecourt, and Passchendaele and was wounded in action in July 1916. After hostilities ceased, he went to Germany with the Army of Occupation and served on the Rhine until his demobilisation in April 1919. He holds the 1914-15 Star, and the General Service and Victory Medals.
11, John Street, Hulme, Manchester. Z11712

GRANT, R., Driver, R.F.A.
He joined in December 1917, and after a period of training was drafted to France. There he was engaged with his Battery at Albert, Arras, Armentières, Cambrai, Bourlon Wood, Lens, Bullecourt and on the Somme front, and did excellent work. After the Armistice he proceeded to Germany with the Army of Occupation, and was still serving in Cologne in 1920 holding the General Service and Victory Medals. 20, Worth Street, Manchester. Z10600

GRANTHAM, G., Corporal, 25th Manchester Regt.
Joining in January 1917, he proceeded to France a month later, and in March of the same year was wounded and taken prisoner at Cassel. In the following December he was repatriated, owing to an exchange of prisoners, and was discharged as unfit in the same month. He holds the General Service and Victory Medals.
34, Ogilvie Street, Chorlton-on-Medlock, Manchester. X6310A

GRANTHAM, H., Pte., 19th Royal Welch Fusiliers.
Volunteering in May 1915, he shortly afterwards embarked for France, and fought in the engagements at Loos, on the Somme, Arras, Ypres and Cambrai. He was engaged in heavy fighting throughout the German Offensive and Allied Advance of 1918, and returning to England after the close of the war, was demobilised in March 1919. He holds the 1914-15 Star, and the General Service and Victory Medals. Z9152
22, George Street, Holland Street, Newton, Manchester.

GRANTHAM, J., Cpl., 2nd and 17th Manchester Regt.
He enlisted in March 1907, and after being mobilised in August 1914, proceeded to France early in 1915, and took part in the second Battle of Ypres, in which he was wounded. He was discharged at the expiration of his period of service in December of the same year, but rejoining, was again drafted to the Western Front, and in July 1916 was severely wounded in action on the Somme. Evacuated to England, he underwent protracted hospital treatment, and in November 1917 was invalided out of the Service. He holds the 1914-15 Star, and the General Service and Victory Medals.
18, Holstein Street, Ardwick, Manchester. X6309A

GRANTHAM, S., Private, 2nd Wiltshire Regiment.
Joining in January 1918, he proceeded overseas a month later, and fought in the Retreat and subsequent Allied Advance on the Western Front, and was slightly wounded in action at Bapaume, and later gassed at Cambrai. He was demobilised in November 1919, and holds the General Service and Victory Medals.
34, Ogilvie Street, Chorlton-on-Medlock, Manchester. X6310

GRANTHAM, J., L/Cpl., 2nd K.O. (R. Lancaster Regt.)
Volunteering in August 1914, he was engaged on important home duties until 1916, Then, crossing to France, he was in action at Beaumont-Hamel. Transferred to Salonika in February 1917, he took part in the operations in many sectors of the Macedonian front, and did valuable work with his unit until December 1918, when he was invalided home suffering from malaria. He was discharged unfit in February of the succeeding year, and holds the General Service and Victory Medals. 18, Holstein Street, Ardwick, Manchester. X6309B

GRANTHAM, T., Private, 1/7th Manchester Regt.
Volunteering in August 1914, he embarked for Egypt two months later, and took part in the defence of the Suez Canal. Proceeding to the Dardanelles in the following year, he took part in the first landing at Gallipoli, and in June 1915 was wounded in the third Battle of Krithia. Transferred to France in January 1916, he was in action at Vimy Ridge, Ypres, where he was again wounded in 1917, Arras, and in the second Battle of the Marne. He was demobilised on his return to England in February 1919, and holds the 1914-15 Star, and the General Service and Victory Medals. 34, Ogilvie Street, Chorlton-on-Medlock, Manchester. X6310C

GRANTHAM, W. H., Sapper, R.E.
He volunteered in 1915, and proceeding to France in the following February was engaged on important duties in connection with operations at Vimy Ridge, Beaumont-Hamel, Arras and Passchendaele. He did valuable work until his demobilisation, which took place on his return to England in January 1919, and holds the General Service and Victory Medals. 34, Ogilvie Street, Chorlton-on-Medlock, Manchester. X6310B

GRATTON, T., Rifleman, K.R.R.C.
He volunteered in June 1915, and two months later was drafted to the Western Front. In this theatre of war he participated in the Battle of Loos, and did good work overseas until he was killed by a shell at St. Eloi in April 1916. He was entitled to the 1914-15 Star, and the General Service and Victory Medals. "Courage, bright hopes, and a myriad dreams, splendidly given." 93, Great Jackson Street, West Gorton, Manchester. Z10234

GRAY, E., Private, 22nd Northumberland Fusiliers.
Joining in June 1916, he proceeded to France in the following October, and was in action at Armentières, the Somme, Ypres and Albert. Later he was evacuated to England, owing to ill-health, and after protracted hospital treatment, was invalided out of the Service in January 1918. He holds the General Service and Victory Medals. 16, Mitton Street, Longsight, Manchester. TZ6311

GRAY, J., Pte., 3rd Oxfordshire and Buckinghamshire Light Infantry.
He joined in April 1916, and embarked for Mesopotamia in the following July. He was in action at Amara, Kut, and was present at the capture of Baghdad, and was engaged in heavy fighting during the final British Advance to Mosul. Returning home he was demobilised in April 1919, and holds the General Service and Victory Medals. 210, Victoria Square, Oldham Road, Manchester. Z9153

GRAY, L., Private, 19th Manchester Regiment.
Two months after volunteering in September 1914, he was sent to France, and there played a prominent part in many important engagements. He was in action on the Somme front, and at Arras, Ypres and Cambrai, subsequently taking part in severe fighting during the Retreat and Advance of 1918. Demobilised in February 1919, he holds the 1914-15 Star, and the General Service and Victory Medals. 62, Collyhurst Street, Collyhurst, Manchester. Z10257

GRAY, N., Private, 1st Cheshire Regiment.
Volunteering at the declaration of war he was drafted to France in September 1914, and took part in the Retreat from Mons and was wounded. He later served in the Battles of the Aisne, La Bassée, Ypres, Neuve Chapelle, and St. Eloi. Transferred to Egypt in March 1915, he served in the defence of the Suez Canal, and in other engagements until December of the same year. He then returned to the Western Front, and fought at Albert, the Somme, Arras, Ypres, and was again wounded at Cambrai in December 1917. After protracted hospital treatment in Manchester Hospital, he was discharged as medically unfit for further service in January of the succeeding year. He holds the Mons Star, and the General Service and Victory Medals. 23, Edmund Street, Openshaw, Manchester. Z6312

GRAY, R., Private, 13th Manchester Regiment.
He volunteered in August 1914, and employed at home on important duties until September 1915, when he was drafted to Salonika. During his service overseas, he took part in several important engagements on the Vardar and Doiran fronts, and was wounded in April 1917. He returned home in March 1919, and when demobilised a month later, was entitled to the 1914-15 Star, and the General Service and Victory Medals. 23, Pearson Street, Newton Heath, Manchester. Z9546

GRAY, R., Private, 8th Manchester Regiment.
He volunteered in September 1914, and after his training was engaged on duties of an important nature at various stations. Owing to ill-health, he was unable to secure his transfer to a theatre of war, but nevertheless did valuable work until February 1918, when he was invalided out of the Service. 25, Edmund Street, Openshaw, Manchester. Z6313

GRAYSON, B., Corporal, Canadian Infantry.
Volunteering in August 1914, he embarked for France in the following December, and was later in action at Neuve Chapelle, Ypres, Festubert, Ploegsteert Wood, the Somme, Arras, Vimy Ridge and Passchendaele, where he was gassed in October 1917. Invalided to the Hamilton Military Hospital, Ontario, he underwent protracted treatment, and in February 1919, was discharged as physically unfit for further service. He holds the 1914-15 Star, and the General Service and Victory Medals. 17, Meadow Street, Ardwick, Manchester. Z6314

GRAYSON, W., Private, Manchester Regiment.
He joined in December 1916, and was retained at home on important duties until March 1918, when he proceeded to France. During his service overseas, he took part in strenuous fighting at Messines Ridge, Cambrai, Le Cateau and Mons, and in various other sectors during the Advance of 1918. He returned home for demobilisation in November 1919, and holds the General Service and Victory Medals. 121, Ryder Street, Collyhurst, Manchester. Z10601

GREATOREX, J., Sapper, R.E. and Private, 7th Leicestershire Regt.
Volunteering in September 1915, he proceeded to the Western Front in the following year, and was in action at Loos, the Somme, Beaumont-Hamel, Bullecourt and Ypres. He also fought throughout the Retreat and subsequent Allied Advance, which terminated hostilities victoriously in November 1918. He was demobilised in February of the succeeding year, and holds the General Service and Victory Medals. 52B, Clayton Street, Hulme, Manchester. Z6315

GREAVES, T., Private, 3/8th Manchester Regt.
He volunteered in May 1915, and was sent for training to the depôt at Ardwick. He remained there for a few months, and did good work. He was employed on various duties until his health broke down, causing him to be discharged in August 1915, as unfit for further military service. 14, Broughton Street, Ancoats, Manchester. Z10258

GREEN, A., Private, 1st Lancashire Fusiliers.
He joined in August 1918, but was not successful in obtaining a transfer overseas owing to the termination of hostilities. After a period of training at Warrington and Aldershot, he was sent to Ireland, where he was employed with his unit on duties of an important nature, and was still serving there in 1920. 20, Iles Street, Oldham Road, Manchester. Z10259

GREEN, C., Private, 2nd Manchester Regiment.
Volunteering in June 1915, he proceeded early in the following year to the Western Front. There he at once participated in strenuous fighting, but had only served overseas for a few months when he was severely wounded at Trones Wood in July 1916. Invalided home he was subsequently discharged in September 1918, as unfit for further service, and holds the General Service and Victory Medals. 41, Bedford Street, Moss Side, Manchester. TZ9547

GREEN, C., Pte., 5th Manchester Regt. and Royal Fusiliers.
He attested in November 1915, and called up in the following August was engaged on important home duties until March 1917, when crossing to France he fought in the Battles of Cambrai, the Somme, Amiens, Bapaume and Ypres. Throughout his service he did excellent work with his unit and remained overseas until the close of hostilities. He was demobilised in January 1919, and holds the General Service and Victory Medals. 45, Crondall Street, Moss Side, Manchester. Z6327

GREEN, C., Private, 8th Lancashire Fusiliers.
Volunteering in March 1915, he embarked for the Dardanelles in the following August, and took part in the Landing at Suvla Bay, and the engagements which followed. After the Evacuation of the Peninsula, he proceeded to Mesopotamia, where he fought in operations in the attempt to relieve Kut. Transferred to France in August 1916, he fought in the Somme Offensive, during which he was unfortunately killed in action on September 26th of the same year. He was entitled to the 1914-15 Star, and the General Service and Victory Medals. 14, Stafford Street, Hulme, Manchester. TZ6321

GREEN, C. F., Private, 5th Manchester Regiment.
Joining in September 1916, he embarked for Egypt in the following January, and was engaged on important duties at Alexandria until March 1917. He was then drafted to France, and was later in action in many important engagements, including that at Cambrai, where he was gassed in December 1917. On recovery he fought in the Retreat and Allied Advance of 1918, and returned to England in February 1919. He was demobilised in the next month, and holds the General Service and Victory Medals. 41, Green Street, Gorton, Manchester. Z6316

GREEN, E., Driver, R.F.A.
Volunteering in September 1914, he was drafted early in the following year to France, where he was in action at Neuve Chapelle, Hill 60, Ypres, Festubert and Loos. He was gassed on the Somme in July 1916, and invalided home, was sent to hospital in Dublin. Upon his recovery he served in Sussex, and was engaged on important duties until January 1919, when he was demobilised, holding the 1914–15 Star, and the General Service and Victory Medals.
54, Sarah Ann Street, Beswick, Manchester.   Z10260

GREEN, F., Private, K.O. (R. Lancaster Regt.)
He volunteered in September 1914, and twelve months later proceeded to France. There he at once took part in heavy fighting at Albert, but in October 1915, was transferred to Salonika, and in this theatre of war participated in further fighting on the Doiran front and during the Serbian Retreat. He remained overseas until March 1919, when he returned home and was demobilised, holding the 1914–15 Star, and the General Service and Victory Medals.
7, Boardman Street, Harpurhey, Manchester.   Z10602

GREEN, F., Driver, R.F.A.
He volunteered in April 1915, and proceeded overseas in November of the following year. In the Western theatre of war he was in action at Ypres, Lens and Loos, also in the Retreat of 1918, and in the final decisive engagements of the war. He was wounded whilst fighting at Ypres in October 1918, and was accidentally wounded at Mons, after the close of hostilities in November 1918. Demobilised in January 1919, he holds the General Service and Victory Medals.
183, Osborne Street, Collyhurst, Manchester.   Z11420

GREEN, G., Private, 16th Manchester Regiment.
Volunteering in 1914, he proceeded later to the Western Front, where he served for a period of two years. During this time he played a prominent part with his unit in several important engagements, including Ypres and Passchendaele, and the capture of Bullecourt and Beaumont-Hamel. He was invalided home as the result of being wounded in action on the Somme, and after spending some time in hospital at Lincoln, was discharged in 1917, as unfit for further service. He holds the 1914–15 Star, and the General Service and Victory Medals.
1, Lamb Street, Longsight, Manchester.   Z10261

GREEN, H., Private, 1/8th Manchester Regiment.
He volunteered in August 1914, and after a brief training was sent to Egypt, where he was in action near the Suez Canal. In April 1915, he proceeded to Gallipoli and took part in the Landing, and in the three Battles of Krithia, where he was wounded in the following June. Evacuated to England, he was sent to hospital in St. Helens, and was eventually invalided out of the Service in October 1916, holding the 1914–15 Star, and the General Service and Victory Medals.
20, Iles Street, Oldham Road, Manchester.   Z10262

GREEN, H., Private, Royal Welch Fusiliers.
He joined in April 1917, and three months later proceeded to Palestine. In this theatre of hostilities he took part in heavy fighting at Gaza, and Jerusalem and later participated in the capture of Jericho and Aleppo. He remained overseas until September 1919, when he returned home for demobilisation, and holds the General Service and Victory Medals.
1, Purdon Street, Ancoats, Manchester.   Z10263

GREEN, H., Sapper, R.E.
Volunteering in August 1914, he was employed on various duties at home stations until September 1915, when he was sent to France. There he was engaged on telephone duties on the lines of communications on the Arras, Passchendaele and Somme fronts, and performed consistently good work. He was later employed as driver on the railway until he was demobilised in September 1919, holding the 1914–15 Star, and the General Service and Victory Medals.
27, Marple Street, Openshaw, Manchester.   Z10264

GREEN, H., Driver, R.A.S.C. (M.T.)
Volunteering in November 1914, he crossed to France a month later, and was engaged on important transport duties at Neuve Chapelle, St. Eloi, Ypres, Festubert, Albert, the Somme, Arras and Ypres. He also served throughout the Retreat and subsequent Allied Advance of 1918, and was demobilised on his return to England in April of the following year. He holds the 1914–15 Star, and the General Service and Victory Medals. 24, Derby Street, Ardwick, Manchester.   TZ6323

GREEN, H., Gunner, R.F.A.
He volunteered in March 1915, and in the following November was sent to a Munition Factory at Stockport, where he was engaged on important duties in connection with the output of shells. Later he was transferred to Messrs. Vickers, and was there employed in the same capacity. Owing to his skill in this work he was unable to secure his transfer overseas, but nevertheless rendered valuable services until January 1919, when he was discharged.
9, Bunyan Street, Ardwick, Manchester.   Z6326

GREEN, H. (M.M.) Sergt., 22nd Manchester Regt.
Volunteering in January 1915, he proceeded to France in November of that year, and fought in the Battles of Loos, St. Eloi, Vimy Ridge, the Somme, Arras, Ypres, and Cambrai, where he was so severely gassed as to cause temporary blindness. After two months hospital treatment, he was transferred to Italy, and fighting until the close of hostilities, was severely wounded during operations on the Piave. In the course of his service, he was awarded the Military Medal for rescuing a Sergeant under intense fire. He holds in addition, the 1914–15 Star, and the General Service and Victory Medals, and was demobilised in February 1919.
50, Pryme Street, Chester Road, Hulme, Manchester.   Z6328

GREEN, J., Private, South Lancashire Regiment.
He volunteered in May 1915, and three months later was drafted to France. In this theatre of war, he took part in many important engagements, including Loos, St. Eloi, Albert, Vimy Ridge, the Somme, Arras, Bullecourt, Ypres, Cambrai, the Aisne, Bapaume and Le Cateau, and was wounded. After serving on the Western Front for over three years, he was demobilised in March 1919, and holds the 1914–15 Star, and the General Service and Victory Medals.
22, Russell Street, Ancoats, Manchester.   Z10265

GREEN, J. (M.M.), Sgt.-Major, 21st Manchester Rgt.
He volunteered in November 1914, and crossing to France in December of the following year, fought in many Battles of importance, including those of Loos, Neuve Chapelle, La Bassée, Givenchy, Festubert, Ypres, Passchendaele and Cambrai. He was awarded the Military Medal for distinguished gallantry and devotion to duty during the Somme Offensive, in which he took a prominent part. Transferred to the Italian front, he did valuable work in operations on the Piave, and served there until the close of hostilities. He was demobilised in January 1919, and holds in addition to the decoration won on the Field, the 1914–15 Star, and the General Service and Victory Medals.
13, Baker Street, Longsight, Manchester.   Z6318A

GREEN, J., Private, 19th Manchester Regiment.
He volunteered in January 1915, and on completion of his training was ten months later sent to the Western Front. There he fought in the Battles of Loos, St. Eloi, Albert and Vimy Ridge, and was severely wounded during an engagement on the Somme, which unfortunately resulted in the loss of a leg. In consequence he was discharged in January 1918, holding the 1914–15 Star, and the General Service and Victory Medals.
11, Dyson Street, Varley Street, Miles Platting, Manchester.   Z10266

GREEN, J., Private, 11th Manchester Regiment.
Volunteering in January 1915, he proceeded a year later to the Western Front, and fought in important engagements in various sectors, including those at St. Eloi, Vermelles, the Somme, Arras, Messines, Lens, Cambrai and Amiens. He was wounded in action in October 1918, but remained in France until demobilised in January 1919, holding the General Service and Victory Medals.
91, Purdon Street, Ancoats, Manchester.   Z10267

GREEN, J., Private, 8th Manchester Regiment.
He volunteered in October 1914, and was later drafted to Gallipoli. In this theatre of hostilities he took part in the Battle of Suvla Bay in August 1915, and after the Evacuation, was sent to Egypt, where he remained until September 1919, when he was sent home and demobilised. During his service overseas he performed consistently good work, and holds the 1914–15 Star, and the General Service and Victory Medals.
7, Raw Street, Collyhurst, Manchester.   Z9548

GREEN, J. H., Private, Lancashire Fusiliers.
Volunteering in August 1914, he embarked for the Dardanelles in the following April and took part in the first Landing at Gallipoli. He also fought in several important engagements on the Peninsula, but was unfortunately so severely wounded at Suvla Bay in August of that year, as to necessitate his return to England. After hospital treatment, he was invalided out of the Service in August 1916, and holds the 1914–15 Star, and the General Service and Victory Medals.
11, Riga Street, Jackson Street, Hulme, Manchester.   Z6322

GREEN, J. R., Private, 12th Manchester Regiment.
He volunteered in August 1914, and proceeding to France four months later took part in operations at Neuve Chapelle, where he was badly wounded in March 1915. Invalided home he underwent hospital treatment, and on recovery returned to the Western Front in June of that year. He then fought at La Bassée, but a month later was again wounded, necessitating his removal to a Base hospital. He was afterwards in action at Neuville St. Vaast, Ypres and Armentières, and was wounded a third time in the Somme Offensive of July 1916. Evacuated to England, he was eventually discharged as physically unfit a year later, and holds the 1914–15 Star, and the General Service and Victory Medals.
8, Broom Street, Ardwick, Manchester.   Z6324

GREEN, J. W., Private, Duke of Cornwall's Light Infantry, and 1st Royal Irish Fusiliers.
Volunteering in November 1915, he crossed to France in the following April, and a month later was wounded in action at Vimy Ridge. On recovery, he fought in many other important engagements, including those at Passchendaele, Bailleul, Kemmel Hill and Ypres, but in September 1918, after treatment at one of the Base hospitals, was evacuated to England, in consequence of ill-health. He was invalided out of the Service in October of the succeeding year, and holds the General Service and Victory Medals.
22, Chadwick Street, West Gorton, Manchester.   Z6317

GREEN, M., Private, 7th Cheshire Regiment.
He volunteered in August 1914, and embarking for Egypt in in the following June, took part in the defence of the Suez Canal. He also saw service on the Gallipoli Peninsula during 1915, and then returned to Egypt, where he participated in the occupation of Sollum and in fighting at Katia. Later he proceeded to Palestine, and was in action at Gaza and Jericho. He returned to England in March 1919, and was demobilised in the next month, and holds the 1914-15 Star, and the General Service and Victory Medals.
13, Baker Street, Ardwick, Manchester.   Z6318B

GREEN, R. J., Special War Worker.
From July 1914 until November 1918, he was engaged on work of National importance at Messrs. Armstrong & Whitworth's. Throughout his period of service with this firm he was employed as a gun borer, and rendered invaluable assistance during the most critical moments of the war.
59, Elizabeth Street, West Gorton, Manchester.   Z10268

GREEN, T., Private, 18th Manchester Regiment.
Volunteering in September 1914, he landed in France in November of the following year, and took part in the Battles of the Somme, Ypres, Passchendaele and the Ancre. He also fought in the Retreat of 1918, and was severely wounded during the subsequent Allied Advance. He holds the 1914-15 Star, and the General Service and Victory Medals, and was demobilised in February 1919.
92, Birch Street, Ardwick, Manchester.   Z6319

GREEN, W. H., Private, 1/8th Manchester Regt.
Mobilised with the Territorials at the declaration of war, he embarked for Egypt in September 1914, and was drafted to the Dardanelles in April 1915. He took part in the first Landing at Gallipoli, and was in action on the Peninsula until the Evacuation was completed at the end of the year. He then returned to England, and in January 1916, was discharged, owing to the expiration of his period of service and medical unfitness. He holds the 1914-15 Star, and the General Service and Victory Medals.
18, Whittaker Street, Chorlton-on-Medlock, Manchester.   TZ6320A

GREEN, W. H., Driver, R.A.S.C.
Volunteering in August 1914, he embarked for the Dardanelles in the following April, and served in the Landing at Gallipoli and the Battle of Cape Helles. He was also engaged on special duties in operations at Krithia, Achi Baba, Chunuk Bair and Suvla, and was in action until the Evacuation of the Peninsu when he was transferred to Egypt. Later he proceeded to Salonika, where he took part in operations on the Vardar front, and was for some time in hospital suffering from malaria. He was demobilised in May 1919, and holds the 1914-15 Star, and the General Service and Victory Medals.
5, Marcus Street, Preston Street, Hulme, Manchester.   Z6329

GREEN, W. P., Sergt., R.A.M.C.
He volunteered in August 1914, and after his training was engaged on important duties as head dispenser at various Military hospitals. He was unable to secure his transfer overseas before the close of hostilities, but nevertheless, did valuable work until demobilised in June 1919.
82, Sloane Street, Moss Side, Manchester.   Z6325

GREENFIELD, W. E., Private, Manchester Regt.
He volunteered in November 1914, and was retained on important duties in England until January 1916, when he procured a transfer to the war zone. Whilst serving on the Western Front he was engaged in fierce fighting in the Somme, Arras, Ypres and Cambrai sectors, and also in the Retreat and Advance of 1918. He was demobilised in March 1919, and holds the General Service and Victory Medals.
26, Houghton Street, Collyhurst, Manchester.   Z10269

GREENHALGH, J., Private, S. Lancashire Regt.
He volunteered in September 1914, and was sent to France in the following March. He was in action in the Battles of Neuve Chapelle, Hill 60, Ypres, and was severely wounded at Loos. He returned to England and after receiving hospital treatment was invalided out of the Service in September 1916. He holds the 1914-15 Star, and the General Service and Victory Medals.
254, Hamilton Street, Collyhurst, Manchester.   Z9154

GREENHALGH, J., Private, Royal Welch Fusiliers.
He joined in June 1917, and on completion of his training was drafted to France. During the Retreat and Advance of 1918, he took part in engagements on the Somme and at Hill

60, St. Eloi, Neuve Chapelle, Arras, Lens, Loos, Bullecourt and Cambrai, before being wounded in action at Ypres. He holds the General Service and Victory Medals, and was demobilised in March 1919.
77, Elizabeth Ann Street, Manchester.   Z11713

GREENHOUGH, G. H., Sergt., East Lancs. Regt., and R.A.S.C. (M.T.)
Mobilised in August 1914, he was drafted a month later to the Western Front. There he played a prominent part in the Battles of the Marne and Ypres, and was later transferred to the R.A.S.C. Whilst engaged as a motor driver and despatch rider he served at Arras, Ypres and on the Somme, and was twice wounded. Invalided home in November 1917, he was after his recovery, employed as motor Instructor and lecturer at Hounslow Barracks, and rendered valuable services in this capacity until he was demobilised in January 1919, holding the 1914 Star, and the General Service and Victory Medals. 33, Ainsworth Street, West Gorton, Manchester. Z9549

GREENHOUGH, T., Private, Manchester Regiment.
He volunteered in October 1914, and served at home until March 1917, when he was drafted to France. Whilst in this theatre of war he took part in several engagements in the Retreat and Advance and was wounded on the Somme in August 1918. Taken to No. 29 Casualty Clearing Station he was later evacuated to England and after treatment in Withington War Hospital was discharged as medically unfit in November 1919. He holds the General Service and Victory Medals.
37, Westmoreland Street, Longsight, Manchester.   Z6331

GREENING, J. C.Q.M.S., South Lancashire Regt.
He volunteered in August 1914, and after a short period of training proceeded to the Western Front, where he was in action during the Retreat from Mons. He also experienced severe fighting in many other sectors of the line, and served in engagements at Le Cateau, St. Eloi, Loos and the Somme. He was wounded at Albert, but remained in France until demobilised in October 1919, and holds the Mons Star, and the General Service and Victory Medals.
3, Windsor Street, Rochdale Road, Manchester.   Z10603

GREENLEES, H., Pte., 9th King's Own Scottish Borderers.
Volunteering in August 1914, he sailed for Gallipoli in the following August and fought in the Landing at Suvla Bay and the Battles of Anzac and Chunuk Bair. Owing to illness he was sent home in December 1915, and after receiving medical treatment was invalided out of the Service in August 1916. He holds the 1914-15 Star, and the General Service and Victory Medals.
8, Ivy Grove, Hulme, Manchester.   Z6330

GREENWOOD, G., Pte., 11th Lancashire Fusiliers.
Volunteering in September 1914, he proceeded overseas a year later. Whilst serving on the Western Front he took an active part in important engagements at Loos, Vermelles, Vimy Ridge, the Ancre, the Somme, Bullecourt, and was unhappily killed in action at Messines in June 1917. He was entitled to the 1914-15 Star, and the General Service and Victory Medals.
" The path of duty was the way to glory."
9, Stanley Street, West Gorton, Manchester.   Z10270A

GREENWOOD, G., Private, 2nd Manchester Regt.
Volunteering in November 1914, he was unsuccessful in obtaining a transfer to the war zone on completion of his training. Throughout the period of his service he was employed at various important stations in England, where he was engaged as a cook, and later performed excellent work as an officer's servant, at Ripon, Southport and Salop. He was demobilised from Ripon in April 1919.
15, Baird Street, Chapel Street, Ancoats, Manchester. Z11615

GREENWOOD, G., Private, Lancashire Fusiliers.
He volunteered in May 1915, and a year later embarked for the Western Front, where he was in action at Vermelles, Vimy Ridge, and in the Somme Offensive. Engaged later in the Battles of Arras and Ypres, he was wounded in 1917, and removed to hospital at Rouen. Evacuated to England he was treated at the King George Military Hospital, and on recovery returned to France to take part in the Battles of Havrincourt, Cambrai and other concluding engagements of the war. He was demobilised in February 1919, and holds the General Service and Victory Medals.
208, Viaduct Street, Ardwick, Manchester.   Z6333

GREENWOOD, J., Sergt., 1st Gloucestershire Regt.
Mobilised on the outbreak of war, he proceeded to France shortly afterwards, and was in action during the Retreat from Mons. He also took part in the Battles of Le Cateau the Marne, the Aisne, La Bassée and was severely wounded at Ypres. Sent home, owing to his injuries, he was in hospital for several months, and was eventually discharged as medically unfit in 1915. He holds the Mons Star, and the General Service and Victory Medals.
25, Cheltenham Street, Chortlon-on-Medlock.   X6332

GREENWOOD, R. H., Pte., 40th Northumberland Fusiliers.

Volunteering in May 1915, he was drafted to Gallipoli in the following October, and took part in operations until the Evacuation of the Peninsula. Proceeding to Egypt in December 1915, he was in action in the Battles of Romani, Raffa, Gaza, and was present at the capture of Jerusalem, after which he was sent to Salonika in September 1918. He fought in the Advance on the Struma and Vardar fronts, and in January 1919, was sent to France, where he served on special duties for some months. He was demobilised in May 1920, and holds the 1914–15 Star, and the General Service and Victory Medals. 20, Pump Street, Hulme, Manchester.　Z6334

GREGG, C. H., Private, East Lancashire Regt.

Mobilised and drafted to the Western Front at the outbreak of war, he fought in the Retreat from Mons, in the Battles of the Marne, the Aisne, Ypres and Hill 60, and was wounded. He died gloriously on the Field of Battle on July 22nd, 1916, during the first British Offensive on the Somme. He was entitled to the 1914–15 Star, and the General Service and Victory Medals.
" And doubtless he went in splendid company."
10, Sand Street, Collyhurst, Manchester.　Z9491

GREGORY, B. (M.M.), Cpl., 2/7th Manchester Regt.

He volunteered in February 1915, and embarking for Egypt five months later served in the Canal zone for a time and proceeded to Gallipoli. There he took part in the Landing at Suvla Bay and other operations until the Evacuation of the Peninsula, when he was drafted to France. Engaged with his unit in the Battles of Nieuport, Ypres, Passchendaele and Cambrai, he was awarded the Military Medal for conspicuous bravery and devotion to duty in conveying ammunition to the firing line under heavy shell-fire on the Somme in March 1918. He was wounded on the Somme in September 1918, during the final Allied Advance, and was invalided to Stockport War Hospital for treatment. Demobilised in March 1919, he also holds the 1914–15 Star, and the General Service and Victory Medals.　Z6335
86, Norton Street, Clove Street, West Gorton, Manchester.

GREGORY, H., Special War Worker.

Throughout the period of hostilities he was engaged on work of National importance at Messrs. Armstrong & Whitworth's. He was employed as a crane driver in the armour plate department, and fulfilled his arduous duties to the entire satisfaction of his firm, and was still working with them in 1920.
8, Truro Street, West Gorton, Manchester.　Z10271

GREGORY, J., Bombardier, R.G.A.

He joined in April 1916, and in the following February sailed for Mesopotamia. In this theatre of war he was in action in several important engagements, including the Battle of Amara, and after hostilities ended was engaged on special duties until his return home for demobilisation in February 1920. He holds the General Service and Victory Medals.
31, Roseberry Street, Gorton, Manchester.　TZ6336

GREGORY, W. H., Lieutenant, Manchester Regt.

He volunteered in 1915, and in the same year was drafted to the Western Front. There he served in the Battles of the Somme, Beaumont-Hamel, Bullecourt, Passchendaele, and Lens, and was gassed in 1917. He received a commission in recognition of his valuable services, and fought with distinction in the Allied Offensive of 1918. He was demobilised in 1919, and holds the 1914–15 Star, and the General Service and Victory Medals.
6, Bridge Street, Chorlton-on-Medlock, Manchester. Z10272

GREGSON, J. J., Private, 23rd Manchester Regt.

Volunteering in December 1914, he sailed for France in January 1916, and fought in the Battles of Albert, Ploegsteert and the Somme. He was also in action at Bullecourt, Ypres, Cambrai and throughout the German Offensive and Allied Advance of 1918. Returning to England he was demobilised in March 1919, and holds the General Service and Victory Medals. 104, Tame Street, Ancoats, Manchester.　Z9155

GREGSON, J. W. E., Private, 2nd K.O. (Y.L.I.)

Joining in August 1918, he completed his training and was engaged on guard and other important duties at various prisoners of war camps. He was unable to secure his transfer overseas before the conclusion of hostilities, and owing to illness was discharged as medically unfit in September 1919.
42, Gregory Street, Ardwick, Manchester.　Z6338

GREGSON, T., Private, K.O. (R. Lancaster Regt.)

Volunteering in August 1914, he was drafted to Gallipoli in the following July, and served as a bomber in the Landing at Suvla Bay. Wounded in December 1915, in the course of operations on the Peninsula he was invalided home and on recovery was sent to France in April 1916. He was in action near Loos, at Vimy Ridge, and was severely wounded on the Somme in 1916. Sent to England for medical treatment he was discharged as medically unfit for further service in March

1917, and holds the 1914–15 Star, and the General Service and Victory Medals.
14, Elliott Street, Bradford, Manchester.　Z6337

GRESTY, A., Private, 1st Manchester Regiment.

He volunteered in October 1914, and crossing to France in the same month fought in the Battle of Ypres and several subsequent engagements. He fell fighting near La Bassée on February 3rd, 1915, and was entitled to the 1914 Star, and the General Service and Victory Medals.
" The path of duty was the way to glory."
17, Gregory Street, West Gorton, Manchester.　Z6339B

GRESTY, H., Pte., 5th King's (Liverpool Regt.)

He joined in October 1917, and landing on the Western Front five months later was almost immediately in action in the second Battle of the Somme. Engaged with his unit in the German Offensive he took part in severe fighting at Amiens, Bapaume, Havrincourt, in the subsequent Allied Advance, and was wounded at Cambrai on September 27th, 1918. Sent home on account of his injuries, he received treatment at the V.A.D. hospital, Southport, and invalided out of the Army in February 1919, holds the General Service and Victory Medals.
17, Gregory Street, West Gorton, Manchester.　Z6339A

GRESTY, J., Private, 1/8th Manchester Regiment.

When war was declared in August 1914, he volunteered, and later was ordered to Salonika. After eleven months' service on the Vardar front he was drafted to Egypt, where he was in action at Katia, El Fasher, Romani, and Magdhaba. He was severely wounded at Katia in April 1916, and in consequence was invalided out of the Army in the following October, holding the 1914–15 Star, and the General Service and Victory Medals.
18, Whitland St., Queen's Park, Manchester.　Z11502

GRESTY, S., Private, R.A.S.C.

Volunteering in January 1916, he was drafted to Mesopotamia five months later, and was engaged on important transport duties during operation on the Tigris, and at the Battle of Kut-el-Amara. He was killed in action at Sanna-i-Yat in September 1917, and was entitled to the General Service and Victory Medals.
" His life for his Country, his soul to God."
12, Pleasant View, Ardwick, Manchester.　Z6340

GRESTY, T., Private, 2nd Manchester Regiment.

He volunteered in September 1914, and proceeding overseas in the following year saw service on the Western Front. There he was in action in the Battle of Ypres, and owing to gas poisoning was sent home, where he received medical treatment. He was invalided out of the Service in 1916, and holds the 1914–15 Star, and the General Service and Victory Medals.
48, Carlisle Street, Hulme, Manchester.　TZ6341

GREY, H., Private, 1st Manchester Regiment.

Volunteering in November 1915, he crossed to France in the same month and took part in heavy fighting at Loos. Severely wounded at St. Eloi he was sent to hospital at Rouen and later evacuated to Eastbourne, where he received further treatment. He was discharged as medically unfit for further service in April 1916, and holds the 1914–15 Star, and the General Service and Victory Medals.　Z6342
25, Charlotte Street, Chorlton-on-Medlock, Manchester.

GRIBBIN, J., Private, 3rd Manchester Regiment.

Joining in December 1916, he was sent to the Western Front in the following March and fought in the Battles of Bullecourt and Passchendaele. He was severely wounded at Gheluvelt in October 1917, and was removed to hospital at Etaples, and later to Havre. After treatment he continued on service in France until the end of the war when he returned home. Demobilised in May 1919, he holds the General Service and Victory Medals.
117, Everton Road, Chorlton-on-Medlock, Manchester.　Z6343

GRICE, H., Sapper, R.E.

He was mobilised when war broke out and embarked for France soon afterwards. In the course of his service overseas he was engaged on important duties in the forward areas and was present at the Battles of La Bassée, Neuve Chapelle, the Somme, Arras and Cambrai. Buried by shell explosion during an engagement, he was sent home suffering from shell-shock, and after treatment was discharged as medically unfit in October 1918. He holds the 1914–15 Star, and the General Service and Victory Medals.
13, Hampden Street, Ardwick, Manchester.　Z6344

GRIFFIN, W., Private, R.A.S.C. (M.T.)

Volunteering in May 1915, he was engaged in convoying guns and motors to the Western Front, until November 1917, when he was drafted to Egypt. Serving with the caterpillar tractors he did good work in the transport of heavy guns during the British Advance through Palestine, in the course of which he was present at the Battles of Gaza and the capture of Jerusalem. He returned to England for demobilisation in April 1919, and holds the 1914–15 Star, and the General Service and Victory Medals.
25, Pump Street, Hulme, Manchester.　Z6345

GRIFFITHS, A., Private, K.O. (Royal L'pool Regt.)
He volunteered in August 1914, and proceeding overseas in
the following July saw much service on the Western Front.
There he was engaged in heavy fighting in the Ypres salient,
at Loos, St. Eloi, Vermelles and on the Somme. He also
fought in the Battles of Beaumont-Hamel, Arras, Ypres and
Passchendaele, where he was wounded. Sent to hospital
in France he was later evacuated to England, and after treatment was invalided out of the Service in June 1918. He holds
the 1914-15 Star, and the General Service and Victory Medals.
48, Owen Street, Hulme, Manchester.   Z6346

GRIFFITHS, H., Private, 12th Manchester Regt.
Volunteering in January 1915, he proceeded eight months
later to Egypt, where he took part in the Suez Canal engagements. He was then sent to Gallipoli and fought at Suvla
Bay, and in the subsequent operations of the campaign.
After the Evacuation he was drafted to France in March 1917,
but was unfortunately killed in action at Arras on May 28th,
1917. He was entitled to the 1914-15 Star, and the General
Service and Victory Medals.
      "His life for his Country, his soul to God."
65, Montague Street, Collyhurst, Manchester.   Z10875B

GRIFFITHS, H., Private, Welch Regt., and R.A.M.C.
He volunteered in May 1915, and in the following March
landed in France. Serving in various parts of the line he
was in action in the Battles of Ploegsteert Wood, Ypres, and
was wounded at Messines. Sent home, owing to his injuries,
he was in hospital for some time, and on recovery was transferred
to the R.A.M.C., with which unit he was engaged on light
duties at Blackpool until discharged on account of service in
April 1918. He holds the General Service and Victory Medals.
49, Marsland Street, Ardwick, Manchester.   Z6349

GRIFFITHS, J., Pte., 1st Welch Regt., and M.G.C.
He joined in July 1916, and after serving on the Western Front
for a few weeks was drafted to Salonika in December 1916.
In this theatre of war he was engaged in fierce fighting on the
Doiran, the Struma and at Monastir. He was severely
wounded on the Doiran front in April 1917, and was in hospital
at Alexandria and Marseilles. Returning home, he was
demobilised in February 1919, and holds the General Service
and Victory Medals.
20, Iles Street, Oldham Road, Manchester.   Z10273

**GRIFFITHS, J., Gunner, R.F.A., and Sapper, R.E.
(I.W.T.)**
Volunteering in December 1914, he sailed for India in January
1915, and served as a gunner for over two years. Transferred
to the Royal Engineers he was sent to Mesopotamia in July
1917, and was engaged with the Inland Water Transport
Section on the Tigris. He was sent back to India, owing to
illness, and on recovery took part in operations against the
rebel tribes on the North West Frontier. Returning home
he was discharged on account of service in November 1919,
and holds the General Service and Victory Medals, and the
India General Service Medal (with clasp, Afghanistan, N.W.
Frontier, 1919).   3, Crayton St., Hulme, Manchester.   Z6352

GRIFFITHS, J. H., Private, 23rd Manchester Regt.
He joined in March 1916, and proceeding to the Western
Front in September of the following year was engaged with
his unit in heavy fighting in the Ypres salient. He gave his
life for King and Country at Houthulst Wood, near Ypres,
in October 1917, and was entitled to the General Service and
Victory Medals.
      "Steals on the ear the distant triumph song."
13, Haughton Street, Bradford, Manchester.   Z6350

GRIFFITHS, M., Private, Lancashire Fusiliers.
He volunteered in January 1915, and on completion of his
training served at Hull and Sutton, at which stations he
performed the duties allotted to him in a highly capable manner.
After only four months' service in the Army, he died of pneumonia at Hull on May 22nd, 1915.
      "His memory is cherished with pride."
19, Heelis Street, Rochdale Road, Manchester.   Z10604A

GRIFFITHS, P. R., Driver, R.A.S.C. (M.T.)
He volunteered in October 1914, and two months afterwards
proceeded to France. Whilst employed as a motor transport
driver, he did excellent service conveying supplies to the
front lines on the Marne and Somme fronts, also at Ypres and
Cambrai. After the Armistice he was engaged on important
transport duties until he was demobilised in August 1919.
He holds the 1914-15 Star, and the General Service and Victory Medals.
51, Francisco Street, Collyhurst, Manchester.   Z9550

GRIFFITHS, R., Private, Royal Welch Fusiliers.
He volunteered in August 1915, and a year later embarked for
Salonika. After a period of service in the Balkans, in the
course of which he fought in the Advance on the Doiran and
Struma fronts, and at the Battle of Monastir, he was sent to
Egypt in March 1917. He served in the Battles of Gaza
(I and II), the fall of Jerusalem, and the capture of Jericho,
Tripoli and Aleppo. Returning to England for demobilisation
in July 1919, he holds the General Service and Victory Medals.
19, New Street, West Gorton, Manchester.   Z6351

GRIFFITHS, T., Rifleman. K.R.R.C.
He volunteered in February 1915, and a month later was
drafted overseas. During his service on the Western Front
he took an active part in an engagement at Hill 60, but was
unfortunately killed in action there in April 1915. He was
entitled to the 1914-15 Star, and the General Service and
Victory Medals.
      "He died the noblest death a man may die,
        Fighting for God, and right, and liberty."
15, Lowe Street, Miles Platting, Manchester.   Z10274A

GRIFFITHS, T. E., Rifleman, 2nd Rifle Brigade.
Volunteering in March 1915, he proceeded to France a month
later, and took part in the Battles of Ypres, Loos, Albert,
Vermelles, the Somme, the Ancre, Arras and Lens. He was
gassed in the second Battle of the Somme, and was admitted
to hospital at Le Havre for treatment. On recovery he returned to England and, demobilised in January 1919, holds
the 1914-15 Star, and the General Service and Victory Medals.
93, Ellesmere Street, Hulme, Manchester.   Z6353

GRIFFITHS, T. G., Driver, R.A.S.C. (M.T.)
He volunteered in February 1916, and drafted to the Western
Front in the same month served in various sectors until the
close of the war. During this period he was engaged in the
transport of ammunition for the Royal Garrison Artillery,
and was present in the Battles of the Somme, Albert, Bullecourt, Cambrai and in the Retreat and Advance of 1918.
After the Armistice he was sent with the Army of Occupation
into Germany, and whilst there was employed in transporting
food supplies. Returning home for demobilisation in September 1919, he holds the General Service and Victory Medals.
42, Dorset Street, Hulme, Manchester.   Z6348

GRIFFITHS, W., Rifleman, Royal Irish Rifles.
Volunteering in November 1914, he was trained at Dublin
and proceeded to France in March 1915. He served on the
Western Front for only two months, and during that time was
engaged in fierce fighting at Neuve Chapelle, and died gloriously
on the Field of Battle at Hill 60 on May 9th, 1915. He was
entitled to the 1914-15 Star, and the General Service and
Victory Medals.
      "Courage, bright hopes, and a myriad dreams splendidly
        given."
19, Heelis Street, Rochdale Road, Manchester.   Z10604B

GRIFFITHS, W., Rifleman, K.R.R.C.
When war broke out in August 1914, he was already serving
in the Army and was at once ordered with the first Expeditionary Force to the Western Front. There he was in action
at Mons, and fell fighting in the Battle of the Marne in September 1914. He was entitled to the Mons Star, and the
General Service and Victory Medals.
                  "Nobly striving,
        He nobly fell that we might live."
15, Lowe Street, Miles Platting, Manchester.   Z10274B

GRIFFITHS, W. J. (M.M.), Private, Lancs. Fusiliers.
He volunteered in April 1915, and proceeding in the following
April to Egypt served at Cairo and Kantara. He also took
part in engagements in the Canal zone, and in May 1917 was
transferred to the Western Front. In this theatre of war he
fought in the Battles of Messines, Passchendaele, Cambrai and
in the Retreat and Advance of 1918. He was awarded the
Military Medal at Ypres in September 1918, for conspicuous
bravery and devotion to duty in delivering Despatches, although severely wounded, under heavy shell-fire. He also
holds the General Service and Victory Medals, and was invalided out of the Service in October 1918.
11, Albion Terrace, Miles Platting, Manchester.   Z6347

GRIMES, P., L/Corporal, 1st Royal Dublin Fusiliers.
He volunteered in March 1915, and two months later was
drafted to the Dardanelles, where he saw much heavy fighting
at Suvla Bay, Chunuk Bair and at the Evacuation of the
Gallipoli Peninsula. He then proceeded to France and played
a prominent part in the Battles of the Ancre, Beaucourt,
Arras, Vimy Ridge (where he was wounded), and Messines.
He was unfortunately killed in action at the Battle of the
Somme (II) on March 21st, 1918, and was entitled to the
1914-15 Star, and the General Service and Victory Medals.
"A valiant Soldier, with undaunted heart he breasted life's
last hill."
8, Southern Street, Hulme, Manchester.   Z11714

GRIMSHAW, H. (M.M.), Sergt., 16th Manchester Regt.
He enlisted in June 1912, and mobilised at the outbreak of
war proceeded to the Western Front in December 1916.
In this theatre of war he fought in several engagements, and
was wounded and gassed at Arras in April 1917. After receiving medical treatment in the Australian Hospital, Rouen,
he returned to the front lines and was in action until June
1918, when he was again wounded during operations at Ypres.
Sent to Wimereux Hospital, Boulogne for treatment, he returned to England in April 1919, and was eventually discharged
in March of the following year. Whilst overseas he was awarded
the Military Medal for conspicuous gallantry and devotion
to duty in the Field. He also holds the General Service and
Victory Medals.
34, Westmoreland Street, Longsight, Manchester.   Z6355

GRIMSHAW, J., Rifleman, 8th Rifle Brigade.
Volunteering in August 1914, in the following May he landed in Fance and fought in the Battles of Hill 60, Ypres, and Loos, and was slightly wounded in 1917. He also was engaged in heavy fighting throughout the German Offensive and subsequent Allied Advance of 1918, and returning home after the Armistice was demobilised in February 1919. He holds the 1914-15 Star, and the General Service and Victory Medals.
14, Vance Street, Oldham Road, Manchester. Z9156

GRIMSHAW, J. H. (M.M.), Pte., 4th Royal Scots.
Volunteering in December 1914, he proceeded to the Dardanelles in the following May, and was engaged in heavy fighting on the Peninsula. Later transferred to Egypt he took part in operations in the Canal zone, and in July 1917 was drafted to France. After fighting in many engagements on the Western Front he was severely wounded at Lens in the next month. Invalided to England he received medical treatment, and was eventually discharged as medically unfit for further service in January 1918. He was awarded the Military Medal for conspicuous bravery and devotion to duty in the Field, and also holds the 1914-15 Star, and the General Service and Victory Medals. Z6356
12, Mornington Street, Chorlton-on-Medlock, Manchester.

GRIMSHAW, S., Private, R.A.V.C.
He joined in September 1916, and six months later was sent to the Western Front, where he rendered most valuable services in attending to sick and wounded horses. He saw severe fighting in the Somme sector, especially at Bray, and remained in France until February 1919. He then proceeded to Germany, and was stationed at Cologne until demobilised in February 1920, holding the General Service and Victory Medals. 12, Marple Street, Ancoats, Manchester. Z10276

GRIMSHAW, W., Private, 2/6th Manchester Regt.
He joined in March 1917, and in the following September was drafted overseas. Whilst serving on the Western Front he was gassed during an engagement at Passchendaele, and also took part in the Battle of the Somme. He was taken prisoner at Péronne in March 1918, and sent to Antwerp, where he was employed in conveying shells to the enemy behind the line. In December 1918 he was released from captivity, and was demobilised in March 1919, holding the General Service and Victory Medals.
9, Rennie Street, West Gorton, Manchester. Z10275

GRIMSHAW, W., A.B., R.N., H.M.S. "Humber."
Having previously served in the Navy, he volunteered in August 1914, and a month later was posted to his ship. He took an active part in the bombardment of the Belgian Coast, and was unhappily killed in action in May 1915, and buried at Malta. He was entitled to the 1914-15 Star, and the General Service and Victory Medals.
"A costly sacrifice upon the altar of freedom."
53, Burton Street, Rochdale Road, Manchester. Z10606

GRIMSHAW, W., Private, King's (Liverpool Regt.)
He joined in March 1917, and after a period of training at Aldershot, was sent to Ireland, where he was employed on garrison and other important duties. In December 1918, he proceeded to Germany, and served with the Army of Occupation at Bonn until January 1920, when he returned home and was demobilised.
47, Baker Street, Longsight, Manchester. TZ9551

GRINDLEY, D., Rflmn., 14th K.R.R.C. and Pte., R.A.S.C.
Volunteering in August 1914, he was drafted in the following year to the Western Front, and fought in several battles, including those of Ypres, and the Somme, where he was wounded in July 1916. Invalided to hospital in London he received medical treatment, and later returning to France was wounded again in the third Battle of Ypres in 1917. Evacuated to England for hospital treatment, he was transferred to the Royal Army Service Corps on recovery, and served at home until his demobilisation in May 1919. He holds the 1914-15 Star, and the General Service and Victory Medals.
40, Libby Street, Lower Openshaw, Manchester. Z6354

GRINDROD, E., Private, South Lancashire Regt.
He volunteered in August 1914, and eighteen months later was ordered overseas. During his service on the Western Front he was in action at Vermelles and Loos, and was wounded in the latter battle. On his recovery he served at Ploegsteert Wood, the Somme, Arras, Ypres, Bullecourt, Cambrai, the Aisne, the Marne and Havrincourt. Demobilised in October 1919, he holds the General Service and Victory Medals.
6, Park Street, West Gorton, Manchester. Z10277

GROCOCK, A. E., Pte., 4th East Yorkshire Regt.
Joining in September 1916, he was drafted overseas in the same month, and served with his unit at Bermuda, West Indies, engaged on garrison and other important duties. Owing to ill-health he returned to England in October 1918, and unhappily died on December 15th of that year, and was laid to rest with full military honours in the Southern Cemetery, Manchester. He was entitled to the General Service Medal.
"His memory is cherished with pride."
14, Athol Street, Hulme, Manchester. Z6357

GROOCOCK, A., Pte., 4th East Lancashire Regt.
He joined in July 1917, and embarking in the following April for France fought in several engagements, including the Battles of Amiens, Bapaume, Havrincourt, Ypres (IV) and the Sambre. Owing to ill-health, he was invalided to hospital, and on recovery was engaged on guard and other duties at various prisoner of war camps until July 1919. He then returned to England, and was demobilised in the next month, holds the General Service and Victory Medals.
51, George Street, Moss Side, Manchester. Z6358

GROOM, E., Private, Welch Regiment.
Joining in August 1916, he proceeded in the following February to Egypt, where he took part in engagements on the Suez Canal and at El Fasher and Romani. He was then transferred to France, and in this sphere of hostilities participated in severe actions on the Somme and Marne fronts, and at Amiens, Bapaume and Cambrai. Subsequently re-enlisting for a period of three years, he was drafted to India, and was still serving there in 1920, holding the General Service and Victory Medals.
12, Romiley Street, Queens Road, Manchester. Z10607B

GROOM, J. R., Rifleman, 8th Rifle Brigade.
He volunteered in August 1914, and after a period of training at Winchester and Aldershot, was drafted in March 1915 to France. In this theatre of war, he played a prominent part with his unit in heavy fighting at Hill 60, and Ypres, and did good work until he fell in action at Hooge on July 30th, 1915. He was entitled to the 1914-15 Star, and the General Service and Victory Medals.
"His life for his Country, his soul to God."
12, Romiley Street, Queens Road, Manchester. Z10607A

GRUNDY, G., Driver, R.F.A.
He volunteered in August 1915, and landing in France three months later, served with his Battery on the front until the termination of hostilities. He fought in several engagements, including the Battles of Loos, Albert, Vimy Ridge, the Somme, Beaumont-Hamel, Arras, Messines, Cambrai, the Marne (II) and Ypres (IV). After the Armistice he proceeded with the Army of Occupation into Germany, and served there until his demobilisation in March 1919. He holds the 1914-15 Star, and the General Service and Victory Medals.
20, Mary Street, Higher Ardwick, Manchester. Z6359

GUILFORD, A., Sapper, R.E.
Joining in March 1917, he completed his training and served on important duties with the Inland Water Transport at various stations in England. He rendered valuable services, but was unable to obtain his transfer to a theatre of war before the cessation of hostilities, and was demobilised in February 1919.
85, Bickley Street, Moss Side, Manchester. Z6360

GUNBY, T., Private, 3rd King's (Liverpool Regt.)
Volunteering in August 1914, he completed his training and crossed to France in the following November. He took part in several engagements, and was wounded at Neuve Chapelle in March 1915. After receiving medical treatment at Rouen Hospital he returned to the trenches, and fought in the Battles of St. Eloi, Hill 60 and Ypres (II). He was unhappily killed in action at Loos on September 15th 1915, and was laid to rest in the Guards Cemetery near Béthune. He was entitled to the 1914-15 Star, and the General Service and Victory Medals.
"His name liveth for evermore."
134, Blackthorn Street, Ardwick, Manchester. Z6361

GUNN, C. F., Cpl., King's Own Scottish Borderers.
A Regular, serving in India at the outbreak of war, he was mobilised and sent to England with the first Indian Contingent in August 1914. Drafted to France in the same year, he took part in the Battles of the Marne, the Aisne and Ypres, and in April 1915, proceeded to the Dardanelles. There he fought in the Battles of Krithia (I, II and III), the Landing at Suvla Bay, and the capture of Chunuk Bair. On the Evacuation of that Peninsula he returned to the Western Front and was engaged in heavy fighting on the Somme, at Arras, and elsewhere. He was also in action in the Retreat and Advance of 1918, and in the course of his service was wounded four times. He holds the 1914 Star, and the General Service and Victory Medals, and was demobilised in February 1919.
15, Mackworth Street, Hulme, Manchester. Z6362

GUTHRIE, P. J., Gunner, R.G.A.
Volunteering in October 1914, he completed his training and was sent in the following January to France. There he fought in several engagements, including the Battles of Neuve Chapelle St. Eloi, Ypres (II), Festubert, Loos, and was wounded during the Somme Offensive in October 1916. After receiving medical treatment at Rouen Hospital he was evacuated to England, to Mill Road, Hospital, Liverpool, and later to Basford House, Seymour Grove, Manchester, where he underwent further treatment. He was invalided out of the Service in March 1919, and holds the 1914-15 Star, and the General Service and Victory Medals.
9, Pine Street, City Road, Hulme, Manchester. Z6364

GUTHRIE, J., Private, 2nd East Lancashire Regt.
He volunteered in September 1914, and at the conclusion of his training was drafted to the Western Front three months later, and serving with his Battalion in various parts of the line did very good work. He gave his life for the freedom of England at the Battles of Hill 60, in May 1915, and was entitled to the 1914–15 Star, and the General Service and Victory Medals. "He joined the great white company of valiant souls."
9, Pine Street, City Road, Hulme, Manchester.   Z6363

GUTTERIDGE, C. J., Pte., 7th Durham Light Infty.
He joined in February 1917, but was unable to procure a transfer overseas before October 1918, when he was drafted to Russia. There he served for eleven months, and during that period was engaged on important guard and patrol duties at Archangel. He returned to England in September 1919, and was demobilised from Ripon, holding the General Service and Victory Medals.
16, Pleasant Street, Harpurhey, Manchester.   Z11503

H

HACKETT, J., Private, 3rd King's (Liverpool Regt.), and Labour Corps.
He volunteered in June 1915, and after two months training, was drafted to the Western Front, where he saw severe fighting in various sectors. After taking part in the Battles of Loos, Albert, the Somme, Arras, Bullecourt, Messines and Passchendaele, and many minor engagements, he was transferred to the Labour Corps in November 1917, and was afterwards engaged in guarding prisoners of war at Ypres. Demobilised in February 1919, he holds the 1914–15 Star, and the General Service and Victory Medals.
163, Cowesby Street, Moss Side, Manchester.   TZ6366

HACKETT, J. F., Gunner, R.F.A.
He joined in January 1917, and after completing a period of training was engaged on important duties as a Signaller at various stations. He was not successful in obtaining his transfer to a theatre of war, but nevertheless, rendered valuable services with his Battery until February 1919, when he was demobilised.
28, Callender Street, Chorlton-on-Medlock, Manchester. Z6367

HACKING, H., Private, Manchester Regiment, and East Yorkshire Regiment.
He joined in June 1918, and after undergoing a period of training, served at various stations, where he was engaged on duties of great importance. Unable to obtain his transfer overseas he nevertheless, did much useful work with his unit until his demobilisation in October 1919.
50, Stockton Street, Moss Side, Manchester.   TZ6368

HACKNEY, H. K. (Mrs.), Special War Worker.
During the whole period of hostilities, this lady was engaged on work of National importance at Messrs. Westinghouse's Munition Factory, Didsbury. There, employed on various responsible duties in connection with the construction of shells and bombs, she rendered very valuable services until her discharge on the signing of the Armistice.
38, Dalton Street, Hulme, Manchester.   Z6369B

HACKNEY, M., L/Corporal, R.A.M.C.
He enlisted in March 1913, and immediately on the outbreak of war in August of the following year, proceeded to the Western Front, where he served through the Retreat from Mons. In January 1915, he was transferred to Egypt, and thence shortly afterwards to Gallipoli, where he saw severe fighting until the Evacuation of the Peninsula. He then returned to France, and again served at Ypres, and the Somme, finally returning home for discharge in 1919. He holds the Mons Star, and the General Service and Victory Medals.
38, Dalton Street, Hulme, Manchester.   Z6369A

HADDON, G., A.B., Royal Navy.
He volunteered in January 1915, and was posted to the "Powerful," on board which vessel he served in the Atlantic Ocean until February 1917. He was then transferred to the "Hope" and later to H.M.S. "Dublin," for patrol duties in the Mediterranean Sea and the Dardanelles. He was finally demobilised in January 1920, and holds the Naval General Service Medal (with four clasps), the 1914–15 Star, and the General Service and Victory Medals.
27, Tongue Street, Ardwick, Manchester.   Z6370

HADFIELD, A. (M.M.), Sergt., 7th Manchester Regt.
Mobilised in August 1914, he was drafted to Egypt in the following month and there served on the Suez Canal until transferred to Gallipoli in the following year. Wounded in action at the Landing at Suvla Bay, he was invalided to hospital at Malta, whence he proceeded, on his recovery to the Western Front. There he took part in the third Battle of Ypres, fought also at La Bassée and Nieuport, and was twice wounded in action on the Somme—in June and September 1918. He was awarded the Military Medal for conspicuous gallantry in the Field, and holding also the 1914–15 Star, and the General Service and Victory Medals. was discharged in July 1920.
79, Harrold Street, Bradford, Manchester   Z6371

HADFIELD, C. F., Sapper, R.E., and Private, King's Own (Royal Lancaster Regiment.)
He volunteered in August 1914, and in April of the following year was drafted to the Western Front, where he was severely wounded in action at Hill 60 in May 1915. Invalided to hospital at Manchester, he was discharged as medically unfit for further service in March 1916, but later, re-enlisted and was stationed in England until finally invalided from the Army in April 1918. He holds the 1914–15 Star, and the General Service and Victory Medals.
43, Randolph Street, Ardwick, Manchester.   Z6372D

HADFIELD, C. F., Pte., K.O. (R. Lancaster Regt.)
He volunteered in August 1914, and after undergoing a period of training was drafted to Gallipoli, where he took part in the Landing at Suvla Bay. There he was unhappily killed in action during severe fighting on August 9th, 1915. He was entitled to the 1914–15 Star, and the General Service and Victory Medals.
"Thinking that remembrance, though unspoken, may reach him where he sleeps."
43, Randolph Street, Ardwick, Manchester.   Z6372A

HADFIELD, F. W., Pte., K.O. (R. Lancaster Regt.)
Having enlisted in July 1914, he was drafted to the Western Front immediately on the outbreak of war in the following month, and there took part in the Retreat from Mons. He also fought in many other important engagements until wounded in action in the second Battle of Ypres and invalided home. On his recovery, however, he returned to France, and was wounded a second time on the Somme in January 1918, and sent to hospital at the Base. He was discharged as medically unfit for further service in March 1918, and holds the Mons Star, and the General Service and Victory Medals.
43, Randolph Street, Ardwick, Manchester.   Z6372C

HADFIELD, J., Private, 1st Border Regiment.
Shortly after volunteering in August 1914, he proceeded to Egypt, where he served on the Suez Canal until transferred to Gallipoli in the following year. He fell fighting in the Landing at Suvla Bay in August 1915. He was entitled to the 1914–15 Star, and the General Service and Victory Medals.
"Nobly striving,
He nobly fell that we might live."
51, Armitage Street, Ardwick, Manchester.   Z6373B

HADFIELD, J., Corporal, Cheshire Regiment.
He volunteered in November 1914, and eighteen months later proceeded to France, where he fought in the Battles of the Somme, Arras, Messines, Ypres and Cambrai. He was severely wounded at Bullecourt in August 1918, and was invalided home to hospital, from whence he was discharged as medically unfit for further service in the following November. He holds the General Service and Victory Medals.
1, Tailor Street, Ancoats, Manchester.   Z9552

HADFIELD, W., Private, 1/8th Manchester Regt.
Volunteering in April 1915, he was drafted to Egypt in the following July, and there saw much severe fighting. After taking part in the engagements at Agagia, Sollum and Katia, he was wounded in action at Romani, and sent to hospital at Cairo. In February 1918, he was transferred to the Western Front, where he fought in the Battle of the Somme, and was again wounded in action at Havrincourt. Invalided home, he unhappily died in June 1918. He was entitled to the 1914–15 Star, and the General Service and Victory Medals.
"The path of duty was the way to glory."
51, Armitage Street, Ardwick, Manchester.   Z6373A

HADFIELD, W. T., Private, Royal Welch Fusiliers.
He joined in September 1918, and shortly afterwards proceeded to the Western Front, where he took part in many important engagements in the Allies' Advance. Demobilised in March 1919, he re-enlisted, however, in the following June, and was drafted to India, where he was still with his unit in 1920. He holds the General Service and Victory Medals.
43, Randolph Street, Ardwick, Manchester.   Z6372B

HADWIN, G., Private, 23rd Manchester Regiment.
He volunteered in December 1914, and was retained on important duties in England until July 1916, when he was drafted to the Western Front. There he took part in the Battles of Arras, Ypres, Passchendaele, Cambrai, the Somme and Le Cateau, and many other important engagements in various sectors, until the cessation of hostilities. He was demobilised in March 1919, and holds the General Service and Victory Medals.
11, Denison Street, Rusholme, Manchester.   TZ6374

HAGAN, F., Drummer, 5th Connaught Rangers.
He volunteered in August 1914, and in the following year was drafted to France, where he took part in the Battles of Ypres, Vimy Ridge, and the Somme. Later he was transferred to Salonika, and saw much heavy fighting, but was unfortunately killed in action on June 21st, 1917. He was entitled to the 1914–15 Star, and the General Service and Victory Medals.
"He died the noblest death a man may die,
Fighting for God, and right, and liberty."
85, Junction Street, Ancoats, Manchester.   Z8942B

HAGGAS, E. H., Sapper, R.E.

He joined in January 1918, and in the following month proceeded overseas. During his service on the Western Front he was severely wounded in the second Battle of the Somme in April 1918, and was invalided home to hospital. After receiving medical treatment he was discharged as unfit for further service in July of the same year, and holds the General Service and Victory Medals.

21, Grantham Street, West Gorton, Manchester.   Z10317

HAGON, E., Trooper, North Somerset Dragoons.

Volunteering in May 1915, he was drafted to the Western Front in December of that year, and there saw much severe fighting until invalided home in February 1916. He returned to France, however, in November 1917, and took part in many important engagements in the Retreat of 1918, and was wounded in action during the Advance. Again sent home, he was discharged as medically unfit for further service in October 1918, and holds the 1914-15 Star, and the General Service and Victory Medals.

17, Norwood Street, Chorlton-on-Medlock, Manchester.   Z6375

HAGUE, J., L/Corporal, 6th South Lancashire Regt.

He volunteered in September 1915, and in May of the following year proceeded to India, where he was engaged on garrison duties near Bombay until transferred to Mesopotamia in September 1916. There he took part in engagements on the Tigris, and at Kut, and also served for a time at Basra. He returned home for demobilisation in March 1919, and holds the General Service and Victory Medals.

18, New Street, West Gorton, Manchester.   TZ6376

HAIGH, H., Trooper, 6th Inniskilling Dragoons, and Private, M.G.C.

He volunteered in September 1914, and in October of the following year was drafted to the Western Front, where he saw severe fighting in various sectors. He took part in the Battles of Loos, the Somme, Ypres and Cambrai, and many other important engagements, served also through the Retreat and Advance of 1918, and was gassed at Cambrai. He was demobilised in February 1919, and holds the 1914-15 Star, and the General Service and Victory Medals.

11, Abbey Street, Hulme, Manchester.   Z6377

HALES, A., L/Corporal, 8th Manchester Regiment.

He volunteered in November 1914, and in the following May was drafted overseas. Whilst in France he fought in the engagements at Festubert, Ploegsteert Wood, Vermelles, Beaumont-Hamel, Arras, Cambrai, and in many subsequent operations in the Retreat and Advance of 1918. He was demobilised in February 1919, and holds the 1914-15 Star, and the General Service and Victory Medals.

14, Linacre Street, Oldham Road, Manchester.   Z10318A

HALES, J., L/Cpl., Loyal North Lancashire Regt.

He was mobilised from the Reserve at the outbreak of war, and in April 1915 proceeded to Gallipoli. Whilst in this theatre of war he took part in the first Battle of Krithia, in the Landing at Suvla Bay and the Evacuation of the Peninsula. In February 1916, he was drafted to the Western Front, and fought in the engagements on the Somme, and at Arras, Bullecourt and Ypres. He gave his life for King and Country in the second Battle of the Somme on April 18th, 1918, and was entitled to the 1914-15 Star, and the General Service and Victory Medals.

"A costly sacrifice upon the altar of freedom."

14, Linacre Street, Oldham Road, Manchester.   Z10318B

HALEY, J., Pte., Queen's Own (Royal West Kent Regt.)

He joined in October 1916, and in March of the following year proceeded to the Western Front, where he saw much heavy fighting. He took part in the Battles of Arras, Ypres and Cambrai, and other important engagements until wounded in action on the Somme, during the Retreat of 1918. Invalided home, he returned to France on his recovery in July of that year, and fought at Amiens, Le Cateau and Cambrai. He afterwards served with the Army of Occupation at Cologne until his return home for demobilisation in October 1919, and holds the General Service and Victory Medals.

15, Alma Street, Hulme, Manchester.   Z6378

HALL, A., L/Corporal, 21st Manchester Regiment.

Joining in June 1917, he was drafted to Italy later in the same year and there saw much severe fighting on the Piave, and the Asiago Plateaux. In September 1918, he was transferred to the Western Front in time to take part in the Allies' Advance, and fought at Havrincourt and Mons, and in various other sectors. He was demobilised in December 1919, and holds the General Service and Victory Medals.

12, Dryden Street, Chorlton-on-Medlock, Manchester.   Z6380

HALL, C., A.B., R.N., H.M.S. "Britannia."

He volunteered in March 1915, and on completion of his training at Devonport, served on shore at Glasgow, Lowestoft, Yarmouth, Liverpool, Cleethorpes, and Grimsby. When posted to his ship H.M.S. "Britannia," he rendered valuable services in connection with the defence of the East Coast. After four years' work in the Navy he was demobilised from Devonport in March 1919.

13, Hughes Street, Ardwick, Manchester.   Z6384

HALL, C., Private, Lancashire Fusiliers.

He joined in September 1917, and after his training embarked for France in March of the following year. Whilst overseas he took part in much of the heavy fighting in the Retreat, and was unhappily killed in action on the Somme on August 22nd, 1918. He was entitled to the General Service and Victory Medals.

"His life for his Country, his soul to God."

5, Pratley Street, Ancoats, Manchester.   Z10319A

HALL, C., Sergt., Northumberland Fusiliers.

He was mobilised at the outbreak of hostilities, and was engaged on important duties as Sergeant Instructor, training recruits. He rendered valuable services, but later, unfortunately contracted a serious illness, and was invalided to hospital and subsequently died in March 1917.

"The path of duty was the way to glory."

5, Pratley Street, Ancoats, Manchester.   Z10319B

HALL, E., Private, Gordon Highlanders.

He volunteered in January 1915, and after his training was drafted to France. Whilst overseas he was in action at Richebourg and Festubert, and also served with the 149th Tunnelling Company at La Boiselle and on other sectors. He was wounded on three occasions, but afterwards rejoined his unit, and continued his service. He holds the 1914-15 Star, and the General Service and Victory Medals, and was demobilised in January 1919.

494, Mill Street, Bradford, Manchester.   Z10321

HALL, E., Corporal, 14th Manchester Regt. and Sherwood Foresters.

He joined in June 1916, and in December of that year was drafted to the Western Front, where he saw much heavy fighting. He took part in the Battles of Arras, Ypres, Cambrai, and the Somme, and other engagements in various sectors until severely wounded in action in the Retreat of 1918. Invalided home, he was finally demobilised in March 1919, and holds the General Service and Victory Medals.

40, Avon Street, Chorlton-on-Medlock, Manchester.   Z6387

HALL, F., Private, 2nd Lancashire Fusiliers.

He joined in January 1916, and in the following December was drafted to France. Whilst overseas he fought at Ypres, the Somme, Nieuport, Givenchy and Loos. He unhappily was killed in action in August 1918, and was entitled to the General Service and Victory Medals.

"He died the noblest death a man may die, Fighting for God, and right, and liberty."

26, Saville Street, Miles Platting, Manchester.   Z10322

HALL, F. W., Private, R.A.M.C.

He joined in January 1916, and after his training served at various stations on important clerical duties. He rendered valuable services, but was not successful in obtaining a transfer overseas, before the termination of hostilities, and was demobilised in January 1919.

3, Link Street, Longsight, Manchester.   Z10324

HALL, G., Private, 1/8th Manchester Regiment.

Mobilised from the Reserve at the outbreak of war, he embarked for Egypt, and served at various stations until proceeding to Gallipoli in April 1915 He fought in the Battles of Krithia and Suvla Bay, and was wounded, but remained on the Peninsula until the Evacuation. Transferred to France in January 1916, he was in action on the Somme and was wounded. On recovery he rejoined his unit, and was engaged in heavy fighting at Arras, Ypres, and throughout the Retreat and Advance of 1918. He was demobilised in March 1919 and holds the 1914-15 Star, and the General Service and Victory Medals.

116, Loom Street, Oldham Road, Manchester.   TZ9157A

HALL, J., Private, 13th Cheshire Regiment.

He joined in May 1916, and proceeding to France shortly afterwards was in action in the Battles of the Somme, Arras, Ypres, and Cambrai. He was engaged in heavy fighting throughout the Offensives of 1918, and after the cessation of hostilities was sent into Germany with the Army of Occupation. Returning home he was demobilised in January 1920, and holds the General Service and Victory Medals.

116, Loom Street, Oldham Road, Manchester.   TZ9157B

HALL, J., Sergt., Lancashire Fusiliers.

He was mobilised at the outbreak of war, and during his service was engaged on important duties at various stations as a tailor. He rendered valuable services, but was not successful in obtaining a transfer overseas before the cessation of hostilities. He was demobilised in 1919.

77, Thornton Street, Manchester.   Z10323

HALL, J., L/Corporal, 2nd Border Regiment.

He volunteered in April 1915, and being in the following August drafted to France fought in engagements at Ploegsteert, the Somme, the Ancre, Bullecourt and Ypres. In December 1917 he proceeded to Italy and was in action on the Asiago Plateau, and the Offensive on the Piave. He returned to England in January 1919, and was demobilised in the following March, holding the General Service and Victory Medals.

39, Francisco Street, Collyhurst, Manchester.   Z9553

HALL, J., Gunner, R.G.A.

He joined in April 1916, and four months later, proceeded to the Western Front. There he saw much severe fighting in various sectors, and took part in the Battles of the Somme, the Ancre, Bullecourt, Lys, Bapaume, the Sambre, and Le Cateau and many minor engagements until the cessation of hostilities. He was demobilised in August 1920, and holds the General Service and Victory Medals.
41, Matthew Street, Ardwick, Manchester.　　Z6381

HALL, J.C., Pte., 7th Manchester Regt. and Labour Corps.

He volunteered in January 1916, and in the following December proceeded to the Western Front, where he saw severe fighting in various sectors. He served through the Battles of Vimy Ridge, and Passchendaele, and other engagements until wounded in action in October 1917, and invalided to hospital at Glasgow. On his recovery, however, he returned to France and served with the Labour Corps at Étaples, and Boulogne, until his demobilisation in February 1919. He holds the General Service and Victory Medals.
10, Lincoln Street, Longsight, Manchester.　　Z6383A

HALL, J. S., Sergt., Somerset Light Infantry.

He joined in July 1917, and on completion of a period of training in December of that year, was drafted to India. There he was engaged on important garrison duties at Rawal Pindi, Peshawar and various other stations, and also served on the North West Frontier. He returned to England for demobilisation in January 1920, and holds the General Service, Victory and India General Service Medal (with clasp, Afghanistan N.W. Frontier, 1919).
10, Lincoln Street, Longsight, Manchester.　　Z6383B

HALL, J. W., Pte., 17th Royal Welch Fusiliers.

He volunteered in March 1915, and in the following November proceeded to the Western Front, where he saw severe fighting in various sectors. He took part in the Battles of the Somme, Arras, and Ypres, and also served through engagements at Nieuport, La Bassée, Givenchy, and many other places. He was demobilised in November 1919, and holds the 1914-15 Star, and the General Service and Victory Medals.
9, Mary's Place, Ancoats, Manchester.　　Z6385

HALL, J. W., L/Corporal, R.A.S.C. and K.R.R.C.

He volunteered in October 1914, and was drafted to the Western Front in May of the following year. After serving for a time at Boulogne, he went into action at Ypres in July 1917, and afterwards took part in the Battles of Passchendaele, Cambrai, and the Somme, and other engagements, and was wounded at Havrincourt in August 1918. He was sent to hospital in Scotland, and finally invalided from the Army in December of that year, and holds the 1914-15 Star, and the General Service and Victory Medals.
8, Emma Street, West Gorton, Manchester.　　Z6386

HALL, T., Private, Durham Light Infantry.

He volunteered in October 1915, and in November 1917 was drafted to the Western Front. During his service in France he took part in much of the severe fighting in the Battles of Cambrai, the Somme, Havrincourt, and the Sambre. Returning home he was demobilised in December 1918, and holds the General Service and Victory Medals.
27, John Street, Bradford, Manchester.　　Z9554

HALL, W., Private, 20th Manchester Regiment.

He volunteered in November 1914, and in the following October landed in France and fought at St. Eloi and Vermelles. Severely wounded in the first Battle of the Somme, he was admitted into hospital, and died from his injuries on July 10th, 1916. He was entitled to the 1914-15 Star, and the General Service and Victory Medals.
"His life for his Country, his soul to God."
3, Bank Street, Hulme, Manchester.　　Z9158

HALL, W., Private, 12th Manchester Regiment.

He volunteered in April 1915, and in August of that year was drafted to Gallipoli, where he took part in the Landing at Suvla Bay, and saw much severe fighting. In December 1915, he was invalided home suffering from dysentery, but on his recovery was sent to the Western Front. He fell in action in the Advance on the Somme on August 4th, 1916, and was buried near Albert. He was entitled to the 1914-15 Star, and the General Service and Victory Medals.
"His life for his Country, his soul to God."
47, Norton Street, West Gorton, Manchester.　　Z6382

HALL, W. T., Corporal, Manchester Regiment.

He volunteered in 1914, and in the following year proceeded to the Western Front. During his service in France he took part in the Battles of Ypres, and the Somme, and was then drafted to Egypt, where he served for about a year, returning to the Western Front in 1917. He was severely wounded in action in the following year, and invalided to hospital in France, and after receiving medical treatment was demobilised in 1919. He holds the 1914-15 Star, and the General Service and Victory Medals.
11, Evans Street, Chorlton-on-Medlock, Manchester. Z10009B

HALL, W., Private, 6th South Lancashire Regt.

He volunteered in August 1914, and in the following May was drafted to the Dardanelles. Here he took part in the Landing at Cape Helles, and was wounded in the Battles of Krithia. Later he served in the engagements at Achi Baba, and in the second Landing on the Peninsula at Suvla Bay. After the Evacuation of Gallipoli he was sent to Mesopotamia via Egypt, and was in action at the Relief of Kut, and was wounded. On recovery he fought at Kut-el-Amara, in the successful attack on the Tigris, and in the capture of Baghdad. He returned to England in March 1919, and holds the 1914-15 Star, and the General Service and Victory Medals.
89, Princess Street, Bradford, Manchester.　　Z11421

HALL, W. T., L/Corporal, 8th Manchester Regt.

He volunteered in 1914, and was retained on important duties at various stations in England until drafted to the East. After serving for a time in Egypt, he saw severe fighting in Mesopotamia, and was finally transferred to the Western Front, where he took part in many important engagements, and was three times wounded in action. He was demobilised in 1919, and holds the General Service and Victory Medals.
6, Melbourne Street, Chorlton-on-Medlock, Manchester. TX6379

HALLAM, G. T., L/Corporal, 22nd Manchester Regt.

He volunteered in October 1914, and twelve months later proceeded to the Western Front, where he fought in various sectors. After taking part in the Battles of St. Eloi, Albert and Vermelles, and many other engagements, he was severely wounded in action in the Advance on the Somme, and invalided home. He was finally discharged as medically unfit for further service in February 1918, and holds the 1914-15 Star, and the General Service and Victory Medals.
5, Teak Street, Beswick, Manchester.　　TZ6389

HALLAM, H., Private, 3rd Loyal N. Lancs. Regt.

A serving soldier, he was mobilised at the outbreak of hostilities, and proceeded to France in 1915. He was in action in the Battles of Festubert, Hill 60, Ypres, Loos, the Somme, and in many other engagements. During his service overseas he was three times wounded and in April 1918 was taken prisoner and held in captivity until the close of hostilities. Repatriated he was demobilised in January 1919, and hold the 1914-15 Star, and the General Service and Victory Medals.
100, Granville Place, Ancoats, Manchester.　　Z9159

HALLAM, J. E., Private, Manchester Regt., and Labour Corps.

He volunteered in 1914 in the Royal Fusiliers, and after his training served at various stations. He was then transferred to the Manchester Regiment, and was drafted to the Western Front. Whilst overseas he was in action at Ypres, Albert and the Somme and in many engagements in the Retreat and Advance of 1918. He was demobilised in the following year, and holds the General Service and Victory Medals.
55, Herbert Street, Ardwick, Manchester.　　Z10325

HALLAM, W., Sapper, R.E.

He joined in July 1916, and after completing a period of training served at various stations, where he was engaged on duties of a highly important nature. He was not successful in obtaining his transfer to a theatre of war, but, nevertheless, rendered valuable services with his Company until February 1919, when he was demobilised.
38, Redvers Street, Ardwick, Manchester.　　Z6388

HALLETT, E., Private, 12th Manchester Regiment.

He volunteered in September 1914, and in November 1915 was drafted to the Western Front, where he played a prominent part in the heavy fighting at Loos, St. Eloi and Albert in 1916. He was also in action at the Battles of the Somme (I), Arras, Messines, Passchendaele, the Somme (II), the Marne (II) and Le Cateau (II). Twice wounded—on the Somme in 1916, and at Passchendaele in 1917—he underwent treatment at a Casualty Clearing Station. He was demobilised in February 1919, and holds the 1914-15 Star, and the General Service and Victory Medals.
39, Baden Street, Ardwick, Manchester.　　Z6390

HALLIDAY, J., Private, M.G.C.

He volunteered in September 1914, and in the following November embarked for France. Whilst on the Western Front he fought at Ypres, Hill 60, Festubert, Albert, Vimy Ridge, the Somme, Arras, Ypres, Cambrai, and in many of the engagements which followed in the Retreat and Advance of 1918. He was demobilised in January of the following year, and holds the 1914-15 Star, and the General Service and Victory Medals. 17, Marcer Street, Ancoats, Manchester. Z10326

HALLIDAY, J., Private, 18th Manchester Regt.

A serving soldier at the outbreak of war he was almost immediately sent to France, and took part in the Retreat from Mons and in several early engagements. He was severely wounded at Festubert in May 1915, and was invalided home after receiving treatment in various hospitals, he was discharged as medically unfit for further duty in January 1916, and holds the Mons Star, and the General Service and Victory Medals.
13, Iron Street, Miles Platting, Manchester.　　Z9555

HALLIWELL, A., Q.M.S., 7th Lancashire Fusiliers, and King's (Liverpool Regiment.)
Volunteering in December 1914, he proceeded overseas on completion of his training at Southport in August 1915. Whilst in Gallipoli he served at Suvla Bay, and in the subsequent engagements of the campaign, and after the Evacuation was drafted to Egypt. On this front he saw heavy fighting on the Suez Canal, and at Agagia, and later was in action in Palestine. On his return home in July 1919, he was demobilised, holding the 1914-15 Star, and the General Service and Victory Medals.
47, Southwell Street, Harpurhey, Manchester. Z11504

HALLIWELL, J., Private, 1st Lancashire Fusiliers.
He volunteered in August 1914, and in February of the following year was drafted to France. During his service on the Western Front he fought in the engagements at Ypres, Festubert, Albert, the Somme and Cambrai, and in various operations in the Retreat and Advance of 1918. Later owing to ill-health he was invalided home and discharged as medically unfit for further duty in November 1918. He holds the 1914-15 Star, and the General Service and Victory Medals.
25, Phelan Street, Collyhurst, Manchester. Z10360

HALLSOR, A., Private, Manchester Regiment.
He joined in August 1916, but owing to his being medically unfit for transfer overseas was engaged on important guard and transport duties on the East Coast. He also served with the King's Own Yorkshire Light Infantry, the South Lancs. Regiment and the Royal Welch Fusiliers, and did consistently good work until his demobilisation in March 1919.
31, Wood Street, Hulme, Manchester. Z6391

HAMER, J., Driver, R.A.S.C. (M.T.)
Volunteering in January 1915, he was quickly drafted to the Western Front, and saw much severe fighting during the Battles of Neuve Chapelle, St. Eloi, Hill 60, Ypres and Loos before being accidentally burnt as the result of his lorry catching fire. He was invalided to hospital at Netley, but on his recovery was sent to German East Africa where he rendered valuable services until his demobilisation in May 1919. He holds the 1914-15 Star, and the General Service and Victory Medals.
44, Dorset Street, Hulme, Manchester. Z6392

HAMERTON, R., Private, 12th Manchester Regt.
He joined in March 1916, and in the following year proceeded to France. In this theatre of war he took part in the Battle of the Somme (II), and in the Retreat, during which he was taken prisoner of war. He was held in captivity in Germany at Chemnitz, and was made to work in the coal mines. Released after the Armistice, he returned home and was demobilised in December 1918, holding the General Service and Victory Medals.
43, Fenwick Street, Hulme, Manchester. Z11715

HAMILTON, G., Private, 2/9th Manchester Regt.
He was mobilised at the outbreak of war, and was at once drafted to France, where he fought in the Retreat from Mons. He also served at La Bassée, Ypres, the Somme and Nieuport, and was wounded and taken prisoner in March 1918 during the German Offensive. He was held in captivity in Germany until December 1919, when he was repatriated, and discharged on account of his wounds in the following month. He holds the Mons Star, and the General Service and Victory Medals.
52, Flower Street, Ancoats, Manchester. Z9470B

HAMILTON, H. K., Sapper, R.E.
He volunteered in 1915, and in the following year was drafted to Egypt, and served with the British Forces in Palestine and Syria. He was engaged on important duties in connection with the operations, and was frequently in the forward areas, notably in the Battle of Gaza, in the capture of Jericho, and at Aleppo. After the Armistice he remained in Egypt until 1919, when he returned to England and was demobilised in October of that year. He holds the General Service and Victory Medals.
11, Fleesen Street, Rusholme, Manchester. Z10327A

HAMILTON, J., Private, R.A.S.C. (M.T.)
He joined in August 1917, and in the following month was drafted to France. Whilst overseas he was engaged on important duties on the lines of communication during the Battles of Cambrai, the Somme and the Marne, Bapaume, Amiens and Le Cateau. He returned to England and was demobilised in October 1919, and holds the General Service and Victory Medals.
54, Inkermann Street, Collyhurst, Manchester. Z10361

HAMILTON, J., Corporal, 12th Manchester Regt.
He volunteered in August 1914, and in the following June was drafted to France, where he took part in the Battles of Loos, Albert, the Somme, Arras, Vimy Ridge and Ypres. He laid down his life for King and Country during a bombing raid near Arras on September 8th, 1917, and was entitled to the 1914-15 Star, and the General Service and Victory Medals.
"And doubtless he went in splendid company."
66, Bradshaw Street, City Road, Hulme, Manchester. Z6393

HAMILTON, T., Pte., 8th South Lancashire Regt.
Volunteering in September 1914, he served at various stations until drafted to France in January 1916. He was in action at Loos, St. Eloi, Albert and on the Somme, where he was severely wounded. Invalided home, he received hospital treatment and was subsequently discharged as unfit for further service in October 1917. He holds the General Service and Victory Medals.
8, Upper Dover Street, Bradford, Manchester. TZ9160

HAMILTON, W. A., Air Mechanic, R.A.F. (late R.N.A.S.)
He joined in 1918, and after his training was engaged on important duties, which demanded a high degree of technical skill. He rendered valuable services, but owing to the cessation of hostilities was unable to proceed overseas, and was demobilised in 1919.
11, Fleesen Street, Rusholme, Manchester. Z10327B

HAMLET, C., Private, 1st East Lancashire Regt.
He volunteered in September 1914, and in July of the following year proceeded to the Western Front. Whilst overseas he fought in the second Battle of Ypres, and was wounded in action at Loos. After his recovery he took part in much of the heavy fighting at Albert, the Somme, Arras, and Vimy Ridge, and was again wounded at Beaumont-Hamel. He subsequently served at Cambrai and in many of the later engagements, and was demobilised in October 1919. He holds the 1914-15 Star, and the General Service and Victory Medals.
2, Grantham Street, West Gorton, Manchester. Z10328

HAMLETT, A., Pte., 8th East Lancashire Regt.
He volunteered in November 1914, and in the following July proceeded to the Western Front, where he took part in the Battle of Loos, and in heavy fighting at Ypres and Festubert. In February 1916 he was transferred to Class W, Army Reserve, and was engaged on important duties as a wire pointer in connection with the manufacture of munitions at Messrs Johnson and Nephews, Forge Lane, Manchester. He was demobilised from the Army in January 1919, and holds the 1914-15 Star, and the General Service and Victory Medals.
119, Cross Street, Bradford, Manchester. Z6394

HAMLETT, A., Private, 4th East Yorkshire Regt.
Volunteering in 1915, he landed in France in the following year and was in action in many parts of the line. He fought in the Somme and Arras sectors, and was taken prisoner at La Fontaine in June 1916. Held in captivity in Germany until the close of hostilities, he was repatriated and was demobilised in 1919. He holds the General Service and Victory Medals. 26, Catherine Street, Manchester. TZ9161

HAMLETT, T., Pte., 8th King's (Liverpool Regt.)
He volunteered in March 1915, and in the following July was drafted to France, where he took part in the severe fighting at Ypres, the Somme, Arras, Bullecourt, Messines, Cambrai, Bapaume, Amiens and Le Cateau. During his service he was twice wounded, at Ypres in 1915, and the Somme in 1916. He was demobilised in March 1919, and holds the 1914-15 Star, and the General Service and Victory Medals.
77, Inkermann Street, Collyhurst, Manchester. Z10362

HAMMOND, A., Sapper, R.E.
Volunteering in December 1914, he was sent to France in the following August and was in action at La Bassée, Givenchy, Festubert, Ypres (I), Albert, Loos, the Somme, Arras, Ypres (III), Messines and Passchendaele. He was twice in hospital suffering from shell-shock, and in November 1917 was drafted to Italy, where he rendered valuable services at the Base until his demobilisation in May 1919. He holds the 1914-15 Star, and the General Service and Victory Medals.
31, Buckingham Street, Moss Side, Manchester. Z6395

HAMMOND, J., Sergt., R.A.S.C.
Volunteering in October 1914, he proceeded to Egypt four months later and served with distinction with the 10th Divisional Train until September 1915. He was then invalided home, and on his recovery was stationed at Dover. In June 1919 he volunteered to go to Russia and did consistently good work there until the following October, when he was again sent home owing to indifferent health. He was eventually demobilised in March 1920, and holds the 1914-15 Star, and the General Service and Victory Medals.
18, Anthony Street, Ardwick, Manchester. Z6396

HAMNETT, J., Trooper, Duke of Lancaster's Own Dragoons.
In August 1914, he volunteered, and a month later was drafted to Egypt, where he was in action on the Suez Canal and served with the Military Mounted Police at Alexandria and Cairo. He was transferred to the Western Front in February 1917 and was in action at Remy, Béthune, Bray, the Somme, Péronne, Arras, Bullecourt, Messines and Ypres. He was in hospital for a short period and was demobilised in February 1919, holding the 1914-15 Star, and the General Service and Victory Medals.
17, Hendham Vale, Collyhurst, Manchester Z11505

HAMNETT, R., Pte., 8th East Lancashire Regt.
Volunteering in October 1914, he proceeded to France in September of the following year, and after taking part in heavy fighting at Loos, St. Eloi, Albert and Vimy Ridge, gallantly laid down his life on July 16th, 1916, during the Battle of the Somme. He was entitled to the 1914–15 Star, and the General Service and Victory Medals.
"His life for his Country, his soul to God."
18, Moor Street, Winslow Road, Rusholme, Manchester. Z6397

HAMPSON, A. E., Private, Royal Fusiliers.
Three months after joining the Army, he proceeded to France in August 1917, and took part in the Battles of Cambrai (where he was wounded), Bapaume and Havrincourt (where he was again wounded in action). In 1920 he was stationed in India on garrison duties, and holds the General Service and Victory Medals.
26, Derby Street, Ardwick, Manchester. Z6398B

HAMPSON, C. H., Special War Worker.
He offered his services to Messrs. Galloways, Ltd., Ardwick, Manchester, in February 1917, and for a period of two years was engaged on very important duties in connection with the output of munitions of war. He rendered valuable services until February 1919.
26, Derby Street, Ardwick, Manchester. Z6398A

HAMPSON, E., Corporal, 2nd Cheshire Regiment.
Volunteering at the commencement of hostilities, he proceeded to France and saw much service in many sectors. He fought at Ypres and Festubert and laid down his life for King and Country in the Battle of Hill 60 in April 1915. He was entitled to the 1914–15 Star, and the General Service and Victory Medals.
"The path of duty was the way to glory."
3, Berry Street, Manchester. Z9162

HAMPSON, H., Pte., 4th King's (Liverpool Regt.)
He volunteered in August 1914, and in February of the following year was sent to France, where he was in action at Ypres, Hill 60, Cambrai, Neuve Chapelle and many other engagements, until the close of hostilities. He returned home, and was demobilised in May 1919, holding the 1914–15 Star, and the General Service and Victory Medals.
18, Hinde Street, Gorton, Manchester. Z10331

HAMPSON, H., Gunner, R.F.A.
Mobilised at the outbreak of hostilities, he was soon drafted to France and was in action in the Retreat from Mons. He also served at La Bassée, Ypres, Nieuport and Loos and in many later engagements. He gave his life for the freedom of England in the Ypres sector in March 1918, and was entitled to the Mons Star, and the General Service and Victory Medals.
"A valiant Soldier, with undaunted heart, he breasted life's last hill."
35, Pilling Street, Newton Heath, Manchester. Z9556

HAMPSON, J., L/Cpl., Canadian Overseas Forces.
He volunteered in February 1915, and was eventually drafted to France, where he took part in much severe fighting at St. Eloi, and Ypres. He was badly wounded in action in March 1916, and was invalided to hospital at Lewisham. Later he returned to the Western Front, but in June 1917 was again invalided home, and until the cessation of hostilities, was engaged as a Corporal Instructor at Whitley Camp until his discharge from the Army in December 1918. He holds the 1914–15 Star, and the General Service and Victory Medals.
11, Mart Street, Bradford, Manchester. Z6400

HAMPSON, J. H., Corporal, 7th Manchester Regt.
He volunteered in November 1914, and in September 1915 was drafted to the Western Front, where he took part in heavy fighting at Neuve Chapelle and Ypres. Later he was in action at the Battles of the Somme and Arras (in both of which engagements he was wounded), and in the Retreat and Advance of 1918, being a third time wounded in October of that year. He was demobilised in 1919, and holds the 1914–15 Star, and the General Service and Victory Medals
21, Bedale Street, Hulme, Manchester. Z6399

HAMPSON, S., Battery Q.M.S., R.F.A.
He volunteered in February 1915, and nine months later was ordered to the Western Front. There he rendered valuable services as a Signaller in important engagements at Ploegsteert Wood, Vimy Ridge, the Ancre, Arras, Ypres, Messines and Bapaume. He was wounded at Ypres in October 1917, and remained in France until demobilised in June 1919, holding the 1914–15 Star, and the General Service and Victory Medals.
115, Crossley Street, Gorton, Manchester. Z11506

HAMPSON, T., 1st Air Mechanic, R.A.F.
He joined in March 1916, in the Lancashire Fusiliers, and after his training was completed, was drafted to the Western Front in December of the same year. He took part in much of the heavy fighting on the Somme and at Albert and was gassed at Albert in November 1917. He was invalided home, and was ultimately demobilised in March 1919. He holds the General Service and Victory Medals.
12, Juno Street, Newton Heath, Manchester. Z9557

HAMPTON, H., L/Corporal, Welch Regiment.
He joined the Cheshire Regiment in February 1918 at the age of sixteen and later in the same year was drafted to France, where he was transferred to the Welch Regiment. He was in charge of a Lewis gun section at Ypres, Armentières and the operations prior to the entry into Mons, and afterwards proceeded with the Army of Occupation to Germany. He was demobilised in October 1919, and holds the General Service and Victory Medals.
14, Crook Street, Miles Platting, Manchester. Z10363

HAMSON, H., Driver, R.F.A.
He was called up from the Reserve at the outbreak of war and at once proceeded with the First Expeditionary Force to France. He was in action at Mons, Le Cateau, the Marne, the Aisne, La Bassée, Ypres, Neuve Chapelle, Hill 60, Ypres (II), the Somme, Arras, Ypres (III), Cambrai, the Marne, Amiens and Le Cateau (II). He served in France until discharged in February 1919, and holds the Mons Star, and the General Service and Victory Medals.
45, Middlewood Street, Harpurhey, Manchester. Z11507

HAMSON, T., Private, Labour Corps.
He joined in June 1917, and after his training, was engaged on important duties as a batman and storekeeper at various stations in England and Wales. Although unsuccessful in obtaining his transfer overseas, he rendered valuable services until his demobilisation in January 1919.
63, Dudley Street, Stratford, Manchester. Z6401

HANBY, F., Corpl., Manchester Regt., and M.G.C.
Volunteering in September 1914, he was quickly drafted to France, where he played a prominent part in the Battles of Ypres, Loos, Vermelles, the Somme, the Ancre and Cambrai, and was twice badly wounded in action. He was demobilised in February 1919, and holds the 1914 Star, and the General Service and Victory Medals.
37, Wellesley Street, West Gorton, Manchester. Z6402

HANCOCK, J. A., L/Corpl., 7th Manchester Regt.
He volunteered in December 1914, and first saw active service in the following June, when he was sent to Gallipoli. After taking part in the Battle of Krithia (III), the Landing at Suvla Bay, the capture of Chunuk Bair and the Evacuation of the Peninsula, he saw much severe fighting in Egypt. In October 1917 he landed in France, where he was in action at the Battles of Cambrai, the Somme (II), the Marne (II), Bapaume and Ypres (IV). Demobilised in February 1919, he holds the 1914–15 Star, and the General Service and Victory Medals. 12, Belleek St., Hulme, Manchester. Z6403

HANCOCK, J. H., Private, 7th Manchester Regt.
He volunteered in August 1914, and in the following year was sent to Egypt, where he took part in the operations on the Peninsula, and was wounded. In 1917 he was transferred to France and was in action on the Somme, at Ypres and Cambrai and in numerous other engagements. He was demobilised in January 1919, and holds the 1914–15 Star, and the General Service and Victory Medals.
6, Mary Place, Ancoats, Manchester. Z9163

HANCOCK, S., Gunner (Signaller) R.F.A.
He joined in November 1917, and underwent a period of training prior to his being drafted to France. There he served as Signaller and Observer to the 119th Battery and took part in the Battles of Havrincourt, Cambrai (II), Ypres (IV), during the Advance of 1918. He was demobilised in July 1919, and holds the General Service and Victory Medals.
45, Robert Street, Newton Heath, Manchester. Z11716

HAND, J. J., L/Corporal, King's (Liverpool Regt.)
He volunteered in August 1914, and in the following June was drafted to the Western Front, where he played an important part in the Battles of Loos, Ypres and Cambrai before being taken prisoner, during the Retreat in March 1918. He was held in captivity for nine months, and was eventually demobilised in March 1919, holding the 1914–15 Star, and the General Service and Victory Medals.
41, Carlisle Street, Hulme, Manchester. Z6405

HAND, T., Private, 4th Cheshire Regiment.
He joined in January 1918, and in the following March was drafted to France, where he was in action on the Arras front and at Poperinghe, Albert, Ypres, Havrincourt and Cambrai. During his service he was twice wounded, first at Kemmel and later at Albert. He was demobilised in October 1919, and holds the General Service and Victory Medals.
10, Teer Street, Ancoats, Manchester. Z10332

HAND, T. H., L/Corporal, Manchester Regiment.
He volunteered in August 1914, and in the following April was sent to France, where he was transferred to the King's (Liverpool Regiment) and took part in the Battles of Ypres, Festubert and Loos. In March 1916 he was invalided home, through an injury received in the trenches. On his recovery, he joined the Royal Welch Fusiliers, and was ordered to Egypt, but whilst on the way on board the s.s. "Arcadian," lost his life when this ship was sunk by an enemy submarine in the Mediterranean on April 15th, 1917. He was entitled to the 1914–15 Star, and the General Service and Victory Medals. 36, Elliott Street, Bradford, Manchester. Z6404

HANDLEY, F., L/Cpl., 1/8th Lancashire Fusiliers.
He volunteered in April 1915, and was sent to Egypt in May 1916. After taking part in the Battles of El Fasher and Magdhaba, he was transferred to France, where he saw much severe fighting until taken prisoner during the second Battle of the Somme in March 1918. Whilst in captivity he was forced to work under our own shell-fire near Bullecourt, and as the result of harsh treatment and poor food, was in hospital for five months suffering from dysentery and dropsy. On his release, he was immediately discharged in December 1918, and holds the General Service and Victory Medals.
2, Allen Street, Hulme, Manchester. TZ6406B

HANDLEY, J., L/Corpl., 7th Manchester Regt. (T.F.)
Mobilised with the Territorials in August 1914, he was sent to Egypt early in the following year, but was quickly drafted to the Dardanelles, where he took part in the Landing at Cape Helles and was wounded in action in May 1915. Later he was transferred to France and was engaged on train ferry construction work at Dunkirk, Dieppe and Oissel and on electrical construction and maintenance at Audruicq with the No. 1 Electrical Section of the R.E. He was demobilised in May 1919, and holds the 1914-15 Star, and the General Service and Victory Medals.
2, Allen Street, Hulme, Manchester. TZ6406A

HANLEY, A., Private, 3rd Manchester Regiment.
He joined in February 1917, and in July was drafted to France, but after only a month on active service was invalided home suffering from general debility and kidney trouble. In September 1917, he was discharged as medically unfit for further duty, and holds the General Service and Victory Medals.
14, Mark Lane, Chorlton-on-Medlock, Manchester. Z6407

HANLEY, G. E., Private, 2nd Manchester Regt.
He volunteered in January 1915, and in the following year landed in France. In the course of his service in this theatre of war he fought in the Battles of Hill 60, Ypres and Loos and later took part in the fighting on the Somme and at Arras, remaining in this seat of war until the conclusion of hostilities. He was demobilised in February 1919, and holds the 1914-15 Star, and the General Service and Victory Medals.
32, Brown Street, Ancoats, Manchester. Z11902

HANLEY, J., Private, 2nd Lancashire Fusiliers.
He volunteered in August 1914, and was sent in the following year to Gallipoli, where he took part in the Landing at Cape Helles, the three Battles of Krithia and the Landing at Suvla Bay, during which he was wounded. In 1917 he was transferred to France and was in action at Arras and Ypres, and was again wounded. After a period in hospital at Boulogne, he was posted to the Labour Corps. He was demobilised in April 1919, and holds the 1914-15 Star, and the General Service and Victory Medals.
10, Vance Street, Oldham Road, Manchester. Z9164

HANLON, J., Private, R.A.M.C.
He joined in April 1917, and later in the same year was sent to Egypt. There he was engaged at Alexandria and Cairo and Kantara on hospital duties for nearly two years. He returned home in February 1919, and was demobilised a month later, holding the General Service and Victory Medals.
169, Victoria Square, Ancoats, Manchester. Z9165

HANNAH, F., Private, R.M.L.I.
He joined in May 1916, and after the completion of his training was posted to H.M.S. "Inflexible," in which he did valuable service until hostilities ceased. His vessel was engaged on important patrol duties in the North Sea, and was in action with German destroyers off the Belgian Coast. He was also present at the bombardment of Kavalla in the Ægean. After returning home, he was demobilised in 1919, and holds the General Service and Victory Medals.
43, Elizabeth Ann Street, Manchester. Z10364

HANNAH, J., Gunner, R.F.A.
A time-serving Soldier, he was immediately drafted to France in August 1914, and took part in the Retreat from Mons. He was also in action at the Battles of the Marne, the Aisne, Ypres, Loos, Givenchy, the Ancre, Arras, Vimy Ridge, Passchendaele and Cambrai. Wounded near Cambrai in March 1918, he was in hospital at Rouen and Penarth (in Wales) until the following December, when he rejoined his Battery. He received his discharge after nineteen years' service in July 1920, and holds the Mons Star, and the General Service and Victory Medals.
27, Pownall Street, Hulme, Manchester. Z6408

HANNAH, J. W., Corpl., 2nd South Lancashire Regt.
Mobilised in August 1914, he was at once drafted to France and served with distinction at the Battle of, and in the Retreat from, Mons. He also took part in the Battles of Le Cateau and La Bassée, where he was badly wounded in action in October 1914. After eight months treatment in the 2nd London General Hospital, he was invalided from the Army in June 1915, and holds the Mons Star, and the General Service and Victory Medals.
15, Chatsworth Street, Hulme, Manchester. Z6409

HANNON, M., Private, Royal Marine Labour Corps.
He joined in August 1917, and was quickly drafted to France, where he was engaged on dangerous work in connection with the treatment of "dud" shells. He was badly poisoned as the result of his hands coming in contact with the T.N.T. composition and was in hospital at Rouen for some time. Demobilised in February 1919, he holds the General Service and Victory Medals.
4, Crawshaw Street, Chorlton-on-Medlock, Manchester. Z6410

HANNON, T., Private, Northamptonshire Regiment.
Joining in July 1917, he was sent to France in April of the following year. He took part in the severe fighting on the Somme, where he was severely wounded. He was invalided home in consequence and after a long period in hospital was discharged from the Army owing to his injuries in May 1919. He holds the General Service and Victory Medals.
14, Jersey Street Dwellings, Ancoats, Manchester. Z10333

HANSHAW, W., Tpr., Duke of Lancaster's Own Dgns.
He volunteered in September 1915, and three months later was sent to Ireland, where he was engaged on important garrison duties and took part during the Rebellion. Although unsuccessful in obtaining his transfer overseas, he, nevertheless, rendered valuable services until his demobilisation in December 1919. 80, Sloane Street, Moss Side, Manchester. Z6411

HANSON, H., Private, Manchester Regiment.
He volunteered in August 1914, and in May of the following year was drafted to the Dardanelles. He took part in the Landing at Suvla Bay, and was severely wounded, having one leg shot off. He unfortunately died of his injuries during the passage to Malta on October 7th, 1915. He was entitled to the 1914-15 Star, and the General Service and Victory Medals.
"The path of duty was the way to glory."
44, Rolleston Street, Ancoats, Manchester. Z10335

HANSON, J. O., Private, 4th Manchester Regiment.
He volunteered in September 1914, and in October of the following year was sent to France, where he took part in the Battle of Loos, and was wounded. On his recovery after treatment in England, he proceeded to Salonika in December 1916, and was engaged in various operations of importance in this theatre of war until January 1919, when he returned home. He was demobilised in the following month, and holds the 1914-15 Star, and the General Service and Victory Medals.
139, Mill Street, Ancoats, Manchester. Z10334A

HANSON, T., Private, R.A.V.C.
He joined in April 1917, and in the same month was drafted to France, where he was engaged at Le Havre on important duties connected with his branch of the Service. After the Armistice he proceeded with the Army of Occupation to Germany. He was demobilised in January 1919, and holds the General Service and Victory Medals.
44, Rolleston Street, Ancoats, Manchester. Z10334C

HARBEN, W., Sapper, R.E.
Mobilised in August 1914, he was immediately sent to France and took an active part in the Battles of Mons, Le Cateau, the Marne, the Aisne, Ypres (I), Neuve Chapelle, Hill 60, Ypres (II), Loos, the Somme, Arras and Vimy Ridge. In November 1917 he was transferred to Italy, and after much severe fighting on the Piave, unfortunately died in December 1917 as the result of septic poisoning. He was entitled to the Mons Star, and the General Service and Victory Medals.
"A costly sacrifice upon the altar of freedom."
24, Garden Walks, Ardwick, Manchester. Z6412

HARBRIDGE, G., Gunner, R.F.A.
Volunteering in January 1915, he was sent to France in July and took part in the Battles of the Somme, Vimy Ridge, Ypres, Passchendaele, and Cambrai. He was also in action with his Battery during the Retreat and Advance of 1918, and after the Armistice, served in Germany with the Army of Occupation. Demobilised in January 1919, he holds the 1914-15 Star, and the General Service and Victory Medals.
22, Tranmere Street, Hulme, Manchester. Z6413

HARBRIDGE, T., Private, Labour Corps.
He first volunteered in 1914, but after a short period of service was discharged. In 1917 however, he rejoined in the Labour Corps and was engaged on important duties at Aldershot. He did consistently good work with his unit until his demobilisation in 1919. 2, James Street, Moss Side, Manchester. Z6414

HARDING, C., Private, Welch Regt., and R.A.S.C.
He volunteered in November 1915, and was shortly afterwards transferred to the Royal Army Service Corps, in which he was engaged at various stations on important transport duties. He was not successful in securing his transfer overseas, and was specially discharged in August 1917 for work in connection with coal mining.
39, Alice Street, Bradford, Manchester. Z9991B

HARDING, D., Private, 19th Manchester Regiment.
Volunteering in April 1915, he was unfortunately taken seriously ill during his training, and after a period of hospital treatment at Southport, was discharged as medically unfit for further service owing to a defective heart in January 1916.
1, Hibbert Street, Hulme, Manchester. Z6417

HARDING, A., Sapper, R.E.

Mobilised at the outbreak of hostilities, he proceeded to France, and was in action in the Retreat from Mons. He also saw service at the Battles of Le Cateau, the Marne, the Aisne, Ypres, Neuve Chapelle, Hill 60, Festubert and Albert, but died gloriously on the Field in the Battle of the Somme in July 1916. He was entitled to the Mons Star, and the General Service and Victory Medals.

"He passed out of the sight of men by the path of duty and self-sacrifice."

12, Holbeck Street, Oldham Road, Manchester.   Z9559B

HARDING, R. D., Private, Manchester Regiment.

He volunteered in September 1915, and in November of the following year was drafted to France, where he took part in heavy fighting at Loos, and Albert. He was also in action at the Battles of the Somme and Arras, and was wounded in both these engagements. Invalided home in July 1917, he was discharged as medically unfit in October, and holds the 1914-15 Star, and the General Service and Victory Medals.

79, Bedford Street, Moss Side, Manchester.   TZ6415

HARDING, S., Sapper, R.E.

He volunteered in February 1915, and on completion of his training was drafted overseas in the following November. During his service on the Western Front, he took part in fierce fighting on the Somme, and at Bray, Montauban, Guillemont, La Bassée, Festubert, Givenchy, Hill 60, Arras, Vimy Ridge, Ypres, and Passchendaele. He was taken prisoner at St. Quentin, and during his captivity was employed on the railway at Cologne. On his release he was demobilised in March 1919, and holds the 1914-15 Star, and the General Service and Victory Medals.

5, Southwell Street, Harpurhey, Manchester.   Z11509

HARDMAN, G., Gunner, R.F.A.

He volunteered in September 1914, and after his training was engaged at various East and South Coast Stations on anti-aircraft duties. He rendered valuable services, but was not successful in obtaining his transfer overseas before the cessation of hostilities, owing to defective eyesight. He was demobilised in February 1919.

13, Buxton Street, West Gorton, Manchester.   Z10336

HARDMAN, J. H., Private, 1/7th Manchester Regt.

He joined in March 1916, and in June of the following year was drafted overseas. During his service on the Western Front, he took part in the Battles of Ypres, and Passchendaele, where he was buried as the result of a shell explosion, and suffered from shell-shock. After protracted hospital treatment in Boulogne and Stockport, he was invalided from the Service in April 1919, and holds the General Service and Victory Medals.

4, Oldenburg Street, Longsight, Manchester.   Z6418

HARDMAN, J. J., Private, 3rd Border Regiment.

Volunteering in August 1914, he was drafted in 1915 to France, where he took part in many important engagements, including those at Neuve Chapelle, the Somme, and Arras, and was wounded twice. He was unfortunately killed in 1918, while lying in hospital at the Base, and was entitled to the 1914-15 Star, and the General Service and Victory Medals.

"A costly sacrifice upon the altar of freedom."

5, Cowleshaw Street, Garratt Street, Manchester.   Z10337B

HARDMAN, R. J., Pte., 10th Loyal N. Lancs. Regt.

He volunteered in September 1914, and in July of the succeeding year proceeded to France. Whilst overseas he took part in the fighting at Albert, Vermelles, Vimy Ridge, and the Somme, but was invalided to hospital in France with heart trouble, and was subsequently discharged as medically unfit for further service in June 1916. He holds the 1914-15 Star, and the General Service and Victory Medals.

122, Parker Street, Bradford, Manchester.   Z9558

HARDMAN, T., Private, 2nd Manchester Regiment.

Having joined in May 1916, he was sent to Egypt in the following year. After much valuable service there for some time, he proceeded to Mesopotamia in 1918, and took part in the operations in that theatre of war. After treatment at Malta for malaria and dysentery he returned home, and was discharged in February 1919, owing to his disabilities. He holds the General Service and Victory Medals.

5, Cowleshaw Street, Garrat Street, Manchester.   Z10337A

HARDMAN, W., Private, Manchester Regiment.

He was mobilised from the Reserve in August 1914, and was immediately sent to France, where he took part in the Retreat from Mons, and the Battle of La Bassée, and was severely wounded. He was invalided home in consequence, and was discharged in September 1915, owing to his injuries, and the expiration of his term of engagement. He holds the Mons Star, and the General Service and Victory Medals.

40, Burns Street, Bradford, Manchester.   Z10338

HARDY, A., Private, Cheshire Regiment.

He joined in March 1918, and did duty with his unit on the Curragh in Ireland. He was not drafted overseas until January 1919, when he was sent to the Army of Occupation in Germany and rendered valuable services there until his demobilisation in November 1919.

153, Heald Grove, Rusholme, Manchester.   Z6416

HARDY, C. T., Pte., Gordon Hldrs. and Labour Corps.

He volunteered in January 1915, and was engaged on important duties with his unit till May 1917, when he was drafted to France. He was on duty with the Labour Corps at Bullecourt, Ypres, and Cambrai, where he was wounded in November of that year. He was discharged in April 1919 in consequence of his service, and holds the General Service and Victory Medals.

9, Drinkwater Street, Harpurhey, Manchester.   Z11422B

HARDY, E., Sergt., South Lancashire Regiment.

He volunteered in 1914, and in the following year was drafted to the Western Front. After serving with distinction in much severe fighting, he was unhappily killed in action by a sniper on July 9th, 1916, during the Battle of the Somme. He was entitled to the 1914-15 Star, and the General Service and Victory Medals.

"A valiant Soldier, with undaunted heart he breasted life's last hill."

9, Caygill Street, Chorlton-on-Medlock, Manchester.   X1344B

HARDY, J. A., A/Corporal, R.A.M.C.

Volunteering in September 1914, he was sent to France nine months later, and first served on the hospital barge running between Béthune and Calais. In November 1917 he was transferred to Queen Mary's Ambulance Train No 14, and rendered valuable services until his demobilisation in February 1919. He holds the 1914-15 Star, and the General Service and Victory Medals.

112, Robert Street, West Gorton, Manchester.   Z6419

HARDY, J. E., Pte., 3rd Canadian Regt., Canadian Overseas Forces.

He volunteered in January 1915, and first served with the Royal Navy on the high seas until September 1916. He then joined the Canadian Forces, and was sent to the Western Front, where he took part in the Battles of Arras and Ypres, and in the Retreat and Advance of 1918. Demobilised in August 1920, he holds the 1914-15 Star, and the General Service and Victory Medals.

153, Heald Grove, Rusholme, Manchester.   Z6421

HARDY, J. T., Private, 25th Manchester Regt.

He volunteered in December 1915, and after a period of duty in England, was sent to France in June 1917. Whilst in this theatre of war, he was in action at the Battles of Ypres, Passchendaele, Lens, Cambrai, and the Somme (II). He was wounded and taken prisoner in March 1918, and was held in captivity until the following December. In January 1919 he was discharged, medically unfit, and holds the General Service and Victory Medals.

2, Walter Street, Hulme, Manchester.   TZ6420A

HARDY, J. T., Trooper, Lancashire Hussars.

He joined in October 1917, and in the following March was drafted to France. He took part in the severe fighting at Lens and Cambrai, and was gassed. He also served in the Retreat and Advance of 1918, and afterwards proceeded with the Army of Occupation to Germany. He was demobilised in September 1919, after his return to England, and holds the General Service and Victory Medals.

5, Pratley Street, Ancoats, Manchester.   Z10319C

HARDY, T., Gunner, R.G.A.

Volunteering in November 1914, he was drafted to France later in the same month, and saw much service there. He did good work as a gunner at Neuve Chapelle, Hill 60, Ypres, Festubert, Loos, Vimy Ridge, the Somme, and Arras, and gave his life for King and Country at Messines Ridge in June 1917. He was entitled to the 1914-15 Star, and the General Service and Victory Medals.

"He died the noblest death a man may die,
Fighting for God, and right, and liberty."

12, Holbeck Street, Oldham Road, Manchester.   Z9559A

HARDY, W., Private, 1st Manchester Regiment.

Mobilised in August 1914, he was shortly afterwards sent to France, where he took part in the Battles of Mons, La Bassée, Ypres, Loos, the Somme, and Arras. He was then transferred to Mesopotamia, and after being in action at Kut, served in Egypt. He was demobilised in June 1919, and holds the Mons Star, and the General Service and Victory Medals.

1, Neild Street, Ancoats, Manchester.   Z10339

HARDY, W. H., Pte., 7th K.O. (R. Lancaster Regt.)

He volunteered in November 1914, and in July of the following year was drafted to France where he was in action at Ypres, Trones Wood, Delville Wood, the Somme, and Arras, and was wounded. He was invalided home, and after a period in hospital, was discharged in July 1918, owing to his injuries. He holds the 1914-15 Star, and the General Service and Victory Medals.

9, Drinkwater Street, Harpurhey, Manchester.   Z11422A

HARE, G., Private, 4th South Wales Borderers.

He joined in July 1918 on attaining military age, and was engaged on important duties at various stations. He was unsuccessful in obtaining his transfer overseas, but did consistently good work with his unit until his demobilisation in January 1919.

6, Peter Street, Openshaw, Manchester.   Z6423

HARE, T. Sapper, R.E.

He volunteered in May 1915, and in April of the following year was drafted to Egypt, where he was stationed on important duties at Khartoum. He was badly injured as the result of the blowing up of a bridge, and was invalided to hospital in Leicester. In July 1918 he was discharged as medically unfit for further service, and holds the General Service and Victory Medals. 68, Stott Street, Hulme, Manchester. Z6422

HARGREAVES, A., Pte., 1/5th Lancashire Fusiliers.

He joined in October 1916, and was drafted to the Western Front, where he saw much severe fighting in the Nieppe Forest sector. He was badly wounded in action at Armentières, during the Retreat of 1918, and was invalided to the Base. On his recovery, he was sent to Salonika in May 1919, and served there for six months. Demobilised in November 1919, he holds the General Service and Victory Medals. 190 Heald Grove, Rusholme, Manchester. Z6427

HARGREAVES, C., Pte., 11th Lancashire Fusiliers.

Mobilised in August 1914, he was quickly drafted to France, and took part in the Battles of Armentières, St. Eloi, Ploegsteert, the Somme, Arras, and Vimy Ridge where he was badly wounded in action in April 1917. After hospital treatment, at Rouen and Northampton, he was discharged as medically unfit for further service, and holds the 1914 Star, and the General Service and Victory Medals. 27, Shrewbridge Street, Ardwick, Manchester. Z6424

HARGREAVES, C. H., Pte., 2/4th S. Lancs. Regt.

Volunteering in December 1915, he was drafted to the Western Front in the following September. Whilst in this theatre of war, he took part in the Battles of Ypres, Cambrai, Armentières, and Lille, and in other important engagements, during the Retreat and Advance of 1918. He was demobilised in September 1919, and holds the General Service and Victory Medals. 190, Heald Grove, Rusholme, Manchester. Z6428

HARGREAVES, E., Sergt., 2/4th S. Lancs. Regt.

Volunteering in November 1914, he was drafted to France in September 1916. Whilst on the Western Front he served with distinction at the Battles of the Somme, Ypres, and Cambrai, and in the Retreat of March 1918. He contracted dysentery, and was sent to the Base. On his recovery he was transferred to the Labour Corps, and did consistently good work until his demobilisation in December 1918, holding the General Service and Victory Medals. 190, Heald Grove, Rusholme, Manchester. Z6430

HARGREAVES, E. (M.M.), Cpl., 15th Royal Scots.

He volunteered in September 1914, and in the following February was drafted to France, where he played a prominent part in the Battles of Ypres (II), the Somme, Arras, Messines, Ypres (III), Cambrai, Havrincourt, and Le Cateau. He was wounded in action on the Somme in July 1916, and at Cambrai in November 1917, when he was invalided home, but returned to France on his recovery. He was awarded the Military Medal for conspicuous bravery in rescuing a wounded officer under heavy shell-fire. Demobilised in February 1919, he also holds the 1914-15 Star, and the General Service and Victory Medals. 27, Shrewbridge St., Ardwick, Manchester. TZ6425

HARGREAVES, J., Sergt., 11th Lancashire Fusiliers.

Volunteering in September 1914, he was drafted to France twelve months later, and served with distinction at the Battles of Loos, Givenchy, the Somme, Arras, Vimy Ridge, and Cambrai. He was wounded on the Somme in July 1916, and at Vimy Ridge in June 1917, and was in hospital on both occasions. On being wounded a third time, he was taken prisoner in April 1918, and was held in captivity until January 1919. He was then repatriated and demobilised, holding the 1914-15 Star, and the General Service and Victory Medals. 34, King Street, Ardwick, Manchester. Z6426

HARGREAVES, W., Sapper, R.E.

He joined in December 1916, and after a period of service in Scotland, was drafted to the Western Front in August 1918. Whilst in this theatre of war, he was engaged on important duties with his unit during the Battles of the Somme, Amiens, Epéhy, and Cambrai. After the cessation of hostilities, he served at Cologne with the Army of Occupation, and was eventually demobilised in October 1919, holding the General Service and Victory Medals. 56, Royal St. Ardwick, Manchester. Z6429

HARGREAVES, W. E., Rifleman, K.R.R.C.

In August 1914, shortly after the outbreak of war he volunteered, and was training at Winchester and Aldershot. Whilst at the latter station he contracted pneumonia, and died in hospital on September 15th, 1914, after only three weeks' service in the Army. " His memory is cherished with pride." 2, Upper Dover Street, Bradford, Manchester. TZ11508

HARLOW, G. H., Private, 2/10th Manchester Regt.

He joined in November 1916, and four months later was drafted to the Western Front, where he took part in the Battles of Arras, Ypres, and Passchendaele. He was first wounded in action at Arras in April 1917, and for the second time at Passchendaele in October 1917, when he was invalided to hospital at Chichester. Demobilised in January 1919, he holds the General Service and Victory Medals. 10, Parkfield Avenue, Rusholme, Manchester. Z6431

HARNEY, G., Private, M.G.C.

He joined in October 1917, and five months later proceeded to the Western Front, where he played a prominent part in much severe fighting during the Retreat and Advance of 1918. In December 1918 he was invalided home with an enlarged heart, and was eventually discharged as medically unfit for further service in October 1919. He holds the General Service and Victory Medals. 13, Jack Street, Ardwick, Manchester. Z4698A

HARPER, G., Leading Seaman, R.N.

He rejoined the Navy at the outbreak of war, and was engaged in H.M.T.B.D. " Brilliant," " Lightfoot," and " Spencer." He served in the Irish Flotilla, and later was attached to the Grand Fleet in the North Sea, and took part in the bombardment of the Belgian Coast, and in the Battle of Jutland. He was afterwards transferred to the Dover Patrol, and did duty in the smoke screen boats in the attack on Zeebrugge. Whilst serving in H.M.T.B.D. " Lightfoot," the vessel was torpedoed, but he was fortunately saved. He was finally engaged in convoying the surrendered enemy submarines to Harwich, and was demobilised in January 1919. He holds the 1914-15 Star, and the General Service and Victory Medals. 23, Alice Street, Bradford, Manchester. Z10340

HARPER, J. R., Private, Lancashire Fusiliers.

Volunteering in January 1915, he was sent to the Western Front in December 1916, and took part in the Battle of Vimy Ridge, where he was badly wounded in action. After hospital treatment in France and at Ramsgate, he returned to France and fought at the second Battle of the Somme (where he was gassed), Amiens, Péronne and Le Cateau. He served on the German Frontier until March 1919, when he returned home for demobilisation. He holds the General Service and Victory Medals. 16, Wilberforce Terrace, Hulme, Manchester. Z6436

HARPER, J. T., Private, Lancashire Fusiliers.

Volunteering in 1914, he was sent to the Dardanelles in the following year, and saw much severe fighting at Suvla Bay and Gallipoli. After the Evacuation of the Peninsula, he was transferred to the Western Front, where he took part in the Battle of the Somme, and was taken prisoner during the Retreat of March 1918, after having been wounded in action in 1916. He was repatriated and discharged in December 1918, and holds the 1914-15 Star, and the General Service and Victory Medals. 8, Richmond Street, Ardwick, Manchester. Z6435

HARPER, T., Private, 8th Manchester Regiment.

Mobilised in August 1914, he was drafted to Egypt in the following month and served at Cairo and Alexandria until early in 1915. He was then sent to the Dardanelles and took part in the Landing at Cape Helles and the three Battles of Krithia before being wounded in action at Achi Baba in June 1915. He was invalided to England, and on his recovery, was engaged on home duties until his demobilisation in February 1919. He holds the 1914-15 Star, and the General Service and Victory Medals. 37' Longridge Street, Longsight, Manchester. Z6432

HARPER, T., Private, R.A.M.C., and R.D.C., and Rifleman, 2/18th Royal Irish Rifles.

He volunteered in November 1915, but on completion of his training was found to be medically unfit for transfer overseas, and was transferred to the Royal Defence Corps. He rendered valuable services whilst engaged on important duties at various stations, and was eventually invalided from the Army in July 1917. 40, Allen Street, Hulme, Manchester. Z6434

HARPER, V., Private, M.G.C.

Volunteering in January 1916, he was quickly drafted to the Western Front, where he was in action at the Battles of Albert, Ploegsteert, the Somme, Vimy Ridge, Ypres, Passchendaele, and Cambrai. He was wounded at Vimy Ridge in May 1916, and at the second Battle of the Marne in July 1918, when he was invalided home. In November 1918 he was discharged as medically unfit for further service, and holds the General Service and Victory Medals. 2, New Street, West Gorton, Manchester. Z6433

HARPHAM, G., Private, Royal Welch Fusiliers.

He joined the Army immediately on attaining military age in May 1918, and on completion of his training, was engaged on important garrison duties at Aldershot, Dublin and Limerick. He was unable to secure his transfer to a theatre of war, but rendered valuable services until his demobilisation in November 1919. 122, Margaret Street, West Gorton, Manchester. Z6437

HARRINGTON, C. H., Private, R. Welch Fusiliers.

Volunteering in September 1914, he was engaged on important duties in England until October 1916. He was then drafted to the Western Front and was in action at La Bassée, Givenchy, Ypres (III), Lens, Cambrai Nieuport, Festubert, and on the Somme. Wounded in January 1918, he was invalided to hospital in London and Manchester, and was eventually demobilised in January 1919, holding the General Service and Victory Medals. 28, Lindum Street, Rusholme, Manchester. Z6438

HARRINGTON, D., Private, 8th Manchester Regt.

He volunteered in October 1914, and in the following July was sent to the Gallipoli Peninsula. After taking part in the Landing at Suvla Bay, he was invalided to hospital in Manchester in August 1915, suffering from gastritis and dysentery. On his recovery he was engaged on important guard duties at prisoner of war camps in the Isle of Man for a time, but later, rejoined his unit for coast defence work in Yorkshire. He was discharged as medically unfit in January 1918, and holds the 1914–15 Star, and the General Service and Victory Medals.
6, Metcalf Street, Miles Platting, Manchester.   TZ6439

HARRIS, C. H., Sergt., 9th K.O. (Royal Lancaster Rgt.)

Volunteering in September 1914, he was sent to France early in the following year and served with distinction at the second Battle of Ypres. In March 1916 he was transferred to the Salonika theatre of war, and took part in much severe fighting on the Doiran front, and in the general Offensives of 1918. He was wounded in action in March 1916, and again in September 1918. Demobilised in April 1919, he holds the 1914–15 Star, and the General Service and Victory Medals.
37, Robert Street, Chorlton-on-Medlock, Manchester.   X6445

HARRIS, E., Driver, R.F.A.

He joined in June 1917, and on completion of his training, was engaged on important duties with his Battery at various stations. He was not successful in obtaining his transfer overseas during hostilities, but after the Armistice, was sent to the Army of Occupation in Germany, where he rendered valuable services until his demobilisation in September 1919.
24, Rose Street, Greenheys, Manchester.   Z6442C

HARRIS, F., Sapper, R.E.

He joined in June 1917, and was retained on important duties in England until August of the following year, when he was drafted to the Western Front. There he saw much severe fighting during the Advance of 1918, took part in the Battles of Bapaume, Havrincourt, Epéhy and Le Cateau, and other engagements, and was gassed at Cambrai in October of that year. He was demobilised on his return home in September 1919, and holds the General Service and Victory Medals.
2, Stanley Avenue, Rusholme, Manchester.   Z6443

HARRIS, G., Gunner, R.F.A.

He volunteered in August 1914, and in the following year was drafted to France, where he saw some heavy fighting at Ypres. In 1916, he proceeded to Salonika, and took part in many engagements and was wounded in action. He contracted malaria in 1918, and was invalided home and was eventually demobilised in April 1919, holding the 1914–15 Star, and the General Service and Victory Medals.
4, Charlton Street, Collyhurst, Manchester.   Z11717

HARRIS, H., Private, 1/7th Manchester Regiment.

Volunteering in December 1915, he proceeded to Egypt on completing a period of training in March of the following year, and there served at Mustapha and other stations. In December 1916, he was transferred to the Western Front, where he took part in many important engagements, including the Battles of Arras, Ypres and Cambrai, and was wounded in August 1917. He fell fighting at Le Cateau on October 20th, 1918. He was entitled to the General Service and Victory Medals.
"And doubtless he went in splendid company."
16, Bonsall Street, Hulme, Manchester.   Z6447

HARRIS, H., Private, 8th Manchester Regiment.

Volunteering in October 1914, he was drafted to Gallipoli in July of the following year, and took part in various operations in the Dardanelles campaign until the Evacuation of the Peninsula. He then proceeded to Egypt, and served with the British Forces under General Allenby in the Offensive on Palestine, notably at Beyrout. He was wounded during his service overseas, and was demobilised after his return to England in July 1919. He holds the 1914–15 Star, and the General Service and Victory Medals.
27, Dawson Street, West Gorton, Manchester.   Z10341

HARRIS, H. N., Private, 19th Manchester Regiment.

Volunteering in May 1915, he was sent to France in the following December, and was wounded in action at Loos in January 1916. On his recovery, he rejoined his unit, and was again wounded at Lens in September 1917. After five months in hospital, he returned to the firing line, and was unhappily killed by a sniper at Courtrai in October 1918. He was entitled to the 1914–15 Star, and the General Service and Victory Medals.
"He died the noblest death a man may die,
Fighting for God, and right, and liberty."
24, Rose Street, Greenheys, Manchester.   Z6442B

HARRIS, H. R., Sapper, R.E.

He joined in November 1916, and proceeded to France in the following January. Whilst in this theatre of war he was engaged in repairing wires in dug-outs until July 1917, when he was taken prisoner at the Battle of Ypres (III). After being held in captivity for twelve months, he was released, and in March 1919 was demobilised, holding the General Service and Victory Medals.
4, Dryden Street, Longsight, Manchester.   Z6441

HARRIS, J., Private, 1st King's (Liverpool Regt.)

He volunteered in November 1914, and in the following March was drafted to France, where he took part in the Battles of Ypres (II), Festubert and Loos. He laid down his life for King and Country at Richebourg on May 16th, 1916, and was entitled to the 1914–15 Star, and the General Service and Victory Medals.
"A valiant Soldier, with undaunted heart he breasted life's last hill."
2, Walters Place, Hyde Street, Hulme, Manchester.   Z6444

HARRIS, J. W., Sergt., 2nd Manchester Regiment.

Mobilised from the Reserve in August 1914, he was drafted to France in the following May, and took part in the Battles of Ypres (II), Albert, and the Somme, where he was badly wounded in action in July 1916. He was invalided home, and after hospital treatment at Epsom, was discharged in May 1917, as medically unfit for further service. He holds the 1914–15 Star, and the General Service and Victory Medals.
13, Bonsall Street, Hulme, Manchester.   Z6446

HARRIS, R., Private, K.O. (R. Lancaster Regt.)

He volunteered in July 1915, and in June of the following year was drafted to France. During his service on the Western Front he fought in the engagements on the Somme, and the Ancre, and at Beaumont-Hamel, Bullecourt, Cambrai and in many of the operations in the Retreat and Advance of 1918. He returned home and was demobilised in January 1919, and holds the General Service and Victory Medals.
10, Haigh Street, West Gorton, Manchester.   Z10342

HARRISON, A., Private, Labour Corps.

He joined in August 1916, and later in the same month was drafted to France, where he was engaged on important duties in the repair of roads and burying the dead, and served at Albert, Vimy Ridge, the Somme and Ypres. He was invalided home with illness resulting from his service in August 1917, and after his recovery did duty on the Regimental Staff in Officers' quarters at various home stations. He holds the General Service and Victory Medals, and was demobilised in November 1919.
125, Cross Street, Bradford, Manchester.   Z9560

HARRISON, C., Private, East Lancashire Regiment.

He joined in May 1916, and in the following February was sent to the Western Front. During his service in France, he fought in the engagements at Arras, Messines, Ypres and Passchendaele, and was later invalided home through illness and discharged as medically unfit for further military service in August 1917. He holds the General Service and Victory Medals.
52, Howarth Street, Chorlton-on-Medlock, Manchester.   Z10343A

HARRISON, C. A., Sergt., Royal Welch Fusiliers.

He volunteered in September 1915, and early in the following year proceeded to France, where he took part in many important engagements, including the Battles of Albert, the Somme (I), Beaucourt, Arras (I), Bullecourt, Messines, Ypres (III), Passchendaele and Cambrai, and the Retreat and Advance of 1918. Returning to England in January 1919, he was then demobilised, and holds the General Service and Victory Medals.
38, Albemarle Street, Moss Side, Manchester.   Z6454

HARRISON, C. E., Private, R.A.S.C.

He volunteered in January 1915, and in the following October embarked for Salonika. Whilst in this theatre of war, he served in various engagements, including those on the Vardar and the Doiran fronts, the capture of Monastir, and the final Advance on the Vardar. After the cessation of hostilities he returned to England and was demobilised in the following June, holding the 1914–15 Star, and the General Service and Victory Medals.
11, Hora Street, Bradford, Manchester.   Z10344

HARRISON, D. (M.M.), Cpl., 2nd Manchester Regt.

Mobilised from the Reserve in August 1914, he was immediately drafted to the Western Front, where he took part in the Battle of, and the Retreat from, Mons. He was also in action at the Battles of the Aisne, Ypres, the Somme, Arras, Passchendaele and Cambrai, and in the Retreat and Advance of 1918, and was wounded at Ypres and on the Somme. He was awarded the Military Medal for conspicuous bravery and devotion to duty in the Field, and was discharged in February 1919. He also holds the Mons Star, and the General Service and Victory Medals.
42, Marsland Street, Ardwick, Manchester.   Z6449

HARRISON, F., Sapper, R.E.

Volunteering in May 1915, he was sent to Egypt after six months' training. Whilst in this theatre of war he rendered valuable services with his unit at various stations, but was admitted to hospital at Alexandria with valvular disease of the heart. In March 1916, he was invalided home, and in the following December was discharged as medically unfit for further service. He holds the 1914–15 Star, and the General Service and Victory Medals.
6, Fountain Street, City Road, Hulme, Manchester.   Z6458

HARRISON, F. H., R.Q.M.S., 8th Manchester Regt.
He volunteered in August 1914, and was engaged on important duties with his unit at various home stations. Although unsuccessful in obtaining his transfer overseas, he, nevertheless, rendered very valuable services until February 1919, when he was demobilised.
195, Earl Street, Longsight, Manchester. Z6456

HARRISON, H., Pte., King's Own Scottish Borderers.
He volunteered in August 1914, and in the following December was drafted to the Western Front, where he played a prominent part in the Battles of Ypres (1914 and 1915), and Loos. In April 1916 he was badly wounded in action during the heavy fighting at Loos, and was invalided to hospital in London. He was discharged as medically unfit for further service in October 1916, and holds the 1914-15 Star, and the General Service and Victory Medals.
13, Victoria Street, Longsight, Manchester. Z6457

HARRISON, H., Corporal, 1st Manchester Regiment.
Having enlisted in August 1912, he was drafted to the Western Front in September 1914, and took part in the Battles of Ypres and Givenchy, where he was wounded in action in December of the same year. On his recovery he was transferred to Mesopotamia, and was in action at Kut-el-Amara, Samara, Baghdad and on the Tigris, being again wounded in April 1916. In September 1917 he proceeded to Egypt and served at Katia, El Fasher and Romani. He received his discharge in August 1919, and holds the 1914 Star, and the General Service and Victory Medals.
10, Metcalfe Street, Miles Platting, Manchester. Z6452

HARRISON, H. E., Private, Labour Corps.
He volunteered in the Manchester Regiment in October 1914, and six months later was discharged as medically unfit. In May 1915, however, he volunteered in the Cheshire Regiment, and after a period of service in England, was drafted to France in February 1917. He was then transferred to the Labour Corps and took an active part in the Battles of Arras, Ypres (III), Cambrai and the Somme (II) and in the Retreat and Advance of 1918. Returning to England in February 1919, he was then demobilised, and holds the General Service and Victory Medals.
48, Gomm Street, Longsight, Manchester. Z6450

HARRISON, J., Private, 1/8th Lancashire Fusiliers.
He volunteered in August 1914, and in January 1916 was drafted to Egypt, where he was in action at Sollum, Katia, El Fasher, Romani and Magdhaba. In July 1917 he was transferred to the Western Front and took part in the Battles of Ypres (III), Cambrai, the Somme and the Marne (II), after which engagement he was employed on special canteen duties owing to heart trouble. He was demobilised in February 1919, and holds the General Service and Victory Medals.
27, Elizabeth Street, Openshaw, Manchester. Z6455

HARRISON, J., Private, 23rd Manchester Regiment.
He volunteered in December 1915, and after a period of service in England, was drafted to the Western Front in January 1917. Whilst in this theatre of war he took part in the Battles of Bullecourt, Armentières and Amiens and in heavy fighting at Beaumont-Hamel. He was wounded in action in October 1917, and again in 1918, on which occasion he was invalided home. After hospital treatment at Manchester and Cleethorpes, he was demobilised in February 1919, and holds the General Service and Victory Medals.
207, Morton Street, Longsight, Manchester. Z6451

HARRISON, J., Private, King's (Liverpool Regt.)
He joined in April 1916, and in the following June was drafted overseas. During his service in France he took part in much of the fighting on the Somme and the Ancre and at Arras, Bullecourt, Ypres, the Marne, Bapaume, Cambrai and Havrincourt. He returned to England and was demobilised in October 1919, and holds the General Service and Victory Medals. 41, Price St., Ancoats, Manchester. Z10346B

HARRISON, J., Private, 3rd Lancashire Fusiliers.
He volunteered at the outbreak of war, and after his training was drafted to the Dardanelles, where he took part in the Landing at Cape Helles. Subsequently he gave his life for King and Country in May 1915, and was entitled to the 1914-15 Star, and the General Service and Victory Medals.
"A costly sacrifice upon the altar of freedom."
21, Copestick Street, Ancoats, Manchester. Z10345

HARRISON, L. J., Private, 3rd Border Regiment.
He volunteered in August 1915, and was sent to France six months later. During his service on the Western Front he took part in the Battles of Albert, Vermelles, the Somme (particularly at Beaumont-Hamel and Beaucourt), Arras, Vimy Ridge, Messines, Passchendaele and Cambrai and in the Retreat and Advance of 1918. He was demobilised in March 1919, and holds the General Service and Victory Medals.
58, St. John's Road, Longsight, Manchester. Z6448

HARRISON, N. A., Private, 2nd Royal Scots.
He volunteered in August 1915, and in the following June was drafted to France. Whilst in this theatre of war he was in action at the Battles of Albert and the Somme, where he was

gassed and buried by the bursting of a shell. He was invalided to England for treatment in hospital, but on his recovery returned to France in September 1917, took part in the Battle of Ypres, and was again wounded and sent to hospital. After three months' treatment in South Wales, he was discharged as medically unfit for further service in January 1918, and holds the General Service and Victory Medals. Z6459
2, Sessay Street, off Hancock Street, Hulme, Manchester.

HARRISON, R., Private, Manchester Regiment.
Volunteering in November 1914, he underwent his training at Morecambe and was then engaged on important duties with his unit. He rendered valuable services, but following his inoculation, septic poisoning unfortunately set in, and he died in May 1915.
"His memory is cherished with pride."
15, Ashmore Street, West Gorton, Manchester. Z6453

HARRISON, S. H., Private, South Lancashire Regt.
Volunteering in August 1914, he proceeded to Mesopotamia in September of the following year. Whilst in this theatre of war he took part in the engagements at Kut-el-Amara, and at the heavy fighting on the Tigris and was present at the Fall of Baghdad. He holds the 1914-15 Star, and the General Service and Victory Medals, and was demobilised after his return to England in February 1919. Z10343B
52, Howarth Street, Chorlton-on-Medlock, Manchester.

HARRISON, T., Private, King's (Liverpool Regt.)
He joined in May 1916, and in the following month was drafted to the Western Front. During his service in France he fought on the Somme and at Vimy Ridge, Bullecourt, Arras, Ypres, Cambrai and Courtrai, and in many later engagements until the Armistice. He holds the General Service and Victory Medals, and was demobilised in February 1920. Z10346A
41, Price Street, Ancoats, Manchester.

HARRISON, W. H., Driver, R.G.A.
He volunteered in July 1915, and after his training served at various stations on important duties with his unit. In November 1917, he was drafted to the Western Front, and took part in much of the heavy fighting at Passchendaele, Cambrai, the Somme, the Marne, Bapaume, Amiens, and Le Cateau. After the Armistice was signed he proceeded to Germany with the Army of Occupation, and was stationed on the Rhine until his return to England for demobilisation in August 1919. He holds the General Service and Victory Medals. 24, Branson Street, Ancoats, Manchester. Z10347

HARROP, A., Pte., Queen's (Royal West Surrey Rgt.)
He joined in March 1916, and after a period of training was drafted to the Western Front. During his service in this theatre of war, he was engaged in the Battles of Arras, Ypres, Passchendaele, Cambrai and the Somme (II), and in August 1918 was badly wounded and gassed in action. He was then invalided to hospital in Scotland, and on his recovery, was demobilised from Heath Park, in February 1919, holding the General Service and Victory Medals. Z6463B
27, Royal Street, Ardwick, Manchester.

HARROP, C. H., Private, 1/6th Royal Scots.
He volunteered in February 1915, and after a period of training was engaged on important munition work at Burnage. He was unable to proceed overseas owing to the important nature of his work, but rendered valuable services until his demobilisation in March 1919.
16, Temple Street, Bradford, Manchester. Z11718B

HARROP, F., Pte., King's Own (Royal Lancs. Regt.)
He volunteered in August 1914, and in the following June was sent to the Dardanelles, where he took part in the third Battle of Krithia, in heavy fighting at Achi-Baba, and in the Landing at Suvla Bay. He was badly wounded whilst burying one of his dead comrades, and in January 1916 was invalided home. Six months later he was discharged as medically unfit, but in January 1918 rejoined in the R.A.S.C., with which unit he rendered valuable services until he was finally demobilised in March 1919, holding the 1914-15 Star, and the General Service and Victory Medals.
17, Berwick Street, Chorlton-on-Medlock, Manchester. Z6461

HARROP, H., Corporal, Royal Welch Fusiliers.
He joined in October 1916, and after undergoing a period of training, was engaged on important duties at various stations. He was medically unfit for service overseas, and was consequently unable to obtain his transfer to a theatre of war, but did much useful work with his unit until his demobilisation in March 1919.
27, Royal Street, Ardwick, Manchester. Z6463A

HARROP, J., Private, 11th Manchester Regiment.
He volunteered in December 1914, and in April of the following year was drafted to Gallipoli, where, after taking part in the Landing at Cape Helles, he fought in the Battles of Krithia and at Suvla Bay. Severely wounded in action in December 1915, and suffering also from heart disease, he was sent home and ultimately invalided from the Army in August 1917. He holds the 1914-15 Star, and the General Service and Victory Medals.
16, Eldon Street, Chorlton-on-Medlock, Manchester. Z6464

HARROP, H. R., 2nd Class Gun Layer, R.N.
Called up from the Reserve at the outbreak of war in August 1914, he was posted to H.M.S. "Prince George," on board which vessel he served in the Mediterranean Sea, and took part in the Dardanelles campaign. In 1916 he was transferred to H.M.S. "Royal Oak" for service in the North Sea with the Grand Fleet, and took part in the Battle of Jutland and other actions. Later he was employed on mine-sweeping and convoy duties in H.M.S. "Totnes," in American, Scandinavian and Russian waters. He was discharged in January 1919, and holds the Naval General Service Medal (with five clasps), the 1914-15 Star, and the General Service and Victory Medals.
8, Frost Street, Hulme, Manchester. Z6466

HARROP, J. A., Private, 1st Manchester Regiment.
Volunteering in January 1915, he proceeded to India in October of that year and was there engaged on garrison duties at various stations. Later he was transferred to Mesopotamia, where he took part in the capture of Kut and in many other important engagements, finally returning to England in May 1919. He was demobilised in the following August, and holds the General Service and Victory Medals.
127, Liverpool Street, Reddish, Manchester. Z6462

HARROP, J. E., Pte,, R.A.M.C., and Driver, R.F.A.
He joined in May 1915, and twelve months later proceeded to Egypt, where he was stationed at Alexandria until April 1917. He was then transferred to the R.F.A., and took part in the Advance into Palestine, where he fought in the Battles of Gaza. Later he was drafted to the Western Front in time to take part in the Retreat of 1918, and unhappily fell in action in the Cambrai sector on September 28th of that year. He was entitled to the General Service and Victory Medals.
"Steals on the ear the distant triumph song."
51, South Street, Longsight, Manchester. Z6460

HARROP, S., Private, Manchester Regiment.
He enlisted in February 1914, and when war broke out in the following August, was quickly drafted to France. There he took part in the fighting at La Bassée, where he was wounded and invalided to the Base. On his recovery he rejoined his unit, and was in action on the Somme, at Arras, and in the Retreat and Advance of 1918. He returned home for leave, but unfortunately contracted an illness and died in February 1919. He was entitled to the 1914 Star, and the General Service and Victory Medals.
"The path of duty was the way to glory."
10, Halifax Street, Bradford, Manchester. TZ11719B

HARROP, T., Sergt., Lancashire Fusiliers.
He was mobilised in August 1914, and served at various stations on important duties with his unit. He was engaged on instructional duties and rendered valuable services, but was not successful in obtaining his transfer overseas owing to his medical unfitness for active service. He was discharged in July 1915, owing to his disabilities.
148, Victoria Square, Oldham Road, Manchester. Z9166

HARROP, W. A., Private, Loyal N. Lancs. Regt.
He volunteered in September 1915, and in March of the following year, proceeded to the Western Front, where, after taking part in engagements at Albert and Ploegsteert Wood, he was severely wounded in action in the Somme Offensive. Invalided home, he was for a considerable period in hospital before being discharged as medically unfit for further service in October 1919. He holds the General Service and Victory Medals.
6, Vulcan Street, Ardwick, Manchester. Z6465

HARROP, W. H., Sergt., 13th King's (Liverpool Rgt.)
He volunteered in September 1914, and was employed as a Sergeant Instructor at various stations until April 1916. He was then released for important work in the railway transport service, and carried out responsible duties until December 1917, when he was discharged.
64, Nicholson Street, Rochdale Road, Manchester. Z9561

HART, C., Stoker Petty Officer, R.N.
He enlisted in September 1910, and after the outbreak of war in August 1914, served in H.M.S. "Bell" and "Tiger" in the North Sea, and many other waters. He took part in the Battles of Heligoland Bight, Falkland Islands, Dogger Bank, the Narrows and Jutland, and in minor actions until the cessation of hostilities. Later he served in H.M.S. "Pegasus" off the coast of Russia, and in 1920 was in H.M.S. "Tuberose" at Devonport. He holds the 1914-15 Star, the General Service Medal (with clasps, Heligoland, Falkland Islands, Dogger Bank and Jutland), and the Victory Medal.
40, Gresham Street, Lower Openshaw, Manchester. Z6533

HART, F., Corporal, 20th Lancashire Fusiliers.
He volunteered in June 1915, and in January of the following year, proceeded to France, where he saw heavy fighting in various sectors of the Front. He took part in the Battles of Ploegsteert Wood and the Somme, and many minor engagements until severely wounded in action at Arras and sent home in March 1917. He was invalided from the Army in March 1918, after a considerable period in hospital at Birmingham, and holds the General Service and Victory Medals.
18, Hewitt Street, Openshaw, Manchester. Z6467

HART, F., Private, Seaforth Highlanders.
Volunteering in January 1915, he proceeded to France in the following March, and took part in the Battles of Neuve Chapelle, and Ypres. He was severely gassed in action in August 1915, and was admitted to hospital, and after his recovery was transferred to the Royal Army Service Corps, Motor Transport section. He then served in many engagements in various sectors until the cessation of hostilities, and was demobilised after his return to England in July 1919. He holds the 1914-15 Star, and the General Service and Victory Medals. 26, James Street, Moss Side, Manchester. Z10348

HART, J. L., Sapper, R.E.
Joining in January 1916, he was sent to the Western Front in the same year, and took part in numerous engagements, including those at Arras, Bullecourt, Passchendaele, Cambrai, Bapaume, Havrincourt and Le Cateau. He was demobilised in September 1919, and holds the General Service and Victory Medals. 23, Raglan Street, Hulme, Manchester. TZ9167

HART, T., Driver, R.A.S.C.
Having volunteered in January 1915, he was shortly afterwards sent to France, and was engaged on important transport work at Armentières, the Somme, Albert, Arras, Péronne and Ypres. He returned home and was demobilised in June 1919, holding the 1914-15 Star, and the General Service and Victory Medals.
55, Harrowby Street, Collyhurst, Manchester. Z9168

HARTLEY, A., Private, 6th Loyal N. Lancs. Regt.
After volunteering in August 1914, he was sent to Gallipoli in the following year and took part in the Landing and the three Battles of Krithia. He was unhappily killed in action at the Landing at Suvla Bay on August 9th, 1915. He was entitled to the 1914-15 Star, and the General Service and Victory Medals.
"Great deeds cannot die :
They, with the sun and moon renew their light for ever."
2, Alfred Street, Sudell Street, Ancoats, Manchester. Z9169

HARTLEY, H., Private, Cheshire Regiment.
He joined in July 1916, and in the same year was sent to France. During about three years there he was in action at Ypres, Hill 60, Festubert, St. Eloi, Neuve Chapelle, the Ancre, the Somme, Arras and Cambrai and in many other engagements. He was demobilised in March 1919, and holds the General Service and Victory Medals.
107, Thornton Street, Manchester. TZ9170

HARTLEY, J., Air Mechanic, R.A.F.
He joined in January 1918, and after his training served at various stations on important duties with his Squadron. His duties, which demanded a high degree of technical skill, were carried out with great efficiency and he rendered valuable services, but was not successful in obtaining his transfer overseas before the cessation of hostilities. He was demobilised in February 1920.
8, Victoria Square, Oldham Road, Manchester. TZ9171

HARTLEY, J., Private, 1/4th Cheshire Regiment.
He joined in November 1916, and in the following July proceeded to Egypt, whence he took part in the Advance into Palestine, and was present at the fall of Jerusalem. In June 1918 he was transferred to the Western Front, where he was again in action in the Advance, taking part in the Battles of the Marne, Amiens, Bapaume, Cambrai and Le Cateau. He was demobilised in September 1919, and holds the General Service and Victory Medals.
234, Viaduct Street, Ardwick, Manchester. Z6468

HARTLEY, R., Private, Lancashire Fusiliers.
Having volunteered in August 1914, he was sent to France in the following November, and was in action at Ypres, Neuve Chapelle, St. Eloi and Hill 60, but was wounded at Ypres and invalided home. On his recovery he returned to France and took part in fighting in the Somme, Ypres, Albert, Passchendaele sectors, and in other important engagements. He also served in the Retreat and Advance of 1918. He was demobilised in April 1920, and holds the 1914 Star, and the General Service and Victory Medals.
18, Upper Dover Street, Bradford, Manchester. TZ9172

HARTLEY, S., Private, R.A.M.C.
He joined in June 1917, and underwent a period of training prior to his being drafted to Russia. Whilst in this theatre of war he saw much active service with the Relief Force until December 1918, when he returned home. He was demobilised in September 1919, and holds the General Service and Victory Medals. 161, Thornton St., Collyhurst, Manchester. TZ11720

HARTNEY, F. W., Sergt., R.F.A.
Mobilised in August 1914, he was immediately drafted to the Western Front, where he fought in the Battle of Mons and the subsequent Retreat. He also took part in the Battles of La Bassée, Ypres, Neuve Chapelle, Hill 60, Loos and the Somme and many minor engagements, and served through the Retreat and Advance of 1918. He returned home in January 1919, and was discharged in the following month, holding the Mons Star, and the General Service and Victory Medals. 27, Hewitt Street, Openshaw, Manchester. Z6469

HARVEY, G., Private, 8th Manchester Regiment.

He volunteered in August 1914, and underwent a period of training prior to being drafted to the Western Front in October 1916. There he saw much severe fighting and took part in the Battles of the Ancre, Arras, Bullecourt, Ypres, and the Somme and other engagements, serving also through the Retreat and Advance of 1918. He was demobilised on his return home in April 1919, and holds the General Service and Victory Medals.

35, Caton Street, Hulme, Manchester. Z6472

HARVEY, H., Sergt., 17th Manchester Regiment.

He volunteered in January 1915, and in November of that year proceeded to the Western Front, and there saw severe fighting in various sectors. He served through the Battles of St. Eloi, Albert, Vermelles and Ploegsteert Wood, and many minor engagements, and was badly gassed in the Somme Offensive of July 1916. He was for some time in hospital at Bath and Blackpool before being invalided from the Army in June 1917, and holds the General Service and Victory Medals.

84, Parkfield Street, Rusholme, Manchester. Z6473

HARVEY, J., Private, R.A.M.C.

He joined in January 1917, and after his training served at several camps on important duties with his unit. He was subsequently transferred to a Military Hospital as Nursing Orderly and rendered skilled and valuable services. Later owing to illness he was discharged as medically unfit for further duty in December 1917.

13, Hope Street, Bradford, Manchester. Z10349

HARVEY, J. A., Pte., Royal Welch Fusiliers.

He joined in February 1916, and after completing a period of training, served at various stations, where he was engaged on duties of a highly important nature. Unable to obtain his transfer to a theatre of war, he nevertheless rendered very valuable services with his unit until October 1919, when he was demobilised.

4, Marie Street, Openshaw, Manchester. TZ6471A

HARVEY, J. H., Pte., K.O. (Royal Lancaster Regt.)

Joining in March 1916, he proceeded to France in the following November, and saw considerable service. He was in action in the Battle of the Somme, and was wounded at Messines Ridge in June 1917. After his recovery he was again severely wounded near St. Quentin in December of the same year. He was then invalided home to hospital and after receiving medical treatment was discharged as physically unfit for further duty in 1918. He holds the General Service and Victory Medals.

11, Thompson Street, North Ardwick, Manchester. Z11350A

HARVEY, J. L., Pte., 3rd Lancashire Fusiliers and 1st King's (Liverpool Regiment).

An ex-Soldier he re-enlisted in August 1914, and in the following year was drafted to Egypt, and stationed on garrison duty at Alexandria. He returned to England, and was demobilised in March 1919, but re-enlisted four months later in the Northumberland Fusiliers and proceeded to France in the following September, and was engaged on important post war work until March 1920, when he was sent home and discharged. He holds the Queen's South African Medal (with four clasps), and the General Service and Victory Medals.

56, Harrowby Street, Collyhurst, Manchester. Z10351

HARVEY, T., Pte., Lancs. Fusiliers and Labour Corps.

Having enlisted in January 1914, he was already in the Army when war was declared in the following August, and was afterwards retained on important duties at various stations. In August 1917, however, he was drafted to the Western Front with the Labour Corps, was present at the Battles of Lens, the Somme and the Marne, and was gassed in April 1918. He was in hospital in London until invalided from the Army in November 1918, and holds the General Service and Victory Medals.

10, Mallow Street, Hulme, Manchester. Z6470

HARVEY, T., Driver, Royal Engineers.

Volunteering in May 1915, he proceeded to France in February 1917, and whilst serving on the Western Front did good work as a driver in many sectors. He was present at the Battles of Arras, Bullecourt, Messines, Ypres and Cambrai, and in various engagements in the Retreat and Advance of 1918. He returned home and was demobilised in May 1919, and holds the General Service and Victory Medals.

95, Ryder Street, Collyhurst, Manchester. Z10365

HARVEY, W., Pte., Argyll and Sutherland H'ldrs.

Volunteering in January 1915, he was drafted to France in the following May, and whilst overseas fought at Ypres and Albert. He died gloriously on the Field of Battle on the Somme on July 27th, 1916, and was entitled to the 1914-15 Star, and the General Service and Victory Medals.

"Nobly striving,
He nobly fell that we might live."

11, Thompson Street North, Ardwick, Manchester. Z10350B

HARWOOD, A., Private, Black Watch.

He volunteered in September 1914, and after his training was engaged in Scotland on important duties with his unit until 1918, when he was sent to France, and was in action on the Somme and the Marne. He was afterwards transferred to the R.A.M.C. He was demobilised in July 1919, and holds the General Service and Victory Medals.

133, Victoria Square, Ancoats, Manchester. Z9173

HASE, G. R., L/Corporal, 8th Manchester Regiment.

Joining in January 1917, he proceeded to the Western Front in June of that year and there took part in the Battle of Messines and was wounded in action at Ypres. Invalided home, he was drafted on his recovery to Salonika, where he saw severe fighting on the Vardar front until the cessation of hostilities. He afterwards served with the Army of Occupation in Germany until his return home for demobilisation in October 1919, and holds the General Service and Victory Medals.

86, Redvers Street, Ardwick, Manchester. Z6474B

HASE, R., N. Private, 9th Cheshire Regiment.

He joined in March 1918, and on completing his training in the following August, was drafted to the Western Front. Whilst in this theatre of war, he saw much severe fighting, taking part in the fourth Battle of Ypres and many other engagements, and was wounded in action. On the cessation of hostilities he was sent with the Army of Occupation into Germany, finally returning home for demobilisation in September 1919. He holds the General Service and Victory Medals. 86, Redvers Street Ardwick, Manchester. Z6474A

HASELDEN, G. H., Private, 2nd Manchester Regt.

He volunteered in September 1914, and in the following December was drafted to France. During his service on the Western Front he took part in many important engagements including, those of Neuve Chapelle, Hill 60, where he was wounded, Loos, Vimy Ridge, the Somme, Arras, Messines and Cambrai. He was also frequently in action in the Retreat and Advance of 1918. He was demobilised in February of the succeeding year, and holds the 1914-15 Star, and the General Service and Victory Medals.

154, Hamilton Street, Collyhurst, Manchester. Z10352

HASELDINE, A., Private, Lancashire Fusiliers.

Volunteering in August 1914, he was drafted to the Western Front in October of the following year, and there saw severe fighting in various sectors. He took part in the Battles of St. Eloi, Vimy Ridge, the Somme, the Ancre, Arras and Passchendaele and many minor engagements until gassed in September 1917, and invalided home. He was finally discharged as medically unfit for further service in March 1918, and holds the 1914-15 Star, and the General Service and Victory Medals.

2, Nuttall Street, Openshaw, Manchester. Z6475

HASEY, F., Private, 1/7th Lancashire Fusiliers.

He volunteered in August 1914, and on completing his training early in the following year, was drafted to the Dardanelles. There he took part in much severe fighting at the Landing at Cape Helles, and the Battles of Krithia (I and II). He was unfortunately killed in action near Suvla Bay in June 1915, and was entitled to the 1914-15 Star, and the General Service and Victory Medals.

" He died the noblest death a man may die,
Fighting for God, and right, and liberty."

1, Mather Street, Hulme, Manchester. Z11721

HASLAM, J., Private, 21st Manchester Regiment.

He volunteered in November 1914, and after his training served at various stations on important duties with his unit. He rendered valuable services, but owing to ill-health, was invalided out in June 1916.

35, Cromwell Avenue, Manley Park, Manchester. Z10353

HASLAM, J., Private, 2/6th Royal Welch Fusiliers.

He joined in May 1916, and after undergoing a period of training, served at various stations, where he was engaged on important coastal defence duties. He was not successful in obtaining his transfer to a theatre of war, but nevertheless, rendered valuable services with his unit until March 1919, when he was demobilised.

27, Mount Street, Hulme, Manchester. Z6476

HASLAM, S., Sapper, R.E.

He joined in October 1916, and after a short period of training was retained on important telegraphic work at various stations. He was unable to obtain his transfer overseas owing to injuries received in an accident, and was for a considerable period in hospital at Bedford, before being discharged in July 1917 as medically unfit for further service.

65, Hinckley Street, Bradford, Manchester. Z6477

HASLAM, W., Private, 1st Border Regiment.

Having volunteered in August 1914, he proceeded in the following year to Mesopotamia, and thence to Egypt. He later served in France, where he took part in important engagements, but was killed in action at Beaumont-Hamel, during the Battle of the Somme on July 1st, 1916. He was entitled to the 1914-15 Star, and the General Service and Victory Medals.

24, Charlton Street, Collyhurst, Manchester. Z9174A

HASSALL, A., Private, Black Watch.
Volunteering in April 1915, he was drafted to Salonika in the following year, and took part in the Capture of Monastir. He later contracted malaria and was invalided home and discharged in August 1918, on account of his disability. He holds the General Service and Victory Medals.
19, Parcel Street, Beswick, Manchester. TZ9175

HASSALL, F., Private, Royal Scots.
He volunteered in March 1915, and in the following October proceeded to the Western Front. Whilst overseas he took part in the fighting at Hooge, where he was wounded in January 1916. He was invalided home to hospital, but rejoined his unit in the following May, and was later in action in the third Battle of Ypres, and was again severely wounded in the Advance in August 1918. He was evacuated to England, and after receiving medical treatment in hospital for about ten months was discharged as physically unfit for further service in June 1919. He holds the 1914-15 Star, and the General Service and Victory Medals.
2, Matilda Street, Ancoats, Manchester. Z10354

HASSALL, G., Private, Royal Fusiliers.
Volunteering in May 1915, he was drafted to the Western Front in October of that year, and there saw heavy fighting in various sectors. After taking part in the Battles of St. Eloi and Albert and many other engagements, he was severely wounded in action on the Somme, and sent to hospital in London. He was finally invalided from the Army in August 1918, and holds the 1914-15 Star, and the General Service and Victory Medals. 59, Cawder Street, Hulme, Manchester. Z6478

HASSALL, J. H., Driver, R.A.S.C.
He joined in January 1917, and in the following August was drafted to France. During his service on the Western Front he did good work as a driver in the Battles of Ypres and the Somme, and was wounded in April 1918. After his recovery he served in many operations in the Retreat and Advance, and was demobilised after his return to England in September 1919. He holds the General Service and Victory Medals.
3, Eliza Ann Street, Collyhurst, Manchester. Z10355

HASSALL, W. H., Private, 21st Manchester Regt.
Three months after volunteering in November 1914, he was drafted to France, where he saw much severe fighting. He took part in important engagements in various sectors, including the Battles of Neuve Chapelle, Hill 60, Ypres, Loos, Albert, the Somme, Arras and Cambrai, and also served through the Retreat and Advance of 1918. He was demobilised in September 1919, and holds the 1914-15 Star, and the General Service and Victory Medals.
5, Dorrington Street, Hulme, Manchester. Z6479

HATCHELL, C., A.B., R.N., H.M.S. "Thunderer."
He joined in February 1916, and was posted to H.M.S. "Thunderer," in which ship he was sent to the North Sea, and was engaged on patrol duties. He remained in this area until he was demobilised in March 1918, holding the General Service and Victory Medals.
49, Burnley Street, Ancoats, Manchester. Z9176

HATCHELL, J, E., Private, 51st Welch Regiment.
He joined in October 1918, and after a short period of training was engaged on important duties with his unit at various stations. He was unable to obtain his transfer overseas before the cessation of hostilities, but in March 1919 proceeded to Germany, where he served for twelve months with the Army of Occupation. He was demobilised on his return home in March 1920. 15, Heaton St., Ardwick, Manchester. Z6480

HATHAWAY, A. E., Private, Manchester Regt.
Joining in January 1918, he was sent to the Western Front later in the same year, and took part in the fighting during the Retreat and Advance of 1918, notably at Amiens and on the Somme. He was demobilised in December 1919, and holds the General Service and Victory Medals.
258, Hamilton Street, Collyhurst, Manchester. Z9177

HATTON, E. (M.M.), Pte., 2/6th King's (L'pool Rgt.)
He joined in November 1916, and in the following April was drafted to the Western Front. There he fought in many important engagements, including the Battles of Arras, Bullecourt, Messines, Ypres, Passchendaele and Cambrai, served also through the Retreat and Advance of 1918, and was wounded in action. He was afterwards sent with the Army of Occupation into Germany, where he was stationed at Cologne and Bonn, until his return home for demobilisation in December 1919. He was awarded the Military Medal for conspicuous bravery in the Field at Havrincourt Wood in September 1918, and holds also the General Service and Victory Medals.
130, Clopton Street, Hulme, Manchester. Z6483C

HATTON, H., Private, K.O (Royal Lancaster Regt.)
He volunteered in August 1915, and after a period of training was retained at various stations, where he was engaged on duties of great importance. Owing to ill-health he was unable to obtain his transfer to the Front, but nevertheless, rendered valuable services with his unit until October 1916, when he was discharged as medically unfit for further service.
9, Hyde View, Grey Street, Ardwick, Manchester. Z6481

HATTON, H., Private, 19th Manchester Regiment.
He volunteered in September 1914, and in November of the following year was sent to the Western Front, where he saw much severe fighting. After taking part in the Battles of Albert, the Somme, Arras, Vimy Ridge, Ypres and Passchendaele and other important engagements, he was taken prisoner when in action on the Somme in September 1918, and whilst in captivity was forced to work in a gas works behind the German lines. Released in January 1919, he was demobilised in the following month, and holds the 1914-15 Star, and the General Service and Victory Medals.
4A, Halsbury Street, Longsight, Manchester. Z6482

HATTON, J., Private, R.A.S.C. (M.T.)
Joining in August 1916, he proceeded to Mesopotamia in the following month, and was there engaged on important transport duties at various places. He was stationed for some time at Baghdad, and was also present at the relief of Kut, and in many other engagements until the cessation of hostilities. He finally returned home for demobilisation in May 1920, and holds the General Service and Victory Medals.
130, Clopton Street, Hulme, Manchester. Z6483A

HATTON, J., Gunner, R.G.A.
Joining in November 1916, he was drafted to the Western Front in April of the following year, and there saw severe fighting in various sectors. He took part in the Battles of Arras, Ypres, Cambrai, Bapaume, Havrincourt and Le Cateau, and other engagements, and fought also in the Retreat and, Advance of 1918. He afterwards served at Cologne and Bonn with the Army of Occupation, and finally returned home for demobilisation in October 1919, holding the General Service and Victory Medals.
130, Clopton Street, Hulme, Manchester. Z6483B

HATTON, W., Corpl., Sherwood Foresters.
Volunteering in September 1915, he served on important coastal defence duties until April 1918, when he proceeded to the Western Front. Whilst in France he took part in much of the severe fighting in the second Battle of the Marne and Cambrai, and in many other engagements of the Retreat and Advance. He returned home, and was demobilised in March 1919, and holds the General Service and Victory Medals.
31, Worth Street, Rochdale Road, Manchester. Z10366

HAUGHTON, A., Private, 8th Border Regiment.
Joining in August 1916, he proceeded to the Western Front after four months' training, and there took part in many important engagements, including the Battles of the Ancre, Arras, Vimy Ridge, Bullecourt, Messines and Cambrai. He was unhappily reported missing, believed to have been killed in action at Ploegsteert in April 1918. He was entitled to the General Service and Victory Medals.
"Whilst we remember, the sacrifice is not in vain."
120, Cross Street, Bradford, Manchester. Z6484

HAUGHTON, A., Private, 22nd Manchester Regt.
He joined in November 1916, and two months later was sent to the Western Front, where he saw much heavy fighting. After taking part in the Battle of Arras and engagements at Courcelles and many other places, he was severely wounded in action at Bullecourt and invalided to hospital at Southampton. He was discharged as medically unfit for further service in June 1917, and holds the General Service and Victory Medals.
24, Mallow Street, Hulme, Manchester. TZ6485

HAUGHTON, J. R., Private, 1st Cheshire Regiment.
He was mobilised at the outbreak of hostilities, and was almost immediately drafted to the Western Front. After about three months' service in France he gave his life for the freedom of England in the first Battle of Ypres on November 20th, 1914. He was entitled to the 1914 Star, and the General Service and Victory Medals.
"His memory is cherished with pride."
14, Ross Street, West Gorton, Manchester. Z10358B

HAUGHTON, M., Private, 2nd Manchester Regt.
He joined in June 1918, and after his training was sent to Germany with the Army of Occupation in January of the following year. He was engaged on important guard duties on the Rhine, being stationed at Bonn and Cologne until February 1920, when he returned to England and was demobilised.
5, Sycamore Street, Gorton, Manchester. Z10357

HAUGHTON, M. A., Special War Worker.
For over three years during the war this lady rendered valuable services as a shell tester at the Belsize Motor Works in Manchester. She carried out her duties with care and efficiency, and was highly commended for her excellent work.
14, Ross Street, West Gorton, Manchester. Z10358A

HAWCROFT, J., Private, 1st Lancashire Fusiliers.
He volunteered in August 1914, and in March of the following year, proceeded to Mesopotamia, where he saw much severe fighting. After taking part in many important engagements in this seat of operations, he was invalided home in December 1917, suffering from paralysis, and was finally discharged as medically unfit for further service in April 1919. He holds the 1914-15 Star, and the General Service and Victory Medals.
16, Ruby Street, Hulme, Manchester. Z6486A

HAWCROFT, J., Private, R.A.V.C.
He joined in May 1917, and after undergoing a period of training, served at various stations, where he was engaged on duties of a highly important nature. He was not successful in obtaining his transfer to a theatre of war, but nevertheless, rendered very valuable services with his unit until August 1919, when he was demobilised.
16, Ruby Street, Hulme, Manchester. Z6486B

HAWKSWORTH, R., Pte., Loyal N. Lancs. Regt.
He joined in December 1915, and sent to Egypt in the following year, saw much service at various stations. Transferred to France in April 1917, he fought in many engagements, and was in action throughout the German Offensive of 1918. Wounded in August he returned home and after receiving hospital treatment was demobilised in March 1919. He holds the General Service and Victory Medals.
63, Lime Street, Miles Platting, Manchester. Z10369

HAWLEY, E., Private, 8th Manchester Regiment.
He volunteered in October 1914, and in April of the following year was drafted to Gallipoli, where he took part in the Landing at Cape Helles. He also saw much severe fighting at Achi Baba, and many other places until November 1915, when he was sent home, suffering from dysentery. He was finally invalided from the Army in May 1917, and holds the 1914-15 Star, and the General Service and Victory Medals.
11, Dalton Terrace, Hulme, Manchester. Z6487

HAWLEY, J. A., Private, 3rd Manchester Regiment.
Joining in March 1917, he was drafted to France two months later, and there saw heavy fighting in various sectors of the Front. After taking part in the Battle of Ypres and many minor engagements, he was wounded in action at Passchendaele in August 1917, and invalided to hospital in London. He was finally demobilised in February 1919, and holds the General Service and Victory Medals.
17, Gladstone Street, West Gorton, Manchester. Z6488

HAWORTH, A., Corporal, 1/8th Manchester Regt.
Volunteering in August 1914, he was sent to the Dardanelles in the following April, and took part in the Landing at Cape Helles, the three Battles of Krithia, the Landing at Suvla Bay, and the Evacuation of the Gallipoli Peninsula. He then proceeded to Egypt, and was in action at Katia, El Fasher, Romani and Rafa, before taking part in the Advance through Palestine with General Allenby's Forces, when he was present at the capture of Jerusalem, Jericho and Aleppo. He was demobilised in April 1919, and holds the 1914-15 Star, and the General Service and Victory Medals.
182, Morton Street, Longsight, Manchester. Z6489

HAWTHORNTHWAITE, F., Pte., Lancashire Fus.
Volunteering in April 1915, he landed in France later in that year, and was in action in the Battles of Ypres and the Somme. Taken prisoner on March 21st, 1918, at the commencement of the German Offensive, he was held in captivity until after the cessation of hostilities. Repatriated, he was demobilised in March 1919, and holds the 1914-15 Star, and the General Service and Victory Medals.
5, Down Street, Ardwick, Manchester. Z10370

HAYES, G., Gunner, R.F.A.
He joined in October 1917, and after his training served at various stations on important coastal guard duties. He rendered valuable services, but was not successful in obtaining a transfer overseas before the cessation of hostilities, and was demobilised in December 1918.
78, Irlam Street, Miles Platting, Manchester. Z9562

HAYES, H., L/Corporal, South Lancashire Regt.
He volunteered in September 1915, and in the following November was drafted to France. Whilst overseas he fought in the engagements at Loos, Albert, Vimy Ridge, the Ancre, and Arras, where he was severely wounded in May 1917. After his recovery he was again in action at Lens, Amiens, Bapaume and Le Cateau. He was demobilised in December 1918, and holds the 1914-15 Star, and the General Service and Victory Medals.
78, Irlam Street, Miles Platting, Manchester. Z9563

HAYES, J., Private, 3rd King's (Liverpool Regt.)
He joined in July 1917, and after completing his training was engaged at various stations on important duties with his unit. He rendered valuable services, but was not successful in obtaining his transfer overseas before the cessation of hostilities, and was demobilised in March 1919.
13, Holme Street, Ancoats, Manchester. Z9178

HAYES, J. R. (M.M.), Pte., 1/10th Manchester Regt.
Volunteering in September 1914, he was sent to France in October 1915, and played a prominent part in the Battles of Albert, the Somme, Arras, Bullecourt, Messines, Passchendaele, Cambrai (I) and Havrincourt. He was awarded the Military Medal for conspicuous bravery and devotion to duty at the second Battle of Cambrai in October 1918, when, although himself badly wounded, he brought in wounded under heavy shell fire. He was invalided from the Army in February 1919, and also holds the 1914-15 Star, and the General Service and Victory Medals.
11, Stanley Avenue, Rusholme, Manchester. Z6490

HAYES, H., Private, 1st Loyal N. Lancashire Regt.
He enlisted in 1913, and, at the outbreak of war in August 1914, was immediately drafted to the Western Front, where he took part in the Battle of, and the Retreat from Mons. He made the supreme sacrifice in November 1914, when he was killed in action at the first Battle of Ypres. He was entitled to the Mons Star, and the General Service and Victory Medals.
"His life for his Country, his soul to God."
53, Sawley Street, Beswick, Manchester. Z6491

HAYES, J. A., Air Mechanic, R.A.F.
He joined in November 1918, and completing his training served at various stations with his Squadron. He was unsuccessful in obtaining his transfer overseas prior to the close of the war, but rendered excellent services until demobilised in January 1919. 367, Collyhurst Road, Collyhurst, Manchester. Z10367

HAYES, J. W., Private, 7th Manchester Regiment.
Volunteering in December 1915, he was sent to France in the following May, and took part in the Battles of the Somme, Vimy Ridge, Passchendaele, Cambrai and Bapaume, and in heavy fighting during the Retreat and Advance of 1918. He was demobilised in January 1919, and holds the General Service and Victory Medals.
57, Halston Street, Hulme, Manchester. Z6492

HAYES, W., Private, King's (Liverpool Regt.)
He volunteered in October 1915, and after a period of service in England, was sent to France in March 1917. He was engaged on important duties in the Somme sector for three months and was then admitted to Netley Hospital with a weak heart. In September 1917 he was discharged as medically unfit, and holds the General Service and Victory Medals.
29, Mount Street, Hulme, Manchester. Z6493

HAYES, W. H., Gunner, R.G.A.
He volunteered in August 1915, and three months later proceeded to France, where he was in action with his Battery at Hill 60, and at the Battles of the Somme, Arras, Bullecourt, Ypres (III), Cambrai, Monchy, Havrincourt and Bapaume. He was wounded in September 1917, again in September 1918, and was gassed in October of that year. Onto occasions he was under treatment at a Casualty Clearing Station. He holds the 1914-15 Star, and the General Service and Victory Medals, and was demobilised in March 1919.
88, Blackthorn Street, Ardwick, Manchester. Z6494

HAYHURST, J., L/Cpl., King's Own Scottish Bord's.
Volunteering in October 1914, he was drafted to France in the following May, and fought in the Battles of Ypres and Festubert. He gave his life for the freedom of England in September 1915, during the Battle of Loos, and was entitled to the 1914-15 Star, and the General Service and Victory Medals.
"He joined the great white company of valiant souls."
14, Russell Street, Ancoats, Manchester. Z10371A

HAYHURST, W., Cpl., King's Own Scottish Bord's.
Volunteering in October 1914, he was sent to France in the following May, and fought in the Battles of Ypres, Festubert, Loos, Ploegsteert, and the Somme. He was also in action at Arras, Bullecourt and Cambrai, and throughout the German and Allied Offensives of 1918. He was demobilised in December of that year, and holds the 1914-15 Star, and the General Service and Victory Medals.
14, Russell Street, Ancoats, Manchester. Z10371B

HAYLES, W., Private, 3rd Lancashire Fusiliers.
He volunteered in August 1915, and in December was drafted to Salonika, where he took part in heavy fighting on the Doiran and Struma fronts, and was present at the recapture of Monastir. In December 1916, he was invalided home, suffering severely from malarial fever, and twelve months later was discharged as medically unfit for further service. He holds the General Service and Victory Medals.
105, Earl Street, Longsight. Manchester. Z6495

HAYMES, F., Private, 4th Border Regiment.
He joined in May 1916, and in the following September was drafted to the Western Front, but after only a month's active service, during which he took part in heavy fighting, was unhappily killed in action on the Somme in October 1916. He was entitled to the General Service and Victory Medals.
"A costly sacrifice upon the altar of freedom."
122, Rutland Street, Hulme, Manchester. Z6496

HAYNES, F. J. (D.C.M.), Sergt., 19th Lancs. Fusiliers.
He volunteered in April 1915, and in the following year was drafted to France, where he took part in the fighting at Loos and Neuve Chapelle, but was gassed at Hill 60. He was later in action on the Somme, and at La Bassée, and at Ypres was badly wounded on March 12th, 1918. He unfortunately died the next day of his injuries. He was awarded the Distinguished Conduct Medal for conspicuous gallantry in leading his Company up the line under shell-fire at Hill 60 in August 1916, and also was entitled to the 1914-15 Star, and the General Service and Victory Medals.
"Steals on the ear, the distant triumph song."
4, Randolph Street, Openshaw, Manchester. TZ9179

HAYWARD, A. E., Private, 13th Manchester Regt.

He volunteered in September 1914, and in the following August was sent to the Western Front, where he saw much severe fighting for three months. In October 1915, he was drafted to Salonika, and took part in the Landing, and in the first operations on the Vardar, during which he was severely shell-shocked. Unfortunately he died from the effects on February 23rd, 1916, and was entitled to the 1914-15 Star, and the General Service and Victory Medals.

" He joined the great white company of valiant souls."

17, Marsland Street, Chorlton-on-Medlock, Manchester. Z6499

HAYWARD, E., Air Mechanic, R.A.F.

He volunteered in the King's (Liverpool Regiment) in September 1914, and on completion of his training was engaged on important duties in Scotland. Later he was transferred to the R.A.F., and carried out special work in connection with the building and testing of aeroplanes. He was also engaged on the manufacture of munitions of war at Newcastle for a time, and rendered valuable services until his demobilisation in January 1919.

144, Earl Street, Longsight, Manchester. Z6498

HAYWARD, G., Pte., 1st N. Staffordshire Regiment.

Volunteering in August 1915, he was drafted to the Western Front in the following year, and fought on the Somme, and in many other engagements of note. Later, owing to ill-health, he returned to England, and after receiving hospital treatment was invalided out of the Service in March 1918. He holds the General Service and Victory Medals.

68, Eliza Ann Street, Rochdale Road, Manchester. Z10372

HAYWARD, S., Private, Labour Corps.

He joined in July 1918, and in the following month was drafted to the Western Front, where he was attached to the R.E. for important duties in connection with the repair of roads in the Amiens, Bapaume, Arras, Albert, Cambrai, Havrincourt and Ypres sectors. In December 1918, he was admitted to hospital at Etaples suffering from general debility, and a month later was invalided from the Army, holding the General Service and Victory Medals.

22, Bradshaw Street, Hulme, Manchester. Z6497

HAYWARD, S. W., 2nd Lieutenant, R.A.F.

He volunteered in August 1915, and after his training served at various stations with his Squadron on important duties which demanded a high degree of technical skill. He was promoted to the rank of Second Lieutenant from that of 1st Air Mechanic on account of his efficiency in the air, and was retained at home on special duties which precluded his transfer to a fighting area. In November 1918 he was demobilised after over three years' valuable service.

19, Vine Street, Newton Heath, Manchester. Z9564

HAZELL, M., Pte., 1st K.O. (Royal Lancaster Rgt.)

He joined in July 1916, and three months later was drafted to the Western Front, where he took part in the Battles of the Somme, Arras, Ypres, Cambrai, the Marne (II), Havrincourt and Le Cateau. He was wounded in action on the Somme in November 1916, at Arras in the following April, and on the Marne in July 1918. Demobilised in February 1919, he holds the General Service and Victory Medals.

24, Alfred Street, West Gorton, Manchester. Z6500

HEAD, R., Driver, R.E.

He volunteered in September 1914, and in the following March was drafted to France, where he was engaged on important transport duties in the forward areas during the Battles of Neuve Chapelle, Ypres, the Somme, Arras and Béthune, and in the Retreat and Advance of 1918. He was demobilised in March 1919, and holds the 1914-15 Star, and the General Service and Victory Medals.

1, Hancock Street, Rusholme, Manchester. TZ6501

HEALD, B., Corporal, R.F.A.

He was mobilised in August 1914, and was shortly afterwards sent to France, where he took part in the fighting at Mons, and in the Retreat, also in the Battles of the Marne, the Aisne, La Bassée, Ypres, Albert, the Somme and Cambrai. He contracted trench fever, and was invalided home and discharged in December 1918, owing to his disability. He holds the Queen's and King's South African Medals, the Mons Star, and the General Service and Victory Medals.

115, Princess Street, Miles Platting, Manchester. Z9180

HEALD, E., Private, 7th King's (Liverpool Regt.)

He joined in June 1918, and in the following October proceeded to the Western Front. After only three weeks' service in France he unfortunately contracted influenza very severely, and was admitted to hospital at Rouen. He was sent home and demobilised in February 1919, and holds the General Service and Victory Medals.

8, Pearson Street, Newton Heath, Manchester. Z9565

HEALD, J. F., Private, 2/7th Manchester Regt.

He volunteered in September 1914, and on completion of his training, acted as a machine gun Instructor for some time before being sent to France in February 1917. After taking part in the Battles of Arras and Vimy Ridge, he was badly wounded in action during a bayonet charge at Ypres in July 1917,

and was invalided home. He was in hospital at Reading for nearly two years, and was eventually discharged as medically unfit for further service in March 1919, holding the General Service and Victory Medals.

67, Dorset Street, Hulme, Manchester. Z6502B

HEALD, J. W. (M.M.), Sapper, R.E.

He joined in September 1916, and proceeded to France two months later. He was in action on the Somme, and at Arras and Cambrai, and was awarded the Military Medal for gallantry and devotion to duty in the Field at Messines. He also served throughout the German and Allied Offensives of 1918, and after the Armistice was sent into Germany with the Army of Occupation. He was demobilised in September 1919, and in addition to the Military Medal, holds the General Service and Victory Medals. 23, Hope St., Bradford, Manchester. Z10373

HEALD, T. G., Sapper, R.E.

He volunteered in January 1916, and twelve months later was drafted to the Western Front, where he was soon slightly wounded. Remaining with his unit, however, he played an important part in the Battles of Arras and Vimy Ridge, and was badly wounded and invalided home. In August 1917, he returned to France, and was in action at the Battles of Ypres (III), and the Somme (II). After the Armistice, he served in Germany with the Army of Occupation until his demobilisation in August 1919, and holds the General Service and Victory Medals.

67, Dorset Street, Hulme, Manchester. Z6502A

HEALD, W., Sapper, R.E.

Volunteering in September 1914, he embarked for the Western Front in the following January, and was engaged on important duties in various parts of the line. He gave his life for the freedom of England at Loos in February 1916, and was entitled to the 1914-15 Star, and the General Service and Victory Medals.

" Whilst we remember, the sacrifice is not in vain."

16, Pollard Street East, Ancoats, Manchester. Z10374

HEALEY, D., Private, West Yorkshire Regiment.

He joined in November 1916, and after a period of training, proceeded to France. Whilst in this theatre of war he took part in the Battles of Arras, Vimy Ridge, Ypres (III), Passchendaele, the Somme (II), and in the Retreat and Advance of 1918, where he was wounded. As a result he was invalided home, and finally discharged in May 1919 as medically unfit for further service. He holds the General Service and Victory Medals. 40, Prescott Street, Hulme, Manchester. Z11722

HEALEY, F., Private, K.O. (Royal Lancaster Regt.

Volunteering in August 1914, he was drafted to Gallipoli in the following April, and after taking part in the Landing at Cape Helles, and in the three Battles of Krithia. He was unfortunately killed in action on August 10th, 1915, during the Landing at Suvla Bay. He was entitled to the 1914-15 Star, and the General Service and Victory Medals.

" Great deeds cannot die :
They, with the sun and moon renew their light for ever."

36, Marple Street, Openshaw, Manchester. Z6534

HEALEY, H., Private, Manchester Regiment.

He joined in April 1916, and in the following January was drafted to the Western Front, where he took part in the Battles of Arras, Vimy Ridge, Ypres and Passchendaele, before being badly gassed and wounded in action. Invalided to England in February 1917, he was discharged five months later as medically unfit for further service and holds the General Service and Victory Medals.

64, George Street, Bradford, Manchester. Z6546

HEALEY, J., Driver, R.F.A.

Volunteering in January 1915, he was drafted to France four months later, and was in action in the Battles of Ypres. the Somme and Cambrai. He was engaged in heavy fighting throughout the German Offensive and Allied Advance of 1918, and returning home after the Armistice was demobilised in February 1919. He holds the 1914-15 Star, and the General Service and Victory Medals.

145, Cobden Street, Ancoats, Manchester. Z10375

HEALEY, J., Private, South Lancashire Regiment.

He volunteered in January 1915, and two months later was drafted to France. Whilst overseas he took part in engagements at St. Eloi, Ypres, Loos and Vermelles, but during fighting at Vimy Ridge was unfortunately killed in action by an enemy sniper in July 1916. He was entitled to the 1914-15 Star, and the General Service and Victory Medals.

" Courage, bright hopes, and a myriad dreams, splendidly given."

103, Teignmouth Street, Rochdale Road, Manchester. Z9566

HEALEY, J., Private, 2nd Manchester Regiment.

He volunteered in August 1914, and in January of the following year was drafted to the Western Front. He fought in the Battles of Neuve Chapelle and Ypres, where he was severely gassed in action, and was invalided home to hospital in September 1915. After receiving prolonged medical treatment, he was discharged as unfit for further duty in February 1917, and holds the 1914-15 Star, and the General Service and Victory Medals.

147, Ludell Street, Rochdale Road, Manchester. Z9567

HEANEY, J., Private, R.A.M.C.

He joined in January 1917, and after a brief period of training was drafted to the Western Front, where he rendered valuable services with his unit during heavy fighting in the Albert, Ypres, Amiens and Hazebrouck sectors. Remaining in France until February 1920, he was then demobilised, and holds the General Service and Victory Medals.
22, Overton Street, Hulme, Manchester. Z6503

HEAP, H., Corporal, 1/4th Seaforth Highlanders.

He volunteered in November 1914, and was quickly drafted to France, where he played an important part in the Battles of Neuve Chapelle and Hill 60, and was wounded in May 1915. After hospital treatment at Rouen, he rejoined his unit and was in action at the Battle of Loos before being again wounded (at Arras) in June 1916. He was invalided home, but on his recovery, returned to France in November 1916, and was in action at Delville Wood, High Wood, Ypres and Passchendaele, where he was wounded a third time. He was again invalided home, and after discharge from hospital in Manchester, was transferred to the R.A.F., and did much good work until his demobilisation in April 1919. He holds the 1914-15 Star, and the General Service and Victory Medals.
10, Emma Street, West Gorton, Manchester. Z6505

HEAP, J. O. P., Sergt., 7th Manchester Regiment.

Volunteering in November 1914, he proceeded to France in the following October, and first saw heavy fighting at Loos, Albert and Vermelles, early in 1916. Later he served with distinction at the Battle of the Somme, but was seriously wounded in action in September 1916. He was invalided home to Grangethorpe Hospital, Fallowfield, Manchester, and after undergoing four operations, was eventually discharged in October 1918, as medically unfit for further service. He holds the 1914-15 Star, and the General Service and Victory Medals.
6, St. Bees Street, Moss Side, Manchester. Z6504

HEAP, T., Private, 3rd King's (Liverpool Regt.)

Joining in March 1917, he embarked for the Western Front in the following month, and fought in various sectors. He was in action in the Battles of Ypres and Cambrai, and throughout the Retreat and Advance of 1918. He was demobilised in February 1919, and holds the General Service and Victory Medals.
14, Dalton Street, Collyhurst, Manchester. Z10368

HEAPS, A., Private, 22nd Manchester Regiment.

He volunteered in November 1914, and in the following October was drafted to the Western Front, where he played an important part in much severe fighting at Loos, St. Eloi and Albert early in 1916. As the result of a serious accident to his knee, he was admitted to hospital at Etaples, and four months after being invalided home, was discharged in October 1917, as medically unfit for further service. He holds the 1914-15 Star, and the General Service and Victory Medals.
2, White Street, Hulme, Manchester. TZ6507

HEAPS, J., Private, Manchester Regt. (Bantams).

He volunteered in November 1914, and first served as a bugler in the Regimental Band at Grantham and Salisbury. In January 1916, he was drafted to the Western Front, and after taking part in heavy fighting at Loos, St. Eloi and Vermelles, was unfortunately killed in action during the Somme Offensive in July 1916. He was entitled to the General Service and Victory Medals.
"He died the noblest death a man may die,
Fighting for God, and right, and liberty."
62, Nellie Street, Ardwick, Manchester. Z6506

HEAPY, G., Private, Lancashire Fusiliers.

Volunteering in November 1914, he served at various stations on important duties until sent to France in June 1916. During his service overseas he fought in the Battles of Vimy Ridge, the Somme, Arras, Lens and Cambrai, and throughout the German Offensive and subsequent Allied Advance of 1918. Returning to England, he was demobilised in March 1919, and holds the General Service and Victory Medals.
73, Burton Street, Rochdale Road, Manchester. Z10452

HEARD, V., Rflmn., 8th London Regt. (P.O. Rifles).

He volunteered in August 1914, and on completion of his training, was engaged on guard duties over important wireless stations in various parts of England. Owing to his being medically unfit he was not transferred overseas, and after three and a half years consistently good work was invalided from the Service in January 1918.
33, York Street, Higher Ardwick, Manchester. Z6509

HEARN, A., Private, Lancashire Fusiliers.

He volunteered in 1914, and after a period of training was drafted to the Western Front in the following year. He played a prominent part in much severe fighting in various sectors, but in 1915 fell gloriously on the Field of Battle whilst gallantly serving his Country. He was entitled to the 1914-15 Star, and the General Service and Victory Medals.
"Nobly striving,
He nobly fell that we might live."
21, Maskell Street, Chorlton-on-Medlock, Manchester. X6510B

HEARN, J., Private, 8th Manchester Regiment.

He volunteered in April 1915, and after twelve months training was transferred to the 1st Monmouthshire Regiment, with which unit he was engaged on important coast defence duties until January 1917. He then took part in heavy fighting at Lens and La Bassée, and in the Battles of Cambrai and St. Quentin. He was wounded at La Bassée in March 1917, and gassed in action at Lens four months later. Demobilised in April 1920, he holds the General Service and Victory Medals.
21, Maskell Street, Chorlton-on-Medlock, Manchester. X6510A

HEARNE, F., Private, 1st Lancashire Fusiliers.

Volunteering in December 1914, he was drafted to the Dardanelles in the following May and after taking part in much heavy fighting on Chocolate Hill, was admitted to hospital in Alexandria, suffering severely from frost bite. In February 1916, he was sent home, and after six months treatment at Harrogate, was discharged in August 1916, as medically unfit for further service. He holds the 1914-15 Star, and the General Service and Victory Medals.
106, Walmer Street, Rusholme, Manchester. Z6511

HEATH, C., Private, Lancashire Fusiliers.

He joined in June 1916, and in the following February was drafted to France. During his service on the Western Front, he played an important part in the Battles of Arras, Ypres (III), Cambrai, the Aisne (III), Bapaume and Le Cateau. He was in hospital for some time suffering severely from trench fever. Eventually demobilised in November 1919, he holds the General Service and Victory Medals.
11, Johnson Street, Ancoats, Manchester. Z6513

HEATH, E., Private, 3rd Sherwood Foresters.

He joined in November 1917, and four months later proceeded to the Western Front, where he saw much severe fighting during the Retreat and Advance of 1918. He was in action at the Battles of Amiens, Bapaume, Cambrai (II), Ypres (IV) and Le Cateau (II), and was wounded on Passchendaele Ridge. In July 1919 he was discharged, and holds the General Service and Victory Medals.
4, Greenhill Street, Chorlton-on-Medlock, Manchester. TZ6515A

HEATH, G., Sergt., R.A.S.C. (M.T.)

Joining in May 1916, he was drafted to Egypt in the following July, but after a period of transport duties there, proceeded to Palestine, where he rendered valuable services with his unit during the Advance of General Allenby's forces. He was present at the fall of Jerusalem, and also at other engagements until hostilities ceased. Demobilised in November 1919, he holds the General Service and Victory Medals.
21, Cuba Street, Hulme, Manchester. Z6512

HEATH, G., Private, 1st East Lancashire Regiment.

He volunteered in August 1914, and in the following November was drafted to France. Whilst overseas he fought at Ploegsteert Wood, and was severely wounded at Armentières, sustaining the loss of one of his legs on March 25th, 1915. He was invalided home to hospital and was discharged as physically unfit for further duty in June 1916. He holds the 1914 Star, and the General Service and Victory Medals.
14, Lindley Street, Newton Heath, Manchester. Z9568A

HEATH, G. W., Private, Border Regiment.

He joined in October 1918, and after a period of training was sent to Ireland, where he rendered valuable services with his unit until August 1919. He then re-enlisted for two years, and was transferred to the 2nd Manchester Regiment, with which he proceeded to Mesopotamia.
7, Galloway Street, Ardwick, Manchester. Z6514

HEATH, T. H., Driver, R.F.A.

Mobilised in August 1914, he immediately proceeded with his Battery to the Western Front, and fought at Mons. Later he took part in the Battles of the Marne, the Aisne, Ypres, Loos, the Somme and Bapaume, and was also in action during the Retreat and Advance of 1918. He received his discharge in April 1919, and holds the Mons Star, and the General Service and Victory Medals.
4, Greenhill Street, Chorlton-on-Medlock, Manchester. TZ5615B

HEATHCOTE, J. W., Private, 2nd E. Lancs. Regt.

He volunteered in January 1915, and in the following April landed in France, where he fought at Loos, St. Eloi, Albert, Vermelles and the Somme. He was killed in action at Bapaume on October 23rd, 1916, and was entitled to the 1914-15 Star, and the General Service and Victory Medals.
"A costly sacrifice upon the altar of freedom."
42, Lowe Street, Oldham Road, Manchester. Z10376

HEATON, E., Private, 5th Manchester Regiment.

Volunteering in December 1914, he was sent to France in November of the following year, and took part in the Battles of the Somme, the Ancre, Arras, Bullecourt, Ypres and Passchendaele, and in heavy fighting at St. Eloi, Albert and Lens, where he was badly wounded in action in August 1917. He was invalided home, and on his recovery, was engaged on special duties until his demobilisation in March 1919. He holds the 1914-15 Star, and the General Service and Victory Medals.
34, Lynn Street, West Gorton, Manchester. Z6517

HEATON, R., Private, Royal Welch Fusiliers.
He joined in March 1916, and drafted to the Western Front
twelve months later, was engaged in heavy fighting in many
parts of the line. He died gloriously on the Field of Battle
at Croisilles on June 27th, 1917, and was entitled to the General
Service and Victory Medals.
  " Steals on the ear the distant triumph song."
70, Albion Street, Miles Platting, Manchester.   Z10377A

HEATON, S., Sapper, R.E.
Volunteering in September 1914, he was engaged on special
duties at various home stations until March 1917, when he
was sent to France. During his service on the Western Front,
he saw severe fighting at La Bassée, Givenchy, Festubert,
Béthune, Nieuport, Ypres, Cambrai, on the Somme, and in
the Retreat and Advance of 1918. He was stationed at Malta
in 1920, and holds the General Service and Victory Medals.
1, Bakewell Street, Ardwick, Manchester.   Z6516

HEATON, T., Private, 21st Manchester Regiment.
Volunteering in August 1915, he was sent to the Western Front
in the following November and fought at Loos, St. Eloi, Albert
and Vimy Ridge. He was unfortunately killed in action at
Mametz Wood in July 1916, during the first British Offensive
on the Somme, and was entitled to the 1914–15 Star, and the
General Service and Victory Medals.
  " His memory is cherished with pride."
21, Iles Street, Oldham Road, Manchester.   Z10118A

HEATON, T., Private, Army Cyclist Corps.
Volunteering in February 1916, he completed his training
and was engaged on important duties as despatch rider at
various stations. He was unsuccessful in obtaining his transfer overseas prior to the close of the war, but rendered valuable
services until demobilised in January 1919.
70, Albion Street, Miles Platting, Manchester.   Z10377B

HEBEL, P., Private, 8th Middlesex Regiment.
He joined in June 1917, and six months later was drafted to
the Western Front. During his service in this theatre of war,
he played a prominent part in the Battles of the Somme (II),
Bapaume, Epéhy, Cambrai (II) and Ypres (IV), and saw much
severe fighting until the cessation of hostilities. He was
demobilised in November 1919, and holds the General Service
and Victory Medals.
17, Callender Street, Chorlton-on-Medlock, Manchester. Z6518

HEDGES, G., Sapper, R.E.
He joined in October 1917, and was quickly drafted to France,
where he rendered valuable services with the Signal Section
of the R.E. He was engaged on the laying of cables in the
Ypres sector, and the setting of mines on the Somme front,
but also saw heavy fighting during the Retreat and Advance
of 1918. Demobilised in June 1919, he holds the General
Service and Victory Medals.
2, Robson Street, Hulme, Manchester.   Z6519-20

HEDGES, H., Private, Lancashire Fusiliers.
He volunteered in August 1914, and twelve months later was
sent to France, where he was in action at Armentières, Albert,
Fricourt, Arras, and on the Somme, before being invalided
home with septic poisoning in December 1916. On his recovery, he was drafted to Egypt, but after ten months service
near Alexandria, returned to the Western Front in October
1917. In January 1918, however, he was again invalided home
suffering from dysentery, and was discharged in the following
June as medically unfit. He holds the 1914–15 Star, and the
General Service and Victory Medals.
21, Walnut Street, Hulme, Manchester.   TZ6522

HEDGES, J., Private, 5th Border Regiment.
Joining in 1916, he was drafted to France on completion of
his training, and took part in the Battles of the Somme (1916
and 1918), Bullecourt and Ypres (III), and was wounded in
action. Early in 1918 he was transferred to a Labour Battalion,
owing to his heart being weak, and did consistently good work
until his demobilisation in 1919. He holds the General Service and Victory Medals.
12, Daniel Street, Hulme, Manchester.   Z6521

HEDLEY, J., Private, East Lancashire Regiment.
Joining in June 1916, he was stationed at various depôts
until proceeding to France in September 1917. Severely
wounded at Messines in the following month he returned
to England, and after receiving hospital treatment, was
engaged on important duties at various stations until demobilised in October 1919. He holds the General Service
and Victory Medals.
23, Francisco Street, Collyhurst, Manchester.   Z10378

HEFFERAN, D., Driver, R.F.A.
He volunteered in January 1915, and in the same year was
sent to Egypt and was engaged at Katia, Suez and Romani.
He was later transferred to Gallipoli, but after taking part in
the Landing at Suvla Bay was sent to Cairo for medical treat-
ment. He was later drafted to France, and was in action at
Ypres, Cambrai, Bapaume, Albert and in other engagements.
He was demobilised in December 1918, and holds the 1914–15
Star, and the General Service and Victory Medals.
8, Dora Street, Rochdale Road, Manchester.   Z9181

HEFFRAN, J., Private, R.A.S.C. (M.T.)
Volunteering in August 1915, he landed in France in the following year, and was engaged on important transport duties
in various parts of the line. He was present at the Battles
of the Somme and Ypres, and saw much service during the
German and Allied Offensives of 1918. He was demobilised
in June 1919, and holds the General Service and Victory Medals.
50, Eliza Ann Street, Rochdale Road, Manchester.   Z10379

HEGAN, H., Rifleman, 7th K.R.R.C.
He volunteered in August 1914, and after a period of duty in
England was drafted to the Western Front in March 1916.
Whilst in this theatre of war, he took part in the Battles of the
Somme, Messines, Ypres (III), Passchendaele, the Somme (II),
Bapaume, Ypres (IV), where he was gassed in September 1918,
and Le Cateau (II). He was demobilised in March 1919
and holds the General Service and Victory Medals.
838, Oldham Road, Newton Heath, Manchester.   Z6523

HEIGHT, J., Private, 8th Manchester Regiment.
Volunteering in September 1914, he was sent to Mesopotamia
in November 1916, and was first engaged on special duties
on board the Hospital Ship " His Presidency " at Amara
on the Tigris. Later he took part in much severe fighting,
and was wounded in a bayonet charge at Kut early in 1917.
He was eventually demobilised in August 1919, and holds
the General Service and Victory Medals.
2, Gorton Street, Ardwick, Manchester.   Z6524

HELICON, J., Private, R.M.L.I.
He joined in June 1918, and after a brief training was engaged
as an engineer with the Marine Royal Engineers at various
places in the South of England. He was unsuccessful in serving
in a theatre of war, but did consistently good work until his
demobilisation in December 1918.
20, Napier Street, Ardwick, Manchester.   Z6525

HELLEY, F., Sergt., K.R.R.C.
He enlisted in April 1914, and at the outbreak of war four
months later was drafted to France, where he served with distinction at the Battles of Mons, Le Cateau, La Bassée, Ypres
Neuve Chapelle and Ypres (II), and in other important engagements throughout hostilities. He was wounded in action at
Ypres in May 1915, and was eventually discharged in December
1918, holding the Mons Star, and the General Service and Victory Medals.
9, Bedale Street, Hulme, Manchester.   Z6526

HELLIER, H., Private, Manchester Regiment.
He volunteered in 1914, and was engaged at various stations
on important duties with his unit. He rendered valuable
services, but was unable to obtain a transfer overseas, and was
discharged in 1917, owing to his age.
127, Granville Place, Ancoats, Manchester.   TZ11723

HELLIWELL, W. H., Private, 1st Manchester Regt.
Volunteering in September 1914, he was drafted to France
two months later and was in action in the Battles of Neuve
Chapelle, Ypres, and Hill 60, where he was wounded. On his
recovery, proceeding to Egypt in November 1915, he was on
duty at various depôts until January 1917, when he returned
to the Western Front. He fought at Arras, Messines, Ypres,
Passchendaele and Cambrai, and throughout the Retreat and
Advance of 1918. He was demobilised in February 1919,
and holds the 1914–15 Star, and the General Service and Victory Medals.
9, Cathcart Street, Ancoats, Manchester.   Z10380

HEMBROUGH, F. W., Rifleman, 6th Rifle Brigade.
Volunteering in September 1915, he first saw active service
at the Landing at Salonika in October 1915. Whilst in the
Balkan theatre of war, he took part in much severe fighting on
the Doiran, Vardar and Struma fronts, and was present at
the recapture of Monastir. In August 1916, he was accidentally
wounded by the explosion of a rifle and unfortunately lost the
sight of his right eye. On his recovery, he rejoined his unit,
and remained in Salonika until December 1918. He was demobilised in February 1919, and holds the 1914–15 Star, and
the General Service and Victory Medals.
26, Hardy Street, West Gorton, Manchester.   Z6527

HEMPSALL, J., Private, 1st Cheshire Regiment.
Joining in June 1918, he was later in the same year sent to
France, and took part in the fighting on the Marne, and at
Bapaume and Havrincourt, during the Advance of 1918.
He was demobilised in October 1919, after seventeen months'
service, and holds the General Service and Victory Medals.
1, William Street, Ancoats, Manchester.   Z9182

HEMPSTOCK, S. W., Gunner, R.G.A.
Mobilised at the commencement of hostilities he proceeded
to the Western Front and fought in the Retreat from Mons,
the Battles of the Marne, the Aisne, La Bassée and Ypres.
He also was in action at Loos, the Somme, Arras, and Cambrai,
and throughout the Retreat and Advance, and was gassed.
Returning home he was demobilised in March 1919, and holds
the Mons Star, and the General Service and Victory Medals.
5, Grantham Street, West Gorton, Manchester.   Z10381

HENDERSON, A., Private, Royal Fusiliers.
He volunteered in May 1915, and was quickly drafted to France, where he took part in heavy fighting at Ypres, Albert, and Vimy Ridge. He was taken prisoner in May 1916, and during his captivity was forced to work immediately behind the firing line. In Feburary 1919 he was repatriated and demobilised, and holds the 1914-15 Star, and the General Service and Victory Medals.
50, York Street, Hulme, Manchester. Z6529

HENDERSON, A. J., Private, R.A.M.C.
He volunteered in August 1914, and two months later was drafted to France, where he rendered valuable service as a nursing orderly at No.1 C.C.S. at Ypres, No. 6 C.C.S. at Rouen, and also in a large hospital at Le Havre. In August 1916 he was invalided to Whalley, near Blackburn, suffering from pleurisy, but on his recovery, was drafted to India, and resumed his former duties as an orderly at Bombay. He was demobilised in February 1919, and holds the 1914 Star, and the General Service and Victory Medals.
27, Callender Street, Chorlton-on-Medlock, Manchester. Z6528A

HENDERSON, J., Private, M.G.C.
He volunteered in July 1915, and in the following January was drafted to France, where he fought on the Somme, and was wounded. On recovery he returned to the Front, and was in action in the third Battle of Ypres. Shortly afterwards he embarked for Egypt, where he served at various stations. Returning to France in March 1918. He was engaged in heavy fighting during the Retreat and Advance, and was twice wounded. He was demobilised in June 1919, and holds the General Service and Victory Medals.
334, Mill Street, Bradford, Manchester. Z10383

HENDERSON, P., Corporal, 1/8th Manchester Regt.
Volunteering at the commencement of hostilities, he landed in France in January 1915, and was in action at La Bassée, Ypres and the Somme, where he was severely wounded. He returned to England, and after receiving hospital treatment, served at various depôts until demobilised in January 1919. He holds the 1914-15 Star, and the General Service and Victory Medals.
16, Flower Street, Ancoats, Manchester. Z10382

HENDERSON, W., A.B., Royal Navy.
He joined in May 1916, and until the close of hostilities served in H.M.T. " Rocksand," " Imperieuse," and other ships. He was engaged in transporting troops and supplies to various theatres of war, frequently passing through areas in which hostile submarines were active. He was demobilised in July 1919, and holds the General Service and Victory Medals.
12, Boslam Street, Ancoats, Manchester. Z10384

HENDERSON, W., Private, 8th Manchester Regt.
Five months after volunteering, he was sent to Egypt in August 1915, and took part in engagements at Mersa-Matruh, Sollum, Katia, El Fasher, Magdhaba, and Rafa. In August 1917, he was transferred to the Western Front, where he was in action at the Battle of Cambrai, and in the Retreat and Advance of 1918. Demobilised in January 1919, he holds the 1914-15 Star, and the General Service and Victory Medals.
27, Callender Street, Chorlton-on-Medlock, Manchester. Z6528B

HENNEGAN, T., Private, Manchester Regiment.
He volunteered in August 1914, and in the following year was sent to Gallipoli. There he took part in the fighting at " C " Beach, but was wounded and sent to Egypt, and from there was invalided home. He was discharged in October 1917, owing to his injuries, and holds the 1914-15 Star, and the General Service and Victory Medals.
36, Masonic Street, Oldham Road, Manchester. Z9183A

HENNESSEY, W., Private, King's (Liverpool Regt.)
He volunteered in September 1914, and in November of the following year was drafted to France, where he took part in the heavy fighting at Loos, St. Eloi, and Vermelles early in 1916. He was gassed near Armentières in March 1916, and in the following July was again badly gassed, and also buried at Sanctuary Wood during the Somme Offensive. He was invalided to hospital at Rhyl, and in September 1916, was discharged as medically unfit for further service, holding the 1914-15 Star, and the General Service and Victory Medals.
19 Bell Street, Openshaw, Manchester. Z6530

HENNIKER, J., Air Mechanic, R.A.F.
He joined in September 1918, but owing to the early cessation of hostilities, was not drafted overseas. During his service he did consistently good work as a gun-tester at the Blandford and Uxbridge Aerodromes, and was eventually demobilised in February 1919.
17, Hibbert Street, Hulme, Manchester. Z6531

HENSHALL, J. H., L/Cpl., 18th Manchester Regt.
Volunteering in September 1914, he was drafted to the Western Front in November 1915, and played a prominent part in the Battles of the Somme, Vimy Ridge, Messines, Ypres, and Passchendaele, and in the Retreat of 1918. He laid down his life for King and Country at Warlencourt, near Bapaume, on August 28th, 1918, and was entitled to the 1914-15 Star, and the General Service and Victory Medals.
" A costly sacrifice upon the altar of freedom."
25, Clifton Street, Newton, Manchester. Z6535

HENSHALL, T., Driver, R.A.S.C.
He joined in September 1916, and in the following March was drafted to the Western Front, where he was present during the Battles of Arras, Vimy Ridge, Bullecourt, Ypres (III), Cambrai, and Le Cateau (II). At the cessation of hostilities, he proceeded to Germany with the Army of Occupation, and remained there until his demobilisation in February 1920. He holds the General Service and Victory Medals.
23, Boston Street, Hulme, Manchester. Z6532

HENSHAW, F., Private, 1st Manchester Regiment.
He was mobilised at the outbreak of war in August 1914, and proceeding to France with the first Expeditionary Force, was unfortunately killed in action during the Retreat from Mons in September of the same year. He was entitled to the Mons Star, and the General Service and Victory Medals.
" Steals on the ear the distant triumph song."
46, Lancaster Street, Hulme, Manchester. Z6536

HENSHAW, J. H., Pte., King's (Liverpool Regt).
He joined in January 1917, and on completion of his training was sent to Ireland, where he was engaged on important garrison duties with his unit. In May 1917 he met with a serious accident, and was admitted to hospital. He was eventually discharged in February 1919, suffering from valvular disease of the heart.
29, Everton Road, Chorlton-on-Medlock, Manchester. Z6537

HEPPINSTALL, J., Driver, R.A.S.C.
Mobilised in August 1914, he was at once drafted to France, where he was engaged on important transport duties in the forward areas during the Battles of La Bassée, Ypres, Neuve Chapelle, and Festubert. In July 1916 he was unhappily killed as the result of a bomb explosion at Vraignes, and was entitled to the 1914 Star, and the General Service and Victory Medals.
" His memory is cherished with pride."
17, Ely Street, Hulme, Manchester. Z6538

HEPPLE, A., Private, 2/8th Manchester Regiment.
Volunteering in December 1914, he was drafted to Salonika in the following year, and was engaged on the Vardar and Doiran fronts. In 1917 he was transferred to France, and was in action at Cambrai, Le Cateau, Ypres, Bapaume, and on the Marne. He was demobilised in February 1919, and holds the 1914-15 Star, and the General Service and Victory Medals.
12, Ernest Street, Ancoats, Manchester. Z9184

HEPWORTH, A. H., Pte., Loyal N. Lancs. Regt.
Volunteering in January 1916, he was drafted to the Western Front in the following August, and fought in the Battles of the Somme, the Ancre, Arras, Ypres, Passchendaele, and Cambrai. He was also engaged in heavy fighting during the Offensives of 1918, and returning home after the Armistice was demobilised in September 1919. He holds the General Service and Victory Medals. 45, Sycamore Street, Manchester. Z10385

HEPWORTH, E., Private, Royal Welch Fusiliers.
He joined in May 1916, and in the following March was sent to the Western Front, where he was in action at Festubert, Givenchy, and in many other engagements of note. He gave his life for the freedom of England at Cambrai on March 22nd, 1918, during the opening phases of the German Offensive. He was entitled to the General Service and Victory Medals.
"The path of duty was the way to glory."
53, Sycamore Street, Oldham Road, Manchester. Z10386

HEPWORTH, J. W., Pte., 2/6th N. Staffordshire Rgt.
He joined in June 1916, and was sent to France in the following December. During his service overseas he was engaged in heavy fighting on the Ancre, at Arras, Albert, Ypres, and Cambrai. He gave his life for King and Country on April 13th, 1918, in action at Messines Ridge. He was entitled to the General Service and Victory Medals.
" His life for his Country, his soul to God."
51, Sycamore Street, Oldham Road, Manchester. Z10387

HEPWORTH, W. R., Rigger, Corporal, R.A.F.
He volunteered in the 7th Manchester Regiment in May 1915, and was afterwards transferred to the Royal Air Force. He was engaged on important special duties at various aerodromes and rendered valuable services. In December 1918, he proceeded to France and remained there until September of the following year, when he returned home, and was demobilised.
7, Hadfield Street, Newton Heath, Manchester. Z9569

HERBERT, T., Gunner, R.F.A.
He enlisted in April 1914, and shortly after the outbreak of war was sent to France, and was in action at Mons, and in the Retreat, also at Ypres, Hill 60, Festubert, Neuve Chapelle, Vimy Ridge, the Somme, Arras, Bullecourt, and Cambrai. He was discharged in 1919, and holds the Mons Star, and the General Service and Victory Medals.
33, Marshall Street, Manchester. Z9185

HERBERT, W. H., Air Mechanic, R.A.F.
He joined in June 1917, and on completion of his training, engaged on special duties with his Squadron at Farnborough, Aldershot, and Blandford. He rendered very valuable services, but was unsuccessful in obtaining his transfer overseas, and was demobilised in July 1919.
38, Percy Street, Hulme, Manchester. Z6539

HERBERTS, J., Private, King's (Liverpool Regt.)

He volunteered in August 1915, and in the following year was drafted to France, where he took part in the fighting on the Somme, at Arras, Ypres, and Cambrai. Owing to ill-health he was invalided home in February 1918, and was stationed at various depôts until demobilised in July 1919. He holds the General Service and Victory Medals.

6, Crook Street, Miles Platting, Manchester.　　Z10453

HERD, E. F., L/Corporal, Lancashire Fusiliers.

Volunteering in January 1916, he was sent to France in May, and played an important part in the Battles of the Somme, Arras, Ypres, and Passchendaele, and in heavy fighting at Festubert, and in the Retreat and Advance of 1918. He was wounded in action at Ypres in September 1916, and again during the Advance in November 1918. Demobilised in May 1919, he holds the General Service and Victory Medals.

23, Tipper Street, Hulme, Manchester.　　TZ6540

HERD, L., Private, Welch Regiment.

He joined in March 1918, but was unsuccessful in obtaining his transfer overseas during the period of hostilities. In March 1919, however, he was sent to the Army of Occupation in Germany, where he rendered valuable services until October of that year. He was then sent to Dublin in Ireland, and remained there until his demobilisation in March 1920.

29, Burns Street, Bradford, Manchester.　　Z6508

HERD, T. H., Seaman, R.N.

He joined in February 1916, and was posted to H.M.S. "Vivid," but, after only two months' service on the high seas, was taken seriously ill, and unhappily died on April 4th, 1916. He was entitled to the General Service and Victory Medals.

"He joined the great white company of valiant souls."

39, Hulton Street, Brooks Bar, Manchester.　　Z6541

HERETY, J., Private, 7th Leicestershire Regiment.

He volunteered in October 1915, and after serving in Wales was drafted overseas in December of the following year. Whilst on the Western Front he did good work with his unit in engagements at Arras, Messines, Ypres, and Lens. During the Battle of the Somme in March 1918, he was taken prisoner, and kept in captivity until the following December. On his release he was sent to hospital in London, suffering from nerves and chest complaint. He was demobilised in June 1919, holding the General Service and Victory Medals.

13, Southwell Street, Harpurhey, Manchester.　　Z11510

HERMAN, W. H., Private, King's (Liverpool Regt.)

He joined in March 1916, and after his training was engaged on important duties with his unit at various stations. He was sent to Aldershot for transfer to the Royal Engineers, but discovered to be unfit for active service, was discharged unfit for further service in May 1917.

32, Simpson Street, Bradford, Manchester.　　Z10388

HERON, M., Pte., 1st King's Shropshire Light Inftry.

Joining in May 1916, he proceeded to the Western Front in the following September, and there saw severe fighting in various sectors. He took part in the Battles of Arras, Vimy Ridge, Bullecourt, Ypres, Passchendaele, and Cambrai, and other important engagements, and served also through the Retreat and Advance of 1918. He was then sent with the Army of Occupation into Germany, finally returning home for demobilisation in September 1919. He holds the General Service and Victory Medals.

42, Redvers Street, Ardwick, Manchester.　　Z6542

HERRING, L., Private, King's (Liverpool Regt.)

Volunteering in April 1915, he was drafted to the Western Front in November of that year, and saw much heavy fighting. He took part in the Battles of St. Eloi, Albert, Vimy Ridge and many minor engagements until severely wounded in action on the Somme in July 1917, and sent to hospital at Boulogne. He was also in hospital in England for a time, before being invalided from the Army in September 1917, and holds the 1914-15 Star, and the General Service and Victory Medals.

10, Ashbury Street, Openshaw, Manchester.　　Z6543

HERRIOTT, J., L/Corporal, Lancashire Fusiliers.

Volunteering in August 1914, he proceeded to Egypt after four months' training, and was thence drafted to Gallipoli shortly afterwards. There, after taking part in the Landing at Cape Helles, he fought in the Battles of Krithia and at Achi Baba and Suvla Bay. He returned to Egypt on the Evacuation of the Peninsula, but in April 1917 was transferred to the Western Front, where he served through the Battles of Ypres and the Somme, and also took part in the Retreat and Advance of 1918. Demobilised in August 1920, he holds the 1914-15 Star, and the General Service and Victory Medals.

15, Gibson Street, Ardwick, Manchester.　　Z6544

HESFORD, J., Rifleman, 5th London Regiment (London Rifle Brigade).

Three months after volunteering in October 1915, he was drafted to the Western Front, where he fought in various sectors. He took part in many important engagements in this theatre of war, including the Battles of St. Eloi, Albert,

Vimy Ridge, the Somme, Arras and Cambrai, and was twice wounded in action—in July 1916, and in March 1918. Invalided home the second time, he returned to France, however, on his recovery, and was again in action until the cessation of hostilities. He was demobilised in January 1919, and holds the General Service and Victory Medals.

31, Leslie Street, Rusholme, Manchester.　　Z6545

HESKETH, T., Pte., King's Shropshire L. Infantry.

He joined in February 1916, and after a period of training was engaged at various stations on important duties with his unit. He was unable to obtain a transfer overseas owing to his being medically unfit, but rendered valuable services until his demobilisation in September 1919.

5, John Street, Hulme, Manchester.　　Z11724

HESLOP, G., Private, Border Regiment.

He volunteered in April 1915, and in January of the following year was drafted to Egypt, where he took part in engagements at Sollum, Jiffjaffa, Katia and Romani, and was afterwards on garrison duty until March 1917. He was then transferred to the Western Front, and there served through the Battles of the Somme, and the Marne, and fought also in the Retreat and Advance of 1918. Demobilised in November of that year, he re-enlisted, however, in September 1919, and was drafted to India, where he was still with his unit in 1920. He holds the General Service and Victory Medals.

44, Council Street, Hulme, Manchester.　　Z6547

HESLOP, W., Private, 2/8th Manchester Regiment.

He volunteered in September 1914, and after his training was engaged on special duties in England for some time. In March 1917, however, he proceeded to the Western Front, and took part in the Battles of Ypres (III), Passchendaele, the Somme (II), Havrincourt, Le Cateau (II) and the Sambre, and in other engagements during the Retreat and Advance of 1918. He holds the General Service and Victory Medals, and was demobilised in February 1919.

18, Baxter Street, Hulme, Manchester.　　Z11725

HESSION, A., Private, South Wales Borderers, and Gunner (Signaller) R.F.A.

He joined in January 1917, and twelve months later proceeded to the Western Front. Whilst in this theatre of war, he saw much severe fighting in various sectors, and took part in many important engagements, including the Battles of Amiens, Bapaume, St. Quentin and Armentières, serving also through the Retreat and Advance of 1918. He was demobilised in March 1919, but, re-engaging for a further period of two years, was still with his Battery in Ireland in 1920. He holds the General Service and Victory Medals.

25, Rumford Street, Hulme, Manchester.　　TZ6548

HEWITT, B. H., Air Mechanic, R.A.F.

Joining in December 1917, he proceeded to France in the following month, and there served in various sectors of the Front. He was present at the Battles of the Somme, Amiens, Bapaume, Havrincourt, Epéhy, Cambrai and Ypres, and many other important engagements until the cessation of hostilities. He returned to England for demobilisation in June 1919, and holds the General Service and Victory Medals.

39, Nut Street, West Gorton, Manchester.　　Z6551

HEWITT, F., L/Corporal, 1/6th Lancashire Fusiliers.

He volunteered in September 1914, and in December of the following year was drafted to Egypt, where he took part in the engagement at Katia, and the capture of El Fasher. After twelve months' service in this seat of operations, he was transferred to the Western Front, and there fought in the Battles of the Somme, the Aisne, Bapaume, Havrincourt and Ypres, and other important actions. He was demobilised in March 1919, and holds the 1914-15 Star, and the General Service and Victory Medals.

11, Overton Street, Hulme, Manchester.　　Z6554

HEWITT, F. H., Private, Royal Marine Engineers.

He joined in October 1917, and was engaged on munition work with Messrs. B. and S. Massy and Co., Manchester, before proceeding to Dover. There he rendered valuable services in the construction of concrete monitors, which were eventually used in the bombardment of the Belgian Coast. He served at Dover until demobilised in November 1918.

42, Crissey St., Miles Platting, Manchester.　　Z11511

HEWITT, H., Private, 27th Winnipeg Regiment (Canadian Overseas Forces).

He volunteered in October 1914, and after four months' training, proceeded to the Western Front, where he saw severe fighting in various sectors. He took part in the Battles of St. Eloi, Hill 60, Ypres, Albert, Vimy Ridge, Passchendaele and Cambrai, and many minor engagements, fought also through the Retreat and Advance of 1918, and was twice wounded in action—at Beaumont-Hamel in November 1916, and in the second Battle of the Somme in March 1918. He was demobilised in March 1919, and holds the 1914-15 Star, and the General Service and Victory Medals.

14, Etruria Street, Longsight, Manchester.　　Z6552

HEWITT, J., Gunner, R.F.A.

Volunteering in January 1915, he was drafted to the Western Front in September of that year and there saw much heavy fighting. After taking part in the Battles of Loos, Albert, Vimy Ridge, the Somme and Arras and other engagements, he was severely wounded in action at Passchendaele, and was for a considerable period in hospital at Rouen and in London. He was invalided from the Army in February 1918, and holds the 1914-15 Star, and the General Service and Victory Medals.
22, Juniper Street, Hulme, Manchester. Z6550

HEWITT, W., Private, 4th King's (Liverpool Regt.)

He joined in April 1916, and in February of the following year was drafted to the Western Front. Whilst in this theatre of war, he fought in many important engagements, including the Battle of Ypres, took part also in the Retreat and Advance of 1918, and was wounded in action on the Somme in October of that year, and was for some time in hospital at the Base. He was demobilised in September 1919, and holds the General Service and Victory Medals.
77, South Street, Longsight, Manchester. Z6549

HEWLETT, W., Private, Lincolnshire Regiment.

Volunteering in September 1914, he was drafted to the Western Front in the following March, and there, after taking part in the second Battle of Ypres, was wounded in action at Hill 60, and invalided home. He returned to France, however, on his recovery, and fought at St. Quentin and in various other sectors until again sent to hospital at Bristol in March 1918. He was discharged as medically unfit for further service in July of that year, and holds the 1914-15 Star, and the General Service and Victory Medals.
3, Kelsall Street, West Gorton, Manchester. Z6553A

HEWLETT, W. E., Gunner, R.F.A.

He joined immediately on attaining military age in March 1919, and after completing a period of training, served at various stations, where he was engaged on duties of great importance. In July 1920, he was drafted to India, and there served at Secunderabad and other places, on garrison duties, and in 1920 was still with his Battery.
3, Kelsall Street, West Gorton, Manchester. Z6553B

HEWSON, W., Private, 8th Border Regiment.

Joining in March 1916, he was sent to France in the following May, and was in action in the Battles of the Somme, Arras, Ypres and Cambrai, where he was wounded. He was invalided home, and after a period in hospital, was discharged as unfit for further service in August 1918. He holds the General Service and Victory Medals.
72, Heyrod Street, Ancoats, Manchester. Z10389

HEYES, F., Private, 8th Lancashire Fusiliers.

Having volunteered in November 1914, he was sent to the Dardanelles in the following year, and served in this area from the Landing at Suvla Bay until the Evacuation. He next proceeded to Egypt, and thence to France, where he was in action at Vimy Ridge, the Somme, Arras, Bullecourt, Messines, Ypres, Passchendaele and Cambrai. He was demobilised in July 1919, and holds the 1914-15 Star, and the General Service and Victory Medals.
65, Long Street, Ancoats, Manchester. Z9186

HEYWOOD, F., Staff-Sergt., R.A.M.C.

He volunteered in June 1915, and twelve months later proceeded to the Western Front, where he served in various sectors. He played an active part in many important engagements in this theatre of war, including the Battles of Vimy Ridge, Cambrai, the Somme, Armentières, Bapaume and Havrincourt, and served also through the Retreat and Advance of 1918. He was afterwards sent with the Army of Occupation into Germany, whence he returned home for demobilisation in January 1919. He holds the General Service and Victory Medals. 12, Webster Street, Greenheys, Manchester. Z6555

HEYWOOD, G., Pte., R.A.S.C., R.D.C. and Pnr., R.E.

He volunteered in May 1915, and after his training was engaged on important duties with the Remount Section until May 1916, when he was invalided from the Army. He re-enlisted, however, in the following August and was engaged in guarding prisoners of war at various stations, until again discharged in February 1917. He joined for a third time in September of that year, but in November was finally discharged as medically unfit for further service.
13, Robert Street, Chorlton-on-Medlock, Manchester. X6559B

HEYWOOD, G. E., Pte., 1st Lancashire Fusiliers and Labour Corps.

Having enlisted in 1912, he was already in the Army when war broke out in August 1914, and in April of the following year was drafted to Gallipoli. There, after taking part in the Landing at Cape Helles, he was wounded in action at the second Battle of Krithia, and was for nine months in hospital. In April 1917 he proceeded to the Western Front with the Labour Corps, and was wounded a second time at the first Battle of Cambrai. He was discharged in May 1919, and holds the 1914-15 Star, and the General Service and Victory Medals.
13, Robert Street, Chorlton-on-Medlock, Manchester. X6559A

HEYWOOD, H., Sapper, R.E. (Signals).

He joined in March 1916, and was engaged on important duties at Bedford till January 1918, when he was sent to France. He was in action at Passchendaele, Lens, Cambrai, and was wounded and gassed. He also served in the Retreat and Advance of 1918 and owing to ill-health was invalided home in August 1918. He was demobilised in November 1919, and holds the General Service and Victory Medals.
6, Duke Street, Bradford, Manchester. Z10390

HEYWOOD, H., Private, R.M.L.I.

He volunteered in October 1914, and in March of the following year was posted to H.M.S. "Birmingham," attached to the Grand Fleet in the North Sea. He also served in H.M.S. "Albemarle" and took part in the Battle of Jutland and many minor actions in these waters. He was still at sea in 1920, in H.M.S. "Southampton" in South American waters, and holds the Naval General Service Medal (with clasp Jutland), the 1914-15 Star, and the General Service and Victory Medals.
22, Hayfield Street, Ardwick, Manchester. Z6556

HEYWOOD, J., Private, Lancashire Fusiliers.

He volunteered at the outbreak of war in August 1914, and in the following year was drafted to the Dardanelles. After much severe fighting he made the supreme sacrifice, falling in action in Gallipoli in August 1915. He was entitled to the 1914-15 Star, and the General Service and Victory Medals.
"He died the noblest death a man may die,
Fighting for God and right and liberty."
39, Napier Street, Ardwick, Manchester. Z6557A

HEYWOOD, J. E., Pte., 17th Royal Welch Fusiliers.

He joined in February 1917, and later in the same year was sent to France, but after being in action at Cambrai and on the Somme, was unhappily killed on the Aisne in May 1918. He was entitled to the General Service and Victory Medals.
"Thinking that remembrance, though unspoken, may reach him where he sleeps."
21, Parcel Street, Beswick, Manchester. TZ9187

HEYWOOD, J. T., Pte., Loyal N. Lancashire Regt.

He volunteered in March 1915, and in the following year was drafted to France, where he took part in the Battles of the Somme, Arras, Bullecourt, Ypres and Cambrai, and was gassed. He returned home and was discharged in consequence in February 1918, holding the General Service and Victory Medals. 19, Tubal St., Ancoats, Manchester. Z9188

HEYWOOD, R., Private, South Wales Borderers.

Joining in December 1917, he was sent to France in the following year and was in action on the Lys, the Aisne and the Marne and at Bapaume, Cambrai and Havrincourt and was wounded at Bapaume in August. He was demobilised in January 1919, and holds the General Service and Victory Medals. 19, Tubal St., Ancoats, Manchester. Z9189

HEYWOOD, S., Private, 2nd Loyal N. Lancs. Regt.

He joined in December 1916, and in March of the following year was sent to Egypt and transferred to the Machine Gun Corps, took part in the fighting at Nebi Samwil during the operations, resulting in the capture of Jerusalem. In June 1918 he proceeded to France, and was in action in the Bapaume sector. He was transferred to the Royal Engineers in September 1918, and was wounded in action in the following month, and was invalided home. He was demobilised in March 1919, and holds the General Service and Victory Medals.
23, Harrowby Street, Collyhurst, Manchester. Z10391

HEYWOOD, S., Air Mechanic, R.A.F.

He volunteered in June 1915, and in January 1917 was drafted to the Western Front, where he was engaged on constructional work at various aerodromes. His duties, which demanded a high degree of technical skill, were carried out in a most satisfactory and efficient manner. He saw much service in the Retreat and Advance of 1918, and was gassed in August 1918. He was demobilised in February 1919, and holds the General Service and Victory Medals.
41, Cobden Street, Ancoats, Manchester. Z10392

HEYWOOD, S., Private, 22nd Manchester Regiment and 2nd Border Regiment.

Volunteering in July 1915, he proceeded to France twelve months later and there saw heavy fighting in various sectors of the Front. After taking part in the Battles of the Somme, Arras and Ypres and many other important engagements in this theatre of war, he was severely wounded in action. He was sent home and invalided from the Army in March 1918, and holds the General Service and Victory Medals.
5, Sandown Street, Ardwick, Manchester. Z6558

HEYWOOD, W., Private, 8th Manchester Regt.

Shortly after volunteering in May 1915, he proceeded to the Western Front, where he saw severe fighting in various sectors. He took part in the Battles of Ypres, Loos, St. Eloi, Vermelles and the Ancre, and many other engagements until the cessation of hostilities, and was wounded in action at Vimy Ridge. He was demobilised on his return home in March 1919, and holds the 1914-15 Star, and the General Service and Victory Medals. 39, Napier Street, Ardwick, Manchester. Z6557B

HEYWOOD, W., 7th Queen's Own (Royal West Kent Regiment).

Joining in January 1918 he was sent to France in the following April. He was in action in the Retreat and Advance of 1918, and was wounded on the Marne in July of that year. He returned home and was demobilised in October 1919, holding the General Service and Victory Medals.
7, Bath Street, Miles Platting, Manchester.　　Z10393

HEYWOOD, W., Private, Manchester Regiment.

Joining in June 1917, he was drafted to the Western Front in November of the same year, and there saw much severe fighting. He took part in the Battles of Cambrai and many other important engagements in various sectors and served also through the Retreat and Advance of 1918. He returned home for demobilisation in October 1919, and holds the General Service and Victory Medals.
10, Helsby Street, Ardwick, Manchester.　　Z6560

HEYWORTH, A. G., Gunner, R.F.A.

Joining in April 1916, he was trained at Colchester and Aldershot, and eight months later proceeded overseas. On the Western Front he took part in severe fighting on the Ancre and at Arras, Nieuport and Ypres, but was unfortunately killed at Dunkerque during a raid on August 17th, 1917. He was entitled to the General Service and Victory Medals.
" Whilst we remember, the sacrifice is not in vain."
6, Middle Wood Street, Harpurhey, Manchester.　　Z11512A

HIBBERT, A., Private, 1st Manchester Regiment.

Mobilised in August 1914, he was shortly afterwards drafted to the Western Front, where he took part in the Battle of Loos and in engagements at Nieuport and many other places. He died gloriously on the Field of Battle on January 1st, 1917. He was entitled to the 1914 Star, and the General Service and Victory Medals.
" Great deeds cannot die :
They, with the sun and moon renew their light for ever."
24, Lawrence Street, West Gorton, Manchester.　　Z6562

HIBBERT, C. A., Private, Cheshire Regiment.

He volunteered in December 1915, and in May of the following year was drafted to France, where he was in action on the Somme, at Albert, Arras, Ypres and Cambrai. He was also engaged in heavy fighting during the Retreat and Advance of 1918, and after the Armistice proceeded with the Army of Occupation into Germany. He was demobilised in September 1919, and holds the General Service and Victory Medals.
8, Francisco Street, Collyhurst, Manchester.　　Z10394

HIBBERT, H., L/Corporal, King's (Liverpool Regt.).

After volunteering in February 1915, he underwent a period of training prior to being drafted to the Western Front in January 1918. There he took part in many important engagements, including the Battles of the Somme, the Aisne, the Marne, Bapaume, Havrincourt, Ypres and Le Cateau, and in further fighting during the Retreat and Advance of 1918. Demobilised in March 1919, he holds the General Service and Victory Medals.
100, Bold Street, Moss Side, Manchester.　　Z6563

HIBBERT, J., Private, King's (Liverpool Regiment) and Royal Welch Fusiliers.

He volunteered in April 1915, and after a period of service at Pembroke Dock was transferred to the Royal Welch Fusiliers proceeding with his new unit to Mesopotamia. There he took part in severe fighting near Kut and on the Tigris and also participated in the capture of Baghdad. Whilst overseas he did excellent work and was demobilised on his return home in February 1919, holding the General Service and Victory Medals.　20, Werneth St., Harpurhey, Manchester.　　Z11513

HIBBERT, J.T.,Rfllmn.,Cameronians (ScottishRifles).

Two months after joining in June 1917, he proceeded to the Western Front, where he saw fighting at Arras and in various other sectors. He was afterwards engaged on important duties with a Labour Company and did much useful work until invalided to hospital at Bristol. He was finally discharged as medically unfit for further service in October 1918, and holds the General Service and Victory Medals.
95, Thomas Street, West Gorton, Manchester.　　Z6564

HIBBERT, J. W., Private, 1st Manchester Regt.

He volunteered in January 1915, and in February of the following year was drafted to Mesopotamia, where he saw severe fighting on the Tigris and took part in the Relief of Kut and the capture of Baghdad. In June 1918 he was transferred to Palestine, and there took part in the Offensive under General Allenby, finally returning home for demobilisation in May 1919. He holds the General Service and Victory Medals.　110, Cross Street, Bradford, Manchester.　　Z6561

HIBBITTS, H., C.Q.M.S., 8th Manchester Regt.

Mobilised in August 1914, he was drafted to Egypt in the following month, and was thence sent to Gallipoli in August 1915. There, after taking part in the Landing at Suvla Bay, he saw much severe fighting until the Evacuation of the Peninsula, when he returned to Egypt in time to serve through the engagement at Katia in April 1916. In February 1917 he was transferred to the Western Front, where he fought in the Battles of Arras and Bullecourt and in the Retreat and Advance of 1918. He was mentioned in Despatches for distinguished service, and holding the 1914–15 Star, and the General Service and Victory Medals, was discharged in March 1919.　20, Grafton St., Ardwick, Manchester.　　Z6565

HICK, J., Guardsman, Coldstream Guards.

Volunteering in January 1915, he was drafted to France in March of the same year and fought in the Battles of Neuve Chapelle, Hill 60, Loos, St. Eloi, Festubert, Vimy Ridge and the Somme. He was wounded at Ypres in 1916, and, invalided home, received hospital treatment. On his recovery he returned to France in 1917, but owing to ill-health was returned to England in the following year. He was demobilised in February 1919, and holds the 1914–15 Star, and the General Service and Victory Medals.
13, Almond Street, Gorton, Manchester.　　Z10395

HICKLIN, J., Drummer, 12th King's(Liverpool Regt.)

He volunteered in November 1914, and in the following year was drafted to the Western Front, where he took part in numerous engagements, including those at Ypres and on the Somme. He also served in the Retreat and Advance of 1918. He was demobilised in January 1919, and holds the 1914–15 Star, and the General Service and Victory Medals.
84, Gibbon Street, Bradford, Manchester.　　Z9190

HICKS, H., Private, 18th Manchester Regiment.

Volunteering in September 1914, he was drafted to the Western Front on completing four months' training, and there saw much severe fighting. He served through the Battles of Neuve Chapelle, St. Eloi, Hill 60, Ypres, Festubert and Albert and many other important engagements in various sectors, and also took part in the Retreat and Advance of 1918. He was demobilised in February 1919, and holds the 1914–15 Star, and the General Service and Victory Medals.
3, Park Place, Hulme, Manchester.　　Z6566

HIGGINBOTTOM, W., Driver, R.A.S.C.

He joined in August 1916, having previously served at Messrs. Hardman and Holding's Chemical Explosives Factory at Manchester. After his training he was engaged on important transport duties at numerous stations and rendered valuable services. He was not successful in obtaining a transfer abroad to a fighting unit, and was demobilised in March 1919.
73, Taylor Street, Bradford, Manchester.　　Z9570

HIGGINS, A., Private, R.A.V.C.

He joined in 1917, and in the same year was drafted to Salonika, where he was engaged in various sectors attending to the sick and wounded horses. He rendered very good services whilst in this theatre of war, and was transferred to the Army Reserve in 1919. He holds the General Service and Victory Medals.　22, Radium Street, Manchester.　　Z11902

HIGGINS, E., Driver, R.A.S.C.

He joined in August 1916, and later in the same year was sent to France, where he was engaged on important transport duties at Ypres and Cambrai. He was afterwards transferred to Egypt and thence to Palestine and took part in the Advance on Jerusalem. He was demobilised in January 1919, and holds the General Service and Victory Medals.
155, Montague Street, Collyhurst, Manchester.　　Z9191

HIGGINS, H., Private, Durham Light Infantry.

Having joined in July 1916, he was drafted to Salonika later in the same year and took part in the severe fighting at Monastir and on the Doiran and Vardar fronts. He returned home, and was demobilised in June 1919, holding the General Service and Victory Medals.
2, Chapel Street, Ancoats, Manchester.　　Z9192

HIGGINS, J., Private, 20th Lancashire Fusiliers.

He volunteered in May 1915, and in the following year proceeded to the Western Front. Whilst overseas he fought in numerous engagements, including those at Albert, Armentières, and Méricourt. He gave his life for the freedom of England on the Somme on October 22nd, 1916, and was entitled to the General Service and Victory Medals.
" He passed out of the sight of men by the path of duty and self-sacrifice."
51, Elizabeth Street, Ancoats, Manchester.　　TZ9571

HIGGINS, T., Private, 3rd Manchester Regt., and Highland Light Infantry.

He volunteered in September 1915, and after undergoing a period of training served at various stations, where he was engaged on duties of great importance. He was not successful in his efforts to obtain his transfer to a theatre of war, but, nevertheless, rendered very valuable services with his unit. He served also with the Black Watch, before being invalided from the Army in July 1918.
23, Allen Street, Hulme, Manchester.　　Z6567

HIGGINSON, H. T., Pte., 3rd Royal Welch Fusiliers.

He joined in October 1916, and in the following March was drafted to France. He was engaged on important duties at Rouen and Le Havre, and was also employed in escorting German prisoners to England. He was demobilised in March 1919, and holds the General Service and Victory Medals.
16, Nancy Street, Chester Road, Hulme, Manchester.　　Z10397

HIGGINSON, J., Corporal, 4th Lancashire Fusiliers.
Volunteering at the outbreak of war in August 1914, he was later drafted to the Western Front, where he took part in many important engagements, including the Battles of the Marne (I), Ypres, Loos and the Somme, and also in strenuous fighting at Vermelles and Passchendaele. He was severely wounded on the Somme in July 1916, and invalided home, spent some time in hospital at Halifax, being eventually demobilised in February 1919. He holds the 1914 Star, and the General Service and Victory Medals.
2, Crawshaw Street, Chorlton on-Medlock, Manchester. Z6569

HIGGINSON, W. H., Rifleman, 2nd Rifle Brigade and Private, 5th (Royal Irish) Lancers.
Volunteering in September 1914, he was drafted to the Western Front in the following year, and was there wounded in action at the Battle of Neuve Chapelle and invalided home in March 1915. He returned to France, however, on his recovery in October of that year, and was again wounded at Loos and sent home. Discharged as medically unfit for further service in December 1916, he re-enlisted in June 1918 and served with the 5th (Royal Irish) Lancers, and also for a short period with the Tank Corps, in Ireland before being finally invalided from the Army in March 1919. He holds the 1914 Star, and the General Service and Victory Medals.
59, Stott Street, Hulme, Manchester. Z6568

HIGGS, M., Private, South Lancashire Regiment.
He volunteered in March 1915, and in September of the same year was sent to France, where he took part in the fighting at Loos, St. Eloi, and Vimy Ridge. He was killed in action in the Battle of the Somme in August 1916, and was buried in a British cemetery. He was entitled to the 1914-15 Star, and the General Service and Victory Medals.
"His life for his Country."
5, Edith Street, West Gorton, Manchester. Z10396

HIGH, A., Private, 2nd South Lancashire Regiment.
He volunteered in August 1914, and in April of the following year was drafted to Gallipoli, where, after taking part in the Landing at Cape Helles, he was wounded in action at Suvla Bay. Invalided to hospital in Egypt, he proceeded, on his recovery in May 1916, to the Western Front, and there served through the Somme Offensive until sent home suffering from dysentery in November of that year. He was finally discharged as medically unfit for further service in January 1918, and holds the 1914-15 Star, and the General Service and Victory Medals.
11, Albert Street, Rusholme, Manchester. TZ6570

HILL, A., Private, 10th East Lancashire Regiment.
He volunteered in August 1914, and in May of the following year was sent to Gallipoli, where he was in action in the Landing at Suvla Bay and was wounded. He was invalided to Malta and later returned home. After a period in hospital, he was discharged as unfit for further service in April 1916, holding the 1914-15 Star, and the General Service and Victory Medals. 11, Broughton St., Ancoats, Manchester. Z10399

HILL, F., Guardsman, Welch Guards.
He volunteered in November 1914, and after his training was engaged at various stations on important duties with his unit. He rendered valuable services, but was discharged in September 1917, owing to being under age.
6, Osborn Street, Oldham Road, Manchester. Z10401

HILL, G. W., Private, R.A.M.C.
Joining in June 1918, he was drafted to the Western Front on completing his training in the following September, and there served in various sectors. He took an active part in the Battles of Havrincourt, Ypres and Cambrai and many other important engagements until the cessation of hostilities, and was then sent with the Army of Occupation into Germany. He was demobilised on his return home in July 1919, and holds the General Service and Victory Medals.
56, Hewitt Street, Openshaw, Manchester. TZ6574

HILL, H., Saddler, R.A.S.C.
He was mobilised at the outbreak of hostilities, and was almost immediately drafted to France, where he served in the Retreat from Mons. He was also present at the Battles of the Marne, the Aisne, Ypres, St. Eloi, Hill 69, Loos, the Somme, Arras, Ypres and Cambrai. After his return home he was discharged in March 1919, and holds the Mons Star, and the General Service and Victory Medals.
25, Mawson Street, Chorlton-on-Medlock, Manchester. Z9573

HILL, J., Private, 8th Manchester Regiment.
He volunteered in November 1915, and six months later was sent to France. In this theatre of war he played a prominent part with his unit in heavy fighting at Ypres, Albert, Loos, Givenchy, Festubert, and Arras, and rendered excellent service until he was unfortunately killed in action at Ypres on October 4th, 1917. He was entitled to the General Service and Victory Medals.
"Whilst we remember, the sacrifice is not in vain."
19, Martha Street, Bradford, Manchester. Z11610A

HILL, J., Pte., Manchester Regt. and Dr., R.A.S.C.
He volunteered in January 1915, and four months later embarked for France. During his service on the Western Front he was present at many important engagements, including

those at Ypres, Festubert and the Somme and in various operations during the Retreat and Advance of 1918. He holds the 1914-15 Star, and the General Service and Victory Medals, and was demobilised in November 1919.
7, Belgrave Street, Newton Heath, Manchester. Z9574

HILL, J. F., Private, 1/6th Manchester Regiment.
Volunteering in June 1915, he was drafted to Egypt shortly afterwards and was engaged on important garrison duties at Cairo. In 1916, however, he proceeded to France and took part in the Battles of the Somme, Arras, Bullecourt, Cambrai Bapaume, Havrincourt and the Sambre. He was present at the entry into Mons on Armistice Day and later was demobilised in January 1919. He holds the 1914-15 Star, and the General Service and Victory Medals.
3, Hurlbutt Street, Hulme, Manchester. Z11726

HILL, J. T., Private, Royal Defence Corps.
He joined in August 1916, and after undergoing a period of training, served at various stations, where he was engaged in guarding prisoners of war and on other important duties. He rendered very valuable services with his Company until May 1917, when he was invalided from the Army. He unfortunately died on August 29th, 1920.
"His memory is cherished with pride."
61, Meadow Street, Ardwick, Manchester. Z6572

HILL, R., Private, 19th Manchester Regiment.
He volunteered in September 1914, and was engaged on important duties with his unit till March 1916, when he was sent to France. He was in action in the Battles of Vimy Ridge, the Somme, Arras, Ypres, Passchendaele, and Cambrai, and was wounded. He also served in the Retreat and Advance of 1918, and returning home after the Armistice was demobilised in January 1919. He holds the General Service and Victory Medals.
16, Lancashire Street, Newton Heath, Manchester. Z10402

HILL, W., Private, Lancashire Fusiliers.
He volunteered in May 1915, and was sent to France in July of the same year. He fought at Loos, St. Eloi, Albert, Vimy Ridge, Arras, Bullecourt, Messines, Ypres, and was wounded. He returned home, and after receiving hospital treatment, was invalided out of the Service in September 1917. He holds the 1914-15 Star, and the General Service and Victory Medals.
6, Osborne Street, Oldham Road, Manchester. Z10400

HILL, W., Private, 7th Manchester Regiment.
After volunteering in August 1914, he underwent a period of training prior to being drafted to the Western Front in September 1916. There he took part in many important engagements, including the Battles of Arras, Vimy Ridge, and Messines, and was gassed at Ypres in August 1917, and sent to hospital at Rouen. He rejoined his unit, however, on his recovery, and was again in action at Cambrai, the Somme, the Marne, Bapaume, and Le Cateau.
5, Auburn Place, Moor St., Rusholme, Manchester. Z6575

HILL, W. G., Driver, R.A.S.C. (M.T.)
Shortly after volunteering in January 1915, he proceeded to the Western Front, where he was engaged chiefly in conveying food and ammunition to the forward areas. He was present at the Battles of Ypres, Loos, the Somme, Passchendaele, and the Marne, and many other important engagements, and served also through the Retreat and Advance of 1918. Demobilised in February 1919, he holds the 1914-15 Star, and the General Service and Victory Medals.
35, Ryder Street, Bradford, Manchester. Z6573

HILL, W. Private, 20th Manchester Regiment.
He volunteered in August 1914, and shortly afterwards was sent to the Western Front, where he saw heavy fighting in various sectors. After taking part in the Battles of the Ancre, Arras, Vimy Ridge, Ypres, Cambrai, and the Somme, and many minor engagements, he was severely wounded in action on the Marne in July 1918, and invalided home. He was finally demobilised in March 1919, and holds the 1914 Star, and the General Service and Victory Medals.
25, Mawson Street, Chorlton-on-Medlock, Manchester. Z6571

HILLARY, J., Private, 6th West Riding Regiment.
He volunteered in October 1914, and later in the same year was sent to France, where he was engaged in heavy fighting at Hill 60, and in other engagements of note. He was wounded and gassed on December 19th, 1915, and admitted into hospital died of his injuries the following day. He was entitled to the 1914-15 Star, and the General Service and Victory Medals.
"A valiant Soldier, with undaunted heart he breasted life's last hill."
5, Teer Street, Ancoats, Manchester. Z10403

HILLIER, H., Pte. (Signr.), 17th Lancashire Fusiliers.
He volunteered in April 1915, and in January of the following year, was drafted to the Western Front. Whilst in this theatre of war he fought in many important engagements, including the Battles of St. Eloi, the Somme, Arras, Ypres, Passchendaele, and Cambrai, and was wounded in action at Ypres in September 1918, and invalided home. On his recovery, however, he returned to France, and was again wounded in October of the same year. He was finally demobilised in February 1919, and holds the General Service and Victory Medals.
10, Royle Street, Chorlton-on-Medlock, Manchester. TX6577

HILLS, W., Private, 13th King's (Liverpool Regt.)
He volunteered in September 1914, and after a period of training was drafted to the Western Front. In this theatre of war he took part in many important engagements including the German attack on Loos, St. Eloi, and Albert, and the Battle of Vimy Ridge, the Somme, and Beaumont-Hamel. He died gloriously on the Field at the Battle of Ypres on July 14th, 1917, and was entitled to the 1914-15 Star, and the General Service and Victory Medals.
"His life for his Country, his soul to God."
7, Birch Street, Hulme, Manchester.   Z6576

HILTON, G., Private, K.O. (Royal Lancaster Regt.)
Volunteering in December 1914, he was drafted to France in the following year, and after taking part in the Battles of St. Eloi and Ypres, was wounded in action at Loos in September 1915. He underwent treatment at the 23rd General Hospital, but on his recovery rejoined his unit, and fought at the Battles of Vermelles, the Somme, Vimy Ridge, and Lens. He was demobilised in February 1919, and holds the 1914-15 Star, and the General Service and Victory Medals.
1, Tempest Street, Ardwick, Manchester.   Z6580

HILTON, G., Private, 13th Manchester Regiment.
Volunteering in January 1915, he was sent to Salonika in the following September, and saw much heavy fighting until November 1916. He was then invalided home with dysentery, but on his recovery, was drafted to France, where he took part in many important engagements, and was badly wounded in action at the fourth Battle of Ypres in September 1918. Again invalided home, he underwent hospital treatment in Manchester, and was eventually discharged as medically unfit for further service in February 1919, holding the 1914-15 Star, and the General Service and Victory Medals.
5, Mulberry Street, Hulme, Manchester.   Z6579

HILTON, J., Sergt., Duke of Lancaster's Own Hussars.
He volunteered in September 1914, and was quickly drafted to Egypt, where he served with distinction in engagements at Mersa-Matruh, and Romani. Later he proceeded to Palestine and whilst with General Allenby's Forces, took part in the three Battles of Gaza, and the capture of Jerusalem, Jaffa, and Tripoli. He was demobilised in March 1919, and holds the 1914-15 Star, and the General Service and Victory Medals.
26, Chatsworth Street, Hulme, Manchester.   Z6581

HILTON, W., Private, Queen's Own (Royal West Kent Regiment).
He volunteered in October 1914, but was retained on important home duties until January 1917, when he was drafted to the Western Front, and took part in much severe fighting before being badly gassed in action at Bullecourt. After six months' treatment at the 24th General Hospital, he rejoined his unit, but later, was again in hospital for four months suffering from dysentery and a weak heart. He was eventually demobilised in February 1919, and holds the General Service and Victory Medals.
4, Westmoreland Street, Longsight, Manchester.   Z6578

HINDLEY, E., Private, 8th Manchester Regiment.
He volunteered in September 1914, and in February of the following year was sent to Gallipoli, where he took part in the Landing at Suvla Bay, and much fighting until the Evacuation. In January 1916, he was transferred to France, and was in action on the Somme, and at Ypres, and Cambrai, and was wounded. He also served in the Retreat and Advance of 1918. He was demobilised in February 1919, and holds the 1914-15 Star, and the General Service and Victory Medals.
1, Back William Street, Ancoats, Manchester.   Z9193

HINDLEY, E., Private, King's (Liverpool Regt.)
Volunteering in September 1914, he was drafted to Egypt later in the same year. He took part in repelling the Turkish attack on the Suez Canal, and in the fighting at Mersa Matruh, Sollum, and El Fasher. He returned home, and was demobilised in February 1919, holding the 1914-15 Star, and the General Service and Victory Medals.
1, Catherine Street, Manchester.   Z11423

HINDLEY, J., Private, Lancashire Fusiliers.
Volunteering in September 1914, he was sent in the following year to France, and thence to Salonika, where he took part in the fighting on the Doiran front. In 1918 he returned to France, but though wounded at Mount Kemmel, served in the Retreat and Advance of 1918. He was demobilised in 1919, and holds the 1914-15 Star, and the General Service and Victory Medals. 6, Catherine St., Manchester.   TZ9194

HINDLEY, J., Private, 2nd Lancashire Fusiliers.
He volunteered in August 1914, and in November of the same year was sent to France. In this theatre of war he was in action at Neuve Chapelle, and was wounded at Armentières. He was invalided home and after a period in hospital was discharged in consequence of his injuries. He holds the 1914-15 Star, and the General Service and Victory Medals.
7, Beattie Street, Oldham Road, Manchester.   Z9195

HINDLEY, L., Private, Lancashire Fusiliers.
Volunteering in August 1914, he proceeded to France in the following year, and was in action on the Somme, and at Ypres. He was later invalided home with shell-shock, and received medical treatment. On his recovery he returned to France, and was engaged in heavy fighting during the Retreat and Advance of 1918. He was demobilised in February 1919, and holds the 1914-15 Star, and the General Service and Victory Medals. 13, Matilda St., Ancoats, Manchester.   Z10407

HINDS, J., Private, 11th Royal Fusiliers.
He volunteered in April 1915, and was sent to France in the following month. He took part in the Battles of Loos, St. Eloi, Albert, the Somme, Arras, Messines, Ypres, and Cambrai. He was unfortunately killed in action on the Cambrai front on April 20th, 1918, during the German Offensive. He was entitled to the 1914-15 Star, and the General Service and Victory Medals.
"Whilst we remember, the sacrifice is not in vain."
15, Moody Street, Bradford, Manchester.   Z10405A

HINDS, J., Private, 3rd Lancashire Fusiliers.
He volunteered in August 1914, and was engaged on important duties with his unit at various stations on the East Coast. He rendered valuable services, but was not successful in obtaining his transfer overseas before the cessation of hostilities. He was demobilised in December 1918.
15, Moody Street, Bradford, Manchester.   Z10404A

HINDS, T., Drummer, 1st Lancashire Fusiliers.
He joined in November 1917, and after completing his training was stationed at Aldershot and Dublin with his unit on guard and other duties. He was unsuccessful in obtaining his transfer to a theatre of war before hostilities ceased, but rendered excellent services throughout. He was still serving in 1920.
15, Wood Street, Bradford, Manchester.   Z10404B

HINDS, W., Private, 4th Manchester Regiment.
He volunteered at the commencement of hostilities, and served at various camps on important duties with his unit. He contracted an illness, in consequence of which he was discharged in May 1915 as medically unfit for further service, and has since died.
"His memory is cherished with pride."
25, Long Street, Ancoats, Manchester.   Z10406

HINDS, W. H., Private, 11th Royal Fusiliers.
Joining in January 1917, he went through a course of training and was afterwards engaged at various stations on important duties. He rendered valuable services, but was not successful in obtaining his transfer to a theatre of war before the cessation of hostilities owing to being under-age. He was demobilised in January 1919. He afterwards re-elisted, and was still serving in 1920.
15, Moody Street, Bradford, Manchester.   Z10405B

HINDSON, T., Private, 3rd Manchester Regiment.
Volunteering in February 1915, he was quickly drafted to the Western Front, and played an important part in the Battles of Hill 60, Ypres (II), Loos, Albert, and Vimy Ridge before being taken prisoner during the Somme Offensive in July 1916. Whilst in captivity he suffered many hardships and was ill with dysentery for some time. He was demobilised on his repatriation in December 1918, and holds the 1914-15 Star, and the General Service and Victory Medals.
8, Marsland Street, Chorlton-on-Medlock, Manchester. Z6582

HINDSON, W., Private, 5th Manchester Regiment.
He joined in September 1916, and was retained on important duties at home until November of the following year. Proceeding to France in that month, he rendered valuable services as a clerk in the orderly room at Cambrai and Etaples. Owing to physical unfitness, he did not participate in any fighting, and was demobilised in March 1919, holding the General Service and Victory Medals.
63, Parkfield Avenue, Rusholme, Manchester.   Z6583

HINES, P., Sergt., Loyal North Lancashire Regt.
He volunteered in August 1914, and was quickly drafted to the Western Front. He took part in several important engagements, including the Retreat from Mons, and the Battles of the Marne, and Ypres I, and was taken prisoner. Whilst held in captivity until December 1919, he was working at Wittenberg Camp as a printer, and after his release was stationed at Tidworth, where he was still serving in 1920. He holds the 1914 Star, and the General Service and Victory Medals.
11, Herbert Street, Ardwick, Manchester.   Z6585

HINES, W., Private, K.O. (Royal Lancaster Regt.)
He volunteered in September 1914, and after a brief period of training, was drafted to the Western Front, where he took part in the Battles of Hill 60, Loos, Vermelles, the Somme, and Vimy Ridge, and in heavy fighting at La Bassée. Badly wounded in action at Lens in August 1917, he was invalided to hospital in Birmingham, and was eventually discharged as medically unfit for further service in July 1918. He holds the 1914-15 Star, and the General Service and Victory Medals.
8, Solent Street, Ardwick, Manchester.   Z6584

HINETT, T., Private, Somerset Light Infantry.

He joined in April 1917, and later in the same year proceeded to France. There he took part in many engagements, including the Battles of Passchendaele, Cambrai, the Marne (II), Havrincourt, and Ypres (IV), where he was badly wounded. As a result he was invalided home and unfortunately lost two toes by amputation. He was discharged in January 1919, and holds the General Service and Victory Medals.
6, School Street, Bradford, Manchester. Z11727

HINSON, C. R., L/Corporal, Lancashire Fusiliers.

He joined in June 1916, and after a period of training served at various home stations on guard and other duties with his unit. He was unsuccessful in obtaining his transfer to a theatre of war, but rendered valuable services until his demobilisation in March 1919.
59, Oliver Street, Openshaw, Manchester. Z6586

HIRST, J., Private, 13th Hussars.

Joining in August 1916, he was drafted to France in September of the following year. He was in action in the Battle of Ypres, and was wounded. On recovery, rejoining his unit, he was engaged in heavy fighting in various sectors, and was wounded and taken prisoner at Mount Kemmel in April 1918. He was held in captivity until the close of hostilities, and then was repatriated. He was demobilised in October 1919, and holds the General Service and Victory Medals.
18, Lime Street, Miles Platting, Manchester. Z10408

HIRST, J., Private, R.A.S.C. (M.T.)

He joined in March 1917, and in the following year was drafted to France, where he was engaged on important transport duties with the ammunition column on the Armentières, Passchendaele and Somme fronts. He was not demobilised until March 1920, and holds the General Service and Victory Medals.
4, Dora Street, Rochdale Road, Manchester. Z9196

HIRST, N., Sapper, R.E.

He joined in August 1917, and after a period of training was retained on important home duties with his unit. He was not successful in obtaining a transfer overseas, but rendered very valuable services until discharged in September 1918 as medically unfit for further duty.
188, Thomas Street, West Gorton, Manchester. TZ6588

HIRST, T., Private, 6th Royal Scots.

He volunteered in December 1914, and twelve months later was drafted to Egypt, where he was in action at Mersa-Matruh, Agagia, and Sollum. In March 1916 he was transferred to the Western Front, and took part in the Battles of Vermelles and the Somme, and in the heavy fighting at St. Eloi. He was invalided home suffering from valvular disease of the heart, and was discharged in October 1916 as medically unfit for further service, holding the 1914-15 Star, and the General Service and Victory Medals.
184, Thomas Street, West Gorton, Manchester. TZ6587

HITCHEN, C., Private, 2nd Border Regiment.

Volunteering at the outbreak of hostilities in August 1914, he was in the following year drafted to the Western Front. Whilst in this theatre of war he took part in the heavy fighting in various sectors, and was later transferred to the Dardanelles, where he was in action at the Battles of Krithia, and the Landing at Suvla Bay, and was wounded in October 1915. On his recovery he again went to France and served in engagements on the Somme, and at Nieuport and St. Quentin, where he was taken prisoner. Held in captivity until February 1919, he was then sent to Ireland, and served until December 1920, when he was invalided out of the Service. He holds the 1914-15 Star, and the General Service and Victory Medals.
23, Pilling Street, Newton Heath, Manchester. Z9575

HITCHEN, J. W., Pte., King's Shropshire Light Infty.

He joined in April 1917, and in the following March was drafted to France. Whilst overseas he took part in much of the heavy fighting in the second Battle of the Somme, at Amiens, Bapaume, and Havrincourt, but was subsequently taken ill and invalided home in September 1918. He was discharged later in the same month, and holds the General Service and Victory Medals.
8, Ardsley Street, Oldham Road, Manchester. TZ9576

HOBDAY, F., Gunner. R.G.A.

He joined in April 1917, and in September of the same year embarked for France. There he served with the 228th Siege Battery in many battles, including those on the Somme, and at Cambrai. He was unfortunately killed in action during an enemy bombardment at Péronne in January 1918. He was entitled to the General Service and Victory Medals.
" Whilst we remember the sacrifice is not in vain."
12, Needwood Street, Collyhurst, Manchester. Z1045B

HOBDAY, F. (Jun.), Private, West Yorkshire Regt.

Joining in November 1917, he was drafted to the Western Front in May of the following year. He took part in the fighting at Cambrai, and in the Retreat and Advance of 1918, being present at the final entry into Mons at dawn on November 11th. After the Armistice he was engaged on clerical duties at the Base until demobilised in November 1919. He holds the General Service and Victory Medals.
12, Needwood Street, Collyhurst, Manchester. Z10454A

HOBEN, J., Pte., 1st K.O. (Royal Lancaster Regt.)

Mobilised on the declaration of war, he proceeded with his Regiment to France, and fought in the Retreat from Mons, the Battles of the Marne, and the Aisne. He was also in action at Ypres, and Festubert, but in May 1915 was sent to Egypt, where he was engaged on garrison duties at Cairo, and other stations. He was invalided home through ill-health in June 1918, and in February of the following year was discharged as medically unfit. He holds the Mons Star, and the General Service and Victory Medals.
24, Limer Street, Rochdale Road, Manchester. Z10455

HOBIN, F., Pte., 12th and 19th Manchester Regt.

Volunteering in October 1915, he embarked for France in the following July, and saw much heavy fighting. He took part in many battles, including those on the Somme, and was wounded. On recovery he returned to the front, and was in action at Delville Wood, Ypres, Cambrai, Amiens, and in the Retreat and subsequent Allied Advance of 1918. Demobilised in February 1919, he holds the General Service and Victory Medals. 64, Branson St., Ancoats, Manchester. Z10409

HOBSON, A., Private, Royal Marine Labour Corps.

He joined in August 1918, and in the following month was drafted to France, where he was stationed at Dunkirk, and rendered valuable services in connection with the loading and unloading of supplies on merchant vessels. He was demobilised in May 1919, and holds the General Service and Victory Medals.
3, Clifford Street, Lower Openshaw, Manchester. Z6589

HOBSON, J., Pte., King's Shropshire Light Infantry.

He joined in March 1916, and six months later proceeded to the Western Front, where he took part in the Battles of Beaumont-Hamel, Arras, Vimy Ridge, Ypres, Passchendaele, and Cambrai, and in the Retreat of 1918. During the subsequent Advance he was gassed in action and admitted to hospital at the Base. On his recovery, he returned to England for demobilisation in January 1919, and holds the General Service and Victory Medals.
232, Greame Street, Moss Side, Manchester. Z6590A

HOBSON, L., Private, 7th Manchester Regiment.

He volunteered in October 1914, and after a period of training was drafted to Gallipoli, where he took part in many important engagements until the Evacuation of the Peninsula. He then proceeded to Egypt, and saw much fighting, including that at the Battles of Katia until 1917, when he was transferred to the Western Front. Whilst in this theatre of war, he served in various sectors until the cessation of hostilities. He was demobilised in February 1919, and holds the 1914-15 Star, and the General Service and Victory Medals.
232, Greame Street, Moss Side, Manchester. Z6590B

HOCKENHULL, G. T., L/Cpl., 17th Manchester Regt.

He joined in August 1916, and in the same year was drafted to the Western Front. He took part in much heavy fighting, including the Battles of the Somme I, Vimy Ridge, Bullecourt, and Messines Ridge, and was wounded. On his recovery, he re-joined his unit, and was in action at Passchendaele, where he was again wounded and sent to England, being discharged as medically unfit in April 1918. He holds the General Service and Victory Medals.
6, Allen Street, Hulme, Manchester. TZ6591

HOCKENHULL, T., Private, 8th Manchester Regt.

He volunteered in November 1914, and in March of the following year was sent to China, and stationed at Singapore. He was engaged on garrison and other important duties, and remained at this station till February 1920, when he returned home, and was demobilised. He holds the 1914-15 Star, and the General Service and Victory Medals.
13, Whatmough Street, Manchester. Z9577B

HODGKINSON, A., Private, Royal Scots.

He volunteered in August 1914, and in September of the following year was drafted to Egypt. He was engaged on various duties at Alexandria, Cairo, and on the Suez Canal defences. Later he proceeded to France, and was in action on the Somme, at Arras, Ypres, Cambrai, and was wounded and taken prisoner in the Retreat of 1918, being held in captivity until after the Armistice. Repatriated, he was demobilised in December 1918, and holds the 1914-15 Star, and the General Service and Victory Medals.
2, Crook Street, Miles Platting, Manchester. Z10456A

HODGKINSON, J., Boy 1st Class, R.N.

He volunteered in March 1915, and during the war was on duty in H.M.S. " Powerful " and " Hampshire " in the North Sea. He took part in the Battle of Jutland, but unhappily lost his life when the " Hampshire " was sunk off the Orkneys on June 5th, 1916. He was entitled to the 1914-15 Star, and the General Service and Victory Medals.
" Thinking that remembrance, though unspoken, may reach him where he sleeps."
2, Crook Street, Miles Platting, Manchester. Z10456B

HODGKINSON, T., Private, Labour Corps and King's (Liverpool Regiment).

He joined in March 1917, and was immediately sent to France, where he was engaged on very important duties with his unit at Etaples, Bapaume, and Havrincourt. He rendered valuable services until invalided home suffering from sciatica, and was subsequently discharged as unfit for further service in April 1918. He holds the General Service and Victory Medals.
7, Guy Street, Ardwick, Manchester.   Z6592

HODGSON, E. J., Private (Signaller), M.G.C.

He volunteered in December 1915, and after a period of training was drafted to Mesopotamia in the following July. Whilst in this theatre of war he saw much fighting, and was present at the capture of Baghdad, and at Amara, and various other important engagements until the cessation of hostilities. Returning home for demobilisation in April 1919, he holds the General Service and Victory Medals.
4, Hancock Street, Rusholme, Manchester.   Z6596A

HODGSON, F. C., Private, K.O. (R. Liverpool Regt.)

He volunteered in 1915, and after a period of training was drafted to Egypt, where he took part in many important engagements. Later he proceeded to India, but unfortunately contracted fever and died on August 25th, 1916. He had been awarded a Serbian decoration for conspicuous bravery, and was entitled to the General Service and Victory Medals.
"Sadly missed by his sorrowing wife and children."
9, Thomas Street, Chorlton-on-Medlock, Manchester. TX6594

HODGSON, S., Private, R.A.V.C.

He joined in July 1916, and on completion of a brief period of training, was drafted to France in the following October, but after only a few weeks service in the Somme sector, was badly wounded in November. He was invalided home and lingered in hospital until November 7th, 1917, when he unhappily died from his wounds. He was entitled to the General Service and Victory Medals.
"He joined the great white company of valiant souls."
34, Marsland Street, Chorlton-on-Medlock, Manchester. Z6595

HODKINSON, A., Sapper, R.E.

He volunteered in January 1915, and was retained on home duties until December 1916, when he proceeded to the Western Front. Whilst in this seat of war he was engaged on very important duties with his unit in the Ypres and Cambrai sectors. He rendered excellent services until he returned to England for demobilisation in March 1919, and holds the General Service and Victory Medals.
145, Heald Grove, Rusholme, Manchester.   Z6597

HODKINSON, E., Private, M.G.C.

Joining in May 1918, he was sent to Ireland on completion of his training, and remained there until after the cessation of hostilities. He was demobilised in March 1919, but later re-enlisted for a period of two years, and after five months valuable services in Russia, was sent to Mesopotamia, where he was still stationed in 1920.
26, Marple Street, Ardwick, Manchester.   Z6593

HODSON, A., Corporal, King's (Liverpool Regt.)

He joined in February 1916, and in the following August proceeded to France. There he fought in many engagements, and was in action on the Somme, at Arras, and Ypres, where he was wounded in July 1917. On recovery he was put on light duties in England until demobilised in August 1919, holding the General Service and Victory Medals.
2, Class Street, Beswick, Manchester.   TZ9197

HOLBROOK, J. (D.C.M.) Sgt., 1/7th Manchester Regt.

He volunteered in September 1914, and being drafted in the same month to Egypt took part in the operations on the Suez Canal. In April 1915 he proceeded to Gallipoli, and served throughout that campaign, afterwards being sent to France. There he fought with distinction in many battles, including those of Vimy Ridge, the Somme, Arras, Messines, and Cambrai, and in the Retreat and Allied Advance of 1918. He was awarded the Distinguished Conduct Medal for conspicuous bravery in bringing in wounded under heavy fire, and in addition holds the 1914–15 Star, and the General Service and Victory Medals. In April 1919 he was demobilised.
4, Stanley Street, Hulme, Manchester.   Z9198

HOLBROOK, J. J., Sergt., R.A.M.C.

He was mobilised in August 1914, and shortly afterwards was sent to France. He served at the Battles of Mons, the Marne, the Aisne, Neuve Chapelle, the Somme, Arras, and Cambrai, and remained in this theatre of war until January 1919, when he returned home, and was discharged. He holds the Mons Star, and the General Service and Victory Medals.
29, Clay Street, Newton Heath, Manchester.   Z9578

HOLCROFT, F., Sergt., 7th Manchester Regiment.

Mobilised with the Territorials in August 1914, he was quickly drafted to Egypt, and served with distinction in the Soudan until the opening of the Gallipoli Campaign. He then played

a prominent part in the Landing at Cape Helles, and in the three Battles of Krithia before being unhappily killed in action at Achi-Baba on June 4th, 1915. He was entitled to the 1914–15 Star, and the General Service and Victory Medals.
"Nobly striving,
He nobly fell that we might live."
30, Berwick Street, Chorlton-on-Medlock, Manchester. Z6598

HOLDCROFT, J., Private, Welch Regiment.

Joining in January 1918, he proceeded in the following June to France, and there fought in the engagements at Ypres, Cambrai, and throughout the Retreat and Advance of 1918. After the Armistice he was sent with the Army of Occupation into Germany, and served on the Rhine until demobilised in December 1919. He holds the General Service and Victory Medals.
75, Cross Street, Bradford, Manchester.   Z10411

HOLDEN, C., Private, R.M.L.I.

He volunteered in January 1915, and first served on board H.M.S. "Himalaya" with the Grand Fleet in the North Sea, where his ship was engaged on important patrol duties. Later he was transferred to H.M.S. "Revenge," and took part in the Battle of Jutland in May 1916. In April 1917, he was discharged as medically unfit for further service, and holds the 1914–15 Star, and the General Service and Victory Medals.
12, Heywood Street, West Gorton, Manchester.   Z6599

HOLDEN, F., Private, King's (Liverpool Regiment).

He joined in August 1916, and on completion of his training, was engaged on important duties with his unit at Shrewsbury. In May 1917, however, he was taken seriously ill with rheumatism and heart trouble, and after three months in the 2nd Western General Hospital at Manchester, was invalided from the Army in August 1917.   Z6600A
26, Georges Avenue, Chester Road, Hulme, Manchester.

HOLDEN, F. A., Driver, R.A.S.C. (M.T.)

He volunteered in August 1915, and after a brief period of training, rendered valuable services with his unit whilst engaged on special transport duties in London. Unfortunately he had a serious nervous breakdown, and after treatment in hospital, was discharged in December 1916 as medically unfit for further service.
40, Lancaster Street, Hulme, Manchester.   Z6601

HOLDER, J., Driver, R.F.A.

He was mobilised in August 1914, and was immediately drafted to France, where he was in action with his Battery at the Battles of Mons, and Le Cateau, and in the subsequent Retreat from Mons. Later he took part in the Battles of Ypres (1914 and 1915), Neuve Chapelle, Loos, Albert, the Somme (1916 and 1918), the Ancre, Arras, Vimy Ridge, Messines, Passchendaele, and Cambrai. He was badly gassed at the commencement of the Retreat of March 1918, and was invalided to hospital in Newcastle, whence he was discharged as medically unfit in May 1918. He holds the Mons Star, and the General Service and Victory Medals.
48, Piggott Street, Greenheys, Manchester.   Z6602

HOLDING, D., Private, R.A.M.C.

He volunteered in August, and in November 1915 was sent to France, where he rendered valuable services as a stretcher-bearer at Loos, Neuve Chapelle, Ypres, La Bassée, Albert, Arras, Passchendaele and Cambrai. He also took part in the Retreat and Advance of 1918, and was demobilised in June 1919, holding the 1914–15 Star, and the General Service and Victory Medals.
33, William Street, West Gorton, Manchester.   Z6603

HOLDSWORTH, T. E., Private, 1st Border Regt.

Enlisting in April 1914, he was sent to France at the outbreak of war in August 1914, and took part in the Battles of Mons, La Bassée and Loos. Unfortunately, during the Somme Offensive in July 1916, he was mortally wounded, and being sent to Netley Hospital, died there later in the same month. He was entitled to the Mons Star, and the General Service and Victory Medals.
"A costly sacrifice upon the altar of freedom."
20, Briscoe Street, Ardwick, Manchester.   Z6604A

HOLDSWORTH, W., Air Mechanic, R.A.F.

Joining in June 1917, after completing his training he served at various stations on important duties, which required a high degree of technical skill. He was not successful in obtaining a transfer overseas before hostilities ceased, but rendered valuable services until demobilised in February 1919. 20, Bath Street, Miles Platting, Manchester. Z10412

HOLDSWORTH, W. H., Pte., 17th Manchester Regt.

He joined in May 1916, and three months later was drafted to the Western Front, where he played a prominent part in the Battles of the Somme, the Ancre, Arras and Cambrai and in heavy fighting at La Bassée, St. Eloi and Vermelles. He was taken prisoner during the Retreat in March 1918, and was held in captivity until the cessation of hostilities. In November 1918 he returned to England, and was engaged on special duties at Barrow-in-Furness until his demobilisation in November 1919. He holds the General Service and Victory Medals. 20, Briscoe Street, Ardwick, Manchester. Z6604B

HOLGATE, C. H., Private, M.G.C.
He joined in August 1916, and in the following February was
drafted to the Western Front, where he took part in the
Battles of Messines and Ypres (III). In October 1917 he
was transferred to Mesopotamia, and after taking part in
further heavy fighting, was engaged on garrison duties at
Baghdad until his demobilisation in February 1920. He
holds the General Service and Victory Medals.
30, Hancock Street, Rusholme, Manchester.   Z6607

HOLGATE, E., Private, Royal Fusiliers.
He joined in July 1917, and in the following month was drafted
to France, where he took part in the Battles of Messines,
Ypres, Passchendaele and Cambrai. He was unfortunately
killed in action in March 1918 during the Retreat of that year,
and was entitled to the General Service and Victory Medals.
" His life for his Country."
55, Francisco Street, Collyhurst, Manchester.   Z9579

HOLGATE, H., Private, 1/7th Manchester Regt.
He enlisted in February 1914, and in May 1915 was drafted
to the Dardanelles, where he saw much severe fighting. After
the Evacuation of the Gallipoli Peninsula, he was transferred
to Egypt, but later served at Mudros. He contracted sand-fly
fever and was admitted to the 16th General Hospital at
Alexandria. Later he also suffered from valvular disease of
the heart, and after being transferred to the 3/4th King's
Shropshire Light Infantry, was sent home and invalided from
the Army in July 1916. He holds the 1914-15 Star, and the
General Service and Victory Medals.
33, Ridgway Road, Moss Side, Manchester.   Z6608

HOLGATE, J. E., Private, M.G.C.
He joined in August 1916, and four months afterwards was
drafted to the Western Front, where he took part in the
Battles of Bullecourt, Messines, Ypres and the Somme (II).
He was wounded in action in this last-named engagement, but
after three months in hospital, rejoined his unit, and during
the Retreat and Advance of 1918, served in the Battles of
Amiens, Bapaume and Le Cateau (II). He later took part in
the march to Germany and was demobilised in February
1919, holding the General Service and Victory Medals.
30, Hancock Street, Rusholme, Manchester.   Z6606

HOLGATE, T., Sergt., Manchester Regiment.
Volunteering in November 1914, he was drafted to France in
January 1916, and four months later was wounded. After
hospital treatment at the Base, he rejoined his unit and served
with distinction at the Battles of the Somme and Ypres (III).
In November 1917 he proceeded to Italy, where he saw much
severe fighting and was wounded in action during the final
offensive on the Piave. He was demobilised in January 1919,
and holds the General Service and Victory Medals.
10, Lucas Street, Openshaw, Manchester.   Z6605

HOLLAND, E. P., Driver. R.F.A.
He volunteered in January 1915, and in June was sent to
France. Whilst on the Western Front he took part in the
Battle of Loos and in heavy fighting at Hill 60, Festubert
and Ypres. In March 1916 he was transferred to Mesopotamia, where he was in action at Kut and Baghdad and in
other important engagements on the Tigris. He was sent
home in July 1918 in order to take up munition work at
Messrs. Armstrong and Whitworth's, where he remained until
his demobilisation from the Army in December of the same
year. He holds the 1914-15 Star, and the General Service
and Victory Medals.
114, Marsland Street, Ardwick, Manchester.   Z6610

HOLLAND, G., Pte., Argyll and Sutherland H'ldrs.
He volunteered in April 1915, and in the following year was
drafted to the Western Front. There he took part in several
engagements, including those at Beaumont-Hamel, Ypres
and Arras, and was wounded in action three times, being
finally invalided home in August 1918. He was discharged
in March 1919 as medically unfit for further service, and holds
the General Service and Victory Medals.
9, Jones Street, Chorlton-on-Medlock, Manchester. Z11728

HOLLAND, J., Private, 6th South Lancashire Regt.
He volunteered in August 1914, and in the following April
was drafted to the Dardanelles, where he took part in the
Landings at Cape Helles and Suvla Bay and in the three
Battles of Krithia. After the Evacuation of the Gallipoli
Peninsula, he proceeded to Mesopotamia and was in action
at Kut and Um-el-Hannah before laying down his life for
King and Country on April 16th, 1916. He was entitled to
the 1914-15 Star, and the General Service and Victory Medals.
" The path of duty was the way to glory."
48, Armitage Street, Ardwick, Manchester.   Z6609A

HOLLAND, J. J., Private, Royal Fusiliers.
Joining in May 1917, he proceeded in the following September
to Egypt, where he fought in the third Battle of Gaza, and
was present at the entry into Jerusalem. Afterwards he was
drafted to the Western Front, and was engaged in heavy
fighting on the Somme and in the second Battle of the Marne,
remaining in France until after the Armistice. Later he was

sent to Ireland, where he did guard duties, but returned to
England in October 1919, and was demobilised, holding the
General Service and Victory Medals.
19, Brougham Street, West Gorton, Manchester.   Z10413

HOLLAND, R., Private, Lancashire Fusiliers.
Volunteering in February 1915, he proceeded to France in
the following July, and was in action at Neuve Chapelle,
Ypres, Loos and the Somme, where he was wounded. On
recovery he returned to the Front and took part in the engagements at Arras, Cambrai and in the Retreat and Advance
of 1918. Returning home, he was demobilised in February
1919, and holds the 1914-15 Star, and the General Service
and Victory Medals.
8, Mary Ellen Street, Collyhurst, Manchester.   Z10414

HOLLAND, T., Staff-Sergt., R.A.S.C.
He volunteered in August 1914, and in the following year
was drafted to the Dardanelles. There he saw much service at
Suvla Bay and Chocolate Hill, but unfortunately contracted
illness, through which he was invalided to hospital at Alexandria. He was subsequently discharged in February 1916,
and holds the 1914-15 Star, and the General Service and
Victory Medals.
22, Shelmerdine Street, Collyhurst, Manchester.   Z9199

HOLLAND, W., L/Corporal, R.A.S.C.
A time-serving Soldier, he was mobilised in August 1914, and
immediately proceeded to France, and after taking part in
the Battles of Mons and Le Cateau, was badly wounded during
the subsequent Retreat from Mons in September. On his
recovery he was engaged in carrying ammunition and food
to the forward areas during the Battles of Ypres (II), Festubert,
Loos, Albert, the Somme (I), Arras, Bullecourt, Cambrai (I),
the Somme (II), Bapaume, Havrincourt and Cambrai (II).
He received his discharge in January 1919, and holds the
Mons Star, and the General Service and Victory Medals.
2, Oak Street, Hulme, Manchester.   TZ11729

HOLLERTON, A., Corporal, R.E.
He volunteered in December 1914, and proceeded to France
in the following March. During his service on the Western
Front he took part in the Battles of Loos, Albert, Vimy
Ridge, the Somme, Arras, Ypres (III), Cambrai (I), the Aisne
(III), the Marne (II), Havrincourt and Cambrai (II). He
was in hospital for a time with trench fever, but again went
into action. Demobilised in March 1919, he holds the 1914-15
Star, and the General Service and Victory Medals.
11, Lavender Street, Hulme, Manchester.   Z6611

HOLLIDAY, G. F., Pte., Loyal N. Lancashire Regt.
He volunteered in January 1916, and in the following December
was drafted to the Western Front, where he played an important part in the Battle of Arras. He then proceeded to
Abbeville in order to take up guard duties in prisoner of war
camps, but later returned to the firing line and was taken
prisoner during the third Battle of the Aisne in May 1918.
He was held in captivity at Chemnitz until the following
December, and in February 1919 was demobilised. Prior
to his joining the Loyal North Lancs. Regiment, he served
in the Manchester Regiment, and now holds the General
Service and Victory Medals.
9, Braham Street, Longsight, Manchester.   Z6612

HOLLINGSWORTH, J., Sapper, R.E.
He volunteered in August 1914, and in January of the following
year crossed to France and during the fighting at Ypres was
wounded. After receiving treatment he was able to return
to the trenches and took part in many other engagements,
including those of Loos, on the Somme, Arras, Havrincourt,
Cambrai and Bapaume. Demobilised in January 1919, he
holds the 1914-15 Star, and the General Service and Victory
Medals. 14, Charles St., Bradford, Manchester.   Z10415

HOLLINGSWORTH, J. J., Pte., King's (L'pool Regt.)
He volunteered in May 1915, and was retained in England
on duties of an important nature until October 1917. He was
then drafted to North Russia, where he saw much heavy
fighting. Returning home in July 1919, he was demobilised
in the following August, and holds the General Service and
Victory Medals.
225, Victoria Square, Ancoats, Manchester.   Z9200

HOLLINGSWORTH, J. T., L/Corporal, R.A.S.C.
He volunteered in December 1914, and in the following January
was drafted to France, where he rendered valuable services
as a Despatch rider and motor driver in the Cambrai, Arras,
Neuve Chapelle and Ypres sectors. He returned to England
for demobilisation in March 1919, and holds the 1914-15
Star, and the General Service and Victory Medals.
151, Clopton Street, Hulme, Manchester.   Z6613

HOLLINS, W., Pte., 10th K.O. (R. Lancaster Regt.)
He volunteered in November 1915, and after a period of
training was retained in England on various important duties,
principally in connection with the defences of London and the
East Coast. He also served as prisoner of war camps and did
consistently good work. He was unsuccessful in obtaining
his transfer overseas and was demobilised in March 1919.
37, Whitley Street, Rochdale Road, Manchester.   Z11730

HOLLINWORTH, J., Pte., 4th South Lancs. Regt.
Volunteering in January 1915, he was drafted to France in
the following November. During his service overseas he was
in action at Ypres, Loos, Albert, Ploegsteert Wood, the Somme,
Beaumont-Hamel and Passchendaele, and was twice wounded,
at Ypres in March 1916 and on the Somme in April 1918.
Returning home on Armistice Day, he was demobilised in
May 1919, and holds the 1914-15 Star, and the General Service
and Victory Medals.
47, Southwell Street, Harpurhey, Manchester.   Z11514

HOLLOWAY, A. W., Private, Manchester Regiment.
He joined in June 1916, and in the following September was
drafted to the Western Front, where he took part in the Battles
of Arras, Bullecourt, Ypres, Lens and Cambrai. He was taken
prisoner during the second Battle of the Somme in March
1918, and whilst in captivity in Germany, was forced to work
in the coal mines. In December 1918 he was repatriated and
demobilised, and holds the General Service and Victory Medals.
4, Patchett Street, Hulme, Manchester.   Z6614

HOLLOWAY, F., Leading Stoker, R.N.
He enlisted in 1912, and from the outbreak of war in August
1914 until 1916 he was engaged on the submarine patrol and
also took part in the Battle of Jutland. In 1917 he was serving
on board H.M.S. " Bullfinch " when she struck a mine off
Kirkwall in Scotland. He was then transferred to H.M.D.
49, and was on escort duties in the English Channel until
the cessation of hostilities. In 1919 he proceeded to the
Baltic on board H.M.S. " Voyager," and was in action with
the Bolsheviks off Kronstadt and Riga. He received his
discharge in September 1920, and holds the 1914-15 Star, and
the General Service (with clasps Jutland and 1914-18) and
Victory Medals.
8, Marsland Street, Ardwick, Manchester.   Z6615

HOLLYWOOD, A. E., Private, Manchester Regt.
He volunteered in December 1915, and was sent to the Western
Front in May of the following year. There he was in action
on the Somme and at Arras, La Bassée, Festubert and Givenchy,
but was wounded at Ypres in June 1917, and invalided home.
He was discharged in September 1917, owing to his injuries,
and holds the General Service and Victory Medals.
111, Naylor Street, Oldham Road, Manchester.   Z9580

HOLLYWOOD, W., Pte., Loyal N. Lancashire Regt.
He joined in April 1916, and in the following June was drafted
to Egypt, where he was in action at Sollum and against the
Senussi Arabs. Later he was transferred to the Western
Front and took part in the Battles of Ypres (III), Lens, the
Somme (II), and the Aisne (III), and in the Retreat and
Advance of 1918. Whilst overseas he was wounded in action,
and after the Armistice served on the Rhine with the Army
of Occupation until his demobilisation at the end of 1920.
He holds the General Service and Victory Medals.
8, Whitfield Street, Ardwick, Manchester.   Z6616

HOLMES, A., Private, 1/4th Seaforth Highlanders.
Volunteering in January 1915, he was sent on active service
later in the same year. Whilst on the Western Front he took
part in the Battles of Neuve Chapelle, Beaumont-Hamel
and Passchendaele and in other important engagements.
He was badly wounded in action, and as a result, was invalided
from the Army in October 1918. He holds the 1914-15
Star, and the General Service and Victory Medals.
84, Ogilvie Street, Chorlton-on-Medlock, Manchester. X6620A

HOLMES, E., Private, 1/8th Manchester Regiment.
Joining in March 1916, he sailed for France in the following
June, and whilst in this theatre of war saw much fighting.
He was in action on the Somme, Arras, Bullecourt, Ypres,
Cambrai and throughout the Retreat and subsequent Allied
Advance of 1918. In November 1919 he was demobilised,
holding the General Service and Victory Medals.
35, Albion Terrace, Varley Street, Manchester.   Z10416

HOLMES, G. H., Private, West Yorkshire Regiment.
He joined in November 1917, and in the following year pro-
ceeding to the Western Front, saw much heavy fighting.
He was in action during the Retreat and Advance of 1918,
and on October 13th, 1918, died gloriously on the Field of
Battle. He was entitled to the General Service and Victory
Medals.
" A valiant soldier, with undaunted heart, he breasted life's
last hill."
59, Herbert Street, Ardwick, Manchester.   Z10417

HOLMES, J. A., Private, 4th Manchester Regiment.
He volunteered in July 1915, and on completion of his training
was engaged on important guard duties at various stations.
He also rendered valuable services on the Regimental Staff, but
unfortunately met with a serious accident whilst on duty,
and was invalided from the Army in August 1917.
27, Hayfield Street, Ardwick, Manchester.   Z6617

HOLMES, W., L/Corporal, R.E.
He joined in August 1916, and in the following April was
sent to France. During his service in this theatre of war
he was in action at La Bassée, Givenchy, Festubert, Béthune,
Nieuport, Dunkirk, Ypres, Passchendaele and in the Retreat

and Advance of 1918. He was gassed at Ypres in December
1917, and was in hospital at Rouen for some time. Demobilised in April 1919, he holds the General Service and Victory
Medals.
24, William Street, West Gorton, Manchester.   Z6618

HOLMES, W., Private, R.A.O.C.
He volunteered in December 1915, but owing to his being
medically unfit for transfer overseas was engaged on important
duties in various places. He first served as a military police-
man in Wales for twelve months, but later acted as a storeman
in the R.A.O.C. stores at Dover, Newcastle and Salisbury.
He was eventually demobilised in March 1919.
13, Lindum Street, Rusholme, Manchester.   TZ6619

HOLMYARD, E., A.B., Royal Navy.
He enlisted in July 1904, and at the outbreak of war in August
1914 proceeded to sea on board H.M.S. " Leviathan " and took
part in the Battles of Heligoland Bight, the Falkland Islands
and the Dogger Bank. He was also engaged on patrol duties
off Bermuda, Jamaica and Nova Scotia until March 1918,
when he was transferred to H.M.T.B. " 042 " for service in
the English Channel. In December 1918 he joined H.M.S.
" Victory," and was stationed at Portsmouth until his discharge in February 1919. He holds the 1914-15 Star, and the
General Service and Victory Medals.
45, Lindum Street, Rusholme, Manchester.   Z6621

HOLT, A., 2nd Lieutenant, R.A.F.
He joined in February 1918, and after a course of training
passed the necessary tests. He then rendered valuable
services with his Squadron at Portland, but was unsuccessful
in obtaining his transfer overseas, and was demobilised in
February 1919.
30, Clayton Street, Hulme, Manchester.   Z6626B

HOLT, A., Private, King's (Liverpool Regiment).
He volunteered in January 1916, and was shortly afterwards
drafted to the Western Front, where he played an important
part in the Battle of Vimy Ridge and was wounded. He was
invalided home, but on his recovery returned to France,
and was in action at Ypres and Loos. In September 1918
he died gloriously on the Field of Battle on the Somme, and
was entitled to the General Service and Victory Medals.
" Nobly striving,"
" He nobly fell that we might live."
33, Rosebery Street, Gorton, Manchester.   TZ6625

HOLT, A., Pte., 3rd Welch Regt., and Gunner, R.F.A.
Volunteering in May 1915, he was sent to the Dardanelles
in the following September and took part in the Battles of
Salt Lake and Chocolate Hill. After the Evacuation of the
Gallipoli Peninsula, he proceeded to Mesopotamia, and after
being in action at Amara, was invalided to hospital with
malarial fever. On his recovery he was drafted to France
in May 1917, and took part in the Battles of the Scarpe,
Havrincourt and Epéhy. During the war he also served for
a time as steward on the s.s. " Canada," and was finally
demobilised in May 1919, holding the 1914-15 Star, and the
General Service and Victory Medals.
9, Leonard Terrace, Green Lane, Ardwick, Manchester. X6624

HOLT, E., Private, Royal Lancaster Regiment.
Volunteering in 1914, he was drafted in the same year to
France, and fought in many engagements, including those at
Ypres, Hill 60, Festubert and on the Somme. At Cambrai,
in November 1917, he was buried in a mine crater, as a result
of which he was rendered unfit for further active service, and
remained in England on light duties until demobilised in 1920.
He holds the 1914-15 Star, and the General Service and
Victory Medals.   10, School Street, Manchester.   Z11424A

HOLT, F., L/Corporal, 1st Manchester Regiment.
Mobilised on the declaration of war, he was shortly afterwards sent to the Western Front, and whilst in this theatre
of war saw much fighting. He was in action at Ypres, St.
Eloi, Hill 60, Festubert, and was wounded; and returning
to hospital in England, was subsequently discharged as
medically unfit in 1917. He holds the 1914 Star, and the
General Service and Victory Medals.
10, School Street, Manchester.   Z11424B

HOLT, F., L/Corporal, 2nd Manchester Regiment.
Mobilised in August 1914, he was at once drafted to France,
where he took part in the Retreat from Mons and the Battles
of La Bassée and Ypres. He was badly wounded in action
at Givenchy in January 1915, and was invalided home. He
remained in hospital until his discharge as medically unfit
for further service in 1917, and holds the Mons Star, and the
General Service and Victory Medals.
24, Barrack Street, Hulme, Manchester.   Z6627

HOLT, G., Corporal, 2nd Manchester Regiment.
Mobilised when war was declared, he was drafted to France
and fought in the Retreat from Mons and in many other
engagements of note. He was also in action at St. Quentin,
and was unfortunately killed in action in the La Bassée
sector in 1915. He was entitled to the Mons Star, and the
General Service and Victory Medals.
" The path of duty was the way to glory."
10, School Street, Manchester.   Z11424C

HOLT, G. A., Private, King's (Liverpool Regt.)
He volunteered in September 1914, and for a time was retained on duties of an important nature in England. In September 1915 he proceeded to France and fought in the Battles of Loos, Vimy Ridge, the Somme, Messines and Ypres. He contracted an illness and on recovery was transferred to the R.E. and served with them on various duties at the Base until demobilised in February 1919. He holds the 1914-15 Star, and the General Service and Victory Medals.
12, Elliott Street, Bradford, Manchester. Z11425A

HOLT, J., Driver, R.A.S.C. (M.T.)
Volunteering in September 1914, he sailed in the following December to France, where he served throughout. He was present during the engagements at Neuve Chapelle, Festubert, Ypres and the Somme, and many others of note, but was sent into hospital in May 1919, through causes due to his service. In August of that year he was demobilised, and holds the General Service and Victory Medals.
33, Birch Street, West Gorton, Manchester. TZ9201

HOLT, J., Private, King's Own Scottish Borderers.
He volunteered in September 1914, and served until April of the following year in England. He then proceeded to France, and during the fierce fighting at Hill 60 in May 1915 was killed in action. He was entitled to the 1914-15 Star, and the General Service and Victory Medals.
" His life for his Country, his soul to God."
12, Elliott Street, Bradford, Manchester. Z11425B

HOLT, J., Private, 6th Batt. Border Regiment.
Volunteering in August 1914, he completed his training and was sent to the Dardanelles. He took part in the Landing at Cape Helles, and the Battles of Krithia and during the fighting at Suvla Bay was killed in action in August 1915. He was entitled to the 1914-15 Star, and the General Service and Victory Medals.
" He died the noblest death a man may die,
Fighting for God and right and liberty."
14, Nancy Street, Chester Road, Manchester. Z10418

HOLT, J., Private, 17th Royal Welch Fusiliers.
He joined in October 1916, and shortly afterwards proceeded to the Western Front. There he saw much fighting in the Ypres sector, at Bapaume and Cambrai, later being invalided home through ill-health. Demobilised in May 1919, he holds the General Service and Victory Medals.
34, Burton Street, Newtown, Manchester. Z10458

HOLT, J. A., Private, R.A.O.C.
He volunteered in August 1914, and four months later was drafted to the Western Front, where he saw much severe fighting at the Battles of Neuve Chapelle, Ypres (II), Loos, the Somme, Arras, Cambrai (1917 and 1918), and in the Retreat and Advance of 1918. After the cessation of hostilities, he served in Germany with the Army of Occupation until his demobilisation in March 1919, and holds the 1914-15 Star, and the General Service and Victory Medals.
30, Clayton Street, Hulme, Manchester. Z6626A

HOLT, J. B., Gunner, R.F.A.
Volunteering in September 1914, he proceeded to France in the following June and took part in the Battles of Loos, Albert, the Somme, the Ancre, Vimy Ridge and Ypres (III), where he was badly wounded and gassed in action in October 1917. He was invalided home, and was in hospital for several months, but on his recovery, served for a short time in England before rejoining his Battery in France, when he was again in action in the Béthune sector. Unfortunately his old wound troubled him, and he was sent to hospital at St. Albans. He was finally discharged in May 1919, and holds the 1914-15 Star, and the General Service and Victory Medals.
22, Hardman Street, City Road, Hulme, Manchester. Z6622

HOLT, T. J., S.S.M. (Warrant Officer), R.A.S.C.
He volunteered in November 1914, and twelve months later was drafted to the Western Front, where he served with distinction with the Mechanical Transport until March 1916. He was then invalided home as the result of a nervous breakdown, and four months later was discharged as medically unfit for further service. He holds the 1914-15 Star, and the General Service and Victory Medals.
17, Ribson Street, Hulme, Manchester. Z6623

HOMAN, F., Private, Lancashire Fusiliers.
He joined in July 1916, and in the same year landed in France. He was engaged in the heavy fighting in the Ypres sector, and was unfortunately killed in action at Passchendaele on October 9th, 1917. He was entitled to the General Service and Victory Medals.
" Great deeds cannot die :
They, with the sun and moon renew their light for ever."
13, Sainsbury Street, Ancoats, Manchester. Z10419

HOME, J., Private, Royal Welch Fusiliers.
He joined in June 1916, and in July of the following year was drafted to the Western Front, where he took part in the Battles of Ypres, Passchendaele, Lens, Cambrai, the Somme (II),

the Marne (II), Amiens and Le Cateau (II). He was also in action at La Bassée, Givenchy and Festubert and in other important engagements during the Retreat and Advance of 1918. After the Armistice he served in Germany with the Army of Occupation and remained there until September 1919. He was then demobilised, and holds the General Service and Victory Medals.
4, Beech Street, Hulme, Manchester. Z6628

HOMER, J. L., Private, 8th Manchester Regiment.
Volunteering in September 1914, he was drafted to the Dardanelles in the following August and took part in the Landing at Suvla Bay. During the Evacuation of the Gallipoli Peninsula in December 1915, he was badly wounded in action and invalided home. After protracted hospital treatment at Winchester, he was discharged as medically unfit for further service in March 1917, and holds the 1914-15 Star, and the General Service and Victory Medals.
3, Nansen Street, Ardwick, Manchester. Z6629A

HOMER, K. A., Pte., Argyll and Sutherland H'ldrs.
He volunteered in January 1915, and on completion of his training, rendered valuable services with his unit whilst engaged on important duties in Scotland and England. He unfortunately contracted blood poisoning in a severe form before he was able to proceed overseas, and after hospital treatment at Southport, was invalided from the Army in June 1916.
3, Nansen Street, Ardwick, Manchester. Z6629B

HOMS, A., Private, M.G.C.
He volunteered in August 1914, and in the following December proceeded to Egypt. He took part in the operations on the Suez Canal, and also served in Palestine at Gaza and other places. In April 1917 he was drafted to the Western Front and was in action on the Somme, Ypres and in the Retreat and Advance of 1918. Demobilised in December 1918, he holds the 1914-15 Star, and the General Service and Victory Medals.
71, Churnett Street, Collyhurst, Manchester. Z10457

HONEY, A., Private, Lancashire Fusiliers.
He enlisted in 1897, and served through the South African campaign. On the outbreak of war in August 1914, he was immediately drafted to France, where he took part in the Battles of Mons and in the subsequent Retreat, the Battles of the Aisne, Armentières, Ypres and Festubert, and was wounded in action in May 1915. Six months later he was sent home and discharged, time expired, after eighteen years' service, and holds the Queen's and King's South African Medals, the Mons Star, and the General Service and Victory Medals.
44, Caroline Street, Hulme, Manchester. Z6630

HONEY, H., Driver, R.F.A.
He volunteered in March 1915, and after a period of duty in England was drafted to France two years later. During his service on the Western Front, he took part in the Battles of Ypres, Passchendaele, the Somme (II), Havrincourt, the Sambre and Le Cateau, and in other important engagements in the Retreat and Advance of 1918. He was demobilised in May 1919, and holds the General Service and Victory Medals.
24, Moulton Street, Hulme, Manchester. Z6631

HOOK, John, Private, Lancashire Fusiliers.
He was mobilised in August 1914, and proceeding to France with the first Expeditionary Force, took part in the Battle of Mons, and the subsequent Retreat. He was also in action at the Battles of the Marne, La Bassée, Ypres and Hill 60, before being killed at Ypres in June 1915. He was entitled to the Mons Star and the General Service and Victory Medals.
" A valiant Soldier, with undaunted heart, he breasted life's last hill."
32, Daniel Street, Hulme, Manchester. Z6633

HOOK, Joseph, L/Corporal, Lancashire Fusiliers.
He volunteered in September 1915, and was quickly drafted to France, where he played a prominent part in the Battles of Albert, the Somme (I), Arras, Vimy Ridge, Ypres, Cambrai (I), the Somme (II), Bapaume, Havrincourt and Cambrai (II). He laid down his life for King and Country during the Battle of the Sambre in November 1918, and was entitled to the 1914-15 Star, and the General Service and Victory Medals.
" He joined the great white company of valiant souls."
32, Daniel Street, Hulme, Manchester. Z6632

HOOTON. H., Pte., 2nd K.O. (R. Lancaster Regt.)
He enlisted in June 1914, and was sent to France at the outbreak of war in the following August. During his service on the Western Front he took part in the Battle of, and the Retreat from, Mons and the Battles of Le Cateau, the Marne, La Bassée, Ypres (1914 and 1915), Neuve Chapelle, Festubert and Loos. In December 1915, he was transferred to Salonika and was in action on the Struma, Vardar and Doiran fronts and at the recapture of Monastir. He received his discharge in February 1919, and holds the Mons Star, and the General Service and Victory Medals.
14, Shakespeare Row, Ardwick, Manchester. Z6634

HOOTON, J., Private, 2/6th Manchester Regiment.
He joined in September 1916, and in the following March was sent to the Western Front. During his service in this theatre of war he was in action in much severe fighting, but in September 1917 was invalided home with a weak heart. After hospital treatment in Colchester and York, he was engaged on special duties at Ripon until October 1918, when he was discharged as medically unfit for further service. He holds the General Service and Victory Medals.
37, Princess Street, Rusholme, Manchester. Z6635

HOPKINS, D. J., Driver, R.A.S.C. (M.T.)
Mobilised in August 1914, he was quickly drafted to France and served through the Retreat from Mons. He was later engaged on important transport duties in the forward areas during the Battles of Ypres (I), Neuve Chapelle, Ypres (II), Albert, the Somme, Arras, Ypres (III), and Cambrai, and also in the Retreat and Advance of 1918. He was discharged in February 1919, and holds the Mons Star, and the General Service and Victory Medals.
25, Etruria Street, Longsight, Manchester. Z6636

HOPKINSON, H. S., Corporal, Army Cyclist Corps.
He joined in September 1917, and in the following March was sent to France. During the Retreat and Advance of 1918, he served with distinction at the Battles of Bapaume, Amiens, Havrincourt, and Le Cateau. After the cessation of hostilities he was stationed at Cologne and Bonn with the Army of Occupation, and was eventually demobilised in October, 1919, holding the General Service and Victory Medals. TZ6637B
25, Hampton Street, Erskine Street, Hulme, Manchester.

HOPKINSON, R., Private, 4th Queen's (Royal West Surrey Regiment and Labour Corps.
He volunteered in January 1915, and a year later proceeded to France. There he at once took part in strenuous fighting and was wounded in July 1916, during the first Battle of the Somme. Evacuated to England, he was sent to hospital at Birmingham, and upon his recovery he returned to France. He was transferred to the Labour Corps, and served for some time until he was invalided home on account of ill-health and eventually discharged in February 1918, holding the General Service and Victory Medals.
10, Boardman Street, Harpurhey, Manchester. Z11515

HOPKINSON, R. H., Sergt., R.A.S.C.
Volunteering in August 1914, he was drafted to France in the following March, and whilst on the Western Front, was engaged on transport duties with the heavy artillery. He was present during the heavy fighting at the Battles of Ypres, Loos, the Somme, Arras, and Cambrai, and in the Retreat and Advance of 1918. He holds the 1914-15 Star, and the General Service and Victory Medals, and was demobilised in April 1919.
25, Hampton Street, Erskine Street, Hulme, Manchester. TZ6637A

HOPPER, T., Private, Royal Welch Fusiliers.
He joined in May 1917, and after a period of training was sent to Ireland where he served on various important duties until the cessation of hostilities. He was not able to obtain a transfer to a fighting unit owing to physical disability, but rendered very valuable services until demobilised in December 1918.
33, Upper Dover Street, Bradford, Manchester. Z9202

HOPSON, J., Private, 11th Manchester Regiment.
He volunteered in August 1914, and twelve months later was drafted to the Gallipoli Peninsula, where he took part in the Landing at Suvla Bay, and was badly wounded in action during the capture of Chunuk Bair. He was invalided to hospital in Liverpool, but, on his recovery, was sent to France, and served at the Battles of Vimy Ridge, Messines, Ypres (III), Lens, the Somme (II), Bapaume, and Mons (II). He was demobilised in June 1919, and holds the 1914-15 Star, and the General Service and Victory Medals.
10, Athol Street, Hulme, Manchester. TZ6638

HOPTON, T. W., Private, 25th Manchester Regt.
He volunteered in May 1915, and in the following November was drafted to the Western Front, where he took part in the Battles of Albert and Vermelles. He was then invalided home suffering from disease of the kidney, and in May 1916, was discharged as medically unfit for further service, holding the 1914-15 Star, and the General Service and Victory Medals.
2, Walter Street, Hulme, Manchester. TZ6420B

HOPWOOD, G., Private, R.A.M.C.
Mobilised in August 1914, and landing in France in the same month he served in the Retreat from Mons, and the subsequent battles. He was also present in the engagements at Hill 60, Festubert, Loos, Vimy Ridge, and on the Somme where he was wounded on July 2nd, 1916. On recovery he returned to his unit, and served on the Western Front until hostilities ceased. Demobilised in May 1919, he holds the Mons Star, and the General Service and Victory Medals.
277, Hamilton Street, Collyhurst, Manchester. Z11426

HOPWOOD, T., Driver, R.F.A.
Having joined in February 1916, he was sent to France in November of the same year and took part in the fighting on the Ancre, and at Arras, Ypres, and Cambrai. He fell fighting

on the Somme in April 1918, and was buried at Heilly Station Cemetery. He was entitled to the General Service and Victory Medals.
"Great deeds cannot die."
20, Vine Street, Newton Heath, Manchester. Z9658A

HORAM, W., Gunner, R.G.A.
He volunteered in January 1915, and was retained at various stations in England until May 1917, when he was drafted to the Western Front. There he took part in many important engagements, including the Battles of Ypres, Passchendaele, and Cambrai, and fought also in the Retreat and Advance of 1918. He was demobilised on his return home in February 1919, and holds the General Service and Victory Medals.
44, Meadow Street, Ardwick, Manchester. Z6639

HORAN, J. H., Private, R.A.M.C.
He joined in October 1916, and served until 1918 on various duties with his unit. He then proceeded to Egypt, and during his service there contracted malaria, but remained in the East until demobilised in January 1920.
5, Tilston Place, Collyhurst, Manchester. Z10420

HORAN, J. W., Private, South Lancashire Regt.
He volunteered in November 1915, and in the following January landed in France. He was in action at Ypres, on the Somme, and was gassed, but after receiving treatment at the Base, was able to return to the trenches, and was in action in various engagements during the Retreat and Advance of 1918. Demobilised in February 1919, he holds the General Service and Victory Medals.
1, Buckland Street, Ancoats, Manchester. Z10421A

HORNBY, C., Stoker, R.N.
Volunteering in August 1914, he was posted to H.M.S. "Fox," in which he served in many waters. He was engaged on various duties in the Red Sea and the Persian Gulf, later proceeding to South Russia, and serving with the naval brigade at Baku. Demobilised in July 1919, he holds the 1914-15 Star, and the General Service and Victory Medals.
2, Fox Street, Ancoats, Manchester. Z10422

HORNBY, F., Private, 8th Manchester Regiment.
Volunteering in October 1914, he was sent to the Dardanelles in August of the following year, and took part in important engagements there. He unluckily contracted an illness and was invalided to Malta and thence home. He was discharged in June 1916, owing to his disability, and holds the 1914-15 Star, and the General Service and Victory Medals.
14, Martha Street, Bradford, Manchester. TZ9581

HORNER, W., Air Mechanic, R.A.F.
He joined in February 1917, and after his training was engaged at various stations on important duties of a highly technical nature with his Squadron. He rendered valuable services, but was not successful in obtaining his transfer overseas before the cessation of hostilities, and was demobilised in March 1919.
5, Stonehewer Street, Ancoats, Manchester. Z9444A

HORNSBY, G., Private, 8th Manchester Regiment.
He volunteered in August 1914, and in April of the following year, was drafted to Gallipoli, where, after taking part in the Landing at Cape Helles, he fought in the Battles of Krithia. On the Evacuation of the Peninsula, he was transferred to the Western Front, and there served through the Battles of Albert, Vimy Ridge, the Somme, Arras, Ypres, and Cambrai, and other engagements, and was severely wounded in action. He was eventually invalided from the Army in April 1919, and holds the 1914-15 Star, and the General Service and Victory Medals.
48, Lancaster Street, Hulme, Manchester. Z6640

HORNSBY, J. H., Private, Lancashire Fusiliers.
He volunteered in August 1914, and in February of the following year was drafted to the Western Front, whence he proceeded shortly afterwards to Gallipoli. There he took part in the first Landing in April 1915, and saw much severe fighting until the Evacuation of the Peninsula, when he returned to France. He took part in the Battles of St. Eloi, and the Somme, and other engagements until wounded in action in 1916, and invalided to hospital at Leeds. He re-joined his unit, however, on his recovery in October of that year, and was in action at Arras, where he was again wounded. Again sent to hospital in England, he returned to France a second time, and was gassed, and a third time wounded at Cambrai. He was finally demobilised in April 1919, and holds the 1914-15 Star, and the General Service and Victory Medals.
36, Lancaster Street, Hulme, Manchester. Z6642

HORNSBY, W. E., Sergt., 5th Manchester Regt.
Volunteering in November 1914, he proceeded to the Western Front in February of the following year, and there saw heavy fighting in various sectors. After taking part in the Battles of Hill 60, Ypres, and Albert, and many other engagements, he was wounded in action on the Somme, and invalided to hospital in London. He afterwards served as an Instructor at Ripon, until his demobilisation in February 1919, and holds the 1914-15 Star, and the General Service and Victory Medals.
45, Tamworth Street, Hulme, Manchester. Z6641

HORROCKS, A. E., Private, 5th Manchester Regt.
He volunteered in 1915, and in November of the same year proceeded to France. He was in action in the Battles of the Somme, Albert, Bullecourt, Beaumont-Hamel, Ypres, Cambrai, and many other engagements until the Armistice. In February 1919, he was demobilised, and holds the 1914–15 Star, and the General Service and Victory Medals.
217, Morton Street, Longsight, Manchester.   Z10424C

HORROCKS, J., Pte., 49th Training Reserve Bn.
He joined in July 1916, and during his training at Whitchurch contracted an illness, through which he was discharged as medically unfit in November of the same year. He was then engaged at Messrs. Crossley Bros'., Works, Gorton, as a tester of aeroplane parts, and subsequently was employed, until the Armistice, on duties in connection with transport of food supplies. 48, Ryder Street, Bradford, Manchester.   Z10423

HORROCKS, T., Private, Labour Corps.
After volunteering in 1915, he passed through his course of military training, but owing to physical weakness was not successful in securing his transfer to a fighting front. He rendered veluable services, however, in various capacities with the Labour Corps at Oswestry, until his demobilisation in 1919.
75, Pierce Street, Ancoats, Manchester.   Z10425

HORSFALL, J., Private, 23rd Royal Fusiliers.
He volunteered in November 1914, and in December of that year crossed to France. There he fought in many engagements, including those at Neuve Chapelle, Hill 60, Loos, the Somme, Arras, Ypres, and Cambrai. He gave his life for King and Country in the second Battle of the Aisne in May 1918, and was entitled to the 1914–15 Star, and the General Service and Victory Medals.
"His life for his Country, his soul to God."
2, Culvert Street, Rochdale, Manchester.   Z10459

HORSEFIELD, J., Private, East Lancashire Regt.
He volunteered in September 1914, and twelve months later, was drafted to the Western Front, whence he was transferred two months later to Salonika. There he saw much severe fighting on the Doiran front, and in January 1918 was invalided home suffering from malaria, having already been for nine months in hospital. He was discharged as medically unfit for further service in May 1918, and holds the 1914–15 Star, and the General Service and Victory Medals.
23, George Street, Hulme, Manchester.   Z6644

HORSFIELD, J., Private, R.A.S.C.
Volunteering in August 1914, he was drafted to France in the following March, and there served in various sectors of the Front. He was chiefly engaged in conveying food and ammunition to the forward areas and took an active part also in the Battle of Loos, and was gassed. Invalided home, he returned to France on his recovery in May 1917, and served at Rouen until his demobilisation in February 1919. He holds the 1914–15 Star, and the General Service and Victory Medals.
11, Charlotte Street, Chorlton-on-Medlock, Manchester. TZ6643

HORSLEY, G., Private, M.G.C.
He joined in February 1917, and in December of that year was drafted to the Western Front, where he saw much heavy fighting. After taking part in the Battles of the Somme, Havrincourt, and Cambrai, and many minor engagements, he was invalided home on account of injuries received in an accident. He was eventually demobilised on October 1919, holding the General Service and Victory Medals.
11, Margaret Street, West Gorton, Manchester.   Z6645

HOSTEY, D., Private, Somerset Light Infantry.
He volunteered in November 1914, and in the following February on the completion of his training at Grantham was drafted to the Western Front. He took an active part in many engagements of importance, including those at Hill 60, Ypres, and the Somme Offensive of 1916, and was wounded on three occasions. After much hospital treatment he was discharged in November 1917 as unfit for further duty, and holds the 1914–15 Star, and the General Service and Victory Medals.
13, Wilkinson Street, Collyhurst, Manchester.   Z10426

HOUGH, T., Private, South Wales Borderers.
He joined in March 1916, and in April of the following year proceeded to the Western Front, where he took part in the Battles of Bullecourt, Passchendaele, Cambrai, the Somme, Bapaume, and Ypres. He died gloriously on the Field of Battle on the Sambre on November 4th, 1918, only seven days before the signing of the Armistice. He was entitled to the General Service and Victory Medals.
"A costly sacrifice upon the altar of freedom."
83, Silver Street, Hulme, Manchester.   TZ6646

HOUGHLAND, W., Corporal, 1/6th Manchester Rgt.
Mobilised in August 1914, he was drafted to the Western Front in the following month, and there took part in many important engagements, including the Battles of the Marne, the Aisne, La Bassée, Ypres, St. Eloi, Festubert, the Somme, the Ancre, Cambrai, and Le Cateau. He also served through the Retreat and Advance of 1918, and was wounded in action in November 1916. He was discharged in February 1919, and holds the 1914 Star, and the General Service and Victory Medals. 6, Stamford Street, Hulme, Manchester.   Z6647

HOUGHTON, B., Private, Royal Welch Fusiliers.
He joined in April 1917, and after a period of training, served at various stations, where he was engaged on duties of a highly important nature. Unable on account of deafness to obtain his transfer to a theatre of war, he nevertheless, rendered very valuable services with his unit until October 1919, when he was demobilised.
7, Kenwyn Street, Newton, Manchester.   Z6648

HOUGHTON, H., Gunner, R.F.A.
Volunteering in July 1915, he was drafted to the Western Front in the following December, and there saw severe fighting in various sectors. He took part in the Battles of St. Eloi, Albert, the Ancre, Arras, Vimy Ridge, Cambrai, the Somme, and Bapaume, and many minor engagements in this theatre of war, and was gassed at Ypres in October 1917. He was demobilised in June 1919, and holds the 1914–15 Star, and the General Service and Victory Medals.
34, Lancaster Street, Hulme, Manchester.   Z6649

HOUGHTON, J., Private, South Lancashire Regt.
He volunteered in September 1914, and in June of the following year proceeded to the Western Front, where, after taking part in the Battles of Loos, and the Somme, he was wounded in action. Invalided to hospital at Birmingham, he returned to France on his recovery and fought in the Battle of Ypres, and in the Retreat of 1918, and was again wounded at Cambrai in August of that year. After a considerable period in hospital at Stockport, he was invalided from the Army in January 1919, holding the 1914–15 Star, and the General Service and Victory Medals.
24, Robert Street, West Gorton, Manchester.   Z6650

HOUGHTON, L., Pte., 4th King's Shropshire Light Infantry.
He joined in December 1916, and after his training served at various stations on important garrison and other duties. He rendered valuable services, but was not successful in obtaining a transfer abroad before the cessation of hostilities. He was demobilised in January 1919.
24, Sycamore Street, Oldham Road, Manchester.   Z10356

HOUGHTON, R. W., Private, Lancashire Fusiliers.
He volunteered in December 1915, and on the completion of his training was drafted to France. There he fought in many notable battles until the close of hostilities, including those at the Somme, Ypres and Dickebusch. On returning home in February 1919 he was demobilised, and holds the General Service and Victory Medals.
9, Railway View, Gorton, Manchester.   Z10427

HOUGHTON, W., Private, 7th Manchester Regt.
Having volunteered in May 1915, he was sent to Egypt later in the same year, and took part in repelling the Turkish attack on the Suez Canal, and in the action at Mersa Matruh. He was then transferred to the Western Front, and was in action at Albert, the Somme, the Ancre, Bullecourt and Ypres, and in numerous other engagements. He was demobilised in February 1919, and holds the 1914–15 Star, and the General Service and Victory Medals.
27, Baguley Street, Miles Platting, Manchester.   Z9582

HOULKER, A., Gunner, R.F.A.
Joining in August 1916, he was drafted to Salonika on completing a period of training in the following December. There he saw much severe fighing on the Doiran front, taking part in many important engagements until the cessation of hostilities, and then served in Russia until his return home for demobilisation in August 1919. He holds the General Service and Victory Medals.
28, Upper Duke Street, Hulme, Manchester.   Z6651

HOUSTON, V., Private, 8th Manchester Regiment.
Volunteering in May 1915, he proceeded to France in the following August, and whilst in this theatre of war fought in many important battles. He was in action at Loos, Ploegsteert Wood, the Somme, and the Ancre, where he was wounded in November 1916. After his recovery he returned to the lines, and was in action at Arras, Ypres, Cambrai, and many engagements in the Retreat and Advance of 1918. He was demobilised in March 1919, and holds the 1914–15 Star, and the General Service and Victory Medals.
2, Beswick Street, West Gorton, Manchester.   Z10428

HOWARD, B., Private, 20th Manchester Regiment.
Volunteering in February 1915, he was drafted to France in the following month, and fought at Hill 60, Ypres, Festubert, and Vimy Ridge. He gave his life for the freedom of England in the Battle of the Somme in December 1916, and was entitled to the 1914–15 Star, and the General Service and Victory Medals.   "A valiant Soldier, with undaunted heart he breasted life's last hill."
73, Knightley Street, Rochdale Road, Manchester.   Z10460

HOWARD, G. W., Private, 51st Welch Regiment.
He joined in July 1918, and after completing his training was engaged on the East Coast Defences until February 1919, when he was drafted to the Army of Occupation in Germany. He was later transferred to Ireland, where he served on important duties until he was demobilised in March 1920.
28, Brass Street, Rochdale Road, Manchester.   Z9584

HOWARD, C. T., Private, 2nd South Lancs. Regt.
He volunteered in September 1914, and in the following January proceeded to the Western Front, where he was wounded in action at Hill 60 in May 1915, and sent to hospital at Rouen. On his recovery he was engaged on important duties on the General Headquarters Staff until again invalided to hospital suffering from septic poisoning. He unhappily died whilst undergoing an operation on October 6th, 1917. He was entitled to the 1914-15 Star, and the General Service and Victory Medals.
"The path of duty was the way to glory."
12, Stott Road, Hulme, Manchester. Z6656

HOWARD, E., Pte., 21st Manchester Regt. and R.D.C.
He joined in March 1916, and three months later proceeded to the Western Front, where he saw much severe fighting. He took part in the Battles of Beaumont-Hamel, Beaucourt, the Ancre and Arras, and many other engagements until wounded in action at Vimy Ridge and invalided home. He afterwards served with the Royal Defence Corps until his demobilisation in March 1919, and holds the General Service and Victory Medals.
74, Warde Street, Hulme, Manchester. TZ6655

HOWARD, E. J., Pte., 8th Royal Welch Fusiliers.
He volunteered in February 1915, and in March of the following year proceeded to Mesopotamia, where during his two years' service he saw much fighting at Sanna-i-Yat, and on the Tigris. Later he was drafted to France, and took part in various engagements, notably Havrincourt and Epéhy, until the close of war. Demobilised in February 1919, he holds the General Service and Victory Medals.
2, Penley Street, Manchester. Z9203

HOWARD, J., Private, South Lancashire Regt.
He volunteered in May 1915, and after undergoing a period of training, served at various stations, where he was engaged on duties of great importance. He was unable to obtain his transfer to a theatre of war on account of ill-health, but, nevertheless, did much useful work with his unit until May 1917, when he was discharged as medically unfit for further service. 76, Armitage Street, Ardwick, Manchester. Z6652

HOWARD, J., Leading Stoker, R.N., H.M.S. "Lion."
He was already in the Royal Navy at the outbreak of war, and was sent to the North Sea in H.M.S. "Lion." He took part in the Battles of the Dogger Bank and Jutland, and in the bombardment of the Belgian Coast, and was afterwards transferred to H.M.S. "Tiger," in which ship he remained until the Armistice. In 1920 he was serving in H.M.S. "High-flyer" in Indian waters, and holds the 1914-15 Star, and the General Service and Victory Medals.
12, Whatmough Street, Oldham Road, Manchester. Z9583

HOWARD, J., Private, Manchester Regiment.
He volunteered in July 1915, and in the same month was drafted to Mesopotamia. After taking a prominent part in the fighting at Kut, he unfortunately contracted fever from which he died on June 30th, 1916. He was entitled to the 1914-15 Star, and the General Service and Victory Medals.
"His memory is cherished with pride."
17, Raglan Street, Ancoats, Manchester. Z9204A

HOWARD, J. E. (Sen.), Pte., 4th Monmouthshire Regiment.
He joined in December 1916, and on completion of a term of training was retained on important duties at various stations. He was not successful in his efforts to obtain his transfer to the Front, owing to ill-health, but rendered very valuable services with his unit until December 1918, when he was invalided from the Army.
9, Unity Street, Ardwick, Manchester. Z6653A

HOWARD, J. E. (Jun.), Pte., 1st London Regt. (Royal Fusiliers).
He volunteered in August 1914, and underwent a period of training prior to being drafted to the Western Front in January 1916. There he saw much severe fighting at Loos, Nieuport, La Bassée, and many other places, took part in the Battles of the Somme, Arras, and Ypres, and was gassed and wounded in action. He was demobilised in November 1919, and holds the General Service and Victory Medals.
9, Unity Street, Ardwick, Manchester. Z6653B

HOWARD, M., L/Corporal, R.E.
Volunteering in February 1915, he was sent in the same month to France, and whilst there saw much heavy fighting. He served at Hill 60, Ypres, Festubert, Loos, and Armentières, where he was severely wounded. He was invalided home, and after hospital treatment was discharged as medically unfit for further duty in August 1916. He holds the 1914-15 Star, and the General Service and Victory Medals.
20, Sudbury Street, Rochdale, Manchester. Z10461

HOWARD, R., Sapper, R.E.
He joined in March 1916, and after three months' training, proceeded to the Western Front. Whilst in this theatre of war he was engaged on important duties in various sectors, and took an active part in the Battles of the Somme, the Ancre, Arras, Bullecourt and Cambrai, and many minor engagements. He was demobilised on his return home in January 1919, and holds the General Service and Victory Medals.
14, Tuley Street, Openshaw, Manchester. Z6654

HOWARD, W. Act. L/Cpl., Loyal N. Lancs. Regt.
Joining in May 1916, he proceeded to France in the following September, and during his service there fought in many important engagements, and was three times wounded and twice gassed. He was in action on the Somme, the Ancre, at Arras, Messines, Ypres, and Cambrai, and in many engagements in the Offensive of 1918. He was demobilised in March 1919, and holds the General Service and Victory Medals.
47, Branson Street, Ancoats, Manchester. Z10429

HOWARTH, A., Private, 2nd Lancashire Fusiliers.
Mobilised in August 1914, he was immediately drafted to the Western Front, where he fought in the Battle of Mons, and the subsequent Retreat. He also took part in the Battles of La Bassée, Ypres, Festubert, the Somme, Arras, Messines, Cambrai, the Marne, and the Aisne, and many other important engagements, and was wounded in action during the Advance of 1918. He was for some time in hospital at Étaples, but on his recovery, re-joined his unit at Brussels, where he remained until his discharge in April 1919. He holds the Mons Star, and the General Service and Victory Medals.
19, Eskrigge Street, Ardwick, Manchester. Z6659

HOWARTH, A., Corporal, 9th Rifle Brigade.
Volunteering in September 1914, he proceeded to the Western Front five months later, and served with distinction in very heavy fighting. After taking part in the Battle of Ypres (II), he died gloriously on the Field of Battle at Loos on September 25th, 1915. He was entitled to the 1914-15 Star, and the General Service and Victory Medals.
"Nobly striving,
He nobly fell that we might live."
70, Whitley Street, Rochdale Road, Manchester. Z11731

HOWARTH, A., Private, 3rd Manchester Regiment.
He volunteered in November 1914, and in May of the following year was drafted to France. During his service in this theatre of war he served in many sectors, and was in action at the Somme, Arras, Bullecourt, Ypres, Cambrai, and in the Retreat and Advance of 1918. In February 1919, he was demobilised, and holds the 1914-15 Star, and the General Service and Victory Medals.
83, Inkerman Street, Collyhurst, Manchester. Z10462

HOWARTH, C., Private, 7th Manchester Regiment.
He enlisted in February 1913, and after war broke out was engaged on duties of an important nature in England until May 1915. He then proceeded to the Dardanelles, and after Landing at West Beach was wounded in June, and sent to hospital at Malta. After returning home he was discharged in September 1916, as medically unfit for further duty. He holds the 1914-15 Star, and the General Service and Victory Medals.
55, Gardner Street, West Gorton, Manchester. Z10430

HOWARTH, E., Private, 10th Lancashire Fusiliers.
Volunteering in November 1915, he was drafted to the Western Front in March of the following year, and there saw severe fighting in various sectors. After taking part in the Battles of St. Eloi, Albert, Vimy Ridge, he was wounded in action on the Somme in August 1916, and invalided home. After his recovery he was engaged on agricultural work at Oxford, until his demobilisation in February 1919, and holds the General Service and Victory Medals.
24, Birch Street, Moss Side, Manchester. Z6657

HOWARTH, H.(Sen.) Pte., K.O. (R. Lancaster Regt.)
Mobilised at the commencement of war, he embarked almost immediately for France, and fought in many battles, including those at Mons and Ypres. He gave his life for the freedom of England at Ypres, on May 9th, 1915, and was entitled to the Mons Star, and the General Service and Victory Medals.
"Whilst we remember, the sacrifice is not in vain."
3, St. Clements Place, Ancoats, Manchester. Z9205B

HOWARTH, H.(Jun.) Pte., K.O. (R. Lancaster Regt.)
Mobilised in August 1914, he was shortly afterwards drafted to France, and fought in the Retreat from Mons, and the Battles of Ypres, Loos, the Somme and Givenchy. He was unhappily killed in action on March 21st, 1917, and was entitled to the Mons Star, and the General Service and Victory Medals.
"The path of duty was the way to glory."
3, St. Clements Place, Ancoats, Manchester. Z9205C

HOWARTH, H., Private, Manchester Regiment.
Volunteering in September 1914, he was drafted in the following August to the Western Front, where he was in action at Ypres, Hill 60, the Somme and Arras. Wounded in May 1917 at Bullecourt, he was sent to hospital in Rouen, and upon his recovery, rejoined his unit, and fought at Cambrai, and in various sectors during the Retreat and Advance of 1918. After the Armistice, he served in Germany with the Army of Occupation until March 1919, when he returned home, and was demobilised, holding the 1914-15 Star, and the General Service and Victory Medals.
32, Pleasant Street, Harpurhey, Manchester. Z11516

HOWARTH, H., Private, 5th Manchester Regiment.
Having joined in January 1916, he was drafted to the Western Front in the following April, and took part in the fighting at Albert, the Somme, Arras, Ypres, Cambrai, Amiens and Bapaume, and was gassed on the Ancre front. He returned home and was attached to the Royal Defence Corps, guarding German prisoners. He was demobilised in November 1919, and holds the General Service and Victory Medals.
18, Vine Street, Newton Heath, Manchester.   Z9585

HOWARTH, J., Private, 12th Manchester Regiment.
Volunteering in August 1914, he proceeded to France in June of the following year, and took part in the Battles of Loos, Vimy Ridge, the Somme (I), Messines, where he was gassed in action, Ypres, (III), Cambrai (I), the Somme (II), Havrincourt, and Cambrai (II). He was also present at the entry into Mons at dawn on Armistice Day. He holds the 1914–15 Star, and the General Service and Victory Medals, and was demobilised in November 1919.
16, Walter Street, Hulme, Manchester.   Z11732

HOWARTH, J., Private, 12th Manchester Regiment.
He volunteered in September 1914, and for twelve months was employed on various duties at home stations. Proceeding in September 1915 to France, he took part in the Battles of the Somme, Arras and Ypres (III), and in many engagements during the Retreat and Advance of 1918. During his service overseas, he did consistently good work, and demobilised in February 1919, holds the 1914–15 Star, and the General Service and Victory Medals.
5, Pleasant Street, Harpurhey, Manchester.   Z11517

HOWARTH, J., Corporal, 2nd Border Regiment.
Volunteering in October 1914, he was retained at home on important duties until November 1915, when he was sent to France. In this theatre of war, he participated in important engagements at Loos, Vimy Ridge, Bullecourt, Havrincourt, Ypres, and on the Somme front. He was later transferred to Italy, and was in action on the Asiago Plateau and the Piave front, where he was wounded. Demobilised in January 1919, he holds the 1914–15 Star, and the General Service and Victory Medals.   57, Southwell St, Harpurhey, Manchester.   Z11518

HOWARTH, J. W., Pte., King's (Liverpool Regt.)
He joined in September 1918, and after completing a period of training, was sent to Ireland, where he was engaged on important duties as a Lewis gunner at various stations. Unable to obtain his transfer to a theatre of war, he nevertheless, rendered valuable services with his unit until November 1919, when he was demobilised.
13, Clifford Street, Lower Openshaw, Manchester.   Z6658A

HOWARTH, R., Private, Royal Fusiliers.
He volunteered in September 1914, and served at various home stations on garrison and other important duties until March 1918, being then drafted to France. Taken prisoner a month later, he was kept in captivity until after the Armistice and was then repatriated and demobilised. He subsequently re-enlisted for service in Russia, where he remained from June to October 1919, when he was finally demobilised, holding the General Service and Victory Medals.
9, Kelsall Street, West Gorton, Manchester.   Z11616

HOWARTH, W., Rifleman, Rifle Brigade.
He was mobilised in August 1914, and was shortly afterwards sent to France, where he was in action at Mons and in the subsequent Retreat, also in the Battles of the Marne, La Bassée, Ypres, Loos, the Somme, Messines and Cambrai. He was severely wounded and taken prisoner in May 1918 during the Retreat of that year. He unfortunately died of his injuries four days later whilst in captivity, and was buried in German territory. He was entitled to the Mons Star, and the General Service and Victory Medals.
        "His memory is cherished with pride."
10, Wragley Street, Miles Platting, Manchester.   Z9586

HOWARTH, W., Private, Welch Regiment.
He volunteered in November 1914, and in April of the following year proceeded to France. There he saw severe fighting in various sectors of the Front and took part in the Battles of Ypres and Loos and many other engagements, and was wounded in action on the Somme. Later he was transferred to Salonika and there served on the Doiran and Struma fronts, until his return home for demobilisation in March 1919. He holds the 1914–15 Star, and the General Service and Victory Medals.
13, Clifford Street, Lower Openshaw, Manchester.   Z6658B

HOWARTH, W., Sergt., 6th K.O. (R. Lancaster Regt.)
Volunteering when war broke out, he proceeded in May of the following year to Egypt, and thence to the Dardanelles, where during the fighting at Suvla Bay, he was wounded. He was sent into hospital at Cairo and on recovery was drafted to Salonika, remaining in this theatre of war until the cessation of hostilities. Returning home, he was demobilised in November 1919, and holds the 1914–15 Star, and the General Service and Victory Medals.
3, St. Clements Place, Ancoats, Manchester.   Z9205A

HOWARTH, W. T., Pte. (Signaller), M.G.C.
He volunteered in August 1914, and after completing a period of training was retained on important duties with his unit at Grantham. In May 1918 he proceeded to the Western Front and took part in engagements in various sectors, and was gassed. Later he was in action throughout the closing operations of the war. He was demobilised in February 1919, and holds the General Service and Victory Medals.
6, Higher Duke Street, Miles Platting, Manchester. Z11904

HOWE, A. H., Private, 1/6th Manchester Regt.
He volunteered in September 1915, and in July of the following year proceeded to the Western Front. There, after taking part in the Battle of the Somme and many minor engagements, he was wounded in action at Arras in April 1917, and invalided to hospital at Newcastle. He returned to France, however, on his recovery, and was again in action at Lens, Cambrai, the Somme and Amiens and fought also in the Retreat and Advance of 1918. He was demobilised in January 1919, and holds the General Service and Victory Medals.
22, Sutherland Street, Hulme, Manchester.   Z6660

HOWE, T., Private, 17th Manchester Regiment.
He volunteered in August 1914, and after undergoing a period of training, served at various stations, where he was engaged on duties of great importance. He was medically unfit for service overseas, and was consequently unable to obtain his transfer to the Front, and in November 1916 was invalided from the Army. He unhappily died at home on February 19th, 1918.
        "Steals on the ear the distant triumph song."
9, Freeman Street, Hulme, Manchester.   Z6661

HOWELL, W., A.B., Royal Navy.
Already in the Navy when war broke out in August 1914, he afterwards served in H.M.S. "Centurion" in the North Sea and various other waters. Engaged chiefly on patrol duties, he also took part in the Battles of Heligoland Bight, the Narrows and Jutland and many minor actions, until the cessation of hostilities. He was discharged in January 1919, and holds the 1914–15 Star, and the General Service and Victory Medals.   14, Dyson Street, Manchester.   Z6662

HOWLLET, T., Private, 21st Manchester Regiment.
He volunteered in September 1914, and in October of the following year was drafted to the Western Front, where he took part in engagements at Loos, St. Eloi, Albert and Vimy Ridge, and also served through the Somme Offensive. He fell fighting at Arras on March 25th, 1917. He was entitled to the 1914–15 Star, and the General Service and Victory Medals.
        "His life for his Country, his soul to God."
236, Viaduct Street, Ardwick, Manchester.   Z3599B

HOWSON, J., Private, 3rd King's (Liverpool Regt.)
He had previously served in India, for six years, but was discharged on account of medical unfitness. In September 1914 he volunteered and was engaged at various stations on important duties with his unit. After rendering very valuable services he was discharged in February 1916.
17, Granville Place, Ancoats, Manchester.   Z9206

HOY, A., Private, 5th Lancashire Fusiliers.
He joined in April 1916, and two months later landed in France. He took part in many important engagements in many sectors of the Front, including those at the Ancre, Arras, Messines and Ypres, where he was wounded in October 1917. After being invalided home he was discharged in September 1918 as medically unfit for further duty. He holds the General Service and Victory Medals.
42, Burton Street, Rochdale Road, Manchester.   Z10463

HOY, A. W., Sergt., 3rd King's (Liverpool Regt.)
Having previously served with the Colours, he re-enlisted in 1915, and was retained at various stations on duties of a highly important nature. He was not successful in obtaining his transfer to a theatre of war, but, nevertheless, rendered very valuable services with his unit. He unfortunately died on May 22nd, 1918, of illness contracted whilst in the Army.
        "He joined the great white company of valiant souls."
9, Cheltenham Street, Chorlton-on-Medlock, Manchester.

HOYES, J., Corporal, Lancashire Fusiliers.
Mobilised in August 1914, he was drafted to Egypt in the following month, and thence proceeded to Gallipoli in April 1915. Wounded in action, he was invalided home in May of that year, but on his recovery in September, proceeded to Mesopotamia, where he served with the Kut Relief Force. Later he was transferred to the Western Front in time to take part in the Retreat and Advance of 1918, and was finally discharged on his return to England in February 1919. He holds the 1914–15 Star, and the General Service and Victory Medals.   36, Fenn Street, Hulme, Manchester.   Z6666

HOYLE, R., Private, 5th Manchester Regiment.
He joined in September 1916, and in March of the following year proceeded to the Western Front, where he was severely wounded in action during heavy fighting at Givenchy. Immediately invalided home, he was in hospital in England until September 1918, when he was discharged as medically unfit for further service. He holds the General Service and Victory Medals.   19, Anson Street, Hulme, Manchester.   Z6664

HOYLE, J., Gunner, R.F.A.
Volunteering in August 1914, he was drafted to Egypt in May of the following year and there saw much severe fighting, taking part in the engagements at Mersa Matruh, Agagia, Sollum, Romani and Magdhaba. In January 1917, he was transferred to the Western Front, where he served through the Battles of Arras, Vimy Ridge, Ypres, Cambrai, and the Somme, and other engagements, until invalided home. He was demobilised in February 1919, and holds the 1914-15, Star, and the General Service and Victory Medals. Z6663
13, Florence Street, Morton Street, Longsight, Manchester.

HOYLE, J., Special War Worker.
He had previously served with the Colours, but was discharged from the Army Reserve in December 1915. He was after-wards engaged on work of National importance at Messrs. Charles Mackintosh and Co.'s, Electrical Engineers, where employed on various responsible duties in connection with the output of munitions of war, he rendered very valuable services. He was still with the firm in 1920.
1, Clyde Street, Chorlton-on-Medlock, Manchester.　X6665

HOYLE, W., Driver, R.F.A.
Volunteering in August 1914, he was drafted to the Western Front in the following May, and whilst in this theatre of war played a prominent part with his Battery in the Battles of Festubert, Vermelles, the Somme, Ypres (III), Passchendaele and Cambrai. He was demobilised in February 1919, and holds the 1914-15 Star, and the General Service and Victory Medals.
14, Fletcher Square, Hulme, Manchester.　Z11733

HOYNE, W., Pte., K.O. (Royal Lancaster Regt.)
He volunteered in November 1915, and in the following May proceeded to France, where he saw severe fighting in various sectors of the Front. He took part in the Battles of Vermelles, Vimy Ridge, the Ancre, Lens, Cambrai and the Marne, and many other important engagements, and was gassed at Ypres in July 1917. He was demobilised in March 1919, and holds the General Service and Victory Medals.
70, Thomas Street, West Gorton, Manchester.　TZ6667

HUDSON, C., Private, 8th Manchester Regiment.
He volunteered in January 1915, and on completion of his training, served with his unit at various stations on guard and other important duties in England and the Isle of Man. He was unsuccessful in obtaining his transfer to a theatre of war, but rendered valuable services until demobilised in December 1919.　144, Bradford St., Hulme, Manchester.　Z11734

HUDSON, J., Pte., Manchester Regiment.
He joined in March 1917, and in the following June was drafted overseas. He served principally at Abbeville and Rouen on guard duties, but unfortunately contracted an illness, through which he was invalided home and subsequently discharged in May 1918. He holds the General Service and Victory Medals.　3, Sidney Street, Bradford, Manchester.　Z9207

HUDSON, L., Driver, R.E.
He joined in May 1916, and after a period of training was retained on important duties at various stations, where he did much useful work with his Company. He was unable to obtain his transfer overseas before the cessation of hostilities, but in May 1919 proceeded with the Army of Occupation to Turkey, where he was stationed at Constantinople. He also served for a time in Salonika, before returning home for de-mobilisation in May 1920.
74, Dale Street, Hulme, Manchester.　TZ6668

HUDSON, W., Private, Royal Irish Fusiliers.
Volunteering in August 1914, he embarked for France in the following October, and was in action at La Bassée, Ypres, and Loos, He then proceeded to Salonika, and after two years' service there was sent to Egypt and served at Cairo and Alex-andria. He was discharged in September 1919, through causes due to his service, and later unfortunately died. He was entitled to the 1914-15 Star, and the General Service and Victory Medals.
　　　　　"Great deeds cannot die."
73, Long Street, Ancoats, Manchester.　Z11411B

HUDSON, W. G., Private, Tank Corps.
He volunteered in September 1915, and in the following year was drafted to France, and thence to Egypt. He took part in the Advance into Palestine, and was in action at Gaza, and present at the entry into Jerusalem. Returning home in November 1919, he was demobilised, holding the General Service and Victory Medals.
6, Bath Street, Newton Heath, Manchester.　Z10431

HUGHES, C., Private, Royal Scots.
He volunteered in December 1914, and in July 1916 was sent to the Western Front, and took part in many battles including that at Vimy Ridge, and was wounded. On recovery he was drafted to Egypt, and whilst en route his ship was torpedoed, but he was fortunately rescued, and later proceeded to France, where he remained until after the Armistice. Demobilised in February 1919, he holds the General Service and Victory Medals.　48, Victoria Road, Gorton, Manchester.　Z10433

HUGHES, C. L., Private, 7th Manchester Regt.
He joined in October 1917, and after completing a period of training was engaged on important duties with his unit at various stations. He was unable to obtain his transfer overseas before the cessation of hostilities, on account of his youth, but later proceeded to the Western Front. He was demobilised on his return to England in February 1919.
7, Baker Street, Longsight, Manchester.　Z6672

HUGHES, E., Private, 1st Manchester Regiment.
He volunteered in August 1914, and in April of the following year was drafted to the Western Front, where he saw heavy fighting in various sectors. After taking part in the Battles of Ypres and Loos, and many minor engagements, he was severely wounded in action on the Somme in July 1916, and invalided to hospital at Glasgow. He was discharged in May 1917, as medically unfit for further service, and holds the 1914-15 Star, and the General Service and Victory Medals.
138, Harrold Street, Bradford, Manchester.　Z6673

HUGHES, E., Private, 12th Manchester Regiment.
Mobilised when war was declared he proceeded with his Regi-ment to France and took part in the memorable Retreat from Mons. He was also in action in many other engagements, including those of Ypres, Vimy Ridge, the Somme, and Arras. In March 1918, he was discharged on account of his service, and holds the Mons Star, and the General Service and Victory Medals.　212, Cobden St., Ancoats, Manchester.　Z10436

HUGHES, E., Private, 1/7th Manchester Regiment.
He volunteered in December 1915, and in July of the following year was drafted to the Western Front. Whilst in this theatre of war, he took part in many important engagements, in-cluding the Battles of the Somme, Arras, Bullecourt, Ypres and Cambrai, and fought also in the Retreat and Advance of 1918. Returning home in February 1919, he was demobilised in the following month, and holds the General Service and Victory Medals.
40, Gregory Street, Ardwick, Manchester.　Z6670

HUGHES, E., Private, 13th Lancashire Fusiliers.
He volunteered in September 1914, and after a short period of training served at various stations, where he was engaged on duties of great importance. He was unable to obtain his transfer overseas on account of ill-health, but nevertheless, rendered valuable services with his unit until May 1915, when he was invalided from the Army.
55, Cawder Street, Hulme, Manchester.　Z6675A

HUGHES, E., Private, East Lancashire Regiment.
He joined in November 1916, and after two months' training, proceeded to Salonika, where he saw much severe fighting. He took part in many important engagements on the Doiran and Vardar fronts until he contracted dysentery, and was invalided to hospital at Curragh. He was ultimately dis-charged, as medically unfit for further service, in September 1919, and holds the General Service and Victory Medals.
55, Cawder Street, Hulme, Manchester.　Z6675B

HUGHES. E. C., Bombardier, R.F.A.
Volunteering in November 1914, he embarked in May of the following year for the Western Front. Whilst there he took part in many engagements, including those at Ypres, Festubert, Loos, and the Somme, and was unhappily killed in action during the fighting in the Ypres sector on April 27th, 1917. He was entitled to the 1914-15 Star, and the General Service and Victory Medals.
　　　"His life for his Country, his soul to God."
7, Ritson Street, West Gorton, Manchester.　Z10434

HUGHES, F., Private, 1st Cheshire Regiment.
Mobilised on the declaration of war, he immediately proceeded with the British Expeditionary Force to France, and during the memorable Retreat from Mons was taken prisoner. He was held in captivity until after hostilities ceased, and in January 1919 was discharged, holding the Mons Star, and the General Service and Victory Medals.
5, Penley Street, Manchester.　TZ9208

HUGHES, F., Private, 8th Lancashire Fusiliers.
Volunteering in August 1914, he was drafted to Gallipoli in April of the following year and there, after taking part in the Landing at Cape Helles, saw much severe fighting. He made the supreme sacrifice, falling in action on June 6th, 1915, at Krithia. He was entitled to the 1914-15 Star, and the General Service and Victory Medals.
　"A valiant Soldier, with undaunted heart he breasted life's last hill."
8, New Square, West Gorton, Manchester.　Z6674

HUGHES, F., Private, 2/9th Durham Light Infantry.
Volunteering in December 1915, he was engaged until February 1917, on important duties in England. He then proceeded to Salonika, and took part in the fighting on the Struma, Vardar and Doiran fronts. Returning home he was de-mobilised in September 1919, holding the General Service and Victory Medals.
16, Rennie Street, West Gorton, Manchester.　Z10435

HUGHES, F., Sergt., 1st Manchester Regiment.

He was already serving in India when war broke out in August 1914, and was immediately drafted to the Western Front. There he took part in the Battles of La Bassée, Hill 60, Ypres, Festubert, Loos and Albert, was wounded in action at Neuve Chapelle, and on being wounded a second time on the Somme, was invalided home. He returned to France, however, on his recovery, and was again twice wounded, in the third and fourth Battles of Ypres. He was finally invalided from the Army in March 1919, and holds the 1914 Star, and the General Service and Victory Medals.
26A, Allen Street, Hulme, Manchester.   Z6681

HUGHES, G., Pte., K.O. (Royal Lancaster Regt.)

After volunteering in August 1914, he underwent a period of training prior to being drafted to the Western Front in February 1917. There he took part in the Battles of the Ancre, Arras, Vimy Ridge, Messines, Ypres and Cambrai, and many minor engagements in various sectors, and was gassed on the Somme in March 1918. Invalided to hospital in England, he was finally demobilised in February 1919. He holds the General Service and Victory Medals.
9, Sorrell Street, Hulme, Manchester.   Z6677

HUGHES, H., Private, 17th Manchester Regiment.

He volunteered in September 1914, and in January of the following year embarked for France, where he took part in engagements at La Bassée, St. Eloi, Loos, Vimy Ridge, and Beaumont-Hamel. During the Battle of the Somme, he was reported missing, and is presumed to have been killed in action in July 1916. He was entitled to the 1914-15 Star, and the General Service and Victory Medals.
"Honour to the immortal dead, who gave their youth that the world might grow old in peace."
11, Lorne Street, Moss Side, Manchester.   Z10464

HUGHES, G. E., L/Corpl., K.O. (R. Lancaster Regt.)

Volunteering in August 1914, he was drafted to the Western Front on completing two months' training, and there fought in the Battles of Neuve Chapelle, Hill 60, Festubert and Loos, and many other important engagements in various sectors. He fell in action in November 1916, near Loos, and was buried in the British Cemetery there. He was entitled to the 1914 Star, and the General Service and Victory Medals.
"He joined the great white company of valiant souls."
8, Ernest Street, Ancoats, Manchester.   Z6032B

HUGHES, H., Private, R.A.S.C. (M.T.)

He volunteered in September 1914, and in January of the following year was drafted to France. In that theatre of war he was engaged on important transport duties at Neuve Chapelle, St. Eloi, Hill 60, Festubert, Loos, Vermelles, the Somme, Arras, Bullecourt, and Bapaume. He was demobilised in April 1919, and holds the 1914-15 Star, and the General Service and Victory Medals.
48, Irlam Street, Miles Platting, Manchester.   Z9587

HUGHES, J., Private, King's (Liverpool Regiment).

He volunteered in June 1916, and in the following October crossed to France. There he was in action in many engagements, including those on the Somme, and at Arras, Messines, Bullecourt, Ypres and Cambrai. He also took part in the Retreat and Advance of 1918, during which time he was wounded. After demobilisation in 1919, he re-enlisted, and in 1920 was still serving. He holds the General Service and Victory Medals.
152, Hamilton Street, Collyhurst, Manchester.   Z10438B

HUGHES, J. E., Pte., 6th K.O.(Royal Lancaster Rgt.)

Joining in July 1916, he was sent in September of the following year to the East. He saw much active service in Mesopotamia, and took part in the fighting at Kut, and on the Tigris. In August 1918, he was invalided to England with malaria, afterwards remaining on light duties until demobilised in March 1919. He holds the General Service and Victory Medals.
54, Tame Street, Ancoats, Manchester.   TZ9209

HUGHES, J. E., Private, 21st Manchester Regt.

He joined in March 1917, and landing in France three months later fought in engagements in the Ypres and Somme sectors. Later he proceeded to Italy, but after serving there for a time returned to the Western Front, and took part in the fighting at Arras and Givenchy and was wounded. He was invalided to hospital in England, and eventually demobilised in February 1919, holding the General Service and Victory Medals.
18, Flower Street, Ancoats, Manchester.   Z10440B

HUGHES, J. W., Private, R.A.M.C.

He volunteered in May 1915, and in January of the following year was drafted to Malta, where he was engaged on various important duties for twelve months. He was then transferred to Salonika, and was engaged on similar work on the Macedonian front, where he rendered valuable services until after the cessation of hostilities. He returned home for demobilisation in March 1919, and holds the General Service and Victory Medals.
70, Blackthorn Street, Ardwick, Manchester.   Z6682

HUGHES, J. W., Gunner, R.F.A.

Volunteering in September 1914, he was drafted in the following year to France, and thence to Salonika. In this theatre of war he saw much heavy fighting on the Doiran and Vardar

fronts. Later he unfortunately died through causes due to his service on June 30th, 1917. He was entitled to the 1914-15 Star, and the General Service and Victory Medals.
"Thinking that remembrance, though unspoken, may reach him where he sleeps."
34, Butterworth Street, Bradford, Manchester.   Z10437B

HUGHES, L., Private, 22nd Manchester Regiment.

He volunteered in May 1915, and shortly afterwards proceeded overseas. During his service on the Western Front, he saw much heavy fighting in various sectors, was in action in the Battle of the Somme, and was badly wounded. In July 1916, he unfortunately died of his wounds. He was entitled to the 1914-15 Star, and the General Service and Victory Medals.
"His memory is cherished with pride."
12, Fielden Street, Oldham Road, Manchester.   Z11905B

HUGHES, P., Pte., 1st Loyal North Lancashire Regt.

Mobilised on the outbreak of war, he was shortly afterwards drafted to France, and fought in the Retreat from Mons, and the Battle of Ypres, where he was wounded. He was invalided home, but on his recovery returned to the trenches, and took part in the fighting until hostilities ceased. Demobilised in June 1919, he holds the Mons Star, and the General Service and Victory Medals.
18, Flower Street, Ancoats, Manchester.   Z10440A

HUGHES, R., Pte., 7th Royal Warwickshire Regt.

He volunteered in August 1914, and in May of the following year was drafted to Gallipoli, where he took part in the third Battle of Krithia and in fighting at Suvla Bay. In October 1915 he was invalided home, suffering from dysentery, but, on his recovery in May 1916, proceeded to the Western Front, and there served through the Battles of the Somme, Arras, Ypres and Cambrai and was twice wounded in action—at Laventie in August 1916, and near Merville in June 1918. He was for a time in hospital in London, before being invalided from the Army in October 1918, and holds the 1914-15 Star, and the General Service and Victory Medals.
13, Derby Street, Ardwick, Manchester.   Z6678

HUGHES, R., Sergt., 2nd Lancashire Fusiliers.

A Reservist, he was mobilised on the declaration of war, and proceeded with his Regiment to France. He was in action in the Retreat from Mons, and at Armentières, and was wounded and invalided home. On recovery he was drafted to the Dardanelles. After the Evacuation of the Peninsula he returned to the Western Front, took part in the fighting there and was wounded on two further occasions. Demobilised in August 1919, he holds the Mons Star, and the General Service and Victory Medals.
34, Butterworth Street, Bradford, Manchester.   Z10437A

HUGHES, R. R., Private, South Lancashire Regt.

He volunteered in April 1915, and after having completed his training proceeded to France, and amongst other places was in action at Loos. He was unfortunately killed by a bomb during the fighting on the Somme on April 29th, 1917, and was entitled to the General Service and Victory Medals.
"The path of duty was the way to glory."
2, Lime Street, Bradford, Manchester.   Z10441

HUGHES, T., Sapper, R.E.

He was already serving in India at the outbreak of hostilities, and was immediately drafted to the Western Front. There he saw much active service in various sectors, and took part in the engagements at Ypres, Passchendaele and Kemmel Hill. He also served for a period in Italy, Serbia and Greece. In May 1919, he was demobilised, and holds the 1914-15 Star, and the General Service and Victory Medals.
12, Fielden Street, Oldham Road, Manchester.   Z11905A

HUGHES, T., Private, East Lancashire Regiment.

Volunteering in September 1914, he was drafted in the following year to France, where he served for about three months. He then proceeded to Salonika and was in action on the Doiran, Struma and Vardar fronts, remaining in the East until after the Armistice. Returning home he was demobilised in February 1919, and holds the 1914-15 Star, and the General Service and Victory Medals.
152, Hamilton Street, Collyhurst, Manchester.   Z10438A

HUGHES, W., Special War Worker.

Throughout the period of hostilities, he was engaged on work of National importance at the Ship Canal Dry Docks at Manchester. There, employed on various responsible duties in connection with the repair of sea-going vessels, he rendered very valuable services during the war, and in recognition of his good work, has received a Certificate of Merit.   TX6680
91, Cottenham Street, Chorlton-on-Medlock, Manchester.

HUGHES, W., Private, Royal Welch Fusiliers.

Volunteering in October 1915, he was drafted to the Western Front in May of the following year, and there saw severe fighting in various sectors. After taking part in engagements at Vermelles and Vimy Ridge, and many other places during the Advance on the Somme, he was invalided home, suffering from shell-shock. In hospital for a time at Liverpool, he was finally discharged in November 1916, as medically unfit for further service, and holds the General Service and Victory Medals. 13, Buckingham Street, Moss Side, Manchester.   Z6679

HUGHES, W., Gunner, R.F.A.

He volunteered in August 1914, and in July of the following year, proceeded to Egypt, where he saw much severe fighting, taking part in the engagements at Mersa Matruh, Agagia and Sollum. In May 1916 he was transferred to the Western Front, and there served through the Battles of the Somme and Arras. He was sent home in July 1917, suffering from bronchitis, and in the following March was invalided from the Army. He holds the 1914-15 Star, and the General Service and Victory Medals.

4, Shakespeare Row, Ardwick, Manchester.   Z6669

HUGHES, W., Private, Seaforth Highlanders.

Five months after joining in June 1916, he was drafted to France, where he saw heavy fighting in various sectors of the Front. He took part in the Battles of the Ancre, Arras, Bullecourt, Ypres and Passchendaele, and also served through engagements at Beaumont-Hamel, Beaucourt, Lens and other places, until severely gassed on the Somme in January 1918. Admitted to hospital in England, he was finally invalided from the Army in July 1918, and holds the General Service and Victory Medals.

3, Sutherland Street, Hulme, Manchester.   Z6676

HUGHES, W. E., L/Corporal, R.A.S.C.

He volunteered in September 1914, and was immediately drafted to the Western Front, Whilst in this theatre of war he rendered valuable services with his unit in various important sectors, including those of Ypres (where he was wounded and gassed in 1915), Arras, Vimy Ridge, and Cambrai. He was demobilised in May 1919, and holds the 1914 Star, and the General Service and Victory Medals.

31, Shakespeare Street, Bradford, Manchester.   Z11735

HUGHES, W. R., Private, R.A.M.C.

Having enlisted in August 1912, he was drafted to the Western Front six months after the outbreak of war two years later. There he was severely wounded in action at Hill 60, but after a considerable period in hospital at Boulogne, re-joined his Company, and was again wounded at Mametz in June 1916. He was for six months in hospital at Rouen, and was then transferred to Palestine, where he remained on various duties until the cessation of hostilities. Discharged in October 1919, he holds the 1914-15 Star, and the General Service and Victory Medals.

32, Westmoreland Street, Longsight, Manchester.   Z6671

HUGHSON, J. H., Private, 1st Manchester Regt.

He enlisted in June 1906, and before the war served in India. He was sent to France in August 1914, and was in action in the Retreat from Mons, the Battles of the Marne, the Aisne, La Bassée, Ypres, Neuve Chapelle, St. Eloi, Albert, Festubert and the Somme. In December 1916 he was transferred to Egypt, and was in action at Magdhaba, Gaza, Jerusalem and Jericho. He was demobilised in February 1919, and holds the Mons Star, and the General Service and Victory Medals.

82, Heyrod Street, Ancoats, Manchester.   Z10442

HULL, R. J., Private, 16th Manchester Regiment.

He volunteered in August 1914, and in November of the following year embarked for the Western Front. There he took part in the Battles of the Somme (I), Arras (I), Ypres (III), and Cambrai (I), and also served through the Retreat and Advance of 1918. After over three years in France he was demobilised in January 1919, and holds the 1914-15 Star, and the General Service and Victory Medals.

26, Pleasant Street, Harpurhey, Manchester.   Z9210A

HULL, S., Private, K.O. (Y.L.I.)

He volunteered in October 1915, when under military age, and after completing his training proceeded to the Western Front, where he was in action at Albert, Ypres and the Somme, during the Retreat and Advance of 1918. He returned home, and was demobilised in February 1919, holding the 1914-15 Star, and the General Service and Victory Medals.

85, Gunson Street, Ancoats, Manchester.   Z10443

HULL, W. R., Telegraphist, R.N., H.M.S. "Robina."

He joined in October 1916, and in July 1917 was sent to sea in H.M.S. "Eske" in which vessel he was engaged on mine-sweeping duties. He was also employed in the mystery ship "Hyderabad" off Sheerness and Harwich and afterwards in H.M.S. "Robina" on patrol work. Returning to shore, he was demobilised in January 1919, and holds the General Service and Victory Medals.

26, Pleasant Street, Harpurhey, Manchester.   Z9210B

HULLEY, G., Private, King's (Liverpool Regt.)

He volunteered in September 1914, and twelve months later proceeded to the Western Front, where he fought in various sectors. After taking part in engagements at Ypres, and on the Ancre, and at many other places, he was severely wounded in action at St. Eloi in March 1916, and was invalided home. He was discharged, as medically unfit for further service in August 1917, and holds the 1914-15 Star, and the General Service and Victory Medals.

49, Forbes Street, West Gorton, Manchester.   Z6683

HULME, A., Pte., 1/7th Manchester Regt. (T.F.)

A Territorial, he was mobilised in August 1914, and proceeded to Egypt in May 1915. After a month's service on the Suez

---

Canal, he was sent to the Dardanelles, and took part in the Battles of Krithia, and in other important engagements until the Evacuation of the Gallipoli Peninsula. He was then transferred to the Western Front, where he fought at Loos, Albert, the Somme, Vimy Ridge, Arras and Ypres, and was four times wounded in action. He holds the 1914-15 Star, and the General Service and Victory Medals, and was demobilised in January 1919.

66, Juniper Street, Hulme, Manchester.   TZ11906

HULME, E., Pte., Queen's (Royal West Surrey Regt.)

After joining in May 1916, he underwent a period of training prior to being drafted to the Western Front in January 1918. There he saw much severe fighting in various sectors and took part in the Battles of the Somme, and the Marne, and many other important engagements, and afterwards served at Etaples and Valenciennes. He was demobilised in March 1919, and holds the General Service and Victory Medals.

91, Dorset Street, Hulme, Manchester.   Z6686

HULME, H., Sergt., 15th York and Lancaster Regt.

He volunteered at the age of fifty-five in September 1914, and was engaged at various stations on important duties with his unit. He was employed as Drill Instructor in training recruits for overseas, and rendered valuable services, though not successful in obtaining his transfer overseas. He unhappily contracted an illness, which caused his discharge as medically unfit for further service, in February 1916.

21, Robert Street, Newton Heath, Manchester.   Z9588

HULME, H. Private, 8th Lancashire Fusiliers.

Volunteering in August 1914, he was drafted to the Dardanelles in April of the following year, and there, after taking part in the Landing at Cape Helles, and the Battles of Krithia, was severely wounded in action at Suvla Bay. In hospital for a time at Cairo he was afterwards invalided home, and was for a few months at Liverpool before being discharged in February 1916, as medically unfit for further service. He holds the 1914-15 Star, and the General Service and Victory Medals.   16, Smithson Street, Hulme, Manchester.   Z6684

HULMES, C., Private, East Lancashire Regiment.

Volunteering in August 1914, in the following month he was drafted to Egypt, and after serving in the Canal zone proceeded to Gallipoli in April 1915. He was in action in many engagements, and after the Evacuation of the Peninsula returned to England. In August 1916, he was drafted to France and served in many sectors and throughout the Retreat and Advance of 1918. He was demobilised in February 1919, and holds the 1914-15 Star, and the General Service and Victory Medals.

14, Gore Street, Hulme, Manchester.   TZ9211

HULMES, J., Private, 3rd Manchester Regiment, 1st Suffolk Regt., and 1st Loyal N. Lancs. Regt.

Volunteering in August 1914, he was sent to France on completing his training in March of the following year, and there saw much severe fighting. After serving through engagements at Vermelles, Cuinchy, Richebourg, and many other places, he was severely gassed at Loos. He was for a considerable period in hospital in France and England before being invalided from the Army in August 1917, and holds the 1914-15 Star, and the General Service and Victory Medals.

39, Armitage Street, Ardwick, Manchester.   Z6685

HULMES, J. W., Private, Northumberland Fusiliers.

He volunteered in August 1914, and in September of the following year was drafted to Gallipoli, where he saw severe fighting at Chocolate Hill and Suvla Bay. On the Evacuation of the Peninsula, however, he was transferred to the Western Front, and there took part in the Battles of the Somme, Arras, Ypres, Passchendaele and Cambrai, and served also through the Retreat and Advance of 1918. He was demobilised in May 1919, and holds the 1914-15 Star, and the General Service and Victory Medals.

43, Ashover Street, Ardwick, Manchester.   Z6687

HULMES, T., Private, Labour Corps.

He joined in August 1916, and in January of the following year proceeded to the Western Front, where he was engaged on important duties in various sectors. Attached to the R.A.V.C., he was also present at the Battles of Ypres, the Somme, the Aisne, Bapaume and Le Cateau, and took an active part in the Retreat and Advance of 1918. He afterwards served with the Army of Occupation in Germany, and finally returned home for demobilisation in February 1919, holding the General Service and Victory Medals.

112, Main Road, Moss Side, Manchester.   TZ6689

HULMES, T., Private, 2nd Manchester Regiment.

He was mobilised in August 1914, and shortly afterwards was sent to France, where he took part in the Retreat from Mons and the Battle of Le Cateau and was wounded. He was invalided home and after a period in hospital was discharged, owing to his injuries in January 1916. He holds the Mons Star, and the General Service and Victory Medals.

116, Edensor Street, Beswick, Manchester.   Z10444

HULSE, J., Private, R.M.L.I.
A Reservist, he was called to the Colours in August 1914, and was posted to H.M.S. " Celtic," on board which vessel he took part in the Battle of the Falkland Islands. He was afterwards engaged on patrol duties in the North Sea and served through many actions in these waters. He was finally discharged in March 1919, and holds the 1914-15 Star, and the General Service (with clasp Falkland Islands), and Victory Medals.
5, Pitt Street, Ancoats, Manchester. Z6690

HULSE, J. D., Air Mechanic, R.A.F.
He joined in February 1918, and on completion of his training was engaged on special duties in connection with the repair of aeroplanes. He rendered valuable services which called for great skill, but was unsuccessful in obtaining his transfer overseas and was demobilised in December 1919.
57, Henry Street, Ardwick, Manchester. Z11907

HULSE, J. W., Private, M.G.C.
He joined in January 1916, and later in the same year was drafted to Mesopotamia. After being in action at Kut-el-Amara, he was transferred to Egypt, and served at Cairo and Alexandria. He returned home in February 1919, when he was demobilised, and holds the General Service and Victory Medals.
17, Percival Street, Newton Heath, Manchester. Z9589

HULSE, W., Sergt., 1/8th Manchester Regiment.
A Territorial, he was mobilised in August 1914, and a month later was drafted to Egypt, where he served at Alexandria and Cairo. He afterwards proceeded to Gallipoli, and took a conspicuous part in many important engagements, until returning to Malta to undergo an operation. On his recovery, he was attached to the Military Police at Alexandria, and did good work. He was demobilised in June 1919, and holds the 1914-15 Star, and the General Service and Victory Medals.
7, Edgeley Street, Ardwick, Manchester. Z11736A

HULSE, W., Pte., Lancashire Fusiliers, and R.A.O.C.
He joined in August 1918, and on completing his training two months later was drafted to France, where he served at Boulogne, Calais, and various other stations. He was engaged on duties of a highly technical nature with the R.A.O.C. whilst overseas, and did much useful work until his return home for demobilisation in March 1920. He holds the General Service and Victory Medals.
7, Edgeley Street, Ardwick, Manchester. Z11736B

HULSTON, J., Private, Labour Corps.
He volunteered in July 1915, and after his training was engaged at various stations on important duties with his unit. He rendered valuable services, but was not successful in obtaining his transfer overseas, and was discharged in December 1917, owing to a defect of the eyes.
7, Teignmouth Street, Rochdale Road, Manchester. Z9590

HULSTON, J. M., Pte., York and Lancaster Regt.
He joined in November 1917, and in January of the following year was drafted to the Western Front, where he took part in numerous engagements, including those at Ypres, and Cambrai. He also served in the Retreat and Advance of 1918. He afterwards contracted an illness and admitted into hospital received treatment. He was demobilised in February 1919, and holds the General Service and Victory Medals.
81, Elliott Street, Bradford, Manchester. Z10445A

HULSTON, J. W., Private, East Lancashire Regt.
Having volunteered in September 1914, and completed his training was sent to Plymouth for duty. He unfortunately met with an accident which resulted in his being discharged as medically unfit for further service in January 1915.
81, Elliott Street, Bradford, Manchester. Z10445B

HULSTON, T., Driver, R.F.A.
Volunteering in April 1915, he was sent to the Western Front in the following October, and fought in the Battles of the Somme, Arras, and Cambrai. He was also engaged in heavy fighting throughout the German Offensive and subsequent Allied Advance of 1918. Returning home, he was demobilised in April 1920, and holds the 1914-15 Star, and the General Service and Victory Medals.
3, Somerset Square, Oldham Road, Manchester. Z9212

HULSTON, T., Private, Leicestershire Regiment.
He joined in August 1917, and after a period of training, was drafted to the Western Front in March of the following year. Whilst in this theatre of war, he saw much severe fighting in various sectors during the Retreat and Advance of 1918, was gassed in September of that year, and admitted to hospital at Trouville, but on his recovery, rejoined his unit, and was again gassed. He afterwards served with the Army of Occupation, and was finally demobilised on his return home in 1919. He holds the General Service and Victory Medals.
21, Marlow Street, Longsight, Manchester. Z6691

HULSTON, W. E., Corporal, Manchester Regiment.
Four months after volunteering in September 1914, he proceeded to the Western Front, where he took part in important engagements in various sectors. He was unhappily killed whilst endeavouring to save the life of an officer during the Somme Offensive of July 1916, and was buried at Trônes Wood.

He was entitled to the 1914-15 Star, and the General Service and Victory Medals.
" He passed out of the sight of men by the path of duty and self-sacrifice."
35, Westmoreland Street, Longsight, Manchester. Z6692A

HULSTON, W. H., Pte., 1/10th Manchester Regt.
He joined in November 1916, and served at various depôts with his unit on important duties. He did not obtain his transfer overseas prior to the cessation of hostilities, but shortly after the Armistice proceeded to France, where he was engaged on guard duties at various prisoners-of-war camps. He was demobilised in November 1919.
34, Gunson Street, off Oldham Road, Manchester. Z9213

HUMPHREYS, E. N., Pte., 4th K.O. (Royal Lancaster Regiment).
He joined in September 1917, and after two months' training was drafted to the Western Front, where he was severely wounded in action in the first Battle of Cambrai in the same month. Invalided to hospital in London, he was finally discharged in February 1918, as medically unfit for further service. He holds the General Service and Victory Medals.
30, Salisbury Street, Moss Side, Manchester. Z6693

HUMPHREYS. H. V., Pte., 4th Lancashire Fusiliers.
He was mobilised in August 1914, and a month later was drafted to the Western Front, where he played an important part in the Battles of the Marne, the Aisne, Hill 60, Loos, Albert, the Somme, Arras, Messines, the Marne (II), Havrincourt, and Le Cateau. He was gassed in action at Hill 60, May 1915, and spent some time in hospital at Rouen, before rejoining his unit He holds the 1914 Star, and the General Service and Victory Medals., and was discharged in February 1919. 27, Power Street, Ardwick, Manchester. Z6695

HUMPHREYS, W., Private, R.A.S.C.
He volunteered in August 1914, and in the following January was drafted to the Western Front, where he was engaged on important transport duties in the forward areas. In May 1915 he was seriously wounded at Ypres, and was invalided home. After twelve months under treatment in hospital at Chester, he was discharged in May 1916 as medically unfit for further service, and holds the 1914-15 Star, and the General Service and Victory Medals.
8, Oliver Street, Chorlton-on-Medlock, Manchester. Z6694

HUMPHRIES, J., Private, 4th Lancashire Fusiliers.
Volunteering in September 1914, he was sent to France in the following November and took part in the heavy fighting at Loos, St. Eloi, Albert, and Vimy Ridge in 1916. He was also in action at the Battles of Vermelles, the Somme, the Ancre, Arras, Ypres, and Lens, and was taken prisoner during the second Battle of the Somme in March 1918. At the cessation of hostilities, he was repatriated, and in March 1919 was demobilised, holding the 1914-15 Star, and the General Service and Victory Medals.
14, Mallow Street, Hulme, Manchester. Z6696

HUNSTON, W. T., Pte., 37th Labour Bn. and K.O. (Royal Lancaster Regt.)
Joining in March 1917, he was drafted to France in the same month, and was engaged at Albert, Loos, the Somme, Arras, Lens, Bullecourt, Mericourt, and La Bassée, owing to ill-health he was invalided home, but returned to France in 1918, and took part in the Retreat and Advance of that year. Afterwards he was employed with the Royal Army Ordnance Corps in the Arras sector. He was demobilised in December 1920, and holds the General Service and Victory Medals.
7, Almond Street, Gorton, Manchester. Z10446

HUNT, H., Private, 16th Lancashire Fusiliers.
Three months after volunteering in November 1914, he was drafted to the Western Front, where he took part in the Battles of Neuve Chapelle, St. Eloi, Hill 60, Ypres (II), Albert, the Somme, the Ancre, Arras, Vimy Ridge, Ypres (III), the Marne (II), Havrincourt, and Cambrai (II). He was demobilised on his return to England in February 1919, and holds the 1914-15 Star, and the General Service and Victory Medals.
6, Gladstone Street, Brook's Bar, Manchester. TZ6697

HUNT, H., Private, 21st Manchester Regiment.
Having volunteered in April 1915, he was sent to the Western Front in January of the following year, and was in action at Loos, Vimy Ridge, and the Somme. He was severely wounded and invalided home, died of his injuries at Springburn Military Hospital, Glasgow, in August 1916 and was buried in Phillip Port Cemetery, Manchester. He was entitled to the General Service and Victory Medals.
" His life for his Country."
11, Clyde Street, Ancoats, Manchester. Z10447B

HUNT, J., L/Corporal, King's (Liverpool Regt.)
He volunteered in August 1914, and after a period of training was engaged on important duties at prisoner-of-war camps. He rendered valuable services, but was unsuccessful in obtaining his transfer overseas, and was invalided from the Army in March 1916.
9, Hamlet Street, Ardwick, Manchester. TX6700

HUNT, H., Private, 2/6th Manchester Regiment.

He joined in May 1916, and after a period of training was drafted to the Western Front in March 1917. During his five months' service in this theatre of war, he took part in the Battles of Bullecourt, Messines, and Ypres (III), where he was badly wounded in action in July 1917, and invalided home to hospital at Stockport. On his recovery, he was retained on important duties in England until his demobilisation in January 1919, holding the General Service and Victory Medals.

13, Etruria Street, Longsight, Manchester.   Z6698

HUNT, R., Sergt., 1/8th Manchester Regiment.

He was mobilised with the Territorials in August 1914, and in the following month was drafted to Egypt, where he took part in heavy fighting in the Suez Canal zone until April 1915. He was then transferred to the Dardanelles, and served with distinction at the 2nd and 3rd Battles of Krithia, being badly wounded during the latter in June 1915. Invalided to England he was transferred to Class W. Army Reserve, on his recovery, and was engaged on work of National importance at Garland's Brook Forge, Ardwick. He holds the 1914–15 Star, and the General Service and Victory Medals.

9, Gregory Street, West Gorton, Manchester.   Z6699

HUNT, W., Private, 6th Manchester Regiment.

He joined in May 1918, and was sent to France in the following October, where he served as a machine-gunner. After the Armistice he proceeded to Namur in Belgium, where he remained till November 1919, when he returned home, and was demobilised, holding the General Service and Victory Medals.

11, Clyde Street, Ancoats, Manchester.   Z10447A

HUNTER, G., Corporal, 16th (The Queen's) Lancers.

A Reservist, he was called to the Colours in August 1914, and immediately drafted to France, where he served with distinction at the Battle of Mons, and in the subsequent Retreat. He was also in action at the Battles of Neuve Chapelle, Loos, the Somme, Arras, Messines, Ypres, Passchendaele, and Cambrai, where he was wounded in 1917. On his recovery, he rejoined his unit and fought throughout the Retreat and Advance of 1918. After the cessation of hostilities he served on the Rhine with the Army of Occupation until his discharge in May 1919, and holds the Queen's and King's South African Medals (with seven bars), the Mons Star, and the General Service and Victory Medals.

127, Cross Street, Bradford, Manchester.   Z6701

HUNTINGTON, C., Pte., 21st Manchester Regt.

He volunteered in November 1914, and on completion of his training in the following year, was drafted to France. During his service on the Western Front, he was transferred to the Labour Corps, with which unit he did consistently good work in various sectors, and was unfortunately injured as the result of an accident. He was demobilised in February 1919, and holds the 1914–15 Star, and the General Service and Victory Medals.

30, Ogilvie Street, Chorlton-on-Medlock, Manchester. X6702

HUNTON, S., Sapper, R.E.

Volunteering in May 1915, he was sent to France in the following August, and was engaged on important duties in connection with road and bridge construction, and on the light railways at Boulogne and Calais. He also took part in the Battles of Arras, Messines, Ypres (where he was wounded in action), and Cambrai, and in the Retreat and Advance of 1918. He was demobilised in September 1919, and holds the 1914–15 Star, and the General Service and Victory Medals.

32, Cuttell Street, Bradford, Manchester.   Z6703

HURD, T., Corporal, 6th Manchester Regiment.

He volunteered in November 1914, and in December of the following year was drafted to France, where he played a prominent part in the Battles of Albert, the Somme, Arras, Ypres (III), and Cambrai, and in the Retreat and Advance of 1918. He was wounded in action during the Somme Offensive in July 1916, and at Arras early in the following year. He holds the 1914–15 Star, and the General Service and Victory Medals, and was demobilised in January 1919.

45, Gladstone Street, West Gorton, Manchester.   Z6704

HURLEY, W. H., L/Corporal, Royal Fusiliers.

Already in the Army at the outbreak of war in August 1914, he was drafted to the Western Front in January 1915, and was continually in action in the Ypres sector until the following June, when he was badly wounded. After hospital treatment in Manchester, and a period of convalescence at Shoreham, he was discharged in July 1916 as medically unfit for further service. He holds the 1914–15 Star, and the General Service and Victory Medals.

3, Overton Street, Hulme, Manchester.   Z6705

HURREN, F. J., Sergt., 1st Loyal N. Lancs. Regt.

He volunteered in January 1915, and in June of the same year was sent to France, and was in action at La Bassée, and Festubert. He fell fighting at the Battle of Loos on September 25th, 1915, and was entitled to the 1914–15 Star, and the General Service and Victory Medals.

"Great deeds cannot die."

6, Drinkwater Street, Harpurhey, Manchester.   Z11427

HURST, E., Private, 22nd Manchester Regiment.

Volunteering in November 1914, he was drafted to the Western Front in November of the following year, and took part in many engagements including those at Loos, St. Eloi, and Vimy Ridge. He was killed in action at the Battle of the Somme in July 1916. He was entitled to the 1914–15 Star, and the General Service and Victory Medals.

"His memory is cherished with pride."

17, Williams Place, Ancoats, Manchester.   Z11417A

HURST, F., Private, 2nd Manchester Regiment.

He joined in October 1916, and shortly afterwards proceeded to the Western Front. In this theatre of hostilities he was employed with his unit on various duties of an important nature, and did uniformly good work. Meeting with an accident in July 1919, he was admitted to hospital, and later evacuated to England, was sent to hospital at Whalley, Blackburn. Eventually demobilised in February 1920, he holds the General Service and Victory Medals.

7, Nelson Place, Rusholme, Manchester.   Z6706

HURST, G., Driver, R.A.S.C.

He joined in August 1917, and in the following November was drafted to the Western Front. Whilst in this theatre of war he rendered valuable services with the remount section, and made repeated journeys from Rouen to the forward areas with horses and mules for various units. He was demobilised in May 1919, and holds the General Service and Victory Medals.

108, Chester Street, Hulme, Manchester.   TZ6707

HURST, J., Private, West Yorkshire Regiment.

He joined in May 1917, and two months later embarked for France, where he was in action in the Battles of Ypres and Cambrai. He fought in many engagements during the German and Allied Offensives of 1918, and was wounded at Cambrai, and lost the sight of his left eye in consequence of his injuries. Returning to England, he received hospital treatment, and subsequently was invalided out of the Service in May 1919. He holds the General Service and Victory Medals.

16, Paris Street, Ancoats, Manchester.   Z9214

HURST, J., Private, 18th Manchester Regiment.

He volunteered in October 1914, and four months later proceeded to the Western Front, where he took part in the Battles of Ypres (II), Loos, Albert, Vimy Ridge, the Somme, and Arras. Severely wounded in action in May 1917, during the last-named engagement, he was in hospital in France and England for twelve months, and was finally discharged as medically unfit for further service in May 1918. He holds the 1914–15 Star, and the General Service and Victory Medals.

16, Stanley Street, Hulme, Manchester.   Z6708

HURST, S., Private, 3rd Manchester Regiment.

Mobilised in August 1914, he quickly proceeded to the Western Front, and played an important part in the Battles of the Marne, the Aisne, La Bassée, Ypres, Neuve Chapelle, St. Eloi, Hill 60, Albert, Vimy Ridge, and the Somme, where he was badly gassed in action in July 1916. He was invalided home, and after treatment in a London hospital, was discharged as medically unfit for further service, holding the 1914 Star, and the General Service and Victory Medals.

14, Moor Street, Winslow Road, Rusholme, Manchester. Z6709

HURSTHOUSE, J. E. (M.S.M.), C.S.M., 8th Manchester Regiment.

Mobilised with the Territorials in August 1914, he was drafted to Egypt in September, and served as a Sergeant there until early in 1915. He was then transferred to the Dardanelles, and played a prominent part in the Landing at Cape Helles, and in the first and second Battles of Krithia. he was badly wounded in action in May 1915, and invalided home on his recovery was promoted to Company Sergeant-Major, and rendered valuable services as an Instructor until his discharge in March 1919. Awarded the Meritorious Service Medal for conspicuously good work, he also holds the 1914–15 Star, and the General Service and Victory Medals.

76, Gibson Street, Ardwick, Manchester.   Z6711

HURSTHOUSE, W., Private, R.A.M.C.

Volunteering in August 1915, he was drafted to the Western Front on completion of his training. During his service in this theatre of war, he played an active part in many important engagements, including the Battles of the Somme and Arras. He was demobilised in 1919, and holds the General Service and Victory Medals.

1, Peel Street, Chorlton-on-Medlock, Manchester.   X6071B

HUSSEY, L., Private, 16th Manchester Regiment.

He volunteered in November 1914, and was engaged on important duties at various stations until July 1916, when he was sent to France. He was engaged in heavy fighting on the Somme, and was wounded at Givenchy. On his recovery he rejoined his unit, and was afterwards in action at Arras and Ypres. He was wounded and taken prisoner at St. Quentin in March 1918, and was held in captivity until the cessation of hostilities. Repatriated, he was demobilised in November 1919, and holds the General Service and Victory Medals.

264, Ridgway Street, Ancoats, Manchester.   Z10448

HUTCHINSON, J. W., Private, Labour Corps.

He joined in December 1917, and in March of the following year was drafted to France, where he was engaged on the construction of light railways, and other important duties. He was present at the Battles of Vimy Ridge, Messines, Ypres, and Cambrai, and served throughout the Retreat and Advance of 1918. He was demobilised in March 1919, and holds the General Service and Victory Medals.

6, Boundary Street, Newton, Manchester. TZ11428

HUTTON, C., Private, 8th Manchester Regiment.

He was mobilised in August 1914, and in the following month he was drafted to Egypt, and thence to Cyprus. In 1915, transferred to the Dardanelles, he took part in the Landing at Cape Helles, the actions at Krithia, Achi Baba, and was wounded and invalided home. On his recovery he was sent to France, and was engaged in the Battles of the Somme, Ypres, and Cambrai, and the Retreat and Advance of 1918, and was again invalided home. He was demobilised in March 1919, and holds the 1914–15 Star, and the General Service and Victory Medals.

10, Howard Street, Ancoats, Manchester. Z10449

HUTTON, E., Private, Manchester Regiment.

He volunteered in September 1914, and twelve months later proceeded to France where he took part in the Battles of the Somme, Arras, Ypres, and Cambrai. He was also in action throughout the Retreat and Advance of 1918. He was mentioned in Despatches for gallantry in the Field and holds the 1914–15 Star, and the General Service and Victory Medals. He was demobilised in March 1919.

34, Seal Street, Collyhurst, Manchester. Z11181A

HUTTON, J. T., Private, South Wales Borderers.

Joining in March 1916, he landed in France in December of the following year, and fought in the Battles of Cambrai and the Somme. He was in action in many engagements during the Retreat and Advance of 1918, serving in many parts of the line. He died gloriously on the Field of Battle on November 4th, 1918, and is buried at Le Cateau. He was entitled to the General Service and Victory Medals.

"He joined the great white company of valiant souls."

33, Boundary Street, Newton, Manchester. Z9215B

HUXLEY, J., Pte., 7th K.O. (Royal Lancaster Regt.)

Volunteering in August 1914, he soon afterwards proceeded to France where he took part in the Battle of Mons, and in the subsequent Retreat; also in the Battles of Ypres, and La Bassée. Wounded in action on the Somme in July 1916, he was invalided home and after spending some time in hospital at Bristol, returned to France and saw further fighting. He was demobilised on his return home, and holds the Mons Star, and the General Service and Victory Medals.

30, Anderton Street, Harpurhey, Manchester. Z11519

HYDE, A., Private, 3rd Manchester Regiment.

Having volunteered in September 1915, he went through a course of training and afterwards served on important duties at various stations with the Military Police. He rendered valuable services, but unfortunately contracted tuberculosis, owing to which he was discharged in November 1916.

8, Hadfield Street, Newton Heath, Manchester. Z9591

HYDE, A., Private, 8th Manchester Regiment.

He volunteered in September 1914, and was engaged on important duties at various depôts until drafted to France in July 1916. He was in action on the Somme, the Ancre, Arras, Messines, Lens, Cambrai, and was wounded on the Somme in August 1918. He was demobilised in March 1919, and holds the General Service and Victory Medals.

8, Hampden Street, W. Gorton, Manchester. Z10450

HYDE, G., Private, 12th Manchester Regiment.

He volunteered in January 1915, and in the following September was drafted to the Gallipoli Peninsula, where he saw much severe fighting for four months. After the Evacuation, he proceeded to Egypt, and was in action on the Suez Canal before being transferred to the Western Front in July 1916. Whilst in France, he took part in the Battles of the Somme (where he was wounded in July 1916), Arras, and Cambrai, and in the Retreat and Advance of 1918. After being wounded he spent some time in hospital in France and England before rejoining his unit. He was demobilised in February 1919, and holds the 1914–15 Star, and the General Service and Victory Medals.

12, Ashbury Street, Openshaw, Manchester. TZ6713

HYDE, H., Private, Border Regiment.

He joined in November 1916, and in the following March was drafted to the Western Front, where he took part in the Battle of Arras, and was seriously wounded in action in April 1917. He was invalided home, and after eight months under treatment in a London Hospital, was discharged as medically unfit for further service in December 1917, holding the General Service and Victory Medals.

47, Welbeck Street, Chorlton-on-Medlock, Manchester. Z6712

HYDE, R., Private, 6th South Lancashire Regiment.

He joined in December 1916, and in the following month embarked for Mesopotamia, where he was in action in the operations, resulting in the capture of Baghdad, and in many other important engagements. He served throughout the final British Advance on Mosul, and returning home was demobilised in March 1919. He holds the General Service and Victory Medals.

31, Nicholson St., Rochdale Rd., Manchester. TZ9216

HYLAND, J., Private, 1st Norfolk Regiment.

He volunteered in December 1915, and after his training, was engaged on important duties in England and Ireland. He rendered valuable services, but was unsuccessful in obtaining his transfer to a theatre of war. During hostilities, he also did duty with the King's Shropshire Light Infantry, the Cheshire Regiment, and the Dorsetshire Regiment, and was demobilised in February 1920.

10, Ravensdale Road, Rusholme, Manchester. Z6241B

HYNES, J., Air Mechanic, R.A.F.

He joined in August 1917, and after his training was engaged at various stations on important duties with his Squadron. He was employed as machine-gun Instructor, and rendered valuable services, but was not successful in obtaining his transfer overseas before the cessation of hostilities. He was demobilised in April 1919.

8, Rigel Street, Ancoats, Manchester. Z10451A

HYNES, J., Driver, R.F.A.

Joining in March 1916, and sent to France in August of the following year he was engaged in heavy fighting at Ypres and Passchendaele, and was gassed. In February 1918, he was transferred to Italy, and was in action on the Asiago Plateau, the Piave, and throughout the final Allied Advance in this theatre of war. He was demobilised in December 1919, and holds the General Service and Victory Medals.

8, Rigel Street, Ancoats, Manchester. Z10451B

HYNES, T., Private, 4th Lancashire Fusiliers.

He joined in April 1917, and after completing his training was engaged with his unit on important duties at various stations in Scotland. He was unable to obtain his transfer to a theatre of war before the Armistice, but rendered valuable services until demobilised in May 1919.

19, Leigh Street, East Ancoats, Manchester. Z10451C

I

IBBERSON, G., Rifleman, 2nd K.R.R.C.

He volunteered in July 1915, and three months later was drafted to the Western Front. There he was in action in engagements at Loos, Albert, the Somme, and Arras, and was wounded and taken prisoner at Nieuport in July 1917. During the period of his captivity he was employed on farm work in Bavaria, and was not released until December 1918. He was demobilised in January 1919, and holds the 1914–15 Star, and the General Service and Victory Medals.

25, Pitt Street, Ancoats, Manchester. Z6714

IBBERSON, G., Private, Royal Fusiliers.

Volunteering in October 1915, he proceeded to the Western Front in the following month, and was there wounded in action at St. Eloi. Admitted to hospital in France, he re-joined his unit, however, on his recovery, and after taking part in engagements at Vimy Ridge, and elsewhere, was wounded a second time at Delville Wood in August 1916, during the Somme Offensive. He was invalided home, but returned to France in March 1917, fought in the Battle of Arras, and was again wounded and taken prisoner near Ypres, in the following month. He was forced, whilst in captivity in Germany to work on the land, and in sugar factories, and was finally demobilised on his release in March 1919. He holds the 1914–15 Star, and the General Service and Victory Medals.

47, Gore Street, Greenheys, Manchester. Z11737

IBBOTSON, C., Private, 17th Manchester Regiment.

At the outbreak of war in August 1914 he volunteered and in the following January was drafted overseas. During his service on the Western Front, he was in action in various sectors of the line, and saw heavy fighting at St. Eloi, Albert, Vimy Ridge, the Somme, the Ancre, Ypres, Cambrai, the Aisne, the Marne, and Havrincourt. He was demobilised in March 1919, and holds the 1914–15 Star, and the General Service and Victory Medals.

24, Georges Avenue, Chester Road, Hulme, Manchester. Z2400A

IDDLES, J., Private, King's (Liverpool Regiment).

Joining in March 1917, he was on completion of his training sent to the Western Front, where he took an active part in engagements in the Arras, Vimy Ridge, Bullecourt, Messines, Ypres, Passchendaele, Lens, Cambrai, the Somme, Amiens, Bapaume, and Havrincourt sectors. Serving in France until demobilised in March 1919, he holds the General Service and Victory Medals.

29, Dale Street, Hulme, Manchester. Z6715

IDDLES, W., L/Cpl., 21st Manchester Regt. and R.E.
He volunteered in December 1914, and in July of the following year was drafted to France, where he saw severe fighting in various sectors of the Front. He took part in the Battles of Loos, Vermelles, Vimy Ridge, the Somme, Bapaume, Cambrai, and the Selle, and many other important engagements, and after the cessation of hostilities, served with the Army of Occupation in Germany. Demobilised on his return home in March 1919, he holds the 1914-15 Star, and the General Service and Victory Medals.
52, Phillip's Street, Hulme, Manchester.   Z11738

IGO, J., Private, R.A.S.C.
He volunteered in January 1915, and in the following April was drafted to France, where he was engaged on important transport duties on the Somme, and at Arras, Nieuport, La Bassée, Ypres, and Cambrai. He remained in this theatre of war till May 1919, when he returned home and was demobilised, holding the 1914-15 Star, and the General Service and Victory Medals. 20, Padgate St., Ancoats, Manchester. TZ9592

ILLINGWORTH, F., Pte., 4th K.O. (R. Lancaster Rgt.)
He volunteered in August 1914, and previously to that had served in the South African Campaign. In November 1914 he proceeded to the Western Front, and was in action at Ypres, Neuve Chapelle, St. Eloi, Ypres II, Festubert, and Loos, and was wounded at Ypres. On his recovery he acted as Sergeant in charge of rations for his Division until invalided out of the Army in November 1917. He holds the Queen's and King's South African Medals, 1914 Star, and the General Service and Victory Medals.
15, Royle Street, Chorlton-on-Medlock, Manchester.   X6716

INGHAM, A. H., Private, Canadian Infantry.
He joined in March 1918, and on completion of his training was two months later drafted overseas. He served on the Western Front for six months, and during that time took an active part in numerous important engagements, and was in action at Ypres, and in the Retreat and Advance of 1918. After the close of hostilities he entered Germany with the Army of Occupation, and was discharged in April 1919, suffering from rheumatism. He holds the General Service and Victory Medals. 25 Phœnix St., Hulme, Manchester.   Z6718

INGHAM, G., Private, 8th Manchester Regiment.
He volunteered in September 1914, and proceeding to Gallipoli in the following year fought at the Landing at Cape Helles, the Battles of Krithia and Achi Baba. On the Evacuation of the Peninsula he was sent to Egypt, and after a period of service in the Canal zone, embarked for France in March 1917, and was in action in the Battles of Ypres, Passchendaele, Cambrai, and was wounded in March 1918. On recovery he took part in several engagements in the concluding stages of the German Offensive and in the Allied Advance of 1918. He holds the 1914-15 Star, and the General Service and Victory Medals, and was discharged on account of service in February 1919. 15, Stockdale St., Ancoats, Manchester.   Z10465

INGHAM, W., Private, 6th Manchester Regt. and Sapper, R.E. (Signal Section).
Volunteering in January 1915, he was retained at various home stations until February 1916, when he was drafted to France. There he was gassed and wounded during the Battles of the Somme, but on his recovery went into action at Vimy Ridge and Lens. He was later transferred to the Royal Engineers, and was engaged on important signalling duties. In March 1919 he was demobilised, and holds the General Service and Victory Medals.
18, Exter Street, Ardwick, Manchester.   Z6717

INGLIS, D., Rifleman, K.R.R.C.
He was mobilised in August 1914, and was immediately afterwards sent to France. After taking part in the fighting at Mons, and in the Retreat, he fought in the Battles of the Marne, Loos, Messines, and Cambrai, and later served in the Retreat and Advance of 1918. He was discharged in March 1919, and holds the Mons Star, and the General Service and Victory Medals.
31, Baguley Street, Miles Platting, Manchester.   Z9593

IRELAND, F., Private, 9th South Lancashire Regt.
He volunteered in September 1914, and in the following February embarked for France, where he fought in the Battles of Neuve Chapelle, Hill 60, Festubert, Loos, St. Eloi, Ploegsteert, the Somme, the Ancre, Ypres, Cambrai, and the Lys. In the latter he was badly wounded in April 1917. After treatment at Bournemouth, he returned to France and served on until January 1919, when he was demobilised. He holds the 1914-15 Star, and the General Service and Victory Medals. 24, Thomas Street, West Gorton, Manchester.   TZ6719

IRONMONGER, G. R., A.B., Royal Navy.
He was serving in H.M.S. Torpedo Boat Destroyer "Verity" on the outbreak of hostilities and continued in that vessel throughout the war. His ship took part in the bombardment of the Dardanelles forts, and in operations covering the landing of troops in Gallipoli. She was also engaged on patrol and other duties in the Mediterranean and Baltic Seas, and had several

encounters with enemy craft. He was wounded in the course of his service. He holds the 1914-15 Star, and the General Service and Victory Medals, and in 1920 was still serving.
13, Raglan Street, Ancoats, Manchester.   Z10466B

IRONMONGER, J. N., L/Cpl., 1/5th Lincolnshire Regt.
Volunteering in May 1915, he was drafted to the Western Front in the following October, and fought in the Battles of Loos, Vermelles, and Vimy Ridge. Gassed in the Battle of the Somme he was admitted to hospital, and on recovery took part in heavy fighting at Arras, Bullecourt, Messines, Lens, Ypres, Cambrai, and in several engagements in the Retreat and Advance of 1918. He was demobilised in January 1919, and holds the 1914-15 Star, and the General Service and Victory. Medals. 13, Raglan St., Ancoats, Manchester.   Z10466A

IRONSIDE, G., Private, East Lancashire Regiment.
Having been previously engaged on work of National importance, he joined the Army in April 1918, and in the following August was drafted to France, where he took part in the final operations during the Advance of that year. He returned home, and was demobilised in February 1919, holding the General Service and Victory Medals.
110, Ravald Street, Miles Platting, Manchester.   Z9594

ISHERWOOD, H., Sapper, R.E.
He joined in January 1917, and on completion of a period of training was drafted overseas eight months later. Whilst serving on the Western Front he experienced fierce fighting in the Passchendaele and Cambrai sectors, and was wounded in action at Forest in October 1918. He remained in France until February 1919, and was demobilised in the following month, holding the General Service and Victory Medals.
10, Tranmere Street, Hulme, Manchester.   Z6720

ISHERWOOD, H. J., Private, Sherwood Foresters.
He joined in March 1917, and on the completion of his training was sent overseas. Serving on the Western Front he saw heavy fighting at Arras and Givenchy, and the Somme, and was wounded at Arras in May 1918. Taken prisoner whilst in hospital he was held in captivity in Germany until the Armistice, when he was repatriated. He was demobilised in 1919, and holds the General Service and Victory Medals.
92, Holland Street, Newton, Manchester.   Z10467C

ISHERWOOD, N. J., Pte., K.O. (R. Lancaster Regt.)
He volunteered in September 1914, and in the following year embarked for the Western Front where he fought in the Battle of Festubert and other engagements, until wounded at Albert in 1916. On recovery he was in action at Messines and Vimy Ridge, and in other operations until the conclusion of hostilities. Returning home for demobilisation in April 1919, he holds the 1914-15 Star, and the General Service and Victory Medals. 92, Holland St., Newton, Manchester.   Z10467A

ISHERWOOD, W., Private, Manchester Regiment.
Volunteering in September 1914, he proceeded overseas in the following year, and saw much service on the Western Front. He fought in the Battles of Festubert, and the Somme, and severely wounded at Albert in 1916, was invalided home where he was under treatment for a year. Discharged as medically unfit in 1917, he holds the 1914-15 Star, and the General Service and Victory Medals.
92, Holland Street, Newton, Manchester.   Z10467B

ISHERWOOD, W., Private (Gunner), M.G.C.
Volunteering in May 1915, he proceeded to France in the following July, and was in action at St. Eloi, Albert, Vimy Ridge, the Somme, Ancre, Messines, Ypres, Cambrai, the Aisne, and the Marne. He was not demobilised until May 1919, and holds the 1914-15 Star, and the General Service and Victory Medals.
54, Irlam Street, Miles Platting, Manchester.   Z9595

J

JACKSON, A., L/Corporal, R.E.
Volunteering in August 1914, he proceeded to France in the following October. Whilst overseas, he served at Neuve Chapelle, La Bassée, Vermelles, Ploegsteert Wood, Beaucourt, Ypres, and Cambrai, and on the Somme Front, and did excellent work employed with his Company on various duties of an important nature. After the Armistice he served in Germany with the Army of Occupation until December 1919, when he was demobilised, holding the 1914 Star, and the General Service and Victory Medals.
15, Napier Street, Ardwick, Manchester.   TZ6734A

JACKSON, A., Private, R.A.M.C.
He volunteered in October 1914, and was employed on clerical duties at Manchester until 1916, when he was drafted to the Western Front. In this theatre of war he served as a stretcher-bearer in the Battles of Loos, Albert, the Somme, Arras, Ypres, and Cambrai, and during many engagements in the Retreat and Advance of 1918. He remained overseas for some time after the Armistice, and was demobilised in September 1919, holding the General Service and Victory Medals.
7, Naylor Street, Hulme, Manchester.   Z6721

JACKSON, A., Driver, R.F.A.
Volunteering in August 1914, he was sent early in the following year to France, where he remained for nearly four years. During this time he served with the 165th Brigade in many important engagements, including the Battles of Ypres, Cambrai, and the Somme. Returning home after the termination of hostilities, he was demobilised in January 1919, and holds the 1914-15 Star, and the General Service and Victory Medals.
9, Prince Street, Ardwick, Manchester.   Z6722

JACKSON, A., L/Corporal, King's (Liverpool Regt.)
He joined in 1916, and after the completion of his training proceeded to the Western Front. In this theatre of war he participated with his unit in the Battles of Ypres III, Ypres IV., and Messines Ridge, and in heavy fighting in many other sectors. He was demobilised on his return home in 1919, and holds the General Service and Victory Medals.   TX6723A
3, Melbourne Street, Chorlton-on-Medlock, Manchester.

JACKSON, A. E., Gunner, R.F.A.
Joining in August 1916, he was drafted to France in the following May. After taking a prominent part with his Battery in severe fighting at Arras, La Bassée, and Givenchy, he was invalided home on account of ill-health. He spent some time in hospital at Bristol and Wells, and upon his recovery, served at Felixstowe, until he was demobilised in February 1919, holding the General Service and Victory Medals.
6, Bainbridge Street, Ardwick, Manchester.   Z6731

JACKSON, B., Gunner, R.G.A.
He joined in June 1916, and in the following November proceeded to the Western Front. There he at once participated in heavy fighting on the Ancre front, but had only served overseas for a few weeks when he was severely wounded on January, 6th 1917, and unfortunately succumbed to his injuries five days later. He was entitled to the General Service and Victory Medals.
"Whilst we remember the sacrifice is not in vain."
20, Pownall Street, Hulme, Manchester.   Z6738

JACKSON, C. W., L/Corporal, 12th Manchester Rgt.
Volunteering in January 1915, he proceeded to France four months afterwards, and took part in the Battles of Loos, Albert, Vermelles, the Somme (I), Arras, Messines, Passchendaele, Cambrai, and the Somme, and in the Retreat of 1918. He was badly wounded in action at Amiens at the commencement of the Advance, and was invalided home. After treatment at the 2nd South African General Hospital, London, he was demobilised in February 1919, and holds the 1914-15 Star, and the General Service and Victory Medals.
31, Napier Street, Ardwick, Manchester.   Z11908

JACKSON, E., Private, R.A.S.C.
Joining in June 1917, he underwent a period of training at Ashton, and was later employed on various duties of an important nature. He performed consistently good work, until his health broke down, and after spending some time in a V.A.D. hospital in London, was discharged in October 1918, as unfit for further service.
12, Fleeson Street, Rusholme, Manchester.   Z6743

JACKSON, F., Sergt., 8th Manchester Regiment.
Mobilised in August 1914, he was drafted in the following month to Egypt, and later, sent to Cyprus, served there until April 1915, when he was transferred to the Dardanelles. In this theatre of war he played a conspicuous part in heavy fighting during the Battles of Cape Helles, and Krithia, and was unhappily killed in action in June 1915, in the Advance on Achi-Baba. He was entitled to the 1914-15 Star, and the General Service and Victory Medals.
"His life for his Country."
10, George Street, Bradford, Manchester.   Z16741

JACKSON, F., Private, 3rd Cameron Highlanders.
He volunteered in September 1914, but was found to be medically unfit for transfer overseas. Retained at home and stationed at Iuvergordon, Inverness, Glasgow, Greenock, and Paisley, he was employed on garrison and other important duties, and rendered valuable services until he was demobilised in February 1919.
29, Pitt Street, Ancoats, Manchester.   Z6737B

JACKSON, F., Rifleman, Royal Irish Rifles.
Volunteering in November 1914, he proceeded three months afterwards to the Western Front. In this theatre of war he at once took part in heavy fighting, and was severely wounded in action at Ypres in May 1915. Admitted to hospital in France, he was later evacuated to England, and after spending some time in hospital at Southend was invalided out of the service in July 1915, holding the 1914-15 Star, and the General Service and Victory Medals.
10, Bradshaw Street, Hulme, Manchester.   Z6726

JACKSON, F., Flight-Sergt., R.A.F.
He joined in May 1916, and two months later was sent to the Western Front. After taking part in heavy fighting on the Somme, and the Ancre fronts, he was invalided to England. On leaving hospital he served at Farnborough, and on the Norfolk Coast, where he carried out highly technical work. After the Armistice he rejoined the Royal Air Force for a period

of two years, but after twelve months service at Edinburgh, Glasgow, and York, was discharged as medically unfit. He holds the General Service and Victory Medals.
21, Hulme Street, Chorlton-on-Medlock, Manchester.   Z6727

JACKSON, G., Sapper, R.E.
He volunteered in October 1915, and after training in Wales, was five months later drafted overseas. Whilst on the Western Front he rendered valuable services, building huts and dug-outs for the troops in the Ypres, Somme, and Cambrai sectors, and was later stationed at Rouen and Lyons, where he served as an orderly. He remained in France until December 1918, and was demobilised in February 1919, holding the General Service and Victory Medals.
73, Cowesby Street, Moss Side, Manchester.   TZ6733

JACKSON, H., Private, South Wales Borderers.
He volunteered in August 1915, but was physically unfit for transfer overseas, and was consequently retained on home service. Whilst stationed at Kinmel Park and Gilstone, he was employed on various duties of an important nature, and was later engaged guarding prisoners of war at Lincoln. He performed very good work during the whole of his service, and was demobilised in October 1919.
42, Owen Street, Hulme, Manchester.   Z6725

JACKSON, H., Sergt., R.F.A.
Mobilised from the Reserve at the commencement of hostilities, he was drafted to France in July 1915, and fought in the Battles of Loos, Albert, Vermelles, and the Somme. He was also engaged in heavy fighting at Arras, Ypres, Cambrai, and throughout the German and Allied Offensives of 1918. Returning home he was discharged in February 1919, and holds the 1914-15 Star, and the General Service and Victory Medals.
221, Victoria Square, Oldham Road, Manchester.   Z9217

JACKSON, H., Gunner, R.G.A.
He joined in March 1917, and embarked for the Western Front three months later. He served in many parts of the line fighting in the engagements at Ypres, Cambrai, and throughout the German Offensive and subsequent Allied Advance of 1918. Returning home after the Armistice, he was demobilised in January 1919, and holds the General Service and Victory Medals.
29, Upper Dover Street, Bradford, Manchester.   Z9218

JACKSON, J., Pte., 8th Loyal N. Lancashire Regt.
Joining in August 1916, he proceeded to France in the following April, and was in action at Arras, Bullecourt, and Messines, where he was wounded in June 1917. On recovery he took part in the Battles of Ypres (III), and Cambrai, and in the German Offensive, and subsequent Allied Advance of 1918, in the course of which he was wounded at Ypres in October. Proceeding after treatment into Germany he served with the Army of Occupation at Bonn, and returned home in October 1919. Demobilised in March 1920, he holds the General Service and Victory Medals.
24, Heyrod Street, Ancoats, Manchester.   Z10469

JACKSON, J., Gunner, R.F.A.
He volunteered in September 1914, and crossing to France in the following July served with his Battery in several engagements in the Ypres salient, and in the Somme Offensive. Owing to illness he was sent home in November 1916, and after treatment was invalided out of the Service in September 1917. He holds the 1914-15 Star, and the General Service and Victory Medals.
203, Morton Street, Longsight, Manchester.   Z10470

JACKSON, J., Private, 1st Cheshire Regiment.
Volunteering in August 1914, he was sent a year later to Gibraltar, where he was engaged on garrison duty until June 1918, He then proceeded to France, and in this theatre of war did good work with his Battalion during the final operations of the war. He returned home for demobilisation in August 1919, and holds the General Service and Victory Medals.
34, Cobden Street, Ancoats, Manchester.   Z10471

JACKSON, J. A., Pte., King's Shropshire Light Infty.
He volunteered in September 1914, and in July of the following year was drafted to Salonika. In this theatre of war he took part in several important engagements on the Vardar, Doiran, and Struma fronts, and in heavy fighting at Monastir. Serving overseas until after the termination of hostilities, he returned home for demobilisation in January 1919, and holds the 1914-15 Star, and the General Service and Victory Medals.
15, Napier Street, Ardwick, Manchester.   TZ6734B

JACKSON, J. O., Driver, R.F.A.
Volunteering in August 1914, he was drafted to France in the following January, and fought in the Battles of Neuve Chapelle, Ypres, Loos, the Somme, Arras, Messines, and Cambrai. He was also in action in many engagements in the German Offensive and was gassed during the subsequent Allied Advance of 1918. On recovery he was sent into Germany with the Army of Occupation, and served on the Rhine until his return to England for demobilisation in May 1919. He holds the 1914-15 Star, and the General Service and Victory Medals.
32, Clyde Street, Ancoats, Manchester.   Z10473

JACKSON, J. H., Gunner, R.F.A.
He joined in December 1917, and completing his training, served at various stations with his unit on important duties. Owing to ill-health, he was unsuccessful in obtaining his transfer overseas, but rendered excellent services until invalided out of the Army in March 1918.
34, Whitfield Street, Ancoats, Manchester. TZ9219

JACKSON, J. T., Private, Manchester Regiment.
Mobilised in August 1914, he proceeded a month later to Egypt, where he served until May 1915. He was then transferred to Gallipoli, and during his service in this theatre of war, participated in strenuous fighting at Krithia, Achi Baba, Lair Bair, and Suvla Bay. In August 1916, he was invalided home on account of ill-health, and after some time in hospital in London, was eventually discharged in November 1917, as unfit for further service. He holds the 1914–15 Star, and the General Service and Victory Medals.
10, Whyatt Street, Bradford, Manchester. Z6736

JACKSON, J. W., Private, Lancashire Fusiliers.
He volunteered in September 1914, and after five months' training was drafted to the Western Front, where he was wounded in action at the second Battle of Ypres in May 1915. He also took part in the Battles of St. Eloi, Loos, Vimy Ridge, the Somme, Arras, Bullecourt, Messines, Passchendaele, and Cambrai, and many other engagements until the cessation of hostilities. He was demobilised in January 1919, and holds the 1914–15 Star, and the General Service and Victory Medals.
29, Congou Street, Ancoats, Manchester. Z11739

JACKSON, L., Private, 2nd Manchester Regiment.
He joined in June 1916, and a few months afterwards was sent to France. There he took part in many important engagements at Neuve Chapelle, Vimy Ridge, Ypres, the Somme, Passchendaele, and Nieuport, and was wounded. He was unhappily killed in action at Péronne on August 28th 1918, and buried in the military cemetery at Brie on the Somme. He was entitled to the General Service and Victory Medals.
" Courage, bright hopes, and a myriad dreams, splendidly given." 102, Cowesby St., Moss Side, Manchester. TZ6732

JACKSON, P., Rifleman, 8th Rifle Brigade.
He volunteered in August 1914, and in the following April proceeded to the Western Front. In this theatre of war he took part in strenuous fighting at Ypres, Loos, Vermelles, Vimy Ridge, and Passchendaele, where he was wounded. Admitted to hospital in Boulogne, he was later evacuated to England, and after a period in hospital at Fulham, was eventually invalided out of the Service in September 1916, holding the 1914–15 Star, and the General Service and Victory Medals.
204, Viaduct Street, Ardwick, Manchester. Z6730

JACKSON, R., Air Mechanic, R.A.F.
He joined in March 1916, but was medically unfit for service in a theatre of war. Retained at home, he was stationed at Farnborough and Kidbrook, engaged on important duties which demanded a high degree of technical skill. He rendered valuable services whilst thus employed until he was discharged in March 1919.
29, Pomfret Street, West Gorton, Manchester. Z6742

JACKSON, R., Private, 2/23rd London Regiment.
Joining in December 1917, he was drafted four months later to France, where he was in action at Havrincourt, Epéhy, Ypres, Messines Ridge, and Comines, and was wounded. Invalided home, he was admitted to hospital at Colchester, and afterwards at Blackburn, subsequently being discharged in November 1919, holding the General Service and Victory Medals. 15, Napier Street, Ardwick, Manchester. TZ6728

JACKSON, R., Cpl., 4th King's (Liverpool Regt.)
Having volunteered in April 1915, he was drafted to the Western Front in August of the same year, and took part in the fighting at Loos, St. Eloi, the Somme, the Ancre, Bullecourt, Ypres, Bapaume, and the Marne. He was demobilised in October 1919, and holds the 1914–15 Star, and the General Service and Victory Medals.
19, Teignmouth Street, Rochdale Road, Manchester. Z9596A

JACKSON, S., Private, 1st Northamptonshire Regt.
Mobilised in August 1914, he was sent to France in the following November, and was wounded in March 1915, during the Battle of Neuve Chapelle. After spending three months in hospital at Carmarthen, he proceeded to Egypt, and was in action at Mersa Matruh, Sollum, Katia, El Fasher, and Magdhaba. Later he took part in further fighting at Rafa, Gaza, Jericho, and Tripoli in Palestine, where he remained until February 1919, when he returned home and was demobilised. He holds the 1914–15 Star, and the General Service and Victory Medals.
13, Coburg Place, Rusholme, Manchester. Z6739A

JACKSON, S. H., Private, 1st Manchester Regt.
Mobilised at the declaration of war, he proceeded to the Western Front, and fought in the Battles of the Marne, the Aisne, and La Bassée. In 1916 he was sent to Mesopotamia, and fought in many engagements of note. Taken prisoner in December 1916, he was held in captivity in Turkey until January 1919, when he was repatriated. He was demobilised in March 1919, and holds the 1914 Star, and the General Service and Victory Medals. 3, Whitby Street, Ancoats, Manchester. Z9220

JACKSON, T., Private, Labour Corps.
Joining the King's Liverpool Regiment in April 1916, he was later transferred to the Labour Corps, and landed in France in September 1917. For upwards of two years he was engaged on important duties in the Ypres, Passchendaele and Cambrai sectors, and also did excellent work in the Retreat and Advance of 1918. Returning to England he was demobilised in February 1919, and holds the General Service and Victory Medals.
7, Alderman Street, Ardwick, Manchester. Z10474

JACKSON, T., Private, 1st Border Regiment.
He volunteered in January 1915, and three months afterwards was drafted to Gallipoli. There he was wounded during severe fighting in the Landing, and sent to hospital at Alexandria. Upon his recovery, he proceeded to France and took part in strenuous fighting at Loos, Albert, Vimy Ridge, the Somme, Arras, Ypres, and Cambrai. After the Armistice he served in Germany with the Army of Occupation until February 1919, when he was demobilised, holding the 1914–15 Star, and the General Service and Victory Medals.
13, Coburg Place, Rusholme, Manchester. Z6739A

JACKSON, T., Rifleman, Rifle Brigade.
Volunteering in 1914, he was later sent to France, but was wounded in action at Neuve Chapelle in May 1915, and invalided home. He was afterwards released in March 1916 from the Colours to take up work of National importance, and rendered valuable services whilst employed as a borer in the gun-making department at Messrs. Kendal and Jenks, Gorton.
3, Melbourne Street, Chorlton-on-Medlock, Manchester. TX6723B

JACKSON, T., Private, R.A.S.C. (M.T.)
He joined in January 1917, but being a skilled tradesman was retained at home, and employed as a motor repairer. Whilst serving at Bedford and Birkenhead, he performed excellent work in this capacity, until he was demobilised in February 1919. 39, Rylance St., Ardwick, Manchester. Z6724

JACKSON, W., Corporal, 2nd Manchester Regt.
Serving at the outbreak of war in August 1914, he was drafted a month later to the Western Front. In this theatre he played a prominent part in many important engagements, including the Battles of Ypres, St. Eloi, Loos, Vimy Ridge, the Somme, Messines Ridge, Cambrai, and Amiens. Severely wounded on the Lys in April 1918, he was invalided home, and remained in hospital at Lincoln until the following September, when he was discharged as unfit for further service. He holds the 1914 Star, and the General Service and Victory Medals.
10, Beswick Street, Ardwick, Manchester. Z6735

JACKSON, W., Pte., 2nd South Wales Borderers.
Joining in October 1917, he proceeded in the following April to the Western Front. There he was in action at Nieppe Forest, Onterstein Ridge, and Ypres, and in other sectors, and after the termination of hostilities, served at Cologne and Remscheid with the Army of Occupation. Returning home he was stationed for some time in Ireland prior to his demobilisation in October 1919, and holds the General Service and Victory Medals.
204, Viaduct Street, Ardwick, Manchester. Z6729

JACKSON, W. J., Private, R.A.S.C.
He joined in June 1916, and a few months afterwards was sent to India. During his service overseas he was employed on various duties of an important nature, and on three occasions was admitted to hospital on account of ill-health. Later returning home he served in Dublin, where he assisted to quell several riots in 1919. He was demobilised in March 1920, holding the General Service and Victory Medals.
8, Union Street, Rusholme, Manchester. TZ6740

JACOBS, R., Rifleman, Royal Irish Rifles.
Volunteering in August 1914, he embarked for France in the following January, and was in action at Neuve Chapelle, St. Eloi, Hill 60, and Ypres. He gave his life for King and Country at Festubert in June 1915, and was entitled to the 1914–15 Star, and the General Service and Victory Medals.
9, Mansfield Street, Miles Platting, Manchester. Z10475

JACQUES, A., Driver, R.F.A.
He volunteered in September 1914, and embarking for Egypt in the following February, was engaged on important duties at Alexandria and Kantara. Transferred to France in March 1917, he served with the Ammunition Column at Arras, Ypres, Passchendaele, Cambrai, and in the Retreat and Allied Advance of 1918. He was demobilised in May of the succeeding year, and holds the 1914–15 Star, and the General Service and Victory Medals. 34, Needwood St., Collyhurst, Manchester. Z10476

JAMES, D., Private, 2/4th Yorkshire Regiment.
He volunteered in September 1915, but was not successful in securing a transfer to a theatre of war. He served at Rhyll, Carmarthen, and Llandudno, and was then sent to Northampton, at which station he was employed in the military tailor's shop, and carried out his work in a highly capable manner. After three and a half years' service in the Army he was demobilised in March 1919.
16, Wigley Street, Ardwick, Manchester. Z6744

JAMES, S., Private, 12th Manchester Regiment.
Volunteering in August 1914, he embarked for France in the following February, and was in action at Cambrai, and the Somme, where he was wounded in November 1916. On recovery, he fought at Hill 60, Festubert, the Ancre, Arras, Bullecourt, Ypres, Lens, Lys, Bapaume, Amiens, and Cambrai, where in October 1918 he was again wounded. He was demobilised on his return to England in February 1919, and holds the 1914-15 Star, and the General Service and Victory Medals.
61, Knightley Street, Rochdale, Manchester.   Z10477B

JAMES, W. G. H., Sapper, R.E.
He joined in September 1916, and on completing his training in June of the following year, was drafted to Egypt, where he was stationed at Kantara, Alexandria, and Port Said. He also took part in the fighting at Rafa, before proceeding into Palestine, and was there present at the fall of Jerusalem. Returning home in March 1920, he was demobilised in the following month, and holds the General Service and Victory Medals. 39, Carlton Terrace, Gorton, Manchester.   Z8689

JAMESON, H., L/Cpl., K.O. (R. Lancaster Regt.)
Volunteering in July 1915, he was drafted to Mesopotamia in February of the following year, and during his service in this theatre of war was wounded in an engagement in January 1918. He was invalided to hospital at Baghdad, and later returning to England was demobilised in March 1919. He holds the General Service and Victory Medals.
51, Crissey Street, Queen's Park, Manchester.   Z11520

JAMIESON, J. (M.M.) Private, 1/8th Manchester Regt.
A serving soldier, having enlisted in February 1914, he embarked for Egypt shortly after the outbreak of hostilities, and in 1915 proceeded to the Dardanelles. He took part in the Landing at Suvla Bay, and many of the subsequent engagements, and in 1917, was transferred to France. Whilst in this theatre of war he fought in many important battles, and was awarded the Military Medal for gallantry and devotion to duty during the Somme Offensive. In addition to the decoration won in the Field, he holds the 1914-15 Star, and the General Service and Victory Medals, and was demobilised in 1919.
100, Tiverton Street, Ardwick, Manchester.   Z10478A

JAMIESON, J., 1st Air Mechanic, R.A.F. (late R.F.C.)
Joining in 1917, he was drafted to France later in the same year, and was engaged on important duties with his Squadron at Ypres, Poperinghe, and Arras. He also served during the Retreat and Allied Advance of 1918, and after the close of hostilities, proceeded with the Army of Occupation to Germany, where he remained for six months. He was demobilised on his return to England in 1919, and holds the General Service and Victory Medals.
100, Tiverton Street, Ardwick, Manchester.   Z10478B

JAMIESON, F., Trooper, 2nd Dragoon Guards, and Private, 1st Cheshire Regiment.
Volunteering in April 1915, he was after a period of training drafted overseas. During his service on the Western Front, he took part in fierce fighting in various sectors of the line, and was in action at Passchendaele and Vimy Ridges. He was later transferred to the Italian front, and served in this theatre of war until the cessation of hostilities. Demobilised in February 1919, he holds the General Service and Victory Medals.
22, St. Leonard Street, Chorlton-on-Medlock, Manchester. X6745

JAMIESON, J., Private, 17th Manchester Regiment.
Volunteering in February 1915, he proceeded to France later in that year, and took part in several battles, including that of the Somme, in which he was severely wounded. Evacuated to England for hospital treatment, he returned to France in December 1916, and was in action at Beaumont-Hamel, Beaucourt, Arras, Messines, Langemarck, Epéhy, and Cambrai. He was demobilised on his return to England in February 1919, and holds the 1914-15 Star, and the General Service and Victory Medals. 64, Boardman St., Harpurhey, Manchester. Z10479

JAMISON, W., Private, Manchester Regiment.
He volunteered in April 1915, and on completing his training in October of the same year, proceeded to Gallipoli, where he saw severe fighting until the Evacuation of the Peninsula. He afterwards proceeded to the Western Front, and there took part in the Battle of Ypres, and many other important engagements, and fought also in the Retreat and Advance of 1918. He was wounded in action whilst overseas, and in 1920 was still with his unit in Ireland. He holds the 1914-15 Star, and the General Service and Victory Medals.
16, Temple Street, Bradford, Manchester.   Z11718A

JAQUIN, J., Private, 7th Manchester Regiment.
He volunteered in August 1914, and after training at Littleborough and Liverpool was sixteen months later sent to the Western Front. There he saw service at Loos, St. Eloi, Albert and Vimy Ridge, and whilst fighting in the Battle of the Somme was taken prisoner. During his period of captivity he was employed on agricultural work, and on his release after the Armistice, was demobilised in December 1918, holding the 1914-15 Star, and the General Service and Victory Medals.
7, Merriner Street, Greenheys, Manchester.   Z6746

JARVIS, A., Rifleman, 6th Liverpool Regt. (Rifles).
He volunteered in December 1915, and in the following June was sent to the Western Front. During his service in France he fought in the third Battle of Ypres, and at Cambrai, and in various engagements in the Retreat and Advance of 1918. After the Armistice he proceeded to Germany with the Army of Occupation, and was stationed at Bonn until October 1919, when he returned home and was demobilised. He holds the General Service and Victory Medals.
17, Pleasant Street, Harpurhey, Manchester.   Z11521

JARVIS, A., Private, 22nd Manchester Regiment.
He volunteered in August 1915, and after his training was engaged on important duties at various stations. Owing to ill-health he was unable to secure his transfer to a theatre of war, but nevertheless did valuable work until April 1917, when he was invalided out of the Service.
19, Windsor Street, Rochdale Road, Manchester.   Z10480

JARVIS, E., Private, 1st Lancashire Fusiliers.
He joined in June 1917, and on completion of his training was six months later drafted overseas. Whilst serving on the Western Front he was in action in various engagements, and saw heavy fighting in the Somme, Nieppe, Aisne, Marne, Passchendaele and Ypres sectors. He was wounded in action at Ypres in September 1918, taken to hospital in Boulogne, and later invalided to England. He was demobilised in August 1919, and holds the General Service and Victory Medals.
30, Augustus Street, Brooks Bar, Manchester.   Z6748A

JARVIS, H., Private, Manchester Regiment.
Volunteering in October 1915, he was drafted to Egypt in the following April and served in various operations in the Suez Canal zone. In February 1917, he was transferred to France, and was in action at Oppy Wood and St. Quentin and was wounded. He was invalided home, but rejoining his unit in March 1918, took part in many engagements in the Retreat and Advance. He was demobilised in April 1919, and holds the General Service and Victory Medals.
17, Pleasant Street, Harpurhey, Manchester.   Z11522

JARVIS, J., Private, 1/8th Lancashire Fusiliers.
At the outbreak of war he volunteered, and a month later was drafted to Egypt, whence after taking part in the Suez Canal engagements he was sent to Gallipoli. In this theatre of war he served for two months, and during that time fought in the three Battles of Krithia, and was wounded in the last engagement. He was invalided to England, and after prolonged hospital treatment was discharged as medically unfit in June 1917. He holds the 1914-15 Star, and the General Service and Victory Medals.
19, Chipping Street, Longsight, Manchester.   Z6747

JARVIS, T., Corporal, R.F.A.
He volunteered in September 1914, and in August of the following year was drafted to the Dardanelles. He took part in the Landing at Cape Helles, and in the fighting at Krithia and Achi Baba, and the Landing at Suvla Bay, and served in this area till the Evacuation, and was wounded. He was afterwards transferred to Palestine, where he was in action at Jaffa, and in the Advance on Jerusalem. He was demobilised in June 1919, on his return home, and holds the 1914-15 Star, and the General Service and Victory Medals.
86, Irlam Street, Newton Heath, Manchester.   Z9597

JEACOCK, C. F. W., Pte., 6th Lancashire Fusiliers.
He joined in August 1916, and in the following February was sent to the Western Front, where he took an active part in numerous engagements, including those at Ypres, the Somme and Cambrai. He was reported missing on March 21st 1918, and later officially reported killed in action on that date. He was entitled to the General Service and Victory Medals.
"Whilst we remember, the sacrifice is not in vain."
7, Sandown Street, Ardwick, Manchester.   Z6749

JEFFERS, E., Private, Lancashire Fusiliers.
He volunteered in April 1915, and crossing to France in the following November, fought at Albert, the Somme, Passchendaele, Ypres and Cambrai. In the course of his service he was for a time attached to the Royal Engineers, and was engaged on important duties in connection with the construction of Military Hospitals at Boulogne. He did valuable work until his demobilisation, which took place on his return to England in February 1919. He holds the 1914-15 Star, and the General Service and Victory Medals.
6, Vale Street, Miles Platting, Manchester.   Z10481

JEFFERS, J., Pte., K.O. (Royal Lancaster Regiment).
Mobilised at the outbreak of hostilities, he was almost immediately drafted to the Western Front, where he took part in the Retreat from Mons. He was severely wounded at Loos in October 1915, and invalided to hospital in Scotland, and was discharged in March of the following year as medically unfit for further service. He holds the Mons Star, and the General Service and Victory Medals.
43, Crissey Street, Queen's Road, Manchester.   Z11523

JEFFREYS, R. D., Private, Manchester Regiment.
In September 1916, he joined the Army but on completion of his training was unable to procure a transfer overseas. He was chiefly engaged on farm work at Ripon and Chester, and did excellent work in looking after the horses. Later he was transferred to the R.A.M.C., and rendered valuable services at Aldershot, and other important stations. He was eventually demobilised in September 1919.
7, Lancaster Street, Hulme, Manchester. Z6751

JEFFRIES, G., Private, 13th Manchester Regiment.
Joining in May 1916, he was drafted overseas later in the same year. During his service on the Western Front, he was engaged in fierce fighting, chiefly in the Ypres sector, and was unfortunately killed in action in the Battle of the Somme in October 1916. He was entitled to the General Service and Victory Medals.
" A valiant Soldier, with undaunted heart he breasted life's last hill."
29, Ely Street, Hulme, Manchester. TZ6750B

JENKINS, G., Private, 2nd Royal Scots.
He volunteered in March 1915, and after training at Edinburgh, was sixteen months later sent to the Western Front. There after only two months' active service he fell fighting at the Battle of the Somme on September 25th, 1916. He was entitled to the General Service and Victory Medals.
" He died the noblest death a man may die,
Fighting for God, and right, and liberty."
93, Nelson Street, Bradford, Manchester. Z6753

JENKINS, J., Private, 5th Durham Light Infantry.
Joining in January 1917, he later embarked for Salonika, where he contracted malaria, necessitating his return to England. On his recovery he was drafted to France in October 1918, and was in action at the Battles of Le Cateau (II) and Selle, in the final operations of the war. He was demobilised in March 1919, and holds the General Service and Victory Medals.
33, Boardman Street, Harpurhey, Manchester. Z10482

JENKINS, J., Private, 16th Lancashire Fusiliers.
Volunteering in December 1914, he was on conclusion of his training three months later drafted to the Western Front, where he was in action in different sectors of the line. After fighting in the Battle of the Somme, he suffered severely from shell-shock, and was invalided to England. After nine months' treatment in hospital he was discharged in August 1917, as unfit for further military service, and holds the 1914–15 Star, and the General Service and Victory Medals.
18, Billington Street, Chorlton-on-Medlock, Manchester. Z6752

JENKINS, S., Corporal, M.G.C.
Volunteering in August 1915, he proceeded to France in the following June, and was in action at Vimy Ridge, the Somme, Arras, Bullecourt, Messines, Ypres, Passchendaele and Cambrai. He also served in the Retreat and Allied Advance of 1918, and was demobilised on his return to England in February of the succeeding year. He holds the General Service and Victory Medals.
13, Crook Street, Harpurhey, Manchester. Z10483

JENKINSON, S. A. (M.M.), 1/1st East Lancashire Regt. and R.A.M.C.
He enlisted in the Army in March 1914, and a month after the outbreak of war was sent to Egypt. After fighting n the Suez Canal engagements he was drafted to Gallipoli, and served through the Campaign there, when returning to Egypt he was in action at El Arish. In March 1917 he was transferred to France, and took part in engagements at Ypres, Passchendaele, Nieuport, the Somme, Epéhy, Bray and La Bassée. He was awarded the Military Medal for conspicuous bravery in evacuating wounded under heavy shell-fire, and also holds the 1914–15 Star, and the General Service and Victory Medals. He was discharged in April 1919.
11, Markham Street, Ardwick, Manchester. TZ6754

JENKINSON, W., Sapper, R.E.
Joining in January 1917, he embarked for France in May of that year, and in the capacity of a signaller served at Arras, Vimy Ridge, Cambrai and Havrincourt Wood. Later he was, transferred to Italy, where he also did valuable work until contracting an illness, he was invalided home. On his recovery he was retained for important home duties, until demobilised in June 1919. He holds the General Service and Victory Medals. 44, Naylor Street, Oldham Road, Manchester. Z10484

JENNINGS, F., Private, 7th Manchester Regiment.
He volunteered in August 1914, and after a course of training was four months later sent to the Western Front, where he took an active part in the Battle of Ypres. In January 1915, he was transferred to Salonika, and saw heavy fighting on the Vardar and the Doiran fronts, and was also in action during the Struma engagement. He was wounded on one occasion, and remained in Salonika until April 1919, when, returning to England, he was demobilised, holding the 1914 Star, and the General Service and Victory Medals.
34, Berwick Street, Chorlton-on-Medlock, Manchester. Z6755C

JENNINGS, F., Private, 9th Manchester Regiment.
Volunteering in February 1915, he was eight months later drafted to Mesopotamia. He served in this theatre of war for three years, and during that period experienced fierce fighting in numerous engagements, including those at Baghdad and Kut-el-Amara, and on the Tigris. In October 1918 he was invalided to England suffering from malaria, and in consequence, was discharged from the Army, holding the 1914–15 Star, and the General Service and Victory Medals.
34, Berwick Street, Chorlton-on-Medlock, Manchester. Z6755B

JENNINGS, H., Private, 11th Manchester Regiment.
He joined in March 1916, and two months later was drafted overseas. Whilst serving on the Western Front he was in action in the Battles of the Somme, Arras, Ypres and Cambrai, and also took an active part in the final Advance prior to the close of hostilities. After the Armistice he proceeded with the Army of Occupation to Germany, and served there until demobilised in October 1919, holding the General Service and Victory Medals.
34, Berwick Street, Chorlton-on-Medlock, Manchester. Z6755A

JEPSON, C. C., Gunner, R.G.A.
Volunteering in September, 1915 he proceeded to the Western Front in the following year, and fought in the Battles of Ypres, Albert, and the Somme. He also served throughout the Retreat and Allied Advance of 1918, and did valuable work until his demobilisation, which took place on his return to England in December of that year. He holds the General Service and Victory Medals.
12, Alder Street, Collyhurst, Manchester. Z10485

JEPSON, R., Private, K.O. (R. Lancaster Regt.)
Volunteering in September 1914, he proceeded in the following month to Mesopotamia. There he was engaged in heavy fighting at Amara, and on the Tigris, and after fourteen months' service on this front was sent to France, where he was in action in the Loos, Albert, the Ancre, Messines and Cambrai sectors He served in France until February 1919, when he was demobilised, holding the 1914–15 Star, and the General Service and Victory Medals.
10, Woodville St., Chorlton-on-Medlock, Manchester. Z6756

JESSON, H., Gunner, R.F.A.
Having volunteered in December 1914, he was quickly drafted to France, and took part in the Battles of Neuve Chapelle, St. Eloi, Hill 60, Ypres, Loos, Albert, Vermelles, Ploegsteert Wood, and the Somme, during which he was seriously wounded in action. He unfortunately died from his wounds at Rouen on November 22nd, 1916, and was entitled to the 1914–15 Star, and the General Service and Victory Medals.
" Nobly striving,
He nobly fell that we might live."
54, Roberts Street, Newton Heath, Manchester. Z11909A

JESSON, P., Private, 2nd Manchester Regiment.
He joined in 1917, and was quickly sent to the Western Front, where he played a prominent part in the Battles of Arras, Bullecourt, Messines, Lens, Bapaume and Cambrai, where he was badly wounded in action in 1918. He was also in action against the Arabs in July 1920, and at the end of that year was still serving. He holds the General Service and Victory Medals.
54, Roberts Street, Newton Heath, Manchester. Z11909B

JEX, W. M., Private, Loyal N. Lancashire Regt., Suffolk Regt. and Labour Corps.
Volunteering in November 1914, he was drafted to the Western Front two months later, and there saw severe fighting in various sectors. Wounded in action at Ypres in 1915, he was invalided home, but on his recovery in November of that year, returned to France, and took part in engagements at Lens, and many other places. He was again admitted to hospital in England in 1917, suffering from dysentery, and afterwards served with the Labour Corps until his demobilisation in February 1919. He holds the 1914–15 Star, and the General Service and Victory Medals. 16, Victoria Street, Longsight, Manchester. Z7305

JOBEY, T. A., Pte., Middlesex and West Yorkshire Regiments.
Having previously been engaged on work of National importance, he joined in February 1917, and after his training served as a tractor driver on agricultural work at various stations. He was not successful in obtaining his transfer overseas before the close of hostilities, but nevertheless rendered valuable services until demobilised in October 1919.
54, Cross Street, Bradford, Manchester. Z10486

JOHNSON, C., Corporal, Royal Irish Fusiliers.
He volunteered in September 1914, and in the following April sailed for Salonika, where he was engaged in heavy fighting in many parts of the line. Contracting fever he was invalided home for treatment, and on his recovery was drafted to France in May 1917. He was in action in various engagements, and later served at the Base on important duties. He was demobilised in April 1919, and holds the 1914–15 Star, and the General Service and Victory Medals.
3, Iron Street, Miles Platting, Manchester. Z9221

JOHNSON, C., Private, 11th Manchester Regiment.
He volunteered in December 1915 and was engaged on important duties with his unit until March 1917, when he was drafted to the Western Front. There he was in action at Ypres and Passchendaele, and also took part in the Retreat and Advance of 1918. He was invalided home, and after a period in hospital was discharged, in consequence of an injured limb in March 1919. He holds the General Service and Victory Medals.
20, Pearson Street, Newton Heath, Manchester. Z9599

JOHNSON, E., L/Corporal, Manchester Regiment.
He volunteered in January 1915, and four months later was drafted to France, where he saw much severe fighting in various sectors and was wounded in action. In November 1915, he was transferred to Mesopotamia, but shortly afterwards contracted malarial fever, and unfortunately died. He was entitled to the 1914–15 Star, and the General Service and Victory Medals.
"A costly sacrifice upon the altar of freedom."
70, Parker Street, Bradford, Manchester. Z11862

JOHNSON, E. G., Pte., 2nd South Lancashire Regt.
He joined the Army in November 1916, and after a course of training was a year later drafted to the Western Front. In this theatre of war he fought in numerous sectors of the Line, and in April 1918, was wounded and taken prisoner at Ploegsteert. He was kept in captivity until December 1918, and was eventually demobilised in June 1920, holding the General Service and Victory Medals.
71, Halston Street, Hulme, Manchester. Z6758

JOHNSON, F., 2nd Air Mechanic, R.A.F.
In January 1918, he joined the R.A.F., but being unfit for active service, was not successful in obtaining a transfer to a theatre of war. He was stationed at Bath and Bristol, and employed as a cook and also on other work, which duties he fulfilled with great ability until demobilised in March 1919.
37, Garibaldi Street, Ardwick, Manchester. Z6759

JOHNSON, F. W., Private, 17th Manchester Regt.
He volunteered in September 1914, and crossing to France in the following July was engaged in heavy fighting at St. Eloi, Vermelles, the Somme, the Ancre, Arras, Bullecourt, Ypres, and in many other important actions. Whilst overseas he contracted influenza, to which unhappily he succumbed in December 1918. He was entitled to the 1914–15 Star, and the General Service and Victory Medals.
"His memory is cherished with pride."
36, Park Street, West Gorton, Manchester. Z10487

JOHNSON, G. F., L/Corporal, 5th Manchester Regt.
He joined in June 1916, and after undergoing a period of training, served at various stations, where he was engaged on important duties as an Instructor. He was not successful in obtaining his transfer to a theatre of war, but, nevertheless, rendered valuable services with his unit until April 1919, when he was demobilised.
82, Russell Street, Moss Side, Manchester. Z11740

JOHNSON, H. (D.C.M.), Private, 10th Loyal North Lancashire Regiment.
Volunteering in September 1914, he proceeded in the following August to the Western Front. There he fought in numerous engagements, including the Battles of Loos and Vimy Ridge, but was reported missing in September 1916, He was awarded the Distinguished Conduct Medal for conspicuous gallantry in the Field, and was also entitled to the 1914–15 Star, and the General Service and Victory Medals.
"Great deeds cannot die:
They, with the sun and moon renew their light for ever."
26, Haydn Avenue, Moss Side, Manchester. Z6771B

JOHNSON, H., L/Corporal, 21st Manchester Regt.
He volunteered in November 1914, and twelve months later proceeded to the Western Front, where he saw severe fighting at Loos, St. Eloi, and many other places. He made the supreme sacrifice, falling in action at Bray on April 27th, 1917, during heavy fighting in the Somme sector. He was entitled to the 1914–15 Star, and the General Service and Victory Medals.
"A costly sacrifice upon the altar of freedom."
63, Russell Street, Moss Side, Manchester. Z11706B

JOHNSON, H., 3rd Air Mechanic, R.A.F.
He joined in October 1918, but was unsuccessful in procuring a transfer overseas before the cessation of hostilities. He served in the R.A.F. for fifteen months, and was stationed at Woking and Cambridge, where he was employed on work requiring exceptional technical knowledge and skill until his demobilisation in January 1919.
49, Caythorpe Street, Moss Side, Manchester. Z6760

JOHNSON, H., Private, Royal Irish Fusiliers.
He volunteered in August 1914, and in September 1915, proceeded to Salonika, where he saw service on the Vardar, the Doiran and the Struma, and at Monastir. He was transferred to Egypt in January 1917, and after serving at Rafa, was drafted to Palestine, where he was in action during the three Battles of Gaza, and at Jerusalem, Jericho and Aleppo. After the last engagement he contracted malaria, and was

sent to Alexandria. He returned to England in August 1919, and was demobilised, holding the 1914–15 Star, and the General Service and Victory Medals. Z6763
18, Northern Street, Erskine Street, Hulme, Manchester.

JOHNSON, J., Driver, R.E.
When war broke out in August 1914, he volunteered, and six months later was sent to the Western Front, where he was in action at Ypres, Arras, Czmbrai, the Somme, Vimy Ridge, and in the final victorious engagements of 1918. During his service in France, he performed excellent work in conveying heavy artillery and stores from the Base to the firing line. He was demobilised in July 1919, and holds the 1914–15 Star, and the General Service and Victory Medals.
13, Lincoln Street, Hulme, Manchester. Z6770

JOHNSON, J., Private, 18th Lancashire Fusiliers.
He volunteered in November 1915, and was retained on Home Service at Brockton, Stafford and Eastbourne, at which stations he was employed as a cook. After undergoing an operation, he was drafted to the Western Front, and served there for ten months, during which period he did excellent work in different sectors of the line. He was demobilised in January 1919, and holds the General Service and Victory Medals.
26, Haydn Avenue, Moss Side, Manchester. Z6771A

JOHNSON, J., Private, Manchester Regiment.
Volunteering in December 1915, he was on conclusion of his training at Ripon, drafted in procuring a transfer to the war zone. He was retained on Home Service for two years, at the end of which time he was, as the result of an accident, discharged unfit for further military duties.
56, Robert Street, West Gorton, Manchester. Z6757

JOHNSON, J., Private, 1st Northamptonshire Regt.
He volunteered in May 1915, and in the following October was drafted to Gallipoli, where he was in action at Suvla Bay, Chocolate Hill and Salt Lake, during which engagement he was wounded. On his recovery he was sent to Egypt, and saw heavy fighting at El Arish, Romani and Gaza. In October 1918 he proceeded to Salonika, and served there for over a year. Returning to England, he was demobilised in February 1919, and holds the 1914–15 Star, and the General Service and Victory Medals.
8, Arbury Strete, Hulme, Manchester. Z6761

JOHNSON, J., Private, Royal Irish Fusiliers.
At the outbreak of hostilities in August 1914, he volunteered, and in the following April proceeded to Gallipoli, where he was in action at Krithia and Suvla Bay. Whilst taking an active part in the capture of Chunuk Bair, he was severely wounded, which resulted in the loss of his left arm. He was invalided to England, and after receiving treatment was discharged as unfit for further service. He holds the 1914–15 Star, and the General Service and Victory Medals.
29, Cawder Street, Hulme, Manchester. Z6762A

JOHNSON, J., Driver, R.G.A.
He volunteered in August 1914, and in the following April proceeded overseas. Whilst serving on the Western Front he was in action at Hill 60, Loos, St. Eloi, Albert, Vimy Ridge, the Somme (I), the Ancre, Messines, Ypres, Cambrai, and the Somme (II), and was wounded in action and gassed at St. Quentin in March 1918. Invalided to England he was eventually demobilised in April 1919, and holds the 1914–15 Star, and the General Service and Victory Medals.
29, Platt Street, Moss Side, Manchester. Z6765

JOHNSON, J., Private, South Lancashire Regiment.
After volunteering in January 1915, he was sent to Mesopotamia in April of the following year, and was in action at Kut-el-Amara, and in the fighting on the Tigris. He also took part in the capture of Baghdad, and was wounded, but continued to serve in this area until November 1919, when he returned home and was demobilised. He holds the General Service and Victory Medals.
16, Whatmough Street, Oldham Road, Manchester. Z9598

JOHNSON, J. E., Corporal, R.A.S.C. (M.T.)
Mobilised in November 1914, he at once proceeded to the Western Front, and was attached to the Motor Transport sector, with which he took part in engagements at Ypres, Neuve Chapelle, and the Somme. In June 1917 he was transferred to Italy, and in this theatre of war served for nearly two years, especially on the Piave front. He was demobilised in March 1919, and holds the 1914 Star, and the General Service and Victory Medals.
2, Ripon Street, Greenheys, Manchester. Z6251B

JOHNSON, J. T., 2nd Corporal, R.E.
He was mobilised at the outbreak of war, and in September 1914 was drafted to France. Whilst overseas, he took part in the Battles of the Marne, the Aisne, Ypres, Neuve Chapelle, Hill 60, and the Somme. He gave his life for King and Country on March 12th, 1917, during the fighting in the Somme sector,, and was entitled to the 1914 Star, and the General Service and Victory Medals.
"He died the noblest death a man may die,
Fighting for God, and right, and liberty."
5, Back, Mount Street, Harpurhey, Manchester. Z11524

JOHNSON, J. W., Pte., Loyal N. Lancashire Regt.
Volunteering shortly after the outbreak of war, he was drafted to France on completion of his training three months later, and was engaged in heavy fighting at the first Battle of Ypres. He was unfortunately killed in action in December 1914, and was entitled to the 1914 Star, and the General Service and Victory Medals.
"Whilst we remember, the sacrifice is not in vain."
13, Stanley Street, West Gorton, Manchester.   Z10489

JOHNSON, P., Private, Labour Corps.
He joined the Army in January 1916, and on completion of his training was retained on important work in England until March 1917, when he obtained a transfer overseas. During his service on the Western Front, he was chiefly engaged in digging trenches and burying the dead, and remained in France until August 1919, when he was demobilised, holding the General Service and Victory Medals.
21, Spruce Street, Hulme, Manchester.   Z6769

JOHNSON, R. H., Private, Manchester Regiment.
He volunteered in August 1915, and embarking for India in the following June was engaged on garrison duty at various military stations, including those of Allahabad and Bangalore. He did valuable work until his demobilisation, which took place on his return to England in May 1919, and holds the General Service Medal.
71, Knightley Street, Rochdale Road, Manchester. Z10490

JOHNSON, S., 1st Air Mechanic, R.A.F.
Joining in June 1917, he proceeded to Farnborough, but on completion of his training there, could not procure a transfer overseas before the termination of the war. He was stationed at Gosport, where he was employed as a rigger, and fulfilled his duties with the utmost skill and ability. He was eventually demobilised in August 1919.
12, Lawson Street, Moss Side, Manchester.   Z6767

JOHNSON, S., Private, 7th Manchester Regiment.
He volunteered in October 1915, and underwent a period of training prior to being drafted to the Western Front in March 1917. There he saw severe fighting in various sectors, took part in the Battles of Cambrai and Le Cateau and other engagements, and also served through the Retreat and Advance of 1918. He was demobilised in April 1919, and holds the General Service and Victory Medals.
35, Prescott Street, Hulme, Manchester.   Z11741

JOHNSON, T., Private, South Lancashire Regiment.
Volunteering in September 1914, he proceeded to France a year later, and fought in the Somme sector. Transferred to Salonika in November 1915, he took part in operations on the Doiran, Struma and Vardar fronts, and returned to England after the close of hostilities. He was demobilised in January 1919, and holds the 1914-15 Star, and the General Service and Victory Medals.
97, Cross Street, Bradford, Manchester.   Z10491

JOHNSON, T., L/Sergt., R.M.L.I.
He was already serving when war broke out, and in April 1915 proceeded to Gallipoli, where he fought in the Battles of Krithia and Suvla Bay. After the Evacuation of the Peninsula, he was sent to France, and took a prominent part in engagements at Albert, Vimy Ridge, and the Ancre. He was unhappily killed in action at Beaumont-Hamel on November 13th, 1916. He was entitled to the 1914-15 Star, and the General Service and Victory Medals.
"A costly sacrifice upon the altar of freedom."
4, Stanley Street, Chorlton-on-Medlock, Manchester. Z6766

JOHNSON, W., Private, 4th K.O. (R.Lancaster Regt.)
He joined in March 1917, and after a period of training was five months later drafted overseas. Whilst serving on the Western Front, he took part in fierce fighting at Cambrai, the Somme, Bapaume, Le Cateau, and in the final decisive engagements of the war. After the close of hostilities he proceeded with the Army of Occupation to Germany, where he was stationed until demobilised in February 1919, holding the General Service and Victory Medals.
29, Cawder Street, Hulme, Manchester.   Z6762B

JOHNSON, W., Guardsman, Coldstream Guards.
During the first eighteen months of the war he was engaged on work of National importance at Mackintosh's Rubber Works, and in April 1916 joined the Army. After training at Caterham, he was unable to obtain a transfer overseas, and was retained on important duties in England, throughout the period of his service. He was stationed at Aldershot until demobilised in January 1919.
45, Hulme Street, Chorlton-on-Medlock, Manchester. Z6764

JOHNSON, W., Private, Lancashire Fusiliers.
Joining in April 1917 he embarked for France in the following September, and was in action at Arras, Messines, Ypres, Bullecourt and Cambrai. He also served in the Retreat and Allied Advance of 1918, at the conclusion of which he proceeded with the Army of Occupation to Germany. He was demobilised in February 1920, and holds the General Service and Victory Medals.
56, Taylor Street, Gorton, Manchester.   Z10492

JOHNSON, W., Air Mechanic, R.A.F.
He volunteered in February 1916, and after his training was engaged on important duties which called for much technical knowledge and skill. Owing to ill-health, he was unable to secure his transfer to a theatre of war, but nevertheless did valuable work with his Squadron until January 1918, when he was discharged as medically unfit.
10, Phelan Street, Collyhurst, Manchester.   Z10493

JOHNSON, W. H., Corporal, Manchester Regiment.
He volunteered in August 1914, and proceeding to France in June of the following year, served with distinction at Ypres and Armentières. He was seriously wounded in action on the Somme in 1916, and was invalided home. After long treatment in various hospitals in the United Kingdom, he was discharged in June 1919, totally disabled, and holds the 1914-15 Star, and the General Service and Victory Medals.
72, Parker Street, Bradford, Manchester.   Z11863

JOHNSON, W. H., Pte., 5th South Lancashire Regt.
He volunteered in August 1914, and completing his training served at various stations until proceeding to France in February 1917. He was in action in many parts of the line, fighting at Ypres, Passchendaele, Cambrai and throughout the Retreat and Advance of 1918. He was demobilised in January 1919, and holds the 1914-15 Star, and the General Service and Victory Medals.
46, George Street, Newton, Manchester.   Z9222

JOHNSTON, J., Private, 3rd South Lancashire Regt.
Volunteering in May 1915, he embarked for France in the following December, and took part in fighting in the vicinity of Armentières. In February 1916 he was invalided home in consequence of ill-health, and after hospital treatment was discharged as medically unfit in September of that year. He holds the 1914-15 Star, and the General Service and Victory Medals.   15, Teer Street, Ancoats, Manchester.   Z10488

JOHNSTON, R., Private, 51st Cheshire Regiment.
He joined in February 1916, and after a course of training was five months later drafted overseas. He served on the Egyptian front for over three years, and during that time was in action in numerous important engagements, including those at Romani, Magdhaba and Gaza. Whilst on the Eastern Front he contracted malaria, and was in hospital at Phaider Pasha. He returned home in December 1919, and was demobilised, holding the General Service and Victory Medals. 26, Erskine Street, Hulme, Manchester. Z6773B

JOHNSTON, R., Battery-Sergt.-Major, R.F.A.
He volunteered for active service in 1915, and in August of that year was drafted to the Western Front. There he took a conspicuous part in the engagements at Loos, the Somme, Albert, Arras, Ypres and Cambrai, and also fought in the Retreat and Advance of 1918. He remained in France until demobilised in March 1919, and holds the 1914-15 Star, and the General Service and Victory Medals.
26, Erskine Street, Hulme, Manchester.   Z6773A

JOHNSTON, W., Private, East Lancashire Regt.
A month after the outbreak of hostilities he volunteered, and in the following July was sent overseas. Whilst on the Western Front he was in action in the Somme, Arras, Ypres and Cambrai sectors, and was severely wounded at Cambrai in November 1917. He was in consequence invalided out of the Army the following month, holding the 1914-15 Star, and the General Service and Victory Medals.
32, Caroline Street, Hulme, Manchester.   Z6772

JOHNSTONE, A., Private, 18th Manchester Regt.
He volunteered in September 1914, and was retained on Home Service until August 1916, when he proceeded to the Western Front, and two months later was wounded in action at Bapaume On his recovery he rejoined his unit, and after taking part in heavy fighting in various sectors was again wounded by a sniper, and taken to hospital at Rouen. He was eventually demobilised in January 1919, and holds the General Service and Victory Medals.
7, Royds Street, Chorlton-on-Medlock, Manchester.   Z6774

JOHNSTONE, H., Private, K.O. (R. Lancaster Regt.)
He volunteered in August 1914, and in July 1915 proceeded to Gallipoli, whence after fighting at Achi Baba and Chocolate Hill he was sent to Salonika. There he was in action in the Servian Retreat in November 1915, and shortly afterwards was drafted to Egypt, and eventually to Mesopotamia. In this theatre of war he saw heavy fighting at Kut-el-Amara, and Baghdad, and was wounded at Sanna-i-Yat and Shati-el-Adhaim. He returned to England in May 1919, and was demobilised, holding the 1914-15 Star, and the General Service and Victory Medals.
4, Mahogany St., Chorlton-on-Medlock, Manchester. Z6777

JOHNSTONE, J. S., Private, 13th Manchester Regt.
He joined the Army in November 1916, and on conclusion of his training was in the following May drafted to Salonika, where he served for nearly two years. During this period he was engaged in action in various sectors of the front, and took part in the operations on the Doiran and the Vardar. He was wounded in the latter engagement, and returning to England in March 1919 was demobilised, holding the General Service and Victory Medals.
209, Earl Street, Longsight, Manchester. Z6775

JOHNSTONE, R., Private, R.A.M.C.
In November 1916 he joined, and two months later proceeded overseas. Whilst serving on the Western Front, he did good work with his unit in the Battles of Arras, Bullecourt, Ypres, Passchendaele, Lens, Cambrai and the Somme, and served in numerous other engagements until the cessation of hostilities. He remained in France until May 1919, when he was demobilised, and holds the General Service and Victory Medals.
12, Wilson Street, Hulme, Manchester. Z6776

JOHNSTONE, W., Gunner, R.F.A.
Mobilised in August 1914, he was immediately drafted to the Western Front, where he saw severe fighting in various sectors. He served through the Battles of the Marne, La Bassée, Ypres, Hill 60, Loos, Vimy Ridge, Cambrai and the Somme, and many other important engagements, and also took part in the entry into Mons at dawn of Armistice Day. He afterwards served with the Army of Occupation in Germany, finally returning home for discharge in July 1920. He holds the 1914 Star, and the General Service and Victory Medals.
26, Edge Street, Hulme, Manchester. Z11742

JOHNSTONE, W. H., A.B., Royal Naval Division.
He volunteered in December 1915, and in November of the following year proceeded to the Western Front with the Hood Battalion, and there saw much severe fighting. He took part in the Battle of Ypres, and many other important engagements in various sectors, was wounded in action at Arras and taken prisoner at Cambrai in December 1917. Held in captivity until after the cessation of hostilities, he was finally discharged in May 1919, and holds the General Service and Victory Medals.
25, Fairhaven Street, West Gorton, Manchester. TZ11743

JONES, A., Gunner, R.F.A.
He was already serving in the Army when war broke out, and at once proceeded with the First Expeditionary Force to France, where he took an active part in fierce fighting at Mons, Armentières, La Bassée, Loos, Albert, Arras, the Somme, Bapaume, Havrincourt, and the Marne. He remained on the Western Front until March 1919, when he was discharged, after seventeen years' service, holding the Mons Star, and the General Service and Victory Medals.
3, Ernest Street, Ancoats, Manchester. Z6819

JONES, A., Private, 17th Manchester Regiment.
Volunteering in September 1914, he was on completion of his training, fourteen months later, drafted to the Western Front, where after eight months' active service he was taken prisoner at Trones Wood, whilst fighting in the Battle of the Somme in July 1916. He was kept in captivity throughout the remaining period of hostilities, and was repatriated in December 1918. He was demobilised in March 1919, and holds the 1914–15 Star, and the General Service and Victory Medals.
10, Cottenham Street, Chorlton-on-Medlock, Manchester. TX6809A

JONES, A., Sapper, R.E.
He joined in August 1917, and three months later was drafted overseas. During his service on the Western Front he did good work at Cambrai and on the Somme, and was engaged in trench digging and removing debris until the close of hostilities. After the Armistice he proceeded with the Army of Occupation to Germany, where he was stationed until demobilised in September 1919. He holds the General Service and Victory Medals.
7, Robson Street, Hulme, Manchester. Z6807

JONES, A., Private, K.O. (Royal Lancaster Regt.)
Volunteering in September 1914, he was on conclusion of his training, four months later, sent to the Western Front, where he was engaged in fierce fighting at St. Eloi, Ypres, Albert, Vermelles, the Somme, Beaucourt, Arras and Messines. He was wounded in action and served in France until August 1918. He was demobilised in December of the same year, and holds the 1914–15 Star, and the General Service and Victory Medals.
6, Hancock Street, Rusholme, Manchester. TZ6799

JONES, A., L/Corporal, 20th Manchester Regiment.
He volunteered in September 1915, and early in the following year was drafted to France. He took part in the fighting at Albert, the Somme, Arras and Ypres, and also in the Retreat and Advance of 1918, but was wounded and taken prisoner at Le Cateau in October of that year. On his release he returned home and was demobilised in December 1918, holding the General Service and Victory Medals.
10, Teignmouth Street, Collyhurst, Manchester. Z9600

JONES, A., Pioneer, R.E.
He volunteered in August 1915, and in January of the following year was drafted to the Western Front. Whilst overseas he served in the engagements at Vimy Ridge, the Ancre, Arras, Messines and Cambrai, and in the second Battle of the Somme. He was invalided home, owing to ill-health, in March 1918, and was discharged later in the same month. He holds the General Service and Victory Medals.
9, Hughes Street, Ardwick, Manchester. Z6804

JONES, A., Tpr., 2nd Dragoon Guards (Queen's Bays).
Joining in February 1918, he obtained his training at various stations, and was afterwards engaged on important home duties. He was not successful in obtaining his transfer overseas before the close of hostilities, but in June 1919, was drafted to Palestine, where he served until January 1920. He was demobilised on his return to England two months later. 5, Lavender Street, Miles Platting, Manchester. Z10496B

JONES, A., L/Corporal, 11th Manchester Regiment.
Volunteering in March 1915, he embarked for Egypt in June of that year, and served in the defence of the Suez Canal. Later, proceeding to the Dardanelles, he took part in the Landing at Suvla Bay, and was in action until the Evacuation of the Peninsula, when he returned to Egypt. Transferred to France in April 1917, he fought at Ypres, Passchendaele, and throughout the Retreat and Advance, which concluded hostilities victoriously in November 1918. He was demobilised in the following March, and holds the 1914–15 Star, and the General Service and Victory Medals.
104, Morton Street, West Gorton, Manchester. Z10494

JONES, A., Private, 2nd Manchester Regiment.
A Reservist, he was mobilised at the declaration of war, and crossing to France, served in the Retreat from Mons, and the Battles of the Marne and the Aisne. Embarking for the Dardanelles in July 1915, he took part in the Landing at Suvla Bay, remaining in this theatre of operations until the Evacuation was completed in January 1916. In the following October he was sent to Mesopotamia, where he took part in important engagements, and from December 1917 until the close of hostilities, was engaged on special duties in India. He was demobilised in February 1919, and holds the Mons Star, and the General Service and Victory Medals.
8, Handel Street, Miles Platting, Manchester. Z10117A

JONES, A., Private, 3rd Manchester Regiment.
Volunteering in December 1915, he landed in France in the following September, and took part in operations at Neuve Chapelle, La Bassée, the Somme and Bray, where he was wounded in January 1917. Evacuated to England, he underwent hospital treatment, and four months later was invalided out of the Service. He holds the General Service and Victory Medals.
80, Lind Street, Ancoats, Manchester. Z10495

JONES, A., Private, Lancashire Fusiliers.
He volunteered in August 1914, and a year later proceeded to Gallipoli, where after taking part in the Suvla Bay Landing, he was wounded and sent to hospital at Mudros. On his recovery he was drafted to France, and was in action in engagements at Arras, and on the Somme. In December 1917 he was invalided to England, suffering from dysentery, and was eventually demobilised in July 1919, holding the 1914–15 Star, and the General Service and Victory Medals.
19, Randolph Street, Ardwick, Manchester. Z6794

JONES, A. E., Rifleman, Rifle Brigade.
He volunteered in November 1914, and after his training, served on the Western Front until the termination of hostilities. During this period he was in action at Ypres, Neuve Chapelle, Hill 60, Loos, St. Eloi, Ploegsteert Wood, Vimy Ridge, the Ancre, Albert, Arras, Cambrai and Amiens, and was wounded, gassed, and suffered from shell-shock. He was demobilised on his return to England in February 1919, and holds the 1914–15 Star, and the General Service and Victory Medals.
4, Rigg Street, Gorton, Manchester. Z10516

JONES, A. E., Private, 2/10th Manchester Regiment.
In August 1915, he volunteered, and in the following March proceeded overseas. Whilst serving on the Western Front he was in action in numerous important engagements in various sectors of the line, and was severely wounded in September 1918, as a result of a shell bursting in the trench. He was invalided to England, and in January 1919 was demobilised, holding the General Service and Victory Medals.
41, St. John's Road, Longhsight, Manchester. Z6802

JONES, A. S., Gunner, 210th Battery, R.F.A.
He joined the Army in 1916, and after a course of training proceeded in the same year to the Western Front, where he did good work with his Battery in different sectors. He was severely wounded in action at Ypres in September 1917, and unfortunately succumbed to his injuries on October 1st, in the same year. He was entitled to the General Service and Victory Medals.
" He passed out of the sight of men by the path of duty and self-sacrifice."
29, Aked Street, Ardwick, Manchester. X6778

JONES, A. W., Private, Royal Scots Regiment.

He volunteered in September 1915, and in December of that year was sent to France. In this theatre of war he saw heavy fighting in numerous engagements, including the Battles of the Somme and Ypres, and also in the Allied Advance of 1918, and was wounded on three occasions. Invalided to England in November 1918, he was demobilised in the following February, and holds the 1914-15 Star, and the General Service and Victory Medals.

39, Thomas Street, West Gorton, Manchester. Z6792

JONES, C., Private, Manchester Regiment.

Volunteering at the outbreak of war, he proceeded a year later to Gallipoli, and was wounded whilst taking part in the Suvla Bay Landing. On his recovery he was transferred to the Labour Corps, and was engaged on important garrison duties at Alexandria and Cairo until after the Armistice. Returning to England in 1919 he was demobilised in the same year, and holds the 1914-15 Star, and the General Service and Victory Medals.

75, Morton Street, Longsight, Manchester. Z6788

JONES, C. W., Gunner, R.G.A.

He joined in May 1917, and after training at Winchester was drafted to the Western Front, where he was engaged in heavy fighting in the Battles of the Aisne, the Marne, Bapaume, Havrincourt, Cambrai and Le Cateau. After the termination of the war he entered Germany with the Army of Occupation, and was stationed at Opladen until demobilised in October 1919. He holds the General Service and Victory Medals.

6, Webster Street, Greenheys, Manchester. Z6779

JONES, D. H., Gunner, Tank Corps.

Volunteering in February 1915, in March of the following year he landed in France and was engaged in heavy fighting at Vermelles, Vimy Ridge, on the Somme and on the Ancre. He was also in action in the Battles of Ypres, Lens, Cambrai, and during the German and Allied Offensives of 1918. Returning to England he was demobilised in February 1919, and holds the General Service and Victory Medals.

44, Sanitary Street, Oldham Road, Manchester. Z9223

JONES, E., Private, 1/8th Manchester Regiment.

He volunteered in December 1915, and ten months later proceeded to the Western Front, after completing his training. There he took an active part in operations at Ypres, the Somme, Amiens, Beauvois, Bapaume and Le Cateau, and remained until 1919. He was demobilised in March of the same year, and holds the General Service and Victory Medals.

20, Spruce Street, Hulme, Manchester. Z6808

JONES, E., Private, 2/5th Lancashire Fusiliers.

Volunteering in July 1915, he was on completion of his training drafted overseas in December 1916. During his service on the Western Front he was in action in many engagements, especially in the Ypres, Cambrai, Givenchy, Festubert, La Bassée, Arras, Bapaume, Havrincourt and Lille sectors. He was present at the entry into Mons in November 1918, and was stationed at Brussels until demobilised in March 1919. He holds the General Service and Victory Medals.

13, Bank Street, Hulme, Manchester. Z6817

JONES, E., Private, Manchester Regiment, Labour Corps, and King's (Liverpool Regiment).

He volunteered in April 1915, and in the following September proceeded to Gallipoli, where he took part in the Suvla Bay Landing. He was then sent to Egypt, and thence to France. In this theatre of war he was in action at Arras, Messines, Ypres, Loos, and the Somme, and was then invalided to hospital in England and discharged as medically unfit in January 1918. Six months later he rejoined in the Marine Labour Corps and was drafted to France, where he was engaged on transport duties at the Docks at Boulogne until April 1919, when he was again discharged. He re-enlisted in the following July in the King's (Liverpool Regiment) and proceeded to France, where he was employed on garrison duties until finally demobilised in March 1920. He holds the 1914-15 Star, and the General Service and Victory Medals.

19, Randolph Street, Ardwick, Manchester. Z6793

JONES, E., L/Corporal, 16th Manchester, Regiment.

In September 1914, he volunteered and in December 1915, was drafted to the Western Front, where he was in action in many engagements, including those at the Somme, and Beaucourt. He was wounded at Suzanne in December 1916, and losing his left arm was in consequence invalided out of the Army in January 1917. He holds the 1914-15 Star, and the General Service and Victory Medals.

35, Dudley Street, Stretford, Manchester. Z6785

JONES, E., Private, 1st Manchester Regiment.

He volunteered in November 1914, and a year later was sent to France, where he took part in engagements in the Arras sector, and was wounded in the Battle of the Somme. On his recovery he was drafted to Mesopotamia, and after fighting at Baghdad and Tekrit, proceeded to Palestine in April 1918. There he was in action at Jerusalem, and served until

February 1919, when returning to England he was demobilised in the following month, holding the 1914-15 Star, and the General Service and Victory Medals.

31, Durham Place, Hulme, Manchester. Z6824

JONES, E., Private, R.A.S.C.

He joined in May 1917, and in the same month was drafted to the Western Front, where he was engaged on important transport duties at Messines, Ypres, Passchendaele and Cambrai. He also took part in the Retreat and Advance of 1918, and after the Armistice proceeded with the Army of Occupation to Germany. He was demobilised in November 1919, and holds the General Service and Victory Medals.

38, Francisco Street, Collyhurst, Manchester. Z9601

JONES, E., Sergt., 6th East Lancashire Regiment.

He volunteered in September 1914, and embarking for the Dardanelles in the following April took part in fierce fighting at the First Landing, and at Suvla Bay, where he was severely wounded. Invalided to Cairo, he shortly afterwards returned to England, and after further hospital treatment was engaged on important home duties until June 1918, when he was discharged as medically unfit for further service. He holds the 1914-15 Star, and the General Service and Victory Medals.

15, Lever Street, Gorton, Manchester. Z10497

JONES, E., Private, Manchester Regiment.

He volunteered in March 1915, and after his training was engaged on important duties at various stations. In September of the same year he was sent to the Munition Factory of Messrs. Johnston and Nephew, Forge Lane, where he did excellent work as a fitter in connection with the repairing of machines used in connection with the output of munitions. He was not successful in obtaining his transfer overseas before the close of hostilities, but nevertheless rendered valuable services until demobilised in February 1919.

63, Cross Street, Bradford, Manchester. Z10498

JONES, E., Drummer, 1st Manchester Regiment.

He joined when only fourteen years of age in October 1917, and after his training was engaged with his Battalion on important duties at various stations. He was unable to secure his transfer overseas, but nevertheless did excellent work, and in 1920 was serving in Ireland.

21, Lancashire Street, Newton Heath, Manchester. Z10499B

JONES, E. A., Flight-Sergt., R.A.F.

He volunteered in August 1914, and served with the Machine Gun Section of the East Surrey Regiment. In November 1914, he proceeded to the Western Front, and was in action during the Battles of the Somme, Arras, Ypres, and Cambrai, and in the Retreat and Advance of 1918. He also took an active part in the raid on Zeebrugge, and was eventually demobilised in February 1919, holding the 1914 Star, and the General Service and Victory Medals.

20, Pendle Street, Openshaw, Manchester. Z6813

JONES, F., A.B., Royal Navy.

Volunteering in 1915, he served with the Auxiliary Cruisers in Home waters until 1916, when he was posted to H.M.S. "Berwick," and later to H.M.T.B. "Hunslet." In these vessels he was engaged in transporting wounded from the Dardanelles, and during the last period of his service in the Navy he rendered valuable service on patrol work. He was demobilised in 1919, and holds the General Service and Victory Medals. TX6809B

10, Cottenham Street, Chorlton-on-Medlock, Manchester.

JONES, F. J., Private, Border Regiment.

Volunteering in July 1915, he embarked for Salonika early in the following year, and took part in operations on the Vardar front. Owing to an illness he was invalided for hospital treatment to Malta and then to England, and after recovery proceeded to France. Whilst in this theatre of war he fought at Ypres, Passchendaele Ridge, Festubert, Cambrai Lens, Albert, Armentières and Arras, and served until the close of hostilities. He was demobilised in March 1919, and holds the General Service and Victory Medals.

30, Kirk Street, Ancoats, Manchester. Z10500

JONES, F. N., Private, 23rd Manchester Regiment.

Volunteering in March 1915, he was on completion of his training drafted to the Western Front, where he served for three years. During that period he did good work with his unit in engagements at Ploegsteert Wood, the Somme, Arras, Ypres, Passchendaele and Cambrai, and was also in action in the Retreat and Advance of 1918. He was demobilised in January 1919, and holds the General Service and Victory Medals.

10, Dryden Street, Chorlton-on-Medlock, Manchester. TZ6825

JONES, G., Private, East Yorkshire Regiment.

He joined the Army in March 1916, and after a period of training at Hull, was four months later drafted to the West Indies. There he served throughout the period of hostilities, and was chiefly employed on important garrison duties. During the last year of his service he contracted tuberculosis, and returning to England in March 1919, was discharged, holding the General Service and Victory Medals. Z6780

8, Cobden Street, Morton Street, Longsight, Manchester.

JONES, G., Private, Manchester Regiment.
Joining in May 1917, he embarked for Mesopotamia in the following July, and took part in engagements at Kut-el-Amara, Baghdad, and the Tigris. Previous to his enlistment, he was engaged on work of National importance in connection with the manuafcture of gun cotton at Messrs. Bailey and Oliver's of Manchester, where he rendered valuable services. He was demobilised in February 1919, and holds the General Service and Victory Medals.
60, Ryder Street, Bradford, Manchester.   Z10501

JONES, G. E., L/Cpl., 2/4th East Yorkshire Regt.
He volunteered in August 1916, and after a period of training at Catterick, was sent in the following November to the West Indies. There he was employed with his unit on garrison and other important duties and performed consistently good work until March 1919. He was demobilised on his arrival home in the following month, and holds the General Service and Victory Medals.
51, Bedford Street, Moss Side, Manchester.   Z6805

JONES, G. D., Sergt., 6th M.G.C.
A Reservist, he was mobilised at the declaration of war, and in August 1914, embarked for India. Later he saw service in Egypt and Salonika, and took part in many notable engagements, including the Serbian Retreat. Transferred to France, he was badly wounded in the German Offensive of March 1918, and on recovery rejoined his unit, and was in action until the close of hostilites. He was demobilised in February 1919, and holds the 1914-15 Star, and the General Service and Victory Medals.
6, Hiram Street, Ancoats, Manchester.   Z10163A

JONES, H. (M.M.), L/Cpl., 1/8th Manchester Regt.
Volunteering in July 1915, he embarked for Egypt in the following April, and took part in the defence of the Suez Canal, and in operations at Katia, and Romani. Transferred to France in March 1917, he fought at Passchendaele, Givenchy, (where he was wounded in January 1918), and Havrincourt Wood, and was again wounded in action at Mormal Forest in the following November. He was awarded the Military Medal for conspicuous bravery and devotion to duty in the Field, and in addition holds the General Service and Victory Medals. He was demobilised in March 1919.
32, Charles Street, Bradford, Manchester.   Z10504

JONES, H., Private, 1/7th East Lancashire Regt.
Volunteering in September 1914, he proceeded to France in the following June, and took part in several important engagements. He died gloriously on the Field of Battle at Loos on November 19th, 1915, and was entitled to the 1914-15 Star, and the General Service and Victory Medals.
"His name liveth for evermore."
37, Prescott Street, West Gorton, Manchester.   Z10502

JONES, H., L/Cpl., 1st South Lancashire Regt.
He joined in November 1916, and three months later proceeded to India, where he served for over two years. During that period he took an active part in numerous Frontier engagements, and served at Quetta, Peshawar, Rawal Pindi and Kharne. In April 1918 he contracted malaria, but remained in India until December 1919, when he returned to England, and was demobilised a month later, holding the General Service and Victory Medals.   TZ6826
10, Dryden Street, Chorlton-on Medlock, Manchester.

JONES, H., Gunner, R.G.A.
He volunteered in March 1915, and on completion of his training was retained on Home Service until June 1916, when he was drafted overseas. Whilst serving on the Western Front he did good work with his Battery in numerous important engagements, principally in the Ypres sector. He remained in France until August 1919, when he was demobilised, holding the General Service and Victory Medals.
18, Gorton Place, Longsight, Manchester.   Z6798

JONES, H. C., Pte., 1st King's Shropshire Light Infty.
Volunteering in August 1914, he proceeded a month later to India, and was engaged on important garrison duties at Rangoon and Singapore until February 1916. Ten months later he was sent to the Western Front, and saw heavy fighting in the Arras, Ypres, and Passchendaele sectors. He was wounded in action on two occasions, and in consequence was invalided to England, and eventually demobilised in March 1919, holding the General Service and Victory Medals.
69, Church Street, Hulme, Manchester.   Z6820

JONES, H. C., Pte., 1/18th East Lancashire Regt.
Volunteering at the outbreak of war in August 1914, he proceeded in April of the following year, to Gallipoli, where he saw much severe fighting. He made the supreme sacrifice, being killed in action in the third Battle of Krithia in June 1915. He was entitled to the 1914-15 Star, and the General Service and Victory Medals.
"He died the noblest death a man may die,
Fighting for God and right and liberty."
44, Peel Street, Hulme, Manchester.   Z11744

JONES, H. G., 1st Air Mechanic, R.A.F.
He joined the Royal Air Force in January 1918, but was not successful in procuring a transfer overseas. He was retained on home defence and stationed at Aldershot, Farnborough, and Bath, where he was engaged in manufacturing and repairing aeroplanes. This responsible work he carried out with the greatest ability until demobilised in March 1919.
36, Whitfield Street, Ardwick, Manchester.   Z6789

JONES, I., Private, K.O. (Y.L.I.) and Labour Corps.
Joining in July 1916, he embarked for France in August of that year, and was engaged on duties of an important nature in connection with road repairs. He did valuable work until his demobilisation, which took place on his return to England in March 1919. He holds the General Service and Victory Medals.
55, Irlam Street, Miles Platting, Manchester.   Z10505

JONES, I., Private, 2nd South Lancashire Regiment.
He volunteered in August 1914, and in the following December was sent to the Western Front. There, after fighting at Neuve Chapelle and Hill 60, he was wounded in the Battle of Ypres. On returning to the firing line he was in action at Loos, Albert, and the Somme, and was again wounded in the latter engagement. Rejoining his unit he took part in heavy fighting at Cambrai, and in the Retreat and Advance of 1918. Demobilised in February 1919, he holds the 1914 Star, and the General Service and Victory Medals.
28, Gregory Street, West Gorton, Manchester.   Z6795

JONES, J., Driver, R.F.A.
Volunteering in August 1914, he proceeded three months later to France, where he saw service at Ypres, Hill 60, and Loos. He was then sent to the East, but after nearly two years was invalided to England with malaria. In March 1918 he returned to the Western Front, and experienced fierce fighting in the final decisive engagements of the war. After the Armistice he proceeded to Germany with the Army of Occupation, and in 1920 was still serving in the Army. He holds the 1914 Star, and the General Service and Victory Medals.
3, Crayton Street, Hulme, Manchester.   Z6830

JONES, J., Private, Royal Defence Corps.
He volunteered in August 1914, and after undergoing a period of training, served at various stations, where he was engaged in guarding prisoners of war, and on other important duties. He rendered very valuable services with his unit during the whole period of hostilities, and was finally discharged in January 1919, as medically unfit for further service.
2, Amy Street, Openshaw, Manchester.   TZ11745B

JONES, J., Driver, R.A.S.C.
Volunteering in March 1915, he proceeded to France two months later, and was engaged as a transport driver in the forward areas until the close of hostilities. He rendered valuable services until demobilised in March 1919, and holds the 1914-15 Star, and the General Service and Victory Medals.
61, Goodier Street, Harpurhey, Manchester.   Z10506

JONES, J., Private, R.A.V.C.
A month after the war broke out he volunteered for active service, and in January 1915, was drafted to the Western Front, where he served for nearly three years. During that time he was stationed at Rouen and Boulogne, and rendered valuable services in attending to the horses. In December 1917 he was discharged as medically unfit, as the result of a kick from a horse. He holds the 1914-15 Star, and the General Service and Victory Medals.
21, Mary Street, Higher Ardwick, Manchester.   Z6827

JONES, J., Driver, R.F.A.
He volunteered in May 1915, and completing his training was stationed at various depôts with his unit on important duties. He was unsuccessful in obtaining his transfer overseas prior to the cessation of hostilities, but rendered excellent services until demobilised in December 1918.
58, Granville Place, Ancoats, Manchester.   Z9224

JONES, J., Private, Manchester Regiment.
Volunteering in September 1915, he proceeded in the following March to the Western Front, and for some time was employed on important duties at Divisional Headquarters. Later he participated in heavy fighting at Loos, Arras, Ypres, and on the Somme, prior to being evacuated to England on account of ill-health. He was eventually discharged in June 1918, as unfit for further service, and holds the General Service and Victory Medals.
12, Hayfield Street, Ardwick, Manchester.   Z6796

JONES, J., Private, King's (Liverpool Regiment).
He joined in March 1917, and two months later was sent to France. In this theatre of war he was in action at Bullecourt, Messines Ridge, Ypres, and Cambrai, and performed good work, but had only served overseas for six months when he was invalided home suffering from gas poisoning. Upon his recovery he was stationed at Aldershot, employed guarding prisoners of war, and was demobilised in November 1919, holding the General Service and Victory Medals.
6, Clarendon Place Chorlton-on-Medlock, Manchester. Z6822

JONES, J. A., Private, R.A.S.C., (M.T.)
Joining in May 1916, he embarked for Salonika in the following August, and was engaged as a wheeler with the mechanical transport. In this capacity he served on the Monastir, Vardar, and Doiran fronts, and did much valuable work. Whilst overseas, he contracted malaria, and was in consequence for some time under hospital treatment, later being invalided home. He was discharged as medically unfit in October 1919, and holds the General Service and Victory Medals.
3, Cromwell Avenue, Manley Park, Manchester.   Z10507

JONES, J. E., Pte., K.O. (Yorkshire Light Infantry).
He joined in October 1917, and after a period of training was sent six months later to France. There he at once took a prominent part in strenuous fighting on the Somme front, and rendered excellent service until he fell gloriously in action at Amiens on August 11th, 1918. He was entitled to the General Service and Victory Medals.
"A costly sacrifice upon the altar of freedom."
12, Nansen Street, Ardwick, Manchester.   Z6782

JONES, J. E., Private, R.A.M.C.
He volunteered in January 1915, and in October of the same year was drafted to the Dardanelles, serving at Cape Helles for three months. He was then sent to Egypt, and was stationed at Alexandria and El Kantara until March 1917, when he was transferred to France. During his service overseas he was employed as a shoeing smith with the 2nd Field Ambulance, and performed consistently good work. He was demobilised in May 1919, and holds the 1914-15 Star, and the General Service and Victory Medals.
10, Cobden Street, Hulme, Manchester.   TZ6800

JONES, J. H., Driver, R.F.A.
He volunteered in October 1915, and was retained at home on important duties until January 1917, when he was drafted to France. There he served at Arras, Vimy Ridge, Bullecourt, Messines Ridge, Ypres, and Cambrai, where he was gassed. He was subsequently in action in various sectors during the Retreat and Advance of 1918, nd when demobilised in March 1919, was entitled to the General Service and Victory Medals.
9, New Street, West Gorton, Manchester.   TZ6811

JONES, J. H., Drummer, 1/5th Royal Welch Fusiliers.
Mobilised at the declaration of war, he was drafted to the Dardanelles early in 1915, and in April of that year took part in the first Landing at Gallipoli, and the Battle of Cape Helles. He also fought in operations at Krithia and Achi Baba, and was in action until the Evacuation of the Peninsula. He then proceeded to Egypt, where he served for a time. In May 1916, he was invalided home in consequence of ill-health, and after undergoing hospital treatment was discharged in the following February. He holds the 1914-15 Star, and the General Service and Victory Medals.
4, Belmont Street, Collyhurst, Manchester.   Z10508

JONES, J. H., Corporal, 3/8th Manchester Regiment.
Volunteering in March 1915, he was medically unfit for transfer to a theatre of war. Retained at home and stationed successively at Margate, Scarborough, and Southport, he was employed on garrison and other important duties. Whilst thus engaged, he did excellent work until October 1918, when he was invalided out of the Service on account of ill-health.
36, Hardy Street, West Gorton, Manchester.   Z6790

JONES, J. W., Gunner, R.F.A.
He joined in November 1918, but had not completed his training when hostilities ceased. He was engaged on important duties with his unit at various stations, and did much valuable work before being demobilised a year later.
19, Crook Street, Harpurhey, Manchester.   Z10590A

JONES, J. W., Private, 11th Manchester Regiment.
Volunteering in January 1915, he proceeded to France in November of that year, and fought in the Somme Offensive, in which he was wounded in July 1916. On recovery, he rejoined his unit in the Field, but was unhappily killed in action at Passchendaele Ridge in January 1917. He was entitled to the 1914-15 Star, and the General Service and Victory Medals.
"A costly sacrifice upon the altar of freedom."
5, Lavender Street, Miles Platting, Manchester.   Z10496A

JONES, J. W., Pte., King's Own Scottish Borderers.
He volunteered in September 1914, and in the following March was drafted to France. In this theatre of war he was in action at St. Eloi, Hill 60, and Ypres, where he was severely wounded. Evacuated to England, he spent six months in hospital at Ipswich, and upon his recovery, returned to France, and took part in further fighting at Loos, Albert, Vimy Ridge, Arras, Cambrai, on the Somme, and on the Aisne, before being killed in action at Havrincourt in September 1918. He was entitled to the 1914-15 Star, and the General Service and Victory Medals.
"His memory is cherished with pride."
16, Brunswick Street, Hulme, Manchester.   Z6816

JONES, O., Private, 30th Royal Welch Fusiliers.
Volunteering in March 1915, he was sent for training to Colchester, after which he did good work whilst employed on

various duties. Later, he underwent an operation, and had two toes cut off, but septic poisoning setting in, he was eventually discharged from the Army in April 1916.
39, Wycliffe Street, Ardwick, Manchester.   Z6801

JONES, P. H., Gunner, R.G.A.
He volunteered in November 1914, and three months later was discharged as unfit for military service. Volunteering for the second time in February 1915, he served for a few months at Lytham, and was employed on various duties, doing excellent work. In July 1915, however, he was again invalided out of the Army as unfit for further service.
99, Gibson Street, Ardwick, Manchester.   Z6786

JONES, R., Rifleman, K.R.R.C.
Having previously served with the Colours and taken part in the South African Campaign, he was mobilised in August 1914, and three months later was drafted to France. There he took part in the Battle of La Bassée, and was wounded during subsequent fighting in January 1915, and sent to hospital at Boulogne. Evacuated to England, he was in hospital in Manchester until October 1915, when he was invalided out of the Army as unfit for further service. He unhappily died on December 20th, 1918, from illness caused by his wounds. He was entitled to the 1914 Star, and the General Service and Victory Medals, in addition to holding the Queen's and King's South African Medals.
45, Riga Street, City Road, Hulme, Manchester.   TZ6818

JONES, S. (M.M.), Corporal, Manchester Regiment.
He volunteered in August 1914, and landing in France in the following January, fought at Loos, Ypres, Albert, and the Somme, at each of which engagements he was wounded. Transferred to Italy in February 1917, he took part in important operations on the Piave, and was in action until August of the succeeding year, when he returned to the Western Front and fought in the Allied Advance. He was awarded the Military Medal for gallantry displayed in rescuing an Officer under intense shell-fire, although himself severely wounded. In addition he holds the 1914-15 Star, and the General Service and Victory Medals, and was invalided out of the Service in December 1919.
21, Lancashire Street, Newton Heath, Manchester.   Z10499A

JONES, S. A., Private, 2/8th Manchester Regiment.
He volunteered in September 1914, and after his training was engaged on duties of an important nature at various stations. Owing to ill-health, he was unable to secure his transfer to a theatre of war, and in December of the same year was invalided out of the Service.
42, Richardson Street, Collyhurst, Manchester.   Z10511

JONES, S. E., Pte., King's Own Scottish Borderers.
He volunteered in August 1914, and in the following April proceeded to the Western Front, where he served for a period of four years. During this time, he took part in many important engagements, including the Battles of Hill 60, Ypres II, Loos, Somme I, Arras, Ypres III, Cambrai, Somme II, Marne II, and Cambrai II. Demobilised on his return home in April 1919, he holds the 1914-15 Star, and the General Service and Victory Medals.
55, Genge's Avenue, Chester Road, Hulme, Manchester.   TZ6829

JONES, T., Private, 1st Manchester Regiment.
Volunteering at the commencement of hostilities, he was sent to the Western Front shortly afterwards, and fought in the Battles of Ypres, and the Somme, where he was wounded. On his recovery, he rejoined his unit and was in action at Vimy Ridge, Givenchy, and throughout the Retreat and Advance of 1918. He was demobilised in January 1919, and holds the 1914-15 Star, and the General Service and Victory Medals.
44, Victoria Square, Oldham Road, Manchester.   TZ9225

JONES, T., A.B., Royal Navy.
Having enlisted in April 1912, he was already in the Navy when war was declared in August 1914, and afterwards served in H.M.S. "Lion" in many waters. He took part in the Battles of Heligoland Bight and Falkland Islands, and many minor engagements, and was wounded in action in the Battle of the Dogger Bank in January 1915. He holds the 1914-15 Star, and the General Service Medal (with five clasps), and Victory Medal, and in 1920 was still at sea.
2, Amy Street, Openshaw, Manchester.   TZ11745A

JONES, T., Private, 8th Manchester Regiment.
Volunteering in August 1914, he was drafted next month to Egypt and served on the Suez Canal until March 1915, when he was sent to Gallipoli. There he participated in the Battles of Krithia, where he was slightly wounded, and after the Evacuation was transferred to France. In this theatre of war he was in action at Albert, Vimy Ridge, and on the Somme, and was again wounded. As a result he was invalided home, admitted to hospital in Stockport, and upon his recovery, was employed on various duties at Scarborough until he was demobilised in February 1919, holding the 1914-15 Star, and the General Service and Victory Medals.
8, Clarendon Place, Chorlton-on-Medlock, Manchester. Z6823

JONES, T., Guardsman, Grenadier Guards, and Private, R.A.M.C.

Joining in March 1918, he embarked for Salonika in the following July, and took part in operations on the Vardar front, remaining overseas until March 1919. He holds the General Service and Victory Medals, and in 1920 was still serving as a medical Orderly at Rochester Row Military Hospital.
28, Lowe Street, Oldham Road, Manchester. Z10512

JONES, T., Sapper, R.E.

He joined in January 1917, and crossing to France two months later, was engaged on duties of an important nature in connection with operations at La Bassée, Nieuport, and Béthune. After the cessation of hostilities, he proceeded with the Army of Occupation to Germany, and was demobilised on his return to England in October 1919. He holds the General Service and Victory Medals. 3, Broughton St., Ancoats, Manchester. Z10509

JONES, T., Sapper, R.E.

He joined in August 1916, and after his training was engaged on duties of an important nature with his unit at various stations. He was not successful in obtaining his transfer to a theatre of war before the close of hostilities, but nevertheless did valuable work until demobilised in February 1919.
70, Heyrod Street, Ancoats, Manchester. Z10510

JONES, T., Private, 7th Royal Welch Fusiliers.

He volunteered in November 1914, and four months later proceeded to the Western Front. There he played a prominent part in many important engagements, including Ypres, Festubert, Loos, Albert, the Somme, Arras, Messines Ridge, Ypres II, and Cambrai, and did excellent work. Returning home after the Armistice, he was demobilised in December 1918, and holds the 1914–15 Star, and the General Service and Victory Medals. 34, Hewitt St., Openshaw, Manchester. Z6812B

JONES, T., Private, 8th Manchester Regiment.

Joining in November 1916, he was drafted in the following May to Egypt, and later proceeded to Palestine. In this theatre of hostilities he participated in several important engagements, was in action at Gaza, and took part in the capture of Jerusalem, Jericho, and Tripoli. He returned home in April 1919, and was demobilised in the following month, holding the General Service and Victory Medals.
14, Solent Street, Ardwick, Manchester. Z6803

JONES, T. A. M., Private, 2/2nd E. Lancashire Regt.

He volunteered in October 1915, and was employed at various home stations on important duties until February 1917, when he was sent to France. In this theatre of war he was in action at Ypres, and Cambrai, and in various sectors during the Retreat and Advance of 1918. Demobilised on his return in April 1919, he holds the General Service and Victory Medals.
55, Morton Street, Longsight, Manchester. Z6787

JONES, T. E., Private, R.A.S.C.

He joined in October 1918, but was not successful in obtaining a transfer overseas owing to the termination of hostilities. After a period of training at Whitchurch, he was sent to Southampton, where he did good work employed on various duties until he was invalided out of the Service on account of ill-health in February 1919.
133, Blackthorn Street, Ardwick, Manchester. Z6783

JONES, T. J., Corporal, R.A.S.C., and R.A.F.

Joining the Royal Army Service Corps in October 1917, he was transferred in the following month to the Royal Air Force, and proceeded to America with the British Aviation Mission. He rendered valuable services whilst employed on important duties, which demanded a high degree of technical skill, and returning home was eventually demobilised in February 1919. He holds the General Service and Victory Medals.
14, Crosscliffe Street, Moss Side, Manchester. Z6806

JONES, W., Private, 12th Manchester Regiment, and Air Mechanic, R.A.F.

Volunteering in June 1915, he proceeded to France in the following January, and fought at Loos and St. Eloi, where he was so severely wounded as to necessitate his return to England. On recovery in December 1917, he was transferred to the Royal Air Force, and was engaged on important home duties with his Squadron until demobilised in April 1919. He holds the General Service and Victory Medals.
12, Dawson Street, West Gorton, Manchester. Z10513

JONES, W.(D.C.M.), C.S.M., 7th Seaforth Highlanders.

He volunteered in 1915, and was later drafted to France. In this theatre of war he played a distinguished part in many important engagements, being in action on the Somme, and at Longueval, Arras, Meteren, Passchendaele, and Messines Ridge, and was twice wounded. He was awarded the Distinguished Conduct Medal for conspicuous gallantry and devotion to duty in the Field, and also received the Médaille Militaire. On his demobilisation in March 1919, he was in addition, entitled to the General Service and Victory Medals.
98, Percival Street, Chorlton-on-Medlock, Manchester. X6797

JONES, W., L/Corporal, 11th Lancashire Fusiliers.

Volunteering in September 1914, he embarked for France a year later and took part in heavy fighting in the Ypres sector. In April 1916, he was sent to England, and owing to his skill

as ammunition worker, was employed in this capacity until March 1917. He was afterwards engaged on important home duties until demobilised in January 1919, and holds the 1914-15 Star, and the General Service and Victory Medals.
10, Harrowby Street, Manchester. Z10514

JONES, W., Driver, R.A.S.C.

He joined in April 1916, and a year later was drafted to France, where he was engaged on important transport duties in the forward areas of the Ypres Salient. Owing to ill-health, in 1918 he was invalided home, and after receiving hospital treatment was discharged in November 1919. He holds the General Service and Victory Medals.
48, Burnley Street, Ancoats, Manchester. Z9226

JONES, W., Driver, R.A.S.C.

He joined in January 1916, and a few months later proceeded to the Western Front. In this theatre of hostilities he was employed as a transport driver and did excellent work whilst serving at Beaumont-Hamel, Arras, Vimy Ridge, Bullecourt, Ypres, Cambrai, Le Cateau, and on the Somme and Ancre fronts. He later served with the Army of Occupation in Germany, and was still in the Army in 1920, stationed in Sussex. He holds the General Service and Victory Medals.
7, Mallow Street, Hulme, Manchester. Z6814A

JONES, W., Private, 7th Lancashire Fusiliers.

Volunteering in August 1915, he was drafted in the following March to France. There he at once took part in strenuous fighting at St. Eloi and Albert, but had only served overseas for a month when he was invalided home on account of ill-health, and sent to hospital in Cardiff. He was discharged in September 1916, as unfit for further service, and holds the General Service and Victory Medals.
14, Lord Street, Hulme, Manchester. TZ6828A

JONES, W., Driver, R.A.S.C.

He volunteered in March 1915, but was medically unfit for service in a theatre of war. Retained at home, he was stationed at various places on the East Coast, and employed on various duties in connection with home defence. He rendered valuable services until he was demobilised in March 1919.
7, Mallow Street, Hulme, Manchester. Z6814B

JONES, W., Sergt., R.E.

Having previously taken part in the South African Campaign, he was mobilised in August 1914, and twelve months later was sent to the Dardanelles, where he was stationed for some time prior to being transferred to France. On the Western Front he served with his Company at Loos, Cambrai, Ypres, La Bassée, Messines Ridge, Hulluch, and on the Somme and Sambre fronts. He was employed on various duties of an important nature, and did excellent work until April 1919, when he returned home and was demobilised, holding the 1914–15 Star, and the General Service and Victory Medals, in addition to the South Africa Medal.
1, Beswick Street, Ardwick, Manchester. Z6784

JONES, W., Private, 8th Lancashire Fusiliers.

He volunteered in August 1914, and after a period of training was drafted in the following April to Gallipoli. During his service in this theatre of war, he participated in heavy fighting during the three Battles of Krithia, and was unhappily killed in action at Suvla Bay in August 1915. He was entitled to the 1914–15 Star, and the General Service and Victory Medals.
"Great deeds cannot die." Z6600B
26, George's Avenue, Chester Road, Hulme, Manchester.

JONES, W., Private, 13th Manchester Regiment.

Volunteering in September 1914, he proceeded in the following year to the Western Front. There he took a prominent part in the Battle of Loos, and other engagements, and was later transferred to Salonika. In this theatre of hostilities he participated in severe fighting on various fronts, and did good work until he was invalided home suffering from malaria. Eventually demobilised in February 1919, he holds the 1914–15 Star, and the General Service and Victory Medals.
41, Bickley Street, Moss Side, Manchester. Z6831

JONES, W. A., Private, 2nd Border Regiment.

He volunteered in July 1915, and after a brief training proceeded two months later to the Western Front. There he participated in strenuous fighting in various sectors, and did good work until he was unfortunately killed by a sniper on the Somme front in November 1916. He was entitled to the 1914–15 Star, and the General Service and Victory Medals.
"Whilst we remember the sacrifice is not in vain."
10, Honduras Street, Chorlton-on-Medlock, Manchester. Z6791

JONES, W. D., Private, R.A.S.C.

Volunteering in April 1915, he was soon afterwards sent to France. There he was employed on important duties and rendered excellent service until he met with an accident at Calais Harbour, and was invalided home. Upon his recovery he proceeded to Salonika where he served for over two years, a part of the time attached to General Headquarters. In June 1918, he was evacuated to England on account of ill-health, and was eventually demobilised in February 1919, holding the 1914–15 Star, and the General Service and Victory Medals. 6, Potter St., Hulme, Manchester. Z6810

JONES, W. H., L/Cpl, 1/6th Sherwood Foresters.
He volunteered in September 1914, and in the following
February was drafted to the Western Front. In this theatre
of war he played a prominent part in heavy fighting at Loos,
Gommecourt, Bellenglise, and in other sectors, and performed
consistently good work. He remained overseas until after
the Armistice, and demobilised on his return home in January
1919, holds the 1914–15 Star, and the General Service and
Victory Medals.
31, Whittaker Street, Chorlton-on-Medlock, Manchester. Z6781

JONES, W. J., L/Corporal, 20th Lancashire Fusiliers.
Mobilised in August 1914, he immediately proceeded to France
and was in action at Mons, Ypres, Loos, Vimy Ridge, the
Somme, the Marne, Arras, Cambrai, Le Cateau, and Havrincourt. He was later invalided home on account of ill-health,
but upon his recovery returned to France and took part in
further fighting in various sectors. Demobilised in February
1919, he holds the Mons Star, and the General Service and
Victory Medals.
6, North Street, Hulme, Manchester.   Z6821

JONES, W. T., Driver, R.F.A.
He volunteered in May 1915, and in the following March was
sent to the Western Front. There he served with his Battery
at Albert, Beaucourt, Arras, Ypres, Cambrai, and on the
Somme, and in various sectors during the Retreat and Advance
of 1918. Wounded in action at Havrincourt in October of
that year, he was invalided home and was eventually discharged in January 1919, holding the General Service and
Victory Medals.
34, Hewitt Street, Openshaw, Manchester.   Z6812A

JOLLEY, S., Private, King's (Liverpool Regiment).
He joined in June 1918, but was not successful in obtaining
a transfer overseas before the termination of hostilities. After
serving at Yarmouth and Kinmel Park, he was sent to Germany in February 1919, and remained with the Army of
Occupation until March 1920, employed as a motor transport
driver, being demobilised on returning home in that month.
40, Lower Chatham St., Chorlton-on-Medlock, Manchester.
                                                  Z6832

JORDAN, A., Private, 8th Manchester Regiment.
He volunteered in August 1914, and in the following April
proceeded to Gallipoli. After taking part in heavy fighting
during the Landing and Evacuation, he was wounded at
Krithia. Upon his recovery, he was transferred to France,
and participated in further fighting at Arras, Bullecourt,
Passchendaele, Cambrai, on the Marne and Somme, and was
wounded on three occasions. Returning home in January
1919, he was demobilised a month later, and holds the 1914–15
Star, and the General Service and Victory Medals.
13, Jones St., Chorlton-on-Medlock, Manchester.   TZ6835

JORDAN, H., Corporal, 2nd East Lancashire Regt.
Volunteering in November 1914, he was drafted four months
later to France. There he was in action at Ypres, Ploegsteert
Wood, and on the Somme front, where he was wounded in
July 1916, and evacuated to England. After nearly twelve
months in hospital, he returned to France, and was again
wounded during the second battle of the Somme. Invalided
home, he was sent to hospital in Bath, and was subsequently
demobilised in February 1919, holding the 1914–15 Star, and
the General Service and Victory Medals.
9, Dorrington Street, Hulme, Manchester.   Z6833

JORDAN, M., Private, K.O. (Royal Lancaster Regt.)
Volunteering in October 1915, he was sent to France on com-
pletion of his training and took part in the Battles of the
Somme, Arras, Bullecourt, Ypres, and Cambrai. He was
also in action during fierce fighting at Albert, Armentières,
Bourlon Wood, and Mericourt, and was wounded and gassed.
Invalided home, he spent some time in hospital at Halifax,
and was eventually demobilised in March 1919, holding the
General Service and Victory Medals.
45, Elizabeth Street, Ancoats, Manchester.   Z11910

JORDAN, W., Private, 12th Manchester Regiment.
Volunteering shortly after the outbreak of war, he proceeded
to the Western Front early in 1915, and took part in operations
at Ypres, and Loos. He fell fighting at Metz Wood, during
the Somme Offensive on July 7th, 1916, and lies buried at
Serre Road Cemetery, Beaumont-Hamel. He was entitled to
the 1914–15 Star, and the General Service and Victory Medals.
                    "Great deeds cannot die."
21, Heaton Street, Ardwick, Manchester.   Z10515

JORDAN, W. H., Private, Suffolk Regiment.
Mobilised in August 1914, he was at once ordered to France,
and participated in the Retreat from Mons, and in the Battles
of the Marne, the Aisne, Ypres, Neuve Chapelle, La Bassée,
Loos, Festubert, and the Somme, where he was wounded in
July 1916. Invalided home he was sent to hospital at Didsbury, and later served at Halton Camp and Crowborough,
until he was discharged in June 1917, as unfit for further
service in consequence of his wounds. He holds the Mons
Star, and the General Service and Victory Medals.
32, Carver Street, Chorlton-on-Medlock, Manchester. Z6834

JOWETT, A. W., Private, 11th Manchester Regt.
He volunteered in October 1914, and in the following May
was sent to the Dardanelles. In this theatre of hostilities he
took part in heavy fighting, and later proceeding to Palestine,
was wounded during the Battle of Gaza. He remained overseas, doing excellent work, until he returned home for demobilisation in February 1919, holding the 1914–15 Star, and the
General Service and Victory Medals.
8, Dryden Street, Upper Plymouth Grove, Longsight, Manchester.   Z6836

JOWETT, J., Private, R.A.M.C.
Volunteering in September 1915, he was too old for service
in a combatant unit, and was posted to the Royal Army
Medical Corps. Proceeding to Malta two months later, he
performed consistently good work employed on various duties
in hospital, until he was invalided home in April 1917 on account
of ill-health, being eventually discharged in the following
October, and subsequently dying at home from a malady
attributed to his military service. He was entitled to the
General Service and Victory Medals.
        "His memory is cherished with pride."
128, Clopton Street, Hulme, Manchester.   Z6837A

JOWETT, J. W., Private, 1st Herefordshire Regt.
Joining in December 1917, he landed in France in the following
July, and fought at Havrincourt, Ypres, and the Selle.
He was with the troops who entered Mons at dawn on November 11th, 1918, and after the signing of the Armistice proceeded
with the Army of Occupation to Germany. He was demobilised in September 1919, and holds the General Service and
Victory Medals.
61, Elizabeth Street, West Gorton, Manchester.   Z10517

JOWETT, S., Bombardier, R.F.A.
Serving in Ireland at the outbreak of war in August 1914, he
was sent in the following month to France where he took part
in the final stages of the Retreat from Mons, and in the Battles
of the Marne and Aisne. He was later transferred to Gallipoli,
and was in action during heavy fighting at Suvla Bay. In
January 1916, he proceeded to Macedonia where he served
on various fronts until June 1920, when he returned home
and was demobilised, holding the Mons Star, and the General
Service and Victory Medals.
128, Clopton Street, Hulme, Manchester.   Z6837B

JOYNSON, D. A., Rifleman, 8th Rifle Brigade.
Volunteering at the commencement of hostilities, in January
1915 he embarked for the Western Front, and was in action
in the Battles of Neuve Chapelle and Ypres. He gave his life
for the freedom of England on July 30th, 1915, at Hooge, and
was entitled to the 1914–15 Star, and the General Service and
Victory Medals.
"A valiant Soldier, with undaunted heart he breasted life's
    last hill."
124, Victoria Square, Oldham Road, Manchester.   Z9227

JOYNSON, E., Private, 2nd Manchester Regiment.
Volunteering in August 1914, he was drafted to France in the
following month, and was in action on the Aisne, and at La
Bassée, Ypres, Neuve Chapelle, and Hill 60. Whilst on leave
he became seriously ill, and was under treatment for six
months in hospital. He then rejoined his unit in France, and
took part in the Battle of the Somme where he was wounded
early in July 1916. He was again invalided home, and was
discharged in July of the following year, and holds the 1914–15
Star, and the General Service and Victory Medals.
10, Cheltenham Street, Collyhurst, Manchester.   Z11525

JOYNSON, J. F., Sapper, R.E.
He volunteered in March 1915, and was employed on various
duties at home stations until February 1916, when he was
drafted to the Western Front. There he served with his
Company at Neuve Chapelle, Albert, Vimy Ridge, Hill 60,
Arras, Ypres, and on the Somme, and did good work. Invalided
home on account of ill-health in July 1918, he was a patient
in hospital at Birmingham for some time, before being demobilised in March 1919, holding the General Service and Victory
Medals. 2, Whitworth St., Longsight, Manchester. Z6839

JOYNSON, P., Private, Royal Welch Fusiliers.
He joined in September 1917, and a month later proceeded
to the Western Front. In this theatre of war he played a
prominent part in strenuous fighting at Cambrai, Amiens, and
on the Somme and Sambre. He was wounded in action at
Ypres in 1918, but remained overseas until November 1919,
when he returned home and was demobilised, holding the
General Service and Victory Medals.
10, Tuley Street, Lower Openshaw, Manchester.   Z6838

JOYNT, J. A., Private, King's Own Scottish Borderers.
He volunteered in February 1915, and after completing his
training was engaged at various stations on important duties
with his unit. He rendered valuable services, but was not
successful in obtaining his transfer overseas. He unfortunately
met with an accident to his eyes, and after treatment in hospital was discharged as medically unfit for further service in
February 1917.
65, Naylor Street, Oldham Road, Manchester.   Z9602

JUBBS, J., Private, King's (Liverpool Regiment).
Volunteering in March 1915, he proceeded to Mesopotamia four months later, and was in action at Kut, and in many other engagements. He laid down his life for King and Country on March 8th, 1917, during the fighting which resulted in the Capture of Baghdad. He was entitled to the 1914-15 Star, and the General Service and Victory Medals.
    " A costly sacrifice upon the altar of freedom."
35, Upper Dover Street, Bradford, Manchester.   Z9228

JUDGE, M., Corporal, 11th Manchester Regiment.
He volunteered in October 1914, and after completing his training was stationed at Cleethorpes and Grantham, employed on various duties, until he was drafted to the Dardanelles in 1915. There he at once participated in heavy fighting, and was severely wounded at Suvla Bay in August 1915, dying shortly afterwards from the effects of his injuries. He was entitled to the 1914-15 Star, and the General Service and Victory Medals.
    " His life for his Country."
5, Hamilton Street, Bradford, Manchester.   TZ6840

JUDSON, J. R., Private, 1/7th Manchester Regt.
Mobilised with the Territorials in August 1914, he was quickly sent to Egypt, where he saw heavy fighting in the Suez Canal zone. Later he proceeded to Palestine and took part in the Advance with General Allenby's Forces. He then returned to Egypt and was stationed at Kantara until his demobilisation in March 1919. He holds the 1914-15 Star, and the General Service and Victory Medals.
5, Samuel Street, West Gorton, Manchester.   TZ11911

JULIAN, F., Private, Royal Welch Fusiliers.
He joined in June 1916, but not being medically fit for service in the front line, was sent to Gibraltar, where he was stationed from August 1917 until June 1919. During this time he was employed with his unit on garrison and other important duties, and performed consistently good work. He was demobilised on his return home in June 1919, and holds the General Service and Victory Medals.
159, Clopton Street, Hulme, Manchester.   Z6841

K

KALE, G., Private, Royal Irish Fusiliers.
He volunteered in August 1914, and was shortly afterwards drafted to the Western Front. There he took part in several engagements, and was badly wounded at Loos, and consequently was invalided home. He was discharged in January 1915 as medically unfit for further service, and holds the 1914 Star, and the General Service and Victory Medals.
35, Neill Street, Gorton, Manchester.   Z10024B

KAY, F., Private, Lancashire Fusiliers.
He volunteered in August 1914, and early in the following year proceeded to the Dardanelles, where he took part in the Landing at Gallipoli, and was wounded. After a period in hospital he was sent to the Western Front in 1916, and was in action in many important sectors. He saw much heavy fighting on the Somme and at Beaumont-Hamel and Ypres III, and was taken prisoner in 1918. He was repatriated after the Armistice, and eventually demobilised in May 1919, and holds the 1914-15 Star, and the General Service and Victory Medals. 47, Bonsall Street, Hulme, Manchester.   Z6846

KAY, F., Driver, R.E.
Volunteering in February 1915, he was sent to France later in the same year and did consistently good work in many sectors of the Front. He was present at the Battles of the Somme (I and II), Beaumont-Hamel, Albert, Arras, Cambrai, Amiens, Bapaume, and Havrincourt, and rendered valuable services during the Retreat and Advance of 1918. He holds the 1914-15 Star, and the General Service and Victory Medals, and was discharged in June 1919.
47, Bonsall Street, Hulme, Manchester.   Z6845

KAY, F. B., Private, R.A.O.C.
He joined in August 1917, and did consistently good work in England during the first part of his service. He was sent to the Eastern theatre of war in April 1918, and saw service in Egypt and Palestine, where he was engaged on special duties with his unit. He returned to England in July 1918, suffering from neurasthenia, and was discharged three months later as medically unfit for further service. He holds the General Service and Victory Medals.
31, Aked Street, Ardwick, Manchester.   X6847

KAY, G., Sapper, R.E.
He joined in October 1916, but owing to his being unfit for service overseas, was retained on special duties with his unit at various important stations in England. He nevertheless rendered valuable services as a gun borer and driller until the termination of hostilities, and was discharged in January 1919, as medically unfit.
26, Marlow Street, Longsight, Manchester.   Z6844

KAY, J., Private, 6th Manchester Regiment.
He volunteered in November 1915, and in June of the following year proceeded to Egypt, where he was engaged on special duties. In April 1917, he was transferred to the Western Front and saw service at the Battles of Messines, Ypres III, and Cambrai, and in other engagements of importance until the termination of hostilities. He holds the General Service and Victory Medals, and was demobilised in May 1919.
25, Freeman Street, Hulme, Manchester.   Z6848

KAY, J. A., 1st Air Mechanic, R.A.F.
Joining in June 1917, he first saw service with the Lancashire Fusiliers, and two months later was transferred to the Royal Air Force. He did consistently good work until his demobilisation in July 1919, but was not successful in his efforts to serve in a theatre of war, owing to physical disability through meeting with an accident.
29, Arnott Street, Hulme, Manchester.   Z6849

KAY, J. E., Corporal, 7th Manchester Regiment.
He was mobilised in August 1914, and was engaged on important guard duties on the East Coast until the end of 1917. He was then drafted to France, and after being transferred to the Labour Corps did consistently good work during the Retreat and Advance of 1918. He holds the General Service and Victory Medals, and was demobilised in February 1919.
70, Earl Street, Longsight, Manchester.   Z6843

KAY, M., Private, 16th Manchester Regiment.
Joining in March 1917, he proceeded to France four months later and took part in much heavy fighting in many sectors. He was in action on the Passchendaele and Cambrai fronts, and made the supreme sacrifice at St. Quentin on March 31st, 1918, during the great Retreat. He was entitled to the General Service and Victory Medals.
    " He died the noblest death a man may die."
59, Barlow Street, Bradford, Manchester.   Z6842

KAY, W., Private, 6th South Lancashire Regiment.
Volunteering in September 1914, he sailed for Gallipoli in the following June, and was in action at Suvla Bay, and in many other engagements of note. Severely wounded in August 1915, he returned to England, and after receiving hospital treatment was discharged unfit for further service in July 1916. He holds the 1914-15 Star, and the General Service and Victory Medals.
77, Oldham Road, Manchester.   Z9229

KAYE, R., Private, Royal Welch Fusiliers.
He volunteered in May 1915, and two months later proceeded to France, where he took part in many important engagements, including the Battles of St. Eloi, Loos, Vermelles, the Somme, Arras, Lens, Bapaume and the Sambre, and was wounded on two occasions—on the Somme in July 1916, and at St. Quentin in April 1918. He returned to England and was discharged in March 1919, holding the 1914-15 Star, and the General Service and Victory Medals.
18, Hughes Street, Ardwick, Manchester.   Z6850

KEANE, J., Sergt., R.A.S.C. (M.T.)
He volunteered in August 1914, and after a brief period of training was drafted to France in the following month. He was engaged on important transport duties at the Base at Rouen and in November 1916 was transferred to East Africa, where he did consistently good work until the cessation of hostilities. He was invalided to England with malaria, and was eventually demobilised in July 1920, holding the 1914 Star, and the General Service and Victory Medals.
13, Granville Street, Chorlton-on-Medlock, Manchester.   Z6851

KEARNEY, A., Private, 1/6th Manchester Regt.
He joined in October 1917, and in March 1918 was drafted to France, where he took part in many important engagements. He was in action on the Somme, and at Beaumont-Hamel, Beaucourt and Havrincourt, and was badly wounded at Mailley-Maillet during the Advance in August 1918. He was invalided to England, and was eventually demobilised in March 1919, holding the General Service and Victory Medals.
98, Rosebery Street, Moss Side, Manchester.   Z6852

KEARNEY, W., Driver, R.F.A.
He was called up from the Reserve in August 1914, and immediately drafted to France. There he took part in the Battles of Mons, Ypres, Loos, the Somme, Arras, Messines, Cambrai and in the Retreat of 1918. He was then transferred to Italy, and saw much fighting on the Piave, but was taken ill in August 1918, and consequently invalided home. He was discharged in November 1918, and holds the Mons Star, and the General Service and Victory Medals.
9, Hope Street, Bradford, Manchester.   Z10608

KEARNS, B., Sergt., Loyal North Lancashire Regt.
He volunteered in September 1914, and was engaged as a Sergt.-Instructor at Felixstowe. He was unable to obtain a transfer overseas owing to his being overage, but did continuously good work at home until he was discharged as medically unfit for further service in April 1918.
49, Sycamore Street, Manchester.   Z10609

KEARNS, J. E., Sergt., R.E.

He volunteered in August 1914, and was shortly afterwards drafted to Egypt, where he took a prominent part in engagements on the Suez Canal. Later he was transferred to the Dardanelles, and saw much heavy fighting and was wounded in action in June 1915. As a result, he was invalided home, and on his recovery served at various stations on important duties until his demobilisation in May 1919. He holds the 1914–15 Star, and the General Service and Victory Medals.
61, Sycamore Street, Manchester.　　Z10610

KEARNS, O., Private, Loyal North Lancashire Regt.

Having previously served in the Army, he re-enlisted in his old Regiment in August 1914, and did consistently good work whilst engaged on special duties at various home stations until October 1916. He was then discharged as medically unfit but, in August 1918, joined the R.A.F., and rendered further valuable services, until finally demobilised in February 1919.
8, Hambro Street, Chapel Street, Ancoats, Manchester. Z6853

KEARSLEY, R., Private, South Lancashire Regt.

He volunteered in August 1914, and underwent a period of training prior to his being drafted to France. There he took part in several engagements, including those at Loos, Albert, Vimy Ridge, the Somme, Ypres (III), Passchendaele, and the second Battle of the Somme, where he was wounded in action in March 1918. As a result, he was invalided home and discharged in October 1918, as medically unfit for further duty, and holds the General Service and Victory Medals.
12, King Street, Hulme, Manchester.　　Z10611

KEATINGE, H., L/Corporal, 19th Manchester Regt.

Volunteering in September 1914, he underwent a period of training and was drafted to the Western Front in November of the following year. He took part in the fighting on the Somme, and was invalided home with trench fever in April 1917. Three months later he returned to France, and fought at Arras, Ypres, Bullecourt and during the Retreat and Advance of 1918. He holds the 1914–15 Star, and the General Service and Victory Medals, and was demobilised in March 1919. 31, Sadler Street, Moss Side, Manchester.　Z6854

KEDIE, J. A., Shoeing Smith, R.F.A.

He volunteered in September 1914, and after doing duty at various camps in England, was drafted to France in June 1915. There he did consistently good work in many sectors, played a prominent part in the Battles of St. Eloi, Loos, Albert, Vimy Ridge, the Somme, Arras, Passchendaele and Cambrai, and was also in action during the Retreat and Advance of 1918. He holds the 1914–15 Star, and the General Service and Victory Medals. and was demobilised in March 1919. 10, Merrimer Street, Greenheys, Manchester.　Z6855B

KEDIE, J. W., Private, 2/4th South Lancashire Regt.

He volunteered in February 1915, and did consistently good work at various camps in England during the first part of his service. In March 1917, he was drafted to France, and took part in many important engagements, including those at Arras and Bullecourt, and made the supreme sacrifice on July 27th, 1917, when he was killed in action at Armentières. He was entitled to the General Service and Victory Medals.
"Whilst we remember, the sacrifice is not in vain."
10, Merrimer Street, Greenheys, Manchester.　Z6855A

KEDIE, P., Driver, R.F.A.

He joined in April 1916, and after undergoing a period of training, was drafted to France in March of the following year. There he was in action with his Battery at numerous important engagements, including the Battles of Arras, Vimy Ridge, Messines, and Passchendaele, and was wounded in the fighting on the Sand Dunes in Belgium in August 1917. He was invalided home, and eventually discharged in August 1918, as physically unfit for further service, and holds the General Service and Victory Medals.
10. Merrimer Street, Greenheys, Manchester.　Z6855C

KEEBLE, L., Bombardier, R.F.A.

Mobilised at the outbreak of war in August 1914, he was immediately drafted to the Western Front, and took part in the Retreat from Mons. He was also in action with his Battery at many subsequent engagements, including the Battles of the Marne, the Aisne, La Bassée, Ypres, Neuve Chapelle, Hill 60, Festubert, Loos, Albert, the Somme, Arras, Vimy Ridge, Messines, Passchendaele and Cambrai, and was wounded and gassed in November 1917. He finally took part in the Retreat and Advance of 1918, and was discharged in February 1919, holding the Mons Star, and the General Service and Victory Medals.
11, Gascoyne Street, Moss Side, Manchester.　　Z6856

KEEFE, H., A.B., Royal Navy.

He volunteered in February 1915, and after a period of training was commissioned to H.M.S. "Doris," in which vessel he served in many waters. He took part in the Naval operations in the Dardanelles, and saw much active service whilst conveying troops to Malta, Egypt, the Syrian Coast, Long Island

and Salonika. He was demobilised in March 1919, and holds the 1914–15 Star, and the General Service (with three clasps) and the Victory Medals.
28, Lancashire Street, Newton Heath, Manchester.　Z10613

KEEFE, J. J., Private, Royal Welch Fusiliers.

Volunteering in August 1914, he proceeded to France after a period of training. Whilst overseas he took part in the Battles of the Somme, Albert, and Ypres (III), where he was wounded and made prisoner of war in July 1917. He was held in captivity in Germany and was forced to work in the coal mines. After the Armistice he was released, and returned home for his demobilisation in January 1919. He holds the General Service and Victory Medals.
90, Churnett Street, Collyhurst, Manchester.　Z10612

KEEFE, M., Private, R.A.S.C.

Volunteering in September 1914, he was drafted to France two months later and was engaged on important transport duties throughout the whole period of hostilities. He rendered valuable services in many sectors of the Front, including the Marne, Ypres and Vermelles, and was wounded whilst taking rations to forward areas. He also suffered from blood-poisoning, and after two months in hospital, was discharged in May 1919, holding the 1914 Star, and the General Service and Victory Medals.
8, Torkworth Avenue, Longsight, Manchester.　Z6858

KEEFE, T., Private, K.O. (Royal Lancaster Regt.)

He joined in February 1917, and after a month's training was drafted to France, where he saw service at the Battles of Arras and Ypres (III). He suffered from nephritis and rheumatism, and after a period in hospital at Rouen, returned to England in December 1917 for treatment. He eventually rejoined his unit in Ireland, and after further service was discharged in May 1919, as physically unfit. He holds the General Service and Victory Medals.
51, Freeme Street, Chorlton-on-Medlock, Manchester. Z6857

KEEL, A., Gunner, R.G.A.

He joined in February 1918, and underwent a period of training at Portsmouth, prior to his being drafted to Gibraltar. There he was engaged on important garrison duty until after the cessation of hostilities. He returned home early in 1920, and was demobilised in the March of that year. He holds the General Service and Victory Medals.
9, Davy Street, Rochdale Road, Manchester.　Z10614

KEELAN, J., Private, 52nd Manchester Regiment.

He joined in October 1918 on attaining military age, and after a period of training was sent to Germany with the Army of Occupation. There he was stationed on the Rhine, and was engaged on important guard duties. He returned home and was demobilised in February 1920.
45, Cyrus Street, Ancoats, Manchester.　Z10615

KEELAN, J., Private, 2nd Manchester Regiment.

He volunteered in February 1915, and four months later was drafted to the Western Front. In this theatre of war he took part in the Battles of Loos, Ypres (II and III), Arras, Passchendaele, Nieuport and La Bassée, and was twice wounded in action. He was demobilised in April 1919, and holds the 1914–15 Star, and the General Service and Victory Medals.
60, Lind Street, Ancoats, Manchester.　Z10616

KEELAN, J., Corporal, 2nd Manchester Regiment.

Volunteering at the outbreak of war, he was drafted to France in November 1914, and fought in the Battles of Neuve Chapelle, Ypres, Loos, St. Eloi and Vimy Ridge. He was unfortunately killed in action in July 1916, during the first Battle of the Somme. He was entitled to the 1914 Star, and the General Service and Victory Medals.
36, Harrison Street, Ancoats, Manchester.　Z9230A

KEELEY, W., Private, 1/7th Manchester Regiment.

He was already in the Army at the outbreak of war in August 1914, and shortly afterwards proceeded to Egypt, where he saw active service until April 1915. He was then transferred to the Dardanelles, and took part in heavy fighting on the Gallipoli Peninsula, being present at the Battles of Krithia (I, II and III), and suffered from shell-shock, He was invalided home and eventually discharged in June 1917, as physically unfit for further service, and holds the 1914–15 Star, and the General Service and Victory Medals.
15, Charlotte Street, Chorlton-on-Medlock, Manchester. Z6859

KEELING, J. W., Guardsman, Grenadier Guards.

He volunteered in January 1915, and after a period of training was drafted to the Western Front, where he was in action at many important engagements, including Ypres (II), and the Somme Offensive of 1916, and was wounded. He re-joined his unit and was again wounded in action in December 1916, when he was invalided to England. He returned to France on his recovery, and during the fighting at the Battle of Cambrai was taken prisoner in November 1917. Repatriated after the Armistice, he was eventually demobilised in February 1919, and holds the 1914–15 Star, and the General Service and Victory Medals.
26, Holstein Street, Ardwick, Manchester.　Z6861

KEELING, W., Pte., 2nd Northumberland Fusiliers.

He enlisted in May 1906, and served with the Colours until 1912. At the outbreak of war in August 1914, he was called up from the Reserve and was immediately drafted to France with the First Expeditionary Force. He took part in the fighting at the Battle of, and in the Retreat from, Mons, and later was in action at the Battles of the Marne, the Aisne, La Bassée, Ypres and St. Eloi. He was taken prisoner in April 1915, at the second Battle of Ypres, and suffered many hardships in Germany. He was repatriated after the Armistice, and eventually discharged in March 1919, holding the Mons Star, and the General Service and Victory Medals.
12, Meadow Street, Ardwick, Manchester. Z6860

KEENAN, J., Private, Cheshire Regiment.

He joined in September 1916, and after a period of training was engaged at various stations on important duties with his unit. He was unable to obtain a transfer overseas owing to his being medically unfit, but rendered valuable services until his discharge in October 1918.
55, Slater Street, Ancoats, Manchester. Z10617

KEIGHTLEY, F. E., Sergt., M.G.C.

He volunteered in November 1914, and shortly afterwards proceeded to the Western Front, where he played a distinguished part in many engagements, and saw much active service in various sectors. He was unfortunately killed in action at Warlencourt on October 18th, 1916, and was entitled to the 1914-15 Star, and the General Service and Victory Medals.
"A costly sacrifice upon the altar of freedom."
83, Percival Street, Chorlton-on-Medlock, Manchester. X6863

KELLER, A. E., Mechanic, R.A.F.

He joined in December 1917, and served in the Balloon section of the R.A.F. on the South-East Coast of England. He was unable to obtain his transfer to a theatre of war owing to medical unfitness, but nevertheless rendered valuable services until his demobilisation in February 1919.
45, Link Street, Longsight, Manchester. Z6864

KELLY, A., Private, South Lancashire Regiment.

Volunteering in March 1915, he was drafted to France in the following September, and fought in the Battle of Loos. Transferred to Salonika, he was in action on the Struma, Vardar, and Doiran fronts, and took part in the capture of Monastir. Owing to ill-health, he was invalided home for hospital treatment, and on his recovery again proceeded to France, and was engaged in heavy fighting at Messines, Ypres, Cambrai, and throughout the Retreat and Advance of 1918. After the Armistice, he was sent into Germany with the Army of Occupation and served there until, returning to England, he was demobilised in April 1919. He holds the 1914-15 Star, and the General Service and Victory Medals.
11, Boundary Street, Newton, Manchester. Z9215A

KELLY, D, W., Private, 7th Manchester Regiment.

He volunteered in November 1915, but owing to his being medically unfit for transfer overseas, was retained on special duties on the East Coast of England. He nevertheless did consistently good work until August 1917, when he was discharged as unfit for further service.
9, Stamford Street, Hulme, Manchester. Z6865

KELLY, E. (D.C.M.), Battery Sergt. Major, R.F.A.

Mobilised at the outbreak of war in August 1914, he was immediately sent to France and took part in the Battle of Mons, and the subsequent Retreat. He also played a distinguished part at the Battles of Le Cateau, the Marne, the Aisne, La Bassée, Ypres, Neuve Chapelle, St. Eloi, Loos, the Somme, Beaumont-Hamel, Arras, Vermelles, Bullecourt and Cambrai, and the Retreat and Advance of 1918. He was awarded the Distinguished Conduct Medal for conspicuous bravery in bringing guns out of action under heavy fire at Bapaume in August 1918, and also the Croix de Guerre for rescuing French soldiers from a blown-up gun pit. In addition, he holds the Mons Star, and the General Service and Victory Medals, and was discharged in December 1919.
4, Heron Street, Hulme, Manchester. Z6875

KELLY, E., Sapper, R.E.

Volunteering at the commencement of hostilities, he was drafted to France, and was in action in many important engagements and was wounded at Ypres in February 1915. Returning home he received hospital treatment and on his recovery embarked for Gallipoli in September 1915. He was engaged in heavy fighting in various sectors, and was severely wounded at Suvla Bay. Invalided home he was in hospital for some months, and then was sent to France, where he served until demobilised in June 1919. He holds the 1914-15 Star, and the General Service and Victory Medals.
12, Queen Street, Bradford, Manchester. TZ9231

KELLY, F. J., Private, Royal Welch Fusiliers.

He joined in February 1917, and after a period of training was drafted to the Western Front in March 1918. There he took part in the Retreat and Advance of that year, and at the cessation of hostilities, proceeded to Egypt, where he was engaged in casual fighting with native tribesmen. He returned

to England, and was demobilised in February 1920, holding the General Service and Victory Medals. X6866-67A
10, Eldon Grove, Chorlton-on-Medlock, Manchester.

KELLY, H., Private, Loyal North Lancashire Regt.

Already in the Army when war broke out in August 1914, he was sent to France with the First Expeditionary Force, and took part in the Battle of, and the Retreat from, Mons. He was also in action at the Battles of Le Cateau, the Aisne, La Bassée and Ypres, where he laid down his life for King and Country in November 1914. He was entitled to the Mons Star, and the General Service and Victory Medals.
"A valiant Soldier, with undaunted heart he breasted life's last hill."
7, Rennie Street, West Gorton, Manchester. Z10619B

KELLY, J., Private, East Yorkshire Regiment.

He joined in May 1916, and in the following November proceeded to the Western Front. There he took part in several engagements, including those at Beaumont-Hamel, Bullecourt (where he was wounded) and Armentières, and in the second Battle of the Somme, when he was again wounded and unfortunately taken prisoner in April 1918. He was held in captivity in Germany, but was repatriated in September 1918, and returned home and was discharged in June 1920, as medically unfit for further service. He holds the General Service and Victory Medals.
47, Hood Street, Ancoats, Manchester. Z11429

KELLY, J., Private, 8th Cheshire Regiment.

He was already in the Army when war broke out in August 1914, and immediately proceeded to France, where he took part in the Battle of Mons, and in the subsequent Retreat, and the Battle of Le Cateau. He died gloriously on the Field of Battle on the Marne on September 10th, 1914, and was entitled to the Mons Star, and the General Service and Victory Medals. "He died the noblest death a man may die, Fighting for God, and right, and liberty."
7, Rennie Street, West Gorton, Manchester. Z10619A

KELLY, J., Private, 3rd Manchester Regiment.

He volunteered in August 1914, and on completing his training in the following February proceeded to Egypt, and thence to the Dardanelles. There he took part in much severe fighting, and was wounded at Suvla Bay in August 1915. On his recovery he was sent to Salonika, and was in action on the Doiran front, but later was transferred to France, and fought on the Somme, at Cambrai, and in the Retreat and Advance of 1918. He was demobilised in March 1919, and holds the 1914-15 Star, and the General Service and Victory Medals.
3, Davy Street, Rochdale Road, Manchester. Z10620

KELLY, J., Private, 8th Manchester Regiment.

He volunteered in August 1914, and on completing his training in the following April, was drafted to the Dardanelles. There he took part in much severe fighting at the Landing at Cape Helles, and in the Battles of Krithia (I, II and III). He gave his life for King and Country during the third Battle of Krithia on June 4th, 1915, and was entitled to the 1914-15 Star, and the General Service and Victory Medals.
"Whilst we remember, the sacrifice is not in vain."
17, Clyde Street, Ancoats, Manchester. Z10621

KELLY, J., Private, 2nd South Wales Borderers.

He volunteered in January 1916, and later in the same year proceeded to the Western Front, where he took part in engagements at Ypres, and was wounded in action. In consequence he was sent to the Base Hospital, but on his recovery, rejoined his unit and fought at Ypres and Messines Ridge, where he was badly gassed. He went to hospital in Boulogne, whence he was demobilised in May 1920. He holds the General Service and Victory Medals.
5, Fox Street, Ancoats, Manchester. Z10622

KELLY, J., Corporal, 22nd Northumberland Fusiliers.

Volunteering in November 1914, he proceeded to France twelve months later and was wounded at Beaumont-Hamel in July 1916, during the Somme Offensive. After treatment at an advanced dressing station, he rejoined his unit, and took part in heavy fighting at La Bassée and Givenchy, and at the Battles of Ypres (III) and Passchendaele, where he was again wounded in October 1917. On this occasion he was invalided to hospital at Leicester and Nottingham, but on his recovery returned to France, and was again in action at La Bassée. Demobilised in March 1919, he holds the 1914-15 Star, and the General Service and Victory Medals.
64, Gresham Street, Openshaw, Manchester. Z6871

KELLY, J., Pte., 1st K.O. (Yorkshire Light Infantry).

He joined in September 1916, and in the following January proceeded to Salonika, where he was in action in many engagements on the Doiran and Vardar fronts. Transferred to France in September 1918, he fought in the Allied Offensive and was wounded at Cambrai in October. Returning home he received treatment, and on recovery served at various stations until demobilised in December 1919. He holds the General Service and Victory Medals.
3, Heyrod Street, Ancoats, Manchester. Z9232

KELLY, James, Private, King's (Liverpool Regt.)
He volunteered in September 1914, and after a period of training was drafted to France, where he was in action at many important engagements, including the Battles of Loos, Albert, Vermelles, and Ploegsteert Wood, but was unhappily killed on the Somme on July 14th, 1916. He was entitled to the 1914–15 Star, and the General Service and Victory Medals.
" Great deeds cannot die."
19, Gregory Street, West Gorton, Manchester. Z6868A

KELLY, Joseph, Private, 2nd Lancashire Fusiliers.
Volunteering in September 1914, he completed a period of training, and was sent to the Western Front in October of the following year. There he took part in many important engagements, including the Battle of Loos, Ploegsteert Wood and Vimy Ridge, and was invalided home with muscular rheumatism in July 1916. He was discharged on the 24th of the following month as physically unfit for further service, and holds the 1914–15 Star, and the General Service and Victory Medals.
19, Gregory Street, West Gorton. Manchester. Z6868B

KELLY, J. E., Rifleman, Royal Irish Rifles, and Private, K.O. (Royal Lancaster Regiment).
He volunteered in August 1915, and four months later proceeded to Mesopotamia, where he took part in the Relief of Kut, and was in action at numerous engagements, including Kut-el-Amara. He later suffered from malaria, and after being invalided to India, was ultimately sent to England, and demobilised in February 1919, holding the 1914–15 Star, and the General Service and Victory Medals.
3, Hibbert Street, Hulme, Manchester. Z6872

KELLY, P., Private, 1st Cheshire Regiment.
He joined in June 1916, and served at various depôts until he embarked for the Western Front in April 1918. He was engaged in heavy fighting throughout the German Offensive and was severely wounded during the Allied Advance. Admitted into hospital he unhappily succumbed to his injuries on August 23rd, 1918. He was entitled to the General Service and Victory Medals.
7, Whitby Street, Ancoats, Manchester. Z9233

KELLY, T., Private, 52nd Manchester Regiment.
He joined in March 1916, and in January of the following year was drafted to the Western Front, where he took part in many important engagements. He was in action at the Battles of Vimy Ridge, Ypres (III), Lens, and the Somme, and later in the Retreat and Advance of 1918. After the cessation of hostilities, he proceeded to Germany, and did duty on the Rhine with the Army of Occupation until his demobilisation in November 1919. He holds the General Service and Victory Medals.
16, Owen Street, Hulme, Manchester. Z6874

KELLY, T., Private, 11th Manchester Regiment.
Volunteering in January 1915, he was drafted to Egypt in the following September, and saw much service on the Western Desert and on the Sinai Peninsula, fighting at Agagia, Sollum, Katia and Romani. Transferred to France he was in action on the Somme, at Arras, Ypres, Cambrai, and throughout the Retreat and Advance of 1918. He was demobilised in April 1919, and holds the 1914–15 Star, and the General Service and Victory Medals.
46, Sandal Street, Newton, Manchester. TZ9234

KELLY, T., L/Corporal, 2nd Lancashire Fusiliers.
He was mobilised in August 1914, and in November of the same year proceeded to France. In this theatre of war he took part in numerous engagements, including the Battles of La Bassée, Ypres and the Somme, and was invalided home and discharged in March 1917. Later he joined the Royal Air Force and did consistently good work in the defence of London until April 1918, when he was again discharged. He holds the 1914 Star, and the General Service and Victory Medals.
3, Harrop Street, Lower Openshaw, Manchester. Z6873

KELLY, T., Sergt. Drummer, 2/7th Manchester Regt.
A Territorial, he was mobilised in August 1914, and was retained on special duties on home stations until March 1917. He then proceeded to France, where he was in action at La Bassée, the Hohenzollern Redoubt and Nieuport. He also served with distinction at the Battles of Ypres and Passchendaele where he was wounded, and was taken prisoner at St. Quentin in March 1918. After a period of captivity in Germany, he was repatriated in December 1918, and three months later was disembodied, holding the General Service and Victory Medals.
10, Eldon Grove, Chorlton-on-Medlock, Manchester. X6866–7B

KELLY, T., Private, 8th Border Regiment.
He volunteered in November 1914, and after a period of training was drafted to the Western Front, where he took part in many important engagements, including the Battles of Loos, Neuve Chapelle, Ypres, the Somme, Passchendaele, Arras and Cambrai, and was wounded during the Somme Offensive of 1916. He was also wounded in the Advance of 1918, and was demobilised in December of that year, holding the General Service and Victory Medals.
54, Norton Street, West Gorton, Manchester. Z6869

KELLY, T. (M.M.), Gunner, R.G.A.
He volunteered in July 1915, and landing in France in the following November was in action at Loos, St. Eloi, on the Somme, and at Arras. He was awarded the Military Medal for conspicuous gallantry during the third Battle of Ypres. He was also engaged in severe fighting throughout the Offensives of 1918, and during his service overseas was wounded. He was demobilised in March 1919, and in addition to the Military Medal, holds the 1914–15 Star, and the General Service and Victory Medals.
45, Sandal Street, Newton Manchester. TZ9235

KELLY, T., Private, Welch Regiment.
He joined in June 1918, and completing his training served at various stations on important duties with his unit. He was unsuccessful in obtaining his transfer overseas prior to the cessation of hostilities, but in February 1919 was drafted to the Army of Occupation in Germany. In August 1919 he returned to the United Kingdom, and was on duty at various depôts in Ireland, until demobilised in March 1920.
60, Francisco Street, Miles Platting, Manchester. TZ9236

KELLY, T. W., Private, 9th East Lancashire Regt.
Volunteering in August 1914, he was drafted overseas in the following year. During his service on the Western Front he fought at Loos, Ypres, and on the Somme, and was wounded and sent to a Base hospital. On his recovery he was transferred to Salonika, and took part in engagements on the Vardar and Doiran fronts, being twice wounded and sent to hospital. Later he returned to France, and was in action during the final engagements in 1918. He was demobilised in March 1919, and holds the 1914–15 Star, and the General Service and Victory Medals.
3, Schofield Street, Ancoats, Manchester. Z10623

KELLY, W., Private, Loyal N. Lancashire Regt.
Volunteering in September 1914, he completed a period of training and was sent to the Western Front in September 1915. Here he took part in many important engagements, including the Battles of Loos, Albert, Vimy Ridge, and the Somme, and was wounded on two occasions. He was invalided home and eventually discharged in September 1917, as physically unfit for further service. He holds the 1914–15 Star, and the General Service and Victory Medals.
37, Caton Street, Hulme, Manchester. Z6876

KELLY, W., Sergt., 10th Lancashire Fusiliers.
He volunteered in December 1915, and in the following July proceeded to the Western Front, where he played a distinguished part in many important engagements. He was in action at the Battles of the Somme, Beaumont-Hamel, Beaucourt, Ypres, Nieuport, La Bassée, Festubert, Messines and Passchendaele, and was promoted to the rank of Sergeant for gallantry in taking a machine gun into action during the Retreat of 1918. He also rendered valuable services in the Advance and was eventually demobilised in September 1919, holding the General Service and Victory Medals.
43, Brunt Street, Rusholme, Manchester. TZ6877

KELSALL, F., Private, 2/5th Manchester Regiment.
Volunteering in February 1915, he completed a period of training, and was sent to France in January 1916. There he was in action in many engagements, including the Battles of La Bassée, Nieuport, Ypres, and the Somme, and later took part in the Retreat and Advance of 1918. He holds the General Service and Victory Medals, and was demobilised in February 1919.
41, Dalton Street, Hulme, Manchester. Z6878

KELSALL, J. H., Private, 8th Manchester Regiment.
He volunteered at the outbreak of war in August 1914, and in November was drafted to France, where he saw much heavy fighting in many sectors. He was in action at the Battles of Neuve Chapelle, La Bassée, Loos, Albert, Vermelles, Ploegsteert Wood, the Somme, Beaumont-Hamel, Messines, Ypres and Cambrai, and later in the Retreat and Advance of 1918. He holds the 1914–15 Star, and the General Service and Victory Medals, and was demobilised in January 1919.
11, Napier Street, Ardwick, Manchester. TZ6879

KELSALL, T., Private, 21st Manchester Regiment.
He voluunteered in March 1915, and after doing important duty in England for some time, was drafted to France in May 1916. There he took part in much heavy fighting in various sectors, and made the supreme sacrifice, being killed in action in July 1916. during the Somme Offensive. He was entitled to the General Service and Victory Medals.
" The path of duty was the way to glory."
56, Ridgway Street, Moss Side, Manchester. Z6880

KELSEY, S., Private, Labour Corps.
He joined in July 1916, and after doing consistently good work in England, was drafted to France in December 1917, and was engaged as a transport driver. He rendered valuable services in many sectors including those of Ypres, Cambrai, the Somme, Lens, La Bassée, and Givenchy, where he was employed taking food to forward areas. He was also present during the Retreat and Advance of 1918, and was demobilised in December of the same year, holding the General Service and Victory Medals.
26, Gore Street, Greenheys, Manchester. TZ6881

KELSHAW, E., Sergt., 8th Manchester Regiment.
Mobilised at the outbreak of war in August 1914, he was drafted to France in the following month and played a distinguished part in numerous engagements. He was in action at the Battles of La Bassée, St. Eloi, Festubert, Hill 60, Ypres (II), the Somme, Arras, Bullecourt and Cambrai, and later, in the Retreat and Advance of 1918. He holds the 1914 Star, and the General Service and Victory Medals, and was discharged in June 1919.
10, Tutbury Street, Ancoats, Manchester. Z6882

KELSHAW, W., Private, 8th Manchester Regiment.
Volunteering in May 1915, he proceeded to Egypt twelve months later, and took part in heavy fighting at El Fasher, Bagdhaba and Romani. In March 1917 he was transferred to the Western Front, where he was in action at the Battles of Arras, Bullecourt, Messines, Ypres (III), Cambrai, the Somme (II), Bapaume, Havrincourt and Ypres (IV), and in other minor engagements during the Retreat and Advance of 1918. He holds the General Service and Victory Medals, and was demobilised in May 1919.
18, Johnson's Buildings, Ancoats, Manchester. Z6883

KENDALL, J., Private, R.A.M.C.
He joined in July 1917, but owing to his being medically unfit was retained on special duties at various stations in England. He nevertheless, rendered valuable services until December 1919, when he was demobilised after being in hospital with influenza for some time.
5, Merrimer Street, Greenheys, Manchester. TZ6884

KENDALL, L., Gunner, R.F.A.
He volunteered in May 1915, and proceeded to France in October of the same year. He was attached to a Trench Mortar Battery, and took part in the fighting in many sectors, including that of Ypres. He also did consistently good work during the Retreat and Advance of 1918, and was demobilised in March 1919, holding the 1914-15 Star, and the General Service and Victory Medals.
9, Temple Street, Bradford, Manchester. Z6885A

KENDRICK, E. G., Private, 2nd Manchester Regt.
Joining in February 1918, he was retained on special duties at important stations in Ireland, where he did consistently good work. Owing to his being medically unfit, he was unable to obtain his transfer to a theatre of war, but, nevertheless, rendered valuable services. He was discharged in February 1920.
22, Leaf Street, Chorlton-on-Medlock, Manchester. Z6886

KENDRICK, R., Private, 2nd Manchester Regiment.
Mobilised at the commencement of hostilities, he proceeded to France and fought in the Retreat from Mons, and in the Battles of Ypres, La Bassée and Givenchy. He was also in action at Vimy Ridge and on the Somme, and was taken prisoner at Messines. He was held in captivity until the cessation of hostilities, and then repatriated, was discharged in March 1919. He holds the Mons Star, and the General Service and Victory Medals.
28, Nelson Street, Rochdale Road, Manchester. Z9237

KENNA, J., L/Corporal, R.A.S.C.
He volunteered in November 1914, and in April of the following year was drafted to the Dardanelles, where he took part in the heavy fighting during the Landing at Suvla Bay, and was wounded. He was invalided to Cairo, and later embarked for France, where he was employed on special duties at Etaples. He holds the 1914-15 Star, and the General Service and Victory Medals, and was demobilised in September 1919. 45, Bonsall Street, Hulme, Manchester. Z6887

KENNA, T., Private, 8th Welch Regiment.
He volunteered in May 1915, and in the following September was drafted to the Dardanelles, where he saw much severe fighting until the Evacuation of the Gallipoli Peninsula. He was then transferred to Mesopotamia, and took part in several engagements, including that of Kut. He returned home and was demobilised in April 1919, holding the 1914-15 Star, and the General Service and Victory Medals.
9, Rockingham Street, Collyhurst, Manchester. Z10624

KENNEDY, F., Rifleman, 1st Rifle Brigade.
Volunteering in September 1914, he proceeded to France three months later, and took part in many important engagements. He was in action at Ypres, Armentières, the Somme, Béthune and Arras, and was invalided home in August 1918, suffering from influenza. He was eventually demobilised in February 1919, and holds the 1914-15 Star, and the General Service and Victory Medals.
51, Dale Street, Hulme, Manchester. Z6889

KENNEDY, G., Private, King's (Liverpool Regt.)
He volunteered in March 1915, and after a period of training was drafted to Salonika, later in the same year, and was killed whilst landing in that theatre of war in October. He was entitled to the 1914-15 Star, and the General Service and Victory Medals.
" Thinking that remembrance, though unspoken, may reach him where he sleeps."
4, Daniel Street, Hulme, Manchester. Z6888A

KENNEDY, J., Private, Border Regiment.
He volunteered in August 1914, and was shortly afterwards drafted to the Western Front, where he took part in the Battles of Loos, and the Somme, and was wounded in action. As a result he was invalided to the Base Hospital, but on his recovery, rejoined his unit, and saw much fighting at Nieuport and Arras. He was again wounded and consequently invalided home. He was demobilised in March 1919, and holds the 1914 Star, and the General Service and Victory Medals.
22, Fox Street, Ancoats, Manchester. Z10625

KENNEDY, J., Private, 8th Manchester Regiment.
He joined in March 1917, and on completing his training in the following September, proceeded to the Western Front. Whilst in this seat of war he took part in the Battles of Cambrai, the Marne (II) and Havrincourt, and in other important engagements during the Retreat and Advance of 1918. He was demobilised in October 1919, and holds the General Service and Victory Medals.
120, Jersey Street Dwellings, Ancoats, Manchester. Z10626

KENNEDY, J., Private, 18th Manchester Regiment.
Volunteering in April 1915, he was drafted to France in the following year, and took part in much heavy fighting on the Passchendaele and La Bassée fronts. He was unfortunately killed in action at Festubert on October 12th, 1916, and was entitled to the General Service and Victory Medals.
" His life for his Country, his soul to God."
82, Beaumont Street, Beswick, Manchester. Z10627

KENNEDY, J., Pte., 2/4th Argyll & Sutherland H'ldrs.
He joined in September 1916, and after his training was completed served on important duties at various stations on the Coast. He rendered valuable services, but was not successful in obtaining a transfer overseas before the cessation of hostilities, and was demobilised in January 1919.
12, Brass Street, Rochdale Road, Manchester. Z9603

KENNEDY, J., Corporal, 2nd Manchester Regt. and K.O. (Y.L.I.)
He volunteered in August 1914, and in February of the following year was drafted to France, where he played a prominent part in the fighting in many sectors. He took part in the Battles of St. Eloi, Hill 60, Loos, Albert, Vimy Ridge, and the Somme, and was wounded in July 1916. He returned to his unit in due course, and was in action on the Arras and Ancre fronts, and was again wounded. He was invalided home in May 1917, and was discharged in November of that year, as physically unfit for further service. He holds the 1914-15 Star, and the General Service and Victory Medals.
28, Orchard Street, Greenheys, Manchester. Z6891

KENNEDY, J., Private, Labour Corps.
Joining in July 1917, he was sent to France two months later, and saw service at Arras, Ypres, Loos, Festubert, and Givenchy, where he was engaged on important duties at ammunition dumps, and on the construction of railway tracks. He also did consistently good work during the Retreat and Advance of 1918, and in March 1919, was demobilised, holding the General Service and Victory Medals.
21, Pump Street, Hulme, Manchester. Z6893

KENNEDY, J., L/Corporal, 2nd Border Regiment.
Volunteering in August 1914, he was drafted to the Dardanelles in July of the following year, and took part in the Landing at Suvla Bay, and the engagement at Chunuk Bair. After the Evacuation of the Gallipoli Peninsula in December 1915, he embarked for France, and later fought at Ypres and Cambrai, and was wounded. He rejoined his Regiment in May 1917, and made the supreme sacrifice in October of that year, being killed in action at Arras. He was entitled to the 1914-15 Star, and the General Service and Victory Medals.
" Whilst we remember, the sacrifice is not in vain."
4, Durham Place, Hulme, Manchester. Z6890

KENNEDY, J. J., Rifleman, Rifle Brigade.
Having previously served in the South African Campaign, he volunteered in November 1915, and served for a time with the R.E. Later he was transferred to the Rifle Brigade and proceeded to France, where he fought in engagements at Amiens, and in the Retreat and Advance of 1918. He was taken prisoner and forced to work behind the German lines until the Armistice, when he was released. He was invalided to Rouen, but unfortunately died in November 1918, through illness contracted whilst in captivity. He was entitled to the Queen's and King's South African Medals (with 7 bars), and the General Service and Victory Medals.
" The path of duty was the way to glory."
16, Bushton Street, Collyhurst, Manchester. Z10628

KENNEDY, P., Private, 2nd Manchester Regiment.
He enlisted in September 1902, and when war broke out in August 1914, was immediately drafted to France. There he took part in the Battles of Mons, Le Cateau, the Marne, the Aisne, Ypres and Festubert, where he was wounded. As a result he was invalided home, and on his recovery, received his discharge, time expired, in December 1915. He holds the Mons Star, and the General Service and Victory Medals.
81, Beaumont Street, Beswick, Manchester. Z10629

KENNEDY, T., Private, 7th South Lancashire Regt.
He volunteered at the outbreak of war in August 1914, and
after a period of training was drafted to the Western Front.
There he took part in many important engagements, and saw
much heavy fighting in various sectors. He was in action at
the Battles of Ypres, the Somme, Vimy Ridge, Nieuport and
Arras, and was invalided home and eventually demobilised
in November 1919, holding the 1914–15 Star, and the General
Service and Victory Medals.
29, Buckland Street, Ancoats, Manchester.   Z6892

KENNEDY, W., Private, 2nd Manchester Regiment.
Volunteering in August 1915, he was immediately drafted
to the Western Front, where he rendered valuable services
during the Battles of Loos. He was engaged on the important
duty of bringing in wounded, when he was killed in action in
September 1915, one month after his arrival in France. He
was entitled to the 1914–15 Star, and the General Service
and Victory Medals.
        "The path of duty was the way to glory."
4, Daniel Street, Hulme, Manchester.   Z6888B

KENNEY, W. H., Corporal, Manchester Regiment.
Volunteering in June 1915, he embarked for the Western
Front two months later, and fought at Loos, Vermelles, Vimy
Ridge, and the Somme. He was also engaged in heavy fighting
in the Ypres salient, and in the Arras and Cambrai sectors,
and in December 1917 was transferred to Italy. Here he saw
much service in many parts of the line, but late in 1918 fell
seriously ill, and died on November 19th, 1918. He was entitled to the 1914–15 Star, and the General Service and Victory
Medals.   43, Long Street, Ancoats, Manchester.   TZ9238

KENNY, C. H., Private, 7th K. (Liverpool Regt.)
He volunteered in September 1915, and after a period of
training and service in England, was drafted to the Western
Front in November of the following year. In this theatre of
war he took part in many important engagements, including
the Battles of Arras, Lens, the Scarpe and Cambrai (II),
and was wounded in action. He also suffered from gastritis,
and after spending some time in hospital near Sheffield, was
finally discharged in March 1919. He holds the General Service and Victory Medals.
18, St. John's Street, Longsight, Manchester.   Z6895

KENNY, E. J., Private, R.A.M.C.
He joined in September 1918, on attaining military age, and
was retained on important hospital duties at various stations in
England. He did consistently good work but was unable
to proceed overseas before the termination of hostilities.
He is still serving in the Army and proceeded to Jamaica in
November 1920.
61, Gibson Street, Ardwick, Manchester.   Z6894

KENNY, H. F., Private, Lancashire Fusiliers.
He was called up from the Reserve at the outbreak of war in
August 1914, and was immediately drafted to the Western
Front, where he took part in the Retreat from Mons. He was
also in action at the Battles of the Marne, the Aisne and Ypres.
In April 1915 he proceeded to the Dardanelles, and served on
the Gallipoli Peninsula until its Evacuation in December of
that year. He saw much heavy fighting during his service
in this theatre of war, and was in action at Suvla Bay and
Krithia. In January 1916 he returned to the Western
Front, and fought at the Battle of the Somme, Arras, Ypres
(III) and Cambrai, and made the supreme sacrifice, being killed
in action in the Ypres sector on June 17th, 1918. He was
entitled to the Mons Star, and the General Service and Victory
Medals.   "Great deeds cannot die."
52, Carlisle Street, Hulme, Manchester.   TZ6896

KENNY, W. H., Driver, R.A.S.C.
He joined in April 1916, and underwent a period of training
prior to his being drafted to France. There he was engaged
on important duties and took an active part in the fighting at
Bapaume and Havrincourt Wood. After hostilities ceased, he
went into Germany with the Army of Occupation and served
there until his demobilisation in February 1919. He holds
the General Service and Victory Medals.
25, Thorn Street, Bradford, Manchester.   Z10630

**KENYON, G., Private, Lancashire Fusiliers, and
South Wales Borderers.**
He joined in February 1918, but owing to his being physically
unfit, was retained on special duties at important stations
in England. He was attached to the R.A.S.C., and did consistently good work distributing foodstuffs and war stores
generally, and, before his demobilisation in January 1920,
also did duty with the Labour Corps.
17, Clayton Street, Hulme, Manchester.   Z6899

KENYON, J., Private, 1st Loyal N. Lancashire Regt.
Volunteering in December 1914, he was drafted to France
in June of the following year, and whilst overseas took part
in the fighting at Loos, and on the Somme. He was wounded
in June 1917 in the vicinity of Loos, but after his recovery
was constantly in action until the cessation of hostilities. He
returned home and was demobilised in February 1919, holding
the 1914–15 Star, and the General Service and Victory Medals.
26, Hayes Street, Newton, Manchester.   Z9604

KENYON, J. R., Private, 8th Lancashire Fusiliers.
He volunteered in October 1914, and after his training served
at various stations on important duties with his unit. He
rendered valuable services until September 1916, when owing
to ill-health he was discharged as medically unfit.
34, Alma Street, Collyhurst, Manchester.   Z11526

KENYON, R., L/Corporal, 12th K. (Liverpool Regt.)
He volunteered in September 1914, and was shortly afterwards
drafted to the Western Front, where he took part in much
heavy fighting. He died gloriously on the Field of Battle at
Ypres (II) on April 2nd, 1915. He was entitled to the 1914
Star, and the General Service and Victory Medals.
        "Great deeds cannot die :
They, with the sun and moon renew their light for ever."
21, North Kent Street, Rochdale Road, Manchester.   Z10631

KENYON, S., Private, King's (Liverpool Regiment).
He volunteered in January 1915, and four months later proceeded to the Western Front, where he took part in much
heavy fighting in various sectors. He served with distinction
at the Battles of Ypres, Loos, Albert, Ploegsteert Wood,
and the Somme, and made the supreme sacrifice in August
1916, when killed in action at Guillemont. He was entitled
to the 1914–15 Star, and the General Service and Victory
Medals.
"A valiant Soldier, with undaunted heart he breasted life's
        last hill."
70, Cawdor Street, Hulme, Manchester.   Z6897

KENYON, T., Private, South Wales Borderers.
Volunteering in May 1915, he was drafted to France in September 1916, and was in action at many important engagements. He saw much severe fighting in various sectors of
the Front, and took part in the Battles of Arras, Vimy Ridge,
Bullecourt and Messines, and was wounded at Ypres (III). He
was eventually invalided home and discharged in August
1918, holding the General Service and Victory Medals.
43, Garibaldi Street, Ardwick, Manchester.   Z6898

KENYON, T., Sapper, R.E.
He volunteered in March 1915, and was shortly afterwards
sent to France, where he was engaged on important duties
in many sectors. He took part in the Battles of Hill 60,
Ypres and Vimy Ridge, and suffered from gas poisoning on
two occasions (in May 1915, and July 1917). He rendered
valuable services, and was eventually discharged at Chatham in
March 1918. He holds the 1914–15 Star, and the General
Service and Victory Medals.
11, Mahogany Street, Chorlton-on-Medlock, Manchester. Z6900

KENYON, T. H., Driver, R.E.
He volunteered in September 1915, and on completing his
training in the following year, was drafted to the Western
Front. There he saw much severe fighting in various sectors,
and took an active part in the Battles of Vimy Ridge, the
Somme, Cambrai, and the Marne, and many other important
engagements. Demobilised in September 1919, he holds the
General Service and Victory Medals.
269, Moreton Street, Longsight, Manchester.   Z10632

KERFOOT, T. B., Private, 2nd Lancashire Fusiliers.
Mobilised at the outbreak of war in August 1914, he immediately proceeded to the Western Front with the British Expeditionary Force, and took part in the Battle of Mons. He
was taken prisoner on August 26th, 1914, after being wounded
at Le Cateau, and was held in captivity at Doeberitz Camp,
Germany, where he suffered many hardships. He was repatriated in December 1918, and eventually discharged in
February of the following year, and holds the Mons Star, and
the General Service and Victory Medals.
51, Earl Street, Longsight, Manchester.   Z6902

KERFORD, W., Private, 14th Manchester Regt.
He joined in June 1916, and in the following October was
drafted to the Western Front, where he saw service on the
Ancre front, at Beaumont-Hamel and Beaucourt, and was
unfortunately killed on April 22nd, 1917, at Loos. He was
entitled to the General Service and Victory Medals.
        "Whilst we remember, the sacrifice is not in vain."
10, Brookside, City Road, Hulme, Manchester.   Z6901

KERR, R., Private, 3rd South Wales Borderers.
He volunteered in September 1914, and twelve months later
was drafted to the Western Front, where he took part in many
important engagements in the Ypres and other sectors. He was
transferred to Salonika, and there saw much severe fighting
until the cessation of hostilities. He was demobilised on his
return home in March 1919, and holds the 1914–15 Star, and
the General Service and Victory Medals.
80, Thornton Street, Collyhurst, Manchester.   Z10633

KERR, W. A., Corporal, 17th South Lancashire Regt.
He joined in February 1917, and after his training served at
various stations on important clerical duties whilst attached
to the Labour Corps. He rendered valuable services, but
was not able to secure a transfer overseas, whilst hostilities
lasted, and was demobilised in May 1919.
71, Nicholson Street, Rochdale Road, Manchester.   Z9605

KERR, J., Private, K.O. (Royal Lancaster Regt.)
Volunteering in September 1914, he was drafted to the Western Front twelve months later, and after taking part in heavy fighting at Loos and St. Eloi, was transferred to the Balkan theatre of war. He was taken prisoner in February 1917, and was held in captivity at Sofia. He was also in hospital at Philippopolis for some time with malarial fever. Repatriated at the cessation of hostilities, he was later sent to India, where he was still serving in 1920, and holds the 1914–15 Star, and the General Service and Victory Medals.
9, Bank Street, Hulme, Manchester. Z6904

KERR, T., Corpl., 1st Duke of Cornwall's Light Infty.
Mobilised from the Reserve in August 1914, he was immediately drafted to France and took part in the Retreat from Mons. He also served in the Battles of Le Cateau, La Bassée, Ypres, and St. Eloi, where he was wounded and invalided to hospital. After his recovery he rejoined his unit in 1918, and was severely wounded and taken prisoner and sent to Germany, where he underwent the amputation of one of his legs. He was repatriated after the Armistice was signed, and discharged in January 1920, holding the Mons Star, and the General Service and Victory Medals.
31, Boardman Street, Harpurhey, Manchester. Z11527

KERRS, J., Private, South Wales Borderers.
Volunteering in June 1915, he was retained on special duties at important stations in England and did consistently good work until February 1916, when he was discharged as physically unfit. He then took up duties of National importance, and rendered valuable services until December 1918.
28, Hazel Street, Hulme, Manchester. TZ6905

KERRY, W., Private, Lancashire Fusiliers.
He volunteered in October 1915, and after a period of training was drafted to the Western Front in March 1916, There he took part in many important engagements, including those at St. Eloi, Vimy Ridge, the Somme, Beaumont-Hamel and Beaucourt, and was wounded at the third Battle of Ypres in August 1917, He returned to his unit after recovery, but was again wounded in the Advance of 1918, and was finally discharged in March of the following year, holding the General Service and Victory Medals.
9, Lime Street, Hulme, Manchester.. Z6906

KERRY, W., Private, Loyal N. Lancashire Regt.
Volunteering in September 1914, he proceeded to France in the following December, and was engaged in much severe fighting in many sectors. He took part in the Battles of La Bassée and Neuve Chapelle, and was wounded in action in 1917. Invalided to England, he was discharged in August of that year as physically unfit for further service, and holds the 1914–15 Star, and the General Service and Victory Medals.
22, James Street, Moss Side, Manchester. Z4608

KERSHAW, J., Private, 18th Manchester Regt.
Volunteering in September 1914, he was drafted to Frnace in November of the following year, and whilst on the Western Front fought in the engagements at Loos, Albert, Vimy Ridge and the Somme. He was taken prisoner at Trones Wood, in July 1916, and sent to Germany and was held in captivity until the Armistice, when he was released. He holds the 1914–15 Star, and the General Service and Victory Medals. and was demobilised in March 1919.
5, Middlewood Street, Harpurhey, Manchester. Z11528

KETTLE, C., Private, Cheshire Regiment.
He volunteered in September 1914, and a year later was sent to the Western Front. During his service overseas he was in action in various parts of the line, fighting in many engagements of note. He died gloriously on the Field of Battle at Thiepval on July 3rd, 1916. He was entitled to the 1914–15 Star, and the General Service and Victory Medals.
"His life for his Country."
3, Hibbert Place, Gunson Street, Manchester. Z9239

KEVILL, J. W., Private, R.A.S.C.
He volunteered in May 1915, and four months later proceeded to the Western Front, where he was engaged on special duties on the clerical staff at the Stationery Depôt at the Base at Boulogne. He did consistently good work until the cessation of hostilities, and was demobilised in June 1919, holding the 1914–15 Star, and the General Service and Victory Medals.
14, Bright Street, Hulme, Manchester. TZ6909

KEVILL, T., Gunner, R.F.A.
Volunteering August 1914, he completed a period of training and was drafted to France in March of the following year. There he was in action with his Battery at numerous engagements, including the Battles of Arras, and the Somme, and was wounded at Armentières in July 1918. He was eventually discharged in March 1919, as medically unfit, and holds the 1914–15 Star, and the General Service and Victory Medals.
32, Durham Place, Hulme, Manchester. Z6910

KEWLEY, T. W., Sergt., 8th Manchester Regiment.
He was mobilised with the Territorials in August 1914, and in the following month was drafted to Egypt. There he saw service on the Suez Canal, and in April 1915, was transferred to the Dardanelles. He played a distinguished part in the Landing on the Gallipoli Peninsula, and later fought at the Battles of Krithia and Suvla Bay, and was wounded. In January 1916 he embarked for France, and was in action at the Battles of Arras, Vimy Ridge, and the third Battle of Ypres. He holds the 1914–15 Star, and the General Service and Victory Medals, and was demobilised in March 1919.
39, Chell Street, Longsight, Manchester. Z6911

KIFORT, J., Signalman, R.N.
He joined in October 1918, and proceeded in H.M.S. "Eaglet" to the Irish Sea, where he was engaged on the important and dangerous duties of mine-sweeping. He did consistently good work during the short time he was serving in the Navy, and was demobilised in February 1919, holding the General Service and Victory Medals.
138, South Street, Longsight, Manchester. TX6903

KILBEG, J., Air Mechanic, R.A.F., and Manchester Regiment.
Volunteering in September 1914, he served with the Royal Air Force during the early part of the war, and in November 1915 proceeded to France with the 12th Manchester Regt. In this theatre of war he took part in many important engagements, including those of the Somme, Beaumont-Hamel, Albert, La Bassée, Givenchy, Festubert, Arras, Ypres, and Bapaume, and was wounded. He was invalided to England and was eventually demobilised in November 1919, holding the 1914–15 Star, and the General Service and Victory Medals.
5, Lindum Street, Rusholme, Manchester. Z6912

KILBRIDE, J., Private, East Lancashire Regiment.
He volunteered in September 1914, and in May of the following year landed in France. During the fighting in the Ypres salient in May 1915, he was taken prisoner, and remained in captivity until the close of the war. Repatriated in December 1918, he was demobilised in the following February, and holds the 1914–15 Star, and the General Service and Victory Medals.
52, Sanitary Street, Oldham Road, Manchester. Z9240

KILBURN, G., Private, Labour Corps.
Volunteering in August 1914, he proceeded to the Western Front in May of the following year, and there took part in the Battle of Ypres, and many other engagements until invalided to hospital at Aberdeen in February 1916. On his recovery, however, he returned to France, and was engaged on important duties in the Cambrai sectors until his demobilisation in March 1919. He holds the 1914–15 Star, and the General Service and Victory Medals.
5, Lime Street, Newton, Manchester. Z10634

KILCOURSE, T. D., Private, 4th Manchester Regt.
Volunteering in August 1914, he was drafted to France in the following October, and was in action at La Bassée, Neuve Chapelle, and Loos, where he was wounded in September 1915. Two months later, after his recovery, he proceeded to India, and was engaged on important garrison duties at Bombay, until sent to Mesopotamia. Whilst in this theatre of war he fought at Kut, Sanna-i-Yat, and in the success on the Tigris, and in subsequent engagements until the cessation of hostilities. He holds the 1914 Star, and the General Service and Victory Medals, and was demobilised, after his return to England, in July 1919.
78, Sudell Street, Rochdale Road, Manchester. Z9606

KILEY, T., Gunner, R.G.A.
He joined in August 1918, and was retained on important duties in Manchester, where he was engaged in the horse lines of the 1st and 2nd Garrison Artillery. He did consistently good work, and was demobilised in March 1920.
3, Lingmoor Street, Chorlton-on-Medlock, Manchester. X6913

KILGOUR, J., Private, Royal (Lancaster Regt.)
Joining in January 1917, he completed his training and served at various stations with his unit on guard and other important duties. Owing to ill-health he was admitted into hospital and subsequently was discharged as unfit for further service in August 1917.
21, Clarence Street, Miles Platting, Manchester. Z9241A

KILGOUR, J., Private, 2nd Cheshire Regiment.
Volunteering in March 1915, he went to France in the following December, and was engaged in heavy fighting at Loos, Ypres, the Somme, and Arras. He was also in action in many important engagements during the German Offensive and Allied Advance of 1918, and returning home after the Armistice, was demobilised in June 1919.
21, Clarence Street, Miles Platting, Manchester. Z9241B

KILKENNY, E., L/Corporal, Leinster Regiment.
Having previously served in the Boer War, he re-enlisted in September 1914, and was drafted to France in January of the following year. After taking a prominent part in the Battles of St. Eloi, Hill 60, Festubert, and Loos, he was sent home in October 1915, and discharged. He holds the Queen's and King's South African Medals (with 3 clasps), the 1914–15 Star, and the General Service and Victory Medals.
152, Thomas Street, West Gorton, Manchester. Z6914

KILLION, D., Private, K.O. (Royal Lancaster Regt.)
He volunteered in March 1915, and in the following July was drafted to France. During his service on the Western Front he fought in the Battles of Loos and the Somme, and was severely wounded in the vicinity of Ypres in August 1916, sustaining the loss of his left leg. He was invalided home, and after receiving medical treatment was discharged as physically unfit in July 1917. He holds the 1914-15 Star, and the General Service and Victory Medals.
5, Crissey Street, Queen's Road, Manchester.   Z11529

KILLORAN, P., Private, 20th Lancashire Fusiliers.
He volunteered in May 1915, and in the following January was drafted to the Western Front where he fought at St. Eloi, Albert, and Ploegsteert. He gave his life for the freedom of England on July 24th, 1916, during the first Battle of the Somme. He was entitled to the General Service and Victory Medals.
"Whilst we remember the sacrifice is not in vain."
140, Tame Street, Ancoats, Manchester.   Z9242

KILNER, W. W., Private, 6th Manchester Regt.
He joined in September 1916, and after undergoing a period of training was drafted to the Western Front. There he took part in much heavy fighting in many sectors, was in action at La Bassée, Givenchy, Festubert, Lens, and Ypres (III), and was wounded. He was invalided to England in June 1917, and was eventually demobilised in April 1919, holding the General Service and Victory Medals.
22, Lindum Street, Rusholme, Manchester.   Z6915

KILROY, A., Sapper, R.E.
He volunteered in October 1914, and after doing consistently good work at various important home stations, was drafted to the Western Front in March 1916. In this theatre of war he saw much heavy fighting, and was present at engagements at Ypres, Neuve Chapelle, Albert, La Bassée, Givenchy, the Somme, and Cambrai, and suffered from gas poisoning. After his recovery, he was stationed at Albert, and rendered valuable services until his demobilisation in February 1919. He holds the General Service and Victory Medals.
13, Hancock Street, Rusholme, Manchester.   Z6916

KING, E., Private, 3rd Devonshire Regiment.
Joining in June 1916, he underwent a period of training and was sent to France in January 1917. He was engaged on special duties in various sectors, and did consistently good work in connection with the construction of dug-outs, the fitting up of trenches and camps, and was present at engagements on the Somme, and at Ypres, Arras, and Cambrai. He also rendered valuable services during the Retreat and Advance of 1918, and was demobilised in February 1919, holding the General Service and Victory Medals.
16, Anthony Street, Ardwick, Manchester.   Z6918

KING, F., Private, 3rd Welch Regiment.
Volunteering in January 1915, he was drafted to Egypt in the following month, and there took part in engagements at Katia, and many other places. He was afterwards transferred to Mesopotamia, where he saw severe fighting at Kut, and was unhappily killed in action in January 1917. He was entitled to the 1914-15 Star, and the General Service and Victory Medals.
"Steals on the ear the distant triumph song."
4, Morville Street, Ancoats, Manchester.   Z10635B

KING, G., Private, K.O. (Royal Lancaster Regt.)
Mobilised at the outbreak of war in August 1914, he was immediately drafted to the Western Front, and took part in the Retreat from Mons. He was also in action at the Battles of Le Cateau, the Marne, La Bassée, and Ypres, and in 1916 was invalided home suffering from disease of the nerves. He holds the Mons Star, and the General Service and Victory Medals, and was discharged in May 1916 as medically unfit for further service. 33, Dorrington St., Hulme, Manchester.   Z6917

KING, J., Driver, R.E.
He volunteered in September 1914, and two months later proceeded to the Western Front, where he did consistently good work in various sectors. He was present at the Battles of Ypres, and Festubert, and later was sent to the Base at Etaples, and was engaged on duties of instruction. In April 1918 he saw heavy fighting on the Somme, was badly wounded and invalided home, and eventually discharged in December 1918, as physically unfit for further service. He holds the 1914 Star, and the General Service and Victory Medals.
57, Naylor Street, Hulme, Manchester.   Z6919

KING, J., Private, 14th Manchester Regiment.
He volunteered in August 1915, and after undergoing a period of training, served at various stations, where he was engaged on duties of a highly important nature. He was not successful in obtaining his transfer to a theatre of war, but nevertheless, rendered valuable services with his unit until August 1919, when he was demobilised.
4, Morville Street, Ancoats, Manchester.   Z10635A

KING, P., Pioneer, R.E.
Joining in February 1916, he was retained on important duties at various stations, on completing a period of training. Owing to defective eyesight, he was not successful in his efforts to obtain his transfer to a theatre of war, but nevertheless, did much useful work with his Company until his demobilisation in December 1919.
14, Hancock Street, Rochdale Road, Manchester.   Z10636

KING, T., L/Corporal, King's (Liverpool Regiment).
He joined in April 1916, and in August of the same year was drafted to France. There he took part in many important engagements, including the Battles of the Somme and Ypres III. He was severely wounded in the head in July 1917, and after being invalided home to the Northern General Hospital, Lincoln, was eventually discharged in April 1918, as unfit for further service, and holds the General Service and Victory Medals.
4, Stone Street, Chester Road, Hulme, Manchester.   Z6921

KING, W. J., Private, 1/8th Manchester Regt.
Volunteering in August 1915, he was drafted to France after four months training, and saw much severe fighting. He took part in the Battles of the Somme, Vimy Ridge, and Cambrai, and in December 1917, was sent to the Base on special duties, in the carrying out of which he rendered valuable services until March 1919. He was then sent home for demobilisation, and holds the 1914-15 Star, and the General Service and Victory Medals.
8, Spruce Street, Hulme, Manchester.   Z6920

KINGSTON, C. W., Pte., South Lancashire Regt.
He joined in January 1917, and after two months' training, was drafted to the Western Front, where he took part in the Battle of Arras, and many minor engagements. He was very severely wounded in action at Bullecourt in June 1917, and as a result, had to have a leg amputated. He was invalided from the Army in October of the same year, and holds the General Service and Victory Medals.
21, Cromwell Avenue, Manley Park, Manchester.   Z10637

KINNINMONT, J., Cpl., 1st Lancashire Fusiliers.
Volunteering in February 1915, he sailed for Gallipoli in the following June, and was wounded two months later in the Landing at Suvla Bay. On recovery he took part in further operations on the Peninsula, and was again wounded in November 1915, and sent home. After treatment he was drafted to France in March 1916, and fought in the Battles of the Somme and Arras, and was wounded for the third time on April 14th, 1917. He later rejoined his Battalion and served in severe fighting at Ypres, and other places until the conclusion of hostilities, when he returned to England. He was demobilised in February 1919, and holds the 1914-15 Star, and the General Service and Victory Medals.
4, Southern Street, Hulme, Manchester.   Z11746

KINSELLA, J., Pte., 2nd Loyal N. Lancashire Regt.
He volunteered in September 1914, and was retained on important guard duties at various camps in England. He was not successful in obtaining his transfer overseas, but nevertheless rendered valuable services until December 1917. He was then transferred to Class W., Army Reserve, and did consistently good work on munitions at Messrs. Schofield's Chemical Works, Clayton, until August 1920, when he was demobilised.
3, Mark Lane, Chorlton-on-Medlock, Manchester.   Z6922

KINSEY, D. H., Sapper, R.E.
He joined in February 1917, and after his training served at various coastal stations on important duties with his unit. He rendered valuable services, but was not successful in obtaining a transfer overseas before the cessation of hostilities, and was demobilised in January 1919.
10, The Brows, Queen's Park, Manchester.   Z11530

KINSEY, W., Private, Loyal N. Lancashire Regt.
He joined in August 1916, and sent to the Western Front in the following May, was in action in the Battles of the Somme and Ypres, where he was wounded. On recovery he rejoined his unit, and was engaged in heavy fighting in many other sectors. He gave his life for King and Country in April 1918, during the German Offensive. He was entitled to the General Service and Victory Medals.
"The path of duty was the way to glory."
48, Abbot's Street, off Ruther Street, Manchester.   Z9243

KIPPAX, J., Private, R.A.M.C.
He volunteered in August 1914, and in March of the following year, was drafted to the Western Front. There he took an active part in the Battles of Vermelles, Arras, Messines, and Ypres, and other important engagements, served also through the Retreat of 1918, and was twice wounded in action—at Festubert in May 1915, and on the Somme in October of the following year. He unhappily died of gas-poisoning in July 1918. He was entitled to the 1914-15 Star, and the General Service and Victory Medals.
"He joined the great white company of valiant souls."
6, Monday Street, Oldham Road, Manchester.   Z10638

KIRK, C. W., Special War Worker.

He volunteered his services at the outbreak of war in August 1914, and being exempt from Military duty, was engaged on work of National importance at Messrs. Armstrong Whitworth and Co., Openshaw. He rendered valuable services throughout the period of hostilities, and was employed chiefly in the manufacture of guns, and did highly commendable work until November 1918.

14, Lord Street, Openshaw, Manchester. Z6923

KIRK, J., Private, 8th Manchester Regiment.

Volunteering in October 1915, he completed a period of training and was drafted to Egypt in June 1916. In this theatre of war he took part in several engagements, including the capture of Magdhaba. In May 1917, he was transferred to the Western Front, and was in action at Passchendaele, Gommecourt, and Le Cateau, and was wounded on two occasions. He was transferred to the 1/5th East Lancs. Regiment in April 1918, and after doing duty with his unit, was demobilised in May 1919, holding the General Service and Victory Medals.

6, Blossom Street, Hulme, Manchester. TZ6924

KIRK, W. T., Sergeant, 8th Lancashire Fusiliers.

He volunteered in August 1914, and in the following April was drafted to Gallipoli. Wounded at the first Landing at Cape Helles, he was evacuated to Alexandria, and after treatment returned to Gallipoli, and fought in operations from the Landing at Suvla Bay in August 1915, until the Evacuation of the Peninsula. Sent to the Western Front he took a prominent part in several battles, including those of Arras, and Cambrai, and was mentioned in Despatches for conspicuous bravery and devotion to duty in leading an attack on an important enemy position in January 1918. Wounded in the course of this engagement he was invalided to England, and on recovery served at home until demobilised in February 1919. He holds the 1914-15 Star, and the General Service and Victory Medals.

2, Phillips Street, Hulme, Manchester. Z11747

KIRKHAM, G., Pte., 10th King's (Liverpool Regt.)

He volunteered in November 1915, and proceeding to France in the following August fought at Ypres and Cambrai, and was twice wounded. He served throughout the German Offensive and Allied Advance of 1918, and on one occasion permitted transfusion of his blood to save a wounded comrade's life. After the Armistice he was sent into Germany with the Army of Occupation, and served there until he returned home, and was demobilised in December 1918. He holds the General Service and Victory Medals.

3, Bell Street, Ancoats, Manchester. TZ9244

KIRKHAM, J., Private, 21st Manchester Regt.

He volunteered in January 1915, and in October of that year, proceeded to the Western Front, where he saw severe fighting in various sectors. After taking part in the Battles of Loos, Vimy Ridge, and the Somme, and many minor engagements, he was invalided home, and on his recovery, was retained on the Regimental Staff in England. He was finally discharged in February 1919, as medically unfit for further service, and holds the 1914-15 Star, and the General Service and Victory Medals. 18, Douro St., Newton Heath, Manchester. Z10639

KIRKHAM, J., Pte., Royal Welch Fusiliers and King's (Liverpool Regt.)

He volunteered in February 1915, and after a period of training, embarked for Salonika with the 2nd King's (Liverpool Regiment). He took part in much fighting on the Struma and Doiran fronts, and later was in action in Bulgaria, where he rendered valuable services. He returned to England in December 1918, and was demobilised in February of the following year, holding the General Service and Victory Medals.

39, Granville Street, Chorlton-on-Medlock, Manchester. Z6925

KIRKHAM, J., Pte., 5th Royal Welch Fusiliers.

He joined in February 1917, and two months later proceeded to the Eastern theatre of war, where he saw service in Egypt and Palestine. He took no part in actual engagements, but nevertheless rendered valuable services at Alexandria, Cairo, Jerusalem, Jericho, Tripoli, and Aleppo, in connection with the supply of food stuffs. He holds the General Service and Victory Medals, and was demobilised in December 1919.

16, Gotha Street, Ardwick, Manchester. Z6926

KIRKHAM, J. T., Pte., 2nd K.O. (R. Lancaster Regt.)

Mobilised at the outbreak of war, he embarked for France, and fought in the Retreat from Mons, and the Battles of Ypres and Loos. Severely wounded on the Somme, he returned home, and after receiving hospital treatment was invalided out of the Service in November 1916. He holds the Mons Star, and the General Service and Victory Medals.

5, St. Clement's Place, Ancoats, Manchester. TZ9245

KIRKHAM, M., Gunner, R.F.A. and R.H.A.

Joining in March 1917, he did consistently good work at various stations in England during the first part of his service. In February 1918, he was drafted to Egypt and was stationed at Cairo and Alexandria, also took part in quelling native riots, and was wounded. He returned to England and was demobilised in March 1920, holding the General Service and Victory Medals. 19, Pump St., Hulme, Manchester. Z6927

KIRKHAM, R., Driver, R.F.A.

Volunteering in August 1914, he was drafted to Salonika on completing his training in the following year, and there saw much severe fighting. He took part in the re-capture of Monastir, and in many other important engagements on the Doiran, Struma, and Vardar fronts, and was wounded in action. He was afterwards transferred to France, where he fought in the Battles of Ypres, and Cambrai, and also served through the Retreat and Advance of 1918. Demobilised in April 1919, he holds the 1914-15 Star, and the General Service and Victory Medals. 29, Elliott St., Bradford, Manchester. Z10640

KIRKLAND, J., Pte., Royal Fusiliers and Spr., R.E.

Joining in April 1916, he was drafted to France three months later, and saw much severe fighting in many sectors, and was in action at Albert and Ypres. He was badly wounded at Beaumont-Hamel during the first battle of the Somme in October 1916, and was later invalided to England, and finally discharged in August 1918 as physically unfit for further service. He holds the General Service and Victory Medals. 2, Bremner Street, Ardwick, Manchester. Z6928 Z6930

KIRKLAND, S. A., Sergt., 1st Manchester Regt.

Volunteering in September 1915, he was sent overseas two months later, and saw much service in France and Flanders. He was engaged in severe fighting in the Somme Offensive, and wounded in July 1916, was evacuated to England. After treatment at Leeds Military Hospital he returned to the Western Front in January 1917, and was in almost continuous action in the Ypres salient, and was again wounded in July 1917, and sent home. On recovery he was stationed at Cleethorpes until his demobilisation in January 1919. He holds the 1914-15 Star, and the General Service and Victory Medals. 14, Hardman Street, Longsight, Manchester. Z11748

KIRKLEY, T. H., Private, R.A.M.C.

Two months after joining in September 1916, he proceeded to the Western Front and was there engaged on important duties in various sectors. He took an active part in the Battles of Arras, Vimy Ridge, Bullecourt, Ypres, and Cambrai, and many other engagements in this theatre of war, and also served through the Retreat and Advance of 1918. He was demobilised on his return home in January 1920, and holds the General Service and Victory Medals. 6, Milne Street, West Gorton, Manchester. TZ11430

KIRKPATRICK, R., Pte., King's (Liverpool Regt.)

He was mobilised in August 1914, and proceeded to France with the 1st Expeditionary Force. After taking part in the Battle of Mons and the subsequent Retreat, he laid down his life for King and Country at the Battle of Hill 60 in May 1915. He was entitled to the Mons Star, and the General Service and Victory Medals.

"Great deeds cannot die:
They, with the sun and moon renew their light for ever."
15, Brown Street, Ancoats, Manchester. Z11913

KIRKWOOD, R., Cpl., 16th Lancashire Fusiliers.

He volunteered in September 1914, and in October of the following year was drafted to the Western Front. Whilst in this theatre of war he took part in many important engagements, including the Battles of Loos, Albert, Vimy Ridge, Bullecourt, Messines and Cambrai, was severely wounded in action and suffered also from shell-shock. Invalided home, he unhappily died in hospital at Huddersfield on November 8th, 1918. He was entitled to the 1914-15 Star, and the General Service and Victory Medals.

"Whilst we remember, the sacrifice is not in vain."
24, Great Jones Street, West Gorton, Manchester. Z10641

KIRWIN, S., Private, 1st Border Regiment.

He volunteered at the outbreak of war in August 1914, and on completion of a period of training in April of the following year was drafted to Gallipoli, where, after taking part in the Landing at Cape Helles, he fought in the Battles of Krithia. He died gloriously on the Field at Krithia in July 1915. He was entitled to the 1914-15 Star, and the General Service and Victory Medals.

"His memory is cherished with pride."
18, Sudbury Street, Rochdale Road, Manchester. Z10642

KITCHEN, J. R., Sapper, R.E.

He volunteered in September 1914, and after undergoing a period of training was drafted to the Western Front in February of the following year. He was present at many engagements, including the Battles of Neuve Chapelle, Hill 60, Ypres (II), and Loos. In January 1916 he was transferred to work of great importance at Hazebrouck Munition Factory, where he was engaged as a brass moulder, and was wounded by German shell-fire in January 1917. After treatment in hospital, he was eventually discharged in September of that year as unfit for further service, and holds the 1914-15 Star, and the General Service and Victory Medals. 10, Oak Street, Hulme, Manchester. TZ6931

KIVEAL, J., Private, 18th Manchester Regiment.
Five months after volunteering in November 1915, he was drafted to the Western Front and saw service at the first Battle of the Somme in 1916, and was severely wounded. He was invalided to England and for nearly two years underwent several operations in hospital, and was finally discharged in June 1918 as physically unfit for military service. He holds the General Service and Victory Medals.
25, Brunswick Street, Hulme, Manchester. Z6932

KNIGHT, A., Pte., Manchester Regt. and Trooper, Yorkshire Hussars.
He volunteered in September 1914, but being medically unfit, was retained on special duties at various stations in the United Kingdom. He was transferred from the Manchester Regiment to the Cameronians (Scottish Rifles) and later did consistently good work with the Yorkshire Hussars until his demobilisation in March 1919.
32, Pump Street, Hulme, Manchester. Z6936

KNIGHT, H., Private, King's (Liverpool Regiment).
After joining in November 1916, he underwent a period of training prior to being drafted to the Western Front in August of the following year. There he saw severe fighting in various sectors and took part in the Battles of Ypres, Cambrai, the Somme, Amiens and Bapaume and many minor engagements. He was sent home and invalided from the Army in September 1918 suffering from shell-shock, and holds the General Service and Victory Medals.
32, Branson Street, Ancoats, Manchester. Z10643

KNIGHT, H. H., Private, 8th Manchester Regt.
Volunteering in March 1915, he was drafted to France in the following June and took part in much heavy fighting in various sectors. He was badly wounded at the Battle of Loos in September 1915, and again at Lens in August 1917 and, after being invalided home, was eventually discharged in February 1918 as physically unfit for further service. He holds the 1914–15 Star, and the General Service and Victory Medals.
10, Mahogany Street, Chorlton-on-Medlock, Manchester. Z6934A

KNIGHT, J., Private, 14th Manchester Regiment.
He volunteered in August 1914, and was drafted to the Western Front in the following May. Whilst in this theatre of war he played an important part in the Battles of Ypres (II), the Somme and Arras and in heavy fighting at La Bassée and Nieuport. He was seriously wounded in action at Arras in May 1917, and was invalided home to hospital at the Royal Infirmary, Manchester, where he unhappily died in January 1918, after long suffering. He was entitled to the 1914–15 Star, and the General Service and Victory Medals.
"His life for his Country, his soul to God."
48, Baguley Street, Miles Platting, Manchester. Z11914

KNIGHT, J., Private, 23rd Manchester Regiment.
He joined in June 1916, and in November of that year was sent to the Western Front, where he took part in many important engagements. He rendered valuable services at Beaumont-Hamel, Vimy Ridge, Beaucourt, Arras and Messines, and made the supreme sacrifice on October 22nd, 1917, being killed in action at Passchendaele, and was entitled to the General Service and Victory Medals.
"He died the noblest death a man may die,
Fighting for God, and right and liberty."
5, Meadow Street, Ardwick, Manchester. Z6933

KNIGHT, J., Driver, R.A.S.C.
He volunteered in January 1915, and in the following October proceeded to France, where he was engaged on important transport duties in connection with the carrying of food to forward areas. He also did consistently good work as cook until his demobilisation in July 1919, and holds the 1914–15 Star, and the General Service and Victory Medals.
10, Mahogany Street, Chorlton-on-Medlock, Manchester. Z6934B

KNIGHT, J. T., Private, 7th Border Regiment.
Volunteering in December 1914, he underwent a period of training and was drafted to the Western Front in August 1915. He unfortunately only saw active service in France for a few weeks before being killed by shrapnel at the Battle of Loos in September 1915. He was entitled to the 1914–15 Star, and the General Service and Victory Medals.
"The path of duty was the way to glory."
22, Union Street, Rusholme, Manchester. Z6937

KNIGHT, R. H., Sergt., 3rd K.O. (R. Lancaster Regt.)
Mobilised at the outbreak of war in August 1914, he was immediately drafted to the Western Front and played a distinguished part in the Retreat from Mons. He was also in action at the Battles of the Marne, La Bassée, Neuve Chapelle and Loos, and was wounded. He returned to his unit in January 1916 and was again in action in many sectors until August 1916, when he was gassed during the Somme Offensive. He was later transferred to Mesopotamia and saw much service in this theatre of war until his return to England for discharge in April 1919. He holds the Mons Star, and the General Service and Victory Medals.
18, Allen Street, Hulme, Manchester. Z6935

KNIGHT, W., A.B. (Gunner), Royal Navy.
He volunteered in September 1914, and did duty in H.M.S. "Ramillies" in the North Sea, where he was engaged escorting transports to various distinations in the war zone. He rendered valuable services throughout the period of hostilities, and was demobilised in January 1919, holding the 1914–15 Star, and the General Service and Victory Medals.
26, Platt Street, Moss Side, Manchester. Z6938

KNOTT, C., Private, Royal Welch Fusiliers.
Three months after joining in July 1916, he was drafted to France and took part in many important engagements in various sectors. He saw much heavy fighting during the time he served on the Western Front, particularly at Vimy Ridge and at Beaucourt on the Somme, but was unfortunately killed in the Ancre sector in February 1917. He was entitled to the General Service and Victory Medals.
"The path of duty was the way to glory."
29, Ely Street, Hulme, Manchester. TZ6750A

KNOTT, J., Sapper, R.E.
He volunteered in August 1914, and during the first part of his service did consistently good work at important stations in England. In 1916 he was drafted to France, where he took part in the first Battle of the Somme and later in the Battle of Ypres (III). He was wounded and invalided to England in 1917, and after being discharged from the Army in August of the following year, he re-enlisted, and in August 1919 proceeded to Egypt, where in 1920 he was still serving. He holds the General Service and Victory Medals.
11, Thomas Street, West Gorton, Manchester. Z6939

KNOTT, J., Private, King's Own Scottish Borderers.
He joined in February 1916, and two months later proceeded to the Western Front, where he took part in many important engagements in various sectors. He suffered severely from trench fever in December 1916, and after a period in hospital in Boulogne, returned to England and was eventually discharged in July 1918 as unfit for further service. He holds the General Service and Victory Medals.
16, Dalton Street, Longsight, Manchester. Z6064B

KNOTT, T., Private, 2nd Seaforth Highlanders.
Volunteering in January 1915, he underwent a period of training and service in England and was drafted to the Western Front in July 1917. There he took part in various important engagements, including those in the Ypres and Somme sectors, and after the cessation of hostilities, proceeded to Germany, where he did duty with the Army of Occupation on the Rhine. In 1920 he was serving with the Army in India, and holds the General Service and Victory Medals.
61, Caton Street, Hulme, Manchester. Z6940

KNOWLES, A., Corporal, 9th Border Regiment.
He volunteered in September 1914, and after a period of training was drafted to Salonika in October of the following year. There he played a prominent part in much heavy fighting and was in action at the Landing in this theatre of war. He also took part in the Advance across the Struma, the capture of Monastir and the Advance on Vardar, but unfortunately contracted malaria, and was invalided to England. He was eventually demobilised in February 1919, and holds the 1914–15 Star, and the General Service and Victory Medals.
55, Thomas Street, Hulme, Manchester. Z6943

KNOWLES, J. W., Air Mechanic, R.A.F.
He joined in September 1918, and was retained with his Squadron at Woodbridge Aerodrome, Suffolk. He did consistently good work as a mechanic, but was unable to obtain his transfer to a theatre of war before the cessation of hostilities. He was demobilised in March 1919.
5, Jane Street, West Gorton, Manchester. Z6942

KNOWLES, S., Private, 6th Cheshire Regiment.
He volunteered in September 1915, and after undergoing a period of training was drafted to France in July 1916. He saw much heavy fighting during the short time he was on the Western Front, and took part in the Advance during the Somme Offensive in August 1916. He was invalided home and eventually discharged in September 1917 as physically unfit for further military service, and holds the General Service and Victory Medals.
12, Mundy Street, Gorton, Manchester. Z6941

KNOX, A., Private, K.O. (Royal Lancaster Regt.)
He volunteered in August 1914, and after a period of training was drafted to the Western Front in June of the following year. He took part in many important engagements, including the Battles of Loos and Albert, and made the supreme sacrifice on November 7th, 1916, when he was killed in action at Beaumont-Hamel, on the Somme. He was entitled to the 1914–15 Star, and the General Service and Victory Medals.
"His life for his Country, his soul to God."
7, William Street, Hulme, Manchester. Z6944

L

LACEY, E., L/Corporal, South Lancashire Regt.

He volunteered in August 1914, and after completing a period of training was drafted in May of the following year to Mesopotamia. There he saw much severe fighting on the Tigris and also took part in numerous engagements at Kut and many other places until the cessation of hostilities. Returning home in February 1919, he was demobilised two months later, and holds the 1914–15 Star, and the General Service and Victory Medals.

30, St. Ann Street, Bradford, Manchester. Z10644

LACEY, J. P., Private, 21st Manchester Regiment.

He volunteered in November 1914, and after completing a period of service was drafted to the Western Front in November of the following year. There he took part in much heavy fighting in various sectors and was in action at the Battles of Ypres, the Somme in 1916 and St. Quentin in the following year. He also rendered valuable services during the Advance of 1918, and was demobilised in February 1919, holding the 1914–15 Star, and the General Service and Victory Medals.

222, Heald Grove, Rusholme, Manchester. Z6945

LAFFIN, J., Corporal, 1st Manchester Regiment.

Volunteering in August 1914, he was drafted to France in December and played a prominent part in the fighting in various sectors, including the Battle of Neuve Chapelle, during which he was severely wounded in action. He unfortunately died from his wounds on March 15th, 1915, and was entitled to the 1914–15 Star, and the General Service and Victory Medals.

"Thinking that remembrance, though unspoken, may reach him where he sleeps."

34, Fenn Street, Hulme, Manchester. Z6946

LAIDLAW, D., Sergt., Manchester Regiment.

He joined in March 1916, and four months later proceeded to the Western Front, where he played a distinguished part in the fighting in various sectors. He was wounded on two occasions, the first at an engagement at Guillemont in 1916 and again after his return to France in July 1918, after carrying out the duties of a Sergeant Instructor at home. He was demobilised in September 1919, and holds the General Service and Victory Medals.

47, Claribel Street, Ardwick, Manchester. Z6947

LAITHWAITE, W., L/Cpl., 16th Manchester Regt.

He volunteered in December 1915, and in March 1917 embarked for France. During his service on the Western Front he took part in much of the heavy fighting at Ypres, and was wounded at Passchendaele and Cambrai in 1917. After his recovery he was in action during the Advance of the following year until the Armistice was signed. He holds the General Service and Victory Medals, and was demobilised in January 1919.

5, Horton Street, Newton Heath, Manchester. Z9607

LAKIN, W., Private, 2nd Manchester Regiment.

Volunteering in September 1914, he proceeded to France in April of the following year, and there saw severe fighting in various sectors of the Front and took part in the Battles of Hill 60, Ypres, Festubert, Loos, Albert, Vermelles and Vimy Ridge. He fell in action on September 28th, 1916, during the Advance on the Somme. He was entitled to the 1914–15 Star, and the General Service and Victory Medals.

"A costly sacrifice upon the altar of freedom."

119, Jersey Street Dwellings, Ancoats, Manchester. Z10645

LALLY, J. (M.M.), Private, K.O. (Y.L.I.)

Volunteering in August 1914, he proceeded to France in the following month and took part in many important engagements. He was in action at the Battles of La Bassée, Ypres (I and II), Hill 60, Vimy Ridge, the Somme (I and II), Arras and the Marne, and was gassed at Le Cateau during the Advance of 1918. He was awarded the Military Medal for conspicuous gallantry in the Field and also holds the 1914 Star, and the General Service and Victory Medals, and was demobilised in January 1919.

38, Blackthorn Street, Ardwick, Manchester. Z6948

LAMB, A., Private, 10th Royal Welch Fusiliers.

He volunteered in November 1915, and in the following year was drafted to France, where he took part in the fighting at Loos, St. Eloi, Albert, Vimy Ridge, the Somme, Arras and Ypres, and was wounded and invalided home. He was demobilised in January 1919, and holds the General Service and Victory Medals.

73, Cheltenham Street, Collyhurst, Manchester. Z9246

LAMB, E., Private, Royal Welch Fusiliers.

Joining in November 1917, he proceeded to the Western Front after two months' training, and was there engaged on important transport duties in various sectors until the cessation of hostilities. He was then sent with the Army of Occupation into Germany, where he was employed on similar duties until his return home in October 1919. Demobilised in the following month, he holds the General Service and Victory Medals.

12, Lawrence Street, Gorton, Manchester. Z10646B

LAMB, J. W., L/Corporal, 6th Border Regiment.

Volunteering in August 1914, he underwent a period of training and was drafted to the Dardanelles in April 1915. After taking part in the Battles of Krithia I, II and III, and the Landing at Suvla Bay, he was invalided to Malta with trench fever and later proceeded to France, where he was in action at the Battles of Vimy Ridge, Albert, the Somme, Arras and Bullecourt, and was wounded. He was invalided to England and eventually discharged in December 1917 as unfit for further service, and holds the 1914–15 Star, and the General Service and Victory Medals.

13, Bury Street, City Road, Hulme, Manchester. Z6949

LAMB, R., Private, 1/8th Manchester Regiment.

He volunteered in April 1915, and in December of the same year proceeded to Egypt, where he served on the Suez Canal until March 1917. He was then transferred to the Western Front and there, after seeing heavy fighting at Nieuport, La Bassée and many other places, was severely wounded in action in March 1918. He unhappily died of wounds in the following month. He was entitled to the 1914–15 Star, and the General Service and Victory Medals.

"The path of duty was the way to glory."

12, Lawrence Street, Gorton, Manchester. Z10646A

LAMB, R. W., Private, 1/7th Manchester Regiment.

He volunteered in August 1914, and was drafted to Egypt after a few weeks' training. There he saw service for six months before proceeding to the Dardanelles in the following April. In this theatre of war he took part in much heavy fighting and made the supreme sacrifice at the third Battle of Krithia, being killed in action on June 4th, 1915. He was entitled to the 1914–15 Star, and the General Service and Victory Medals.

"A valiant Soldier, with undaunted heart, he breasted life's last hill."

10, Brunswick Street, Hulme, Manchester. Z6951

LAMB, T., Trooper, 2nd Dragoon Guards.

He joined in April 1917, and after a short period of training was sent to France, where he took part in many engagements. He was in action at the second Battle of the Somme (where he was gassed), Havrincourt Wood, Cambrai (II) and the Selle, and the entry into Mons. After the Armistice he proceeded to Germany and did duty with the Army of Occupation in Cologne until his return to England for demobilisation in November 1919. He holds the General Service and Victory Medals.

36, Russell Street, Moss Side, Manchester. TZ6952A

LAMB, T. J., L/Corporal, 2/7th Manchester Regt.

Volunteering in October 1914, he was retained on work of National importance as an iron turner at Messrs. Blakeley's Munition Factory, Atherton, Lancs., and did consistently good work during the whole period of the war. He rendered valuable services and in 1920 after his demobilisation in February of the previous year, was still employed by the same firm. 12, Brunswick Street, Hulme, Manchester. Z6950

LAMB, W., Gunner, R.G.A.

He joined in November 1917, and later was drafted to Gibraltar, where he was engaged on important garrison duties. He rendered valuable services during the latter period of hostilities and was not demobilised until March 1919. He holds the General Service Medal.

84, Ogilvie Street, Chorlton-on-Medlock, Manchester. X6620B

LAMBERT, A. E., L/Corpl., Loyal N.Lancashire Regt.

Volunteering in August 1914, he was sent to France in the following January, and took part in heavy fighting at Cuinchy, Givenchy and La Bassée. In May 1915 he proceeded to Egypt with the 2nd Cheshire Regiment and was engaged on important duties there until July 1916. He was eventually demobilised in January 1919, and holds the 1914–15 Star, and the General Service and Victory Medals.

18, Amos Street, Ancoats, Manchester. Z10647

LAMBERT, F., Driver, R.A.S.C. (M.T.)

He joined in May 1918, and after completing his training was engaged on transport duties at various depôts, and rendered valuable services. Unsuccessful in obtaining his transfer overseas before the close of the war, in November 1918, he was sent with the Army of Occupation into Germany and served as a motor driver on the General Headquarter Staff at Bonn and Cologne until his return home for demobilisation in February 1920.

54, Russell Street, Moss Side, Manchester. Z11749B

LAMBERT, J. W., Corporal, 2nd Duke of Lancaster's Own Dragoons.

He volunteered in January 1915, and on the conclusion of his training was engaged on home service duties at various stations in England and Scotland and Ireland. Employed on important clerical duties in the stores, he did excellent work but was unable to procure his transfer to a theatre of war before the cessation of hostilities, and was demobilised in July 1919.

54, Russell Street, Moss Side, Manchester. Z11749A

LAMBERT, R., Private, Lancashire Fusiliers.
He volunteered in September 1914, and in the following year was drafted to France, but after taking part in the Battle of Loos, was transferred to Salonika in January 1916. Whilst in the Balkan theatre of war, he was in action during the heavy fighting in the Doiran, Struma and Vardar fronts and at the recapture of Monastir. He was demobilised in January 1919, and holds the 1914–15 Star, and the General Service and Victory Medals.
7, Perrin Street, Ancoats, Manchester. Z10648

LANCASTER, F., Driver, R.F.A.
He volunteered in August 1914, and after undergoing a period of training was drafted to the Eastern theatre of war in May 1915. He saw service at Kut-el-Amara in Mesopotamia, whilst with the relieving forces, and later took part in the fighting on the Tigris. In January 1917 he proceeded to Palestine and was in action at the Battles of Gaza I. II and III, and during the offensive in this theatre of war. He holds the 1914–15 Star, and the General Service and Victory Medals, and after his return home was demobilised in January 1919.
25, Cawder Street, Hulme, Manchester. Z6955

LANCASTER, G. E., Private, Manchester Regiment.
He volunteered in January 1915, and after a period of training was sent to the Western Front in November of the same year. There he took part in many engagements, including the Somme Offensive of 1916, and was badly wounded. After being invalided to England he returned to France, and rejoining his unit, was later transferred to Salonika. He holds the 1914–15 Star, and the General Service and Victory Medals, and returning home, was demobilised in February 1919.
26, Turner Street, Rusholme, Manchester. Z6954A

LANCASTER, J., Private, 20th Lancashire Fusiliers.
He volunteered in May 1915, and after completing a period of training was drafted to the Western Front in May of the following year. There he took part in much heavy fighting, but was unfortunately killed in action at the first Battle of the Somme on July 25th, 1916. He was entitled to the General Service and Victory Medals.
" Thinking that remembrance, though unspoken, may reach him where he sleeps."
26, Turner Street, Rusholme, Manchester. Z6954B

LANCASTER, N., L/Corporal, 5/7th K.O. (Royal Lancaster Regiment).
Having volunteered in August 1914, he first saw active service in the following April, when he took part in the Landing at Cape Helles in the Dardanelles. He was also in action at the Battles of Krithia (I, II and III), the Landing at Suvla Bay and at Chocolate Hill. After the Evacuation of the Gallipoli Peninsula, he proceeded to the Western Front, where he served at St. Eloi and Loos, in the Battles of the Somme, Arras, Vimy Ridge and Ypres (III), and was badly wounded in October 1917. Invalided to England, he was discharged in January 1918 as medically unfit for further service, and holds the 1914–15 Star, and the General Service and Victory Medals.
11, Eliza Ann Street, Rochdale Road, Manchester. Z10649

LANCASTER, N., Pte. K.O. (Royal Lancaster Regt.)
He volunteered in August 1914, and in September of the following year was sent to the Dardanelles, where he took part in the three Battles of Krithia and the Landing at Suvla Bay. In consequence of contracting malaria he was invalided home, and was discharged in November 1917, owing to his disability. He holds the 1914–15 Star, and the General Service and Victory Medals.
20, Sanitary Street, Oldham Road, Manchester. Z11531B

LANCASTER, S., Gunner, R.F.A.
Volunteering in November 1914, he completed a period of training and did duty with his Battery at important stations in England for some time. He later suffered from ill-health and after doing consistently good work sketching X-ray results for the R.A.M.C., was discharged in November 1917 as medically unfit for futher military service.
93, Crondall Street, Moss Side, Manchester. Z6953

LANCASTER, W., Sapper, R.E.
Volunteering in August 1914, he proceeded to Egypt in January of the following year, and was in action at Jifjaffa, Katia and El Fasher. In May 1916 he was transferred to Salonika, where he was engaged in the heavy fighting on the Vardar, Struma and Doiran fronts until hostilities ceased. He was demobilised in June 1919, and holds the 1914–15 Star, and the General Service and Victory Medals.
20, Sanitary Street, Oldham Road, Manchester. Z11531A

LANCE, M., Private, Labour Corps.
He joined in March 1918, and in the following June was sent to the Western Front, where he was engaged on the important duties of road mending and the unloading of shells. He rendered valuable services at Havrincourt, Ypres (IV), Cambrai (II) and Le Cateau (II), and was demobilised in March 1919, holding the General Service and Victory Medals.
4, Gregory Street, West Gorton, Manchester. Z6956

LANDER, G. W., Private, Labour Corps.
He joined in May 1916, and five months later was drafted to the Western Front, where he was present at many important engagements. He rendered valuable services on the Ancre front and at Arras, Ypres and the Somme, and made the supreme sacrifice in August 1918, being unfortunately killed at Bapaume during the great Offensive of that year. He was entitled to the General Service and Victory Medals.
" His memory is cherished with pride."
94, Thomas Street, West Gorton, Manchester. Z6957B

LANDER, U., Private, Royal Scots.
Volunteering in January 1915, he proceeded to France four months later and took part in many important engagements. He was in action at the Battles of Festubert, Loos, St. Eloi, Albert, the Somme, Bullecourt, Ypres and the Selle, and suffered severely from gas poisoning. He was invalided to England and discharged in August 1918 as physically unfit for further service, and holds the 1914–15 Star, and the General Service and Victory Medals.
94, Thomas Street, West Gorton, Manchester. Z6957A

LANDER, S., Private, King's (Liverpool Regt.)
He joined in February 1917, and after a period of training and duty in England was drafted to France in November of the following year. He was transferred to the Royal Engineers and rendered valuable services as an electrician, until his return home for demobilisation in May 1919. He holds the General Service and Victory Medals.
94, Thomas Street, West Gorton, Manchester. Z6957C

LANE, T., Private, 5th Loyal N. Lancashire Regt.
He volunteered in September 1914, but owing to his being medically unfit was not successful in obtaining his transfer to a theatre of war. He nevertheless rendered valuable services during the four months he was with his unit, and was discharged in December 1914, as unfit for military duties.
10, Gregory Street, West Gorton, Manchester. Z6959

LANE, W., Driver, R.A.S.C.
Volunteering in August 1914, he was sent to France in June of the following year, and was engaged on important transport duties in many sectors of the Front. He was present at the Battles of the Somme, Ypres, Loos, Albert Arras and Passchendaele and in the Retreat and Advance of 1918, and was often under fire whilst taking rations to forward areas. He was in hospital in France for a time and was eventually demobilised in January 1919, holding the 1914–15 Star, and the General Service and Victory Medals.
3, Brackley Street, Hulme, Manchester. Z6958

LANG, D., Sergt., Loyal North Lancashire Regt.
He volunteered at the outbreak of war, and in August 1915 proceeded to Gibraltar, where, throughout, he was engaged on important garrison and guard duties until the cessation of hostilities. He did not return home until February 1919, when he was demobilised, holding the General Service and Victory Medals.
3, Pearson Street, Newton Heath, Manchester. Z9608

LANG, H., Private, 8th South Lancashire Regt.
He volunteered in March 1915, and after undergoing a period of training was sent to France in February of the following year. There he took part in many important engagements, including the Battles of Vimy Ridge and Messines, and was gassed at the latter place in July 1917. He was invalided to England, and after a few months in hospital was discharged in November 1917 as physically unfit for further service. He holds the General Service and Victory Medals.
36, Lord Street, Hulme, Manchester. TZ6960

LANGDON, A., Corporal, Black Watch.
Volunteering in December 1914, he completed a period of training, and was drafted to Egypt in January 1916. There he saw service on the Suez Canal, and was also in action at Romani and El Arish. From January to July 1918, he took a prominent part in engagements on the Doiran and Vardar fronts at Salonika, and was then transferred to France, where he fought at Passchendaele, Bapaume, the Sambre and Le Cateau and later proceeded to Germany with the Army of Occupation. He suffered from dysentery and temporary blindness during his service in the East, and was demobilised in February 1919, holding the General Service and Victory Medals.
62, Palmerston Street, Moss Side, Manchester. TZ6961

LANGFORD, T., Private, 8th Manchester Regt.
Mobilised in August 1914, he proceeded to Egypt in the following month and was stationed at Khartoum. In April 1915 he was transferred to the Dardanelles and took part in the fighting on the Gallipoli Peninsula, being in action at the Battles of Krithia III, Seddil Bahr and the Landing at Suvla Bay. He returned to England after the Evacuation, and after a period of illness in hospital, rejoined his Regiment in February 1917, but unhappily died of fever, contracted abroad, two months later. He was entitled to the 1914 Star, and the General Service and Victory Medals.
" His memory is cherished with pride."
14, Alder Street, Hulme, Manchester. TZ6962

LANGLEY, D., Cpl., 7th K.O. (R. Lancaster Regt.)

He volunteered in August 1914, and after undergoing a period of training was drafted to the Western Front in July of the following year. In this theatre of war he played a prominent part in many engagements, including the Somme Offensive of 1916 and the Battles of Arras, Ypres and Cambrai and later, the Retreat and Advance of 1918. He holds the 1914-15 Star, and the General Service and Victory Medals, and was demobilised in April 1919.

262, Ridgway Street, Ancoats, Manchester. Z6964

LANGLEY, G., Pte., 2/5th Durham Light Infantry.

He joined in August 1917, and three months later was drafted to Salonika, where he was in action on the Doiran and Vardar fronts. He saw much heavy fighting in this theatre of war and suffered from malaria. After recovery he rejoined his unit and was again in action until the cessation of hostilities. He eventually returned to England and was demobilised in March 1919, holding the General Service and Victory Medals.

124, Viaduct Street, Ardwick, Manchester. Z6963

LANGRON, M., Private, South Lancashire Regt.

He volunteered in August 1914, and after undergoing a period of training was drafted to the Dardanelles early in the following year. There he took part in much heavy fighting, including the Landing at Suvla Bay. After the Evacuation of the Gallipoli Peninsula, he embarked for France and was in action during the Somme Offensive of 1916 and other engagements of importance. He was discharged in September 1918 after being wounded on two occasions, and holds the 1914-15 Star, and the General Service and Victory Medals.

22, Melbourne Street, Chorlton-on-Medlock, Manchester. X6965

LANGSHAW, W., Private, 17th Manchester Regt.

Volunteering in September 1914, he completed his training and was drafted to the Western Front in November of the following year. In this theatre of war he took part in much severe fighting in various sectors, including the Somme, and made the supreme sacrifice in July 1916, being killed in action at Montauban. He was entitled to the 1914-15 Star, and the General Service and Victory Medals.

"He died the noblest death a man may die."

3, North Street, Hulme, Manchester. Z6966

LANGSTON, G. F., Corporal, R.E.

He volunteered in July 1915, and after undergoing a period of training, was drafted to Mesopotamia in April of the following year. There he was engaged on important duties with the Royal Engineers at Basra Electricity Station, but was unfortunately taken ill, and died of small-pox in April 1918. He was entitled to the General Service and Victory Medals.

"His memory is cherished with pride."

88, Stockton Street, Moss Side, Manchester. Z6967A

LANGTON, A. (M.S.M.), Sergt., Tank Corps.

He volunteered in November 1914, and proceeding to France in 1916, served with distinction at the Battles of the Somme, Messines, Ypres, Cambrai, Havrincourt, and Valenciennes, and in heavy fighting at Neuve Chapelle, Richebourg, St. Vaast, Festubert, Adinfer Wood, Courcelles, Norueuil, Quéant, Canal de l'Escat Masnières and Achiet-le-Grand. He was wounded at Ypres in August 1917, and on two occasions his tank was struck by shells and put out of action. He was awarded the Meritorious Service Medal and mentioned in Despatches for conspicuous bravery in the Field, and was demobilised in February 1919. He also holds the General Service and Victory Medals.

15, Elias Street, Manchester. Z11915

LANGTON, H. (Mrs.), Worker, Q.M.A.A.C.

After doing consistently good work of National importance at No. 2 Filling Factory, Aintree, for some time, she joined the Queen Mary Army Auxiliary Corps, and was engaged as a tailoress in the camp workshop at Kinmel Park. She also rendered valuable services at various other important stations, and was discharged in December 1918.

38, Marsland Street, Ardwick, Manchester. Z6968B

LANGTON, J., Pte., 1st Loyal N. Lancashire Regt.

He volunteered in November 1914, and four months later was sent to the Western Front, where he played an important part in the Battles of Hill 60, Ypres (II), Festubert, Loos, Arras, Ypres (III), and Cambrai. He was badly wounded in action at Loos, and was eventually demobilised in October 1919, holding the 1914-15 Star, and the General Service and Victory Medals. 10, Hancock St., Rochdale Rd., Manchester. Z10650

LANGTON, M., Private, 2nd Manchester Regt.

Volunteering in July 1915, he proceeded to France in the following January, and took part in the Battles of Albert, Ploegsteert, the Somme, Arras, Bullecourt, Messines, Ypres (III), Passchendaele (when he was wounded and gassed in action in November 1917), and in the Retreat and Advance of 1918. After the cessation of hostilities, he served at Cologne with the Army of Occupation, and was demobilised in March 1919, holding the General Service and Victory Medals.

4, Haigh Street, West Gorton, Manchester. Z10651

LANGTON, R., Private, Border Regiment.

He joined in February 1916, and in June of the following year was drafted to the Western Front, where he played a prominent part in heavy fighting at Nieuport. Unfortunately he was killed in action in September 1917, and was entitled to the General Service and Victory Medals.

"Great deeds cannot die :
They, with the sun and moon renew their light for ever."

41, Albion Street, Miles Platting, Manchester. Z10652

LANGTON, R. A., Manchester Regt. and Lancashire Fusiliers.

He volunteered in August 1914, and after doing duty at important stations in England during the first part of his service, was drafted to the Western Front in December 1916. There he was in action in various sectors with the Manchester Regiment, but was later transferred to the Lancashire Fusiliers, and took part in the Battles of Arras, Vimy Ridge, Bullecourt, and Messines, and was wounded on two occasions. He was invalided home in July 1917, and afterwards, transferred to the Royal Engineers, served until his demobilisation in February 1919 as a boilermaker at Sandwich, Kent. He holds the General Service and Victory Medals.

38, Marsland Street, Ardwick, Manchester. Z6968A

LANIGAN, E., Private, 18th Lancashire Fusiliers.

Volunteering in January 1915, he completed his training and was drafted to the Western Front in December of the same year. There he took part in numerous important engagements, including the Battles of Albert, Ploegsteert Wood, the Somme I, Beaucourt, and Arras I, and was unfortunately killed in action on the Ypres front on December 11th, 1917. He was buried at Ypres Church Cemetery, and was entitled to the General Service and Victory Medals. Z6970

"He died the noblest death a man may die.
Fighting for God and right and liberty."

6, Little Rumford Street, Chorlton-on-Medlock, Manchester.

LANIGAN, P., Private, 15th Lancashire Fusiliers.

He joined in July 1917, and was drafted to the Western Front in the following December. In this theatre of war he took part in many engagements, including those at Ypres, Arras, Amiens, St. Quentin, and the Sambre, and after the Armistice proceeded to Germany, where he did duty with the Army of Occupation on the Rhine. He returned to England, and was demobilised in October 1919, holding the General Service and Victory Medals. Z6969

6, Little Rumford Street, Chorlton-on-Medlock, Manchester.

LARKIN, J., Private, 5th King's (Liverpool Regt.)

Joining in September 1916, he was retained on special duties with his unit at important stations in England, but was unable to obtain his transfer to a theatre of war on account of being medically unfit. He nevertheless rendered valuable services, and was discharged in April 1917.

34A, Lingmoor St., Chorlton-on-Medlock, Manchester. X6971

LARNER, G., Trooper, 5th (Princess Charlotte of Wales) Dragoon Guards.

He joined in June 1916, and after his training served at various stations on important duties with his unit. He rendered valuable services, but was not successful in obtaining his transfer overseas, and was discharged in April 1918 as medically unfit for further service.

43, Victoria Square, Oldham Road, Manchester. Z9247

LARRAD, T., Private, 7th Manchester Regiment.

He volunteered in November 1914, and in the following month proceeded to Egypt, where he saw service on the Suez Canal, and at Mersa Matruh, Sollum, Katia, and Romani, and was wounded in August 1916. He was invalided to England, and in June 1917 was drafted to France, where he was in action at Ypres III and IV., Cambrai I, and the third Battle of the Aisne, and was again wounded. He holds the 1914-15 Star, and the General Service and Victory Medals, and was demobilised in June 1919.

30, Lancaster Street, Hulme, Manchester. Z6972

LAST, V. E., Private, R.A.S.C.

He volunteered in January 1915, and did consistently good work in England during the first part of his service. In May 1917 he was drafted to France and was engaged on important transport duties in various sectors, including Messines, Ypres, Lens, and Cambrai, and was badly wounded on two occasions. He was taken prisoner in December 1917, and after the cessation of hostilities was repatriated and eventually demobilised in March 1920, holding the General Service and Victory Medals.

28, Nelly Street, Ardwick, Manchester. Z6973

LATER, G. N., Private, 1/7th Gordon Highlanders.

Three months after volunteering in January 1915, he was drafted to the Western Front, where he was in action at various important engagements. He saw much heavy fighting at Hill 60, Ypres II, Festubert, Albert, Ploegsteert Wood, Vimy Ridge, the Somme, Beaucourt, and Beaumont-Hamel, and made the supreme sacrifice on January 7th, 1917, being killed in action at Courcelette. He was entitled to the 1914-15 Star, and the General Service and Victory Medals.

"A costly sacrifice upon the altar of freedom."

74, Everton Road, Chorlton-on-Medlock, Manchester. Z6974B

LATER, S., Private, 5th Middlesex Regiment.

He joined in April 1918, but being physically unfit for service overseas, was retained on special duties at various important stations in England. He, nevertheless, rendered valuable services, and was finally discharged from the Army in June 1919.

74, Everton Road, Chorlton-on-Medlock, Manchester.   Z6974A

LATHAM, A., L/Corporal, 1/5th Border Regiment.

Joining in March 1917 he was drafted to France three months later and took part in the third battle of Ypres, and other engagements of importance on the Western Front. He also rendered valuable services during the Retreat and Advance of 1918, and after the Armistice proceeded to Germany, where he did duty with the Army of Occupation on the Rhine. He was demobilised in September 1919 on his return to England, and holds the General Service and Victory Medals.

40, Robert Street, West Gorton, Manchester.   Z6976

LATHAM, J., Sapper, R.E.

Having joined in April 1916, he was drafted to France later in the same year, and took part in numerous engagements, including those on the Ancre front, and at Arras, Messines, Ypres, Cambrai, Lys, the Aisne, and Bapaume. He was demobilised in September 1919, and holds the General Service and Victory Medals.

139, Victoria Square, Ancoats, Manchester.   Z9248

LATHAM, S. H., Police Steward, Royal Navy.

He joined in June 1916, and after doing duty in the North Sea on board H.M.S. "Olympic" was engaged in carrying troops from Canada to Liverpool. He was later transferred to a Labour Battalion, and was employed on police work and unloading ships at Le Havre until his discharge in December 1917, as unfit for further service. He holds the General Service and Victory Medals.

4, Coburg Street, Rusholme, Manchester.   Z6975

LATHWOOD, T. A., Private, Lancashire Fusiliers.

He volunteered in September 1914, and after a course of training was drafted to the Dardanelles in April 1915. There he took part in much heavy fighting on the Gallipoli Peninsula, and was wounded at the Battle of Krithia. He returned to England after the Evacuation, and was transferred to a Labour Battalion, and rendered valuable services as a storeman at Barry Docks until his demobilisation in January 1919. He holds the 1914-15 Star, and the General Service and Victory Medals. 6, Dundas Street, Ancoats, Manchester.   TZ6977

LAVERY, A., Private, Labour Corps.

He volunteered in December 1915, and in the following July was drafted to France, where he was engaged on ammunition carrying and trench digging work. He was present during the Battle of the Somme in 1916, and afterwards rendered valuable services in this sector throughout hostilities. Demobilised in September 1919, he holds the General Service and Victory Medals.

7, Shepley Street, Harpurhey, Manchester.   Z10653

LAW, J., Private, 1st Lancashire Fusiliers.

Volunteering in August 1914, he underwent a period of training, and was drafted to the Dardanelles in May of the following year. He took part in much severe fighting on the Gallipoli Peninsula, and was wounded in August 1915. He was eventually invalided to England, and on his recovery was sent to France in June 1916. There he was in action at many important engagements, including those at Loos, Ypres, and the Somme. He was transferred to the Royal Air Force in October 1917, and after doing consistently good work in the workshops at Rouen was demobilised in March 1919, holding the 1914-15 Star, and the General Service and Victory Medals.

3, Bradshaw Street, Hulme, Manchester.   Z6980

LAW, J., Corporal, 11th Hussars.

He volunteered in August 1914, and proceeded to France in the following month. In this theatre of war he played a prominent part in many important engagements, including the Battles of Ypres I and III, Hill 60, Loos, Albert, the Somme I and II, Arras and Lens, and later the Retreat and Advance of 1918. He finally did duty with the Army of Occupation on the Rhine until his return to England for demobilisation in May 1919. He holds the 1914 Star, and the General Service and Victory Medals, as well as those for the South African War of 1899-1902.

14, Stanley St., Hulme, Manchester.   Z6979

LAW, T., A.B., Royal Navy.

He enlisted in April 1912 and at the outbreak of war in August 1914 proceeded to the North Sea, where he was engaged on important patrol and escort duties. He also took part in the Battles of the Falkland Isles, Heligoland and Dogger Bank, and was also in action at the Battle of Jutland in May 1916. He first did duty in H.M.S. "Bollone," and later saw service in H.M.S. "Constance" on coastal work. He holds the 1914-15 Star, and the General Service and Victory Medals, and in 1920 was serving in H.M.S. "Tiger."

17, Whitworth Street, Longsight, Manchester.   Z6978

LAWLER, J., Sergt., 2nd Lancashire Fusiliers.

He volunteered in August 1914, and did consistently good work at home during the first period of his service. In March 1916 he was drafted to France, where he played a conspicuous part in the fighting in various sectors. He was in action at Ypres, the Somme, La Bassée, Arras, Nieuport, and Vimy Ridge, and was demobilised in February 1920, holding the General Service and Victory Medals.

17, Buckland Street, Ancoats, Manchester.   Z6981

LAWLER, T., Private, Lancashire Fusiliers.

He volunteered in October 1914, and proceeding to France in the following year, was in action at the Battles of Neuve Chapelle, St. Eloi, Hill 60, Ypres (II), Loos, Albert, Vimy Ridge and the Somme, and was wounded in July 1916. On August 7th, 1916, he was unfortunately killed in the last-named sector, and was entitled to the 1914-15 Star and the General Service and Victory Medals.

"Great deeds cannot die."

17, Beasley Street, Gorton, Manchester.   Z10654

LAWLEY, V.W., Pte., King's Own Scottish Borderers.

He volunteered in September 1914, and in the following year was drafted to France where he was in action at Loos, Albert, Vermelles, Ploegsteert Wood, and the Somme. He fell fighting at Beaucourt on September 14th, 1916. He was entitled to the 1914-15 Star, and the General Service and Victory Medals.

"His life for his Country, his soul to God."

2, Victoria Square, Oldham Road, Manchester.   Z9249

LAWLOR, T., Sapper, R.E.

Volunteering in August 1914, he was drafted to France in January 1916, and took part in heavy fighting at La Bassée, Ypres, the Somme, and Richebourg, St. Vaast, where he was wounded and invalided home. On his recovery, he returned to the Western Front, served at Ypres, Nieuport, and on the Somme, and was wounded a second time at Corbie. He was again invalided home and was eventually discharged as medically unfit for further service in March 1919, holding the General Service and Victory Medals.

34, Brown Street, Ancoats, Manchester.   TZ11916

LAWSON, B., Private, Royal Welch Fusiliers.

He joined in September 1916, and three months later proceeded to the Western Front, where he took part in many important engagements. He saw much heavy fighting at Loos, La Bassée, Givenchy, Festubert, Ypres, the Somme, Arras and Albert, and made the supreme sacrifice on August 27th, 1918, being killed in action on the Somme. He was entitled to the General Service and Victory Medals.

"The path of duty was the way to glory."

4, Gaspard Street, Rusholme, Manchester.   Z6982A

LAWSON, F., Sergt., 16th Lancashire Fusiliers.

He volunteered in November 1914, and twelve months later was drafted to the Western Front, where he first saw heavy fighting at Ploegsteert Wood, St. Eloi, and Vimy Ridge. Unfortunately he was badly wounded in action at the end of the Somme Offensive in November 1916, and was invalided home. On his recovery, he rendered valuable services as an Instructor of recruits, and was eventually demobilised in February 1919, holding the 1914-15 Star, and the General Service and Victory Medals.

9, Egerton Street, West Gorton, Manchester.   Z10655

LAWSON, J., Private, 18th Manchester Regt. (T.F.)

Volunteering in September 1914, he served for some time with his unit in England, and was drafted to France in July 1916. There he took part in much heavy fighting and was wounded in the first Battle of the Somme. After a period in hospital at Rouen he was brought to England and was finally discharged in October 1917 as physically unfit for further service. He holds the General Service and Victory Medals.

35, Kingston Street, Hulme, Manchester.   Z6983

LAWSON, W. (M.M.), Private, R.A.M.C.

Mobilised at the outbreak of war in August 1914, he was immediately sent to the Western Front, where he rendered valuable services at the Battle of Mons, and in the subsequent Retreat. He was also present at numerous other engagements of importance, including the Battles of Le Cateau, Ypres, La Bassée, the Somme, Passchendaele, Givenchy, Cambrai, Lens, and Festubert, and later in the Retreat and Advance of 1918, and was wounded on the Somme. He was awarded the Military Medal for conspicuous bravery and devotion to duty at Ypres, and also holds the Mons Star, and the General Service and Victory Medals. He was demobilised in September 1919.

4, Gaspard Street, Rusholme, Manchester.   Z6982B

LAWSON, W., Pioneer, R.E.

He volunteered in November 1914, and after his training was engaged on the Mersey defences until March 1917. He was then drafted to the Western Front, and saw severe fighting at Armentières, Bapaume, Ypres, and on the Somme. In June 1918 he was invalided home with valvular disease of the heart, and a month later was discharged as medically unfit for further service, holding the General Service and Victory Medals.

18, Ancoats Grove North, Ancoats, Manchester.   Z10656

LAWTON, E., Private, 11th East Lancashire Regt.
He joined in December 1917, and was drafted to France in the following April. There he saw much heavy fighting in various sectors, and took part in the Battles of Amiens, Bapaume, and Havrincourt. He was unfortunately killed in action at Armentières on September 20th, 1918, during the great Advance, and was entitled to the General Service and Victory Medals.
" Thinking that remembrance, though unspoken, may reach him where he sleeps."
1, Jack Street, Ardwick, Manchester. Z6985

LAWTON, J. H., Gunner, R.F.A.
He volunteered in January 1915, and after undergoing a period of training was drafted to France in February 1916. In this theatre of war he was in action with his Battery at many important engagements, including those at St. Eloi, Vermelles, the Somme, and Arras, and was wounded. He returned to England, and after doing police duty was transferred to work of National importance at Messrs. Vickers, Barrow-in-Furness, until the cessation of hostilities. He holds the General Service and Victory Medals, and was demobilised in March 1919.
11, Tuley Street, Openshaw, Manchester. Z6986

LAWTON, J. W., Private, 2nd Manchester Regt.
He volunteered in January 1915, having previously served throughout the South African War, and in May of the same year was sent to the Western Front. Whilst overseas he was in action in the engagements at Ypres, Albert, and Vimy Ridge, and in much of the heavy fighting on the Somme. He was invalided home with heart trouble in February 1918, and subsequently died of valvular disease of the heart in December of the same year. He was entitled to the 1914-15 Star, and the General Service and Victory Medals.
" His memory is cherished with pride."
96, Kemp Street, Ancoats, Manchester. TZ9609

LAWTON, T., Sergt., Royal Welch Fusiliers.
Volunteering in March 1915, he was sent to France early in the following year, and played a distinguished part in numerous engagements. He saw much heavy fighting in various sectors, notably at the Battles of the Somme and Ypres, and was wounded. After being invalided home he returned to the Western Front, and made the supreme sacrifice on September 25th, 1917, being killed in action during the Battle of Cambrai. He was entitled to the General Service and Victory Medals.
" Fighting for God, and right and liberty."
26, Viaduct Street, Ardwick, Manchester. Z6984

LAWTON, W., L/Corporal, Lancashire Fusiliers.
He volunteered in December 1914, and in February of the following year was drafted to France, where he fought with the Machine Gun Section in the Battles of Neuve Chapelle, Ypres, and Loos, in which he was wounded. After his recovery he served in the Military Police at Grantham, and was discharged in August 1917. Subsequently he worked as a miner at Mostyn Colliery until the end of the war. He holds the 1914-15 Star, and the General Service and Victory Medals.
12, Werneth Street, Harpurhey, Manchester. Z11532

LAXTON, F. T., Private, R.M.L.I.
He volunteered in November 1914, and was retained on garrison duties at Deal until July 1915. Owing to ill-health he was confined to hospital for some time, and in March 1916 was discharged as medically unfit for further service.
9, Heald Grove, Rusholme, Manchester. Z6987

LEACH, A. E., C.S.M., King's (Liverpool Regt.)
Volunteering in September 1914, he proceeded to France in January of the following year. There he was engaged on special duties as a musketry and drill Instructor, and did consistently good work until the cessation of hostilities. He returned to England, and was demobilised in April 1919, holding the 1914-15 Star, and the General Service and Victory Medals.
31, St. John Street, Longsight, Manchester. Z6990A

LEACH, E., Private, 20th Manchester Regiment.
Having volunteered in November 1914, he was drafted to the Western Front in the following year, and after taking part in the Battles of Loos, Albert, and Ploegsteert Wood, laid down his life for King and Country at the opening of the Somme Offensive on July 1st, 1916. He was entitled to the 1914-15 Star, and the General Service and Victory Medals.
" A costly sacrifice upon the altar of freedom."
67, Bath Street, Miles Platting, Manchester. Z10657B

LEACH, H., Private, 9th East Surrey Regiment.
He joined in May 1916, and was drafted to France in the following July. Whilst on the Western Front, he played a prominent part in the Battles of the Somme, Arras, Bullecourt (where he was wounded in May 1917), Ypres (III), and Cambrai, and in the Retreat and Advance of 1918. He was demobilised in January 1919, and holds the General Service and Victory Medals.
67, Bath Street, Miles Platting, Manchester. Z10657A

LEACH, J. E., Private, K.O. (R. Lancaster Regt.)
Volunteering in November 1914, he underwent a period of training, and was drafted to the Western Front in September of the following year. There he took part in many important engagements, including those at Loos, and Hooge, and suffered

from frost-bitten feet. After a period in hospital at Boulogne and Poperinghe, he returned to England, and was discharged in April 1918, as no longer physically fit for military service, and holds the 1914-15 Star, and the General Service and Victory Medals.
49, Nelson Street, Bradford, Manchester. Z6989

LEADBEATER, E., Pte., 22nd Manchester Regt.
He volunteered in May 1915, and after a period of training was drafted to the Western Front in January 1916. In this theatre of war he saw much heavy fighting in various sectors, and rendered valuable services with his unit at Loos, and other engagements of importance. He was unfortunately killed in action at Mailly-Maillet on March 6th, 1916, and was entitled to the General Service and Victory Medals.
" Great deeds cannot die :
They, with the sun and moon renew their light for ever."
25, Gladstone Street, West Gorton, Manchester. Z6991A

LEADBEATER, H., R.Q.M.S., 12th Army Cyclist Cps.
He volunteered in October 1914, and was drafted to the Dardanelles in April of the following year. There he played a distinguished part during the fighting at the third Battle of Krithia, and the Landing at Suvla Bay. After the evacuation of the Gallipoli Peninsula, he proceeded to Salonika, and saw service on the Doiran and Vardar fronts, until the cessation of hostilities. He holds the 1914-15 Star, and the General Service and Victory Medals, and was demobilised in March 1919. 25, Gladstone St., West Gorton, Manchester. Z6991C

LEADBEATER, W., Corporal, Lancashire Fusiliers.
Mobilised at the outbreak of war in August 1914, he proceeded to France and played a prominent part at the Battle of Mons, and in the subsequent Retreat. He was also in action at the Battles of the Marne, the Aisne, Ypres (I and II), La Bassée, Hill 60, and Albert, and made the supreme sacrifice on July 1st, 1916, during the Somme Offensive. He was entitled to the Mons Star, and the General Service and Victory Medals.
" His life for his Country, his soul to God."
25, Gladstone Street, West Gorton, Manchester. Z6991B

LEADSOM, T. S., Gunner, R.G.A.
He volunteered in February 1915, and after doing consistently good work at various stations in England, was drafted to India in March 1916. There he was engaged on important garrison and other duties at Rawal Pindi, Lahore, and Bombay, and was invalided home with malaria in July 1917. He rendered valuable services, and was ultimately discharged in August 1918 as medically unfit for further duty, and holds the General Service and Victory Medals.
15, Coach Terrace, Gorton, Manchester. Z6992

LEAH, G., Private, 2nd Manchester Regiment.
Mobilised in August 1914, he was drafted to France with the 1st Expeditionary Force, and after taking part in the Battle of, and the Retreat from Mons, was wounded at Ypres in October 1914. He was sent to England, but on his recovery, returned to France, and took part in the Battles of Hill 60, Festubert and Ypres (II). Again wounded in action at Hill 60, in 1916, he was invalided home, but after hospital treatment, once more returned to the Western Front, and was wounded for the third time at Cambrai in 1918. He received his discharge in 1919, and holds the Mons Star, and the General Service and Victory Medals.
10, Catherine Street, Manchester. Z11431

LEAH, J., L/Corporal, 9th Manchester Regiment.
Volunteering in January 1915, he embarked for the Western Front in the following October and fought in the Battles of Vimy Ridge, and the Somme, and was taken prisoner on July 1st, 1916. Whilst in captivity he was compelled to work on a farm, and in loading and unloading ammunition waggons. Repatriated from Germany in January 1919, he was demobilised a month later, and holds the 1914-15 Star, and the General Service and Victory Medals.
31, Ann Street, Hulme, Manchester. Z11750

LEATHER, A., Private, 11th King's (Liverpool Regt.)
He volunteered in November 1914, and after a period of training was drafted to the Western Front in February of the following year. There he took part in various engagements of importance, including the Battles of St. Eloi and Ypres II, and was wounded by shrapnel. He was invalided to England in consequence, and after spending some time in hospital was discharged in March 1916, as unfit for further service. He holds the 1914-15 Star, and the General Service and Victory Medals.
6, Oak Street, Hulme, Manchester. TZ6993

LEATHERBARROW, J. W., Pte., King's (Liverpool Regt.) and Labour Corps.
Volunteering in December 1915, he did duty with his unit in England for a time, and in March 1917 was sent to France, where he was engaged on special work of importance in various sectors. He did consistently good work at Albert, Poperinghe, Amiens, Villers-Bretonneux, and Flexicourt, whilst attached to the Labour Corps until October 1918, when he returned to England. He was demobilised in March 1919, and holds the General Service and Victory Medals.
5, Overton Street, Hulme, Manchester. Z6994

LEATHERBARROW, W., Private, 17th (Duke of Cambridge's Own) Lancers.
He joined in April 1916, and for the first five months did duty in Ireland. He was then drafted to the Western Front, and took part in many important engagements, including the Battles of the Somme and Ypres III, and was wounded and gassed. He was invalided to England, and after a period in hospital was discharged in April 1918 as unfit for further military service, and holds the General Service and Victory Medals.
13, Brunswick Street, West Gorton, Manchester.   Z6995

LEATHWHITE, G. H., Private, 53rd Cheshire Regt.
He joined in April 1918, and was retained on special duties at important stations in England. He was unable to obtain his transfer overseas on account of physical unfitness, but, nevertheless, rendered valuable service and was eventually discharged from the Army in October 1919, suffering from hernia.
25, Stanley Street, Hulme, Manchester.   Z6996

LEE, A., L/Corporal, Manchester Regiment.
Joining in March 1916, he proceeded to France later in the same year, and after playing an important part in heavy fighting on the Somme, at St. Eloi, Albert, Vimy Ridge, Festubert, Neuve Chapelle, Hill 60, and Passchendaele, was wounded in action at Ypres, and invalided home. After hospital treatment in Birmingham, he was demobilised in 1919, and holds the General Service and Victory Medals.
18, Roberts Street, Newton Heath, Manchester.   Z10659

LEE, B., Private, 1st Manchester Regiment.
Volunteering in September 1914, he proceeded to the Western Front early in the following year, and took part in the Battles of Ypres, and the Somme. He was badly wounded in action in December 1916, and was invalided home. After lengthy hospital treatment at Dover, he was discharged in December 1917, as medically unfit for further service, and holds the 1914-15 Star, and the General Service and Victory Medals.
29, Marlow Street, Longsight, Manchester.   Z10660

LEE, E., Private, 12th Somerset Light Infantry.
Three months after joining the Army in August 1917, he proceeded to the Western Front, but after taking part in severe fighting at La Bassée, Passchendaele, and on the Somme, was transferred to Palestine. In this theatre of war he served with General Allenby's Forces at the Capture of Tripoli and Aleppo, and throughout the Advance of 1918. He was in hospital at Cairo for a time with malarial fever, and was demobilised in April 1920, holding the General Service and Victory Medals.
169, Cobden St., Ancoats, Manchester.   Z10661

LEE, E., Private, Royal Marine Labour Corps.
Joining in July 1917, he was shortly afterwards drafted to France, where he was engaged on special duties in connection with the loading of ships at Le Havre and Dunkirk. He did consistently good work until the cessation of hostilities, and was demobilised in April 1919, holding the General Service and Victory Medals.
18, Westminster St., Chester Rd., Hulme, Manchester. TZ7003B

LEE, H., Private, South Lancashire Regiment.
He volunteered in April 1915, and in the following December was sent to the Western Front, where he saw much heavy fighting in various sectors. He was in action at the Battles of the Somme, and Ploegsteert Wood, and was badly wounded in the latter engagement, which necessitated his removal to England. He was in hospital for seven months and was eventually discharged in May 1917 as physically unfit for further service. He holds the 1914-15 Star, and the General Service and Victory Medals.
93, Victoria Street, Longsight, Manchester.   Z7002

LEE, H., Driver, R.E.
He joined in March 1916, and in the following November proceeded to the Western Front, where he played an important part in the Battles of Arras, Ypres (III), Cambrai (I), Bapaume, Amiens, Havrincourt, and Cambrai (II). After the cessation of hostilities, he served in Germany with the Army of Occupation until September 1919, when he returned home for demobilisation, holding the General Service and Victory Medals.
6, Nancy Street, Chester Road, Manchester.   Z10662

LEE, H., Private, 3rd Manchester Regiment.
He joined in September 1917, but owing to his being medically unfit for transfer overseas, was retained on important guard and general duties at various home-stations. He rendered valuable services with his unit until his demobilisation in November 1919.
47, Sycamore Street, Manchester.   Z10663

LEE, H., Pte., King's Shropshire Light Infantry.
Four months after joining in November 1916, he proceeded to France and took part in many important engagements, including the Battles of the Somme, Ypres and Messines. He rendered valuable services during the later stages of the war, and after the Armistice, did duty in Germany with the Army of Occupation on the Rhine. He holds the General Service and Victory Medals, and was demobilised in October 1919.
3, Roseberry Street, Gorton, Manchester.   Z6997

LEE, J., Private, Manchester Regiment.
Having attested under the Derby Scheme, he was called up in June 1917, and in the following month proceeded to the Western Front, where he was in action at many engagements of importance. He took part in the Battles of Ypres (III), Lens and Cambrai, and in December 1917 was transferred to Italy, where he saw service on the Piave and the Asiago Plateaux. He holds the General Service and Victory Medals, and was demobilised in June 1919.
10, Patchett Street, Hulme, Manchester.   Z6999

LEE, J., Private, Royal Scots and Gunner, R.G.A.
He joined in March 1917 and in the following August was drafted to Palestine, where he was in action during much severe fighting, and was taken prisoner by the Turks. He succeeded in making his escape and by swimming the River Jordan reached our lines. In May 1918 he was invalided home, and after five months in hospital at Southampton, was discharged as medically unfit for further service in September 1918, holding the General Service and Victory Medals.
15, Neill Street, Gorton, Manchester.   Z10664

LEE, J., Private, 6th Manchester Regiment.
Volunteering in May 1915, he was sent to Egypt in July and took part in heavy fighting against the Senussi Arabs at Agagia and El Fasher. In August 1916 he was transferred to the Western Front, where he was in action at the Battles of the Somme, Bullecourt, Lens, the Lys, the Aisne (III), the Marne (II), Amiens and the Selle. He was demobilised in February 1919, and holds the 1914-15 Star, and the General Service and Victory Medals.
58, Grey Street, Ancoats, Manchester.   Z10665A

LEE, J., Corporal, Manchester Regiment.
He volunteered in November 1914, and after a period of training was drafted to the Western Front in November of the following year. There he played a prominent part in the fighting in many sectors, and was in action on the Somme and the Ancre fronts and at the Battle of Ypres (III). He was transferred to Italy in October 1917, and saw service on the Piave and Asiago Plateaux until August of the following year. He then returned to France and was in action at the Battles of Le Cateau (II) and Havrincourt. He was in hospital for a time suffering from a poisoned arm, and was mentioned in Despatches for distinguished services in the Field at the third Battle of Ypres in 1917. He holds the 1914-15 Star, and the General Service and Victory Medals, and was demobilised in March 1919.   TZ7003A
18, Westminster Street, Chester Road, Hulme, Manchester.

LEE, S., Special War Worker.
He was engaged at Messrs. Armstrong & Whitworth's, Ltd., Openshaw, Manchester, and was employed as station attendant in the electrical department. His duties, which were of a responsible and important nature, were carried out in a commendable manner, and he rendered valuable services during the war.
91, Dale Street, Miles Platting, Manchester.   Z9250

LEE, S., Private, 22nd Manchester Regiment.
Volunteering in November 1914, he was drafted in October of the following year to the Western Front, where he took part in the heavy fighting on the Somme in 1916, and was wounded. He was later transferred to the Royal Engineers, but was afterwards re-transferred to his old Regiment. He was demobilised in February 1919, and holds the 1914-15 Star, and the General Service and Victory Medals.
46, Nicholson Street, Rochdale Road, Manchester. Z11533

LEE, T., Air Mechanic, R.A.F.
He joined in June 1917, and in the following month was sent to France, where he was engaged chiefly on aircraft construction and repairs. He was stationed at various bases on the Verdun, Lille and Ypres fronts until the cessation of hostilities, and did consistently good work. He returned to England in April 1919, and in 1920 was still serving with his Squadron. He holds the General Service and Victory Medals.   Z7001
18, Westminster Street, Chester Road, Hulme, Manchester.

LEE, T. H., Private, Manchester Regiment.
He joined in July 1916, and after undergoing a period of training was drafted to the Western Front in March of the following year. There he was in action at various engagements, including Nieuport and the third Battle of Ypres in 1917, and was wounded. He was invalided to England, and after some time in hospital, returned to France in 1918, and took part in the Advance of that year. He holds the General Service and Victory Medals, and was demobilised in September 1919.
47, Randolph Street, Ardwick, Manchester.   Z7000

LEE, W., Sapper, R.E.
He volunteered in August 1914, and in the following May was drafted to the Western Front, where he took part in the Battles of Ypres, the Somme, Arras and Cambrai and in heavy fighting at Nieuport, La Bassée and Givenchy. Returning to England in March 1919, he was then demobilised, and holds the 1914-15 Star, and the General Service and Victory Medals.
13, Schofield Street, Ancoats, Manchester.   Z10670

LEE, T. G., Sergt., R.E.
Mobilised with the Territorials in August 1914, he was sent to Egypt a month later and saw service in the Suez Canal and the Desert zones until April 1915. He was then transferred to the Dardanelles, played a prominent part in the Landing at Cape Helles and the three Battles of Krithia, and was wounded in action in July 1915. He also suffered severely from dysentery, but on his recovery proceeded to France and served with distinction in the Passchendaele and Cambrai sectors. He was demobilised in March 1919, and holds the 1914-15 Star, and the General Service and Victory Medals.
4, Nancy Street, Chester Road, Hulme, Manchester. Z10667

LEE, W., Private, 12th Manchester Regiment.
He volunteered in January 1915, and five months later proceeded to France, where he saw much severe fighting in various sectors. He took part in the Battles of Loos, the Somme, Arras, Messines, Ypres (III) and Passchendaele and was wounded. He rendered valuable services as a bomb thrower and made the supreme sacrifice in October 1917, being killed in action at Ypres. He was entitled to the 1914-15 Star, and the General Service and Victory Medals.
"The path of duty was the way to glory."
23, Clifton Street, Newton, Manchester. Z6998

LEE, W., Private, 17th Manchester Regiment.
He volunteered in September 1914, and in December the following year was drafted to the Western Front. He fought at Loos, Vermelles, Albert, the Somme and the Ancre, and was gassed and later contracted fever. After hospital treatment at Blackpool he was discharged in February 1917, owing to his disabilities, and holds the 1914-15 Star, and the General Service and Victory Medals.
40, Whitland Street, Queen's Park, Manchester. Z11534

LEE, W., Private, Welch Regiment.
Volunteering in January 1915, he was drafted to Egypt twelve months later, and after being in action at Katia, Romani and Magdhaba, proceeded to Palestine. In this theatre of war he took part in the three Battles of Gaza, the capture of Jerusalem and in the Advance of General Allenby's Forces. He was demobilised in November 1919 on returning home, and holds the General Service and Victory Medals.
58, Gray Street, Ancoats, Manchester. Z10665B

LEE, W., Driver, R.F.A.
Volunteering in January 1915, he was sent to France in June and whilst on the Western Front, took part in the Battles of Loos, Albert, Vermelles, the Somme, Arras, Vimy Ridge, Bullecourt, Messines, Ypres (III), Passchendaele, Cambrai and Bapaume and in the Retreat and Advance of 1918. He was twice wounded in action on the Somme in 1916 and at Cambrai in 1918, when he was invalided home. He was discharged in May 1919 from Liverpool Military Hospital, and holds the 1914-15 Star, and the General Service and Victory Medals.
3, Cathcart Street, Ancoats, Manchester. Z10668

LEE, W. S., Corporal (Signaller) R.E.
He volunteered in September 1914, and in the following March was sent to Egypt, where he took part in the fighting on the Suez Canal. Later he took part in the Landing at Gallipoli, the three Battles of Krithia and other engagements until invalided home suffering from dysentery. On his recovery, he was transferred to Mesopotamia, and during his service in this seat of war, was in engagements at Amara and the capture of Baghdad. He was demobilised in August 1919, and holds the 1914-15 Star, and the General Service and Victory Medals.
6, Nancy Street, Chester Road, Manchester. Z10669

LEECH, D., Private, 8th King's (Liverpool Regt.) Liverpool Irish.
He volunteered in February 1916, and five months later proceeded overseas. In the course of his service in France he was in action in the Battles of Arras, Vimy Ridge, Messines, Lens, Passchendaele and Cambrai and in the Retreat and Advance of 1918, and entered Mons the day the Armistice was signed. Sent into Germany with the Army of Occupation, he served on the Rhine for upwards of a year, and returning to England for demobilisation in September 1919, holds the General Service and Victory Medals.
27, John Street, Hulme, Manchester. Z11751

LEECH, F. W., Gunner, R.F.A.
He volunteered in November 1915, and after undergoing a period of training, was drafted to France in February of the following year. He was in action with his Battery at many important engagements, including the Battles of the Somme, Ypres, and Messines, and was sent to hospital at the Base in 1918. He holds the General Service and Victory Medals, and was demobilised in February 1919.
38, Bellew Street, Ardwick, Manchester. Z6988

LEECH, J. Private, 11th Manchester Regiment.
He volunteered at the outbreak of hostilities in August 1914, and on completion of his training was drafted to Gallipoli, where he took part in the Landing at Suvla Bay. After a short period of service he was unfortunately killed in action on August 14th, 1915. He was entitled to the 1914-15

Star, and the General Service and Victory Medals.
"His life for his Country, his soul to God."
48, Harvest Street, West Gorton, Manchester. Z10658

LEECH, J. F., Sergt., 8th Manchester Regiment.
Volunteering in February 1915, he proceeded to France in January of the following year, and took part in an engagement at Neuve Chapelle, and was badly wounded in May 1916. He was invalided to England, and after suffering for some time in various hospitals, was sent to a Training Reserve Battalion in January 1917, and did consistently good work as a tailor until his demobilisation in February 1919. He holds the General Service and Victory Medals.
63, Devonshire Street, Hulme, Manchester. Z7005

LEECH, W. (M.M.), 1st Lieutenant, M.G.C.
He volunteered in November 1914, and after a period of training was drafted to France in June 1915. In this theatre of war he played a distinguished part in many engagements, including Loos, St. Eloi, Vermelles, Vimy Ridge and the Somme, and was awarded the Military Medal for conspicuous bravery and devotion to duty in the Field. He was also promoted from Sergeant to the rank of Sergt-Major, and later was in action at Arras, Ypres (III) and Lens. He was gazetted 2nd Lieut., and returning to France took a prominent part in the fighting during the Retreat and Advance of 1918. He proceeded to Germany after the Armistice, and did duty with the Army of Occupation on the Rhine, and was promoted to 1st Lieut. In addition to the Military Medal, he holds the 1914-15 Star, and the General Service and Victory Medals, and was demobilised in November 1919.
130, Newcastle Street, Hulme, Manchester. Z7004A and TZ1265/66F

LEEMING, A. E., Sapper, R.E.
He joined in May 1916, and after serving with the R.E. for a time in England was drafted to the Eastern theatre of war, where he saw much severe fighting at Salonika. He did consistently good work in various sectors, and was wounded accidentally whilst mine-laying, and after three months in hospital, was sent to England and demobilised in January 1919. He holds the General Service and Victory Medals.
24, Rose Street, Greenheys, Manchester. Z6442A

LEEMING, R., Corporal, 6th Manchester Regiment.
Having previously served in the Boer War, he rejoined in September 1914, and did consistently good work with his unit in England during the first part of his service. At the latter end of 1916 he was drafted to France, was transferred to the Royal Engineers, and rendered valuable services at Ypres (III), Ploegsteert Wood and Nieppe Forest. He was demobilised in July 1919, and in addition to the Queen's South African Medal, holds the General Service and Victory Medals.
69, Old Elm Street, Chorlton-on-Medlock, Manchester. X7006

LEEMING, R. E., Private, 51st Welch Regiment.
He joined in March 1917, and drafted to France in the following year, took part in the fighting at Cambrai. After the Armistice he proceeded with the Army of Occupation to Germany, but later returned home and was sent to Ireland. He was demobilised in March 1920, and holds the General Service and Victory Medals.
20, Sandal Street, Ancoats, Manchester. Z9251

LEES, D., Bombardier, R.G.A.
Volunteering in November 1914, he underwent a period of training and was drafted to France in March 1915. There he was in action with his Battery at many important engagements, including the Battles of Ypres (II and III), Festubert, Albert, the Somme, Arras, Bullecourt and Cambrai and later in the Retreat and Advance of 1918. He, however, made the supreme sacrifice on October 7th, 1918, when he was killed in action at the second Battle of Cambrai, and was entitled to the 1914-15 Star, and the General Service and Victory Medals.
"Great deeds cannot die."
103, Norton Street, West Norton, Manchester. Z7008

LEES, F., Sergt., Lancashire Fusiliers.
Volunteering in August 1914, he was drafted to the Western Front in the following March and served with distinction at the Battles of Neuve Chapelle, Hill 60, Ypres (II), Festubert, Loos, the Somme, Vimy Ridge, Ypres (III) and Cambrai. After taking part in the Retreat of 1918, he was unfortunately killed in action on July 19th of that year. He was entitled to the 1914-15 Star, and the General Service and Victory Medals.
"A costly sacrifice upon the altar of freedom."
5, Rigg Street, Gorton, Manchester. Z9890B

LEES, R., Private, 8th Cheshire Regiment.
He joined in June 1917, and, on completion of his training served at various stations on important duties with his unit. He was not able to obtain a transfer to a theatre of war during the period of hostilities, but, in February 1919, proceeded to Germany and did important garrison duties until March 1920, when he returned to England. He was still serving in the Army at the end of 1920.
34, Gotley Street, Ancoats, Manchester. Z10671B

LEES, F., Corpl., Argyll and Sutherland Highlanders.
He volunteered in March 1915, and in the following August was drafted overseas. During his service on the Western Front he took part in much heavy fighting, including the Battles of Loos, Albert, Somme, Arras, Bullecourt, Ypres (III) and Cambrai, and was gassed in December 1917. Later he returned to his unit, and was in action throughout the Retreat and Advance of 1918. After the cessation of hostilities he returned to England, and was demobilised in March 1919, holding the 1914–15 Star, and the General Service and Victory Medals. 62, Chapelfield Road, Ardwick, Manchester. Z10671A

LEES, J. E., Private, 1/6th Manchester Regiment.
Volunteering in June 1915, he proceeded to Egypt in the following December, and after taking part in engagements at Agagia, Sollum, Katia, El Fasher, Romani and Magdhaba, advanced into Palestine and fought at the Battles of Gaza (I and II). In July 1917 he was transferred to the Western Front, where he was in action at the Battles of Cambrai, the Somme (II), Bapaume, Havrincourt and Ypres (IV), and was badly wounded here in 1918. Invalided to England, he spent some time in hospital at Liverpool, and was discharged as medically unfit for further service in January 1919, holding the 1914–15 Star, and the General Service and Victory Medals. 3, Etruria Street, Longsight, Manchester. Z7010

LEES, S., Private, K.O. (Royal Lancaster Regt.)
Volunteering in August 1915, he underwent a period of training and was drafted to France in December 1916. There he took part in many important engagements, including the Battles of the Somme, Arras, Ypres (III) and Cambrai. He also rendered valuable services during the Retreat of 1918, and was wounded on the Somme in March, and after a period in hospital, was demobilised in December 1918, holding the General Service and Victory Medals. 15, Spurgeon Street, West Gorton, Manchester. Z7009

LEES, T., Private, 2/4th Yorkshire Regiment.
He joined in November 1917, and shortly afterwards was drafted to France, where he was engaged on the important duties of road repairing in the Ypres, Bapaume, Albert and Amiens sectors. He did consistently good work until August 1918, when he was discharged from the Army suffering from chronic bronchitis. He holds the General Service and Victory Medals. He was twice wounded during his service on the Western Front. 24, Daniel Street, Hulme, Manchester. Z7007

LEIGH, E., Private, 7th E. Lancashire Regiment.
He volunteered in September 1914, and proceeding to France in the following July took part in the Battles of Loos, Vermelles, the Somme, the Ancre, Arras, Bullecourt, Ypres (III), Lens, Cambrai, the Marne (II) and Havrincourt. He was three times wounded in action, at Loos in October 1915, at Vimy Ridge seven months afterwards and at Arras in May 1917, when he unfortunately lost the sight of his left eye, but on his recovery rejoined his unit and served in France until March 1919. He was then demobilised, and holds the 1914–15 Star, and the General Service and Victory Medals. 6, Junction Street, West Gorton, Manchester. Z10672

LEIGH, R., Sergt., R.A.S.C.
He volunteered in January 1915, and was retained on special duties in England until May 1916. He then proceeded to Egypt, where he was stationed at Kantara before taking part in the Advance into Palestine, when he rendered valuable services with his unit at Deir-el-Belah, Karm, Beersheba and Haifa. Demobilised in May 1919, he holds the General Service and Victory Medals. 3, Tipping Street, Lower Openshaw, Manchester. Z7012

LEIGH, S. E., Private, K.O. (Royal Lancaster Regt.)
He volunteered in September 1914, and in the following March proceeded to France. Whilst in this theatre of war he saw much active service in various sectors of the Front. He took part in the heavy fighting at Hill 60, Loos, Vimy Ridge and the Somme, where he was wounded and sent to England. Later he was engaged on important duties attached to the Military Police until demobilised in December 1919. He was also wounded in action at the Battle of Loos in 1915, and holds the 1914–15 Star, and the General Service and Victory Medals. 281, Hamilton Street, Collyhurst, Manchester. Z11432

LEIGH, T., Private, Lancashire Fusiliers.
Volunteering in September 1914, he was in the following year sent to Egypt, and was engaged on important signal duties at Alexandria and Cairo. He unfortunately contracted an illness, owing to which he was invalided home and discharged in March 1917. He holds the 1914–15 Star, and the General Service and Victory Medals. 240, Hamilton Street, Collyhurst, Manchester. Z9252

LEIGH, T. B., Private, 1/6th Manchester Regt.
Volunteering in November 1914, he completed a period of training, and was drafted to the Dardanelles early in the following year. There he took part in many important engagements, including the Landings at Cape Helles and Suvla Bay. After the Evacuation of the Gallipoli Peninsula in January 1916, he proceeded to France and was in action at

the Battles of the Somme, Arras, Bullecourt, Messines and Ypres and made the supreme sacrifice on September 17th, 1917, being killed during heavy fighting at Passchendaele. He was entitled to the 1914–15 Star, and the General Service and Victory Medals. 24, Heald Avenue, Rusholme, Manchester. TZ7011

LEIGHTON, S., Driver, R.F.A.
He volunteered in December 1915, and after a period of training was retained on important duties with his Battery at various stations. He later proceeded to the Western Front, and saw much service, taking an active part in the Battles of Havrincourt, Ypres IV and the Sambre. He returned to England after the cessation of hostilities, and was demobilised in February 1919, holding the General Service and Victory Medals. 71, Bath Street, Miles Platting, Manchester. Z10673

LEISHMAN, G., Corporal, E. Lancs. Regt., and R.E.
Mobilised at the outbreak of hostilities, he was at once drafted to France, and was in action in the Retreat from Mons. He was wounded in November, but after being in various hospitals, in October 1915, sailed to the Dardanelles. After the Evacuation of the Peninsula he proceeded to Mesopotamia and fought at Kut-el-Amara and Baghdad. He returned home in December 1918, and was demobilsed in April of the following year. He holds the Mons Star, and the General Service and Victory Medals. 1, Needwood Street, Collyhurst, Manchester. Z9610

LENGDEN, H. J., Private, 2nd Lancashire Fusiliers.
He was called up from the Reserve in August 1914, and shortly afterwards sent to France. During his service in this theatre of war he took part in much severe fighting in various sectors, and was in action at the Battle of Ypres, where he was gassed in May 1915. He was discharged in December 1916, as time-expired, and holds the 1914–15 Star, and the General Service and Victory Medals. 179, Cheltenham Street, Collyhurst, Manchester. Z10674

LENNON, J., Gunner, R.F.A.
He volunteered in May 1915, and four months later proceeded to Salonika, where he was in action with his Battery in various sectors. He took part in many important engagements in this theatre of war, including the Offensive on the Doiran front in 1916 and the 1st and 2nd Battles of the Vardar, and was wounded in action. He holds the 1914–15 Star, and the General Service and Victory Medals, and was eventually demobilised in May 1919. 10, Higher Temple Street, Chorlton-on-Medlock, Manchester. X7013

LEONARD, A., Private, 23rd Manchester Regt.
He volunteered in July 1915, and in the following December was drafted to India, where he was engaged at various stations on important duties, and remained till 1918. After much valuable service later at Singapore, he returned home, and was demobilised in March 1919, holding the General Service Medal. 1, Crissy St., Queen's Park, Manchester. Z11535

LEONARD, E., Private, 3/8th Manchester Regt.
He volunteered in September 1915, and after a period of training was retained on important duties with his unit at various stations. He was not successful in obtaining a transfer to a theatre of war owing to his being over-age, and after rendering valuable services, was discharged in September 1916. 6, Haigh Street, West Gorton, Manchester. Z10675

LEONARD, H., Private, Queen's Own (Royal West Kent Regiment).
He joined in June 1916, and on completion of his training was drafted to France, where he saw much service in various sectors. He fought throughout the Battles of Ypres III, Passchendaele, Lens, Cambrai, and later took part in the Retreat and Advance of 1918. After the cessation of hostilities, he was sent to Egypt, where he served on important duties until demobilised in August 1919. He holds the General Service and Victory Medals. 51, Montague Street, Collyhurst, Manchester. Z10676

LEONARD, J., Pte., K.O. (Royal Lancaster Regt.)
He volunteered in November 1915, and proceeding to France two months later, went into action at Loos. Later he took part in the Battles of Albert, Vimy Ridge and the Somme, where he was in October 1916. On his recovery he returned to the firing line and was wounded and taken prisoner at the Battle of Cambrai in November 1917. After fifteen months in captivity in Germany, he was repatriated and demobilised in January 1919, holding the General Service and Victory Medals. 2, Chapman Grove, Hulme, Manchester. Z7015

LEONARD, J., Sapper, R.E.
He joied in January 1917, and three months later proceeded to France, where he was engaged on important duties in bridge construction in connection with the operations and was frequently in the forward areas, notably at Messines, Ypres, and Passchendaele. He was taken prisoner in 1918 and was sent to Germany, and was compelled to work in the iron ore mines until repatriated in December 1918, after the cessation of hostilities. He was demobilised in March of the following year, and holds the General Service and Victory Medals. 22, Ainsworth Street, West Gorton, Manchester. Z9611

LEONARD, T., Driver, R.A.S.C.

Mobilised at the outbreak of war in August 1914, he immediately proceeded to the Western Front, where he was present at the Battle of Mons and in the subsequent Retreat. He also rendered valuable services at the Battles of Le Cateau, La Bassée, Ypres, Hill 60 and Festubert, and in February 1916 was transferred to Salonika, where he saw heavy fighting on the Doiran and Vardar fronts. He returned to England in February 1919, and was demobilised in the following March, holding the Mons Star, and the General Service and Victory Medals. 3, Hawthorn St., Ardwick, Manchester. Z7014

LEONARD, T., Driver, R.A.S.C. (M.T.)

He volunteered in April 1915, and was immediately sent to the Western Front, where he saw much service. He was attached to the Motor Transport Section and did good work in conveying food and ammunition to the forward areas during the Battles of Loos, the Somme, Vimy Ridge, Arras and Messines. In June 1917 he was discharged as medically unfit for further military service, and holds the 1914–15 Star, and the General Service and Victory Medals. 48, Howarth Street, Chorlton-on-Medlock, Manchester. Z10678

LEONARD, T. E., Private, 9th S. Lancashire Regt.

He volunteered in September 1914, and on completion of his training was drafted to the Western Front, where he saw much heavy fighting, until December 1915. He then proceeded to Salonika and took part in the Advance across the Struma and Doiran and in other engagements until February 1918, when he was invalided home suffering from fever. In March 1919 he was demobilised, and holds the 1914–15 Star, and the General Service and Victory Medals. 17, Marcer Street, Newton, Manchester. Z10677

LEONARD, V. A., Private, 16th Manchester Regt.

He volunteered in January 1915, and in the following July was drafted to the Western Front, where he took part in heavy fighting at Nieuport, Ypres and La Bassée and at the Battles of the Somme and Arras. He was badly wounded in May 1917, and admitted to hospital at the Base, but on his recovery, rejoined his unit and was in action at Messines and Givenchy. He holds the 1914–15 Star, and the General Service and Victory Medals, and was demobilised in January 1919. 39, Clare Street, Chorlton-on-Medlock, Manchester. Z11917

LESLIE, J., Pte., 1/10th King's (Liverpool Regt.) (Liverpool Scottish).

He joined in September 1916, and two months later proceeded to France. He took part in many important engagements, but was unfortunately killed at Lens in October 1917 whilst engaged on road mending. He did consistently good work during the time he served on the Western Front, and was entitled to the General Service and Victory Medals.
" Thinking that remembrance, though unspoken, may reach him where he sleeps." Z7016B
9, Dewsbury Place, Plymouth Grove, Longsight, Manchester.

LESSER, T. B., L/Cpl., 2nd West Yorkshire Regt.

Joining in July 1917, he underwent a period of training, and was drafted to France in February of the following year. There he took part in many engagements of importance, including the Battles of Cambrai (II), Ypres (IV) and Bullecourt. He rendered valuable services, and was demobilised in March 1919, holding the General Service and Victory Medals. 6, Bath Street, Hulme, Manchester. Z7017

LESTER, G., Private, R.M.L.I.

He volunteered in December 1915, and did duty in H.M.S. " Tiger," patrolling the high seas. He was also engaged on escorting duties, and rendered valuable services in the search for enemy submarines until the cessation of hostilities. He holds the 1914–15 Star, and the General Service and Victory Medals, and was demobilised in July 1920. 12, Eskrigge Street, Ardwick, Manchester. Z7019

LESTER, J., Private, 3rd Manchester Regiment.

He volunteered in October 1915, and in the following March proceeded to the Western Front. During his service in this theatre of war he took part in many important engagements, including the Battles of the Somme (I), Beaumont-Hamel, Arras (I), Bullecourt and Ypres (III) where he was taken prisoner and held in captivity until December 1918. He was demobilised in March 1919, and holds the General Service and Victory Medals. 33, Grantham St., West Gorton, Manchester. Z10679

LESTER, J. H., Private, Royal Fusiliers.

He volunteered in November 1914, and on completing a period of training, was drafted to France in April 1915. He first served at a R.A.S.C. depôt at Boulogne until June 1917, after which date he took part in much heavy fighting in various sectors, and was in action at Nieuport, Ypres and Passchendaele. He suffered from gas poisoning during his service on the Western Front, and made the supreme sacrifice in April 1918, being killed in action in the Ypres sector. He was entitled to the 1914–15 Star, and the General Service and Victory Medals.
" And doubtless he went in splendid company."
59, Norton Street, West Gorton, Manchester. Z7018

LETHBRIDGE, T., Private, 2nd Hampshire Regt.

Volunteering in September 1914, he underwent a period of training and was drafted to Egypt shortly afterwards. He saw service on the Suez Canal and later proceeded to the Dardanelles, where he took part in the Landing at Suvla Bay in August 1915. He was transferred to the Western Front after the Evacuation of the Gallipoli Peninsula and was in action at the Battles of Arras, Vimy Ridge, Messines, Lens, Ypres, Passchendaele and Cambrai, and was gassed in February 1918 on the Somme. He holds the 1914–15 Star, and the General Service and Victory Medals, and was demobilised in April 1919. 21, Sutherland Street, Hulme, Manchester. TZ7020

LEVAGGI, J., Corporal, K.O. (R. Lancaster Regt.)

Joining in March 1916, he was drafted to the Western Front on completing his training. He saw much severe fighting in this theatre of war, and was in action at the Battles of Vimy Ridge and the Somme, and was twice wounded during this period. Later he was sent to Ireland, where he was engaged on important duties until demobilised in September 1919. He holds the General Service and Victory Medals. 68, Loom Street, Ancoats, Manchester. Z11433

LEVER, B., Private, 3rd Manchester Regiment.

Having first enlisted in 1900, he was called from the Reserve in August 1914, and early in the following year proceeded to France. During his service in this theatre of war he took part in many engagements in various sectors of the Front. He was wounded in action at Neuve Eglise in February 1916, and was invalided to England. He was discharged as medically unfit in July 1917, holding the 1914–15 Star, and the General Service and Victory Medals. 12, Harvest Street, West Gorton, Manchester. Z10680

LEVER, H., L/Corporal, R.E.

He volunteered in January 1916, and two months later proceeded to France, where he did consistently good work whilst attached to the gas section of the R.E. He saw service at Vermelles, Ploegsteert Wood, Vimy Ridge, the Somme, Arras, Messines, Passchendaele, Amiens, Bapaume and Lille, and later did duty at the Base at Calais. He holds the General Service and Victory Medals, and was demobilised in October 1919. 4, Hancock St., Rusholme, Manchester. Z6596B

LEVER, T. H., Private, 1st K.O. (R. Lancaster Regt.)

He volunteered in February 1915, and later in the same year was drafted to France, where he took part in the Battles of Albert, the Somme, Arras and Ypres and in heavy fighting at Mametz Wood, Delville Wood, Beaumont-Hamel and Nieuport. He was badly wounded in action, and as a result, was invalided from the Army in October 1917, holding the 1914–15 Star, and the General Service and Victory Medals. 14, Churnett Street, Collyhurst, Manchester. Z10681

LEWELL, J., Private, East Yorkshire Regiment.

He volunteered in May 1915, and in the following August was drafted to the West Indies, where he was engaged on special duties at Bermuda. He also saw service in India, and after doing consistently good work in that part of the British dominions, returned to England and was demobilised in March 1919. He holds the General Service Medal. 30, Augustus Street, Brook's Bar, Manchester. Z6748B

LEWIS, A., Private, 2nd Wiltshire Regiment.

He joined in 1916, and after undergoing a period of training was drafted to the Western Front, where he was in action at numerous important engagements, and was wounded at the Battle of Ypres on July 1917. He had his right leg badly fractured, and unfortunately lost his left arm by amputation, in consequence of the severe injuries sustained. He was eventually discharged in 1919, and holds the General Service and Victory Medals. X7024A
15, Geoffrey Street, Chorlton-on-Medlock, Manchester.

LEWIS, E., Private, South Wales Borderers.

He joined in 1917, and on completion of his training was drafted to the Western Front in April 1918. After a short period of service in this seat of war, he was gassed at Merville during the Advance, and was invalided to England. He was discharged as medically unfit for further military service in 1918, and holds the General Service and Victory Medals. 5, Tiverton Street, Ardwick, Manchester. Z10682A

LEWIS, E., Sapper, R.E.

He volunteered in June 1915, and on completion of his training was retained on important duties with his unit at various stations. In 1917 he proceeded to the Western Front, where he took part in the engagements at Arras, and in the Retreat and Advance of 1918. After the cessation of hostilities he returned to England, and was demobilised in March 1919, holding the General Service and Victory Medals. 5, Tiverton Street, Ardwick, Manchester. X10682D

LEWIS, E. (Miss), Worker, Land Army.

She volunteered her services in 1918, and was immediately engaged on work of National importance. She served on farms in various parts of Wiltshire, and did consistently good work of an agricultural nature until the cessation of hostilities, when she relinquished her duties. 7022/23D
2, Rosamond Place, Chorlton-on-Medlock, Manchester.

LEWIS, E. L., Battery-Sergt.-Major, R.F.A.
He enlisted in 1906, and at the outbreak of war in August 1914 was sent to the Western Front, where he played a distinguished part in the fighting in many sectors. He was in action with his Battery at the Battle of Ypres II, and after being wounded was transferred to Salonika in October 1915. In that theatre of war he saw service on the Vardar and Doiran fronts and took part in the general advance across the Struma, and the capture of Monastir. He holds the 1914 Star, and the General Service and Victory Medals, and in 1920 was still serving in the Army.
2, Rosamond Place, Chorlton-on-Medlock, Manchester.
X7022/23F

LEWIS, F., Private, 2/6th South Staffordshire Regt.
He volunteered in October 1914, and was immediately sent to France. During his service in this theatre of war he took an active part in the fighting at the Battles of Ypres (II), Hill 60, and the Somme, where he was badly wounded, and invalided to England. He was discharged in October 1916 as medically unfit for further duty, and holds the 1914-15 Star, and the General Service and Victory Medals.
31, Pilling Street, Newton Street, Manchester.
Z10683

LEWIS, F. Private, 2/4th York and Lancaster Regt.
He joined early in 1918, and after a period of training was drafted to the Western Front, where he took part in many of the concluding Battles of the war. He rendered valuable services and made the supreme sacrifice on September 2nd, 1918, during the great Advance, being killed in action near Bullecourt. He was entitled to the General Service and Victory Medals.
X7022/23B
"The path of duty was the way to glory."
2, Rosamond Place, Chorlton-on-Medlock, Manchester.

LEWIS, G., Private, 22nd Manchester Regiment.
At the outbreak of war in August 1914, he immediately volunteered, and on completion of his training, was drafted to the Western Front, where he saw much severe fighting in various sectors. He laid down his life for King and Country at the opening of the Somme Offensive on July 1st, 1916, and was entitled to the 1914-15 Star, and the General Service and Victory Medals.
"A costly sacrifice upon the altar of freedom."
15, Geoffrey Street, Chorlton-on-Medlock, Manchester. X7024B

LEWIS, G., L/Corporal, K.O. (R. Lancaster Regt.)
Mobilised at the outbreak of war in August 1914, he was shortly afterwards drafted to the Western Front, where he took part in the Battle of Mons and many other engagements of importance, including the Battles of Ypres (I) and St. Eloi. He was unhappily killed in action at Hill 60, on May 8th, 1915, and was entitled to the Mons Star, and the General Service and Victory Medals.
X7022-23C
"He died the noblest death a man may die."
2, Rosamund Place, Chorlton-on-Medlock, Manchester.

LEWIS, J., Rifleman, Rifle Brigade.
He volunteered in August 1914, and in February 1915 was drafted to the Western Front. There he took part in numerous engagements, and saw much heavy fighting in various sectors, until May 13th, 1916, when he made the supreme sacrifice, being killed in action at Ypres. He was entitled to the 1914-15 Star, and the General Service and Victory Medals.
"Honour to the immortal dead who gave their youth that the world might grow old in peace."
6, Rose Street, Old Trafford, Manchester.
Z7027

LEWIS, J., Private, Army Cyclists Corps.
He joined in May 1916, and after doing duty at various stations in England, was drafted to France in October 1918. Whilst on the Western Front he was engaged on important duties as a despatch rider on the General Headquarters Staff, and saw service on the Somme, and at Amiens and Le Cateau. After the Armistice, he proceeded to Germany, and did duty with the Army of Occupation until his return to England for demobilisation in November 1919. He holds the General Service and Victory Medals.
53, Dorset Street, Hulme, Manchester.
Z7026

LEWIS, J. H., Private, 1/8th Manchester Regiment, and Sapper, R.E.
Mobilised with the Territorials in August 1914, he proceeded to Egypt a month later and saw heavy fighting in the Suez Canal zone. In 1915 he was sent to the Dardanelles, but being wounded at the Landing at Suvla Bay in August, was admitted to hospital at Alexandria. On his recovery, he rejoined his unit and fought at Gaza in Palestine. He was then transferred to the Western Front, and was in action at the Battles of Ypres (III) and Passchendaele, where he was gassed in September 1917. After treatment at the Base, he returned to the line, served at Cambrai, Nieuport, Dunkirk, and on the Somme, and in the Retreat and Advance of 1918. He was demobilised in August 1919, and holds the 1914-15 Star, and the General Service and Victory Medals.
11, Carmen Street, Ardwick, Manchester.
Z7021

LEWIS, J., Corporal, 18th Manchester Regiment.
Volunteering in September 1914, he underwent a period of training and was drafted to France in November of the following year. There he played a prominent part in numerous engagements, and was in action at the Battles of Ypres, Vimy Ridge, the Somme and Trones Wood, and was wounded on two occasions. He also rendered valuable services during the Retreat and Advance of 1918, and was demobilised in February 1919, holding the 1914-15 Star, and the General Service and Victory Medals.
10, Gibson Street, Ardwick, Manchester.
Z7025

LEWIS, J. R., Private, 7th Manchester Regiment.
He volunteered in May 1915, and was drafted to France in the following year. In this theatre of war he took part in many important engagements, including the Battles of Arras, Ypres (III) and Cambrai, and later served in the fighting at the second Battle of Cambrai, where he was wounded in October 1918. He was demobilised in March 1919, and holds the General Service and Victory Medals.
19, Great Jones Street, West Gorton, Manchester.
Z10684

LEWIS, J. W., Private, Manchester Regiment.
He volunteered in September 1914, and in the following year was drafted to Salonika, where he rendered valuable services as a stretcher bearer during heavy fighting on Doiran, Vardar and Struma fronts. In July 1918, however, he was transferred to France, and took part in many important engagements in the Advance, including the second Battle of Cambrai. He holds the 1914-15 Star, and the General Service and Victory Medals, and was demobilised on his return home in January 1919. 31, Bennett Street, Openshaw, Manchester. Z7028

LEWIS, L. L., Battery-Sergt.-Major, R.F.A.
Mobilised at the outbreak of war in August 1914, he immediately proceeded to France, and played a distinguished part in the Battle of Mons and many subsequent engagements of importance. In May 1915, he was transferred to Salonika, and was in action with his Battery during the Serbian Retreat. He also saw much heavy fighting on the Doiran front, and later rendered valuable services in Egypt, India and Russia. He was discharged in February, 1920, and holds the Mons Star and the General Service and Victory Medals. X7022-23A
2, Rosamond Place, Chorlton-on-Medlock, Manchester.

LEWIS, S. T. V. (D.C.M. and M.M.) B.S.M., R.F.A.
He enlisted in 1903, and at the outbreak of war in August 1914, embarked for France from India. He saw much heavy fighting in various sectors of the Western Front, and was in action with his Battery at the Battles of Hill 60, (where he was wounded), Loos, the Somme, Ypres and Passchendaele. He was awarded the Distinguished Conduct Medal, and the Military Medal for conspicuous bravery and devotion to duty in the Field on two occasions, and also holds the 1914 Star, and the General Service and Victory Medals, and was in 1920 still serving in the Army. X7022-23E
2, Rosamond Street, Chorlton-on-Medlock, Manchester.

LEWIS, W., Wheeler, R.A.O.C.
He volunteered in the R.A.S.C. in November 1915, and after a period of training was transferred to the R.A.O.C. as a wheeler. In October 1916, he proceeded to the Western Front, where he took part in many important engagements, including the Battle of the Somme, and the Retreat and Advance of 1918. After the cessation of hostilities, he served in Germany with the Army of Occupation until July 1919, when he was demobilised, holding the General Service and Victory Medals.
31, Longridge Street, Longsight, Manchester.
Z10685

LEWIS, W., Gunner, R.F.A.
He volunteered in May 1915, and in the same year was drafted to the Western Front. Whilst in this theatre of war he took part in many important engagements, including the Battles of Arras, Ypres and the Somme. During his period of service he was once wounded, and was demobilised in February 1919, holding the 1914-15 Star, and the General Service and Victory Medals. 62, Birtles Street, Collyhurst, Manchester. Z10686

LEYLAND, W., Private, 8th Manchester Regiment.
He volunteered in 1914, and was retained on special duties with his unit at important stations in England. Owing to his being unfit he was unable to obtain his transfer to a theatre of war, but nevertheless rendered valuable services until his discharge on medical grounds in 1917.
12, Thomas Street, Chorlton-on-Medlock, Manchester. TX7029

LIGGETT, H., L/Corporal, Lancashire Fusiliers.
Volunteering in August 1914, he was engaged on important clerical duties until June 1916, when he proceeded to France. Whilst overseas he fought at Vimy Ridge, on the Somme, at Arras, Bullecourt, Ypres, Cambrai, the Aisne, Havrincourt and Le Cateau, and returned home in May 1919, when he was demobilised, holding the General Service and Victory Medals.
96, Irlam Street, Miles Platting, Manchester.
Z9612

LIGHTFOOT, C. T., Driver, R.A.S.C. (M.T.)
He volunteered in May 1915, and four months later proceeded to the Western Front, where he was engaged on special duties in connection with the fumigation of uniforms by motive power. He did consistently good work in the Ypres, Loos, Albert, the Somme and Cambrai sectors, and was demobilised in May 1919, holding the 1914–15 Star, and the General Service and Victory Medals.
19, Runcorn Street, Hulme, Manchester.   TZ7030

LILLEY, J. W., Rifleman, 2nd Rifle Brigade.
Mobilised at the outbreak of war in August 1914, he was sent to France four months afterwards, and took part in heavy fighting at La Bassée and Neuve Chapelle, where he was badly wounded in September 1915. He was invalided home, but, on his recovery in April 1916, was drafted to Salonika, and was in action on the Doiran front. In October 1918 he was taken seriously ill, and again invalided home, and was discharged as medically unfit for further service in September 1918. Unfortunately he died in March 1920, and was entitled to the 1914–15 Star, and the General Service and Victory Medals.
"His memory is cherished with pride."
29, John Street, Ardwick, Manchester.   Z7032B

LILLEY, P., Pte., 3rd Border Regt., and Sapper, R.E.
Volunteering in November 1915, he underwent a period of training and was drafted to the Western Front in January 1917. There he took part in much severe fighting in various sectors and was in action at Ypres, La Bassée, Arras, the Somme and Lille, and throughout the Retreat and Advance of 1918. He was wounded in action on the Somme, and finally demobilised in February 1919, holding the General Service and Victory Medals.
15, Bremner Street, Ardwick, Manchester.   Z7031A

LILLEY, S., Private, 7th Lancashire Fusiliers.
Two months after volunteering in October 1914, he proceeded to the Western Front, where he saw severe fighting in various sectors, and took part in the Battles of St. Eloi, Hill 60, Loos, Albert, and Vimy Ridge. He made the supreme sacrifice, falling in action in October 1916, during the Advance on the Somme. He was entitled to the 1914–15 Star, and the General Service and Victory Medals.
"His life for his Country, his soul to God."
1, Irlam Street, Miles Platting, Manchester.   Z10688

LILLEY, T. (M.M.), L/Corporal, 15th Royal Scots.
He volunteered in October 1914, and in December of the following year, was drafted to France, but after taking a prominent part in the Battle of the Somme, and in heavy fighting at Neuve Chapelle and Loos, was unhappily killed in action at Lens in April 1917. He had been awarded the Military Medal for conspicuous bravery and devotion to duty during the Somme Offensive in 1916, and was also entitled to the 1914–15 Star, and the General Service and Victory Medals.
"He joined the great white company of valiant souls."
15, Bremner Street, Ardwick, Manchester.   Z7031B

LILLEYMAN, C., Leading Stoker, R.N.
After previous service in the Mercantile Marine, he volunteered at the outbreak of hostilities and from January 1915 was engaged in H.M.S. "Lion," "Tiger" and "Essex" on important duties with the Fleet in the North Sea. He was present at the Battle of Jutland in May 1916, and was wounded there. He continued his valuable service in those waters until January 1919, and was demobilised in the following May, holding the 1914–15 Star, and the General Service (with four clasps), and the Victory Medals.
5, Geoffrey Street, Chorlton-on-Medlock, Manchester.   Z7033

LILLEYMAN, T., Sapper, R.E.
He joined in September 1917, and was retained on special duties at Sandwich and Richborough, where he did consistently good work. He was unable to obtain his transfer to a theatre of war, but nevertheless, rendered valuable services in the workshops until his demobilisation in April 1919.
5, Pollitt Street, West Gorton, Manchester.   Z7042

LILLIS, J. T., Sergt., King's (Liverpool Regiment).
Volunteering in September 1914, he crossed to France five months later and served in various parts of the line for four years. During this period he fought in the Battles of Neuve Chapelle, Ypres and Hill 60, and was wounded in May 1915. After treatment in a Base Hospital he was in action in the Somme Offensive, at Cambrai and in several other engagements until the end of the war. Returning home he was demobilised in February 1919, and holds the 1914–15 Star, and the General Service and Victory Medals.
10, Bloom Street, Hulme, Manchester.   Z11752

LIMBRICK, H. G., Trooper, Oxfordshire Hussars, and 3rd Hussars.
He joined in January 1918, and in the following July was drafted to France, where he took part in the Battles of the Marne, Amiens, Bapaume, the Scarpe, Havrincourt, Cambrai (II), Ypres (IV), and Le Cateau, during the Advance of 1918. He rendered valuable services and was demobilised in October 1919, holding the General Service and Victory Medals.
44, Riga Street, City Road, Hulme, Manchester.   TZ7034A

LINGHAM, A., Sergt., K.O. (R. Lancaster Regiment).
He volunteered in July 1915, and early in the following year, was drafted to France, where he served with distinction at La Bassée, Givenchy, Loos, Festubert, Ypres, and Vimy Ridge, before being seriously wounded during the Somme Offensive in 1916. He was invalided home and after long hospital treatment in Surrey was discharged as medically unfit for further service in March 1918. He holds the General Service and Victory Medals.
35, Halsbury Street, Longsight, Manchester.   Z7035

LINIHAN, J. E., Private, 1st Manchester Regiment.
He was called up from the Reserve at the outbreak of war in August 1914, and was immediately drafted to France. There he took part in many important engagements in various sectors of the Front. In December 1915, he was transferred to Mesopotamia, and was in action during the relief of Kut, and the fighting on the Tigris, where he was unfortunately killed in action in 1916. He was entitled to the 1914–15 Star, and the General Service and Victory Medals.
"He died the noblest death a man may die,
Fighting for God, and right, and liberty."
24, Chatham Street, Bradford, Manchester.   Z10687

LIPTROT, A. P., Private, 7th King's (Liverpool Regt.)
Joining in June 1916, he was drafted to France in the following October after a period of training, and saw heavy fighting on the Somme. He unfortunately met with an accident which incapacitated him from further active service, and he returned to England, where he was engaged guarding prisoners of war until his demobilisation in January 1919. He holds the General Service and Victory Medals.
30, Rumford Street, Hulme, Manchester.   TZ7036

LITSTER, J., Private, 8th Manchester Regiment.
He volunteered in August 1914, and after a period of training, was drafted to the Dardanelles early in the following year. He took part in the heavy fighting during the Landing on the Gallipoli Peninsula and was later in action at the Battles of Krithia (I, II and III), and was badly wounded in June 1915. He was invalided to England, and after a long period in hospital was discharged in August 1918, as unfit for further service. He holds the 1914–15 Star, and the General Service and Victory Medals.
26, Boundary Street East, Chorlton-on-Medlock, Manchester.   Z7038

LITSTER, R., Private, 1/4th S. Lancashire Regt.
He volunteered in 1915, and on completion of his training was drafted to the Western Front, where he was wounded at the Battle of Passchendaele. On his recovery, he rejoined his unit but was reported missing after heavy fighting on the Lys on April 11th, 1918. He is now presumed to have been killed in action on that date, and was entitled to the General Service and Victory Medals.
"Steals on the ear the distant triumph song."
43, New York Street, Chorlton-on-Medlock, Manchester. Z7037

LITTLE, A. (M.M.), Sergt., 7th Lancashire Fusiliers.
Volunteering in September 1914, he first rendered valuable services as an Instructor of recruits, but in August 1915, proceeded to the Dardanelles, and took part in the Landing at Suvla Bay. During the subsequent Evacuation of the Gallipoli Peninsula, he was recommended for the Distinguished Conduct Medal for great gallantry. He then served in Palestine for a time, until in January 1917 was transferred to the Western Front, and played a prominent part in the Battles of Arras, Bullecourt, Ypres (II), Passchendaele and Cambrai, where he was badly gassed in November 1917, and invalided home. He was awarded the Military Medal for conspicuous bravery in taking food to his Company under heavy fire at Nieuport, and also holds the 1914–15 Star, and the General Service and Victory Medals. In November 1918, after hospital treatment in France and England, he was discharged as medically unfit for further service.
51, Brunt Street, Rusholme, Manchester.   TZ7039

LITTLE, D. (M.M.), Corporal, 22nd Manchester Regt.)
Volunteering in November 1914, he proceeded to France in November of the following year after a period of training. He saw much service in this theatre of war, and was wounded in July 1916, at Mametz whilst bringing in his Officer through heavy shell-fire, for which gallant act he was awarded the Military Medal. He was taken prisoner at High Wood, and held in captivity until the signing of the Armistice. He was eventually demobilised in February 1919, and holds the 1914–15 Star, and the General Service and Victory Medals.
15, Theodore Street, Ardwick, Manchester.   Z7040

LITTLE, J., Private, 8th Manchester Regiment.
He volunteered in March 1915, and after undergoing a period of training, was retained on important duties at various stations. He was not successful in his efforts to obtain his transfer to a theatre of war, but nevertheless, rendered very valuable services with his unit until February 1919, when he was demobilised.
31, Laurence Street, West Gorton, Manchester.   Z10690

LITTLE, J. A., Private, 2nd South Lancashire Regt.
He joined in July 1916, and after completing a period of training was drafted to the Western Front in August 1917. There he took part in many important engagements, including the Battles of the Somme (II), Ploegsteert Wood, Lens, Givenchy, Bapaume, Amiens and Ghent, and was wounded on three occasions. He was invalided to England, and later demobilised in February 1919, holding the General Service and Victory Medals.
101, Nelson Street, Bradford, Manchester. Z7043

LITTLE, T. W., Private, 2nd Manchester Regt.
Shortly after volunteering in March 1915, he was drafted to the Western Front, where after taking part in the Battle of Hill 60, he was wounded in action in July of the same year. Invalided home, he was for a considerable period in hospital, but on his recovery, returned to France and was again in action at Albert, and on the Somme. He was invalided from the Army and holds the 1914-15 Star, and the General Service and Victory Medals.
14, Tomlinson Street, Bradford, Manchester. Z10689

LITTLEMORE, J. P., Sapper, R.E.
Volunteering in October 1914, he was shortly afterwards drafted to Egypt, where he saw service on the Suez Canal, and at Mersa Matruh, Sollum and Katia. He was transferred to France in March 1916, and was present at many important engagements, including those at Beaucourt, the Somme, Bullecourt, Arras and Cambrai, and later in the Advance of 1918. After the cessation of hostilities he proceeded to Germany, where he did duty with the Army of Occupation until his demobilisation in February 1919. He holds the 1914-15 Star, and the General Service and Victory Medals.
16, Platt Street, Moss Side, Manchester. Z7041

LITTLER, J., Pte., K.O. (Royal Lancaster Regt.)
He volunteered in September 1914, and after a period of training was drafted in the following year to the East, where he took part in the first Landing at Salonika. He afterwards fought in many important engagements on the Vardar and Doiran fronts, including the recapture of Monastir, and was wounded in action in April 1917. He finally returned home for demobilisation in March 1919, and holds the 1914-15 Star, and the General Service and Victory Medals.
25, Park Street, West Gorton, Manchester. Z10691

LITTLER, W. E., Gunner, R.F.A.
Volunteering in January 1915, he was drafted to the Western Front on completing a period of training in the following August and there saw severe fighting in the Battles of Arras, Ypres and Cambrai, and many other important engagements in this theatre of war, and served also through the Retreat and Advance of 1918. He was demobilised on his return home in June 1919, and holds the 1914-15 Star, and the General Service and Victory Medals.
18, Seal Street, Collyhurst, Manchester. Z10692

LITTLEWOOD, H., Pte., 2nd Lancashire Fusiliers.
He volunteered at the outbreak of war in August 1914, and in April of the following year was drafted to the Western Front, where he saw much severe fighting, taking part in several important engagements. He made the supreme sacrifice, being killed in action on July 7th, 1915 at Loos. He was entitled to the 1914-15 Star, and the General Service and Victory Medals.
"He joined the great white company of valiant souls."
1, Buckland Street, Ancoats, Manchester. Z10421B

LITTLEWOOD, W., Petty Officer, R.A.F.
He volunteered in September 1914, and was retained on important duties at Hendon Aerodrome, where he was engaged chiefly on machine repairs. He did consistently good work until September 1915, when he was discharged as physically unfit for further service.
33, Hastings Street, Chorlton-on-Medlock, Manchester. Z7044

LIVESEY, F., Air Mechanic, R.A.F.
He joined in May 1917, but owing to his high degree of technical knowledge was retained on important structural and repairing work at various Aerodromes in England. He was unable to obtain his transfer overseas before the cessation of hostilities, but rendered valuable services until his demobilisation in April 1919.
1, Hinckley Street, Bradford, Manchester. Z7045

LIVESEY, H., Private, 7th Lancashire Fusiliers.
He volunteered in September 1914, and was drafted to the Dardanelles in April of the following year, after serving for a time in Egypt. He took part in much heavy fighting on the Gallipoli Peninsula, and was in action at Sedd-el-Bahr, and Krithia (III), where he was badly wounded. He was invalided to England and eventually discharged in December 1916, as unfit for further service. He holds the 1914-15 Star, and the General Service and Victory Medals.
6, Alder Street, Hulme, Manchester. Z7047

LIVESEY, S., Private, 7th King's (Liverpool Regt.)
He joined in June 1918, and after undergoing a period of training, served at various stations, where he was engaged on duties of great importance. Owing to the early cessation of hostilities he was unable to obtain his transfer to a theatre of war, but was afterwards sent with the Army of Occupation into Germany. He was demobilised on his return to England in October 1919.
34, Moody Street, Bradford, Manchester. Z9995B

LIVESEY, T., Pte., 12th King's (Liverpool Regt.)
He volunteered in September 1914, and after completing a period of training was sent in August of the following year to the Western Front, where he saw much severe fighting. He died gloriously on the Field of Battle at Loos on September 25th, 1915, after only a few weeks' active service, and was buried at Estaires. He was entitled to the 1914-15 Star, and the General Service and Victory Medals.
"And doubtless he went in splendid company."
52, Phelan Street, Collyhurst, Manchester. Z10693

LIVESEY, W., L/Corporal, 2/5th Manchester Regt.
Joining in February 1917, he proceeded to the Western Front in the following December, and took part in much heavy fighting in this theatre of war. He was also in action during the Retreat of 1918, and was taken prisoner in March of that year. He was repatriated after the cessation of hostilities, and eventually demobilised in February 1919, holding the General Service and Victory Medals.
4, Meadow Street, Ardwick, Manchester. Z7046

LIVESTY, A., Private, 6th Manchester Regiment.
He volunteered in November 1915, and was shortly afterwards drafted to the Western Front, where he took part in many important engagements. He saw much heavy fighting in various sectors, and was in action at the Battles of Loos, Albert, Vimy Ridge and the Somme, and made the supreme sacrifice in February 1917, being killed in action on the Ancre front. He was entitled to the 1914-15 Star, and the General Service and Victory Medals.
"His life for his Country, his soul to God."
27, Fernley Street, Moss Side, Manchester. Z7048

LLEWELLYN, E., Gunner, R.F.A.
Volunteering in March 1915, he did consistently good work in England during the first part of his service and was drafted to France in March 1917. There he was in action with his Battery at many important engagements, including the Battles of Messines, Ypres, and the Somme, and in the Retreat and Advance of 1918. He was wounded at Ypres and suffered from gas poisoning on two occasions. After being invalided to England, he was demobilised in June 1919, holding the General Service and Victory Medals.
64, Forbes Street, West Gorton, Manchester. TZ7050

LLEWELLYN, H., Gunner, R.F.A.
He volunteered in November 1915, and in June of the following year was drafted to India, where he was engaged on important garrison duties. In July 1917 he was transferred to Mesopotamia, and was in action with his Battery at Kut-el-Amara, Tekrit, and other engagements of importance until June 1918. He returned to England, and was eventually demobilised in September 1919, holding the General Service and Victory Medals.
8, John Street, Openshaw, Manchester. Z7049

LLOYD, A., L/Cpl., 9th Loyal N. Lancashire Regt.
He volunteered in September 1915, and was retained on important duties at various stations in England until March 1917, when he was drafted to the Western Front. There he unfortunately fell fighting in the Battle of Arras on April 10th, 1917, after only two or three weeks' service in France. He was entitled to the General Service and Victory Medals.
"A valiant Soldier, with undaunted heart he breasted life's last hill."
11, Upper Vauxhall Street, Rochdale Road, Manchester. Z10694

LLOYD, A. R., Sergt., Manchester Regiment.
Volunteering in September 1914, he was drafted to France in October of the following year, and played a distinguished part in the heavy fighting in various sectors and was gassed. He was in action at Ypres, the Somme, Vimy Ridge and Passchendaele, and was later transferred to the Intelligence Corps. He rendered valuable services during the Retreat and Advance of 1918, and after the Armistice served with the Army of Occupation on the Rhine. He holds the 1914-15 Star, and the General Service and Victory Medals, and was demobilised in July 1919.
38, Prince Street, Ardwick, Manchester. Z7057

LLOYD, C. J., Pte., 14th Royal Welch Fusiliers.
He joined in March 1918, and after a period of training was drafted to the Western Front in the following October. There he took part in the heavy fighting at Havrincourt Wood, and the second Battle of Cambrai, and after the cessation of hostilities returned to England and was demobilised in January 1919. He holds the General Service and Victory Medals.
12, Gregory Street, West Gorton, Manchester. Z7051

LLOYD, D., Private, King's (Liverpool Regiment).
Volunteering in September 1914, he was drafted to Egypt in September of the following year, and saw service at Mersa Matruh, Agagia, Sollum, Jifjaffa, Katia, Romani, Rafa, and the Battles of Gaza. He later served with General Allenby at the taking of Jerusalem and Jericho. He returned to England for demobilisation and re-joined for service in France in connection with exhumation duties. He was finally discharged in March 1920, and holds the 1914-15 Star, and the General Service and Victory Medals. Z7061
52, George's Avenue, Chester Road, Hulme, Manchester.

LLOYD, E., Private, 8th Border Regiment.
After volunteering in November 1914, he underwent a period of training, prior to being drafted to the Western Front in January 1916. There he took part in engagements at Loos, St. Eloi, Ploegsteert Wood, Vimy Ridge and many other places, and was unhappily killed in action in October 1916, during the Somme Offensive. He was entitled to the General Service and Victory Medals.
"Courage, bright hopes, and a myriad dreams, splendidly given."
30, School Street, West Gorton, Manchester. Z10696B

LLOYD, G. S., Private, 1st Manchester Regiment.
He volunteered in January 1915, and in July of the following year, proceeded to the Western Front, where he saw severe fighting in various sectors. He took part in the Battles of the Somme, the Ancre, Bullecourt, Ypres, Cambrai, the Aisne, Havrincourt and Le Cateau, and many minor engagements, and suffered from shell-shock whilst in France. Demobilised on his return home in September 1919, he holds the General Service and Victory Medals.
30, School Street, West Gorton, Manchester. Z10696A

LLOYD, H., Farrier Sergt., R.E.
He volunteered in September 1914, and did good work in England during the first part of his service. In March 1917 he was drafted to the Western Front, and was present at the Battles of Arras, Vimy Ridge, Bullecourt, Messines, but on July 2nd, 1917 was killed in action at the last-named engagement. He was entitled to the General Service and Victory Medals.
"Thinking that remembrance, though unspoken, may reach him where he sleeps."
18, George's Avenue, Chester Road, Hulme, Manchester. Z7060

LLOYD, H., Private, Royal Dublin Fusiliers.
Joining in November 1916, he underwent a period of training, and was drafted to the East in February 1917. He saw service in the Advance on the Doiran front in Salonika, and later was transferred to Egypt and Palestine. He was in action at Gaza, and the capture of Jerusalem and Jericho, and in August 1918, proceeded to France, where he took part in the Advance of that year. After the cessation of hostilities he was sent to Germany, and did duty with the Army of Occupation until his return to England for demobilisation in February 1919. He holds the General Service and Victory Medals.
3, Dalby Street, Longsight, Manchester. Z7058

LLOYD, I., Private, 1st Lancashire Fusiliers.
He volunteered at the outbreak of war in August 1914, and in May of the following year was drafted to Gallipoli, where he saw severe fighting at West Beach, and was wounded in action. Invalided to hospital in Egypt he was transferred, on his recovery to the Western Front, and there, after taking part in the Battle of Vimy Ridge and other engagements, was wounded a second time at Ypres. He was sent home and afterwards served in Ireland until March 1918, when he was discharged as medically unfit for further service. He holds the 1914-15 Star, and the General Service and Victory Medals.
29, Neill Street, Gorton, Manchester. Z10695

LLOYD, J., Gunner, R.H.A.
He had already completed twenty-one years' service in the Army at the outbreak of war, when he was mobilised in August 1914, and was immediately drafted to the Western Front, where he was in action with his Battery at the Battle of Mons, and in the subsequent Retreat. He also rendered valuable services on the Marne, and at La Bassée, Loos and Neuve Chapelle, and was discharged as time-expired in October 1915. He re-joined however, in July of the following year, and was drafted to Mesopotamia, where he saw service at Kut-el-Amara and Sanna-i-Yat. He was eventually demobilised in May 1919, after his return and holds the Mons Star, and the General Service and Victory Medals.
125, Thomas Street, Miles Platting, Manchester. Z7059

LLOYD, J., Private, 4th Manchester Regiment.
He volunteered in September 1914, but was retained on special duties with his unit at various stations in England, and was discharged, owing to rheumatism. He was called up again in January 1917, and was attached to the Royal Air Force, with which he did good work in the construction of aeroplanes. He was later sent to North Africa, where he was engaged as a flight mechanic. He holds the General Service and Victory Medals, and was demobilised in March 1919.
23, Lavender Street, Hulme, Manchester. TZ7056

LLOYD, J. E., Sapper, R.E.
Volunteering in February 1915, he was retained on important duties at various stations in England, but was not successful in obtaining his transfer to a theatre of war. He nevertheless rendered valuable services, and after a period in hospital was discharged in July 1916, as unfit for further service.
30, Alder Street, Hulme, Manchester. Z7055

LLOYD, J. S., Private, 1/10th Manchester Regiment.
He joined in November 1916, and after a period of training was drafted to France in February of the following year. There he was in action at Arras, Vimy Ridge, Bullecourt, Passchendaele, Messines and Cambrai, and was wounded during the Advance of 1918. He was demobilised in February 1919, and holds the General Service and Victory Medals.
13, Stanley Avenue, Rusholme, Manchester. Z7053

LLOYD, J. T., Private, 1st Manchester Regiment.
Four months after joining in June 1916, he proceeded to the Western Front, where he took part in various important engagements in the Somme and Ancre sectors. He returned home, however, after only a short period of active service, and was engaged on garrison duties in Ireland until after the cessation of hostilities. Demobilised in May 1919, he holds the General Service and Victory Medals.
30, School Street, West Gorton, Manchester. Z10696C

LLOYD, O.E. (D.C.M.),Corpl.,1/10th ManchesterRegt.
He joined in October 1917, and two months later proceeded to the Western Front, where he played a prominent part in the fighting in many sectors. He was in action at Cambrai, and the Somme, and was gassed. He was awarded the Distinguished Conduct Medal for conspicuous bravery and devotion to duty in the Field, and also holds the General Service and Victory Medals. He was discharged in March 1918, owing to the effects of gas-poisoning.
22, Hardman Street, Moss Side, Manchester. Z7054

LLOYD, P., Gunner, R.F.A.
He volunteered in September 1914, and after undergoing a period of training was drafted to the East in February 1915. There he was in action with his Battery at many important engagements in Egypt and Palestine, including those on the Suez Canal, and at Mersa Matruh, Sollum, El Fasher, Magdhaba, Rafa, Gaza (I and III), Jerusalem, Jericho and Aleppo. He returned home and was demobilised in June 1919, holding the 1914-15 Star, and the General Service and Victory Medals.
9, Heyrod Street, Ancoats, Manchester. Z7106

LLOYD, R., Private, King's (Liverpool Regiment).
He was mobilised at the outbreak of war in August 1914, and was immediately drafted to the Western Front, where he took part in the Battle of Mons, He was also in action at many subsequent engagements, and was invalided to England. He returned to France in June 1916, and was taken prisoner in the following August. After the signing of the Armistice, he was repatriated and eventually discharged in November 1918, holding the Mons Star, and the General Service and Victory Medals.
11, Woburn Place, Chorlton-on-Medlock, Manchester. TX7052

LOCKE, C., Sapper, R.E.
He volunteered in 1914, and on completing a period of training in the following year, proceeded to Gallipoli, where he saw much severe fighting. He made the supreme sacrifice, being killed in action at Suvla Bay in 1915. He was entitled to the 1914-15 Star, and the General Service and Victory Medals.
"He died the noblest death a man may die, Fighting for God, and right, and liberty."
39, Bridge Street, Chorlton-on-Medlock, Manchester. Z10697

LOCKER, F., Private, 21st Manchester Regiment.
He volunteered in May 1915, and after a period of training was drafted to the Western Front in June of the following year. There he took part in many important engagements, including the Battles of the Somme, Vimy Ridge, Arras, Messines and Ypres, and made the supreme sacrifice in October 1917, being killed in action at Passchendaele. He was entitled to the General Service and Victory Medals.
"And doubtless he went in splendid company."
60, Redvers Street, Ardwick, Manchester. Z7062

LOCKETT, J., Private, K.O. (Royal Lancaster Regt.)
He volunteered in September 1914, and was engaged with his unit at home on important duties until October 1916, when he was sent to France. There he was in action at Arras, Bullecourt, Ypres and Cambrai and was gassed and invalided home. After a period in hospital, he was discharged, owing to his disability in February 1918, and holds the General Service and Victory Medals.
211, Victoria Square, Oldham Road, Manchester. Z9253

LOCKETT, R., Corporal, R.A.S.C.
He volunteered in September 1914, and was drafted to France in the following year. Whilst there he served in various engagements, including those at Neuve Chapelle, St. Eloi, Hill 60, Ypres, Loos, Albert, Arras and Cambrai, and in many of the operations in the Retreat and Advance of 1918. Returning home he was demobilised in 1919, and holds the 1914-15 Star, and the General Service and Victory Medals.
2, Elizabeth Ann Street, Manchester. Z9613

LOCKETT, G., Rflmn., Rifle Brigade, and A.B., R.N.
He volunteered in September 1914, and after three months' service with the Rifle Brigade was discharged as medically unfit in December 1914. In April 1915 he joined the Navy, and did duty in H.M.S. "Adventure" on patrolling duties in the North Sea. He fought at the Battle of Jutland in H.M.S. "Cordelia" and finally did convoy work between England and America, whilst serving on board H.M.S. "Cumberland." He holds the 1914–15 Star, and the General Service and Victory Medals, and was demobilised in February 1919.
18, Alice Street, Hulme, Manchester. Z7063

LOCKLEY, R., Private, 3rd Lancashire Fusiliers.
He volunteered in March 1915, and whilst with the Colours, served in various theatres of war. Drafted to Gallipoli in April 1915, he fought in the Landings at Cape Helles and Suvla Bay, and in the capture of Chunuk Bair. After the Evacuation of the Peninsula he proceeded to Egypt in January 1916, and took part in the capture of El Fasher and the Battle of Romani. He left Egypt in December 1916, and landing in France in the following month, was engaged in the Battles of Arras, Ypres, Cambrai, the Somme, and was wounded in March 1918, and on recovery saw heavy fighting in the concluding stages of hostilities. After the Armistice he was sent with the Army of Occupation into Germany, where he was stationed until his return home for demobilisation in April 1919. He holds the 1914–15 Star, and the General Service and Victory Medals.
16, Peel Street, Hulme, Manchester. Z11753

LOCKLIN, J., Driver, R.A.S.C. (M.T.)
Volunteering in April 1915, he was drafted to the Western Front two months later and was engaged on important transport duties in various sectors. He rendered valuable services in many engagements, including the Battles of Loos, Albert, Ploegsteert Wood, the Somme, Arras, Bullecourt, Messines, Ypres and Cambrai, and later in the Retreat and Advance of 1918. After the Armistice he proceeded to Germany, where he did duty with the Army of Occupation on the Rhine. He was demobilised in June 1919, and holds the 1914–15 Star, and the General Service and Victory Medals.
5, Billington Place, Chorlton-on-Medlock, Manchester. Z7064

LODGE, A., Air Mechanic, R.A.F.
He joined in September 1917, but on account of his being under military age, was not transferred to a theatre of war. On completion of his training however, he rendered valuable services with his Squadron in Ireland, and was eventually demobilised in 1919.
2, Witton Street, Ancoats, Manchester. Z11912C

LODGE, J., Private, 9th Loyal N. Lancashire Regt.
Volunteering in January 1915, he served in England with his unit for a time, and in July 1916, proceeded to France. There he took part in many engagements of importance, including the Battles of the Somme, Beaumont-Hamel, Arras, Messines, Ypres and Cambrai, and the Retreat and Advance of 1918. He also served with the Military Police for a short period, and was eventually demobilised in February 1919, holding the General Service and Victory Medals.
14, Renshaw Street, West Gorton, Manchester. Z7065A

LODGE, J. H., Corporal, R.A.V.C.
He volunteered in 1915, and in the following year was drafted to Salonika, where he saw severe fighting in the Balkans. He was chiefly engaged on important work in connection with the treatment of sick and wounded horses, and remained in this theatre of war until after the cessation of hostilities. He holds the General Service and Victory Medals, and was demobilised in March 1919.
2, Witton Street, Ancoats, Manchester. Z11912B

LODGE, J. H. (Jun.), Sapper, R.E.
Joining in April 1917, he underwent a period of training, and was then engaged on special duties as a pattern machine maker. Owing to the important nature of his work he was not drafted overseas, but rendered valuable services with his unit until his demobilisation in 1919.
2, Witton Street, Ancoats, Manchester. Z11912A

LODGE, W., Private, 21st Manchester Regiment.
He volunteered in July 1915, and after completing a period of training was drafted to France in May of the following year. In that theatre of war he took part in much heavy fighting, and was in action at the Battles of the Somme (I and II), Beaumont-Hamel, Arras, Messines and Ypres, and was wounded on three occasions. He finally took part in the Advance of 1918, and suffered from gas poisoning. He holds the General Service and Victory Medals, and was demobilised in April 1919.
14, Renshaw Street, West Gorton, Manchester. Z7065B

LOFT, F. Pte., 2nd Border Rgt., and Driver, R.F.A.
Mobilised in August 1914, he was immediately drafted to the Western Front, where he fought in the Retreat from Mons. He also took part in the Battle of La Bassée, and many minor engagements, before being severely wounded in action at Ypres in March 1915, and invalided home. On his recovery, however, twelve months later, he proceeded to Salonika, and was there in action on the Doiran and Struma fronts until the cessation of hostilities. Returning home in December 1918, he was discharged in the following month, and holds the Mons Star, and the General Service and Victory Medals.
70, Churnett Street, Collyhurst, Manchester. Z10698

LOFTUS, J., Private, King's (Liverpool Regiment).
Joining in November 1916, he proceeded to France six months later, and there saw severe fighting in various sectors of the Front. He took part in the Battles of Ypres and Cambrai, and many other important engagements in this theatre of war, and served also through the Retreat and Advance of 1918. He was demobilised on his return home in September 1919, and holds the General Service and Victory Medals.
21, Linacre Street, Oldham Road, Manchester. Z10699

LOGAN, F., Private, 11th East Lancashire Regt.
He joined in January 1918, and after undergoing a period of training was drafted to the Western Front in the following June. There he was engaged in much heavy fighting at important engagements, but was unfortunately killed by a sniper at Armentières on September 5th, 1918. He was entitled to the General Service and Victory Medals.
"His memory is cherished with pride."
10, Bank Street, Bradford, Manchester. Z7104

LOGAN, J. W., Private, Cheshire Regiment.
Volunteering in August 1915, he was sent to the Western Front after two months' training, and there saw heavy fighting in various sectors. After taking part in the Somme Offensive, and in engagements at Ypres, Nieuport and many other places, he was severely wounded in action at Arras in May 1917, and admitted to hospital in England. He was invalided from the Army in September 1918, and holds the 1914–15 Star, and the General Service and Victory Medals.
15, Buckland Street, Ancoats, Manchester. Z11918

LOMAS, A., Driver, R.A.S.C. (M.T.)
He joined in October 1916, and after completing four months' training, proceeded to the Western Front. Whilst in this theatre of war he was engaged on important duties in various sectors, and took an active part in the Battles of Arras, Vimy Ridge, Bullecourt, Ypres, Cambrai, Bapaume and Le Cateau, and many other engagements. He was demobilised in December 1919, and holds the General Service and Victory Medals.
17A, Irlam Street, Miles Platting, Manchester. Z10700

LOMAS, A., Gunner, R.G.A., and Private, R.A.O.C.
He joined in July 1916, and on completing his training in February of the following year, was drafted to the Western Front, where he took part in many important engagements until December 1917. He was then transferred to Italy, where he was again in action until the cessation of hostilities. Demobilised on his return home, he re-enlisted however, shortly afterwards, and proceeded to Russia with the Relief Force. He was finally demobilised in December 1919, and holds the General Service and Victory Medals.
4, Corby Street, West Gorton, Manchester. Z11387B

LOMAS, A., Private, Cheshire Regiment.
He joined in March 1916, and in the following May proceeded to France, where he was in action in the Somme sector, and at Ypres, Kemmel, La Clytte, High Wood, Albert, Arras, Fricourt and the Scarpe. From 1917 he was engaged with the Royal Engineers. He was invalided home in 1918, owing to eye trouble, and was demobilised in January 1919, holding the General Service and Victory Medals.
101, Jersey Street Dwellings, Manchester. Z11536

LOMAS, G. A., Private, 1/7th Manchester Regiment.
Mobilised at the outbreak of war in August 1914, he was immediately drafted to France, and took part in the Battles of the Marne, Ypres, Vimy Ridge, and the Somme, and other engagements of importance, but was unfortunately killed by shell-fire at Ablainzeville in March 1918, during the Retreat. He was entitled to the 1914 Star, and the General Service and Victory Medals.
"He passed out of the sight of men by the path of duty and self-sacrifice."
127, Everton Road, Chorlton-on-Medlock, Manchester. Z7067

LOMAS, H., Air Mechanic, R.A.F.
Joining in October 1916, he was retained with his Squadron at various important aerodromes in England and did consistently good work in the repair shops. He was unable to obtain his transfer to a theatre of war, but, nevertheless, rendered valuable services until he was demobilised in February 1919.
28, Hancock Street, Rusholme, Manchester. Z7066

LOMAS, H., Private, 25th Manchester Regiment.
He volunteered in August 1915, and two months later proceeded to the Western Front, where he took part in many important engagements. He saw much heavy fighting in various sectors, and was in action at the Battles of Loos, St. Eloi, Albert, Vermelles, Vimy Ridge, the Somme, Beaumont-Hamel, Arras, Bullecourt, Ypres (III) and Cambrai. He also rendered valuable services during the Retreat and Advance of 1918, and was wounded on the Sambre. He holds the 1914–15 Star, and the General Service and Victory Medals, and was demobilised in February 1919.
28, Hancock Street, Rusholme, Manchester. Z7068

LOMAS, J., Private, K.O. (Royal Lancaster Regt.)

He joined immediately on attaining military age in August 1919 and after a short period of training was retained at various stations, where he was engaged on duties of great importance, being medically unfit for service abroad. Invalided from the Army in December 1919, he re-enlisted, however, shortly afterwards, and twelve months later was still with his unit.
4, Corby Street, West Gorton, Manchester. Z11387C

LOMAX, A., Private, 7th Lincolnshire Regiment.

He joined in August 1916, and was drafted to France in the following November after a period of training. In this theatre of war he took part in much heavy fighting, and was present at many important engagements on the Western Front. On April 23rd, 1917, he made the supreme sacrifice, being killed in action at the first Battle of Arras. He was entitled to the General Service and Victory Medals.
" Honour to the immortal dead, who gave their youth that the world might grow old in peace."
39, Stott Street, Hulme, Manchester. Z7070

LOMAX, D., Corporal, R.A.S.C. (M.T.)

Volunteering in January 1915, he was drafted to Egypt in the following month and was there engaged on important duties at various stations. He afterwards took part in the Advance into Palestine, where he was present at the capture of Jerusalem, and on the cessation of hostilities was sent with the Army of Occupation into Turkey. He also served for a time in France, before returning home for demobilisation in November 1919, and holds the 1914-15 Star, and the General Service and Victory Medals.
7, Broughton Street, Ancoats, Manchester. Z10701

LOMAX, G., Private, R.A.M.C.

He enlisted in August 1904, and at the outbreak of war in August 1914 was sent to the Western Front, where he was engaged on important transport duties in various sectors. He was present at many engagements, including the Battles of the Marne, Ypres, St. Eloi, Loos, Vermelles, and Cambrai, and later in the Retreat and Advance of 1918. He was demobilised in February of the following year, and holds the 1914 Star, and the General Service and Victory Medals. He also served through the South African war of 1899-1902, and possesses the Queen's and King's South African Medals.
16, Walworth Street, Ardwick, Manchester. Z7069

LOMAX, J., Private, 4th Royal Scots.

He volunteered in November 1914, and in May of the following year was sent to the Dardanelles. He took part in the Landing at Cape Helles, and the Battles of Krithia. He was killed in action during the attack on Achi Baba on June 22nd, 1915. He was entitled to the 1914-15 Star, and the General Service and Victory Medals.
" The path of duty was the way to glory."
5, Werneth Street, Harpurhey, Manchester. Z11537A

LOMAX, J. R., Private, Queen's Own (Royal West Kent Regiment).

He was mobilised in August 1914, and was engaged on important duties with his unit at various stations till September 1916, when he was drafted to the Western Front. He fought in the Battles of Albert and the Somme. He was reported as having been taken prisoner, and later to have been killed in action on November 1st, 1918. He was entitled to the General Service and Victory Medals.
" Great deeds cannot die."
5, Werneth Street, Harpurhey, Manchester. Z11537B

LOMAX, N., Private, M.G.C.

He joined in May 1917, and on completion of his training was drafted to Egypt in the following March. Whilst in this theatre of war, he served with the 7th Indian Division at Kantara, and in the Suez Canal zone. He also took part in the Advance through Palestine, and was at Beyrout for a time. Demobilised in February 1919, he holds the General Service and Victory Medals.
8, Wright Street, Oldham Road, Manchester. Z10702

LONG, A., L/Corporal, R.A.M.C.

He was mobilised at the outbreak of war in August 1914, and was immediately drafted to the Western Front, where he did consistently good work at various Field Dressing Stations, attending the wounded. He was present during many engagements in various sectors, and also served on board hospital ships, conveying wounded between France and England. He holds the 1914 Star, and the General Service and Victory Medals, and was discharged in December 1918.
10, Ravensdale Road, Rusholme, Manchester. TZ7072

LONG, G. F., Private, 7th Manchester Regiment.

He volunteered in November 1914, and after doing duty for a time in England was drafted to France in February 1916. There he was engaged on special duties, but although unable to take part in actual fighting on account of disability, did good service in the Ypres, Vimy Ridge, Arras, the Somme, Beaumont-Hamel, Cambrai and Bullecourt sectors, and during the Retreat and Advance of 1918. He holds the General Service and Victory Medals, and was demobilised in February 1919.
22, George Street, Moss Side, Manchester. Z7071

LONG, C. W., Sergt., E. Lancaster Regt., and R.A.F.

He volunteered in September 1914, and in November of the following year was drafted to Salonika. Whilst in this theatre of war he fought in the General Offensive on the Doiran front, and in the Advance across the Struma, and also took part in the Retreat from Serbia. Invalided home with fever, he was sent after his recovery to France in February 1918, and was engaged on important duties at an aeroplane workshop at Rouen, until the cessation of hostilities. He was demobilised in February 1919, and holds the 1914-15 Star, and the General Service and Victory Medals.
2, Grosvenor Street, Newton Heath, Manchester. Z9614

LONG, W., Private, Manchester Regiment.

He volunteered in September 1914, and in the following April took part in the Landing at Cape Helles on the Gallipoli Peninsula, and was wounded in August 1915. On his recovery in the following November, he was transferred to the Signal section as a Pioneer and was sent to Salonika, where he was in action throughout the Balkan campaign. In June 1915 he was mentioned in Despatches and recommended for the Distinguished Conduct Medal for conspicuous bravery in the Field. He was demobilised in February 1919, and holds the 1914-15 Star, and the General Service and Victory Medals.
139, Hamilton Street, Collyhurst, Manchester. Z10703

LONGBOTTOM, H. V., Petty Officer, R.N.

Mobilised at the outbreak of war in August 1914, he proceeded to the North Sea in H.M.S. " Endros " and was engaged on important patrol and escort duties. He also rendered valuable services on the Channel patrol, and was discharged in February 1918, as no longer physically fit for active service. He holds the 1914-15 Star, and the General Service and Victory Medals.
19, Dorrington Street, Hulme, Manchester. TZ7073

LONGDEN, A., Private, Lancashire Fusiliers.

He joined in February 1917, and on completion of his training was engaged on important garrison duties at Belfast, Cork and Dublin, in Ireland. Although not successful in obtaining his transfer to a theatre of war, he did consistently good work with his unit, and in 1920 was still serving.
8, Boslam Street, Ancoats, Manchester. Z10704

LONGDEN, W., A.B., R.N.V.R.

He joined in April 1918, having been previously engaged on work of National importance as a miner at a Bradford Colliery. He proceeded to France in August 1918, and during the Advance served as a Lewis gunner with the Drake Battalion of the Royal Naval Division, and saw severe fighting at Cambrai. He holds the General Service and Victory Medals, and was demobilised in December. 1918.
7, Clyde Street, Ancoats, Manchester. Z10705

LONGFELLOW, S., Corporal, R.A.S.C. (M.T.)

Volunteering in May 1915, he proceeded to the Western Front two months later, and played a prominent part during the fighting in many sectors. He was engaged on important transport duties and was present at many engagements, including the Battles of Loos, Albert, the Somme, Beaumont-Hamel, Arras, Messines, Ypres and Cambrai. He suffered from shell-shock, and was discharged in May 1919, as unfit for further service. He holds the 1914-15 Star, and the General Service and Victory Medals.
5, Etruria Street, Longsight, Manchester. Z7074

LONGFIELD, H., Private, Lancashire Fusiliers.

Volunteering in September 1914, he underwent a period of training, and was drafted to the Western Front in March of the following year. There he was engaged on important duties as a stretcher-bearer, but was unfortunately killed during an air raid at Lens in September 1917. He was entitled to the 1914-15 Star, and the General Service and Victory Medals.
" His memory is cherished with pride."
14, Upper Plymouth Grove, Longsight, Manchester. Z7075

LONGMIRE, W. H., Corporal, 8th Manchester Regt.

He was mobilised at the outbreak of war in August 1914, and was drafted to France in the following November. There he played a prominent part in many engagements of importance, and was in action at Ypres, St. Eloi, Vermelles, Arras, Bullecourt, Nieuport, Albert, Cambrai and Bapaume, and rendered valuable services during the Advance of 1918. He holds the 1914 Star, and the General Service and Victory Medals, and was discharged in April 1919.
7, Gleave Street, West Gorton, Manchester. Z7076

LONGSDALE, J., Private, Lancashire Fusiliers.

Volunteering in September 1914, he proceeded to France in the following February and took part in many engagements of importance. He saw much heavy fighting in various sectors and was in action at the Battles of Hill 60, Ypres, Vermelles, Ploegsteert Wood, the Somme, the Scarpe, Messines, Cambrai, the Aisne, Bapaume, Havrincourt, and the Marne (II). He was demobilised in July 1919, and holds the 1914-15 Star, and the General Service and Victory Medals.
28, Harrison Street, Ancoats, Manchester. Z7107

LONGSHAW, G., Sapper, R.E.
Volunteering in January 1915, he embarked for France in the following September, and during his service on the Western Front was engaged in the forward areas whilst operations were in progress at Loos, Ypres, and the Somme. He then proceeded to Egypt, and was stationed at Alexandria and Cairo, and later served in Syria. On his return home, he was demobilised in February 1919, and holds the 1914-15 Star, and the General Service and Victory Medals.
19, Percival Street, Newton Heath, Manchester. Z9615

LONGSHAW, H., Pte., K.O. (R. Lancaster Regt.)
He volunteered in April 1915, and was eventually sent to the Western Front after a period of service at home stations. He took part in the Battles of Cambrai (I), Havrincourt, Epéhy and Cambrai (II), and in heavy fighting at Rainecourt and Bourlon Wood. Demobilised in August 1919, he holds the General Service and Victory Medals.
9, Roberts Street, Newton Heath, Manchester. Z10707

LONGSHAW, J. E., Private, 6th Manchester Regt.
Volunteering in August 1914, he was drafted to Egypt in the following year and was engaged on the Suez Canal. He contracted enteric fever and was invalided home. On his recovery he was sent to France and transferred to the Labour Corps, with which unit he served at Boulogne. He was demobilised in February 1919, and holds the 1914-15 Star, and the General Service and Victory Medals.
58, Cowgill Street, Chorlton-on-Medlock, Manchester. Z9254

LONGSHAW, P. W., Pte., 2nd Sherwood Foresters.
Mobilised at the outbreak of war in August 1914, he was immediately drafted to France and took part in the Battle of, and the Retreat from, Mons. He was also in action at subsequent engagements, including the Battles of the Marne and the Aisne, and was reported missing, and later presumed killed on October 20th, 1914. He was entitled to the Mons Star, and the General Service and Victory Medals.
" He passed out of the sight of man by the path of duty and self-sacrifice."
147, Rosebery Street, Moss Side, Manchester. TZ7078

LONSDALE, H., Private, Manchester Regiment.
He joined in November 1918, on attaining military age, and after a period of training was drafted to Germany in January of the following year. There he was engaged on important garrison duties with the Army of Occupation on the Rhine, and was demobilised in May 1920, on his return to England.
5, Anson Street, Hulme, Manchester. Z7077B

LONSDALE, R., Private, West Riding Regiment.
He volunteered in September 1914, and after a period of training was drafted to France in May 1915. He took part in much heavy fighting, but was unfortunately killed in action at Ypres in July of the same year, two months after his landing on the Western Front. He was entitled to the 1914-15 Star, and the General Service and Victory Medals.
" He joined the great white company of valiant souls."
5, Anson Street, Hulme, Manchester. Z7077A

LOOKER, B., Private, 19th Manchester Regiment.
Volunteering in September 1914, he was drafted to France in November of the following year. During his service on the Western Front, he played a prominent part in the Battles of the Somme, Ypres, Cambrai and Bapaume, and in other important engagements. He was twice wounded in action on the Somme in July 1916, and at Ypres twelve months later. He holds the 1914-15 Star, and the General Service and Victory Medals, and was demobilised in December 1918.
27, Sycamore Street, Newton, Manchester. Z10708

LORD, F., Private, 8th Manchester Regiment.
He joined in October 1916, and two months later proceeded to the Western Front, where he was in action at Arras, Vimy Ridge, Ypres (III), and the Retreat and Advance of 1918. After the Armistice he was sent to Germany and did duty with the Army of Occupation on the Rhine, until his return to England for demobilisation in March 1919. He holds the General Service and Victory Medals.
47, William Street, Hulme, Manchester. Z7079

LORD, J. W., Pte., King's (Liverpool Regiment), and Loyal North Lancashire Regiment.
He joined in January 1917, and after a period of training was drafted to France in the following July. There he took part in much heavy fighting at Ypres (III), and was wounded in the leg. He suffered the loss of a foot by amputation, and after being invalided to England was finally discharged in September 1918, as unfit for further service. He holds the General Service and Victory Medals.
55, Pownall Street, Hulme, Manchester. Z7080

LORD, W., Staff-Sergt., King's African Rifles.
He volunteered in August 1914, and was sent to France in January of the following year. He was in action at St. Eloi, the Somme, Arras and Ypres, and wounded at Guillemont, was invalided home. In March 1918 he proceeded to Africa and served at various stations. He was demobilised in June 1920, and holds the 1914-15 Star, and the General Service and Victory Medals.
204, Cheltenham Street, Collyhurst, Manchester. Z11538

LOSEBY, T., Private, 1st Manchester Regiment.
Joining in January 1917, he completed his training and was engaged on Home Service duties with his unit. He did good work at various prisoners of war camps, but was unsuccessful in securing his transfer overseas before the conclusion of hostilities, and was demobilised in November 1919.
18, Abram Street, Hulme, Manchester. Z11754

LOVELL, E. W., Gunner, R.F.A.
Volunteering in November 1915, he was drafted to France in March of the following year, and was engaged in heavy fighting at Loos, Albert, the Somme, Ypres, and later returned to England for special work. In December 1918 he was sent to the Army of Occupation in Germany, and served there until he returned home, and was demobilised in August 1919. He holds the General Service and Victory Medals.
58, Southwell Street, Harpurhey, Manchester, Z11539

LOW, F., L/Corporal, Military Police.
He volunteered in November 1915, and after a period of training was drafted to East Africa, where he was engaged on important Police duties in both British and German territory. He rendered valuable services during the period of the war, and returning to England, was demobilised in April 1919. He holds the General Service and Victory Medals.
10, May Street, Lower Openshaw, Manchester. TZ7081

LOWDE, J., Sapper, R.E.
He volunteered in October 1915, and in the following month proceeded to Salonika, where he saw service on the Doiran front, in the Advance across the Struma, and at the capture of Monastir. He was also present at the Battle of Vardar (II), and suffered from malaria. Returning to England after the cessation of hostilities, he was demobilised in May 1919, and holds the 1914-15 Star, and the General Service and Victory Medals.
8, Edlin Street, Morton Street, Longsight, Manchester. Z7082

LOWE, A., Private, 14th King's (Liverpool Regt.)
He joined in June 1916, and in the following February was drafted to France, where he was wounded in action at the Battle of Bullecourt. After treatment at the Casualty Clearing Station at Achiet-le-Grand, he was sent home in September 1917, and five months later was discharged owing to his being under military age. He holds the General Service and Victory Medals.
51, Laurence Street, West Gorton, Manchester. Z10709

LOWE, C., Private, Labour Corps.
Joining in August 1916, he ws sent to France in the following October and was engaged on important duties in connection with the repair of roads, and other work of importance. He rendered valuable services in many sectors of the Western Front, including Ypres, Cambrai and Lens. He holds the General Service and Victory Medals, and was demobilised in February 1919.
14, Gomm Street, Ardwick, Manchester. Z7083

LOWE, C. H., Sapper, R.E.
Joining in September 1917, he was shortly afterwards sent to France, where he was engaged at various stations, including Cherbourg, Havre, Rouen and Boulogne, on important duties connected with his branch of the Service. He returned home in March 1919, and was demobilised, holding the General Service and Victory Medals.
27, Clare Street, Chorlton-on-Medlock, Manchester. TZ9255

LOWE, H., Sapper, R.E.
He joined in July 1916, but owing to his being physically unfit for service over-seas, was retained on important duties at various stations in England. He, nevertheless, did consistently good work until June 1917, when he was discharged as unfit for further military duties.
16, Ashmore Street, West Gorton, Manchester. Z7084

LOWE, J., Private, Lancashire Fusiliers.
He joined in March 1917, and after training was drafted to the Western Front in the following May. There he took part in many important engagements, including those at Bullecourt, Ypres III, Lens and Bapaume, and was gassed at Zonnebeke in February 1918. He was invalided to England, and was eventually discharged in the following December as unfit for further service. He holds the General Service and Victory Medals. 2, Nelly St., Ardwick, Manchester. Z7087

LOWE, J. A., Driver, R.A.S.C.
He volunteered in September 1915, and after training at Aldershot was drafted to France in March of the following year. There, as a gunner in the Royal Field Artillery, he was in action with his Battery at St. Eloi, Albert, and the Battle of the Somme, and suffered from shell-shock. He was invalided home, and after a period in hospital was sent to his depôt in April 1917, and did important guard and other duties until his demobilisation in January 1919. He was entitled to the General Service and Victory Medals, but unfortunately died at home in January 1920.
69, Norton Street, West Gorton, Manchester. Z7085

LOWE, J. H., Pte., 1/4th Loyal N. Lancashire Regt.

Joining in February 1917, he completed a period of training at Grimsby, and was drafted to France in July 1918. There he was in action at many of the concluding engagements of the war, including La Bassée, and Givenchy, and was wounded in October of the same year. He was eventually demobilised in February 1919, and holds the General Service and Victory Medals. 43, Wilson St., Ardwick, Manchester. Z7088

LOWE, S., Private, 1/8th Manchester Regiment.

He joined in July 1916, and proceeded to the Western Front in February of the following year after a period of training. In this theatre of war he was in action at numerous engagements and suffered from gas poisoning at Givenchy. He was invalided home, and after spending some time in various hospitals was eventually discharged in April 1919, and holds the General Service and Victory Medals.
3, Eskridge Street, Ardwick, Manchester. Z7086

LOWE, S., Rifleman, Rifle Brigade.

Volunteering in January 1915, he proceeded to Egypt in May of that year, and there saw severe fighting on the Suez Canal, and at Katia, and many other places. He was later transferred to Mesopotamia, where he was wounded in action at the Relief of Kut in January 1917, and afterwards served at Cyprus. He was also in action on the Western Front, before returning home for demobilisation in January 1919, and holds the 1914-15 Star, and the General Service and Victory Medals.
11, Close Street, Chorlton-on-Medlock, Manchester. Z11919A

LOWENS, R. J., C.S.M., 9th Loyal N. Lancs. Regt.

He volunteered in November 1914, and in the following year was drafted to the Western Front, where he took part in the fighting at Ypres and on the Somme, and was twice wounded. He was invalided home and discharged in February 1918, owing to his injuries. He holds the 1914-15 Star, and the General Service and Victory Medals.
14, Luke Street, Collyhurst, Manchester. Z9256

LOWICK, S. C., Private, 11th Cheshire Regiment.

He volunteered in January 1915, and was drafted to France in July of the following year. In this theatre of war he saw active service on the Ancre front, and took part in the Battles of Arras, Vimy Ridge, Messines, Ypres, the Somme, and Cambrai. He was reported missing, but it was later discovered that he had been taken prisoner during the second Battle of the Somme in March 1918, and died from wounds on November 23rd of that year. He was entitled to the General Service and Victory Medals.
"His memory is cherished with pride."
5, St. Clement's Place, West Gorton, Manchester. Z7090

LOWTHER, A., Private, Manchester Regiment.

He volunteered in May 1915, and after his training was completed embarked for India in February 1917. On his way out, however, he contracted an illness and was detained in Africa. He was subsequently invalided home in May 1917, and discharged two months later as medically unfit for further duty. He holds the General Service Medal.
24, Wilton Street, Newton Heath, Manchester. Z9616

LOYND, A., Stoker, R.N.

He enlisted in May 1909, and at the outbreak of war in August 1914 proceeded to the North Sea, where he was engaged on important patrol duties in H.M.S. "Temeraire." He was also in action at Heligoland, the Dogger Bank and Jutland, and in the early part of the war fought at the Battle of the Falkland Isles. He rendered valuable services until the cessation of hostilities, and in 1920 was still serving in the Navy. He holds the 1914-15 Star, and the General Service and Victory Medals.
4, Solent Street, Ardwick, Manchester. Z7091

LUBY, J., Private, 21st West Yorkshire Regiment.

He volunteered in December 1915, and in the following year was drafted to the Western Front. Whilst in this theatre of war he took part in heavy fighting at St. Eloi, and in other important engagements, including the Battles of the Somme and Ypres. He was gassed in action in April 1918, during the Retreat, and was also present in the Advance of that year. Demobilised in December 1919, he holds the General Service and Victory Medals.
25, Windsor Street, Rochdale Road, Manchester. Z10710

LUCAS, F., Private, 1/7th Lancashire Fusiliers.

He enlisted in April 1911, and at the outbreak of war in August 1914 proceeded to the Eastern Front, where he took part in the fighting on the Suez Canal. In 1915 he proceeded to the Dardanelles, and was in action at the Landing at Suvla Bay, and other engagements of importance on the Gallipoli Peninsula. He was transferred to France in March 1917, and saw much heavy fighting at Givenchy, Bapaume, La Bassée, Nieuport, and Passchendaele, and later in the Retreat and Advance of 1918, and was gassed on two occasions. He holds the 1914-15 Star, and the General Service and Victory Medals, and was discharged in February 1919.
50, Owen Street, City Road, Hulme, Manchester. Z7094

LUCAS, F., Bombardier, R.F.A.

Joining in March 1916, he underwent a period of training, and was drafted to the Western Front in October of the following year. There he was in action with his Battery at numerous important engagements, including the Battles of Cambrai, and the Somme II, and was wounded in March 1918. He also rendered valuable services during the Advance of 1918, at Cambrai II, and the Selle, and after the Armistice proceeded to Germany, where he did duty with the Army of Occupation on the Rhine. He was demobilised in November 1919, and holds the General Service and Victory Medals. 19, Walter St., Hulme, Manchester. TZ7093

LUCAS, J. W., Private, 12th Manchester Regiment.

Volunteering in September 1914, he underwent a period of training, and was drafted to France in July of the following year. There he took part in much heavy fighting in various sectors, and was in action at Loos, Ypres, Festubert, and Hooge, and later after returning from leave, made the supreme sacrifice on July 7th, 1916, being killed in action during the Somme Offensive. He was entitled to the 1914-15 Star, and the General Service and Victory Medals.
"Nobly striving,
He nobly fell that we might live."
31, Hope Street, Hulme, Manchester. TZ7092

LUCAS, W. C., Private, 7th Gordon Highlanders.

After volunteering in February 1915, he underwent three months training before being drafted to France. Whilst on the Western Front, he was in action at the Battles of Hill 60, Ypres (II), Loos, the Somme, and Cambrai, and in heavy fighting at La Bassée, and Neuve Chapelle. He was twice wounded, and on the second occasion was taken prisoner in March 1918. He spent some time in hospital in Germany, and was eventually repatriated in January 1919, when he was demobilised, holding the 1914-15 Star, and the General Service and Victory Medals.
47, Naylor Street, Oldham Road, Manchester. Z10711

LUCKCUCK, J. A., Pte., K.O. (R. Lancaster Regt.)

He joined in October 1918, and after his training was sent to Ireland, where he was engaged at Dublin, the Curragh Camp, Mount Joy and Kingston, on important duties with his unit, and rendered valuable services. He was not successful in obtaining his transfer to a fighting area before the cessation of hostilities, and was demobilised in November 1919.
48, Jersey St. Dwellings, Ancoats, Manchester. Z9257

LUCKMAN, E., Pte., 2nd York and Lancaster Regt.

He volunteered in November 1915, and in October of the following year was sent to France. In July 1917 he was wounded at Loos, and invalided home. After receiving hospital treatment he was discharged as medically unfit for further service in April 1918, and holds the General Service and Victory Medals.
7, Rocester Street, Harpurhey, Manchester. Z11540

LUCY, J., Sergt., 5th Manchester Regiment.

He volunteered in September 1914, and early in the following year was drafted to France, where he served with distinction at the Battles of Neuve Chapelle, St. Eloi, Hill 60, Ypres, Festubert, Loos, Albert, Ploegsteert, the Somme, and the Ancre. He then took part in heavy fighting at Salonika, and was finally engaged as a drill Instructor. Demobilised in 1919, he holds the 1914-15 Star, and the General Service and Victory Medals.
12, Pilling Street, Newton Heath, Manchester. Z10712

LUDLAM, H., Pte., 4th York and Lancaster Regt.

He joined in May 1916, and in the following August was drafted to the Western Front, where he took part in numerous engagements. During his service in this theatre of war he was wounded on three occasions. He was demobilised in January 1919, and holds the General Service and Victory Medals.
57, Carisbrook Street, Harpurhey, Manchester. Z11541

LUKES, W., Gunner, R.H.A., and R.F.A.

Mobilised in India at the outbreak of war in August 1914 he landed in France in April 1915, and was in action with his Battery at Neuve Chapelle, Hill 60, Ypres II, Festubert, and Loos. In December 1915 he was transferred to Mesopotamia and took part in many important engagements, including Ali-el-Gharb, Um-el-Hannah, Sanna-i-Yat, and Kut-el-Amara. He suffered from malaria, and at the expiration of eight years' service was discharged in March 1920, holding the 1914-15 Star, and the General Service and Victory Medals.
4, Gay Street, Jackson Street, Hulme, Manchester. Z7095

LUNN, H. A., Private, R.A.S.C.

He volunteered in April 1915, and after completing a period of training, was drafted to Egypt, where he was engaged on important duties at various stations. He was afterwards transferred to the Western Front, and there did much good work in many sectors until the cessation of hostilities. He was eventually demobilised, and holds the General Service and Victory Medals.
23, Chapel Street, West Gorton, Manchester. TZ11920

LUTLEY, J. R., Private, 3rd Cheshire Regiment.
He joined in May 1918, and was retained on special duties at important stations in England and Ireland. He was unable to obtain his transfer to a theatre of war before the cessation of hostilities, but nevertheless rendered valuable services until his demobilisation in September 1919.
9, Williams Place, Ancoats, Manchester.   Z7096

LUTLEY, T. H., Private, Labour Corps.
He joined in May 1918, and shortly afterwards proceeded to the Western Front, where he was engaged on special duties in connection with the filling up of shell holes, and the removal of shells from various fronts. He did consistently good work until May 1919, when he was discharged, and holds the General Service and Victory Medals.
9, Williams Place, Ancoats, Manchester.   Z7097

LUTTRELL, J., Private, Devonshire Regiment.
He was mobilised in August 1914, and quickly proceeded to France, where he played an important part in the Battles of Le Cateau, La Bassée, Ypres (I), Ypres (II), the Somme, Arras, Vimy Ridge, Messines, Ypres (III), Cambrai, and Ypres (IV). He was also in action throughout the Retreat and Advance of 1918. Demobilised in February 1919, he unfortunately died a short time afterwards, and was entitled to the 1914 Star, and the General Service and Victory Medals.
" His memory is cherished with pride."
40, Richardson Street, Collyhurst, Manchester.   Z10713A

LYLE, W. H., Pte., 2nd King's Shropshire Light Inftry.
He joined in August 1916, but owing to his being too old for transfer to a theatre of war, was engaged on important duties on the East and West Coasts, and in the Channel Islands. He rendered very valuable services with his unit until his demobilisation in February 1919.
16, Phelan Street, Collyhurst, Manchester.   Z10714

LYNCH, A. T., L/Corporal, 4th Royal Fusiliers.
Volunteering in March 1915, he underwent a period of training and was drafted to the Western Front in May of the following year. In this theatre of war he took part in heavy fighting in various sectors, and was in action at the Battles of the Somme, Beaumont-Hamel, Arras, Bullecourt, and Ypres III, and later in the Retreat and Advance of 1918, and was wounded at Le Cateau II. He holds the General Service and Victory Medals, and was demobilised in January 1919.
27, Oliver Street, Bradford, Manchester.   Z7101

LYNCH, D., Corporal, K.O. (Royal Lancaster Regt.)
He enlisted in 1908, and was serving in India at the outbreak of war in August 1914. He embarked for France shortly afterwards and took a prominent part in numerous engagements, including the Battles of Neuve Chapelle and Ypres II, and was invalided home in May 1915, through wounds. He proceeded to the Dardanelles in August of that year, and was in action at the Landing at Suvla Bay, and the engagement at Chunuk Bair. In February 1916 he was transferred to Mesopotamia, and rendered valuable services during the attempted Relief of Kut, and the later fighting. He made the supreme sacrifice, being killed in action in February 1917, and was entitled to the 1914-15 Star, and the General Service and Victory Medals.
" Great deeds cannot die."
25, Boundary Street, Newton, Manchester.   TZ7105

LYNCH, D., Tpr., Queen's Own Worcester Hussars.
Joining in June 1917, he underwent a period of training, and was retained on special duties at important stations in Ireland. He was unable to serve in a theatre of war owing to ill-health, but nevertheless rendered valuable services until discharged in March 1919, as unfit for further military duties.
118, Bennett's Street, Ardwick, Manchester.   Z7099

LYNCH, J., Private, 4th Yorkshire Regiment.
He joined in September 1916, and after a period of service at various home stations, was drafted to the Western Front in July 1918, in time to take part in much severe fighting during the Advance. He returned to England for his demobilisation in September 1919, and holds the General Service and Victory Medals.
57, Bath Street, Miles Platting, Manchester.   Z10715

LYNCH, J., Sapper, R.E.
Volunteering in August 1914, he was drafted to the Western Front early in the following year. During his service in this theatre of war, he took part in the Battles of the Somme, Arras, Vimy Ridge, Lens, and Cambrai, and in heavy fighting at Beaumont-Hamel, Mericourt, and Albert. He was demobilised in January 1919, and holds the 1914-15 Star, and the General Service and Victory Medals.
37, Thornton Street, Manchester.   Z10716B

LYNCH, J. A., Private, R.A.M.C.
He volunteered in September 1914, and was sent to the Western Front in May of the following year. He did consistently good work in this theatre of war, and was attached to the 28th Field Ambulance. He was present at numerous engagements, including the Battles of Ypres II, Festubert, Loos, Albert, Ploegsteert Wood, Vermelles, the Somme, and Beaumont-Hamel, and was wounded and gassed. In February 1917 he was transferred to the East, and saw service in Egypt and Palestine, being present at the Battles of Gaza, the entry into

Jerusalem and Jericho, and the capture of Tripoli and Aleppo. He was demobilised in May 1919, and holds the 1914-15 Star, and the General Service and Victory Medals.
27, Oliver Street, Bradford, Manchester.   Z7102

LYNCH, J. F., Private, Manchester Regiment.
Joining in June 1918, after completing his training he was engaged at various stations with his unit. He rendered valuable services, but was not successful in obtaining his transfer overseas before hostilities ceased. He was demobilised in November 1919.
155, Hamilton Street, Collyhurst, Manchester.   Z9258A

LYNCH, J. J., Private, Highland Light Infantry.
Mobilised at the outbreak of hostilities he was quickly drafted to France, and took part in the Retreat from Mons. He also served at La Bassée, Ypres, Nieuport, Givenchy, and Vimy Ridge, and in many later engagements, until the cessation of hostilities. Returning home, he was demobilised in January 1919, and holds the Mons Star, and the General Service and Victory Medals.
42, Flower Street, Ancoats, Manchester.   Z9617

LYNCH, T., Private, Manchester Regiment.
He volunteered in August 1914, and shortly afterwards was sent to France, where he took part in the Battle of Mons, and other engagements. He was reported missing, and later killed in action on July 17th, 1916. He was entitled to the Mons Star, and the General Service and Victory Medals.
" Steals on the ear the distant triumph song."
155, Hamilton Street, Collyhurst, Manchester.   Z9258B

LYNCH, T. H., Corporal, 1/4th Seaforth Highlanders.
He joined in November 1916, and after a period of training was drafted to the Western Front in the following April. There he played a prominent part in the Battles of Arras, Bullecourt, and Ypres III, and was wounded and taken prisoner in July 1917. After working in the salt mines he was repatriated in February 1919, and demobilised in the same month, holding the General Service and Victory Medals.
34, Queen's Street, Higher Ardwick, Manchester. Z7098

LYNCH, W., Corporal, R.E. (Signal Section).
Joining in November 1916, he was drafted to France in May of the following year, and played a prominent part in the fighting in various sectors, during which he was wounded. He was present at engagements at Ypres, Passchendaele, Lens, Bapaume, and Havrincourt, and after the Armistice proceeded to Germany where he did duty with the Army of Occupation on the Rhine. He returned to England in September 1919, and was demobilised in the following month, and holds the General Service and Victory Medals.
130, Newcastle Street, Hulme, Manchester.   Z7004B

LYNCH, W., Private, M.G.C.
He volunteered in June 1915, and after a period of training was drafted to the Western Front in November 1916. He saw active service at the first Battle of Arras, but owing to ill-health was later invalided home. He was detained for six months at the 3rd Southern General Hospital, Oxford, and after convalescence was discharged in June 1918, as medically unfit for further service. He holds the General Service and Victory Medals.
36, Welbeck Street, Chorlton-on-Medlock, Manchester. Z7100

LYONS, H., Private, Royal Inniskilling Fusiliers.
He joined in July 1917, and after a period of training was drafted to France in the following year. There he took part in many of the concluding engagements of the war, notably the Battle of Ypres, and rendered valuable services during the Advance of 1918, and was wounded. He returned to England, and was demobilised in 1919, holding the General Service and Victory Medals.
50, Thompson Street, Ardwick, Manchester.   Z7103B

LYONS, J., Corporal, King's (Liverpool Regiment).
He joined in September 1917, but owing to his being medically unfit for transfer overseas, was retained on important duties at home stations. He did consistently good work and gained quick promotion to the rank of Corporal, but in July 1918, was discharged as unfit for further service.
109, Mills Street, Ancoats, Manchester.   Z10717

LYONS, J., Private, R.A.M.C.
He volunteered in August 1915, and two months later was drafted to the Western Front, where he took an active part in heavy fighting, and was badly gassed in action during the Somme Offensive in July 1916. In the following month he was discharged as medically unfit for further service, and holds the 1914-15 Star, and the General Service and Victory Medals.
34, Paget Street, Collyhurst, Manchester.   Z10718

LYONS, M., Private, 8th Manchester Regiment.
He volunteered in December 1915, and completing his training was engaged at various stations on important duties with his unit. He rendered valuable services, but was not successful in obtaining his transfer overseas before the cessation of hostilities, and in March 1917 was transferred to the Royal Army Medical Corps. In June 1919 he proceeded to Russia and remained there until the Evacuation in October of that year. He holds the General Service Medal.
33, Nicholson Street, Rochdale Road, Manchester. Z11542

LYONS, T. W., L/Cpl., 1/7th Manchester Regiment.
Volunteering in August 1914, he first saw service in Egypt, and later was drafted to the Dardanelles, where he was in action at the Landing at Suvla Bay. In 1917 he was transferred to the Western Front, and after taking part in many engagements in this theatre of war was invalided to England suffering from wounds received at Nieuport. He was discharged as unfit for further service in October 1918, and holds the 1914–15 Star, and the General Service and Victory Medals.
50, Thompson Street, Ardwick, Manchester. Z7103A

M

MACAULAY, R., Pte., 15th Highland Light Infantry.
Joining in November 1916, he proceeded to the Western Front in the following year, and there saw fighting in various sectors. He took part in the Battles of the Somme, and Armentières, and many other important engagements, and also fought in the Retreat and Advance of 1918. He was demobilised on his return to England in October 1919, and holds the General Service and Victory Medals.
51, Bothal Park, Rose, Lanarkshire, Scotland. Z7132

MACBETH, G., Private, 15th Royal Scots.
He volunteered in September 1914, and underwent a period of training prior to being drafted to the Western Front in June 1916. There he took part in the Battles of the Somme, Arras, Ypres, Passchendaele, and Armentières, and many other engagements until invalided home, suffering from rheumatism. He re-joined his unit in France, however, in October 1918, and was in action until the cessation of hostilities. He was demobilised in March 1919, and holds the General Service and Victory Medals.
30, George's Avenue, Chester Road, Hulme, Manchester. Z7128

MACBRIDE, F., Private, Border Regiment.
He volunteered in August 1914, and in the following year proceeded to the Dardanelles, where he was wounded in action at the Landing at Suvla Bay. Invalided to hospital at Alexandria, he was transferred to the Western Front on his recovery in 1916, and was there again wounded in the Somme Offensive of July of that year. He rejoined his unit on his recovery, and was wounded a third time at Ypres in 1917, afterwards taking part in the Retreat and Advance of 1918. He was demobilised in May 1919, and holds the 1914–15 Star, and the General Service and Victory Medals.
58, Bennett Street, Ardwick, Manchester. Z7129A

MACBRIDE, J. A., Private, Manchester Regiment.
Volunteering in December 1914, he was drafted to the Western Front in June of the following year, and there took part in important engagements in various sectors. He made the supreme sacrifice, falling in action at Ypres on December 8th, 1915. He was entitled to the 1914–15 Star, and the General Service and Victory Medals.
" He died the noblest death a man may die,
Fighting for God and right and liberty."
58, Bennett Street, Ardwick, Manchester. Z7129C

MACBRIDE, W. Private, 4th Royal Scots.
He volunteered at the outbreak of war in August 1914, and in May of the following year was drafted to the Dardanelles, where he saw much severe fighting. He died gloriously on the Field of Battle in Gallipoli on June 28th, 1918. He was entitled to the 1914–15 Star, and the General Service and Victory Medals.
" Great deeds cannot die ;
They, with the sun and moon renew their light for ever."
58, Bennett Street, Ardwick, Manchester. Z7129B

MACDONALD, W., Pte., 1st King's (L'pool Regt.)
He joined in February 1916, and two months later was drafted to the Western Front, where he took part in heavy fighting at St. Eloi, and the Ancre. He was also in action at the Battles of Arras, Lens, and Cambrai, where he was badly wounded. Invalided to England he was discharged in March 1918 as medically unfit for further service, and holds the General Service and Victory Medals.
14, Tongue Street, Ardwick, Manchester. Z7152

MACHIN, J., Private, 1st Manchester Regiment.
Joining in May 1916, he proceeded to Egypt in the following month, and there served at Cairo, Alexandria, Khartoum, and various other stations. Later he took part in the Advance into Palestine, and was present at the Capture of Jerusalem, Jericho, and Tripoli, and in many other important engagements, until the cessation of hostilities. He served also for a short time in Italy, before returning home for demobilisation in December 1919, and holds the General Service and Victory Medals. 65, Long Street, Ancoats, Manchester. Z7112

MACHIN, W., Private, Manchester Regiment and 4th King's (Liverpool Regiment).
Three months after joining in June 1916, he proceeded to the Western Front, where he saw severe fighting in various sectors, taking part in the Battles of the Somme, Ypres, and Cambrai, and many other important engagements. He died gloriously on the Field of Battle on the Somme in April 1918. He was entitled to the General Service and Victory Medals.
" He joined the great white company of valiant souls."
22, Herbert Street, Ardwick, Manchester. Z7163

MACK, A., Sergt., 2/6th Manchester Regiment.
Mobilised with the Territorials in August 1914, he proceeded to France in April of the following year, and there saw severe fighting in various sectors of the front. After taking part in the Battles of Vimy Ridge, Ypres, and Passchendaele, and many other important engagements, he was invalided home in December 1917, suffering from trench fever, and was in hospital at Newcastle. Serving after his recovery, as a musketry Instructor, he re-engaged for a further period on the cessation of hostilities, and was finally demobilised in February 1920. He holds the 1914–15 Star, and the General Service, Victory, and Territorial Efficiency Medals.
47, Russell Street, Moss Side, Manchester. TZ7166

MACK, G. W., Private, 3rd Cheshire Regiment.
He joined in November 1916, and after a period of training served at various stations on important duties in connection with the stores. He was not successful in obtaining his transfer overseas before hostilities ended, but rendered valuable services until demobilised in January 1919.
36, Alma Street, Collyhurst, Manchester. Z11547

MACK, M., Private, 2/5th Lancashire Fusiliers.
He volunteered in January 1916, and embarking for France four months later served in various parts of the line. He went into action with his Battalion in several engagements in the Ypres Salient and on the Somme, and was severely wounded. Admitted to a Base hospital he was later evacuated to England for further treatment, and on recovery was engaged on home service duties. He was demobilised in January 1919, and holds the General Service and Victory Medals.
16, Marsh Street, Ancoats, Manchester. Z10755

MACK, R., Pioneer, R.E.
Joining in June 1918, he completed his training, and was engaged on important duties with his unit at various depôts in the South of England. He rendered valuable services, but was unable to procure his transfer to a theatre of war before hostilities were concluded, and was demobilised in January 1919.
4, Rigel Street, Ancoats, Manchester. Z10754

MACKIE, T., Private, Lancashire Fusiliers.
After joining in September 1916, he underwent a short period of training prior to being drafted to Salonika in January of the following year. There he saw much severe fighting on the Macedonian front until transferred to the Western Front, in time to take part in the Allies' Advance of 1918. He was afterwards stationed at Bonn until his return home for demobilisation in May 1919, and holds the General Service and Victory Medals. 4, South Street, Ardwick, Manchester. Z7173

MACKIN, T., Gunner, R.G.A.
He joined in October 1917, and crossing to the Western Front in the following March fought in the Battle of the Somme II, and several engagements during the German Offensive. He also took part in operations at Amiens, Bapaume, Havrincourt, Cambrai II, and Le Cateau, in the subsequent Allied Advance of 1918. He then proceeded with the Army of Occupation into Germany, and was stationed at Cologne until his return home for demobilisation in December 1919. He holds the General Service and Victory Medals.
53, Dalton Street, Collyhurst, Manchester. Z10359

MADDEN, A., Gunner, R.G.A., and Private, R.A.S.C.
He volunteered in August 1914, and in December of the following year proceeded to the Western Front, where he served in various sectors. He saw much heavy fighting on the Somme until wounded in action in the Offensive of August 1916, and invalided home. He returned to France, however, on his recovery in November of that year and served with the Royal Army Service Corps until his demobilisation in April 1919. He holds the 1914–15 Star, and the General Service and Victory Medals. 1 Raw St., Collyhurst, Manchester. Z11926

MADDEN, D., Private, Monmouthshire Regiment.
He was mobilised in August 1914, and was immediately drafted to the Western Front, where he served through the fighting at Mons, and afterwards took part in other important engagements. He died gloriously on the Field of Battle in February 1915. He was entitled to the Mons Star, and the General Service and Victory Medals.
" The path of duty was the way to glory."
25, Brown Street, Ancoats, Manchester. TZ11927A

MADDEN, J., Private, 6th Manchester Regiment.
He joined in November 1917, and in the following month proceeded to the Western Front. Whilst overseas he took part in much of the heavy fighting at Cambrai and in various engagements in the Retreat and Advance of 1918 until the Armistice was signed. He returned to England and was demobilised in October 1919, and holds the General Service and Victory Medals.
13, Williams Place, Ancoats, Manchester. Z8913A

MALLARD, J. E., L/Corporal, 16th Manchester Regt.
Mobilised from the Reserve at the declaration of war, he was sent to France in September of the following year and fought in the Battles of Loos, Albert and Ploegsteert. He was unfortunately killed in action on July 30th, 1916, during the first Battle of the Somme. He was entitled to the 1914-15 Star, and the General Service and Victory Medals.
"His memory is cherished with pride."
22, Woodward Street, Ancoats, Manchester.   Z9632A

MALLING, H., Private, 4th Manchester Regiment.
Volunteering in August 1914, he was retained on important home duties until November 1915, when he was sent to the Western Front, where he saw much heavy fighting. He took part in engagements in various sectors of the Front, and fought in the Battles of Arras (I), Ypres (III), Cambrai (I), the Somme, Bapaume, Havrincourt and Le Cateau, and remained in this sector until the cessation of hostilities. He was demobilised in February 1919, and holds the 1914-15 Star, and the General Service and Victory Medals.
61, Nelson Street, Bradford, Manchester.   Z7219

MALONE, E., Sapper, R.E.
Volunteering in August 1914, he landed in France in the following June and was engaged on important duties during operations at Festubert, Vimy Ridge, and was wounded on the Somme in September 1916. On recovery he rejoined his unit and was present at the Battles of Bullecourt, Lens, Cambrai, and was taken prisoner in April 1918. Repatriated after the Armistice, he was subsequently demobilised, but re-enlisted in July 1919 and sent to Turkey, and was still serving there in 1920. He holds the 1914-15 Star, and the General Service and Victory Medals.
36, Anslow Street, Rochdale Road, Manchester.   Z10780

MALONEY, D., Private, R.A.V.C.
He joined in June 1917, and was immediately drafted to France. In this theatre of war he was engaged on important duties attending to the horses whilst stationed at Amiens, Etaples and Boulogne, where he rendered valuable services until returning home for demobilisation in February 1919. He holds the General Service and Victory Medals.
1, Halton Street, Chorlton-on-Medlock, Manchester. Z7213

MALONEY, J., Pte., 11th and 42nd Manchester Regt.
He volunteered in September 1914, and embarking for Gallipoli in the following June took part in the Landing at Suvla Bay and many other engagements. Sent to Egypt in 1916, he served in the Canal zone and in operations during the advance through Palestine. Transferred in March 1917 to the Western Front, he was in action at Ypres, the Somme II, and in the Retreat and Advance of 1918, and returned home for demobilisation in February 1919. He holds the 1914-15 Star, and the General Service and Victory Medals.
69, Montague Street, Collyhurst, Manchester.   Z10781

MALONEY, L., Private, K.O. (R. Lancaster Regt.)
Volunteering in November 1915, he proceeded to France in the following year and was in action at Loos, St. Eloi, Albert, and on the Somme. He also fought in the engagements at Bullecourt, Messines, Ypres and throughout the German and Allied Offensives of 1918. During his active service he was twice wounded. He was demobilised in January 1919, and holds the General Service and Victory Medals.
29, Baguley Street, Miles Platting, Manchester.   Z9633

MALPAS, W., Private, Lancashire Fusiliers.
He volunteered in November 1915, and in the following September embarked for Egypt, where he was engaged on garrison and other duties for some months. Proceeding to the Western Front in March 1917, he was in action in the Battles of Bullecourt and Ypres, and was gassed on September 9th, 1917, and invalided home. After treatment he served at various depôts in England until demobilised in April 1919. He holds the General Service and Victory Medals.
28, Edge Street, Hulme, Manchester.   Z11761

MALTBY, G., Private, 11th Manchester Regiment.
Joining in March 1917, he was drafted to the Western Front later in that year and fought in many important engagements. Owing to ill-health he returned to England, and after receiving treatment in hospital was invalided out of the Service in August 1918. He subsequently died on March 17th, 1919, and was entitled to the General Service and Victory Medals.
"He passed out of the sight of men by the path of duty and self-sacrifice."
14, Lindley Street, Newton Heath, Manchester.   Z9568B

MANFORD, J., 1st Class Stoker, Mechanician, R.N.
At the outbreak of war he was serving as a Private in the Howe Battalion of the Royal Naval Division, and immediately proceeded to France, where he saw much severe fighting. In April 1915 he was transferred to the Dardanelles, took part in the Landing at Cape Helles and the three Battles of Krithia, and was wounded in action in June 1915. After treatment in hospital, he returned to Gallipoli in October 1915, and served there until the Evacuation of the Peninsula three months later. He then qualified as a Stoker-Mechanician on H.M.S.

"Indus" at Devonport and afterwards served on board the motor-lighter "X223," on submarine chasing duties in the English Channel. He received his discharge in March 1919, and holds the 1914 Star, and the General Service and Victory Medals.   Z7215
23, St. Clements Place, Grey Street, West Gorton, Manchester.

MANFORD, J. J., 1/7th Manchester Regiment.
He volunteered in August 1914, and after a period of training was sent to the Dardanelles, where he took part in the Battles of Krithia, and was wounded in June 1915. On his recovery he proceeded to the Western Front, and was in action at the Battles of Arras. He was demobilised in February 1919, and holds the 1914-15 Star, and the General Service and Victory Medals.
19, Francis Street, Chorlton-on-Medlock, Manchester. TZ7214

MANFORD, W., Private, 11th Manchester Regt.
Volunteering in September 1914, he embarked in the following year for Gallipoli and took part in the Landing at Suvla Bay and other actions until the Evacuation of the Peninsula. He was then sent to Egypt, and after serving there for several months, proceeded to the Western Front in August 1916, fought in many important battles, including those of Ypres and in the Retreat and Advance of 1918. He returned to England in 1919, and was demobilised in February of that year, and holds the 1914-15 Star, and the General Service and Victory Medals.
37, Clayton Street, Ancoats, Manchester.   Z10782

MANION, W., Private, R.A.M.C.
He joined in October 1916, and in the following April was drafted to Egypt, where he served at Alexandria and Cairo. He was also present at various engagements in Palestine, including the capture of Jerusalem. In June 1918 he was invalided to hospital in England suffering from malarial fever, and was finally discharged as medically unfit for further service in August 1919. He holds the General Service and Victory Medals.
27, Bremmer Street, Stockport Road, Chorlton-on-Medlock, Manchester.   Z7220

MANLEY, J., Private, South Lancashire Regiment.
He volunteered in December 1914, and after completing a period of training was retained on important duties at various home stations until January 1917, when he proceeded to the Western Front. During his service in this seat of war he took part in much severe fighting in many sectors of the Front, including the Battles of Passchendaele and Armentières, where he was wounded. On his recovery he again proceeded to the fighting area, and was wounded and gassed at Ypres. He was invalided home and discharged in October 1918, and holds the General Service and Victory Medals.
26, Armitage Street, Ardwick, Manchester.   Z7216

MANNING, J., Gunner, R.F.A.
He volunteered in August 1914, and crossing to France in November of the following year served with his Battery on this Front until the end of the war. During this period he fought in the Battles of Loos, Albert, the Somme, Arras, Bullecourt, Ypres (III), Cambrai and in the Retreat and Advance of 1918. He returned home for his demobilisation in February 1919, and holds the 1914-15 Star, and the General Service and Victory Medals.
45, Elizabeth Street, West Gorton, Manchester.   Z10783

MANNING, J. E., Gunner, R.F.A.
He volunteered in May 1915, and on completing his training in July of the following year, was drafted to Mesopotamia, where he saw much service during heavy fighting on the Tigris. Afterwards he was transferred to India, where he rendered valuable services until demobilised in October 1919. He holds the General Service and Victory Medals.
13, Ashbourne Street, West Gorton, Manchester.   Z7218

MANNING, R., Driver, R.F.A.
Volunteering in August 1914, he quickly proceeded to the Western Front and took part in much severe fighting with his Battery in various sectors. He was seriously wounded in action at Festubert, and unfortunately died in hospital in 1915. He was entitled to the 1914-15 Star, and the General Service and Victory Medals.
"His life for his Country, his soul to God."
18, Morton Street, Chorlton-on-Medlock, Manchester. X7217

MANNION, T., Gunner, R.G.A.
He joined in March 1916, and after his training was drafted to the Western Front in the same year. He took an important part in many of the Battles, including those at Messines Ridge, Ypres, Passchendaele and Cambrai, where he was taken prisoner in December 1917. During his period of captivity he was chiefly engaged on railway duties in Munster until the cessation of hostilities, when he returned to England and was demobilised in February 1919. He holds the General Service and Victory Medals.
9, Neptune Street, Ancoats, Manchester.   Z7221

MANNION, F., Private, King's (Liverpool Regt.)
Volunteering in August 1914, he completed his training and served with his unit at various stations engaged on guard and other duties. He did good work, but was unable to obtain his transfer overseas on account of medical unfitness, and was discharged in consequence in April 1916.
15, Diggles Street, Ancoats, Manchester. Z10784

MANSFIELD, S. (O.B.E.), British Warrant Officer (Indian Army).
Previously to joining the Army in August 1917, he was employed on important munition work, and in recognition of his valuable services in this connection was appointed an Officer of the Order of the British Empire. After his enlistment he served for a time in India, and was then transferred to Mesopotamia, where he was engaged in the workshops and docks with the Royal Engineers at Basra. He was demobilised in June 1920, and holds the General Service and Victory Medals. 29, Link St., Longsight, Manchester. Z7222

MANSFIELD, S., Private, 17th Lancashire Fusiliers.
He volunteered in April 1915, and in the following December proceeded to France. During his service in this theatre of war he took part in much of the severe fighting, and was in action at the Battles of Neuve Chapelle, Albert and the Somme, where he was wounded and gassed in July 1916. On his recovery he again went into the fighting area, and took part in the 2nd Battle of the Somme, where he was killed in action on May 22nd, 1918. He was entitled to the 1914-15 Star, and the General Service and Victory Medals.
"He died the noblest death a man may die,
Fighting for God and right and liberty."
25, Upper Dover Street, Bradford, Manchester. TZ7116

MANUEL, C., Gunner, R.N.V.R.
He joined in November 1916, and after completing his training was posted to a vessel in which he served on look-out and other duties until the end of hostilities. His ship was engaged in carrying foodstuffs and other cargoes between West African ports, the United Kingdom and the Argentine. In November 1918, he sailed for Salonika, and after a period of service in Greek waters, returned home for demobilisation in April 1919. He holds the General Service and Victory Medals.
34, Burn Street, Bradford, Manchester. Z10786

MAPE, J., Private, Cheshire Regiment.
He joined in January 1916, and was retained on important duties at various stations with his unit until March 1917, when he was sent to France. Whist in this theatre of war he took part in the fighting at Arras, and was later invalided home suffering from influenza. On his recovery he was engaged on garrison duties until his demobilisation in September 1919. He holds the General Service and Victory Medals.
76, Gibbons Street, Bradford, Manchester. Z7120

MARCHANT, C. E., Private, R.A.S.C.
He joined in June 1917, and three months later embarked for France, where he saw much service in the Ypres salient and the Arras and Cambrai sectors, driving a staff car. He saw heavy fighting throughout the Retreat and Advance of 1918, and in the following year became seriously ill. Admitted into hospital, he died in March 1919, and was entitled to the General Service and Victory Medals.
"His memory is cherished with pride."
48, Brunt Street, Rusholme, Manchester. Z9634

MARCHANT, J., Driver, R.A.S.C. (M.T.)
He volunteered in the Royal Army Medical Corps in September 1915, and was retained at home on important duties with his unit. Later he was transferred to the Royal Army Service Corps, and in March 1918, proceeded to the Western Front, where he rendered good services as a motor transport driver, and was engaged in conveying ammunition to various sectors of the Front. He remained in this theatre of war until June 1919, when he returned to England, and was demobilised. He holds the General Service and Victory Medals.
3, Lindum Street, Rusholme, Manchester. Z7223

MARKHAM, H., Private, 3rd Manchester Regt.
He joined in July 1918, and two months later was drafted to the Western Front, where he did consistently good work until after the cessation of hostilities. He then proceeded to Germany with the Army of Occupation, but was later recalled for service with a mobile column in Ireland. In 1920 he was still with his unit, and holds the General Service and Victory Medals. 39, Link St., Longsight, Manchester. Z7224B

MARKHAM, W., Private, King's (Liverpool Regt.)
He volunteered in August 1914, and in the following November was drafted to the Western Front. During his service in this theatre of war, he took part in the Battles of Ypres, Loos, the Somme, Arras, Passchendaele, Cambrai, Havrincourt, and Le Cateau. He was also in action in other important engagements in the Retreat and Advance of 1918, and was wounded a few days before the cessation of hostilities. After hospital treatment at Rouen, he was demobilised in February 1919, and holds the 1914-15 Star, and the General Service and Victory Medals.
39, Link Street, Longsight, Manchester. Z7224A

MARKS, W., Private, Cheshire Regiment.
Joining in May 1918, he embarked for France two months later, and fought in many of the principal battles during the Allied Advance of that year, at the conclusion of which he proceeded with the Army of Occupation to Germany. He was demobilised on his return to England in September 1919, and holds the General Service and Victory Medals.
17, Sun Street, Newton Heath, Manchester. Z10789

MARNEY, D., Private, 8th Manchester Regiment.
Volunteering in August 1914, he was sent to the Western Front in the following July, and took part in the Battles of Albert, the Somme (during which he was in action at Beaucourt and Beaumont-Hamel), Arras, and Vimy Ridge, where he was badly wounded in April 1917. He was admitted to hospital at Evesham, and on his recovery was retained on important duties at home until demobilised in April 1919. He holds the 1914-15 Star, and the General Service and Victory Medals.
3, Dalton Street, Chorlton-on-Medlock, Manchester. Z7225

MARRIAN, W., Private, 6th Manchester Regiment.
Volunteering in October 1914, he completed his training, and served with his unit at several stations. He did good work on coastal defence duties on the South East Coast, and at the prisoners-of-war camp in the Isle of Man. He was not sent overseas owing to medical unfitness, and was discharged in consequence in July 1917.
43, George Street, Moss Side, Manchester. Z11762

MARRS, J., Corporal, R.A.M.C.
Volunteering in September 1915, he proceeded to France two months later, and rendered valuable services with the 97th Field Ambulance at the Loos, St. Eloi, Albert, and on the Ancre. He also played an active part in the Battles of the Somme, Arras, Cambrai, Bapaume, and the Marne. Demobilised on returning to England in January 1919, he holds the 1914-15 Star, and the General Service and Victory Medals.
30, Carver Street, Hulme, Manchester. TZ7226

MARSDEN, A., Private, 5th Devonshire Regiment.
He joined in February 1917, and in November of the same year was drafted to the East. In this theatre of war he saw much service, and took part in the operations on the Suez Canal, and later in the fighting at Baghdad. He was unhappily killed in the Jaffa sector on April 10th, 1918, and was entitled to the General Service and Victory Medals.
"Honour to the immortal dead, who gave their youth that the world might grow old in peace."
89, Carisbrooke Street, Harpurhey, Manchester. Z11549A

MARSDEN, C., Private, 3rd King's (Liverpool Regt.)
He joined in April 1918, and on completion of his training was engaged on special guard duties in prisoner-of-war camps at Aldershot. He was unsuccessful in obtaining his transfer overseas, but did consistently good work with his unit until taken seriously ill and admitted to hospital, whence he was discharged in August 1919.
79, Henry Street, Ardwick, Manchester. Z7227

MARSDEN, G., Sergt., 2nd Sherwood Foresters.
He was in the Army when war was declared, and almost immediately proceeded to France. He fought in the Retreat from Mons, and at the Battles of Le Cateau, La Bassée, Ypres, and Neuve Chapelle, and was wounded. In March 1915, he was discharged as time expired, and holds the Mons Star, and the General Service and Victory Medals.
569, Collyhurst Road, Manchester. Z11550

MARSDEN, J., Private, 8th Manchester Regiment.
He volunteered in October 1915, and served at various stations until drafted to Egypt in the following May. He was on duty in the Canal zone for a time and then was transferred to France, and was in action in the Battles of Arras and Vimy Ridge. He gave his life for the freedom of England in December 1917 at Ypres, and was entitled to the General Service and Victory Medals.
"His life for his Country his soul to God."
109, Naylor Street, Oldham Road, Manchester. Z9635

MARSDEN, J., Gunner, R.G.A.
Joining in September 1917 he crossed to France in March of the following year, and served in many sectors of the Front. He remained in the devastated area until demobilised in November 1919, and holds the General Service and Victory Medals.
89, Carisbrooke Street, Harpurhey, Manchester. Z11549B

MARSDEN, J. D., Private, 18th Manchester Regt.
He volunteered in March 1915, and after a period of training in England and Wales, was sent to France in July 1916. During the Battle of the Somme, he was in action at Montauban, Guillemont (where he was wounded), and Trônes Wood, and was taken prisoner in the same sector in 1917. Whilst in captivity in Silesia, he suffered many hardships, and was eventually repatriated and demobilised in March 1919. He holds the General Service and Victory Medals.
4, Grove Street, Rusholme, Manchester. Z7229

MARSDEN, W., Pte., 1st Vol. Bn., Manchester Regt.
He joined in September 1916, and during his service did consistently good work whilst engaged as a Special Constable on night duty, when he acted as guard over munition factories. He unfortunately met with a serious accident whilst on duty and was discharged in August 1917.
8, Lyme Street, Chorlton-on-Medlock, Manchester.   Z7228

MARSDEN, W., Driver, R.E.
He volunteered in September 1915, and in the following January proceeded overseas. After several months service in Egypt and Sinai, he was drafted to France in March 1917, and was engaged on important duties in connection with the Battles of Arras, Vimy Ridge, Messines, Ypres, Cambrai, and in the Retreat and Advance of 1918. He was sent into Germany after the Armistice, and served with the Army of Occupation until his return to England in January 1919. Demobilised a month later he holds the General Service and Victory Medals.
42, Allen Street, Hulme Manchester.   Z11763A

MARSDEN, W. A., Private, Royal Welch Fusiliers.
He joined in September 1917, and landing in France in the following April saw heavy fighting at Albert, High Wood, and other places during the German Offensive. He gave his life for the freedom of England at Montauban on August 26th, 1918, and was entitled to the General Service and Victory Medals.
"His life for his Country, his soul to God."
42, Allan Street, Hulme, Manchester.   Z11763B

MARSH, A. T., Private, 1st Border Regiment.
He joined in June 1917, and on completion of his training later in the same year, was drafted to Mesopotamia, where he saw much severe fighting during the Advance towards Mosul. He was in an Australian Base Hospital for some time owing to a serious illness. Demobilised in November 1919, he holds the General Service and Victory Medals.
97, Junction Street, Ancoats, Manchester.   Z7121

MARSH, D., Private, Manchester Regiment, and Royal Welch Fusiliers.
He volunteered in March 1915, and in December proceeded to the Western Front, where he was wounded in action at Suzanne in January 1916. He was invalided home, but, on his recovery, rejoined his unit, and was in action at Beaumont-Hamel, Beaucourt, La Bassée, Hill 60, Arras, Festubert, and Albert. Later he was transferred to Egypt, and after heavy fighting in the Suez Canal zone, proceeded to Palestine, and took part in the Battles of Gaza, and the capture of Jerusalem. In June 1918, he returned to France, was again wounded in July at Festubert, and in the following month was taken prisoner on the Somme. Repatriated in April 1919, he was then demobilised, and holds the 1914–15 Star, and the General Service and Victory Medals.
74, Higher Chatham Street, Chorlton-on-Medlock, Manchester.   Z7231

MARSH, G., L/Corporal, 1st Essex Regiment.
Volunteering in August 1914, he was drafted to France in the following May, and took part in the Battles of Ypres (II), and Loos, and in heavy fighting at St. Eloi, and Albert, where he was wounded in April 1916. After three months in hospital at Rouen, he rejoined his unit, and was in action at the Battles of the Somme, the Ancre, Ypres (III), Cambrai, Amiens, and Le Cateau, and in other important engagements during the Retreat and Advance of 1918. He then served in Germany with the Army of Occupation for two months, and was demobilised in January 1919, holding the 1914–15 Star, and the General Service and Victory Medals.
21, Robson Street, Hulme, Manchester.   Z7230A

MARSH, J., Private, Royal Welsh Fusiliers.
He joined in April 1917, and sent to France in the following September, proceeded to Egypt in the next month. He served at various stations on guard and other duties, and in September 1918 was drafted to Salonika, where he was on duty until February 1919. He then returned to England, and was demobilised in September of that year, holding the General Service and Victory Medals.
10, Nicholson Street, Rochdale Road, Manchester.   Z9636

MARSH, M. (Miss), Worker, Q.M.A.A.C.
She joined in August 1917, and during her service did consistently good work as a cook in a disembarkation camp at Dover. She rendered very valuable services in this capacity until her demobilisation in September 1919.
21, Robson Street, Hulme, Manchester.   Z7230B

MARSHALL, F., Private, Cheshire Regiment.
He volunteered in February 1915, and in April was drafted to France, where he took part in the Battles of Hill 60, Festubert, Vermelles, the Somme, Arras, and Bullecourt. Unfortunately he was killed in action at the third Battle of Ypres in July 1917, and was entitled to the 1914–15 Star, and the General Service and Victory Medals.
"He died the noblest death a man may die,
Fighting for God and right and liberty."
99A, Forbes Street, West Gorton, Manchester.   TZ7237

MARSHALL, F. E., Gunner, R.F.A.
Volunteering in February 1915, he was quickly drafted to the Western Front, and was in action with his Battery at the Battles of St. Eloi, Ypres, Festubert, Loos, the Somme, Arras, Vimy Ridge, Messines, and Cambrai. In December 1916 he was badly injured as the result of an accident. He remained in France until his demobilisation in May 1919, and holds the 1914–15 Star, and the General Service and Victory Medals.
4, Brougham Street, West Gorton, Manchester.   Z7235

MARSHALL, J., Private, 1/8th Manchester Regt.
Having previously served with the Territorials, he volunteered in September 1914, and in the following April embarked for the Dardanelles, and took part in the first Landing on the Peninsula, and the Battles of Krithia and Achi Baba. Owing to a severe wound received in action at Suvla Bay in August 1915, he was invalided home, and after hospital treatment was discharged as medically unfit in September 1917. He holds the 1914–15 Star, and the General Service and Victory Medals. 110, Beaumont St., Beswick, Manchester.   Z10788

MARSHALL, J. E., Driver, R.A.S.C.
Joining in March 1917, he was sent to Egypt three months later and served in that theatre of war for over two years. During this period he was engaged on important transport duties in the British Advance through Palestine, and was present at the Battle of Gaza, and the capture of Damascus. Retained on special duties after hostilities ended, he returned home in October 1919, was demobilised a month later. He holds the General Service and Victory Medals.
14, Howard Avenue, Ardwick, Manchester.   Z11764

MARSHALL, R., Driver, R.A.S.C.
He joined in April 1918, and after his training was engaged on important transport duties at various home stations. He was not successful in securing his transfer overseas before the conclusion of hostilities, but afterwards proceeded with the Army of Occupation to Germany. He was demobilised on his return to England in November 1919.
82, Long Street, Ancoats, Manchester.   TZ11436

MARSHALL, T., Private, Cheshire Regiment.
He volunteered in November 1915, and after three months training, was drafted to the Western Front, where he played a prominent part in the heavy fighting at Albert, and La Bassée during the Somme Offensive. He was badly wounded in action in July 1916, and was evacuated to England for hospital treatment. On his recovery, he did consistently good work until invalided from the Army in March 1918, and holds the General Service and Victory Medals.
99A, Forbes Street, West Gorton, Manchester.   TZ7238

MARSHALL, W., Corporal, King's (Liverpool Regt.)
Three months after volunteering, he proceeded to France in July 1915, and served with distinction at the Battles of Loos, Albert, the Somme (I), Arras, Vimy Ridge, Ypres (III), Cambrai and the Somme (II). He was also in action at St. Eloi, and during the Retreat, and fought at the Battles of Havrincourt and Le Cateau during the Advance of 1918. After the cessation of hostilities, he took part in the march into Germany, and was demobilised in January 1919, holding the 1914–15 Star, and the General Service and Victory Medals.
4, Vulcan Street, Ardwick, Manchester.   Z7239

MARSHALL, W., L/Corpl., 2nd Royal Welch Fusiliers.
Volunteering in May 1915, he crossed to France in June of the succeeding year, and fought in engagements at Loos, the Somme, Cambrai, Péronne, La Bassée, Vimy Ridge, Ypres, and Passchendaele. In June 1918, he was so severely wounded in action on the Somme, as to necessitate his return to England, and after hospital treatment was invalided out of the Service in the following March. He holds the General Service and Victory Medals.
91, Montague Street, Collyhurst, Manchester.   Z10787

MARSHALL, W., Private, 8th Manchester Regiment.
Volunteering in September 1914, he completed six months' training, and then proceeded to France in the following February. After taking part in the Battles of Neuve Chapelle, St. Eloi, Hill 60, and Ypres (II), he died gloriously on the Field of Battle at Festubert in May 1915. He was entitled to the 1914–15 Star, and the General Service and Victory Medals.
"Nobly striving,
He nobly fell that we might live."
31, Lomas Street, Ancoats, Manchester.   Z7236

MARSHALL, W. E., Pte., 2nd Lancashire Fusiliers.
Having volunteered in April 1915, he first saw active service in the Dardanelles, where he took part in much severe fighting until the Evacuation of the Gallipoli Peninsula. He then served in Egypt for a time before proceeding to the Western Front, where he played a prominent part in many important engagements, and was wounded in action in 1916 and in 1918. He returned home for demobilisation in November 1919, and holds the 1914–15 Star, and the General Service and Victory Medals.
12, Franchise Street, Ardwick, Manchester.   X7232-3

MARSHALL, W., Gunner, R.F.A.

He volunteered in October 1915, and in the following January was sent to Mesopotamia, where he was in action with his Battery in many important engagements. He took part in the Battles of Um-el-Hannah, Sanna-i-Yat, Kut-el-Amara, and was present at the Occupation of Baghdad, and Mosul. Demobilised on his return to England in April 1919, he holds the General Service and Victory Medals.

37, Geoffrey Street, Chorlton-on-Medlock, Manchester. Z7234

MARSHALL, W. F., C.S.M., 13th King's (L'pool Regt.)

Volunteering in September 1914, he was drafted to the Western Front in the following March, and took an active part in the Battles of St. Eloi, Hill 60, and Loos. Found unfit for service in the trenches he was engaged on important work at prisoners-of-war camps for a year, and was then sent to the Base after being transferred to the Labour Corps. In January 1918 he returned to England and served on special duties until demobilised in May 1919. He holds the 1914–15 Star, and the General Service and Victory Medals.

17, Allen Street, Hulme, Manchester. Z11765

MARSLAND, J., Private, King's (Liverpool Regt.)

Volunteering in September 1915, he was first drafted to Mesopotamia in the following January, and after a period of garrison duty there, was transferred to Salonika. He saw much severe fighting in the Balkan theatre of war until March 1917, when he was invalided home with malarial fever. After hospital treatment at Salford, he was discharged as medically unfit for further service in March 1918, and holds the General Service and Victory Medals.

55, Milton Street, Bradford, Manchester. TZ7240

MARTIN, A., Stoker, R.N.

He enlisted in September 1912, and at the outbreak of war in August 1914, proceeded to the North Sea on board H.M.S. "New Zealand," and took part in the Battles of Heligoland Bight, and the Dogger Bank. He also cruised in Australian and South African waters, but was invalided from the Royal Navy in March 1916, owing to chronic chest trouble, and holds the 1914–15 Star, and the General Service and Victory Medals.

43, Wigley Street, Ardwick, Manchester. Z7241

MARTIN, A., L/Cpl., K.O. (Royal Lancaster Regt.)

Volunteering at the outbreak of war he was drafted to France in January 1915, after the completion of his training, and took a prominent part in the second Battle of Ypres, where he fell gallantly fighting on May 8th, 1915. He was entitled to the 1914–15 Star, and the General Service and Victory Medals.

"Courage, bright hopes, and a myriad dreams splendidly given."

2, Crossby's Buildings, Miles Platting, Manchester. Z9272

MARTIN, C., Private, Border Regiment.

He joined in June 1916, and in April of the following year was drafted to the Western Front, where he played an important part in the Battles of Arras, Messines, Ypres, Passchendaele, Cambrai, the Aisne (III), and the Marne, and in other engagements during the Retreat and Advance of 1918. In February 1919 he proceeded to Ireland on garrison duty, and remained there until his demobilisation in the following September. He holds the General Service and Victory Medals.

10, Deramore Street, Rusholme, Manchester. Z7244

MARTIN, C. H., Private, 6th Manchester Regt.

He joined in March 1916, and in April of the following year proceeded to France. Here he fought in numerous engagements during the Retreat of 1918, and was taken prisoner. Whilst in captivity he was made to work behind the German lines until the Armistice. He was then released and eventually demobilised in March 1920, holding the General Service and Victory Medals.

555, Collyhurst Road, Manchester. Z11551

MARTIN, E., Private, Durham Light Infantry.

He joined the 54th Training Reserve Battalion in March 1917, and on being transferred to the Durham Light Infantry, was drafted to France in April 1918. During his service on the Western Front, he took part in much severe fighting in the Ypres sector, and in the Retreat and Advance of 1918. At the cessation of hostilities he was invalided home, but on his recovery, served on Salisbury Plain. He was demobilised in November 1919, and holds the General Service and Victory Medals. 16, Talbot St., Ardwick, Manchester. Z7242

MARTIN, E. J., Pte., 2nd East Lancashire Regt.

He volunteered in June 1915, and in September of the following year embarked for France. During his service on the Western Front he fought in the Battles of the Somme, Nieuport, and Arras, but fell gloriously on the Field of Battle at Passchendaele Ridge on November 20th, 1917. He was entitled to the General Service and Victory Medals.

"He passed out of the sight of men by the path of duty and self-sacrifice."

10, Walter Street, Ancoats, Manchester. Z9273

MARTIN, G., Sapper, R.E.

Volunteering in November 1915, he was drafted to East Africa on completion of his training and rendered valuable services with his unit, whilst engaged on important duties. Unfortunately he contracted malarial fever, and was invalided home. He was demobilised in February 1919, and holds the General Service and Victory Medals.

12, Hargreaves Street, Chorlton-on-Medlock, Manchester. X7246A

MARTIN, G., Private, 4th Seaforth Highlanders.

Volunteering in August 1914, he was shortly afterwards drafted to the Western Front, where he took part in several engagements. He died gloriously on the Field of Battle at Hill 60, on May 9th, 1915, and was entitled to the 1914–15 Star, and the General Service and Victory Medals.

"His name liveth for evermore."

26, Thorn Street, Bradford, Manchester. Z10792

MARTIN, H., Gunner, R.F.A.

He volunteered in August 1914, and embarking for Mesopotamia in the following March, took part in fighting at Kut-el-Amara, and in the capture of Baghdad. He did valuable work until his demobilisation, which took place on his return to England in August 1919. He holds the 1914–15 Star, and the General Service and Victory Medals.

6, Saville Street, Miles Platting, Manchester. Z10793

MARTIN, H., Sergt., 11th Manchester Regiment.

He volunteered in August 1914, and in the following May was sent to Egypt, where he played a prominent part in heavy fighting in the Suez Canal zone. In September 1915, he was transferred to the Western Front, and served with distinction at the Battles of the Somme, Arras, Messines, and Ypres, in which sector he was badly wounded in action in December 1917. After nine months in hospital in France, he was sent home and discharged in November 1918 as medically unfit, and holds the 1914–15 Star, and the General Service and Victory Medals.

23, Arthur Street, Hulme, Manchester. Z7247

MARTIN, H., Sapper, R.E.

He volunteered in May 1915, and in the following November was drafted to France. During his service on the Western Front he played an important part in heavy fighting at St. Eloi, Festubert, Loos, Messines, Lens, and Cambrai, and on the Ancre, and the Scarpe. He was badly wounded in action at Cambrai in August 1918, and spent some time in hospital. Demobilised in January 1919, he holds the 1914–15 Star, and the General Service and Victory Medals.

20, Solent Street, Ardwick, Manchester. Z7245

MARTIN, J., Sapper, R.E.

Joining in January 1918, he embarked for Mesopotamia a month later, and was engaged on duties of an important nature at Baghdad. He rendered valuable services until his demobilisation, which took place on his return to England in January 1920. He holds the General Service and Victory Medals.

91, Inkermann Street, Collyhurst, Manchester. Z10790

MARTIN, J., Pte., 8th Manchester Regt. (Volunteer Battalion).

Being ineligible for active service, he joined the Volunteer Battalion of the Manchester Regiment in August 1914, and after training was engaged on guard and other important duties at home stations. He rendered valuable services, but in consequence of ill-health was discharged in November 1916.

256, Hamilton Street, Collyhurst, Manchester. Z11437

MARTIN, J, P., Pte., 1st K.O. (R. Lancaster Regt.)

He enlisted in June 1914, and in the following December embarked for the Western Front. He was in action in many engagements in the Ypres salient, and was severely wounded at St. Julien. Admitted into hospital it was found necessary to amputate his left leg, and returning home he was invalided out in September 1915. He holds the 1914–15 Star, and the General Service and Victory Medals.

22, Law Street, Rochdale Road, Manchester. Z9637

MARTIN, J. W., Private, 16th Manchester Regt.

After volunteering in September 1914, in the 1st City Battalion, he underwent a period of training prior to being drafted to France in November 1915. He took part in heavy fighting at Albert and St. Eloi, and was wounded and taken prisoner at Trones Wood during the Somme Offensive in July 1916. Whilst in captivity in Germany he suffered many hardships, and was forced to do arduous work on the land. He was repatriated and demobilised in December 1918, and holds the 1914–15 Star, and the General Service and Victory Medals.

21, Devonshire Street, Hulme, Manchester. TZ7248

MARTIN, T., Private, 8th East Lancashire Regt.

Having volunteered in November 1914, he was sent to France in the following July, and played a prominent part in the Battles of Loos, Albert, Ploegsteert, and the Somme, where he was badly wounded in action in July 1916. He was invalided to Epsom Military Hospital, and after ten months' treatment, was discharged in May 1917 as medically unfit for further service. He holds the 1914–15 Star, and the General Service and Victory Medals.

112, Tame Street, Ancoats, Manchester. Z7118

MARTIN, T. F., Driver, R.A.S.C. (M.T.)
He volunteered in April 1915, and in the following March was sent on active service. Whilst on the Western Front, he was engaged on important transport duties, and saw heavy fighting at St. Eloi, Vermelles, Ploegsteert, Vimy Ridge, Beaumont-Hamel, and Beaucourt. Unfortunately he died from exposure on December 21st, 1916, and was entitled to the General Service and Victory Medals.
"He joined the great white company of valiant souls."
14, Tunstall Street, Longsight, Manchester.   Z7243

MASON, A., Private, Royal Welch Fusiliers.
He joined in May 1916, and on completion of his training, was engaged on special duties in England and Wales. Owing to indifferent health, he was not successful in obtaining his transfer overseas during hostilities, but rendered valuable services. He was demobilised in April 1919, but soon afterwards re-enlisted, and in 1920 was stationed in India.
5, Mytton Street, Hulme, Manchester.   Z7253

MASON, A., Private, 2nd Border Regiment.
Joining in August 1916, he was sent to France in the following November and took part in the Battles of Bullecourt, Messines, Ypres III, and Passchendaele. In November 1917, he was transferred to Italy, and was in action during the heavy fighting on the Piave whilst attached to the Honourable Artillery Company. After the cessation of hostilities, he served with the Army of Occupation at Innsbrück, Austria. He was demobilised in February 1919, and holds the General Service and Victory Medals, and an Italian Decoration.
17, Braham Street, Longsight, Manchester.   Z7252

MASON, C., Private, Cheshire Regiment, King's (Liverpool Regt.), and 1st Air Mechanic, R.A.F.
Volunteering in December 1915, he proceeded to the Western Front in the following March, and was engaged on duties of an important nature at St. Omer, and at other places. Owing to a wound, he was for a time under treatment at the Base, but on recovery rejoined his Squadron, and served overseas until 1919. He then returned to England, and was demobilised in March of that year, and holds the General Service and Victory Medals.
89, Kendall Street, Bradford, Manchester.   Z10796

MASON, G., Sapper, R.E.
Volunteering in October 1914, he was drafted to the Western Front in the following May, and played an important part in the Battles of Loos, Vermelles, the Somme, and Vimy Ridge. He was also engaged on the dangerous work of laying mines under the German trenches, and at strategic points, and in fixing electric lights in dugouts. He holds the 1914–15 Star, and the General Service and Victory Medals, and was demobilised in February 1919.
3A, Wycliffe Street, Ardwick, Manchester.   Z7249

MASON, G.H., Pte., King's Shropshire Light Infantry.
Mobilised at the outbreak of war in August 1914, he proceeded to France in the following October, and took part in much severe fighting. He was in action at the Battles of Ypres I, St. Eloi, Loos, Vermelles, Vimy Ridge, and Cambrai, and in the Retreat and Advance of 1918. He holds the 1914 Star, and the General Service and Victory Medals, and was discharged in February 1919.
33, Everton Road, Chorlton-on-Medlock, Manchester.   Z7255

MASON, J., Corporal, 1/8th Lancashire Fusiliers.
He was mobilised with the Territorials in August 1914, and within a month was sent to Egypt, where he saw heavy fighting in the Suez Canal zone. In May 1915 he was transferred to the Dardanelles and took part in the Battles of Krithia and other important engagements. After the Evacuation of the Gallipoli Peninsula he returned to Egypt, but three months later contracted dysentery and was in hospital at Lemnos. In April 1916 he was discharged as medically unfit for further service, and holds the 1914–15 Star, and the General Service and Victory Medals.
3, Marple Street, Ardwick, Manchester.   Z7251

MASON, R., Corporal, Royal Welch Fusiliers.
Having volunteered in April 1915, he was sent to France six months later and was wounded in action at Neuve Chapelle in February 1916. Invalided to hospital at Blackburn, he returned to the Western Front on his recovery in the following July and took part in the Battles of the Somme, Ypres (III), and Passchendaele, and in heavy fighting at Beaumont-Hamel, La Bassée and Givenchy. He remained overseas until his demobilisation in October, 1919, and holds the 1914–15 Star, and the General Service and Victory Medals.
29, Dalby Street, Longsight, Manchester.   TZ7254

MASON, S., Private, Manchester Regiment.
He was mobilised in August 1914, and proceeding to France with the First Expeditionary Force, took part in the Battle of and the Retreat from Mons. He also fought at the Battle of Ypres (I) and made the supreme sacrifice in the same sector on April 4th, 1915. He was entitled to the Mons Star, and the General Service and Victory Medals.
"A valiant Soldier, with undaunted heart, he breasted life's last hill."
21, Lime Bank Street, Ardwick, Manchester.   Z7250

MASON, T., Private, 8th Manchester Regiment.
He volunteered in June 1915, and embarking for France in the following October, served on that front until the close of hostilities. During this period he was in action at St. Eloi, Loos, Albert, Arras, Bullecourt, Ypres, Lens, Cambrai, Le Cateau, Havrincourt Wood and the Marne, and did much valuable work. He was demobilised in January 1919, and holds the 1914–15 Star, and the General Service and Victory Medals. 13, Gray Street, Ancoats, Manchester.   Z10794

MASON, W., Private, Loyal N. Lancashire Regiment.
He volunteered in February 1915, and three months later was drafted to the Western Front. In this theatre of war he played an important part in the Battles of Hill 60, Ypres (II), and Loos before gallantly laying down his life for King and Country during the heavy fighting at Vimy Ridge on May 16th, 1916. He was entitled to the 1914–15 Star, and the General Service and Victory Medals.
"Nobly striving,
He nobly fell that we might live."
57, Phillips Street, Hulme, Manchester.   TZ7256

MASON, W., Private, 3rd Manchester Regiment.
Volunteering in November 1914, he crossed to France in the following March, and was in action at Neuve Chapelle, Hill 60, Ypres and Loos, where he was wounded. Evacuated to England, he underwent hospital treatment, but returned to the Western Front on recovery in 1916, and took part in the Battles of Vimy Ridge, and the Somme. In February 1918, he was again sent to England in consequence of ill-health, and in June of the same year was invalided out of the Service. He holds the 1914–15 Star, and the General Service and Victory Medals.
10, Jersey Street Dwellings, Ancoats, Manchester.   Z10795

MASSAM, A., Pte., K.O. (Royal Lancaster Regt.)
Mobilised in August 1914, he was quickly drafted to France, and took part in the Battles of the Aisne (I), Ypres (I), Hill 60, Loos, the Somme, the Ancre and Ypres (III). He was badly wounded in action at Givenchy in January 1915, and was gassed in the Ypres sector in November 1917. He holds the 1914 Star, and the General Service and Victory Medals, and was demobilised in April 1919.   Z7257
16, Spring Gardens, Chancery Lane, Ardwick, Manchester.

MASSEY, A. (D.C.M.), Sergt., Manchester Regt.
He volunteered shortly after the outbreak of war, and until drafted to France in July 1917, was engaged as a musketry Instructor. In the course of his overseas service, he fought in engagements at Arras, Vimy Ridge, Passchendaele, and in the Retreat of 1918, in which he was wounded. He was awarded the Distinguished Conduct Medal in October of that year, for gallantry and devotion to duty displayed after his Officers had fallen at Neuvilly, in taking command of his Company and leading them successfully to their objective under heavy fire. He was demobilised in February 1919, and also holds the General Service and Victory Medals.
26, Duke Street, Bradford, Manchester.   Z10797

MASSEY, A., Corporal, R.A.M.C.
He volunteered in August 1914, and landing at Gallipoli in the following April, was engaged with the 1st Field Ambulance in operations in that theatre of war until the Evacuation of the Peninsula, and was twice wounded. After treatment in England he was transferred to the Royal Air Force and served as a 1st Class Air mechanic at Farnborough, did duties as a Bandsman until demobilised in February 1919. He holds the 1914–15 Star, and the General Service and Victory Medals.
80, Russell Street, Moss Side, Manchester.   Z11766

MASSEY, A., Private, 2nd Border Regiment.
He volunteered in August 1914, and in the following December proceeded to the Western Front, where he saw service at Sailly-Sailly, Neuve Chapelle, Laventie, Givenchy, Armentières and Festubert. He was severely wounded later when again in action at Neuve Chapelle, and was invalided home to hospital. Owing to the loss of his eye and other disabilities as the result of his injuries he was discharged as physically unfit for further duty in November 1915, and holds the 1914–15 Star, and the General Service and Victory Medals.
15, Kirk Street, Ancoats, Manchester.   Z9274

MASSEY, E., Private, Manchester Regiment.
Joining in April 1916, he was drafted to the Western Front in August, and immediately went into action on the Somme. He later took part in the Battle of Cambrai, but was unhappily killed during heavy fighting at St. Quentin in March 1918. He was entitled to the General Service and Victory Medals.
"Great deeds cannot die :
They, with the sun and moon renew their light for ever."
51, Prince Street, Ardwick, Manchester.   Z7258B

MASSEY, F., Private, 7th Manchester Regiment.
He volunteered in September 1914, and after a period of service at home stations, was sent to France in March 1917. He took part in the Battle of Arras and was then seriously wounded in action at Givenchy in July of the same year. As a result, he unfortunately suffered amputation of one of his legs, and in January 1918 was invalided from the Army. He holds the General Service and Victory Medals.
7, Whittaker Street, Chorlton-on-Medlock, Manchester.   Z7259

MASSEY, E., Pte., 1st K.O. (R. Lancaster Regt.)
A Reservist, he was called to the Colours at the outbreak of war in August 1914, and proceeding to France immediately, took part in the Battle of Mons and the subsequent Retreat. Later he was in action at the Battles of the Marne, the Aisne, Ypres, Neuve Chapelle, Festubert and Albert, where he was badly wounded in April 1916. He was invalided to hospital at Hastings, and in the following August was discharged as medically unfit for further service, holding the Mons Star, and the General Service and Victory Medals.
10, Heyrod Street, Ancoats, Manchester. Z7114

MASSEY, J. R., Private, Manchester Regiment.
Volunteering in September 1914, he embarked for France in the following March, and took part in the Battles of Loos, Festubert, Vimy Ridge, the Somme, Arras, Bullecourt, Messines, Ypres and Cambrai. He also served throughout the Retreat and Allied Advance of 1918, and did valuable work until his demobilisation, which took place on his return to England in March 1919. He holds the 1914-15 Star, and the General Service and Victory Medals.
27, Hamilton Street, Collyhurst, Manchester. Z10791

MASSEY, T., Private, R.M.L.I.
He volunteered in January 1915, and in the following November was posted to H.M.S. " Indefatigable." After taking part with his ship in various operations, and serving on important patrol duties in the North Sea, he lost his life in the Battle of Jutland, when his vessel was sunk in action on May 31st, 1916. He was entitled to the 1914-15 Star, and the General Service and Victory Medals.
" The path of duty was the way to glory."
37, Reather Street, Miles Platting, Manchester. Z9275

MASTERMAN, J. E., Air Mechanic, R.A.F.
He joined in November 1917, and on completion of his training was sent to Palestine, where he rendered valuable services with his Squadron. He was present at the capture of Tripoli and Aleppo by General Allenby's Forces, and after the cessation of hostilities was stationed at Alexandria. Demobilised in August 1919, he holds the General Service and Victory Medals.
10, Albemarle Street, Moss Side, Manchester. Z7260

MATHER, C. A., Private, 22nd Manchester Regt.
He joined in August 1916, and in the following January was drafted to France, where he served in engagements at Bullecourt and Passchendaele Ridge. He was sent to Italy in November 1917, and was in action in various operations against the Austrians until March of the following year, when he was invalided home on account of illness. After convalescence he returned to Italy in August 1918, and remained there until the cessation of hostilities. Returning to England he was demobilised in October 1919, and holds the General Service and Victory Medals. Z9276
9, Thistle Street, Gayler Street, Miles Platting, Manchester.

MATHER, J., Gunner, R.F.A.
He was mobilised with the Territorials in August 1914, and a month later was drafted to India, where he rendered valuable services with his Battery whilst engaged on garrison duties. From July 1915, until the following December, he was in hospital with malarial fever, but on his recovery returned to duty and remained in the East until April 1919. He was then sent home for demobilisation, and holds the General Service and Victory Medals. and the Territorial Force War Medal. 57, Naylor Street, Hulme, Manchester. Z7262

MATHER, S. G., Private, East Lancashire Regt.
Volunteering in September 1914, he proceeded to the Western Front twelve months later, but after taking part in the Battle of Loos, was sent to Salonika with reinforcements. Whilst in the Balkan theatre of war, he was in action during heavy fighting on the Doiran, Struma and Vardar fronts, and was in hospital for a time with malarial fever. Demobilised in May 1919, he holds the 1914-15 Star, and the General Service and Victory Medals.
15, Rex Street, Jackson Street, Hulme, Manchester. Z7261

MATHESON, J. S., Pte., King's Own Scottish Bord'rs.
Volunteering in August 1914, he was sent to France in the following year and was wounded in action at the Battle of Loos in September 1915. After treatment at the 20th General Hospital at Camiers, he rejoined his unit and took part in the Battle of the Somme, where he was badly wounded at Martinpuich in August 1916. On this occasion he was invalided home and was eventually discharged in March 1918, as medically unfit for further service. He holds the 1914-15 Star, and the General Service and Victory Medals. Z7263
21, Bremner Street, Chorlton-on-Medlock, Manchester.

MATHEWS, G. J., Corporal, 21st Manchester Regt.
He joined in July 1917, and in the following November was drafted to France, and thence to Italy. Whilst in this seat of operations he took part in engagements on the Asiago Plateau and the Piave, and was wounded in action and sent to hospital. On his recovery, he was employed in guarding prisoners at the camps at Montello, Asiago, and on the Piave. He returned home and was demobilised in January 1920, holding the General Service and Victory Medals. Z7268
3, Ernest Street, Morton Street, Longsight, Manchester.

MATLEY, D., Private, M.G.C.
He volunteered in the Royal Warwickshire Regiment in February 1915, and after a period of training proceeded to the Western Front. In this theatre of war he took part in several engagements, including those at Ypres, Lens and Cambrai, and was wounded in action. In consequence he was sent home to hospital, but on his recovery was transferred to the Machine Gun Corps, and returned to France, where he remained until his demobilisation in February 1919. He holds the General Service and Victory Medals.
39, Rowen Street, Ardwick, Manchester. Z7264

MATTHEWS, A., Corporal, 23rd Manchester Regt., and 1st Air Mechanic, R.A.F.
Volunteering in November 1914, he was drafted to France after a period of training. He took part in the Battles of Neuve Chapelle, Festubert, the Somme, Arras, Messines, Ypres and Passchendaele. About March 1918 he was transferred to the R.A.F., and served at Rouen until his demobilisation in February 1919. He holds the 1914-15 Star, and the General Service and Victory Medals.
7, Robert St., Chorlton-on-Medlock, Manchester. TX7265-6A

MATTHEWS, D. H., Private, R.A.M.C.
Mobilised on the declaration of war he was shortly afterwards drafted to France, and served throughout the Retreat from Mons, and in the Battles of Le Cateau, the Marne and Aisne. He took part in several other engagements, including that of Ypres, where he was gassed, and later in May 1917, proceeded to Italy and was present during the fighting on the Piave and the Asiago Plateaux. Returning home he was demobilised in January 1919, and holds the Mons Star, and the General Service and Victory Medals.
56, Middlewood Street, Harpurhey, Manchester. Z11552

MATTHEWS, F. J., L/Corpl., 20th Manchester Regt.
He volunteered in November 1914, and on completing his training in the following year proceeded to France. There he took part in many engagements, was wounded in action at Fricourt in March 1916, and was invalided to the Base before being sent home. On his recovery he was transferred to the Rifle Brigade and later to the Labour Corps, and was engaged on important duties until his discharge in February 1918. He holds the 1914-15 Star, and the General Service and Victory Medals.
46, Princes Street, Rusholme, Manchester. Z7269

MATTHEWS, H., Private, 7th Manchester Regiment.
A serving soldier, having enlisted in January 1914, he embarked for Egypt in the following September, and a year later proceeded to the Dardanelles, where he took part in the concluding operations of the Gallipoli campaign. He was invalided home in consequence of ill-health, and on recovery in January 1917, was drafted to France. In this theatre of war he fought at Arras, Albert, Ypres, Passchendaele, St. Quentin and throughout the Retreat and Allied Advance of 1918. He was demobilised in the following January, and holds the 1914-15 Star, and the General Service and Victory Medals.
31, Drinkwater Street, Harpurhey, Manchester. Z11438

MATTHEWS, W., Pte., K.O. (Royal Lancaster Regt.)
Volunteering in May 1915, he was sent to Gallipoli shortly afterwards, and saw service there until the Evacuation of the Peninsula, when he proceeded to Egypt. In March 1916, he proceeded to Mesopotamia, and took part in operations at Kut-el-Amara until his Battalion was transferred to India in January 1917. Engaged on important duties at various stations he returned to England for demobilisation in February 1920, and holds the 1914-15 Star, and the General Service and Victory Medals.
13, Back Pump Street, Hulme, Manchester. Z11768

MATTHEWS, W. V., Pte., 1/4th S. Lancashire Regt.
He joined in September 1916, and embarking for France in the following July was in action in several engagements in the Ypres salient. Reported missing on September 20th, 1917, he was later presumed to have been killed in the attack on Pommern Redoubt on that date. He was entitled to the General Service and Victory Medals.
" Steals on the ear, the distant triumph song."
23, Fairhaven Street, West Gorton, Manchester. TZ11767

MAWSON, F., Private, 21st Manchester Regiment.
He volunteered in November 1914, and in the following November was drafted overseas. In the course of service on the Western Front he fought in various parts of the line, and was severely wounded in the Battle of the Somme on July 21st, 1916. Admitted to the 13th General Military Hospital, Boulogne, he was later evacuated to England for treatment, and was subsequently invalided out of the Army in October 1917. He holds the 1914-15 Star, and the General Service and Victory Medals.
17, Athol Street, Hulme, Manchester. Z11769

MAY, H.. C.Q.M.S., 5th Lancashire Fusiliers.
He volunteered in February 1915, and after a period of training was engaged at various stations on important clerical duties with his unit. He was not successful in obtaining his transfer overseas, but rendered valuable services until his demobilisation in January 1920.
99, Thomas Street, Miles Platting, Manchester. TZ7270

MAY, D., Q.M.S., Northern Nigerian Regiment.
In September 1914, he volunteered in the Legion of Frontiersmen, but later was transferred to the Montgomery Yeomanry, with which Regiment he was engaged on many important duties. In April 1918 he was drafted to Africa with the Northern Nigerian Regiment, and saw much service at Sierra Leone until his demobilisation in July 1919. He holds the General Service and Victory Medals. Z2453B
13, Higher Chatham Street, Chorlton-on-Medlock, Manchester.

MAY, J., Corporal, Manchester Regiment.
He volunteered in September 1914, and in the following January was drafted to Egypt, and later to the Dardanelles, where he saw much heavy fighting. After the Evacuation of the Gallipoli Peninsula, he was transferred to France, took part in engagements at Loos, and during the Somme Offensive, and was badly wounded in action. In consequence he was invalided home and finally discharged in April 1917, as medically unfit for further service. He holds the 1914-15 Star, and the General Service and Victory Medals. Z2453C
13, Higher Chatham Street, Chorlton-on-Medlock, Manchester.

MAYCOCK, A. E., Corporal, 18th Manchester Regt.
Volunteering in August 1914, he proceeded overseas in the following March. During his service on the Western Front, he took part in many engagements, including those at Loos, St. Eloi, Vimy Ridge, the Somme, the Ancre, Arras, Messines and Cambrai, but unfortunately had a breakdown and was invalided home. On his recovery, he was engaged on the East Coast on outpost duties. In March 1920 he was demobilised, and holds the 1914-15 Star, and the General Service and Victory Medals.
5, Bickley Street, Moss Side, Manchester. Z7271

MAYER, G., Air Mechanic, R.A.F.
He volunteered in November 1915, and after completing his training was engaged as superintendent at the Sheet Metal Works, Amesbury. Owing to the important nature of his work, he was unable to obtain a transfer overseas, but rendered valuable services, and was demobilised in April 1919.
11, Dorset Street, Ardwick, Manchester. Z7272

MAYHEAD, A. H., Sergt., R.A.S.C.
He was mobilised in August 1914, and immediately drafted to the Western Front, where he played a prominent part in the Battles of Mons, the Aisne, Ypres, (I and II), Neuve Chapelle, Vimy Ridge, and the Somme. He was invalided home suffering from dysentery, but on his recovery, proceeded to the East, and saw much fighting at the capture of Jericho, and in the Advance with General Allenby's Forces. He returned home and was discharged in July 1919, holding the Mons Star, and the General Service and Victory Medals.
8, Westminster Street, Chester Road, Hulme, Manchester. TZ7273

MAYLETT, H., Private, 16th Manchester Regiment.
Volunteering in November 1914, he proceeded overseas in the following year. During his service on the Western Front, he took part in much heavy fighting at Loos, St. Eloi, Vimy Ridge and Trones Wood, where he was wounded and taken prisoner in 1916. He was held in captivity in Germany and suffered many hardships. After the Armistice, he was released and returned home for his demobilisation in December 1918. He holds the 1914-15 Star, and the General Service and Victory Medals.
120, Edensor Street, Beswick, Manchester. Z7274

MAYO, J., Corporal, 3rd Manchester Regiment.
He enlisted in October 1908, and after the outbreak of war in August 1914, rendered valuable services as a drill Instructor until he became time-expired in 1915. He then joined the Royal Navy and was chiefly engaged on dangerous mine-sweeping duties in the English Channel, but also served with the Dover Patrol during the bombardment at Zeebrugge and Ostend. In May 1918 he was discharged in order to take up work of National importance as a steel smelter at Messrs. Armstrong and Whitworth's. He holds the 1914-15 Star, and the General Service and Victory Medals.
8, Haughton Street, Bradford, Manchester. Z7275

MAYOR, F., Sergt., R.A.M.C.
Volunteering in September 1914, he proceeded to Egypt in the same month, and was stationed at Alexandria, served in the General Military Hospital there until March 1915, when he was sent to Gallipoli. He did good work with his Corps from the first Landing until the Evacuation of the Peninsula, after which he was sent to Salonika in March 1916. Engaged as a hospital orderly he was also on duty in the operating theatre at a Base hospital and returning to England in September 1918, served in a similar capacity in various hospitals. He was demobilised in September 1919, and holds the 1914-15 Star, and the General Service and Victory Medals.
48, Warde Street, Hulme, Manchester. Z11770

MAYORS, A., Private, 7th Manchester Regiment.
Joining in May 1916, he proceeded overseas in the following March. Whilst on the Western Front, he took part in heavy fighting at Bullecourt, Ypres, (III), and Cambrai, where he was wounded and consequently invalided home. On his recovery, he returned to France, and was in action in the Re-

treat and Advance of 1918 at Cambrai (II), Havrincourt Wood and Le Cateau (II). He was demobilised in November 1919, and holds the General Service and Victory Medals.
42, Mercer Street, Hulme, Manchester. Z7276

MCALLISTER, J. P., Private, Lancashire Fusiliers.
He volunteered in June 1915, and sailing for Egypt in the following year served in the Battle of Katia and other engagements until 1917, when he was sent to France. There he took part in heavy fighting on the Somme, and owing to illness was sent home. After treatment in Runcorn Hospital, he was discharged in February 1919, as medically unfit for further service. He holds the General Service and Victory Medals.
54, Alexandra Place, Manchester. Z11434

MCALROY, F., Corporal, 18th Manchester Regt.
He volunteered in July 1915, and in May of the following year, was drafted to the Western Front, where he saw severe fighting in various sectors. He took part in the Battles of the Somme, Arras, Ypres, Amiens, Bapaume, Havrincourt and Cambrai, and many other important engagements in this theatre of war, and was for three months in hospital at Etaples suffering from trench fever. He was demobilised in May 1919, and holds the General Service and Victory Medals.
125, Armitage Street, Ardwick, Manchester. Z7123

MCANDRY, B., Private, King's (Liverpool Regiment).
He joined in May 1917, and on completing three months' training proceeded to France, where he saw severe fighting in various sectors of the Front, took part in many important engagements, and was wounded in action. He contracted pneumonia whilst in this theatre of war, was sent home and was for a considerable period in hospital before being invalided from the Army in February 1920. He holds the General Service and Victory Medals.
12, Westmoreland Street, Longsight, Manchester. Z7124

MCANEARY, J., Private, Royal Defence Corps.
He volunteered at the outbreak of war in August 1914, and after completing a period of training, served at various stations, where he was engaged on duties of a highly important nature. He rendered very valuable services with his Company until February 1917, and was then invalided from the Army, as medically unfit for further military service.
4, Pump Street, Hulme, Manchester. Z7125

MCARDLE, E., Gunner, R.F.A.
He volunteered in August 1914, and after completing his training was engaged at Portsmouth, the Isle of Wight, and Scotland, on important duties connected with explosives. He rendered valuable services but was not successful in obtaining his transfer overseas before the cessation of hostilities, and was demobilised in November 1918.
8, Milton Street, Ancoats, Manchester. Z9259

MCARTHUR, A., Corporal, R.F.A.
Shortly after volunteering in September 1914, he proceeded to the Western Front, where he fought in many important engagements, including the Battles of Ypres, Hill 60, Loos, Albert and the Somme. In November 1916, he was transferred to Mesopotamia, and there took part in the Relief of Kut, the capture of Baghdad and Tekrit and engagements at Ramadieh and Mosul. He afterwards served for two months in Egypt, before returning home for demobilisation in February 1919, and holds the 1914-15 Star, and the General Service and Victory Medals.
28, Industrial Street, Stockport Road, Manchester. Z7126

MCARTHUR, N., Corporal, R.F.A.
He volunteered in May 1915, and in April of the following year proceeded to the Western Front. Whilst in this theatre of war he saw much severe fighting in various sectors and took part in the Battles of the Somme, the Ancre, Arras, Ypres, Passchendaele, the Marne, Bapaume, Havrincourt and Cambrai, and other engagements during the Retreat and Advance of 1918. Demobilised in June 1919, he holds the General Service and Victory Medals.
31, Cranworth Street, Chorlton-on-Medlock, Manchester. Z7127

MCCABE, F. W., C.Q.M.S., Border Regt. and R.E.
Volunteering in November 1914, he was drafted to the Western Front in May of the following year and there saw much severe fighting. He took a prominent part in the Battles of St. Eloi, Albert, Vimy Ridge, the Somme, Arras, Ypres and Cambrai, and many minor engagements in various sectors, was gassed at Loos in March 1916, and later served with the R.E. He was demobilised in September 1919, and holds the 1914-15 Star, and the General Service and Victory Medals.
30, Brunswick Street, Hulme, Manchester. Z7130

MCCABE, H., Driver, R.A.S.C.
He volunteered in September 1915, and in the same year was drafted to Egypt. There he saw much service and took part in the Advance to Palestine, and was present at the entry into Jerusalem. Demobilised in December 1918, he holds the 1914-15 Star, and the General Service and Victory Medals.
6, Marshall Street, New Cross, Manchester. Z11543

M^CCABE, P., Private, 7th Manchester Regiment.

He was mobilised in August 1914, and later in the same year was sent to Egypt, where he was engaged at Romani. He afterwards proceeded to Palestine, and served at Gaza, Rafa, and in the Advance to and in the capture of Jerusalem, and was once wounded. He returned home and was demobilised in June 1919, holding the 1914-15 Star, and the General Service and Victory Medals.

38, Bengal Street, Oldham Road, Manchester. Z9261

M^CCABE, T. E., Private, K.O. (R. Lancaster Regt.)

Three months after volunteering in September 1915, he was drafted to the Western Front, where he saw severe fighting in various sectors. After taking part in the Battles of Vermelles, Vimy Ridge, the Somme, the Ancre, Arras, Bullecourt, Ypres and Cambrai and many minor engagements, he was sent home and invalided from the Army in August 1917, suffering from heart disease. He unhappily died at home in November of that year. He was entitled to the 1914-15 Star, and the General Service and Victory Medals.

" His memory is cherished with pride."

26, Harrison Street, Ancoats, Manchester. Z7122

M^CCADDEN, J., Private, 15th Sherwood Foresters.

He volunteered in June 1915, and in January of the following year was drafted to France, where he saw much severe fighting in various sectors of the Front. After taking part in engagements at High Wood, Trones Wood, Thiépval, and many other places on the Somme, he was sent home and discharged, being under age for military service. He holds the General Service and Victory Medals.

52, Gibbon Street, Bradford, Manchester. Z7119

M^CCAFFERY, D., Private, 3rd (King's Own) Hussars.

He volunteered in January 1916, and in June of that year proceeded to the Western Front, where he saw much severe fighting at Arras and Nieuport, and in various other sectors. He was afterwards engaged on important duties at various stations, in Ireland and finally returned home for demobilisation in October 1920. He holds the General Service and Victory Medals.

13, Buckland Street, Ancoats, Manchester. Z5789

M^CCAFFREY, J., Private, 6th Border Regiment.

Volunteering in November 1914, he was drafted to Gallipoli in the following September, and served in operations until the Evacuation of the Peninsula, when he proceeded to Egypt. After a period of service in the Canal zone he was sent to France in July 1916, and fought in the Battles of Arras, Thiépval, Ypres, Cambrai, and was taken prisoner in April 1918, during the German Offensive. Released from captivity in the following November, he was demobilised in September 1919, and holds the 1914-15 Star, and the General Service and Victory Medals.

5, Mansfield Street, Miles Platting, Manchester. Z10719

M^CCALL, H., Private, K.O. (Y.L.I.)

He joined in November 1916, and after five months' training was sent to the Western Front. There, being medically unfit for service in the firing line, he was stationed at Trouville and various other places, where he was engaged in guarding prisoners of war, and on other important duties. He was demobilised on returning home in April 1919, and holds the General Service and Victory Medals.

4, Thornhill Street, Hulme, Manchester. TZ7131

M^CCALL, J., Private, Loyal North Lancashire Regt.

He volunteered in August 1914, and was sent overseas in the following February. Serving with his unit on the Western Front, he was engaged in heavy fighting in the Battle of Loos, and was wounded near La Bassée. Sent home on account of his injuries he returned to France after treatment, and shortly after rejoining his Battalion was wounded for the second time and admitted to a Base Hospital. On recovery he was in action in several engagements until taken prisoner in March 1918. Repatriated in March 1919, he was demobilised two months later, and holds the 1914-15 Star, and the General Service and Victory Medals.

14, Whittaker Street, Gorton, Manchester. Z10721

M^CCARTHY, F., Private, 1/7th Manchester Regt.

Having enlisted in 1912, he was drafted to Egypt shortly after the outbreak of war in August 1914, and there served at various stations until April 1915. He was then transferred to Gallipoli, where, after taking part in the Landing at Cape Helles, he fought in the Battles of Krithia and Achi Baba. On the Evacuation of the Peninsula, he proceeded to the Western Front, and served through the Battles of the Somme and Ypres. He was wounded in action whilst overseas, and in September 1918, was sent home and invalided from the Army, suffering from the effects of trench fever. He holds the 1914-15 Star, and the General Service and Victory Medals.

42, Carter Terrace, Greenheys, Manchester. Z7133

M^CCARTHY, F. W., A.B., Royal Navy.

He was serving at the outbreak of war in H.M.S. " Hampshire," which vessel was engaged on patrol and other duties in the North Sea and other waters. His ship was in action in the Battles of Heligoland Bight, the Dogger Bank and Jutland, and was sunk off the Orkney Islands when carrying Lord

Kitchener to Russia on June 6th, 1916, and he was unfortunately drowned. He was entitled to the 1914-15 Star, and the General Service and Victory Medals.

" Thinking that remembrance, though unspoken, may reach him where he sleeps."

9, Stanley Street, West Gorton, Manchester. Z10270B

M^CCARTHY, H., Gunner, R.F.A.

Joining in May 1917, he landed on the Western Front four months later, and was in action in several engagements in the Ypres Salient. He also fought in the German Offensive, and in several battles, including those of Amiens, Bapaume, Epéhy, and Havrincourt, during the subsequent Allied Advance of 1918. Returning to England for demobilisation in March 1919, he holds the General Service and Victory Medals.

29, Elizabeth Street, West Gorton, Manchester. Z10724

M^CCARTHY, J., Private, South Lancashire Regt.

Volunteering in 1914 he proceeded overseas in the following year. During his services in France he fought in many sectors and was wounded in August 1915. On recovery he returned to the trenches, and served until the conclusion of hostilities. Demobilised in December 1919 he holds the 1914-15 Star, and the General Service and Victory Medals.

10, Ella Street, Harpurhey, Manchester. Z11544

M^CCARTHY, W., Rifleman, 10th Rifle Brigade.

He volunteered in September 1914, and served at home until December of the following year, when he was drafted to France. There was heavy fighting at Albert, Ploegsteert, the Somme, and in numerous engagements during the Retreat and Advance of 1918. Retained for special duties after the Armistice he returned home some months later, and was demobilised in August 1919. He holds the 1914-15 Star, and the General Service and Victory Medals.

41, Dickens Street, Queen's Road, Manchester. Z10723

M^CCLEAN, J., L/Corporal, Loyal N. Lancashire Regt.

He joined in February 1918, and on completion of a period of training, was retained at various stations, where he was engaged on duties of great importance. He was not successful in obtaining his transfer to a theatre of war, but nevertheless rendered valuable services with his unit until January 1919, when he was demobilised.

45, Edensor Street, Beswick, Manchester. Z11921

M^CCLEAN, R. Private, K.O. (R. Lancaster Regt.)

He volunteered in February 1915, and three months later crossed to France, where he served in several engagements, including the Battle of Loos. Sent to Egypt in October 1915, he was stationed at Alexandria for a month, and then proceeded to Salonika. Whilst in the Balkans he was engaged on signalling and outpost duties on the Doiran front, and was present at the Capture of Monastir. Owing to illness he was sent to Malta for treatment, and on recovery, embarked for the Western Front in February 1917, and fought in the Battles of Arras, Ypres, Cambrai, the Marne, and in other operations until the close of the war. He holds the 1914-15 Star, and the General Service and Victory Medals, and was demobilised in July 1919. Z10726

M^CCLELLAN, G.(D.C.M.),C.S.M.,2nd ManchesterRgt.

A Reservist, he was called to the Colours at the outbreak of war in August 1914, and was immediately drafted to the Western Front, where he fought in the Retreat from Mons. He also took a prominent part in the Battles of the Marne, the Aisne, La Bassée, Ypres, Neuve Chapelle, Festubert, Loos, the Somme, Arras, Vimy Ridge, and Cambrai, and was twice wounded in action—at Albert in June 1916, and on the Aisne in May 1918. He was awarded the Distinguished Conduct Medal for conspicuous gallantry in the Field, and holds also the Mons Star, and the General Service and Victory Medals. He was invalided from the Army in November 1918.

5, Alliott Grove, Hulme, Manchester. TZ7134

M^CCLENNON, J., Private, 8th Border Regiment.

He joined in September 1917, and embarking for the Western Front in the following March was engaged in severe fighting at Ploegsteert Wood, Kemmel Hill, and the Aisne. During the Allied Advance he was wounded on the Marne in August 1918, and after treatment in France was evacuated to England for further medical attention a month later. He was demobilised in October 1919, and holds the General Service and Victory Medals.

16, Coulman Street, Rochdale Road, Manchester. Z10727

M^CCLURE, H., Sergt., 7th Manchester Regiment.

He joined in December 1914, and was retained on important duties at various stations until March 1917, when he was drafted to the Western Front. After taking part in the Battles of Arras, Bullecourt, Messines, and Passchendaele, and many minor engagements, he was severely wounded in action at Ypres in October 1917, and invalided to hospital at Manchester. He was ultimately discharged as medically unfit for further service in April 1919, and holds the General Service and Victory Medals.

28, Dryden Street, Chorlton-on-Medlock, Manchester.TZ7135

McCLURE, J. W., L/Corpl., 4th Loyal N. Lancs. Regt.
He joined in December 1916, and three months later, proceeded to Palestine, where he took part in the Battles of Gaza and the Capture of Jerusalem and Jericho. In February 1918 he was transferred to the Western Front and there fought in the Battles of the Marne, Amiens, Bapaume, Havrincourt, Epéhy, Cambrai and Ypres. He was sent with the Army of Occupation into Germany, on the cessation of hostilities, and there served at Cologne and Bonn until his return home for demobilisation in December 1919. He holds the General Service and Victory Medals.
28, Dryden Street, Chorlton-on-Medlock, Manchester. TZ7136

McCONNELL, J., Pte., K.O. (Royal Lancaster Regt.)
Volunteering in June 1915, he proceeded to the Western Front in December of that year, and there saw severe fighting at St. Eloi until invalided home, suffering from trench feet. On his recovery in October 1916, however, he was drafted to Mesopotamia, where he served at Ctesiphon, Kirkuk, and many other places until after the cessation of hostilities. Returning home in February 1919, he was demobilised in the following month, and holds the 1914–15 Star, and the General Service and Victory Medals.
31, Kingston Street, Hulme, Manchester. Z7137

McCORMACK, J., Private, 3rd and 9th King's Own (Royal Lancaster Regiment).
He volunteered in April 1915, and five months later was drafted to Gallipoli, where he saw much severe fighting. In December of that year he was sent to hospital at Mudros, suffering from dysentery, and was thence invalided home. On his recovery in August 1917, he proceeded to Mesopotamia, but five months later was sent to India, suffering from enteric fever. Later he served for a time in Salonika, before returning home for demobilisation in May 1919, and holds the 1914–15 Star, and the General Service and Victory Medals.
12, Mulberry Street, Hulme, Manchester. Z7138

McCORMICK, D., Pte., K.O. (Royal Lancaster Regt.)
Two months after volunteering in October 1915, he was sent to the Western Front, where he saw severe fighting in various sectors. He took part in the Battles of St. Eloi, Vermelles, the Somme, the Ancre, Ypres and Bapaume, and many minor engagements, until sent home suffering from injuries incurred in an accident. After a considerable period in hospital at Leeds, he was invalided from the Army in February 1919, holding the 1914–15 Star, and the General Service and Victory Medals.
16, Hughes Street, Ardwick, Manchester. Z7139

McCORMICK, H., Private, K.O. (R. Lancaster Regt.)
He volunteered in October 1914, and in September of the following year was drafted to the Western Front. There he saw much severe fighting, and took part in the Battles of Loos, St. Eloi, Albert, Vimy Ridge, the Somme, Arras, Bullecourt, Ypres, Cambrai, the Aisne and the Marne, and many other important engagements until the cessation of hostilities. He was then sent with the Army of Occupation to Germany, finally returning home for demobilisation in March 1919. He holds the 1914–15 Star, and the General Service and Victory Medals.
46, Dover Street, Chester Road, Hulme, Manchester. Z7141

McCORMICK, J., Worker, Q.M.A.A.C.
Joining in February 1917, she served throughout the course of hostilities on important duties at various stations, and rendered valuable services until demobilised in September 1919. 1, Southwell Street, Harpurhey, Manchester. Z11545

McCORMICK, J., Private, Lancashire Fusiliers.
Volunteering in September 1915, he proceeded overseas in the following May and served in France for over three years. He took part in several engagements in the Somme Offensive and was wounded at Arras in May 1917. Rejoining his unit on recovery he was in action in the Battles of Ypres, Cambrai, in those of the German Offensive, and at Amiens, Bapaume, Havrincourt, during the subsequent Allied Advance, in the course of which he was wounded at Cambrai in September 1918. After treatment he was employed on special duties in France until his return home for demobilisation in September 1919. He holds the General Service and Victory Medals.
66, Sycamore Street, Oldham Road, Manchester. Z10728

McCORMICK, J. T., Private, 9th Border Regiment.
He volunteered in October 1914, and sailing for Gallipoli in the following year took part in heavy fighting at the Landing at Suvla Bay and the capture of Chunuk Bair, where he was gassed. On the Evacuation of the Peninsula he was sent to France in 1916, and served in the Battles of Vimy Ridge, Mericourt, Bullecourt and was wounded on the Somme in 1917. After treatment he was in action in the Battle of Amiens and other engagements of the concluding stages of the war. He was discharged on account of service in October 1918, and holds the 1914–15 Star and the General Service and Victory Medals.
1, Horne Street, Gorton, Manchester. Z10729A

McCORMICK, W., Private, 1st Manchester Regiment.
He volunteered in October 1914, and crossing to the Western Front in the following year fought in several engagements, including the Battles of Neuve Chapelle and Ypres. Sent home in 1916, owing to physical unfitness for active service, he was discharged in July 1916, and holds the 1914–15 Star, and the General Service and Victory Medals.
1, Horne Street, Gorton, Manchester. Z10729B

McCORMICK, W. H., Private, 13th Manchester Regt.
Volunteering in 1915, he sailed for Salonika in the same year, and saw much service on the Balkans. He was in action in the Advance on the Doiran and Struma fronts, and was present at the capture of Monastir. In 1920 he was still serving with the Colours, and holds the 1914–15 Star, and the General Service and Victory Medals.
1, Horne Street, Gorton, Manchester. Z10729C

McCORMICK, W. H., Private, 13th Manchester Regt.
Volunteering in December 1914, he proceeded to the Western Front in April of the following year, but in the following month was transferred to Salonika. There he saw much severe fighting on the Doiran, Struma and Vardar fronts, taking part in many important engagements until the cessation of hostilities. Returning home in February 1919, he was demobilised in the following month, and holds the 1914–15 Star, and the General Service and Victory Medals.
37, Markham Street, Ardwick, Manchester. Z7140

McCORMICK, W. P., Sergt., 12th Manchester Regt.
He volunteered in September 1914, and in the following year was drafted to the East, where he took part in the first Landing at Salonika. There he was present at the re-capture of Monastir and saw much severe fighting on the Struma and other fronts, until wounded in action in April 1917, during the Advance on the Doiran. He was for a considerable period in hospital at Malta, and in England before being invalided from the Army in March 1919, and holds the 1914–15 Star, and the General Service and Victory Medals.
11, Fletcher Square, Hulme, Manchester. TZ7142

McCORRICK, J., Private, 12th Manchester Regt.
Volunteering in 1914, he proceeded to France in the following year, and was in action in the Battles of Neuve Chapelle, St. Eloi, Hill 60, Ypres and Festubert. He was wounded in 1916, and invalided home for treatment, returned to the Western Front on recovery, and fought on the Somme, at Mericourt, Arras, Cambrai and Bourlon Wood. He was discharged on account of service in February 1918, and holds the 1914–15 Star, and the General Service and Victory Medals.
63, Kemp Street, Manchester. Z10722.

McCOWAN, A., Corporal, 20th Manchester Regt.
He volunteered in August 1914, and in March of the following year was drafted to the Western Front, where he saw severe fighting in various sectors. He took part in the Battles of Ypres, and the Somme, and many minor engagements, was wounded in action at Arras and admitted to hospital at the Base and on rejoining his unit was a second time wounded at Givenchy, and invalided home. He returned to France, however, on his recovery, and was finally demobilised in January 1919, holding the 1914–15 Star, and the General Service and Victory Medals.
2, Unity Street, Ancoats, Manchester. Z11922

McCOY, D., Private, 4th Lancashire Fusiliers.
He volunteered in January 1915, and two months later was drafted to the Western Front, where he saw severe fighting in various sectors. He took part in the Battles of Ypres and the Somme, and many other engagements until wounded in action at Delville Wood, and sent to hospital at Cardiff. He was invalided from the Army in January 1917, but later re-enlisted and served in England for twelve months, being finally demobilised in August 1919. He holds the 1914–15 Star, and the General Service and Victory Medals.
12, Oram Street, Miles Platting, Manchester. Z11923

McCOY, J. T., Private, 8th Manchester Regiment.
He volunteered in January 1916, and in the following April landed in France. Serving in various parts of the line he was in action at St. Quentin, and was gassed near La Bassée in August 1917. On recovery he fought at Nieuport, and in many battles during the Retreat and Advance of 1918. He holds the General Service and Victory Medals, and was demobilised in February 1919.
38, Gunson Street, Miles Platting, Manchester. Z10730

McCRACKEN, S., Air Mechanic, R.A.F.
He joined in October 1918, and after a period of training served at various stations, where he was engaged on duties, which required a high degree of technical skill. He was unable, owing to the early cessation of hostilities, to obtain his transfer to a theatre of war, but nevertheless, rendered valuable services with his Squadron until November 1919, when he was demobilised.
18, Cadogan Street, Moss Side, Manchester. Z7144

McCRACKEN, J., Private, Royal Scots.
He volunteered in October 1914, and in June of the following year, proceeded to the Western Front, where after seeing severe fighting at La Bassée and Givenchy, he was wounded in action in the Somme Offensive of July 1916. He was invalided home, but on his recovery, returned to France, was again in action at Arras and was taken prisoner in April 1917. Held in captivity until after the cessation of hostilities, he was demobilised on his release in January 1919, and holds the 1914-15 Star, and the General Service and Victory Medals.
5, Nansen Street, Ardwick, Manchester.   Z7143

McCRACKEN, W., Pte., 9th King's (Liverpool Regt.)
Three months after joining in June 1916, he was drafted to France, where he saw heavy fighting in various sectors of the Front. After taking part in the Battles of the Somme, Arras, Ypres and Cambrai, and many other important engagements, he was wounded in action on the Somme during the Retreat of March 1918, and invalided home. He was finally demobilised in January 1919, and holds the General Service and Victory Medals.
11, Dougall Street, Hulme, Manchester.   Z7145

McCULLAGH, C., Pte., King's (Liverpool Regt.) and Military Police.
He joined in March 1916, and underwent a period of training prior to being drafted to the Western Front in May of the following year. There, after taking part in many important engagements, including the Battles of Messines, Ypres, Cambrai, the Somme, Amiens, Bapaume and Le Cateau, he was transferred to the Military Police and was engaged as an escort to prisoners of war. He was demobilised in March 1919, and holds the General Service and Victory Medals.
11, Cawdor Street, Hulme, Manchester.   Z7146

McCULLOCH, J., Sergt., 3rd Hampshire Regiment.
Mobilised in August 1914, he was drafted to Egypt in the following month and thence to Gallipoli in April of the following year. There, after taking part in the Landing at Cape Helles, he took part in the Battles of Krithia and Achi Baba, and was wounded in action. He afterwards served in Palestine, before being transferred to the Western Front in March 1917, and after seeing severe fighting near St. Quentin, was invalided home. He then served as a Sergeant Instructor until discharged in December 1918. He was awarded the Royal Humane Society's Medal for bravery in saving life at Alexandria, and holds also the 1914-15 Star, and the General Service and Victory Medals.
4, Coalbrook Street, Ardwick, Manchester.   Z7147

McCULLOUGH, W., Private, 8th Manchester Regt.
Volunteering in July 1915, he embarked for Egypt in the following year, and served at El Arish, Kantara and in the Canal zone. In March 1917, he was drafted to the Western Front, where he took part in the Battles of Arras, Ypres, Passchendaele and Cambrai, and in the Retreat and Advance of 1918. Returning to England for demobilisation in March 1919, he holds the General Service and Victory Medals.
2, Vale Street, North Porter Street, Miles Platting, Manchester,   Z10731

McCURDY, S., R.E.
He volunteered in May 1915, and in March of the following year was drafted to Egypt, where he saw severe fighting at Romani and many other places. He also served in Palestine, and took part in the first Battle of Gaza before being transferred to the Western Front. There he served through the Battles of Arras, Passchendaele, Havrincourt and Valenciennes, and many other engagements, fought also in the Advance of 1918, and was wounded in action at St. Pol. He was demobilised in March 1919, and holds the General Service and Victory Medals.
8, Durham Place, Hulme, Manchester.   Z7148

McDERMOTT, A., Private, Royal Welch Fusiliers.
He volunteered in July 1915, and was retained on important duties in England until June of the following year, when he proceeded to the Western Front. After taking part in the Battles of the Somme, Arras, Vimy Ridge, Bullecourt, Messines and Ypres, and many minor engagements in various sectors, he was taken prisoner at Cambrai, and held in captivity until after the cessation of hostilities. He was demobilised in March 1919, and holds the General Service and Victory Medals.
7, Long Street, Ancoats, Manchester.   Z7149

McDERMOTT, J., Corporal, 23rd Manchester Regt.
After volunteering in August 1914, he underwent a period of training prior to being drafted to the Western Front in July 1916. Whilst in this theatre of war he saw much severe fighting, took part in the Battles of Arras, Ypres and Cambrai, and many other important engagements, and was gassed on the Somme in 1916. He was demobilised on returning home in December 1919, and holds the General Service and Victory Medals. 5, Baines Place, Ancoats, Manchester.   Z7150

McDERMOTT, J. W., Sapper, R.E.
He volunteered in October 1915, and in November 1917 was drafted to France. Whilst overseas he was engaged on important duties in connection with the operations, and was frequently in the forward areas, notably at Arras, Ypres, Cambrai, Amiens, Bapaume and Havrincourt. He was demobilised in November 1919, and holds the General Service and Victory Medals.
3, Trickett's Place, Oldham Road, Manchester.   TZ9618

McDONALD, B., Private, 16th Cheshire Regiment.
He volunteered in October 1915, and proceeding overseas in the following January saw active service on the Western Front. Taking part in heavy fighting in the Somme Offensive, he was seriously wounded in the course of operations, and invalided home for treatment. On recovery he rejoined his Battalion in France, but owing to illness was sent to hospital at Rouen, and later evacuated to Scotland for treatment, after which he was transferred to the South Lancashire Regiment, and retained on Home Service. He was demobilised in December 1918, and holds the General Service and Victory Medals. 15, Dearden Street, Ancoats, Manchester.   Z10732

McDONALD, C., Private, 1/6th Manchester Regt.
Two months after volunteering in September 1914 he was drafted to Egypt, where he saw much fighting on the Suez Canal. He unhappily lost his right eye as the result of being thrown from his horse at Mersa Matruh, and was for a considerable period in hospital at Cairo, Alexandria, Malta and in England. Invalided from the Army in June 1916, he re-enlisted, however, in October of the following year, but was finally discharged in October 1918, as medically unfit for further service, suffering from neurasthenia. He holds the 1914-15 Star and the General Service and Victory Medals.
20, Dover Street, Chester Road, Hulme, Manchester.   Z7154

McDONALD, J., Pte., 6th K.O. (R. Lancaster Regt.)
Volunteering in September 1914, he was drafted to Egypt in October of the following year, and served there until January 1916, when he was sent to Mesopotamia. In this theatre of war he took part in several operations on the Tigris and at Kut-el-Amara, and was wounded in the Battle of Sanna-i Yat on April 9th, 1916. Invalided home owing to his injuries he was under treatment in Manchester, and was subsequently discharged as medically unfit in October 1916. He holds the 1914-15 Star, and the General Service and Victory Medals.
16, Wilkinson Street, Collyhurst, Manchester.   Z10735

McDONALD, J. J., Pte., 8th Manchester Regt. and South Lancashire Regt.
Shortly after volunteering in August 1914, he was drafted to Egypt, where he served at various stations. He was severely injured in an accident at Mustapha, and as a result, was in hospital at Cairo, where he underwent the amputation of a finger. On his recovery in October 1915, he was transferred to the Western Front, whence he was sent in the following month to Salonika. There he took part in the recapture of Monastir, and in much fighting on the Doiran and Struma fronts, until invalided to Malta suffering from malaria. He finally returned home and was discharged as medically unfit for further service in September 1917, and holds the 1914-15 Star, and the General Service and Victory Medals.
20, Holt Street, Morton Street, Longsight, Manchester.   Z7151

McDONALD, R., Pte., 2nd Cheshire Regt. and Spr., R.E.
He joined in January 1917, and was drafted in the following November to France, where he served at Nieuport, Ypres and in the second Battle of the Somme, during which he was taken prisoner. Held in captivity in Germany until December 1918, he was then released and on his return was demobilised in the following month, holding the General Service and Victory Medals.
9, Gibson Street, Newton Heath, Manchester.   Z9619

McDONALD, T., Pte., 13th Royal Welch Fusiliers.
He volunteered in April 1915 and sent overseas in the following January served in various sectors of the Western Front. He took part in severe fighting at Loos, and was wounded and admitted to hospital. On recovery he returned to the trenches, and, wounded for the second time, was invalided to hospital in England. After treatment he was discharged as medically unfit for further service in July 1918, and holds the General Service and Victory Medals.
8, Morville Street, Ancoats, Manchester.   Z10733

McDONALD, T., Private, 1/10th King's (Liverpool Regt.) Liverpool Scottish.
Volunteering in August 1915, he was sent to the Western Front in the following December and took part in several engagements until wounded on the Somme on July 31st, 1916. After treatment in hospital at Etaples he returned to the trenches and was again wounded in the Battle of Ypres in 1917. On recovery he was in action in many engagements through the German Offensive and subsequent Allied Advance of 1918, after which he was retained on special duties in France for nearly a year. Demobilised in October 1919, he holds the 1914-15 Star, and the General Service and Victory Medals.
16, Temple Street, Bradford, Manchester.   TZ11719A

McDONALD, T., Driver, R.A.S.C.
A Reservist, he was mobilised on the outbreak of hostilities, and proceeding to France shortly afterwards served on important transport duties during the Retreat from Mons and in the Battles of Le Cateau and Ypres. Sent to England owing to illness in October 1915, he received hospital treatment, after which he was stationed in the South of England. Demobilised in March 1919, he holds the Mons Star, and the General Service and Victory Medals.
31, Naylor Street, Oldham Road, Manchester.   Z10734

McDONALD, W., Sapper, R.E.
Joining in October 1916, he underwent his training and was then posted to the Kent Fortress Company, with which unit he was engaged on special electrical work. He was unsuccessful in obtaining his transfer overseas, but rendered valuable services throughout hostilities. He was in hospital for some time with influenza and was eventually demobilised in March 1919.
5, George's Avenue, Chester Road, Hulme, Manchester. Z7155

McDONALD-HAY, J., Private, 7th Manchester Regt.
He volunteered in June 1915, but owing to his being physically unfit for transfer overseas was retained on important coast defence duties. He did consistently good work for twelve months, but unfortunately became further disabled through his military service and was invalided from the Army in July 1916. He holds the King's Certificate.
10, Overton Street, Hulme, Manchester.   TZ7153

McDONNELL, J., Gunner, R.G.A.
Volunteering in October 1914, he was sent to Gallipoli in the following August and served in operations from the Landing at Suvla Bay until the Evacuation of the Peninsula. Proceeding to the Western Front in July 1916, he fought in the Battles of the Somme and Arras, and was wounded at Ypres in 1917. Evacuated to England, he was under treatment in Birmingham, and on recovery was drafted to Ireland, where he was stationed until discharged as medically unfit for further service in December 1918. He holds the 1914–15 Star, and the General Service and Victory Medals.
16, Marple Street, Ancoats, Manchester.   Z10736

McDONNELL, T. J. M., Sergt., R.E.
He volunteered in February 1915, and was immediately drafted to the Western Front. He saw much severe fighting in this theatre of war, and was in action at the Battles of Hill 60, Arras, the Somme, Ypres (III), Passchendaele and Cambrai, where he was wounded and invalided to hospital in England. On his recovery he was stationed at Chatham, where he did good work until he was demobilised in March 1919. He holds the 1914–15 Star, and the General Service and Victory Medals.   Z7156
78, Higher Chatham Street, Chorlton-on-Medlock, Manchester.

McDONOUGH, A., Air Mechanic, R.A.F.
He volunteered in June 1915, and embarking for France in October of the following year, was engaged on observation duties with his Squadron in the forward areas. He did good work during the Battles of the Somme, Beaumont-Hamel, Ypres and Passchenadele and in the German Offensive. In June 1918 he returned to England and was sent to Ireland, where he served for upwards of a year. Demobilised in February 1919, he holds the General Service and Victory Medals. 23, Drinkwater St., Harpurhey, Manchester. Z11435

McDONOUGH, J., Private, 1st Manchester Regiment.
He volunteered in August 1914, and in the following April sailed for Gallipoli, where he served in operations from the first Landing on the Peninsula until the Evacuation. Drafted in 1916 to Egypt, he was wounded at El Fasher in May of that year, and, invalided home, received treatment at Pendleton War Hospital. On recovery he was sent to India in December 1916, and after two years' service there proceeded to Siberia. Owing to illness he was evacuated to England in April 1919, and in the following July was demobilised. He holds the 1914–15 Star, and the General Service and Victory Medals.
8, Jones Street, Chorlton-on-Medlock, Manchester. Z11756

McDONOUGH, J., Private, Manchester Regiment.
Volunteering in February 1916, he proceeded overseas three months later and saw active service on the Western Front. He fought in the Battles of Vimy Ridge, the Somme, Arras, Bullecourt, Messines, Ypres and Cambrai, and in many of those during the Retreat and Advance of 1918. After the Armistice he was retained in France on special duties. Returning to England for demobilisation in December 1919, he holds the General Service and Victory Medals.
45, Hamilton Street, Collyhurst, Manchester.   Z10737A

McDONOUGH, M., Private, M.G.C.
He joined in March 1916, and three months later crossed to the Western Front. In this theatre of war he was in action in the Battles of Vimy Ridge, the Somme, Arras, Bullecourt, Messines, Ypres, Cambrai, and in those of the Retreat and Advance of 1918. Retained on special duties in France after the Armistice, he returned to England for demobilisation in November 1919, and holds the General Service and Victory Medals.
45, Hamilton Street, Collyhurst, Manchester.   Z10737C

McDONOUGH, J., Private, Lancashire Fusiliers.
He joined in March 1918, and on the completion of his training served with his Battalion at various depôts and did excellent work. He was unable to obtain his transfer overseas before the conclusion of hostilities, but was, however, sent to France in March 1919, and was engaged on special duties at various prisoners of war camps for several months. He returned to England in January 1920, when he was demobilised.
45, Hamilton Street, Collyhurst, Manchester.   Z10737B

MACDOUGALL, F., Private, Lancashire Fusiliers.
He volunteered in May 1915, and three months later crossed to the Western Front, where he fought in the Battles of Loos, Albert, the Somme and Arras. In September 1917 he was sent to Salonika and among other operations in the Balkans took part in the Advance on the Vardar. Owing to illness he was invalided home early in 1918, and after treatment in hospital was discharged as medically unfit in April 1918. He holds the 1914–15 Star, and the General Service and Victory Medals. 13, Aspden St., Ancoats, Manchester. Z10738

McDOWELL, J. C., L/Corporal, S. Lancashire Regt.
Volunteering in March 1915, he was drafted to France in the following July and was in action at Ypres and in the Battle of Loos. Sent to Salonika in October 1915, he was engaged with his unit in the Allied Offensive on the Doiran front and in the advance on the Struma and Vardar. Sent home on account of ill-health in July 1918, he returned to the Western Front on recovery, and fought in the Battle of Cambrai. Transferred later to the Labour Corps, he was stationed at Boulogne and engaged in loading and unloading military supplies for several months. He was demobilised in February 1919, and holds the 1914–15 Star, and the General Service and Victory Medals.
70, Cross Street, Bradford, Manchester.   Z10739

McELROY, J., Private, 18th Cheshire Regiment.
Joining in June 1916, he was sent overseas two months later and served on the Western Front for over three years. During this period he fought in the Somme Offensive, and was wounded at Arras in May 1917. On recovery he took part in the Battles of Ypres, Cambrai, Bapaume, Havrincourt, Le Cateau and others in the Retreat and subsequent Allied Advance of 1918. Engaged on special duties in France after the Armistice, he returned home for demobilisation in November 1919, and holds the General Service and Victory Medals.
5, Anslow Street, Rochdale Road, Manchester.   Z10740

McEVILLEY, H., Private, 3rd Manchester Regiment.
He volunteered in November 1914, and was engaged on home service duties until August 1916, when he embarked for France. There he was in action in the Battles of the Ancre, Arras, Ypres and Cambrai and in those of the Retreat and Advance of 1918. He was demobilised in March 1919, and holds the General Service and Victory Medals.
49, Beaumont Street, Beswick, Manchester.   Z10742

McEVILLY, P., Private, Manchester Regiment.
Volunteering in October 1914, he proceeded to the Western Front in December of the following year and fought in the Somme Offensive and in several engagements in the Ypres salient. He was invalided home in March 1917, owing to illness, and was under treatment for nine months. Discharged as medically unfit for further service in March 1918, he holds the 1914–15 Star, and the General Service and Victory Medals.
31, Clayton Street, Ancoats, Manchester.   Z10741

McEVOY, J. H., Gunner, R.F.A., and Sapper, R.E.
He volunteered at the outbreak of hostilities, but was retained on important home duties with his Battery at various stations until 1916, when he proceeded to France and took part in fierce fighting at Ypres and Hill 60, where he was wounded. On his recovery he was transferred to the R.E. and did good work with his unit until December 1918. He returned to England and was discharged as medically unfit for further service in May 1919. He holds the General Service and Victory Medals.
9, Lingmoor St., Chorlton-on-Medlock, Manchester. X1026D

McEVOY, P., Private, Royal Scots.
He joined in April 1916, and after completing his training was sent to the Western Front in the same year. Whilst in this theatre of war he took part in much fierce fighting at the Battles of Arras (I), Ypres (III) and the Somme (II), and in the Retreat and Advance of 1918. He also took part in the Advance into Germany, where he remained until he was demobilised in February 1919. He holds the General Service and Victory Medals.
7, Dougall Street, Hulme, Manchester.   Z7157

McEWAN, J., Private, 8th Manchester Regiment.
He volunteered in August 1914, and in September of the following year proceeded to Egypt. Whilst in this theatre of war he was in action against the Senussi Arabs when they were repulsed at Mersa Matruh, and also fought at Katia and at the capture of El Fasher. He was drafted to the Western Front in August 1916, and served in the Battles of the Somme, the Ancre, Bullecourt, Ypres and Bapaume. He was demobilised in March 1919, and holds the 1914–15 Star, and the General Service and Victory Medals.
109, Teignmouth Street, Rochdale Road, Manchester. Z9620

M^CFALL, W., Private, R.A.V.C.

He joined in June 1916, and two months later embarked for France, where he was engaged on important veterinary duties and was present at the engagements at Vimy Ridge, the Somme, Arras, Ypres, Cambrai, Amiens, Havrincourt and Bapaume. He remained in France after the cessation of hostilities until October 1920, when he returned home and was demobilised. He holds the General Service and Victory Medals.
22, Hadfield Street, Newton Heath, Manchester. Z9621

M^CFARLANE, J., Private, K.O. (R. Lancaster Regt.)

Mobilised in August 1914, he was shortly afterwards drafted with his Regiment to France and fought in the Retreat from Mons and at Ypres, where he was wounded. Later he proceeded to Egypt, took part in the operations on the Suez Canal and was again wounded and sent into hospital at Cairo and thence to Malta. He returned home and was demobilised in March 1919, holding the Sudan, Sudan (Khedive's) and Queen's and King's South African Medals, the Mons Star, and the General Service and Victory Medals.
130, Oldham Road, Manchester. Z11546

M^CFARLANE, M., Stoker, R.N.

He volunteered in April 1914, and was posted to H.M.S. " Bellona," which vessel was engaged on patrol duties in the North Sea. She was in action in the Battles of Heligoland Bight and had other encounters with enemy craft. Contracting illness in the course of his service, he was admitted to hospital and discharged as medically unfit in December 1914, holding the 1914-15 Star, and the General Service and Victory Medals.
27, Burton Street, Rochdale Road, Manchester. Z10743A

M^CFARLANE, T., Private, 6th Border Regiment.

Volunteering in August 1914, he was drafted overseas in the following year and saw service in various theatres of war. Sent to Gallipoli he took part in operations until the Evacuation of the Peninsula, and in January 1916 proceeded to Egypt, There he was in action in the Battles of Katia and Romani and the capture of El Fasher, and in December 1916 was sent to the Western Front. Whilst in this theatre of war he fought in the Battles of Arras, Bullecourt, Messines, Ypres, Cambrai and in several of those in the Retreat and Advance of 1918. He holds the 1914-15 Star, and the General Service and Victory Medals, and in 1920 was still serving.
27, Burton Street, Rochdale Road, Manchester. Z10743C

M^CFARLANE, W., Gdsmn., 2nd Grenadier Guards.

He volunteered in August 1914, and crossing to France in the same year fought in several engagements until wounded on the Somme in October 1916. On recovery he returned to the firing line and was in action in the Battles of Arras, Vimy Ridge, Messines, Ypres, Cambrai and at Bapaume, Le Cateau and the Lys, in the Retreat and subsequent Allied Advance of 1918. He was demobilised in December 1918, and holds the 1914 Star, and the General Service and Victory Medals.
27, Burton Street, Rochdale Road, Manchester. Z10743B

M^CGAHAN, J. W., L/Corporal, R.E.

Volunteering in September 1914, he was drafted to the Western Front in the following January and served in various sectors. Engaged in the Tunnelling Section of his Corps, he did good work in the Battles of Hill 60, Ypres, Loos, the Somme, Messines, Cambrai and in the Retreat and Advance of 1918. Returning to England for demobilisation in December 1918, he holds the 1914-15 Star, and the General Service and Victory Medals.
11, Elliott Street, Bradford, Manchester. Z10744

M^CGAHEY, J., Private, Lancashire Fusiliers.

He enlisted in March 1913, and immediately on the outbreak of hostilities in August 1914, proceeded to the Western Front, where he served through the Battle of, and Retreat from, Mons, also the Battles of the Marne and the Aisne(I). He was later transferred to the Dardanelles, where he took part in the Landing at Suvla Bay and other engagements until the Evacuation of the Gallipoli Peninsula. He was invalided home in December 1915, and finally received his discharge as medically unfit for further service in July 1916. He holds the Mons Star, and the General Service and Victory Medals.
14, Clifford Street, Lower Openshaw, Manchester. Z7158

M^CGARRY, M., Guardsman, Irish Guards.

He was mobilised in August 1914, and was quickly drafted to France. During his service in this theatre of war he was in action at the Battle of, and in the Retreat from, Mons. Later he took an active part in the Battles of the Aisne and Ypres (I). He was then invalided to hospital in England suffering from shell-shock, and in August 1916 was discharged as medically unfit for further service, holding the Mons Star, and the General Service and Victory Medals.
14, Marsland Street, Chorlton-on-Medlock, Manchester. Z7159

M^CGARVEY, J., Private, 11th Lancashire Fusiliers.

Volunteering in September 1914, he was sent to the Western Front in the following September and was almost immediately in action in the Battle of Loos. He also fought in the Battles of the Somme, Arras and Ypres, and afterwards, stationed at Boulogne, was engaged there on special duties for a year. He was demobilised in February 1919, and holds the 1914-15

Star, and the General Service and Victory Medals.
89, Inkermann Street, Collyhurst, Manchester. Z10725

M^CGINN, E., Gunner, R.F.A.

He volunteered in July 1915, and after a period of training served at various stations on important duties with his Battery. He proceeded to France in March 1917, where he saw much fighting and was wounded. Later he was transferred to Salonika, and was in action during the heavy fighting on the Doiran front. He returned home and was demobilised in March 1919, and holds the General Service and Victory Medals. 34, Carlisle St., Hulme, Manchester. Z7160

M^CGINN, M., Gunner, R.F.A. and Sapper, R.E. (Signal Section).

Enlisting in November 1909, he was mobilised when war broke out and crossed to France soon afterwards. He served with his Battery in the Retreat from Mons and the Battles of Ypres, Loos and the Somme, and in 1917 was transferred to the Royal Engineers. Engaged as a field linesman in the forward areas, he was present in heavy fighting on the Somme, and the Ancre and was wounded near Cambrai on March 21st, 1918. He was demobilised in February 1919, and holds the Mons Star, and the General Service and Victory Medals.
53, Fielden Street, Oldham Road, Manchester. Z11757

M^CGLONE, D., Private, 2nd Manchester Regiment.

He joined in August 1917, and on completing his training was engaged on important home service duties with his Battalion. Owing to his being under age for active service he was unable to obtain his transfer overseas before the termination of the war, but in February 1920 was sent to Mesopotamia, and was stationed at Baghdad. He was still serving with the Colours in 1920.
37, Grantham Street, West Gorton, Manchester. Z10745

M^CGLYNN, P., Sergt., 2nd Manchester Regiment.

Mobilised from the Army Reserve on the outbreak of war, he proceeded to France with the first Expeditionary Force, and fought in the Retreat from Mons, and the Battles of Le Cateau, the Marne, and the Aisne. He was wounded at La Bassée in October 1914, and on recovery took an active part in severe fighting at Loos, Albert, Vermelles, and Vimy Ridge, where he was again wounded in May 1916. Evacuated to England he received hospital treatment, and was engaged on home service duties. Still serving in 1920, he holds the Mons Star, and the General Service and Victory Medals.
23, Garrick Street, Ancoats, Manchester. Z10746

M^CGLYNN, R., Private, Lancashire Fusiliers.

He volunteered in November 1914, and in the following June was drafted to the Western Front, where he took part in the severe fighting in various sectors of the Front. He fought in important engagements until August 1915, when he was unfortunately killed in Action at Loos. He was entitled to the 1914-15 Star, and the General Service and Victory Medals.
" The path of duty was the way to glory."
63, Long Street, Ancoats, Manchester. Z7111A

M^CGLYNN, W., Private, Lancashire Fusiliers.

He volunteered in August 1914, and shortly afterwards was drafted to the Western Front, where he saw much fighting, and was in many important engagements, including the Battles of Ypres I, Neuve Chapelle, St. Eloi, Hill 60, Vermelles, Vimy Ridge, and the Somme, where he was killed in Action in December 1916. He was entitled to the 1914-15 Star, and the General Service and Victory Medals.
" His life for his Country, his soul to God."
63, Long Street, Ancoats, Manchester. Z7111B

M^CGRATH, E., Rifleman, K.R.R.C.

He volunteered in March 1915, and crossing to France three months later was engaged with his unit in the Battles of Loos, St. Eloi, and Albert. He gave his life for King and Country in the Battle of the Somme on September 9th, 1916, and was buried at the British Military Cemetery at Combles. He was entitled to the 1914-15 Star, and the General Service and Victory Medals.
" Nobly striving,
He nobly fell that we might live."
130, Knightly Street, Rochdale Road, Manchester. Z10747A

M^CGRATH, J., Rifleman, K.R.R.C.

Volunteering in September 1914, he was drafted to the Western Front five months later, and fought in the Battles of Neuve Chapelle, Hill 60, Ypres, Festubert, and Loos. He fell fighting at St. Eloi in March 1916, and was entitled to the 1914-15 Star, and the General Service and Victory Medals.
" He passed out of the sight of men by the path of duty and self sacrifice."
18, Dalton Street, Collyhurst, Manchester. Z10748A

M^CGRATH, J., Guardsman, 3rd Dragoon Guards.

He joined in March 1916, and after completing a term of training was engaged on very important duties with his unit at various stations. He rendered valuable services, but was unsuccessful in obtaining his transfer to a theatre of war before the cessation of hostilities, owing to his being under age. He was, however, sent to India in October 1919, and was engaged on important garrison duties, and was still serving there in 1920.
122, Tame Street, Ancoats, Manchester. Z7117A

McGRATH, J. W., Rifleman, 3rd Rifle Brigade.
He volunteered in September 1914, and in the following
January proceeded overseas. Serving with his Battalion in
various parts of the line in France and Flanders, he was in
action in the Battles of Hill 60, Ypres, Loos, St. Eloi, the
Somme, Arras, and Cambrai, and was wounded and gassed
at Armentières in March 1918. On recovery he was attached
to the Royal Army Ordnance Corps, with which unit he served
until the end of hostilities. He was demobilised in March
1919, and holds the 1914–15 Star, and the General Service and
Victory Medals.
130, Knightley Street, Rochdale Road, Manchester. Z10747B

McGRATH, M., Private, 12th Manchester Regt.
He volunteered in September 1914, and was drafted to France
in the following June. Whilst in this theatre of war he took
part in much of the fierce fighting in various sectors, and was
in action at the Battles of Loos, Albert, the Somme I, Bullecourt, Ypres III, and in the Retreat and Advance of 1918. He
remained in France until after the cessation of hostilities, and
was demobilised in February 1919, holding the 1914–15 Star,
and the General Service and Victory Medals.
122, Tame Street, Ancoats, Manchester. Z7117B

McGRATH, W., Private, 4th Manchester Regiment.
Volunteering in September 1914, he was engaged with his
Battalion on important duties at various stations until November 1916, when he was drafted to the Western Front. There
he took part in the Battles of Arras, Bullecourt, Ypres, and
in the German Offensive and subsequent Allied Advance of
1918. Returning home for demobilisation in March 1919, he
holds the General Service and Victory Medals.
18, Dalton Street, Collyhurst, Manchester. Z10748B

McGREAVY, J. F., L/Cpl., 1st Manchester Regt.
He volunteered in August 1914, and in the following month
was drafted to France, when he fought in many important
engagements. He was in action at La Bassée, Armentières,
Ypres, Hill 60, and Festubert, but was unfortunately killed
by a sniper at Loos in March 1916. He was entitled to the
1914 Star, and the General Service and Victory Medals.
"A valiant soldier with undaunted heart he breasted life's
last hill."
37, Teignmouth Street, Collyhurst, Manchester. Z9622A

McGUIRE, A., 1st Air Mechanic, R.A.F.
He joined in April 1916, and after passing his trade test served
on the London defences, and later was transferred to Edinburgh, where he was engaged in the testing and repair of
aeroplanes. His duties, which demanded a high degree of
technical skill were carried out in an efficient manner, and he
rendered valuable services, but was not successful in obtaining
his transfer overseas. He contracted an illness, owing to which
he was discharged in November 1918.
52, Francisco Street, Miles Platting, Manchester. Z9263

McGUIRE, J. B., Private, 6th Manchester Regt.
He volunteered in August 1914, and in April of the following
year was drafted to Gallipoli, where he took part in the
Landing at Cape Helles, and saw much severe fighting. He
made the supreme sacrifice, falling in action in the third Battle
of Krithia on June 5th, 1915. He was entitled to the 1914–15
Star, and the General Service and Victory Medals.
"He died the noblest death a man may die,
Fighting for God and right and liberty."
35, Oliver Street, Openshaw, Manchester. Z7162A

McGUIRE, T., Private, 8th Manchester Regiment.
He volunteered in October 1915, and was retained on important duties at various stations in England until August 1918,
when he was drafted to the Western Front. There he served
at Arras, and in various other sectors, and was engaged chiefly
in guarding prisoners of war. He returned home for demobilisation in March 1919, and holds the General Service and
Victory Medals.
35, Oliver Street, Openshaw, Manchester. Z7162B

McGUIRE, T., Private, 2nd Manchester Regiment.
He volunteered in August 1914, and in the following March
was sent overseas. In the course of his service in France he
was in action in the Battles of Neuve Chapelle, St. Eloi, and
the Somme, and was wounded at Beaumont-Hamel in November 1916. On recovering he fought at Arras, and in several
engagements in the Ypres Salient. He died gloriously on the
Field of Battle on September 16th, 1917, and was entitled to
the 1914–15 Star, and the General Service and Victory Medals.
136, Gunson Street, Miles Platting, Manchester. Z10749

McGUNIGALL, J., L/Corporal, Royal Scots.
Volunteering in October 1914, he was engaged on important
military police duties in various parts of England and Scotland,
and in January 1918, embarked for the Western Front. There
he was in action in several important engagements, including
those in the Retreat and Advance of 1918. He was demobilised
in December of that year, and holds the General Service and
Victory Medals.
2, Hooley Street, Ancoats, Manchester. Z10750

McHALE, A., Private, 4th Manchester Regiment.
A Regular, he was mobilised on the outbreak of hostilities,
and shortly afterwards proceeded to the Western Front. There
he was in action in the Retreat from Mons, and the Battles of
the Marne, Ypres, St. Eloi, Hill 60, Loos, Albert, Vermelles,
Ploegsteert Wood, and was wounded at Bullecourt. Sent
home on account of his injuries he was treated in the London
Military Hospital, and was subsequently discharged on account
of service in September 1918. He holds the Mons Star, and
the General Service and Victory Medals.
2, Wragby Street, Miles Platting, Manchester. Z11758

McHALE, A., Private, East Lancashire Regiment.
He volunteered in January 1916, and crossing to France two
months later was almost immediately engaged in severe fighting
at Loos. Seriously wounded, he was sent home for treatment,
and was in hospital for several months. He was invalided out
of the Army in February 1918, and holds the General Service
and Victory Medals.
17, Whalley Street, Ancoats, Manchester. Z10752

McHUGH, J., Sergt., 6th Manchester Regiment.
Mobilised in August 1914, he was drafted to Egypt in the
following month, and there served on the Suez Canal. In
1915 he was transferred to Gallipoli, where, after taking part
in the Landing at Cape Helles, he fought in the Battles of
Krithia, and Achi Baba. Sent to Egypt on the Evacuation
of the Peninsula, he finally returned home and was discharged,
time-expired, in 1917. He holds the 1914–15 Star, and the
General Service Victory, and Long Service and Good Conduct
Medals. 5, Molyneux St., Longsight, Manchester. Z7164

McINNES, A., Private, 6th Manchester Regiment.
He volunteered in June 1915, and in January of the following
year, proceeded to Egypt, where he took part in engagements
at Sollum, Katia, El Fasher, Romani, Magdhaba, and many
other places. In February 1917 he was transferred to the
Western Front, and there fought on the Ancre front, and was
severely wounded in action near Ypres in March 1917. He
was invalided from the Army in May of that year, and holds
the General Service and Victory Medals.
36, Russell Street, Moss Side, Manchester. TZ6952E

McINNES, D., Private, 3rd Lancashire Fusiliers.
He volunteered in September 1914, and after completing a
period of training, served at various stations, where, engaged
on duties of great importance, he rendered very valuable
services with his unit. He was not successful in obtaining
his transfer to a theatre of war, and in September 1916, was
discharged on compassionate grounds.
36, Russell Street, Moss Side, Manchester. TZ6952D

McINNES, H., Private, 15th Royal Scots.
Volunteering in October 1914, he was drafted to the Western
Front in December of the following year, and there saw severe
fighting at Loos, St. Eloi, Ploegsteert Wood, and many other
places. He unhappily fell in action in the Advance on the
Somme on July 1st, 1916. He was entitled to the 1914–15
Star, and the General Service and Victory Medals.
"Courage, bright hopes, and a myriad dreams, splendidly
given."
36, Russell Street, Moss Side, Manchester. TZ6952C

McINTYRE, C. T., Driver, R.F.A.
Volunteering in June 1915, he sailed for Egypt in the following
January, and was in action in the Canal zone, at Mersa Matruh,
Agagia, and at the occupation of Sollum. In March 1917,
he proceeded to the Western Front, where he took part in the
Battles of Ypres, Cambrai, and in those of the Retreat and
Advance of 1918. He holds the General Service and Victory
Medals, and was demobilised in April 1919.
61, Elizabeth Street, West Gorton, Manchester. Z10753

McINTYRE, J., Sergt., R.A.O.C.
He volunteered in September 1914, and was retained on
important duties at various stations in England until January
1916, when he proceeded to the Western Front. There he
was present at the Battles of Vimy Ridge, the Somme, Arras,
Bullecourt and Ypres, and many other engagements, and also
took an active part in the Retreat and Advance of 1918. He
afterwards served with the Army of Occupation in Germany,
before returning home for demobilisation in June 1919, and
holds the General Service and Victory Medals.
2, Pickering Street, Hulme, Manchester. Z7165B

McINTYRE, R., Driver, R.A.S.C.
Joining in December 1916, he proceeded to German East
Africa on completing a period of training four months later.
There he served at Dar-es-Salaam, Delagoa Bay, and various
other places, where, engaged on duties of a highly important
nature, he rendered very valuable services. Invalided home
in January 1919, suffering from fever, he was in hospital in
London until discharged in June of that year as medically
unfit for further service. He holds the General Service and
Victory Medals.
2, Pickering Street, Hulme, Manchester. Z7165A

M^CINTYRE, W., Gunner, R.F.A.

He volunteered in December 1914, and in April of the following year proceeded to the Western Front, where he saw much heavy fighting. He took part in engagements at Fricourt, Beaucourt, Menin Road, St. Quentin, and many other places, and also served through the Battles of Ypres, Loos, Albert, Vermelles, Vimy Ridge, St. Quentin, and Armentières. Finally demobilised in January 1919, he holds the 1914-15 Star, and the General Service and Victory Medals.
16, John Street, Bradford, Manchester. Z11864

M^CKAY, J. E., Private, Cheshire Regiment.

He joined in May 1916, and in July of the following year crossed to the Western Front. In the course of his service there he was in action in the Battles of Ypres, Passchendaele, Cambrai, and in the German Offensive, and subsequent Allied Advance of 1918, and was wounded. Sent home, owing to his injuries, he received treatment in hospital, and in March 1919, was discharged on account of service. He holds the General Service and Victory Medals.
9, Worrall Street, Collyhurst, Manchester. Z10756

M^CKAY, L. H., Lieut., Loyal (N. Lancashire Regt.)

He volunteered at the outbreak of war in August 1914, and was retained on important duties in England until January 1916, when he proceeded to the Western Front. There, after much severe fighting, he was wounded in action at St. Eloi in March 1916, and invalided home. On his recovery, however, he returned to France, and was again wounded on two occasions, and was for a considerable period in hospital. He was finally demobilised in March 1919, and holds the General Service and Victory Medals.
26, Great Southern Street, Moss Side, Manchester. Z7167

M^CKEEVER, J., A.B., Royal Naval Division.

He volunteered in June 1915, and in November of the following year, proceeded with the Royal Marines to the Western Front, where he saw much severe fighting. He took part in the Battles of the Ancre, Arras, and Cambrai, and other important engagements, was wounded in action at Gavrelle in April 1917, and in March 1918, was taken prisoner near Ypres. Held in captivity until after the cessation of hostilities, he was finally demobilised in February 1919, holding the General Service and Victory Medals.
83, George Street, Moss Side, Manchester. TZ7168

M^CKEEVER, J., Driver, R.A.S.C.

Volunteering in May 1915, he was drafted to Egypt in December of that year, and there took part in the engagements at Mersa Matruh. He was for a time in hospital at Alexandria and Cairo, before being transferred to Palestine in February 1916, and afterwards proceeded to Mesopotamia, where he was again in action on the Tigris, and at Kut. He finally returned home for demobilisation in August 1919, and holds the 1914-15 Star, and the General Service and Victory Medals.
104, George Street, Moss Side, Manchester. Z6862

M^CKEIRNON, M., Seaman, R.N., and Private, King's (Liverpool Regiment).

He volunteered in August 1914, and attached to the Grand Fleet, served in various patrol boats in the North Sea for nearly twelve months. Discharged in 1915, he enlisted in the Army in July of that year, and two months later was drafted to the Western Front, where he served with the Labour Corps in various sectors. He was present at the Battles of Arras, Ypres, and Cambrai, and many other engagements in this theatre of war, and also took an active part in the Retreat of 1918. He was invalided from the Army in November of that year, and holds the 1914-15 Star, and the General Service and Victory Medals.
39, Pump Street, Hulme, Manchester. Z7169

M^CKENNA, A., Private, R.A.M.C.

Volunteering in August 1915, he was drafted to France three months later, and served as a stretcher bearer with the 96th Field Ambulance. He did excellent work in the Battles of the Somme, Arras, Vimy Ridge, Ypres, and in those of the German Offensive. Invalided home in July 1918, on account of illness, he was admitted to Netley Hospital, and subsequently discharged as medically unfit in August 1919. He holds the 1914-15 Star, and the General Service and Victory Medals.
5, Worth Street, Rochdale Road, Manchester. Z10757

M^CKENNA, C. W., Corporal, 2nd Manchester Regt.

Volunteering in February 1915, he proceeded to Mesopotamia in the following month, and there saw much severe fighting. He took part in the Capture of Amara, in engagements at Ali-el-Gharb, Um-el-Hannah, Sanna-i-Yat, and the Tigris, and was also present at the Relief of Kut and was wounded in action. Returning home in September 1919, he was demobilised in the following month, and holds the 1914-15 Star, and the General Service and Victory Medals.
16, Spurgeon Street, West Gorton, Manchester. Z7109

M^CKENNA, J., Private, R.M.L.I.

He volunteered in September 1914, and after training at Plymouth and Cardiff was posted to H.M.S. "Donegal," which ship was engaged in escorting vessels carrying troops and food supplies from Canada, Nova Scotia, to the various theatres of war. His vessel was twice torpedoed in the Irish Sea, but escaped serious damage. On the conclusion of hostilities he was sent to Ireland, and in 1920 was still stationed there. He holds the 1914-15 Star, and the General Service and Victory Medals.
11, Alder Street, Rochdale Road, Manchester. Z10758

M^CKENNA, J., Guardsman, 1st Grenadier Guards.

He joined in October 1917, and in the following February was drafted to the Western Front. Whilst overseas he fought at Havrincourt, Maubeuge, and Canal du Nord, and in various other sectors of France before the cessation of hostilities. He returned home, and was demobilised in January 1919, holding the General Service and Victory Medals.
44, Rusholme Grove, Rusholme, Manchester. Z9623

M^CKENNA, J., Gunner, R.F.A.

Volunteering in January 1915, he was drafted to Egypt on completing his training in the following June, and there saw much severe fighting. He took part in engagements on the Suez Canal, and at Katia, Romani, Magdhaba, and many other places, before being transferred to the Western Front in February 1917. There he served through the Battles of Ypres and Passchendaele, and was gassed and wounded in action in September 1917. Invalided home, he was finally discharged, as medically unfit for further service in October 1918, and holds the 1914-15 Star, and the General Service and Victory Medals.
9, Hannah Street, Ardwick, Manchester. Z7170

M^CKENNA, J., H., Private, 8th Manchester Regt.

Volunteering in November 1915, he completed his training, and was selected for work on munitions. Engaged in the manufacture of shells at various factories in England and Scotland, he rendered valuable services, but was unable to secure his transfer overseas before the termination of the war. He was demobilised in February 1919.
8, Worth Street, St. Michaels, Manchester. Z10759

M^CKENZIE, C., A.B., Royal Navy.

He joined in February 1917, and in the following May was posted to H.M.S. "Tiger," which ship, attached to the Grand Fleet, was engaged on patrol and other important duties in the North Sea. His vessel had several encounters with enemy craft whilst hostilities were in progress. He was demobilised in April 1919, and holds the General Service and Victory Medals.
2, Heelis Street, Rochdale Road, Manchester. Z10760

M^CKENZIE, F., Pte., 11th King's (Liverpool Regt.)

Volunteering in October 1914, he was sent to France in May of the following year, and was in action at Ypres, Festubert, Albert, the Somme, Arras, Bullecourt and Cambrai. He also served in the Retreat and Advance of 1918. He was demobilised in February 1919, and holds the 1914-15 Star, and the General Service and Victory Medals.
43, Buxton Street, Manchester. Z9264

M^CKEOWN, J., Corporal, K.O. (R. Lancaster Regt.)

Volunteering in August 1914, he landed in France in the same month, and was engaged in heavy fighting in the Retreat from Mons, and the Battles of the Marne, Neuve Chapelle, Festubert, and Loos. He gave his life for King and Country in the Battle of the Somme on July 1st, 1916, and was entitled to the Mons Star, and the General Service and Victory Medals.
"He died the noblest death a man may die,
Fighting for God and right and liberty."
39, Edge Street, Hulme, Manchester. Z11759

M^CKEVITT, J., Private, South Lancashire Regt.

Joining in April 1918, he was drafted to France two months later and took part in the final operations of the German Offensive. He was also in action in numerous engagements in the subsequent Allied Advance, which brought the war to a close, and in January 1919, proceeded to Egypt. Serving there for over a year he was engaged on garrison duty at Alexandria, and returned home in February 1920. He was demobilised in the following April, and holds the General Service and Victory Medals.
50, Bath Street, Miles Platting, Manchester. Z10761A

M^CKEW, G. E., Gunner, R.G.A.

He volunteered in January 1915, and in November of the following year was drafted to the Western Front. Whilst in this theatre of war he saw much severe fighting, took part in the Battles of Ypres and the Somme, and many other engagements, and was gassed. He was invalided home, and afterwards served at various stations until his demobilisation in November 1919. He holds the General Service and Victory Medals. 13, Walter Street, Ancoats, Manchester. Z7171

M^CKIDDIE, E., Sergt., 1st K.R.R.C.

Shortly after volunteering in August 1914, he proceeded to the Western Front, where he took part in the Battles of Neuve Chapelle and Ypres, and many other important engagements in various sectors. He fell fighting at Festubert in June 1915. He was entitled to the 1914 Star, and the General Service and Victory Medals.
"Nobly striving,
He nobly fell that we might live."
1, Whitfield Street, Ardwick, Manchester. X7172

McKINLEY, C. J. (D.C.M.), Corporal, R.A.S.C.
Having previously served in the South African Campaign he volunteered in September 1914, and was engaged at various stations, including the Isle of Man, on important duties with his unit. He rendered valuable services, but was not successful in obtaining his transfer to a fighting area before the cessation of hostilities, and was demobilised in November 1919. He was awarded the Distinguished Conduct Medal for conspicuous gallantry during the South African War, and also holds the Queen's South African Medal.
8, Heywood Street, West Gorton, Manchester. Z9265

McKINNEY, D., Pte., 3rd Royal Welch Fusiliers.
Joining in December 1916, he proceeded to the Western Front on completion of a period of training in May of the following year. There he took part in many important engagements, including the Battles of Bullecourt, Cambrai, the Marne, and Le Cateau, fought also in the Retreat and Advance of 1918, and suffered from shell-shock. He was afterwards transferred to the Labour Corps, with which he served until his demobilisation in November 1919. He holds the General Service and Victory Medals.
11, Sorrell Street, Hulme, Manchester. Z7174

McKINNEY, J., Driver, R.A.S.C.
He joined in March 1916, and after completing a term of training, served at various stations, where he was engaged on duties of great importance. He was medically unfit for active service, and was consequently unable to obtain his transfer to a theatre of war, but did much useful work with his Company until invalided from the Army in October 1917. He re-enlisted, however, in the following April, and was finally demobilised in February 1919.
11, Sorrell Street, Hulme, Manchester. Z7175

McKINNON, W., Private, 4th Royal Scots.
Volunteering in August 1914, he completed his training and served with his unit at various stations engaged on important duties. He did good work, but was unable to obtain his transfer to a theatre of war on account of medical unfitness, and was discharged in consequence in August 1916.
7, Anslow Street, Rochdale Road, Manchester. Z10764

McKNIGHT, J., Private, Lancashire Fusiliers.
He joined in February 1918, and after a short period of training was engaged on important duties at various stations. Owing to ill-health he was not successful in his efforts to obtain his transfer to the Front, but nevertheless, rendered valuable services with his unit until November 1919, when he was demobilised.
37, Dorrington Street, Hulme, Manchester. Z7176

McKNIGHT, J., Pte., Argyll and Sutherland Hldrs.
He volunteered in March 1915, and after a course of training was two months later drafted overseas. Whilst on the Western Front he took an active part in severe fighting in the Albert and Arras sectors, and during the Battle of the Somme had both legs blown off. He was in hospital at Rouen, and then at Chester, and was subsequently invalided out of the Army in March 1918. He holds the 1914-15 Star, and the General Service and Victory Medals.
12, St. Ann Street, Bradford, Manchester. X11885B

McKNIGHT, W., Private, 1st Manchester Regiment.
Volunteering in October 1915, on completion of his training in February 1916 drafted to India. He served there for eighteen months, and during that time carried out the various duties assigned to him with great ability. In 1917 he contracted malaria, to which he unfortunately succumbed on September 17th, 1917. He was entitled to the General Service and Victory Medals.
"His memory is cherished with pride."
12, St. Ann Street, Bradford, Manchester. X11885A

McKNIGHT, W. J., Pte., King's (Liverpool Regt.)
After having served on transport duties in the Mercantile Marine from August 1914 he joined the King's Liverpool Regiment in February 1916, and later in the same year was sent to France, where he took part in the Battles of the Somme and Ypres. He was later invalided home, and after a period in hospital was demobilised in December 1918, and holds the General Service, Mercantile Marine War, and Victory Medals.
7, Herbert Street, Bradford, Manchester. Z9266

McLAREN, J., Private, Liverpool Scottish and Air Mechanic, R.A.F.
He joined in September 1916, and landing in France three months later took part in heavy fighting in the Ypres salient, and was wounded. Evacuated to England he underwent medical treatment in Glasgow War Hospital, and on recovery was transferred to the Royal Air Force. He was engaged on work of a highly technical nature with the Balloon Section, and throughout rendered valuable services until his demobilisation in February 1919. He holds the General Service and Victory Medals.
7, Berkshire Street, Ancoats, Manchester. Z10765

McLAREN, J., Private, 2nd Manchester Regiment.
Volunteering in January 1915, he was drafted to the Western Front in December of that year, and there saw severe fighting in various sectors. After taking part in the Battles of Vimy Ridge and the Somme, and many minor engagements, he was wounded in action at Arras in April 1917, and was for a considerable period in hospital at Rouen, and in England. He was invalided from the Army in January 1919, and holds the 1914-15 Star, and the General Service and Victory Medals.
13, Northern Street, Erskine Street, Hulme, Manchester. Z7177

McLAUGHLIN, J., Pte., King's (Liverpool Regt.)
Joining in March 1916, he was drafted to France in the following month, and there saw severe fighting in various sectors of the Front. After taking part in the Battles of Vimy Ridge, the Somme, Arras, and Bullecourt, and many minor engagements he was gassed at Ypres in July 1917, and invalided home. After his recovery he served with the Labour Corps in England until demobilised in March 1919, holding the General Service and Victory Medals.
13, Rex Street, Jackson Street, Hulme, Manchester. Z7180

McLEAN, A. C., Private, 1st Manchester Regiment.
He volunteered in August 1915, and in June of the following year, proceeded to Mesopotamia, where he took part in the Capture of Baghdad and Tekrit. In March 1918 he was transferred to Palestine, and there saw severe fighting at Tripoli, Aleppo, and many other places until the cessation of hostilities. He also served for a time in the Soudan, and suffered from dysentery, whilst overseas. He finally returned home for demobilisation in June 1919, and holds the General Service and Victory Medals.
17, Welbeck Street, Chorlton-on-Medlock, Manchester. Z7178

McLEAN, J., Private, 1st Lancashire Fusiliers.
Volunteering in August 1914, he was engaged on important duties with his unit at various stations throughout the duration of the war. He rendered valuable services, but was not successful in obtaining a transfer overseas before the termination of hostilities, and was demobilised in January 1919.
22, Fletcher Street, Newton Heath, Manchester. Z9624

McLEARY, W., Private, 18th Manchester Regt.
He volunteered in November 1914, and twelve months later proceeded to the Western Front, where he saw much heavy fighting. He took part in many important engagements in this theatre of war, including those at Loos and St. Eloi in 1916, and was three times wounded in action—at Vimy Ridge in May 1916, on the Somme in July of that year, and at Ypres in October 1917. Invalided home, he was for a time in hospital at Manchester before being demobilised in February 1919, and holds the 1914-15 Star, and the General Service and Victory Medals. 10, Lingard St., Hulme, Manchester. Z7179A

McLEISH, J., Private, K.O. (R. Lancaster Regt.)
Volunteering in August 1914, he was drafted to France in the following February, and served with his unit in heavy fighting in the Ypres salient. Reported missing on May 8th of the same year, he was later presumed to have been killed in action on that date. He was entitled to the 1914-15 Star, and the General Service and Victory Medals.
"He passed out of the sight of men by the path of duty and self-sacrifice."
10, Lime Street, Newton, Manchester. Z10032-33A

McLENAHAN, J., Sergt., R.M.L.I.
Enlisting in 1907, he was mobilised on the declaration of war, and was posted to H.M.S. "Bulwark," which vessel was engaged on patrol and other duties in the North Sea. He was killed when his ship was destroyed by an accidental explosion off Sheerness with heavy loss of life on November 24th, 1914, and was entitled to the 1914-15 Star, and the General Service and Victory Medals.
"The path of duty was the way to glory."
13, Goole Street, Bradford, Manchester. Z11760

McLOUGHLIN, G. Private, (Signaller), King's Own (Royal Lancaster Regt.)
He was already serving in India when war broke out in August 1914, and in October of the following year was drafted to Salonika. There he saw much severe fighting and took part in many important engagements on the Vardar, Doiran and Struma fronts until the cessation of hostilities. Returning home in February 1919, he was discharged in the following month, and holds the 1914-15 Star, and the General Service and Victory Medals.
8, Pine Street, City Road, Hulme, Manchester. Z7182B

McLOUGHLIN, J., Private, K.O. (Y.L.I.)
He volunteered in August 1914, and landing in France shortly afterwards, fought through the Retreat from Mons. He also took part in numerous other engagements, notably those of Le Cateau, the Marne, the Aisne, Ypres, La Bassée, Neuve Chapelle, Hill 60, Festubert, Loos, St. Eloi, and Albert. He made the supreme sacrifice during the Somme Offensive on July 1st, 1916, and was entitled to the Mons Star, and the General Service and Victory Medals.
"Nobly striving,
He nobly fell that we might live."
17, Limer Street, Rochdale, Road, Manchester. Z10766A

McLOUGHLIN, J., Private, K.O. (R. Lancaster Regt.)
He volunteered in August 1914, and after completing his training was drafted to France, where he took part in important engagements. He fell fighting at Hill 60 in May 1916 and was entitled to the 1914-15 Star, and the General Service and Victory Medals.
" Thinking that remembrance, though unspoken, may reach him where he sleeps."
17, Gunson Street, Ancoats, Manchester.   Z9267A

McLOUGHLIN, J., Private, 9th Border Regiment.
He volunteered in July 1915, and in the same year was sent to Salonika, where he took part in the fierce fighting during the advance on the Vardar, Doiran and Struma fronts. He returned home in May 1919, and was demobilised, holding the 1914-15 Star, and the General Service and Victory Medals.
47, Princess Street, Miles Platting, Manchester.   Z9268

McLOUGHLIN, J., Corporal, R.F.A.
Twelve months after volunteering in January 1915, he proceeded to the Western Front, where he saw heavy fighting in various sectors. He took part in the Battles of Ploegsteert Wood, the Somme, Arras, Messines, Ypres, Cambrai and Le Cateau and many other engagements, served also through the Retreat and Advance of 1918, and was wounded in action near Ypres in 1916. Demobilised in May 1919, he holds the General Service and Victory Medals.   X7181A
14, Melbourne Street, Chorlton-on-Medlock, Manchester.

McLOUGHLIN, J., Private, 8th Manchester Regt.
Volunteering in April 1915, he was drafted to the Dardanelles in the following August and there, after taking part in the Landing at Suvla Bay, saw much severe fighting until the Evacuation of the Gallipoli Peninsula. He was then transferred to the Western Front, where he fought in the Battles of Arras, Vimy Ridge, Messines and Ypres and other engagements, and was gassed and wounded in action at Amiens in 1918. He was demobilised in February 1919, and holds the 1914-15 Star, and the General Service and Victory Medals.   X7181B
14, Melbourne Street, Chorlton-on-Medlock, Manchester.

McLOUGHLIN, M., Pte., K.O. (R. Lancaster Regt.)
Volunteering in July 1915, he proceeded to Mesopotamia in December of that year and there saw much fighting at Kut and was wounded in action. He was afterwards transferred to the Western Front, where he took part in the Battles of Vimy Ridge and the Somme and engagements at Loos, St. Eloi and many other places. He contracted pneumonia and unfortunately died in November 1916 and was buried at Lille. He was entitled to the 1914-15 Star, and the General Service and Victory Medals.
" His memory is cherished with pride."
8, Pine Street, City Road, Hulme, Manchester.   Z7182A

McLOUGHLIN, M., Pte., Royal Marine Labour Corps.
Joining in October 1917, he completed his training and was sent in the following month to France. There he was stationed at Calais, engaged in unloading ships until the cessation of hostilities. He rendered valuable services throughout and returning home in April 1919 was demobilised a month later. He holds the General Service and Victory Medals.
17, Limer Street, Rochdale Road, Manchester.   Z10766B

McMAHON, E., Private, East Surrey Regiment.
He joined in January 1917, and was retained on important duties in England until April of the following year, when he was drafted to the Western Front. Whilst in this theatre of war he saw much severe fighting, took part in the Battles of the Somme, the Lys, the Aisne and the Marne and many minor engagements, and was wounded in action at Cambrai in August 1918. Invalided home, he was for a considerable period in hospital before being discharged in November 1919 as medically unfit for further service. He holds the General Service and Victory Medals.
31, Riga Street, City Road, Hulme, Manchester.   TZ7184B

McMAHON, J., Pte., 7th Manchester Regiment.
He volunteered in May 1915, and after completing his training proceeded to Egypt, where he served for upwards of a year. In 1916, he was drafted to France and took part in the Battles of Ypres, the Somme, and many others. He also fought in the Retreat and Advance of 1918, and returned to England for his demobilisation in April 1919. He holds the 1914-15 Star, and the General Service and Victory Medals.
20, Retford Street, Chorlton-on-Medlock, Manchester.   Z10767

McMAHON, J., Pte., 2nd Manchester Regiment.
Mobilised in August 1914, he was drafted to the Western Front in the following month and there saw much heavy fighting in various sectors. He took part in the Battles of the Marne, the Aisne, Ypres and St. Eloi and many other important engagements, he was severely gassed whilst in action at Hill 60 in May 1915, and was in hospital at Rouen and in England. He was invalided from the Army in August 1916, and holds the 1914 Star, and the General Service and Victory Medals.
31, Riga Street, City Road, Hulme, Manchester.   TZ7184A

McMAHON, M., Driver, R.F.A.
He volunteered at the outbreak of war in August 1914, and in February of the following year was sent to the Western Front. There he took part in many important engagements in various sectors, including the Battles of Neuve Chapelle, Ypres and Festubert, was wounded in action and was buried by an explosion at Loos in January 1916. He was invalided from the Army in December of that year, suffering from shell-shock, and holds the 1914-15 Star, and the General Service and Victory Medals.
8, William Street, Hulme, Manchester.   Z7185

McMAHON, W., Cpl., Northumberland Fusiliers.
Volunteering in November 1915, he was in September of the following year drafted to Mesopotamia and took a prominent part in the fighting at Kut-el-Amara. He also served in the relief force advance from Ali-el-Gharb, and was in action at Sanna-i-Yat, in the success on the Tigris and in various subsequent operations until the Armistice. He returned home and was discharged in March 1919, holding the General Service and Victory Medals.
8, Bright Street, Rochdale Road, Manchester.   Z9625

McMAHON, W., Corporal, 11th Manchester Regt.
He volunteered in August 1914, and in July of the following year was drafted to the Dardanelles, where he saw much heavy fighting at Suvla Bay. Mortally wounded in action, he died in Gallipoli on August 8th, 1915, after only a few weeks' overseas service. He was entitled to the 1914-15 Star, and the General Service and Victory Medals.
" And doubtless he went in splendid company."
112, Cross Street, Bradford, Manchester.   Z7183

McMAHON, W., Pte., 11th S. Lancashire Regt.
He volunteered in April 1915, and in January of the following year proceeded to the Western Front, where he took part in the Battles of the Somme, Vimy Ridge and Ypres and many other important engagements. He died gloriously on the Field of Battle on March 21st, 1918, during the Allied Retreat. He was entitled to the General Service and Victory Medals.
" Steals on the ear the distant triumph song."
4, Dearden Street, Hulme, Manchester.   TZ7186

McMEEKAN, H., Sapper, R.E.
Volunteering in May 1915, he underwent a period of training prior to being drafted to the Western Front in June of the following year. There he took an active part in the Battles of Bullecourt, Ypres, Cambrai, Amiens, Bapaume, Cambrai, Le Cateau and the Sambre and many other important engagements, and fought also in the Retreat and Advance of 1918, taking part in the march into Germany. He was demobilised on his return home in 1919, and holds the General Service and Victory Medals.
1, Dorrington Street, Hulme, Manchester.   Z7187

McMINN, C., Pte., 2nd K.O. (Royal Lancaster Regt.)
A serving Soldier since 1910, he was drafted to France in January 1915, and was in action in the Battles of Neuve Chapelle, Ypres and Festubert. In January 1916 he was sent to the Balkan front and fought in the Offensive on the Doiran, the advance across the Struma and in the recapture of Monastir. Returning to England, he was demobilised in May 1919, and holds the 1914-15 Star, and the General Service and Victory Medals.
82, Teignmouth Street, Collyhurst, Manchester.   Z9626

McMORINE, P. A,, Corpl., 6th Manchester Regt.
Joining in February 1916, he was drafted to France in August of that year and there saw severe fighting in various sectors of the Front. He took part in the Battles of the Somme, Arras and Ypres, and many minor engagements until admitted to hospital at Rouen, suffering from trench fever. He was also in hospital in England for a time, but on his recovery, returned to the Western Front and served through the Battles of the Marne, Havrincourt and Le Cateau and in other engagements during the Retreat and Advance of 1918. He was demobilised in September 1919, and holds the General Service and Victory Medals.
67, Caythorpe Street, Moss Side, Manchester.   Z7188

McNAB, J. S., Corporal, R.G.A.
He was mobilised at the outbreak of hostilities, and served with his Battery at various stations engaged on important duties as a gunnery Instructor. He did good work, but was not successful in securing his transfer overseas before the close of the war owing to medical unfitness, and was discharged in consequence in April 1919.
139, Mill Street, Ancoats, Manchester.   Z10334B

McNALLY, G., Private, Loyal N. Lancashire Regt.
He joined in June 1915, and in July of the following year proceeded to the Western Front, where he saw much heavy fighting. He took part in the Battles of the Somme, Ypres and Cambrai and many other important engagements in various sectors until the cessation of hostilities, and then proceeded with the Army of Occupation into Turkey, where he was stationed at Constantinople. He was demobilised on returning home in October 1919, and holds the General Service and Victory Medals.
13, Lythgoe Street, Moss Side, Manchester.   Z7190

McNAB, W., Sergt., 1st Lancashire Fusiliers, and M.G.C.

He volunteered in August 1914, and sailing for Egypt in the following February served there until drafted to the Dardanelles two months later. He took part in the first Landing on the Peninsula, and was wounded in April 1915. Sent to hospital in Egypt, he received treatment and on recovery was transferred to the Western Front, and was again wounded on the Somme in July 1916. In March 1917, owing to ill health, he returned to England and was engaged on important instructional duties until demobilised in March 1919. He holds the 1914-15 Star, and the General Service and Victory Medals. 48, Gunson St., Miles Platting, Manchester. Z10768

McNALLY, P., Sapper, R.E.

Volunteering in February 1915, he was shortly afterwards sent to France, where he took part in the Battles of Neuve Chapelle, Ypres and Festubert. He was unhappily killed in action at Fricourt, near Albert, on February 8th, 1916. He was entitled to the 1914-15 Star, and the General Service and Victory Medals.

"Nobly striving,
He nobly fell that we might live."
2, Gatley Street, Ancoats, Manchester. Z9269A

McNALLY, T., Private, 11th Lancashire Fusiliers.

Volunteering in November 1914, he was drafted to France in September of the following year, and fought in several important engagements. He was unhappily killed in action near Albert in the fierce fighting on the Somme on July 9th, 1916, and was entitled to the 1914-15 Star and the General Service and Victory Medals.
7, Bowden Street, Newton Heath, Manchester. Z9627

McNALLY, W., Corporal, Cheshire Regiment.

He volunteered in November 1915, and after completing a period of training served at various stations, where he was engaged on duties of great importance as a gas Instructor. He was unable to obtain his transfer overseas, but on several occasions escorted drafts to France. He rendered very valuable services until his demobilisation in February 1919, and holds the General Service and Victory Medals.
2, Hazel Grove, Longsight, Manchester. TZ7189

McNAMARA, T., Private, 12th Lancashire Fusiliers.

He volunteered in September 1914, and in the following year was drafted to the Western Front, where he was in action at Loos. In 1916 he was transferred to Salonika and served on the Vardar and Doiran fronts, but contracted malaria and was invalided home. After a period in hospital he was discharged, owing to his disability, in February 1918, and holds the 1914-15 Star, and the General Service and Victory Medals. 18, Nelson St., Rochdale Rd,. Manchester. Z9270

McNICHOLLS, W. Pte., Royal Irish Fusiliers.

Volunteering in September 1914, he proceeded to the Western Front in June of the following year, and there saw much heavy fighting. After taking part in the Battles of Loos, Vimy Ridge, the Somme, the Ancre, Arras and Passchendaele and many minor engagements in various sectors, he was severely wounded in action at Cambrai in December 1917. He was sent home and invalided from the Army in January 1918, and holds the 1914-15 Star, and the General Service and Victory Medals.
24, Westminster Street, Chester Rd., Hulme, Manchester. TZ7191

McNULTY, E., Private, King's (Liverpool Regt.)

Five months after joining in October 1916, he was drafted to the Western Front. Whilst in this theatre of war he saw much severe fighting in various sectors, took part in the Battles of Arras, Vimy Ridge, Bullecourt, Ypres, Passchendale and Cambrai and many other engagements and also served through the Retreat and Advance of 1918. Demobilised in March 1919, he holds the General Service and Victory Medals.
25, Carlton Terrace, Gorton, Manchester. Z7192

McPARLAND, A., Pte., King's Own Scottish Bord'rs.

He volunteered in September 1914, and in the following year was sent to the Western Front, where he took part in the Battle of Ypres and was wounded in action in 1915. Invalided to hospital at Belfast, he returned to France on his recovery and was again wounded in the Somme Offensive of July 1916, and sent home. He again rejoined his unit, however, and was wounded in action on two further occasions, the last and fourth time in the Retreat of March 1918. He was demobilised in May 1919, and holds the 1914-15 Star, and the General Service and Victory Medals.
1, Buxton Street, Chorlton-on-Medlock, Manchester. Z7193

McPHAIL, C. S., Private, 17th Manchester Regt.

Volunteering in August 1914, he was sent to the Western Front in March of the following year, and there fought in various sectors. He took part in the Battles of Ypres, Vimy Ridge, the Somme and many other important engagements, was wounded in action at Arras in May 1917, and was for a time in hospital at the Base. He was demobilised in January 1919, and holds the 1914-15 Star, and the General Service and Victory Medals.
25, Gibson Street, Newton Heath, Manchester. Z11924

McRAE, A., Driver, R.F.A.

He volunteered in September 1914, and in the following June was drafted to the Western Front. During his service overseas he was engaged as a Despatch rider in various sectors, but in 1916 proceeded to Salonika and subsequently to Egypt. Suffering from malaria, he was in hospital at Cairo, and after the Armistice was signed sailed for England. He was demobilised in March 1919, and holds the 1914-15 Star, and the General Service and Victory Medals.
16, Grange Street, Bradford, Manchester. Z9628

McSWEENEY, J., Rifleman, Royal Irish Rifles.

He volunteered in May 1915, and in August of the following year was drafted to Salonika, where he saw much heavy fighting. After taking part in many important engagements on the Doiran front he was severely wounded in action in April 1917, and was for a time in hospital suffering also from malaria. He afterwards served with the Labour Corps until his return home for demobilisation in May 1919, and holds the General Service and Victory Medals.
28, Park Street, Hulme, Manchester. Z7194

McVETY, J., Private, 1st Lancashire Fusiliers.

He volunteered in May 1915, and sailing in the following September for Egypt, took part in operations at Mersa Matruh and other places until drafted to France in February 1916. In this theatre of war he fought in the Battles of Loos, St Eloi, Vermelles, Albert, and was unhappily killed in action at Vimy Ridge, in July of that year. He was entitled to the 1914-15 Star, and the General Service and Victory Medals.
"His memory is cherished with pride."
61, Knightley Street, Rochdale Road, Manchester. Z10477A

McWHARTER, J., Sapper, R.E.

Mobilised in August 1914, he was immediately drafted to the Western Front, where he served through the fighting at Mons. He also took an active part in the Battles of Ypres, Givenchy, Loos, the Somme and Arras and many other important engagements in various sectors until the cessation of hostilities. Discharged in November 1919, he holds the Mons Star, and the General Service and Victory Medals.
4, Barnes Place, Ancoats, Manchester. Z11925B

McWILLIAM, G., Private, King's (Liverpool Regt.)

He volunteered in September 1914, and was drafted to France in the following year. After being in action on the Ancre and at Passchendaele, he was severely wounded at Ypres and was invalided home, and after a period in hospital was discharged, owing to his injuries, in February 1916. He holds the 1914-15 Star, and the General Service and Victory Medals.
14, Shelmerdine Street, Collyhurst, Manchester. Z9271

McWILLIAM, R., Sergt., 7th Manchester Regiment.

Mobilised in August 1914, he was immediately drafted to Egypt and served for a time in H.M.S. "Enterprise," in the Red Sea and Suez Canal. Later he was transferred to Gallipoli, where he made the supreme sacrifice, being killed in action in the third Battle of Krithia on June 4th, 1915. He was entitled to the 1914-15 Star, and the General Service and Victory Medals.
"The path of duty was the way to glory."
33, Sutherland Street, Hulme, Manchester. TZ7195

McWILLIAMS, T., Sergt., R.G.A.

Volunteering in February 1915, he proceeded to the Western Front seven months later and there saw severe fighting in various sectors. After taking part in the Battles of the Somme, Arras, Vimy Ridge, Bullecourt and Ypres and many minor engagements, he was taken prisoner at St. Quentin in March 1918, and held in captivity until after the cessation of hostilities. He was discharged on his release in December 1918, and holds the 1914-15 Star, and the General Service and Victory Medals.
9, Leach Street, Gorton, Manchester. Z7196

MEAD, W., Private, R.A.M.C.

Volunteering in August 1915, he proceeded to the Western Front in the following November and whilst overseas served in many important engagements, including those at Loos, Vermelles, Albert, the Somme, Ploegsteert Wood and the Ancre. He was invalided home in March 1917, with severe bronchitis, and was discharged as medically unfit for further duty in the same month. He holds the 1914-15 Star, and the General Service and Victory Medals.
25, Woburn Place, Chorlton-on-Medlock, Manchester. Z9277

MEADE, J., Cpl., 24th and 11th Manchester Regts.

He joined in July 1916, and on completing his training in the following November was drafted to France. There he took part in several engagements, including those on the Somme, at Arras, Beaumont-Hamel, Cambrai and Bapaume. He was taken seriously ill with double pneumonia and pleurisy, and invalided to Rouen. He was demobilised in September 1919, and holds the General Service and Victory Medals.
11, Brunswick Street, Hulme, Manchester. Z7277

MEADOWCROFT, J., Pte., King's (Liverpool Regt.) and Air Mechanic, R.A.F.
He joined in February 1917, in the King's Liverpool Regiment, and after his training was completed was transferred to the Royal Air Force about six months later. He was engaged on important duties with his Squadron at various stations and served as a rigger on aeroplanes, and subsequently on the Regimental Staff on important clerical work. He rendered valuable services throughout, and was demobilised in October 1919. 7, Enoch St., Miles Platting, Manchester. Z9278

MEAKIN, A., Private, K.O. (Y.L.I.)
He joined in November 1917, and proceeded to France in March of the following year. During his service overseas he took part in the general Retreat on the Somme in March 1918, and in the advance of the succeeding August. He was severely wounded in an engagement in this month and was invalided home to hospital. After about eight months' treatment in hospital he rejoined his Regiment and was subsequently demobilised in August 1919. He holds the General Service and Victory Medals.
15, Sidney Street, Bradford, Manchester. TZ9279

MEAKIN, J., Sapper, R.E.
Mobilised in August 1914, he was immediately drafted to the Western Front, where he took part in the fighting at Mons. He also served through the Battles of Loos and the Somme and other important engagements, and was wounded in action at Ypres in July 1917. He was in hospital at the Base, but on his recovery, rejoined his unit and was again wounded at Ypres in September 1918. He was discharged in December 1919, and holds the Mons Star, and the General Service and Victory Medals.
13, Roseberry Street, Gorton, Manchester. Z11928

MEAKINS, W. E. (M.M.), Corporal, 17th (Duke of Cambridge's Own) Lancers.
He was serving in India at the commencement of hostilities, and in September 1914 proceeded to France. He fought in the Battles of La Bassée, Ypres, Neuve Chapelle, Loos, the Somme, Passchendaele and Cambrai. He was also in action during the Retreat and Advance of 1918, and was awarded the Military Medal for conspicuous gallantry in the Field. He was demobilised in March 1919, and holds the 1914 Star, and the General Service and Victory Medals.
10, Williams Place, Ancoats, Manchester. Z9638

MEALING, J., Private, 7th Lancashire Fusiliers.
He volunteered in August 1914, and in the following May was drafted to the Dardanelles, where he took part in much heavy fighting at Krithia, and was wounded and invalided to Alexandria. On his recovery, he proceeded to Egypt and took part in many important engagements, including that at Romani, and was twice wounded in action. He returned home, and was demobilised in February 1919, holding the 1914–15 Star, and the General Service and Victory Medals.
12, Georges Avenue, Chester Road, Hulme, Manchester. Z7278

MEALING, W., Private, 1st Manchester Regiment.
He volunteered in January 1916, and in the following September proceeded to Mesopotamia, where he saw much heavy fighting, and was wounded at Baghdad. As a result, he was invalided to India, but, on his recovery, rejoined his unit and was drafted to Palestine. There he took part in many engagements, including the fall of Jerusalem and in the Advance with General Allenby's forces in 1918. He returned home and was demobilised in September 1919, holding the General Service and Victory Medals.
13, Pump Street, Hulme, Manchester. Z7279

MEARS, J., H., Sergt. R.E.
He volunteered in February 1915, and after completing his training proceeded to France. There he played a prominent part in engagements at Festubert, Ypres, Hill 60, Loos, Albert, Vimy Ridge, the Somme, Beaucourt, Arras, Ypres III, Cambrai and in the Retreat and Advance of 1918. After hostilities ceased, he served in Germany with the Army of Occupation until his demobilisation in February 1919. He holds the 1914–15 Star, and the General Service and Victory Medals. 78, Dorset St., Hulme, Manchester. Z7280

MEDLICOTT, H. R., Private, 1/5th Manchester Rgt.
He volunteered in November 1915, and after a period of training proceeded to Egypt, where he took part in many engagements. Later he was transferred to France and saw much fighting at the Battles of Ypres (III), Monchy and Passchendaele, but was shortly afterwards invalided home suffering from trench fever. He was demobilised in February 1919, and holds the General Service and Victory Medals.
97, Earl Street, Longsight, Manchester. Z7282

MEDLICOTT, W., Private, 3rd Border Regiment.
Volunteering in August 1914, he was retained at home for a time on important duties. In 1916 he was drafted to France, where he took part in much heavy fighting at Ploegsteert Wood, on the Somme, at Beaucourt, Beaumont-Hamel, Messines, Ypres, Passchendaele and Havrincourt Wood, and was wounded in action on three occasions. He was demobilised in February 1919, and holds the General Service and Victory Medals. 97, Earl St., Longsight, Manchester. Z7281

MEDLOCK, J., Driver, R.A.S.C.
He volunteered in October 1915, and in the following June proceeded to Salonika, where he was engaged on important duties on the Struma, Monastir and Doiran fronts. Later he went to Egypt, saw much service at Tripoli and Aleppo, and was also on garrison duties at Cairo and Alexandria. He returned home and was demobilised in June 1919, holding the General Service and Victory Medals.
23, Redver's Street, Ardwick, Manchester. Z7283

MEEHAN, E., Private, Queen's Own (Royal West Kent Regiment).
He volunteered in September 1914, and in the following May sailed for Mesopotamia. In this theatre of war he took part in the capture of Amara and in operations in the attempts to relieve Kut, and, owing to illness, was sent to Bombay for medical treatment. On recovery he served on garrison and other duties in India until March 1919, when he returned home for demobilisation. He holds the 1914–15 Star, and the General Service and Victory Medals.
39, James Street, Moss Side, Manchester. Z11771

MEEHAN, J., Private, 11th Manchester Regt. and Air Mechanic, R.A.F.
Volunteering in January 1915, he embarked for the Dardanelles in the following September, and served in the Peninsula until the Evacuation in December of the same year. He then proceeded to Egypt, and was engaged on important duties until transferred to France in July 1916. After taking part in fighting on the Somme, at Albert and Thiépval, he was twice wounded, and invalided home. After hospital treatment he returned to the Western Front, and, transferred to the Royal Air Force, served in France until the conclusion of hostilities. He was demobilised in February 1919, and holds the 1914–15 Star, and the General Service and Victory Medals.
26, Burton Street, Newtown, Manchester. Z10799

MEEHAN, T., Private, 8th Manchester Regiment.
He volunteered in January 1915, and after his training served at various stations on important duties with his unit. He rendered valuable services, but was not successful owing to medical reasons, in obtaining a transfer abroad and was discharged in December 1918 as unfit for further military duty. 24, Chorlton Street, Collyhurst, Manchester. Z9174B

MEEK, J., Sapper, R.E.
He volunteered in November 1914, and in the following year proceeded to France. In this theatre of war he served as a farrier, and also took part in several engagements, including those at Ypres, on the Somme, at Arras, Cambrai and in the Retreat and Advance of 1918. He was demobilised in February 1919, and holds the 1914–15 Star, and the General Service and Victory Medals.
58, Gibson Street, Ardwick, Manchester. Z7285

MEEK, W., Private, 17th Manchester Regt., King's (Liverpool Regt.), and Labour Corps.
Volunteering in November 1915, he proceeded to the Western Front in the following July. In this seat of war he took part in much heavy fighting at Ypres, Albert and Delville Wood, and was badly wounded in action on the Somme in September 1916. As a result he was invalided home, and on his recovery was engaged on agricultural duties in Warwickshire. He was demobilised in March 1919, and holds the General Service and Victory Medals. Z7284
19, Bremner Street, Stockport Road, Ardwick, Manchester.

MEGSON, A., Private, 8th Middlesex Regiment.
He joined in September 1917, and underwent a period of training prior to his being drafted overseas. Whilst on the Western Front he took part in several engagements, including the second Battle of the Somme, and the Advance of 1918. He was demobilised in November 1919, and holds the General Service and Victory Medals. X7286
2, Franchise Street North, Chorlton-on-Medlock, Manchester.

MELIA, F., Private, King's (Liverpool Regiment).
Joining in January 1917, he proceeded to France in June of the succeeding year, and took part in many important engagements, including those at Cambrai, Havrincourt and Ribecourt during the Allied Advance of 1918. At the conclusion of hostilities he was sent to Germany with the Army of Occupation, and was stationed at Bonn. He was demobilised in January 1919, and holds the General Service and Victory Medals.
40, Neill Street, Gorton, Manchester. Z10800A

MELIA, J., Private, 1/7th Manchester Regiment.
Volunteering in August 1914, he embarked in the following May for the Dardanelles. He was in action throughout the Gallipoli campaign, and after the Evacuation of the Peninsula proceeded to Egypt and took part in fighting at Katia, where he was wounded. Evacuated to England, he underwent hospital treatment, and on recovery served on important home duties until demobilised in June 1919. He holds the 1914–15 Star, and the General Service and Victory Medals.
40, Neill Street, Gorton, Manchester. Z10800B

MELLOR, A., Private, 4th Manchester Regiment.
He volunteered in January 1916, and was shortly afterwards
drafted to Egypt. There he took part in much fighting at
Sollum, Jifjaffa, Katia, Romani, Magdhaba, and later served
with General Allenby in Palestine, where he was in action at
Gaza (II) and Tripoli. He returned home and was demobilised
in January 1920, holding the General Service and Victory
Medals.
9, Lancaster Street, Hulme, Manchester.   Z7294

MELLOR, A., Rifleman, Rifle Brigade.
He volunteered in September 1914, and in the following June
was drafted to France, where he took part in many engagements, including that of the Somme. During the heavy fighting at Bucquoy in May 1917 he was wounded and invalided
home. On his recovery he returned to France, but was again
wounded in action at Epéhy in September 1918, and sent home.
He was demobilised in January 1919, and holds the 1914–15
Star, and the General Service and Victory Medals.
60, Burnley Street, Ancoats, Manchester.   Z7580

MELLOR, A. (M.M.) Private, 2/7th Manchester Regt.
He joined in May 1916, and on completing his training in the
following year, was drafted to France. There he played a
distinguished part in engagements at Arras, Vimy Ridge,
Bullecourt, Messines, Ypres and Cambrai, and was awarded
the Military Medal for conspicuous bravery and devotion to
duty in bringing in wounded under heavy shell-fire during the
Battle of the Somme (II). He was taken prisoner on the
Lys in April 1918, and was held in captivity in Germany, where
he was forced to work in the iron mines. After the Armistice
he was released and returned home for his demobilisation in
January 1919. He also holds the General Service and Victory
Medals. 10, Meadow Street, Ardwick, Manchester.   Z7287

MELLOR, A., A.B., Royal Navy.
He joined the Navy in 1909, and when war broke out in August
1914 quickly proceeded to the North Sea. He served as a
seaman-gunner on board H.M.S. " Temeraire " and " Reso-
lution " and took part in the Battle of Heligoland Bight and
in several minor engagements. He did continuously good
work throughout hostilities, and received his discharge in
March 1919, holding the 1914–15 Star, and the General Service
and Victory Medals.
11, Britannia Street, Openshaw, Manchester.   Z7288

MELLOR, E., Stoker, R.N.
He volunteered in January 1915, and after his training was
posted to H.M.S. " Lion," which vessel was engaged on
important duties in the North Sea and other waters. His
ship also took part in several Naval actions, including the
Battle of Jutland on May 31st, 1916. He rendered valuable
services until his demobilisation, which took place on his
return to shore in January 1920. He holds the 1914–15
Star, and the General Service and Victory Medals.
70, Lime Street, Newton, Manchester.   Z10801

MELLOR, G. E., Private, 5th Manchester Regiment.
Volunteering in January 1915, he was drafted to France in
the following April. Whilst in this theatre of war he took
part in several engagements, including those at Ypres, the
Somme, the Ancre, Arras, Ypres, Cambrai, Amiens and
Havrincourt, and was gassed in action. After the Armistice
he proceeded to Germany with the Army of Occupation, and
served there until his demobilisation in August 1919. He
holds the 1914–15 Star, and the General Service and Victory
Medals.
2, North Street, Hulme, Manchester.   Z7295

MELLOR, J., Gunner, R.F.A.
He volunteered in May 1915, and in October of that year was
drafted to Gallipoli, where he saw much severe fighting until
the Evacuation of the Peninsula. He then proceeded to
Egypt, served on the Suez Canal, and afterwards in Palestine,
before being transferred to the Western Front in 1916. There
he took part in many important engagements, including the
Battles of Ypres, Cambrai and the Somme, also fought in
the Retreat and Advance of 1918, and was severely wounded
in action at Le Cateau in October of that year. He was in
hospital for a time in England, before being invalided from
the Army in January 1919, and holds the 1914–15 Star, and
the General Service and Victory Medals.
10, Meadow Street, Ardwick, Manchester.   Z7296

MELLOR, J., Sergt., R.F.A.
Volunteering in February 1915, in the following January
he embarked for Egypt and saw much service in the Canal
zone. Transferred to France in June 1916, he fought in the
Battles of Ypres, the Somme, Cambrai, and throughout the
Retreat and Advance of 1918, and was wounded. He was
demobilised in December 1918, and holds the General Service
and Victory Medals.
38, Grosvenor Street, Newton Heath, Manchester. Z9639

MELLOR, J., Private, 2nd East Lancashire Regt.
He volunteered in June 1915, and on completing his training
in November of that year, was sent to Gallipoli. On the
evacuation of the Peninsula, two months later, he was transferred to the Western Front, where he saw heavy fighting in

various sectors. After taking part in the Battles of the Somme,
Arras, Ypres and Cambrai and other engagements, he fought
also in the Retreat and Advance of 1918, and was wounded in
action at Ypres in October of that year. Invalided home,
he was discharged in January 1919, as medically unfit for
further service, and holds the 1914–15 Star, and the General
Service and Victory Medals.
10, Meadow Street, Ardwick, Manchester.   TZ7291

MELLOR, J., Private, 3/8th Manchester Regiment.
He joined in June 1918, on attaining military age, and after
his training served at various stations in Wales on important
duties with his unit. He rendered valuable services until
invalided to hospital with a severe illness, and was subsequently
demobilised in November 1919.
1, Lelia Street, Ancoats, Manchester.   Z9280

MELLOR, J. W., Corpl., R.A.S.C. (M.T.)
Volunteering in April 1915, he crossed to France in June of
the following year, and was stationed at a Base for some months.
In October 1916, he proceeded to Egypt, and served as a
blacksmith in the workshops of his unit at Alexandria. Owing
to ill-health he was sent home in July 1918, and after treatment
was discharged as medically unfit in October of that year.
He holds the General Service and Victory Medals.
17, Bloom Street, Hulme, Manchester.   Z11772

MELLOR, S., Private, K.O. (Royal Lancaster Regt.)
He volunteered in August 1914, and was retained on important duties at home until drafted to Salonika in April
1916. After seeing much service on the Doiran and Struma
fronts, he was transferred to Mesopotamia, where he took part
in the relief of Kut, and in many other important engagements.
Invalided home, suffering from fever, he unhappily died on
the voyage in the " Varsovia " on May 3rd, 1917, and was
buried at sea. He was entitled to the General Service and
Victory Medals.
" Whilst we remember, the sacrifice is not in vain."
55, Granville Street, Chorlton-on-Medlock, Manchester. Z7289

MELLOR, W., Private, 18th Manchester Regiment.
Three months after volunteering in September 1915, he proceeded to the Western Front, where he saw severe fighting
in various sectors, taking part in many important engagements.
He was unfortunately reported missing and presumed to have
been killed in action at Trones Wood on July 30th, 1916,
during the Advance on the Somme. He was entitled to the
1914–15 Star, and the General Service and Victory Medals.
" A valiant Soldier, with undaunted heart he breasted life's
last hill."
35, Gorton Road, Openshaw, Manchester.   TZ7290

MELLOR, W., Chief Petty Officer, R.N.
Having enlisted in 1891, he was already in the Navy when war
was declared in August 1914, and was posted to H.M.S.
" Galatea," for service with the Grand Fleet in the North
Sea. He was chiefly engaged on patrol duties and was present
when the first Zeppelin was brought down at sea. He also
served for a time in H.M.S. " Caroline," and whilst on board
this vessel was promoted to the rank of Chief Petty Officer
in March 1917. Discharged in April 1919, he holds the 1914–15
Star, and the General Service, Victory, and Long Service and
Good Conduct Medals.
14, Park Street, Manchester.   Z7297

MELLOR, G., Private, 2nd Manchester Regiment.
Mobilised in August 1914, he proceeded to the Western Front
in time to take part in the Battle of, and Retreat from, Mons.
He also fought in the Battles of Ypres and Neuve Chapelle
and other engagements, and was severely wounded in action
at La Bassée. Invalided home, he was for a considerable
period in hospital, before being discharged in February 1919,
as medically unfit for further service, and holds the Mons Star,
and the General Service and Victory Medals.
18, Eskrigge Street, Ardwick, Manchester.   Z11929

MENZIES, T. M. M., Sergt., Gordon Highlanders.
Joining in August 1916, he proceeded to France on completing
his training in the following December, and there saw severe
fighting in various sectors of the Front. After taking part
in many important engagements on the Somme, he was
wounded in action at Arras, and was for a considerable period
in hospital at Etaples, and in England. On his recovery
he was stationed at Aberdeen, where he was engaged in training
recruits until his demobilisation in February 1919. He holds
the General Service and Victory Medals.
7, Granville Street, Moss Side, Manchester.   Z7298

MERCER, E., Private, R.A.M.C.
He joined in 1917, and underwent a period of training prior
to being drafted to Salonika in 1918. There he was engaged
on important duties at the 29th General Hospital until March
1919, when transferred to a Field Ambulance, he was transferred to the Caucasus. Later he served with the Army
of Occupation at Constantinople, before returning home for
demobilisation in 1920, and holds the General Service and
Victory Medals.
6, Halifax Street, Chorlton-on-Medlock, Manchester. X7299

MERCER, F., Corporal, 2nd Manchester Regiment.
Mobilised in August 1914, he was immediately drafted to the Western Front, where he took part in the fighting at Mons. He also served through the Battles of Le Cateau, Neuve Chapelle, Ypres and Loos, and other engagements, until gassed and wounded in action on the Somme in July 1916. He was invalided home, but on his recovery proceeded to Egypt, whence he returned to France, however, in March 1917, and was again in action at Ypres, Nieuport and the Somme. He was discharged in December 1918, and holds the Mons Star, and the General Service and Victory Medals.
58, Gresham Street, Openshaw, Manchester. Z7300

MEREDITH, T., Private, Loyal N. Lancashire Regt.
He joined in March 1916, and was sent in the following September to France, where he was in action in many parts of the line, fighting in many engagements of note. He gave his life for King and Country in the Péronne sector on September 18th, 1918 and was entitled to the General Service and Victory Medals.
"His life for his Country, his soul to God."
31, Bedford Street, Moss Side, Manchester. Z9442A

MEREDITH, V. C., 1st Cl. Petty Officer, R.N.
He volunteered at the outbreak of war in August 1914, and afterwards served in H.M.S. "Victory" and "Calgaria" in various waters. He was engaged chiefly on escort duties in the Atlantic Ocean and also with the Grand Fleet in the North Sea, and took part in many important actions in these waters. He was still at sea with the Australian Navy in 1920, and holds the Naval General Service Medal (with four clasps), the 1914–15 Star, and the General Service and Victory Medals.
8, Rover Street, Moss Side, Manchester. Z7301

MERRICK, J., 1st Air Mechanic, R.A.F.
He joined in September 1918, and after completing a period of training, served at various stations, where he was engaged on important duties which called for a high degree of technical skill. He was not successful in his efforts to obtain his transfer to a theatre of war, on account of the early cessation of hostilities, but, nevertheless, rendered valuable services with his Squadron until November 1919, when he was demobilised.
49, Watson Street, West Gorton, Manchester. Z7302

MERRICK, J., Private, 8th Manchester Regiment.
Volunteering in October 1914, he proceeded to France in the following June, and took part in operations at Loos, St. Eloi, Albert, Vermelles, Vimy Ridge, the Somme, Arras, Bullecourt, Messines, Ypres and Cambrai. He served also throughout the Retreat and Allied Advance which terminated hostilities in November 1918, and was wounded. He was demobilised in March 1919, and holds the 1914–15 Star, and the General Service and Victory Medals.
122, Jersey Street Dwellings, Ancoats, Manchester. Z10802

MERRILL, T., Pte., R.A.M.C., and Gunner, R.G.A.
He volunteered in November 1914, and after a short period of training was engaged on important duties as a hospital orderly at various stations until November 1915. He was then invalided from the Army, but re-enlisted, however, shortly afterwards, and served in Ireland on various duties, not being able to obtain his transfer to the Front on account of ill-health. Nevertheless, he did much good work with his Battery until finally discharged in October 1918, as medically unfit for further service.
147, Hartington Street, Moss Side, Manchester. TZ7303

MERRON, C., Pte., 8th Manchester Rgt., and R.A.M.C.
Joining in June 1916, he proceeded to the Western Front on completion of three months' training, and there took part in important engagements in various sectors, including the Battles of the Somme, Ypres and Cambrai. He was afterwards transferred to the R.A.M.C., and served on an ambulance train in France until after the cessation of hostilities. He was discharged on his return home in December 1919, and holds the General Service and Victory Medals.
12, Sandown Street, Ardwick, Manchester. Z7304A

MERRON, D., Private, Border Regiment.
He joined in August 1916, and after completing his training, served at various stations in Ireland, where he was engaged on duties of a highly important nature. He was unable to obtain his transfer overseas before the cessation of hostilities, but in February 1920 was drafted to the East. He served on garrison duties for a time in India, and in December 1920 was still with his unit at Kut, in Mesopotamia.
12, Sandown Street, Ardwick, Manchester. Z7304B

MERRY, E., Sergt., 1st East Lancashire Regiment.
He enlisted in March 1912, and when war was declared, proceeded with his Regiment to France. He was in action in the Retreat from Mons, and in the Battles of Le Cateau, the Marne, the Aisne, La Bassée and Ypres, and was wounded and invalided home. On recovery he returned to the Western Front, and took part in many other engagements, but was again wounded at Vermelles. After receiving treatment at the Base he rejoined his unit and served until hostilities

ended. He holds the Mons Star, and the General Service and Victory Medals, and in 1920 was still in the Army.
36, Dysen Street, Miles Platting, Manchester. Z11495D

MESSENGER, T., Private, R.A.M.C.
He joined in October 1916, and before proceeding to France gave valuable assistance to the injured in the great explosion at Silvertown on January 19th, 1917, when sixty-nine munition workers were killed. In the following month he was drafted to the Western Front, and served at Arras, Bullecourt, Messines Ypres, Passchendaele and Cambrai, also in many engagements in the Retreat and Advance of 1918. He was demobilised in August 1919, and holds the General Service and Victory Medals. 85, Blossom Street, Ancoats, Manchester. Z9281

METCALF, J. G., Private, 8th Manchester Regt.,
A Reservist, he was called to the Colours in August 1914, and in April of the following year was drafted to Gallipoli. There, after taking part in the Landing at Cape Helles, he fought in the Battles of Krithia, and at Suvla Bay, and many other places until the Evacuation of the Peninsula. He was then transferred to the Western Front, where he took part in the Battles of the Somme, Arras, Bullecourt, Ypres and Cambrai, and served also through the Retreat and Advance of 1918. He was discharged in March 1919, and holds the 1914–15 Star, and the General Service and Victory Medals.
28, Neptune Street, Ancoats, Manchester. Z6033B

METCALF, W., Corporal, Military Foot Police.
He volunteered in November 1914, and after his training was engaged on important Police duties at various stations. Owing to medical unfitness, he was unable to secure his transfer to a theatre of war, and in December 1917, was invalided out of the Service.
9, Ryder Street, Bradford, Manchester. Z10803

MIDDLETON, A., L/Corporal, R.E.
Volunteering in September 1914, he landed in France in the following April, and fought in the Battles of Loos, Albert, the Somme, Ypres, Passchendaele and Cambrai. He was unfortunately killed in action at Epéhy on March 22nd, 1918, at the commencement of the German Offensive. He was entitled to the 1914–15 Star, and the General Service and Victory Medals.
"A costly sacrifice upon the altar of freedom."
6, Juno Street, Newton Heath, Manchester. Z9640

MIDDLETON, H., Private, 16th Lancashire Fusiliers.
He volunteered in November 1914, and crossing to France in the following year fought in the Battles of Neuve Chapelle, Hill 60, Ypres, Festubert, and in several engagements in the Somme Offensive. He was unfortunately killed on the Somme in 1916 and was entitled to the 1914–15 Star, and the General Service and Victory Medals.
"And doubtless he went in splendid company."
33, Elizabeth Ann Street, Manchester. Z11773

MIDDLETON, S., Pte., King's (Liverpool Regiment).
He joined in November 1916, and after undergoing a period of training, served at various stations, where he was engaged on duties of great importance. He was not successful in his efforts to obtain his transfer to a theatre of war, but nevertheless rendered very valuable services with his unit until April 1919, when he was demobilised.
47, Prescott Street, West Gorton, Manchester. Z7306

MILES, A. J., Private, 22nd Manchester Regiment.
Joining in October 1916, he proceeded to the Western Front after two months' training, and there saw much heavy fighting in various sectors. After taking part in many important engagements, he was so severely wounded in action at Lens in August 1917, as to necessitate the amputation of his right leg. He was for a considerable period in hospital at Norwich, before being invalided from the Army in July 1918, and holds the General Service and Victory Medals.
33, Everton Road, Chorlton-on-Medlock, Manchester. Z7307A

MILES, F. T., Private, King's (Liverpool Regt.)
Joining in September 1917, he proceeded to the Western Front two months later, and there saw much severe fighting. He took part in several important engagements in various sectors until December 1917, when he was wounded in action in the first Battle of Cambrai, and admitted to hospital. He was finally demobilised in April 1919, and holds the General Service and Victory Medals.
33, Everton Road, Chorlton-on-Medlock, Manchester. Z7307B

MILLAR, J., Corporal, King's (Liverpool Regiment).
He volunteered in March 1915, and in November of the following year was drafted to Salonika, where he saw much severe fighting on the Doiran and other fronts until June 1918. He was then transferred to France, and there took part in the second Battle of Le Cateau and many other important engagements during the Allied Advance. He was demobilised on his return to England in May 1919, and holds the General Service and Victory Medals.
157, Clopton Street, Hulme, Manchester. Z7308A

MILLAR, T., Private, R.A.M.C.

Shortly after volunteering in August 1914, he proceeded to Egypt, whence he was drafted in the following year to the Dardanelles. There he took part in the first Landing at Gallipoli, and also served through the Battles of Krithia and many other engagements until the Evacuation of the Peninsula. He was then transferred to the Western Front, where he served in various sectors until after the cessation of hostilities. He was demobilised in May 1919, and holds the 1914–15 Star, and the General Service and Victory Medals.
157, Clopton Street, Hulme, Manchester.   Z7308B

MILLAR, T., Private, M.G.C.

He joined in August 1918, and after completing a short period of training, served at various stations, where he was engaged on duties of a highly important nature. He was not successful in obtaining his transfer to the Front, being too old for active service, but nevertheless, did much useful work with his Company until January 1919, when he was demobilised.
157, Clopton Street, Hulme, Manchester.   Z7308C

MILLARD, G. W., Pte., K.O. (R. Lancaster Regt.)

He volunteered in October 1914, and on completing a period of training in the following year was drafted to the Dardanelles. There he gave his life for King and Country, being killed in action whilst landing at Gallipoli on August 4th, 1915. He was entitled to the 1914–15 Star, and the General Service and Victory Medals.
"Thinking that remembrance, though unspoken, may reach him where he sleeps."
9, Goole Street, Bradford, Manchester.   Z11930

MILLER, A., Private, 16th Manchester Regiment.

He volunteered in June 1915, and in April of the following year proceeded to France, where he saw severe fighting in various sectors of the Front. He was in action at Beaumont-Hamel, Achiet-le-Grand, Varennes, and many other places, and also took part in many important engagements, including the Battles of the Somme. Demobilised in April 1919, he holds the General Service and Victory Medals.
18, Jack Street, Ardwick, Manchester.   Z7309

MILLER, A., Private, 12th Manchester Regiment.

Volunteering in January 1915, he crossed to France in July of the succeeding year, but unhappily was killed in action on the Somme on August 4th, 1916, during his first engagement. He was entitled to the General Service and Victory Medals.
"A valiant Soldier, with undaunted heart he breasted life's last hill."   Z10804A
27, February Street, Chorlton-on-Medlock, Manchester.

MILLER, A., Corporal, Manchester Regiment.

He volunteered in February 1915, and landing in France in August of the following year, was badly gassed on the Somme. Evacuated to England, he underwent hospital treatment, and a year later returned to the Western Front, and was in action at Bullecourt and Guillemont. He was also engaged for a time on important duties at a prisoner of war camp, and did valuable work until after the conclusion of hostilities. He was demobilised in August 1919, and holds the General Service and Victory Medals.
13, Rockingham Street, Collyhurst, Manchester.   Z10805

MILLER, A. R., Sapper, R.E.

Volunteering in February 1915, he was drafted to Egypt twelve months later, and there was engaged on important duties in connection with the lines of communication. He served at Kantara, Port Said, and many other stations in this seat of operations, and did much useful work with his Company. Returning home in July 1919, he was demobilised in the following month, and holds the General Service and Victory Medals.
132, Maine Road, Moss Side, Manchester.   Z7315

MILLER, E., L/Corporal, 2nd Manchester Regiment.

With a previous record of twelve years' service in the Army, he was mobilised with the Reserves in August 1914, and sent at once to France. During the famous Battle of Mons he was both wounded and taken prisoner by the enemy. After two and a half years' imprisonment in Germany he made a plucky attempt to escape, but was recaptured and subjected to brutal treatment by his captors. He was released after the Armistice, but had to spend some time in hospital in London, owing to his brutal treatment before he was discharged in February 1919. In addition to the Mons Star, and the General Service and Victory Medals, he holds the South African and Long Service Medals. 9, Webster Place, Ancoats, Manchester.   Z9282

MILLER, E. (M.M.), Sergt., M.G.C.

Volunteering in August 1914, he was engaged on important home duties until March 1916, when crossing to France he was in action at Loos, Albert, the Somme, Arras and Ypres. In March 1917 he was awarded the Military Medal for conspicuous bravery and devotion to duty at Irles. He later fought at Cambrai, and in the second Battle of the Somme, in which he was severely wounded. After being treated at a Casualty Clearing Station, he was invalided to a hospital in York, and

after recovery was retained for home service, until demobilised in March 1919. He holds in addition to the decoration won in the Field, the General Service and Victory Medals.
24, Kendall Street, Bradford, Manchester.   Z10806

MILLER, F., Private, Hampshire Regiment.

He volunteered in January 1915, and embarking for France three months later took part in several engagements. In July of the same year he was drafted to Salonika and was in action against the Bulgarians until the signing of the Armistice. He was demobilised on his return to England in January 1919, and holds the 1914–15 Star, and the General Service and Victory Medals. 13, Bradbury Street, Ancoats, Manchester. Z10807

MILLER, F., Driver, R.A.S.C.

He volunteered in September 1914, and after completing a term of training, served at various stations, where he was engaged on duties of great importance. He was medically unfit for service overseas, and was consequently unable to obtain his transfer to a theatre of war, but did much useful work with his Company, until his demobilisation in September, 1919.
27, Leigh Place, Ardwick, Manchester.   Z7310

MILLER, H., Gunner, R.F.A.

Volunteering in June 1915, he proceeded to the Western Front in the following November, and there saw severe fighting in various sectors. After taking part in engagements at Loos, St. Eloi, Albert and Vimy Ridge, he was severely wounded in action during the Somme Offensive, and was admitted to hospital at Rouen, where he unhappily died in September 1916. He was entitled to the 1914–15 Star, and the General Service and Victory Medals.
"His memory is cherished with pride."
23, Waterloo Grove, Greenheys, Manchester.   Z7312

MILLER, J., Special War Worker.

During the whole period of hostilities, he was engaged on work of great importance in the Post Office, where employed as a postman, he thus released a younger man for service with the Colours. He did much good work until the signing of the Armistice, and his services were very highly valued.
8, Goolden Street, Chorlton-on-Medlock, Manchester. TX7311

MILLER, J., Private, Labour Corps.

Volunteering in January 1915, he proceeded to the Western Front in May of that year, and there saw heavy fighting in various sectors. After taking part in engagements at La Bassée and many other places, he was severely wounded in action at Nieuport in February 1917, and admitted to hospital in London. He was finally invalided from the Army in November 1917, and holds the 1914–15 Star, and the General Service and Victory Medals.
30, Gibson Street, Newton Heath, Manchester.   Z11931

MILLER, J., Private, 22nd Manchester Regiment.

Volunteering in August 1914, he embarked for France in November of that year, and fought at Armentières, La Bassée, Ypres, Hill 60, Loos, Albert and Arras, where in May 1917, he was wounded. On recovery he rejoined his unit in the Field, and was in action throughout the Retreat and Allied Advance of 1918. He was demobilised in May 1919, and holds the 1914 Star, and the General Service and Victory Medals.
28, Aspden Street, Ancoats, Manchester.   Z10808

MILLER, J., Private, R.A.M.C.

He joined in September 1916, and after his training was retained on important duties in the hospitals at various stations. He was not successful in his efforts to obtain his transfer to a theatre of war, but nevertheless rendered very valuable services with his Company until June 1919, when he was demobilised.   37, Phillips St., Hulme, Manchester.   TZ7313

MILLER, J. S., Sergt., 17th South Lancashire Regt.

He joined in August 1916, and on completion of a period of training was retained at various stations, where he was engaged on important transport duties. Unable to obtain his transfer to the Front, he nevertheless did much useful work with his unit until his demobilisation in August 1919.
12, Arbury Street, Hulme, Manchester.   Z7314

MILLER, T. H., Private, Lancashire Fusiliers.

Joining in 1917, he embarked for the Western Front in the following year, and after taking part in the Retreat of 1918, was taken prisoner in October of that year, during the subsequent Allied Advance. Repatriated after the conclusion of hostilities, he was demobilised in 1919, and holds the General Service and Victory Medals.   Z10804B
27, February Street, Chorlton-on-Medlock, Manchester.

MILLIGAN, J., Private, 11th Manchester Regiment.

Volunteering in October 1914, he proceeded to Gallipoli in July of the following year, and there took part in severe fighting at Suvla Bay and many other places. Invalided to hospital at Alexandria, suffering from dysentery, he unfortunately died there on November 14th, 1915. He was entitled to the 1914–15 Star, and the General Service and Victory Medals.
"A costly sacrifice upon the altar of freedom."
Heald Grove, Rusholme, Manchester.   Z7316

MILLER, W. W., Private, King's (Liverpool Regt.), and Rifleman, Cameronians (Scottish Rifles).
He joined in March 1916, and after his training served at various stations on important duties with his unit. In October 1918 he was drafted to India and was engaged on important work at several garrison outposts. He holds the General Service Medal, and in 1920 was still serving in India.
12, Montague Street, Collyhurst, Manchester. Z9283

MILLIGAN, J., Gunner, R.G.A.
Joining in July 1918, he proceeded to France a month later and took part in the Allied Advance of that year, which ended victoriously on November 11th. After the Armistice, he was drafted to Malta, where he was engaged on garrison duty until 1919. He then returned to England, and was demobilised in March of that year, and holds the General Service and Victory Medals.
17, Bath Street, Miles Platting, Manchester. Z10809

MILLIKIN, R., Driver, R.F.A.
He volunteered in April 1915, and in January of the following year was drafted to Egypt, whence he was transferred two months later to the Western Front. There, after taking part in the Battles of Vimy Ridge, the Somme, Arras, Ypres and Cambrai and engagements at St. Eloi, Albert, and many other places, he contracted trench fever, and was for a considerable period in hospital at Rouen and in England. He was finally demobilised in June 1919, holding the General Service and Victory Medals.
63, Mawson Street, Chorlton-on-Medlock, Manchester. Z7317

MILLINGTON, A., L/Corpl., Loyal N. Lancashire Rgt.
Already in the Army, he was sent to France in August 1914, and played an important part in the Battle of Mons and the subsequent Retreat, and in the Battle of Le Cateau. He was taken prisoner during the heavy fighting on the Aisne in September 1914, and whilst in captivity in Germany, suffered many hardships, being forced to work on the land. Repatriated in December 1918, he was discharged in the following month, and holds the Mons Star, and the General Service and Victory Medals.
23, Hazel Street, Hulme, Manchester. TZ7320

MILLINGTON, J., Pte., 7th K.O. (R. Lancaster Regt.)
He joined in July 1916, and was sent to France in the following September in time to take part in the latter stages of the Somme Offensive. Later he was in action at the Battles of Bullecourt, Messines, Lens, Cambrai (I), the Somme (II), the Aisne (III), Amiens, Havrincourt, Cambrai (II) and Le Cateau. After hostilities ceased, he served in Germany with the Army of Occupation and was eventually demobilised in November 1919, holding the General Service and Victory Medals.
14, Clement Street, Moss Lane, Hulme, Manchester. Z7319

MILLINGTON, J. A., Private, 2nd Cheshire Regt.
He volunteered in October 1914, and in the following December was sent to France, where he took part in the Battle of Ypres, and was wounded. He was also in action at Loos, Bapaume and Havrincourt, and was later invalided home. He was demobilised in February 1919, and holds the 1914-15 Star, and the General Service and Victory Medals.
6, Marcus Street, Preston Street, Hulme, Manchester. Z7318

MILLINGTON, P., Pte., 1/7th Manchester Regt.
Volunteering in August 1914, he embarked for Egypt a month later, and in the following April proceeded to the Dardanelles, where he took part in the first Landing at Gallipoli. He was unfortunately killed in action at the third Battle of Krithia on June 5th, 1915, and lies buried in the 11th Casualty Clearing Station Cemetery at Cape Helles. He was entitled to the 1914-15 Star, and the General Service and Victory Medals.
"A costly sacrifice upon the altar of freedom."
32, Eliza Ann Street, Rochdale Road, Manchester. Z10810

MILLS, A. H., Corporal, 2nd Manchester Regiment.
He joined in May 1917, and on completion of his training was engaged on important duties in England until April 1918. He then proceeded to France, and during the Retreat and Advance of that year played a prominent part in the Battles of the Somme (II), the Lys, the Marne (II), Amiens, Cambrai (II) and Le Cateau (II). After hostilities ceased, he took part in the march into Germany and was eventually demobilised in February 1919, holding the General Service and Victory Medals.
30, Fernley Street, Moss Side, Manchester. Z7323

MILLS, H., Private, 10th South Lancashire Regt.
He volunteered in April 1915, and landing in France in the following November, was in action at Loos, La Bassée, the Somme, Vimy Ridge, Ypres, Beaumont-Hamel, Passchendaele and Cambrai. He also served throughout the Retreat and Allied Advance of 1918, and did valuable work until his demobilisation, which took place on his return to England in February 1919. He holds the 1914-15 Star, and the General Service and Victory Medals.
12, Heelis Street, Rochdale Road, Manchester. Z10811

MILLS, H., L/Corpl., 3rd (King's Own) Hussars.
He enlisted in September 1913, and proceeding to France at the outbreak of war served through the Battle of, and the Retreat from, Mons. He also took part in the Battles of the Marne, the Aisne, Ypres (1914 and 1915), the Somme, Arras and Cambrai, and in the Retreat and Advance of 1918. He was wounded in action whilst on the Western Front, and after the cessation of hostilities served with the Army of Occupation in Germany until September 1919. He received his discharge twelve months later, and holds the Mons Star, and the General Service and Victory Medals.
5, Platt View, Rusholme, Manchester. Z7326

MILLS, H. F., Private, R.A.M.C.
He volunteered in September 1914, and was retained on special duties at home stations until April 1916. He was then sent to the Western Front and rendered valuable services at the 55th General Hospital for twenty seven months. In July 1918 he returned to England for important work in various hospitals, and was demobilised in March 1919, holding the General Service and Victory Medals.
140, Warde Street, Hulme, Manchester. Z7324

MILLS, J., Private, Royal Scots Fusiliers.
Mobilised from the Reserve in August 1914, he immediately proceeded to France and took part in the Retreat from Mons, and the Battles of the Marne, La Bassée and Ypres, where he was taken prisoner in November 1914. Unfortunately he died on January 1st, 1915, from a serious illness whilst in captivity in Germany. He was entitled to the Mons Star, and the General Service and Victory Medals.
"A costly sacrifice upon the altar of freedom."
6, Rose View, Longsight, Manchester. Z7327B

MILLS, J., Private, 4th K.O. (Royal Lancaster Regt.)
Joining in May 1916, he landed in France in the following August, and took part in operations at Ypres, the Somme, Nieuport, La Bassée and Arras, where in May 1917, he was wounded. Evacuated to England, he underwent treatment at various hospitals and was eventually demobilised in January 1919. He holds the 1914-15 Star, and the General Service and Victory Medals.
4, Flower Street, Ancoats, Manchester. Z10814B

MILLS, J., Private, Welch Regiment.
Volunteering in November 1914, he proceeded overseas in the following September, and was in action at Loos, St. Eloi and Albert. He fell fighting on the Somme in August 1916, and was entitled to the 1914-15 Star, and the General Service and Victory Medals.
"Whilst we remember the sacrifice is not in vain."
8, Hancock Street, Rochdale Road, Manchester. Z10812

MILLS, J., Corpl., K.O. (Royal Lancaster Regiment.)
He volunteered in November 1914, and in September of the following year, was drafted to the Western Front, where he played a prominent part in heavy fighting at Ypres, La Bassée, Givenchy and Arras. He laid down his life for King and Country at Ypres on March 2nd, 1916, and was entitled to the 1914-15 Star, and the General Service and Victory Medals.
"The path of duty was the way to glory."
83, Cowesby Street, Moss Side, Manchester. TZ7321

MILLS, J., 1st Air Mechanic, R.A.F.
He joined in December 1916, and on passing the necessary qualifications, was engaged on special duties as a skilled fitter in the workshops at several aerodromes. Owing to his being under age, he was not successful in obtaining his transfer overseas, but rendered very valuable services. In 1920 he was stationed in Scotland.
45, Ashover Street, Ardwick, Manchester. Z7322

MILLS, J. P., Pioneer, R.E.
He volunteered on the outbreak of war, and crossing to France shortly afterwards took part in the concluding operations of the Retreat from Mons. Later he served at Ypres, the Somme and Loos, where he was so badly gassed as to necessitate his return to England. After hospital treatment he was discharged as medically unfit in July 1916. He holds the Mons Star, and the General Service and Victory Medals.
4, Flower Street, Ancoats, Manchester. Z10814A

MILLS, N., Private, 10th Essex Regiment.
He joined in January 1917, and served with the 5th Manchester Regiment and the Sherwood Foresters, before being transferred to the Essex Regiment. In May 1918 he was sent to France and during the Retreat and Advance took part in the Battles of the Marne (II) and Bapaume. He was wounded in action in September 1918, and invalided home, being discharged in April 1919 as medically unfit for further service. He holds the General Service and Victory Medals.
20, Albert Grove, Longsight, Manchester. Z7325B

MILLS, R., Private, Manchester Regiment.
Volunteering in November 1915, he was sent to France in the following May and took part in the Battles of Vimy Ridge (where he was wounded in action) and the Somme. He was then transferred to the Labour Corps, and served through the Battles of Cambrai, Bapaume and Havrincourt, and in other important engagements during the Retreat and Advance of 1918. Demobilised on his return to England in March 1919, he holds the General Service and Victory Medals.
20, Albert Grove, Longsight, Manchester. Z7325A

MILLS, W., Pte., Lancashire Fusiliers, and Sapper, R.E.

Joining in March 1916, he was drafted to France two months later, and fought at Albert, the Somme, Arras, Messines Ridge, Ypres and Cambrai, where in 1917 he was wounded. On recovery he was transferred to the Royal Engineers, and engaged on pontoon building and road making until after the cessation of hostilities. He was discharged on account of service in February 1919, and holds the General Service and Victory Medals.

5, Stockdale Street, Ancoats, Manchester.   Z10815A

MILLS, W. H., Sergt., 6th Loyal N. Lancashire Regt.

Volunteering in August 1914, he shortly afterwards embarked for Egypt, and served at Cairo and Alexandria until April 1915, when he proceeded to the Dardanelles and took part in the Gallipoli campaign. After the Evacuation of the Peninsula he was drafted to Mesopotamia with a relief force for Kut, and served in that theatre of war until January 1919. He then returned to England, and was demobilised a year later, and holds the 1914–15 Star, and the General Service and Victory Medals.

34, Hewitt Street, Gorton, Manchester.   Z10816

MILLS, W., Pte., R.A.M.C., and Lancashire Fus.

Joining in November 1916, he embarked for Salonika in the following March, and was engaged on important ambulance duties on the Doiran and Vardar fronts. After the Armistice he proceeded to France and was engaged on important transport duties for some months. He was demobilised in October 1919, and holds the General Service and Victory Medals.

8, Hancock Street, Rochdale Road, Manchester.   Z10813

MILLWARD, C., Private, Border Regt., and M.G.C.

He volunteered in June 1915, and after a period of service at home stations, was drafted to the Western Front in 1917. During his service in this theatre of war, he took part in the Battles of Arras, Bullecourt, Ypres (III) and the Somme (II). In 1918 he was invalided to England, owing to a defective heart, and was engaged on light duties until his demobilisation in February 1919. He holds the General Service and Victory Medals.

3, Sadler Street, Hulme, Manchester.   Z7328

MILLWARD, H., Rifleman, Rifle Brigade.

He volunteered in September 1914, and in the following January was drafted overseas. Serving in France and Flanders he took part in several engagements, and was wounded at Hill 60, on May 11th, 1915. On recovery he was in action in the Somme Offensive, and in the Battles of Arras and Ypres, where he was wounded again on October 14th, 1917. After treatment he fought at Cambrai, and was taken prisoner on the 21st March 1918, and held in captivity until the Armistice, when he was repatriated from Germany. He was demobilised in March 1919, and holds the 1914–15 Star, and the General Service and Victory Medals.

30, Haughton Street, Collyhurst, Manchester.   Z10817

MILLWARD, J., Private, 23rd Manchester Regiment.

Volunteering in May 1915, he was sent to France in the following July and took part in the Battles of Loos, Albert and Vermelles, where he gallantly laid down his life for King and Country in May 1916. He was entitled to the 1914–15 Star, and the General Service and Victory Medals.

"Honour to the immortal dead, who gave their youth that
    the world might grow old in peace."

2, Gray Street, Hulme, Manchester.   Z7329

MILLWARD, J., Private, King's (Liverpool Regt.)

He joined in November 1916, and in the following April was drafted to the Western Front, where he served as a Lewis gunner. He took part in the Battles of Arras, Vimy Ridge, Ypres, Passchendaele and Cambrai, where he was taken prisoner in November 1917. During his captivity at Posen in Germany, he suffered many hardships and was eventually repatriated, and demobilised in July 1919, holding the General Service and Victory Medals.   Z7331B

41, Higher Ormond Street, Chorlton-on-Medlock, Manchester.

MILLWARD, R., Private, 7th Manchester Regiment.

Volunteering in October 1915, he was sent to Egypt in May 1916, and took part in heavy fighting against the Senussi Arabs. In January 1918 he was transferred to the Western Front, and after serving through the Battles of the Somme (II), the Aisne (III) and the Marne (II), was unhappily killed in action at Albert in April 1918. He was entitled to the General Service and Victory Medals.   Z7331A

"His memory is cherished with pride."

41, Higher Ormond Street, Chorlton-on-Medlock, Manchester.

MILLWOOD, E., Bombardier, R.G.A.

He volunteered in November 1914, and proceeded to the Western Front in the following August. After taking part in the Battles of Loos, Albert, Ploegsteert and the Somme (where he was wounded in July 1916), he was transferred to Salonika. Whilst in the Balkan theatre of war, he was in action during the heavy fighting on the Doiran, Struma and Vardar fronts. He was demobilised in March 1919, and holds the 1914–15 Star, and the General Service and Victory Medals.

28, Boundary Street East, Chorlton-on-Medlock, Manchester.   Z7330B

MILLWOOD, T. E., Private, 7th Manchester Regt.

On attaining military age, he joined the Army in May 1917, and on completion of his training was engaged on important duties at home stations. He was unsuccessful in obtaining his transfer overseas during hostilities, but rendered valuable services. In 1920 he was still with his unit, and was stationed in Ireland.   Z7330A

28, Boundary Street East, Chorlton-on-Medlock, Manchester.

MILNER, A., Private, R.A.M.C.

He joined in January 1913, and proceeded to Egypt in September 1914. After taking an active part in heavy fighting in the Suez Canal zone, he was transferred to the Dardanelles, where he served at the Battle of Achi-Baba, and in other important engagements until the Evacuation of the Gallipoli Peninsula. He then returned to Egypt, but later took part in the Advance into Palestine. In March 1917 he was transferred to the Western Front and was gassed in action at Ypres in September of the same year. Discharged in March 1919, he holds the 1914–15 Star, and the General Service and Victory Medals. 18, Rose St., Old Trafford, Manchester.   Z7332

MILNER, E., Private, 8th Manchester Regiment.

He volunteered in September 1914, and completing his training was drafted to France in July 1916, and was in action at La Bassée, Festubert, Givenchy, Béthune, the Somme, Albert and Arras, where he met with an accident and was invalided home in November 1917. In January 1919 he proceeded to Mesopotamia, and served at Basra and Baghdad. He was demobilised in April 1919, and holds the General Service and Victory Medals. 5, Harold St., Bradford, Manchester.   Z11553

MILNER, J., L/Corpl., 1st K.O. (R. Lancaster Regt.)

Enlisting in April 1913, he was mobilised when war broke out, and landing on the Western Front with the first Expeditionary Force was in action in the Retreat from Mons, in the course of which he was wounded and taken prisoner on August 26th, 1914. Whilst in captivity in Germany he was employed on agricultural work for two years, and then as a plate layer on the railways, until repatriated in December 1918. He later served with his Regiment at home, and demobilised in April 1920, holds the Mons Star, and the General Service and Victory Medals. 19, Phillips St., Hulme, Manchester. Z11774

MILWARD, H., Air Mechanic, R.A.F.

He joined in July 1918, and on the completion of his training served with his Squadron at various aerodromes in the south of England and in Scotland. Engaged as a fitter and turner of aero engines—work demanding a high degree of technical skill— he rendered valuable services, but was unable to obtain his transfer to a theatre of war before hostilities ended, and was demobilised in June 1919.

61, Milton Street, West Gorton, Manchester.   Z10818A

MINSHULL, A., Private, Labour Corps.

Joining in February 1917, he was sent to the Western Front a month later, and served there for over two years. During this period he was engaged on light railway construction in the forward areas, and saw heavy fighting at Poperinghe and Ypres. He was wounded near Ypres on July 25th, 1918, during the Allied Advance, which brought the war to a close in the following November. Returning home for demobilisation in October 1919, he holds the General Service and Victory Medals. 51, Fitz George Street, Collyhurst, Manchester.   Z10819B

MINSHULL, J., Private, 1/8th Manchester Regt.

Volunteering in 1914, he sailed for Gallipoli in the following year, and took part in the first Landing at Cape Helles, and was wounded during operations at the Landing at Suvla Bay. Sent to hospital he was later evacuated to England, and after treatment was invalided out of the Service in 1917. He holds the 1914–15 Star, and the General Service and Victory Medals. 53, Piercy Street, Ancoats, Manchester.   Z10820A

MINSHULL, J., Gunner, R.F.A.

He joined in November 1919, and on completion of his training served with his Battery until his embarkation for India in the same year. Engaged on garrison and other important duties he did good work at Mhow and other stations, and in 1920 was still serving abroad.

53, Piercy Street, Ancoats, Manchester.   Z10820B

MINSHULL, T., Sapper, R.E.

Joining in 1917, he completed his training and was engaged on important Home Service duties, and was later drafted to India. There he was employed on garrison and other duties, and rendered valuable services. He holds the General Service Medal, and in 1920 was still stationed in the East.

53, Piercy Street, Ancoats, Manchester.   Z10820C

MINTOFT, G., Rifleman, Rifle Brigade.

He volunteered in 1914, and on completion of his training in the following year, was drafted to the Western Front, where he saw much severe fighting in various sectors. He took part in the Battles of Loos and Ypres, and was three times wounded in action. As a result of his wounds he was discharged in October 1917, as medically unfit for further service, and holds the 1914–15 Star, and the General Service and Victory Medals.

65, Richmond Street, Moss Side, Manchester.   Z7333

MISKELLY, S., Private, 18th Manchester Regiment.
He volunteered in September 1914, and after a period of service at home, was drafted to France in November of the following year. Whilst on the Western Front, he played a prominent part in the Battles of the Somme, Ypres and St. Quentin, and in the Retreat and Advance of 1918. Demobilised on his return to England in March 1919, he holds the 1914–15 Star, and the General Service and Victory Medals.
4, Ivy Grove, Hulme, Manchester. Z6870

MITCHELL, A., Private, Manchester Regiment.
Having volunteered in September 1914, he was retained in England on important duties for fourteen months. He then proceeded to France, but within a few weeks was wounded in action, and admitted to hospital at Rouen. On his recovery he rejoined his unit and was taken prisoner in July 1916, during the Somme Offensive. Whilst in captivity in Germany he was forced to work in the mines and suffered great privations. He was repatriated at the cessation of hostilities, and was demobilised in March 1919, holding the 1914–15 Star, and the General Service and Victory Medals.
12, Emily Street, Ardwick, Manchester. TZ7339

MITCHELL, A., Private, Labour Corps.
Joining in July 1917, he was drafted to France in the same month. He was engaged on road making and trench construction, and served at Arras, Lille and the Somme. He also took part in the Retreat and Advance of 1918. He was demobilised in October 1919, and holds the General Service and Victory Medals.
9, Brown Street, Miles Platting, Manchester. Z11554

MITCHELL, A. H., L/Corporal, R.E.
He volunteered in April 1915, and proceeding to France five months later, saw much severe fighting before being badly wounded in action during the Somme Offensive in September 1916. He was invalided to hospital in Scotland, and on his recovery served with an Officers' Training Battalion at Bisley until February 1918. He then carried out special duties with the R.E. Cross Channel Service until his demobilisation in February 1919. He holds the 1914–15 Star, and the General Service and Victory Medals.
2, Carver Street, Hulme, Manchester. Z7336

MITCHELL, C. (Miss), Special War Worker.
For some time during the war this lady rendered valuable services as a rivetter in connection with the manufacture of munitions of war at Messrs. Vickers, Ltd., Barrow-in-Furness. She carried out her responsible work in a very skilful manner, and relinquished her duties in November 1918.
227, Earl Street, Longsight, Manchester. Z7335

MITCHELL, F., Sergt., K.O. (Royal Lancaster Regt.)
He volunteered in September 1914, and in the following August crossed to France and took part in heavy fighting at Ypres and in the Battle of Loos. In October 1915 he proceeded to Salonika and in the course of his service in the Balkans, fought in the Offensive on Lake Doiran, in the Advance on the Struma and in the capture of Monastir. Returning to England for demobilisation in February 1919, he holds the 1914–15 Star, and the General Service and Victory Medals.
6, Bushton Street, Collyhurst, Manchester. Z10822

MITCHELL, G. R., Pte., 51st South Wales Borderers.
He joined the Army on attaining military age in June 1918, but was unsuccessful in obtaining his transfer overseas during hostilities. In December 1918, however, he was sent to the Army of Occupation. in Germany, and rendered valuable services with his unit at Bonn until September 1919. He was then transferred to Ireland, and was stationed at Carrickfergus until his demobilisation in March 1920.
33, Mark Lane, Chorlton-on-Medlock, Manchester. Z7334

MITCHELL, H., Driver, R.F.A.
He volunteered in January 1915, but owing to a physical disability, was retained on important guard duties and remount work with his Battery at various stations. He did consistently good work until August 1918, when he was invalided from the Army, owing to his disability having been aggravated by his military service.
7, Ashwood Street, Openshaw, Manchester. Z7338

MITCHELL, H., Rifleman, K.R.R.C.
Volunteering in August 1914, he was drafted to the Western Front in the following January and fought in the Battles of Ypres and the Somme, and was wounded on July 1st, 1916. Returning to the firing line on recovery, he was in action in several engagements, and on January 4th, 1917, was mentioned in Despatches for conspicuous gallantry in the Field. Taken prisoner at Nieuport on July 10th, 1917, he was held in captivity in Germany until the Armistice, after which he was repatriated. He was demobilised in February 1919, and holds the 1914–15 Star, and the General Service and Victory Medals.
7, Hooley Street, Ancoats, Manchester. Z10821

MITCHELL, H., Private, 8th Manchester Regiment.
He volunteered in September 1914, and in the following July was drafted to France. Whilst overseas he fought in the Battles of Loos, Albert, Vimy Ridge, the Somme (I), Arras, Bullecourt, Ypres (III), the Aisne (III), the Marne (II) and Le Cateau (II). He holds the 1914–15 Star, and the General

Service and Victory Medals, and was demobilised in February 1919. 10, Ernest Street, Ancoats, Manchester. Z9284

MITCHELL, J., Private, 16th Manchester Regiment.
He joined in September 1916, and after completing his training sailed for France. There he was in action on the Somme, and was wounded on April 18th, 1917, in the Battle of Arras. Invalided home, on account of his injuries, he received hospital treatment at Woking, and on recovery returned to the Western Front where he saw heavy fighting in several actions. Reported missing on April 27th, 1918, he was later believed to have been killed in action on that date. He was entitled to the General Service and Victory Medals.
"A valiant Soldier, with undaunted heart, he breasted life's last hill."
12, Adelaide Street, Bradford, Manchester. Z10823

MITCHELL, J., Bombardier, R.G.A.
He volunteered in November 1914, and three months later proceeded to the Western Front with the 26th Heavy Battery. Whilst in this theatre of war he took part in the Battles of Neuve Chapelle, St. Eloi, Hill 60, Festubert, Loos, Albert, Vermelles, the Somme, Arras, Messines, Ypres (III) and Cambrai, and in the Retreat and Advance of 1918. He was wounded in action at the Battle of Loos in September 1915, and was demobilised in March 1919, holding the 1914–15 Star, and the General Service and Victory Medals.
227, Earl Street, Longsight, Manchester. Z7337

MITCHELL, T., Private, 1st Border Regiment.
Volunteering at the beginning of 1915, he was quickly drafted to the Dardanelles, and whilst taking part in the first Landing on the Gallipoli Peninsula was unfortunately killed in action in April of the same year. He was entitled to the 1914–15 Star, and the General Service and Victory Medals.
"He died the noblest death a man may die," Fighting for God, and right, and liberty."
8, Back Pump Street, Hulme, Manchester. Z7340

MITCHELL, W., Pte., 8th and 26th Manchester Regt.
He volunteered in November 1914, and completing his training served at various stations with his unit on important duties. He became seriously ill, and admitted into hospital, unhappily died in March 1916.
"His memory is cherished with pride."
17, Gaggs Street, Newton, Manchester. Z9641

MITCHELL, W. R., 1st Air Mechanic, R.A.F.
At the outbreak of war he volunteered his services at the Westinghouse, Manchester, and did valuable work there until January 1918. He then joined the R.A.F. and on completion of h s training, was engaged as a skilled fitter in the workshops at various aerodromes in England and Wales. He was unsuccessful in obtaining his transfer overseas, and was demobilised in October 1919.
11, Normanby Street, Manchester. Z7341

MOFFAT, J. A., Private, 7th Manchester Regiment.
Volunteering in November 1914, he was sent to France in October 1915, and took part in the Battles of Albert, Ploegsteert, the Somme (I), Arras, Vimy Ridge, Bullecourt, Passchendaele, Cambrai, and the Somme (II). He was three times wounded in action—on the Somme in July 1916, at Bullecourt in May of the following year, and again on the Somme in March 1918, on which occasion he was invalided home. He was demobilised in March 1919, and holds the 1914–15 Star, and the General Service and Victory Medals.
23, Callender Street, Chorlton-on-Medlock. Manchester. Z7342

MOFFATT, S., Corporal, 8th Manchester Regiment.
Volunteering in February 1915, he was drafted overseas in the following year and saw much service in France and Flanders. He took part in severe fighting on the Somme, at Albert, Bourlon Wood and Cambrai, and through the German Offensive, and was wounded near Arras in 1918. Invalided home on account of his injuries he received hospital treatment in Liverpool, and was discharged as medically unfit later in 1918. He holds the General Service and Victory Medals.
123, Victoria Square, Manchester. TZ11775

MOISER, C. R., L/Corporal, 21st Manchester Regt.
He volunteered in September 1915, and in March of the following year was drafted to the Western Front. There he took part in the Battle of the Somme, and in many other important engagements in various sectors until severely wounded in action on the Marne in July 1918, and invalided home, suffering also from shell-shock. He was for a considerable period in hospital in England, and was finally demobilised in April 1919, holding the General Service and Victory Medals.
5, Pollitt Street, West Gorton, Manchester. Z11932

MOLE, W., Private, R.A.M.C.
He volunteered in November 1915, and was retained on important duties in England until February 1917, when he proceeded to Salonika. There he was engaged on important duties on various fronts, serving in a Field Hospital, at an Advance Dressing Station, and later at the 80th General Hospital, where he did much good work. He was demobilised on his return home in March 1919, and holds the General Service and Victory Medals.
22, Spruce Street, Hulme, Manchester. Z7343

MOLLARD, E., Pte., King's Own Scottish Borderers.
Shortly after joining in April 1916, he was drafted to the Western Front, where he saw heavy fighting in various sectors. He took part in the Battles of Albert, the Somme, the Ancre, Vimy Ridge and Ypres, and many other important engagements, until severely gassed and invalided home. He was discharged in September 1917 as medically unfit for further service, and holds the General Service and Victory Medals.
4, Daniel Street, Hulme, Manchester.   Z7344

MOLLOY, C., Private, 4th Manchester Regiment.
Shortly after volunteering in August 1914, he proceeded to the Western Front, where he saw much severe fighting in various sectors. He served through the Battles of Ypres, Neuve Chapelle and Hill 60, and many minor engagements, until wounded in action in the second Battle of Ypres in May 1915. He was for a time in hospital at Manchester, before being invalided from the Army in December of that year, and holds the 1914 Star, and the General Service and Victory Medals. 6, Broom Street, Ardwick, Manchester.   Z7345

MOLLOY, D., Gunner, R.F.A.
He was mobilised at the outbreak of hostilities, and in the following month was drafted to Egypt, where he was stationed at Alexandria. In June 1917 he sailed for France, and on arrival took part in various engagements, and was severely wounded at La Bassée in October 1917. He was in consequence sent home to hospital, and subsequently invalided out of the Service in February 1919. He holds the General Service and Victory Medals.
1, Day Street, off Oldham Road, Manchester.   Z9285

MOLLOY, H., Private, K.O. (R. Lancaster Regt.)
Mobilised at the outbreak of war in August 1914, he was immediately drafted to the Western Front, where he fought in the Retreat from Mons. He afterwards took part in the first and second Battles of Ypres, and many minor engagements, and was severely gassed in 1915. Invalided to hospital at Manchester, he unhappily died there on July 30th, 1915. He was entitled to the Mons Star, and the General Service and Victory Medals.
        "The path of duty was the way to glory."
2, Gorton Place, Longsight Street, Manchester.   Z7346

MOLLOY, J., Sergt., Loyal North Lancashire Regt.
He volunteered at the outbreak of war, and in June 1915 sailed for the Dardanelles. He gave his life for his King and Country at the Landing at Suvla Bay in August of the same year, and was entitled to the 1914-15 Star, and the General Service and Victory Medals.
        "And doubtless he went in splendid company."
37, Whitfield Street, Chorlton-on-Medlock, Manchester. TZ9286

MOLLOY, J. E., Sergt., 18th Manchester Regiment.
Volunteering in August 1914, he was drafted to India on completing a period of training in February of the following year. There he was engaged on important garrison duties at Allahabad, Cawnpore, Agra and various other stations, and rendered valuable services with his unit. Returning home in October 1919, he was demobilised in the following month, and holds the General Service and Victory Medals.
56, Gore Street, Greenheys, Manchester.   TZ9347

MOLLOY, R., Private, King's (Liverpool Regiment).
Volunteering in September 1914, he was drafted to the Western Front twelve months later, and there saw severe fighting in various sectors. He took part in the Battles of the Somme, the Ancre, Arras, Bullecourt and Ypres, and many minor engagements, was wounded in action at Cambrai in November 1917, and taken prisoner. Held in captivity until December 1918, he was finally invalided from the Army in May 1919, and holds the 1914-15 Star, and the General Service and Victory Medals.
35, Brunswick Street, Hulme, Manchester.   Z7348

MOLLOY, T., Driver, R.A.S.C. (M.T.)
He joined in September 1917, and in the following December was drafted to France. During his service on the Western Front he fought in the Battles of Arras and Bullecourt, and was wounded at Ypres in September 1917. After his recovery he rejoined his Corps, and was again severely wounded at Amiens in August 1918. He was then invalided home to hospital, and later discharged as unfit for further duty in December 1919. He holds the General Service and Victory Medals.
213, Victoria Square, Oldham Rd., Manchester.   TZ9287

MOLLOY, W. H., Private, 6th Manchester Regt.
Volunteering in August 1914, he was drafted to the Western Front in October of the following year, and fought at Loos, Ploegsteert, Vimy Ridge, the Somme, Messines, Ypres and Cambrai. He returned to England, and was discharged on account of his service in February 1918, holding the 1914-15 Star, and the General Service and Victory Medals.
6, Strand Street, Ancoats, Manchester.   Z9642

MOLYNEAUX, C. E., Sergt., 8th King's Own (Royal Lancaster Regiment).
He volunteered in September 1914, and was drafted to France in the following year, and took part in numerous engagements,

including those at Loos, St. Eloi, Albert, Vimy Ridge, the Somme, Arras, Cambrai and Poperinghe. During his service in this theatre of war he was wounded on three occasions. He was demobilised in March 1919, and holds the 1914-15 Star, and the General Service and Victory Medals.
9, Middlewood Street, Harpurhey, Manchester.   Z11555

MONK, T., Private, Essex Regiment.
He joined in June 1918, and in August of that year, was drafted to the Western Front, where he served at Etaples, and in various other sectors, and was engaged, after his training, on duties of great importance. On the cessation of hostilities he was sent with the Army of Occupation into Germany, finally returning home for demobilisation in February 1919. He holds the General Service and Victory Medals.
19, Watson Street, Hulme, Manchester.   Z7349

MONKS, H., Private, R.A.S.C. (M.T.)
Joining in September 1916, he was engaged on transport duties at various home stations until November 1918, when he was sent to the Western Front. Engaged as a fitter in the travelling workshops, he did excellent work in the Arras and Ypres sectors, and after the Armistice was retained in France for a year. He returned to England in November 1919, was demobilised in the following month, and holds the General Service and Victory Medals.
31, Gardner Street, Gorton, Manchester.   Z10824

MONKS, J. T., Private, 3rd Border Regiment.
He volunteered in January 1916, and on the conclusion of his training was engaged on guard and other duties at stations in the North and West of England. He was not sent overseas owing to medical unfitness, and was discharged in consequence in September 1916.
17, Rennie Street, West Gorton, Manchester.   Z10825

MONTGOMERY, H., L/Cpl., Military Foot Police.
He volunteered in October 1915, and on completing his training in March of the following year, proceeded to the Western Front, where he served in various sectors. Engaged on duties of great importance, he was unfortunately severely wounded in a fracas with German prisoners near Calais, and was invalided to hospital in England. He was finally discharged as medically unfit for further service in June 1918, and holds the General Service and Victory Medals.
12, Rumford Street, Hulme, Manchester.   TZ7350

MOODY, J., Private, Royal Berkshire Regiment.
He volunteered in April 1915, and in January of the following year was drafted to France, where he saw heavy fighting in various sectors. After taking part in the Battles of Vimy Ridge and the Somme, and engagements at Loos, St. Eloi, Albert and many other places, he was severely wounded in action at Arras, and sent to hospital at Bristol. He was invalided from the Army in July 1917, and holds the General Service and Victory Medals.
134, Blackthorn Street, Ardwick, Manchester.   Z7351

MOON, J., Private, Loyal North Lancashire Regt.
He joined in November 1915, and in the following June was drafted to the Western Front, where he took part in many important engagements in various sectors, including the Battles of the Ancre, Arras and Vimy Ridge. He died gloriously on the Field of Battle at Ypres in July 1917, and was buried at Rouen. He was entitled to the General Service and Victory Medals.
        "His life for his Country, his soul to God."
67, Upton Street, Chorlton-on-Medlock, Manchester. Z7352

MOON, T. H., Private, R.A.S.C.
He volunteered in November 1914, and in the following year was drafted to Salonika, where he saw much severe fighting on the Vardar and Doiran fronts. In February 1918 he was transferred to the Western Front, and there, after taking part in many important engagements, was killed in action on the Sambre in November 1918, shortly before the cessation of hostilities. He was entitled to the 1914-15 Star, and the General Service and Victory Medals.
        "Steals on the ear the distant triumph song."
67, Upton Street, Chorlton-on-Medlock, Manchester. Z7353

MOONEY, F., Private, Labour Corps.
Joining in February 1917, he proceeded to the Western Front in the following month and was there engaged in guarding prisoners of war, and on other important duties in various sectors. He served at Etaples and Boulogne, and was also present at the Battles of Arras, Ypres and Cambrai, and other engagements. Demobilised in September 1919, he holds the General Service and Victory Medals.
44, Chelford Street, Chorlton-on-Medlock, Manchester. Z7354

MOONEY, M. A. (Mrs.), Special War Worker.
During the war this lady offered her services for Government work, and was engaged at Messrs. Briggs, Jones and Gibsons' Army Clothing Factory. Her duties which consisted in the manufacture of uniforms were carried out with efficiency, and to the entire satisfaction of the firm. After the Armistice was signed she relinquished her position owing to the cessation of hostilities.
35, Stonehewer Street, Rochdale Road, Manchester. Z9288

MOONEY, J., Private, 2/8th Manchester Regiment.
He joined in September 1916, and in February of the following year was drafted to the Western Front. Whilst in this theatre of war he took part in many engagements, including the Battles of Arras, Bullecourt and Ypres, was wounded in action at Cambrai in November 1917, and taken prisoner on the Somme during the Retreat of 1918. Held in captivity in Germany until after the cessation of hostilities, he was finally demobilised in March 1919 holding the General Service and Victory Medals. 17, Gladstone St,. West Gorton, Manchester. Z7355

MOONEY, J., Corporal, 2nd Manchester Regiment.
Mobilised in August 1914, he was immediately drafted to the Western Front, where he took part in the Battle of Mons, and the subsequent Retreat. After serving also through the Battles of the Marne, the Aisne, La Bassée, and Givenchy, he was wounded in action at Ypres, and invalided to hospital at Liverpool. On his recovery, however, he returned to France and unhappily fell fighting at the second Battle of Ypres on May 13th, 1915. He was entitled to the Mons Star, and the General Service and Victory Medals.
"The path of duty was the way to glory."
6, Heron Street, Hulme, Manchester. Z7356

MOONEY, J. W., Private, K. (Liverpool Regiment).
Volunteering in September 1914, he served on Home Defence duties for upwards of two years, and in July 1916 embarked for France. Whilst in this theatre of war he was in action with his Battalion in several engagements, including those of the Somme Offensive, and was taken prisoner at Oppy Wood on May 11th, 1917. He died in captivity a week later, and was entitled to the General Service and Victory Medals.
"His memory is cherished with pride."
19, Mary Street, Gorton, Manchester. Z10826

MOONEY, T., Private, Lancashire Fusiliers.
He volunteered in December 1915, and underwent a period of training prior to being drafted to the Western Front in November of the following year. There he saw severe fighting at Neuve Chapelle, La Bassée, Albert, and various other places and also took part in many important engagements, including the Battles of Arras, Ypres, Passchendaele, Cambrai and the Somme. He was demobilised in June 1919, and holds the General Service and Victory Medals.
11, Matlock Street, Ardwick, Manchester. Z7357

MOORE, A., Private, King's (Liverpool Regiment).
Joining in February 1916, he proceeded to the Western Front in the following month, and was there engaged on important duties in various sectors, being over age for service in the firing line. He was stationed at Neuve Chapelle, Ypres, La Bassée, St. Quentin, Arras, Albert and Lille, and many other places in this theatre of war, and finally returned home for demobilisation in February 1919. He holds the General Service and Victory Medals.
35, Baker Street, Ardwick, Manchester. Z7358

MOORE, F., Private, 12th Manchester Regiment.
He volunteered at the commencement of hostilities, and proceeding to France in January 1915, was engaged in heavy fighting in many parts of the line. Severely wounded in March 1915, he returned home to hospital, where it was found necessary to amputate one of his feet. After receiving protracted hospital treatment he was invalided out in February 1918, and holds the 1914-15 Star, and the General Service and Victory Medals.
21, Pilling Street, Newton Heath, Manchester. Z9643

MOORE, G., Private, 1st Dorsetshire Regiment.
He volunteered in September 1914, and after doing duty at various home stations embarked for France in February 1917. Whilst overseas he took part in engagements at Arras, Nieuport, La Bassée and the Somme, and in various operations during the Retreat and Advance of 1918, and was demobilised in April 1919, and holds the General Service and Victory Medals.
51, Baguley Street, Miles Platting, Manchester. Z9289

MOORE, G. A., Driver, R.A.S.C. (M.T.)
Joining in May 1916, he proceeded to Salonika after two months training, and was there engaged on important duties at various stations, where he did much useful work. He was also for a considerable period in hospital suffering from malaria, and was finally sent home and invalided from the Army in September 1918. He holds the General Service and Victory Medals. 10, Crofton Street, Moss Side, Manchester. Z7362

MOORE, J., Pte., 8th K.O. (Royal Lancaster Regt.)
He joined in November 1917, and was retained on important duties at home until August 1918, when he was drafted to the Western Front. There, after taking part in severe fighting he was wounded in action at Gommecourt in the following month and was later engaged on duties at the Base in France. He was demobilised in November 1919, and holds the General Service and Victory Medals.
8, St. Leonard Street, Chorlton-on-Medlock, Manchester. X7360

MOORE, J. A., Driver, R.A.S.C.
He joined in December 1917, and after two months' training proceeded to the Western Front, where he was engaged on important duties in various sectors. After taking an active part in the Battles of the Somme, the Lys and the Aisne,

and other engagements, he was sent home and invalided from the Army on account of deafness caused by gun-fire. He holds the General Service and Victory Medals.
80, Birch Lane, Longsight, Manchester. TZ7363

MOORE, S. J., Private, Manchester Regiment.
Volunteering in December 1915, he was sent to France on completing his training in April of the following year, and there saw much heavy fighting. After taking part in the Battles of Albert, the Somme, and Arras, he was wounded in action, and admitted to hospital. He re-joined his unit, however, on his recovery, fought in the third Battle of Ypres, and was so severely wounded at Cambrai as to necessitate the amputation of his left arm. He was invalided from the Army in April 1918, and holds the General Service and Victory Medals.
16, Avenham Street, Hulme, Manchester. Z7359

MOORE, T., Private, 8th Manchester Regiment.
He volunteered in October 1915, and in September of the following year, was drafted to the Western Front. Whilst in this theatre of war he saw much severe fighting in various sectors, took part in the Battles of Arras, Bullecourt, Messines and Cambrai, and other engagements, and served also through the Retreat and Advance of 1918. Demobilised in March 1919, he holds the General Service and Victory Medals.
21, Heyrod Street, Ancoats, Manchester. Z7115

MOORE, T., Corporal, 2nd Manchester Regiment.
Having enlisted in 1911, he was already serving in India when war broke out in August 1914, and in April of the following year was drafted to the Western Front. There he was unhappily reported missing, believed to have been killed in action at the second Battle of Ypres on April 26th, 1915, only a few days after landing in France. He was entitled to the 1914-15 Star, and the General Service and Victory Medals.
"He joined the great white company of valiant souls."
24, James Street, Moss Side, Manchester. Z7361

MOORE, T., Private, Manchester Regiment.
Shortly after volunteering in June 1915, he was drafted to the Western Front, where he saw heavy fighting in various sectors. After taking part in many important engagements, he was severely wounded in action in the Somme Offensive of July 1916 and invalided home. He was for a considerable period in hospital, before being discharged as medically unfit for further service in April 1918, and holds the 1914-15 Star, and the General Service and Victory Medals.
8, Leonard Street, Openshaw, Manchester. Z7364

MOORE, W., Driver, R.A.S.C.
Volunteering on the outbreak of war, he was sent to the Western Front shortly afterwards, and served there throughout the war. Engaged on important transport duties he did valuable work during the Retreat from Mons, and the Battles of La Bassée, Loos, Ypres, the Somme, Nieuport, and in those of the concluding stages of hostilities. He was demobilised in May 1919, and holds the Mons Star, and the General Service and Victory Medals.
19, Whalley Street, Ancoats, Manchester. Z10828

MOORES, A., Private, K.O. (R. Lancaster Regt.)
He volunteered in November 1914, and embarking for France five months later fought in the Battles of Ypres and Loos. He gave his life for the freedom of England at Ypres on March 2nd, 1916, and was entitled to the 1914-15 Star, and the General Service and Victory Medals.
"Whilst we remember, the sacrifice is not in vain."
1, Sun Street, Newton Heath, Manchester. Z10139B

MOORES, A., Private, Highland Light Infantry.
Volunteering in August 1914, he proceeded to Mesopotamia in October of the following year, and took part in several operations for the relief of Kut. He was also in action at the Battle of Kut-el-Amara, the second attack on Kut, in several engagements on the Tigris, and in the capture of Baghdad, and was wounded three times—twice at Kut in 1915, and at Baghdad in 1916. He returned to England for demobilisation in January 1920, and holds the 1914-15 Star, and the General Service and Victory Medals.
4, Needwood Street, Collyhurst, Manchester. Z10830

MOORES, A., L/Corporal, K.O. (R. Lancaster Regt.)
Volunteering in August 1914, he proceeded to Mesopotamia in December of that year, and there took part in many important engagements. He made the supreme sacrifice, falling in action in August 1916, near Amara, where he was buried. He was entitled to the 1914-15 Star, and the General Service and Victory Medals.
"He died the noblest death a man may die,
Fighting for God, and right, and liberty."
9, Heron Street, Chorlton-on-Medlock, Manchester. Z7368

MOORES, F., Air Mechanic, R.A.F.
He joined in February 1918, and crossing to France two months later was engaged with his Squadron in the forward areas. Engaged on duties of a highly technical nature he did good work in aerodromes at Bapaume, Havrincourt, Cambrai and other places in the final stages of the war, and returned to England in December 1918. Demobilised in the following February, he holds the General Service and Victory Medals.
13, Alma Street, Queen's Road, Manchester. Z10829

MOORES, A. B., Private, Manchester Regiment, and 1st South Lancashire Regiment.

He joined in April 1917, and after completing a period of training, served at various stations, where he was engaged on duties of great importance. He was not successful in obtaining his transfer to a theatre of war, but in November 1918 was sent to Ireland, where he rendered valuable services, and was still with his unit in 1920.

41, Claribel Street, Ardwick, Manchester.   Z7365A

MOORES, E., Corporal, 8th Manchester Regiment.

He volunteered in August 1914, and after a period of home service, was drafted to France in February 1916. He first saw heavy fighting at Loos, St. Eloi and Albert, and later played a prominent part in the Battles of Vermelles, the Somme Vimy Ridge, Ypres and Cambrai. Invalided to England with yellow jaundice, he was in hospital at Ashton before being demobilised in February 1919, and holds the General Service and Victory Medals.

110, Thomas Street, West Gorton, Manchester.   Z7366

MOORES, H., Sergeant, 11th Manchester Regiment.

He volunteered in October 1915, and was drafted overseas three months later. Serving with his Battalion in various sectors of the Western Front he was in action in the Somme Offensive, and the Battles of Arras, Ypres and Cambrai. He also took part in heavy fighting in the Retreat and was wounded at Cambrai on October 11th, 1918, in the Allied Advance, which terminated hostilities. He holds the General Service and Victory Medals, and was demobilised in January 1919. 39, Gardener Street, West Gorton, Manchester. Z10831

MOORES, H., Private, 13th Manchester Regiment.

He volunteered in September 1914, and served at various stations until drafted to Salonika in January 1916. In this theatre of war he was in action in many engagements both on the Struma and Doiran fronts. Contracting malaria, he returned to England, and after receiving hospital treatment was discharged as unfit for further service in March 1918. He holds the General Service and Victory Medals.

9, Hadfield Street, Newton Heath, Manchester.   Z9644

MOORES, J., Gunner, R.F.A.

He was already in the Army when war broke out in August 1914, having enlisted in July 1908, and was immediately drafted to the Western Front. During his service overseas he took part in the Battle of and the Retreat from Mons, and the Battles of the Marne, the Aisne, and La Bassée, Ypres, Neuve Chapelle, Hill 60, Albert, and the Somme. He was killed in action at the Battle of Arras on April 6th, 1917, and was entitled to the Mons Star, and the General Service and Victory Medals.

"He passed out of the sight of men by the path of duty and self-sacrifice."

38, Milton Street, West Gorton, Manchester.   Z5885A

MOORES, J. E., Private, South Lancashire Regiment.

Volunteering in March 1915, he was sent to France in the following September, and during his service on the Western Front, saw much severe fighting. He took part in the Battles of the Somme and Ypres, and in the Retreat and Advance of 1918. He holds the 1914–15 Star, and the General Service and Victory Medals, and was demobilised on his return to England in March 1919.

42, Meridian Street, Higher Ardwick, Manchester.   Z7365B

MOORES, J. P., Private, 17th Manchester Regiment.

He joined in February 1916, and, after a period of training, was drafted to Salonika later in that year. In this theatre of war, he was engaged on important duties with his unit on the Macedonian front, and also saw service in Turkey. After rendering valuable services, he was demobilised in November 1919, and holds the General Service and Victory Medals.

6, Bloom Street, Hulme, Manchester.   TZ7369

MOORES, P., Private, 2/8th Manchester Regiment.

He volunteered in February 1915, but after completing a term of training was retained on home service, and was engaged on important duties with his unit. He was not able to obtain his transfer to a theatre of war, but, nevertheless, rendered valuable services until his discharge in March 1917, owing to valvular disease of the heart.

4, Goburg Place, Manchester.   Z7367

MOORES, R., Rifleman, Rifle Brigade.

Volunteering in September 1914, he was sent to France in the following January, and fought in several engagements, including the Battles of St. Eloi and Hill 60. He died gloriously on the Field of Battle at Hooge on 14th May, 1915, and was entitled to the 1914–15 Star, and the General Service and Victory Medals.

"His life for his Country."

1, Sun Street, Newton Heath, Manchester.   Z10139C

MOORES, W., Private, 25th Manchester Regiment.

He joined in January 1916, and was quickly drafted to France, where he took part in much severe fighting. He fought in many important engagements, including the Battles of the Somme, Arras, Bullecourt, Messines, and Ypres, where he was killed in action on October 22nd, 1917. He was entitled to the General Service and Victory Medals.

"And doubtless he went in splendid company."

4, Heyrod Street, Ancoats, Manchester.   Z7113B

MOORES, W. A., 4th Lancashire Fusiliers.

He volunteered in September 1914, and on completion of his training was drafted to the Dardanelles, and took part in the Landing at Suvla Bay. He remained in this seat of war until the Evacuation of the Gallipoli Peninsula, when he was invalided to hospital suffering from dysentery. On his recovery he proceeded to the Western Front, and took part in the fighting at Ypres, and in the Retreat and Advance of 1918, and was wounded on two occasions. He was demobilised in January 1919, and holds the 1914–15 Star, and the General Service and Victory Medals.

16, Tempest Street, Ardwick, Manchester.   Z7365C

MOOREY, J. H., Driver, R.A.S.C.

He joined in May 1916, and was immediately drafted to France, where he was engaged with the transport section in conveying ammunition to the various fighting sectors. He also served through the Battles of Ypres, Cambrai, and the Somme, and in the Retreat and Advance of 1918, and remained in France until demobilised in May 1919. He holds the General Service and Victory Medals.

60, Avon Street, Chorlton-on-Medlock, Manchester.   Z6109A

MOORHOUSE, J. A., Pte., 4th Lancashire Fusiliers.

He volunteered in August 1914, and in the following May sailed for Gallipoli, where he took part in various operations, including the Landing at Suvla Bay, the capture of Chunuk Bair, and the Evacuation of the Peninsula. In January 1916, he was sent to the Western Front, and fought at Albert and other places in the Somme area. He fell fighting at Armentières on May 15th, 1916, and lies buried in the neighbouring British Military Cemetery. He was entitled to the 1914–15 Star, and the General Service and Victory Medals.

"Courage, bright hopes, and a myriad dreams, splendidly given."

51, Melbourne Street, Hulme, Manchester.   Z11776A

MOORHOUSE, S., Private, 1st Bedfordshire Regt.

He volunteered in January 1916, and on completion of his training embarked for India in May 1916. Serving with his Battalion at various stations he did excellent work on garrison and other duties for over four years, returning home for demobilisation in December 1920. He holds the General Service Medal.

12, Spring Street, Chorlton-on-Medlock, Manchester. Z10832

MOORHOUSE, T., Private, Leinster Regiment.

He volunteered in August 1914, and in March of the following year was drafted to France, where he saw much active service. He took part in engagements at Neuve Chapelle, Hill 60, Ypres, and Loos, and was wounded at Vimy Ridge. After his recovery he fought again on the Somme, at Arras, Bullecourt, Messines, Passchendaele, Cambrai, and in the Retreat and Advance of 1918. He was demobilised in May 1919, and holds the 1914–15 Star, and the General Service and Victory Medals. 9, Sparkle's Street, Ancoats, Manchester. Z9290

MOORHOUSE, T. A., Acting Q.M.S., M.G.C.

Volunteering in August 1914, he was sent to Egypt in the next month, and was stationed at Cairo and Alexandria, until invalided home owing to illness in May 1915. Discharged on medical grounds in the following month he joined the King's Own (Royal Lancaster Regiment) in July 1916, and in December of that year embarked for France. There he served in the Battles of Ypres and Passchendaele, and was wounded in the Ypres Salient on January 8th, 1917. On recovery he was drafted to Mesopotamia in the following October, and in that theatre of war did good work until the conclusion of hostilities. He returned to England in August 1919, and demobilised two months later, holds the 1914–15 Star, and the General Service and Victory Medals.

51, Melbourne Street, Hulme, Manchester.   Z11776B

MORAN, A., Private, 1st Manchester Regiment.

He volunteered in February 1915, and in the following June was sent to India, where he saw service until November of that year. He was then drafted to Mesopotamia, and, during his period of service in this theatre of war, was present at the attack on Kut-el-Amara, and in engagements on the Um-el-Hannah Front, where he was killed in action on February 2nd, 1916. He was entitled to the 1914–15 Star, and the General Service and Victory Medals.

"He joined the great white company of valiant souls."

30, Devonshire Street, Hulme, Manchester.   TZ7108

MORAN, J., Private, King's (Liverpool Regiment).

He joined in January 1917, and was immediately drafted to the Western Front. Whilst in this theatre of war he took part in many important engagements in various sectors of the Front, including the Battles of Bullecourt, Messines, Ypres, Passchendaele, Cambrai (I), the Somme (II), Amiens, Bapaume, Havrincourt, Cambrai (II), and Le Cateau (II). He was demobilised in February 1919, and holds the General Service and Victory Medals.

7, Stockton Street, Chorlton-on-Medlock, Manchester. Z7374

MORAN, J., Private, East Lancashire Regiment.
Volunteering in August 1914, he completed his training at Hull and proceeded to the Western Front in the following April, and was in action in the Battles of Hill 60, Ypres, and Festubert. He fell fighting in June 1915, and was entitled to the 1914-15 Star, and the General Service and Victory Medals.
" Great deeds cannot die."
15, Iles Street, Oldham Road, Manchester.   Z10834

MORAN, J., Private, 11th Manchester Regiment.
Joining in February 1916, he was quickly sent to France. There he took part in the heavy fighting at the Battles of Albert, the Somme, and Arras, where he was wounded in action in 1917. He was invalided to hospital in England, and finally demobilised in January 1919, holding the General Service and Victory Medals.
19, Watson Street, Hulme, Manchester.   Z7373

MORAN, J., Sapper, R.E.
He joined in November 1917, and after a period of training, was first engaged on very important duties with his unit at various stations in England. He was also engaged on special work in prisoners-of-war camps, and rendered very valuable services until demobilised in November 1919.
3, Clayburn Street, Hulme, Manchester.   Z7370

MORAN, J. M., Sergt., King's Royal Rifle Corps.
He volunteered in September 1914, and crossing to France in the same year served with his Battalion in several engagements, until wounded at Ploegsteert Wood in June 1915. Sent home on account of his injuries he returned to the Western Front in April 1916, and was engaged in heavy fighting in various parts of the line. Owing to illness he was invalided to England, where, after treatment, he was discharged as medically unfit in April 1917. He holds the 1914 Star, and the General Service and Victory Medals.
56, North Kent Street, Rochdale Road, Manchester. Z10833

MORAN, M., Private, Lancashire Fusiliers.
He volunteered in July 1915, and after his training served at various stations on important duties with his unit. He rendered valuable services, but was not successful in obtaining his transfer overseas, whilst hostilities were in progress, and was demobilised in February 1919.
203, Victoria Square, Oldham Road, Manchester.   Z9291

MORAN, P., Private, 7th Loyal N. Lancashire Regt.
He volunteered shortly after the outbreak of war in August 1914, and was drafted to the Western Front in the following June. A month later, he was badly gassed in action at Neuve Chapelle, and after hospital treatment at Etaples, was invalided home in March 1916. He was eventually discharged as medically unfit for further service in August 1917, and holds the 1914-15 Star, and the General Service and Victory Medals.
10, Cowper Street, Bradford, Manchester.   TX7371

MORAN, T., Sergt., 19th Manchester Regiment.
He volunteered in October 1914, and in November of the following year was drafted to France, where he served with distinction at Loos, St. Eloi, Albert, Vimy Ridge, and on the Somme. He was badly wounded in action in July 1916, and after treatment in hospital at Rouen was invalided to Lincoln. After his demobilisation in February 1919, he tried to follow his old trade as a printer, but unfortunately had to forsake his work, and died as the result of his wounds in January 1920. He was entitled to the 1914-15 Star, and the General Service and Victory Medals.
" His memory is cherished with pride."
6, College Street, Greenheys, Manchester.   Z7372B

MORAN, W., Private, Lancashire Fusiliers.
Volunteering in October 1914, he was drafted to the Western Front in the following April, and was engaged in severe fighting in the Battles of Ypres, Loos the Somme, and Beaucourt. Severely wounded at Arras, he was removed to hospital, where he died from the effects of his injuries in May 1917. He lies buried in the British Cemetery at Arras, and was entitled to the 1914-15 Star, and the General Service and Victory Medals.
" A costly sacrifice upon the altar of freedom."
5, Stockdale Street, Ancoats, Manchester.   Z10815B

MORAN, W., Private, 7th Manchester Regiment.
He volunteered in January 1915, and, on completion of his training, was engaged on important duties with his unit at various stations. Later he was sent to France, where he took part in the Battles of Cambrai, the Somme (II), the Marne, and Le Cateau (II). He then returned home and was demobilised in August 1919, holding the General Service and Victory Medals. 6, College Street, Greenheys, Manchester. Z7372A

MORELAND, P., Stoker, R.N., H.M.S. " Exmouth."
Mobilised in August 1914, he proceeded to Belgium with the Royal Naval Division, and took part in the Defence of Antwerp. Later he was transferred to the Dardanelles, where he was badly wounded in action during the Landing at Suvla Bay in August 1915. On his recovery, he saw service in Egypt until the cessation of hostilities. He received his discharge in February 1919, and holds the 1914 Star, and the General Service and Victory Medals.
64, Exeter Street, Ardwick, Manchester.   Z7375

MORETON, T., Private, 7th Manchester Regiment.
He volunteered in January 1916, and was retained on important duties with his unit until May 1917, when he was drafted to France. During his service in this seat of war, he took an active part in the fighting at Arras, Ypres, and Cambrai. He was killed in action in September 1918, and was entitled to the General Service and Victory Medals.
"Honour to the immortal dead, who gave their youth that the world might grow old in peace."
78, Rutland Street, Hulme, Manchester.   TZ7376

MOREY, T. G., Private, Lancashire Fusiliers.
He joined in June 1917, and was quickly drafted to the Western Front. During his service in this theatre of war, he saw much heavy fighting, and was badly wounded and gassed at the Battle of Cambrai in November 1917. Invalided to hospital in England, he was under treatment for six months. He was eventually demobilised in September 1919, and holds the General Service and Victory Medals.
15, John Street, Rusholme, Manchester.   Z7378

MOREY, W. Sergt., R.F.A.
Volunteering in May 1915, he was drafted to France in July, and served with distinction at the Battles of Loos, Albert, the Somme (I), Arras, Messines, Ypres (III), Cambrai (I), and the Somme (II). He was wounded in action in each of the three last-named engagements, and was finally invalided to hospital at Stockport. Demobilised in January 1919, he holds the 1914-15 Star, and the General Service and Victory Medals.
5, Auburn Place, Moor Street, Rusholme, Manchester. Z7377

MORGAN, F., Driver, R.F.A.
Joining in May 1917, he completed his training, and served with his Battery at various depôts. Among other important duties he was engaged in guarding ammunition and in looking after horses, and rendered valuable services. He was unsuccessful in his efforts to obtain his transfer overseas before the end of the war, and was demobilised in September 1919.
5, Dickens Street, Queen's Road, Manchester.   Z10836

MORGAN, J., Private, Royal Scots Fusiliers.
He volunteered in November 1914, and proceeding overseas in the following year saw active service in France. In the course of operations in this theatre of war he fought in the Battle of Festubert, and was wounded and sustained shell-shock at Flers. Invalided home, owing to his injuries, he was admitted to the 1st Southern General Hospital, Stourbridge, and after a prolonged course of treatment was discharged as medically unfit for further service in September 1917. He holds the 1914-15 Star, and the General Service and Victory Medals.
11, Almond Street, Gorton, Manchester.   Z10835

MORGAN, J. (M.M.), L/Cpl., 22nd Manchester Regt.
Twelve months after volunteering in November 1914, he was drafted to the Western Front, where he played a prominent part in the Battles of the Somme, Arras, Vimy Ridge, Messines, Ypres (III), Cambrai, the Aisne (III) and Havrincourt, and in heavy fighting at St. Eloi, Beaumont-Hamel, Beaucourt, and on the Ancre. Badly wounded in action at Havrincourt in September 1918, he was invalided home and underwent treatment at Portsmouth and Manchester. He was awarded the Military Medal for conspicuous bravery in the Field, he also holds the 1914-15 Star, and the General Service and Victory Medals, and was demobilised in October 1919.
13, Lavender Street, Hulme, Manchester.   Z7379

MORGAN, T., Private, 20th Manchester Regiment.
Volunteering in November 1914, he embarked for the Western Front in the following November, and took part in heavy fighting at Loos and St. Eloi. He was also in action in the Battles of Albert, Vimy Ridge and the Somme, and was wounded in July 1916. Evacuated to England he was under treatment for a protracted period, and was subsequently invalided out of the Service in August 1917. He holds the 1914-15 Star, and the General Service and Victory Medals.
37, Eliza Ann Street, Rochdale Road, Manchester. Z10837

MORGAN, W., Corporal, 16th Manchester Regiment.
Volunteering in August 1915, he was sent to the Western Front in February of the following year. Whilst overseas he fought in the early stages of the Battle of the Somme, and was severely wounded in Trones Wood on July 8th, 1916. He was invalided home to hospital, and after receiving medical treatment, was transferred in October 1917 to the Royal Army Pay Corps, and engaged on light duties until January 1920, when he was demobilised. He holds the General Service and Victory Medals.
17, Whitby Street, Ancoats, Manchester.   Z9292

MORGAN, W. A., Private, K.O. (R. Lancaster Regt.)
He volunteered at the commencement of hostilities, and embarking for the Western Front soon afterwards was in action in the Retreat from Mons, and the Battles of the Marne, the Aisne and at Meteren. Wounded on October 19th, 1914 at Le Toquet, during an hostile air-raid, he was sent to hospital in England and received prolonged medical treatment. He was ultimately discharged as medically unfit in May 1916, and holds the Mons Star, and the General Service and Victory Medals. 18, Strand Street, Ancoats, Manchester.   TZ11777

MORGAN, W. G., Private, 2nd Gloucestershire Regt.
He volunteered in March 1915, and in January of the following
year was drafted to Salonika, where he played an important
part in the strenuous fighting on the Doiran, Vardar and Struma
fronts. He was in hospital for some time with malarial fever,
but on his recovery, rejoined his unit and continued to serve
in the Balkan theatre of war until April 1919. He then came
home for demobilisation, and holds the General Service and
Victory Medals.
29, Brunswick Street, Hulme, Manchester.   Z7380

MORLEY, B. J., Corporal, R.H.A.
Volunteering in August 1914, he proceeded overseas two months
later and served with his Battery in various parts of the line
in France and Flanders. Carrying out the duties of a " spotter "
in the anti-Aircraft section, he did good work in several
engagements, including those of Ypres (I and II), Arras and
Vimy Ridge, and in August 1917, was sent home to serve at
the London Headquarters, Air Defence Centre, as an Instructor. In this capacity he rendered excellent services until
demobilised in March 1919, and holds the 1914 Star, and the
General Service and Victory Medals.
75, Welcomb Street, Hulme, Manchester.   Z11778

MORLEY, G., Corporal, R.G.A.
He was mobilised from the Reserve when war broke out, and
sent to France shortly afterwards took part in the Retreat
from Mons. He also fought in numerous battles, including
those of the Marne, the Aisne, La Bassée, Ypres, Neuve Chapelle, Hill 60, Loos, St. Eloi, the Somme, Arras and in the
Retreat and Advance of 1918. He returned home for demobilisation in January 1919, and holds the Mons Star, and
the General Service and Victory Medals.
79, Inkermann Street, Collyhurst, Manchester.   Z10838

MORRELL, S., Driver, R.A.S.C.
He was sent to Salonika within a month after volunteering
in October 1915, and during his four months service in the
Balkan theatre of war, was engaged on important duties
with a Labour Battalion and saw heavy fighting on the Vardar
front. In March 1916 he was invalided home with chest
trouble, and in April was discharged as medically unfit for
further service, holding the 1914-15 Star, and the General
Service and Victory Medals.
28, Dorset Street, Hulme, Manchester.   Z7381

MORREY, W., Pioneer, R.E.
He volunteered in January 1916, and was quickly drafted
to France, where he first saw heavy fighting during the German
attacks at Loos, St. Eloi and Albert. Later he took part in
the Battle of Vimy Ridge, but was badly gassed in action on
the Somme on June 26th, 1916. Unfortunately he died on
the following day, and was entitled to the General Service
and Victory Medals.
          " A costly sacrifice upon the altar of freedom."
158, Beresford Street, Moss Side, Manchester.   Z7382

MORRIS, A., Driver, R.A.S.C.
He volunteered in August 1914, and in September of the
following year was drafted to the Western Front, where he
was engaged on important transport duties during the Battles
of the Somme (I), Arras, Vimy Ridge, Ypres (III), Cambrai (I),
the Somme (II), Amiens, Bapaume and Cambrai (II). He
was demobilised in March 1919, and holds the 1914-15 Star,
and the General Service and Victory Medals.
49, Wood Street, Hulme, Manchester.   TZ7396

MORRIS, A., Leading Aircraftsman, R.A.F.
He joined in December 1917, and on completion of his training
was engaged on special duties as a tin-plate worker at various
home stations. He rendered valuable services, but was not
successful in obtaining his transfer overseas, and was demobilised in November 1919.
2, Pownall Street, Hulme, Manchester.   Z7384

MORRIS, A. E., Private, 9th East Lancashire Regt.
Volunteering in September 1914, he was sent to France
twelve months later. After a period of service in this theatre
of war, he was drafted to Salonika, and took part in much
severe fighting on the Struma and Vardar fronts. In March
1918, he was invalided home with malarial fever, and on his
recovery, was engaged on guard duties over prisoners of war
in Yorkshire. He was demobilised in March 1919, and holds
the 1914-15 Star, and the General Service and Victory Medals.
2, Pownall Street, Hulme, Manchester.   Z7385

MORRIS, A. H., Driver, R.F.A.
Volunteering in November 1914, he proceeded to France in
August 1915, and took part with his Battalion in the Battles
of Loos, Albert, Ploegsteert,the Somme, the Ancre, Vimy
Ridge, Passchendaele and Cambrai, where he was badly gassed
in action. After hospital treatment at Rouen and Bristol
he was engaged on important work at various depôts until
his demobilisation in December 1918, and holds the 1914-15
Star, and the General Service and Victory Medals.
20, Anson Street, Hulme, Manchester.   Z7394

MORRIS, C., Private, R.A.V.C.
He volunteered in January 1916, and in September was
drafted to France. During his service on the Western Front
he did consistently good work with his unit at the R.A.V.C.

depôt at Boulogne. In November 1918 he was invalided home
through disability caused by his war service, and in the following
month was discharged as medically unfit. He holds the
General Service and Victory Medals.
2, Earl Street, Rusholme, Manchester.   Z7383B

MORRIS, D., Private, 8th Lancashire Fusiliers.
He volunteered in October 1914, and six months later proceeded to the Dardanelles, where he took part in the Landings
at Cape Helles and Suvla Bay, and in the three Battles of
Krithia. After the Evacuation of the Gallipoli Peninsula,
he served in Egypt until December 1916, when he was transferred to the Western Front. He then took part in the Battles
of Arras, Vimy Ridge, Ypres (III), and Cambrai, before being
invalided home with trench fever. He holds the 1914-15
Star, and the General Service and Victory Medals, and was
demobilised in February 1919.   Z7399
12, Higher Temple Street, Chorlton-on-Medlock, Manchester.

MORRIS, E., Pte., 1st King's Shropshire Light Infty.
Mobilised at the outbreak of war, he embarked for France and
fought in the Retreat from Mons, the Battles of Le Cateau,
the Marne, the Aisne and Ypres. He was also in action at
Neuve Chapelle, the Somme, Cambrai, and throughout the
Retreat and Advance of 1918, and was twice wounded. He
was demobilised in March 1919, and holds the Mons Star, and
the General Service and Victory Medals.
22, Pearson Street, Newton Heath, Manchester.   Z9645

MORRIS, E., Private, 1st South Staffordshire Regt.
He volunteered in September 1914, and landing in France
two months later was in action at Neuve Chapelle, Hill 60,
Ypres (II), Loos, St. Eloi, and was wounded in July 1916,
during the Somme Offensive. On recovery he returned to
the front line trenches, and saw heavy fighting at Arras,
Ypres (III), and Cambrai (I) where he was taken prisoner
in November 1917. He remained in captivity until the signing
of the Armistice when he was repatriated and demobilised in
February of the following year. He holds the 1914 Star, and
the General Service and Victory Medals.
38, Sarah Ann Street, Beswick, Manchester.   Z10885

MORRIS, E., Sergt., King's Own Scottish Borderers.
Already in the Army in August 1914, he was sent to France
immediately, and served with distinction at the Battle of, and
in the Retreat from, Mons. He also took part in the Battles
of La Bassée, Ypres, Neuve Chapelle and Loos, where he was
badly wounded in action and taken prisoner. Whilst in
captivity in Westphalia, he spent some time in hospital,
and was eventually sent to Holland, whence he was repatriated
in November 1918. He then joined the Tank Corps, and in
1920 was still serving, holding the Mons Star, and the General
Service and Victory Medals.
4, Platt Street, Moss Side, Manchester.   Z7398B

MORRIS, F., Private, 2nd K.O. (R. Lancaster Regt.)
He volunteered in August 1914, and in November was drafted
to France. During his service in this theatre of war he played
an important part in the Battles of Neuve Chapelle, and Hill
60, where he was taken prisoner in April 1915. Whilst in
captivity in Germany, he suffered many hardships and was
repatriated in November 1918. Two months later he volunteered for service in Russia and saw heavy fighting on the
Archangel front until the Evacuation in November 1919.
In 1920 he was stationed in Ireland, having engaged for
twelve years, and holds the 1914 Star, and the General Service
and Victory Medals.
2, Pownall Street, Hulme, Manchester.   Z7386

MORRIS, H., Private, 18th Manchester Regiment.
Volunteering in September 1914, he was engaged on important
duties in England until November 1915. He then proceeded
to France, but after two months heavy fighting, laid down
his life for King and Country at Loos on January 28th, 1916.
He was entitled to the 1914-15 Star, and the General Service
and Victory Medals.
          " The path of duty was the way to glory."
44, Albemarle Street, Moss Side, Manchester.   TZ7391

MORRIS, H., Private, South Lancashire Regiment.
He volunteered in January 1916,and in the following November
was drafted to the Western Front, where he first saw heavy
fighting at Beaumont-Hamel. Later he took part in the
Battles of Arras, Vimy Ridge and Ypres (III), and was
seriously wounded in action. Unfortunately he died in
hospital on August 6th, 1917, and was entitled to the General
Service and Victory Medals.
          " His life for his Country, his soul to God."
2, Earl Street, Rusholme, Manchester.   Z7383A

MORRIS, J., Private, 17th Manchester Regiment.
Joining in October 1916, he crossed to the Western Front
in the following January, and after fighting in many important
engagements, was taken prisoner in the Battle of Arras in
April 1917. Sent to Germany he remained in captivity
until the termination of hostilities, when he was repatriated
according to the terms of the Armistice. He holds the General
Service and Victory Medals, and was demobilised in December
1918.
68, Canning Street, Ancoats, Manchester.   Z10839

MORRIS, H. T., Corporal, 1st Seaforth Highlanders.
He volunteered in August 1914, and first saw active service in July 1915, when he was sent to the Dardanelles and took part in the Landing at Suvla Bay. After the Evacuation of the Gallipoli Peninsula, he proceeded to Palestine and played a prominent part in the three Battles of Gaza and the capture of Jerusalem. In January 1918 he was transferred to the Western Front and was in action at Soissons, Passchendaele and the Menin Road, where he was badly wounded. After hospital treatment at Boulogne, he was sent home and demobilised in January 1919, holding the 1914–15 Star, and the General Service and Victory Medals.
26, Platt Street, Moss Side, Manchester. Z7397

MORRIS, J. A., Gunner, R.F.A.
Volunteering in July 1915, he was sent to France in the following year and fought in the Battles of Ypres, and was wounded. On his recovery he rejoined his unit and was in action at Lens, Albert and Cambrai, where he was wounded in 1918. Returning to England he received hospital treatment and was subsequently demobilised in March 1919. He holds the General Service and Victory Medals.
1, Webster Place, Ancoats, Manchester. TZ9646

MORRIS, J. E., Private, Labour Corps.
Joining in February 1917, he was quickly drafted to France, and during his service on the Western Front he was engaged on special duties at Rouen and in the Ypres, Cambrai, Armentières and Bapaume sectors. He was demobilised in January 1919, and holds the General Service and Victory Medals.
9, Raglan Street, Hulme, Manchester. TZ7110

MORRIS, J. W., Private, King's (Liverpool Regt.)
He volunteered in August 1914, and in the following year embarked for France. During his service on the Western Front he fought at Armentières, Ypres, Mailly, Albert, Trones Wood, Longueval, Oppy and Guillemont, where he was taken prisoner in 1916. After being interned in Germany he was repatriated, according to the terms of the Armistice, in December 1918, and demobilised in the following April. He holds the 1914–15 Star, and the General Service and Victory Medals.
55, Thornton Street, Manchester. TZ9294

MORRIS, M., Private, King's (Liverpool Regiment).
He joined in May 1916, and after completing his training served with his unit at various stations engaged on guard and other important duties. He was not successful in securing his transfer to a theatre of war owing to his being over military age, but, nevertheless, rendered valuable services until his demobilisation in May 1919.
4, Buxton Street, West Gorton, Manchester. Z10841

MORRIS, N., Private, Royal Scots.
He joined in November 1916, and three months later proceeded to the Western Front, where he was in action at the Battles of Arras, Vimy Ridge, Ypres (III), Lens, the Somme II), the Marne (II), Amiens, Havrincourt, Le Cateau (II) and the Selle. After hostilities ceased, he was sent to Germany with the Army of Occupation, but in January 1919 was drafted to India. In 1920 he was stationed at Rangoon, and holds the General Service and Victory Medals.
4, Platt Street, Moss Side, Manchester. Z7398A

MORRIS, R., Corporal, Royal Scots.
Mobilised in August 1914, he was immediately drafted to the Western Front, where he took part in the Battle of Mons and the subsequent Retreat. Later he fought in the Battles of the Aisne, Ypres, St. Eloi, Loos, Albert and Vimy Ridge, and was wounded in action in the Somme Offensive of 1916, and invalided home. On his recovery, however, he returned to France and was again in action at Arras, Ypres, Cambrai, the Somme, and Le Cateau, and in the Retreat and Advance of 1918. He afterwards served with the Army of Occupation in Germany, and later was drafted to Burma, where, in 1920, he was still with his unit at Rangoon. He holds the Mons Star, and the General Service and Victory Medals.
4, Platt Street, Moss Side, Manchester. Z7398C

MORRIS, R. E., Private, 22nd Manchester Regt.
Volunteering in May 1915, he was drafted to the Western Front in November of that year, and there saw fighting in various sectors. After taking part in the Battles of the Somme, Arras, Ypres and Cambrai and many minor engagements, he was transferred in December 1917 to Italy, where he was again in action until the cessation of hostilities. Returning home in January 1919, he was demobilised in the following month, and holds the 1914–15 Star, and the General Service and Victory Medals.
35, Whittaker Street, Chorlton-on-Medlock, Manchester. Z7387

MORRIS, R. S., Sergt., R.A.P.C.
He volunteered in December 1915, and after undergoing a period of training served at various stations, where he was engaged on important clerical duties in the pay office. He was not successful in obtaining his transfer overseas, but, nevertheless, rendered valuable services with his unit until February 1919, when he was demobilised.
4, Platt Street, Moss Side, Manchester. Z7398D

MORRIS, S., Driver, R.A.S.C. (M.T.)
Three months after volunteering in November 1914, he proceeded to the Western Front, where he was engaged in con-

veying food and ammunition to the forward areas in various sectors. He was present at the Battles of Neuve Chapelle, St. Eloi, Hill 60, Loos, the Somme, Arras, Ypres, Passchendaele and Cambrai and many other engagements, took an active part also in the Retreat and Advance of 1918, and was wounded in action at Arras in June 1916. He was demobilised in May 1919, and holds the 1914–15 Star, and the General Service and Victory Medals.
45, Brunt Street, Rusholme, Manchester. TZ7389

MORRIS, T., Sergt., King's (Liverpool Regiment).
Re-enlisting in November 1914, he was drafted to Egypt in September of the following year and there served at Cairo, Alexandria and many other stations. He was engaged on important clerical duties nd also in superintending military stores whilst in this seat of operations, and finally returned home for demobilisation in April 1919. He holds the Queen's and King's South African Medals (with three bars), the 1914–15 Star, and the General Service and Victory Medals.
7, Welton Place, Moor Street, Rusholme, Manchester. Z7392

MORRIS, T., Private, Labour Corps.
He joined in January 1917, and in the following March was sent to France. Whilst overseas he served at Ypres, on the Somme and at La Bassée, and for a time was stationed at Boulogne. He returned home, and was demobilised in January 1919, holding the General Service and Victory Medals.
15, Frederick Place, Rochdale Road, Manchester. Z9293

MORRIS, T. E., Private, Argyll and Sutherland Highlanders.
Volunteering in January 1915, in the following November he embarked for the Western Front and fought at Loos, Albert, Ploegsteert, Vermelles, the Somme and Arras. He was also engaged in heavy fighting at Messines, Ypres, Cambrai, throughout the German Offensive and Allied Advance of 1918, and was wounded. Returning home, he was demobilised in May 1919, and holds the 1914–15 Star, and the General Service and Victory Medals.
22, Pearson Street, Newton Heath, Manchester. Z9647

MORRIS, T. C., Private, 2nd Border Regiment.
Two months after volunteering in September 1914, he proceeded to France, where he saw heavy fighting in various sectors of the Front. He took part in the Battles of Ypres, Festubert and Loos and many minor engagements in this theatre of war until severely wounded in action at Neuve Chapelle. He was finally invalided from the Army in November 1917, and holds the 1914–15 Star, and the General Service and Victory Medals.
18, Abbey Grove, Hulme, Manchester. Z7393

MORRIS, T.P., Driver, R.A.S.C., and Pte., Labour Corps.
Volunteering in November 1914, and on completing his training in the following March proceeded to the Western Front. There, engaged on various important duties, he was present at the Battles of Vermelles and the Ancre front, and was gassed at Festubert in May and at Loos in October 1915. Later he served with the Labour Corps in various sectors, finally returning home for demobilisation in February 1919. He holds the 1914–15 Star, and the General Service and Victory Medals. Z7390
47, Higher Chatham Street, Chorlton-on-Medlock, Manchester.

MORRIS, W., Private, Border Regiment.
Joining in April 1916, he was drafted to the Western Front on completing his training in August of that year, and there served in various sectors. Owing to ill-health, he was unfit for service in the firing-line, but, engaged in guarding prisoners of war and on important duties on the lines of communication, he did much useful work in the Somme, Ancre and Passchendaele sectors. Demobilised in February 1919, he holds the General Service and Victory Medals.
6, Riga Street, City Road, Hulme, Manchester. TZ7395

MORRIS, W., Private, Manchester Regiment.
After volunteering in August 1914, he was retained on important duties at various stations in England until January 1916. He was then drafted to the Western Front, where he saw much severe fighting at Loos and many other places. He died gloriously on the Field of Battle on July 7th, 1916, during the Somme Offensive. He was entitled to the General Service and Victory Medals.
"And doubtless he went in splendid company."
2, Earl Street, Rusholme, Manchester. Z7383C

MORRIS, W.H., Private, 2nd K.O.(R.Lancaster Regt.)
Volunteering in February 1915, he proceeded to the Western Front after three months' training, and was there wounded in action at the Battle of Loos in September 1915. Invalided home, he was in hospital for a few months at Sheffield, and in August 1916 was drafted to Salonika, where he fought on the Doiran front. Admitted to hospital at Malta, suffering from malaria, he returned to Salonika, however, on his recovery, but was shortly afterwards sent to England. In August 1918, he was again drafted to France, where he was in action until the cessation of hostilities. He was demobilised in February 1919, and holds the 1914–15 Star, and the General Service and Victory Medals.
2, Pownall Street, Hulme, Manchester. Z7388

MORRIS, W., Driver, R.A.S.C.
Volunteering in February 1916, he completed his training and served at Messrs. A. V. Roe's Aeroplane Works, engaged as a costing clerk. He did good work, but was not successful in obtaining his transfer overseas owing to medical unfitness, and was discharged in consequence in September 1917.
479, Collyhurst Road, Rochdale Road, Manchester.   Z10840

MORRIS, W., Driver, R.F.A.
He volunteered in September 1914, and crossing to France two months later was in action at the Battles of Ypres I and II, Hill 60, and was wounded on the Somme in March 1916. On recovery he was drafted with his Battery to Salonika, where he fought in several engagements on the Doiran front and contracting malaria was invalided to England in 1918. He was subsequently discharged in October of that year in order to resume his pre-war occupation as a miner. He holds the 1914-15 Star, and the General Service and Victory Medals.   34, Edensor Street, Beswick, Manchester.   Z10842

MORRIS, W., Air Mechanic, R.A.F.
He joined in September 1916, and after completing his training was engaged at various stations on important duties with his Squadron. He rendered valuable services as a Drill Instructor, but was not successful in obtaining his transfer overseas before the cessation of hostilities. He was demobilised in November 1919.   16, Beecher Street, Queen's Park, Manchester.   Z11556

MORRISEY, T., Gunner, R.F.A.
Mobilised in August 1914, he was immediately drafted to the Western Front, where he took part in the fighting at Mons. He also served through the Battles of La Bassée and Ypres and may other important engagements, until transferred to Mesopotamia in March 1916. There he was again in action and was present at the Relief of Kut and the capture of Baghdad, afterwards returning to France, where he fought in the Battles of the Somme, and was wounded in action at Cambrai in November 1917. Discharged, time-expired, in March 1919, he holds the Mons Star, and the General Service and Victory Medals.
25, Buckland Street, Ancoats, Manchester.   Z11933

MORRISON, J. (M.M.), Private, M.G.C.
Volunteering in December 1915, he proceeded to France on the completion of his training in the following June and during his service on the Western Front took a prominent part in the Battles of the Somme, the Ancre, Arras and Ypres. In August 1917, he was taken prisoner and sent to Bavaria, where he was compelled to work on agricultural duties. He was awarded the Military Medal for conspicuous bravery and devotion to duty, in carrying an important Despatch up the line at Cambrai in August 1917, and holds in addition the General Service and Victory Medals. After his release from Germany in December 1918, he was demobilised later in the same month.
22, Naylor Street, Miles Platting, Manchester.   Z9295A

MORRISON, T., Gunner, R.F.A.
He volunteered in March 1915, and in the following October was drafted to France. During his service on the Western Front he did good work as a gunner in the Battles of Neuve Chapelle, Ypres and the Somme. He was severely wounded in action on August 2nd, 1916, and was admitted to hospital at Etaples, where he died the same day from his injuries. He was entitled to the 1914-15 Star, and the General Service and Victory Medals.
"Great deeds cannot die."
22, Naylor Street, Miles Platting, Manchester.   Z9295B

MORRISON, W., Private, 24th Manchester Regt.
He volunteered in September 1914, and after a period of training was drafted to the Western Front in November of the following year. There he took part in engagements at Loos, St. Eloi, Vimy Ridge and many other places until wounded in action in the Somme Offensive of 1916 and sent to hospital at Rouen and later, Aberdeen. In 1917 he proceeded to Italy and there saw much severe fighting on the Piave and the Asiago Plateau until the cessation of hostilities. He was demobilised on his return home in March 1919, and holds the 1914-15 Star, and the General Service and Victory Medals.
35, Birch Street, Moss Side, Manchester.   Z7400

MORRISY, J., Sergt., 10th Manchester Regiment.
He volunteered in August 1914, and in October of the following year was drafted to the Western Front, where he saw heavy fighting in various sectors. After taking part in the Battles of Vimy Ridge, the Somme and Bullecourt and many minor engagements, he was severely gassed at Messines in June 1917, and admitted to hospital at Glasgow. He was invalided from the Army in August 1917, and holds the 1914-15 Star, and the General Service and Victory Medals.
20, Albemarle Street, Moss Side, Manchester.   Z7401

MORROW, E., Private, King's (Liverpool Regiment).
He joined in March 1917, and proceeding shortly afterwards to the Western Front, fought in the Battles of Ypres (III), Passchendaele, Bullecourt and Messines. He also took part in many notable engagements during the Retreat and Advance of 1918, and returned to England for his demobilisation in

October of the succeeding year. He holds the General Service and Victory Medals.
6, Redford Street, Newton Heath, Manchester.   Z10844/45A

MORROW, H., Private, K.O. (R. Lancaster Regt.)
Volunteering in February 1915, he landed in France three months later and fought at Ypres, Loos and Vermelles, and in December of that year he was drafted to Egypt and stationed at Alexandria for a time. He proceeded to Salonika in January 1916, and took part in the advance across the Struma and in operations on the Doiran front. Contracting malaria, he was invalided to England, and after receiving treatment was demobilised in April 1919. He holds the 1914-15 Star, and the General Service and Victory Medals.
6, Redford Street, Newton Heath, Manchester.   Z10844/45B

MORT, G., Private, Royal Defence Corps.
He volunteered in December 1914, and after completing a period of training served at various stations, where he was engaged in guarding prisoners of war and on other important duties and rendered very valuable services. He was for a time in hospital at Taunton, suffering from dysentery, and was finally invalided from the Army in October 1918.
7, Gladstone Street, Brook's Bar, Manchester.   Z7402B

MORT, J. W., Private, 7th Gordon Highlanders.
Shortly after volunteering in August 1914, he proceeded to Egypt, where he served at Cairo and on the Suez Canal until April of the following year. He was then transferred to Gallipoli, where, after taking part in the Landing at Cape Helles, he fought in the three Battles of Krithia and at West Beach and various other places. In October 1915 he was invalided home, suffering from dysentery, but on his recovery in January 1917, was sent to the Western Front, where he served through the Battles of the Ancre, Arras, Ypres, Passchendaele, Cambrai, the Somme, the Marne and Epéhy and fought also in the Retreat and Advance of 1918. Demobilised in March 1919, he holds the 1914-15 Star, and the General Service and Victory Medals.
7, Gladstone Street, Brook's Bar, Manchester.   Z7402

MORT, T., Private, 12th Manchester Regiment.
Volunteering in October 1914, he landed in France in the following July, and was in action at Loos, St. Eloi, Vimy Ridge, and was severely wounded in the first Battle of the Somme. On his recovery he rejoined his Battalion and fought in the Arras sector and in the Ypres salient, where he was again wounded. Returning home, he received hospital treatment, and was invalided out of the Service in April 1918. He holds the 1914-15 Star, and the General Service and Victory Medals.
11, Holbeck Street, Oldham Road, Manchester.   Z9648

MORTIQUE, J., Private, Royal Dublin Fusiliers.
He was mobilised from the Reserve at the outbreak of war, and sent shortly afterwards to France, where he fought through the Retreat from Mons and the Battles of the Marne, the Aisne and La Bassée. He was wounded at Ypres in November 1914, and on recovery took part in operations at Festubert, Albert, and was again wounded on the Somme in August 1916. Invalided to England in 1917, he received hospital treatment and was eventually discharged as medically unfit for further service in May 1919. He holds the Mons Star, and the General Service and Victory Medals.
8, Juno Street, Oldham Road, Manchester.   Z10846B

MORTIQUE, W., Private, 23rd Manchester Regt.
He volunteered in November 1914, and embarking for the Western Front in the following July fought in operations at Loos, Albert, the Somme, Arras, Messines, and Ypres (III). He gave his life for the freedom of England in the Battle of Passchendaele on October 28th, 1917, and was entitled to the 1914-15 Star, and the General Service and Victory Medals.
"Nobly striving,
He nobly fell that we might live."
8, Juno Street, Oldham Road, Manchester.   Z10846A

MORTIQUE, W., L/Corporal, South Lancashire Regt.
A serving soldier since June 1912, he was drafted to the Western Front at the outbreak of hostilities and was wounded in the Retreat from Mons. He also fought in the second Battle of Ypres, when he was again wounded, and was hit a third time on the Somme in July 1916. He was invalided home to hospital, and after receiving medical treatment was discharged as physically unfit for further duty in June 1919. He holds the Mons Star, and the General Service and Victory Medals.
134, Slater Street, Rochdale Road, Manchester.   Z9296

MORTON, C., Pte., 2nd Lincolnshire Regt. and M.G.C.
Volunteering in August 1914, he was drafted shortly afterwards to France and fought in the Battles of Ypres, and La Bassée. He was seriously wounded during operations at Festubert in October of the same year, and evacuated to England, received prolonged hospital treatment. He was eventually discharged as medically unfit for further military service in November 1916, and holds the Mons Star, and the General Service and Victory Medals.
148, Cobden Street, Ancoats, Manchester.   Z10847

MORTON, J., Gunner, M.G.C.

A Reservist, he was mobilised when war broke out and sent to France in the following March. He fought in the Battles of Neuve Chapelle, St. Eloi, Ypres (II) and others until January 1916, when he was drafted to Mesopotamia. In this theatre of war he took part in the Battles of Kut, Um-el-Hannah, and was wounded during the attempted relief of Kut in March 1916. On recovery he rejoined his unit and was engaged in operations at Kut-el-Amara, and the capture of Baghdad in March 1918. After the Armistice he remained in the middle East for a time and returned to England in December 1919. He was demobilised a month later, and holds the 1914–15 Star, and the General Service and Victory Medals.
7, Rigel Street, Ancoats, Manchester. Z10848

MORTON, J., Private, Labour Corps.

He joined in November 1917, and on the completion of his training served with his Company at several stations in the North of England. Engaged on guard and other duties at various prisoners of war camps, he rendered valuable services, but was unable to secure his transfer overseas before the cessation of hostilities. He was demobilised in March 1919.
7, Rigel Street, Ancoats, Manchester. Z10849

MORTON, J., Private, 1/8th Manchester Regiment.

Mobilised on the outbreak of war, he was drafted to Egypt in the same year, and after a period of service there proceeded to Gallipoli in 1915. Wounded in the Landing at Suvla Bay he was sent to hospital at Birmingham, and on recovery was drafted to France in 1917. He was in action in the Battles of Messines, Ypres and Passchendaele, and owing to ill-health was invalided home in the same year. After treatment, he was discharged as medically unfit for further service in October 1918, and holds the 1914–15 Star, and the General Service and Victory Medals.
39, Spire Street, Ardwick, Manchester. Z10850A

MOSELY, A., Private, 7th Manchester Regiment.

After volunteering in October 1914, he underwent a period of training prior to being drafted to the Western Front in June 1916. There he took part in important engagements in various sectors, including the Battles of the Ancre, Arras, Bullecourt, and Messines, and was severely wounded in action at Ypres in July 1917. Invalided to hospital at Birmingham, he unhappily died there in May 1919. He was entitled to the General Service and Victory Medals.
" Thinking that remembrance, though unspoken, may reach him where he sleeps."
39, Hulme Street, Chorlton-on-Medlock, Manchester. Z7403

MOSS, H., Private, 17th Manchester Regiment.

He volunteered in September 1914, and after completing a period of training, was drafted to the Western Front in November of that year. There he saw much heavy fighting in various sectors, took part in engagements at Trones Wood, Albert, and many other places, and was severely wounded in action on the Somme in July 1916. He was for a considerable period in hospital at Birmingham, before being invalided from the Army in November 1917, and holds the 1914–15 Star, and the General Service and Victory Medals.
42, White Street, Hulme, Manchester. Z7404

MOSS, F. W., Corporal, 8th Manchester Regiment.

He was mobilised from the Reserve at the outbreak of hostilities, and in February 1915, proceeded to the Dardanelles, where he took part in the Landing at Cape Helles, in the first and second Battles of Krithia, and was wounded at Suvla Bay in August. After his recovery he was again in action in the Evacuation of the Peninsula, and in February 1916, was drafted to France. Whilst in this theatre of war he fought at Albert, Ploegsteert Wood, on the Somme, at Bullecourt, Messines and Cambrai, and in many operations in the Retreat and Advance of 1918. He returned home in February of the following year, and was demobilised a month later, holding the 1914–15 Star, and the General Service and Victory Medals.
39, Buxton Street, Manchester. Z9297

MOSS, J., Private, 15th South Lancashire Regiment.

He volunteered in September 1914, and at the conclusion of his training was engaged on important duties with his unit at various stations. Owing to ill-health, he was unable to secure his transfer to a theatre of war, but did valuable work until August 1917, when he was invalided out of the Service.
14, Diggles Street, Ancoats, Manchester. Z10851

MOSS, W. E., Private, Loyal North Lancashire Regt.

Volunteering in September 1914, he embarked for the Western Front early in the following year, and fought at Arras and the Somme, where in August 1916, he was wounded. He was invalided home, and on recovery was drafted to Salonika, where he took part in operations on the Vardar front. Transferred to Palestine, he participated in heavy fighting at Beersheba, and the capture of Jerusalem, and later returning to France served in the Allied Advance which terminated hostilities on November 11th, 1918. He was demobilised in the following year, and holds the 1914–15 Star, and the General

Service and Victory Medals.
52, Kemp Street, Manchester. Z11164–5A

MOSSMAN, H., Driver, R.A.S.C.

He volunteered in November 1915, and after his training was engaged on important duties at various stations. He was not successful in obtaining his transfer overseas before the cessation of hostilities, but nevertheless did valuable work until demobilised in January 1919.
72, York Avenue, Manley Park, Manchester. Z10852

MOSTYN, G., Driver, R.A.S.C. (M.T.)

Two months after volunteering in November 1914, he proceeded to France, where he was engaged on important duties in various sectors of the Front. He was present at the Battles of Neuve Chapelle, Hill 60, Ypres, Festubert, Albert, and the Somme, and other engagements, served also through the Retreat and Advance of 1918, and was wounded in action at Passchendaele in September 1917. He was demobilised in March 1919, and holds the 1914–15 Star, and the General Service and Victory Medals.
38, Bell Street, Openshaw, Manchester. Z7405

MOTT, A., Driver, R.A.S.C.

He volunteered in December 1914, and in the following October proceeded to France, where he fought in the Battles of Ypres and the Somme. Transferred to Salonika in October 1916, he was in action in many engagements on the Doiran, Struma, and Vardar fronts, and in January 1918 was sent to Italy. He was there engaged in heavy fighting on the Piave, and took part in the final Allied Advance in this theatre of war. Returning home, he was demobilised in May 1919, and holds the 1914–15 Star, and the General Service and Victory Medals.
141, Sudell Street, Rochdale Road, Manchester. Z9649

MOTTERSHEAD, A., Pte., 3rd N. Staffordshire Regt.

He volunteered in May 1915, proceeding to the Dardanelles later in that year, was wounded at Suvla Bay whilst attending to a Sergeant of his Company, who was also wounded. He was invalided home, and in 1916 proceeded to France, where he was gassed in action in the Ypres sector, and again in 1917 at Lens. He was also wounded near Arras, whilst carrying Despatches, and lost one of his fingers, thus rendering his hand useless. He was then sent home and discharged from the Army in 1918, and holds the 1914–15 Star, and the General Service and Victory Medals.
6, Kirk Street, Ancoats, Manchester. Z11557

MOTTERSHEAD, F. (D.C.M.), Pte., Manchester Regt.

Volunteering in August 1914, he embarked for Egypt in September of that year, and proceeded to the Dardanelles in the following April. He served on the Peninsula throughout the Gallipoli Campaign, and was awarded the Distinguished Conduct Medal for conspicuous gallantry and devotion to duty in destroying enemy mines. Later he was drafted to Mesopotamia, and thence to Palestine, where he took part in the Battles of Gaza. In 1917, owing to a severe wound he was invalided home, and after receiving medical treatment was discharged in November of that year. He holds in addition to the decoration won in the Field the 1914–15 Star, and the General Service and Victory Medals.
19, Hamilton Street, Collyhurst, Manchester. Z10853

MOTTERSHEAD, J. A., Pioneer, R.E.

He volunteered in November 1915, and after four months' training, proceeded to the Western Front, where he was engaged on important duties with the Signal section in various sectors. He took an active part in the Battles of the Somme, Ypres, and Cambrai, and other engagements, served also through the Retreat and Advance of 1918, and was twice wounded in action. Demobilised in March 1919, he holds the General Service and Victory Medals.
89, Higher Chatham Street, Chorlton-on-Medlock, Manchester Z7406

MOTTERSHEAD, R., Pte., King's (Liverpool Regt.)

Joining in January 1917, he crossed to France three months later, and attached to the 2/2nd London Field Ambulance, was engaged on important ambulance duties at Arras, Ypres, Messines, Cambrai, and Havrincourt Wood. He also served in the Retreat and Allied Advance, entering Mons at dawn on November 11th, 1918, and afterwards proceeded with the Army of Occupation to Germany. He was demobilised in December 1919, and holds the General Service and Victory Medals. 2, Belmont St., Collyhurst, Manchester. Z10854

MOULDING, H., L/Corporal, 1st Manchester Regt.

Mobilised at the outbreak of war in August 1914, he proceeded to the Western Front in the following month, and there, after much severe fighting, was wounded in action and taken prisoner in the first Battle of Ypres. He was held in captivity in Germany until the cessation of hostilities, and during this period suffered many hardships. He was for a considerable time in hospital at Aldershot, after his release, and in May 1920, was invalided from the Army, holding the 1914 Star, and the General Service and Victory Medals.
40, Percy Street, Hulme, Manchester. TZ7407

MOULTON, A. R., Private, Labour Corps.
He joined in May 1916, and underwent a period of training prior to being drafted to the Western Front in December 1917. There he was engaged on important duties in various sectors, at Ypres, Albert, Arras, the Somme, and many other places, and also took an active part in the Retreat and Advance of 1918. He afterwards served with the Army of Occupation in Germany, before returning home for demobilisation in October 1919, and holds the General Service and Victory Medals.
15, Brunt Street, Rusholme, Manchester. TZ7410

MOULTON, S., Private, 11th East Lancashire Regt.
Shortly after joining in January 1918, he proceeded to the Western Front, where he saw severe fighting in various sectors, and took part in the Battles of the Aisne and the Marne, and other important engagements. He unhappily fell in action at Vieux-Berquin on August 29th, 1918, during the Allies' Advance. He was entitled to the General Service and Victory Medals.
"His memory is cherished with pride."
5, Markham Street, Ardwick, Manchester. TZ7408

MOULTON, W., Sergt., K.O. (R. Lancaster Regt.)
Mobilised in August 1914, he was immediately drafted to the Western Front, where he took part in the Battle of Mons. He afterwards fought in the Battles of the Marne, the Aisne, Neuve Chapelle, Ypres, and Loos, and many minor engagements until March 1916. He was then sent home and discharged, in order to take up munition work. He holds the Mons Star, and the General Service and Victory Medals.
22, Tipper Street, Hulme, Manchester. Z7409

MOUNTAIN, C. H., Pte., Argyll and Sutherland H'ldrs.
He volunteered in February 1915, and was retained on important duties in England until January 1917, when he was drafted to the Western Front. There he took part in many important engagements in various sectors, including the Battles of Passchendaele, Cambrai, and the Somme, and took part also in the march into Germany. He was demobilised on his return home in February 1919, and holds the General Service and Victory Medals.
19, Carlisle Street, Hulme, Manchester. Z7411

MOUNTFORD, D. E., Driver, R.E.
Volunteering in January 1915, he was drafted to Gallipoli after a period of training, and there took an active part in the three Battles of Krithia and other engagements. He was invalided to hospital at Malta in September 1915, suffering from dysentery, but on his recovery in the following December proceeded to the Western Front. There he was present at the Battles of Albert, the Somme, Arras, Messines, the Marne, and Cambrai, served also through the Retreat and Advance of 1918, and was afterwards engaged on important duties with the Labour Corps. Demobilised in June 1919, he holds the 1914-15 Star, and the General Service and Victory Medals.
26, Ogden Street, Hulme, Manchester. Z7412

MOUNTNEY, J., Private, 8th Manchester Regiment.
He volunteered in December 1914, and after completing a period of training, served at various stations, where he was engaged in guarding prisoners of war, and on other important duties. Unable to obtain his transfer overseas, he nevertheless rendered valuable services with his unit, and was for a time in hospital suffering from rheumatism, before being invalided from the Army in October 1917.
14, Cornbrook Road, Chester Road, Hulme, Manchester. Z7413

MOYLAN, J., Private, 4th K.O. (R. Lancaster Regt.)
He volunteered in September 1914, and in the following year was drafted to the Dardanelles, where he took part in the Battles of Krithia and many other engagements until the Evacuation of the Gallipoli Peninsula. He was then transferred to Egypt and served at Agagia and Sollum, before proceeding to the Western Front in February 1918. After seeing much severe fighting in various sectors, he was gassed at St. Quentin and invalided to hospital at Weymouth. He was discharged in March 1919, as medically unfit for further service, and holds the 1914-15 Star, and the General Service and Victory Medals.
29, Easton Street, Hulme, Manchester. Z7414

MOYLIN, T. (M.M.), Corporal, 8th King's Own (Royal Lancaster Regiment).
Mobilised in August 1914, he proceeded to the Western Front in time to take part in the Retreat from Mons, and later saw severe fighting in various other sectors. He served through the Battles of Ypres, and the Somme, and other important engagements, and was four times wounded in action—at High Wood, Delville Wood, Bullecourt, and Cambrai. He was awarded the Military Medal for great gallantry and devotion to duty displayed in taking charge of his Company, when all his officers were killed and received the Bar for conspicuous bravery in the Field at Monchy. Holding also the Mons Star, and the General Service and Victory Medals, he was discharged in February 1919.
35, River Street, Hulme, Manchester. Z7415A

MOZR, A., Private, Lancashire Fusiliers.
He joined in June 1917, and after undergoing a period of training, served at various stations, where he was engaged on duties of a highly important nature. He was not successful in his efforts to obtain his transfer to a theatre of war, but nevertheless, rendered valuable services with his unit until March 1919, when he was demobilised.
9, Sedden Street, Rusholme, Manchester. Z7416

MUDD, J., Private, 28th Manchester Regiment.
He joined in June 1916, and crossing to France four months later served there for upwards of three years. During this period he was in action in the Battles of the Somme, Beaucourt, Arras, Ypres, Passchendaele, Cambrai, the Marne, and in the Retreat and Advance of 1918, after which he was sent into Germany. There he was engaged on garrison and other duties with the Army of Occupation for some months, and returned to England for demobilisation in September 1919. He holds the General Service and Victory Medals.
107, Henry Street, Ardwick, Manchester. Z11779

MUGGLESTONE, F., Pte., 12th Lancashire Fusiliers.
Volunteering in September 1914, he was drafted to Salonika in December of the following year and saw much fighting on the Doiran and Struma fronts. In August 1918, he proceeded to France and fought in many engagements during the Allied Advance. Returning home, he was demobilised in February 1919, and holds the 1914-15 Star, and the General Service and Victory Medals.
4, Grosvenor Street, Newton Heath, Manchester. Z9650

MUIRHEAD, E., Private, 3rd Manchester Regiment.
Mobilised in August 1914, he was immediately drafted to the Western Front, where he took part in the Battle of Mons and the subsequent Retreat. He also fought in the Battles of La Bassée and Ypres, and many other engagements until taken prisoner during a German attack on Loos in 1916. Held in captivity until after the cessation of hostilities, he was forced during this time, to work in the mines, and, on his release in January 1919, was invalided from the Army. He holds the Mons Star, and the General Service and Victory Medals.
3, Charlotte Street, Chorlton-on-Medlock, Manchester. TZ7418

MUIRHEAD, W., Private, 1/4th Cheshire Regiment.
Volunteering in December 1915, he proceeded to France in April of the following year, and there saw heavy fighting in various sectors of the Front. After taking part in engagements at Beaumont-Hamel, and many other places on the Somme, he was wounded in action at Thiépval, and admitted to hospital at Etaples. On his recovery, however, in February 1917, he rejoined his unit and fought in the Battles of Arras, Ypres and Cambrai, and was severely wounded in action a second time. He was for a time in hospital at Birmingham, before being invalided from the Army in January 1918, and holds the General Service and Victory Medals.
5, Charlotte Street, Chorlton-on-Medlock, Manchester. Z7417

MUIRHEAD, W., Pte., 12th York and Lancaster Regt.
Four months after joining in June 1916, he proceeded to the Western Front, where he saw heavy fighting in various sectors. After taking part in engagements at Albert, and many other places on the Somme, he was severely wounded in action, and invalided home in December 1916. He was for a considerable period in hospital before being discharged as medically unfit for further service in July 1918, and holds the General Service and Victory Medals.
19, Braham Street, Longsight, Manchester. Z7419

MULCHAY, E., Pte., King's Own Scottish Borderers.
Volunteering in September 1914, he was drafted to the Western Front in December of that year, and there took part in the Battles of Neuve Chapelle, Hill 60, and Festubert, and many minor engagements. He made the supreme sacrifice, falling in action at Loos in September 1915. He was entitled to the 1914-15 Star, and the General Service and Victory Medals.
"A costly sacrifice upon the altar of freedom."
3, Beswick Street, Ardwick, Manchester. Z7420

MULDOON, T., Sergt., 15th South Lancashire Regt.
Volunteering in June 1915, he completed his training and served at various stations with his unit on important duties. He was unsuccessful in obtaining his transfer overseas, but rendered valuable services until demobilised in February 1919.
16, Robinson Street East, Ancoats, Manchester. TZ9651

MULLANEY, D., Private, 2nd Manchester Regiment.
Having previously served twelve years in the Army, he volunteered in December 1915, and was engaged on important guard and general duties at various stations. He rendered valuable services until his discharge in November 1916, as medically unfit for further duty.
29, Lord Street, Openshaw, Manchester. Z7422

MULLEN, E., Private, 3rd Manchester Regiment.
He volunteered at the outbreak of war in August 1914, and on completing his training in February of the following year, proceeded to the Western Front. Whilst in this theatre of war, he took part in many important engagements, including the Battles of Ypres, Vimy Ridge, and the Somme, and was severely wounded in action at Arras. He was for a time in hospital at Chatham, and was finally invalided from the Army in April 1919, holding the 1914-15 Star, and the General Service and Victory Medals.
31, Brown Street, Ancoats, Manchester. Z7421

MULLEN, F., Private, Loyal N. Lancashire Regt.

Volunteering in September 1914, he proceeded to the Western Front twelve months later, and there, after taking part in the Battle of Loos, was wounded in action at Vimy Ridge in May 1916. Invalided home, he returned to France, however, on his recovery, and was shortly afterwards wounded a second time on the Somme, and admitted to hospital at Bradford. Again rejoining his unit in January 1917, he was again wounded in action at Ypres, and invalided to England. He was finally demobilised in May 1920, and holds the 1914–15 Star, and the General Service and Victory Medals.

3, Ashbourne Street, West Gorton, Manchester.   Z11935

MULLEN, G., Private, 8th Loyal N. Lancashire Regt.

He volunteered in 1915, and in June of the following year was drafted to the Western Front, where he saw severe fighting in various sectors. He took part in the Battles of the Somme, Arras, Messines, and Ypres, and many minor engagements until wounded in action at Passchendaele. He afterwards served with the Labour Corps at Cambrai, and other places, finally returning home for demobilisation in March 1919. He holds the General Service and Victory Medals.

87, Old Elm Street, Chorlton-on-Medlock, Manchester. X1182A

MULLEN, J.,Private, 2nd Welch Regimentand M.G.C.

He volunteered in May 1915, and on completing his training in October of that year, proceeded to the Western Front, where he saw much severe fighting until wounded in action at Ypres, and sent to hospital at the Base. He re-joined his unit, however, on his recovery, and was again in action at Nieuport, La Bassée, and many other places, and was wounded a second time on the Somme. He was invalided home, but later returned to France and fought in the Battle of Cambrai, and other important engagements. He was demobilised in May 1919, and holds the 1914–15 Star, and the General Service and Victory Medals.

26, Brown Street, Ancoats, Manchester.   Z11934

MULLIGAN, F. J., Corporal, 11th Manchester Regt.

Volunteering in September 1914, he embarked for the Dardanelles in the following March, and took part in the Landing at Gallipoli, and the Battles of Cape Helles, Krithia, and Achi Baba. Transferred to France after the Evacuation of the Peninsula, he fought at Albert, and the Somme, but in February 1917, owing to a severe illness, was invalided to England for hospital treatment, and in November of the same year was discharged. Unfortunately he died on March 6th, 1920, and was entitled to the 1914–15 Star, and the General Service and Victory Medals.

"He joined the great white company of valiant souls."

18, Phelan Street, Collyhurst, Manchester.   Z10855

MULLIGAN, W., Private, South Lancashire Regt.

He volunteered in October 1914, and crossing to France in the following March, fought at Ypres, Hill 60, Loos, Vimy Ridge, the Somme, Arras, Bullecourt, Messines, Ypres, and Cambrai. He also served in the Retreat and Allied Advance of 1918, and did valuable work until his demobilisation, which took place on his return to England in April 1919. He holds the 1914–15 Star, and the General Service and Victory Medals.

68, Long Street, Ancoats, Manchester.   TZ11493

MULLIN, C., Sergt., King's Own Scottish Borderers.

He volunteered in August 1914, and was shortly afterwards drafted to France. There he fought at La Bassée, Ypres, Neuve Chapelle, Loos, Albert, Vimy Ridge, the Somme, the Ancre, Beaumont-Hamel, Arras, Cambrai, and in the Retreat and Advance of 1918. After hostilities ceased he served in Germany with the Army of Occupation until he was demobilised in September 1918. He holds the 1914 Star, and the General Service and Victory Medals.

1, Humphrey Street, Chorlton-on-Medlock, Manchester. Z7423

MULLIN, C., Private, Royal Welch Fusiliers.

He volunteered in October 1914, and after a period of training was sent to Ireland, where he was engaged on important garrison duties whilst stationed in Belfast. He was unable to obtain a transfer overseas owing to medical reasons, but rendered valuable services until his demobilisation in February 1919.

1, Humphrey Street, Chorlton-on-Medlock, Manchester. Z7424

MULLIN, J. F., Sergt., 1st Manchester Regiment.

He volunteered in February 1915, and in the following year was drafted to Mesopotamia. There he took part in engagements at Kut, Um-el-Hannah, Sanna-i-Yat, and on the Tigris, and at the capture of Tekrit. He was then sent to Egypt, and later served at Jerusalem and Jericho in Palestine. He was demobilised in June 1919, and holds the General Service and Victory Medals.

34, Hancock Street, Rusholme, Manchester.   Z7425

MULLIN, T., Private, Lancashire Fusiliers.

Volunteering in 1914, he embarked for France in September of the succeeding year and fought in engagements at Ypres, Arras, and Armentières. He died gloriously on the Field of Battle in March 1918, whilst fighting on the Somme during the German Offensive, and was entitled to the 1914–15 Star, and the General Service and Victory Medals.

"His life for his Country, his soul to God."

15, Cross Street, Chorlton-on-Medlock, Manchester.   Z10856

MULLINDER, W., Gunner, R.F.A.

He volunteered in September 1914, and crossing to France in the following April was in action at Hill 60, Ypres, Loos, St. Eloi, Vimy Ridge, the Somme, Arras, Bullecourt, Messines, Passchendaele and Cambrai. He also served in the Retreat of 1918, and in October of that year was so severely wounded during the subsequent Allied Advance as to necessitate his return to England. After protracted hospital treatment, he was demobilised in February 1919, and holds the 1914–15 Star, and the General Service and Victory Medals.

11, Kertch Street, Ancoats, Manchester.   TZ10857

MULROY, J., Sapper, R.E.

Joining in April 1918, and completing his training, he was stationed at various depôts with his unit on important duties. He was unable to obtain his transfer to a theatre of war prior to the termination of hostilities, but rendered excellent services until demobilised in February 1919.

6, Prescott Street, West Gorton, Manchester.   TZ9652

MULRYAN, M., Private, 13th K. (Liverpool Regt.)

Volunteering in November 1914, he embarked for France in the same month, and was in action at St. Eloi, Ypres, the Somme, Vimy Ridge, and Cambrai. He gave his life for the freedom of England at Arras, in March 29th, 1918, and was entitled to the 1914–15 Star, and the General Service and Victory Medals.

"His name liveth for evermore."

49, Hinde Street, Gorton, Manchester.   Z10858

MULVANEY, F., Cpl., 2nd Lancashire Fusiliers.

He joined in April 1917 in the South Wales Borderers, and was engaged at various stations on important duties with his unit. He rendered valuable services, but was unable to obtain a transfer overseas before the cessation of hostilities. In 1919 he was transferred to the 2nd Lancashire Fusiliers and proceeded to India where, in 1920, he was still serving.

6, Small Street, Chorlton-on-Medlock, Manchester.   Z7426

MULVANEY, W., Private, 1st Dorsetshire Regt.

He joined in May 1916, and in the following October was drafted to the Western Front. In this theatre of war he took part in many engagements, including those at Ypres and Cambrai, and was wounded in action. As a result, he was invalided home, but on his recovery, returned to France and saw much fighting during the Advance of 1918. He was demobilised in December 1918, and holds the General Service and Victory Medals.

38, Helsby Street, Ardwick, Manchester.   Z7428

MULVANY, M. (Miss), Special War Worker.

During the war this lady volunteered her services as a nurse at a private hospital, Cheetham Hill, Manchester. She rendered valuable services and carried out her duties in a very efficient manner until the cessation of hostilities in November.

1918. 18, Ferry St., Ardwick, Manchester.   Z7427

MULVEY, C., Driver, R.F.A.

He volunteered in August 1914, and in October of the following year proceeded to France. There he took part in engagements at Loos, Albert, the Somme, Arras, Ypres, Passchendaele, Cambrai, and in the Retreat and Advance of 1918, and was gassed in action. He was demobilised in April 1919, and holds the 1914–15 Star, and the General Service and Victory Medals.

5, Hardy Street, West Gorton, Manchester.   Z7429A

MULVEY, C., Private, 16th S. Lancashire Regiment.

He volunteered in November 1915, and was engaged on important duties at various stations with his unit. He was not successful in obtaining a transfer overseas, but rendered valuable services until his demobilisation in March 1919.

5, Hardy Street, West Gorton, Manchester.   Z7429B

MULVEY, M., Private, 3rd Manchester Regiment.

Volunteering in August 1914, he was drafted to France in the following December, and fought in the first Battle of Ypres. He afterwards proceeded to Egypt, and was in action against the Senussi Arabs. In January 1916 he returned to the Western Front, but during his service suffered severely from frost-bite. He was invalided home and subsequently discharged as physically unfit for further duty in December 1917. He holds the 1914–15 Star, and the General Service and Victory Medals. 142, Victoria Square, Ancoats, Manchester. TZ9298

MULVEY, W., Private, 2nd E. Lancashire Regt.

He volunteered in August 1914, and on completing his training in the following January, was drafted to France, where he saw much fighting at Ypres, La Bassée, Loos, and Arras. He was unfortunately killed in action on the Somme in October 1916, and was entitled to the 1914–15 Star, and the General Service and Victory Medals.

"Whilst we remember, the sacrifice is not in vain."

20, Sparkle Street, Ancoats, Manchester.   Z7430

MUMFORD, C., Sergt., South Lancashire Regiment.

Volunteering in April 1915, he was drafted to Mesopotamia in the following year. Whilst in this seat of operations he took part in much fighting at Kut, on the Tigris, and at the capture of Baghdad. After hostilities ceased, he was engaged as an instructor of signalling until he returned home, and was demobilised in May 1919. He holds the General Service and Victory Medals. 41, Hancock Street, Rusholme, Manchester. Z7431

MUMFORD, S. J., Gunner, R.F.A.
He volunteered in January 1915, and in the following June was drafted to France. There he took part in many engagements, including those at Loos, Albert, the Somme, Kemmel Hill, and in the Advance of 1918, and was wounded in action. He was invalided home suffering from a nervous breakdown, and was discharged in February 1919. He holds the 1914-15 Star, and the General Service and Victory Medals. X1128A
9, Cheltenham Street, Chorlton-on-Medlock, Manchester.

MUNDELL, J. H., Private, 1/7th K. (Liverpool Regt.)
He joined in June 1918, and on completing his training in the following October proceeded to Russia. There he was engaged on important garrison duties at Archangel until he was demobilised in September 1919. He holds the General Service and Victory Medals.
4, Greenhill Street, Chorlton-on-Medlock, Manchester. TZ7432

MUNRO, A., L/Corporal, 5th Manchester Regiment.
He volunteered in November 1914, and on completing his training, was drafted to the Western Front, where he took part in several engagements, and was wounded in action on the Somme. As a result, he was invalided home, but, on his recovery, returned to France, and saw much fighting at Béthune, Arras, Armentières, being again wounded, and as a result one of his legs had to be amputated. He was sent home to hospital, and finally discharged in July 1918, holding the 1914-15 Star, and the General Service and Victory Medals.
55, Hall Street, Greenheys, Manchester. TZ7433

MURDOCH, A., Private, Gordon Highlanders.
He was mobilised in August 1914, and immediately drafted to the Western Front, where he took part in the Battle of Mons, and was taken prisoner during the subsequent Retreat. He was held in captivity in Germany, and suffered many hardships, being forced to work in the salt and coal mines during the remaining period of war. He was released after the Armistice, and received his discharge in December 1918. He holds the Mons Star, and the General Service and Victory Medals. 17, Wenlock St., Hulme, Manchester. Z7435

MURDOCH, G., Corporal, 7th Manchester Regiment.
Volunteering in August 1914, he was drafted overseas later in the same year. Whilst on the Western Front he took part in engagements at Neuve Chapelle, Ypres (II), Loos, Albert, Vimy Ridge, the Somme, Beaucourt, Arras, Messines, Lens, Cambrai, the Somme (II), and in the Retreat and Advance of 1918. He was demobilised in January 1919, and holds the 1914-15 Star, and the General Service and Victory Medals.
31, Hancock Street, Rusholme, Manchester. Z7436

MURDOCH, R., Rifleman, Rifle Brigade, and Private, 10th London Regiment.
He volunteered in January 1916, and in the following July proceeded to France. In this theatre of war he saw much heavy fighting on the Somme, at Arras, Passchendaele and in many other sectors, and was severely wounded in September 1918. As a result he was invalided home, and on his recovery rejoined his unit, but was shortly afterwards demobilised in February 1919, holding the General Service and Victory Medals.
20, Ogden Street, Hulme, Manchester. TZ7434

MURNEY, T., Sergt., R.A.F.
Having enlisted in July 1913, he was mobilised when war was declared, and crossed to France with the first British Expeditionary Force. He took part in the Retreat from Mons, and the Battles of Ypres, Arras, the Somme, and Passchendaele, but in October 1917, was invalided home for hospital treatment in consequence of ill-health. He was discharged as medically unfit in July 1918, and holds the Mons Star, and the General Service and Victory Medals.
46, Dickens Street, Miles Platting, Manchester. Z10859

MURNEY, W., Private, R.A.V.C.
He joined in November 1917, and after his training was engaged on duties of an important nature at various stations. During his service he contracted an illness, to which unhappily he succumbed in May 1919.
"His memory is cherished with pride."
57, Knightley Street, Rochdale Road, Manchester. Z10860

MURPHY, A. (M.M.), Sergt., R.F.A.
He volunteered in August 1914, and in the following May was drafted to the Western Front. There he played a distinguished part in several engagements, including those at Loos, Albert, the Somme, Arras, Messines, and in the Retreat and Advance of 1918, being gassed and twice wounded in action. He was awarded the Military Medal for conspicuous bravery and devotion to duty in the Field near Ypres in April 1917, and also holds the 1914-15 Star, and the General Service and Victory Medals. He was demobilised in July 1919.
57, Morton Street, Longsight, Manchester. Z7439

MURPHY, A. J., Private, 7th Manchester Regiment.
He volunteered in May 1915, and on completing his training in the following February, was drafted to Egypt, and saw much fighting at Solluм, Katia, and Romani. Later he was transferred to France, and took part in engagements at Ypres, Passchendaele, and on the Somme (II), being badly gassed in action and finally invalided home. He was demobilised in February 1919, and holds the General Service and Victory Medals.
14, Pine Street, City Road, Hulme, Manchester. Z7438

MURPHY, B. T., Private, R.A.M.C.
Mobilised at the outbreak of war in August 1914, he proceeded to France with the 1st Expeditionary Force, and served through the Retreat from Mons. He also took an active part in the Battles of Le Cateau, the Marne, the Aisne, La Bassée, Ypres (I), Neuve Chapelle, St. Eloi, Hill 60, Ypres (II), Festubert, Loos, and Albert. In May 1916 he received his discharge on completion of seven years' colour service, and holds the Mons Star, and the General Service and Victory Medals.
26, Ribstone Street, Hulme, Manchester. TZ7444

MURPHY, C., Pte., K.O. (Royal Lancaster Regt.)
He volunteered in June 1915, and in August of the following year was drafted to Mesopotamia, where he took part in heavy fighting at Kut-el-Amara. He was badly wounded in action near Baghdad in March 1917, and was admitted to hospital, but on his recovery, rejoined his unit after a forced march of 100 miles, and was present at the capture of Tekrit. Demobilised in February 1919, he holds the General Service and Victory Medals.
36, William Street, Hulme, Manchester. Z7443

MURPHY, D., Private, 16th Manchester Regiment.
He volunteered in January 1915, and in the following December landed in France. Serving with his unit in various parts of the line he was in action in the Battles of the Somme, Arras, Nieuport, Ypres, and in other engagements until the close of the war. Proceeding into Germany after the Armistice he served in the Army of Occupation for several months, and returning from Cologne, was demobilised in June 1919. He holds the 1914-15 Star, and the General Service and Victory Medals.
16, Fox Street, Ancoats, Manchester. Z10861

MURPHY, E., Private, K.O. (Royal Lancaster Regt.)
Volunteering in August 1914, he was drafted to the Western Front in the following January, and took part in the Battles of Ypres, Loos, and Albert. He laid down his life for King and Country during the Somme Offensive in July 1916, and was entitled to the 1914-15 Star, and the General Service and Victory Medals.
"Great deeds cannot die:
They, with the sun and moon renew their light for ever."
68, Birch Street, Ardwick, Manchester. Z7442

MURPHY, G., Private, R.A.M.C.
Volunteering in January 1916, he was retained on important duties at home stations until May 1918 He then proceeded to the Western Front, and was engaged on special work at Boulogne and Amiens, until admitted to hospital at Rouen with fever. On his recovery, he himself rendered valuable services in various hospitals, and was eventually demobilised in October 1919, holding the General Service and Victory Medals.
61, Dorset Street, Hulme, Manchester. Z7445

MURPHY, G., Private, Labour Corps.
Joining in March 1917, he was quickly drafted to the Western Front, and whilst in this theatre of war rendered valuable services with his unit in various sectors. He was present at the Battles of Ypres (III), Cambrai (I and II), and Havrincourt, during heavy fighting at Ploegsteert, and Vermelles, and at the entry into Mons on Armistice Day. Demobilised in February 1919, he holds the General Service and Victory Medals.
42, Meridian Street, Higher Ardwick, Manchester. Z7448

MURPHY, H., Private, R.A.S.C.
He joined in January 1916, and in the following October was drafted to France, where he took part in many engagements. He served on the Somme, at Ypres, Delville Wood, Arras, and Messines Ridge, and was invalided home with dysentery contracted during this period. He was discharged as medically unfit for further duty in November 1918, and holds the General Service and Victory Medals.
16, Mary Street, Ancoats. Z9299

MURPHY, H., Private, 12th Somerset Light Infantry.
He joined in April 1918, and proceeded to the Western Front in the following August, but, within a month of his going into action, fell gallantly on the Field of Battle on the Somme, on September 2nd, 1918. He was buried near Péronne, and was entitled to the General Service and Victory Medals.
"A valiant Soldier, with undaunted heart he breasted life's last hill."
23, Hewitt Street, Openshaw, Manchester. Z7440

MURPHY, J., Private, 8th Manchester Regiment.
Volunteering in August 1914, he was drafted to Egypt in the following month and later to Gallipoli, where he fought in the first landing on the Peninsula, and was wounded on June 4th, 1915, in the third Battle of Krithia. Evacuated to England on account of his injuries he received medical treatment, and on recovery was engaged on home service duties until discharged on medical grounds in May 1918. He holds the 1914-15 Star, and the General Service and Victory Medals.
117, Jersey Street Dwellings, Ancoats, Manchester. Z10864

MURPHY, J., Private, 7th South Lancashire Regt.
Volunteering in September 1914, he was sent to the Western Front in the following July, and was engaged as a sniper in the Battles of Ypres, Festubert, and Loos. Later in the year he was severely wounded at Festubert, and subsequently died from his injuries in December 1915. He was entitled to the 1914–15 Star, and the General Service and Victory Medals.
"Whilst we remember, the sacrifice is not in vain."
2, Tailor Street, Ancoats, Manchester.   Z9653

MURPHY, J., Private, K.O. (R. Lancaster Regt.)
Volunteering in February 1915, he was drafted to the Western Front in the following April, and took part in the heavy fighting at Ypres. He was reported missing after an engagement on May 8th, 1915, and subsequently was officially notified as having been killed in action on that date. He was entitled to the 1914–15 Star, and the General Service and Victory Medals.
"A costly sacrifice upon the altar of freedom."
27, Nicholson Street, Rochdale Road, Manchester.   L9300

MURPHY, J., Private, R.A.S.C.
Volunteering in November 1914, he was sent to France in the following year, and whilst overseas served in the engagements at Neuve Chapelle, St. Eloi, Hill 60, Ypres, Festubert, Armentières, Albert, the Somme, Arras, Péronne, St. Quentin and Mericourt. Owing to illness he returned to England in 1917, to undergo an operation in hospital. He holds the 1914–15 Star, and the General Service and Victory Medals, and was demobilised in February 1919.
46, Jersey Dwellings, Manchester.   Z9301

MURPHY, J., Private, 53rd Welch Regiment.
He joined immediately on attaining military age in August 1918, but was unsuccessful in obtaining his transfer overseas before the cessation of hostilities. In March 1919, however, he was sent to the Army of Occupation in Germany and rendered valuable services with his unit on the Rhine until his demobilisation in March 1920.
1, Alder Street, Hulme, Manchester.   TZ7446

MURPHY, J., Private, K.O. (R. Lancaster Regt.)
Volunteering in May 1915, he was sent to Egypt in the following July and saw severe fighting in the Suez Canal zone until December 1915, when he was transferred to the Dardanelles. He was badly wounded in action during the Evacuation of the Gallipoli Peninsula in January 1916, and was invalided home. On his recovery he was retained on special duties until his discharge as medically unfit in September 1918. Previous to the war he had served as a Corporal for four years in the Regular Army, and holds the 1914–15 Star, and the General Service and Victory Medals.
36, Bedale Street, Hulme, Manchester.   Z7437

MURPHY, J., Private, 6th East Lancashire Regt.
He volunteered in August 1914, and in the following November was sent to Egypt, but later proceeded to Mesopotamia. Whilst in this theatre of war, he took part in the Battles of Basra and Kut-el-Amara, the capture of Baghdad, and in heavy fighting on the Tigris. He was three times wounded in action and was invalided home in October 1917. Three months later he was discharged as medically unfit for further service, and holds the 1914–15 Star, and the General Service and Victory Medals.
5, Higher Chatham Street, Hulme, Manchester.   Z7441A

MURPHY, J. J., Sapper, R.E.
He joined in February 1916, and in the following September was drafted to Mesopotamia, where he played an important part as head sapper in charge of bridge building operations at Kut and Baghdad, and during the Offensive on the Tigris. He was demobilised in May 1920, and holds the General Service and Victory Medals.
5, Higher Chatham Street, Hulme, Manchester.   Z7441B

MURPHY, L., L/Corporal, 20th Manchester Regt.
He volunteered in September 1914, and three months later was sent overseas. Whilst on the Western Front he took part in the Battles of Neuve Chapelle, Hill 60, Ypres, Festubert, Albert, Vimy Ridge, and was seriously wounded on the Somme in July 1916. Sent home to hospital he received treatment at Bristol and Ripon, and was later employed on light duties until discharged as medically unfit for further service in February 1919. He holds the 1914–15 Star, and the General Service and Victory Medals.
17, Iles Street, Oldham Road, Manchester.   Z10862

MURPHY, M., Driver, R.A.S.C.
He joined in April 1918, and was quickly drafted to the Western Front, where he was engaged on important transport duties in the forward areas during the Battles of Amiens, Havrincourt and Le Cateau (II). After the cessation of hostilities, he served on the railways at Bonn in Germany, and did consistently good work with the Army of Occupation until his demobilisation in September 1919. He holds the General Service and Victory Medals.
8, Birch Street, Moss Side, Manchester.   Z7447

MURPHY, M. J., Sergt., 3rd Cheshire Regiment.
He first volunteered at the age of fifteen years in August 1915, but within a month was discharged owing to his youth.

In February 1918, however, he rejoined, and quickly gained promotion to Sergeant, rendering valuable services at various stations in England. He was not successful in obtaining his transfer overseas, and was demobilised in September 1919.
17, Rial Street, Hulme, Manchester.   Z7449

MURPHY, R., Private, 2nd Manchester Regiment.
Mobilised at the commencement of hostilities, he landed in France and fought in the Retreat from Mons, and in many other engagements of note. He was severely wounded in the Battle of La Bassée, and unhappily died from his injuries on October 14th, 1914. He was entitled to the Mons Star, and the General Service and Victory Medals.
"And doubtless he went in splendid company."
7, League Street, Rochdale Road, Manchester.   Z9654

MURPHY, T., Private, Manchester Regiment.
Mobilised on the outbreak of war, he embarked for France shortly afterwards, and fought in the Retreat from Mons, and in the Battles of Le Cateau, La Bassée, and Ypres. He was also engaged in heavy fighting at Neuve Chapelle, St. Eloi, Hill 60, Loos, Vimy Ridge, and was wounded on the Somme. Evacuated to England he was under treatment at the Western General Hospital, London, and invalided out of the Service in August 1917, holds the Mons Star, and the General Service and Victory Medals.
13, Cathcart Street, Ancoats, Manchester.   Z10865

MURPHY, T. H. (M.M.), L/Corporal, 1st Loyal North Lancashire Regiment.
He volunteered in April 1915, and was drafted to France later in the same year. He was engaged in heavy fighting in the Battle of the Somme, where he fell in action on July 15th, 1916. He was awarded the Military Medal for his conspicuous gallantry and devotion to duty, and was also entitled to the 1914–15 Star, and the General Service and Victory Medals.
"Great deeds cannot die :
They, with the sun and moon renew their light for ever."
32, Rosecester Street, Harpurhey, Manchester.   Z11558

MURPHY, W., Private, Northumberland Fusiliers.
He volunteered in September 1914, and after his training served at various stations on important coastal defence duties. He rendered valuable services but was not able to secure a transfer overseas before the cessation of hostilities, and was demobilised in February 1919.
50, Sanitary Street, Oldham Road, Manchester.   Z9302

MURRAY, C., Rifleman, Royal Irish Rifles.
He volunteered in June 1915, and a month later landed on the Western Front in several sectors of which he was engaged on important duties with his Battalion. Owing to illness he was sent home and after treatment at Northampton War Hospital served in Scotland and Ireland, until his discharge on medical grounds in December 1917. He holds the 1914–15 Star, and the General Service and Victory Medals.
17, Edgely Street, Ardwick, Manchester.   Z11780

MURRAY, G., Private, M.G.C.
He joined in May 1917, and in the following November was drafted to India, where he did consistently good work with his unit, whilst engaged on garrison duties. Unfortunately he contracted malarial fever, and was in hospital for some time. He returned to England for demobilisation in December 1919, and holds the General Service and Victory Medals.
24, Alfred Street, West Gorton, Manchester.   Z7450

MURRAY, J., Private, 8th Manchester Regiment.
He joined in February 1917, and four months later was drafted to the Western Front, where he played an important part in the Battles of Ypres (III) and the Somme (II), and was wounded in action at Havrincourt during the Advance of 1918. After a few weeks in hospital, he was engaged on guard duties at prisoner of war camps at Péronne and Charleroi. He holds the General Service and Victory Medals, and was demobilised in October 1919.
23, Marsland Street, Chorlton-on-Medlock, Manchester. Z7451

MURRAY, J., Private, Royal Scots.
Volunteering in January 1915, he proceeded to Egypt a year later, and whilst there took part in operations including the occupation of Sollum. In November 1916, he was transferred to the Western Front, and was in action in many engagements on the Somme, and was wounded in February 1917. Invalided to England he was treated for his injuries at Stockport, and subsequently discharged as medically unfit in July 1917. He holds the General Service and Victory Medals.
75, Burns Street, Bradford, Manchester.   Z10866

MURRAY, J., L/Corporal, Border Regiment.
He volunteered in November 1914, and in February 1916, was drafted to France. During his service on the Western Front he was in action at Loos, St. Eloi and Vimy Ridge, before being badly wounded on the Somme in August 1916. He was invalided home, where he unfortunately underwent a severe operation, and had part of his shoulder removed. He received his discharge as medically unfit in November 1917, and holds the General Service and Victory Medals. In 1920 he was still under treatment for his wound. Z4453
19, St. Clements Place, Grey Street, West Gorton, Manchester.

MURRAY, J., Private, 22nd Manchester Regiment.
He volunteered in November 1917, and twelve months later proceeded to the Western Front, where he was wounded whilst on special wiring duties. After three months in a Field Ambulance he rejoined his unit, but a short time afterwards was invalided home for hospital treatment. On his recovery, he was transferred to the Labour Corps and again sent to France in January 1918, when he carried out special bridge and trench construction work in various sectors. He was demobilised in April 1919, and holds the 1914-15 Star, and the General Service and Victory Medals.
50, Ridgway Street, Moss Side, Manchester.   Z7452

MURRAY, J., Private, Lancashire Fusiliers.
Joining in August 1917, he was engaged on special duties at various home stations and rendered valuable services with his unit until April 1918. He was then taken seriously ill with bronchitis and invalided from the Army.
27, Teak Street, Ardwick, Manchester.   Z7454

MURRAY, M., Private, 22nd Manchester Regiment.
He volunteered in July 1915, and crossing to France in the following October did good work with his unit in the Battles of Loos, St. Eloi, Albert, Vimy Ridge, and was wounded on the Somme in July 1916. Returning to the trenches on recovery he saw heavy fighting on the Ancre, and in the Arras sector. He was killed in action near Arras on March 28th, 1917, and lies buried in the British Cemetery at Croisilles. He was entitled to the 1914-15 Star, and the General Service and Victory Medals.
"Nobly striving:
He nobly fell that we might live."
15, Upper Vauxhall St., Rochdale Rd., Manchester.   Z10863

MURTHWAITE, G. W., Pte., East Yorkshire Regt.
He volunteered in 1915, and in the same year sailed to the Bermuda Islands, where he was engaged on important garrison duties at various stations. He rendered valuable services throughout the duration of hostilities, and was demobilised in March 1919, after his return to England. He holds the General Service Medal.
25, Kirk Street, Ancoats, Manchester.   Z9303

MUSGROVE, S., Private, 22nd Manchester Regt.
Volunteering in November 1914, he was drafted to the Western Front seven months later and took part in the Battles of Loos, St. Eloi, Albert and Vimy Ridge. He gave his life for the freedom of England in the Battle of the Somme in July 1916, and was entitled to the 1914-15 Star, and the General Service and Victory Medals.
"Honour to the immortal dead, who gave their youth that the world might grow old in peace."
23, Hewitt Street, Gorton, Manchester.   Z10867

MYCOCK, H., Corporal, Loyal N. Lancashire Regt.
Having enlisted in 1910, he was stationed in India, when war broke out in August 1914, and was quickly sent to German East Africa, where he played a prominent part in much severe fighting. In November 1916, he was transferred to the Western Front, and served through the Battles of Ypres, Lens and Cambrai, and the Retreat and Advance of 1918. He was chiefly engaged with the Lewis Gun Section, and was three times wounded in action. He received his discharge in January 1919, and holds the 1914-15 Star, and the General Service and Victory Medals.
5, Aden Street, Ardwick, Manchester.   Z7455

MYCOCK, J. W., Private, East Lancashire Regt.
He volunteered in November 1914, and in the following June was sent to Gallipoli. There he took part in the Landing at Suvla Bay, and was shortly after removed to hospital at Malta suffering from sun-stroke. Evacuated to England he was under medical treatment at Reading, and on recovery was engaged on special duties with his Battalion until December 1918, when he was discharged on account of service. He holds the 1914-15 Star, and the General Service and Victory Medals.
9, Ross Street, West Gorton, Manchester.   Z10868A

MYCOCK, J. W., Private, 11th Manchester Regt.
Volunteering in January 1915, he sailed for Gallipoli in the following June and served at the Landing at Suvla Bay, and the Battles of Krithia and other operations until the Evacuation of the Peninsula, when he returned to England. In January 1917, he embarked for France, and in this theatre of war fought at the Battles of Arras, Vimy Ridge, Bullecourt, Messines, Lens, Cambrai, the Somme, the Aisne, (III) and the Marne (II). After the cessation of hostilities he was retained in France on special duties for some months, and on his return home was demobilised in May 1919. He holds the 1914-15 Star, and the General Service and Victory Medals.
9, Gray Street, Ancoats, Manchester.   Z10869

MYERS, A., Private, M.G.C.
He volunteered in March 1915, and after a period of important home duties, was drafted to France in July 1917. He saw much severe fighting whilst attached to the Tank Corps as a Gunner, but was unhappily killed in action at Ypres on October 1st, 1917. He was entitled to the General Service and Victory Medals.
"A costly sacrifice upon the altar of freedom."
95, Darncombe Street, Moss Side, Manchester.   Z7458A

MYERS, A. R., Private, 4th Manchester Regiment.
He volunteered in December 1915, and was engaged on Home Service duties until his embarkation for the Western Front in January 1917. Whilst overseas he fought in the Battles of Arras, Bullecourt, Messines and Ypres, and wounded on August 29th, 1917, was sent home to hospital. After receiving treatment at St. Luke's Hospital, Bradford, he was discharged on medical grounds in October 1918, and holds the General Service and Victory Medals.
79, Cromwell Avenue, Manley Park, Manchester.   Z10870

MYERS, R., Sergt., 7th Manchester Regiment.
Mobilised in August 1914, he was quickly drafted to the Western Front, where he served with distinction at the Battle of, and in the Retreat from, Mons. He also took part in the Battles of Le Cateau, La Bassée, Ypres (1914 and 1915), Neuve Chapelle and Loos, and was wounded in action in February 1916. Invalided to England, he spent some time in hospital, and, on his recovery, carried out special postal duties until his discharge in February 1919, holding the Mons Star, and the General Service and Victory Medals.
22, Chatsworth Street, Hulme, Manchester.   Z7459

MYERS, T., Private, Lancashire Fusiliers.
Volunteering January 1915, he was drafted to the Western Front in May of the following year, and was in action at Vermelles and Vimy Ridge. In October 1916, he was invalided home with a severe attack of fever, and after hospital treatment in Essex, was retained on special agricultural duties in various parts of England. He holds the General Service and Victory Medals, and was demobilised in March 1919.
8, George Street, West Gorton, Manchester.   Z7456

MYERS, T., Private, Manchester Regt. and M.G.C.
He joined in December 1916, and proceeding to the Western Front in the following April, was in action at the Battles of Arras, Bullecourt, Lens, Cambrai, the Somme (II), the Aisne (III), Bapaume, Havrincourt, Epéhy, and the Selle. Returning to England in February 1920, he was then demobilised, and holds the General Service and Victory Medals.
8, George Street, West Gorton, Manchester.   Z7457

MYERS, T. E., Private, Loyal N. Lancashire Regt.
He joined in May 1917, and in the following July was sent to India, where he was engaged on important garrison duties. He rendered valuable services with his unit whilst so employed, but was eventually taken seriously ill with fever. Invalided to England, he was discharged as medically unfit in June 1919, and holds the General Service and Victory Medals.
95, Darncombe Street, Moss Side, Manchester.   Z7458B

MYERS, W., Private, 1/7th Manchester Regiment.
A Territorial, he was mobilised at the outbreak of war in August 1914, and a month later was sent to Egypt, where he rendered valuable services until April 1915. He was then transferred to the Dardanelles, and after taking part in the Landing at Cape Helles, was wounded in action at the third Battle of Krithia in June 1915. He spent some time in hospital at Malta, and was sent home to Eastbourne for convalescence. In February 1916 he was discharged, time expired, and holds the 1914-15 Star, and the General Service and Victory Medals.
8, Sessay Street, Hancock Street, Hulme, Manchester.   Z7460

MYERSCOUGH, J. E., Armourers' Crew, R.N.
Volunteering in August 1915, he was posted to a ship on the completion of his training at Devonport, and served in that vessel for over three years. During this period his ship was engaged in patrol and other duties off the East African Coast, and took part in the bombardment of enemy ports in German East Africa. He was demobilised on returning to shore in March 1919, and holds the General Service and Victory Medals.
1, Moody Street, Bradford, Manchester.   Z10871

N

NAAN, T., Sapper, R.E.
Joining in March 1916, he crossed in the following July to the Western Front, and there saw much active service. He was present at many battles, including those of the Somme, Beaumont-Hamel, Ypres, and Cambrai, but suffered severely from shell-shock during April 1918. He was invalided home, and remained in hospital until demobilised in May 1919. He holds the General Service and Victory Medals.
8, Heron Street, Hulme, Manchester.   Z7461

NADEN, T., Rflmn., The Cameronians (Scottish Rifles).
Volunteering in September 1914, he proceeded to France in the following month, and during his service in this theatre of war was frequently in action. He fought in many Battles, including those of Neuve Chapelle, St. Eloi, Cambrai, and the Scarpe, and was wounded at Festubert, and gassed at Lens. Demobilised in February 1919, he holds the 1914 Star, and the General Service and Victory Medals.
15, Bell Street, Openshaw, Manchester.   Z7462

NALLY, J., Private, 2nd Lancashire Fusiliers.
Mobilised in August 1914, he was drafted in the following January to the Western Front. In this theatre of war he took part in many important engagements, including Ypres, Albert, Ploegsteert Wood, the Somme and Arras, and in many sectors during the Retreat and Advance of 1918. He was gassed at Ypres, but remained overseas until February 1919, when he was discharged, holding the 1914–15 Star, and the General Service and Victory Medals.
20, Woodward Street, Ancoats, Manchester. Z9655

NASH, G., Corporal, Manchester Regiment.
He volunteered in August 1914, and in the following year was sent to Gallipoli, where he was wounded during the Landing at Suvla Bay. In July 1916 he proceeded to Egypt, and after serving there for over a year, embarked for France, and fought in the Retreat and Allied Advance of 1918. Invalided home through ill-health he received hospital treatment, and was eventually discharged in November 1918. He holds the 1914–15 Star, and the General Service and Victory Medals.
28, Derby Street, Ardwick, Manchester. TZ7463

NAVEN, J., Air Mechanic, R.A.F.
Volunteering in September 1914, he embarked in August of the following year for France, and served in many sectors of the Front. He was principally engaged in repairing the engines of aeroplanes, and was present during the fighting at Loos, the Somme, Arras, Amiens, and Cambrai. Returning home in March 1919, he was demobilised, and holds the 1914–15 Star and the General Service and Victory Medals.
9, Marshall Street, Ardwick, Manchester. TZ7464

NAVEN, R., Private, R.A.M.C.
Volunteering in June 1915, he was drafted to Egypt in the same year, and served with the Field Ambulance in the Canal region, and during operations at Mersa Matruh. He did good work at various other places whilst hostilities were in progress, and returned home after the Armistice. Demobilised in February 1919, he holds the 1914–15 Star, and the General Service and Victory Medals.
2, Jessie Ann, Miles Platting, Manchester. Z11781

NAYLOR, E., Private, 8th Manchester Regiment.
He volunteered in September 1914, and after having completed his training, served at various stations on Coastal Defence duties, and in guarding German prisoners. He rendered very valuable services until September 1917, when he was discharged from the Army on account of the important nature of his civil employment.
21, Hughes Street, Ardwick, Manchester. Z7468

NAYLOR, J., Private, 1/7th Manchester Regiment.
He volunteered in August 1914, and in the following June crossed to France. Whilst in this theatre of war he took part in many notable battles, including those of Vimy Ridge, Ploegsteert Wood, the Somme and Ypres, and was wounded three times as well as gassed. He was invalided home in May 1918, and after receiving hospital treatment, was discharged as medically unfit in February 1919. He holds the 1914–15 Star, and the General Service and Victory Medals.
211, Earl Street, Longsight, Manchester. Z7470

NAYLOR, J., Pte., King's Own Scottish Borderers.
Volunteering in August 1914, he sailed in the following January for France, and there fought in many battles. He was in action at Ypres and Loos, and during the first Battle of the Somme was wounded and invalided home. After receiving hospital treatment, he was discharged as medically unfit owing to wounds in December 1916. and holds the 1914–15 Star, and the General Service and Victory Medals.
124, Heald Grove, Rusholme, Manchester. Z7465

NAYLOR, J., Gunner, R.F.A.
Volunteering in November 1914, he embarked for France in March 1915, and whilst there saw much heavy fighting. He took part in the operations at Hill 60 and Passchendaele, but met with an accident, after which he was employed on important duties as a shoeing smith at Le Havre until demobilised in February 1919. He holds the 1914–15 Star, and the General Service and Victory Medals.
15, Garibaldi Street, Ardwick, Manchester. Z7466

NAYLOR, L., Corporal, R.A.M.C.
He joined in September 1916, and after a course of training served as nursing orderly in various hospital ships. He assisted in tending the wounded from the Dardanelles, Egypt and France, later helping to fit up a military hospital at Etaples. He was discharged in December 1918, through causes due to his service, and holds the General Service and Victory Medals.
45, Elliott Street, Bradford, Manchester. Z7467

NAYLOR, W., Driver, R.A.S.C. (M.T.)
Volunteering in May 1915, he proceeded to France a year later and served with the ammunition column in many sectors of the Front. He was present during the fighting at Ypres, Arras and Albert, and served right through the concluding stages of the war. He was demobilised in June 1919, and holds the General Service and Victory Medals.
34, Stott Street, Hulme, Manchester. Z7471

NAYLOR, R., Private, 1/8th Manchester Regiment.
He volunteered in August 1914, and in the following year was drafted to the Dardanelles, where he was in action at Krithia in June. After the Evacuation of the Peninsula he proceeded to Egypt, and was later sent to France. There he took part in the fighting at Vimy Ridge and in the Advance of 1918, and with the Allied Forces crossed the German frontier. Demobilised in March 1919, he holds the 1914–15 Star, and the General Service and Victory Medals.
2, Peel Street, Chorlton-on-Medlock, Manchester. X7469

NEAL, D. (Sen.), Pioneer, R.E.
He volunteered in August 1914, and after a course of training was found to be unfit and was discharged. He rejoined, however, in October 1917, but shortly afterwards contracted pneumonia, from which he died in June 1918.
"Whilst we remember, the sacrifice is not in vain."
39, Clare Street, Chorlton-on-Medlock, Manchester. Z9305A

NEAL, D. (Jun.), Private, 7th Manchester Regiment.
Volunteering in August 1914, he was retained on special home duties until June 1916. He then proceeded to the Western Front, where he saw much heavy fighting, and during the Battle of Arras was wounded. He was invalided to hospital, but unhappily died from his injuries in April 1917. He was entitled to the General Service and Victory Medals.
"Honour to the immortal dead, who gave their youth that the world might grow old in peace."
39, Clare Street, Chorlton-on-Medlock, Manchester. Z9305B

NEALON, J., Corporal, Lancashire Fusiliers.
He was serving in India when war broke out, and in April 1915 was drafted to Gallipoli, where he fought at Krithia and Achi Baba. He was wounded at Suvla Bay in August 1915, and invalided home. In February 1916 he was sent to France, and after taking part in engagements at Loos, the Somme, Arras, Ypres and Messines, was again wounded at Cambrai in April 1918. He was discharged from the Army in December 1918, and holds the 1914–15 Star, and the General Service and Victory Medals.
1, Francisco Street, Collyhurst, Manchester. Z10872

NEAVE, H., Rifleman, K.R.R.C.
He joined in October 1915, at sixteen and a half years of age, but was discharged in September 1916. He rejoined, however, in the following February in the Monmouthshire Regiment and did guard and various other duties on the South-East Coast. In February 1918 he proceeded to France and served in the King's Royal Rifle Corps on the Somme, the Marne and the Aisne and in the Retreat and Advance of 1918, and was wounded. Later he went with the Army of Occupation into Germany and was not demobilised until June 1919. He holds the General Service and Victory Medals.
23, Molyneux Street, Longsight, Manchester. Z7472

NEAVES, J. W., Private, 22nd Manchester Regt.
He volunteered in November 1914, and a year later was drafted to the Western Front, where he fought in important engagements at Albert, the Somme, Arras, Nieuport, Ypres, St. Quentin and Cambrai. He was wounded in action on three occasions, and also experienced fierce fighting in the Retreat of 1918, and in the subsequent Allied Advance. In March 1919 he was demobilised, holding the 1914–15 Star, and the General Service and Victory Medals.
42, Phelan Street, Collyhurst, Manchester. Z10873

NEEDHAM, A. (D.C.M.), Sergt., R.E.
He joined the Army as a boy in 1892, afterwards served in the Volunteers, and was mobilised with the Territorial Force in August 1914. Proceeding to the Dardanelles a month later, he served throughout this campaign and was awarded the Distinguished Conduct Medal for conspicuous gallantry and devotion to duty in the Field. He was subsequently stationed in Egypt and was employed on various duties of an important nature until May 1918, when he was invalided home on account of ill-health, and was eventually discharged in November 1918, holding the 1914–15 Star, the General Service and Victory Medals, the Medal for Long Service and Good Conduct in addition to the Distinguished Conduct Medal. 15, Sadler Street, Moss Side, Manchester. Z9656

NEEDHAM, J., Leading Stoker, R.N., H.M.S. "Lion."
He enlisted in June 1912, and during the period of hostilities served in H.M.S. "Lion." He took part in the fighting at Heligoland Bight, the Dogger Bank and later in the great Battle of Jutland, afterwards serving on convoy and escort duties in the North Sea, until after the war. Returning to shore, he was discharged in December 1919, and holds the 1914–15 Star, and the General Service and Victory Medals.
10, Mundy Street, Gorton, Manchester. Z7473

NEILD, F. A., Private, 6th Manchester Regiment.
He volunteered in July 1915, and embarking for France two months later, was engaged in heavy fighting in the Battles of Loos, St. Eloi, Vermelles and the Somme. He gave his life for King and Country on July 1st, 1916, and lies buried near Albert. He was entitled to the 1914–15 Star, and the General Service and Victory Medals.
"Whilst we remember, the sacrifice is not in vain."
8, Peter Street, Hulme, Manchester. Z11782

NEILD, J., Sergt., M.G.C.
He volunteered in August 1914, and in the same month was
sent to Egypt, later proceeding to Gallipoli and serving
throughout that campaign. Afterwards he returned to
Egypt and remained there until drafted to France in 1917.
In this theatre of war he saw much fighting and took part in
the Retreat and Allied Advance of 1918. Returning to
England for demobilisation in March 1919, he holds the
1914-15 Star, and the General Service and Victory Medals.
131, Devon Street, Ardwick, Manchester.   Z7474

NEILD, W., Gunner, R.F.A.
He volunteered in September 1914, but was retained for
duty in England until February 1916. He then proceeded
to France and took part in the fighting at Ploegsteert Wood
and on the Somme, where he was wounded in July 1916.
On recovery he returned to the fighting area and served in
many further engagements, including those during the Retreat
and Advance of 1918. Returning home, he was demobilised
in April 1919, and holds the General Service and Victory
Medals.
12, Hawthorne Street, Ardwick, Manchester.   Z7475

NESBITT, S., Private, 21st Manchester Regiment.
Joining in January 1917, he completed his training and crossed
to France in the following May. Whilst in this theatre of
war he saw much heavy fighting, and was in action at Arras,
Ypres and Cambrai and on the Somme, and in the Retreat
and subsequent Allied Advance of 1918. He was demobilised
in March 1919, and holds the General Service and Victory
Medals.
19, Hinckley Street, Bradford, Manchester.   Z7476

NEVILLE, T., Private, East Lancashire Regiment.
Joining in March 1917, he underwent a period of training at
Rhyl and Ripon, and eight months later was sent to India.
He served there for over two years, and during that time was
engaged on important garrison duties at Bangalore, which he
fulfilled in a very able manner. On his return to England
in March 1920, he was demobilised, holding the General
Service and Victory Medals.
22, Aspden Street, Ancoats, Manchester.   Z10874

NEVIN, P. J. (M.M.), Driver, R.A.S.C.
He volunteered in October 1914, and served for a time on
important duties in England. Proceeding to France in
February 1916, he served with distinction during the engagements at Vimy Ridge, the Somme, Beaumont-Hamel, Arras,
Ypres and Cambrai, and was gassed. He was awarded the
Military Medal for conspicuous bravery in bringing in wounded
under heavy enemy fire on March 18th, 1918, and in addition
holds the General Service and Victory Medals. He was
discharged in November 1918, as medically unfit through
gas-poisoning and illness.
26, Gotha Street, Ardwick, Manchester.   Z7477

NEVISON, W., Private, 11th Manchester Regiment.
He volunteered in December 1914, and in the following September was sent to Egypt. After taking part in the Suez
Canal engagements he was transferred to Gallipoli, where
he served at Suvla Bay and in subsequent battles until the
Evacuation of the Peninsula. In March 1917 he was drafted
to France, and was in action at Nieuport, Ypres, Passchendaele,
the Somme and La Bassée. He was demobilised in May 1919,
and holds the 1914-15 Star, and the General Service and
Victory Medals.
65, Montague Street, Collyhurst, Manchester.   Z10875A

NEWALL, A., Private, Northumberland Fusiliers.
He volunteered in August 1914, and in the following June
was drafted to France, where he was in action at Arras, Ypres
and Lens. Later transferred to Italy he took part in many
important engagements on the Asiago and Piave fronts,
remaining in this theatre of war until February 1919. He
was demobilised a month later and holds the 1914-15 Star,
and the General Service and Victory Medals.   Z9657
2, St. George's Buildings, Stonehewer Street, Manchester.

NEWALL, H. B., Pte.(Signaller) King's (L'pool Regt.)
He volunteered in August 1915, and in November of the following year was drafted to Salonika, where he saw much service
on the Doiran and Struma fronts, and contracted malaria.
In June 1918 he proceeded to France, and took part in the
fighting at Valenciennes, the 2nd Battle of Le Cateau and
many other engagements until the close of war. Returning
home, he was demobilised in February 1919, and holds the
General Service and Victory Medals.
29, Caroline Street, Hulme, Manchester.   Z7478

NEWBIGGIN, J., Sergt., 2nd Lancashire Fusiliers.
Volunteering in August 1914, he served on the completion
of his training, at various stations on important duties with
his unit. Owing to medical unfitness he was not able to
obtain a transfer overseas, but rendered valuable services
until discharged in February 1916, after hospital treatment.
42, Wilson Street, Ardwick, Manchester.   Z7479

NEWCOMBE, W. H., Private, Labour Corps.
He joined in September 1916, and in the following January
crossed to France. He served in many sectors of the Front

in the repair of roads, and was present during the fighting at
Cambrai, Ypres, Havrincourt and Armentières. He returned
home and was demobilised in March 1919, holding the General
Service and Victory Medals.
42, Meadow Street, Ardwick, Manchester.   Z7480

NEWISS, F., Gunner, R.F.A.
He volunteered in January 1915, and in the following September embarked for the Western Front. There he took part
in the heavy fighting on the Somme and at Arras and Ypres,
but during the Battle of Cambrai was wounded in December
1917. He was invalided home and after receiving hospital
treatment was discharged as medically unfit in March 1918.
He holds the 1914-15 Star, and the General Service and Victory Medals.
39, Greenheys Lane, Moss Side, Manchester.   Z7482

NEWMAN, J., Gunner, R.F.A.
He had previously served in the South African War, and volunteering in December 1914 proceeded overseas in the following
April. During his service in France he took part in many
important battles, including those of Loos, Vimy Ridge, the
Somme, Arras and Ypres. He was demobilised in January
1919, and holds the 1914-15 Star, and the General Service
and Victory Medals.
4, Woodhouse Street, Openshaw, Manchester.   Z7483

NEWNES, T. J., Private, 6th Manchester Regiment.
Volunteering in May 1915, he crossed in the following August
to France, where he saw much active service. He took part
in the fighting at Loos, Ploegsteert Wood, the Somme, Beaucourt, Arras, Ypres, Cambrai, Amiens, Bapaume and Le Cateau,
and in the Retreat and Advance of 1918. Afterwards he
proceeded with the Army of Occupation into Germany,
remaining there until demobilised in February 1919. He
holds the 1914-15 Star, and the General Service and Victory
Medals.   4, Ridley Grove, Greenheys, Manchester.   Z7481

NEWSOME, H., Private, R.A.S.C.
He volunteered in November 1915, and was retained for home
duties until January 1917. He then proceeded to Salonika,
where he served on important duties in the workshops of the
R.A.S.C. until November of the following year. Afterwards
he was sent to Mesopotamia and remained in the East until
his return home for demobilisation in September 1919.
He holds the General Service and Victory Medals.
3, Bedson Street, Bradford, Manchester.   Z7484

NEWTON, A., Private, Army Cyclist Corps.
Almost immediately after volunteering at the outbreak of
war he reached France and took part in the Battles of Neuve
Chapelle, St. Eloi, Hill 60, Ypres (II), Festubert, Loos, Albert,
Ploegsteert, the Somme (I), the Ancre, Arras, Bullecourt,
Ypres (III), Lens and Cambrai. During the Retreat and
Advance of 1918, he was in action at Amiens, Bapaume,
Cambrai, Ypres and Le Cateau. He was demobilised in
April 1919, and holds the 1914 Star, and the General Service
and Victory Medals.
14, Franchise Street, Ardwick, Manchester.   Z1092A

NEWTON, C. J., Private, 2/5th Lancashire Fusiliers.
Volunteering in November 1915, he embarked for France in
the following February, and whilst in this theatre of war saw
much fighting. He was in action on the Somme, but was
wounded at Givenchy and invalided home. On recovery
he served with the Labour Corps on light duties until discharged as medically unfit in November 1918. He holds the
General Service and Victory Medals.
5, Hadfield Street, Chorlton-on-Medlock, Manchester.   TZ7487B

**NEWTON, D. H., Sergt., Cheshire Regiment, and
Labour Corps.**
He joined in August 1916, and after a period of training at
Kinmel Park was sent to Lincolnshire, where he was attached
to the R.A.S.C., and employed on important duties in connection with forage. He later served at Oswestry, engaged on
military police duties until he was demobilised in June 1919.
Although medically unfit for service overseas, he rendered
very valuable services.
20, Vine Street, Newton Heath, Manchester.   Z9658B

NEWTON, E., Special War Worker.
This worker was engaged on work of National importance at
Messrs. Woods' Ocean Iron Works, Salford, and was employed
on important and responsible duties in connection with shell
making. He rendered invaluable services to his Country in
the most critical moments of the war, and gave complete
satisfaction to his employers.
14, Cathcart Street, Ancoats, Manchester.   Z10876

NEWTON, J., Private, 42nd M.G.C.
He joined in May 1917, and after a year's training and service
at home, was drafted to France. There he saw much fighting
at Armentières, Cambrai, Bapaume, and Havrincourt, and
after hostilities ceased proceeded with the Army of Occupation
into Germany. In October 1919 he was demobilised on his
return home, and holds the General Service and Victory Medals.
8, Foster Street, City Road, Hulme, Manchester   Z7485

NEWTON, J., Private, R.M.L.I.
Joining in March 1918, he completed his training and served with his unit at various stations in the South of England. Amongst other duties he was engaged in loading and unloading munitions at naval depôts, and did good work. He was not successful in securing his transfer overseas before the conclusion of hostilities, and was demobilised in January 1919.
10, Scott Street, Hulme, Manchester. Z11783

NEWTON, J., Private, 3rd Manchester Regiment.
He volunteered in November 1915, and being drafted in the following January to Mesopotamia, served with the Kut Relief Forces at Um-el-Hannah, Sanna-i-Yat, and on the Tigris. In January 1917 he was sent to Egypt, and with General Allenby's Forces took part in the Advance to Jerusalem. For a short time he was in hospital through ill-health, but on recovery returned to his unit. Demobilised in October 1919, after his return home, he holds the General Service and Victory Medals.
8, Foster Street, City Road, Hulme, Manchester. Z7486

NEWTON, R., Private, Labour Corps, and Air Craftsman, R.A.F.
He joined a T. R. Battalion in March 1917, and after a course of training served for a time on coastal defence duties with the Labour Corps. Later, transferred to the R.A.F., he was engaged on duties of a highly technical nature, but was not able to obtain a transfer overseas before hostilities ceased. In December 1919 he was demobilised. TZ7487A
5, Hadfield Street, Chorlton-on-Medlock, Manchester.

NEWTON, R., Sergt., 2nd Dragoon Guards.
When war was declared he was serving in the Army and at once proceeded with the first Expeditionary Force to France. There he played a conspicuous part in the Battles of Mons, Neuve Chapelle, Ypres, Loos, the Somme, Arras and Cambrai, and was also in action in the Retreat and Advance of 1918. In January 1919 he returned home, and was stationed at Oswestry and the Curragh until discharged in October 1919, holding the Mons Star, and the General Service and Victory Medals. 2, Tailor Street, Ancoats, Manchester. Z10877

NEWTON, T., Private, 2nd Manchester Regiment.
Mobilised on the declaration of war, he was shortly afterwards drafted to France, and fought in the Retreat from Mons, and many subsequent engagements. He was also in action at Loos, Ypres, on the Somme, Arras and Givenchy, but was unhappily killed in action in March 1917. He was entitled to the 1914–15 Star, and the General Service and Victory Medals.
"His memory is cherished with pride."
8, St. Clement's Place, Ancoats, Manchester. Z7581

NEWTON, W., Private, 2nd East Yorks Regiment.
He joined the Army in July 1916, and on completion of a period of training at Catterick was later in the same year drafted to the West Indies. There he was employed on important garrison duties, and later was sent to South America, where he also rendered valuable services. On returning to England in January 1920, he was demobilised, holding the General Service Medal. Z10878
33, Windsor Street, Rochdale Road, Collyhurst, Manchester.

NICHOLLS, H. (Sen.) Bandsman, 1/8th Lancashire Fus.
Volunteering in August 1914, he was unable to procure a transfer overseas on the conclusion of his training at Crowborough, but served with the Labour Corps at Guildford and Gloucester, at which stations he was engaged on important and responsible work in the stores department. After nearly five years' service in the Army he was demobilised in April 1919. 32, Eliza Ann Street, Rochdale Road, Manchester.
Z10879C

NICHOLLS, H. (Jun.), Sergt., 6th Lancashire Fusiliers.
He volunteered in January 1915, and was retained on important duties in England, until January 1917, when he was drafted overseas. During his service on the Western Front he took a prominent part in engagements on the Ancre front, and was unhappily killed in action at Arras on May 19th, 1917. He was entitled to the General Service and Victory Medals.
"Whilst we remember the sacrifice is not in vain."
32, Eliza Ann Street, Rochdale Road, Manchester. Z10879A

NICHOLLS, J., Private, 8th East Lancashire Regt.
Volunteering in September 1914, he proceeded in the following June to the Western Front, and in this theatre of war participated in many severe actions in various sectors in France and Belgium. He performed consistently good work until he was invalided home in July 1917, on account of ill-health, and after spending some time in hospital at Cardiff was discharged in November 1917, holding the 1914–15 Star, and the General Service and Victory Medals.
25, Cross Street, Bradford, Manchester. Z9659

NICHOLLS, J., Private, Royal Defence Corps.
He volunteered in October 1914, but owing to ineligibility for general service was posted to the Royal Defence Corps. On the completion of his training he was engaged on guard and other duties at various prisoner of war camps and hospitals, and rendered valuable services until December 1918, when he was discharged. 8, Oak St., Hulme, Manchester. TZ11784

NICHOLLS, P., Pte., 18th King's (Liverpool Regt.)
He joined in March 1917, and in the same month was drafted to France. During his service overseas he fought in the third Battle of Ypres, on the Somme and at Cambrai, and in various engagements in the Retreat and Advance of 1918. He was sent home suffering from the effects of fever contracted in December 1918, and was demobilised in February of the following year. He holds the General Service and Victory Medals. 24, Clayton St., Hulme, Manchester. Z7488

NICHOLLS, S., Private, 9th Manchester Regiment.
Volunteering in October 1914, he was drafted to Salonika in September of the following year, and whilst in this theatre of war was engaged with the Transport Section in conveying rations and ammunition up to the front lines. He served in numerous engagements, but was severely wounded, and was invalided to hospital in Salonika. After his recovery he did duty with the Transport in the Balkans until the conclusion of hostilities, and returning to England was demobilised in April 1919. He holds the 1914–15 Star, and the General Service and Victory Medals.
37, Adelaide Street, Hulme, Manchester. TZ7489

NICHOLLS, W., Private, 19th Manchester Regiment.
In April 1915 he volunteered, and eight months later proceeded to the Western Front, where he took an active part in numerous important engagements in different sectors of the war zone. He was engaged in severe fighting at Carnoy, the Somme and Bray, and remained in France until February 1919, when he was demobilised, holding the 1914–15 Star, and the General Service and Victory Medals.
7, Drinkwater Street, Harpurhey, Manchester. Z11441

NICHOLLS, W. Trooper, Westmoreland and Cumberland Hussars.
He joined in February 1917, and after a period of training at Cupar and Fife, proved to be unsuccessful in procuring a transfer to a theatre of war. He was retained on Home Defence, and was engaged on important guard duties at Cork, Killarney and Maryborough, and throughout the period of his service carried out his work with great ability. He was demobilised in October 1919.
32, Eliza Ann Street, Rochdale Road, Manchester. Z10879B

NICHOLSON, A., Pte., K.O. (Royal Lancaster Regt.)
He volunteered in November 1914, and in the following September was drafted to France, when he saw much service. He took part in the fighting at Loos, Albert and Vimy Ridge, and was wounded in the Battle of the Somme in July 1916, and was shortly afterwards again wounded at Guillemont in December of the same year. He was also in action at Beaumont-Hamel, Beaucourt, Arras, Bullecourt, Messines and Ypres, where he received his third wound and was invalided to hospital at Rouen. He again rejoined his unit and fought at Cambrai, the Somme, Bapaume and Ypres, and in the final operations until the Armistice was signed. He was demobilised in February 1919, and holds the 1914–15 Star, and the General Service and Victory Medals.
3, Gladstone Street, Brooks Bar, Manchester. Z7490

NICHOLSON, J., Pte., 8th King's (Liverpool Regt.)
He volunteered in February 1915, and three months later was drafted to France. There he took part in many important engagements, including Ypres, Albert, the Somme, Beaumont-Hamel, Arras, Cambrai and Passchendaele, and in many sectors during the Retreat and Advance of 1918. He was demobilised on his return home in March 1919, and holds the 1914–15 Star, and the General Service and Victory Medals.
14, Teignmouth Street, Collyhurst, Manchester. Z9660

NICHOLSON, P., Private, Lancashire Fusiliers.
Volunteering in September 1914, he crossed to France in the following September, and served there for a month. He was then drafted to Salonika, and in this theatre of war took part in the Serbian Retreat of December 1915, and in other engagements in the Balkans, and was mentioned in Despatches for bravery in the Field. Invalided to England on account of wounds received in action in May 1918, he received hospital treatment and was discharged as medically unfit for further service in November of that year. He holds the 1914–15 Star, and the General Service and Victory Medals.
56, Ravald Street, Miles Platting, Manchester. Z11785

NICHOLSON, T. H., Private, Labour Corps.
He joined in June 1917, and in the same month was drafted to France. During his service overseas he was engaged on important duties in road and trench repairs, and was frequently in the battle areas, notably at Ypres, Passchendaele, Cambrai and Givenchy. He returned home and was demobilised in March 1919, holding the General Service and Victory Medals.
4, Chapel Grove, Lower Openshaw, Manchester. Z7491

NICKEAS, T., Private, 8th Manchester Regiment.
He joined in July 1916, and after his training served at various stations on important duties with his unit. He rendered valuable services, but owing to serious heart trouble was discharged as medically unfit for further duty in March 1917.
28, Devonshire Street, Hulme, Manchester. TZ7495

NICKEAS, G. E., L/Corpl., 2nd E. Lancashire Regt.
He volunteered in May 1915, and in January of the succeeding year proceeded to Egypt, where he served in various operations until October 1917. when he was drafted to the Western Front. Whilst in France he took part in much of the heavy fighting at Ypres, and was severely wounded and invalided home to hospital. He rejoined his unit in France in February 1918, and was in action in the Retreat and Advance of that year. He was demobilised in February 1919, and holds the General Service and Victory Medals.
25, Thomas Street, West Gorton, Manchester. Z7492

NICKERSON, L. A., Pte., K.O. Scottish Borderers.
He enlisted in July 1914 in the Bedfordshire Regiment, but was two years afterwards transferred to the King's Own Scottish Borderers, and embarked for France in June 1916. Whilst on the Western Front he fought on the Ancre, at Albert and Vimy Ridge, and was wounded at Messines in July 1917. After his recovery he rejoined his unit and was in action on the Scarpe and the Sambre, and in the final operations until the Armistice was signed. He holds the General Service and Victory Medals, and was discharged in November 1918.
62, Nellie Street, Ardwick, Manchester. Z7493

NICKLESS, W., Private, 2nd E. Lancashire Regt.
Joining in September 1916, he embarked for France in March of the following year. During his service on the Western Front he took part in much of the severe fighting at Vimy Ridge, Bullecourt, Messines, Ypres, Passchendaele and Cambrai, and was almost continuously in action in the Retreat and Advance of 1918. He holds the General Service and Victory Medals, and was demobilised in February 1919.
4, Marcus Grove, Rusholme, Manchester. Z7494

NIELD, H., Special War Worker.
From the outbreak of hostilities until the Armistice was signed he was engaged on important and responsible work at Messrs. James Hill's Works at Oldham, Manchester. His duties which consisted in transporting ammunition to the stations for shipment overseas, were carried out with commendable efficiency, and his valuable services were highly appreciated. 18, Markham St., Ardwick, Manchester. Z7496

NIGHTINGALE, A., Private, 8th Manchester Regt.
He joined in May 1917, and in the following August was drafted to France. Owing to physical disability he was unable to take part in the fighting, but was engaged on important and responsible guard duties over German prisoners and ammunition dumps. He served principally at Ypres, Etaples, Péronne and Soissons until the cessation of hostilities, and in February 1919 returned home. He was then demobilised and holds the General Service and Victory Medals. Z7497
2, Blackburn Street, Marple Street, Hulme, Manchester.

NIHILL, W. Private, 12th Manchester Regt.
He volunteered in July 1915, and in the following April was drafted to France, where he saw much fighting. He fought at Albert, Vermelles, Ploegsteert Wood and Vimy Ridge, and died gloriously on the Field of Battle during the Somme Offensive on July 6th, 1916. He was entitled to the General Service and Victory Medals.
"A costly sacrifice upon the altar of freedom."
29, Foster Street, City Road, Hulme, Manchester. Z7498

NIMS, F. W., Corporal, Middlesex Regiment.
He volunteered in 1915, and on completion of his training was in the following year drafted to India. He was stationed there for over three years, and during that time served at Lucknow, where he performed the various duties allotted to him in a highly capable manner. He also rendered valuable services as a signaller, and on his return to England in 1919, was demobilised, holding the General Service and Victory Medals. Z10880B
34, Lamb Street, Richmond Grove, Longsight, Manchester.

NIMS, H. H., Sergt., Middlesex Regiment.
Volunteering at the outbreak of hostilities in August 1914, he proceeded overseas in the following year. Whilst serving on the Western Front he fought with distinction in the engagements in the Ypres, Somme, Albert and Cambrai sectors, and was wounded in action. He remained in France until demobilised in 1919, and holds the 1914–15 Star, and the General Service and Victory Medals. Z10880A
34, Lamb Street, Richmond Grove, Longsight, Manchester.

NIXON, A., Private, Royal Fusiliers.
He joined in May 1917, and after his training was completed proceeded to France in February of the succeeding year. Whilst in this theatre of war he took part in much severe fighting in the Retreat of 1918, and was taken prisoner in May. He was held in captivity until after the Armistice, when he was released and was then sent to Mesopotamia, but unfortunately contracted an illness from the effects of which he subsequently died on June 26th, 1920. He was entitled to the General Service and Victory Medals.
"Thinking that remembrance, though unspoken, may reach him where he sleeps."
118, Bennett's Street, Ardwick, Manchester. Z7502

NIXON, J., Gunner, R.F.A.
Volunteering in 1914, he was sent overseas in September of that year, and in 1916 was transferred to the Trench Mortar Section. He was gassed at Bullecourt, and reported missing, and was afterwards presumed to have been killed in action in that engagement, but was later found to be a prisoner of war. With the help of some French civilians, he managed to escape from his captors, and reached the British lines early in 1919. He holds the 1914 Star, and the General Service and Victory Medals. X7499
78, Higher Temple Street, Chorlton-on-Medlock, Manchester.

NIXON, J., Private, 5th King's (Liverpool Regiment).
When war broke out he was engaged on important mining work at Bradford Colliery, Manchester, and consequently was not released for military service until April 1917. He did not succeed in securing a transfer overseas, but nevertheless, performed excellent work at Oswestry and Pembroke Docks. He also rendered valuable services in connection with coast defence, and was demobilised in December 1918.
122, Edensor Street, Beswick, Manchester. Z10881

NIXON, J. W., Pioneer, R.E.
He joined in September 1917, and in the following month was drafted to France, where he was engaged on important duties in connection with the operations, and was in the front line at Ypres, attached to an Australian Division. He also served at Rouen with the Railway Operating Division, and at various other places. After the cessation of hostilities he remained in France until November 1919, when he returned home and was demobilised. He holds the General Service and Victory Medals.
27, Berwick Street, Chorlton-on-Medlock, Manchester. Z7501

NIXON, R., Private, Loyal N. Lancashire Regiment.
He volunteered in September 1914, and a year later was sent to France. He was in action at Vimy Ridge, the Somme, the Ancre, Beaumont-Hamel, Arras, Ypres, Cambrai, Bapaume Amiens and the second Battle of Le Cateau. Returning home he was demobilised in February 1919, and holds the 1914–15 Star, and the General Service and Victory Medals.
36, Gibbon Street, Bradford, Manchester. Z7500

NIXON, R., Rifleman, 8th Rifle Brigade.
He volunteered in September 1914, and in the following January was drafted to the Western Front, where he took part in the engagements at Neuve Chapelle, Hill 60, Loos and the Somme. He was wounded at Hill 60 and Loos, and very severely in July 1916 in the Battle of the Somme, and was invalided home to hospital. After receiving protracted medical treatment he was discharged as physically unfit for further duty in January 1918, and holds the 1914–15 Star, and the General Service and Victory Medals.
14, Beattie Street, Oldham Road, Manchester. Z9304

NOBLETT, G., Private, Lancashire Fusiliers.
He volunteered in August 1914, and in July of the following year proceeded to the Western Front, where after taking part in numerous engagements in various sectors he contracted bronchitis. On recovering from this illness he was transferred to the 218th Divisional Employment Company in June 1917, and was engaged on important duties until the Armistice was signed, notably at Douai. He holds the 1914–15 Star, and the General Service and Victory Medals, and was demobilised in January 1919.
9, Holt Street, Bradford, Manchester. Z7503

NODEN, C., Corporal, M.G.C.
He joined in February 1917, and after his training was engaged on Home Service duties prior to proceeding to the Western Front in March of the following year. There he was in action in the Battles of the Marne (II), Havrincourt Wood, Epéhy, Le Cateau (II) and others during the German Offensive and subsequent Allied Advance of 1918. He was demobilised in October 1919, and holds the General Service and Victory Medals. 7. Walter Street, Hulme, Manchester. Z11786

NOLAN, D., Private, K.O. (Royal Lancaster Regt.)
He volunteered in August 1914, and in the following November was sent to Salonika. After taking part in the operations on the Doiran front, he proceeded in May 1915 to Mesopotamia, and was in action at Kut, Sanna-i-Yat and Baghdad, and was wounded. On recovery he rejoined his unit and remained in the East until his return for demobilisation in February 1919. He holds the 1914–15 Star, and the General Service and Victory Medals.
3, Vance Street, Oldham Road, Manchester. Z9306

NOLAN, J., Corporal, 19th Lancashire Fusiliers.
He volunteered in June 1915, and in the following December proceeded to the Western Front. After being in action at Loos, Albert, Vimy Ridge, Arras, Bullecourt, Messines and Ypres, he was gassed at Nieuport in April 1918, and taken captive to Germany. After his release, he was engaged at various camps in England on guard duties over German prisoners of war. He holds the 1914–15 Star, and the General Service and Victory Medals, and was demobilised in September 1919. 8, Bury St., City Road, Hulme, Manchester. Z7504

NOLAN, M., L/Corporal, East Lancashire Regiment.
He joined in January 1916, and after serving for about two years as an Instructor in musketry was drafted to Salonika in December 1917. He died gloriously on the Field of Battle on the Doiran front, on February 28th, 1918, and was buried at Coral Hill Cemetery in Greece. He was entitled to the General Service and Victory Medals.
" His life for his Country, his soul to God."
52, Middlewood Street, Harpurhey, Manchester. Z11559

NORBURY, J., Sapper, R.E.
He enlisted in the Border Regiment in March 1917, and was drafted to France in June of the same year. He was then transferred to the Royal Engineers and was engaged on special duties in connection with the main water supply to various hospitals, notably those at St. Omer, Calais, Arras and Cambrai. He was demobilised in February 1919, and holds the General Service and Victory Medals.
21, Higher Chatham Street, Chorlton-on-Medlock, Manchester. Z7505

NORMAN, G. F. (M.M.),Private, Lancashire Fusiliers.
At the outbreak of hostilities in August 1914, he was already serving, and was at once ordered to the Western Front. There he fought with distinction in the Battles of Mons, Le Cateau, La Bassée, Ypres (I, II, and III), Vimy Ridge, the Somme, Arras, Bullecourt and Messines, and in the Retreat and Advance of 1918. He was awarded the Military Medal for conspicuous gallantry in the Field, and was discharged in February 1919, holding also the Mons Star, and the General Service and Victory Medals.
79, Ryder Street, Collyhurst, Manchester. Z10882

NORMAN, J., Private, 26th Manchester Regiment.
He joined in June 1916, and in the following February crossed over to France, where he saw considerable service. He took part in much of the heavy fighting at Arras and Ypres, and in August 1917 was very severely wounded and invalided home to hospital. After his recovery he was retained on home defence duties in Wales, and was subsequently demobilised in May 1919. He holds the General Service and Victory Medals. 42, Ashover Street, Ardwick, Manchester. Z7508

NORMAN, J. E., Driver, R.A.S.C. (M.T.)
He was mobilised at the outbreak of hostilities, and was almost immediately drafted to France, where he was present at the Retreat from Mons. He also served at La Bassée, Albert, Ypres, Armentières, St. Eloi, Hill 60, Festubert, and Cambrai. He was blown up at Arras, and from 1917 acted as Despatch Rider until the cessation of hostilities. In April 1919 he returned home and was discharged, holding the Mons Star, and the General Service and Victory Medals.
5, Exmouth Street, Ancoats, Manchester. Z7507

NORMAN, J. E., A.B., Mercantile Marine.
He was already in the Merchant Service at the outbreak of hostilities, and during the war did duty in various ships, and was engaged in conveying food supplies across the seas, passing frequently through mine-infested areas. On two occasions his ship was torpedoed, but fortunately he was rescued on each occasion. He also served in the Admiralty Voluntary Service in connection with gunnery, and was retained until October 1920. He holds the General Service and the Mercantile Marine War Medals, and in 1920 was still in the Mercantile Marine.
29, John Street, Ardwick, Manchester. Z7032A

NORMAN, J. W., Special War Worker.
During the war he held a responsible position at Messrs. Allen and Harrison's Munition Works at Hulme, Manchester, and was engaged on highly dangerous duties in the T.N.T. shell filling department. This work severely affected his health, but he continued his service. He was physically unfit for joining the Army owing to varicose veins, but did valuable work of National importance at home, and in 1920 he was still in the employ of this firm.
211, Warde Street, Hulme, Manchester. Z7506A

NORMAN, M. (Mrs.), Special War Worker.
In October 1914 this lady offered her services, and was engaged at Messrs. Wood and Harris'at Manchester in the manufacture of khaki suits. After about a year's service she went to the Munition Works in Bangor Street, Hulme, and was engaged on important duties in connection with the output of 6-inch shells. She rendered valuable services until December 1918, when, owing to the cessation of hostilities, she was discharged.
211, Warde Street, Hulme, Manchester. Z7506B

NORMOYLE, W., Private, 21st Manchester Regt.
He volunteered in April 1915, and thirteen months later was sent to the Western Front, where he was wounded in the Battle of Bullecourt. On returning to the firing line he was in action in engagements at the Vimy Ridge, Beaumont-Hamel, Somme, Arras, Messines, Cambrai and Amiens sectors. He was discharged in August 1917 as medically unfit for further service, holding the General Service and Victory Medals.
61, Irlam Street, Miles Platting, Manchester. Z10883

NORMOYLE, W., Private, 21st Manchester Regt.
Volunteering in February 1915, he proceeded two months later to the Western Front. He served in that theatre of war for over two years, and during that time took part in heavy fighting

at Loos, Vermelles, Vimy Ridge, the Somme and Bullecourt. He was severely wounded in action at Arras in May 1917, and in consequence was invalided out of the Army in August 1917, holding the 1914-15 Star, and the General Service and Victory Medals.
61, Irlam Street, Miles Platting, Manchester. Z10884

NORMYLE, W., Gunner, Tank Corps.
He joined in May 1916, and early in the following year was sent to the Western Front. In this theatre of war he participated in heavy fighting at Bullecourt, Ypres and Cambrai, and was also in action at many places during the Advance prior to the Armistice. He remained overseas until September 1919, when he was demobilised, holding the General Service and Victory Medals.
28, Pearson Street, Newton Heath, Manchester. Z9661

NORRIS, J., Sapper, R.E.
He joined in October 1916, and after his training served at various stations on important duties with his unit. He rendered valuable services, but owing to medical reasons was unable to obtain a transfer overseas, and was demobilised in January 1919.
3, Olive Grove, Hulme, Manchester. Z7509

NORRIS, W. H., Sapper, R.E.
He volunteered in April 1915, and after his training served at various stations on important duties with his unit. He was engaged on the barge boats in conveying food supplies for the troops, and did valuable work. In November 1917 he was discharged on account of service.
10, Watson Street, West Gorton, Manchester. Z7510

NORRIS, O. S., Private (Shoeing Smith), M.G.C.
He volunteered in June 1915, and in the following July was drafted to France, where he saw service at Ypres and Loos. He contracted dysentery and was treated in hospital at Rouen and afterwards invalided home. On recovery in January 1916 he was engaged on important duties at various home stations until December 1918, when he was demobilised. He holds the 1914-15 Star, and the General Service and Victory Medals.
53, Barlow Street, Bradford, Manchester. Z7511

NORTH, B., Private, 2nd Manchester Regiment.
Volunteering in August 1914, he was drafted to France in March of the following year, and whilst overseas fought in various engagements. He was in action at La Bassée, Givenchy, Loos, Ypres and the Somme, and in many subsequent battles before the cessation of hostilities. He holds the 1914-15 Star, and the General Service and Victory Medals, and was demobilised in January 1919.
19, Walter Street, Ancoats, Manchester. Z7512

NORTON, A. H., Private, 7th Manchester Regiment.
He enlisted the day before war was declared, and in October 1914 was drafted to Egypt. In February of the following year he was sent to the Dardanelles, and was severely wounded in the third Battle of Krithia. He was one of a batch of six runners who were sent with a vital message during the fierce fighting, and he alone returned alive with the reply Despatch, his Captain being killed as he handed him the message. He was then invalided to hospital at Lemnos and Malta, and thence to England. He was discharged as medically unfit for further duty in June 1916, and holds the 1914-15 Star, and the General Service and Victory Medals.
15, Harper Place, Hulme, Manchester. TZ7513

NORTON, A. N., Private, 7th Manchester Regiment.
He volunteered in November 1914, and in April of the following year was drafted to the Western Front. There he experienced fierce fighting in different sectors of the line, and was in action at Festubert, Loos, Vimy Ridge, the Somme, Arras, Bullecourt, Messines, Ypres, Passchendaele and Cambrai. He was wounded on one occasion and also served in the Retreat and Advance of 1918. Demobilised in December 1918, he holds the 1914-15 Star, and the General Service and Victory Medals.
109, Ryder Street, Collyhurst, Manchester. Z10886

NOWELL, S., Private, Labour Corps.
He volunteered in August 1915, and in the following November was drafted to the Western Front. During his service in France he was engaged in various sectors until December 1917, when he was blown up and suffered severely from shell-shock. He was invalided home, and discharged as medically unfit for further duty in March 1918, and holds the General Service and Victory Medals.
2, Dennison Street, Rusholme, Manchester. TZ7514

NUTTALL, F., Private, 16th Welch Regiment.
He joined in February 1917, and on conclusion of his training was two months later drafted overseas. Whilst serving on the Western Front he took an active part in severe fighting at Arras and Bullecourt, and was unfortunately killed in action at Cambrai in November 1917. He was entitled to the General Service and Victory Medals.
" A valiant Soldier, with undaunted heart he breasted life's last hill."
4, Chesshyre Street, Ancoats, Manchester. Z11048B

NUTTALL, J., Driver, R.A.S.C.
He joined in August 1917, and on completion of his training at Aldershot, proceeded to Salonika in January 1918. Eight months later, whilst engaged in heavy fighting on the Vardar front he was severely wounded and invalided to England. On his recovery he was retained on Home Service, and was eventually demobilised in September 1919, holding the General Service and Victory Medals.
4, Chesshyre Street, Ancoats, Manchester.　　Z10887

NUTTALL, T., Drummer, Lancashire Fusiliers.
He volunteered in June 1915, and after his training served at various stations on important duties with his unit. He rendered valuable services, but was not successful in obtaining a transfer overseas before the cessation of hostilities, and was demobilised in February 1919.
26, Devonshire Street, Hulme, Manchester.　　TZ7515

NUTTALL, W., Private, York and Lancaster Regt.
He volunteered in December 1914, and in July of the following year was drafted to France, where he fought at Loos, Vimy Ridge, Albert, the Somme, Arras, Ypres and Cambrai, and was gassed in action. He also took part in the 2nd Battles of the Somme, the Marne, Cambrai and Le Cateau, in the Retreat and Advance of 1918. He was demobilised in February of the following year, and holds the 1914–15 Star, and the General Service and Victory Medals.
8, Sandal Street, Ancoats, Manchester.　　Z7582

NUTTALL, W., L/Corpl., K.O. (R. Lancaster Regt.)
He volunteered in January 1915, and was sent to France two months later. Whilst on the Western Front he took part in the Battles of Festubert and Loos, and in March 1916 proceeded to Salonika. In this theatre of war he saw service on the Doiran front, in the Advance across the Struma, and in the Offensive on the Vardar. He contracted dysentery and after the Armistice was invalided home to hospital suffering from that complaint. He was discharged as medically unfit for further service in December 1918, and holds the 1914–15 Star, and the General Service and Victory Medals.　　Z7516
33, Lower Chatham Street, Chorlton-on-Medlock, Manchester.

NUTTALL, W. A., Private, 7th Manchester Regt.
Having previously served in the South African War he was mobilised in September 1914, and immediately drafted to Egypt, where he served at Alexandria, and in the Sudan. In April 1915 he was transferred to Gallipoli and fought in the Battles of Cape Helles and Krithia. He was severely wounded at Achi Baba in May 1915, and succumbed to his injuries two days later. He was entitled to the Queen's and King's South African Medals, 1914–15 Star, and the General Service and Victory Medals.
30, Lancashire Street, Newton Heath, Manchester.　　Z10888

NUTTER, C., Driver, R.F.A.
He volunteered in September 1915, and in February of the following year proceeded to France, where he did good work as a driver in engagements at St. Eloi, Vermelles, the Somme, Arras and Lens. He was severely injured on the Somme through a kick from a horse, which was terrified by the bursting of shells during the battle in June 1916, and was invalided home and subsequently discharged in March 1918. He holds the General Service and Victory Medals.
12, Thorpe Street, Ardwick, Manchester.　　Z7517

O

OAKES, A. W., Private, Manchester Regiment.
He volunteered in February 1916, and in the following July proceeded to India and was engaged on important garrison duties at Rawal Pindi, Kirkee, Cawnpore and other stations. During his service he was transferred from the King's Own Royal Lancaster Regiment to the Royal Irish Rifles. He returned to England in October 1919, and in 1920 was serving in the Manchester Regiment, and holds the General Service Medal.　131, Hillkirk Street, Ardwick, Manchester.　Z7518B

OAKES, F. S., Private, R.A.S.C. (M.T.)
He volunteered in May 1915, and ten days after enlisting proceeded to France. Whilst overseas he was engaged as Mechanical Storekeeper in the Motor Transport section, and served at Rouen, Abbeville, Calais, and also was present at many operations in the Retreat and Advance of 1918. Returning home he was demobilised in April 1919, and holds the 1914–15 Star, and the General Service and Victory Medals.
131, Hillkirk Street, Ardwick, Manchester.　　Z7518A

OAKES, W., Air Mechanic, R.A.F.
After having served as a packing case manufacturer on important Government work, he joined the Army in January 1917, and was engaged as a mechanic in the Royal Air Force in the production of aeroplane parts. He also did important work in the Quarter-Master's Stores, and rendered valuable services. Owing to illness caused by the burning at night of the aerodrome in which he was stationed, he was invalided to hospital, and subsequently discharged as unfit for further duty in July 1919.
106, Marsland Street, Ardwick, Manchester.　　TZ7519

OAKES, J., Private, Border Regiment.
He volunteered in August 1914, and in March of the following year was drafted to France, where he fought in engagements at Neuve Chapelle, Ypres, Givenchy, Loos and Bullecourt. In November 1917 he was sent to Italy and was in action on the Piave, and wounded in the Battle of the Asiago Plateau. After his recovery he continued his service in Italy until January 1919, when he was sent to England and demobilised. He holds the 1914–15 Star, and the General Service and Victory Medals.　24, Marsland Street, Ardwick, Manchester.　Z7520

OAKLEY, R., Private, Sherwood Foresters.
He joined in July 1916, and proceeding to the Western Front in the following February, fought in the Battles of Arras, Bullecourt, Ypres, Passchendaele, Cambrai, and was gassed. On recovery he was in action in the German Offensive and subsequent Allied Advance, during which he was taken prisoner at Bapaume in August 1918. Held in captivity in Germany, he was demobilised after his repatriation in January 1919, and holds the General Service and Victory Medals.
21, Heald Avenue, Rusholme, Manchester.　　Z11787

OARTON, H., Driver, R.A.S.C.
He volunteered in September 1915, and in March of the following year was drafted to the Western Front. Whilst overseas he served on the Belgian Coast and in engagements at Vimy Ridge, and Ypres. He was severely wounded in action in 1917, and was invalided to hospital in France, and in July 1918 to hospital in Scotland. After the Armistice he remained at home, and was demobilised in June 1919, holding the General Service and Victory Medals.
72, Bennett Street, Ardwick, Manchester.　　Z7521B

OARTON, W., Private, Manchester Regiment.
He joined in November 1916, and after his training was completed embarked for France in December of the following year. During his service on the Western Front he served through the Allied Retreat in March 1918, and was in action at the commencement of the Advance in the following August. He gave his life for the freedom of England on the 23rd of that month, and was entitled to the General Service and Victory Medals.
"The path of duty was the way to glory."
22, Bennett Street, Ardwick, Manchester.　　Z7521A

O'BRIEN, E., Private, 2/5th Manchester Regiment.
Volunteering in March 1915, he was retained at home on important duties until September 1916, when he proceeded to France. There he was in action at Beaumont-Hamel, Arras, Albert, Vimy Ridge, Ypres, and Passchendaele, and was taken prisoner during an engagement on the Somme in March 1918. He was interned in Germany until December 1918, and was eventually demobilised in April 1919, holding the General Service and Victory Medals.
80, Sudell Street, Rochdale Road, Manchester.　　Z9662

O'BRIEN, F. J., Pte., 11th Loyal N. Lancashire Regt.
Volunteering in November 1914, he proceeded to Gallipoli in August of the following year, and whilst in this theatre of war took part in the Landing at Suvla Bay and in the attack on Chunuk Bair. He died gloriously whilst fighting at "Chocolate Hill" on November 27th, 1915, and was entitled to the 1914–15 Star, and the General Service and Victory Medals.
"Whilst we remember, the sacrifice is not in vain."
2, Napier Street, Ardwick, Manchester.　　Z7525

O'BRIEN, G., Private, 11th Manchester Regiment.
He volunteered in September 1915, and in the following December was drafted to Egypt, where he was stationed on important duties at Cairo until November 1916, when he proceeded to the Western Front. During his service in France he fought in the Somme sector, and at Arras, and died gloriously on the Field in the third Battle of Ypres in September 1917. He was entitled to the General Service and Victory Medals.
"A costly sacrifice upon the altar of freedom."
71, Birch Street, Ardwick, Manchester.　　Z7522B

O'BRIEN, J., Private, Lancashire Fusiliers.
He volunteered in August 1914, but a few months later was invalided out of the Service on account of ill-health. He, however, rejoined in 1917, and proceeding shortly afterwards to France, participated in strenuous fighting in the Somme sector, and at Arras, Armentières and Cambrai. As a result of being wounded at Albert he was invalided home and subsequently discharged in consequence of his injuries and shell-shock. He holds the General Service and Victory Medals.
35, Jersey Street Dwellings, Manchester.　　Z11560C

O'BRIEN, J., Private, Lancashire Fusiliers.
Volunteering at the outbreak of hostilities, he was drafted to Gallipoli on the completion of his training in April 1915. During his service on the Peninsula he fought in all the Battles of Krithia, and was severely wounded in the last in June 1915. He was sent to hospital in Gallipoli, and was later invalided home, and subsequently discharged as medically unfit for further military service in June 1916. He holds the 1914–15 Star, and the General Service and Victory Medals.
137, Armitage Street, Ardwick, Manchester.　　Z7524B

O'BRIEN, H., Private, 2nd Manchester Regiment.
He was mobilised at the outbreak of hostilities, and was almost immediately drafted to France. After taking part in the Retreat from Mons, he was in action in the Battle of the Marne and was wounded at Ypres. He was invalided home, but returning later fought at Hill 60, and was then sent to Mesopotamia. He was unfortunately killed in action in an engagement on March 4th, 1916, and was entitled to the Mons Star, and the General Service and Victory Medals.
" The path of duty was the way to glory."
10, Stott Street, Hulme, Manchester. Z7527

O'BRIEN, J., Private, 2nd Manchester Regiment.
When war was declared in August 1914, he was already serving in the Army, and was accordingly sent with the first Expeditionary Force to France. There he was in action at St. Eloi, Festubert and Neuve Chapelle, and was mortally wounded in the Battle of Ypres on October 27th, 1914. He was entitled to the 1914 Star, and the General Service and Victory Medals. " Great deeds cannot die."
45, Kemp Street, Manchester. Z10889

O'BRIEN, J., Private. Loyal N. Lancashire Regt.
He volunteered in August 1914, and in the following December was drafted to France, where he fought in the Battles of Neuve Chapelle and Loos, and was severely wounded and invalided home to hospital. After his recovery he was sent to German East Africa, and later proceeding to Egypt, took part in the British Advance into Palestine under General Allenby, and was wounded in the Battle of Gaza. Subsequently he returned to the Western Front, and was wounded a third time during the Advance on July 29th, 1918. He was discharged as time expired in August 1920, and holds the 1914-15 Star, and the General Service and Victory Medals.
12, Goodiers Street, Ancoats, Manchester. Z7586

O'BRIEN, J. E., Private, 4th Manchester Regiment.
Volunteering in August 1914, he embarked for Gallipoli in April of the following year, and during his service on the Peninsula took part in the first Landing, in all the Battles of Krithia, and in the attack on Chunuk Bair. After the Evacuation of the Dardanelles he proceeded to Egypt, and was engaged on the Suez Canal, at Katia, in the Capture of El Fasher and at Romani. In July 1917 he was sent to the Western Front, and was severely wounded in action in the third Battle of Ypres in November of the same year. He was invalided home to hospital and discharged as medically unfit for further service in January 1918. He holds the 1914-15 Star, and the General Service and Victory Medals.
137, Armitage Street, Ardwick, Manchester. Z7524A

O'BRIEN, R. F., Sergt., 13th K. (Liverpool Regt.)
He volunteered early in August 1914, and in the following March proceeded to the Western Front. Whilst in France he took part in, and was wounded, in the second Battle of Ypres, and also fought at Albert, Vimy Ridge, and on the Somme. He was severely wounded again at Beaucourt in November 1916 and was invalided home to hospital, and subsequently discharged as medically unfit for further service in February 1917. He holds the 1914-15 Star, and the General Service and Victory Medals.
3, Queen's Street, Higher Ardwick, Manchester. Z7526

O'BRIEN, S., Rifleman, King's Royal Rifle Corps.
He volunteered in September 1914, and in the following March was drafted to France. During his service on the Western Front he fought in the second Battle of Ypres, at Festubert and Albert, and was wounded on the Somme in July 1916. After his recovery he rejoined his unit and was again wounded in the third Battle of Ypres in November 1917. He was invalided to hospital in Scotland, and after receiving medical treatment was discharged as physically unfit for further military duty in August 1918. He holds the 1914-15 Star, and the General Service and Victory Medals.
128, Tame Street, Ancoats, Manchester. Z7523

O'BRIEN, T., Private, 8th Manchester Regiment.
He joined in November 1916, and after a period of training was drafted to the Western Front, where he was in action at Lens, Loos, Hill 60, and Neuve Chapelle, and was wounded at Ypres in July 1917. Invalided home, he later returned to France and after taking part in further fighting, was again wounded at Ypres in October 1918. Evacuated to England he was discharged shortly afterwards, holding the General Service and Victory Medals.
35, Jersey Street Dwellings, Manchester. Z11560A

O'BRIEN, T., Corporal, 13th K. (Liverpool Regt.)
He volunteered in December 1915, and on conclusion of a period of training at Oswestry was drafted overseas in the following year. During his service in France he was engaged in fierce fighting in the Somme sector, and was unhappily killed in action at Guillemont on August 16th, 1916. He was entitled to the General Service and Victory Medals.
" His life for his Country."
74, Bold Street, Chorlton Road, Old Trafford, Manchester. Z10981

O'BRIEN, W., Private, King's (Liverpool Regiment).
Volunteering in September 1914, he afterwards was sent to France, and in this theatre of war played a prominent part in many important engagements, including the Battles of Ypres, Festubert, Hill 60 and St. Eloi. He was wounded at Loos in October 1915, was sent home and returning to France upon his recovery, was again in action at Albert, Lens, Armentières, Cambrai and Bourlon Wood. Demobilised in 1919, he holds the 1914-15 Star, and the General Service and Victory Medals.
35, Jersey Street Dwellings, Manchester. Z11560B

O'BRYAN, J. T., Private, E. Lancashire Regiment.
He volunteered in January 1915, and on completion of his training at Preston, was drafted overseas in the following year. During his service on the Western Front he was wounded in the Battle of Ypres, and invalided to hospital in London. On his recovery he returned to France, but was unhappily killed in action on July 1st, 1916, during the Somme Offensive. He was entitled to the General Service and Victory Medals.
" His life for his Country, his soul to God."
12, Pratley Street, Ravald Street, Ancoats, Manchester. Z10890

O'CONNELL, J. T., Private, Lancashire Fusiliers.
He joined in August 1916, and after a period of training was three months later sent to the Western Front, where he served for over two years. During that time he was in action in many important engagements, including those on the Somme and at Lens, Ypres, Cambrai, the Aisne, the Marne, Amiens, Bapaume, Havrincourt and Le Cateau. He was demobilised in February 1919, and holds the General Service and Victory Medals. 49, Burton St., Rochdale Rd., Manchester. Z10892

O'CONNOR, A., Pte., R.A.S.C., and Manchester Regt.
He joined in November 1918, in the Royal Army Service Corps, and after his training was transferred to the Manchester Regiment, and was engaged on important duties at various stations. He rendered valuable services, but owing to physical disabilities was invalided to hospital and subsequently discharged in February 1920.
105, Broadfield Road, Moss Side, Manchester. Z7532

O'CONNOR, J. (M.M.), Corporal, R.E.
Volunteering in November 1914, he served on the Western Front from January 1916 until June 1919. During this period he was engaged on important duties in connection with the operations, and was frequently in the forward areas, notably in the Battles of the Somme and Cambrai, and in various engagements in the Retreat and Advance of 1918. He was awarded the Military Medal for conspicuous bravery and devotion to duty, and holds in addition the General Service and Victory Medals. He was demobilised in June 1919, and has since been employed in France in attending to the British Soldiers' graves.
105, Broadfield Road, Moss Side, Manchester. Z7531

O'CONNOR, J. F., Private, 7th Lancashire Fusiliers.
He volunteered in September 1914, and in April of the following year was sent to the Dardanelles. He took part in the first Landing at Gallipoli, and was also in action in the third Battle of Krithia, but was reported missing after the engagement, and later was presumed to have been killed in action on June 4th, 1915. He was entitled to the 1914-15 Star, and the General Service and Victory Medals.
" His memory is cherished with pride."
65, Park Street, Hulme, Manchester. Z7530B

O'CONNOR, M., Private, Border Regiment.
He volunteered in November 1914, and in February 1916 was drafted to France. During his service on the Western Front he fought at Albert, and Vimy Ridge, but died gloriously on the Field in the Battle of the Somme on July 30th, 1916. He was entitled to the General Service and Victory Medals.
" A costly sacrifice upon the altar of freedom."
10, Billington Street, Chorlton-on-Medlock, Manchester. Z7528

O'CONNOR, P., Signaller, R.F.A.
In April 1918 he joined the Army, and after a period of training at Preston was drafted overseas in the following November. During his four months' service in France he performed good work as a signaller, and on his return to England was engaged on important telephonic duties. He was demobilised in November 1919, and holds the General Service and Victory Medals. 323, Mill Street, Bradford, Manchester. Z10893

O'CONNOR, T., Private, 6th E. Lancashire Regt.
Volunteering in November 1914, he was unfortunately unable to continue his training owing to defective eyesight, and was discharged in January 1915. After considerable improvement in this respect he rejoined in July 1918, and was engaged on important duties at various stations until April 1919, when he was again discharged for the same cause.
37, Mark Street, Hulme, Manchester. Z7529

OFFICER, T., L/Corporal, 1st Border Regiment.
He joined in November 1916, and was employed on various duties at different home stations until December 1917. He was then drafted to the Western Front, where he participated in heavy fighting on several Fronts, and did good work until he fell in action near Merville on April 11th, 1918. He was entitled to the General Service and Victory Medals.
" His life for his Country."
82, Leather Street, Miles Platting, Manchester. Z9307

OFSEANEY, J., Private, K.O. (Y.L.I.)
Joining in December 1917, he underwent a course of training at York, and in March 1918 was sent to Malta. There he was employed with his unit on garrison and other duties of an important nature, and rendered excellent service until he returned home for demobilisation in March 1919, holding the General Service and Victory Medals.
14, Stonehewer Street, Rochdale Road, Manchester. Z9308

O'GARA, P., Private, 22nd Manchester Regiment.
He volunteered in January 1915, and after his training was engaged on important duties until February of the following year, when he was drafted to India. He suffered from chest trouble, and after rendering valuable services at various garrison outposts in India unfortunately died of bronchial pneumonia in April 1917., He was entitled to the General Service Medal.
27, Wood Street, Hulme, Manchester. Z7533

OGDEN, A., Private, 21st Manchester Regiment.
Volunteering in November 1914, he was drafted a year later to the Western Front, where he took part in numerous engagements, including the Battles of Vermelles and High Wood. He was wounded in action on the Somme in July 1916, and in consequence was discharged as medically unfit for further military duties in April 1918. He holds the 1914-15 Star, and the General Service and Victory Medals.
15, Tonge Street, Ancoats, Manchester. Z10894A

OGDEN, A. E., Private, 5/20th Manchester Regt.
He volunteered in January 1915, and in the following November was sent to the Western Front, where he saw heavy fighting in the Albert, Somme, Beaumont-Hamel and Bullecourt sectors. He died gloriously on the Field of Battle at Maricourt on July 18th, 1916, and was entitled to the 1914-15 Star, and the General Service and Victory Medals.
"He died the noblest death a man may die,
Fighting for God, and right, and liberty."
217, Morton Street, Longsight, Manchester. Z10424D

OGDEN, E., Private, R.A.S.C.
He joined in December 1915, and after a period of training was engaged at various stations on important duties with his unit. He was unable to obtain a transfer overseas owing to his being medically unfit, but rendered valuable services until his discharge in February 1918.
22, Roseberry Street, Gorton, Manchester. Z11938

OGDEN, G., Pte., 1st Manchester Rgt., and Sapr.,R.E.
He was mobilised at the outbreak of hostilities, and was almost immediately drafted to France, where he took part in the Retreat from Mons. He also served in the Battles of the Marne, the Aisne, La Bassée, Ypres, Neuve Chapelle, St. Eloi, Hill 60, and Vimy Ridge, and was wounded in the Battle of the Somme in October 1916. He was invalided home to hospital and after his recovery did garrison duty at various stations until his demobilisation in March 1919. He holds the Mons Star, and the General Service and Victory Medals.
174, Viaduct Street, Ardwick, Manchester. Z7539

OGDEN, H., Private, Border Regiment.
Volunteering in January 1915, he was drafted later in the same year to France, where he served in the Battles of Albert, Ypres, and Cambrai. In 1916 he was transferred to Salonika, and was engaged in severe fighting in various sectors of the Front until the cessation of hostilities. On his return to England in 1919 he was demobilised, holding the 1914-15 Star, and the General Service and Victory Medals.
217, Morton Street, Longsight, Manchester. Z10424A

OGDEN, H., Private, Manchester Regiment.
He volunteered in October 1914, and in September of the following year was drafted to the Western Front. Whilst in France he took part in many important engagements, including those at Albert, the Somme, Messines and Passchendaele, and was gassed in action at Cambrai in November 1917. After his recovery he was in action in the Retreat and Advance of 1918. He was demobilised in March 1919, and holds the 1914-15 Star, and the General Service and Victory Medals.
21, Tunstall Street, Longsight, Manchester. Z7535

OGDEN,H.,Pte., 8th Manchester Rgt., and Sapr.,R.E.
He volunteered in November 1914, and for over two years was engaged on important guard duties at various munition works. In February 1917 he was drafted to France, and served in the forward areas whilst operations were in progress, notably at Arras, Ypres, Cambrai, and the Somme. After the Armistice was signed he proceeded to Germany and was stationed on the Rhine until March 1919, when he returned to England, and was demobilised. He holds the General Service and Victory Medals.
7, Bunyan Street, Ardwick, Manchester. Z7540

OGDEN, T., Corporal, R.E.
He volunteered in May 1915, but was not successful in procuring a transfer to the fighting area. During his period of service he was stationed at Colchester, Bristol, Salisbury Plain, Codford and Oswestry, where he was employed on important clerical duties. He was eventually demobilised from Bristol in December 1918.
217, Morton Street, Longsight, Manchester. Z10424B

OGDEN, M., Private, 21st Manchester Regiment.
He volunteered in December 1915, and on completion of his training was drafted to the Western Front in May of the following year. After taking part in the Battle of Vimy Ridge, he was unfortunately killed in action on the Somme in July 1916. He was entitled to the General Service and Victory Medals.
"His memory is cherished with pride."
15, Tonge Street, Ancoats, Manchester. Z10894B

OGDEN, O. O., Private, 16th Manchester Regiment.
In May 1915, he volunteered for active service, and seven months later was ordered to the Western Front, where he was in action in the Somme sector, and was wounded at Maricourt in June 1916. On his return to the firing line he did good work with his unit at Arras, Ypres and Passchendaele, and in the Retreat and Advance of 1918. After the Armistice he served at Charleroi until demobilised in February 1919, and holds the 1914-15 Star, and the General Service and Victory Medals.
22, Shipley Street, Harpurhey, Manchester. Z10895

OGDEN, S. H., Private, Manchester Regiment.
He volunteered in November 1914, and in May 1917 proceeded to France. Whilst overseas he took part in the Battles of Arras, Ypres, the Somme Retreat, and in various engagements in the Advance up to October 1918, when he was wounded in the Somme sector. He was invalided home to hospital, and later discharged from the Army as medically unfit for further duty in August 1919. He holds the General Service and Victory Medals.
30, Libby Street, Lower Openshaw, Manchester. Z7538

OGDEN, T., Petty Officer, R.N.
A serving Sailor since June 1901, he sailed to the South Atlantic in September 1914, and was in action in the Battle of the Falkland Islands. He later returned to the North Sea, and fought in the Battles of the Dogger Bank, Jutland and Heligoland Bight. During his service he did duty in the "Defiance," and also in submarines, and was wounded in December 1916, when his vessel was torpedoed. He holds the 1914-15 Star and the General Service and Victory Medals, and in 1920 was still in the Navy. 29, Matthew St., Ardwick, Manchester. Z7536

OGDEN, W., Private, 1st Manchester Regiment.
He enlisted in June 1912, and soon after the declaration of war was drafted to France, where he took part in the Battles of La Bassée, Ypres, St. Eloi, Loos, Vermelles, and the Somme. During his service he was three times wounded, in September 1914, and at Ypres in May 1915, and again when buried through shell explosion on the Ancre front. He was then invalided home to hospital, and discharged later as medically unfit for further duty in May 1917. He holds the 1914 Star, and the General Service and Victory Medals.
15, Wellesley Street, West Gorton, Manchester. TZ7537

O'GRADY, H., Private, York and Lancaster Regt.
He joined in January 1918, and in the following June landed in France, where he was in action in many parts of the line during the German Offensive and subsequent Allied Advance of 1918. Severely wounded in August 1918, he returned to England, and after receiving hospital treatment was demobilised in February 1919. He holds the General Service and Victory Medals.
29, Stonehewer Street, Rochdale Road, Manchester. Z9148

O'HAGAN, G., Private, 5th Royal Irish (Lancers).
He enlisted in April 1907, and when war broke out proceeded with his Regiment to France, and fought in the Retreat from Mons, and the Battles of the Marne and the Aisne. He was also in action at Ypres, Loos, and the Somme, and was severely wounded in October 1917. Invalided home, he was discharged as medically unfit in July 1918, and holds the Mons Star, and the General Service and Victory Medals.
35, Allen Street, Hulme, Manchester. TZ7541

O'HANLON, J., Private, 1/7th Manchester Regt.
He volunteered in August 1915, and in the following May was drafted to the East, where he took part in the operations on the Suez Canal. In March 1917 he proceeded to the Western Front, and there fought in numerous engagements, including the Battles of the Somme, and Ypres, and in the Retreat of 1918, during which he was wounded. After receiving hospital treatment, he was demobilised in January 1919, and holds the General Service and Victory Medals.
36, George Street, Newton, Manchester. Z7584

O'HARE, B., Guardsman, Welch Guards.
He joined in June 1918, but was not successful in obtaining a transfer to a theatre of war before the termination of hostilities. Later, however, he was sent to Germany and served with the Army of Occupation at Cologne and Bonn, performing consistently good work until he was demobilised in November 1919. 25, Masonic Street, Miles Platting, Manchester. Z9309B

O'HARE, J. T., Guardsman, Irish Guards.
Joining in June 1918, he was after a period of training, employed on garrison and other important duties in London and Warley. Owing to the termination of fighting, he was not sent overseas, but rendered valuable services at home until he was demobilised in January 1919.
25, Masonic Street, Miles Platting, Manchester. Z9309A

OLBINSON, G. E., L/Corpl., Lancashire Fusiliers.
He volunteered in December 1915, and in April of the following year was drafted to France, where during the fighting on the Ancre he was wounded. He was invalided home, and on recovery returning to the Western Front, served in the Armentières sector until the Armistice. Demobilised in February 1919, he holds the General Service and Victory Medals.
54, Caroline Street, Hulme, Manchester. Z7542

OLDERSHAW, R., Private, Lancashire Fusiliers.
Volunteering in July 1915, he was drafted overseas in February of the following year, and whilst serving on the Western Front, took part in important engagements at Loos, Albert, Vermelles, Vimy Ridge, the Somme, Beaumont-Hamel, Ypres and Cambrai. He was wounded in action on two occasions, and was demobilised in February 1919, but re-enlisted in January 1920. He holds the General Service and Victory Medals.
87, Jersey Street Dwellings, Ancoats, Manchester. Z10896

OLDFIELD, A., Corporal, 6th Manchester Regiment.
He volunteered in July 1915, and was first drafted to Egypt, where he served for about a year. Proceeding to France in December 1916, he saw service in many sectors of the Front, and was engaged on important duties as a butcher until demobilised in February 1919. He holds the 1914-15 Star, and the General Service and Victory Medals.
13, Palmerston Street, Moss Side, Manchester. Z7543C

OLDFIELD, B., C.Q.M.S., Rifle Brigade.
Having served for twenty one years, he re-joined on the outbreak of war and in May of the following year proceeded to France. He served with the 7th Service Battalion, but was seriously wounded in November 1915, and died at Etaples from his injuries shortly afterwards. He was entitled to the 1914-15 Star, and the General Service and Victory Medals, and was already in possession of the Indian and South African Medals.
"A costly sacrifice upon the altar of freedom."
3, Grove Street, Rusholme, Manchester. Z7544

OLDFIELD, J. W., Private, R.A.S.C., and Rifleman, Royal Irish Rifles.
Volunteering in August 1914, he was drafted in the following month to France and served at Boulogne on important duties for two years. He then proceeded up the line and took part in the fighting at Messines and Ypres, where he was wounded in August 1917. He was invalided home, and after receiving hospital treatment, was demobilised in February 1919, holding the 1914-15 Star, and the General Service and Victory Medals.
13, Palmerston Street, Moss Side, Manchester. Z7543A

OLDFIELD, S., Private, 10th Lancashire Fusiliers.
He volunteered in March 1915, and in the following July sailed for France, where he saw much service. He was in action at Loos, Vimy Ridge, Beaumont-Hamel, Beaucourt, Arras, Ypres, and Cambrai, and in the Retreat and Allied Advance of 1918. He was demobilised in February 1919, and holds the 1914-15 Star, and the General Service and Victory Medals.
13, Palmerston Street, Moss Side, Manchester. Z7543B

OLDHAM, A., Private, 8th Manchester Regiment.
He was called up from the Reserve in August 1914, and in the following year was sent to Gallipoli. There he took part in numerous engagements and was wounded at Suvla Bay in August 1915. He proceeded to France in January 1916, and experienced fierce fighting in the Somme Offensive, and in the Battle of Ypres. He was discharged in March 1918, and holds the 1914-15 Star, and the General Service and Victory Medals.
34, Dalton Street, Collyhurst Road, Manchester. Z10897

OLDHAM, A., Private, 19th Manchester Regiment.
He volunteered in January 1916, and was drafted overseas four months later. Landing in France he was in almost continuous action in the Somme Offensive, and was wounded at Guillemont on July 23rd, 1916, Rejoining his Battalion on recovery he was engaged in heavy fighting in the Battles of Arras, Messines, Ypres, and the Somme (II), and was wounded again at Gommecourt on May 1st, 1918. Invalided home for treatment he returned to the Western Front in the following October and after the Armistice proceeded into Germany with the Army of Occupation, and was stationed at Cologne. He was demobilised in September 1919, and holds the General Service and Victory Medals.
84, Church Street, Hulme, Manchester. Z11788

OLDHAM, C., Sergt., 4th Manchester Regiment.
He volunteered in September 1914, and after a period of training was sent to India in the following March. Whilst there he was engaged on important transport duties at various stations, and did excellent work. In March 1918 he proceeded to Russia, where he was frequently in action. Returning home in April 1919, he was demobilised, and holds the General Service and Victory Medals.
81, Thomas Street, Miles Platting, Manchester. TZ7547

OLDHAM, G., Private, 6th Lancashire Fusiliers.
He joined in August 1917, and on conclusion of his training was drafted to the Western Front, where he was in action in many important engagements in different sectors of the war zone. He also fought in the Battle of Arras, and was taken

prisoner in May 1918. He remained in captivity until October 1919, and on his release was demobilised a month later, holding the General Service and Victory Medals.
6, Boughton Street, Ancoats, Manchester. Z10898

OLDHAM, I., Private, 15th Lancashire Fusiliers.
Volunteering in August 1914, he was drafted to France in the following May and fought in the engagements at Ypres, Festubert, Loos, Vermelles, Albert, Ploegsteert Wood, and Vimy Ridge. He gave his life for King and Country in the Battle of the Somme in July 1916, and was entitled to the 1914-15 Star, and the General Service and Victory Medals.
"He passed out of the sight of men by the path of duty and self-sacrifice."
24, Beecher Street, Queens Park, Manchester. Z11561A

OLDHAM, J., Private, 3rd Manchester Regiment.
He volunteered in February 1915, and seven months later proceeded to Gallipoli, where he was in action at Suvla Bay. He was invalided to England in December 1915, suffering from frost-bite, which resulted in the amputation of three toes. On his discharge from hospital he rendered valuable services in the Royal Defence Corps at Liverpool and Palling-on-Sea. He was demobilised in February 1919, and holds the 1914-15 Star, and the General Service and Victory Medals.
58, Beaumont Street, Beswick, Manchester. Z10899

OLDHAM, J., Private, South Wales Borderers.
Volunteering in August 1914, he embarked for Salonika in September of the following year, and took part in the fighting on the Doiran and Vardar fronts. During the Advance across the Struma he was unfortunately killed in action on October 23rd, 1916. He was entitled to the 1914-15 Star, and the General Service and Victory Medals.
"Whilst we remember the sacrifice is not in vain."
73, Thomas Street, Miles Platting, Manchester. Z7546

OLDHAM, J., L/Corporal, 7th E. Lancashire Regt.
He volunteered in September 1914, and after a year's service at home, was drafted to France, where he was wounded during the fighting at Loos. On recovery he returned to the firing line and fought in many engagements, notably on the Menin Road, where he was again wounded. He was taken to No. 153 Clearing Station, but unhappily succumbed to injuries on September 23rd, 1917. He was entitled to the 1914-15 Star, and the General Service and Victory Medals.
"The path of duty was the way to glory."
40, Boundary Street East, Chorlton-on-Medlock, Manchester. TX7545A

OLDHAM, J. W., L/Corpl., K.O. (R. Lancaster Regt.)
Volunteering in January 1915, he proceeded ten months later to the Western Front, where he was wounded in the Ypres salient in March 1916. He was sent back to hospital in England, but on recovery was retained on Home Service, and performed excellent work in connection with stores at Kinmel Park and Abergele. He was demobilised in March 1919, holding the 1914-15 Star, and the General Service and Victory Medals.
65, Beaumont Street, Beswick, Manchester. Z10900

OLDHAM, W., Air Mechanic, R.A.F. (late R.F.C.)
Having previously been rejected three times, he joined in October 1917, and after the completion of his training was drafted to France. There he served on various important duties with his unit, and was stationed for a time at Le Havre, Rouen and Etaples. Returning home, he was demobilised in November 1919, and holds the General Service and Victory Medals.
40, Boundary Street East, Chorlton-on-Medlock, Manchester. TX7545B

OLDLAND, G., Private, Manchester Regiment.
He had previously served for twenty-one years and on the declaration of war volunteered for further service. He was engaged on important duties in training and instructing recruits and rendered very valuable services. Owing to ill-health he was sent to hospital, and on March 24th, 1919, died of consumption.
114, Thomas Street, Miles Platting, Manchester. Z7548

OLDRICH, J. A., Private, Manchester Regt., and King's (Liverpool Regiment).
Volunteering in January 1915, he embarked in the following year for France, where he saw much active service. He took part in the Battles of the Somme, St. Quentin, and numerous other engagements, including those during the German Offensive of 1918, until the cessation of hostilities. Demobilised in February 1919, he holds the General Service and Victory Medals. 18, Whittaker St., Chorlton-on-Medlock, Manchester. TZ6320B

O'LEARY, J., Private, Hampshire Regiment.
He enlisted in November 1906, and in March 1915 was drafted to the Dardanelles, where during the heavy fighting against the Turks he was wounded. He was first sent into hospital at Cairo, and eventually to England, and after receiving treatment was discharged as medically unfit in February 1916, owing to wounds. He holds the 1914-15 Star, and the General Service and Victory Medals.
13, Princess Street, Rusholme, Manchester. Z7549

O'LEARY, T., Private, 1st Manchester Regiment.
He had previously served for twelve years, and at the commencement of war volunteered in the Cheshire Regiment, but was shortly afterwards discharged as unfit. Later he rejoined, and in January 1915, proceeded to France, and was in action at Neuve Chapelle, Loos, and Albert. Sent in March 1916, to Mesopotamia, he saw much fighting at Kut, and was unhappily killed in action on the Tigris in March 1916. He was entitled to the 1914-15 Star, and the General Service and Victory Medals.

"He died the noblest death a man may die,
Fighting for God, and right, and liberty."
81, Norton Street, West Gorton, Manchester. Z7550

OLIVER, C. V., A.B., Royal Navy.
He volunteered in September 1914, and was posted to H.M.S. "Tiger," in which he served throughout the war. He was in action in the Battle of Heligoland Bight, the Falkalnd Isles, the Dogger Bank, and later in the great Battle of Jutland, and afterwards was engaged on various important duties until after the conclusion of hostilities. In 1920 he was still serving and holds the 1914-15 Star, and the General Service and Victory Medals. 5, Roy St., Ardwick, Manchester. Z7552B

OLIVER, E. J., Private, King's (Liverpool Regt.)
He volunteered in August 1915, and in May of the following year proceeded with his Regiment to France. There he fought at Vimy Ridge, the Somme, Arras, Ypres and Cambrai, and in the Retreat and Advance of 1918, and was afterwards transferred to the 75th Canadian Forestry Corps, with which he served until demobilised in February 1919. He holds the General Service and Victory Medals.
10, Barlow Street, Lower Openshaw, Manchester. Z7551

OLIVER, H., Private, 8th Manchester Regiment.
Joining in October 1916, he crossed to France in the following January, and whilst there fought in many engagements. He was in action at Arras, Ypres, Lens, the Scarpe and Cambrai, and was wounded on the Scarpe. Returning home in March 1919, he was demobilised, and holds the General Service and Victory Medals.
8, Rowen Street, Ardwick, Manchester. Z7556

OLIVER, J., Stoker, R.N.
He joined in July 1918, on attaining the required age, and was sent to Chatham, where he was engaged on important work. He also served at other Naval stations, notably at Harwich, and was employed as a stoker, but was not able to obtain a transfer to a fighting unit on account of his age. In 1920 he was still serving.
5, Roy Street, Ardwick, Manchester. Z7552A

OLIVER, T. E., Private, 3rd Manchester Regiment.
A Reservist, he was mobilised when war broke out, and crossing to the Western Front shortly afterwards was engaged in heavy fighting in the first Battle of Ypres. Severely wounded in this action he was sent to hospital at Bristol, and then to Seymour Road Second Western General Hospital. Discharged as medically unfit for further service in September 1916, he holds the 1914 Star, and the General Service and Victory Medals.
31, Burns Street, Bradford, Manchester. TZ11789

OLIPHANT, F., Pte., 10th Durham Light Infantry.
He volunteered in August 1915, and after a period of training served at various stations on important guard and other duties throughout the war. He was not successful in obtaining his transfer overseas before hostilities ceased, but rendered valuable services until demobilised in January 1919.
72, Everton Road, Chorlton-on-Medlock, Manchester. Z7555

OLIPHANT, R., Pioneer, R.E.
He volunteered in August 1915, and in the same month sailed for France, where he was engaged on making roads. He served at Albert, Ypres, Cambrai, Armentières, Passchendaele and Havrincourt, but in April 1918 was discharged through causes due to his service. He holds the 1914-15 Star, and the General Service and Victory Medals.
72, Everton Road, Chorlton-on-Medlock, Manchester. Z7554

OLLERTON, H., Private, 2nd Manchester Regt.
Mobilised on the outbreak of war, he was at once drafted with his Regiment to France, and during the memorable Retreat from Mons was killed in action early in September 1914. He was entitled to the Mons Star, and the General Service and Victory Medals.

"His name liveth for evermore."
22, Mallow Street, Hulme, Manchester. TZ7553

OLSEN, W., Driver, R.A.S.C. (M.T.)
He joined in July 1918, on attaining military age, and after his training served on various important duties. Later he proceeded to Germany, where he was engaged in transporting supplies to the Army of Occupation at Cologne. After rendering valuable services he was demobilised in December 1919. 49, Walnut Street, Hulme, Manchester. Z7557

OLVER, W. P., Private, 2/6th Manchester Regt. and King's (Liverpool Regt.)
Volunteering in February 1915, he proceeded overseas in the following April, and whilst in France saw much heavy fighting.

He was in action at Hill 60, Ypres, Loos, Vimy Ridge, the Somme and Arras, and was wounded, and sent into hospital at Rouen. On recovery, he returned to the trenches, and took part in many other engagements until hostilities ended. Demobilised in February 1919, he holds the 1914-15 Star, and the General Service and Victory Medals.
37, Addison Street, Chorlton-on-Medlock, Manchester. Z7558

O'NEIL, F., Private, 19th (Queen Alexandra's Own Royal) Hussars.
Volunteering in August 1914, he landed in France in the same month, and was in action in the Retreat from Mons, and the Battles of the Marne, La Bassée, Ypres, Neuve Chapelle, and was gassed in May 1915. On recovery he fought in several engagements, including those at Loos, Vimy Ridge, Cambrai, the Somme, and in the Retreat and Advance of 1918. Returning to England in December 1918, he was demobilised a month later, and holds the Mons Star, and the General Service and Victory Medals.
122, Bedford Street, Hulme, Manchester. Z11790

O'NEILL, A. V., Gunner, R.F.A.
Volunteering in February 1915, he embarked on the completion of his training to the Western Front, and there took part in many fierce engagements, including those at La Bassée, Givenchy and Festubert. For a time he was stationed at Dunkirk, but was invalided home through ill-health in February 1918, and in the following May was discharged as medically unfit. He holds the General Service and Victory Medals. 12, Walworth Street, Ardwick, Manchester. Z7559

O'NEILL, F. J., Gunner, R.F.A.
Volunteering at the outbreak of war, he embarked in the following month for Egypt, and during the operations on the Suez Canal was wounded. After receiving hospital treatment he was able to rejoin his unit, and in October 1916 proceeded to France, where he fought in many Battles, including those of the Somme and Ypres, and was twice wounded. After hostilities ended he was drafted to India, and was engaged on important garrison duties until his return home for demobilisation in November 1919. He holds the 1914-15 Star, and the General Service and Victory Medals.
23, Redvers Street, Ardwick, Manchester. Z7563

O'NEILL, G., Private, 13th Cheshire Regiment.
He was mobilised in August 1914, and shortly afterwards was sent to France, where he took part in the Retreat from Mons, the Battles of Armentières, Ypres, Hill 60, Albert, Vimy Ridge, the Somme, Arras and Cambrai. He was also in action throughout the Retreat and Advance of 1918, and during his service in France was wounded on four occasions. He was demobilised in June 1919, and holds the Mons Star, and the General Service and Victory Medals.
5, Newman Street, Ancoats, Manchester. TZ11562

O'NEILL, J., Private, 2nd Manchester Regiment.
Mobilised at the commencement of war, he was drafted with the First Expeditionary Force to France, and fought in the Retreat from Mons, and many of the subsequent Battles, during the course of which he was twice wounded. In 1915 he was transferred to the R.F.A. (Trench Mortar Battery) with which he proceeded to Salonika, and took part in the fighting on the Doiran front. Returning home in February 1919, he was demobilised, and holds the Mons Star, and the General Service and Victory Medals.
17, Helsby Street, Ardwick, Manchester. Z7561

O'NEILL, J., Private, Lancashire Fusiliers.
Volunteering in August 1914, he served after a course of training on important guard and garrison duties in Ireland. He was not successful in obtaining a transfer to a fighting unit before hostilities ceased, but rendered very valuable services throughout, and was demobilised in December 1918.
5, Collinge Street, Newton, Manchester. Z7585

O'NEILL, J., Private, King's (Liverpool Regiment).
He joined in February 1917, and a month later was drafted to France, where he served for eleven months. During that time he took an active part in severe fighting at Arras, Bullecourt, Ypres and Cambrai. In February 1918 he returned home, and after undergoing an operation contracted influenza, and was sent to hospital in London. He was demobilised in January 1919, and holds the General Service and Victory Medals. 43, Great Jackson St., West Gorton, Manchester.
Z10902

O'NEILL, J., Private, 13th Manchester Regiment.
He volunteered in May 1915, and on completion of his training four months later, was drafted to Salonika. There he took an active part in fierce fighting in numerous important engagements, chiefly on the Doiran, Struma, Monastir, and Vardar fronts. He was wounded in action in April 1917, and returned to England in October 1919. Two months later he was demobilised, holding the 1914-15 Star, and the General Service and Victory Medals.
58, Heyrod Street, Ancoats, Manchester. Z10903

O'NEILL, J., Private, 8th Manchester Regiment.
He volunteered in September 1914, and was drafted overseas in the following May. Serving with his unit on the Western Front he took part in the Battles of Ypres, Loos, Vermelles, the Somme, and was wounded at Bullecourt in June 1917. After treatment he rejoined his Battalion and served at Lens, Cambrai and other places until invalided home owing to medical unfitness for further service, in consequence of which he was discharged in July 1918. He holds the 1914–15 Star, and the General Service and Victory Medals.
7, Knoll Street, Rochdale Road, Manchester.   Z11791

O'NEILL, J., Private, Loyal North Lancashire Regt.
He volunteered in August 1914, and after a course of training was drafted to the Western Front. He served there for a short period, and was then sent to Gallipoli, where he was unfortunately killed in action at Suvla Bay on November 27th, 1915. He was entitled to the 1914–15 Star, and the General Service and Victory Medals.
"Honour to the immortal dead, who gave their youth that the world might grow old in peace."
113, Gunson Street, Ancoats, Manchester.   Z10901

O'NEILL, P., Private, 2nd Manchester Regiment.
Volunteering in August 1914, he crossed in the following December to France. There he fought in notable engagements at Neuve Chapelle, Ypres, Loos and St. Eloi, but was killed in action during the Somme Offensive in July 1916. He was entitled to the 1914–15 Star, and the General Service and Victory Medals.
"His life for his Country."
27, Hulme Street, Ancoats, Manchester.   Z7560

O'NEILL, P., Corporal, 3rd Border Regiment.
At the outbreak of hostilities in August 1914, he was already serving, and was immediately drafted to the Western Front. On this Front he was in action in the Battles of Mons, Ypres, St. Eloi, Neuve Chapelle, Festubert, Maricourt, Loos and Vimy Ridge, and fell fighting in the Battle of the Somme on July 1st, 1916. He was entitled to the Mons Star, and the General Service and Victory Medals.
"Courage, bright hopes, and a myriad dreams splendidly given."
11, Almond Street, Gorton, Manchester.   Z10904

O'NEILL, R., Driver, R.G.A.
He volunteered in October 1915, and in December of the same year was drafted to the Western Front. During his service in this theatre of war he fought in many engagements, including those on the Somme, and at Arras, Ypres and Cambrai, and in the Retreat and Advance of 1918, and was wounded twice. Demobilised in February 1919, he holds the General Service and Victory Medals.
4, Peter Street, Openshaw, Manchester.   Z7562B

O'NEILL, T., Private, 8th Manchester Regiment.
He volunteered in August 1914, and after a course of training was drafted in the following year to Gallipoli, where during the Landing at Suvla Bay he was unhappily killed in action in May 1915. He was entitled to the 1914–15 Star, and the General Service and Victory Medals.
"His life for his Country, his soul to God."
26, Daniel Street, Hulme, Manchester.   Z7564

O'NEILL, W., Signaller, R.F.A.
He volunteered in May 1915, and in July of the following year sailed for France, where he took part in much of the heavy fighting. He was present during the Battles of the Somme, Arras, Bullecourt, and many others until hostilities ceased, and returned home in March 1919. He was demobilised in that year and holds the General Service and Victory Medals.
4, Peter Street, Openshaw, Manchester.   Z7562A

ORCHARD, E., Sergt., 20th Lancashire Fusiliers
He volunteered in September 1914, and in the following year was sent to France, where he was in action at Hill 60, Ypres, St. Eloi, Vimy Ridge, the Somme, Arras, Bullecourt, Cambrai, the Marne, Bapaume and Havrincourt, and was wounded. He was demobilised in February 1919, and holds the 1914–15 Star, and the General Service and Victory Medals.
4, Holme Street, Ancoats, Manchester.   Z7566

ORCHARD, H. J., Private, 7th E. Lancashire Regt.
He volunteered in September 1914, and was drafted to France in the following year. After being in action at Loos, he was then sent to Salonika, where he took part in the fighting on the Doiran front, and was also in the Advance across the Struma, and later contracted malaria. He was demobilised in March 1919, after his return home, and holds the 1914–15 Star, and the General Service and Victory Medals.
5, Park Street, Hulme, Manchester.   Z7565

ORFORD, T., Sapper, R.E.
He was mobilised in August 1914, and shortly afterwards was sent to France, where he was in action at Mons, and in the subsequent Retreat and also at La Bassée, and was wounded at Ypres. After his recovery he took part in the Battles of Neuve Chapelle, Festubert and Loos, but was again wounded.

He afterwards served in the Somme, Arras, Ypres and Amiens sectors, and was demobilised in December 1918. He holds the Mons Star, and the General Service and Victory Medals.
8, Bradshaw Street, Hulme, Manchester.   Z7567

ORMAN, J. A., Private, Lancashire Fusiliers.
He volunteered in September 1914, and was retained on important duties at Barrow-in-Furness until December 1915, when he was sent overseas. During his service on the Western Front he was wounded on three occasions, whilst fighting in the Battles of Ypres and the Somme. He also took part in engagements at St. Eloi, Albert, Arras, Vimy Ridge, and in the 1918 Retreat and Advance. Demobilised in April 1919 he holds the 1914–15 Star, and the General Service and Victory Medals. 4, Crook St., Miles Platting, Manchester. Z10905

ORME, A., Private, 1st King's (Liverpool Regt.)
Volunteering in August 1914, he proceeded in January of the following year to France, where he served for four years. During that time he was engaged in severe fighting at Ypres, Festubert, Neuve Chapelle, Loos, Vimy Ridge, the Somme, Beaumont-Hamel, Arras, Delville Wood, Guillemont, Bapaume and Cambrai. He was demobilised in March 1919, and holds the 1914–15 Star, and the General Service and Victory Medals.
59, Thornton Street, Manchester.   Z10906

ORME, G., Rifleman, 6th London Regiment (Rifles).
He joined in March 1917, and after a period of service in Ireland proceeded overseas in the following year. Whilst on the Western Front he experienced fierce fighting in many sectors, and was in action on the Somme and at Albert, Arras, Armentières, Cambrai, and Bourlon Wood. He remained in France until 1919, when he was demobilised, holding the General Service and Victory Medals.
37, Thornton Street, Manchester.   Z10716A

ORME, W., Private, 3rd Welch Regiment.
He joined the Army in July 1916, but on account of ill-health was unable to secure a transfer overseas. He was, however, retained on home defence duties, and throughout the period of hostilities rendered valuable services whilst stationed at Hartlepool, Redcar and in South Wales. He was eventually demobilised from Ripon in March 1919.
9, Montague Street, Collyhurst, Manchester.   Z10907

ORMROD, A. E., Private, 1/7th Manchester Regt.
He volunteered in May 1915, and three months later proceeded to the Western Front. In this theatre of hostilities he played a prominent part in many important engagements, including Loos, St. Eloi, Ploegsteert Wood, and Vimy Ridge, and in actions on the Ancre and Somme fronts, before he was unfortunately killed by a shell in March 1918. He was entitled to the 1914–15 Star, and the General Service and Victory Medals.
"Whilst we remember the sacrifice is not in vain."
21, Prescott Street, West Gorton, Manchester.   Z9310A

ORMROD, A. E., Private, R.A.V.C.
He joined in October 1917, and in the following year was drafted to France. Whilst there he was stationed at Calais, and was engaged in attending to convalescent horses. Remaining on this duty until October 1919 he returned home and was demobilised in October 1919, holding the General Service and Victory Medals.
14, Alpha Street, Hulme, Manchester.   Z7568

ORMROD, J.R., Private, 4th King's (Liverpool Regt.)
Volunteering in May 1915, he was drafted in the following August to France. During his service overseas, he participated in strenuous fighting at Loos, Albert, Vermelles, and on the Somme and Ancre fronts, as well as Arras, Messines Ridge and Ypres, and did good work until he was unhappily killed by a sniper on the Somme front in April 1918. He was entitled to the 1914–15 Star, and the General Service and Victory Medals.
"Great deeds cannot die."
21, Prescott Street, West Gorton, Manchester.   Z9310B

O'ROURKE, H., Private, King's (Liverpool Regt.)
He joined in May 1918, but previously to that time had rendered valuable services in the manufacture of shells at Messrs. Belsize and Co's. After a month's training he was ordered to the Western Front, where he was in action at Ypres, Lens and Cambrai, and in the 1918 Retreat and in the final Allied Advance. He served in France until demobilised in January 1919, holding the General Service and Victory Medals.
9, Cuttell Street, Bradford, Manchester.   Z10908

OSBALDESTON, J. S., Driver, R.A.S.C. (M.T.)
He was mobilised in October 1914, and at once proceeded to France, where he performed excellent work in conveying ammunition and supplies to the forward lines. He was in action at Ypres, the Somme, Arras and Cambrai, and in the Retreat and Advance of 1918. In 1916 he was employed for eight months as chauffeur to Marshal Foch, and in the latter part of 1918 served as an ambulance driver. He was discharged in May 1919, holding the 1914 Star, and the General Service and Victory Medals.
29, Howarth Street, Chorlton-on-Medlock, Manchester. Z10909

OSBORNE, A., Private, 2nd Manchester Regiment.
Having volunteered in June 1915, he was sent to France later in the same year, and took part in the fighting at Loos, St. Eloi, the Somme, the Ancre, Messines and Ypres. In 1917 he was transferred to Italy, and was engaged in the operations on the Asiago Plateau. He was demobilised in March 1919, after his return home, and holds the 1914–15 Star, and the General Service and Victory Medals.
14, Bank Street, Hulme, Manchester.   Z7569

OSBORNE, A. E., Private, 1st King's (Liverpool Regt.)
He volunteered in January 1915, and in November of the same year was drafted to France. After he had seen heavy fighting at Loos and St. Eloi, he unhappily was killed at Albert on March 14th, 1916. He was entitled to the 1914–15 Star, and the General Service and Victory Medals.
" A valiant Soldier, with undaunted heart he breasted life's last hill."
10, Eagle Street, Hulme, Manchester.   Z7570

O'SHAUGHNESSY, J., Pte., 6th Connaught Rangers.
Volunteering in November 1915, he was trained at Cork, and four months later was drafted overseas. During his three years' service on the Western Front he took part in many engagements in various sectors of the Line, including those at Loos, St. Eloi, Albert, the Somme, Arras, Ypres, Cambrai and Amiens. He remained in France until January 1919, and was demobilised a month later, holding the General Service and Victory Medals.
52, Knightley Street, Rochdale Road, Manchester. Z10910

O'TOOLE, J, Private, 1st Manchester Regiment.
He volunteered in November 1914, and on completion of his training at Ashton, and Cleethorpes, was two months later sent to the Western Front. There, after only two months' active service, he fell fighting in the Battle of Neuve Chapelle on March 10th, 1915. He was entitled to the 1914–15 Star, and the General Service and Victory Medals.
" Great deeds cannot die :
They with the sun and moon renew their light for ever."
9, Montague Street, Collyhurst Street, Manchester. Z10911

OUTHWAITE, A., Private, Royal Welch Fusiliers.
Volunteering in August 1914, he proceeded overseas in the following January. Whilst on the Western Front he took part in many engagements, including the Battles of Ypres, Loos, the Somme and Arras. In January 1919 he returned home and was demobilised, holding the 1914–15 Star, and the General Service and Victory Medals.
43, Baguley Street, Miles Platting, Manchester. Z11939

OVEN, A., Private, 20th Manchester Regiment.
Having joined in October 1916, he was sent to France in the following year and took part in the fighting on the Ancre and at Arras, Messines and Passchendaele. He was unfortunately killed in action at Lens in October 1917. He was entitled to the General Service and Victory Medals.
" Whilst we remember, the sacrifice is not in vain."
19, Napier Street, Ardwick, Manchester.   TZ7571C

OVEN, H., Sergt., Royal Irish Fusiliers.
He volunteered in August 1914, and in the following year was sent to Gallipoli. In that theatre of war he took part in the Landing at Cape Helles, the first two Battles of Krithia and the Landing at Suvla Bay, but was unfortunately killed in action during the attack on Chunuk Bair in August 1915. He was entitled to the 1914–15 Star, and the General Service and Victory Medals.
" His life for his Country."
19, Napier Street, Ardwick, Manchester.   TZ7571A

OVEN, J. S., Private, M.G.C.
Having volunteered in August 1914, he was sent to France in December of the same year and was in action at La Bassée, Ypres, St. Eloi, Hill 60, Festubert, Loos, Albert, Vimy Ridge, the Somme, Arras, Messines, Lens and the Lys. He also served in the Retreat and Advance of 1918, but was unfortunately killed in action on the Somme in November 1918. He was entitled to the 1914–15 Star, and the General Service and Victory Medals.
" Steals on the ear the distant triumph song."
19, Napier Street, Ardwick, Manchester.   TZ7571B

OVENS, W., L/Corpl., 17th Manchester Regiment.
He volunteered in September 1914, and in the following year was drafted to France, where he took part in the fighting at Albert, Vermelles and Vimy Ridge. He unhappily fell fighting on the Somme on August 3rd, 1916. He was entitled to the 1914–15 Star, and the General Service and Victory Medals.
" His memory is cherished with pride."
42, Albemarle Street, Moss Side, Manchester.   Z7572

OWEN, D., Private, 8th South Lancashire Regiment.
He volunteered in January 1915, and after a period of training was drafted overseas in the following December. During his service on the Western Front he was engaged in fierce fighting in the Battles of Ypres, the Somme and Albert, and was unfortunately killed in action on July 9th, 1916. He was

entitled to the 1914–15 Star, and the General Service and Victory Medals.
" His life for his Country."
8, Sutton Street, Ancoats, Manchester.   Z10912

OWEN, F., Private, 8th Manchester Regiment.
Joining in June 1916, he was retained on important duties in England until February 1917, when he was sent to Mesopotamia. During his service in this theatre of war he saw much heavy fighting and did good work with his unit in engagements at Kut-el-Amara, Um-el-Hannah, the Tigris and Baghdad. On returning home he was demobilised in April 1919, and holds the General Service and Victory Medals.
8, Tonge Street, Ancoats, Manchester.   Z10913

OWEN, F., Sergt., R.F.A.
He was mobilised in 1914, and in the same year proceeded to Egypt. He served at Cairo and El Kantara and was afterwards transferred to the Dardanelles, where he took part in the Landing at Cape Helles and the actions at Krithia and Achi Baba, and remained there until the Evacuation. In 1917 he was drafted to France and was in action at Arras, Messines and Cambrai. He also took part in the Retreat and Advance of 1918, and was wounded. He was invalided home and discharged in June 1918 owing to his injuries, and holds the 1914–15 Star, and the General Service and Victory Medals.
14, Wilson Street, Bradford, Manchester.   Z7576

OWEN, F., Private, R.A.M.C.
He volunteered in August 1915, and later in the same year was sent to France, where he was engaged on important duties at St. Eloi, Loos, Albert, the Somme, Vimy Ridge, Arras and Ypres, and was wounded. He also took part in the Retreat and Advance of 1918, and afterwards proceeded with the Army of Occupation to Germany. He was demobilised in June 1919, and holds the 1914–15 Star, and the General Service and Victory Medals.
40, Percy Street, Hulme, Manchester.   TZ7577

OWEN, G. E., Driver, R.E.
Having volunteered in September 1914, he was sent to the Dardanelles in the following year, but, after seeing heavy fighting there was transferred later to Salonika and was engaged on the Vardar front. In 1917 he proceeded to Egypt, where he remained until June 1919, when he returned home. He was demobilised in the following month, and holds the 1914–15 Star, and the General Service and Victory Medals.
11, Whitby Street, Ancoats, Manchester.   Z7583

OWEN, H., Private, 8th Manchester Regiment.
He joined in August 1916, and on conclusion of a period of training was two months later sent to the Western Front. There he experienced severe fighting in many sectors and took an active part in important engagements on the Somme, and at Arras, Bullecourt, Ypres, Cambrai, the Marne, Bapaume and Le Cateau. He was demobilised in November 1919, and holds the General Service and Victory Medals.
36, Gray Street, Ancoats, Manchester.   Z10914

OWEN, J., Private, Lancashire Fusiliers.
When war was declared in August 1914, he volunteered, and after training at Southport was ordered to the Western Front. Whilst serving in France, he performed excellent work with his unit, chiefly in the La Bassée, Loos, Albert and the Ancre sectors. In July 1918, owing to ill-health, he was discharged as medically unfit for further service, holding the 1914 Star, and the General Service and Victory Medals.
5, Pexton Street, Collyhurst, Manchester.   Z10915

OWEN, J., L/Corporal, 18th Manchester Regiment.
He volunteered in August 1914, and in May of the following year was sent to the Western Front. There he took part with his unit in severe engagements on many fronts, including Vermelles, Vimy Ridge, the Somme, Arras and Ypres, and rendered excellent service until he made the supreme sacrifice, being killed in action on April 23rd, 1917. He was entitled to the 1914–15 Star, and the General Service and Victory Medals.
" His memory is cherished with pride."
30, Crasen Street, Bradford, Manchester.   Z9311

OWEN, J. J., Private, Worcestershire Regiment.
Having volunteered in August 1914, he was sent to France in November of the same year, and saw much fighting. He gave his life for the freedom of England in the Battle of Neuve Chapelle on March 10th, 1915. He was entitled to the 1914 Star, and the General Service and Victory Medals.
" He died the noblest death a man may die,
Fighting for God and right and liberty."
1, Goldsmidt Street, Chorlton-on-Medlock, Manchester. Z7574B

OWEN, J. J., Private, 12th Manchester Regiment.
He volunteered in January 1915, and proceeding to France later in the same year, was in action on the Somme and at Ypres and Mametz Wood, and was wounded. He was invalided home, and after a period in hospital was discharged in August 1917 owing to his injuries, and holds the 1914–15 Star, and the General Service and Victory Medals.
1, Goldschmidt Street, Chorlton-on-Medlock, Manchester.
Z7574A

OWEN, S., Corporal, 20th Manchester Regiment.
Having volunteered in October 1914, he was sent to France in the following year and took part in the fighting at Albert, Arras, Ypres, Bullecourt and Cambrai, and in other engagements. He was afterwards attached to the Headquarters Staff on clerical duty and was not demobilised until June 1919. He holds the 1914-15 Star, and the General Service and Victory Medals.
43, Baker Street, Longsight, Manchester. Z7575

OWEN, T., Private, 10th Manchester Regiment.
He joined in January 1916, and two months afterwards proceeded to France. In this theatre of war he took a prominent part in strenuous fighting at Nieuport, La Bassée, Loos, Vimy Ridge, Arras and on the Somme front. He was later admitted to hospital at the Base, suffering from fever, from the effects of which he died in May 1918. He was entitled to the General Service and Victory Medals.
" A costly sacrifice upon the altar of freedom."
62, Victoria Square, Oldham Road, Manchester. TZ9312

OWENS, J., Private, R.A.S.C. (M.T.)
He joined in October 1916, and in January of the following year was drafted to France, where he was engaged in the transport of ammunition and supplies to the various Fronts. He unfortunately contracted an illness of which he died suddenly on November 9th, 1918, and was buried in the cemetery at Lille. He was entitled to the General Service and Victory Medals.
" The path of duty was the way to glory."
3, Whitfield Place, Ardwick, Manchester. Z7578

OXX, A., Private, Welch Regiment.
Volunteering in April 1915, he was sent to France in October of the same year and took part in the fighting on the Somme and at Bullecourt. He contracted an illness and was invalided home. After a period in hospital he was discharged owing to his disability, in June 1918, and holds the 1914-15 Star, and the General Service and Victory Medals.
41, Sarah Street, Bradford, Manchester. Z7579

P

PACE, T., Sergt., 6th K.O. (Royal Lancaster Regt.)
Volunteering in August 1914, he was drafted in the following May to the Dardanelles, where he took a conspicuous part in heavy fighting, and was wounded. Invalided home, he was sent to hospital in Aberdeen, and upon his recovery proceeded to Mesopotamia. There he was in action on various Fronts and performed excellent work until he returned home and was demobilised in November 1919, holding the General Service and Victory Medals.
8, Padgate Street, Ancoats, Manchester. TZ9663

PACEY, H., Bombardier, R.F.A.
A Reservist, he was called to the Colours in August 1914, and was immediately drafted to the Western Front, where he fought in the Retreat from Mons. He also took part in the Battles of the Marne, the Aisne, Ypres, Givenchy, Albert, the Somme and Passchendaele, and many other important engagements and was for a time in hospital at Havre. Discharged in May 1919, he holds the Mons Star, and the General Service and Victory Medals.
5, Hey Street, Bradford, Manchester. Z10916

PACKER, W., Private, King's (Liverpool Regiment).
He volunteered in March 1915, and in January of the following year was drafted to France, where he saw severe fighting in various sectors of the Front. He took part in the Battles of Vermelles, Albert, the Somme, Arras, Bullecourt, Ypres, Cambrai, Amiens, Bapaume, Havrincourt and Le Cateau, and many minor engagements until the cessation of hostilities. He was demobilised in August 1919, and holds the General Service and Victory Medals.
56, Gray Street, Ancoats, Manchester. Z10917

PACKHAM, R., Private, 4th King's (Liverpool Regt.)
He volunteered in September 1914, and proceeded to France in the following February. He took part in the Battles of Hill 60 and Ypres (II), and was afterwards engaged at Vimy Ridge and in the 1st Battle of the Somme. In this he was severely wounded, and being invalided to England underwent treatment at various hospitals until discharged as unfit for further service in February 1917. He holds the 1914-15 Star, and the General Service and Victory Medals.
14, Milton Street. Hulme, Manchester. TZ7589

PACKHAM, S., Private, 4th King's (Liverpool Regt.)
Volunteering in August 1914, he was sent to France two months later and saw heavy fighting in the Battles of La Bassée, Ypres (I and II), Hill 60 and Festubert. In November 1915 he was invalided to England on account of illness, and after prolonged treatment in hospitals at Oxford and Liverpool, was discharged as medically unfit in June 1917. He holds the 1914-15 Star, and the General Service and Victory Medals.
28, Prescott Street, Hulme, Manchester. Z11792

PADLEY, P., Corporal, East Lancashire Regiment.
After volunteering in April 1915, he passed through his training and was drafted to the Western Front in the following December. He saw heavy fighting at Loos, in the Ypres sector and at Arras. On June 16th, 1918, he was severely wounded in action during the German Advance on the Lys, and died of his wounds two days later. He was entitled to the 1914-15 Star, and the General Service and Victory Medals.
" His life for his Country."
62, Markham Street, Ardwick, Manchester. Z7590

PAERSCH, H. A., Private, 7th Manchester Regt.
He volunteered in January 1916, and shortly afterwards was sent to the Western Front. In this theatre of hostilities he took part with his unit in several severe engagements, including Ypres, Albert and the Somme, and was later in action in many sectors during the Retreat and Advance of 1918. He was demobilised in February 1919, and holds the General Service and Victory Medals.
45, Bishop Street, Moss Side, Manchester. Z9670A

PAERSCH, L. F., Sergt.-Major, 7th Manchester Regt.
Mobilised in August 1914, he was retained at home on duties of an important nature until December 1916, when he proceeded to France. There he played a distinguished part in strenuous fighting on many Fronts, and was in action at Ypres, Messines Ridge, Cambrai and on the Somme, rendering valuable services until he returned home. He was discharged in February 1919, and holds the General Service and Victory Medals.
45, Bishop Street, Moss Side, Manchester. Z9670C

PAERSCH, O., Private, 7th Manchester Regiment.
He joined in August 1916, and after a brief training was sent in the following month to the Western Front. During his service overseas, he was attached to the Labour Corps and performed consistently good work whilst engaged on important duties on the lines of communication. He was demobilised in March 1919, and holds the General Service and Victory Medals.
45, Bishop Street, Moss Side, Manchester. Z9670B

PAGE, J. C., Private, R.A.S.C.
He joined in September 1917, and served with his unit at various stations in the United Kingdom. He rendered valuable services, but owing to medical unfitness was not successful in obtaining his transfer overseas, and after doing good work was discharged in March 1918.
13 Brindle Street, Hulme, Manchester. TZ7591

PAILIN, J., Private, 2nd Cheshire Regiment.
Volunteering in January 1916, he was drafted overseas after a short period of training. During his service in Gibraltar, he was engaged on important garrison duty and did consistently good work with his unit. He was demobilised in November 1919, and holds the General Service and Victory Medals.
37, Congou Street, Ancoats, Manchester. Z11940B

PAILIN, T. H., Trooper, Duke of Lancaster's Own Dragoons.
He volunteered in January 1916, and was shortly afterwards drafted to France, where he took part in many engagements, including that of Ypres. He died gloriously on the Field of Battle on the Somme on August 21st, 1918. He was entitled to the General Service and Victory Medals.
" Whilst we remember, the sacrifice is not in vain."
37, Congou Street, Ancoats, Manchester. Z11940A

PALETHORPE, W., Private, King's (Liverpool Regt.)
He volunteered at the outbreak of war in August 1914, and on completing a period of training in April of the following year, was drafted to the Western Front. After taking part in the Battles of Ypres, Festubert and Loos and many minor engagements, he was severely gassed whilst in action at St. Eloi in April 1916, and was invalided home. He was discharged two months later as medically unfit for further service, and holds the 1914-15 Star, and the General Service and Victory Medals.
9, Sycamore Street, Newton, Manchester. Z10918

PALFREYMAN, B., (Sen.), Pte., 4th Monmouthshire Regiment (T.F.)
He joined in July 1918, and served with his unit at various stations in England. He rendered valuable services, but was not successful in obtaining his transfer overseas before the cessation of hostilities, and after doing good guard work on the East Coast, was demobilised in December 1918.
21, Mark Street, Hulme, Manchester. Z7592B

PALFREYMAN, B. (Jun.), Private, King's (Liverpool Regiment) and Lancashire Fusiliers.
He joined in February 1917, and after being sent to a training Battalion, served with his unit at various stations near the East Coast of England. He did good service, but was not successful in obtaining his transfer overseas before the cessation of hostilities. After being demobilised in March 1919, he re-enlisted later, and joining the Lancashire Fusiliers, went with them to India, where he was still serving in 1920.
21, Mark Street, Hulme, Manchester. Z7592A

PALIN, G., L/Corpl., King's Shropshire Light Infantry.
Having enlisted in July 1914, he was sent to France on the outbreak of war, with the Expeditionary Force, and saw much heavy fighting. He was in the great Retreat from Mons, and was engaged later at La Bassée (III), the first Battle of Ypres, at Givenchy, Festubert, Loos and Lens, also in the Somme Offensive of 1916. In the course of these actions he was twice wounded, and a third time at Arras in April 1918. Invalided to England in consequence, he was discharged in the next month as unfit for further service. He holds the Mons Star, and the General Service and Victory Medals. 8, Gaspard St., Rusholme, Manchester.   Z7593

PALMER, C., Sergt., K.O. (Royal Lancaster Regt.)
Volunteering in August 1914, he passed through training, and proceeded to France in the following May. After seeing fighting at Loos, Hulluch and Givenchy, he was transferred in May 1916 to Salonika, where he took part in the Doiran offensive and the action on the Struma. He was then unfortunately attacked with malaria and dysentery, and after treatment at various hospitals in England, on his recovery did duty on home service. He holds the 1914-15 Star, and the General Service and Victory Medals, and was demobilised in February 1919.
4, Lancaster Street, Hulme, Manchester.   Z7596

PALMER, C., Driver, R.F.A.
He volunteered in June 1915, and proceeded with his Battery to Egypt in the following January. He took part in engagements at Kantara, the three Gaza Battles, and the fighting at Jaffa, also in the capture of Jerusalem and Jericho, and serving right through the final operations on the Palestine front, was demobilised in March 1919, and holds the General Service and Victory Medals.
34, Libby Street, Lower Openshaw, Manchester.   Z7595

PALMER, J., L/Sergt., 21st Manchester Regiment.
He volunteered in March 1915, and was drafted to France almost immediately. He did good service in many engagements, notably at Ploegsteert Wood and in the Somme Offensive of 1916. Later he fought at Beaumont-Hamel, where he received a severe wound, and being sent to hospital in France, was placed, on his recovery, in charge of details at a Base camp. He holds the 1914-15 Star, and the General Service and Victory Medals, and was demobilised in 1919.
36, Dalton Street, Hulme, Manchester.   Z7594

PALMER, T., A.B., Royal Navy.
He joined in February 1918, and was posted to H.M.S. "St. Vincent." Proceeding to the North Sea, he was engaged on patrol, escort and other important duties with the fourth Battle Squadron of the Grand Fleet. He was demobilised in March 1919, and holds the General Service and Victory Medals.
2, Whitland Street, Queen's Park, Manchester.   Z11563

PANTER, E., Shoeing Smith, R.F.A.
Volunteering in September 1914, he was drafted to the Western Front after two months' training and there saw severe fighting in various sectors. He took part in the Battles of Ypres, Neuve Chapelle, St. Eloi, Festubert, Vermelles, the Somme, and Arras and many other important engagements until the cessation of hostilities. He was demobilised on his return home in June 1919, and holds the 1914 Star, and the General Service and Victory Medals.
8, School Street, West Gorton, Manchester.   Z10919

PANTER, S., Private, Manchester Regiment.
He joined in August 1916, and in the following month was drafted to France, where he took part in engagements on the Somme and at Ypres and La Bassée. He was invalided to the Base suffering from acute bronchitis, from which he unfortunately died in February 1918. He was entitled to the General Service and Victory Medals.
"His memory is cherished with pride."
11, Clare Street, Chorlton-on-Medlock, Manchester. Z11919B

PARISH, J. C., Sergt., Canadian Light Infantry.
After volunteering in Canada in 1915, he came to England for training, and was sent to France in August of the next year, in time to take part in the first Battle of the Somme, in which he was gassed. On his recovery he did good service in the actions of Vimy and Messines Ridges, Ypres (III) and Cambrai (I), also in the Retreat and Advance of 1918. He continued to serve after the Armistice and was not demobilised until March 1920. He holds the General Service and Victory Medals. 84, Gibson St., Ardwick, Manchester.   Z7597A

PARISH, W. A., Stoker, R.N.
He joined in June 1916, and after a month's training at a Southern Depôt, served in the North Sea Fleet. He took part in many Naval engagements in one of which, in December 1917, he was wounded, but recovered, and served later in operations on the Belgian Coast aboard the T.B.D. "Penn." After the Armistice he proceeded in August 1919, with the Baltic Fleet to Russia, and was eventually demobilised in March 1920. He holds the General Service and Victory Medals.
84, Gibson St., Ardwick, Manchester.   Z7597B

PARK, A., Private, 8th East Lancashire Regiment.
Having volunteered in October 1914, he was drafted to the Western Front in the following July. He was heavily engaged in the Ypres sector, in the Somme Offensive, near Arras and Verdun, also at Passchendaele Ridge and the Battle of Cambrai (I). Afterwards he took part in the Retreat and Advance of 1918, and in the latter of these was severely wounded. After treatment at a Welsh hospital, he was discharged in November 1918, and holds the 1914-15 Star, and the General Service and Victory Medals.
30, Pump Street, Hulme, Manchester.   Z7598

PARK, J. H. H., Pte., K.O. (Royal Lancaster Regt.)
He joined in December 1917, and after training proceeded to France in the following June. He did good service in the Machine Gun Section of his unit in many different actions during the Retreat and Advance of 1918, and serving through all the final stages of the campaign, was demobilised in January 1919. He holds the General Service and Victory Medals. 8, Sadler Street, Moss Side, Manchester.   Z7599

PARK, W. H., Private, 22nd Manchester Regiment.
He volunteered in November 1914, and after some months of training was drafted to France in November 1915. He did good service as Driver in the Transport section of his Battalion in engagements at Loos, on the Somme, and near Arras. He had the misfortune to lose his leg by shell fire when conveying supplies for his Battalion, and was discharged in consequence as unfit for further service in February 1918. He holds the 1914-15 Star, and the General Service and Victory Medals.
4, Samuel Street, West Gorton, Manchester.   Z7599B

PARKER, A., Driver, R.E.
Joining in April 1918, he was later sent to France, where he was employed as a Pioneer and later as a Signaller with the Signal section of the Royal Engineers. After the Armistice he proceeded into Germany and served with the Army of Occupation until December 1919, when he returned home and was demobilised, holding the General Service and Victory Medals.
164, Crossley Street, Gorton, Manchester.   Z11971

PARKER, A., Private, King's (Liverpool Regiment).
He joined in February 1916, and proceeded to France in the following April. He saw heavy fighting at St. Eloi, Vermelles, in the first Battle of the Somme, and in the capture of Bullecourt. Later, in July 1918 near Conty, he was very badly gassed, and being invalided home, was, after treatment at various hospitals in the North of England, discharged in August 1919. He holds the General Service and Victory Medals.
58, Napier Street, Ardwick, Manchester.   Z7602

PARKER, G.T., Sergt., 1st Royal Warwickshire Regt.
He was mobilised in August 1914, and immediately ordered to France, where he participated in the Retreat from Mons and was wounded. Invalided home, he was sent in June 1915 to Egypt, and was in action on the Suez Canal, and at Mersa Matruh, Agagia, Sollum, Katia, El Fasher, Romani and Magdhaba, where he was wounded for the second time. Upon his recovery he was employed on garrison and other important duties at Alexandria and Cairo until February 1919. He was demobilised on his return home in the following month, holding the Mons Star, and the General Service and Victory Medals.
44, Parkfield Avenue, Rusholme, Manchester.   Z9664

PARKER, H., Private, Manchester Regiment, and Queen's (Royal West Surrey Regiment).
Joining in September 1916, he was sent to France in April of the following year, and was in action at Arras, La Bassée, Givenchy, Festubert, Nieuport, Dunkirk, Ypres and Passchendaele. He was wounded on the Somme in November 1918, and returning home received hospital treatment. He was discharged as unfit for further service in September 1919, and holds the General Service and Victory Medals.
43, Southwell Street, Manchester.   Z11565

PARKER, H., Private, 13th Manchester Regiment.
Mobilised on the outbreak of war, he proceeded to France with the Expeditionary Force, and fought in the Retreat from Mons, also in engagements at Loos, at Ypres, and many other places. While helping to stem the German Advance of 1918, he was wounded on the Somme front, and on recovery in a Base Hospital was sent to Salonika, where he was again wounded in action. Being evacuated to Hospital in England, he was finally demobilised in May 1919, and holds the Mons Star, and the General Service and Victory Medals.
1, Roseberry Street, Gorton, Manchester.   Z7603

PARKER, J., Private, R.A.V.C.
He joined in November 1917, and after training, did service with his Corps at a London Depôt. He was not successful in obtaining his transfer overseas before the cessation of hostilities, but some months after the Armistice, was sent to Germany with the Army of Occupation, in which he was posted to a Labour Corps and for work at an ammunition dump, and other duties. He was finally demobilised in March 1920.
33A, Napier Street, Ardwick, Manchester.   TZ7601

PARKER, J., Private, Royal Naval Division.

He volunteered in November 1915, and served with the Hood Battalion in Gallipoli until the Evacuation of the Peninsula, in the course of which he was wounded in January 1916. Transferred on recovery to the Nelson Battalion he was sent to France in December 1916, and was in action in several parts of the line. Taken prisoner at Cambrai in December 1917, he returned to England as an exchanged prisoner of war in June 1918, and was later sent to France, where he was engaged with his unit until his return to England for demobilisation in February 1919. He holds the 1914–15 Star, and the General Service and Victory Medals.

6, Watson Street, Hulme, Manchester. Z11793

PARKER, L. (D.C.M.), Sergt., R.E.

He volunteered in August 1914, and was retained on important duties in England until January 1916, when he was drafted to Mesopotamia. There he saw much severe fighting, took part in engagements at Um-el-Hannah, the Tigris, Kut, and many other places, and was wounded in action at the capture of Baghdad. He was awarded the Distinguished Conduct Medal for conspicuous bravery displayed at Baghdad in February 1917, and holds also the General Service and Victory Medals. He was demobilised on his return home in September 1919. 11, Rigel Street, Ancoats, Manchester. Z10921

PARKER, R., Private, K.O. Scottish Borderers.

Volunteering soon after the outbreak of hostilities, he proceeded to France in the following April, and did good service in his Battalion as Transport in connection with engagements on the Somme and Ancre fronts, at Passchendaele Ridge, and at Cambrai. He continued to serve through the final operations, and after the Armistice went with the Army of Occupation to Germany. He was demobilised in April 1919, and holds the 1914–15 Star, and the General Service and Victory Medals.

18 Nelson Street Bradford, Manchester. Z7605

PARKER, S., Private, 10th Manchester Regiment.

After volunteering in May 1915, he passed through a considerable period of training at various stations in the South of England, and was sent to France in March 1917. He saw heavy fighting in the Battles of Ypres (III) and Cambrai (I), and later took part in the Retreat and Advance of 1918, being in action at Amiens, Bapaume, Havrincourt and Le Cateau. On his return to England after the Armistice, he was demobilised in March 1919, and holds the General Service and Victory Medals.

164, Crossley Street, Gorton, Manchester. Z7604

PARKER, T., Private, Royal Welch Fusiliers.

After volunteering in December 1915, he underwent a period of training prior to being drafted to the Western Front in July 1917. There, after taking part in much severe fighting, he gave his life for King and Country, falling in action near Ypres in September 1917. He was entitled to the General Service and Victory Medals.

"Great deeds cannot die :
They with the sun and moon renew their light for ever."

254, Mill Street, Bradford, Manchester. Z10920

PARKER, T., Corpl., K.O. (Royal Lancaster Regt.)

After volunteering in February 1915, he was sent to France in the next month and saw much hard fighting, being in engagements at Ypres, Festubert, Givenchy, and La Bassée, in that year, and being wounded once. Later in action near Arras he was again wounded, but after treatment at a hospital in Scotland, returned to France and fought again at Lens and Cambrai. In April 1918 being wounded a third time, on the Somme, he was sent to a Base hospital, and on his recovery was given the duty of guarding German prisoners until his demobilisation in June 1919. He holds the 1914–15 Star, and the General Service and Victory Medals.

3, Lime Street, Hulme, Manchester. Z7600

PARKER, W., Private, Lancashire Fusiliers.

He volunteered in August 1914, and proceeding to the Gallpoli Peninsula in the following April, took part in the Landing at Cape Helles, and in the three Battles of Krithia. In October 1915, he was transferred to the Western Front, and fought at the Battles of Albert, the Somme, Arras, Vimy Ridge, Ypres, and Passchendaele, where he was badly wounded in action and invalided home. He holds the 1914–15 Star, and the General Service and Victory Medals, and was demobilised in January 1919.

33A, Napier Street, Ardwick, Manchester. Z11941

PARKER, W. A., Acting Captain, Tank Corps.

He volunteered in October 1914, and proceeded to France in March of the following year. He was in action in the Battles of the Somme and Cambrai, where he was wounded. On his recovery he rejoined his unit and fought in many engagements during the Retreat and Advance of 1918. He was still serving in 1920, and holds the 1914–15 Star, and the General Service and Victory Medals.

87, Carisbrooke Street, Harpurhey, Manchester. Z11564A

PARKER, W. H., Private, R.A.F.

He joined in May 1917, and after his training was engaged at Blandford on important duties with his Squadron. He was employed on clerical work and rendered valuable services, but was not successful in obtaining his transfer overseas owing to his being overage for active service. He was demobilised in December 1919.

87, Carisbrooke Street, Harpurhey, Manchester. Z11564B

PARKES, J., Private, 11th Lancashire Fusiliers.

He was mobilised in August 1914, and in the following year was drafted to the Western Front, where he was engaged in heavy fighting at St. Eloi, Ypres, Neuve Chapelle, Festubert, and the Somme. He also fought in the Battles of Arras, Bullecourt, Beaumont-Hamel, Albert, Cambrai, throughout the Offensive of 1918, and was three times wounded. He was demobilised in February 1919, and holds the 1914–15 Star, and the General Service and Victory Medals.

61, Baguley Street, Miles Platting, Manchester. Z11566

PARKES, W., Private, 5th Manchester Regiment.

Volunteering in August 1914, he proceeded to the Western Front four months later and served there until the close of the war. He was in action in the Battles of St. Eloi, Festubert, Loos, Albert, Vimy Ridge, the Somme, Arras, Ypres, Lens, Cambrai, the Marne, and in the Retreat and Advance of 1918. After the Armistice he was sent with the Army of Occupation into Germany for a time, and returning home for demobilisation in January 1919, holds the 1914–15 Star, and the General Service and Victory Medals.

21, Edgeley Street, Ardwick, Manchester. Z11794

PARKES, W. C., Private, 13th Lancashire Fusiliers.

He volunteered in September 1914, and on completing his training in January of the following year, proceeded to the Western Front. There, after taking part in the Battles of Hill 60 and Loos, and other engagements, he was wounded in action on the Somme, and was admitted to hospital at Rouen. On his recovery, however, he re-joined his unit, and was again in action in the Battles of Arras, Ypres, Cambrai, the Marne, Bapaume, Havrincourt, and Le Cateau, before returning home for demobilisation in March 1919. He holds the 1914–15 Star, and the General Service and Victory Medals.

105, Kendall Street, Bradford, Manchester. Z10927

PARKIN, A. E., Sapper, R.E.

He joined in March 1916, and after a considerable period of training was sent to France in May 1917. He did good service in engagements on the Lys front, in the Ypres sector, and at Nieuport, Arras, Albert, and Cambrai, being once wounded. After serving through the Retreat and Advance of 1918 until the Armistice, he was not demobilised until November 1919, and holds the General Service and Victory Medals.

9, Matlock Street, Ardwick, Manchester. Z7608

PARKIN, C. F., Air Mechanic, R.A.F. (late R.F.C.)

He joined in June 1918, and after a very short period of training, was sent to France in the following month. He did good work at various aerodromes in different areas of the Western Front until August 1919, when he returned to England. He was still serving in 1920 in Kent, and holds the General Service and Victory Medals.

19, Upper Plymouth Grove, Longsight, Manchester. Z7610

PARKIN, E., L/Corporal, 1st Grenadier Guards.

He volunteered on the outbreak of war, and was sent to France in September 1914. He took part in much of the heavy fighting of that period of the Campaign, but in October of the same year died gloriously on the Field of Battle at Dixmude. He was entitled to the 1914 Star, and the General Service and Victory Medals. His body lies in the military cemetery at Dixmude.

"A valiant Soldier with undaunted heart he breasted life's last hill."

6, Solent Street, Ardwick, Manchester. Z7607

PARKIN, E., Private, King's (Liverpool Regiment).

He volunteered in September 1914, and in February of the following year, proceeded to the Western Front. Whilst in this theatre of war he took part in many important engagements, including the Battles of Neuve Chapelle, Ypres, Festubert, the Somme and Cambrai, served also through the Retreat and Advance of 1918, and was wounded in action at Ypres in July 1917, and was for a time in hospital at Etaples. Demobilised in March 1919, he holds the 1914–15 Star, and the General Service and Victory Medals.

12, Clyde Street, Ancoats, Manchester. Z10924

PARKIN, J. H., Corporal, R.A.S.C.

He joined in September 1916, and was sent to France in the following month. He did good service in this responsible rank with the Mechanical Transport, in connection with engagements on the Somme, at Messines Ridge, and Cambrai. Later he took part in the Retreat and Advance of 1918 until the Armistice, and was not demobilised until December 1919. He holds the General Service and Victory Medals.

6, Solent Street, Ardwick, Manchester. Z7606

PARKIN, J. S., Driver, R.A.S.C.
Volunteering in January 1916, he proceeded in the following
May to the Western Front. In this theatre of war, he served
with his Company on the Somme front, and at Beaumont-
Hamel, Arras, Ypres, and in various sectors during the Advance
of 1918. He did good work whilst engaged on important
duties, and was demobilised on returning home in June 1919,
holding the General Service and Victory Medals.
41, Princess Street, Miles Platting, Manchester.   Z9313

PARKIN, T., Private, M.G.C.
He volunteered in December 1915, and in September of the
following year, proceeded to Mesopotamia, where he saw much
severe fighting. He took part in the Relief of Kut, and the
Capture of Baghdad, Kirkuk, and various other places, and
also fought in numerous engagements on the Tigris. Returning
home in August 1919, he was demobilised in November of
that year, and holds the General Service and Victory Medals.
25, Grantham Street, West Gorton, Manchester.   Z10923

PARKIN, W., Private, Labour Corps.
He volunteered in December 1915, and was sent to France in
the following June. He rendered valuable services in the
Labour Battalion of the Manchester Regiment in connection
with the Somme Offensive of that Summer, in the course of
which he was severely wounded, and after treatment at a
Base Hospital, and also in England, returned to duty in France.
He was finally demobilised in March 1919, and holds the
General Service and Victory Medals.
19, Upper Plymouth Grove, Longsight, Manchester.   Z7609

PARKIN, W., Corporal, 7th Loyal N. Lancashire Regt.
Having enlisted in July 1909, he was drafted to the Western
Front immediately on the outbreak of war in August 1914,
and there fought in the Battle of Mons, and the subsequent
Retreat. He also took part in the Battles of the Marne, the
Aisne, Albert, Ploegsteert Wood, and the Somme, and other
engagements, and was three times wounded in action—at
Ypres, where he was also gassed, in May 1915, at Beaumont-
Hamel in July 1916, and at High Wood in November of that
year. Invalided home, he was finally discharged as medically
unfit for further service in September 1917, and holds the
Mons Star, and the General Service and Victory Medals.
23, Grantham Street, West Gorton, Manchester.   Z10922

PARKINSON, C., Private, King's (Liverpool Regt.)
He joined in March 1918, and completing his training was
engaged on important duties with his unit at various stations.
He rendered valuable services, but was not successful in
obtaining his transfer overseas before the cessation of hostilities. He was demobilised in March 1919.
559, Collyhurst Road, Manchester.   Z11567

PARKINSON, E. F., Sapper, R.E.
He volunteered in August 1914, and was retained at home
on various duties until December 1915, when he was drafted
to Salonika. There he served for some months on the Vardar
front, but in June 1916 was transferred to France and stationed
in Boulogne. Returning to England shortly afterwards, he
was employed on important duties at different stations until
he was discharged in March 1919. He holds the 1914-15 Star,
and the General Service and Victory Medals.
80, Jersey Street, Ancoats, Manchester.   TZ9665

PARKINSON, G. H., L/Corpl., King's (Shropshire Light Infantry).
After volunteering in January 1915, he underwent a period of
training prior to being drafted to the Western Front in September of the following year. There, after taking part in the
Battles of Arras and Ypres, and many other important engagements, he fell fighting at Cambrai in December 1917. He was
entitled to the General Service and Victory Medals.
" Thinking that remembrance, though unspoken, may reach
him where he sleeps."
17, Sycamore Street, Newton, Manchester.   Z10926A

PARKINSON, J., L/Corporal, S. Lancashire Regt., and Labour Corps.
He joined in August 1916, and proceeded to France in the
following November. He was in action in the Somme sector
and near Cambrai, and later in June 1917, was badly wounded
at Messines Ridge, and evacuated to hospital in England.
On recovery, being now unfit for the fighting line, he was
transferred to the Labour Corps for light duty at home, and
was eventually demobilised in August 1919. He holds the
General Service and Victory Medals.
8, Markham Street, Ardwick, Manchester.   Z7611

PARKINSON, J., Private, 1/4th Seaforth Highlanders.
Volunteering in January 1915, he was sent two months later
to France. Wounded in the following May at Neuve Chapelle,
he was invalided home and sent to hospital in Leicester,
returning to France in June 1916. Whilst taking part in the
Battle of the Somme, his health broke down, and he was again
invalided home, and was subsequently discharged from hospital in Manchester in January 1917, as unfit for further service,

eventually dying at home on June 7th, 1919, from the effects
of an illness attributed to his military service. He was entitled to the 1914-15 Star, and the General Service and Victory
Medals.
" His memory is cherished with pride."
5, Pearson Street, Newton Heath, Manchester.   Z9666

PARKINSON, R., Private, Royal Welch Fusiliers.
He volunteered in November 1914, and three months after-
wards proceeded to the Western Front. In this theatre of
war he took part in many important engagements, including
Hill 60, Ypres, the Somme, Festubert, Vimy Ridge, Arras,
Bullecourt, Cambrai, Bapaume, and the Lys, and was wounded.
He remained overseas until March 1919, when he was demob-
ilised, holding the 1914-15 Star, and the General Service and
Victory Medals.
38, Woburn Place, Chorlton-on-Medlock, Manchester. Z9314

PARKINSON, R., Private, Loyal N. Lancashire Regt.
He joined in 1916, and proceeded to the Western Front in the
same year. He saw much heavy fighting in various engagements of that period of the war, notably near Armentières,
Albert, Festubert, and St. Eloi. In July 1917, he gave his
life for King and Country in the Field near Ypres, and was
entitled to the General Service and Victory Medals.
" His memory is cherished with pride."
24, Malaga Street, Ancoats, Manchester.   Z7613

PARKINSON, T., A.B., R.N., H.M.S. "President III."
He joined in July 1916, and underwent a course of training
in H.M.S. " Vivid " at Portsmouth. Two months later he
was posted to H.M.S. " President III," and whilst serving in
this vessel was employed on transport duties in the English
Channel. He rendered excellent service until he was demobilised in February 1919, holding the General Service and Victory
Medals.
5, Pearson Street, Newton Heath, Manchester.   Z9667

PARKINSON, T., Stoker, R.N.
He was mobilised at the outbreak of war in August 1914, and
was immediately drafted to the Western Front, where, attached to the Royal Naval Division, he saw much severe
fighting. He was wounded and taken prisoner in the Defence
of Antwerp, and was interned in Holland until January 1918.
He was then released and invalided from the Navy, and holds
the 1914 Star, and the General Service and Victory Medals.
181, Morton Street, Longsight, Manchester.   Z10925

PARKINSON, W., Private, 13th Manchester Regt.
Joining in July 1917, he proceeded to Salonika in the following
month, and there saw much severe fighting. He took part in
many important engagements on the Doiran and Vardar
fronts, whilst in this theatre of war, and suffered from shell-
shock. He finally returned to England for demobilisation
in December 1919, and holds the General Service and Victory
Medals. 17, Sycamore St., Newton, Manchester.   Z10926B

PARKINSON, W. H., 21st Manchester Regiment.
After joining in October 1916, he proceeded, after training,
to France in the following January, and saw heavy fighting
in actions near Vimy Ridge and Bullecourt, also in the Arras
sector. At this last place on May 15th, 1917, he died a
glorious death on the Field of Battle, and was entitled to
the General Service and Victory Medals.
" The path of duty was the way to glory."
6, Upper Dover Street, Bradford, Manchester.   TZ7612

PARNELL, A. R., Gunner, R.G.A.
He volunteered in May 1915, and proceeded with his Battery
to France in the following year. He took part in an engagement near Vimy Ridge, also in the great Somme Offensive of
July 1916. He afterwards was in action near Arras, and did
good service all through the final operations until the Armistice.
He was demobilised in February 1919, and holds the General
Service and Victory Medals.
21, Curry Street, Polygon Street, Ardwick, Manchester. Z7614

PARNELL, E. H., Private, 5th Manchester Regt.
After volunteering in November 1914, he passed through his
training, and was drafted to the Western Front towards the
end of the next year. He fought at Loos, St. Eloi, and Vermelles, and also took part in the 1st Battle of the Somme.
During this engagement on July 20th, 1916, while bringing
in wounded near Albert, he died a valiant soldier's death, and
was entitled to the 1914-15 Star, and the General Service and
Victory Medals.
" Great deeds cannot die."
11, Brunt Street, Rusholme, Manchester.   Z7615

PARR, G. W., Private, King's (Liverpool Regt.)
He joined in October 1916, and was drafted to the Western
Front in the following December. He at once saw fighting
on the Ancre Front, and later at Arras, Vimy Ridge, and
Bullecourt, where he was wounded. On recovery he rejoined
and took part in the Battles of Ypres III, and Cambrai I, also
in the Retreat and Advance of 1918 fighting again at Cambrai.
He was demobilised in February 1918, and holds the General
Service and Victory Medals.
11, Hardman Street, City Road, Hulme, Manchester.   Z7616

PARR, J., Private, King's Own Scottish Borderers.
He volunteered at the outbreak of hostilities, and, after his training, proceeded to France in the following March. He fought in the Battle of Hill 60, in which he was severely wounded, and after treatment at a Base hospital in France, and later in England, rejoined his Regiment in Edinburgh, and did service as Secretary for the Royal Defence Corps until discharged in April 1918. He holds the 1914-15 Star, and the General Service and Victory Medals.
13, Westmoreland Street, Longsight, Manchester. Z7617

PARR, J. H., Driver, R.A.S.C. (M.T.)
Shortly after volunteering in September 1914, he was drafted to France, where he was engaged on important duties in various sectors of the Front. He was present also at the Battles of Ypres, Arras, Vimy Ridge, Passchendaele, and Cambrai, and many other engagements until the cessation of hostilities. He returned home for demobilisation in May 1919, and holds the 1914-15 Star, and the General Service and Victory Medals.
32, Burton Street, Newtown, Manchester. Z10929

PARR, T., Private, Queen's Own (R. West Kent Rgt.)
Joining in January 1917, he proceeded to the Western Front on completion of four month's training, and there saw severe fighting in various sectors. He took part in the Battles of Arras, Vimy Ridge, Bullecourt, Messines, Ypres, Passchendaele and Cambrai, and many minor engagements, and served also through the Retreat and Advance of 1918. Demobilised on his return home in May 1919, he holds the General Service and Victory Medals.
55, Hamilton Street, Collyhurst, Manchester. Z10928

PARRATT, A., 10th Lancashire Fusiliers.
Having enlisted in January 1914, he was sent for training, and drafted to France in August 1915. He fought in the Battle of Loos, and afterwards in the great Somme Offensive of 1916 in which he was wounded, but, on recovery, took part in actions at Beaumont-Hamel and Beaucourt, where he was again wounded in November 1916. Being then invalided to England, he remained under treatment until finally demobilised in March 1919. He holds the 1914-15 Star, and the General Service and Victory Medals.
31, Bedale Street, Hulme, Manchester. Z7618

PARROTT, J., Private, 11th Lancashire Fusiliers.
Volunteering in August 1914, he was sent three months later to France, where he participated in heavy fighting at Neuve Chapelle, Hill 60, Ypres, Loos, St. Eloi, Arras, Ypres II, Cambrai, Amiens, Bapaume, and Havrincourt. He served overseas until the termination of hostilities, and performed uniformly good work. Demobilised in January 1919, he holds the 1914-15 Star, and the General Service and Victory Medals.
4, Holbeck Street, Oldham Road, Manchester. Z9668

PARROTT, J., Private, 4th Manchester Regiment.
A veteran soldier, who had seen service in the South African War, he volunteered in August 1914, and served with his unit at various stations in England. He rendered valuable services but, owing to his age, was not successful in obtaining his transfer overseas before the cessation of hostilities, and after doing good work, was demobilised in February 1919. He holds the Queen's South African Medal.
43, Woburn Place, Chorlton-on-Medlock, Manchester. X7619

PARROTT. J. A., Private, 2/10th Manchester Regt.
He joined in May 1916, and after training, was drafted to the Western Front in June 1917, in time to take part in the great Battles of Messines Ridge, and Ypres III. Not long after this last engagement, on October 9th, 1917, he was killed in action near Passchendaele Ridge, thus giving his life for his Country. He was entitled to the General Service and Victory Medals.
"He died the noblest death a man may die,
Fighting for God and right and liberty."
77, Hinckley Street, Bradford, Manchester. Z7620B

PARROTT, R. F., Private, 17th Manchester Regt.
After volunteering in September 1914, he proceeded to France in the following May, and was in action at Ypres, Loos, Albert, and Vimy Ridge. Later he fought in the 1st Battle of the Somme, and during it, on July 3rd, 1916, was dangerously wounded. He was sent to hospital at Paignton in Devonshire, and there succumbed to his wounds on July 27th. His body lies in Phillip's Park Cemetery, near Manchester. He was entitled to the 1914-15 Star, and the General Service and Victory Medals.
"The path of duty was the way to glory."
77, Hinckley Street, Bradford, Manchester. Z7620A

PARRY, C. J., Private, 2nd Lancashire Fusiliers.
Volunteering in August 1914, he was drafted to the Western Front on completing his training three months later, and there took part in the Battle of Ypres, and many engagements. He died gloriously on the Field of Battle at La Bassée in February 1915, after only three months' active service. He was entitled to the 1914-15 Star, and the General Service and Victory Medals.
"He passed out of the sight of men by the path of duty and self-sacrifice."
5, Moody Street, Bradford, Manchester. Z10931B

PARRY, C. J., Private, 2nd Lancashire Fusiliers.
A Reservist, he was mobilised on the outbreak of war, and after training proceeded to France in January 1915. He served in the Ypres Sector, but on February 12th, of that year was killed while on guard duty at Le Bizeh, near Ypres, thus giving his life for King and Country. He was entitled to the 1914-15 Star, and the General Service and Victory Medals.
"Thinking that remembrance, though unspoken, may reach him where he sleeps."
58, Tame Street, Ancoats, Manchester. TZ7622B

PARRY, E., Private, 8th Manchester Regiment.
He volunteered in September 1915, and on completing a period of training in the following year, proceeded to Egypt, where he was engaged on important duties at various stations. In 1917 he was transferred to the Western Front, and there saw severe fighting at Loos and Delville Wood, and took part also in the Battle of the Somme. He was demobilised on his return home in February 1919, and holds the General Service and Victory Medals.
103, Thornton Street, Collyhurst, Manchester. Z10930

PARRY, G., Pte., Lancashire Fus., and Labour Corps.
He volunteered in May 1915, and proceeded to France in the following August. He took part in actions in the Ypres sector, and afterwards fought at Arras, and in the Battles of Vimy Ridge, and Ypres III in 1917. In June 1918 he was transferred to a Prisoners of War Company, and served with it until demobilised in June 1919. He holds the 1914-15 Star, and the General Service and Victory Medals.
12, Beresford St., Great Western St., Moss Side, Manchester. X7621

PARRY, J., Corporal, 3rd Royal Welch Fusiliers.
A Reservist, he was mobilised on the outbreak of war, and proceeding to France with the Expeditionary Force, took part in the Retreat from Mons, and in the great Battles of the Marne and the Aisne, which followed it. In the last of these he was severely wounded, and being invalided to hospital in England, on his recovery did duty at a depôt in the North West of England as cook, and afterwards in Ireland, from which country he was discharged in February 1919. He holds the Mons Star, and the General Service and Victory Medals.
28, Pitt Street, Ancoats, Manchester. Z7623

PARRY, J. F., Private, 2/24th Queen's (Royal West Surrey Regiment).
He volunteered in November 1915, and after his training, was drafted to France in the following June. In December of that year he was transferred to Salonika, and took part in the Doiran Advance, and the operations on the Vardar, being chiefly engaged in patrol and raiding work. In June 1917 he was sent to Palestine, and was in the 3rd Gaza Battle, and the capture of Jerusalem. After this he was drafted to France in July 1918, and was wounded at Epéhy in the Great Advance. He was finally demobilised in February 1919, and holds the General Service and Victory Medals.
31, Hyde Street, Hulme, Manchester. Z7624

PARRY, J. W., Private, 1st Manchester Regiment.
He volunteered in March 1915, but was medically unfit for transfer to a theatre of war. Retained at home, he served at Heaton Park, Grantham, and Salisbury Plain, and did excellent work whilst engaged on various important duties. He was invalided out of the Army on account of ill-health in September 1916.
10, Somerset Place, Oldham Road, Manchester. Z9315

PARRY, W. F., Private, 23rd Royal Fusiliers.
He joined in April 1917, and after undergoing a period of training, served at various stations, where he was engaged on duties of a highly important nature. He was unable to obtain his transfer overseas before the cessation of hostilities, but afterwards proceeded with the Army of Occupation into Germany. He was finally demobilised on his return to England in December 1919.
5, Moody Street, Bradford, Manchester. Z10931C

PARSON, W., L/Corporal, 9th E. Lancashire Regt.
Volunteering in October 1915, he was drafted in the following June to France, and there took part in numerous important engagements, including the Battles of the Somme, Arras, Cambrai, and Ypres. He later was in action in various sectors during the Retreat and Advance of 1918, prior to being demobilised in February 1919, holding the General Service and Victory Medals.
8, Harry Street, London Road, Manchester. Z9316

PARSONAGE, E., Private., 2/10th Manchester Regt.
He joined in August 1916, and after training, proceeded to France in the following March. He took part in the capture of Bullecourt, also in the Battles of Ypres III (including Passchendaele Ridge), and Cambrai I. Being shortly afterwards attacked by serious illness, he was invalided home, and later, discharged from hospital as unfit for further service, in April 1918. He holds the General Service and Victory Medals.
130, Bedford Street, Hulme, Manchester. TZ7625

PARSONS, C. J., Rifleman, Northern Rifles.
After volunteering in May 1915, he was sent, before the end of the Summer, to Gallipoli, and took part in the Suvla Bay operations. In the course of these he contracted a serious illness, and was sent to hospital at Alexandria. On recovering he served there in the Military Police until June 1917, when he again became ill, and died in hospital at Alexandria on July 31st, 1918. He was entitled to the 1914-15 Star, and the General Service and Victory Medals.
"He passed out of the sight of men by the path of duty and self-sacrifice."
37, Bennett Street, Hyde Road, Ardwick, Manchester. Z7626

PARTINGTON, D., Private, 19th R. Welch Fusiliers.
He volunteered in March 1915, and in the January following, proceeded to the Western Front. In this theatre of war, he was in action with his unit at Albert, Ploegsteert, Arras, Bullecourt, on the Somme front, and at Ypres, where he was gassed. He later took part in heavy fighting during the Advance of 1918, and in December of the same year was invalided home, admitted to hospital at Oswestry, and eventually discharged in March 1919, suffering from the effects of gas poisoning. He holds the General Service and Victory Medals.
24, Pearson Street, Newton Heath, Manchester. Z9669

PARTINGTON, E., L/Corporal, Lancashire Fusiliers.
After volunteering in January 1915, he passed through a considerable period of training and service in England, and was drafted to France in April 1917. He fought in the Battles of Vimy and Messines Ridges, and of Ypres III, in which he was wounded. Suffering also from gas poisoning and trench fever, he was invalided to hospital in England in April 1918, and eventually demobilised in February 1919. He holds the General Service and Victory Medals.
71, Park Street, Hulme, Manchester. Z7627

PARTINGTON, J., Sapper, R.E.
He volunteered in June 1917, and was sent for training to a depôt in the South of England. Owing to being found medically unfit, he was not successful in obtaining his transfer overseas, and after doing good work, was discharged on that account in December of the same year.
74, Long Street, Ancoats, Manchester. Z7628

PARTINGTON, J. E., Pte., 1/4th Gloucestershire Regt.
He joined in June 1917, and five months later was drafted to Italy. Whilst in this theatre of war he saw much severe fighting and took part in many important engagements on the Piave and the Asiago Plateaux until the cessation of hostilities. Returning to England in November 1919 he was demobilised in that month, and holds the General Service and Victory Medals.
13, Teer Street, Ancoats, Manchester. Z9918B

PARTINGTON, S., Private, 1/9th Manchester Regt.
He joined the Army in May 1913, and when war broke out in August 1914 was retained for a time at various home stations. In April 1915, however, he was drafted to the Dardanelles, where he took part in the Landing at Cape Helles and in the Battles of Krithia. He made the supreme sacrifice, being killed in action in May 1915, and was entitled to the 1914-15 Star, and the General Service and Victory Medals.
"Great deeds cannot die :
"They with the sun and moon renew their light for ever."
35, Queen Street, West Gorton, Manchester. Z11942

PARTINGTON, T. N., Pte., King's (Liverpool Regt.,) and Sapper, R.E.
He volunteered in September 1914, but shortly after completing his training was invalided from the Army in January 1915. He re-enlisted, however, in July 1917, and was retained on important duties on the Anti-Aircraft Defence at Portsmouth and various other stations, where he rendered very valuable services, being unable to obtain his transfer overseas. He was demobilised in February 1919.
5, Perrin Street, Ancoats, Manchester. Z10932

PARTLAN, R., Private, East Lancashire Regiment.
Having enlisted in June 1914, he was already in the Army when war broke out two months later, and after completing his training was retained on important duties at various stations. Owing to ill-health he was unable to obtain his transfer to a theatre of war, but, nevertheless, rendered valuable services with his unit until June 1916, when he was invalided from the Army.
26, Park Street, West Gorton, Manchester. Z10933

PARTLAND, W., Private, King's (Liverpool Regt.), and Labour Corps.
He joined in February 1917, and was sent to France in the same month. He was in action near Cambrai, and was afterwards transferred to the Labour Corps, in which he did good service both before and after the Armistice until his demobilisation in September 1919. He holds the General Service and Victory Medals.
3, Percival Street, Longsight, Manchester. Z7629

PARTRIDGE, G. L/Corpl., 12th Gloucestershire Regt.
He volunteered in May 1915, and twelve months later proceeded to the Western Front, where he took part in the

Battles of Loos, the Somme, Arras and Ypres and many other engagements and fought also in the Retreat of 1918. He unhappily fell in action at Cambrai on August 26th of that year during the Advance. He was entitled to the General Service and Victory Medals.
"Honour to the immortal dead who gave their youth that the world might grow old in peace."
62, Howarth Street, Chorlton-on-Medlock, Manchester. Z10934

PARTRIDGE, J. R., Private, 8th King's Shropshire Light Infantry.
After volunteering in August 1914, he passed through a considerable period of training, and was drafted to Mesopotamia in September of the next year. He took part in two operations for the Relief of Kut and many subsequent engagements on that Front. In May 1917, in an action on the Tigris, he received severe wounds, of which he afterwards died. He was entitled to the 1914-15 Star, and the General Service and Victory Medals.
"Honour to the immortal dead who gave their youth that the world might grow old in peace."
42, Fenn Street, Hulme, Manchester. Z7630

PASCALL, E., Private, 5th Royal Welch Fusiliers.
He volunteered in November 1914, and after training and service in England, proceeded to Egypt in June 1916. He took part in engagements on the Palestine front at Magdhaba and Rafa, and was in the second and third Gaza Battles, also in the capture of Jerusalem (where he was wounded), Jericho and Aleppo. After the Armistice he returned home and was demobilised in August 1919. He holds the General Service and Victory Medals.
18, Dryden Street, Chorlton-on-Medlock, Manchester. TZ7631

PASSMAN, R., Sergt., 2nd Loyal N. Lancashire Regt.
Mobilised on the outbreak of war, he proceeded to France in September 1914, and fought in the desperate Battle of Ypres (I). He was then transferred to Gallipoli and took part in the three Krithia engagements, also in the Suvla Bay Landing, and the capture of Chunuk Bair. After doing good work in his responsible rank, he was sent to England and discharged on account of service in December 1915. He holds the 1914-15 Star, and the General Service and Victory Medals.
84, Church Street, Hulme, Manchester. Z7632

PATCHETT, H., Driver, R.A.S.C.
He joined in February 1916, and after training proceeded to France in the following August. He did good service with the transport in engagements on the Somme, near Arras (where he was gassed), at the capture of Bullecourt and in the third Battle of Ypres, in which he was wounded a second time. On recovery he took part in the action of Cambrai (I), and later in the Retreat and Advance of 1918. He was demobilised in January 1919, and holds the General Service and Victory Medals.
39, Green Street, West Gorton, Manchester. Z7633B

PATCHETT, W., Gunner, R.F.A.
He joined in April 1917, and served with his unit at various stations in England. Owing to his youth he was not successful in obtaining his transfer overseas before the cessation of hostilities, but after the Armistice joined the Army of Occupation on the Rhine and remained with it until April of that year, when he was sent home. He was still serving in Scotland in 1920.
39, Green Street, Gorton, Manchester. Z7633A

PATIENT, T. C., Driver, R.A.S.C.
Mobilised on the outbreak of war, he proceeded with his Corps to France in the Expeditionary Force, and did good service in the Retreat from Mons, also in the Battles of Neuve Chapelle and Ypres (II). He carried out his difficult and often dangerous work in connection with supply until May 1916, when he was discharged on account of service, and holds the Mons Star, and the General Service and Victory Medals.
25, Dorrington Street, Hulme, Manchester. TZ7634

PATRICK, J., Sapper, R.E.
He volunteered at the outbreak of war in August 1914, and after training was retained on important duties at various stations in England until February 1917. He was then drafted to the Western Front, where he took part in the Battles of Arras, Messines and Ypres, fought also in the Retreat and Advance of 1918, and was gassed at Passchendaele in November 1917. Demobilised in June 1919, he holds the General Service and Victory Medals.
10, Garrick Street, Ancoats, Manchester. Z10935

PATTEN, C., Private, 1/8th Manchester Regiment.
Called up from the Reserve at the outbreak of war in August 1914, he was drafted in the following February to Gallipoli. There he took part in the operations during the Landing, and later fell in action on June 4th, 1915, during the third Battle of Krithia. He was entitled to the 1914-15 Star, and the General Service and Victory Medals.
"The path of duty was the way to glory."
5, Penley Street, Manchester   TZ9317

PATTERSON, H., Private, Royal Welch Fusiliers.
He joined in April 1918, and after undergoing a period of training served at various stations, where he was engaged on duties of great importance. He was not successful in obtaining his transfer to a theatre of war, but, nevertheless, rendered valuable services with his unit until February 1919, when he was demobilised.
184, Hamilton Street, Collyhurst, Manchester.   Z10936B

PATTERSON, H., Private, R.A.M.C.
He joined in May 1917, and after training at various hospitals, was sent to Egypt in the following December. He did valuable work at various places on the Palestine front, in connection with both illness and wounds, going as far as Damascus and Beyrout, and, serving on for many months after the Armistice, was not demobilised until March 1920. He holds the General Service and Victory Medals.
23, Wycliffe Street, Ardwick, Manchester.   Z7635

PATTERSON, W., Private, Royal Welch Fusiliers.
Joining in January 1917, he proceeded to Salonika on completing two months' training and there saw much severe fighting. He took part in the recapture of Monastir and in many other important engagements on the Vardar and Struma fronts until the cessation of hostilities. Returning home in February 1919, he was demobilised in the following month, and holds the General Service and Victory Medals.
184, Hamilton Street, Collyhurst, Manchester.   Z10936A

PATTERSON, W., Private, Lancashire Fusiliers, and R.A.V.C.
He joined in May 1916, and after completing a period of training was retained at various stations, where he was engaged on duties of a highly important nature. He was not successful in his efforts to obtain his transfer to the Front, but, nevertheless, rendered very valuable services, and in December 1920 was still with his unit.
184, Hamilton Street, Collyhurst, Manchester.   Z10936C

PAULL, H., Corporal, West Somerset Hussars.
After volunteering in October 1914, he passed through his training and saw service on many different fronts. In September 1915 he was drafted to Gallipoli and took part in the Suvla Bay Landing. After the Evacuation he was transferred to Egypt and fought in many actions on the Palestine front, including the first two Gaza Battles and the capture of Jerusalem. He was then in March 1918, sent to France, and in the Retreat and Advance of that year fought at Amiens, Bapaume, Havrincourt and Lille. He was demobilised in April 1919, and holds the 1914-15 Star, and the General Service and Victory Medals.   Z7636
120, Higher Cambridge St., Chorlton-on-Medlock, Manchester.

PAYNE, E., Sergeant, 1/8th Lancashire Fusiliers.
He volunteered in August 1914, and in March of the next year sailed for Gallipoli. Taking part in operations on the Peninsula, including the first Landing at Cape Helles and that at Suvla Bay and the capture of Chunuk Bair, he was wounded in January 1916 during the Evacuation. After treatment he was drafted to France in April 1917, and fought in the Battles of Messines, Cambrai and in the early stages of the German Offensive, during which he was taken prisoner on April 5th, 1918, and held in captivity in Germany. Repatriated in December 1918, he was demobilised in the following month, and holds the 1914-15 Star, and the General Service and Victory Medals.
36, Prescott Street, Hulme, Manchester.   Z11795

PAYNE, J., Sapper, R.E.
He joined in May 1917, and went through long training in England, not being sent to France until October 1918. He was in time to render good service in the engagement of Le Cateau (II) and on the Sambre just before the Armistice. After thus taking part in the victorious Advance, he was eventually demobilised in September 1919, and holds the General Service and Victory Medals.
49, Thomas Street, Hulme, Manchester.   Z7637

PAYNE, W., Private, 16th Lancashire Fusiliers.
He volunteered in June 1915, and proceeded to France in the following December. He saw heavy fighting at Albert (where he was wounded), in the Battles of Somme (I) and Ypres (III), and also at Havrincourt in the Retreat and Advance of 1918, in the course of which he was again wounded. After treatment at a Base hospital in France, he returned to England, and was finally demobilised in March 1919. He holds the 1914-15 Star, and the General Service and Victory Medals.
34, Ogden Street, Hulme, Manchester.   TZ7638

PEACH, A., Private, 4th South Wales Borderers.
He volunteered in April 1915, and, after training and service in England, proceeded to Mesopotamia in August 1917. He unfortunately contracted pneumonia on his way to that front, and after six months' treatment at a British hospital, died at sea on his way home in a transport ship, and was buried in the Red Sea, thus giving his life for his Country. He was entitled to the General Service and Victory Medals.
"Whilst we remember, the sacrifice is not in vain."
9, Dewsbury Place, Longsight, Manchester.   Z7016A

PEACH, S., Corporal, 1/4th S. Lancashire Regiment.
He volunteered at the outbreak of war in August 1914, and in February of the following year was drafted to the Western Front. Whilst in this theatre of war he took part in the Battles of Ypres, Festubert, Albert and Cambrai and many other important engagements, fought also in the Retreat and Advance of 1918, and was wounded in action in the Somme Offensive of July 1916. He was demobilised in March 1919, and holds the 1914-15 Star, and the General Service and Victory Medals.
36, Phelan Street, Collyhurst, Manchester.   Z10937

PEACHEY, A., Private, King's (Liverpool Regt.)
After volunteering in September 1915, he was sent to France in the following November and fought in almost every one of the important engagements on that front, being in action at St. Eloi, Albert and Ploegsteert Wood. He also took part in the great Somme Offensive of 1916, in which he was twice wounded, but on recovery served again in engagements at Arras, Bullecourt, Ypres and Cambrai, also through the Retreat and Advance of 1918, seeing fighting at Havrincourt, and on the Aisne and the Marne. After this hard service, he was demobilised in December 1918, and holds the 1914-15 Star, and the General Service and Victory Medals.
23, Holme Street, Ancoats, Manchester.   Z7639

PEACOCK, A., Private, 4th Lancashire Fusiliers.
He volunteered in August 1914, and early in 1915 was sent to the Western Front. During his service overseas he participated in heavy fighting at Ypres, La Bassée and Nieuport, before he was killed in action on the Somme on July 9th, 1916. He was entitled to the 1914-15 Star, and the General Service and Victory Medals.
"Thinking that remembrance, though unspoken, may reach him where he sleeps."
32, Elias Street, Miles Platting, Manchester.   Z9318

PEACOCK, E. Sergeant, 1/8th Manchester Regt.
Volunteering in August 1914, he was drafted to India and served for some time in Calcutta before proceeding to Hong Kong. He was later transferred to Mesopotamia, and after taking part in heavy fighting at Kut-el-Amara, was employed on draft conducting duties between Singapore and France. He returned home for demobilisation in January 1919, and holds the General Service and Victory Medals.
32, Elias Street, Miles Platting, Manchester.   Z9319

PEACOCK, H., Private, 10th Border Regiment.
He volunteered in November 1914, and in April of the following year was drafted to Gallipoli, where he took part in the Battles of Krithia and engagements at Suvla Bay. In November 1915 he was transferred to the Western Front, where he was again in action at the Battles of Albert, Ploegsteert Wood, the Somme and Bullecourt, fought also in the Retreat and Advance of 1918, and was wounded in action at Ypres in August 1917. He afterwards served with the Army of Occupation in Germany, finally returning home for demobilisation in July 1919. He holds the 1914-15 Star, and the General Service and Victory Medals.   7, Dalton St., Collyhurst, Manchester.   Z10938

PEAK, A., Private, 8th Manchester Regiment.
Mobilised on the outbreak of war, he was sent to Egypt in September 1914, and after service there, saw fighting at Gallipoli in the following summer. He then unfortunately fell ill, and being invalided home in December 1915, on his recovery did duty on garrison work on the East Coast of England until December 1917, and afterwards at a prisoners of war camp in the Isle of Man. He was finally demobilised in March 1919, and holds the 1914-15 Star, and the General Service and Victory Medals.
2, Goodier's Buildings, Ancoats, Manchester.   TZ7587A

PEAKE, A., Private, 16th Manchester Regiment.
He volunteered in December 1915, and after training and service in England, proceeded to France at the end of the following year. He saw service in the Ypres sector and on the Somme front, but then, unfortunately, contracted a bad form of influenza, which resulted in his being invalided home to hospital. On recovery he returned to France and fought again at Cambrai, also in the Advance of 1918, and was demobilised from Belgium in February 1919. He holds the General Service and Victory Medals.
40, Mornington Street, Longsight, Manchester.   Z7640

PEAKE, W., Sergt., Loyal North Lancashire Regt.
He volunteered in September 1914, and proceeded in the next month to the Western Front, on which he at once saw heavy fighting at La Bassée and in the following March at St. Eloi, where he was wounded. On recovery he fought at Loos, on the Ancre front, at Ploegsteert Wood, and in the capture of Bullecourt. In the Battle of Messines Ridge, in June 1917, he was again wounded, but served again and was finally demobilised in March 1919. He holds the 1914 Star, and the General Service and Victory Medals.
107, Bell Street, Openshaw, Manchester.   Z7641

PEAKE, W. G., Corporal, R.F.A.
He volunteered in September 1914, and was sent to Egypt in the following year. He took part in many engagements in that region, and in January 1917 was transferred to the Western Front, where he fought in the third Battle of Ypres. In the Retreat of 1918, on March 21st, he died gloriously on the Field of Battle, and was entitled to the 1914–15 Star, and the General Service and Victory Medals.
" And doubtless he went in splendid company."
8, Goodier Street, Ancoats, Manchester.   TZ7587B

PEARCE, S., Private, 19th Manchester Regiment.
He volunteered in August 1914, and after a period of training and service in England proceeded to the Western Front in September of the next year. He did much service in the trench warfare of that period of the campaign, notably at La Bassée and Givenchy. On July 3rd, 1916, in the first Battle of the Somme, he gave his life for King and Country, and was entitled to the 1914–15 Star, and the General Service and Victory Medals.
" His memory is cherished with pride."
7, Walmer Place, Longsight, Manchester.   Z7642

PEARCY, F., Private, R.A.S.C.
He joined in April 1918, having previously been engaged on work of National importance, and on completing his training in September of the same year, was drafted to the Western Front. After seeing much severe fighting in this theatre of war, he was wounded in action at Le Cateau in November 1918, and was invalided to hospital at Manchester, where he remained for eight months. Demobilised in October 1919, he holds the General Service and Victory Medals.
67, Lime Street, Miles Platting, Manchester.   Z10939

PEARSON, A., Private, 3rd Cheshire Regiment.
Volunteering in February 1915, he was drafted to Egypt in the following month and there served on the Suez Canal until transferred to the Dardanelles. He was afterwards sent to Mesopotamia, where he saw much severe fighting until wounded in action, and invalided to India and thence home. On his recovery, however, he proceeded to the Western Front and there took part in the Battles of Ypres and the Somme, and was again wounded in action. He was finally discharged as medically unfit for further service in April 1918, and holds the 1914–15 Star, and the General Service and Victory Medals.
45, Stewart Street, Gorton, Manchester.   Z10940

PEARSON, A., Private, 8th Manchester Regiment.
He volunteered in October 1914, and after training, was drafted to the Egyptian front in the following July. After taking part in the later operations at Gallipoli and in those on the Palestine front, he was transferred to France in April 1917, and fought in the Battles of Messines Ridge, and Ypres (III). Later on September 7th, 1918, he was killed in the Ypres sector by an enemy's bomb, thus giving his life for the great cause. He was entitled to the 1914–15 Star, and the General Service and Victory Medals.
" His memory is cherished with pride."
7, Horsly Street, Chorlton-on-Medlock, Manchester. TX7647

PEARSON, C., Private, 10th South Lancashire Regt.
Mobilised in August 1914, he was immediately drafted to the Western Front, where he took part in the fighting at Mons. He afterwards fought in the Battle of Ypres and many other important engagements until severely wounded in action in that sector in December 1915. Invalided home, he was retained in England after his recovery, and was finally discharged in February 1919. He holds the Mons Star, and the General Service and Victory Medals.
114, Jersey Street Dwellings, Ancoats, Manchester. Z10941

PEARSON, E., Pte., 18th (Queen Mary's Own) Hussars.
He joined in May 1916, and after a period of training in England was sent in June 1917 to India. During the voyage his ship was torpedoed in the Mediterranean, but he was landed safely in Malta. On arrival in India he took part in the Afghan frontier campaign against the hostile tribes, and serving there throughout the war was not demobilised until December 1919. He holds the General Service and Victory Medals, and the India General Service Medal (with clasp Afghanistan N.W. Frontier, 1919).
37, Bedford Street, Moss Side, Manchester.   TZ7649

PEARSON, F., Private, East Lancashire Regiment.
After volunteering in September 1914, he proceeded to the Western Front in the following March, and saw heavy fighting at St. Eloi, Hill 60, Ypres and Loos. In December of the same year he was transferred to Salonika, and there took part in the operations on the Struma and at Monastir, later in the Doiran Advance, and the Battles on the Vardar River, which concluded the campaign on that front. He was demobilised in February 1919, and holds the 1914–15 Star, and the General Service and Victory Medals.
1, Peter Street, Ardwick, Manchester.   Z7646

PEARSON, J., Private, Manchester Regiment.
He joined in October 1916, and was drafted to France in the following January. He was in action at Arras, and in the Battle of Ypres (III) and also took part in much other fighting, being chiefly engaged with the anti-aircraft section of his Battalion. After serving through the remainder of the

campaign, he was discharged in October 1919, owing to a physical disability, caused while serving, and holds the General Service and Victory Medals.
103, Heald Grove, Rusholme, Manchester.   TZ7648

PEARSON, J. A., Cpl., 2/6th Royal Warwickshire Regt.
Volunteering in August 1914, he passed through his training and was drafted to the Western Front in the following May. He fought in the Battles of Ypres (II) and Loos, was in action at Albert, and later took part in the Somme Offensive of 1916, and in engagements at Beaumont-Hamel, Arras, Messines Ridge and Cambrai. He fell fighting on the Somme front in March 1918, while taking his part in resisting the German Advance of that Spring, and was entitled to the 1914–15 Star, and the General Service and Victory Medals.
" His life for his Country."
81, Earl Street, Longsight, Manchester.   Z7645A

PEARSON, J. W., Private, 9th Cheshire Regiment.
He volunteered in July 1915, and being too young to proceed at once overseas, did service after his training at various stations in England. He eventually proceeded to the Western Front in January 1918, and fought through the Retreat and Advance of that year, taking part in all the final operations until the Armistice. He was demobilised in April 1919, and holds the General Service and Victory Medals.
81, Earl Street, Longsight, Manchester.   Z7645B

PEARSON, R., A.B., R.N., H.M.S. " Mounsey."
He joined the Royal Navy in July 1910, and after the outbreak of war in August 1914, served in H.M.S. " Mounsey," in which vessel he took part in the Battles of Heligoland Bight and Dogger Bank. He later proceeded to the Dardanelles, and after the Evacuation served with the Grand Fleet in the North Sea, and participated in the Battle of Jutland. He was subsequently employed on patrol and other duties until he returned to Devonport, from which station he was discharged in January 1920, holding the 1914–15 Star, and the General Service and Victory Medals.
15, Teignmouth Street, Collyhurst, Manchester.   Z9422B

PEARSON, S., Corporal, Royal Dublin Fusiliers.
After volunteering in September 1914, and receiving training in England, he was sent in July 1915 to the Dardanelles, and took part in the Suvla Bay Landing, and in the operations which succeeded it. He then unfortunately contracted fever, and was invalided home. On recovery he proceeded to France in August 1916, and fought in the latter stages of the Somme Offensive, during which he was badly wounded at Beaumont-Hamel in November, and being evacuated to hospital in England was finally discharged as unfit for further service in January 1918. He holds the 1914–15 Star, and the General Service and Victory Medals.
50, Gore Street, Greenheys, Manchester.   TZ7644

PEARSON, W., Pte., 7th Loyal N. Lancashire Regt.
After volunteering in September 1914, he proceeded to France in the following January, and at once took part in the Battles of Neuve Chapelle and Hill 60. Later he was in action at Festubert and fought in the Somme Offensive, also at Bullecourt, Messines Ridge, and in the third Battle of Ypres. Serving through the Retreat and Advance of 1918, he returned to England shortly before the Armistice, and was demobilised in January 1919. He holds the 1914–15 Star, and the General Service and Victory Medals.
25, Gatley Street, Ancoats, Manchester.   Z7643

PEARTON, J. E., Private, 3rd Welch Regiment.
Volunteering in March 1915, he was drafted to the Western Front on completing his training three months later, and there saw heavy fighting in various sectors. After taking part in the Battles of Loos and Vimy Ridge, and other important engagements, he was severely wounded in action on the Somme in July 1916, and sent home. He was invalided from the Army in September 1919, and holds the 1914–15 Star, and the General Service and Victory Medals.
33, Great Nelson Street, West Gorton, Manchester. Z10942

PEARTON, T. W., Private, 5th Manchester Regt.
He joined in September 1916, and was drafted to the Western Front in the following December. He saw heavy fighting in the Somme Sector, and at Arras. Later in the third Battle of Ypres he was dangerously wounded, and being sent to a Base hospital, succumbed to his wounds on October 28th, 1917. He was entitled to the General Service and Victory Medals, and was buried in Wimereux Cemetery, near Boulogne.
" His life for his Country, his soul to God."
12, Marsland Street, Ardwick, Manchester.   Z7650

PECK, G., Pte., Manchester Regt. and A/M., R.A.F.
After volunteering in January 1916, he was sent for training to various stations in the North of England, and proceeded to France in January 1917. Soon after his arrival there he was transferred to the Royal Air Force, and rendered valuable services, being a mechanic by trade, in aeroplane repairing and constructional work. Attacked by severe influenza when home on leave he received treatment in hospital, and on recovery returned to France and continued his work to the end of the war, being finally demobilised in August 1919. He holds the General Service and Victory Medals.
10, Webster Street, Greenheys, Manchester.   Z7651

PEDDER, C. G. (M.S.M.), Staff Sergt. Major, R.A.S.C.

An ex-soldier, who had served in the South African war, he was mobilised on the outbreak of hostilities, and proceeded to France in September 1914. He did great service first with the ambulance, and afterwards on food supply, was promoted to Company Sergt.-Major, and then to Staff Sergt.-Major, was twice mentioned in Despatches, and was awarded the Meritorious Service Medal for his excellent work in the Field. After the Armistice he was sent, in March 1919, to Ireland, where he was still serving in 1920, and will now have completed twenty-three years' service in the Army. In addition to the Meritorious Service Medal, he holds the Queen's South African, the 1914 Star, and the General Service and Victory Medals, as well as the Long Service Medal.
38, Halston Street, Hulme, Manchester. Z7652

PEDDER, M., Pte., 2nd Northumberland Fusiliers.

He volunteered in 1915, and in the following year proceeded to Mesopotamia, where he saw much severe fighting. He took part in engagements at Ali-el-Gharb, Um-el-Hannah, Sanna-i-Yat, the Tigris and many other places, and also served at the Relief of Kut. He was afterwards transferred to India, and was engaged on garrison duties at various stations until his return home for demobilisation in March 1919. He holds the General Service and Victory Medals.
64, Buckley Street, St. Michael's, Manchester. Z10943

PEDLEY, J. R., C.S.M., Manchester Regiment.

He was already serving in India when war broke out in August 1914, and was immediately drafted to the Western Front, where he was wounded in action at Givenchy in March 1915. Invalided home, he proceeded on his recovery to Mesopotamia, and there took a prominent part in many important engagements, and was again wounded on two occasions. He was then sent to hospital in India, and was afterwards in command of a clearing camp for convalescents until his return home in 1919. He then served in Ireland, and was finally discharged in June 1920, holding the 1914–15 Star, and the General Service and Victory Medals.
15, Fisher Street, Newton, Manchester. Z10058B

PEERS, W., Private, 2nd Border Regiment.

He volunteered in October 1914, and on completing his training in the following year, was drafted to France. There he took part in the Battles of Neuve Chapelle, St. Eloi, Loos, Albert and Ploegsteert. He was unfortunately killed in action during the raids along the Somme on May 9th, 1916, and was entitled to the 1914–15 Star, and the General Service and Victory Medals.
"A costly sacrifice upon the altar of freedom."
52, Buckley Street, St. Michaels, Manchester. Z10944

PEET, A., Private, 3rd Manchester Regiment.

He joined in September 1918, but was not successful in obtaining a transfer to a theatre of war owing to the termination of hostilities. Retained at home, he served at Filey and Bisley, and rendered excellent service whilst employed on various duties of an important nature, until he was demobilised in November 1919.
42, Parkfield Avenue, Rusholme, Manchester. Z9671

PEET, H. G., Rifleman, 4th Rifle Brigade.

Having volunteered in August 1914, he passed through his training, and was drafted to France in the following December. He saw heavy fighting at St. Eloi, where he was wounded, and on his recovery, in the Battle of Ypres (II), in which he was gassed, but fought afterwards in the Somme Offensive, where he was again wounded in September 1916. In spite of these wounds he was engaged later at Arras and Messines Ridge, and serving on, was demobilised immediately after the Armistice. He holds the 1914–15 Star, and the General Service and Victory Medals.
26, Armitage Street, Ardwick, Manchester. Z7653

PEGG, J. W., Private, Manchester Regiment.

Having enlisted in 1911, he was serving in India on the outbreak of war, and proceeded to France in April 1915. He took part in the Battles of Hill 60, and Ypres (II), and after treatment in hospital for illness, proceeded to Salonika in January 1916. In the following October he was in action on the Doiran front, where he was wounded, but recovered and fought in the Advance on the Vardar, which concluded that campaign. He was finally demobilised in April 1919, and holds the 1914–15 Star, and the General Service and Victory Medals. 30, Ryder Street, Bradford, Manchester. Z7654

PELOW, J., Private, Royal Irish Fusiliers.

After volunteering in October 1915, and receiving training in Ireland, he proceeded to France in the following February, and saw heavy fighting at various points of the front, being wounded at Hulluch, in April 1916. Later, he took part in the Battles of Messines Ridge and Ypres (III), during which he was again wounded. In the Retreat of 1918, on March 30th, he fell fighting on the Somme front, and was entitled to the General

Service and Victory Medals.
"A costly sacrifice upon the altar of freedom."
97, Crondall Street, Moss Side, Manchester. Z7655

PEMBERTON, W., Pte., Loyal N. Lancashire Regt.

He joined in May 1916, and after a short training was drafted to the Western Front in the following August, in time to take part in the later stages of the Somme Offensive. During this, in October of that year, he was severely wounded, and after treatment at a Base Hospital, was sent to England, where he underwent many operations, and was discharged as unfit for further service in September 1918. He was still threatened in 1920 with amputation owing to his wound. He holds the General Service and Victory Medals.
14, Towson Street, Russell Street, Hulme, Manchester. TZ7656

PENDLEBURY, J., L/Corporal, M.G.C.

He joined in January 1917, and after training was sent in the following October to Mesopotamia, where he did good service in the operations which succeeded the capture of Baghdad. In October 1918 he broke down in health and had a severe attack of pneumonia, but recovered and continued to serve on that front until his demobilisation in September 1919. He holds the General Service and Victory Medals.
51, Wood Street, Hulme, Manchester. Z7657

PENNEY, A. E., Sergt., 11th Manchester Regiment.

Having previously served in South Africa, he volunteered in August 1914, and early in the following year was drafted to the Dardanelles, where he saw much heavy fighting at the Landing at Suvla Bay, and was wounded in action, and consequently invalided home. On his recovery he proceeded to France, and took a prominent part in engagements at La Bassée, Warlencourt, Bucquoy, Albert and St. Quentin. He was demobilised in March 1919, and holds the Queen's and King's South African Medals, the 1914–15 Star, and the General Service and Victory Medals.
65, Kirk Street, Ancoats, Manchester. Z10946

PENNEY, J., L/Corporal, 16th Cheshire Regiment.

He volunteered in June 1915, and proceeded to France in the following December. He saw heavy fighting at Albert, Ploegsteert Wood, and in the Somme offensive, in which he was wounded. Later he was wounded again in action at Arras in April 1917, but recovered and fought in the Battles of Ypres (III), and Cambrai (I). In the Advance of 1918 he was wounded a third time at Ypres in September. He was then invalided home, and finally demobilised in May 1919. He holds the 1914–15 Star, and the General Service and Victory Medals.
92, Tame Street, Ancoats, Manchester. TZ7658A

PENNEY, J., Private, 52nd Cheshire Regiment.

He joined in April 1918, and served with his unit at various stations in England. He was not successful in obtaining his transfer overseas before the cessation of hostilities, but after the Armistice was sent in December 1918 to the Army of Occupation on the Rhine, and served at Cologne until September 1919, being finally demobilised in February 1920.
92, Tame Street, Ancoats, Manchester. TZ7658B

PENNEY, T. H., Corporal, M.G.C.

He joined in February 1916, and proceeded to France in the following July. He took part in engagements at Beaumont-Hamel, Arras, and Bullecourt, and later in the Battle of Ypres III, in which he was wounded in August 1917. On recovery he served through the Retreat and Advance of 1918, being wounded a second time near Havrincourt Wood in September of that year. After the Armistice he returned to England, and was demobilised in February 1919. He holds the General Service and Victory Medals.
92, Tame Street, Ancoats, Manchester. TZ7659

PENNILL, W., Private, 22nd Manchester Regiment.

He volunteered in November 1914, and after a period of training and service at home, was sent in December 1915 to India, where he did garrison duty until June 1917. He was then transferred to Hong Kong, and after three months to Siberia, where he was attached to the Middlesex Regiment, and served in the Army against the Bolshevists until March 1919. He was then invalided home suffering from bronchitis, and demobilised in May 1919. He holds the 1914–15 Star, and the General Service and Victory Medals.
1, Violet Street, Hulme, Manchester. TZ7660

PENNINGTON, F., Private, 9th Lancashire Fusiliers.

He volunteered in August 1914, and in the following April proceeded to the Dardanelles, but met with an accident before landing, and was sent home. On his recovery, he was drafted to France, and took part in severe fighting at Beaumont-Hamel during the Somme Offensive, where he was badly wounded in July 1916. In consequence he was invalided home and discharged in May 1917 as medically unfit for further service. He holds the 1914–15 Star, and the General Service and Victory Medals.
103, Kendall Street, Bradford, Manchester. Z10945

PENNINGTON, F., Driver, R.A.S.C.
After volunteering in August 1914, he received short training, and proceeded to France in the following October. He did good service in the great Battle of Ypres I, and also, later, at Vermelles, where he was gassed and suffered shell-shock in May 1916, but after treatment at a Base hospital recovered, and resumed his valuable work of supply in engagements at Messines Ridge and Cambrai. Serving on to the end of the Campaign he was finally demobilised in September 1919, and holds the 1914 Star, and the General Service and Victory Medals.
24, Everton Road, Chorlton-on-Medlock, Manchester. Z7661A

PENNINGTON, J. H., Private, King's Own Scottish Borderers, and Labour Corps.
He joined in May 1916, and proceeded to the Western Front in the following August. Shortly after his arrival he was transferred to the Labour Corps, and did good work in the forward areas. In January 1917, near Arras he was killed by a shell striking the hut in which he was sleeping, thus giving his life for his Country. His body lies in the Cemetery at Arras. He was entitled to the General Service and Victory Medals.
"His name liveth for evermore."
21, Everton Road, Chorlton-on-Medlock, Manchester. Z7661B

PENNY, W., Private, 22nd Manchester Regiment.
After volunteering in November 1914, he was sent for training to various places in England, and proceeded to France in October 1915. He saw heavy fighting at Loos, St. Eloi, and Albert, and later in the Somme Offensive of 1916. During this Battle on July 3rd of that year, he gave his life for King and Country, and was entitled to the 1914-15 Star, and the General Service and Victory Medals.
"And doubtless he went in splendid company."
12, Carlisle Street, Hulme, Manchester. TZ7662

PENTLAND, T., Sergt., Lancashire Fusiliers.
Having enlisted in November 1914, in the Duke of Lancaster's Own Dragoons, he was, after his training, transferred to the Lancashire Fusiliers, and proceeded in September 1915, to France, where he did good service in the fighting of that Autumn. On January 10th, 1916 he died gloriously on the Field of Battle near Beaumont-Hamel on the Ancre front. His body lies in Beaumont-Hamel Cemetery. He was entitled to the 1914-15 Star, and the General Service and Victory Medals.
"The path of duty was the way to glory."
TZ7663

PERCIVAL, D., Private, 1/8th Manchester Regt.
Volunteering in October 1915, he was drafted overseas in the following March. During his service on the Western Front, he took part in the Battles of Vimy Ridge, the Somme (I), Arras, Ypres, Cambrai, the Somme (II), Bapaume, and Le Cateau (II). He was demobilised in January 1919, and holds the General Service and Victory Medals.
35, Branson Street, Ancoats, Manchester. Z10947

PERCIVAL, G., Private, King's (Liverpool Regt.)
Volunteering in October 1915, he was drafted to Egypt in the following April, and was in action in the Battle of Katia. He also took part in the capture of Magdhaba, Jericho, Tripoli, and Aleppo, during the British Advance through Palestine and Syria. Returning home on the conclusion of hostilities he was demobilised in March 1919, and holds the General Service and Victory Medals.
33A, Peel Street, Hulme, Manchester. Z11796

PERCIVAL, J., Private, 1st Manchester Regiment.
He joined in September 1916, and on completing his training in the following year, was drafted to India, thence to Mesopotamia. In this theatre of war he served about four weeks and then proceeded to Palestine, where he took part in several engagements, including the Capture of Jerusalem. He returned home and was demobilised in May 1919, and holds the General Service and Victory Medals.
44, Harvest Street, West Gorton, Manchester. Z10948

PERCIVAL, J., Private, 52nd Welch Regiment.
He joined in July 1918, and after training served with his unit at various stations in the United Kingdom. He was not successful in obtaining his transfer overseas before the cessation of hostilities, but immediately after the Armistice was sent to the Army of Occupation on the Rhine, and served in it until January 1920, when he was transferred to Ireland and finally demobilised in March 1920.
39, Sandal Street, Newton, Manchester. Z7588

PERCY, G., Private, Border Regiment.
He joined in September 1917, and completing his training was stationed at various depôts with his unit on guard and other duties. He was unsuccessful in obtaining his transfer overseas prior to the cessation of hostilities, but was drafted to Russia in May 1919. He saw much service against the Bolshevist Forces, and returned home in September 1919. He was demobilised in the following month, and holds the General Service Medal.
11, Crissey Street, Queen's Road, Manchester. Z11568

PERKINS, F., 1st Class Stoker, R.N.
He was mobilised in August 1914, and quickly proceeded to the North Sea on board H.M. Submarine "K12." He took part in the Battles of Heligoland Bight and Jutland, and was also engaged on important patrol duties off the Coast of Belgium. He was discharged in April 1920, and holds the 1914-15 Star, and the General Service and Victory Medals.
49, Saville Street, Miles Platting, Manchester. Z10950

PERKINS, G., Private, 7th South Lancashire Regt.
He volunteered in April 1915, and later in the same year was drafted to France. There he took part in the Battles of Loos, Albert, Vimy Ridge, the Somme, Arras, and Bullecourt. He died gloriously on the Field of Battle at Messines on June 7th, 1917, and was entitled to the 1914-15 Star, and the General Service and Victory Medals.
"The path of duty was the way to glory."
6, Diggles Street, Ancoats, Manchester. Z10951A

PERKINS, W., Private, 2nd Manchester Regiment.
Volunteering in March 1915, he was drafted to France in the following year. Whilst overseas he took part in many engagements including those at Ypres, on the Somme, at Nieuport, and La Bassée, and was wounded. In consequence he was invalided home, but, on his recovery, returned to France and was in action at Arras. He was demobilised in January 1919, and holds the General Service and Victory Medals.
6, Tavery Street, Ancoats, Manchester. Z10949

PERRIN, A., L/Cpl., 13th Manchester Regt. and R.E.
After volunteering in December 1914, he passed through his training, and was drafted to the Western Front in the following August. He saw heavy fighting at Loos and Albert, and in November of the same year was transferred to Salonika, where he took part in the Offensive on the Doiran front, and the actions on the Struma River, and against Monastir. He was then attacked by illness, and being invalided home in November 1916, was on his recovery transferred to the Royal Engineers, in which Corps he served on defence work in the North of Ireland, until his demobilisation in March 1919. He holds the 1914-15 Star, and the General Service and Victory Medals.
50, Gonm Street, Longsight, Manchester. Z7665

PERRIN, E., Private, Manchester Regiment.
He volunteered in November 1914, and after training proceeded in August 1915 to Gallipoli, where he took part in the Suvla Bay Landing, and in the further operations which succeeded it. After the Evacuation he went to Egypt, and was transferred from there to France in September 1916, in time to join the later stages of the Offensive on the Somme. He gave his life for his Country on this front in October 1916, and holds the 1914-15 Star, and the General Service and Victory Medals.
"His name liveth for evermore."
27, Helsby Street, Ardwick, Manchester. Z6215B

PERRIN, J., Private, 26th Manchester Regiment.
He volunteered in August 1914, and after his training served with his unit at various stations in the United Kingdom. He rendered valuable services, but was not successful in obtaining his transfer overseas before the cessation of hostilities, and after doing good work, was eventually demobilised in November 1919. 24, Princess St., Rusholme, Manchester. Z7664

PERRIN, T., Private, 2nd Manchester Regiment.
He was called up from the Reserve in August 1914, and immediately drafted to France, where he was wounded at the Battle of Mons, and invalided home. On his recovery he returned to the Western Front, but was shortly afterwards sent to Mesopotamia and saw much heavy fighting. He was unfortunately killed in action at the Relief of Kut on March 8th, 1916. He was entitled to the Mons Star, and the General Service and Victory Medals.
"He passed out of the sight of men by the path of duty and self-sacrifice."
34, Butterworth Street, Bradford, Manchester. Z10952

PERRIS, R., Driver, R.F.A.
He volunteered in November 1915, and after a period of training proceeded to Salonika. In this seat of operations he took part in engagements on the Struma and Doiran fronts, and at the Recapture of Monastir. He returned home and was demobilised in January 1919, holding the General Service and Victory Medals.
31, Seal Street, Collyhurst, Manchester. Z10953

PERRY, J. R., Pte., 6th K.O. (R. Lancaster Regt.)
After volunteering in August 1914, he was sent in the following June to Gallipoli, and took part in the 3rd Krithia Battle, in which he was wounded. After treatment at a hospital in England he recovered in December 1915 and proceeded to Mesopotamia. He was in action at Kut-el-Amara, and served in the Kut Relief Force. On April 9th, 1916, he was reported missing, and later officially presumed killed in action. He was entitled to the 1914-15 Star, and the General Service and Victory Medals.
"Nobly striving,
He nobly fell that we might live."
11, Hibbert Street, Hulme, Manchester. Z2481A

PERRY, E., Private, 16th Manchester Regiment.
After volunteering in June 1915, he was drafted to France in the following January, and at once saw heavy fighting at Loos, also, later at Albert, where he was wounded on April 23rd. On recovery he took part in the Somme Offensive, and was unfortunately taken prisoner in July of the same year. After nearly two years' imprisonment in Germany, he was, on his release demobilised in March 1919, and holds the General Service and Victory Medals.
20, Hibbert Street, Hulme, Manchester. Z7670

PERRY, J., Private, Manchester Regiment.
He volunteered in July 1915, and crossing to France in the following December was engaged in heavy fighting in the Somme Offensive, and the Battle of Arras. He died gloriously on the Field of battle in January 1917, and was entitled to the 1914-15 Star, and the General Service and Victory Medals.
"Thinking that remembrance, though unspoken, may reach him where he sleeps."
60, Lowe Street, Miles Platting, Manchester. TZ11755B

PERRY, L., Private, Manchester Regiment.
Volunteering in November 1914, he proceeded to the Western Front in the following July, and was in action in several engagements on the Somme. He also fought in the Battle of Arras, and was wounded and taken prisoner on July 16th, 1917. He died from the effects of his injuries, whilst in a German prisoner-of-war camp, on October 19th, 1918, and was entitled to the 1914-15 Star, and the General Service and Victory Medals.
"He passed out of the sight of men by the path of duty and self-sacrifice."
60, Lowe Street, Miles Platting, Manchester. TZ11755A

PERRY, R., Driver, R.F.A.
He volunteered in August 1914, and after some months of training, was sent to Salonika, where he did good service as a shoeing smith of Artillery horses, taking part in the Doiran offensive, and the operations on the Vardar River. In April 1918, he was invalided home, and was discharged on account of service in November of that year. He holds the 1914-15 Star, and the General Service and Victory Medals.
27, Cawdor Street, Hulme, Manchester. TZ7667

PERRY, S., Corporal, R.F.A.
After volunteering in February 1915, he proceeded to France in the following November, and was in action at Loos, St. Eloi, Albert, and Vimy Ridge. He afterwards fought at Beaumont-Hamel and Arras, and in the Battles of Ypres III, including Passchendaele Ridge, and Cambrai I. He served through the Retreat and Advance of 1918, seeing fighting at Bapaume, Havrincourt Wood, and Le Cateau. He concluded his service by doing duty as shoeing smith until demobilised in February 1919. He holds the 1914-15 Star, and the General Service and Victory Medals.
31, Cawdor Street, Hulme, Manchester. Z7668

PERRY, T., Driver, R.F.A.
After volunteering in November 1914, he was sent to France in June of the next year, and fought in the Battle of Ypres II, also at Festubert, Givenchy, and La Bassée. He also took part in actions at Loos, and in the Somme Offensive in which he was wounded, but soon recovered, and was engaged at Arras, Vimy Ridge, Bullecourt, and the 3rd Battle of Ypres. Serving all through the later stages of the Campaign, he was finally demobilised in January 1919, and holds the 1914-15 Star, and the General Service and Victory Medals.
19, Sutherland Street, Hulme, Manchester. Z7669

PERRY, W., Pte., Cheshire Regt., and Labour Corps.
He joined in August 1916, and proceeded at once to France, doing duty on the line of communication on the Somme and Ancre Fronts, and also near Passchendaele Ridge, and Cambrai, having been transferred to the Labour Battalion attached to his Regiment. He subsequently went to Germany and served in the Army of Occupation on the Rhine, being eventually demobilised in October 1919. He holds the General Service and Victory Medals. Z7666
20, Ambrose Street, Pottery Lane, Openshaw, Manchester.

PETERSEN, A., Sergt., 13th Warwickshire Regt., and M.G.C.
After volunteering in August 1914, he went through training and service in England, and was drafted to the Western Front in February 1916. He did good service in his responsible rank, and saw much hard fighting, being wounded twice, and suffering also from shell-shock and trench fever. His wounds were gained in the Somme Offensive of 1916, his other disablement in the 3rd Battle of Ypres, and after it. Notwithstanding these he served on through all the final operations, being in action at Arras and Cambrai, and was eventually demobilised in January 1919. He holds the General Service and Victory Medals.
83, Percival Street, Chorlton-on-Medlock, Manchester. TX7671

PETTITT, W. G., Driver, R.A.S.C.
Volunteering in August 1914, he was sent in the following month to Egypt, and took part in the operations on the Suez Canal, and later in the action at Mersa Matruh. He then unfortunately contracted fever, and after treatment at hospital in Egypt, was invalided home. On recovery in August 1916, he proceeded to Salonika, where he joined in the

Doiran offensive, the Struma River engagement, and the Capture of Monastir. Being again attacked with fever, he was sent home, and discharged as unfit for further service in March 1918. He holds the 1914-15 Star, and the General Service and Victory Medals.
38, Buckingham Street, Moss Side, Manchester. Z7672

PETTY, A., Sergt., Duke of Wellington's (West Riding Regiment).
Having enlisted in January 1914, he was serving in the Army at the outbreak of hostilities, and was sent to France in August of that year. He took part in the desperate Battle of Ypres I, and in fighting round Arras, but then unfortunately suffered from frost bite. After some months of hospital treatment in England, he recovered, and returning to France, served in the Somme offensive of 1916, the capture of Bullecourt, and the Retreat and Advance of 1918. He was eventually demobilised in November 1919, and holds the 1914 Star, and the General Service and Victory Medals.
31, Glebe Street, Gorton, Manchester. Z7673

PHAIR, R., Private, 86th Labour Corps.
He joined in March 1917, and proceeded in his Corps to France in the same month. He did good service on the Somme front, and near Vimy Ridge, Ypres, Arras, and Cambrai. He carried on his valuable duties in the Advance of 1918, and after the Armistice went with the Army of Occupation to the Rhine. He was demobilised in January 1919, and holds the General Service and Victory Medals.
5, Abbey Grove, Hulme, Manchester. Z7674

PHAUP, W., Private, 8th Border Regiment.
After volunteering in September 1915, he passed through some months of training and service in England, and was drafted to the Western Front in February 1917. On the 23rd of April in that year he died a glorious death in the Battle of Arras, thus giving his life for the great cause of freedom. He was entitled to the General Service and Victory Medals.
"A valiant Soldier, with undaunted heart he breasted life's last hill."
24, Neptune Street, Ancoats, Manchester. Z7675

PHEASEY, J. E., 7th Manchester Regiment.
He volunteered in July 1915, and served with his unit at various stations in the United Kingdom. He rendered valuable services, but, owing to a physical disability, was not successful in obtaining his transfer overseas, and after doing good work, was discharged as medically unfit in February 1917.
32, Hardy Street, West Gorton, Manchester. Z7676

PHEASEY, T., Sergt., 1/7th Manchester Regiment.
After volunteering in August 1914, and undergoing training, he was sent in April of the next year to Gallipoli, and took part in the famous landing, and in the three Krithia Battles, which succeeded it, also in the Suvla Bay operation. After the Evacuation he went to Egypt, and fought on the Suez Canal, and in the actions at Katia, El Fasher, and Romani. Being transferred to France, he was in engagements at Arras, Ypres, and Cambrai, also in the Retreat of March 1918, on the Somme, in which he was wounded, but after some months treatment at a Base hospital recovered, and went with the Army of Occupation to the Rhine, being eventually demobilised in October 1919. He holds the 1914-15 Star, and the General Service and Victory Medals.
124, Armitage Street, Ardwick, Manchester. Z7677

PHELAN, D. D., Sergt., South Lancashire Regt.
He volunteered in August 1915, and after training at a depot in North Wales, served at various stations in England. He rendered valuable services, but was not successful in obtaining his transfer overseas before the cessation of hostilities, and after doing much useful and responsible work, especially as a Government Clerk, was eventually demobilised in July 1919.
7, Hardman St., City Road, Hulme, Manchester. Z7679

PHELAN, J., L/Corporal, 1/8th Manchester Regt.
After volunteering in August 1915, and passing through his training, he proceeded to France in the following June, and saw service at once in the Somme offensive, in which he was severely wounded, but, after long treatment in hospital, recovered, and returning to France in June 1917, took part in the engagements at Ypres III, Cambrai I, and the Retreat of March 1918 on the Somme. In this he was gassed, and after being sent to a Base hospital, concluded his service as officers' mess orderly, being demobilised in June 1919. He holds the General Service and Victory Medals.
38, Houghton Street, Bradford, Manchester. Z7678

PHILBIN, M., Private, 18th Royal Irish Regiment.
Having volunteered immediately after the outbreak of war, he proceeded to France with the Expeditionary Force, and took part in the Retreat from Mons, and the great Battle of the Marne which succeeded it. Later he fought at Ypres, where he was wounded in May 1915, and on recovery, at Armentières where he was again wounded in July of the same year. After hospital treatment, he was transferred to Salonika in November 1915, and was in action in the Doiran Advance, and on the Struma River. Serving on this front to the end of the war, he was demobilised in February 1919, and holds the Mons Star, and the General Service and Victory Medals.
6, Somerset Square, Ardwick, Manchester. Z7680

PHILLINGHAM, A., Private, Manchester Regt.
He joined in February 1917, and was sent to France in the following July, but in September of the same year was transferred to Italy, and took part in the 1st Piave Battle, and the action on the Asigao Plateau. In September 1918 he returned to France, and in the final Advance of October was wounded, and being invalided to hospital in Scotland, was finally discharged on account of wounds in March 1919, and holds the General Service and Victory Medals.
31, Whyatt Street, Bradford, Manchester.　　　Z7682C

PHILLINGHAM, H., Sapper, R.E.
Volunteering in September 1914, he passed through his training and proceeded to France in the following July. He rendered good service at Loos in that year, and in the great Somme offensive of 1916, also in the Battle of Ypres III in 1917. On March 21st of the next year, during the Retreat, he was badly gassed, and being invalided to hospital in Scotland, on his recovery, remained on home service in the South of England until his demobilisation in February 1919. He holds the 1914–15 Star, and the General Service and Victory Medals.
31, Whyatt Street, Bradford, Manchester.　　　TZ7682A

PHILLINGHAM, J., Private, Lancashire Fusiliers.
He volunteered in September 1914, and on completing his training in the following May was drafted to France, where he took part in the Battles of Ypres, Festubert, St. Eloi, Vimy Ridge, and the Somme. In January 1917 he was transferred to Egypt, and later saw much fighting in Palestine at Gaza, and the fall of Jerusalem. He was serving in Ireland in 1920, and holds the 1914–15 Star, and the General Service and Victory Medals.
13, Gardener Street, West Gorton, Manchester.　　　Z10954

PHILLINGHAM, J., Private, Manchester Regiment.
He joined in May 1916, and two months later was drafted to India, where he was engaged on important garrison duties. Later he was transferred to China for garrison duty, but shortly afterwards contracted malarial fever, which resulted in his being invalided home. He was discharged in May 1919, and holds the General Service and Victory Medals.
9, Whyatt Street, Bradford, Manchester.　　　Z10955

PHILLINGHAM, P., Sapper, R.E.
He volunteered in September 1915, and was sent to the Western Front almost immediately. Here he did good service in construction work in the Ypres sector, and other forward areas for two years. Being then unfortunately attacked by severe illness, he was invalided home and discharged as medically unfit in December 1917. He holds the 1914–15 Star, and the General Service and Victory Medals.
31, Whyatt Street, Bradford, Manchester.　　　TZ7682B

PHILIP, J., Private, 4th East Lancashire Regiment.
He joined in September 1917, and after training, served in his unit at various stations in England, and rendered valuable services, especially in connection with clerk's work, and the issuing of rations, but was not successful in obtaining his transfer overseas before the cessation of hostilities, and was afterwards sent on garrison duty to Ireland, where he was still serving in 1920.
7, Watson Street, West Gorton, Manchester.　　　Z7684

PHILLIP, A., Private, 2nd Manchester Regiment.
Volunteering on the outbreak of war, he proceeded to France with the Expeditionary Force, and fought in the Retreat from Mons, also in the desperate Battle of Ypres I, and at Neuve Chapelle, Ypres II, and Albert. Later he was engaged in the Somme offensive, at Arras, and in the 3rd Battle of Ypres, in which he was badly gassed, and being evacuated to hospital in England, was invalided out of the Service in January 1918. He holds the Mons Star, and the General Service and Victory Medals.
18, Mellow Street, Hulme, Manchester.　　　TZ7685

PHILLIPS, A. J., Private, Royal Welch Fusiliers.
After volunteering in June 1915, he was sent to France in the following January, and saw much heavy fighting at Vermelles, and Vimy Ridge, and in the Somme offensive of July 1916, in which he was wounded. On recovery he fought at Arras, and in the Battle of Ypres III, in which he was wounded a second time, so severely as to necessitate his removal to hospital in England, and his discharge in July 1919. He holds the General Service and Victory Medals.
20, Teak Street, Beswick, Manchester.　　　Z7686

PHILLIPS, C., Tpr., Duke of Lancaster's Own Dragoons.
After volunteering in September 1914, he passed through a considerable period of training in England, and was sent to France in September of the same year. He saw service in the Ypres sector, and later at Armentières, Loos, Albert, and Vimy Ridge. He was then unfortunately attacked with a serious complaint, and being invalided to hospital in Scotland, was discharged in July 1916 as unfit for further service. He holds the Queen's and King's South African Medals, as well as the 1914–15 Star, and the General Service and Victory Medals.
20, Industrial Street, Stockport Road, Chorlton-on-Medlock, Manchester.　　　Z7688

PHILLIPS, F., Pte., King's Shropshire Light Infantry.
He joined in June 1917, and proceeded to France in the following September. He took part in actions near Messines Ridge, and in the 1st Battle of Cambrai, also in the Retreat and Advance of 1918 until the Armistice, after which, on his return home, he was demobilised in January 1919. He holds the General Service and Victory Medals.
18, Lever Street, Bradford, Manchester.　　　TZ7687

PHILLIPS, H., Corporal, South Wales Borderers.
Volunteering in April 1915, he was retained at home on important duties until December 1916, when he was sent to the Western Front. There he took part in strenuous fighting at Arras, Bullecourt, Messines Ridge, Lens, Cambrai, Bapaume, Havrincourt, and on the Aisne, Marne, and Somme fronts. He rendered valuable services whilst overseas, and was demobilised in March 1919, holding the General Service and Victory Medals.
32, Rhodes Street, Miles Platting, Manchester.　　　TZ9322

PHILLIPS, H., Private, M.G.C.
After volunteering in September 1915, he was sent to France in the following January, and did good work in the great Somme offensive of July 1916, and later in the Battles of Ypres, III, and Cambrai I. He fought right through the Retreat and Advance of 1918 until the Armistice, and was demobilised in January 1919. He holds the General Service and Victory Medals.
41, South Street, Longsight, Manchester.　　　Z7683

PHILLIPS, J., Sergt., Manchester Regiment.
Volunteering in March 1915, he was drafted to France in the following August. During his service on the Western Front he took a prominent part in the Battles of Vimy Ridge, the Somme, Arras, Bullecourt, Messines, Ypres (III), Passchendaele, and Cambrai, in engagements in the Retreat and Advance of 1918, and was wounded in action at Loos. He was demobilised in February 1919, and holds the 1914–15 Star, and the General Service and Victory Medals.
89, Ryder Street, Collyhurst, Manchester.　　　Z10528B

PHILLIPS, T. H., Driver, R.A.S.C. (M.T.)
He joined in December 1916, and after training, was sent to the Western Front in the following August. He carried on the difficult and often dangerous work of supply in connection with action at Albert and Cambrai, also in the Retreat and Advance of 1918, at Bapaume, Havrincourt, Cambrai again, and the entry into Mons. He afterwards served with the Army of Occupation on the Rhine, and was not demobilised until March 1920. He holds the General Service and Victory Medals.
53A, Chapman Street, Hulme, Manchester.　　　Z7689

PHILLIPS, W., Gunner, R.G.A.
He joined in April 1917, and after completing his training served with his Battery at various stations engaged on important duties. He rendered valuable services, but was unable to obtain his transfer to a theatre of war, on account of medical unfitness. He was discharged in consequence in August of the same year.
26, Russell Street, Moss Side, Manchester.　　　Z11797

PHILLIPSON, E., Private, Royal Fusiliers.
He joined in June 1917, and later in the same year proceeded to France where he met with an accident, and was invalided home. On his recovery he was transferred to the Labour Corps, went to Germany with the Army of Occupation, but through the effects of his accident, was confined to hospital again, and then sent home. He was demobilised in November 1919, and holds the General Service and Victory Medals.
229, Morton Street, Longsight, Manchester.　　　Z10956A

PHILLIPSON, H., Private, 22nd Manchester Regt.
He volunteered in November 1914, and in the following year was drafted to France. There he took part in many engagements, including the Battles of the Somme, Bullecourt and Beaumont-Hamel, and was wounded in action. As a result, he was invalided home, and discharged in 1917, as medically unfit for further service. He holds the 1914–15 Star, and the General Service and Victory Medals.
229, Morton Street, Longsight, Manchester.　　　Z10956B

PHILLIPSON, H., Gunner, R.F.A.
He joined in February 1916, and was shortly afterwards drafted to France. There he took part in much severe fighting, and was badly wounded in action near Béthune, which resulted in his being invalided home, and discharged in August 1918, as medically unfit for further service. He holds the General Service and Victory Medals.
229, Morton Street, Longsight, Manchester.　　　Z10956C

PHIPPS, A. (Mrs.), Worker, Q.M.A.A.C.
She volunteered in July 1917, and at once went overseas, and did good service at a Base Headquarters in France, as waitress to girl clerks. She then unluckily contracted illness which resulted in her being sent to hospital in London. On recovery she again carried on her work at a large camp in England, and was finally demobilised in August 1919. She holds the General Service and Victory Medals.
3, Princess Street, Rusholme, Manchester.　　　Z7690A

PHIPPS, W., Gunner, R.F.A.
He volunteered n March 1915, and for a time was employed in England as a transport driver. He was sent with his Battery to France in June 1917, and did good service in engagements at Lens and Bapaume, also in the Retreat and Advance of 1918, right through the final operations until the Armistice. He was eventually demobilised in May 1919, and holds the General Service and Victory Medals.
31, Princess Street, Rusholme, Manchester. Z7690B

PHIPSON, W., Sergt., R.A.M.C.
Having enlisted originally in 1910, he proceeded to France very soon after the outbreak of war, and rendered valuable service with the Field Ambulance in most of the important engagements of the campaign, often under circumstances of great difficulty and danger. He was eventually discharged iu February 1919, as medically unfit, and holds the 1914 Star, and the General Service and Victory Medals.
15, Kinmore Street, Chorlton-on-Medlock, Manchester.
X1269A. X1270A.

PHOENIX, E., Sergt., Military Police.
He volunteered in July 1915, and was at first attached to the R.F.A., but being found unfit for service overseas, was transferred to the Military Police, in which Force he rendered valuable services at various camps in England until his discharge on the ground of health in February 1918.
6, Ridgway Street, Moss Side, Manchester. Z7691

PICKBUR, C., Private, Manchester Regiment and Labour Corps.
After volunteering in December 1914, he passed through a considerable period of training and service in England, and was drafted to France in April 1916. He saw heavy fighting in the neighbourhool of Arras and Lens, and was then transferred to the Labour Corps, in which he rendered valuable services in railway construction, road repairing and other useful work. He was demobilised in April 1919, and holds the General Service and Victory Medals.
10, Wycliffe Street, Ardwick, Manchester. Z7692

PICKER, F., Private, 13th Manchester Regiment.
He joined in March 1916, and was sent in the following September to Salonika, where he took part in the Offensive of July 1917 on the Doiran front. He was then affected by a severe attack of malarial fever, and being invalided to Malta in January 1918, was sent later to hospital in England, and finally demobilised in February 1919. He holds the General Service and Victory Medals.
28, Theodore Street, Ardwick, Manchester. Z7693B

PICKER, W. T., Sergt., 2/7th Manchester Regiment.
After volunteering in September 1914, he did valuable work as an Instructor at various centres in England, and eventually proceeded to France in March 1917. He saw much heavy fighting in that year, and in March 1918, during the Retreat on the Somme, he gave his life for his Country in the Field. He was entitled to the General Service and Victory Medals.
"Whilst we remember, the sacrifice is not in vain."
25, Theodore Street, Ardwick, Manchester. Z7693A

PICKERING, A., Private, 8th Manchester Regt.
Volunteering in April 1915, he was drafted to Egypt in the following November, and took part in heavy fighting in the Suez Canal sector. In February 1916 he wa transferred to the Western Front, where he was in action at the Battles of Albert, the Somme (I), Arras, Vimy Ridge, Cambrai, and the Somme (II). During the las^t named engagement he was badly wounded, and as a result, lost the sight of an eye. He was discharged as medically unfit for further service, and holds the 1914-15 Star, and the General Service and Victory Medals.
13, Teer Street, Ancoats, Manchester. Z10957

PICKERING, E., Pte., 4th Northumberland Fusiliers.
He joined in September 1916, and was quickly drafted to the Western Front, where he saw heavy fighting at Messines, La Bassée, Givenchy, Festubert, Béthune, Bapaume, Lens and Arras, and was wounded in action at Ploegsteert. He was taken prisoner at Armentières in April 1918, and during his captivity in Germany, was forced to work in the mines at Essen. Repatriated in November 1918, he was demobilised twelve months' later and holds the General Service and Victory Medals. 10, Drinkwater Street, Harpurhey, Manchester. Z11142

PICKERING, S., Private, 22nd Manchester Regt.
He volunteered in June 1915, and proceeded to France in the following August. He saw much severe fighting on that front, commencing with the Battle of Loos, and was actually wounded three times at Ploegsteert Wood in May 1916, on the Somme in the following November, and at Bullecourt in May 1917. Notwithstanding these wounds he fought at Cambrai and in the Somme Retreat of 1918, after which he was invalided home, and discharged in August 1918, as unfit for further service. He holds the 1914-15 Star, and the General Service and Victory Medals.
73, Phillips Street, Hulme, Manchester. TZ7694

PICKFORD, E. D., Private, 26th Manchester Regt.
He volunteered in September 1914, and after training served at various stations in the United Kingdom. He was not successful in obtaining his transfer overseas, but being transferred

to special war work rendered valuable services in connection with the construction of aeroplanes until his demobilisation in February 1919. 22, Marple St., Ardwick, Manchester. Z7697

PICKFORD, J., Private, 1/7th Manchester Regiment.
He volunteered in March 1915, and proceeded in the following July to the Western Front, where he took part in many engagements, being in action at Loos, Albert, on the Somme, and at Beaumont-Hamel. He afterwards fought at Arras and Bullecourt, in the Battles of Messines Ridge, Ypres (III) and Cambrai (I), and through the Retreat and Advance of 1918, being finally demobilised in February 1919. He holds the 1914-15 Star, and the General Service and Victory Medals.
68, Henry Street, West Gorton, Manchester. Z7696

PICKINS, H. F., Pte., 8th K.O. (R. Lancaster Regt.)
After volunteering in November 1914, and passing through training, he was sent to France in the following September, and saw heavy fighting at Loos, Albert, and in the first Battle of the Somme. Later he was in action at Arras, Bullecourt and Messines Ridge, also in the Battles of Ypres (III) and Cambrai (I). While taking part in operations near Amiens in the Retreat of 1918, he was severely wounded, and after some months' treatment at a Base Hospital was discharged in May 1919. He holds the 1914-15 Star, and the General Service and Victory Medals.
6, Blackburn Street, Marple Street, Hulme, Manchester. Z7695

PICKLES, R., Private, 3rd Lancashire Fusiliers.
He volunteered in March 1915, and three months later proceeded to the Dardanelles, where he took part in the third Battle of Krithia, and the Landing at Suvla Bay, and was badly wounded in October 1915. On his recovery he was unfit for further service overseas, and was therefore retained on special canteen and guard duties at various stations. He was demobilised in March 1919, and holds the 1914-15 Star, and the General Service and Victory Medals.
73, Branson Street, Ancoats, Manchester. Z10958

PIERCE, T., Private, K.O. (Royal Lancaster Regt.)
A Reservist, he was mobilised on the outbreak of war, and proceeded to France in September 1914, after seeing heavy fighting at Ypres, Ploegsteert Wood, on the Somme, and at Arras, during which he was wounded three times. He was transferred in March 1916 to Egypt and was in action in the Sinai Desert. In August 1918 he returned to France and serving right through the final operations, was discharged in February 1919, and holds the 1914 Star, and the General Service and Victory Medals.
31, Clifford Street, Lower Openshaw, Manchester. Z7699

PIERCE, W., Lieut., 1st Lancashire Fusiliers.
This Officer, having enlisted in 1912, was serving in India on the outbreak of war and proceeded to France in October 1914. He took part in many important engagements including those of Hill 60, Loos and Somme (I). Later he fought at Ypres and Cambrai, and in the Retreat of 1918, in which he was wounded on the Somme, and also gassed, but served on through the final stages of the war, and after the Armistice was in the Army of Occupation on the Rhine. He was not demobilised until January 1920, and holds the 1914 Star, and the General Service and Victory Medals.
38, Birch Street, Ardwick, Manchester. Z7698

PIGGOTT, T., Corporal, Military Mounted Police.
He volunteered in February 1915, and after a few months' service in Ireland, proceeded to France in the following September, and did good work in connection with engagements near Arras, Ypres, Messines and Cambrai. In November 1917 he was transferred to Italy, and was engaged on the Piave front. Returning to France in March 1918, he was in the Retreat of that Spring, and then unfortunately contracted trench fever, which resulted in his being sent to a Base Hospital. On recovery he did duty with the Mounted Police at a French Coast Station until demobilised in July 1919. He holds the Queen's and King's South African Medal, the 1914-15 Star, and the General Service and Victory Medals.
7, Hibbert Street, Rusholme, Manchester. Z7700

PIKE, C., Private, 8th Manchester Regiment.
He was mobilised at the outbreak of war, and later proceeded to the Western Front. In this theatre of war he played a prominent part with his unit in heavy fighting at Ypres, Hill 60, Albert and Festubert, and was wounded at Ypres in March 1916. Invalided home, he was sent to hospital at Bolton, but upon his recovery returned to France, where he remained until he was discharged in February 1919, holding the 1914-15 Star, and the General Service and Victory Medals.
25, Gunson Street, Ancoats, Manchester. Z9672

PILLING, J. H., Private, 7th Loyal N. Lancashire Regt.
Having volunteered in November 1915, he was drafted to France in the following February, and saw heavy fighting at St. Eloi, Hill 60, Ypres (II), Vermelles and Ploegsteert Wood. Later he took part in the Somme Offensive of July 1916, during which he was wounded at Mametz Wood in July, and being invalided to England received treatment at various hospitals until his demobilisation in March 1919. He holds the General Service and Victory Medals.
80, Bird Lane, Longsight, Manchester. TZ7681

PILLING, W., Private, King's (Liverpool Regt.), and Labour Corps.

Having volunteered in January 1915, he proceeded to France in the following August, and on his arrival was transferred to the Labour Battalion attached to his unit. and thus he did good work for fourteen months and then unfortunately met with an accident, which resulted in his being invalided to hospital in England. On his recovery he remained on Home Service until demobilised in January 1919. He holds the 1914–15 Star, and the General Service and Victory Medals.

12, Riga Street, City Road, Hulme, Manchester.   Z7701

PILSTON, H., Corporal, Border Regiment.

After volunteering in August 1914, he underwent training and proceeded in the following February to the Western Front, where he saw heavy fighting in the Battles of Neuve Chapelle, Hill 60, and Ypres (II). He was also in action at Festubert, and being severely wounded there was evacuated to Hospital in England. On recovery he did good service at recruiting centres in England until discharged as medically unfit in February 1916. He holds the 1914–15 Star, and the General Service and Victory Medals.

40, Ainsworth Street, West Gorton, Manchester.   Z7702

PIMBLETT, A. E., Private, King's (Liverpool Regt.)

After volunteering in August 1914, he went through his training and was drafted in November of the next year to the Western Front, where he took part in heavy fighting at Loos, in the Ypres sector, and many other places. Later, in the Retreat of 1918, he was severely wounded at St. Quentin, and on his recovery was sent to the Russian front, where he remained until demobilised in February 1919. He holds the 1914–15 Star, and the General Service and Victory Medals.

13, Chatsworth Street, Hulme, Manchester.   Z7703

PIMLETT, W. H., Pte., King's Shropshire Light Infty.

He joined in March 1917, and proceeded atmosl immediately to France. He saw heavy fighting in the Battles of Arras, Vimy Ridge, Ypres (III) and Cambrai (I). Later in the Retreat of 1918 on the Somme, he was badly wounded, and being evacuated to hospital in Ireland, was eventually discharged as unfit for further service in June 1918. He holds the General Service and Victory Medals.

17, Watson Street, Hulme, Manchester.   Z7704

PIMLY, J., Pte., 1st K.O. (Royal Lancaster Regt.)

After volunteering in August 1914, he proceeded to France in the following November, and fought in the desperate Battle of Ypres in which he was badly wounded, but after treatment at a Base Hospital recovered, and rejoining his unit was in action at Loos, St. Eloi, on the Somme, and at Bullecourt. He was afterwards gassed in the Battle of Cambrai, and being sent to hospital in France, on his recovery did duty at the Base until demobilised in March 1919. He holds the 1914 Star, and the General Service and Victory Medals.

26, Lord Street, Hulme, Manchester.   TZ7705

PIMLOTT, H., Private, Lancashire Fusiliers.

Volunteering in September 1914, he was quickly drafted to Egypt, where he took part in heavy fighting in the Suez Canal zone. He then proceeded to the Dardanelles, and served in many important engagements on the Gallipoli Peninsula. Returning to Egypt, he was in action at Mersa Matruh, Sollum, Katia, Romani and Magdhaba, but in December 1916, was transferred to the Western Front, where he played a prominent part in the Battles of the Ancre, Vimy Ridge, Bullecourt, Ypres, Passchendaele, Lens, Cambrai, and the Somme. He holds the 1914–15 Star, and the General Service and Victory Medals, and was demobilised in March 1919.

10, Lorne Street, Moss Side, Manchester.   TZ10959

PIMLOTT, H., L/Corporal, R.E.

He volunteered in April 1915, and proceeded to France in the following October. He rendered valuable services in the Battle of Loos, in which he was wounded, but continued his important work in other engagements, and in May 1916 was badly gassed near Vimy Ridge. As a result of this he was invalided to England and remained on Home Service until his demobilisation in March 1919. He holds the 1914–15 Star, and the General Service and Victory Medals.

22, Ridgway Street, Moss Side, Manchester.   Z7706

PIMLOTT, R., Private, Loyal N. Lancashire Regt., and King's (Liverpool Regiment).

He enlisted in July 1895, and served through the South African campaign. Proceeding to France in January 1915, he took part in the Battles of Neuve Chapelle, and Festubert, but later invalided home on account of ill-health was discharged as unfit for further service. He, however, joined the King's (Liverpool Regiment) in July 1918, and served at Purfleet on important duties until April 1920, when he was demobilised holding the 1914–15 Star, and the General Service and Victory Medals, in addition to the South African Medals.

1, Whitfield Street, Chorlton-on-Medlock, Manchester. TZ9320

PINDER, A., Private, K.O. (R. Lancaster Regiment).

He volunteered in February 1915, and two months later was drafted to France, where he was in action at Ypres and was wounded at Loos. Upon his recovery he rejoined his unit,

but was taken prisoner in July 1916, during the Battle of the Somme. He escaped from captivity on November 11th, 1918, the date of the signing of the Armistice, and eventually arrived in England. Subsequently demobilised in July 1919, he holds the 1914–15 Star, and the General Service and Victory Medals.

1, St. Georges Buildings, Stonehewer St., Manchester. Z9673

PINDER, S. H., Private, Manchester Regiment.

He joined in November 1916, and was sent to France two months later. After being in action in this theatre of war at Ypres, he was transferred to Italy, and there participated in several important engagements on various fronts. He performed exceedingly good work, and returning to England, was eventually demobilised in December 1919. He holds the General Service and Victory Medals.

41, Masonic Street, Oldham Road, Manchester.   Z9321

PINDER, T. H., Private, 7th Lancashire Fusiliers.

Having volunteered in November 1914, he went through his training, and was drafted to Gallipoli in the following July. Immediately upon his arrival there he took part in the Suvla Bay Landing, and in the course of the action died gloriously on the Field of Battle in August 1915. He was entitled to the 1914–15 Star, and the General Service and Victory Medals. "A valiant Soldier, with undaunted heart he breasted life's last hill."

34, Park Street, Hulme, Manchester.   Z7707

PINKNEY, D., L/Corporal, M.G.C.

Joining in May 1917, he was at first posted to the 14th Hussars, and then transferred to the Oxford and Buckinghamshire Light Infantry, with which Regiment he proceeded to India in November of the same year. On arrival there he was transferred to the Machine Gun Corps, and did good service on the North West Frontier, and in the Afghanistan operations of 1919. He was finally demobilised in January 1920, and holds the General Service and Victory Medals, and the India General Service Medal (with clasp, Afghanistan, N.W. Frontier, 1919).

42, Booth Street East, Chorlton-on-Medlock, Manchester. Z7708

PITMAN, S., Private, 1/8th Manchester Regiment.

He joined in August 1916, and in the following year was drafted to the Western Front, where he took part in the Battles of Bullecourt, Lens and Cambrai, in heavy fighting at St. Quentin, Loos and Armentières, and was wounded. Unfortunately he was killed in action at Albert on June 16th, 1918, and was entitled to the General Service and Victory Medals.

"His life for his Country, his soul to God."

62, Granville Place, Ancoats, Manchester.   Z10960

PITTS, W., Driver, R.F.A.

He joined in January 1918, and in the following March was drafted to the Western Front, where he took part in the Retreat and Advance of 1918, during hich he was in action at Lens, Cambrai, the Scarpe and Mons. After the cessation of hostilities, he served on the Rhine with the Army of Occupation until his demobilisation in October 1919. He holds the General Service and Victory Medals.

15, Duke Street, Bradford, Manchester.   Z10961

PLAITER, H. R., Private, 8th Manchester Regt.

Volunteering in September 1914, he was sent to Gallipoli in the following May, and after taking part in the three Krithia Battles was in the Suvla Bay Landing, in which he was severely wounded. After treatment at a hospital in England, he recovered, and in December 1916 went to France with the Royal Warwickshire Regiment, seeing service on the Ancre front, and at Arras, Messines Ridge and Ypres. In November 1917 he was transferred to Italy, but returned to France in April 1918, and concluded his service on that front, being demobilised in January 1919. He holds the 1914–15 Star, and the General Service and Victory Medals.

7, Park Street, Hulme, Manchester.   Z7710

PLAITER, J., Private, Lancashire Fusiliers.

Volunteering in August 1914, he went through training and proceeded to the Western Front in September of the following year. He saw heavy fighting at St. Eloi, Vermelles, Vimy Ridge, and in the Somme Offensive of 1916. Later he fought at Beaumont-Hamel, Beaucourt and Arras, in the Battles of Ypres (III) and at Lens, also in the Retreat and Advance of 1918, being in action near Amiens in August of that year. He was demobilised in February 1919, and holds the 1914–15 Star, and the General Service and Victory Medals.

4, Bradshaw Street, Hulme, Manchester.   Z7711

PLANT, J., Private, 2nd Manchester Regiment.

Called up from the Reserve in August 1914, he proceeded to France with the First Expeditionary Force, and was badly wounded during the Retreat from Mons. He was invalided home, but on his recovery returned to the Western Front, and took part in the Battles of Ypres (II) where he was gassed, and Loos.. In January 1916 he was transferred to Salonika, where he saw heavy fighting on the Doiran and Struma fronts, and at the re-capture of Monastir. He was again sent home through ill-health, and was discharged as medically unfit for further service in December 1916, holding the Mons Star, and the General Service and Victory Medals.

3, Worth Street, Rochdale Road, Manchester.   Z10964

PLANT, J., Private, 9th East Lancashire Regiment.
He was mobilised in August 1914, and quickly drafted to France where he took part in the Battle of Mons. Later he was transferred to Salonika, and saw much fighting on the Vardar, Doiran and Struma fronts. He returned home and was discharged in May 1919, and holds the Mons Star, and the General Service and Victory Medals.
49, Brown Street, Ancoats, Manchester. Z11943

PLATT, A., Private, 1st East Lancashire Regiment.
After volunteering in March 1915, he was drafted to the Western Front in the following July, and saw much heavy fighting, being three times wounded, once in the Somme Offensive in July 1916, and twice later in the Ypres sector in October and November 1917. He was then invalided to England, and after treatment at a Hospital in the North West, was finally demobilised in August 1919, and holds the 1914-15 Star, and the General Service and Victory Medals.
7, Meadow Street, Ardwick, Manchester. TZ7715

PLATT, A., Private, 7th Manchester Regiment.
Having enlisted in January 1914, he underwent special training on the outbreak of war, and was drafted to Gallipoli in April 1915. After taking part in the famous Landing, and in the Krithia Battles, which followed, he was sent when the Evacuation was completed, to France, and fought on the Somme, in the Battle of Ypres (III), and during the Advance of 1918, and at Havrincourt and Epéhy. He was demobilised in April 1919, and holds the 1914-15 Star, and the General Service and Victory Medals. 85, Earl St., Longsight, Manchester. Z7714

PLATT, D., Private, 7th East Lancashire Regiment.
He joined in August 1916, and after a considerable period of training and service in England proceeded to France in December 1917, and saw much service in the trenches near Cambrai, in the Ypres sector, and on the Somme. He was wounded at Passchendaele Ridge in February 1918, but after treatment at a Base Hospital, rejoined, and was badly gassed in action at Villers-Bretonneux in April of the same year. Invalided to hospital in England, he recovered, and returning to France in August, continued his service to the end of the campaign, being finally demobilised in February 1919. He holds the General Service and Victory Medals. Z7713A
10, Halsbury Street, Stockport Road, Longsight, Manchester

PLATT, E. (Mrs.), Special War Worker.
This lady volunteered in June 1915, for work of National importance, and was most usefully employed at a shell factory, where she carried out her duties faithfully as a finisher and turner, right on through the war until the Armistice, being discharged in November 1918.
10, Halsbury Street, Longsight, Manchester. Z7713B

PLATT, J., King's (Liverpool Regiment).
Volunteering in September 1914, he was after training drafted to France in September of the next year, and in the following month was transferred to Salonika, where he took part in actions on the Vardar, and later in the Doiran Offensive. In June 1918 he returned to France, and did good service with the Lewis Gun Section of his unit at Arras and Cambrai, and in the Retreat and Advance of 1918. After the Armistice he was demobilised in February 1919, and holds the 1914-15 Star, and the General Service and Victory Medals.
22, Lever Street, Bradford, Manchester. TZ7712

PLATT, J., Private, Labour Corps.
He joined in June 1917, and proceeding to France in the following month rendered valuable services with the 42nd Labour Battalion. He was engaged on special duties on the lines of communication in the Cambrai, Bapaume, Passchendaele and Le Cateau sectors, and saw severe fighting. He holds the General Service and Victory Medals, and was demobilised in March 1919. 57, Beaumont St., Beswick, Manchester. Z10962

PLATT, J., Private, South Wales Borderers.
He joined in March 1918, immediately on attaining military age, and on completion of his training, did consistently good work with his unit at various home stations. He was unsuccessful in obtaining his transfer overseas during hostilities, but later was sent to India, where he was still serving in 1920.
25, Kemp Street, Manchester. Z10963A

PLATT, J., Private, Lancashire Fusiliers.
Volunteering in September 1914, he was drafted to the Western Front in the following year, but was soon invalided home as medically unfit for service overseas. He was then engaged on special duties at home stations until 1917, when he was discharged, and holds the 1914-15 Star, and the General Service and Victory Medals.
23, Kemp Street, Manchester. Z10963B

PLATT, W., Private, 6th East Lancashire Regiment.
Volunteering in March 1915, he proceeded to Gallipoli, and after taking part in the great Landing and the engagements which followed it, was transferred to France in November 1916, and fought at Arras and Bullecourt, also in the Battle of Ypres (III). In this action he gave his life for King and Country on the Field of Battle, and was entitled to the 1914-15 Star, and the General Service and Victory Medals.
"Great deeds cannot die."
7, Meadow Street, Ardwick, Manchester. TZ7716

PLIMMER, J., Private, 22nd Manchester Regiment.
He volunteered in November 1914, and a year later was drafted overseas. During his service on the Western Front he took an active part in engagements at St. Eloi, Albert, Vimy Ridge, the Somme, Arras, Messines, Passchendaele, Cambrai, Bapaume, the Scarpe, Le Cateau, and the Sambre, and was wounded in action on three occasions. He was eventually demobilised in March 1919, and holds the 1914-15 Star, and the General Service and Victory Medals.
7, Sussex Street, West Gorton, Manchester. Z9323

PLUMMER, W., Private, K.O. (R. Lancaster Regt.)
He volunteered in August 1914, and in September of the following year was drafted to the Western Front, where he took part in the Battles of Loos and the Somme, during which engagements he was twice wounded—in July and August 1916. He was also in action at Guillemont and Festubert, where he was again wounded in April 1918. He holds the 1914-15 Star, and the General Service and Victory Medals, and was demobilised in April 1919.
14, Ross Street, West Gorton, Manchester. Z10358C

PLUMPTON, W. E., Air Mechanic, R.A.F. (late R.F.C.
Volunteering in December 1914, he was at first posted to the Manchester Regiment, but was discharged at medically unfit in February 1915. Re-enlisting in June 1916 in the Royal Air Force, he went for training to a Southern centre in England, and proceeded in the same year to the Western Front, where he did good service at many aerodromes in the forward areas. After his demobilisation in March 1919, he unfortunately contracted illness, and died in hospital in September of the same year. He was entitled to the General Service and Victory Medals.
"A costly sacrifice upon the altar of freedom."
24, Small Street, Stockport Road, Manchester. Z7717

PLUNKETT, C. W., Sapper, R.E.
He volunteered in April 1915, and proceeded to France in the following November. He took part in much heavy fighting at Loos, Albert, in the Somme Offensive of 1916, and at Arras. He also rendered good service in the Battles of Ypres (III) and Cambrai (I), as well as in the Retreat and Advance of 1918. Serving right on to the end of the campaign he was finally demobilised in June 1919, and holds the 1914-15 Star, and the General Service and Victory Medals.
5, Thornhill Street, Hulme, Manchester. TZ7718A

PLUNKETT, G. E., Pte., K.O. (R. Lancaster Regt.) and Manchester Regiment.
Volunteering in April 1915, he served for a month only in the K.O.R.L. Regiment, and was then transferred to the Manchester Regiment, in which he concluded his training. He then proceeded to Gallipoli, where he took part in the third Krithia Battle, and the Suvla Bay operations. After the Evacuation he was sent to Mesopotamia, and served all through the fighting on that front, being wounded at Baghdad. He was finally demobilised in February 1919, and holds the 1914-15 Star, and the General Service and Victory Medals.
5, Thornhill Street, Hulme, Manchester. TZ7718B

POFF, G. G., Driver, R.A.S.C. (M.T.)
After volunteering in November 1914, he proceeded to the Western Front in the following April. He rendered good service in connection with engagements at Ypres, Festubert, Loos, Albert, and on the Somme, also at Cambrai and in the Retreat and Advance of 1918. Continuing to carry out the important duties of supply all through the final stages of the campaign, he went to Cologne with the Army of Occupation and was demobilised in March 1919. He holds the 1914-15 Star, and the General Service and Victory Medals.
40, Lillian Street, Beswick, Manchester. Z7719

POINTON, W., Private, 5th Manchester Regiment.
He joined in January 1917, and after training proceeded to the Western Front in the following June. He was in action at Nieuport and Dunkirk, doing duty as stretcher bearer, and later in the Battle of Ypres (III), including Passchendaele Ridge. In this same sector on November 21st, 1917, he was killed in the Field, while bringing in wounded men, and was entitled to the General Service and Victory Medals.
"His memory is cherished with pride."
26, Williams Street, Ardwick, Manchester. Z7720

POKE, J. B. (M.M.), Cpl., 1/8th Manchester Regt.
Volunteering in August 1914, he was sent to Egypt in the following month, and served on the Suez Canal, where he was wounded in action in June 1915. After treatment in hospital at Malta, he proceeded to France in April 1916, and fought at Vimy Ridge in the Somme Offensive, and in the third Battle of Ypres, in which action he gained the Military Medal for conspicuous gallantry in the Field. Later he took part in the Battle of Cambrai, and the Retreat and Advance of 1918, seeing heavy fighting at Bapaume and Havrincourt, also in the fourth Battle of Ypres in September of that year. In this engagement he was severely wounded, and being invalided to hospital in Yorkshire was finally demobilised in March 1919. He holds in addition to the Military Medal, the 1914-15 Star, and the General Service and Victory Medals.
27, Pownall Street, Hulme, Manchester. Z7721

POLLITT, A., Rifleman, Royal Irish Rifles.

Volunteering in March 1915, he landed in France in the same year and took part in heavy fighting in many notable engagements, including the second Battle of Ypres. He also fought in the Somme Offensive, and was unfortunately killed in action on July 1st, 1916. He was entitled to the 1914–15 Star, and the General Service and Victory Medals.

"Nobly striving,
He nobly fell that we might live."

8, Juliet Street, Ardwick, Manchester.　　Z11798A

POLLITT, I., Private, Cheshire Regiment.

He joined in September 1916, having been previously employed as a miner at Bradford Colliery since the outbreak of war. In April 1917 he was sent to Gibraltar, where he was first engaged on important guard duties on the Spanish Frontier, but later did special work on the Regimental Staff. He was demobilised in November 1919, and holds the General Service and Victory Medals.

9, Hope Street, Bradford, Manchester.　　Z10965

POMFRET, A., Private, Welch Regiment.

He joined in July 1918, and owing to his youth was not successful in obtaining his transfer overseas before the cessation of hostilities, but in February 1919 was sent to join the Army of Occupation on the Rhine, in which he served as a Lewis gunner until November of that year. He then proceeded to Ireland, where he did duty at various centres until his demobilisation in March 1920.

108, Cross Street, Bradfield, Manchester.　　Z7722

POMFRETT, J., Private, 17th Manchester Regiment.

Volunteering in October 1915, he proceeded to the Western Front in the following January and first saw heavy fighting at Loos and Albert. He also took part in the Battles of the Somme, Arras and Ypres (III), where he was badly wounded. Invalided to England, he spent some time in hospital at Reading before returning to France, when he served as a machine gunner at Cambrai, and Le Cateau. He holds the General Service and Victory Medals, and was demobilised in January 1919.

11, Edensor Street, Reswick, Manchester.　　Z10966

POOLE, D., Driver, R.F.A.

He volunteered in August 1914, and in the following year was drafted to the Western Front, where he took part in the Battles of St. Eloi, Hill 60, Ypres and Festubert, and was wounded. Invalided to England, he underwent a period of hospital treatment, but on his recovery returned to France, and served at the Battles of the Somme, Arras, Vimy Ridge, and Cambrai, and in heavy fighting at Albert, Armentières and Albert. He was badly gassed in action at La Bassée, and was again invalided home. In 1919 he was demobilised, and holds the 1914–15 Star, and the General Service and Victory Medals.

55, Pierce Street, Ancoats, Manchester.　　Z10967

POOLE, E., Sapper, R.E.

He joined in April 1918, and proceeded to the Western Front very shortly afterwards. He did good service in the laying of railways in connection with engagements in the Ypres sector, near Cambrai, and on the Somme, carrying on his important and often dangerous work through the final stages of the campaign. He was demobilised in April 1919, and holds the General Service and Victory Medals.

82, Marsland Street, Ardwick, Manchester.　　Z7727

POOLE, E., Private, 9th K.O. (R. Lancaster Regt).

After volunteering in December 1914, and undergoing training, he proceeded to France in September 1915, and two months afterwards was transferred to Salonika. Here he took part in the Doiran Advance, and later in the operations on the Vardar River, during which he unfortunately contracted malarial fever, and being invalided to the Base Hospital, was sent to England and discharged in February 1919. He holds the 1914–15 Star, and the General Service and Victory Medals.

15, Green Street, Gorton, Manchester.　　TZ7723

POOLE, J., Private, Lancashire Fusiliers.

He joined in December 1917, and after training, proceeded to France in the following May, and fought in the final operations connected with the Retreat and Advance, being in action at Bapaume, Havrincourt (where he was gassed in September 1918), and at Cambrai. Immediately after the Armistice he returned to England and was demobilised in December 1918. He holds the General Service and Victory Medals.

28, Gotha Street, Ardwick, Manchester.　　Z7724

POOLE, M., Private, 1st Manchester Regiment.

After joining in November 1917, and passing through his training, he was drafted to the Western Front in the following May, and fought in the Lys sector, also later, in the Battle of Cambrai (II), in which he was wounded in October 1918. This resulted in his being invalided to England, and finally discharged in October 1919 as unfit for further service. He holds the General Service and Victory Medals.

52, Henry Street, West Gorton, Manchester.　　Z7726

POOLE, T., Private, 2/8th Manchester Regiment.

After volunteering in October 1914 he passed through a considerable period of training and service in England, and

proceeded to France in July 1916, in time to take part in the 1st Battle of the Somme. He afterwards fought at Beaumont-Hamel and at Arras. In action near this last place on April 12th, 1918, he gave his life for the great cause, and was entitled to the General Service and Victory Medals.

"The path of duty was the way to glory."

52, Henry Street, West Gorton, Manchester.　　Z7725

POOLE, T. J., Bombardier, R.F.A.

After volunteering in January 1916, he went through his training, and proceeded with his Battery to France in the following January. He took part in severe fighting at Bapaume, Arras, and Lens, where he was badly wounded in August 1917. After a long period of treatment at a Base Hospital, he was finally demobilised in July 1919, and holds the General Service and Victory Medals.

57, Everton Road, Chorlton-on-Medlock, Manchester.　Z7728B

POOLE, W., Private, 1/6th Cheshire Regiment.

He joined in September 1917, and after his training, served on coast defence work in the Isle of Man. He was not successful in obtaining his transfer overseas before the cessation of hostilities, but in April 1919 proceeded to France, and did duty at various prisoners of war camps until his demobilisation in November 1919.

57, Everton Road, Chorlton-on-Medlock, Manchester.　Z7728A

POPE, F. J., Private, King's (Liverpool Regiment).

After volunteering in September 1914, he was sent to France in the following November, and saw much heavy fighting at La Bassée, and in the desperate Battle of Ypres (I). In November 1915 he was transferred to Salonika, where he took part in the Offensive on the Doiran front, and the operations on the River Struma. He then unfortunately contracted illness, and being invalided home, was finally discharged in December 1918. He holds the 1914 Star, and the General Service and Victory Medals.

10, Tipping Street, Lower Openshaw, Manchester.　　Z7730

POPE, T. W., Private, 75th Labour Corps.

He joined in February 1916, and was at once sent to France, where he did good service at important Bases, carrying on the valuable duties of his Corps with credit. Being then attacked by sudden illness, he was invalided home and discharged as unfit for further service, in 1918. He holds the General Service and Victory Medals.

21, Humphrey Street, Chorlton-on-Medlock, Manchester.　Z7729

PORTER, G., Sergt., Royal Welch Fusiliers.

Volunteering in April 1915, he proceeded to France in the following July and after serving for some time at a Base, went into the fighting line. In action near Festubert he was badly wounded, and after treatment at a Base Hospital, was evacuated to England, and eventually discharged as unfit for further service in July 1918. He holds the 1914–15 Star, and the General Service and Victory Medals.

70, Upper Moss Lane, Hulme, Manchester.　　Z7731

PORTER, J., Pte., Royal Fusiliers and Sapper, R.E.

He joined in July 1917, and after training at a Northern centre, was transferred to the Royal Engineers, and proceeded in January 1918 to Italy, where he was engaged in railway work. He continued his service there until finally demobilised in March 1919, and holds the General Service and Victory Medals.　39, Bennett Street, Ardwick, Manchester.　Z7732

PORTER, W., Private, King's (Liverpool Regiment).

He volunteered in December 1915, and after a period of service in England was drafted to the Western Front in March 1916. Whilst in this theatre of war he took part in the Battles of the Somme (I), Arras, Vimy Ridge, Cambrai and the Somme (II), and was in action throughout the Retreat and Advance of 1918. He was demobilised in March 1919, and holds the General Service and Victory Medals.

4, Drinkwater Street, Harpurhey, Manchester.　　Z11443

POSCHA, F. A., Rifleman, K.R.R.C.

Volunteering in August 1914, he was four months later sent to the Western Front, where he was in action in the Ypres sector, and was gassed in May 1915. He returned to his unit in the following September, and after two months' further service in France, was transferred to Salonika, where he served on the Struma front. In March 1917 he was drafted to Malta and nine months later was transferred to the R.A.S.C. (M.T. Section). He was discharged from the Army in February 1918, and holds the 1914–15 Star, and the General Service and Victory Medals.

44, Nicholson Street, Rochdale Road, Manchester.　　Z9324

POSTILL, H. D., Pte., Manchester Regt. (Bantams' Battalion).

He volunteered in the Bantams' Battalion in January 1916, and on completion of his training was engaged on important duties with his unit at various home stations. Despite his efforts, he was unable to obtain his transfer overseas, and was discharged as medically unfit in June 1917, after rendering valuable services.

36, Neill Street, Gorton, Manchester.　　Z10968

POTTER, C. W., Private, 7th Manchester Regt.
He volunteered in April 1915, and was eventually drafted to the Western Front in March 1917. During his service in this theatre of war, he took part in the Battles of Arras, Bullecourt, Ypres (III), Cambrai and the Somme (II), and was badly gassed. He was also in action in the Retreat and Advance of 1918, and was recommended for the Military Medal for carrying Despatches under heavy fire. Demobilised in April 1919, he holds the General Service and Victory Medals.
6, Corby Street, West Gorton, Manchester. Z10970

POTTER, F., Private, 7th Royal Sussex Regiment.
He joined in June 1916, and after training, was drafted to France in the following February. He took part in actions at Nieuport and Dunkirk, also in the 3rd Battle of Ypres, including Passchendaele Ridge. He served through the Retreat of 1918, and early in the victorious Advance was dangerously wounded in the Somme sector, on September 7th of that year. He succumbed to his wounds shortly after in the Base Hospital at Rouen. His body lies in the Military Cemetery there. He was entitled to the General Service and Victory Medals.
" He passed out of the sight of men by the path of duty and self-sacrifice."
9, Lindum Street, Rusholme, Manchester. TZ7736B

POTTER, J., Private, R.A.V.C.
He volunteered in November 1914, and on completion of his training was seven months later drafted to France. In this theatre of war he experienced fierce fighting in engagements at Loos, Albert, the Somme, Arras, Bullecourt, Ypres and Cambrai, and in the Retreat and Advance of 1918. He remained in France until March 1919, and was demobilised in the following month, holding the 1914-15 Star, and the General Service and Victory Medals.
41, Buxton Street, Manchester. TZ9325

POTTER, J. P., Rifleman, 5th London Regiment (London Rifle Brigade).
He volunteered in March 1915, and after a period of training and service in England was sent to France in August 1916, in time to take part in the later stages of the Somme Offensive; in this he was severely wounded, and after treatment at a Base Hospital, was invalided to England, and discharged as unfit for further service in September 1917. He holds the General Service and Victory Medals.
14, St. Leonard Street, Chorlton-on-Medlock, Manchester. X774B3

POTTER, O. A., Private, 53rd Manchester Regt.
He joined in August 1918, and on completion of his training was sent to Germany in the following February. He rendered valuable services as a clerk on the Deputy Assistant Provost Marshal's Staff at Bonn, and was eventually demobilised in October 1919.
6, Corby Street, West Gorton, Manchester. Z10969

POTTER, W., Private, 22nd Manchester Regiment.
He joined in June 1918, and after a brief period of training was sent to France, where he did duty at Le Havre. Later he rendered valuable services with his unit in Italy, Egypt and Australia, and was eventually demobilised in March 1920, holding the General Service and Victory Medals.
176, Queen's Road, Gorton, Manchester. Z10971

POTTER, W., Corporal, R.E.
Volunteering in June 1915, he passed through his training and after a period of service in England was sent in October 1917 to Egypt. He took part in the 2nd and 3rd Gaza Battles in the march on Jerusalem, and in the capture of Jericho. He then unfortunately contracted fever, and after being sent to hospital at Alexandria was finally demobilised in August 1919. He holds the General Service and Victory Medals.
22, Ribston Street, Hulme, Manchester. Z7733

POTTER, W., Pte., 6th Loyal N. Lancashire Regt.
He joined in November 1916, and was sent in the next year to Mesopotamia, where he took part in the operations which followed on the capture of Baghdad, including the occupation of Kirkuk. After this he unfortunately contracted fever and dysentery, but continued his service on that front until July 1919. He was finally demobilised in March 1920, and holds the General Service and Victory Medals. Z7735
105, Cottenham Street, Chorlton-on-Medlock, Manchester.

POTTS, J., Private, Cheshire Regiment.
Mobilised at the outbreak of hostilities, he proceeded to France with the Expeditionary Force, and took part in the Retreat from Mons, and in the great Battles of Ypres (I) and Ypres (II). Later, during the Offensive on the Somme he gave his life for King and Country on July 27th, 1916, and was entitled to the Mons Star, and the General Service and Victory Medals.
" He joined the great white company of valiant souls."
21, Hope Street, Ardwick, Manchester. Z7738B

POTTS, S., Pioneer, R.E.
He joined in April 1918, and after his training served at various centres in England. Owing to medical unfitness, he was not successful in obtaining his transfer overseas before the cessation of hostilities, and after rendering valuable services was discharged in August 1919, on account of service.
21, Hope Street, Chorlton-on-Medlock, Manchester. Z7738A

POTTS, M. H., Gunner, R.G.A.
He joined in October 1917, and after training, proceeded with his Battery to the Western Front in February 1918. During the Retreat of that year, on March 24th, he was killed by a bomb from an enemy aeroplane, while on his way up to the firing line. He was entitled to the General Service and Victory Medals.
" His memory is cherished with pride."
6, Prospect Street, West Gorton, Manchester. Z7737

POTTS, S., Rifleman, Rifle Brigade.
After volunteering in September 1914, he proceeded to the Western Front in the following December, and took part in heavy fighting at Loos, St. Eloi and Vimy Ridge, where he was wounded in several places in June 1916. After a short time in hospital he recovered, rejoined his unit, and fought on the Somme, at Arras, Ypres and Cambrai, also through the Retreat and Advance of 1918, being in action at Amiens, Bapaume and Cambrai again. He was demobilised in February 1919, and holds the 1914-15 Star, and the General Service and Victory Medals.
7, Sorrell Street, Hulme, Manchester. Z7739

POULTON, S., Gunner, R.G.A.
Joining in December 1916, he was sent to France with his Battery in the following March, and saw heavy fighting at Arras in the capture of Bullecourt, and in the Battles of Messines Ridge, Ypres (III) and Cambrai (I). He also served through the Retreat and Advance of 1918 until the Armistice, and was demobilised in March 1919. He holds the General Service and Victory Medals.
16, Callender Street, Chorlton-on-Medlock, Manchester. Z7741

POVAH, T., Private, King's (Liverpool Regiment).
He joined in September 1916, and was drafted to the Western Front in the following year. He took part in engagements at Ypres, in the Somme sector, near Arras, and at Lens, where he was both wounded and gassed. After a period of treatment in hospital he recovered, rejoined his unit, and served through all the final stages of the campaign, being eventually demobilised in September 1919. He holds the General Service and Victory Medals.
8, John Street, Chorlton-on-Medlock, Manchester. Z7742

POVEY, H., Gunner, R.F.A.
He volunteered in September 1915, and in the following February was drafted to the Western Front, but was badly wounded in action at Ypres two months later. After hospital treatment in France and at Fulham, he was discharged in July 1917 as medically unfit for further service, and holds the General Service and Victory Medals.
48, Lind Street, Ancoats, Manchester. Z10972

POWELL, A., Private, Cheshire Regt. and R.A.O.C.
He joined in October 1918, but being under age for transfer overseas, was engaged on important duties at various home stations. He rendered valuable services with his unit, and was eventually demobilised in October 1919.
6, King Street, Hulme, Manchester. Z10973

POWELL, A., Pte., 2nd East Lancashire Regiment.
After joining in September 1917, he passed through a short period of training, and was sent to India in the following December. He served during the remainder of the war at Bangalore, carrying out various duties until December 1918, when he returned to England and was demobilised in February 1919. He holds the General Service and Victory Medals.
75, Cowcill Street, Chorlton-on-Medlock, Manchester. Z7745

POWELL, G., Corporal, 8th Manchester Regiment.
Volunteering in September 1914, he underwent training and proceeded in the following July to Gallipoli, where he took part in the Suvla Bay Landing. In this he was badly wounded in August of that year, and being invalided home was discharged as unfit for further service in April 1916. He had the misfortune to be killed by a fire engine in the streets of Manchester on June 8th, 1919. He held the 1914-15 Star, and the General Service and Victory Medals.
65, Park Street, Hulme, Manchester. Z7530A

POWELL, G. E., Lieutenant, R.M.L.I.
This officer, after volunteering in October 1914, proceeded to the Western Front in the same month, and saw much heavy fighting all through the campaign, doing good service in many important engagements, in different sectors of the line. He carried on his responsible work through the final stages of the war, and was not demobilised until November 1919. He holds the 1914 Star, and the General Service and Victory Medals.
5, Rosebery Street, Moss Side, Manchester. Z7743B

POWELL, J., Driver, R.A.S.C.
After joining in October 1916, he was sent to France in the following April, and carried out the important and often dangerous duties of supply in connection with engagements at Arras, Vimy Ridge, and Bullecourt, also in the Battles of Messines Ridge and Cambrai (I). Later he served through the Retreat and Advance of 1918 until the Armistice, and was not demobilised until July 1919. He holds the General Service and Victory Medals.
82, George Street, Hulme, Manchester. Z7746

POWELL, J., Private, 8th Lancashire Fusiliers.
Volunteering in September 1914, he underwent a period of
training and was then sent to the Gallipoli Peninsula. Unfortunately he was killed in action whilst landing at Suvla
Bay on August 7th, 1915, and was entitled to the 1914-15
Star, and the General Service and Victory Medals.
                    " Nobly striving,
          He nobly fell that we might live."
138, Knightley Street, Rochdale Road, Manchester.   Z10974

POWELL, J., Corporal, Manchester Regiment.
He volunteered in November 1915, and after serving at various
important home stations, was sent to the Western Front in
the following year. Whilst in France he did excellent work
as a Lewis gunner in the Arras sector until wounded in June
1917. After a protracted hospital treatment in Etaples,
he was invalided to England, and demobilised in January 1919,
holding the General Service and Victory Medals.
15, Iron Street, Miles Platting, Manchester.   Z9674

POWELL, L. C., Sergt., R.A.F. (late R.F.C.)
He volunteered in November 1914, and served at various
aerodromes in the United Kingdom, rendering important
services as Instructor, and also in connection with repairs to
aircraft and the testing of their engines. He was not successful
in obtaining his transfer overseas before the cessation of
hostilities, and after doing much valuable work was demobilised
in April 1919.
20, Richmond Street, Moss Side, Manchester.   Z7747

POWELL, P., Private, K.O. (R. Lancaster Regt.)
Having volunteered in August 1915, he was drafted after a
short period of training to the Western Front in the following
December, and at once became engaged in heavy fighting at
Loos. Later, after taking part in actions at Vimy Ridge and
in the Somme Offensive, he was invalided to England with
trench fever, but after six months' treatment, recovered,
returned to France, and fought at Arras, Messines Ridge,
Ypres and Cambrai, also in the Retreat and Advance of 1918
until the Armistice. Demobilised in March 1919, he holds the
General Service and Victory Medals.
4, Milton Square, Lingard Street, Hulme, Manchester.   Z7744

POWELL, W., Private, 7th Manchester Regiment.
He joined in April 1916, and was drafted to the Western
Front in the same month. After taking part in several
actions of that Spring, he was engaged in the Somme Offensive
of the following Summer. During this at High Wood in August
1916, he made the great sacrifice in the cause of freedom, and
was entitled to the General Service and Victory Medals.
          " And doubtless he went in splendid company."
5, Rosebery Street, Moss Side, Manchester.   Z7743A

POWELL, W., Private, 8th Manchester Regiment.
After volunteering in August 1914, he underwent training,
and was sent to Gallipoli in the following April. He took
part in the famous Landing, and in the actions which succeeded
it. In the 3rd Krithia Battle on June 8th, 1915, he gave his
life for King and Country, and was entitled to the 1914-15
Star, and the General Service and Victory Medals.
          " He died the noblest death a man may die,
            Fighting for God and right, and liberty."
48, Lancaster Street, Hulme, Manchester.   Z7748

POWER, F., Private, Lancashire Fusiliers.
He volunteered in August 1914, and on completion of his
training, was drafted to the Dardanelles early in the following
year. After taking part in the Landing at Cape Helles, he
laid down his life for King and Country on July 13th, 1915.
He was entitled to the 1914-15 Star, and the General Service
and Victory Medals.
" Thinking that remembrance, though unspoken, may reach
          him where he sleeps."
9, James Place, Thornton Street, Collyhurst, Manchester.
                                                    Z10975

POWER, G., Private, 16th Manchester Regiment.
Volunteering in August 1914, he was drafted to the Western
Front in the following June, and took part in much heavy
fighting, being engaged at Loos, St. Eloi, Arras and in the Somme
Offensive of 1916. Later he fought at Bullecourt, Messines
Ridge, Ypres and Cambrai. In the Retreat of 1918 he was
unfortunately taken prisoner in March, near St. Quentin.
Being released after the Armistice he was discharged in December 1918, and holds the 1914-15 Star, and the General Service
and Victory Medals.
34, Ledge Street, Ancoats, Manchester.   Z7750

POWER, J., Gunner, R.F.A. (Trench Mortar Bty.)
Having volunteered in August 1914, he proceeded to France
in the following July, and did good service in a Trench Mortar
Battery at Loos, in the Somme Offensive, and later at Arras,
and in the Battles of Ypres (III) and Cambrai (I). He also
took part in the Retreat and Advance of 1918, seeing fighting
at Beaumont-Hamel, Havrincourt and Epéhy. Serving on
through the final stages he was demobilised in February 1919,
and holds the 1914-15 Star, and the General Service and
Victory Medals.   Z7749
68, Higher Chatham Street, Chorlton-on-Medlock, Manchester

POWER, P., Sapper, R.E.
He volunteered in January 1915, and in June of the same year
was sent to France, where he took part in the Battle of the
Somme. Wounded, he was invalided to England, and after
receiving hospital treatment, was discharged as medically
unfit for further service in May 1918. He holds the 1914-15
Star, and the General Service and Victory Medals.
15, Goodier Street, Harpurhey, Manchester.   Z11569

POWER, W., 66th Training Reserve Battalion.
He joined in July 1917, and was sent for training to a depôt
in North Wales. After doing good service for two months,
he unfortunately developed serious illness, which resulted in
his discharge as medically unfit in September of the same year.
24, Dearden Street, Hulme, Manchester.   TZ7751

POYNTER, J., Rifleman, 7th Rifle Brigade.
Having volunteered in August 1914, he underwent training
and was drafted to France in the following May. He saw
much heavy fighting in the Battles of Ypres (II) and Loos,
also in 1916 at Albert, at Vimy Ridge, on the Somme, and on
the Ancre front, at Beaucourt and Beaumont-Hamel. On
April 9th, 1917, he fell fighting near Arras, and was entitled
to the 1914-15 Star, and the General Service and Victory
Medals.
          "His memory is cherished with pride."
12, Caygill Street, Chorlton-on-Medlock, Manchester. TX7752

PRATT, E. A., Sergt., King's (Liverpool Regt.)
After joining in May 1916, he passed through a considerable
period of training and service in England, and proceeded to
France in January 1918. He took part in the Retreat of
1918, during which in March of that year he was both wounded
and gassed. On recovery he rejoined and fought in the Battles
of Ypres (IV), and Le Cateau (II), also through all the final
engagements, and was eventually demobilised in May 1919.
He holds the General Service and Victory Medals.
17, Mulberry Street, Hulme, Manchester.   Z7753

PRATT, G. H., Private, 2nd East Lancashire Regt.
Volunteering in August 1914, he was drafted to the Western
Front in the following January, and played a prominent part
in the Battles of St. Eloi, Ypres (II), Loos, Albert and Vimy
Ridge. He was unhappily killed in action at Thiepval during
the Somme Offensive in August 1916, and was entitled to the
1914-15 Star, and the General Service and Victory Medals.
" He joined the great white company of valiant souls."
14, Hampden Street, West Gorton, Manchester.   Z10976

PRATT, H., Private, 1st Manchester Regiment.
He joined in May 1917, and served with his unit at various
stations in England. He rendered valuable services, but owing
to medical unfitness, was not successful in obtaining his transfer overseas before the cessation of hostilities, and after giving
much help in transport work, was eventually demobilised in
October 1919.
11, Overton Street, Hulme, Manchester.   Z7754

PRATT, J., Private, Manchester Regiment.
After volunteering in May 1915, he underwent training at
various centres in the North West of England, and was sent
to India in the following March. Here he was engaged in
garrison duties, and though suffering from malarial fever,
resumed them on his recovery, and serving on to the end of
the war was finally demobilised in March 1919, and holds the
General Service and Victory Medals.
87, Blackthorn Street, Ardwick, Manchester.   Z7755A

PREEDY, J. H., Private, Lancashire Fusiliers.
Joining in July 1918, he served with his unit at various stations
in the United Kingdom. He was not successful in obtaining
his transfer overseas before the cessation of hostilities, but
rendered valuable services in Ireland, and was still at Dublin
in 1920.
43, Lavender Street, Hulme, Manchester.   Z7756

PRENDERGAST, J., Private, R.A.V.C.
He joined in June 1917, and was sent to France in the following
September. He rendered valuable services on the lines of
communication on the Somme, and after being discharged as
surplus to his unit, worked for nine months at a Base Veterinary Hospital, attending to the charger of the Commander-
in-Chief. Eventually demobilised in September 1919, he
holds the General Service and Victory Medals.
37, Marsland Street, Chorlton-on-Medlock, Manchester. Z7757

PRENDERGAST, T., Private, Manchester Regiment.
He volunteered in November 1914, and was drafted to France
in January 1916. After taking part in heavy fighting at
Neuve Chapelle, he was wounded in action during the Somme
Offensive in July 1916. On his recovery he served at the
Battle of Ypres (III), and in the Retreat and Advance of
1918. He was demobilised in May 1919, and holds the General
Service and Victory Medals.
41, Back of Mount Street, Harpurhey, Manchester.   Z10977

PRENDEGROSS, J., Private, 2nd Manchester Regt.
Volunteering in August 1914, he was retained on home defence duties until November 1916, when he succeeded in obtaining a transfer to the Western Front. There he saw heavy fighting in the Ypres, Somme, Nieuport, La Bassée, Givenchy, and Arras sectors. He remained in France until demobilised in January 1919, and holds the General Service and Victory Medals. 62, Nelson Street, Rochdale Road, Manchester. Z9326

PRESCOTT, S. J., Pte., 2nd Royal Welch Fusiliers.
He joined in July 1918, and after a brief period of training was drafted to the Western Front, where he was wounded in action at the 4th Battle of Ypres during the Advance. In 1920 he was stationed at Limerick in Ireland, and holds the General Service and Victory Medals.
53, Elizabeth Street, West Gorton, Manchester. Z10978

PRESCOTT, G. W., Pte., 21st Royal West Kent Regt.
He joined in March 1918, and served with his unit at various stations in Ireland. He rendered valuable services, but owing to medical unfitness, was not successful in obtaining his transfer overseas, and was discharged on that account in June 1919. He succumbed to a fatal complaint, which was doubtless aggravated by his service, on October 5th of the same year, and lies buried in Gorton Cemetery.
"His life for his Country."
36, Thomas Street, West Gorton, Manchester. Z7758

PRESTON, G., Private, King's (Liverpool Regiment).
He joined in 1917, and was quickly drafted to France. During his service on the Western Front he took part in the Battles of Bullecourt, Lens and Epéhy and in heavy fighting at Mericourt, Armentières, Péronne and Loos. He was invalided home sick, and spent some time in hospital before being demobilised in May 1919, holding the General Service and Victory Medals.
35, Alexandra Place, Manchester. Z11409D-444D

PRESTON, H., Private, 1/7th Manchester Regt.
Mobilised on the outbreak of war, he was sent to Egypt in September 1914, and took part in the famous Landing on Gallipoli in the following April, also in the Suvla Bay operations. After the Evacuation he was transferred to France, and was unfortunately taken prisoner at Cambrai in 1917 and sent to Germany. On his release after the Armistice, he was demobilised in January 1919, and holds the 1914-15 Star, and the General Service and Victory Medals.
105, Broadfield Road, Moss Side, Manchester. Z7759

PRESTON, H. A., Driver, R.A.S.C.
A Reservist, he was mobilised on the outbreak of war, and proceeding to France with the Expeditionary Force, took part in the Retreat from Mons, during which he was both wounded by shrapnel fire, and kicked by a mule. On recovery he rendered good service at Hill 60, and other engagements. Later he suffered from shell-shock, and after doing good work at various Base Camps, was invalided out of the Service in May 1916. He holds the Mons Star, and the General Service and Victory Medals.
28, Hyde Street, Hulme, Manchester. Z7760

PRICE, C., Private, 26th Manchester Regiment.
He joined in November 1916, and served with his unit at various stations in England. He rendered valuable services, notably as cook, but owing to a physical disability was not successful in obtaining his transfer overseas before the cessation of hostilities, and was discharged on account of service in November 1918.
18, Etruria Street, Longsight, Manchester. Z7763B

PRICE, C., Special War Worker.
Being unfit for service owing to a physical disability, he volunteered in March 1915 for work of National importance, and rendered valuable aid at large munition works in the neighbourhood of his own home, holding a responsible position in them, and was assisted by his wife. He continued his important duties until discharged in February 1919.
33, Carlton Street, Moss Side, Manchester. Z7762

PRICE, E., Sergeant, R.A.S.C.
Volunteering in October 1914, he underwent training at various stations in England, and was sent to France in December 1915. He carried out his important and responsible duties in connection with engagements at Arras, Ypres, Passchendaele Ridge, Lens and Cambrai, also through the Retreat and Advance of 1918, until after the Armistice. He was eventually demobilised in May 1919, and holds the 1914-15 Star, and the General Service and Victory Medals.
68, Rutland Street, Hulme, Manchester. TZ7770

PRICE, E., Sapper, R.E.
He joined in June 1916, and being sent to France in the following October, rendered valuable services to his Corps in the later stages of the Somme Offensive, also at Beaucourt, Arras and Bullecourt, in the Battle of Ypres (III), and in the severe fighting around Lens. Later he served through the Retreat and Advance of 1918, being engaged in the second Battles of the Marne and Cambrai. After the Armistice he was in the Army of Occupation on the Rhine, and was demobilised in February 1919. He holds the General Service and Victory Medals.
54, Cawdor Street, Hulme, Manchester. Z7771

PRICE, E. J., Private, 2nd Manchester Regiment.
When war was declared in August 1914, he was called up from the Reserve, and proceeded to France later in the same year. After only a few weeks' service on the Western Front he was severely wounded in action at Givenchy in December 1914, and invalided to England. On leaving hospital he was sent to Cleethorpes, and was discharged from the Army in May 1916, holding the 1914 Star, and the General Service and Victory Medals.
7, Garratt Street, Newton End, Manchester. Z9675

PRICE, F., Private, 12th Manchester Regiment.
Volunteering in September 1914, he proceeded to France in the following month, and took part in the desperate Battle of Ypres, and later in heavy fighting at St. Eloi and Loos. He was then attacked by severe illness, due to exposure, and being evacuated to hospital in England, was invalided out of the Service in May 1916. He holds the 1914 Star, and the General Service and Victory Medals.
21, Marshall Street, Ardwick, Manchester. Z7772A

PRICE, H., Private, K.O. (Royal Lancaster Regt.)
He volunteered in November 1914, and three months later proceeded to the Western Front, where he took part in the Battles of Neuve Chapelle, Ypres (III), Festubert, Loos, Vermelles, the Somme, the Ancre, Vimy Ridge, Bullecourt, Cambrai, the Marne (II), Havrincourt and Le Cateau (II). He was wounded in action at Bullecourt in May 1917 and at Havrincourt in September of the following year. He was demobilised in July 1919, and holds the 1914-15 Star, and the General Service and Victory Medals.
3, Thompson Street, West Gorton, Manchester. Z10979

PRICE, H., Private, 8th Manchester Regiment.
After volunteering in August 1914, he underwent training and proceeded, in April 1915, to Gallipoli, where he took part in the famous Landing, and later in the Suvla Bay operations. After the Evacuation he went to France in February 1916, and fought at Albert, in the first Battle of the Somme, and at Arras, Bullecourt, Messines Ridge, and Ypres, also at Cambrai. He served in the Retreat of 1918, and at the commencement of the Advance was sent to hospital in England, suffering from an affection of the feet. He was finally demobilised in February 1919, and holds the 1914-15 Star, and the General Service and Victory Medals.
18, Etruria Street, Longsight, Manchester. Z7763A

PRICE, H., Private, 8th Manchester Regiment.
He volunteered in April 1915, and served with his unit at several stations in the North of England. Owing to medical unfitness, he was not successful in obtaining his transfer overseas, but after being discharged on that account in August 1915, was engaged in special war work rendering valuable services at a Manchester Factory in the construction of aeroplanes until the end of the war.
32, Bunyan Street, Ardwick, Manchester. Z7765

PRICE, J., Private, 23rd Manchester Regiment.
He volunteered in January 1915, and after training proceeded to France in the following December. He saw much heavy fighting in the Somme Offensive of 1916, in the Battle of Vimy Ridge, the capture of Bullecourt, and later at Messines and Passchendaele Ridges. Being wounded in the Battle of Cambrai in December 1915, he was transferred to the Labour Corps, and being again wounded was sent to hospital in England, and finally demobilised in February 1919. He holds the 1914-15 Star, and the General Service and Victory Medals.
11, Mulberry Street, Hulme, Manchester. Z7769

PRICE, J., Pte., 3rd K.O. (Y.L.I.)
He joined in September 1916, and after four months' training was drafted to the Western Front, where he played a prominent part in the Battle of Arras, Ypres (III), Cambrai and Hazebrouck. He was demobilised on his return to England in February 1919, and holds the General Service and Victory Medals.
21, Nancy Street, Chester Road, Hulme, Manchester. Z10980

PRICE, J. T., Corporal, Welch Regiment.
He volunteered in October 1914, and proceeding to the Dardanelles in the following April, took part in the Landings at Cape Helles and Suvla Bay, and was in action at the three Battles of Krithia. After the Evacuation of the Gallipoli Peninsula, he was invalided home suffering severely from frostbite, and was discharged in August 1916, as medically unfit for further service. He holds the 1914-15 Star, and the General Service and Victory Medals.
22, Back Mount Street, Harpurhey, Manchester. Z10981

PRICE, P., Private, R.A.M.C.
He volunteered in September 1915, but on completion of his training was not successful in procuring a transfer to the war zone. During his period of service he was stationed at Sheffield and Blackpool, and performed the various duties assigned to him in a highly capable manner. He was demobilised in January 1919. Z8012B
56, Higher Chatham Street, Chorlton-on-Medlock, Manchester.

PRICE, R., Private, 16th Manchester Regiment.
After volunteering in March 1915, he passed through his training, and proceeded to the Western Front in May of the following year. He took part in the first Battle of the Somme, in which he was severely wounded on July 1st, 1916, and being invalided to England, underwent treatment at many different hospitals in the neighbourhood of Manchester, and was finally discharged as unfit for further service in June 1918. He holds the General Service and Victory Medals.
29, John Street, Hulme, Manchester. TZ7766

PRICE, T., Private, 8th Lancashire Fusiliers.
He volunteered in September 1914, and was sent almost immediately to Egypt, where he took part in the operations on the Suez Canal in February 1915, and in other actions on that front. After this he unfortunately contracted severe illness, of which he died in hospital at Cairo on April 8th, 1915. His body lies in Cairo Cemetery. He was entitled to the 1914–15 Star, and the General Service and Victory Medals.
" Thinking that remembrance, though unspoken, may reach
him where he sleeps."
14, Lord Street, Hulme, Manchester. TZ6828B

PRICE, W., Driver, R.F.A.
He volunteered in February 1915, and served at various stations in England. Owing to medical unfitness, he was not successful in obtaining his transfer overseas, and after doing much useful work in connection with the supply of rations for troops, was finally discharged on account of service in May 1918.
9, Hambro Street, Chapel Street, Ancoats, Manchester. Z7764

PRICE, W., 1st Air Mechanic, R.A.F. (late R.F.C.)
Volunteering in September 1914, he served at first on motor transport work in England, and was sent with the Air Force to Salonika in September 1915. Here he did good service on raids over the enemy lines in the Doiran and Struma regions, until wounded whilst coming down in an aeroplane. He returned home in December 1918, and being demobilised in the following month, holds the 1914–15 Star, and the General Service and Victory Medals.
8, Brenner Street, Stockport Road, Manchester. Z7767

PRICE, W., Private, R.M.L.I.
After joining in June 1916, he was sent to the Western Front in December of the same year, and took part in the Battle of Messines and Passchendaele Ridges and Cambrai (I). Later he served through the Retreat and Advance of 1918s and returning to England shortly after the Armistice, was demobilised in February 1919. He holds the General Service and Victory Medals.
18, Napier Street, Ardwick, Manchester. Z7768

PRICE, W. E., Private, Welch Regiment.
He joined in August 1918, on attaining military age, and although not successful in obtaining his transfer overseas before the cessation of hostilities, was sent to the Army of Occupation on the Rhine in the month after the Armistice. In this he served until April 1919, when he was transferred to Ireland, and did garrison duty there until his demobilisation in March 1920.
18, Etruria Street, Longsight, Manchester. Z7763

PRIEST, A., Private, 11th East Lancashire Regt.
Volunteering in October 1914, he was drafted to France in the following March, and was wounded in action at the second Battle of Ypres in April 1915. On his recovery he took part in heavy fighting at La Bassée, Givenchy, Festubert, and on the Somme, and was taken prisoner in April 1917. Whilst in captivity he suffered many hardships, and being forced to work immediately behind the lines, was wounded near Lille in April 1918. He was repatriated and discharged in February 1919, and holds the 1914–15 Star, and the General Service and Victory Medals.
10, Wilkinson Street, Rochdale Road, Manchester. Z10982

PRIEST, W. J., Private, Lancashire Fusiliers.
Volunteering in March 1915, he was sent in the following August to the Western Front, and saw heavy fighting at Loos, and other places in that year. In March 1916, he was badly gassed and invalided to hospital in England, but recovered, returned to France, and fought in the first Battle of the Somme, and later at Nieuport, La Bassée, Ypres, and Passchendaele, also in the Retreat and Advance of 1918. He was not demobilised until October 1919, and holds the 1914–15 Star, and the General Service and Victory Medals.
49, Ashover Street, Hyde Road, Ardwick, Manchester. Z7773

PRIESTNALL, T. W., Pte., 2nd Lancashire Fusiliers.
He volunteered on the outbreak of war, and after a very short period of training, was drafted to the Western Front early in September 1914. He at once took part in heavy fighting at this critical time in the campaign. In the desperate struggle of the first Battle of Ypres, he died a Soldier's glorious death on the Field and was entitled to the 1914 Star, and the General Service and Victory Medals.
" His name liveth for evermore."
51, Pownall Street, Hulme, Manchester. Z6203B

PRINCE, J., Private, M.G.C.
Volunteering in November 1914, he proceeded to France in the following December, and took part in many of the early engagements of the war. In the Retreat of 1918 he was taken prisoner on March 22nd, and after a years' captivity in Germany was demobilised on his release in March 1919. He holds the 1914–15 Star, and the General Service and Victory Medals.
38, Woburn Place, Chorlton-on-Medlock, Manchester.
X7776B. X7777B

PRINCE, J., Private, 20th Manchester Regiment.
Volunteering in June 1915, he trained at Prees Heath, Southport, and Salisbury, and proceeded in March 1916 to the Western Front. He served on this Front for three years and during that time took part in severe fighting on the Somme, and at Bray, Ypres, Passchendaele, Cambrai, La Bassée and Loos. He remained in France until demobilised in March 1919, and holds the General Service and Victory Medals.
105, Naylor Street, Oldham Road, Manchester. Z9678

**PRINCE, J., Private, South Lancashire Regt. and
8th Manchester Regt.**
He volunteered in January 1915, and served with his unit at various stations in the United Kingdom. He rendered valuable services, but was not successful in obtaining his transfer overseas before the cessation of hostilities, and after doing good work on guard and other duties was eventually discharged in March 1919. X7776C. X7777C
38, Woburn Place, Chorlton-on-Medlock, Manchester.

PRINCE, J. H., Air Mechanic, R.A.F. (late R.F.C.)
He joined in May 1918, and did excellent work at various air centres, especially in Scotland. He rendered valuable services, but was not successful in obtaining his transfer overseas before the cessation of hostilities, and after carrying out important duties in connection with the transport of foodstuffs, and the loading of aircraft was demobilised in March 1919. 30, Lister Street, Longsight, Manchester. Z7775

PRINCE, R. W., Cpl., 2nd East Lancashire Regt.
At the outbreak of hostilities in August 1914, he volunteered for active service, and in February 1916, proceeded overseas. Whilst on the Western Front, he did good work with his unit at the Battles of the Somme, Ypres, La Bassée, Nieuport and Arras. After the Armistice he entered Germany with the Army of Occupation, and was stationed at Cologne. He was demobilised in June 1919, and holds the General Service and Victory Medals.
67, Woodward Street, Ancoats, Manchester. Z9676

PRINCE, T., Gunner, R.F.A.
He volunteered in September 1914, and nine months later proceeded to Egypt, and then to Gallipoli, in which campaign, he was in action at Suvla Bay. After the Evacuation of the Peninsula, he was drafted to France, and was wounded on two occasions whilst fighting in the Battle of the Somme in 1916. He was invalided home and discharged as medically unfit for further service in September 1917, holding the 1914–15 Star, and the General Service and Victory Medals.
83, Ravald Street, Miles Platting, Manchester. Z9677

PRINCE, T., Private, 1st Manchester Regiment.
Having enlisted in 1905, he was serving in India on the outbreak of war and was drafted to France in the following October. He took part in action at La Bassée, the desperate Battle of Ypres (I), and afterwards fought at Neuve Chapelle and Givenchy. In August 1916, he was transferred to Mesopotamia, and was heavily engaged in the operations for the relief of Kut. He was then sent to Egypt, where he was in action on the Suez Canal, and other places. Demobilised in February 1919, he holds the 1914 Star, and the General Service and Victory Medals.
7, Willaston Street, Ardwick, Manchester. Z7774

PRINCE, T., (D.C.M.), L/Cpl., 1/7th Lancashire Fus.
Volunteering in November 1914, he proceeded to France before the end of the year, and saw much heavy fighting at Hill 60, in the second Battle of Ypres, at Loos, and Ploegsteert Wood. Later he was in the Somme Offensive of 1916, and in the Battles of Arras, and Vimy and Messines Ridges. On September 5th, 1918, at the commencement of the victorious Advance, he won the Distinguished Conduct Medal for conspicuous gallantry in action at Neuville, Bonjourval. Eventually demobilised in February 1919, he holds in addition to the Distinguished Conduct Medal, the 1914–15 Star, and the General Service and Victory Medals. X7776A. X7777A
38, Woburn Place, Chorlton-on-Medlock, Manchester.

PRINCE, W. (D.C.M.), Pte., 1/7th Lancashire Fus.
He volunteered in 1914, and first saw active service in the Dardanelles, where he took part in the Landings at Cape Helles and Suvla Bay and in heavy fighting on Gallipoli. He was awarded the Distinguished Conduct Medal for conspicuous bravery in capturing Turkish prisoners single-handed, and after the Evacuation of the Peninsula, was transferred to France. Whilst on the Western Front, he served at the Battles of the Somme and Ypres, and in the Retreat and Advance of 1918, and was twice wounded. He also holds the 1914–15 Star, and the General Service and Victory Medals, and was demobilised in February 1919.
15, Evans Street, Chorlton-on-Medlock, Manchester. Z10983

PRINGLE, H., Private, King's (Liverpool Regt.)
He joined in September 1917, and after training was drafted in the following March to the Western Front. He took part in the Retreat and Advance of 1918, being in action at Bapaume Amiens, Havrincourt and Cambrai (II), where he was wounded in September of that year, and, being evacuated to hospital in England, was eventually demobilised in January 1919. He holds the General Service and Victory Medals.
89, Earl Street, Longsight, Manchester. Z7778A

PRINGLE, J., Private, 1/6th Manchester Regiment.
After volunteering in September 1914, he was sent to Gallipoli in the following April, and took part in the famous Landing. and in the first, and third Krithia Battles which succeeded it. Later, in the course of the Suvla Bay operations, he was severely wounded, and being invalided to hospital in England, was discharged in December 1916, as unfit for further service. He holds the 1914-15 Star, and the General Service and Victory Medals.
89, Earl Street, Longsight, Manchester. Z7778B

PRIOR, F., Private, 8th Manchester Regiment.
He volunteered in August 1914, and after a period of service at home stations, was drafted to France in June 1916. Whilst on the Western Front, he took part in the Battles of the Somme, Vimy Ridge and Messines, and in heavy fighting at La Bassée and Nieuport. He was demobilised in April 1919, and holds the General Service and Victory Medals.
2, Neill Street, Gorton, Manchester. Z10984B

PRIOR, T., Sapper, R.E.
Volunteering in December 1914, he was retained on important duties in England on completion of his training. Despite his efforts, he was unsuccessful in obtaining his transfer to a theatre of war, but rendered valuable services with his unit until his demobilisation in August 1919.
2, Neill Street, Gorton, Manchester. Z10984A

PRITCHARD, C., Pte., 1st King's (Liverpool Regt.)
Volunteering in August 1914, he proceeded in May 1915 to Egypt, and after serving in the Suez Canal engagements was drafted to Gallipoli. There he took part in the Suvla Bay Landing, and then was sent to France, where he fought in the Battles of Ypres, and the Somme. In 1916 he proceeded to Palestine, and whilst engaged in severe fighting at Romani was wounded. On his return home he was demobilised in January 1919, and holds the 1914-15 Star, and the General Service and Victory Medals.
83, Woodward Street, Ancoats, Manchester. Z9679A

PRITCHARD, H., Gunner, R.F.A.
Volunteering in December 1915, he proceeded with his Battery to France in the following March, and did good service in actions at St. Eloi, Albert, Vimy Ridge and Arras, also in the first Battle of the Somme. Later he was engaged at Passchendaele Ridge, and Cambrai, and served through the Retreat and Advance of 1918, seeing heavy fighting on the Marne, and at Bapaume and Le Cateau. Demobilised in March 1919, he holds the General Service and Victory Medals.
52, Chipping Street, Longsight, Manchester. Z7780

PRITCHARD, V. E., Private, Cheshire Regiment.
He volunteered in January 1916, and after training at Prees Heath proceeded to Ireland, where he served at the Curragh Camp. He was not successful in procuring a transfer overseas but throughout the period of his service carried out his duties with the utmost ability. He was demobilised in February 1919.
83, Woodward Street, Ancoats, Manchester. TZ9679B

PRITCHARD, W., Private, Royal Welch Fusiliers.
Mobilised at the outbreak of hostilities, he proceeded to France with the Expeditionary Force, and took part in the Retreat from Mons, also in action at La Bassée, St. Eloi, Festubert, and Loos in 1915. In the next Spring he was in severe fighting at Albert and Vimy Ridge, and being severely wounded in this last engagement was invalided to hospital in England in June 1916, and finally discharged in December 1917. He holds the Mons Star, and the General Service and Victory Medals.
4, Whittaker Street, Hulme, Manchester. TZ7779

PROCTER, H., Private, 51st Cheshire Regiment.
He joined in April 1917, and served with his unit at various stations in the United Kingdom. He rendered valuable services but was not successful in obtaining his transfer overseas before the cessation of hostilities, and after carrying out many important duties, was finally demobilised in November 1919.
32, Vulcan Street, Ardwick, Manchester. Z7783

PROCTER, W. E., Private, Military Foot Police.
Joining in November 1916, he served in his Force at various stations in the United Kingdom. He rendered valuable services, but was not successful in obtaining his transfer overseas before the cessation of hostilities, and after doing much valuable work, especially in guarding prisoner of war camps, was demobilised in February 1919.
16, Greenhill Street, Chorlton-on-Medlock, Manchester. Z7781

PROCTOR, S., Private, 4th Yorkshire Regiment.
He joined in 1916, and served with his unit at various stations. He rendered valuable services, but was not successful in obtaining his transfer overseas, and being found to be suffering from serious disability was discharged on that account in 1917.
38, Rosebery Street, Moss Side, Manchester. Z7782

PROPHET, G. A., Gunner, R.F.A.
Having volunteered in September 1914, he underwent training at an East Coast station, and was sent with his Battery to Egypt in the following May. He took part in engagements on the Suez Canal, and in the Suvla Bay Landing in Gallipoli. Being after the Evacuation transferred to the Palestine front, he fought in the Gaza Battles and was present at the capture of Jerusalem. Serving to the end of the campaign on that Front he was finally demobilised in May 1919, and holds the 1914-15 Star, and the General Service and Victory Medals.
3, Willaston Street, Ardwick, Manchester. Z7785

PROPHET, J. W., Pte., Loyal N. Lancashire Regt.
He joined in April 1917, and twelve months later was drafted to the Western Front, where he took part in several important engagements during the Retreat and Advance of 1918 until badly wounded on the Somme in October. He was invalided to hospital at Hereford and was discharged in February 1919, holding the General Service and Victory Medals.
21, Clayton Street, Newtown, Manchester. Z10985

PROPHET, R., Private, Lancashire Fusiliers.
He joined in December 1916, and was drafted in the following June to the Western Front. He took part in the first Battle of Cambrai, and saw much heavy fighting in the Retreat and Advance of 1918, serving right through until the Armistice. He then went to Germany in the Army of Occupation on the Rhine, being finally demobilised in October 1919. He holds the General Service and Victory Medals.
40, Victoria Street, Longsight, Manchester. Z7784

PROSSER, F., Sapper, R.E.
After volunteering in October 1914, he passed through his training and served for some time in England. He proceeded to France in 1916, and did good service in connection with actions at Albert in that year, and in 1917 at Arras, also in the capture of Bullecourt, the severe fighting round Lens, and the Battle of Cambrai (I). Serving through the remainder of the campaign, he was finally demobilised in October 1919, and holds the General Service and Victory Medals.
12, Kirk Street, Ancoats, Manchester. Z7740

PRYCE, F., Air Mechanic, R.A.F.
He joined in May 1916, and after a period of valuable service in England was drafted to France in November 1917. He played an important part in the Battles of Cambrai and Ypres, and in the Retreat and Advance of 1918, and was eventually demobilised in September 1919, holding the General Service and Victory Medals.
69, Elizabeth Street, West Gorton, Manchester. Z10986

PUGH, J. T., Private, 2nd Manchester Regiment.
Volunteering in October 1914, he was sent to France in the following April. Whilst on the Western Front he was in action at the Battles of Ypres, Loos Albert, the Somme and Arras, and in the Retreat and Advance of 1918, and was three times wounded. He was demobilised in February 1919, on returning to England, and holds the 1914-15 Star, and the General Service and Victory Medals.
13, Lavender Street, Miles Platting, Manchester. Z10987

PULLER, E. G., Corporal, 2nd Reserve Cavalry.
A Reservist, who had enlisted originally in the 6th Inniskilling Dragoons in October 1902, he was mobilised on the outbreak of war, and served with his unit at various stations in the United Kingdom. Owing to ill-health he was not successful in obtaining his transfer overseas and on completion of his twelve years' service joined the Cavalry Reserve, in which he rendered valuable service as an Instructor until he unfortunately contracted a serious illness, and died on June 20th, 1916.
"His life for his Country, his soul to God."
23, New York Street, Chorlton-on-Medlock, Manchester. TX7786

PURCELL, E., Gunner, R.G.A.
Volunteering in October 1915, he was in training at Gosport for four months, at the end of which time he was drafted to British East Africa. There he served for three years, and during that time took an active part in fierce fighting at Dodoma, Dar-es-Salaam, Mrogoro and Tanga. He contracted malaria, and was sent to hospital at Nairobi. On returning to England in March 1919, he was demobilised, and holds the General Service and Victory Medals.
22, Shelmerdine Street, Collyhurst, Manchester. Z9328

PURCELL, H., Pte., Manchester Regt. and Dr., R.A.S.C.
He volunteered in April 1915, and in the following February was drafted to France, where after taking part in heavy fighting at La Bassée, he was badly wounded during the Somme Offensive in July 1916. He was invalided home, and on his recovery, was transferred to the R.A.S.C., and was engaged on special duties on the East Coast. He holds the General Service and Victory Medals, and was demobilised in August 1919. 8, King Street, Hulme, Manchester. Z10988

PURSLOW, G., Private, 2nd East Lancashire Regt.
Volunteering in September 1914, he was drafted to France in the same month and fought in many important engagements. He was in action at Ypres, on the Somme, at Delville Wood, and gave his life for King and Country during the fighting at Beaumont-Hamel in 1916. He was entitled to the 1914 Star, and the General Service and Victory Medals.
   " His life for his Country, his soul to God."
14, Boardman Street, Harpurhey, Manchester.   Z11570

PURSLOW, W. H., Private, Lancashire Fusiliers.
A serving Soldier, he was drafted to the Western Front with the First Expeditionary Force in August 1914, and took part in the Battles of Mons, Le Cateau, the Marne and the Aisne. He was unhappily killed in action at La Bassée on October 18th 1914, and was entitled to the Mons Star, and the General Service and Victory Medals.
   " The path of duty was the way to glory."
103, Ryder Street, Collyhurst, Manchester.   Z10584B

PURVIS, J., A.B., Royal Navy.
After volunteering in March 1915, he did service on Transport ships in the North Sea, and the Mediterranean from October of that year until May 1918, when he lost his life in the torpedoing of H.M.S. " Ansonia " by enemy submarine. In addition to having been awarded three torpedo badges, he was entitled to the 1914-15 Star, and the General Service and Victory Medals.
   " Whilst we remember, the sacrifice is not in vain."
24, Eagle Street, Hulme, Manchester.   Z7787

PUSILL, H., (Miss), Worker, Q.M.A.A.C
She joined in February 1918, and in the following June was drafted to France. Whilst on the Western Front, she rendered valuable services as a motor trimmer at Le Havre, Honfleur, and Camiers. She was demobilised in January 1919, and holds the General Service and Victory Medals.
60, Collyhurst Street, Collyhurst, Manchester.   Z10989

PYGOTT, T. (M.M.), Sergt., 18th Manchester Regt.
He volunteered in January 1915, and in the following November proceeded to France, where he fought in the Battles of Albert, Vermelles, the Somme, and was gassed at Beaucourt in November 1916. On recovery he returned to the trenches, and was in action at Arras and Cambrai in which engagement he was awarded the Military Medal for conspicuous gallantry and devotion to duty, whilst out on patrol, in capturing forty German prisoners. He later took part in the second Battle of the Somme, and gave his life for the freedom of England at Béthune on July 23rd, 1918, and was entitled to the 1914-15 Star, and the General Service and Victory Medals.
   " His memory is cherished with pride."
7, Towson Street, Hulme, Manchester.   Z11799

PYE, A., Corporal, 7th Manchester Regiment.
Volunteering in May 1915, he was sent to Egypt in the following January, and served there until April 1917, when he was transferred to France, and took part in the 3rd Battle of Ypres, and in the Retreat and Advance of 1918, being in action at Havrincourt Wood. After this engagement he joined the Head-quarters Staff until his demobilisation in February 1919. He holds the General Service and Victory Medals.
18, Sadler Street, Moss Side, Manchester.   Z7788

PYE, G., Private, 9th South Lancashire Regiment.
Volunteering in December 1915, he proceeded to France in the following February, and was in action at Loos, Vimy Ridge, and Armentières, where he was severely wounded. After some months treatment at a hospital in England, he recovered, and returned to France in March 1917, he did good service in pioneer work, and was badly gassed near La Bassée and invalided home. On recovery he served with a Pioneer Battalion on the Egyptian Front until his demobilisation in 1919. He holds the General Service and Victory Medals.
11, Boston Street, Hulme, Manchester.   Z7789

Q

QUARMBY, E., Private, 1/7th Manchester Regt.
Having enlisted in April 1912, he was mobilised at the outbreak of hostilities, and proceeded in September 1914 to the Egyptian front, where he took part in actions on the Suez Canal, and at other engagements. He returned to England in May 1916, being a time-expired soldier, but did valuable war work, making tools and gauges for the Navy until March 1917, when he was finally discharged, and holds the 1914-15 Star, and the General Service and Victory Medals.
42, William Street, West Gorton, Manchester.   Z7790

QUAYLE, E., Sergt., 23rd Manchester Regiment.
He volunteered in February 1915, and six months later proceeded to the Western Front, where he was in action on the Somme, and at Bullecourt and Ypres. He was wounded at Carnoy and on the Somme, and in September 1917 was drafted to Italy, where he served with distinction, until after the close of hostilities. Demobilised in February 1919, he holds the 1914-15 Star, and the General Service and Victory Medals. 37, Teignmouth St., Collyhurst, Manchester.   Z9622B

QUIGLEY, C., Driver, R.A.S.C. (M.T.)
Having volunteered in April 1915, he passed through his training, and was sent in February 1916 to Mesopotamia, where he did valuable work at the Base at Basra, also later at Amara, and Baghdad. Being then attacked by fever he was sent to hospital in India, but on recovery returned to Mesopotamia, and was in the Advance to Tekrit in November 1917. Serving on to the end of the campaign, he was demobilised in March 1919, and holds the General Service and Victory Medals.
3, Pump Street, Hulme, Manchester.   Z7791A

QUIGLEY, C. W., Private, Manchester Regiment.
Volunteering in December 1915, he was drafted to France in the following September, and took part in engagements at Arras, Festubert, Ypres and Passchendaele Ridge. In an action near Cambrai in March 1918 he was severely wounded, and being evacuated to hospital in England remained under treatment until his demobilisation in March 1919. He holds the General Service and Victory Medals.
3, Pump Street, Hulme, Manchester.   Z7791B

QUILTY, J., Private, Labour Corps.
He joined in October 1917, and was sent to France in the following December. He did good service in his Corps, chiefly in connection with the loading of munitions, and other important duties, and was in the Arras sector of the front. In October 1918 he was invalided home suffering from illness, and remained in hospital until demobilised in March 1919. H eholds the General Service and Victory Medals.
11, Durham Place, Hulme, Manchester.   Z7792

QUINLAN, D., Private, 7th Manchester Regiment.
He volunteered in December 1914, and in the following year was drafted overseas. He took part in heavy fighting at the Landing at Gallipoli, and after the Evacuation of the Peninsula proceeded to the Western Front. In this theatre of war he served in numerous engagements, was in action at Cambrai, and was wounded. He was demobilised in 1918, and holds the 1914-15 Star, and the General Service and Victory Medals.
11, Robert Street, Chorlton-on-Medlock, Manchester.   X7793

QUINLAN, E., Private, 2nd Border Regiment.
Having enlisted in June 1913, he was mobilised on the outbreak of war and proceeded to France in the following October. He fought in the desperate Battle of Ypres (I), and afterwards at Sailly, where he was severely wounded. On recovery he was sent in July 1915 to Gallipoli, where he was again wounded in September of that year. After hospital treatment he was transferred to Salonika, and in action there was wounded a third time, and suffering in addition from dysentery and malaria, was invalided home, and afterwards transferred to the Labour Corps, from which he was discharged in June 1918. He holds the 1914-15 Star, and the General Service and Victory Medals.
8, Hargreaves Street, New York Place, Chorlton-on-Medlock, Manchester.   TX7794

QUINN, A., Private, 8th Manchester Regiment.
After volunteering in June 1915, he proceeded in the following month to the Western Front, where he saw much heavy fighting at Loos, Albert, Vermelles and in the 1st Battle of the Somme. Later he was invalided home suffering from shell-shock and after treatment in hospital was retained on Home Service, in which he did guard duties at large military centres until demobilised in August 1919. He holds the 1914-15 Star, and the General Service and Victory Medals.
13, Fletcher's Square, Hulme, Manchester.   TZ7797

QUINN, A., Private, 16th Manchester Regiment.
Having volunteered in June 1915, he passed through a considerable period of training, and service in England and was drafted to France in December 1916. He saw much heavy fighting at Arras, Vimy and Messines Ridges, and in the Battle of Ypres (III). He was wounded near the Ypres sector in September 1917, and again wounded and also taken prisoner at St. Quentin in March 1918. After his release from captivity in Germany he was demobilised in August 1919, and holds the General Service and Victory Medals.
57, Barlow Street, Bradford, Manchester.   Z7795

QUINN, G., Private, South Wales Borderers.
He joined in August 1918, and served with his unit at various stations in England. He was not successful in obtaining his transfer overseas before the cessation of hostilities, but in March 1919 was sent to the Army of Occupation on the Rhine, and served in it until August of the same year, when he was transferred to Ireland and did garrison duty in that Country until his demobilisation in March 1920.
32, Gorse Street, Hulme, Manchester.   Z7796

QUINN, H., L/Cpl., 1st Argyll and Sutherland Hldrs.
He volunteered in February 1915, and on the completion of his training was drafted to France, where he served in many parts of the line, including the Albert sector. Transferred to Salonika in November 1917, he was in action on the Doiran, Vardar and Struma fronts, and was engaged in heavy fighting during the final Allied Advance in the Balkans. Returning home he was demobilised in May 1919, and holds the General Service and Victory Medals.
23, Middlewood Street, Harpurhey, Manchester.   Z1157

QUINN, H., Sergt., 2nd Manchester Regiment.
When war was declared in August 1914, he was already serving in the Army, and accordingly was ordered immediately to the Western Front. There he played a conspicuous part in the fighting at Mons, La Bassée, Ypres, Givenchy, Nieuport, the Somme and Arras, but was taken ill with pneumonia and died on June 29th, 1918. He was entitled to the Mons Star, and the General Service and Victory Medals.
"Thinking that remembrance, though unspoken, may reach him where he sleeps."
13, Frederick Place, Rochdale Road, Manchester.   Z9329

QUINN, J., Private, 2nd Manchester Regiment.
Volunteering in November 1914, he proceeded to France in the following April, and saw heavy fighting in the Battles of Ypres (II) and Loos, where he was wounded in October, but recovered and fought later at St. Eloi and Vimy Ridge. In July 1916 he was transferred to Egypt, and was in action on the Suez Canal, and at Mersa Matruh, Sollum, Katia and Romani. In June 1918 he returned to France, and being wounded in the Battle of Cambrai (II) was invalided home, and finally demobilised in April 1919. He holds the 1914-15 Star, and the General Service and Victory Medals.
25, Foster Street, City Road, Hulme, Manchester.   Z7798

QUINN, J., Private, King's (Liverpool Regiment).
He volunteered in August 1914, and in May of the following year was drafted to the Western Front, where he was in action at Festubert and Albert before being badly wounded at Gommecourt on the Somme in 1916. He was invalided to England, and on his recovery was engaged on light duties at home stations until his discharge in December 1918, holding the 1914-15 Star, and the General Service and Victory Medals.
72, Cobden Street, Ancoats, Manchester.   Z10990

QUINN, J. M., Sergt., Lincolnshire Regiment.
He volunteered in November 1914, and was engaged on special duties at home stations until May 1917. He was then drafted to the Western Front, where he served with distinction at the Battles of Arras, Ypres (III) and Havrincourt, and was wounded in action in September 1917. He holds the General Service and Victory Medals, and was discharged as medically unfit for further service in July 1918.
6, Woodley Street, Queen's Road, Manchester.   Z10991

QUINN, T., Private, Welch Regt., and R.A.M.C.
Joining in July 1916, he first served with the Welch and Devonshire Regiments, and the R.A.S.C., with which last named unit he was engaged on important transport duties. Later he was transferred to the Labour Corps, but was not successful in serving in a theatre of war. He did consistently good work, however, until his demobilisation in June 1919.
14, Marple Street, Ancoats, Manchester.   Z10992

QUINN, W., Driver, R.F.A.
Volunteering soon after the outbreak of war he served at various stations in the United Kingdom. He rendered valuable services, but was not successful in obtaining his transfer overseas before the cessation of hostilities, and after doing much valuable transport, as well as coast defence work, was demobilised in January 1919.
12, Forbes Street, West Gorton, Manchester.   Z7799

QUINT, S. E., A.B., Royal Navy.
Volunteering in September 1914, he went for training and patrol work to Chatham, and in May 1915 was posted to Harwich, from which Port he worked in H.M.S. "St. Scirol" in mine-sweeping with the Southern part of the North Sea as area. He continued to serve in this ship until he unfortunately was killed at sea in April 1918. He was entitled to the 1914-15 Star, and the General Service and Victory Medals.
"He passed out of the sight of men by the path of duty and self-sacrifice."
18, Patchett Street, Hulme, Manchester.   TZ7800

QUINTON, W., Private, 1st Manchester Regiment.
He joined in October 1916, and was drafted in the following December to Mesopotamia. After a short period of service there he was transferred to the Palestine front, and took part in the operations leading up to the capture of Jerusalem. After this he was seized with illness, and after treatment at a Base Hospital, returned home and was finally demobilised in November 1919. He holds the General Service and Victory Medals. 102, Victoria Street, Longsight, Manchester. Z7801

R

RABY, J. T., Private, Royal Welch Fusiliers.
He joined in April 1916, and served at Borden Camp before proceeding overseas in February 1917. Whilst on the Western Front he was transferred to the Royal Dublin Fusiliers, and was engaged in action at Arras, Messines, Ypres and Cambrai. He was wounded at Cambrai, and invalided to England in January 1918. On his recovery he was stationed at Aldershot and Limerick before being demobilised in January 1919. He holds the General Service and Victory Medals.
38, Lostock Street, Miles Platting, Manchester.   Z9330

RACE, J., Sapper, R.E.
He volunteered in August 1914, and in the following December was drafted to the Western Front. During his service in France he was in action at Neuve Chapelle, Ypres, Festubert, Albert, Ploegsteert, the Somme, Arras and Ypres. He gave his life for King and Country in the third Battle of the Aisne in May 1918, and was entitled to the 1914 Star, and the General Service and Victory Medals.
"He passed out of the sight of men by the path of duty and self-sacrifice."
3, Linacre Street, Oldham Road, Manchester.   Z10993

RADFORD, S., Private., 1st Lincolnshire Regt.
He joined in August 1917, and after training was sent in January 1918 to India, where he did service on garrison duty at various stations. Being then attacked by fever he was invalided home, and underwent treatment in hospital until his discharge in October 1919. He holds the General Service and Victory Medals.
49, Normanby Street, Moss Side, Manchester.   Z7802

RAFFERTY, A., Private, Labour Corps.
He joined in May 1917, and after service in England was sent to France in the following September. He did good service in his Corps in the region of Hazebrouck and Hesdin, carrying out the various duties assigned to him with diligence and care until the end of the campaign, and afterwards. He was demobilised in June 1919, and holds the General Service and Victory Medals.
54, Lomas Street, Ancoats, Manchester.   Z7803

RAFFERTY, J., Private, K.O. (R. Lancaster Regt.)
Volunteering in August 1914, he went for training to a Southern station, and was sent in June 1915 to the Dardanelles, where he was engaged with the transport section of his Battalion in the conveyance of machine guns. He took part in the actions of Krithia and Suvla Bay, and being then attacked by illness was sent to hospital at Mudros, where he died in October 1915. His body lies in Mudros Cemetery. He was entitled to the 1914-15 Star, and the General Service and Victory Medals.
"The path of duty was the way to glory."
5, Herbert Street, Ardwick, Manchester.   Z7804

RAFFERTY, J., Sapper, R.E.
At the outbreak of hostilities he was already serving, and at once proceeded with the first Expeditionary Force to the Western theatre of war. There he took part in the Battles of Mons, La Bassée, Ypres, Nieuport, the Somme, Arras, Vimy Ridge and Givenchy. When the war terminated he entered Germany with the Army of Occupation, and served at Cologne until discharged in January 1919. He holds the Mons Star, and the General Service and Victory Medals.
59, Victoria Square, Oldham Road, Manchester.   Z9331

RAINSBURY, E., Private, Manchester Regiment.
Having volunteered in October 1914, he was drafted to France in December of the following year, but, after taking part in important engagements at Ypres and Festubert, was unhappily killed in action at Fricourt in July 1916, during the Somme Offensive. He was entitled to the 1914-15 Star, and the General Service and Victory Medals.
"He died the noblest death a man may die,
Fighting for God and right and liberty."
70, Duke Street, Lower Broughton, Manchester.   Z10996

RALPH, H. F., Cpl., Queen's (Royal West Surrey Regiment).
He volunteered in September 1914, and proceeded to the Western Front in the next month. He did good service in the desperate Battle of Ypres (I), and later at St. Eloi, and Hill 60. In September 1915 he gave his life for King and Country in the heavy fighting at Loos. His body lies in the Military Cemetery there. He was entitled to the 1914 Star, and the General Service and Victory Medals.
"Great deeds cannot die."
13, Poplar Street, Ardwick, Manchester.   Z6210B

RALPHS, E., Stoker, R.N.
Joining in September 1917, he was posted in the following November to H.M. Mine-sweeper "William Griffin" and aboard this vessel did valuable service as a mine-sweeper round the Shetland Islands during the rest of the war. Volunteering to serve for another twelve months after the Armistice he was demobilised in October 1919, and holds the General Service and Victory Medals.
9, Edensor Place, Chorlton-on-Medlock, Manchester. Z7806B

RALPHS, W., Private, 6th Manchester Regiment.
Joining in May 1916, he passed through training in England and was drafted to France in March 1917. He fought in the Battle of Vimy Ridge, and at the capture of Bullecourt, also took part in engagements at Ypres and in the Nieuport sector, where he was wounded in July 1917, but quickly recovered, and was in action at Cambrai, and later in the Retreat of March 1918, in which he was captured near St. Quentin. After nine months' captivity in Germany, he was after his release, demobilised in September 1919. He holds the General Service and Victory Medals.
9, Edensor Place, Chorlton-on-Medlock, Manchester. Z7806A

RAMELL, J., Gunner, R.G.A.
He volunteered in September 1914, but was retained on important duties at home until August 1918, when he was drafted to the Western Front. There he did good work with his Battery in numerous engagements, and saw heavy fighting at Havrincourt, Cambrai and Ypres. He served in France until February 1919, and was demobilised a month later, holding the General Service and Victory Medals.
21, Sanitary Street, Oldham Road, Manchester.   Z9332

RAMELL, W., L/Cpl., Loyal N. Lancashire Regt.
In July 1916 he joined the Army, and on conclusion of his training was drafted overseas seven months later. He served on the Western Front for nine months, and during that time took an active part in engagements at Arras, Bullecourt, Messines and Ypres, but fell fighting at Cambrai on November 30th, 1917. He was entitled to the General Service and Victory Medals.
          "His life for his Country, his soul to God."
33, Jersey Street Dwellings, Ancoats, Manchester.   Z9333

RAMSAY, G., Sergt., M.G.C.
An ex-soldier, he re-enlisted at the outbreak of war, and was immediately drafted to France, where he fought in the Retreat from Mons. Proceeding to Mesopotamia he served in various engagements, and later was transferred to Egypt, where he was in action in many parts of the line. He also saw much service in Russia. In May 1919 he was demobilised after returning to England, and on May 30th of the following year he unfortunately died. He was entitled to the Mons Star, and the General Service and Victory Medals.
          "Steals on the ear the distant triumph song."
157, Thornton Street, Collyhurst, Manchester.   Z10995

RAMSDALE, E., Private, 3/8th Manchester Regt.
He volunteered in October 1915, and served with his unit at various stations in England and Wales. He rendered valuable services, but owing to a physical disability, was not successful in obtaining his transfer overseas before the cessation of hostilities, and after doing much valuable work, chiefly at prisoner of war camps, was demobilised in April 1919.
32, Churchill Street, Openshaw, Manchester.   TZ7809

RAMSDEN, A., Private, Welch Regiment.
He joined in September 1917, and after training was drafted to France in June of the next year, in time to take part in the 2nd Battle of the Aisne, and in the operations which followed it, notably those at Bapaume, Havrincourt Wood and in the Battles of Cambrai (II) and Ypres (IV), in which he was severely wounded. After treatment at a Base Hospital he was invalided home, and remained in hospital until his demobilisation in October 1919. He holds the General Service and Victory Medals.
30, Garibaldi Street, Ardwick, Manchester.   Z7807

RAMSDEN, F., Pte., Loyal North Lancashire Regt.
Volunteering in October 1914, he passed through his training and was drafted in April 1915 to the Egyptian front, from which in the following June he was sent to Gallipoli, where he was wounded in action. After being in hospital at Malta, and in Scotland, he recovered, and proceeded to France in April 1916. Whilst taking part in the Somme Offensive of July, he was again wounded, and being invalided home was discharged in January 1917 as unfit for further service. He was still under treatment in 1920, and holds the General Service and Victory Medals.
21, Lord Street, Openshaw, Manchester.   Z7808

RAMSDEN, J., L/Cpl. (Lewis Gnr.), The Welch Regt.
He volunteered in July 1915, and in December 1917 was drafted to France, where he was in action at Cambrai, Arras and was gassed at La Bassée in September 1918 during the Allied Advance. He was invalided to Hospital at Le Tréport, and returning to England in 1919, was demobilised in September of the same year. He holds the General Service and Victory Medals. 25, Granville Place, Ancoats, Manchester.   Z10994

RAMSEY, J. W., Private, Lancashire Fusiliers.
Volunteering soon after the outbreak of war, he was drafted to the Western Front in September 1915, and whilst in action on the Ancre front, in the following November, was severely wounded. After being invalided to a hospital in the Midlands, he remained under treatment until his final demobilisation in April 1919. He holds the 1914-15 Star, and the General Service and Victory Medals.
59, Ridgway Street, Moss Side, Manchester.   Z7810

RAMSHEAD, T., Private, 1st Lancashire Fusiliers.
He was already in the Army when war broke out in August 1914, and early in the following year proceeded to the Dardanelles, where he took part in severe fighting at Krithia, Suvla Bay and Chunuk Bair, and was badly wounded. As a result he was invalided home and finally discharged in January 1916 as medically unfit for further service. He holds the 1914-15 Star, and the General Service and Victory Medals.
7, Daniel Street, Ancoats, Manchester.   Z11944

RATCHFORD, D., Private, Royal Marine Engineers.
He volunteered in September 1914, and was later transferred to the Labour Corps. He was engaged on important duties on the South Coast in laying oil pipes for the use of H.M.S.

ships, and rendered valuable services. He was not successful in obtaining a transfer overseas during the war, and was demobilised in December 1918.
44, Park Street, W. Gorton, Manchester.   Z10997

RATCLIFFE, A. C., Driver, R.A.S.C. (M.T.)
He joined in May 1916, and was sent in the following December to France, where he did good service driving motor tractors for the conveyance of heavy guns to change of position, notably in the region of Albert, Ypres, Arras and Béthune. He took part in the Retreat and Advance of 1918, carrying on his important duties at Thiepval, Cambrai and Le Cateau. He was demobilised in January 1919, and holds the General Service and Victory Medals.
78, Meadow Street, Moss Side, Manchester.   Z7811

RATCLIFFE, C., Corporal, Seaforth Highlanders.
Volunteering in January 1915, he passed through a considerable period of training and service in England, and on attaining sufficient age was drafted to the Western Front in November 1916. He saw service in the Somme sector, and near Arras, and Béthune, and later took part in the Retreat and Advance and was twice wounded. Serving through all the final operations, he was eventually demobilised in June 1919, and holds the General Service and Victory Medals.
12, Bentley Street, Hulme, Manchester.   TZ7812

RATCLIFFE, J., Corporal, Manchester Regiment.
He was mobilised from the Reserve in August 1914, and was immediately drafted to France, where he took part in the Retreat from Mons. He also served in the first Battle of Ypres, and wounded at Festubert, was sent to hospital at the Base. After his recovery he was again wounded at St. Quentin in 1916, and a third time in the Advance in September 1918. He was invalided home, and demobilised in April of the following year, and holds the Mons Star, and the General Service and Victory Medals.
6, Berkshire Street, Ancoats, Manchester.   Z10998

RATCLIFFE, R., Private, R.A.M.C.
Volunteering in November 1914, he went through his training and proceeded to the Western Front in the following June. He did good service as stretcher-bearer in engagements at Loos, Albert, Ploegsteert Wood and in the Somme Offensive. Later he carried on his important duties in the actions of Arras, Ypres (III), Cambrai (I) and in the Retreat and Advance of 1918, being also with the Army of Occupation on the Rhine. Demobilised in February 1919, he holds the 1914-15 Star, and the General Service and Victory Medals.
61, Heald Avenue, Rusholme, Manchester.   TZ7813

RATHBONE, H. Pte., 1/8th K. (Liverpool Regt.)
After volunteering in May 1915, he underwent training in England, and was drafted in June 1916 to the Western Front, in time to take part in the great Somme Offensive. Later he fought at Messines Ridge and in the Battle of Ypres (III), during which, on September 20th, 1917, he was both wounded and gassed at St. Julien. After being invalided home, he remained under treatment in hospital until his discharge in October 1918. He holds the General Service and Victory Medals.
6, Marple Street, Openshaw, Manchester.   Z7815

RATHBONE, T., Private, Suffolk Regiment.
He joined in January 1918, and embarking for France in the following June, took part in various important engagements in the Allied Advance. After the Armistice he was sent into Germany with the Army of Occupation, remaining there until September 1919, when he returned home and was demobilised. He holds the General Service and Victory Medals.
5, Tiverton Grove, Ardwick, Manchester.   Z10999B

RATHBONE, W. E., Private, Manchester Regiment.
After volunteering in July 1915, he proceeded to France in the following November and saw heavy fighting doing good service as a sniper, at Loos, near Arras, in the Ypres sector and in the first Battle of the Somme. In this engagement he was severely wounded, and being evacuated to hospital in England remained under treatment until discharged as unfit for further service in July 1917. He holds the 1914-15 Star, and the General Service and Victory Medals.
99, Marsland Street, Ardwick, Manchester. Z7814 Z10999A

RATHBONE, W. G., Corporal, Manchester Regiment.
He joined in March 1916, and after a period of training was drafted to the Western Front later in the same year. He did valuable work with his unit during the various battles and engagements of 1917, notably at Arras, Ypres, and Cambrai. He was unfortunately killed in action at the commencement of the Retreat of 1918, and was entitled to the General Service and Victory Medals.
          "Whilst we remember, the sacrifice is not in vain."
                                                      C1235

RATHMILL, G. B., Corporal, R.A.S.C.
He joined in March 1918, and was engaged on transport and other important duties at various stations until February 1919. He was then transferred to the South Lancashire Regiment and proceeded to the Army of Occupation in Turkey. He was demobilised in March 1920.
79, Holland Street, Newton, Manchester.   Z11000

RATICAN, J., Private, York and Lancaster Regt., Worcestershire Regiment, and Labour Corps.

Enlisting in March 1917 in the Worcestershire Regiment, he proceeded to France in the following September. Being too young to be sent into the firing line, he was given duty at the Base and then transferred to the Labour Corps, in which he did good service until demobilised in July 1919. After demobilisation he re-enlisted in the York and Lancaster Regiment, and was still serving in Persia in 1920. He holds the General Service and Victory Medals.

71, Birch Street, Ardwick, Manchester. Z7522A

RATTIGAN, M., Bombardier, R.G.A.

He volunteered in November 1914, and proceeded to France late in the following year. He fought in the Battle of the Somme, and was severely wounded and gassed. Invalided home, he received hospital treatment and subsequently was discharged as unfit for further service in January 1919. He holds the 1914-15 Star, and the General Service and Victory Medals.

28, Harrowby Street, Collyhurst, Manchester. Z11001

RAW, T., Private, Royal Welch Fusiliers.

Volunteering in June 1915, he passed through a long period of training and service in England, and was sent to Egypt in March 1918. There he was engaged on garrison duty at Alexandria, Cairo and other places, and continuing to serve until the end of the war, was demobilised in March 1919. He holds the General Service Medal.

18, Delhi Grove, Greenheyes, Manchester. Z7816

RAWLINS, H., Private, R.A.M.C.

Volunteering in March 1915, he passed through his training in England, and was sent to France in June 1917. in the Field Ambulance. He rendered good service in connection with engagements at Ypres, Pilkem, Armentières and in the Retreat of 1918, Aveluy Wood and Albert. Later he carried on his important duties through the final Advance, notably at Le Catelet and Le Cateau, and was eventually demobilised in July 1919. He holds the General Service and Victory Medals.

1, Derby Street, Hulme, Manchester. Z7817

RAWSON, T., Corporal, 7th Manchester Regiment.

He volunteered in May 1915, and in the following March proceeding to Egypt, served in many engagements during the British Advance through Palestine. He was in action in the first and second Battles of Gaza, and in September 1917 was drafted to the Western Front. Whilst in this theatre of war he fought in both the engagements at Cambrai, and was severely wounded in the latter in October 1918, and invalided home. He was demobilised later in January 1919, and holds the General Service and Victory Medals.

18, Back Mount Street, Harpurhey, Manchester. Z11572

RAY, W., Private, Lancashire Fusiliers.

He volunteered at the outbreak of hostilities and was drafted to France in May 1915. He fought in many important engagements, including those at Festubert, Loos and Vermelles, and was wounded in the Battle of the Somme in November 1916. After his recovery he was again in action on the Ancre and at Cambrai, and died gloriously on the Field of Battle at Bapaume in August 1918. He was entitled to the 1914-15 Star, and the General Service and Victory Medals.

" A valiant Soldier, with undaunted heart, he breasted life's last hill."

1, Nelson Street, West Gorton, Manchester. Z11002

RAYBONE, A., Private, South Staffordshire Regt.

Volunteering in August 1914, he proceeded to France in the following November and fought in the first and second Battles of Ypres. Later he saw much hard service, being wounded four times in the first Battle of the Somme in July 1916, at Delville Wood in 1917, in an enemy air raid at Boulogne, and in the final Advance of September 1918. As a result of this last wound he was invalided home and eventually demobilised in March 1919. He holds the 1914-15 Star, and the General Service and Victory Medals.

48, Burnley Street, Ancoats, Manchester. Z7992

RAYNER, E., Private, 7th South Wales Borderers.

He joined in March 1917, and after a period of training was four months later ordered to Salonika. In this theatre of war he experienced fierce fighting in different sectors of the Front, and was in action during the operations on the Doiran and the Vardar. On his return to England in December 1919, he was demobilised, and holds the General Service and Victory Medals.

282, Victoria Square, Oldham Road, Manchester. Z9334A

RAYNER, S., Private, 5th Manchester Regiment.

Joining in March 1917, he proceeded overseas six months later and served on the Western Front for two years. During that period he took an active part in many engagements of importance, including those at Ypres and Cambrai and was also in action during the victorious Allied Advance in 1918. He remained in France until demobilised in November 1919, and holds the General Service and Victory Medals.

282, Victoria Square, Oldham Road, Manchester. Z9334B

RAYNES, F., Private, K.O. (Royal Lancaster Regt.)

Volunteering in November 1914, he was drafted in September of the next year to the Western Front and saw heavy fighting at Loos, in the Ypres sector, and the first Battle of the Somme, in which he was wounded in three places. After four months' treatment at a Base hospital, he recovered, rejoined his unit and fought at Arras and Messines Ridge. He then contracted trench fever, and being sent to hospital in England, was invalided out of the Service in June 1918. He holds the 1914-15 Star, and the General Service and Victory Medals.

4, Mansfield Street, Chorlton-on-Medlock, Manchester. TX7818

RAYNER, F., Air Mechanic, R.A.F. (Balloon Section).

He joined in December 1917, and after his training served at various stations on important duties which demanded a high degree of technical skill. He rendered valuable services but was not successful in obtaining a transfer overseas before the cessation of hostilities, and was demobilised in April 1919.

17, Great Jackson Street, West Gorton, Manchester. Z11003

RAYNOR, J. H., A.B., Royal Navy.

Volunteering in June 1915, he served in H.M.S. " Arduna " in the North Sea from November 1915 to June 1916, then in the Mediterranean until December 1917, and afterwards until the end of the war, in the Atlantic except for a short period of hospital treatment for defective eyesight, taking part in many Naval engagements. Demobilised in February 1919, he holds the 1914-15 Star and the General Service and Victory Medals.

32, Viaduct Street, Ardwick, Manchester. Z7819

RAYSON, G. F., L/Corporal, 20th Hussars.

He was mobilised in August 1914, and immediately drafted to France, where he took a prominent part in the Battles of Mons and Ypres (I). He died gloriously on the Field of Battle at Ypres in November 1915, and was entitled to the Mons Star, and the General Service and Victory Medals.

" The path of duty was the way to glory."

7, Milton Street, Ancoats, Manchester. Z11945

REA, J. (D.C.M.), R.S.M., 7th King's Own Scottish Borderers.

Volunteering in August 1914, he embarked for the Western Front in the following June and was actively engaged in various parts of the line. He took part in the Battle of Loos, during which he was awarded the Distinguished Conduct Medal on September 25th, 1915, for conspicuous bravery and devotion to duty, in operating his machine gun after all the other machine guns in his section had been put out of action. He loaded his gun from his bandolier and continued firing the whole of the afternoon and held up the enemy He also fought in the Somme Offensive, and was wounded in July 1916. On recovery he served at Arras and in the Retreat and Advance of 1918, and entered Mons at dawn on Armistice Day. He was demobilised in May 1919, and holds the 1914-15 Star, and the General Service and Victory Medals.

59, Church Street, Hulme, Manchester. Z11800

READ, H., Private, Cheshire Regiment.

Volunteering in September 1915, he served at first in the King's Shropshire Light Infantry at various stations in England and Wales, and was afterwards transferred to the Cheshire Regiment. He was not successful in obtaining his transfer overseas before the cessation of hostilities, but joined the Army of Occupation on the Rhine in November 1918, and remained with it until his demobilisation in October 1919.

33, Granville St., Chorlton-on-Medlock, Manchester. Z7822

READ, J., Private, 8th Manchester Regiment.

He volunteered in November 1915, and after undergoing a period of training, served at various stations, where he was engaged on duties of great importance. Unable, owing to ill-health, to obtain his transfer overseas, he nevertheless rendered valuable services with his unit until August 1916, when he was invalided from the Army.

29, Granville St., Chorlton-on-Medlock, Manchester. Z7820

READ, J., Private, 3rd Manchester Regiment.

He joined in June 1917, and after completing a term of training was retained as a machine-gunner on important coastal defence duties at various stations. He was not successful in obtaining his transfer to a theatre of war, but nevertheless, did much useful work with his unit until May 1919, when he was demobilised.

29, Prescott Street, West Gorton, Manchester. Z7821

READE, L. L., Sapper, R.E.

Volunteering in January 1915, he was drafted to the Dardanelles in June of that year, and there saw much severe fighting, particularly at Suvla Bay. On the Evacuation of the Gallipoli Peninsula, he was invalided to hospital at Malta, and after his recovery, was engaged on important duties in connection with the making of instruments for wireless telegraphy. He was demobilised in February 1919 and holds the 1914-15 Star, and the General Service and Victory Medals.

8, Marsland Street, Ardwick, Manchester. Z4664B

READE, T. J., Gunner, R.G.A.
He joined in November 1917, and in April of the following
year, proceeded to France, where he saw severe fighting in
various sectors of the Front. He took part in the Battles of
Bapaume, Havrincourt, Cambrai, and Le Cateau, and many
other important engagements until the cessation of hostilities.
Demobilised on his return home in February 1919, he holds the
General Service and Victory Medals.
9, Hinckley Street, Bradford, Manchester.   Z7823

READEY, J., Corporal, 3rd Cheshire Regiment.
He volunteered in July 1915, and after completing his training,
served at various stations, where he was engaged on important
duties as a signaller on the General Headquarters Staff. He
was unable to obtain his transfer to the Front, but nevertheless, rendered very valuable services with his unit until March
1919, when he was demobilised.
8, Brampton Street, Ardwick, Manchester.   Z7824A

READEY, J., Sapper, R.E.
He volunteered in June 1915, and after his training was
retained at various stations, where he was engaged on duties
of a highly important nature. He was not successful in his
efforts to obtain his transfer to a theatre of war, being over
age for active service, but, nevertheless, did much useful work
with his Company until demobilised in January 1919.
8, Brampton Street, Ardwick, Manchester.   Z7824B

REDDICEN, H., Private, King's (Liverpool Regt.)
He joined in November 1916, and in October of the following
year proceeding to the Western Front, and was in action in the
engagements at Messines and Cambrai, where he was taken
prisoner in November 1917. He was first sent to a Prisoners-
of-War Camp in Germany, and was afterwards compelled to
work behind the enemy lines at Tournai, where he was employed
in loading up railway waggons with ammunition. He was
released after the Armistice was signed, and demobilised in
February 1919, and holds the General Service and Victory
Medals. 42, Hope St., Bradford, Manchester.   Z11004

**REDFERN, A., Pte., 12th Manchester Regt. and
and R.A.O.C.**
Volunteering in October 1914, he proceeded to the Western Front
in September of the following year, and there saw severe
fighting in various sectors. He took part in many important
engagements in this theatre of war, and was twice wounded
in action—on the Somme in July 1916, and at Ypres in 1918.
He was invalided from the Army in March 1919, and holds
the 1914–15 Star, and the General Service and Victory Medals.
31, Carter Terrace, Greenheys, Manchester.   TZ7825

REDFERN, E., Sergt., 2nd Cheshire Regiment.
Six months after joining in February 1916, he proceeded to
the Western Front, where he saw much heavy fighting. He
took part in the Battles of Arras, Bullecourt, Ypres, and
Cambrai, and other engagements in various sectors, served
also through the Retreat and Advance of 1918, and was wounded
in action at Amiens in August of that year. He was demobilised in January 1920, and holds the General Service and
Victory Medals.
10, Hawthorn Street, Ardwick, Manchester.   Z7827

REDFERN, F., Cpl., 3rd and 21st Manchester Regt.
Three months after volunteering in March 1915, he was drafted
to the Western Front, where he took part in the Battles of the
Somme, Bullecourt, and Ypres, and other engagements, and
was wounded in action. In November 1917 he was transferred
to Italy, and there saw severe fighting on the Piave until his
return to France, where he was again wounded during the
Retreat of March 1918. He was recommended for a decoration for conspicuous bravery in the Field on the Piave, and
holding the 1914–15 Star, and the General Service and Victory
Medals, was demobilised in May 1919.   Z7734A
14, St. Leonard Street, Chorlton-on-Medlock, Manchester.

REDFERN, J., Air Mechanic, R.A.F. (late R.F.C.)
He volunteered in January 1915, but on completion of his
training in March of that year, was invalided from the Service.
He was then engaged on important munition work at Woolwich Arsenal and at Glasgow until January 1918, when he
re-enlisted. Retained on duties of a highly technical nature
on the Defence of London, he rendered valuable services with
his Squadron until demobilised in January 1919. He holds
the General Service and Victory Medals.
10, Hill Street, Chorton-on-Medlock, Manchester.   Z7826

REDFERN, J. H., L/Cpl., 3/8th Manchester Regt.
He volunteered in April 1915, and after undergoing a period
of training, served at various stations, where he was engaged
on duties of great importance. Although unable to obtain
his transfer to a theatre of war, he rendered valuable services
with his unit until January 1919, when he was demobilised.
12, Meadow Street, Ardwick, Manchester.   Z7828

REDFORD, H., Cpl., King's Shropshire Light Infty.
He volunteered in October 1914, and in January 1916 was
drafted to France. He fought in many important engagements,
including these at Vermelles, Vimy Ridge, the Somme, Arras,
Bullecourt, Messines, Ypres, Cambrai, and was wounded on
the Somme in March 1918. He was invalided home to hospital

and subsequently was discharged at Fermoy as medically
unfit for further duty in December 1918. He holds the General
Service and Victory Medals.
121, Mill Street, Ancoats, Manchester.   Z11005

REDIKIN, W., Private, Manchester Regiment.
He joined in October 1916, and on completion of his training
was sent in January 1917 to the Western Front. After taking
part in the Battle of the Somme he proceeded nine months
later to Italy, and was engaged in severe fighting on the Piave
front. After the cessation of hostilities he proceeded to
Ireland, and was stationed at Cork. In 1920 he was still serving in the Army, and holds the General Service and Victory
Medals.
5, Day Street, Oldham Road, Manchester.   Z9335

REDMAN, J. C., Pte., 3rd King's (Liverpool Regt.)
He volunteered in June 1915, and in the following November
was drafted to France. He was in action at Loos, Albert, and
was wounded, and buried under débris in a trench, in the
Battle of the Somme in July 1916. After his recovery he was
engaged in heavy fighting at Arras, Ypres, Passchendaele,
Cambrai, Amiens, Havrincourt, and Le Cateau. He was
demobilised in September 1919, and holds the General Service
and Victory Medals.
11, Wrght Street, Oldham Road, Manchester.   Z11006

REDMAN, S., Private, K.O. (R. Lancaster Regt.)
He volunteered in September 1914, and was drafted in the
following April to France. He fought in the Battles of Ypres
II, Loos, and other engagements, and in December 1915, proceeded to Egypt, where he served for a time, and was then
transferred to Salonika. In this theatre of war he took part
in the Advance across the Struma, and in engagements on the
Doiran front, and invalided home with malaria, he received
medical treatment and was eventually demobilised in November
1919. Owing to a recurrence of the fever in August 1920, he
was admitted into Frodsham Military Hospital, where he unfortunately died on October 7th of that year. He was entitled
to the 1914–15 Star, and the General Service and Victory
Medals.
        " A costly sacrifice upon the altar of freedom."
13, Kirkham Street, Bradford Road, Manchester.   Z11801

REDSTON, A. H., Private, 12th Manchester Regt.
He volunteered in September 1914, and in March of the following year proceeded to France. He fought in the Battles of
Ypres, Festubert, Albert, and was wounded in the Battles of
the Somme in July 1916. After his recovery he was again in
action at the third Battle of Ypres, and was wounded at
Passchendaele in November 1917. He received hospital
treatment and rejoining his unit served in many engagements
in the Retreat and Advance of 1918. He was demobilised in
April 1919, and holds the 1914–15 Star, and the General
Service and Victory Medals.
66, Heyrod Street, Ancoats, Manchester.   Z11007

REECE, R. H., Private, 4th South Lancashire Regt.
He volunteered in November 1914, and in August of the following year was drafted overseas. Whilst serving on the Western
Front, he was in action in many engagements, and was gassed
during the Battle of Ypres in July 1917. On returning to the
firing line he served at Cambrai, and in the Retreat and Advance
of 1918. Remaining in France until his demobilisation in
March 1919, he holds the 1914–15 Star, and the General Service
and Victory Medals.
5, Norbury St., Gaylor St., Miles Platting, Manchester. TZ9336

REED, A., Rifleman, Cameronians (Scottish Rifles).
He joined in April 1916, and after a period of training, was
engaged on important duties at various stations. He was
unable, on account of ill-health, to obtain his transfer to a
theatre of war, and was for a considerable period in hospital.
He unhappily died of consumption in September 1919.
        " Steals on the ear the distant triumph song."
36, Kippax Street, Moss Side, Manchester.   Z7829

REED, J., Private, 1st Manchester Regiment.
Volunteering in August 1914, he proceeded overseas in the
following March, and was in action in the Battles of Neuve
Chapelle and Loos. He was then drafted to Mesopotamia, and
fought at Kut-el-Amara, Um-el-Hannah, and in the attempt
to relieve Kut in March 1916. He was invalided home owing
to ill-health in 1918, and discharged as medically unfit for
further military service in July of that year. He holds the
1914–15 Star, and the General Service and Victory Medals.
27, Montague Street, Collyhurst, Manchester.   Z11008

REED, J. S., Air Mechanic, R.A.F.
He volunteered in December 1914, and in October of the
following year proceeded to Egypt, where he saw much severe
fighting. He took part in engagements at Katia, El Arish,
Romani, and many other places, and was wounded in action
in 1916, and admitted to hospital at Alexandria. He rejoined his Squadron, however, on his recovery, and proceeded
into Palestine, where he fought in the Battles of Gaza, and the
Capture of Jerusalem. He was demobilised on his return
home in March 1919, and holds the 1914–15 Star, and the
General Service and Victory Medals.
15, Olive Grove, Hulme, Manchester.   Z7831

REED, J. E., Private, 2nd Royal Welch Fusiliers.
He was mobilised at the outbreak of war, and drafted to France, took part in the Retreat from Mons. He also served at La Bassée, Ypres, Givenchy, Loos, on the Somme, and in many engagements during the German and Allied Offensives of 1918. He holds the Mons Star, and the General Service and Victory Medals, and was demobilised in January 1919.
55, Saville Street, Miles Platting, Manchester.   Z11009

REED, W. R., Driver, R.F.A.
Volunteering in August 1914, he was drafted to the Western Front in July of the following year, and there saw severe fighting in various sectors. After serving through many important engagements, he was wounded in action at Albert in June 1916, and admitted to hospital at Rouen. On his recovery, however, he re-joined his Battery, and took part in the Battles of Ypres and the Somme.   Demobilised in January 1919, he holds the 1914-15 Star, and the General Service and Victory Medals.
43, Lowe Street, Miles Platting, Manchester.   Z7830

REEVES, F., Sergt., 17th Manchester Regiment.
He volunteered in February 1915, and was drafted to the Western Front in the following November. He fought in the Battles of the Somme, Arras, and Ypres, and was wounded in May 1918, during the German Offensive. Invalided to hospital in England on his recovery he proceeded to the Army of Occupation in Germany, where he served until May 1919, when he was demobilised, holding the 1914-15 Star, and the General Service and Victory Medals.
13, Leach Street, Gorton, Manchester.   Z11445

REEVES, J. O., Corporal, Lancashire Fusiliers.
Volunteering in April 1915, he embarked for Egypt in the following January, and served at Cairo and Alexandria, and in the Canal zone.   Transferred to France in June 1918 he was in action in many engagements during the Retreat and Advance and was wounded. Invalided home he received hospital treatment, and was discharged as medically unfit for further service in March 1919. He holds the General Service and Victory Medals.
6, Sycamore Street, Gorton, Manchester.   Z11010

REEVES, J. R., Pte., K. Shropshire Light Infantry.
Joining in May 1918, he was sent to the Western Front in the following September, and fought in many parts of the line.   He died gloriously on the Field of Battle at Le Cateau on October 17th, 1918, and was entitled to the General Service and Victory Medals.
"A costly sacrifice upon the altar of freedom."
34, Howarth Street, Bradford, Manchester.   Z11011

REGAN, F. A., Private, 5th Lancashire Fusiliers.
Volunteering in February 1915, he was drafted to Egypt in the following November, and served at various stations. Transferred to France in August 1917, he was engaged in heavy fighting in various sectors. He gave his life for the freedom of England on September 6th, 1917, in the third Battle of Ypres, and was entitled to the 1914-15 Star, and the General Service and Victory Medals.
"His life for his Country."
7, Rockingham Street, Collyhurst, Manchester.   Z11012

REID, J., Sergeant, 18th Manchester Regiment.
Volunteering in August 1914, he proceeded in the following January to the Western Front, where he was in action at Ypres, Loos, Nieuport, and La Bassée. He was wounded in the Battle of the Somme, and sent to hospital in Belfast. On his recovery he returned to France, but was again wounded at Merville, and in consequence was invalided out of the Army as medically unfit in November 1918. He holds the 1914-15 Star, and the General Service and Victory Medals.
32, Flower Street, Ancoats, Manchester.   Z9680

REID, J. R., L/Corpl., 1/8th Manchester Regiment.
He volunteered in April 1915, and proceeding to Egypt in January of the following year, took part in engagements at Katia, El Fasher, Romani, and Rafa. He also served in Palestine, and fought in the first Battle of Gaza, before being transferred to the Western Front in April 1917. There he took part in the Battles of Arras, Ypres, and Cambrai, and many other engagements, and was twice wounded in action —at Achiet-le-Petit in March 1918, and near Havrincourt in August of that year. Demobilised in February 1919, he holds the General Service and Victory Medals.
9, Meadow Street, Ardwick, Manchester.   Z7832

REID, W., Private, K.O. (Yorkshire Light Infantry).
He was mobilised at the outbreak of war in August 1914, and at once proceeded to France, where he served throughout the period of hostilities. He took part in fierce fighting in the Battles of Mons, Le Cateau, the Aisne, La Bassée, Ypres, I, II, and III, Messines, Hill 60, Loos, the Somme, Bapaume, the Marne and Cambrai.   He was discharged from the Army in April 1919, and holds the Mons Star, and the General Service and Victory Medals.
99, Abbott Street, Reather Street, Manchester.   Z9337

REILLY, J., Private, 13th Manchester Regiment.
Volunteering in September 1914, he was drafted to the Western Front in the following year, and there saw severe fighting in various sectors. After taking part in the Battles of Hill 60, Ypres, Festubert, Albert, the Somme, and Cambrai, and many minor engagements, he was transferred in 1918 to Salonika, where he was wounded in action on the Doiran Front   He was demobilised on his return home in February 1919, and holds the 1914-15 Star, and the General Service and Victory Medals.
25, Hambro' Street, Ancoats, Manchester.   Z7833

REILLY, J., Driver, R.G.A.
He joined in June 1916, and on completing his training in January of the following year was drafted to the Western Front.   Whilst in this theatre of war he took part in many important engagements, including the Battles of Arras, Bullecourt, Messines, Ypres, and Passchendaele, fought also in the Retreat and Advance of 1918, and was gassed at Cambrai in November 1917.   He was demobilised in March 1919, and holds the General Service and Victory Medals.
9, Somerset Street, Ardwick, Manchester.   Z7834

RELPH, F., Private, 21st Manchester Regiment.
Three months after joining in June 1917, he proceeded to the Western Front, where he took part in many important engagements in various sectors. He made the supreme sacrifice, falling in action at Avesnes in November 1918, only a few days before the signing of the Armistice. He was entitled to the General Service and Victory Medals.
"The path of duty was the way to glory."
6, Copinger Street, Greenheys, Manchester.   Z7805

REMMOS, A., Private, R.M.L.I.
He volunteered in August 1914, and was posted to H.M.S. "Mars," on board which vessel he served in the North Sea for a short period, proceeding to the Western Front later in the same month.   In February 1915, however, he was commissioned to H.M. Monitor "30" for duty in the White Sea, and afterwards served in H.M.S. "Jupiter" in the Mediterranean until June 1916. Later he was on board H.M.S. "Roxburgh" and H.M.T. "Desna" in the Pacific Ocean, and off the south coast of America, until after the cessation of hostilities.   He was awarded the Russian Order of St. Stanislas for distinguished service, and holds also the 1914 Star, and the General Service (with five clasps), and Victory Medals.
He was demobilised in January 1919.
63, Barlow Street, Chorlton-on-Medlock, Manchester.   Z7835

REMMOS, O., Pte., Royal Scots, and Middlesex Regt.
He volunteered in June 1915, and after his training, was engaged on important duties at various stations until January of the following year, when he was invalided from the Army. He re-enlisted, however, in January 1917, and in June of that year proceeded to the Western Front, where he took part in the Battles of Ypres, Cambrai, and the Somme, and other engagements, and fought also in the Retreat and Advance of 1918. Demobilised in March 1919, he holds the General Service and Victory Medals.
19, Ross Street, Ardwick, Manchester.   Z7836

RENNIE, E., Private, 8th Manchester Regiment.
He joined in October 1916, and after a course of training was sent overseas in December 1917.   He served on the Western Front for only three months, and during that time fought in the Retreat of 1918, and was severely wounded in the second Battle of the Somme in March 1918. He was invalided to England and retained on home service until demobilised in February 1919, holding the General Service and Victory Medals.
2, Teignmouth Street, Collyhurst, Manchester.   Z9681

RENSHAW, F. T., Pte., Border Regt. and King's Own (Royal Lancaster Regt.)
He joined in September 1916, and after undergoing a period of training was retained at various stations, where he was engaged on duties of great importance.   Being too young for active service, he was unable to obtain his transfer to the Front, but nevertheless, rendered valuable services with his unit until January 1919, when he was invalided from the Army, on account of deafness.
9, Dalton Street, Hulme, Manchester.   Z7211B

RENSHAW, W., Gunner, R.F.A.
Volunteering in September 1914, he was drafted to the Western Front after two months' training, and there took part in the Battles of Ypres, Hill 60, Loos, Vermelles, the Somme, Arras and Cambrai, and many minor engagements. He was killed in action in August 1918, at Amiens, where he was buried. He was entitled to the 1914 Star, and the General Service and Victory Medals.
"His life for his Country, his soul to God."
24, Tonge Street, Ardwick, Manchester.   Z7837

RESTRICK, E., Private, 25th Manchester Regt. and Tank Corps.
After volunteering in December 1915, he underwent a period of training, prior to proceeding to the Western Front in August 1917.   Whilst in this theatre of war he took part in important engagements in various sectors, including the Battles of Cambrai, and served also through the Retreat and Advance of 1918. Demobilised in May 1919, he holds the General Service and Victory Medals.
12, Braham Street, Longsight, Manchester.   Z7838

REVETT, J., Private, Middlesex Regiment.
Volunteering in March 1915, he was drafted two months
later to the Western Front. There he saw service at Festubert,
Loos, St. Eloi, the Somme, Arras, Bullecourt, Ypres and
Cambrai, and fell fighting in the Battle of the Aisne in May
1918. He was entitled to the 1914–15 Star, and the General
Service and Victory Medals.
" Nobly striving,
He nobly fell that we might live."
19, Teignmouth Street, Rochdale Road, Manchester.　Z9596C

REVETT, W., Corporal, R.A.S.C.
He volunteered for active service in November 1914, but was
not successful in obtaining a transfer overseas. He did excellent work at important stations in England, including
Grantham, Salisbury Plain and Morecambe, but in November
1918, contracted influenza and died in the Military Hospital
at Boston.
19, Teignmouth Street, Rochdale Road, Manchester.　Z9596B

REYNOLDS, C. R., Private, 1st Norfolk Regiment.
Mobilised in August 1914, he was immediately drafted to the
Western Front, where he served as bomber in the Battle of,
and Retreat from, Mons. He also took part in the Battles
of La Bassée, Ypres, Neuve Chapelle and Festubert, and other
important engagements, and was severely wounded in action
at Delville Wood during the Somme Offensive of July 1916.
He was for a considerable period in hospital at Stockport
and Manchester, before being invalided from the Army in
April 1918, and holds the Mons Star, and the General Service
and Victory Medals.
11, Hancock Street, Rusholme, Manchester.　TZ7843

REYNOLDS, J., Private, 8th Manchester Regiment.
He volunteered in January 1916, and in the following October
proceeded to the Western Front, where he saw much heavy
fighting in the Somme sector. After taking part in several
important engagements, he was severely wounded in action
in February 1917, and invalided home. He returned to France
however, on his recovery, and was engaged in guarding prisoners of war in various sectors with the Labour Corps until
his demobilisation in September 1919. He holds the General
Service and Victory Medals.
663, Sixth Street, Trafford Park, Manchester.　Z7844

REYNOLDS, J., Private, Lancashire Fusiliers.
Shortly after volunteering in August 1914, he was drafted to
France, where he saw severe fighting in various sectors of
the Front. He took part in the Battles of Ypres, Loos, Arras,
Messines, Passchendaele, Cambrai and Le Cateau, and many
other important engagements, served also through the Retreat
and Advance of 1918, and was wounded in action on the Somme.
He was demobilised in February 1919, and holds the 1914
Star, and the General Service and Victory Medals.
23, Woburn Place, Chorlton-on-Medlock, Manchester.　X7842

REYNOLDS, J., Private, King's (Liverpool Regt.)
He volunteered in November 1915, and in December of the
following year was drafted to the Western Front, where
he saw severe fighting in various sectors. He took part in
the Battles of Arras, Cambrai and the Somme, and other engagements, served also through the Retreat and Advance
of 1918, and was wounded in action at Havrincourt. He
was invalided from the Army in April 1919, and holds the
General Service and Victory Medals.
21, Clifford Street, Lower Openshaw, Manchester.　Z7841

**REYNOLDS, J., Private, Border Regt. and 4th Loyal
North Lancashire Regt.**
Joining in April 1917, he was drafted to the Western Front
in October of that year, and there saw much severe fighting.
He took part in important engagements in various sectors,
including the Battles of Cambrai, the Somme, the Marne
and Ypres, and served also through the Retreat and Advance
of 1918. Demobilised in April 1919, he holds the General
Service and Victory Medals.
31, Wesley Street, Ardwick, Manchester.　Z7839

REYNOLDS, J., Private, King's (Liverpool Regt.)
Volunteering in February 1915, he landed in France in the
following May, and was in action at Festubert, Loos and St.
Eloi, and was severely wounded. Returning home he received
hospital treatment, and ultimately was discharged as unfit
for further service in February 1916. He holds the 1914–15
Star, and the General Service and Victory Medals.
6, Diggle Street, Ancoats, Manchester.　Z10951B

REYNOLDS, J., Pte., 2nd K.O. (R. Lancaster Regt.)
A serving soldier, he proceeded to France in November 1914,
and was in action at Ypres, Hill 60, the Somme and Arras.
He also took part in the Battle of Cambrai, and was present
throughout the German Offensive and subsequent Allied
Advance. During his service overseas he was wounded,
and returning home after the Armistice was demobilised in
March 1919. He holds the Queen's and King's South African
Medals, the 1914–15 Star, and the General Service and Victory
Medals.　Z11013
23, Woburn Place, Chorlton-on-Medlock, Manchester.

REYNOLDS, M., Private, Manchester Regiment.
He volunteered in January 1915, and after three months
training, proceeded to the Western Front, where he saw heavy
fighting in various sectors. After taking part in the Battles
of Ypres, Loos, the Somme and Arras, and other important
engagements, he was severely wounded in action at Messines,
and invalided home. He was discharged in September 1917,
as medically unfit for further service, and holds the 1914–15
Star, and the General Service and Victory Medals.
8, Clifford Street, Lower Openshaw, Manchester.　Z7840

REYNOLDS, T., Private, Border Regiment.
Three months after joining in March 1916, he was drafted to
the Western Front, where he fought in various sectors. He
served through the Battles of the Somme, the Ancre, Arras,
Vimy Ridge, Ypres, Cambrai, the Marne, Cambrai II and Le
Cateau, and many other important engagements, and took
part also in the Retreat and Advance of 1918. He was afterwards sent with the Army of Occupation into Germany,
finally returning home for demobilisation in September 1919.
He holds the General Service and Victory Medals.
8, Ashbury Street, Openshaw, Manchester.　TZ6073A

RHODES, H., Pte., Welch Regt. and Labour Corps.
He joined in November 1916, and in December of the following
year proceeded to France, where he saw severe fighting
in various sectors of the Front. He took part in the Battle
of the Somme, and in many other important engagements
in various sectors and was wounded in action on the Marne
in June 1918. On his recovery he served with the Labour
Corps until November 1919, when he was demobilised, holding
the General Service and Victory Medals.
32, Dorset Street, Hulme, Manchester.　Z7845

**RHODES, H., Sapper, R.E. and Pte., Argyll and
Sutherland Highlanders.**
Volunteering in February 1915, he was drafted to the Western
Front in November of the same year, and was there engaged
on important duties in various sectors. He also took part
in the Battles of Vermelles, the Somme and Vimy Ridge,
and many other important engagements until the cessation
of hostilities, and on his return home in February 1919, was
demobilised. He holds the 1914–15 Star, and the General
Service and Victory Medals.
63, Jenkinson St., Chorlton-on-Medlock, Manchester.　Z7846

RICE, J., Private, 12th South Lancashire Regt.
He joined in June 1918, and completing his training was
stationed at various depôts with his unit on important duties.
He did not obtain his transfer overseas prior to the Armistice,
but was drafted to Russia in February 1919, and saw much
service there until returning home in the following December.
He was demobilised in the same month, and holds the General
Service and Victory Medals.
10, Lowe Street, Miles Platting, Manchester.　Z11014

RICE, J., Pte., 8th King's Own (Scottish Borderers).
A month after the outbreak of war, he volunteered, and in
June 1915, was drafted to the Western Front. There he was
principally in action in the Loos sector, and was unfortunately
killed there on September 25th, 1915. He was entitled to
the 1914–15 Star, and the General Service and Victory Medals.
" Honour to the immortal dead who gave their youth that
the world might grow old in peace."
4, Brass Street, Rochdale Road, Manchester.　Z9682

RICE, W., Private, K.O. (Royal Lancaster Regt.)
He volunteered in January 1915, and underwent a period of
training prior to his being drafted overseas. During his service
on the Western Front he took part in the Battles of Ypres,
the Somme and Nieuport. He was demobilised in January
1919, and holds the General Service and Victory Medals.
23, Gibson Street, Newton Heath, Manchester.　Z11946

RICHARD, A., Private, 9th Cheshire Regiment.
He joined immediately on attaining military age in June 1918,
and after completing a period of training, was engaged on
important duties at various stations. He was unable to obtain his transfer overseas before the cessation of hostilities,
but in March 1919, proceeded to Germany, where he served
with the Army of Occupation at Bonn. He was demobilised
on his return home in March 1920.
21, Halsbury Street, Longsight, Manchester.　Z7847

RICHARDS, J., Corporal, 1st Royal Welch Fusiliers.
Having enlisted in March 1910, he proceeded to the Western
Front three months after the outbreak of war in August
1914, and was there wounded in action in December of the
same year. Invalided home, he returned to France, however,
after two months in hospital, and was again wounded at Ypres
in March 1915. After taking part in many important engagements, he was taken prisoner at Zillebeke in October 1916,
and was held in captivity in Germany until the cessation of
hostilities. Discharged in March 1919, he holds the 1914
Star, and the General Service and Victory Medals.
58, Princess Street, Rusholme, Manchester.　TZ7851

RICHARDS, E. H., Private, M.G.C.

He joined in January 1917, and on completing his training in August of that year, was drafted to the Western Front, where he took part in the Battles of Lens, Cambrai, and the Aisne, and other important engagements. He fell fighting near Arras in March 1918, during the Allies' Retreat. He was entitled to the General Service and Victory Medals.

"He joined the great white company of valiant souls."

51, Pownall Street, Hulme, Manchester.   Z7848

RICHARDS, G., Corporal, R.A.S.C. (M.T.)

He volunteered in April 1915, and after undergoing a period of training, was retained at various stations, where he was engaged on important repair work. He was not successful in obtaining his transfer to a theatre of war, but nevertheless, rendered valuable services with his Company until March 1919, when he was demobilised.

32 Pomfret Street, West Gorton, Manchester.   Z7849

RICHARDS, G., Private, Labour Corps.

After joining in September 1916, he underwent a period of training prior to being drafted to the Western Front in April of the following year. There he was engaged in repairing the roads and railways in various sectors, took an active part in the Battles of Arras, Vimy Ridge, Messines, Ypres, Passchendaele, Cambrai, the Somme and Amiens, and also served through the Retreat and Advance of 1918. He was demobilised in February 1919, and holds the General Service and Victory Medals.

148, Beresford Street, Moss Side, Manchester.   Z7850

RICHARDS, J. C., Private, 4th Yorkshire Regiment, and Sapper, R.E.

Two months after joining in September 1916, he proceeded to the Western Front, where he was engaged on important duties in various sectors. He also took an active part in the Battles of Ypres, Cambrai, and the Somme, and after serving through the Retreat and Advance of 1918, was injured in an accident in November of that year. He was demobilised in June 1919, and holds the General Service and Victory Medals.
15, Norwood Street, Chorlton-on-Medlock, Manchester. Z7852B

RICHARDS, J. M., 1st Air Mechanic, R.A.F.

He joined in April 1916, having previously been engaged on Government work at Messrs. Ford's Motor Works, Trafford Park, and after a period of training served at various stations, where he was engaged on duties of a highly technical nature. He was unable to obtain his transfer overseas, but, nevertheless, rendered valuable services with his Squadron until April 1919, when he was demobilised.

15, Norwood Street, Chorlton-on-Medlock, Manchester. Z7852A

RICHARDS, T., Private, 1st Cheshire Regiment.

He joined in August 1917, and in April of the following year proceeded to the Western Front, where he saw much severe fighting. He made the supreme sacrifice, falling in action in the third Battle of the Aisne in May 1918, only a few days after landing in France. He was entitled to the General Service and Victory Medals.

"And doubtless he went in splendid company."

34, Welbeck Street, Chorlton-on-Medlock, Manchester. Z7853

RICHARDS, W., L/Cpl. K. (Liverpool Regiment).

Volunteering in September 1914, he was sent to Egypt in the following January, and was in action during the Turkish attack on the Suez Canal and at Sollum and Jifjaffa on the Western Desert. Transferred to France in May 1916, he fought in the Battles of Vermelles and Vimy Ridge and was unfortunately killed in action in July 1916 during the first Battle of the Somme. He was entitled to the 1914-15 Star, and the General Service and Victory Medals.

"He joined the great white company of valiant souls."

23, Savoy Street, Great Jackson Street, West Gorton, Manchester.   Z11015

RICHARDSON, C., A.B., R.N., H.M.S. "Walker."

He volunteered in August 1914, and was in action in H.M.S. "Venetia" in engagements at Coronel, Falkland Islands, Dogger Bank and Heligoland. He was wounded in the Battle of Jutland and also served on the North Mediterranean and Black Seas. In June 1916 he was washed overboard in the North Sea and remained in the water for four and a half hours before being rescued. In 1920 he was still serving in the Navy, and holds the 1914-15 Star, and the General Service and Victory Medals.

12, Padgate Street, Ancoats, Manchester.   TZ9683

RICHARDSON, E., Private, Border Regiment, and Air Mechanic, R.A.F.

Having enlisted in August 1913, he was drafted to the Western Front shortly after the outbreak of war twelve months later, and there saw much severe fighting. After taking part in the Battle of Ypres and other engagements, he was severely wounded in action at Festubert in June 1915 and invalided home. On his recovery he was transferred to the R.A.F. and was retained on important duties in England, where he was still with his Squadron in 1920. He holds the 1914 Star, and the General Service and Victory Medals.

20, Hutton Street, Hulme, Manchester.   TZ7855

RICHARDSON, E., Pte., K.O. (R. Lancaster Regt.)

He volunteered in November 1915, and embarking for the Western Front three months later, was in action in many parts of the line. He died gloriously on the Field of Battle at Delville Wood on August 19th, 1916, during the first British Offensive on the Somme, and was entitled to the General Service and Victory Medals.

"Courage, bright hopes and a myriad dreams splendidly given."

23, Dougall Street, Hulme, Manchester.   Z11016B

RICHARDSON, F., Private, 1st Manchester Regt.

He volunteered in June 1916, and three months later embarked for Mesopotamia. In this theatre of war he was engaged in operations on the Tigris, the Offensive at Kut-el-Amara and many other actions. Contracting influenza, he was invalided to hospital at Alexandria, where he unfortunately died on December 2nd, 1918, and lies buried in Ramleh Military Cemetery. He was entitled to the General Service and Victory Medals.

"Whilst we remember, the sacrifice is not in vain."

8, Granville Place, Ancoats, Manchester.   TZ11803

RICHARDSON, F. N., Private, R.A.S.C.

Having enlisted in February 1911, he proceeded to Egypt shortly after war was declared in August 1914, and there served at various stations until April of the following year. He was then transferred to Gallipoli, where, after taking part in the Landing at Cape Helles, he saw much severe fighting until the Evacuation of the Peninsula, when he was sent to Malta. He returned to Alexandria before being drafted to the Western Front, where he was in action in the Battles of the Somme, Amiens and Bapaume, and also served through the Retreat and Advance of 1918. He was discharged in February 1919, and holds the 1914-15 Star, and the General Service and Victory Medals.

13, Gorse Street, Hulme, Manchester.   Z7856

RICHARDSON, P., Private, K. (Liverpool Regt.)

Volunteering in February 1916, he proceeded to France in the following September, but shortly afterwards returned to England owing to ill-health. He continued to render excellent services, however, until the close of hostilities, on guard and other important duties at various stations. He was demobilised in December 1918, and holds the General Service and Victory Medals.

23, Dougall Street, Hulme, Manchester.   Z11016A

RICHARDSON, S., Private, Labour Corps.

Shortly after joining in March 1917, he was drafted to France, where he was engaged in repairing roads and on other important duties in various sectors of the Front. He was also present at the Battles of Arras, Ypres, Passchendaele and Kemmel Hill and many other engagements, and finally returned home for demobilisation in November 1919. He holds the General Service and Victory Medals.

28, Bremner Street, Chorlton-on-Medlock, Manchester. Z7854

RICHARDSON, S., Gunner, 2nd Cheshire Regiment.

Volunteering in August 1914, he was drafted to Egypt in the following May and served in the Canal zone and was in action at Katia. Later transferred to France, he was in action in many parts of the line and fought in numerous engagements during the German and Allied Offensives of 1918. He was demobilised in January 1919, and holds the 1914-15 Star, and the General Service and Victory Medals.

4, Saville Street, Miles Platting, Manchester.   Z11018

RICHARDSON, T., Pte., 10th Loyal N. Lancs. Regt.

Volunteering in September 1914, he was sent to the Western Front in the following June and was in action in the Battles of Loos, St. Eloi, Albert, Vimy Ridge and Ploegsteert. Severely wounded on the Somme in August 1916, he returned home, and after receiving hospital treatment was attached to the Labour Corps with which he was on duty until the close of the war. He was demobilised in March 1919, and holds the 1914-15 Star, and the General Service and Victory Medals.

8, Edensor Street, Beswick, Manchester.   Z11017

RICHARDSON, T. A., 1st Air Mechanic, R.A.F.

He joined in May 1916, and after completing a period of training, was retained at various stations, where he was engaged on duties which required a high degree of technical skill. Unable to obtain his transfer to a theatre of war, he nevertheless, did much useful work with his Squadron until October 1919, when he was demobilised.

25, Percy Street, Hulme, Manchester.   Z7857

RICHARDSON, W. Pte., 9th Loyal N. Lancs. Regt.

Volunteering in June 1915, he landed in France in the following November and was in action at Loos, St. Eloi, Albert, the Somme and Ypres, and was wounded at Messines. On his recovery he rejoined his unit and was engaged in heavy fighting throughout the German Offensive and Allied Advance of 1918. He was demobilised in April 1919, and holds the 1914-15 Star, and the General Service and Victory Medals.

7, Middlewood Street, Harpurhey, Manchester.   Z11573

RICHMOND, J. W., Corporal, Labour Corps.
Joining in June 1916, in the following month he embarked for France and was engaged on important duties in the Ypres salient and in the La Bassée sector. He rendered excellent services throughout the Retreat and Advance of 1918 and returning home after the Armistice, was demobilised in July 1919. He holds the General Service and Victory Medals.
37, Stewart Street, Gorton, Manchester. Z11019

RICHMOND, S., Private, R.A.M.C.
Volunteering in September 1914, he served at various stations until proceeding to France in March 1917. During his service overseas he was engaged on important duties attending the sick and wounded troops at the 32nd Stationary Hospital, Boulogne, rendering excellent services throughout. He was demobilised in March 1919, and holds the General Service and Victory Medals.
38, Elizabeth Street, West Gorton, Manchester. Z11020

RIDDEOUGH, F., Private, R.M.L.I.
Volunteering in May 1915, he was sent to France in the following August and was engaged in heavy fighting at Festubert, Loos, Albert, the Somme, Arras, Bullecourt, Messines, Ypres and Cambrai. He was taken prisoner in April 1918 and sent to Germany. On his release he returned home and was demobilised in December 1918, holding the 1914–15 Star, and the General Service and Victory Medals.
12, Love Lane, Ancoats, Manchester. Z11021A

RIDDEOUGH, R., Pte., Loyal N. Lancashire Regt.
He joined in June 1916, and in the following August was sent to France. He fought in numerous engagements, including those on the Somme, at Arras, Bullecourt, Ypres, Cambrai, Bapaume, and was wounded in November 1917. On recovery he was in action throughout the Retreat and Advance of 1918, and returning home was demobilised in March 1919. He holds the General Service and Victory Medals.
12, Love Lane, Ancoats, Manchester. Z11021B

RIDEHALGH, A., Pte., 2nd East Lancashire Regt.
He volunteered in November 1915, and in the following year was drafted to France, where he took part in numerous engagements, including the Battle of the Somme. He fell fighting at the Battle of Ypres on July 31st, 1917. He was entitled to the General Service and Victory Medals.
"Whilst we remember, the sacrifice is not in vain."
14, February Street, Chorlton-on-Medlock, Manchester. Z11022

RIDEHALGH, J. D., Pte., King's Shropshire Light Infantry.
He volunteered in December 1915, and in the following year embarked for the Western Front. He was in action in the Battle of the Somme and was gassed at Messines. He was invalided home, and after a period in hospital was discharged as medically unfit for further service in 1918, holding the General Service and Victory Medals.
14, February St., Chorlton-on-Medlock, Manchester. Z11022A

RIDGWAY, G., Private, South Wales Borderers.
He joined in 1917, and later in the same year was ordered to the Western Front. During his service there he took an active part in engagements at Ypres, Hill 60, the Somme, Lens, Albert, Arras, Cambrai, Bourlon Wood and Armentières. He was wounded in action on one occasion, but served in France until the close of hostilities. Demobilised in 1919, he holds the General Service and Victory Medals.
25, Elizabeth Ann Street, Manchester. Z9685A

RIDGWAY, J. G., Private, 22nd Manchester Regt.
He volunteered in November 1914, and twelve months later proceeded to the Western Front. There he saw heavy fighting in various sectors, and after taking part in engagements at Loos and St. Eloi, was severely gassed at Albert in April 1916, and invalided home. He was for a time in hospital before being discharged in May 1917 as medically unfit for further service, and holds the 1914–15 Star, and the General Service and Victory Medals.
67, Milton Street, West Gorton, Manchester. Z7858

RIDGWAY, T., Private, 1st East Lancashire Regt.
Having previously served with the Colours he re-enlisted in October 1914, and in March of the following year, was drafted to the Western Front. After taking part in the Battle of Ypres and many other important engagements, he was transferred in 1917 to Italy, where he was again in action. He was wounded in action whilst overseas, and in November 1917 was sent home suffering from malaria. He was invalided from the Army in the following month and holds the 1914–15 Star, and the General Service and Victory Medals.
54, Carlisle Street, Hulme, Manchester. Z7859

RIDGWAY, W., Private, 6th South Lancashire Regt.
He volunteered in September 1914, and in the following year proceeded to Gallipoli. After taking an active part in operations at Krithia, Chocolate Hill, Suvla Bay, Achi Baba and Chunuk Bair, he was unhappily killed in action in 1915. He was entitled to the 1914–15 Star, and the General Service and Victory Medals.
"He passed out of the sight of men by the path of duty and self-sacrifice."
25, Elizabeth Ann Street, Manchester. Z9685B

RIDING, T. (M.M.), Air Mechanic, R.A.F.
He volunteered in August 1914, and crossing to France soon afterwards, fought in the Retreat from Mons and many other actions, and was wounded at the Battle of Loos. On recovery he served on the Somme and, engaged as an observer, took part in the bombing raids on Mannheim, and was badly gassed. He was awarded the Military Medal for gallantry and devotion to duty in the Field, and also holds the Mons Star, and the General Service and Victory Medals. He was demobilised in February 1919.
80, Mawson Street, Chorlton-on-Medlock, Manchester. TX11804

RIDING, W. H., Pte., 1/8th Lancashire Fusiliers.
Shortly after volunteering in August 1914 he was drafted to Egypt, where he was wounded in action during severe fighting on the Suez Canal in April 1915. He was for a time in hospital, but on his recovery rejoined his unit and again fought in engagements at Agagia, Katia and El Fasher. In December 1916, he was transferred to the Western Front and there took part in the Battles of Ypres, Cambrai, Bapaume and Havrincourt, and many minor engagements. He was demobilised in January 1919, and holds the 1914–15 Star, and the General Service and Victory Medals.
32, Lancaster Street, Hulme, Manchester. Z7860

RIDINGS, J. E., Special War Worker.
During the period of the war he was engaged as a clerk and checker by the London & North Western Railway Company at Manchester. He was unable to obtain a release from the railway authorities in order to join the Army, but, nevertheless, performed excellent work in this capacity in which he was employed.
12, Holbeck Street, Oldham Road, Manchester. Z9684

RIDLEY, A., Private, 3rd Manchester Regiment.
Volunteering in July 1915, he landed in France in the following September, and took part in several engagements, including the Battle of Ypres where he was wounded. He was invalided home, and on his recovery returned to the Western Front and was in action throughout the German Offensive and Allied Advance of 1918. He was demobilised in February 1919, and holds the 1914–15 Star, and the General Service and Victory Medals.
19, Martha Street, Bradford, Manchester. TZ11610B

RIELEY, R., Sergt., 1/7th Manchester Regiment.
He volunteered in August 1914, and in April of the following year was drafted to Gallipoli, where, after taking part in the Landing at Cape Helles, he saw much severe fighting until the Evacuation of the Peninsula. He was then transferred to the Western Front, and there having fought in many important engagements, was killed in action at Le Cateau in October 1918. He was entitled to the 1914–15 Star, and the General Service and Victory Medals.
"His memory is cherished with pride."
23, Ely Street, Hulme, Manchester. TZ5740A

RIGBY, J., Private, Lancashire Fusiliers.
He joined in April 1917, and on completing a period of training in October of that year was drafted to India. There he was engaged on important garrison duties at Lahore and various other stations, and rendered valuable services during the period of hostilities. He holds the General Service and Victory Medals, and in 1920 was still with his unit.
37, Rylance Street, Ardwick, Manchester. Z7861

RIGBY, W., Corporal, R.E. (T.F.)
Mobilised at the outbreak of war, he proceeded to Egypt in September 1914, but seven months later was transferred to the Dardanelles, where he took part in the Landing at Cape Helles and the three Battles of Krithia. After the Evacuation of the Gallipoli Peninsula he returned to Egypt and served in the heavy fighting at Katia and Romani. In April 1917 he was sent to France and was in action at the Battles of Vimy Ridge, Ypres (III), Passchendaele, The Aisne (III), the Marne (II), Havrincourt, Ypres (IV) and Le Cateau (II). He was demobilised in March 1919, and holds the 1914–15 Star, and the General Service and Victory Medals.
17, Lavender Street, Hulme, Manchester. Z7862

RIGG, C., Private, 7th Manchester Regiment.
He volunteered in June 1915, and five months later was sent to Salonika, where he took part in heavy fighting on the Vardar, Doiran and Struma fronts during the Balkan campaign. He suffered severely from malarial fever whilst in this theatre of war, and was demobilised in July 1919. In November 1919, however, he enlisted in the Royal Navy as a stoker, and in 1920 was waiting to be posted to a ship. He holds the 1914–15 Star, and the General Service and Victory Medals.
25, Durham Place, Hulme, Manchester. Z7863

RILES, E., Driver, R.A.S.C.
He joined in September 1916, and after a period of training was engaged at various stations on important duties with the Remount section. He was unable to obtain a transfer overseas owing to his being medically unfit, but rendered valuable services until his demobilisation in May 1919.
51, Meadow Street, Ardwick, Manchester. Z7864

RILEY, C., Staff Sergt., R.F.A.
He volunteered in September 1915, and in the following year proceeded to France. Whilst in this seat of war he played a prominent part in several engagements, including the Battles of the Somme, Ypres and Cambrai, and in heavy fighting during the Retreat and Advance of 1918. He did continuously good work throughout, and was demobilised in November 1919. He holds the General Service and Victory Medals.
5, Thompson Street North, Ardwick, Manchester. Z7867

RILEY, E., Private, 4th Lancashire Fusiliers.
He volunteered in August 1914, and in the following year was drafted to the Dardanelles, where he took part in the Landing at Suvla Bay, and was wounded in action in October 1915. As a result, he was invalided home, but on his recovery proceeded to France, and was engaged on important duties. He also saw service in Italy, but returned to France and after hostilities ceased, was demobilised in March 1919. Five months later, however, he re-enlisted in the R.A.S.C. and in 1920 was serving at Cologne with the Army of Occupation, and holds the 1914-15 Star, and the General Service and Victory Medals. 15, Stanley St., Hulme, Manchester. Z7865B

RILEY, E., Sergt. Instructor, 8th Manchester Regt.
He volunteered in August 1914, and in the following month was sent to Egypt. In January 1915 he was transferred to the Dardanelles, where he took part in the Landing at Cape Helles, and the Battles of Krithia. In November 1915 he returned home, and was engaged on instructional duties at various stations until he was discharged in February 1919. He holds the 1914-15 Star, and the General Service and Victory Medals.
4, Johnsons Buildings, Ancoats, Manchester. Z11025A

RILEY, F., Sapper, R.E.
In March 1916 he joined the Army, and six months later was drafted to Salonika. There he was engaged in action on the Struma, the Doiran and the Vardar, and later was sent to Athens, where he was engaged on garrison duties. He also served on the Italian Front, and saw heavy fighting in various sectors of the line. Demobilised in February 1919, he holds the General Service and Victory Medals.
117, Hamilton Street, Collyhurst, Manchester. Z9338

RILEY, G., Private, 7th Lancashire Fusiliers.
He volunteered in December 1914, and proceeding to France in the following year played an important part in the Battles of Loos, Albert and the Somme, and in heavy fighting at St. Eloi. He was badly gassed in action, and invalided home and in June 1917, was discharged as medically unfit for further service. He holds the 1914-15 Star, and the General Service and Victory Medals.
15, Stanley Street, Hulme, Manchester. Z7865A

RILEY, G., Private, K.O. (Royal Lancaster Regt.)
He volunteered in September 1914, and after his training was engaged on important duties at home stations for some time. In May 1917, however, he was drafted to France, and took part in the Battles of Messines, Lens and the Somme (II). He was invalided home suffering severely from frostbite, and in March 1918, was discharged as medically unfit for further service. He holds the General Service and Victory Medals.
13, Tuley Street, Lower Openshaw, Manchester. Z7866A

RILEY, H., Private, R.A.M.C.
Volunteering in June 1915, he completed a course of training and was then engaged as a 2nd Class Nursing Orderly in military hospitals at Manchester, Stockport, Pendleton, Blackpool and London. He was not successful in obtaining a transfer overseas, but did consistently good work until his demobilisation in August 1919.
36, Phillips Street, Hulme, Manchester. TZ7869

RILEY, J., Private, 19th Cheshire Regiment.
He volunteered in December 1915, and five months later was drafted to France. During his service on the Western Front, he took part in the Battles of the Somme (I), Arras, Ypres (III), Cambrai (I), the Somme (II), Bapaume (II) and Cambrai (II), and in other important engagements in the Retreat and Advance of 1918. After the cessation of hostilities he proceeded to Germany with the Army of Occupation, and was eventually demobilised in September 1919, holding the General Service and Victory Medals.
25, Ely Street, Hulme, Manchester. Z7870

RILEY, J., Private, K.O. (Royal Lancaster Regt.)
Volunteering in August 1914, he proceeded to France in June of the following year, and was in action at Festubert, Loos, the Somme, Bullecourt, Messines and Ypres. He was also engaged in heavy fighting throughout the Retreat and Advance of 1918, and during this service in France acted as Lewis gunner, and was wounded on five occasions. He was invalided home in October 1918, and discharged twelve months later. He holds the 1914-15 Star, and the General Service and Victory Medals.
77, Cross Street, Bradford, Manchester. Z11023

RILEY, J., Private, 3rd Manchester Regiment.
He volunteered in August 1914, and whilst engaged on important duties with his unit on the East Coast was wounded

at Cleethorpes during an air raid in April 1917. Admitted into hospital, he received treatment, and was discharged in November 1917 as unfit for further service.
6, Bridenville Street, Collyhurst, Manchester. Z11026

RILEY, J. J., Private, Royal Welch Fusiliers.
Having joined in May 1916, he was sent to France in March of the following year. During his service on the Western Front, he took part in the Battles of Arras, Ypres, Passchendaele, Cambrai, the Somme (II), the Aisne (III). In June 1918 he was taken seriously ill and after being in hospital at Rouen until September of the same year, was invalided to Edinburgh, where he underwent further treatment for four months. He was demobilised in November 1919, and holds the General Service and Victory Medals.
20, Fawcett Street, Hulme, Manchester. TZ7871

RILEY, J. W., Drummer, 8th Manchester Regt.
He enlisted in March 1913, and in September 1914 was sent to Egypt. After serving for a short time in Cairo and Alexandria he was transferred to Cyprus. He later returned home and in September 1917 proceeded to France, where he was in action at Arras, Ypres, Cambrai and Bapaume. He was demobilised in June 1919, and holds the 1914-15 Star, and the General Service and Victory Medals.
4, Johnsons Buildings, Ancoats, Manchester. Z11025B

RILEY, L., Air Mechanic, R.A.F.
He volunteered in March 1915, and on completion of his training was first engaged on important duties at Nottingham. Later he was sent to London for special work in connection with the aircraft defences of the City. He was unsuccessful in obtaining his transfer overseas, but rendered valuable services until his demobilisation in February 1919, and holds the General Service and Victory Medals.
69, Longridge Street, Collyhurst, Manchester. Z7873

RILEY, N. E., 2nd Lieut., 2nd K.O. (Y.L.I.)
He volunteered in the Grenadier Guards in November 1914, and served as a Sergeant with this unit in France for nine months, during which time he played a prominent part in much severe fighting. He then came home to take up his commission, and later returned to the 2nd King's Own (Yorkshire Light Infantry) on the Western Front, where he gallantly laid down his life for King and Country at Cambrai on May 21st, 1918, one month after landing in this theatre of war for the second time. He was entitled to the 1914-15 Star, and the General Service and Victory Medals.
"A costly sacrifice upon the altar of freedom."
23, Carlisle Street, Hulme, Manchester. Z7872

RILEY, T., Private, South Wales Borderers.
He volunteered in November 1915, and whilst training at Aldershot met with a gun accident, which unfortunately resulted in the loss of his left eye. In consequence he was discharged from the Army as medically unfit for further military service in November 1916.
2, Stanley Street, Hulme, Manchester. Z8926B

RILEY, W., Private, K.O. (R. Lancaster Regiment).
After volunteering in August 1914, he spent five months in training, and was then drafted to France, where he took part in the Battles of Neuve Chapelle, Hill 60, Loos, Vermelles and Vimy Ridge. He died gloriously on the Field of Battle during the Somme Offensive in July 1916, and was entitled to the 1914-15 Star, and the General Service and Victory Medals.
"And doubtless he went in splendid company."
13, Tuley Street, Lower Openshaw, Manchester. Z7866B

RILEY, W., Private, 5th Lancashire Fusiliers.
Volunteering in April 1915, in November of the same year he was drafted to France, and fought in numerous engagements, including the Battles of Albert, the Somme, Arras, Ypres, Passchendaele and Cambrai. He also served in the Retreat and Advance of 1918. He was demobilised in April 1919, and holds the 1914-15 Star, and the General Service and Victory Medals.
39, Worth Street, Rochdale Road, Manchester. Z11024

RILEY, W. H., L/Corporal, 7th Manchester Regt.
He volunteered in August 1914, and proceeding to Gallipoli in the following May was badly wounded in action in July 1915. After six months in hospital, he was sent to France in November 1916 and was gassed at the Battle of Messines in June 1917. He was invalided home in December of that year, and was discharged in February 1918 as medically unfit for further service, holding the 1914-15 Star, and the General Service and Victory Medals.
14, Walden Street, Longsight, Manchester. Z7868

RILEY, W. T., Private, 21st Manchester Regiment.
He volunteered in November 1914, and in the following year was drafted to the Western Front, where he played a prominent part in the Battles of Hill 60, Ypres (II), Festubert, Loos, Albert, the Somme, Arras and Cambrai. He then proceeded to Italy, and was in action during heavy fighting on the Piave front. He was demobilised in July 1920, and holds the 1914-15 Star, and the General Service and Victory Medals.
44, Clayton Street, Hulme, Manchester. Z7874

RILEY, W. V., Private, Manchester Regiment.

He volunteered in April 1915, at the age of seventeen years, and was drafted to the Western Front in November 1916. He went into action with the Lewis Gun Section of his unit, and was mortally wounded at the Battle of Arras, unfortunately dying at No. 41 C.C.S. on April 14th, 1917. He was entitled to the General Service and Victory Medals.
"Honour to the immortal dead, who gave their youth that the world might grow old in peace."
281, Morton Street, Longsight, Manchester. Z7875

RIMMER, J., Private, Loyal N. Lancashire Regt.

Volunteering in September 1914, he served for a short time on the Western Front, and was then sent to Gallipoli. There he took part in fierce fighting at Krithia and Suvla Bay, and was unhappily killed in action in August 1915. He was entitled to the 1914–15 Star, and the General Service and Victory Medals.
"Great deeds cannot die:
They, with the sun and moon, renew their light for ever."
1, Hadfield Street, Newton Heath, Manchester. Z9686

RIPPINGHAM, W., Private King's (Liverpool Regt.)

Joining in October 1917, he was drafted to France in May of the following year, and took part in numerous engagements during the German and Allied Offensives of 1918. He was unfortunately killed in action at Arras on August 21st, 1918. He was entitled to the General Service and Victory Medals.
"His life for his Country."
5, Kertch Street, Ancoats, Manchester. TZ11027

RISBY, M., Private, Sherwood Foresters.

He joined in March 1916, and in the following May was drafted to France. He took part in the severe fighting at Albert and on the Somme, where he was badly wounded. He was invalided home, and after a period in hospital was discharged as medically unfit for further service in September 1916. He holds the General Service and Victory Medals.
44, Dickens Street, Miles Platting, Manchester. Z11028

RITSON, H., Lieutenant, Manchester Regiment.

He volunteered in August 1914, and in February of the following year proceeded to the Western Front. He was engaged in heavy fighting at Neuve Chapelle, St. Eloi, Festubert, Loos, Vimy Ridge, the Somme, Arras, Bullecourt, Ypres and Passchendaele. He also served throughout the Retreat and Advance of 1918, and during his service in this theatre of war was twice wounded. He was demobilised in February 1919, and holds the 1914–15 Star, and the General Service and Victory Medals.
49, Hendham Vale, Collyhurst, Manchester. Z11486B

RITSON, W., Private, R.A.S.C.

He volunteered in June 1915, and crossing to France in the following year served in various parts of the line for three years. During this period he was engaged in the transport of rations, and other supplies to the firing line, and was present at several battles, including those of the Somme, Ypres and Péronne. Serving until the end of hostilities he returned home in 1919, and discharged later in that year as medically unfit for further service, holds the General Service and Victory Medals. 89, Morton St., Longsight, Manchester. Z7876A

RITSON, W. H., Private, Manchester Regiment.

He joined in 1916, and drafted to the Western Front in the same year fought in the Battles of Albert, Arras, Ypres and Cambrai. With his Battalion he was also in action in several engagements in the German Offensive, and subsequent Allied Advance, which brought the war to an end in November 1918. After the Armistice he was retained in France for several months, and on returning home was demobilised in October 1919. He holds the General Service and Victory Medals. 89, Morton St., Longsight, Manchester. Z7876B

RIVETT, J., Private, 5th Manchester Regiment.

Joining in October 1916, he was drafted to France in the following month. He was in action at Arras, the Somme, Nieuport, and was wounded. He was afterwards engaged on important duties at Etaples. Returning home after the Armistice he was demobilised in March 1919, and holds the General Service and Victory Medals.
6, Churnett Street, Collyhurst, Manchester. Z11029

ROACH, G., Private, 6th South Lancashire Regt.

Volunteering in August 1914, he embarked for Gallipoli in June 1915, and was severely wounded at the Landing at Suvla Bay in August of that year. Transferred to France in February 1916, he fought at Vimy Ridge, and Neuve Chapelle, where he was again wounded in the following April. On recovery, he proceeded to Salonika in August 1916, and taking part in heavy fighting, was wounded on two further occasions, on the Doiran and Vardar fronts. He was demobilised after returning to England in April 1919, and holds the 1914–15 Star, and the General Service and Victory Medals.
14, Hurlbutt Street, Hulme, Manchester. TZ7878

ROACH, T. W., Private, 22nd Manchester Regiment.

He volunteered in August 1914, and proceeding to France in November of the following year, was engaged in the fighting at Albert, Vimy Ridge, and the Somme, where in July 1916, he was severely wounded. Invalided home, he underwent treatment at the Northern General Hospital, Sheffield, where he remained for twelve months. Returning to the Western Front in July 1917, he was in action until the close of hostilities, and in 1920 was still in France employed on important work with the Graves Registration Commission. He holds the 1914–15 Star, and the General Service and Victory Medals.
14, Hurlbutt Street, Hulme, Manchester. TZ7877

ROACH, W., Private, 21st Cheshire Regiment.

He joined in July 1916, and in the following October was sent to the Western Front. He was in action in the Battles of Arras, Bullecourt, Ypres, Cambrai, and the Somme. Owing to ill-health he was invalided home in August 1918, and served at various depôts until demobilised in March 1919. He holds the General Service and Victory Medals.
21, Dalton Street, Collyhurst, Manchester. Z11030

ROBERTON, A., Private, Highland Light Infantry.

A Reservist, he was mobilised at the declaration of war, and crossing to France shortly afterwards took part in heavy fighting in the Retreat from Mons, and other early engagements. He was unfortunately killed in action in October 1914, and was entitled to the Mons Star, and the General Service and Victory Medals.
"His memory is cherished with pride."
68, Walnut, Street, Hulme, Manchester. Z7880A

ROBERTON, H., Private, 7th Manchester Regiment.

Joining in June 1917, he completed his training and crossed to the Western Front, where he took part in heavy fighting during the third Battle of Ypres. He was unfortunately killed in action in the following October, and was entitled to the General Service and Victory Medals.
"Thinking that remembrance, though unspoken, may reach him where he sleeps."
68, Walnut Street, Hulme, Manchester. Z7880B

ROBERTS, A., Corporal, 19th Manchester Regt. and Tank Corps.

He volunteered in January 1915, and was drafted in the following November to the Western Front, where he was in action during operations at Loos, Vimy Ridge, Albert, and was wounded on the Somme. Invalided home he received medical treatment at Torquay Military Hospital, and on recovery was transferred to the Tank Corps. Returning to the Western Front he fought in the Battles of Cambrai (II), and the Somme (II), and was unhappily killed at Amiens in the Allied Advance on August 11th, 1918, and was entitled to the 1914–15 Star, and the General Service and Victory Medals.
"His name liveth for evermore."
215, Morton Street, Longsight, Manchester. Z7886

ROBERTS, A., Private, 3rd Loyal North Lancashire Regt. and Royal Inniskilling Fusiliers.

He joined in January 1917, and on completion of his training at Felixstowe, was three months later drafted overseas. During his service on the Western Front, he was engaged in action at Messines and Ypres, and was severely wounded in the latter engagement. In consequence he was discharged from the Army as medically unfit for further duties in April, 1918, and holds the General Service and Victory Medals.
14, Dora Street, Rochdale Road, Manchester. Z9341

ROBERTS, A. E., A/Corporal, 11th Manchester Regt. and M.G.C.

Volunteering in October 1914, he completed his training, and sailed for Gallipoli in the following June. In this theatre of war, he took part in the Landing at Suvla Bay and other engagements and was wounded. Evacuated to England, he was transferred to the Machine Gun Corps on recovery, and drafted to the Western Front in June 1916, fought in several battles during the Somme Offensive, and in the Retreat and Advance of 1918. Returning home, he was demobilised in March 1919, and holds the 1914–15 Star, and the General Service and Victory Medals.
7, Sadler Street, Moss Side, Manchester. Z7899

ROBERTS, A. L., L/Cpl., 7th Lancashire Fusiliers.

He volunteered in August 1914; and embarking for Egypt in the following month served with his Battalion on important duties until February of the succeeding year, when he was sent to Gallipoli. He took part in the first Landing on the Peninsula in April 1915, and in other operations which followed. Wounded in action in June of that year he was sent to hospital in Egypt, where he died from the effects of his injuries later in that month. He was entitled to the 1914–15 Star, and the General Service and Victory Medals.
"A costly sacrifice upon the altar of freedom."
17, Tranmere Street, Hulme, Manchester. Z7895B

ROBERTS, E., L/Corporal, Border Regiment.

He volunteered in June 1915, and at the conclusion of his training proceeded to France in the following September. He was in action in various parts of the line, and fought at the Battles of Arras, Passchendaele, the Somme, Ypres, and Cambrai. He gave his life for the freedom of England in the second Battle of the Somme in March 1918, and was entitled to the General Service and Victory Medals.
"His life for his Country, his soul to God."
14, Dark Lane, Ardwick, Manchester. Z7885

ROBERTS, D., Private, 13th Manchester Regiment.
Volunteering in September 1914, he was sent in the following January to the Western Front, and fought in several engagements, including the Battles of La Bassée, Ypres, St. Eloi, Albert, Vimy Ridge, the Somme, and the Ancre. He was transferred in January 1917, to Mesopotamia, and took part in operations at Amara, Kut (I), Kut-el-Amara, Um-el-Hannah, Sanna-i-Yat, and on the Tigris. Returning to England in December 1918, he was demobilised a month later, and holds the 1914–15 Star, and the General Service and Victory Medals.
55, Greecham Street, Openshaw, Manchester. Z7884

ROBERTS, D. C., Sapper, R.E.
Volunteering in August 1914, he served on home duties after completing his training, and was sent to France in February 1916. Whilst overseas he was engaged on special duties whilst operations were in progress at Albert, the Somme, Beaucourt, Arras, and was gassed at Passchendaele. On recovery he returned to the forward areas, and was in action at Bapaume and Cambrai during the closing stages of the war. He later went into Germany with the Army of Occupation, and was stationed at Cologne. He returned to England in June 1919, and was demobilised a month later, and holds the General Service and Victory Medals.
69, Bath Street, Hulme, Manchester. Z11805

ROBERTS, E., Private, 2/7th Manchester Regiment.
Volunteering in January 1916, he was drafted in the following January to the Western Front, and took part in many important engagements, including those of Arras, Vimy Ridge, Bullecourt, Messines and Ypres(III). Owing to ill-health he was invalided home to Edinburgh Military Hospital, where he underwent treatment, and on recovery returned to France. He fought in the Battles of the Aisne (III), the Marne (II), Cambrai, and several others until the cessation of hostilities. He was demobilised in January 1919, and holds the General Service and Victory Medals.
16, Marsden Street, Chorlton-on-Medlock, Manchester. Z7891A

ROBERTS, E., Private, 1/16th Manchester Regt.
He volunteered in September 1915, and embarking for France in the following January fought in the Battles of Loos, St. Eloi, Vermelles, the Somme, Arras and Cambrai. In August 1917, owing to ill-health he was admitted into hospital at Rouen, and later returned to England, received further medical treatment in Netley Hospital. On recovery he was transferred to the Royal Engineers, and was engaged on home duties. He was afterwards transferred to the Royal Army Service Corps with which unit he served on transport work, and rendered valuable services. He was demobilised in August 1920, and holds the General Service and Victory Medals.
29, Wigley Street, Ardwick, Manchester. Z7883

ROBERTS, E., Private, Oxfordshire and Buckinghamshire Light Infantry.
He volunteered in August 1914, and in June of the following year was sent to Gallipoli. He took part in the Landing at Suvla Bay, and in many of the subsequent engagements until the Evacuation of the Peninsula in January 1916. He then proceeded to Egypt, and served at Alexandria, Kantara and Hill 70. In June 1916, he was transferred to France, and was in action on the Somme, the Ancre, Bullecourt, Messines, Ypres, Bapaume, and was twice wounded. He was demobilised in March 1919, and holds the General Service and Victory Medals.
10, Park Street, West Gorton, Manchester. Z11034

ROBERTS, E. S., Private, 21st Royal Fusiliers.
Volunteering in August 1914, he was drafted in the following January to the Western Front, and serving as a signaller, took part in several Battles, including those of Neuve Chapelle, Hill 60, Ypres, Loos, St. Eloi, and was wounded on the Somme. Admitted into hospital at Rouen he received medical treatment, and on recovery was transferred to the Italian front in November 1917. In this theatre of war he was in action in operations on the Asiago Plateau, and in the British Offensive on the Piave. Returning home he was demobilised in February 1919, and holds the 1914–15 Star, and the General Service and Victory Medals.
139, Rosebery Street, Moss Side, Manchester. Z7887

ROBERTS, F. I. (Miss) Worker, Q.M.A.A.C.
She volunteered in October 1918, and sent in the following month to France was attached to the Royal Engineers and engaged as a store-keeper at Boulogne, Camiers and Etaples. She rendered valuable services and returning to England in 1919, was demobilised in July of that year. She holds the General Service and Victory Medals.
41, Plymouth Street, Chorlton-on-Medlock, Manchester. Z7889

ROBERTS, I., Sergeant, R.E.
Volunteering in November 1914, he embarked in the following September for France and served with his unit until the close of the war. During this period he was engaged on important duties during operations on the Somme, at Ypres, Passchendaele, Vimy Ridge, and in the German Offensive, and subsequent Allied Advance of 1918. He did good work throughout, and was demobilised on his return to England, in March

1919. He holds the 1914–15 Star, and the General Service and Victory Medals.
22, Greenhill Street, Chorlton-on-Medlock, Manchester. Z7902

ROBERTS, J., Corporal, R.E.
Volunteering in April 1915, he was drafted to the Western Front in the following month, and was in action in the Battles of Festubert, Loos, Vimy Ridge, Ploegsteert Wood, Bullecourt, Messines, Ypres and Cambrai. He was also engaged in heavy fighting throughout the Retreat and Advance of 1918, and returning home was demobilised in April 1919, holding the 1914–15 Star, and the General Service and Victory Medals.
28, Gray Street, Ancoats, Manchester. Z11033

ROBERTS, J., Private, Manchester Regiment.
He was mobilised in August 1914, and proceeded in June 1915 to Gallipoli, where he served until the Evacuation of the Peninsula. He then was drafted to Egypt, and took part in engagements on the Suez and at El Arish. In March 1917, he was sent to the Western Front, and whilst fighting in the Battle of Ypres was gassed. On rejoining his unit he took an active part in the Allied Advance of 1918. He was discharged in March 1919, and holds the 1914–15 Star, and the General Service and Victory Medals.
31, Masonic Street, Oldham Road, Manchester. Z9342

ROBERTS, J. A., Private, R.A.M.C.
He volunteered in March 1915, and sent to Egypt in the following June served on the Suez Canal. He later proceeded to Palestine, where he was engaged as hospital orderly at Gaza and Jerusalem, and also as a stretcher bearer in the Field. He was demobilised in January 1919, and holds the 1914–15 Star, and the General Service and Victory Medals.
89, Montague Street, off Collyhurst Street, Manchester. Z11031

ROBERTS, J. F., Private, King's (Liverpool Regt.)
He joined in September 1917, and on completion of his training served with his unit at various stations engaged on important duties. He did good work, but was not successful in securing his transfer to a theatre of war, before the cessation of hostilities. He proceeded to Ireland in September 1918, and was employed on garrison and other duties. Owing to ill-health he was sent to the Victoria Hospital, Bandon, Cork, and after receiving medical treatment was invalided out of the Service in January 1919.
6, Dorrington Street, Hulme, Manchester. Z7894

ROBERTS, J. H.,Rifleman, King's Royal Rifle Corps.
Volunteering in August 1914, he was sent in the following year to the Western Front, and was in action during operations at Le Cateau and many other engagements. He gave his life for the freedom of England in the Battle of the Somme, in August 1916, and was entitled to the 1914–15 Star, and the General Service and Victory Medals.
"His memory is cherished with pride."
21, Parker Street, Hulme, Manchester. Z7896

ROBERTS, J. R., Private, 1st Manchester Regiment.
He volunteered in January 1915, and in June of the same year was sent to the Dardanelles, where he took part in the Landing at Suvla Bay, and many other engagements. After the Evacuation of the Peninsula, he proceeded to Egypt, and was stationed at Kantara. In 1917, he was transferred to France, and was in action on the Somme, Arras, Monchy, Bullecourt, and in many important engagements during the Offensives of 1918. He was wounded and invalided home, and received hospital treatment. He was demobilised in January 1919, and holds the 1914–15 Star, and the General Service and Victory Medals.
24, Hinde Street, Gorton, Manchester. Z11032

ROBERTS, J. R., Private, 10th Manchester Regt.
Joining in June 1917, he proceeded to France later in the same year, and took part in the fighting at Amiens, Bapaume, Havrincourt and Cambrai. He was also engaged in heavy fighting during the Retreat and Advance of 1918, and returning home after the Armistice was demobilised in January 1919, holding the General Service and Victory Medals.
3, Osborne Street, Oldham Road, Manchester. Z11037A

ROBERTS, J. T., Private, 1/8th Manchester Regt.
He volunteered in August 1914, and in the following May was drafted to Egypt, thence to the Dardanelles, where he fought at Krithia and Suvla Bay. After the evacuation of the Gallipoli Peninsula, he returned to Egypt, and was wounded during fighting on the Suez Canal. In consequence he was sent to the Base Hospital, and on his recovery proceeded to France. He was again in action and fought at Ypres, and on the Somme. Later he was demobilised in January 1919, holding the 1914–15 Star, and the General Service and Victory Medals.
2, Morris Street, Ancoats, Manchester. Z11947

ROBERTS, L., Private, 3rd Manchester Regiment.
He volunteered in August 1914, and four months later was sent to the Western Front. There he was in action in important engagements in different sectors of the line, and saw heavy fighting at Neuve Chapelle. He was wounded at Hill 60 in May 1915, and in consequence was discharged as medically unfit for further military service. He holds the General Service and Victory Medals.
14, Dora Street, Rochdale Road, Manchester. Z9340B

ROBERTS, J.W., Rifleman, 2/6th K.(Liverpool Regt.)
He joined in October 1916, and crossing to France in the following January fought in several engagements, notably those of Ploegsteert and Armentières, where he was severely wounded, and in consequence lost the sight of his right eye. Invalided home to No. 2 V.A.D. Hospital, Exeter, in July 1917, he underwent prolonged medical treatment, and was eventually discharged as medically unfit for further service in January 1918. He holds the General Service and Victory Medals.
98, Tame Street, Ancoats, Manchester.   Z7882

ROBERTS, R., Private, K.O. (R. Lancaster Regt.)
He volunteered in August 1914, and landing in France in the following March fought in many important engagements, including the Battles of Hill 60, Loos, Albert, the Somme, Arras, Ypres (III) and Cambrai. Seriously wounded during the second Battle of the Somme, he was evacuated to England for hospital treatment, and eventually discharged as medically unfit for further service in April 1918. He holds the 1914–15 Star, and the General Service and Victory Medals.
27, Humphrey Street, Chorlton-on-Medlock, Manchester. Z7897

ROBERTS, R., Driver, R.A.S.C. (M.T.)
He joined in December 1917, and at the conclusion of his training served at various stations, engaged on transport and other important duties with his unit. He did good work, but was not successful in securing his transfer overseas before the close of the war, and was demobilised in February 1919.
48, Bell Street, Openshaw, Manchester.   Z7892

ROBERTS, R., Driver, R.F.A.
Volunteering in August 1914, he proceeded to Egypt in the following April, and took part in the defence of the Suez Canal, and in operations at Katia. Transferred to Salonika in December 1915, he saw service on the Doiran and Vardar fronts, and in November 1917, embarked for France. Whilst in action on the Somme in March 1918, he was severely wounded and returning to England was invalided out of the Service in April of that year. He holds the 1914–15 Star, and the General Service and Victory Medals.
14, Dora Street, Rochdale Road, Manchester.   Z9340A

ROBERTS, R., Private, 8th Manchester Regiment.
Joining in August 1916, he embarked for Egypt at the conclusion of his training, and in December of the same year took part in the capture of Madghaba. Transferred to France in August 1917, he fought in several important engagements, but was unfortunately killed in action at Ploegsteert Wood in May 1918. He was entitled to the General Service and Victory Medals.
" His name liveth for evermore."
56, Park Street, Hulme, Manchester.   Z7879

ROBERTS, R., L/Corporal, 18th Manchester Regt.
Volunteering in August 1914, he served with his unit at various depôts until drafted in 1916 to the Western Front, where he was engaged in heavy fighting in many parts of the line. He was reported missing during the Somme Offensive on October 12th, 1916, and was later presumed to have been killed in action on that date. He was entitled to the General Service and Victory Medals.
" His life for his Country, his soul to God."
1A, Lillian Square, Ardwick, Manchester.   X7893

ROBERTS, R. W., Driver, R.A.S.C.
He volunteered in August 1914, and landing in France later in that month served through the Retreat from Mons, and the Battles of La Bassée, Hill 60, Festubert, Vimy Ridge, the Somme, Beaumont-Hamel, Messines and Passchendaele. He also did good work in the Retreat and Advance of 1918, and after the Armistice was engaged on special work at Abbeville. He returned to England for demobilisation in April 1919 and holds the Mons Star, and the General Service and Victory Medals. 137, Cowesby St., Moss Side, Manchester. Z11806

ROBERTS, S., Private, 8th Manchester Regiment.
Joining in May 1916, he proceeded to France in the following July, and was in action in the Battles of the Somme, the Ancre, Bullecourt, Ypres and Cambrai. He served throughout the German Offensive and Allied Advance of 1918, and was demobilised in March 1919, holding the General Service and Victory Medals.
10, Cheshire Street, Ancoats, Manchester.   Z11036

ROBERTS, T., Private, Border Regiment.
Volunteering in August 1914, he sailed for Gallipoli in the following July, and took part in the Landing at Suvla Bay and several other engagements until the Evacuation of the Peninsula. Transferred in June 1916, to the Western Front, he fought in many important Battles, notably those of the Somme, Ypres, Arras, Cambrai, and in the Retreat and Advance of 1918. After the Armistice he served with his Battalion on special duties until his return home for demobilisation in April 1919. He holds the 1914–15 Star, and the General Service and Victory Medals.
33, Bennett Street, Openshaw, Manchester.   Z7898

ROBERTS, T. A., Cpl., South Wales Borderers.
He volunteered in September 1915, and embarking for Salonika in the following February, fought in several engagements on the Doiran front, and took part in the British Advance across

the Struma. Invalided home in April 1917, owing to ill-health, he underwent prolonged medical treatment, and on recovery was drafted to the Western Front in July 1918. In this theatre of war, he was in action at Ypres, Arras, the Somme, and on account of illness was again admitted into hospital. He returned to England in February 1919, and demobilised a month later, holds the General Service and Victory Medals.
33, Brunt Street, Rusholme, Manchester.   Z7900

ROBERTS, T. A., Private, 1st Manchester Regt.
Joining in May 1916, he was sent in July of the following year to the Western Front, and took part in many important engagements, including the Battles of Vimy Ridge, Ypres, Passchendaele, Cambrai, and in the Retreat and Advance of 1918. After the Armistice, he proceeded with the Army of Occupation into Germany and served on the Rhine until his return to England in July 1919. He was later drafted to Ireland, where he was still serving in 1920. He holds the General Service and Victory Medals.
17, Tranmere Street, Hulme, Manchester.   Z7895A

ROBERTS, V., Special War Worker.
He offered his services during the war for work of National importance, and was employed at Messrs. Mandleburg's Airship Works, Cheetham, Manchester, from October 1917 until May 1918. During this period he was engaged as a marker out in the balloon department, and carried out his work in a capable and efficient manner.
2, Jessel Street, Chorlton-on-Medlock, Manchester.   Z7888

ROBERTS, W., Corporal, R.E.
Volunteering in August 1915, he completed his training, and served with his unit at various depôts engaged on important clerical and other duties. He did good work, but was not successful in securing his transfer overseas before the close of the war, and was demobilised in February 1919.
189, Acomb Street, Moss Side, Manchester.   Z7901

ROBERTS, W., Private, Royal Inniskilling Fusiliers.
He had previously seen service in the South African War, and volunteering in September 1914, was engaged on Home Service duties until the following April, when he was drafted to Gallipoli. In this theatre of war he took part in the first Landing on the Peninsula, and fought in the Battles of Krithia and Achi Baba. He gave his life for the freedom of England during heavy fighting at the Landing of Suvla Bay in August 1915. He held the Queen's and King's South African Medals (with seven bars), and was also entitled to the 1914–15 Star, and the General Service and Victory Medals.
" His memory is cherished with pride."
41, Ryder Street, Bradford, Manchester.   Z7881

ROBERTS, W., Pte., K.O. (Royal Lancaster Regt.)
He volunteered in November 1914, and crossing in the following June to the Western Front, took part in several engagements, including the Battles of Loos, St. Eloi, Vimy Ridge, Albert and Vermelles. He gave his life for King and Country during the Somme Offensive on July 24th, 1916, and was entitled to the 1914–15 Star, and the General Service and Victory Medals.
" Nobly striving,
He nobly fell that we might live."
99, Carmen Street, Ardwick, Manchester.   Z7890

ROBERTS, W., Private, 2nd Manchester Regiment.
Volunteering in 1914, he was sent to France in the following year, and was in action at Ypres, Festubert, and Hill 60. He was wounded and invalided home. On his recovery he returned to France in 1916, and was engaged in heavy fighting at Albert, the Somme, Arras, Cambrai and throughout the Offensives of 1918. He was demobilised in 1919, and holds the 1914–15 Star, and the General Service and Victory Medals.
7, Pierce Street, Ancoats, Manchester.   Z11035

ROBERTS, W., Sapper, R.E.
He volunteered in January 1915, and embarked for France in September of that year. Whilst overseas, he was engaged on important duties in connection with operations at Ypres, the Somme, Gommecourt, Beaumont-Hamel and Passchendaele, where he was badly wounded in November 1917. Evacuated to England, he underwent protracted hospital treatment, and in February of the succeeding year was invalided out of the Service. He holds the 1914–15 Star, and the General Service and Victory Medals.
25, Clare Street, Chorlton-on-Medlock, Manchester.   TZ9339

ROBERTSHAW, F.(M.M.), Sergt., 1st Grenadier Gds.
He was mobilised at the outbreak of war, and drafted with the First Expeditionary Force to France, fought in the Retreat from Mons. He also took part in many other important engagements, notably those of La Bassée, Ypres, Neuve Chapelle and Cambrai. He was awarded the Military Medal for conspicuous bravery and devotion to duty in the Field in taking ammunition to the front line trenches under heavy shell fire. After the Armistice he returned to England, and in 1920 was still serving on special duties at the Tower of London. He also holds the Mons Star, and the General Service and Victory Medals.
121, Bedford Street, Hulme, Manchester.   Z7903B

ROBERTSHAW, F., Stoker Petty Officer, R.N.
Mobilised in August 1914, he was posted shortly afterwards to H.M.S. " Temeraire," which vessel served on patrol and other important duties in the North Sea, and fought in the Battles of Jutland in May 1916. In January 1918, he was transferred to H.M.S. "Bellerophon," which ship after hostilities ceased was sent to New Zealand, where as a Diving Instructor he was still serving in 1920. He rendered valuable services throughout the war, and holds the 1914–15 Star, and the General Service and Victory Medals.
121, Bedford Street, Hulme, Manchester. Z7903

ROBINSON, B., Sergt., K.O. (R. Lancaster Regt.)
Volunteering in August 1914, he embarked for the Dardanelles in the following June, and in August 1915, was severely wounded during the Landing at Suvla Bay. Invalided home, he underwent hospital treatment, and in the following December proceeded to France, where in March 1916, he was again wounded. Evacuated to England, he was in hospital for some months, and returning later to France took part in the Retreat and Allied Advance of 1918, and was wounded a third time. In the course of his overseas service, he was mentioned in Despatches for his splendid work and gallantry in the Field. He was demobilised in March 1919, and holds the 1914–15 Star, and the General Service and Victory Medals.
5, Nelson Place, Rusholme, Manchester. TZ7916

ROBINSON, C., Gunner, R.F.A.
He joined in December 1916, and after his training was engaged on important duties at various stations with his unit. Owing to ill-health, he was unable to secure his transfer to a theatre of war, but rendered valuable services until September 1918, when he was discharged as medically unfit for further service.
21, Purley Street, Ardwick, Manchester. Z7915

ROBINSON, C. H., Private, 1/7th Manchester Regt.
Volunteering in May 1915, he embarked for Egypt in the following February, and took part in the defence of the Suez Canal, and the Battle of Romani. Transferred to France in March 1917, he was in action at Nieuport, Ypres, Passchendaele, the Somme, and in the Allied Retreat and Advance, which terminated hostilities in November 1918. He was demobilised in March of the ensuing year, and holds the General Service and Victory Medals.
41, Royal Street, Ardwick, Manchester. Z7913

ROBINSON, C. H., Driver, R.A.S.C.
He joined in August 1918, and after his training was engaged on important transport duties at various stations. He was not successful in obtaining his transfer overseas before the close of hostilities, but nevertheless rendered valuable services until demobilised in September 1919.
17, Mark Lane, Chorlton-on-Medlock, Manchester. Z7910

ROBINSON, D., Private, Labour Corps.
He volunteered in November 1914, and completed his training at Conway with the Lancashire Fusiliers. In May 1916, he proceeded to France and was transferred to the Labour Corps engaged on guard duties at prisoners of war camps. He was demobilised in April 1919, and holds the General Service and Victory Medals.
16, Thorton Street, Openshaw, Manchester. Z11041

ROBINSON, E., Private, 19th Manchester Regiment.
Volunteering in August 1914, he served at home after completing his training and crossed to France in September of the following year. There he took part in the Battles of Loos, Albert, the Somme, the Ancre, Arras and Ypres (III), and in October 1917 was transferred to the Italian front. In this theatre of war he fought in operations on the Piave and Asiago Plateaux, and in the final Offensive of October 1918. He was demobilised after returning to England, in April 1919, and holds the 1914–15 Star, and the General Service and Victory Medals.
10, Ernest St., Morton St., Longsight, Manchester. Z11807

ROBINSON, F., L/Corporal, 18th Manchester Regt.
Volunteering in September 1914, he was engaged at Grantham and Salisbury with his unit on important duties till November 1916, when he was drafted to France. He was in action at Beaumont-Hamel, Beaucourt and Arras, where he was wounded. He was invalided home, and after receiving hospital treatment was discharged in November 1917, owing to his injuries, He holds the General Service and Victory Medals.
28, Sudbury Street, Rochdale Road, Manchester. Z11040

ROBINSON, F., Corporal, Manchester Regiment.
Volunteering in November 1915, he was sent to France in December of the following year, and was wounded at the Battle of Ypres in 1917. On recovery he rejoined his unit and fought in various sectors, and was taken prisoner during the Retreat of March 1918. He was held in captivity until the cessation of hostilities, and then was repatriated. He was demobilised in December 1918, and holds the General Service and Victory Medals.
9, Marple Street, Miles Platting, Manchester. Z11042

ROBINSON, G., L/Corporal, 12th Manchester Regt.
Volunteering in November 1914, he crossed to France in the following July, and took part in the Battles of Loos, Albert, and the Somme. He was unfortunately killed in action at

Arras in June 1917, and was entitled to the 1914–15 Star, and the General Service and Victory Medals.
" His name liveth for evermore."
72, Barrack Street, Hulme, Manchester. Z7925

ROBINSON, G., Private, Lancashire Fusiliers.
He volunteered in August 1914, and in the following January embarked for the Western Front. Whilst in this theatre of war he fought at Ypres, the Somme, Vimy Ridge and Cambrai, where he was severely wounded in February 1917. Evacuated to England, he underwent hospital treatment, and in November of the succeeding year was invalided out of the Service. He holds the 1914–15 Star, and the General Service and Victory Medals. 41, Roseberry Street, Gorton, Manchester. Z7924

ROBINSON, G. A., Air Mechanic, R.A.F.
Joining in March 1917, he embarked for the Western Front a month later, and fought in engagements at Arras, Bullecourt, and Messines. In August of the same year he was invalided home in consequence of ill-health, and was for some time under treatment at the 1st General Military Hospital, Aberdeen. After recovery he served on Home duties and was eventually demobilised in March 1919. He holds the General Service and Victory Medals.
8, Milton Street, West Gorton, Manchester. Z7906

ROBINSON, G. B., Driver, R.F.A.
Volunteering in April 1915, he crossed to France in the following March, and took part in operations at St. Eloi, Vimy Ridge, the Ancre, Beaumont-Hamel, Arras and Ypres. Owing to injuries received through a kick from a horse, he was for some time under hospital treatment, first at Le Havre, and later at Brighton, and after his recovery was transferred to the Labour Corps and returned to the Western Front. He did valuable work until his demobilisation, which took place on his arrival in England in March 1919. He holds the General Service and Victory Medals.
55, New York Street, Chorlton-on-Medlock, Manchester. Z17918

ROBINSON, G. F., A.B., Royal Navy.
He joined in June 1917, and after his training saw service at sea in H.M.S. " Powerful " and " Revenge." He took part with his ship in several Naval actions, including those at Heligoland Bight, and the bombardment of the Belgian Coast, and was also present at the surrender of the German Fleet at Scapa Flow. He was demobilised in November 1919, and holds the General Service and Victory Medals.
107, Cross Street, Bradford, Manchester. Z7923

ROBINSON, G. P., Private, South Lancashire Regt.
He volunteered in September 1914, and after his training served at various stations in England prior to being drafted to France in the following year. During his service overseas he was engaged in heavy fighting at Loos, Vimy Ridge, and the Somme, and was wounded at Thiepval in July 1916. On recovery he returned to the line and fought at the Battle of Arras, and was again wounded at Passchendaele in July 1917. Evacuated to England, he received medical treatment at Exeter Hospital, and was afterwards employed on home duties until demobilised in February 1919. He holds the 1914–15 Star, and the General Service and Victory Medals.
1, Corporation Terrace, Chapman Street, Manchester. Z11808

ROBINSON, H., Pioneer, R.E.
Joining in June 1917, he crossed to France in September of that year, and was engaged on important duties in connection with operations at Cambrai, Amiens and Bapaume. He also served throughout the Retreat and Allied Advance of 1918, and was demobilised on his return to England in November 1919. He holds the General Service and Victory Medals.
14, Leigh Street, Ancoats, Manchester. Z9689

ROBINSON, H., Cpl., K.O. (Royal Lancaster Regt.)
He volunteered in August 1914, and was engaged on important home duties until February 1916, when crossing to France, he was in action at Loos, St. Eloi, Albert, the Somme and Arras. In September 1917, he was blown up by shell explosion, and twice wounded, and evacuated to England, underwent protracted hospital treatment. He was invalided out of the Service in March 1918, and holds the General Service and Victory Medals. 6, Clayton Street, Hulme, Manchester. Z7920

ROBINSON, H., Private, 2/5th Manchester Regiment.
Joining in September 1916, he proceeded to France in the following March, and took part in operations at La Bassée, Givenchy, Festubert and Ypres. He was unfortunately killed in action at Nieuport on August 31st, 1917, and was entitled to the General Service and Victory Medals.
" Thinking that remembrance, though unspoken, may reach him where he sleeps."
45, Normanby Street, Moss Side, Manchester. Z7928

ROBINSON, J., Private, King's (Liverpool Regt.)
He volunteered in June 1915, and embarking for the Western Front two months later, fought in the Battles of Loos and Hill 60. He died gloriously on the Field of Battle at St. Eloi on March 8th, 1916, and was entitled to the 1914–15 Star, and the General Service and Victory Medals.
" Whilst we remember, the sacrifice is not in vain."
28, Fernely Street, Hulme, Manchester. Z7926

ROBINSON, J., Private, 19th Lancashire Fusiliers.
He volunteered in September 1914, and was sent to France
in the following February. He took part in numerous engagements, including those at Neuve Chapelle, Hill 60, Ypres,
Loos, Vimy Ridge, the Somme, Arras and Messines. He was
killed in action at the third Battle of Ypres in 1917. He was
entitled to the 1914-15 Star, and the General Service and
Victory Medals.
           " His memory is cherished with pride."
12, Worrall Street, Collyhurst, Manchester.   Z10320B

ROBINSON, J., L/Cpl., K.O. (R. Lancaster Regt.)
He volunteered in October 1914, and two months later proceeded to France and fought in the Battles of Neuve Chapelle
and Ypres, where he was wounded in May 1915. On recovery
he was engaged in other actions and was gassed at Loos in
October of that year. He subsequently took part in operations on the Somme, at Cambrai, Bapaume and in the Retreat
and Advance of 1918. He was demobilised in January 1919,
and holds the 1914-15 Star, and the General Service and
Victory Medals.
8, Blossom Street, Hulme, Manchester.   Z11809

ROBINSON, J., Private, 21st Manchester Regiment.
Volunteering in November 1915, he crossed to France a year
later, and was engaged in the fighting at Arras, Messines,
Ypres and Cambrai. In the course of his service he contracted
a severe illness, and after treatment at a Casualty Clearing
Station, was evacuated to the Central London Military Hospital.
He was discharged as medically unfit in February 1918, and
holds the General Service and Victory Medals.   Z7922B
10, Ernest Street, Morton Street, Longsight, Manchester.

ROBINSON, J., Rifleman, Rifle Brigade.
He joined in April 1918, and after his training was engaged on
duties of an important nature at various stations. He was
not successful in obtaining his transfer overseas before the
close of hostilities, but in April 1919, joined the Army of
Occupation in Germany, where he served for ten months.
He was demobilised in March 1920.   TZ7921
218, Upper Brook Street, Chorlton-on-Medlock, Manchester.

ROBINSON, J., Private, 8th Manchester Regiment.
A serving soldier, he was drafted to Egypt in September 1914,
and was engaged on important duties on that Front until
the following March, when he embarked for the Dardanelles,
and took part in the first Landing at Gallipoli and the Battle
of Cape Helles. He was unfortunately killed during the
third Battle of Krithia and Achi Baba, in March 1915, and
was entitled to the 1914-15 Star, and the General Service
and Victory Medals.
           " A costly sacrifice upon the altar of freedom."
7, Hughes Street, Ardwick, Manchester.   Z7917

ROBINSON, J., Private, 17th Lancashire Fusiliers.
Joining in June 1917, he embarked for France in October
of the succeeding year, and took part in the concluding operations of the Allied Advance, which terminated hostilities
victoriously in November 1918. He was afterwards engaged
on guard and other important duties at prisoner of war camps
at Calais, Boulogne and Etaples, and did valuable work until
November 1919, when he returned to England and was demobilised. He holds the General Service and Victory Medals.
3, Pitt, Street, Ancoats, Manchester.   Z7911

ROBINSON, J., Staff-Sergeant, R.G.A.
Volunteering shortly after the outbreak of war, he proceeded
to France in September 1914, and was in action at La Bassée,
Ypres, Neuve Chapelle, Hill 60, Albert and Vimy Ridge,
where he was badly gassed in May 1916. Evacuated to
England he underwent three months' hospital treatment,
at the conclusion of which he returned to the Western Front,
and took part in the final operations of the Somme Offensive.
Later he fought at Arras, Passchendaele, Cambrai and throughout the Retreat and Allied Advance of 1918. He was demobilised in January of the succeeding year, and holds the
1914 Star, and the General Service and Victory Medals.
21, Pomfret Street, West Gorton, Manchester.   Z7909

ROBINSON, J., 1st Air Mechanic, R.A.F.
Joining in November 1916, he embarked for Egypt in the
following March, and was engaged on duties of an important
nature with his Squadron at Cairo and Alexandria. He did
valuable work until his demobilisation, which took place on
his return to England in March 1919. He holds the General
Service and Victory Medals.
33, Carver Street, Chorlton-on-Medlock, Manchester.   Z7908

ROBINSON, J., L/Corporal, 23rd Manchester Regt.
Volunteering in November 1914, he was engaged on important
home duties until January 1916, when crossing to France he
fought in engagements at Ploegsteert Wood, Neuve Chapelle
and Festubert. Whilst in the trenches he contracted an
illness and in July of the same year was invalided home to
hospital. Three months later he was discharged as medically
unfit for further service, and holds the General Service and
Victory Medals.
10, Johnson's Buildings, Ancoats, Manchester.   Z7907

ROBINSON, J. W., Private, 7th K. (Liverpool Regt.
He volunteered in October 1915, and in February of the following year was drafted to the Western Front. He was in action
on the Somme, at Arras, Ypres and Cambrai. He was unfortunately killed in action in the Ypres salient on August
29th, 1918, and was buried in St. Martin's British Cemetery
near Arras. He was entitled to the General Service and
Victory Medals.
           " A costly sacrifice upon the altar of freedom."
61, Beaumont Street, Beswick, Manchester.   Z11043

ROBINSON, M., Private, Manchester Regiment.
Joining in June 1916, he embarked for France in December
of that year, and was engaged in heavy fighting at Arras and
Zonnebeke. He also took part in many other important
battles, and remained on the Western Front until the conclusion of hostilities. He was demobilised in September
1919, and holds the General Service and Victory Medals.
10, Thistle Street, Gayler Street, Miles Platting, Manchester.
           TZ9343

ROBINSON, R. W., Pte., 2/1st E. Lancashire Regt.
He volunteered in 1915, and shortly afterwards was drafted
to the Western Front, where in May of the same year he was
severely wounded at the second Battle of Ypres. Evacuated
to England, he underwent three months' hospital treatment,
and in 1916 returned to France. On rejoining his unit he
again went into action, but was so badly gassed as to necessitate his return to England, and after protracted hospital
treatment was discharged as medically unfit in December 1919.
He holds the 1914-15 Star, and the General Service and Victory
Medals.   45, Naylor St., Hulme, Manchester.   Z7919

ROBINSON, S. M., L/Corporal, 1st Manchester Regt.
Volunteering in January 1915, he proceeded to France five
months later, and took part in the Battle of Loos. Transferred
to Mesopotamia in January 1916, he was in action at Amara,
Kut-el-Amara and Um-el-Hannah, and was severely wounded
at Es Sinn in March 1916, in the second attempt to relieve
Kut. On recovery he rejoined his unit in the Field, and was
in action until the close of hostilities. He was demobilised
on his return to England in April 1919, and holds the 1914-15
Star, and the General Service and Victory Medals.
42, Milton Street, West Gorton, Manchester.   Z7905

ROBINSON, T., Private, 15th Royal Scots.
He volunteered shortly after the outbreak of war, and in
December 1915 embarked for the Western Front. In the
course of his service he fought in the Battles of Loos, St.
Eloi, Albert and the Somme, where he was so severely wounded
as to necessitate his return to England for hospital treatment.
On recovery he was re-drafted to France, and after taking
part in heavy fighting at Arras, was taken prisoner at the third
Battle of Ypres in July 1917. Repatriated after the close of
hostilities he was demobilised in January 1919, and holds the
1914-15 Star, and the General Service and Victory Medals.
10, Ernest Street, Morton Street, Longsight, Manchester.
           Z7922A

ROBINSON, T., Private, Labour Corps.
He joined in March 1917, and in September of the same year
was sent to France. During his service in this theatre of war
he was engaged on important duties principally in the Ypres
salient, and rendered valuable services. He was demobilised
in February 1919, and holds the General Service and Victory
Medlas.
37, Albion Street, Miles Platting, Manchester.   Z11038

ROBINSON, T. A., Gunner, R.G.A.
Volunteering in June 1915, he embarked for Egypt in the
following January, and fought in several engagements, notably
the Battle of Romani. Later he served in the Palestine
campaign, during which he took part in the Battles of Gaza,
and the capture of Jerusalem and Jericho. Whilst overseas,
he contracted malaria, and in consequence was for some
weeks in hospital at Jerusalem. He was demobilised in
March 1919, and holds the General Service and Victory Medals.
5, New Lorne Street, Moss Side, Manchester.   Z7927

ROBINSON, W., Private, R.A.S.C. (M.T.)
Volunteering in January 1915, he proceeded to France a month
later, and was engaged as chauffeur to his Colonel and served
in the Ypres, Somme, Arras, La Bassée and Bapaume sectors.
He did valuable work until his demobilisation, which took
place on his return to England in January 1919, and holds
the 1914-15 Star, and the General Service and Victory Medals.
70, Lewis Street, Miles Platting, Manchester.   Z9690

ROBINSON, W., Private, 2nd Manchester Regiment.
He volunteered in January 1915, and after his training served
on the Western Front until the close of hostilities. During
this period he took part in the Battles of Albert, the Somme,
Arras, Messines, Passchendaele and Cambrai, and in the
Retreat and Allied Advance of 1918, at the conclusion of
which he proceeded with the Army of Occupation to Germany.
He was demobilised in June 1919, and holds the 1914-15 Star,
and the General Service and Victory Medals.
8, St. Bees Street, Moss Side, Manchester.   Z7904

ROBINSON, W. A., Private, 12th Manchester Regt.
Volunteering in January 1915, he proceeded to France in the following June, and was in action at Loos, where he was wounded. On returning to the line he was again wounded in the Somme Offensive, but after treatment rejoined his unit, and fought at Albert, Arras and Bullecourt, where he was wounded a third time. He received a fourth wound during the second Battle of the Somme in March 1918, which resulted in his being invalided home for hospital treatment. He was discharged as medically unfit five months later, and holds the 1914-15 Star, and the General Service and Victory Medals.
23, Baird Street, Chapel Street, Ancoats, Manchester. Z7912

ROBINSON, W. E., Pte., 9th East Lancashire Regt.
He volunteered in September 1914, and crossing to France a year later, served on that Front until October 1915, when he embarked for Salonika. In the next month he took part in the Serbian Retreat, and later fought on the Doiran front, where he was severely wounded. Shortly after rejoining his unit, he contracted malaria and in consequence was under hospital treatment for a further period. He was demobilised on his return to England in April 1919, and holds the 1914-15 Star, and the General Service and Victory Medals.
132, Higher Cambridge Street, Chorlton-on-Medlock, Manchester. Z7914

ROBINSON, W. G., L/Corporal, Tank Corps.
He joined in June 1918, and crossing to France in the following August took part in many important battles during the Allied Advance of that year. He did valuable work until his demobilisation, which took place on his return to England in February 1919. He holds the General Service and Victory Medals.
29, Bennett Street, Openshaw, Manchester. Z7929

ROBINSON, W. H., Sergt., 9th Lancashire Fusiliers.
Volunteering in May 1915, he was drafted to the Dardanelles, and took part in the Landing at Suvla Bay, and in many other important engagements. He was later transferred to Egypt, and in March 1916 proceeded to the Western Front, where he was in action at Loos, St. Eloi and Albert. He was reported missing on the Somme in September 1916, and later was presumed to have been killed in action on that date. He was entitled to the 1914-15 Star, and the General Service and Victory Medals.
"He died the noblest death a man may die, Fighting for God, and right, and liberty."
22, Drinkwater Street, Harpurhey, Manchester. Z11446

ROBINSON, W. Private, 23rd Manchester Regt
Volunteering in January 1915, he was drafted to France in the following April, and was in action at Neuve Chapelle, Hill 60, Ypres, Festubert, Loos, Albert and the Somme, where he was wounded in August 1916. He was invalided home, and after receiving hospital treatment returned to France and was engaged as Despatch Rider. Owing to ill-health he was again invalided home, and was discharged in December 1917, as unfit for further service, holding the 1914-15 Star, and the General Service and Victory Medals.
44, Sarah Ann Street, Beswick, Manchester. Z11039

ROCCA, F., Gunner, R.G.A.
Joining in May 1917, he completed his training and served with his unit at various stations engaged on important duties. He did good work, but was not successful in securing his transfer overseas, owing to medical unfitness, and was demobilised in December 1918.
11, Platt Street, Moss Side, Manchester. Z7930

ROCHE, J. A., Driver, R.A.S.C. (M.T.)
He joined in December 1916, and was drafted in the following August to the Western Front, where he was attached to the R.G.A., and engaged on important duties as a Caterpillar tractor driver during operations at Cambrai, Arras (II), Bapaume, Amiens and Passchendaele. He was wounded in the second Battle of the Somme in March 1918, and on recovery was sent with the Army of Occupation into Germany and served there until his return home for demobilisation in November 1919. He holds the General Service and Victory Medals. 16, New Lorne Street, Moss Side, Manchester. Z7931

ROCHFORD, W., Rifleman, K.R.R.C.
Volunteering in November 1914, he was drafted to France in the following August, and whilst overseas took part in the fighting in the Ypres sector, and was wounded in March 1916. He was invalided home, but later rejoined his unit on the Western Front in January 1917, and was again wounded in action at Messines in June of the same year, and sent to hospital in England. After his recovery he returned to France and served from August to November 1918 in the Advance. He was demobilised in March of the following year, and holds the 1914-15 Star, and the General Service and Victory Medals.
46, Burn Street, Bradford, Manchester. Z11044

RODGERS, A. E., Private, 4th Manchester Regt.
He volunteered in January 1915, and after his training served on the Western Front until the close of hostilities. During this period he fought in the Battles of Loos, La Bassée, Givenchy, Festubert, Neuve Chapelle, the Somme, Ypres, Cambrai and in the Retreat and Allied Advance of 1918, at the conclusion

of which he proceeded with the Army of Occupation into Germany. He was demobilised in March 1919, and holds the General Service and Victory Medals.
4, Naylor Street, Newton, Manchester. Z9344

RODGERS, F., Private, 22nd Manchester Regiment.
He volunteered in November 1914, and after his training was engaged on important duties with his unit at various stations. He was not successful in obtaining his transfer to a theatre of war, in consequence of ill-health, and in July 1915, was invalided out of the Service. Afterwards, however, he obtained work of National importance in connection with the building of the Hollinwood Aerodrome, and rendered valuable services until after the close of hostilities.
25, Whatmough Street, Newton, Manchester. Z9691

RODGERS, J., Rifleman, Rifle Brigade.
He volunteered in October 1914, and after his training served at various stations on important duties with his unit. Owing to ill-health, he was unable to secure his transfer to a theatre of war, and in May 1915, was discharged as medically unfit for further military service.
187, Victoria Square, Ancoats, Manchester. Z9345

RODGERS, J., Private, 7th Manchester Regiment.
Volunteering in August 1915, he proceeded to the Western Front on the completion of his training in November of the same year. Whilst in France he took part in the heavy fighting at Loos and in the Ypres salient, and died gloriously on the Field of Battle on the Somme in July 1916. He was entitled to the 1914-15 Star, and the General Service and Victory Medals.
"Courage, bright hopes, and a myriad dreams, splendidly given."
33, Taunton Street, Ancoats, Manchester. Z11046

RODGERS, J., Seaman Gunner, R.N.
A Reservist, mobilised when war broke out and posted to H.M.S. "Undaunted," which ship sank three enemy destroyers off the Dutch Coast in October 1914, and also took part in the Battle of Jutland, and was present at the sinking of the German raider "Blücher." He was afterwards transferred to H.M.S. "Coventry," which vessel was engaged on patrol and other important duties in the North Sea until the end of hostilities. He was demobilised in January 1919, and holds the 1914-15 Star, and the General Service and Victory Medals.
8, Wilson Street, Bradford, Manchester. Z7932

RODGERS, J., Private, East Lancashire Regiment.
Volunteering in January 1915, he embarked for Egypt four months later, and proceeded thence to the Dardanelles. After taking part in many important engagements on the Gallipoli Peninsula, he was transferred to the Western Front, and served with the Labour Corps on the Somme and at Cambrai. He was demobilised on his return to England in February 1919, and holds the 1914-15 Star, and the General Service and Victory Medals.
49, Fielden Street, Oldham Road, Manchester. Z9346A

RODGERS, J. T., Private, 11th Manchester Fusiliers.
Volunteering in September 1914, he embarked for France a year later, and was in action at Loos, Neuve Chapelle and Ypres. He gave his life for King and Country at Vimy Ridge on April 24th, 1916, and lies buried in a military cemetery at St. Eloi. He was entitled to the 1914-15 Star, and the General Service and Victory Medals.
"A costly sacrifice upon the altar of freedom."
49, Fielden Street, Oldham Road, Manchester. Z9346B

RODGERS, R., Pte., 23rd Manchester Regiment.
He joined in March 1916, and after his training was completed proceeded to France in July of the same year. He gave his life for the freedom of England in the Battle of the Somme on August 25th, 1916, and was entitled to the General Service and Victory Medals.
"His life for his Country, his soul to God."
78, Heyrod Street, Ancoats, Manchester. Z11045

ROE, E., Private, 7th Manchester Regiment.
Joining in 1916, he proceeded to the Western Front on the completion of his training in the following year. After taking part in several important engagements he was unhappily killed during the severe fighting at Albert in September 1918. He was entitled to the General Service and Victory Medals.
"Whilst we remember, the sacrifice is not in vain."
470, Claremont Road, Rusholme, Manchester. Z11047C

ROE, H., Driver, R.A.S.C. (M.T.)
Volunteering in October 1914, he was sent in the following December to the Western Front, and engaged on important transport duties during operations at the Somme, Ypres, Arras, La Bassée, Givenchy, Cambrai and Hill 60. In February 1915 he was recommended for the Distinguished Conduct Medal for conspicuous gallantry and devotion to duty whilst driving under heavy shell-fire during the Battle of Neuve Chapelle. Shortly afterwards he was invalided home suffering from shell-shock, and received treatment in the Royal Herbert Hospital, London. He was ultimately discharged as medically unfit for further military service in June 1916, and holds the 1914-15 Star, and the General Service and Victory Medals.
18, Birch Street, Hulme, Manchester. Z7933

ROE, G., Private, 16th Manchester Regiment.
He volunteered in 1914, and after the completion of his training was drafted overseas in the following year. During his service in France he fought in many important engagements in various sectors, and gave his life for King and Country at Fresnoy, on the Arras Front, in April 1918. He was entitled to the 1914-15 Star, and the General Service and Victory Medals.
"The path of duty was the way to glory."
470, Claremont Road, Rusholme, Manchester.   Z11047B

ROE, J., Private, 2nd Manchester Regiment.
Mobilised at the outbreak of war he was sent to France in September 1911, and was wounded in an engagement in the same month. After his recovery he fought at Armentières and Hill 60, and was again wounded in the Battle of the Somme, in November 1916. Later he rejoined his unit, and fought at Arras, Cambrai, Bullecourt and the Marne, and in various subsequent operations in the Retreat and Advance of 1918. He holds the 1914 Star, and the General Service and Victory Medals, and in January 1919 was demobilised.
4, Chesshyre Street, Ancoats, Manchester.   Z11048A

ROE, W., Private, King's (Liverpool Regiment).
He joined in 1916, and later in the same year was drafted to France. Whilst overseas he took part in the Battle of the Somme, where he was wounded, and was invalided home. Returning to the Western Front in the following year, he fought in the engagements at Arras and Ypres, and was again wounded and sent to England. After his recovery he proceeded to Egypt and served in this country until the cessation of hostilities. He was demobilised on returning home in 1919, and holds the General Service and Victory Medals.
470, Cleamont Road, Rusholme, Manchester.   Z11047

ROGALSKI, W., Corporal, 31st Middlesex Regiment, and Labour Corps.
He joined in October 1916, and served with his unit on Home Service duties until August 1918, when he was sent to France. In this theatre of war he was employed in making and repairing roads behind the lines in the Somme, Ypres, Cambrai and La Bassée sectors until the cessation of hostilities. After the Armistice he was engaged in a similar capacity until he returned home for his demobilisation in December 1919. He holds the General Service and Victory Medals.
29, Cowesby Street, Moss Side, Manchester.   Z7934

ROGERS, A., Gunner, R.G.A.
He joined in June 1916, and after serving at Gosport and in London, was discharged in the following November as physically unfit for military service. He subsequently died at home in January 1918, from an illness attributed to his Army service.
"His memory is cherished with pride."
2, Bell Street, Lower Openshaw, Manchester.   Z7938

ROGERS, G., Driver, R.F.A.
Volunteering in July 1915, he completed his training and sailed for Mesopotamia two months later. In this theatre of war he took part in operations in the attempted Relief of Kut, and in several other engagements until invalided to hospital in India, owing to illness. After receiving protracted medical treatment he returned to England and was discharged in May 1919. He holds the 1914-15 Star, and the General Service and Victory Medals.
20, Seymour Street, Hulme, Manchester.   Z7942

ROGERS, J., Private, 20th Lancashire Fusiliers.
Volunteering in April 1915, he sailed for the Dardanelles in the following September, and served there for a period of two months when he was invalided home owing to ill-health. On recovery he was drafted in July 1916 to the Western Front and fought in the Somme Offensive and at Guillemont in September of that year. He was wounded in the Battle of St. Quentin in April 1917, and after receiving medical treatment returned to England in June 1918. He was discharged as medically unfit for further military service two months later and holds the 1914-15 Star, and the General Service and Victory Medals.
56, Williams Street, Hulme, Manchester.   Z7941

ROGERS, J. A., Private, 1/8th Manchester Regt.
He joined in March 1917, and proceeding in the following June to the Western Front, was in action at the Battles of Ypres (III), and Cambrai where he was wounded and taken prisoner in November 1917. Sent to Germany he remained in captivity until the cessation of hostilities when he was repatriated and admitted into Grangethorpe Military Hospital suffering from the effects of his wounds. He was discharged in September 1919 as medically unfit for further military service, and holds the General Service and Victory Medals.
30, Hewitt Street, Openshaw, Manchester.   Z7940

ROGERS, J. H., Private, 21st Welch Regiment, and 16th King's (Liverpool Regiment).
Joining in June 1916, he was sent in the following March to the Western Front, and took part in several engagements,

including the Battles of Ypres (III), Passchendaele, Messines, Vimy Ridge, Hill 60, Arras, Albert, and the Somme. In January 1918, he was invalided home owing to ill-health, and after receiving medical treatment in Manchester War Hospital, was eventually discharged on account of service in January of the succeeding year. He holds the General Service and Victory Medals.
8, Spurgeon Street, West Gorton, Manchester.   Z7936

ROGERS, J. W., Private, 10th Cheshire Regiment.
He volunteered in September 1914, and served with his unit on Home duties until March 1916, when he was drafted to the Western Front. In this theatre of war he was in action in operations at Loos, Albert and Ypres, where he was severely wounded in June of that year. Evacuated to England for hospital treatment he was later discharged from the Service on account of his injuries, but unhappily died shortly afterwards in March 1917. He was entitled to the General Service and Victory Medals.
"The path of duty was the way to glory."
92, Gibson Street, Ardwick, Manchester.   Z1144A

ROGERS, J. W., Private, 21st (Empress of India's) Lancers.
He was mobilised when war broke out, and shortly afterwards embarking with the First Expeditionary Force for France took part in the Retreat from Mons. He also fought in the Battles of the Marne, and many other engagements until returning to England in October 1915, when he was discharged from the Service as a time-expired man. He holds the Mons Star, and the General Service and Victory Medals.
7, Jane Street, West Gorton, Manchester.   Z7937

ROGERS, R., Gunner, R.F.A.
He volunteered in September 1914, and crossing to France early in the succeeding year, took part in operations at Ypres, Hill 60, Festubert, Neuve Chapelle, St. Eloi, Cambrai, Albert, Arras, Bullecourt, Méricourt and Bourlon Wood. Unfortunately he was killed in action near Cambrai in 1917, and was entitled to the 1914-15 Star, and the General Service and Victory Medals.
"His life for his Country, his soul to God."
19, Elizabeth Street, Ancoats, Manchester.   TZ9692

ROGERS, W., Private, 11th Lancashire Fusiliers.
Joining in November 1917, he completed his training, and crossed to France in the following April. In this theatre of war he saw heavy fighting in different parts of the line during the German Offensive. He was unhappily killed in action on May 28th, 1918, and was entitled to the General Service and Victory Medals.
"He joined the great white company of valiant souls."
91, Silver Street, Hulme, Manchester.   Z7935

ROGERS, W. J., Private, 7th E. Lancashire Regt.
He volunteered in September 1914, and landing in France three months later fought in several engagements including those at Neuve Chapelle, Hill 60, Ypres (II) and Festubert. He was invalided home in July 1915, owing to illness, and after receiving medical treatment was discharged in February of the succeeding year as medically unfit for further service. He holds the 1914-15 Star, and the General Service and Victory Medals.
91, Silver Street, Hulme, Manchester.   Z7935B

ROGERS, W. J., Driver, R.F.A.
He joined in January 1916, and in the following August was drafted to Egypt. During his service overseas he took part in the Battles at Magdhaba and Rafa, and in the Advance to Palestine, where he fought in the second Battle of Gaza, and was present at the entry into Jerusalem and the Capture of Jericho. After the Armistice he was engaged on important garrison duties at Alexandria until February 1920, when he returned to England. He was demobilised in the ensuing month, and holds the General Service and Victory Medals.
14, Phelan Street, Collyhurst, Manchester.   Z11049

ROGERS, W. J., Sergeant, 4th Cheshire Regiment.
Volunteering in March 1915, he was drafted in the following October to the Western Front, where he took part in several engagements, notably those of Loos, Albert, and the Somme. He was unhappily killed in action in July 1916, and was entitled to the 1914-15 Star, and the General Service and Victory Medals.
"Whilst we remember, the sacrifice is not in vain."
22, Milton Street, West Gorton, Manchester.   Z7939

ROGERSON, H., Private, 8th East Surrey Regt.
He joined in February 1916, and in the following November proceeded to France. During his service on the Western Front he fought in the Battle of the Somme, and was wounded at St. Leger in March 1917, at Cambrai in the following December, and at Trones Wood during the Advance in September 1918. He was invalided home, and later in the same month was discharged as medically unfit for further service. He holds the General Service and Victory Medals.
18, Middlewood Street, Harpurhey, Manchester.   Z11574

ROGERSON, T., Pte., 2nd K.O. Scottish Borderers.
He was mobilised in August 1914, and was almost immediately drafted to France, where he took part in the Retreat from Mons. He also served at Loos, Ypres, Nieuport and the Somme, and was severely wounded and invalided home. After his recovery he rejoined his unit and was in action at Arras and in various later operations until the cessation of hostilities. He holds the Mons Star, and the General Service and Victory Medals, and was demobilised in January 1919.
4, Sutton Street, Ancoats, Manchester.   Z11050

ROLES, C., Private, 20th Manchester Regiment.
He volunteered in November 1914, and after completing his training served with his unit until owing to physical unfitness for general service, he was sent to Newcastle in August 1915. Employed as a plumber in shipyards he was engaged on work of National importance, and for over three years carried out his duties in an efficient and capable manner. He was demobilised in November 1918.
31, Birch Street, Moss Side, Manchester.   TZ7943

ROLLEY, J., Driver, R.F.A.
Volunteering in May 1915, he proceeded to Egypt in the following January, and served on the Suez Canal for a time. Sent to France in March 1917 he was in action at La Bassée and Nieuport, and served at Dunkirk, but was killed in action during the third Battle of Ypres in October 1917. He was entitled to the General Service and Victory Medals.
" Great deeds cannot die."
36, Lind Street, Ancoats, Manchester.   Z11052

ROLLEY, T., Private, Labour Corps.
He joined in September 1917, on attaining military age, and after his training embarked for France in November of the following year. Whilst overseas he was engaged on important duties repairing roads at Boulogne, until April 1919, when he returned home and was demobilised.
36, Lind Street, Ancoats, Manchester.   Z11051

ROLLINSON, J. J., Pte., 4th South Lancashire Regt.
Volunteering in August 1914, he was drafted to France a year later, and took part in several engagements on the Somme and in the Ypres salient until invalided home owing to illness in August 1917. Returning to the Western Front in the following December he was transferred to the Machine Gun Corps, with which unit he was in action during the Retreat and Advance of 1918. After the Armistice he was sent with the Army of Occupation, and served in Germany until sent home for demobilisation in March 1919. He holds the 1914-15 Star, and the General Service and Victory Medals.
1, Auburn Place, Rusholme, Manchester.   Z7944

RONAN, W., Pte., 4th K.O. (Royal Lancaster Regt.)
Mobilised in August 1914, he was immediately drafted to the Western Front, where he served until the termination of hostilities. He took part in the Battle of Mons and subsequent Retreat, and later participated in the Battles of La Bassée, Ypres and the Somme, and in heavy fighting at Nieuport, Givenchy, Messines Ridge and Vimy Ridge. He was demobilised in January 1919, and holds the Mons Star, and the General Service and Victory Medals.
21, Sparkle Street, Ancoats Manchester.   TZ9347

ROONEY, J., Private, 3rd Manchester Regiment.
He was mobilised in August 1914, and in the following December was drafted to France, and was in action at Neuve Chapelle and Loos. In January 1916 he sailed to Mesopotamia, and after serving in various operations in this theatre of war was sent home and discharged as time expired in May 1916. He holds the 1914-15 Star, and the General Service and Victory Medals.
38, Lind Street, Ancoats, Manchester.   Z11054

ROONEY, W., Private, Lancashire Fusiliers.
He joined in April 1916, and in the following October proceeded to the Western Front. Whilst in France he took part in the heavy fighting on the Somme, and at Beaumont-Hamel, Beaucourt, Bullecourt and Arras, and was severely wounded at Givenchy in May 1917. He was invalided home and subsequently was discharged as medically unfit for further duty in December of the same year. He holds the General Service and Victory Medals.
1, Howell Street, Collyhurst, Manchester.   Z11053

ROONEY, M., L/Sergt., 7th K.O. (R. Lancaster Regt.)
A Reservist, he was mobilised on the outbreak of hostilities, and proceeding to France in September 1914, served there until the end of the war. He fought in the final stages of the Retreat from Mons, in the Battles of Neuve Chapelle, Ypres, Festubert, Ploegsteert Wood, the Somme, Arras, and was wounded at Messines in June 1917. On recovery he was engaged in heavy fighting at Cambrai, and during the Retreat and Advance of 1918. Returning to England for demobilisation in February 1919, he holds the Mons Star, and the General Service and Victory Medals.
126, Tame Street, Ancoats, Manchester.   Z7945

ROPER, E., Gunner, R.G.A.
He joined in May 1916, and after serving on the Humber River Defences, was engaged on important duties as an Instructor in signalling at various stations. He also served with the heavy batteries at several depôts. Later he was invalided to hospital owing to illness, and subsequently discharged as medically unfit for further service in May 1917.
19, Lancashire Street, Newton Heath, Manchester.   Z11055B

ROPER, E. A., Stoker, Mercantile Marine.
He joined in April 1918, and was posted to H.M.S. "Moldavia," which was torpedoed in the English Channel in June of the same year. Fortunately he was saved and was transferred to H.M.S."Heroic"and was engaged in conveying troops to Malta and Greece. Later after serving for two months in barracks at Malta he joined H.M.S. " Biarritz " and was employed in mine-laying between Mudros and the Dardanelles. He was demobilised in April 1919 from H.M.S. " Eaglet," and holds the General Service, Mercantile Marine War and Victory Medals.
19, Lancashire Street, Newton Heath, Manchester.   Z11055A

ROPER, L., Private, Royal Scots.
Volunteering in April 1915, he proceeded to Egypt in the following year, and after serving on important duties in that country was drafted to the Western Front. Whilst in France he fought at Arras, Vimy Ridge, and the Somme, and in various later operations in the Retreat and Advance of 1918. He returned to England and was demobilised in June 1919, and holds the General Service and Victory Medals.
18, Tilstine Place, Rochdale Road, Manchester.   Z11056

ROSCOE, J. W., Driver, R.E.
He volunteered in September 1914, and was engaged on Coastal Defence duties until February 1917, when he was sent to France. There he saw much service in the forward areas whilst heavy fighting was in progress, and in May 1919 was sent into Germany to the Army of Occupation. He returned home in January 1920, and demobilised a month later, holds the General Service and Victory Medals.
99, Dale Street, Hulme, Manchester.   Z7946

ROSE, J., Private, 17th Manchester Regiment.
Volunteering in September 1914, he embarked for the Western Front in the following year and was in action in several engagements until wounded at Montauban on July 1st, 1916, during the Somme Offensive. Invalided home on account of his injuries he was sent to France after treatment in February 1917, and later owing to medical unfitness for active service returned to England, where he was engaged on Home Defence duties until discharged in March 1919. He holds the 1914-15 Star, and the General Service and Victory Medals.
19, Kay Street, Ardwick Green, Manchester.   TX7947

ROSE, S., Private, 1st Manchester Regiment.
He joined in February 1916, and after a period of training was drafted to Mesopotamia. In this theatre of war he took part with his unit in several severe engagements, and did excellent work until he fell fighting at Kut on December 18th, 1916. He was entitled to the General Service and Victory Medals.
" Whilst we remember, the sacrifice is not in vain."
10, Horner Street, Chorlton-on-Medlock, Manchester.   TZ11700B

ROSEBY, W. F., Driver, R.A.S.C.
He volunteered in February 1915, and a month later proceeded to France, where he served on important transport duties in the forward areas. He did good work during the Battles of Neuve Chapelle, St. Eloi, Hill 60, Ypres, Festubert, Albert, Vimy Ridge, the Somme, Arras, Messines, and was gassed in November 1917, at Ypres. Admitted to a Base hospital in February 1918, he was later evacuated to the Lister Road War Hospital, Higher Broughton, and after treatment served with his unit at home. He was demobilised in February 1919, and holds the 1914-15 Star, and the General Service and Victory Medals.
50, Blackthorn Street, Ardwick, Manchester.   Z7948

ROSEWELL, A., Sergt., 1/7th Manchester Regt.
He volunteered in March 1915, and two months later proceeded to Gallipoli, where he participated in heavy fighting at Suvla Bay. After the Evacuation he was transferred to France, and was in action on the Somme and at Albert, Arras, Vimy Ridge, Messines, Cambrai and Bapaume. He rendered valuable services overseas, and was unhappily killed in action near Bapaume on August 21st, 1918. He was entitled to the 1914-15 Star, and the General Service and Victory Medals.
" His life for his Country."
112, Bickley Street, Moss Side, Manchester.   Z11810

ROSS, J., Private, 7th Border Regiment.
He volunteered in August 1914, and in the next month was sent to France. In the course of service in this theatre of war he fought in the Battles of Ypres, Neuve Chapelle, Hill 60, Loos, the Somme, the Ancre, Passchendaele, and was wounded at Arras in September 1917. His injuries necessitated the amputation of his left arm, and he was sent to Roehampton Military Hospital, where he was under treatment for several months. Discharged as physically unfit for further military service in September 1918, he holds the 1914 Star and the General Service and Victory Medals.
14, Marple Street, Openshaw, Manchester.   TZ7949B

ROSS, D., Private, 19th Manchester Regiment.
Volunteering in August 1915, he was drafted to the Western Front in the following February and was in action in several engagements until severely wounded near Arras. Sent home in consequence of his injuries he was treated in the 1st London General Hospital, and was ultimately discharged as medically unfit for further service in October 1916. He holds the General Service and Victory Medals.
19, Cawdor Street, Hulme, Manchester.   Z7950

ROSS, T., Pte., Duke of Cornwall's Light Infantry.
He joined in April 1917, and embarking for the Western Front two months later was in action in the Battles of Ypres (III), Lens, Cambrai, and the Somme. During the German Offensive he was engaged in heavy fighting, in the course of which he was wounded near Bapaume in April 1918, and sent to Grosvenor Square War Hospital, London, for treatment and later to the Isle of Wight. After convalescence, he was demobilised in February 1919, and holds the General Service and Victory Medals.
19, Cawdor Street, Hulme, Manchester.   Z7951

ROSS, T., Private, Cheshire Regiment.
Joining in May 1917, he was sent to Ireland and Salisbury to complete his training, and afterwards was engaged on various important duties with his unit. He was not successful in obtaining his transfer overseas before hostilities ceased, but in November 1918, proceeded with the Army of Occupation into Germany. After his return home he was demobilised in February 1920.
1, Magdala Street, Newton, Manchester.   Z11057

ROSS, T., Private, Manchester Regiment.
He volunteered in January 1915, and in April of the following year after much good service he was discharged as medically unfit. In August 1917 he re-enlisted in the Royal Engineers, and was engaged with them at Grantham, Bristol and other stations on important duties until demobilised in March 1919.
62, Able Street, Collyhurst, Manchester.   Z11058

ROSSI, F., Cpl., 18th Infantry Regt. (Italian Army).
He volunteered in January 1915, and in the following May was drafted to the Italian front. He saw much active service, and was severely wounded in the Trentino on May 31st, 1916. He was awarded the Italian Military Medal and Iron Cross for conspicuous gallantry in the Field, and also holds the Victory Medal. In September 1918 he was discharged as medically unfit for further duty.
69, Blossom Street, Ancoats, Manchester.   Z11447A

ROSSI, J., Private, 4th Yorkshire Regiment.
He volunteered in December 1915, and in November of the following year embarked for France, where he took part in the fierce fighting in the Arras sector. He was afterwards engaged in R.T.O.'s. Offices at Boulogne, on important duties, remaining there until demobilised in March 1919. He holds the General Service and Victory Medals.
30, Gunson Street, Miles Platting, Manchester.   Z11059

ROSSI, J., Private, South Wales Borderers.
Joining in February 1918, he completed his course of training at Prees Heath, and in September crossed to France. He was unhappily killed in action during the fierce fighting at Cambrai a few weeks later. He was entitled to the General Service and Victory Medals.
"His life for his Country, his soul to God."
69, Blossom Street, Ancoats, Manchester.   Z11447B

ROSTRON, H., Gunner, R.F.A.
Joining in 1916, he sailed for Mesopotamia in the same year, and in the course of service there, took part in several operations including those for the attempted relief of Kut. He was later sent to Egypt, and after a period of service at Cairo was stationed with his Battery in Syria. Returning home on the conclusion of hostilities, he was demobilised in 1919, and holds the General Service and Victory Medals.
14, Exmouth Street, Ancoats, Manchester.   Z7952

ROTHWELL, A., Drummer, 17th Manchester Regt.
Volunteering in September 1914, he proceeded to France in October of the following year and served with his unit in the Battles of Loos, Vimy Ridge, and the Somme. He gave his life for the freedom of England at Trones Wood in July 1916, and was entitled to the 1914-15 Star, and the General Service and Victory Medals.
"Great deeds cannot die."
59, Gibson Street, Ardwick, Manchester.   Z7954A

ROTHWELL, F., Corporal, M.G.C.
Mobilised in August 1914, he was at once drafted to France and took part in the Battle of Mons, and the subsequent Retreat, also in the Battles of the Marne, La Bassée, Ypres I, Neuve Chapelle, St. Eloi, and Ypres (II), being wounded on two occasions. He later proceeded to Gallipoli, where he was again wounded in action, and after a short spell of service in Egypt, returned to France, and was wounded for the fourth time. Invalided home in December 1916, he was eventually discharged in May 1917, as unfit for further service, and holds the Mons Star, and the General Service and Victory Medals.
9, Allen Street, Hulme, Manchester.   Z11811

ROTHWELL, F., Private, Tank Corps.
He joined in March 1918, and on the conclusion of his training was engaged on important duties with his unit in the South of England. He rendered valuable services, but was unable to procure his transfer overseas before the termination of the war, and was demobilised in October 1919.
39, Addison Street, Chorlton-on-Medlock, Manchester. Z7953B

ROTHWELL, W., Cpl., Loyal N. Lancashire Regt.
He volunteered in August 1914, and was drafted overseas in the following January. Serving in several sectors of the Western Front he fought at Neuve Chapelle, St. Eloi, Hill 60, Loos, and was wounded in the Battle of the Somme in October 1916. Admitted to the Canadian Hospital at Rouen he was later sent to the Derby Hospital, Warrington, for further treatment, and returning to France on recovery was in action at Arras and Ypres, and was again wounded in October 1917. After convalescence he took part in the Battles of Cambrai and the Somme, and in several others during the Retreat and Advance of 1918. He was demobilised in March 1919, and holds the 1914-15 Star, and the General Service and Victory Medals.
39, Addison St., Chorlton-on-Medlock, Manchester. Z7953A

ROTHWELL, W., Gunner, R.G.A.
Volunteering in May 1915, he embarked for France in the following August, and was in action at Loos, the Somme, Vimy Ridge, Albert, Cambrai, Ypres, Bullecourt, and Messines, where in June 1917 he was badly gassed. After hospital treatment, he returned to the line, and served until the close of hostilities. He was demobilised in December 1918, and holds the 1914-15 Star, and the General Service and Victory Medals. 92, Irlam St., Miles Platting, Manchester.   Z9693

ROTHWELL, W., Private, 19th Manchester Regt.
Volunteering in September 1914, he was sent to France in October of the following year, and was in action in the Battles of Loos, Ypres, and the Somme. He was reported missing at Guillemont in July 1916, and was later presumed to have been killed in action there. He was entitled to the 1914-15 Star, and the General Service and Victory Medals.
"Steals on the ear the distant triumph song."
59, Gibson Street, Ardwick, Manchester.   Z7952B

ROUGHSEDGE, H., Bandsman, 20th Manchester Rgt.
He volunteered in October 1914, and after a year's service in England proceeded to France. There he fought in many notable engagements, including those at Loos, Albert, Vimy Ridge, and the Somme, where he was twice wounded. On recovery he rejoined his unit, and took part in the fighting at Arras, Bullecourt, Messines, and other engagements until hostilities ceased. Returning home he was demobilised in February 1919, and holds the 1914-15 Star, and the General Service and Victory Medals.
59, Beswick Street, Ancoats, Manchester.   Z11060

ROURKE, J. E., Private, 8th Manchester Regiment.
He volunteered in January 1915, and crossed to the Western Front six months later. Serving with his unit in several sectors he saw heavy fighting in the Battles of Albert, the Somme, Arras, and was wounded at Vimy Ridge in April 1917. On recovery he was engaged in the Battles of Ypres and Passchendaele, and was wounded for the second time at Péronne in March 1918. Invalided home on account of his injuries he was under treatment at the 5th Southern General Hospital, Southampton, for some months. Demobilised in January 1919, he holds the 1914-15 Star, and the General Service and Victory Medals.
29, Gatley Street, Ancoats, Manchester.   Z7956

ROURKE, J. F., Private, 26th Manchester Regt.
Volunteering in August 1915, he sailed for Egypt in November of the following year, and fought in the Battles of Katia and Romani, and the Capture of El Fasher. He was also in action in the Battles of Gaza (I and II), was present at the fall of Jerusalem and the Capture of Jericho, and Aleppo, and was invalided home from Palestine owing to illness. After treatment at Bellahouston War Hospital, Glasgow, he was discharged from the Army on medical grounds in February 1919, and holds the General Service and Victory Medals.
24, Newman Street, Ancoats, Manchester.   Z7955

ROURKE, T., A.B., Royal Navy.
He was in the Navy at the declaration of war, and subsequently saw service with the Grand Fleet in H.M.S. "Tiger," until January 1915, when he was unfortunately killed in action at the Dogger Bank. He was entitled to the 1914-15 Star, and the General Service and Victory Medals.
"He passed out of the sight of men, by the path of duty and self-sacrifice."
5, Stand Street, Ancoats, Manchester.   TZ9348

ROUTLEDGE, W. T., Private, 19th Cheshire Regt.
Joining in March 1916, he embarked for the Western Front two months later and was transferred to the Labour Corps in the following year. Serving with his Company he did good work during heavy fighting in the Ypres salient, and on the Somme, in which sectors he was engaged in the construction of light railways. He was demobilised in September 1919, and holds the General Service and Victory Medals.
116, Chester Street, Hulme, Manchester.   TZ7957

ROWAN, T., Private, 1st Manchester Regiment.
He joined in March 1916, and landing in France three months later served in various sectors of the Front until the end of hostilities. During this period he took part in several engagements of the Somme Offensive, and in the Battles of Arras, Bullecourt, Messines, Ypres III, Passchendaele, Cambrai, and those of the German Offensive, and subsequent Allied Advance of 1918. He was demobilised in January of the succeeding year, and holds the General Service and Victory Medals.
27, Long Street, Ancoats, Manchester.   Z7993

ROWBOTHAM, A., Sergt. Major, Manchester Regt.
He volunteered in August 1914, and in November of the following year was drafted to France, where he took a prominent part in much severe fighting. He was engaged in the Battle of Vimy Ridge, and was wounded at Carnoy. After rejoining his unit he was again in action in the opening stages of the Somme Offensive, and was severely wounded on July 1st. After much hospital treatment he was discharged in December 1917 in consequence of his injuries. He holds the 1914-15 Star, and the General Service and Victory Medals.
9, Howell Street, Collyhurst, Manchester.   Z11061

ROWCROFT, J. T., Gunner, R.F.A.
A Reservist, he was mobilised at the declaration of war, and shortly afterwards proceeding to France took part with his Battery in the Retreat from Mons, and the Battles of Ypres (II), and Albert. Returning to England in March 1916, as time-expired, he rejoined a month later and was sent again to the Western Front, where he fought in the Battle of Messines, and was gassed at Menin Road. On Recovery he rejoined his Battery, and was in action during the German Offensive, and was wounded at Havrincourt in the subsequent Allied Advance in September 1918. Invalided home to hospital, he was subsequently discharged on account of service in April 1919. He holds the Mons Star, and the General Service and Victory Medals.
6, Dearden Street, Hulme, Manchester.   Z7958

ROWDEN, H., Driver, R.F.A.
Volunteering in December 1915, he was sent in January 1917 to the Western Front, and took part in heavy fighting on the Ancre, and in the Battles of Arras, Cambrai I, the Somme II, Amiens, and St. Quentin. Admitted into hospital owing to illness he shortly afterwards rejoined his Battery, and fought until the end of the war. Returning to England he was demobilised in June 1919, and holds the General Service and Victory Medals.
27, Thorne Street, Bradford, Manchester.   Z7959

ROWE, S., Private, 7th East Lancashire Regiment.
He volunteered in September 1914, and in the following June was drafted to France, where he took part in the Battle of Loos, and was badly wounded. As a result he was invalided home, and on his recovery was retained at various home stations on important duties. He was demobilised in March 1919, and holds the 1914-15 Star, and the General Service and Victory Medals.
12, Reather Street, Miles Platting, Manchester.   Z11948

ROWEN, B., Private, 8th Manchester Regiment.
He volunteered in March 1915, and at the conclusion of his training served with his unit at various stations engaged on important duties. He rendered valuable services as a cook, but was not successful in securing his transfer overseas on account of physical unfitness, and was discharged in January 1919. 124, Tame Street, Ancoats, Manchester.   Z7960

ROWLAND, E., Driver, R.F.A.
Volunteering in August 1915, he crossed to France in the following January, and served with his Battery in various sectors of this front. He fought at the Battles of Vimy Ridge, Lens, Ypres, and Le Cateau, and contracting trench fever was invalided to England and underwent treatment in Nottingham Hospital. On recovery he was demobilised in February 1919, and holds the General Service and Victory Medals.
21, Elton Street, Chorlton-on-Medlock, Manchester. Z7962A

ROWLAND, H., Corporal, 13th Lancashire Fusiliers.
He joined in June 1916, and in the following August was drafted to the Western Front. There he played a prominent part in severe fighting on the Somme Front, and was wounded. Invalided home as a result, he spent some time in hospital at Glasgow, and upon recovering returned to France, where he took part in further fighting at Ypres, Cambrai, Arras, Vimy Ridge, and on the Somme. Gassed in action in November 1917, he was again invalided home and admitted to hospital in Liverpool, being eventually demobilised in August 1919, holding the General Service and Victory Medals.
4, Whitworth Street, Longsight, Manchester.   TZ11812

ROWLAND, T., Driver, R.A.S.C.
Joining in June 1915, he was retained in England on various important transport duties until May 1917. He then proceeded to the Western Front, and did excellent service at Albert, the Somme, Bertincourt, and in the Retreat and Allied Advance of 1918. He returned home and was demobilised in February 1919, holding the General Service and Victory Medals.
21, Derby Street, Gorton, Manchester.   Z11062

ROWLAND, J. E., Private, 1/7th Manchester Regt.
He volunteered in October 1915, and embarking for Egypt in the following May served in operations in the Canal zone, notably those of Katia, and Romani. Transferred in March 1917 to the Western Front, he fought on the Somme, and in several other engagements, and was wounded during the Allied Advance in September 1918. Invalided home for hospital treatment he was subsequently discharged on account of service in February 1919. He holds the General Service and Victory Medals.
102, Clopton Street, Hulme, Manchester.   Z7961

ROWLANDS, J. F., Driver, R.A.S.C. (M.T.)
He joined in March 1917, and was quickly drafted to France, where he served at Arras, and in the Retreat and Advance of 1918. He was demobilised in March 1919, but re-enlisted three months later, and was sent to Russia. There he was awarded the Russian Order of St. George for bravery in bringing transports out of action under difficult circumstances. He was demobilised in September 1920, and holds the General Service and Victory Medals.
18, Higham Street, Oldham Road, Manchester.   Z11868C

ROWLES, J., Gunner, R.G.A.
Enlisting in 1911, he was mobilised when war broke out and drafted to France in September of the following year. In this theatre of war he served with his Battery in numerous engagements, including those at Loos, Albert, Vermelles, Ploegsteert, Vimy Ridge, the Somme, Beaumont-Hamel, Beaucourt, Arras, Ypres III, Passchendaele, and Cambrai. He was wounded on the Somme during the Allied Advance in August 1918, and, evacuated to England, received treatment at Tunbridge Wells Hospital. He was subsequently discharged on account of service in July 1919, and holds the 1914-15 Star, and the General Service and Victory Medals.
16, Bank Street, Hulme, Manchester.   Z7965A

ROWLES, N., Private, 1st Wiltshire Regiment.
He volunteered in July 1915, and served on special Home Service duties until April 1917, when he was sent to the Western Front. There he fought in several engagements, including the Battles of Arras, Messines, Cambrai, the Marne, and was severely gassed at Ypres in November 1917. On recovery he rejoined his Battalion in the front line trenches, and was wounded during the second Battle of the Somme in April 1918. After receiving medical treatment he returned to England for his demobilisation in March 1919, and holds the General Service and Victory Medals.
37, Sawley Street, Beswick, Manchester.   Z7963-64B

ROWLES, T., A.B., Royal Navy.
He was serving at the outbreak of hostilities in H.M.S. " Manners," which vessel was engaged on patrol and other important duties in the North Sea, and off the Belgian Coast. She was in action in the Battles of Heligoland Bight, the Narrows, Jutland, and had many other encounters with enemy craft during the course of the war. He was demobilised in February 1919, and holds the 1914-15 Star, and the General Service and Victory Medals.
16, Bank Street, Hulme, Manchester.   Z7965B

ROWLEY, A. E., Private, 13th Canadian Infantry (Royal Highlanders of Canada).
Joining in June 1917, he proceeded in the following March to the Western Front, where he was in action during the second Battle of the Somme. He also fought in several engagements in the Retreat and Advance of 1918, notably those at Havrincourt, Ypres IV., and Cambrai II. After the Armistice he proceeded with the Army of Occupation into Germany, and was stationed at Cologne until March 1919. He then returned to England and was demobilised three months later, and holds the General Service and Victory Medals.
2, Guy Street, Ardwick, Manchester.   Z7968

ROWLEY, G., Corporal, 13th Manchester Regiment.
He volunteered in September 1914, and on completion of his training served at home for a time and embarked in the following September for France. He took part in the Battles of Loos, La Bassée, and other engagements until drafted to Salonika three months later. In this theatre of war he fought in the Battles of the Vardar, Struma, and Monastir, and was wounded at Horse Shoe Hill on the Doiran front in April 1917. Sent to hospital in Malta, he was afterwards evacuated to England, where he underwent further treatment in Fulham Hospital. He was eventually discharged on account of service in January 1919, and holds the 1914-15 Star, and the General Service and Victory Medals.
12, Randolph Street, Openshaw, Manchester.   Z7966

ROWLEY, W. H., Sapper, R.E.
He joined in August 1917, and after having completed his training was retained at Chatham with the Searchlight Section in connection with the aerial defence of London. Owing to ill-health he was not able to obtain a transfer overseas, and was for a time in hospital. In January 1919 he was discharged as medically unfit for further duty.
44, Crissey Street, Miles Platting, Manchester.   Z11576

ROWLEY, H. B., A.B., R.N., H.M.S. "Trent" and Private, Royal Welch Fusiliers.

He volunteered in September 1914, and was posted to H.M.S. "Trent," in which vessel he served until it was torpedoed in the English Channel in July 1915. He was severely injured and subsequently discharged from the Royal Navy. Later joining the Royal Welch Fusiliers, he served in France, was wounded in action on the Ancre front, and was invalided home as the result. Eventually discharged in May 1917, as unfit for further service, he holds the 1914-15 Star, and the General Service and Victory Medals.

19, Exeter Street, Ardwick, Manchester. Z7967

ROWLINSON, J. (D.C.M.), Corporal, K.O. (Royal Lancaster Regiment.)

Volunteering in August 1914, he proceeded shortly afterwards to France, where he took part in the Retreat from Mons, and the Battles of the Aisne, Armentières, La Bassée, Neuve Chapelle, Hill 60, and Ypres. He was awarded the Distinguished Conduct Medal for gallantry during the Retreat, rescuing two comrades under heavy fire. Early in 1916 he was sent to Mesopotamia, and after participating in several important engagements, contracted malaria, from the effects of which he died in November 1916. He was entitled to the Mons Star, and the General Service and Victory Medals in addition to the Distinguished Conduct Medal.
"Great deeds cannot die."

219, Crossley Street, Gorton, Manchester. Z11813

ROWLINSON, J., Sergt., Manchester Regiment.

Volunteering in October 1914, he crossed to France in November of the following year, and fought in the Somme Offensive, in which he was wounded. After treatment at a Base hospital, he returned to the line, and was in action at Arras, Vimy Ridge, and Ypres. Later he contracted a severe illness, and evacuated to England, underwent protracted hospital treatment. He was discharged as medically unfit for further service in March 1918, and holds the 1914-15 Star, and the General Service and Victory Medals.

71, Crosscliffe Street, Moss Side, Manchester. Z7969

ROWLINSON, T., Corporal, R.E.

An ex-soldier, with a previous good record of service in the South African War, he volunteered in August 1914, and embarking for the Dardanelles early in the following year, did valuable work during the Landing at Gallipoli, and the first, second, and third Battles of Krithia. After the Evacuation of the Peninsula, he proceeded to Salonika, and was engaged on important duties in connection with operations on the Doiran, Struma, and Vardar fronts. In the course of his service he was invalided to Cairo, suffering from malaria, and was under hospital treatment for three months. He was demobilised in January 1919, and holds the 1914-15 Star, and the General Service and Victory Medals.

23, Seddon Street, Rusholme, Manchester. TZ9694

ROWLINSON, T., Private, Lancashire Fusiliers.

He volunteered in August 1914, and in the following June embarked for the Western Front. Whilst in this theatre of war he fought in the Battles of Loos, St. Eloi, Albert, the Somme, Arras, Bullecourt, Passchendaele, Cambrai, the Marne (II), and Bapaume. In August 1918, in consequence of ill-health, he was invalided home, and discharged, unfit for further service, in the next month. He holds the 1914-15 Star, and the General Service and Victory Medals.

2, Gleave Street, West Gorton, Manchester. Z7970

ROWSON, H., Private, 1/8th Lancashire Fusiliers and Royal Welch Fusiliers.

Volunteering in 1915 he was drafted to Egypt in 1916, and served at Port Said, Suez, Kubri, Kantara, and other stations in the Canal zone. He was in action in the Battle of Romani, and saw much fighting during the advance across the Sinai Peninsula to El Arish. In 1917, on being discovered to be under military age he was sent home, and was transferred to the Royal Welch Fusiliers. He was stationed at various depôts and rendered excellent services until demobilised in 1919. He holds the General Service and Victory Medals.

47, Granville Place, Ancoats, Manchester. Z11062

ROYLANCE, F., Gunner, R.F.A.

He volunteered in December 1915, and in the following August was drafted to the Western Front. In this theatre of war he served with his Battery in many important engagements, including the Battles of St. Eloi, Ypres III, and the second Battle of the Somme, performing consistently good work. He was demobilised in January 1919, and holds the General Service and Victory Medals.

1, Bright Street, Hulme, Manchester. Z11814

ROYLE, E. R., Air Mechanic, R.A.F.

He volunteered in August 1915, and for two years was engaged in England on important duties with his Squadron. He proceeded to the Western Front in August 1917, and was wounded in December of that year in the third Battle of Ypres. After his recovery he was stationed in Ireland until demobilised in April 1919. He holds the General Service and Victory Medals.

3, Osborne Street, Oldham Road, Manchester. Z11037B

ROYLE, A., Private, 19th Manchester Regiment.

Volunteering in May 1915, he embarked for France in the following March, and was in action at St. Eloi, Ploegsteert Wood, St. Quentin, Arras, the Somme, Cambrai, and Vimy Ridge. In June 1918, he contracted a severe illness, but after being treated at the 42nd Casualty Clearing Station, was able to rejoin his unit, and fight until the close of hostilities. He was demobilised in March 1919, and holds the General Service and Victory Medals.

7, Tuley Street, Lower Openshaw, Manchester. Z7974

ROYLE, E., Air Mechanic, R.A.F.

Joining in January 1917, he proceeded to France two months later, and was engaged on important work in connection with the repair of aeroplanes at Boulogne. In September of the following year, he sustained severe injuries in an accident, and evacuated to England was for some time under hospital treatment. After being demobilised in February 1919, he rejoined for a further period of service, and in 1920 was stationed at Gosport. He holds the General Service and Victory Medals.

31, Barlow Street, Bradford, Manchester. Z7971

ROYLE, H., Sapper, R.E.

Volunteering in September 1915, he was drafted to France in the following June, and saw service in many sectors of the Front. He was chiefly engaged on the lines of communication, and also did good service at the Battles of the Somme, the Ancre, Messines, Ypres, Cambrai, and Bapaume. After returning home in July 1919 he was demobilised, and holds the General Service and Victory Medals.

17, Ellen Street, West Gorton, Manchester. Z11064

ROYLE, H. C., Private, 7th Manchester Regiment.

Volunteering in May 1915, he embarked for Egypt in the following January, and took part in operations at Sollum, Katia, El Fasher, and the Battle of Romani. Transferred to France in February 1917, he was in action at Arras, Ypres, Cambrai, and in the Retreat and Allied Advance, which terminated hostilities victoriously in November 1918. He was demobilised in February of the succeeding year, and holds the General Service and Victory Medals.

30, Pomfret Street, West Gorton, Manchester. Z7972

ROYLE, L., Pioneer, R.E.

He volunteered in August 1915, and after his training served on the Western Front until the close of hostilities. During this period, he was engaged on road construction and bridge building, and did valuable work in this capacity on the Somme, at Arras, Ypres, Cambrai, and in the Retreat and Allied Advance of 1918. He was demobilised in March of the following year, and holds the 1914-15 Star, and the General Service and Victory Medals.

42, Clifford Street, Lower Openshaw, Manchester. Z7975

ROYLE, M., Private, Manchester Regiment.

Having enlisted in May 1910, he was mobilised when war broke out, and crossing immediately to France took part in the memorable Retreat from Mons. Later he was in action at Ypres, and the Somme, and in 1917, was severely wounded at the third Battle of Ypres. Evacuated to England, he underwent protracted hospital treatment, and after his recovery was engaged on important home duties until demobilised in November 1919. He holds the Mons Star, and the General Service and Victory Medals.

27, Down Street, Ardwick, Manchester. Z7976

ROYLE, S., Private, 2nd K.O. Scottish Borderers.

Volunteering in June 1915, he proceeded to France in the following December, and was in action at La Bassée and Verdun, where he was taken prisoner in April 1916. During his captivity in Germany, he was employed as a farm labourer, and whilst engaged on this work contracted pneumonia, from the effects of which he died on November 5th, 1918. He was entitled to the 1914-15 Star, and the General Service and Victory Medals.
"Thinking that remembrance, though unspoken, may reach him where he sleeps."

4, Durham Place, Hulme, Manchester. Z7973

ROYLE, T., Private, 17th Manchester Regiment.

He volunteered in November 1915, and after his training served on the Western Front until the close of hostilities. During this period, he was in action at Trones Wood, the Somme, where, in July 1916, he was wounded, Arras, Bullecourt, Ypres and Cambrai, and was again wounded at St. Quentin in the German Offensive in March 1918. On recovery he rejoined his unit in the Field, and served throughout the Allied Advance of that year. He was demobilised in February 1919, and holds the General Service and Victory Medals.

44, Teignmouth Street, Collyhurst, Manchester. Z9695

RUAN, G., Private, 1st Manchester Regiment.

Joining in November 1916, he was engaged on important home duties until June 1918, when crossing to France, he was employed on road repairing during the Allied Advance of that year. He returned to England in the following October, but was later sent with the Army of Occupation to Germany. He was demobilised in October 1919, and holds the General Service and Victory Medals.

24, Bedale Street, Hulme, Manchester. Z7977

RUDD, R., Private, 11th Manchester Regiment.

Volunteering in September 1915, he embarked for France in the following January, and in May 1916, was badly wounded at Festubert. He underwent treatment at the 32nd Casualty Clearing Station and afterwards at the 2nd Canadian General Hospital, and on recovery rejoined his unit in the Field. In October 1918, during the Allied Advance, he was again severely wounded at Cambrai, and invalided home. He was demobilised in February 1919, and holds the General Service and Victory Medals.

67, Everton Road, Chorlton-on-Medlock, Manchester.   Z7978

RUDDEN, O.,Pte.,Cheshire Regt., and Labour Corps.

Joining in November 1916, he embarked in February of the following year for the Western Front and saw much service there. He was present during the engagements at Arras, Bullecourt, Ypres, Cambrai, the Marne, the Aisne and Bapaume. After his return to England he was demobilised in January 1919, and holds the General Service and Victory Medals.

10, Tonge Street, Ancoats, Manchester.   Z11065

RUDDLE, G., Private, 18th Manchester Regiment.

He volunteered in September 1914, and in the following June embarked for Egypt and thence to the Dardanelles. After taking part in the Landing at Suvla Bay, he fought in many engagements on the Peninsula, and after the Evacuation was completed, proceeded to the Western Front and was in action on the Somme, at La Bassée, Albert, Cambrai, Ypres and Passchendaele. He died gloriously on the Field of Battle in July 1917, and was entitled to the 1914-15 Star, and the General Service and Victory Medals.

"Nobly striving,
He nobly fell that we might live."

15, Willaston Street, Ardwick, Manchester.   Z7979

RUDYARD, J., Private, King's (Liverpool Regiment).

Volunteering in November 1914, he proceeded to France in the following July, and fought in the Battles of Loos, Vimy Ridge, the Somme and Bullecourt. He was unfortunately killed whilst on night patrol at Arras in March 1917, and lies buried in the British Cemetery at Bray. He was entitled to the 1914-15 Star, and the General Service and Victory Medals.

"He passed out of the sight of men by the path of duty and self-sacrifice."

21, Albion Terrace, Miles Platting, Manchester.   Z7980

RULE, S., Private, 11th Lancashire Fusiliers.

Volunteering in September 1914, he embarked for France in November of the following year, and fought in engagements at Loos, St. Eloi, Albert, the Somme, Arras, Ypres and Cambrai. He was also for a time engaged on special duties with the Labour Corps, and was stationed at the Base. He was demobilised on his return to England in February 1919, and holds the 1914-15 Star, and the General Service and Victory Medals.

28, Dora Street, Rochdale Road, Manchester.   Z9349

RUSHTON, W., Private, 4th Manchester Regiment.

Joining in May 1917, he embarked for India in the following July, and was engaged on important duties at various military stations, including those of Bangalore and Singapore. In October 1918 he contracted malaria, and, evacuated to England, underwent hospital treatment until March 1919, when he was discharged as medically unfit for further service. He holds the General Service Medal.

3, Belgrave Street, Hulme Manchester.   Z7981

RUSSELL, M., Private, 4th Manchester Regiment.

Volunteering in September 1914, he was sent a year later to France. During his service overseas, he was engaged with his unit in strenuous fighting at Loos, Albert and on the Somme front, also at Arras, Passchendaele, Cambrai, Havrincourt and Le Cateau. He performed very good work, remaining on the Western Front until January 1919. Demobilised two months later, he holds the 1914-15 Star, and the General Service and Victory Medals.

16, George Street, Moss Side, Manchester.   Z11815

RUSSELL, P., Private, K.O. (Royal Lancaster Regt.)

He volunteered in August 1914, and in July of the following year was drafted to Gallipoli. Upon reaching Mudros he contracted an illness through which he was invalided home. On his recovery he was retained in England until discharged as medically unfit for further service in February 1918. He holds the 1914-15 Star, and the General Service and Victory Medals.

20, Wright Street, Oldham Road, Manchester.   Z11066

RUSSELL, S., Stoker, R.N.

He volunteered in June 1915, and after his training saw service in H.M.S. "Liverpool," "Ariadne" and "Bellona." He was engaged with his vessel on important patrol duties off the Italian Coast and in the North Sea, and was frequently in action with enemy craft. After four years' valuable work he returned to shore for his demobilisation, which took place in March 1919, and holds the 1914-15 Star, and the General Service and Victory Medals.

20, Naylor Street, Newton, Manchester.   Z9350

RUSTAGE, W., Private, South Wales Borderers.

He volunteered in June 1915, and in the following year was sent to France. Whilst in this theatre of war he fought in many notable battles, and was twice wounded. He was unfortunately killed in action on April 21st, 1917, and was entitled to the General Service and Victory Medals.

"A valiant Soldier, with undaunted heart, he breasted life's last hill."

9, Evans Street, Chorlton-on-Medlock, Manchester.   Z11067A

RUTHVEN, C., Private, Royal Welch Fusiliers.

He volunteered in July 1915, but in the course of his training was found to be medically unfit, and on these grounds was invalided out of the Service a month later.

5, Ely Street, Hulme, Manchester.   Z7982

RUTLAND, G., Private, 1st N. Staffordshire Regt.

Joining in July 1917, he embarked for the Western Front in the following March, and took part in the second Battles of the Somme and Cambrai, where in September 1918, he received an injury, which confined him to hospital for four weeks. On recovery, he was engaged on important duties in France until November 1919, when he returned to England and was demobilised. He holds the General Service and Victory Medals.

5, Derby Street, Hulme, Manchester.   Z7983

RUTTER, I., Private, 5th Manchester Regiment.

He volunteered in September 1914, and after his training was engaged on duties of an important nature at various stations. He did valuable work, but was not sent overseas owing to his being over age for military service. He was discharged in consequence in November 1915.

22, Roe Street, Ancoats, Manchester.   Z9687B

RUTTER, J., Private, King's (Liverpool Regiment).

Joining in March 1917, he proceeded to France in the following January and took part in operations at Armentières, Arras, Béthune and Bray, where he was severely wounded. After being treated in hospital at Etaples, he rejoined his unit and served until hostilities closed victoriously on November 11th, 1918. He was demobilised in January 1920, and holds the General Service and Victory Medals.

22, Rose Street, Ancoats, Manchester.   Z9687A

RYALL, R. P., Trooper, 7th (Princess Royal's) Dragoon Guards.

Volunteering in September 1914, he embarked for France in the following April and took part in many important battles, including that of Cambrai, where he was wounded in November 1917. On recovery he returned to the Line, and was in action until the close of hostilities. He was demobilised in March 1919, and holds the 1914-15 Star, and the General Service and Victory Medals.

33, Ann Street, Hulme, Manchester.   Z7984

RYAN, D., Corporal, King's (Liverpool Regiment).

Mobilised in August 1914, he was retained at home on important duties up to December 1915, and then proceeded to France. There he played a prominent part in heavy fighting at St. Eloi, Loos, Albert and Vimy Ridge and was afterwards sent to Egypt. Proceeding later to Salonika, he took part in the advance on the Doiran front and remained overseas until March 1919, when he returned home and was demobilised. He holds the 1914-15 Star, and the General Service and Victory Medals.

77, Victoria Buildings, Ancoats, Manchester.   Z9351

RYAN, E., Private, 2/10th Manchester Regiment.

Joining in May 1916, he embarked for France in the following February, and in May 1917 was so severely wounded at Arras as to necessitate his return to England for hospital treatment. After recovery he returned to France, and was engaged on important duties at various prisoners of war camps until after the close of hostilities. He was demobilised in September 1919, and holds the General Service and Victory Medals.

60, Higham Street, Miles Platting, Manchester.   Z9688

RYAN, J., Sergt., 6th South Lancashire Regiment.

A Reservist, he was mobilised at the declaration of war, and in September 1915 embarked for Mesopotamia. He took part in engagements at Kut-el-Amara, Um-el-Hannah, Sanna-i-Yat, the capture of Baghdad and many others, until the close of hostilities. He was demobilised in March 1919, and holds the 1914-15 Star, and the General Service and Victory Medals.

61, Pilling Street, Rochdale Road, Manchester.   Z9352A

RYAN, J., Gunner, R.G.A.

Joining in June 1916, he proceeded to France in September of that year, and took part in the final operations of the Somme Offensive. Later he was in action at Beaumont-Hamel, Arras and Vimy Ridge, where he was wounded. On recovery he fought in the Retreat and Allied Advance of 1918. He was demobilised in August of the following year, and holds the General Service and Victory Medals.

60, Green Street, Gorton, Manchester   TZ7985

RYAN, J. (Jun.), Private, Welch Regiment.
Joining in September 1917, he proceeded to France in the following March, and took part in several important engagements during the Retreat and Allied Advance of 1918, at the conclusion of which he was sent with the Army of Occupation to Germany. He was demobilised in October 1919, and holds the General Service and Victory Medals.
61, Pilling Street Rochdale Road, Manchester.   Z9352B

RYAN, J., 1st Class Stoker, R.N., and Pte., King's (Liverpool Regiment).
He volunteered in August 1914, and after his training was posted to H.M.S. "Jupiter," which vessel was engaged on patrol and other duties in co-operation with the Grand Fleet in the North Sea. In April 1915, his ship assisted in covering the Landing of troops at Gallipoli and took part in the bombardment of the Dardanelles Forts until the Evacuation of the Peninsula. He was then engaged with his ship in the Sea of Marmora, and was awarded the Russian Order of St. Stanislaus for good work in the Black Sea. He was also for a time with his vessel in the Mediterranean, and was twice wounded. Demobilised in January 1919, he joined the Army in the following July, and in 1920 was serving with the Army of Occupation in Germany. He holds the 1914-15 Star, and the General Service and Victory Medals.
16, Durham Place, Hulme, Manchester.   Z7986

RYAN, M., Pioneer, R.E.
He joined in January 1917, and a month later embarked for the Western Front. Whilst in this theatre of war he was engaged on important duties in connection with road and bridge construction in the Arras, Nieuport and the Somme sectors. He was discharged through causes due to his service in April 1919, and holds the General Service and Victory Medals. 40, Sand St., Rochdale Rd., Manchester.   Z9353

RYAN, M., Private, 2nd Manchester Regiment.
Volunteering in August 1914, he landed in France in the following January, and was in action at Neuve Chapelle, Hill 60 and Ypres, where he was unfortunately killed in April 1915. He was entitled to the 1914-15 Star, and the General Service and Victory Medals.
"A valiant Soldier, with undaunted heart, he breasted life's last hill."
36, Harrison Street, Ancoats, Manchester.   Z9220B

RYAN, M., Pte., 11th (Prince Albert's Own) Hussars.
He was mobilised at the outbreak of hostilities, and was immediately drafted to France, where he took part in the Retreat from Mons. He also served at Ypres, the Somme and Givenchy. Afterwards he proceeded to Mesopotamia and did excellent work in many engagements in this theatre of war. During his service he was wounded on one occasion. He holds the Mons Star, and the General Service and Victory Medals. and was demobilised in January 1919 after his return to Ireland.
30, Whalley Street, Ancoats, Manchester.   Z11068

RYAN, T. (D.C.M.), Sapper, R.E.
He volunteered in May 1915, and later in the same year was sent to the Western Front, where he took a prominent part in the fighting in the Neuve Chapelle and Loos sectors, and was wounded in action in November 1918. He was shortly afterwards transferred to the King's (Liverpool Regiment), and served with the 55th Division. He was awarded the Distinguished Conduct Medal for conspicuous bravery in the Field, and was demobilised in July 1919, also holding the 1914-15 Star, and the General Service and Victory Medals. 19, Shakespeare Street, Bradford, Manchester.   X11886

RYAN, T., Sergeant, 8th Manchester Regiment.
He volunteered in August 1914, and in January of the following year proceeded to France. Whilst overseas he fought at Ypres, Givenchy, Loos, Vimy Ridge, the Somme, Arras and in many later engagements until the conclusion of hostilities. He returned home and was demobilised in March 1919, and holds the 1914-15 Star, and the General Service and Victory Medals. 16, Flower St., Ancoats, Manchester.   Z11069

RYAN, W., Private, 11th Manchester Regiment.
He volunteered in November 1914, and embarking for the Dardanelles in the following year, was unhappily killed whilst landing at Suvla Bay in August 1915. He was entitled to the 1914-15 Star, and the General Service and Victory Medals.
"Whilst we remember, the sacrifice is not in vain."
17, Gunson Street, Ancoats, Manchester.   Z9267B

RYDER, A. E., L/Corporal, Border Regiment.
Volunteering in August 1914, he embarked for the Dardanelles in the following year, and took part in the first Landing at Gallipoli, and the Battles of Cape Helles, Krithia and Achi Baba and Suvla. Transferred to France after the Evacuation of the Peninsula, he fought at Loos, St. Eloi, the Somme, the Ancre, and Arras where in May 1918 he was wounded and taken prisoner. Repatriated after the close of hostilities, he was demobilised in March 1919, and holds the 1914-15 Star, and the General Service and Victory Medals.
53, Carmen Street, Ardwick, Manchester.   Z7988

RYDER, C. (M.M.), Sgt., 1st K.O. (R. Lancaster Regt.)
Mobilised on the outbreak of war he proceeded with the British Expeditionary Force to France and fought gallantly at Mons, Le Cateau, the Marne, the Aisne and the first and second Battles of Ypres. He was also in action at Albert, Ploegsteert Wood, the Somme, Arras, Bullecourt, Ypres, and in the Retreat and Advance of 1918, and was wounded on three occasions. He was awarded the Military Medal for conspicuous bravery and judgment in capturing an enemy position near Givenchy in August 1918, and in addition holds the Mons Star, and the General Service and Victory Medals. In January 1919 he was demobilised.
7, Phelan Street, Collyhurst, Manchester.   Z11071

RYDER, E., Private, 1/5th Essex Regiment.
He volunteered in January 1915, and sailing for Salonika in the following October, took part in the Battle of the Vardar and the advance on the Doiran and Struma fronts. Sent to Egypt in November 1916, he served in the British Advance through Palestine during which he was in action in the Battles of Gaza (I and II), the capture of Jericho and was present at the entry into Jerusalem. Returning home in July 1919, owing to illness, he received hospital treatment, and discharged medically unfit for further service in August 1919, and holds the 1914-15 Star, and the General Service and Victory Medals. 20, Seak Street, Beswick, Manchester.   Z7990

RYDER, J., Private, 24th Manchester Regiment.
He volunteered in November 1914, and in September of the following year proceeded to the Western Front, where he saw much service. He fought at Albert, and was wounded in the Battle of the Somme in July 1916, and after his recovery was again in action at Bullecourt, Messines, Passchendaele and in many later operations in the Retreat and Advance of 1918. He returned to England in February of the following year, and was demobilised in the succeeding month, holding the 1914-15 Star, and the General Service and Victory Medals. 7, Phelan Street, Collyhurst, Manchester.   Z11070

RYDER, J. H., Private, 1/7th Manchester Regiment.
Volunteering in April 1915, he was drafted to Egypt in the following January and fought in the Battles of Romani and Gaza and in March 1917 proceeded to France. There he was in action in several engagements in the Ypres salient, and was wounded at Passchendaele in July 1917. Returning to the trenches on recovery, he was wounded for the second time in the Battle of Cambrai, and after treatment served during the German Offensive and subsequent Allied Advance, and was gassed at Ypres in September 1918. He returned home for demobilisation in June 1919, and holds the General Service and Victory Medals.   Z7987
11, Whitworth St., Stanley Grove, Longsight, Manchester.

RYDER, R., Private, R.M.L.I.
He joined in April 1918, and after completing his training was engaged on special duties at Scapa Flow. He rendered valuable services, but owing to his age, was unable to secure his transfer to a ship afloat or to a theatre of war before hostilities ceased, and was demobilised in February 1919.
8, Garden Walks, Ardwick, Manchester.   Z7989

RYDER, T., Private, 6th Manchester Regiment.
He volunteered in September 1914, and in August of the following year was drafted to the Western Front. Whilst in France he fought in the Battles of Loos, Albert and the Somme, where he was wounded on July 1st, 1916. After his recovery he was again in action at Ypres and Cambrai and in many engagements in the Retreat and Advance of 1918. He holds the 1914-15 Star, and the General Service and Victory Medals. and was demobilised in March 1919.
4, Phelan Street, Collyhurst, Manchester.   Z11072

RYDINGS, J., Private, R.A.S.C.
He joined in October 1916, and two months later embarked for Salonika. Whilst in this theatre of war he was engaged on important duties in connection with transport on the Doiran front. He contracted malaria, and after being invalided home in June 1918, was discharged as medically unfit for further service in the following September. He holds the General Service and Victory Medals.
50, Bath Street, Miles Platting, Manchester.   Z10761B

RYDINGS, R., Private, M.G.C.
He volunteered in March 1915, and on the completion of his training served with his unit in the South of England on duties connected with home defence. He did excellent work, but was unsuccessful in securing his transfer overseas before the end of the war owing to medical unfitness for general service, and was demobilised in September 1919.
40, Canning Street, Hulme, Manchester.   Z7991

RYNHAM, W. J., Private, 22nd Manchester Regt.
He joined in June 1916, and in the following January, after completing his training, was drafted to the Western Front. Whilst overseas he fought at Arras, the capture of Vimy Ridge, Ypres, Cambrai and in many engagements in the Retreat and Advance of 1918. He holds the General Service and Victory Medals, and was demobilised in February 1919.
35, Milton Street, West Gorton, Manchester.   Z11073

S

SABOR, M., Driver, R.A.S.C.
He joined in April 1917, and after completing a period of training was retained on important duties with his unit at various stations. He was not able to obtain a transfer to a theatre of war during the period of hostilities owing to his being medically unfit, but rendered valuable services until discharged from the Army in February 1918.
28, Gorton Street, Ardwick, Manchester.   Z7998

SADLER, A., Air Mechanic, R.A.F.
He joined in March 1918, and after a period of training was engaged at Farnborough on duties which called for a high degree of technical skill. Owing to the early cessation of hostilities he was unable to obtain a transfer overseas, but rendered valuable services until his demobilisation in September 1919.
17, Elizabeth Street, West Gorton, Manchester.   Z11074A

SADLER, A. C., 2nd Class Boy, R.N.
He volunteered at the beginning of August 1915, and being posted to H.M.S. "Powerful," was sent to Devonport for training. Unfortunately he contracted fever after only a few days in the Service, and died on August 22nd, 1915, in the Royal Naval Hospital at Plymouth.
" His memory is cherished with pride."
19, Sarah Street, Bradford, Manchester.   Z7999

SADLER, D., Corporal, R.F.A.
He volunteered in November 1914, and on completing his training in the following June was drafted to Egypt, where he took part in engagements at Mersa Matruh, Agagia, Sollum, Katia, El Fasher and the capture of Magdhaba. In 1917 he was transferred to France and saw much fighting in the Retreat and Advance of 1918. He was demobilised in March 1919, and holds the 1914-15 Star, and the General Service and Victory Medals.
17, Elizabeth Street, West Gorton, Manchester.   Z11074B

SADLER, H., Sergt., M.G.C.
He volunteered in March 1915, and two months later was drafted to Mesopotamia. In this theatre of war he took a prominent part in engagements at Amara, Kut, Um-el-Hannah and on the Tigris. He was demobilised in February 1919, and holds the 1914-15 Star, and the General Service and Victory Medals.
17, Elizabeth Street, West Gorton, Manchester.   Z11074C

ST. GEORGE, H., Pte., 6th South Lancashire Regt.
Volunteering in August 1914, he was drafted to Egypt in the following May. During his service in this theatre of war he took part in several engagements, and was badly wounded in action in June 1917. As a result he was invalided home and finally discharged in September 1917, medically unfit. He holds the 1914-15 Star, and the General Service and Victory Medals. 20, Fox St., Ancoats, Manchester.   Z10236

SALE, E., Private, 8th Manchester Regiment.
He volunteered in 1915, and was retained on important home duties with his unit until 1916, when he proceeded to the Western Front. During his service in this theatre of war he took part in the Battle of the Somme (I), where he was unhappily killed in action in the same year. He was entitled to the General Service and Victory Medals.
" His memory is cherished with pride."
8, Halifax Street, Chorlton-on-Medlock, Manchester. X8000

SALISBURY, A. E., Driver, R.A.S.C.
Volunteering in May 1915, he was drafted to France in the following August. During his service on the Western Front he was engaged on important transport duties and was present at the Battles of Ypres and the Somme. He was afterwards transferred to the Italian Front in time to take part in the Offensive on the Piave and the Asiago Plateaux. He returned for demobilisation in April 1919, and holds the 1914-15 Star, and the General Service and Victory Medals.
3, Gloucester Place, Longsight, Manchester.   Z8001

SALISBURY, F. E., 1st Class Seaman Gunner, R.N.
He joined in October 1916, and after a period of training at the Crystal Palace and Devonport, was posted to the s.s. "Singleton Abbey," in which ship he rendered valuable services off the coasts of Scotland. Later he was transferred to the s.s. "Eltham" and the "Sheaf Don," and continued to do consistently good work until his demobilisation in January 1919, holding the General Service and Victory Medals.
114, South Street, Longsight, Manchester.   Z8002

SALSBURY, J. W., Driver, R.H.A.
Mobilised at the declaration of war, he crossed to France and took part in the Retreat from Mons and the Battles of the Marne, Ypres, the Somme, Loos, Messines and Cambrai. He also served throughout the Retreat and Allied Advance which terminated hostilities victoriously in November 1918. He was demobilised in the following February, and holds the Mons Star, and the General Service and Victory Medals.
8, Tailor Street, Ancoats, Manchester.   9696Z

SALT, J., Sergt., 6th South Lancashire Regiment.
Volunteering in August 1914, he was sent to Egypt in September of the following year and served with distinction on the

Suez Canal, in engagements against the Senussi Arabs and in heavy fighting at Katia and Rafa. Later he was transferred to Mesopotamia and took a prominent part in the Advance in that seat of war. He suffered severely from malarial fever, and was eventually demobilised in May 1919, holding the 1914-15 Star, and the General Service and Victory Medals.
5, Johnson's Buildings, Ancoats, Manchester.   Z8003

SALT, R., Private, K.O. (Royal Lancaster Regt.)
He joined in February 1917, and was quickly drafted to France. Whilst on the Western Front he took an active part in the Battle of Ypres (III), during which he was gassed, and invalided to hospital in England. On his recovery he was sent to Ireland, where he remained on important garrison duties until demobilised in August 1919. He holds the General Service and Victory Medals.
62, Juniper Street, Hulme, Manchester.   TZ8004

SALTHOUSE, E., Gunner, R.F.A.
He joined in September 1916, and after a period of training was drafted to India in the following February. Whilst in this Country he was engaged on important garrison duties with his Battery until October 1919, when he was sent to England suffering from malaria, and was demobilised in December of that year. He holds the General Service and Victory Medals.
20, Edge Street, Hulme, Manchester.   TZ8006

SALTHOUSE, E. K., Pte., 3rd Manchester Regt.
He joined in June 1916, and early in the following year was drafted to the Western Front, where he took part in much heavy fighting. He died gloriously on the Field of Battle at Arras on April 9th, 1917, and was entitled to the General Service and Victory Medals.
" Nobly striving,
He nobly fell that we might live."
15, Alder Street, Collyhurst, Manchester.   Z11075

SALTHOUSE, W. B., Private, R.A.S.C. (M.T.)
Joining in May 1916, he was sent to Egypt in the following February. During his service in this theatre of war he rendered valuable services with the Motor Transport section, and in the repair shops. He was also present at various engagements in Palestine, including the Battle of Jaffa and the capture of Jerusalem. Returning to Egypt, he served there until demobilised in August 1919, holding the General Service and Victory Medals.
80, Prince Street, Ardwick, Manchester.   Z8005

SAMUEL, A., Sergeant, R.E.
He enlisted in 1899, and after the outbreak of war in August 1914, served at various stations, where he was engaged on duties of a highly important nature. He was not successful in his efforts to obtain his transfer to a theatre of war, but, nevertheless, rendered very valuable services with his Company until March 1919, when he was discharged.
52, Haydn Avenue, Moss Side, Manchester.   Z8007

SANDBACH, J., L/Corporal, 4th Manchester Regt.
He was mobilised at the outbreak of war in August 1914, and was afterwards engaged on important duties as a Signal Instructor at various stations. He was unable to obtain his transfer to the Front, but, nevertheless, rendered valuable services with his unit until November 1916, when he was discharged, time-expired.
226, Ridgway Street, Ancoats, Manchester.   Z8008

SANDERS, L., Driver, R.E.
Mobilised in August 1914, he was immediately drafted to the Western Front, where he took an active part in the Battle of Mons and the subsequent Retreat. He also served in the Battle of the Marne and was wounded in action on the Aisne in September 1914, and invalided home. On his recovery, however, in May 1915, he returned to France and was again in action at Loos, Albert, Vimy Ridge and the Somme. Discharged in February 1917, time-expired, he re-enlisted, however, shortly afterwards, and was retained in England until finally demobilised in February 1919. He holds the Mons Star and the General Service and Victory Medals.
16, St. Clement's Place, West Gorton, Manchester. Z8009

SANDERS, W., Private, Labour Corps.
He joined in August 1918, but was not successful in obtaining a transfer overseas before the termination of hostilities. Whilst stationed at Oswestry, Chester, Stockport and Bootle, he was employed on various duties of an important character, and rendered excellent services until he was demobilised in March 1919.
77, Robert Street, West Gorton, Manchester.   Z11816

SANDERSON, J., Private, 1st Manchester Regiment.
He volunteered in December 1915, and in September of the following year was drafted to Mesopotamia, where he saw much severe fighting until wounded in action at Basra in January 1917. He was in hospital at Sheikh Saad and Amara, and was later invalided to India, where he was in hospital at Bombay and Colombo. On his recovery in July 1918, he proceeded to China and was there engaged on important garrison duties until his return home for demobilisation in October 1919. He holds the General Service and Victory Medals. 5, Birch St., Hulme, Manchester.   Z8010

SANDS J., Sapper, R.E.
He volunteered in November 1914, and in the following August was drafted to Gallipoli, where, after taking part in the Landing at Suvla Bay, he served at the capture of Chunuk Bair and in many other engagements. On the Evacuation of the Peninsula, he was sent to Egypt and thence into Palestine, where he took an active part in the Battles of Gaza and the capture of Jerusalem. He was transferred in June 1918, to the Western Front, and there served in the Allies' Advance, afterwards proceeding with the Army of Occupation into Germany. He was demobilised on his return home in July 1919, and holds the 1914–15 Star, and the General Service and Victory Medals.
35, Bunyan Street, Ardwick, Manchester.   Z8011

SANSOME, H., Private, 1st Lancashire Fusiliers.
He joined in April 1916, and underwent a period of training prior to being drafted to the Western Front in February of the following year. There, after taking part in the Battles of Arras and Ypres, and many minor engagements in various sectors, he was severely wounded in action at Passchendaele, in October 1917. He was for a considerable period in hospital at Bristol and Taunton before being invalided from the Army in July 1919, and holds the General Service and Victory Medals.
56, Higher Chatham Street, Chorlton-on-Medlock, Manchester.
                                                Z8012A

SARGEANT, R., Gunner, M.G.C.
Volunteering in January 1916, he proceeded to France in the following June. Whilst in this theatre of war he took part in several engagements, including those at Vimy Ridge, the Somme, Ypres (III), Cambrai and in the Retreat and Advance of 1918, and was wounded in action. After hostilities ceased, he went to Turkey, where in 1920 he was still serving. He holds the General Service and Victory Medals.
15, Hamilton Street, Collyhurst, Manchester.   Z11077

SARGEANT, R., Corporal, King's (Liverpool Regt.)
Volunteering in March 1915, he was engaged on important home duties until March 1917, when crossing to France, he fought in engagements at Bullecourt, Messines, Ypres, and Cambrai. He also served in the Retreat and Allied Advance of 1918, and after the close of hostilities was engaged in conveying German prisoners of war back to their own country. He was demobilised in November 1919, and holds the General Service and Victory Medals.
39, Simpson Street, Bradford, Manchester.   TZ9697

SARGENT, H., L/Corporal, M.G.C.
Volunteering in September 1914, he was drafted overseas after a period of training. During his service on the Western Front he took part in several engagements, including those at Nieuport, on the Somme, and at Ypres, where he was badly wounded in January 1918. In consequence he was invalided home and later demobilised in February 1919. He holds the General Service and Victory Medals.
57, Charlotte Street, West Gorton, Manchester.   TZ11949

SARGENT, J. W., Private, R.A.V.C.
He volunteered in September 1914, and was employed at home on various duties until November 1915, when he was sent to Salonika. There he served up to the end of 1916, and was then transferred to Malta. He performed excellent work whilst engaged on important duties, but in July 1917, contracted malaria, and as a result was invalided home. Demobilised in February 1919, he holds the 1914–15 Star, and the General Service and Victory Medals.
1, Melbourne Street, Hulme, Manchester.   Z11817

SARGENT, W. H., Private, 24th Welch Regiment.
He was called up from the Reserve in August 1914, and immediately drafted to the Western Front, where he took part in several engagements, and was wounded. As a result he was invalided home, but on his recovery, proceeded to the Dardanelles. There he saw much severe fighting, and was wounded and suffered from dysentery, being again invalided home. Later he was sent to Palestine and received his third wound at the Mount of Olives, and was consequently invalided to hospital in Alexandria. He returned home and was demobilised in February 1919, holding the 1914 Star, and the General Service and Victory Medals.
8, St. Ann Street, Bradford, Manchester.   Z11078

SARSON, G., Private, Royal Sussex Regiment.
Volunteering in September 1915, he was drafted to France in the following January. In this seat of war he took part in several engagements, including the Battles of the Somme, Ypres, Arras, Cambrai, La Bassée, and Lille. He was demobilised in March 1919, and holds the General Service and Victory Medals. 45, Naylor St., Oldham Rd., Manchester.   Z11076

SARSON, P., Private, R.M.L.I.
He volunteered in November 1914, and in the following year was drafted to the Dardanelles, where he took part in much heavy fighting at Suvla Bay, and Chunuk Bair. After the Evacuation of the Gallipoli Peninsula he proceeded to France, and fought at the Battles of Albert, the Somme, Arras, Ypres,

and Vimy Ridge. Whilst acting as a stretcher bearer on the Arras sector, he was unfortunately killed in action in April 1917. He was entitled to the 1914–15 Star, and the General Service and Victory Medals.
"He joined the great white company of valiant souls."
27, Copper Street, Rochdale, Manchester.   Z11079

SATTIN, L., Private, Royal Fusiliers.
He joined in February 1916, and in the following year proceeded to Egypt, where he served for a time at Alexandria and Cairo. Later he took part in many engagements in Palestine in the Jordan Valley, but was unfortunately taken ill with fever and invalided to Alexandria. He returned home and was demobilised in February 1919, holding the General Service and Victory Medals. 62, Downing St., Ardwick, Manchester. Z9775–6A

SAUNDERS, J., Bombardier, R.G.A.
He volunteered in August 1914, and underwent a period of training prior to his being drafted to France. Whilst in this theatre of war he took part in several engagements, including the Battles of the Somme, Albert and Ypres, and was wounded in action in July 1916. He was discharged in October 1918 on compassionate grounds, and holds the General Service and Victory Medals.
1, Heelis Street, Rochdale Road, Manchester.   Z11080

SAUNDERS, J., Private, 20th Lancashire Fusiliers.
He volunteered in May 1915, and after his training was engaged on duties of an important nature with his unit at various stations. Owing to medical unfitness, he was unable to secure his transfer to a theatre of war, and in December of the same year was invalided out of the Service.
171, Thornton Street, Manchester.   Z9355

SAUNDERS, R. D., Pioneer, R.E.
Volunteering in August 1915, he crossed to France in the next month, and was engaged on important duties in connection with operations on the Somme, at Passchendaele and Cambrai. He did valuable work until October 1916, when in consequence of ill-health, he was invalided home and discharged. He holds the 1914–15 Star, and the General Service and Victory Medals.
3, Alfred Street, Collyhurst, Manchester.   Z9354

SAVAGE, J., Rifleman, 1st Rifle Brigade.
He volunteered in September 1914, and in July of the following year, was drafted to the Western Front, where he took part in the Battles of Loos and Vimy Ridge, and was wounded in action on the Somme in August 1916. He rejoined his unit, however, on his recovery, and fought in the Battles of the Ancre, and Ypres, and other engagements, and was wounded at Arras in May 1917, and at Cambrai in November of that year. Invalided home, he was for a time in hospital, before being discharged as medically unfit for further service in February 1919. He holds the 1914–15 Star, and the General Service and Victory Medals.
204, Morton Street, Longsight, Manchester.   Z8013

SAVAGE, W., Private, King's (Liverpool Regiment).
He joined in August 1916, and in the following month was drafted overseas. During his service on the Western Front, he took part in the Battles of the Ancre, Arras, Ypres, Cambrai, the Somme (II), Bapaume, and Havrincourt. He was demobilised in October 1919, and holds the General Service and Victory Medals.
38, Beaumont Street, Beswick, Manchester.   Z11081

SAXBY, H., Private, King's (Liverpool Regiment).
Two months after joining in June 1916, he proceeded to the Western Front, where he saw severe fighting in various sectors and took part in engagements at Vimy Ridge, Lens, and many other places. He was for six months in hospital, suffering from heart failure, and afterwards served with the Army of Occupation in Germany. He finally returned home for demobilisation in November 1919, and holds the General Service and Victory Medals.
32, Crofton Street, Rusholme, Manchester.   Z8014

SAXON, A., Bombardier, R.G.A.
Volunteering in January 1915, he proceeded to the Western Front on completing four months' training, and there took part in the Battles of Hill 60, Loos, Vermelles, the Ancre, Vimy Ridge, and Cambrai, and other important engagements. He died gloriously on the Field of Battle on the Lys, in April 1918, and was buried at Doullens. He was entitled to the 1914–15 Star, and the General Service and Victory Medals.
"And doubtless he went in splendid company."
37, Sawley Street, Beswick, Manchester.   Z7963–4C

SAXON, G., Private, 2/8th Manchester Regiment.
He re-enlisted in December 1914, and was retained at various stations, where he was engaged on duties of a highly important nature. Being over age for active service, he was unable to obtain his transfer to a theatre of war, but did much useful work with his unit until October 1918, when he was invalided from the Army. He holds the Egyptian Medal and Khedive's Bronze Star, and the Queen's South African Medal (with four bars). 6, Brunswick St., Hulme, Manchester.   Z8017

SAXON, J., Gunner, R.F.A.
After joining in June 1915, he underwent a period of training prior to being drafted to the Western Front in July of the following year. Whilst in this theatre of war, he took part in many important engagements, including the Battles of the Somme, Arras, Bullecourt, Ypres and Passchendaele, fought also in the Retreat and Advance of 1918, and was gassed at Cambrai in November 1917. He was demobilised in March 1919, and holds the General Service and Victory Medals.
31, Queen's Street, Higher Ardwick, Manchester.　　Z8015

SAXON, R., Private, 11th Lancashire Fusiliers.
He volunteered in January 1915, and later in the same year was drafted to France. There he took part in several engagements, including those at Ploegsteert Wood, La Boiselle (where he was first wounded), Armentières, Ypres (III), Messines Ridge, the Somme (II), and Kemmel, and was again wounded. As a result, he was invalided home, and finally discharged in May 1918 as medically unfit for further duty. He holds the 1914–15 Star, and the General Service and Victory Medals.
36, Edensor Street, Beswick, Manchester.　　Z11082

SAXON, T., Gunner, R.G.A.
Having enlisted in September 1907, he was already in the Army when war was declared in August 1914, and was shortly afterwards drafted to India. There he was engaged on important duties as a range-finder at Bombay and various other stations, and rendered very valuable services with his Battery. He was still serving in India in 1920, and holds the General Service and Victory Medals.
37, Sandey Street, Beswick, Manchester.　　Z7963–4A

SAXON, W. J., Private, 23rd Manchester Regiment.
He volunteered in January 1915, and twelve months later proceeded to France, where he saw severe fighting in various sectors of the Front. He took part in many important engagements during the Somme Offensive of 1916, and afterwards served through the Battles of Arras, Bullecourt, Ypres, and Passchendaele. He was demobilised in February 1919, and holds the General Service and Victory Medals.
104, Granville Place, Ancoats, Manchester.　　Z8016

SAXTON, J. W., Gunner, R.G.A.
He volunteered in September 1914, and whilst stationed on the South Coast was engaged on important anti-submarine duties. In 1916 he was released from the Army for work of National importance, and, employed in the manufacture of "T.N.T." explosives, rendered valuable services. Later recalled to the Colours, he was stationed on the East Coast until demobilised in February 1919.
19, Taylor Street, Gorton, Manchester.　　Z11083

SCARLETT, L., Private, R.A.M.C.
Volunteering in November 1915, he was quickly drafted to the Western Front and took an active part in the heavy fighting at Loos and Albert early in 1916. Later he served at the Battles of the Somme, Arras, Vimy Ridge, Ypres(III), Cambrai, the Lys, Ypres (IV), and the Sambre, and in other important engagements during the Retreat and Advance of 1918. After the cessation of hostilities, he proceeded to Germany with the Army of Occupation, and was eventually demobilised in June 1919, holding the 1914–15 Star, and the General Service and Victory Medals.
75, Henry Street, Ardwick, Manchester.　　Z11950

SCHAFER, F. W., Driver, R.A.S.C. (M.T.)
Volunteering in June 1915, he was drafted to the Western Front in November of that year, and was there engaged in conveying food and ammunition to the forward areas. He was present at the Battles of Albert, the Somme, Arras, Messines, and Ypres, and many other engagements in various sectors. He was invalided from the Army in November 1917, and holds the 1914–15 Star, and the General Service and Victory Medals.
37, Parkfield Avenue, Rusholme, Manchester.　　TZ8018

SCHELDT, E. G., Private, Middlesex Regiment.
He joined in December 1916, and was retained on important duties in England until January 1918, when he was drafted to the Western Front. There, attached to the Labour Corps, he was engaged on important duties on the lines of communication at Cambrai, Arras, Bapaume, Havrincourt, and Le Cateau, and also took an active part in the Retreat and Advance of 1918. He was demobilised in May 1919, and holds the General Service and Victory Medals.
6, St. Saviour Street, Chorlton-on-Medlock, Manchester. Z8019

SCHOFIELD, C., Private, 8th Manchester Regiment.
After volunteering in September 1915, he was engaged on important duties at various stations in England until December of the following year. He was then drafted to India, and was there engaged on garrison duties at Singapore, Allahabad, and elsewhere, being medically unfit for active service. He afterwards served in China, and finally returned home for demobilisation in February 1920, holding the General Service and Victory Medals.
26, Lord Street, Openshaw, Manchester.　　Z8020

SCHOFIELD, A. E. (M.M.), Sergt., 7th Manchester Rgt.
Volunteering in January 1915, he was drafted to Gallipoli in the following April, and there, after taking part in the Landing at Cape Helles, fought in the Battles of Krithia, and at Suvla Bay. On the Evacuation of the Peninsula, he was transferred to the Western Front, where he served through the Battles of Albert, Vermelles, the Somme, Arras, Ypres, and Cambrai, and also took part in the Retreat and Advance of 1918. He was awarded the Military Medal for conspicuous gallantry and devotion to duty displayed in the Field near the Selle in October 1918, and holds also the 1914–15 Star, and the General Service and Victory Medals. He was demobilised in February 1919.
14, Salisbury Street, Moss Side, Manchester.　　Z8022

SCHOFIELD, H., Pte., 5th (Royal Irish) Lancers.
Having enlisted in July 1909, he was drafted to the Western Front immediately on the outbreak of war in August 1914, and there took part in the Battle of, and Retreat from, Mons. He also fought in the Battles of the Marne, the Aisne, La Bassée, Ypres, Neuve Chapelle, Hill 60, Loos, the Somme, Arras, Bullecourt, and Passchendaele, and was wounded in action at Cambrai in November 1917. Invalided home, he was finally discharged, as medically unfit for further service in December 1918, and holds the Mons Star, and the General Service and Victory Medals.
37, Gregory Street, West Gorton, Manchester.　　Z8021

SCHOFIELD, J. A., Private, Monmouthshire Regt.
He joined in May 1916, and after a period of training was engaged for a time on coastal defence. In May 1918 he proceeded to France and took part in the second Battle of the Somme, and in the Retreat and Advance of 1918. Later he served on the General Headquarters Staff at Boulogne until his demobilisation in October 1919. He holds the General Service and Victory Medals.
15, Abbey Field Street, Openshaw, Manchester.　　Z11084–5

SCHOFIELD, W., Private, 1/10th King's (Liverpool Regt.) and R.A.S.C.
He joined in September 1916, and after three months' training was drafted to the Western Front, where he saw much service in the Somme and other sectors until gassed at St. Julien, and invalided home. After his recovery he served with the Horse Transport Section of the Royal Army Service Corps at Blackheath, returning to France in November 1918. He was demobilised in December 1919, and holds the General Service and Victory Medals.
9, Shrewbridge Street, West Gorton, Manchester.　　Z8023

SCHOFIELD, W. H., Pte., Royal Welch Fusiliers.
He joined in March 1917, and in February of the following year was drafted to Egypt, where he was engaged on important garrison duties, being medically unfit for active service. He served at Sollum, Alexandria, and various other stations in this seat of operations until his return home for demobilisation in April 1919. He holds the General Service and Victory Medals. 17, Norway Street, Ardwick, Manchester.　　Z8028

SCHOFIELD, T., Private, South Wales Borderers.
He joined in May 1918, and after completing a period of training, served at various stations, where he was engaged on duties of great importance. Being over age for active service, he was not successful in obtaining his transfer overseas, but did much useful work with his unit until December 1918, when he was demobilised.
19, Bonsall Street, Hulme, Manchester.　　Z8024

SCHOLES, J., Private, 18th Manchester Regiment.
He volunteered in September 1914, and was retained on important duties at various stations in England until 1916. He was then sent to the Western Front, where, after seeing much severe fighting, he was wounded in action and blown up by the explosion of a shell in May 1916. He was invalided home, but returned to France, however, on his recovery in January 1918, and was there engaged in guarding prisoners of war at Péronne. He was demobilised in March 1919, and holds the General Service and Victory Medals.
11, Granville Place, Ancoats, Manchester.　　Z8029

SCHOLES, J., Private, K.O. (R. Lancaster Regt.)
Volunteering in August 1914, he was drafted to the Western Front in September of the following year, and there took part in the Battle of Loos, and many other important engagements. He was afterwards transferred to Salonika, and there saw much severe fighting on the Doiran and Vardar fronts until the cessation of hostilities. Returning home in March 1919, he was demobilised in August of the following year, and holds the 1914–15 Star, and the General Service and Victory Medals.
21, Hampton Place, Erskine Street, Hulme, Manchester.TZ8025

SCHOLES, J. W., Private, 21st Manchester Regt.
After volunteering in December 1914, he underwent a period of training prior to being drafted to Salonika in June 1916. There he took part in the re-capture of Monastir, and in much severe fighting on the Doiran front until July 1917, when he was transferred to Egypt. He proceeded thence into Palestine and was present at the Capture of Jerusalem, Jericho, and Tripoli, and served also in the Offensive of September 1918, under General Allenby. He was demobilised on his return home in June 1919, and holds the General Service and Victory Medals. 3, Heron Street, Hulme, Manchester.　　Z8026

SCHOLES, L., Private, 16th (The Queen's) Lancers.
He volunteered in September 1915, and after a period of training was engaged at various stations on important duties with his unit. He was unable to obtain a transfer overseas owing to his being medically unfit, but rendered valuable services until his discharge in December 1916.
24, Beecher Street, Queen's Park, Manchester. Z11561B

SCHOLES, T., Private, 1st Manchester Regiment.
Having enlisted in February 1911, he was already serving in India when war broke out in August 1914, and was immediately drafted to the Western Front. There he saw severe fighting in various sectors, took part in the Battles of Givenchy, Ypres, and Neuve Chapelle, and many other important engagements, and was wounded in action at Ypres in July 1917. He was sent home and invalided from the Army in September of that year, and holds the 1914 Star, and the General Service and Victory Medals.
7, William Street, Hulme, Manchester. Z8027

SCOTT, A., Sergeant, R.A.S.C. (M.T.)
Volunteering in September 1914, he was drafted to France in June of the following year, and was there severely wounded whilst conveying ammunition to the forward areas in November 1915. He was for a time in hospital in Scotland, and after his recovery was retained on important duties in England, where he rendered valuable services until invalided from the Army in December 1918. He holds the 1914-15 Star, and the General Service and Victory Medals.
115, Broadfield Road, Moss Side, Manchester. TZ8030

SCOTT, A., Corporal, 14th King's (Liverpool Regt.)
He volunteered in August 1914, and on completing his training in the following January was drafted to France, where he took part in the Battles of Ypres, the Somme, Nieuport, Albert, and Messines. Later he was transferred to Mesopotamia, and saw much fighting at Kut and Amara. He returned home, and was demobilised in April 1919, and holds the 1914-15 Star, and the General Service and Victory Medals.
42, Clare Street, Chorlton-on-Medlock, Manchester. Z11951

SCOTT, A., Gunner, R.F.A., and Pte., Labour Corps.
Having enlisted in November 1913, he was already in the Army when war was declared in August of the following year, and six months later was drafted to Egypt. There he was stationed on the Suez Canal until August 1915, and then served for a time in England prior to proceeding to the Western Front, where he was twice wounded in action during the Somme Offensive of 1916, and admitted to hospital at Le Havre. Later he fought at Messines, Cambrai, and in other sectors until invalided home suffering from shell-shock. On his recovery he served with the Labour Corps at Shrewsbury until his demobilisation in February 1919, and holds the 1914-15 Star, and the General Service and Victory Medals.
18, Carver Street, Hulme, Manchester. Z8033

SCOTT, A., Private, Labour Corps, and Sapper, R.E.
He volunteered in 1915, and on completing his training later in the same year was drafted to the Western Front, where he served in various sectors. He was engaged on duties of great importance whilst in this theatre of war, and finally returned home, and was discharged as medically unfit for further service in November 1917. He holds the 1914-15 Star, and the General Service and Victory Medals.
9, Caygill St., Chorlton-on-Medlock, Manchester. X1344A

SCOTT, G., Private, 1st Manchester Regiment.
He volunteered at the outbreak of war in August 1914, and in March of the following year was drafted to the Western Front. Whilst in this theatre of war he saw much severe fighting, and took part in the Battles of Neuve Chapelle, Ypres, Loos, the Somme, and Bullecourt, and many minor engagements in various sectors. Demobilised in March 1919, he holds the 1914-15 Star, and the General Service and Victory Medals.
9, Oak Street, Hulme, Manchester. TZ8031

SCOTT, J., Bandsman, Connaught Rangers.
He volunteered in August 1915, at the age of fourteen years, and was engaged on important duties with his unit at various home stations for about three years, during which time he rendered valuable services. Later he was drafted to India, where, in 1920, he was still serving.
25, Brown Street, Ancoats, Manchester. TZ11927B

SCOTT, J., Private, South Lancashire Regiment.
He volunteered in August 1914, and on completing his training in the following year was drafted to Mesopotamia, where he took part in the Relief of Kut, and the Capture of Baghdad, and many other important engagements. Invalided home, suffering from enteric fever, he afterwards proceeded to the Western Front in time to serve through the Retreat of March 1918. He fell fighting at Messines in May of that year. He was entitled to the 1914-15 Star, and the General Service and Victory Medals.
"His memory is cherished with pride."
40, Gorton Road, Openshaw, Manchester. TZ8032

SCOTT, R., Private, 3rd Essex Regiment.
He joined in January 1918, and after a period of training was drafted to the Western Front in August of that year, and was there severely wounded in action at Epéhy Wood in the following month. Invalided home, he was in hospital for a time at Southport before being discharged as medically unfit for further service in March 1919. He holds the General Service and Victory Medals.
19, Welbeck St., Chorlton-on-Medlock, Manchester. Z8034B

SCOTT, R. E., Gunner, R.F.A.
He joined in March 1916, and after his training served on important duties with his unit at various stations. He was not successful in obtaining his transfer overseas before the close of hostilities, but nevertheless did valuable work until demobilised in November 1919.
13, Dennison Street, Rusholme, Manchester. TZ8400B

SCOTT, W., Private, 17th Manchester Regiment.
Joining in October 1916, he proceeded to the Western Front three months later, and there saw much severe fighting in various sectors. After taking part in the Battles of Arras, Ypres, and Passchendaele, and other engagements, he was taken prisoner at St. Quentin in the Retreat of March 1918, and held in captivity in Germany until after the cessation of hostilities. He was demobilised in November 1919, and holds the General Service and Victory Medals.
19, Welbeck Street, Chorlton-on-Medlock, Manchester. Z8034A

SCOTT, W., A. B., Royal Naval Reserve.
He joined in February 1918, and after a period of training at Devonport was posted to H.M.S. "Berwick," and served in the North Sea. He was engaged on important and dangerous mine-sweeping duties, and also saw service on board H.M.S. "Pitchley." He was demobilised in October 1919, and holds the General Service Medal (with two clasps), and the Victory Medal.
5, Metcalf Street, Miles Platting, Manchester. Z11577

SCOTT, W. H., Private, R.A.M.C.
He joined in June 1916, and in the following year was drafted to the Western Front. There he was transferred to the Labour Corps, and engaged on many important duties, but took an active part in the heavy fighting at Ypres, Cambrai, the Somme (II), and in the Retreat and Advance of 1918. He was demobilised in December 1919, and holds the General Service and Victory Medals.
101, Cross Street, Bradford, Manchester. Z11086

SCRAFTON, T., Gunner, R.G.A.
Volunteering in August 1915, he was drafted to the East two months later, and there took part in the first Landing at Salonika, where he saw much severe fighting on the Doiran and Struma fronts, and at Monastir. He was for a time in hospital in this seat of operations, suffering from malaria, and was wounded in action in December 1916. Later he was transferred to Egypt, whence he proceeded into Palestine, and served at the Capture of Jerusalem and Jericho, and in the engagements at Haifa and Aleppo. He was demobilised on his return home in October 1919, and holds the 1914-15 Star, and the General Service and Victory Medals.
47, Chipping Street, Longsight, Manchester. Z8035

SCREETON, J. F., Private, R.A.O.C.
He joined in January 1917, and after undergoing a period of training, served at various stations, where he was engaged on duties of a highly important nature. He was not successful in obtaining his transfer to a theatre of war, but, nevertheless, rendered valuable services with his Company until February 1919, when he was demobilised.
11, Dalton Street, Chorlton-on-Medlock, Manchester. Z8036

SCULLY, J., Private, 12th Sherwood Foresters.
He joined in July 1917, and in the following January proceeded to the Western Front. In this theatre of war he took part in the Battles of the Marne (II), and Cambrai (II), and in other important engagements during the Retreat and Advance of 1918. After hostilities ceased he remained in France on important duties with the Labour Corps, in the prison camps at Abbeville until January 1920, when he was demobilised. He holds the General Service and Victory Medals.
77, Cowcill Street, Hulme, Manchester. Z11952

SCULLY, M., Private, 8th South Staffordshire Regt.
He volunteered in February 1915, and in the following October sailed for Gallipoli, where he took part in various operations. After the Evacuation of the Peninsula he was sent to Egypt, where he served in the Canal zone until June 1916. He was then drafted to France, and fought in the Somme Offensive, in the course of which he was wounded in July 1916, and sent home on account of his injuries. After treatment at Cambridge he returned to the Western Front in the following October, and drafted to Italy, shortly afterwards saw much service in that theatre of war. He was demobilised in February 1919, and holds the 1914-15 Star, and the General Service and Victory Medals.
77, Cowcill St., Chorlton-on-Medlock, Manchester. Z9356

SEAL, J., Gunner, R.G.A.
He joined in March 1916, and was shortly afterwards drafted to the Western Front. In this theatre of war he took part in much heavy fighting on the Somme, at Beaucourt, Arras, Vimy Ridge, Ypres, Cambrai, and in the Retreat and Advance of 1918. He contracted influenza, and was in hospital for some time, but on his recovery returned home and was demobilised in February 1919. He holds the General Service and Victory Medals.
3, Halton Street, Hulme, Manchester. Z8037

SEAL, W. T., Private, Lancashire Fusiliers.

Joining in February 1916, he was drafted overseas two months later. Whilst on the Western Front he saw much fighting at Albert, Vermelles, Vimy Ridge, the Somme, Arras, Ypres, Passchendaele, and Cambrai, where he was taken prisoner in November 1917. He was held in captivity in Germany for about twelve months, being released after the Armistice, he returned home. He was demobilised in November 1918, and holds the General Service and Victory Medals.
8, Pickering Street, Hulme, Manchester.   TZ8038

SEARLE, R., Corporal, R.A.F.

He joined in August 1916, and underwent a period of training prior to his being drafted to France. There he was engaged with the 19th Squadron on duties which demanded a high degree of technical skill. He was injured in the hand by a propeller, and was in hospital for some time. He was demobilised in March 1919, and holds the General Service and Victory Medals.
91, Temple Street, Chorlton-on-Medlock, Manchester. X8039

SEARSON, J. (D.C.M.), Sergt., K.O. (Royal Lancaster Regiment).

Having previously served in the South African War, during which he was awarded the Distinguished Conduct Medal for conspicuous bravery and devotion to duty in the Field, he rejoined in September 1914, and proceeded to France in the following July. He saw much fighting at Loos, St. Eloi, Albert, and Vimy Ridge, and was unfortunately killed in action on the Somme in July 1916. He was entitled to the 1914-15 Star, and the General Service and Victory Medals.
" Great deeds cannot die :
They with the sun and moon renew their light for ever."
35, Brunswick Street, Hulme, Manchester.   Z8040B

SEARSON, R., Corporal, K.O. (R. Lancaster Regt.)

He was mobilised in August 1914, and immediately drafted to France where he saw much fighting at Mons, on the Marne, the Aisne, and at Neuve Chapelle, and La Bassée, where he was badly wounded in 1915. As a result he was invalided home, and on his recovery, was retained on important duties in Plymouth until discharged in March 1919. He holds the Mons Star, and the General Service and Victory Medals.
35, Brunswick Street, Hulme, Manchester.   Z8040A

SEATON, E., Corporal, 9th East Lancashire Regt.

Volunteering in September 1914, he was drafted overseas in the following year. During his service in Egypt he was engaged on important duties at Alexandria, Cairo, and Kantara, until January 1918, when he contracted malarial fever. As a result he was invalided to hospital, and finally discharged in February 1919. He holds the 1914-15 Star, and the General Service and Victory Medals.
7, Copestick Street, Ancoats, Manchester.   Z11087

SEDDON, J. H., Private, 19th Manchester Regt.

Volunteering in September 1914, he crossed to France in December of the following year, and saw heavy fighting at Loos, Arras, Vimy Ridge, Bullecourt, Ypres, Passchendaele, and the Somme. He was wounded at Havrincourt in April 1918, and sent home owing to his injuries, received treatment at Brighton. Discharged in September 1918, as medically unfit for further service, he holds the 1914-15 Star, and the General Service and Victory Medals.
34, Temple St., Chorlton-on-Medlock, Manchester.   Z9357

SEDDON, W. T., Private, King's (Liverpool Regt.)

He volunteered in February 1915, and three months later was drafted to France. Here he took part in engagements at Festubert, Loos, Vermelles, on the Somme, and at Arras. He returned home on leave, but unfortunately contracted influenza and died in hospital in July 1918. He was entitled to the 1914-15 Star, and the General Service and Victory Medals.
" His memory is cherished with pride."
33, Matthew Street, Ardwick, Manchester.   Z8041

SEDGWICK, E., Private, 6th Manchester Regt.

He volunteered in August 1914, and later in the same year was drafted to Egypt, where he took part in engagements on the Suez Canal. Later he was transferred to the Dardanelles and saw much heavy fighting at the Landing at Suvla Bay, where he was wounded and invalided to Alexandria. On his recovery he was again in action in Egypt at Agagia, Sollum and Romani, but, in December 1916, was sent to the Western Front. There he fought at the Battles of the Ancre, at Arras, Vimy Ridge, Ypres (III), Passchendaele, Lens, Cambrai, the Somme (II), and in the Retreat and Advance of 1918. He was demobilised in February 1919, and holds the 1914-15 Star, and the General Service and Victory Medals.
24, Lorne Street, Moss Side, Manchester.   Z11088

SELBY, G. D., Private, Cheshire Regiment.

He joined in July 1916, and in the following September proceeded to Salonika. In this seat of operations he took part in much fighting on the Doiran and Struma fronts. He

contracted malarial fever, and was invalided home and finally discharged in February 1919. He holds the General Service and Victory Medals.
21, Elton Street, Chorlton-on-Medlock, Manchester. Z7962B

SELLARS, A., Private, 2nd Manchester Regiment.

He joined in March 1918, immediately on attaining eighteen years of age, and after a period of training was drafted to the Western Front. During his service in this seat of war he was chiefly engaged in bringing prisoners from various sectors to the Base. He was demobilised in October 1919, and holds the General Service and Victory Medals.
2, Lind Street, Ancoats, Manchester.   Z11089

SELLARS, G., Corporal, 9th Black Watch.

Volunteering in June 1915, he was drafted to France three months later. Whilst on the Western Front he took part in much fighting at Loos, Albert the Somme, Arras, Ypres, Cambrai and in the Retreat and Advance of 1918, and was wounded in action. Later he proceeded to Mesopotamia with the Machine Gun Corps, and took part in engagements at Baghdad against the Kurds. He returned home, and was demobilised in November 1919, holding the 1914-15 Star, and the General Service and Victory Medals.
5, Guy Street, Ardwick, Manchester.   Z8043

SELLARS, W. J., Corporal, King's (Liverpool Regt.)

He joined in April 1916, and in the following August proceeded to the Western Front. There he took part in the Battles of the Somme and Ypres, and was wounded in action and consequently invalided to the Base. On his recovery he returned to his unit and saw much fighting during the Retreat and Advance of 1918. After hostilities ceased, he was sent to Egypt, where he served until his demobilisation in November 1919. He holds the General Service and Victory Medals. 82, Robert St., West Gorton, Manchester. Z8042

SEMMENS, W., A.B., Royal Navy.

He volunteered in June 1915, and after a period of training proceeded to the North Sea on board H.M. Mine-sweeper "Eclipse." He was engaged on important and dangerous mine-sweeping duties until 1917, when he unfortunately met with an accident which resulted in his discharge in June 1917, as medically unfit for further duty. He holds the 1914-15 Star, and the General Service and Victory Medals.
11, Newton Street, Hulme, Manchester.   Z8044

SENIOR, C. B., Q.M.S., Essex Regiment.

He joined in March 1916, and was engaged on important duties with his unit at various stations. He was unable to obtain a transfer overseas, but rendered valuable services. On March 6th, 1919, he unfortunately died from the effects of pneumonia.
" His memory is cherished with pride."
15, Derby Street, Hulme, Manchester.   Z8045

SENIOR, J. Private, 13th Manchester Regt.

He volunteered in September 1914, and was shortly afterwards drafted to the Western Front, where he played a prominent part in the Battles of Neuve Chapelle, Ypres, Loos, St. Eloi, the Somme, the Ancre, Arras, Vimy Ridge, Lens, the Selle and the Sambre. He was demobilised in February 1919, and holds the 1914 Star, and the General Service and Victory Medals. 7, Major St., Ardwick, Manchester.   Z8046

SENIOR, R., Private, 16th Manchester Regiment.

Volunteering in January 1915, he was drafted overseas later in the same year. Whilst on the Western Front he took part in the Battles of Loos, Vimy Ridge, the Somme and Arras, where he was badly wounded in May 1917. In consequence he was invalided home, but on his recovery returned to France and fought at Ypres (III), Cambrai, the Somme (II), and was again wounded and sent home, being finally discharged in July 1918 as medically unfit for further duty. He holds the 1914-15 Star, and the General Service and Victory Medals. 9, Gay Street, Jackson Street, Hulme, Manchester. Z8047

SENIOR, W., L/Cpl., E. Lancashire Regt. and R.E.

He volunteered in June 1915, and was engaged on home service duties until February 1917, when he proceeded to the Western Front. In this theatre of war he acted as a Driver and did excellent work with the transport in the forward areas and during the Retreat and Advance of 1918. Returning to England, he was demobilised in March 1919, and holds the General Service and Victory Medals.
12, Dalton Street, Hulme, Manchester.   TX8695

SERMON, G., Sapper, R.E.

He joined in March 1917, and sailing for Salonika three months later, served there for upwards of three years. During this period he was engaged with his unit in the Balkans, where he did good work whilst operations were in progress and was present at several engagements, including the Battles of the Vardar (I and II). Retained on special duties in the Balkans after the Armistice, he returned home in November 1919, and was demobilised a month later. He holds the General Service and Victory Medals.
93, Dale Street, Miles Platting, Manchester.   TZ9358A

SERMON, S., Private, Labour Corps.
Volunteering in October 1915, he was sent to France in the following January, and was engaged on road making and the construction of trenches. Transferred to the King's (Liverpool Regiment) in 1916, he fought in the Battles of the Somme, Arras and Ypres, and was wounded. On recovery he was in action at Cambrai and in numerous engagements in the Retreat and Advance of 1918, and after the Armistice proceeded with the Army of Occupation into Germany. Returning home he was demobilised in October 1919, and holds the General Service and Victory Medals.
81, Dale Street, Miles Platting, Manchester.   Z9359

SERVAN, A., Sergt., 2nd Manchester Regiment.
He was mobilised in August 1914, and immediately drafted to France. There he took a conspicuous part in the Battle of Mons and in the subsequent Retreat and the Battles of Le Cateau, the Marne, the Aisne, La Bassée, Ypres (I), Neuve Chapelle, Hill 60 and Ypres (II). He suffered from rheumatism and bronchitis, and in consequence was invalided home. In April 1916 he was discharged as medically unfit for further service, and holds the Mons Star, and the General Service and Victory Medals.
38, Trafford Street, Hulme, Manchester.   Z8048

SEVILLE, J. W., Sergt., King's (Liverpool Regt.)
He volunteered in August 1914, and was shortly afterwards drafted to France. In this theatre of war he served with distinction in several engagements, including those on the Somme and at Arras and Ypres, being twice wounded and gassed in action. Later he was employed on important duties in charge of prisoners of war at Boulogne. He was demobilised in February 1919, and holds the 1914 Star, and the General Service and Victory Medals.
21, Mount Street, Hulme, Manchester.   Z8049

SEWELL, A., Private, York and Lancaster Regt.
He volunteered in September 1915, and two months later was drafted to France, where he took part in several engagements, including that of St. Eloi. He made the supreme sacrifice, being killed in action at Vermelles in May 1916. He was entitled to the 1914-15 Star, and the General Service and Victory Medals.
"A valiant Soldier, with undaunted heart, he breasted life's last hill."
13, Fernley Street, Moss Side, Manchester.   Z8050

SHAILE, F., Rifleman, Rifle Brigade.
He volunteered in 1915, and later in the year proceeded to France. There, after fighting at Ypres, St. Eloi, Festubert, Albert, Vimy Ridge and Armentières, he was unluckily killed on August 16th, during the Somme Offensive of 1916. He was entitled to the 1914-15 Star, and the General Service and Victory Medals.
"Great deeds cannot die."
5, School Street, Manchester.   Z11448A

SHALLIKER, R., Private, Labour Corps.
He joined in March 1916, and after a period of training proceeded to France and was attached to the R.E. He was engaged on important duties trench digging, wiring and making gun positions at Arras, Villiers-au-Bois, Douai, Condé, Bertincourt, Gouzeaucourt, Haplincourt, Fins, Beauvillers and Gommecourt. He was demobilised in July 1919, and holds the General Service and Victory Medals.
7, Queen Street, Hulme, Manchester.   Z8051

SHALLIKER, S., Sapper, R.E.
Volunteering in March 1915, he proceeded overseas later in the same year. During his service on the Western Front he took part in engagements at St. Eloi, Albert, Vimy Ridge and on the Somme, where he was badly wounded in July 1916. As a result, he was invalided home, and on his recovery was retained on important duties until his demobilisation in February 1919. He holds the 1914-15 Star, and the General Service and Victory Medals.
19, Ann Street, Hulme, Manchester.   Z8052

SHALLOW, W., Pte., 12th King's (Liverpool Regt.)
He joined in February 1917, and underwent a period of training prior to his being drafted overseas. Whilst on the Western Front he took part in the Battles of the Somme (II), Arras, Vimy Ridge and Havrincourt and in the Retreat and Advance of 1918. He was also present at the entry into Mons on Armistice Day. He was demobilised in March 1919, and holds the General Service and Victory Medals.   Z8053
36, Higher Chatham Street, Chorlton-on-Medlock, Manchester.

SHANN, W., Private, 1st Manchester Regiment.
He volunteered at the outbreak of hostilities in August 1914, and was shortly afterwards drafted to France, where after a very short period of service he was unfortunately killed in action in the Battle of La Bassée on October 19th, 1914. He was entitled to the 1914 Star, and the General Service and Victory Medals.
"His life for his Country."
6, Virginia Street, Rochdale, Manchester.   Z11090

SHARKEY, W., Private, R.A.S.C.
He joined in March 1917, and after a period of training was drafted to Palestine. There he took part in many important engagements, including the Battles of Gaza and the capture

of Jerusalem. He returned to England and was demobilised in March 1920, holding the General Service and Victory Medals.
16, Haigh Street, West Gorton, Manchester.   Z11091

SHARKY, J., Private, 18th Manchester Regiment.
Joining in February 1916, he was drafted a few months afterwards to France. At once participating in heavy fighting on the Somme, he was wounded there in July 1916. He subsequently fought at Passchendaele Ridge, Guillemont, High Wood, Cambrai and in many sectors during the Retreat and Advance of 1918. Returning home after the Armistice, he was demobilised in January 1919, and holds the General Service and Victory Medals.
6, Fielden Street, Oldham Road, Manchester.   Z11818

SHARMAN, G. W. (M.M.), Sergeant, R.G.A.
He joined in March 1916, and in the following August was drafted to the Western Front, where he played a prominent part in the Battles of Beaumont-Hamel, Beaucourt, the Ancre, Arras, Bullecourt, Messines, Ypres (III), Passchendaele and Cambrai, and was gassed in action. He was awarded the Military Medal for conspicuous bravery and devotion to duty in bringing in wounded under heavy shell-fire at Passchendaele. Demobilised in January 1919, he also holds the General Service and Victory Medals.
17, Cadogan Street, Moss Side, Manchester.   Z8054

SHARP, G. R., Private, King's (Liverpool Regt.)
He volunteered in September 1915, and was retained on important duties at home stations until January 1917, when he was sent to France. After taking part in heavy fighting on the Somme and the Ancre and in the Battles of Vimy Ridge and Ypres (III), he was invalided to England with trench fever. In August 1917 he was discharged as medically unfit for further service, and holds the General Service and Victory Medals.
73, Hinckley Street, Bradford, Manchester.   Z8057

SHARP, W., Private, 2/9th Lancashire Fusiliers.
Volunteering in March 1915, he was later transferred to the 2/8th Manchester Regiment, and was engaged on important duties at various stations. He rendered valuable services with his unit until September 1916, when, owing to a physical disability, he was invalided from the Army.
1, Arthur Street, Gorton, Manchester.   Z8055

SHARP, W., Private, 3rd East Lancashire Regiment.
He volunteered in February 1915, and in the following August was drafted to the Western Front, where he took part in the Battle of Loos and in heavy fighting at La Bassée, Givenchy, Festubert, Neuve Chapelle and Arras. He was badly wounded in action on the Somme in July 1916, and was invalided to hospital at Woolwich. In April 1917 he was discharged as medically unfit for further service, and holds the 1914-15 Star, and the General Service and Victory Medals.
3, Willaston Street, Ardwick, Manchester.   Z8056

SHARPES, S., Gunner, R.F.A.
He volunteered in January 1915, and was retained at home on important duties until May 1916, when he proceeded to the Western Front. In this theatre of war he served with his Battery at Ypres, Arras, Bapaume, Cambrai and in many severe engagements during the Retreat and final Advance in 1918. He remained overseas for some time after the Armistice, and was eventually demobilised in August 1919, holding the General Service and Victory Medals.
10, Shakespeare Street, Bradford, Manchester.   Z11819

SHARPLES, A. W., Driver, R.F.A.
Mobilised in August 1914, he proceeded to the Western Front with the first Expeditionary Force and took part in the Battles of Mons and Le Cateau and in the subsequent Retreat from Mons. He was also in action at the Battles of the Marne, the Aisne, La Bassée, Ypres (I), Neuve Chapelle, Hill 60, Loos, the Somme, Ypres (III), Passchendaele and Cambrai and in the Retreat and Advance of 1918. He received his discharge in February 1919, and holds the Mons Star, and the General Service and Victory Medals.
9, Coach Terrace, Gorton, Manchester.   Z8058

SHARPLES, E.Y., Pte., 1/6th Manchester Rgt.(T.F.)
He volunteered in August 1914, and on completion of his training was sent to the Gallipoli Peninsula, where he took part in the Landing at Cape Helles and in the Battles of Krithia. He was badly wounded in action in June 1915, and was invalided home. After long treatment in hospital he was eventually discharged in September 1918 as medically unfit for further service, and holds the 1914-15 Star, and the General Service and Victory Medals.
82, Exeter Street, Ardwick, Manchester.   Z8060A

SHARPLES, F., Private, Labour Corps.
He joined the 9th S. Lancs. Regiment in January 1917, and after a brief period of training was drafted to the Western Front, where he was badly wounded in action at Arras. On his recovery he rejoined the 9th Cheshire Regiment, but was later transferred to the Labour Corps, owing to the effects of his wounds. He then did consistently good work until his demobilisation in April 1919, and holds the General Service and Victory Medals.
29, Bedford Street, Moss Side, Manchester.   TZ8063

SHARPLES, G., Private, 2/10th Manchester Regt.
He joined in March 1916, and four months later proceeded to the Western Front, where he took part in the Battles of the Somme, the Ancre, Arras, Vimy Ridge, Bullecourt, Ypres (III), the Marne (II), Amiens and Bapaume. He was badly wounded in action at the second Battle of Cambrai in October 1918, and was invalided to hospital in Leeds. On his recovery he was sent to a remount depôt at Sheffield and rendered valuable services there until his demobilisation in September 1919, holding the General Service and Victory Medals.
46, Lower Chatham Street, Chorlton-on Medlock, Manchester.
Z8062

SHARPLES, J., Private, 2nd Lancashire Fusiliers.
He joined in February 1916, and on completion of his training was sent to the Western Front, where he served at the Battle of Arras, and was wounded and taken prisoner. He was held in captivity in Germany and suffered many hardships until the cessation of hostilities. He was demobilised in August 1919, holding the General Service and Victory Medals.
10, Long Street, Ancoats, Manchester. Z11449

SHARPLES, P., Private, K.O. (R. Lancaster Regt.)
Volunteering in August 1915, he was shortly afterwards transferred to the Rifle Brigade and proceeded to Egypt in March 1916. He was then engaged on important clerical duties at Cairo and Alexandria and did consistently good work. Unfortunately he suffered severely from sunstroke, and was in hospital for four months. He holds the General Service and Victory Medals, and was demobilised in February 1920.
82, Exeter Street, Ardwick, Manchester. Z8060B

SHARPLES, W., Private, 2nd Manchester Regt.
He volunteered in January 1916, and in the following May was drafted to Mesopotamia, where he took part in the Battles of Sanni-a-Yat and Kut (I), and was present at the capture of Baghdad and Tekrit. In June 1918 he was transferred to Egypt and was engaged on important garrison duties at Cairo and Alexandria. Demobilised in August 1919, he holds the General Service and Victory Medals.
10, Paris Street, Ancoats, Manchester. Z8059

SHARPLES, W., Driver, R.A.S.C.
He joined in January 1918, and on completion of his training was engaged on special duties with the remount service at various stations in Scotland. He was unsuccessful in obtaining his transfer overseas, but did consistently good work until his demobilisation in December 1919. Z8061
46, Lower Chatham St., Chorlton-on-Medlock, Manchester.

SHAW, A., Private, 1st Lancashire Fusiliers.
He volunteered in September 1914, and a year later was drafted overseas. Serving for a time on the Western Front, he was drafted to Salonika in November 1915, and among other operations in the Balkans was in action in the advance on the Doiran and Struma fronts and at the capture of Monastir. Sent to hospital, owing to illness, he returned to France on recovery in December 1917, and fought in the Battle of Cambrai and at Ypres and other places through the German Offensive and subsequent Allied Advance of 1918. He was demobilised in March 1919, and holds the 1914–15 Star, and the General Service and Victory Medals.
137, Suddell Street, Ancoats, Manchester. Z9360

SHAW, A., Special War Worker.
During the whole period of hostilities, he rendered valuable services on the manufacture of munitions at Messrs. Armstrong and Whitworth's. In March 1919 he joined the Royal Marine Labour Corps and proceeded to France for special work in connection with the repair of the machinery on transport and troopships during the demobilisation period. He was demobilised in December 1919.
49, Lord Street, Openshaw, Manchester. TZ8072

SHAW, A., Corporal, 15th Lancashire Fusiliers.
He volunteered in January 1915, and on completion of his training was engaged on important duties as an Instructor of musketry, bomb-throwing and observation outpost work. Owing to the vital importance of his duties he was not drafted overseas, but rendered valuable services until his demobilisation in September 1919. He then re-enlisted, however, for twelve months special service with a Chinese Labour Corps in France, and was finally demobilised in 1920.
1, Brookside, City Road, Hulme, Manchester. Z8066

SHAW, C., Corporal, 2nd Monmouthshire Regiment.
He joined in July 1916, and after his training rendered valuable services on the clerical staff of the Records Office at Lowestoft. Although unsuccessful in obtaining his transfer overseas, he did consistently good work until his demobilisation in February 1919. 5, Chatsworth Street, Hulme, Manchester. Z8070

SHAW, E., Private, Lancashire Fusiliers.
Volunteering in September 1914, he was sent to France in the following January. Whilst on the Western Front he played an important part in the Battles of Festubert, Givenchy, Loos, the Somme and Ypres (III), where he was badly wounded in action in July 1917. He was invalided home and four months later was discharged as medically unfit for further service, holding the 1914–15 Star, and the General Service and Victory Medals.
2, Wilkinson St., Rochdale Rd., Collyhurst, Manchester. Z11092

SHAW, F., Corporal, Royal Dublin Fusiliers.
Joining in March 1916, he embarked for France in June of the following year and fought in the Battles of Arras, Bullecourt, Ypres and Passchendaele. He fell fighting near Beaumont-Hamel on November 13th, 1917, and lies buried in the British Military Cemetery at Albert. He was entitled to the General Service and Victory Medals.
" A costly sacrifice upon the altar of freedom."
5, Ellesmere Place, Stockport Rd., Longsight, Manchester.
Z8805B

SHAW, F., Sergt., Cheshire Regiment.
He volunteered in September 1914, and first rendered valuable services as an Instructor of recruits. In December 1915, however, he was sent to Gibraltar, where he was engaged on important garrison duties throughout the remaining period of hostilities. He was demobilised in August 1919, and holds the General Service and Victory Medals.
106, Margaret Street, West Gorton, Manchester. Z8065

SHAW, H., Sergt., 8th Manchester Regiment.
Mobilised in August 1914, at the outbreak of war, he immediately proceeded to Egypt, and there served at Alexandria and Cairo. Later he was drafted to the Dardanelles, where he took part in the engagements at Cape Helles, Krithia and Achi Baba. After the Evacuation of the Peninsula, he was invalided to hospital, but, on his recovery, proceeded to France and was engaged on clerical duties at the Record Office in Rouen, until demobilised in April 1919. He holds the 1914–15 Star, and the General Service and Victory Medals.
43, Worth Street, Rochdale Road, Manchester. Z11094

SHAW, H., Driver, R.H.A.
Volunteering in January 1915, he was sent to the Western Front five months later and served in various sectors until the end of the war. During this period he was in action in the Battles of Albert, the Somme, Ypres, Cambrai and in those of the Retreat and Advance of 1918, and entered Mons the day the Armistice was signed. He was demobilised in December 1918, and holds the 1914–15 Star, and the General Service and Victory Medals.
1, Belgrave Street, Newtown Heath, Manchester. Z9698

SHAW, H., Private, 2nd Manchester Regiment.
Volunteering in June 1915, he was sent to France in the following October and saw much severe fighting in various sectors. He was badly wounded in action at the third Battle of Ypres in July 1917, and was invalided to hospital in England. On his recovery he proceeded to Germany with the Army of Occupation and was engaged on special duties guarding prisoners. He was demobilised in November 1919, and holds the 1914–15 Star, and the General Service and Victory Medals.
64, Longridge Street, Longsight, Manchester. Z8074

SHAW, H., Cpl., Duke of Lancaster's Own Dragoons.
He joined the Yeomanry in 1913, and at the outbreak of war in August 1914, was retained on special duties in England and met with a serious accident in September 1915. After serving at the Irish Rebellion in 1916, he proceeded to France in May of that year and first rendered valuable services as a Corporal Shoeing-smith on the Staff of the Director of Remounts. Later he served as a Despatch Rider with the Military Police, and was attached to the 2nd Cavalry Corps. He received his discharge in 1919, and holds the General Service and Victory Medals.
63, Robert St., Chorlton-on-Medlock, Manchester. X8075

SHAW, I., Rifleman, 1st Rifle Brigade.
Called up from the Reserve in August 1914, he immediately proceeded to the Western Front, where he took an important part in the Retreat from Mons and in the Battles of the Marne, the Aisne, La Bassée, Ypres (I) and Neuve Chapelle. He laid down his life for King and Country in the last-named sector on April 1st, 1915, and was entitled to the Mons Star, and the General Service and Victory Medals.
" Nobly striving,
He nobly fell that we might live."
44, Roseberry Street Gorton, Manchester. TZ8073

SHAW, J., Private, and K.O. (R. Lancaster Regt.)
He volunteered in February 1915, and was shortly afterwards drafted to the Western Front. During his short period of service there he took part in the Battle of Hill 60, where he was unfortunately killed in action on May 5th, 1915. He was entitled to the 1914–15 Star, and the General Service and Victory Medals.
" He joined the great white company of valiant souls."
45, Sycamore Street, Newton, Manchester. Z9784B

SHAW, J., Private, East Lancashire Regiment.
He volunteered in September 1914, and proceeding to France in November of the following year served in various engagements until sent to Salonika in 1916. Taking part in operations in the Balkans, he was wounded on the Bulgarian frontier in October 1916, and after treatment rejoined his unit and was in action in serveral parts of the Macedonian front until the cessation of hostilities. Returning home for demobilisation in March 1919, he holds the 1914–15 Star, and the General Service and Victory Medals.
3, Hey Street, Bradford, Manchester. TZ9699

SHAW, J., Private, 1/5th Manchester Regiment.

He volunteered in 1915, and in October of the same year was drafted to France, where he first saw heavy fighting at Loos, Albert, and Vimy Ridge. Later he took part in the Battles of the Somme (I), Bullecourt, Ypres (III), Cambrai, the Somme (II), Amiens and Bapaume and in other important engagements during the Retreat and Advance of 1918. Unfortunately he was killed in action by a sniper at Villers-la-Fosse on September 2nd, 1918. He was entitled to the 1914-15 Star, and the General Service and Victory Medals.

"His life for his Country, his soul to God."

5, Chatsworth Street, Hulme, Manchester. Z8071

SHAW, J., L/Corporal, Manchester Regiment.

He volunteered in August 1914, and in the following year was drafted to the Western Front, where he played a prominent part in the heavy fighting in various sectors, and was wounded in action during the Somme Offensive in July 1916. After hospital treatment at the Base, he was transferred to Egypt and served there for twelve months. He then returned to France and took part in the Advance of 1918. Demobilised in December 1918, he holds the 1914-15 Star, and the General Service and Victory Medals.

16, Amy Street, Openshaw, Manchester. Z8067

SHAW, J. J., Private, R.A.S.C. (M.T.)

He volunteered in 1914, and was immediately drafted to France, where he took an active part in many important engagements in various sectors of the Front. He was present at the Battles of the Somme, Arras and Cambrai and the Offensive of 1918. Later he was invalided to England and finally discharged in April 1919. He holds the 1914-15 Star, and the General Service and Victory Medals.

9, Evans Street, Oxford Road, Chorlton-on-Medlock, Manchester. Z11067B

SHAW, J. O., Private, 17th Manchester Regiment.

Volunteering in May 1915, he was sent to Egypt in the following January and took part in the engagements at Sollum, Romani and Magdhaba. Later he proceeded to Palestine, where he was in action at the three Battles of Gaza and at the capture of Jerusalem and Jericho. He was in hospital at Alexandria with malarial fever on several occasions and was eventually demobilised in July 1919, holding the General Service and Victory Medals.

7, Norseman Street, Ardwick, Manchester. Z8064

SHAW, J. W., Private, 1st Manchester Regiment.

Volunteering in August 1914, he was shortly afterwards sent to France, where he was in action at Givenchy, Loos, La Bassée, Ypres the Somme, Vimy Ridge and St. Eloi. In January 1916 he was transferred to Mesopotamia and took part in heavy fighting at Kut and Sanna-i-Yat. Reported as having been taken prisoner during an action on the Tigris, he was later stated to have been killed in June 1916. He was entitled to the 1914-15 Star, and the General Service and Victory Medals.

"His memory is cherished with pride."

11, Gower Street, Hulme, Manchester. Z11820

SHAW, L., Private, 1st Border Regiment.

He joined in July 1917, and after a period of training was retained on important duties with his unit at various stations. In October 1918 he proceeded to the Western Front, and there did good work as a Signaller, until he was wounded whilst going into action on the Somme. He was demobilised in February 1919, and holds the General Service and Victory Medals. 5, Coulman St., Rochdale Rd., Manchester. Z11093

SHAW, R., Private, R.A.S.C.

He joined in April 1917, and five months later was drafted to the Western Front, where he was engaged on important transport duties in the forward areas. He was present at the Battles of Cambrai (I), the Somme (II), the Aisne (III), the Marne (II), Bapaume, Havrincourt and Cambrai (II), and at other engagements during the Retreat and Advance of 1918. Demobilised in August 1919, he holds the General Service and Victory Medals.

18, Bickley Street, Moss Side, Manchester. Z8069

SHAW, T., Sapper, R.E.

He joined in 1917, and on completion of his training was drafted to the Western Front, where he was engaged on special duties with his unit at Douai and Lille. He rendered valuable services as a plumber, and returning to England in 1919, was then demobilised, holding the General Service and Victory Medals.

15, Thompson Street, Chorlton-on-Medlock, Manchester. Z8077

SHAW, W., Private, King's (Liverpool Regiment).

He volunteered in July 1915, and shortly afterwards proceeded to the Western Front. Whilst in this theatre of war he took part in many important engagements in various sectors of the Front. He did good work whilst attached to the Army Service Corps until the cessation of hostilities. He was accidentally killed at Cologne in Germany in 1919, and was entitled to the General Service and Victory Medals.

"His memory is cherished with pride."

51, Harrowby Street, Collyhurst, Manchester. Z11578

SHAW, W., Driver, R.F.A.

Volunteering in August 1914, he proceeded in the following May to the Dardanelles, where he was in action with his Battery in the second and third Battles of Krithia, Suvla Bay and Chunuk Bair. Early in 1916 he was invalided home on account of ill-health, and later was sent to France. In this theatre of war he was again in action, at Bapaume, Amiens, on the Aisne front, and at Havrincourt and Ypres. Evacuated to England suffering from gas-poisoning, he was invalided out of the Army in February 1919, holding the 1914-15 Star, and the General Service and Victory Medals.

34, Rhodes Street, Miles Platting, Manchester. TZ9361

SHAW, W., Private, 2nd Manchester Regiment.

He volunteered in August 1914, and in the following June was drafted to the Western Front, where he took part in the Battles of Loos, Vermelles, Ypres, Arras, Cambrai, the Somme (II) and Amiens. He was also in action during heavy fighting at La Bassée, St. Eloi, Givenchy and in the Retreat and Advance of 1918. After the cessation of hostilities, he proceeded to Germany with the Army of Occupation and remained there until his demobilisation in April 1919. He holds the 1914-15 Star, and the General Service and Victory Medals.

43, Owen Street, Hulme, Manchester. Z8068

SHAW, W., Private, King's (Liverpool Regiment).

Having attested under the Derby scheme, he was called up for service in February 1916, and was quickly drafted to France. Whilst in this theatre of war, he took part in the Battles of Arras, Vimy Ridge, Bullecourt, Ypres (III), Passchendaele and Cambrai and in the Retreat and Advance of 1918. After the cessation of hostilities, he proceeded to Germany with the Army of Occupation, and was eventually demobilised in October 1919, holding the General Service and Victory Medals.

1, Cuba Street, Hulme, Manchester. Z8076

SHAWCROSS, T., Private, 17th Manchester Regt.

He volunteered in December 1915, and in the following July was drafted to the Western Front, where he first saw heavy fighting during the Somme Offensive. Later he was in action at La Bassée, Givenchy, Festubert, Albert, and Guillemont, before being badly wounded at the Battle of Arras in April 1917. He was then invalided home, and after hospital treatment in Southampton and Manchester, was discharged in April 1918 as medically unfit for further service. He holds the General Service and Victory Medals.

18, Lindrum Street, Rusholme, Manchester. Z8078

SHAY, M., Driver, R.A.S.C.

He joined in 1918, and after a short period of training was drafted to the Western Front. There he was engaged in conveying food and ammunition to the forward area in various sectors of the Front until the cessation of hostilities. He was demobilised in December 1919, and holds the General Service and Victory Medals.

13, Cross Street, Chorlton-on-Medlock, Manchester. Z11095

SHELBOURNE, A. F., Private, S. Lancashire Regt.

He volunteered in May 1915, and three months later was drafted to the Western Front, where he took part in the Battles of Loos and Vermelles, and in heavy fighting at St. Eloi. Unfortunately, he was killed in action in August 1916, during the Somme Offensive, and was entitled to the 1914-15 Star, and the General Service and Victory Medals.

"The path of duty was the way to glory."

30, Margaret Street West, Gorton, Manchester. Z8079

SHELDON, A., Private, 22nd Manchester Regiment.

Volunteering in June 1915, he proceeded to the Western Front five months later and took part in severe fighting, during the German attack of Loos early in 1916. He laid down his life for King and Country at Albert on March 9th, 1916, and was entitled to the 1914-15 Star, and the General Service and Victory Medals.

"He died the noblest death a man may die,
Fighting for God and right and liberty."

42, Henry Street, West Gorton, Manchester. Z8080B

SHELDON, J. H., C.S.M., 20th Lancashire Fusiliers.

He volunteered in June 1915, and was drafted to France in the following January. Whilst on the Western Front, he served with distinction at the Battles of Albert, the Somme, Arras, Bullecourt, Ypres (III), and Cambrai, and in the Retreat and Advance of 1918. He was wounded in action at Cambrai in September 1918, and was eventually demobilised in May 1919, holding the General Service and Victory Medals.

42, Henry Street, West Gorton, Manchester. Z8080A

SHELMERDINE, J., Private, 1st Manchester Regt.

He joined in March 1916, and on completion of his training, was drafted to Mesopotamia in the following September. During his service in this theatre of war, he took part in the relief of Kut, and the capture of Baghdad, Tekrit and Mosul. Later he marched to the Relief of Baku in the Caucasus, but returned to Kantara in Egypt. He returned to England via Italy and France, and was demobilised in May 1919, holding the General Service and Victory Medals.

88, Stockton Street, Moss Side, Manchester. Z6967B

SHELMERDINE,W.E.,Pte.,25th King's(L'pool Rgt.)
He joined in October 1916, and six months later proceeded to the Western Front, where he was badly wounded in action at Ypres, and was invalided home. On his recovery, he rejoined his unit in France and saw further heavy fighting. Later he was transferred to Egypt, and remained there until his demobilisation in March 1920, holding the General Service and Victory Medals.
24, Easton Street, Hulme, Manchester. Z8081

SHENNAN, A., Driver, R.A.S.C.
He joined in February 1917, and shortly afterwards proceeded to France. During his service overseas he was engaged on important transport duties, and was present at the Battles of Messines, Ypres III, Passchendaele, Cambrai, and in the Retreat and Advance of 1918. He was demobilised in May 1919, and holds the General Service and Victory Medals.
9, Tunstall Street, Longsight, Manchester. Z8082

SHENNAN, D., Sapper, R.E.
He volunteered in March 1915, but, whilst in training at Morecambe, was found to be physically unfit for military duty and was therefore discharged in the following month after a praiseworthy effort to serve his Country.
26, St. John's Avenue, Longsight, Manchester. Z8083

SHENTON, H. L., Pte., 10th Loyal N. Lancashire Regt.
He joined in January 1917, and shortly afterwards proceeded to France, where he took part in severe fighting in various sectors of the Front. He fought in many important engagements until April 1917, when he was wounded in action at the Battle of Arras, and invalided to England. Later, after a period of hospital treatment, he was discharged as unfit for further service in December 1917. He holds the General Service and Victory Medals.
170, Hartington Street, Moss Side, Manchester. TZ8084

SHEPHARD, G., Private, 3rd Manchester Regiment.
He volunteered in August 1915, and in November of the following year, proceeded to France. There he underwent a medical examination at Le Havre, where he was for a short time in hospital before being invalided home. He was finally discharged in February 1918, as medically unfit for further service, and holds the General Service and Victory Medals.
13, Whittacker Street, Gorton, Manchester. Z11098

SHEPHERD, E. R., Telegraphist, R.N.
He volunteered in the Merchant Service in September 1914, and underwent a period of training on the "Warspite," but was soon transferred to the Royal Navy. After further training in electricity and wireless telegraphy in the "Vernon" and "Impregnable," he proceeded to the North Sea in March 1915, and took part in important Naval operations until July 9th, 1917. He was then unfortunately killed when H.M.S. "Vanguard" blew up at Scapa Flow. He was entitled to the 1914-15 Star, and the General Service and Victory Medals.
75, Caythorpe Street, Moss Side, Manchester. Z8087

SHEPHERD, F., Private, Seaforth Highlanders.
He volunteered at the outbreak of hostilities in August 1914, and after a period of training proceeded to France in the following June. During his service in this theatre of war, he took part in heavy fighting at Vermelles, La Bassée, and Givenchy until October 1915, when he was wounded at Loos. On his recovery, he was transferred to Salonika, and was in action during the heavy fighting on the Doiran and Struma fronts, remaining in this seat of war until January 1920. He then returned home, and was demobilised in February, holding the 1914-15 Star, and the General Service and Victory Medals.
10, Bremner Street, Ardwick, Manchester. Z8086

SHEPHERD, J., Private, 12th Manchester Regiment.
He volunteered in August 1914, and in the following year proceeded to France. Whilst in this theatre of war he saw much fighting in various sectors of the Front, and took part in the Battles of St. Eloi, Ypres (II), the Somme (I), Loos, Arras, Messines, Ypres (III), the Somme (II), Amiens, Le Cateau (II), and others of importance until the cessation of hostilities. He was demobilised in March 1919, and holds the 1914-15 Star, and the General Service and Victory Medals.
17, Upper Vauxhall Street, Rochdale Road, Manchester. Z11096

SHEPHERD,W. R.V.,Pte.,11th Lancashire Fusiliers.
Volunteering in September 1914, he proceeded in the following September to the Western Front. There he took part in several engagements, including the Battles of Armentières, Vimy Ridge, the Somme, and Guillemont, where he was taken prisoner, and held in captivity for over two years. He was released after the Armistice, and demobilised in April 1919, holding the 1914-15 Star, and the General Service and Victory Medals. 5, Stretford Street, Hulme, Manchester. Z8085

SHEPLEY, J., Private, 2nd Manchester Regiment.
He was called up from the Reserve in August 1914, and immediately proceeded to France, where he saw much active service. He served throughout the Battle and Retreat from Mons, and later took part in the fierce fighting at the Battles of Hill 60, the Somme (I), Arras, Ypres and Cambrai. During this period of service on the Western Front, he was wounded on two occasions. He was discharged in November 1919, and holds the Mons Star, and the General Service and Victory Medals. 204, Cobden Street, Ancoats, Manchester. Z11097

SHEPLEY, A. V., Sergt., 8th Lancashire Fusiliers.
He volunteered in November 1914, and was drafted to France in the following year. He first saw heavy fighting at St. Eloi and Albert, where he was slightly wounded, and later played a distinguished part in the Battles of the Somme, Arras, Ypres (III), and Cambrai and was badly gassed. On his recovery in England, he returned to France, but was badly wounded during a raid at Passchendaele in February 1918, and was again invalided home. He was discharged as medically unfit for further service in October 1918, and holds the 1914-15 Star, and the General Service and Victory Medals.
48, Percy Street, Hulme, Manchester. TZ8088

SHEPPARD, J. H., Private, 51st Welch Regiment.
He joined in April 1918, and on completion of his training was sent to Ireland, where he was engaged with his unit on important garrison duties. Later in the following year he proceeded with the Army of Occupation into Germany, and after service there, returned to Ireland until demobilised in March 1920.
26, Robert Street, West Gorton, Manchester. Z8089

SHEPPARD, T., Private, 19th Lancashire Fusiliers.
He volunteered in April 1915, and later in the same year was drafted to France. During his service in this theatre of war, he took part in much heavy fighting at the Battles of Loos, Albert, Somme (I), Beaumont-Hamel, Arras, Bullecourt and Ypres, where he was gassed in September 1917. On his recovery, he was again in action throughout the Retreat and Advance of 1918, and remained in this seat of war until the cessation of hostilities. He was demobilised in February 1919, and holds the 1914-15 Star, and the General Service and Victory Medals.
10, New Street, West Gorton, Manchester. TZ8090

SHERIDAN, J., Sergeant, Royal Irish Regiment.
Enlisting in August 1904, he was stationed in Ireland when war broke out, and was almost immediately drafted to France. There he fought in several engagements during the Retreat from Mons, and in the Battles of Le Cateau, the Marne, the Aisne and La Bassée, and was wounded at Vieille Chapelle in October 1914. Sent home on account of his injuries he received medical treatment, and on recovery served at the Command Depôt, Tipperary, until June 1916, when he was discharged on account of service. He holds the Mons Star, and the General Service and Victory Medals.
14, Brass Street, Rochdale Road, Manchester. Z9700

SHERIDAN, J., Private, 9th Manchester Regiment.
Volunteering in August 1914, he sailed for Egypt a month later, and was engaged on important duties there for upwards of two years, when he was invalided home owing to illness in May 1916. On recovery he crossed to France in the following February, and took part in the Battles of Arras, Bullecourt, Messines, Ypres, Passchendaele, Cambrai, and in the Retreat and Advance of 1918. He returned home for demobilisation in February 1919, and holds the 1914-15 Star, and the General Service and Victory Medals.
30, Strand Street, Ancoats, Manchester. TZ9701A

SHERIDAN, J., Private, R.A.V.C.
He volunteered in June 1915, and on the conclusion of his training was engaged on important duties with his unit at various depôts. He rendered valuable services in attending to sick horses, but was unable to obtain his transfer to a theatre of war before the conclusion of hostilities, owing to medical unfitness, and was discharged in consequence in March 1918.
24, Strand Street, Ancoats, Manchester. TZ9701B

SHERIFF, F., C.S.M., 13th King's (Liverpool Regt.)
He volunteered in September 1914, and was retained on important duties in England until March 1915, when he proceeded to the Western Front. During his services in this theatre of war, he played a prominent part in many engagements, including the Battles of Neuve Chapelle, Ypres, Loos, and the Somme, where he was severely wounded, and died from the effects of his wounds on August 31st, 1916. He was entitled to the 1914-15 Star, and the General Service and Victory Medals.
"He died the noblest death a man may die,
Fighting for God, and right, and liberty."
24, Finlay Street, Newton, Manchester. TZ7996

SHERRATT, A., Private, Manchester Regiment.
He joined in April 1916, and in the following month was drafted to Mesopotamia. Whilst in this theatre of war he saw service at Kut, took part in the capture of Baghdad, and was wounded. On his recovery he rejoined his unit and remained in the East until he was demobilised in October 1919. He holds the General Service and Victory Medals.
39, Rostron Street, Ardwick, Manchester. Z8091

SHERRIFF, N., Private, 11th Manchester Regiment.
Joining in May 1916, he was drafted to France in November of that year, and there saw severe fighting in various sectors. He took part in the Battles of the Ancre, Bullecourt, Cambrai, the Somme, Havrincourt, Le Cateau and the Selle, and many minor engagements in this theatre of war, and was wounded in action at Ypres in October 1917. Demobilised in July 1919, he holds the General Service and Victory Medals.
26, James Street, West Gorton, Manchester. Z11099

SHERROTT, E., Private, 6th Manchester Regiment.

He volunteered in September 1914, and in October of the following year was drafted to the Western Front, where he took part in severe fighting at Neuve Chapelle, La Bassée, Festubert and many other places, and also served in the Somme Offensive. He died gloriously on the Field of Battle on November 28th, 1916, at Beaumont-Hamel, where he is buried. He was entitled to the 1914–15 Star, and the General Service and Victory Medals.

"A valiant Soldier, with undaunted heart he breasted life's last hill."

90, Naylor Street, Newton, Manchester.　　Z11579

SHERVILL, G., Private, 4th Royal Berkshire Regt.

Mobilised from the Army Reserve in August 1914, he was engaged on Military Police duties until the following November, when he embarked for the Western Front. In this theatre of war he was in action at the first Battle of Ypres, and in other engagements in the Ypres salient, and owing to injuries accidentally sustained was invalided home in February 1915. After treatment he was discharged as physically unfit in April of the same year, and holds the 1914 Star, and the General Service and Victory Medals.

6, Alfred Street, Collyhurst, Manchester.　　Z9363

SHERWIN, J., Private, 7th Manchester Regiment.

He joined in April 1916, and was retained on important duties with his unit at various stations until March 1917, when he proceeded to France. During his short period of service in this theatre of war, he saw heavy fighting at Festubert, Passchendaele and Ypres, where he was unfortunately killed on October 9th, 1917. He was entitled to the General Service and Victory Medals.

"His memory is cherished with pride."

1, Rose Street, Old Trafford, Manchester.　　Z8092

SHIELDS, E., Private, York and Lancaster Regt.

Joining in July 1917, he was drafted to the Western Front in the following month and there saw much heavy fighting in various sectors. He took part in the Battles of Ypres and Cambrai, and other important engagements, served also through the Retreat of 1918, and was wounded in action in September of that year. Invalided home, he was for some time in hospital, before being demobilised in February 1919, and holds the General Service and Victory Medals.

14, Dickens Street, Miles Platting, Manchester.　　Z11100B

SHIELDS, J., Private, R.A.V.C., and R.A.S.C.

He joined immediately on attaining military age in July 1918, and after undergoing a period of training, served at various stations, where he was engaged on duties of great importance. Owing to the early cessation of hostilities, he was not successful in obtaining his transfer overseas, but, nevertheless, rendered valuable services with his Company until demobilised in December 1919.

14, Dickens Street, Miles Platting, Manchester.　　Z11100A

SHIERS, R., Corporal, 19th Manchester Regiment.

He volunteered in July 1915, and later in the same year proceeded to the Western Front. Whilst in this theatre of war he took part in many important engagements in various sectors of the front, including the Battles of Loos, Albert, the Somme, Arras, Vimy Ridge, Bullecourt, Messines and Ypres (IV), and was wounded at Cambrai in December 1917. After his recovery, he was again in action, and served throughout the Retreat and Advance of 1918. He was demobilised in February 1919, and holds the 1914–15 Star, and the General Service and Victory Medals.

6, New Square, West Gorton, Manchester.　　Z8093

SHIPLEY, J., Corporal, Labour Corps.

Shortly after joining in July 1917, he proceeded to France, where he saw severe fighting in various sectors of the Front. He was engaged on various important duties whilst in this theatre of war, and also took an active part in the Battle of the Somme, and many other engagements. He was demobilised on his return home in February 1919, and holds the General Service and Victory Medals.

64, North Kent Street, Rochdale Road, Manchester.　　Z11101

SHIPPAM, G., Private, 3rd Manchester Regiment.

He joined in February 1916, and proceeded to France in the following October. He saw much severe fighting in this theatre of war, and was in action in the Somme sector, where he was gassed and invalided home. On his recovery he returned to the Western Front, and served at Bapaume with the Labour Corps until again invalided home suffering from the effects of gas poisoning, and was finally discharged in December 1918, holding the General Service and Victory Medals.

7, Tipper Street, Hulme, Manchester.　　Z8094

SHIREMAN, C., Worker, Q.M.A.A.C.

She joined in May 1917, and in the following month was sent to France. During over two years' service in this theatre of war she did excellent work engaged on various duties, and was demobilised on returning home in September 1919. She holds the General Service and Victory Medals.

21, Harrowby Street, Collyhurst, Manchester.　　Z11969

SHIRLEY, C., Private, 2/8th Manchester Regiment.

He volunteered in August 1914, and on completion of his training was retained at home for work of National importance owing to his abilities. For two years he was engaged on special duties at Messrs. Cammell-Lairds, Shipbuilders, Birkenhead, and later went to the Lancashire and Yorkshire Railway as a tool grinder. He rendered valuable services throughout and was demobilised from the Army in November 1918.

18, Garden Walks, Ardwick, Manchester.　　Z8095B

SHIRLEY, J., Private, 2/8th Manchester Regiment.

He joined in November 1916, and three months later was drafted to the Western Front. There he took part in several important engagements, including Arras, Bullecourt, Passchendaele and Cambrai, and did good work until he fell gloriously on the Field of Battle at St. Quentin on March 25th, 1918. He was entitled to the General Service and Victory Medals.

"A costly sacrifice upon the altar of freedom."

16, Heald Avenue, Rusholme, Manchester.　　Z11821

SHIRLEY, J., Private, 2nd Manchester Regiment.

He volunteered at the outbreak of hostilities in August 1914, and immediately proceeded to Egypt, where he took part in the attacks on the Suez Canal. Later he was transferred to Gallipoli, and whilst in this theatre of war, saw much fighting. He took part in the Landings at Cape Helles and Suvla Bay, the Battles of Krithia, and in the capture of Chunuk Bair. After the Evacuation of the Peninsula, he was sent to Salonika, and was in action on the Doiran front, where he was wounded in August 1916, and invalided to hospital. On his recovery, he was again in action on the Doiran and Struma fronts until the cessation of hostilities, when he returned to England, and was demobilised, holding the 1914–15 Star, and the General Service and Victory Medals.

18, Garden Walks, Ardwick, Manchester.　　Z8095A

SHIRLEY, T., Private, 11th Manchester Regiment.

Volunteering in July 1915, he proceeded to the Dardanelles three months later, and there saw severe fighting until the Evacuation of the Gallipoli Peninsula. He was then sent to Egypt, whence he was transferred in July 1916, to the Western Front, and there took part in the Battles of the Somme and Arras and other important engagements. He was invalided from the Army in April 1918, and holds the 1914–15 Star, and the General Service and Victory Medals.

18, Diggles Street, Ancoats, Manchester.　　Z11102

SHOESMITH, F., Private, 1st Lincolnshire Regt.

He joined in April 1917, and in March of the following year was drafted to the Western Front, where he saw severe fighting in various sectors. He took part in the Battles of Ypres, Passchendaele and the Somme, and many other engagements, and was wounded in action in June 1918. He was a second time wounded at Cambrai, and unhappily died in hospital on October 9th of the same year. He was entitled to the General Service and Victory Medals.

"A costly sacrifice upon the altar of freedom."

8, Walmer Place, Longsight, Manchester.　　Z8096

SHONGITHARM, F., Private, Manchester Regt.

He volunteered in August 1915, and on completing his training in the following year, was drafted to the Western Front, where he saw much severe fighting. After taking part in the Advance on the Somme, and in the Battle of Bullecourt and many other important engagements in various sectors, he was taken prisoner in 1918. He was held in captivity until the cessation of hostilities, and was finally demobilised in January 1919, holding the General Service and Victory Medals.

1, South Place, Longsight, Manchester.　　Z8097

SHOREMAN, B., Private, 2nd Manchester Regt.

Volunteering in January 1915, he proceeded overseas four months later and saw much service in France and Flanders. He was in action in the Battles of Loos, Vermelles, and the Somme, in the course of which he was wounded in November 1916. After convalescence he fought at Arras, Bullecourt, Ypres and Lens, Cambrai, and in several other important engagements until the close of the war. Demobilised in February 1919, he holds the 1914–15 Star, and the General Service and Victory Medals.

9, Franklin Street, Rochdale Road, Manchester.　　Z9702

SHOREMAN, C. E., Pte., 6th K.O. (R. Lancaster Regt.)

He volunteered in August 1914, and in the following year was drafted to Gallipoli, where he took part in the third Battle of Krithia, and in severe fighting at Suvla Bay. On the Evacuation of the Peninsula he was transferred to Mesopotamia, and there served through engagements at Ali-el-Gharb and Sanna-i-Yat, and took part also in the Relief of Kut, and the capture of Baghdad. He finally returned home for demobilisation in February 1919, and holds the 1914–15 Star, and the General Service and Victory Medals.

3, Frost Street, Hulme, Manchester.　　Z8098

SHORROCKS, J. T., Driver, R.F.A.

Volunteering in May 1915, he was drafted to Egypt in the following month and there served on the Suez Canal and at Kantara, and many other places. In March 1916, he was transferred to the Western Front, where he was engaged on important duties with an ammunition column at Bapaume, Albert, the Marne, and in various other sectors. He was demobilised on his return home in January 1919, and holds the 1914–15 Star, and the General Service and Victory Medals.
69, Cawdor Street, Hulme, Manchester.   Z8099

SHORT, A., Gunner, R.G.A.

He volunteered in January 1916, and was retained on important duties in England until 1917, when he was drafted to the Western Front. There he saw much severe fighting in various sectors and took part in the Battles of Ypres and Passchendaele, and many other important engagements until the cessation of hostilities. He was finally demobilised in April 1920, and holds the General Service and Victory Medals.
8, Norway Grove, South Reddish, Manchester.   X8100

SHORTLE, W., Private, 2nd Manchester Regiment.

Volunteering on the outbreak of war he was drafted to France soon afterwards, and took part in the Retreat from Mons, and in the Battles of Ypres (I and II). He fell fighting on July 10th, 1915, near Ypres, and was entitled to the Mons Star, and the General Service and Victory Medals.
"A costly sacrifice upon the altar of freedom."
13, Gunson Street, Ancoats, Manchester.   Z9364

SHUFFLEBOTTOM, E. (D.C.M.), Sergt., R.F.A.

Mobilised in August 1914, he was immediately drafted to the Western Front, where after taking part in the Retreat from Mons, he fought in the Battles of the Marne, the Aisne, Festubert, Loos, the Somme, Arras, Bullecourt and Messines, and many minor engagements. He unhappily fell in action on July 31st, 1917, in the third Battle of Ypres. He had been awarded the Distinguished Conduct Medal for conspicuous gallantry in the Field, and was entitled also to the Mons Star, and the General Service and Victory Medals.
"His memory is cherished with pride."
4, Spruce Street, Hulme, Manchester.   Z8101

SHUFFLEBOTTOM, G., Private, 1st K. (Liverpool Regiment), and Labour Corps.

He volunteered in December 1915, and was retained on important duties in England until February 1917, when he was engaged on important duties in various sectors, was present at the Battles of Ypres, Cambrai and the Somme, and took an active part also in the Retreat and Advance of 1918. He afterwards served with the Army of Occupation in Germany, where he was stationed at Bonn until his return home for demobilisation in March 1920. He holds the General Service and Victory Medals.
14, Naylor Street, Oldham Road, Manchester.   Z11103B

SHUFFLEBOTTOM, J., Gunner, R.G.A.

He volunteered in August 1914, and crossed to France two months later and was engaged with his Battery in the Battles of Ypres, St. Eloi and Hill 60. In June 1915, he proceeded to Egypt and in that theatre of war fought in the Battles of Katia and Romani, the capture of Magdhaba, at Gaza, the fall of Jerusalem, and in other operations during the British Advance through Palestine. He holds the 1914 Star, and the General Service and Victory Medals, and in 1920 was still serving abroad. 128, Teignmouth St., Rochdale Rd., Manchester. Z9703

SHUFFLEBOTTOM, S., Private, Loyal N. Lancashire Regiment, Welch Regt., and K. (Liverpool Regt.)

After volunteering in December 1915, he underwent a period of training prior to being drafted to the Western Front in September 1917. There he took part in many important engagements and saw severe fighting at La Bassée, Festubert, Kemmel and the Marne, and many other places, until wounded in action at Béthune, and invalided to hospital in London. He returned to France, however, in July 1919, and was stationed at Calais until finally discharged in December 1919. He holds the General Service and Victory Medals.
14, Naylor Street, Oldham Road, Manchester.   Z11103A

SHUFFLETON, J., Private, 12th K. (Liverpool Regt.)

Shortly after volunteering in September 1914, he was drafted to the Western Front, where he saw severe fighting in various sectors. He took part in the Battles of La Bassée, St. Eloi, Ypres, Loos, Bullecourt, and Cambrai, and many other important engagements in this theatre of war, and was twice wounded in action—at Lens in August, and on the Somme in October 1916. Demobilised in February 1919, he holds the 1914 Star, and the General Service and Victory Medals.
89, Burton Street, Rochdale Road, Manchester.   Z11104

SHUTTLEWORTH, H., Private, Welch Regiment.

He volunteered in February 1916, and in the same year sailed for Salonika. During operations in the Balkans he was engaged in heavy fighting on the Doiran and Vardar fronts, and in the Advance across the Struma, and was present at the capture of Monastir. Returning to England for demobilisation in February 1919, he holds the General Service and Victory Medals
37, Baguley Street, Miles Platting, Manchester.   Z9704

SHUTTLEWORTH, J., Private, 1/7th Lancashire Fusiliers.

He volunteered in August 1914, and shortly afterwards was drafted to Egypt, where he was in action on the Suez Canal, before being transferred to Gallipoli in the following year. There he saw much severe fighting at Suvla Bay, and many other places, and was wounded in action and invalided to Alexandria. He afterwards proceeded to the Western Front, where he took part in many important engagements, was a second time wounded in July 1917, during the third Battle of Ypres, and was for a time in hospital in France. He was demobilised in March 1919, and holds the 1914–15 Star, and the General Service and Victory Medals.
16, Gresham Street, Lower Openshaw, Manchester.   Z8102

SIBBIT, F., Private, Seaforth Highlanders.

Joining in February 1916, he was drafted to the Western Front on completing his training in September of the same year, and there saw severe fighting in various sectors. He served through engagements at St. Eloi and Beaumont-Hamel, was wounded in action on the Somme, and was for a time in hospital in France. On his recovery, however, he rejoined his unit and was again in action at La Bassée, Givenchy, Nieuport and Arras. Demobilised in October 1919, he holds the General Service and Victory Medals.
4, Yarwood Buildings, Ardwick, Manchester.   Z8103

SIBBLES, O., Private, 23rd Royal Fusiliers.

He volunteered in December 1915, and after six months' training was drafted to the Western Front. There he served as a Despatch rider in various sectors, and took part also in the Battles of the Somme, Arras, Vimy Ridge, Ypres, Passchendaele and Cambrai, and other important engagements. Mortally wounded in action on the Somme during the Retreat af 1918, he unhappily died in hospital at Manchester in May of that year. He was entitled to the General Service and Victory Medals.
"Whilst we remember, the sacrifice is not in vain."
29, Ferry Street, Ardwick, Manchester.   Z8104

SIDDALL, E., Private, Manchester Regiment.

He volunteered at the outbreak of war in August 1914, and in the following year was drafted to the Dardanelles, where he saw severe fighting at Suvla Bay and various other places. He was also stationed for a time at Mudros and in Egypt, before being transferred to the Western Front in July 1916, and there took part in many engagements during the Somme Offensive and was severely wounded in action at Thiepval in September 1916. He was for a considerable period in hospital at Boulogne and in England, before being invalided from the Army in July 1917, and holds the 1914–15 Star, and the General Service and Victory Medals.
87, Cobden Street, Ancoats, Manchester.   Z11106

SIDDALL, G., Private, K.O. (Royal Lancaster Regt.)

After volunteering in November 1915, he was retained on important duties at various stations in England until September 1917, when he was drafted to the Western Front. There he saw much severe fighting, took part in the Battles of Cambrai, the Somme, the Marne and Bapaume, and other engagements and was gassed whilst in action at Cambrai in November 1917. He was demobilised on his return home in September 1919, and holds the General Service and Victory Medals.
23, Park Street, West Gorton, Manchester.   Z11105

SIDDALL, J., Private, 2nd K.O. (Y.L.I.)

He volunteered in August 1914, and after a period of training was engaged at various stations on important duties with his unit. He was not successful in obtaining a transfer overseas, but rendered valuable services until his demobilisation in January 1919.
7, Barnes Place, Ancoats, Manchester.   Z11953

SIDDON, R. H., L/Corporal, Grenadier Guards.

He volunteered in December 1914, and in the following March proceeded to the Western Front, where he took part in the Battles of St. Eloi, Ypres (II), Loos, Albert, Ploegsteert, the Somme, Beaucourt, Arras, and Ypres (III). He died gloriously on the Field of Battle in November 1917, and was entitled to the 1914–15 Star, and the General Service and Victory Medals.
"A valiant Soldier, with undaunted heart he breasted life's last hill."
17, Henry Street, Ardwick, Manchester.   Z11954

SIDDON, W. A. (M.M.), Pte., Loyal N. Lancashire Regt.)

He volunteered in September 1914, and on completing his training in the following January, was drafted to the Western Front. There he played a prominent part in the Battles of Neuve Chapelle, Hill 60, Festubert, Loos, Albert, Vermelles, Vimy Ridge, the Somme, Beaucourt, and the Ancre, and was awarded the Military Medal for conspicuous bravery and devotion to duty in the Field. In April 1917 he made the supreme sacrifice, being killed in action at the Battle of Arras. He was also entitled to the 1914–15 Star, and the General Service and Victory Medals.
"He died the noblest death a man may die,
Fighting for God, and right, and liberty."
17, Henry Street, Ardwick, Manchester.   Z11955

SIDWELL, C., Corporal, Rifle Brigade.
Volunteering in August 1914, he was sent to France in March of the following year, and there saw heavy fighting in various sectors of the Front. After taking part in engagements at Passchendaele, he was severely wounded in action at Ypres, and was invalided home, where he was in hospital at Birmingham and Sheerness. He was finally discharged as medically unfit for further service in June 1916, and holds the 1914–15 Star, and the General Service and Victory Medals. TZ8105
6, Westminster Street, Chester Road, Hulme, Manchester.

SIMCOCK, J., Private, 1/7th Manchester Regiment.
He volunteered in May 1915, and in the following September proceeded to Gallipoli, where he served until the Evacuation. He was then transferred to France, and in this theatre of war was in action at Albert, Beaumont-Hamel, Bullecourt, Passchendaele, Cambrai, Amiens, Bapaume and Havrincourt, where he was wounded in September 1918. Invalided home, he was in hospital at Southport, and was eventually demobilised in December 1918, holding the 1914–15 Star, and the General Service and Victory Medals.
86, Bickley Street, Moss Side, Manchester. Z11822

SIMKIN, F., Private, 2/7th Manchester Regiment.
He joined in September 1916, and after his training was retained on important duties in England, where he was present at the explosion at the Silvertown Munition Factory. He was shortly afterwards drafted to the Western Front, and there after much severe fighting was killed in action at Bullecourt on April 10th, 1917. He was entitled to the General Service and Victory Medals.
　"A costly sacrifice upon the altar of freedom."
20, Linson Street, Bradford, Manchester. Z8106

SIMMONS, J., Private, King's (Liverpool Regt.), and Gunner (Signaller), R.G.A.
He joined in April 1916, and was retained on important duties in England until June 1917, when he proceeded to the Western Front. There he saw severe fighting in various sectors, took part in the Battles of Ypres, Passchendaele and the Somme and the Retreat and Advance of 1918, and was wounded in action. He was demobilised on his return home in February 1919, and holds the General Service and Victory Medals.
41, Elliott Street, Bradford, Manchester. Z11107

SIMMONS, J. (M.M.), Gunner, R.G.A.
Volunteering in January 1916, he was drafted to the Western Front in the following May and there saw much severe fighting. He took part in the Battles of the Somme, Bullecourt, Messines, Ypres, Passchendaele and Cambrai and many other important engagements in various sectors. He unhappily contracted pneumonia and died on November 3rd, 1918, in the 1st Australian General Hospital at Rouen. He had been awarded the Military Medal for conspicuous bravery displayed on the Field in rescuing the wounded under heavy shell-fire on the Somme in March 1918, and was also entitled to the General Service and Victory Medals.
　"The path of duty was the way to glory."
12, Mundy Street, Gorton, Manchester. Z8115

SIMMONS, W. H., Corporal, R.A.M.C.
Volunteering in August 1915, he was drafted to the Western Front in November of that year, and there served as a stretcher-bearer in various sectors. He was present at the Battles of the Somme, Arras, Ypres and Passchendaele and many minor engagements, and also took an active part in the Retreat and Advance of 1918. He was demobilised in March 1919, and holds the 1914–15 Star, and the General Service and Victory Medals. 4, Walmer Place, Longsight, Manchester. Z8114

SIMNOR, R., Sergt., K.O. (Royal Lancaster Regt.), and Royal Welch Fusiliers.
Having enlisted in 1904, he was called up from the Reserve at the outbreak of war in August 1914, and was immediately drafted to the Western Front, where he fought in the Battle of Mons and the subsequent Retreat, and was wounded in action. Invalided home, he returned to France, however, on his recovery in March 1915, and took a prominent part in the Battle of Hill 60, and other engagements until wounded a second time at Ypres. Again sent home, he proceeded to Egypt in March 1916, and was stationed at Cairo and in the Sahara until his return to England for discharge in March 1919. He holds the Mons Star, and the General Service and Victory Medals.
11, Cuttell Street, Bradford, Manchester. Z11108

SIMNOR, W., Private, 2nd Manchester Regiment.
He volunteered in May 1915, and on completing his training in December of that year, proceeded to Mesopotamia, where he served for twelve months. He was then transferred to Palestine and was there engaged on important transport duties at various stations and was also in hospital for a time, suffering from dysentery. He was demobilised on his return home in March 1919, and holds the 1914–15 Star, and the General Service and Victory Medals.
1, North Street, Hulme, Manchester. Z8116

SIMONS, O., Rifleman, Rifle Brigade.
He volunteered in July 1915, and on completing his training in March of the following year, proceeded to the Western Front, where he fought in various sectors. He took part in the Battles of Albert, Vimy Ridge and the Somme and many other important engagements, and was twice wounded in action—at Guillemont in August 1916, and at Arras in April 1917—and was gassed at Ypres in September of that year. He was invalided from the Army in March 1918, and holds the General Service and Victory Medals.
14, Nancy Street, Chester Road, Hulme, Manchester. Z11109

SIMONS, O. (Miss), Worker, Q.M.A.A.C.
She joined in May 1918, and after completing two months' training, was drafted to the Western Front. There she was engaged on duties of great importance at General Headquarters at Montreuil and Wimereux and rendered very valuable services until her return home for demobilisation in July 1919. She holds the General Service and Victory Medals.
19, Princess Street, Chester Road, Hulme, Manchester. Z11110

SIMONS, W., Private, 7th Lancashire Fusiliers.
He volunteered at the outbreak of war in August 1914, and twelve months later was drafted to Mesopotamia, where he saw much severe fighting. He served through numerous engagements on the Tigris and also took part in the Relief of Kut and the capture of Baghdad, before being invalided to India, suffering from malaria and dysentery. He was in hospital at Bombay and Madras, and finally returned home for discharge in November 1919. He holds the 1914–15 Star, and the General Service and Victory Medals.
19, Princess Street, Chester Road, Hulme, Manchester. Z11111

SIMPSON, E. W., Private, 1/3rd Manchester Regt.
He volunteered in November 1915, and in October of the following year proceeded to Egypt, where at Katia, Romani and on the Suez Canal. In March 1917 he was transferred to the Western Front, and after taking part in many important engagements in this theatre of war, proceeded to Italy, where he saw much severe fighting on the Piave. He was demobilised on his return home in March 1919, and holds the General Service and Victory Medals.
102, Clopton Street, Hulme, Manchester. TZ8111

SIMPSON, F., Pte., K.O. (Y.L.I.)
He volunteered in April 1915, and after a period of training proceeded to the Western Front in January of the following year. There he took part in many important engagements in various sectors, including the Battles of the Somme and Ypres, and also fought in the Retreat and Advance of 1918. He returned home for demobilisation in February 1919, and holds the General Service and Victory Medals.
45, Burnley Street, Ancoats, Manchester. Z7997

SIMPSON, H., Corporal, R.G.A.
After volunteering in May 1915, he underwent a period of training prior to being drafted to the Western Front in August of the following year. He took part in the Battles of the Somme, Arras and Messines Ridge and many minor engagements until gassed and wounded in action at Passchendaele in November 1917. On his recovery he was transferred to the Chinese Labour Corps, and served in the Record Office in France until his demobilisation in January 1919. He holds the General Service and Victory Medals.
50, Wedgwood Street, Newton Heath, Manchester, Z8107

SIMPSON, H., Private, 17th Manchester Regiment.
Volunteering in September 1915, he was drafted to the Western Front in April of the following year, and there took part in severe fighting at Albert, St. Eloi, Vimy Ridge and many other places. He died gloriously on the Field of Battle on July 6th, 1916, during the Somme Offensive. He was entitled to the General Service and Victory Medals.
　"He joined the great white company of valiant souls."
76, Harrowby Street, Collyhurst, Manchester. Z11113–4B

SIMPSON, H., 1st Air Mechanic, R.A.F.
He joined in February 1917, and after undergoing a period of training, served at various stations, where he was engaged on duties of a highly technical nature. He was not successful in obtaining his transfer to a theatre of war, but nevertheless, rendered valuable services with his Squadron until April 1919, when he was demobilised.
156, Hamilton Street, Collyhurst, Manchester. Z11113–4A

SIMPSON, J., Private, 2/7th Manchester Regiment.
He joined in May 1916, and in June of the following year was drafted to the Western Front. Whilst in this theatre of war, he saw severe fighting in various sectors and took part in the Battles of Messines, Ypres, Cambrai, the Somme, the Aisne, the Marne and Bapaume, and many other engagements until the cessation of hostilities. He was demobilised in September 1919, and holds the General Service and Victory Medals. 2, Smedley Road, Cheetham, Manchester. Z11580

SIMPSON, J., Gunner, R.G.A.
Joining in May 1917, he crossed to the Western Front in the following September, and served in various sectors until the end of hostilities. During this period he was in action in the Battles of Cambrai, the Somme (II), the Aisne (III), the Marne, and at Havrincourt, Le Cateau and other places in the German Offensive and subsequent Allied Advance of 1918. He was demobilised in September 1919, and holds the General Service and Victory Medals. Z9705
3, Moor Street, Wilmslow Road, Rusholme, Manchester.

SIMPSON, T. W., Driver, R.A.S.C.

Volunteering in February 1915, he was drafted to France after three months' training, and was there engaged on important duties in various sectors of the Front. He was present at the Battles of Ypres, Loos, Vimy Ridge, the Somme, Arras, Passchendaele, Cambrai, the Marne, Bapaume and Havrincourt and many minor engagements until the cessation of hostilities. Demobilised in May 1919, he holds the 1914-15 Star, and the General Service and Victory Medals.

48, Haughton Street, Bradford, Manchester.   Z8112

SIMPSON, L., Driver, R.A.S.C., and Sergt., R.M.A.

He volunteered in October 1914, and on completing a period of training in February of the following year was drafted to the Western Front, where he took an active part in the Battles of Neuve Chapelle, Ypres and Arras and other engagements. He was afterwards engaged on important duties as a Police Sergeant and gunner on board H.M.S. " Princess Thiera," on escort duty between Europe and Canada. He was gassed in action on the Somme whilst in France, and was finally demobilised in February 1919, holding the 1914-15 Star, and the General Service and Victory Medals.

12, Chunnett Street, Collyhurst, Manchester.   Z11112

SIMPSON, T., Private, South Lancashire Regiment, and Trooper, Pembroke (Castlemartin) Hussars.

He volunteered in March 1915, and on completing his training in September of that year, was drafted to the Western Front, where he took part in the Battle of Loos and minor engagements. In December 1915 he was transferred to Salonika, and there saw much severe fighting on the Doiran, Struma and Vardar fronts, and was present at the recapture of Monastir. He was discharged on his return home in February 1919, and holds the 1914-15 Star, and the General Service and Victory Medals.

24, Edmund Street, Openshaw, Manchester.   Z8113

SIMPSON, W., Private, R.A.M.C.

He joined in October 1916, and in June of the following year proceeded to Egypt, where he served at Cairo, Alexandria, Mustapha and various other stations. He was there engaged on important duties as a nursing orderly and did much good work until sent home in November 1918, owing to the loss of his right eye in an accident. He was invalided from the Army in March 1919, and holds the General Service and Victory Medals.

8, Wellesley Street, West Gorton, Manchester.   Z8110

SIMPSON, W. A., Private, R.A.P.C.

He volunteered in December 1915, and after undergoing a period of training, served at various stations, where he was engaged on important clerical duties. He was unable to obtain his transfer overseas on account of ill-health, but nevertheless, rendered valuable services wtih his unit until March 1918, when he was invalided from the Army.

21, Carlton Terrace, Gorton, Manchester.   Z8109

SIMPSON, W. W., Private, 1st K. (Liverpool Regt.)

Four months after volunteering in September 1914, he was drafted to the Western Front, where he saw heavy fighting in various sectors. After taking part in engagements at Givenchy, Festubert and many other places, he was severely wounded in action at Vermelles in July 1915, and admitted to hospital in France. He was also in hospital in England before being invalided from the Army in April 1916, and holds the 1914-15 Star, and the General Service and Victory Medals.

17, Industrial Street, Chorlton-on-Medlock, Manchester. Z8108

SINCLAIR, E., Private, Royal Fusiliers.

He volunteered in October 1915, and in February of the following year proceeded to the Western Front. Whilst in this theatre of war he took part in many important engagements, including the Battles of Albert, Arras, Bullecourt and Cambrai, and also fought in the Retreat and Advance of 1918. He was afterwards sent with the Army of Occupation to Germany, where he was stationed at Cologne until his return home for demobilisation in April 1919. He holds the General Service and Victory Medals.

5, Grosvenor Street, Hulme, Manchester.   TZ8117A

SINCLAIR, J., Corporal, Royal Fusiliers.

Four months after volunteering in July 1915, he was drafted to the Western Front, where he saw severe fighting in various sectors, and took part in the Battles of Albert, the Somme and Bullecourt, and many other engagements. He died gloriously on the Field of Battle at Ypres on June 24th, 1917.
He was entitled to the 1914-15 Star, and the General Service and Victory Medals.

" His life for his Country, his soul to God."

5, Grosvenor Street, Hulme, Manchester.   TZ8117B

SINGLETON, R., L/Cpl., 2/8th Lancashire Fusiliers.

Volunteering in February 1915, he landed in France in the following October and took part in the Battles of Loos, St. Eloi, the Somme, Bullecourt and was wounded at Ypres in October 1917. Sent home owing to his injuries he received protracted hospital treatment in Liverpool, and was subsequently discharged as medically unfit in March 1919. He holds the 1914-15 Star, and the General Service and Victory Medals.

33, Kingston Street, Hulme, Manchester.   Z9365

SINGLETON, S., Private, 20th Manchester Regt.

He volunteered in November 1914, and twelve months later was drafted to the Western Front, where he saw severe fighting in various sectors. He was for a time in hospital in France suffering from debility and in September 1917 was invalided home. He returned to the Western Front, however, on his recovery in April of the following year, but was finally discharged as medically unfit for further service in November 1918. He holds the 1914-15 Star, and the General Service and Victory Medals.

50, Princess Street, Rusholme, Manchester.   Z8118

SINGLETON, T., Driver, R.F.A.

Volunteering in January 1915, he proceeded to the Western Front in July of that year, and there saw severe fighting in various sectors. He took part in the Battles of Loos, the Somme, Bullecourt and Ypres, and many minor engagements until gassed whilst in action at Passchendaele in July 1917, and invalided home. On his recovery he was retained on important duties in England until his demobilisation in February 1919. He holds the 1914-15 Star, and the General Service and Victory Medals.

7, Diggles Street, Ancoats, Manchester.   Z11115

SKADE, H., Private, 5/20th Manchester Regiment.

After volunteering in January 1915, he underwent a period of training prior to being drafted to India in February of the following year. There he was engaged on garrison duties at Allahabad and various other stations until February 1918, and was then transferred to Siberia, where he served at Vladivostock, Omsk and elsewhere. Returning home in February 1919, he was invalided from the Army in May of that year, and holds the General Service and Victory Medals.

17, Jersey Street Dwellings, Ancoats, Manchester.   Z11116

SKARRATTS, G., Private, 2nd Manchester Regt.

He volunteered in December 1914, and six months later proceeded to Mesopotamia, where he saw much severe fighting. He took part in important engagements at Basra and many other places in this seat of operations, and served also at the Relief of Kut, and the capture of Baghdad. He was for some time in hospital at Bombay, suffering from fever, and finally, returning home in October 1919, was demobilised in the following month. He holds the 1914-15 Star, and the General Service and Victory Medals.

54, Lind Street, Ancoats, Manchester.   Z11117

SKELLY, A., Gunner, R.G.A.

Volunteering in August 1915, he proceeded to the Western Front five weeks later, and there took part in important engagements in the Loos sector until November of that year. He was then transferred to Salonika, where he saw much severe fighting on the Doiran and Struma fronts, and was present at the recapture of Monastir. Returning home in January 1918, he was demobilised in April 1919, and holds the 1914-15 Star, and the General Service and Victory Medals.

2A, Argyle Street, Marple Street, Hulme, Manchester. Z8119

SKELLON, W., Private, 6th Leicestershire Regt.

After volunteering in September 1915, he was retained on important duties at various stations in England until February 1917. He was then drafted to the Western Front, where he saw severe fighting in various sectors and took part in the Battles of Ypres, Cambrai, the Somme, Havrincourt and Epéhy, and many other engagements. Demobilised in March 1919, he holds the General Service and Victory Medals.

57, Church Street, Hulme, Manchester.   Z8120

SKELTON, T., Private, R.A.S.C.

Joining in April 1917, he proceeded to the Western Front in the following month, and was there engaged on duties of great importance at Le Havre and Rouen, where he rendered valuable services. Contracting malaria, he was invalided to hospital in England, and there unhappily died in July 1918. He was entitled to the General Service and Victory Medals.

" Steals on the ear the distant triumph song."

20, Caroline Street, Hulme, Manchester.   Z8122

SKELTON, W. H. J., Private, M.G.C.

He volunteered in November 1914, and after four months' training was drafted to the Western Front, where he took part in the Battle of St. Eloi and many minor engagements. Later in 1915, however, he was transferred to Salonika, and was there engaged on important duties at various stations, and was for a time in hospital suffering from malaria. Returning home in January 1919, he was demobilised in the following month, and holds the 1914-15 Star, and the General Service and Victory Medals.

14, Violet Street, Hulme, Manchester.   TX8121

SKERRETT, J. W., Private, 3rd Manchester Regt.

He volunteered in November 1914, and in the following March proceeded overseas. Serving with his Battalion on the Western Front he fought in the Battles of Neuve Chapelle, Ypres (II and III), Loos, Vimy Ridge, the Somme and Passchendaele, and in July 1917 was sent home owing to illness. After treatment he was invalided out of the Army in October 1918, and holds the 1914-15 Star, and the General Service and Victory Medals.

7, Strand Street Ancoats Manchester.   Z9706

SKERRITT, H., Driver, R.F.A.
He volunteered in September 1914, and was shortly afterwards
drafted overseas. During his service on the Western Front
he took part in engagements at Loos, Ypres, the Somme
(II), Lens and in the Retreat and Advance of 1918, being
wounded in action on three occasions and invalided to hospital.
He was demobilised in January 1919, and holds the 1914
Star, and the General Service and Victory Medals.
12, Sutherland Street, Barracks Street, Hulme, Manchester.
Z8123

SKEVY, G. A., Sergeant, R.E.
Volunteering in August 1914, he proceeded to France three
months later. In this theatre of war he took a prominent
part in several engagements, including those at Ypres (I),
Hill 60, Ypres (II), Ploegsteert, the Somme, Vimy Ridge and
in the Retreat and Advance of 1918, and was wounded and
gassed in action. He was demobilised in March 1919, and
holds the 1914 Star, and the General Service and Victory
Medals. 36, Milton Street, West Gorton, Manchester. TZ8124

SKIDMORE, W. Private, 1/8th Manchester Regt.
He volunteered in August 1914, and in the following April
was drafted to the Dardanelles, where he saw much heavy
fighting in the Battles of Krithia (I, II and III), at the Landing
at Suvla Bay and the capture of Chunuk Bair, and was wounded
in action. As a result he was invalided to the Base, thence
to Malta and home. On his recovery he proceeded to France,
and took part in engagements at Arras, Ypres, Cambrai,
the Somme (II) and Le Cateau (II). He was demobilised in
February 1919, and holds the 1914–15 Star, and the General
Service and Victory Medals.
90, Viaduct Street, Ardwick, Manchester. Z8125

SKILLERN, C., Gunner, R.F.A.
He joined in October 1917, but during his training suffered
severely from rheumatism, and was invalided to hospital.
He was under treatment until he was demobilised in May 1919.
24, Elizabeth Street, Openshaw, Manchester. Z8126

SKINKIS, F., Private, M.G.C.
He joined in August 1918, and after completing a period of
training served at various stations, where he was engaged
on duties of great importance. Owing to the early cessation
of hostilities, he was unable to obtain his transfer overseas,
but nevertheless, rendered very valuable services, and in
1920 was still with his Company, having engaged for a period
of twelve years.
3, Hancock Street, Rochdale Road, Manchester. Z11119

SKIPPERS, J., Private, 16th Manchester Regiment.
Volunteering in March 1915, he was drafted to France in the
following January. Whilst overseas he saw much fighting
at Loos, and Vimy Ridge, and was wounded in action at
Trônes Wood, and consequently invalided home. On his
recovery he was transferred to the Labour Corps, and returning
to the Western Front, was present during engagements at
Arras, Ypres (III), Cambrai and in the Retreat and Advance
of 1918. He was demobilised in March 1919, and holds the
General Service and Victory Medals.
116, Earl Street, Longsight, Manchester. Z8127

SKITT, A., Driver, R.A.S.C. (M.T.)
He joined in April 1916, and was quickly drafted to France.
There he was engaged with the Mechanical Transport, convey-
ing supplies to the forward areas during the Battles of the
Somme, Arras, Ypres, and in the Retreat and Advance of
1918. He was demobilised in January 1919, and holds the
General Service and Victory Medals.
10, Anthony Street, Ardwick, Manchester. Z8128

SKITT, R. (M.M.), Sergt., Manchester Regiment.
He was called up from the Reserve in August 1914, and immediately drafted to France, where he fought at Mons and in
the subsequent Retreat. He also served with distinction
at the Battles of Ypres (II), Loos and the Somme, and was
wounded in action in May 1915. He was discharged time-
expired in 1916, but rejoined and again proceeded to France,
taking part in the Battles of Arras, Messines, Cambrai and in
the Retreat and Advance of 1918. He was awarded the
Military Medal for conspicuous bravery and devotion to duty
in capturing two German machine guns in September 1918.
He also holds the Mons Star, and the General Service and
Victory Medals, and was demobilised in 1919.
13, Amy Street, Longsight, Manchester. Z8129

SLACK, A., Sergt., Lancashire Fusiliers.
He volunteered in September 1914, and was engaged as a
drill Instructor at Aldershot before proceeding to France
in September 1915. In this theatre of war he saw much fighting at Loos, Lens, Vimy Ridge, the Somme, Messines, Ypres
and Cambrai, where he was wounded in action in March 1918.
As a result, he was invalided home, and on his recovery remained as an Instructor until his demobilisation in February
1919. He holds the 1914–15 Star, and the General Service
and Victory Medals.
33, Boundary Street, Newton, Manchester. TZ8130A

SLACK, C., Rifleman, 1st Rifle Brigade.
A Reservist, he was called to the Colours at the outbreak of
war in August 1914, and in June of the following year, was

drafted to Egypt, where he saw much severe fighting. After
serving through engagements at Romani, Magdhaba and
Rafa, he proceeded into Palestine, and there took part in the
Battles of Gaza and Aleppo, and the capture of Jerusalem,
Jericho and Tripoli. Returning home in January 1919, he
was demobilised in the following month, and holds the 1914–15
Star, and the General Service and Victory Medals.
31, Phelan Street, Collyhurst, Manchester. Z11120

SLACK, F. E., Private, 8th Manchester Regiment.
He joined in May 1916, and two months later crossed to France.
There he was engaged with his unit in the Battles of the Somme,
Arras, Messines and was wounded at Ypres in October 1917.
On recovery he took part in several engagements in the German
Offensive and subsequent Allied Advance of 1918, in the course
of which he was wounded at Bapaume in August of that year.
He was demobilised in January 1919, and holds the General
Service and Victory Medals.
26, Princess Street, Miles Platting, Manchester. Z9366

SLACK, J., Private, Manchester Regiment.
He joined in October 1917, at the age of eighteen years, and
after completing his training in the following March was
drafted to France, where he took part in much heavy fighting
at Cambrai, and in the Retreat. He made the supreme
sacrifice, being killed in action in April 1918, and was entitled
to the General Service and Victory Medals.
"Honour to the immortal dead, who gave their youth that
the world might grow old in peace."
33, Boundary Street, Newton, Manchester. TZ8130B

SLATER, F., Private, South Lancashire Regiment.
He volunteered in August 1914, and in the following year
proceeded to France. There he took part in much fighting
on the Somme, and at Ypres, where he was wounded in 1917,
and consequently invalided home. On his recovery he returned to France, and was in action in the Retreat of 1918,
being again wounded and sent home in March. He was
demobilised in March 1919, and holds the 1914–15 Star, and
the General Service and Victory Medals.
93, Thomas Street, West Gorton, Manchester. Z8132

SLATER, H., Private, 8th Manchester Regiment.
Volunteering in December 1915, he proceeded overseas in
the following March. Whilst on the Western Front he took
part in engagements on the Somme, at Ypres, Passchendaele,
Cambrai and in the Retreat and Advance of 1918, and was
wounded in action. He was demobilised in November 1919,
and holds the General Service and Victory Medals.
24, Gregory Street, West Gorton, Manchester. Z8133

SLATER, W., Private, Labour Corps.
He joined in April 1916, and underwent a period of training
prior to his being drafted to France. There he was engaged
on important duties at the ammunition dumps in various
sectors, including those of Ypres, Passchendaele, Cambrai,
the Somme, Epéhy and Arras. He was invalided home with
heart trouble, and was demobilised in January, 1919. He
holds the General Service and Victory Medals.
36, Markham Street, Ardwick, Manchester. Z8131

SLATTERY, F., Gunner, R.N.
He was mobilised in August 1914, and commissioned to H.M.S.
"Cochrane" and served in the North Sea and Mediterranean.
He took part in many engagements, and did continuously
good work throughout hostilities. He was discharged in
July 1919, owing to his ears being seriously affected by gun-
fire. He holds the 1914–15 Star, and the General Service
(with five clasps) and Victory Medals.
48, Canning Street, Hulme, Manchester. Z8134

SLATTERY, P., Private, 1/8th Manchester Regt.
He was mobilised when war broke out, and sailing for Gallipoli
in March 1915, fought in the first Landing on the Peninsula,
and in the first and second Battles of Krithia. He fell fighting
on May 15th, 1915, and was entitled to the 1914–15 Star,
and the General Service and Victory Medals.
"The path of duty was the way to glory."
14, Harrold Street, Miles Platting, Manchester. TZ9367

SLING, W., Private, 8th Manchester Regiment.
He volunteered in August 1914, and two months later was
drafted to France. In this theatre of war he took part in
several engagements, including the Battles of St. Eloi, Albert,
Ypres, Armentières, the Somme, Arras, Bullecourt, Cambrai,
Bapaume and the Marne (II), and was wounded in action at
Albert in May 1916. He was discharged in November 1918,
and holds the 1914 Star, and the General Service and Victory
Medals. 20, Newman St., Ancoats, Manchester. Z8135

SLOANE, H., Private, Lancashire Fusiliers.
Enlisting in July 1914, he was mobilised on the outbreak of
hostilities, and proceeding to France in September 1914,
was in action in the final operations of the Retreat from Mons.
He also took part in the Battles of Hill 60, Ypres, Loos, the
Somme, Messines and Cambrai, and in several of those in the
Retreat during which he was wounded in June 1918. Invalided home on account of his injuries he received hospital
treatment and was discharged in the same month as medically
unfit for further service. He holds the Mons Star, and the
General Service and Victory Medals.
13, Whatmough Street, Manchester. Z9577A

SLOANE, J., Private, R.A.S.C.

He volunteered in April 1915, and after a period of training proceeded to France, where he was engaged with the Remount Section on important duties at Calais. Later he was transferred to Italy, and saw much service on the Asiago Plateau and the Piave. After hostilities ceased, he returned home and was demobilised in June 1919, holding the General Service and Victory Medals.

48, Armitage Street, Ardwick, Manchester.   Z6609B

SLOANE, J. H., Private, 1/8th Manchester Regt.

He volunteered in October 1915, and in the following March proceeded to Egypt, where he took part in engagements at Agagia, Sollum, Katia, Romani and the capture of Magdhaba. Advancing with General Allenby into Palestine, he was in action at the Battles of Gaza (I, II and III). Later he was transferred to France, and fought on the Somme (II), the Marne (I) and at Havrincourt, where he was wounded in August 1918, and consequently invalided home. He was demobilised in April 1919, and holds the General Service and Victory Medals.

48, Armitage Street, Ardwick, Manchester.   Z6609C

SMALLSHAW, W., Private, Sherwood Foresters.

He was mobilised in August 1914, and immediately drafted to the Western Front, where he fought through the Retreat from Mons and in the Battles of the Marne, the Aisne and La Bassée. He was unfortunately killed in action in the Ypres sector on October 20th, 1914. He was entitled to the Mons Star, and the General Service and Victory Medals.

"The path of duty was the way to glory."

26A, Allen Street, Hulme, Manchester.   Z8136

SMALLWOOD, J., Private, 12th Manchester Regt.

He volunteered in September 1914, and after four months' training, was drafted to the Western Front, where he saw heavy fighting in various sectors. He took part in the Battles of Ypres, Festubert and the Somme, and in engagements at Hooge, Bray, La Bassée, Givenchy and many other places, and was twice wounded in action—at Hill 60, in November 1915, and at Passchendaele in October 1917. He was invalided home and was finally demobilised in March 1920, holding the 1914-15 Star, and the General Service and Victory Medals.

46, Churnett Street, Collyhurst, Manchester.   Z11121

SMALLWOOD, W., Pte., 19th Lancashire Fusiliers.

He volunteered in April 1915, and did continuously good work with his unit at various stations for about three months, when owing to ill-health, he was discharged in July 1915 as medically unfit for further service.

15, Hewitt Street, Openshaw, Manchester.   Z8137

SMALLWOOD, W., Private, K. (Liverpool Regt.)

He volunteered in December 1915, and after a period of training was sent to Ireland, where he was engaged on important guard and coastal duties, and rendered valuable services. He also served with the Labour Corps, but was not successful in obtaining a transfer to a theatre of war. He was demobilised in December 1918.

49, Edensor Street, Beswick, Manchester.   Z8138

SMEATON, E., Private, E. Lancashire Regiment.

Two months after volunteering in November 1914, he proceeded to the Western Front, where he took part in various important engagements, including the Battles of Neuve Chapelle and St. Eloi. He made the supreme sacrifice, falling in action on May 9th, 1915, at Hill 60. He was entitled to the 1914-15 Star, and the General Service and Victory Medals.

"And doubtless he went in splendid company."

10, Stretton Street, Collyhurst, Manchester.   Z10279A

SMEATON, G., Private, 5th S. Lancashire Regiment.

He volunteered in April 1915, and twelve months later proceeded to Salonika, where he saw much heavy fighting, taking part in the recapture of Monastir and in other important engagements on the Doiran and Struma fronts. He was very severely wounded in action in April 1918, and was in hospital at Malta before being invalided home, where he unhappily died of wounds on September 28th of that year. He was entitled to the General Service and Victory Medals.

"Courage, bright hopes, and a myriad dreams, splendidly given."

6, Kendall Street, Bradford, Manchester.   Z11122

SMETHURST, A., C.Q.M.S., Loyal N. Lancashire Regt.

He volunteered in September 1914, and twelve months later proceeded to the Western Front, where after taking a prominent part in the Battles of Loos and Vimy Ridge, he was wounded in action on the Somme in September 1916. Invalided home, he was transferred on his recovery in May of the following year, to Class W of the Reserve, and was engaged on munition work at Bootle until his demobilisation in January 1919. He re-enlisted, however, in the Labour Corps in September of that year, and was sent to Le Havre, whence he proceeded to Tsing Tau. He finally returned home for demobilisation in May 1920, and holds the 1914-15 Star, and the General Service and Victory Medals.

54, Nicholson Street, Rochdale Road, Manchester.   Z11581

SMETHURST, C. R., Private, 3rd Manchester Regt.

He joined in March 1916, and later in the same year proceeded to France, where he took part in several engagements, and was wounded in action at Bullecourt in June 1917. In consequence he was invalided home, but, on his recovery, returned to France, and was attached to the 9th Manchester Regiment. He was again wounded at Roisel in March 1918, and later served with the R.E. (Signal Section). He was demobilised in October 1919, and holds the General Service and Victory Medals. 48, Boston Street, Hulme, Manchester.   Z8140

SMETHURST, H., Private, R.A.S.C.

He volunteered in November 1914, and was engaged as a transport driver at home before proceeding to the Western Front in January 1916. Here he served as a clerk at the supply dumps in the forward areas during engagements at Givenchy, Festubert, Béthune, Ypres and in the Retreat and Advance of 1918. He was demobilised in March 1919, and holds the General Service and Victory Medals.

9, Cowesby Street, Moss Side, Manchester.   TZ8139

SMETHURST, W., Driver, R.A.S.C. (M.T.)

Volunteering in August 1914, he was drafted a year later to France. In this theatre of hostilities he was engaged as a motor transport driver carrying supplies to the front line in many sectors, including Loos, Albert, Arras, Ypres, Cambrai, Havrincourt and the Somme, and performed consistently good work. He was demobilised in May 1919, and holds the 1914-15 Star, and the General Service and Victory Medals.

77, Bedford Street, Hulme, Manchester.   Z11823

SMITH, A. (M.M.) Sergt., 2nd Manchester Regt.

He was called up from the Reserve in August 1914, and quickly drafted to the Western Front, where he played a distinguished part in the fighting at Mons, Ypres and the Somme, and was wounded in action in 1916. He was awarded the Military Medal for conspicuous bravery and devotion to duty in the Field. After recovering from his wound he returned to his unit and was unfortunately killed in action at Vimy Ridge on December 29th, 1917. He was entitled to the Mons Star, and the General Service and Victory Medals.

"Great deeds cannot die:
They with the sun and moon renew their light for ever."

35, River Street, Hulme, Manchester.   Z7415B

SMITH, A., Sapper, R.E.

Volunteering in December 1914, he was drafted shortly afterwards to Egypt, where he served on the Suez Canal. Later in the same year he was sent to the Dardanelles and there, after taking part in the Landing at Cape Helles saw much severe fighting until the Evacuation of the Peninsula. He then returned to Egypt, whence he proceeded into Palestine and took part in the first Battle of Gaza, before being transferred to the Western Front in April 1917. There he fought in the Battles of Ypres, Passchendaele, the Somme and Epéhy, and many other engagements, and also served through the Retreat and Advance of 1918. Demobilised in March 1919, he holds the 1914-15 Star, and the General Service and Victory Medals.

116, Norton Street, West Gorton, Manchester.   Z11146

SMITH, A., Driver, R.G.A.

Having enlisted in February 1914, he was already in the Army when war broke out in August of that year, and in April 1915, was drafted to the Western Front. There he saw severe fighting in various sectors, took part in the Battles of the Somme, Arras, Messines, Ypres, Cambrai, the Aisne and the Marne, and many minor engagements, and also served through the Retreat and Advance of 1918. He was afterwards stationed at Bonn with the Army of Occupation, and in April 1919 was transferred to India, where he was still with his Battery in 1920. He holds the 1914-15 Star, and the General Service and Victory Medals.

7, Ryder Street, Bradford, Manchester.   Z11144

SMITH, A., Private, 1st K.O. (Royal Lancaster Regt.)

He enlisted in July 1907, and five months after the outbreak of war in August 1914, proceeded to the Western Front, where he saw much severe fighting. After taking part in the Battles of St. Eloi and Hill 60, and many minor engagements, he was wounded in action and taken prisoner at Ypres. Held in captivity in Germany until December 1918, he was finally discharged in April of the following year, holding the 1914-15 Star, and the General Service and Victory Medals.

74, Heyrod Street, Ancoats, Manchester.   Z11138

SMITH, A., Private, Loyal N. Lancashire Regiment.

He volunteered in September 1914, and in July of the following year was drafted to the Western Front, where he took part in the Battles of Loos and Albert, and also saw severe fighting at Ypres and many other places. He fell in action at Vimy Ridge in May 1916, and was buried at St. Eloi. He was entitled to the 1914-15 Star, and the General Service and Victory Medals.

"He passed out of the sight of men by the path of duty and self-sacrifice."

10, Heatley Street, Miles Platting, Manchester.   Z11131

SMITH, A., Private, 2nd Black Watch.

Volunteering in September 1914, he was drafted to Mesopotamia on completing four months' training, and there saw much heavy fighting. After taking part in many important engagements, he was severely wounded in action at Kut and was in hospital in India and Egypt before being invalided home. He was finally demobilised in May 1919, and holds the 1914-15 Star, and the General Service and Victory Medals.
34, Davies Street, Ancoats, Manchester. Z11133

SMITH, A., Sapper, R.E.

He joined in September 1917, and was engaged on important duties with his unit at various stations. He rendered valuable services but was unable to obtain a transfer overseas before the cessation of hostilities. Later he proceeded to Germany with the Army of Occupation, and served there until his demobilisation in March 1920.
6, Ogilvie Street, Chorlton-on-Medlock, Manchester. X8162

SMITH, A., Gunner. R.G.A.

He joined in July 1916, and on completing his training was drafted to Salonika. In this seat of operations he took part in engagements on the Vardar and Doiran fronts, but contracted malaria, and was invalided home in April 1919. He was demobilised in September 1919, and holds the General Service and Victory Medals.
61, Parkfield Avenue, Rusholme, Manchester. Z8153

SMITH, A., Driver, R.A.S.C.

Joining in August 1916, he embarked for Salonika four months later, and was engaged on important transport duties during operations in the Balkans. Sent to France in 1918, he did good work in the Ypres salient and in the Retreat and Advance of that year, and returned to England after the Armistice. He was demobilised in September 1919, and holds the General Service and Victory Medals.
23, Masonic Street, Miles Platting, Manchester. Z9368

SMITH, A., Private, South Wales Borderers.

He joined in April 1917, and served with his Battalion at home until sent to the Western Front in March 1918. Whilst overseas he took part in heavy fighting in the German Offensive, and reported missing on May 30th, 1918, was later presumed to have been killed in action on that date. He was entitled to the General Service and Victory Medals.
"Great deeds cannot die :
They with the sun and moon renew their light for ever."
21, Ravald Street, Miles Platting, Manchester. Z9707A

SMITH, A., Wheeler, R.A.S.C.

He joined in June 1916, and after a period of training was engaged at various stations on important duties with his unit. He was not successful in obtaining a transfer overseas, but rendered valuable service as a wheelwright until his demobilisation in January 1919.
7, Derby Street, Ardwick, Manchester. Z8141

SMITH, A., Private, King's (Liverpool Regiment).

He enlisted in January 1912, and when war broke out in August 1914, quickly proceeded to France, where he took part in much heavy fighting at Mons, and in several other Battles. He was badly wounded at Loos in 1916, and in consequence was invalided home, being discharged in December 1917 as medically unfit for further duty. He holds the Mons Star, and the General Service and Victory Medals.
16, Union Street, Rusholme, Manchester. Z8157

SMITH, A. E., Gunner, R.G.A.

Volunteering in November 1914, he sailed for Salonika in the following August, and saw much service in the Balkans. He did good work with his Battery in engagements on the Doiran front, and in the Advance across the Struma and the Vardar. Contracting illness he was sent home early in 1918 and was invalided out of the Service in June of that year. He holds the 1914-15 Star, and the General Service and Victory Medals.
56, Woburn Place, Chorlton-on-Medlock, Manchester. Z9369

SMITH, A.W.J.(M.M.), Sergt., 2nd Grenadier Guards.

Volunteering on the outbreak of war, he was drafted to France in September 1914, and fought in several engagements until wounded at Ypres in November 1914. On recovery he took an active part in the Somme Offensive, and was awarded the Military Medal in November 1916, for conspicuous gallantry in bringing in the wounded under heavy shell-fire. He was also in action in the Battles of Arras, Bullecourt, Cambrai, Bapaume and Le Cateau and other places in the Retreat and Advance of 1918. Demobilised in January 1919, he holds the 1914 Star, and the General Service and Victory Medals.
56, Woburn Place, Chorlton-on-Medlock, Manchester. Z9370

SMITH, C., Private, Labour Corps.

He volunteered in June 1915, and in the following December was drafted overseas. Serving with his Company on the Western Front he did good work in the forward areas, and saw heavy fighting at Loos, Arras, the Somme, and in other sectors. Returning home for demobilisation in January 1919, he holds the 1914-15 Star, and the General Service and Victory Medals.
5, Frederick Place, Rochdale Road, Manchester Z9371

SMITH, C., Private, 1st South Wales Borderers.

He volunteered in May 1915, and in the following year proceeded to France. There he took part in the Battles of the Somme, Arras, Ypres and Passchendaele, and was wounded in action in 1916. He was demobilised in March 1919, and holds the General Service and Victory Medals.
2, Collinge Street, Newton, Manchester. Z7994

SMITH, C. C., Corporal, R.E.

Volunteering in March 1915, he was sent to the Western Front in the following October and served there for upwards of four years. During this period he was engaged with his unit on important duties in connection with operations in the advanced areas, and was present at the Battles of the Somme, Arras, Bullecourt, Cambrai and the Aisne. He also took part in the Retreat and Advance of 1918, and returning home for demobilisation in March 1919, holds the 1914-15 Star, and the General Service and Victory Medals.
12, Hadfield Street, Ancoats, Manchester. TZ9708

SMITH, D., Private, 4th Manchester Regiment.

He volunteered in August 1914, and was engaged on home service duties until August 1917, when he was sent to France. Whilst in this theatre of war he served in various sectors, and took part in the Battles of Arras, Messines, Ypres and Passchendaele. He gave his life for King and Country on November 13th, 1917, and was entitled to the General Service and Victory Medals.
"Steals on the ear the distant triumph song."
17, Raglan Street, Ancoats, Manchester. Z9204B

SMITH, D. H., Private, King's (Liverpool Regt.)

Shortly after joining in March 1916, he was drafted to France, where he saw severe fighting in various sectors of the Front. He took part in the Battles of the Somme, Ypres and the Marne, and many other important engagements in this theatre of war, and was gassed whilst in action in December 1916 He was demobilised in January 1919, and holds the General Service and Victory Medals. Z11136
1, Dawson Buildings, Chester Road, Hulme, Manchester.

SMITH, D. S., Private, 7th Lancashire Fusiliers.

Joining in January 1917, he was drafted overseas shortly afterwards. Whilst on the Western Front he took part in engagements on the Ancre, at Arras, Albert, Ypres and the Somme (II), and was badly wounded near Cambrai in August 1918. As a result he was invalided home and was in hospital in Wales and at Manchester until demobilised in December 1919. He holds the General Service and Victory Medals.
23, Cowesby Street, Moss Side, Manchester. Z8149

SMITH, E., Private, 11th East Lancashire Regt.

He joined in January 1918, and on completing his training in June of that year, was drafted to the Western Front, where he saw severe fighting at Havrincourt, Cambrai and many other places. He died gloriously on the Field of Battle near Armentières on September 13th, 1918, and was buried at Nieppe. He was entitled to the General Service and Victory Medals.
"Honour to the immortal dead, who gave their youth that the world might grow old in peace."
25, Iles Street, Oldham Road, Manchester. Z11132B

SMITH, E., Private, 9th Lancashire Fusiliers.

Volunteering in August 1914, he sailed for Gallipoli in the following June, and was in action at the Landing at Suvla Bay, and other operations until the Evacuation of the Peninsula, when he was sent to Egypt. After a short term of service in the Canal zone he proceeded to France in January 1917, and fought at Arras, Ypres and Passchendaele. Wounded on October 4th, 1917, he was sent home on account of his injuries and was under hospital treatment for several months. He was discharged as medically unfit for further service in December 1918, and holds the 1914-15 Star, and the General Service and Victory Medals.
115, Montague Street, Collyhurst, Manchester. Z9372

SMITH, E., Private, 1st Cheshire Regiment.

He volunteered in March 1915, and after completing a period of training, was drafted later in the same year to Gibraltar. There he was engaged on important garrison duties for nearly four years, during which period he rendered valuable services with his unit. He returned to England for demobilisation in February 1919, and holds the General Service and Victory Medals. 6, South Street, Hulme, Manchester. Z8164

SMITH, F., Corporal, 1/8th Manchester Regiment.

He volunteered at the outbreak of war in August 1914, and in the following year was drafted to the Dardanelles, where after taking part in the Landing at Cape Helles, he saw much severe fighting until the Evacuation of the Peninsula. He was then sent to Egypt, whence he was transferred shortly afterwards to the Western Front, and took part in the Battles of the Somme, Arras, Vimy Ridge, Ypres and Cambrai, and many other engagements. He was killed in action at Mormal Forest on November 6th, 1918, only five days before the signing of the Armistice. He was entitled to the 1914-15 Star, and the General Service and Victory Medals.
"Nobly striving, he nobly fell that we might live."
6, Clough Street, Newton, Manchester. Z11123

SMITH, E., Air Mechanic, R.A.F.
He volunteered in January 1916, and after undergoing a period of training, served at various stations, where he was engaged on duties of a highly technical nature. He was unable to obtain his transfer to a theatre of war on account of defective eyesight, but nevertheless rendered valuable services with his Squadron until February 1919, when he was demobilised.
26, Mitton Street, Longsight, Manchester.   Z8115

SMITH, F., Private, 13th Manchester Regiment.
He volunteered in September 1914, and after a period of training, was drafted to Salonika, where he took part in many engagements. Later he was transferred to France, and was in action at Ypres, Ploegsteert and Delville Wood. During hostilities he also saw service in Serbia. He was demobilised in February 1920, and holds the General Service and Victory Medals. 5, John Street, Bradford, Manchester.   Z11865

SMITH, F., Rifleman, K.R.R.C.
He joined in July 1916, and after undergoing a period of training, served at various stations, where he was engaged on duties of great importance. He was unable to obtain his transfer to the Front on account of ill-health, but nevertheless rendered valuable services with his unit until May 1918, when he was invalided from the Army, suffering from debility.
5, Haigh Street, West Gorton, Manchester.   Z11127

SMITH, F., Private, R.M.L.I.
He joined in May 1918, and after completing a term of training served at various stations, where he was engaged on duties of great importance. Owing to the early cessation of hostilities he was unable to obtain his transfer overseas, but, nevertheless, rendered valuable services with his unit until March 1919, when he was discharged as medically unfit for further service.
81, Robert Street, West Gorton, Manchester.   Z8160A

SMITH, F., Private, 9th Lancashire Fusiliers.
He volunteered in August 1914, and embarking for Gallipoli in the following year fought at the Landing at Suvla Bay and in other engagements on the Peninsula. Owing to illness he was invalided home in January 1916, and after treatment at Cardiff and Barry Dock Hospitals. proceeded to the Western Front. He was in action in the Somme Offensive, in the course of which he was gassed and sent to England, receiving medical treatment. Invalided out of the Army in February 1917, he holds the 1914–15 Star, and the General Service and Victory Medals. 26, Gunson Street, Miles Platting Manchester. Z9373

SMITH, F., Private, 3rd (King's Own) Hussars.
Joining in March 1917, he landed in France a year later, and took part in heavy fighting in several engagements during the German Offensive. He was also in action in the subsequent Allied Advance of 1918, and sent in February of the following year into Germany, served with the Army of Occupation for upwards of a year. He returned to England for demobilisation in November 1919, and holds the General Service and Victory Medals. 50, Higham Street, Miles Platting, Manchester. Z9709

SMITH, F., Driver, R.A.S.C. (M.T.)
Two months after joining in March 1916, he was sent to the Western Front, where he was engaged on important duties in various sectors. Attached to the R.F.A. he was present at the Battles of the Somme, Arras, Ypres and Cambrai, and many other engagements, and also took an active part in the Retreat and Advance of 1918. He afterwards served with the Army of Occupation in Germany, finally returning home for demobilisation in September 1919. He holds the General Service and Victory Medals.
11, Earl Street, Hulme, Manchester.   TZ8161

SMITH, F., Private, 16th Lancashire Fusiliers.
He joined in July 1917, and in January of the following year, proceeded to the Western Front. Whilst in this theatre of war he saw much severe fighting, took part in the Battles of the Somme and the Marne, and other engagements in various sectors, and was gassed whilst in action. He was for a time in hospital at Rouen and Glasgow, and on his recovery in May 1919, was drafted with the Army of Occupation to Turkey, where he served at Constantinople. He was demobilised on his return home in December 1919, and holds the General Service and Victory Medals.
16, Edmund Street, Openshaw, Manchester.   Z8147

SMITH, F. J., Sergt., R.F.A.
Volunteering in August 1914, he was drafted to Gallipoli in the following May, and served with his Battery from the Landing at Suvla Bay until the Evacuation of the Peninsula. In January 1916 he was sent to Mesopotamia, in which theatre of war he took part in heavy fighting in operations for the relief of Kut, and was present at the capture of Baghdad. Returning to England, he was demobilised in March 1919, and holds the 1914–15 Star, and the General Service and Victory Medals.
12, Sutton Street, West Gorton, Manchester.   TZ9374

SMITH, G., Private, 7th Seaforth Highlanders.
He volunteered in October 1915, and after completing four months' training, was drafted to the Western Front, where he saw much severe fighting at Albert, and many other places. He made the supreme sacrifice, falling in action on October

12th, 1916, during the Advance on the Somme. He was entitled to the General Service and Victory Medals.
    "He died the noblest death a man may die,
    Fighting for God, and right, and liberty."
43, Derby Street, Hulme, Manchester.   Z8163

SMITH, G., Sapper, R.E.
Volunteering in March 1915, he proceeded to the Western Front in October of that year, and there served in various sectors. After taking an active part in the Battles of Loos, Albert and Ploegsteert Wood, and many other engagements, he was severely wounded in action in August 1916 during the Somme Offensive, and was invalided to hospital in England. He was finally discharged in February 1917, as medically unfit for further service, and holds the 1914–15 Star, and the General Service and Victory Medals.
39, Boslam Street, Ancoats, Manchester.   Z11135

SMITH, G., Rifleman, 19th Rifle Brigade.
Volunteering in December 1914, he was drafted to Egypt in the following month, and there saw much severe fighting. After taking part in engagements on the Suez Canal and at Mersa Matruh, Sollum, Katia, El Fasher, Romani and Magdhaba, he proceeded into Palestine, where he was again in action at the Battles of Gaza, at the capture of Jerusalem, Jericho and Tripoli, and at Aleppo. Returning home on the cessation of hostilities he was demobilised in May 1919, and holds the 1914–15 Star, and the General Service and Victory Medals. 12, Melbourne Street, Hulme, Manchester. Z8159

SMITH, G. E., Pte., 9th Loyal N. Lancashire Regt.
He volunteered in December 1915, and twelve months later was drafted to the Western Front, where he saw heavy fighting in various sectors. He took part in the Battles of Messines, Ypres and Cambrai, and many minor engagements until severely wounded in action on the Somme in March 1918. Invalided home he was finally discharged as medically unfit for further service in November 1918, and holds the General Service and Victory Medals.
17, Rex Street, Jackson Street, Hulme, Manchester. Z8165

SMITH, H., Sergt., Border Regt. and Labour Corps.
He volunteered in December 1914, and in May of the following year was drafted to France, where he took part in the Battle of Loos and many other important engagements. He afterwards served with the Labour Corps in various sectors, and was engaged chiefly in guarding prisoners of war until after the cessation of hostilities. Returning home in February 1919, he was demobilised in the following month, and holds the 1914–15 Star, and the General Service and Victory Medals.
15, Elizabeth Street, Greenheys, Manchester.   Z8167

SMITH, H., Pte., 1st Loyal North Lancashire Regt.
He volunteered in January 1916, and in August of that year was drafted to the Western Front. Whilst in this theatre of war he saw severe fighting in various sectors, and took part in the Battles of the Somme and Passchendaele, and in engagements at Nieuport, Givenchy and many other places. Invalided home in August 1918, he was retained in England until his demobilisation in August 1919, and holds the General Service and Victory Medals.
Radnor Hotel, Radnor Street, Hulme, Manchester.   Z8166

SMITH, H., L/Cpl., King's Own Scottish Borderers.
He volunteered in August 1914, and embarking for France in the following July was in action in the Battle of Loos. He fell fighting on September 25th, 1915, and was entitled to the 1914–15 Star, and the General Service and Victory Medals.
    "His life for his Country, his soul to God."
21, Ravald Street, Miles Platting Manchester.   Z9707B

SMITH, H., Private, 8th Manchester Regiment.
He joined in January 1917, and after completing his training was engaged on important duties with his unit at various stations. He rendered valuable services, but was not successful in securing his transfer overseas before the termination of hostilities, and was discharged on account of service in February 1919.
90, Irlam Street, Miles Platting, Manchester.   Z9710

SMITH, H., Private, 3rd Border Regiment.
He joined in July 1917, and six months later was sent to the Western Front. There he took part in strenuous fighting on the Somme and Marne fronts, and at Bapaume, Havrincourt, Cambrai and Mons. After the Armistice he served in Germany with the Army of Occupation until October 1919, when he returned home and was demobilised, holding the General Service and Victory Medals.
4, Mather Street, Hulme, Manchester.   Z11824

SMITH, H., Corporal, R.F.A.
Having enlisted in January 1908, he was already serving in the East when war broke out in August 1914. He saw much severe fighting in Mesopotamia during the period of hostilities, and took part in engagements at Amara, Um-el-Hannah and the Tigris, and served also at the Relief of Kut and the capture of Baghdad and Tekrit. Returning home in August 1918 he was discharged in February of the following year, and holds the 1914–15 Star, and the General Service and Victory Medals.
32, Myrtle Grove, Ardwick, Manchester.   Z8158

SMITH, H., Private, 1/7th Lancashire Fusiliers.
Volunteering in April 1915, he was drafted to France in September of that year, and there saw severe fighting in various sectors of the Front. He took part in the Battles of Albert, the Somme, Ypres and Cambrai, and many other important engagements, served also through the Retreat and Advance of 1918, and was wounded in action at Arras in April 1917. He was demobilised in March of the following year, and holds the 1914-15 Star, and the General Service and Victory Medals.
12, Gatley Street, Ancoats, Manchester.　　Z8155A

SMITH, H., L/Corporal, K.O. (R. Lancaster Regt.)
Volunteering in August 1914, he was drafted to the Western Front in February of the following year, and there fought in various sectors. He took part in the Battles of St. Eloi, Hill 60, Festubert and Vimy Ridge, and minor engagements, and was twice wounded in action in the Somme Offensive of 1916. He was invalided home, but returned to France on his recovery, and was again in action at the Battles of Arras, Ypres, Cambrai and the Selle. Demobilised in February 1919, he holds the 1914-15 Star, and the General Service and Victory Medals.
56, Cheetham Street, Lower Openshaw, Manchester.　Z8144

SMITH, J., Private, 6th Border Regiment.
He volunteered in August 1914, and in the following year, was drafted to the Dardanelles, where he saw much severe fighting at Suvla Bay, and was wounded. He was unhappily reported missing and, later, killed in action at Chocolate Hill on August 9th, 1915. He was entitled to the 1914-15 Star, and the General Service and Victory Medals.
"Thinking that remembrance, though unspoken, may reach him where he sleeps."
20, Granville Place, Ancoats, Manchester.　　Z11134

SMITH, J., Sapper, R.E.
He volunteered in 1915, and on completing his training in the following year, proceeded to the Western Front, where he was engaged on important duties in the Somme sector until wounded in action in August 1916, and invalided home. He returned to France, however, in 1916, and took an active part in the Battles of Arras and Cambrai, and many other engagements. Demobilised in January 1919, he holds the General Service and Victory Medals.
119, Victoria Square, Oldham Road, Manchester.　Z11584

SMITH, J., Private, 4th Seaforth Highlanders.
Two months after volunteering in January 1915, he proceeded to the Western Front, where he saw much severe fighting. After taking part in the Battles of Neuve Chapelle and Hill 60, and many minor engagements, he was wounded in action and invalided home. He was afterwards retained on important duties with a Labour Battalion in England until September 1919, when he was discharged as medically unfit for further service. He holds the 1914-15 Star, and the General Service and Victory Medals.
15, Taylor Street, Gorton, Manchester.　　Z11139A

SMITH, J., Private, 1/7th Gordon Highlanders.
After volunteering in August 1914, he underwent a period of training prior to being drafted to the Western Front in January 1916. There he saw severe fighting in various sectors, and took part in the Battles of the Somme, Arras and Ypres, and many other important engagements until the cessation of hostilities. He unfortunately contracted influenza, and died at Castle Douglas on December 13th, 1918. He was entitled to the General Service and Victory Medals.
"Steals on the ear the distant triumph song."
3, Saville Street, Miles Platting, Manchester.　Z11128

SMITH, J., Sapper, R.E.
He joined in September 1917, and after undergoing a period of training, was retained on important duties at various stations. He was not successful in his efforts to obtain his transfer to a theatre of war, but nevertheless rendered valuable services with his Company until December 1919, when he was demobilised.
15, Taylor Street, Gorton, Manchester.　　Z11139B

SMITH, J., Private, Labour Corps.
After volunteering in November 1914, he underwent a period of training prior to being drafted to the Western Front in September 1916. There he saw severe fighting in various sectors, took part in the Battles of Arras, Bullecourt, Ypres and Cambrai, and many other engagements, and served also through the Retreat and Advance of 1918. He was demobilised in February 1919, and holds the General Service and Victory Medals.
138, Tame Street, Ancoats, Manchester.　　Z8143A

SMITH, J., Private, 1st K.O. (R. Lancaster Regt.)
Volunteering in August 1914, he was drafted to the Western Front after three months' training, and there saw much severe fighting. He took part in the Battles of St. Eloi, the Somme and the Ancre, and many other engagements, and was three times wounded in action—at Ypres in May and June 1915, and at Arras in May 1917. Invalided to hospital in London, he was finally discharged as medically unfit for further service in December 1917. He holds the 1914 Star, and the General Service and Victory Medals.
5, Melbourne Street, Hulme, Manchester.　　TZ8156

SMITH, J., Sapper, R.E.
He joined in July 1916, and after completing a period of training, served at various stations, where he was engaged on important coastal defence duties. He was not successful in his efforts to obtain his transfer to a theatre of war, but, nevertheless, rendered valuable services with his Company until November 1919, when he was demobilised.
7, Beta Street, Hulme, Manchester.　　Z8168

SMITH, J., Private, 2/8th Manchester Regiment.
Joining in November 1916, he crossed to the Western Front in the following February, and fought in the Battles of Arras, Bullecourt, Messines, Ypres. Reported missing in October 1917, he was later presumed to have been killed in action at Ypres, and was entitled to the General Service and Victory Medals.
"His life for his Country, his soul to God."
9, Cheltenham Street, Collyhurst, Manchester.　Z9375

SMITH, J., Private, 13th Manchester Regiment.
Volunteering in August 1914, he was sent to France in September of the following year, and served in the Battle of Loos, and in several other engagements until December 1915, when he proceeded to Salonika. In the Balkans he took part in operations including the Advance on the Doiran and Struma fronts, and contracting fever was sent to hospital at Manchester for treatment in September 1916. He was discharged as medically unfit for further service in August 1917, and holds the 1914-15 Star, and the General Service and Victory Medals.
28, Naylor Street, Newton, Manchester.　　Z9376

SMITH, J., Private, 22nd Manchester Regiment.
He volunteered in January 1915, and was retained on important duties in England until March 1916, when he was drafted to Egypt. After taking part in engagements at Sollum, Katia, El Fasher and Romani, he proceeded into Palestine, where he was again in action at the capture of Jerusalem and Jericho. He finally returned home for demobilisation in March 1920, and holds the General Service and Victory Medals.
12, Gatley Street, Ancoats, Manchester.　　Z8155B

SMITH, J., Private, 9th Black Watch.
He volunteered in November 1915, and in April of the following year proceeded to the Western Front, where he saw severe fighting in various sectors and was twice wounded in action. After taking part in the Battles of the Somme, Vimy Ridge, Messines and Ypres, and other engagements, he was taken prisoner in the Retreat of March 1918, and was held in captivity until after the cessation of hostilities. He was demobilised on his release in February 1919, and holds the General Service and Victory Medals.
8, Fenn Street, Hulme, Manchester.　　TZ8169

SMITH, J., Private, 2nd South Lancashire Regt.
Three months after joining in November 1916, he proceeded to the Western Front, and there saw heavy fighting in various sectors. He took part in the Battles of the Ancre, Arras, Bullecourt, Messines and Ypres, and many minor engagements until so severely wounded in action in the second Battle of the Somme as to necessitate the amputation of his right foot. He was for a considerable period in hospital in France and England, before being invalided from the Army in August 1919, and holds the General Service and Victory Medals.
11, Lilford Street, West Gorton, Manchester.　TZ8182

SMITH, J. A., Driver, R.A.S.C. (H.T.)
He joined in January 1918, and after completing a period of training served at various stations, where he was engaged on duties of a highly important nature. He was not successful in obtaining his transfer to the front, but nevertheless, rendered very valuable services, and in 1920 was still with his Company.
138, Tame Street, Ancoats, Manchester.　　Z8143B

SMITH, J. D., Sergt., R.E., and R.A.P.C.
He volunteered in March 1915, and after his training was retained on important clerical duties at various stations. He was also attached for a time to the R.A.F., and although unsuccessful in his efforts to obtain his transfer overseas, rendered very valuable services during the period of hostilities. He was demobilised in March 1919.
82, Earl Street, Longsight, Manchester.　　Z8142A

SMITH, J. F. S., Air Mechanic R.A.F.
He joined in August 1918, and after completing a term of training served at various stations, where he was engaged on duties of a highly technical nature. He was unable to obtain his transfer overseas on account of the early cessation of hostilities, but nevertheless, rendered valuable services with his Squadron until demobilised in February 1919.
19, Cromwell Avenue, Manley Park, Manchester.　Z11125

SMITH, J. H., L/Corporal, E. Lancashire Regiment.
Joining in March 1916, he was drafted to the Western Front in October of that year, and there took part in the Battles of the Somme, Ypres, and Cambrai and many minor engagements in various sectors. He died gloriously on the Field of Battle on November 27th, 1917. He was entitled to the General Service and Victory Medals.
"He joined the great white company of valiant souls."
13, Matlock Street, Ardwick, Manchester.　　Z8146

SMITH, J. F., Private, Manchester Regiment.
He volunteered in September 1914, and served at various stations in England until drafted to the Western Front in January 1916. There he took part in the Somme Offensive until wounded in action at Arras, in September 1916, and invalided to hospital at Manchester. He returned to France, however, on his recovery, fought in the Battle of Cambrai, and other importuat engagements, and was a second time wounded at La Bassée in 1918. He was finally demobilised in March 1919, and holds the General Service and Victory Medals.
180, Heald Grove, Rusholme, Manchester. Z8172-3A

SMITH, J. H., Private, 8th Manchester Regiment.
He joined in May 1916, and in February of the following year proceeded to the Western Front, where he saw much severe fighting. After taking part in the Battles of the Ancre, Arras, Messines, Ypres and Cambrai, and other engagements, he was wounded in action on the Somme, and invalided home. On his recovery, however, in September, 1918 he was drafted to Egypt, where he was engaged on garrison duties at Cairo until his return to England for demobilisation in November 1919. He holds the General Service and Victory Medals.
25, Iles Street, Oldham Road, Manchester. Z11132A

SMITH, J. H.C., Gunner, R.F.A.
He volunteered in August 1915, and after undergoing a period of training, served at various stations, where he was engaged on duties of great importance. Being over age for active service, he was unable to obtain his transfer to a theatre of war, but nevertheless, did much useful work with his Battery until December 1918, when he was demobilised.
34, Ashover Street, Ardwick, Manchester. Z8145

SMITH, J. J., Private, 7th Manchester Regiment.
He volunteered in August 1914, and in April of the following year was drafted to Gallipoli, where he took part in the Landing at Suvla Bay, and in the same month was severely wounded in action, losing his leg. He was for a considerable period in hospital in England, before being invalided from the Army in December 1916, and holds the 1914-15 Star, and the General Service and Victory Medals.
20, Stamford Street, Hulme, Manchester. Z8170

SMITH, J. T., Pte., 1/8th King's (Liverpool Regt.)
Three months after joining in February 1916, he was drafted to the Western Front, where he saw much severe fighting. After being wounded in action near Ypres in May 1916, he was taken prisoner at Arras, in November of that year, and whilst in captivity was forced to work in the salt mines in Germany. Released in January 1919, he was demobilised in September of that year, and holds the General Service and Victory Medals.
180, Heald Grove, Rusholme, Manchester. Z8172-3B

SMITH, J. V., Driver, R.E.
He volunteered in March 1915, and after two months' training was drafted to Egypt, where he saw severe fighting on the Suez Canal. In February 1916 he was transferred to the Western Front, where there took an active part in the Battles of Albert, Vimy Ridge, the Somme, Bullecourt, the Lys and Le Cateau, and was severely injured in May 1918 in an accident. Demobilised in February 1919, he holds the 1914-15 Star, and the General Service and Victory Medals.
20, Portugal Street, Ancoats, Manchester. Z11583

SMITH, J. W., Stoker, R.N.
He volunteered in August 1914, and was posted to H.M.S. "Victoria," attached to the Grand Fleet in the North Sea. There he was engaged on mine-sweeping and other important duties and took part in the Battle of Jutland and many minor actions, until the cessation of hstilities. He was demobilised in November 1919, and holds the 1914-15 Star, and the General Service (with five clasps) and Victory Medals.
9, Phoenix Street, Hulme, Manchester. Z8171

SMITH, J. W., Private, 8th Manchester Regiment.
He volunteered in October 1914, and sailing for Gallipoli in the following January, fought in the first Landing on the Peninsula, the Battle of Krithia, the Landing at Suvla Bay, and in other operations until the Evacuation of the Peninsula. Sent to the Western Front in January 1916, he was in action at Albert, and Vermelles, and was wounded on the Somme in November 1915. On recovery he served with his his unit in the Battles of Bullecourt, Lens, Messines, and in the Retreat and Advance of 1918. He holds the 1914-15 Star, and the General Service and Victory Medals, and was demobilised in July 1919. 42, Chapel Street, Ancoats, Manchester. Z9362B

SMITH, J. W., Private, 8th Manchester Regiment.
Volunteering in September 1914, he completed his training, and was engaged on Coast Defence duties at Southport and Blackpool, and rendered valuable services. Contracting blood poisoning he was sent to hospital and after treatment was discharged as medically unfit in May 1916.
42, Chapel Street, Ancoats, Manchester. Z9362A

SMITH, J. W., Sergt., 8th Manchester Regiment.
Mobilised with the Territorials in August 1914, he was drafted to Gallipoli in the following year, and was there wounded in action in the third Battle of Krithia in June 1915. He was

invalided home, but on his recovery in May 1916, proceeded to the Western Front, where he took part in the Somme Offensive of that year. A second time invalided to England, suffering from debility, he afterwards was sent to Italy, and was in action on the Piave until the cessation of hostilities. He was discharged on his return home in March 1919, and holds the 1914-15 Star, and the General Service and Victory and Territorial Efficiency Medals.
3, Derby Street, Ardwick, Manchester. Z8148

SMITH, M. M., Private, 2/10th Manchester Regt.
He joined in August 1916, and on completing his training in the following year was drafted to France. In this theatre of war he took part in the Battles of Arras, Messines, Bullecourt, and Ypres (III). He was invalided home suffering from shell-shock, and on his recovery served at the War Office until he was demobilised in April 1919. He holds the General Service and Victory Medals.
3, Sycamore Street, Newton, Manchester. Z11126

SMITH, N., Private, York and Lancaster Regiment.
Mobilised in August 1914, he was drafted overseas shortly afterwards. Whilst on the Western Front he took part in the Battles of Hill 60, and Loos, where he was badly wounded in 1915. In consequence he was invalided home and finally discharged in August 1916, as medically unfit for further duty. He holds the 1914-Star, and the General Service and Victory Medals.
21, Stewart Street, Gorton, Manchester. Z11140

SMITH, N. (Mrs.), Special War Worker.
At the outbreak of war in August 1914, this lady immediately offered to do work of National importance and was engaged at Messrs. T. Rycroft & Co., in connection with the manufacture of articles of Army clothing. She carried out her duties in a very able manner, and rendered valuable services until after the cessation of hostilities.
3, Poynton Street, Ardwick, Manchester. X8174

SMITH, P. (M.M.), Private, 22nd Manchester Regt.
Twelve months after volunteering in November 1914, he was drafted to the Western Front, and first saw heavy fighting at Loos, St. Eloi and Albert. He also took part in the Battles of Vermelles, the Somme, Arras, Vimy Ridge and Bullecourt, where he was wounded in action in May 1917, and was awarded the Military Medal for conspicuous bravery and devotion to duty during a German attack. On his recovery, he was transferred to Italy, and was in action on the Asiago Plateau and the Piave. Demobilised in February 1919, he holds the 1914-15 Star, and the General Service and Victory Medals.
5, Henry Street, Moor Street, Rusholme, Manchester. Z8175

SMITH, R., Private, Manchester Regiment.
He was already in the Army when war broke out in August 1914, and in the following year was drafted to the Dardanelles, where he took part in much severe fighting and was wounded. On his recovery he proceeded to France and was in action on the Somme, at Arras, Albert and Armentières, and was wounded at Cambrai. He was discharged in March 1919, and holds the 1914-15 Star, and the General Service and Victory Medals.
62, Kemp Street, Manchester. Z11142

SMITH, R., Private, 10th King's (Liverpool Regt.)
He joined the Liverpool Scottish in September 1916, and was quickly drafted to the Western Front, where he took part in the Battles of Arras, Bullecourt, Ypres (III), and Lens, and in heavy fighting on the Somme and the Ancre. He died gloriously on the Field of Battle at Cambrai in November 1917, and was entitled to the General Service and Victory Medals.
"The path of duty was the way to glory."
43, Forbes Street, West Gorton, Manchester. Z8150

SMITH, R. A., Corporal, Labour Corps.
He joined in March 1917, and was speedily drafted to the Western Front, where he was engaged on special road and trench construction work in the Ypres, Somme, La Bassée, Albert and Cambrai sectors. He also rendered valuable services with his unit during the Retreat and Advance of 1918, and was eventually demobilised in November 1919, holding the General Service and Victory Medals.
34, Randolph Street, Openshaw, Manchester. Z8183

SMITH, S., Private, R.A.S.C.
He joined in 1917, but after a very short period of service, was discharged as medically unfit for military duty later in the same year.
3, Peel Street, Chorlton-on-Medlock, Manchester. X8176

SMITH, S., Private, 8th Manchester Regiment.
He joined in April 1916, and was drafted overseas two months later. Serving with his Battalion in various sectors of the Western Front he fought in the Battles of Vimy Ridge, the Somme, Arras, Bullecourt, Ypres and Cambrai, and owing to illness was invalided home early in 1918. After receiving treatment at Whitworth Military Hospital, Manchester, he was discharged on medical grounds in April 1918, and holds the General Service and Victory Medals.
39, Dale Street, Miles Platting, Manchester. Z9377

SMITH, S., Private, 3/2nd Welch Regiment.

He volunteered in May 1915, and on completing his training in the following March proceeded to France. There he took part in several engagements, including the Battles of the Somme Arras, Passchendaele and Cambrai, and was badly wounded in March 1918. As a result he was invalided home, and on his recovery was transferred to the Royal Defence Corps, and was engaged on guard duties in the prison camps. He was demobilised in March 1919, and holds the General Service and Victory Medals.

94, Gunson Street, Miles Platting, Manchester.　　Z11130

SMITH, S. C., Private, 2/8th Manchester Regiment.

He joined in October 1916, and in the following March was drafted to France. Whilst in this theatre of war he took part in the Battles of Messines, Ypres (III) and Cambrai, and in the Retreat and Advance of 1918. After hostilities ceased, he went to Germany with the Army of Occupation, and served there until his demobilisation in October 1919. He holds the General Service and Victory Medals.

12, Alma Street, Collyhurst, Manchester.　　Z11582

SMITH, S. D., Private, Loyal North Lancaster Regiment and M.G.C.

He joined in July 1917, and in March of the following year was drafted to the Western Front, where he took part in much severe fighting at Arras, Vimy Ridge, Havrincourt, Cambrai, Epéhy, and on the Somme, during the Retreat and Advance of 1918. After the cessation of hostilities, he served in Germany with the Army of Occupation until September 1919, when he was demobilised, holding the General Service and Victory Medals.

8, Baker Street, Longsight, Manchester.　　Z8154

SMITH, T., Private, 8th Manchester Regiment.

He volunteered in September 1914, and in the following April was sent to Gallipoli, where he was badly wounded in action during the Landing at Cape Helles. Invalided to hospital in Cardiff, he was under treatment there for nine months, but in September 1916, was drafted to France, and took part in the Battles of Beaumont-Hamel, Arras, Bullecourt, Ypres (III), Cambrai (1917 and 1918) and St. Quentin, and in the Retreat and Advance of 1918. He holds the 1914–15 Star, and the General Service and Victory Medals, and was demobilised in February 1919.

27, Patchett Street, Hulme, Manchester.　　Z8177

SMITH, T., Private, 1st Highland Light Infantry.

He was called up from the Reserve in August 1914, and immediately drafted to France, where he took part in the Battle of Mons, and the subsequent Retreat and the Battle of Le Cateau. He was unfortunately killed in action near the Marne on September 17th, 1914, and was entitled to the Mons Star, and the General Service and Victory Medals.

" A valiant Soldier, with undaunted heart he breasted life's last hill."

61, Green Street, Gorton, Manchester.　　Z11141

SMITH, T., Private, 2nd King's (Liverpool Regt.)

He volunteered in May 1915, and on completing his training in the following year, proceeded to France. There he took part in the Battles of the Somme, Beaumont-Hamel, Beaucourt, Delville Wood and Ypres, where he was wounded in action in July 1917. As a result he was invalided home, but on recovery returned to France, and was again wounded at Cambrai in 1918, and once more sent home. He was demobilised in September 1919, and holds the General Service and Victory Medals.

51, Boardman Street, Harpurhey, Manchester.　　Z11137

SMITH, T., Private, 2nd Manchester Regiment.

He volunteered in August 1914, and after a period of training in Ireland, was drafted to France. Whilst in this seat of war he took part in several engagements, including the Battles of Ypres, Loos, and the Somme. He was demobilised in March 1920, and holds the 1914 Star, and the General Service and Victory Medals.

123, Thorton Street, Collyhurst, Manchester.　　Z11124

SMITH, W., L/Corporal, 9th Manchester Regiment.

He joined in March 1916, and in the following November was drafted overseas. During his service in Mesopotamia, he took part in several engagements, including those at Kut-el-Amara, and the capture of Baghdad. He returned home and was demobilised in June 1919, holding the General Service and Victory Medals.

383, Collyhurst Road, Collyhurst, Manchester.　　Z11147

SMITH, W., L/Corporal, 11th Manchester Regt.

He volunteered in February 1915, and in March of the following year was sent to France. In this theatre of war he was in action at Vermelles, the Somme, Arras and Bullecourt. He also fought in the Battles of the Aisne, the Marne, Le Cateau and other places, in the Retreat and subsequent Allied Advance, in the course of which he was wounded at Cambrai in October 1918. He was demobilised in January 1919, and holds the General Service and Victory Medals.

2, Woburn Place, Chorlton-on-Medlock, Manchester.　　Z9378

SMITH, W., Private, 14th King's (Liverpool Regt.)

He volunteered in August 1914, and a year afterwards proceeded to France, where he took part in the Battle of Loos. Transferred to Salonika, he was engaged with his unit on the Doiran and Struma fronts, and was wounded at Monastir. He later participated in further fighting on the Doiran and Vardar fronts, and did excellent work until he returned home, being eventually demobilised in April 1919, holding the 1914–15 Star, and the General Service and Victory Medals.

59, Church Street, Hulme, Manchester.　　Z11825

SMITH, W., Private, York and Lancaster Regt.

He joined in February 1918, and in the following July was sent to the Western Front, where he saw severe fighting during the Advance of 1918. He was in action at Bullecourt, Bucquoy, Cambrai, Vaux, Marcoing and Havrincourt, and was wounded and gassed in September 1918. After spending two months in hospital in France, he proceeded to Germany with the Army of Occupation and remained there until his demobilisation in November 1919. He holds the General Service and Victory Medals.

6, Stone Street, Chester Road, Hulme, Manchester.　　Z8184

SMITH, W., Private, 12th Manchester Regiment.

He volunteered in November 1914, and in the following July was sent to the Western Front, where he played a prominent part in the Battles of Loos, Albert, Vimy Ridge, and the Somme and in heavy fighting at St. Eloi, Armentières, and on the Ancre. He was wounded at Loos in January 1916, and spent a short time in hospital at the Base. Unfortunately he was killed in action near Arras on February 12th, 1917, and was entitled to the 1914–15 Star, and the General Service and Victory Medals.

" Great deeds cannot die."

9, Hardman Street, City Road, Hulme, Manchester.　　Z8181

SMITH, W., Sapper, R.E.

He volunteered in August 1914, and after a period of service in England, was drafted to the Western Front, where he first saw heavy fighting during the German attack on Albert. He then took part in the Somme Offensive until August 1916, when he was wounded by a shell explosion. He quickly recovered, but was again wounded and admitted to hospital at Havre. Later he rejoined his unit, and was gassed in action at the third Battle of Ypres in July 1917. On this occasion he was invalided home and underwent treatment in various hospitals. Demobilised in March 1919, he holds the General Service and Victory Medals.

26, Allen Street, Hulme, Manchester.　　Z8178

SMITH, W., Private, Labour Corps.

He volunteered in September 1915, and was quickly drafted to the Western Front, where he was attached to the Royal Engineers, and did consistently good work at Dieppe, and in the Ypres sector. He rendered valuable services until his demobilisation in March 1919, and holds the 1914–15 Star, and the General Service and Victory Medals.

81, Robert Street, West Gorton, Manchester.　　Z8160B

SMITH, W., Cpl., 4th King's Own Scottish Borderers.

He volunteered in September 1914, and early in the following year was sent to the Dardanelles, where he took part in the Landing at Cape Helles, and in the three Battles of Krithia. After an attack on Achi-Baba on July 12th, 1915, he was reported missing, and is now presumed to have been killed in action on that date. He was entitled to the 1914–15 Star, and the General Service and Victory Medals.

' A costly sacrifice upon the altar of freedom."

82, Earl Street, Longsight, Manchester.　　Z8142B

SMITH, W. E., Sergeant, 8th Manchester Regiment.

He volunteered in August 1914, and in the following year was drafted to the Dardanelles, where he played a prominent part at the Landing at Cape Helles, and in several engagements. After the Evacuation of the Gallipoli Peninsula, he proceeded to France, and saw much fighting at Vimy Ridge, the Somme, Arras, Bullecourt, Messines, Ypres, and in the Retreat and Advance of 1918, and was wounded in action. He was demobilised in February 1919. and holds the 1914–15 Star, and the General Service and Victory Medals.

190, Hamilton Street, Collyhurst, Manchester.　　Z11129

SMITH, W. E., Private, 2nd Manchester Regiment.

He joined in March 1916, and after a period of training was drafted to France in the following January. During his service on the Western Front, he was engaged on special duties as a Company runner and saw much severe fighting in various sectors. He was in hospital sick for some time, and was eventually demobilised in February 1919, holding the General Service and Victory Medals.

4, Dryden Street, Longsight, Manchester.　　Z8152

SMITH, W. H., Private, 8th Lancashire Fusiliers.

Volunteering in September 1914, he was retained at home on important duties before being drafted to France in December 1916. In this theatre of war he took part in the Battles of Arras, Ypres (III) and Cambrai, and in the Retreat and Advance, being wounded and gassed in action in March 1918. He was demobilised in April 1919, and holds the General Service and Victory Medals.

13, Shepley Street, Harpurhey, Manchester.　　Z11145

SMITH, W. H., Private, East Lancashire Regiment.
He volunteered in April 1915, and underwent a period of training prior to his being drafted to Mesopotamia. There he took part in several engagements, including those at the Relief of Kut, on the Tigris, and at the capture of Baghdad, where he was wounded. In consequence he was invalided to Egypt, but on his recovery, returned to Mesopotamia, and served until after hostilities ceased. He was serving in India in 1920, and holds the 1914–15 Star, and the General Service and Victory Medals.
101, Cross Street, Bradford, Manchester. Z11143

SMITH, W. H., Pte., King's Own Scottish Borderers.
He joined in November 1916, and in the following February was drafted to the Western Front, where he was in action at the Battles of Arras, Vimy Ridge, Bullecourt, Ypres, Cambrai (I), the Marne (II), Havrincourt and Cambrai (II). He was in hospital with hernia in France and England, and was eventually demobilised in March 1919, holding the General Service and Victory Medals.
31, Orchard Street, Greenheys, Manchester. Z8179

SMITH, W. H., Private, Royal Welch Fusiliers.
He joined in November 1916, and four months later proceeded to Salonika, where he saw much severe fighting during the Advance on the Doiran front. In April 1918 he was invalided to Malta suffering from a serious attack of malarial fever and dysentery, and was then sent to hospital in London. He was discharged as medically unfit for further service in July 1918, and holds the General Service and Victory Medals.
15, Marshall Street, Ardwick, Manchester. Z8180

SMITHEMAN, A., Driver, R.F.A.
He volunteered in October 1915, and on completion of his training was sent to France, but after seeing heavy fighting at Cuinchy, was transferred to Salonika. In 1917, however, he was drafted to Palestine, where he took part in the three Battles of Gaza and the capture of Beersheba. He was also in action during the Advance with General Allenby's Forces. Demobilised in March 1919, he holds the General Service and Victory Medals. 33, Gorse St., Hulme, Manchester. TZ8185

SMYTH, W., Private, M.G.C.
He volunteered in August 1914, and after a period of service in England was drafted to Salonika in December 1915. Whilst in the Balkan theatre of war, he took part in the Advances of the Doiran and Vardar fronts, and was admitted to hospital suffering from malarial fever. He was then invalided home, and eventually demobilised in March 1919, holding the 1914–15 Star, and the General Service and Victory Medals.
4, Ridley Grove, Greenheys, Manchester. Z8186

SNAITH, H., Sapper, R.E.
He volunteered in the Royal Fusiliers in October 1914, but during his training was transferred to the R.E. and in November 1915, drafted to the Western Front, where he took part in several important engagements. He died gloriously on the Field of Battle in the Arras sector on July 2nd, 1916, and was entitled to the 1914–15 Star, and the General Service and Victory Medals.
"Whilst we remember, the sacrifice is not in vain."
338, Mill Street, Bradford, Manchester. Z11148

SNAPE, G., Corporal, 2nd Lancashire Fusiliers.
He was mobilised in August 1914, and immediately drafted to the Western Front, where he took part in the Battles of Mons and Le Cateau. He was taken prisoner during the Retreat from Mons, and whilst in captivity in Germany at Sennelager, suffered many hardships, and was made to work on the land. He was released after the Armistice and returned home for his discharge in December 1919. He holds the Mons Star, and the General Service and Victory Medals.
41, Cyrus Street, Ancoats, Manchester. Z11149

SNOWDEN, F., Private, 8th Manchester Regiment.
He volunteered in August 1914, and in the following April was drafted to the Western Front, where he was in action at the Battles of Hill 60, Loos, the Somme, Arras, Passchendaele and Bapaume. He was admitted to hospital in Boulogne, suffering from bronchial-asthma, and after being invalided home, spent some time in convalescent homes at Llandudno and Southport. He was demobilised in May 1919, and holds the 1914–15 Star, and the General Service and Victory Medals.
2, St. Clements Place, Gray Street, West Gorton, Manchester. Z8187

SNOWDON, L. L., L/Corporal, 17th Manchester Regt.
He volunteered in September 1914, and on completion of his training was sent overseas in the following April. During his service on the Western Front he took part in many important engagements, including the Battles of Hill 60, Ypres (II), Loos, St. Eloi, Albert and the Somme, where he was wounded, and invalided to hospital in July 1916. After a period of treatment he was discharged in November 1916, as medically unfit for further military service, and holds the 1914–15 Star, and the General Service and Victory Medals.
5, Dalby Street, Longsight, Manchester. Z8188

SOCKETT, A. E., Sapper, R.E.
He joined in September 1916, and after a period of training was sent to France in the following January. During his

voyage overseas his ship, the "Transylvania," was torpedoed, but he was rescued, and sent to a rest camp. Later he was drafted to Egypt, and there served on the Suez Canal. He also fought in Palestine, at the Capture of Jerusalem, when he was invalided to hospital in England, suffering from fever. He was finally discharged in June 1919, holding the General Service and Victory Mdeals. TZ8189
12, Mitton Street, Stanley Grove, Longisght, Manchester.

SOCKETT, E., Private, 2nd Lancashire Fusiliers.
He volunteered in August 1914, at the outbreak of hostilities, and after a period of training was drafted to the Western Front. Whilst in this seat of war he took part in much heavy fighting including the Battles of Ypres and Somme (I), where he was unfortunately killed in action in October 1916. He was entitled to the 1914–15 Star, and the General Service and Victory Medals.
"His memory is cherished with pride."
19, Buxton Street, Chorlton-on-Medlock, Manchester. Z2472A

SOCKETT, R. W., Pte., 1/7th K. (Liverpool Regt.)
He joined in February 1917, and three months later proceeded to the Western Front, where he took part in the Battles of the Somme (II), Bapaume, Havrincourt, Cambrai (II), Ypres (IV), and the Sambre, and in other important engagements during the Retreat and Advance of 1918, including the entry into Mons at dawn of Armistice day. After hostilities ceased, he served with the Army of Occupation in Germany until his demobilisation in March 1920, and holds the General Service and Victory Medals.
16, Bloom Street, Hulme, Manchester. TZ8190

SOLOMON, J., Private, Manchester Regiment.
He joined in July 1916, and after a period of training, was engaged at various stations on important duties with his unit. He was unable to obtain a transfer overseas owing to his being medically unfit but rendered valuable services until his discharge in January 1918.
13, Jersey Street Dwellings, Ancoats, Manchester. Z11150

SOLOMON, L., Private, Wiltshire Regiment.
He volunteered in April 1915, and after a period of training was drafted to Mesopotamia, where he saw heavy fighting. He took part in the engagements at Kut, and Baghdad, and in others of importance, until being severely wounded in action in 1917. He was discharged in October 1917, as medically unfit for further service, and holds the General Service and Victory Medals.
23, Cheetham Street, Lower Openshaw, Manchester. Z8191

SONLEY, T., Sapper, R.E.
Having previously served for twelve years with the Colours in India, he re-enlisted in February 1918, and was retained at various stations, where he was engaged on duties of great importance. He was not successful in obtaining his transfer to a theatre of war, but nevertheless, rendered valuable services with his Company until January 1919, when he was demobilised.
2, Gay Street, Jackson Street, Hulme, Manchester. Z8192

SOUTER, A. C., Private, 2nd Manchester Regiment.
He volunteered in January 1916, and four months later proceeded to France, where he served as a signaller during the Battle of the Somme. In 1917 he was transferred to Italy, and took part in many engagements, but was badly wounded on the Piave. As a result, he was invalided home, and finally discharged in 1918, as unfit for further service. He holds the General Service and Victory Medals.
21, Cuttell Street, Bradford, Manchester. Z11151B

SOUTER, J. C., Pte., Cheshire Regt., and Sapper, R.E.
Volunteering in December 1914, he was quickly drafted to Gibraltar, where he was engaged on important duties. In April 1917, he proceeded to France, was transferred to the R.E. and was employed on road making and bridge building. Later he took part in engagements at Arras (where he was wounded), Ypres, Cambrai, and in the Retreat and Advance of 1918. He was demobilised in March 1919, and holds the General Service and Victory Medals.
21, Cuttell Street, Bradford, Manchester. Z11151A

SOUTH, F., Private, Border Regiment.
He joined in May 1916, and twelve months later proceeded to the Western Front, where he took part in the Battle of Ypres, and was wounded in action in July 1917. Invalided to hospital at Dover, he returned to France, however, on his recovery, fought in the Retreat and Advance of 1918, and was again wounded on the Somme, and sent to hospital at Birmingham. He was demobilised in November 1919, and holds the General Service and Victory Medals.
3, Glebe Place, Gorton, Manchester. Z8193

SOUTHALL, H. H., L/Cpl., 9th Lancashire Fusiliers.
He volunteered at the outbreak of war in August 1914, and in June of the following year was drafted to the Dardanelles, where he saw much severe fighting. He made the supreme sacrifice, falling in action at Suvla Bay in August 1915. He was entitled to the 1914–15 Star, and the General Service and Victory Medals.
"Great deeds cannot die:
They, with the sun and moon renew their light for ever."
60, Nelson Street, Bradford, Manchester. Z8195A

SOUTHALL, A., Private, 1/8th Lancashire Fusiliers and Rifleman, 21st Rifle Brigade.
Volunteering in November 1915, he proceeded to Egypt on completing a period of training in July of the following year, and there took part in engagements on the Suez Canal, and at Kantara, Romani, and many other places. In October 1918, he was transferred to India, where he was engaged on garrison duties at various stations, finally returning home for demobilisation in June 1919. He holds the General Service and Victory Medals.
60, Nelson Street, Bradford, Manchester.   Z8195B

SOUTHERN, H., Pte., Loyal N. Lancashire Regt.
Volunteering in January 1915, he proceeded to the Western Front in June of that year, and there saw severe fighting in various sectors. He took part in the Battles of Loos, Vimy Ridge, the Somme, Arras, Messines, Ypres and Cambrai, and many other engagements, served also through the Retreat and Advance of 1918, and suffered from shell-shock whilst in France. He was demobilised in March 1919, and holds the 1914-15 Star, and the General Service and Victory Medals.
8, Prospect Street, West Gorton, Manchester.   Z8194

SOUTHWARD, A., Private, Manchester Regiment.
He volunteered in September 1914, and in the following March proceeded to the Western Front. In this seat of war he took part in the Battles of Ypres (II), the Somme, Ypres (III), and in the Retreat and Advance of 1918, and was wounded in action. He was demobilised in March 1919, and holds the 1914-15 Star, and the General Service and Victory Medals.
35, Clayton Street, Bradford, Manchester.   Z11152

SOUTHWELL, F. E., Private, Labour Corps.
Volunteering in August 1915, he proceeded to France in the following month, and there served in various sectors of the Front. He was engaged whilst overseas on bridge-repairing and road-making, and other inportant duties and rendered very valuable services until after the cessation of hostilities. He returned home for demobilisation in March 1919, and holds the 1914-15 Star, and the General Service and Victory Medals.
2, Dalton Street, Longsight, Manchester.   Z8196

SOUTHWORTH, P. W., Rifleman, K.R.R.C.
He volunteered in November 1914, and twelve months later, proceeded to the Western Front. Whilst in this theatre of war, he saw much severe fighting, took part in the Battles of Albert, Arras, Bullecourt, Ypres, Cambrai, Bapaume and Havrincourt, and other engagements in various sectors, and was wounded in action on the Somme in November 1916. He was demobilised in January 1919, and holds the 1914-15 Star, and the General Service and Victory Medals.
10, Newman Street, Ancoats, Manchester.   Z8197

SOWDEN, B., Private, 7th Border Regiment.
Four months after joining in July 1916, he was drafted to the Western Front, where he saw severe fighting in various sectors, and took part in the Battles of the Ancre, Arras, and Vimy Ridge. He unhappily died in April 1917, of poisoning, caused by injuries received in an accident near Arras. He was entitled to the General Service and Victory Medals.
    "His memory is cherished with pride."
1, Milton Square, Lingard Street, Hulme, Manchester. Z8198

SPACEY, J., Sergt., South Wales Borderers.
Volunteering in November 1914, he proceeded to the Dardanelles in the following April, served with distinction at the Landing at Cape Helles, and at the Battles of Krithia (I, II and III), and Achi-Baba, and was three times wounded. After the Evacuation of the Gallipoli Peninsula, he was sent to the Western Front, and took part in the Battles of the Somme and Arras, where he was badly wounded and gassed in 1917. As a result, he was invalided and discharged in November 1914, medically unfit, and holds the 1914-15 Star, and the General Service and Victory Medals.
12, Belmont Street, Collyhurst, Manchester.   Z11153

SPARLING, R. F. (D.C.M.), Private, 9th (Queen's Royal) Lancers.
Mobilised in August 1914, he was immediately drafted to the Western Front, where he fought in the Battle of Mons, and the subsequent Retreat. He also took part in the Battles of Le Cateau, the Marne, La Bassée, Neuve Chapelle, St. Eloi, Albert, the Somme, Passchendaele and Cambrai, and minor engagements, before being transferred to Italy. There he fought on the Piave and Asiago Plateaux, but returned to France in time to serve through the Retreat of March 1918, when he was taken prisoner on the Somme. He was forced whilst in captivity, to work in the coal mines, and was finally discharged on his release in December 1918. He was awarded the Distinguished Conduct Medal for conspicuous bravery in the Field, and holds the Mons Star, and the General Service and Victory Medals.
39, Baker Street, Ardwick, Manchester.   Z8200

SPARLING, Vᵣ., L/Corporal, 21st Manchester Regt.
He volunteered in November 1914, and after a period of training was drafted to France, where he fought in various sectors of the Front. He took part in the fierce fighting in the Battles of Albert, the Somme, Messines, and Ypres. Later he took part in the Advance into Germany. He was demobilised in

February 1919, and holds the 1914-15 Star, and the General Service and Victory Medals.
16, Abbey Grove, Hulme, Manchester.   Z8199

SPARROW, J., Private, 16th Manchester Regiment and Labour Corps.
He volunteered in September 1914, and in the following year was drafted to France. In this seat of war he took part in the Battles of Albert and the Somme. He was then transferred to the Labour Corps, and was engaged on important duties until he was demobilised in November 1919, holding the 1914-15 Star, and the General Service and Victory Medals.
27, Clayton Street, Hulme, Manchester.   Z8201

SPEAKMAN, F., Air Mechanic, R.A.F. and Pte., Labour Corps.
He joined in January 1917, and after his training served at various stations on important duties with the Royal Air Force. He was later transferred to the Labour Corps, and was engaged on garrison duties. He rendered valuable services, but was not successful in obtaining a transfer to a theatre of war, owing to his being medically unfit, and was demobilised in January 1919.
10, Coral Street, Chorlton-on-Medlock, Manchester. TX8202B

SPEAKMAN, J., Private, Cheshire Regiment.
He joined in April 1919, at the age of seventeen, and after a period of training was sent to Constantinople, where he was engaged on important garrison duties, and in 1920 was still serving with the Army of Occupation.
10, Coral St., Chorlton-on-Medlock, Manchester. TX8202A

SPEAKMAN, J., Private, 20th Manchester Regt.
He joined in August 1916, and in the following January proceeded to the Western Front, where he took part in several engagements, including the Battles of Arras, Bullecourt, and Ypres III, and in the Retreat and Advance of 1918. After hostilities ceased, he went into Germany with the Army of Occupation, and served there until his demobilisation in October 1919. He holds the General Service and Victory Medals. 18, Juno St., Ancoats, Manchester. Z11154

SPELLACY, J., Air Mechanic, R.A.F.
He volunteered in October 1914, and, after a period of training was drafted to France, where he was engaged in the repairing of engines at Albert, Amiens, and Rouen. He rendered very valuable services with the Royal Air Force until demobilised in March 1919. He holds the 1914-15 Star, and the General Service and Victory Medals.
15, Hamilton Street, Hulme, Manchester.   Z8203

SPELMAN, J., Private, 21st Manchester Regt.
Volunteering in August 1914, he was drafted overseas in the following January. Whilst on the Western Front he saw much fighting at the Battles of Ypres, the Somme, Arras, Nieuport, and Cambrai, but was badly wounded and invalided to Rouen. He was demobilised in February 1919, and holds the 1914-15 Star, and the General Service and Victory Medals.
1A, Buckland Street, Ancoats, Manchester.   Z11155

SPENCE, J., Private, 1st Manchester Regiment.
He joined in February 1916, and in the following month proceeded to India, where he was engaged on important garrison duties. Later he was transferred to Mesopotamia, and took part in engagements at Amara, Kut, and Baghdad, and contracted malarial fever. He returned home and was demobilised in December 1919, holding the General Service and Victory Medals.
2, Elizabeth Street, West Gorton, Manchester.   Z11156

SPENCER, H., Private, 1/7th Manchester Regt.
He joined in May 1918, and on completion of his training was drafted to France. Whilst in this theatre of war he took part in many important engagements towards the close of hostilities, including the Battles of Havrincourt, Cambrai, Ypres, Le Cateau, the Selle, and the Sambre. He was demobilised in October 1919, and holds the General Service and Victory Medals.
1, Sherwood Street, Rochdale Road, Manchester.   Z11158

SPENCER, J., Private, 13th Manchester Regiment.
He volunteered in October 1914, and after a period of training was drafted to the Western Front, where he saw active service in various sectors, and took part in the Battles of the Somme and Arras. In March 1918, he was transferred to Salonika, and saw service on the Doiran front. He contracted fever, and was invalided to hospital, and finally demobilised in March 1919, holding the 1914-15 Star, and the General Service and Victory Medals.
81, Chester Street, Hulme, Manchester.   Z8207

SPENCER, S., Pte., 1st K.O. (Royal Lancaster Regt.)
He volunteered in April 1915, and shortly afterwards proceeded to the Western Front. In this seat of war he took an active part in many important engagements, including the Battles of Loos, Albert, Vimy Ridge, Beaucourt, Arras, and Bullecourt, but was unfortunately killed at Vimy Ridge on June 3rd, 1917, during a bombing raid. He was entitled to the 1914-15 Star, and the General Service and Victory Medals.
    "His life for his Country his soul to God."
484, Mill Street, Bradford, Manchester.   Z11157

SPENCER, E., Sergt.-Major, 8th Manchester Regt.
He volunteered at the outbreak of hostilities in August 1914, and proceeded to Gallipoli, where he took part in the engagements at Krithia. Later he was transferred to Egypt, and saw service there until April 1916, when he was discharged as time-expired. In July of that year he rejoined, and was again in action on the Western Front, where he took part in much heavy fighting. He later took part in the closing operations of the war, marched into Germany with the Army of Occupation, and was demobilised in February 1919, holding the 1914-15 Star, and the General Service and Victory Medals.
71, Temple Street, Chorlton-on-Medlock, Manchester. X8204

SPENCER, J., Private, 10th Border Regiment.
He volunteered in August 1914, and in the following May was drafted to the Dardanelles, where he took part in the Landing at Suvla Bay, and in other engagements until the Evacuation of the Gallipoli Peninsula, when he contracted an illness, and was invalided to Malta. On his recovery, he was engaged for a time on important guard duties. Later he was sent to Ireland and saw service there until December 1918, when he was discharged, holding the 1914-15 Star, and the General Service and Victory Medals.
57, Church Street, Bradford, Manchester. Z8205

SPENCER, J., Pte., 1/5th K.O. (R. Lancaster Regt.)
He joined in July 1916, and shortly afterwards proceeded to France. During his service in this theatre of war, he took part in many important engagements, including the Battles of Albert and the Somme. He was then sent to England suffering from trench fever. On his recovery he again proceeded to the Western Front, and saw much fighting at Armentières, Festubert, and Givenchy. He was demobilised in September 1919, after serving in Germany for a time, and holds the General Service and Victory Medals.
139A, Clopton Street, Hulme, Manchester. TZ8206

SPENCER, T., Pte., R.A.S.C., and R.Welch Fusiliers).
He volunteered in September 1915, and later in the same year proceeded to Egypt. Whilst in this theatre of war he saw much service at Alexandria and Kantara, and also took part in the Battle of Gaza, the capture of Jerusalem in Palestine. Later he was engaged on important patrol duties attached to the Royal Naval Air Service during the riots in Egypt. After the cessation of hostilities, he returned to England, and was demobilised in August 1919. He holds the 1914-15 Star, and the General Service and Victory Medals.
6, Cuba Street, Hulme, Manchester. Z8208

SPILLING, C., Private, 17th Lancashire Fusiliers.
He volunteered in January 1915, and, on completion of his training was drafted to France. Whilst in this theatre of war he took part in many important engagements, including the Battles of Albert, and the Somme I, where he was wounded in action in August 1916. On his recovery he returned to the fighting area, but was wounded a second time at Cambrai in 1917, and was invalided to London. He was finally discharged in February 1918 as medically unfit for further service, and holds the General Service and Victory Medals.
11, Rennie Street, West Gorton, Manchester. Z11159

SPINK, H., Private, Black Watch.
He volunteered in August 1914, and three months later proceeded to France, when he immediately went into action at the Battles of Ypres (I). He was wounded at Givenchy in January 1915, but, of after hospital treatment at Cambridge, returned to France, and was again wounded at the 2nd Battle of Ypres in May 1915. Invalided to England, he underwent treatment in Birmingham until July of the same year, when he once more returned to the Western Front. Three months later he was wounded for the 3rd time at Loos, and was again invalided home. In January 1916, he was transferred to Class W, Army Reserve, and sent on munition work at Sheffield until demobilised in January 1919, holding the 1914 Star, and the General Service and Victory Medals.
31, Ferneley Street, Hulme, Manchester. Z8209

SPRAGG, J., Private, K.O. (Royal Lancaster Regt.)
Volunteering in November 1915, he was drafted to France in the following month. During his service on the Western Front he saw much severe fighting, and was in action at the Battles of the Somme I, Ancre, Arras, Vimy Ridge, and other important engagements. He dislocated his knee cap whilst in the trenches, and was invalided to England. After a period of treatment in hospital, he returned to France, and was attached to the Labour Corps. He remained in this theatre of war until the cessation of hostilities, and was demobilised in September 1919, holding the General Service and Victory Medals. 4, Towson St., Russell St., Hulme, Manchester. TZ8210

SPRATT, J., Private, Manchester Regiment.
Volunteering in August 1914, he proceeded to Gallipoli in the following December, and took part in the early engagements on the Peninsula, and was wounded. On recovery he was drafted to the Western Front in June 1915, and fought in the Battle of the Somme, Arras, Cambrai, Ypres, and taken

prisoner in August 1917, remained in captivity until repatriated in December of the succeeding year. He was demobilised in the same month, and holds the 1914-15 Star, and the General Service and Victory Medals.
27, Almond Street, Collyhurst, Manchester. Z9711

SPRATT, P., Private, 23rd Manchester Regiment.
He volunteered in June 1915, and at the conclusion of his training was sent to the Western Front in the following December. In this theatre of war he fought in many important engagements, and was unhappily killed in action during the Somme Offensive on July 25th, 1916. He was entitled to the 1914-15 Star, and the General Service and Victory Medals.
"Thinking that remembrance, though unspoken, may reach him where he sleeps."
28, Chariton Street, Collyhurst, Manchester. Z9379

SPRIGGS, W., Sergt., 23rd Manchester Regiment.
He volunteered in August 1914, and, after his training was drafted to the Western Front. He saw much heavy fighting whilst overseas, particularly at the Battles of Loos, the Somme, Arras I, and Ypres, where he was gassed. On his recovery he rendered very valuable services until demobilised in February 1919, and holds the 1914-15 Star, and the General Service and Victory Medals.
6, Walter Street, Ancoats, Manchester. Z7995

SPURR, F., 2nd Lieutenant, R.A.F.
He joined in September 1915, having previously been engaged at Messrs. Mather and Platt's, in connection with the buying of materials for manufacture into munitions of war. After a period of training at Farnborough, he rendered valuable services as a pilot with his Squadron on the air defences of London, and was often in action with enemy aircraft. He was demobilised in December 1918, and holds the General Service Medal. 104, Clifton St., Bradford, Manchester. Z8211

SPURR, G., Private, South Lancashire Regiment.
Volunteering in January 1915, he was drafted six months later to the Western Front, and was in action at St. Eloi, where he was wounded and invalided home as a result. After spending some time in hospital at Asyut, he was sent to Egypt, and was in action at Assiott. Later returning to France, he served on the Somme, and was again wounded and also gassed. Invalided home for the second time, he was sent to hospital in Dublin, where he remained until discharged in December 1916, as unfit for further service. He holds the 1914-15 Star, and the General Service and Victory Medals.
87, Garratt Street, Oldham Road, Manchester. Z11826

SQUIRE, W., Private, Royal Scots.
He volunteered in December 1914, and twelve months later was sent to France, where he took part in heavy fighting at St. Eloi and Albert, before being wounded during the Somme Battle in July 1916. Remaining in action, he was again wounded two months later at Montauban. On his recovery, he rejoined his unit, served at the Battles of Arras, Vimy Ridge, and Ypres, and was badly wounded for the third time at Martinpuich in September 1917. As a result, he unfortunately lost his left eye, and after treatment at Etaples and Rouen, was sent home for special duties. He was discharged in January 1919, and holds the 1914-15 Star, and the General Service and Victory Medals.
212, Viaduct Street, Ardwick, Manchester. Z8212

STACEY, J., Private (Bugler), 6th Manchester Regt.
He volunteered in August 1914, and after a period of training was retained at home on account of ill-health. In October 1916, however, he was drafted to Egypt, and during his service in this seat of war took part in the capturing of Magdhaba. Later he was transferred to the Western Front, and was engaged in the heavy fighting at the Battles of Cambrai I, Somme II, the Marne II, and in the Retreat of 1918. He was unfortunately killed in action near Albert on August 23rd, 1918, and was entitled to the General Service and Victory Medals.
"A costly sacrifice upon the altar of freedom."
Z11181A

STAFFORD, L., Sapper, R.E.
He volunteered in April 1915, and shortly afterwards proceeded to France, where he fought on various sectors of the Front. He took part in the Battles of St. Eloi, Hill 60, Vimy Ridge, Arras, Ypres III, and was gassed. On his recovery he returned to the fighting area, and was in action at the Battles of the Somme (II), Havrincourt, Le Cateau, and the Sambre, where he was wounded in November 1918. He was demobilised in January 1919, and holds the 1914-15 Star, and the General Service and Victory Medals.
26, Hardman St., City Road, Hulme, Manchester. Z8214

STAFFORD, W., Sapper, R.E.
He volunteered in February 1915, and was immediately sent to France, where he took part in many important engagements, including those at Neuve Chapelle and St. Eloi. He was unfortunately killed by a German mine on April 22nd, 1915, whilst working in the field at Givenchy, and was entitled to the 1914-15 Star, and the General Service and Victory Medals.
"Whilst we remember the sacrifice is not in vain."
14, Prescott Street, Hulme, Manchester. Z8213

STAHLER, A., Private, 23rd Manchester Regiment.
He volunteered in October 1915, and crossing to France in the following January took part in the Battles of Albert, Ploegsteert, the Somme, Arras, Bullecourt, Ypres III, and Cambrai. He also fought in several engagements during the German Offensive, and was taken prisoner in the subsequent Allied Advance in August 1918. He was repatriated in December 1918, and demobilised a month later, holds the General Service and Victory Medals.
1, Harry Street, London Road, Manchester.   Z9380

STAIT, T. H., L/Cpl., 4th Rifle Brigade, and 2nd Oxfordshire and Buckinghamshire Lgt.Infantry.
Volunteering in September 1914, he proceeded to France three months later, and took part in the Battles of Ypres (II), the Somme (I), Cambrai (I), St. Quentin, Ypres (III), the Somme (II), Cambrai (II), Villers-Bretonneux, Le Cateau (II), and Nesle. He was in hospital in France and England with trench feet, but on his recovery, rejoined his unit on the Western Front. He was demobilised in March 1919, and holds the 1914-15 Star, and the General Service and Victory Medals.
96, Blackthorn Street, Ardwick, Manchester.   Z8215

STALEY, J. E., Private, 17th Manchester Regiment.
He volunteered in April 1915, and later in the same year was drafted to the Western Front, where he saw much active service. He took part in the heavy fighting at the Battles of Loos, St. Eloi, Albert, and the Somme, where he was unfortunately killed in action on the 10th July 1916. He was entitled to the 1914-15 Star, and the General Service and Victory Medals.
"The path of duty was the way to glory."
15, Sudbury Street, Rochdale Road, Manchester.   Z11160

STALKER, D., Private, 9th King's (Liverpool Regt.)
He joined in September 1916, and was retained on important duties at various stations until January 1917. He then proceeded to the Western Front, and took part in the Battles of Arras I, Bullecourt, and Messines. Invalided home in June 1917, he was discharged as medically unfit for further service in the Army in September, and holds the General Service and Victory Medals.
61, Earl Street, Longsight, Manchester.   Z8216

STANDEN, G. S., Guardsman, 3rd Coldstream Gds.
He joined in October 1916, and five months later was drafted to the Western Front, where he took part in the Battles of Bullecourt, Messines, Ypres (III), and Lens, before laying down his life for King and Country in the Ypres sector on September 11th, 1917. He was entitled to the General Service and Victory Medals.
"His memory is cherished with pride."
112, Welcomb Street, Hulme, Manchester.   Z8217

STANIFORTH, H., Private, Manchester Regiment.
He was called up from the Reserve in August 1914, and immediately drafted to the Western Front, where he took part in the Battle of La Bassée, and in other severe fighting until wounded at Ypres in March 1915. Invalided to hospital he was discharged as medically unfit for service in October 1915. Later, however, he was called up again, and was engaged on important duties with the Royal Garrison Artillery in the Isle of Wight until June 1920, when he was finally discharged. He holds the 1914-15 Star, and the General Service and Victory Medals.
26, Gorton Road, Lower Openshaw, Manchester.   Z8219

STANIFORTH, H., Pte., 16th Lancashire Fusiliers.
He joined in May 1916, and in October of the same year was drafted to France, where he saw much heavy fighting. He took part in engagements on various sectors of the Front, and fought in the Battles of Arras I, Bullecourt, Ypres III, and Cambrai. Later he was in action throughout the Retreat and Advance of 1918, and was demobilised in August 1919. He holds the General Service and Victory Medals.
67, North Greaves Street, Cheetham, Manchester.   Z11161

STANIFORTH, T. H., Pte., 8th Manchester Regt.
He joined in October 1916, and after a period of training was sent to France. During his service in this theatre of war he took part in many important engagements, including the Battles of Bullecourt, Lens, Cambrai, the Scarpe, and the Sambre. After the cessation of hostilities, he returned home and was demobilised in March 1919, holding the General Service and Victory Medals.
3, Wycliffe Street, Ardwick, Manchester.   Z8218

STANKER, E., Private, Royal Fusiliers.
He joined in April 1917, and after a term of training was drafted to France in the same year. There he took part in many notable engagements, including those at Cambrai and on the Somme front, where he was wounded in April 1918. On his recovery, he again proceeded to the fighting area, and was later gassed at Valenciennes during the Advance. Invalided to hospital in Scotland, he remained there until demobilised in December 1919, holding the General Service and Victory Medals.
12, Westminster St., Chester Rd., Hulme, Manchester. TZ8220

STANLEY, A., Driver, R.F.A.
Mobilised in August 1914, he was immediately drafted to the Western Front, where he took part in the Battle of Mons, and the subsequent Retreat. He afterwards fought in the Battles of the Marne, the Aisne, La Bassée, Ypres, Neuve Chapelle, Hill 60, Albert, the Somme, Arras, and Cambrai, and many minor engagements until invalided home in March 1918, suffering from shell-shock. He was discharged in October of that year, as medically unfit for further service, and holds the Mons Star, and the General Service and Victory Medals.
38, Hardy Street, West Gorton, Manchester.   Z8222

STANLEY, C., Private, South Lancashire Regiment.
He volunteered in September 1914, and in the same year was sent to France. During his service in this theatre of war he took part in much heavy fighting. He was in action throughout the Battles of St. Eloi, Ypres, Hill 60, and Festubert, and was wounded. On his recovery he returned to France, and served there until the cessation of hostilities, being wounded on two other occasions. He was demobilised in February 1919, and holds the 1914-15 Star, and the General Service and Victory Medals.
29, Cross Keys Street, Manchester.   Z11585

STANLEY, F. S., Private, Lancashire Fusiliers.
He volunteered at the outbreak of war in August 1914, and in April of the following year, was drafted to the Dardanelles, where he took part in the three Battles of Krithia and the fighting at Suvla Bay. On the Evacuation of the Gallipoli Peninsula, he proceeded to Egypt, and was there in action at Agagia, Sollum, Katia, and Romani, and various other places until January 1917. He was then transferred to the Western Front, where, after fighting in the Battles of Arras, Vimy Ridge, Messines, Passchendaele, Cambrai, and Le Cateau, he fell in action on the Selle on October 22nd, 1918. He was entitled to the 1914-15 Star, and the General Service and Victory Medals.
"And doubtless he went in splendid company."
55, Wood Street, Hulme, Manchester.   TZ6023A

STANLEY, F. W., Private, 9th Cheshire Regiment.
He joined in October 1918, and after five months' training was drafted to France and thence to Germany, where he served with the Army of Occupation at various stations. Returning home in August 1919, he was afterwards engaged in guarding prisoners of war in the Isle of Man until November of that year, when he was demobilised.
12, Ridley Grove, Greenheys, Manchester.   Z8221

STANLEY, J., L/Corporal, R.E.
Volunteering in March 1915, he proceeded to the Western Front in July of the same year, and there saw much severe fighting in the Loos sector. In November 1917 he was transferred to Italy, where he was engaged on important duties on the lines of communication until invalided home suffering from bronchitis. He was for a considerable period in hospital, before being demobilised in May 1919, and holds the 1914-15 Star, and the General Service and Victory Medals.
13, Riga Street, Jackson Street, Hulme, Manchester. Z8223

STANLEY, T., Sergt., 16th Lancashire Fusiliers.
Volunteering in October 1914, he was sent in the following year to the Western Front, where he fought in the Battles of Albert, Arras, Vimy Ridge, and was wounded on the Somme in April 1917. On recovery he rejoined his Battalion, and took part in the third Battle of Ypres, and was again wounded at Nieuport in August of the same year. Evacuated to Leeds War Hospital he received medical treatment, and was eventually discharged as medically unfit for further service in January 1918. He holds the 1914-15 Star, and the General Service and Victory Medals.
2, Naylor Street, Newton, Manchester.   Z9381

STANSFIELD, G. T., Private, 3rd Royal Scots.
He joined in June 1916, and after undergoing a period of training, served at various stations in Ireland, where he was engaged on duties of great importance. He was not successful in obtaining his transfer to a theatre of war, but nevertheless rendered valuable services with his unit until his demobilisation in March 1919.
21, Hewitt Street, Openshaw, Manchester.   Z8225

STANSFIELD, J., Pioneer, R.E.
Joining in January 1918, he proceeded to the Western Front on completing his training in April of the same year, and was there engaged on important duties with the Telegraph Construction Company in various sectors. On the cessation of hostilities he was sent with the Army of Occupation into Germany, where he was stationed at Cologne until his return home for demobilisation in October 1919. He holds the General Service and Victory Medals.
51, Edensor Street, Beswick, Manchester.   Z8224

STANTON, J., Private, Lancashire Fusiliers.
Volunteering in March 1915, he was employed on various duties at home stations until June 1916, when he was sent to France. In this theatre of war he was in action at Ploegsteert Wood, the Somme, Bullecourt, Lens, Cambrai, Amiens, and Havrincourt, and during the fourth Battle of Ypres. He returned home for demobilisation in January 1919, and holds the General Service and Victory Medals.
62, Bath Street, Hulme, Manchester.   Z11972

STANTON, W., Private, 23rd Manchester Regiment.

He volunteered in October 1915, and landing in France in the following May served on this Front until the end of the war. During this period he took part in heavy fighting in the Battles of Neuve Chapelle, the Somme, Arras, Ypres, Vimy Ridge, Passchendaele, Messines, and in the Retreat and Advance of 1918. After the Armistice he proceeded with the Army of Occupation into Germany, and was stationed at Cologne until his return home for demobilisation in March 1919. He holds the General Service and Victory Medals.
18, Wragby Street, Miles Platting, Manchester. Z9712

STARK, T. M., Corporal, R.A.F.

He volunteered in February 1915, and in October of that year proceeded to France, where he was engaged on duties of a highly technical nature in various sectors of the Front. He was present at the Battles of Arras, Ypres, Passchendaele and Cambrai, and other important engagements in this theatre of war, and also served through the Retreat and Advance of 1918. Demobilised in February 1919, he holds the 1914-15 Star, and the General Service and Victory Medals.
18, John Street, Ardwick, Manchester. Z8226

STARKEY, J., Private, 1st Manchester Regiment.

Having previously fought in the South African Campaign, he re-enlisted in August 1914, at the outbreak of hostilities. Early in the following year he proceeded to France, where he was in action at the Battle of Neuve Chapelle, and was gassed. After a period of treatment he was invalided to England, and discharged as medically unfit in June 1917. He holds the Queen's and King's South African Medals, the 1914-15 Star, and the General Service and Victory Medals.
48, Nicholson Street, Rochdale Road, Manchester. Z11586

STARMER, A. C., Gunner, R.F.A.

Having enlisted at the age of thirteen, he was already in the Army when war broke out in August 1914, and in April of the following year was drafted to Egypt, where he served for two years. He was then transferred to the Western Front, and there, after taking part in the Battles of Ypres and the Somme, was severely wounded in action in April 1918. He was for a time in hospital at Manchester, before being invalided from the Army in November 1918, and holds the 1914-15 Star, and the General Service and Victory Medals.
41, Molyneux Street, Stockport Road, Manchester. Z8227

STARR, J. H., Pte. (Signaller), Manchester Regt. and East Yorkshire Regt.

Volunteering in November 1915, he was drafted to the Western Front on completing his training two months later, and there saw much severe fighting until wounded in action in the Somme Offensive in August 1916. He was invalided home, but on his recovery in February of the following year, returned to France, and was again in action at Cambrai, and in the Retreat of 1918. Again sent to England, suffering from shell-shock, he was finally discharged in February 1919, as medically unfit for further service. He holds the General Service and Victory Medals. 3, Prince Street, Ardwick, Manchester. Z8228

STATHAM, C. H., Pte., South Wales Borderers and Royal Welch Fusiliers.

He joined in April 1917, and twelve months later proceeded to the Western Front, where he saw much severe fighting in the Retreat of 1918, and was wounded in action on the Somme in May of that year. He was for a time in hospital, but on his recovery rejoined his unit, and took part in the Battles of Cambrai and Le Cateau, and other engagements during the Advance. He was afterwards transferred to Egypt, and was there stationed at Cairo until his return home for demobilisation in March 1920. He holds the General Service and Victory Medals. 11, Cedar Street, Hulme, Manchester. TZ8229

STATON, J. H., Cpl., 4th K.O. (R. Lancaster Regt.)

Having previously served in the Boer War, he was mobilised in August 1914, but was not drafted to France until July 1916. He then took a prominent part in the Battles of the Somme, and Arras, and in other important engagements until the cessation of hostilities. After hostilities ceased, he proceeded to Germany with the Army of Occupation, and was stationed at Cologne. Returning to England in February 1920, he was discharged, and holds the Queen's and King's South African Medals, and the General Service and Victory Medals.
33, Brown Street, Ancoats, Manchester. Z11956

STEAD, G., Sergeant, R.A.F.

He volunteered at the outbreak of war in August 1914, and was retained on important duties of a highly technical nature in England until April 1917. He was then drafted to the Western Front, where he was unhappily killed whilst on flight observation with his Squadron over Arras in May of the same year, after only about two weeks' active service. He was entitled to the General Service and Victory Medals.
"Whilst we remember, the sacrifice is not in vain."
27, Ossory Street, Rusholme, Manchester. Z3564D

STEAD, H., Driver, R.A.S.C. (M.T.)

Joining in November 1916, he was drafted to Salonika after two months' training and was there engaged in conveying ammunition to the forward areas. He also took an active part in important engagements on the Macedonian front until the cessation of hostilities, and then proceeded to Turkey, where he served with the Army of Occupation at Constantinople. He was demobilised on his return home in December 1919, and holds the General Service and Victory Medals.
33, Claribel Street, Ardwick, Manchester. Z8230

STEADMAN, A., L/Corporal, R.E.

He volunteered in August 1914, and in June of the following year, was drafted to the Western Front, where he served in various sectors. He was present at the Battles of Loos, Albert, Arras, Bullecourt and Ypres, and many other engagements, took part also in the Retreat and Advance of 1918, and was wounded in action in the Somme Offensive of 1916. On the cessation of hostilities, he was sent with the Army of Occupation into Germany, finally returning home for demobilisation in February 1919. He holds the 1914-15 Star, and the General Service and Victory Medals.
8, Dorrington Street, Hulme, Manchester. TZ8231-2C

STEADMAN, C. (D.C.M.), Pte., 6th S. Lancashire Rgt.

Volunteering in August 1914, he was drafted to Gallipoli in April of the following year, but after much severe fighting in this seat of operations, was transferred to Salonika. There he served on the Doiran and Vardar fronts, and was wounded in action before proceeding, in January 1916, to Mesopotamia, where he took part in engagements at Kut and was so severely wounded as to necessitate the amputation of an arm. He was awarded the Distinguished Conduct Medal for conspicuous bravery in the Field at Kut, and holds also the 1914-15 Star, and the General Service and Victory Medals. He was sent home and invalided from the Army in October 1916.
8, Dorrington Street, Hulme, Manchester. TZ8231-2B

STEADMAN, H. R., Gunner, R.F.A.

After volunteering in May 1915, he underwent a period of training prior to being drafted to the Western Front in January 1917. There he took part in many important engagements, including the Battles of Arras, Vimy Ridge and the Somme, served also through the Retreat and Advance of 1918, and was twice gassed—near Bullecourt and again at Cambrai. Demobilised in February 1919, he holds the General Service and Victory Medals. 8, Dorrington St., Hulme, Manchester. TZ8231-2

STEADMAN, W., Private, 7th Manchester Regt.

He joined in May 1916, and after a period of training was drafted to the Western Front, where he took part in the Battles of Arras, Vimy Ridge, Bullecourt, Ypres and Lens. He made the supreme sacrifice, being killed in action in the Cambrai sector in January 1918. He was entitled to the General Service and Victory Medals.
"His life for his Country, his soul to God."
8, Dorrington Street, Hulme, Manchester. TZ8231/2A

STEARS, T., Driver, R.E.

He volunteered in December 1915, and was engaged on important duties for about six months and was then discharged. He rejoined, however, in October 1917, and in the following February proceeded to France, where he took part in many engagements, including the Retreat and Advance of 1918. After hostilities ceased he went to Germany with the Army of Occupation and served there until his demobilisation in July 1919. He holds the General Service and Victory Medals.
19, Tranmere Street, Hulme, Manchester. Z8233

STEEL, G., Private, King's Own Scottish Borderers.

He volunteered in September 1914, and after completing a period of training was drafted to France, where he saw much active service. He took part in many important engagements in various sectors of the Front, fought in the Battles of Neuve Chapelle, Loos, Vimy Ridge, and was in action at the capture of Bullecourt. He was afterwards transferred to Italy and saw service in this seat of war until invalided to hospital suffering from sickness, and was finally demobilised in 1919. He holds the 1914-15 Star, and the General Service and Victory Medals.
10, Norbury Street, Longsight, Manchester. Z11162A

STEEL, J. T., Petty Officer, R.N.A.S. (Armoured Car Section).

He volunteered in October 1914, and shortly afterwards was drafted to the Dardanelles, where he was in action during the second and third Battles of Krithia, and the Landing at Suvla Bay. On the Evacuation of the Gallipoli Peninsula, he was sent to Egypt, and was present at the occupation of Sollum and other important engagements until he returned for demobilisation in 1918. He holds the 1914-15 Star, and the General Service and Victory Medals.
10, Norbury Street, Longsight, Manchester. Z11162B

STEELE, T. W., Private, 16th Manchester Regt.

He joined the Army in June 1914, and when war broke out in the following August, was quickly drafted to France, where he took part in the Battles of Ypres, Hill 60 and Loos, and was taken prisoner in October 1915. He was held in captivity in Germany, where he suffered severely from ill-health, and in July 1916 was repatriated and invalided home to hospital. On his recovery, he was engaged on guard duties at Cleethorpe's prisoners of war camp. He was discharged in February 1917 as medically unfit for further service, and holds the 1914 Star, and the General Service and Victory Medals.
68, Juniper Street, Hulme, Manchester. TZ8234

STELFOX, E., L/Corporal, 12th Manchester Regt.
He volunteered in September 1914, and in the following year was drafted to France, where he took part in several engagements, including the Battles of the Somme, Arras, Bullecourt and Messines. He was unfortunately killed in action at Albert in July 1917, and was entitled to the 1914–15 Star, and the General Service and Victory Medals.
"The path of duty was the way to glory."
20, Botham Street, Hulme, Manchester. Z8235

STEPHENSON, W., Private, Border Regiment.
Volunteering in January 1915, he was sent in February of the following year to the Western Front, where he saw heavy fighting at Loos, and was later wounded at the Battle of Vimy Ridge in May 1916. On recovery he returned to the Front line trenches and was gassed during the Somme Offensive and admitted into hospital. After receiving medical treatment he was transferred to the Labour Corps engaged in unloading transports at Boulogne until sent home in March 1918. He was discharged as medically unfit for further military service in the next month, and holds the General Service and Victory Medals.
55, Lord Street, Openshaw, Manchester. Z9713

STEVENS, A. E., Gunner, R.F.A.
He volunteered in March 1915, and underwent a period of training prior to his being drafted overseas. Whilst on the Western Front he took part in engagements at Ypres, Nieuport, on the Somme and at Kemmel Hill. He was also engaged on special duties, and was demobilised in March 1919, holding the General Service and Victory Medals.
16, Royds Street, Chorlton-on-Medlock, Manchester. Z8236

STEVENS, H., Special War Worker.
He was engaged throughout the war on work of National importance at Messrs. Gallaway's. He was employed on the manufacture of shells, and owing to the special nature of his work, was exempted from military service. He was also employed with Messrs. B. Thomas, Worsley Street, Hulme, Manchester, and rendered valuable services until December 1919. 2, Embden Grove, Hulme, Manchester. TZ8237

STEVENS, J. W., Private, M.G.C.
He volunteered in August 1914, but was shortly afterwards discharged owing to medical unfitness. Later he rejoined, and after a period of training proceeded to France, where he took part in several engagements, including the Battle of Cambrai, and was wounded in action. As a result, he was invalided home, and on his recovery served at various stations on important duties. He was demobilised in January 1919, and holds the General Service and Victory Medals.
12, Potter Street, Preston St., Hulme, Manchester. Z8238

STEVENS, R., Private, 11th Border Regiment.
He joined in July 1916, and in the following December proceeded to France. In this theatre of war he took part in many important engagements, including Arras, Albert, Ypres, Vimy Ridge, Lille and Verdun. After the Armistice he served with the Army of Occupation in Germany until September 1919, when he returned home and was demobilised, holding the General Service and Victory Medals.
4, Groom Street, Ancoats, Manchester. Z11827

STEVENSON, W. E., Corporal, Lancashire Fusiliers.
Volunteering in January 1915, he proceeded in the following April to the Western Front, where he served for nearly four years. During that time he was engaged in fierce fighting at St. Eloi, Ypres, Loos, Albert, Vimy Ridge, the Somme, the Ancre, Messines, Cambrai, the Marne, and Le Cateau, and also took part in the advance into Germany. He was demobilised in February 1919, and holds the 1914–15 Star, and the General Service and Victory Medals.
12, School Street, Bradford, Manchester. X11880

STEWARD, C., Private, Gordon Highlanders.
He volunteered in September 1914, and after completing a period of training was sent in the following year to India. He was engaged on important garrison duties, also took part in the fighting on the North-West Frontier and remained there until the cessation of hostilities. He was demobilised in August 1919, and holds the General Service and Victory Medals, and the India General Service Medal (with clasp Afghanistan, N.W. Frontier, 1919).
90, Holland Street, Newton, Manchester. Z11163A

STEWARD, J., Private, Lancashire Fusiliers.
He joined in June 1916, and after a period of training was drafted to the Western Front. During his service in this theatre of war he took part in many important engagements in various sectors of the Front. He was unfortunately killed in action on October 31st, 1918, and was entitled to the General Service and Victory Medals.
"And doubtless he went in splendid company."
90, Holland Street, Newton, Manchester. Z11163B

STEWARDSON, S., Cpl., 11th Lancashire Fusiliers.
He volunteered in August 1914, and twelve months later was drafted to the Western Front, where he was engaged in various

sectors. He saw much heavy fighting and took part in the Battles of the Somme (I), Vimy Ridge and Ypres, and was wounded. On his recovery he returned to France and was in action at Cambrai before being again invalided to England. He was demobilised in June 1919, and holds the 1914–15 Star, and the General Service and Victory Medals.
46, Burton Street, Newton, Manchester. Z11166

STEWART, C., Sapper, R.E.
He volunteered in November 1914, and in the following year was drafted to the Western Front. There he took part in many engagements with the 106th Field Company, including those at Ypres, Armentières and Cambrai. He was demobilised in February 1919, and holds the 1914–15 Star, and the General Service and Victory Medals.
11, Thompson Street, Hulme, Manchester. Z8244

STEWART, E. G., L/Cpl., Cameron Highlanders and Royal Fusiliers.
Joining in February 1916, he was drafted after the completion of his training to the Western Front, where he participated in heavy fighting at Ypres and Kemmel Hill and St. Eloi, and was wounded and gassed. Returning home, he was eventually demobilised in February 1919, but four months later, having volunteered for service in Russia, proceeded to that theatre of hostilities and remained there until September 1919. He was awarded a Russian Decoration, and when finally demobilised in December 1919, was also entitled to the General Service and Victory Medals.
19, Upper Plymouth Grove, Longsight, Manchester. Z11828

STEWART, F. C., Pte., Black Watch and M.G.C.
He volunteered in July 1915, and twelve monthss later was drafted to Salonika, where he was in action during the heavy fighting on the Doiran front and at the recapture of Monastir. In July 1918 he was transferred to the Western Front, but was admitted to hospital suffering from malarial fever. He was demobilised in February 1919, and holds the General Service and Victory Medals.
4, Dorrington Street Hulme, Manchester. Z8241

STEWART, H., Private, 20th Manchester Regt.
He volunteered in August 1915, and drafted to France in the following March, served with his unit in many important engagements, notably those at Loos, St. Eloi, Albert and Vimy Ridge. He died gloriously on the Field of Battle during the Somme Offensive on October 20th, 1916, and was entitled to the General Service and Victory Medals.
"His life for his Country, his soul to God."
21, Dora Street, Rochdale Road, Manchester. Z9382

STEWART, H. D., Private, Cheshire Regiment.
He volunteered in December 1915, and was engaged on important duties as a storekeeper with the Royal Engineers. He was unable to obtain a transfer overseas owing to his being medically unfit, but rendered valuable services until his demobilisation in February 1919.
16, Gladstone Street, Brooks Bar, Manchester. TZ8243

STEWART, J., Private, 21st Manchester Regt.
He volunteered in November 1914, and in the following year was drafted to the Western Front, where he was in action at Arras, Albert, Mericourt and Vimy Ridge. He was badly wounded at Mametz Wood during the Somme Offensive in 1916, and unfortunately had to suffer amputation of his left foot and the toes of his right foot. He holds the 1914–15 Star, and the General Service and Victory Medals, and was invalided from the Army in 1917.
52, Kemp Street, Manchester. Z11164/5B

STEWART, J., Pte., 12th King's (Liverpool Regt.)
Volunteering in January 1915, he was drafted overseas later in the same year. Whilst on the Western Front he took part in engagements at St. Eloi, Albert, Vermelles, the Somme, Arras, Ypres and in the Retreat and Advance of 1918. He was demobilised in February 1919, and holds the 1914–15 Star, and the General Service and Victory Medals.
54, Harrison Street, Ancoats, Manchester. Z8240

STEWART, J. A. C. (Miss), Member, V.A.D.
She joined in June 1917, and for over two years did continuously good work at the 1st New Zealand General Hospital, Brockenhurst, Hants. She carried out her duties in a very efficient manner and gave great satisfaction. She was demobilised in February 1919.
Glen Cottage, North Street, Alloa, Scotland. TZ8239

STEWART, S., Private, 7th Manchester Regiment.
He enlisted in May 1916, and underwent a period of training prior to his being drafted to France. There he took part in several engagements, including the Battles of Passchendaele and Cambrai, where he was badly gassed in November 1917. As a result he was invalided home and discharged as medically unfit for further service in October 1918. He holds the General Service and Victory Medals.
4, Dorrington Street, Hulme, Manchester. Z8242

STEWART, W., Pte., 7th Manchester Regt. (T.F.)
He enlisted in the Territorials in March 1907, and shortly after the outbreak of war in August 1914, was drafted to Egypt, where he served until May 1915. He was then transferred to the Gallipoli Peninsula, and was badly wounded in action at Seddul Bahr in July 1915. Invalided to hospital in England, he was discharged as medically unfit for further service in May 1916, and holds the 1914-15 Star, and the General Service and Victory Medals.
11, Thompson Street, Hulme, Manchester. Z8245

STINTON, R., Private, King's (Liverpool Regiment).
He joined in February 1916, and in the following July proceeded to France. In this theatre of war he took part in the Battles of the Somme, the Ancre, Arras, Vimy Ridge, Ypres, Passchendaele, Lens, Cambrai and the Somme (II), where he was gassed in action in March 1918. He also contracted trench fever, and in consequence was invalided home to hospital at Preston. He was demobilised in September 1919, and holds the General Service and Victory Medals.
18, Walmer Place, Longsight, Manchester. Z8246

STIRLING, W., Private, 3rd Manchester Regiment.
He volunteered in September 1914, and was quickly drafted to France. In this theatre of war he took part in many engagements, including the Battles of Neuve Chapelle, Loos, Givenchy and Ypres (II) and was badly wounded in action in June 1915. As a result, he was invalided home, and on his recovery served at home on important duties until his demobilisation in June 1919. He holds the 1914 Star, and the General Service and Victory Medals.
21, Granville Street, Chorlton-on-Medlock, Manchester. Z8247

STIRRUP, J., Special War Worker.
He volunteered in August 1914, for work of National importance, and was employed by the Great Central Railway Coy. His duties consisted in the manufacture of ambulance coaches, transport wagons and shells, and he also did good work as a blacksmith. Owing to the importance of his work he was unable to join the Army, but, nevertheless, rendered valuable services until discharged in November 1918, and was awarded a Medal for his services.
54, Ryder Street, Bradford, Manchester. Z11167

STOCKDALE, P., 1st Air Mechanic, R.A.F.
He joined in May 1917, and after a period of training served as a rigger, whilst attached to a Balloon section. He was engaged on the London air defences, and was on duty during several air raids. He rendered valuable services until his demobilisation in April 1919, and holds the General Service Medal.
11, Pink Street, Ardwick, Manchester. Z8248

STOCKS, N., Lieut., 1/7th Manchester Regt. and Royal Warwickshire Regt.
He was mobilised in August 1914, and in the following month proceeded to Egypt, where he took a conspicuous part against the Turkish attacks on the Suez Canal. Later he was sent to the Dardanelles and saw much heavy fighting, being wounded at the Battle of Krithia (III), and invalided to hospital in Alexandria. He then rejoined his unit and fought with distinction on the Suez and at Romani, but later was sent to France and took part in the Battle of the Somme. In January 1918 he was drafted to Italy and was in action on the Asiago Plateau, where in September 1918 he was wounded. He was invalided home, and was discharged in July 1920, holding the 1914-15 Star, and the General Service and Victory Medals. 10, Palmerston St., Moss Side, Manchester. Z8249

STOCKTON, F., Pte., Queen's (Royal West Surrey Regiment).
He joined in May 1917, and in November of that year proceeded to the Western Front, and there saw severe fighting in various sectors. After taking part in many important engagements, he was invalided home suffering from shell-shock and trench fever, and was for a considerable period in hospital. On his recovery, however, he was sent with the Army of Occupation into Germany and finally returned to England, and was discharged in September 1919 as medically unfit for further service. He holds the General Service and Victory Medals. 132, Sowerby St., Moss Side, Manchester. Z8251B

STOCKTON, T., Gunner, R.F.A.
He volunteered in November 1915, and in October of the following year proceeded to France, where he saw severe fighting in various sectors of the Front. He took part in the Battles of Arras, Ypres and Cambrai and many minor engagements, served also through the Retreat and Advance of 1918, and was wounded in action near Ypres in September of that year. He was demobilised in February 1919, and holds the General Service and Victory Medals.
6, Hewitt Street, Openshaw, Manchester. Z8250

STOCKTON, W., 2nd Lieutenant, R.F.A.
Five months after volunteering in July 1915, he proceeded to the Western Front, where he saw much severe fighting in various sectors. He took a prominent part in the Battles of the Somme, Arras and Ypres, and many other important engagements until wounded in action at La Bassée in October

1918 and invalided to hospital in England. He was finally demobilised in March 1919 and holds the 1914-15 Star, and the General Service and Victory Medals.
132, Sowerby Street, Moss Side, Manchester. Z8251A

STOKES, E., Private, 16th South Lancashire Regt.
He volunteered in December 1915, and after completing a period of training served at various stations, where, attached to the Labour Corps, he was engaged on duties of great importance. He was not successful in obtaining his transfer to a theatre of war, but, nevertheless, rendered valuable services with his unit until March 1919, when he was demobilised.
7, Fleeson Street, Rusholme, Manchester. Z8252B

STOKES, H., Private, 1/8th Manchester Regiment.
Mobilised in August 1914, he was shortly afterwards drafted to Egypt, whence he proceeded in the following year to the Dardanelles. There he saw much severe fighting, taking part in many important engagements, and was twice wounded in action—in June and September 1915. Invalided home, he was retained on his recovery, at various stations in England until January 1919, when he was discharged. He holds the 1914-15 Star, and the General Service and Victory Medals.
7, Fleeson Street, Rusholme, Manchester. Z8252A

STOLE, W., Private, 39th Royal Fusiliers.
Joining in February 1918, he was drafted to Egypt on completing three months' training and was there stationed at Kantara and on the General Headquarters Staff at Cairo. He was for a time in hospital at Alexandria, suffering from malaria and also served in Palestine, where he was in hospital at Jericho. He finally returned home for demobilisation in March 1919, and holds the General Service and Victory Medals.
34, Robert Street, Chorlton-on-Medlock, Manchester. X8253

STONE, W., Private, 7th Manchester Regiment.
He volunteered in January 1916, and after four months' training was drafted to the Western Front, where he was wounded in action in the Somme Offensive of the same year. He was invalided home, but, on his recovery, returned to France in time to take part in the Retreat and Advance of 1918. He was finally sent to England for demobilisation in September 1919, and holds the General Service and Victory Medals. 17, Broadfield St., Moss Side, Manchester. Z8254

STONE, W. E., Private, 4th Lancashire Fusiliers.
He was called up from the Reserve in August 1914, and shortly afterwards proceeded to the Western Front. Whilst in this theatre of war he took part in many important engagements, including the Battles of Neuve Chapelle, Hill 60, and Ypres (II). Later he was transferred to the R.E. and went to Belgium, where he served until the cessation of hostilities. He was demobilised in May 1919, and holds the 1914-15 Star, and the General Service and Victory Medals.
35, Shepley Street, Harpurhey, Manchester. Z11168

STONELAKE, D. W., Corporal, 1st Welch Regt.
Shortly after volunteering in March 1915, he proceeded to the Western Front, where he saw severe fighting in various sectors. He took part in engagements at Neuve Chapelle, St. Eloi and many other places in this theatre of war, and was twice wounded in action—at Ypres and again at Vimy Ridge. He was for a considerable period in hospital in England before being invalided from the Army in September 1919, and holds the 1914-15 Star, and the General Service and Victory Medals.
80, Great Jackson Street, West Gorton, Manchester. Z8255

STONIER, J., Air Mechanic, R.A.F.
Joining in April 1917, he completed his training and served with his squadron at various aerodromes engaged on important work of a highly technical nature. He rendered valuable service, but was not successful in securing his transfer overseas before the close of the war. After the Armistice, however, he was sent to Germany to the Army of Occupation, and was stationed at Cologne. He was demobilised in December 1919.
54, Vine Street, Newton Heath, Manchester. Z9714

STONIER, J. E., Corporal, South Lancashire Regt.
He volunteered in September 1914, and twelve months later was drafted to the Western Front. Whilst in this theatre of war he saw much severe fighting in various sectors, took part in the Battles of the Somme, Messines and Ypres, and many other engagements, and was three times wounded in action —on the Ancre in November 1916, and on the Somme and the Aisne in March and June 1918. He was finally demobilised in January 1919, and holds the 1914-15 Star, and the General Service and Victory Medals.
3, William Street, Rusholme Road, Chorlton-on-Medlock, Manchester. TX8256

STORAH, W., Aircraftsman, R.A.F.
He volunteered in April 1915, and after a period of training was sent to France, where he was engaged on important duties with the Kite Balloon Section, and was present at several important engagements. He also rendered valuable services at St. Omer and Calais, and was demobilised in April 1920, holding the General Service and Victory Medals.
47, Branson Street, Ancoats, Manchester. Z11169

STORMES, A. E., Rifleman, K.R.R.C.
Volunteering in November 1914, he was drafted to the Western Front in April of the following year, and there took part in the Battles of Ypres, Albert, Vimy Ridge, the Somme, the Ancre, Arras, Cambrai and Amiens, and many other important engagements. He unfortunately fell fighting at Ypres in November 1918, only a few days before the cessation of hostilities. He was entitled to the 1914–15 Star, and the General Service and Victory Medals.
" His memory is cherished with pride."
10, Watson Street, Hulme, Manchester.　　　Z8257

STOTT, A., Pte., Lancashire Fus. and Border Regt.
Shortly after volunteering in August 1914, he proceeded to Egypt, whence he was sent, in May of the following year, to the Dardanelles. Wounded in action in the following month, he was invalided to hospital at Cairo and afterwards to England, but on his recovery was drafted to the Western Front, where he was wounded a second time during the fighting on the Ancre. He was again sent home, but returned to France in August 1917, and there, after taking part in the Battles of Ypres, Cambrai and the Somme, was taken prisoner near Armentières. Held in captivity until the cessation of hostilities he was finally demobilised in April 1919, holding the 1914–15 Star, and the General Service and Victory Medals.
43, Allen Street, Hulme, Manchester.　　　Z8258

STOTT, A., Pte., R.A.S.C. (M.T.) and Sapper, R.E.
He volunteered in November 1915, and after three months' training was drafted to the Western Front, where he was engaged on important duties in various sectors. He also took an active part in the Battles of Vermelles, the Somme and Vimy Ridge, and many other engagements until the cessation of hostilities. He was demobilised on his return to England in August 1919, and holds the General Service and Victory Medals.
7, St. John Street, Longsight, Manchester.　　　Z8259

STOUT, G., Private, Lancashire Fusiliers.
Volunteering in February 1915, he embarked in the following July for the Western Front and was in action at the Battles of Loos, Vimy Ridge, the Somme, Arras, Bullecourt, Messines, Ypres, Passchendaele and Cambrai. He also fought in the German Offensive and subsequent Allied Advance of 1918, and returning home after the Armistice, was demobilised in February 1919. He holds the 1914–15 Star, and the General Service and Victory Medals.
10, Heath Street, Ancoats, Manchester.　　　Z9715

STRAFFORD, A., Sergt., 3rd Manchester Regt.
A Reservist, he was called to the Colours at the outbreak of war in August 1914, and was retained at various stations, where he was engaged on duties of a highly important nature. He was not successful in his efforts to obtain his transfer to a theatre of war, but, nevertheless, rendered valuable services with his unit until February 1919, when he was discharged.
79, Higher Ormond Street, Chorlton-on-Medlock, Manchester.　　　Z8260

STRAHAND, G., Gunner, R.F.A.
Volunteering in March 1915, he proceeded five months later to France, where he served with his Battery in the Battles of Ypres (II), the Somme and Ypres (III). He was invalided home in December 1917, suffering from gas poisoning and, admitted to hospital in Manchester, died from the effects on April 11th, 1918. He was entitled to the 1914–15 Star, and the General Service and Victory Medals.
" The path of duty was the way to glory."
8, Milton Street, Bradford, Manchester.　　　Z11829JB

STRAHAND, J., Private, York and Lancaster Regt.
He joined in December 1917, and in the following May was drafted to the Western Front. In this theatre of war he took part in several engagements during the final Advance of 1918, and was wounded and taken prisoner on October 13th of that year. He unfortunately died from the effects of his wounds at a field dressing station on the following day, and was buried in St. Vaast Cemetery. He was entitled to the General Service and Victory Medals.
" Thinking that remembrance, though unspoken, may reach him where he sleeps."
8, Milton Street, Bradford, Manchester.　　　Z11829A

STRAND, G., Gunner, R.F.A.
He volunteered in August 1914, and crossing to France in the following March fought in many important battles, including those of Neuve Chapelle, Hill 60, Ypres (II and III), Festubert, Loos, Albert, Vimy Ridge, the Somme, Arras, Bullecourt and Cambrai. He was severely wounded in the German Offensive and subsequently died from the effects of his injuries on April 16th, 1918. He was entitled to the 1914–15 Star, and the General Service and Victory Medals.
" His name liveth for evermore."
50, Jersey Street Dwellings, Ancoats, Manchester.　　　Z9383B

STRAND, J., Private, York and Lancaster Regt.
He joined in November 1917, and embarking in the following June for the Western Front, saw heavy fighting during the German Offensive and fought in many important battles in the subsequent Allied Advance. He was unfortunately killed at the entry into Mons on Armistice Day, and was entitled to the General Service and Victory Medals.
" The path of duty was the way to glory."
50, Jersey Street Dwellings, Ancoats, Manchester.　　　Z9383A

STRANGE, H., Stoker, R.N.
Volunteering in August 1914, he completed his training and was posted to H.M.S. " Bristol," which ship was engaged on patrol and other important duties in the Mediterranean, and was in action with enemy craft off Brindisi and Trieste. Returning home, he was demobilised in July 1919, and holds the 1914–15 Star, and the General Service and Victory Medals.
96, Bold Street, Moss Side, Manchester.　　　Z9716

STRATH, F. (D.C.M.), Sergt., 1st Lancashire Fus.
Volunteering in July 1915, he was drafted to Gallipoli two months later, and there saw much severe fighting, and was wounded in action. On the Evacuation of the Peninsula, he was transferred to the Western Front, where he took part in the Battles of Albert, Vimy Ridge and Arras, and was again wounded on the Somme and invalided to hospital at Nottingham. He returned to France, however, on his recovery in July 1917, and was wounded in action for the third time at Cambrai in March of the following year and was again sent home. He was awarded the Distinguished Conduct Medal for conspicuous bravery and devotion to duty in the Field at Arras in April 1917, and holds also the 1914–15 Star, and the General Service and Victory Medals. He was demobilised in January 1919.
5, Bradshaw Street, Hulme, Manchester.　　　TZ8262

STRATH, H., Private, 11th Manchester Regiment.
He volunteered in August 1914, and in October of the following year was drafted to Salonika, where he saw much severe fighting. After taking part in many important engagements on the Vardar and Struma fronts, he was wounded in action on the Doiran front in April 1917, sent to hospital at Malta and thence invalided home. He was finally demobilised in February 1919, and holds the 1914–15 Star, and the General Service and Victory Medals.
9, Stone Street, Chester Road, Hulme, Manchester.　　　Z8261

STREET, C., Private, 4th Manchester Regiment.
Joining in September 1916, he proceeded to the Western Front in the following month and there saw much severe fighting in various sectors. He took part in the Battles of Ypres, Cambrai and the Somme and many other important engagements, and served also through the Retreat and Advance of 1918. He was afterwards sent with the Army of Occupation into Germany, but returned home for demobilisation in December 1918, holding the General Service and Victory Medals.　15, Emily St., Ardwick, Manchester.　　　TZ8265

STREET, H., Private, 7th Manchester Regiment.
He joined in October 1916, and in the following January proceeded to France. Whilst in this theatre of war he took part in much heavy fighting in various sectors of the Front. He was in action throughout the Battles of Arras, Vimy Ridge, Bullecourt, Ypres (III) and Passchendaele, and the Retreat and Advance of 1918. Later he was transferred to Egypt, and was engaged on important garrison duties at Cairo until December 1919. He was demobilised in January 1920, and holds the General Service and Victory Medals.
19, Wrigley Street, West Gorton, Manchester.　　　Z11450

STREET, J., Corporal, R.A.F. (Late R.F.C.)
After joining in August 1916, he underwent a period of training at various stations before being drafted to Italy in the following year. There, engaged on duties of a highly technical nature near Venice, he rendered very valuable services with his Squadron until after the cessation of hostilities. He was demobilised on his return to England in February 1919, and holds the General Service and Victory Medals.
11, Fir Street, Hulme, Manchester.　　　Z8267

STREET, J., Private, 4th Manchester Regiment.
He volunteered in August 1914, and in December of that year was drafted to the Western Front, where he took part in the Battle of Ypres, and many other important engagements in various sectors. He died gloriously on the field of Battle at Loos on September 25th, 1915. He was entitled to the 1914–15 Star, and the General Service and Victory Medals.
" He died the noblest death a man may die,
Fighting for God and right and liberty."
15, Emily Street, Ardwick, Manchester.　　　TZ8266

STREET, P., Corporal, Lancashire Fusiliers.
He volunteered at the outbreak of war in August 1914, and in April of the following year was drafted to Gallipoli, where he was severely wounded in action shortly after landing. He was sent to hospital at Malta, and was thence invalided home, where, after his recovery, he was retained on important duties at various stations. He was finally demobilised in February 1919, and holds the 1914–15 Star, and the General Service and Victory Medals.
28, Silk Street, Hulme, Manchester.　　　Z8263

STREET, W., Private, 4th Royal Scots.

He volunteered in August 1914, and was retained on important duties in England until September 1916, when he proceeded to Egypt. There he took part in the Advance into Palestine, where after fighting in the Battles of Rafa and Gaza, he made the supreme sacrifice, falling in action on November 2nd, 1917. He was entitled to the General Service and Victory Medals.
"A valiant Soldier, with undaunted heart he breasted life's last hill."
28, Aked Street, Ardwick, Manchester. Z8264

STRETCH, J., Private, M.G.C.

He joined in June 1916, and after a period of training proceeded to France. There he took part in many engagements, including the Battles of Arras, Messines, Ypres, Cambrai, the Somme (II.), Amiens, and St. Quentin, and was gassed and twice wounded in action. He was demobilised in July 1919, and holds the General Service and Victory Medals.
2, Henry St., Moor St., Rusholme, Manchester. TZ8268

STRINGER, A., L/Corporal, Manchester Regiment.

Volunteering in August 1914, he proceeded to France three months later, but was wounded in action at the 1st Battle of Ypres in November 1914. After hospital treatment at the Base, he rejoined his unit and took part in the Battles of Ypres (II), the Somme, and Cambrai, where he was wounded in action in 1917. He was invalided to hospital in Edinburgh, but on his recovery, returned to the Western Front, and took part in the Retreat and Advance of 1918. He holds the 1914 Star, and the General Service and Victory Medals, and was demobilised in April 1919.
18, Victoria Street, Longsight, Manchester. Z8269

STRINGER, W., Private, 7th and 8th King's Own Scottish Borderers.

Volunteering in September 1914, he was drafted to France early in 1915, and took part in the Battles of Neuve Chapelle, St. Eloi, and Hill 60, where he was wounded in action and invalided home. On his recovery he returned to the Western Front, and served at the Battles of the Somme, the Ancre, Arras, Vimy Ridge, and Cambrai, and was again badly wounded at Loos in 1918. He holds the 1914-15 Star, and the General Service and Victory Medals, and was discharged as medically unfit for further service in October 1918.
6, Pilling Street, Newton Heath, Manchester. Z11170

STRONG, H., Sapper, R.E.

Joining in January 1917, he was drafted overseas in the following March. Whilst on the Western Front he took part in the Battles of Arras, Ypres, Passchendaele, and Cambrai, where he was badly wounded in action in November 1917. As a result he was invalided home and discharged in February 1918 as medically unfit. He holds the General Service and Victory Medals.
8, Anthony Street, Ardwick, Manchester. Z8270B

STUBBINS, J. A., Private, 9th Lancashire Fusiliers.

He volunteered in December 1915, and in the following June was drafted to France. Whilst overseas he took part in several engagements, including the Battles of the Somme (where he was in action at Beaumont-Hamel, and Beaucourt), Bullecourt, Messines, Ypres, Bapaume, and the Selle. He was demobilised in March 1919, and holds the General Service and Victory Medals.
45, Heald Avenue, Rusholme, Manchester. TZ8271

STUBBS, C., Private, 2nd South Lancashire Regt.

He volunteered in September 1914, and on completing his training in the following January, proceeded to the Western Front. There he took part in the Battles of Neuve Chapelle, Hill 60, Ypres (II), and the Somme, where he was badly wounded. In consequence he was invalided home and discharged on account of wounds in November 1917. He holds the 1914-15 Star, and the General Service and Victory Medals.
2, Rosamond Place, Chorlton-on-Medlock, Manchester. TX1035B

STUBBS, W., Private, Manchester Regiment.

He volunteered in November 1914, and twelve months later proceeded to the Western Front, where he took part in many important engagements in various sectors. He made the supreme sacrifice, being killed in action on March 25th, 1916, and was buried at Corbie. He was entitled to the 1914-15 Star, and the General Service and Victory Medals.
"Great deeds cannot die."
They with the sun and moon renew their light for ever."
47, Milton Street, Bradford, Manchester. Z11171-2-3B

STURGEON, W., Private, 16th Manchester Regt.

Volunteering in March 1915, he was drafted to France in the following November, and took part in heavy fighting at La Bassée, Loos, Givenchy, and Festubert. He was later in action at Guillemont and Montauban during the Somme Offensive, and was badly wounded in July 1916. After hospital treatment in Leicester, he returned to the Western Front, and served at the 2nd Battle of the Somme, and at Nieuport and Dunkirk. He was again admitted to hospital, suffering from trench fever, and was eventually demobilised in February 1919, holding the 1914-15 Star, and the General Service and Victory Medals.
131, Beresford Street, Moss Side, Manchester. Z8272

SUFFIELD, W., L/Cpl., K.O. (R. Lancaster Regt.)

He volunteered in September 1915, and in the following year was drafted to Salonika. There he took part with his unit in heavy fighting on various fronts, remaining in this theatre of war up to 1918. He was then sent to the Dardanelles, where he was employed on special duties until he returned home for demobilisation in April 1919, holding the General Service and Victory Medals.
27, Broadfield Street, Moss Side, Manchester. Z8273

SULLIVAN, A., L/Cpl., K.O. (R. Lancaster Regt.)

He was mobilised in August 1914, and immediately drafted to the Western Front, where he took part in the Battle of Mons, and was wounded in action. As a result, he was invalided home, but on his recovery, returned to France and fought at Albert, Vimy Ridge, the Somme, Arras, and in the Retreat and Advance of 1918. He suffered from tuberculosis and was sent home, and discharged in September 1918. He unhappily died in January 1920, and was entitled to the Mons Star, and the General Service and Victory Medals.
"His memory is cherished with pride."
37, Park Street, Hulme, Manchester. Z8275

SULLIVAN, D., Sergeant, Manchester Regiment.

Three months after volunteering in January 1915, he was drafted to the Dardanelles, where, after taking part in the first Landing at Gallipoli, he saw much severe fighting until the Evacuation of the Peninsula. He was then transferred to the Western Front, and there served through the Battle of Vimy Ridge, and was severely wounded in action in the Somme Offensive. He was invalided from the Army in November 1917, and holds the 1914-15 Star, and the General Service and Victory Medals.
38, Richardson Street, Collyhurst, Manchester. Z11176

SULLIVAN, E. A., Sapper, R.E.

He joined in May 1917, and after a period of training was drafted in January of the following year to Egypt. There he was engaged on duties of great importance at Kantara, and various other stations, and rendered valuable services with his Company until his return to England for demobilisation in February 1920. He holds the General Service and Victory Medals. 27, North Kent St., Rochdale Rd., Manchester. Z11175

SULLIVAN, F. A., Private, Manchester Regiment.

Volunteering in February 1915, he was sent to the Dardanelles in September of that year, and there saw much severe fighting until the Evacuation of the Gallipoli Peninsula. He was then transferred to the Western Front, where he was unhappily killed in action near Albert in September 1916, during the Somme Offensive. He was entitled to the 1914-15 Star, and the General Service and Victory Medals.
"His life for his Country, his soul to God."
5, Alderman Street, Ardwick, Manchester. Z11174

SULLIVAN, F. J., Private, 2nd S. Lancashire Regt.

He volunteered in March 1915, and in the following August was drafted to the Western Front, where he fought at St. Eloi, Ploegsteert, and Vimy Ridge. He was unfortunately killed in action on the Somme on July 3rd, 1916, and was entitled to the 1914-15 Star, and the General Service and Victory Medals.
"A valiant Soldier, with undaunted heart he breasted life's last hill."
24, Lord Street, Hulme, Manchester. TZ8274A

SULLIVAN, J., 2nd Lieut., Loyal N. Lancashire Regt.

He volunteered in September 1914, and in the following July proceeded to the Western Front, where he took part in engagements at St. Eloi, Vimy Ridge, Arras, and Cambrai. He was then transferred to the Durham Light Infantry, but later was unfortunately killed in action in the Ypres sector in October 1918. He was entitled to the 1914-15 Star, and the General Service and Victory Medals.
"Whilst we remember the sacrifice is not in vain."
8, Woodville Street, Chorlton-on-Medlock, Manchester. Z8278

SULLIVAN, J., Private, 7th Lancashire Fusiliers.

He was mobilised with the Territorials in August 1914, and in the following month proceeded to Egypt. Later he was transferred to the Dardanelles, where he took part in much heavy fighting, and was wounded in action at the Battle of Krithia in June 1915. As a result he was invalided to Alexandria, but, on his recovery, rejoined his unit. In 1917, he was sent to the Western Front, and was in action at the Battles of Bullecourt, Ypres III, Bapaume, St. Quentin, the Somme (II), Cambrai (II), and Ypres (IV). He was demobilised in June 1919, and holds the 1914-15 Star, and the General Service and Victory Medals.
15, Clayburn Street, Hulme, Manchester. Z8277

SULLIVAN, J., Sapper R.E.

Volunteering in October 1914, he was drafted overseas two months later. During his service in France he took part in the Battles of Neuve Chapelle, and Ypres II, where he was badly gassed and invalided to Rouen. On his recovery, he was engaged on important duties until after the cessation of hostilities. He was demobilised in June 1919, and holds the 1914-15 Star, and the General Service and Victory Medals.
16, Park Place, Hulme, Manchester. Z8276

SULLIVAN, J. E., 2nd Lancashire Fusiliers.
He was mobilised when war broke out and drafted shortly afterwards to France. There he took part in the Retreat from Mons, and was wounded and taken prisoner in September 1914. He remained in captivity in Germany until the cessation of hostilities, and during this period was compelled to work in iron works at Sennelager and Jefannalager. Repatriated in December 1918, he was demobilised in that month, and holds the Mons Star, and the General Service and Victory Medals.
6, Bright Street, Rochdale Road, Manchester. Z9717

SULLIVAN, T., Private, 20th Manchester Regiment.
He volunteered in August 1914, and in the following March proceeded to the Western Front. There he took part in several engagements, including the Battles of Hill 60, Festubert, Albert, the Somme, Bullecourt, Passchendaele, Cambrai, and in the Retreat and Advance of 1918. He was demobilised in February 1919, and holds the 1914-15 Star, and the General Service and Victory Medals.
16, Lord Street, Hulme, Manchester. TZ8274B

SULLIVAN, T., Private, Cheshire Regiment.
He joined in April 1916, and after a period of training was engaged at various stations on important duties with his unit. He was not successful in obtaining a transfer overseas, but rendered valuable services until his demobilisation in April 1919. 19, Brunswick Street, Hulme, Manchester. Z8279

SUMMERS, F., Private, 4th King's (Liverpool Regt.)
He volunteered in August 1914, and in the following April was drafted to the Gallipoli Peninsula, where he took part in the Landing at Cape Helles, and the Battles of Krithia. He died gloriously on the Field of Battle at Chunuk Bair on August 28th, 1915, and was entitled to the 1914-15 Star, and the General Service and Victory Medals.
"A costly sacrifice upon the altar of freedom."
10, Somerset Square, Ardwick, Manchester. Z8280B

SUMMERS, G., Private, Manchester Regiment.
Volunteering in December 1915, he was drafted overseas in the following year. Whilst on the Western Front he took part in many engagements, including those at Ypres and Péronne, and was wounded and invalided home. On his recovery, he returned to France, but was seriously wounded at the Battle of Cambrai in 1917, and was sent to the Base hospital where he unfortunately died from the effects of his wounds on October 21st, 1918. He was entitled to the General Service and Victory Medals.
"Great deeds cannot die:
They with the sun and moon renew their light for ever."
20, Viaduct Street, Ardwick, Manchester. Z8281

SUMMERS, J., Private, 4th King's (Liverpool Regt.)
He was mobilised in August 1914, and immediately drafted to France. There he took part in the Battle of Mons, and in the subsequent Retreat, and the Battles at La Bassée, Ypres (I), Hill 60, Festubert, Albert, the Somme, and Beaucourt. Later he was transferred to Mesopotamia, where he was unfortunately killed in action at Kut (II) on February 10th, 1917. He was entitled to the Mons Star, and the General Service and Victory Medals.
"His life for his Country, his soul to God."
10, Somerset Square, Ardwick, Manchester. Z8280A

SUMNER, A., Private, 7th Manchester Regiment.
He was mobilised with the Territorials in August 1914, and in the following month was drafted to Egypt, where he was stationed at Khartoum and Alexandria. In May 1915 he was transferred to the Dardanelles and saw much heavy fighting at Seddul Bahr, Krithia, and in the Evacuation of the Gallipoli Peninsula. He then returned to Egypt, and was engaged along the Suez Canal until March 1917, when he was sent to France. There he fought at Bullecourt, Havrincourt, and in the Retreat of 1918, and was wounded in action at Gommecourt, which resulted in his being invalided home. He was demobilised in January 1919, and holds the 1914-15 Star, and the General Service and Victory Medals.
41, Mercer Street, Hulme, Manchester. Z8283

SUMNER, F., Private, 1/7th Manchester Regiment.
He was mobilised in August 1914, and was shortly afterwards drafted to Egypt, but later proceeded to the Dardanelles. There he saw much fighting at Seddul Baharb, Krithia III, and after the evacuation of the Gallipoli Peninsula, proceeded to France. In this theatre of war he took part in the Battles of Béthune, at Epéhy, Havrincourt, Cambrai (II), Le Cateau (II), and in other engagements during the Retreat and Advance of 1918. He was demobilised in January 1919, and holds the 1914-15 Star, and the General Service and Victory Medals.
41, Mercer Street, Hulme, Manchester. Z8282

SUNDERLAND, W., Gunner, R.G.A.
He volunteered in 1915, and after a period of training was sent in the following year to France. Remaining overseas for a period of three years, he served in many sectors, including Ypres, Cambrai, and Hill 60, and did very good work whilst engaged on various duties, being once wounded. He was demobilised in 1919, and holds the General Service and Victory Medals.
28, Robert Street, Chorlton-on-Medlock, Manchester. Z11830

SUPER, W., Driver, R.E.
He volunteered in January 1916, and after a period of training was drafted to France, where he took part in several engagements, including the Battles at Vimy Ridge, Ypres (III), Lens, Cambrai, the Somme (II), the Marne (II), Bapaume, Amiens, Ypres (IV), and Le Cateau (II), and was present at the entry into Mons on Armistice Day. After the cessation of hostilities, he went to Germany with the Army of Occupation. He was demobilised in August 1919, and holds the General Service and Victory Medals.
5, Argyle Street, Hulme, Manchester. Z8284

SURREY, T., Private, R.A.M.C. (T.F.)
Volunteering in September 1915, he served at various home stations until March 1917, and then proceeded with the 66th Division to the Western Front. There he was stationed with his Company in many sectors, including Festubert, Nieuport, Ypres, and the Somme, and was taken prisoner at Templeux in March 1918. Kept in captivity in Westphalia until the termination of hostilities, he was then repatriated, and was eventually demobilised in March 1919, holding the General Service and Victory Medals.
17, Macclesfield Street, Hulme, Manchester. Z11831

SURRIDGE, A., Private, South Lancashire Regt.
He volunteered in August 1914, and in September of the following year, was drafted to the Western Front, where he took part in several important engagements, and was wounded in action at the Battle of Loos. In April 1916, however, he was transferred to Salonika, and there saw severe fighting on the Doiran, Struma, and Vardar fronts until invalided home in 1917. He was afterwards retained on various duties with the Royal Defence Corps in England until demobilised in February 1920, holding the 1914-15 Star, and the General Service and Victory Medals. 33, Simpson St., Bradford, Manchester. Z11177

SUTCLIFFE, A., Private, Labour Corps.
He volunteered in August 1914, and was engaged on important duties at various stations with his unit. He was unable to obtain a transfer overseas owing to his being medically unfit, but rendered valuable services until his demobilisation in October 1919.
26, William Street, West Gorton, Manchester. Z8285

SUTCLIFFE, J., Private, 2nd Manchester Regt.
He joined in August 1918, and sailing in the following October for Egypt, served with his unit at Cairo and Alexandria, engaged on garrison and other important duties. He rendered valuable services throughout, and returning to England in 1920, was demobilised in April of that year. He holds the General Service and Victory Medals.
1, Alfred Street, Collyhurst, Manchester. Z9384

SUTHERLAND, W., Sapper, R.E.
He joined in September 1917, and after undergoing a period of training, served at various stations, where he was engaged on duties of a highly important nature. He was not successful in obtaining his transfer overseas, but nevertheless rendered valuable services until September 1918, when he was invalided from the Army, suffering from an illness contracted whilst with the Colours.
18, Victoria Street, Longsight, Manchester. Z8286

SUTTON, D., Air Mechanic, R.A.F. (late R.N.A.S.)
He joined in November 1916, and after his training was engaged on duties of a highly technical nature in England until April 1918. He then proceeded to the Western Front, and there served at Boulogne, and various other stations, where he did much useful work with his Squadron until after the cessation of hostilities. He was demobilised on his return home in February 1919, and holds the General Service and Victory Medals. 26, Gatley Street, Ancoats, Manchester. Z8287

SUTTON, F., Driver, R.F.A.
He volunteered in October 1914, and after concluding a period of training, served at various stations, where he was engaged on duties of a highly important nature. He was not successful in obtaining his transfer to a theatre of war on account of ill-health, but, nevertheless, rendered valuable services with his Battery until September 1918, when he was invalided from the Army. 11, Park Street, West Gorton, Manchester. Z11178

SUTTON, G. W., Private, 21st Manchester Regt.
Volunteering in August 1914, he was sent in the following year to the Western Front. In this theatre of war he fought in several engagements, notably those of Neuve Chapelle, Ypres, Vimy Ridge, and the Somme. In the course of his service he was engaged for a short period with the Labour Corps, and returning to his unit took part in operations in the closing stages of the war. He was demobilised in February 1919, and holds the 1914-15 Star, and the General Service and Victory Medals.
16, Cross Street, Newton Heath, Manchester. Z9718

SUTTON, P., Private, King's (Liverpool Regiment.)
Joining in April 1916, he completed his training and served with his unit at various stations engaged on important duties. He did good work, but was not successful in securing his transfer overseas before the cessation of hostilities, and was demobilised in March 1919.
45, Francisco Street, Collyhurst, Manchester. Z9720

SUTTON, J., L/Corporal, Border Regiment.
He volunteered in November 1914, and landing in France shortly afterwards saw heavy fighting at Ypres. Sent home in January 1915, owing to ill-health, he was admitted into the 2nd Western General Hospital, Manchester, where he received treatment and returned to the Western Front in March 1916. He fought in the Battles of Givenchy, Ploegsteert, the Somme, Bullecourt, and was wounded at Passchendaele in 1917. Again evacuated to England to Gosport Hospital, he was eventually discharged as medically unfit for further service in August 1918. He holds the 1914 Star, and the General Service and Victory Medals.
25, John Street, Bradford, Manchester. Z9719

SUTTON, J., Private, East Lancashire Regiment.
He volunteered in September 1914, and in March of the following year proceeded to Egypt, where he served on the Suez Canal. Later in 1915 he was transferred to Salonika, and there saw much severe fighting on the Vardar and Doiran fronts until drafted to India in January 1918. There he served at various stations, was wounded in action, and was also in hospital, suffering from dysentery. Invalided home in September 1918, he was demobilised in June 1919, and holds the 1914-15 Star, and the General Service and Victory Medals.
14, Sorrell Street, Hulme, Manchester. Z1009A

SWAIN, F., L/Corporal, 1/7th Manchester Regt.
He volunteered in November 1914, and on completing his training in the following year, proceeded to the Western Front, where he took part in the Somme Offensive and was shortly afterwards wounded in action. Invalided home, he returned to France, however, on his recovery in 1917, and took part in many important engagements, fought also in the Retreat and Advance of 1918, and was wounded a second time at Ypres. He was demobilised on his return to England in 1919, and holds the 1914-15 Star, and the General Service and Victory Medals.
14, Back Tiverton Street, Ardwick, Manchester. Z11179

SWALES, T. (M.M.) Private, 11th Manchester Regt.
He volunteered in August 1914, and in the following June was drafted to Gallipoli. In this theatre of hostilities he was in action at Suvla Bay, and after the Evacuation served in Egypt at Alexandria, and other places. Later proceeding to France, he took part in heavy fighting on the Somme, at Arras, Bullecourt, Ypres, and Passchendaele, and was wounded and gassed. He was awarded the Military Medal for bravery and consistent devotion to duty in the Field, and when demobilised in January 1919, was also entitled to the 1914-15 Star, and the General Service and Victory Medals.
22, Heath Street, Ancoats, Manchester. Z11832

SWANWICK, H. V., Private, Manchester Regiment.
Volunteering in September 1914, he was drafted to the Western Front twelve months later, and there saw much severe fighting until blown up by an explosion during the Somme Offensive in October 1916, and invalided home. He returned to France, however, on his recovery in October 1918, and took part in several important engagements in the final stages of the war. Demobilised in February 1919, he holds the 1914-15 Star, and the General Service and Victory Medals.
34, Seal Street, Collyhurst, Manchester. Z11181B

SWANWICK, T., Corporal, M.G.C.
He volunteered in September 1914, and was retained on important duties in England until drafted, in February 1916, to the Western Front, where he took part in severe fighting at Loos, St. Eloi, and Vermelles, and many other places. He gave his life for King and Country in July 1916, during the Advance on the Somme. He was entitled to the General Service and Victory Medals.
"The path of duty was the way to glory."
9, Park Street, West Gorton, Manchester. Z11180

SWARBRICK, H., Private, M.G.C., and Tank Corps.
He joined in September 1916, and after completing a period of training, served at various stations, where he was engaged as a mechanic on the construction and repair of tanks. He was unable to obtain his transfer overseas on account of heart disease, and in November 1918, after rendering very valuable services, was invalided from the Army. He has unhappily since died.
"Steals on the ear the distant triumph song."
136, Clopton Street, Hulme, Manchester. TZ8288

SWEENEY, J., Private, 10th Lancashire Fusiliers.
He volunteered in August 1914, and twelve months later, proceeded to the Western Front, where he saw heavy fighting at Festubert, and in September 1915, was severely wounded in action at Ypres. He was for a considerable period in hospital at Norwich, and was finally invalided from the Army in April 1917. He holds the 1914-15 Star, and the General Service and Victory Medals.
16, Culvert Street, Rochdale Road, Manchester. Z11182

SWEETMAN, J., Private, 12th Manchester Regiment.
Volunteering in February 1915, he was sent five months later to France. There he played a prominent part with his unit in many important engagements, including Loos, Vermelles the Somme, Arras, Ypres, and Cambrai. Invalided home on account of ill-health in January 1918, he was admitted to

hospital in Beckenham, and was subsequently discharged in July 1918 as unfit for further service. He holds the 1914-15 Star, and the General Service and Victory Medals.
12, Church Street, Hulme, Manchester. Z11833

SWEETMAN, W. C., Private, 8th Border Regiment.
Volunteering in January 1916, he embarked for France three months later and was in action on the Somme, at Beaumont-Hamel, Arras, Messines, and Cambrai. He also took part in the Retreat of 1918, and in September of that year was severely wounded at Havrincourt Wood during the subsequent Allied Advance. Evacuated to England, he underwent hospital treatment, and in March 1919, was invalided out of the Service. He holds the General Service and Victory Medals.
59, Teignmouth Street, Collyhurst, Manchester. Z9721

SWEETSER, C. W., Private, 2/8th Manchester Regt.
A Reservist, he was mobilised on the declaration of war, and proceeding to France with the 1st British Expeditionary Force, fought in the Retreat from Mons, at the Battles of the Marne, the Aisne and Ypres. He was also in action in many other important engagements, and took part in the heavy fighting during the Retreat and Allied Advance of 1918. He was demobilised in February 1919, and holds the Mons Star, and the General Service and Victory Medals.
6, Ashmore Street, West Gorton, Manchester. Z11617

SWIFT, J. H., Private, 1/8th Manchester Regiment.
He volunteered at the outbreak of war in August 1914, and in May of the following year proceeded to Gallipoli, where he took part in the fighting at West Beach. On the Evacuation of the Peninsula, he was sent to Egypt, and there served on the Suez Canal, and at Katia, before being transferred to the Western Front. He took part in many important engagements in this theatre of war until wounded in action at Loos, and admitted to hospital at Birmingham. He was invalided from the Army in February 1918, and holds the 1914-15 Star, and the General Service and Victory Medals.
23, Whalley Street, Ancoats, Manchester. Z11183

SWINBURNE, J., Sergt., 1st Lancashire Fusiliers.
A serving soldier, having enlisted in March 1914, he embarked for the Dardanelles in May 1915, and took part in the Landing at Gallipoli, and the Battle of Cape Helles. He also served in many of the engagements which followed, including the Battles of Krithia and Achi Baba, and was in charge of a wiring party during operations at Suvla Bay. After the Evacuation of the Peninsula, he proceeded to Egypt, where he participated in the defence of the Suez Canal. Transferred to France in March 1916, he fought on the Somme, and was wounded at Beaumont-Hamel in the same year. On recovery, he rejoined his unit, and was in action throughout the Retreat and Allied Advance of 1918, towards the close of which he was again wounded. He afterwards served with the Army of Occupation in Germany until April 1919, when he returned to England, and was demobilised. He holds the 1914-15 Star, and the General Service and Victory Medals.
46, Lostock St., Miles Platting, Manchester. Z9385

SWINDELL, J. A., Private, R.A.V.C.
He joined in April 1918, and after a period of training served at various stations in Ireland, where he was engaged on duties of a highly important nature. He was unable, on account of ill-health to obtain his transfer to a theatre of war, but, nevertheless, rendered valuable services with his Company until invalided from the Army in July 1919.
72, Long Street, Ancoats, Manchester. Z11451

SWIRE, F., Private, Royal Welch Fusiliers.
He volunteered in July 1915, and after undergoing a period of training, was retained on important transport duties at various stations. He was not successful in obtaining his transfer to a theatre of war, but, nevertheless, rendered valuable services with his unit until January 1919, when he was demobilised. 5, Kay St., Chorlton-on-Medlock, Manchester. X8289

SWITZER, W. H., Sergt., 2nd S. Lancashire Regt.
Mobilised in August 1914, he was immediately drafted to the Western Front, where, after serving through the Retreat from Mons, he took part in the Battles of La Bassée, Ypres, Hill 60, Loos, Albert, and Vimy Ridge, and other engagements. He fell fighting in July 1916, during the Advance on the Somme. He was entitled to the Mons Star, and the General Service and Victory Medals.
"Whilst we remember the sacrifice is not in vain."
2, Eskrigge Street, Ardwick, Manchester. Z8290

SYKES, J., Sapper, R.E.
A Reservist, he was called to the Colours in August 1914, and in February of the following year was drafted to the Western Front, where he was engaged on important duties in various sectors. He was present at the Battles of Ypres, Loos, Albert, and the Somme, and other engagements until wounded in action at Arras in April 1917, and invalided home. On his recovery, however, he returned to France in time to take an active part in the Retreat and Advance of 1918. He was discharged in March 1919, and holds the 1914-15 Star, and the General Service and Victory Medals.
11, Braham Street, Longsight, Manchester. Z8292

SYKES, A., Private, 24th Royal Fusiliers.

Joining in April 1916, he proceeded to France on completing a period of training in July of that year. There he saw much severe fighting in various sectors, and took part in the Battles of the Somme, the Ancre, Bullecourt, and Ypres, and many other important engagements until the cessation of hostilities. He was demobilised on his return home in August 1919, and holds the General Service and Victory Medals.
23, Craven Street, Upper Moss Lane, Hulme, Manchester Z8296

SYKES, J. E., Private, Royal Welch Fusiliers, and Air Mechanic, R.A.F.

Having previously been employed on munition work at Messrs. Galloway's, he joined the Colours in May 1917, and after a period of training was sent to Ireland, where he was engaged on important duties at various stations. He was unable to obtain his transfer to the Front, but, nevertheless, rendered valuable services with his Squadron until his demobilisation in October 1919.
20, Gomm Street, Longsight, Manchester.   Z8293

SYKES, R., Pte., King's Own Scottish Borderers.

He volunteered in September 1914, and in June of the following year was drafted to the Western Front, where he saw severe fighting in various sectors, taking part in the Battle of Loos, and other important engagements. In January 1916, however, he was sent home in order to continue his former occupation of engineer at the National Shell Factory, Barnsley. He was demobilised in December 1918, and holds the 1914-15 Star, and the General Service and Victory Medals.
116, Chester Street, Hulme, Manchester.   TZ8291

SYKES, W., Private, 1/8th Manchester Regiment.

Having enlisted in February 1914, he was already in the Army when war broke out in August of that year, and later proceeded to the Dardanelles, where he took part in the Landing at Cape Helles, and also fought at Suvla Bay. He died gloriously on the Field of Battle on August 7th, 1915. He was entitled to the 1914-15 Star, and the General Service and Victory Medals.
    "A costly sacrifice upon the altar of freedom."
9, Juliet Street, Ardwick, Manchester.   Z8295

SYKES, W. H., Private, Labour Corps.

He joined in April 1916, and on completion of a period of training in October of the same year proceeded to the Western Front. Whilst in this theatre of war, he was engaged on duties of great importance in various sectors, being too old for service in the firing line, and did much useful work during the period of hostilities. He was demobilised in January 1919, and holds the General Service and Victory Medals.
27, Carlisle Street, Hulme, Manchester.   Z8294

T

TABBRON, W. (D.C.M.), C.S.M., 7th Manchester Regiment.

Mobilised with the Territorials in August 1914, he was in the following month drafted to Egypt, where he played a prominent part in the fighting on the Suez Canal and at Agagia, Katia and Romani. In March 1917 he was transferred to France, and there fought in the Battles of Bullecourt, Ypres, the Somme, the Marne, Le Cateau and Cambrai, and in other engagements. For conspicuous bravery in the Field at Havrincourt Wood in August 1917, when he captured a machine-gun and thirty-two prisoners, he was awarded the Distinguished Conduct Medal, and on his return home was demobilised in March 1919. In addition to the Distinguished Conduct Medal, he holds the 1914-15 Star, and the General Service and Victory Medals.   Z8298
22, Higher Chatham St., Chorlton-on-Medlock, Manchester.

TABBRON, L., Corporal, M.G.C.

He volunteered in May 1915, and after a period of training was sent overseas in February 1916. He served in Egypt on the Suez Canal, and also took part in various engagements, including those at Katia, Romani and El Fasher. Transferred to the Western Front, he fought with distinction at Ypres, La Bassée, Albert, the Somme and Cambrai, and on his return home was demobilised in March 1919, holding the General Service and Victory Medals.   Z8297
22, Higher Chatham St., Chorlton-on-Medlock, Manchester.

TABNER, J., Private, King's (Liverpool Regiment.)

He joined in March 1917, and was at once drafted to the Western Front. There he did excellent work with a Labour Battalion on water patrols and on road-making, and took an active part in several engagements, including those at Ypres, Passchendaele, Cambrai, and in the Retreat and Advance of 1918. On returning home he was demobilised in April 1919, and holds the General Service and Victory Medals.
68, Marsland Street, Ardwick, Manchester.   Z8299

TABNER, W., Sapper, R.E.

He volunteered in January 1915, and proceeding to France in the following September, was first engaged on important duties with his unit in various sectors. Later, however,

he took part in the Battles of Messines and Ypres and in heavy fighting during the Retreat and Advance of 1918. He was demobilised in December 1918, and holds the 1914-15 Star, and the General Service and Victory Medals.
343, Mill Street, Bradford, Manchester.   Z11184

TAGGART, R. H., 1st Air Mechanic, R.A.F.

Joining in 1917, he was, after completing his training, retained on important duties at various stations with his Squadron, and later was sent to Ireland. He was unable to obtain his transfer overseas owing to ill-health, but rendered valuable services, requiring a high degree of technical skill, before being demobilised in 1919.
1, Royle Street, Chorlton-on-Medlock, Manchester. X8300

TAIT, D., Private, 10th Lancashire Fusiliers.

He joined in April 1916, and in the following July proceeded to the Western Front. In this theatre of war he fought in various sectors of the line, and played a distinguished part in the fierce fighting in the Ypres salient and in the Battles of the Somme, Festubert and Cambrai, where he was severely wounded, as a result of which he suffered amputation of his right leg. He was discharged on his returning home in December 1918, and holds the General Service and Victory Medals. 25, Hope St., Hulme, Manchester.   TZ8301

TAKER, J. E., Driver, R.A.S.C.

After joining in March 1916, he was retained on important duties at home with his unit until October 1917, when he was drafted to the Western Front. There he did excellent work as a waggon driver, and was present at the Battle of Cambrai, where he was gassed. Later he was invalided home to undergo an operation in the Royal Infirmary, Manchester. He was eventually demobilised in February 1919, and holds the General Service and Victory Medals.
40, Clifford Street, Chorlton-on-Medlock, Manchester. Z8302

TALBOT, J., Private, 1st Manchester Regiment.

Having volunteered in September 1914, he was drafted to the Western Front three months later, and after playing a prominent part in the Battle of Neuve Chapelle, laid down his life for King and Country at the Battle of St. Eloi in March 1915. He was entitled to the 1914-15 Star, and the General Service and Victory Medals.
                "Nobly striving,
            He nobly fell that we might live."
67, Knightley Street, Rochdale Road, Manchester. Z11185A

TALBOT, J., Sergt., 22nd Manchester Regiment.

He volunteered in November 1914, and after a period of valuable services in England, was sent to India in February 1916. He was then engaged on important garrison duties at Allahabad, Fyzabad, Fort William and Calcutta, and did consistently good work there until October 1919. Returning home he was demobilised a month later, and holds the General Service and Victory Medals.
23, Buxton Street, West Gorton, Manchester.   Z11186

TALBOT, S., Sapper, R.E.

Volunteering in December 1914, he, in the same month, proceeded to France, where he served for about four years. During this period he was engaged on important duties in the forward areas, and took part in the Battles of Vimy Ridge, Cambrai and Arras. Although wounded three times, he rejoined his unit after recovery, and did excellent work whilst in action, and on returning home was demobilised in January 1919, holding the 1914-15 Star, and the General Service and Victory Medals.
72, Gibbons Street, Bradford, Manchester.   Z8304

TALBOT, T., Pte., 11th Loyal N. Lancashire Regt.

Volunteering in August 1914, he proceeded to France a year later and was in action at Loos, St. Eloi, Festubert and Albert. He was taken prisoner at Béthune in May 1916, and during his captivity was employed in the collieries at Münster and Westphalia. Repatriated at the close of hostilities, he was demobilised in April 1919, and holds the 1914-15 Star, and the General Service and Victory Medals.
27, Clay Street, Newton Heath, Manchester.   Z9722

TALBOT, T. H., Private, Lancashire Fusiliers.

He enlisted in August 1914, and in the following year was drafted to the Western Front. Whilst in this theatre of hostilities, he fought with distinction in the second Battle of Ypres, and in the Somme Offensive of July 1916, but unfortunately was severely wounded during heavy fighting in the Ypres sector in November 1917, and eventually succumbed to his injuries. He was entitled to the 1914-15 Star, and the General Service and Victory Medals.
"A valiant Soldier, with undaunted heart, he breasted life's last hill."
14, Kensington Street, Moss Side, Manchester.   Z8303

TALLON, E., Private, 3rd South Lancashire Regt.

He volunteered in May 1915, and on completion of his training was placed in a draft for France. Before he could embark however, he was taken seriously ill, and after a period of treatment in Liverpool General Infirmary, was discharged in August 1916 as medically unfit for further service.
38, Hewitt Street, Gorton, Manchester.   Z11187

TANKERARD, J., Corporal, 3rd Manchester Regt.
Volunteering in September 1914, he proceeded to France in the following January, and during his service on the Western Front played a prominent part in the Battles of Neuve Chapelle, St. Eloi, Hill 60, Ypres (II), Loos, the Somme, Arras, Vimy Ridge, Bullecourt, Messines, Ypres (III), Passchendaele and Cambrai. He was also in action throughout the Retreat and Advance of 1918, but was badly wounded a few days before the cessation of hostilities. He was then in hospital for eighteen months, and was eventually invalided from the Army in May 1920, holding the 1914-15 Star, and the General Service and Victory Medals.
100, Long Street, Ancoats, Manchester. Z11416D

TANT, H. A., Private, 17th Manchester Regiment.
After volunteering in September 1914, he was retained at home until November of the following year. He then proceeded to the Western Front, where he took part in the Battles of the Somme and Arras, and was badly wounded in action in March 1917. He was in hospital at Camieres for eight months, and was then invalided home, where he was under treatment at Canterbury, Liverpool and Manchester until his discharge as medically unfit for further service in April 1918. He holds the 1914-15 Star, and the General Service and Victory Medals.
17, Albion Street, Miles Platting, Manchester. Z11188

TAPLEY, D. C. (Mrs.), Member, V.A.D.
This lady offered her services in 1914, and for five years rendered valuable services as a member of the V.A.D. in Manchester. She was attached to the Military Hospitals, and did excellent work in conveying and attending to the wounded between Mayfield Station, Manchester, and the Hospitals. On relinquishing her post in 1919, she was awarded the Red Cross Proficiency Badge.
180, Oxford Road, Chorlton-on-Medlock, Manchester. X8305A

TAPLEY, R., Corporal, R.A.S.C. (M.T.)
From August 1914 until August 1915, he rendered valuable services with the British Red Cross Society, conveying wounded to various hospitals. He then volunteered in the R.A.S.C. and was quickly drafted to France, where he was engaged on convoy duties in the forward areas and did consistently good work. He was demobilised in September 1919, and holds the 1914-15 Star, and the General Service and Victory Medals.
180, Oxford Road, Chorlton-on-Medlock, Manchester. X8305B

TARPEY, J., Private, 8th Manchester Regiment.
He was mobilised with the Territorials in August 1914, and in the following month was despatched to Egypt, where he took part in several engagements on the Suez Canal. In March 1915 he was transferred to Gallipoli and fought gallantly in the Landing on the Peninsula, also at the three engagements of Krithia, and at Achi Baba, and was buried by an explosion in September 1915. He was rescued and invalided home, and afterwards transferred to the R.A.F., in which unit he served at Farnborough until demobilised in February 1919. He holds the 1914-15 Star, and the General Service and Victory Medals.
21, Gregory Street, West Gorton, Manchester. Z8306

TARRANT, C., Corporal, Military Foot Police.
Volunteering in May 1915, he was sent to Egypt six months later and rendered valuable services during the engagements at Romani. He then proceeded to Palestine and was present at the capture of Jerusalem, Jaffa, Haifa, Beyrout and Damascus. He was demobilised in September 1919, and holds the 1914-15 Star, and the General Service and Victory Medals.
1, Pollard Buildings, Savoy St., West Gorton, Manchester. Z11189

TASKER, A., Private, Manchester Regiment.
He volunteered in July 1915, and embarking for the Dardanelles in the following October, took part in the final operations of the Gallipoli campaign. After the Evacuation of the Peninsula, he proceeded to Egypt and in March 1916 to France. In this theatre of war he fought in the Somme Offensive and at Ypres, where in 1917 he was so severely wounded as to necessitate his return to England. After hospital treatment, he was demobilised in May 1919, and holds the 1914-15 Star, and the General Service and Victory Medals.
12, Whyatt Street, Bradford, Manchester. Z9723

TASKER, C. H., Corporal, R.E.
Volunteering in August 1914, he was retained on important duties with his unit at various home stations until October 1916, when he was drafted to the Western Front. There he took part in many severe engagements, including those at Loos, Neuve Chapelle, La Bassée, Givenchy, Ypres and Passchendaele. Owing to being over age he was sent to England in December 1917, and was stationed at Aldershot and Newark until demobilised in February 1919. He did excellent work, and holds the General Service and Victory Medals. 6 Lord St., Openshaw, Manchester. Z8308

TASKER, G., Private, 3rd Royal Scots.
He volunteered in November 1915, and in the following March proceeded to France, where he served for about three years. There he played an important part in the Battles of St. Eloi, Albert, Vimy Ridge and the Somme, and was wounded.

Invalided home for eight months, he rejoined his unit and again fought gallantly in the severe fighting at Arras, Ypres, the Somme, the Marne, and Cambrai. On his return he was demobilised in February 1919, and holds the General Service and Victory Medals.
9, Lingard Street, Hulme, Manchester. Z8307

TASKER, J. (M.M.), Sergeant, M.G.C.
Having volunteered in October 1914, he was drafted to the Western Front and served with distinction at the Battles of Ypres (II), Festubert, Loos, Albert, the Somme, Arras, Ypres (III), Passchendaele and Cambrai and in the Retreat and Advance of 1918. After the cessation of hostilities he was stationed at Cologne with the Army of Occupation for seven months. He was awarded the Military Medal for conspicuous bravery in bringing in wounded under heavy shell-fire at Passchendaele in November 1917. Demobilised in June 1919, he also holds the 1914-15 Star, and the General Service and Victory Medals.
39, Grantham Street, West Gorton, Manchester. Z11190

TASKER, J. H., Private, 21st Manchester Regt.
Joining in March 1916, he was in the following September sent to the Western Front. In this theatre of war he took part in severe fighting in different sectors of the line, and fought with distinction on the Somme and the Ancre fronts. Later he was engaged at Beaumont and Beaucourt, and unhappily was killed in action in May 1917 at Arras. He was entitled to the General Service and Victory Medals.
"Whilst we remember, the sacrifice is not in vain."
9, Lingard Street, Hulme, Manchester. Z8309

TASKER, O., Private, 7th East Lancashire Regt.
He volunteered in October 1914, and was quickly drafted to France, where he played a prominent part in the Battles of Neuve Chapelle, Hill 60, Ypres (II), Festubert, Albert, the Somme and Bullecourt. In June 1917 he was transferred to the R.E. as a Sapper and then served at the Battle of Cambrai and in the Retreat and Advance of 1918. Returning to England in February 1919, he was demobilised a month later, and holds the 1914-15 Star, and the General Service and Victory Medals.
39, Grantham Street, West Gorton, Manchester. Z11191

TASSAKER, J., Private, 1st Cheshire Regiment.
He volunteered at the outbreak of war in August 1914, and in the following May was sent to the Dardanelles, where he took part in the third Battle of Krithia and in heavy fighting at "W" Beach, Suvla Bay and Seddul Bahr. After the Evacuation of the Gallipoli Peninsula, he was transferred to Egypt and rendered valuable services whilst engaged on police duties at Katia, Cairo and Alexandria. Later he proceeded to France and remained there until his demobilisation in November 1919, holding the 1914-15 Star, and the General Service and Victory Medals.
13, Broughton Street, Ancoats, Manchester. Z11192

TATEHAM, W., Special War Worker.
He volunteered in August 1914, and for some time was engaged on important National work as a wood-cutter for the Army huts sent overseas. Later he was engaged on the Great Central Railway, where he rendered valuable services, and throughout the period of hostilities did excellent work. He relinquished his duties in November 1918.
22, Broom Street, Ardwick, Manchester. Z8310

TATTERSALL, J., Private, South Lancashire Regt.
After volunteering in August 1914, he was in the following October despatched to France. Whilst on the Western Front he took part in the fierce fighting at and around Ypres and in the Battles of La Bassée, Neuve Chapelle and Festubert, and unfortunately was killed by a sniper during the Battle of Loos in October 1915. He was entitled to the 1914 Star, and the General Service and Victory Medals.
"His life for his Country, his soul to God."
57, Wellington Street, West Gorton, Manchester. Z8311

TATTERSALL, J.W. (D.S.M.) Leading Seaman, R.N.
He was already in the Royal Navy when war broke out, and served aboard H.M.S. "Indefatigable" on important patrol duties off the Coast of Scotland. On May 31st, 1916, his ship took part in the Battle of Jutland, in which he was twice wounded and his ship was sunk. He was then awarded the Distinguished Service Medal for conspicuous bravery and devotion to duty during this action. Invalided to a hospital in Liverpool, he underwent treatment, and in August of the same year was discharged as medically unfit. He also holds the 1914-15 Star, and the General Service and Victory Medals.
88, John Street, Nelson, Manchester. Z9386

TATTON, J. E., Private, South Lancashire Regt.
Volunteering in August 1914, he embarked for India shortly afterwards, and was engaged on duties of an important nature at Calcutta. He did valuable work, and returned to England in January 1920, was demobilised two months later. He holds the General Service Medal.
18, Stonehouse Street, Ancoats, Manchester. Z9529/30B

TAYLOR, A., Pte., 1st and 4th Lancashire Fusiliers.

A Reservist, having served in the South African War, he was mobilised at the declaration of war, and crossing at once to France took part in the Retreat from Mons, in which he was wounded, and the Battles of the Marne, the Aisne, and Ypres, where he was again wounded. On recovery he rejoined his unit in the Field, and was in action at Armentières, Neuve Chapelle, Hill 60, Ploesgteert Wood, Loos and St. Eloi. In March 1916 he returned to England and was discharged, owing to the expiration of his period of service, and holds the Mons Star, and the General Service and Victory Medals.

29, Clay Street, Newton Heath, Manchester.   Z9724

TAYLOR, A., Private, 3rd Manchester Regiment.

He volunteered in August 1914, and seven months later was drafted to the Western Front, where he took part in the Battle of Ypres (II), and was twice wounded in action. As a result he was invalided from the Army in March 1916, but in April 1917 rejoined in the Tank Corps and rendered valuable services at Borden Camp. He was finally demobilised in March 1919, and holds the 1914–15 Star, and the General Service and Victory Medals.

57, Gardner Street, West Gorton, Manchester.   Z11203B

TAYLOR, A., Private, Border Regiment.

He joined in February 1917, and in the following June was drafted to France. Owing to ill-health he was placed on the lines of communication with the Labour Corps on the Somme and Passchendaele fronts, and, after a severe engagement, was in July 1918, unfortunately reported missing, and later was presumed to have been killed in action. He was entitled to the General Service and Victory Medals.

"Great deeds cannot die."

13, Dorset Street, Ardwick, Manchester.   Z8312

TAYLOR, A., Private, King's (Liverpool Regiment).

After joining in February 1917, he was in the following month sent to the Western Front. In this theatre of war he was engaged in the severe fighting on the Ypres salient and on the Ancre front, and took a prominent part in the Battles of the Somme, Cambrai and Bapaume. He also was in action at Bullecourt and Havrincourt, and on his return home was demobilised in October 1919, and holds the General Service and Victory Medals.

30, Harrison Street, Ancoats, Manchester.   Z8313

TAYLOR, A., Private, 2/7th Manchester Regiment, and 2nd East Lancashire Regiment.

He joined in August 1917, and in the following February proceeded to the Western Front. He took an important part in various severe engagements, including those at Amiens the Somme, St. Quentin, the Marne, and Cambrai, and was gassed at Gavrelle Wood in August 1918. In October of that year he was taken prisoner of war whilst fighting at Cambrai, and was held in captivity at Geissen until the Armistice was signed. On his return to England he was demobilised in September 1919, and holds the General Service and Victory Medals.

19, Charles Street, Bradford, Manchester.   TZ8328

TAYLOR, A., Private, Welch Regiment.

Volunteering in April 1915, he was in the following June drafted to the Dardanelles, where he took a distinguished part in the Landing at Suvla Bay and in the severe fighting at Krithia and Achi Baba. In November 1915 he was invalided home, and was in hospital for three months, after which he served in the Record Office of Cardiff General Hospital, until discharged in November 1916. He holds the 1914–15 Star, and the General Service and Victory Medals.

51, Elliott Street, Bradford, Manchester.   Z8329

TAYLOR, A., Private, 4th Manchester Regiment.

He volunteered in August 1914, and was retained on important duties at various stations with his unit until January 1915, when he was discharged owing to illness. In June 1916 he re-enlisted and joined the 8th Lancashire Fusiliers, and proceeded to Margate for duty, but was later transferred to the Royal Defence Corps, and did excellent work guarding German prisoners in the Isle of Man, until demobilised in March 1919.

4, Milton Street, Bradford, Manchester.   TZ8330A

TAYLOR, A., Private, 8th Manchester Regiment.

Joining in September 1916, he was drafted to France in the following January and played a prominent part in the Battles of Arras, Vimy Ridge, Bullecourt, Ypres (III), Cambrai, the Somme (II), Bapaume and Havrincourt. He did excellent work with his unit throughout, and was demobilised on his return to England in February 1919, holding the General Service and Victory Medals.

47, Congou Street, Ancoats, Manchester.   Z8322

TAYLOR, A., L/Corporal, 18th Manchester Regiment.

He volunteered in April 1915, and after completing his training was retained on important duties at various stations with his unit. Owing to ill-health, he was unable to obtain his transfer overseas, but rendered valuable services connected with staff work at Blackpool, in looking after convalescent soldiers, before being demobilised in September 1919.   Z8338

23, Clarendon Place, Chorlton-on-Medlock, Manchester.

TAYLOR, A., Corporal, Rifle Brigade.

Volunteering in September 1914, he was in the following year sent to the Western Front. In this theatre of war he played a distinguished part in the fierce fighting on the Arras, Ypres and the Somme fronts, and was present at the capture of Bullecourt. He also fought in the engagements from August to November 1918, which culminated in the signing of the Armistice. On his return he was demobilised in January 1919, and holds the 1914–15 Star, and the General Service and Victory Medals.

3, Leonard Street, Lower Openshaw, Manchester.   Z8314

TAYLOR, A., Private, 1/8th Manchester Regiment.

A Territorial, he was mobilised in August 1914, and proceeded to Egypt in the following month, He took part in the taking of Cyprus from the Turks, and was afterwards sent back to Egypt, and stationed at Cairo. Later he was transferred to the Dardanelles, where he fought gallantly in the fierce fighting at the Landing on the Peninsula, and was wounded at Krithia, but was in action again in July 1915, being then severely wounded. He was sent to hospital in England, and was retained there until discharged in November 1917, holding the 1914–15 Star, and the General Service and Victory Medals.

77, Morton Street, Longsight, Manchester.   Z8315

TAYLOR, A., Gunner, R.F.A.

Volunteering in September 1914, he proceeded to France in the following July and took part in the Battles of Givenchy, the Somme, Arras and Vimy Ridge, and in heavy fighting at La Bassée, Beaumont-Hamel and Albert. He died gloriously on the Field of Battle at Ypres on July 20th, 1917, and was entitled to the 1914–15 Star, and the General Service and Victory Medals.

"His memory is cherished with pride."

6, Heron Place, Hulme, Manchester.   Z8342

TAYLOR, A. E., Pte., Loyal N. Lancashire Regt.

He was mobilised at the outbreak of war, and in August 1914 was drafted to the Western Front with the British Expeditionary Force. He fought in the Battles of Mons, the Marne, the Aisne, La Bassée, Ypres and Neuve Chapelle, and was severely wounded at Albert. In consequence of his wounds he was finally discharged in October 1917, holding the Mons Star, and the General Service and Victory Medals.

7, Bonsall Street, Hulme, Manchester.   Z8339

TAYLOR, A. R., Sapper, R.E. and Private, 7th Manchester Regiment.

Having attested under the Derby Scheme, he was called to the Colours in November 1916, and first served with the R.E. In March 1917 he was drafted to France, and after being transferred to the 7th Manchester Regiment, took part in the Battles of Arras, Bullecourt, Ypres and Cambrai, and in the Retreat and Advance of 1918, during which he was wounded in action in September 1918. He was invalided home and eventually demobilised in February 1919, holding the General Service and Victory Medals.

48, Avon Street, Chorlton-on-Medlock, Manchester. Z8357

TAYLOR, B., Corporal, 13th Manchester Regiment.

He volunteered in October 1914, and was retained on important home duties for a year. In October 1915 he was sent to Salonika, and with his unit played an important part in the fighting on the Doiran front, at the Battles of the Struma and in the Advance on the Vardar. He unfortunately was taken ill and sent to hospital, where he succumbed to malaria in December 1917. He was entitled to the 1914–15 Star, and the General Service and Victory Medals.

"His memory is cherished with pride."

14, Marple Street, Openshaw, Manchester.   TZ7949A

TAYLOR, C., Corporal, 11th Manchester Regiment.

Volunteering shortly after the outbreak of war in August 1914, he was sent to France later in the same year, but after a short period of heavy fighting there was transferred to the Dardanelles, where he took part in the Landing at Suvla Bay and in other important engagements. After the Evacuation of the Gallipoli Peninsula, he returned to the Western Front, took part in the Battles of the Somme and Arras and was wounded. In 1917 he proceeded to Egypt, but later returned to France for the third time and remained there until his demobilisation in March 1919. He holds the 1914–15 Star, and the General Service and Victory Medals.

5, Groom Street, Ancoats, Manchester.   Z11208

TAYLOR, E., Driver, R.F.A.

Having enlisted in February 1913, he was in September of the following year despatched to Egypt, and afterwards to Gallipoli. There he took part in the Battle of Krithia and remained on the Peninsula until the Evacuation in December 1915. He again served in Egypt and was in action at Romani, and Katia, but was transferred to France in 1917, where he played a conspicuous part in various engagements, including those at Ypres, Cambrai, Le Quesnoy, Mormal Forest and St. Emilie. On his return home he was discharged in May 1919, and holds the 1914–15 Star, and the General Service and Victory Medals.

155, Clopton Street, Hulme, Manchester.   TZ8334

TAYLOR, C. F., Special War Worker.
Owing to defective eyesight, he was rejected for service in the Army, but from the outbreak of hostilities until the signing of the Armistice, was engaged on work of National importance at Messrs. Armstrong and Whitworths'. His duties, which were in connection with the manufacture of gun parts, required much skill and were carried out in a very able manner throughout.
33, Buxton Street, Gorton, Manchester. Z11198

TAYLOR, E., Gunner, R.G.A.
Volunteering in April 1915, he was drafted overseas after completing his training. During his service on the Western Front he took part in several engagements in various sectors and did consistently good work with his Battery. He was demobilised in November 1919, and holds the General Service and Victory Medals.
2, Goole Street, Bradford, Manchester. Z11957

TAYLOR, E., L/Corporal, 2nd Border Regiment.
Mobilised in August 1914, he was immediately drafted to the Western Front, where he took a prominent part in the Battles of Ypres and Neuve Chapelle and in heavy fighting at Arras, and was wounded in action. In November 1915 he was discharged, time-expired, and was then engaged on work of National importance until after the cessation of hostilities. He holds the 1914 Star, and the General Service and Victory Medals.
17, Milton Street, Ancoats, Manchester. Z8319

TAYLOR, F., Private, 3rd Manchester Regiment.
He volunteered in May 1915, and in the following January was sent to Mesopotamia. There he took a prominent part in the severe fighting at Kut (I and II), Um-el-Hannah and on the Tigris, and afterwards suffered from dysentery. He was sent to hospital, but on recovery was transferred to Palestine, and was again in action at the second and third Battles of Gaza, and entered Jerusalem under General Allenby. On his return home he was demobilised in May 1919, and holds the General Service and Victory Medals.
3, Edlin Street, Morton Street, Longsight, Manchester. Z8316

TAYLOR, F., Private, 2/6th Manchester Regiment.
He volunteered in March 1915, and three months later was sent to France, where he was in action at the Battles of Loos, Albert, the Somme, Arras, Vimy Ridge and Ypres, before being taken prisoner at Cambrai in November 1917. During his captivity in Germany he suffered many hardships, and was forced to work in the salt mines. He was repatriated after the Armistice, and was eventually demobilised in November 1919, holding the 1914-15 Star, and the General Service and Victory Medals.
488, Mill Street, Bradford, Manchester. Z11197

TAYLOR, F., Private, Royal Welch Fusiliers.
He volunteered in August 1914, and in November of the following year took part in the landing at Salonika. Later he was in action on the Vardar, Doiran and Struma fronts and at the recapture of Monastir before being transferred to Egypt, where he was stationed at Alexandria, Mustapha and Port Said. He then proceeded to Palestine and served at Jerusalem, Bethlehem and Jaffa. Demobilised in April 1919, he holds the 1914-15 Star, and the General Service and Victory Medals.
130, Jersey Street Dwellings, Ancoats, Manchester. Z11193

TAYLOR, G., Pte., 6th Loyal N. Lancashire Regt.
He volunteered in November 1915, and in the following January was sent to India, but was immediately transferred to Mesopotamia. In this theatre of hostilities he took an active part in the Advance through Baghdad to Mosul, and whilst at Kieffrie he contracted malaria. He was invalided home in April 1919, and demobilised in the following October, holding the General Service and Victory Medals.
153, Clopton Street, Hulme, Manchester. Z8333B

TAYLOR, F. J., Pte., 6th King's Own Scottish Bdrs.
Volunteering in August 1914, he was sent to France in the following May and played a prominent part in the Battles of Ypres, Festubert, Loos, the Somme (I), Arras, Zonnebeke, Passchendaele, Cambrai and the Somme (II). He was badly wounded in action at Moislains in May 1918 during the Retreat, and after hospital treatment in France, was invalided to Southampton. He holds the 1914-15 Star, and the General Service and Victory Medals, and was discharged from Liverpool Hospital in April 1919.
55, Jenkinson Street, Chorlton-on-Medlock, Manchester. Z8337

TAYLOR, G., Pte., 1st Loyal N. Lancashire Regt.
Having previously served in the Boer War, he rejoined in September 1914, and was sent to France a month later. Whilst on the Western Front he took part in the Battle of La Bassée and in heavy fighting at Nieuport before being invalided home in March 1915. After treatment in various hospitals, he was drafted to Gibraltar for garrison duty, and in June 1918, returned to Newcastle in order to undertake work of National importance on munitions. He was eventually demobilised in February 1919, and holds the Queen's and King's South African Medals, the 1914 Star, and the General Service and Victory Medals.
39, Laurence Street, West Gorton, Manchester. Z11196

TAYLOR, G. H., A.B., Royal Navy.
He joined in May 1917, and in June was sent to France with the Hood Battalion of the Royal Naval Division. Whilst on the Western Front, he took part in the Battles of Ypres, Passchendaele and Cambrai and in heavy fighting during the Retreat and Advance of 1918. After the cessation of hostilities he proceeded to Germany with the Army of Occupation and remained there until his demobilisation in June 1919. He holds the General Service and Victory Medals.
12, Gibson Street, Ardwick, Manchester. Z8336

TAYLOR, G. R., Gunner, R.F.A.
Volunteering in May 1915, he was drafted to France ten months later, and first saw fierce fighting during the German attacks on Loos, St. Eloi and Albert. He also took part in the Battles of the Somme (I), Passchendaele, Cambrai (I and II) and Le Cateau, and after the cessation of hostilities proceeded to Germany with the Army of Occupation. He returned to England for his demobilisation in April 1919, and holds the General Service and Victory Medals.
8, Ernest Street, Morton Street, Longsight, Manchester. Z8317

TAYLOR, H., Special War Worker.
Being ineligible for service with the Colours owing to medical unfitness, he obtained work of National importance at Messrs Mather and Platts, where he was engaged as an electro plater for two years. Later he left this work to take up a post at Messrs, Vickers, and for a further period of two and a half years did valuable work as a turner, resigning at the close of hostilities.
38, Kemp Street, Oldham Road, Manchester. TZ9387

TAYLOR, H., Private, 1/8th Manchester Regiment.
Mobilised with the Territorials in August 1914, he was in the following month sent to Egypt, where he served on the Suez Canal. He later took part in the Landing at Gallipoli, and in the three Battles of Krithia, and was wounded in August 1915. On his recovery he was transferred to France, and fought with distinction in the Battle of Vimy Ridge, where he was gassed. He was sent to hospital in London, and later was retained on home duties until demobilised in December 1918. He holds the 1914-15 Star, and the General Service and Victory Medals.
27, Ogden Street, Hulme, Manchester. TZ8323

TAYLOR, H., Private, Welch Regiment.
He volunteered in December 1914, and on completion of his training was drafted to the Gallipoli Peninsula in April of the following year. After taking part in the Landings at Cape Helles and Suvla Bay, and in other important engagements, he was unfortunately killed in action on August 11th, 1915. He was entitled to the 1914-15 Star, and the General Service and Victory Medals.
"A costly sacrifice upon the altar of freedom."
4, Milton Street, Bradford, Manchester. TZ8330B

TAYLOR, H., Private, K.O. (R. Lancaster Regt.)
He volunteered in April 1915, and in September was drafted to the Western Front, where he played a prominent part in much severe fighting in various sectors. He was badly wounded in action at Ypres early in 1917, and was invalided home. After hospital treatment at Etaples, and in England, he was discharged in May 1917, as medically unfit for further service, and holds the 1914-15 Star, and the General Service and Victory Medals.
39, Gorse Street, Hulme, Manchester. Z8327

TAYLOR, H., Private, 26th Manchester Regiment.
He joined the Manchester Regiment in June 1916, and was drafted to France on completion of his training. He was transferred to the 4th King's (Liverpool Regiment) and was wounded in action at the Battle of Arras in April 1917. On his recovery he joined the 19th King's (Liverpool Regiment), but was again wounded in December of the same year at Kemmel. After hospital treatment in France, he was transferred to the 2/5th Lincolnshire Regiment, and was unfortunately killed in action at Kemmel Hill on April 15th, 1918. He was entitled to the General Service and Victory Medals.
"The path of duty was the way to glory."
35, Curry Street, Ardwick, Manchester. TX8326

TAYLOR, H. (Mrs.), Special War Worker.
This lady offered her services in June 1916, and carried out work of National importance, in the Belle Vue Munition Works, Manchester. She was employed as an examiner of Stokes Bombs, and throughout her services did excellent work, and on relinquishing her duties in March 1919, received a special letter of acknowledgment for services rendered.
28, Birch Street, Moss Side, Manchester. Z8353B

TAYLOR, H. H., Corporal, 2/6th Manchester Regt.
Volunteering in January 1915, he, after completing his training, was retained on important duties at various stations with his unit. Owing to ill-health, he was unable to obtain his transfer overseas, but rendered valuable service, as a mastercook, before being demobilised in November 1919. He had previously served in the Boer war, and holds the Queen's South African Medal (with 4 Bars).
28, Birch Street, Moss Side, Manchester. Z8353A

TAYLOR, J., Private, 1st Lancashire Fusiliers.
Volunteering in August 1914, he embarked for the Dardanelles in the following April and took part in the first Landing at Gallipoli, and the Battles of Cape Helles, Krithia, Achi Baba and Suvla. In September 1915, he was wounded, and invalided home to hospital, underwent treatment. He proceeded to France in January 1916, and served on that front until the close of hostilities, fighting at Loos, the Somme, Arras, Ypres, Cambrai, Amiens, Bapaume and Le Cateau. He was demobilised in May 1919, and holds the 1914-15 Star, and the General Service and Victory Medals.
15, Clay Street, Newton Heath, Manchester.   Z9725

TAYLOR, J., Sergeant, 3rd Royal Welch Fusiliers.
He joined in March 1918, and in the following June was sent to France, where he served with distinction with the 18th Welch Regiment in heavy fighting on the Cambrai and La Bassée fronts. After the cessation of hostilities, he proceeded to Germany with the Army of Occupation and was stationed at Bonn. He gained quick promotion to Sergeant for consistently good work, and was demobilised in October 1919, holding the General Service and Victory Medals.
36, Howarth Street, Bradford, Manchester.   Z11204

TAYLOR, J., Driver, R.F.A.
Mobilised in August 1914, he was sent to France with the First Expeditionary Force, and took part in the Battle of, and the Retreat from, Mons, and the Battles of Le Cateau, the Aisne, La Bassée, Ypres (I), Neuve Chapelle, St. Eloi and Ypres (II). In February 1916, he was transferred to Salonika, where he saw heavy fighting during the Balkan campaign. He received his discharged in January 1919, and holds the Mons Star, and the General Service and Victory Medals.
20, Diggles Street, Ancoats, Manchester.   Z11206

TAYLOR, J., Corporal, 23rd King's (Liverpool Regt.)
He joined in May 1917, but owing to his low medical category, was unfit to take part in actual fighting. He first rendered valuable services as a orderly room clerk, but afterwards carried out important guard duties at prisoner of war camps in the Isle of Man and Wales. In November 1918, he proceeded to France for work of a similar nature, and was stationed at Fromelles and Etaples until his demobilisation in October 1919.
40, Sycamore Street, Newton End, Manchester.   Z11200

TAYLOR, J., L/Corporal, Lancashire Fusiliers.
He volunteered in August 1914, and proceeding to France on completion of his training, took a prominent part in the Battles of Ypres (II), Loos, Vimy Ridge, the Somme, Arras, Bullecourt, Messines, Ypres (III) and Cambrai, and in the Retreat and Advance of 1918. Whilst on the Western Front, he was four times wounded in action—at Loos in September 1915, at Vermelles eight months later, on the Somme in July 1916, and at Arras in May of the following year. He was demobilised in February 1919, and hold the 1914-15 Star, and the General Service and Victory Medals.
83, Ryder Street, Collyhurst, Manchester.   Z10581A

TAYLOR, J., Private, 12th Manchester Regiment.
He volunteered in September 1914, and in the following July was drafted to the Western Front. There he fought with distinction in the Battles of Loos, St. Eloi and Vimy Ridge, and also on the Albert front, and at Vermelles, where he was wounded. He was sent to hospital in Boulogne, but was eventually removed to England and discharged in July 1916, in consequence of his injuries. He holds the 1914-15 Star, and the General Service and Victory Medals.
14, Marple Street, Ardwick, Manchester.   Z8325

TAYLOR, J., Sapper, R.E.
Volunteering in June 1915, he was for a period retained on important duties at home with his unit, but in April 1916, was drafted to France. There he took a prominent part in the Somme Offensive and was wounded, but after recovery, was once more in action, and was gassed and again wounded. He was sent to hospital, and also suffered from dysentery, and was ultimately discharged in September 1918, holding the General Service and Victory Medals.
20, Ridgway Street, Moss Side, Manchester.   Z8356

TAYLOR, J., Private, 18th Manchester Regiment.
He volunteered in July 1915, and proceeding to France in the following March, took part in the Battle of the Somme, during which he was twice wounded—in July and October 1916. In April 1917 he was very badly wounded in action at the Battle of Arras, and after six months' treatment at Rouen, was invalided to hospital in Glasgow, where he remained until August 1918. He was then discharged as medically unfit for further service, and holds the General Service and Victory Medals.
16, Teak Street, Beswick, Manchester.   Z8355

TAYLOR, J., Private, 3rd Manchester Regiment.
He volunteered in January 1915, and after a period of training was retained at various stations on important duties. Owing to physical disabilities he was not successful in obtaining his transfer overseas, but did excellent work, prior to being discharged as medically unfit for further service in May 1916.
51, Long Street, Ancoats, Manchester.   Z8318

TAYLOR, J., Private, 1/4th Manchester Regiment.
He volunteered in August 1914, and after four months' training was drafted to the Western Front, but was almost immediately killed in action during heavy fighting in the Ypres sector. He was entitled to the 1914-15 Star, and the General Service and Victory Medals.
    "He died the noblest death a man may die,
        Fighting for God, and right, and liberty."
17, Charles Street, Bradford, Manchester.   TZ8331B

TAYLOR, J., Gunner, R.F.A.
After volunteering in August 1914, he was retained at various home stations for some time, but in September 1916 was drafted to Salonika, where he served for more than two years. During this period he took a distinguished part in several engagements, including the re-capture of Monastir, and the Advance on the Doiran front in April 1917. He suffered from fever, and was sent to hospital. On his return home, he was demobilised in May 1919, and holds the General Service and Victory Medals.
82, Park Street, Hulme, Manchester.   Z8350

TAYLOR, J., Private, Cheshire Regiment.
Volunteering in September 1914, he was quickly drafted to France, but after two months' heavy fighting was admitted to hospital, suffering from hæmorroids. On his recovery, he was transferred to Gibraltar, where he rendered valuable services with the Regimental Police. He was eventually discharged in March 1919, and holds the 1914 Star, and the General Service and Victory Medals.
1, Dalton Street, Longsight, Manchester.   Z8340A

TAYLOR, J. E., Pte., K.O. (Royal Lancaster Regt.)
He volunteered in August 1914, and early in the following year was sent to the Dardanelles, where he took part in the Landings at Cape Helles and Suvla Bay, and in the Battles of Krithia. After the Evacuation of the Gallipoli Peninsula, he proceeded to Mesopotamia, and was in action at Kut-el-Amara, Baghdad, Sheik Saad and Tuz Khurmath. He was demobilised in February 1919, holding the 1914-15 Star, and the General Service and Victory Medals, but later re-enlisted in the King's Shropshire Light Infantry, and in 1920 was still serving.
24, Wood Street, Harpurhey, Manchester.   Z11210A

TAYLOR, J. E., Special War Worker.
In January 1915, he undertook work of National importance for the Admiralty in the munition department of the Chloride Electrical Works at Clifton Junction. Later he was engaged on special electrical work at Huddersfield, at Messrs. Taylor Brothers, Trafford Park, and at the Tramcar Works, Manchester. He rendered valuable services at each of these places until the cessation of hostilities.
27, Lavender Street, Hulme, Manchester.   Z8347

TAYLOR, J. H., Private, Lancashire Fusiliers.
He volunteered in December 1915, and in the following November crossed to France. Whilst in this theatre of war, he was in action on the Somme, at Arras, Bullecourt, Messines, Ypres, Lens and Lys, and early in 1918 was badly wounded. Invalided home, he was discharged in May of that year, and holds the General Service and Victory Medals.
9, Chester, Street Ardwick, Manchester.   Z9388

TAYLOR, J. H., Driver, R.A.S.C. (M.T.)
He joined in June 1917, and was retained on important duties at various home stations for a year. In June 1918 he proceeded to the Western Front, where he did excellent work as a mechanical transport driver, in taking ammunition and foodstuffs to the front lines. He was present at various engagements, including Havrincourt and Le Cateau (II), and on returning home, was demobilised in June 1919, holding the General Service and Victory Medals.
5, Melbourne Place, Hulme, Manchester.   Z8354

TAYLOR, J. H., Private, 7th Manchester Regt.
He volunteered in May 1915, and proceeding to Egypt twelve months later, took part in engagements at Katia and El Fasher, but was invalided home in December 1916 with dysentery. After hospital treatment in London, he was sent to France in June 1917, and was soon in action at the Battle of Messines. He was wounded at the Battle of Ypres, but quickly returned to duty and fought at Passchendaele and Cambrai, where he was again wounded. On his recovery, he served throughout the Retreat and Advance of 1918 until wounded for the third time at the second Battle of Cambrai. He was then admitted to hospital at Chatham, and was discharged in December 1918, holding the General Service and Victory Medals.
15, Cedar Street, Hulme, Manchester.   Z8341

TAYLOR, N. E., Private, Border Regiment.
Joining in March 1917, he was in the following August drafted to the Western Front, where he served for about fifteen months. During this period he took part in severe fighting in the Ypres salient, and on the Marne, and the Somme fronts, and played a distinguished part in the Battles of Bapaume, Cambrai and Le Cateau (II). After the Armistice, he went to Germany with the Army of Occupation and was stationed at Cologne. On his return home, he was demobilised in September 1919, and holds the General Service and Victory Medals.
8, Ernest Street, Morton Street, Longsight, Manchester. Z8321

TAYLOR, J. T., Pte., K.O. (R. Lancaster Regt.)
He volunteered in December 1915, and after being retained on important home duties for a year was drafted to France. In this theatre of war he served in many sectors, and took a conspicuous part in the Battles of Ypres (III) and Cambrai, where he was wounded and sent home to hospital. He was again in action at La Bassée, and was made prisoner of war in April 1918. He was taken to Lille Camp behind the German lines, where he worked on the loading and unloading of trains. Released after the Armistice, he returned home and was demobilised in March 1919, and holds the General Service and Victory Medals.
9, Boundary Street, Newton, Manchester. Z8332

TAYLOR, J. T., Pte., 4th King's (Liverpool Regt.)
He joined in April 1916, and on completion of his training, was drafted to the Western Front. After taking part in the third Battle of Ypres, he made the supreme sacrifice in the same sector on November 24th, 1917. He was entitled to the General Service and Victory Medals.
" A valiant Soldier, with undaunted heart he breasted life's last hill."
48, Eliza Ann Street, Rochdale Road, Manchester. Z11194

TAYLOR, P., Private, 3rd Border Regiment.
He joined in August 1916, and was quickly sent to France, where he played a prominent part in the Battles of Arras, Vimy Ridge, Bullecourt, Ypres (III) and the Somme (II), and was in action in June 1918 during the Retreat. He was then invalided home and was eventually demobilised in September 1919, holding the General Service and Victory Medals.
25, William Street, Harpurhey, Manchester. Z8346

TAYLOR, P., Sergt., R.E.
Volunteering in November 1914, he was drafted to France almost immediately, and played a prominent part in the Battles of Ypres (II), Hill 60, the Somme, Arras, Cambrai and St. Quentin, where he was badly wounded in action in March 1918. He was invalided home, and was eventually demobilised in March 1919, holding the 1914-15 Star, and the General Service and Victory Medals.
14, Carisbrook Street, Harpurhey, Manchester. Z11587

TAYLOR, R., Private, Lancashire Fusiliers.
He volunteered in April 1915, and later in the same year was drafted to the Western Front, where he took part in the Battles of the Somme, Ypres, and Cambrai and in the Retreat and Advance of 1918. He was wounded at Ypres in 1917, and was demobilised in February 1919, but two months later rejoined in the M.G.C., was sent to India, and was in action on the North West Frontier. In 1920 he was still serving in the East, and holds the 1914-15 Star, and the General Service and Victory Medals, and the India General Service Medal (with clasp Afghanistan, N.W. Frontier, 1919).
57, Gardner Street, West Gorton, Manchester. Z11203A

TAYLOR, R., Private, 12th Manchester Regiment.
He volunteered in September 1914, and proceeding to France in the following July, took part in the Battle of Loos before being seriously wounded in action in the Ypres sector in December 1915. He was invalided home and underwent treatment at No.11 General Military Hospital at Northampton, until July 1917, when he was discharged as medically unfit for further service. He holds the 1914-15 Star, and the General Service and Victory Medals.
86, Heyrod Street, Ancoats, Manchester. Z11209

TAYLOR, R., Sergt., Black Watch.
Volunteering in July 1915, he was for about two years retained on important duties at various stations with his unit, and afterwards proceeded to Ireland, where he served for a few weeks. Being transferred to France, he took an active part in various engagements, including those at Ypres, Cambrai, the Somme, the Marne, and in the Retreat and Advance of 1918. He rendered valuable service, and was demobilised in March 1919, holding the General Service and Victory Medals.
18, Collins Street, Hulme, Manchester. Z8352

TAYLOR, R. H., Private, Manchester Regiment.
Six months after volunteering, he was drafted to France in July 1915, and served as a signaller at the Battles of Loos, the Somme, Messines, Ypres, Passchendaele and Cambrai, and in the Retreat and Advance of 1918. He was also engaged on special duties at prisoners of war camps, and was eventually demobilised in February 1919, holding the 1914-15 Star, and the General Service and Victory Medals.
32, Francisco Street, Collyhurst, Manchester. Z11201

TAYLOR, S., Private, 12th Manchester Regiment.
Having volunteered in August 1914, he was drafted to France early in the following year, and whilst on the Western Front played an important part in the Battles of Neuve Chapelle, Loos, Ypres (II), and the Somme, where he was unhappily killed in action on July 7th, 1916. He was entitled to the 1914-15 Star, and the General Service and Victory Medals.
" The path of duty was the way to glory."
31, Marcer Street, Ancoats, Manchester. Z11205

TAYLOR, T., Private, Manchester Regiment.
Volunteering in August 1914, he proceeded to France in November of that year, and was in action at La Bassée,

Festubert and Neuve Chapelle. Later he was invalided home in consequence of ill-health, and after recovery was engaged on important home service duties until January 1917, when he was discharged as medically unfit. He holds the 1914 Star, and the General Service and Victory Medals.
2, Rowbotham Street, Miles Platting, Manchester. Z9389

TAYLOR, T., Private, 15th Royal Fusiliers and Durham Light Infantry.
Joining in May 1917, he was in the following December sent to Ireland, where he served until April 1918. He then proceeded to France, and whilst with his unit in the Champagne sector, was unhappily killed in action during a raid in May 1918. He was entitled to the General Service and Victory Medals.
" He passed out of the sight of men by the path of duty and self-sacrifice."
153, Clopton Street, Hulme, Manchester. Z8333A

TAYLOR, T., Private, 9th Lancashire Fusiliers.
He volunteered in January 1915, and after a period of training was in the following April drafted with his unit to Gallipoli. There he fought with distinction at the first Landing on the Peninsula, and in the Battles of Krithia (I, II and III), but was unfortunately killed in action whilst fighting valiantly at Suvla Bay in August 1915. He was entitled to the 1914-15 Star, and the General Service and Victory Medals.
" His life for his Country, his soul to God."
19, Charles Street, Bradford, Manchester. Z8331A

TAYLOR, T., Private, Lancashire Fusiliers.
Joining in May 1915, he was for nearly two years retained on important duties at various home stations, but in March 1917 was drafted to France. There he fought in different sectors, and took a distinguished part in the Battles of Ypres, Vimy Ridge and Passchendaele, and in the heavy fighting on the Arras and Somme fronts. He was also in action at Bullecourt, but unhappily was killed whilst fighting at Ypres on November 15th, 1917. He was entitled to the General Service and Victory Medals.
" Honour to the immortal dead who gave their youth that the world might grow old in peace."
1, Rose Street, Old Trafford, Manchester. Z8348

TAYLOR, T., Private, 26th Manchester Regiment.
He joined in July 1916, but on account of his youth was not eligible for transfer to a theatre of war. On completion of his training, he rendered valuable services with the Western Command Labour Corps until May 1918, when he was invalided from the Army with valvular disease of the heart.
31, Gorse Street, Hulme, Manchester. Z8344

TAYLOR, T. H., Pte., K.O. (R. Lancaster Regt.)
Volunteering in November 1914, he was drafted to France on completion of his training, but shortly afterwards was transferred to Salonika. In this theatre of war he played a prominent part in the heavy fighting during the Retreat from Serbia, and was awarded the Serbian Star (2nd Class with swords), for conspicuous bravery. Later he returned to the Western Front, and laid down his life for King and Country at the Battle of the Lys on April 9th, 1918. He was also entitled to the 1914-15 Star, and the General Service and Victory Medals.
" His memory is cherished with pride."
16, Ismay Street, Chorlton-on-Medlock, Manchester. TX8343

TAYLOR, W., Private, 23rd Manchester Regiment.
He volunteered in January 1915, and on completing his training in the following year, proceeded to the Western Front. In this theatre of war he took part in several engagements, including those at Loos (where he was wounded in 1916), Ypres, Arras and Beaumont-Hamel. He was demobilised in June 1919, and holds the General Service and Victory Medals.
54, Flower Street, Ancoats, Manchester. Z11958

TAYLOR, W., Guardsman, Grenadier Guards.
He joined in April 1917, and on completion of his training was engaged on important duties at Aldershot, the Crystal Palace and Whitehall, London. He rendered valuable services with his unit, but was unsuccessful in obtaining his transfer overseas, and was demobilised in November 1919.
22, Elizabeth Street, West Gorton, Manchester. Z11202

TAYLOR, W., Private, M.G.C.
Volunteering in November 1915, he proceeded to France seven months later, and was wounded in action during the Somme Offensive in November 1916. On his recovery he took part in the Battles of the Ancre, Arras, Vimy Ridge, Messines and Ypres (III), but was then transferred to India. He then carried out important garrison duties at Bangalore until his return home for demobilisation in March 1920. He holds the General Service and Victory Medals.
11, Beswick Street, West Gorton, Manchester. Z11195

TAYLOR, W., L/Corporal, 1st Lancashire Fusiliers.
He joined in July 1917, and after completing his training was stationed at Withernsea in Yorkshire, on important duties connected with Coast Defence, and later was sent to Aldershot. He was unable to obtain his transfer overseas, but did excellent work before being demobilised in November 1919.
123, Beresford Street, Moss Side, Manchester. Z8351

TAYLOR, W., L/Corporal, 3rd Welch Regiment.

He volunteered in September 1914, and first saw heavy fighting during the Landing at Cape Helles in the Dardanelles in the following April. Later he took part in the Battles of Krithia (I, II and III), and the Landing at Suvla Bay. After the Evacuation of the Gallipoli Peninsula, he was sent to Mesopotamia, where he served at the Battle of Kut (II), and was wounded in action in February 1917. He holds the 1914-15 Star, and the General Service and Victory Medals, and was demobilised in April 1919.
85, Beaumont Street, Beswick, Manchester. Z11199

TAYLOR, W., Private, 2nd Cheshire Regiment.

Joining in May 1917, he was in the following August drafted to Palestine, where he served for eighteen months. During this period he saw much fighting and took an important part in the Battle of Gaza (III), and in other engagements, including those at Jerusalem, Jericho, Tripoli and Aleppo. On his return to England he was demobilised in February 1919, and holds the General Service and Victory Medals.
18, Halton Street, Hulme, Manchester. Z8349

TAYLOR, W. H., Private, Manchester Regiment.

Volunteering at the commencement of hostilities, he was drafted to France, and took part in the Retreat from Mons, and the Battles of Le Cateau, La Bassée and Ypres, where he was wounded in May 1915. On recovery he fought at Loos, the Somme, Cambrai, Arras, and throughout the Retreat and Allied Advance, which terminated hostilities victoriously in November 1918. He was demobilised in January of the succeeding year, and holds the Mons Star, and the General Service and Victory Medals.
15, Worsley Street, Oldham Street, Manchester. Z9390

TAYLOR, W. H., Private, 16th Manchester Regt.

He volunteered in May 1915, and in the following April was sent to France, where he took part in the Battles of the Somme, Arras, Vimy Ridge, Ypres (III), and Passchendaele, and in heavy fighting at Neuve Chapelle, La Bassée, Givenchy, Festubert, and during the Retreat and Advance of 1918. He was twice wounded in action at—Arras in May 1917, and on the Somme in August 1918, on both occasions being admitted to hospital at the Base. He holds the General Service and Victory Medals, and was demobilised in January 1919.
26, Randolph Street, Openshaw, Manchester. Z8320

TEAL, H., Private, 2nd Lancashire Fusiliers.

He joined in March 1918, but was unsuccessful in obtaining his transfer to a theatre of war. He rendered valuable services with his unit in England until the cessation of hostilities, when he re-engaged for a period of three years, and was sent to India in March 1919. In 1920 he was stationed at the Napier Barracks, Lahore.
4, Dyson Street, Miles Platting, Manchester. Z11211

TEANBY, W., Private, 2nd South Lancashire Regt.

He joined in August 1917, and proceeded to France three months later, but was wounded at Ploegsteert in April 1918, and invalided home. On his recovery he returned to the Western Front, and whilst attached to the Pioneer Battalion of the 11th South Lancs. Regiment, rendered valuable services at Cambrai. He was demobilised in July 1919, and holds the General Service and Victory Medals.
4, Longworth Street, Hulme, Manchester. Z8358

TEASDALE, W., Cpl., 2nd North Staffordshire Regt.

He volunteered in August 1914, and on completion of his training was retained on special duties in the North of England. He rendered valuable services as a physical training Instructor, but was unsuccessful in obtaining his transfer overseas until after the Armistice. He then proceeded to France, where he carried out work of a similar nature at Boulogne, but was unfortunately taken seriously ill, and died of consumption on September 30th, 1919.
"His memory is cherished with pride."
32A, Napier Street, Ardwick, Manchester. Z8359

TEBAY, J., Private, 1st Manchester Regiment.

He volunteered in November 1914, and proceeded to France six months later. Whilst on the Western Front he took part in the Battles of Ypres (II), Festubert, Loos and Albert, and was wounded. He died gloriously on the Field of Battle during the Somme Offensive in July 1916, and was entitled to the 1914-15 Star, and the General Service and Victory Medals.
"A costly sacrifice upon the altar of freedom."
1, Hutton Street, Hulme, Manchester. TZ8360

TEBB, H., Telegraphist, R.N.

Volunteering in January 1915, he was posted to H.M.S. "King George V." and took part in the Battles of the Dogger Bank and Jutland. He was also in action during the engagement off Heligoland and later served in H.M.T.B. "Meteor" with the Dover Patrol, as escort to ships sailing between England and France. In 1920 he was still in the Royal Navy, and holds the 1914-15 Star, and the General Service (with six clasps) and Victory Medals.
19, Aked Street, Ardwick, Manchester. Z8361

TEERS, J., Signalman, R.N.

Volunteering in November 1914, he was commissioned to H.M.S. "Eclipse," and throughout the whole period of hostilities, rendered valuable services whilst engaged on dangerous patrol duties with this ship in the North Sea. He was demobilised in March 1919, and holds the 1914-15 Star, and the General Service (with four clasps), and Victory Medals.
22, Barrack Street, Hulme, Manchester. Z8362

TEERS, J., Sergeant, Royal Scots.

He joined in January 1915, and was retained for a few months on important duties at various home stations. In September 1915 he was drafted to Egypt, and took part in the fighting at Mersa Matruh, Agagia and Sollum, but in March 1916 was transferred to France. There he played a distinguished part in many important Battles, including those of the Somme, Arras, the Ancre, Messines, Nieuport, Passchendaele, Amiens, Cambrai and Le Cateau. He also fought in the engagements at Beaumont-Hamel and St. Quentin, and later entered Germany with the Army of Occupation. He was demobilised in April 1919, and holds the 1914-15 Star, and the General Service and Victory Medals.
73, York Street, Hulme, Manchester. Z8363A

TEERS, J., Sapper, R.E.

He joined in November 1918, and after completing his training was retained on important duties at Sandwich with his unit. There he was engaged chiefly in making Army Huts for troops at the Front, and although unable to obtain his transfer overseas, rendered valuable services prior to being demobilised in January 1919.
73, York Street, Hulme, Manchester. Z8363B

TEMPLE, C., Private, 18th Manchester Regiment.

He joined in May 1916, and after a period of training was drafted to France in the following January and was in action at Loos, Ypres, Nieuport, and on the Somme. He also took part in heavy fighting in Italy, and was eventually demobilised from there in January 1919, holding the General Service and Victory Medals.
2, Saville Street, Miles Platting, Manchester. Z11212

TETLOW, F., Sergeant, R.E.

He volunteered in November 1915, and in the following month proceeded to the Western Front. There he was attached to the Railway Operative Department, and did excellent work in connection with the loading of trucks, general railway goods, and railway repairs. He also carried out other duties, and whilst in France was stationed at Armentières, Rouen, Boulogne, and Charleroi. He was demobilised in May 1919, and holds the 1914-15 Star, and the General Service and Victory Medals.
37, Dudley Street, Stretford, Manchester. Z8364

TETLOW, J., Private, 2nd Royal Fusiliers.

Joining in June 1917, he embarked for France in the following October, and fought in engagements at Ypres and Cambrai, where in December 1917, he was badly wounded. After recovery he returned to the line, and was in action until hostilities ceased in November 1918. He was demobilised in December of the succeeding year, and holds the General Service and Victory Medals.
217, Victoria Square, Oldham Road, Manchester. Z9391

THACKWELL, G. A., Pte., King's (Liverpool Regt.)

He joined in March 1916, and after being transferred to the Labour Corps, was sent to France, where he rendered valuable services in the forward areas in the Ypres, Cambrai, Arras and Vimy Ridge sectors. He was wounded near St. Quentin, and was invalided home, but on his recovery returned to the Western Front, and was engaged on guard duties at prisoner of war camps. After hostilities ceased, he served in Germany with the Army of Occupation, and was eventually demobilised in November 1919, holding the General Service and Victory Medals. 5, Naylor St., Oldham Road, Manchester. Z11213

THELEN, C., Private, Labour Corps.

He joined in June 1917, and after a period of training was retained on important duties at Oswestry with his unit. He was unable owing to physical disabilities, to obtain his transfer overseas, but rendered valuable services before being demobilised in February 1919.
45, Granville St., Chorlton-on-Medlock, Manchester. Z8365

THELWELL, F., Private, Northumberland Fusiliers.

He joined in October 1915, and after completing his training, was sent to France. In this theatre of war he fought with his unit in various sectors of the line and took a prominent part in the Battle of Arras and was badly wounded. He was sent to hospital, and after his recovery was demobilised in January 1919, holding the General Service and Victory Medals.
11, Marsden St., Chorlton-on-Medlock, Manchester. TX8366

THELWELL, W., Private, King's (Liverpool Regt.)

He joined in April 1916, but owing to his being too young for transfer overseas, was retained on important duties at various stations and rendered valuable services until his demobilisation in January 1919. Unfortunately he contracted pneumonia shortly afterwards and died at home.
"His memory is cherished with pride."
105, Kendall Street, Bradford, Manchester. Z11214B

THELWELL, T., Private, 13th Lancashire Fusiliers.
He volunteered in January 1915, and on completion of his training was transferred to Class W, Army Reserve. For fifteen months he was engaged at Messrs. Morris', Government Chemical Factory, Openshaw, and then went to Messrs. Cook's, Aeroplane Works at Lincoln. At both these places he did consistently good work and rendered valuable services until his demobilisation in December 1918.
105, Kendall Street, Bradford, Manchester.   Z11214A

THEOBALD, F. W., Private, 19th Manchester Regt.
Volunteering in March 1915, he underwent his training and was then engaged on special duties at home stations. He rendered valuable services until March 1916, when he was discharged as medically unfit for further military duty owing to bronchitis.
27, Birtles Street, Collyhurst, Manchester.   Z11215

THEOBALD, S., Private, 7th Manchester Regiment.
A Territorial, he was mobilised at the outbreak of war, and in September 1914 was drafted to Egypt, and afterwards transferred to the Dardanelles. There he landed at Cape Helles, fought at Krithia and Achi Baba, and being wounded, was invalided home. Later he was sent to France and played a distinguished part in the Battles of Ypres and Passchendaele, and was again badly wounded. In July 1918 he was discharged as medically unfit, holding the 1914-15 Star, and the General Service and Victory Medals.
15, Coalbrook Street, Ardwick, Manchester.   Z8367

THEOBALD, W., Private, 4th Lancashire Fusiliers.
He volunteered in September 1915, but on completion of his training was retained on special work in England until early in 1917. He was then sent to France, and after taking part in the Battles of Bullecourt, Ypres, Cambrai and the Somme, was engaged on guard duties with the 158th Prisoner of War Company at Candas. He holds the General Service and Victory Medals, and was demobilised in February 1919.
162, Hamilton Street, Collyhurst, Manchester.   Z11216

THICKETT, J. H., Private, 3rd Welch Regiment.
Joining in April 1916, he was in the following June drafted to France, where he served for three years. During this time he fought with distinction in the Battles of Vimy Ridge, the Somme (I), the Ancre, Ypres (III), Cambrai (I and II) and at Havrincourt. He was gassed and invalided to hospital in Kent for two months, but rejoined his unit, and after the Armistice proceeded to Germany with the Army of Occupation to guard prisoners. He was demobilised in June 1919, and holds the General Service and Victory Medals.
36, Pryme Street, off Chester Road, Hulme, Manchester.   Z8368

THIRKETTLE, J., Pte., 1st and 5th King's (L'pool R.)
He joined early in 1916, and later in the same year was sent to France, where he was in action at Festubert, St. Eloi and Neuve Chapelle, and at the Battles of the Somme, Bourlon Wood, Ypres and Cambrai. He was wounded in 1917, and in April 1918 was taken prisoner, but succeeded in escaping from captivity a few days prior to the cessation of hostilities. He was demobilised in 1919, and holds the General Service and Victory Medals.
6, Elliott Street, Ancoats, Manchester.   Z8369

THOMAS, A. E., Private, 22nd Manchester Regt.
He volunteered in August 1915, and three months later was sent to France, where he first saw heavy fighting during the German attacks at Loos, St. Eloi and Albert. He was also in action at Ypres and Vermelles, but was unfortunately killed at the opening of the Somme Offensive on July 1st, 1916. He was entitled to the 1914-15 Star, and the General Service and Victory Medals.
"Great deeds cannot die:
They with the sun and moon renew their light for ever."
19, Harrowby Street, Hulme, Manchester.   Z8373

THOMAS, E. (M.S.M.), Driver, R.A.S.C.
Volunteering in October 1914, he was retained on important duties at home stations until 1917, when he was drafted to Russia. He then saw much severe fighting, and was awarded the Meritorious Service Medal for conspicuous bravery in carrying rations to the forward areas under heavy shell-fire. He was demobilised in August 1919, and also holds the General Service and Victory Medals.
31, Windsor Street, Rochdale Road, Manchester.   Z11217

THOMAS, E., Pte., 2nd K.O. (R. Lancaster Regt.)
Volunteering in August 1914, he shortly afterwards crossed to France, and took part in the final operations of the Retreat from Mons and the Battles of La Bassée, Ypres, Messines Ridge and the Somme. He gave his life for King and Country at Loos in October 1916, and was entitled to the Mons Star, and the General Service and Victory Medals.
"The path of duty was the way to glory."
34, Flower Street, Ancoats, Manchester.   Z9726

THOMAS, G. P., A.B., Royal Navy.
Mobilised in August 1914, he served on board H.M.S. "Roxburgh" and "Liverpool" during hostilities, and was engaged in important Naval operations in the North Sea, the Dardanelles, the Sea of Marmora and the Mediterranean. He also cruised off the coasts of Russia and in the Black Sea,

and did consistently good work. He received his discharge in March 1919, and holds the 1914-15 Star, and the General Service (with five clasps) and Victory Medals.
8, Lingard Street, Hulme, Manchester.   Z8371

THOMAS, H., Driver, R.A.S.C. (M.T.)
He joined in June 1916, and proceeded to France in the following August. During his service on the Western Front he was engaged in carrying supplies to the forward areas, and took an active part in the Battles of Arras, Vimy Ridge, Ypres (III) and Cambrai, and in the Retreat and Advance of 1918. He holds the General Service and Victory Medals, and was demobilised in June 1919.
16, Alma Street, Collyhurst, Manchester.   Z11588

THOMAS, H., Private, 8th Border Regiment.
Volunteering in August 1914, he was retained for more than a year on important duties at various home stations, but in November 1915 was drafted to Egypt, where he took part in the fighting on the Suez Canal. In July 1916 he was transferred to France and fought with distinction in the Battles of the Somme and at Beaumont-Hamel, and was wounded. Later he was again in action at Ypres and Passchendaele Ridge. He was discharged as medically unfit for further service in November 1917, and holds the 1914-15 Star, and the General Service and Victory Medals.
32, Abram Street, Hulme, Manchester.   Z8372

THOMAS, J. A., Private, 1/7th Manchester Regt.
He volunteered in March 1915, and was quickly drafted to the Western Front, where he played a prominent part in the Battles of Loos, Albert, the Somme, Arras, Vimy Ridge, Bullecourt, Messines and Ypres (III). He died gloriously on the Field of Battle at Lens on September 8th, 1917, and was entitled to the 1914-15 Star, and the General Service and Victory Medals.
"His life for his Country, his soul to God."
44, Grimshaw Lane, Newton Heath, Manchester.   Z11218

THOMAS, J. F., Private, 1/8th Manchester Regt.
Mobilised with the Territorials in August 1914, he was sent to Egypt in the following month, and was stationed at Cairo. In June 1915 he was discharged as medically unfit for further service, but shortly afterwards succeeded in joining the R.E. He was then engaged on special duties in Yorkshire, and did consistently good work until his demobilisation in 1919. He holds the 1914-15 Star, and the General Service and Victory Medals.
79, Junction Street, Ancoats, Manchester.   Z11589

THOMAS, J. J., Private, 6th East Lancashire Regt.
He volunteered in April 1915, and in the following August was drafted to Egypt, where he took part in the fighting on the Suez Canal, and at Katia. Being transferred to Mesopotamia he fought at Kut and the capture of Baghdad, and in other engagements. Later he was sent to India, where he was demobilised in October 1919. He holds the 1914-15 Star, and the General Service and Victory Medals.
47, Brown Street, Ancoats, Manchester.   Z8370

THOMAS, J. W., Private, 4th Yorkshire Regiment.
He volunteered in August 1914, and on completion of his training was engaged on special duties at various home stations near London. Despite his efforts, he was unsuccessful in obtaining his transfer overseas, but did consistently good work until his demobilisation in February 1919.
39, Alexandra Place, Manchester.   Z11409-44B

THOMAS, S. C., Gunner, R.F.A.
A Reservist, he was mobilised at the declaration of war, and crossing to France, took part in the Retreat from Mons and the Battles of Le Cateau, the Marne and La Bassée. He was unhappily killed in action at the Battle of Ypres on November 13th, 1914, and lies buried in the churchyard there. He was entitled to the Mons Star, and the General Service and Victory Medals.
"His name liveth for evermore."
33, Boundary Street, Newton, Manchester.   Z9023

THOMAS, S. R., Sapper, R.E.
Volunteering in June 1915, he was sent to Egypt in the following April, but after taking part in an engagement at Magdhaba, was transferred to Salonika, where he was taken ill with malaria and invalided to Malta. On his recovery he returned to Egypt, and later served at the capture of Tripoli in Palestine. He then rejoined his unit in Salonika, and was eventually demobilised in March 1919, holding the General Service and Victory Medals.
48, Longridge Street, Longsight, Manchester.   Z8375B

THOMAS, W. H., Private, 21st Manchester Regt.
He volunteered in June 1915, and in the following August proceeded to France, where he fought gallantly at the Battles of Loos, the Ancre and Ypres (III). He also took an important part in the fierce fighting on the Albert front, and in the Somme Offensive of July 1916. Unfortunately he was killed in action at Lens in October 1917, and was entitled to the 1914-15 Star, and the General Service and Victory Medals.
"His memory is cherished with pride."
85, Henry Street, Ardwick, Manchester.   Z8374

THOMAS, W. J., A.B., Royal Navy.
He first joined the King's Royal Rifle Corps, but afterwards transferred to the Navy and was posted to H.M.S. "Queen Elizabeth." He then took part in the Battles of the Dogger Bank, Jutland and Heligoland Bight, and was also on patrol duties in the North Sea. He was demobilised in 1919, and holds the 1914–15 Star, and the General Service and Victory Medals. 39, Alexandra Place, Manchester. Z11409–44C

THOMASON, G. H., Pte., 3rd Lancashire Fusiliers.
Volunteering in April 1915, he proceeded to France in July of the following year, and took part in the Somme Offensive, in which he was gassed. On recovery he fought at Arras, Ypres, Cambrai, St. Quentin and throughout the Retreat and Allied Advance, which brought hostilities to a victorious close on November 11th, 1918. He holds the General Service and Victory Medals, and in 1920 was still serving. 4, Ward Street, Oldham Road, Manchester. Z9396

THOMASON, W. T., Private, 8th Manchester Regt.
Mobilised with the Territorials in August 1914, he quickly proceeded to Egypt and saw heavy fighting in the Suez Canal sector. In April 1915, he was sent to the Dardanelles, where he took part in the Landings at Cape Helles and Suvla Bay. After the Evacuation of the Gallipoli Peninsula, he came to England, but in February 1917 was drafted to France, and was in action at the Battles of Arras and Cambrai, and throughout the Retreat and Advance of 1918. He holds the 1914–15 Star, and the General Service and Victory Medals, and was demobilised in March 1919. 8, Janet Street, Miles Platting, Manchester. Z11223

THOMPSON, A., Pte., 2nd Northumberland Fusiliers.
He volunteered in October 1915, and was engaged on important home duties until March 1917, when he embarked for India, and served at various stations. Transferred to Mesopotamia in April 1919, he did valuable work, and was demobilised on his return to England in October of the same year. He holds the General Service Medal. 11, Almond Street, Collyhurst, Manchester. Z9727A

THOMPSON, A. E., Sapper, R.E.
He joined in September 1916, and six months later was drafted to the Western Front, where he took part in the Battles of Bullecourt, Hill 70, Lens, Cambrai, Amiens, Bapaume, Havrincourt and Epéhy. He returned to England in February 1919, and in the following month was demobilised, holding the General Service and Victory Medals. 21, Birtles Street, Collyhurst, Manchester. Z11219

THOMPSON, A. R., Corporal, R.A.S.C.
He joined in October 1917, and after a period of training was retained with his unit on important duties at Bath, Chatham and Tunbridge. He was, owing to age and ill-health, unable to obtain his transfer overseas, but rendered valuable services before being demobilised in May 1919. 99, Bedford Street, Moss Side, Manchester. Z8376

THOMPSON, C., Pte., 1st K.O. (R. Lancaster Regt.)
He was mobilised in August 1914, and immediately drafted to France, where he took part in the Battles of Mons, the Marne, La Bassée, Ypres and the Somme, and in much heavy fighting at Nieuport and Givenchy. He died gloriously on the Field of Battle in August 1918, and was entitled to the Mons Star, and the General Service and Victory Medals.
"The path of duty was the way to glory."
15, Sparkle Street, Ancoats, Manchester. Z11959

THOMPSON, C. F., Pte., 5th E. Lancashire Regt.
Volunteering in January 1916, he proceeded to the Western Front in the following May, and fought on the Somme, at Arras, Ypres and Cambrai. He gave his life for the freedom of England at Bapaume on September 23rd, 1918, and was entitled to the General Service and Victory Medals.
"Great deeds cannot die."
11, Almond Street, Collyhurst, Manchester. Z9727B

THOMPSON, C. F., Sergt., 2nd S. Lancashire Regt.
He was mobilised at the outbreak of war, and in August 1914 was drafted to the Western Front. There he took part in the Battle of Mons, and the subsequent Retreat, and fought with distinction in the Battles of Le Cateau (I.), and the Marne (I.), where he was taken a prisoner of war in September. He was taken to Hanover and employed in repairing roads and drains, and was released in December 1918. He received his discharge in February 1919, and holds the Mons Star, and the General Service and Victory Medals. Z8381 6, Leamington Street, Chorlton-on-Medlock, Manchester.

THOMPSON, F., L/Cpl., 9th K.O. (R.Lancaster Regt.)
Joining in February 1916, he was drafted to France in the following November, and took part in the Battles of Arras, Bullecourt, Ypres (III) and Cambrai, and in the Retreat and Advance of 1918. He was unfortunately killed in action at Cambrai on September 27th of that year, and was entitled to the General Service and Victory Medals.
"The path of duty was the way to glory."
569, Collyhurst Road, Manchester. Z11590

THOMPSON, G., Driver, R.A.S.C. (M.T.)
Volunteering in March 1915, he was retained for a period on important duties at various home stations, and in January

1917 was drafted to Salonika. There he served on the Doiran front, and took part in the Battle of the Struma, the capture of Monastir, and in other engagements, including the Advance across the Vardar. He contracted fever and was taken to hospital, but rejoined his unit, and saw further fighting on the Vardar. He was demobilised in April 1919, and holds the General Service and Victory Medals. 19, Pickering Street, Hulme, Manchester. Z8384

THOMPSON, G. A., L/Cpl., 1/8th Manchester Regt.
A Territorial, he was mobilised in August 1914, and quickly drafted to Egypt, where he was stationed at Cairo and Alexandria. Later he proceeded to the Dardanelles, took part in the Landing at Suvla Bay, and was wounded. After treatment on the Isle of Imbros and at Malta he returned to Egypt, but shortly afterwards was transferred to the Western Front. He was then in action at Fricourt, Bapaume and Ypres, but was unhappily killed at La Baraque, near St. Quentin, on September 2nd, 1918, and was entitled to the 1914–15 Star, and the General Service and Victory Medals.
"He joined the great white company of valiant souls."
93, Curzon Street, Gorton, Manchester. Z8380

THOMPSON, H., Private, R.A.M.C.
He volunteered in January 1916, and twelve months later was drafted to the Western Front, where he was engaged on special duties as an officer's Orderly at several hospitals. He rendered valuable services in this capacity until March 1919, when he was demobilised, holding the General Service and Victory Medals. 30, Lorne Street, Moss Side, Manchester. Z11220

THOMPSON, H., Cpl., 2nd South Lancashire Regt.
He volunteered in August 1914, and after a period of training proceeded to France. In this theatre of war he fought in many important engagements, including the Battles of Neuve Chapelle, St. Eloi, Hill 60, Ypres (II.), Albert, Vimy Ridge, Cambrai (I.) and the Somme (I and II). He was wounded and sent home to hospital, but returned to France, and was attached to the Labour Corps. He was demobilised in February 1919, and holds the 1914–15 Star, and the General Service and Victory Medals. 10, Dorset Street, West Gorton, Manchester. Z8377

THOMPSON, J., Pte., K.O. Shropshire Light Infantry.
He volunteered in February 1916, and after his training was engaged on duties of an important nature at various stations. Owing to ill-health he was unable to secure his transfer to a theatre of war, and in July of the same year was invalided out of the Service. 11, Almond Street, Collyhurst, Manchester. Z9727C

THOMPSON, J., L/Cpl., 22nd Manchester Regiment.
He volunteered in November 1914, and early in the following year was drafted to the Western Front, where he was in action at the Battles of Ypres and the Somme. In 1917 he was transferred to Italy and saw heavy fighting on the Asiago and the Piave. He was demobilised in March 1919, and holds the 1914–15 Star, and the General Service and Victory Medals. 14, Windsor Street, Rochdale Road, Manchester. Z11221

THOMPSON, J., Private, 16th Lancashire Fusiliers.
He joined in June 1918, and was quickly drafted to the Western Front, where he took part in heavy fighting at St. Quentin, Albert and Ypres during the Advance of that year. Returning to England in February 1919 he was then demobilised, and holds the General Service and Victory Medals. 8, Rennie Street, West Gorton, Manchester. Z11222

THOMPSON, J., Pte., 8th Loyal N. Lancashire Regt.
A Reservist, he was mobilised in August 1914 on the outbreak of war, and went to France with the 1st Expeditionary Force. He fought in the Battle of Mons, and in the Retreat, and played a distinguished part in many of the important Battles of the campaign, including the Marne (I.), La Bassée, Ypres (I.), Neuve Chapelle, Festubert, Loos, Somme (I.), Arras, Ypres (III.) and Cambrai (I.). He was taken prisoner in March 1918, and was sent to Lemberg to work in the salt mines. After returning home, he was discharged as unfit for further service in January 1919, and holds the Mons Star, and the General Service and Victory Medals. 12, Peter Street, Ardwick, Manchester. Z8379A

THOMPSON, J., Special War Worker.
He closed his works during the war and was employed on various work of National importance. He was employed as a shell turner, as assistant fireman and chief inspector, and served at Messrs. Armstrong, Whitworths Works. Apart from these duties he undertook the work of a special constable, and rendered very valuable services. 105, George Street, Manchester. X8387

THOMPSON, J., Pte., 16th South Lancashire Regt.
He joined in April 1917, and on completion of his training was engaged on important transport duties at various home stations. He served principally in the Dockyards at Liverpool, Manchester and Barrow-in-Furness, and although unsuccessful in obtaining his transfer overseas, did consistently good work until his demobilisation in July 1919. 34, Granville Street, Moss Side, Manchester. Z8382

THOMPSON, J., Private, 16th Lancashire Fusiliers.
He volunteered in November 1914, and for a year was retained on important home duties at various stations. He was then drafted to the Western Front, where he played a conspicuous part in the Battles of Vimy Ridge, and the Somme (I), in the severe fighting on the Albert front, and was twice wounded. He was sent to hospital at home, and in April 1917 was discharged as medically unfit for further service, and holds the 1914-15 Star, and the General Service and Victory Medals.
95, Silver Street, Hulme, Manchester. TZ8383

THOMPSON, J., Private, 2nd Sherwood Foresters.
He volunteered in November 1915, and twelve months later was drafted to France, where he played a prominent part in the Battles of Arras, Ypres (III), the Somme (II), the Marne (II) and in the Retreat. He was taken prisoner in July 1918, and was repatriated after the cessation of hostilities. Demobilised in November 1919, he holds the General Service and Victory Medals.
35, Adelaide Street, Hulme, Manchester. Z8385A

THOMPSON, J. W., Private, 3rd South Lancashire Regiment, and Royal Defence Corps.
He volunteered in July 1915, and on completion of his training was transferred to the Royal Defence Corps, with which unit he was engaged on special guard duties at various stations. He did consistently good work until November 1917, when he was discharged as medically unfit for further service.
5, Moody Street, Bradford, Manchester. Z10931A

THOMPSON, N., Private, 28th Manchester Regt.
He joined in June 1916, and early in the following year was transferred to the R.F.C., and sent to France, where he served on the Somme with the 29th Balloon Section. After the conclusion of the war, he proceeded into Germany and was stationed at various places with his section. He was, however, placed in a low category, sent home and discharged in July 1919. He holds the General Service and Victory Medals.
37, St. Leonard Street, Chorlton-on-Medlock, Manchester. X8388

THOMPSON, R., Private, 4th Cheshire Regiment.
He volunteered in July 1915, and in the following February was despatched to Egypt, where he took part in the fighting at Agagia, Sollum, Katia, and Romani, after which he suffered from dysentery and was sent to hospital in Cairo. In March 1917 he was transferred to France, and there fought with distinction at Armentières and Hollebeke. On returning from France in December 1917, he was retained on important duties for a period at home, and discharged in April 1918, holding the General Service and Victory Medals.
9, Meriner Street, Greenheys, Manchester. Z8386

THOMPSON, T., Private, M.G.C.
He volunteered in March 1915, and after his training was engaged on important duties at home for some time. In August 1916, however, he proceeded to France and took part in the Battles of the Somme (where he was wounded in action shortly after landing on the Western Front), Arras, Vimy Ridge, Bullecourt, Messines, Ypres (III), Passchendaele and Cambrai, and in the Retreat and Advance of 1918. After the cessation of hostilities, he served at Cologne with the Army of Occupation, but later proceeded to India and in 1920, was stationed at Dinapore. He holds the General Service and Victory Medals.
12, Peter Street, Ardwick, Manchester. TZ8379B

THOMPSON, T. H., Private, 3rd Manchester Regt.
He volunteered in September 1914, and a year later proceeded to the Dardanelles, where he took an important part in the fierce fighting at Suvla Bay, after which he was invalided home with dysentery. In August 1916 he was sent to Mesopotamia and fought at Kut-el-Amara, and was wounded at Baghdad. Invalided to Poona, India, he was retained there for a year, and on his return to England was discharged in April 1918. He holds the 1914-15 Star, and the General Service and Victory Medals.
12, Adelaide Street, Hulme, Manchester. Z8389

THOMPSON, W., Private, Lancashire Fusiliers.
Volunteering in January 1915, he embarked for Egypt four months later, and took part in the defence of the Suez Canal. Later he served in the Advance through Palestine, participating in several important engagements, including those at Jaffa and Jerusalem. Transferred to France in August 1917, he fought at Ypres, Passchendaele and Messines, where in the following October he was so severely wounded as to necessitate his return to England. After hospital treatment he was discharged as medically unfit in January 1918, and holds the 1914-15 Star, and the General Service and Victory Medals.
47, Francisco Street, Collyhurst, Manchester. Z9728

THOMPSON, W., Private, R.A.M.C.
Joining in May 1917, he at first was retained on important duties at various stations, and was later drafted to France. In this theatre of war he did excellent work with his unit in caring for the wounded, particularly at Etaples, and for some time acted as orderly in the 46th General Hospital,

where he was serving at the time of the air raids. On his return he was demobilised in January 1919, and holds the General Service and Victory Medals.
8, Eskrigge Street, Ardwick, Manchester. Z8378

THOMPSON, W., Bombardier, R.F.A.
He was mobilised in August 1914, and immediately drafted to France, where he took part in the Battles of Mons, Ypres, Givenchy, Loos, the Somme, Arras, Messines and Cambrai and was badly wounded in December 1917. After hospital treatment at Rouen and Trouville, he was discharged in January 1919, but, later volunteered for the North Russian Relief Force. He was finally demobilised in October 1919, and holds the Mons Star, and the General Service and Victory Medals.
130, Oldham Road, Manchester. Z11591

THOMPSON, W. H., Sergt., 9th E. Lancashire Regt.
He volunteered in September 1914, and crossing to France in the following August, fought in many important engagements, including the Battle of Loos. In January 1916 he was sent to Salonika, where he took part in the Advance on the Doiran front, the capture of Monastir, and in the Offensive on the Vardar. He returned to England in January 1919, and was demobilised a month later, and holds the 1914-15 Star, and the General Service and Victory Medals.
33, Peel Street, Hulme, Manchester. Z11834

THOMSON, W., A.B., Royal Navy.
Already in the Royal Navy at the outbreak of war, he was sent to the North Sea, and served with a destroyer flotilla off the Belgian Coast. He fought at the Battles of Heligoland Bight and the Dogger Bank, and whilst in action in May 1916 at the Battle of Jutland was wounded in H.M.S. "Defence." After being in hospital at Plymouth and Portsmouth, he was discharged in April 1918, and holds the 1914-15 Star, and the General Service and Victory Medals.
18, Bradshaw Street, Hulme, Manchester. Z8390

THOMSON, W. N., A.B., Royal Navy.
Mobilised at the declaration of war, he was posted to H.M.S. "Cressy," which ship was torpedoed off the Hook of Holland on September 22nd, 1914. He was reported missing, but was afterwards found to have been picked up by a Dutch merchant ship. Later he was posted to another vessel, which was engaged in convoying troopships from Australia, and also served with a Flotilla Patrol off the West Coast of Africa, and in the North Sea. He was demobilised in January 1919, and holds the 1914-15 Star, and the General Service and Victory Medals.
12, Hague Street, Newton Heath, Manchester. Z9729

THORBURN, G., Private, 7th Manchester Regiment.
After volunteering in August 1914, he was in the following month sent to Egypt, where he saw fighting at Katia and Romani. Drafted to the Dardanelles in August 1915, he played an important part in the Landing at Suvla Bay, and also fought at Chunuk Bair, remaining in Gallipoli until the Evacuation was accomplished. After further service in Egypt he was recalled home to take up work of National importance, and was discharged in March 1917, holding the 1914-15 Star, and the General Service and Victory Medals.
4, Wilberforce Terrace, Hulme, Manchester. Z8391

THORLEY, P., Driver, R.F.A.
Volunteering in August 1914, he was sent to France five months later and was in action at Hill 60, Ypres (II), Loos and Albert. Wounded in the Battle of the Somme in September 1916, he received treatment at Etaples Hospital, and on recovery rejoined his unit and took part in heavy fighting at Arras, the Somme (II), Cambrai and in the Retreat and Advance of 1918, entering Mons on Armistice Day. Returning to England he was demobilised in March 1919, and holds the 1914-15 Star, and the General Service and Victory Medals.
7, Athol Street, Hulme, Manchester. Z11835

THORN, R., 1st Air Mechanic, R.A.F.
He joined in May 1916, and after a period of training was retained at various stations with his Squadron. He was unable to obtain his transfer overseas, owing to ill-health, but rendered excellent services whilst engaged on important duties which demanded a high degree of technical skill, at various aerodromes, including Farnborough and Dumfries, before being demobilised in February 1919.
22, Moulton Street, Hulme, Manchester. Z8393

THORN, W., Driver, R.F.A.
Volunteering in September 1914, he was in the same month despatched to Egypt, where he took part in the fighting on the Suez Canal, and served in the desert. In April 1915 he was sent to Gallipoli, and played a distinguished part in the Battles of Krithia (I, II and III) and Suvla Bay. After the Evacuation, he was transferred to France in December 1915, and fought at St. Eloi, Albert, the Somme, Arras, Ypres, Cambrai, the Marne, Havrincourt and Le Cateau. On his return he was demobilised in June 1919, and holds the 1914-15 Star, and the General Service and Victory Medals.
8, Caygill Street, Chorlton-on-Medlock, Manchester. Z8392

THORNHILL, A., Private, 69th Labour Corps.
He joined in April 1916, and in the following month was drafted to France, where he served for about two and a half years. During this period he was stationed at various places, and retained on important duties, including the making of roads, and the repairing of trenches and bridges. He was demobilised in February 1919, and holds the General Service and Victory Medals.
35, Westmoreland Street, Longsight, Manchester.   Z6692B

THORNHILL, A., Private, 6th Manchester Regt.
He volunteered in June 1915, and after undergoing a period of training served at various stations, where he was engaged on duties of great importance. Unable, owing to ill-health, to obtain his transfer to a theatre of war, he, nevertheless, did much useful work with his unit until October 1917, when he was invalided from the Service.
19, Tilstone Place, Rochdale Road, Manchester.   Z11224

THORNHILL, H., Private, Border Regiment.
Volunteering in August 1914, he proceeded to France in the following October, and fought in different sectors of the line. He took a distinguished part in various engagments, but unhappily was killed in action whilst fighting gallantly at Ypres in December 1914. He was entitled to the 1914 Star, and the General Service and Victory Medals.
"And doubtless he went in splendid company."
35, Westmoreland Street, Longsight, Manchester.   Z6692C

THORNHILL, S., Private, Manchester Regiment.
He volunteered in August 1914, and in the following November was sent to France. Whilst in this theatre of war he saw heavy fighting during the fierce onslaught of the enemy in the Ypres salient at the close of 1914, and played an important part in several other engagements, including that at Hill 60, where he died gloriously on the Field of Battle on April 2nd, 1915. He was entitled to the 1914 Star, and the General Service and Victory Medals.
"Whilst we remember, the sacrifice is not in vain."
30, Ashworth Street, Openshaw, Manchester.   Z8394A

THORNTON, D., Private, Northumberland Fusiliers.
He joined in September 1916, and on completing his training in March of the following year, proceeded to the Western Front, where he saw much heavy fighting. After taking part in the Battles of Arras, Vimy Ridge, Bullecourt and Messines, and many other engagements, he was severely wounded in action, and taken prisoner at Ypres in July 1918. He unhappily died whilst still in captivity on November 9th of that year, only two days before the signing of the Armistice. He was entitled to the General Service and Victory Medals.
"A costly sacrifice upon the altar of freedom."
4, Sun Street, Newton Heath, Manchester.   Z11225B

THORNTON, E., 1st Cl. Stoker, R.N.
He volunteered in October 1915, and was posted to H.M.S. "King George V," on board which vessel he served with the Grand Fleet in the North Sea. He took part in several bombardments of the Belgian Coast, and fought also in the Battle of Jutland, and many minor Naval engagements. He was demobilised in January 1919, and holds the 1914-15 Star, and the General Service Medal (with four clasps), and Victory Medal. 4, James Place, Miles Platting, Manchester.   Z11226

THORNTON, J., L/Corporal, Scottish Borderers.
He volunteered in September 1914, and after four months' training proceeded to the Western Front, where he took part in the Battles of Neuve Chapelle, Hill 60, Ypres and Festubert, and many minor engagements. He died gloriously on the Field of Battle at Loos on September 25th, 1915. He was entitled to the 1914-15 Star, and the General Service and Victory Medals.
"His memory is cherished with pride."
4, Sun Street, Newton Heath, Manchester.   Z11225A

THORNTON, J., Rifleman, 10th K.R.R.C.
He joined in February 1916, and in July of the same year was drafted to France, where he saw severe fighting in various sectors of the Front. After taking part in the Battles of Vimy Ridge, the Somme, Arras, Bullecourt and Messines, and many minor engagements, he was taken prisoner in August 1917, and held in captivity until the cessation of hostilities. Demobilised on his return home in January 1919, he holds the General Service and Victory Medals.
449, Collyhurst Road, Rochdale Road, Manchester.   Z11227

THORNTON, S., Sergeant, 1st Lancashire Fusiliers.
Volunteering at the outbreak of war, he completed his training and was sent to the Dardanelles in April 1915. After taking part in the Landing at Cape Helles, and the three Battles of Krithia, he fought at Suvla Bay and Chunuk Bair, and remained in action until the Evacuation of the Peninsula. Sent to Egypt, he served on the Suez Canal, and on the Western Desert at Sollum and Katia. In May 1916 he was drafted to France, and fought in the Battle of the Somme, being in action at Beaumont-Hamel and Beaucourt. He also took part in the first Battle of Arras, and was wounded in the third Battle of Ypres. Invalided home, he spent some time in hospital at Exeter, and was discharged as unfit in April 1918, holding the 1914-15 Star, and the General Service and Victory Medals.
40, Haughton Street, Bradford, Manchester.   TZ11973-4-5

THORNTON, S. J., Sergeant, South Lancashire Regt.
Volunteering at the age of sixteen in February 1915, he was sent in the following February to the Western Front. In this theatre of war he fought in many important Battles, including those of Lens, Albert, and was seriously wounded at Cambrai. He unhappily succumbed to his injuries in a Field Dressing Station on December 29th, 1917, and was laid to rest in Poperinghe Cemetery. He was entitled to the General Service and Victory Medals.
"Courage, bright hopes, and a myriad dreams splendidly given."
61, Garratt Street, Miles Platting, Manchester.   Z9730

THORNTON, T., Private, Manchester Regiment.
He was mobilised at the outbreak of war, and proceeding shortly afterwards to France took part in the Retreat from Mons, and the Battles of Ypres (I and II), and the Somme. Sent to Egypt in January 1917, he served there until February 1918, when he was drafted to Salonika. He did good work during operations in the Balkans, and returning to France in June 1918, was engaged on important duties in the closing stages of the war. He was demobilised in October 1919, and holds the Mons Star, and the General Service and Victory Medals.
32, Johnson Street, Bradford, Manchester.   Z9731

THORP, C. P., Air Mechanic, R.A.F.
He joined in January 1917, and after completing a period of training, served at various stations, where he was engaged on duties which called for a high degree of technical skill. He was not successful in obtaining his transfer overseas, but, nevertheless, rendered valuable services with his Squadron until March 1919, when he was demobilised.
21, Bath Street, Miles Platting, Manchester.   Z11228A

THORP, F., Private, 8th Manchester Regiment.
He joined in June 1916, and having completed a term of training, was retained on important duties at various stations. Unable, on account of ill-health, to obtain his transfer to a theatre of war, he, nevertheless, did much useful work with his unit until December 1917, when he was discharged as medically unfit for further service.
21, Bath Street, Miles Platting, Manchester.   Z11228B

THORP, J. H., Pte., K.O. (Royal Lancaster Regt.)
Volunteering in August 1914, he was in the following month despatched to the Western Front. In this theatre of hostilities he was engaged in severe fighting, particularly in the Battles of La Bassée and Hill 60, and whilst in action at Ypres unfortunately fell mortally wounded in July 1915. He was entitled to the 1914 Star, and the General Service and Victory Medals.
"His life for his Country."
4, Ancoats Street, Chancery Lane, Ardwick, Manchester. Z8396

THORPE, H., Pte., 16th and 6th Manchester Regt.
He volunteered in August 1914, and was retained at home on important duties until June 1915, when he was drafted to the Dardanelles. There he took part in the fighting at Suvla Bay, but was wounded, and sent to hospital in Cairo, where he remained until December 1916. In the following January he was transferred to France, and fought with distinction in the Battle of Ypres, but contracting trench fever was invalided home, and eventually demobilised in March 1919. He holds the 1914-15 Star, and the General Service and Victory Medals.
15, Clayton Street, Hulme, Manchester.   Z8399

THORPE, J., Private, 1st Lancashire Fusiliers.
Volunteering at the outbreak of war, he proceeded to Egypt in May 1915, and shortly afterwards was sent to Gallipoli, where he fought at Suvla Bay. After further service in Egypt he was drafted to France in February 1917, and was in action at Ypres, the Somme, Cambrai, La Bassée and Nieuport. He also served in Germany with the Army of Occupation, and was not demobilised until November 1919. He holds the 1914-15 Star, and the General Service and Victory Medals.
5, Mary Street, Ancoats, Manchester.   Z8395

THORPE, W., Private, 10th Essex Regiment.
He joined in April 1918, and in the following August was sent to the Western Front. Whilst in this theatre of war, he served in various sectors, and took an important part in the fighting on the Arras front, and in other engagements, including that at Douai, and the Battle of Cambrai. After the Armistice, he was attached to the R.A.M.C., and on his return home was demobilised in December 1919, holding the General Service and Victory Medals.
17, Meadow Street, Ardwick, Manchester.   Z8397

THORPE, W. E., Sapper, 430th Field Company, R.E.
Volunteering in October 1915, he was in the following year despatched to the Western Front. There he was engaged on important duties in the forward areas on the Ancre front, and at Bullecourt, and was also employed in many parts of the line, in mining operations, and on defensive works for troops in the front lines. He was demobilised in July 1919, and holds the General Service and Victory Medals.
14, Dalton Street, Hulme, Manchester.   Z8398

THREADGOLD, J., Private, Labour Corps.
Joining in March 1917, he was drafted to the Western Front in the following month, and was there engaged on important duties in various sectors. He was present at the Battles of Ypres and Cambrai, and many other engagements in this theatre of war, and also took part in actions in the Retreat of 1918. Invalided home in August of that year, he was in hospital at Manchester, before being demobilised in February 1919, and holds the General Service and Victory Medals.
8, Alma Street, Collyhurst, Manchester.   Z11593

THRELFALL, T., Rifleman, Winchester Rifle Brigade.
He volunteered in September 1914, and soon proceeded to the Western Front, where he fought in the Battles of La Bassée and Ypres. In December of the same year, however, he was unhappily killed in action near Ypres, and was buried near by. He was entitled to the 1914 Star, and the General Service and Victory Medals.
"His memory is cherished with pride."
120, Thomas Street, West Gorton, Manchester.   Z8436

THROUP, H., Private, R.A.S.C.
Volunteering in August 1914, he was retained on important duties at various stations with his unit, until July 1917, when he proceeded to France. There he was stationed at Le Havre, and was engaged in conveying horses to the front lines, but owing to ill-health was invalided home in September 1917, and after hospital treatment, was employed on home service duties, until demobilised in March 1919. He holds the General Service and Victory Medals.
13, Dennison Street, Rusholme, Manchester.   TZ8400A

THURSTON, G. W., Private, R.A.S.C.
He volunteered in August 1914, and in the same month was sent to France, where he served for more than four years and a half. During this period he was engaged chiefly in taking food stuffs to the troops in the front lines, and whilst on these important duties was present during the heavy fighting on various fronts, including Passchendaele, the Somme and Cambrai. On his return he was demobilised in March 1919, and holds the 1914 Star, and the General Service and Victory Medals.
5, Welton Place, Moor Street, Rusholme, Manchester.   Z8401

THURSTON, H., Driver, R.H.A.
He volunteered in August 1914, and landing in France a month later served with his Battery in various sectors of the Front until the close of hostilities. During this period he fought in the Battles of Neuve Chapelle, Hill 60, Ypres (II and III), Ploegsteert, the Somme, and in the Retreat and Advance of 1918. He returned home for his demobilisation in March 1919, and holds the 1914 Star, and the General Service and Victory Medals.
20, Princess Street, Miles Platting, Manchester.   Z9392

TIANI, A., Private, 8th Manchester Regiment.
Joining in February 1917, he was drafted in the following April to the Western Front, and fought in the Battles of Arras, Vimy Ridge, Bullecourt, Messines, Cambrai, and was wounded during the second Battle of the Marne in July 1918. On recovery he rejoined his unit and was in action at Amiens, Le Cateau, and several other engagements in the Allied Advance of 1918. Returning home for demobilisation in September 1919, he holds the General Service and Victory Medals.
24, Victoria Square, Ancoats, Manchester.   Z9393

TICKLE, F. C., Private, East Lancashire Regiment.
He volunteered in September 1914, and twelve months later, proceeded to the Western Front, where he took part in the Battle of Loos and various minor engagements. In December 1915, however, he was transferred to Salonika, and there saw severe fighting on the Doiran front, and was wounded in action in April 1917. He was for a considerable period in hospital at Malta, and in England, and was finally demobilised in February 1919, holding the 1914-15 Star, and the General Service and Victory Medals.
26, Haughton Street, Bradford, Manchester.   Z11229

TICKLE, J., Gunner, R.F.A.
Shortly after volunteering in August 1914, he was drafted to Egypt, where he was engaged on important duties at Alexandria, and also took part in the capture of El Fasher. Later in 1916, he was transferred to the Western Front, and there fought in the Battles of Vimy Ridge and Ypres, and many other engagements, and also served through the Retreat and Advance of 1918. Demobilised in February 1919, he holds the 1914-15 Star, and the General Service and Victory Medals.
21, Alderman Street, Ardwick, Manchester.   Z11230

TIDESWELL, H., Private, K.O. (R. Lancaster Regt.)
Joining in June 1916, he was in the following November despatched to the Western Front, where he saw heavy fighting, and took part in the Battles of Arras (I), the Somme (I), Ypres (III), Cambrai (I), and the Marne (II), and the British Retreat and Advance of 1918. He suffered from septic poisoning, and was in hospital for three months, but rejoined his unit, and entered Germany with the Army of Occupation, where he was employed in guarding prisoners. On his return he was demobilised in August 1919, and holds the General Service and Victory Medals.
10, Sorrell Street, Hulme, Manchester.   TZ8402

TIDSWELL, J., Sergt., 11th Manchester Regt. and M.G.C.
Volunteering in August 1914, he proceeded to Gallipoli in the following June and took part in the Landing at Suvla Bay, and the Battle of Krithia, and was slightly wounded several times. After the Evacuation of the Peninsula he was sent to Malta for hospital treatment, and returning to England in August 1916, was drafted to the Western Front two months later. He served with the Machine Gun Corps during operations on the Ancre in January 1917, and several other engagements until the close of the war. He was demobilised in February 1919, and holds the 1914-15 Star, and the General Service and Victory Medals.
30, Halston Street, Hulme, Manchester.   Z9394

TIERNEY, J., Private, 22nd Manchester Regiment.
He volunteered in September 1914, and after completing a period of training served at various stations, where he was engaged on duties of a highly important nature. Owing to ill-health, he was unable to obtain his transfer to the Front, but did much useful work with his unit until May 1916, when he was invalided from the Service.
30, Anslow Street Rochdale Road, Manchester.   Z11231

TIGHE, J., Private, 17th Manchester Regiment.
He volunteered in September 1914, and after a period of training was drafted to France in November 1915. In this theatre of war he served in many sectors of the line, and fought at Loos and St. Eloi, and on the Albert and the Somme fronts, but was unfortunately killed in action at Trones Wood in July 1916. He was entitled to the 1914-15 Star, and the General Service and Victory Medals.
"His memory is cherished with pride."
3, Ross Street, Ardwick, Manchester.   Z8403A

TIGHE, W., L/Cpl., 4th Manchester Regt. and M.G.C.
Joining in November 1916, he was retained on important home duties until November 1917, when he proceeded to France. After taking part in the fighting on the Somme and Cambrai fronts, he was transferred to Italy in February 1918, and fought on the Piave. Later he was again on the Western Front, and transferred to the Machine Gun Corps, was in action in the Battle of the Somme (II). Wounded there in the Spring of 1918, he was invalided home, and served at Grantham until demobilised in March 1919. He holds the General Service and Victory Medals.
3, Ross Street, Ardwick, Manchester.   Z8403B

TILSON, J. R., Private, 19th Manchester Regiment.
He volunteered in August 1915, and on completing his training in May of the following year was drafted to the Western Front. Whilst in this theatre of war he took part in important engagements in various sectors, including the Battles of the Somme, and Arras, and was twice wounded in action—at Trones Wood in July 1916, and again at St. Quentin in 1917. He was for a time in hospital at Bradford, and was finally invalided from the Army in March 1918, holding the General Service and Victory Medals. 13, Howarth St., Bradford, Manchester. Z11232

TIMMIS, C. E., Private, East Lancashire Regiment.
He volunteered in August 1914, and in the following month was sent to France, where he served for more than two and a half years. During this period he played a prominent part in various engagements, including those at St. Eloi, Loos, Vermelles, and Bullecourt, and also in the Battles of Ypres (I), the Marne (II), Arras, and the Somme, where he was wounded. He was sent home to hospital, but rejoined his unit, and served in France until 1919. On his return he was demobilised in March of that year, and holds the 1914 Star, and the General Service and Victory Medals.
13, Beswick Street, Ardwick, Manchester.   Z8404

TIMPERLEY, A., Driver, R.A.S.C.
Volunteering in November 1915, he was in the following year despatched to France, and was present at the Battles of Ypres and La Bassée. During the fierce fighting he was chiefly engaged in conveying ammunition to the troops, and was wounded twice, and sent home to hospital. He was demobilised in October 1919, and holds the General Service and Victory Medals. 2, Wolsey St., Ancoats, Manchester. Z8405

TIMPERLEY, G., Sapper, R.E.
He volunteered in August 1914, and was quickly drafted to Egypt. During his service in this seat of war he was stationed at Alexandria and Cairo. Later he was transferred to the Western Front, and took part in the Battle of Ypres, and the Retreat and Advance of 1918. He was discharged in April 1919, and holds the 1914-15 Star, and the General Service and Victory Medals.
186, Hamilton Street, Collyhurst, Manchester.   Z11233

TIMPERLEY, W., Private, 8th Manchester Regt.
He volunteered in December 1915, and in the following May was drafted to France. There he at once took part in heavy fighting, and after two months' service, was wounded and taken prisoner during the Battle of the Somme. Interned in Germany until after the Armistice, he was then repatriated, and was eventually demobilised in February 1919, holding the General Service and Victory Medals.
27, Briscoe Street, Ardwick, Manchester.   Z11967

TIMPERLEY, W., Pte., 20th Lancashire Fusiliers.

He joined in June 1915, and in the following December was drafted to the Western Front. Whilst in this theatre of war he fought with distinction in the Battles of Albert, Vimy Ridge, and the Somme (I), and was wounded at Arras, and gassed at Cambrai. He was invalided home, and was eventually discharged as unfit for further service in April 1918, holding the 1914–15 Star, and the General Service and Victory Medals.

27, Mark Lane, Chorlton-on-Medlock, Manchester. Z8406

TIMPERLEY, W., Private, 2nd Manchester Regt.

Volunteering in 1914, he proceeded to France, and took part in the early Battles of the campaign, fighting gallantly at Mons, Ypres (I), and the Somme (I), where he was wounded, and taken a prisoner of war. He was interned in Poland, Westphalia, and at Friedrichsfelde, and after the Armistice was released, and on returning home was demobilised in December 1918, holding the Mons Star, and the General Service and Victory Medals.

27, Briscoe Street, Ardwick, Manchester. X8407

TINSLEY, C. E., Private, 15th Royal Scots.

He volunteered in October 1914, and on completion of his training was retained on important duties with his unit at various stations. In January 1916, however, he proceeded to the Western Front, where he saw much active service. He took part in the Battles of Albert, the Somme (I), and Beaumont-Hamel, and was wounded. On his recovery, he returned to France, and served throughout the engagements at Arras (I), Bullecourt, Ypres (III) and Cambrai, and was again wounded. As a result, he was invalided to hospital and discharged in April 1918, as medically unfit for further military service. He holds the 1914–15 Star, and the General Service and Victory Medals.

11, Wrigley Street, West Gorton, Manchester. Z11234B

TINSLEY, S., Private, 11th Royal Scots.

He volunteered in January 1915, and shortly afterwards proceeded to the Western Front. In this theatre of war, he took part in many important engagements in various sectors. He fought in the Battles of Ypres (II), Festubert, Albert, and the Somme, where he was wounded. On his recovery he returned to the fighting area, and was in action at Arras and Ypres (III). He was unfortunately killed in action near Passchendaele on November 4th, 1917. He was entitled to the 1914–15 Star, and the General Service and Victory Medals.

"A costly sacrifice upon the altar of freedom."

11, Wrigley Street, West Gorton, Manchester. Z11234A

TIPPETTS, W., Private, 5th and 6th Royal Scots.

He volunteered in January 1915, and after a period of service was retained on important duties at home until July 1916, when he was sent to France. There he saw severe fighting in various engagements, including those at Loos, Neuve Chapelle, Ypres (III), Passchendaele, La Bassée, Cambrai, Albert and Arras, but unhappily whilst fighting on the Somme fell mortally wounded in August 1918. He was entitled to the General Service and Victory Medals.

"The path of duty was the way to glory."

47, Aked Street, Ardwick, Manchester. Z8408

TIPTON, J. H., Private, 13th Manchester Regiment.

Volunteering in September 1914, he was in the following August despatched to France, where he fought in the Battle of Loos. Transferred to Salonika in November 1915, he took a prominent part in the fighting on the Doiran front, in the capture of Monastir, and in the Struma and Vardar Advances. Owing to ill-health he was invalided home in July 1918, and was eventually discharged in December of that year, holding the 1914–15 Star, and the General Service and Victory Medals.

43, Elliott Street, Bradford, Manchester. Z8409

TITLEY, P., Private, 19th Manchester Regiment.

He volunteered in July 1915, and, on completion of his training in March 1916, was drafted to the Western Front. During his service in this theatre of war he took part in many important engagements, and was unhappily killed in action on the Somme in July 1916. He was entitled to the 1914–15 Star, and the General Service and Victory Medals.

"Steals on the ear the distant triumph song."

14, Harrowby Street, Collyhurst, Manchester. Z11235

TITTERINGTON, J. W., Private, Manchester Regt. and York and Lancaster Regiment.

He joined in April 1916, and on completion of his training served at various stations on important duties with his unit. In June 1917 he proceeded to France, where he took part in the heavy fighting on the Somme and Arras fronts, and was wounded and invalided to England in August 1917. He was discharged in March 1918 as medically unfit for further service, and holds the General Service and Victory Medals.

19, Douro Street, Newton Heath, Manchester. Z11236

TITTLE, H., Private, 1st Lancashire Fusiliers.

He volunteered in August 1914, and sailing for Egypt in the following May served in the Canal zone until drafted to Gallipoli. In this theatre of war he took part in the Landing at West Beach and Suvla Bay, and several other engagements until the Evacuation of the Peninsula when he proceeded to the Western Front. There he saw heavy fighting at Loos, and in the Battles of Arras, the Somme, Albert, Monchy le Preux where he was unhappily killed in April 1917. He was entitled to the 1914–15 Star, and the General Service and Victory Medals.

"A costly sacrifice upon the altar of freedom."

26, Oram Street, Miles Platting, Manchester. Z9395B

TITTLE, J. E., Private, 27th Manchester Regiment.

He volunteered in April 1915, and at the conclusion of his training served with his unit at various stations engaged on important duties. He did good work but was not successful in securing his transfer overseas owing to medical unfitness, and was discharged in consequence in December of the succeeding year.

26, Oram Street, Miles Platting, Manchester. Z9395A

TITTLE, R. E., Private, M.G.C.

Volunteering in January 1916, he completed his training and served at home until drafted in November of the following year to the Western Front. There he took part in many important battles, including those of Ypres, and the Somme, and returned to England after the Armistice. In 1919 he was sent to India, and stationed in the Punjab, was engaged on garrison and other important duties. He was still serving there in 1920, and holds the General Service and Victory Medals. 26, Oram St., Miles Platting, Manchester. Z9395

TOBONI, F., Private, Royal Welch Fusiliers.

He joined in April 1916, and on completion of his training was drafted to France. Whilst in this theatre of war he took part in much heavy fighting in various sectors. He was in action at the Battles of Arras, Ypres, and other important engagements. During his period of service he was wounded on three occasions. He was discharged in December 1918, and holds the General Service and Victory Medals.

60, Loom Street, Ancoats, Manchester. Z11452A

TOBONI, J., Private, Labour Corps.

He joined the 66th Training Reserve Battalion in April 1917, and, after a period of training in Wales, was transferred to the Labour Corps, with which unit he rendered valuable services at various stations. He was unsuccessful in obtaining his transfer overseas, and was discharged as medically unfit for further military duty in April 1918.

60, Loom Street, Ancoats, Manchester. Z11452B

TODD, A., Drummer, East Lancashire Regiment.

He volunteered in September 1914, and after a period of training was drafted to the Western Front. There he served in various sectors of the line, taking part in the Battles of Festubert and Loos, and was severely wounded. He was invalided home, and on recovery was retained in England until discharged in January 1919. He holds the 1914–15 Star, and the General Service and Victory Medals.

34, Ryder Street, Bradford, Manchester. Z1240B

TODD, F., Private, Royal Welch Fusiliers.

Joining in July 1918, after completing his training, he was drafted in the following January to Germany, and served with the Army of Occupation until July 1919, when he was transferred to the Lancashire Fusiliers. Enlisting for a further period of three years, he was sent to Ireland, where he was in 1920 still serving.

30, Juniper Street, Hulme, Manchester. TZ8411C

TODD, H., Private, East Yorkshire Regiment.

He joined in July 1915, and in the following February was sent to France. Whilst in this theatre of war he played an important part in the severe fighting on the Ancre Front, and in the Battles of Vimy Ridge, and the Somme I, where he was wounded and taken a prisoner of war in August 1916. He was confined at Freiderichsfeldt, and after the signing of the Armistice was released, and on returning home was demobilised in February 1919. He holds the General Service and Victory Medals.

1, Sorrell Street, Hulme, Manchester. Z8413A

TODD, H. B. (Sen.), Private, Lancashire Fusiliers.

He joined in June 1915, and after a period of training was drafted in January 1916 to France, where he took part in many important engagements. He fought with distinction in the fierce Battles of Ypres III and IV, the Somme I and II, in action also at Albert, Arras I, Vimy Ridge, and the Marne II. In 1918 he served through the British Retreat and Advance, and on his return was demobilised in February 1919, holding the General Service and Victory Medals.

30, Juniper Street, Hulme, Manchester. TZ8411A

TODD, H. B., Private, Lancashire Fusiliers.

Joining in January 1917, he was drafted in the following May to the Western Front, where he served for more than two years. During this period he took a distinguished part in the Battles of Passchendaele, and Cambrai I, and in other engagements, including Havrincourt, and the Sambre, and in the Retreat and Advance of 1918, and was twice wounded. After the Armistice he entered Germany with the Army of Occupation, and was stationed at Bonn until October 1919, when he was demobilised, holding the General Service and Victory Medals.

30, Juniper Street, Hulme, Manchester. TZ8411B

TODD, F. T., Private, 5th King's (Liverpool Regt.)
He volunteered in September 1915, and after a period of training, served at various stations on important duties with his unit. He was unable to obtain a transfer overseas owing to his being medically unfit, but rendered valuable services until he was discharged in November 1917.
51, Burton Street, Rochdale Road, Manchester.   Z11237

TODD, J., Driver, R.F.A.
Volunteering in August 1914, he was for a period retained on home duties with his unit, and in December 1915, proceeded to Egypt. There he served at various stations, and took part in many engagements including those at Sollum, Katia, Magdhaba, Gaza I and III, Jericho, and Aleppo, and was wounded. He was sent to hospital in Alexandria, where he remained until his return to England, and was demobilised in February 1919. He holds the 1914-15 Star, and the General Service and Victory Medals.
3, Goburg Place, Rusholme, Manchester.   TZ8410. Z11970

TODD, W., Sergt., 6th York and Lancaster Regt.
He volunteered in August 1914, and in the following April was sent to Gallipoli. There he took a distinguished part in the very severe fighting which characterised the Landing on the Peninsula, and was in action at Krithia, and in the Battle of Suvla Bay, where he was wounded. He was sent to hospital on board H.M.S. "Aluni," but unfortunately succumbed to his injuries in August 1915. He was entitled to the 1914-15 Star, and the General Service and Victory Medals.
19, John Street, Bradford, Manchester.   TZ8412

TODHUNTER, T., Driver, R.A.S.C.
He volunteered in April 1915, and four months later proceeded to Egypt, where he took part in engagements at Mersa Matruh, Katia and Romani. He then advanced with General Allenby's Forces into Palestine, and was present at the Battles of Gaza, the Capture of Jerusalem, Jericho, and Tripoli, and in the Offensive of September 1918. He holds the 1914-15 Star, and the General Service and Victory Medals, and was demobilised in October 1919.
14, Crayton Street, Hulme, Manchester.   Z11238

TOFT, C., Private, King's (Liverpool Regiment).
Joining in April 1916, he crossed to the Western Front in the following August and took part in several engagements in the Somme Offensive. He fell fighting on October 12th, 1916, and was entitled to the General Service and Victory Medals.
"He died the noblest death a man may die,
Fighting for God and right and liberty."
2, Victoria Square, Oldham Road, Manchester.   Z9397A

TOFT, W., Private, K.O. (Royal Lancaster Regt.)
He joined in March 1916, and proceeding in the following July to France fought in several battles during the Somme Offensive. He gave his life for the freedom of England near Beaumont-Hamel on October 8th, 1916, and was laid to rest in Boulogne Cemetery. He was entitled to the General Service and Victory Medals.
"He joined the great white company of valiant souls."
2, Victoria Square, Oldham Road, Manchester.   Z9397B

TOLTON, F., Private, K.O. (Royal Lancaster Regt.)
A Reservist, he was mobilised at the outbreak of war, and in August 1914 went to France with the Expeditionary Force. He fought in the Battle of Mons, and in the subsequent Retreat, and played a prominent part in the Battles of Ypres, Arras, Cambrai, and the Somme I, during which he was wounded. Later he fought in the Retreat and Advance of 1918, and on his return was discharged in February 1919. He holds the Mons Star, and the General Service and Victory Medals.
35, Berwick St., Chorlton-on-Medlock, Manchester.   Z8414

TOMKIN, F. H., Private, 1st Seaforth Highlanders.
He volunteered in August 1914, and after completing his training served with his unit at various stations engaged on important duties. He did good work, but was unable to secure his transfer to a theatre of war, owing to medical unfitness, and was discharged in consequence in February 1915.
57, Heald Avenue, Rusholme, Manchester.   Z11836

TOMKINSON, G., Private, 8th Lancashire Fusiliers.
Volunteering in September 1914, he was drafted to Egypt two months later, and took part in heavy fighting at Mersa Matruh, the Occupation of Sollum, and was wounded in the Capture of El Fasher in May 1916. On recovery he was sent to the Western Front in the following August and fought in the Battles of Beaucourt, Messines, Cambrai, and at Bapaume, the Sambre, and in the Retreat and subsequent Allied Advance of 1918. Returning home in July 1919, he was demobilised in the following month, and holds the 1914-15 Star, and the General Service and Victory Medals.
3, Prescott Street, Hulme, Manchester.   Z11837

TOMKINSON, H., A.B., Royal Naval Division.
Joining in July 1917, he was in the following October despatched to the Western Front, where he served for fifteen months. During this period he took an important part in the Battles of Cambrai, and the Somme. Wounded in the last engagement, he was sent to hospital in Rouen, and later was invalided home,

being eventually discharged as medically unfit in August 1919. He holds the General Service and Victory Medals.
30, Ashover Street, Ardwick, Manchester.   Z8415

TOMKINSON, T. A., Driver, R.F.A.
He volunteered in August 1914, and in the following February was drafted to Egypt, where he served for two and a half years. During this period he took part in the fighting on the Suez Canal, and also in other engagements, including those at Mersa Matruh, Katia, El Fasher, Romani, Rafa, and Gaza I. He was transferred to France in August 1917, and fought in the Battle of Cambrai I, but in June 1918 was gassed on the Marne. On recovery he rejoined his unit, and was in action in the Advance of 1918. He was demobilised in March 1919, and holds the 1914-15 Star, and the General Service and Victory Medals.
23, Callender Street, Chorlton-on-Medlock, Manchester.   Z8416

TOMLIN, C., Driver, R.E.
Volunteering in February 1915, he proceeded in the following June to France, where he saw severe fighting. He took part in the Battles of Loos, St. Eloi, Vimy Ridge, the Somme, the Ancre, Ypres III, Passchendaele, and Cambrai, and was in several other engagements, including the fierce fighting on the Arras front. He was present at the entry into Mons, and on his return was demobilised in March 1919, holding the 1914-15 Star, and the General Service and Victory Medals.
48, Sutherland Street, Hulme, Manchester.   Z8419

TOMLINSON, E., Private, Sherwood Foresters.
He joined in January 1917, and after a period of training was retained at home on important duties with his unit until March 1918, when he was sent to France. There he played a prominent part in the Battles of the Somme II, and the Marne II, where he was gassed, taken a prisoner of war, and sent into Germany to work in the coal mines. Released after the Armistice, he was demobilised in 1919, and holds the General Service and Victory Medals.
18, Patchett Street, Hulme, Manchester.   TZ8420A

TOMLINSON, F. (D.C.M.), Bombardier, R.F.A.
He was a time-serving soldier at the outbreak of war, and in December 1914, was despatched to the Western Front. In this theatre of war he fought in the Battles of Neuve Chapelle, St. Eloi, Ypres II, Festubert, Loos, Albert, the Somme, and Givenchy. Transferred to India in June 1916, he three months later, was drafted to Palestine, where he took an important part in several engagements, including those at at Gaza III, Jerusalem, Jericho, and Aleppo, and for conspicuous bravery in the Field was awarded the Distinguished Conduct Medal. He afterwards served with the Army of Occupation in Jerusalem and was still serving in 1920. In addition to the Distinguished Conduct Medal, he holds the 1914-15 Star, and the General Service and Victory Medals.
18, Patchett Street, Hulme, Manchester.   TZ8420B

TOMLINSON, J., Trooper, 2nd Life Guards.
Joining in August 1918, he completed his training, and was retained on important duties with his unit at various stations. He was unable to obtain his transfer overseas, owing to physical disabilities, but rendered valuable services before being demobilised in November 1919.
7, Fountain St., City Rd., Hulme, Manchester.   TZ8421

TOMLINSON, J., Private, M.G.C.
Joining in January 1917, he embarked for Mesopotamia three months later, and was in action in heavy fighting at Kut-el-Amara, and other places until transferred to Egypt in January 1918. In this theatre of war he fought in the Battle of Gaza and several other engagements during the Advance through Palestine, including the Capture of Jerusalem. Returning home in February 1919 he crossed to Ireland and was stationed there until his demobilisation in the following June. He holds the General Service and Victory Medals.
66, Nicholson Street, Rochdale Road, Manchester.   Z9732

TOMLINSON, J. H., Gunner, R.F.A.
He joined in April 1916, and embarking for South Africa a month later served at Cape Town for a time. He was drafted to India in December of the same year and took part in heavy fighting on the North West Frontier, and was afterwards transferred to the Persian Gulf, where he served until later in 1919. He then returned to England, and was demobilised in December of that year, and holds the General Service and Victory Medals, and the India General Service Medal (with clasp Afghanistan, N.W. Frontier, 1919).
8, Whatmough Street, Oldham Road, Manchester.   Z9733

TOMLINSON, W., Rifleman, K.R.R.C. and Private, Labour Corps.
He volunteered in September 1914, and in the following year was drafted to France. During his service in this seat of war he saw much heavy fighting, and was in action at the Battles of Albert, the Somme, Cambrai, and Arras, where he met with an accident, and was invalided to hospital at Rouen. As a result, he was discharged in September 1918, medically unfit for further military service, and holds the 1914-15 Star, and the General Service and Victory Medals.
86, Lind Street, Ancoats, Manchester.   Z11239

TOMLINSON, W., Private, Lancashire Fusiliers.

He volunteered in September 1914, and was retained on home duties for a year, after which he was drafted to the Western Front. There he was engaged in various sectors of the line, and took an important part in engagements of Vimy Ridge, Passchendaele and Mormal Wood. Wounded three times he was finally invalided home, and demobilised in February 1919, holding the 1914-15 Star, and the General Service and Victory Medals.

46, Warde Street, Hulme, Manchester.   TZ8422

TOMLINSON, W., Private, Royal Irish and Royal Dublin Fusiliers.

He volunteered in December 1915, and proceeding to France in the following July, took part in the Battles of the Somme, Albert, Arras, Ypres and Havrincourt and in heavy fighting at La Bassée, Givenchy, Festubert, and in the Retreat and Advance of 1918. He was twice wounded in action on the Somme—in September 1916, and again two years later. He holds the General Service and Victory Medals, and was demobilised in April 1919.

31, Southwell Street, Harpurhey, Manchester.   Z11592

TOMPKINS, W., Corporal, R.E.

Volunteering in September 1914, he was in the following May sent to Egypt, and afterwards took part in the severe fighting at the Landing in Gallipoli and at Suvla Bay. He remained on the Peninsula until the Evacuation, and was then transferred to the Western Front, where he fought with distinction in the Battles of Loos, St. Eloi, Albert, Vimy Ridge, the Somme (I), Arras (I), Ypres (III), including Passchendaele, and Cambrai (I), also in other engagements, but whilst holding a signalling class at Magincarbe, was unhappily killed on May 28th, 1918. He was entitled to the 1914-15 Star, and the General Service and Victory Medals.

"Great deeds cannot die."

14, Birch Street, Hulme, Manchester.   Z8423

TONER, O., Corporal, R.F.A.

He volunteered in September 1915, and in the following year proceeded to the Western Front. In this theatre of war he took part in several engagements, including those at Albert, Vimy Ridge, the Somme, Arras, Beaumont-Hamel, Ypres, Messines, Passchendaele, Cambrai and in the Retreat and Advance of 1918. He was demobilised in April 1919, and holds the General Service and Victory Medals.

80, Hamilton Street, Collyhurst, Manchester.   Z11240

TONGE, C., Sergt., 8th Lancashire Fusiliers.

He volunteered in November 1914, and was retained at home for some time as a musketry Instructor. In March 1916 he was drafted to France, and played a prominent part in engagements at Vimy Ridge, the Somme and Ypres, where he was badly wounded in October 1917, and invalided home. He was discharged in February 1918, and holds the General Service and Victory Medals.

7, Duke Street, Bradford, Manchester.   Z11241

TONGE, R., L/Corporal, 1/7th Lancashire Fusiliers.

He volunteered in August 1914, and in the following month proceeded to Egypt, where he served until May 1915. He was then transferred to Gallipoli, and took part in the severe fighting during the Landing on the Peninsula. Unfortunately after the Battle of Krithia (III), he was on June 4th, 1915 reported missing, and later, was presumed to have been killed in action on that date. He was entitled to the 1914-15 Star, and the General Service and Victory Medals.

"His life for his Country."

13, Fountain Street, Erskine Street, Hulme, Manchester.   TZ8424

TOOLAN, H., Private, 1st King's (Liverpool Regt.)

Joining in April 1916, he was retained on important duties at various stations with his unit until November 1916, when he was despatched to the Western Front. There he fought in the engagements on the Arras and the Ancre fronts, and in the Battle of Vimy Ridge, but after the last engagment was reported missing, and finally, was presumed to have been killed in action there in April 1917. He was entitled to the General Service and Victory Medals.

"His life for his Country, his soul to God."

59, Dalton Street, Hulme, Manchester.   Z5782B

TOOLE, P., Private, Lancashire Fusiliers.

He volunteered in September 1914, and served at home until 1917, when he was drafted to the Western Front. In this theatre of war he took part in the Battles of Vimy Ridge and Messines, and was wounded in May 1917. On recovery he rejoined his unit, and went into action on the Somme, the Marne and was wounded again at Havrincourt in September 1918. He returned to England for his demobilisation in February 1919, and holds the General Service and Victory Medals. 90, Charlton Street, Collyhurst, Manchester.   Z11838

TOOLE, W., Private, South Staffordshire Regiment.

Volunteering in August 1914, he was drafted overseas shortly afterwards. Whilst on the Western Front he acted as scout for his Battalion, and took part in engagements at Ypres,

---

Neuve Chapelle, Festubert (where he was wounded), Loos, and Albert, and was again badly wounded in action. In consequence, he was invalided home and finally discharged in March 1917 as medically unfit for further duty. He holds the 1914 Star, and the General Service and Victory Medals.

17, Hope Street, Bradford, Manchester.   Z11242

TOOLE, W., Private (Driver), Manchester Regiment.

He volunteered in November 1914, and after a period of training was drafted to France in November 1915. In this sphere of activities he served in many important engagements, including those on the Somme and at Ypres, Cambrai, La Bassée, Givenchy, Festubert, and Vimy Ridge. Later he was transferred to Italy, where he was engaged in conveying ammunition to the troops on the Piave front, and was present at the fighting on the Asiago Plateau. He was mentioned in Despatches, and for taking ammunition to the front lines under heavy shell-fire, was recommended for a decoration. On returning home he was demobilised in March 1919, and holds the 1914-15 Star, and the General Service and Victory Medals. 21, Halsbury Street, Longsight, Manchester.   Z8425

TOOMEY, P. (M.M.), Private, Queen's (Royal West Surrey Regiment).

A Reservist, he was mobilised at the outbreak of war, and proceeded to France in August 1914. After fighting in the Battles of Mons, the Marne (I), La Bassée (I), Neuve Chapelle, Hill 60, Ypres, (II), Festubert, and Loos, he was wounded, but on his recovery was again in action in several engagements, including Messines, the Somme (I), Arras (I) and Cambrai (I), and was wounded a second time. For conspicuous bravery in the Field in December 1917 he was awarded the Military Medal. He also took part in the Retreat and Advance of 1918, and was demobilised in January 1919. In addition to the Military Medal he holds the Mons Star, the General Service and Victory Medals.

14, Heyrod Street, Ancoats, Manchester.   Z7113A

TOOMEY, R., Pioneer, R.E.

He joined in January 1917, and four months later was drafted to France. There he took part in several important engagements, including that of Havrincourt. He was taken ill and consequently invalided home and discharged in January 1918 as medically unfit for further service. He holds the General Service and Victory Medals.

18, Flower Street, Ancoats, Manchester.   Z11243

TORKINGTON, H., Private, R.A.M.C. (T.F.)

Volunteering in April 1915, he was after completing his training retained on important duties at various stations with his unit. Owing to reasons of health, he was unable to obtain his transfer overseas, but rendered valuable services as an orderly in different hospitals before being demobilised in March 1919.

62, Henry Street, West Gorton, Manchester.   Z8417

TOWERS, E., Corporal, R.E.

He volunteered in August 1914, and on completing his training in the following year, was drafted to France. There he took part in the Battles of the Somme, and Ypres, and in the Retreat and Advance of 1918, and was wounded in action at Cambrai. As a result, he was invalided to Rouen, and on his recovery returned home for his demobilisation in April 1919. He holds the 1914-15 Star, and the General Service and Victory Medals.

317, Mill Street, Bradford, Manchester.   Z11244

TOWERS, R., Private, Royal Scots.

He volunteered in August 1914, and early in the following year proceeded to the Western Front. There he took part in several engagements, including the Battles of St. Eloi, Ypres (II), Hill 60, Loos, the Somme, Ypres (III), Cambrai, Amiens, Bapaume and in the Retreat and Advance of 1918, and was wounded in action. He was discharged in November 1918, and holds the 1914-15 Star, and the General Service and Victory Medals.

40, Richardson Street, Collyhurst, Manchester.   Z10713B

TOWERS, W., Private, 17th Manchester Regiment.

He volunteered in January 1915, and in the following December was sent to France. There he served in various sectors of the line, and took a prominent part in the severe fighting in the Ypres salient, especially at Dickebusch, and in the Battle of Loos, where he was wounded. He was invalided home, and in consequence of his injuries was discharged in March 1916, holding the 1914-15 Star, and the General Service and Victory Medals.

17, Anthony Street, Ardwick, Manchester.   Z8418

TOWLE. G. F., Corporal, R.F.A.

He was mobilised in August 1914, and quickly proceeded to France. Whilst in this theatre of war he took part in the Retreat from Mons, the Battles of Ypres, Neuve Chapelle, Loos, the Somme, Vimy Ridge, Bullecourt and the Advance of 1918, and was twice wounded in action. He was discharged in June 1919, and holds the Mons Star, and the General Service and Victory Medals.

39, Spire Street, Ardwick, Manchester.   Z10850B

TOWLER, A. H., Private, Cheshire Regiment.

He joined in September 1916, and on completing his training in the following year was drafted to France. There he served as a Lewis gunner, and took part in engagements at Cambrai, the Somme (II), and in the Retreat and Advance of 1918. He made the supreme sacrifice, being killed in action at the Battle of Ypres (IV) on October 14th, 1918. He was entitled to the General Service and Victory Medals.

"Steals on the ear the distant triumph song."

23, Worth Street, Rochdale Road, Manchester. Z11245

TOWLER, J. W., Driver, R.E.

Joining in July 1917, he was in the following October despatched to the Western Front, where he served for nearly two years. During this period he took part in the Battles of Cambrai (I), the Somme (II), Amiens, Ypres, (IV), and the Selle, and in the Retreat and Advance of 1918 at Havrincourt. After the Armistice he entered Germany with the Army of Occupation, and on returning home was demobilised in July 1919, holding the General Service and Victory Medals.

40, Meridian Street, Higher Ardwick, Manchester. Z8426

TOWNDROW, A., Private, Royal Welch Fusiliers.

Volunteering in February 1915, he crossed to France four months later, and fought in the Battles of Festubert, Albert, the Somme, Arras, Passchendaele, and was wounded at Cambrai in November 1917. On recovery he returned to the front line trenches and took part in the Retreat and Advance of 1918. After the Armistice he served in Germany with the Army of Occupation for a period of two months, and then returned home. He was discharged on account of service in April 1919, and holds the 1914-15 Star, and the General Service and Victory Medals.

2, Harlbutt Street, Hulme, Manchester. Z11839

TOWNLEY, F., Private, Lancashire Fusiliers.

He volunteered in December 1916, and after completing his training served with his unit at various stations engaged on important duties. He rendered valuable services, but was not successful in securing his transfer overseas on account of medical unfitness, and was discharged in consequence in December of the following year.

3, George Street, Moss Side, Manchester. Z11840

TOWNLEY, J., Lieutenant, 7th Cheshire Regiment.

He volunteered in December 1915, and after a period of training was retained on home duties for about two years, at the end of which he was drafted to Egypt. There he took part in the fighting in the Eastern campaign, notably at the capture of Jerusalem and Jericho, and also served at Tripoli. He suffered from dysentery, and was sent to hospital in Cairo, but later was invalided home, and unfortunately died at Worsley Hall Road Red Cross Hospital, Worsley, on April 1st, 1919. He was entitled to the General Service and Victory Medals.

19, Cadogan Street, Moss Side, Manchester. Z8427

TOWNS, H. L. A., Private, 16th Manchester Regt.

Volunteering in July 1915, he completed his training and was retained on important duties at various stations with his unit. Owing to ill-health he was unable to obtain his transfer overseas, but did excellent work particularly as clerk in the Army Pay Corps before being demobilised in February 1919.

33, Crondall Street, Moss Side, Manchester. Z8428

TOWNSEND, H., Private, King's (Liverpool Regt.)

He joined in April 1916, and immediately proceeded to France, where he served for more than three and a half years. During this time he took a prominent part in the Battles of Loos, St. Eloi, Vimy Ridge, the Somme (I), Arras (I), Messines, Ypres (III), Passchendaele, and Cambrai, and also in the British Retreat and Advance of 1918. He did excellent work with his unit, and on his return was demobilised in December 1919, holding the General Service and Victory Medals.

14, Dundas Street, Ancoats, Manchester. Z8429

TOWNSEND, H., Private, Manchester Regiment.

Volunteering in January 1915, he embarked four months later for the Western Front, and went into action at Ypres almost immediately. Severely wounded during a bombing raid in that sector, he recovered and fought at Mametz Wood in 1916. Invalided home, he was discharged as unfit in September 1917, and holds the 1914-15 Star, and the General Service and Victory Medals.

5, Oswald Street, Ancoats, Manchester. TZ8430

TOWNSEND, W., Gunner, R.G.A.

He volunteered in August 1914, and after a period of training was drafted to Mesopotamia, where he saw much heavy fighting at Kut and Amara. In 1917 he was sent to India for garrison duty, but early in the following year proceeded to France, where he fought in the Retreat and Advance of 1918. He was demobilised in September 1919, and holds the 1914-15 Star, and the General Service and Victory Medals.

21, Combrook Park Road, Stretford, Manchester. Z10186-7A

TOWNSON, J., Private, Gloucestershire Regiment.

He joined in February 1916, and after a period of training was in the following August despatched to the Western

Front. There he took part in various engagements, including the Battle of the Somme (I) and Bullecourt, and the final British Advance of August 1918, and was gassed. He rendered excellent services and on his return was demobilised in February 1919, holding the General Service and Victory Medals.

65, Hampden Street, Ardwick, Manchester. Z1314A

TOZER, F. J., Private, 20th Manchester Regiment.

Volunteering in November 1914, he was retained on home duties for a year, and was then drafted to the Western Front, where he served for over three years. During that time he took a distinguished part in the Battles of Loos, St. Eloi, Albert, Ypres (III), and Cambrai, and in the fierce fighting on the Ancre, Vermelles and Somme fronts. Wounded at Loos in 1916, he was afterwards transferred to the Labour Corps, and did good work in repairing bridges and roads. On his return he was demobilised in February 1919, and holds the 1914-15 Star, and the General Service and Victory Medals.

25, Lynn Street, West Gorton, Manchester. Z8431

TRACEY, W., Private, 9th Manchester Regiment.

He volunteered in October 1914, and in the following May was sent to Egypt, whence a few months later he proceeded to the Dardanelles. During the operations on the Peninsula he fought at Cape Helles, but was invalided home owing to ill-health in November 1915. After some time in hospital he was discharged as medically unfit in December 1917, and holds the 1914-15 Star, and the General Service and Victory Medals.

13, Granville Street, Chorlton-on-Medlock, Manchester. Z8432

TRACEY, W., Private, 7th Manchester Regiment.

Volunteering in November 1914, he met with an accident in the course of his training and was admitted into the Devonport Military Hospital, where he received prolonged medical treatment. Proceeding to France in June 1917, with the 1st Cavalry Division, he was engaged on important duties on the lines of communication on the Somme, Passchendaele and Cambrai fronts. He was demobilised in March 1919, and holds the General Service and Victory Medals.

14, Holbeck Street, Oldham Road, Manchester. Z9734

TRANTER, W., Driver, R.F.A.

He volunteered in August 1914, and in the following July was drafted to France. During his service overseas he took part in the Battles of Loos, Ypres, Béthune, the Somme, Arras, Nieuport and Bullecourt, and was wounded in action at Cambrai. As a result, he was invalided to the Base, and after his recovery was demobilised in November 1919. He holds the 1914-15 Star, and the General Service and Victory Medals.

29, Taunton Street, Ancoats, Manchester. Z11246

TRANTER, W. E., Private, 9th Seaforth Highlanders.

Three months after volunteering in February 1915, he crossed to France and was in action at Ypres, Arras, Loos and Neuve Chapelle. Wounded in 1916 during the Somme Offensive, he soon rejoined his unit and fought at the Battles of Ypres, Passchendaele and Cambrai. Serving right through the Retreat and Advance of 1918, he proceeded to Germany with the Army of Occupation and was not demobilised until September 1919. He holds the 1914-15 Star, and the General Service and Victory Medals.

46, King Street, Ardwick, Manchester. Z8433

TRAVIS, G., Private, Royal Welch Fusiliers.

He volunteered in May 1915, and landing in France in the following August, fought in many important battles, notably those of Loos, St. Eloi and Albert. He gave his life for King and Country at the Battle of Arras in April 1916, and was entitled to the 1914-15 Star and the General Service and Victory Medals.

"And doubtless he went in splendid company."

17, John Street, Bradford, Manchester. Z9735B

TRAVIS, J., Private, 8th Manchester Regiment.

Joining in January 1918, he was drafted overseas in the following April, and served with his unit on the Western Front. There he took part in the Battle of Amiens and in other operations in the closing stages of the war. After the Armistice he was retained on special duties in guarding and escorting prisoners of war to the German Frontier. Returning home, he was demobilised in March 1919, and holds the General Service and Victory Medals.

17, John Street, Bradford, Manchester. Z9735A

TRAVIS, R., Private, 1/4th South Lancashire Regt.

He volunteered in November 1914, and after a period of training was despatched to France in August 1915. In this theatre of war he took a prominent part in the Battle of the Somme, and afterwards, being transferred to the 69th Labour Corps, was stationed at Rouen, and chiefly engaged in the making and repairing of roads and other important duties. On his return he was demobilised in February 1919, and holds the 1914-15 Star, and the General Service and Victory Medals.

58, Boston Street, Hulme, Manchester. TZ8434

TRAVIS, W. H., Private, 7th Manchester Regiment.

Volunteering in August 1914, he embarked for Gallipoli early in the following year and took part in the first Landing and the Battles of Krithia. He was severely wounded in July 1915, and evacuated to England, received protracted medical treatment. On recovery he was engaged on home service duties until discharged on account of service in February 1919. He holds the 1914–15 Star, and the General Service and Victory Medals.
13, Energy Street, Bradford, Manchester.   Z9736

TRAVIS, W. P., Private, 1/8th Manchester Regt.

He volunteered in March 1915, and crossing to France three months later served in various parts of the Line for four years. During this period he fought at Ypres and in the Battles of Loos, St. Eloi, Albert, Vimy Ridge, the Somme, Beaucourt, Arras, Messines and Cambrai. He was also in action in the German Offensive and in several battles, including those of Amiens, Le Cateau and the Sambre, in the subsequent Allied Advance of 1918. He holds the 1914–15 Star, and the General Service and Victory Medals. and was demobilised in March 1919.
17, John Street, Bradford, Manchester.   Z9735C

TRAYNOR, A., Private, M.G.C.

Volunteering in September 1914, he was drafted overseas in the following year. During his service on the Western Front he took part in several engagements, including those at Armentières, the Somme, Vimy Ridge, Messines, Ypres and in the Retreat and Advance of 1918, and was twice wounded in action. He was demobilised in March 1919, and holds the 1914–15 Star, and the General Service and Victory Medals.
12, Dundas Street, Ancoats, Manchester.   Z11247A

TREACHER, H., Private, 6th Manchester Regiment.

Serving with the Territorials on manœuvres at the outbreak of war, he was in January 1915 sent to the Western Front, where he played a distinguished part in the fierce Battles of Neuve Chapelle, St. Eloi, Ypres, the Somme and Cambrai, and was twice wounded. After recovery he was again in action, but unhappily, whilst taking a position at Cambrai with a raiding party, he fell mortally wounded in October 1918. He was entitled to the 1914–15 Star, and the General Service and Victory Medals.
"Steals on the ear the distant triumph song."
36, Rial Street, Hulme, Manchester.   Z8435

TRELFORD, J., Pte., 1st Loyal North Lancashire Regt.

Volunteering in August 1914, he was in the following month despatched to the Western Front and fought in the Retreat from Mons and in the Battles of the Marne (I), and La Bassée. Whilst fighting at Festubert, he died gloriously on the Field of Battle on December 22nd, 1914. He was entitled to the Mons Star, and the General Service and Victory Medals.
"Nobly striving,
He nobly fell that we might live."
21, William Street, West Gorton, Manchester.   Z8437

TRIMBLE, J. F., Corporal, King's Shropshire Light Infantry.

Having served from 1912 to 1914 in India, he volunteered for further service in the December following the outbreak of war, and was quickly sent to the Western Front. After a short time, however, he was invalided home, but recovered, rejoined his unit and fought on the Ancre front at Beaumont-Hamel. He subsequently was in action at Arras, Ypres, Cambrai, Bapaume, the Scarpe and Havrincourt. Demobilised in April 1919, he holds the 1914–15 Star, and the General Service and Victory Medals.
19, Wellbeck Street, Chorlton-on-Medlock, Manchester. Z8438

TROTMAN, H., Driver, R.F.A.

He enlisted in 1909, and on the outbreak of war proceeded to France, where he fought in the Battle of Mons and in the subsequent Retreat. He also took part in the severe fighting at Le Cateau, La Bassée, Béthune, Givenchy, Festubert and Nieuport, Arras, Albert, the Somme and Passchendaele, and the second and third Battles of Ypres, and was wounded. In 1918 he was in action in the Retreat and Advance, and after the Armistice entered Germany with the Army of Occupation. On his return he was demobilised in March 1919, and holds the Mons Star, and the General Service and Victory Medals. 16, Wilson Street, Ardwick, Manchester.   Z8439

TROY, J. J., Cpl., 6th K.O. (R. Lancaster Regt.)

Volunteering in August 1914, he was sent in the following April to Gallipoli, where he fought in the Battles of Krithia (II and III), and Suvla Bay, and was wounded. In March 1916 he was drafted to Mesopotamia and there played an important part in the severe fighting at Kut, and was again wounded and sent to hospital in Karachi, India. On his return to England he was demobilised in January 1920, and holds the 1914–15 Star, and the General Service and Victory Medals. He, however, re-enlisted for a period of service and in 1920 was serving in Ireland.
19, Hardman Street, City Road, Hulme, Manchester. Z8440

TROYANOWSKI. J., Pte., Loyal N. Lancashire Regt.

He joined in November 1916, and in the following March was despatched to France, where he served for nearly two years.

During this period he took an active part in the severe fighting on the Arras, Bullecourt and Passchendaele fronts and in the Battles of Vimy Ridge, Ypres (III), and Cambrai (I), and was badly wounded. He was invalided home and retained in Leeds General Hospital until demobilised in February 1919. He holds the General Service and Victory Medals.
10, Lingard Street, Hulme, Manchester.   Z8441

TRUIN, H., Private, R.A.M.C.

Volunteering in April 1915, he was drafted in the following month to France and was attached to a field ambulance, as a stretcher-bearer and orderly in the advanced dressing stations at Ypres, Passchendaele, the Somme, La Bassée, Givenchy, Festubert, Cambrai, Lens and Loos. He did valuable work in the care of the wounded, and after the Armistice, entered Germany with the Army of Occupation, and was stationed at Cologne. On his return he was demobilised in June 1919, and holds the 1914–15 Star, and the General Service and Victory Medals.
1, Brunt Street, Rusholme, Manchester.   Z8442

TRUMAN, B., Sergt., K.R.R.C.

Volunteering in August 1914, he was drafted overseas a month later and served with his unit on the Western Front. He fought at the Battles of the Marne, and was wounded in action at La Bassée. Evacuated to England for hospital treatment, he was transferred to the Labour Corps on recovery, and, sent to France, was engaged on important duties in the forward areas. Owing to ill-health, following his wounds, he was invalided home in December 1916, and subsequently discharged unfit for further service in December of the succeeding year. He holds the 1914 Star, and the General Service and Victory Medals.
72, Phillips Street, Hulme, Manchester.   Z11841A

TRUMAN, H. B., Corporal, K.R.R.C.

He volunteered in December 1915, and served at home until November 1917, when he was drafted to the Western Front. Wounded at Passchendaele a month later, he was sent to a Base hospital for treatment, and rejoining his unit on recovery, was in action in the German Offensive and was wounded in May 1918. He was evacuated to England, and after receiving treatment at Sutton Coldfield Military Hospital, Birmingham, was discharged as medically unfit for further service in September 1918. He holds the General Service and Victory Medals.
72, Phillips Street, Hulme, Manchester.   Z11841B

TUCKER, J., Private, 18th Manchester Regiment.

He volunteered in November 1915, and was retained on important duties at various stations with his unit until May 1916, when he proceeded to France. Whilst on the Western Front he served in different sectors of the Line and fought with distinction in engagements at Combles and Guillemont, but unhappily fell mortally wounded in the latter action on July 30th, 1916. He was entitled to the General Service and Victory Medals.
"He passed out of the sight of men by the path of duty and self-sacrifice."
92, Old Elm Street, Ardwick, Manchester.   TX8443

TULEY, I., Sergt., 8th Manchester Regiment.

He volunteered in August 1914, and underwent a period of training prior to his being drafted to France. There he played a prominent part in engagements at Albert, the Somme, Beaumont-Hamel, Arras, Ypres, Cambrai, Bapaume and Le Cateau (II). He was demobilised in February 1919, and holds the General Service and Victory Medals.
18, Charles Street, Manchester.   Z11248

TURLEY, F., Private, Lancashire Fusiliers.

Joining in May 1916, he was retained on important duties at various stations with his unit, and for a considerable period was engaged on the North-East Coast defences. Owing to physical disabilities he was not successful in obtaining his transfer overseas, but did excellent work before being demobilised in February 1919.
13, Towson Street, Russell Street, Hulme, Manchester. TZ8444

TURLEY, W., Driver, R.A.S.C.

He volunteered in August 1914, and after a period of training was drafted to Egypt, and thence to the Dardanelles. There he took an active part in much heavy fighting at Cape Helles and Suvla Bay. After the Evacuation of the Gallipoli Peninsula, he was sent to Salonika and was again in action on the Doiran front. He returned home and was demobilised in April 1919, holding the 1914–15 Star, and the General Service and Victory Medals.
40, Southwell Street, Harpurhey, Manchester.   Z11594

TURNBULL, J. J., A.B., Royal Navy.

He volunteered in August 1914, and was posted to a torpedo boat destroyer, which vessel was engaged on important patrol duties off the West Indies. His ship also took part in the Battle of Jutland, and afterwards served with the Naval Police stationed at Dover, until the end of the war. He was demobilised in March 1919, and holds the 1914–15 Star, and the General Service and Victory Medals.
110, Parker Street, Bradford, Manchester.   Z9737

TURNBULL, W., A,B., Royal Navy.
Having joined the Royal Navy in 1902, he was serving when war was declared, and in the course of hostilities his ship was engaged on patrol and other duties in various waters. He was in action with his ship in the Battles of Heligoland Bight, the Dogger Bank, the Falkland Islands and Jutland, and was also engaged in covering the landing of troops in German New Guinea. He was discharged on account of service in January 1919, and holds the 1914–15 Star, and the General Service and Victory Medals.
43, John Street, Chorlton-on-Medlock, Manchester. Z11842

TURNER, A., Bombardier, R.F.A.
He joined in January 1917, and in the following July was sent to the Western Front, where he served for over a year. In this theatre of war he took a prominent part in several engagements, including those at Passchendaele, Cambrai (I) and Amiens, and fought in the Battles of the Somme (II). Later he was recalled home, and after serving in the Pay Office at Dover, was demobilised in September 1919, holding the General Service and Victory Medals.
36, Russell Street, Moss Side, Manchester. TZ6952B

TURNER, A., Private, R.A.M.C.
Volunteering in December 1915, he was retained at home on important duties until the following July, when he was despatched to France, where he served for about eight months. During this period he took a distinguished part in the Battles of the Somme (I) and Arras (I), and was in action at Beaucourt, but in March 1917 was invalided home. Afterwards he was drafted to Egypt, but unfortunately was drowned, through his ship being torpedoed in the Mediterranean Sea on May 4th, 1917. He was entitled to the General Service and Victory Medals.
"Honour to the immortal dead, who gave their youth that the world might grow old in peace."
12, New Square, West Gorton, Manchester. Z8445

TURNER, A. E., Driver, R.A.S.C. (M.T.)
He volunteered in April 1915, and served at home until drafted to France in February 1917. Whilst on the Western Front he was engaged on important transport duties in the forward areas, and was present during engagements at Albert, the Somme, Ypres (III), Cambrai and in the Retreat and Advance of 1918. He returned to England for his demobilisation in March 1919, and holds the General Service and Victory Medals.
8, Harrold Street, Miles Platting, Manchester. Z9398

TURNER, C., S.M., 6th Manchester Regiment.
He volunteered in December 1915, and for two years was retained on important home duties. In 1917, however, he acted as a special messenger, conveying official Despatches between the War Office and the General Headquarters in France, and in this capacity rendered valuable services, until the cessation of hostilities. He was demobilised in January 1920, and holds the General Service and Victory Medals.
50, Clayton Street, Hulme, Manchester. Z8447A

TURNER, C. H., Private, 16th Manchester Regt.
He joined in January 1917, and on completing his training in the following year, was drafted to the Western Front. In this theatre of war he took part in several engagements, including the Battles of the Somme (II), Ypres and La Bassée. After the cessation of hostilities he went to Germany with the Army of Occupation and served on the Rhine until his demobilisation in February 1919. He holds the General Service and Victory Medals.
15, Flower Street, Ancoats, Manchester. Z11249

TURNER, E. P., Private, R.A.M.C.
Volunteering in August 1914, he was drafted in the same month to the Western Front, where he acted as a Despatch rider. There he took part in the Retreat from Mons, and in several other engagements, but was seriously wounded in January 1915, whilst delivering Despatches near Armentières. He was invalided home, and in consequence of his injuries was eventually discharged later in the year. He holds the Mons Star, and the General Service and Victory Medals.
14, Ravensdale Road, Rusholme, Manchester. Z8449A

TURNER, F. H., Private, Labour Corps.
He volunteered in September 1915, and on completion of his training served with his Company at various stations. In 1917 he was engaged on agricultural work in the North of England, and after a year returned to his unit. He rendered valuable services, but owing to physical unfitness was unable to secure his transfer overseas before the termination of the war, and was demobilised in September 1919.
123, Broadfield Road, Moss Side, Manchester. Z11843

TURNER, H., L/Cpl., R.G.A., and Military Police.
He joined in December 1917, and in the following June proceeded to Italy, where he served on the Piave. Transferred to Egypt in October 1919, he was retained at various stations on garrison duty, and afterwards, being attached to the Military Police, did excellent work at Alexandria. On his return to England he was demobilised in January 1920, and holds the General Service and Victory Medals.
14, Alderley Street, Hulme, Manchester. Z8450

TURNER, J., Private, Durham Light Infantry.
He joined in October 1916, and two months later was drafted to France, where he took part in engagements on the Ancre, and at Merville. He was reported missing, and is now presumed to have been killed in action in the Lys sector on April 9th, 1918. He was entitled to the General Service and Victory Medals.
"Honour to the immortal dead, who gave their youth that the world might grow old in peace."
12, Dundas Street, Ancoats, Manchester. Z11247B

TURNER, J., Private, 7th Manchester Regiment.
Volunteering in May 1915, he proceeded overseas in the following January. During his service on the Western Front he took part in the Battles of the Somme, Arras, Ypres, and Cambrai, and in the Retreat and Advance of 1918. He was demobilised in March 1919, and holds the General Service and Victory Medals.
68, Gunson Street, Miles Platting, Manchester. Z10223B

TURNER, J., Private, 8th Manchester Regiment.
He volunteered in August 1914, and in May of the following year proceeded to the Dardanelles, where he saw severe fighting at Suvla Bay and many other places, until wounded in action. Invalided to Malta, he unfortunately contracted fever, and was for nine months in hospital there and in England. On his recovery in November 1916, however, he was drafted to the Western Front, when he was again in action until the cessation of hostilities. Demobilised in December 1918, he holds the 1914–15 Star, and the General Service and Victory Medals.
1A, Adelaide Street, Bradford, Manchester. Z11250

TURNER, J. H., Private, Royal Scots.
He volunteered in January 1915, and was retained on important home duties until the following December, when he was despatched to Egypt. In the next month he was transferred to the Western Front, where he served in various sectors, and took part in the Battles of Loos, the Somme, Cambrai I, and in the severe fighting in the Ypres salient. During this period he was wounded three times. He was finally sent to hospital in Surrey, and Birmingham, in March 1918, and was eventually discharged in July 1918, holding the 1914–15 Star, and the General Service and Victory Medals.
26, Ferneley Street, Hulme, Manchester. Z8451

TURNER, J. W., Driver, R.A.S.C.
Volunteering in June 1915, he was kept in England until the beginning of 1918. There, however, he obtained his transfer to Egypt, but four months later was sent to France, where he served with the 52nd Division in the British Advance, engaged in the transport of food and stores to the front lines. He was demobilised in September 1919, and holds the General Service and Victory Medals.
25, Randolph Street, Ardwick, Manchester. Z8448

TURNER, L. H., Private, Manchester Regiment.
He volunteered in 1915, and in the same year was despatched to the Western Front, where he fought in the Battle of Ypres II. In 1916 he was transferred to Italy and played an important part in the fighting on the Asiago front until 1917, when he was again sent to France, being present in the final Allied Advance from August to October 1918, during which he was wounded. He was sent home to hospital, and was discharged in 1919, holding the 1914–15 Star, and the General Service and Victory Medals.
14, Ravensdale Road, Rusholme, Manchester. Z8449B

TURNER, N., Private, 8th Manchester Regiment.
Volunteering in August 1914, he was in the following February drafted to the Western Front, where he served for more than four years. During this period he fought with distinction in the Battles of Loos, Vimy Ridge, Arras I, Messines, Ypres, and Cambrai, and in other engagements including Bullecourt, and was wounded and gassed. He was demobilised in April 1919, and holds the 1914–15 Star, and the General Service and Victory Medals.
1, Crook Street, Ancoats, Manchester. Z8446

TURNER, S., L/Corporal, 2/5th Manchester Regt.
He volunteered in September 1915, and in the following May proceeded to France. Whilst on the Western Front he saw severe fighting on the Ancre and Arras fronts, and in the Ypres salient. He also took a distinguished part in the Battles of Vimy Ridge, the Somme I, Cambrai I, the Marne II, Le Cateau II, and in other engagements, including Havrincourt and Bapaume during the Retreat and Advance of 1918, and was wounded at Arras in 1917. On his return he was demobilised in October 1919, and holds the General Service and Victory Medals. 24, Viaduct St., Ardwick, Manchester. Z8452

TURNER, T., Private, 2nd Manchester Regiment.
Joining in January 1917, he was sent in the following July to France, but owing to sudden illness was detained in hospital and operated on. After recovery he re-joined his unit, and entered Germany with the Army of Occupation, serving there until March 1919, when he returned to England, and was demobilised. He holds the General Service and Victory Medals.
50, Clayton Street, Hulme, Manchester. Z8447B

TURRELL, J., Private, 3rd Manchester Regiment.
He volunteered at the outbreak of war in August 1914, and in June of the following year was drafted to the Western Front, where he took part in many important engagements in the Somme, and other sectors. He was afterwards transferred to Italy, and there saw much severe fighting until the cessation of hostilities. He was demobilised on his return home in August 1919, and holds the 1914–15 Star, and the General Service and Victory Medals.
12, Gardner St., West Gorton, Manchester.   Z11251

TURTLE, H., Private, 2/6th Manchester Regiment.
Joining in May 1916, he was in the following February sent to France, and took part in the Battles of Vimy Ridge, and Ypres III, and in the fierce fighting on the Arras front. Later he was in action in the Retreat of March 1918, but was reported missing. He was entitled to the General Service and Victory Medals.
"Courage, bright hopes, and a myriad dreams splendidly given."
84, Stott Street, Hulme, Manchester.   Z8453

TURTON, C., Private, Labour Corps.
He joined in March 1917, and in the same month was despatched to France, where he served for about two years. In this theatre of war he did valuable work on road repairs behind the lines, and also in the transport of ammunition to the front lines at Ypres, Passchendaele, Cambrai, the Somme, La Bassée, Givenchy, and Béthune, and during the Retreat and Advance of 1918. On his return he was demobilised in February 1919, and holds the General Service and Victory Medals.
10, Walmer Street, Longsight, Manchester.   Z8454

TUSTIN, R. G., L/Corporal, R.A.M.C.
Volunteering in August 1915, he completed his training and was retained on important duties at various stations with his unit. He was unable owing to ill-health to obtain his transfer overseas, but rendered valuable services in caring for the wounded in various hospitals as orderly, before being demobilised in March 1919.
24, Edward Streeet, Moss Side, Manchester.   Z8455

TWEEDALE, C., Rifleman, Rifle Brigade.
He volunteered in March 1915, and in the following October proceeded to France, where he served for four years. During this time he fought in the Battles of Neuve Chapelle, Ypres II, Festubert, La Bassée, Albert, Arras, Ypres III, Passchendaele, Vimy Ridge, and Cambrai, and was in action at Givenchy, Beaucourt, and Beaumont-Hamel. He also took part in the Somme Offensive of 1916, and in the Retreat of 1918, during which he was wounded. Sent to hospital in France, he was finally invalided home, and discharged in November 1919. He holds the 1914–15 Star, and the General Service and Victory Medals. 10, Birch Street, Hulme, Manchester.   Z8456

TWEEDALE, W., Pte., Northumberland Fusiliers.
Volunteering in the Royal Fusiliers in May 1915, he was sent to France in October and fought at Loos, Albert, and Vimy Ridge. Transferred to the Royal West Kent Regiment, he was wounded during the Somme Offensive of 1916, and invalided home. Recovering, he proceeded to Mesopotamia in February 1917, and attached to the Northumberland Fusiliers, fought at Ramadieh, and was present at the capture of Baghdad and Mosul. Returning home, he was demobilised in April 1919, and holds the 1914–15 Star, and the General Service and Victory Medals.
2, Sabin Street, Longsight, Manchester.   Z8457

TWEMLO, A., Gunner, R.G.A.
Volunteering in November 1915, he was drafted with his Battery in the following year to the Western Front. In this theatre of war he took part in heavy fighting in the Battles of Ypres, Arras, Albert, Bullecourt, Armentières, and Vimy Ridge. He gave his life for King and Country at Cambrai, on August 31st, 1916, and was entitled to the General Service and Victory Medals.
"Whilst we remember the sacrifice is not in vain."
9, Kirk Street, Ancoats, Manchester.   Z9399

TWIGG, F., Private, 5th Manchester Regiment.
He joined in August 1916, and in the following November was despatched to France. There he was engaged in various sectors, and took part in the fierce fighting in the Ypres salient, and in the Battles of the Somme, Cambrai, and the Marne II, but unhappily was killed in August 1918, whilst on patrol duty during the Allied Offensive of that year. He was entitled to the General Service and Victory Medals.
"And doubtless he went in splendid company."
102, Birch Street, Ardwick, Manchester.   Z8458

TWIGG, J. E. (D.C.M.), Sergt., 1/8th Manchester Regiment.
A month after volunteering in August 1914, he was sent to Egypt, and in the following year to the Dardanelles, where he fought at Krithia. For conspicuous gallantry in holding a position for seven hours under heavy fire he was promoted to the rank of Sergeant, mentioned in despatches and awarded the Distinguished Conduct Medal. Before proceeding to France in March 1917, he served at Cyprus, and on the Suez Canal. Whilst on the Western Front he fought at La Bassée, Nieuport,
Ypres, Cambrai, and the Somme, but wounded on the Somme during the Retreat of 1918, was invalided home and discharged shortly afterwards. In addition to the Distinguished Conduct Medals, he holds the 1914–15 Star, and the General Service and Victory Medals.
9, Spurgeon Street, West Gorton, Manchester.   Z8459

TYCE, J., Corporal, K.O. (Royal Lancaster Regt.)
Volunteering in November 1914, he was drafted to the Western Front on completing his training in the following year. Whilst in this theatre of war, he saw much severe fighting in various sectors, and took part in the Battles of St. Eloi, Hill 60, Ypres, Messines, and Passchendaele, and many other important engagements. He was demobilised in February 1919, and holds the 1914–15 Star, and the General Service and Victory Medals.   86, Kemp Street, Manchester.   Z11252

TYERS, W., Private, 1st Manchester Regiment.
He volunteered in September 1914, and was retained on important duties in England until drafted to the Western Front in the following year. There he took part in the Battles of St. Eloi, Loos, Vermelles, Albert, Vimy Ridge, the Somme, and the Ancre, and many minor engagements, and was wounded in action at Neuve Chapelle in March 1915. He was discharged in December 1916, in order to take up munition work, and holds the 1914–15 Star, and the General Service and Victory Medals.
67, Knightley Street, Rochdale Road, Manchester.   Z11185B

TYLER, R. W., Pte., 14th South Lancashire Regt. and 23rd Cheshire Regt.
He joined in November 1916, and after a period of training proceeded to France in the following May. In this zone of hostilities, he took an important part in the Battles of Ypres III, Cambrai I, the Marne I, and in other engagements, but was gassed at the Somme II in March 1918. He was afterwards transferred to the 14th South Lancashire Regiment, and on his return was demobilised in September 1919, holding the General Service and Victory Medals.
16, Caroline Street, Hulme, Manchester.   Z8460

TYRRELL, J. H., Corporal, 2/4th Yorkshire Regt.
Joining in September 1916, and completing a period of training he was drafted in the following September to France, and played a prominent part in the Battle of Cambrai I, and in the Retreat and Advance of 1918. On his return he was demobilised in February 1919, and holds the General Service and Victory Medals.
31, Derby Street, Ardwick, Manchester.   Z8461

TYSON, A., Sapper, R.E.
He joined in September 1916, and in April of the following year proceeded to the Western Front, where he served in various sectors. He was present at the Battles of Bullecourt, Ypres, Cambrai, the Somme, Bapaume, and the Scarpe, and many minor engagements in this theatre of war, and was wounded in action. Demobilised in November 1919, he holds the General Service and Victory Medals.
8, Edith Street, West Gorton, Manchester.   Z10214B

TYSON, E., Sergt., 3rd Coldstream Guards.
He volunteered in January 1915, and in the following month was drafted to the Western Front, where he took a prominent part in the Battle of Loos, and was wounded. He was found to be under age, and was sent home and discharged. Later, on attaining military age, he rejoined in the Buffs (East Kent Regiment), and was again sent to France in December 1918, and served there until his demobilisation in February 1919. He holds the 1914–15 Star, and the General Service and Victory Medals.
1, Roseberry Street, Gorton, Manchester.   Z11960

U

UNWIN, A. W., Private, Royal Scots.
He volunteered in October 1914, and was employed at various home stations on important duties until November 1915, when he proceeded to France. There he was in action at Albert, Vimy Ridge, Bullecourt, Ypres, Cambrai, and Arras, and did excellent work. In August 1918 he was transferred to Malta, and served there until January 1919, when he returned home and was demobilised, holding the 1914–15 Star, and the General Service and Victory Medals.
21, Dawson Street, West Gorton, Manchester.   Z8463

UNWIN, G., Private, 1/8th Manchester Regiment.
He volunteered in December 1914, and a month later was drafted to Egypt, where he served for a short time before being sent to Gallipoli. He served throughout the Campaign on the Peninsula, and on his return to Egypt was in action at Kantara. In January 1917 he was transferred to France and took part in engagements at Ypres, the Somme, La Bassée, and Nieuport. He was wounded whilst fighting at Gommecourt, and in consequence was invalided out of the Army in October 1918, holding the 1914–15 Star, and the General Service and Victory Medals.
29, Stewart Street, Gorton, Manchester.   Z11253

UNWIN, H., Private, 8th Manchester Regiment and Sapper, R.E.
Volunteering in September 1915, he was stationed at Codford, Southport, and Yarmouth, engaged on various duties until he was claimed out in April 1917, on account of being under age. He then worked on munitions at Messrs. Galloway's, Manchester, and rejoined the Colours in April 1918. After a further spell of home service he was drafted in the following November to Germany, and served with the Army of Occupation on the Rhine until November 1919, and was then demobilised.
3, Hoylake Street, West Gorton, Manchester.   Z8462

UNWIN, H., L/Corporal, 1/7th Manchester Regt.
In August 1914 he volunteered, and later in the same year was sent to Egypt, where he served at Khartoum, until drafted to Gallipoli. There he took part in many engagements, but prior to the Evacuation of the Peninsula was ordered to Malta, where he was employed on important garrison duties. Owing to ill-health he was discharged from the Army in 1916, and holds the 1914-15 Star, and the General Service and Victory Medals. 21, Tiverton St., Ardwick, Manchester.   Z11254B

UNWIN, I., Private, 19th Manchester Regiment.
Volunteering in 1915, he was on conclusion of his training drafted overseas in the following year. During his service on the Western Front he was in action in the Battle of the Somme, but fell fighting at Delville Wood in 1916. He was entitled to the General Service and Victory Medals.
"A valiant soldier, with undaunted heart he breasted life's last hill."
21, Tiverton Street, Ardwick, Manchester.   Z11254A

UPCHURCH, C., Air Mechanic, R.A.F.
He joined in August 1918, but was not successful in obtaining a transfer overseas owing to the termination of hostilities. Whilst stationed at Blandford and Wendover, he was employed on important duties which demanded a high degree of technical skill, and rendered valuable services until he was demobilised in March 1919.
62, Milton Street, West Gorton, Manchester.   TZ8464

V

VAHEY, T., Private, 8th Manchester Regiment.
He volunteered in May 1915, and twelve months later was sent to Egypt, where he served until March 1917, being stationed on the Suez Canal and in the Desert. Transferred to the Western Front, he was in action at Epéhy, Havrincourt, Ypres, Nieuport, and Givenchy, and was wounded at Festubert, and invalided home. After a time in hospital in York, he returned to France, and was wounded for the second time at Givenchy in April 1918. Again invalided home, he was sent to hospital at Hereford, and was eventually demobilised in March 1919, holding the General Service and Victory Medals.
34, Garibaldi Street, Ardwick, Manchester.   Z8465A

VAIL, G., Sergt., Seaforth Highlanders.
He volunteered in August 1914, and rendered valuable services whilst employed as an instructor at Castle Hill, Edinburgh, until May 1917, when he was drafted to France. In this theatre of hostilities he played a conspicuous part in heavy fighting at Ypres, Albert, Rheims, Givenchy, and on the Somme front. Demobilised on his return home in March 1919, he holds the General Service and Victory Medals.
14, Hey Street, Bradford, Manchester.   Z8466

VALENTINE, H., Private, 2/4th E. Yorkshire Regt., and Gunner, R.G.A.
He joined in July 1916, and after a period of training at Catterick, proceeded to Bermuda. There he was employed with his unit on garrison and other important duties and performed consistently good work until he returned to England for demobilisation in October 1919, holding the General Service and Victory Medals.
16, Marsden St., Chorlton-on-Medlock, Manchester. Z7891B

VANES, A. (Miss), Special War Worker.
This lady volunteered for work of National importance, and from February 1916 until December 1918, was employed at the National Projectile Factory, Dudley. She was engaged there, turning shells, and rendered valuable services during the whole period of her employment.
29, Brunswick St., West Gorton, Manchester.   TZ5991A

VARDEN, T. G., L/Corporal, Lancashire Fusiliers.
Volunteering in August 1914, he was drafted to Gallipoli early in the following year, and took part in the first Landing and the Capture of Chunuk Bair, and other engagements. On the evacuation of the Peninsula he proceeded to France in January 1916, and fought in the Battles of the Somme, Arras, Bullecourt, Ypres, and in the German Offensive. Wounded near Ypres in May 1918, he returned to England and received treatment at Platt Field Military Hospital, Manchester. He was invalided out of the Army in November 1918, and holds the 1914-15 Star, and the General Service and Victory Medals.
1, Oak Street, Hulme, Manchester.   Z11844

VARETTO, J., Private, King's (Liverpool Regiment).
He joined in August 1917, and served in Co. Cork, Dublin, and Liverpool, engaged on garrison and other important duties. He was not successful in obtaining a transfer to a theatre of war, but nevertheless rendered excellent services until he was demobilised in April 1919.
53, Sanitary Street, Oldham Road, Manchester.   Z9400

VARLEY, G. C., Private, Manchester Regiment, and 8th Lancashire Fusiliers.
Joining in May 1917, he was later drafted to the Western Front, and in this theatre of war took part in several important engagements, including the Battles of Ypres, Cambrai, and the Somme, where he was wounded. He spent some time in hospital in Rouen, and upon his recovery, rejoined his unit, afterwards proceeding to Germany with the Army of Occupation. He returned home in November 1919, and was demobilised, holding the General Service and Victory Medals. C8467B

VARLEY, R., Private, King's (Liverpool Regiment).
He volunteered in November 1914, and in the following year was sent to France, where he participated with his unit in the Battles of the Somme, and Ypres. He was reported missing in November 1917, during the Battle of Cambrai, and was later presumed to have been killed at that time. He was entitled to the 1914-15 Star, and the General Service and Victory Medals.
"His life for his Country."   C8467A

VARLEY, W., Private, 11th Manchester Regiment.
Volunteering in September 1914, he served at Grantham, and in Surrey, prior to being drafted to Gallipoli in July 1915. He had only been overseas for a few weeks, when he made the supreme sacrifice, being killed in action at Suvla Bay on August 19th, 1915. He was entitled to the 1914-15 Star, and the General Service and Victory Medals.
"Great deeds cannot die."
69, Edensor Street, Beswick, Manchester.   Z8468

VASEY, W., Private, Lancashire Fusiliers.
He volunteered in October 1914, and in the following April was sent to Gallipoli. There he participated in heavy fighting during the Landing, and in the Battles of Krithia and Suvla Bay. After the Evacuation, he served on the Western Front, and was in action at St. Eloi, Vimy Ridge, the Somme, and Arras, from which place he was invalided home, suffering from shell-shock. He was admitted to hospital in London, and was eventually discharged in August 1917, as unfit for further service. He holds the 1914-15 Star, and the General Service and Victory Medals.
16, Addison Street, Chorlton-on-Medlock, Manchester. Z8469

VAYRO, S. N., Private, R.A.S.C.
He joined in January 1917, and six months later was drafted to the Western Front. In this theatre of war he was employed on important duties in connection with transport service, and rendered valuable services, during which he was wounded and also gassed. He returned home for demobilisation in November 1919, and holds the General Service and Victory Medals.
5, Darncombe Street, Moss Side, Manchester.   Z8470

VEAR, T., L/Corporal, R.E.
Volunteering in August 1914, he was sent a month later to Egypt, where he was stationed on the Suez Canal. In April 1915, he was drafted to Gallipoli and served with his Company during the Landing, and in the Battles of Krithia, where he was wounded. After spending some time in hospital at Alexandria and Cairo, he proceeded to France and saw further service on the Somme, and at Ypres, Cambrai, and Le Cateau. He was demobilised in February 1919, and holds the 1914 Star, and the General Service and Victory Medals.
18, Seddon Street, Rusholme, Manchester.   Z8471

VENTRIS, A. E., Gunner, R.F.A.
He joined in November 1916, and two months later proceeded to the Western Front. There he took part with his Battery in several important engagements on the Ancre front, and at Arras, Vimy Ridge, Bullecourt, Messines Ridge, Ypres, and Cambrai. He was unfortunately killed in action at Monchy on February 6th, 1918, and was buried in the British Cemetery at Arras. He was entitled to the General Service and Victory Medals.
"His memory is cherished with pride."
8, Chipping Street, Longsight, Manchester.   Z8472

VERITY, E., Pte., 5th Manchester Rgt., and R.A.S.C.
He was employed at Messrs. Johnstone and Nephew's Works, Bradford, in the manufacture of barbed wire, before he attained the age of eighteen in January 1918, when he joined the Colours. After serving for some time on coast defence duty at Scarborough, he was transferred to the Royal Army Service Corps, and whilst stationed at the Remount Depôt in Hampshire, was engaged on important duties, until he was discharged in January 1919, on account of ill-health, eventually dying at home a year later from an illness attributed to his military service.
82, Princess Street, Bradford, Manchester.   Z8474

VERITY, J. W., Sapper, R.E.
He volunteered in November 1915, and on completion of his training was drafted overseas in February 1916. During nearly three years' service on the Western Front he was engaged in action in different sectors of the line, and saw heavy fighting at Vimy Ridge, where he was gassed. He was demobilised in January 1919, and holds the General Service and Victory Medals. 14, Chell Street, Longsight, Manchester. Z8473

VERNON, C. A., Sergeant, R.E.
Volunteering in October 1914, he was retained in England until February 1917, and employed in training recruits at Crowborough and Colchester. During his service on the Western Front, he played a conspicuous part in many important engagements, and whilst fighting at Ypres in November 1917, was badly gassed and sent to the American War Hospital for four months. He was demobilised in February 1919, and holds the General Service and Victory Medals. 6, Lythgoe Street, Moss Side, Manchester. Z8477A

VERNON, C. C., Private, 7th Leicestershire Regt.
He volunteered in November 1914, and proceeded in December 1916, to the Western Front, where he was in action at La Fontaine and Croiselles. In October 1917, whilst engaged in severe fighting at Ypres, he was wounded and invalided to England. He was subsequently discharged as medically unfit for further military duties in August 1918, holding the General Service and Victory Medals. 13, Ossory Street, Miles Platting, Manchester. Z8475

VERNON, H., Private, Manchester Regiment.
Mobilised in August 1914, he was sent to Egypt a month later, and served at Alexandria until invalided home in December 1914. On his recovery he was engaged on coast defence duties at Southport and Margate, until August 1915, when he was drafted to France. On this front, he was in action at Loos, Vimy Ridge, the Somme, Messines, Ypres, and Cambrai, and also in the Retreat and Advance of 1918. He was discharged in January 1919, holding the 1914-15 Star, and the General Service and Victory Medals. 90, Cross Street, Bradford, Manchester. Z11255

VERNON, J., Gunner, R.F.A.
Volunteering in September 1914, he was retained on important duties at home until January 1916, when he was drafted to the Western Front. There he did excellent work as a gunner in engagements at Vermelles, Vimy Ridge, the Somme, Arras, Ypres, and Passchendaele, and in the Retreat and Advance of 1918, and was gassed at Passchendaele in November 1917. He was demobilised in February 1919, and holds the General Service and Victory Medals. 115, Earl Street, Longsight, Manchester. Z8476

VERNON, J. F., Gunner, R.F.A.
He volunteered in March 1915, and after serving at various important home stations was drafted overseas in March 1917. During his two years' service on the Western Front he performed good work as a gunner in many engagements, including those at Arras, Ypres, the Somme, Bapaume, and Le Cateau. He remained in France until demobilised in March 1919, and holds the General Service and Victory Medals. 35, Savoy Street, West Gorton, Manchester. Z11256

VERNON, T. S., Bombardier, R.F.A.
He volunteered at the outbreak of war in August 1914, and two months later was ordered to the Western Front. After taking part in many important engagements he was gassed at Bullecourt in May 1917, and sent to hospital in England for three months. On his recovery he was drafted to the Egyptian front, and served in this theatre of war until March 1919, when he returned home and was demobilised, holding the 1914 Star, and the General Service and Victory Medals. 6, Lythgoe Street, Moss Side, Manchester. Z8477B

VESEY, W. T., Corporal, 2/6th Manchester Regt.
A month after war was declared he volunteered and in March 1917 was sent overseas. During his service on the Western Front, he served at La Bassée, Givenchy, Festubert, Nieuport, and Dunkerque. In July 1917, he was severely wounded in action at Nieuport, and in consequence received his discharge from the Army in January 1918. He holds the General Service and Victory Medals. 51, Normanby Street, Moss Side, Manchester. Z8478

VESTY, J., Driver, R.F.A.
Joining in May 1917, he proceeded four months later to the Western Front, where he was in action in various engagements, in different sectors of the war zone. He did good work with his Battery at Cambrai, and also in the 1918 Retreat, and the final Allied Advance. After the Armistice, he entered Germany with the Army of Occupation, and served at Bonn until demobilised in September 1919. He holds the General Service and Victory Medals. 30, Juno Street, Ancoats, Manchester. Z11257

VICKERMAN, A., Private, King's (Liverpool Regt.)
On attaining the age of eighteen he joined the Army in January 1918, but was unsuccessful in obtaining a transfer to the fighting area before the cessation of hostilities. Immediately after the Armistice was declared, however, he proceeded with the Army of Occupation to Germany, and served there until demobilised in May 1919. 3, Belmont Street, Collyhurst, Manchester. Z11258B

VICKERMAN, F., Private, Gloucestershire Regt.
He volunteered in May 1915, and six months later proceeded overseas. During his service on the Western Front he took an active part in severe fighting in the Battles of Loos, Albert, the Somme, Arras, Bullecourt, and Ypres, and was unfortunately killed in action at Messines in June 1917. He was entitled to the 1914-15 Star, and the General Service and Victory Medals.
"Whilst we remember the sacrifice is not in vain."
3, Belmont Street, Collyhurst, Manchester. Z11258A

VICKERS, D., A/Cpl., Manchester Regt. and 2nd Lincolnshire Regt.
He volunteered in June 1915, and in the following December was drafted to the Western Front. There he was in action in many sectors, and was severely wounded in the Battle of the Somme in July 1916. He was invalided to England, and on his discharge from hospital was stationed at Ashton until September 1917, when he was discharged as medically unfit for further service. He holds the 1914-15 Star, and the General Service and Victory Medals. 4, Small Street, Ardwick, Manchester. Z8480

VICKERS, H., Private, 7th Manchester Regiment.
Volunteering in May 1915, he proceeded in December 1915 to Egypt, and after taking part in the Suez Canal engagements was drafted to Gallipoli. There he was in action at Suvla Bay, and was later transferred to the Western Front, where he saw heavy fighting at La Bassée, Givenchy, Nieuport, Ypres, Passchendaele, and the Somme. He was demobilised in January 1919, and holds the General Service and Victory Medals. 34, Wardle Street, Newton, Manchester. Z8482

VICKERS, J. W., Special War Worker.
From the outbreak of war in August 1914, until January 1919, he was engaged on work of National importance at Messrs. Vickers', where he was employed in making guns, and throughout the period of his service carried out his duties with the utmost skill and ability, giving complete satisfaction to his employers. 61, Rylance Street, Ardwick, Manchester. Z8481

VICKERS, W., Private, 2nd Manchester Regiment and R.A.F.
He volunteered in September 1914, and two months later was drafted overseas. During his ten months' service on the Western Front he was in action at Neuve Chapelle, St. Eloi, Hill 60 and Ypres, and was wounded in the Battle of Loos in September 1915. On his discharge from hospital he joined the R.A.F. and was employed on engineering work at Bristol until demobilised in May 1919, holding the 1914 Star, and the General Service and Victory Medals. 21, Chell Street, Longsight, Manchester. Z8479

VINTER, J. W., Corporal, 2nd Sherwood Foresters.
He volunteered in August 1914, and in the following month proceeded to the Western Front. There he took an active part in engagements at Ypres, Neuve Chapelle, Arras, Ypres (III) and Armentières. He also served in the Retreat until June 1918, when owing to shattered nerves he was discharged from the Army as medically unfit for further military duties, holding the 1914 Star, and the General Service and Victory Medals. 36, Rhodes St., Miles Platting, Manchester. TZ9401

VOELLNER, A., Pte., 3rd Loyal N. Lancashire Regt.
He volunteered in February 1915, and on conclusion of his training at Felixstowe, was in the following October drafted to Gibraltar, where he was employed on important garrison duties. In February 1918 he returned to England and for two years rendered valuable services in the Tank Corps at Wareham and Swanage. He was demobilised in February 1920, and holds the General Service and Victory Medals. 53, Beaumont Street, Beswick, Manchester. Z11259

VOELLNER, Walter, Pte., 2/10th Manchester Regt.
Joining in January 1917, he trained at Ripon and Scarborough, and five months later proceeded to the Western Front. There he saw heavy fighting in the Battle of Ypres and in the Passchendaele sector. On the conclusion of hostilities he was sent to Germany with the Army of Occupation, and served on the Rhine until demobilised in March 1920, holding the General Service and Victory Medals. 53, Beaumont Street, Beswick, Manchester. Z11260

VOELLNER, William, Pte., 2/8th Manchester Regt.
He joined the Army in August 1916, and on completion of a period of training at Ripon was sent overseas in May of the following year. He served on the Western Front for over two years, and during that time did good work with his unit in important engagements at Arras, Ypres, Cambrai, the Somme, Amiens, Bapaume, Havrincourt and Le Cateau. He was demobilised in October 1919, and holds the General Service and Victory Medals. 53, Beaumont Street, Beswick, Manchester. Z11261

W

WADDELL, J. A., Private, Labour Corps.
Joining in March 1918, and proceeding to France in the same month, he was present during the severe fighting on the Somme, and in the subsequent Retreat and Advance of 1918. He was invalided home through ill-health, and after receiving hospital treatment was discharged in February 1919, He holds the General Service and Victory Medals.
17, Halton Street, Hulme, Manchester.   Z8487

WADDINGTON, J. H., Private, M.G.C.
He joined in November 1917, and in March of the following year proceeded to the Western Front, where he took part in the severe fighting throughout the Offensives of 1918 until the Armistice. Afterwards he was sent with the Army of Occupation into Germany, and on his return was on duty in Ireland until demobilised in March 1920. He holds the General Service and Victory Medals.
34, Laurence Street, West Gorton, Manchester.   Z11262B

WADDINGTON, J. W., Private, Manchester Regt.
He volunteered in January 1915, and after the completion of his training was retained on important duties with his unit at Grantham, Chatham and other stations. He was not successful in securing his transfer overseas while hostilities continued, but rendered valuable services until his discharge through medical unfitness in February 1916.
34, Laurence Street, West Gorton, Manchester.   Z11262A

WADDINGTON, W., Special War Worker.
Throughout the period of hostilities he was engaged on special transport work in connection with the forwarding of munitions from Manchester on the Cheshire Lines Railway. His valuable and expert services were much appreciated.   TX6809C
10, Cottenham St., Chorlton-on-Medlock, Manchester.

WADE, G. B., Sergt., 1st. Bn. Grenadier Guards.
He volunteered in November 1915, and in the following year was drafted overseas. During his service in France he fought in many notable battles, including those of the Somme and the Offensives of 1918, Arras, and was wounded on four occasions. After the Armistice he was sent with the Army of Occupation into Germany, and after valuable service there returned home for demobilisation in 1919. He holds the General Service and Victory Medals.
11, Eldon Street, Chorlton-on-Medlock, Manchester.   X8488

WADSWORTH, J., Driver, R.F.A.
He joined in February 1916, and after a course of training proceeded to the Western Front, where he took part in much strenuous fighting in the Ypres sector. Shortly afterwards he was sent to Italy, where he saw much valuable service, and later to Egypt, where he was stationed near the Nile. He returned home for demobilisation in December 1919. He holds the General Service and Victory Medals.
103, Sloane Street, Moss Side, Manchester.   Z8489

WAGGETT, W., Private, 21st Manchester Regt.
He volunteered in November 1914, and afterwards was transferred to the Grenadier Guards, In January 1915 he was drafted to France, where he took an active part in many engagements of importance until July 1918, when he was invalided home. After hospital treatment at Withington, he was discharged in October 1918, and holds the 1914-15 Star, and the General Service and Victory Medals.
27, St. John's Road, Longsight, Manchester.   Z8490

WAGSTER, J., Pte., 10th (Prince of Wales' Own Royal) Hussars.
Volunteering in September 1914, he proceeded to France in November. Whilst in this theatre of war he took part in many fierce engagements, including those at Ypres, Festubert, and Loos, and was twice wounded. After receiving treatment at the Base he returned to the Line, but was unhappily killed in action on February 6th, 1916. He was entitled to the 1914-15 Star, and the General Service and Victory Medals.
"Honour to the immortal dead, who gave their youth that the world might grow old in peace."
97, Chester Street, Hulme, Manchester.   TZ8491

WAGSTER, W., Sergt., R.F.A.
Volunteering in August 1914, he crossed to France in the following month, and whilst there saw much heavy fighting at La Bassée, St. Eloi, Ypres, Vermelles, and Albert. In July 1916 he proceeded to Egypt and took part in the Battles of Romani, Magdhaba, Rafa, Gaza, and the capture of Jerusalem. After valuable services in both seats of war, he returned home, and was demobilised in February 1919, holding the 1914 Star, and the General Service and Victory Medals.
3, Beecher Street, Queen's Park, Manchester.   Z11595

WAINWRIGHT, G. B., Pte., 2nd South Lancashire Regiment.
He volunteered in August 1915, and in the following December landed in France. There he took part in many great battles, including those at St. Eloi, Loos, Vimy Ridge, the Somme, Arras, Messines, Ypres, Passchendaele, Cambrai,

and in the Retreat and Advance of 1918. He was wounded on three occasions. In October 1918 he was discharged on account of his injuries, and holds the General Service and Victory Medals.
11, Diggles Street, Ancoats, Manchester.   Z11264

WAINWRIGHT, R., Cpl., 1st South Wales B'ders.
He volunteered in May 1915, and after a course of training served at various stations on guard and other important duties. Owing to ill-health he was not fit for duty in the trenches, but after the Armistice rendered valuable services in the Military Police in Salonika and Turkey until November 1919, when he returned home for demobilisation.
13, Norway Street, Ardwick, Manchester.   Z8492

WAKEFIELD, G., L/Cpl., Royal Irish Fusiliers.
He volunteered in August 1914, and was sent to Ireland for training. Afterwards he proceeded to the Dardanelles and took part in the Battles of Krithia and the Landing at Suvla Bay, where he was unhappily killed in action in August 1915. He was entitled to the 1914-15 Star, and the General Service and Victory Medals.
"He died the noblest death a man may die,
    Fighting for God and right and liberty."
3, Fountain Street, City Road, Hulme, Manchester. Z6150A

WAKEFIELD, J., Private, Lancashire Fusiliers.
Volunteering in April 1915, and proceeding to the Western Front in the following June, he fought at Ypres, the Somme, Arras, Messines and Cambrai, and in the Retreat of 1918 was taken prisoner. He was made to work behind the German lines until the Armistice, and was then repatriated. He was demobilised in January 1919, and holds the 1914-15 Star, and the General Service and Victory Medals.
31, Franciso Street, Collyhurst, Manchester.   Z11265

WAKEFIELD, J., Private, South Lancashire Regt.
Volunteering in September 1914, he was drafted in the following year to the Western Front. He was in action at Neuve Chapelle, Festubert, Givenchy, Loos, the Somme, Kemmel, Ploegsteert Wood, Hébuterne and Grandicourt. In November 1916 he was invalided home and transferred to the R.A.S.C. and in December 1917 returned to France and was present during the Allied Retreat and Advance of 1918. Demobilised in April 1919, he holds the 1914-15 Star, and the General Service and Victory Medals.
39, Hendham Vale, Collyhurst, Manchester.   Z11596

WAKES, J. A., Gunner, R.F.A.
He volunteered in September 1914, and in the following year proceeded to the Dardanelles, where he took part in the Landing at Suvla Bay. He was afterwards drafted to Mesopotamia and was in action at Kut and Baghdad and in many other engagements until hostilities ceased, and whilst in the theatre of war was wounded three times. Returning home he was demobilised in April 1919, and holds the 1914-15 Star, and the General Service and Victory Medals.
56, Ravald Street, Miles Platting, Manchester.   Z9738

WAKES, W. H., Private, 9th Lancashire Fusiliers.
Volunteering in August 1914, he was drafted in the following year to the Dardanelles and took part in the Landing at Suvla Bay and other operations in the Gallipoli campaign. Afterwards he proceeded to Egypt and was on duty at Kantara and in the Suez Canal zone. In July 1916 he was sent to France and fought at Arras, Ypres, Passchendaele, Lens, Cambrai and the Somme, where he was wounded in March 1918. After receiving hospital treatment he was subsequently demobilised in February 1919, and holds the 1914-15 Star, and the General Service and Victory Medals.
171, Montague Street, Collyhurst, Manchester.   Z8851

WALKER, A., Driver, R.A.S.C.
He volunteered in May 1915, and in August of the same year, after completing his training, was drafted to Salonika. He was engaged on important transport duties on the Doiran, Struma and Vardar fronts, and did valuable work there until hostilities ceased. He returned home, and was demobilised in April 1919, holding the 1914-15 Star, and the General Service and Victory Medals.
99, Montague Street, Collyhurst, Manchester.   Z11274

WALKER, A., Private, 2nd Manchester Regiment.
He joined in February 1919, and after a period of training was sent to Ireland, where he was engaged on important guard and other duties. In January 1920 he was drafted to Mesopotamia and took part in much fighting there until July 24th, 1920, when he was reported missing.
"His memory is cherished with pride."
43, Royal Street, Ardwick, Manchester.   TZ8495B

WALKER, A. (Mrs.), Special War Worker.
This lady volunteered in April 1915, and for five years was engaged on important duties as cook at Levenshulme Auxiliary Military Hospital, Manchester. She was awarded the British Red Cross and the Brook House Hospital Medals for her valuable services, and continued her splendid work until April 1920.
3, Coach Terrace, Gorton, Manchester.   TZ8497A

WALKER, Annie M., Worker, W.A.A.C.
She volunteered for service in the W.A.A.C. in September 1918, and from that date until January 1919 was engaged on important store-keeping and clerical duties with her unit at Chadderton. She discharged her responsible duties throughout with great efficiency.
167, Victoria Square, Ancoats, Manchester. Z8852

WALKER, A. T., Private, 12th Manchester Regt.
He joined in June 1916, and in the following October was drafted to the Western Front. There he took part in many important engagements, including those at Messines Ridge, Ypres, High Wood and the Offensives of 1918. After returning home in February 1919 he was demobilised, and holds the General Service and Victory Medals.
139, Morton Street, Longsight, Manchester. Z8503

WALKER, C., Private, 21st Manchester Regiment.
He joined in May 1916, and in January of the following year proceeded to the Western Front. During the heavy fighting at Bullecourt he was badly wounded, and after being invalided home and receiving hospital treatment, was discharged as medically unfit for further duty in April 1918. He holds the General Service and Victory Medals.
6, Laurence Street, West Gorton, Manchester. Z11267

WALKER, C. H., Private, Royal Welch Fusiliers.
He volunteered in October 1914, and after completing his training was retained at Bedford, Southwold and other stations on coast guard, police and other important duties. He was not successful in obtaining his transfer overseas before hostilities ceased, but rendered valuable services until demobilised in October 1919.
3, Coach Terrace, Gorton, Manchester. TZ8497B

WALKER, E., Private, Manchester Regiment.
He had previously served with the Colours, and in June 1916 rejoined. He embarked for France in the following August, and whilst there took part in many engagements, including those on the Somme, at Arras, Messines, Ypres and the Lys where he was wounded and taken prisoner in April 1918. He was sent to Germany and worked in the salt mines until the Armistice, when he was repatriated. He returned home and was demobilised in December 1918, and holds the Queen's South African and the General Service and Victory Medals.
13, Elliott Street, Bradford, Manchester. Z11270

WALKER, F., Sergt., K.O. (Royal Lancaster Regt.)
Volunteering in September 1914, he crossed to France in the following December and fought at Neuve Chapelle, Ypres, Festubert and the Somme. He was also in action in many other engagements, including those at Arras, Cambrai, Amiens, Bapaume, and was unhappily killed in action in the second Battle at Le Cateau in October 1918. He was entitled to the 1914-15 Star, and the General Service and Victory Medals.
"His life for his Country, his soul to God."
1, Argyll Street, Marple Street, Hulme, Manchester. Z8509

WALKER, F., Corporal, 8th Manchester Regiment.
He volunteered in May 1915, and in April of the following year proceeded to Egypt and saw much service in the Suez Canal zone. In April 1917 he was drafted to the Western Front and was in action on the Somme and at Ypres, and in March 1918 was wounded and sent into hospital. Demobilised in March 1919, he holds the General Service and Victory Medals. 43, Royal Street, Ardwick, Manchester. TZ8495A

WALKER, F., Rifleman, 2nd Rifle Brigade.
Volunteering in June 1915, he sailed for France in the following October, and was in action at Loos and on the Somme, where in July 1916 he was taken prisoner. He was held in captivity until November 1918, and was then released and subsequently demobilised, holding the 1914-15 Star, and the General Service and Victory Medals. Later he joined the Navy in May 1919, and in 1921 was serving on board H.M.S. "Sidouyx." 29, Alder St., Hulme, Manchester. TZ8493

WALKER, G., Private, 8th Manchester Regiment.
He volunteered in December 1914, and in the following November proceeded overseas. Whilst in France he fought in many notable battles, including those of Loos, the Somme, Arras, Ypres, Cambrai and St. Quentin, where he was wounded in August 1918. Demobilised in February 1919, he holds the 1914-15 Star, and the General Service and Victory Medals.
91, Thomas Street, Miles Platting, Manchester. Z8504

WALKER, G., Private, 6th Royal Irish Fusiliers.
A Reservist, he was mobilised in August 1914, and in the following year was drafted to the Dardanelles and took part in the first Landing on the Peninsula. He was in action at Krithia and later gave his life for the freedom of England at Suvla Bay on August 17th, 1915. He was entitled to the 1914-15 Star, and the General Service and Victory Medals.
"A costly sacrifice upon the altar of freedom."
4, Grantham Street, West Gorton, Manchester. Z11268

WALKER, G., Private, Highland Light Infantry.
He had previously served in India, and in the South African campaign, and on the outbreak of hostilities voluntarily re-enlisted. He was engaged on guard and various other important duties and rendered valuable services until March 1916, when he was discharged as medically unfit. He holds the Indian General Service and the Queen's and King's South African Medals.
19, Ogden Street, Hulme, Manchester. TZ8494

WALKER, J., Sergeant, K.R.R.C.
He volunteered in November 1914, and in the following December crossed to France, and was in action at Neuve Chapelle, Hill 60, Ypres and Festubert. Later he was invalided home through shell-shock, and after receiving hospital treatment was discharged as medically unfit in April 1916. He holds the 1914-15 Star, and the General Service and Victory Medals.
29, Hora Street, Bradford, Manchester. Z11273

WALKER, J., Private, Loyal N. Lancashire Regt.
He volunteered in August 1914, and in June of the following year was drafted to Gallipoli. Here he was in action at Krithia, Anzac and the Landing at Suvla Bay. In 1916 he was sent to Mesopotamia, and served with the Kut Relief Force, at Baghdad, Tekrit, Mosul and in other important engagements. He was demobilised in 1919, and holds the 1914-15 Star, and the General Service and Victory Medals.
12, Renshaw Street, West Gorton, Manchester. Z8501A

WALKER, J., Private, South Lancashire Regiment.
Volunteering in April 1915, he was retained in England on duties in connection with the output of munitions until April 1917. He then proceeded to France, where after four months' active service he was killed in action on July 21st. He was entitled to the General Service and Victory Medals.
"His memory is cherished with pride."
3, Rockingham Street, Collyhurst, Manchester. Z11275

WALKER, J., Private, 7th Manchester Regiment.
He joined in October 1916, and in November of the following year landed in France, and served for a time at the Base. Later he took part in the fighting, and was wounded at Gommecourt in March 1918, and invalided home. After receiving hospital treatment he was discharged as medically unfit in March 1919, and holds the General Service and Victory Medals.
1, Swallows Place, Ancoats, Manchester. Z11271

WALKER, J., Private, East Lancashire Regiment.
He volunteered in February 1915, and in the following July embarked for France, where he saw much fighting. He took part in engagements at Vimy Ridge, the Somme, Beaucourt, and Arras, and was unfortunately killed in action in April 1917. He was entitled to the 1914-15 Star, and the General Service and Victory Medals.
"His life for his Country, his soul to God."
64, Barrack Street, Hulme, Manchester. Z8506

WALKER, J., Private, M.G.C.
He volunteered in October 1915, and in November of the same year embarked for the Western Front. Here he was in action at Loos and the Somme, where he was gassed and invalided home. On recovery he returned to the trenches and fought at Arras, Cambrai, the Lys, the Scarpe, and many other engagements. Demobilised in January 1919, he holds the 1914-15 Star, and the General Service and Victory Medals.
8, Major Street, Ardwick, Manchester. Z8500

WALKER, J., L/Sergt., 15th Royal Scots.
He volunteered in September 1914, and for a time was retained in England on duties of an important nature. In January 1916 he landed in France, and was in action on the Somme and at Ypres, but in April 1917 was unfortunately wounded and taken prisoner. He was held in captivity until after the Armistice, and was then released and finally demobilised in March 1919, holding the General Service and Victory Medals.
22, Marsland Street, Ardwick, Manchester. Z8499

WALKER, J. D., Private, Cheshire Regiment.
He joined in January 1917, and in the following October was drafted to Gibraltar, where he served on important garrison duties throughout. Returning home in February 1919, he was demobilised, and holds the General Service Medal.
9, Spring Street, Chorlton-on-Medlock, Manchester. Z11266

WALKER, M., Private, Manchester Regiment.
He volunteered in August 1915, and after a course of training served at various stations on important duties with his unit. He was not successful in obtaining his transfer overseas before hostilities ended, but rendered valuable services until demobilised in March 1919.
41, Francisco Street, Collyhurst, Manchester. Z9739

WALKER, P., L/Cpl., 2/5th Manchester Regiment, and Sherwood Foresters.
Joining in August 1916, he landed in France the same year, and was in action at Vimy Ridge and the Somme, and was wounded and invalided home. On recovery he returned to the trenches, and was again wounded and taken prisoner, being held in captivity until March 1919, when he was repatriated and demobilised. He holds the General Service and Victory Medals. Z8496
15, Whittaker Street, Chorlton-on-Medlock, Manchester.

WALKER. P., Pte.,20th Hussars,and 1st Suffolk Rgt.
He volunteered in August 1914, and in March of the following year was sent to France, and took part in the fighting at Hill 60, Ypres and Loos. He was then transferred to Salonika, where he was in action on the Vardar, Struma and Doiran fronts, and in the capture of Monastir. He was demobilised in October 1919, and holds the 1914–15 Star, and the General Service and Victory Medals.
6, Middlewood Street, Harpurhey, Manchester.   Z11512B

WALKER, R., Private, Durham Light Infantry.
He joined in March 1917, and later in the same year was drafted to France, and was in action on the Somme, and at Vermelles and Ypres. Returning home after the cessation of hostilities he was demobilised in September 1919, and holds the General Service and Victory Medals.
50, William Street, West Gorton, Manchester.   Z8498

WALKER, T., Corporal, 8th Manchester Regiment, and A.B., Royal Navy.
He was serving at the outbreak of war, and in May 1915 was sent to Gallipoli, and took part in the Battles of Krithia and the Landing at Suvla Bay. He remained in this area till the Evacuation, after which he returned to England and was discharged in April 1916, as time expired. Immediately afterwards, however, he joined the Royal Navy and served in H.M.S. "Adventurer." He was engaged in H.M.S. "Hyacinth" on patrol off the Coast of East Africa, and in the Mediterranean, and later in the North Sea. He was demobilised in April 1919, and holds the 1914–15 Star, and the General Service and Victory Medals.
17, Durham Place, Hulme, Manchester.   Z8505

WALKER, T., Private, Royal Inniskilling Fusiliers.
He joined in July 1917, and in May of the following year was sent to France, where he took part in the Retreat and Advance of 1918. He was killed in action at Bailleul near Ypres on August 31st, 1918, and was entitled to the General Service and Victory Medals.
"He joined the great white company of valiant souls."
1, Handel Street, Miles Platting, Manchester.   Z9421

WALKER, T., L/Corporal, 12th Manchester Regt.
He volunteered in January 1915, and was sent to France in the following year. He was in action at Beaumont-Hamel and Beaucourt, and was taken prisoner on the Ancre front in March 1917. During his captivity he was employed behind the German lines in conveying ammunition to the front. After the Armistice he was released, and returning home was demobilised in March 1919, holding the General Service and Victory Medals.
17, Moor Street, Windsor Road, Rusholme, Manchester. Z8508

WALKER, T. A., Private, Connaught Rangers.
He was serving at the outbreak of war, and was immediately afterwards sent to France. He was in action at Mons, and was taken prisoner during the Retreat and was sent to Germany. He was released after the Armistice, and discharged in September 1919, holding the Mons Star, and the General Service and Victory Medals.
30, Gibson Street, Ardwick, Manchester.   Z8507

WALKER, W., Private, Lancashire Fusiliers.
He joined in May 1917, and after his training was engaged at various stations on important duties with his unit. He rendered valuable services, but was not successful in obtaining his transfer overseas. Later, owing to ill-health he was discharged in October 1918.
12, Renshaw Street, West Gorton, Manchester.   Z8501B

WALKER, W., Private, M.G.C.
He volunteered in October 1914, and served for a time on special duties in England, proceeding to the Western Front in 1916. Whilst there he fought in many notable battles, including those on the Somme, and at Ypres, where he was gassed. After receiving treatment at the Base he returned to the trenches and took part in fighting in the Retreat and Advance of 1918. Demobilised in January 1919, he holds the General Service and Victory Medals.
8, Juliet Street, Ardwick, Manchester.   Z11798B

WALKER, W., Pte., 4th Border Regt., and Spr., R.E.
He joined in March 1917, on attaining military age, and in the following year embarked for France. There he took part in the fighting in many sectors of the Front until the Armistice, returning home for demobilisation in December 1919. He holds the General Service and Victory Medals.
27, Lord Street, Openshaw, Manchester.   Z8502

WALKER, W., Private, Border Regiment.
A Reservist, he was mobilised on the declaration of war, and proceeded with the original Expeditionary Force to France, and fought in the Retreat from Mons, and in the Battles of the Marne and Aisne. He was also in action in many other engagements, and was wounded at Cambrai in 1917. On recovery he served with the Military Police until hostilities ceased. Returning home he was demobilised in January 1919, holding the Mons Star, and the General Service and Victory Medals.
13, Elliott Street, Bradford, Manchester.   Z11272

WALKER, W. H., Sapper, R.E.
Joining in September 1917, he served after a course of training, at various stations on important engineering work. Owing to medical unfitness he was not successful in obtaining his transfer overseas, and was discharged in February 1918, after rendering valuable services.
12, Renshaw Street, West Gorton, Manchester.   Z8501C

WALKLETT, E., Private, Tank Corps.
He was mobilised in August 1914, and in March of the following year was drafted to France, where he was in action at Hill 60, Loos, the Somme and Bullecourt. During the latter part of the war he was engaged on repair work at Treport, and rendered excellent services. He was demobilised in March 1919, and holds the 1914–15 Star, and the General Service and Victory Medals.
112, Edensor Street, Beswick, Manchester.   Z11276

WALL, G. T., Private, Royal Irish Fusiliers.
He was mobilised in August 1914, and immediately afterwards was sent to France, where he was in action in the Retreat from Mons, the Battles of Le Cateau, Ypres, Neuve Chapelle, Loos, Albert, the Somme, Beaumont-Hamel, Arras and Cambrai. He was taken prisoner during the Retreat on the Somme in 1918, and was held in captivity until the cessation of hostilities. On his release he returned home, and was demobilised in August 1919, holding the Mons Star, and the General Service and Victory Medals.
14, Matlock Place, Hulme, Manchester.   Z8510

WALL, J., Sergt., R.A.S.C. (M.T.)
He volunteered in April 1915, and after completing his training was engaged at various stations on important duties with his unit. He rendered valuable services but was not successful in obtaining his transfer overseas before the cessation of hostilities, and was demobilised in January 1919.
6, Rocester Street, Harpurhey, Manchester.   Z11597

WALL, J. N., Pte., 8th Loyal N. Lancashire Regt.
He volunteered in August 1914, and in the following year was drafted to France, where he was in action at Loos, St. Eloi, Albert and Vimy Ridge. He unfortunately died from gas poisoning, having been badly gassed during a trench raid on June 27th, 1916. He was entitled to the 1914–15 Star, and the General Service and Victory Medals.
"Whilst we remember the sacrifice is not in vain."
11, Lingard Street, Hulme, Manchester.   TZ8514

WALL, L., Driver, R.A.S.C.
Volunteering in November 1914, he was sent to France in March of the following year. He was engaged on important transport duties at Ypres, St. Quentin, La Bassée, Albert and Cambrai. After the Armistice he proceeded with the Army of Occupation to Germany, and served at various stations on the Rhine. He was demobilised in April 1919, and holds the 1914–15 Star, and the General Service and Victory Medals.
1, Thompson Street, Hulme, Manchester.   Z8511

WALL, T., Private, Border Regiment.
He volunteered in September 1914, and was drafted to Gallipoli in the following April. He was in action in the Landing at Cape Helles, the three Battles of Krithia, and was wounded and sent to hospital at Alexandria. He shortly afterwards returned to Gallipoli, and was engaged in heavy fighting at the Landing at Suvla Bay, and in the Capture of Chunuk Bair. In 1916 he proceeded to France, where he became seriously ill and was invalided home. On his recovery, he returned to the Western Front, and was in action at the Ancre, Arras and Ypres. He was again wounded and sent to the Base, and was in hospital at Boulogne. He later returned to the front line and took part in the fighting at the Marne and Amiens. and in many other engagements during the Retreat and Advance of 1918. He was demobilised in December 1918, and holds the 1914–15 Star, and the General Service and Victory Medals.
73, Edensor Street, Beswick, Manchester.   Z8512

WALL, W, H., Private, 1st East Yorkshire Regt.
Volunteering in September 1914, he was sent to France in July of the following year, and took part in numerous engagements on the Ypres front. He was unfortunately killed whilst on outpost duty on November 15th, 1915. He was entitled to the 1914–15 Star, and the General Service and Victory Medals.
"His life for his Country."
22A, Clarence Street, Hulme, Manchester.   TZ8513

WALLACE, J., Gunner, R.G.A.
Joining in June 1917, he was sent to France later in the same year. He fought in many engagements, including those at Ypres, Cambrai, the Somme, Amiens, Bapaume, Havrincourt, Le Cateau, and was gassed. He was demobilised in January 1919, and holds the General Service and Victory Medals.
13, Alfred Street, Collyhurst, Manchester.   Z8853

WALLEY, J., Private, K.O. (R. Lancaster Regt.)
He was mobilised in August 1914, and was sent to France in the same month. He fought in the Retreat from Mons, and was wounded. On recovery rejoining his unit he was engaged in heavy fighting in many sectors, and was taken prisoner at Ypres in May 1915. He was held in captivity until the close of hostilities, and was then repatriated. Later he served with the Army of Occupation on the Rhine. He was demobilised in February 1920, and holds the Mons Star, and the General Service and Victory Medals.
27, Nelson Street, Rusholme, Manchester.   Z8515

WALLEY, N., Private, 2nd Manchester Regiment.
Volunteering in August 1914, he was sent to France in November of the same year, and was in action at La Bassée, Ypres and St. Eloi. In March 1916, transferred to Salonika, he was engaged in heavy fighting in many parts of the line. Contracting malaria he was invalided home in November 1918, and after receiving hospital treatment was demobilised in May 1919. He holds the 1914 Star, and the General Service and Victory Medals.
18, Union Street, Rusholme, Manchester.   Z8516

WALLWORK, H., Private, Sherwood Foresters.
He volunteered in May 1915, and in the following September was drafted to the Western Front. He fought in the Battles of St. Eloi, Vimy Ridge, the Somme, Arras, Bullecourt, Ypres, Cambrai, and the Marne. He was reported missing at Cambrai in April 1918, and later was presumed to have been killed in action. He was entitled to the 1914-15 Star, and the General Service and Victory Medals.
" His memory is cherished with pride."
1, Brief Street, Ancoats, Manchester.   TZ9740

WALLWORK, T., Driver, R.F.A.
Volunteering in September 1914, he was drafted to the Western Front in August of the following year, and was in action at Loos, Albert, Ploegsteert Wood, and the Somme. He also fought at Beaucourt, and was wounded at Ypres in November 1917. He was engaged in heavy fighting throughout the Retreat and Advance of 1918, and returning home after the Armistice was demobilised in February 1919. He holds the 1914-15 Star, and the General Service and Victory Medals.
20, Jack Street, Ardwick, Manchester.   Z8517

WALMSLEY, F. E. M., Pte., King's Own (Royal Lancaster Regiment).
He joined in July 1916, and later in the same year was sent to France, where he fought in the Battles of the Somme Vimy Ridge, Arras, Bapaume, Ypres, Lens and Mericourt. He was wounded at Ypres in 1917, and on recovery rejoined his unit and was in action in many parts of the line. He was unfortunately killed in action during heavy fighting. He was entitled to the General Service and Victory Medals.
" A costly sacrifice upon the altar of freedom."
73, Thornton Street, Manchester.   Z11279B

WALMSLEY, G. A., Private, Lancashire Fusiliers.
Joining in June 1916, he was sent to France later in the same year, and was in action on the Somme, at Albert, Arras, Beaumont-Hamel, Ypres and Cambrai. He also fought in many engagements during the German Offensive and subsequent Allied Advance of 1918, and was wounded. He was demobilised in 1919, and holds the General Service and Victory Medals.
73, Thornton Street, Manchester.   Z11279A

WALPOLE, J. G., Sergt., 1st Royal Scots.
He volunteered in September 1914, and in the following month was drafted to the Western Front. He took part in numerous engagements, including the Battles of La Bassée, Ypres, Neuve Chapelle, Loos, St. Eloi, Albert, the Somme, Arras, Messines and Cambrai. He also served in the Retreat of 1918, and was wounded, and taken prisoner in March 1918. He was repatriated after the Armistice, and was demobilised in March 1919, holding the 1914 Star, and the General Service and Victory Medals.
18, Gatley Street, Ancoats, Manchester.   Z8519

WALPOLE, J. J., Pte., 7th South Lancashire Regt.
Volunteering in April 1915, he was sent to France in July of the following year, and was in action at Arras, Beaumont-Hamel and Messines. He was wounded and invalided home in June 1917, and after receiving hospital treatment served at various stations until demobilised in May 1919, and holds the General Service and Victory Medals.
36, Gatley Street, Ancoats, Manchester.   Z8518

WALSH. A., Private, King's (Liverpool Regiment).
He volunteered in October 1915, and was engaged with his unit at various stations on important duties until June 1917, when he was sent to the Western Front. He served in many parts of the line and was invalided home in October 1918, owing to heart trouble. After receiving hospital treatment he was discharged unfit for further service in the following month. He holds the General Service and Victory Medals.
70, Princess Street, Rusholme, Manchester.   Z8523

WALSH, B., Private, 4th Manchester Regiment.
He volunteered in November 1914, and early in the following year, drafted to France, was in action at La Bassée. He was wounded at Hill 60, and invalided home for treatment. On

his recovery he proceeded to Gallipoli, and took part in the Landing at Suvla Bay, and the fighting at Chocolate Hill, and owing to ill-health returned to England. In June 1916 he returned to France, and was engaged on the Somme, at Ypres and Cambrai, and was twice wounded. He returned home and after a period in hospital, was invalided out of the Service in October 1918. He holds the 1914-15 Star, and the General Service and Victory Medals.
17, Matlock, Street, Ardwick, Manchester.   Z8521

WALSH, C., Private, 8th Royal Dublin Fusiliers.
He volunteered in March 1915, and later in the same year embarked for the Western Front. He was in action at Loos, Albert, the Somme, Arras, Ypres and Cambrai, and was twice wounded. He was killed in action on the Somme on March 21st, 1918, during the opening phases of the German Offensive. He was entitled to the 1914-15 Star, and the General Service and Victory Medals.
" He died the noblest death a man may die,
Fighting for God, and right, and liberty."
18, Adelaide Street, Hulme, Manchester.   Z8525

WALSH, F., Private, Welch Regiment.
Volunteering in August 1914, he was sent to France in October of the same year. He was engaged in heavy fighting at La Bassée, Armentières, Ypres, Hill 60, Vermelles, St. Eloi, Albert, Vimy Ridge, Arras, the Scarpe, Bullecourt and Messines, and was wounded at St. Eloi in 1915. In 1917 he proceeded to Egypt, and was in action at Siwa and was then sent to Palestine. He was engaged at Gaza, Jerusalem, the capture of Jericho and Tripoli. He was demobilised in September 1919, and holds the 1914 Star, and the General Service and Victory Medals.
63, Burton Street, Rochdale Road, Manchester.   Z11286

WALSH, H. J., Private, 8th Manchester Regiment.
He volunteered in August 1914, and in January of the following year was sent to France, where he was in action in the Battles of Neuve Chapelle, Ypres and was wounded at Loos. Invalided home, he received hospital treatment, and in 1916 returning to France was in action at Beaucourt, Vimy Ridge, Ypres, Cambrai, and the Somme. He also served in the Retreat and Advance of 1918, and was again wounded. He was demobilised in February 1919, and holds the 1914-15 Star, and the General Service and Victory Medals.
7, Phœnix Street, Hulme, Manchester.   Z8524

WALSH, J., Private, 1st Manchester Regiment.
Volunteering in August 1914, he landed in France in the following month, and fought in the Retreat from Mons. He was also in action in the Battles of the Marne, La Bassée, Ypres and St. Eloi. He was killed in action near Hill 60 on April 10th, 1915. He was entitled to the Mons Star, and the the General Service and Victory Medals.
" The path of duty was the way to glory."
5, Oak Street, Hulme, Manchester.   Z11845

WALSH, J., Private, 2nd Manchester Regiment.
He enlisted in February 1908, and in August 1914, was sent to France. He was in action in the Battles of the Marne, La Bassée, Ypres, Hill 60, Festubert, Albert, the Somme, Arras, Bullecourt, Passchendaele and Bapaume. He was wounded at Wulveringham in December 1914, and at Ypres in May 1915. He was discharged as medically unfit for further service in November 1918, and holds the 1914 Star, and the General Service and Victory Medals.
18, Edge Street, Hulme, Manchester.   TZ8522

WALSH, J., Corporal, R.A.F.
He volunteered in October 1915, and in the following June was drafted to the Western Front. He fought in many engagements, including the Battles of Albert, the Somme, Arras, Ypres, Cambrai, and was gassed. He also was in action throughout the Retreat and Advance of 1918. He was demobilised in November 1919, and holds the General Service and Victory Medals.
1, Bright Street, Rochdale Road, Manchester.   Z9741

WALSH, J., Private, 2nd South Lancashire Regt.
Volunteering in August 1914, he was sent to France in April of the following year, and was in action at Ypres, Loos, the Somme, Arras and Cambrai. He also served throughout the Retreat and Advance of 1918, and was wounded. After the Armistice he proceeded with the Army of Occupation to Germany, and served at various stations. He was demobilised in February 1919, and holds the 1914-15 Star, and the General Service and Victory Medals.
49, Lostock Street, Miles Platting, Manchester.   Z8854A

WALSH, J. F., Private, 42nd Manchester Regt.
He volunteered in November 1914, and was drafted to France in December of the following year. He took part in the fighting on the Somme, the Ancre, at Ypres, Cambrai, and the Marne, and was engaged in heavy fighting throughout the Retreat and Advance of 1918. He was demobilised in June 1919, and holds the 1914-15 Star and the General Service and Victory Medals.
34, Stockton Street, Chorlton-on-Medlock, Manchester.   Z8529

WALSH, J. F., Private, 2nd Manchester Regt.
Having previously served for twenty-one years in Africa, India, China and other parts, he again volunteered in August 1914, and in the following September was sent to the Western Front. He was in action at La Bassée, Ypres, and was wounded and invalided home in February 1915. On his recovery, proceeding to Gallipoli, he took part in the Landing at Suvla Bay, the Battles of Krithia, and remained in this area until the Evacuation. In February 1916, he was transferred to Egypt, where he served on important duties at various stations. In July of the same year he returned to France, and fought on the Somme, at Arras, Bullecourt, Passchendaele, and was again wounded. He was sent home, and after receiving hospital treatment was discharged in March 1918, holding the South African Medal, the 1914 Star, and the General Service and Victory Medals.
5, Earl Street, Hulme, Manchester. TZ8528

WALSH, J. R., Special War Worker.
He offered his services for work of National importance, and was engaged at Messrs. Vickers, Miles Platting, Manchester, from the outbreak of war until the Armistice, employed as boiler-man in the chemical department. He carried out his work in a most commendable manner, rendering valuable services throughout.
117, Thomas Street, Miles Platting, Manchester. Z8526

WALSH, J. T., Private, 1st King's (Liverpool Regt.)
He volunteered in September 1914, and was drafted to Egypt in the following April. He was in action on the Western Desert, at Mersa Matruh and Sollum, and at Maghdaba in the Sinai Peninsula. He was sent to Cairo, where he was engaged on guard and other important duties till June 1919, when he returned home and was demobilised. He holds the 1914-15 Star, and the General Service and Victory Medals.
3, Thorn Street, Bradford, Manchester. Z11285

WALSH, J. W., Driver, R.H.A.
He was mobilised in August 1914, and shortly afterwards was sent to France. He fought in the Retreat from Mons, the Battles of Le Cateau, the Marne, La Bassée, Ypres, Festubert, Loos, the Somme, Beaumont-Hamel and Beaucourt. He was demobilised in 1919, and holds the Mons Star, and the General Service and Victory Medals.
39, Boardman Street, Harpurhey, Manchester. Z11280

WALSH, L., Sapper, R.E.
He joined in October 1917, and afrer his training was engaged at various stations on important duties with his unit. He rendered valuable services, but was not successful in obtaining his transfer overseas before the cessation of hostilities. He was demobilised in October 1919.
71, Buiton Street, Rochdale Road, Manchester. Z11283

WALSH, R., Private, 9th Manchester Regiment.
He volunteered in November 1914, and in December of the following year was sent to France. He was in action on the Somme, and at Bray and Carnoy. He was wounded and invalided home, and after receiving hospital treatment was transferred to the Lincolnshire Regiment. He was discharged as unfit for further service in August 1917, and holds the 1914-15 Star, and the General Service and Victory Medals.
9, Fielden Street, Oldham Road, Manchester. Z8855

WALSH, W., Private, Loyal N. Lancashire Regt.
Volunteering in September 1914, he was sent to the Dardanelles in August of the following year. He took part in the Landing at Suvla Bay, the Battle of Chunuk Bair, and remained in this area till the Evacuation, and was then drafted to Egypt. In April 1916 he proceeded to France, and was in action at Ploegsteert Wood, the Somme, and Messines. He was invalided home in February 1918, and on his recovery, transferred to the R.A.M.C. He served at vaiious stations until demobilised in June 1919. He holds the 1914-15 Star, and the General Service and Victory Medals.
49, Lostock Street, Miles Platting, Manchester. Z8854B

WALSH, W., Private, Lancashire Fus., and Spr., R.E.
He volunteered in September 1914, and was engaged with his unit on important duties until March 1917, when he was sent to the Western Front. He was in action in the Battles of Arras, and was wounded at Ypres. He was invalided home, and after a period in hospital was discharged as unfit for further service in December 1917. He holds the General Service and Victory Medals.
7, Caulman Street, Rochdale Road, Manchester. Z11281

WALSH, W., Private, 9th Border Regiment.
He volunteered in November 1914, and in the following year landed in France. He was in action on the Somme, at Ypres, La Bassée and Lens. In 1917 he was transferred to Salonika, where he was engaged in heavy fighting on the Doiran and Struma fronts, and took part in the final Allied Advance in the Balkans. He was demobilised in February 1919, and holds the 1914-15 Star, and the General Service and Victory Medals.
7, Caulman Street, Rochdale Road, Manchester. Z11284

WALSH, W., Private, 8th Manchester Regiment.
Volunteering in January 1915, he went through a course of training, and was stationed at various depôts with his unit on guard and other important duties. He rendered valuable services, but was not successful in obtaining his transfer overseas before the cessation of hostilities. He was demobilised in November 1919.
20, Hope Street, Hulme, Manchester. Z8527

WALSH, W.. Private, R.A.S.C.
Joining in April 1916, he completed his training, and served at various military centres on transport and other duties of an important nature. He was not successful in obtaining his transfer to a theatre of war, but rendered excellent services until demobilised in September 1919.
12, Bakewell Street, Ardwick, Manchester. Z8520

WALTERS, G., Private, 11th Essex Regiment.
Joining in March 1917, he was drafted to the Western Front in the following January, and whilst engaged in heavy fighting in the Ypres salient, was gassed. He returned to England, and after receiving hospital treatment served at various stations until demobilised in January 1919. He holds the General Service and Victroy Medals.
48, Reather Street, Miles Platting, Manchester. Z8856

WALTOCK, G. A., Corporal, 8th Manchester Regt.
He joined in 1916, and in the following year was sent to France, where he was in action in many parts of the line, including the Bapaume and Cambrai sectors. Wounded, he returned to England for treatment, and on his recovery served at the Whitworth Institute, on the Recruiting Staff until demobilised in 1919. He holds the General Service ana Victory Medals.
46, Greville Street, Rusholme, Manchester. Z4696B

WALTON, A., Private, Tank Corps.
He joined in June 1917, and landing in France twelve months later was engaged on important repair work in various parts of the line, including the Arras sector. He saw much service during the Allied Advance, and returning home after the close of hostilities was demobilised in December 1919. He holds the General Service and Victory Medals.
33, Zinc Street, Rochdale Road, Manchester. Z11291

WALTON, G., Sapper, R.E.
Volunteering at the commencemeut of hostilities, he embarked for the Western Front in December 1914, and was in action at Ypres, Hill 60, Festubert and Loos. Transferred to Italy in January 1916, he was engaged in heavy fighting on the Piave and the Asiago Plateau, and served throughout the Allied Advance of 1918 in this theatre of war. He was demobilised in March 1919, and holds the 1914-15 Star, and the General Service and Victory Medals.
12, Palmerston Street, Moss Side, Manchester. TZ8531

WALTON, H., Private, King's (Liverpool Regt.)
Volunteering in December 1914, he completed his training, and served at various stations on important duties with his unit. In November 1916, he was released from military service, and was engaged as a turner at an iron works, and rendered excellent services. Later he became seriously ill, and unfortunately died on July 10th, 1918.
"His memory is cherished with pride."
73, Harold Street, Bradford, Manchester. Z8530

WALTON, H., Private, Manchester Regiment.
Volunteering in September 1914, in the following August he proceeded to the Dardanelles, and was in action in the Landing at Suvla Bay, and in many other engagements until the Evacuation of the Peninsula. Later, drafted to France, he fought at Arras, Bullecourt and Messines, and in June 1917 was sent home and transferred to the Reserve, Class W. Until April 1919, he was employed at the Rolls Royce Works, as a grinder on the manufacture of the component parts of aircraft. He holds the 1914-15 Star, and the General Service and Victory Medals.
20, Hardy Street, West Gorton, Manchester. TZ8533

WALTON, J., Private, King's (Liverpool Regiment).
He joined in April 1918, and completing his training was stationed at various military centres on important duties. He was not successful in obtaining his transfer overseas prior to the close of the war, but in February 1919, was sent with the Army of Occupation to Germany. Returning home he was demobilised in February 1920.
42, Beaumont Street, Beswick, Manchester. Z11290

WALTON, J., Sergt., 20th Manchester Regiment.
Volunteering in November 1914, he was sent to France in the following year, and fought in the Battles of Ypres, Hill 60, Festubert, St. Eloi and the Somme. Transferred to Italy in 1916, he was engaged in heavy fighting in various sectors, and returned to the Western Front, later in 1917. He served in many engagements during the German and Allied Offensives of 1918, and during his service overseas was once wounded. He was killed in action on October 4th, 1918, and was entitled to the 1914-15 Star, and the General Service and Victory Medals.
"A valiant Soldier, with undaunted heart he breasted life's last hill."
15, Marshall Street, New Cross, Manchester. Z11598

WALTON, J., Private, 6th Yorkshire Regiment.
Volunteering in June 1915, he proceeded to Gallipoli in the following October, and was in action at Suvla Bay and Chocolate Hill. After the Evacuation of the Peninsula, he was sent to Egypt and served at Alexandria on garrison duties until June 1916, when he embarked for France. He was engaged on guard and other important duties at various stations, and returning home was demobilised in February 1919. He holds the 1914–15 Star, and the General Service and Victory Medals.
10, Mansfield Street, Miles Platting, Manchester.   Z11288

WALTON, J. A., A.B., Royal Navy.
Volunteering in January 1915, he was posted to H.M.S. "Thunderer," and was engaged in the North Sea on patrol, escort and other important duties, and rendered excellent services throughout. In 1920 he was on duty in H.M.S. "Curlew" at the China Station, and holds the 1914–15 Star, and the General Service and Victory Medals.
9, William Street, West Gorton, Manchester.   Z8532

WALTON, J. F., Private, 14th K. (Liverpool Regt.)
He volunteered in September 1914, and was engaged on important work at various stations until proceeding to France in September 1918. Here he served at prisoners of war camps on guard duties, rendering excellent services. He was demobilised in February 1919, and holds the General Service and Victory Medals.
42, Beaumont Street, Beswick, Manchester.   Z11289

WALTON, M. J. (D.S.M.), Petty Officer, 1st Cl., R.N.
Mobilised at the commencement of hostilities, he was posted to H.M.S. "Kent," and proceeding to the South Atlantic, was in action in the Battle of the Falkland Islands. He was awarded the Distinguished Service Medal for gallantry and devotion to duty and also took part in the sinking of the "Dresden" off Juan Fernandez Island. In January 1917, he returned home and until 1919 he was engaged as Captain's coxswain of the Signal School Boat, and then was sent to Russia where he saw much service. Returning home, he was demobilised in March 1920, and in addition to the Distinguished Service Medal, holds the 1914–15 Star, and the General Service and Victory Medals.
9, William Street, West Gorton, Manchester.   Z8535

WALTON, R., L/Corporal, Lancashire Fusiliers.
Volunteering in November 1914, he embarked for Gallipoli in the following May, and after a short period of service there became seriously ill. He was invalided to Malta, and later returned home. After receiving hospital treatment, he was discharged as unfit for further service in November 1919. He holds the 1914–15 Star, and the General Service and Victory Medals.
17, Upper Plymouth Grove, Longsight, Manchester.   Z8534

WALTON, T., Corporal, 12th Manchester Regiment.
Volunteering in January 1915, he was drafted to the Western Front in the following August, and fought at Ypres and was wounded. On his recovery he returned to the Front, and was in action on the Somme, and in various other sectors. Severely wounded he returned to England, and after receiving hospital treatment was invalided out in November 1918. He holds the 1914–15 Star, and the General Service and Victory Medals.
34, South Porter Street, Ancoats, Manchester.   Z11287

WARBURTON, A., Private, 6th Lancashire Fusiliers.
Volunteering in May 1915, he landed in France two months later, and was engaged in heavy fighting at Festubert, Loos, Vermelles, the Somme, and the Ancre. He gave his life for the freedom of England at Arras in April 1917, and was entitled to the 1914–15 Star, and the General Service and Victory Medals.
"A costly sacrifice upon the altar of freedom."
45, Higher Sheffield Street, Ardwick, Manchester.   Z8538A

WARBURTON, C., Sapper, R.E.
Volunteering at the declaration of war, he was sent to Egypt shortly afterwards, and was engaged on guard and other important duties at Alexandria and other stations until 1916, when he proceeded to France. Here he was in action in the first Battle of the Somme, and throughout the German Offensive and Allied Advance of 1918. He was demobilised in February 1919, and holds the 1914–15 Star, and the General Service and Victory Medals.
99, Broadfield Road, Moss Side, Manchester.   Z5724A

WARBURTON, C., Private, Labour Corps.
Joining in January 1917, he was sent to the Western Front four months later, and was engaged on important duties in the front lines. He saw much service throughout the Retreat and Advance of 1918, and returning home after the cessation of hostilities was demobilised in March 1919. He holds the General Service and Victory Medals.
45, Higher Sheffield Street, Ardwick, Manchester.   Z8538B

WARBURTON, C. F., Gunner, R.F.A.
He volunteered in September 1914, and embarked for France in the following May. He fought in the Battles of Festubert, Loos, St. Eloi, Vimy Ridge, the Somme, Arras, Messines and Ypres, and was wounded and gassed at Cambrai in November 1917. Invalided home, he received hospital treatment, and was discharged as unfit for further service in October 1918. He holds the 1914–15 Star, and the General Service and Victory Medals.   Z11292A
129, Jersey Street Dwellings, Ancoats, Manchester.

WARBURTON, G., Private, 1/8th Manchester Regt.
A Territorial, mobilised at the outbreak of war he proceeded to Gallipoli in May 1915, and was wounded during the Landing at Cape Helles. On his recovery he rejoined his unit and fought in many other engagements. Wounded a second time in August 1915, he returned home, and after receiving hospital treatment was transferred to the Royal Army Medical Corps. He was invalided out of the Service in March 1919, and holds the 1914–15 Star, and the General Service and Victory Medals.
26, Pearson Street, Newton Heath, Manchester.   Z9742

WARBURTON, J. P., Driver, R.A.S.C.
Volunteering in April 1915, he was sent to the Western Front shortly afterwards, and was engaged on important transport duties in many parts of the line. He was present at many engagements and rendered excellent services throughout the Offensives of 1918. After the Armistice, he served with the Army of Occupation in Germany until he returned to England, and was demobilised in February 1919. He holds the 1914–15 Star, and the General Service and Victory Medals.
2, Lincoln Street, Longsight, Manchester.   TZ8539

WARBURTON, R., Corporal, R.A.F.
Joining in February 1917, he embarked for France later, and served at various aerodromes on important duties with his Squadron. He saw much service during the German Offensive and Allied Advance of 1918, and in 1920 was still serving. He holds the General Service and Victory Medals.
113, Broadfield Road, Moss Side, Manchester.   Z8537C

WARBURTON, R., Private, 2/5th Manchester Regt.
Joining in September 1916, he landed in France twelve months later, and was in action in the Battles of Arras, Vimy Ridge, Messines, Ypres, and Cambrai. He was taken prisoner in the second Battle of the Somme in March 1918, and was held in captivity until the close of hostilities. Repatriated, he received hospital treatment on account of ill-health contracted whilst a prisoner, and was eventually demobilised in March 1920. He holds the General Service and Victory Medals.
50, Haughton Street, Bradford, Manchester.   Z8536

WARBURTON, R., Sergeant, Cheshire Regiment.
He was mobilised at the outbreak of hostilities, and during the war was engaged in the training of recruits with his Regiment at Mundesley Camp. He was afterwards appointed Sergeant in charge of a prisoners of war camp in South Wales. He was not successful in obtaining his transfer overseas before fighting ceased, but rendered excellent services until his demobilisation in April 1919. He holds the Egyptian Medal for his earlier service.
113, Broadfield Road, Moss Side, Manchester.   Z8537A

WARBURTON, R. B., Private, 8th Manchester Regt.
Volunteering in September 1914, he was sent to Gallipoli in the following April, and was in action in the Landing at Cape Helles. He was wounded and returning to England, received hospital treatment. Subsequently he was invalided out of the Service in August 1916, and holds the 1914–15 Star, and the General Service and Victory Medals.
113, Broadfield Road, Moss Side, Manchester.   Z8537B

WARD, A. W., Sergeant, Tank Corps.
He volunteered in August 1914, and seven months later proceeded overseas. He served on the Western Front until the end of 1915, when he was wounded at Ypres and sent back to hospital in Cambridge. In 1916, he returned to France and performed excellent work in connection with the construction of tanks until after the close of hostilities. He was demobilised in 1919, and holds the 1914–15 Star, and the General Service and Victory Medals.
22, Marlow Street, Longsight, Manchester.   Z11846

WARD, B., Private, 1st Loyal N. Lancashire Regt.
A month after the outbreak of war he volunteered, and four months later was drafted to the Western Front. There he was in action at Neuve Chapelle, St. Eloi, Hill 60, Ypres and Festubert, and fell fighting at Loos on September 25th, 1915. He was entitled to the 1914–15 Star, and the General Service and Victory Medals.
"A valiant Soldier, with undaunted heart he breasted life's last hill."
10, Coverdale Street, Ardwick, Manchester.   Z8549

WARD, C., Driver, R.A.S.C.
He volunteered in August 1914, and on completion of his training was three months later drafted overseas. During his service on the Western Front, he took an active part in many important engagements, principally in the Ypres sector. In 1916 he was transferred to Egypt, and was engaged on important garrison duties at Alexandria. On returning home in April 1919, he was demobilised and holds the 1914 Star, and the General Service and Victory Medals.
1, Wesley Street, West Gorton, Manchester.   Z11296

WARD. C. H., Sergt., 5th Manchester Regiment.

Volunteering in November 1914, he proceeded a year later to the Western Front, and took a conspicuous part in many important engagements, including those at St. Eloi, Albert, Vimy Ridge, Beaumont-Hamel, the Somme, Arras, Bullecourt, Ypres, Cambrai and Bapaume. He was wounded in action at Bullecourt in May 1917, and was demobilised in March 1919, holding the 1914-15 Star, and the General Service and Victory Medals. 18, Milne St., West Gorton, Manchester. Z11294

WARD, G., Private, 1st Royal Warwickshire Regt.

He volunteered in October 1914, and shortly afterwards was ordered to the Western Front, where he was in action at Messines, Ypres and Nieuport, and was gassed at Ypres. He was invalided to England, ond on his recovery, rendered valuable services, working at munitions at the Broughton Copper Company. He was demobilised in January 1919, and holds the 1914 Star, and the General Service and Victory Medals. 47, Laurence Street, West Gorton, Manchester. Z11297

WARD, G., Private, 2nd Manchester Regiment.

When war was declared in August 1914, he volunteered, and in February of the following year was drafted overseas. Whilst serving on the Western Front, he took part in fierce fighting at Albert, Ypres, Festubert, St. Eloi, Loos, the Somme, the Ancre, Bullecourt, Ypres, Cambrai, the Aisne, Havrincourt and Le Cateau, and was wounded in action on three occasions. He was demobilised in December 1918, and holds the 1914-15 Star, and the General Serivce and Victory Medals. 14, Park Street, West Gorton, Manchester. Z11293

WARD, G. H., Private, 11th Manchester Regiment.

He volunteered in January 1915, and in the following October was sent to Gallipoli, where he served until the Evacuation of the Peninsula. He was then drafted to Egypt, but shortly afterwards was transferred to the Western Front. There he saw heavy fighting in the Somme and Arras sectors, and remained in France until demobilised in February 1919, holding the 1914-15 Star, and the General Service and Victory Medals. 78, Lowe Street, Miles Platting, Manchester. Z8544A

WARD, H., L/Corporal, 1/8th Manchester Regt.

He volunteered in August 1914, and on conclsuion of his training in April 1915, proceeded to Gallipoli. There he was an action at Krithia, and in the subsequent engagements of the campaign. After the Evacuation of the Peninsula he served in Egypt for a time, but was invalided home, and in May 1916 was discharged as medically unfit for further military service. He holds the 1914-15 Star, and the General Service and Victory Medals. 24, Vulcan Street, Ardwick, Manchester. Z11300

WARD, H.. Private, Worcestershire Regiment.

Joining in June 1917, he proceeded to India in the following November, and was engaged on important garrison duties at Poona. In December 1918 he was sent to Salonika, and served there during the demobilisation period. Transferred to Russia he was stationed at Tiflis and Baku, and on being sent to Turkey, served with the Army of Occupation at Constantinople. Returning home he was demobilised in December 1919, and holds the General Service and Victory Medals. 5, Howard Street, Ancoats, Manchester. Z11295

WARD, H. J., Corporal, 1st East Lancashire Regt.

A month after the outbreak of war he volunteered and in October 1914 was ordered to France. On this Front he was in action at La Bassée, Neuve Chapelle, Hill 60, Loos and Cambrai, but was wounded at Lens in August 1917. On his recovery he returned to the Western Front, and served there until after the close of hostilities. He was demobilised in December 1919, and holds the 1914 Star, and the General Service and Victory Medals. 7, Rowen Street, Ardwick, Manchester. Z8550

WARD, J., Private, 3rd Manchester Regiment.

He volunteered in November 1914, and in June 1916 proceeded to France, where he was wounded a month later in the Battle of the Somme. On returning to the firing line he saw heavy fighting at Delville Wood, Albert, La Bassée, Arras, Ypres and Lille, and in the Retreat and Advance of 1918. He was also present at the Entry into Mons, and was demobilised in March 1919, holding the General Service and Victory Medals. 13, Heelis Street, Newton, Manchester. Z11299

WARD. J., L/Corporal, 11th M.G.C.

He joined the Army in April 1918, but on completion of his training at Clipstone, was unsuccessful in procuring a transfer to a theatre of war. He was, however, sent to Ireland, and engaged on important guard duties, which he fulfilled in a highly capable manner. He was eventually demobilised from Prees Heath in September 1919. 17, Nansen Street, Ardwick, Manchester. Z8545

WARD, J., L/Sergeant, 8th Lancashire Fusiliers.

Joining in June 1916, he was retained on home service, as owing to ill-health, he was unable to secure a transfer to the fighting area. On conclusion of his training at Whitley, he proceeded to Oswestry, at which station he performed good work as caterer to the Sergeants' Mess. After nearly three years' service in the Army he was demobilised in March 1919. 75, Masonic Street, Oldham Road, Manchester. Z8857

WARD, J. A., Driver, R.F.A.

He volunteered in October 1914, and a year later was ordered to the Western Front. In this theatre of war he took part in fierce fighting in the Battles of Loos, Albert, the Somme, Arras, Ypres, Cambrai and the 1918 Retreat, and also did good work with his Battery in the final victorious engagements of the war. In February 1919 he was demobilised, holding the 1914-15 Star, and the General Service and Victory Medals. 91, Tame Street, Ancoats, Manchester. Z8543

WARD, J. E., Private, Cheshire Regiment.

Volunteering in April 1915, he proceeded in the following July to India, where he served for three months. At the end of that time he was sent to Egypt, and stationed at Alexandria and Cairo until March 1916, when he was transferred to Mesopotamia. A month later he was wounded in action at Kut, and was unfortunately killed during the Advance on Baghdad in April 1917. He was entitled to the 1914-15 Star, and the General Service and Victory Medals.

"His life for his Country, his soul to God."

21, Chapel Street, West Gorton, Manchester. TZ8540

WARD, J. J., L/Corporal, 6th Manchester Regt.

He was mobilised in August 1914, and a month later was sent to Egypt, whence, after serving at Alexandria and Cairo, he was drafted in April 1915 to Gallipoli. There he took part in the Landing on the Peninsula, and was wounded in the Battle of Krithia in June 1915. He was sent to hospital in Malta, and on his recovery returned to England and was discharged as a time-expired man in May 1916. He holds the 1914-15 Star, and the General Service and Victory Medals. 45, Mercer Street, Hulme, Manchester. Z8551

WARD, J. T., Private, 8th K.O. (R. Lancaster Regt.)

He volunteered in August 1915, and on conclusion of his training was five months later drafted overseas. During his service on the Western Front he saw heavy fighting, especially at St. Eloi, but in April 1916 was invalided home and sent to hospital in Nottingham. Four months later he was discharged from the Army suffering from heart disease. He holds the General Service and Victory Medals. 1, Gatley Street, Ancoats, Manchester. Z8541

WARD, R., Private, 1st Lancashire Fusiliers.

Volunteering in June 1915, he was in March of the following year ordered to France. On this Front he did good work with his unit at Albert and Ploegsteert Wood, but fell fighting valiantly on the Somme on October 27th, 1916. He was entitled to the General Service and Victory Medals.

"He died the noblest death a man may die,
Fighting for God, and right, and liberty."

1, Gatley Street, Ancoats, Manchester. Z8542

WARD, T., Private. Manchester Regiment.

He volunteered in January 1915, and in the following November was sent to the Western Front, where he took part in the Battles of Ypres, Loos, the Somme, Bullecourt and Messines. He was severely wounded in action at Passchendaele in October 1917, and invalided to England. On his discharge from hospital he served at Grimsby until demobilised in February 1919, holding the 1914-15 Star, and the General Service and Victory Medals. 25, Wesley Street, Ardwick, Manchester. Z8546

WARD, T., Private, 12th Manchester Regiment.

He joined the Army in March 1917, and a year later proceeded to the Western theatre of war. There, after six months' service, he was wounded and taken prisoner at Cambrai in September 1918. He was kept in captivity until January 1919, and returning to England on his release was eventually demobilised in the following October, holding the General Service and Victory Medals. 78, Lowe Street, Miles Platting, Manchester. Z8544B

WARD, W., Sapper, R.E.

Joining in June 1916, he proceeded after a period of training to the Western Front in August 1916. During over three years in France he did good work with his Company in different sectors of the Front, and saw fighting at Arras, Bullecourt, Messines and Ypres, and in the Retreat and Advance of 1918. In October 1919 he was demobilised, holding the General Service and Victory Medals. 28, Gatley Street, Ancoats, Manchester. Z8548

WARD, W., Air Mechanic, R.A.F.

At the outbreak of war in August 1914 he volunteered, and in February of the following year was drafted to the Western Front, where he was engaged in fierce fighting in numerous sectors of the line, including Ypres, the Somme, Arras, Givenchy, La Bassée and Cambrai. He remained in France until demobilised in October 1919, holding the 1914-15 Star, and the General Service and Victory Medals. 14, Padgate Street, Ancoats, Manchester. TZ9743

WARD, W. R., Private, 3rd Lancashire Fusiliers.
He volunteered in September 1914, and three months later was ordered overseas. Whilst serving on the Western Front he took an active part in engagements at Neuve Chapelle, Hill 60, Festubert, Albert, the Somme, Arras, Ypres, Cambrai, the Somme (II), Amiens and Havrincourt. After the Armistice he proceeded with the Army of Occupation to Germany, where he served until demobilised in April 1919, holding the 1914-15 Star, and the General Service and Victory Medals.
10, Eskrigge Street, Ardwick, Manchester.   Z8547

WARDEN, W., Private, Manchester Regiment.
He volunteered in September 1914, and was retained at home on important duties until November 1915, when he was sent to France. After taking part in several engagements, he was wounded on the Somme in July 1916, and was sent to hospital in London. Upon recovering he returned to the Western Front, was again wounded at Ypres, and admitted to hospital in Rouen. He was later wounded a third time and was afterwards transferred to Italy, where he served until demobilised in February 1919. He holds the 1914-15 Star, and the General Service and Victory Medals.
31, Neden Street, Openshaw, Manchester.   TZ6471B

WARDLE, H., Private, 2nd South Lancashire Regt.
Volunteering in September 1914, he was drafted in the following April to France. There he took part in fighting at Ypres, Festubert, Hill 60, St. Eloi, Vimy Ridge, and on the Somme, and was wounded at Beaumont-Hamel in August 1916. Evacuated home, he spent some time in hospital in Scotland, and upon his recovery, returned to France, where he saw further fighting. He was again invalided home in August 1917 on account of ill-health, and was eventually discharged in the following October. He holds the 1914-15 Star, and the General Service and Victory Medals.
8, Elliott Street, Ancoats, Manchester.   Z11618

WARDLE, H,, Private, 2/8th Manchester Regiment.
He volunteered in October 1914, and proceeded in the following June to Gallipoli. During his service in this theatre of hostilities, he was employed on various duties, and did good work until he was invalided home on account of ill-health in November 1915. He was subsequently discharged in March 1917 as unfit for further military service, and holds the 1914-15 Star, and the General Service and Victory Medals.
8, Chell Street, Longsight, Manchester.   Z4645A

WARDLE, J., Sergeant, 16th Manchester Regt.
Volunteering in September 1914, he was retained at home on various duties of an important nature until May 1917, when he was then sent to France. In this theatre of war he played a prominent part in several engagements, and after three months' service overseas was invalided home on account of ill-health. Sent to hospital at St. Albans, he remained there for some time, and was eventually demobilised in February 1919, holding the General Service and Victory Medals.
31, St. John Street, Longsight, Manchester.   Z6990B

WARDLE, R., Private, 2nd Manchester Regiment, and K.O. (Royal Lancaster Regiment).
He volunteered in August 1914, and in the following March was drafted to the Western Front. There he was wounded in action at Neuve Chapelle, and admitted to hospital at Rouen, being later evacuated to England. After spending nine months in hospital at Liverpool, he was sent to Salonika, and whilst in action on the Doiran front, was again wounded. Upon his recovery he rejoined his unit, and saw further fighting on the Vardar front. Demobilised on returning home in March 1919, he holds the 1914-15 Star, and the General Service and Victory Medals.
34, Cedar Street, Russell Street, Hulme, Manchester.   TZ8553

WARDLE, S., Private, 1st East Lancashire Regt.
He joined in April 1918, and after a period of training, proceeded to France. During his service in this theatre of hostilities, he participated with his unit in the fourth Battle of Ypres, and was later invalided home, suffering from fever. He was eventually discharged in January 1919, and holds the General Service and Victory Medals.   TZ8552
26, Melbourne Street, Chorlton-on-Medlock, Manchester.

WARDLE, W., Private, Labour Corps.
Volunteering in February 1915, he was drafted three months afterwards to the Western Front, and there served with his Company at Festubert, Loos, Vimy Ridge, the Somme, Beaumont-Hamel, Arras, Bullecourt, Messines, Ypres and Cambrai. After being employed on various duties, he was demobilised in May 1919, and holds the 1914-15 Star, and the General Service and Victory Medals.
7, Hamilton Street, Collyhurst, Manchester.   Z11301

WARDLEY, T., Pte., E. Lancs. Regt., and Spr.,R.E.
He volunteered in November 1915, and five months later was drafted to France. In this theatre of war he played a prominent part with his unit in many important engagements, including Albert, Vimy Ridge, Arras, Ypres, Cambrai, Le

Cateau, the Ancre and the Marne. He was wounded on the Marne in July 1918, and spent some time in hospital at Rouen, and was also for a short period in hospital at Etretat, suffering from fever. He was demobilised in April 1919, and holds the General Service and Victory Medals.
49, Lavender Street, Hulme, Manchester.   TZ8554

WAREHAM, J., Private, 19th Manchester Regt.
Volunteering in July 1915, he was retained at home on important duties until September 1916, when he was sent to the Western Front. There he was in action on the Somme, and at Albert, Amiens, La Bassée and Ypres, and was severely wounded at Arras in April 1917. Invalided home, he spent some time in hospital at Stockport and Manchester, and was eventually discharged in February 1918 as unfit for further service. He holds the General Service and Victory Medals.
79, Norton Street, West Gorton, Manchester.   Z8555

WARHURST, A.(M.M.) L/Cpl.,2/5th Lancashire Fus.
Shortly after volunteering in August 1915, he was released in order to resume his pre-war occupation on the railway. Rejoining the Colours in August 1917, however, he was drafted two months later to France, and there took part in severe fighting at Givenchy, La Bassée and Festubert. He was awarded the Military Medal for conspicuous bravery in capturing a machine gun post under heavy fire at Tournai in October 1918, and when demobilised in March 1919, was also entitled to the General Service and Victory Medals.
9, Marcus Street, Preston Street, Hulme, Manchester. Z8557

WARHURST, A., Driver, R.A.S.C. (M.T.)
He volunteered in April 1915, and two weeks later was sent to Egypt. There he was stationed at Alexandria, Cairo and Heliopolis, and was afterwards sent to Palestine. During his service overseas he was employed as a motor transport driver, and did excellent work in this capacity until he returned home for demobilisation in March 1919. He holds the General Service and Victory Medals.
57, Hyde Street, Hulme, Manchester.   Z8556

WARING, J., Air Mechanic, R.A.F.
He joined in May 1916, but was not successful in obtaining a transfer overseas. Retained at home, he served for some time in England, and was later sent to Scapa Flow, where he was engaged on important duties, which demanded a high degree of technical skill. He rendered very valuable services until he was demobilised in February 1919.
28, Prince Street, Ardwick, Manchester.   Z8558

WARK, A., Gunner, R.F.A., and Private, R.A.M.C.
Mobilised in August 1914, he proceeded in the following September to Egypt. After serving for some time on the Suez Canal, he was sent to Gallipoli, where he was wounded in action at Krithia. Sent to hospital in Cairo, he later returned to Gallipoli, and remained there until the Evacuation. Ordered back to Egypt, he was in action on the Suez Canal again and at El-Arish, Katia, El Fasher, and Romani. In March 1917 he was transferred to France and saw further fighting at Péronne, St. Quentin, Ypres and Roulers. After the Armistice he served in Cologne with the Army of Occupation until January 1919, when he was demobilised, holding the 1914-15 Star, and the General Service and Victory Medals.
75, Crosscliffe Street, Moss Side, Manchester.   Z8559A

WARK, H., Private, 2/5th Manchester Regiment.
Joining in September 1916, he proceeded in the following March to France. There he took part in several severe engagements, including those at Nieuport and Ypres, where he was wounded. Upon his recovery, he rejoined his unit, was in action during the Retreat in 1918, and was unhappily killed during heavy fighting at La Bassée on March 21st, 1918. He was entitled to the General Service and Victory Medals.
          " Great deeds cannot die."
75, Crosscliffe Street, Moss Side, Manchester.   Z8559B

WARNER, H., Pte., King's Own Scottish Borderers.
He volunteered in August 1914, and three months later was drafted to the Western Front, where he was wounded in the first Battle of Ypres. He was also in action at Loos, Vimy Ridge, the Somme, Arras and Messines, was wounded at Loos and Cambrai, and invalided to England. On his return to France in April 1918 he was in action on the Marne, and was present at the Entry into Mons. He was demobilised in February 1919, holding the 1914 Star, and the General Service and Victory Medals.
10, Violet Street, Hulme, Manchester.   Z11847

WARNER, J., Driver, R.A.S.C.
Volunteering in April 1915, he was unable to procure a transfer overseas owing to medical unfitness and was stationed for a time at Woolwich, where he rendered valuable services conveying food and supplies to the various depots. He was afterwards transferred to Aldershot, at which station he served until his health broke down in 1918. In November of that year he died in Connaught Military Hospital.
          " His memory is cherished with pride."
20, Abbey Field Street, Openshaw, Manchester.   Z8561

WARNER, J. T., Private, R.M.L.I.
He volunteered in November 1915, and eighteen months later proceeded overseas. During his service on the Western Front, he fought in the Battles of Arras, Vimy Ridge, Ypres, Passchendaele, Lens, Cambrai and the Somme, and was wounded and gassed at Cambrai in March 1918. On returning to the firing line he was in action in the engagements prior to the close of hostilities, and in June 1919 was demobilised, holding the General Service and Victory Medals.
53, Markham Street, Ardwick, Manchester.   Z8560

WARREN, A., Pte., 8th K.O. (R. Lancaster Regt.)
He joined in July 1916, and proceeding to France before the close of the year, fought at Albert, Arras and Cambrai. He was wounded at Armentières in April 1917, and on the Somme in the following year. He continued his service in France and was not demobilised until July 1919. He holds the General Service and Victory Medals.
5, School Street, Manchester.   Z11448B

WARREN, E., Driver, R.E.
When war was declared he was already serving, and at once proceeded with the First Expeditionary Force to France. There he was in action in the Battles of Mons, the Marne, La Bassée, Ypres, Hill 60, the Somme, the Ancre, Arras, Lens, Cambrai and the Scarpe, and fell fighting in April 1918. He was entitled to the Mons Star, and the General Service and Victory Medals.
" Courage, bright hopes, and a myriad dreams splendidly given."
13, Edith Street, West Gorton, Manchester.   Z11302

WARREN, G., Private, King's (Liverpool Regt).
He joined in October 1917, and two months later was sent to France, where he did good work as a Lewis gunner in the Battles of Cambrai, the Aisne and the Lys. He was also in action in the Retreat of 1918, and during the Advance was wounded and gassed and invalided home. In January 1919 he proceeded to Egypt, and served on the Suez and at Ismailia until April 1920, when he returned to England and was demobilised. He holds the General Service and Victory Medals.
93, Elliott Street, Bradford, Manchester.   Z11304A

WARREN, J., Private, Lancashire Fusiliers.
Volunteering in August 1915, he was after a course of training drafted overseas in September 1916. Whilst serving on the Western Front, he experienced severe fighting at Ypres, the Somme and Arras, and in the Retreat of 1918, and also took an active part in the final engagements of the war. He was mentioned in Despatches in February 1918 for conspicuous devotion to duty. He was demobilised in January 1919, and holds the General Service and Victory Medals.
40, John Street, Chorlton-on-Medlock, Manchester.   Z8562

WARREN, J. W., Gunner, R.F.A.
At the outbreak of hostilities in August 1914, he volunteered and in May 1915 was ordered to Gallipoli. There he was in action at Suvla Bay, and in the subsequent engagements of the campaign. After the Evacuation of the Peninsula he was sent to Egypt, where he fought in the Battles of Rafa and Gaza. On being transferred to Palestine, he served at Jerusalem until after the termination of the war. Returning to England in November 1919, he was demobilised, holding the 1914-15 Star, and the General Service and Victory Medals.
46, Lowe Street, Miles Platting, Manchester.   Z11303

WARREN, W. H., Driver, R.A.S.C.
He volunteered in February 1915, and in the following December was sent to the Western Front, where he rendered valuable services in conveying supplies to the forward areas. He saw heavy fighting in engagements in the Somme, Arras, Ypres and Cambrai sectors, and also in the Retreat and Advance of 1918. He was demobilised in May 1919, and holds the 1914-15 Star, and the General Service and Victory Medals.
93, Elliott Street, Bradford, Manchester.   Z11304B

WARRENDER, E., Private, R.A.M.C.
Volunteering in May 1915, he was three months later drafted to Mesopotamia, where he served for nine months. During that time he performed excellent work as a stretcher bearer at Kut-el-Amara and Baghdad, until invalided home in May 1916, suffering from consumption. He was discharged from the Army as medically unfit in August 1916, but unhappily died at Baguley Sanatorium on December 26th, 1918. He was entitled to the 1914-15 Star, and the General Service and Victory Medals.
" Whilst we remember the sacrifice is not in vain."
5, Harry Street, London Road, Manchester.   Z8858

WARRINER, E., Sapper, R.E.
He volunteered in December 1914, and on completion of a period of training was drafted overseas in February of the following year. During his service in Mesopotamia, he did good work with his Battery in numerous engagements, including those at Amara, Kut-el-Amara and the Tigris. On returning to England in April 1919 he was demobilised, and holds the 1914-15 Star, and the General Service and Victory Medals.
28, Kingston Street, Hulme, Manchester.   Z8850

WARRINER, J. W., Pte., K.O. (R. Lancaster Regt).
He joined the Army in November 1917, and on completion of his training was four months later drafted to the Western Front. In this theatre of war he saw severe fighting in the Retreat of 1918, but whilst taking part in the Allied Advance was unfortunately killed in action on August 24th, 1918. He was entitled to the General Service and Victory Medals.
" The path of duty was the way to glory."
69, Eliza Ann Street, Collyhurst, Manchester.   Z11305

WARRINGTON, G. W., Gunner, R.G.A.
Joining in September 1916, he was sent three months later to the Western Front, but after fighting in the Ancre, the Somme, Beaumont-Hamel, Beaucourt and Arras sectors, his health broke down and he was sent to the Base at Etaples, where he served until the close of hostilities. In February 1919 he proceeded with the Army of Occupation to Germany, and served there until demobilised in September 1919. He holds the General Service and Victory Medals.
125, Beresford Street, Moss Side, Manchester.   Z8565

WARRINGTON, J., Private, 8th Manchester Regt.
He joined in October 1916, and on conclusion of his training was drafted overseas in January 1917. During his service on the Western Front, he was in action in engagements at Arras, Messines, Ypres and Cambrai, and was gassed at Bapaume in August 1918. He was sent to hospital in England, and on his discharge from there was demobilised in February 1919, holding the General Service and Victory Medals.
6, Roy Street, Ardwick, Manchester.   Z8563

WARRINGTON, W., Pte., 7th Lancashire Fusiliers.
Volunteering in October 1914, he proceeded in the following year to Gallipoli, where he was wounded in action in August 1915. On his recovery he served on the Peninsula until the Evacuation, and was then sent to Cairo for six months. At the end of that time he was transferred to the Western Front, where in November 1918 he received a second wound, which resulted in the loss of his right eye. After protracted hospital treatment, he was demobilised in February 1919, and holds the 1914-15 Star, and the General Service and Victory Medals.
21, Mulberry Street, Hulme, Manchester.   TZ8564

WASHINGTON, J., Corporal, 8th Manchester Regt.
He volunteered in November 1914, and in February 1916 was sent to the Western Front, where he was in action in the Battles of Ploegsteert Wood, the Somme, Beaucourt, Arras, and Vimy Ridge. In May 1917, he was invalided home. suffering from trench fever, and on his discharge from hospital was employed as a drill Instructor at Cleethorpes. He was demobilised in February 1919, and holds the General Service and Victory Medals.
12, Bloom Street, Hulme, Manchester.   TZ8566

WATERFALL, E. V., Worker, Women's Land Army.
She joined the Land Army in May 1918, and was employed at Eaton Hall Farm, Congleton, Cheshire, where she rendered valuable services in dairy work and hay making. She also worked at farms at Garstang and Aintree, and carried out her duties with the greatest ability. She was not demobilised until June 1920.   TX8567-8-9-70-1-2E
8, Heywood Street, Ardwick, Manchester.

WATERFALL, G., Bombardier, R.F.A.
He volunteered in June 1915, and on completion of his training was drafted overseas in the following November. Whilst on the Western Front he was in action at Vimy Ridge and the Somme, and was then transferred to Salonika, where he took part in the recapture of Monastir. He also fought on the Doiran front, and in September 1917 was sent to Palestine and later to Syria. On returning home he was demobilised in July 1919, and holds the 1914-15 Star, and the General Service and Victory Medals.   TX8567-8-9-70-1-2B
8, Heywood Street, Chorlton-on-Medlock, Manchester.

WATERFALL, R. U., Pte., 3rd King's (L'pool Regt.)
Volunteering at the outbreak of war in August 1914, he was medically unfit for service overseas, and was therefore retained on home defence. Throughout the period of hostilities he was stationed in Ireland, where he performed excellent work as an officer's servant, groom and chauffeur. He was eventually demobilised in January 1919.   TX8567-8-9-70-1-2C
169, Prince Street, Ardwick, Manchester.

WATERFALL, S. Private, Manchester Regiment and King's Own (Royal Lancaster Regiment).
He joined in November 1917, and after a period of training was later in the same year drafted to the Western Front. There he took an active part in numerous important engagements, in different sectors of the line, and was gassed in the Battle of the Aisne in 1918. He was also severely wounded at La Bassée in the same year, and unfortunately lost his right leg. In May 1919 he was demobilised, holding the General Service and Victory Medals.   TX8567-8-9-70-1-2A
8, Heywood Street, Ardwick, Manchester.

WATERFALL, T. J. (D.C.M.), Sergt., Grenadier Gds.
Mobilised in August 1914, he was at once ordered to the Western Front, where he served with distinction in many important engagements. He was in action in the Battles of Mons, Ypres, La Bassée, Neuve Chapelle, Festubert, Givenchy, Loos and the Somme, and was wounded on two occasions. He was awarded the Distinguished Conduct Medal for conspicuous gallantry in the Field, and was discharged in August 1919, also holding the Mons Star, and the General Service and Victory Medals. TX8567-8-9-70-1-2F
8, Heywood Street, Ardwick, Manchester.

WATERFALL, W. B., Private, R.A.S.C.
He volunteered in August 1914, and later in the same year proceeded to the Western Front, where he did good work as a despatch rider. After taking part in numerous engagements, including the Battle of the Somme, he was transferred to Italy, and there experienced fierce fighting on the Piave front, and was wounded in action in November 1917. He was demobilised in February 1919, and holds the 1914 Star, and the General Service and Victory Medals.
85, Carman Street, Ardwick, Manchester.
TX8567-8-9-70-1-2D

WATERHOUSE, A., Private, 2nd Manchester Regt. and 1st King's (Liverpool Regt.)
Volunteering in November 1914, he was on completion of his training sent overseas in March 1915. Whilst serving in the Western theatre of war, he experienced severe fighting in different sectors of the front, and was in action in the Battles of Loos, the Somme and Vimy Ridge. He was demobilised in February 1919, and holds the 1914-15 Star, and the General Service and Victory Medals.
27, Mark Street, Hulme, Manchester. TZ8575B

WATERHOUSE, J. (D.C.M.), Sergt., 1/8th Manchester Regiment.
He was mobilised in August 1914, and a month later was drafted to Egypt, where he served for over two years. In March 1917, he was transferred to the Western Front, where he played a conspicuous part in many engagements, but was unhappily killed in action on August 30th, 1918. He was awarded the Distinguished Conduct Medal for gallantry in the Field and devotion to duty, and was also entitled to the 1914-15 Star, and the General Service and Victory Medals.
"He joined the great white company of valiant souls."
27, Mark Street, Hulme, Manchester. TZ8575C

WATERHOUSE. J. W., Private, Labour Corps.
He joined the Army in February 1916, and shortly afterwards was ordered overseas. He served on the Western Front for over two years, and during that time did good work with his unit in the Albert, Vimy Ridge and Havrincourt sectors. In November 1918 he was discharged as medically unfit for further military duties, and holds the General Service and Victory Medals.
34, Trafford Street, Hulme, Manchester. Z8576

WATERHOUSE, T., Pte., K. Shropshire Light Inftry.
A Reservist, he was called up when war was declared in August 1914, and at once proceeded with the First Expeditionary Force to the Western Front. Whilst taking part in severe fighting during the Retreat from Mons, he was unfortunately killed in September 1914. He was entitled to the Mons Star, and the General Service and Victory Medals.
"A costly sacrifice upon the alter of freedom."
20, Gorse Street, Hulme, Manchester. Z8573

WATERHOUSE, W. (M.M.), Cpl., 1st Border Regt.
Joining in September 1916, he was attached to the 7th Manchester Regiment, and on conclusion of his training was drafted overseas in the following year. During his service on the Western Front he fought in numerous engagements, and was wounded in action. He was awarded the Military Medal for exceptional bravery in the Field, and after the cessation of hostilities, rejoined for a further period of four years, and was drafted to India. He also holds the General Service and Victory Medals.
27, Mark Street, Hulme, Manchester. TZ8575A

WATERHOUSE, W., Pte., 2nd K.O. (R. Lancaster Rgt.)
He volunteered in November 1914, and six months later proceeded to France, where he did excellent work as a bomber in the Battles of Ypres and Loos. In November 1915 he was transferred to Salonika, and was engaged in heavy fighting on the Doiran, Vardar and Struma fronts, and at Monastir, On returning home in March 1919 he was demobilised, holding the 1914-15 Star, and the General Service and Victory Medals.
17, Albion Terrace, Miles Platting, Manchester. Z8574

WATERS, G., Private, 16th Manchester Regiment.
Volunteering in January 1915, he trained at Heaton Park, and in July 1916 was sent to the Western Front. There he was in action at the Battle of the Somme, and was wounded and invalided to England. Three months later he returned to the fighting line, and saw service in the Neuve Chapelle and Vimy Ridge sectors. He remained in France until demobilised in November 1919, holding the 1914-15 Star, and the General Service and Victory Medals.
183, Cobden Street, Ancoats, Manchester. Z11306

WATERS, G. F., Private, Cheshire Regiment.
He joined in April 1917, but was unsuccessful in procuring a transfer to the war zone before the cessation of hostilities. He was retained on home service and stationed at Kinmel Park, Clacton-on-Sea, and in Ireland. In January 1919, he was drafted to Germany, and served with the Army of Occupation on the Rhine until demobilised in April 1920.
33, Syndall Street, Ardwick, Manchester. Z8577A

WATERS, H., Private, 1st Manchester Regiment.
Joining in April 1916, he was sent in the following October to Egypt, where he served in Alexandria, Cairo, and on the Suez Canal. In 1917 he proceeded to Palestine and saw heavy fighting at Gaza, Jericho and Jerusalem. Transferred to Mesopotamia, he was in action in engagements at Kut-el-Amara, and on the Tigris. On his return to England he was demobilised in July 1919, holding the General Service and Victory Medals.
33, Syndall Street, Ardwick, Manchester. Z8577B

WATERSON, J., Private, 2nd Manchester Regiment.
When war broke out in August 1914, he was already serving in the Army and was at once ordered to France with the First Expeditionary Force. He took an active part in the Battle of Mons and was unfortunately killed in action on the Marne on September 9th, 1914. He was entitled to the Mons Star, and the General Service and Victory Medals.
"His life for his Country, his soul to God."
16, Hayfield Street, Ardwick, Manchester. Z8578B

WATERSON, T. S., Corporal, R.E.
He enlisted in September 1913, and two years later was drafted to the Western Front, where he performed excellent work in connection with bridge building, water supply, and the construction of gun pits and defences. He experienced fierce fighting in engagements on the Somme, at Guillemont, Cambrai and Havrincourt, and in the Retreat and Advance of 1918. After the Armistice he served in Germany with the Army of Occupation, until discharged in June 1919, and holds the 1914-15 Star, and the General Service and Victory Medals.
20, Marsland Street, Ardwick, Manchester. Z8578A

WATSON, E. E., Signalman, R.N., H.M.S. "Saumarez."
He volunteered in February 1915, and on being posted to his ship was engaged for twelve months on patrol work off the English Coast. He also served on the West African Coast, the Mediterranean and Black Seas, and in the Grecian Archipelago. After the Armistice was signed he assisted in bringing the surrendered German Fleet to Scapa Flow. In 1920 he was still serving in the Navy, and holds the General Service and Victory Medals.
27, Great Jones Street, West Gorton, Manchester. Z11307

WATSON. J., Gunner, 20th R.F.A.
When war was declared in August 1914, he was already in the Army, and consequently immediately proceeded to the Western Front, where he was unfortunately killed in action during the Retreat from Mons in August 1914. He was entitled to the Mons Star, and the General Service and Victory Medals.
"Honour to the immortal dead who gave their youth that the world might grow old in peace."
5, Humphrey St., Chorlton-on-Medlock, Manchester. Z8580

WATSON, J., Private, 42nd Lancashire Fusiliers.
He volunteered in July 1915, and after training at Codford and Whitley six months later was drafted to Egypt. There he saw fierce fighting at the Suez Canal, Kantara, and El Arish, but was taken ill with bronchitis and double pneumonia. On returning to England in January 1918, he was engaged on important guard duties until discharged in September 1918, as medically unfit for further service. He holds the General Service and Victory Medals.
26, Law Street, Rochdale Road, Manchester. Z11308

WATSON, R., Private. K.O. (Royal Lancaster Regt.)
Mobilised in August 1914, he was immediately drafted to the Western Front, where he took part in the fighting at Mons. He also fought in the Battles of Le Cateau, La Bassée, Ypres, Festubert, Loos, the Somme, Arras and Passchendaele, and other important engagements in various sectors, and was gassed during the Advance of 1918. Admitted to hospital at Putney, he was invalided from the Army in September of that year, and holds the Mons Star, and the General Service and Victory Medals.
9, Crook Street, Harpurhey, Manchester. Z11309

WATSON, R. W., Corporal, 8th Manchester Regt., and M.G.C.
Volunteering in January 1915, he proceeded to France in August of that year, and there saw severe fighting in various sectors of the Front. He took part in the Battles of Vimy Ridge, the Somme, Arras, Ypres, Passchendaele, Cambrai and Bapaume, and many other important engagements, and served also through the Retreat and Advance of 1918. He was for a time in hospital in France and England, suffering from dysentery, and was finally demobilised in January 1919, holding the 1914-15 Star, and the General Service and Victory Medals.
18, Gladstone Street, Brooks' Bar, Manchester. TZ8581

WATSON, J. W., Gunner, R.F.A.

Joining in April 1917, he was on completion of a course of training in July 1917 drafted to Mesopotamia, where he served for nearly three years. During that time he did good work with his Battery in various sectors of the front, and fought in engagements at Kut, Um-el-Hannah, Sanna-i-Yat, the Tigris and Baghdad. On his return to England in February 1920, he was demobilised, holding the General Service and Victory Medals. 20, Link Street, Longsight, Manchester. Z8579

WATTS, D., Private, 1st Manchester Regiment.

Mobilised in August 1914, he was drafted to the Western Front in the following month and there saw much severe fighting, taking part in the Battles of the Marne, the Aisne, Armentières and Ypres. He died gloriously on the Field of Battle at La Bassée in December 1914. He was entitled to the 1914 Star, and the General Service and Victory Medals.
"He joined the great white company of valiant souls."
91, Knightley Street, Rochdale Road, Manchester. Z11278

WATTS, G., Corporal, 7th Lincolnshire Regiment.

After joining in May 1917, he underwent a period of training prior to being drafted to the Western Front in March of the following year. There he saw much severe fighting in the Ypres sector until gassed in June 1918, and admitted to hospital at Rouen, and later at Cardiff. He returned to France however, on his recovery, and was again in action at the Battles of Cambrai and Ypres. He was afterwards engaged in guarding prisoners of war, until his demobilisation in November 1919, and holds the General Service and Victory Medals.
10, Riga Street, City Road, Manchester. Z8583

WATTS, J., Private, 7th Seaforth Highlanders.

He volunteered in January 1915, and in November of that year, proceeded to the Western Front, where, after taking part in the Battles of Albert and the Somme, he was wounded in action at Arras in April 1917, and invalided home. On his recovery, however, he returned to France, and served through the second Battle of the Somme, and the Marne, and was again wounded at Cambrai in October 1918, and admitted to hospital in Cheshire. Demobilised in February 1919, he holds the 1914-15 Star, and the General Service and Victory Medals.
10, Haughton Street, Bradford, Manchester. Z8582

WATTS, J., Private, Loyal N. Lancashire Regt.

He volunteered in September 1914, and twelve months later, was drafted to France, where he saw heavy fighting in various sectors of the Front. He took part in the Battles of Loos, Vimy Ridge, the Somme, Arras, Bullecourt, Messines and Ypres and many minor engagements, and was severely wounded in action in October 1917. He was for a considerable period in hospital in England, before being invalided from the Army in March 1919, and holds the 1914-15 Star, and the General Service and Victory Medals.
4, Redford Street, Newton Heath, Manchester. Z11310A

WATTS, T., Private, 23rd Manchester Regiment.

Volunteering in July 1915, he was drafted to the Western Front six months later, and there served with a Trench Mortar Battery in various sectors. He took part in the Battles of the Somme, Ypres and Cambrai and many other important engagements and fought also in the Retreat and Advance of 1918. Returning home in January 1919, he was invalided from the Army in March of that year, and holds the General Service and Victory Medals.
55, Francisco Street, Collyhurst, Manchester. Z9744

WATTS, W. (D.C.M.) Sgt., K. O. (R.Lancaster Regt.)

Mobilised in August 1914, he was immediately drafted to the Western Front, where, after fighting at Mons, he took a prominent part in the Battles of Le Cateau, Neuve Chapelle, St. Eloi, Hill 60, Ypres, Loos and Vimy Ridge, and other engagements. He fell in action on July 1st, 1916, in the Advance on the Somme. He had been awarded the Distinguished Conduct Medal for conspicuous bravery in the Field at La Bassée, and a Russian decoration for distinguished service in the same engagement, and was also entitled to the Mons Star, and the General Service and Victory Medals.
"His memory is cherished with pride."
4, Redford Street, Newton Heath, Manchester. Z11310B

WAYWELL, W. H., Private, 10th Manchester Regt.

He joined in July 1916, and after completing a short period of training, was retained on important duties at various stations, where he did much useful work with his unit. Admitted to hospital at Colchester in November 1916, he unfortunately died there in the following month, of an illness contracted during his service with the Colours.
"Steals on the ear the distant triumph song."
22, Cookson Street, Bradford, Manchester. Z11311

WEARING, A. E., Private, 23rd Cheshire Regiment.

He joined in November 1916, and was retained on important duties with his unit in England until February 1918, when he proceeded to the Western Front. There he saw much severe fighting at Armentières and in various other sectors, and took part also in many important engagements during the Retreat and Advance of 1918. Demobilised on his return home in February 1919, he holds the General Service and Victory Medals. 6, Sadler St., Moss Side, Manchester. Z8584

WEATHERILT, J., Private, Royal Welch Fusiliers.

He volunteered in April 1915, and in March of the following year proceeded to the Western Front. Whilst in this theatre of war, he took part in many important engagements, including the Battles of Ypres, Passchendaele, Cambrai and the Somme, fought also in the Retreat and Advance of 1918, and was gassed in March of that year. He afterwards served with the Army of Occupation in Germany, where he was stationed at Cologne until his return home for demobilisation in April 1919. He holds the General Service and Victory Medals.
22, Montague Street, Collyhurst, Manchester. Z8860

WEATHERILT, T., Private, Royal Welch Fusiliers.

He joined in October 1916, and after seven months' training in Ireland, proceeded to the Western Front, where he saw severe fighting in various sectors. He took part in the Battles of Arras, Passchendaele and the Somme, and other important engagements, served also through the Retreat and Advance of 1918, and was gassed at Ypres in October 1917. On the cessation of hostilities, he was sent with the Army of Occupation into Turkey, finally returning home for demobilisation in December 1919. He holds the General Service and Victory Medals.
22, Montague Street, Collyhurst, Manchester. Z8861

WEAVER, G. C., Private, Royal Munster Fusiliers.

Three months after joining in June 1916, he proceeded to the Western Front, where he took part in important engagements in various sectors. Later he was transferred to Italy, and was there again in action, seeing much severe fighting on the Piave and the Asiago Plateaux. After the cessation of hostilities, he was stationed at Vienna until his return home for demobilisation in May 1920, and holds the General Service and Victory Medals.
2, Hazel Grove, Longsight, Manchester. TZ8586

WEAVER, H., Private, 1/8th Lancashire Fusiliers.

Volunteering in August 1914, he was drafted to the Western Front in June of the following year, and there took part in the Battle of Loos, where he was wounded, and other engagements until transferred to Egypt in November 1915. During his twelve months' service in this seat of operations, he fought in action at Katia and Romani, and in the capture of El Fasher, afterwards returning to France. He then served through the Battles of Arras, Ypres, the Somme, the Marne and Le Cateau, and other engagements until the cessation of hostilities, and was finally discharged in February 1920. He holds the 1914-15 Star, and the General Service and Victory Medals.
11, Ashbury Street, Openshaw, Manchester. Z8585

WEAVER, W., Private, 2nd Manchester Regiment.

He volunteered at the outbreak of war in August 1914, and on completing his training in the following January, proceeded to the Western Front. There, after much heavy fighting in various sectors, he was severely wounded in action at Ypres in May 1915, and sent home. Invalided from the Army in September 1916, he holds the 1914-15 Star, and the General Service and Victory Medals.
205, Victoria Square, Ancoats, Manchester. Z11599

WEBB, A. G., Rifleman, K.R.R.C.

He joined in June 1918, and after undergoing a period of training, served at various stations, where he was engaged on important coastal defence duties. Owing to the early cessation of hostilities, he was not successful in obtaining his transfer overseas, but nevertheless, rendered valuable services with his unit until November 1919, when he was demobilised.
36, Brougham Street, West Gorton, Manchester. Z8589

WEBB, C., Air Mechanic, R.A.F.

He joined in August 1918, and after completing a term of training, was retained at various stations, where he was engaged on duties of a highly technical nature. He was unable to obtain his transfer to the Front on account of ill-health, but nevertheless, did much useful work with his Squadron until demobilised in March 1919.
12, Meriner Street, Chorlton-on-Medlock, Manchester. Z8587

WEBB, H. J., Private, Royal Fusiliers.

Joining in March 1916, he was drafted to the Western Front after three months' training, and there saw severe fighting in various sectors. He took part in the Battles of the Somme, the Ancre, Vimy Ridge, Ypres, Bapaume and the Scarpe and many minor engagements, and was wounded in action—at Arras in April 1917, and at Cambrai in November of that year. Demobilised in August 1919, he holds the General Service and Victory Medals.
36, Brougham Street, West Gorton, Manchester. Z8588

WEBB, J., Driver, R.F.A.

He volunteered in September 1914, and after a short period of training was engaged in conveying horses to and from France until March 1917. He was then drafted to the Western Front, where he saw much severe fighting, and was twice wounded in action—at Nieuport in July 1917, and in the third Battle of Ypres later in that year. Invalided home, he was retained, on his recovery, on important duties with the Anti-Aircraft section until his demobilisation in January 1919. He holds the 1914 Star, and the General Service and Victory Medals.
128, Slater Street, Rochdale Road, Manchester. Z8859

WEBB, F., Pte., Loyal N. Lancs. Rgt. and Labour Corps.
He joined in July 1916, and after his training served at various stations, where he was engaged on duties of great importance. He was not successful in obtaining his transfer to a theatre of war, on account of ill-health, but rendered very valuable services with his unit until March 1919, when he was demobilised. 6, Rose View, Longsight, Manchester. Z7327A

WEBB, J. B., Private, K.O. (Royal Lancaster Regt.)
Already in the Army when war was declared in August 1914, he was immediately drafted to the Western Front, where he fought in the Retreat from Mons. He also took part in the Battles of Ypres and the Somme and many other important engagements in various sectors, served also through the Retreat and Advance of 1918, and was wounded in action near Valenciennes in October of that year. Discharged in February 1919, he holds the Mons Star, and the General Service and Victory Medals.
36, Masonic Street, Oldham Road, Manchester. Z9183B

WEBSTER, A., Private, 2nd Manchester Regiment.
Mobilised in August 1914, he was immediately drafted to the Western Front, where he saw much severe fighting and took part in the Battles of Mons, and Le Cateau. He made the supreme sacrifice, falling in action in September 1914, during the Retreat from Mons. He was entitled to the Mons Star, and the General Service and Victory Medals.
"And doubtless he went in splendid company."
17, Rylance Street, Ardwick, Manchester. Z8590

WEBSTER, F., Guardsman, 1st Grenadier Guards.
He volunteered in August 1914, but after only a few weeks' service was invalided from the Army in the following month. He re-enlisted, however, in March 1917, and was immediately drafted to the Western Front, where he fought in the Battles of Ypres, and Havrincourt and other engagements and was gassed at Arras in May 1917. Finally demobilised in March 1919, he holds the General Service and Victory Medals.
91, Dale Street, Hulme, Manchester. Z8593

WEBSTER, F., Pte., 8th and 18th Manchester Regt.
Volunteering in March 1915, he proceeded to France three months later, and there saw heavy fighting in various sectors of the Front. He took part in the Battles of Loos, the Ancre, and many minor engagements until severely wounded in action at Arras in April 1917 and invalided home. He was finally discharged in April 1918, as medically unfit for further service, and holds the 1914-15 Star, and the General Service and Victory Medals.
4, Hyde View, Grey Street, West Gorton, Manchester. Z8492

WEBSTER, J., L/Cpl., 8th K.O. Scottish Borderers.
He volunteered in August 1914, and in April of the following year proceeded to the Western Front, where he saw heavy fighting in various sectors. After taking part in the Battles of Ypres and Albert and many other important engagements, he was severely wounded in action on the Somme in July 1916, and admitted to hospital in Birmingham. He was finally invalided from the Army in March 1917, and holds the 1914-15 Star, and the General Service and Victory Medals.
70, Rutland Street, Hulme, Manchester. TZ8594

WEBSTER, V. (Miss), Member, W.R.N.S. and W.R.A.F.
She joined in October 1918, and after completing a period of training, was engaged on important munition work at Messrs. Crossley's, Manchester. She also served at various other stations on various duties and rendered very valuable services until August 1919, when she was demobilised.
4, Hyde View, Grey Street, West Gorton, Manchester. Z8591

WEEDEN, J., Private, 16th Lancashire Fusiliers.
Joining in November 1916, he proceeded to the Western Front two months later, and there saw much severe fighting. He served through the Battles of Arras, Vimy Ridge, Ypres Cambrai, Armentières, Bapaume and Havrincourt, and many other engagements in various sectors, and was for a time in hospital at Rouen and in London, suffering from dysentery. Demobilised in December 1919, he holds the General Service and Victory Medals.
1, Galloway Street, Ardwick, Manchester. Z8595

WEETMAN, W. W., Pte., 1st Lancashire Fusiliers.
He volunteered in February 1915, and in April of the same year proceeded to the Dardanelles, where he saw much heavy fighting until the Evacuation of the Gallipoli Peninsula. He was then transferred to the Western Front, and there took part in many important engagements, and was severely wounded in action on the Somme. Invalided home, he was finally discharged in June 1918, as medically unfit for further service, and holds the 1914-15 Star, and the General Service and Victory Medals.
41, Denton Street, Hulme, Manchester. Z8596

WEIGH, R., Gunner, R.F.A.
He joined in April 1917, and after undergoing a period of training, served at various stations, where he was engaged on duties of great importance. He was not successful in obtaining his transfer to the Front, but nevertheless, rendered valuable services with his unit until October 1918, when he was transferred to Class W. of the Army Reserve.
36, Hancock Street, Rusholme, Manchester. Z8597

WEILDING, T., L/Corporal, R.E.
Volunteering in August 1914, he was drafted to Gallipoli in April of the following year, and there, after taking part in the Landing at Cape Helles, was present at the Battles of Krithia and other engagements. He was unhappily killed in action on September 3rd, 1915, and was buried near Cape Helles. He was entitled to the 1914-15 Star, and the General Service and Victory Medals.
"His life for his Country, his soul to God."
121, Bedford Street, Hulme, Manchester. Z8598

WEIR, J., Private, 11th Manchester Regiment.
He volunteered in September 1914, and on completing his training in the following year was drafted to Gallipoli, where he saw much severe fighting until the Evacuation of the Peninsula. He was then transferred to the Western Front, and there took part in important engagements in various sectors, including the Battles of Ypres. He was demobilised in February 1919, and holds the 1914-15 Star, and the General Service and Victory Medals.
176, Cobden Street, Ancoats, Manchester. Z11312

WEIR, R., Driver, R.A.S.C. (M.T.)
Shortly after volunteering in October 1914, he proceeded to the Western Front, where he was engaged on important duties in various sectors. He was present at the Battles of Ypres, Neuve Chapelle, St. Eloi, Hill 60, Festubert, Loos, Albert, the Somme, and Cambrai, and many minor engagements, and also took part in the Retreat and Advance of 1918. He holds the 1914 Star, and the General Service and Victory Medals, and in 1920 was still serving.
2, Gatley Street, Ancoats, Manchester. Z9269B

WELCH, C., Private, 23rd Welch Regiment.
He joined in January 1917, and after a period of training was retained on important duties at various stations. He was unable to obtain his transfer overseas before the cessation of hostilities, but in December 1918, proceeded to Germany, where he served with the Army of Occupation for ten months. He was demobilised on his return home in October 1919.
24, Anslow Street, Rochdale Road, Manchester. Z11314

WELCH, G., Gunner, R.F.A.
He volunteered in September 1914, and in June of the following year was drafted to the Western Front, where he saw severe fighting at Ypres, Kemmel, Armentières, and many other places. After taking part also in the Battles of Albert, Vimy Ridge, and the Somme, he was transferred in June 1917 to Mesopotamia, and was there engaged on important duties with the Royal Army Medical Corps. He was demobilised on his return home in May 1919, and holds the 1914-15 Star, and the General Service and Victory Medals.
9, Welton Place, Moor Street, Rusholme, Manchester. Z8600

WELCH, R., Private, M.G.C.
Volunteering in January 1916, he underwent a period of training prior to being drafted to Mesopotamia in March of the following year. There he took part in the Capture of Baghdad, and in other important engagements, and was stationed also at Amara and Kut, before being transferred to India. He finally returned home for demobilisation in January 1919, and holds the General Service and Victory Medals. 21, Clarence St., Miles Platting, Manchester. Z9241C

WELCH, R., Private, 1/10th King's (Liverpool Regt.)
He joined in August 1916, and in January of the following year was drafted to the Western Front, where he took part in the Battles of the Ancre, Arras, and Vimy Ridge, and many minor engagements. He died gloriously on the Field of Battle at Ypres on July 31st, 1917. He was entitled to the General Service and Victory Medals.
"The path of duty was the way to glory."
50, Markham Street, Ardwick, Manchester. Z8599

WELCH, S., L/Corporal, K.R.R.C.
He volunteered in August 1914, and three months later proceeded to the Western Front, where he saw severe fighting in various sectors. After taking part in the first Battle of Ypres, he was wounded in action in January 1915, and invalided home, but on his recovery returned to France. There he was again in action at the Battles of Festubert, Albert, the Somme, Arras, Ypres, and Cambrai, and other engagements until the cessation of hostilities. Demobilised in February 1919, he holds the 1914 Star, and the General Service and Victory Medals.
114, Lind Street, Ancoats, Manchester. Z11313

WELCH, W., Private, King's (Liverpool Regiment).
He volunteered in August 1915, and proceeding to France in October, first saw heavy fighting during the German attacks at Festubert, Loos, and St. Eloi early in 1916. Later he took part in the Battles of the Somme, the Ancre, Arras, Vimy Ridge, Bullecourt, Ypres (III), and Cambrai. He was invalided home to hospital at Oswestry, where he unfortunately died from hemorrhage of the lungs in September 1918. He was entitled to the 1914-15 Star, and the General Service and Victory Medals.
"A costly sacrifice upon the altar of freedom."
24, Auslow Street, Rochdale Road Manchester. Z11315

WELLOCK, C. S., Private, Border Regiment.
He volunteered in August 1914, and proceeding to France twelve months later, took part in the Battles of Loos, the Somme and Ypres, and in heavy fighting in other sectors. He was badly wounded and invalided home to hospital at Bradford, but on his recovery was sent to Mesopotamia, where he participated in several important engagements. During his active service he was wounded in action on seven different occasions, and also suffered from trench fever. He holds the 1914-15 Star, and the General Service and Victory Medals, and was demobilised in November 1919.
8, Apsley Square, Ardwick, Manchester. TX8601A

WELLINGS, A., Private, 13th Manchester Regt.
He volunteered in November 1914, and was drafted overseas in September of the following year. During his service on the Western Front, he was in action at Armentières, but in December 1915, was sent to Salonika, where he took part in heavy fighting on the Struma, Vardar, and Doiran fronts until November 1918. He then returned to Le Havre in France, and was engaged on important hospital duties. He was demobilised in January 1919, and holds the 1914-15 Star, and the General Service and Victory Medals.
11, Howell Street, Collyhurst, Manchester. Z11316A

WELLINGS, J., Sergeant, 2nd Manchester Regt.
He enlisted in June 1913, and at the outbreak of war in August 1914, was sent to France with the first Expeditionary Force, and was wounded in action at the Battle of Mons. Later he served with distinction at Arras (where he was again wounded in September 1915), and in other important engagements. He was wounded for the third time at Laventie in June 1916, and on this occasion was invalided home. Two months later he was discharged as medically unfit for further service, and holds the Mons Star, and the General Service and Victory Medals.
26, Gladstone Street, West Gorton, Manchester. Z8602

WELLINGS, R., Driver, R.A.S.C.
He volunteered in August 1914, and on completion of his training was retained on important transport duties at various home stations. Owing to heart disease, he was unsuccessful in obtaining his transfer overseas, but did consistently good work until his discharge as medically unfit in January 1919. Unfortunately he died from his infirmity at the Royal Infirmary, Manchester, on October 10th, 1919.
"His memory is cherished with pride."
62, Chapelfield Road, Ardwick, Manchester. Z8603

WELLINGS, T., Sergeant, 26th Middlesex Regiment.
He volunteered in August 1914, and was engaged on important duties as an instructor at Aldershot, where he rendered valuable services until January 1916. He was then sent to Hong-Kong in China, but in March 1917, was transferred to Russia, and did consistently good work at Vladivostok. He holds the General Service and Victory Medals, and was demobilised in December 1919.
11, Howell Street, Collyhurst, Manchester. Z11316B

WELLINGS, W., Private, M.G.C.
Volunteering in April 1915, he was quickly drafted to France, and took part in the Battles of Loos, Vermelles, the Somme, the Ancre, Arras, Bullecourt, Ypres (III), Cambrai, the Aisne (III), the Marne, Bapaume, and Le Cateau (II). He returned to England in February 1919, and was then demobilised, holding the 1914-15 Star, and the General Service and Victory Medals. 19, Holme Street, Ancoats, Manchester. Z8604

WELLOCK, H., Private, Labour Corps.
He joined in January 1917, and was quickly drafted to France, where he was engaged on important trench digging and railway construction duties at Albert, Grandecourt and Arras. After a short period of valuable service, he was unfortunately killed on June 4th, 1917, and was entitled to the General Service and Victory Medals.
"The path of duty was the way to glory."
23, Parker Street, Ardwick, Manchester. Z11317

WELLOCK, J., Sgt., L. N. Lancs. Regt., and R.A.S.C.
He volunteered in September 1914, and was drafted to the Western Front in the following year. He served with distinction at Armentières, Pont Nieppe, Ploegsteert Wood, and Vimy Ridge, and was wounded in action on the Somme in July 1916. He holds the 1914-15 Star, and the General Service and Victory Medals. and was demobilised in February 1919.
8, Apsley Square, Ardwick, Manchester. TX8601B

WELLS, G. E., Private, 20th Lancashire Fusiliers.
He volunteered in July 1915, and on completion of his training was drafted to the Western Front, where he took part in the Battles of the Somme, Arras, Ypres, and Cambrai, and in heavy fighting at Albert and Gouzeaucourt. Unfortunately he was killed in action near Corbie on March 26th, 1918, during the Retreat, and was entitled to the General Service and Victory Medals.
"A valiant soldier, with undaunted heart he breasted life's last hill."
85, Granville Place, Ancoats, Manchester. Z9745A

WELLS, H., Private, 3rd Welch Regiment.
On attaining military age, he joined the Welch Regiment in September 1918, and was quickly drafted to the Western

Front, where he was engaged on important duties. After the cessation of hostilities, he served for a time with the Army of Occupation in Germany, but was later transferred to Ireland. He was demobilised in April 1920, and holds the General Service and Victory Medals.
46, Hazel Street, Hulme, Manchester. TZ8606

WELLS, P., Sergeant, 2/6th Manchester Regiment.
He joined in February 1916, and early in the following year was drafted to France, where he served with distinction at the Battles of Arras, Ypres, and Passchendaele. He was then sent to Marseilles, and was engaged on special duties as an orderly room sergeant. In February 1919 he was demobilised, and holds the General Service and Victory Medals.
156, Cowesby Street, Moss Side, Manchester. Z11848

WELLS, R., Private, 13th King's (Liverpool Regt.)
He joined in July 1916, and five months later was in action on the Western Front, where he took part in the Battles of the Ancre, Bullecourt, Ypres (III), Cambrai (I), the Marne (II), Havrincourt and Cambrai (II), and in the other important engagements during the Retreat and Advance of 1918. After the cessation of hostilities, he served in Germany with the Army of Occupation, and was eventually demobilised in November 1919, holding the General Service and Victory Medals. 46, Hazel St., Hulme, Manchester. TZ8605

WELLS, T., Private, 1st South Lancashire Regt.
He joined in 1918, and on completion of his training was drafted to Ireland, where he was engaged on important garrison duties. He rendered valuable services with his unit, but was unsuccessful in obtaining his transfer to a theatre of war, and was demobilised in 1919.
86, Granville Place, Ancoats, Manchester. Z9745C

WELSBY, J. E., Sergt., Military Foot Police.
He volunteered in October 1915, and after being stationed at Aldershot and in Dorset, was sent to Ireland, and did consistently good work at Cork and Dublin. He also did duty on the boat service between Ireland and England, but, owing to an attack of pneumonia which rendered him medically unfit, was not successful in obtaining his transfer overseas, and was demobilised in September 1919. Z8607 Z11318
32, Holstein Street, Chorlton-on-Medlock, Manchester.

WELSH, J., Private, 20th Manchester Regiment.
Volunteering in March 1915, he proceeded to France in December, and first saw heavy fighting at St. Eloi, and Albert. Later he took part in the Battles of the Somme, Ypres (III), the Marne (II), and Cambrai (II), and was twice wounded in action —on the Somme in July 1916, and at Cambrai in September 1918. He was in hospital in France and Wales, and after the cessation of hostilities, re-engaged in the Army for a period of three years, and was serving in Mesopotamia in 1920. He holds the 1914-15 Star, and the General Service and Victory Medals. 11, George Street, Hulme, Manchester. Z8610

WELSH, J., Private, 8th South Lancashire Regt.
He volunteered in March 1915, and six months later was drafted to the Western Front, where he took part in the Battles of Loos, Albert and the Somme, and was badly wounded in July 1916. After hospital treatment at Brighton, he was transferred to Class W. Army Reserve, but in July 1917 was discharged as medically unfit for further service. In September 1918, however, he rejoined and was engaged on important duties until February 1919, when he was finally demobilised, holding the 1914-15 Star, and the General Service and Victory Medals.
26, Lavender Street, Miles Platting, Manchester. Z11319

WELSH, P., Private, 8th Manchester Regiment.
He volunteered in August 1914, and in the following April was drafted to the Gallipoli Peninsula, where he took part in the Landing at Cape Helles, and in the three Battles of Krithia. Badly wounded in action in June 1915, he spent three months in hospital at Port Said before being invalided to Warrington for further treatment. He was discharged as medically unfit for further service in December 1916, and holds the 1914-15 Star, and the General Service and Victory Medals.
11, George Street, Hulme, Manchester. Z8609

WELSH, T., Private, 2nd Manchester Regiment.
A serving soldier, he was drafted to France with the first Expeditionary Force, but was unhappily killed in action at the Battle of Mons in August 1914, after a short, but distinguished period of active service. He was entitled to the Mons Star and the General Service and Victory Medals.
"A valiant Soldier, with undaunted heart he breasted life's last hill."
11, George Street, Hulme, Manchester. Z8608

WELSH, T., Driver, R.A.S.C.
He volunteered in January 1915, and was sent to France twelve months afterwards. During his service on the Western Front, he was engaged on important transport duties in the forward areas, and saw heavy fighting on the Somme, the Lys and the Ancre, and at St. Eloi, Arras, Bullecourt, Messines, Amiens and Bapaume. He holds the General Service and Victory Medals, and was demobilised on his return to England in March 1919.
18, Victoria Square, Ancoats, Manchester. Z8862

WELSH, W., Sergt., Manchester Regiment.
He volunteered in August 1914, and twelve months later was sent to the Dardanelles, where he took part in the Landing at Suvla Bay, and was wounded. After the Evacuation of the Gallipoli Peninsula, he was stationed at Kantara, El Foden and Alexandria in Egypt until May 1916. He was then transferred to the Western Front, where he served with distinction at the Battles of the Somme, Arras, Messines, Ypres and Cambrai, and in the Retreat and Advance of 1918. He was wounded in action on two other occasions—at Ypres in 1917, and at Cambrai during the Advance. He holds the 1914-15 Star, and the General Service and Victory Medals, and was demobilised on his return home in May 1919.
16, Baguley Street, Miles Platting, Manchester. Z9746

WELSH, W., Private, 17th Manchester Regiment.
He volunteered in October 1915, and first saw active service at Loos, where he was in action during the German attack in March 1916. He also fought at St. Eloi, Albert, Vermelles and Vimy Ridge, and was wounded on the Somme in July 1916. Unfortunately he died gloriously on the Field of Battle shortly afterwards, and was entitled to the General Service and Victory Medals.
"Whilst we remember, the sacrifice is not in vain."
35, Elizabeth Ann Street, Manchester. Z9747A

WENFORD, G., Private, R.A.M.C.
Mobilised in August 1914, he was immediately drafted to France, where he rendered valuable services as a first-class nursing Ordely at Rouen and Le Tréport. In August 1918 he was sent home for similar duties at the 2nd Western General Hospital, and was finally discharged in July 1919, holding the 1914 Star, and the General Service and Victory Medals.
17, James St., Moss Side, Manchester. Z8611

WENTWORTH, E., Private, King's (Liverpool Regt.).
He joined in March 1916, and two months later was drafted to the Western Front, where he played a prominent part in the Battles of the Somme, Bullecourt and Ypres (III), and in heavy fighting during the Retreat and Advance of 1918. He returned to England for his demobilisation in January 1919, and holds the General Service and Victory Medals.
45, Albion Terrace, Varley Street, Manchester. Z11320

WEST, C., Rifleman, K.R.R.C.
He volunteered in November 1914, and in the following month was drafted to the Western Front, where he took part in the Battles of Neuve Chapelle and Hill 60, and was wounded in each of these engagements. He also fought at the Battles of Ypres (II) and Loos, but was unfortunately killed in action on the Somme (II) in April 1918. He was entitled to the 1914-15 Star, and the General Service and Victory Medals.
"His life for his Country, his soul to God."
30, Hibbert Street, Hulme, Manchester. Z8612

WEST, J., Private, Lancashire Fusiliers.
He joined in March 1918, and was quickly sent to Ireland, where he was engaged on important garrison duty. Owing to the early cessation of hostilities he was unable to obtain a transfer to a theatre of war, but rendered valuable services, and in 1920 was still serving.
50, Rylance Street, Ardwick, Manchester. Z8613

WEST, J., L/Corporal, K.R.R.C.
He was mobilised in August 1914, and in the following month proceeded to France, where he took part in the Retreat from Mons and the Battles of the Marne, La Bassée, Ypres, Neuve Chapelle, St. Eloi, Hill 60, Ypres II, Loos, Vimy Ridge, the Somme and Arras, and was badly wounded. As a result he was invalided home and discharged in June 1917, holding the Mons Star, and the General Service and Victory Medals.
63, Hewitt Street, Gorton, Manchester. Z11321

WEST, W., Rifleman, 16th K.R.R.C.
He volunteered in September 1914, and early in the following year was drafted to the Western Front. In this seat of war he took part in many engagements, including the Battles of Ypres (II), Festubert, Albert, Vermelles, the Somme, Arras, Bullecourt, Ypres (III) and Cambrai and in the Retreat and Advance of 1918. He was demobilised in March 1919 and holds the 1914-15 Star, and the General Service and Victory Medals.
53, Oliver St., Openshaw, Manchester. Z8614

WESTBROOK, F., Corporal, M.G.C.
Volunteering in August 1914, he proceeded to France in July of the following year and played a prominent part in the heavy fighting at St. Eloi and at the Battles of the Somme and Ypres, and was twice wounded in action. He was mentioned in Despatches for conspicuous bravery on the Somme in July 1916, when he stuck to his gun after all his comrades had been killed. In March 1918 he was taken prisoner at Arras and was held in captivity at Mecklenberg in Germany. Repatriated in December 1918, he was demobilised a month later, and holds the 1914-15 Star, and the General Service and Victory Medals.
22, Kay St., Chorlton-on-Medlock, Manchester. X8615B

WESTBROOK, J. P., Pte., Loyal N. Lancashire Regt.
He joined in November 1917, and after a period of training was drafted to France, where he took part in the Retreat and Advance of 1918 and in the Battle of Ypres (IV). After the Armistice he went to Germany with the Army of Occupation and served there until his demobilisation in December 1919. He holds the General Service and Victory Medals.
22, Kay St., Chorlton-on-Medlock, Manchester. TX8616

WESTBROOK, T., Private, 1/8th Manchester Regt.
Volunteering in April 1915, he was sent to Egypt in the following January and saw service on the Suez Canal. In March 1917 he was transferred to the Western Front, and after taking part in heavy fighting on the Somme and at La Bassée and Ypres, was wounded and gassed during the Retreat of 1918. On his recovery he rejoined his unit and was in action at the Battles of Havrincourt, Epéhy and Bapaume. He holds the General Service and Victory Medals, and was demobilised in March 1919.
22, Kay St., Chorlton-on-Medlock, Manchester. X8615A

WESTBROOK, W., Private, 8th Manchester Regt.
He volunteered in June 1915, and later in the same year proceeded to the Western Front. There he took part in many engagements, including the Battles of Arras, the Somme, Péronne and Havrincourt, whence he was invalided home suffering from trench fever. On his recovery he returned to France and saw much fighting at Le Cateau (II) and was near Mons on Armistice Day. Whilst in France he also served with the 21st and 23rd Manchester Regiments, and was demobilised in June 1919, holding the 1914-15 Star, and the General Service and Victory Medals. TX7265/6B
7, Robert Street, Chorlton-on-Medlock, Manchester.

WESTMORLAND, F., Pte., 1st Gloucestershire Regt.
After working as a miner in Bradford Colliery, he volunteered in May 1915, and in the same year was drafted to the Western Front, where he took part in the Battles of Loos and Vimy Ridge. He was reported missing during the Battle of the Somme and afterwards officially reported killed in action on September 8th, 1916. He was entitled to the 1914-15 Star, and the General Service and Victory Medals.
"A costly sacrifice upon the altar of freedom."
28, Lever Street, Bradford, Manchester. Z8617

WESTWOOD, E. (M.M.) Sgt., 13th R.Welch Fusiliers.
Volunteering in May 1915, he was drafted overseas in the following July. Whilst on the Western Front he took a prominent part in the Battles of Loos, Vermelles, Vimy Ridge, Arras, Bullecourt, Ypres, Cambrai, the Marne (II) and Havrincourt. He was awarded the Military Medal for conspicuous bravery and devotion to duty in the Field in November 1916. He also holds the 1914-15 Star, and the General Service and Victory Medals, and was demobilised in March 1919. 16, Johnson's Buildings, Ancoats, Manchester. Z8619

WESTWOOD, W., Sapper, R.E. (Signal Section).
He joined in June 1916, and on completing his training in the following January, proceeded to France, where he took part in the Battles of Arras, Ypres (III), Cambrai (I and II) and Le Cateau (II) and in other important engagements during the Retreat and Advance of 1918. After the Armistice he went to Germany with the Army of Occupation and served at Cologne until his demobilisation in September 1919. He holds the General Service and Victory Medals.
3, Dearden Street, Hulme, Manchester. TZ8618

WETTON, G., Special War Worker.
He undertook work of National importance shortly after the outbreak of war and was engaged on the construction of aeroplanes at the Aero Factory at Newton, Manchester. He carried out his duties in a very skilful manner and rendered valuable services until the cessation of hostilities in November 1918. 75, Naylor St., Oldham Road, Manchester. Z9748

WHAITE, H., Private, Manchester Regiment.
He volunteered in August 1915, and in November was drafted to the Western Front, where he took part in the Battles of the Somme (I) and Passchendaele, and in the Retreat of 1918, during which he was wounded in action and invalided to hospital. On his recovery he was in action throughout the final Advance. He was demobilised in March 1919, and holds the 1914-15 Star, and the General Service and Victory Medals. 100, Victoria St., Longsight, Manchester. Z8620

WHALEN, F. W., 2nd Border Regiment.
He joined in June 1917, and shortly afterwards was drafted to France. During his service on the Western Front he took part in the heavy fighting at the Battle of Cambrai (I). Later he was transferred to Italy, where he was in action on the Piave front until May 1918, when he was invalided to hospital in England suffering from shell-shock. He was discharged as medically unfit for further service in July 1918, and holds the General Service and Victory Medals.
5, Garatt Street, Newton End, Manchester. Z11849

WHALLEY, E., Pte., Oxfordshire and Buckinghamshire Light Infantry.
He volunteered in September 1915, and in the following June proceeded to France, where he took part in the heavy fighting on the Somme. After a short period of service he was unfortunately killed in action on September 3rd, 1916. He was entitled to the General Service and Victory Medals.
"He joined the great white company of valiant souls."
1, Matilda Street, Ancoats, Manchester. Z11322

WHALLEY, F., Air Mechanic, R.A.F.
He joined in November 1917, and after a period of service was retained on important duties with his Squadron at Aldershot. Owing to medical unfitness he was not successful in obtaining a transfer to a theatre of war, but did consistently good work during the period of hostilities. He was still serving in 1920.
51, Halston Street, Hulme, Manchester. Z8621

WHALLEY, J., Private, Durham Light Infantry, and Sapper. R.E.
Volunteering in July 1915, he was sent to France in the following May and took part in heavy fighting at Armentières. He was also in action at the Battles of Ploegsteert, the Somme (I), Ypres (III), Cambrai, the Somme (II), Bapaume, Havrincourt, Ypres (IV) and Le Cateau (II). He holds the General Service and Victory Medals, and was demobilised on his return to England in March 1919.
87, Hinckley Street, Bradford, Manchester. Z8623

WHALLEY, J., Private, 2nd Lancashire Fusiliers.
He volunteered in August 1914, and on completion of his training was drafted to the Western Front, where he played a prominent part in the Battles of St. Eloi, Ypres (II), Albert, the Somme (II), Havrincourt, Bullecourt and Cambrai (II). He returned to England in March 1919, and was demobilised in the following month, holding the 1914-15 Star, and the General Service and Victory Medals.
35, Charles Street, Bradford, Manchester. Z8622

WHALLEY, L., Private, Loyal N. Lancashire Regt.
He volunteered in August 1914, and proceeding overseas in the following May served on the Western Front for fifteen months, during which time he was in action at Messines and Albert, and was twice wounded. Later he was transferred to Palestine, and was present at the Capture of Jerusalem, Jaffa and Jericho. He was discharged in April 1918 as medically unfit for further service, and holds the 1914-15 Star, and the General Service and Victory Medals.
5, Lime Street, Bradford, Manchester. ZT11850

WHARTON, M., Private, 3rd K. (Liverpool Regt.)
He joined in July 1918, and on completion of his training served in Ireland and England, where he was engaged on important garrison and guard duties with his unit. He was not able to obtain a transfer to a theatre of war during the period of hostilities, but, nevertheless, rendered valuable services until demobilised in November 1919.
46, Redvers Street, Ardwick, Manchester. Z8625

WHARTON, R. E., Private, 1st Manchester Regt.
He joined in June 1917, and shortly afterwards proceeded to France, where he saw service in various sectors of the Front. In December 1917, he was transferred to India, and was engaged on important garrison duties until January 1919. He then returned to England, and was demobilised in the following month, and holds the General Service and Victory Medals.
16, Dearden St., Hulme, Manchester. TZ8624

WHATLEY, T., Corporal, M.G.C.
He joined in July 1916, and in the following April was sent to France, where he served with distinction in the Battles of Bullecourt and Passchendaele. In November 1917 he was transferred to Italy and took part in heavy fighting on the Piave and the Asiago Plateaux. Admitted to the 62nd General Hospital in November 1918 suffering from a serious illness, he was invalided home in January 1919, when he was discharged, and holds the General Service and Victory Medals.
102, South Street, Longsight, Manchester. Z8626

WHATMOUGH, F., Private, 12th Manchester Regt.
Volunteering in September 1914, he proceeded to France in the following July and saw much heavy fighting in various sectors of the Front. He was in action throughout the Battles of Loos, St. Eloi, Albert, Vimy Ridge and the Somme, where he was badly wounded in July 1916. As a result he was invalided to hospital and finally discharged in January 1917. He holds the 1914-15 Star, and the General Service and Victory Medals.
75, Edensor Street, Beswick, Manchester. Z8627

WHATMOUGH, G., Gunner, R.F.A.
He volunteered in September 1914, and after a period of training was drafted to the Western Front. He saw much service in various sectors, and took part in the engagements at Ypres (II), Kemmel and Loos. In September 1915 he was sent to Salonika and took part in the advance across the Struma front. He was demobilised in February 1919, and holds the 1914-15 Star, and the General Service and Victory Medals.
13, Long St., Ancoats, Manchester. Z11323

WHEATCROFT, D., Pte., K.O. (R. Lancaster Regt.)
He volunteered in September 1914, and after his training was retained on important duties with his unit. He did valuable work until May 1915, when owing to an unfortunate accident, in which he was badly hurt, he was discharged from the Service after a period of treatment at the General Military Hospital in Sunderland.
32, Garibaldi Street, Ardwick, Manchester. Z8628

WHEATCROFT, E., Pte., 8th Manchester Regiment.
Volunteering in August 1914, he completed his training and

was engaged on important coast defence duties with his unit at various stations. He rendered valuable services until August 1916, when he was discharged as medically unfit for duty owing to his age and general indisposition.
34, Garibaldi Street, Ardwick, Manchester. Z8465B

WHEATCROFT, S. E., Private, 8th Manchester Rgt.
He volunteered in January 1915, and three months later was drafted to the Dardanelles, where he took part in the Landings at Cape Helles and Suvla Bay and in the three Battles of Krithia. After the Evacuation of the Gallipoli Peninsula he proceeded to Egypt and fought at Matia, Sollum and Romani. In March 1917 he was transferred to the Western Front, but after taking part in the Battles of Ypres (III), the Somme (II), Epéhy and Havrincourt, was badly gassed in action at Givenchy in September 1918, and was invalided home. He was demobilised in April 1919, and holds the 1914-15 Star, and the General Service and Victory Medals.
34, Garibaldi Street, Ardwick, Mnachester. Z8465C

WHEDDOW, W. E., 16th Manchester Regiment.
He volunteered at the outbreak of hostilities in August 1914, and was first retained on important duties with his unit. In January 1916 he proceeded overseas and took part in many engagements in various sectors of the Western Front. He was in action at the Battles of the Somme, Vimy Ridge and Bullecourt and later in the Offensive of 1918, where he was wounded in August. As a result, he was invalided to hospital and finally demobilised in April 1919. He holds the General Service and Victory Medals.
20, Scott Street, Hulme, Manchester. Z8629

WHEELDON, T., Private, 1st Border Regiment.
He volunteered in December 1914, and in March of the following year was drafted to the Dardanelles, where he fought at the Landing at Cape Helles and the Battles of Krithia and Achi Baba. He was wounded three times, and on the last occasion was invalided home. On his recovery in March 1916 he was sent to France and was in action in the Battle of the Somme, where he was wounded. He again went into action and was wounded for the fifth time on the Somme, a few months later. As a result he was invalided to England and discharged as medically unfit for further service in December 1917. He holds the 1914-15 Star, and the General Service and Victory Medals.
5, Loftus Street, Bradford, Manchester. Z8630

WHEELER, V. A., Gunner, R.F.A.
Mobilised in August 1914, he quickly proceeded to France and went with his Battery to the relief of the Royal Naval Division at Antwerp. Later he took part in the Battles of La Bassée, Ypres (I), Neuve Chapelle, Festubert, Loos, Albert, the Somme, Arras, Bullecourt and Ypres (III). In November 1917 he was transferred to Italy, where he was in action on the Piave and Asiago Plateaux. He was slightly gassed at Loos in September 1915, and eventually received his discharge in February 1919, holding the 1914-15 Star, and the General Service and Victory Medals.
15, Drayton Street, Hulme, Manchester. TZ8632

WHEELER, W., Driver, R.F.A.
He volunteered in August 1914, and on completion of his training was drafted to France, where he saw much service in various sectors of the Front. He took part in many important engagements, including the Battles of Loos, the Somme (I), Vimy Ridge, Ypres, Cambrai and St. Quentin. In May 1918 he was wounded in action and invalided to hospital. He was demobilised in February 1919, and holds the 1914-15 Star, and the General Service and Victory Medals.
33, Mark Street, Hulme, Manchester. Z6631

WHEELTON, S. (M.S.M.), Manchester Regiment, and M.G.C.
A Territorial, he was mobilised in August 1914, and quickly proceeded to Egypt, where he saw heavy fighting in the Suez Canal zone. In 1915 he was sent to the Dardanelles, took part in the Landing at Suvla Bay and after the Evacuation of the Gallipoli Peninsula, returned to Egypt. Later he advanced into Palestine, but in March 1917 was transferred to the Western Front, and was in action at the Battles of Ypres (III), Passchendaele and the Somme (II), and in heavy fighting at La Bassée, Nieuport and Dunkirk. He was awarded the Meritorious Service Medal and mentioned in Despatches for conspicuously good work throughout hostilities, and also holds the 1914-15 Star, and the General Service and Victory Medals and the Territorial Force Efficiency Medal. He was demobilised on his return to England in March 1919.
4, Montague Street, Collyhurst, Manchester. Z11600

WHELAN, J., Private, 1st Border Regiment.
Joining in April 1917, he was drafted to the Western Front on completion of his training, but after taking part in the Battles of Ypres (III), and Cambrai, was badly wounded in action and invalided home. On his recovery he was sent to Dublin in Ireland and did consistently good work whilst on transport duties with the South Lancashire Regiment. He was demobilised in September 1919, and holds the General Service and Victory Medals.
10, Mark Street, Hulme, Manchester. Z8633

WHELAN, J. C., Private, 19th Manchester Regt.
He joined early in 1916, and was quickly drafted to France, where he was in action at Ypres, Festubert, Armentières and Albert, before being wounded and taken prisoner during the Somme Offensive in July 1916. He received three separate wounds, but stuck to his post until falling into enemy hands. During his captivity he suffered many hardships and was repatriated in January 1919. He was then discharged, and holds the General Service and Victory Medals.
131, Granville Place, Ancoats, Manchester. Z8634

WHELAND, F., Private, 4th King's (Liverpool Regt.)
He volunteered in July 1915, and five months later was drafted to the Western Front, where he was first in action during the German attack at Loos early in 1916. Later he took part in the Battles of the Somme and Arras, but was unfortunately killed at the 3rd Battle of Ypres on July 31st, 1917. He was entitled to the 1914-15 Star, and the General Service and Victory Medals.
" Nobly striving,
He nobly fell that we might live."
42, Park Street, Hulme, Manchester. Z8635

WHETTALL, L., L/Cpl., 6th King's Shropshire L.I.
Volunteering in September 1914, he proceeded to France in the following July and played a prominent part in the Battles of Loos, Albert, Vermelles, Ploegsteert, the Somme, Arras, Ypres (III) and Cambrai and in the Retreat and Advance of 1918. He laid down his life for King and Country near Havrincourt on September 27th, 1918, and was entitled to the 1914-15 Star, and the General Service and Victory Medals.
" The path of duty was the way to glory."
27, Jackson Street, Openshaw, Manchester. Z8636B

WHETTALL, W. W., Pte., 1st Loyal N. Lancs. Regt.
He volunteered in September 1914, and on completion of his training was drafted to France in June of the following year. After taking part in heavy fighting at Festubert, he died gloriously on the Field of Battle at Loos in September 1915. He was entitled to the 1914-15 Star, and the General Service and Victory Medals.
" He died the noblest death a man may die,
Fighting for God and right and liberty."
27, Jackson Street, Openshaw, Manchester. Z8636A

WHILES, F., Private, 2nd East Lancashire Regt.
Volunteering in October 1915, he was drafted to France five months later, and during his service in this theatre of war took part in heavy fighting at St. Eloi, Beaucourt and Beaumont-Hamel. He was also in action at the Battles of Vermelles, Bullecourt, Passchendaele and Cambrai, where he was badly wounded in November 1917. Invalided home, he spent some time in No. 3 Western General Hospital at Preston, and was eventually demobilised in November 1919, holding the General Service and Victory Medals.
90, Bickley Street, Moss Side, Manchester. Z11851A

WHILES, T. W., Private, 1/7th Manchester Regt.
He volunteered in August 1914, and proceeding to the Dardanelles early in the following year, took part in the Landings at Cape Helles and Suvla Bay, and was wounded during the Evacuation of the Gallipoli Peninsula. On his recovery, he was sent to the Western Front and fought at the Battles of Ploegsteert, the Somme, Messines, Lens and Cambrai. He was demobilised in January 1919, and holds the 1914-15 Star, and the General Service and Victory Medals.
90, Bickley Street, Moss Side, Manchester. Z11851B

WHIMPENNY, F., Gunner, R.F.A.
Mobilised in August 1914, he proceeded to France with the 34th Battery, and was wounded in action almost immediately at the Battle of Mons. After hospital treatment at the Base, he rejoined his Battery and took part in the Battles of La Bassée, Ypres (I), Neuve Chapelle, Arras (where he was wounded for the second time), Ypres (III), Passchendaele and the Somme. He then served at Cologne and Bonn with the Army of Occupation, and received his discharge in June 1919, holding the Mons Star, and the General Service and Victory Medals.
18, Granville Street, Chorlton-on-Medlock, Manchester. Z8637

WHITAKER, J. H., Private, 53rd Manchester Regt.
Although forty-four years of age, he volunteered in November 1915, and on completion of his training was engaged on special duties with his unit at various home stations. He was not successful in obtaining his transfer overseas, but rendered valuable services until his demobilisation in May 1919.
13, Ovil St., Hancock St., Hulme, Manchester. Z8638

WHITAKER, T., Private, 1/7th Manchester Regt.
Mobilised with the Territorials in August 1914, he was sent to Egypt within a month. Later, however, he proceeded to the Dardanelles and saw much severe fighting during the Gallipoli campaign. After the Evacuation of the Peninsula, he returned to Egypt and was in action at the Battle of Romani. In February 1917 he was transferred to the Western Front, where he was engaged on special duties at Dunkirk. He holds the 1914-15 Star, and the General Service and Victory Medals. and was demobilised in February 1919.
14, Craven Street, Hulme, Manchester. Z8639

WHITTALL, J. T., Private, 23rd Manchester Regt.
He joined in September 1917, and proceeding to France two months later, played a prominent part in the Battles of Cambrai, the Somme (II), and the Marne. He laid down his life for King and Country in July 1918, and was entitled to the General Service and Victory Medals.
Great deeds cannot die :
They with the sun and moon renew their light for ever."
14, Tonge Street, Ancoats, Manchester. Z11333

WHITE, C., Corporal, North Lancashire Regiment.
He was mobilised in August 1914, and quickly drafted to the Western Front, where he played a prominent part in the Battles of La Bassée, Ypres and Loos and in heavy fighting at other important places. He was badly wounded in action, and invalided home, and as a result, was discharged in 1916 as medically unfit for further service, holding the 1914 Star, and the General Service and Victory Medals.
8, Oram Street, Manchester. Z11601

WHITE, H., Private, 21st Manchester Regiment.
He volunteered in December 1914, and after a period of training was drafted to the Western Front, where he was in action at the Battles of Ypres (II), Albert, the Somme, Arras, Vimy Ridge, Ypres (III), Passchendaele and Cambrai. In November 1917 he was transferred to Italy and fought on the Asiago Plateau and the Piave, but in March 1918 returned to France, and was in action throughout the Retreat and Advance. Demobilised on his return to England in January 1919, he holds the 1914-15 Star, and the General Service and Victory Medals.
77, Norton Street, West Gorton, Manchester. Z8640

WHITE, H., Private, 7th Manchester Regiment.
Volunteering in May 1915, he proceeded to the Dardanelles on completion of his training and took part in heavy fighting on Gallipoli until the Evacuation of the Peninsula in January 1916. He was then sent to Egypt, but later in the same year was drafted to Salonika, where he was in action at important engagements on the Struma front. In October 1917 he was transferred to Palestine and then served through the advance with General Allenby's Forces. He holds the 1914-15 Star, and the General Service and Victory Medals, and was demobilised in July 1919.
15, Marsden Street, Newton Heath, Manchester. Z9752

WHITE, H., Private, King's (Liverpool Regiment).
He joined in September 1917, and was drafted to France four months later. He was in action at Béthune, La Bassée, and Nieuport, and after the cessation of hostilities, rendered valuable services whilst engaged on reconstruction work. He holds the General Service and Victory Medals, and was demobilised on his return to England in February 1920.
12, Ashbourne Street, West Gorton, Manchester. Z8641

WHITE, J., Private, 23rd Manchester Regiment.
Volunteering in January 1915, he proceeded to France later in the same year. He was badly wounded during the Somme Offensive in July 1916, and was invalided to the 2nd Western General Hospital in Manchester. On his recovery he returned to the Western Front, and was in action in other important engagements. He holds the 1914-15 Star, and the General Service and Victory Medals. and was demobilised in 1918.
36, Rochester Street, Harpurhey, Manchester. Z11602

WHITE, J., Driver, R.F.A.
Volunteering in August 1914, he proceeded to France early in the following year and took part with his Battery in the Battles of Neuve Chapelle, St. Eloi, Ypres, Festubert, Loos, the Somme, Arras, Bullecourt, Lens, Cambrai, Havrincourt and Epéhy. He was demobilised in 1919, and holds the 1914-15 Star, and the General Service and Victory Medals.
18, Worth Street, St. Michaels, Manchester. Z11326A

WHITE, J. H., Private, 16th Lancashire Fusiliers.
He volunteered in September 1914, and in December of the following year was drafted to the Western Front, where he took part in the Battles of Albert, Ploegsteert, the Somme, Bullecourt and Ypres (III). He was badly wounded in action in September 1917, and after hospital treatment in France, was invalided home seven months later. He was eventually demobilised in May 1919, and holds the General Service and Victory Medals.
11, Linacre Street, Oldham Road, Manchester. Z11325

WHITE, J. W., Pte., King's Shropshire Light Infty.
He joined in 1917, and on completion of his training was drafted to the Western Front, where he saw much severe fighting during the Retreat and Advance, and was wounded in action at the Battle of Valenciennes in November 1918. In 1920 he was still in the Army, and holds the General Service and Victory Medals.
18, Worth Street, St. Michaels, Manchester. Z11326B

WHITE, M.(Mrs.), Assist. Administrator, Q.M.A.A.C.
She joined in November 1917, and was quickly sent to Ireland, where she was stationed at Holywood Camp and engaged on important duties. She was inspecting the food supplies for the staff, and rendered valuable services until her demobilisation in March 1919.
1, Dalton Street, Longsight, Manchester. Z8340B

WHITE, S., Driver, R.A.S.C.
He volunteered in September 1914, and on completing his training in the following May, was drafted to France. There he took part in the Battles of Loos, St. Eloi, Vimy Ridge, the Somme, Arras, Bullecourt, Messines, Ypres (III), Passchendaele and Cambrai and in the Retreat and Advance of 1918. He was demobilised in January 1919, and holds the 1914–15 Star, and the General Service and Victory Medals.
12, Kertch Street, Ancoats, Manchester. Z8642

WHITE, T., L/Corporal, Loyal N. Lancashire Regt.
He joined in February 1917, and later in the same year was drafted to France, where he took part in some heavy fighting near Cambrai, and was badly wounded in action. As a result he was invalided home, but on his recovery, was transferred to the Royal Army Service Corps, and engaged on important clerical duties. He was demobilised in November 1919, and holds the General Service and Victory Medals.
30, Albion Street, Miles Platting, Manchester. Z11324

WHITE, T. H., Private, Loyal N. Lancashire Regt.
He joined in May 1916, and two months later was drafted to France, where he took part in the Battle of the Somme, and was wounded. In consequence he was invalided home, but on his recovery, returned to France, and was in action at Beaumont-Hamel, Givenchy, and La Bassée, being gassed in action and sent to hospital in Boulogne. After hostilities ceased he went to Germany with the Army of Occupation and served there until his demobilisation in October 1919. He holds the General Service and Victory Medals.
10, Gower Street, Hulme, Manchester. Z8643

WHITEHEAD, A., Sapper, R.E.
He joined in April 1918, and during his training with his unit was engaged at various stations. Owing to the early cessation of hostilities he was unable to obtain a transfer overseas, but after the Armistice went to Germany, with the Army of Occupation, and served there until his demobilisation in October 1919.
210, Morton Street, Longsight, Manchester. Z8644

WHITEHEAD, A., Private, 8th Manchester Regt.
He volunteered in September 1914, and in the following year was drafted to the Dardanelles, where he saw much severe fighting. After the evacuation of the Gallipoli Peninsula, he was transferred to France, and took part in several engagements and was wounded in action at Ypres in October 1917. He was demobilised in January 1919, and holds the 1914–15 Star, and the General Service and Victory Medals.
124, Parker Street, Bradford, Manchester. Z9750

WHITEHEAD, E., Private, 8th Manchester Regt.
He joined in April 1917, and whilst in training at Preston was taken ill and invalided to hospital. He unfortunately died from weakness in September 1917.
" Steals on the ear the distant triumph song."
13, Mozart Street, Ancoats, Manchester. Z11328B

WHITEHEAD, F. W., Pte., 8th Manchester Regt.
He was mobilised with the Territorials in August 1914, and quickly sent to Egypt, where he was engaged on important duties at Cairo and Alexandria. Later he was transferred to the Dardanelles, and took part in much severe fighting, and was badly wounded. As a result he was invalided home and discharged in March 1918 as medically unfit for further service. He holds the 1914–15 Star, and the General Service and Victory Medals. 22, Glee St., Ancoats, Manchester. Z11327

WHITEHEAD, H., Sapper, R.E.
He volunteered in August 1914, and after completing his training, was drafted to France, where he served at the Base before proceeding to Egypt. In this seat of operations he took part in many engagements on the Suez Canal, and in Palestine until the cessation of hostilities. Later he was sent to Russia, where in 1920 he was still serving. He holds the General Service and Victory Medals.
1, Lord Street, Openshaw, Manchester. TZ8645

WHITEHEAD, H., Private, M.G.C.
Volunteering in August 1914, he underwent a period of training prior to his being drafted to France. There he took part in the Battles of the Somme and Ypres, and was wounded in action and admitted to hospital at the Base, before being invalided home. On his recovery he served on important duties until his demobilisation in January 1919. He holds the General Service and Victory Medals.
51, Masonic Street, Oldham Road, Manchester. Z8863

WHITEHEAD, H., Private, Welch Regiment.
He joined in September 1917, and on completion of his training, was engaged on important duties with his unit, and did consistently good work. Before being able to obtain his transfer overseas, he was unfortunately taken seriously ill with bronchitis, and as a result was discharged in April 1918, as medically unfit for further service.
8, Cowper Street, Bradford, Manchester. Z11852

WHITEHEAD, J., Sergeant, 8th Manchester Regt.
He volunteered in September 1914, and in April of the following year was drafted to the Dardanelles, where he served with distinction at the Landing at Cape Helles and Suvla Bay. He then did consistently good work as an instructor until Decem-

ber 1915, when he was invalided home owing to a breakdown in health. On his recovery he was retained on special duties at various home stations, and was eventually demobilised in January 1919, holding the 1914–15 Star, and the General Service and Victory Medals.
142, Barmouth Street, Bradford, Manchester. Z9749

WHITEHEAD, L., L/Corporal, Rifle Brigade.
He volunteered in August 1914, and in the following May was drafted to the Western Front. There he took part in the Battles of Ypres (II) and (III), Vimy Ridge, Arras, Amiens, St. Quentin, Passchendaele, Cambrai, and in the Retreat and Advance of 1918. He was present at the entry into Mons on Armistice Day, and was demobilised in May 1919. He holds the 1914–15 Star, and the General Service and Victory Medals.
8, Lind Street, Ancoats, Manchester. Z11329

WHITEHEAD, S., Private, 22nd Manchester Regt.
Joining in May 1916, he was drafted to France in the following August. Whilst overseas he took part in several engagements, including the Battles of the Somme, Arras, Bullecourt, Ypres ((III), Cambrai, and Havrincourt. He was demobilised in March 1919, and holds the General Service and Victory Medals.
13, Mozart Street, Ancoats, Manchester. Z11328A

WHITEHEAD, T., Private, 2/8th Manchester Regt.
He volunteered in September 1914, and was retained on important duties at various home stations until March 1917, when he was drafted to France. There he took part in much heavy fighting at Ypres, St. Quentin, and La Motte, where he was taken prisoner. He was released after the Armistice, returned home, and was demobilised in February 1919, holding the General Service and Victory Medals.
124, Parker Street, Bradford, Manchester. Z9751

WHITEHEAD, T., Private, K. (Liverpool Regiment). and Labour Corps.
He joined in February 1916, and was quickly drafted to France, where he was attached to the Labour Corps, and chiefly engaged on important duties in the forward areas at Messines, Ypres, and Nieuport. He was demobilised in September 1919, and holds the General Service and Victory Medals.
19, Hibbert Street, Hulme, Manchester. Z8646

WHITEHILL, G., Corporal, Middlesex Regiment.
Volunteering in November 1915, he was drafted overseas after a period of training. Whilst on the Western Front he took part in engagements at Ypres, Armentières, Nieuport, and in the Retreat and Advance of 1918. He was demobilised in May 1919, and holds the General Service and Victory Medals.
12, Thompson Street, Ardwick, Manchester. Z8647

WHITEHOUSE, S., Rifleman, 4th Rifle Brigade.
He volunteered in August 1914, and in the following February was drafted to France, where he took part in the Battles of Neuve Chapelle, Hill 60, Ypres (II), (where he was first wounded), St. Eloi, Loos, and on the Somme. Later he was transferred to Salonika, and saw much fighting on the Struma and Vardar fronts, being again wounded in action in July 1917. He returned home and was demobilised in July 1919, holding the 1914–15 Star, and the General Service and Victory Medals.
12, Whitland Street, Queen's Park, Manchester. Z11603

WHITELEGG, A., A.B., Royal Navy.
He volunteered in December 1914, and after a period of training proceeded to the North Sea, where he served in several of H.M. ships. He took part in the Battles of Dogger Bank and Jutland, and in minor engagements. Later he served on board a mine-sweeper engaged on dangerous duties and was wounded in May 1918, when his ship struck a mine. He was fortunately rescued, and in February 1919 was demobilised, holding the 1914–15 Star, the General Service (with three clasps), and Victory Medals, and a mine-sweeping Badge.
9, Emily Street, Ardwick, Manchester. TZ8648

WHITELEGG, J. W., Sergeant, R.A.M.C.
He volunteering in September 1914, and was engaged on important duties at Bethnal Green Military Hospital. He was unable to obtain a transfer overseas owing to his being medically unfit, but rendered valuable services until his demobilisation in August 1919.
11, Craig Street, Ardwick, Manchester. Z8649

WHITELEY, J. E., Private, Durham Light Infantry.
He joined in August 1916, and on completing his training in the following year was drafted to Salonika. In this seat of operations he took part in many engagements on the Doiran and Struma fronts, and at Monastir. Later he was sent to Russia, where he was engaged on important duties whilst stationed in Archangel. He was demobilised in August 1919, and holds the General Service and Victory Medals.
6, Dyson Street, Miles Platting, Manchester. Z11330

WHITEMAN, W. H., Private, K. (Liverpool Regt.)
He volunteered in 1914, but was shortly afterwards discharged owing to medical unfitness. In June 1915, however, he rejoined, and later in the same year proceeded to the Western Front, where he took part in the Battles of Ypres, Hill 60, Festubert, the Somme, Arras, Bullecourt, Lens, Péronne, and Albert. He was eventually demobilised after the Armistice, and holds the 1914–15 Star, and the General Service and Victory Medals. 5, Raidium Street, Manchester. Z11604

WHITFIELD, A., V., Sergt., 19th Manchester Regt.
Volunteering in December 1915, he was drafted overseas in the following June. Whilst on the Western Front, he took a prominent part in the Battles of Arras, Ypres (III), and Cambrai, and in the Retreat and Advance of 1918. He was demobilised in April 1919, and holds the General Service and Victory Medals.
34, Milton Street, West Gorton, Manchester.   TZ8650

WHITING, G. E., Private, K. (Liverpool Regiment).
Having previously been engaged on munition work, he joined the Army in February 1918, and served at various stations on important duties with his unit. Owing to the early cessation of hostilities, he did not proceed overseas, but rendered valuable services until his discharge in November 1918.
33, Avon Street, Chorlton-on-Medlock, Manchester.   Z1286B

WHITNEY, F. M., A.B., Royal Navy.
He enlisted in March 1912, and at the outbreak of war in August 1914, immediately put to sea and was first engaged off the Belgian Coast. Early in 1915 he took part in the Battles of the Dogger Bank and then proceeded to the Dardanelles, where he was on board H.M.S. " Irresistible " when this ship was sunk at the Battles of the Narrows in March 1915. He also served on board H.M.S. " Blake," " Harwich," " Setter," " Lucifer," and " Teazer," and in 1920 was still in the Royal Navy, holding the 1914-15 Star, and the General Service and Victory Medals.
27, Mark Street, Hulme, Manchester.   Z8651

WHITNEY, G., Pte., King's Shropshire Light Infty.
He volunteered in November 1914, and in October of the following year, was drafted to Salonika, where he took part in the first landing. Later he was in action during severe fighting on the Vardar, Doiran, and Struma fronts. In September 1918 he was admitted to hospital at Malta suffering severely from dysentery and malarial fever, and was then invalided home. He was discharged in January 1919 as medically unfit for further service, and holds the 1914-15 Star, and the General Service and Victory Medals.
3, Riga Street, Hulme, Manchester.   Z8652

WHITTAKER, A., Private, 3rd Manchester Regt,
He joined in February 1917, and two months later was drafted to the Western Front, where he took part in the Battles of the Ancre, Arras, Vimy Ridge, Bullecourt, Messines, Ypres (III), and Passchendaele. Unfortunately he contracted jaundice and died at Rouen Military Hospital on August 14th, 1917. He was entitled to the General Service and Victory Medals.
    " His life for his Country, his soul to God."
2, Milton Square, Lingard Street, Hulme, Manchester. TZ8655

WHITTAKER, H., Private, R.A.S.C.
He joined in March 1918, and was quickly drafted to the Western Front, where he rendered valuable services as a skilled baker at Calais and Boulogne. During an air-raid on the former town he was badly gassed. He returned to England for demobilisation in November 1919, and holds the General Service and Victory Medals.
43, Hyde Street, Hulme, Manchester.   Z8656

WHITTAKER, J., Private, 9th Border Regiment.
Volunteering in August 1914, he proceeded to the Western Front twelve months later, but after a short period of severe fighting in this theatre of war, was transferred to Salonika. Whilst on the Balkan front, he was in action on the Doiran, Struma, and Vardar. He was demobilised in February 1919, and holds the 1914-15 Star, and the General Service and Victory Medals. 45, Randolph Street, Ardwick, Manchester. Z11852

WHITTAKER, J. W., Pte., 22nd Manchester Regt.
Having volunteered in August 1915, he was drafted to the Western Front in December, and was wounded in action during the Somme Offensive in 1916. Invalided to England, he remained in hospital at Colchester for several months, and then returned to France. He was again wounded at Ypres, and invalided home, but on his recovery once more rejoined his unit in France, and served in much severe fighting until the cessation of hostilities. He was demobilised in February 1919, and holds the 1914-15 Star, and the General Service and Victory Medals.
33, Beresford Street, Moss Side, Manchester.   Z11332

WHITTAKER, S., Private, 2nd Border Regiment.
He volunteered in August 1914, and was sent to France in the following March. After taking part in the Battles of Festubert, Loos, and Givenchy, he was badly wounded in action at the commencement of the Somme Offensive in July 1916, and was invalided home. On his recovery, he was incapacitated for further service overseas, and was therefore retained on special duties at home stations. He holds the 1914-15 Star, and the General Service and Victory Medals, and was demobilised in April 1919. 14, Gorton Place, Longsight, Manchester. Z8654

WHITTAKER, T., Gunner, R.F.A.
He joined early in January 1917, and on completion of his training, was engaged on special duties on the South and West of England. He rendered valuable services with his Battery, but was unsuccessful in obtaining his transfer to a theatre of war, and was demobilised in November 1919.
18, Ward Street, Gorton, Manchester.   Z1133

WHITTAKER, T., Private, 8th Manchester Regt.
He volunteered in May 1915, and after a period of training, was retained on important guard and general duties at various home stations. He was unsuccessful in obtaining his transfer overseas before the cessation of hostilities, but did consistently good work with his unit until his demobilisation in January 1919. 48, Oliver St., Openshaw, Manchester.   Z8657

WHITTAKER, W., Private, South Lancashire Regt.
Volunteering in June 1915, he was drafted to Egypt in the following January, and rendered valuable services as a signaller with his unit. Unfortunately he contracted enteric fever in a very severe form, and was in hospital for nearly two years before being invalided home. He was eventually demobilised in April 1919, and holds the General Service and Victory Medals.
14, Haydn Avenue, Moss Side, Manchester.   Z8653

WHITTER, C. E., Pte., 7th East Lancashire Regt.
After volunteering in September 1914, he was quickly drafted to the Western Front, where he took part in the Battles of Ypres (I), Neuve Chapelle, Hill 60, Ypres (II), Loos, and Albert, but died gloriously on the Field of Battle on the Somme on July 7th, 1916. He was entitled to the 1914 Star, and the General Service and Victory Medals.
    " His life for his Country, his soul to God."
16, Hyde View, Grey St., West Gorton, Manchester.   Z8658

WHITTERANCE, E. W., Private, 1st Border Regt.
He volunteered in August 1914, and six months later was drafted to the Western Front, where he was wounded at the Battle of Neuve Chapelle in March 1915. After hospital treatment in England, he rejoined his unit, and was almost immediately wounded at the Battle of Loos in the following September. He was wounded for the third time at the commencement of the Somme Offensive in July 1916, but later proceeded to Italy, where he was badly injured by a heavy fall of rock. He was invalided home and finally discharged as medically unfit in August 1920, holding the 1914-15 Star, and the General Service and Victory Medals.
1, Ridgway Street, Moss Side, Manchester.   Z8659A

WHITTERANCE, W., Pte., 21st Yorkshire Hussars.
He joined in July 1916, and on completion of his training was drafted to Ireland, where he was engaged on important garrison duties at various stations. He was unable to obtain his transfer to a theatre of war, but rendered valuable services with his unit until his demobilisation in November 1919.
1, Ridgway Street, Moss Side, Manchester.   Z8659B

WHITTINGHAM, A., Private, 2nd Welch Regt.
He volunteered in April 1915, and after a few weeks' training, was drafted to the Western Front, where he was in action at Neuve Chapelle and Ypres. He died gloriously on the Field of Battle at Loos in September 1915, and was entitled to the 1914-15 Star, and the General Service and Victory Medals.
    " His life for his Country, his soul to God."
8, Anthony Street, Ardwick, Manchester.   Z8270

WHITTINGHAM, G., Pte., 17th Manchester Regt.
He volunteered in November 1915, and twelve months later was drafted to the Western Front. After taking part in the Battles of Arras, and in heavy fighting at St. Eloi, he was unhappily killed in action at Héninel on April 23rd, 1917. He was entitled to the General Service and Victory Medals.
    " A costly sacrifice upon the altar of freedom."
40, South Porter Street, Ancoats, Manchester.   Z11335A

WHITTINGHAM, J., Corporal, Welch Regiment.
Volunteering in May 1915, he was drafted to the Western Front in the following January and played a prominent part in the Battles of Arras, and Ypres, and in heavy fighting in other important sectors. Whilst in France, he was three times buried as the result of shell explosions, but was fortunately unwounded. He was demobilised in February 1919, and holds the General Service and Victory Medals.
40, South Porter Street, Ancoats, Manchester.   Z11335B

WHITTINGHAM, T., Driver, R.F.A.
He volunteered in December 1914, and on completion of his training, was engaged on important duties with his Battery until February 1917, when he was transferred to the Royal Air Force. He was not successful in obtaining his transfer overseas, but rendered valuable services until his demobilisation in March 1919.
30, Harvest Street, West Gorton, Manchester.   Z11334

WHITTINGHAM, W., Private, Worcestershire Regt.
He joined in February 1916, and in the following November was drafted to the Western Front, where he took part in much severe fighting in the Albert, Arras, and Somme sectors. Later he rendered valuable services with the Divisional Supply Column, and was eventually demobilised in April 1919, holding the General Service and Victory Medals.
40, South Porter Street, Ancoats, Manchester.   Z11335C

WHITTLE, E., Sapper, R.E.
He joined in October 1917, and after completing his training was engaged on special duties at various stations. He was unsuccessful in obtaining his transfer overseas, but rendered valuable services as a turner on motor repair work until his demobilisation in December 1919.
17, Jobling Street, Bradford, Manchester.   Z8661

WHITTLE, C., Private, K.O.Y.L.I.

He was mobilised in August 1914, and proceeded to France with the first Expeditionary Force. After taking part in the Battle of, and the Retreat from, Mons, and in other important engagements during the early days of the war, he was unfortunately killed in action by a sniper at the Battle of La Bassée in October 1914. He was entitled to the Mons Star, and the General Service and Victory Medals.

"The path of duty was the way to glory."

23, Margaret Street, West Gorton, Manchester. Z8660A

WHITTLE, J., Gunner, R.F.A.

Volunteering in May 1915, he proceeded to Egypt in the following October, and took part in the Battles of Mersa Matruh, El Fasher, and Magdhaba, and in other important engagements along the Suez Canal. In 1917 he was sent on to Palestine, but after being in action at the Battles of Gaza, was transferred to the Western Front. He then fought at the Battles of the Somme (II), Bapaume, the Scarpe, and Cambrai, and was badly wounded at Le Cateau (II) in October 1918. As result he was invalided from the Service in February 1918, and holds the 1914-15 Star, and the General Service and Victory Medals.

23, Margaret Street, West Gorton, Manchester. Z8660B

WHITTLE, T., Private, Suffolk Regiment.

A Reservist, he was called to the Colours at the outbreak of war, and was drafted to France in November 1914. After taking a prominent part in the Battles of Le Bassée, Ypres, and Neuve Chapelle, he was invalided home in March 1915, owing to a severe attack of trench fever. He was discharged as medically unfit for further service in July 1915, and holds the 1914 Star, and the General Service and Victory Medals.

151, Sudell Street, Rochdale Road, Manchester. Z9754

WHITTON, R., Private, Lancashire Fusiliers.

He volunteered in September 1914, and five months later was drafted to India, where he was engaged on important garrison duties at Lucknow, and succeeded in gaining a British Red Cross Society first aid certificate. Later he served on the North West Frontier, but in April 1918, was transferred to China, and was stationed at Hong Kong and at Singapore. He returned to England in May 1919, and was demobilised in the following November, holding the General Service and Victory Medals. 34, Lostock St., Miles Platting, Manchester. Z8864

WHITWORTH, E., Sapper, R.E.

He joined in May 1917, and two months later was drafted overseas. During his service on the Western Front he saw much heavy fighting, and took part in the Battles of Ypres III, and Cambrai. Later he was in action throughout the Retreat and Advance of 1918, remaining in this seat of war until after the cessation of hostilities. He was demobilised in May 1919, and holds the General Service and Victory Medals.

28, Houghton Street, Collyhurst, Manchester. Z11336

WHITWORTH, G., Private, East Lancashire Regt.

He volunteered in September 1914, and in the following February was sent to Salonika, and took part in the fighting on the Vardar front. Later he was transferred to the Western Front, where he fought in the Battles of Vimy Ridge, the Somme I, the Ancre, Arras, Bullecourt, Messines, Ypres III, and Lens. He was invalided to England, suffering from malarial fever, and was finally discharged as medically unfit for further military service in October 1917. He holds the 1914-15 Star, and the General Service and Victory Medals.

38, Ancoats Grove, North Ancoats, Manchester. Z8662

WHITWORTH, J., Private, R.A.M.C.

He volunteered in November 1915, and was retained on important duties with his unit at Aldershot. Owing to being accidentally poisoned he was admitted to hospital at Eastbourne, and finally discharged in February 1916, as medically unfit for further military service.

16, Whitworth Street, Longsight, Manchester. Z8663

WHITWORTH, J., Corporal, 8th Manchester Regt.

He volunteered in September 1914, and in the following month proceeded overseas. Whilst on the Western Front he took part in many important engagements, including the Battles of Ypres, Hill 60, Loos, and Vermelles. Later he saw service on the Ancre front, and at the Capture of Bullecourt. In January 1919 he was invalided to hospital suffering from Dysentery and was finally discharged in May 1919. He holds the 1914-15 Star, and the General Service and Victory Medals. 11, Bell Street, Openshaw, Manchester. Z8665

WHORK, T., Private, R.A.M.C.

He joined in May 1917, and two months later was drafted to Egypt, where he was chiefly engaged with his unit attending to the sick and wounded in hospital at Alexandria. He did good work until after the cessation of hostilities, and returning to England was demobilised in September 1919, and holds the the General Service and Victory Medals.

57, Stonehewer Street, Rochdale Road, Manchester. Z11605

WHYATT, E., Private, 23rd Manchester Regiment.

He volunteered in August 1914, and after completing a period of training was drafted to the Western Front in March of the following year. There he saw much heavy fighting in various sectors, and was in action at the Battles of Ypres, the Somme, La Bassée, Nieuport, and Givenchy. He was demobilised in France in January 1919, and holds the 1914-15 Star, and the General Service and Victory Medals.

23, Sparkle Street, Ancoats, Manchester. Z8880

WHYATT, E., Drummer, Irish Guards.

Joining in October 1913, he was mobilised at the outbreak of hostilities in August 1914, and was retained on important duties with his unit at various stations until early in 1915, when he proceeded overseas and took part in many important engagements in various sectors of the Front. He fought in the Battles of St. Eloi, Ypres (II), and Loos, and was wounded. After the cessation of hostilities, he returned to England, and in 1920 was still serving at Chelsea Barracks. He holds the General Service and Victory Medals.

14, Dalton Street, Longsight, Manchester. Z8666

WIDDOWS, J., Private, R.A.V.C.

Joining in February 1916, he was immediately drafted to France, and was stationed at Rouen and Albert, where he did good consistent work with the Royal Army Veterinary Corps until August 1917, when he was discharged as medically unfit for further service. He holds the General Service and Victory Medals. 10, Mary Street, Hulme, Manchester. Z8667

WIDDOWSON, G., Private, R.M.L.I.

Volunteering in August 1914, he first saw active service in the Dardanelles during the Gallipoli Campaign, and after the Evacuation of the Peninsula, proceeded to German West Africa in 1916. Later in the same year, however, he was sent to German East Africa, where he saw heavy fighting until 1917, when he was transferred to Palestine, and took part in the Advance with General Allenby's Forces. Finally he served in Italy and returned to England after the cessation of hostilities. In 1920 he was still in the Marines, and holds the 1914-15 Star and the General Service and Victory Medals.

89, Morton Street, Longsight, Manchester. Z7876C

WIGGLESWORTH, E.,Pte.,K.O. (R. Lancaster Rgt.)

Volunteering at the outbreak of hostilities in August 1914, he proceeded in the following year to the Dardanelles. There he took part in the fighting at Cape Helles, the Battles of Krithia, and the Landing at Suvla Bay, and was invalided to England. In March 1916, he proceeded to the Western Front, and was in action throughout the Battles of the Somme, Arras, Ypres, and Cambrai, and was wounded at Delville Wood, in 1916. Later he was in action in the Retreat and Advance of 1918, and was demobilised in March 1919, holding the 1914-15 Star, and the General Service and Victory Medals.

43, Elliott Street, Bradford, Manchester. Z8668

WIGHTMAN, C., Pte., 14th Royal Welch Fusiliers.

He joined in August 1917, and on completion of his training, was sent to France in the following year. During the Retreat and Advance of 1918, he took part in strenuous fighting in the Villers-Bretonneux, Arras, Armentières, Albert, and Cambrai sectors, and was gassed in action. After the cessation of hostilities, he was transferred to Ireland, and in 1920 was stationed at Cork. He holds the General Service and Victory Medals. 15, Elias Street, Manchester. Z11606B

WIGHTMAN, C., Private, 18th Manchester Regt.

He volunteered in November 1914, and in December of the following year, was drafted to the Western Front, where he saw severe fighting at La Bassée, Givenchy, and Festubert. He also took part in the Battles of the Somme, Arras, Ypres, and Passchendaele, and was twice wounded in action—on the Somme in July 1916, and at Arras in 1917. In March 1918, he was taken prisoner at St. Quentin, and during his captivity was forced to work in the stone quarries. Repatriated in December 1918, he was then demobilised and holds the 1914-15 Star, and the General Service and Victory Medals. 12, Mary Ellen Street, Collyhurst, Manchester. Z11337

WIGHTMAN, T., Private, 21st Manchester Regt.

He joined in October 1916, and in the following year was sent to France, where he took part in heavy fighting at Arras, Villers-Bretonneux, Trones Wood, St. Quentin, Ham, Albert, Mervillers, Cambrai, Nesle, and Le Cateau. Later he was transferred to the Border Regiment, and proceeded to Germany with the Army of Occupation. He returned home for demobilisation in November 1919, and holds the General Service and Victory Medals. 15, Elias Street, Manchester. Z11606A

WIGLEY, J., Private, 9th East Lancashire Regt.

He volunteered in September 1914, and in May of the following year was drafted to the Western Front, where he saw severe fighting in various sectors. He was afterwards transferred to Salonika, and there took part in many important engagements on the Doiran and Struma fronts, until invalided home in August 1916, suffering from malaria. On his recovery, however, in November 1917, he returned to France, and was again in action in the first Battle of Cambrai, and in the Retreat and Advance of 1918. Demobilised in March 1919, he holds the 1914-15 Star, and the General Service and Victory Medals. 65, Pilling Street, Rochdale Road, Manchester. Z8865

WIGNALL, A., Stoker, Royal Naval Reserve.
He volunteered in September 1914, and in April of the following
year, proceeded to Gallipoli, where he took part in the Landing
at Cape Helles. He saw much severe fighting in this seat of
operations until wounded in action during the Evacuation of
the Peninsula, and invalided home. After his recovery he was
stationed at Scapa Flow, until his demobilisation in December
1919, and holds the 1914-15 Star, and the General Service and
Victory Medals.
4, Redford Street, Newton Heath, Manchester.   Z11338

WIGNALL, P. R., Q.M.S., 16th Lancashire Fusiliers.
Three months after joining in June 1916, he was drafted to the
Western Front, where he saw severe fighting in various sectors.
He took part in the Battles of the Somme, Ypres, and Cambrai,
and many other important engagements, served also through
the Retreat and Advance of 1918, and was wounded in action.
He was afterwards sent with the Army of Occupation into
Germany, finally returning home for demobilisation in Sep-
tember 1919. He holds the General Service and Victory Medals.
4, Latimer Street, Longsight, Manchester.   Z11339

WILCOCK, A., Private, 4th Yorkshire Regiment.
He volunteered in November 1914, and in June of the following year proceeded to France, where he saw much heavy
fighting. He took part in important engagements in various
sectors of the Front, including the Battles of Loos, the Somme,
Ypres and Passchendaele, and in February 1918 was invalided
to hospital in England, suffering from dysentery. He was
discharged as medically unfit for further service in January
1919, and holds the 1914-15 Star, and the General Service
and Victory Medals.
10, Matlock Street, Ardwick, Manchester.   Z8669

WILCOCK. R., L, Corporal, 21st Manchester Regt.
He volunteered in January 1915, and in November of that
year proceeded to the Western Front. Whilst in this theatre
of war he took part in many important engagements, including
the Battles of Albert, Ploegsteert Wood, Vimy Ridge, the
Somme, Bullecourt, Messines, Ypres and Cambrai, and was
wounded at Beaumont-Hamel in November 1916. In January 1918 he was transferred to Italy, where he was again
in action on the Piave and the Asiago Plateaux, and was
gassed in June of that year. Demobilised on his return home
in February 1919, he holds the 1914-15 Star, and the General
Service and Victory Medals.
32, Queen's Street, Higher Ardwick, Manchester.   Z8670

WILCOX, F., Corporal, 6th Manchester Regiment.
He volunteered in September 1914, and on completing his
training in February of the following year was drafted to
Egypt, where he took part in engagements on the Suez Canal
and at Mersa Matruh, Sollum, Katia and Romani. Transferred in June 1917 to the Western Front, he was unhappily
killed in action there on July 31st of that year, only seven
weeks after landing in France. He was entitled to the 1914-15
Star, and the General Service and Victory Medals.
"His memory is cherished with pride."
37, Lancaster Street, Hulme, Manchester.   TZ8671

WILCOX, G., Private, Northumberland Fusiliers.
He joined in March 1917, and twelve months later proceeded
to the Western Front, where he saw heavy fighting in various
sectors. He took part in many important engagements
whilst in this theatre of war, and was twice wounded in action
—on the Somme in March, and in May 1918. Sent
home in August of that year, he was invalided from the Army
in October 1918, and holds the General Service and Victory
Medals.   3, Gaylor St., Miles Platting, Manchester.   TZ8866A

WILCOX, H., Rifleman, 9th Rifle Brigade.
Volunteering at the outbreak of war in August 1914, he was
drafted to the Western Front on completion of his training
in January of the following year, and there took part in many
important engagements. Severely wounded in action at
Ypres in June 1915, he unhappily died of wounds on October
31st of that year. He was entitled to the 1914-15 Star, and
the General Service and Victory Medals.
"Whilst we remember, the sacrifice is not in vain."
3, Gaylor Street, Miles Platting, Manchester.   TZ8856B

WILCOX, R., Private, R.A.M.C.
He joined in April 1916, and was retained on important duties
in England until December of the following year, when he
was drafted to the Western Front. Whilst in France, he
served in the hospitals at Rouen and Boulogne and various
other stations, and did much useful work. Invalided home
in August, he was discharged in October 1918 as medically
unfit for further service, on account of heart trouble, and
holds the General Service and Victory Medals.
1, League Street, Reather Street, Manchester.   Z9755

WILD, R., Driver, R.A.S.C. (M.T.)
Two months after joining in August 1916, he proceeded to
German East Africa. Whilst in this seat of operations, he
was engaged on important transport duties, conveying food
and ammunition to the forward areas and served also at
Dar-es-Salaam and various other stations. He finally returned
home in October 1919, and was demobilised in that month,
holding the General Service and Victory Medals.
28, Wovenden Street, Openshaw, Manchester.   Z8672

WILD, T., Driver, R.F.A.
He volunteered in September 1914, and twelve months later
proceeded to France, where he saw severe fighting in various
sectors of the Front. He took part in the Battles of the Somme,
Arras, Ypres and Cambrai, and many other important engagements, and fought also in the Retreat and Advance of
1918. He afterwards served with the Army of Occupation
in Germany, finally returning home for demobilisation in
April 1919. He holds the 1914-15 Star, and the General
Service and Victory Medals.
39, Able Street, Collyhurst, Manchester.   Z11340

WILDE, G., Private, 1st Manchester Regiment.
He joined in October 1916, and in June of the following year
was drafted to Mesopotamia, where he took part in the Relief
of Kut, the capture of Baghdad and the Occupation of Basra.
Transferred in June 1918 to Egypt, he was there engaged on
garrison duties at Alexandria and Cairo. He unfortunately
died of pneumonia on December 15th, 1918 at Jaffa, where he
was buried. He was entitled to the General Service and
Victory Medals.
"Steals on the ear the distant triumph song."
49, Dale Street, Miles Platting, Manchester.   Z8867

WILDE, H., L/Cpl., 2/7th King's (Liverpool Regt.)
Joining in August 1916, he was drafted to the Western Front
in February of the following year, and there took part in the
Battles of Arras, Bullecourt, Messines and Ypres. Severely
gassed at Passchendaele in November 1917, he was invalided
to hospital in England, but on his recovery, returned to France
and was again in action in the Battles of the Somme, the
Marne, Bapaume, Havrincourt, Cambrai and Le Cateau.
Demobilised in February 1919, he holds the General Service
and Victory Medals.
59, Baden Street, Ardwick, Manchester.   Z8673

WILDE, J., Pte., Cheshire Rgt., and R. Defence Corps.
He volunteered in October 1914, and after undergoing a
period of training, was retained at various stations, where he
was engaged on duties of great importance. He was not successful in obtaining his transfer to a theatre of war, but
nevertheless, rendered very valuable services with his unit
until January 1919, when he was discharged.
112, Marsland Street, Ardwick, Manchester.   TZ8674

WILDE, O. H., Gunner, R.G.A.
He volunteered in April 1915, and in May of the following year
was drafted to the Western Front. There he saw much heavy
fighting in various sectors, took part in the Battles of Albert,
the Somme, Arras, Vimy Ridge, Ypres, Passchendaele and
Bullecourt, and many minor engagements, and served also
through the Retreat and Advance of 1918. Demobilised in
March 1919, he holds the General Service and Victory Medals.
15, Overton Street, Hulme, Manchester.   Z8675

**WILDE, R., Private, 11th Manchester Regiment,
and 18th Lancashire Fusiliers.**
Volunteering in January 1915, he was drafted to Mesopotamia
in September of that year, and there took part in numerous
engagements at Kut, Sanna-i-Yat and the Tigris. In July
1916, he was transferred to the Western Front, where he fought
in the Somme Offensive and contracted trench fever. He
was for a considerable period in hospital in England, before
being invalided from the Army in September 1917, and holds
the 1914-15 Star, and the General Service and Victory Medals.
1, Lilford Street, West Gorton, Manchester.   TZ8676

WILDMAN, B., Private, Lancashire Regiment.
He volunteered in January 1915, and after completing a period
of training was engaged on important duties at various stations.
Owing to ill-health, he was unable to obtain his transfer to
a theatre of war, but, nevertheless, rendered valuable services
with his unit until June 1916, when he was invalided from
the Army.
4, Sycamore Street, Gorton, Manchester.   Z11341

WILKES, F. P., Private, M.G.C.
He joined in March 1917, and underwent a period of training
prior to being drafted to the Western Front twelve months
later. There he saw severe fighting in various sectors, and
took part in the Battles of the Somme and Ypres, and many
other important engagements until the cessation of hostilities.
Demobilised on his return home in February 1919, he holds
the General Service and Victory Medals.
12, Mark Street, Hulme, Manchester.   Z8677

WILKINSON, A., Sergeant, Manchester Regiment.
Four months after joining in August 1916, he was drafted
to the Western Front, where he saw severe fighting in various
sectors. He took a prominent part in the Battles of Messines,
Ypres, Passchendaele, Cambrai and St. Quentin, and many
other engagements, served also through the Retreat and
Advance of 1918, and was wounded in action. He was afterwards sent with the Army of Occupation into Germany,
finally returning home for demobilisation in October 1919.
He holds the General Service and Victory Medals.
51, Prince Street, Ardwick, Manchester.   Z7258A

WILKINSON, F., Corporal, 22nd Manchester Regt.
He joined in February 1917, and in October of the same year proceeded to the Western Front, where he saw severe fighting at Ypres and Passchendaele. He was afterwards transferred to Italy, and was there again in action on the Asiago Plateau and the Piave, where he took part in many engagements. In March 1919 he was sent to Egypt and was there stationed at Cairo, finally returning home in January 1920, for demobilisation in the following month. He holds the General Service and Victory Medals.
10, Rex Street, Jackson Street, Hulme, Manchester. TZ8683A

WILKINSON, G., Private, 1/4th Border Regiment.
He joined in August 1916, and after five months' training was drafted to India, where he was engaged as a hospital orderly, and on other important duties. He served at Bangalore, Bombay, Calcutta and various other stations, whilst overseas, and finally returned to England for demobilisation in January 1920. He holds the General Service and Victory Medals. 8, Hardy Street, West Gorton, Manchester. Z8680

WILKINSON, G., W., Sergeant, R.A.V.C.
Volunteering in April 1915, he was drafted to the Western Front in August of that year, and was there engaged on important duties in various sectors. He played a prominent part in the Battles of Albert, Vimy Ridge, Arras, Ypres and Cambrai, and many other engagements, and served also through the Retreat and Advance of 1918. He was mentioned in Despatches for distinguished service in the Field on the Somme in April 1918, and holds the 1914-15 Star, and the General Service and Victory Medals. He was demobilised in April 1919.
14, Bank Street, Hulme, Manchester. Z8685

WILKINSON, H., Sapper, R.E.
He joined in October 1917, and on completing his training in February of the following year, proceeded to the Western Front. There he was engaged on important duties on the railways in various sectors, and also took an active part in the Retreat and Advance of 1918. He returned to England for demobilisation in January 1919, and holds the General Service and Victory Medals.
5, Clement Street, Hulme, Manchester. Z8684

WILKINSON, H., C.Q.M.S., R.A.S.C. (M.T.)
He joined in 1916, and later in the same year proceeded to Mesopotamia. He served for two years in this seat of operations, and during that period took a prominent part in the capture of Baghdad, and in many other important engagements. He was afterwards sent into North Persia, where he was still with his Company in 1920. He holds the General Service and Victory Medals.
14, Tiverton Street, Ardwick, Manchester. Z11344

WILKINSON, H., Private, 20th E. Yorkshire Regt.
He volunteered in August 1915, and in January of the following year proceeded to the Western Front, where he took part in the Battles of Vermelles, the Somme, Arras and Bullecourt, and many minor engagements. He died gloriously on the Field of Battle at Ypres on July 24th, 1917. He was entitled to the General Service and Victory Medals.
"His life for his Country, his soul to God."
3, Gatley Street, Ancoats, Manchester. Z8682

WILKINSON, J., Private, 7th Leicestershire Regt.
Shortly after joining in August 1916, he was drafted to the Western Front, where he saw severe fighting in various sectors. He took part in the Battles of the Somme, Arras, Ypres and Cambrai, and in engagements at Loos, Armentières, Hill 60, and many other places until taken prisoner in May 1918. Held in captivity in Germany until December of that year, he was finally demobilised in March 1919, holding the General Service and Victory Medals.
57, Granville Place, Ancoats, Manchester. Z11343

WILKINSON, J., Sapper, R.E.
A Reservist, he was called to the Colours in August 1914, and in December of that year was drafted to the Western Front, where he was engaged on important duties in various sectors. He took an active part in the Battles of Neuve Chapelle, Ypres, Festubert, Albert, the Somme, Bullecourt and Cambrai, and other important engagements, and also served through the Retreat and Advance of 1918. He was demobilised in February 1919, and holds the 1914-15 Star, and the General Service and Victory Medals.
15, Linacre Street, Oldham Road, Manchester. Z11346

WILKINSON, J. H., Private, K. (Liverpool Regt.), and Labour Corps.
Joining in March 1916, he proceeded to France in the following month, and there saw severe fighting in various sectors of the Front. He took part in the Battles of the Somme, Arras and Ypres, and other important engagements, and afterwards served with the Labour Corps in the Ancre and Cambrai sectors. Demobilised in February 1919, he holds the General Service and Victory Medals.
5, Holbeck Street, Oldham Road, Manchester. Z9756

WILKINSON, R., Private, Border Regiment.
Volunteering in August 1914, he proceeded to Gallipoli in April of the following year, and there saw severe fighting at Suvla Bay, and various other places until the Evacuation of the Peninsula. He was then transferred to the Western Front where he was again in action at the Battles of the Somme, the Ancre, Arras, Cambrai and Bapaume, and other engagements, was gassed and wounded in action at Ypres in June 1917, and wounded again in the following October at Poelcappelle. Demobilised in January 1919, he holds the 1914-15 Star, and the General Service and Victory Medals.
5, Cleveland Street, West Gorton, Manchester. Z8681

WILKINSON, S., (Mrs.), Special War Worker.
Throughout the war this lady was engaged on work of National importance at Messrs. Charles Mackintosh's, Brook Street, Manchester. There she was employed chiefly in making waterproof sheets and capes, and other articles of equipment for the Army, and rendered very valuable services until the cessation of hostilities.
6, Markham Street, Ardwick, Manchester. Z8679

WILKINSON, S., Private, 8th Manchester Regt.
He joined in December 1916, and in June of the following year was drafted to the Western Front, where he saw severe fighting in various sectors. He took part in many important engagements in this theatre of war, fought also in the Retreat and Advance of 1918, and was wounded in action at Ypres in November 1917. Demobilised in January 1919, he holds the General Service and Victory Medals.
15, Linacre Street, Oldham Road, Manchester. Z11345

WILKINSON, T., Private, 1st Manchester Regt.
A Reservist, he was called to the Colours in August 1914, and in January of the following year was drafted to the Western Front, where he took part in the Battles of Neuve Chapelle, Hill 60, Ypres and Festubert and other engagements. Transferred in January 1916 to Mesopotamia, he there served at Um-el-Hannah and Sanna-i-Yat, and was unhappily killed in action at the Relief of Kut on January 9th, 1917. He was entitled to the 1914-15 Star, and the General Service and Victory Medals.
"A costly sacrifice upon the altar of freedom."
10, Leigh Street East, Ancoats, Manchester. Z9757

WILKINSON, W., Private, R.A.M.C.
He volunteered in December 1914, and was retained on important duties in England until January 1917, when he proceeded to the Western Front. There he served at Festubert, Givenchy and in various other sectors, until admitted to hospital at Etaples, and later invalided home. He was finally demobilised in April 1919, and holds the General Service and Victory Medals.
10, Rex Street, Jackson Street, Hulme, Manchester. TZ8683B

WILKINSON, W., Private, 6th Cheshire Regiment.
Volunteering in August 1914, he proceeded to the Western Front after three months' training, and there saw much severe fighting. He took part in the Battles of Armentières, Festubert, the Somme, Arras and Ypres, and many other engagements, was wounded in action at Givenchy in June 1916, and twelve months later, was taken prisoner at Passchendaele. Held in captivity until after the cessation of hostilities, he was demobilised in February 1919, holding the 1914 Star, and the General Service and Victory Medals.
33, Southwell Street, Harpurhey, Manchester. Z11607

WILKINSON, W. H., Private, 2nd Cheshire Regt.
After volunteering in December 1914, he underwent a period of training prior to being drafted to Egypt in March 1916. There he was engaged on garrison duties at Alexandria and Cairo, and took part also in the fighting at Romani before proceeding into Palestine, where he served through the Battles of Gaza and the capture of Jerusalem. He also saw service in Bulgaria, and finally returned home for demobilisation in April 1919. He holds the General Service and Victory Medals. 57, Branson Street, Ancoats, Manchester. Z11342

WILLAN, J. F., Private, Royal Welch Fusiliers.
Joining in May 1916, he proceeded to France in November of that year, and there saw heavy fighting in various sectors of the Front. After taking part in the Battle of Arras, he was severely wounded in action at Ypres in July 1917, and invalided home, but on his recovery returned to the Western Front. He then served through the Battles of Cambrai and the Somme, and was again wounded during the Retreat of 1918. Finally demobilised in February 1919, he holds the General Service and Victory Medals.
29, Francisco Street, Collyhurst, Manchester. Z11347

WILLAN, J. F., Pte., 17th Royal Welch Fusiliers.
He volunteered in December 1915, and was retained in England until January 1917, when he proceeded to the Western Front. There he took part in important engagements in various sectors until wounded in action at Ypres in July 1917, and admitted to hospital, where he remained for three months. On his recovery, however, he rejoined his unit, but was a second time wounded in December 1917. He was finally discharged in February 1918 as medically unfit for further service, and holds the General Service and Victory Medals.
7, Upper Plymouth Grove, Longsight, Manchester. Z8686

WILLAN. W. A., Pte. (Signaller), R. Welch Fusiliers.
He joined in September 1916, and after completing a period of training, served at various stations, where he was engaged on duties of a highly important nature. He was not successful in obtaining his transfer to the Front, on account of ill-health, but, nevertheless, rendered valuable services with his unit until November 1917, when he was invalided from the Army.
19, Great Jackson Street, West Gorton, Manchester. Z11348

WILLDIG, J., Private, Royal Scots.
He volunteered in November 1914, and underwent a period of training before being drafted to Egypt in June 1916. After taking part in engagements at Romani and many other places, he proceeded into Palestine and there fought in the Battles of Gaza and the capture of Jerusalem. In August 1918 he was transferred to the Western Front, and was again in action until the cessation of hostilities. He was demobilised in March 1919, and holds the General Service and Victory Medals.
94, Rutland Street, Hulme, Manchester. TZ8687

WILLETTS, B., Private, 18th Lancashire Fusiliers.
Volunteering in January 1915, he was sent to the Western Front in December of that year, and there saw severe fighting in various sectors. He took part in important engagements at Festubert, Givenchy, Béthune and many other places in this theatre of war, and was twice wounded in action—at Arras and Péronne. Invalided home in September 1918, he was finally demobilised in February 1919, holding the 1914-15 Star, and the General Service and Victory Medals.
2, Godson Street, West Gorton, Manchester. TZ8688B

WILLETTS, W., Private, 2nd Manchester Regiment.
Joining in May 1917, he was drafted to the Western Front on completing a period of training six months later, and there saw much severe fighting. He took part in the third Battle of Ypres, and in many other important engagements, fought also in the Retreat and Advance of 1918, and was among the troops to enter Mons at dawn of Armistice Day. He was demobilised in December 1919, and holds the General Service and Victory Medals.
2, Godson Street, West Gorton, Manchester. TZ8688A

WILLEY, J., Private, 1/10th Manchester Regiment.
He joined in July 1918, and on completing his training in November of that year, was drafted to France, where he served at Charleroi. Later he proceeded with the Army of Occupation into Germany, and was stationed at Cologne for twelve months. He was demobilised on his return to England in December 1919, and holds the General Service and Victory Medals.
35, Adelaide Street, Hulme, Manchester. Z8385B

WILLIAMS, A., Private, 2nd Manchester Regiment.
Joining in July 1916, he proceeded to France in December of that year, and there saw heavy fighting in various sectors. He took part in the Battle of Ypres and in minor engagements at Nieuport and many other places until severely wounded in action at Passchendaele, and admitted to hospital in France. He was invalided from the Army in July 1918, but has since re-enlisted, and in 1920 was with his unit in Mesopotamia. He holds the General Service and Victory Medals.
82, Naylor Street, Oldham Road, Manchester. Z8868B

WILLIAMS, A., Private, 17th Manchester Regt., and 1st Border Regiment.
He volunteered in September 1914, and after a period of training was drafted in November of the following year to the Western Front. There he took part in the Battles of the Somme, Arras and Ypres, and many other important engagements in various sectors, and fought also in the Retreat and Advance of 1918. He was finally demobilised in July 1919, and holds the 1914-15 Star, and the General Service and Victory Medals.
19, Richmond Street, Moss Side, Manchester. Z8700

WILLIAMS, B., Private, Queen's Own (Royal West Kent Regiment).
He joined in 1916, and on completing his training in the following year proceeded to the Western Front. Whilst in this theatre of war he saw severe fighting in various sectors, took part in the Battles of Arras, Bullecourt, Ypres, and many other important engagements, and was wounded in action on the Somme. Demobilised on his return home in 1919, he holds the General Service and Victory Medals.
9, Elizabeth Ann Street, Manchester. Z9758

WILLIAMS, B. W., Sergt., Lancashire Fusiliers, and 4th Border Regiment.
He volunteered in 1915, and after a period of training served at various stations, until discharged ten months later as under-age. He re-enlisted, however, in 1918, and was engaged on important duties with his unit, being unable to obtain his transfer to a theatre of war. He was finally demobilised in March 1919.
26, Higher Temple Street, Chorlton-on-Medlock, Manchester. Z8690B

WILLIAMS, C., Private, Royal Welch Fusiliers.
He joined in July 1918, immediately on attaining military age, and after a short period of training was retained on im-

portant duties at various stations. He was unable to obtain his transfer overseas on account of ill-health, and was for a time in hospital before being invalided from the Army in January 1919.
15, Adelaide Street, Hulme, Manchester. Z8712B

WILLIAMS, C., Private, 3/7th Lancashire Fusiliers.
He volunteered in July 1915, and after undergoing a period of training, served at various stations, where he was engaged on important munition work. He was not successful in obtaining his transfer overseas, but, nevertheless, rendered valuable services with his unit until March 1917, when he was invalided from the Army, on account of injuries sustained in an accident.
15, Adelaide Street, Hulme, Manchester. Z8712A

WILLIAMS, E., Pte., 1st Manchester Regt. and M.F.P.
Mobilised in August 1914, he was immediately drafted to the Western Front, where he fought in the Battle of Mons and the subsequent Retreat. He also took part in the Battles of Le Cateau, the Marne, the Aisne, La Bassée, Ypres and Neuve Chapelle before being transferred to Gallipoli, where he was in action at Suvla Bay. He afterwards served in Mesopotamia, and was present in the engagements at Sanna-i-Yat, at the Relief of Kut and the capture of Baghdad. Returning home in April 1919, he was discharged in March of the following year, and holds the Mons Star, and the General Service and Victory Medals.
15, Nuttall Street, Chorlton-on-Medlock, Manchester. TZ8713

WILLIAMS, E., Sapper, R.E.
He joined in July 1917, and was retained on special duties in connection with searchlights at various important stations in England. He was unable to obtain his transfer overseas, but nevertheless did consistently good work until the cessation of hostilities, and was demobilised in May 1919.
24, Elizabeth Street, West Gorton, Manchester. Z11350

WILLIAMS, E., Pte., 2nd Loyal N. Lancashire Regt.
He volunteered in August 1914, and after a period of training was drafted to the Egyptian theatre of war. He also took part in much heavy fighting on the Gallipoli Peninsula, including the Landing at Suvla Bay, and was later transferred to the Western Front, where he fought in various sectors. After taking part in the Battle of Ypres he was unfortunately killed on the Somme on July 10th, 1918, during the Advance of that year, and was entitled to the 1914-15 Star, and the General Service and Victory Medals.
"Whilst we remember, the sacrifice is not in vain."
31, Copestick Street, Ancoats, Manchester. Z11354

WILLIAMS, E., Private, South Wales Borderers.
Joining in April 1918, he was drafted to France three months later, and took part in much heavy fighting during the great Advance of that year. He was in action on the Aisne, at Armentières and in various other engagements of importance and was invalided to England suffering from gas poisoning. After some time in hospital he was eventually demobilised in September 1919, and holds the General Service and Victory Medals. 131, Barmouth Street, Bradford, Manchester. Z9759

WILLIAMS, F., Sapper, R.E.
Volunteering in March 1915, he proceeded to France in August of the same year, and was present at numerous engagements of importance, including the Battles of Loos, St. Eloi, Albert, Vimy Ridge, the Somme, Beaucourt, Arras, Messines and Cambrai. He also did consistently good work during the Retreat and Advance of 1918, and after the cessation of hostilities did duty with the Army of Occupation on the Rhine. He holds the 1914-15 Star, and the General Service and Victory Medals, and was demobilised in December 1918.
16, Link Street, Longsight, Manchester. Z8709

WILLIAMS, F. F., Private, 9th Lancashire Fusiliers.
Joining in April 1917, he was drafted to the Western Front in the following June, and took part in many important engagements. He saw much heavy fighting in various sectors, and was in action at the Battle of Passchendaele in September 1917, where he was badly wounded. He was invalided home in consequence, and after a period in hospital at Derby was discharged in July 1919 as unfit for further military service. He holds the General Service and Victory Medals.
18, Redvers Street, Ardwick, Manchester. Z8697

WILLIAMS, G., Sergt., 8th King's (Liverpool Regt.)
He enlisted in 1888, and after serving through the Boer War of 1899-1902, during which he was wounded, he re-enlisted in September 1914, and was drafted to the East. He was attached to the R.A.S.C., and served with the Camel Corps in Egypt for three months, and later did duty in Palestine. He rendered valuable services in this theatre of war until the cessation of hostilities and was eventually demobilised in August 1919. In addition to the Queen's and King's South African Medals, he holds the 1914-15 Star, the General Service and Victory Medals, and the India General Service Medal (with clasps N.E. Frontier, 1891).
24, Shaftesbury Street, Chorlton-on-Medlock, Manchester.
TX8705-06B

WILLIAMS, G. (Jun.), Cpl., 6th Manchester Regt.

Joining in December 1916, he did consistently good work at various important stations in England during the first part of his service, and in January 1918 was drafted to France. In this theatre of war he played a prominent part in many engagements, including the Battles of the Somme (II), La Bassée, Havrincourt Wood, Cambrai (II), Ypres (IV) and Le Cateau (II), and finally did duty in Belgium guarding prisoners of war. He holds the General Service and Victory Medals, and was demobilised in November 1919.
24, Shaftesbury Street, Chorlton-on-Medlock, Manchester.
TX8705–06A

WILLIAMS, H., Private, South Lancashire Regt.

He volunteered in September 1915, and after a period of service in England was drafted to the Western Front in December 1916. There he took part in heavy fighting in various sectors, and was in action at Ypres, and other engagements of importance, and was badly wounded at St. Julien. He was invalided to England, and from September 1917 until August 1919 was confined to hospital and ultimately discharged as no longer physically fit for service. He holds the General Service and Victory Medals.
15, Turner Street, Rusholme, Manchester.   Z8701

WILLIAMS, H., Rifleman, K.R.R.C.

He was already serving in the Army at the outbreak of war in August 1914, and in the following month was drafted to the Western Front. He took part in much heavy fighting in various sectors, and was wounded at La Bassée in January 1915. He returned to his unit in due course, and was wounded on two further occasions, at Ypres and on the Somme, and after being invalided to England was finally discharged in March 1916 as unfit for further service. He holds the 1914 Star, and the General Service and Victory Medals.
12, Lincoln Street, Longsight, Manchester.   Z11619

WILLIAMS, H., Private, South Lancashire Regt.

Volunteering in September 1914, he was drafted to France two months later, and was in action at numerous engagements during the early stages of the war. He was transferred to the Dardanelles in April 1915, and fought at the Landing of Cape Helles, and at the Battles of Krithia and Achi Baba. After the Evacuation of the Gallipoli Peninsula he proceeded to Mesopotamia, where he took part in the fighting during the Offensive in this theatre of war, and was present at the capture of Baghdad. He was eventually demobilised in April 1919, and holds the 1914 Star, and the General Service and Victory Medals. 45, Francisco Street, Collyhurst, Manchester. Z9760

WILLIAMS, H. O., Private, 7th Manchester Regt.

Mobilised in August 1914, he proceeded to France in the following month, and took part in many important engagements. He was in action at the Battles of the Marne, La Bassée, Ypres, Hill 60, Loos, Vimy Ridge and the Somme, and was wounded and gassed. He returned to his unit after recovery, and was again in action at Arras, Ypres and Cambrai. He was discharged in March 1919, and holds the 1914 Star, and the General Service and Victory Medals.
25, Platt Street, Moss Side, Manchester.   Z8699

WILLIAMS, J., Sapper, R.E.

Volunteering early in 1915, he was quickly drafted to the Western Front, and took a prominent part in the Battles of St. Eloi, and Hill 60. Unfortunately he was killed in action during the last named engagement in April 1915, after only a short but valuable period of active service. He was entitled to the 1914–15 Star, and the General Service and Victory Medals.
"A valiant Soldier, with undaunted heart he breasted life's last hill."
41, Percy Street, Hulme, Manchester.   TZ8710

WILLIAMS, J., Corporal, R.A.M.C.

He volunteered in September 1915, and after a period of training at various stations was drafted to the Western Front in August of the following year. He rendered valuable services on the Somme and at St. Quentin and Roubaix, and was injured by being buried through a shell explosion. He returned to England in February 1918, and after some time in hospital was demobilised in May 1919, holding the General Service and Victory Medals.
50, Burton Street, Newton, Manchester.   Z11356

WILLIAMS, J., Private, Cheshire Regiment.

He enlisted in December 1912, and, at the outbreak of war in August 1914, proceeded to the Western Front, where he took part in the Retreat from Mons. He was also in action at subsequent engagements, and was wounded at the Battle of La Bassée in October 1914. After recovery he returned to France, and was wounded at Cambrai in September 1918, during the great Advance. He was invalided to England and was eventually demobilised in September 1919, holding the Mons Star, and the General Service and Victory Medals.
3, Ashworth Street, Openshaw, Manchester.   Z8394B

WILLIAMS, J., Private, Manchester Regiment.

Mobilised at the outbreak of war in August 1914, he was quickly sent to the Western Front, and took part in the Retreat from Mons. He was also in action at numerous other engagements of importance, including the Battles of Le Cateau, the

Marne, La Bassée and Ypres. In December 1915 he was transferred to Mesopotamia, and was wounded in severe fighting at Kut in March 1916. He also saw fighting in Egypt and Palestine, and after rendering valuable services in this theatre of war was discharged in March 1919, holding the Mons Star, and the General Service and Victory Medals.
82, Naylor Street, Newton, Manchester.   Z8868A

WILLIAMS, J. E., Leading Aircraftsman, R.A.F.

He joined in April 1918, and later in the same year proceeded to Egypt, and was stationed at Cairo, Alexandria and Kantara. He also saw service in France and at Malta, and did consistently good work until his demobilisation in February 1920, and holds the General Service and Victory Medals.
21, Taylor Street, Gorton, Manchester.   Z11355

WILLIAMS, J. R., 1st Air Mechanic, R.A.F.

He joined in March 1917, and after a period of service in England was sent to France in April 1918. There he did consistently good work in various sectors of the Front, including those of the Marne, Bapaume, Havrincourt and Cambrai. He rendered valuable services of a highly technical character, and was demobilised in February 1919, holding the General Service and Victory Medals.
151, Earl Street, Longsight, Manchester.   Z8693

WILLIAMS, J. S., Private, King's (Liverpool Regt.)

Joining in February 1916, he completed a period of training, and was later in the year drafted to France, where he was in action in many important engagements. He saw service at St. Julien and Ypres, and suffered from gas poisoning. He returned home, but was afterwards sent to Ireland, and was engaged on important duties with the R.A.S.C. for a time. Before his demobilisation in November 1918, he again saw service in France, and holds the General Service and Victory Medals.   Z11353
2, Lamb Street, Richmond Grove, Longsight, Manchester.

WILLIAMS, J. T., Private, 2nd Lancashire Fusiliers.

Mobilised from the Reserve in August 1914, he was immediately drafted to the Western Front, and took part in the Retreat from Mons. He was also in action at the Battles of Ypres, Neuve Chapelle, Hill 60, Festubert, Loos, the Somme, Mericourt, Lens, Arras, Albert, Armentières, Cambrai and Valenciennes, and had both legs broken. He holds the Mons Star, and the General Service and Victory Medals. and was discharged in January 1919.
8, Jersey Street Dwellings, Manchester.   Z11352

WILLIAMS, J. W., L/Cpl., 7th E. Lancashire Regt.

Mobilised in August 1914, he proceeded to France in the following October, and was in action at many engagements of importance. He took part in much heavy fighting at the Battles of La Bassée, Ypres, Hill 60, Festubert, Albert, the Somme, Beaumont-Hamel, Arras, Bullecourt and Messines, and made the supreme sacrifice, being killed in action at the last-named engagement on June 17th, 1917. He was entitled to the 1914 Star, and the General Service and Victory Medals.
"Great deeds cannot die."
24, Hardy Street, West Gorton, Manchester.   Z8694A

WILLIAMS, L., Sapper, R.E.

He volunteered in November 1914, and four months later was drafted to the Western Front, where he was engaged on special duties with his unit. He took part in the Battles of Albert, the Somme, Vimy Ridge and Ypres. He was twice wounded in action—at Bray near Albert, and at Armentières. Invalided home early in 1918, he was discharged in April of that year, and holds the 1914–15 Star, and the General Service and Victory Medals.
13, Green Street, Greenheys, Manchester.   Z8698

WILLIAMS, M. (Mrs.), Worker, Q.M.A.A.C.

She joined in 1918, and during the remaining period of hostilities, was engaged on important duties as a storekeeper with the Army Auxiliary Corps at various places. She rendered valuable services until her demobilisation in 1919.
26, Higher Temple Street, Chorlton-on-Medlock, Manchester.
Z8690A

WILLIAMS, P., Private, 22nd Manchester Regt.

He volunteered in November 1914, and after serving for a time in England, was drafted to the Western Front in March 1916. He took part in many important engagements and was in action at Loos, St. Eloi, the Somme, Arras and Verdun. In August 1917 he was transferred to Italy, where he saw service on the Asiago Plateau and the Piave. He holds the General Service and Victory Medals, and was demobilised in January 1919.
51, Middlewood Street, Harpurhey, Manchester.   Z11608

WILLIAMS, R., Private, 19th Lancashire Fusiliers.

Volunteering in January 1915, he was drafted to the Western Front twelve months later and first saw heavy fighting at Loos and St. Eloi during the German attacks on these places. Later he was badly wounded in action at the Battle of the Somme in July 1916, and was invalided home. After a long period in hospital, he was discharged as medically unfit for further service in July 1917, and holds the General Service and Victory Medals.
59, Sanitary Street, Oldham Road, Manchester.   Z8869

WILLIAMS, P., Air Mechanic, R.A.F.

He joined in September 1918, and was retained on special duties at various Aerodromes in England. He was not successful in obtaining his transfer to a theatre of war before the cessation of hostilities, but nevertheless rendered valuable services with his Squadron until his demobilisation in February 1919. 26, Elizabeth Street, West Gorton, Manchester. Z11351

WILLIAMS, R. T., Private, 2nd and 12th King's (Liverpool Regiment).

He volunteered in November 1914, and in July of the following year was drafted to the Western Front, where he took part in many important engagements. He was in action at the Battles of Loos, Albert, and the Somme, and in January 1917 was transferred to India, after recovering from dysentery contracted in France. There he was engaged on important garrison duties, and was in action with the native tribesmen on the North Western Frontier. He was demobilised in November 1919, and holds the 1914–15 Star, and the India General Service Medal (with clasp, Afghanistan, N.W. Frontier 1919), and the General Service and Victory Medals.
42, Blackthorne Street, Ardwick, Manchester. Z8702

WILLIAMS, S. P., Private, 9th Cheshire Regiment.

He joined in June 1918, on attaining military age, and after a period of training, did duty at various important stations in England and Ireland. In January 1919 he was sent to Germany and was engaged on special garrison duties with the Army of Occupation on the Rhine. He rendered valuable services, and was demobilised in November 1919.
16, Wragley Street, Miles Platting, Manchester. Z9761

WILLIAMS, T., L/Cpl., 19th Manchester Regiment.

Volunteering in September 1914, he underwent a period of training, and was drafted to the Western Front in November of the following year. In this theatre of war he took part in many important engagements, and saw much fighting at Albert, Vermelles, Ploegsteert Wood, and Vimy Ridge, and was wounded in action at Carnoy in 1916. He was invalided home and was discharged in March of that year, as physically unfit for further service, holding the 1914–15 Star, and the General Service and Victory Medals.
8, Matlock Place, Hulme, Manchester. Z8714

WILLIAMS, T., Gunner, R.F.A.

He volunteered in September 1915, and was retained on special duties, chiefly in the horse lines at various stations in England. He was unable to obtain his transfer overseas on account of physical unfitness, but nevertheless did consistently good work until the cessation of hostilities. He was demobilised in January 1919.
12, Beswick Street, West Gorton, Manchester. Z11349

WILLIAMS, T., Sergeant, Cheshire Regiment.

He re-enlisted in June 1916, after having seen service during the Boer War of 1899–1902, and in India, and proceeded to France in January 1917. He went into action with the Queen's (Royal West Surrey Regiment), played a distinguished part in many engagements, including the Battles of Arras, Ypres, Messines and St. Quentin, and later in the Retreat and Advance of 1918. He was invalided home in January 1919, and acted as a Company Quartermaster-Sergeant on the demobilisation staff at Heaton Park until June 1919, when he was demobilised. He holds the Queen's and King's South African Medals, and the General Service and Victory Medals.
27, Avon Street, Chorlton-on-Medlock, Manchester. TZ8692

WILLIAMS, T., Gunner, R.F.A.

He volunteered in December 1915, and was drafted to Salonika in September of the following year after undergoing a period of training. In this theatre of war he was in action with his Battery on the Doiran and Vardar fronts, where he was chiefly engaged on 4'5 Howitzers and 18-pounders. He rendered valuable services until the cessation of hostilities, and was demobilised in August 1919, holding the General Service and Victory Medals.
15, Clayton Street, Hulme, Manchester. TZ8708

WILLIAMS, T., Sergt., 8th Lancashire Fusiliers.

He volunteered in 1915, and was retained on important duties at various stations in England. He was not successful in obtaining his transfer overseas, but nevertheless did consistently good work on the defences of the East Coast until his demobilisation in 1919.
28, Higher Temple Street, Chorlton-on-Medlock, Manchester. X8704

WILLIAMS, T., Pte., K.O. (Royal Lancaster Regt.)

He joined in November 1918, on attaining military age, and after doing duty in Dublin until February of the following year, embarked for India in November 1919. There he was engaged on important garrison and other duties, and in 1920 was still serving in Burma.
65, Dorset Street, Hulme, Manchester. Z8696

WILLIAMS, T. H., Driver, R.A.S.C. (M.T.)

He volunteered in October 1914, and was immediately drafted to France, where he was engaged on important transport duties. He saw much active service on the Western Front, and took part in many engagements, including those at Ypres, Neuve Chapelle, Hill 60, and Loos, and was badly wounded at Ypres. He was discharged in September 1915, as physi-

cally unfit and holds the 1914 Star, and the General Service and Victory Medals.
33, Watson Street, West Gorton, Manchester. Z8691

WILLIAMS, T. H., Private, R.A.M.C.

Mobilised at the outbreak of war in August 1914, he was immediately drafted to France, and rendered valuable services at the Battle of Mons. He was also present at numerous other engagements, including the Battles of the Marne, Ypres, Hill 60, Festubert, St. Eloi, the Somme, Arras, Bullecourt, Cambrai, the Aisne (III), Le Cateau and Havrincourt. He was discharged in February 1919, and holds the Mons Star, and the General Service and Victory Medals.
5, Hadfield Street, Newton Heath, Manchester. Z9762

WILLIAMS, W., Corporal, M.G.C.

Joining in June 1916, he was drafted to the Western Front in the following January, and played a prominent part in many important engagements. He was in action at Passchendaele, where he was wounded and during the Advance of 1918 was again wounded at Cambrai in October. He rendered valuable services and was demobilised in October 1919, holding the General Service and Victory Medals.
8, Rumford Place, Chorlton-on-Medlock, Manchester. TZ8707

WILLIAMS, W., Private, R.A.M.C.

Two months after joining in October 1916, he was drafted to the Western Front, where he was engaged on important duties in various sectors. He served at Calais, Rouen, Boulogne, and many other stations, and did much useful work with his Company during the period of hostilities. Demobilised in November 1919, he holds the General Service and Victory Medals. 24, Hardy Street, West Gorton, Manchester. Z8694B

WILLIAMS, W., Private, K.O. (R. Lancaster Regt.)

Volunteering in August 1914, he proceeded to France in March of the following year, and after a period of training took part in much heavy fighting in various sectors. He was in action at the Battles of St. Eloi and Hill 60, and made the supreme sacrifice in May 1915, being killed at the last-named engagement whilst rendering valuable services. He was entitled to the 1914–15 Star, and the General Service and Victory Medals, and already held the Queen's South African Medal for services in the Boer War.

"Whilst we remember, the sacrifice is not in vain."
49, Wood Street, Hulme, Manchester. TZ8711

WILLIAMS, W. R., Gunner, R.F.A.

He volunteered in November 1914, and was drafted to France in the following May. There he was in action with his Battery at numerous engagements, including those at Messines, and in the Ypres salient. He was wounded at the third Battle of Ypres in August 1917, and after being invalided home, was discharged in January 1918, as no longer physically fit for service. He holds the 1914–15 Star, and the General Service and Victory Medals.
34, Dorset Street, Hulme, Manchester. TZ8703

WILLIAMSON, A., Private, R.A.S.C. (M.T.)

He volunteered in 1914, and in March 1915 was sent to Mesopotamia, where he was engaged on important duties which required a high degree of technical skill. He saw much service during the Advance in this theatre of war, and did consistently good work until the cessation of hostilities. He returned to England for demobilisation in August 1919, and holds the 1914–15 Star, and the General Service and Victory Medals.
15, Robson Street, Hulme, Manchester. Z8715

WILLIAMSON, B., Private, R.A.S.C.

He joined in June 1918, and was drafted to the Western Front in September of the same year after a period of training. He saw service during the concluding stages of hostilities, and after the Armistice proceeded to Germany, where he did duty with the Army of Occpation on the Rhine. He was eventually demobilised in April 1920, and holds the General Service and Victory Medals.
25, Edgely Street, Ardwick, Manchester. Z11854A

WILLIAMSON, E., Private, 7th Manchester Regt.

Three months after volunteering in June 1915, he was drafted to the Western Front, and took part in heavy fighting in various sectors. He saw much active service at St. Eloi, Albert, Vimy Ridge, the Somme, Beaucourt, Arras, Ypres and Cambrai, and was unfortunately killed in action at the second Battle of the Somme in March 1918, during the Retreat. He was entitled to the 1914–15 Star, and the General Service and Victory Medals.

"Great deeds cannot die."
27, Edgely Street, Ardwick, Manchester. Z11855B

WILLIAMSON, H., Private, K.O.(Y.L.I.)

He volunteered in October 1915, and after undergoing a period of training was sent to the Western Front in November of the following year. There he took part in many important engagements, including the Battles of the Somme and Arras, and was wounded in action on two occasions. He was invalided to England, and was discharged in January 1918, as unfit for further military service. He holds the General Service and Victory Medals.
13, Nicholson Street, Rochdale Road, Manchester. Z8870

WILLIAMSON, H., Private, Suffolk Regiment.

He joined in March 1917, and in the following November was drafted to France, where he took part in many of the final engagements of the war. He was in action at the third Battle of Ypres, and later rendered valuable services during the Retreat and Advance of 1918. He was eventually demobilised in England in October 1919, holding the General Service and Victory Medals.

42, Bennett Street, Ardwick, Manchester. Z8716

WILLIAMSON, J. R., Rifleman, 9th Cameronians (Scottish Rifles).

He was mobilised in August 1914, and was immediately drafted to the Western Front, where he took part in many important engagements. He saw much heavy fighting in various sectors and rendered valuable services at the Battles of Ypres, St. Eloi, Loos, Albert, the Somme, Arras, Messines and Cambrai, and later in the Retreat of 1918, but was unfortunately killed in action at Amiens during the final Advance and was entitled to the 1914 Star, and the General Service and Victory Medals.

"His memory is cherished with pride."

25, Edgely Street, Ardwick, Manchester. Z11855A

WILLIAMSON, J. W., Private, R.A.M.C.

He joined in July 1917, and was retained on special duties at various important stations in the United Kingdom. He did consistently good work as orderly at the Curragh Hospital, and rendered valuable services attending the sick and wounded. He was eventually demobilised in February 1919, having been unsuccessful in obtaining his transfer to a theatre of war.

10, Fountain Street, City Road, Hulme, Manchester. Z8718

WILLIAMSON, R., Private, M.G.C.

Volunteering in August 1914, he served for a time with the Hussars, and was later transferred to the Machine Gun Corps, and drafted to the Western Front in December 1915. There he was in action during the Somme Offensive of 1916, and later saw much severe fighting at the Battle of Arras. He was unfortunately killed in action on April 11th, 1917, and was entitled to the 1914-15 Star, and the General Service and Victory Medals.

"A costly sacrifice upon the altar of freedom."

75, South Street, Longsight, Manchester. Z8717

WILLIAMSON, R., C.S.M., 1st Manchester Regt.

Volunteering in August 1914, he proceeded to Mesopotamia five months later, and whilst in the theatre of war served with distinction at the Battles of Amara, Nasiryeh, Um-el-Hannah, Sanna-i-Yat, Kut-el-Amara, and in other important engagements on the Tigris. He returned to England for his demobilisation in January 1919, and holds the 1914-15 Star, and the General Service and Victory Medals.

25, Edgely Street, Ardwick, Manchester. Z11854B

WILLIAMSON, R., Driver, R.A.S.C.

Volunteering in August 1914, he proceeded to France in January of the following year, and was engaged on important transport duties in many sectors. He rendered valuable services at Lens, St. Quentin, Bapaume, Cambrai, the Somme, Ypres, Bullecourt, Albert and St. Eloi, and was demobilised in April 1919, holding the 1914-15 Star, and the General Service and Victory Medals.

38, Love Lane, Ancoats, Manchester. Z11357

WILLIAMSON, T., Pte., 10th Lancashire Fusiliers.

Volunteering in September 1914, he underwent a period of training and was drafted to France in August 1915. In this theatre of war he took part in many engagements, including the Battle of Loos (where he was gassed), and later was in action at Messines, Ypres, Lens, the Somme, and in the Retreat and Advance of 1918. He rendered valuable services, and was demobilised in February 1919, holding the 1914-15 Star, and the General Service and Victory Medals.

44, Owen Street, Hulme, Manchester. Z8720

WILLIAMSON, T. E., Private, Labour Corps.

He joined in February 1917, and in due course was drafted to France, where he took an active part in many engagements of importance. He saw much heavy fighting at Arras, Bullecourt, Ploegsteert Wood, Ypres (III), Cambrai, and in the Retreat of 1918, and made the supreme sacrifice in September 1918, during the Advance of that year. He was entitled to the General Service and Victory Medals.

"He died the noblest death a man may die."

28, Walnut Street, Hulme, Manchester. TZ8719A

WILLIAMSON, W., Private, 2/10th Royal Scots.

He joined in October 1916, and for some time was engaged on important guard duties on the East Coast. In August 1918, he proceeded to North Russia, and saw active service at Archangel and other important places in this theatre of war until his return to England for demobilisation in June 1919. He holds the General Service and Victory Medals.

8, Cheltenham Street, Collyhurst, Manchester. Z8871

WILLIAMSON, W. H., Private, Manchester Regt.

He was mobilised in August 1914, and in the following month was drafted to France, where he saw active service with the 23rd Royal Fusiliers. He was in action at the Battles of Neuve Chapelle, Ypres (II), and many other engagements of importance, and was invalided home in November 1915, suffering from trench fever and nephritis. He was eventually discharged in January 1919, and holds the 1914 Star, and the General Service and Victory Medals.

7, Nuttall Street, Chorlton-onMedlock, Manchester. Z8721

WILLIS, A., Private, Royal Welch Fusiliers.

He joined in December 1916, and three months later was drafted to Palestine, where he played an important part in the three Battles of Gaza, and was present at the capture of Jerusalem, Jericho, Tripoli and Aleppo during the Advance of General Allenby's Forces. He was demobilised in December 1920, and holds the General Service and Victory Medals.

172, Victoria Square, Oldham Road, Manchester. Z8872

WILLIS, J. N., Gunner, R.F.A.

He volunteered in September 1915, and was drafted to the Western Front in the following January. He was in action with his Battery at many engagements of importance, including the Battles of the Somme in 1916, La Bassée and Nieuport in 1917 and Ypres (IV) in the following year. He suffered from trench fever, and was invalided to England, and demobilised in February 1919, after a period in hospital. He holds the General Service and Victory Medals.

128, Victoria Street, Longsight, Manchester. Z8722

WILLIS, T., Private, 2nd Lancashire Fusiliers.

He volunteered in September 1914, and was drafted to France in May of the following year after undergoing a period of training. In this theatre of war he took part in much heavy fighting in various sectors, and was in action at numerous engagements, including the Battles of Festubert, Loos, St. Eloi, Albert, the Somme and Arras. He was then sent to the Base at Abbeville and Rouen, suffering from deafness, and was finally discharg   in March 1918, as unfit for further service. He holds the 14-15 Star, and the General Service and Victory Medals, in addition to the Queen's and King's South African Medals for services during the Boer War of 1899-1902.

10, Beaumont Street, Beswick, Manchester. Z11358

WILLMER, H., Leading Aircraftsman, R.A.F.

He joined in February 1918, on attaining military age, and was retained on special duties with his Squadron at important aerodromes in England and Scotland. He was unable to obtain his transfer to a theatre of war, but nevertheless did consistently good work until his demobilisation in April 1919.

17, Cuba Street, Hulme Manchester. Z8723B

WILLMER, W., 2nd Lieut., R.A.F. (late Royal Scots).

Volunteering originally with the Royal Scots in November 1914, he was later transferred to the Royal Air Force and proceeded to the East in January 1916. He played a distinguished part in aerial engagements in Palestine, and was wounded in action at Gaza. In August 1917, after recovery from wounds, he crashed whilst fighting an enemy aeroplane and was invalided to Cairo. He returned to his Squadron in February 1918, and rendered valuable services in Palestine as an observer until the cessation of hostilities. He was demobilised in February 1919, and holds the General Service and Victory Medals.

17, Cuba Street, Hulme, Manchester. Z8723A

WILLOTT, J., Pioneer, R.E. and Private, 16th and 17th Manchester Regiment.

He volunteered in September 1914, and after a period of important duties in England, was sent to France in July 1916. Whilst on the Western Front, he took part in the Battles of the Somme (I), Arras, Ypres (III), Cambrai, and the Somme (II), and was in action throughout the Retreat and Advance of 1918. He was demobilised in February 1919, and holds the General Service and Victory Medals.

19, Marple Street, Ardwick, Manchester. Z8724

WILLOUGHBY, C. W., L/Cpl., 20th Manchester Rgt.

Volunteering in November 1914, he completed a period of training, and was drafted to the Western Front in the following year. There he was in action at the Battles of Loos, Albert, Givenchy, the Somme, Beaumont-Hamel, Beaucourt, Arras, Bullecourt and Ypres (III), and in November 1917, saw service in Italy, where he took part in the fighting on the Piave, and the Asiago Plateaux. He returned to the Western Front in March 1918, and rendered valuable services during the Retreat and Advance of 1918, and was wounded. He was eventually demobilised in January 1919, and holds the 1914-15 Star, and the General Service and Victory Medals.

26, Rumford Street, Hulme, Manchester. TZ8725

WILLOUGHBY, W., Bombardier, R.F.A.

He volunteered in June 1915, and served in the Remount section of the R.F.A. breaking horses in and taking them to France from the Midland Remount Depôt. He rendered valuable services during the period of hostilities, and was demobilised in July 1919, holding the 1914-15 Star, and the General Service and Victory Medals.

37, St. Ann Street, Bradford, Manchester. Z11359

WILLOX, J. A., Sapper, R.E.
He joined in 1916, and was retained on important duties in connection with anti-aircraft searchlights at various stations in England. He was not successful in his efforts to serve overseas, but nevertheless rendered valuable services until the cessation of hostilities, and was demobilised in March 1919.
6, Tiverton Place, Ardwick, Manchester.　　　Z11360

WILLSHAW, A., Pte., King's Own (Scottish Bdrs.)
He volunteered in September 1914, and proceeded to France in the following January. In this theatre of war, he saw much active service in various sectors, and fought at the Battles of Ypres, Neuve Chapelle, Hill 60, La Bassée, Festubert and Loos and was badly wounded at the last engagement. He was in consequence discharged in June 1916, but unfortunately died in February of the following year. He was entitled to the 1914–15 Star, and the General Service and Victory Medals.
"His memory is cherished with pride."
3, King Street, Hulme, Manchester.　　　Z9818B

WILMOTT, A. E., Private, R.M.L.I.
He enlisted in July 1907, and at the outbreak of war in August 1914, saw active service on the high seas. He was present at important engagements in the Cameroons, and in 1916 fought at Jutland. He was wounded on three occasions in East Africa, and later proceeded to Scapa Flow, where he rendered valuable services until the cessation of hostilities. He was eventually discharged in September 1920, and holds the 1914–15 Star, and the General Service and Victory Medals.
52, Hinde Street, Gorton, Manchester.　　　Z11361–62A

WILMOTT, H. P., Private, M.G.C.
He joined in June 1917, and later in the same year proceeded to the Western Front, where he was in action at many important engagements, and was wounded at the Battle of Passchendaele in 1917. He was transferred to Italy before the cessation of hostilities, and whilst in action in this theatre of war was again wounded. Returning to England, he was demobilised in October 1919, and holds the General Service and Victory Medals.
52, Hinde Street, Gorton, Manchester.　　　Z11361–62B

WILMOTT, W., Gunner, R.F.A.
He was already serving in the Army at the outbreak of war in August 1914, and was drafted to France, where he was in action with his Battery at Mons. He also took part in many other engagements of importance, including the Battles of Ypres, Beaumont-Hamel, Bourlon Wood, the Somme, Vimy Ridge, Arras, Cambrai, Armentières and St. Eloi; and was wounded three times and gassed. He proceeded to Germany after the Armistice and did duty with the Army of Occupation until his discharge in January 1920, and holds the Mons Star, and the General Service and Victory Medals.
52, Hinde Street, Gorton, Manchester.　　　Z11361–62C

WILSHAW, A. D., Sapper, R.E.
Volunteering in September 1915, he was sent to France later in the same year, and was chiefly engaged on work of excavation at Ypres until 1916. He also did consistently good work in the Arras sector until February 1918, and was then invalided to England, suffering from shell-shock, and discharged as unfit for further service three months later. He holds the 1914–15 Star, and the General Service and Victory Medals.
9, Temple Street, Bradford, Manchester.　　　Z6885B

WILSON, A., Pte., 8th Argyll and Sutherland Hldrs.
He volunteered in March 1915, and after training for nine months was drafted to the Western Front. There he took part in important engagements until January 1916, when he returned home on account of age and gastric trouble. He was in hospital for nine months, and on recovery was retained with his unit, and was engaged on special duties until his discharge in June 1918, as unfit for further service. He holds the 1914–15 Star, and the General Service and Victory Medals.
52, Forbes Street, West Gorton, Manchester.　　　TZ8733

WILSON, A., Private, Lancashire Fusiliers.
He joined in February 1916, and after a period of training was transferred for duty with a Labour Battalion. He did consistently good work at various important stations in England, but was not successful in obtaining his transfer overseas on account of being physically unfit, and was eventually demobilised in February 1919.
14, Garratt Street, Newton End, Manchester.　　　Z11856C

WILSON, A., Pte., (Signaller), 20th Lancashire Fus.
He volunteered in May 1915, and after undergoing a period of training was drafted to France in the following year. There he took part in many important engagements, including those at Albert, Messines, Arras, Neuve Chapelle, Armentières, the Somme, Lens, Loos and Cambrai, and was wounded during the Retreat in May 1918. He rendered valuable services, and was demobilised in 1919, holding the General Service and Victory Medals.
2, Worth Street, St. Michaels, Manchester　　　Z11367B

WILSON, A., Private, 10th King's (Liverpool Regt.)
He joined in December 1916, and in the following year was drafted to the Western Front. In this theatre of war he took part in the Battles of Cambrai (I), the Somme (II) and Ypres

(IV), and after the cessation of hostilities returned home. He was then transferred to the Cameron Highlanders and proceeded to India, where in 1920 he was still serving. He holds the General Service and Victory Medals.
10, Mary Street, Gorton, Manchester.　　　Z11961

WILSON, A., Private, 8th Manchester Regt. and R.A.M.C.
He volunteered in September 1915, and nine months later was sent to Egypt, where he took part in severe fighting on the Suez Canal and at Katia, Kantara, El Fasher and Romani. In March 1917 he was drafted to the Western Front, but after taking part in engagements at Havrincourt and Epéhy, was wounded in action and invalided home later in the same year. On his recovery, he was transferred to the R.A.M.C., with which unit he did excellent work as a nursing Orderly until his demobilisation in September 1919. He holds the General Service and Victory Medals.　　　Z11365
7, Upper Vauxhall Street, Rochdale Road, Manchester.

WILSON, C., Private, 4th Royal Scots.
Volunteering in September 1914, he was drafted to France in the following February with the Black Watch, and was later transferred to the Royal Scots. He saw much active service in many sectors, and took part in the Battles of Neuve Chapelle, Ypres, Festubert and Loos, and was wounded whilst carrying Despatches under heavy fire. He was invalided home, and on recovery served on the Regimental Staff in Officers quarters in Scotland, until his demobilisation in November 1919. He holds the 1914–15 Star, and the General Service and Victory Medals.
102, Clifton Street, Bradford, Manchester.　　　Z8732

WILSON, D., Corporal, 14th King's (L'pool Regt.)
He volunteered in September 1914, and after training for twelve months was drafted to the Western Front, where he played a prominent part in many important engagements. He was in action at Loos and Ypres, and in January 1916 proceeded to the Balkans, where he took part in the Offensive on the Doiran front. He made the supreme sacrifice on September 14th, 1916, being killed in action at Machucova. He was entitled to the 1914–15 Star, and the General Service and Victory Medals.
"He died the noblest death a man may die,
Fighting for God, and right, and liberty."
16, Wilson Street, Hulme, Manchester.　　　Z8742

WILSON, D., Private, R.N.D.
He joined in February 1916, and wsa drafted to France in the following month. There he took part in much heavy fighting in various sectors, including that at the Battle of Ypres, and after rendering valuable services during the Retreat of 1918, was unfortunately killed in action in the Advance in August of that year, and was entitled to the General Service and Victory Medals.
"The path of duty was the way to glory."
41, Ravald Street, Miles Platting, Manchester.　　　Z9763B

WILSON, E., Private, Devonshire Regiment.
He joined in February 1916, and later in the same year was drafted to Egypt, where he took part in various important engagements and was wounded at Jiffaffa. He was invalided to hospital at Cairo, and upon recovery was transferred to the Western Front in 1917. In this theatre of war he saw much active service, and was finally demobilised in January 1919, holding the General Service and Victory Medals.
14, Garratt Street, Newton End, Manchester.　　　Z11856B

WILSON, F., Gunner, R.F.A.
He was mobilised in August 1914, and shortly afterwards proceeded to Egypt, where he saw service with the Ammunition Column. In April 1915 he embarked for the Dardanelles, and was in action with his Battery at numerous important engagements on the Gallipoli Peninsula until its Evacuation in December. He then returned to Egypt, but owing to ill-health, was invalided to England, and discharged in November 1916 as physically unfit for further service. He holds the 1914–15 Star, and the General Service and Victory Medals.
31, Cross Street, Bradford, Manchester.　　　Z9764

WILSON, F. J., Private, South Lancashire Regt.
Volunteering in January 1915, he underwent a period of training, and was drafted to the Western Front in February of the following year. There he was in action at important engagements in various sectors, and took part in the Battles of Ypres, the Somme, La Bassée, Nieuport and Arras, and later rendered valuable services during the Retreat and Advance of 1918. He was demobilised in January 1919, and holds the General Service and Victory Medals.
22, Oram Street, Miles Platting, Manchester.　　　Z8873

WILSON, H., Private, 10th Border Regiment.
He volunteered in August 1914, and was retained on special duties at important stations in England. He was engaged on work in connection with searchlights, and rendered valuable services, but was not successful in obtaining his transfer to a theatre of war on account of being physically unfit. He was eventually discharged in May 1918.
52, Lomas Street, Ancoats, Manchester.　　　Z11454

WILSON, G., Cpl., K.O. (R. Lancaster Regiment).
He enlisted in July 1912, and at the outbreak of war in August 1914, was immediately drafted to the Western Front with the 1st British Expeditionary Force. He was in action at the Battle of Mons and played a prominent part in subsequent engagements, including the Battles of the Marne and the Aisne, but made the supreme sacrifice on September 15th, 1914, being killed in action during heavy fighting in the last named engagement. He was entitled to the Mons Star, and the General Service and Victory Medals.
"Great deeds cannot die."
11, Drinkwater Street, Manchester. Z11453

WILSON, H., L/Corporal, Royal Welch Fusiliers.
Volunteering in April 1915, he was soon drafted to the Western Front, and whilst in this theatre of war, took part in the Battles of Loos, Albert, the Somme, Bullecourt, Arras and Cambrai, and in heavy fighting at Bourlon Wood, Aveluy Wood, Mericourt, Bray, Corbie, Lille and the Forêt du Mormal. He was demobilised in February 1919, and holds the 1914-15 Star, and the General Service and Victory Medals.
85, Granville Place, Ancoats, Manchester. Z9745B

WILSON. H., Private, Royal Scots.
Volunteering in November 1914, he underwent a period of training, and was drafted to Egypt in the following year. He took part in many important engagements and was wounded at Jifjaffa in April 1916. He was invalided to hospital in Cairo, but in 1917 proceeded to the Western Front. In this theatre of war he saw much active service, and was wounded in action on the Somme. He holds the 1914-15 Star, and the General Service and Victory Medals, and was demobilised in January 1919.
14, Garratt Street, Newton End, Manchester. Z11856A

WILSON, H., Private, 51st Manchester Regiment.
He joined in June 1918, on attaining military age, and was drafted to France in the following November. After the cessation of hostilities, he proceeded to Germany, and was engaged on important garrison duties with the Army of Occupation on the Rhine. He rendered valuable services until November 1919, when he was demobilised, and holds the General Service and Victory Medals.
117, Upper Medlock Street, Hulme, Manchester. Z8743

WILSON, H. J., 2nd Lieutenant, Essex Regiment.
He volunteered in October 1915, and after a period of training proceeded to the Western Front in October of the following year. There he played a distinguished part in many important engagements, including the Battles of Arras, Messines, Ypres (III), Cambrai, the Somme (II), and the Marne (II), and later rendered valuable services during the Retreat and Advance of 1918. He was unhappily killed in action on September 19th, 1918, and was entitled to the General Service and Victory Medals.
"His life for his Country, his soul to God."
13, Leigh Place, Stockport Road, Manchester. Z8728

WILSON, J., Gunner, R.F.A.
Five months after joining in April 1915, he was drafted to India, and was engaged on important garrison and other duties at Calcutta. He rendered valuable services during the period of hostilities, and in 1920 was still serving out there. He holds the General Service and Victory Medals.
21, Ryland Street, Ardwick, Manchester. Z8738

WILSON, J., Private, Royal Scots.
He volunteered in April 1915, and after a period of training was drafted to France in April of the following year. In this theatre of war he took part in much heavy fighting, and was in action at numerous engagements, including the third Battle of Ypres, and in the Retreat and Advance of 1918. He returned to England after the Armistice, and was demobilised in December 1918, holding the General Service and Victory Medals.
41, Ravald Street, Miles Platting, Manchester. Z9763A

WILSON, J., Private, 7th South Lancashire Regt.
Volunteering in June 1915, he proceeded to France six months later, and took part in many important engagements in various sectors of the front. He was in action at the Battles of Albert, the Somme (where he was wounded) and Arras, but unfortunately died on December 10th, 1917 at No.2 General Hospital, Rouen, from influenza. He was entitled to the 1914-15 Star, and the General Service and Victory Medals.
"His memory is cherished with pride."
42, Leigh Street East, Ancoats, Manchester. Z9765

WILSON, J., Sergt., 8th Manchester Regiment.
Mobilised at the outbreak of war in August 1914, he proceeded to the Dardanelles in April of the following year, and was first in action during the Landing on the Gallipoli Peninsula. He played a distinguished part in the heavy fighting in this theatre of war, and was wounded in November. He was invalided home, but unhappily died of his wounds in July 1917, and was entitled to the 1914-15 Star, and the General Service and Victory Medals.
"A costly sacrifice upon the altar of freedom."
31, Cross Street, Bradford, Manchester. Z9766

WILSON, J., Tpr., Duke of Lancaster's Own Dragoons.
He volunteered in March 1915, and six months later was sent to Egypt, where he was in action during the Battles of Mersa-Matruh, Agagia, El Fasher, Romani, Maghdaba and Rafa. Later he proceeded to Palestine, and took part in the Battles of Gaza and the capture of Jerusalem, Jericho and Aleppo. He was demobilised in April 1919, and holds the 1914-15 Star, and the General Service and Victory Medals.
30, Albemarle Street, Moss Side, Manchester. Z8739

WILSON, J., Private, 1/8th Manchester Regiment.
Volunteering in September 1914, he underwent a period of training, and was drafted to the Western Front in February of the following year. There he took part in many engagements of importance, including the Battles of Hill 60, Ypres (II and III), Loos, Albert, Vimy Ridge, the Somme, Arras and Cambrai and later rendered valuable services during the Retreat and Advance of 1918. He holds the 1914-15 Star, and the General Service and Victory Medals, and was demobilised in March 1919.
9, Albany Street, West Gorton, Manchester. Z8731

WILSON, J., Private, Royal Welch Fusiliers.
One month after volunteering in April 1915, he was drafted to the Dardanelles, and took part in much heavy fighting on Gallipoli. He was present at the Landing at Suvla Bay in August of that year, and at other engagements of importance until the Evacuation of the Peninsula in December, during which he made the supreme sacrifice. He was entitled to the 1914-15 Star, and the General Service and Victory Medals.
"Thinking that remembrance, though unspoken, may reach him where he sleeps."
21, Eskrigge Street, Ardwick, Manchester. Z8735

WILSON. J., Private, 1st Lancashire Fusiliers.
Volunteering in August 1914, he completed a period of training and was drafted to the Dardanelles early in the following year. There he was in action at many engagements of importance, and took part in much heavy fighting. In 1916 he proceeded to France after the Evacuation of the Gallipoli Peninsula, and saw much service in various sectors of the Western Front, being present at the Battles of Ypres, Albert and the Somme, and later, in the Retreat and Advance of 1918, and was wounded in action. He holds the 1914-15 Star, and the General Service and Victory Medals, and was demobilised in 1919.
67, Junction Street, Ancoats, Manchester. Z8730

WILSON, J., Corporal, R.A.M.C.
Mobilised at the outbreak of war in August 1914, he was sent to France immediately afterwards, and served with the Field Ambulance during the Retreat from Mons. He was also present at many subsequent engagements, and was gassed at the Battle of Loos in September 1915. He was invalided home, but on his recovery was drafted to the East in January 1916, and did consistently good work in both Egypt and Palestine, until the cessation of hostilities. He was wounded in March 1918, was discharged in February of the following year, holding the Mons Star, and the General Service and Victory Medals.
11, Sidney Street, Bradford, Manchester. Z8729

WILSON, J., Pte., 11th, 19th, and 22nd Lancs. Fus.
He volunteered in September 1914, and twelve months later was sent to France, where he played an important part in the Battles of Albert, the Somme, Arras, Cambrai (I and II) and Le Cateau. He was three times wounded in action—at Albert in June 1916, at Cambrai in November 1917, and at Le Cateau, just prior to the cessation of hostilities. Demobilised on returning to England in March 1919, he holds the 1914-15 Star, and the General Service and Victory Medals.
2, Metcalfe Street, Miles Platting, Manchester. Z8727

WILSON, J. F., Private, Manchester Regiment,
Mobilised in August 1914, he was drafted to France a month later and took part in much severe fighting before being transferred to Salonika. In the Balkan theatre of war, he was in action on the Doiran, Struma and Vardar fronts, and was wounded in April 1917. He returned to the Western Front in February 1918, and served at the Battles of the Aisne (II) and the Marne (III), but was sent home in July of that year. He was discharged in March 1919, and holds the 1914 Star, and the General Service and Victory Medals.
10, Beswick Street, West Gorton, Manchester. Z11366

WILSON, J. H., Corporal, R.A.S.C. (M.T.)
Mobilised in August 1914, he was immediately drafted to the Western Front, and played a prominent part during the Battle of, and the Retreat from, Mons. He did consistently good work whilst engaged in the transport of supplies to the trenches in various important sectors, was also present at the Battles of the Marne, Ypres, Neuve Chapelle and Loos, and later conveyed wounded to hospital after the Battles of the Somme, Arras and Cambrai. He was gassed during the Retreat in March 1918, was invalided to England, and ultimately discharged in November 1918. He holds the Mons Star, and the General Service and Victory Medals.
44, Cookson Street, Ancoats, Manchester. Z11364

WILSON, J. H., Private, 8th Manchester Regiment.
Mobilised with the Territorials at the outbreak of war in
August 1914, he proceeded to Egypt with the 42nd Division
and was stationed at Cairo and Alexandria. In 1915 he was
transferred to the Dardanelles, and was in action at Cape
Helles, Krithia, Achi-Baba, and was badly wounded in August
of that year. He was invalided to England, and being unfit
for further active service, was retained on important duties
at various camps and depôts in England until his demobilisation in January 1919, after being transferred to the R.A.S.C.
He holds the 1914-15 Star, and the General Service and
Victory Medals.
5, Belmont Street, Collyhurst, Manchester.   Z11368

WILSON, J. R., Gunner, R.F.A.
Two months after joining in July 1916 he proceeded to the
Western Front, and was in action with his Battery at many
important engagements. He took part in the Battles of
Arras, Vimy Ridge, Bullecourt, Messines, Passchendaele and
Cambrai, and rendered valuable services during the Retreat
of 1918, during which he was wounded in April. He returned
to France in September of the same year, and was again in
action during the Advance, and after the Armistice proceeded
to Germany, where he did duty with the Army of Occupation on the Rhine. He returned to England for demobilisation, and holds the General Service and Victory Medals.
57, Parkfield Avenue, Rusholme, Manchester.   TZ8734

**WILSON, J. T. (M.M., M.S.M.), Sergt, 6th King's
Own Scottish Borderers.**
He volunteered in September 1914, and was first engaged as
an Instructor of recruits until January 1915, for which work
he was awarded the Meritorious Service Medal. He then
proceeded to France and played a prominent part in the
Battles of Neuve Chapelle, Hill 60, Ypres (II), Festubert,
Albert, the Somme (where he was wounded in action), Arras,
Bullecourt, Messines, and Cambrai (where he was gassed in
November 1917) and in the Relief and Advance of 1918.
After the cessation of hostilities he served on the Rhine with
the Army of Occupation until his demobilisation in March
1919. He was awarded the Military Medal for conspicuous
bravery in carrying wounded under heavy shell-fire
during the Somme Offensive in July 1916, and also holds the
1914-15 Star, and the General Service and Victory Medals.
41, Derby Street, Ardwick, Manchester.   Z8737

WILSON, J. W., Private, Manchester Regiment.
He volunteered in November 1914, and was retained on important duties in England until March 1917. He was then
sent to Palestine, and took part in the heavy fighting during
General Allenby's Advance, in which he was present
at the capture of Jerusalem and Jaffa, and was wounded in
action at the occupation of Tripoli in October 1918. He holds
the General Service and Victory Medals, and was demobilised
in April 1919.
61, Loom Street, Ancoats, Manchester.   Z11455

WILSON, M., Pte., 8th Loyal N. Lancashire Regt.
Volunteering in September 1914, he completed a period of
training, and was drafted to the Western Front in September
of the following year. In this theatre of war he took part in
many engagements of importance, including those at Vimy
Ridge, the Somme and Thiepval. He was invalided home
with nephritis in September 1916, and after recovery, rejoined
his unit, but was eventually discharged in September 1917
as unfit for further military service. He holds the 1914-15
Star, and the General Service and Victory Medals.
1, Lavender Street, Miles Platting, Manchester.   Z11363

WILSON, N., Private, 18th Manchester Regiment.
Volunteering in September 1915, he proceeded to France two
months later and took part in many important engagements.
He saw much heavy fighting at the Battles of Loos, St. Eloi,
Albert and Vimy Ridge and made the supreme sacrifice on
July 9th, 1916 during the Somme Offensive. He was entitled
to the 1914-15 Star, and the General Service and Victory
Medals.
" He passed out of the sight of men by the path of duty and
   self-sacrifice."
10, Lingard Street, Hulme, Manchester.   Z7179B

WILSON, P. J., Private, 17th Manchester Regt.
He volunteered in September 1915, and after a period of training was drafted to France in July 1916. He was unfortunately
killed in action during the only engagement in which he took
part, the Battle of the Somme on July 30th, a few weeks after
his landing on French soil. He was entitled to the General
Service and Victory Medals.
" Honour to the immortal dead, who gave their youth that the
   world might grow old in peace."
25, Phelan Street, Collyhurst, Manchester.   Z11369

WILSON, R., Private, K.O. (Y.L.I.)
He joined in November 1916, and completing his training
was drafted to France in February 1917. There he took
part in heavy fighting in various important sectors and was
in action at the Battles of Passchendaele, Cambrai, the Somme
(II), Arras, La Bassée and Givenchy. He also rendered
valuable services during the Retreat and Advance of 1918,

and was demobilised in January of the following year, holding
the General Service and Victory Medals.
10, Mitton Street, Longsight, Manchester.   Z8726

WILSON, T., Private, R.A.M.C.
Joining in March 1917, he was drafted to the Western Front
in the following December and was engaged as a stretcher-
bearer in various sectors. He was wounded at Ypres during
the Retreat of 1918, and after spending some time in hospital
at Rouen and Étaples, was invalided to England and eventually demobilised in September 1919. He holds the General
Service and Victory Medals.   TX8740
23, Lingmoor Street, Chorlton-on-Medlock, Manchester.

WILSON, T., Private, R.A.S.C. (M.T.)
He volunteered in November 1915, and after a short period
of training was sent to France in February 1916. He did
consistently good work as a motor mechanic throughout
the whole time he was on the Western Front, his duties being
chiefly in connection with the driving and repairing of motor
ambulances. He saw service at Loos, Albert, Vimy Ridge,
Lens and Cambrai. He holds the General Service and Victory
Medals, and was demobilised in May 1919.
37, Matthew Street, Ardwick, Manchester.   Z8736

WILSON, W., Private, 17th Lancashire Fusiliers.
Volunteering in September 1915, he was drafted to France
in the following January and took part in many important
engagements, including those at Loos, St. Eloi, Ploegsteert
Wood, the Somme, Arras, Cambrai, the Marne, Bapaume, Havrincourt and Épéhy, and was wounded in action at Arras in
1917. He rendered valuable services, and was demobilised
in March 1919, holding the General Service and Victory
Medals. 2, Worth St., St. Michaels, Manchester.   Z11367A

WILSON, W. H., Pte., K.O. (R. Lancaster Regt.)
He joined in October 1916, and two months later proceeded
to France, where he took part in many important engagements and saw much heavy fighting in various sectors. In
December 1917 he was transferred to Egypt, and was engaged
as a motor transport driver, but through the excessive heat
suffered from heart failure, and in 1920 was still under treatment in hospital. He holds the General Service and Victory
Medals. 6, Marne Rd., Moss Side, Manchester.   Z8741

WIMBURY, B., Pioneer, R.E.
He joined in February 1917, and was engaged on important
duties at various stations in England during the first period
of his service. He was drafted to France in December of the
same year and was present at many important engagements,
including those on the Somme and at Havrincourt, Beaumont-
Hamel and Beaucourt, and was wounded later at Bullecourt.
He was invalided to England and finally demobilised in
November 1919, holding the General Service and Victory
Medals. 52, Norton St., West Gorton, Manchester.   Z8744

WINDELER, J. A., Guardsman, Grenadier Guards.
Joining in December 1916, he proceeded to France in February
of the following year, after a short period of training, and
took part in numerous important engagements in various
sectors of the Front. He saw much heavy fighting at Péronne,
Arras, Ypres, Cambrai, the Somme, Amiens, and Bapaume,
and was wounded in action. He was eventually invalided to
England and later discharged in April 1918 as unfit for further
military service. He holds the General Service and Victory
Medals. 12, Hancock St., Rusholme, Manchester.   Z8745

WINDER, C., Private, 1st Manchester Regiment.
He volunteered in December 1915, and underwent a period
of training prior to his being drafted to Egypt. In this seat
of operations he saw much active service and later took part
in several engagements in Palestine, including the fall of
Jerusalem. He returned home after a period in hospital
at Cairo, and was demobilised in July 1919, holding the
General Service and Victory Medals.
2, Goole Street, Bradford, Manchester.   Z11962

WINDER, J., Private, 8th Lancashire Fusiliers.
He volunteered in November 1915, and after completing a
period of training was drafted to the Western Front in 1916.
He saw much heavy fighting in various sectors, including those
of Arras and Ypres, and was twice wounded in action. He
also took part in the Retreat and Advance of 1918, and was
eventually demobilised in January 1919, holding the General
Service and Victory Medals.
8, Goole Street, Bradford, Manchester.   Z11370

WINDRAM, F., Pte., 1st King's (Liverpool Regt.)
Six months after volunteering in June 1915, he was drafted
to the Western Front, and was in action at many important
engagements. He took part in the Battles at Vimy Ridge
and in the Somme Offensive of 1916, and was invalided to England through wounds. He returned to France in April
1917, and fought in the Battles of Arras, Vimy Ridge and
Ypres (III), and was wounded a second time and gassed.
After being discharged from hospital, he was eventually
demobilised in April 1919, and holds the 1914-15 Star, and
the General Service and Victory Medals.
8, Fountain Street, City Road, Hulme, Manchester. Z8746

WINFIELD, C., Corporal, 11th Manchester Regt.
He volunteered in August 1914, and in April of the following year was drafted to the Dardanelles, where he played a prominent part in the heavy fighting on the Gallipoli Peninsula, and was wounded on two occasions. After the Evacuation, he proceeded to the Western Front and was in action with a trench mortar battery at the Battles of Loos, Albert, Vimy Ridge, the Somme, Arras, Bullecourt and Cambrai, and rendered valuable services until August 1918. He was demobilised in December of the same year, and holds the 1914-15 Star, and the General Service and Victory Medals.
11, Edith Street, West Gorton, Manchester. Z11371

WINGRAVE, D. A., Private, M.G.C.
He joined in November 1916, and after a period of training was drafted to France, where he took part in several engagements, including the Battles of Arras and Ypres. After hostilities ceased, he went to Germany with the Army of Occupation and served there until his demobilisation in August 1919. He holds the General Service and Victory Medals. 5, Goole St., Bradford, Manchester. Z11963

WINN, G., Private, 2nd Manchester Regiment.
He joined in August 1914, and was retained on important duties at various stations in England. He was unable to obtain his transfer to a theatre of war, but, nevertheless, rendered valuable services until his discharge in November 1915, as physically unfit for military duty.
21, Hancock Street, Rusholme, Manchester. TZ8747

WINNINGTON, C., Private, 1st Manchester Regt.
He volunteered in October 1914, and in the following January was sent to France, where he took part in many important engagements. He was in action at the Battles of Ypres, Loos, St. Eloi, Albert, the Somme, Arras and Cambrai, and later at Amiens, Havrincourt and Le Cateau, during the Advance of 1918. After his return from France he was discharged in July 1919, suffering from malaria and rheumatism, and holds the 1914-15 Star, and the General Service and Victory Medals.
13, Upper Vauxhall Street, Rochdale Rd., Manchester. Z11372

WINSTANLEY, A., Pte., K.O. (R. Lancaster Regt.)
Volunteering in January 1915, he was soon drafted to the Western Front, and took part in many engagements, including the Battles of Neuve Chapelle, St. Eloi, Ypres (II), La Bassée, Givenchy, Festubert, Albert, Vimy Ridge and Beaumont-Hamel, and was wounded in action at La Boiselle in 1916. He was sent to Salonika in September 1916, after a period in hospital, and saw much service on the Doiran and Struma fronts and at the 1st and 2nd Battles of the Vardar. Returning to England, he was demobilised in March 1919, and holds the 1914-15 Star, and the General Service and Victory Medals.
26, Birch Street, Hulme, Manchester. Z8749

WINSTANLEY, J., Pte., 4th King's (L'pool Regt.)
Volunteering in September 1914, he completed a period of training and was drafted to France, where he took part in many engagements of importance. He was in action at Loos, St. Eloi and on the Somme, and was wounded. He returned to his unit on recovery, and later was engaged in much heavy fighting at Arras and made the supreme sacrifice on May 20th, 1917, being killed in action on that date. He was entitled to the 1914-15 Star, and the General Service and Victory Medals.
"And doubtless he went in splendid company."
1, Metcalf Street, Miles Platting, Manchester. TZ8748

WINT, J., Private, Manchester Regiment.
Mobilised at the outbreak of war in August 1914, he proceeded to France shortly afterwards and took part in much heavy fighting in various sectors. He was in action at Ypres and Neuve Chapelle and other engagements of importance, and in 1915 was transferred to Salonika. He saw much service in this theatre of war and was in action on the Doiran front and on the Struma, and later suffered from malaria. He was finally discharged in December 1918, and holds the 1914 Star, and the General Service and Victory Medals.
8, Byrom Street, Longsight, Manchester. TZ8750

WINTER, W. G., Private, 28th Manchester Regt.
He joined in March 1918, and was drafted to the Eastern theatre of war after a period of training. He saw active service in Egypt and took part in many engagements, including those on the Suez Canal and at Mersa-Matruh and elsewhere. He holds the General Service and Victory Medals, and was demobilised in 1919 on his return to England.
35, Elizabeth Street, Manchester. Z9747B

WINTER, W. H., Private, 6th Leicestershire Regt.
He volunteered in October 1915, and after a period of training was drafted to the Western Front in December 1916. He took part in much severe fighting in this theatre of war and was present at the Battles of Arras (where he was wounded) and Passchendaele, and was unfortunately killed in action at the second Battle of the Somme on March 22nd, 1918. He was entitled to the General Service and Victory Medals.
"He joined the great white company of valiant souls."
10, Jones Street Chorlton-on-Medlock, Manchester. Z11857

WINTERBOTTOM, A., Private, Lancashire Fusiliers.
He was already serving in the Army at the outbreak of war in August 1914, and was drafted to the Dardanelles, where he was engaged in much heavy fighting on the Gallipoli Peninsula, including the action at Cape Helles. He returned to England and was later sent to Palestine and saw service in this theatre of war until 1917, when he was transferred to the Western Front, and was gassed after taking part in important engagements. He was invalided to England and finally demobilised in February 1919, holding the 1914-15 Star, and the General Service and Victory Medals.
53, Alexandra Place, Manchester. Z8874

WINTERBOTTOM, G., L/Cpl., 1/7th Manchester Rgt.
He was already serving with the Colours at the outbreak of war in August 1914, and in due course was drafted to the Dardanelles. There he took part in much heavy fighting, and was in action during the Landing on the Gallipoli Peninsula. He also fought at the Battles of Krithia (I and II), and made the supreme sacrifice on May 12th, 1915, being killed in action He was entitled to the 1914-15 Star, and the General Service and Victory Medals.
"A valiant soldier, with undaunted heart, he breasted life's last hill."
53, Alexandra Place, Manchester. Z8875

WISELEY, W., Private, Lancashire Fusiliers.
He volunteered in February 1915, and served at Conway and Salisbury Plain before proceeding to France in May 1916. In this theatre of war he took part in many engagements, including the Battles of Ploegsteert Wood and Vimy Ridge. He was severely wounded on the Somme, and after a period in hospital, unhappily died of his wounds on August 30th, 1916. He was entitled to the General Service and Victory Medals.
"Thinking that remembrance, though unspoken, may reach him where he sleeps."
69, Elliott Street, Bradford, Manchester. Z8751

WISEMAN, H., Private, King's (Liverpool Regt.)
One month after joining in February 1916, he proceeded to France and took part in many important engagements. He was in action at Loos, St. Eloi, Albert, Vimy Ridge, the Somme, Arras, Messines, Ypres and Cambrai and rendered valuable services during the Retreat and Advance of 1918. He returned to England after the Armistice and was demobilised in February 1919, holding the General Service and Victory Medals. TZ8752
4, Wiggin Street, Wilmslow Road, Rusholme, Manchester.

WITHERS, A. E., Sergt., 11th Manchester Regt.
Volunteering in September 1914, he proceeded to the Dardanelles in the following year and took a distinguished part in the fighting at Suvla Bay and Chunuk Bair. After the Evacuation of the Gallipoli Peninsula he was sent to Egypt and saw service in that theatre of war until July 1916, when he was transferred to France. There he was in action on the Somme and at Bullecourt, and made the supreme sacrifice at the Battle of Messines in May 1917 being killed in action. He was entitled to the 1914-15 Star, and the General Service and Victory Medals.
"Great deeds cannot die: They, with the sun and moon renew their light for ever."
99, Cross Street, Bradford, Manchester. Z8754

WITHERS, E., Private, 4th Manchester Regiment.
He volunteered in March 1915, and after a period of training was drafted to the Western Front, where he took part in many important engagements and saw much heavy fighting in various sectors of France and Belgium until 1918. He was then transferred to the Italian front and was in action during the British Offensive on the Piave. He holds the 1914-15 Star, and the General Service and Victory Medals. and in 1920 was still serving in the Army.
27, St. Ann Street, Bradford, Manchester. X8753

WITHERS, E.. Private, 4th Manchester Regiment.
He joined in March 1917, and on conclusion of his training was two months later ordered overseas. During his service on the Western Front he was in action in numerous important engagements in different sectors of the war zone. On being transferred to the Labour Corps, he performed excellent work with that unit and was eventually demobilised in January 1920, holding the General Service and Victory Medals.
27, St. Ann Street, Bradford, Manchester. X11883

WITHERS, F., Private, R.A.M.C.
He volunteered in October 1915, and after a period of training was drafted to the Balkans in June of the following year. He rendered valuable services in Salonika and was attached later to the 1st Royal Serbian Army, and was present at engagements on the Struma and the Vardar and at Monastir. He suffered from ill-health, and was invalided home in February 1919, and in the following May was demobilised, holding the General Service and Victory Medals.
34, George Street, Bradford, Manchester. Z8755

WITHINGTON, H., Pte., K.O. (R. Lancaster Regt.)
Joining in November 1916, he completed his training and was engaged on important duties in connection with the conveyance of enemy prisoners to England during 1917. He proceeded to Ireland in 1918, and served in Dublin for eight months and later was drafted to India, where in 1920 he was still stationed. He holds the General Service and Victory Medals. 61, Ainsworth St., West Gorton, Manchester. Z9767

WITHINGTON, T., Driver, R.F.A.
Mobilised at the outbreak of war in August 1914, he proceeded to the Western Front in the following month and was present during the Retreat from Mons. He was also in action with his Battery at subsequent engagements of importance, including the Battles of the Marne, the Aisne, Ypres (I, II, and III), Arras and Cambrai, and was wounded in May 1915. He also suffered from trench fever after the Battle of Cambrai, and was eventually invalided to England and discharged in February 1919, holding the Mons Star, and the General Service and Victory Medals.
7, Lavender Street, Hulme, Manchester. TZ8756

WITTER, G., Private, 19th Lancashire Fusiliers.
He volunteered in April 1915, and six months later was drafted to the Western Front, where he took part in many important engagements. He was in action at Loos and was wounded in February 1916, but on his recovery saw service at the Battles of Vimy Ridge, the Somme, Beaucourt, Beaumont-Hamel, Arras and was gassed at the third Battle of Ypres. He returned to his unit after a period in hospital, and was again in action at Cambrai and on the Somme, where he was a second time wounded. He was taken prisoner in April 1918, during the Retreat and after the Armistice was repatriated and later discharged in September 1919. He holds the 1914-15 Star, and the General Service and Victory Medals.
528, Claremont Road, Rusholme, Manchester. TZ8757

WOLF, A. R., Corporal, 8th Royal Fusiliers.
One month after joining in June 1916, he was drafted to France and played a prominent part in the heavy fighting on the Western Front. He was in action at the Battles of the Somme, Beaumont-Hamel, Beaucourt, Arras, Vimy Ridge, and Cambrai, and was invalided home suffering with trench fever. He returned to France within six months, and was again in action at the Battle of Cambrai in November 1917, where he was taken prisoner and kept in captivity until the cessation of hostilities. He was eventually demobilised in September 1919, and holds the General Service and Victory Medals. 12, Towson Street, Russell Street, Hulme, Manchester. Z8758

WOLFE, J., Private, 2nd Manchester Regiment.
Mobilised at the outbreak of war in August 1914, he proceeded to France with the 1st Expeditionary Force and took part in the Battle of Mons and the subsequent Retreat. He was also in action at the Battles of Le Cateau, La Bassée, and Ypres and was taken prisoner. He was forced to work in the saw mills in Germany until the cessation of hostilities, and was repatriated and finally discharged in December 1919, holding the Mons Star, and the General Service and Victory Medals.
16, Daniel Street, Hulme, Manchester. Z8759

WOLSTENCROFT, E. (M.M.), L/Corporal, 22nd Manchester Regiment.
He volunteered in December 1914, and in the following October was drafted to France, where he took part in much heavy fighting at Albert, the Somme, Arras and Beaumont-Hamel. He was awarded the Military Medal for conspicuous bravery and devotion to duty in the Field on July 3rd, 1916. He made the supreme sacrifice, being killed in action at Trones Wood on March 14th, 1917, and was also entitled to the 1914-15 Star, and the General Service and Victory Medals.
"Whilst we remember, the sacrifice is not in vain."
14, Lime Street, Bradford, Manchester. Z11964

WOLSTENCROFT, G. T., Cpl., 8th Manchester Regt.
Volunteering in September 1914, he completed a period of training and was drafted to the Dardanelles in April 1915. There he played a prominent part in much heavy fighting and was in action during the Landing on the Gallipoli Peninsula and later at the Battles of Krithia, Suvla Bay and Chunuk Bair. He was taken ill during the Evacuation in December 1915, and was invalided home. After serving on demobilisation work at Heaton Park, Manchester, he was himself demobilised in January 1919, and holds the 1914-15 Star, and the General Service and Victory Medals.
12, Culvert Street, Rochdale Road, Manchester. Z11375

WOLSTENCROFT, J., Private, Manchester Regt.
He joined in June 1918, and after completing his training was sent to Germany in January of the following year. He did duty with the Army of Occupation at Bonn for nine months and returned to England in October 1919, when he was demobilised.
51, Fitzgeorge Street, Collyhurst, Manchester. Z10819A

WOLSTENCROFT, J. T., Pte., S. Lancaster Regt.
He joined in March 1916, and after doing duty in England for a time, was drafted to the Western Front in August 1917.

There he took part in many important engagements, including the Battles of Ypres (III) and Cambrai and later during the Retreat and Advance of 1918. He holds the General Service and Victory Medals, and was demobilised in July 1919.
22, Boslam Street, Ancoats, Manchester. Z11374

WOLSTENCROFT, T. S., Pte., 13th Manchester Rgt.
He volunteered in September 1914, and after a period of training was drafted to Salonika. There he took part in many important engagements in the Balkans, and was in action on the Vardar and Doiran fronts. He continued his service until the cessation of hostilities, and returning to England was discharged in December 1918. He holds the 1914-15 Star, and the General Service and Victory Medals.
21, Long Street, Ancoats, Manchester. Z11373

WOOD, A., Private, 21st Manchester Regiment.
Volunteering in November 1914, he first served at various important stations in England, and in November 1915 proceeded to France, where he was in action at numerous engagements. He took part in the heavy fighting at Albert and Delville Wood, and made the supreme sacrifice on July 14th, 1916, being killed in action during the Somme Offensive. He was entitled to the 1914-15 Star, and the General Service and Victory Medals.
11, Sandal Street, Newton, Manchester. TZ8485

WOOD, A., Private, R.A.S.C.
He joined in October 1916, and three months later proceeded to Mesopotamia, where he was engaged on important transport duties. He saw service at Baghdad, Ramadieh, Tekrit and Mosul, and suffered from malaria and dysentery. He was treated at New South Wales Military Hospital, India, and later in Lancashire, on his return to England. He was demobilised in October 1919, and holds the General Service and Victory Medals.
51, Carmen Street, Ardwick, Manchester. Z8769

WOOD, A., Private, West Riding Regiment.
Joining in December 1917, he underwent a period of training and was drafted to France in May 1918. In this theatre of war he took part in many of the concluding engagements, being in action at the Battles of the Marne (II), Amiens, Bapaume, Havrincourt Wood and Cambrai (II), and was wounded. He was invalided home and eventually discharged in May 1919, as unfit for further service, and holds the General Service and Victory Medals.
28, Henry Street, West Gorton, Manchester. Z8761

WOOD, A. N., Private, R.A.S.C.
He joined in June 1916, and in the following year was drafted to the Western Front, where he was engaged on important transport duties in many sectors. He did consistently good work until the cessation of hostilities, finishing his services at various stations in England, and was demobilised in March 1920. He holds the General Service and Victory Medals.
5, Piercy Street, Ancoats, Manchester. Z11379

WOOD, C., Private, 24th Manchester Regiment.
Three months after joining in February 1916, he proceeded to the Western Front and took part in many important engagements. He was in action at the Battles of the Somme, Passchendaele, Bullecourt and Cambrai, and was wounded on three occasions. He was demobilised in May 1919, and holds the General Service and Victory Medals.
11, Sandal Street, Newton, Manchester. TZ8486

WOOD, C., L/Corporal, 21st Manchester Regiment.
He joined in June 1916, and after completing his training was sent to the Western Front in March 1917. There he took part in many important engagements, including those at Arras and Bullecourt, but on August 29th, 1917, was killed in action in the Ypres salient. He was entitled to the General Service and Victory Medals.
"Fighting for God, and right, and liberty."
45, Buxton Street, Manchester. Z8876

WOOD, D., Sergt., 2nd Royal Welch Fusiliers.
A time-serving soldier since 1907, he proceeded to the Western Front from India at the outbreak of hostilities and played a prominent part in the fighting in various sectors. He was invalided to England suffering from frost-bite in 1915, and in November of that year was drafted to Egypt. He saw service in this theatre of war and later served in Palestine with General Allenby. He returned to England for demobilisation in April 1919, and holds the 1914 Star, and the General Service and Victory Medals.
14, Tranmere Street, Hulme, Manchester. Z8771

WOOD, E., Private, King's (Liverpool Regiment).
He volunteered in November 1915, and after completing his training was drafted to France, where, on account of his being unfit for the Service in forward areas, he was retained as a telephone operator at the First Army School of Trench Mortar Guns. He was stationed at St. Omar, Le Havre and elsewhere at the Base and was eventually demobilised in January 1919, holding the General Service and Victory Medals.
49, Gore Street, Greenheys, Manchester. TZ8763

WOOD, F., Driver, R.A.S.C. (M.T.)
He joined in January 1917, and was retained on special duties with the R.A.S.C. at various important stations in England. He was unable to obtain his transfer to a theatre of war, but, nevertheless, did consistently good work until his demobilisation in March 1919.
68, Teignmouth Street, Collyhurst, Manchester.   Z9768

WOOD, F., Private, Labour Corps.
Joining in June 1917, he was drafted to France in January 1918, after a period of training and did consistently good work in various sectors. He was present at Vimy Ridge, Bapaume, Havrincourt, Arras, Albert, Bullecourt, Cambrai and Lille, but owing to paralysis eventually lost the use of both legs. He was in consequence discharged as unfit in February 1919, and holds in addition to the General Service and Victory Medals the Medals for the South African War.
56, Buckley Street, St. Michaels, Manchester.   Z11382

WOOD, G., Driver, R.A.S.C.
Mobilised at the outbreak of war in August 1914, he was immediately sent to the Western Front, and was present at the Battle of Mons. He did consistently good work in connection with the transport of food and ammunition, and also served in the Battles of the Marne, the Aisne, Ypres, Neuve Chapelle, St. Eloi, Loos, Vimy Ridge, the Somme, Passchendaele and Cambrai, and later in the Retreat and Advance of 1918. He holds the Mons Star, and the General Service and Victory Medals, and was discharged in March 1919.
25, Mark Street, Hulme, Manchester.   Z8765

WOOD, G., Gunner, R.G.A.
He joined in May 1918, but was exempted from serving overseas on account of his being indispensable in matters pertaining to coal rationing. He nevertheless rendered valuable services, and was not demobilised until February 1919.
11, Sandal Street, Newton, Manchester.   TZ8484

WOOD, G. H., Private, R.A.M.C.
He joined in August 1917, and was retained on special duties as an Instructor in hospital work at various stations in England. He rendered valuable services, but was unable to obtain a transfer overseas, and was discharged in December 1918.   22, Strand Street, Ancoats, Manchester.   TZ9769

WOOD, H., Private, 12th M.G.C.
Joining in June 1916, he proceeded to France two months later and took part in many engagements in various sectors. He rendered valuable services at the Battles of Arras, Albert and Ypres (III), and later fought at the second Battle of Cambrai during the Advance of 1918. He proceeded to Germany after the cessation of hostilities and served with the Army of Occupation on the Rhine until his return to England for demobilisation in October 1919. He holds the General Service and Victory Medals.
3, Dearden Street, Hulme, Manchester.   Z8768

WOOD, H., Private, 5th M.G.C.
He joined in September 1917, and after completing a period of training was drafted to the Western Front in April 1918. There he was in action at Havrincourt, the Somme (II) and Cambrai (II), during the Advance of that year, and after the Armistice proceeded to Germany, where he did duty with the Army of Occupation on the Rhine. He was demobilised in March 1919, and holds the General Service and Victory Medals.
11, Riall Street, Hulme, Manchester.   Z8764

WOOD, J., Private, 19th Manchester Regiment.
He volunteered in November 1915, and was drafted to France in June of the following year. In this theatre of war he took part in numerous engagements of importance, including the Battles of the Somme (where he was wounded), Albert, Ypres and Cambrai. He suffered from gas poisoning, but after a period in hospital re-joined his Regiment, and was transferred to a Labour Corps for light duty until his demobilisation in March 1919. He holds the General Service and Victory Medals.
2, Tipper Street, Hulme, Manchester.   Z8772

WOOD, J., Private, 12th Cheshire Regiment.
Volunteering in March 1915, he underwent a period of training, and was drafted to Salonika in October of the same year. He took part in important engagements on the Vardar and Doiran fronts, at the capture of Monastir, and in the General Advance in this theatre of war, and was wounded on two occasions. Returning to England he was demobilised in November 1919, and holds the 1914-15 Star, and the General Service and Victory Medals.
4, Hampden Street, West Gorton, Manchester.   Z11377

WOOD, J., Sapper, R.E.
Volunteering in January 1915, he proceeded to the Western Front in the following August, and took part in the Battles of Loos, the Somme and Ypres. In October 1917, he was transferred to Italy, and served with distinction on the Piave, and in other heavy fighting in this theatre of war. He was demobilised in February 1919, and holds the 1914-15 Star, and the General Service and Victory Medals.
43, Longridge Street, Longsight, Manchester.   Z8707

WOOD, J. A., Pte., Welch Regt. (Cyclist Battalion).
He joined in November 1916, and was retained on special duties at important stations in England. He was not successful in obtaining his transfer to a theatre of war, but nevertheless rendered valuable services and was demobilised in January 1919.
46, Richardson Street, Collyhurst, Manchester.   Z11381

WOOD, J. H., Pte., 1/6th King's (Liverpool Regt.)
He volunteered in August 1914, and after a brief training was drafted to Egypt in the following month and saw active service there until January 1915. In April he was transferred to the Dardanelles, and took part in much heavy fighting at Suvla Bay on the Gallipoli Peninsula and was wounded. He proceeded to the Western Front in May 1917, and whilst in action at the third Battle of Ypres, made the supreme sacrifice, being killed in July 1917. He was entitled to the 1914-15 Star, and the General Service and Victory Medals.
"The path of duty was the way to glory."
48, Wood Street, Hulme, Manchester.   Z8762

WOOD, J. W., Driver, R.F.A.
He volunteered in October 1914, and after undergoing a period of training was sent to France in April 1915. There he was in action with his Battery at numerous engagements, and saw much heavy fighting at Loos, Albert, the Somme, Arras, Bullecourt, Ypres and Cambrai, and later during the Retreat and Advance of 1918. He holds the 1914-15 Star, and the General Service and Victory Medals, and was demobilised in May 1919.
17, Rock Street, Higher Openshaw, Manchester.   Z11376

WOOD, L., Private, Lancashire Fusiliers.
Volunteering in August 1914, he did consistently good work at various camps in England during the first part of his service and was drafted to the Western Front in December 1915. There he took part in numerous engagements of importance, and made the supreme sacrifice, being killed in action at St. Eloi on February 14th, 1916. He was entitled to the 1914-15 Star, and the General Service and Victory Medals.
"His life for his Country, his soul to God."
10, Haughton Street, Collyhurst, Manchester.   Z11378A

WOOD, S., Private, 2/5th Lancashire Fusiliers.
He joined in June 1916, and was drafted to the Western Front in the following September. In this theatre of war he took part in many important engagements, including the Battles of Beaumont-Hamel, Beaucourt, Arras, Vimy Ridge, Messines and Passchendaele, and was in hospital for three months suffering from concussion of the brain. He was later transferred to a Labour Battalion, and did duty behind the lines until his return to England for demobilisation in April 1919. He holds the General Service and Victory Medals.
26, Pownall Street, Hulme, Manchester.   Z8767

WOOD, T., Sapper, R.E.
He was called up from the Reserve in August 1914, and proceeded to the Western Front in March of the following year. There he rendered valuable services with the Searchlight Section of the anti-aircraft guns in various sectors and did consistently good work on the Somme in 1916, and at other engagements of importance until the cessation of hostilities. He was demobilised in April 1919, and holds the 1914-15 Star, and the General Service and Victory Medals.
8, Hooley Street, Ancoats, Manchester.   Z11380

WOOD, W., A B., Royal Navy.
He was already serving in the Navy at the outbreak of war in August 1914, and at once went to sea. He took part in the engagement off the Falkland Isles and the Battle of Jutland in May 1916, and later served in various destroyers in the North Sea on mine-sweeping duties. He did duty in H.M.S. "Victory" and in 1920 was serving in H.M.S. "Emperor of India." He holds the 1914-15 Star, and the General Service (with five clasps) and the Victory Medals.
82, Teignmouth Street, Collyhurst, Manchester.   Z9770

WOOD, W. A., Private, 8th Manchester Regiment.
An ex-sailor, he volunteered in June 1915, and after doing duty in the Isle of Man guarding prisoners of war, was drafted to India in January 1916, and was engaged on important garrison and other duties for nearly four years. He rendered valuable services, and in February 1919, returned to England, where he was demobilised in the following month. He holds the General Service and Victory Medals.
10, Forest Street, Erskine Street, Hulme, Manchester..   Z8766

WOOD, W. C., Gunner, R.F.A.
He volunteered in May 1915, and after a period of training was retained on special duties in England, owing to his possessing a high degree of technical skill. He rendered valuable services with the Linotype Machine Co., Ltd., Broadheath, Manchester, from April 1916, to the cessation of hostilities, and was demobilised in December 1918.
6, Galloway Street, Hulme, Manchester.   Z8760

WOODBINE, J., Private, 6th Manchester Regt.
Volunteering in November 1915, he was retained on special duties with his unit at important stations in England, but owing to his being physically unfit was unable to obtain his transfer overseas. He nevertheless rendered valuable services guarding prisoners of war, and was eventually discharged in September 1916.
91, Victoria Square, Oldham Road, Manchester.   TZ8993B

WOODBURY, J. (M.M.), Cpl.,23rd Manchester Regt.
He volunteered in August 1915, and was drafted to France
in January of the following year. In this theatre of war he
played a prominent part in many important engagements,
and was in action at the Battles of Loos, St. Eloi, Vermelles,
Vimy Ridge, the Somme, Arras, Bullecourt, Messines, Ypres
and Cambrai and was wounded. He also served during the
Retreat and Advance of 1918, and was awarded the Military
Medal for conspicuous gallantry and devotion to duty in the
Field. He was demobilised in February 1919, and also holds
the General Service and Victory Medals.
17, Long Street, Ancoats, Manchester. Z11383

WOODBURY, J. G., Corporal, King's (L'pool Regt.)
He joined in September 1916, and proceeded to France in
February of the following year. after a period of training.
He played a prominent part in many important engagements,
including those at Arras, Bullecourt, Ypres and Cambrai,
and later, in the Retreat and Advance of 1918. He was sent
to Germany after the cessation of hostilities, and did important
garrison duties at Bonn and Cologne with the Army of Occupation. He holds the General Service and Victory Medals.
and was demobilised in March 1919.
29, Pitt Street, Ancoats, Manchester. Z6737A

WOODBURY, J. G., Pte., 51st King's (L'pool Regt.)
Joining in April 1918, he underwent a period of training,
and was sent to Germany in February of the following year.
There he did important garrison duties with the Army of Occupation on the Rhine, and eventually returned to England for
demobilisation in October 1919.
10, Wesley Street, Ancoats, Manchester. Z11384

WOODCOCK, E., Sergt., 1st Manchester Regt.
He volunteered in September 1914, and did consistently good
work at various stations in England during the first part of
his service. In February 1916 he proceeded to India, where he
was engaged on important garrison duties at Allahabad,
Fyzabad and Bangalore, and in May 1917, and was transferred
to Mesopotamia. In this theatre of war he played a distinguished part in many engagements, notably at Kut-el-
Amara. He was demobilised in April 1919 on his return home,
and holds the General Service and Victory Medals.
1, Etruria Street, Longsight, Manchester. Z8773

WOODCOCK, W., Private, Royal Defence Corps.
Volunteering in September 1914, he was engaged on important
guard and escort duties with the Royal Defence Corps at various
stations in England, and rendered valuable services. He was
unable to obtain his transfer overseas, owing to physical unfitness, and was discharged in November 1918 suffering from
myalgia. 8A, Chapel St., Ancoats, Manchester. Z8877

WOODHALL, T., Private, 77th Labour Corps.
He joined in March 1916, and in the following month embarked
for France. There he was engaged on the unloading of
munition ships, and later did consistently good work in connection with the repair of roads behind the lines at Loos,
Neuve Chapelle, La Bassée, Givenchy, Douai, Ypres, the
Somme, and Cambrai. He was demobilised in October 1919,
and holds the General Service and Victory Medals.
13, Markham Street, Ardwick, Manchester. Z8774

WOODHEAD, E., Private, 13th Manchester Regt.
Volunteering in September 1914, he proceeded to France after
a period of training and fought at Loos and other engagements
of importance until November 1915, when he was transferred
to Salonika. He saw much service in this theatre of war, and
was in action in the Advance across the Struma, the Capture
of Monastir, and the Battles on the Doiran front. He returned
to England in August 1918, and was again sent to France,
where he took part in the final Advance. He holds the 1914-
15 Star, and the General Service and Victory Medals, and
was demobilised in February 1919.
13, Bentley Street, Clayton Street, Hulme, Manchester. Z8775

WOODINGS, E. J., L/Cpl., 12th Manchester Regt.
He volunteered in September 1914, and after a period of service
in England was drafted in November 1915, to the Western
Front, where he took part in many important engagements.
He was in action at Arras, and in the Offensive on the Somme,
and received a special letter cof commendation for his gallant
conduct in the Field from the Brigadier-General commanding
the 21st Brigade. He made the last great sacrifice on September 9th, 1918, being killed in action during the great Advance,
and was entitled to the 1914-15 Star, and the General Service
and Victory Medals.
"Nobly striving,
He nobly fell that we might live."
19, Forrest Street, Erskine Street, Hulme, Manchester. Z8776A

WOODINGS, J. W., Driver, R.E. (Signal Section).
He volunteered in December 1915, and in the following August
was sent to France, where he was engaged on important duties
in various sectors. He was transferred to Italy in November
1917, after taking part in the fighting on the Arras front, and
the Battles of the Somme, and saw service on the Piave. He
eventually returned to England, and was demobilised in April
1919, holding the General Service and Victory Medals.
19, Forrest Street, Erskine Street, Hulme, Manchester. Z8776B

WOODLEY, J., Private, 2nd Manchester Regiment.
Mobilised at the outbreak of war in August 1914, he was drafted
to the Western Front in the following month and took part in
many important engagements. He was in action at the Battles
of La Bassée, Ypres, Neuve Chapelle, Hill 60, Albert, Arras,
the Somme, and Passchendaele, and during the Retreat and
Advance of 1918. He holds the 1914-15 Star, and the General
Service and Victory Medals, and in 1920 was serving with his
unit in India.
125, Montague Street, Collyhurst, Manchester. Z8878

WOODMAN, H., Private, 14th Gloucestershire Regt.
He joined in April 1916, and after a period of training was
drafted to France in January 1917. In this theatre of war he
took part in many important engagements, including those at
Albert, the Somme, Ypres III, and Havrincourt, and was
wounded on two occasions. He was also in action during the
Retreat and Advance of 1918, and after a month in hospital
returned to his unit, and was eventually demobilised in January
1919 He holds the General Service and Victory Medals.
46, Percival St., Chorlton-on-Medlock, Manchester. X8777B

WOODMAN, J., Private, King's (Liverpool Regt.)
He joined in 1916 on attaining military age, and served at
important stations in England until September 1918. He
was then sent to France, and after much heavy fighting in the
Advance of that year was gassed on the Sambre in November
1918. He was invalided to England, and was discharged in
July 1919 as unfit for further service. He holds the General
Service and Victory Medals.
46, Percival St., Chorlton-on-Medlock, Manchester. X8777A

WOODROW, D. (Mrs.), Worker, Q.M.A.A.C.
She joined in June 1918, and served with the Queen Mary's
Army Auxiliary Corps at Chadderton Camp, Oldham, where
she was engaged chiefly in the cook-house. She was later
attached to the Royal Army Service Corps, and did consistently
good work at Liverpool until November 1919, when she was
discharged.
153, Heald Grove, Rusholme, Manchester. Z8778A

WOODROW, J., Private, 2nd Worcestershire Regt.
A time-serving soldier, he was mobilised in August 1914, and
proceeded to the Western Front with the British Expeditionary
Force. He took part in the Retreat from Mons, and was badly
wounded in action at Ypres. After being invalided to England
he returned to France, and was wounded on three further
occasions, whilst fighting at Festubert, and the Battles of the
Somme. He was taken prisoner in April 1918 during the
Retreat, and died in captivity in the following October. He
was entitled to the Mons Star, and the General Service and
Victory Medals.
"His memory is cherished with pride."
153, Heald Grove, Rusholme, Manchester. Z8778B

WOODS, A., Private, Lancashire Fusiliers.
He volunteered in October 1914, and after a period of training
was drafted to the Dardanelles in July 1915. He took part
in many engagements on the Gallipoli Peninsula, and was
wounded. After being invalided to Alexandria and Malta,
he returned to the Dardanelles, and was later sent home suffering from fever. He proceeded to France in October 1916, and
was in action at Loos, Albert, Ypres, the Somme, and Cambrai,
and in January 1918, was claimed out as being under age. He
was officially demobilised in February 1919, and holds the
1914-15 Star, and the General Service and Victory Medals.
2, Lloyd Place, Rusholme, Manchester. Z8781

WOODS, A. E., Gunner, R.F.A.
He joined in February 1918, but owing to his being medically
unfit was retained on special duties at important stations in
England. He, nevertheless, rendered valuable services and
was discharged in August 1918 on account of ill-health.
15, Hughes Street, Ardwick, Manchester. Z8784

WOODS, F., Guardsman, Grenadier Guards.
Mobilised at the outbreak of war in August 1914, he was im-
mediately drafted to the Western Front, and took part in the
Retreat from Mons. He was also in action at numerous subse-
quent engagements, including the Battles of Ypres, the Somme,
Arras, Bullecourt, and Passchendaele, and during the Retreat
and Advance of 1918. He proceeded to Germany after the
Armistice and did duty with the Army of Occupation on the
Rhine. He was discharged in January 1919, and in addition
to the South African Medals, holds the Mons Star, and the
General Service and Victory Medals.
28, Glebe Street, Gorton, Manchester. Z8780

WOODS. H., Corporal, R.A.M.C.
A time-serving soldier who had served 17 years with the
Colours, he was mobilised at the outbreak of war in August
1914, and immediately drafted to France. There he played a
prominent part in the Battle of Mons, and in the Battles of the
Marne. the Aisne, La Bassée, Ypres, Neuve Chapelle, St. Eloi,
and Loos, and was invalided home suffering from rheumatism
and sciatica. After some time in hospital he was discharged
in January 1916 as medically unfit for further service, and
holds the Queen's and King's South African Medals, the Mons
Star, and the General Service and Victory Medals.
15, Northern St., Erskine St., Hulme, Manchester. Z8783

WOODS, G. R., Private, 417th Agricultural Co., Labour Corps.
He joined in March 1917, and was retained on special agricultural duties in various parts of the country. He did consistently good work until the signing of the Armistice, and was demobilised in January 1919.
14, Riga Street, City Road, Hulme, Manchester. TZ8782

WOODS, J. H., Air Mechanic, R.A.F.
He joined in October 1918, and was retained on special duties at important stations in England. He was unable to obtain his transfer to a theatre of war, but, nevertheless, rendered valuable services as a motor driver to the Royal Air Force, and was demobilised in October 1919.
20, New Street, West Gorton, Manchester. Z8779

WOODS, W. Private, South Lancashire Regt.
Joining in April 1916, he proceeded to France three months later, and saw service on the Somme and Ancre fronts. He was also engaged in much heavy fighting at the Battles of Arras, Ypres, and Cambrai, and was wounded and taken prisoner in November 1917. He was repatriated after the cessation of hostilities, and eventually demobilised in January 1919, holding the General Service and Victory Medals.
52, Lythgoe Street, Moss Side, Manchester. Z8785

WOODWARD, A., Private, Lancashire Fusiliers.
He volunteered in November 1914, and after a course of training was drafted to the Dardanelles in June 1915. He took part in the heavy fighting at Suvla Bay, Chunuk Bair, and other engagements of importance on the Gallipoli Peninsula. After the Evacuation he proceeded to the Western Front, and was in action at the Battles of Arras, Messines, Ypres, and Cambrai, and was wounded in the Advance of 1918. He also served with the Army of Occupation on the Rhine, and, returning to England, was demobilised in May 1919. He holds the 1914-15 Star, and the General Service and Victory Medals.
132, Cross Street, Bradford, Manchester. Z8778

WOODWARD, A. J. (M.M.), Sergt., Lancashire Fus.
Volunteering in September 1914, he was drafted to France in due course and played a distinguished part in the fighting in various sectors. In 1915 he was transferred to the Balkans, and saw much active service in Salonika. He was awarded the Military Medal for conspicuous bravery and devotion to duty in the Field, and also holds the 1914-15 Star, and the General Service and Victory Medals. He was demobilised in 1919 on his return home.
6, Franchise St., Chorlton-on-Medlock, Manchester. TX8788D

WOODWARD, G. F., Pte., 23rd Manchester Regt.
He volunteered in 1915, and after completing his training, was drafted to the Western Front later in the same year. He took part in much heavy fighting in various sectors, and made the supreme sacrifice on August 20th, 1916, being killed in action during the Somme Offensive of that year. He was entitled to the 1914-15 Star, and the General Service and Victory Medals.
" And doubtless he went in splendid company."
6, Franchise St., Chorlton-on-Medlock, Manchester. TX8788C

WOODWARD, J. G., Sergt., R.E. (Signal Section).
A Reservist, he was called to the Colours at the outbreak of war in August 1914, and was at once sent to France, where he played a distinguished part in many engagements of importance. He was in action at Mons, the Marne, the Aisne, Ypres I, II, and III, Neuve Chapelle, Arras, and Cambrai, and was both wounded and gassed. He also fought during the Retreat and Advance of 1918, and was mentioned in Despatches for conspicuous gallantry in November 1914. He holds the Mons Star, and the General Service and Victory Medals, and was discharged in April 1919.
31, Mawson Street, Ardwick Green, Manchester. Z8790

WOODWARD, J. L., Private, Labour Corps.
He volunteered in 1915, but owing to his being physically unfit for service in a theatre of war was retained on special duties in Ireland. He nevertheless rendered valuable services and was demobilised in 1919.
6, Franchise Street, N., Chorlton-on-Medlock, Manchester. TX8788A

WOODWARD, J. P., Sergt., M.G.C.
He enlisted in June 1913, and six months after the outbreak of war in August 1914, proceeded to the Western Front, where he played a prominent part in the fighting in many sectors. He was in action at St. Eloi, Hill 60, Festubert, and Loos, and in March 1916, was transferred to Salonika, where he rendered valuable services on the Doiran, Vardar, and Struma fronts. He holds the 1914-15 Star, and the General Service and Victory Medals., and after his return home was discharged in June 1920.
2, Purdon Street, Ancoats, Manchester. Z11385

WOODWARD, W., Corporal, R.A.S.C.
He came from America and volunteered in May 1915, for service in France. There he was engaged on important work in connection with the transport of food and ammunition, and the carrying of wounded in various sectors until the cessation of hostilities. He was demobilised in 1919, and holds the 1914-15 Star, and the General Service and Victory Medals.
6, Franchise St., Chorlton-on-Medlock, Manchester. TX8788B

WOODWARD, W. J., Sergt., K.O. (R. Lancaster Regt.)
Volunteering in June 1915, he was drafted to France three months later, and took a distinguished part in many important engagements on the Western Front. He was in action at Loos, St. Eloi, Vimy Ridge, Vermelles, the Somme, Beaumont-Hamel, and Beaucourt, and was wounded. He returned to France in February 1917, after a period in hospital, and was again in action, and saw service at the Battles of Ypres III, where he was wounded a second time, and invalided to England. Recovering, he rejoined his unit in January 1918, and rendered valuable services in the Retreat and Advance of that year. He holds the 1914-15 Star, and the General Service and Victory Medals, and was demobilised in February 1919.
118, Dorset Street, Hulme, Manchester. Z8786

WOODWORTH, G., Sapper, R.E.
He volunteered in October 1915, and after a period of training was sent to the Western Front, where he was engaged on important duties in various sectors of France and Belgium. He did consistently good work until the cessation of hostilities, and was demobilised in May 1919, holding the General Service and Victory Medals.
24, Melbourne St., Chorlton-on-Medlock, Manchester. X8789

WOODWORTH, R., Private, 8th Manchester Regt.
He joined in January 1917, and being unfit for service overseas was retained on important duties at various stations in England. He, nevertheless, rendered valuable services until the Armistice, and was demobilised in January 1919.
16, Dougill Street, Hulme, Manchester. Z11386

WOODWORTH, W., Sergt., R.E.
A time-serving soldier, he was drafted to Egypt at the outbreak of hostilities in August 1914, and played a distinguished part in operations in that theatre of war. He rendered valuable services in many important engagements, but becoming time-expired, was discharged as a time-expired man in January 1916. He holds the General Service and Victory Medals.
12, Hargreaves St., Chorlton-on-Medlock, Manchester. X7246B

WOOLFE, G. T., Private, 2nd Manchester Regiment.
He volunteered in August 1914, and after completing his training, was drafted to the Dardanelles in April of the following year. He took part in the heavy fighting during the Landing on the Gallipoli Peninsula, but was unfortunately killed in action one month after his arrival in this theatre of war, and was entitled to the 1914-15 Star, and the General Service and Victory Medals.
" He died the noblest death a man may die."
6, Daniel Street, Hulme, Manchester. Z8794

WOOLFORD, J. H., Pte., 21st Manchester Regt.
He volunteered in August 1914, and was retained at home during the first period of his service. He was, however, drafted to France in June 1916, and took part in many important engagements, including the Battles of the Somme, Beaucourt, Arras, Vimy Ridge, and Messines. He was unhappily killed in October 1917 in action at Passchendaele Ridge. He was entitled to the General Service and Victory Medals.
" And doubtless he went in splendid company."
23, Purley Street, Ardwick, Manchester. Z8795

WOOLLAMS, A., Private, K.O. (R. Lancaster Regt.)
He joined in February 1916, and was sent to France in the following April. There he took part in many engagements of importance, including those at St. Eloi, the Somme, Arras, Bullecourt, Messines, and Ypres, and later was employed as a fitter at the Base. He holds the General Service and Victory Medals, and was not demobilised until December 1919.
4, Corby Street, West Gorton, Manchester. Z11387D

WOOLLAMS, T., Private, Royal Welch Fusiliers.
Joining in November 1917, he completed a period of training and was drafted to the Western Front in May of the following year. After taking part in the Retreat and Advance of 1918, he was sent to the near East after the Armistice, and saw service in Salonika and Turkey. He returned to England and was demobilised in January 1920, holding the General Service and Victory Medals.
4, Corby Street, West Gorton, Manchester. Z11387A

WOOLLEY, A. (Mrs.), Special War Worker.
This lady volunteered her services in August 1915, and was engaged on important duties at the 2nd General Western Military Hospital, Manchester. She gave entire satisfaction. and did not relinquish her duties until April 1920.
4, Coach Terrace, Longsight, Manchester. Z8791

WOOLLEY, S. E., Private, 1/4th Hampshire Regt.
He joined in December 1916, and after a period of training was drafted to India in March 1917. There he was engaged on important garrison duties until February 1918, when he was transferred to Mesopotamia. In this theatre of war he took part in various engagements in the Advance on Baghdad, and at one time was employed at a Prisoners of War Camp. He returned to England, and was eventually demobilised in May 1920, holding the General Service and Victory Medals.
47, Crosscliffe Street, Moss Side, Manchester. Z8793

WOOLLEY, J. W., L/Corporal, 6th Border Regt.
He volunteered in March 1915, and was retained on special
duties at important stations in England. He was unable to
obtain his transfer to a theatre of war, but nevertheless
rendered valuable services until his demobilisation in January
1919. He holds the South African Medals.
4, Coach Terrace, Longsight, Manchester.   Z8791B

**WOOLLEY, R. C., Private, 14th Argyll and Suther-
land Highlanders.**
Volunteering in September 1915, he proceeded to France in
September of the following year after a period of training and
saw service on the Ancre front. He also took part in the
Battles of Arras, Ypres, the Somme, Cambrai, Bapaume, and
Havrincourt, and was engaged in guarding prisoners of war
until the close of hostilities. He was demobilised in February
1919, and holds the General Service and Victory Medals.
77, Edensor Street, Beswick, Manchester.   Z5813A

WOOLLEY, W., Private, 20th Manchester Regt.
Volunteering in November 1914, he completed his training
and was drafted to the Western Front in November of the
following year. In this theatre of war he took part in many
important engagements, and saw much heavy fighting at
Loos and Albert. Unhappily on May 8th, 1916, he was killed
in action at La Neuville. He was entitled to the 1914-15
Star, and the General Service and Victory Medals.
"His life for his Country, his soul to God."
6, Rob Roy Street, Hulme, Manchester.   TZ8792

WORDLEY, H., Sergt., R.A.S.C.
He volunteered in November 1914, and in the following March
was drafted to France, where he was chiefly engaged on important transport duties. He did consistently good work at
Boulogne, where he arranged the distribution of food stuffs
for forward areas. He also rendered valuable services, whilst
on road repair work, and was demobilised in April 1919,
holding the 1914-15 Star, and the General Service and Victory
Medals.   84, Park Street, Hulme, Manchester.   Z8796

WORRALL, A., Private, Labour Corps.
He joined the Manchester Regiment in August 1916, and, after
a few months' duty at various stations in England, was drafted
to France. There he took an active part in many important
engagements, including the Battles of Vimy Ridge, and Passchendaele, and was wounded at the latter engagement in
October 1917. He was transferred to a Labour Corps in
May 1918, and was eventually demobilised in February 1919,
and holds the General Service and Victory Medals.
19, Marie Street, Openshaw, Manchester.   TZ8798

WORRALL, J., Private, Manchester Regiment.
Volunteering in January 1915, after having seen previous
service with the Colours, he did duty on the Regimental Staff
in the Officers' Quarters of the Manchester Regiment. He did
consistently good work until about twelve months before the
Armistice, when he was transferred to Class W, Army Reserve,
and was employed by Messrs. Muir and Co., of Salford, on work
of National importance. He was demobilised in January
1919, and holds the India General Service Medals (with clasp
Burmah).
32, George Street, Bradford, Manchester.   Z8797

WORSLEY, J., Driver, R.F.A.
He was called from the Reserve at the outbreak of war in August
1914, and in January 1915 was drafted to France, where he
was in action with his Battery at many important engagements.
He took part in the Battles of Ypres and Loos, and was transferred to Salonika in December 1915. In this theatre of war
he saw much active service on the Struma and Doiran fronts,
and returning to England, was discharged in March 1919,
holding the 1914-15 Star, and the General Service and Victory
Medals. 29, Jersey St. Dwellings, Ancoats, Manchester. Z11388

WORSLEY, T., L/Cpl., 4th K.O. (R. Lancaster Regt.)
Mobilised from the Reserve at the outbreak of war in August
1914, he was drafted to France in the following month, and
took part in the Retreat from Mons. He was also in action at
subsequent engagements, and was wounded at the first Battle
of Ypres. After being invalided home, he rejoined his Regiment in April 1915, and saw further heavy fighting at the
Battles of Ypres II, the Somme, and La Bassée, and was discharged time-expired in December 1916. He holds the Mons
Star, and the General Service and Victory Medals.
93, Stott Street, Hulme, Manchester.   Z8799

WORSTENCROFT, C., Cpl., 3rd East Lancs. Regt.
He volunteered in September 1914, and was drafted to the
Western Front in March of the following year after a period of
training. There he played a prominent part in the Battles of
Ypres (II), Festubert, Loos, St. Eloi, Vimy Ridge, and the
Somme, and was wounded in August 1917, at the third Battle
of Ypres. He returned to his unit after recuperation, and was
in action at the first Battle of Cambrai, where he received his
second wound, and was invalided to England. He was again
drafted to France in April 1918, and saw service at Bapaume,
the Scarpe, Cambrai II, and Le Cateau II, during the great Advance. He holds the 1914-15 Star, and the General Service
and Victory Medals, and was demobilised in February 1919.
8, Pownall Street, Hulme, Manchester.   Z8800

WORSWICK, A., Private, K.O. (R. Lancaster Regt.)
Volunteering in January 1915, he was drafted to France in the
following month, and took part in the second Battle of Ypres,
where he was badly wounded. In October 1915, he was sent
to the Dardanelles, and was engaged in much heavy fighting
on the Gallipoli Peninsula until the Evacuation. He then
embarked for Mesopotamia, where he was in action on the
Tigris, and at Kut-el-Amara, and suffered from sunstroke. He
was invalided to India, and returning eventually to England,
was demobilised in November 1919, holding the 1914-15 Star,
and the General Service and Victory Medals.
84, Armitage Street, Ardwick, Manchester.   Z8802

WORSWICK, C. R., Private, Labour Corps.
He volunteered in December 1915, and was retained on important duties in Ireland, where he did guard and other duties,
and also worked on various farms. He was unable to proceed
to a theatre of war, but, nevertheless, did consistently good
work until September 1918, when he was discharged as physically unfit for further service.
27, Bremner Street, Ardwick, Manchester.   Z8801

WORSWICK, J., Private, 8th Manchester Regt.
He volunteered early in 1915, and in due course was drafted to
France, where he took part in many important engagements.
He was in action at the Battles of Neuve Chapelle, St. Eloi,
Hill 60, Ypres, and Loos, and rendered valuable services until
the Armistice. He holds the 1914-15 Star, and the General
Service and Victory Medals. and was demobilised in December
1918.   21, Hastings Rd., Chorlton-on-Medlock, Manchester.
                                                      X8803

WORTHINGTON, G., Corporal, Royal Fusiliers.
Volunteering in June 1915, he underwent a period of training
in Scotland, and was sent to France in September 1916. He
did consistently good work as a clerk on the 19th Army Corps
Staff, behind the lines at Ypres, Cambrai, the Somme, Neuve
Chapelle, Amiens, and Havrincourt, and was demobilised in
January 1919, holding the General Service and Victory Medals.
5, Ellesmere Place, Longsight, Manchester.   Z8805A

WORTHINGTON, G., Pte., 8th Manchester Regt.
He volunteered in August 1914, and after a period of training
was drafted to the Dardanelles in April of the following year.
There he took part in much heavy fighting on the Gallipoli
Peninsula, including the Battles of Krithia (I, II, and III),
Suvla Bay, and Chunuk Bair, and made the supreme sacrifice,
being killed in action on August 7th, 1915. He was entitled
to the 1914-15 Star, and the General Service and Victory
Medals.
"He passed out of the sight of men by the path of duty and
self-sacrifice."
5, Ward Street, Gorton, Manchester.   Z11389

**WORTHINGTON, G., Private, 2nd King's Own
Scottish Borderers.**
Volunteering in August 1914, he was drafted to France on
completion of his training, and took part in many engagements
of importance, including the Battles of Loos, and Ypres, and
was wounded in action. He was invalided to England, and
after a period in hospital, was eventually discharged in September 1917 as physically unfit for further service. He holds
the 1914-15 Star, and the General Service and Victory Medals.
5, Milton Street, Ancoats, Manchester.   Z8483

WORTHINGTON, P., Private, Manchester Regt.
Volunteering in August 1914, he underwent a period of training
and was drafted to Egypt early in the following year. He was
shortly afterwards transferred to the Dardanelles, and took
part in much severe fighting on the Gallipoli Peninsula. He
made the supreme sacrifice on June 4th, 1915, when he was
killed in action at the 3rd Battle of Krithia, soon after his
arrival in this theatre of war. He was entitled to the 1914-15
Star, and the General Service and Victory Medals.
"Honour to the immortal dead who gave their youth that the
world might grow old in peace."
13, Marsden St., Newton Heath, Manchester.   Z9753

WORTHINGTON, T., Pte., 6th Loyal N. Lancs. Regt.
He volunteered in September 1914, and shortly afterwards
proceeded to the Dardanelles, where he took part in many
engagements and saw much heavy fighting on the Gallipoli
Peninsula. He rendered valuable services, but was unfortunately killed in August 1915, and was entitled to the 1914-15
Star, and the General Service and Victory Medals.
"Courage, bright hopes, and a myriad dreams splendidly
given."
32, Oliver Street, Bradford, Manchester.   Z8806

WORTHINGTON, W., Private, 3rd Border Regt.
Four months after joining in August 1916, he was drafted to
France, and took part in many important engagements,
including those at Neuve Chapelle, La Bassée, Givenchy, and
Festubert, and was gassed at the Battle of Ypres in July 1917.
He was invalided to England, and in April of the following
year was discharged as medically unfit for further service, and
holds the General Service and Victory Medals.
86, Gresham St., Lower Openshaw, Manchester.   Z8804

WORTHINGTON, W. R., Pte., 2/7th Manchester Rgt.

He volunteered in July 1915, and after a period of training and service at various camps in England, was drafted to the Western Front, where he took part in engagements at Neuve Chapelle and La Bassée. He saw much active service in many important sectors, and suffered from shell-shock, and after the cessation of hostilities was demobilised in April 1919. He holds the General Service and Victory Medals.

35, St. Leonard St., Chorlton-on-Medlock, Manchester. X8807

WREN, J., Private, 18th Manchester Regiment.

Volunteering in June 1915, he underwent a period of training before being drafted to France in February 1916, and took part in many engagements. He was in action at the Battles of Vimy Ridge, the Somme (where he was wounded), Messines, Ypres, Passchendaele, and Cambrai, and during the Retreat and Advance of 1918, rendered valuable services, and was gassed whilst saving the life of an officer. He was demobilised in January 1919, and holds the General Service and Victory Medals.

11, David Street, Bradford, Manchester. TZ8808

WREN, J., Private, King's (Liverpool Regiment).

He volunteered in September 1914, and in the following August was drafted to the Western Front, where he took part in much severe fighting, and was gassed at Loos in January 1916. He was invalided home, but on his recovery, was sent to Salonika, and after being wounded in action in September 1916, contracted malaria, and was again sent home. He underwent treatment in Netley Hospital, and was eventually sent back to France, where he was gassed at Cambrai in September 1918, and invalided to England for the third time. He was discharged in December of the same year, and holds the 1914–15 Star, and the General Service and Victory Medals.

20, Beaumont Street, Bradford, Manchester. Z9771

WRENCH, T., Private, 4th King's (Liverpool Regt.)

Volunteering in June 1915, he proceeded to France in September 1916, after a period of training, and was in action at many important engagements. He took part in much heavy fighting at the Battles of Beaumont-Hamel, Arras, Ypres (III), and Cambrai, and later in the Retreat and Advance of 1918. He holds the General Service and Victory Medals, and was demobilised in March 1919.

50, Queen's St., Higher Ardwick, Manchester. Z8809

WRENSHALL, F., Private, 18th Lancashire Fusiliers.

He volunteered in February 1915, and after undergoing a period of training was drafted to France in December of the same year. There he took part in many important engagements, including the Battles of Ploegsteert Wood, the Somme, Messines and Passchendaele. He was also in action during the Retreat and Advance of 1918, and rendered valuable services until the Armistice. Demobilised in April 1919, he holds the 1914–15 Star, and the General Service and Victory Medals.

11, Garrick Street, Ancoats, Manchester. Z10064A

WRIGHT, A., L/Cpl., 15th King's (Liverpool Regt.)

Three months after volunteering in November 1915, he was drafted to the Western Front, and saw much heavy fighting in various sectors. He was in action at the Battles of Arras, Vermelles, the Somme, Beaumont-Hamel, Arras, and Ypres, and was wounded. Returning to France after three months in hospital at Southport, he was again in action on the Somme, and at Arras, and Cambrai, and the Selle during the Advance of 1918. He was eventually demobilised in January 1919, and holds the General Service and Victory Medals.

119, Henry Street, Ardwick, Manchester. Z11858

WRIGHT, A., Sapper, R.E.

He joined in January 1916, and after training at Chatham was sent to France, where he saw heavy fighting on the Ancre front. He also took part in the Battles of Arras, Ypres (III), Cambrai, the Marne (II), Havrincourt, and Le Cateau (II), and rendered valuable services until the cessation of hostilities. He holds the General Service and Victory Medals, and was demobilised in March 1919.

53, New York St., Chorlton-on-Medlock, Manchester. Z8813

WRIGHT, D., Private, Lancashire Fusiliers.

Volunteering in August 1914, he proceeded to the Western Front after a period of training, and from January 1915, until the cessation of hostilities, took part in many important engagements. He was in action at the Battles of St. Eloi, Ypres, and the Somme, and was badly wounded at Lens in August 1917. He rejoined his unit in France after a period in hospital at Liverpool, and was eventually demobilised in July 1919, holding the 1914–15 Star, and the General Service and Victory Medals. 21, Marshall St., Ardwick, Manchester. Z7772B

WRIGHT, E., Driver, R.F.A.

He volunteered in November 1914, and was sent to France in the following April. Whilst on the Western Front, he was in action with his Battery at many important engagements, including Festubert and Arras, and was wounded by shell-fire in May 1917. He rendered valuable services, and was demobilised in May 1919, holding the 1914–15 Star, and the General Service and Victory Medals.

10, Mary Street, Ardwick, Manchester. TZ8819

WRIGHT, F., Staff Sergeant, R.A.S.C.

Volunteering in August 1914, he was drafted to France in the following February, and did consistently good work whilst in charge of a Field Bakery at Calais, Boulogne, and Rouen. He rendered valuable services throughout the whole period of hostilities, and was demobilised in January 1919, holding the 1914–15 Star, and the General Service and Victory Medals.

10, Mary Street, Higher Ardwick, Manchester. Z8810

WRIGHT, F. T., Sergeant, M.G.C.

He enlisted in July 1900, and after the outbreak of war in August 1914, did consistently good work in England during the first part of his service. He proceeded to France in February 1917, and played a distinguished part in many important engagements, including the Battles of Vimy Ridge, Bullecourt, Passchendaele, and Cambrai, and rendered valuable services during the Retreat and Advance of 1918. He was discharged in February 1919, and holds the General Service and Victory Medals.

7, Gregory Street, West Gorton, Manchester. Z8814

WRIGHT, G. A., Sapper, R.E.

Mobilised at the outbreak of war in August 1914, he was immediately sent to France, where he was in action in the Retreat from Mons. He also took part in many subsequent engagements of importance, including the Battles of the Aisne, La Bassée, Ypres, Hill 60, Loos, Albert, and Vimy Ridge, and made the supreme sacrifice on June 7th, 1916, being killed whilst out with a wiring party. He was entitled to the Mons Star, and the General Service and Victory Medals.

"The path of duty was the way to glory."

16, Platt Street, Moss Side, Manchester. Z8820

WRIGHT, H., C.S.M., 9th Cheshire Regiment.

Mobilised at the outbreak of war in August 1914, he did consistently good work in England until July 1915, when he proceeded to France. In this theatre of war he played a distinguished part in the fighting at Loos, Messines, and on the Somme front, and in November 1917, was transferred to Italy. There he was in action in many important engagements until the cessation of hostilities, when he returned to England, and was discharged in February 1919. He holds the 1914–15 Star, and the General Service and Victory Medals.

3, Sorrell Street, Hulme, Manchester. TZ8821

WRIGHT, H., Driver, R.A.S.C. (M.T.)

He volunteered in May 1915, and six months later proceeded to the Western Front, where he was engaged on important transport duties at Loos and St. Eloi. He then embarked for German East Africa, and was for some time stationed at Durban and Lindi, where he did consistently good work. He suffered from malaria, and was eventually invalided to England and discharged in November 1917 as medically unfit for further service. He holds the 1914–15 Star, and the General Service and Victory Medals.

26, Newport Street, Rusholme, Manchester. Z9772B

WRIGHT, J., Corporal, 2/8th Manchester Regiment.

He volunteered in September 1914, and after a period of service in England, was drafted to the Western Front in March 1917. There he took a prominent part in the Battles of Vimy Ridge, Ypres, and Passchendaele, and was wounded in action. He was invalided to hospital, and was eventually discharged in February 1918, as physically unfit for further service. He holds the General Service and Victory Medals.

13, Greenhill St., Chorlton-on-Medlock, Manchester. Z8822

WRIGHT, J., Private, Royal Berkshire Regiment.

He joined in May 1918, and after a period of training was drafted to the Western Front in the following October. There he arrived in time to take part in the Advance of 1918, and was in action at the Battle of Le Cateau (II), and various other concluding engagements of the war. He holds the General Service and Victory Medals, and was demobilised in February 1919. 7, Wentworth St., Beswick, Manchester. Z8823

WRIGHT, J., Private, 8th Welch Regiment.

He volunteered in April 1915, and was shortly afterwards drafted to the Dardanelles, where he was in action at the Battles of Krithia (I and II). He also took part in the heavy fighting at Suvla Bay, Chocolate Hill, and Chunuk Bair, and after the Evacuation of the Gallipoli Peninsula, was invalided home suffering from dysentery. He was eventually discharged in September 1917, no longer physically fit for service, and holds the 1914–15 Star, and the General Service and Victory Medals.

9, Haigh Street, West Gorton, Manchester. Z11392

WRIGHT, J., Private, 5th Cheshire Regiment.

He volunteered in August 1914, and after undergoing a period of training was drafted to the Western Front in February of the following year. There he took part in many important engagements, including the Battles of Neuve Chapelle, and Ypres (II), and was wounded during the Somme Offensive in July 1916. He was invalided home and eventually demobilised in February 1919, holding the 1914–15 Star, and the General Service and Victory Medals.

99, Fitzgeorge St., Collyhurst, Manchester. Z11391

WRIGHT, J., Gunner, R.F.A.

He was mobilised at the outbreak of war in August 1914, and in April 1915, was drafted to the Dardanelles, where he was in action with his Battery at the Landing on the Gallipoli Peninsula. He took part in much heavy fighting at the third battle of Krithia, and other subsequent engagements until the Evacuation in December 1915. In February 1916 he proceeded to France; and fought on the Somme, and at Ypres, and Cambrai, and was seriously wounded. He eventually lost one arm by amputation, and returning to England, was discharged in March 1919, holding the 1914-15 Star, and the General Service and Victory Medals.

14, Patchett Street, Hulme, Manchester. Z8824

WRIGHT, J., Sapper, R.E.

Volunteering in September 1914, he was drafted to the Dardanelles after a period of training, and served with the 11th Division Mediterranean Expeditionary Force. He did consistently good work at the Landing at Suvla Bay, and other subsequent engagements on the Gallipoli Peninsula, and after the Evacuation, was sent to France, where he saw active service on the Somme, and was wounded in September 1916. He was eventually demobilised in February 1919, and holds the 1914-15 Star, and the General Service and Victory Medals.

48, Nellie Street, Ardwick, Manchester. Z8815

WRIGHT, J., Private, Manchester Regiment.

He volunteered in August 1914, and proceeded to France in the following year. There he took part in many important engagements, including the Battle of Ypres in 1915, the first Battle of the Somme in 1916, and the third Battle of Ypres in 1917. He also rendered valuable services in the Retreat and Advance of 1918, and was demobilised in May 1919, holding the 1914-15 Star, and the General Service and Victory Medals.

3, Lewis St., Miles Platting, Manchester. TZ8811

WRIGHT, J., Pte., 16th South Lancashire Regt.

He joined in February 1916, but, being medically unfit for transfer to a theatre of war, was retained on special duties at important stations in England. He, nevertheless, rendered valuable services until the cessation of hostilities, and was demobilised in June 1919.

106, Charlton St., Collyhurst, Manchester. Z8879

WRIGHT, P., Gunner, R.G.A.

He volunteered in August 1914, and after a period of training was drafted to the Dardanelles in April 1915. He was in action with his Battery at the Landing on the Gallipoli Peninsula, and later saw service at the Battles of Krithia (I, II and III), and at Chunuk Bair. After the Evacuation, he was sent to France in February 1916, and took part in the Battles of the Somme, Beaumont-Hamel, Messines, and Cambrai, and later in the Retreat and Advance of 1918. He holds the 1914-15 Star, and the General Service and Victory Medals, and was demobilised in February 1919.

5, Callender St., Chorlton-on-Medlock, Manchester. Z1203B

WRIGHT, R., Private, Lancashire Fusiliers.

He joined in March 1917, and after a period of training was drafted to France, where he was in action at the Battles of Arras, La Bassée, Béthune, and Cambrai, and was wounded and gassed in August 1918, during the Advance of that year. He was invalided to England, and eventually demobilised in October 1919, holding the General Service and Victory Medals.

128, Thornton St., Collyhurst, Manchester. Z11390

WRIGHT, R. L., Pte., 10th Loyal N. Lancashire Regt.

He joined in September 1914, and on completing his training was drafted to France in July 1915. In this theatre of war he took part in many important engagements, including the Battles of Loos, St. Eloi (1916), Albert, the Somme, Pozières, Arras, Passchendaele, and St. Quentin, and during the Advance of 1918 fought at the Battles of Amiens, Bapaume, Le Cateau (II), and at Sambre. He was demobilised in April 1919, and holds the 1914-15 Star, and the General Service and Victory Medals. 56, Carlisle St. Hulme, Manchester. Z8825

WRIGHT, R. W., Private, 1/7th Manchester Regt.

Volunteering in August 1914, he proceeded to the Dardanelles in April of the following year, and took part in the Landing on the Gallipoli Peninsula. He saw much heavy fighting in this theatre of war, and was wounded in action at the 3rd Battle of Krithia in June 1915. He was invalided home, and discharged as unfit for further military service in December 1916. He holds the 1914-15 Star, and the General Service and Victory Medals.

1, Gladstone Street, West Gorton, Manchester. Z8818

WRIGHT, S., Private, 1/8th Lancashire Fusiliers.

Mobilised with the Territorials at the outbreak of war in August 1914, he was drafted to Egypt in the following month, and in April 1915, saw service at the Dardanelles, where he was in action at the Battles of Krithia (I, II, and III), and other subsequent engagements until the Evacuation of the Gallipoli Peninsula. He was sent to France in January 1916, and fought at the Battles of Vimy Ridge, the Somme (I), Beaumont-Hamel, Arras, and Ypres, and was wounded in action and taken prisoner at the 2nd Battle of the Somme in

March 1918. He was repatriated after the Armistice and eventually demobilised in April 1919, holding the 1914-15 Star, and the General Service and Victory Medals.

25, Foster Street, City Road, Hulme, Manchester. Z8826

WRIGHT, T., Driver, R.E.

He volunteered in February 1915, and later in the same year was drafted to France, where he was engaged in the transport of supplies to his unit. He was present at the Battles of Loos, the Somme, Arras, Messines, and Cambrai, and rendered valuable services during the Retreat and Advance of 1918. He holds the 1914-15 Star, and the General Service and Victory Medals, and was demobilised in February 1919.

7, Albion Terrace, Miles Platting, Manchester. Z8812

WRIGHT, W. (M.M.), Pte., 1/7th Royal Warwickshire Regiment.

He joined in June 1916, and was drafted to France in the following December. There he took part in the fighting on the Somme, and at Arras, and was transferred to Italy in 1917. In this theatre of war, he rendered distinguished services whilst in action on the Piave, and was awarded the Military Medal for conspicuous bravery and devotion to duty in the Field. He also holds the General Service and Victory Medals, and was demobilised in October 1919, having been wounded on two occasions during his service.

12, Emery Street, Hall Road, Stockport. Z9772A

WRIGHT., W., Private, 1st East Yorkshire Regt.

Mobilised from the Reserve at the outbreak of war, he was drafted to France two months later, and took part in many important engagements, including the Battles of La Bassée, Ypres (I), Neuve Chapelle, and Hill 60, and made the supreme sacrifice in July 1915, being killed in action at the second Battle of Ypres. He was entitled to the 1914 Star, and the General Service and Victory Medals.

"His life for his Country, his soul to God."

57, Syndall Street, Ardwick, Manchester. Z8827

WRIGHT, W., Sapper, R.E.

Volunteering in February 1915, he was drafted to France in the following November, and served with the bridge construction section of the Royal Engineers in various sectors. He was present during the fighting at Loos, and made the supreme sacrifice in February 1916, being killed in action, and was entitled to the 1914-15 Star, and the General Service and Victory Medals.

"Whilst we remember, the sacrifice is not in vain."

30, Dark Lane, Ardwick, Manchester. TZ8816

WRIGHT, W. A., Private, Labour Corps.

He joined in July 1918, and in the following month proceeded to the Western Front with a Labour Battalion. He served in the railway repair section during the Advance of 1918, and did consistently good work until the Armistice. He afterwards served on the regimental staff in officers' quarters until his demobilisation in November 1919, and holds the General Service and Victory Medals.

12, Marsland Street, Ardwick, Manchester. Z8817

WRIGHT, W. A., Private, Labour Corps.

He joined in March 1917, and was immediately afterwards sent to France, where he was engaged on important duties in many sectors. He was present during the Battles of Arras, Vimy Ridge, Bullecourt and Ypres (III), and was gassed on the Somme. He was invalided to Scotland, but unfortunately died in May 1918 as the result of gas poisoning, and was entitled to the General Service and Victory Medals.

"His memory is cherished with pride."

14, Mark Street, Hulme, Manchester. TZ8719B

WRIGLEY, A., L/Cpl., 2nd Manchester Regt. and Border Regt.

He enlisted in March 1905, and at the outbreak of hostilities in August 1914, was immediately drafted to Egypt, where he saw service on the Suez Canal. In 1915 he was transferred to the Dardanelles and was in action at many important engagements on the Gallipoli Peninsula, including the Landing at Suvla Bay. After the Evacuation, he proceeded to the Western Front and saw much heavy fighting at Loos, La Bassée, Ypres, Arras, Albert, the Somme and Cambrai, and was wounded and suffered from shell-shock. Returning to England, he was discharged medically unfit in May 1918, and holds the 1914-15 Star, and the General Service and Victory Medals. 19, Matlock St., Ardwick, Manchester. Z8831

WRIGLEY, S., Sergt., 8th Manchester Regiment.

Joining in May 1916, he did consistently good work with his unit in England during the first part of his service, and in February 1917 was drafted to the Western Front. There he played a distinguished part in many important engagements, including those at Messines, Lens and Cambrai and later rendered valuable services in the Retreat and Advance of 1918. He was badly wounded at Amiens in August 1918, and was eventually invalided to England and discharged in October 1919. He holds the General Service and Victory Medals. 9, Apsley Grove, Ardwick, Manchester. Z8828

WRIGLEY, W., Pte., 6th South Lancashire Regt.
Volunteering in January 1915, he completed a period of training and was sent to France in June of the following year. There he was in action at many engagements, including the Battles of the Somme and Arras, and was wounded. He was transferred to Mesopotamia in February 1917 and took part in the second Battle of Kut, and later in the Advance on Baghdad, where he was again wounded in action. He holds the General Service and Victory Medals, and was demobilised in April 1919.
13, Neptune Street, Ancoats, Manchester.   Z8829

WRIGLEY, W. J., Pte., 14th King's (L'pool Regt.)
He volunteered in March 1915, and later in the same year proceeded to France, where he was in action at numerous engagements, including those at St. Eloi, Bullecourt, Albert and the Somme. He rendered valuable services and at one time acted as escort to prisoners of war at Calais. He was eventually demobilised in July 1919, and holds the 1914-15 Star, and the General Service and Victory Medals.
21, Lingmoor St., Chorlton-on-Medlock, Manchester. X8830

WROE, G., Private, Middlesex Regiment.
Volunteering in September 1915, he proceeded to France two months later and took part in many important engagements. He saw much heavy fighting in various sectors, and was in action at the Battles of Loos, Vermelles, St. Eloi, Albert and Ploegsteert Wood and made the supreme sacrifice, being killed by shell-fire at Arras in May 1916. He was entitled to the 1914-15 Star, and the General Service and Victory Medals.
"He died the noblest death a man may die."
95, Knightley Street, Rochdale Road, Manchester.   Z11393

WROE, T. R., Private, Manchester Regiment.
He volunteered in January 1915, and after training at various camps, was drafted to France in the following November. He rendered valuable services in this theatre of war and was wounded on the Somme in July 1916 whilst on ammunition column duties. He unfortunately died of wounds on the 26th of that month, and was entitled to the 1914-15 Star, and the General Service and Victory Medals.
"The path of duty was the way to glory."
45, Milton Street, Bradford, Manchester.   Z11171/73A

WROE, W., Special War Worker.
Being physically unfit for service in a theatre of war, he volunteered his services in September 1914, and was engaged on important duties in connection with the construction of aeroplanes at Messrs. Boulton and Pauls' of Norwich. He did consistently good work throughout the period of hostilities and gave entire satisfaction to his employers. He relinquished his duties in November 1918.
5, Bremner Street, Stockport Road, Chorlton-on-Medlock, Manchester.   Z8832

WYCH, J., Sapper, R.E.
He joined in August 1916, and four months later proceeded to France, where he was engaged on important duties in connection with searchlight work in various sectors of the Front until the cessation of hostilities. He rendered valuable services, and after the Armistice, did duty in Germany with the Army of Occupation on the Rhine. He was demobilised in September 1919, and holds the General Service and Victory Medals. 1, Lincoln St., Longsight, Manchester.   Z8833B

WYCH, W., Private, Cheshire Regiment.
Joining in February 1916, he was drafted to the Western Front in the following month, and was engaged on important duties with a Labour Battalion in the Arras and Cambrai sectors. He did consistently good work until the cessation of hostilities, and was demobilised in August 1919, holding the General Service and Victory Medals.
1, Lincoln Street, Longsight, Manchester.   Z8833A

WYNNE, H. R., Private, 7th Manchester Regiment.
Volunteering in August 1914, he did duty at important coastal stations during the first part of his service, and was drafted to Egypt in February 1917. He saw service in this theatre of war for a short time and was transferred to the Western Front in the following April. There he was in action at numerous engagements, including the Battles of Messines, Lens, Cambrai, (I and II) and Bapaume and the Retreat and Advance of 1918. He holds the General Service and Victory Medals and was demobilised in February 1919.
5, Elivington Street, Hulme, Manchester.   Z8835

WYNNE, P., A.B., Royal Navy.
Mobilised at the outbreak of war in August 1914, he proceeded to sea and was engaged on important patrol duty in the English Channel on board H.M.S. "Sunfish." In June 1916 he was transferred to and served in H.M.S. "Francol," doing duty in the North Sea until the cessation of hostilities, and rendered valuable services. He was demobilised in October 1919, and holds the 1914-15 Star, and the General Service (with five clasps) and Victory Medals.
30, Sycamore Street, Manchester.   Z11394

WYNNE, R., Private, 8th King's (Liverpool Regt.)
Mobilised in August 1914, he proceeded to France in the following month and took part in many important engage-

ments. He was in action at the Battles of La Bassée, Ypres, Neuve Chapelle, Hill 60, Loos, Albert, the Somme and Messines, and was wounded in action in August 1917. He was invalided home, but in due course returned to the Western Front and saw service at Cambrai (I and II), the Somme (II) and Havrincourt, and was again wounded. He was eventually demobilised in January 1919, and holds the 1914 Star, and the General Service and Victory Medals.
11, Blackthorn Street, Ardwick, Manchester.   Z8834

Y

YAPP, R. J., Air Mechanic, R.A.F.
He joined in January 1917, and first did duty with the 14th South Lancashire Regiment, but, later, was transferred to the Royal Air Force. He did consistently good work with his Squadron at various important aerodromes in England, but was not successful in obtaining his transfer overseas before the cessation of hostilities. He was demobilised in 1919.
38, Darncombe Street, Moss Side, Manchester.   Z11859

YARDLEY, W. H. (M.M.), L/Corporal, K.O. (Royal Lancaster Regiment.)
He volunteered in May 1915, and later in the same year was drafted to the Western Front, when he first saw heavy fighting at Neuve Chapelle and Ypres. He also played a prominent part in the Battles of Loos and the Somme, but was badly wounded in action and invalided home. In May 1917 he was discharged as medically unfit for further service and shortly afterwards unfortunately died. He had been awarded the Military Medal for great bravery and devotion to duty during the Somme Offensive in October 1916, and was also entitled to the 1914-15 Star, and the General Service and Victory Medals.
"His memory is cherished with pride."
31, Heaton Street, Ardwick, Manchester.   Z11395

YARWOOD, J. E., Private, 14th Royal Scots.
He volunteered in January 1915, and after doing duty at various stations in Scotland for a time was sent to France in January 1917. There he was in action at the Battles of Arras, Vimy Ridge, Bullecourt and Ypres (III), and returning to England in April 1919 for demobilisation, had to go into hospital on account of his suffering from tuberculosis. He unhappily died in November 1919, and was entitled to the General Service and Victory Medals.
"He joined the great white company of valiant souls."
11, Dalton Street, Hulme, Manchester.   Z8836B

YARWOOD, J. W., Private, 11th Manchester Regt.
He volunteered in September 1914, and after a period of training was drafted to the Dardanelles early in the following year. There he took part in much heavy fighting on the Gallipoli Peninsula, particularly at the Landing at Suvla Bay. He also took part in the capture of Chunuk Bair and Chocolate Hill, and after the Evacuation proceeded to Egypt, where he saw service on the Suez Canal and at Mersa Matruh, Agagia and Sollum. In August 1916 he was transferred to the Western Front and took part in the Battles of the Somme, Beaumont-Hamel, Beaucourt, Arras and the capture of Vimy Ridge, and was severely wounded. He was invalided home and finally discharged in May 1917 as unfit for further service, and holds the 1914-15 Star, and the General Service and Victory Medals.
45, Birch Street, Hulme, Manchester.   Z8838

YARWOOD, J. W., Private, R.A.S.C.
Volunteering in May 1915, he was drafted to France in the following October and was present at numerous engagements. He was employed on important transport duties, saw service at Ypres, Arras, Passchendaele and Lille and was wounded. He returned to England in 1918, and did much good work at various stations in Wales until his demobilisation in February 1919. He holds the General Service and Victory Medals. 14, Tipper St., Hulme, Manchester.   TZ8837

YARWOOD, T. W., Private, 2nd Lancashire Fusiliers.
He volunteered in August 1914, and after a period of training was drafted to France in the following January. There he took part in many engagements of importance, including those at Neuve Chapelle, St. Eloi and the second Battle of Ypres. He suffered from gas poisoning on two occasions, and unfortunately died of wounds sustained in July 1915. He was entitled to the 1914-15 Star, and the General Service and Victory Medals.
"A costly sacrifice upon the altar of freedom."
11, Dalton Street, Hulme, Manchester.   Z8836A

YATES, A. H., Private, 7th Manchester Regiment.
He volunteered in January 1915, and after a period of training was drafted to France in June 1916. In this theatre of war he took part in the Battles of the Somme, Arras, Bullecourt and Ypres (III), and was wounded and gassed in August 1917. He also rendered valuable services during the Retreat and Advance of 1918, and was eventually demobilised in February 1919, holding the General Service and Victory Medals. 58, Lame Street, Ancoats, Manchester.   TZ7622A

YATES, A., Corporal, 7th Lancashire Fusiliers.
Volunteering in June 1915, he proceeded to France in May 1916 after a period of training and played a prominent part in the Battles of the Somme, Arras and Bullecourt, and was wounded at Passchendaele in the following October. He was invalided to England, but returned to the Western Front, where he was wounded a second time at the second Battle of the Marne. He also served at Havrincourt and Le Cateau (II) during the Advance of 1918, and was again wounded. He was demobilised in February of the following year, and holds the General Service and Victory Medals.
18, Cobden Street, Hulme, Manchester.   TZ8839

YATES, E., Staff Sergeant, R.A.M.C.
Volunteering in August 1914, he did consistently good work at various important stations in England during the first part of his service, and in March 1917 proceeded to Mesopotamia. There he took a distinguished part in many engagements, including the capture of Baghdad, Ramadieh, Tekrit, Khan Baghdadie and the Occupation of Mosul. He was in hospital with malaria at Hamadam in Persia, and was eventually demobilised in September 1919, holding the General Service and Victory Medals.
7, Gladstone Street, Brook's Bar, Manchester.   TZ8844

YATES, E., Private, 1st Sherwood Foresters.
He joined in August 1916, and after a period of training and duty in England, was drafted to France in March 1918. There he took part in much heavy fighting during the Retreat and was wounded in action on the Marne in May of that year. He was invalided to England and was demobilised in March 1919, holding the General Service and Victory Medals.
14, Tunstall Street, Longsight, Manchester.   Z8845

YATES, G. G., Sergeant, R.F.A.
Joining in August 1916, he proceeded to France in the following November and played a distinguished part in many important engagements. He was in action with his Battery at the Battles of Arras, Ypres (III), and Cambrai and later rendered valuable services during the Retreat and Advance of 1918. He was wounded at Cambrai, and returning to England for treatment in hospital, he was finally demobilised in September 1919 after acting as a Signal Instructor at Cosham Barracks, Portsmouth. He holds the General Service and Victory Medals
142, Newcastle Street, Hulme, Manchester.   Z8841

YATES, J., L/Corporal, Lancashire Fusiliers.
He volunteered in August 1914, and after a period of training was sent to France in September 1916. There he was in action in heavy fighting at Loos and on the Somme, and was wounded in December 1916. He returned to his unit from a Base hospital and again fought at various engagements, including the Battles of Ypres (III), Cambrai, La Bassée, and Lille, and was invalided to England suffering with nephritis. He was demobilised in April 1919, after a period of guard duty at a prisoner of war camp, and holds the General Service and Victory Medals.
15, Marcer Street, Ancoats, Manchester.   Z11397

YATES, J., Private, 9th Lancashire Fusiliers.
At the outbreak of hostilities in August 1914, he volunteered and after a course of training was in April of the following year drafted overseas. He served at Gallipoli for four months, and after taking part in several engagements, was unhappily killed in action in August 1915. He was entitled to the 1914-15 Star, and the General Service and Victory Medals.
"His life for his Country."
14, School Street, Bradford, Manchester.   X11882

YATES, J., Sergeant, 4th Manchester Regiment.
He volunteered in January 1915, and did consistently good work in England during the first portion of his service. He was drafted to the Western Front in May 1917, and took a distinguished part in many important engagements, including those at Vimy Ridge, Cambrai, Havrincourt and the Sambre. He rendered valuable services until the cessation of hostilities, and was demobilised in March 1919, holding the General Service and Victory Medals.
16, Bright Street, Hulme, Manchester.   Z11860

YATES, M., Sergt., R.A.M.C.
Volunteering in August 1914, and completing a period of training, he was drafted to the Western Front in February of the following year. He did consistently good work in this theatre of war at advanced dressing stations in many sectors, including those of Loos, Neuve Chapelle, Arras, La Bassée, Givenchy and Ypres, and rendered valuable services during the Retreat and Advance of 1918. After the Armistice, he proceeded to Germany with the Army of Occupation, and in 1920 was still serving on the Rhine. He holds the 1914-15 Star, and the General Service and Victory Medals.   Z8840
31, Granville Street, Chorlton-on-Medlock, Manchester

YATES, P., Private, 10th Manchester Regiment.
He joined in August 1916, and was sent to France three months later. There he saw active serve at Arras, Bullecourt and Vimy Ridge, and rendered valuable services on the Somme. He was later transferred to a prisoners of war camp at Abbeville, where he remained until his demobilisation in May 1919. He holds the General Service and Victory Medals.
4, Hibbert Street, Hulme, Manchester.   Z8843

YATES, S. H., Pte., 7th East Lancashire Regt.
He volunteered in November 1914, but owing to his being unfit for transfer overseas, was retained on important duties at various stations in England. He, nevertheless, rendered valuable services until the cessation of hostilities, and was discharged in December 1918.
7, Jack Street, Ardwick, Manchester.   Z8842

YEOMANS, F., Private, 2nd Sherwood Foresters.
Mobilised at the outbreak of war in August 1914, he was immediately drafted to France and took part in the Battle of Mons and the subsequent Retreat. He was also in action at Le Cateau, the Marne, La Bassée, and was wounded and taken prisoner at the last-named engagement in October 1914. He was employed in the mines and quarries in Germany until his repatriation in November 1918, and was discharged in the following month. He holds the Mons Star, and the General Service and Victory Medals.
72, Bickley Street, Moss Side, Manchester.   Z11861

YEOMANS, G., L/Corporal, R.A.M.C.
Volunteering in May 1915, he proceeded to France in February 1917, after doing duty at important stations in England and was engaged as a first-class nursing orderly at the General Military Hospitals at Rouen and Amiens. In February 1918 he was transferred to Egypt, and after doing consistently good work at the Alexandria General Hospital, returned to the Western Front in April 1918, and was stationed at Albert Military Hospital. He finally returned to England, and was demobilised in February 1919, holding the General Service and Victory Medals.
72, Bickley Street, Moss Side, Manchester.   Z11862

YORK, G. A., Corporal, R.A.S.C.
Joining in November 1916, he proceeded to Egypt in January of the following year and saw service in the East. He was engaged on important transport duties at various engagements in Palestine and was present at the taking of Jerusalem, the Battles of Gaza and the capture of Jericho and Tripoli and rendered valuable services in the Offensive under General Allenby. He holds the General Service and Victory Medals, and in 1920 was still serving in Palestine.
18, Stonehouse Street, Ancoats, Manchester.   Z9529/30C

YOUD, F., Sergt., 13th Manchester Regiment.
He volunteered in September 1914, and proceeding to France in the following April played a distinguished part in the Battles of Ypres and Festubert, where he was wounded in May. In October 1915 he proceeded to Salonika, and was in action on the Doiran and Vardar fronts, at Monastir and on the Struma, and rendered valuable services until January 1919, when he returned to England. He was demobilised in the following month, and holds the 1914-15 Star, and the General Service and Victory Medals.
16, Juno Street, Ancoats, Manchester.   Z11398

ADDENDA

ADAMS, E. H., Sergt., 8th Manchester Regiment.
Volunteering in August 1914, he proceeded to the East in the following month, and after serving at Cyprus, was in action in Egypt, where he was wounded in May 1915. Invalided to Malta, he was then sent home, but in June 1916 returned to Egypt. He was transferred in the following March to France, where he was twice wounded and gassed, and contracted trench fever. Sent to England, he was transferred to the Dragoon Guards, and served in Ireland until demobilised in March 1919. He holds the 1914–15 Star, and the General Service and Victory Medals.
4, Nelson Street, West Gorton, Manchester. Z1101

ALLEN, J. T., Private, 19th Manchester Regiment.
He volunteered in November 1915, and in June of the following year, was drafted to the Western Front, where he saw much heavy fighting. After taking part in the Battles of Ypres, Passchendaele and the Somme, he was wounded and taken prisoner at Messines, and whilst in captivity at Metz was forced to work in the mines. Released in December 1918 he was demobilised twelve months later, and holds the General Service and Victory Medals.
21, Thorn Street, Bradford, Manchester. TZ1079

APPLEYARD, E., L/Cpl., 1st Manchester Regiment.
He joined in October 1916, and three months later proceeded to India, where he was stationed at Bangalore until July 1917. He was then transferred to Mesopotamia, and thence, shortly afterwards to Palestine, where he took part in the third Battle of Gaza, and in the capture of Jerusalem and Jericho. Demobilised on returning home in October 1919, he holds the General Service and Victory Medals.
88, Great Jackson Street, West Gorton, Manchester. TZ1100

BELSHAW, R. I., Pte., King's (Liverpool Regt.)
He joined in January 1918, and two months later crossed to France. There he took part in severe fighting at Arras, Bullecourt, Ypres and Lens, and was badly wounded in August 1918. Invalided home, he was sent to hospital in Weymouth, and after undergoing an operation for the amputation of his right arm was eventually discharged in May 1919. He holds the General Service and Victory Medals.
8, Osborne Street, Oldham Road, Manchester. Z1007A

BELSHAW, W., Pte., Argyll and Sutherland Hldrs.
He volunteered in January 1915, and after a course of training served at various stations on important duties with his unit. Owing to medical unfitness he was not able to obtain a transfer to a fighting unit, and in September 1916 was discharged after having rendered much valuable service.
8, Osborne Street, Oldham Road, Manchester. Z1007B

BENSON, F. R., Private, Lancashire Fusiliers.
He volunteered in 1915, and in the same year proceeded to France. There he fought in the Battles of Hill 60, Ypres, Festubert, the Somme, Arras, Armentières and later was drafted to Italy, where he saw much heavy fighting against the Austrians. He returned to England and was discharged in May 1918, and holds the General Service and Victory Medals.
32, Catherine Street, Manchester. Z1063

BURNS, D., Stoker, 1st Class, R.N.
He joined in July 1918, and in the following month was posted to H.M.S. "Ambrose," attached to the Grand Fleet in the North Sea. In March 1919 he was transferred to the Mediterranean waters, and later served for twelve months in Chinese waters. He was demobilised in October 1920, and holds the General Service, with clasp 1918, and Victory Medals.
41, Sandal Street, Newton, Manchester. Z1093B

BURNS, G. P. (D.C.M.), Pioneer, R.E.
Called up from the Reserve in August 1914, he was immediately drafted to the Western Front, where, after serving at Mons, he took an active part in the Battles of Le Cateau, the Marne, the Aisne and La Bassée. He fell fighting on October 30th, 1914 at Ypres, where he was buried. He had been awarded the Distinguished Conduct Medal for conspicuous bravery in the Field, and was also entitled to the Mons Star, and the General Service and Victory Medals.
"A costly sacrifice upon the altar of freedom."
41, Sandal Street, Newton, Manchester. Z1093A

BURNS, W., Private, 7th Manchester Regiment.
He joined in September 1916, and in March of the following year proceeded to France, where he saw severe fighting in various sectors of the Front. He took part in the Battles of Arras, Ypres, Cambrai, the Somme, Amiens, Bapaume, Havrincourt and Cambrai (II), and many minor engagements, and was demobilised on returning home in October 1919. He holds the General Service and Victory Medals.
41, Sandal Street, Newton, Manchester. Z1093C

CHORLTON, H., Private, Royal Fusiliers.
Joining in 1917, he was later drafted to France, where he participated in the second Battle of the Somme, and in various engagements during the Retreat and Advance in 1918. In August of that year he was wounded and gassed, and as a result evacuated to England. After he recovered, he was employed on various duties at the Prisoners of War Camp, Feltham, and was demobilised in 1919, holding the General Service and Victory Medals.
10, Cheltenham Place, Chorlton-on-Medlock, Manchester. X1014

CLARKE, F., Private, 2nd Lancashire Fusiliers.
He was mobilised in August 1914, and saw service in various theatres of war. In Egypt he was engaged in several actions near the Suez Canal, and at Katia, and during the time he was in France he took part in severe fighting at Nieuport, Loos, Ypres, La Bassée and on the Somme front. He also served in Mesopotamia, was invalided home from Kut, and admitted to hospital at Moston. Demobilised in January 1919, he holds the 1914–15 Star, and the General Service and Victory Medals.
21, Fraser Street, Oldham Road, Manchester. Z1006

CROWTHER, W., Private, 2nd Manchester Regt.
Called up from the Reserve in August 1914, he was drafted to France in the following October. In that theatre of war he took part in the Battles of Ypres (I) and Neuve Chapelle, and was also engaged during heavy fighting at Kemmel Hill, where he was unhappily killed in March 1915. He was buried in the cemetery near where he fell, and was entitled to the 1914 Star, and the General Service and Victory Medals.
"His life for his Country."
30, Rhodes Street, Miles Platting, Manchester. Z1000

DERVIN, J., A.B., Royal Naval Division.
Volunteering in August 1914, he served with the "Anson" Battalion in France until February 1915, when he proceeded to Gallipoli. There he participated in the Battles of Krithia, the Suvla Bay Landing and the capture of Chunuk Bair, and was in hospital for some time suffering from dysentery. He was later transferred to H.M.S. "Thunderer," in which vessel he served until his demobilisation in January 1919. He holds the 1914 Star, and the General Service and Victory Medals. 25, Holme Street, Ancoats, Manchester. Z1011

DEVINE, W., Private, M.G.C.
He volunteered in August 1914, and three months later was sent to France, where he took part in the Battles of Ypres (I), Neuve Chapelle and St. Eloi, and was wounded at Hill 60 in April 1915. Two months afterwards he was drafted to Gallipoli, was in action during the Suvla Bay Landing, and in various operations up to the Evacuation, when he was sent to Mesopotamia. There he took part in the Battles of Kut, Sanna-i-Yat and the capture of Tekrit. In March 1918 he was invalided home suffering from fever, and was eventually demobilised in October 1919, holding the 1914 Star, and the General Service and Victory Medals.
57, Burton Street, Rochdale Road, Manchester. Z1061

FERRIS, C. W., Corporal, 4th Lancashire Fusiliers.
Three months after joining in August 1916, he was sent to the Western Front, where he saw much severe fighting. He took part in the Battles of Arras, Ypres, Cambrai and Havrincourt, and many other important engagements in this theatre of war. Demobilised in February 1919, he holds the General Service and Victory Medals.
66, Boardman Street, Harpurhey, Manchester. Z1077

FINNEY, C., Sapper, R.E.
He joined in October 1917, and after a period of training was retained at various stations, where he was engaged on duties of a highly important nature. He was not successful in obtaining his transfer to a theatre of war, but nevertheless, rendered valuable services with his Company until March 1919, when he was demobilised.
74, Granville Place, Ancoats, Manchester. TZ1095

FITZPATRICK, J., Pte., K.O. (R. Lancaster Regt.)
He volunteered in May 1915, and after his training was retained on important duties in England until November of the following year, and was then drafted to France, where he saw severe fighting in the Ancre and Arras sectors, and was wounded at Ypres in February 1917. He unhappily died of pneumonia in hospital in Cumberland on March 2nd of that year, and was entitled to the General Service and Victory Medals.
"Steals on the ear the distant triumph song."
69, Thornton Street, Collyhurst Street, Manchester. Z1078

FLANAGAN, T., Private, 11th Manchester Regt.
Six months after volunteering in January 1915, he was sent to Egypt, and thence to the Dardanelles, where he saw heavy fighting at Suvla Bay. He afterwards fought on the Western Front, and after taking part in several engagements, was severely wounded on the Somme in September 1916. He was invalided from the Army in December 1917, and holds the 1914-15 Star, and the General Service and Victory Medals.
49, Naylor Street, Oldham Road, Manchester.   Z1099

FLEET, E., Private, 2nd South Lancashire Regt.
Mobilised on the outbreak of war, he was shortly afterwards drafted to France, where he saw much severe fighting. He was in action at Ypres, but was unhappily killed in action in the Somme sector on August 28th, 1915. He was entitled to the 1914 Star, and the General Service and Victory Medals.
"The path of duty was the way to glory."
25, Stewart Street, Gorton, Manchester.   Z1081B

FLEET, S., Private, 25th King's (Liverpool Regt.)
He joined in March 1917, and was quickly sent to France, where he saw much service. He was engaged on important duties at Dieppe, Tincourt, Le Havre and Rouen, and saw heavy fighting at Aveluy Wood and Cambrai. He was in hospital at Etaples for some time suffering from hemorrhage, and was eventually demobilised in November 1919, holding the General Service and Victory Medals.
25, Stewart Street, Gorton, Manchester.   Z1081A

FLETCHER, J., Private, 8th Manchester Regt.
He volunteered in November 1914, and in the following January proceeded to the Western Front, where he played a prominent part in many important engagements. He served at Givenchy, Neuve Chapelle, Ypres, Guillemont and Valenciennes, and was gassed in action at Arras. He was demobilised in January 1919, and holds the 1914-15 Star, and the General Service and Victory Medals.
35, Whalley Street, Ancoats, Manchester.   Z1012

FLETCHER, J., Driver, R.F.A. and R.H.A.
Mobilised in August 1914, he quickly proceeded to France, and served through the Retreat from Mons. He was also in action at the Battles of Neuve Chapelle, Loos, The Somme, Arras and Cambrai. He returned to England for his discharge in April 1919, and holds the Mons Star, and the General Service and Victory Medals.
20, Stonehewer Street, Rochdale Road, Manchester. Z1096

FRANCE, J. A., Private, Royal Irish Regiment.
Volunteering in May 1915, he was retained at various home stations on important duties before proceeding to the Western Front in September 1917. In this theatre of war he served with the Royal Irish Fusiliers, and took part in much fighting during the Retreat and Advance of 1918. Demobilised in September 1919, he holds the General Service and Victory Medals.   12, Hewitt Street, Gorton, Manchester.   Z1089C

GARTSIDE, O. S., Private, 7th Manchester Regt.
He volunteered in March 1915, and was quickly drafted to France. There he took part in several engagements, including the Battles of Neuve Chapelle, Ypres, Festubert, St. Eloi, Albert, the Somme, Arras, Ypres (III), Cambrai, the Somme (II) and the Retreat and Advance of 1918. He was demobilised in November 1919, and holds the 1914-15 Star, and the General Service and Victory Medals.
10, South Street, Hulme, Manchester.   Z1098

GILL, W., Corporal, 1/8th Lancashire Fusiliers.
He volunteered in May 1915, and in the following year was drafted to Egypt, where he saw much fighting at Katia, El Fasher, Romani and Magdhaba. Later he was transferred to France, and took part in the Battles of Arras, Bullecourt, Ypres (III), Cambrai, Lens, Amiens and Bapaume. He was unfortunately killed in action in September 1918, and was entitled to the General Service and Victory Medals.
"He nobly fell that we might live."
50, Sherwood Road, Rochdale Road, Manchester. Z1092

GRIFFITHS, H., Private, R.A.M.C.
Volunteering in May 1915, he served at Cardiff with the 3rd Welch Regiment until August 1916, when he crossed to France. There he participated in heavy fighting at Ploegsteert Wood, Messines, Ypres and Cambrai, and in March 1917 was evacuated home on account of ill-health. He was later transferred to the R.A.M.C., and employed as a nursing orderly at Blackpool until he was invalided out of the Army in April 1918. He holds the General Service and Victory Medals. 49, Morsland St., Ardwick, Manchester. Z1065-6B

GRIMSHAW, T. H., Sergt., 4th Lancashire Fus.
Volunteering in August 1914, he proceeded to the Dardanelles in the following year, and served with distinction at the Battles of Krithia and the Suvla Bay Landing. After the Evacuation of Gallipoli, he was sent to France, when he was in action at Loos, Lens, the Somme, Albert, Arras, Cambrai, Havrincourt and Bapaume, and was wounded. He was recommended for a decoration for great bravery at Amiens during the Advance, and was demobilised in April 1919, holding the 1914-15 Star, and the General Service and Victory Medals.   Z1075A
50, Buckley Street, St. Michaels, Rochdale Road, Manchester.

HAMER, J., A.B., Royal Navy.
He volunteered in February 1915, and quickly proceeded to the North Sea on board H.M.S. "Aster." He rendered valuable services with this vessel in these waters for some time, but whilst cruising off Malta, he was unfortunately killed when his ship struck a mine on July 4th, 1917. He was entitled to the 1914-15 Star, and the General Service and Victory Medals.
"A costly sacrifice upon the altar of freedom."
44, Dorset Street, Hulme, Manchester.   Z1088

HAMLETT, W. H., Private, 1st Manchester Regt.
Mobilised from the Reserve in August 1914, he was sent to France in February 1915, and fought in the Battles of Hill 60, Ypres (II), Loos, Albert, the Somme and Vimy Ridge before being sent to Egypt. Later he advanced into Palestine, and was in action at the Battles of Gaza (I, II and III) and the capture of Jerusalem. He received his discharge in May 1919, but later re-enlisted for three years, and holds the 1914-15 Star, the General Service and Victory Medals, and the Long Service and Good Conduct Medal.
41, Congou Street, Ancoats, Manchester.   Z1094

HAMNETT, J., L/Cpl., 6th K.O. (R. Lancaster Regt.)
He volunteered in July 1915, and six months later was drafted to Egypt, where he served with his unit in various engagements. He was afterwards transferred to Mesopotamia, and saw further service in that theatre of war. After taking part in the second Battle of Kut, he was unfortunately killed in action on April 13th, 1917, and was entitled to the General Service and Victory Medals.
"Great deeds cannot die."
59, Percy Street, Ancoats, Manchester.   Z1005

HARRISON, A., Private, 11th E. Lancashire Regt.
He joined in July 1918, and was quickly sent to France, where he rendered valuable services whilst engaged on guard duties over German prisoners at Abbeville. In February 1919 he was attached to the R.A.M.C. at Poperinghe, where he did excellent work until his demobilisation in November 1919. He holds the General Service and Victory Medals.
10, Small Street, Chorlton-on-Medlock, Manchester. Z1002

HEALEY, J., Pte., 2nd Lancashire Fusiliers and 3rd Leicestershire Regiment.
Mobilised in August 1914, he immediately proceeded to France, and took part in the Battles of Mons, Le Cateau, the Marne, the Aisne, La Bassée and Ypres, where he was wounded in November 1914. After being again wounded at Neuve Chapelle in March 1915, he was sent to the Dardanelles, and was in action at the Battles of Krithia (II and III) and Suvla Bay, where he was wounded for the third time in August 1915, and invalided home. Eventually discharged in March 1919, he holds the Mons Star, and the General Service and Victory Medals.
5, Beattie Street, Oldham Road, Manchester.   Z1008

HODSON, W. G., Special War Worker.
In August 1915, he offered his services for work of National importance at Messrs. Peacocks of Gorton, and was engaged on special duties as a planer for over three years. During this time he did splendid work, and gave entire satisfaction to his employers until he relinquished his duties in November 1918. 14, Taylor Street, Gorton, Manchester. Z1082

HOUGHTON, J., Gunner, R.G.A.
He volunteered in April 1915, and twelve months later was drafted to the Western Front, where he was in action with his Battery at the Battles of the Somme, Arras and Ypres. He died gloriously on the Field of Battle during the Retreat on the Somme in May 1918, and was entitled to the General Service and Victory Medals.
"He nobly fell that we might live."
12, Anthony Street, Ardwick, Manchester.   Z1069B

HUDSON, Joseph (M.M.), Pte., Duke of Cornwall's L.I.
He joined in February 1917, and twelve months later was drafted to Italy, but after a short period of heavy fighting there was transferred to France. He was then in action at Merville and on the Somme, and throughout the Retreat and Advance of 1918, and was awarded the Military Medal for conspicuous bravery in the Field. Demobilised in October 1919, he also holds the General Service and Victory Medals.
275, Hamilton Street, Collyhurst, Manchester.   Z1084A

HUDSON, J., Private, East Lancashire Regiment.
Volunteering in February 1915, he first saw active service in Gallipoli, where he took part in heavy fighting. After the Evacuation of the Peninsula, he proceeded to Mesopotamia, and served under General Townsend until April 1916, when he was transferred to Egypt. Advancing into Palestine, he was in action at Gaza, Jaffa, Bethlehem and Jerusalem. He was demobilised in February 1919, and holds the 1914-15 Star, and the General Service and Victory Medals.
275, Hamilton Street, Collyhurst, Manchester.   Z1084C

HUDSON, John, Private, Royal Scots.
He volunteered in February 1915, and in June was sent to Egypt, where he served at Alexandria, Cairo, Khartoum and Kantara before being transferred to France in June 1916. A month later he was badly wounded on the Somme, and was invalided home, but returned to the Western Front in January 1917, and fought at Vimy Ridge, and during the Retreat and Advance of 1918. Demobilised in March 1919, he holds the 1914-15 Star, and the General Service and Victory Medals. 275, Hamilton Street, Collyhurst, Manchester. Z1084B

HUGHES, J., Cpl., King's Own Scottish Borderers.
Volunteering in November 1915, he was sent to France five months later, and was wounded in action at Ypres in the same year. He also took a prominent part in heavy fighting at Albert and Grandecourt on the Somme. He was in hospital at Etaples and in Norfolk for some time after being wounded, but returned to France and served there until hostilities ceased. Demobilised in January 1919, he holds the General Service and Victory Medals. 60, Cobden Street, Ancoats, Manchester. Z1010

HULME, J., Private, 8th Manchester Regiment.
Having previously served with the Colours, he re-enlisted immediately on the outbreak of war in August 1914, and in the following May was drafted to the Dardanelles. He made the supreme sacrifice, falling in action during the Landing at Suvla Bay on August 7th, 1915. He was entitled to the 1914-15 Star, and the General Service and Victory Medals. "Courage, bright hopes, and a myriad dreams, splendidly given." 40, Clare Street, Chorlton-on-Medlock, Manchester. TX1060

JACKSON, E., 2nd Lieut., 4th S. Lancashire Regt.
He volunteered in the ranks of the King's Own (Royal Lancaster Regiment) in November 1915, and on the completion of his training qualified for a commission, and was sent to France in December 1916. Whilst overseas he took an important part in heavy fighting in several engagements in the Ypres Salient and at Albert. He fell fighting on April 25th, 1917, and was buried at Etaples. He was entitled to the General Service and Victory Medals. "And doubtless he went in splendid company." 37, Rolleston Street, Ancoats, Manchester. Z1072A

JACKSON, F. W., Pte., K.O. (R. Lancaster Regt.)
Volunteering in September 1914, he embarked for the Western Front in the following July, and took part in heavy fighting in the Ypres salient. Sent home owing to illness he returned to France on recovery, and served as a Lewis gunner in several engagements. He died gloriously on the Field of Battle at Ypres on July 31st, 1917, and was entitled to the 1914-15 Star, and the General Service and Victory Medals. "Nobly striving, He nobly fell that we might live." 37, Rolleston Street, Ancoats, Manchester. Z1072B

JACKSON, J., Private, Royal Welch Fusiliers.
He volunteered in May 1915, and after completing his training at Aldershot was drafted to India, where he rendered valuable services with his unit whilst engaged on garrison duties at Nowshera and other important stations. He returned home in December 1919, and was demobilised a month later, holding the General Service and Victory Medals. 55, Thornton Street, Collyhurst Street, Manchester. Z1076

JONES, H., Private, 3rd Manchester Regiment.
He volunteered in January 1916, and was sent to Cleethorpes for important coast defence work. He rendered valuable services until April of the same year, when he was badly wounded during an air-raid whilst on duty. After hospital treatment in Grimsby, he was discharged as medically unfit in August 1916. 4, Beswick Street, West Gorton, Manchester. TZ1086

JONES, J. J., Private, Delhi Light Infantry.
Volunteering in March 1915, he was sent to France in June, and served with the Indian contingent. He was in action at Loos, Albert, the Somme, Arras, Bullecourt, Ypres and Cambrai, where he was wounded. After hospital treatment at Rouen, he fought in the Battles of Bapaume, Cambrai (II) and Le Cateau. In 1921 he was still serving at Cologne with the Army of Occupation, and holds the 1914-15 Star, and the General Service and Victory Medals. 48, Piggott Street, Greenheys, Manchester. Z1097

KAMURZURNA, W., Pte., Lancs. Fus. and R.A.M.C.
He joined in June 1916, and in the following August proceeded overseas and was in action at Ploegsteert Wood, Ypres, Beaumont-Hamel and Messines Ridge. Severely wounded and gassed he was invalided home and after his recovery was transferred to the Royal Army Medical Corps. He served on important duties at Manchester Hospital until September 1919, when he was demobilised. He holds the General Service and Victory Medals. 5, Heelis Street, Newton, Manchester. Z1015

KEENAN, W., Private, Royal Irish Fusiliers.
Having volunteered in January 1915, he was quickly sent to France, where he took part in the Battles of Loos, the Somme, Ypres, and Cambrai. Wounded in action at Cambrai he was in hospital at the Base for some time but later fought at Arras, La Bassée and Nieuport. He was demobilised in February 1919, and holds the 1914-15 Star, and the General Service and Victory Medals. 9, Price Street, Ancoats, Manchester. Z1009

KEMP, A., Driver, Canadian Horse Artillery.
Volunteering in August 1914, he was drafted to England with the first Canadian Contingent and proceeded thence to France in February of the following year. There he took part in the Battles of Ypres, Vimy Ridge, the Somme, Arras, the Marne and Cambrai and other engagements and was twice wounded. Invalided from the Army in October 1918, he holds the 1914-15 Star, and the General Service and Victory Medals. 49, Marsland Street, Ardwick, Manchester. TZ1065-6A

KERSHAW, M., Private, 1st Border Regiment.
Having enlisted in May 1913, he was sent to France in January 1915, and took part in the Battles of Hill 60 and Loos. Badly wounded in action at Arras in April 1916, he was taken to the 23rd Canadian General Hospital, where he unfortunately suffered amputation of his right arm. After further hospital treatment at Birmingham, he was discharged in November 1918, holding the 1914-15 Star, and the General Service and Victory Medals. 5, New Street, Ardwick, Manchester. Z1087

KIRBY, F. (D.C.M.), Sergt., R.G.A. and Manchester Regiment.
He first volunteered in the Manchester Regiment in March 1915, and was drafted to France ten months later. Whilst on the Western Front he served with distinction at the Battles of the Somme, Vimy Ridge and Passchendaele, and in the Retreat and Advance of 1918. After hostilities ceased he proceeded to Germany with the Army of Occupation and was eventually demobilised in November 1919. He was awarded the Distinguished Conduct Medal for conspicuous bravery on the Somme and also holds the General Service and Victory Medals. 12, Pendle Street, Openshaw, Manchester. Z1102

LINDLEY, F., Rifleman, 4th Rifle Brigade.
Volunteering in August 1914, he proceeded to the Western Front in January of the following year and there saw severe fighting in various sectors. He took part in the Battles of Ypres, the Somme, Arras and Amiens, and many other important engagements and was wounded in April 1915. He was demobilised in January 1919, and holds the 1914-15 Star, and the General Service and Victory Medals. 34, Simpson Street, Lower Broughton, Manchester. Z1017

LITTLEWOOD, A., L/Cpl., 1st K.O. (R. Lancaster R.)
Mobilised in August 1914, he was immediately drafted to the Western Front, where he took part in the fighting at Mons. He also served through the Battles of Ypres, and the Somme and many minor engagements, until severely wounded in action. Invalided from the Army in November 1916, he holds the Mons Star, and the General Service and Victory Medals. 4, Simpson Street, Lower Broughton, Manchester. Z1044

MADDOCKS, C., Private, 7th Manchester Regt.
Volunteering in May 1915, he embarked in the following year for Egypt and served there for a time until drafted to Salonika in March 1916. There he was engaged in several operations in the Balkans, but owing to his contracting fever was invalided home in May 1918. After treatment at Queen Mary's Hospital, Liverpool, he was discharged as medically unfit for further service in October 1918, and holds the General Service and Victory Medals. 7, Wesley Street, Gorton, Manchester. Z1083

MAGUIRE, J. (M.S.M.), R.Q.M.S., 10th Manchester Regiment.
He volunteered in September 1914, and completing his training in the following year was drafted to France. There he played a distinguished part in the Battles of Loos, St. Eloi, Vimy Ridge, the Somme, Beaumont-Hamel, Arras and Ypres. He was awarded the Meritorious Service Medal for conspicuous services under fire. Owing to an accident he was invalided home, and on his recovery retained at various stations for important duties. Demobilised in March 1920, he holds also the 1914-15 Star, and the General Service and Victory Medals. 64, Collyhurst Street, Collyhurst, Manchester. Z1090

MANNION, J., Munition Worker and Pte., Labour Corps.
During the war he was engaged on work of National importance at Messrs. Morris's Chemical Works, Manchester, where he rendered valuable services. Owing to scarcity of chemicals the factory had to close down in December 1917, and later he joined the Army, being employed in the Labour Corps. Unfortunately his health broke down, and he was discharged in February 1920. 34, Beaumont Street, Beswick, Manchester. Z1074

MᶜCALL, T., Private, 6th Leicestershire Regiment.
He enlisted in August 1916, and three months later was drafted to France, where he took part in several engagements, including those in the Ypres and La Bassée sectors. In March 1918 he was taken prisoner during the Advance, and was held in captivity in Germany eight months. Repatriated after the Armistice, he was demobilised in April 1919, holding the General Service and Victory Medals.
16, Lawrence Street, Gorton, Manchester.   Z1080

MᶜHALE, J. F., Private, 4th Cheshire Regiment.
He joined in December 1916, and after six months' training was drafted to the Western Front, where he served in various sectors. Engaged chiefly in conducting prisoners of war whilst overseas, he rendered very valuable services with his unit until his return home for demobilisation in October 1919. He holds the General Service and Victory Medals.
19, Whalley Street, Ancoats, Manchester.   Z1013

MILLINGTON, J. H., Pte., 2/6th Lancashire Fuslrs.
Volunteering in January 1915, he was drafted overseas in the following May. Whilst on the Western Front he took part in many engagements, including those in the Somme, Ypres, Loos, La Bassée, Arras, Givenchy and Nieuport sectors. He was demobilised in February 1919, and holds the 1914-15 Star, and the General Service and Victory Medals.
30, Simpson Street, Lower Broughton, Manchester.   Z1018

MILLINGTON, S., Private, King's (Liverpool Regt.)
He volunteered in August 1914, and underwent a short period of training prior to his being drafted to Salonika, where he saw much heavy fighting. He made the supreme sacrifice, being killed in action in February 1916, and was entitled to the 1914-15 Star, and the General Service and Victory Medals.
"Thinking that remembrance, though unspoken, may reach him where he sleeps."
1, Clayton Street, Newtown, Manchester.   Z1091

MOORE, W., Gunner, R.F.A.
He volunteered in February 1915, and in the same year was drafted to Egypt, where he saw much heavy fighting on the Suez Canal. Later he was transferred to France, and took part in the Battles of Loos, Ypres, Vimy Ridge, the Somme and Passchendaele. He was demobilised in May 1919, and holds the 1914-15 Star, and the General Service and Victory Medals.
173, Cheltenham Street, Collyhurst, Manchester.   Z1085

MURPHY, H., Private, K.O. (R. Lancaster Regt.)
Called up from the Reserve in August 1914, he was immediately drafted to the Western Front, where he fought at the Battles of Mons, the Marne, the Aisne, Ypres (I and II), La Bassée, Neuve Chapelle, Loos, Albert and the Somme. Invalided home with bronchitis he was in hospital for some time, but on his recovery returned to France and was in action at Cambrai, and in the Retreat and Advance of 1918. Discharged in 1918 he re-enlisted in January 1919 in the R.A.S.C., and served on transport work until demobilised in October 1920. He holds the Mons Star, and the General Service and Victory Medals.
8, Rob Roy Street, Hulme, Manchester.   TZ1001B

MURPHY, R., Private, 1st Cheshire Regiment.
Mobilised in August 1914, he was immediately drafted to France. There he took part in the Battles of La Bassée, Hill 60, Festubert, Loos and Vimy Ridge. He made the supreme sacrifice, being killed in action at the Battle of the Somme on September 11th, 1916, and was entitled to the Mons Star, and the General Service and Victory Medals.
"A valiant Soldier, with undaunted heart he breasted life's last hill."
8, Rob Roy Street, Hulme, Manchester.   TZ1001A

MYCOCK, J. W., Private, Manchester Regiment.
Volunteering in December 1915, he underwent a period of training and was retained on important duties with his unit at various stations. Early in November 1918 he proceeded to France, and served with the Army of Occupation until demobilised in February 1919. He holds the General Service and Victory Medals.
25, Drinkwater Street, Harpurhey, Manchester.   Z1068

OLIVER, J., Private, 22nd Manchester Regiment.
He volunteered in November 1914, and completing his training in the following year was drafted to the Western Front. In this theatre of war he took part in several engagements, including the Battles of Delville Wood, Vimy Ridge, Beaucourt and Arras, and was twice wounded in action. He was demobilised in February 1919, and holds the 1914-15 Star, and the General Service and Victory Medals.
10, Castleton Street, Bradford, Manchester.   TZ1064

RICHARDS, J., Private, 2nd Manchester Regiment.
Called up from the Reserve in August 1914, he quickly proceeded to France, where he fought in the Battles of Mons, the Marne and La Bassée and was wounded at Le Cateau in August 1914, and at Festubert in October 1915. He after-

wards transferred to the Admiralty Company of the R.E. serving in France until September 1918. He was invalided from the Army in the following month, and holds the Mons Star, and the General Service and Victory Medals.
7, Back Hadfield Street, Ancoats, Manchester.   TZ1071

RODGERS, W. P., Lieutenant, Manchester Regt.
He volunteered in October 1914, and in the following February was drafted to Egypt. There he participated in engagements on the Suez Canal, and at Mersa Matruh, Agagia, Katia and Rafa. Proceeding later into Palestine, he took part in the Battles of Gaza, and the capture of Jerusalem and Jericho. He remained in this theatre of war until May 1920, when he returned home and was demobilised, holding the 1914-15 Star, and the General Service and Victory Medals.
72, Duke Street, Lower Broughton, Manchester.   Z1027

RYDER, J., Private, K.O. (R. Lancaster Regt.)
He joined in January 1916, and five months later proceeded to the Western Front. In this theatre of war he took part in heavy fighting at Ypres, on the Somme front, at Arras, Nieuport, Givenchy, Delville Wood and Messines Ridge. He was wounded in 1918, but remained overseas until February 1919, when he was demobilised, holding the General Service and Victory Medals.
10, Simpson Street, Lower Broughton, Manchester.   Z1043

SALISBURY, P., Private, 6th Welch Regiment.
Joining in October 1916, he was drafted to France on completion of his training. He did excellent work whilst engaged with his unit in heavy fighting on various fronts, and died gloriously on the Field of Battle at Lens in August 1917. He was entitled to the General Service and Victory Medals.
"Whilst we remember, the sacrifice is not in vain."
11, Leamington Avenue, Chorlton-on-Medlock, Manchester.
   Z1003-4

SCOTT, T., Private, 2nd K.O. (R. Lancaster Regt.)
He joined in 1916, and later in the same year proceeded to the Western Front. There he took a prominent part with his unit in numerous severe engagements, including Ypres, La Bassée, Arras, Givenchy, Delville Wood, Messines Ridge, Passchendaele, and on the Somme front. He returned home and was demobilised in February 1919, and holds the General Service and Victory Medals.
28, Simpson Street, Lower Broughton, Manchester.   Z1042

SCRUTON, F., Driver, R.E. (Signal Section).
He joined the Royal Engineers in September 1920, and after completing his training as a signaller at Devonport, was drafted to India. There he was employed with his Company on various duties of an important nature, and in 1921 was still stationed in the East.
193, Morton Street, Longsight, Manchester.   Z1062B

SCRUTON, F., A.B., Royal Naval Reserve.
He joined in April 1917, but was medically unfit for duty at sea or in a theatre of war. Retained on home service he was stationed in Suffolk, and later in Ireland, and rendered valuable services whilst employed on various duties, until he was demobilised in December 1918.
193, Morton Street, Longsight, Manchester.   Z1062A

SKIDMORE, D., Private, Border Regiment.
He volunteered in August 1914, and twelve months later proceeded to Gallipoli in H.M.T. "Royal Edward," which vessel was sunk in the Ægean Sea. Fortunately rescued, he afterwards saw much severe fighting in the Peninsula, and was later transferred to France, where he took part in the Battles of Arras, Ypres and Cambrai, and was wounded at Givenchy in 1916. Demobilised in January 1919, he holds the 1914-15 Star, and the General Service and Victory Medals.
21, Sutton Street, Ancoats, Manchester.   Z1073

STEARNS, C. E., Leading Seaman, R.N.
Having volunteered in January 1915, he underwent a period of training and was posted to H.M.S. "Collingwood," in which vessel he saw much service in many waters. He took part in the Battle of Jutland, and did consistently good work throughout the period of hostilities. In 1920 he was still serving on board H.M.S. "Hearty," and holds the 1914-15 Star, and the General Service and Victory Medals.
12, Hewitt Street, Gorton, Manchester.   Z1089A

STEARNS, W. R., 16th Manchester Regt. (Pals.)
Volunteering in August 1914, he underwent a period of training and in the following year proceeded to France. Whilst in this theatre of war, he took part in the Battles of Loos, St. Eloi, Vimy Ridge, and the Somme. He made the supreme sacrifice, being killed in action in July 1916, and was entitled to the 1914-15 Star, and the General Service and Victory Medals.
"His life for his Country, his soul to God."
12, Hewitt Street, Gorton, Manchester.   Z1089B

SWINDELLS, T. E., Pte., K.O. (R. Lancaster Regt.)
He volunteered in August 1915, and in the following June was sent to the Western Front. In this theatre of hostilities he was in action during the Battles of the Somme (I), the Ancre, Arras, Ypres (III), Lens, Somme (II) and Aisne (III). He was also engaged in various sectors during the Retreat and Advance in 1918, and was demobilised in March 1919, holding the General Service and Victory Medals.
88, Duke Street, Lower Broughton, Manchester. Z1016

TIPPER, J. J., Private, K.O. (R. Lancaster Regt.)
Having volunteered in June 1915, he was shortly afterwards drafted to the Dardanelles, and took part in the Landing at Suvla Bay, the capture of Chunuk Bair and minor engagements. After the Evacuation of the Gallipoli Peninsula, he was invalided home with frost-bite, but on his recovery in August 1916, was transferred to France, where he was in action on the Somme. He died gloriously on the Field of Battle on October 19th, 1916, and was entitled to the 1914-15 Star, and the General Service and Victory Medals.
"Whilst we remember, the sacrifice is not in vain."
50, Buckley Street, St. Michaels, Manchester. Z1075B

WALSH, J., Private, 11th Manchester Regiment.
Mobilised from the Reserve in August 1914, he completed a period of training and proceeded to Gallipoli, where he took part in the Battles of Krithia, and the capture of Chunuk Bair. After the Evacuation of the Peninsula, he was transferred to Egypt, and served at Katia, and El Fasher. Later in 1916 he was drafted to France, and was in action on the Somme before being wounded and invalided to England in September 1916. After a long period of hospital treatment he was eventually discharged in July 1919, holding the 1914-15 Star, and the General Service and Victory Medals.
59, Burton Street, Rochdale Road, Manchester. TZ1070

WHITWORTH, S., Engine Room Artificer, R.N.
He joined in May 1917, and was posted to H.M.S. "Phelous," in which vessel he was engaged on patrol duties in the Eastern Mediterranean in the vicinity of the Dardanelles. Later he was transferred to H.M.S. "Europa" for similar work in the North Sea, and rendered valuable services until demobilised in July 1919, holding the General Service and Victory Medals.
24, Ashover Street, Ardwick, Manchester. Z1067

WOOD, A., Private, Yorkshire Regiment.
Volunteering in November 1915, he served at Catterick Bridge before proceeding to France in March 1917. Whilst in this seat of operations, he took part in the Battles of Arras, Bullecourt, Ypres (III), and the Somme (II). Later in 1918 he contracted an illness, and as a result, was invalided to hospital in England, and eventually demobilised in February 1919. He holds the General Service and Victory Medals.
12, Anthony Street, Ardwick, Manchester. Z1069A

YOUNG, A., Sergt., Loyal North Lancashire Regt.
He volunteered in November 1914, and in November of the following year proceeded to the Western Front, where he played a distinguished part in many engagements. He was in action at Loos, St. Eloi, Albert, the Somme (I and II), Arras, Ypres (III) and Cambrai, and made the supreme sacrifice on September 18th, 1918, being killed in action at Havrincourt during the Advance. He was entitled to the 1914-15 Star, and the General Service and Victory Medals.
"His memory is cherished with pride."
9, Haughton Street, Bradford, Manchester. Z1272B

YOUNG, D., Private, 2nd Manchester Regiment.
He volunteered in September 1914, and after a period of training was sent to France in May of the following year. In this theatre of war he was engaged in much severe fighting and was in action at the Battles of Ypres, Loos, the Somme and Arras. He made the supreme sacrifice in April 1917, being killed in action at Vimy Ridge. He was entitled to the 1914-15 Star, and the General Service and Victory Medals.
"His life for his Country."
18, Francisco Street, Collyhurst, Manchester. Z11399

YOUNG, E., Private, Lancashire Fusiliers.
He volunteered in January 1915, and after undergoing a period of training was drafted to the Dardanelles in August 1915. He took part in the fighting at Suvla Bay, and was invalided home with frost-bite. He later proceeded to the Western Front, where he saw much service at Ypres, and after being wounded, made the supreme sacrifice in April 1918, being killed in action at Cambrai. He was entitled to the 1914-15 Star, and the General Service and Victory Medals.
"Whilst we remember, the sacrifice is not in vain."
39, Ravald Street, Miles Platting, Manchester. Z9773

YOUNG, F., Private, 1/4th South Lancashire Regt.
Volunteering in November 1914, he completed a period of training and was drafted to France in the following year. There he took part in many engagements of importance, and was in action at the Battles of Ypres (II), Vimy Ridge, the Somme, St. Quentin, La Bassée and Passchendaele, and was

gassed at Cambrai during the Advance of 1918. He holds the 1914-15 Star, and the General Service and Victory Medals, and was demobilised in February 1919.
6, Williams Place, Ancoats, Manchester. Z11457/A

YOUNG, G., Private, 1/7th Manchester Regiment.
He was mobilised at the outbreak of war in August 1914, and was drafted to the Dardanelles in April of the following year. There he took part in many important engagements on the Gallipoli Peninsula, including the Landing at Suvla Bay. After the Evacuation in December 1915 he proceeded to the Western Front, where he saw much heavy fighting at the Battles of the Somme, Arras, Bullecourt, Messines and Ypres (III), and made the supreme sacrifice, being killed in action on September 8th, 1917. He was entitled to the 1914-15 Star, and the General Service and Victory Medals.
"Great deeds cannot die."
17, Heyrod Street, Ancoats, Manchester. TZ8847B

YOUNG, J., Private, 2nd Manchester Regiment.
He was mobilised from the Reserve in August 1914, and was immediately drafted to the Western Front, where he took part in the Battle of Mons and the subsequent Retreat. He was also in action at the Battles of the Marne, the Aisne, Ypres and Neuve Chapelle, but was unfortunately killed in action at Hill 60 on June 15th, 1915, and was entitled to the Mons Star, and the General Service and Victory Medals.
"The path of duty was the way to glory."
17, Heyrod Street, Ancoats, Manchester. TZ8847C

YOUNG, J. H., Air Mechanic, R.A.F.
He joined in October 1917, and after passing his trade test, was transferred from Farnborough to London, where he did consistently good work in the repairing of aeroplanes. He also served on the London defence section against enemy aircraft, and was eventually demobilised in February 1919, after rendering valuable services. He holds the General Service and Victory Medals.
87, Cross Street, Bradford, Manchester. Z11400

YOUNG, J. W., Sapper, R.E.
He joined in November 1916, and after completing his training was drafted to Mesopotamia in April 1917. There he took part in many important engagements in this theatre of war, including Kut-el-Amara, Basra and Baghdad, and rendered valuable services until his return to England for demobilisation in March 1920. He holds the General Service and Victory Medals. 10, Henry St., Ardwick, Manchester. Z8846

YOUNG, T., Rifleman, K.R.R.C.
He was mobilised in August 1914, and immediately drafted to France, where he took part in the Battles of Mons and Loos, and was slightly gassed in action. In consequence he was transferred to India and was engaged on important garrison duties, but later was sent back to France and fought at Ypres and Arras. He was demobilised in March 1919, and holds the Mons Star, and the General Service and Victory Medals.
43, Brown Street, Ancoats, Manchester. Z11965

YOUNG, W., Sergt., 25th Royal Fusiliers.
He volunteered in February 1915, and in the following April was drafted to East Africa, where he saw service at Bukoba, Mushi and Mombassa, and did consistently good work in this theatre of war. He returned to England and was discharged in March 1918 as unfit for further service and has since died through disease contracted in the East African theatre of war. He was entitled to the 1914-15 Star, and the General Service and Victory Medals.
"And doubtless he went in splendid company."
6, Williams Place, Ancoats, Manchester. Z11457B

YOUNG, W., (M.M.), C.S.M., 11th Lancashire Fus.
Volunteering in September 1914, he proceeded to France in the following March and played a distinguished part in numerous engagements of importance. He was in action at the Battles of Neuve Chapelle, Hill 60, Ypres (II), Festubert, Albert, the Somme, Arras, Vimy Ridge, Bullecourt and Messines, and was awarded the Military Medal for conspicuous bravery and devotion to duty in the Field. He was also mentioned in Despatches by Sir Douglas Haig and later by his Divisional Commander. He was wounded on four occasions, and also suffered from gas poisoning. In addition to the Military Medal he holds the 1914-15 Star, and the General Service and Victory Medals, and was demobilised in March 1919.
17, Heyrod Street, Ancoats, Manchester. TZ8847A

YOUNG, W., Sergt., 2nd Manchester Regiment.
Already in the Army at the outbreak of war, he proceeded to France with the first Expeditionary Force, but died gloriously for the freedom of England at the Battle of Mons in August 1914. He was entitled to the Mons Star, and the General Service and Victory Medals.
"Honour to the immortal dead, who gave their youth that the world might grow old in peace."
46, Dale Street, Hulme, Manchester. Z884

YOUNGBLUTT, A., Pte., Loyal N. Lancs. Regt.

Mobilised in August 1914, he proceeded to France in the following month and took part in the Battle of Loos in September 1915, when he was wounded and sent to hospital in England. He returned to France after recovery, and was wounded in the Somme Offensive of 1916, and again at Mametz Wood during the Advance of 1918. Invalided home once more, he was finally discharged in December as unfit for further service, and holds the 1914 Star, and the General Service and Victory Medals.

21, Whyatt Street, Bradford, Manchester.   Z11401

YOUNGBLUTT, J., Corporal, R.F.A.

He volunteered in January 1915, and after a period of training proceeded to France in November of that year. There he played a prominent part in many engagements, including the first Battle of the Somme in July 1916 and the third Battle of Ypres in the following year. He also rendered valuable services during the Retreat and Advance of 1918, and was demobilised in December, holding the 1914–15 Star, and the General Service and Victory Medals.

19, Whyatt Street, Bradford, Manchester.   Z11396

Z

ZIRFAS, H. L., Bombardier, R.F.A.

He enlisted in October 1907, and at the outbreak of war in August 1914, was immediately drafted to France, where he took part in the Retreat from Mons. He was also in action with his Battery at many subsequent engagements, including the Battles of La Bassée, Ypres and Messines. He was invalided to England through wounds received in action in 1915, but returned to the Western Front and served throughout the Retreat and Advance of 1918. He holds the Mons Star, and the General Service and Victory Medals, and was discharged in October 1919.

35, Down Street, Ardwick, Manchester.   Z8849

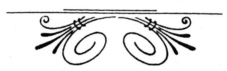

Printed at Intype London Ltd

Printed in the United Kingdom
by Lightning Source UK Ltd.
127377UK00001B/103-200/A